At JetEx, we make use of our limitless budgetary facilities to provide our customers with highly enhanced and truly customized service that covers the wide range of their travel needs. Turn to JetEx for incomparable experience.

It all starts with us here in Dubai !

24 hrs Flight Service Operations
Tel: +971 4 268 9910

The Registry of Aruba
International Air Safety Office, Inc.

The Aircraft Registry of Choice

8750 NW 36 St, Suite#210 • Miami, Florida 33178 • Tel: +1.305.471.9889 • Fax: +1.305.471.8122 • admin@airsafetyfirst.com • www.airsafetyfirst.com

Ministry of Transport & Tourism

DEPARTMENT OF CIVIL AVIATION
SABANA BERDE 73-B
ORANJESTAD, ARUBA

ARE YOU CONSIDERING REGISTERING YOUR AIRCRAFT IN A CREDIBLE **CATEGORY 1** ASSESSED COUNTRY, FOR POLITICAL FISCAL, ECONOMIC, COMMERCIAL OR ANY OTHER REASON?

Worldwide Private Aircraft Owners and Operators, Commercial Jet and Regional Airlines, International Leasing Companies, Banks, Financial Groups, value our services for high safety oversight standards, superior customer service, efficiency, cost containment, financial benefits, premier tax advantages, reliability, maintenance conformity, regulations compliance to **EASA & FAA** standards, quickness and much more... **Call us today.**

For more information and a Brochure, please contact:

International Air Safety Office
8750 NW 36th Street, Suite 210
Miami, Florida 33178 USA
Tel: +1305- 471-9889
Fax: +1305- 471-8122 or 8561
E-mail: admin@airsafetyfirst.com
Website: www.airsafetyfirst.com

ONE STEP FOR SAFETY, QUALITY AND DEPENDABILITY

Aruba Registry welcomes all Aircraft Owners and Operators, because we have the know how and the know who!

Member of

Isle of Man
Aircraft Registry

The first dedicated high quality business aircraft register in Europe

Isle of Man Aircraft Registry
Hamilton House, Peel Road, Douglas, Isle of Man, IM1 5EP, British Isles

Isle of Man Government
Reiltys Ellan Vannin

tel **+44 (0)1624 682358** fax **+44 (0)1624 682355**
email **aircraft@gov.im** web **www.iomaircraftregistry.com**

C-FPTM   Diamond D-Jet   photo: Bill Shull

N505EA   Eclipse EA500   photo: Barry Ambrose BIZAV

N403CM   Citation Mustang   photo: Jean-Luc Altherr

jp Biz-Jet 2008
& Turboprops
By Brian Gates

41st Edition
ISBN 978-1-898779-31-5
48 Colour photographs
Published by:

BUCHair (U.K.) Ltd
P.O. Box 89, Reigate, Surrey, RH2 7FG
Tel: +44 (0)1737 224747
Fax: +44 (0)1737 226777
Email: sales@buchairuk.co.uk
Web: www.buchairshop.co.uk

Printed in Great Britain
Copyright © BUCHair (U.K.) Ltd 2008

Whilst every effort is made to ensure that the information in this directory is accurate and up to date, the publishers cannot undertake responsibility for errors or omissions or their consequences

No part of this publication may be reproduced, stored in a retrieval system, or transmitted, in any form or by means, mechanical, photocopying, recording and/or otherwise, without the prior written permission of the publishers.

Where to get the products of BUCHair (UK) Ltd, and Bucher & Co Zurich

Australia & NZ	Aviation Worldwide, 24 Happy Valley Road, 7.O.R.D, Oamaru, New Zealand

Austria:	Freytag & Berndt, Reisebuchhandlung, Brunner Strasse 69, A1231 Viena Phone: (1) 5338685

Canada:	Aviation World, 195 Carlingview Drive, Rexdale, Ontario, M9W 5E8 Phone: (416) 674-5959 Fax: (416) 674-5915 Email: avworld@interlog.com Web www.interlog.com/-avworld

Denmark:	Nyboder Boghandel, ApS, 114 Store Kongensgade, DK-1264 Copenhagen K Phone: 33 32 33 20 Fax: 33 32 33 62

Finland:	Aviation Shop, Kajanuksenkatu 12, SF-00250 Helsinki Phone: (09) 449 801 Fax: (09) 149 6163

France:	La Maison Du Livre, 76 Boulevard Malesherbes, F-75008 Paris Phone: (1) 45 22 74 16 Fax: (1) 42 93 81 23

Ireland:	Greene's Bookshop , Unit 7, 78 Furze Road, Sandyford Industrial Est., Dublin 18 Phone: 01 2938801 Fax: 01 2938803

Italy:	La Bancarella Aeronautica S.A.S., Via G Fattori 116/A, I-10141 Torino Phone: (011) 7793586 Fax: (011) 772 5447

Japan:	Nishiyama Yosho Co Ltd Narityata Bldg 7-13 Ginza, 3 Chrome,Chuo-ku, Tokyo 104-0061 Phone: (03) 3562-0840 Fax: (03) 3562-0828

Netherlands:	Boekhandel Venstra B.V., Binnenhof 50, Postbus 77, NL-1180 AB Amstelveen Phone: (020) 641 98 80 Fax: (020) 640 02 52 Luchtvaart Hobby Shop, Molenweg 249, 1436 BV Aaismeerderbrug Web: Aviationmegastore.com

Portugal:	Ocean Wings, Rua Jose Lins do Rego, 3 - D1700-262 Lisboa Portugal Phone: +351 21 793 24 57 email: oceanwings@netcabo.pt Web: www.oceanwings.pt

Switzerland:	Bucher & Co Publikationen, Postfach 44, CH8058 Zurich Flughafen Phone: (044)874 1 747 Fax: (044)874 1 757 Email jp@buchair.ch Web: buchairnet.com Shop: BUCHairSHOP, Schaffhauserstrasse 76, CH-8152 Glattbrugg Shop Flughafen: BUCHairSHOP, Terrasse, Terminal B, Zurich Flughafen

Spain:	La Aeroteca Libreria Miguel Creus, C/Montseny, 22 E08012 Barcelona Spain Phone: (93) 218 17 39 Fax: (93) 217 05 66

Sweden:	Stenvalls, Box 17111, S-20010 Malmo, Sweden, Shop Foreningsgatan, 12, Malmo Phone: 040 127703 Fax: 040 127706 Email: info@stenvalls.com web: www.stenvalls.com

UK:	BUCHair UK Ltd, PO Box 89, Reigate, Surrey, RH2 7FG Phone: 01737 224747 Fax: 01737 226777 Email: sales@buchairuk.co.uk Web: www.buchairshop.co.uk And all good aviation shops: Aviation Shop, Manchester The aviation Hobby Shop, West Drayton Aviationretaildirect, Heathrow, The aviation Bookshop, Tunbridge Wells Air Trans, Birmingham & West Midlands, Air Supply, Leeds Ian Allan Bookshops, Midland Counties.

USA:	BUCHair(USA), Inc. PO Box 750515, Forest Hills, NY 11375-0515 Phone: (718) 263 8748 Fax: (718) 275 6190 Email: best_of_flight@buchair.com Web: buchair.com

INTRODUCTION

The U.S. dollar has been at its weakest for sometime, and this has contributed to a new delivery and sales bonanza for the International market, especially Europe and Middle East (Dubai), but also to the ever expanding markets of Eastern Europe (Russia), India & China. VLJs too, initially the Eclipse & Mustang are making an impact with 200 units already delivered. 2008 will see further expansion of the VLJ market with other types coming on stream.

FIRST FLIGHTS

Falcon 2000DX	19 Jun 07	Embraer Phenom 100	26 Jul 07
Citation XLS	7 Aug 07	Hawker 900XP	24 Aug 07
Lineage 1000	26 Oct 07		

This 41st edition is in the usual format. South America & Mexico remain difficult areas with little official information available. An * against a registration indicates at the time of going to press it was a reserved registration only. Generally, 90% of these are taken up.
This edition will be the last under my editorship. Administrative changes are currently on going to ensure the continuation of BIZ-JET.

briangatesbizJet@aol.com

1 January 2008

ACKNOWLEDGEMENTS

I am indebted to the following for their invaluable help: Air Britain News, Aviation Letter, Corporate Monthly, BISP, Anton Heumann, Pierre Parvaud, Walter Hager, Jean Luc-Altherr, Paul Suter, Steve Garner, turboprops by BuchAir UK Ltd and to many individuals & Companies that provided a little but essential data.

FRONT COVER

Photo provided by Aviation Partners Inc – " The future is on the Wing"
" Performance Enhancement Blended Winglets Technology"
Aviation Partners Inc. 13200 S E 30th Street, Bellevue, WA 98005, USA.

Contents

VLJs	17

BizJets

BizJets by Country	23
BizJets Written Off Section	279
BizJets Cross Reference	309

BizTurboprops

BizTurboprops by Country	357
BizTurboprops Written Off Section	531
BizTurboprops Cross Reference	561

BizJet Reports

Business Jets - By Country within Continent includes Civil And Military

Total Jets 16631

Africa

Code	Country	Count
7T =	ALGERIA	7
D2 =	ANGOLA	17
TY =	BENIN	2
A2 =	BOTSWANA	2
XT =	BURKINA FASO	2
TJ =	CAMEROON	4
TT =	CHAD	1
9Q =	CONGO KINSHASA	8
J2 =	DJIBOUTI	1
SU =	EGYPT	19
3C =	EQUATORIAL GUINEA	4
TR =	GABON	9
9G =	GHANA	1
TU =	IVORY COAST	4
5Y =	KENYA	4
5A =	LIBYA	13
5R =	MADAGASCAR	4
7Q =	MALAWI	1
TZ =	MALI	3
5T =	MAURITANIA	1
3B =	MAURITIUS	4
CN =	MOROCCO	13
V5 =	NAMIBIA	5
5U =	NIGER	1
5N =	NIGERIA	33
9X =	RWANDA	1
S9 =	SAO TOME & PRINCIPE	3
6V =	SENEGAL	1
ZS =	SOUTH AFRICA	126
ST =	SUDAN	4
3D =	SWAZILAND	5
5H =	TANZANIA	2
5V =	TOGO	3
TS =	TUNISIA	3
5X =	UGANDA	1
9J =	ZAMBIA	1
Z =	ZIMBABWE	1

Total for Continent 314

Australasia

Code	Country	Count
VH =	AUSTRALIA	110
ZK =	NEW ZEALAND	7
P2 =	PAPUA NEW GUINEA	1

Total for Continent 118

Central America

Code	Country	Count
P4 =	ARUBA	53
C6 =	BAHAMAS	2
8P =	BARBADOS	1
VP- =	CAYMAN ISLANDS	115
TI =	COSTA RICA	1
HI =	DOMINICAN REPUBLIC	1
TG =	GUATEMALA	5
HR =	HONDURAS	1
HP =	PANAMA	3

Total for Continent 182

Europe

Code	Country	Count
OE =	AUSTRIA	188
EW =	BELARUS	1
OO =	BELGIUM	43
T9 =	BOSNIA-HERZEGOVINA	1
LZ =	BULGARIA	11
9A =	CROATIA	1
5B =	CYPRUS	3
OK =	CZECH REPUBLIC / CZECHIA	17
OY =	DENMARK	62
EI =	EIRE	13
ES =	ESTONIA	8
OH =	FINLAND	18
F =	FRANCE	186
4L =	GEORGIA	1
D =	GERMANY	335
G =	GREAT BRITAIN	229
SX =	GREECE	21
HA =	HUNGARY	4
M =	ISLE OF MAN	20
I =	ITALY	131
YL =	LATVIA	5
LY =	LITHUANIA	2
LX =	LUXEMBOURG	37
Z3 =	MACEDONIA	2
9H =	MALTA	2
ER =	MOLDOVA	1
3A =	MONACO	3
PH =	NETHERLANDS	35
LN =	NORWAY	19
SP =	POLAND	5

CS	=	PORTUGAL	176
YR	=	ROMANIA	9
RA	=	RUSSIA / RUSSIAN FEDERATION	17
T7	=	SAN MARINO	2
YU	=	SERBIA	10
OM	=	SLOVAKIA	4
S5	=	SLOVENIA	10
EC	=	SPAIN	127
SE	=	SWEDEN	46
HB	=	SWITZERLAND	138
TC	=	TURKEY	56
UR	=	UKRAINE	9
Total for Continent			**2008**

Far East

V8	=	BRUNEI	3
XU	=	CAMBODIA	2
B	=	CHINA	50
B-	=	CHINA - HONG KONG	9
B-	=	CHINA - MACAU	4
B	=	CHINA - TAIWAN	2
VT	=	INDIA	81
PK	=	INDONESIA	25
JA	=	JAPAN	82
UN	=	KAZAKHSTAN	6
HL	=	KOREA	19
9M	=	MALAYSIA	14
XY	=	MYANMAR	1
AP	=	PAKISTAN	22
RP	=	PHILIPPINES	18
HS	=	THAILAND	14
EZ	=	TURKMENISTAN	1
UK	=	UZBEKISTAN	1
Total for Continent			**354**

Middle East

EK	=	ARMENIA	1
4K	=	AZERBAIJAN	3
A9	=	BAHRAIN	18
EP	=	IRAN	22
YI	=	IRAQ	7
4X	=	ISRAEL	31
JY	=	JORDAN	9
9K	=	KUWAIT	6
OD	=	LEBANON	5
A4	=	OMAN	5
A7	=	QATAR	15
HZ	=	SAUDI ARABIA	64
YK	=	SYRIA	3
A6	=	UNITED ARAB EMIRATES	42
7O	=	YEMEN	1

Total for Continent	**232**

North America

VP-	=	BERMUDA	149
C	=	CANADA	418
XA	=	MEXICO	616
N	=	USA	11664
Total for Continent			**12847**

South America

LV	=	ARGENTINA	78
CP	=	BOLIVIA	5
PP	=	BRAZIL	352
CC	=	CHILE	26
HK	=	COLOMBIA	13
HC	=	ECUADOR	6
ZP	=	PARAGUAY	3
OB	=	PERU	9
CX	=	URUGUAY	1
YV	=	VENEZUELA	83
Total for Continent			**576**

NOTE - Totals for current aircraft in production include pre-delivery inventory stock, so will give a slightly inflated figure

BizJets- totals by type   Total Jets   16631

Model	Count	Model	Count	Model	Count
390 Premier 1	135	Challenger 850	15	Eclipse EA500	136
390 Premier 1A	95	Citation	290	EMB-135ER	6
AC 690A-TU	1	Citation 1/SP	280	EMB-135EW	1
Adam A700	4	Citation Bravo	337	EMB-135LR	7
Airbus A300	2	Citation Eagle	30	EMB-135LR Legacy	1
Airbus A310	12	Citation Eagle 400SP	1	EMB-145LR	4
Airbus A318 Elite	3	Citation Eagle II	7	EMB-145RS	1
Airbus A319	46	Citation Eagle SP	3	Embraer Legacy 600	117
Airbus A320	6	Citation Encore	149	Embraer Lineage 100	2
Airbus A321	1	Citation Encore+	45	Epic Elite	1
Airbus A330	2	Citation Excel	375	Epic Victory	1
Airbus A340	9	Citation Excel XLS	290	F 28-1000	11
Astra C-38A	2	Citation Excel XLS+	2	F 28-1000C	1
Astra-1125	33	Citation II	595	F 28-3000	3
Astra-1125SP	34	Citation II/SP	69	F 28-3000C	1
Astra-1125SPX	52	Citation III	197	F 28-3000M	1
B 707	29	Citation Longwing SP	5	F 28-4000	6
B 720	2	Citation Mustang	56	F 28-4000VIP	1
B 727	67	Citation OT-47B	5	Falcon 10	153
B 737	66	Citation S Super II	1	Falcon 100	34
B 747	23	Citation S/II	155	Falcon 10MER	5
B 757	17	Citation Sovereign	205	Falcon 20	3
B 767	8	Citation Stallion	2	Falcon 200	33
B 777	2	Citation UC-35A	20	Falcon 2000	231
BAC 1-11	24	Citation UC-35B	2	Falcon 2000DX	2
BAe 1000A	31	Citation UC-35C	7	Falcon 2000EX	29
BAe 1000B	9	Citation UC-35D	11	Falcon 2000EX EASY	121
BAe 125/800A	154	Citation V	260	Falcon 2000LX EASY	3
BAe 125/800B	49	Citation V Ultra	248	Falcon 20-5	14
BAe 125/800SP	1	Citation VI	41	Falcon 20-5B	17
BAe 125/C-29A	4	Citation VII	119	Falcon 20C	67
BAe 125/CC3	6	Citation X	292	Falcon 20C-5	6
BAe 146	14	CitationJet	354	Falcon 20D	23
BAe U-125A	32	CitationJet CJ-1	201	Falcon 20D-5	2
BBJ	89	CitationJet CJ1+	66	Falcon 20D-5B	2
BBJ2	20	CitationJet CJ-2	241	Falcon 20DC	12
Beechjet 400	62	CitationJet CJ2+	95	Falcon 20E	31
Beechjet 400A	350	CitationJet CJ-3	234	Falcon 20E-5	8
Beechjet 400T	13	CitationJet CJ-4	1	Falcon 20E-5B	5
C-135B	5	Compair Jet	1	Falcon 20ECM	2
C-9C	3	Corvette	17	Falcon 20EW	20
Caravelle 3	1	DC 10	1	Falcon 20F	47
Challenger 300	198	DC 8	13	Falcon 20F-5	31
Challenger 5000	1	DC 9	14	Falcon 20F-5B	32
Challenger 600	5	Diamond 1	16	Falcon 20GF	1
Challenger 600S	74	Diamond 1A	63	Falcon 20SNA	1
Challenger 601	64	Diamond D-Jet	2	Falcon 20SP	1
Challenger 601-3A	133	Do 328-310 ENVOY	1	Falcon 50	238
Challenger 601-3R	59	Dominie T1	3	Falcon 50 SURMAR	4
Challenger 604	363	Dominie T2	7	Falcon 50-4	3
Challenger 605	45	Dornier Do328JET	18	Falcon 50-40	1
Challenger 700	1	Eclipse 500	7	Falcon 50EX	102
Challenger 800	16	Eclipse Concept Jet	1	Falcon 7X	25

Model	Count	Model	Count	Model	Count
Falcon 900	60	Hawker 800XP2	41	Learjet 25G	3
Falcon 900A	1	Hawker 800XPi	46	Learjet 25XR	15
Falcon 900B	117	Hawker 850XP	94	Learjet 28	5
Falcon 900C	24	Hawker 850XPi	2	Learjet 29	4
Falcon 900DX	20	Hawker 900XP	51	Learjet 31	38
Falcon 900EX	118	Hawker U-125A	1	Learjet 31A	206
Falcon 900EX EASY	83	HFB 320	6	Learjet 35	59
Fokker 100	4	HS 125/	4	Learjet 35A	480
Fokker 70	5	HS 125/1A	10	Learjet 35ZR	1
Galaxy-1126	13	HS 125/1A-522	10	Learjet 36	15
Gardian	5	HS 125/1B	1	Learjet 36A	35
Global 5000	61	HS 125/1B-S522	1	Learjet 40	97
Global Express	205	HS 125/3A	3	Learjet 40XR	4
Global Express XRS	8	HS 125/3A-R	1	Learjet 45	341
Grob G-180 SPn	2	HS 125/3A-RA	8	Learjet 45XR	14
Guardian HU-25A	12	HS 125/3B	5	Learjet 55	117
Guardian HU-25B	4	HS 125/3B-RA	1	Learjet 55B	8
Guardian HU-25C	9	HS 125/3B-RC	3	Learjet 55C	14
Guardian HU-25D	1	HS 125/400	1	Learjet 60	328
Gulfstream 2	67	HS 125/400A	21	Learjet 60XR	10
Gulfstream 2B	41	HS 125/400B	5	Learjet C-21A	58
Gulfstream 2TT	15	HS 125/403A	1	Learjet U36A	4
Gulfstream 3	179	HS 125/403B	7	McDonnell 220	1
Gulfstream 4	192	HS 125/600A	24	MD-11	2
Gulfstream 4/Tp 102	1	HS 125/600B	9	MD-87	5
Gulfstream 4/Tp 102B	2	HS 125/700A	172	MS 760 Paris	45
Gulfstream 4/Tp 102C	1	HS 125/700A-2	1	PD 808	3
Gulfstream 4SP	291	HS 125/700B	28	Phenom 100	5
Gulfstream C-20A	2	HS 125/731	56	Phenom 300	3
Gulfstream C-20B	5	HS 125/F3A	1	Regional Jet	3
Gulfstream C-20C	2	HS 125/F3B-RA	2	Sabre-	8
Gulfstream C-20D	3	HS 125/F400A	8	Sabre T-39N	14
Gulfstream C-20E	2	HS 125/F400B	2	Sabre-40	22
Gulfstream C-20F	1	HS 125/F403A	1	Sabre-40/Tp 86	1
Gulfstream C-20G	6	HS 125/F403B	2	Sabre-40A	29
Gulfstream C-37A	11	HS 125/F600A	10	Sabre-40R	4
Gulfstream C-37B	1	HS 125/F600B	3	Sabre-50	1
Gulfstream G100	29	Javelin 100	1	Sabre-60	87
Gulfstream G150	49	Jayhawk T-1A	179	Sabre-60A	9
Gulfstream G200	170	Jet Commander	15	Sabre-65	75
Gulfstream G300	12	Jet Commander-A	3	Sabre-75	3
Gulfstream G300MPA	2	Jet Commander-B	4	Sabre-75A	43
Gulfstream G350	13	Jet Commander-C	1	Sabre-80A	6
Gulfstream G400	22	JetStar	1	Sabreliner CT-39A	13
Gulfstream G450	121	JetStar 2	33	Sabreliner CT-39B	2
Gulfstream G500	5	JetStar-6	3	Sabreliner CT-39E	3
Gulfstream G550	199	JetStar-731	20	Sabreliner CT-39G	8
Gulfstream II SP	100	JetStar-8	7	Sabreliner T-39A	1
Gulfstream SRA-1	3	Learjet	4	Sabreliner T-39D	4
Gulfstream U-4	5	Learjet 23	23	Sentinel R1	5
Gulfstream V	180	Learjet 24	37	SJ 30-2	6
Gulfstream V-SP	1	Learjet 24A	7	Spectrum 33 VLJ	1
HA-420 HondaJet	1	Learjet 24B	30	Sport-Jet	1
Hawker	3	Learjet 24D	57	TriStar 100	2
Hawker 1000	12	Learjet 24E	15	TriStar 500	4
Hawker 4000	20	Learjet 24F	10	Vantage	1
Hawker 400XP	211	Learjet 24XR	13	VFW 614	1
Hawker 750	6	Learjet 25	38	Westwind-1123	13
Hawker 800	20	Learjet 25B	74	Westwind-1124	155
Hawker 800SP	36	Learjet 25C	14	Westwind-1124N	3
Hawker 800XP	380	Learjet 25D	137	Westwind-Two	84

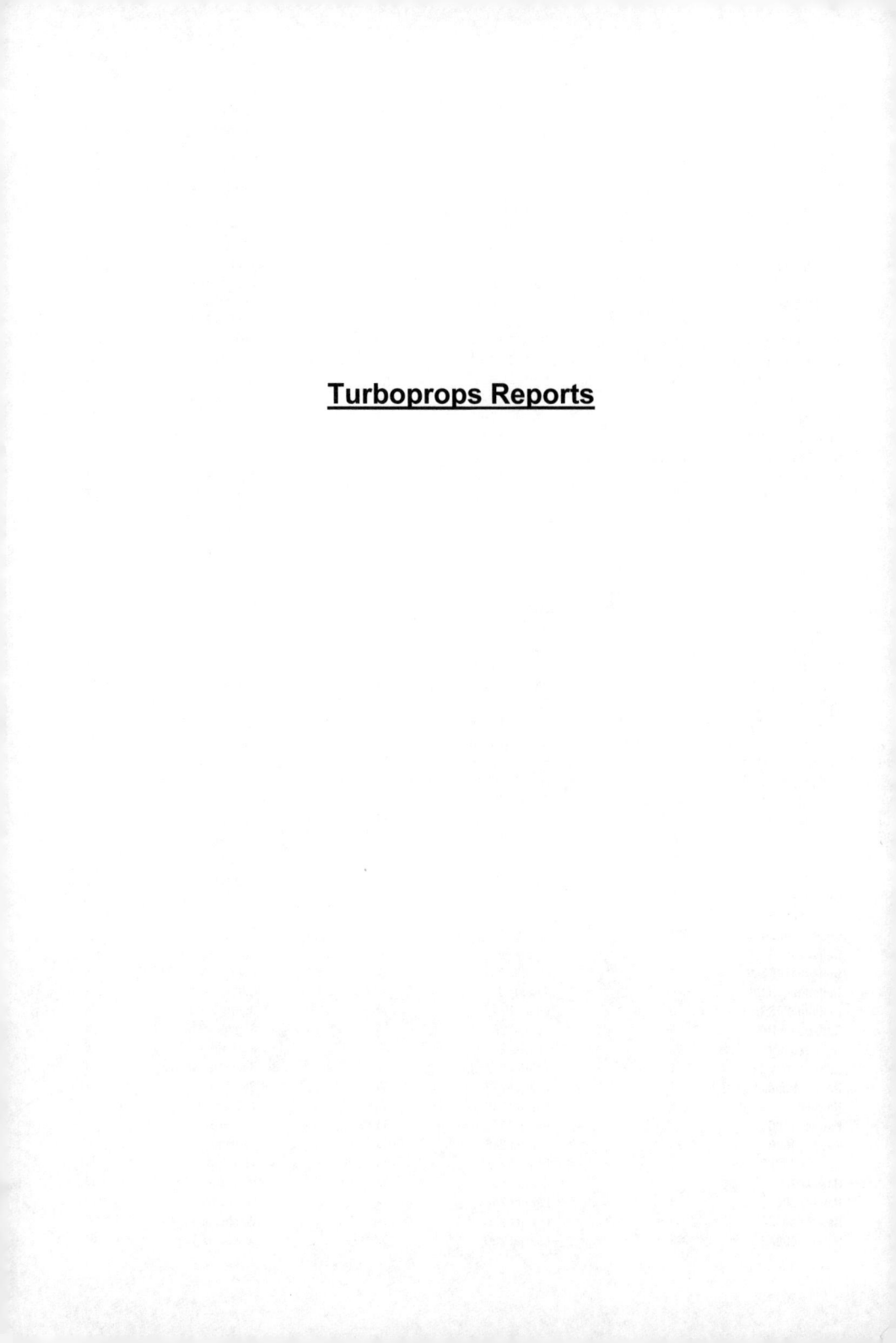

Turboprops Reports

Business TurboProps - By Country within Continent includes Civil And Military

Total Props 10839

Africa

7T =	ALGERIA		14
D2 =	ANGOLA		31
A2 =	BOTSWANA		12
XT =	BURKINA FASO		3
TJ =	CAMEROON		2
TL =	CENTRAL AFRICAN REPUBLIC		1
TT =	CHAD		1
TN =	CONGO BRAZZAVILLE		2
9Q =	CONGO KINSHASA		8
SU =	EGYPT		4
E3 =	ERITREA		1
TR =	GABON		3
TU =	IVORY COAST		1
5Y =	KENYA		35
5A =	LIBYA		5
5R =	MADAGASCAR		1
7Q =	MALAWI		1
TZ =	MALI		1
5T =	MAURITANIA		2
3B =	MAURITIUS		1
CN =	MOROCCO		18
C9 =	MOZAMBIQUE		4
V5 =	NAMIBIA		14
5N =	NIGERIA		10
S9 =	SAO TOME & PRINCIPE		4
6V =	SENEGAL		1
ZS =	SOUTH AFRICA		204
ST =	SUDAN		4
5H =	TANZANIA		8
5V =	TOGO		3
5X =	UGANDA		1
9J =	ZAMBIA		8
Z =	ZIMBABWE		8

Total for Continent 416

Australasia

VH =	AUSTRALIA		205
ZK =	NEW ZEALAND		15
P2 =	PAPUA NEW GUINEA		8

Total for Continent 228

Central America

P4 =	ARUBA		2
C6 =	BAHAMAS		2
VP- =	CAYMAN ISLANDS		1
TI =	COSTA RICA		10
HI =	DOMINICAN REPUBLIC		4
YS =	EL SALVADOR		2
TG =	GUATEMALA		26
HR =	HONDURAS		5
6Y =	JAMAICA		1
PJ =	NETHERLANDS ANTILLES		3
YN =	NICARAGUA		1
HP =	PANAMA		53
VQ =	TURKS & CAICOS ISLANDS		1

Total for Continent 111

Europe

OE =	AUSTRIA		16
OO =	BELGIUM		15
LZ =	BULGARIA		5
9A =	CROATIA		4
5B =	CYPRUS		1
OK =	CZECH REPUBLIC / CZECHIA		13
OY =	DENMARK		29
EI =	EIRE		3
OH =	FINLAND		10
F =	FRANCE		212
D =	GERMANY		159
G =	GREAT BRITAIN		85
SX =	GREECE		15
HA =	HUNGARY		3
TF =	ICELAND		4
M =	ISLE OF MAN		4
I =	ITALY		56
YL =	LATVIA		1
LY =	LITHUANIA		1
LX =	LUXEMBOURG		24
3A =	MONACO		2
PH =	NETHERLANDS		25
LN =	NORWAY		25
SP =	POLAND		8
CS =	PORTUGAL		3
YR =	ROMANIA		3
RA =	RUSSIA / RUSSIAN FEDERATION		4
YU =	SERBIA		4
OM =	SLOVAKIA		2
S5 =	SLOVENIA		2
EC =	SPAIN		41
SE =	SWEDEN		30
HB =	SWITZERLAND		75
TC =	TURKEY		17
UR =	UKRAINE		4

Total for Continent   905

Far East

S2	=	BANGLADESH	2
XU	=	CAMBODIA	1
B	=	CHINA	11
B-	=	CHINA - HONG KONG	2
B	=	CHINA - TAIWAN	3
VT	=	INDIA	81
PK	=	INDONESIA	24
JA	=	JAPAN	100
UN	=	KAZAKHSTAN	3
HL	=	KOREA	7
9M	=	MALAYSIA	9
AP	=	PAKISTAN	11
RP	=	PHILIPPINES	26
S7	=	SEYCHELLES	3
4R	=	SRI LANKA	2
HS	=	THAILAND	26
VN	=	VIETNAM	1

Total for Continent   312

Middle East

A9	=	BAHRAIN	1
EP	=	IRAN	24
4X	=	ISRAEL	29
JY	=	JORDAN	1
A4	=	OMAN	1
HZ	=	SAUDI ARABIA	3
A6	=	UNITED ARAB EMIRATES	6

Total for Continent   65

North America

VP-	=	BERMUDA	5
C	=	CANADA	506
XA	=	MEXICO	269
N	=	USA	6911

Total for Continent   7691

South America

LV	=	ARGENTINA	107
CP	=	BOLIVIA	13
PP	=	BRAZIL	397
CC	=	CHILE	33
HK	=	COLOMBIA	179
HC	=	ECUADOR	18
ZP	=	PARAGUAY	16
OB	=	PERU	30
CX	=	URUGUAY	4
YV	=	VENEZUELA	314

Total for Continent   1111

Totals by Type Biz Turboprops

Model	Count	Model	Count	Model	Count
120ER Brasilia	13	King Air 350	558	Mitsubishi MU-2J	51
120RT(VC-97)Brasilia	3	King Air 350 (LR-2)	5	Mitsubishi MU-2K	44
2000 Starship	1	King Air 350C	1	Mitsubishi MU-2L	27
2000A Starship	4	King Air 350ER	1	Mitsubishi MU-2M	19
680T Turbo Commander	7	King Air 90	60	Mitsubishi MU-2N	27
680V Turbo Commander	31	King Air A100	121	Mitsubishi MU-2P	33
680W Turbo Commander	31	King Air A90	248	MU-2 Marquise	102
681 Turbo Commander	27	King Air B100	126	MU-2 Solitaire	44
681B Turbo Commander	16	King Air B200	1058	P-180 Avanti	100
AP68TP-600 Viator	1	King Air B200C	48	P-180 Avanti II	44
ATR 42	5	King Air B200CT	9	PA-31T Cheyenne 1	182
BAe HS 748-2A	3	King Air B200GT	30	PA-31T Cheyenne 1A	17
BAe Jetstream 31	8	King Air B200S	7	PA-31T Cheyenne II	400
BAe Jetstream 32	1	King Air B200T	18	PA-42 Cheyenne 400LS	40
BAe Jetstream 41	8	King Air B300	7	PA-42 Cheyenne III	81
Beech 1900C	9	King Air B300C	20	PA-42 Cheyenne IIIA	58
Beech 1900C-1	9	King Air B90	133	PA-46 Turbo Malibu	1
Beech 1900D	38	King Air C-12A	3	PA-46-400TP Meridian	2
Beech C-12J	1	King Air C-12C	91	PA-46-500TP Meridian	325
CASA 212-200	2	King Air C-12D	29	PC-12 Spectre	1
CASA 212-300	1	King Air C-12F	57	Pilatus PC-12	75
Cheyenne II-XL	77	King Air C-12J	6	Pilatus PC-12/45	498
Cheyenne T-1040	10	King Air C-12L	3	Pilatus PC-12/47	201
Conquest 1	208	King Air C-12R	26	Pilatus PC-12/47E	1
Conquest II	322	King Air C-12U	9	Pilatus PC-12M	1
DHC 6-300	4	King Air C90	442	Pilatus PC-12M Eagle	1
DHC 7-103	1	King Air C90-1	40	Reims/Cessna F406	86
DHC 8-102	1	King Air C90A	225	Rockwell 690	55
DHC 8-202	4	King Air C90B	428	Rockwell 690A	191
Dornier 228-100	1	King Air C90GT	113	Rockwell 690AT	1
Dornier 228-201	1	King Air C90SE	2	Rockwell 690B	195
Dornier 228-212	4	King Air E90	299	SA-226AT Merlin 4	12
Dornier 328-100	6	King Air F90	194	SA-226AT Merlin 4A	27
Dornier 328-110	3	King Air F90-1	30	SA-226T Merlin 3	30
Dornier 328-130	1	King Air JC-12C	2	SA-226T Merlin 3A	34
Fairchild F-27F	3	King Air JC-12D	1	SA-226T Merlin 3B	61
Fokker 50	2	King Air LC-90	5	SA-227AT Merlin 4C	43
Fokker 60UTA-N	2	King Air RC-12D	19	SA-227TT Merlin 300	6
Fokker F 27-200	1	King Air RC-12G	3	SA-227TT Merlin 3C	25
Grob G160 Ranger	1	King Air RC-12H	5	SA-227TT Merlin 4C	2
Gulfstream 1	78	King Air RC-12K	8	SA-26AT Merlin 2B	50
Gulfstream 1000	95	King Air RC-12N	13	SA-26T Merlin 2A	11
Gulfstream 1000B	9	King Air RC-12P	12	SAAB 2000	7
Gulfstream 1C	2	King Air TC90	26	SAAB 340A	4
Gulfstream 840	109	King Air U-21J	5	SAAB 340B/Tp 100	2
Gulfstream 900	39	King Air UC-12B	41	SAAB 340B-SAR	2
Gulfstream 980	79	King Air UC-12F	11	TBM 700	106
Ibis Ae 270P Spirit	4	King Air UC-12M	11	TBM 700A	4
Jetcruzer 500	1	King Air UC-90	1	TBM 700B	98
Kestrel F1C3	1	King Air/Catpass 250	33	TBM 700C	2
King Air 100	75	Kodiak 100	1	TBM 700C2	102
King Air 1300	15	Mitsubishi LR-1	13	TBM 850	100
King Air 200	728	Mitsubishi MU-2B	8	Xingu 121A	10
King Air 200C	36	Mitsubishi MU-2D	4	Xingu 121E (VU-9)	8
King Air 200T	24	Mitsubishi MU-2E	5	Xingu II 121A1	7
King Air 300	216	Mitsubishi MU-2F	49		
King Air 300LW	21	Mitsubishi MU-2G	11		

Biz-Jet Database

If you need more information then call us for a quote.

We can supply a database updated monthly or a simple report.

Demo available to download on
www.buchairuk.co.uk

Data Includes:

Registration
Registration Country
Construction Number
Aircraft Type
Engine Manufacturer
Engine Model
Year of manufacturer
Base of Operation
Operator/Owners Name
Operator/Owners Address
Contact
Telephone Number
Fax Number
Purchase date
History of Aircraft

BUCHair UK Ltd, 78 High Street,
Reigate, Surrey, RH2 9AP
Tele: +44 (0)1737 224747   Fax: +44 (0)1737 226777
Email sales@buchairuk.co.uk

VLJ - By Country

C	=	**CANADA**			*Total*	**3**

Civil

☐ C-FPTM	07	Diamond D-Jet	0002	Diamond Air, London, ON.	
☐ C-GROL	07	Epic Elite	001J	Aircraft Resources Canada Ltd. Calgary, AB. (Ff 7 Jun 07).	
☐ C-GVLJ	06	Diamond D-Jet	0001	Diamond Air, London, ON. (Ff 18 Apr 06).	

D	=	**GERMANY**			*Total*	**2**

Civil

| ☐ D-IEGO | 07 | Citation Mustang | 510-0048 | Triple Alpha Luftfahrt GmbH. Duesseldorf. | N..... |
| ☐ D-ISRM | 07 | Citation Mustang | 510-0035 | Inovex Charter GmbH. Pforzheim. | N4202M |

G	=	**GREAT BRITAIN**			*Total*	**2**

Civil

| ☐ G-EXLT* | 08 | Citation Mustang | ... | FlyExAlt Ltd. | N..... |
| ☐ G-LEAI | 08 | Citation Mustang | 510-0052 | London Executive Aviation Ltd. Stansted. | N..... |

N	=	**USA**			*Total*	**197**

Civil

☐ N3MT	08	Eclipse EA500	000135	Eclipse Aviation Corp. Albuquerque, NM.	
☐ N4FF	06	Citation Mustang	510-0007	Furtco/Chalk Hill Winery, Healdsburg, Ca.	N510FF
☐ N17AE	06	Eclipse EA500	000017	Air Repair Inc. Keene, NH.	
☐ N21EK	08	Eclipse EA500	000133	Eclipse Aviation Corp. Albuquerque, NM.	
☐ N22EM	07	Citation Mustang	510-0047	MM Air Inc/MMI Hotel Management, Flowood, Ms.	N.....
☐ N23PJ	07	Eclipse EA500	000065	Pegasus Jet LLC. Scottsdale, Az.	
☐ N24YY	07	Citation Mustang	510-0010	Oakmont Management LLC. Burbank, Ca.	N654EA
☐ N33NP	07	Citation Mustang	510-0037	Cessna Finance Corp. Wichita, Ks.	N.....
☐ N38DA	07	Eclipse EA500	000083	Baccarat Air LLC. Missoula, Mt.	
☐ N50EJ	07	Eclipse EA500	000087	PS Aviation LLC. Concord, Ca.	
☐ N50HS	06	Citation Mustang	510-0013	Van Voorst Lumber Co. Union Hill, Il.	N.....
☐ N54KJ	07	Eclipse EA500	000091	SWU LLC. Boston, Ma.	
☐ N54PV	07	Citation Mustang	510-0028	California Natural Products, Sacramento, Ca.	N.....
☐ N55BX	07	Eclipse EA500	000029	Boxer Property Management Corp. Houston, Tx.	
☐ N62RC	06	Eclipse EA500	000043	Cizek Partners LLC/Cizek Homes, Omaha-Millard, Ne.	
☐ N67NV	08	Eclipse EA500	000131	Eclipse Aviation Corp. Albuquerque, NM.	
☐ N71MT	07	Eclipse EA500	000069	MAG Aviation Sales/MAG Management Corp. Akron, Oh.	
☐ N75EA	07	Eclipse EA500	000116	Eclipse Aviation Corp. Albuquerque, NM.	
☐ N75ES	07	Citation Mustang	510-0024	TechSpec Inc. Latrobe, Pa.	N.....
☐ N80HQ	07	Citation Mustang	510-0021	Jane Air Inc/Elizabeth Howell, Southampton, UK.	N.....
☐ N80TF	07	Eclipse EA500	000032	Circuit Breakers Sales Co. Denton, Tx.	
☐ N104TG	05	Javelin 100	001	Aviation Technology Group, Englewood, Co. (Ff 30 Sep 05).	
☐ N105LB	07	Eclipse EA500	000118	Eclipse Aviation Corp. Albuquerque, NM.	
☐ N109DJ	06	Eclipse EA500	000006	DayJet, Gainesville, Fl.	
☐ N110DJ	06	Eclipse EA500	000007	DayJet, Gainesville, Fl.	
☐ N112EA	07	Eclipse EA500	000038	Freeway ApS. Viborg, Denmark.	
☐ N112EJ	07	Eclipse EA500	000112	Eclipse Aviation Corp. Albuquerque, NM.	
☐ N115DJ	07	Eclipse EA500	000020	DayJet, Gainesville, Fl.	
☐ N116DJ	07	Eclipse EA500	000021	DayJet, Gainesville, Fl.	
☐ N117EA	07	Eclipse EA500	000104	Eclipse Aviation Corp. Albuquerque, NM.	
☐ N117UH	07	Eclipse EA500	000117	Eclipse Aviation Corp. Albuquerque, NM.	
☐ N119DJ	07	Eclipse EA500	000022	DayJet, Gainesville, Fl.	
☐ N126DJ	06	Eclipse EA500	000002	DayJet, Gainesville, Fl.	
☐ N130DJ	07	Eclipse EA500	000023	DayJet, Gainesville, Fl.	
☐ N131DJ	07	Eclipse EA500	000033	DayJet, Gainesville, Fl.	
☐ N132DJ	07	Eclipse EA500	000034	DayJet, Gainesville, Fl.	
☐ N134DJ	07	Eclipse EA500	000035	DayJet, Gainesville, Fl.	
☐ N135DJ	07	Eclipse EA500	000036	DayJet, Gainesville, Fl.	
☐ N136DJ	07	Eclipse EA500	000037	DayJet, Gainesville, Fl.	
☐ N136EA	08	Eclipse EA500	000136	Eclipse Aviation Corp. Albuquerque, NM.	
☐ N139DJ	07	Eclipse EA500	000054	DayJet, Gainesville, Fl.	
☐ N141DJ	07	Eclipse EA500	000055	DayJet, Gainesville, Fl.	
☐ N142DJ	07	Eclipse EA500	000056	DayJet, Gainesville, Fl.	
☐ N145DJ	07	Eclipse EA500	000057	DayJet, Gainesville, Fl.	
☐ N146DJ	07	Eclipse EA500	000058	DayJet, Gainesville, Fl.	
☐ N147DJ	07	Eclipse EA500	000059	DayJet, Boca Raton, Fl.	

| *Reg* | *Yr* | *Type* | *c/n* | *Owner/Operator* | *Prev Regn* |

Reg	Yr	Type	c/n	Owner/Operator	Prev Regn
☐ N148DJ	07	Eclipse EA500	000061	DayJet, Boca Raton, Fl.	
☐ N150DJ	07	Eclipse EA500	000062	DayJet, Boca Raton, Fl.	
☐ N152DJ	07	Eclipse EA500	000071	DayJet, Gainesville, Fl.	
☐ N153DJ	07	Eclipse EA500	000072	DayJet, Gainesville, Fl.	
☐ N156DJ	07	Eclipse EA500	000073	DayJet, Tallahassee, Fl.	
☐ N158DJ	07	Eclipse EA500	000074	DayJet, Gainesville, Fl.	
☐ N160DJ	07	Eclipse EA500	000077	DayJet, Gainesville, Fl.	
☐ N161DJ	07	Eclipse EA500	000078	DayJet, Gainesville, Fl.	
☐ N162DJ	07	Eclipse EA500	000079	DayJet, Tallahassee, Fl.	
☐ N163DJ	07	Eclipse EA500	000081	DayJet, Gainesville, Fl.	
☐ N164MW	07	Eclipse EA500	000122	Eclipse Aviation Corp. Albuquerque, NM.	
☐ N168TT	07	Eclipse EA500	000042	James Teng & Sons Inc. Wilmington, De.	
☐ N175JE	07	Eclipse EA500	000111	Eclipse Aviation Corp. Albuquerque, NM.	
☐ N197AR	07	Eclipse EA500	000114	Eclipse Aviation Corp. Albuquerque, NM.	
☐ N199ML	06	Citation Mustang	510-0002	199ML LLC/Power Equipment Co. Jeffco, Co.	N510KS
☐ N218JT	07	Eclipse EA500	000047	John Travolta/Constellation Productions Inc. Ocala, Fl.	
☐ N227G	07	Eclipse EA500	000124	Eclipse Aviation Corp. Albuquerque, NM.	
☐ N229BW	06	Eclipse EA500	000004	SPJ Aircraft LLC. Portland, In.	
☐ N233MT	07	Eclipse EA500	000093	Maran Desarrollos SA. Calexico, Ca.	(N457TB)
☐ N245MU	06	Citation Mustang	510-0006	MUK Aviation Corp/Gutierrez & Assocs. Opa Locka, Fl.	N.....
☐ N261DC	08	Eclipse EA500	000127	Eclipse Aviation Corp. Albuquerque, NM.	
☐ N277G	07	Eclipse EA500	000102	Eclipse Aviation Corp. Albuquerque, NM.	
☐ N316CP	06	Eclipse EA500	000089	Vinci Aviation Co. Fort Lauderdale, Fl.	N44EJ
☐ N317BH	07	Eclipse EA500	000013	Efficient Marketing LLC. St George, Ut.	
☐ N317DJ	07	Eclipse EA500	000095	D & J Aviation LLC. Las Vegas, Nv.	
☐ N320LA*	06	Eclipse EA500	000016	Transport Partners LLC. Bedford, Ma.	N15ND
☐ N322JG	08	Eclipse EA500	000130	Eclipse Aviation Corp. Albuquerque, NM.	
☐ N322LA	06	Spectrum 33 VLJ	0001	W/o Spanish Fork, Ut. USA. 25 Jul 06.	
☐ N325RR	06	Citation Mustang	510-0025	SJS Jet Aviation/Sterling Group Worldwide LLC. Concord, NC	N.....
☐ N327CM	07	Citation Mustang	510-0027	Cessna Aircraft Co. Wichita, Ks.	N.....
☐ N333MY	07	Eclipse EA500	000103	Eclipse Aviation Corp. Albuquerque, NM.	
☐ N350SJ	06	Sport-Jet	001	Robert Bornhofen, Monument, Co. (Ff 11 May 06).	
☐ N355BM	07	Eclipse EA500	000092	BL Aircraft Services Inc. Bloomfield Hills, Mi.	
☐ N370EA	08	Eclipse EA500	000125	Eclipse Aviation Corp. Albuquerque, NM.	
☐ N370EJ	07	Epic Victory	001	RL4U LLC/Epic Aircraft, Bend, Or. (Ff 6 Jul 07).	
☐ N370P	07	Eclipse EA500	000066	OurPlane Corp. Buffalo, NY.	
☐ N382EA	07	Eclipse EA500	000082	Eclipse Aviation Corp. Albuquerque, NM.	
☐ N396DM	06	Citation Mustang	510-0008	David Miller, Dallas, Tx.	N.....
☐ N403CM	06	Citation Mustang	510-0003	Mustang Management Group LLC/Scott Aircraft Inc. Fresno, Ca.	N.....
☐ N404CM	06	Citation Mustang	510-0004	FSI Leasing LLC. Centre Hall, Pa.	
☐ N406CM	06	Citation Mustang	510-0015	TVPX Inc. Concord, Ma.	N.....
☐ N416CM	06	Citation Mustang	510-0016	Caroom Aviation LLC. Las Vegas, Nv.	N.....
☐ N417CG	07	Eclipse EA500	000094	Kingsway Aviation LLC. Valdosta, Ga.	
☐ N420HA	03	HA-420 HondaJet	P001	Honda Aircraft Co. Greensboro, NC. (Ff 3 Dec 03)	
☐ N429CC	07	Eclipse EA500	000060	MBA Graphics of Delaware Inc. Lakeland, Fl.	
☐ N443HC	07	Citation Mustang	510-0012	Hill Construction Corp. San Juan, PR.	N.....
☐ N444RL	07	Eclipse EA500	000040	A-Ron Resources LLC. Van Nuys, Ca.	
☐ N456MF	07	Eclipse EA500	000050	Big Fork Logistics LLC. Big Fork, Mt.	
☐ N457TB	07	Eclipse EA500	000088	Hamster LLC/Dr Juris Bunkis, Rancho Santa Margarita, Ca.	
☐ N464PG	07	Eclipse EA500	000096	Grupo Provivenda SA. Panama City, Panama.	
☐ N489JC	07	Eclipse EA500	000044	J C Cheek Contractors Inc. Kosciusko, Ms.	
☐ N500CD	07	Eclipse EA500	000045	Tradewinds Management/Continental Development Corp. Blaine	
☐ N500DG	08	Eclipse EA500	000129	Eclipse Aviation Corp. Albuquerque, NM.	
☐ N500EA	02	Eclipse 500	EX500-100	Wfu. Retired after 55 flights with TT 54 hours on 22 Oct 03.	
☐ N500UK	07	Eclipse EA500	000051	EA51 Inc. Blackpool, UK.	
☐ N500VK	06	Eclipse EA500	000010	VK Aircraft Sales LLC. St Petersburg, Fl.	
☐ N501DX	07	Eclipse EA500	000110	Eclipse Aviation Corp. Albuquerque, NM.	
☐ N502EA	04	Eclipse 500	EX500-101	Wfu. Airframe not completed, subsequently painted N500EA.	
☐ N502EA	05	Eclipse 500	EX500-103	Eclipse Aviation Corp. Albuquerque, NM.	
☐ N502ET	07	Eclipse EA500	000052	Everair LLC. Niagara Falls, NY.	
☐ N502LT	07	Eclipse EA500	000027	Leader Technologies Inc. Albuquerque, NM.	
☐ N502TS	07	Eclipse EA500	000097	HTS CAP SA. Luxembourg.	
☐ N503EA	04	Eclipse 500	EX500-108	Eclipse Aviation Corp. Albuquerque, NM.	
☐ N504EA	05	Eclipse 500	EX500-109	Eclipse Aviation Corp. Albuquerque, NM.	
☐ N504RS	06	Eclipse EA500	000005	Gen Cor LLC. Goose Creek, SC.	

Reg	Yr	Type	c/n	Owner/Operator	Prev Regn
N505EA	05	Eclipse 500	EX500-106	Eclipse Aviation Corp. Albuquerque, NM.	
N506EA	05	Eclipse 500	EX500-107	Eclipse Aviation Corp. Albuquerque, NM.	
N508JA	06	Eclipse EA500	000001	Jet-Alliance/David Crowe LLC. Westlake Village, Ca.	
N509JA	07	Eclipse EA500	000084	Jet Alliance LLC. Westlake Village, Ca.	
N510CE	05	Citation Mustang	510-0001	Cessna Aircraft Co. Wichita, Ks. (Ff 29 Aug 05).	
N510GH	07	Citation Mustang	510-0036	Sigma Partners, San Ramon, Ca.	N.....
N510GJ	08	Citation Mustang	510-0083	Cessna Aircraft Co. Wichita, Ks.	N.....
N510JH	07	Citation Mustang	510-0051	Cessna Aircraft Co. Wichita, Ks.	N.....
N510VV	06	Citation Mustang	510-0014	Mustang V S A, San Jose, Costa Rica.	N.....
N510WC*	06	Citation Mustang	510-0017	Black Knight Air Inc. Farmington, Mo.	N17MU
N513EA	07	Eclipse EA500	000009	RiRo Ventures Ltd. Road Town, Tortola, BVI.	
N514EA	07	Eclipse EA500	000053	Eclipse Aviation Corp. Albuquerque, NM.	
N515MP	07	Eclipse EA500	000015	Next Jet AB. Stockholm, Sweden.	
N516EA	07	Eclipse EA500	000106	Eclipse Aviation Corp. Albuquerque, NM.	
N519EJ	06	Eclipse EA500	000019	Robert H Yarbrough, Pagosa Springs, Co.	
N522DK	07	Eclipse EA500	000105	Eclipse Aviation Corp. Albuquerque, NM.	
N528DM	07	Citation Mustang	510-0031	Archer Daniels Midland Co. Decatur, Il.	N.....
N528EA	08	Eclipse EA500	000128	Eclipse Aviation Corp. Albuquerque, NM.	
N531EA	07	Eclipse EA500	000031	Echo Aviation LLC. Ridgeland, Ms.	
N539RM	07	Eclipse EA500	000101	Lakeshore Leasing Ltd. Gross Pointe Shore, Mi.	
N541LB	07	Eclipse EA500	000041	Beathe Jet Hawaii LLC. Anchorage, Ak.	
N546BW	06	Eclipse EA500	000025	Ecipse 25 LLC/Miller Development, Charleston, SC.	
N549AF	06	Eclipse EA500	000049	Archie Fraser, Edmonton, AB. Canada.	
N551WH	07	Citation Mustang	510-0055	Cessna Aircraft Co. Wichita, Ks.	N.....
N561EA	07	Eclipse EA500	000024	RFC Aviation LLC. Telluride, Co.	
N568PB	07	Eclipse EA500	000067	Parish Financial Services Inc. Covington, La.	
N570EA	07	Eclipse EA500	000070	Eclipse Vision Aircraft/Micnic Eclipse LLC. Brooksville, Fl.	
N570RG	06	Eclipse EA500	000048	Kingsley Management Corp. Provo, Ut.	
N575CC	07	Eclipse EA500	000075	Covington Associates, Boston, Ma.	
N576EA	07	Eclipse EA500	000076	Eclipse Aviation Corp. Albuquerque, NM.	
N580WC	07	Eclipse EA500	000080	Oxley Aviation P/L. Coopers Plains, QLD. Australia.	
N591ES	07	Citation Mustang	510-0042	JetCom Aviation Inc. Fort Lauderdale, Fl.	N.....
N598EA	07	Eclipse EA500	000098	Jet Squared LLC/Pathway Com-Tel, Joshua, Tx.	
N600DE	06	Citation Mustang	510-0005	GOODE Ski Technologies, Ogden, Ut.	N.....
N612KB	06	Eclipse EA500	000026	Kiernan Companies LLC. Coronado, Ca.	
N615RH	07	Eclipse EA500	000068	Heidrich Aviation LLC. Bloomfield Hills, Mi.	(N370P)
N651FC	06	Eclipse EA500	000012	Rolf Illsley Revocable Trust, San Rafael, Ca.	
N696NA	07	Eclipse EA500	000123	Eclipse Aviation Corp. Albuquerque, NM.	
N700AJ	03	Adam A700	0001	Wfu. Cx USA 8 Jun 07.	N700JJ
N700LJ	06	Adam A700	0002	Adam Aircraft Industries Inc. Englewood, Co. (Ff 6 Feb 06).	
N703AJ	06	Adam A700	0003	Adam Aircraft Industries Inc. Englewood, Co. (Ff 9 Apr 07).	
N704AJ	07	Adam A700	0004	Adam Aircraft Industries Inc. Englewood, Co.	
N705PT	06	Eclipse EA500	000014	SABENA Flight Academy NV. Brussels, Belgium.	
N706PT	07	Eclipse EA500	000107	Eclipse Aviation Corp. Albuquerque, NM.	
N717HD	07	Eclipse EA500	000113	Gray & Co. Metairie, La.	
N717LK	07	Eclipse EA500	000064	Kolssak Jets Inc. Wheeling, Il.	
N725JB	07	Citation Mustang	510-0030	Sweatmore IV LLC/DMB Associates Inc. Scottsdale, Az.	N.....
N727HD	07	Eclipse EA500	000115	Gray & Co. Metairie, La.	
N761JP	07	Citation Mustang	510-0045	Air1 Aviation LLC. Duesseldorf, Germany.	N.....
N768JF	07	Eclipse EA500	000030	Milestown Services LLC. Newport Coast, Ca.	
N777VE	07	Eclipse EA500	000011	Straubel Investments LLC. Davenport, Ia.	
N777ZY	07	Eclipse EA500	000109	Eclipse Aviation Corp. Albuquerque, NM.	
N778TC	07	Eclipse EA500	000085	Jetko LLC/Terry Tuell Concrete Inc. Fresno, Ca.	
N778VW	07	Eclipse EA500	000063	M & M Aircraft Sales Co. Indian Harbour Beach, Fl.	
N800EJ	08	Eclipse EA500	000134	Eclipse Aviation Corp. Albuquerque, NM.	
N812MJ	07	Eclipse EA500	000108	Eclipse Aviation Corp. Albuquerque, NM.	
N814WS	07	Citation Mustang	510-0032	Walter Scott & Partners Ltd. Edinburgh, Scotland	N4107D
N815WT	07	Eclipse EA500	000119	Eclipse Aviation Corp. Albuquerque, NM.	
N816KD	06	Eclipse EA500	000003	Capital Holdings 182 LLC. Cleburne, Tx.	
N821ND	07	Citation Mustang	510-0038	MSTG 38 LLC. Los Altos Hills, Ca.	N411SW
N827DK	06	Citation Mustang	510-0018	BNP Assocs/Strategic Organizational Management, Danbury, Ct.	N.....
N855MS	07	Eclipse EA500	000121	Eclipse Aviation Corp. Albuquerque, NM.	
N858GS	07	Eclipse EA500	000039	D Gregory Scott, Van Nuys, Ca.	
N875NA	06	Eclipse EA500	000018	Group Four Aviation Partners LLC. Palwaukee, Il.	
N888TF	07	Citation Mustang	510-0023	Winter Park Construction, Sanford, Fl.	N.....

Reg	Yr	Type	c/n	Owner/Operator	Prev Regn
☐ N910SY	07	Citation Mustang	510-0009	Kimball International Transit Inc. Huntingburg, In.	N.....
☐ N911MX	07	Eclipse EA500	000099	Eclipse Aviation Corp. Albuquerque, NM.	
☐ N941NC	06	Eclipse EA500	000008	Dlorah Inc. Rapid City, SD.	
☐ N946CM	07	Citation Mustang	510-0046	Cessna Aircraft Co. Wichita, Ks.	N.....
☐ N953JB	08	Eclipse EA500	000126	Eclipse Aviation Corp. Albuquerque, NM.	
☐ N963JG	07	Eclipse EA500	000028	SABENA Airline Training Center Inc. Mesa, Az.	
☐ N964S	08	Eclipse EA500	000132	Eclipse Aviation Corp. Albuquerque, NM.	
☐ N990NA	07	Eclipse EA500	000086	Cardone Record Services Inc. Mount Prospect, Il.	
☐ N1693L	07	Citation Mustang	510-0026	JDI Holdings LLC. Washington, NJ.	N.....
☐ N1749L	07	Citation Mustang	510-0054	Cessna Aircraft Co. Wichita, Ks.	N.....
☐ N2243W	07	Citation Mustang	510-0011	Bank of Utah, Salt Lake City, Ut. (trustor New Zealand ?).	(VH-SJP)
☐ N2427N	07	Citation Mustang	510-0019	Greenback Holdings LLC. Fort Lauderdale, Fl.	N.....
☐ N2486B	07	Eclipse EA500	000090	S V Air LLC. Palo Alto, Ca.	
☐ N5184U	07	Eclipse Concept Jet	SE-400-001	Swift Engineering Inc. San Clemente, Ca. (Ff 2 Jul 07).	
☐ N6100	07	Eclipse EA500	000046	Four Country LLC/Marc Glassman Inc. Cuyahoga County, Oh.	
☐ N9922F	07	Eclipse EA500	000100	VLJ Express LLC. Eagle, Id.	
☐ N13616	07	Citation Mustang	510-0049	Globe Aero Ltd. Lakeland, Fl.	N.....
☐ N24329	07	Citation Mustang	510-0020	Eastwalk International Inc. Panama.	N.....
☐ N27052	07	Eclipse EA500	000120	Eclipse Aviation Corp. Albuquerque, NM.	
☐ N27369	05	Citation Mustang	712001	Cessna Aircraft Co. Wichita, Ks. (Ff 23 Apr 05).	
☐ N41861	04	Compair Jet	04001	Ronald Lueck, Merritt Island, Fl.	

OE = AUSTRIA Total 1
Civil

| ☐ OE-FID | 07 | Citation Mustang | 510-0040 | Intersky Luftfahrt GmbH. Bregenz. | N4009F |

OY = DENMARK Total 1
Civil

| ☐ OY-LPU | 07 | Citation Mustang | 510-0022 | JAI Aviation ApS. | N4089Y |

PH = NETHERLANDS Total 1
Civil

| ☐ PH-TXI | 07 | Citation Mustang | 510-0050 | Bikkair BV. Rotterdam. | N..... |

PP = BRAZIL Total 10
Civil

☐ PP-MIS	07	Citation Mustang	510-0043		N4030W
☐ PP-NNN*	07	Citation Mustang	510-0041		N4021E
☐ PP-XOG*	08	Phenom 100	50000004	Embraer SA. Sao Jose dos Campos, SP.	
☐ PP-XOH*	08	Phenom 100	50000003	Embraer SA. Sao Jose dos Campos, SP.	
☐ PP-XOJ	07	Phenom 100	50000002	Embraer SA. Sao Jose dos Campos, SP. (Ff 21 Dec 07).	
☐ PP-XOM	07	Phenom 100	50000001	Embraer SA. Sao Jose dos Campos, SP. (Ff 27 Sep 07).	
☐ PP-XPH	07	Phenom 100	50099801	Embraer SA. Sao Jose dos Campos, SP. (Ff 26 Jul 07).	
☐ PP-XVI*	08	Phenom 300	50599801	Embraer SA. Sao Jose dos Campos, SP.	
☐ PP-XVJ*	08	Phenom 300	50500001	Embraer SA. Sao Jose dos Campos, SP.	
☐ PP-XVK*	08	Phenom 300	50500002	Embraer SA. Sao Jose dos Campos, SP.	

VH = AUSTRALIA Total 2
Civil

| ☐ VH-CCJ | 07 | Citation Mustang | 510-0033 | CCJ P/L. Ascot, QLD. | N..... |
| ☐ VH-NEQ | 07 | Citation Mustang | 510-0029 | GetJets P/L. Palm Beach, QLD. | N45SP |

XA = MEXICO Total 2
Civil

| ☐ XA-JRT | 07 | Citation Mustang | 510-0034 | | N4155B |
| ☐ XB-RYE | 07 | Citation Mustang | 510-0039 | | N4159Z |

Total VLJ   221

jp airline-fleets international

Industry Standard Fleet Reference Directory

Published annually in May

Fleet lists covering
around 200 Countries
Listing every Commercial Operator
and their aircraft (over 3,000lb MTOW)
72+ Colour Photographs

Data Includes

Operator, Address, Telephone, Fax, Email, Founded, Head, Number of Employees, IATA code, IATA number, ICAO code, ICAO callsign, Operational Base(s)

Aircraft Reg'n, Aircraft Type, Construction Number, Line Number, Year of Manufacture, Previous Reg'n, Delivery Date, Engine Type, Max Take-Off Weight, Seating Configuration

jp airline-fleet Database

All the data from the book described above (and more!) available electronically.

Instant and simple access to over 6,000 operators and over 60,000 aircraft

Data is available

- With Regular Updates – Monthly, Quarterly, Half-yearly – or "one-off"
- As subsets – by manufacturer, geographical region or any combination.
- In the file format of your choice
- Printed Reports, Mailing Labels
- Custom Reports and Analysis
- With our FREE professional software to sort, search, select etc
- Demo available to download from www.buchairuk.co.uk

For further details, please contact

BUCHair (UK) Ltd

P O Box 89, Reigate, Surrey, RH2 7FG, UK
Tel: +44 1737 224747
Fax: +44 1737 226777

Email: sales@buchairuk.co.uk
Website: www.buchairshop.co.uk

BizJet - Country Index

Country	Code	Page	Country	Code	Page
ALGERIA	7T	276	KOREA	HL	53
ANGOLA	D2	41	KUWAIT	9K	277
ARGENTINA	LV	59	LATVIA	YL	269
ARMENIA	EK	43	LEBANON	OD	235
ARUBA	P4	247	LIBYA	5A	275
AUSTRALIA	VH	252	LITHUANIA	LY	60
AUSTRIA	OE	235	LUXEMBOURG	LX	60
AZERBAIJAN	4K	274	MACEDONIA	Z3	273
BAHAMAS	C6	35	MADAGASCAR	5R	275
BAHRAIN	A9C	24	MALAWI	7Q	276
BARBADOS	8P	276	MALAYSIA	9M	277
BELARUS	EW	44	MALI	TZ	252
BELGIUM	OO	239	MALTA	9H	276
BENIN	TY	252	MAURITANIA	5T	276
BERMUDA	VP-B	254	MAURITIUS	3B	274
BOLIVIA	CP	33	MEXICO	XA	259
BOSNIA-HERZEGOVINA	T9	252	MOLDOVA	ER	44
BOTSWANA	A2	23	MONACO	3A	273
BRAZIL	PP	241	MOROCCO	CN	32
BRUNEI	V8	259	MYANMAR	XY	269
BULGARIA	LZ	61	NAMIBIA	V5	259
BURKINA FASO	XT	269	NETHERLANDS	PH	240
CAMBODIA	XU	269	NEW ZEALAND	ZK	271
CAMEROON	TJ	250	NIGER	5U	276
CANADA	C	25	NIGERIA	5N	275
CAYMAN ISLANDS	VP-C	256	NORWAY	LN	58
CHAD	TT	525	OMAN	A4O	23
CHILE	CC	32	PAKISTAN	AP	23
CHINA	B	24	PANAMA	HP	53
CHINA - HONG KONG	B-H	25	PAPUA NEW GUINEA	P2	247
CHINA - MACAU	B-M	25	PARAGUAY	ZP	271
CHINA - TAIWAN	B	25	PERU	OB	235
COLOMBIA	HK	53	PHILIPPINES	RP	248
CONGO KINSHASA	9Q	277	POLAND	SP	249
COSTA RICA	TI	250	PORTUGAL	CS	33
CROATIA	9A	276	QATAR	A7	24
CYPRUS	5B	275	ROMANIA	YR	269
CZECH REPUBLIC / CZECHIA	OK	238	RUSSIA / RUSSIAN FEDERATION	RA	248
DENMARK	OY	239	RWANDA	9XR	277
DJIBOUTI	J2	58	SAN MARINO	T7	252
DOMINICAN REPUBLIC	HI	53	SAO TOME & PRINCIPE	S9	250
ECUADOR	HC	53	SAUDI ARABIA	HZ	54
EGYPT	SU	249	SENEGAL	6V	276
EIRE	EI	43	SERBIA	YU	270
EQUATORIAL GUINEA	3C	274	SLOVAKIA	OM	239
ESTONIA	ES	44	SLOVENIA	S5	250
FINLAND	OH	238	SOUTH AFRICA	ZS	271
FRANCE	F	44	SPAIN	EC	41
GABON	TR	250	SUDAN	ST	249
GEORGIA	4L	274	SWAZILAND	3D	274
GERMANY	D	36	SWEDEN	SE	248
GHANA	9G	276	SWITZERLAND	HB	50
GREAT BRITAIN	G	47	SYRIA	YK	269
GREECE	SX	249	TANZANIA	5H	275
GUATEMALA	TG	250	THAILAND	HS	53
HONDURAS	HR	53	TOGO	5V	276
HUNGARY	HA	53	TUNISIA	TS	250
INDIA	VT	258	TURKEY	TC	250
INDONESIA	PK	241	TURKMENISTAN	EZ	44
IRAN	EP	43	UGANDA	5X	276
IRAQ	YI	269	UKRAINE	UR	252
ISLE OF MAN	M	61	UNITED ARAB EMIRATES	A6	23
ISRAEL	4X	274	URUGUAY	CX	35
ITALY	I	55	USA	N	61
IVORY COAST	TU	252	UZBEKISTAN	UK	252
JAPAN	JA	57	VENEZUELA	YV	270
JORDAN	JY	58	YEMEN	7O	276
KAZAKHSTAN	UN	252	ZAMBIA	9J	276
KENYA	5Y	276	ZIMBABWE	Z	271

Business Jets - By Country

AP = PAKISTAN — Total 22

Civil

Reg	Yr	Type	c/n	Owner/Operator	Prev Regn
☐ AP-BEH	92	B 737-33A	25504	Government of Pakistan, Karachi.	N25997
☐ AP-BEK	92	Learjet 31A	31A-062	Government of Baluchistan, Quetta.	N8180Q
☐ AP-BEX	93	Beechjet 400A	RK-80	Government of Punjab, Lahore. (status ?).	EX-269
☐ AP-BGI	71	HS 125/400B	25269	Royal Airlines Pvt Ltd. Karachi.	N1276A
☐ AP-BHD	05	Citation Bravo	550-1102	Shaheen Air International, Karachi.	N627L
☐ AP-BHE	98	Citation Bravo	550-0843	Shaheen Air International, Karachi.	N36792
☐ AP-BHQ	04	Hawker 400XP	RK-392	Government of Punjab, Lahore.	N50145
☐ AP-BHY	06	Learjet 45	45-316	Government of Sind, Karachi.	ZS-OXY
☐ AP-BJL	87	BAe 125/800A	258095	Lynx Aviation Pvt Ltd. Karachi.	N601FJ
☐ AP-MIR	84	Challenger 601	3023	Princely Jets Pvt Ltd. Karachi.	N639GA
☐ AP-MMM	07	Gulfstream G150	239		N7226P
☐ AP-PAL	07	Hawker 400XP	RK-526	AG Aviation Services Ltd.	N7226P

Military

Reg	Yr	Type	c/n	Owner/Operator	Prev Regn
☐ 0233	93	Citation V	560-0233	Pakistan Army, Rawalpindi.	N1288A
☐ 1003	01	Citation Bravo	550-1003	Pakistan Army, Rawalpindi.	N777UU
☐ 68-19635	68	B 707-351C	19635	Pakistan Air Force, Islamabad.	AP-BAA
☐ 68-19866	68	B 707-340C	19866	Pakistan Air Force, Islamabad.	AP-AWY
☐ J 468	82	Falcon 20F	468	Pakistan Air Force, Sargodha. 'Lohdi'	F-WMKG
☐ J 469	82	Falcon 20F	469	Pakistan Air Force, Sargodha. 'Iqbal'	F-WMKI
☐ J 753	72	Falcon 20E	277	Pakistan Air Force, Islamabad.	F-WPXD
☐ J 754	98	Citation Excel	560-5004	Pakistan Air Force, Islamabad.	N504BM
☐ J 755	98	Gulfstream 4SP	1325	Pakistan Air Force, Islamabad.	(N24EE)
☐ J 756	07	Gulfstream G450	4090	Pakistan Air Force, Islamabad.	N490GA

A2 = BOTSWANA — Total 2

Civil

Reg	Yr	Type	c/n	Owner/Operator	Prev Regn
☐ A2-MCG	97	Beechjet 400A	RK-140	Motor Centre P/L.	ZS-OCG

Military

Reg	Yr	Type	c/n	Owner/Operator	Prev Regn
☐ OK1	91	Gulfstream 4	1173	Government/Botswana Defence Force, Gaborone. 'Puna'	N17587

A4O = OMAN — Total 5

Civil

Reg	Yr	Type	c/n	Owner/Operator	Prev Regn
☐ A4O-AA	05	Airbus A320-232	2566	Government of Oman, Seeb.	F-WWDG
☐ A4O-AB	91	Gulfstream 4	1168	Government of Oman, Seeb.	N462GA
☐ A4O-AC	92	Gulfstream 4	1196	Government of Oman, Seeb.	N420GA
☐ A4O-OMN	01	B 747-430	32445	Government of Oman, Seeb.	D-ARFO
☐ A4O-SO	79	B 747SP-27	21785	Government of Oman, Seeb.	N351AS

A6 = UNITED ARAB EMIRATES — Total 42

Civil

Reg	Yr	Type	c/n	Owner/Operator	Prev Regn
☐ A6-AIN	99	BBJ-7Z5	29268	The Royal Jet Group, Abu Dhabi.	N1786B
☐ A6-AUH	03	BBJ2-8EX	33473	Government of Abu Dhabi Amiri Flight.	N379BC
☐ A6-CGK	84	Citation III	650-0048	Execujet Middle East Ltd. Dubai.	VP-CGK
☐ A6-DAS	00	BBJ-7Z5	29858	Government of Abu Dhabi Amiri Flight.	N1786B
☐ A6-DEJ	99	Gulfstream V	564	Priyan Foundation/Dana Executive Jets, Dubai.	N54PR
☐ A6-DFR	01	BBJ-7BC	30884	Government of Abu Dhabi Amiri Flight.	VP-BFE
☐ A6-DHG	06	Global 5000	9226	Nakheel Aviation LLC. Dubai.	C-FJNX
☐ A6-DPW	06	Embraer Legacy 600	14500955	Nakheel Aviation LLC. Dubai.	PT-SFD
☐ A6-EJA	00	Learjet 60	60-200	Execujet Middle East Ltd. Dubai.	(OY-TCG)
☐ A6-ELC	06	Hawker 850XP	258781	Elite Jets, Dubai.	N37261
☐ A6-ESH	99	Airbus A319-133XCJ	910	Government of Sharjah.	D-AWFR
☐ A6-HEH	04	BBJ2-8AJ	32825	Dubai Air Wing, Dubai.	N.....
☐ A6-HHH	87	Gulfstream 4	1011	Dubai Air Wing, Dubai.	N17581
☐ A6-HRM	98	B 747-422	26903	Dubai Air Wing, Dubai.	N108UA
☐ A6-HRS	98	BBJ-7EO	29251	Dubai Air Wing, Dubai.	
☐ A6-IFA	05	Challenger 604	5641	Execujet Middle East Ltd. Dubai.	N641DA
☐ A6-INF	86	Gulfstream 3	491	Infinity Aviation, Dubai.	N51FF
☐ A6-KNH	05	Challenger 300	20050	Execujet Middle East Ltd. Dubai.	N350TG
☐ A6-KWT	06	Embraer Legacy 600	14500973	United Aviation, Kuwait City, Kuwait.	N135SH
☐ A6-MAA	90	BAe 125/800A	NA0462	RAK Airways, Ras Al Khaimah.	N800DN
☐ A6-MAF	07	Falcon 900EX EASY	183	Majid Al Futtaim Group LLC. Dubai.	F-WWFG
☐ A6-MAH	97	Hawker 800XP	258328	Empire Aircraft Sales, Sharjah.	VH-SCY
☐ A6-MAJ	03	Learjet 60	60-270	Nakheel Aviation LLC. Dubai.	(A6-MSC)

Reg	Yr	Type	c/n	Owner/Operator	Prev Regn
☐ A6-MBH	01	Challenger 604	5520	MB Aviation Ltd/Elite Jets, Dubai.	VP-CBR
☐ A6-MMM	98	B 747-422	26906	Dubai Air Wing, Dubai.	N109UA
☐ A6-MRM	01	BBJ2-8EC	32450	Dubai Air Wing, Dubai.	
☐ A6-MRS	06	BBJ2-8EO	35238	Dubai Air Wing, Dubai.	
☐ A6-NKL	05	Embraer Legacy 600	14500944	Nakheel Aviation LLC. Dubai.	PT-SCP
☐ A6-NMA	99	Gulfstream 4SP	1381	Royal Jet, Abu Dhabi.	VP-BYS
☐ A6-RJA	02	Gulfstream G300MPA	1503	The Royal Jet Group, Abu Dhabi.	N403GA
☐ A6-RJB	03	Gulfstream G300MPA	1505	The Royal Jet Group, Abu Dhabi.	N405GA
☐ A6-RJH	81	Learjet 35A	35A-429	The Royal Jet Group, Abu Dhabi.	UAE 800
☐ A6-RJI	79	Learjet 35A	35A-265	The Royal Jet Group, Abu Dhabi.	801
☐ A6-RJX	99	BBJ-7AK	29865	The Royal Jet Group, Abu Dhabi.	HB-IIO
☐ A6-RJY	99	BBJ-7Z5	29857	The Royal Jet Group, Abu Dhabi.	A6-LIH
☐ A6-RJZ	99	BBJ-7Z5	29269	The Royal Jet Group, Abu Dhabi.	A6-SIR
☐ A6-RZJ	06	390 Premier 1A	RB-177	Rizon Jet BSC. Manama, Bahrain.	(A6-RZA)
☐ A6-SMS	07	Falcon 900DX	616	Fujairah Aviation Centre, Fujairah.	F-WWFM
☐ A6-SUN	07	Embraer Legacy 600	14501001	Nakheel Aviation LLC. Dubai.	PT-SKS
☐ A6-TBF	06	Hawker 850XP	258792	Elite Jets, Dubai.	N792XP
☐ A6-UAE	97	B 747-48E	28551	Dubai Air Wing, Dubai.	V5-NMA
☐ A6-YAS	99	B 747-4F6	28961	Government of Abu Dhabi Amiri Flight.	

A7 = QATAR
Total 15

Civil

Reg	Yr	Type	c/n	Owner/Operator	Prev Regn
☐ A7-AAF	88	Airbus A310-304	473	Qatari Government Amiri Flight, Doha. 'Al Sad'	F-ODSV
☐ A7-AAG	98	Airbus A320-232	927	Qatari Government Amiri Flight, Doha.	F-WWBA
☐ A7-AAM	02	Global Express	9126	Qatari Government Amiri Flight, Doha.	C-GZPT
☐ A7-AAN	05	Challenger 300	20042	Qatari Government Amiri Flight, Doha.	C-FDSR
☐ A7-AFE	94	Airbus A310-308	667	Qatari Government Amiri Flight, Doha.	F-WQTO
☐ A7-ASA	73	Citation 1/SP	501-0446	Sheikh Abdulla Al Thani, Doha. (was s/n 500-0097).	N888MJ
☐ A7-CJA	01	Airbus A319-133XCJ	1656	Qatari Government Amiri Flight, Doha.	D-AVYT
☐ A7-CJB	03	Airbus A319-133XCJ	2341	Qatari Government Amiri Flight, Doha.	F-W...
☐ A7-CJI	07	CitationJet CJ1+	525-0646	HBK Group, Doha.	N5154J
☐ A7-GEY	06	Global Express	9230	Qatari Government Amiri Flight, Doha.	C-FJMV
☐ A7-HHH	03	Airbus A340-541	495	Qatari Government Amiri Flight, Doha.	F-WWTQ
☐ A7-HHJ	00	Airbus A319-133XCJ	1335	Qatari Government Amiri Flight, Doha. 'Al Rayal'	A7-ABZ
☐ A7-HHK	93	Airbus A340-211	026	Qatari Government Amiri Flight, Doha.	F-WWJQ
☐ A7-HHM	04	Airbus A320-202	605	Qatari Government Amiri Flight, Doha.	F-WWCS
☐ A7-HJJ	04	Airbus A330-202	487	Qatari Government Amiri Flight, Doha.	F-WWYM

A9C = BAHRAIN
Total 18

Civil

Reg	Yr	Type	c/n	Owner/Operator	Prev Regn
☐ A9C-BA	80	B 727-2M7	21824	Government of Bahrain Royal Flight. 'Al Bahrain'	N740RW
☐ A9C-BAH	98	Gulfstream 4SP	1353	Government of Bahrain Royal Flight, Sheikh Isa AB.	(N555KC)
☐ A9C-BG	77	Gulfstream 2TT	202	Government of Bahrain Royal Flight, Sheikh Isa AB.	N17586
☐ A9C-BXA	99	Citation Excel	560-5046	Bexair-Bahrain Executive Air Services, Muharraq.	N966MT
☐ A9C-BXB	00	Challenger 604	5477	Bexair-Bahrain Executive Air Services, Muharraq.	N477AT
☐ A9C-BXD	96	Challenger 601-3R	5194	Bexair-Bahrain Executive Air Services, Muharraq.	N601R
☐ A9C-BXG	01	Challenger 604	5485	Bexair-Bahrain Executive Air Services, Muharraq.	LX-FBY
☐ A9C-BXH	00	Challenger 604	5476	Bexair-Bahrain Executive Air Services, Muharraq.	N343K
☐ A9C-BXI	06	Citation Excel XLS	560-5658	Bexair-Bahrain Executive Air Services, Muharraq.	N5135A
☐ A9C-BXJ	06	Citation Excel XLS	560-5676	Bexair-Bahrain Executive Air Services, Muharraq.	N5265N
☐ A9C-HAK	87	B 747SP-31	23610	Government of Bahrain Royal Flight, Sheikh Isa AB.	A6-ZSN
☐ A9C-HMH	79	B 747SP-21	21649	Government of Bahrain Royal Flight. 'Gulf of Bahrain'	A9C-HHH
☐ A9C-HMK	02	B 747-4PB	33684	Government of Bahrain Royal Flight, Sheikh Isa AB.	
☐ A9C-MAN	07	Embraer Legacy 600	14500978	Bexair-Bahrain Executive Air Services, Dubai, UAE.	PT-SHM
☐ A9C-MTC	06	Embraer Legacy 600	14500975	Bexair-Bahrain Executive Air Services, Dubai, UAE.	(PH-CEL)
☐ A9C-RJA	07	390 Premier 1A	RB-195	Rizon Jet BSC. Manama.	N74065

Military

Reg	Yr	Type	c/n	Owner/Operator	Prev Regn
☐ A9C-BDF	01	BAe 146/RJ-85	E2390	Bahrain Defence Force, Sheikh Isa AB.	G-3-390
☐ A9C-HWR	97	BAe 146/RJ-85	E2306	Bahrain Defence Force, Sheikh Isa AB.	EI-CNK

B = CHINA
Total 50

Civil

Reg	Yr	Type	c/n	Owner/Operator	Prev Regn
☐ B-3642	04	Citation Excel XLS	560-5539	Flight Inspection Centre, ATM Bureau,	N4007J
☐ B-3643	04	Citation Excel XLS	560-5540	Flight Inspection Centre, ATM Bureau,	N4008S
☐ B-3644	05	CitationJet CJ-1	525-0551	Civil Aviation Flight University of China, Guanghan.	N1279A
☐ B-3645	05	CitationJet CJ-1	525-0552	Civil Aviation Flight University of China, Guanghan.	N1279V
☐ B-3647	05	CitationJet CJ-1	525-0554	Civil Aviation Flight University of China, Guanghan.	N1290N
☐ B-3648	05	CitationJet CJ-1	525-0555	Civil Aviation Flight University of China, Guanghan.	N1287B

Reg	Yr	Type	c/n	Owner/Operator	Prev Regn
B-3649	05	CitationJet CJ-1	525-0557	Civil Aviation Flight University of China, Guanghan.	N1287F
B-3650	05	CitationJet CJ-1	525-0558	Civil Aviation Flight University of China, Guanghan.	N1288N
B-3668	01	CitationJet CJ-1	525-0471	PanAm International Aviation Academy,	N471CJ
B-3669	00	CitationJet CJ-1	525-0380	PanAm International Aviation Academy,	N83DC
B-3901	07	Hawker 850XP	258856	DeerJet Aviation Ltd. Beijing.	N7256C
B-3902	07	Hawker 850XP	258858	Hangzhou Daoyuan Chemical Fire Group, Beijing.	N71958
B-3990	99	Hawker 800XP	258408	DeerJet Aviation Ltd. Beijing.	N30319
B-3991	00	Hawker 800XP	258470	DeerJet Aviation Ltd. Beijing.	N42830
B-3992	00	Hawker 800XP	258501	DeerJet Aviation Ltd. Beijing.	N5001S
B-3993	01	Hawker 800XP	258525	Thai Air Charter, Bangkok, Thailand.	N4425R
B-3997	01	Hawker 800XP	258575	DeerJet Aviation Ltd. Beijing.	N3215M
B-4005	96	Challenger 800	7138	Government/China United Airlines, Beijing.	C-FZAT
B-4006	96	Challenger 800	7149	Government/China United Airlines, Beijing.	C-FZIS
B-4007	97	Challenger 800	7180	Government/China United Airlines, Beijing.	C-GATM
B-4010	97	Challenger 800	7189	Government/China United Airlines, Beijing.	C-GATY
B-4011	97	Challenger 800	7193	Government/China United Airlines, Beijing.	C-GBFR
B-4018	01	B 737-33A	25502	Government of China, Beijing.	
B-4019	01	B 737-33A	25503	Government of China, Beijing.	
B-4020	95	B 737-34N	28081	Government of China, Beijing.	
B-4021	95	B 737-34N	28082	Government of China, Beijing.	
B-4101	85	Citation S/II	S550-0049	CAAC Special Services Division, Beijing.	N1270K
B-4102	85	Citation S/II	S550-0050	CAAC Special Services Division, Beijing.	N1270S
B-4108	97	CitationJet	525-0204	Broad Air Conditioning/China Southern Airways, Baiyun.	(N323LM)
B-4599	78	Learjet 36A	36A-034	Geological Survey, Chinese Government, Beijing.	HY-985
B-6165	06	Airbus A319-115XCJ	2935	Shenzhen Airlines, Shenzhen-Baoan.	D-AVWM
B-7019	00	Citation Excel	560-5118	Yuanda Group/China Southern Airways, Baiyun.	N1241K
B-7021	01	Citation X	750-0157	CAAC Special Services Division, Beijing.	N52081
B-7022	92	Citation VI	650-0220	CAAC Special Services Division, Beijing.	B-4106
B-7024	81	Citation II	550-0301	Zhongfei Airlines, Xian.	B-4103
B-7025	82	Citation II	550-0297	Zhongfei Airlines, Xian.	B-4104
B-7026	81	Citation II	550-0305	Zhongfei Airlines, Xian.	B-4105
B-7777	07	CitationJet CJ1+	525-0655		N1367D
B-8020	96	Falcon 2000	27	CITIC Group, Beijing.	F-GSYC
B-8021	07	Falcon 900DX	613	CITIC Group, Beijing.	F-WWFQ
B-8080	89	Gulfstream 4	1100	DeerJet Aviation Ltd. Beijing.	N100GX
B-8081	06	Gulfstream G200	135	Huang Huang Group, Shanghai.	N435GA
B-8082	91	Gulfstream 4	1157	Huang Huang Group, Shanghai.	N157FQ
B-8083	01	Gulfstream G200	037	DeerJet Aviation Ltd. Beijing.	N204AB
B-8085	05	Gulfstream G200	114	Everbest Technology Enterprise Co. Hong Kong.	N833BA
B-8087	07	Gulfstream G200	174		N674GA
HY-984	85	Learjet 36A	36A-053	Geological Survey, Chinese Government, Beijing.	N39418
HY-986	85	Learjet 35A	35A-601	Geological Survey, Chinese Government, Beijing.	
HY-987	85	Learjet 35A	35A-602	Geological Survey, Chinese Government, Beijing.	
HY-988	85	Learjet 35A	35A-603	Geological Survey, Chinese Government, Beijing.	

B-H = CHINA - HONG KONG Total 9

Civil

Reg	Yr	Type	c/n	Owner/Operator	Prev Regn
B-KGV	05	Gulfstream G550	5111	Adon Ltd. Hong Kong.	N981GA
B-KHK	05	Gulfstream G450	4018	Metrojet Ltd. Hong Kong.	N618GA
B-KID	05	Gulfstream G550	5115	Donizetti International Ltd. Hong Kong.	N835GA
B-KMJ	03	Gulfstream G200	090	Metrojet Ltd. Hong Kong.	N790GA
B-KSJ	01	Gulfstream G200	036	Metrojet Ltd. Hong Kong.	N408LN
B-LBL	05	Challenger 604	5604	Jet Leader Ltd. Hong Kong.	(N78RX)
B-LLL	05	Challenger 604	5622	Hong Kong Natural Win Co. Hong Kong.	C-FFLA
B-LMJ	06	Gulfstream G200	153	Metrojet Ltd. Hong Kong.	N653GA
B-LUE	07	Gulfstream G550	5147	Sky FarEast Ltd. Hong Kong.	N647GA

B-M = CHINA - MACAU Total 4

Civil

Reg	Yr	Type	c/n	Owner/Operator	Prev Regn
B-M..	07	Hawker 900XP	HA-28		N31958
B-M..	07	Hawker 900XP	HA-36		N34956
B-MAC	95	Challenger 601-3R	5178	Jet Asia Ltd. Macau.	CS-MAC
B-MAI	89	Challenger 601-3A	5049	Jet Asia Ltd. Macau.	N888JA

B = CHINA - TAIWAN Total 2

Military

Reg	Yr	Type	c/n	Owner/Operator	Prev Regn
3701	99	B 737-8AR	30139	Taiwan Air Force, Taipei.	
B-20001	99	Astra-1125SPX	119	AIDC-Aerospace Industrial Development Corp.Taipei.	

C = CANADA　　　　　　　　　　　　　　　Total 415
Civil

Reg	Yr	Type	c/n	Owner/Operator	Prev Regn
☐ C-F...	07	Challenger 605	5744	Bombardier Inc. Dorval, PQ.	
☐ C-FABF	86	Citation S/II	S550-0101	Provincial Airlines Ltd. St Johns, NS.	N101QS
☐ C-FACO	90	Citation V	560-0053	Northwestern Utilities Ltd. Edmonton, AB.	C-GCUW
☐ C-FALI	00	Citation Encore	560-0573	Irving Oil Transport Ltd. Saint John, NB.	N162TF
☐ C-FAMJ	00	Citation Bravo	550-0931	Omega Air Corp. Richmond, BC.	N233DW
☐ C-FANJ	07	CitationJet CJ-3	525B-0201	Skyservice Business Aviation Inc. Dorval, PQ.	N5260Y
☐ C-FANS	06	Learjet 45	45-303	Ainsworth Lumber Co. Vancouver, BC.	N40043
☐ C-FBCL	05	Learjet 45XR	45-288	London Air Services Ltd. Vancouver, BC.	N5014F
☐ C-FBCR	93	Challenger 601-3A	5117	Skyservice Aviation Inc. Dorval, PQ.	N80BF
☐ C-FBDR	97	Global Express	9003	Bombardier Inc. Dorval, PQ.	C-FJGX
☐ C-FBDS	79	Citation 1/SP	501-0094	BDK Air Ltd. Villeneuve, AB.	N159LC
☐ C-FBEL	84	Challenger 601	3028	Skyservice Aviation Inc. Dorval, PQ.	C-GLXB
☐ C-FBFP	75	Learjet 35	35-038	Canada Global Air Ambulance Ltd. Winnipeg, MT.	VH-ELJ
☐ C-FBLJ	04	Learjet 45	45-270	Skyservice Aviation Inc. Dorval, PQ.	N4004Q
☐ C-FBNA	84	Citation III	650-0046	IMP Group Ltd/Execaire Inc. Toronto, ON.	N650TT
☐ C-FBNS	98	Challenger 604	5364	Bank of Nova Scotia, Toronto, ON.	C-GLXK
☐ C-FBNW	81	Falcon 10	190	CEC Flightexec, Buttonville, ON.	N190L
☐ C-FBOC	04	Global 5000	9151	IMP Group Ltd/Execaire Inc. Dorval, PQ.	
☐ C-FBOM	93	Challenger 601-3A	5124	Execaire Inc/IMP Group Ltd-Bank of Montreal, Toronto, ON.	C-GLXD
☐ C-FBUR	92	BAe 125/800A	258232	Burmac Corp/Skycharter Ltd. Toronto-Pearson, ON.	N723HH
☐ C-FBVF	81	Falcon 50	48	Skyservice Aviation Inc. Toronto-Pearson, ON.	N247BC
☐ C-FBXL	02	Citation Excel	560-5298	Airsprint Inc. Calgary, AB.	C-GSEC
☐ C-FCDE	98	Challenger 604	5392	Skyservice Business Aviation Inc. Toronto, ON.	C-FLPC
☐ C-FCIB	95	Challenger 601-3R	5181	Execaire Inc/IMP Group Ltd. Toronto-Pearson, ON.	N602D
☐ C-FCLJ	78	Learjet 36A	36A-037	Executive Aircraft Ltd & Robert Jens, Richmond, BC.	C-GRJL
☐ C-FCMG	98	Learjet 60	60-133	Aviation Starlink Inc. Dorval, PQ.	C-FBCD
☐ C-FCNR	88	Gulfstream 4	1065	Canadian National Railway Co. Dorval, PQ.	N599CN
☐ C-FCPR	07	Citation Sovereign	680-0157	Canadian Pacific Railway Co. Calgary, AB.	N5226B
☐ C-FCRF	89	Hawker 800SP	NA0447	Harvard Oil & Gas Inc. Calgary, AB.	C-FSCH
☐ C-FCRH	81	Falcon 50	56	Harvard Oil & Gas Inc. Calgary, AB.	(N844J)
☐ C-FCSI	06	Challenger 300	20114	Skyservice Aviation Inc. Dorval, PQ.	C-FIEP
☐ C-FCSS	81	HS 125/700A	NA0325	161768 Canada Inc/Decair, Dorval, PQ.	C-GQGM
☐ C-FCXL	02	Citation Excel	560-5234	RJM Aviation Ltd/Airsprint, Calgary, AB.	N.....
☐ C-FDAX	91	Astra-1125SP	058	Sobeys Group Inc. Halifax, NS.	N1125E
☐ C-FDDD	85	Hawker 800SP	258038	Hawker West Inc. Calgary, AB.	C-GTNT
☐ C-FDHD	05	Citation Sovereign	680-0032	Omega Air Corp. Richmond, BC.	N132SV
☐ C-FDJC	85	Citation III	650-0080	Chartright Air Inc. Toronto-Pearson, ON.	N69LD
☐ C-FDMB	76	Citation	500-0341	MBE Jet Ltd. Red Deer, AB.	C-GVKL
☐ C-FDMM	07	390 Premier 1A	RB-198	MBE Jet Ltd. Calgary, AB.	N7198H
☐ C-FDOL	06	Challenger 300	20093	Skyservice Aviation Inc. Dorval, PQ.	C-FGWR
☐ C-FEAE	82	HS 125/700A	NA0328	ACASS Canada Ltd. Montreal-Trudeau, PQ.	N192A
☐ C-FEMA	85	Citation S/II	S550-0040	Manitoba Emergency Aero-Medical Services, Winnipeg, MT.	(N1269D)
☐ C-FEMT	77	Learjet 36A	36A-024	Fox Flight Inc. Toronto City, ON.	N978E
☐ C-FEPG	92	Citation V	560-0182	Air Partners Corp. Calgary, AB.	C-FCRH
☐ C-FETB	61	B 720-023B	18024	Pratt & Whitney Canada Inc. Montreal. PQ. (PW530 testbed)	OD-AFQ
☐ C-FETJ	90	Citation V	560-0082	Canadian Forest Products Ltd. Vancouver, BC.	N950WA
☐ C-FEVC	01	Citation Bravo	550-1023	LeFevre & Co Property Agents, Victoria, BC.	N4405
☐ C-FEXD	76	Falcon 10	78	CEC Flightexec, London, ON.	N199SA
☐ C-FFEV	85	Falcon 100	204	Air Nunavut Ltd. Frobisher, NT.	XA-UDP
☐ C-FGFI	94	Falcon 900B	138	Grant Forest Products Inc. Earlton, ON.	VH-FHR
☐ C-FGJC	01	Learjet 60	60-210	Aviation Starlink Inc. Dorval, PQ.	N700JE
☐ C-FHGC	00	Challenger 604	5453	Jetport Inc. Hamilton, ON.	N453AD
☐ C-FHNS	05	Gulfstream G100	156	Jetport Inc. Hamilton, ON.	N996GA
☐ C-FHPM	89	Gulfstream 4	1103	Barrick Gold Corp. Toronto, ON.	N3KN
☐ C-FHRL	03	Gulfstream G100	150	Jetport Inc. Hamilton, ON.	N750GA
☐ C-FHYL	01	Challenger 604	5506	London Air Services Ltd. Vancouver, 'Spirit of Enterprise'	C-GJFI
☐ C-FICA	82	Falcon 100	196	CEC Flightexec, Buttonville, ON.	N125CA
☐ C-FICU	79	Learjet 35A	35A-249	Canadian Global Air Ambulance Ltd. Winnipeg, MT.	N300DA
☐ C-FIGD	67	Falcon 20C	109	Government/National Research Council, Ottawa, ON.	117506
☐ C-FIGO	87	BAe 125/800A	258087	Execaire Inc/IMP Group Ltd. Dorval, PQ.	C-GAWH
☐ C-FIMO	84	Citation III	650-0065	Skyservice Business Aviation Inc. Dorval, PQ.	N500E
☐ C-FIPE	97	Hawker 800XP	258319	Enbridge Pipelines Ltd. Calgary, AB.	N2291X
☐ C-FJBO	97	Citation Bravo	550-0812	Regional Aviation Ltd. Campbell River, BC.	N5223P
☐ C-FJCZ	92	Citation II	550-0700	Department of Transport, Montreal, PQ.	

Reg	Yr	Type	c/n	Owner/Operator	Prev Regn
C-FJGG	94	Learjet 60	60-038	Skyservice Aviation Inc. Toronto-Pearson, ON.	N638LJ
C-FJHS	95	Hawker 800XP	258283	Chartright Air Inc. Toronto-Pearson, ON.	N82EA
C-FJJC	91	Challenger 601-3A	5096	Fox Aviation Inc. Dorval, PQ.	C-FNNS
C-FJMX	06	Global Express	9232	Bombardier Inc. Downsview, ON.	
C-FJNS	90	Challenger 601-3A	5059	Skyservice Aviation Inc. Dorval, PQ.	N627KR
C-FJOI	00	Falcon 900EX	69	Future Electronics Inc. Dorval, PQ.	N969EX
C-FJOJ	79	Westwind-1124	271	Fast Air Ltd. Winnipeg, MT.	C-FREE
C-FJWZ	91	Citation II	550-0685	Department of Transport, Ottawa, ON.	(N6778T)
C-FJXN	91	Citation II	550-0684	Department of Transport, Ottawa, ON.	(N6778L)
C-FKBC	97	Citation V Ultra	560-0409	Air Partners Corp. Calgary, AB.	N390BA
C-FKCE	91	Citation II	550-0686	Department of Transport, Edmonton, AB.	(N6778V)
C-FKDX	91	Citation II	550-0687	Department of Transport, Hamilton, ON.	(N6778Y)
C-FKEB	91	Citation II	550-0688	Department of Transport, Ottawa, ON.	(N6779D)
C-FKGN	85	Hawker 800SP	258052	VIH Execujet Ltd. Sidney, BC.	N221HB
C-FKJM	83	Challenger 601	3012	Skyservice Aviation Inc. Calgary, AB.	N878RM
C-FKLB	92	Citation II	550-0699	Department of Transport, Hamilton, ON.	
C-FLLA	07	Global Express	9235	Bombardier Inc. Downsview, ON.	
C-FLLF	07	Global Express XRS	9236	Bombardier Inc. Downsview, ON.	
C-FLLN	07	Global Express XRS	9238	Bombardier Inc. Downsview, ON.	
C-FLLV	07	Global Express XRS	9240	Bombardier Inc. Downsview, ON.	
C-FLRJ	01	Learjet 45	45-156	Skyservice Aviation Inc. Dorval, PQ.	N156AV
C-FLSF	06	Challenger 605	5706	Bombardier Inc. Dorval, PQ.	C-GLXF
C-FLTI	07	Global Express	9244	Bombardier Inc. Downsview, ON.	
C-FLZA	92	Citation II	550-0701	Department of Transport, Moncton, NB.	
C-FMCI	97	Citation Bravo	550-0816	Mountain Cabelevision Ltd. Hamilton, ON.	N5225K
C-FMFL	82	Falcon 50	96	McCain Foods Ltd. Florenceville, NB.	N4AC
C-FMFM	92	Citation II	550-0702	Department of Transport, Montreal, PQ.	
C-FMFN	07	Global 5000	9247	Bombardier Inc. Downsview, ON.	
C-FMFO	07	Global 5000	9248	Bombardier Inc. Downsview, ON.	
C-FMGE	07	Global 5000	9249	Bombardier Inc. Downsview, ON.	
C-FMGK	07	Global Express	9250	Bombardier Inc. Downsview, ON.	
C-FMGL	99	Learjet 45	45-088	London Air Services Ltd. Vancouver, BC.'Spirit of Tong'	N454MK
C-FMGV	07	Challenger 850	8069	Bombardier Inc. Dorval, PQ.	
C-FMHA	06	Learjet 40	45-2043	MH Aviation Ltd/AirSprint Inc. Calgary, AB.	N4001G
C-FMHL	92	Astra-1125SP	066	Kelowna Flightcraft Air Charter Ltd. Kelowna, BC.	N419MK
C-FMJM	82	Citation II	550-0444	Image Air Charter Inc. Toronto, ON.	N71GA
C-FMKZ	07	Global Express	9252	Bombardier Inc. Downsview, ON.	
C-FMLB	07	Global Express	9253	Bombardier Inc. Downsview, ON.	
C-FMLI	07	Global 5000	9255	Bombardier Inc. Downsview, ON.	
C-FMLQ	07	Global Express	9256	Bombardier Inc. Downsview, ON.	
C-FMLT	07	Global 5000	9257	Bombardier Inc. Downsview, ON.	
C-FMLV	07	Global Express	9258	Bombardier Inc. Downsview, ON.	
C-FMOS	01	Citation Bravo	550-0982	Skyservice Aviation Inc. Dorval, PQ.	C-GVIJ
C-FMUI	07	Global 5000	9261	Bombardier Inc. Downsview, ON.	
C-FMUN	07	Global Express	9262	Bombardier Inc. Downsview, ON.	
C-FMUO	07	Challenger 5000	9263	Bombardier Inc. Downsview, ON.	
C-FNCT	80	Citation II	550-0155	Department of Transport, Moncton, ON.	(N155FF)
C-FNDK	07	Global 5000	9265	Bombardier Inc. Downsview, ON.	
C-FNDN	07	Global Express	9264	Bombardier Inc. Downsview, ON.	
C-FNDT	07	Global Express	9268	Bombardier Inc. Downsview, ON.	
C-FNEU	93	Challenger 601-3A	5119	Chartright Air Inc. Toronto-Pearson, ON.	N601FS
C-FNHZ	85	Citation 1/SP	501-0689	Wayne D Gray, Charlottetown, PEI.	N288MM
C-FNMC	66	Learjet 24	24-106	1737994 Ontario Inc. Kemptville, ON.	N888MC
C-FNNS	90	Challenger 601-3A	5068	Nortel Networks Ltd. Toronto, ON.	N66NT
C-FNNT	96	Challenger 604	5317	Skyservice Aviation Inc. Toronto-Pearson, ON.	C-GGPK
C-FNRG	02	Learjet 45	45-223	Skyservice Aviation Inc. Calgary, AB.	(D-CTAN)
C-FNRP	07	Global 5000	9269	Bombardier Inc. Downsview, ON.	
C-FNRR	07	Global Express	9270	Bombardier Inc. Downsview, ON.	
C-FNSN	07	Global 5000	9271	Bombardier Inc. Downsview, ON.	
C-FNSV	07	Global Express	9272	Bombardier Inc. Downsview, ON.	
C-FNXL	07	Citation Excel XLS	560-5686	Airsprint Inc. Calgary, AB.	N86XL
C-FNZZ	07	Global 5000	9273	Bombardier Inc. Downsview, ON.	
C-FOAB	07	Global Express	9274	Bombardier Inc. Downsview, ON.	
C-FOAD	07	Global 5000	9275	Bombardier Inc. Downsview, ON.	
C-FOAI	07	Challenger 300	20166	Bombardier Inc. Dorval, PQ.	
C-FOAQ	07	Challenger 300	20168	ACASS Canada Ltd. Hamilton, ON.	

Reg	Yr	Type	c/n	Owner/Operator	Prev Regn
☐ C-FOAU	07	Challenger 300	20170	Bombardier Inc. Dorval, PQ.	(C-FOMU)
☐ C-FOBJ	07	Challenger 300	20173	Bombardier Inc. Dorval, PQ.	
☐ C-FOBK	07	Challenger 605	5719	Bombardier Inc. Dorval, PQ.	C-G...
☐ C-FOBQ	85	Citation S/II	S550-0036	1304453 Alberta Ltd. Calgary, AB.	C-FRGY
☐ C-FOGI	07	Challenger 605	5723	Bombardier Inc. Dorval, PQ.	C-G...
☐ C-FOKD	07	Global Express	9276	Bombardier Inc. Downsview, ON.	
☐ C-FOKF	07	Global Express	9277	Bombardier Inc. Downsview, ON.	
☐ C-FOKH	07	Global Express	9278	Bombardier Inc. Downsview, ON.	
☐ C-FOKJ	07	Global 5000	9279	Bombardier Inc. Downsview, ON.	
☐ C-FOMU	07	Challenger 605	5725	Bombardier Inc. Dorval, PQ.	C-G...
☐ C-FOQR	07	Challenger 300	20174	Bombardier Inc. Dorval, PQ.	
☐ C-FOQW	07	Challenger 300	20175	Bombardier Inc. Dorval, PQ.	
☐ C-FORB	07	Challenger 300	20176	Bombardier Inc. Dorval, PQ.	
☐ C-FORJ	86	Citation III	650-0104	Image Air Charter Ltd. Toronto, ON.	C-GOXB
☐ C-FOSB	07	Challenger 300	20177	Bombardier Inc. Dorval, PQ.	
☐ C-FOSG	07	Challenger 300	20178	Bombardier Inc. Dorval, PQ.	
☐ C-FOSM	07	Challenger 300	20179	Bombardier Inc. Dorval, PQ.	
☐ C-FOSQ	07	Challenger 300	20180	Bombardier Inc. Dorval, PQ.	
☐ C-FOSW	07	Challenger 300	20181	Bombardier Inc. Dorval, PQ.	
☐ C-FOSX	07	Challenger 300	20182	Bombardier Inc. Dorval, PQ.	
☐ C-FOTF	07	Challenger 300	20183	Bombardier Inc. Dorval, PQ.	
☐ C-FOYE	07	Challenger 605	5728	Bombardier Inc. Dorval, PQ.	C-G...
☐ C-FPCE	00	Hawker 800XP	258500	Sunwest Aviation Ltd. Calgary, AB.	C-FPCP
☐ C-FPEP	88	Westwind-Two	441	Chartright Air Inc. Toronto-Pearson, ON.	C-FZEI
☐ C-FPHS	90	B 737-53A	24970	Pacific Sky Aviation, Vancouver, BC.	C-GBGL
☐ C-FPJT	89	Citation V	560-0017	Partner Jet Inc. Toronto-Pearson, ON.	N560H
☐ C-FPQT	07	Challenger 605	5731	Bombardier Inc. Dorval, PQ.	C-G...
☐ C-FPQV	07	Challenger 605	5732	Bombardier Inc. Dorval, PQ.	C-G...
☐ C-FPQW	07	Challenger 605	5733	Bombardier Inc. Dorval, PQ.	C-G...
☐ C-FPQY	07	Challenger 605	5734	Bombardier Inc. Dorval, PQ.	C-G...
☐ C-FPRP	81	Learjet 35A	35A-390	Skyservice Aviation Inc. Dorval, PQ.	C-FJEF
☐ C-FPSV	07	Challenger 605	5738	Bombardier Inc. Dorval, PQ.	C-G...
☐ C-FPUB	72	Learjet 25B	25B-090	L & C Canada Coastal Aviation Inc. Victoria, BC.	N754CA
☐ C-FPUI	95	Citation X	750-0002	Skyservice Business Aviation Inc. Calgary, AB.	N752VP
☐ C-FPWB	94	CitationJet	525-0062	Arctic Financial Ltd. Yellowknife, NT.	C-GINT
☐ C-FPXD	68	B 727-171C	19859	First Air, Carp, ON.	N1727T
☐ C-FPZZ	07	Challenger 300	20184	Bombardier Inc. Dorval, PQ.	
☐ C-FQCF	07	Challenger 300	20185	Bombardier Inc. Dorval, PQ.	
☐ C-FQOA	07	Challenger 300	20187	Bombardier Inc. Dorval, PQ.	
☐ C-FQOF	07	Challenger 300	20188	Bombardier Inc. Dorval, PQ.	
☐ C-FQOI	07	Challenger 300	20189	Bombardier Inc. Dorval, PQ.	
☐ C-FQOK	07	Challenger 300	20190	Bombardier Inc. Dorval, PQ.	
☐ C-FQOL	07	Challenger 300	20191	Bombardier Inc. Dorval, PQ.	
☐ C-FQOM	07	Challenger 300	20192	Bombardier Inc. Dorval, PQ.	
☐ C-FQOQ	07	Challenger 300	20193	Bombardier Inc. Dorval, PQ.	
☐ C-FQQG	07	Challenger 605	5740	Bombardier Inc. Dorval, PQ.	
☐ C-FQQK	07	Challenger 605	5742	Bombardier Inc. Dorval, PQ.	C-G...
☐ C-FQQO	07	Challenger 605	5743	Bombardier Inc. Dorval, PQ.	C-G...
☐ C-FQQW	07	Challenger 605	5745	Bombardier Inc. Dorval, PQ.	C-G...
☐ C-FRCI	06	Challenger 604	5650	Skyservice Aviation Inc. Dorval, PQ.	C-FIEX
☐ C-FRGY	95	Learjet 60	60-061	FN Aircraft LP. Calgary, AB.	N219DC
☐ C-FRJZ	97	Astra-1125SPX	087	Jetport Inc. Hamilton, ON.	4X-CUU
☐ C-FRQA	07	Challenger 300	20194	Bombardier Inc. Dorval, PQ.	
☐ C-FRQC	08	Challenger 300	20195	Bombardier Inc. Dorval, PQ.	
☐ C-FRQH	08	Challenger 300	20196	Bombardier Inc. Dorval, PQ.	
☐ C-FRQK	08	Challenger 300	20197	Bombardier Inc. Dorval, PQ.	
☐ C-FRQM	08	Challenger 300	20198	Bombardier Inc. Dorval, PQ.	
☐ C-FRST	01	Citation Bravo	550-1011	Jet-Share Aviation Inc. Toronto, ON.	N51870
☐ C-FRYS	05	Learjet 45	45-275	McCain Foods Ltd. Florenceville, NB.	N40082
☐ C-FSCI	07	Challenger 605	5717	Bombardier Inc. Dorval, PQ.	C-GLYH
☐ C-FSDL	04	Learjet 45	45-255	London Air Services Ltd. Vancouver, BC.	N40081
☐ C-FSJR	99	Challenger 604	5413	Shaw Communications Inc. Calgary, AB.	C-GLXM
☐ C-FSNC	04	Citation Encore	560-0676	Syncrude Canada Ltd. Fort McMurray, AB.	N277WS
☐ C-FTEN	02	Citation X	750-0188	Telus Communications Ltd. Vancouver, BC.	N5163K
☐ C-FTFC	91	Challenger 601-3A	5091	The Futura Corp. Vancouver, BC.	(N715BD)
☐ C-FTIL	01	Citation Excel	560-5253	Skyservice Aviation Inc. Dorval, PQ.	N73SG

Reg	Yr	Type	c/n	Owner/Operator	Prev Regn
C-FTKX	99	CitationJet CJ-1	525-0364	FlightWx Inc. Waterloo, ON.	N525DE
C-FTMI	73	Citation	500-0069	Central Aviation Ltd. Springbank, AB.	N255RD
C-FTOM	02	Citation Encore	560-0633	Kal Aviation Group Inc. Vernon, BC.	N427CD
C-FTOR	96	Citation VII	650-7067	Jet Share Aviation Inc. Toronto, ON.	N502T
C-FTVC	93	Hawker 800SP	258243	North Cariboo Flying Service Ltd. Calgary, AB.	C-FLPH
C-FTWO	76	Westwind-1124	199	Top Aces Consulting Inc. Dorval, PQ.	N199WW
C-FTWR	77	Westwind-1124	207	Top Aces Consulting Inc. Dorval, PQ.	N207WW
C-FTXL	06	Citation Excel XLS	560-5672	Airsprint Inc. Calgary, AB.	N5207V
C-FURG	86	Challenger 601	3063	Government of Quebec, Sainte-Foy, PQ. (Air Ambulance)	C-GLYH
C-FVSL	98	Learjet 45	45-024	London Air Services Ltd. Vancouver, BC.'Spirit of London'	C-FBCL
C-FWBK	01	CitationJet CJ-1	525-0425	Island Valley Airways Ltd. Richmond, BC.	N335J
C-FWXL	07	Citation Excel XLS	560-5691	Airsprint Inc. Calgary, AB.	N5264E
C-FXCN	00	Challenger 604	5474	Skyservice Aviation Inc. Dorval, PQ.	C-FXPB
C-FXHN	00	Learjet 45	45-126	Skyservice Business Aviation Inc. Dorval, PQ.	N420FX
C-FXTC	05	CitationJet CJ-3	525B-0037	Albatros Aircraft Corp. Calgary, AB.	N52653
C-FYMM	06	Citation Encore	560-0705	Syncrude Canada Ltd. Fort McMurray, AB.	N52639
C-FYUL	01	Citation Bravo	550-1028	Monarch Air Ltd. Lethbridge, AB.	N442LV
C-FZOP	75	Falcon 10	44	Air Nunavut Ltd. Frobisher, NT.	(N90AB)
C-FZQP	78	Learjet 35A	35A-168	Skyservice Aviation Inc. Dorval, PQ.	C-GPDO
C-G...	06	CitationJet CJ1+	525-0637	Woodwards Oil Ltd. Goose Bay, NF.	(N779RB)
C-GAAA	82	HS 125/700A	NA0327	LID Brokerage & Realty Co (1977) Ltd. Calgary, AB.	N810SC
C-GAGU	06	Citation Sovereign	680-0100	Agrium Inc. Calgary, AB.	C-GAZU
C-GAJS	81	Learjet 35A	35A-380	Canadian Global Air Ambulance Ltd. Winnipeg, MT.	N903WJ
C-GAPC	89	Citation V	560-0033	Sunwest Aviation Ltd. Calgary, AB.	N4333W
C-GAPT	00	Citation X	750-0131	Centaero Aviation Ltd. Windsor, ON.	N131CX
C-GAWH	03	Challenger 604	5557	Clearwater Fine Foods Inc. Bedford, NS. (600th Challenger).	C-FZSO
C-GAWJ	80	Westwind-1124	277	Top Aces Consulting Inc. Dorval, PQ.	N277WW
C-GAWR	07	Citation Excel XLS	560-5717	IMP Group Ltd/Execaire Inc. Dorval, PQ.	N52369
C-GAWU	96	Citation V Ultra	560-0351	IMP Group Ltd/Execaire Inc. Winnipeg, MT.	C-GAWR
C-GAZU	02	Falcon 900C	198	Cathton Holdings Ltd. Edmonton, AB.	N198FJ
C-GBAP	99	Hawker 800XP	258444	Air Partners Corp. Calgary, AB.	LX-ARC
C-GBBB	83	Gulfstream 3	368	Chartright Air Inc. Toronto-Pearson, ON.	(N112GS)
C-GBBX	90	Citation II	550-0650	Air Georgian Ltd. Toronto, ON.	N823CT
C-GBCI	84	Falcon 20F-5	478	2106701 Ontario Inc/Novajet, Toronto, ON.	N39RP
C-GBFP	74	Learjet 25B	25B-167	Adlair Aviation (1983) Ltd. Cambridge Bay, NT. 'Ernie Lyall'	
C-GBIS	88	BAe 125/800A	258117	Chartright Air Inc. Toronto-Pearson, ON.	N826CT
C-GBKB	99	Challenger 604	5420	Morningstar Leasing Ltd. Edmonton, AB.	N604TS
C-GBLX	03	Global Express	9112	Skyservice Aviation Inc. Dorval, PQ.	C-GJTP
C-GBNX	90	Citation V	560-0074	Manitoba Provincial Government, Winnipeg, MT.	N593MD
C-GBPM	98	CitationJet	525-0287	Westcorp Inc. Edmonton, AB.	N73PM
C-GBSW	00	Astra-1125SPX	130	Sobeys Group Inc. Halifax, NS.	N100GA
C-GCCU	87	BAe 125/800A	NA0406	Sunwest Aviation Ltd. Calgary, AB.	C-FSCI
C-GCDS	04	Global Express	9137	Execaire Inc/IMP Group Ltd. Dorval, PQ.	C-GZPW
C-GCFG	84	Challenger 601	3022	NAV Canada, Ottawa, ON.	C-GLXS
C-GCFI	84	Challenger 601	3020	NAV Canada, Ottawa, ON.	C-GLXO
C-GCGS	88	BAe 125/800A	NA0416	Perimeter Aviation Ltd. Winnipeg, MT.	N353WG
C-GCGT	07	Hawker 850XP	258828	Aviation Starlink Inc. Dorval, PQ.	N7128T
C-GCIX	98	Citation VII	650-7092	Image Air Charter Ltd. Toronto, ON.	(N792VP)
C-GCMP	01	Learjet 45	45-153	Aviation CMP Inc. Dorval, PQ.	N30137
C-GCNR	97	Challenger 604	5339	Canadian National Railway Co. Dorval, PQ.	N604CU
C-GCPM	94	Gulfstream 4SP	1238	P M Air Inc. Toronto-Pearson, ON.	N415PG
C-GCUL	99	Citation X	750-0090	Canadian Utilities Ltd. Edmonton, AB.	N193ZP
C-GCXL	00	Citation Excel	560-5096	Airsprint Inc. Calgary, AB.	N5202D
C-GDBC	89	BAe 125/800A	NA0457	Partner Jet Inc. Toronto-Pearson, ON.	C-GKGD
C-GDBF	83	Challenger 601	3014	Chartright Air Inc. Vancouver, BC.	N698RT
C-GDDR	82	Challenger 600S	1048	Pal Air Ltd. Calgary, AB.	C-FSIP
C-GDII	96	Hawker 800XP	258316	IMP Group Ltd/Execaire Inc. Dorval, PQ.	N516GP
C-GDJH	80	Learjet 35A	35A-353	Canadian Global Air Ambulance Ltd. Vancouver, BC.	N3819G
C-GDLI	95	Challenger 601-3R	5179	Skyservice Aviation Inc. Dorval, PQ.	N168LA
C-GDLR	79	Citation II	550-0062	Sunwest Aviation Ltd. Calgary, AB.	(N77SF)
C-GDMI	00	Learjet 45	45-096	Uniform Yankee Juliet Air Inc. Toronto-Pearson, ON.	N5009T
C-GDPG	05	Global 5000	9178	IMP Group Ltd/Execaire Inc. Dorval, PQ.	C-FCUX
C-GDSH	03	Citation Encore	560-0647	Derek Stimson Holdings Ltd. Lethbridge, AB.	N647CE
C-GDSR	80	Westwind-1124	313	Fast Air Ltd. Winnipeg, MT.	N611WW
C-GDWS	95	CitationJet	525-0109	Lindenhome Corp. Edmonton, AB.	N393N
C-GEIV	93	Gulfstream 4SP	1224	Skyservice Aviation Inc. Dorval, PQ.	N124TS

Reg	Yr	Type	c/n	Owner/Operator	Prev Regn
☐ C-GENW	07	Falcon 2000EX EASY	129	Enbridge Inc. Calgary, AB.	N129EX
☐ C-GERS	03	Global 5000	9127	Bombardier Inc. Dorval, PQ. (Ff 7 Mar 03).	
☐ C-GESO	06	Challenger 300	20110	Imperial Oil Ltd. Dorval, PQ.	C-FIEA
☐ C-GFCL	96	Citation V Ultra	560-0346	West Wind Aviation Inc. Saskatoon, SK.	N346CC
☐ C-GFEE	80	Citation 1/SP	501-0169	Jalair S E C, Sherbrooke, PQ.	D-IBWG
☐ C-GFHR	04	Challenger 300	20016	FHR Real Estate Corp. Toronto, ON.	N777VC
☐ C-GFIL	06	Challenger 300	20107	Skyservice Aviation Inc. Dorval, PQ.	C-FIDZ
☐ C-GGBL	01	Challenger 604	5489	London Air Services Ltd. Vancouver, BC.	N604BD
☐ C-GGFP	91	Falcon 50	227	Grant Executive Jets Inc. Earlton, ON.	(N37LQ)
☐ C-GGHZ	99	Astra-1125SPX	117	Chartright Air Inc. Toronto-Pearson, ON.	C-FTDB
☐ C-GGMI	01	Falcon 900EX	87	Magna International Inc. Buttonville, ON.	N487MA
☐ C-GGMP	07	Hawker 900XP	HA-11	Morningstar Partners Ltd. Edmonton, AB.	N211XP
☐ C-GGWH	98	Challenger 604	5371	Sunwest Aviation Ltd. Calgary, AB.	N371CL
☐ C-GHGC	88	Challenger 601-3A	5019	Sky Service FBO Inc. Toronto, ON.	N575CF
☐ C-GHJJ	95	Learjet 31A	31A-102	Helijet International Inc. Richmond, BC.	N681AF
☐ C-GHJU	96	Learjet 31A	31A-120	Helijet International Inc. Richmond, BC.	N200TJ
☐ C-GHKY	97	Challenger 604	5343	Shaw Communications Inc. Calgary, AB.	C-GAUK
☐ C-GHML	97	Challenger 604	5360	CEC Flight Exec, London, ON.	C-GZEK
☐ C-GHMP	01	Learjet 45	45-183	Aviation CMP Inc. Dorval, PQ.	N511WP
☐ C-GHYD	80	Westwind-1124	278	Image Air Charter Inc. Toronto, ON.	N10S
☐ C-GIBU	00	Hawker 800XP	258507	IMP Group Ltd/Execaire Inc. Dorval, PQ.	N507BW
☐ C-GIOH	89	Challenger 601-3A	5034	Imperial Oil Ltd. Toronto-Pearson, ON.	C-GLXK
☐ C-GIPZ	03	Challenger 300	20005	Aviation CMP Inc. Dorval, PQ.	N850EJ
☐ C-GIRE	74	Learjet 35	35-004	Skyservice Aviation Inc. Dorval, PQ.	N74MJ
☐ C-GIRL	07	CitationJet CJ1+	525-0641	Anderson Air Ltd. Vancouver, BC.	N5214K
☐ C-GIWO	81	Learjet 35A	35A-407	Canadian Global Air Ambulance Ltd. Toronto, ON.	C-GIWD
☐ C-GIWZ	98	Citation X	750-0041	Uniform Yankee Juliet Air Inc. Toronto-Pearson, ON.	C-GIWD
☐ C-GJBJ	83	HS 125/700A	NA0335	Skyservice Aviation Inc. Dorval, PQ.	N702E
☐ C-GJCJ	01	Challenger 300	20001	Bombardier Inc. Dorval, PQ. (Ff 14 Aug 01).	
☐ C-GJCY	04	Learjet 45	45-239	Skyservice Aviation Inc. Dorval, PQ.	N45LJ
☐ C-GJEI	01	Citation Encore	560-0588	Irving Oil Transport Ltd. Saint John, NB.	N5243K
☐ C-GJET	74	Falcon 10	25	2106701 Ontario Inc/Nova Jet, Toronto, ON.	N177BC
☐ C-GJKI	05	Citation Sovereign	680-0071	Irving Oil Transport Ltd. Saint John, NB.	N5061P
☐ C-GJKK	02	Hawker 800XP	258605	ATCON Logistics Inc. Miramichi, NB.	C-GJKI
☐ C-GJLB	97	Falcon 50EX	270	Tidnish Holding Ltd. Halifax, NS.	N148M
☐ C-GJPG	92	Falcon 900B	110	Jim Pattison Industries Ltd. Vancouver, BC.	N110FJ
☐ C-GJRB	99	Citation Excel	560-5026	CEC Flight Exec, London, ON.	(N17UG)
☐ C-GJVK	73	Citation	500-0103	Dale Kirkwood, Springbank, AB.	PT-KIR
☐ C-GKAU	81	Citation II	550-0280	Skyservice Aviation Inc. Dorval, PQ.	N7SN
☐ C-GKCI	98	Falcon 50EX	272	Irving Oil Transport Ltd. Saint John, NB.	N272F
☐ C-GKEG	07	Citation Excel XLS	560-5729	Anderson Air Ltd. Vancouver, BC.	N5264N
☐ C-GKMS	89	Learjet 31	31-006	Albatros Aircraft Corp. Calgary, AB.	N26LC
☐ C-GKPP	89	BAe 125/800A	NA0439	Ledair Ltd. Dorval, PQ.	N74PQ
☐ C-GKTM	83	Learjet 55	55-076	Samuel Son & Co Ltd/Kim-Tam, Toronto, ON.	N30GL
☐ C-GLBJ	82	HS 125/700A	NA0312	161768 Canada Inc/Decair, St Hubert, PQ.	N412DP
☐ C-GLGB	01	Citation Bravo	550-0994	Omega Air Corp. Richmond, BC.	N580SH
☐ C-GLIG	81	HS 125/700A	NA0302	Air 700 Ltd. Vancouver, BC.	C-GEPF
☐ C-GLMI	00	Citation Excel	560-5097	Airsprint Inc. Kitchener-Waterloo, ON.	N5226B
☐ C-GLMK	79	Citation II	550-0100	Air Tindl Ltd. Yellowknife, NT. (was 551-0143)	N140DA
☐ C-GLOJ	84	Challenger 601	3034	ACASS Canada Ltd. Dorval, PQ.	C-GSAP
☐ C-GLRJ	97	Learjet 45	45-019	Skyservice Aviation Inc. Dorval, PQ.	C-GCMP
☐ C-GLRS	04	Learjet 45	45-249	Bombardier Transport Canada Inc. Montreal, PQ.	N40075
☐ C-GLXC	07	Falcon 900EX EASY	190	Aviation Starlink Inc. Dorval, PQ.	N190FJ
☐ C-GMGB	91	Challenger 601-3A	5093	Image Air Charter Inc. Toronto, ON.	C-GGMP
☐ C-GMII	03	Falcon 50EX	335	Magna International Inc. Buttonville, ON.	N535EX
☐ C-GMKZ	03	Citation Excel	560-5309	Magna International Inc. Buttonville, ON.	N309XL
☐ C-GMLR	93	BAe 125/800A	258239	Millar Western Industries Ltd. Edmonton, AB.	N84CT
☐ C-GMMA	90	Learjet 35A	35A-655	Wal-Mart Stores Inc. Toronto-Pearson, ON.	N785JM
☐ C-GMMI	94	Challenger 601-3R	5151	Image Air Charter Inc. Toronto, ON.	N333MX
☐ C-GMMY	88	Learjet 35A	35A-644	Wal-Mart Stores Inc. Toronto-Pearson, ON.	N54SB
☐ C-GMNC	99	Citation X	750-0097	IMP Group Ltd/Execaire Inc. Ottawa, ON.	C-GIGT
☐ C-GMRO	00	Learjet 45	45-086	Uniform Yankee Juliet Air Inc. Toronto-Pearson, ON.	N386K
☐ C-GMTI	00	CitationJet CJ-1	525-0398	Manitoulin Transport Inc. Gore Bay, ON.	N398CJ
☐ C-GMTR	89	BAe 125/800A	NA0435	Sunwest Aviation Ltd. Calgary, AB.	N800BA
☐ C-GNCB	00	Global Express	9088	AIC Ltd. Hamilton, ON.	C-FDLR
☐ C-GNEQ	06	Citation Sovereign	680-0064	Hughes Air Corp. Calgary, AB.	N5214L

Reg	Yr	Type	c/n	Owner/Operator	Prev Regn
☐ C-GNET	99	Falcon 50EX	281	Ledcor Industries Ltd. Vancouver, BC.	N17AN
☐ C-GNLQ	96	Citation V Ultra	560-0390	Hughes Air Corp. Calgary, AB.	N560SE
☐ C-GNWM	82	Citation II	550-0410	Northwest International Jet Ltd. Edmonton, AB.	N46MF
☐ C-GOAG	97	Falcon 900EX	15	Sunwest Aviation Ltd. Calgary, AB.	N914JL
☐ C-GOHB	06	Falcon 2000EX EASY	90	Aviation Starlink Inc. Dorval, PQ.	N190EX
☐ C-GOHJ	78	HS 125/700A	NA0239	Aviation Starlink Inc. Dorval, PQ.	C-GNOW
☐ C-GOIL	82	Falcon 50	87	Skyservice Aviation Inc. Toronto-Pearson, ON.	C-GLRP
☐ C-GOJC	81	Falcon 10	182	Craig Evan Corp. London, ON.	N809F
☐ C-GPAW	06	Citation Excel XLS	560-5681	Pratt & Whitney Canada Inc. Montreal, PQ.	N5221Y
☐ C-GPCZ	06	Challenger 300	20096	Sunwest Aviation Ltd. Calgary, AB.	C-FHMI
☐ C-GPDQ	99	Learjet 45	45-041	Skyservice Aviation Inc. Calgary, AB.	N541LJ
☐ C-GPFC	96	Challenger 604	5310	Power Corp of Canada/Execaire-IMP Group Ltd. Dorval, PQ.	C-GPGD
☐ C-GPGA	97	Citation Bravo	550-0807	Air Georgian Ltd. Vancouver, BC.	C-FANS
☐ C-GPGD	99	Challenger 604	5432	Power Corp of Canada/Execaire-IMP Group Ltd. Dorval, PQ.	C-FDRS
☐ C-GPLN	72	Citation Eagle	500-0016	Hawkeye Aviation Holdings Ltd. Kelowna, BC.	N9AX
☐ C-GPMW	07	CitationJet CJ-3	525B-0206	Westcorp Inc. Edmonton, AB.	N52086
☐ C-GPOP	84	Citation III	650-0042	Expressair/102662 Canada Inc. Ottawa-Gatineau, PQ.	N342AS
☐ C-GPOS	95	CitationJet	525-0129	1147967 Alberta Ltd. Grand Prairie, AB.	N229CJ
☐ C-GPOT	06	Falcon 900DX	607	Potash Corp of Saskatchewan Inc. Saskatoon, SK.	N907DX
☐ C-GPPI	04	Global 5000	9158	Skyservice Aviation Inc. Toronto-Pearson, ON.	(N858TS)
☐ C-GPSI	84	Challenger 601	3027	Swanberg Air Inc. Grand Prarie, AB.	(N603LX)
☐ C-GQBQ	89	Challenger 601-3A	5051	Government of Quebec, Sainte-Foy, PQ.	N190SB
☐ C-GQCC	81	Citation II	550-0285	Algonquin Airlink Inc. Toronto-Pearson, ON.	N989TV
☐ C-GQJJ	82	Citation 1/SP	501-0236	Alta Flights (Charters) Inc. Edmonton, AB.	N711VF
☐ C-GQPA	98	Challenger 604	5379	ACASS Canada Ltd. Dorval, PQ.	N604CA
☐ C-GQPJ	75	Citation Stallion	501-0643	Quikjets Operating Ltd. Edmonton, AB. (was 500-0293).	N54TS
☐ C-GQWI	87	Challenger 601-3A	5016	ACASS Canada Ltd. Dorval, PQ.	N868CE
☐ C-GRCC	94	Citation V Ultra	560-0269	Skyservice Aviation Inc. Dorval, PQ.	N357EC
☐ C-GREK	73	Citation	500-0082	Triventure Estimating & Consulting, Calgary, AB.	N428RJ
☐ C-GRFO	77	Learjet 35A	35A-100	Skyservice Aviation Inc. Dorval, PQ.	N558E
☐ C-GRFT	74	Citation	500-0154	Black Eagle Aviation Ltd. Springbank, AB.	PT-WFT
☐ C-GRGE	80	Falcon 50	29	Chartright Air Inc. Toronto-Pearson, ON.	N529MM
☐ C-GRHC	79	Citation II	550-0046	Omega Air Corp. Richmond, BC.	(N3292M)
☐ C-GRIS	73	Falcon 10	2	Skycharter Ltd. Toronto-Pearson, ON.	N103JM
☐ C-GROG	07	Hawker 850XP	258852	Aviation Starlink Inc. Dorval, PQ.	N7302P
☐ C-GRPB	06	Citation Excel XLS	560-5618	IMP Group Ltd/Execaire Inc. Halifax, NS.	N618EL
☐ C-GRPF	94	Challenger 601-3R	5168	Skyservice Aviation Inc. Toronto-Pearson, ON.	C-GLYC
☐ C-GSEC	05	Citation X	750-0246	IMP Group Ltd/Execaire Inc. Dorval, PQ.	N5214K
☐ C-GSKL	74	Learjet 25B	25B-179	Skycharter Ltd. Toronto-Pearson, ON.	C-GBQC
☐ C-GSMR	99	Falcon 2000	88	Chartright Air Inc. Toronto-Pearson, ON.	C-GSCL
☐ C-GSSC	06	CitationJet CJ-3	525B-0118	Sanjel Corp. Calgary, AB.	N51143
☐ C-GSSK	85	Citation S/II	S550-0027	Alta Flights (Charters) Inc. Edmonton, AB.	N5WC
☐ C-GSUN	05	Citation Sovereign	680-0068	Suncor Energy Inc. Calgary, AB.	(N68HQ)
☐ C-GSUW	06	Challenger 850	8047	Suncor Energy Inc. Calgary, AB.	C-FGKZ
☐ C-GSUX	02	Citation X	750-0205	Suncor Energy Inc. Calgary, AB.	N4005T
☐ C-GSWP	82	Learjet 55	55-019	Sunwest Aviation Ltd. Calgary, AB.	N141SM
☐ C-GSWQ	99	Learjet 45	45-022	Sunwest Aviation Ltd. Calgary, AB.	(XA-RUR)
☐ C-GTDE	76	Learjet 35	35-057	Skyservice Aviation Inc. Dorval, PQ.	N35MR
☐ C-GTDK	81	Citation II	550-0292	West Wind Aviation LP. Regina, SK.	C-FTOC
☐ C-GTDM	83	Learjet 35A	35A-498	Uniform Yankee Juliet Air Inc. Toronto-Pearson, ON.	N400FF
☐ C-GTDO	03	Gulfstream G100	151	TDL Group Ltd/Jetport Inc. Mount Hope, ON.	N751GA
☐ C-GTGO	01	Citation Encore	560-0576	Air Partners Corp. Calgary, AB.	N280JR
☐ C-GTJL	77	Learjet 35A	35A-124	Sunwest Aviation Ltd. Calgary, AB.	N8LA
☐ C-GTNG	74	Citation	500-0169	1161071 Alberta Ltd. Calgary, AB.	N75GM
☐ C-GTOG	03	Citation Encore	560-0648	Anderson Air Ltd. Vancouver, BC.	N820QS
☐ C-GTOL	83	Citation 1/SP	501-0320	Technisonic Industries Ltd. Hamilton, ON.	C-GPTI
☐ C-GTOR	78	HS 125/700A	NA0221	Partner Jet Inc. Toronto-Pearson, ON.	N705JH
☐ C-GTPL	06	Falcon 2000EX EASY	87	Trans Canada Pipelines Ltd. Calgary, AB.	N287F
☐ C-GTRG	06	CitationJet CJ1+	525-0636	Visionaire Services Inc. Red Deer, AB.	N5066U
☐ C-GTRL	05	Gulfstream G200	112	Partner Jet Inc. Toronto-Pearson, ON.	N112GA
☐ C-GTWV	77	Westwind-1124	226	Top Aces Consulting Inc. Dorval, PQ.	N226WW
☐ C-GUAC	80	Learjet 35A	35A-309	Fox & Associates Inc/Fox Flight Inc. Toronto-Pearson, ON.	D-CHPD
☐ C-GUPC	02	Citation Excel	560-5284	Skyservice Business Aviation Inc. Dorval, PQ.	N560JP
☐ C-GVGM	82	Citation II	550-0344	1156006 Alberta Ltd. Calgary, AB.	N550GM
☐ C-GVMP	07	Hawker 900XP	HA-15	Morningstar Partners Inc. Edmonton, AB.	N915XP
☐ C-GVVA	74	Learjet 35	35-002	Sunwest Aviation Ltd. Calgary, AB.	N35SC

Reg	Yr	Type	c/n	Owner/Operator	Prev Regn
☐ C-GVVZ	98	Learjet 45	45-020	Sunwest Aviation Ltd. Calgary, AB.	N45NP
☐ C-GWFG	91	Learjet 35A	35A-669	West Fraser Air Ltd. Vancouver, BC.	N893CF
☐ C-GWFM	97	Falcon 50EX	264	McCain Capital Corp. Toronto, ON.	N900CH
☐ C-GWLE	83	BAe 125/800B	258007	IMP Group Ltd/Execaire Inc. Winnipeg, MT.	C-GWLL
☐ C-GWLL	01	Challenger 604	5484	IMP Group Ltd/Execaire Inc. Dorval, PQ.	N684TS
☐ C-GWPB	05	Gulfstream G200	119	Partner Jet Inc. Toronto-Pearson, ON.	N419GA
☐ C-GWWW	07	Challenger 850	8057	Chartright Air Inc. Toronto-Pearson, ON.	C-FHCN
☐ C-GXBB	98	Falcon 50EX	278	1432766 Ontario Inc. Waterloo, ON.	N623QW
☐ C-GXCG	98	Citation V Ultra	560-0481	9022-6317 Quebec Inc. St Hunbert, PQ.	C-GXCO
☐ C-GXCO	01	Citation Excel	560-5200	Exco Technologies Ltd. Toronto-Buttonville, ON.	N5109R
☐ C-GXPR	06	Global 5000	9211	Jetport Inc. Hamilton, ON. (status ?).	C-FIPH
☐ C-GYMM	98	Citation V Ultra	560-0484	Syncrude Canada Ltd. Fort McMurray, AB.	N5125J
☐ C-GYPV	01	390 Premier 1	RB-16	1336194 Premier LP. Calgary, AB.	N444SS
☐ C-GZPX	00	Challenger 604	5458	Skyservice Aviation Inc. Toronto-Pearson, ON.	N458MS
Military					
☐ 144601	82	Challenger 600S	1040	CC144, DND, 412 (Transport) Squadron, Uplands, ON.	C-GLYM
☐ 144614	85	Challenger 601	3036	CC144, DND, 412 (Transport) Squadron, Uplands, ON.	C-GCUP
☐ 144615	85	Challenger 601	3037	CC144, DND, 412 (Transport) Squadron, Uplands, ON.	C-GCUR
☐ 144616	85	Challenger 601	3038	CC144, DND, 412 (Transport) Squadron, Uplands, ON.	C-GCUT
☐ 144617	02	Challenger 604	5533	DND, 412 (Transport) Squadron, Uplands, ON.	C-GKGR
☐ 144618	02	Challenger 604	5535	DND, 412 (Transport) Squadron, Uplands, ON.	C-GKGS
☐ 15001	87	Airbus A310-304	446	Canadian Armed Forces, 437 Squadron, 8 Wing, Trenton.	C-GBWD

CC = CHILE   Total   26

Civil

Reg	Yr	Type	c/n	Owner/Operator	Prev Regn
☐ CC-CAB	05	Hawker 850XP	258769	Servicios Los Condores SA.	N769XP
☐ CC-CHE	03	CitationJet CJ-2	525A-0171		N271CJ
☐ CC-CLC	80	Citation II	550-0104	Inversiones y Rentas Los Cedros Ltda. Santiago.	301
☐ CC-CMS	04	Learjet 40	45-2009	Inversiones y Rentas Los Cedros Ltda. Santiago.	N40LJ
☐ CC-CPS	06	Citation X	750-0268	Quinenco SA-Inversiones Punta Brava SA. Santiago.	N5262W
☐ CC-CRT	06	Hawker 400XP	RK-493	Servicios Aereos y Terrestres SA. Santiago.	(CS-DMO)
☐ CC-CTC	76	Sabre-60	306-112	Aguos Clara Inc. Santiago.	N740RC
☐ CC-CVO	98	CitationJet	525-0243	Transportes Aereos Inca Ltda. Santiago.	CC-PVJ
☐ CC-CWK	06	Gulfstream G150	219	Cardal AG/Aerocardal Ltda. Santiago.	N219GA
☐ CC-CWW	84	Citation S/II	S550-0002	Cardal AG/Aerocardal Ltda. Santiago.	N211VP
☐ CC-DAC	93	Citation VI	650-0233	Directorate of Civil Aviation, Santiago.	N1303H
☐ CC-DGA	90	Citation II	550-0657	Directorate of Civil Aviation, Santiago.	N3986G
☐ CC-LLM	01	Citation Bravo	550-0996	Club Aero de Cabineros de Chile, Santiago.	N5270W
☐ CC-PGK	06	CitationJet CJ1+	525-0632	Aeroservicio SA. Santiago.	N1314N

Military

Reg	Yr	Type	c/n	Owner/Operator	Prev Regn
☐ 303	87	Citation III	650-0131	Chilean Navy, Santiago.	E-303
☐ 351	76	Learjet 35	35-050	Fuerza Aerea Chilena, Santiago.	CC-ECO
☐ 352	76	Learjet 35	35-066	Fuerza Aerea Chilena, Santiago.	CC-ECP
☐ 361	01	CitationJet CJ-1	525-0463	Fuerza Aerea Chilena, Grupo Aviacion 5, El Tepual.	N1284D
☐ 362	01	CitationJet CJ-1	525-0464	Fuerza Aerea Chilena, Grupo Aviacion 5, El Tepual.	N1284P
☐ 363	01	CitationJet CJ-1	525-0465	Fuerza Aerea Chilena, Grupo Aviacion 5, El Tepual.	N1285P
☐ 364	03	CitationJet CJ-1	525-0507	Fuerza Aerea Chilena, Grupo Aviacion 5, El Tepual.	N.....
☐ 902	67	B 707-351C	19443	Fuerza Aerea Chilena, Gr 10, Santiago.	CC-CCK
☐ 903	65	B 707-330B	18926	Fuerza Aerea Chilena, Gr 10, Santiago. 'Aguila'	CC-CEA
☐ 904	65	B 707-385C	19000	Fuerza Aerea Chilena, Gr 10, Santiago. 'Condor'	905
☐ 911	89	Gulfstream 4	1089	Fuerza Aerea Chilena, Gr 10, Santiago.	N53MU
☐ 921	70	B 737-58N	28866	Fuerza Aerea Chilena, Gr 10, Santiago.	

CN = MOROCCO   Total   13

Civil

Reg	Yr	Type	c/n	Owner/Operator	Prev Regn
☐ CN-TDE	74	Corvette	5	CASA Air Services, Casablanca. (status ?). (stored Toulouse)	F-BVPA
☐ CN-THL	78	Corvette	39	CASA Air Services, Casablanca.	F-GJLB
☐ CN-TJB	00	Learjet 45	45-112	Tafarayt Jet, Casablanca.	N415FX
☐ CN-TLB	98	CitationJet	525-0312	Groupe Addoha, Casablanca.	F-GTMD

Military

Reg	Yr	Type	c/n	Owner/Operator	Prev Regn
☐ CN-ANL	76	Gulfstream 2TT	182	Government of Morocco, Rabat.	N17589
☐ CN-ANM	69	Falcon 20ECM	165	Ministry of Defence, Kenitra.	CN-MBH
☐ CN-ANN	68	Falcon 20ECM	152	Ministry of Defence, Kenitra.	CN-MBG
☐ CN-ANO	80	Falcon 50	12	Government of Morocco, Rabat.	F-WZHC
☐ CN-ANS	61	B 707-138B	18334	Government of Morocco, Rabat. 'Africa Crown'	N58937
☐ CN-ANU	82	Gulfstream 3	365	Government of Morocco, Rabat.	HZ-AFO
☐ CN-ANV	89	Citation V	560-0025	Government of Morocco, Rabat.	(N12285)

Reg	Yr	Type	c/n	Owner/Operator	Prev Regn

Reg	Yr	Type	c/n	Owner/Operator	Prev Regn
☐ CN-ANW	89	Citation V	560-0039	Government of Morocco. Rabat.	
☐ CN-ANZ	88	Falcon 100	212	Government of Morocco, Rabat.	CN-TNA

CP = BOLIVIA Total 5
Civil

Reg	Yr	Type	c/n	Owner/Operator	Prev Regn
☐ CP-2317	74	Sabre-40A	282-136	Aerojet SA. Cochabamaba.	N112ML

Military

Reg	Yr	Type	c/n	Owner/Operator	Prev Regn
☐ FAB 001	76	Sabre-60	306-115	President of Bolivia, Esc 810, La Paz.	(XA-LEI)
☐ FAB 008	75	Learjet 25B	25B-192	Fuerza Aerea Boliviana, Esc 810, La Paz. (photo survey)	
☐ FAB 010	76	Learjet 25D	25D-211	Fuerza Aerea Boliviana, Esc 810, La Paz.	
☐ FAB 098	87	BAe 146-100	E1076	Fuerza Aerea Boliviana, La Paz.	N76HN

CS = PORTUGAL Total 176
Civil

Reg	Yr	Type	c/n	Owner/Operator	Prev Regn
☐ CS-AYY	80	Citation 1/SP	501-0183	Hersal, Cascais-Tires.	(N8NC)
☐ CS-DCK	74	Falcon 20E	297	Masterjet Aviacao Executive SA. Paris-le Bourget, France.	(N297AG)
☐ CS-DDV	87	Citation S/II	S550-0147	Airjetsul, Cascais-Tires.	OO-OSA
☐ CS-DDZ	91	Learjet 31	31-034	OMNI Aviacao y Tecnologia Ltda. Cascais-Tires.	N394SA
☐ CS-DFB	91	Falcon 900	94	NTA/European NetJets, Lisbon.	N94WA
☐ CS-DFC	01	Falcon 2000	148	NTA/European NetJets, Lisbon.	F-WWVC
☐ CS-DFD	01	Falcon 2000	174	NTA/European NetJets, Lisbon.	F-WWMA
☐ CS-DFE	03	Falcon 2000	205	NTA/European NetJets, Lisbon.	F-WWVS
☐ CS-DFF	04	Falcon 2000EX EASY	41	NTA/European NetJets, Lisbon.	F-WWGW
☐ CS-DFG	04	Falcon 2000EX EASY	44	NTA/European NetJets, Lisbon.	F-WWGA
☐ CS-DFH	91	Falcon 900	91	NTA/European NetJets, Lisbon.	N991EJ
☐ CS-DFK	05	Falcon 2000EX EASY	65	NTA/European NetJets, Lisbon.	F-WWMN
☐ CS-DFL	02	Falcon 900EX EASY	97	NTA/European NetJets, Lisbon.	F-WNCO
☐ CS-DFM	02	Citation Excel	560-5257	NTA/European NetJets, Lisbon.	N5196U
☐ CS-DFN	02	Citation Excel	560-5283	NTA/European NetJets, Lisbon.	N.....
☐ CS-DFO	03	Citation Excel	560-5314	NTA/European NetJets, Lisbon.	N5000R
☐ CS-DFP	03	Citation Excel	560-5315	NTA/European NetJets, Lisbon.	N5095N
☐ CS-DFQ	03	Citation Excel	560-5334	NTA/European NetJets, Lisbon.	N5093L
☐ CS-DFR	03	Citation Excel	560-5355	NTA/European NetJets, Lisbon.	N5200Z
☐ CS-DFS	04	Citation Excel	560-5372	NTA/European NetJets, Lisbon.	N5091J
☐ CS-DFT	04	Citation Excel XLS	560-5512	NTA/European NetJets, Lisbon.	N52433
☐ CS-DFU	04	Citation Excel XLS	560-5520	NTA/European NetJets, Lisbon.	N5269A
☐ CS-DFV	04	Citation Excel XLS	560-5543	NTA/European NetJets, Lisbon.	N5165T
☐ CS-DFW	03	Hawker 800XP	258664	NTA/European NetJets, Lisbon.	N664XP
☐ CS-DFX	03	Hawker 800XP	258656	NTA/European NetJets, Lisbon.	N656XP
☐ CS-DFY	03	Hawker 800XP	258663	NTA/European NetJets, Lisbon.	N663XP
☐ CS-DFZ	04	Hawker 800XP	258673	NTA/European NetJets, Lisbon.	N673XP
☐ CS-DGO	00	Citation X	750-0140	TINAirlines Transportes Aereos Ltda. Cascais.	D-BLUE
☐ CS-DGQ	04	CitationJet CJ-2	525A-0200	Masterjet Aviacao Executiva SA. Lisbon.	F-GZUJ
☐ CS-DGR	94	Citation VII	650-7045	Airjetsul, Cascais-Tires.	N745VP
☐ CS-DHA	02	Citation Bravo	550-1005	NTA/European NetJets, Lisbon.	N5247U
☐ CS-DHB	01	Citation Bravo	550-1009	NTA/European NetJets, Lisbon.	N5155G
☐ CS-DHC	02	Citation Bravo	550-1013	NTA/European NetJets, Lisbon.	N5166U
☐ CS-DHD	02	Citation Bravo	550-1017	NTA/European NetJets, Lisbon.	N51666
☐ CS-DHE	02	Citation Bravo	550-1022	NTA/European NetJets, Lisbon.	N5168Y
☐ CS-DHF	02	Citation Bravo	550-1025	NTA/European NetJets, Lisbon.	N5172M
☐ CS-DHG	02	Citation Bravo	550-1034	NTA/European NetJets, Lisbon.	N52086
☐ CS-DHH	02	Citation Bravo	550-1043	NTA/European NetJets, Lisbon.	N52235
☐ CS-DHI	03	Citation Bravo	550-1048	NTA/European NetJets, Lisbon.	N5253S
☐ CS-DHJ	04	Citation Bravo	550-1082	NTA/European NetJets, Lisbon.	N5180C
☐ CS-DHK	04	Citation Bravo	550-1090	NTA/European NetJets, Lisbon.	N51038
☐ CS-DHL	04	Citation Bravo	550-1092	NTA/European NetJets, Lisbon.	N52645
☐ CS-DHM	04	Citation Bravo	550-1093	NTA/European NetJets, Lisbon.	N5263D
☐ CS-DHN	04	Citation Bravo	550-1098	NTA/European NetJets, Lisbon.	N5132T
☐ CS-DHO	04	Citation Bravo	550-1099	NTA/European NetJets, Lisbon.	N5180C
☐ CS-DHP	05	Citation Bravo	550-1104	NTA/European NetJets, Lisbon.	N52144
☐ CS-DHQ	05	Citation Bravo	550-1109	NTA/European NetJets, Lisbon.	N1281A
☐ CS-DHR	05	Citation Bravo	550-1114	NTA/European NetJets, Lisbon.	N1298Y
☐ CS-DIY	06	CitationJet CJ-3	525B-0146	Hersal, Cascais-Tires.	N300GM
☐ CS-DKA	01	Gulfstream 4SP	1480	NTA/European NetJets, Lisbon.	N482QS
☐ CS-DKB	01	Gulfstream V	642	NTA/European NetJets, Lisbon.	N510QS
☐ CS-DKC	04	Gulfstream G550	5057	NTA/European NetJets, Lisbon.	N957GA
☐ CS-DKD	05	Gulfstream G550	5081	NTA/European NetJets, Lisbon.	N581GA

Reg	Yr	Type	c/n	Owner/Operator	Prev Regn
☐ CS-DKE	05	Gulfstream G550	5094	NTA/European NetJets, Lisbon.	N594GA
☐ CS-DKF	05	Gulfstream G550	5099	NTA/European NetJets, Lisbon.	N699GA
☐ CS-DKG	06	Gulfstream G550	5127	NTA/European NetJets, Lisbon.	N527GA
☐ CS-DKH	07	Gulfstream G550	5150	NTA/European NetJets, Lisbon.	N43GA
☐ CS-DKI	07	Gulfstream G550	5166	NTA/European NetJets, Lisbon.	N966GA
☐ CS-DKJ	07	Gulfstream G550	5174	NTA/European NetJets, Lisbon.	N974GA
☐ CS-DLA	93	Falcon 900B	120	NTA/European NetJets, Lisbon.	F-WQBM
☐ CS-DLB	06	Falcon 2000EX EASY	80	NTA/European NetJets, Lisbon.	F-WWGQ
☐ CS-DLC	06	Falcon 2000EX EASY	98	NTA/European NetJets, Lisbon.	F-WWGP
☐ CS-DLD	06	Falcon 2000EX EASY	109	NTA/European NetJets, Lisbon.	F-WWGX
☐ CS-DLE	07	Falcon 2000EX EASY	127	NTA/European NetJets, Lisbon.	F-WWGQ
☐ CS-DLF	07	Falcon 2000EX EASY	134	NTA/European NetJets, Lisbon.	F-WWGV
☐ CS-DLG	07	Falcon 2000EX EASY	144	NTA/European NetJets, Lisbon.	F-WWGW
☐ CS-DMA	04	Hawker 400XP	RK-401	NTA/European NetJets, Lisbon.	N36701
☐ CS-DMB	04	Hawker 400XP	RK-403	NTA/European NetJets, Lisbon.	N36803
☐ CS-DMC	04	Hawker 400XP	RK-404	NTA/European NetJets, Lisbon.	N37204
☐ CS-DMD	04	Hawker 400XP	RK-407	NTA/European NetJets, Lisbon.	N36607
☐ CS-DME	04	Hawker 400XP	RK-408	NTA/European NetJets, Lisbon.	N37108
☐ CS-DMF	04	Hawker 400XP	RK-410	NTA/European NetJets, Lisbon.	N37310
☐ CS-DMG	04	Hawker 400XP	RK-417	NTA/European NetJets, Lisbon.	N36907
☐ CS-DMH	05	Hawker 400XP	RK-425	NTA/European NetJets, Lisbon.	N37325
☐ CS-DMI	05	Hawker 400XP	RK-437	NTA/European NetJets, Lisbon.	N37737
☐ CS-DMJ	05	Hawker 400XP	RK-443	NTA/European NetJets, Lisbon.	N36646
☐ CS-DMK	05	Hawker 400XP	RK-464	NTA/European NetJets, Lisbon.	N36764
☐ CS-DML	05	Hawker 400XP	RK-465	NTA/European NetJets, Lisbon.	N37165
☐ CS-DMM	06	Hawker 400XP	RK-472	NTA/European NetJets, Lisbon.	N36632
☐ CS-DMN	06	Hawker 400XP	RK-475	NTA/European NetJets, Lisbon.	N61675
☐ CS-DMO	06	Hawker 400XP	RK-494	NTA/European NetJets, Lisbon.	N72594
☐ CS-DMP	07	Hawker 400XP	RK-508	NTA/European NetJets, Lisbon.	N70158
☐ CS-DMQ	06	Hawker 400XP	RK-512	NTA/European NetJets, Lisbon.	N37339
☐ CS-DMR	06	Hawker 400XP	RK-516	NTA/European NetJets, Lisbon.	N74116
☐ CS-DMS	07	Hawker 400XP	RK-519	NTA/European NetJets, Lisbon	N72539
☐ CS-DMT	04	Hawker 400XP	RK-532	NTA/European NetJets, Lisbon.	N532XP
☐ CS-DMU	07	Hawker 400XP	RK-538	NTA/European NetJets, Lisbon.	N538XP
☐ CS-DMV*	07	Hawker 400XP	RK-549	NTA/European NetJets, Lisbon.	N34249
☐ CS-DMW*	07	Hawker 400XP	RK-550	NTA/European NetJets, Lisbon.	N3500R
☐ CS-DMX*	07	Hawker 400XP	RK-555	NTA/European NetJets, Lisbon.	N31975
☐ CS-DMY*	07	Hawker 400XP	RK-556	NTA/European NetJets, Lisbon.	N3186B
☐ CS-DMZ*	08	Hawker 400XP	RK-559	NTA/European NetJets, Lisbon.	N.....
☐ CS-DNJ	98	Hawker 800XP	258399	NTA/European NetJets, Lisbon.	N899QS
☐ CS-DNK	99	Hawker 800XP	258430	NTA/European NetJets, Lisbon.	N31590
☐ CS-DNL	99	Hawker 800XP	258439	NTA/European NetJets, Lisbon.	N31596
☐ CS-DNM	99	Hawker 800XP	258422	NTA/European NetJets, Lisbon.	N822QS
☐ CS-DNN	99	Hawker 800XP	258435	NTA/European NetJets, Lisbon.	N835QS
☐ CS-DNO	00	Hawker 800XP	258457	NTA/European NetJets, Lisbon.	N41984
☐ CS-DNP	00	Falcon 2000	109	NTA/European NetJets, Lisbon.	N2218
☐ CS-DNQ	00	Falcon 2000	115	NTA/European NetJets, Lisbon.	F-WWVK
☐ CS-DNR	00	Falcon 2000	120	NTA/European NetJets, Lisbon.	F-WWVP
☐ CS-DNS	01	Falcon 2000	139	NTA/European NetJets, Lisbon.	F-WWVR
☐ CS-DNT	00	Hawker 800XP	258468	NTA/European NetJets, Lisbon.	N43436
☐ CS-DNU	00	Hawker 800XP	258479	NTA/European NetJets, Lisbon.	N44779
☐ CS-DNV	00	Hawker 800XP	258499	NTA/European NetJets, Lisbon.	N51099
☐ CS-DNW	02	Citation Excel	560-5221	NTA/European NetJets, Lisbon.	N5094D
☐ CS-DNX	00	Hawker 800XP	258511	NTA/European NetJets, Lisbon.	N5011J
☐ CS-DNY	01	Citation Excel	560-5216	NTA/European NetJets, Lisbon.	N5103J
☐ CS-DNZ	01	Citation Excel	560-5235	NTA/European NetJets, Lisbon.	N5086W
☐ CS-DOA*	08	Hawker 400XP	RK-561	NTA/European NetJets, Lisbon.	N.....
☐ CS-DRA	04	Hawker 800XP	258686	NTA/European NetJets, Lisbon.	N61746
☐ CS-DRB	04	Hawker 800XP	258690	NTA/European NetJets, Lisbon.	N36990
☐ CS-DRC	04	Hawker 800XP	258714	NTA/European NetJets, Lisbon.	N61944
☐ CS-DRD	05	Hawker 800XP	258721	NTA/European NetJets, Lisbon.	N36621
☐ CS-DRE	05	Hawker 800XPi	258725	NTA/European NetJets, Lisbon.	N30355
☐ CS-DRF	05	Hawker 800XPi	258730	NTA/European NetJets, Lisbon.	N37060
☐ CS-DRG	05	Hawker 800XPi	258741	NTA/European NetJets, Lisbon.	N36841
☐ CS-DRH	05	Hawker 800XPi	258746	NTA/European NetJets, Lisbon.	N6046J
☐ CS-DRI	05	Hawker 800XPi	258756	NTA/European NetJets, Lisbon.	N37056

Reg	Yr	Type	c/n	Owner/Operator	Prev Regn
☐ CS-DRJ	05	Hawker 850XPi	258760	NTA/European NetJets, Lisbon.	N37160
☐ CS-DRK	06	Hawker 800XPi	258765	NTA/European NetJets, Lisbon.	N61285
☐ CS-DRL	06	Hawker 800XPi	258770	NTA/European NetJets, Lisbon.	N36970
☐ CS-DRM	06	Hawker 800XPi	258771	NTA/European NetJets, Lisbon. 'NetJets 100 Europe'	N6171U
☐ CS-DRN	05	Hawker 800XPi	258772	NTA/European NetJets, Lisbon.	N672XP
☐ CS-DRO	06	Hawker 800XPi	258775	NTA/European NetJets, Lisbon.	N37105
☐ CS-DRP	06	Hawker 800XPi	258779	NTA/European NetJets, Lisbon.	N37179
☐ CS-DRQ	06	Hawker 800XPi	258783	NTA/European NetJets, Lisbon.	N37146
☐ CS-DRR	06	Hawker 800XPi	258786	NTA/European NetJets, Lisbon.	N36986
☐ CS-DRS	06	Hawker 800XPi	258795	NTA/European NetJets, Lisbon.	N37295
☐ CS-DRT	06	Hawker 800XPi	258802	NTA/European NetJets, Lisbon.	N7102Z
☐ CS-DRU	06	Hawker 800XPi	258821	NTA/European NetJets, Lisbon.	N73721
☐ CS-DRV	06	Hawker 800XPi	258825	NTA/European NetJets, Lisbon.	N3725Z
☐ CS-DRW	06	Hawker 800XPi	258829	NTA/European NetJets, Lisbon.	N73729
☐ CS-DRX	06	Hawker 800XPi	258834	NTA/European NetJets, Lisbon.	N71934
☐ CS-DRY	07	Hawker 800XPi	258840	NTA/European NetJets, Lisbon.	
☐ CS-DRZ	07	Hawker 850XP	258847	NTA/European NetJets, Lisbon.	N74476
☐ CS-DSA*	08	Falcon 7X	30	NTA/European NetJets, Lisbon.	F-WWZR
☐ CS-DUA*	07	Hawker 750	HB-6	NTA/European NetJets, Lisbon.	N3206V
☐ CS-DUB*	07	Hawker 750	HB-7	NTA/European NetJets, Lisbon.	N3207V
☐ CS-DUC*	08	Hawker 750	HB-8	NTA/European NetJets, Lisbon.	N.....
☐ CS-DUD*	08	Hawker 750	HB-11	NTA/European NetJets, Lisbon.	N.....
☐ CS-DXB	05	Citation Excel XLS	560-5553	NTA/European NetJets, Lisbon.	N12778
☐ CS-DXC	05	Citation Excel XLS	560-5559	NTA/European NetJets, Lisbon.	N1281N
☐ CS-DXD	05	Citation Excel XLS	560-5568	NTA/European NetJets, Lisbon.	N6779D
☐ CS-DXE	05	Citation Excel XLS	560-5578	NTA/European NetJets, Lisbon.	N1299H
☐ CS-DXF	05	Citation Excel XLS	560-5586	NTA/European NetJets, Lisbon.	N1299K
☐ CS-DXG	05	Citation Excel XLS	560-5595	NTA/European NetJets, Lisbon.	N5135K
☐ CS-DXH	06	Citation Excel XLS	560-5615	NTA/European NetJets, Lisbon.	N5266F
☐ CS-DXI	06	Citation Excel XLS	560-5621	NTA/European NetJets, Lisbon.	N1300J
☐ CS-DXJ	06	Citation Excel XLS	560-5627	NTA/European NetJets, Lisbon.	N51396
☐ CS-DXK	06	Citation Excel XLS	560-5633	NTA/European NetJets, Lisbon.	N13218
☐ CS-DXL	06	Citation Excel XLS	560-5640	NTA/European NetJets, Lisbon.	N1319X
☐ CS-DXM	06	Citation Excel XLS	560-5683	NTA/European NetJets, Lisbon.	N1130X
☐ CS-DXN	06	Citation Excel XLS	560-5685	NTA/European NetJets, Lisbon.	N11963
☐ CS-DXO	06	Citation Excel XLS	560-5692	NTA/European NetJets, Lisbon.	N1198V
☐ CS-DXP	07	Citation Excel XLS	560-5702	NTA/European NetJets, Lisbon.	N1275T
☐ CS-DXQ	07	Citation Excel XLS	560-5704	NTA/European NetJets, Lisbon.	N1281R
☐ CS-DXR	07	Citation Excel XLS	560-5748	NTA/European NetJets, Lisbon.	N585QS
☐ CS-DXS*	07	Citation Excel XLS	560-5754	NTA/European NetJets, Lisbon.	(N578QS)
☐ CS-DXT*	08	Citation Excel XLS	560-5765	NTA/European NetJets, Lisbon.	N5233J
☐ CS-DXU*	07	Citation Excel XLS	560-5775	NTA/European NetJets, Lisbon.	N.....
☐ CS-DXV*	07	Citation Excel XLS	560-5782	NTA/European NetJets, Lisbon.	N.....
☐ CS-DXW*	08	Citation Excel XLS	560-5787	NTA/European NetJets, Lisbon.	N.....
☐ CS-DXX*	08	Citation Excel XLS	560-5789	NTA/European NetJets, Lisbon.	N.....
☐ CS-DXY*	08	Citation Excel XLS	560-5791	NTA/European NetJets, Lisbon.	N.....
☐ CS-DXZ*	08	Citation Excel XLS	560-5794	NTA/European NetJets, Lisbon.	N.....
☐ CS-TFI	99	Learjet 45	45-021	AeroNorte, Braga.	HB-VMB
☐ CS-TFN	90	Falcon 900B	66	Vinair Aeroservicios SA. Cascais-Tires.	CS-TMK
☐ CS-TLP	04	Falcon 2000EX EASY	39	Heliavia Transporte Aereo Ltda. Lisbon.	F-WWGU
☐ CS-TLU	00	Airbus A319-133XCJ	1256	OMNI Aviacao e Tecnologia Ltda. Cascais-Tires.	F-GSVU
☐ CS-TLW	01	Learjet 45	45-144	OMNI Aviacao e Tecnologia Ltda. Cascais-Tires.	D-CEMM
☐ CS-TLY	07	Falcon 7X	15	Vinair Aeroservicios SA. Cascais-Tires.	F-WWUL
Military					
☐ 17103	69	Falcon 20D	217	Portuguese Air Force, Esc 504, Montijo, Lisbon.	8103
☐ 17401	89	Falcon 50	195	Portuguese Air Force, Esc 504, Montijo, Lisbon.	7401
☐ 17402	89	Falcon 50	198	Portuguese Air Force, Esc 504, Montijo, Lisbon.	7402
☐ 17403	91	Falcon 50	221	Portuguese Air Force, Esc 504, Montijo, Lisbon.	7403

CX = URUGUAY   *Total*   **1**

Civil

Reg	Yr	Type	c/n	Owner/Operator	Prev Regn
☐ CX-CBS	76	HS 125/600A	256067	Aeromont Ltda. Montevideo.	(N157RP)

C6 = BAHAMAS   *Total*   **2**

Civil

Reg	Yr	Type	c/n	Owner/Operator	Prev Regn
☐ C6-JET	97	Astra-1125SPX	095	Advanced Aviation Ltd, Freeport.	N98AD
☐ C6-LVU	03	CitationJet CJ-2	525A-0170	Russell Jedinak/RJT Ltd. Nassau.	N915RJ

D = GERMANY Total 333
Civil

Reg	Yr	Type	c/n	Owner/Operator	Prev Regn
☐ D-....	00	CitationJet CJ-1	525-0366	L U Bettermann GmbH.	N850GM
☐ D-....	06	Falcon 900EX EASY	178		N900EX
☐ D-AAAI	07	Embraer Legacy 600	14500991	Cirrus Airlines Luftfahrt GmbH. Saarbruecken.	PT-SKL
☐ D-AAAZ	05	Global 5000	9170	Cirrus Luxaviation SA. Luxembourg.	C-FCSY
☐ D-AAMA	88	Challenger 601-3A	5023	Jet Air Flug GmbH. Zweibrucken.	N623CW
☐ D-AAOK	04	Challenger 604	5585	Cirrus Airlines Luftfahrt GmbH. Saarbruecken.	OE-IMB
☐ D-ABCD	03	Challenger 604	5565	Knorr-Bremse GmbH/Cirrus Aviation GmbH. Munich.	N604KB
☐ D-ACBG	07	Embraer Legacy 600	14501016	Cirrus Airlines Luftfahrt GmbH. Saarbruecken.	PT-SVD
☐ D-ADAM	78	VFW 614	G17	DLR Flugbetriebe, Oberpfaffenhofen.	D-BABP
☐ D-ADCA	05	Gulfstream G550	5114	Daimler Chrysler AG. Stuttgart.	N834GA
☐ D-ADCB	06	Gulfstream G550	5142	Daimler Chrysler AG. Stuttgart.	N42GA
☐ D-ADLR*	05	Gulfstream G550	5093	DLR Flugbetriebe, Oberpfaffenhofen.	N593GA
☐ D-ADNA	99	Airbus A319-133XCJ	1053	Daimler Chrysler AG. Stuttgart.	D-AVYN
☐ D-ADNB	00	Global Express	9071	Daimler Chrysler AG. Stuttgart.	C-GHDQ
☐ D-ADND	99	Challenger 604	5403	Daimler Chrysler AG. Stuttgart.	N604DC
☐ D-ADNE	99	Challenger 604	5422	Daimler Chrysler AG. Stuttgart.	N605DC
☐ D-AEKT	06	Global Express	9213	Daimler Chrysler AG. Stuttgart.	(VP-CAH)
☐ D-AETV	99	Challenger 604	5417	Air Independence GmbH. Munich.	N605MP
☐ D-AEUK	05	Challenger 604	5632	Challenge Air GmbH. Cologne.	N604CG
☐ D-AGSI	01	Falcon 900EX	78	Aero-Dienst GmbH. Nuremberg.	G-DAEX
☐ D-AHEI	00	Challenger 604	5463	Daimler Chrsyler AG. Stuttgart.	N463AG
☐ D-AHLE	00	Challenger 604	5462	Daimler Chrysler AG. Stuttgart.	N462PG
☐ D-AIFR	07	Airbus A319-115XCJ	3073	Sonair SA/China SONANGOL International, Luanda, Angola.	D-AVXP
☐ D-AIMM	08	Airbus A318 Elite	3333	Airbus Industrie, Hamburg.	
☐ D-AIND	03	Challenger 604	5572	Air Independence GmbH. Munich.	(N472TS)
☐ D-AJAD	00	Falcon 900EX	64	Deutsche Telekom AG. Cologne-Bonn.	N900VM
☐ D-AJAG	02	Challenger 604	5528	Deutsche Telekom AG. Cologne-Bonn.	N528DT
☐ D-AJGK	01	Gulfstream 4SP	1459	Windrose Air Flugcharter GmbH. Berlin.	(D-AJJJ)
☐ D-AKUE	95	Challenger 601-3R	5173	Ullmann Krockow Esch/Challenge Air GmbH. Cologne.	N181JC
☐ D-AMBI	06	Falcon 900EX EASY	176	ACD Aviation Services Ltd/Vibro Air, Moenchengladbach.	(LX-GDX)
☐ D-ANKE	01	Challenger 604	5494	Jet Connection Business Flight AG. Frankfurt.	N494JC
☐ D-AONE	06	Embraer Legacy 600	14500988	Cirrus Airlines Luftfahrt GmbH. Saarbruecken.	PT-SKD
☐ D-APAA	03	Airbus A319-132LR	1947	PrivatAir SA/Airbus Industrie, Toulouse, France.	D-AVWI
☐ D-APAB	03	Airbus A319-132LR	1955	PrivatAir SA. Hamburg.	D-AVWD
☐ D-APAC	03	Airbus A319-132LR	1727	PrivatAir SA/DLH Shuttle, Dusseldorf.	D-AVWQ
☐ D-APAD	03	Airbus A319-132LR	1880	PrivatAir SA/DLH Shuttle, Dusseldorf.	D-AVYM
☐ D-ARKK	03	Gulfstream G450	4004	Windrose Air Flugcharter GmbH. Berlin.	(N8875)
☐ D-ARTE	90	Challenger 601-3A	5060	Jet Connection Business Flight AG. Frankfurt.	(D-ADLA)
☐ D-ARTN	05	Embraer Legacy 600	14500941	Cirrus Aviation GmbH. Saarbruecken.	PT-SCM
☐ D-ASIE	00	Challenger 604	5475	Aero-Dienst GmbH. Nuremberg.	N475AD
☐ D-ASTS	98	Challenger 604	5378	ACM Air Charter GmbH. Baden-Baden.	C-GDBZ
☐ D-ATNR	04	Global Express XRS	9159	Cirrus Aviation GmbH. Saarbruecken (Ff 16 Jan 05).	C-FCOI
☐ D-ATON	07	Embraer Legacy 600	14501017	ATON GmbH. Fulda.	PT-SVK
☐ D-ATTT	05	Challenger 604	5609	Windrose Air Flugcharter GmbH. Berlin.	N604JC
☐ D-ATWO	07	Embraer Legacy 600	14501010	Cirrus Airlines Luftfahrt GmbH. Saarbruecken.	PT-SKZ
☐ D-AUCR	06	Falcon 900DX	606	Nalex Co.	F-WWFF
☐ D-AUKE	98	Challenger 604	5389	Ullmann Krockow Esch/Challenge Air GmbH. Cologne.	N604JE
☐ D-AWKG	97	Falcon 900EX	20	Adolf Wuerth GmbH. Niederstetten.	F-WQBK
☐ D-AZEM	03	Falcon 900EX EASY	133	Zeman Flugtechnik GmbH. Munich.	F-WQBJ
☐ D-BADA	05	Dornier Do328JET	3224	ADAC Luftrettung GmbH. Munich.	D-BDXB
☐ D-BADC	04	Dornier Do328JET	3216	ADAC Luftrettung GmbH. Munich.	D-BDXO
☐ D-BADO	06	Challenger 300	20116	SAP/DH Flugcharter GmbH. Mannheim.	C-FIOC
☐ D-BAMA	98	Falcon 2000	70	Jet Air Flug GmbH. Zweibrucken.	P4-IKR
☐ D-BAMM	05	Falcon 2000EX EASY	74	BASF AG. Speyer.	F-WWGK
☐ D-BASE	06	Falcon 2000EX EASY	111	ThyssenKrupp GmbH. Duesseldorf.	F-WWMH
☐ D-BERT	04	Falcon 2000EX EASY	30	Bertlesmann AG. Paderborn.	F-WWGG
☐ D-BEST	97	Falcon 2000	50	Bauhaus GmbH. Mannheim.	F-WWME
☐ D-BETA	05	Challenger 300	20079	Cirrus Airlines Luftfahrt GmbH. Saarbruecken.	C-FGCJ
☐ D-BFFB	06	Falcon 2000EX EASY	93	ACM Air Charter GmbH. Baden-Baden.	F-WWGH
☐ D-BJET	04	Dornier Do328JET	3207	Private Wings Flugcharter GmbH. Berlin-Tempelhof.	N328FJ
☐ D-BKLI	03	Citation X	750-0219	Daimler Chrysler/LIDL Dienstleistung GmbH. Bad Wimpfen.	N5192E
☐ D-BLDI	03	Citation X	750-0218	Daimler Chrysler/LIDL Dienstleistung GmbH. Bad Wimpfen.	N5223X
☐ D-BMVV	05	Falcon 2000EX EASY	42	BMW GmbH. Munich.	F-GUTC
☐ D-BONN	07	Falcon 2000EX EASY	118	Deutsche Telekom AG. Cologne-Bonn.	F-WWGC

Reg	Yr	Type	c/n	Owner/Operator	Prev Regn
D-BOOK	05	Falcon 2000EX EASY	70	Bertelsmann AG. Paderborn.	F-WWGE
D-BOSS	04	Falcon 2000EX EASY	33	BASF AG. Speyer.	D-BILL
D-BSMI	05	Challenger 300	20071	Execujet Europe GmbH. Zurich, Switzerland.	N371TS
D-BSNA	82	Challenger 600S	1066	Fondsprojekt Josef Esch GmbH/Challenge Air GmbH. Cologne.	N51TJ
D-BTEN	99	Citation X	750-0085	ACM Air Charter GmbH. Baden-Baden.	(N985QS)
D-BUBI	07	Challenger 300	20145	Triple Alpha Luftfahrt GmbH. Duesseldorf.	C-FLQG
D-BUSY	82	Challenger 600S	1070	Jet Executive International Charter GmbH. Duesseldorf.	N670CL
D-C...	84	Citation III	650-0037		(D-CLDF)
D-CAAA	05	Citation Excel XLS	560-5555	Daimler Chrysler AG. Stuttgart.	(D-CLDI)
D-CAAE	84	Learjet 55	55-095	Air Alliance Express GmbH. Siegerland.	N55RT
D-CABB	92	Gulfstream G100	059	Vibro Air Flugservice GmbH. Moenchengladbach.	LX-GOL
D-CAIR	06	Citation Excel XLS	560-5620	Airtrans GmbH. Schwaebisch Hall.	N5264E
D-CAJK	06	Citation Excel XLS	560-5670	Helicopter Travel Munich GmbH.	(D-CCWD)
D-CALL	98	Citation Bravo	550-0834	Hamburger Air Charter GmbH. Hamburg.	N834CB
D-CAMS	93	Citation V	560-0243	Triple Alpha GmbH/Club Airways, Geneva, Switzerland.	N39N
D-CAPO	78	Learjet 35A	35A-159	Jet Executive International Charter GmbH. Duesseldorf.	(N135CK)
D-CARL	81	Learjet 35A	35A-387	GFD fuer Flugzieldarstellungen mbH. Hohn.	
D-CASA	00	Citation Encore	560-0544	Adolf Wuerth GmbH. Niederstetten.	N701DK
D-CATL	83	Learjet 55	55-051	FAI rent-a-jet AG. Nuremberg.	N55KD
D-CAUW	01	Citation Encore	560-0578	A W Aerowest GmbH. Hannover.	(D-CSUN)
D-CAVE	81	Learjet 35A	35A-423	Deutsche Rettungsflugwacht, Karlsruhe/Baden-Baden.	(N335GA)
D-CBBB	05	Citation Excel XLS	560-5567	Daimler Chrysler AG. Stuttgart.	(D-CKLI)
D-CBEN	94	Citation V Ultra	560-0282	Adolf Wuerth GmbH. Niederstetten.	N51055
D-CBIZ	94	Citation VII	650-7039		OY-GGG
D-CBPL	87	Citation III	650-0149	Eheim GmbH/SFD-Stuttgarter Flugdienst GmbH. Stuttgart.	(CS-DNE)
D-CCAA	80	Learjet 35A	35A-315	Deutsche Rettungsflugwacht, Karlsruhe/Baden-Baden.	N662AA
D-CCAB	97	Citation Bravo	550-0827	Albert Berner GmbH. Kuenzelsau.	N51042
D-CCCA	78	Learjet 35A	35A-160	Jet Executive International Charter GmbH. Duesseldorf.	
D-CCCB	90	Learjet 35A	35A-663	Maschinenfabrik E Mollers GmbH. Beckum.	N91480
D-CCCF	80	Citation II	550-0189	CCF Manager Airline GmbH. Cologne.	HB-VGP
D-CCEU	90	Citation III	650-0190	Air Traffic GmbH. Duesseldorf.	N260VP
D-CCGG	02	Learjet 60	60-256	GAS Air Service GmbH. Muenster-Osnabrueck.	OY-LJK
D-CCGN	82	Learjet 55	55-017	Juliane Griesemann/Quick Air Jet Charter GmbH. Cologne.	N760AQ
D-CCHB	76	Learjet 35A	35A-089	Bauhaus GmbH. Mannheim.	N3547F
D-CCJS	07	Citation Sovereign	680-0175	MSR-Flug Charter GmbH. Greven.	N52144
D-CDDD	06	Citation Excel XLS	560-5623	Daimler Chrysler AG. Stuttgart.	N5244F
D-CDEF	07	Learjet 60	60-331	DCA GmbH.	N4001G
D-CDSF	81	Learjet 35A	35A-421	DSF Flugdienst AG. Siegerland.	I-VULC
D-CEBM	01	Citation Encore	560-0569	EBM Papst Mulfingen GmbH. Mulfingen.	N600LF
D-CEEE	06	Citation Excel XLS	560-5630	Daimler Chrysler AG. Stuttgart.	N51612
D-CEFD	06	CitationJet CJ-3	525B-0120	EFD Eisele Flugdienst GmbH. Stuttgart.	N5211A.
D-CEIS	90	Beechjet 400A	RK-10	Suedzucker AG/Haberlein Metzer Reise Service, Mannheim.	(D-CLSG)
D-CEJA	00	Learjet 60	60-173	Execujet Europe AG. Berlin-Texel.	OY-LJF
D-CEMG	98	Citation V Ultra	560-0463	SFD Stuttgarter Flugdienst GmbH. Stuttgart.	N48LQ
D-CEXP	86	Learjet 35A	35A-616	Air Alliance Express GmbH. Siegerland.	N876C
D-CFAI	81	Learjet 35A	35A-365	FAI rent-a-jet AG. Nuremberg.	G-GJET
D-CFAX	77	Learjet 35A	35A-135	FAI rent-a-jet AG. Nuremberg.	N135GJ
D-CFCF	81	Learjet 35A	35A-413	ADAC/Senator Aviation Charter GmbH. Hamburg.	N27KG
D-CFFB	97	Learjet 60	60-107	Hansgrohe GmbH. Nuremberg.	N107LJ
D-CFFF	06	Citation Excel XLS	560-5634	Daimler Chrysler AG. Stuttgart.	N51612
D-CFGG	81	Learjet 36A	36A-048		N32AJ
D-CFLG	05	Learjet 60	60-290	Air Alliance Express GmbH. Siegerland.	N260DB
D-CFTG	78	Learjet 35A	35A-204	Juliane Griesemann/Quick Air Jet Charter GmbH. Cologne.	(N277AM)
D-CGBR	85	Learjet 55	55-122	Jet Executive International Charter GmbH. Duesseldorf.	OE-GRO
D-CGEO	99	Learjet 60	60-160	Windrose Air Flugcharter GmbH. Berlin.	D-CDNY
D-CGFA	78	Learjet 35A	35A-179	GFD fuer Flugzieldarstellungen mbH. Hohn.	N801PF
D-CGFB	79	Learjet 35A	35A-268	GFD fuer Flugzieldarstellungen mbH. Hohn.	N2U
D-CGFC	80	Learjet 35A	35A-331	GFD fuer Flugzieldarstellungen mbH. Hohn.	N435JW
D-CGFD	77	Learjet 35A	35A-139	GFD fuer Flugzieldarstellungen mbH. Hohn.	N15SC
D-CGFE	89	Learjet 36A	36A-062	GFD fuer Flugzieldarstellungen mbH. Hohn.	N4291N
D-CGFF	89	Learjet 36A	36A-063	GFD fuer Flugzieldarstellungen mbH. Hohn.	N1048X
D-CGFG	79	Learjet 35A	35A-222	GFD fuer Flugzieldarstellungen mbH. Hohn.	N789KW
D-CGFH	86	Learjet 35A	35A-607	GFD fuer Flugzieldarstellungen mbH. Hohn.	N68MJ
D-CGFI	86	Learjet 35A	35A-612	GFD fuer Flugzieldarstellungen mbH. Hohn.	N36BP
D-CGFJ	88	Learjet 35A	35A-643	GFD fuer Flugzieldarstellungen mbH. Hohn.	N643MJ
D-CGGB	04	Learjet 40	45-2018	Cirrus Airlines Luftfahrt GmbH. Saarbruecken.	OE-GGB

Reg	Yr	Type	c/n	Owner/Operator	Prev Regn
D-CGGG	01	Learjet 31A	31A-227	GAS Air Service GmbH. Muenster-Osnabrueck.	N40073
D-CGRC	79	Learjet 35A	35A-223	Jet Executive International Charter GmbH. Duesseldorf.	N215JW
D-CGTF	04	Learjet 60	60-281	Air Executive Charter GmbH. Munich.	OE-GTF
D-CHDC	07	Citation Sovereign	680-0150	Heidelberg Cement AG. Heidelberg.	N......
D-CHDE	89	Citation V	560-0031	Aerowest Flugcharter GmbH. Hanover.	N1229F
D-CHEF	01	Hawker 800XP	258514	Elbe Air Lufttransport AG. Paderborn.	N4021Z
D-CHEP	92	Citation II	550-0697	Triple Alpha Luftfahrt GmbH. Duesseldorf.	HB-VMP
D-CHHH	06	Citation Excel XLS	560-5674	Augusta Air GmbH. Augsburg.	N51160
D-CHIP	07	Citation Sovereign	680-0156	Comfort Air GmbH. Munich.	N5235G
D-CHLE	01	Learjet 60	60-211	Daimler Chrysler AG. Stuttgart.	N5012Z
D-CHMC	99	Citation Bravo	550-0874	Homac Aviation Executive, Friedrichshafen.	LX-EJH
D-CHSP	04	Citation Excel XLS	560-5536	Bluebird Aviation GmbH. Dusseldorf.	N25XL
D-CHSW	94	Beechjet 400A	RK-84	Augusta Air GmbH. Augsburg.	N8138M
D-CHZF	99	Citation Bravo	550-0866	SFD Stuttgarter Flugdienst GmbH. Stuttgart.	N866CB
D-CIAO	81	Citation II	550-0255	ACH Hamburg Flug GmbH. hamburg.	I-JESO
D-CINS	07	Learjet 45	45-347	Aero Dienst GmbH. Nuremberg.	N40050
D-CITA	95	Learjet 60	60-069	Senator Aviation Charter GmbH. Hamburg.	N60CE
D-CITY	78	Learjet 35A	35A-177	Helmut Idzkowiak/Senator Aviation Charter GmbH.Hamburg.	N174CP
D-CJAK	06	CitationJet CJ-3	525B-0075	MAP Management + Planning GmbH. Vienna, Austria.	N528JC
D-CJJJ	86	Citation S/II	S550-0086	Travel Air Flug GmbH. Duesseldorf.	N11SU
D-CJPG	77	Learjet 35A	35A-108	Juliane Griesemann/Quick Air Jet Charter GmbH. Cologne.	(N86PQ)
D-CKDM	07	Gulfstream G150	235		N635GA
D-CKJS	06	CitationJet CJ-3	525B-0086	MSR-Flug Charter GmbH. Muenster-Osnabrueck.	N51993
D-CLAT	06	CitationJet CJ-3	525B-0085	Liebherr-Aerospace Lindenberg GmbH. Friedrichshafen.	N51881
D-CLBA	91	Beechjet 400A	RK-25	LBA-Luftfahrt Bundesamt, Braunschweig.	(VR-CDA)
D-CLBB	74	Falcon 20E-5	315	Elbe Air Lufttransport AG. Paderborn.	F-GSXF
D-CLBC	86	BAe 125/800B	258050	Elbe Air Lufttransport AG. Paderborn.	G-OURA
D-CLBD	99	Hawker 800XP	258405	Elbe Air Lufttransport AG. Paderborn.	N866RB
D-CLBG	04	Hawker 800XP	258682	Elbe Air Lufttransport AG. Paderborn.	4X-CRU
D-CLBH	06	Hawker 850XP	258812	Elbe Air Lufttransport AG. Paderborn.	N812XP
D-CLBR	66	Falcon 20C	52	Challenge Aero, Kiev, Ukraine.	N852TC
D-CLDF	98	Citation VII	650-7085	EFS/Love Dynamic Flight GmbH. Duesseldorf.	N785CC
D-CLLL	07	Citation Excel XLS	560-5722	Augusta Air GmbH. Augsburg.	N5165T
D-CLUE	89	Citation III	650-0174	GEG Grundstueckscentwicklungs H H Goettsch KG. Cologne.	N674CC
D-CLUX	06	Learjet 40	45-2061	Cirrus Airlines Luftfahrt GmbH. Saarbruecken.	N5016Z
D-CMAX	81	Learjet 55	55-011	FAI rent-a-jet AG. Nuremberg.	SE-RCK
D-CMEI	91	Citation V	560-0117	Siegfried Meister/Lech Air GmbH Lech AFB.	(N6804F)
D-CMES	07	Citation Sovereign	680-0162	Lech Air GmbH. Oberpfaffenhofen.	N5218T
D-CMET	75	Falcon 20E-5	329	Deutsches Zentrum fuer Luft und Raumfahrt GmbH.	F-WRQV
D-CMHS	07	CitationJet CJ-3	525B-0161	HTM Helicopter Travel Munich GmbH. Munich.	N5268M
D-CMIX	03	Citation Bravo	550-1050	Dr Schenk Flugbetrieb GmbH. Munich.	A9C-BXC
D-CMMI	04	Citation Excel XLS	560-5538	Dr Schenk Flugbetrieb GmbH. Munich.	OE-GCM
D-CMMP	07	Citation Excel XLS	560-5719	SFD Stuttgarter Flugdienst GmbH. Stuttgart.	N12UD
D-CMPI	95	Citation VII	650-7055	SFD Stuttgarter Flugdienst GmbH. Stuttgart.	N817MZ
D-CMRM	00	Learjet 31A	31A-213	Aero-Dienst GmbH. Nuremberg.	
D-CMSC	00	Learjet 45	45-097	SAP AG Systeme, Mannheim.	N5017J
D-CNCJ	99	Citation VII	650-7102	ACM Air Charter GmbH. Baden-Baden.	N5223X
D-CNIK	03	Learjet 40	45-2006	Cirrus Airlines Luftfahrt GmbH. Saarbruecken.	N50111
D-CNOB	06	CitationJet CJ-3	525B-0119	Atlas Air Service GmbH. Gandersee.	N5257V
D-COBO	06	CitationJet CJ-3	525B-0107	OBO Jet Charter GmbH. Arnsberg.	N709PG
D-COKE	81	Learjet 35A	35A-447	Private Wings Flugcharter GmbH. Berlin-Tempelhof.	N300FN
D-CONE	77	Learjet 35A	35A-111	Air Alliance Express GmbH. Siegerland.	I-LIAD
D-CONU	86	Learjet 55	55-124	FAI rent-a-jet AG. Nuremberg.	SX-BTV
D-COOL	83	Learjet 55	55-052	Premium Aviation GmbH. Munich.	N551DB
D-CPDR	07	Learjet 40	45-2080	Silver Bird Charterflug GmbH. Bremen.	N40076
D-CPMU	94	Learjet 60	60-032	Premium Aviation GmbH. Munich.	OE-GNL
D-CPPP	98	Citation Bravo	550-0865	Windrose Air Flugcharter GmbH. Berlin.	N505X
D-CPRO	98	Learjet 31A	31A-155	Proair Charter Transport GmbH. Frankfurt.	N525GP
D-CRAH	07	CitationJet CJ-3	525B-0154	Fresner Flug GmbH. Leer.	N......
D-CRAN	93	Learjet 60	60-019	Senator Aviation Charter GmbH. Hamburg.	HB-VKI
D-CREY	90	Citation III	650-0192	Triple Alpha Luftfahrt GmbH. Duesseldorf. 'Ladybird'	N78EM
D-CRHR	87	Citation III	650-0142	EFS Flug Service GmbH. Duesseldorf. (status ?).	(N492BA)
D-CRIS	98	Astra-1125SPX	107	Fondsprojekt Josef Esch GmbH/Challenge Air GmbH. Cologne.	N997GA
D-CROB	02	Learjet 60	60-261	Cirrus Airlines Luftfahrt GmbH. Saarbruecken.	N4003Q
D-CRON*	07	Citation Excel XLS	560-5762		N51780
D-CRRR	90	Citation III	650-0187	EFS Flug Service GmbH. Duesseldorf.	LN-AAA

Reg	Yr	Type	c/n	Owner/Operator	Prev Regn
☐ D-CSAP	92	Learjet 31A	31A-057	SAP AG Systeme, Mannheim.	N9147Q
☐ D-CSFD	99	Citation Excel	560-5022	SFD Stuttgarter Flugdienst GmbH. Stuttgart.	HZ-FYZ
☐ D-CSIE	00	Learjet 31A	31A-207	Aero-Dienst GmbH. Nuremberg.	N50126
☐ D-CSIM	04	Learjet 60	60-274	Aero-Dienst GmbH. Nuremberg.	N4003K
☐ D-CSIX	97	Learjet 60	60-120	Rainer Wenz, Wiesbaden.	(N141MB)
☐ D-CSMB	06	Citation Bravo	550-1130	S M Aviation Service GmbH. Neuburg.	N5125J
☐ D-CSMS	98	Learjet 45	45-017	SMS Industrie GmbH.	D-CESH
☐ D-CSPJ	07	Grob G-180 SPn	90003	Grob Aerospace, Tussenhausen-Mattsies. (Ff 29 Oct 07).	
☐ D-CSPN	05	Grob G-180 SPn	90001	Grob Aerospace, Tussenhausen-Mattsies. (Ff 20 Jul 05).	D-ISPN
☐ D-CSUL	01	Learjet 45	45-189	Silke & Roland Sulz GbR/Proair Aviation GmbH. Filderstadt.	N800MA
☐ D-CSWM	99	Citation Bravo	550-0884	LGM Luftfahrt GmbH. Mosbach.	VP-CGL
☐ D-CTEC	06	CitationJet CJ-3	525B-0101	Aero Business Charter GmbH. Egelsbach.	N52113
☐ D-CTLX	05	Citation Excel XLS	560-5569	Daimler Chrysler AG. Stuttgart.	N.....
☐ D-CTRI	80	Learjet 35A	35A-346	Air Alliance GmbH. Siegerland.	EC-IIC
☐ D-CTTT	05	Citation Excel XLS	560-5573	Augusta Air GmbH. Augsburg.	(OE-GAL)
☐ D-CTWO	89	Learjet 31	31-011		HB-VJI
☐ D-CUBA	07	CitationJet CJ-3	525B-0169	Air Service GmbH. Essingen.	N5250P
☐ D-CUNO	84	Learjet 55	55-108	FAI rent-a-jet AG. Nuremberg.	(D-CMAX)
☐ D-CUPI	06	Citation Sovereign	680-0066	Jet Air Flug GmbH. Kiev, Ukraine.	OE-GUP
☐ D-CURT	91	Learjet 31A	31A-042	Air Traffic GmbH. Duesseldorf. 'Erich Morillo'	D-CGGG
☐ D-CUUU	07	CitationJet CJ-3	525B-0197	Windrose Air Flugcharter GmbH. Berlin.	N5262X
☐ D-CVHA	05	Citation Sovereign	680-0050	Viessmann Werke GmbH. Allendorf.	N5257V
☐ D-CVHB	07	Citation Excel XLS	560-5688	Viessmann Werke GmbH. Allendorf.	N50639
☐ D-CVHI	01	Citation Excel	560-5195	MAP Management + Planning GmbH, Vienna, Austria.	N51143
☐ D-CVII		Citation VII	...		
☐ D-CVIP	84	Learjet 55	55-109	WDL Aviation GmbH. Koeln.	N348HM
☐ D-CVJN	07	Learjet 40	45-2091	Vistajet Luftfahrt GmbH.	N5009T
☐ D-CVJP	07	Learjet 40	45-2079	Air Executive Charter GmbH. Munich.	N40082
☐ D-CVVV	07	Citation Excel XLS	560-5723	Augusta Air GmnH. Augsburg.	N5260M
☐ D-CWAY	84	Learjet 55	55-107	Silver Bird Charterflug GmbH. Bremen.	N304AT
☐ D-CWDL	83	Learjet 55	55-084	WDL Aviation GmbH. Koeln.	I-FLYJ
☐ D-CWHS	06	Learjet 60	60-246	Cirrus Airlines Luftfahrt GmbH. Saarbruecken.	N5035F
☐ D-CWWW*	07	Citation Excel XLS	560-5788	Augusta Air GmbH. Augsburg.	N.....
☐ D-IAGG	01	390 Premier 1	RB-35	Vibro Air Flugservice GmbH. Moenchengladbach.	N435K
☐ D-IAHG	95	CitationJet	525-0126	AHG Handel & Logistics GmbH.	D-IMPC
☐ D-IAJJ	75	Citation	500-0245	Travel Air Flug GmbH. Duesseldorf.	(N245BC)
☐ D-IAMO	03	CitationJet CJ-2	525A-0166	Windrose/Bizair Flug GmbH. Berlin-Tempelhof.	N5218R
☐ D-IAOA	93	CitationJet	525-0024	Triple Alpha Luftfahrt GmbH. Duesseldorf.	F-HAOA
☐ D-IATT	02	390 Premier 1	RB-48	Vibro Air Flugservice GmbH. Moenchengladbach.	N51480
☐ D-IBBA	93	CitationJet	525-0025	Aerocharter L U Bettermann OHG. Menden.	D-IOBO
☐ D-IBBB	03	390 Premier 1	RB-82	Amola GmbH. Darmstadt.	N61882
☐ D-IBBS	06	CitationJet CJ2+	525A-0313	Atlas Air Service GmbH. Gandersee.	N5157E
☐ D-IBCT	06	CitationJet CJ2+	525A-0328	Aero GmbH. Bielefeld.	(N65PZ)
☐ D-IBJJ	02	CitationJet CJ-2	525A-0125	Elbe Aviation Lufttransport AG. Hamburg.	N525CG
☐ D-IBMS	99	CitationJet	525-0309	Brose Fahrzeugteile GmbH. Coburg.	
☐ D-ICAC	79	Citation II/SP	551-0010	Oldenburg Kunstoff Technik GmbH. Kassel.	(N460JR)
☐ D-ICEE	95	CitationJet	525-0096	Krause/Private Flight GmbH. Bayreuth.	(EC-...)
☐ D-ICEY	05	CitationJet CJ1+	525-0611	Lenoxhandels u Speditions GmbH. Hamburg.	N52645
☐ D-ICIA	73	Citation	500-0086	Uniwest Air BV. Lelystad, Holland.	LX-YKH
☐ D-ICMS	02	CitationJet CJ-2	525A-0108	Brose Fahrzeugteile GmbH. Coburg.	N5136J
☐ D-ICOL	99	CitationJet	525-0353	Colloseum II Handels und Beteilings mbH. Moenchengladbach.	N5211Q
☐ D-ICSS	95	CitationJet	525-0121	EFD-Eisele Flugdienst GmbH. Stuttgart.	TC-EMA
☐ D-ICTA	81	Citation II/SP	551-0051	Flugbereitschaft GmbH. Karlsruhe.	(D-IHAT)
☐ D-ICWB	99	CitationJet	525-0349	BFD-Brandenburger Flugdienst GmbH. Berlin-Schoenefeld.	
☐ D-IDAG	96	CitationJet	525-0144	DAS-Direct Air Service GmbH. Mannheim.	N5200R
☐ D-IDAS	00	CitationJet CJ-1	525-0389	Donau Air Service GmbH. Mengen.	N389CJ
☐ D-IDBA	06	390 Premier 1A	RB-164	Premier Flug GmbH.	N36864
☐ D-IDMH	03	CitationJet CJ-2	525A-0174	Herrenknecht AG. Lahr.	N5076K
☐ D-IEAR	79	Citation II/SP	551-0018	(status ?). (was 550-0373).	N387MA
☐ D-IEFA	07	CitationJet CJ2+	525A-0358	EFD-Eisele Flugdienst GmbH. Stuttgart.	N5061F
☐ D-IEGA	73	Citation	500-0081		I-PEGA
☐ D-IEIR	83	Citation 1/SP	501-0259	Karl Georg Theurer, Stuttgart.	(N225WT)
☐ D-IEPR	06	CitationJet CJ1+	525-0625	Dieter Eifler Elekrto GmbH. Saarbruecken.	(VH-ODJ)
☐ D-IETZ	07	CitationJet CJ-3	525A-0363	Aero Business Charter GmbH. Egelsbach.	D-IEBJ
☐ D-IFDH	03	CitationJet CJ-1	525-0517	Flugbetrieb Gesellschaft Dix mbH. Diepholz.	N52626
☐ D-IFDN	07	CitationJet CJ2+	525A-0343	Dix Flugbetrieb GmbH. Paderborn.	N5108G

| Reg | Yr | Type | c/n | Owner/Operator | Prev Regn |

Reg	Yr	Type	c/n	Owner/Operator	Prev Regn
☐ D-IFIS	06	CitationJet CJ2+	525A-0340	SFD Stuttgarter Flugdienst GmbH. Stuttgart.	N5086W
☐ D-IFLY	05	CitationJet CJ2+	525A-0330	Tamsen Sea & Air GmbH. Stuhr.	N5231S
☐ D-IFMC	01	390 Premier 1	RB-27	GEMU Gebr Muller GmbH. Schwaebisch Hall.	N3216P
☐ D-IFMG	04	390 Premier 1	RB-109	Forum Air GmbH.	N50078
☐ D-IGIT	01	CitationJet CJ-2	525A-0032	Triple Alpha Luftfahrt GmbH. Duesseldorf.	D-IOBO
☐ D-IGME	98	CitationJet	525-0279	Charter Service Hetzler GmbH. Frankfurt.	
☐ D-IGRO	04	CitationJet CJ-2	525A-0230	Atlas Air Service GmbH. Gandersee.	N5136J
☐ D-IHEB	94	CitationJet	525-0064	Fortuna-Werbung GmbH/Silver Cloud Air GmbH. Speyer.	N2649S
☐ D-IHHN	01	CitationJet CJ-2	525A-0041	Triple Alpha Luftfahrt GmbH. Duesseldorf.	N43ND
☐ D-IHRA	02	CitationJet CJ-2	525A-0168	Triple Alpha Luftfahrt GmbH. Duesseldorf.	N767W
☐ D-IIMC	07	390 Premier 1A	RB-196	MSR-Flug Charter GmbH. Muenster-Osnabrueck.	N37346
☐ D-IJOA	01	CitationJet CJ-2	525A-0034	Air Evex GmbH. Duesseldorf.	N5211F
☐ D-IKJS	01	CitationJet CJ-2	525A-0029	MSR-Flug Charter GmbH. Muenster-Osnabrueck.	N92CJ
☐ D-IKOP	93	CitationJet	525-0016	Jet Executive International Charter GmbH. Duesseldorf.	N216CJ
☐ D-ILAM	02	CitationJet CJ-2	525A-0070	Liebherr-Aerospace Lindenberg GmbH. Friedrichshafen.	N5157E
☐ D-ILAT	97	CitationJet	525-0209	Liebherr-Aerospace Lindenberg GmbH. Friedrichshafen.	
☐ D-ILDL	03	CitationJet CJ-2	525A-0167	Daimler Chrysler AG. Stuttgart.	N51806
☐ D-ILIF	00	CitationJet CJ-1	525-0411	Air Alliance Express GmbH. Siegerland.	N535RF
☐ D-ILLY	01	CitationJet CJ-1	525-0442	Jetline Flug GmbH. Stuttgart.	D-IFIS
☐ D-IMAC	00	CitationJet CJ-1	525-0396	Dr Schenk Flugbetrieb GmbH. Munich.	N51575
☐ D-IMAX	04	CitationJet CJ-2	525A-0195	Fortuna-Werbung GmbH/Silver Cloud Air GmbH. Speyer.	N51942
☐ D-IMMD	97	CitationJet	525-0211	Makro-Medien-Dienst GmbH. Ostfildern.	
☐ D-IMME	82	Citation II/SP	551-0400	Commander Flugdienst GmbH. Hamburg. (was 550-0359).	N280JS
☐ D-IMMI	99	CitationJet	525-0303	Dr Schenk Flugbetrieb GmbH. Munich.	N51612
☐ D-IMPC	06	CitationJet CJ1+	525-0639	Schroeder & Offen GmbH. Hamburg.	(D-ICPO)
☐ D-INCS	01	CitationJet CJ-1	525-0466	Canair Luftfahrtunternehmen, Hamburg.	(D-ILLL)
☐ D-INER	03	CitationJet CJ-1	525-0516	Triple Alpha Liftfahrt GmbH. Duesseldorf.	N525CF
☐ D-INFS	98	CitationJet	525-0286	Nordfrost Kuehl u Lagerhaus GmbH.	D-ICEY
☐ D-INOB	04	CitationJet CJ-2	525A-0196	Atlas Air Service GmbH. Gandersee.	N5166T
☐ D-IOBO	06	CitationJet CJ2+	525A-0332	OBO Jet Charter GmbH. Arnsberg.	D-IOBU
☐ D-IOHL	05	CitationJet CJ-2	525A-0233	Ohlair Charterflug KG. Kiel-Holtenau.	D-IBBE
☐ D-IOWA	06	CitationJet CJ1+	525-0624	Waldmann Lichttechnik GmbH. Villingen.	N5141F
☐ D-IPCS	98	CitationJet	525-0264	MSR-Flug Charter GmbH. Muenster-Osnabrueck.	EC-HBC
☐ D-IPMI	04	CitationJet CJ-1	525-0533	Papier Mettler, Morbach.	(D-IPMM)
☐ D-IPVD	04	CitationJet CJ-2	525A-0218	GIL-Gebaude u Industrieguter Leasing GmbH. Mannheim.	N.....
☐ D-IRKE	95	CitationJet	525-0123	Triple Alpha Luftfahrt GmbH. Duesseldorf.	N5223P
☐ D-IRON	96	CitationJet	525-0168	Geisers Stahlbau GmbH. Duesseldorf.	N51522
☐ D-IRUP	88	Citation II	551-0572	Triple Alpha Luftfahrt GmbH. Duesseldorf. (was 550-0572).	N719EH
☐ D-IRWR	95	CitationJet	525-0118	Bizair Flug GmbH. Berlin-Tempelhof.	N118AZ
☐ D-ISAG	07	390 Premier 1A	RB-221		N31921
☐ D-ISAR	05	390 Premier 1A	RB-148	Euroflug Freiburg Gerhard Frenzel, Freiburg.	N6148Z
☐ D-ISCH	02	CitationJet CJ-2	525A-0052	Gerhard Schubert GmbH. Nordlingen.	N51881
☐ D-ISEC	80	Citation II/SP	551-0201	EFS Flug Service GmbH. Duesseldorf. (was 550-0131).	N550GB
☐ D-ISGW	94	CitationJet	525-0070	MSR-Flug Charter GmbH. Muenster-Osnabrueck.	N26504
☐ D-ISHW	98	CitationJet	525-0289	Siemag Verwaltungs GmbH. Hilchenbach.	
☐ D-ISJM	05	CitationJet CJ1+	525-0602	Secura Vermogensverwaltungs GmbH/JABJ, Cologne-Bonn.	N74UK
☐ D-ISJP	01	CitationJet CJ-2	525A-0030	Juergen Persch, Siegerland.	N302DM
☐ D-ISKM	76	Citation Eagle	500-0313	Marxer Anlagen u Maschinenbrau GmbH. Friedberg.	N313BA
☐ D-ISUN	03	CitationJet CJ-2	525A-0143	Challengeline LS GmbH. Business Jets,	N.....
☐ D-ISWA	98	CitationJet	525-0236	Herbert Waldmann Lichttechnik GmbH. Villingen-Schwenningen.	
☐ D-ISXT	02	390 Premier 1	RB-50	Sixt Autovermietung GmbH. Paderborn.	N390NS
☐ D-ITAN	00	CitationJet CJ-1	525-0399	Transavia GmbH. Speyer.	(VP-CTN)
☐ D-ITIP	01	CitationJet CJ-1	525-0494	Aircraft Investment GmbH. Moenchen Gladbach.	N71HR
☐ D-ITOR	07	CitationJet CJ2+	525-0364	Hoermann KG Verkaufsgesellschaft, Paderborn.	N5090V
☐ D-IURS	99	CitationJet	525-0343	WB Jet Charter GmbH.	N5244F
☐ D-IVVA	03	CitationJet CJ-2	525A-0147	Jetline Flug GmbH. Stuttgart.	VP-BJR
☐ D-IWAN	04	CitationJet CJ-2	525A-0223	CCC Air GmbH. Hanover.	N.....
☐ D-IWBL	07	CitationJet CJ2+	525A-0355	Hans Dutzi/Air Traffic GmbH. Duesseldorf.	N5079V
☐ D-IWHL	93	CitationJet	525-0029	HL & Partner Marketing Services GmbH. Hamburg.	(N525KT)
☐ D-IWIL	97	CitationJet	525-0221	Charterflug Rademacher GmbH. Rhede.	
☐ D-IWIN	05	CitationJet CJ-2	525A-0231	Silver Cloud Air GmbH. Speyer.	N5211A
☐ D-IWIR	02	CitationJet CJ-2	525A-0102	Wirten Group GmbH. Windhagen.	N888KL
☐ D-IWWW	03	390 Premier 1	RB-89	MSR-Flug Charter GmbH. Muenster-Osnabrueck.	N61589

Military

Reg	Yr	Type	c/n	Owner/Operator	Prev Regn
☐ 10+21	89	Airbus A310-304	498	Bundesrepublik Deutschland, Cologne. 'Konrad Adenauer'	D-AOAA
☐ 10+22	89	Airbus A310-304	499	Bundesrepublik Deutschland, Cologne. 'Theodor Heuss'	D-AOAB

Reg	Yr	Type	c/n	Owner/Operator	Prev Regn
☐ 12+02	85	Challenger 601	3040	Luftwaffe, FBS, Cologne.	N608CL
☐ 12+03	85	Challenger 601	3043	Luftwaffe, FBS, Cologne.	N609CL
☐ 12+04	85	Challenger 601	3049	Luftwaffe, FBS, Cologne.	C-FQYT
☐ 12+05	86	Challenger 601	3053	Luftwaffe, FBS, Cologne.	N604CL
☐ 12+06	86	Challenger 601	3056	Luftwaffe, FBS, Cologne.	N612CL
☐ 12+07	86	Challenger 601	3059	Luftwaffe, FBS, Cologne.	N614CL

D2 = ANGOLA   Total   17

Civil

Reg	Yr	Type	c/n	Owner/Operator	Prev Regn
☐ D2-...	99	Learjet 45	45-066		N94CK
☐ D2-EBA	99	Citation V Ultra	560-0502	Aeromercado Ltda. Luanda.	N1298X
☐ D2-EBN	00	Learjet 45	45-069	Angola Air Services, Luanda.	SU-MSG
☐ D2-ECB	85	Gulfstream 3	474	Government of Angola, Luanda. 'Cunene'	N311GA
☐ D2-ECE	02	Citation Bravo	550-1008	Aeromercado Ltda. Luanda.	N40435
☐ D2-EDC	73	Citation	500-0071	MRI Angola, Luanda.	(D2-AJL)
☐ D2-EFM	71	HS 125/400B	25260		ZS-JIH
☐ D2-EVD	67	B 727-29C	19403	SONANGOL Aeronautica - Helipetrol, Luanda.	CB-02
☐ D2-EVG	67	B 727-29C	19402	SONANGOL Aeronautica - Helipetrol, Luanda.	N70PA
☐ D2-EXR	70	HS 125/403B	25215	Intertransit, Luanda. (status ?)	ZS-NPV
☐ D2-FEZ	69	HS 125/F3B-RA	25171	Gira Globo Ltda Aeronautica, Luanda.	(N171AV)
☐ D2-FFH	70	HS 125/F400A	25219	Gira Globo Ltda Aeronautica, Luanda.	(ZS-OZU)
☐ D2-GES	06	Citation Bravo	550-1135		N5180C
☐ D2-JMM	66	Falcon 20-5	54	American Consulting Business SA Ltd. Tortola, BVI.	N405JW
☐ D2-MAN	69	B 707-321B	20025	Government of Angola, Luanda.	N707KS
☐ D2-TPR	74	B 707-3J6B	20715	Government of Angola, Luanda.	B-2404

Military

Reg	Yr	Type	c/n	Owner/Operator	Prev Regn
☐ T-501	07	Embraer Legacy 600	14500981	Government of Angola, Luanda.	PT-SHT

EC = SPAIN   Total   127

Civil

Reg	Yr	Type	c/n	Owner/Operator	Prev Regn
☐ EC-EDC	65	Falcon 20C	6	Audeli SA. Madrid-Torrejon. (status ?).	N750SS
☐ EC-EDN	77	Citation 1/SP	501-0010	Instituto Cartografic de Catelunya, Barcelona-El Prat.	VH-POZ
☐ EC-EHC	66	Falcon 20DC	46	Audeli SA. Madrid-Torrejon. (status ?).	N46VG
☐ EC-FZP	94	CitationJet	525-0065	Gestair Executive Jet SA. Madrid-Torrejon.	EC-704
☐ EC-GIE	96	CitationJet	525-0133	Gestair Executive Jet SA. Madrid-Torrejon.	EC-261
☐ EC-GJF	79	Citation 1/SP	501-0107	Jose Maria Caballe Horta, Alicante.	(N75471)
☐ EC-GNK	96	Falcon 2000	37	Gestair Executive Jet SA. Madrid-Torrejon.	F-WWMH
☐ EC-GOV	97	Citation V Ultra	560-0419	Gestair Executive Jet SA. Madrid-Torrejon.	N5233J
☐ EC-GSL	81	Westwind-Two	353	Gestair Executive Jet SA. Burgos.	C-GRGE
☐ EC-GTS	72	Citation	500-0037	Clipper National Air SA. Barcelona-El Prat.	N407SC
☐ EC-HCX	72	Falcon 20C	184	Audeli SA. Madrid-Torrejon.	OE-GCJ
☐ EC-HGI	88	Citation II	550-0596	Transportes Aereos del Sur SA. Seville. 'L'Altet'	D-CAWA
☐ EC-HIA	75	Corvette	19	Wondair on Demand Aviation SL. Valencia.	F-GEPQ
☐ EC-HIN	97	CitationJet	525-0197	Air Link Solutions, Madrid.	N525KH
☐ EC-HOB	99	Falcon 900EX	43	Executive Airlines SA. Barcelona.	F-WQBK
☐ EC-HPQ	74	Citation	500-0157	Airnor - Aeronaves del Noroeste SL. Ponteareas.	EC-HFY
☐ EC-HRH	73	Citation	500-0116	PRT Aviation SL. Barcelona-El Prat.	D-IATC
☐ EC-HRO	00	Citation Bravo	550-0938	CIRSA/Executive Airlines SA. Barcelona-El Prat.	N5VN
☐ EC-HRQ	82	HS 125/700B	257166	Executive Airlines SA. Barcelona.	EC-HRQ
☐ EC-HTR	00	Beechjet 400A	RK-293	Universal Jet SL. Barcelona.	N4293K
☐ EC-HVQ	01	CitationJet CJ-1	525-0436	Gestair Executive Jet SA. Madrid-Torrejon.	N5141F
☐ EC-HVV	82	Falcon 100	193	Dominguez Toledo SA/Mayoral Executive Jet, Malaga.	(N30TN)
☐ EC-HYI	01	Falcon 2000	150	Gestair Executive Jet SA. Madrid-Torrejon.	F-WWVH
☐ EC-IAX	80	Citation II	550-0156	TRAGSA-Empresa de Transformacion Agraria SA. Madrid.	N205SC
☐ EC-IBA	74	Citation	500-0178	Airnor - Aeronaves del Noroeste SL. Ponteareas.	HB-VKK
☐ EC-IBD	01	Global Express	9060	Gestair Executive Jet SA. Madrid-Torrejon.	(EC-FPI)
☐ EC-IEB	02	CitationJet CJ-2	525A-0064	TAG Aviation Espana SA. Madrid-Torrejon.	N5135K
☐ EC-IFS	02	Global Express	9089	Gestair Executive Jet SA. Madrid-Torrejon.	C-GHZH
☐ EC-IIR	02	Embraer Legacy 600	145540	FADESA/Audeli Air Express, Madrid-Torrejon.	PT-SAI
☐ EC-ILK	99	Learjet 45	45-064	Mango, Punto Fa SL. Barcelona.	N800UA
☐ EC-IMF	82	Citation II	550-0443	Aerodynamics Malaga SL. Malaga.	D-CGAS
☐ EC-INJ	79	Citation 1/SP	501-0086	Clipper National Air SA. Barcelona-El Prat	(N554T)
☐ EC-INS	87	Learjet 55B	55B-133	Gestair-Sky Service Aviation SL. Madrid-Torrejon.	N810V
☐ EC-IOZ	02	390 Premier 1	RB-61	Gestair Executive Jet SA. Madrid-Torrejon. (status ?)	N61161
☐ EC-IRZ	99	Gulfstream V	582	Gestair Executive Jet SA. Madrid-Torrejon.	N271JG
☐ EC-ISP	79	Citation 1/SP	501-0084	Ibiza Flight, Ibiza.	G-CITI
☐ EC-ISQ	03	Citation Excel	560-5353	Industrias Titan SA. Barcelona-Sabadell.	(N678QS)

Reg   Yr Type   c/n   Owner/Operator   Prev Regn

41

Reg	Yr	Type	c/n	Owner/Operator	Prev Regn
☐ EC-IUQ	98	Global Express	9007	Iberostar Group. Palma.	N907GX
☐ EC-IVJ	00	CitationJet CJ-1	525-0429	Executive Airlines SA. Palma di Mallorca.	N429PK
☐ EC-JBB	98	Falcon 900C	182	TAG Aviation Espana SA. Madrid-Torrejon.	N168HT
☐ EC-JBH	87	Falcon 200	511	Mayoral Executive Jet, Malaga.	F-WQBK
☐ EC-JFD	01	CitationJet CJ-1	525-0448	Executive Airlines SA. Barcelona.	N448JC
☐ EC-JFT	99	Citation V Ultra	560-0506	Wondair on Demand Aviation SL. Valencia.	G-OGRG
☐ EC-JGN	04	Gulfstream G200	103	Gestair Executive Jet SA. Madrid-Torrejon.	N203GA
☐ EC-JIL	04	Global Express	9146	Mango MNG Bird SL. Barcelona.	C-FAHQ
☐ EC-JIU	02	CitationJet CJ-1	525-0486	Sky Helicopteros SA. Palma-Son Bonet.	N334BD
☐ EC-JJH	69	Falcon 20-5	176	Gestair Executive Jet SA. Madrid-Torrejon.	F-WQBM
☐ EC-JJU	01	CitationJet CJ-2	525A-0033	SOKO Aviation SL. Madrid-Cuatro Vientos.	(D-IETZ)
☐ EC-JKL	84	Diamond 1A	A084SA	FlyLink Express SA. Madrid-Cuatro Vientos.	N160H
☐ EC-JMS	04	CitationJet CJ-2	525A-0216	Jetnova de Aviacion Ejecutiva SA. Murcia.	OY-GGR
☐ EC-JNY	05	Hawker 850XP	258748	Gestair Executive Jet SA. Madrid-Torrejon.	N748XP
☐ EC-JNZ	99	Falcon 900C	181	TAG Aviation Espana SA. Madrid-Torrejon.	N833AV
☐ EC-JON	80	Citation II	550-0190	Aerotaxi Los Valles SL. Madrid.	F-GZLC
☐ EC-JPK	05	Gulfstream G550	5078	Gestair Executive Jet SA. Madrid-Torrejon.	N578GA
☐ EC-JPN	05	Hawker 400XP	RK-428	Marina Aeroservice SA/Universal Jet SL. Barcelona.	OE-GYR
☐ EC-JQE	05	Gulfstream G200	125	Executive Airlines SA. Barcelona.	N221GA
☐ EC-JSH	02	CitationJet CJ-1	525-0508	SOKO Aviation SL. Madrid-Cuatro Vientos.	N508CJ
☐ EC-JTH	80	Citation II/SP	551-0031	Clipper National Air SA. Barcelona-El Prat.	N5TQ
☐ EC-JVB	01	Learjet 60	60-243	Wondair on Demand Aviation SL. Valencia.	OY-LGI
☐ EC-JVF	05	Citation Excel XLS	560-5564	Executive Airlines SA. Barcelona.	N560TM
☐ EC-JVI	98	Falcon 2000	61	Gestair Executive Jet SA. Madrid-Torrejon.	F-GJTH
☐ EC-JVM	99	Learjet 60	60-161	BKS Air, Getxo.	D-CDNZ
☐ EC-JVR	91	Falcon 900B	106	Gestair Executive Jet SA. Madrid-Torrejon.	N333EC
☐ EC-JXC	75	Citation	500-0278	Airnor - Aeronaves del Noroeste SL. Ponteareas.	OY-PCW
☐ EC-JXE	05	Gulfstream G100	158	Executive Airlines SA. Barcelona.	N995GA
☐ EC-JXI	05	Citation Excel XLS	560-5593	Jetnova de Aviacion Ejecutiva SA. Murcia.	N593XL
☐ EC-JXR	97	Falcon 2000	55	Gestair Executive Jet SA. Madrid-Torrejon.	F-GJTG
☐ EC-JYG	06	Citation Sovereign	680-0087	SOKO Aviation SL. Madrid-Cuatro Vientos.	(N666BK)
☐ EC-JYQ	02	Learjet 60	60-249	SOKO Aviation SL. Madrid-Cuatro Vientos.	D-CLUB
☐ EC-JYR	05	Gulfstream G550	5116	Executive Airlines SA. Barcelona.	N836GA
☐ EC-JYT	06	Challenger 604	5648	Jet Personales SA. Madrid-Torrejon.	C-FHDV
☐ EC-JYY	05	Learjet 40	45-2026	SOKO Aviation SL. Madrid-Cuatro Vientos.	OE-GVI
☐ EC-JZK	05	Citation Excel XLS	560-5554	Corporate Jets XXI, Barcelona.	JY-AW1
☐ EC-K..	07	Citation Excel XLS	560-5753		N52653
☐ EC-K..	07	CitationJet CJ2+	525A-0381		N52627
☐ EC-KBC	06	Gulfstream G200	145	TAG Aviation Espana SA. Madrid-Torrejon.	N645GA
☐ EC-KBR	06	Gulfstream G550	5124	TAG Aviation Espana SA. Madrid-Torrejon.	N524GA
☐ EC-KBZ	91	Citation II	550-0678	Gestair Executive Jet SA. Madrid-Torrejon.	SE-RCI
☐ EC-KCA	06	Gulfstream G200	150	Gestair Executive Jet SA. Madrid-Torrejon.	N698GA
☐ EC-KES	03	CitationJet CJ-2	525A-0155	SOKO Aviation SL. Madrid-Cuatro Vientos.	N105PT
☐ EC-KEY	97	Gulfstream 4SP	1331	Executive Airlines SA. Barcelona.	N878G
☐ EC-KFA	97	Falcon 900C	169	Corporate Jets XXI, Barcelona.	VP-BGC
☐ EC-KFQ	07	Embraer Legacy 600	14500995	FlyLink Express SA. Madrid-Cuatro Vientos.	PT-SKO
☐ EC-KFS	06	Global Express	9208	Jet Personales SA. Madrid-Torrejon.	C-FIHN
☐ EC-KGE	76	Citation	500-0312	Air Taxi & Charter International SL.	(F-HBMS)
☐ EC-KGX	78	Citation 1/SP	501-0061	Pirinair Express SL. Zaragoza.	SE-RBZ
☐ EC-KHH	06	390 Premier 1A	RB-160	Jusair Aviacion SL.	N36890
☐ EC-KHP	01	Citation Bravo	550-0955	Gestair Executive Jet SA. Madrid-Torrejon.	HB-VMW
☐ EC-KHT	04	Embraer Legacy 600	14500863	Aerodynamics Malaga SL. Malaga.	G-YIAN
☐ EC-KJH	02	Global Express	9094	TAG Aviation Espana SA. Madrid-Torrejon.	A6-EJB
☐ EC-KJJ	82	Citation II	550-0415	Taxi Fly/Pronair Airlines SL. Murcia.	F-GJYD
☐ EC-KJR	82	Citation II/SP	551-0412	Nord Jet SA.	OY-PDN
☐ EC-KJS	07	Gulfstream G550	5151	Executive Airlines SA. Barcelona.	N921GA
☐ EC-KJV	96	CitationJet	525-0143	Wondair on Demand Aviation SL. Valencia.	D-IALL
☐ EC-KKB	07	Citation Encore+	560-0768	Labaro Grupo Inmobiliara SA/Bestfly, Madrid.	N179RP
☐ EC-KKC	06	Citation Sovereign	680-0117	SOKO Aviation SL. Madrid-Cuatro Vientos.	N5094D
☐ EC-KKD	07	Hawker 400XP	RK-533	Gestair Executive Jet SA. Madrid-Torrejon.	N533HB
☐ EC-KKE	93	CitationJet	525-0044	Wondair on DEmand Aviation SL. Valencia.	D-IDBW
☐ EC-KKK	07	Citation Encore+	560-0770	Gestair Executive Jet SA. Madrid-Torrejon.	N5093Y
☐ EC-KKN	00	Global Express	9084	TAG Aviation Espana SA. Madrid-Torrejon.	VP-COU
☐ EC-KKO	01	Citation Bravo	550-0992	Transportes Aereos del Sur SA. Seville.	D-COFY
☐ EC-KLL	07	Gulfstream G200	171	Executive Airlines SA. Barcelona.	N671GA
☐ EC-KLS	07	Gulfstream G550	5162	Executive Airlines SA. Barcelona.	N662GA

Reg	Yr	Type	c/n	Owner/Operator	Prev Regn
☐ EC-KMF	07	Gulfstream G150	233	Executive Airlines SA. Barcelona.	N633GA
☐ EC-KMK	07	Citation Sovereign	680-0178	TAG Aviation Espana SA. Madrid-Torrejon.	N5163K
☐ EC-KMS	07	Gulfstream G150	237	TAG Aviation Espana SA. Madrid-Torrejon.	N537GA
☐ EC-KMT	07	Hawker 900XP	HA-33	Gestair Executive Jet SA. Madrid-Torrejon.	N933XP
Military					
☐ T 17-1	68	B 707-331B	20060	47 Grupo Mixto, 471 Esc. Torrejon.	N275B
☐ T 17-2	64	B 707-331C	18757	47 Grupo Mixto, 471 Esc. Torrejon.	N792TW
☐ T 17-3	77	B 707-368C	21367	47 Grupo Mixto, 471 Esc. Torrejon.	N7667B
☐ T 18-1	88	Falcon 900	38	45-40, 45 Grupo, 451 Esc. Torrejon.	F-WWFE
☐ T 18-2	91	Falcon 900	90	45-41, 45 Grupo, 451 Esc. Torrejon.	F-WWFG
☐ T 18-3	89	Falcon 900	77	45-42, 45 Grupo, 451 Esc. Torrejon.	N107BK
☐ T 18-4	89	Falcon 900	74	45-43, 45 Grupo, 451 Esc. Torrejon.	N108BK
☐ T 18-5	89	Falcon 900	73	45-44, 45 Grupo, 451 Esc. Torrejon.	N109BK
☐ T 22-1	90	Airbus A310-304	550	45-50, 45 Grupo, 451 Esc. Torrejon.	F-WEMP
☐ T 22-2	90	Airbus A310-304	551	45-51, 45 Grupo, 451 Esc. Torrejon.	F-WEMQ
☐ TM 11-1	71	Falcon 20E	253	47-21. 47 Grupo Mixto, 471 Esc. Torrejon.	T 11-1
☐ TM 11-2	71	Falcon 20D	222	47-22. 47 Grupo Mixto, 471 Esc. Torrejon.	EC-BXV
☐ TM 11-3	70	Falcon 20D	219	47-23. 47 Grupo Mixto, 472 Esc. Torrejon.	EC-BVV
☐ TM 11-4	75	Falcon 20E	332	47-24. 47 Grupo Mixto, 472 Esc. Torrejon.	EC-CTV
☐ TR 20-01	92	Citation V	560-0161	403-11, 403 Esc. Madrid-Cuatro Vientos.	(XA-CYC)
☐ TR 20-02	92	Citation V	560-0193	403-12, 403 Esc. Madrid-Cuatro Vientos.	N1282K
☐ U 20-1	82	Citation II	550-0425	01-405, Armada, 4a Escuadrilla, Rota.	(LN-FOX)
☐ U 20-2	83	Citation II	550-0446	01-406, Armada, 4a Escuadrilla, Rota.	N1248N
☐ U 20-3	88	Citation II	550-0592	01-407, Armada, 4a Escuadrilla, Rota.	N1302N
☐ U 21-01	97	Citation VII	650-7079	01-408, Armada, 4a Escuadrilla, Rota.	N779VP

EI = EIRE *Civil* Total 13

Reg	Yr	Type	c/n	Owner/Operator	Prev Regn
☐ EI-CIR	80	Citation II/SP	551-0174	Aircraft International Renting Ltd. Dinard. (was 550-0128).	N60AR
☐ EI-DXW	06	Learjet 60	60-300	Airlink Airways Ltd. Shannon.	G-CJMC
☐ EI-GDL	04	Gulfstream G550	5068	Westair Aviation Ltd. Shannon. 'Born Free'	N968GA
☐ EI-IAW	01	Learjet 60	60-218	Voltage Plus Ltd/Westair Aviation Ltd. Shannon.	N8084J
☐ EI-IRE	01	Challenger 604	5515	Starair (Ireland) Ltd. Dublin.	N515DM
☐ EI-KJC	06	Hawker 850XP	258805	Airlink Airways Ltd. Shannon.	N71025
☐ EI-MAX	01	Learjet 31A	31A-233	Airlink Airways Ltd. Shannon.	N233BX
☐ EI-REX	98	Learjet 60	60-149	Airlink Airways Ltd. Shannon.	N260CA
☐ EI-VIV	06	Learjet 60	60-305	Airlink Airways Ltd. Shannon.	OH-VIV
☐ EI-WJN	79	HS 125/700A	257062	Westair Aviation Ltd. Shannon.	N416RD
☐ EI-WXP	98	Hawker 800XP	258382	Westair Aviation Ltd. Shannon.	SE-DYE
Military					
☐ 251	91	Gulfstream 4	1160	Irish Air Corps. Casement-Dublin.	N17584
☐ 258	03	Learjet 45	45-234	Irish Air Corps. Casement-Dublin.	N5009T

EK = ARMENIA *Civil* Total 1

Reg	Yr	Type	c/n	Owner/Operator	Prev Regn
☐ EK-52526	01	CitationJet CJ-2	525A-0026	Blue Airways, Yerevan.	D-IHAP

EP = IRAN *Civil* Total 22

Reg	Yr	Type	c/n	Owner/Operator	Prev Regn
☐ EP-AGA	77	B 737-286	21317	Government of Iran, Teheran.	
☐ EP-AGB	00	Airbus A321-231	1202	Government of Iran, Teheran.	F-WQSS
☐ EP-AGY	73	Falcon 20E	286	Iran Asseman Airlines, Teheran.	F-WRQU
☐ EP-AKC	74	Falcon 20E	301	National Cartographic Centre, Teheran.	F-WNGL
☐ EP-FIC	75	Falcon 20E	334	Iran Asseman Airlines, Teheran.	F-WRQU
☐ EP-FID	75	Falcon 20E	338	CAO/Iran Asseman Airlines, Teheran.	F-WMKG
☐ EP-FIF	75	Falcon 20E	320	Iran Asseman Airlines, Teheran.	YI-AHG
☐ EP-IPA	71	Falcon 20E	251	Department of Police, Teheran.	EP-FIE
☐ EP-PAZ	76	F 28-1000	11104	Government of Iran, Teheran.	F-GIAK
☐ EP-SEA	77	Falcon 20E	367	Iran Asseman Airlines, Teheran.	F-WRQR
☐ EP-TFA	82	Falcon 50	101	Government of Iran, Teheran.	5-9012
☐ EP-TFI	83	Falcon 50	120	Government of Iran, Teheran.	5-9011
Military					
☐ 1001	78	B 707-386C	21396	Government of Iran, Teheran.	EP-NHY
☐ 1003	76	JetStar 2	5203	Government of Iran, Teheran. (status ?).	EP-VLP
☐ 15-2235	75	Falcon 20E	318	Revolutionary Guard, Teheran. (status ?).	EP-FIG
☐ 5-3021	76	Falcon 20E	350	Iranian Air Army, Mehrabad.	5-4040
☐ 5-9001	69	JetStar-8	5137	Government of Iran, Teheran.	1004
☐ 5-9003	76	Falcon 20F	354	Iranian Air Force, 1st Transport Base, Mehrabad.	F-WRQR

☐ 5-9003		JetStar 2	...	Government of Iran, Tehran.	
☐ 5-9013	83	Falcon 50	122	Government of Iran, Teheran.	YI-ALE
☐ 5-9014		Falcon 20	...	noted Tehran 9/06.	
☐ 5-9015		Falcon 20	...	noted Tehran 9/06.	

ER = MOLDOVA Total 1
Civil

☐ ER-LGA	81	Learjet 35A	35A-406	Nobil Air SRL. Chisinau.	I-KELM

ES = ESTONIA Total 8
Civil

☐ ES-LUX	04	CitationJet CJ-2	525A-0213	United Capital, Tallinn.	(OE-FJR)
☐ ES-PVC	95	Learjet 60	60-051	Avies Air Co. Tallinn.	D-CHER
☐ ES-PVD	90	Learjet 55C	55C-143	Avies Air Co. Tallinn.	D-CMAD
☐ ES-PVH	98	Learjet 31A	31A-162	Avies Air Co. Tallinn.	N125GP
☐ ES-PVP	06	Learjet 60	60-302	Avies Air Co. Tallinn.	(OE-GJA)
☐ ES-PVS	00	Learjet 60	60-190	Avies Air Co. Tallinn.	EI-IAU
☐ ES-PVT	82	Learjet 55	55-061	Avies Air Co. Tallinn.	D-CFUX
☐ ES-SKY	07	Citation Excel XLS	560-5700		N52235

EW = BELARUS Total 1
Civil

☐ EW-001PA	02	BBJ2-8EV	33079	Government of Belarus, Minsk.	N375BC

EZ = TURKMENISTAN Total 1
Civil

☐ EZ-B021	92	BAe 1000B	259029	Government of Turkmenistan, Ashkhabad.	G-5-751

F = FRANCE Total 186
Civil

☐ F-....	90	Citation II	550-0625	Aero Capital SAS, Paris-le Bourget.	N6846T
☐ F-BJET	59	MS 760 Paris-1A	39	Your Aircraft Source LLC. Calhoun, Ga. USA. (status ?).	F-WJAA
☐ F-BLKL	64	MS 760 Paris-3	01	Association Potez Paris Jet III, Paris-Le Bourget. (rebuild)	F-WLKL
☐ F-BVPK	74	Corvette	7	Aero Stock, Paris-Le Bourget.	N611AC
☐ F-BVPN	75	Falcon 20E-5B	311	Dassault Falcon Service, Paris-Le Bourget.	F-WRQS
☐ F-BVPR	75	Falcon 10	5	AVDEF, Nimes-Garons. (out of service).	F-WVPR
☐ F-BXAS	75	AC 690A-TU	11240	Ste. Turbomeca, Pau.	F-WXAS
☐ F-BXQL	61	MS 760 Paris-2B	105	Your Aircraft Source LLC. Calhoun, Ga. USA. (status ?).	N76OQ
☐ F-GBRF	75	Falcon 10	38	Aero Services Executive, Paris-Le Bourget.	N20ET
☐ F-GBTM	78	Falcon 20GF	397	Institut National des Sciences de l'Universe du CNRS, Creil.	F-WBTM
☐ F-GDLR	78	Falcon 10	121	AVDEF-Aviation Defence Service, Nimes-Garons.	HB-VFT
☐ F-GELT	86	Falcon 100	211	CATEX SA. St Etienne.	F-WZGT
☐ F-GESP	00	Falcon 2000	119	Dassault Falcon Service, Paris-Le Bourget.	D-BDNL
☐ F-GFDH	75	Corvette	13	EADS Airbus SA. Toulouse-Blagnac.	N601AN
☐ F-GFMD	81	Falcon 10	136	Aero Services Executive, Paris-Le Bourget.	F-WZGS
☐ F-GFPF	75	Falcon 10	68	Aero Services Executive, Paris-Le Bourget.	N80MP
☐ F-GGAL	86	Citation III	650-0117	Avialair/Gilbert Gross, Paris-Le Bourget.	N1321N
☐ F-GGGA	88	Citation II	550-0586	Aero Vision SARL. Toulouse-Blagnac.	N1301N
☐ F-GGGT	89	Citation II	550-0611	CFPR-Cie Financiere et de Participations Roullier, Dinard.	(N1242K)
☐ F-GGVB	79	Falcon 50	11	Unijet SA. Paris-Le Bourget.	N5739
☐ F-GHDX	79	Falcon 10	140	GIE Flying Bird. Quimper.	N88WL
☐ F-GHPB	88	Falcon 100	215	Aero Jet Corporate, Paris-Le Bourget.	F-WZGY
☐ F-GILM	76	Corvette	32	Airbus France SAS, Toulouse-Blagnac.	EC-DUF
☐ F-GIPH	82	Falcon 100	194	Regourd Aviation/Occitania SA. Paris-Le Bourget.	N61FC
☐ F-GJAP	76	Corvette	31	Airbus France SAS, Toulouse-Blagnac.	EC-DYE
☐ F-GJAS	74	Corvette	8	Aero Vision SARL, Toulouse-Blagnac.	6V-AEA
☐ F-GJBZ	97	Falcon 50EX	269	Cora SA/Air BG, Paris-Le Bourget.	(F-GPBG)
☐ F-GJDB	67	Falcon 20C	76	AVDEF-Aviation Defence Service, Nimes-Garons.	F-GGFO
☐ F-GJXX	89	Citation V	560-0070	Ste J C Decaux, Toussus le Noble.	
☐ F-GKGA	75	Corvette	11	Airbus France SAS, Toulouse-Blagnac.	F-WFPD
☐ F-GKHJ	87	Falcon 900	11	Aero Services Executive, Paris-Le Bourget.	N251SJ
☐ F-GKID	76	Citation	500-0319	Loca Air SA. Perpignan.	N94MA
☐ F-GKIR	77	Citation	500-0361	Soc de Location pour l'Industrie Aerienne-Solid Air, Paris.	N90EB
☐ F-GLEC	76	Corvette	30	Airbus France SAS, Toulouse-Blagnac.	(F-GKGB)
☐ F-GLSJ	82	Falcon 50	107	Unijet SA. Paris-Le Bourget.	N253SJ
☐ F-GLTK	89	Citation II	550-0609	Knauf Trade SNC/Alsair SA. Colmar.	N344A
☐ F-GMDL	00	CitationJet CJ-1	525-0400	Dominique Libert, Agen.	(N88798)
☐ F-GMIR	06	CitationJet CJ2+	525A-0322	WG Motorsport SA. Cannes.	(LX-WGR)
☐ F-GMOF	75	Corvette	12	Aero Stock, Paris-Le Bourget.	TJ-AHR
Reg	*Yr*	*Type*	*c/n*	*Owner/Operator*	*Prev Regn*

Reg	Yr	Type	c/n	Owner/Operator	Prev Regn
☐ F-GMOH	87	Falcon 900B	7	DFS/Management Executive Jet Services, Paris-Le Bourget.	3B-XLA
☐ F-GMOT	82	Falcon 50	111	Occitania, Paris-Le Bourget.	N50AH
☐ F-GNCP	78	Citation II	550-0004	Fortis Lease France, Puteaux.	N312GA
☐ F-GNDZ	74	Falcon 10	17	Unijet SA. Paris-Le Bourget. (in storage).	EC-949
☐ F-GOPM	74	Falcon 20E-5B	302	Aero Services Executive, Paris-Le Bourget.	F-WQBM
☐ F-GOYA	96	Falcon 900EX	11	SNC Artemis Conseil, Paris-Le Bourget.	F-WWFI
☐ F-GPAA	67	Falcon 20EW	103	AVDEF-Aviation Defense Service, Nimes-Garons.	G-FRAV
☐ F-GPAB	71	Falcon 20EW	254	AVDEF-Aviation Defense Service, Nimes-Garons.	G-FRAC
☐ F-GPAD	73	Falcon 20EW	280	AVDEF-Aviation Defense Service, Nimes-Garons.	(F-GPAE)
☐ F-GPFD	90	Falcon 100	221	SNC Sporto et Cie. Paris-Le Bourget.	OE-GHA
☐ F-GPGL	83	Falcon 100	203	Trans Helicopteres/Polygone 69 SA. Lyon-Bron.	I-FJDC
☐ F-GPLA	76	Corvette	28	Aero Vision SARL. Toulouse-Blagnac.	(OO-TTL)
☐ F-GPLF	98	CitationJet	525-0291	Business Express Luftfahrt GmbH. Graz, Austria.	N51744
☐ F-GPNJ	99	Falcon 900EX	50	Aero Services Executive, Paris-Le Bourget.	F-WWFS
☐ F-GPPF	81	Falcon 50	65	Laboratoires Pierre Fabre SA. Paris-Le Bourget.	N1EV
☐ F-GPSA	83	Falcon 50	123	Ste Gefco & Cie/Air Gefco, Paris-Le Bourget.	N211EF
☐ F-GPUJ	03	CitationJet CJ-2	525A-0169	Unijet SA. Paris-Le Bourget.	N5262W
☐ F-GRUJ	06	CitationJet CJ-3	525B-0117	Unijet SA. Paris-Le Bourget.	N5212M
☐ F-GSGL	07	CitationJet CJ-3	525B-0178	IXAir SA/Polygone SA. Lyon-Bron.	N5203S
☐ F-GSLZ	86	Falcon 100	208	Toperline, Nancy-Essey.	F-WQBJ
☐ F-GSMC	76	Citation	500-0308	Wing Aviation, Paris-Le Bourget.	F-GMLH
☐ F-GSNA	04	Falcon 900EX EASY	145	Exair SA. Luxembourg.	(LN-SEH)
☐ F-GTOD	80	Falcon 10	155	Olivier Dassault/DARTA Aero Charter, Paris-Le Bourget.	N725PA
☐ F-GTRY	00	CitationJet	525-0359	Air Ailes, Colmar-Houssen.	
☐ F-GUAJ	86	Falcon 50	169	Aero Services Executive, Paris-Le Bourget.	I-SNAB
☐ F-GVML	00	Global Express	9081	Unijet SA. Paris-Le Bourget.	C-GZTZ
☐ F-GVMV	06	Global Express	9202	GIE LVMH Services, Paris-Le Bourget.	C-FHPB
☐ F-GVNG	06	Falcon 2000EX EASY	114	Dassault Aviation, Paris-Le Bourget.	F-WWMK
☐ F-GVRB*	08	Falcon 7X	34	Dassault Falcon Service, Paris-Le Bourget.	F-WWZV
☐ F-GVUJ	07	CitationJet CJ-3	525B-0156	Unijet SA. Paris-Le Bourget.	N5145V
☐ F-GVYC	06	Citation Excel XLS	560-5682	Lyreco SAS, Marly les Valenciennes.	N50549
☐ F-GXMC	89	Falcon 50	190	EUR Mascaralain, Paris-Le Bourget.	CS-TMJ
☐ F-GXRK	97	CitationJet	525-0229	IXAir SA. Paris-Le Bourget.	LX-FOX
☐ F-GXRL	01	CitationJet CJ-2	525A-0019	IXAir SA. Paris-Le Bourget.	S5-BBB
☐ F-GXRM	94	Falcon 900B	142	DEA Transport SNC. Paris-Le Bourget.	N100FF
☐ F-GYCA	70	Falcon 20E-5B	240	SNC Laboratoire ASL. Avignon-Caumont.	HB-VMN
☐ F-GYCP	94	Falcon 900B	135	Omni Aviation SA. Paris-Le Bourget.	VP-BPW
☐ F-GYFC	07	CitationJet CJ-3	525B-0176	Promod SA. Lille-Lesquin.	N5188N
☐ F-GYMC	74	Falcon 20E-5	307	Lov'Air Aviation, Paris-Le Bourget.	F-GYPB
☐ F-GYRB	02	Falcon 900EX	113	DFS UK Ltd. Paris-Le Bourget.	(F-HRBS)
☐ F-GYSL	75	Falcon 20F-5B	341	Lov'Air Aviation SARL. Paris-Le Bourget.	F-OHCJ
☐ F-HACA	80	Citation II	550-0182	Champagne Airlines, Reims-Champagne.	N107CF
☐ F-HACP	05	Learjet 45	45-287	Aero Services Executive, Paris-Le Bourget.	CS-TLT
☐ F-HAGH	03	CitationJet CJ-1	525-0518	Sodiflers SAS et autres, Laval.	D-IETZ
☐ F-HAIR	80	Falcon 50	37	Groupe Jean Claude Darmon, Paris-Le Bourget.	F-GMCU
☐ F-HAJD	03	CitationJet CJ-1	525-0523	Star Service International, Orleans.	N51246
☐ F-HAJV	89	Citation II	550-0622	ASEC-Aero Saint Exupery SA. Blois Le Breuil.	LX-VAZ
☐ F-HALM	84	Falcon 50	134	Aero Services Executive, Paris-Le Bourget.	(OY-CKH)
☐ F-HALO	02	CitationJet CJ-1	525-0484	Jet Invest SAS, Marseilles.	N484CJ
☐ F-HAMG	03	CitationJet CJ-2	525A-0193	Dalia Airlines SA. Marseilles.	D-IKAL
☐ F-HAPM	05	Falcon 50EX	346	Michelin Air Services, Clermont Ferrand.	N346EX
☐ F-HAPN	05	Falcon 50EX	347	Michelin Air Services, Clermont Ferrand.	F-WWHC
☐ F-HAPP	00	CitationJet CJ-2	525A-0009	Air Taxi SAT, Blois Le Breuil.	N525LC
☐ F-HASC	97	CitationJet	525-0177	Socri Aero SARL. Cannes.	G-OWRC
☐ F-HAST	05	390 Premier 1A	RB-149	DARTA Aero Charter, Paris-Le Bourget.	N36979
☐ F-HAXA	97	Falcon 900EX	12	AXA Reassurance SA/Unijet SA. Paris-Le Bourget.	F-WQBL
☐ F-HBBM	80	Falcon 50	16	Bernard Magrez SA. Paris-Le Bourget.	F-WQBL
☐ F-HBFP	04	Hawker 800XP	258689	Unijet SA. Paris Le-Bourget.	N36689
☐ F-HBMB	81	Citation II	550-0324	Aero Vision SARL, Toulouse-Blagnac.	HB-VLQ
☐ F-HBOL	02	Falcon 900EX	107	Unijet SA. Paris-Le Bourget.	F-WWFE
☐ F-HBPP	04	CitationJet CJ-3	525B-0013	World Liner Inc. Seychelles/Air Taxi SAT, Paris-Le Bourget.	N831V
☐ F-HCBM	06	Falcon 900EX EASY	174	Dassault Aviation, Paris-Le Bourget.	F-WWFR
☐ F-HCGD	07	Learjet 45	45-328	Chalair Aviation SAS. Caen-Carpiquet.	N40081
☐ F-HCIC*	08	CitationJet CJ-3	525B-0224		N.....
☐ F-HDGT	90	Citation II	550-0634	Blueaero SARL. La Rochelle.	SE-DVT
☐ F-HEKO	02	CitationJet CJ-2	525A-0080	Econocom International NV/Eco Jet Leasing SA.	N525TK

Reg	Yr	Type	c/n	Owner/Operator	Prev Regn
F-HEOL	04	CitationJet CJ-2	525A-0219	Domair SNC/Air Ailes, Colmar-Houssen.	N5247U
F-HFBY	06	Global 5000	9188	Bouyghes Transport Air Service, Paris-Le Bourget.	C-FECN
F-HITM	06	Hawker 400XP	RK-501	SAS Air ITM/Intermarche, Lorient.	N501XP
F-HLIM	04	Citation Encore	560-0683	SAS SELIA-Service Limagrain Adherents, Clermont-Ferrand.	N51042
F-HMJC	98	CitationJet	525-0250	Malet Jet Team SARL. Toulouse.	HB-VMT
F-OHFO	97	Falcon 50EX	267	Adolf Wuerth GmbH. Niederstetten, Germany.	(D-BETI)
F-OHJX	99	Airbus A319-112	1086	National Air Services, Jeddah, Saudi Arabia.	F-GYFN
F-OHJY	99	Airbus A319-112	1124	National Air Services, Jeddah, Saudi Arabia.	F-WIHG
F-ONYY	06	CitationJet CJ2+	525A-0320	Air Alize SARL. Noumea-Magenta, Guadaloupe.	N5188A
F-WFBW	05	Falcon 7X	01	Dassault Aviation, Bordeaux. (FBW-Fly By Wire Ff 5 May 05)	
F-WQBL	05	Falcon 2000EX EASY	76	Dassault Aviation, Paris-Le Bourget.	A6-SMS
F-WSKY	05	Falcon 7X	3	Dassault Aviation, Bordeaux. (Ff 20 Sep 05).	
F-WTDA	05	Falcon 7X	2	Dassault Aviation, Bordeaux. (Ff 5 Jul 05).	(F-HNFG)
F-WWFF	07	Falcon 900EX EASY	198	Dassault Aviation, Bordeaux.	
F-WWFP	07	Falcon 900EX EASY	191	Dassault Aviation, Bordeaux.	
F-WWFW	08	Falcon 900EX EASY	200	Dassault Aviation, Bordeaux.	
F-WWFY	07	Falcon 900EX EASY	201	Dassault Aviation, Bordeaux.	
F-WWGA	08	Falcon 2000EX EASY	152	Dassault Aviation, Bordeaux.	
F-WWGE	07	Falcon 2000EX EASY	148	Dassault Aviation, Bordeaux.	
F-WWGI	07	Falcon 2000EX EASY	138	Dassault Aviation, Bordeaux.	
F-WWGJ	07	Falcon 2000EX EASY	149	Dassault Aviation, Bordeaux.	
F-WWGL	07	Falcon 2000EX EASY	150	Dassault Aviation, Bordeaux.	
F-WWGM	07	Falcon 2000EX EASY	125	Dassault Aviation, Bordeaux.	(D-BONN)
F-WWGO	07	Falcon 2000EX EASY	142	Dassault Aviation, Bordeaux.	
F-WWGR	07	Falcon 2000LX EASY	143	Ven Air Ltd. Dublin, Ireland.	
F-WWGY	07	Falcon 2000DX	601	Dassault Aviation, Bordeaux. (Ff 19 Jun 07).	
F-WWMD	07	Falcon 2000EX EASY	151	Dassault Aviation, Bordeaux.	
F-WWUK	07	Falcon 7X	14	Dassault Aviation, Bordeaux.	
F-WWUL	07	Falcon 7X	15	Dassault Aviation, Bordeaux.	
F-WWUN	07	Falcon 7X	17	Dassault Aviation, Bordeaux.	
F-WWUO	07	Falcon 7X	18	Dassault Aviation, Bordeaux.	
F-WWUP	07	Falcon 7X	19	Dassault Aviation, Bordeaux.	
F-WWUQ	07	Falcon 7X	20	Dassault Aviation, Bordeaux.	
F-WWUR	07	Falcon 7X	21	Dassault Aviation, Bordeaux.	
F-WWUS	07	Falcon 7X	22	Dassault Aviation, Bordeaux.	
F-WWVB	07	Falcon 900DX	619	Dassault Aviation, Bordeaux.	
F-WXEY	03	Falcon 2000EX	6	Dassault Aviation, Bordeaux.	F-W...

Military

Reg	Yr	Type	c/n	Owner/Operator	Prev Regn
101	77	Falcon 10MER	101	Marine Nationale, SIMMAD, Lann-Bihoue.	F-WPXJ
129	79	Falcon 10MER	129	Marine Nationale, SIMMAD, Lann-Bihoue.	F-WZGA
132	83	Falcon 50 SURMAR	132	Marine Nationale, Flotille 24F, Lanne Bihoue.	I-EDIK
133	79	Falcon 10MER	133	Marine Nationale, SIMMAD, Nimes-Garon.	F-ZGTI
143	80	Falcon 10MER	143	Marine Nationale, SIMMAD, Lann-Bihoue.	F-WZGO
185	81	Falcon 10	185	Marine Nationale, SIMMAD, Lann-Bihoue.	F-WQBJ
30/F-ZVMB	80	Falcon 50 SURMAR	30	Marine Nationale, Flotille 24F, Lanne-Bihoue.	F-WQFZ
32	75	Falcon 10MER	32	Marine Nationale, SIMMAD, Lann-Bihoue.	F-W...
36	80	Falcon 50 SURMAR	36	Marine Nationale, Flotille 24F, Lanne Bihoue.	F-ZJTL
48	82	Gardian	448	Aeronavale, Flotile 25F, BA-190 Tahiti.	F-ZWVF
65	83	Gardian	465	Aeronavale, Flotille 25F, BA-190 Tahiti.	F-ZJTS
7	80	Falcon 50 SURMAR	7	Marine Nationale, Flotille 25, Lanne-Bihoue.	F-WQBN
72	83	Gardian	472	Aeronavale, Flotille 25F, BA-190 Tahiti.	F-Z...
77	83	Gardian	477	Aeronavale, Flotille 25F, BA-190 Tahiti.	F-Z...
80	84	Gardian	480	Aeronavale, Flotille 25F, BA-190 Tahiti.	F-ZJSA
F-RAEA	72	Falcon 20E	260	A de l'Air, (stored Chateaudun).	F-WMKJ
F-RAEB	68	Falcon 20C	167	A de l'Air, (stored Chateaudun).	F-RAFL
F-RAEC	76	Falcon 20F	342	A de l'Air, (stored Chateaudun).	F-RAEG
F-RAEF	72	Falcon 20E	268	A de l'Air, (stored Chateaudun).	F-RAFK
F-RAFC	65	DC 8F-55F	45819	A de l'Air, ET 3/60, Roissy.	F-BNLD
F-RAFE	64	DC 8-53	45570	A de l'Air, SARIGUE ELINT, EE/51, Evreaux-Fauville.	F-ZARK
F-RAFF	69	DC 8-72CF	46370	A de l'Air, (stored Chateaudun).	OH-LFY
F-RAFI	79	Falcon 50	5	A de l'Air, ETEC 00.065, Villacoublay.	(F-WZHB)
F-RAFJ	82	Falcon 50	78	A de l'Air, ETEC 00.065, Villacoublay.	F-GEOY
F-RAFK	81	Falcon 50	27	A de l'Air, ETEC 00.065, Villacoublay.	F-WGTG
F-RAFL	80	Falcon 50	34	A de l'Air, ETEC 00.065, Villacoublay.	F-WEFS
F-RAFP	85	Falcon 900	2	A de l'Air, ETEC 00.065, Villacoublay.	F-GFJC
F-RAFQ	86	Falcon 900	4	A de l'Air, ETEC 00.065, Villacoublay.	F-WWFA

Reg	Yr	Type	c/n	Owner/Operator	Prev Regn
☐ F-RBFA	01	Airbus A319-115XCJ	1485	A de l'Air, COTAM, Esterel Squadron, Villacoublay.	
☐ F-RBFB	01	Airbus A319-115XCJ	1556	A de l'Air, COTAM, Esterel Squadron, Villacoublay.	
☐ F-UKJA	70	Falcon 20SP	182	A de l'Air, 339-JA, (stored Chateaudun).	F-BVFV
☐ F-UKJC	81	Falcon 20SNA	451	A de l'Air, 339-JC, (stored Chateaudun).	F-UGWN
☐ F-ZACA	71	Falcon 20E	252	CEV, Bretigny.	I-GIAZ
☐ F-ZACB	67	Falcon 20C	96	CEV, Cazaux.	F-GERT
☐ F-ZACC	68	Falcon 20C	124	CEV, Bretigny. (stored).	F-WJMJ
☐ F-ZACD	68	Falcon 20C	131	CEV, Bretigny.	F-WJMK
☐ F-ZACG	67	Falcon 20C	86	CEV, Cazaux.	F-WRGQ
☐ F-ZACR	68	Falcon 20C	138	CEV, Bretigny.	F-BUIC
☐ F-ZACT	67	Falcon 20C	79	CEV, Bretigny.	F-BNRH
☐ F-ZACV	73	Falcon 20E	288	CEV, Bretigny.	F-BUYE
☐ F-ZACX	69	Falcon 20C	188	CEV, Bretigny.	F-BRPK
☐ F-ZACY	72	Falcon 20E	263	CEV, Bretigny.	F-BSBU
☐ F-ZACZ	78	Falcon 20F	375	CEV, Bretigny.	F-GBMD
☐ F-ZVMT	69	DC 8-72CF	46043	A de l'Air, SARIGUE ELINT, EE/51, Evreaux-Fauville.	F-RAFD

G = GREAT BRITAIN   Total 227
Civil

Reg	Yr	Type	c/n	Owner/Operator	Prev Regn
☐ G-BLRA	84	BAe 146-100	E1017	BAe Systems (Corporate Air Travel) Ltd. Warton.	N117TR
☐ G-BVCM	93	CitationJet	525-0022	Kenmore Aviation Ltd. Edinburgh.	(N1329N)
☐ G-BYHM	92	BAe 125/800B	258233	Club 328 Ltd. Southampton.	VP-BTM
☐ G-CBHT	99	Falcon 900EX	48	TAG Aviation Charter UK Ltd. Farnborough.	G-GPWH
☐ G-CBRG	02	Citation Excel	560-5266	Queensway Aviation Ltd. Belfast, N Ireland.	N5245D
☐ G-CDCX	02	Citation X	750-0194	Peter Harris/Pen-Avia Ltd. Luton.	N194CX
☐ G-CDFS	01	Embraer EMB-135ER	145431	CityLynx Travel Ltd. Farnborough.	EI-ORK
☐ G-CDLT	04	Hawker 800XP	258710	GAMA Aviation Ltd. Farnborough.	N37010
☐ G-CDNK	05	Learjet 45	45-280	Air Partner Private Jets Ltd. Stansted.	N40079
☐ G-CDSR	05	Learjet 45XR	45-286	Air Partner Private Jets Ltd. Stansted.	N50126
☐ G-CEDK	05	Citation X	750-0252	The Duke of Westminster, Hawarden-Chester.	N252CX
☐ G-CERX	06	Hawker 850XP	258810	Hangar 8 Ltd. Oxford-Kidlington.	OE-GJA
☐ G-CEUO	78	Citation II	550-0033	Unique Air International Ltd. Farnborough.	LX-GDL
☐ G-CHAI	94	Challenger 601-3R	5152	TAG Aviation Charter UK Ltd. Farnborough.	G-FBFI
☐ G-CIEL	02	Citation Excel	560-5247	Enerway Ltd/London Executive Aviation, Luton.	N57RL
☐ G-CITJ	94	CitationJet	525-0084	Centreline Air Charter Ltd. Bristol.	D-ITSV
☐ G-CJA.	05	Dornier Do328JET	3220	Corporate Jet Services Ltd. Southampton.	
☐ G-CJAB	04	Dornier Do328JET	3200	Corporate Jet Services Ltd. Southampton.	OE-HAA
☐ G-CJAD	01	CitationJet CJ-1	525-0435	Davis Aircraft Operations, Edinburgh.	N525AD
☐ G-CJAG	04	390 Premier 1	RB-122	Corporate Jet Services Ltd. Southampton.	N3722Z
☐ G-CJAH	05	390 Premier 1	RB-131	Corporate Jet Services Ltd. Southampton.	N36731
☐ G-CJDB	07	CitationJet CJ1+	525-0648	Breed Aircraft Ltd. Jersey, C.I.	N5152X
☐ G-CJMB	06	Challenger 850	8055	Corporate Jet Management Ltd. Farnborough.	N850RJ
☐ G-CJMD	07	Embraer Legacy 600	14500994	Corporate Jet Management Ltd. Farnborough.	P4-SAO
☐ G-CMAF	07	Embraer Legacy 600	14501011	TAG Aviation Charter UK Ltd. Farnborough.	PT-...
☐ G-CTEN	07	Citation X	750-0281		N50639
☐ G-DCTA	88	BAe 125/800B	258130	Direct Air Executive Ltd. Oxford-Kidlington.	G-OSPG
☐ G-DGET	05	Challenger 604	5608	TAG Aviation Charter UK Ltd. Farnborough.	C-FDWU
☐ G-DJAE	76	Citation	500-0339	Billion-Air Ltd. Westonn, Ireland.	G-JEAN
☐ G-DWJM	81	Citation II	550-0296	MAS Airways Ltd. Biggin Hill.	G-BJIR
☐ G-ECJI	80	Falcon 10	161	Fleet International Aviation&Maritime Finance Ltd. Northolt.	I-CREM
☐ G-EDCJ	95	CitationJet	525-0105	Air Charter Scotland Ltd. Edinburgh.	N305CJ
☐ G-EDCK	03	CitationJet CJ-1	525-0510	Air Charter Scotland Ltd. Edinburgh.	(N278CA)
☐ G-EDCL	02	CitationJet CJ-2	525A-0083	Air Charter Scotland Ltd. Edinburgh.	N975DN
☐ G-EDCS	06	Hawker 400XP	RK-487	Mountain Aviation Ltd. Edinburgh.	N487XP
☐ G-EEBJ	04	CitationJet CJ-2	525A-0202	Skyblue Business Services LLP.	N719WP
☐ G-EGNS*	07	Gulfstream G550	5167		N967GA
☐ G-EJEL	90	Citation II	550-0643	Elliott Brick Co. Leeds-Bradford.	N747CR
☐ G-ELNX	01	Regional Jet	7508	CityLynx Travel Ltd. Farnborough.	VH-KXJ
☐ G-ELOA	00	Citation Excel	560-5106	TAG Aviation Charter UK Ltd. Farnborough.	HB-VND
☐ G-EMLI	98	Challenger 604	5383	Twinjet Aircraft Sales Ltd. Luton.	N383DT
☐ G-ESTA	80	Citation II	550-0127	Executive Aviation Services Ltd. Staverton.	G-GAUL
☐ G-EVLN	91	Gulfstream 4	1175	Metropix Ltd. Luton.	N18WF
☐ G-EVRD	06	390 Premier 1A	RB-172	Commercial Aviation Charters Ltd. Farnborough.	N7102U
☐ G-FCDB	01	Citation Bravo	550-0985	Eurojet Aviation Ltd. Birmingham.	N.....
☐ G-FECR	07	Embraer Legacy 600	14501020	London Executive Aviation Ltd. Stansted.	PT-...
☐ G-FFRA	68	Falcon 20EW	132	F R Aviation Ltd. Hurn.	N902FR
☐ G-FINK	93	BAe 1000A	259037	Barbaro Toni Fink, Southend.	XA-RGG

Reg	Yr	Type	c/n	Owner/Operator	Prev Regn
G-FIRM	00	Citation Bravo	550-0940	Marshall Executive Aviation, Cambridge.	N5263S
G-FJET	82	Citation II	550-0419	London Executive Aviation Ltd. Stansted.	G-DCFR
G-FNES	05	Falcon 900EX EASY	159	Finesse Executive Ltd/Matrix Aviation Ltd. Douglas, IOM.	(N900SG)
G-FRAD	75	Falcon 20EW	304	F R Aviation Ltd. Hurn.	9M-BDK
G-FRAF	74	Falcon 20EW	295	F R Aviation Ltd. Hurn.	N911FR
G-FRAH	69	Falcon 20EW	223	F R Aviation Ltd. Durham Tees Valley.	G-60-01
G-FRAI	72	Falcon 20EW	270	F R Aviation Ltd. Durham Tees Valley.	N901FR
G-FRAJ	66	Falcon 20EW	20	F R Aviation Ltd. Durham Tees Valley.	N903FR
G-FRAK	69	Falcon 20EW	213	F R Aviation Ltd. Durham Tees Valley.	(N213FC)
G-FRAL	68	Falcon 20EW	151	F R Aviation Ltd. Durham Tees Valley.	N904FR
G-FRAO	69	Falcon 20EW	214	F R Aviation Ltd. Hurn.	N906FR
G-FRAP	69	Falcon 20EW	207	F R Aviation Ltd. Hurn.	N908FR
G-FRAR	69	Falcon 20EW	209	F R Aviation Ltd. Hurn.	N909FR
G-FRAS	67	Falcon 20EW	82	F R Aviation Ltd. Durham Tees Valley.	117501
G-FRAT	67	Falcon 20EW	87	F R Aviation Ltd. Durham Tees Valley.	117502
G-FRAU	67	Falcon 20EW	97	F R Aviation Ltd. Durham Tees Valley.	117504
G-FRAW	67	Falcon 20EW	114	F R Aviation Ltd. Durham Tees Valley.	117507
G-FRBA	70	Falcon 20EW	178	F R Aviation Ltd. Hurn.	OH-FFA
G-FRYL	03	390 Premier 1	RB-97	Hawk Air Ltd. Farnbotough.	N6197F
G-FTSL	99	Challenger 604	5416	Farglobe Transport Services Ltd. Farnborough.	N161MD
G-GALX	06	Falcon 900EX EASY	163	Charter Air Ltd. Farnborough, UK.	F-WWFX
G-GEDY	03	Falcon 2000	208	Victoria Aviation Ltd. Cairo, Egypt.	F-WWVV
G-GHPG	99	Citation Bravo	550-0897	MCP Aviation (Charters) Ltd/LEA, Stansted.	EI-GHP
G-GMAA	01	Learjet 45	45-167	GAMA Aviation Ltd. Farnborough.	N5012V
G-GMAB	93	BAe 1000B	259034	GAMA Aviation Ltd. Farnborough.	N81HH
G-GOMO	99	Learjet 45	45-055	Air Partner Private Jets Ltd. Biggin Hill.	G-OLDF
G-GSSO	03	Gulfstream G550	5019	TAG Aviation Charter UK Ltd. Farnborough.	SE-RDX
G-HARK	06	Challenger 604	5646	Corbridge Ltd. Guernsey, C.I.	N646JC
G-HCSA	06	CitationJet CJ2+	525A-0334	Hangar 8 Ltd. Oxford-Kidlington.	N52699
G-HGRC	07	CitationJet CJ2+	525A-0360	Hangar 8 Ltd. Oxford-Kidlington.	N13474
G-HMEI	84	Falcon 900B	1	Executive Jet Group Ltd. Paris, France.	F-HOCI
G-HMEV	86	Falcon 900	5	Maughold Ltd.	(D-ACDC)
G-HMMV	99	CitationJet	525-0358	European Business Jets, Cambridge.	N51564
G-HRDS	03	Gulfstream G550	5032	Fayair (Jersey) Ltd. Stansted.	N932GA
G-HSXP	07	Hawker 850XP	258827	TAG Aviation Charter UK Ltd. Farnborough.	N7077S
G-IDAB	00	Citation Bravo	550-0917	Eassda Ireland Ltd. Belfast, Northern Ireland.	(SE-RBY)
G-IFTE	78	HS 125/700B	257037	Albion Aviation Management Ltd. Biggin Hill.	G-BFVI
G-IKOS	00	Citation Bravo	550-0957	Medox Enterprises Ltd. Limassol, Cyprus.	N957PH
G-IMAC	86	Challenger 601	3065	GAMA Aviation Ltd. Farnborough.	LX-GDC
G-IOOX	04	Learjet 45	45-243	100% Aviation Ltd/David Richards BAR Racing, Oxford.	N4004Q
G-IPAL	00	Citation Bravo	550-0935	Pacific Aviation Ltd. Dublin, Ireland.	EI-PAL
G-IPAX	01	Citation Excel	560-5228	Pacific Aviation Ltd. Dublin, Ireland.	EI-PAX
G-ITIG	06	Falcon 2000EX EASY	102	TAG Aviation Charter UK Ltd. Farnborough.	F-WWMD
G-IUAN	98	CitationJet	525-0324	RF Celada SpA. Milan, Italy.	N5163C
G-IWDB	03	Hawker 800XP	258618	Bizair Ltd/Markoss Aviation UK Ltd. Biggin Hill.	N82GK
G-JANV	01	Learjet 45	45-124	Jannaire LP. Manchester.	N124AV
G-JBIS	82	Citation II	550-0447	24/7 Jet Ltd. Southend.	HB-VIS
G-JBIZ	79	Citation II	550-0073	24/7 Jet Ltd. Southend.	VP-CTJ
G-JCBC	04	Gulfstream G550	5060	J C Bamford (Excavators) Ltd. East Midlands.	N960GA
G-JETA	79	Citation II	550-0094	Icon Two Ltd/Jet Options Ltd. Birmingham.	G-RDBS
G-JETC	81	Citation II	550-0282	SJL Aviation LLP/London Executive Aviation, Stansted.	G-JCFR
G-JETF	06	Falcon 2000EX EASY	78	TAG Aviation Charter UK Ltd. Farnborough.	I-JETF
G-JETI	86	BAe 125/800B	258056	Ford Motor Co. Stansted.	G-5-509
G-JETJ	80	Citation II	550-0154	G-JETJ Ltd. Liverpool.	G-EJET
G-JETO	82	Citation II	550-0441	Jet Options Ltd. Birmingham.	N80LA
G-JJMX	07	Falcon 900EX EASY	184	J-MAX Air Services Ltd. Blackpool.	F-WWFN
G-JJSI	86	BAe 125/800B	258058	GAMA Aviation Ltd. Farnborough.	G-OMGG
G-JMAX	99	Hawker 800XP	258456	J-MAX Air Services Ltd. Blackpool.	N41762
G-JMDW	80	Citation II	550-0183	Phoenix Air Ltd. Farnborough.	HB-VGS
G-JOPT	91	Citation V	560-0159	Jet Options Ltd. Birmingham.	D-CLEO
G-JPSX	03	Falcon 900EX EASY	132	Sorven Aviation Ltd/Group 4 Securities, Staverton.	F-WWFJ
G-JTNC	75	Citation	500-0264	Eurojet Aviation Ltd. Birmingham.	G-OEJA
G-KALS	06	Challenger 300	20106	MCP Continental Ltd. Luton.	C-FIDX
G-KDMA	00	Citation Encore	560-0553	Forest Aviation Ltd. Gamston.	N5145V
G-KWIN	04	Falcon 900EX EASY	52	Quinn Aviation Ltd. Cambridge.	F-WWMA
G-LAOR	98	Hawker 800XP	258384	Select Plant Hire Co. Southend.	N955MC

Reg	Yr	Type	c/n	Owner/Operator	Prev Regn
☐ G-LCYA	01	Falcon 900EX	105	London City Airport Jet Centre Ltd. London City.	F-WWFC
☐ G-LDFM	02	Citation Excel	560-5242	MAS Airways Ltd. Biggin Hill.	TC-LMA
☐ G-LGAR	05	Learjet 60	60-286	TAG Aviation Charter UK Ltd. Farnborough.	N262DB
☐ G-LGKO	05	Challenger 604	5610	TAG Aviation Charter UK Ltd. Farnborough.	C-FEFW
☐ G-LLOD	03	Learjet 45	45-236	Stephen Lloyd, Doncaster-Sheffield.	N66DN
☐ G-LOFT	76	Citation	500-0331	Fox Tango (Jersey) Ltd.	LN-NAT
☐ G-LUXY	82	Citation II/SP	551-0421	Mitre Aviation Ltd. Shoreham. (was 550-0422).	3A-MRB
☐ G-LVLV	98	Challenger 604	5372	GAMA Aviation Ltd. Farnborough.	(N413LV)
☐ G-LXRS	06	Global Express	9200	Profred Partners Ltd. Lyneham.	C-FEBX
☐ G-MATF	90	Gulfstream 4	1109	GAMA Aviation Ltd. Farnborough.	EC-IKP
☐ G-MDBA*	02	Falcon 2000	184		N71AX
☐ G-MEET	06	Learjet 40	45-2054	TAG Aviation Charter UK Ltd. Farnborough.	N50111
☐ G-MGYB	06	Embraer Legacy 600	14500972	Haughey Air Ltd. Belfast, N I.	PT-SFZ
☐ G-MOOO	03	Learjet 40	45-2007	LPC Aviation Ltd. Manchester.	N40PX
☐ G-NMAK	05	Airbus A319-115XCJ	2550	Al Kharafi/Twinjet Aircraft Sales Ltd. Luton.	D-AVYH
☐ G-NSJS	07	Citation Sovereign	680-0161	Ferncroft Ltd. Jersey, C.I.	N5268V
☐ G-OBCC	99	Citation V Ultra	560-0497	MAS Airways Ltd. Biggin Hill.	OE-GCD
☐ G-OCJT	02	CitationJet CJ-2	525A-0113	Standard Aviation Ltd. Newcastle.	N525VV
☐ G-OCSC	01	Challenger 604	5505	Ocean Sky (UK) Ltd. Manchester.	(D-ARTE)
☐ G-OCSD	04	Challenger 604	5591	Ocean Sky (UK) Ltd. Manchester.	N604CD
☐ G-OEBJ	01	CitationJet CJ-1	525-0423	European Business Jets, Cambridge.	N292SG
☐ G-OEWD	04	390 Premier 1	RB-126	Bookajet Aircraft Management Ltd. Farnborough.	N3726G
☐ G-OFOA	83	BAe 146-100	E1006	Formula One Management Ltd. Biggin Hill.	EI-COF
☐ G-OFOM	90	BAe 146-100	E1144	Formula One Management Ltd. Biggin Hill.	N3206T
☐ G-OJAJ	07	Falcon 2000EX EASY	132	BG Aviation Ltd/Baugur UK Ltd. Farnborough.	F-WWGN
☐ G-OJMW	02	Citation Bravo	550-1042	Horizon Air Charter LLP. Staverton.	G-ORDB
☐ G-OJWB	04	Hawker 800XP	258674	Hangar 8 Ltd. Oxford-Kidlington.	N841WS
☐ G-OLDD	88	BAe 125/800B	258106	Air Partner Private Jets Ltd. Stansted.	N888SS
☐ G-OLDK	06	Learjet 45XR	45-311	Air Partner Private Jets Ltd. Stansted.	N40078
☐ G-OLDT	05	Learjet 45XR	45-265	Air Partner Private Jets Ltd. Stansted.	N5017J
☐ G-OLDW	06	Learjet 45XR	45-294	Air Partner Private Jets Ltd. Stansted.	N5014E
☐ G-OMEA	05	Citation Excel XLS	560-5610	Marshall Executive Aviation, Cambridge.	LX-GDX
☐ G-OMJC	03	390 Premier 1	RB-88	Manhattan Jet Charter Ltd. Farnborough.	N4488F
☐ G-OMRH	04	Citation Bravo	550-1086	McAir Services LLP. Hawarden.	N58HK
☐ G-OODM	03	CitationJet CJ-2	525A-0190	Hangar 8 Ltd. Oxford-Kidlington.	N680JB
☐ G-ORHE	74	Citation	500-0220	Eassda Ireland Ltd. Belfast, Northern Ireland.	(N619EA)
☐ G-OROO	07	Citation Excel XLS	560-5724	Rooney Air Ltd.	N5263U
☐ G-OXLS	06	Citation Excel XLS	560-5675	EBJ/Go XLS Ltd. Guernsey, C.I.	N5266F
☐ G-PHTO	04	390 Premier 1	RB-125	Bookajet Aircraft Management Ltd. Farnborough.	N312SL
☐ G-PKRG	05	Citation Excel XLS	560-5613	Parkridge (Aviation) Ltd. Gamston.	N613XL
☐ G-PPLC	90	Citation V	560-0059	Sterling Aviation/Skydrift Air Charter Ltd. Norwich.	F-GKHL
☐ G-PREI	02	390 Premier 1	RB-60	Craft Air SA/Manhattan Air Ltd. Farnborough.	LX-PRE
☐ G-PRKR	05	Challenger 604	5617	TAG Aviation Charter UK Ltd. Farnborough.	C-FEYU
☐ G-PWNS	96	CitationJet	525-0153	Hangar 8 Ltd. Gloucester-Staverton, UK.	VP-CNF
☐ G-RBRO	06	Embraer Legacy 600	14500982	LEA/Platinum Associates Ltd. Luton.	PT-SHV
☐ G-RCEJ	85	BAe 125/800B	258021	Albion Aviation Management Ltd. Biggin Hill.	VR-CEJ
☐ G-RDMV	00	Hawker 800XP	258496	Clearwater Aviation Ltd. Belfast, N.I.	N175TM
☐ G-REDS	01	Citation Excel	560-5167	Bridge Aviation Ltd. Hawarden.	N250SM
☐ G-REYG*	07	Falcon 900EX EASY	193	Spanacre Ltd.	F-WWFU
☐ G-REYS	00	Challenger 604	5467	Greyscape Ltd/TAG Aviation (UK) Ltd. Farnborough.	(VP-CAR)
☐ G-RRAZ	06	Embraer Legacy 600	14500954	Raz Air Ltd/London Executive Aviation, Stansted.	G-RUBN
☐ G-RSXL	07	Citation Excel XLS	560-5699	MAS Airways Ltd. Biggin Hill.	N5148N
☐ G-RWGW	02	Learjet 45	45-213	Woodlands Air LLP. Manchester.	G-MUTD
☐ G-SEAJ*	95	CitationJet	525-0113	Centreline Air Charter Ltd. Bristol.	N111AM
☐ G-SFCJ	98	CitationJet	525-0245	Sureflight Aviation Ltd. Birmingham.	N33CJ
☐ G-SIRA	04	Embraer Legacy 600	14500832	Amsair Aircraft Ltd. Stansted.	OE-IAS
☐ G-SIRO	06	Falcon 900EX EASY	172	Condor Aviation LLP/Ogden & Sons plc. Leeds-Bradford.	F-WWFL
☐ G-SIRS	01	Citation Excel	560-5185	London Executive Aviation Ltd. Stansted.	N51042
☐ G-SOVA	90	Citation II	550-0649	Mitre Aviation Ltd. Biggin Hill.	N649DA
☐ G-SOVB	01	Learjet 45	45-138	Sovereign Air Ltd. Doncaster-Robin Hood.	N138AX
☐ G-SOVC	01	Learjet 45	45-161	Cumulus Investment Holdings Ltd. Doncaster-Sheffield.	N161AV
☐ G-SPUR	92	Citation II	550-0714	London Executive Aviation Ltd. Stansted.	N593EM
☐ G-STCC	05	Challenger 604	5623	Ocean Sky (UK) Ltd. Manchester.	N623HA
☐ G-STOB	06	Hawker 400XP	RK-502	STA (2006) Ltd. Carlisle.	N502XP
☐ G-STUF	07	Learjet 40	45-2074	TAG Aviation Charter UK Ltd. Farnborough.	N40012
☐ G-SVSB	06	Citation Sovereign	680-0094	Ferron Trading/Aviation Beauport Ltd. Jersey, C.I.	N5263D

Reg	Yr	Type	c/n	Owner/Operator	Prev Regn
☐ G-SXTY	05	Learjet 60	60-280	TAG Aviation Charter UK Ltd. Farnborough.	OE-GKP
☐ G-SYLJ	05	Embraer Legacy 600	14500937	TAG Aviation Charter UK Ltd. Farnborough.	PT-SCI
☐ G-TAGA	06	Challenger 604	5659	TAG Aviation Charter UK Ltd. Farnborough.	C-FJCB
☐ G-TAYC	06	Gulfstream G450	4060	TAG Aviation Charter UK Ltd. Farnborough.	N460GA
☐ G-TBAE	83	BAe 146-200	E2018	BAe Systems (Corporate Air Travel) Ltd. Warton.	G-JEAR
☐ G-TBEA	03	CitationJet CJ-2	525A-0191	Xclusive Jet Charter Ltd. Bournemouth-Hurn.	N776LB
☐ G-UYGB	07	Challenger 300	20169	Air Partner Private Jets Ltd. Biggin Hill.	C-FOAT
☐ G-VIPI	92	BAe 125/800B	258222	Executive Jet Charter Ltd. Staverton.	G-5-745
☐ G-VONJ	03	390 Premier 1	RB-66	Von Essen Aviation Ltd/Manhattan Air Ltd. Farnborough.	N931BR
☐ G-VUEA	91	Citation II	550-0671	A D Aviation Ltd. Hawarden-Chester.	G-BWOM
☐ G-VUEM	81	Citation Eagle II	501-0178	Frandley Aviation Partnership LLP. Hawarden-Chester.	G-FLVU
☐ G-VUEZ	78	Citation II	550-0008	A D Aviation Ltd. Hawarden-Chester.	N70XA
☐ G-WAIN	04	Citation Bravo	550-1100	Ferron Trading/Aviation Beauport Ltd. Jersey, C.I.	N110BR
☐ G-WCCI	03	Embraer Legacy 600	145505	Altarello Ltd/London Executive Aviation, Luton.	G-REUB
☐ G-WCIN	00	Citation Excel	560-5088	TAG Aviation Charter UK Ltd. Farnborough.	VP-BSD
☐ G-WINA	03	Citation Excel	560-5343	Inclination 1 LLP/London Executive Aviation, Stansted.	N5145V
☐ G-WVLS*	07	Falcon 2000LX EASY	141	Trinity Aviation Ltd.	F-WWGK
☐ G-WYNE	93	BAe 125/800B	258240	Mercury Air Ltd. Jersey, Channel Islands.	(G-OURC)
☐ G-XBEL	07	Citation Excel XLS	560-5698	Aviation Beauport Ltd. Jersey, C.I.	N5091J
☐ G-XBLU	07	Citation Sovereign	680-0143	Datel Holdings Ltd.	N1318X
☐ G-XLMB	02	Citation Excel	560-5259	Aviation Beauport Ltd. Jersey, C.I.	N52526
☐ G-ZIZI	99	CitationJet	525-0345	Ortac Air Ltd. Guernsey, C.I.	N5185V
☐ G-ZXZX	97	Learjet 45	45-005	GAMA Aviation Ltd. Farnborough.	N455LJ

Military

Reg	Yr	Type	c/n	Owner/Operator	Prev Regn
☐ XS709/M	65	Dominie T1	25011	RAF, 55 (R) Squadron, Cranwell.	
☐ XS711/L	65	Dominie T2	25024	RAF, 55 (R) Squadron, Cranwell.	
☐ XS712/A	65	Dominie T2	25040	RAF, 55 (R) Squadron, Cranwell.	
☐ XS713/C	65	Dominie T1	25041	RAF, 55 (R) Squadron, Cranwell.	
☐ XS727/D	65	Dominie T2	25045	RAF, 55 (R) Squadron, Cranwell.	
☐ XS728/E	65	Dominie T2	25048	RAF, 55 (R) Squadron, Cranwell.	
☐ XS730/H	65	Dominie T2	25050	RAF, 55 (R) Squadron, Cranwell.	
☐ XS731/J	66	Dominie T1	25055	RAF, 55 (R) Squadron, Cranwell.	
☐ XS737/K	66	Dominie T2	25076	RAF, 55 (R) Squadron, Cranwell.	
☐ XS739/F	66	Dominie T2	25081	RAF, 55 (R) Squadron, Cranwell.	
☐ ZD620	82	BAe 125/CC3	257181	RAF, 32 (The Royal) Squadron, Northolt.	G-5-16
☐ ZD621	82	BAe 125/CC3	257190	RAF, 32 (The Royal) Squadron, Northolt.	
☐ ZD703	82	BAe 125/CC3	257183	RAF, 32 (The Royal) Squadron, Northolt.	G-5-20
☐ ZD704	82	BAe 125/CC3	257194	RAF, 32 (The Royal) Squadron, Northolt.	G-5-870
☐ ZE395	83	BAe 125/CC3	257205	RAF, 32 (The Royal) Squadron, Northolt.	G-5-19
☐ ZE396	84	BAe 125/CC3	257211	RAF, 32 (The Royal) Squadron, Northolt.	G-5-12
☐ ZE700	86	BAe 146/CC2	E1021	RAF, 32 (The Royal) Squadron, Northolt.	G-6-021
☐ ZE701	86	BAe 146/CC2	E1029	RAF, 32 (The Royal) Squadron, Northolt.	G-5-03
☐ ZH763	80	BAC 1-11/539GL	263	QINETIQ Ltd. Boscombe Down.	G-BGKE
☐ ZJ690	01	Sentinel R1	9107	Royal Air Force, 5 Squadron, Waddington.	C-GJRG
☐ ZJ691	02	Sentinel R1	9123	Royal Air Force, 5 Squadron, Waddington.	C-FVZM
☐ ZJ692	02	Sentinel R1	9131	Royal Air Force, 5 Squadron, Waddington.	C-FZWW
☐ ZJ693	02	Sentinel R1	9132	Royal Air Force, 5 Squadron, Waddington.	C-FZXC
☐ ZJ694	02	Sentinel R1	9135	Royal Air Force, 5 Squadron, Waddington.	C-FZYL

HA = HUNGARY Total 4

Civil

Reg	Yr	Type	c/n	Owner/Operator	Prev Regn
☐ HA-JET	75	Citation	500-0349		N1GG
☐ HA-LKN	04	Falcon 900EX EASY	143	OTP Bank/Air Invest, Budapest.	F-WWFV
☐ HA-YFE	83	Diamond 1A	A046SA	Fotex RT/Plaza-Park Kft-Pannon Air Service Ltd. Budapest.	N109PW
☐ HA-YFH	07	Hawker 400XP	RK-528	Plaza Centers (Europe) BV. Budapest.	N528XP

HB = SWITZERLAND Total 138

Civil

Reg	Yr	Type	c/n	Owner/Operator	Prev Regn
☐ HB-AEU	03	Dornier Do328JET	3199	Swiss Jet AG. Zurich.	OE-HCM
☐ HB-IAH	98	Falcon 900EX	28	TAG Aviation SA. Geneva.	F-WWFZ
☐ HB-IAJ	02	Falcon 2000EX	3	Altona SA/TAG Aviation SA. Geneva.	F-WWGC
☐ HB-IAU	03	Falcon 2000EX	14	CAT Aviation AG. Zurich.	F-WWGM
☐ HB-IAW	95	Falcon 2000	16	Starjet Establishment for Aviation, Lugano-Agno.	F-WWMB
☐ HB-IAX	96	Falcon 2000	33	Rabbit Air AG. Zurich.	F-WWME
☐ HB-IAZ	96	Falcon 2000	30	TAG Aviation SA. Geneva.	F-WWMB
☐ HB-IBH	96	Falcon 2000	42	TAG Aviation SA. Geneva.	F-WWMG
☐ HB-IDJ	97	Challenger 800	7136	TAG Aviation SA. Geneva.	VP-CRJ

Reg   Yr   Type   c/n   Owner/Operator   Prev Regn

Reg	Yr	Type	c/n	Owner/Operator	Prev Regn
HB-IEE	89	B 757-23A/W	24527	PrivatAir SA. Geneva.	HB-IHU
HB-IFJ	01	Falcon 900EX	92	B-Jet SA/Albinati Aeronautics SA. Geneva.	F-WWFK
HB-IFQ	92	Falcon 900B	121	Malaysian Jet Services, Kuala Lumpur, Malaysia.	9M-BAB
HB-IGH	69	DC 8-72	46067	Al Nassar Ltd/Jet Aviation Business Jets AG. Zurich.	VP-BJR
HB-IGI	00	Falcon 900EX	83	Fast Bird AG/CAT Aviation AG. Zurich.	F-WWFY
HB-IGL	88	Falcon 900B	58	SIMU Trade Consulting GmbH/TAG Aviation SA. Geneva.	OE-ILS
HB-IGM	02	Gulfstream G550	5004	G-5 Executive AG. Zurich.	N904GA
HB-IGQ	03	Falcon 2000EX	9	Alpcom SA/Dasnair SA. Geneva.	(N209EX)
HB-IGY	01	Falcon 900EX	95	Advanced Aviation Services Ltd/CAT Aviation AG. Zurich.	F-WWFO
HB-IHQ	98	Global Express	9011	ExecuJet Europe AG. Zurich.	VP-BJJ
HB-IIQ	99	BBJ-7AK	30752	PrivatAir SA. Munich, Germany.	HB-IIQ
HB-IIR	04	BBJ2-86Q	30295	PrivatAir SA. Zurich.	
HB-IIS	99	Gulfstream V	572	Jetclub AG. Zurich.	P4-FAZ
HB-IKR	91	Gulfstream 4	1159	Loyd's Business Jets Ltd/Jetclub AG. Zurich.	N458FA
HB-IKS	89	Challenger 601-3A	5042	Air Charter AG/Kraus und Naimer, Basle.	N28UA
HB-IKZ	00	Global Express	9054	Heliz Air Services AG/TAG Aviation SA. Geneva.	N700LA
HB-IMJ	97	Gulfstream V	517	G-5 Executive AG. Zurich.	N517GA
HB-IMY	89	Gulfstream 4	1084	Sit Set AG. Geneva.	(N448GA)
HB-INJ	01	Global Express	9086	Japat AG. Basle.	C-GHZC
HB-IPP	07	Airbus A318 Elite	2910	Comlux Aviation AG. Zurich.	D-AIJA
HB-ITF	93	Gulfstream 4SP	1202	GAMA Aviation SA. Zurich.	N369XL
HB-IUT	99	Galaxy-1126	007	TAG Aviation SA. Geneva.	(C-GRJZ)
HB-IUW	95	Falcon 900B	150	Inter Retail AG/Jet Aviation Business Jets AG. Zurich.	N335MC
HB-IUX	99	Falcon 900EX	54	Montres Rolex SA/Air King Jet SA. Geneva.	F-WWFY
HB-IVL	97	Gulfstream V	513	Private Jet Services, Basle.	N513GA
HB-IVO	98	Falcon 2000	62	Icebird Ltd. Lugano/Jet Aviation Business Jets AG. Zurich.	F-WWMF
HB-IVR	96	Challenger 604	5318	Interline SA/Execujet Charter AG. Moscow-Vnukovo.	HB-IKQ
HB-IVS	94	Challenger 601-3R	5166	Becket Holdings Inc/Jetclub AG. Zurich.	N601A
HB-IVZ	99	Gulfstream V	577	Capelink Establishment, Vaduz.	N577GA
HB-IWX	04	Embraer Legacy 600	14500841	Swiss Eagle AG. Bern-Belp.	OE-IWP
HB-IWY	91	Gulfstream 4	1176	International Private Jet Service AG. Geneva.	N9253V
HB-JEB	01	Gulfstream G200	032	TAG Aviation SA. Geneva.	N406LM
HB-JEC	04	Challenger 300	20029	Legendair AG. Reinach.	N129LJ
HB-JED	03	Embraer Legacy 600	145644	DiaMed SA/DiamAir SA. Bern-Belp.	PT-SAR
HB-JEE	03	Gulfstream G550	5025	Venturi Enterprises/Aviation 604 AG. Cairo, Egypt.	N925GA
HB-JEG	04	Falcon 2000EX EASY	34	Comlux Aviation AG. Zurich.	F-WWGM
HB-JEI	90	Falcon 900	86	Clear Sky SA/Dasnair SA. Geneva.	F-GVAE
HB-JEL	05	Embraer Legacy 600	14500933	PrimeAir AG/Comlux Aviation AG. Zurich.	PT-SCB
HB-JEM	05	Challenger 604	5613	HB-JEM GmbH. Vnukovo, Russia.	C-FEPR
HB-JEN	98	Global Express	9015	Radar 9015 Ltd/ExecuJet Charter AG. Zurich.	N708KS
HB-JEP	04	Gulfstream G550	5070	Farner Airwings AG. Solothurn.	N870GA
HB-JEQ	05	Gulfstream G450	4027	G-5 Executive AG. Zurich.	N627GA
HB-JER	99	Global Express	9017	Rolex SA. Geneva.	VP-BDD
HB-JES	98	Gulfstream V	556	MWM AG/Jetclub AG. Zurich.	N556AR
HB-JEV	03	Gulfstream G550	5040	G-5 Executive AG. Zurich.	(N13J)
HB-JEX	04	Global Express	9145	TAG Aviation SA. Geneva.	N914DT
HB-JEY	05	Global Express	9173	Comlux Aviation AG. Zurich.	C-FCUA
HB-JEZ	02	Citation X	750-0179	TAG Aviation SA. Zurich.	OE-HFE
HB-JFO	06	Challenger 300	20137	TAG Aviation SA. Geneva.	N301TG
HB-JGK	79	JetStar 2	5233	Dynacore SA. Geneva.	OD-KMI
HB-JGR	05	Challenger 604	5624	Swiss Eagle AG. Bern-Belp.	OY-MKS
HB-JGS	04	Embraer Legacy 600	14500854	G-5 Executive AG. Zurich.	VP-CNG
HB-JGU	94	Citation X	750-0001	Swiss Eagle AG. Berne-Belp.	N754SE
HB-JGV	99	BBJ-7BC	30330	G-5 Executive AG. Zurich.	VP-BJB
HB-JGY	05	Global Express XRS	9167	Comlux Aviation AG. Zurich.	(OE-LNX)
HB-JJA	05	B 737-7AK/W	34303	PrivatAir SA. Geneva.	N1780B
HB-JKA	98	Gulfstream V	554	Servair Private Charter AG. Zurich.	N450BE
HB-JRA	02	Challenger 604	5529	Swiss Air Ambulance, Zurich.	C-GJZB
HB-JRB	02	Challenger 604	5530	Swiss Air Ambulance, Zurich.	C-GJZD
HB-JRC	02	Challenger 604	5540	Swiss Air Ambulance, Zurich.	C-GKMU
HB-JRP	07	Challenger 605	5709	Comlux Aviation AG. Zurich.	C-GSCB
HB-JRQ	06	Challenger 604	5651	Albinati Aeronautics SA. Geneva.	N651JC
HB-JRR	06	Global 5000	9198	Comlux Aviation AG. Zurich.	C-FECZ
HB-JRS	05	Global 5000	9174	Albinati Aeronautics SA. Geneva.	C-FCUF
HB-JRT	99	Challenger 604	5442	Sonnig AG. Geneva.	YL-WBD
HB-JRV	88	Challenger 601-3A	5035	Sonnig AG. Geneva.	N202W

Reg	Yr	Type	c/n	Owner/Operator	Prev Regn
☐ HB-JSO*	07	Falcon 7X	12	Montres Rolex SA. Geneva.	F-WWUI
☐ HB-JSR	94	Falcon 900B	130	Dasnair SA. Geneva.	G-HAAM
☐ HB-JSS*	07	Falcon 7X	16		F-WWUM
☐ HB-JSU	07	Falcon 900DX	612	Japat AG. Basle.	F-WWFJ
☐ HB-JSV	91	Falcon 50	215	Cx HB- 10/07 to ?	(D-BOOI)
☐ HB-JSW	05	Falcon 900DX	601	ExecuJet Europe AG, Zurich. (First flight 13 May 05).	F-WWFA
☐ HB-JSX	04	Falcon 900EX EASY	141	Dasnair SA. Geneva.	N141EX
☐ HB-JSY	01	Falcon 900EX	96	Cayley Aviation Ltd/Swiss Jet AG. Zurich.	N900ZA
☐ HB-JSZ	06	Falcon 7X	4	Dasnair SA. Geneva.	F-WWUA
☐ HB-VCN	80	Sabre-65	465-32	Sonnig AG. Geneva.	N303A
☐ HB-VDO	79	Citation II/SP	551-0133	Sonnig AG. Geneva.	I-JESA
☐ HB-VHV	89	BAe 125/800A	258153	CAT Aviation AG. Zurich.	G-5-627
☐ HB-VJB	78	Citation 1/SP	501-0067	AFLAG AG/Sius Electronics SA. Zurich.	VR-BLW
☐ HB-VKW	93	BAe 125/800B	258246	Sky Jet AG. Zurich.	N387H
☐ HB-VLF	94	Hawker 800	258264	Robert Bosch GmbH. Stuttgart, Germany.	G-5-806
☐ HB-VLG	94	Hawker 800	258265	Robert Bosch GmbH. Stuttgart, Germany.	G-5-809
☐ HB-VLZ	98	Citation V Ultra	560-0446	Sky Work AG. Bern-Belp.	N51038
☐ HB-VMJ	85	Citation S/II	S550-0029	Work in Progess-WIP Trading AG. Basel.	N608LB
☐ HB-VML	00	Learjet 45	45-084	Sun Heli Estab. Vaduz/ExecuJet Europe AG. Zurich.	N5009V
☐ HB-VMO	99	Citation Excel	560-5061	Fly Away Jet SA/Sky Work AG. Bern-Belp.	N5200R
☐ HB-VMU	99	Citation Excel	560-5066	Jet Aviation Business Jets AG. Zurich.	N134SW
☐ HB-VMV	92	Citation V	560-0166	Sonnig AG. Geneva.	N166JV
☐ HB-VMX	00	Citation Bravo	550-0946	Jet Aviation Business Jets AG. Zurich.	N52229
☐ HB-VMY	01	Citation Bravo	550-0964	Jet Aviation Business Jets AG. Zurich.	N52234
☐ HB-VNA	95	Citation V Ultra	560-0280	GE Lisca AG/Speedwings SA. Geneva.	PH-MDC
☐ HB-VNB	94	Citation V Ultra	560-0271	Speedwings SA. Geneva.	N49TT
☐ HB-VNE	01	Beechjet 400A	RK-318	Sirius AG. Zurich.	N3185K
☐ HB-VNG	85	Falcon 200	502	Sphinx Wings AG. Solothurn.	N64YR
☐ HB-VNH	01	Citation Excel	560-5172	Servair Private Charter AG. Zurich.	N5086W
☐ HB-VNI	01	Citation Excel	560-5154	Good Aero Ltd/TAG Aviation SA. Mannheim, Germany.	N154XL
☐ HB-VNK	98	CitationJet	525-0271	Primjet SA/Albinati Aeronautics SA. Geneva.	N860DB
☐ HB-VNL	00	CitationJet CJ-1	525-0375	Girard-Perregaux SA. Geneva.	N375KH
☐ HB-VNM	80	Falcon 20F-5B	426	Altria Corporate Services SA. Moscow, Russia.	I-BAEL
☐ HB-VNP	02	CitationJet CJ-1	525-0499	Mathys Aviation Ltd. Bettlach Grenchen.	N5200Z
☐ HB-VNS	01	Citation Excel	560-5209	Speedwings SA. Geneva.	N501XL
☐ HB-VNU	75	Citation	500-0282	Jetclub AG. Zurich.	N510RC
☐ HB-VNV	99	Learjet 60	60-179	Jetclub AG. Zurich.	C-FCNR
☐ HB-VNW	98	Citation V Ultra	560-0457	Cirrus Swiss Eagle AG. Bern-Belp.	G-GRGS
☐ HB-VNY	05	Citation Excel XLS	560-5576	Fine Jet AG/Jetclub AG. Zurich.	N5245U
☐ HB-VNZ	00	Citation Bravo	550-0906	Jet Aviation Business Jets AG. Zurich.	D-CSSS
☐ HB-VOA	99	Astra-1125SPX	111	GE Lisca AG/Libra Travel AG. Altenrhein.	OE-GAM
☐ HB-VOB	05	Hawker 800XPi	258733	MSC Aviation SA. Geneva.	N333XP
☐ HB-VOC	95	Citation V Ultra	560-0301	Sonnig AG. Geneva.	N560AG
☐ HB-VOD	00	CitationJet CJ-1	525-0415	Jet Aviation Business Jets AG. Zurich.	D-IUWE
☐ HB-VOE	01	CitationJet CJ-2	525A-0017	Speedwings SA. Geneva.	N172CJ
☐ HB-VOF	06	CitationJet CJ-1	525-0623	CJet SA. Geneva.	N5124F
☐ HB-VOG	04	CitationJet CJ-1	525-0544	Cirrus Swiss Eagle AG. Bern-Belp.	OE-FUJ
☐ HB-VOH	98	Citation Bravo	550-0864	Sky Work AG. Bern-Belp.	D-CCWD
☐ HB-VOI	06	390 Premier 1A	RB-152	Share Plane AG. Interlaken.	N3732Y
☐ HB-VOJ	06	Hawker 850XP	258799	Johnson Controls AG. Basle.	
☐ HB-VOL	06	CitationJet CJ2+	525A-0341	Speedwings SA. Geneva.	N241CJ
☐ HB-VOM	06	Citation Excel XLS	560-5642	Astron Aviation AG. Zurich.	D-CRUW
☐ HB-VON	04	Citation Excel XLS	560-5528	Jetclub AG. Zurich.	N456SL
☐ HB-VOO	92	BAe 1000A	259030	Sonnig AG. Geneva.	LN-SUU
☐ HB-VOR	01	CitationJet CJ-1	525-0473	Speedwings SA. Geneva.	LX-MRC
☐ HB-VOS	07	390 Premier 1A	RB-187	Ahrenkiel Consulting Services, Bern-Belp.	N7187J
☐ HB-VOW*	07	CitationJet CJ-3	525B-0209		N5262B
☐ HB-VOZ	97	CitationJet	525-0193	Swiss Eagle AG. Bern-Belp.	D-ILCB
☐ HB-VOZ	98	Learjet 60	60-148	Dajrisa AG/JetClub AG. Zurich.	N648TS
☐ HB-VWA	07	CitationJet CJ2+	525A-0383	ARionics AG. Staefa.	N5120U
☐ HB-VWF	07	CitationJet CJ1+	525-0650	Waltair AG/Swiss Eagle AG. Bern-Belp.	N51511
Military					
☐ T-783	81	Falcon 50	67	Swiss Air Force, Bern-Belp.	HB-IEP
☐ T-784	02	Citation Excel	560-5269	Swiss Air Force, Bern-Belp.	HB-VAA

HC = ECUADOR   Total   6
Civil

| ☐ HC-BSS | 68 | Falcon 20C | 150 | Aero Express del Ecuador, Guayaquil. | TG-RBW |

Military

☐ FAE-001A	76	Sabre-60	306-117	Aviacion del Ejercito. (status ?).	N22MY
☐ FAE-043	65	Sabre-40R	282-43	Ministry of National Defence, Quito.	N4469F
☐ FAE-047	72	Sabre-40A	282-109	Ministry of National Defence, Quito.	N77AT
☐ FAE-049	73	Sabre-60	306-68	Ministry of National Defence, Quito.	N265DP
☐ IGM-628	90	Citation II	550-0628	Aviacion del Ejercito,	N183AB

HI = DOMINICAN REPUBLIC   Total   1
Civil

| ☐ HI-766SP | 98 | Beechjet 400A | RK-208 | | N890BH |

HK = COLOMBIA   Total   13
Civil

☐ HK-2485W	79	Westwind-Two	239	Ingenio del Cauca SA. Bogota.	HK-2485
☐ HK-4204	80	Westwind-Two	306	Petroleum Helicopters de Colombia SA. Bogota.	HK-4204X
☐ HK-4250X	00	Citation Bravo	550-0961	Central Charter de Colombia SA. Bogota.	HK-4250X
☐ HK-4304	95	Citation V Ultra	560-0355	Central Charter de Colombia SA. Bogota.	N67GU
☐ HK-4446W	91	Beechjet 400A	RK-26	Colombiana SA. Bogota.	HK-4446X

Military

☐ FAC-0001	99	BBJ-74V	29272	Fuerza Aerea Colombiana, ETE, Bogota-El Dorado.	N7378P
☐ FAC-0002	70	F 28-1000	11992	Fuerza Aerea Colombiana, ETE, Bogota-El Dorado.	FAC-0001
☐ FAC-1201	67	B 707-373C	19716	Fuerza Aerea Colombiana, Esc 711, Bogota-El Dorado.	HL7425
☐ FAC-1211	88	Citation II	550-0582	Fuerza Aerea Colombiana, Esc 713, Bogota-El Dorado.	(N1301A)
☐ FAC-5760	95	Citation OT-47B	560-0350	Fuerza Aerea Colombiana, Bogota-El Dorado.	N2500N
☐ FAC-5761	96	Citation OT-47B	560-0374	Fuerza Aerea Colombiana, Bogota-El Dorado.	N1066W
☐ FAC-5763	95	Citation OT-47B	560-0365	Fuerza Aerea Colombiana, Bogota-El Dorado.	N2500D
☐ FAC-5764	96	Citation OT-47B	560-0381	Fuerza Aerea Colombiana, Bogota-El Dorado.	N5373D

HL = KOREA   Total   19
Civil

☐ HL7222	92	Gulfstream 4	1188	Korean Air Lines, Cheju.	N482GA
☐ HL7501	95	Citation V Ultra	560-0292	Korean Air Lines, Cheju.	N1295N
☐ HL7502	95	Citation V Ultra	560-0294	Korean Air Lines, Cheju.	N1295Y
☐ HL7503	95	Citation V Ultra	560-0297	Korean Air Lines, Cheju.	N1296N
☐ HL7504	95	Citation V Ultra	560-0300	Korean Air Lines, Cheju.	N1297V
☐ HL7577	95	Challenger 601-3R	5182	Regional Aviation Administration, Seoul.	C-FVZC
☐ HL7748	05	Global Express	9179	Samsung Techwin Co. Seoul.	C-FCVC
☐ HL7749	05	Global Express	9184	Samsung Techwin Co. Seoul.	C-FEAE
☐ HL7770	01	BBJ-7EG	32807	Samsung Techwin Co. Seoul.	N375BJ

Military

☐ 258-342	98	Hawker 800XP	258342	Republic of Korea Air Force,	N2320J
☐ 258-343	97	Hawker 800XP	258343	Republic of Korea Air Force,	N1102U
☐ 258-346	97	Hawker 800XP	258346	Republic of Korea Air Force,	N23204
☐ 258-350	98	Hawker 800XP	258350	Republic of Korea Air Force,	N23207
☐ 258-351	98	Hawker 800XP	258351	Republic of Korea Air Force,	N23208
☐ 258-352	98	Hawker 800XP	258352	Republic of Korea Air Force,	N2321S
☐ 258-353	98	Hawker 800XP	258353	Republic of Korea Air Force,	N2321V
☐ 258-357	98	Hawker 800XP	258357	Republic of Korea Air Force,	N2321Z
☐ 701	99	Challenger 604	5429	Maritime National Police Agency, Seoul.	N604KM
☐ 85101	85	B 737-3Z8	23152	Government of South Korea, Seoul.	

HP = PANAMA   Total   3
Civil

☐ HP-....	69	Gulfstream 2	68	Ciro World, Panama City. (status ?).	N308EE
☐ HP-....	68	Gulfstream 2	21	Brazilia Airways Inc. Panama City.	N244DM
☐ HP-1A	69	Gulfstream II SP	78	Government of Panama, Panama City.	N90HH

HR = HONDURAS   Total   1
Civil

| ☐ HR-PHO | 81 | Westwind-1124 | 333 | Government of Honduras, Tegucigalpa. | HR-CEF |

HS = THAILAND   Total   14
Civil

☐ HS-CDY	02	Citation X	750-0184	The Royal Group, Bangkok.	I-JETX
☐ HS-CFS	81	Learjet 35A	35A-366	Chiron Flight Services, Bangkok.	N350DA
☐ HS-CMV	95	B 737-4Z6	27906	Government of Thailand, Bangkok.	55-555
Reg	*Yr*	*Type*	*c/n*	*Owner/Operator*	*Prev Regn*

Reg	Yr	Type	c/n	Owner/Operator	Prev Regn
☐ HS-CPG	07	Hawker 850XP	258833	Siam Land Flying Co. Don Muang.	N72233
☐ HS-DCG	96	Citation VII	650-7071	Aerothai, Bangkok.	N1130N
☐ HS-HRH	91	B 737-448	24866	99-904. Government of Thailand, Bangkok.	EI-BXD
☐ HS-MCL	06	CitationJet CJ-3	525B-0383		N13001
☐ HS-RBL	92	Citation II	550-0707	Siam Winery Trading Plus Co. Bangkok.	OE-GDM
☐ HS-TPD	00	Beechjet 400A	RK-294	Directorate of Civil Aviation, Bangkok.	N5049E

Military

Reg	Yr	Type	c/n	Owner/Operator	Prev Regn
☐ 40208	88	Learjet 35A	35A-635	Royal Thai Air Force, 605 Sqn 6 Wing. (status ?).	60505
☐ 55-555	06	BBJ2-8Z6/W	35478	Royal Thai Air Force, Bangkok.	N369BJ
☐ 60201	83	B 737-2Z6	23059	Royal Thai Air Force, Bangkok.	22-222
☐ 60202	91	Airbus A310-324	591	HS-TYQ, Royal Thai Air Force, Bangkok.	44-444
☐ 60221	03	Airbus A319-115XCJ	1908	HS-TYR. Royal Thai Air Force, Bangkok.	D-AIJO

HZ = SAUDI ARABIA Total 64

Civil

Reg	Yr	Type	c/n	Owner/Operator	Prev Regn
☐ HZ-124	92	Airbus A340-211	004	RESA, Riyadh.	D-ACME
☐ HZ-AB1	83	TriStar 500	1247	Al-Anwa Establishment, Riyadh.	JY-HKJ
☐ HZ-AB3	80	B 727-2U5	22362	Al-Anwa Establishment, Riyadh.	V8-BG1
☐ HZ-AFA2	96	Challenger 604	5320	Bin Shuaileh Group/Abdul Aziz bin Fahd,	N605CC
☐ HZ-AFAS	93	MD-11	48533	Bin Shuaileh Group/Abdul Aziz bin Fahd,	HZ-AFA1
☐ HZ-AFN	82	Gulfstream 3	364	Saudia Special Flight Services, Jeddah.	N1761D
☐ HZ-AFR	83	Gulfstream 3	410	Saudia Special Flight Services, Jeddah.	N350GA
☐ HZ-AFT	87	Falcon 900B	21	Saudia Special Flight Services. (at Geneva since 3/06).	(HZ-R4A)
☐ HZ-AFU	87	Gulfstream 4	1031	Saudia Special Flight Services, Jeddah.	N434GA
☐ HZ-AFV	87	Gulfstream 4	1035	Saudia Special Flight Services, Jeddah.	N435GA
☐ HZ-AFW	88	Gulfstream 4	1038	Saudia Special Flight Services, Jeddah.	N438GA
☐ HZ-AFX	90	Gulfstream 4	1143	Saudia Special Flight Services, Jeddah.	N410GA
☐ HZ-AFY	91	Gulfstream 4	1166	Saudia Special Flight Services, Jeddah.	HZ-SAR
☐ HZ-AFZ	89	Falcon 900B	61	Saudia Special Flight Services, Jeddah.	HZ-AB2
☐ HZ-AIJ	82	B 747SP-68	22750	Saudi Royal Family, Riyadh.	
☐ HZ-ARK	05	Gulfstream G550	5074	International Jet Club Ltd. Farnborough, UK.	N574GA
☐ HZ-BIN	07	Hawker 900XP	HA-23	Salem Aviation, Jeddah, Saudi Arabia.	N923XP
☐ HZ-BL1	00	CitationJet CJ-1	525-0371	Salem Aviation, Jeddah.	N175SB
☐ HZ-DME	89	Falcon 900	76	Sheikh Mustafa Idrees, Jeddah.	N54SK
☐ HZ-HA1	78	Gulfstream 2TT	216	Harth Trading Establishment, Jeddah.	HZ-ND1
☐ HZ-HM11	69	DC 8-72	46084	Saudi Armed Forces Medical Services, Riyadh. (stored Dallas)	HZ-MS11
☐ HZ-HM1A	83	B 747-3G1	23070	Saudi Royal Family, Riyadh.	N1784B
☐ HZ-HM1B	78	B 747SP-68	21652	Saudi Royal Family, Riyadh.	HZ-HM1
☐ HZ-HM7	93	MD-11	48532	Saudi Royal Family, Riyadh.	N9093P
☐ HZ-HMED	94	B 757-23A	25495	Saudi Armed Forces Medical Services, Riyadh.	
☐ HZ-HMS	98	Airbus A340-213X	204	Government of Saudi Arabia, Jeddah.	D-ASFB
☐ HZ-HR3	82	B 727-2Y4	22968	Saudi Oger Ltd. Riyadh.	HZ-RH3
☐ HZ-KSDC	01	Falcon 2000	142	NetJets Middle East, Jeddah.	F-WWVV
☐ HZ-KSRC	00	Hawker 800XP	258481	NetJets Middle East, Jeddah.	N43926
☐ HZ-MBA	66	B 727-21	19006	Express Camel Aviation,	HZ-OCV
☐ HZ-MF1	02	BBJ-7FG	33405	Saudi Ministry of Finance & Economy, Riyadh.	N373JM
☐ HZ-MF2	02	BBJ-7FG	33499	Saudi Ministry of Finance & Economy, Riyadh.	
☐ HZ-MF3	03	Gulfstream G300	1520	Saudi Ministry of Finance & Economy, Riyadh.	N520GA
☐ HZ-MF4	03	Gulfstream G300	1525	Saudi Ministry of Finance & Economy, Riyadh.	N425GA
☐ HZ-MF5	03	Gulfstream G300	1532	Saudi Ministry of Finance & Economy, Riyadh.	N532GA
☐ HZ-MFL	90	Gulfstream 4	1128	Saudia Special Flight Services, Jeddah.	N429GA
☐ HZ-MIS	81	B 737-2K5	22600	Sheikh Mustafa Idrees, Jeddah.	D-AHLH
☐ HZ-MS1C	82	Learjet 35A	35A-467	Saudi Armed Forces Medical Services, Riyadh.	HZ-MS1
☐ HZ-MS3	83	Gulfstream 3	385	Saudi Armed Forces Medical Services, Riyadh.	N1761K
☐ HZ-MS4	98	Gulfstream 4SP	1365	Saudi Armed Forces Medical Services, Riyadh.	HZ-MS04
☐ HZ-MS5A	01	Gulfstream V	644	Saudi Armed Forces Medical Services, Riyadh.	N644GA
☐ HZ-MS5B	99	Gulfstream V	583	Saudi Armed Forces Medical Services, Riyadh.	HZ-MS5
☐ HZ-NSA	87	Airbus A310-304	431	ARABASCO-Arabian Aircraft Services Co Ltd. Jeddah.	P4-ABU
☐ HZ-OFC5	07	Falcon 900EX EASY	180	Olayan Finance Co. Luton, UK.	F-WWFD
☐ HZ-PCA	76	Gulfstream 2	179	ARABASCO-Arabian Aircraft Services Co Ltd. Jeddah.	HZ-CAD
☐ HZ-SJP3	97	Challenger 604	5346	Jounaou & Parskevaides, Farnborough, UK.	N604JP
☐ HZ-SKI	78	B 727-212	21460	Precision International Services Ltd. Bouremouth-Hurn, UK.	P4-SKI
☐ HZ-TAA	99	BBJ-7P3	29188	JABJ AG/H R H Talal bin Abdul Aziz,	N1779B
☐ HZ-WBT3		B 747-4J6	25880	Kingdom Establishment, Riyadh.	N747BZ
☐ HZ-WBT5	85	BAe 125/800A	258032	ROTANA, Jeddah.	N526M
☐ HZ-XY7	04	Airbus A320-214	2165	National Air Services, Jeddah.	F-WWBT

Military

Reg	Yr	Type	c/n	Owner/Operator	Prev Regn
☐ HZ-101	01	BBJ-7DP	32805	Royal Saudi Air Force, Riyadh.	HZ-102
☐ HZ-102	01	BBJ2-8DP	32451	Royal Saudi Air Force, Riyadh.	HZ-101
☐ HZ-103	88	Gulfstream 4	1037	Royal Saudi Air Force, Riyadh.	HZ-ADC
☐ HZ-105	88	BAe 125/800B	258118	Royal Saudi Air Force, Riyadh.	105
☐ HZ-106	81	Learjet 35A	35A-374	Royal Saudi Air Force, Riyadh.	
☐ HZ-107	81	Learjet 35A	35A-375	Royal Saudi Air Force, Riyadh.	
☐ HZ-109	89	BAe 125/800A	258146	Royal Saudi Air Force, Riyadh.	G-5-825
☐ HZ-110	89	BAe 125/800B	258148	Royal Saudi Air Force, Riyadh.	RSAF-110
☐ HZ-130	89	BAe 125/800B	258164	Royal Saudi Air Force, Riyadh.	130
☐ HZ-133	05	Citation Bravo	550-1115	Royal Saudi Air Force, Riyadh.	N4002Y
☐ HZ-134	05	Citation Bravo	550-1116	Royal Saudi Air Force, Riyadh.	N4060Y
☐ HZ-135	06	Citation Bravo	550-1126	Royal Saudi Air Force, Riyadh.	N12993
☐ HZ-136	06	Citation Bravo	550-1127	Royal Saudi Air Force, Riyadh.	N1298P

I = ITALY   Total   131

Civil

Reg	Yr	Type	c/n	Owner/Operator	Prev Regn
☐ I-AEAL	72	Citation	500-0053	Itali Airlines SRL. Pescara.	HB-VGO
☐ I-AIRW	90	Learjet 31	31-025	Soc. Air Vallee SpA. Aosta.	N39399
☐ I-ALHO	01	Hawker 800XP	258561	Soc. ALBA Servizi Trasporti SpA. Milan.	N16300
☐ I-ALKA	82	Citation II	550-0351	Air One Executive SpA. Pescara.	(N167WE)
☐ I-ALPG	81	Citation II/SP	551-0355	Action Air SRL. Milan.	N551AS
☐ I-ALVC	06	Hawker 400XP	RK-515	Romeo Group SpA.	N3735U
☐ I-AMCY	74	Citation	500-0192	Easy Way SRL/Airclub SpA. Ciampino.	(N70WA)
☐ I-ARIF	02	Falcon 2000	203	Soc. Aer Marche SpA. Ancona-Falconara	F-WWVQ
☐ I-ARON	73	Citation	500-0095	Aeroitalia SRL. Roma-Ciampino.	M950AM
☐ I-AROO	79	Citation II	550-0081	Unifly Servizi Aerei SRL. Roma-Ciampino.	N254AM
☐ I-ASER	98	Beechjet 400A	RK-204	Soc. Aliserio SpA. Milan.	N2357K
☐ I-AUNY	81	Citation 1/SP	501-0213	TAI-Trasporti Aerei Italiani SRL. Pescara.	N6785D
☐ I-AVEB	84	Diamond 1A	A087SA	SLAM Lavori Aerei SRL. Naples.	N870AM
☐ I-AVGM	84	Citation II	550-0492	ENAV Flight Inspection, Roma-Ciampino.	(N1254G)
☐ I-AVRM	84	Citation II	550-0491	ENAV Flight Inspection, Roma-Ciampino.	(N1254D)
☐ I-AVSS	93	Beechjet 400A	RK-66	SLAM Lavori Aerei SpA. Naples.	N6048F
☐ I-AVVM	85	Citation S/II	S550-0062	ENAV Flight Inspection, Roma-Ciampino.	N12715
☐ I-AZFB	83	HS 125/700A	NA0341	Air Four SpA. Milan.	N700KG
☐ I-BEAU	87	Falcon 900	23	Soc. SARAS/Sirio SpA. Milan.	F-WWFK
☐ I-BENN	98	Citation Bravo	550-0859	Soc. Benetton/Benair SpA. Treviso.	(N550KH)
☐ I-BENT	99	Citation Excel	560-5053	Soc. Benetton/Benair SpA. Treviso.	N5231S
☐ I-BLUB	92	Citation VI	650-0216	Vitrociset SpA. Roma.	N68269
☐ I-BMFE	73	Learjet 25C	25C-146	Gruppo Compagnie Aeronautiche SRL. Parma.	N6KJ
☐ I-BNTN	02	Falcon 2000	191	Soc. Benetton/Benair SpA. Treviso.	F-WQBJ
☐ I-BOAT	01	CitationJet CJ-1	525-0450	Ferretti SpA/Sirio SpA.. Milan.	N5156D
☐ I-CABD	99	CitationJet	525-0354	Interfly SRL. Brescia.	OE-FCA
☐ I-CAEX	01	Falcon 900EX	91	Soc. CAI, Roma-Ciampino.	F-WQBJ
☐ I-CAFD	88	Falcon 50	183	Eurofly Service SpA. Turin.	F-WWHF
☐ I-CCCH	06	Challenger 300	20094	Sirio SpA. Milan.	C-FGWW
☐ I-CDOL	05	Citation Excel XLS	560-5584	Eurofly Service SpA. Turin.	G-CDOL
☐ I-CFLY	98	Learjet 31A	31A-167	C Fly SRL/Air Four SpA. Milan.	LX-OMC
☐ I-CIGB	80	Citation 1/SP	501-0163	Jonathan SARL/Datamat,	(I-AGIK)
☐ I-CLAD	74	Citation	500-0223	EX.AV Executive Aviation SRL. Turin.	(N89319)
☐ I-CMAB	07	Citation Excel XLS	560-5731	Aliven SRL. Verona.	N51995
☐ I-CMAL	03	Citation Excel	560-5344	Aliven SRL. Verona.	N51055
☐ I-CMCC	00	Citation Encore	560-0542	Hi Fly Service SRL/Euraviation SRL. Milan.	N12MY
☐ I-DAGF	99	CitationJet	525-0347	Sirio SpA. Milan.	N1133G
☐ I-DAGS	91	Challenger 601-3A	5085	Finzeta Due SRL/Eurofly Service SpA. Turin.	D-ACTE
☐ I-DAKO	05	Falcon 900EX EASY	160	Unifly Servizi Aerei SRL. Roma-Ciampino.	F-WWFS
☐ I-DARK	85	Falcon 50	151	Soc. CAI, Roma-Ciampino.	F-WQBM
☐ I-DDVF	01	Falcon 2000	161	Sirio SpA. Milan.	F-WWVA
☐ I-DEAC	97	CitationJet	525-0194	Aviomar SRL. Milan.	(N194VP)
☐ I-DEAS	00	Gulfstream V	593	Soc. ALBA Servizi Trasporti SpA. Milan.	(I-MPUT)
☐ I-DEUM	02	CitationJet CJ-2	525A-0095	Eurojet Italia SRL. Milan.	N5221Y
☐ I-DFSL	01	Learjet 45	45-158	Air Four SpA. Milan.	LX-DSL
☐ I-DIES	88	Falcon 900	30	Soc. CAI, Roma-Ciampino.	F-WGTH
☐ I-DLOH	99	Hawker 800XP	258450	De Longhi SpA/Soc Nauta SRL. Treviso.	D-CTAN
☐ I-DMSA	07	390 Premier 1A	RB-201	Sirio SpA. Milan.	N801BP
☐ I-ECJA	05	Airbus A319-115LRCJ	2440	Eurofly Service SpA. Turin.	F-ONAS
☐ I-EDEM	96	CitationJet	525-0155	Air Class SRL. Milan.	N155CJ

Reg	Yr	Type	c/n	Owner/Operator	Prev Regn
☐ I-ELYS	04	Learjet 40	45-2016	Eurofly Service SpA. Turin.	N40078
☐ I-ERJA	77	Citation 1/SP	501-0006	Air Four SpA. Milan.	N93TJ
☐ I-ERJD	00	Learjet 45	45-068	Air Four SpA. Milan.	
☐ I-ERJE	02	Learjet 45	45-226	Air Four SpA. Milan.	N40085
☐ I-ERJG	04	Learjet 40	45-2015	Air Four SpA. Milan.	N40077
☐ I-ERJJ	06	Learjet 40	45-2053	Eurojet Italia SRL. Milan.	N5018G
☐ I-FARN	80	Citation	500-0401	Aliven SRL. Verona.	N2651
☐ I-FDED	06	Hawker 400XP	RK-500	Locat SpA. Bologna.	N500XP
☐ I-FEEV	86	Citation III	650-0105	Air One Executive SpA. Pescara.	N67BG
☐ I-FJTC	01	Citation Bravo	550-0988	Fly Jet SRL. Turin.	N32FJ
☐ I-FLYA	79	Citation 1/SP	501-0099	Soc. Alma Fly SRL. Como.	N3170A
☐ I-FLYD	81	Citation II	550-0393	Unifly Servizi Aerei SRL. Roma-Ciampino.	N12GK
☐ I-FLYP	99	Falcon 2000	103	Eurofly Service SpA. Turin.	F-WWVX
☐ I-FLYS	92	Falcon 900B	115	Eurofly Service SpA. Turin.	LX-MEL
☐ I-FLYV	00	Falcon 2000	108	Eurofly Service SpA. Turin.	F-WWVC
☐ I-FLYW	97	Falcon 900EX	27	Eurofly Service SpA. Turin.	N626CC
☐ I-FORR	04	Learjet 40	45-2019	Sirio SpA. Milan.	G-FORN
☐ I-FORU	08	Learjet 40	...		
☐ I-FRAI	78	Citation 1/SP	501-0077	DJet Service SRL.	(N678JG)
☐ I-GFVF	06	Hawker 400XP	RK-499	Eurojet Italia SRL. Milan.	N499XP
☐ I-GIWW	99	Citation Bravo	550-0871	Editoriale Domus SpA/Soc. Ariete 21 SRL. Milan.	N871CB
☐ I-GOCO	07	Learjet 40	45-2078	Sirio SpA. Milan.	N40079
☐ I-GURU	05	Learjet 40	45-2059	Sirio SpA. Milan.	N695BD
☐ I-IMMG	01	CitationJet CJ-2	525A-0038	Aliven SRL. Verona.	N5235G
☐ I-IMMI	00	CitationJet CJ-1	525-0379	Aliven SRL. Verona.	N5188A
☐ I-IPIZ	91	Beechjet 400A	RK-29	Italfly SRL. Trento.	N15693
☐ I-JAMJ	06	Falcon 2000EX EASY	108	Sirio SpA. Milan.	F-WWGW
☐ I-JAMY	97	Falcon 2000	54	Sirio SpA. Milan.	D-BOND
☐ I-KREM	02	Hawker 800XP2	258608	Interjet SRL. Bologna.	N500BN
☐ I-LALL	00	CitationJet CJ-2	525A-0005	Interfly SRL. Brescia.	OY-LLA
☐ I-LUXO	05	Gulfstream G550	5071	Luxottica Leasing SRL. Treviso.	(N550GA)
☐ I-LVNB	02	CitationJet CJ-2	525A-0073	Aliven SRL. Verona.	N5165T
☐ I-MESK	78	Citation II/SP	551-0003	Giorgio Forno, Nairobi. Kenya.	(5Y-GGG)
☐ I-MTVB	99	Citation Bravo	550-0932	Miroglio UK Ltd. London/Fly Jet SRL, Turin.	G-MIRO
☐ I-NATS	03	Falcon 2000EX	11	Natuzzi Trade Service SRL./Sirio SpA. Milan.	F-WWGJ
☐ I-NUMI	91	Falcon 900	89	Soc. CAI, Roma-Ciampino.	F-WWFB
☐ I-OTEL	77	Citation 1/SP	501-0048	Italfy SRL. Caproni-Trento.	(I-DAEP)
☐ I-PABL	04	Citation Bravo	550-1083	Unifly Servizi Aerei SRL. Roma-Ciampino.	N5201M
☐ I-PARS	05	Learjet 40	45-2034	Sirio SpA. Milan.	N5018G
☐ I-PBRA	04	Falcon 50EX	339	Sirio SpA. Milan.	5B-CKN
☐ I-PIAL	69	PD 808	504	Soc. Rinaldo Piaggio, Genoa.	
☐ I-PNCA	81	Citation II	550-0235	Unifly Servizi Aerei SRL. Roma-Ciampino.	N67SG
☐ I-PRAD	98	Learjet 60	60-145	Soc. ALBA Servizi Trasporti, Milan.	LX-PRA
☐ I-PZZR	05	Hawker 800XP	258722	Aliparma SRL. Parma.	N37322
☐ I-RAGW	76	Citation Eagle	500-0311	Air Umbria SRL. Perugia.	LN-AAF
☐ I-RELT	73	Sabre-40A	282-133	Conair Jet Sales Inc. Fort Lauderdale, Fl. USA. (status ?).	N41NR
☐ I-RODJ	85	Falcon 50	155	Soc. CAI, Roma-Ciampino.	F-WQBM
☐ I-RONY	00	Hawker 800XP	258506	Soc. ALBA Servizi Trasporti SpA. Milan.	N50166
☐ I-RPLY	01	Learjet 60	60-212	Air Four SpA. Milan.	LX-RPL
☐ I-RVRP	00	CitationJet CJ-1	525-0397	Esair SRL. Turin.	N5163C
☐ I-SDFC	03	Challenger 300	20013	Same Deutz-Fahr Group/Sirio SpA. Milan.	N315LJ
☐ I-SEAE	02	Falcon 2000	200	Servizi Aerei SpA. Roma-Ciampino.	F-WWVN
☐ I-SEAS	07	Falcon 900EX EASY	192	Servizi Aerei SpA. Roam-Ciampino.	F-WWFR
☐ I-SNAW	95	Falcon 2000	12	Servizi Aerei SpA. Roma-Ciampino.	(F-GLHJ)
☐ I-SNAX	89	Falcon 900	69	Servizi Aerei SpA. Milan.	F-WWFD
☐ I-SRAF	92	BAe 1000B	259012	Soc. ALBA Servizi Trasporti SpA. Milan.	N512LR
☐ I-TAKA	04	Citation Excel XLS	560-5537	RHEA SRL. Turin.	N5152X
☐ I-TCGR	95	Falcon 900B	154	Sirio SpA. Milan.	LX-LFA
☐ I-TLCM	90	Falcon 900	81	Servizi Aerei SpA. Roma-Ciampino.	N81GN
☐ I-TOIO	82	Citation 1/SP	501-0252	Soc. Jolly Hotels, Valdagno (Vicenza).	N574CC
☐ I-TOPB	96	Beechjet 400A	RK-133	Euraviation SRL/Sirio SpA. Milan.	N133BP
☐ I-TOPD	97	Beechjet 400A	RK-163	Euraviation SRL/Sirio SpA. Milan.	N163BJ
☐ I-TOPH	06	Hawker 850XP	258809	Euraviation SRL/Sirio SpA. Milan.	N70409
☐ I-ULJA	78	Falcon 20F-5B	380	Air One Executive SpA. Pescara.	N3848U
☐ I-UUNY	77	Citation	500-0358	Unifly Servizi Aerei SRL. Roma-Caimpino.	SE-DEP
☐ I-VITH	01	Beechjet 400A	RK-309	Aliparma SRL. Parma.	N3239A

| Reg | Yr | Type | c/n | Owner/Operator | Prev Regn |

Reg	Yr	Type	c/n	Owner/Operator	Prev Regn
❏ I-ZACK	07	Citation Encore+	560-0767	Cia Generale Ripresa Aerea, Parma.	N5247U
❏ I-ZUGR	05	Falcon 50EX	341	Soc. Flynor Jet SpA. Milan.	F-WWHW
Military					
❏ MM61950	69	PD 808-VIP	508	AMI, 14 Stormo, 8 Gruppo, Pratica di Mare. (status ?).	
❏ MM61954	69	PD 808-TP	512	AMI, 14 Stormo, 8 Gruppo, Pratica di Mare. (status ?).	
❏ MM62012	74	DC 9-32	47595	AMI, 306 Grupo, Roma-Ciampino. (ex 31-12). (status ?).	N54635
❏ MM62026	89	Falcon 50	193	AMI, 93 Grupo, Roma-Ciampino.	F-WWHH
❏ MM62029	91	Falcon 50	211	AMI, 93 Grupo, Roma-Ciampino.	F-WWHR
❏ MM62171	99	Falcon 900EX	45	AMI, 93 Grupo, Roma-Ciampino.	F-WWFJ
❏ MM62172	99	Falcon 900EX	52	AMI, 93 Grupo, Roma-Ciampino.	F-WWFV
❏ MM62174	00	Airbus A319-115XCJ	1157	AMI, Government of Italy, Roma-Ciampino.	D-AACI
❏ MM62209	02	Airbus A319-115XCJ	1795	AMI, Government of Italy, Roma-Ciampino.	D-AWOR
❏ MM62210	02	Falcon 900EX	116	AMI, 93 Grupo, Roma-Ciampino.	F-WWFO
❏ MM62243	05	Airbus A319-115XCJ	2507	AMI, Government of Italy, Roma-Ciampino.	D-AVIP
❏ MM62244	05	Falcon 900EX EASY	149	AMI, Government of Italy, Roma-Ciampino.	F-WWFH
❏ MM62245	05	Falcon 900EX EASY	156	AMI, Government of Italy, Roma-Ciampino.	F-WWFO

JA = JAPAN   Total   82
Civil

Reg	Yr	Type	c/n	Owner/Operator	Prev Regn
❏ JA....	07	CitationJet CJ2+	525A-0380	JAC USA Inc. NYC. USA.	N5192U
❏ JA001A	96	Citation V Ultra	560-0349	Aero Asahi Corp. Tokyo-Haneda.	N1127P
❏ JA001G	92	Gulfstream 4	1190	JCAB Flight Inspection, Tokyo-Haneda.	N403GA
❏ JA001T	06	CitationJet CJ2+	525A-0311	Japan Aerospace Corp. Tokyo.	N1317X
❏ JA002A	02	Citation Encore	560-0597	Aero Asahi Corp. Tokyo-Haneda.	N597KC
❏ JA002G	94	Gulfstream 4SP	1244	JCAB Flight Inspection, Tokyo-Haneda.	N404GA
❏ JA005G	99	Global Express	9034	JCAB Flight Inspection, Tokyo-Haneda.	N700HF
❏ JA006G	00	Global Express	9082	JCAB Flight Inspection, Tokyo-Haneda.	N700AY
❏ JA01CP	97	Learjet 31A	31A-144	Chunichi Press, Nagoya.	N144LJ
❏ JA01TM	97	Citation V Ultra	560-0403	Aero Asahi Corp. Tokyo-Haneda.	N1202D
❏ JA02AA	99	Citation V Ultra	560-0518	Aero Asahi Corp. Tokyo-Haneda.	N1295B
❏ JA119N	90	Citation V	560-0067	Naha Nikon Air Service Co. Nagoya.	N45BA
❏ JA120N	90	Citation V	560-0072	Kawasho Corp. Tokyo.	(N772KC)
❏ JA30DA	83	Diamond 1	A053SA	Diamond Air Service Co/MHI, Nagoya. (Flying Laboratory).	D-CDRB
❏ JA359C	07	CitationJet CJ2+	525A-0359	Japan Aerospace Corp. Tokyo.	N12742
❏ JA525A	01	CitationJet CJ-1	525-0449	Auto Panther, Kagoshima,	(JA001T)
❏ JA525B	02	CitationJet CJ-2	525A-0156	Auto Panther, Kagoshima.	N256CJ
❏ JA525C	05	CitationJet CJ-2	525A-0244	Showa Lease,	N13087
❏ JA525J	05	CitationJet CJ-1	525-0549	KM Investment, Oita.	N549CJ
❏ JA525Y	04	CitationJet CJ-1	525-0535	Yomiuri Shimbun,	N535CJ
❏ JA560Y	05	Citation Encore	560-0694	Jomiuri Shimbun	N4018S
❏ JA8248	79	Diamond 1	A002SA	Mitsubishi Heavy Industries, Nagoya.	JQ8003
❏ JA8380	76	Citation 1/SP	501-0027	Konno Kiseki & Partner, Miyagi.	N54DS
❏ JA8420	94	CitationJet	525-0056	Itogumi Construction Co. Sapporo Hokkaido.	N56NZ
❏ JA8431	74	Gulfstream 2	141	Diamond Air Service Co/MHI, Nagoya.	N17584
❏ JA8493	83	Citation 1/SP	501-0324	San-Kei Press Ltd. Haneda.	N2651J
❏ JA8570	88	Falcon 900	53	JCG-Japanese Coast Guard, Tokyo-Haneda.	N438FJ
❏ JA8571	88	Falcon 900	56	JCG-Japanese Coast Guard, Tokyo-Haneda.	N440FJ
Military					
❏ 01-5060	96	Beechjet 400T	TX-10	060. JASDF, 41st Flight Training Squadron, Miho AB.	N3221Z
❏ 02-3013	99	BAe U-125A	258370	013. JASDF, Air Rescue Wing, Hyakuri.	N23566
❏ 02-3014	99	BAe U-125A	258381	014. JASDF, Air Rescue Wing, Chitose.	N23566
❏ 05-3255	98	Gulfstream U-4	1359	255, JASDF, Air Defense Command HQ Squadron, Iruma AB.	N359GA
❏ 12-3015	00	BAe U-125A	258407	015. JASDF, Air Rescue Wing, Hyakuri.	N30562
❏ 12-3016	00	BAe U-125A	258427	016. JASDF, Air Rescue Wing, Hyakuri.	N31833
❏ 12-3017	00	BAe U-125A	258445	017. JASDF, Air Rescue Wing,	N40708
❏ 12-3018	00	BAe U-125A	258493	018. JASDF, Air Rescue Wing, Chitose.	N40933
❏ 20-1101	90	B 747-47C	24730	Government of Japan, Tokyo.	JA8091
❏ 20-1102	91	B 747-47C	24731	Government of Japan, Tokyo.	JA8092
❏ 21-5011	01	Beechjet 400T	TX-11	011, JASDF, 41st Flight Training Squadron, Miho AB.	N50561
❏ 21-5012	01	Beechjet 400T	TX-12	012, JASDF, 41st Flight Training Squadron, Miho AB.	N50512
❏ 22-3019	00	BAe U-125A	258469	019. JASDF, Air Rescue Wing,	N43079
❏ 22-3020	01	BAe U-125A	258513	020, JASDF, Air Rescue Wing,	N50513
❏ 29-3041	92	BAe U-125A	258215	041. JASDF-Japanese Air Self Defence Force, Iruma.	G-JFCX
❏ 32-3021	01	BAe U-125A	258533	021, JASDF, Air Rescue Wing,	N50733
❏ 39-3042	92	BAe U-125A	258227	042. JASDF-Japanese Air Self Defence Force, Iruma.	G-BUUW
❏ 41-5051	93	Beechjet 400T	TX-1	051, JASDF, 41st Flight Training Squadron, Miho AB.	N82884
❏ 41-5052	93	Beechjet 400T	TX-2	052, JASDF, 41st Flight Training Squadron, Miho AB.	N82885

Reg	Yr	Type	c/n	Owner/Operator	Prev Regn
☐ 41-5053	93	Beechjet 400T	TX-3	053, JASDF, 41st Flight Training Squadron, Miho AB.	N82886
☐ 41-5054	94	Beechjet 400T	TX-4	054, JASDF, 41st Flight Training Squadron, Miho AB.	N3195K
☐ 41-5055	94	Beechjet 400T	TX-5	055, JASDF, 41st Flight Training Squadron, Miho AB.	N3195Q
☐ 41-5063	02	Beechjet 400T	TX-13	JASDF, 41st Flight Training Squadron, Miho AB.	N50543
☐ 42-3022	02	BAe U-125A	258610	JASDF,	N61320
☐ 49-3043	94	BAe U-125A	258242	043. JASDF-Japanese Air Self Defence Force, Iruma.	G-BVFE
☐ 51-5056	95	Beechjet 400T	TX-6	056, JASDF, 41st Flight Training Squadron, Miho AB.	N3195X
☐ 51-5057	95	Beechjet 400T	TX-7	057, JASDF, 41st Flight Training Squadron, Miho AB.	N3228M
☐ 51-5058	95	Beechjet 400T	TX-8	058, JASDF, 41st Flight Training Squadron, Miho AB.	N3228V
☐ 52-3001	93	BAe U-125A	258245	001. JASDF, Air Rescue Wing, Komaki.	G-JHSX
☐ 52-3002	94	BAe U-125A	258247	002. JASDF, Air Rescue Wing, Hyakuri.	G-5-813
☐ 52-3003	94	BAe U-125A	258250	003. JASDF, Air Rescue Wing, Komaki.	G-BVRG
☐ 52-3023	03	BAe U-125A	258629	JASDF,	N61729
☐ 62-3004	95	BAe U-125A	258268	004. JASDF, Air Rescue Wing, Komaki.	N809H
☐ 62-3024	04	BAe U-125A	258685	JASDF,	N36685
☐ 71-5059	95	Beechjet 400T	TX-9	059, JASDF, 41st Flight Training Squadron, Miho AB.	N1069L
☐ 72-3005	96	BAe U-125A	258288	005. JASDF, Air Rescue Wing, Nyutabaru.	N816H
☐ 72-3006	96	BAe U-125A	258305	006. JASDF, Air Rescue Wing, Hyakuri.	N305XP
☐ 75-3251	95	Gulfstream U-4	1270	251, JASDF, Air Defence Command HQ Squadron, Iruma AB.	N442GA
☐ 75-3252	95	Gulfstream U-4	1271	252, JASDF, Air Defence Command HQ Squadron, Iruma AB.	N452GA
☐ 82-3007	97	BAe U-125A	258306	007, JASDF, Air Rescue Wing, Matsushima.	N1103U
☐ 82-3008	97	BAe U-125A	258325	008, JASDF, Air Rescue Wing, Komatsu.	N1112N
☐ 85-3253	96	Gulfstream U-4	1303	253, JASDF, Air Defence Command HQ Squadron, Iruma AB.	N435GA
☐ 9201	86	Learjet U36A	36A-054	JMSDF, 91 Kokutai, Iwakuni.	N1087Z
☐ 9204	90	Learjet U36A	36A-059	JMSDF, 91 Kokutai, Iwakuni.	N1087Z
☐ 9205	90	Learjet U36A	36A-060	JMSDF, 91 Kokutai, Iwakuni.	N1088A
☐ 9206	93	Learjet U36A	36A-061	JMSDF, 91 Kokutai, Iwakuni.	N2601B
☐ 92-3009	98	BAe U-125A	258333	009, JASDF, Air Rescue Wing, Nyutabaru.	N3261Y
☐ 92-3010	98	BAe U-125A	258341	010, JASDF, Air Rescue Wing, Chitose.	N3251M
☐ 92-3011	98	BAe U-125A	258348	011, JASDF, Air Rescue Wing, Naha.	N2175W
☐ 92-3012	99	BAe U-125A	258360	012, JASDF, Air Rescue Wing, Komatsu.	N3189H
☐ 95-3254	97	Gulfstream U-4	1326	254, JASDF, Air Defence Command HQ Squadron, Iruma AB.	N325GA
☐ JA500A	02	Gulfstream V	683	LAJ 500. Japanese Coast Guard,	N683GA
☐ JA501A	02	Gulfstream V	689	LAJ 501. Japanese Coast Guard,	N689GA
☐ N71907	06	BAe U-125A	258797	..., JASDF, Air Rescue Wing,	

JY = JORDAN Total 9
Civil

Reg	Yr	Type	c/n	Owner/Operator	Prev Regn
☐ JY-ABH	93	Airbus A340-211	009	Government of Jordan, Amman.	V8-AM1
☐ JY-AFH	77	Sabre-75A	380-57	Arab Wings Ltd. Amman.	HZ-RBH
☐ JY-AFP	78	Sabre-75A	380-62	Arab Wings Ltd. Amman.	
☐ JY-AW3	97	Challenger 604	5362	Arab Wings Ltd. Amman.	N995MA
☐ JY-AW4	00	Hawker 800XP	258520	Arab Wings Ltd. Amman.	VP-CEA
☐ JY-AW5	01	Hawker 800XP	258539	Arab Wings Ltd. Amman.	VP-BKB
☐ JY-JAS	78	Sabre-75A	380-64	Jordan Aviation, Amman. (status ?).	N942CC
☐ JY-RY1	83	Challenger 601	3017	Raja Jet Executive Charters, Amman.	A6-EJD
☐ JY-TWO	99	Challenger 604	5443	Government of Jordan, Amman.	N605JA

J2 = DJIBOUTI Total 1
Civil

Reg	Yr	Type	c/n	Owner/Operator	Prev Regn
☐ J2-KBA	67	B 727-191	19394	Government of Djibouti, Djibouti.	N727X

LN = NORWAY Total 19
Civil

Reg	Yr	Type	c/n	Owner/Operator	Prev Regn
☐ LN-...	07	Citation Sovereign	680-0183		N5130J
☐ LN-AIR	06	Challenger 300	20141	Sundt Air A/S. Gardemoen.	N341TS
☐ LN-AKA*	06	Citation Encore+	560-0764		N764CE
☐ LN-AKR	07	Falcon 900EX EASY	185	Aker A/S-Sundt Air A/S. Gardermoen.	F-WWFV
☐ LN-AOC	05	Falcon 900EX EASY	155	Sundt Air A/S. Gardemoen.	(LN-SEH)
☐ LN-AVA	03	CitationJet CJ-2	525A-0199	Bergen Air Transport A/S. Bergen.	I-GOSF
☐ LN-BWG	96	Challenger 604	5328	Block Watne Group/Flyfort A/S. Oslo-Gardemoen.	N328BX
☐ LN-ESA	87	BAe 125/800B	258094	EuroSky AS/Guard Air A/S. Skien.	(LN-BEP)
☐ LN-EXL	06	Citation Excel XLS	560-5666	Sundt Air A/S. Oslo.	N51780
☐ LN-HOT	05	CitationJet CJ-3	525B-0065	Jet Air KS.	N105CQ
☐ LN-IDB		Citation Excel	...	Hesnes Air A/S. Sandjeford-Torp.	
☐ LN-SSS	07	Citation Sovereign	680-0133	Sundt Air A/S. Gardemoen.	(LN-TIH)
☐ LN-SUN	01	Challenger 604	5517	Sundt Air A/S. Oslo.	N517RH
☐ LN-SUV	00	Citation Bravo	550-0951	Sundt Air A/S. Oslo.	N51KR

Reg	Yr	Type	c/n	Owner/Operator	Prev Regn
☐ LN-SUX	02	Citation Excel	560-5271	Sundt Air A/S. Oslo.	N5103J
☐ LN-XLS	05	Citation Excel XLS	560-5608	Sundt Air A/S. Oslo.	N5103J

Military

Reg	Yr	Type	c/n	Owner/Operator	Prev Regn
☐ 0125	67	Falcon 20-5B	125	RNAF, 717 Squadron, Rygge.	LN-FOE
☐ 041	66	Falcon 20-5B	41	RNAF, 717 Squadron, Rygge.	LN-FOI
☐ 053	66	Falcon 20-5B	53	RNAF, 717 Squadron, Rygge.	LN-FOD

LV = ARGENTINA   Total   78
Civil

Reg	Yr	Type	c/n	Owner/Operator	Prev Regn
☐ LQ-BFS	03	Learjet 40	45-2003	Gobierno Provincia de Santiago del Estero.	N404MK
☐ LQ-MRM	78	Citation	500-0386	Argentine Federal Police, Buenos Aires.	LV-PAX
☐ LV-...	99	Challenger 604	5407		N604GG
☐ LV-...	80	Learjet 35A	35A-343		N998GC
☐ LV-...	73	Learjet 25B	25B-110		N343RK
☐ LV-...	99	Citation Excel	560-5025		N584CC
☐ LV-AHX	90	Citation V	560-0090	Banco Macro Bansud SA. Buenos Aires.	N30PQ
☐ LV-AIT	81	Learjet 35A	35A-408	Direccion de Aeronautica, Ushaia, Tierra del Fuego.	LV-POG
☐ LV-AIW	03	Citation Excel	560-5350	Tango Jet SA/Tango Sur, Buenos Aires.	N325FN
☐ LV-AMB	94	CitationJet	525-0045	Royal Air SA. Buenos Aires.	N525AP
☐ LV-APL	81	Citation II/SP	551-0361	Banco Macro Bansud SA. Buenos Aires. (was 550-0330).	LV-PNB
☐ LV-ARD	03	Learjet 45XR	45-232	Gobierno Provincia de Salta.	N45XR
☐ LV-AXN	99	CitationJet	525-0327	Royal Class SA. Buenos Aires.	(N398EB)
☐ LV-AXZ	71	HS 125/400B	25251	SASA-Sudamericana de Aviacion SA. Buenos Aires.	5-T-30-065
☐ LV-B..	81	Learjet 35A	35A-373		N971K
☐ LV-BAS	83	Challenger 600S	1053	Pertrans SA. Buenas Aires.	N54SU
☐ LV-BAW	81	Learjet 35A	35A-386	Baires Fly SA. Buenos Aires.	N999FA
☐ LV-BBG	04	Hawker 800XP	258707	Lineas Aereas CAS SA. Buenos Aires.	LV-PJL
☐ LV-BCO	83	Citation II	550-0458	Alianza Inversora SA.	N664SS
☐ LV-BCS	04	Citation Excel XLS	560-5541	Perez Companc. Gregorio,	N560JC
☐ LV-BDM	97	Learjet 31A	31A-145	Direccion Provincial de Salta,	(N696RB)
☐ LV-BEM	05	Hawker 400XP	RK-456	Gobierno Provincia de Chubut, Rawson.	N61256
☐ LV-BEU	05	Citation Bravo	550-1120	Gobierno Provincia de Tucuman.	N112BR
☐ LV-BFE	99	Learjet 31A	31A-183		N183ML
☐ LV-BFG	92	Learjet 31A	31A-054	Frente de Onda SA.	N54TN
☐ LV-BFM	77	Citation 1/SP	501-0031	Aviajet SA. Buenos Aires.	N510AJ
☐ LV-BFR	95	Learjet 60	60-059	Banco Macro Bansud SA. Buenos Aires.	N159SC
☐ LV-BHP	01	Challenger 604	5493	Inversora Consultatio SA. Buenos Aires.	N604VK
☐ LV-BIB	07	Citation Excel XLS	560-5696	Sudflug SA.	N5105F
☐ LV-BID	80	Citation	500-0404	Air Genesis SA. Buenos Aires.	N789DK
☐ LV-BIE	93	Learjet 35A	35A-674	Tenil SA. Buenos Aires.	N674LJ
☐ LV-BIY	81	Falcon 20F-5B	444	La Estrella SA de Seguro de Retiro, Buenoas Aires.	N244FJ
☐ LV-JTD	71	B 737-287	20523	Aerolineas Executive Jet SA. Buenos Aires.	LV-PRQ
☐ LV-JTZ	70	Learjet 24D	24D-234	C T Air SA/Manuel Tienda Leon. Buenos Aires.	LV-PRA
☐ LV-LRC	75	Learjet 24D	24D-316	Gobierno Provincia de la Rioja, La Rioja.	T-03
☐ LV-OEL	80	Learjet 25D	25D-307	Macair Jet SA. Buenos Aires.	LV-PEU
☐ LV-RED	91	Citation V	560-0126	Aguila del Sur SA. Buenos Aires.	LV-PFN
☐ LV-WDR	93	Citation V	560-0227	Royal Class SA. Buenos Aires.	LV-PGR
☐ LV-WEJ	93	Citation II	550-0724	Gobierno Provincia de Buenos Aires.	LV-PGU
☐ LV-WGY	94	Citation V	560-0246	Banco Patagonia SA.	LV-PHD
☐ LV-WJN	87	Citation II	550-0558	Banco del Buen Ayre SA. Buenos Aires.	N558AG
☐ LV-WJO	94	Citation II	550-0728	Gobierno Provincia de Corrientes.	LV-PHN
☐ LV-WLG	81	Learjet 25D	25D-345	Medical Jet SA. Buenos Aires.	LV-PHU
☐ LV-WLR	72	Westwind-1123	183	Charter Jet SRL. Buenos Aires.	N51990
☐ LV-WLS	95	Citation V Ultra	560-0289	Gobierno Provincia de Santa Cruz.	LV-PHY
☐ LV-WMM	66	Falcon 20C	29	Air Service SA. Buenos Aires.	LV-PLD
☐ LV-WMT	95	Citation V Ultra	560-0305	Royal Class SA. Buenos Aires.	LV-PLE
☐ LV-WND	73	Sabre-40A	282-131	Executive Jet SA. Buenas Aires.	N82R
☐ LV-WOC	79	Learjet 25D	25D-269	Heli-Air SA. Buenos Aires.	LV-PLL
☐ LV-WRE	81	Learjet 25D	25D-355	Helyjet SA. Buenos Aires.	N355AM
☐ LV-WSS	96	Gulfstream 4SP	1297	Aguila del Sur SA. Buenos Aires. 'Santa Marguerita III'	N420GA
☐ LV-WTN	95	Citation VII	650-7054	Ledesma S A A I. Buenos Aires.	N7243U
☐ LV-WTP	96	Beechjet 400A	RK-118	Gym SA. Buenos Aires.	LV-PMH
☐ LV-WXD	82	Citation II/SP	551-0396	Digital Air Taxi SA. Buenos Aires.	N45GA
☐ LV-WXX	74	Sabre-60	306-91	Patria Cargas Aereas SA. Buenos Aires.	(N45MM)
☐ LV-WXY	82	Learjet 25D	25D-357	Helyjet SA. Buenos Aires.	N27KG
☐ LV-WYL	75	Westwind-1123	182	M G Montoto, Buenos Aires.	(N123SE)
☐ LV-YGC	65	HS 125/1A-522	25046	Aviajet SA. Buenos Aires.	N125AD
Reg	Yr	Type	c/n	Owner/Operator	Prev Regn

Reg	Yr	Type	c/n	Owner/Operator	Prev Regn
☐ LV-YHC	92	Citation II	550-0715	Gobierno Provincia de San Juan.	LV-PNL
☐ LV-YMB	93	Learjet 31A	31A-081	Editorial Sarmiento SA. Buenos Aires.	N83WN
☐ LV-YRB	74	Citation	500-0191	Ecodyma Empresa Constructora SA. Buenos Aires.	N701BR
☐ LV-ZSZ	79	Learjet 35A	35A-235	American Jet SA. Buenos Aires.	N166HE
☐ LV-ZTH	71	Learjet 25C	25C-071	Federal Aviation SA. Buenos Aires.	N97AM
☐ LV-ZTR	00	Hawker 800XP	258462	Puyel SA. Buenos Aires.	LV-PIW
☐ LV-ZZF	76	Learjet 35	35-049	Baires Fly SA. Buenos Aires.	N899WA

Military

Reg	Yr	Type	c/n	Owner/Operator	Prev Regn
☐ 5-P-20-0741		F 28-3000C	11145	Armada-Argentina, Buenos Aires. 'Canal de Beagle'	LV-RRA
☐ 5-T-21-0742		F 28-3000M	11350	Armada-Argentina, Buenos Aires. 'Islas Malvinas'	PH-EXX
☐ AE-175	74	Sabre-75A	380-13	Ejercito/Comision Especial do Adquisiciones, Buenos Aires.	N65761
☐ AE-185	77	Citation	500-0356	Ejercito Argentina, Buenos Aires. 'Alvarez de Condarco'	N36848
☐ T-01	92	B 757-23A	25487	FAA=Fuerza Aerea Argentina, Buenos Aires.	
☐ T-02	83	F 28-4000	11203	FAA=Fuerza Aerea Argentina, Buenos Aires.	T-50
☐ T-03	70	F 28-1000	11028	FAA=Fuerza Aerea Argentina, Buenos Aires.	T-04
☐ T-10	98	Learjet 60	60-140	FAA=Fuerza Aerea Argentina, Buenos Aires.	N140LJ
☐ T-22	77	Learjet 35A	35A-136	Grupo 1 de Aerofotografico, II Brigada Aerea, Parana.	
☐ T-23	80	Learjet 35A	35A-319	Grupo 1 de Aerofotografico, II Brigada Aerea, Parana.	
☐ T-25	82	Learjet 35A	35A-484	Escuadron Verificacion Radio Ayudos, Parana.	VR-18
☐ T-26	81	Learjet 35A	35A-369	Escuadron Verificacion Radio Ayudos, Parana.	T-24
☐ T-50	71	F 28-1000	11048	FAA=Fuerza Aerea Argentina, Buenos Aires.	LV-LZN

LX = LUXEMBOURG   Total   37

Civil

Reg	Yr	Type	c/n	Owner/Operator	Prev Regn
☐ LX-AAA	02	Global Express	9133	Global Jet Luxembourg SA. Luxembourg.	G-XPRS
☐ LX-AAM	03	Falcon 2000EX	8	Global Jet Luxembourg SA. Luxembourg.	OE-HRA
☐ LX-AFD	07	Falcon 900DX	615	Global Jet Luxembourg SA. Luxembourg.	F-WWFX
☐ LX-AKI	00	Falcon 50EX	306	Global Jet Luxembourg SA. Luxembourg.	F-WWHH
☐ LX-COS	96	Falcon 900B	159	Global Jet Luxembourg SA. Cannes, France.	LX-NAN
☐ LX-EAR	98	Learjet 31A	31A-160	Global Jet Luxembourg SA. Luxembourg.	(D-CPRO)
☐ LX-FAZ	96	Challenger 604	5307	Global Jet Luxembourg SA. Farnborough, UK.	C-GIDG
☐ LX-FMR	86	Falcon 50	165	Global Jet Luxembourg SA. Cannes, France.	HZ-HM3
☐ LX-FTA	03	Falcon 900C	201	Northgas, Moscow/Global Jet Luxembourg SA.	N210FJ
☐ LX-GBY	98	Hawker 800XP	258392	Bouygues Transport Air Service, Paris-Le Bourget, France.	G-0504
☐ LX-GCA	98	CitationJet	525-0235	Serlux SA. Luxembourg.	I-ESAI
☐ LX-GES	89	Falcon 900B	78	Gedair SA. Luxembourg.	N522KM
☐ LX-GEX	98	Global Express	9013	Global Jet Luxembourg SA. Luxembourg.	C-GZSM
☐ LX-GJL	02	Falcon 900C	197	Global Jet Luxembourg SA. Luxembourg.	(LX-MAM)
☐ LX-GJM	06	Global Express	9189	Global Jet Luxembourg SA. Luxembourg.	C-FEAQ
☐ LX-GVV	00	BBJ-7BC	30791	Global Jet Luxembourg SA. Luxembourg.	N191QS
☐ LX-IIH	00	CitationJet CJ-1	525-0391	Italtrieste International Holding SA. Luxembourg.	N5130J
☐ LX-IMZ	05	Learjet 45XR	45-266	Husky Luxembourg SA.	(LX-IMS)
☐ LX-JCD	00	Citation Excel	560-5104	Jean Claude Decaux International, Toussus Le Noble, France.	(F-GXXX)
☐ LX-LAR	89	Learjet 35A	35A-653	Luxembourg Air Ambulance SA/Ducair SA. Luxembourg.	HB-VJL
☐ LX-LFB	88	Falcon 900B	62	Luxflight Executive SA. Luxembourg.	(OO-LFQ)
☐ LX-LOU	04	Learjet 60	60-277	Luxembourg Air Ambulance SA/Ducair SA. Luxembourg.	N40079
☐ LX-LOV	95	CitationJet	525-0102	Jet Corporate Consulting SA. Luxembourg.	TC-CRO
☐ LX-OKR	07	Hawker 850XP	258855	Madeleine Ltd/Global jet Luxembourg SA. Luxembourg.	N7225U
☐ LX-ONE	81	Learjet 35A	35A-417	Luxembourg Air Ambulance SA/Ducair SA. Luxembourg.	N281CD
☐ LX-PAK	06	Global Express	9197	Aigleemont, Paris-Le Bourget, France.	C-FEBS
☐ LX-PCT	95	Learjet 31A	31A-112	JABJ AG/Powder Coating Technologies International SA.	N5082S
☐ LX-PMA	06	Challenger 300	20097	Premiair SA. Luxembourg.	C-FHMM
☐ LX-PMR	02	390 Premier 1	RB-64	Premiair SA. Luxembourg.	N6164U
☐ LX-SVW	01	Falcon 2000	133	Global Jet Luxembourg SA. Luxembourg.	F-WQBK
☐ LX-THS	88	Falcon 50	185	Trans Helicopteres Services/Air Bouriez Group, Lyon-Bron.	F-GKBZ
☐ LX-TQJ	07	Challenger 300	20159	Global Jet Luxembourg SA. Luxembourg.	C-FMXQ
☐ LX-TWO	87	Learjet 35A	35A-628	Luxembourg Air Ambulance SA/Ducair SA. Luxembourg.	N628GZ
☐ LX-VIP	00	Global Express	9076	Global Jet Luxembourg SA. Luxembourg.	N700XT
☐ LX-YSL	99	CitationJet	525-0322	Berlys Aero SA/Yves St Laurent, Paris-Le Bourget, France.	N52LT
☐ LX-ZAK	06	Global 5000	9204	Global Jet Luxembourg, Luxembourg.	OE-IAK
☐ LX-ZAV	01	Challenger 604	5523	Global Jet Luxembourg SA. Luxembourg.	N523CL

LY = LITHUANIA   Total   2

Civil

Reg	Yr	Type	c/n	Owner/Operator	Prev Regn
☐ LY-DSK	06	Hawker 850XP	258811	Aurela Co Ltd. Vilnius.	N71881
☐ LY-HER	03	390 Premier 1	RB-83	Vespera UAB. Vilnius.	N88EU

LZ = BULGARIA   Total   11
Civil

Reg	Yr	Type	c/n	Owner/Operator	Prev Regn
☐ LZ-...	99	Learjet 60	60-167	Hypo Luftfahrzeug Leasing GmbH. Klagenfurt. (lessor ?).	N167XX
☐ LZ-ABV	04	Citation Bravo	550-1103	Air VB/AVB-2004 Ltd, Sofia.	N1276Z
☐ LZ-BVE	07	Learjet 60	60-329	Air VB/AVB-2004 Ltd. Sofia.	N50111
☐ LZ-BVV	00	Learjet 60	60-203	Air VB/AVB-2004 Ltd. Sofia.	N770BG
☐ LZ-DIN	95	CitationJet	525-0090	Venid Air,	(N525KF)
☐ LZ-FIB	99	Galaxy-1126	011	BH Air Ltd-Balkan Holidays, Sofia.	(N223AM)
☐ LZ-OOI	01	Falcon 2000	123	Government of Bulgaria, Avio Detachment 28, Sofia.	F-WWVS
☐ LZ-VTS	67	Learjet 24	24-156	Vivas Air, Sofia.	N712R
☐ LZ-YUM	83	Challenger 600S	1085	Petrol Holding Aviation-Naftex Bulgaria/Air Lazur, Sofia.	OE-HET
☐ LZ-YUN	01	Challenger 604	5508	Air Lazur, Sofia.	P4-FAY
☐ LZ-YUP	04	Challenger 604	5602	Air Lazur, Sofia.	HB-JRW

M = ISLE OF MAN   Total   20
Civil

Reg	Yr	Type	c/n	Owner/Operator	Prev Regn
☐ M-AGIC	07	Citation Sovereign	680-0138	Trust Air Ltd/Westair Flying Services Ltd, Blackpool.	N51984
☐ M-BIGG*	07	Challenger 605	5722	Signal Aviation Ltd.	C-FOGE
☐ M-BWFC	06	Citation Excel XLS	560-5690	Bakewell Industries Ltd. Douglas.	N560FC
☐ M-CHEM	07	Falcon 2000EX EASY	128	Ineos/CTC Aviation Services Ltd. Bournemouth-Hurn.	VP-BOE
☐ M-DASO	97	Falcon 50EX	268	Bramptonia Ltd. Luton.	G-DASO
☐ M-ELON	06	CitationJet CJ-3	525B-0148	Sleepwell Aviation Inc. Douglas.	N148CJ
☐ M-FALC	98	Falcon 900EX	31	Noclaf Ltd. Luton.	HZ-OFC4
☐ M-GULF	88	Gulfstream 4	1082	Earth One Ltd.	(N82BR)
☐ M-HAWK	00	Hawker 800XP	258494	Ineos/CTC Aviation Services Ltd. Bournemouth-Hurn.	VP-BXP
☐ M-HDAM	85	BAe 125/800B	258037	ABG Air Ltd. Farnborough.	70-ADC
☐ M-ICRO	07	CitationJet CJ2+	525A-0347	Pektron Aviation Ltd. Gamston.	N5262X
☐ M-LLGC	06	Global 5000	9227	TAG Aviation Charter UK Ltd. Farnborough.	(N200LS)
☐ M-NEWT	07	Challenger 300	20151	Sterling Aviation Properties, Luton.	C-FLQX
☐ M-RURU	95	Falcon 900B	140	Rozita Ltd. Guernsey, C.I.	N900UT
☐ M-SAIR	94	Falcon 900B	141	W A Developments International Ltd. Carlisle,.	C-GHML
☐ M-TAGB*	07	Challenger 300	20172	TAG Aviation Charter UK Ltd. Farnborough.	C-FPMU
☐ M-XONE	01	CitationJet CJ-2	525A-0031	Newshore Ltd. Jersey, C.I.	VP-BFC
☐ M-XXRS*	05	Global Express	9169	TAG Aviation Charter UK Ltd. Kiev, Ukraine.	G-XXRS
☐ M-YNJC	06	Embraer Legacy 600	14500961	NewJetCo (Europe) Ltd/ASCE Ltd. Stansted.	G-ONJC
☐ M-YSKY	07	390 Premier 1A	RB-209	Pool Aviation Ltd. Blackpool.	N209BP

N = USA   Total   11467
Civil

Reg	Yr	Type	c/n	Owner/Operator	Prev Regn
☐ N1	89	Gulfstream 4	1071	FAA, Washington, DC. 'Spirit of America'	N410GA
☐ N1AG	88	Beechjet 400	RJ-35	Gossett Aviation LLC/Gossett Suzuki, Memphis, Tn.	N137MM
☐ N1AK*	02	Citation V	560-0205	Pruhs Corp. Anchorage, Ak.	N205VP
☐ N1AP	02	Citation X	750-0176	Arnold Palmer, Youngstown, Pa.	N51806
☐ N1BN	03	Gulfstream G550	5036	Iliad Leasing Inc/Odyssey Aviation, West Palm Beach, Fl.	N936GA
☐ N1BR	93	Learjet 31A	31A-086	Synfuel Management LLC. Lexington-Blue Grass, Ky.	N969
☐ N1BS	99	Citation X	750-0081	Bank of Stockton, Portland, Or.	N810X
☐ N1C	96	Falcon 2000	40	Maverick Air LLC/C & S Aviation LLC. Addison, Tx.	F-W...
☐ N1CA	04	Hawker 800XP	258672	Coin Acceptors Inc. St Louis, Mo.	N672XP
☐ N1CC	79	Gulfstream 2B	257	CCI Pilot Services LLC/Tonkawa Inc. St Paul, Mn.	N56D
☐ N1CF	98	Citation V Ultra	560-0473	Schermerhorn Construction LLC. Queensbury, NY.	N473SB
☐ N1CG	81	Learjet 55	55-014	ICG LLC. Denver, Co.	N551CG
☐ N1CH	05	CitationJet CJ-3	525B-0064	KOAV LLC/Clayton Homes Inc. Knoxville, Tn.	N5263S
☐ N1CR	05	390 Premier 1A	RB-146	Roberts Properties Inc. Atlanta-DeKalb, Ga.	N6146J
☐ N1D*	83	Falcon 200	495	WDA LLC. Linthicum Heights, Md.	N800EG
☐ N1DA	75	Citation	500-0288	Donald Anderson, Roswell, NM.	(N502BA)
☐ N1DC	01	Gulfstream V	651	Ark-Air Flight Inc. Dallas, Tx.	N651GV
☐ N1DE	90	Learjet 31	31-016	Champion Air LLC. Statesville, NC.	N92LJ
☐ N1DG	04	Global 5000	9156	LPL Management Group Inc. Startford, Ct.	N156DG
☐ N1DH	94	Challenger 601-3R	5145	Den-Star Management Inc. Minneapolis, Mn.	N145LJ
☐ N1DW	88	Challenger 601-3A	5025	Air Orange Inc. Orange County, Ca.	N93DW
☐ N1EB	99	Gulfstream 4SP	1367	Premiere Radio Networks, Sherman Oaks, Ca.	N422ML
☐ N1ED	00	Learjet 31A	31A-218	DeBartolo Corp/San Francisco Forty-Niners,Youngstown ,Oh.	N30050
☐ N1EG	02	390 Premier 1	RB-43	Malibu Leasing Corp. Aspen, Co.	
☐ N1FE	01	Global Express	9091	FEDEX, Memphis, Tn.	N700XM
☐ N1FJ	07	Citation Sovereign	680-0166	Roadlink Transportation Inc. Livingston, Mt.	N5086W
☐ N1GH	80	Citation II	550-0201	Victor X LLC. Newport Beach, Ca.	N566TX
☐ N1GM	76	Sabre-60	306-120	Victory Christian Ministries International, Clinton, Md.	N265SR

Reg	Yr	Type	c/n	Owner/Operator	Prev Regn
☐ N1GN	03	Gulfstream G550	5023	Greg Norman Arcraft Leasing Inc. West Palm Beach, Fl.	N923GA
☐ N1HA	79	Citation II/SP	551-0021	One Hotel Alpha LLC/Aker Plastics Inc. Plymouth, In.	N55LS
☐ N1HC	02	Gulfstream G550	5009	Hardesty-Gulfstream LLC. Tulsa, Ok.	N909GA
☐ N1HF	82	Falcon 20F-5	474	Harbison-Fischer Inc. Fort Worth, Tx.	N211HF
☐ N1HP	00	Learjet 45	45-082	Helmerich & Payne Inc. Tulsa, Ok.	N40082
☐ N1HS	05	Citation Excel XLS	560-5596	Erickson Petroleum Corp. St Paul, Mn.	N82GM
☐ N1HZ	88	Challenger 601-3A	5030	Herzog Contracting Corp. St Joseph, Mo.	N816SP
☐ N1JB	05	Hawker 400XP	RK-424	Auto Team Management Inc. Orlando, Fl.	N24XP
☐ N1JC	83	Diamond 1A	A059SA	New Braunfels Aviation Ltd. New Braunfels, Tx.	N126GA
☐ N1JG	82	Learjet 55	55-055	Half Moon Transportation LLC. Allentown, Pa.	N852PA
☐ N1JK	07	Falcon 2000EX EASY	130	Pegasus South LLC. New Orleans, La.	F-WWGA
☐ N1JM	99	Learjet 31A	31A-196	JM 500 LLC/James McMurray Racing, Statesville, NC.	N136BX
☐ N1JN	98	Gulfstream V	538	Nicklaus Design LLC/Air Bear Inc. West Palm Beach, Fl.	N601MD
☐ N1JW	82	Falcon 100	200	JRW Aviation Inc. Dallas, Tx.	N808L
☐ N1KA	06	CitationJet CJ-3	525B-0076	CMH Homes Inc. Knoxville, Tn.	N.....
☐ N1KE	99	Gulfstream V	574	Nike Inc/Aero Air LLC. Hillsboro, Or.	N674GA
☐ N1KT	78	Westwind-1124	230	Murray Energy Corp. Pepper Pike, Oh.	N102U
☐ N1LB	00	Gulfstream 4SP	1448	Lehman Brothers/Executive Fliteways Inc. Ronkonkoma, NY.	N448GA
☐ N1LT	77	Sabre-75A	380-59	Aircraft Turbine & Support Inc. Tulsa, Ok. (status ?).	N27LT
☐ N1LW	81	Gulfstream 3	329	Lester Woemer/LJW Asset Management LLC. West Palm Beach.	N327JJ
☐ N1M	87	Challenger 601-3A	5008	United Aircraft Holdings LLC. Charlotte, NC.	N601EG
☐ N1MC	99	Astra-1125SPX	112	Jernigan Air LLC. Birmingham, Al.	N633GA
☐ N1MJ	77	JetStar 2	5217	486MJ Inc. Daphne, Al.	N486MJ
☐ N1MM	81	Citation II	550-0269	Erin Air Inc. Seattle, Wa.	N28RC
☐ N1NA	00	Challenger 604	5447	Carlisle Air Corp/Westwind Air Inc. Portsmouth, NH.	N323BX
☐ N1NC	05	Falcon 2000EX EASY	48	Broad River Aviation Inc. Fort Lauderdale, Fl.	N48NC
☐ N1NL	81	Citation II	550-0271	Neil F Lampson Inc. Kennewick, Wa.	N729MJ
☐ N1PB	98	Citation Excel	560-5013	Francis S Baldwin Jr. Longboat Key, Fl.	N1243C
☐ N1PG	99	Gulfstream 4SP	1374	Proctor & Gamble Co. Cincinnati-Lunken, Oh.	N7PG
☐ N1PR	81	Gulfstream 3	341	Paragon Ranch Inc. Broomfield, Co.	N263C
☐ N1QH	71	HS 125/731	NA763	Riley Aviation Co. Claremont, Ca.	N19H
☐ N1RB	00	Learjet 45	45-119	Bank of Agriculture & Commerce, Stockton, Ca.	N316SR
☐ N1RF	07	Citation Sovereign	680-0163	J Russell Flowers LLC. St Louis, Mo.	N5267J
☐ N1RL	99	Challenger 600	10004	Indianapolis Motor Speedway Corp. Indianapolis, In.	N400MJ
☐ N1S	87	Falcon 900	28	Sunoco Inc. Philadelphia, Pa.	N86MC
☐ N1SA	01	Global Express	9100	Stanford Financial Group Co. Houston, Tx.	N700CX
☐ N1SF	99	Gulfstream V	598	Gulf States Toyota Inc. Houston, Tx.	N598GA
☐ N1SL	91	Gulfstream 4	1167	Sara Lee Corp. Chicago-Midway, Il.	N49SL
☐ N1SN	00	Gulfstream 4SP	1433	Sky Night LLC/LandAir Transport, Greeneville, Tn.	N433GA
☐ N1SV	80	Citation II	550-0150	Viersen Air Services LLC. Okmulgee, Ok.	N2668A
☐ N1TF	04	Gulfstream G550	5035	Gulf States Toyota Inc. Houston, Tx.	N935GA
☐ N1TG	07	Citation Sovereign	680-0147	147 Sovereign Investments LLC. Dayton, Nv.	N102TG
☐ N1TM	02	Gulfstream 4SP	1490	Marsico Aviation LLC. Denver, Co.	(N4900S)
☐ N1TS	99	Global Express	9046	First Virtual Air LLC/Siebel Systems Inc. San Jose, Ca.	N700BV
☐ N1TY	80	Citation II	550-0171	Gulfport Jet Aviation LLC. Concord, NC.	N19AJ
☐ N1UA	90	Astra-1125SP	044	University of Alabama, Tuscaloosa, Al.	N844GA
☐ N1UM	77	Citation 1/SP	501-0011	University of Mississippi, Oxford, Ms.	N650AC
☐ N1UP	92	Citation VI	650-0224	Foresight Management LLC. Wilmington, De.	(N7UL)
☐ N1WP	87	Gulfstream 4	1030	AMSI/Wm Pennington/WNP Aviation Inc. Reno, Nv.	(N811JK)
☐ N1XH	03	390 Premier 1	RB-76	Thayer Lodging Group Inc. Fort Lauderdale, Fl.	N6076Y
☐ N1XL	81	Learjet 35A	35A-392	Northstar Aviation LLC. St Croix, USVI.	N18DY
☐ N1XT	02	390 Premier 1	RB-36	JB Services Inc. Wilmington, De.	
☐ N1Z	03	Gulfstream G200	084	Niznick Enterprises Inc. Las Vegas, Nv.	N414KD
☐ N1ZC	06	Citation Sovereign	680-0085	Zachary Construction Corp. San Antonio, Tx.	N5202D
☐ N2	02	Citation Excel	560-5333	FAA, Oklahoma City, Ok.	N533XL
☐ N2AT	97	Falcon 2000	51	ALLTEL Corp. Little Rock, Ar.	N82AT
☐ N2BA	76	Learjet 35	35-051	Silver Lining Leasing Inc. Pensacola, Fl.	(N123MJ)
☐ N2BD	00	Falcon 900EX	72	Becton-Dickinson & Co. Teterboro, NJ.	F-WWFH
☐ N2BG	02	Gulfstream G200	064	Boyd Gaming/California Hotel & Casino, Las Vegas, Nv.	(N706QS)
☐ N2CC	98	Gulfstream 4SP	1343	CCI Pilot Services LLC/Tonkawa Inc. St Paul, Mn.	N99SC
☐ N2DD	76	Learjet 24E	24E-335	N2DD Inc. Newark, De.	N8AE
☐ N2DF	70	Gulfstream 2B	95	Suburban Properties 3 LLC. Detroit, Mi.	N889DF
☐ N2DH	90	Citation III	650-0193	Den-Star Management Inc. Minneapolis, Mn.	N650CC
☐ N2FE	91	Challenger 601-3A	5095	FEDEX, Memphis, Tn.	N95FE
☐ N2FQ	86	Falcon 50	167	SK Aviation LLC/Sweeney Development Co. St Helena, Ca.	N2T
☐ N2FU	90	Learjet 31	31-027	Formula One Management Ltd. Biggin Hill, UK.	N30LJ

Reg	Yr	Type	c/n	Owner/Operator	Prev Regn
❏ N2G	97	Hawker 800XP	258354	CCA Financial LLC. Ashland, Va.	
❏ N2GG	81	Citation II	550-0286	Pro Aviation Inc. Wadsworth, Il.	N78BA
❏ N2HB	05	Citation Excel XLS	560-5579	Hilliard Leasing LLC. Clewiston, Fl.	N5253S
❏ N2HL	03	Gulfstream G200	091	Leach Capital LLC. San Francisco, Ca.	(N19HL)
❏ N2HP	07	Learjet 45	45-330	Helmerich & Payne Inc. Tulsa, Ok.	N45XT
❏ N2HZ	06	390 Premier 1A	RB-186	Herzog Contracting Corp. St Joseph, Mo.	N37086
❏ N2JR	73	Citation 2B	131	BGI Aviation LLC/Blair Group Inc. St Petersburg, Fl.	N759A
❏ N2JW	02	Challenger 604	5549	Williams Bailey Law Firm/Excel Three LLC. Houston, Tx.	N540JW
❏ N2KZ	82	HS 125/700A	NA0324	Hotel Hotel Aircraft Inc. Chesterfield, Mo.	N507F
❏ N2N	99	Gulfstream V	586	Steven Jobs/Glass Aviation Inc. San Jose, Ca.	N586GA
❏ N2NA	80	Gulfstream 3	309	NASA, Washington, DC.	N1NA
❏ N2NL	81	Sabre-65	465-63	Stewart Lubricants & Service Co. Birmingham, Al.	N2N
❏ N2PG	99	Gulfstream 4SP	1378	Procter & Gamble Co. Cincinnati-Lunken, Oh.	N378GA
❏ N2QG	91	BAe 125/800A	NA0467	Boyd Atlantic City Inc. Atlantic City, NJ.	(N103BG)
❏ N2RC	95	Citation V Ultra	560-0319	Rico Marketing Corp. Flint-Bishop, Mi.	LV-WOE
❏ N2RM	74	Citation	500-0153	Coastal Atlantic Aviation Investments, Suffolk, Va.	N153JP
❏ N2SA	89	Gulfstream 4	1104	Stanford Aircraft LLC. Miami, Fl.	N700GD
❏ N2T	04	Global Express	9162	Oakley Inc/N2T Inc. Hillsboro, Or.	C-FCOZ
❏ N2UJ	07	Citation Sovereign	680-0179	Cessna Finance Corp. Wichita, Ks.	N5200Z
❏ N2UP	93	Citation VI	650-0227	Mid-America Aviation LLC. Oklahoma City, Ok.	(N2UX)
❏ N2WC	83	Diamond 1	A047SA	White Rock Aircraft LLC. Little Rock, Ar.	N333TS
❏ N2ZC	00	Citation Excel	560-5156	Zachary Construction Corp. San Antonio, Tx.	N5155G
❏ N3	03	Citation Excel	560-5341	FAA, Oklahoma City, Ok.	N5061W
❏ N3AS	04	Learjet 45	45-247	Shamrock Foods Co. Scottsdale, Az.	N50154
❏ N3AV	81	Westwind-Two	361	Avjet Corp. Burbank, Ca.	N610HC
❏ N3BL	64	Learjet 23	23-003	Alpha Jet International Inc. Bartow, Fl.	N3BL
❏ N3BM	04	Falcon 2000EX EASY	38	Morris Communications Corp. Augusta, Ga.	F-WWGT
❏ N3CJ	02	CitationJet CJ-3	711	Cessna Aircraft Co. Wichita, Ks.	
❏ N3CT	05	CitationJet CJ-3	525B-0041	InnCal Inc. Stockton, Ca.	N525PC
❏ N3DP	81	Gulfstream 3	334	Green Chair Productions Inc. Van Nuys, Ca.	N700SB
❏ N3FA	89	Citation V	560-0023	Falwell Aviation/Truck Body Aviation Inc. Lynchburg, Va.	N345MB
❏ N3FE	89	Challenger 601-3A	5054	FEDEX, Memphis, Tn.	N619FE
❏ N3GN	78	Citation 1/SP	501-0090	R-Air Inc. Wilmington, De.	N41JP
❏ N3HB	92	Falcon 900B	126	Hamilton Companies LLC. Denver, Co.	N94NA
❏ N3JM	06	CitationJet CJ-3	525B-0102	JMA Energy LLC. Oklahoma City, Ok.	N812JM
❏ N3K	07	390 Premier 1A	RB-218	Haggerty Equipment Leasing Inc. Las Vegas, Nv.	
❏ N3MB	81	Learjet 35A	35A-335	Pace American of Indiana/Pair Corp. Middlebury, In.	(N880CH)
❏ N3PC	99	Challenger 604	5411	Trinity Broadcasting of Florida Inc. Pembroke Park, Fl.	N604TS
❏ N3PG	05	Gulfstream G550	5091	Procter & Gamble Co. Cincinnati-Lunken, Oh.	N591GA
❏ N3PW	81	Falcon 10	179	Edgington Transport LLC. Pleasanton, Ca.	N100RR
❏ N3QG	88	BAe 125/800A	NA0420	Marina District Development LLC. Atlantic City, NJ.	N803X
❏ N3RC	94	BAe 125/800A	258253	Richard Childress Racing Enterprises Inc. Lexington, NC.	N801CE
❏ N3RP	77	Sabre-75A	380-42	Qualint LLC. Wesley Chapel, Fl.	N6YL
❏ N3SA	91	Gulfstream 4	1171	Stanford Aircraft LLC. Miami, Fl.	N686CG
❏ N3ST	01	CitationJet CJ-2	525A-0045	Beehawk Aviation Inc/Thomas Enterprises Inc. Smyrna, Ga.	N5214L
❏ N3VF	77	Falcon 20F-5	363	VF Corp. Greensboro-Highpoint, NC.	N363FJ
❏ N3VJ	91	Learjet 31A	31A-035	Bergen Jet LLC/Venture Jets Inc. Lititz, Pa.	N618RF
❏ N3WB	94	CitationJet	525-0053	3 Generation Air LLC/Diversified Partners LLC. Scottsdale,	(N603JC)
❏ N3WT	79	Citation 1/SP	501-0088	Eagle Ventures LLC. Mobile, Al.	(N23TZ)
❏ N4AZ		McDonnell 220	1	Fuel Fresh Inc. Tempe, Az.	N220N
❏ N4CJ	07	CitationJet CJ-4	714001	Cessna Aircraft Co. Wichita, Ks.	
❏ N4CP	02	Gulfstream G550	5005	Pfizer Inc. Mercer County Airport, NJ.	N805GA
❏ N4CR	66	HS 125/1A-522	25109	Trail's Productions Inc. Thousand Oaks, Ca.	N201H
❏ N4CS	80	Sabre-65	465-27	Career Sports Management Inc. Atlanta-DeKalb, Ga.	N39TR
❏ N4DA	05	Learjet 45	45-283	Adam Aviation LLP. College Station, Tx.	
❏ N4EA	82	Learjet 35A	35A-458	Rolex/Woodhill Aviation Corp. Palwaukee, Il.	N86RX
❏ N4ES	70	HS 125/F400A	25243	Azair Inc. Birmingham, Al.	VP-CTS
❏ N4FE	99	Learjet 45	45-032	FEDEX, Memphis, Tn.	
❏ N4GA	05	CitationJet CJ-3	525B-0055	AOPA-Aircraft Owners & Pilots Association, Frederick, Md.	N5151D
❏ N4GX	99	Global Express	9048	Sierra Aviation Inc. Kansas City, Mo.	N700BY
❏ N4J	77	Learjet 35A	35A-110	RR Investments Inc/Million Air, Dallas, Tx.	(N12EP)
❏ N4JB	00	Citation Excel	560-5125	Breco International, Harare, Zimbabwe.	N5124K
❏ N4JS	99	Citation Excel	560-5035	John F Scarpa Inc. Pleasantville, NJ.	N35XL
❏ N4MH	78	Westwind-1124	232	Genesis Aircraft Marketing LLC. Bethany, Ok.	N773AW
❏ N4MM	91	Citation V	560-0109A	Morgan McClure Motorsports Inc. Abingdon, Va.	(N560RD)
❏ N4NR	79	Gulfstream 2B	255	Wilmington Aero Ventures Inc. Wilmington, De.	N442A

Reg	Yr	Type	c/n	Owner/Operator	Prev Regn
☐ N4NT	70	Sabre-60	306-48	Sabre Fifty Inc. Opa Locka, Fl.	N4228A
☐ N4PG	94	Gulfstream 4SP	1259	Procter & Gamble Co. Cincinnati-Lunken, Oh.	N1PG
☐ N4QB	71	HS 125/F400A	25255	River Run Projects LLC. Nashua, NH.	(N255TS)
☐ N4QG	04	Falcon 2000EX	28	WFBNW NA. Salt Lake City, Ut. (trustor ?).	(N28EX)
☐ N4QN	93	Citation VII	650-7031	Blessey Travel LLC. Big Sky, Mt.	N40N
☐ N4QP	98	CitationJet	525-0272	F B Aire LLC/Fletcher Bright Co. Chattanooga, Tn.	N4GA
☐ N4SA	96	Hawker 800XP2	258303	Stanford Financial Group Co. Houston, Tx.	N621CH
☐ N4SQ	80	Westwind-Two	307	Sunquest Executive Air Charter Inc. Van Nuys, Ca.	N494BP
☐ N4T	06	Global Express	9195	Scout Aviation II LLC/Atticus Capital LLC. NYC.	N195GX
☐ N4TL	01	Citation Encore	560-0587	Toyota-Lexus/Morningstar Aviation II Inc. Greenville, SC.	(N587K)
☐ N4UB	77	Gulfstream 2B	207	Kingfisher Airlines Ltd/U B Ltd. Bangalore, India "Sidharta"	VP-CUB
☐ N4VF	85	Falcon 50	160	V F Corp. Greensboro-Highpoint, NC.	N487F
☐ N4WC	72	HS 125/F400A	NA771	W & P Supply Corp. Miami, Fl.	N298NM
☐ N4WG	76	Westwind-1124	200	Owners Jet Services Ltd. DuPage, Il.	N1124X
☐ N4Y	86	Citation III	650-0137	Heartland Aviation Inc. Eau Claire, Wi.	N874G
☐ N4ZL	97	Citation V Ultra	560-0448	Flying Tigers LLC/Ozark Management Inc. Jefferson City, Mo.	C-GSUM
☐ N5CA	81	Falcon 10	187	ABI LLC. Van Nuys, Ca.	(N600AP)
☐ N5DA	03	Gulfstream G550	5021	Adam Aviation LLP. College Station, Tx.	N921GA
☐ N5DL	78	Gulfstream II SP	226	CLG Properties LLC. Moorpark, Ca.	N1902L
☐ N5FE	00	Learjet 45	45-079	FEDEX, Memphis, Tn.	
☐ N5FF	02	Citation X	750-0192	Frederick Furth/Furthco, Healdsburg, Ca.	N51817
☐ N5GF	95	Gulfstream 4SP	1277	685TA Corp/American Home Products, Teterboro, NJ.	N426GA
☐ N5GU	04	CitationJet CJ-3	525B-0009	LKM Inc. Wilmington, De.	N777NJ
☐ N5HQ	79	Westwind-1124	266	SCI Air LLC/Steven Counts Inc. Ocala, Fl.	N7HM
☐ N5LK	75	Citation	500-0274	Kerman Holdings LLC. Wilmington, De.	N70TF
☐ N5MC	93	Gulfstream 4SP	1218	McCaw Communications Inc. Seattle, Wa.	N418SP
☐ N5NC	00	Learjet 31A	31A-211	Air Operations LLC/Noland Co. Newport News, Va.	N574BA
☐ N5NG	02	Gulfstream 4SP	1485	Northrop Grumman Aviation Inc. Van Nuys, Ca.	N485GA
☐ N5NR	05	Citation Excel XLS	560-5557	L & F Arrow LLC/L & F Distributors, McAllen, Tx.	N551CS
☐ N5PG	04	Gulfstream G550	5046	Procter & Gamble Co. Cincinnati-Lunken, Oh.	N946GA
☐ N5RD	91	Gulfstream 4	1156	RDC Marine Inc. Houston, Tx.	N156TS
☐ N5SA	98	Gulfstream V	527	WEKEL SA. Bogota, Colombia.	N527GA
☐ N5T	99	Citation X	750-0104	Azlon LLC. Austin, Tx.	N51478
☐ N5TR	81	Citation II	551-0351	Housey Aviation LLC. Southfield, Mi. (was 550-0322).	N322CS
☐ N5UD	05	CitationJet CJ1+	525-0620	Wallan Aviation, Riyadh, Saudi Arabia.	N620CJ
☐ N5UU	00	Global Express	9029	Final Sequel Newco LLC. Dulles, Va.	N929TS
☐ N5VF	86	Falcon 50	166	V F Corp. Greensboro-Highpoint, NC.	N316PA
☐ N5VG	90	Learjet 31	31-014	Wal-Mart Stores Inc. Rogers, Ar.	PT-OFJ
☐ N5VJ	87	Falcon 900B	27	Yet Again Inc. Dulles, Va.	N91EW
☐ N5VP	77	Citation 1/SP	501-0046	Air East Charters of Ashoskie Inc. Ashoskie, NC.	N405CC
☐ N5VS	05	Gulfstream G550	5088	Cartera Inversiones Venezolanas CA. Caracas, Venezuela.	N588GA
☐ N5WF	78	Citation 1/SP	501-0082	Mociva Inc. Carlsbad-Palomar, Ca.	XB-ERX
☐ N5WN	07	CitationJet CJ-3	525B-0204	Universal Hyundai Nissan, Orlando, Fl.	N5066F
☐ N5WT	79	Citation II/SP	551-0149	Walter Woltosz, Palmdale, Ca. (was 550-0107).	(N715PS)
☐ N5XP	01	Learjet 45	45-118	Xpress Air Inc. Chattanooga, Tn.	N50163
☐ N5YD	02	CitationJet CJ-2	525A-0121	Inversiones Chocolido CA. Caracas, Venezuela.	N121YD
☐ N6BX	89	Falcon 900B	79	Baxter Healthcare Corp/Allegiance Healthcare, Waukegan, Il.	N901FJ
☐ N6D	06	Global Express	9191	XRS Holdings LLC. Chicago, Il.	N91NG
☐ N6FE	01	Learjet 45	45-098	FEDEX, Memphis, Tn.	
☐ N6FR	97	Citation Bravo	550-0828	Fall River Group Inc. Fall River, Wi.	N5058J
☐ N6GD*	06	Embraer Legacy 600	14500983	GNG LLC. Gulfport, Fl.	N473MM
☐ N6GV	79	Sabre-65	465-9	AG Atlantic Investment Inc. Ocean City, Md.	(N769EG)
☐ N6HF	80	Citation II	550-0260	HCF Realty Inc. St Clair Shores, Mi.	N8CF
☐ N6JB	93	Challenger 601-3A	5131	Palmer Aviation Leasing LLC. Germantown, Tn.	(N405DP)
☐ N6JR	06	390 Premier 1A	RB-161	Roush Fenway Racing LLC. Willow Run, Mi.	(N606JR)
☐ N6JW	73	Gulfstream 2	138	Walter Industries Inc. Tampa, Fl.	
☐ N6MF	01	Beechjet 400A	RK-315	Tamco Roofing Products/Midwest Flight LLC. Joplin, Mo.	N3215J
☐ N6MW	82	Challenger 600S	1057	M A Inc. Oshkosh, Wi.	N78SR
☐ N6NR	04	Hawker 800XP	258701	Rockwell Automation Inc. Milwaukee, Wi.	N501XP
☐ N6NY	97	Citation V Ultra	560-0439	LJ Associates Inc/LJ Aviation, Latrobe, Pa.	VP-CSC
☐ N6SS	66	HS 125/1A-522	25100	J-Bird Air Service Corp. Rosedale, NY.	N44TQ
☐ N6TM	03	Citation Bravo	550-1067	Liberty Mutual Insurance Co. Bedford, Ma.	N5085E
☐ N6VB	04	Global Express	9144	Paramount Pictures Corp. Van Nuys, Ca.	C-FAGV
☐ N6VF	84	Falcon 20F-5B	486	V F Corp. Greensboro-Highpoint, NC.	F-GEFS
☐ N6VG	75	Falcon 10	62	P & G LC. Van Nuys, Ca.	N12LB
☐ N6ZE	03	CitationJet CJ-2	525A-0141	Six Zulu Echo LLC/Alltel Corp. Little Rock, Ar.	N141JV

Reg	Yr	Type	c/n	Owner/Operator	Prev Regn
☐ N7AB	96	Citation VII	650-7068	Coral Aviation Inc. Cape Coral, Fl.	N111BZ
☐ N7CC	04	CitationJet CJ-3	525B-0007	Intrust Financial Corp. Wichita, Ks.	N5239J
☐ N7CH	07	CitationJet CJ-3	525B-0202	CMH Homes Inc. Knoxville, Tn.	N51896
☐ N7CQ	93	CitationJet	525-0004	IBL Aircraft LLC. Marysville, Ca.	N7CC
☐ N7DJ	79	Westwind-1124	265	Robert Lanphere, Beaverton, Or.	N167J
☐ N7EJ	76	Learjet 24E	24E-343	Fabair LLC. Milwaukee, Wi.	(N602JF)
☐ N7EN	80	Citation Eagle II	501-0302	Gulfstream Nautical LC. Naples, Fl. (was 500-0402).	N801EL
☐ N7FE	99	Learjet 45	45-099	FEDEX, Memphis, Tn.	(N545RS)
☐ N7GF	66	Learjet 23	23-093	Avitrans Inc. Wilmington, De.	N80775
☐ N7GJ	72	Citation	500-0021	WFBNW NA. Salt Lake City, Ut. (trustor ?).	XA-JLV
☐ N7GX	83	Falcon 50	139	Dura Automotive Systems Inc. Pontiac, Mi.	N1S
☐ N7GZ	03	CitationJet CJ-2	525A-0145	Duval Asphalt Products Inc. Cincinnati, Oh.	N.....
☐ N7HB	98	Citation Excel XLS	560-5607	Hunt Building Co. El Paso, Tx.	N52038
☐ N7JM	90	Gulfstream 4	1132	Life in the Word/Joyce Meyer Ministries Inc. St Louis, Mo.	N71NR
☐ N7KC	83	Falcon 200	479	Arnie Barn Inc/Falcon 200 Inc. Nashville, Tn.	N240RS
☐ N7KG	73	Sabre-40A	282-111	Tulsa Technology Center, Tulsa, Ok.	(N246GS)
☐ N7MZ	81	Citation 1/SP	501-0217	SMDA LLC/Ozark Management Inc. Jefferson City, Mo.	N500TW
☐ N7NE	04	CitationJet CJ-3	525B-0025	Norfolk Iron & Metal Co/NIM Air LLC. Norfolk, Ne.	N5201J
☐ N7NN	98	Citation Bravo	550-0851	Knauss Ventures LLC. Las Vegas, Nv.	
☐ N7PS*	88	Challenger 601-3A	5027	Thundervolt LLC. Scottsdale, Az.	N420ST
☐ N7PW	80	Diamond 1	A027SA	General Aviation Services LLC. Lake Zurich, Il.	N27TJ
☐ N7QM	04	CitationJet CJ-2	525A-0214	Caladero SL. Zaragoza, Spain.	N1DM
☐ N7RX	05	Gulfstream G450	4017	IMS Health Inc. Oxford, Ct.	N917GA
☐ N7SB	02	Citation X	750-0209	OPA LLC/Business Resources International Inc. Winnetka, Il.	N52229
☐ N7SJ	05	SJ 30-2	007	Action Aviation Holdings Inc. Wilmington, De.	N70SJ
☐ N7SN	01	Learjet 31A	31A-226	Sevenson Enviromental Services Inc. Niagara Falls, NY.	N226LJ
☐ N7TK	79	Citation 1/SP	501-0116	Timothy Mellon, Lyme, Ct.	(N90MT)
☐ N7UF	00	Gulfstream 4SP	1422	Frank & Victoria Fertitta Trust, Las Vegas, Nv.	N999GP
☐ N7XE	00	CitationJet CJ-1	525-0419	D & H Airways LLC. Fort Collins, Co.	N7NE
☐ N7YA	99	Citation Bravo	550-0880	Rolling Green Enterprises LLC. Edina, Mn.	N5112K
☐ N7ZG	84	Citation III	650-0031	Brundage Management Co. San Antonio, Tx.	N1ZC
☐ N7ZH	80	Learjet 35A	35A-348	Robert Bouwer, Daytona Beach, Fl.	N35DL
☐ N7ZU	82	Citation II	550-0433	Aegis Security Inc. Harrisburg, Pa.	N131GA
☐ N8AF	64	Sabre-40	282-24	SI Air Cargo Co. San Antonio, Tx.	N40DW
☐ N8BX	91	Falcon 900B	111	Baxter Healthcare Corp/Allegiance Healthcare, Waukegan, Il.	N472FJ
☐ N8DX	76	Citation Eagle	500-0303	Shelter Charter Services Inc. Atlanta, Ga.	C-GDWS
☐ N8HQ	88	Beechjet 400	RJ-50	C C Medflight Inc. Lawrenceville, Ga.	N406GJ
☐ N8JC	01	Citation X	750-0154	Jepson Associates Inc. Savannah, Ga.	N5206T
☐ N8JQ	97	Citation X	750-0020	CNH America LLC. Waukegan, Il.	N8JC
☐ N8JR	96	Learjet 60	60-084	JRM Air LLC/JR Motorsports LLC. Statesville, NC.	N306R
☐ N8LE	83	Diamond 1A	A042SA	Diamond Jet LLC/Belew Group, Lebanon, Tn.	(N420FA)
☐ N8LT	80	Falcon 10	173	Aviation Enterprises Inc. Atlanta-Hartsfield, Ga.	(N34LT)
☐ N8MC	90	Gulfstream 4	1129	Monaco Coach Corp. Eugene, Or.	N1129X
☐ N8MF	99	Galaxy-1126	006	Famiglio & Assocs. Sarasota, Fl.	N81TT
☐ N8SP	01	Challenger 604	5518	SPX Corp. Charlotte, NC.	C-GLXM
☐ N8TG	99	Learjet 31A	31A-190	Kitty Hawk Aircraft Services LLC. Hayden, Id.	N316AC
☐ N8VB	99	Global Express	9021	Viacom Inc. Van Nuys, Ca.	C-GEYY
☐ N8VF	87	Falcon 900B	12	VF Corp. Greensboro-Highpoint, NC.	N77CE
☐ N8YM	85	Beechjet 400	RJ-4	T & S Aircraft Sales of Texas LLC. Dallas, Tx.(was A1004SA).	(N401TJ)
☐ N9AZ	76	HS 125/600A	256063	Rellet Services Inc. Vero Beach, Fl.	5N-...
☐ N9CH	01	Learjet 45	45-129	C W Hurd Jr. Santa Teresa, NM.	N4003W
☐ N9CN	01	Citation Encore	560-0602	Nearburg Producing Co. Dallas, Tx.	N5206T
☐ N9CR	84	Citation II/SP	551-0500	Cedar Ridge Estates, Macon, Ga.	N501MC
☐ N9CU	96	Learjet 60	60-075	Aircraft Holding & Leasing LLC. Sarasota, Fl. (status ?).	N675LJ
☐ N9DC	78	Citation II	550-0031	WSD LLC. Coalinga, Ca.	N22GA
☐ N9FE	04	Learjet 45	45-240	FEDEX, Memphis, Tn.	N50579
☐ N9GU	68	JetStar-731	5119	Dezer Development, Sunny Isles Beach, Fl.	N1DB
☐ N9GY	88	Citation S/II	S550-0159	Flight Investment LLC. Paso Robles, Ca.	N9GT
☐ N9KL	81	Gulfstream 3	321	SPW LLC/Ozark Management Inc. Jefferson City, Mo.	(N91KL)
☐ N9NG	03	Citation X	750-0213	Northrop Grumman Aviation Inc. Baltimore, Md.	N50715
☐ N9PW	90	Beechjet 400A	RK-7	Pelican Bay Equipment Leasing LLC. Naples, Fl.	(N848TC)
☐ N9RA	79	Learjet 25D	25D-277	Royal Air Freight Inc. Pontiac, Mi.	N81MW
☐ N9RD	77	Westwind-1124	220	Dowdy Plane Aviation Sales & Service, Orlando, Fl.	N106BC
☐ N9SC	98	Gulfstream V	552	SCI Texas Funeral Services Inc. Houston, Tx.	N652GA
☐ N9SS	80	Citation II/SP	551-0214	Thomas G Somermeier Jr. Santa Monica, Ca. (was 550-0163).	N178HH
☐ N9TE	80	Falcon 50	17	Tensor Engineering, Melbourne, Fl	(N114TD)

Reg	Yr	Type	c/n	Owner/Operator	Prev Regn
☐ N9UD	06	CitationJet CJ2+	525A-0317	Claxton Aviation LLC. Wilmington, De.	N.....
☐ N9UP	89	BAe 125/800A	NA0433	W C Leasing LLC. Franklin Lakes, NJ.	N919P
☐ N9WV	02	Falcon 900EX	108	JCL Corp. Bentonville, Ar.	G-JCBX
☐ N9WW	97	Beechjet 400A	RK-142	W W Williams Co. Columbus, Oh.	N142BJ
☐ N9ZD	80	Learjet 35A	35A-306	White Industries Inc. Bates City, Mo. (status ?).	(N63602)
☐ N10AH	90	Learjet 35A	35A-657	Kokomo Aviation Inc. Indianapolis, In.	N1CA
☐ N10AU	99	Citation V Ultra	560-0512	Auburn University, Auburn, Al.	N29WE
☐ N10C	78	HS 125/700A	NA0235	Robert Hewitt, Victoria, Tx.	N700GB
☐ N10EG	79	Citation II	550-0055	Collins & Ware Inc. Midland, Tx.	(N1466K)
☐ N10EH	85	Gulfstream 3	436	Sinclair Oil Corp. Salt Lake City, Ut.	N436GA
☐ N10EU	04	Falcon 2000EX EASY	46	Riverbank Investments Inc. Luton, UK.	N21HE
☐ N10F	74	Falcon 10	12	King Schools Inc/King Leasing Corp. San Diego, Ca.	(N76TJ)
☐ N10FE	95	Challenger 601-3R	5188	FEDEX, Memphis, Tn.	N575CF
☐ N10FG	76	Citation Eagle	500-0295	Kindle Ford Mercury Lincoln Inc. Cape May, NJ.	N44HC
☐ N10FN	75	Learjet 36	36-015	Flight Capital LLC. Madison, Ms.	N14CF
☐ N10J	07	Learjet 45	45-337	Penn National Gaming Inc. Wyomissing, Pa.	
☐ N10JA	78	Citation II	550-0219	Flying Safe LLC. Chicago, Il. (was 551-0008).	N550PM
☐ N10JP	95	Falcon 2000	23	JP Air Transportation LLC/Pattco Inc. Louisville, Ky.	N23FJ
☐ N10JY	99	Learjet 45	45-063	Millennium Aviation New York LLC. Rochester, NY.	N10J
☐ N10LR	79	Citation II/SP	551-0122	DJL Properties Inc. Baker, Or. (was 550-0059).	(N2662F)
☐ N10LX	70	Sabre-60	306-59	Lockheed Martin Tactical Defence Systems, Goodyear, Az.	N20GX
☐ N10LY	83	Citation II	550-0466	First Air Leasing Inc. Greenville, SC.	N412MA
☐ N10MB	99	Learjet 60	60-176	Fly Becky's Air LLC. Houston-Hooks, Tx.	N176MB
☐ N10MZ	06	Gulfstream G550	5141	ZWA Inc. Teterboro, NJ.	N541GA
☐ N10NC	80	Falcon 10	172	Hayward Enterprises Inc. Fort Lauderdale, Fl.	N172CP
☐ N10NL	00	Learjet 45	45-128	O'Neal Steel Inc. Birmingham, Al.	
☐ N10QS	07	Hawker 4000	RC-22	Hawker Beechcraft Corp. Wichita, Ks.	
☐ N10R	99	Learjet 45	45-042	Brown Shoe Co. St Louis, Mo.	
☐ N10RQ	78	Gulfstream 2	232	Starwood Aviation Inc. Carson City, Nv.	N508T
☐ N10SA	76	HS 125/600A	256065	Stanford Aircraft LLC. Miami, Fl.	N4SA
☐ N10SE	05	Learjet 40	45-2032	RAM Aircraft LLC/Star Distributors Inc. Memphis, Tn.	N5015U
☐ N10SL	06	Global 5000	9221	The Tornante Company LLC. Camarillo, Ca.	C-FIPT
☐ N10SV	06	Embraer Legacy 600	14500974	ACM/Aircraft Guaranty Holdings & Trust LLC. Houston, Tx.	PT-SHD
☐ N10TB	91	Citation V	560-0143	Tim-Bar Corp. Harrisburg, Pa.	N744WW
☐ N10TC	84	Citation II	550-0495	Fantasy Air Ltd. Boring, Or.	(N400MC)
☐ N10TD	91	Citation V	560-0096	SBM Cleaning LLC. Corvallis, Or.	(N96JJ)
☐ N10TN	80	HS 125/700A	257085	Cando Air Inc. Bridgewater, Ma.	RP-C1714
☐ N10UC	80	HS 125/700A	NA0284	Heritage Aviation LLC/Global Publishing Inc. Jacksonville.	(N311MG)
☐ N10UF	78	Learjet 35A	35A-166	Horsham Valley Airways Inc. Horsham, Pa.	N719JB
☐ N10UH	00	Citation Bravo	550-0925	Lifeguard Air Ambulance/University of Alabama, Birmingham.	N550PF
☐ N10VG	73	Learjet 25B	25B-125	Grancor Aviation Inc. Phoenix, Az.	(N11MC)
☐ N10VT	82	Citation II	550-0364	Fralin Heywood, Roanoke, Va.	N180FW
☐ N10XQ	07	Gulfstream G200	169	ECA Trans LLC/Energy Corp of America, Denver, Co.	4X-CVF
☐ N10YJ	87	BAe 125/800A	258099	Jones International Aviation Inc. Englewood, Co.	OY-MCL
☐ N11A	97	Challenger 604	5354	ARAMARK Services Inc. Philadelphia, Pa.	N604BM
☐ N11AF	76	HS 125/600B	256057	Arnoni Aviation Ltd. Houston, Tx.	N602CF
☐ N11AM	97	Learjet 60	60-118	International Associates of Machinists, Washington, DC.	N301BC
☐ N11BV	95	Falcon 2000	21	Nereid LLC/Silicone Valley Express, San Jose, Ca.	N390GS
☐ N11FH	78	Citation II	550-0012	Dove Air Inc. Asheville, NC.	C-GHOL
☐ N11LB	04	CitationJet CJ-3	525B-0019	G & G Aviation LLC. Carlsbad, Ca.	N79LB
☐ N11LK	96	Challenger 601-3R	5193	WFBNW NA. Salt Lake City, Ut. (trustor ?).	(N601HJ)
☐ N11LN	79	Westwind-1124	261	Newcastle Capital Group LLC. Dallas, Tx.	N39JN
☐ N11LX	74	Sabre-60	306-75	Lockheed Martin Tactical Defense Systems, Goodyear, Az	N509AB
☐ N11MN	76	Citation	500-0266	Jet Mavericks LLC. Indianapolis, In.	N40RF
☐ N11TM	78	Citation 1/SP	501-0060	Westwood Development Corp. Portland, Or.	N573L
☐ N11TS	99	Learjet 60	60-151	NTS Development Co. Louisville, Ky.	N9ZM
☐ N11UB	98	Beechjet 400A	RK-212	MCFH Inc. Davis-Woodland, Ca.	N299AW
☐ N11UF	79	Learjet 35A	35A-237	Horsham Valley Airways Inc. Horsham, Pa.	N300TE
☐ N11UL	00	Hawker 800XP	258498	WFBNW NA. Moscow-Vuukovo, Russia.	N809TA
☐ N11WF	99	Beechjet 400A	RK-236	Flowers Foods Inc. Thomasville, Ga.	N2349V
☐ N11WM	99	Falcon 900EX	58	AzaAir Inc. Seattle, Wa.	N958EX
☐ N12AM	74	Citation	500-0235	Jet Sales & Leasing LLC. Galesburg, Il.	N235CC
☐ N12AR	06	Falcon 2000EX EASY	97	N12AR LLC/ALLTEL Corp. Little Rock, Ar.	F-WWGA
☐ N12BW	72	Sabre-40A	282-99	Barry Wehmiller Group Inc. St Louis, Mo.	N100FG
☐ N12CQ	93	Citation V	560-0231	Paloma Packing Inc. Santa Maria, Ca.	N501E
☐ N12CV	78	Citation 1/SP	501-0081	NTSS LLC. Henderson, Nv.	(N12CQ)
Reg	Yr	Type	c/n	Owner/Operator	Prev Regn

Reg	Yr	Type	c/n	Owner/Operator	Prev Regn
☐ N12EP	80	Falcon 10	175	Kenneth Padgett, Vero Beach, Fl.	XA-LOK
☐ N12F	90	BAe 125/800A	258182	Wolfe Enterprises Inc. Columbus, Oh.	N128RS
☐ N12FN	75	Learjet 36	36-016	Flight Capital LLC. Madison, Ms.	N616DJ
☐ N12GP	69	Gulfstream 2	63	BCBG Max Azria Group Inc. Vernon, Ca.	(N20GP)
☐ N12GS	06	CitationJet CJ-3	525B-0122	Blue Sky Inc. Coatesville, Pa.	N.....
☐ N12GY	99	CitationJet CJ-1	525-0374	C J L Enterprises Inc. Phoenix, Az.	N12GS
☐ N12L	98	Citation Excel	560-5002	TCF National Bank, Minneapolis, Mn.	N562XL
☐ N12MG	01	Beechjet 400A	RK-331	Scotts Miracle-Gro/The Scotts Co. Columbus, Oh.	N5031D
☐ N12MW	99	Falcon 2000	97	Daggett Investment/Dakota Investment Corp. Teterboro, NJ.	N922J
☐ N12ND	99	Astra-1125SPX	116	Paradise Development Group Inc. Clearwater, Fl.	N456PR
☐ N12NV	95	Beechjet 400A	RK-103	Cutter Southwest Aircraft Sales LLC. Phoenix, Az.	(N422LX)
☐ N12NZ	99	Gulfstream 4SP	1376	Apollo Management LP. Ronkonkoma, NY.	N376GA
☐ N12PA	03	Hawker 800XP	258642	Poly Jet LLC/Poly-Flex Inc. Dallas-Love Field, Tx.	N642XP
☐ N12RN	95	Citation V Ultra	560-0316	Island Aircraft Associates Inc. Dallas, Tx.	(N5251Y)
☐ N12RP	79	Learjet 35A	35A-278	Stevens Aviation Inc. Greenville, SC.	N17GL
☐ N12SS	06	Challenger 300	20138	SJS Two LLC. Scottsdale, Az.	N247SS
☐ N12U	89	Gulfstream 4	1112	United Technologies Corp. Hartford, Ct.	N12UT
☐ N12VU	06	Learjet 45	45-324	Pella Corp. Pella, Ia.	N50126
☐ N12WF	99	Beechjet 400A	RK-228	Flowers Foods Inc. Thomasville, Ga.	N3228V
☐ N12WH	98	Citation 1/SP	501-0064	Willard Hanzlik/Nuevo Aviation Inc. Austin, Tx.	N96DS
☐ N13BK	76	Falcon 10	94	Steen Aviation Inc. Shreveport, La.	N54RS
☐ N13FE	66	DC 9-14	45706	NC Aircraft LLC. Hendersonville, NC.	N5NE
☐ N13FH	97	CitationJet	525-0185	Globe Aero Ltd. Lakeland, Fl.	N83TR
☐ N13GW	73	Westwind-1123	162	Jet Set Aircraft, Bogota, Colombia. (status ?).	XA-SDW
☐ N13JS	06	Global 5000	9212	Turnberry Associates, Fort Lauderdale, Fl.	C-FIPJ
☐ N13KD	79	Citation 1/SP	501-0119	Charles Kaady, Portland, Or.	N53EZ
☐ N13ST	78	Citation 1/SP	501-0285	Mike & Hank DeShazer, Spring, Tx. (was 500-0366).	N100BX
☐ N13SY	96	Beechjet 400A	RK-111	Southern Air Systems/SY Air LLC. Tampa, Fl.	N412WP
☐ N13VP	79	Citation II	550-0263	K3C Inc/Sierra Industries Inc. Uvalde, Tx.(was 551-0009)	D-IMTM
☐ N14CG	82	Falcon 50	100	Beta Aircraft Corp. Teterboro, NJ.	N102FJ
☐ N14CN	81	Westwind-Two	359	California Natural Products, Stockton, Ca.	C-GRGE
☐ N14DM	76	Learjet 24E	24E-341	Future Care Consultants Inc. Fort Lauderdale, Fl.	(N103JW)
☐ N14FE	98	Learjet 45	45-038	FEDEX, Memphis, Tn.	(N454RR)
☐ N14FN	73	Learjet 25C	25C-126	Columbus Trading Aviation Inc. Wilmington, De.	(N162AC)
☐ N14GD	01	Challenger 604	5490	GG Aircraft LLC/Gordon Gund, Trenton, NJ.	N604GD
☐ N14NA	92	Falcon 900B	124	The Anschutz Corp. Englewood, Co.	VP-BWS
☐ N14RM	80	Citation II/SP	551-0169	Guardian American Security, Southfield, Mi. (was 550-0126).	N700YM
☐ N14SA	97	Hawker 800XP2	258339	Stanford Financial Group Co. Houston, Tx.	SE-DVD
☐ N14T	01	Learjet 31A	31A-222	Rutherford Aviation LLC. Rutherfordton, NC.	N770CH
☐ N14TU	93	Learjet 60	60-026	VGR Aviation LLC/Vector Group Ltd. Wilmington, De.	N14T
☐ N14VA	79	Citation 1/SP	501-0137	Vision Flight Services LLC/Minor Tire & Wheel, Decatur, Il.	N46SC
☐ N15AS	94	Falcon 2000	3	Flight Proficiency Service Inc. Dallas, Tx.	N2000A
☐ N15AW	73	Citation	500-0139	Flight Source International Inc. Sarasota, Fl.	N3771U
☐ N15AX	84	BAe 125/800B	258002	Air-X LLC. Opa Locka, Fl.	N882CW
☐ N15BV	03	CitationJet CJ-1	525-0527	Momentum Holdings LLC. Carlsbad, Ca.	N527CJ
☐ N15C	05	CitationJet CJ-3	525B-0023	Spiral Colorado LLC/15C LLC. Chandler, Az.	N77M
☐ N15CV	97	Citation Bravo	550-0819	Cache Valley Electric Co. Logan, Ut.	N1259B
☐ N15CY	80	Citation 1/SP	501-0152	Theodor Huber, Wiesbaden, Germany.	VP-CCD
☐ N15EH	77	Learjet 35A	35A-126	Sinclair Oil Corp. Salt Lake City, Ut.	N744GL
☐ N15ER	79	Learjet 25D	25D-267	Richardson Investments Inc. San Antonio, Tx.	
☐ N15FE	98	Learjet 45	45-039	FEDEX, Memphis, Tn.	N456AS
☐ N15FX*	85	Falcon 50	157	McKesson Information Solutions Inc. Atlanta-DeKalb, Ga.	N901MK
☐ N15GT	06	Challenger 300	20120	Thornburg Mortgage Advisory Corp. Santa Fe, NM.	C-FIOJ
☐ N15H	77	Falcon 20F-5B	368	Wilson Aviation LLC. Glacier International, Mt.	N23A
☐ N15HE	82	Gulfstream 3	369	Flight Services Group Inc. Bridgeport, Ct.	N17ND
☐ N15HF	70	Sabre-60	306-60	Williams International LLC. Waterford, Mi.	N15H
☐ N15JA	78	Citation II	550-0035	Carlyle Capital Markets Inc. Dallas, Tx.	(N50GG)
☐ N15JH	74	Citation Eagle	500-0174	JH690 Inc. Lake St Louis, Mo.	N16LG
☐ N15LN	92	Citation VII	650-7013	John R Lawson Rock & Oil Inc. Madera, Ca.	N2NT
☐ N15LV	97	CitationJet	525-0191	Florida Custom Coach Inc. Leesburg, Fl.	C-FIMA
☐ N15RH	83	Learjet 35A	35A-497	Camden Aviation Inc. St Charles, Il.	N21DA
☐ N15RL	01	Citation X	750-0165	Levi, Ray & Shoup Inc. Springfield, Il.	N5257V
☐ N15SK	96	Citation V Ultra	560-0395	Teterboro Aviation Inc. Teterboro, NJ.	(N19MU)
☐ N15SL	71	Falcon 20F-5	256	Tensor Engineering, Melbourne, Fl.	N868DS
☐ N15SN	88	Citation II	550-0566	Century Airconditioning Transportation LLC. Houston, Tx.	N15SP
☐ N15SS*	01	CitationJet CJ-1	525-0455	JFS Aviation LLC. Reston, Va.	N75FC

Reg	Yr	Type	c/n	Owner/Operator	Prev Regn
❏ N15TT	00	Citation X	750-0127	Cleo J Thompson, Ozona, Tx.	N52639
❏ N15UC	99	Gulfstream V	589	The United Co. Bristol-Tri Cities, Tn.	(N15UQ)
❏ N15WH	76	Learjet 35A	35A-085	AirNet Systems Inc. Columbus, Oh.	
❏ N15XM	81	Citation II	550-0308	John R Lawson Rock & Oil Inc. Madera, Ca.	N30SA
❏ N15YD	06	CitationJet CJ2+	525A-0336	Constructora Sambil CA. Caracas, Venezuela.	N336CJ
❏ N15ZZ	07	CitationJet CJ-3	525B-0221	Cessna Aircraft Co. Wichita, Ks.	N.....
❏ N16DK	01	390 Premier 1	RB-19	DEKA Research & Development Corp. Manchester, NH.	N65TB
❏ N16GH	86	BAe 125/800A	258065	G-H Holdings LLC/Glen Hill Investments LLC. Nashville, Tn.	N65FA
❏ N16GS	06	Citation Sovereign	680-0096	Great Southern Wood Preserving, Dothan, Al.	N5200Z
❏ N16HC	66	Learjet 24	24-126	Dodson International, Rantoul, Ks.	(N345SF)
❏ N16HD	91	Beechjet 400A	RK-16	Westheimer Aviation LLC. Shawnee, Ok.	XA-MGM
❏ N16HL	78	Citation 1/SP	501-0059	Owners Jet Services Ltd. DuPage, Il.	ZS-EHL
❏ N16KK	74	Learjet 25B	25B-174	Royal Air Freight Inc. Pontiac, Mi.	N412SP
❏ N16LJ	86	Learjet 55	55-126	Have Plane Will Travel LLC. Golden, Co.	N7260J
❏ N16MF	89	Beechjet 400	RJ-65	Davidson Companies, Great Falls, Mt.	N1565B
❏ N16MK	66	Jet Commander	84	Westar Aviation Inc. Miami, Fl. (status ?).	N600ER
❏ N16NK	99	Gulfstream V	585	Business Aircraft Corp. Coral Gables, Fl.	N18NK
❏ N16NL	77	Citation 1/SP	501-0043	Oakbrooke Aviation LLC. Heathrow, Fl.	N10NL
❏ N16PC	06	Learjet 45	45-319	Southern Company Services Inc. Atlanta, Ga.	
❏ N16PL	81	Citation II	550-0265	Aviation Enterprises Inc. Bedford, Ma.	CN-TKK
❏ N16PQ	99	Learjet 45	45-050	Corporate Creations Network Inc. Wilmington, De.	N16PC
❏ N16RP	85	Citation S/II	S550-0047	Rose Aviation LLC. Cresskill, NJ.	I-CEFI
❏ N16RW	81	Challenger 600S	1013	Central Services LLC. St Louis, Mo.	N72SR
❏ N16SM	07	Hawker 900XP	HA-40	Hawker Beechcraft Corp. Wichita, Ks.	
❏ N16SU	84	Citation III	650-0025	Speciality Travel Services Inc. Oak Creek, Wi.	(N522GS)
❏ N16TS	78	Citation II	550-0030	N12CF LLC/GroWest Nurseries, Riverside, Ca. (was 551-0077).	N4TS
❏ N16VG	80	Citation 1/SP	501-0157	Gordon Rosenburg, San Ardo, Ca.	(N88BR)
❏ N16YD*	98	Challenger 604	5367	Arch Coal Inc. St Louis, Mo.	N898CC
❏ N17A	80	Learjet 36A	36A-046	Avstar Inc. Seattle, Wa.	N146MJ
❏ N17AH	80	Learjet 25D	25D-316	Spirit Wing Aviation Ltd. Guthrie, Ok. (Ff FJ44-2C 9 Jan 03)	(N782JR)
❏ N17AN	99	Citation Excel	560-5030	AON Corp/Globe Leasing Inc. Palwaukee, Il.	N899BC
❏ N17AZ	76	Learjet 35A	35A-080	Duty Free Aviation LLC. Fort Lauderdale, Fl.	N10AZ
❏ N17CJ	06	390 Premier 1A	RB-171	Sycamore LLC. Wilmington, De.	
❏ N17CN	06	CitationJet CJ-3	525B-0128	Cecil Atkission Motors, Kerrville, Tx.	N.....
❏ N17CX	06	Citation X	750-0267	Howson&Simon/Wing and a Prayer Inc. Stockton, Ca.	N5267G
❏ N17DD	89	BAe 125/800A	NA0437	Camco Aviation Group LLC. Indianapolis, In.	C-FFTM
❏ N17DM	82	Citation II	550-0417	VIP's Industries Inc. Salem, Or.	ZS-LHW
❏ N17FX*	98	Falcon 900EX	29	McKesson Information Solutions Inc. Atlanta-DeKalb, Ga.	N900MK
❏ N17GX	99	Global Express	9045	Howson&Simon/Wing and a Prayer Inc. Stockton, Ca.	C-GFKY
❏ N17HA	78	Citation 1/SP	501-0072	Titan Air LLC. Pasco, Wa.	N1HA
❏ N17JK	94	Gulfstream 4SP	1235	TransMeridian Aviation LLC. St Paul, Mn.	N500EP
❏ N17KD	76	Citation	500-0337	Mark Hankins Ministries, Alexandria, La.	(F-GNAB)
❏ N17KJ	77	Gulfstream II SP	200	Not Yours LLC. Teterboro, NJ.	(N200UJ)
❏ N17KW	68	Gulfstream 2	28	K W Plastics Co. Troy, Al.	N68DM
❏ N17LJ	76	Learjet 36	36-017	Premier Jets Inc. Hillsboro, Or.	(N361PJ)
❏ N17LK	84	Gulfstream 3	431	Robinson Leasing Inc. Driggs, Id.	P4-AEA
❏ N17MK	65	BAC 1-11/410AQ	054	Business Jet Services Ltd. Dallas-Love, Tx.	N17VK
❏ N17NC	80	Gulfstream 3	318	Saturn Productions Inc. Burbank, Ca.	N500WW
❏ N17PL	97	Citation V Ultra	560-0412	Farmington Aviation Inc/Trumpf Inc. Plainville, Ct.	N513EF
❏ N17TE	07	Challenger 605	5724	Bombardier Aerospace Corp. Windsor Locks, Ct.	C-FOMS
❏ N17TJ	75	Falcon 10	43	Premier Air Center Inc. Alton/St Louis, Il.	F-GIQP
❏ N17TZ	99	Challenger 604	5437	Turner Enterprises Inc/Flying T LLC. Atlanta, Ga.	N17TE
❏ N17UC	04	Challenger 300	20011	The United Co. Bristol-Tri Cities, Tn.	(N311DB)
❏ N17VP	84	Citation II	550-0483	Trebor Air LLC. Greenville, NC.	N17FS
❏ N17WG	74	Falcon 10	35	Hawker Air LP/Jones & Granger, Houston, Tx.	N726MR
❏ N18AN	93	Gulfstream 4SP	1228	AON Aviation Inc. Palwaukee, Il.	N464QA
❏ N18AX	76	Learjet 35A	35A-087	Omni Air International Inc. Tulsa, Ok.	(N862BD)
❏ N18BA	82	HS 125/700A	NA0316	M & V Airplane LLC. San Antonio, Tx.	(N501F)
❏ N18BH	67	JetStar-731	5099	JetStar One LLC. San Leon, Tx.	(N117J)
❏ N18CC	78	HS 125/700A	NA0222	Starlight Aviation Inc. Round Rock, Tx.	C-GNAZ
❏ N18CG	98	Falcon 2000	57	Corning Inc. Hamilton, NY.	N2132
❏ N18DF	05	Falcon 900EX EASY	158	Cintas Corp. Cincinnati, Oh.	N15FF
❏ N18FM	72	Citation	500-0014	N18FM LLC. Tulsa, Ok.	N800W
❏ N18FX*	95	Falcon 900B	152	McKesson Corp. San Francisco, Ca.	N902MK
❏ N18GA	97	CitationJet	525-0216	Griffin Industries Inc. Cold Springs, Ky.	
❏ N18GB	94	Citation VII	650-7048	New Albertson's Inc. Boise, Id.	N51176

Reg	Yr	Type	c/n	Owner/Operator	Prev Regn
N18HC	81	Citation 1/SP	501-0223	J & S Wings LLC. Tuscaloosa, Al.	(N26HA)
N18HJ	88	Citation II	550-0587	Kinnarps AB. Falkoping, Sweden.	N1301S
N18HN	71	Falcon 20F-5	257	Holly Corp/Navajo Refining Co. Dallas-Love, Tx.	HB-VKO
N18MV	96	Falcon 2000	24	Short Hills Aviators LLC. Morristown, NJ.	N876SC
N18MX	78	Falcon 10	117	Air Quest LLC/One Quest Capital Management, Holland, Mi.	N923DS
N18MZ	87	Falcon 900B	32	SP Leasing LLC/Steel Partners Ltd. NYC.	N10MZ
N18NA	88	Citation II	550-0580	Go Flying High LLC. San Marcos, Tx.	N912BD
N18RF	04	390 Premier 1	RB-127	Goldleaf Development LLC. Madison, Wi.	N3727H
N18SK	74	Falcon 10	34	Falconshare LLC. Danbury Municipal, Ct.	N220M
N18TF	01	CitationJet CJ-2	525A-0014	WMCR Holding LLC. Saginaw, Mi.	N110MQ
N18TM	02	Global Express	9090	SDA Enterprises Inc. West Palm Beach, Fl.	C-GIOD
N18WZ	00	Global Express	9059	Rank Services Ltd. Auckland, NZ.	N18WF
N19DD	83	Challenger 600S	1081	Challenger LLC. Fort Worth, Tx.	N199D
N19DU	99	Hawker 800XP	258448	Whitney Aviation LLC. Greenville, SC.	N19DD
N19ER	79	Citation II	550-0048	GWW LLC. Lompoc, Ca.	N10BF
N19HU	91	Citation V	560-0135	Batair LLC/Louisville Bats Baseball, Louisville, Ky.	N560RL
N19LJ	71	Learjet 24XR	24XR-233	Horizon Aircraft Maintenance LLC. Wichita, Ks.	N143GB
N19LT	90	Learjet 31	31-019	Wal-Mart Stores Inc. Rogers, Ar.	PT-OFL
N19MK	05	Citation Sovereign	680-0052	MOKI Corp. Teterboro, NJ.	N12925
N19QC	94	Citation VI	650-0238	650 Leasing Corp. Wilmington, De.	N19UC
N19R	83	Diamond 1A	A043SA	Express Air LLC. Granite City, Il.	N322DM
N19RP	81	Learjet 35A	35A-363	Roaring Fork Partners LLC. Aspen, Co.	N183JC
N19SV	92	Citation VII	650-7002	SuperValu Inc. Minneapolis, Mn.	N95CC
N19VF	87	Falcon 900B	29	VF Corp. Greensboro-Highpoint, NC.	C-GTCP
N19ZA	86	Citation S/II	S550-0094	Vision A101 LLC. Stockton, Ca.	N1H
N20AU	01	Citation Bravo	550-1012	Auburn University, Auburn, Al.	N.....
N20CC	98	Citation V Ultra	560-0467	Aircraft Operators Inc. Destin, Fl.	N98NA
N20CF	77	Falcon 10	106	Contract Freighters Inc. Joplin, Mo.	N103MM
N20CL	84	Falcon 200	497	Mari LLC/Bloomington Aircraft Rentals Inc. Bloomington, Mn.	N720HC
N20CR	83	Learjet 55	55-097	RVDH Development Corp/Shopko Stores Inc. Green Bay, Wi.	N40CR
N20CS	87	Citation S/II	S550-0138	CSPAN Aviation Leasing LLC. Fort Pierce, Fl.	N522BE
N20CZ	77	Citation 1/SP	501-0262	Aircraft Owners LLC. Destin, Fl.	N20CC
N20DA	61	MS 760 Paris-2B	102	FM Aero Inc. Calhoun, Ga.	N99HB
N20DK	78	Learjet 35A	35A-143	International Auto Brokers Inc. Paradise Valley, Az.	OE-GER
N20EG	99	Global Express	9038	Aero Toy Store LLC. Fort Lauderdale, Fl.	N738TS
N20FJ	67	Falcon 20C	119	Wextrust Capital LLC. Chicago, Il.	F-GHFP
N20FM	76	HS 125/F600A	256058	N20FM LLC. Tampa, Fl.	N658KA
N20G	93	Challenger 601-3R	5136	Goodyear Tire & Rubber Co. Akron, Oh.	N51GY
N20GP	02	CitationJet CJ-2	525A-0131	N83 Charlie Inc. Fort Wayne, In.	N51564
N20H	69	Gulfstream II SP	51	Hubbard Broadcasting Inc. St Paul, Mn.	N20HE
N20HF	68	Falcon 20D-5	191	Lily Aviation LLC. Colleyville, Tx.	OE-GCR
N20LW	75	Falcon 10	48	ConeJet LLC/Cone Management Inc. Nashville, Tn.	LX-EPA
N20NL	04	390 Premier 1	RB-106	CNS Corp. Quincy, Il.	N61706
N20NY	66	Falcon 20C	61	Air Force Systems Command, Bedford, Ma.	N299NW
N20PA	85	Diamond 1A	A089SA	Lane Aviation/Pepsi-Cola Bottling Co. Colorado Springs, Co.	N88CR
N20RM	77	Citation 1/SP	501-0025	Jetquest LLC. Helena, Ar.	N21BS
N20RZ	69	Learjet 25	25-024	Gimli Son LLC/Trinity Air Ambulance, Fort Lauderdale, Fl.	N20HJ
N20SM	96	Citation V Ultra	560-0353	State of Mississippi, Jackson, Ms.	N353Z
N20TA	65	Learjet 23	23-062	Merit Capital LLC. Carson City, Nv. (status ?).	N670MF
N20UA	67	Falcon 20-5B	91	PRMR LLC/Premier Bancshares Inc. Jefferson City, Mo.	(N200SS)
N20VL	94	CitationJet	525-0069	Aviation II Inc. Tulsa, Ok.	N20FL
N20WN	77	Falcon 20F	370	Air Century Inc. Miami, Fl.	N269SR
N20XP	00	Learjet 31A	31A-197	Xpress Air Inc. Chattanooga, Tn.	
N20YL	95	Astra-1125SP	076	EAP Operating Inc. Fort Worth, Tx.	N699MQ
N20ZC	94	Beechjet 400A	RK-86	Z Air LLC/The Zimmermann Agency, Tallahassee, Fl.	N757CE
N21AC	95	Learjet 60	60-070	N21AC LLC. Lexington, Ky.	N5035R
N21BD	02	Learjet 45	45-188	Columbus Transportation LLC. Columbus, Ga.	
N21CV	95	Citation V Ultra	560-0340	Old Dominion Freight Lines Inc. High Point, NC.	N5267T
N21DX	79	Westwind-1124	269	Deeluxe Transport Inc/Diamond Manufacturing Co. Wyoming, Pa	N50SL
N21EG	86	Citation S/II	S550-0087	Karibou Aviation LLC. New Hope, Mn.	N1274Z
N21EL	99	Hawker 800XP	258396	Private Wings LLC. Miami, Fl.	N23585
N21EP	77	Citation 1/SP	501-0040	N21EP LLC/Infiniti Aviation LLC. Scottsdale, Az.	N501E
N21FN	70	Learjet 25	25-062	Hampton University, Newport News, Va.	N25ME
N21HR	81	Westwind-Two	335	AIM Aircraft Leasing LLC. Franklin, Tn.	EC-GIB
N21LG	92	Citation V	560-0197	CFAM GP LLC/Lionstone Group, Houston, Tx.	XA-SJC
N21LL	83	Citation III	650-0016	Jordyn Holdings IV LLC. Sarasota, Fl.	N316CW

Reg	Yr	Type	c/n	Owner/Operator	Prev Regn
N21NW	81	Learjet 25D	25D-351	North West Geomatics Ltd. San Angelo, Tx.	N425RA
N21RA	02	CitationJet CJ-2	525A-0092	Green King Inc. Wilmington, De.	N.....
N21SF	77	Westwind-1124	214	Starflite/John Beeson, Houston, Tx.	N46BK
N21SL	99	Citation Bravo	550-0877	Schweitzer Engineering Laboratories Inc. Pullman, Wa.	N5085J
N21VC	95	CitationJet	525-0106	Seastar Inc/Ritron Inc. Carmel, In.	(N444H)
N21XP	01	390 Premier 1	RB-9	CTW Trading LLC. Tulsa, Ok.	XA-ZUL
N22	95	Gulfstream V	501	Ford Motor Co. Detroit, Mi.	N501GV
N22AF	91	Citation V	560-0129	C H C LLC. Memphis, Tn.	
N22AX	00	Learjet 45	45-101	Stepping Stones 1030 Accommodations, Burlington, NC.	N410BX
N22CS	80	Sabre-65	465-24	Career Sports Management Inc. Atlanta-DeKalb, Ga.	N271MB
N22EL	77	Citation 1/SP	501-0045	Santangelo Law Offices PC. Fort Collins, Co.	N833JL
N22FM	83	Citation II	550-0461	Symbolic Aviation Inc. La Jolla, Ca.	N12507
N22FW	84	Falcon 20F-5	485	SRCG Holdings Inc/Richardson Aviation Inc. Fort Worth, Tx.	(N23SJ)
N22G	93	Learjet 60	60-022	Goodyear Tire & Rubber Co. Akron, Oh.	N2602Z
N22GM	05	Learjet 40	45-2038	GM Aviation/Multi Inversiones, Guatemala City, Guatemala.	
N22GR	99	Citation Bravo	550-0892	Carlton Forge Works, Paramount, Ca.	(N84CF)
N22HS	85	Falcon 200	507	Falcon 200 Aviation LLC. NYC.	N50LG
N22LC	03	Falcon 900EX EASY	136	Lowe's Companies Inc. North Wilkesboro, NC.	F-WWFN
N22LQ	99	Citation V Ultra	560-0521	Taylor Fresh Foods Inc. Salinas, Ca.	N22LC
N22LX	02	CitationJet CJ-2	525A-0109	Lexicon Inc. Little Rock, Ar.	N301EL
N22LZ	78	Westwind-1124	236	Websta's Aviation Services Inc. St Croix, USVI.	(N236TS)
N22MS	78	Learjet 35A	35A-209	Evergreen Equity Inc. McMinnville, Or.	N711DS
N22NB	77	Sabre-75A	380-56	Construction Partners Inc. Dothan, Al.	N14JD
N22NF	89	Hawker 800SP	NA0432	Sunwest Aero LLC/SunTX Capital Partners, Dallas, Tx.	N810LX
N22NG	02	Citation X	750-0204	Northrop Grumman Aviation Inc. Hawthorne, Ca.	N5197M
N22PC	88	Citation II	550-0583	DW Aviation LLC. Bloomfield, Mi.	(N228G)
N22RD	77	Westwind-1124	203	N22RD Inc. Corpus Christi, Tx.	N880Z
N22RG	97	Citation X	750-0031	Greenhill Aviation LLC. NYC.	N5061W
N22SF	04	Challenger 604	5589	State Farm Insurance Companies, Bloomington, Il.	N604SF
N22SM	03	Hawker 800XP	258655	Select Medical Corp. Harrisburg, Pa.	(N16SM)
N22T	92	Falcon 900B	119	Aplomado Inc. Portland, Or.	N477FJ
N22UL	85	Citation S/II	S550-0039	JL Diversified LLC/Lion Raisins, Selma, Ca.	
N22VK	05	390 Premier 1A	RB-140	CTE II LLC/Cherokee Ford Inc. Marietta, Ga.	N3540R
N22VS	08	Hawker 900XP	HA-47	Hawker Beechcraft Corp. Wichita, Ks.	
N23A	79	Learjet 35A	35A-233	Max Quest LLC. Van Nuys, Ca.	(N428TB)
N23AJ	06	Citation Bravo	550-1128	Rani SA Aviation Inc. South Africa.	N.....
N23BY	65	Learjet 23	23-009	Robert Younkin, Rogers, Ar.	N49CK
N23CJ	67	HS 125/3A-RA	25152	North American Tactical Aviation Inc. Lincoln Park, NJ.	N50MJ
N23FM	00	Falcon 50EX	296	Federal Mogul Corp. Southfield, Mi.	N50FJ
N23LM	99	Citation Excel	560-5062	Omega Management Services Inc. Scottsdale, Az.	N22KW
N23M	99	Gulfstream V	579	3M Co. St Paul, Mn.	N579GA
N23NG	01	Citation Excel	560-5133	Northrop Grumman Aviation Inc. Hawthorn, Ca.	N.....
N23RZ	74	Learjet 25B	25B-164	Forza Aviation Inc. Key Biscayne, Fl.	OB-1430
N23SB	90	Challenger 601-3A	5074	MBG LLC. Seattle, Wa.	C-GLXH
N23SP	04	390 Premier 1	RB-124	Stone Power Sales & Service Inc. Casper, Wy.	N6124W
N23SR	01	Learjet 60	60-229	Sears Roebuck & Co. Chicago-Midway, Il.	
N23TJ	76	Falcon 10	89	Storm Recovery Workforce LA LLC. Hammond, La.	(N888WJ)
N23VG	96	Learjet 31A	31A-123	F-90 LLC. Chattanooga, Tn.	N23NP
N23VK	80	Citation 1/SP	501-0175	VK Aviation & Trading GmbH. Egelsbach, Germany.	VP-BVK
N23VP	76	Falcon 10	91	MWM Leasing LLCThird Coast Aviation LLC. Nashville, Tn.	N790US
N23WA	01	390 Premier 1	RB-18	Hale-Whit Air LLC/Hale-Halsell Co. Tulsa, Ok.	LX-POO
N23YC	00	Citation Bravo	550-0923	W G Yates & Sons Construction Co. Philadelphia, Pa.	N676PB
N23YZ	03	Citation Encore	560-0638	YZ Corp. Palm Beach, Fl.	N1269P
N24AJ	74	Citation	500-0221	JMB Air Services Inc. Mobile, Al.	XC-GUH
N24BC	07	CitationJet CJ1+	525-0651	Happy Landings LLC. Camarillo, Ca.	N5267D
N24E	90	Citation II	550-0651	Million Air Richmond, Richmond, Va.	(N1311K)
N24EP	01	Citation Excel	560-5213	Excel Ventures LLC. La Jolla, Ca.	N1130G
N24ET	67	Learjet 24	24-148	Florida Aircraft Sales LLC. Lighthouse Point, Fl.	N41MP
N24FW	76	Learjet 24E	24E-329	Dr Fr Louden-Hans Flisk, Sykeston, ND.	N329TJ
N24G	93	Learjet 60	60-018	Goodyear Tire & Rubber Co. Akron, Oh.	N4016G
N24GF	03	Citation Encore	560-0639	Grede Foundries Inc. Milwaukee, Wi.	N639CV
N24HX	92	Citation V	560-0165	Charles Anderson, Jacksonville, Tx.	C-GAPD
N24JD	91	Citation V	560-0140	Goodwyn Sales LLC. Memphis, Tn.	(N75GV)
N24JG	89	BAe 125/800A	NA0441	Jeff Gordon Inc. Charlotte, NC.	N79NP
N24KL	79	Westwind-1124	237	Orlando Financial Corp. Mount Dora, Fl.	N28TJ
N24KT	95	Citation VII	650-7052	Jostens Inc. Minneapolis, Mn.	N24NB

Reg	Yr	Type	c/n	Owner/Operator	Prev Regn
N24LG	65	Learjet 24A	24A-011	Younkin Boreing Inc. Hot Springs, Ar.	N225LJ
N24NG	01	Citation Excel	560-5124	Northrop Grumman Aviation Inc. Hawthorn, Ca.	N5207A
N24NJ	65	Learjet 24	24-050	Wing Financial LLC. Las Vegas, Nv.	N24ET
N24PH	05	Citation Excel XLS	560-5571	Pamplemousse LLC. Key Biscayne, Fl.	N5211F
N24PR	88	Astra-1125	026	Progress Rail Services Corp. Albertville, Al.	N9VL
N24QT	06	Citation Encore+	560-0762	Quik Trip Corp. Tulsa, Ok.	N68NC
N24S	74	Learjet 24D	24D-297	Metropolitan Air Inc. Baltimore, Md.	N8094U
N24SA	66	Learjet 24XR	24XR-117	Sundance Aviation Inc. Yukon, Ok.	N140EX
N24SM	01	Hawker 800XP	258567	Select Medical Corp. Harrisburg, Pa.	N74PC
N24SR	01	Learjet 60	60-234	Sears Roebuck & Co. Chicago-Midway, Il.	N5013J
N24TH	06	Gulfstream G450	4071	Chelsea Aviation LP. Dallas-Love, Tx.	N471GA
N24TK	73	Learjet 24D	24D-268	Baja Jets LLC. Las Vegas, Nv.	N98WJ
N24UD	00	Citation Excel	560-5147	Bridgeview Aviation LLC/Motley Rice Inc. Mount Pleasant, SC.	N52059
N24VP	07	Learjet 40	45-2081	WFBNW NA. Salt Lake City, Ut. (trustor ?).	
N24WX	66	Learjet 24	24-101	T H Leasing Inc. Wilmington, De. (status ?).	XA-SGU
N24XC	05	Gulfstream G450	4032	Hermes Express LLC. Bedford, Ma.	N632GA
N24YA	69	Learjet 24B	24B-206	Arvest Bank Group Inc. Springdale, Ar.	N116RM
N24YP	03	390 Premier 1	RB-95	Yates Petroleum Corp. Artesia, NM.	N6195S
N24YS	68	Gulfstream 2B	16	Fry's Electronics Inc. San Jose, Ca.	N38GL
N25AM	80	Learjet 25D	25D-321	CPN Television Inc. Clearwater, Fl.	
N25AN	79	Learjet 35A	35A-259	AirNet Systems Inc. Columbus, Oh.	HK-3983X
N25AZ	65	B 727-30	18370	Aviation Consultants, Johannesburg, RSA.	7P-DPT
N25BB	90	BAe 125/800A	NA0455	Aero Comondu LLC. Mexico.	N195KC
N25CU	03	Hawker 400XP	RK-361	United Bottling Management LLC. Birmingham, Al.	N61661
N25EC	69	Learjet 25	25-026	Millennium Aircraft Holdings Ltd. Republic Airport, NY.	N281R
N25FM	70	Learjet 25	25-063	Royal Air Freight Inc. Pontiac, Mi.	N24LT
N25FS	97	Citation Bravo	550-0823	Sarob/KFE Partnership Inc. San Diego, Ca.	(N823CB)
N25GG	02	Challenger 604	5536	BCMC Air LLC/Booth Creek Management Corp. Vail, Co.	N536MP
N25GJ	71	Gulfstream II SP	97	L & L Manufacturing Co. Long Beach, Ca.	N55HY
N25GZ	84	Citation S/II	S550-0011	SP Express Inc. Wilmington, De.	N211QS
N25LJ	66	Learjet 24	24-123	Avstar Inc. Seattle, Wa.	N35EC
N25LZ	03	CitationJet CJ-2	525A-0177	Lima Zulu Aircraft Corp. Burbank, Ca.	N55KT
N25MB	78	Citation 1/SP	501-0078	Santa Elena Aviation Inc. Yorklyn, De.	N501EK
N25MC	02	390 Premier 1	RB-49	Mercury Travel Inc. Denver-Centennial, Co.	N5049U
N25MD	70	Learjet 25	25-054	Royal Air Freight Inc. Pontiac, Mi.	N509G
N25MT	73	Learjet 25C	25C-129	SFG Commercial Aircraft Leasing Inc. South Bend, Or.	N25MR
N25MX	97	CitationJet	525-0220	Jan M Smith, Childress, Tx.	C-GHPP
N25NB	80	Learjet 25D	25D-326	Swing Wing Inc. Veedersburg, In.	N771CB
N25NY	80	Learjet 25D	25D-304	Savage Aviation Inc. Lebanon, Tn.	
N25PW	81	Learjet 25D	25D-342	Patterson & Wilder/P & W Aviation Inc. Pelham, Al.	(N325PJ)
N25QT	01	Citation Encore	560-0613	Quik Trip Corp. Tulsa, Ok.	N448H
N25RE	77	Learjet 25D	25D-227	Aerojet Charters Inc. Reno, Nv.	N227EW
N25SB	92	Challenger 601-3A	5115	Anjet Handels u Transport GmbH. Vienna, Austria.	C-GLYC
N25SJ	88	Falcon 50	186	SSM Genpar Inc. Portland, Or.	N450K
N25UJ	77	Learjet 25D	25D-215	Airojet Charters Inc. Fort Lauderdale, Fl.	N325JL
N25UT	72	Citation	500-0049	Universal Turbine Parts Inc. Prattville, Al. (status ?).	PT-LDH
N25V	80	Challenger 600S	1015	4KS Aviation III Inc. Dallas, Tx.	144608
N25VC	80	Sabre-65	465-15	NCI Operating Corp. Houston, Tx.	N465TS
N25W	03	Hawker 800XP	258626	Watkins Associated Industries Inc. Lakeland, Fl.	N626XP
N25WJ	73	Learjet 25B	25B-105	Indiana Aircraft Charter LLC. Scherville, In.	LY-AJB
N25XP	99	Beechjet 400A	RK-247	BB&T/Branch Banking & Trust Co. Winston-Salem, NC.	N20FL
N26AT	73	Learjet 25B	25B-130	ATI Jet Sales LLC. El Paso, Tx.	N25PL
N26CB	01	Citation Bravo	550-1001	Brown Transport Inc/Metal Flow Corp. Holland, Mi.	N.....
N26CV	98	Citation Bravo	550-0861	Murphy Co. Eugene, Or.	N26CB
N26DV*	00	CitationJet CJ-1	525-0414	Vogel Paint & Wax Co. Orange City, Ia.	N726TM
N26FN	75	Learjet 36	36-011	Flight Capital LLC. Madison, Ms.	N26MJ
N26GP	78	Learjet 35A	35A-157	WestJet LLC. Galesburg, Il.	ZS-MWW
N26HG	89	Citation II/SP	551-0614	Harry Glauser, Houston, Tx.	D-ILAN
N26HH	81	Citation II	550-0316	Clayton Leasing Inc. Houston, Ms.	N741JC
N26KL	84	Westwind-Two	409	Ashton Woods Transportation LLC. Roswell, Ga.	N217BM
N26ME	82	HS 125/700A	NA0315	F B L Jetco LLC. Issaquah, Wa.	N869KM
N26MJ	00	Citation X	750-0139	Independence Airlines Inc. Manchester, NH.	N5196U
N26PA	99	Beechjet 400A	RK-256	Professional Airways LLC. Plymouth, Ma.	N387AT
N26QB	95	CitationJet	525-0117	Master Craft Industrial Equipment Co. Tifton, Ga.	N26CB
N26QT	98	Citation V Ultra	560-0498	QuikTrip Corp. Tulsa, Ok.	(N24QT)
N26RL	97	CitationJet	525-0207	ZZ Enterprises, Kings Beach, Ca.	N31SG

Reg	Yr	Type	c/n	Owner/Operator	Prev Regn
☐ N26SC	80	HS 125/700A	NA0283	Swiss Colony Inc. Janesvillee, Wi.	N93GR
☐ N26TN	86	Westwind-1124	418	B E & K Inc. Birmingham, Al.	N26T
☐ N26TZ	80	Westwind-1124	293	Air Nova Inc. Wilmington, De.	N26T
☐ N26WJ	87	Falcon 50	181	MJBW Aviation LLC. Fort Worth, Tx.	N600CH
☐ N26WP	01	Falcon 50EX	312	Weyerhaeuser Co. Tacoma, Wa.	F-WWHP
☐ N26XP	00	Beechjet 400A	RK-280	BB&T/Branch Banking & Trust Co. Winston-Salem, NC.	N4480W
☐ N27AJ	74	Falcon 10	31	International Union of Bricklayers & Allied Craftworkers, Va	(N29AA)
☐ N27AX	90	Learjet 35A	35A-662	Omni Air Transport Services Corp. Tulsa, Ok.	N35UK
☐ N27BJ	71	Learjet 24B	24B-227	CBG LLC. Wilsonville, Or.	N28AT
☐ N27BL	78	Learjet 35A	35A-163	AirNet Systems Inc. Columbus, Oh.	YV-173CP
☐ N27CD	90	Gulfstream 4	1136	Schering Plough Corp. Morristown, NJ.	N401GA
☐ N27CJ	98	CitationJet	525-0311	MGR Aviation LLC. Jackson, Mi.	N270J
☐ N27FL	99	Hawker 800XP	258426	Encanto Investments Inc. Tortola, BVI.	N426XP
☐ N27JJ	93	Beechjet 400A	RK-59	Gaylord Sports Management, Scottsdale, Az.	N5PF
☐ N27L	72	Citation	500-0038	Joe Durant, Estancia, NM.	(N207L)
☐ N27MJ	77	Learjet 36A	36A-027	Flight Capital LLC. Madison, Ms.	N484HB
☐ N27R	94	Falcon 2000	5	R J Reynolds Tobacco Co. Winston-Salem, NC.	F-WWMB
☐ N27SF	73	Citation	500-0064	Seneca Foods Corp. Penn Yan, NY.	N564CC
☐ N27SL	70	Gulfstream 2	84	Wiley Sanders Truck Lines Inc. Troy, Al.	N5101T
☐ N27TB	85	Citation S/II	S550-0082	BOS Dairies LLC. Bakersfield, Ca.	N282QS
☐ N27TT	77	Learjet 35A	35A-122	AirNet Systems Inc. Columbus, Oh.	OE-GMP
☐ N27TZ	77	Westwind-1124	213	Akins Ford, Winder, Ga.	4X-CLK
☐ N27UM	71	HS 125/731	25249	Marathon Hawker LLC. Boca Raton, Fl.	(N303BX)
☐ N27VP	97	Citation X	750-0027	Precision Jet Management Inc. Syracuse, NY.	N854WC
☐ N27WW	77	Citation 1/SP	501-0264	Wildwood Industries Inc. Bloomington, Il. (was 500-0353).	N353WB
☐ N27X	96	Challenger 604	5319	Rainier Aviation Inc/Sloan Capital Companies, Seattle, Wa.	N5319
☐ N27XP	00	Beechjet 400A	RK-266	MCM Transport Inc/McMurray Fabrics, Aberdeen, NC.	N10FL
☐ N28CK	97	CitationJet	525-0210	Charter Jet Transport Inc. Charlotte, NC.	XA-CAH
☐ N28DM	07	CitationJet CJ-3	525B-0142	Machavia Inc/Doug Mockett & Co. Torrance, Ca.	N.....
☐ N28FR	07	CitationJet CJ-3	525B-0153	Asia Today Ltd. Hong Kong.	N5145P
☐ N28GA	97	CitationJet	525-0215	Griffin Industries Inc. Cold Springs, Ky.	
☐ N28GP	00	Hawker 800XP	258489	Genuine Parts Co. Atlanta, Ga.	
☐ N28KA	95	Challenger 601-3R	5174	Lear 45-086 Holding Corp. Fort Lauderdale, Fl.	(N386K)
☐ N28MH	06	CitationJet CJ-3	525B-0110	Bear Air LLC. Duncansville, Pa.	N.....
☐ N28MJ	79	Learjet 35A	35A-224	M & J Leisure Ltd. Ogden, Ut.	N40RW
☐ N28NP	99	Astra-1125SPX	118	Perlmutter Investment Co. Waukegan, Il.	N529GA
☐ N28PT	93	CitationJet	525-0017	Eagle Holding Corp. Las Vegas, Nv.	N525AE
☐ N28R	95	Falcon 2000	7	R J Reynolds Tobacco Co. Winston-Salem, NC.	F-WWME
☐ N28TS	73	HS 125/600A	256009	M F R Associates LLC. Wilmington, De.	(N183RM)
☐ N28TX	92	Citation VII	650-7007	Bell Helicopter Textron Inc. Fort Worth, Tx.	N944L
☐ N28WL	73	Citation	500-0077	Magic 2 LLC/Nightline Inc. Miami, Fl.	N147SC
☐ N28ZF*	90	BAe 125/800A	NA0458	Core Projects Inc/Zinkin Properties, Fresno, Ca.	N941HC
☐ N29B	00	Hawker 800XP	258518	Batelle Memorial Institute, Columbus, Oh.	
☐ N29CL	84	Westwind-Two	404	Word of Life Ministries Inc. Shreveport, La.	N404W
☐ N29ET	05	CitationJet CJ1+	525-0601	NST Investments LLC. Sheridan, Wy.	N601CJ
☐ N29GP	97	Hawker 800XP	258344	Genuine Parts Co. Atlanta, Ga.	
☐ N29LJ	01	Learjet 60	60-240	Suzuki del Caribe Inc. San Juan, PR.	N5019V
☐ N29NW	82	Learjet 55	55-029	RCP's Lear LLC. Skillman, NJ.	(N55PJ)
☐ N29PB	68	Sabre-60	306-18	Commercial Aviation Enterprises Inc. Delray Beach, Fl.	N12PB
☐ N29QC	04	Citation Encore	560-0675	Questar Pipeline Co. Salt Lake City, Ut.	N.....
☐ N29RE	06	Learjet 40	45-2069	Allen Investments Inc. Stuart, Fl.	N29RN
☐ N29SM	02	Learjet 45	45-214	Sterling Motors Ltd. Santa Ana, Ca.	N214LF
☐ N29SN	99	Learjet 31	31A-194	Basic Construction Inc/Gold Star Aviation, Springdale, Ar.	N29SM
☐ N29TE	69	Falcon 20D-5	202	Tensor Engineering, Melbourne, Fl.	N9TE
☐ N29WE	05	Citation Sovereign	680-0042	Whelen Engineering, Groton, Ct.	N5090V
☐ N29XA	86	Citation S/II	S550-0096	Interflight Inc. West Palm Beach, Fl.	N29X
☐ N30AD	03	CitationJet CJ-2	525A-0165	Blue Yonder Holdings Inc. Fort Lauderdale, Fl.	N5243K
☐ N30AF	84	Citation III	650-0049	Poppy Air LLC. Syosset, NY.	(N650AN)
☐ N30AV	78	Citation II	550-0026	Hersey Mountain Air Inc/American Veladur Metal, Concord, NH.	(N2231B)
☐ N30FT	98	Falcon 50EX	271	Intercon Inc. NYC.	N30FE
☐ N30GF	83	Westwind-1124	401	Pelair Transport LLC. Houston, Tx.	N980S
☐ N30GJ	00	Learjet 60	60-204	Publix Supermarkets Inc. Lakeland, Fl.	I-NATZ
☐ N30GR	90	Citation II	550-0656	BossGo Aviation LLP. Pampa, Tx.	
☐ N30HD	02	CitationJet CJ-2	525A-0062	Roth Aircraft Inc. Sanford, Fl.	N5125J
☐ N30HJ	79	Learjet 35A	35A-226	White Industries Inc. Bates City, Mo. (status ?).	N1127M
☐ N30JD	80	Citation II	550-0205	International Development Group Ltd. Kootenai, Id.	(N88727)
Reg	Yr	Type	c/n	Owner/Operator	Prev Regn

Reg	Yr	Type	c/n	Owner/Operator	Prev Regn
☐ N30LB	96	Falcon 900EX	8	Great American Insurance Co. Cincinnati-Lunken, Oh.	F-WWFB
☐ N30LF	07	Falcon 2000DX	602	Dassault Falcon Jet Corp. Teterboro, NJ.	F-WWMC
☐ N30LJ	76	Learjet 25D	25D-209	Midsouth Services Inc. Clearwater, Fl.	N18NM
☐ N30MP	66	B 727-21	18998	MP Aviation LLC. Costa Mesa, Ca.	N111JL
☐ N30MR	78	Westwind-1124	225	Midwest Trophy Manufacturing Co. Del City, Ok.	N1124U
☐ N30PA	79	Learjet 35A	35A-245	Big Sur Waterbeds Inc. Denver, Co.	N1526L
☐ N30PC	03	Learjet 45	45-235	Southern Company Services Inc. Atlanta, Ga.	N50145
☐ N30PR	68	Gulfstream II SP	35	Rutherford Oil Co. Houston, Tx.	N830TL
☐ N30RL	90	Citation II	550-0653	Roseburg Lumber Co. Roseburg, Or.	N36854
☐ N30SJ	02	SJ 30-2	003	Sino Swearingen Aircraft Co. San Antonio, Tx.	
☐ N30UD	06	CitationJet CJ-3	525B-0131	Cessna Aircraft Co. Wichita, Ks.	N331CJ
☐ N30WR	83	Gulfstream 3	380	Rollins Inc/LOR Inc. Atlanta, Ga.	N159B
☐ N30XL	90	Beechjet 400A	RK-5	Advanced Flightworks LLC. Austin, Tx.	N495CW
☐ N31AA	69	Learjet 25	25-041	JODA LLC. Chesterfield, Mo.	(N25RE)
☐ N31CJ	01	CitationJet CJ-1	525-0474	Baird Air LLC. Springfield, Mo.	N.....
☐ N31D	01	Falcon 900C	191	Sentry Aviation Services LLC. Stevens Point, Wi.	F-WWFM
☐ N31DP	76	Learjet 35	35-062	CJPJ Associates Inc. Little Falls, NJ.	N310BA
☐ N31EP	68	HS 125/731	NA714	Inversiones 714 Inc. Wilmington, De.	N811JA
☐ N31FF	92	Learjet 31A	31A-053	J H Siroonian Inc. Fresno, Ca.	(N555JS)
☐ N31GA	81	Citation II	550-0221	Rainbow International Airlines, St Thomas, USVI.	N31GA
☐ N31GQ	97	Learjet 31A	31A-147	Grupo Q Holdings, Road Town, BVI.	N45KK
☐ N31HD	97	CitationJet	525-0261	Hillsboro Air Services Inc. Hillsboro, Or.	(N61CV)
☐ N31JB	99	CitationJet	525-0352	Jeff Burton Auto Sports Inc. Concord, NC.	N99JB
☐ N31LJ	94	Learjet 31A	31A-097	Alpine Air Inc. Charleston, WV.	N50207
☐ N31LW	73	Citation	500-0083	Top Flight Aviation LLC. Picayune, Ms.	VP-CHH
☐ N31MC	79	Learjet 35A	35A-270	Jagee Travel LLC. Fort Worth, Tx. (status ?).	FAV-0013
☐ N31MJ	99	Learjet 31A	31A-185	Marcone Investments LLC. St Louis, Mo.	N110SC
☐ N31MW	99	Learjet 31A	31A-171	Whiskey Tango LLC. Midland, Tx.	N129FX
☐ N31NF	97	Learjet 31A	31A-151	Comtide Investments LLC. Columbus, Oh.	N583LJ
☐ N31NS	95	Citation V Ultra	560-0286	Zero Five Kilo Corp. Wilson, Wy.	N57MB
☐ N31PV	97	Learjet 31A	31A-130	Fabrica de Jabon Valdes, Guatemala City, Guatemala.	N5013N
☐ N31TK	92	Learjet 31A	31A-059	Wal-Mart Stores Inc. Rogers, Ar.	(N67MP)
☐ N31TR	79	B 727-212RE	21948	Triarc Companies Inc. Stewart, NY.	VR-COJ
☐ N31UJ	95	Learjet 31A	31A-116	Aerorutas SATA, Buenos Aires, Argentina.	N112HV
☐ N31V	97	Learjet 45	45-015	Silver Lane Aviation LLC/Siegler & Co Inc. NYC.	
☐ N31WR	80	Learjet 35A	35A-313	AirNet Systems Inc. Columbus, Oh.	TR-LZI
☐ N31WS	75	Learjet 35	35-027	Extrapoint LLC/DD Marketing Inc. Pueblo, Co.	
☐ N31WU	99	Learjet 31A	31A-175	OB Air LLC. Mercer Island, Wa.	N27AL
☐ N32AA	99	Beechjet 400A	RK-242	Advance Aircraft Co. Roanoke, Va.	N2322B
☐ N32B	88	Falcon 900	59	Black & Decker Corp. Baltimore, Md.	N442FJ
☐ N32BC	96	Hawker 800XP	258321	Brunswick Corp. Waukegan, Il.	N691H
☐ N32BD	98	Gulfstream V	548	Black & Decker Corp. Baltimore, Md.	N245TJ
☐ N32DD	76	Learjet 24E	24E-331	Foster Racing/Dunnerstock Development Inc. Fayetteville, Ar.	XA-REA
☐ N32FJ	93	Citation VII	650-7032	Crescent Property Services Inc. Fort Worth, Tx.	XA-XIS
☐ N32FM	81	Citation 1/SP	501-0210	Imperial Transport Inc. NYC.	N67848
☐ N32GM	69	HS 125/731	NA728	23 West End Properties LLC. Franklin, Mi.	N410PA
☐ N32HH	00	Learjet 31A	31A-201	PHI Inc/Petroleum Helicopters Inc. Phoenix, Az.	N776PH
☐ N32HM	78	Learjet 35A	35A-187	Bradshaw Aviation LLC. Keller, Tx.	N755GL
☐ N32HP	83	Diamond 1A	A074SA	A & B Consultants LLC. Vicksburg, Ms.	N19GA
☐ N32KB	72	HS 125/731	NA773	S S K Hawker Group LLC/O E M Controls Inc. Shelton, Ct.	C-FPPN
☐ N32KJ	84	Learjet 55	55-093	Lone Palm Air LLC.	N725K
☐ N32KM	06	Citation Excel XLS	560-5715	El Dorado Aircraft LLC/Stebbins Five Companies, Longview, Tx	N.....
☐ N32MJ	85	Gulfstream 3	460	Magic Johnson Entertainment Inc. Van Nuys, Ca.	N460PG
☐ N32NG	97	Citation X	750-0039	Precision Jet Management Inc. Syracuse, NY.	N22NG
☐ N32PA	77	Learjet 36A	36A-025	Phoenix Air Group Inc. Cartersville, Ga.	N800BL
☐ N32PE	80	Learjet 35A	35A-327	Blue Canyon Inc. Smyrna, Tn.	N32PF
☐ N32RZ	79	Learjet 35A	35A-238	White Industries Inc. Bates City, Mo. (status ?).	N500HZ
☐ N32SG	02	390 Premier 1	RB-90	Sauvage Fuels Inc. Billings, Mt.	
☐ N32SM	83	Citation II	550-0478	Valley Air Service Inc. DuPage, Il.	N17WC
☐ N32TK	81	Citation II	550-0313	Sky View Aviation Inc. Orlando, Fl.	N32TM
☐ N32TM	00	Gulfstream G200	023	Sterling Advisors LP. Palwaukee, Il.	N414DK
☐ N32TX	84	Citation S/II	S550-0026	Therma-Tron-X Inc. Sturgeon Bay, Wi.	N24PF
☐ N33BC	95	Hawker 800XP	258292	Brunswick Corp. Waukegan, Il.	N673H
☐ N33D	05	Falcon 2000	224	Warbler 1 LLC/Dow Chemical Co. Saginaw, Mi.	N33FJ
☐ N33DT	94	CitationJet	525-0080	Delta Tango Inc. Des Moines, Ia.	N80CJ
☐ N33EK	81	Citation II	550-0281	Reid Tool Supply Co. Muskegon, Mi.	N31RK

Reg   Yr   Type   c/n   Owner/Operator   Prev Regn

Reg	Yr	Type	c/n	Owner/Operator	Prev Regn
N33FW	97	CitationJet	525-0203	Duke Realty Services LP/Aire Corr LLC. Indianapolis, In.	N525GP
N33JW	74	Sabre-60	306-92	Government of Democratic Republic of Congo, Kinshasa.	N74AB
N33L	00	Citation VII	650-7118	KGC Aviation LLC/Fairway Chevrolet, Las Vegas, Nv.	N5264U
N33LC	02	Falcon 50EX	326	Lowe's Companies Inc. North Wilkesboro, NC.	N37LC
N33M	99	Gulfstream V	594	3M Co. St Paul, Mn.	N594GA
N33NJ	80	Learjet 35A	35A-305	National Jets Inc. Fort Lauderdale, Fl.	N3VG
N33NL	03	Hawker 800XP	258643	Nick Corp. Lawrence, Ma.	(N843TS)
N33PJ	06	390 Premier 1A	RB-179	Phillips & Jordan Inc. Knoxville, Tn.	N7079N
N33PT	78	Learjet 25D	25D-240	Bankair Inc. West Columbia, SC.	(N339BA)
N33RL	98	Citation VII	650-7106	Levi, Ray & Shoup Inc. Springfield, Il.	N71NK
N33RZ	76	Sabre-75A	380-47	Air N33RZ Inc. Southfield, Mi.	N25BX
N33SJ	66	JetStar-731	5087	Craig Aviation Inc. Carlsbad-Palomar, Ca.	N75MG
N33TP	75	Learjet 24D	24D-321	Cinema Aircraft Restoration LLC. Las Vegas, Nv.	(N351MH)
N33TR	80	Sabre-65	465-47	Trinity Industries Inc. Dallas, Tx.	N265A
N33TS	00	Citation Encore	560-0549	Devco Properties LLC. New Castle, De.	N11TS
N33TW	81	Westwind-1124	316	PDMA II Aviation Inc. Naples, Fl.	N93KE
N33VC	96	Hawker 800XP2	258310	Silver Lake Aviation LLC. Salt Lake City, Ut.	PT-WMG
N33WW	78	Citation 1/SP	501-0065	Bodmer Financing Co. Zurich, Switzerland.	N2888A
N34AM	65	Sabre-40	282-31	Sabre Investments Ltd. St Louis, Mo.	N577VM
N34DZ	06	CitationJet CJ1+	525-0640	DLZ Corp. Columbus, Oh.	N5076L
N34FS	84	Westwind-Two	417	Roundtree Aviation LLC. Shreveport, La.	(N99WF)
N34GB	84	Learjet 55	55-114	Reinalt-Thomas Corp. Scottsdale, Az.	N72608
N34GG	78	HS 125/700A	257034	Hawker 700 LLC. Lake Oswego, Or.	N402GJ
N34GN	02	390 Premier 1	RB-58	Hawker Pacific P/L. Milperra, NSW.	N5158B
N34S	67	Gulfstream 2	5	Lockton Enterprises Inc. Houston, Tx.	N655TJ
N34TJ	75	Falcon 10	41	Ace Air Inc/Ace Transportation Inc. Lafayette, La.	(N550BG)
N34TN	78	Learjet 25D	25D-249	Williams Development & Construction, Houston, Tx.	XA-FMU
N34U	00	Global Express	9070	United Technologies Corp. Hartford, Ct.	N700XR
N34WP	02	Citation Excel	560-5232	Weyerhaeuser Co/Paccar Inc. Tacoma, Wa.	N451W
N34WR	77	JetStar 2	5207	Nevada Sky Inc. Asheville, NC.	N176BN
N35AJ	75	Learjet 35	35-010	Butler National Inc. Newton, Ks.	N888DE
N35AX	79	Learjet 35	35A-280	Superior Air Charter Inc. Medford, Or.	87-0026
N35BG	81	Learjet 35A	35A-402	Tashi Corp. Medford, Or.	N7AB
N35CC	81	Sabre-65	465-59	Crown Controls Corp. New Bremen, Oh.	N8500
N35CD	99	Gulfstream V	603	Schering Plough Corp. Morristown, NJ.	N539GA
N35CR	74	Westwind-1123	176	Websta's Aviation Services Inc. St Croix, USVI.	N27AT
N35CY	82	Learjet 35A	35A-473	Yelvington Transport Inc. Daytona Beach, Fl.	N777LB
N35D	72	Westwind-1123	156	G W Taylor/Taylor Aircraft, Halfway, Mo. (status ?).	N566MP
N35DL	80	Learjet 25D	25D-317	Lyons Magnus Inc. Fresno, Ca.	N25CY
N35ED	79	Learjet 35A	35A-215	E H Darby & Co/Alpha Jet International, Muscle Shoals, Al.	N80GD
N35ET	99	Citation Bravo	550-0879	Bright World Inc. Minnetonka, Mn.	N4M
N35GC	79	Learjet 35A	35A-266	T & A Aviation LLC. Miami, Fl.	N922GL
N35GZ	85	Gulfstream 3	465	Trans Gulf Corp. Clearwater, Fl.	N33NT
N35HS	96	Citation VII	650-7072	Diversified Human Resources Inc. Phoenix, Az.	N8494C
N35JN	82	Learjet 35A	35A-469	Taxi Jet Air Del Norte Inc. Houston, Tx.	N71MH
N35LH	85	Westwind-Two	413	Liberty Homes Inc. Goshen, In.	N413WW
N35NA	81	Learjet 35A	35A-381	Pinnacle Air Executive Jet, Springdale, Ar.	N300CM
N35NK	82	Learjet 35A	35A-491	B & E Houck Leasing LLC. Fort Pierce, Fl.	N394JP
N35RZ	94	Falcon 900B	137	RZ Aviation LLC/Ritz Camera Centers Inc. Leesburg, Va.	(N98DQ)
N35SA	80	Learjet 35A	35A-326	Precision Funding Inc. Little Rock, Ar.	N612DG
N35SE	06	Citation Excel XLS	560-5656	Sklar Exploration Co. Shreveport, La.	N52369
N35TJ	77	Learjet 35A	35A-137	Aston Aviation Leasing LLC. Brentwood, Tn.	N41FN
N35TK	05	CitationJet CJ1+	525-0610	Allied Resources Inc/Gregg's Restaurants, Providence, RI.	N51817
N35UA	91	Learjet 35A	35A-665	UltraAir LLC. Omaha, Ne.	N291K
N35WB	80	Learjet 35A	35A-350	La Stella Corp. Pueblo, Co.	(N88NE)
N35WE	78	Learjet 35A	35A-156	Chipola Aviation Inc. Panama City, Fl.	N190DA
N35WP	74	HS 125/600B	256029	Schubach Aviation Inc. Carlsbad-Palomar, Ca.	N629TS
N35WR	79	Learjet 35A	35A-234	Wholesale Printing Products Inc. El Paso, Tx.	
N36BL	94	Learjet 31A	31A-094	Bolavi Aviation/Ambulatory Surgical Centers, Westfield, Ma.	N817BD
N36DA	85	Gulfstream 3	450	Exeter Reverse 1031 Exchange Service, Ontario, Ca.	N801MJ
N36EP	01	Falcon 2000	172	JSM at Falcon LLC/Edgewood Properties Inc. Morristown, NJ.	N272EJ
N36GV	02	Gulfstream V	674	LFG P/L-W/S G-V Corp. Sydney, Australia.	(N26GV)
N36HA	99	Challenger 604	5441	5441-604 Corp. Fort Lauderdale Executive, Fl.	N33PA
N36LG	06	Global Express	9225	Westfield Aviation Inc. Sydney, NSW. Australia.	C-FJMP
N36PJ	81	Learjet 36A	36A-047	Maritime Sales & Leasing Inc. Newnan, Ga.	OE-GMD
N36PN	68	Gulfstream 2B	42	B & G Leasing LLC. Southfield, Mi.	N1164N

Reg	Yr	Type	c/n	Owner/Operator	Prev Regn
❏ N36PT	01	Citation Bravo	550-0966	Akio Hirato, Hillsboro, Or.	N51806
❏ N36RG	95	CitationJet	525-0139	Meridian Air Management Inc. Avalon Manor, NJ.	N76AE
❏ N36RR	67	Gulfstream 2B	4	Capital Consortium Group LLC. Columbia, SC.	N8490P
❏ N36RZ	67	Sabre-60	306-2	Ricardo Aramendia, Kenner, La.	(N27RZ)
❏ N36SF	78	Westwind-1124	233	Starflite/William J Ware, Houston, Tx.	N67DF
❏ N36TH	04	Falcon 2000EX EASY	53	Chelsea Aviation LP. Dallas-Love, Tx.	F-WWMB
❏ N36UP	02	Learjet 31A	31A-238	Thunderstone Aviation LLC. Boca Raton, Fl.	
❏ N36WJ	79	Falcon 10	126	Lake Air Inc. Fort Lauderdale, Fl.	N26WJ
❏ N37BE	83	Westwind-1124	396	Baldor Electric Co. Fort Smith, Ar.	8P-BAR
❏ N37BG	02	CitationJet CJ-2	525A-0123	Integrated Aviation Services LLC. Scottsdale, Az.	N5203S
❏ N37BM	94	Learjet 31A	31A-096	Beach Air Travel Inc. Floyd Knobs, In.	N30TK
❏ N37CB	83	Diamond 1A	A035SA	Diversified Capital Investments LLC. Central City, Ky.	N702JH
❏ N37ER	81	Falcon 50	47	Falcon Leasing of South Florida LLC. Boca Raton, Fl.	(N81CH)
❏ N37FA	76	Learjet 35A	35A-091	J & S Properties LLC. Chicago, Il.	(N900JV)
❏ N37MH	80	Citation II	550-0153	Charlie Brown Air Corp. State College, Pa.	N27MH
❏ N37NY	88	B 737-4YO	23976	ITT Flight Operations Inc/New York Knicks, Allentown, Pa.	N773RA
❏ N37TA	75	Learjet 35	35-034	RLO Aviation Inc. Peoria, Il.	
❏ N37WH	94	Gulfstream 4SP	1243	Miami Dolphins/Huizenga Holdings Inc. Fort Lauderdale, Fl.	(N39WH)
❏ N38AE	81	Westwind-Two	318	Time Compression Inc. New Castle, De.	N10FG
❏ N38BA	03	Gulfstream V	682	Greenmark Enterprises Ltd. Roadtown, BVI.	N551M
❏ N38CP	97	Learjet 60	60-108	Celeritas Holdings Management LLC. Cincinnati, Oh.	N60RY
❏ N38DD	82	Citation II	550-0340	Resort Air LLC. Honolulu, Hi.	ZP-TWN
❏ N38KW	07	Citation Excel XLS	560-5716	Progress Energy Inc. Raleigh-Durham, NC.	N.....
❏ N38M	07	CitationJet CJ-3	525B-0253	Cessna Aircraft Co. Wichita, Ks.	N.....
❏ N38MG	89	Learjet 31	31-009	Meridian Transportation Resources LLC. Seattle, Wa.	N727CP
❏ N38NA	94	Citation II	550-0729	North American Jet LLC. Tulsa, Ok.	(N128GH)
❏ N38NS	97	Citation V Ultra	560-0411	Mountain Shadow Ventures LLC. Port Hadlock, Wa.	PT-WNF
❏ N38PS	78	Learjet 35A	35A-206	Southern Jet Inc. Warner Robbins, Ga.	(N46KB)
❏ N38SA	76	Citation	500-0297	Tropic Winds Hotel/Stanley L Allen, Myrtle Beach, SC.	N48DA
❏ N38SC	99	CitationJet	525-0330	Collins/Goodman Development Co. Tyrone, Ga.	N331MS
❏ N38SK	92	Learjet 31A	31A-050	Devlin Air Charters LLC/SK Logistics Inc. St Augustine, Fl.	N92UG
❏ N38SW	99	Challenger 604	5423	SLW Aviation Inc. Houston, Tx.	N238SW
❏ N38TT	81	Citation II	550-0268	Island One Resort, Orlando, Fl. (was 551-0311)	N500FX
❏ N38WF*	02	Global Express	9128	First American Exchange LLC. Glendale, Ca.	N18WF
❏ N38WP	99	Falcon 50EX	292	Weyerhaeuser Co/Paccar Inc. Tacoma, Wa.	N292EX
❏ N39CB	76	Sabre-60	306-116	CC2B LLC. San Jose, Ca.	N44WD
❏ N39CD	84	Challenger 601	3030	Air Castle Worldwide Jet Charter Inc. Millville, NJ.	N34CD
❏ N39CJ	93	CitationJet	525-0039	TVPX Inc. Concord, Ma.	N1958E
❏ N39CK	68	Learjet 25	25-005	Kalitta Charters LLC. Detroit-Willow Run, Mi.	XA-SDQ
❏ N39DK	82	Learjet 35A	35A-480	AirNet Systems Inc. Columbus, Oh.	(N484)
❏ N39EL	72	Learjet 24D	24D-251	By Jet Inc. Carson City, Nv.	N69XW
❏ N39FN	74	Learjet 35	35-006	Flight Capital LLC. Madison, Ms.	N39DM
❏ N39FS	62	Sabreliner CT-39A	276-33	BAe Systems Flight Systems Inc. Mojave, Ca. (status ?).	N24480
❏ N39GA	05	Citation Excel XLS	560-5549	Cloudscape Inc. Ruidoso, NM.	CS-DXA
❏ N39H	04	Hawker 800XP	258695	Bob Air LLC/Thompson & Co of Tampa Inc. Tampa, Fl.	N695XP
❏ N39HF	93	Beechjet 400A	RK-65	E L K Air Partners LLC. Adrian, Mi.	(N81TT)
❏ N39HH	79	Citation 1/SP	501-0132	HRH Aviation Inc. Dover, De.	N717JL
❏ N39HJ	81	Learjet 35A	35A-337	Hop-A-Jet Inc. Fort Lauderdale, Fl.	N710AT
❏ N39KM	69	Learjet 24B	24B-198	Aero-Jet Aviation Inc. Fort Lauderdale, Fl.	N21XB
❏ N39NP	98	Falcon 900EX	39	Blue Ridge Air Inc. Greater Wilmington, De.	VP-BID
❏ N39PJ	77	Learjet 35A	35A-128	First Private Bank & Trust, Encino, Ca.	N257AL
❏ N39RC	99	Citation Excel	560-5041	Warehouse Management Inc. Cincinnati-Lunken, Oh.	N1XL
❏ N39RE	88	Challenger 601-3A	5020	AiRush Inc/Rush Enterprises Inc. San Antonio, Tx.	N604CF
❏ N39RG	67	Sabre-40	282-82	Tulsa Technology Center, Tulsa, Ok.	XB-EQR
❏ N39TW	91	Learjet 31A	31A-047	Liquid Magnetix Corp. Stony Brook, NY.	N31UK
❏ N39WP	99	Falcon 50EX	294	Weyerhaeuser Co/Paccar Inc. Tacoma, Wa.	F-WWHV
❏ N40	68	B 727-25QC	19854	FAA R&D Flight Program, Atlantic City, NJ.	N8171G
❏ N40AJ	77	Citation 1/SP	501-0275	Impact Racing Products, Brownsburg, In. (was 500-0362).	(N41AJ)
❏ N40AN	79	Learjet 35A	35A-271	AirNet Systems Inc. Columbus, Oh.	LV-OAS
❏ N40BD	77	Learjet 35A	35A-140	Newcastle Corp. Wichita Falls, Tx.	N72TP
❏ N40CJ	04	CitationJet CJ-1	525-0540	James Vannoy & Sons Construction Co. Jeffferson, NC.	N5127M
❏ N40DK	84	Learjet 55	55-092	Corporate Jets Inc. Allegheny County, Pa.	N500FA
❏ N40FC	87	Citation III	650-0143	Frank's Casing Crew & Rental Tools, Lafayette, La.	N312CF
❏ N40GA	83	Diamond 1A	A040SA	Pennco Inc/Pennco Air LLC. Wilmington, De.	N188ST
❏ N40GG	78	Westwind-1124	229	Circus Air Inc. Zellwood, Fl.	N162E
❏ N40GS	88	Hawker 800SP	NA0421	Go See LLC/Darby Advisors, Easton, Md.	N804X

Reg	Yr	Type	c/n	Owner/Operator	Prev Regn
☐ N40GT	73	Sabre-40A	282-126	Big Sky Sabre 40 LLC. Kansas City, Mo.	XA-SNI
☐ N40KJ	03	Learjet 40	45-2002	Apple Six Hospitality Air LLC. Richmond, Va.	
☐ N40KW	98	Citation X	750-0040	Triad Hospitals Inc. Dallas, Tx.	N740VP
☐ N40LJ	07	Learjet 40	45-2084	Learjet Inc. Wichita, Ks.	
☐ N40LX	95	Learjet 40	45-001	Learjet Inc. Wichita, Ks. (Ff 31 Aug 02).	N45XL
☐ N40MF	00	Citation Bravo	550-0921	Dot Foods Inc. Mount Sterling, Il.	N5073G
☐ N40ML	04	Learjet 40	45-2024	40ML Aviation Inc. Fort Lauderdale, Fl.	N424LF
☐ N40NB	07	Learjet 40	45-2087	Nelson Brothers Management Services, Birmingham, Al.	
☐ N40ND	75	Falcon 10	21	Shamrock Charter LLC. Fort Lauderdale, Fl.	N6OND
☐ N40NJ	73	Sabre-40A	282-134	ZMP Corp. Huntsville, Al.	N134JJ
☐ N40PC	04	Learjet 45	45-259	Southern Company Services Inc. Atlanta, Ga.	
☐ N40PK	79	Learjet 35A	35A-260	Med Air LLC. Lawrenceville, Ga.	
☐ N40TH	03	Falcon 2000EX	7	Sony Corporate Services Inc. Teterboro, NJ.	D-BIRD
☐ N40XR	05	Learjet 40	45-2028	JetCare International Ltd. Bournemouth-Hurn, UK.	
☐ N41AU	90	Astra-1125	041	Novellus Systems Inc/NVLS 1 LLC. Tulatin, Or.	(N29UC)
☐ N41AV	69	Gulfstream II SP	61	PHRM Leasing LLC/FlightWorks, Kennesaw, Ga.	N61LH
☐ N41C	83	Westwind-1124	398	Trey Aviation LLC. Addison, Tx.	N59AP
☐ N41DP	03	Challenger 300	20010	Dean Phillips Inc. Essendon, VIC. Australia.	C-GZEB
☐ N41EA	96	CitationJet	525-0131	Executive Citation/Aequitas Capital Management, Portland, Or	N800AJ
☐ N41GA	78	Citation II	550-0042	Cloudscape Inc. Ruidoso, NM.	C-FLBC
☐ N41GT	79	Citation 1/SP	501-0297	Tobin Aviation Enterprises, Abilene, Tx. (was 500-0394).	N35LD
☐ N41HF	95	Hawker 800	258274	Fath Aviation Ltd/Fath Properties, Cincinnati, Oh.	N4428
☐ N41HL	76	Citation	500-0338	Magna Tech Manufacturing Co. Muncie, In.	(N404JW)
☐ N41LF	02	CitationJet CJ-1	525-0501	Ludwig Law Firm Aviation Rental Inc. Little Rock, Ar.	N501CJ
☐ N41MH	65	Falcon 20C	14	Threshold Technologies Inc. Ontario, Ca.	N91JF
☐ N41ND	06	CitationJet CJ-3	525B-0134	The Nordam Group Inc. Tulsa, Ok.	N52691
☐ N41NK	78	Learjet 25D	25D-238	Okun Air LLC. Indianapolis, In.	N300TL
☐ N41NW	75	Learjet 35	35-041	IDM Aviation Services LLC. Austin, Tx.	(N694PG)
☐ N41NY	59	MS 760 Paris	41	JSI Holdings Inc. Calhoun, Ga.	41
☐ N41PC	01	Learjet 45	45-190	Southern Company Services Inc. Atlanta, Ga.	
☐ N41PG	96	CitationJet	525-0175	Duke Realty Services LP/Aire Corr LLC. Indianapolis, In.	N175CP
☐ N41RG	76	Sabre-60	306-119	Circle B Enterprises Inc. Ocilla, Ga.	N109MC
☐ N41SM	81	Citation II	550-0231	American Care Air Inc. Poway, Ca.	N148DR
☐ N41TF	01	Learjet 45	45-175	Gulf States Toyota Inc. Houston, Tx.	N30SF
☐ N41VP	02	Citation Encore	560-0626	Citation Technology Partners LLC. Hayward, Ca.	N.....
☐ N41WJ	81	Citation II	550-0237	Advanced Aviation LLC. Rancho Palos Verde, Ca.	ZS-NHO
☐ N41YP	95	CitationJet	525-0122	Yankee Pacific LLC. Portsmouth, NH.	N102AF
☐ N42AA	06	CitationJet CJ-3	525B-0140	Adkins Aviation LLC/Timberline Corp. Cornelius, NC.	N51612
☐ N42AJ	92	Beechjet 400A	RK-55	Alan Jay Logistics LLC. Sebring, Fl.	N404CC
☐ N42AS	68	HS 125/F3A	25150	Aero Toy Store LLC. Fort Lauderdale, Fl.	VP-BKY
☐ N42CM	76	Westwind-1124	189	Robinson Air Crane Inc. Opa Locka, Fl.	N200DL
☐ N42DC	80	Sabre-65	465-25	First State Trucking Inc. Salisbury, Mo.	N812WN
☐ N42EH	74	Falcon 10	28	New Time LLC. Minnetonka, Mn.	(N655DB)
☐ N42EL	05	390 Premier 1A	RB-145	El Dorado Hotel & Casino, Reno, Nv.	N37245
☐ N42FB	00	Hawker 800XP	258467	First Tennessee Equipment Finance, Memphis, Tn.	N5732
☐ N42FL	87	Westwind-1124	429	Structure Management Aviation LLC. Chicago, Il.	C-FROY
☐ N42G	74	Falcon 10	20	Daily Transport LLC. Glacier Park, Kalispell, Mt.	N113FJ
☐ N42GJ	06	Challenger 300	20085	John J McNamara Jr PA. Morristown, NJ.	C-FGCZ
☐ N42HN	83	Learjet 35A	35A-507	C C Medflight Inc. Lawrenceville, Ga.	N42HP
☐ N42NA	82	Falcon 50	128	Stensrud Ventures Management Co. Carlsbad, Ca.	N223DD
☐ N42ND	96	Citation V Ultra	560-0400	University of Notre Dame, Notre Dame, In.	N916CG
☐ N42PH	81	Citation II	550-0304	BK Aviation Group LLC. Schaumburg, Il.	(N70PH)
☐ N42SC	07	390 Premier 1A	RB-212	CLC Group Inc/Charles L Cabe Interests Inc. Dallas, Tx.	
☐ N42SK	99	Falcon 50EX	290	660 AH Corp. Madison, NJ.	(N302WY)
☐ N42SR	83	Diamond 1	A038SA	Source One Aviation LLC. Myrtle Beach, SC.	(N212PA)
☐ N42ST	96	Falcon 2000	39	Seagate Air LLC. San Jose, Ca.	N151AE
☐ N42TS	79	HS 125/700A	257067	Q-Jet Aviation LLC. Houston, Tx.	N267TS
☐ N42US	80	Falcon 10	171	US Aircraft Sales Inc/Aughrim Holding Co. Hillsboro, Or.	PT-OIC
☐ N42WJ	82	Falcon 20F-5	427	R-Plane Inc. Houston, Tx.	I-ACTL
☐ N43BD	05	Hawker 400XP	RK-441	Bear Creek Aviation LLC. Cincinnati, Oh.	N610PR
☐ N43BH	06	CitationJet CJ1+	525-0633	525-0633 LLC. Orlando, Fl.	(N28FM)
☐ N43DR	82	Learjet 25D	25D-353	Roever Evangelistic Associates Inc. Fort Worth, Tx.	N71AX
☐ N43EC	80	Falcon 10	168	Sequoia Properties Inc. Palwaukee, Il.	N175BL
☐ N43FC	98	Citation VII	650-7087	Frank's Casing Crew & Rental Tools, Sugar Land, Tx.	N149WC
☐ N43HF	04	Citation Excel XLS	560-5519	Mach Chasers LLC/Aviation Consulatants Inc. San Luis Obispo.	N52655
☐ N43MF	80	Learjet 35A	35A-284	ATI Jet/Med Flight Air Ambulance Inc. Albuquerque, NM.	OO-GBL

Reg	Yr	Type	c/n	Owner/Operator	Prev Regn
N43MH	90	Astra-1125SP	043	Bellair Construction Management Corp. Clearwater, Fl.	N1M
N43NR	94	Learjet 60	60-043	Jupiter Aviation LLC. Darby, Pa.	C-GHKY
N43NW	04	CitationJet CJ-1	525-0543	Harley Air Co. New Bern, NC.	N5200U
N43PJ	79	Learjet 28	28-004	Conover Aviation LLC. Bend, Or.	N28AY
N43PR*	98	BBJ-75V	28581	Town & Country Food Markets Inc. Wichita, Ks.	N781TS
N43R	97	Challenger 604	5334	Rockwell Automation Inc. Milwaukee, Wi.	N604RC
N43RC	93	Citation V	560-0245	Rohrer Corp. Wadsworth, Oh.	N508KD
N43RJ	01	Gulfstream G100	136	TVPX Inc. Concord, Ma.	N68GX
N43RP	81	Westwind-Two	332	Petty Air LLC. Harrisburg, NC.	N332DF
N43SA	79	Citation II	550-0086	U S Customs Service, New Orleans NAS, La.	(XC-JCY)
N43SF	04	Challenger 604	5594	State Farm Insurance Companies, Bloomington, Il.	N594SF
N43SP	82	Citation 1/SP	501-0243	Charter Services Inc. Mobile, Al.	N2624Z
N43TS	69	HS 125/731	NA721	Aero Toy Store LLC. Fort Lauderdale, Fl.	N777GD
N43VS	85	Citation S/II	S550-0069	Kurt Manufacturing Co. Minneapolis, Mn.	(N12720)
N43W	82	Westwind-Two	374	H L Brown Operating LLC. Midland, Tx.	N33MK
N43WL	64	Sabre-40	282-15	Desert Laboratories/DLI Aviation LLC. St George, Ut.	N43W
N44AS	79	Citation II	550-0047	Julrich Aviation Inc. Jeffco Airport, Co.	N66VM
N44CE	89	Gulfstream 4	1125	Law Offices of Peter Angelos, Baltimore, Md.	N49PP
N44CK	00	CitationJet CJ-1	525-0401	Koury Aviation Inc. Liberty, NC.	N142EA
N44DD	79	Sabre-60	306-146	DDD Aero LLC. Concord, NH.	N31CR
N44EG	87	Falcon 900	14	Bloomberg Services LLC. Morristown, NJ.	(N47EG)
N44EL	94	Learjet 60	60-036	U S Epperson Underwriting Co. Boca Raton, Fl.	N60LR
N44EV	76	Learjet 36A	36A-022	Chipola Aviation Inc. Panama City, Fl.	N36PD
N44FG	98	Citation V Ultra	560-0470	AFG Industries Inc. Blountville, Tn.	
N44FJ	03	CitationJet CJ-2	525A-0178	Williams International LLC. Waterford, Mi.	N80AX
N44FM	79	Citation 1/SP	501-0156	Supreme Indiana Management LLC. Goshen, In.	N123FG
N44GT	93	Citation V	560-0252	Groendyke Transport Inc. Enid, Ok.	N252CV
N44HH	92	BAe 125/800A	NA0474	Aldercrest Development Corp. Old Bridge, NJ.	(N823KG)
N44JC	01	Falcon 2000	164	J M Cox Resources LP. Midland-Odessa, Tx.	F-WWVY
N44LC	98	Falcon 50EX	275	Lowe's Companies Inc. North Wilkesboro, NC.	(N44EQ)
N44LG	02	Learjet 31A	31a-237	Alyeska Ocean Inc. Anacortes, Wa.	N84MJ
N44LQ	98	Citation V Ultra	560-0482	Guardian Financial Management Inc. Burnsville, Mn.	N44LC
N44LV	96	Citation V Ultra	560-0397	Air Pronto LLC/Loves Country Stores Inc. Oklahoma City, Ok.	N560RC
N44LX	89	Gulfstream 4	1114	Trans-Exec Air Service Inc. Van Nuys, Ca.	N314GA
N44M	06	Citation Sovereign	680-0083	Seward Prosser Mellon, Latrobe, Pa.	N50612
N44MK	77	Citation 1/SP	501-0272	Solley Air LLC. Birmingham, Al.	N700JA
N44MM	84	Diamond 1A	A080SA	Mike Moser Inc. Rogers, Ar.	N275HS
N44MQ	94	Citation VII	650-7043	ATM Aviation Services LLC. Coraopolis, Pa.	N44M
N44PR	73	Westwind-1123	169	Websta's Aviation Services Inc. St Croix, USVI.	N1100D
N44QG	03	Learjet 45	45-237	Quad/Air Inc. Waukesha, Wi.	N45QG
N44SF	04	Challenger 604	5601	State Farm Insurance Companies, Bloomington, Il.	C-GLXB
N44SH	04	Citation Sovereign	680-0023	44SH LLC/Bob Howard Pontiac GMC Inc. Oklahoma City.	N52235
N44SW	94	Citation II	550-0733	Steel Warehouse Co. South Bend, In.	N550TR
N44ZF	87	Gulfstream 4	1029	Zyman Group, Opa Locka, Fl.	VP-BKH
N45AC	87	Gulfstream 4	1036	Ashton Air Inc. Seattle, Wa.	N152A
N45AE	81	Learjet 35A	35A-422	GCA Aviation LLC. Tulsa, Ok.	N86BL
N45AF	78	Citation Eagle II	501-0284	Ardenbrook Inc/Matthews Properties Inc. Fremont, Ca.	N729PX
N45AU	04	Learjet 45	45-262	AGG Learjet P/L. Sydney, QLD. Australia.	VH-VVI
N45AX	03	Learjet 45	45-206	Omni Air Transport Services Corp. Tulsa, Ok.	(PR-...)
N45BE	90	Citation II	550-0664	Chief Industries Inc. Grand Island, Ne.	N70PC
N45BK	69	Learjet 25	25-036	Sterling Bank, Houston, Tx. (status ?).	N15M
N45BR	98	Citation X	750-0045	Universal Forest Products Inc. Grand Rapids, Mi.	N5109R
N45BS	73	Learjet 25B	25B-111	Premier Jets Inc. Hillsboro, Or.	(N25PJ)
N45BZ	05	Learjet 45	45-290	Bozzutos Inc/Logistics Business Services LLC. Windsor Locks.	N260DB
N45ED	66	Learjet 24	24-104	E H Darby & Co/Alpha Jet International, Muscle Shoals, Al.	N924ED
N45EJ	00	Learjet 45	45-080	Coral Aircraft LLC/Marathon Aircraft Corp. North Platte, Ne.	(N451DZ)
N45ET	00	Gulfstream 4SP	1405	Bright Flight Inc. Carlsbad, Ca.	N310GA
N45FG	75	Learjet 36	36-010	Fremont Group/Bechtel Corp. Oakland, Ca.	N50SF
N45FJ	93	CitationJet	525-0003	Cessna Finance Corp. Wichita, Ks.	N44FJ
N45GD	88	BAe 125/800A	NA0430	Grand Duke Air LLC/Pearce-Friedal Developers Inc. Dulles, Va	N50BN
N45GP	86	Citation S/II	S550-0110	Sunbelt Properties, Birmingham, Al.	(N116LD)
N45H	90	Astra-1125SP	050	45 Hotel Corp/Howard Industries Inc. Columbus, Oh.	N501JT
N45HC	01	Learjet 45	45-174	Harbert Aviation Inc. Birmingham, Al.	
N45HF	00	Learjet 45	45-121	HNT Properties LLC/Tenaska, Omaha, Ne.	(N666BG)
N45HG	07	Learjet 45	45-343	Asphalt Materials Inc. Indianapolis, In.	
N45HK	07	Learjet 45	45-349	VP 429 LLC/Virginia Air Exchange Inc. Chicago, Il.	

Reg	Yr	Type	c/n	Owner/Operator	Prev Regn
N45JB	86	Falcon 200	505	Barron Aircraft Management SA. Cannes, France.	N221FJ
N45KB	92	Citation V	560-0191	N45KB LLC. Seattle, Wa.	N2JW
N45KG	82	HS 125/700A	257189	Kaman Corp. Hartford-Bradley, Ct.	N8KG
N45KH	06	Learjet 45	45-313	K H Family Enterprises Inc. Norfolk, Va.	
N45KR	84	Gulfstream 3	433	Kelray Investments Inc. Addison, Tx.	N579TG
N45KX	03	Learjet 45	45-233	Carmax Auto Superstores Inc. Glan Allen, Va.	N5000E
N45LJ	07	Learjet 45	45-361	Learjet Inc. Wichita, Ks.	
N45LR	98	Learjet 45	45-013	Bullock Charter Inc. Princeton, Ma.	D-CFWR
N45ME	79	Citation II	550-0080	Sacramento Aviation Management Co. Sacramento, Ca.	N22511
N45MH	06	CitationJet CJ2+	525A-0344	PGM Air Inc. Morristown, NJ.	N5200Z
N45ML	82	Citation II	550-0367	Air Suz LLC/Mallory Group, Memphis, Tn.	N3MB
N45MM	78	Citation 1/SP	501-0070	GRL Investments LLC. Kalispell, Mt.	N628ZG
N45MR	07	Learjet 45	45-345	Superior Aviation LLC. Fort Wayne, In.	N5017J
N45MW	00	Learjet 45	45-115	Eagle Rock Air/Double Diamond Resorts, Dallas-Love, Tx.	(N405MW)
N45NB	03	390 Premier 1	RB-91	Air King Aviation LLC. Chattanooga, Tn.	N24YD
N45NC	00	Falcon 50EX	302	National City Corp/NCC Services, Cleveland, Oh.	N302FJ
N45NF	05	Citation Excel XLS	560-5563	Samuel Roberts Noble Foundation, Ardmore, Ok.	N5226B
N45NM	04	Learjet 45	45-253	HM International LLC. Tulsa, Ok.	N4008G
N45NP	02	Learjet 45	45-204	News Press & Gazette Co/NPG Aircraft Inc. St Joseph, Mo.	VH-ZZH
N45NS*	00	Citation Bravo	550-0949	Mid Ohio Aviation Inc/Seaman Corp. Wooster, Oh.	N550KG
N45PD	99	Learjet 31A	31A-186	Diloreto Construction & Development, Reno, Nv.	N45PK
N45PF*	97	CitationJet	525-0206	Oasis Services LLC. Southfield, Mi.	N17VB
N45PH	83	Challenger 601	3004	Willis Leasing Finance Corp. Sausalito, Ca.	N501PC
N45PK	06	Citation Excel XLS	560-5614	Pike Electric Inc. Mount Airy, NC.	N5206T
N45RC	90	Citation V	560-0071A	Avatar Holdings LLC. Dallas, Tx.	N2728N
N45RK	92	Beechjet 400A	RK-43	Actuant Corp. Milwaukee, Wi.	N56400
N45SJ	96	Falcon 900EX	7	Sid Richardson Carbon & Gasoline Co. Fort Worth, Tx.	N907FJ
N45ST	04	Gulfstream G550	5056	Beehawk Aviation Inc/Thomas Enterprises, Smyrna, Ga.	N956GA
N45TE	96	Citation V Ultra	560-0405	Berry Petroleum Co. Bakersfield, Ca.	N45TP
N45TK	07	Learjet 45	45-338	Speedbird Aviation LLC/Kelley Automotive, Fort Wayne, In.	
N45TL	77	Citation 1/SP	501-0016	TLR Inc. Santa Ana, Ca.	N17TJ
N45TP	04	Citation Encore	560-0668	Zurich Insurance Services Inc. Jacksonville, Fl.	(N560TP)
N45UG	01	Learjet 45	45-198	Universal Underwriters Service Corp. Kansas City, Mo.	N5048K
N45VB	00	Learjet 45	45-043	Riverbend Enterprises Inc. Idaho Falls, Id.	D-CRAN
N45VM	00	Citation Bravo	550-0918	JD Air Inc. Hackensack, NJ.	N5109R
N45VS	01	Learjet 45	45-170	N811BP Inc. Fort Lauderdale, Fl.	N45UP
N45XP	07	Learjet 45	45-355	Learjet Inc. Wichita, Ks.	N4008G
N45XR	07	Learjet 45XR	45-332	Learjet Inc. Wichita, Ks.	
N46E	04	Learjet 40	45-2010	Hunt Consolidated Inc. Dallas, Tx.	N50163
N46F	03	Challenger 604	5574	Hunt Consolidated Inc. Dallas, Tx.	N574F
N46GA	90	Citation V	560-0061	Frederick Air Charter LLC. Frederick, Md.	D-CNCI
N46HA	99	Falcon 2000	91	Wahovia Bank NA. Charlotte, NC.	F-WWVK
N46MF	81	Learjet 35A	35A-377	Med Flight Air Ambulance Inc. Albuquerque, NM.	N18WE
N46MK	83	Falcon 100	206	Merillat Industries Inc. Adrian, Mi.	N367F
N46NR*	82	Citation II	550-0363	Maranantha World Revival Ministries, Chicago, Il.	N741T
N46NT	01	CitationJet CJ-2	525A-0046	Cheyenne Aircraft LLC. Searcy, Ar.	N46JW
N46PJ	78	Citation II/SP	551-0027	George Tracey & David Agar, Dublin-Weston, Ireland.	N522CC
N46VE	00	Citation Excel	560-5077	Greenfield Builders Inc/V & E Aviation LLC. Indianapolis, In	N221LC
N46WC	92	BAe 1000B	259028	Weldbend Corp. Argo, Il.	D-CBWW
N47	04	Global 5000	9160	FAA, Atlantic City, NJ.	C-FCOJ
N47AN	84	Citation III	650-0054	Affordable Equity Partners Inc. Columbia, Mo.	N17AN
N47EG	05	Falcon 900EX EASY	154	Bloomberg Services LLC. Morristown, NJ.	F-WWFM
N47FH	93	CitationJet	525-0047	Dodeca Resources Inc. Hidale, Ut.	N47TH
N47HF	03	Citation Excel	560-5347	Applied Technologies Flight Inc. Paso Robles, Ca.	N.....
N47HV	73	HS 125/600A	256014	Aracel Inc. Tortola, BVI. (status ?).	N47HW
N47HW	84	BAe 125/800A	258023	Walsh Oil Co.. Fort Worth Meacham, Tx.	N1910J
N47LP	81	Falcon 20F-5	457	High Valley Air Service Inc. Colorado Springs, Co.	N4362M
N47MR	72	Learjet 25B	25B-101	Mojave Executive Jet 1 LLC. Mojave, Ca.	N821AW
N47NM	05	Citation Bravo	550-1112	State of New Mexico, Santa Fe, NM.	N5202D
N47PW	92	Citation V	560-0186	Pioneer Wings LLC. Scottsdale, Az.	N583N
N47SE	80	Sabre-65	465-34	AIG Aviation Inc. Atlanta, Ga.	N65TS
N47SM	88	Citation II	550-0568	Shank's Mare LLC/Wick Communications Co. Sierra Vista, Az.	N83KE
N47TL	81	Citation 1/SP	501-0200	Sunset Vacations Corp. Kissimmee, Fl.	7Q-YTL
N47TR	97	Learjet 31A	31A-136	BIK Rentals Inc. Concord, NC.	N131DA
N47VL	65	Sabre-40R	282-48	Jett Racing & Sales Inc. Laredo, Tx.	XA-RGC
N47XL	07	Citation Excel XLS	560-5747	Cessna Aircraft Co. Wichita, Ks.	N5040E

Reg	Yr	Type	c/n	Owner/Operator	Prev Regn
N48AL	90	BAe 125/800A	258167	Lakha Air LLC/Lakha Investments, Seattle, Wa.	N825DA
N48BV	85	Citation S/II	S550-0032	Regent Air Service Inc. Truckee, Ca.	N232WC
N48CG	96	Falcon 2000	41	Corning Inc. Hamilton, NY.	N2073
N48CT	73	Learjet 24XR	24XR-274	Aero Prodin S.A. Guatemala City, Guatemala.	(TG-...)
N48DD	66	HS 125/731	25115	Jet Services Enterprises Inc. Bethany, Ok.	N420JC
N48DK	78	Citation II/SP	551-0095	S & K Aviation Inc. Lake in the Hills, Il. (was 550-0049).	N402TJ
N48FB	95	Falcon 2000	11	Skylands Aviation LLC. Pontiac, Mi.	N248JF
N48FN	71	Learjet 24D	24D-238	Hampton University, Newport News, Va.	N49DM
N48FW	00	Citation Bravo	550-0948	Lucas Oil Products Inc. Corona, Ca.	N49FW
N48G	97	Falcon 50EX	258	Civic Center Corp/Anheuser Busch, Chesterfield, Mo.	VP-BST
N48GL	88	Gulfstream 4	1052	Royal Jet Inc. San Diego, Ca.	N722MM
N48GP	76	Learjet 35A	35A-069	L3 Communications Flight Capital LLC. Newport News, Va.	N10AQ
N48GR	69	Learjet 25	25-048	G & R Machinery Sales LLC. Pharr, Tx.	XA-TCY
N48GX	00	Galaxy-1126	017	Southeast Frozen Foods Co. Miami, Fl.	4X-CVF
N48HF	03	Citation X	750-0220	Mach McKenzie LLC. Greenwich, Ct.	N52613
N48KH	81	Citation II	550-0295	Kir-Nie Aviation Corp. Quincy, Il.	N339MC
N48KR	82	Falcon 50	127	Kroger Co. Cincinnati, Oh.	N129JE
N48L	66	Learjet 24A	24A-107	Royal Air Freight Inc. Pontiac, Mi.	
N48LB	79	HS 125/700A	257064	Casillas Aviation Corp. Tulsa, Ok.	N395RD
N48MF	98	Beechjet 400A	RK-218	AirJet Services LLC/Edward DeSeta & Assocs. Wilmington, De.	N3068M
N48NS	00	Citation Bravo	550-0939	Tower House Consultants Ltd. Southampton, UK.	VP-BNS
N48PL	97	Beechjet 400A	RK-138	Flyaway Inc. Fort Worth, Tx.	N40PL
N48SD	83	Westwind-Two	399	Valy Aviation Corp. Wilmington, De.	N78WW
N48SE	92	Beechjet 400A	RK-48	Blue Sky Aviation LLC/Indiana Sugars Inc. Burr Ridge, Il.	N94HT
N48TC	01	390 Premier 1	RB-13	Tool Crib Aero Inc. Grand Forks, ND.	
N48TF	04	Learjet 45	45-248	Gulf States Toyota Inc. Houston, Tx.	N4004Y
N48VC*	05	390 Premier 1	RB-132	Vermeer Manufacturing Co. Pella, Ia.	N9LV
N48WA	73	Learjet 25B	25B-136	Divine Aviation LLC. Van Nuys, Ca.	N753CA
N48WK	97	Falcon 2000	48	Las Brias LLC/Quail K LLC. Scottsdale, Az.	N701WG
N48WS	77	Sabre-60A	306-124	Lucio Luzzardi, Paradise Valley, Az.	N60RS
N48Y	84	BAe 125/800A	258009	Genesis Energy Inc. Houston, Tx.	N45Y
N49BE	78	Learjet 35A	35A-192	Mayo Aviation Inc. Englewood, Co.	N49PE
N49CT	81	Westwind-1124	314	Blue Sky Aviation LLC. Wichita, Ks.	N2HZ
N49FW	97	Citation X	750-0021	Advocate Aircraft Taxation Co. Indianapolis, In.	N61KB
N49GS	76	Learjet 24F	24F-336	White Cloud Aviation LLC. Seattle, Wa.	N9LD
N49KR	82	Falcon 50	104	Kroger Co. Cincinnati, Oh.	N725PA
N49KW	02	Citation Bravo	550-1021	PPAL Inc. Kalamazoo, Mi.	N5174W
N49LD	92	Citation V	560-0175	McKee Foods Transportation LLC. Chattanooga, Tn.	N1279Z
N49MN	88	Astra-1125	019	Astralee Terra Winery, Napa, Ca.	N49MW
N49RF	94	Gulfstream 4SP	1246	NO&AA/U S Department of Commerce, MacDill AFB. Fl.	N407GA
N49U	79	Citation II	550-0082	Helicopters Inc. Calokia, Il.	N21DA
N49VC	07	Gulfstream G200	161	American Family Mutual Insurance Co. Madison, Wi.	(N361GA)
N49WA	73	Learjet 25B	25B-142	Fleet Unlimited Inc/Spirit Aviation, Van Nuys, Ca.	N70CE
N49WL	81	Learjet 35A	35A-457	O & S LLC. Waterford, Mi.	N113LB
N50AE	03	Hawker 800XP	258650	American Electric Power Co. Columbus, Oh.	N650XP
N50AK	78	Learjet 35A	35A-172	PPH Inc. Dover, De.	(ZS-ZZZ)
N50AM	72	Citation	500-0041	Phoenix Helicopters LLC. Dover, De.	N50AS
N50BH	82	Gulfstream 3	359	Crystal Jet Aviation Inc/Trans World Entertainment, NY.	(N25MT)
N50BL	78	Falcon 50	2	BNB LLC/Brunner & Lay Inc. Franklin Park, Il.	F-GSER
N50BV	77	Falcon 20F	365	J & R Aviation LLC. Warwick, RI.	N50BH
N50CK	74	Learjet 25B	25B-157	Michigan Air Freight LLC. Ypsilanti, Mi.	N57CK
N50CR	69	Sabre-50	287-1	Rockwell Collins Inc. Cedar Rapids, Ia.	N287NA
N50CV	95	Citation V Ultra	560-0293	River City Flying Service LLC. Hailey, Id. (status ?).	N131WC
N50DR	94	Citation V	560-0248	RWB Enterprises Inc. Norfolk, Va.	(N226U)
N50DS	04	Global 5000	9140	First Southeast Aviation Corp. Tampa, Fl.	N140AE
N50EE	02	Gulfstream G400	1500	Idaho Associates LLC. Spartanburg, SC.	(N55GJ)
N50EF	84	Diamond 1A	A081SA	Eastern Foods Inc/Robert Brooks, Atlanta, Ga.	N750TJ
N50FD	82	Westwind-1124	381	Sallie Mae Inc. Dulles, Va.	N381W
N50FF	91	Falcon 50	220	Maltese Journeys Inc. Portland, Or.	N528JR
N50FN	76	Learjet 35A	35A-070	Flight Capital LLC. Madison, Ms.	N543PA
N50FX	87	Falcon 50	175	Ozark Management Inc. Jefferson City, Mo.	N530AR
N50GP	98	Citation V Ultra	560-0477	Gate Asphalt Co. Jacksonville, Fl.	N5085E
N50HA	04	Gulfstream G500	5067	Wachovia Bank NA/Hawkaire, Charlotte, NC.	N967GA
N50HC	90	Falcon 50	208	Group Holdings OR Inc. Fort Worth, Tx.	N50AE
N50HD	82	Falcon 50	83	Architectural Air LLC. Washington-Dulles, Va.	N881M
N50HM	85	Falcon 50	153	Health Management Associates Inc. Naples, Fl.	N16CP

Reg	Yr	Type	c/n	Owner/Operator	Prev Regn
N50HT	80	Falcon 10	163	Henneman Engineering Inc. Champaign, Il.	N83JJ
N50JP	80	Citation II	550-0143	Waipunalei Inc. Marbella, Panama.	N150RD
N50KC	01	Gulfstream V	659	Air Tiger LLC/Key Air Inc. Oxford, Ct.	N589GA
N50KD	85	Falcon 50	145	Daniel J Harrison III, Houston, Tx.	(TC-...)
N50KR	81	Falcon 50	58	Kroger Dedicated Logistics Co. Cincinnati-Lunken, Oh.	N744X
N50LB	06	Falcon 900DX	608	Hangar Acquisition Corp. Cincinnati, Oh.	F-WWFN
N50LK	07	Learjet 60	60-316	Precious Jet Ltd/Pacific Flight Services P/L. Singapore.	N5017J
N50M	81	Westwind-1124	327	Air Herrig LLC. Sarasota, Fl.	4X-CRU
N50MJ	78	Learjet 35A	35A-164	N50MJ LLC. Nashville, Tn.	N248HM
N50MW	85	Falcon 200	503	Transportation Systems Architects Inc. Omaha, Ne.	(N50MX)
N50NF	90	Citation II	550-0636	OnFlight Inc. Cincinnati, Oh.	N4EW
N50NM	97	Falcon 50EX	266	Motley Rice LLC/MRRM PA.. Charleston, SC.	VP-BPA
N50PL*	94	CitationJet	525-0083	Sargent Stutts Aviation LLC. Rome, Ga.	(N421CP)
N50PM	03	390 Premier 1	RB-80	Mallen Industries Inc. Hilton Head, SC.	N50280
N50PN	01	390 Premier 1	RB-11	Hawker Beechcraft Corp. Wichita, Ks.	N50PM
N50QJ	91	BAe 125/800A	NA0469	Gruffy LLC/Lyon Aviation Inc. Pittsfield, Ma.	N500J
N50QS	07	Hawker 4000	RC-20	Hawker Beechcraft Corp. Wichita, Ks.	
N50RW	74	Learjet 25B	25B-135	MBI LLC. Arlington, Va.	(N1RW)
N50SF	88	Falcon 50	180	Speciality Financial Corp. Reno, Nv.	N2254S
N50SJ	04	SJ 30-2	005	Sino Swearingen Aircraft Co. San Antonio, Tx.	
N50SN	00	Falcon 50EX	310	First Quality Enterprises Inc. Farmingdale, NY.	N50FQ
N50TC	98	BBJ-72T	29024	Tracinda Corp. Van Nuys, Ca.	N1787B
N50TG	04	Falcon 2000EX EASY	49	Lake Capital Management LLC. Palwaukee, Il.	F-GUDC
N50TQ	93	Astra-1125SP	065	Timberland Equities LLC. Fort Lauderdale, Fl.	N50TG
N50UG	05	Hawker 850XP	258749	Corporacion 731CP CA. Caracas, Venezuela.	N36669
N50US	80	Citation II	550-0181	Citation 550 LLC. Wilmington, De.	N550GP
N50VC	05	CitationJet CJ1+	525-0609	Mistral Aviation Inc. Guernsey, Channel Islands.	N5161J
N50XJ	81	Falcon 50	80	Aspect Energy LLC. Denver, Co.	N50BZ
N50YP	05	Falcon 50EX	344	Villages Equipment Co. Leesburg, Fl.	N344EX
N51B	99	Beechjet 400A	RK-261	NACCO Industries Inc. Cleveland, Oh.	N3261A
N51C	90	Citation V	560-0084	Captain Bly Inc. Rochester, Mn.	C-GHEC
N51CD	96	CitationJet	525-0163	Sanjenis Aircraft Services LLC. Ridgefield, Ct.	N5138F
N51EB	87	Beechjet 400	RJ-28	Sherr & Co. Hickory, NC.	N700LP
N51EF	98	Citation V Ultra	560-0487	Symphony Aviation LLC. Palm Beach International, Fl.	N43KW
N51EM	84	Citation III	650-0030	JDI Holdings LLC/United Bank Card, Hampton, NJ.	N380CW
N51FE	82	Falcon 50	121	McKinley Aircraft Holdings Inc. Akron-Canton, Oh.	N121FJ
N51FK	95	Citation V Ultra	560-0307	FLKY Aviation LLC/FKI Security Group, Louisville, Ky.	N139WC
N51FL	00	Gulfstream V	646	Star Aircraft Leasing SA. Monaco.	N524GA
N51FT	82	Citation 1/SP	501-0317	Computer Service Professionals Inc. Jefferson City, Mo.	N706DC
N51GS	99	CitationJet	525-0317	General Shale Building Materials Inc. Bristol, Tn.	N317CJ
N51JJ	05	CitationJet CJ-3	525B-0068	Jets Rents Aviation SARL. Marmaz, France.	N.....
N51JV	84	Citation III	650-0050	AMS Construction Co. Dallas, Tx.	(D-CVHA)
N51LC	80	Learjet 35A	35A-302	AirNet Systems Inc. Columbus, Oh.	N631CW
N51MF	05	Gulfstream G500	5100	Ferrell Aircraft Holdings LLC. Opa Locka, Fl.	N820GA
N51MN	95	Falcon 2000	14	MediaNews Services Inc. Denver, Co.	N70KS
N51ND	96	Citation V Ultra	560-0364	Quest II LLC. Moline, Il.	N560A
N51SE	04	Global Express	9138	Liberty Mutual Insurance Co. Bedford, Ma.	C-GZRA
N51TV	83	Westwind-Two	402	Texas Television Inc. Corpus Christi, Tx.	N999LC
N51V	88	Falcon 50	189	Starflight 50 LLC. Belle Chasse, La.	N51VT
N51VL	85	Learjet 55	55-116	SP Aviation Inc. Hayward, Ca.	N51V
N51VR	99	Challenger 604	5426	Dark Blue Aviation Ltd. Majuro, Marshall Islands.	JY-ONE
N52AG	02	CitationJet CJ-2	525A-0075	ICM Inc. Colwich, Ks.	HP-1461
N52AL	88	Beechjet 400	RJ-38	ALP Air LLC/Azalea Management & Leasing Inc. Asheville, NC.	N438DA
N52AW	96	Beechjet 400A	RK-115	Executive Charters Inc. Kinston, NC.	(N369EA)
N52CK	85	Citation S/II	S550-0076	N52CK LLC. San Diego, Ca.	N89TD
N52CT	87	Learjet 55B	55B-131	PRA Development & Management Corp. Philadelphia, Pa.	N7260K
N52DC	00	Falcon 2000	116	Dow Chemical Co. Midland, Mi.	N2216
N52ET	05	CitationJet CJ-3	525B-0018	Burlingame Industries Inc. Ontario, Ca.	N51896
N52FN	81	Learjet 35A	35A-424	Flight Capital LLC. Madison, Ms.	N508GP
N52FT	85	Citation S/II	S550-0056	Texas Citation S/II Management LLC. San Antonio, Tx.	N550F
N52GA	80	HS 125/700A	NA0270	Carnac Holdings Inc. Houston, Tx.	PK-CTC
N52JA	75	Falcon 10	59	Sportsmed Aviation LLC. Birmingham, Al.	N633WW
N52LT	82	Citation II	550-0355	Tristen Aviation LLC. Van Nuys, Ca.	N355DF
N52MK	97	Gulfstream 4SP	1337	Michael Kittredge, Hobe Sound, Fl.	N637GA
N52N	85	Falcon 100	197	East Hampton Airlines, Farmingdale, NY.	N888G
N52PK	93	CitationJet	525-0052	North Park Transportation Co. Billings, Mt.	N252CJ

Reg	Yr	Type	c/n	Owner/Operator	Prev Regn
☐ N52PM	74	Citation	500-0222	Aircraft Properties, Whitefish Bay, Wi.	N636SC
☐ N52RF	78	Citation II	550-0021	NO&AA/U S Department of Commerce, Stewart, NY.	N900LJ
☐ N52SM	92	BAe 1000A	NA1009	Sierra Pacific Industries Inc. Anderson, Ca.	N125CJ
☐ N52TL	77	Citation 1/SP	501-0053	Citizens Telephone Co. Brevard, NC.	N14EA
☐ N52WF	99	Citation V Ultra	560-0528	ThyssenKrupp-Waupaca Inc. Waupaca, Wi.	
☐ N53BB	80	Citation Eagle II	501-0146	Tour America Inc. Wilmington, De.	N194RC
☐ N53DF	01	Challenger 604	5507	Sierra Land Group Inc. Burbank, Ca.	C-GLXB
☐ N53FL	68	Learjet 25	25-017	Airmark International, Corona, Ca.	N128JS
☐ N53FP	82	Citation II	550-0434	Heartland Aviation Inc. Eau Claire, Wi.	(D-CVAU)
☐ N53FT	81	Citation II	550-0276	Red Wing Aeroplane Co. Bay City, Wi.	C-GGFW
☐ N53G	79	Learjet 35A	35A-274	First Star Inc. Van Nuys, Ca.	N274JS
☐ N53GH	82	HS 125/700A	NA0314	G Howard & Assocs Inc. Ronkonkoma, NY.	(N106AE)
☐ N53GX	00	Global Express	9053	Mills Pride LP/White Rose Aviation Inc. W Palm Beach, Fl.	N700LJ
☐ N53HJ	82	Learjet 55	55-037	JODA LLC/Worldwide Jet Charter Inc. Fort Lauderdale, Fl.	PT-OBR
☐ N53KV	93	CitationJet	525-0030	M & J Leasing LLC. Cumberland, Wi.	(N93KV)
☐ N53LB	96	Hawker 800XP2	258332	Blanco Industries LLC. Raleigh-Durham, NC.	N36H
☐ N53LM	80	Westwind-1124	311	Lattimore Aviation LLC. McKinney, Tx.	N788MA
☐ N53MS	93	Beechjet 400A	RK-64	Image Air LLC. Warsaw, In.	N8164M
☐ N53NA	04	Embraer Legacy 600	145770	DC 3 Entertainment LP. Hillsboro, Or. 'The Lisa Marie'	N3005
☐ N53NW	05	CitationJet CJ-3	525B-0053	Nationwide Homes Inc. Lake Havasu City, Az.	N.....
☐ N53PE	97	Citation V Ultra	560-0464	Platt Electric Supply Inc. Beaverton, Or.	N420DM
☐ N53PJ	60	MS 760 Paris-1R	53	DFX LLC. Calhoun, Ga.	No 53
☐ N53RD	81	Citation	500-0415	STG Realty Ventures Inc. Santa Rosa, Ca.	N50KR
☐ N53RG	81	Citation II	550-0257	Airlec Ast Espace SA. Bordeaux, France.	N187TA
☐ N53SF	03	CitationJet CJ-3	525B-0001	Lauralis Training LLC/Bomasada Group, Houston. (FF 8 Aug 03)	(N929SF)
☐ N53WF	99	Citation Excel	560-5057	ThyssenKrupp-Waupeca Inc. Waupeca, Wi.	N240B
☐ N54	93	Learjet 60	60-009	FAA, Oklahoma City, Ok.	N26029
☐ N54AP	01	Learjet 31A	31A-220	A R Arena Products Inc. Rochester, NY.	N521WH
☐ N54AX	01	Gulfstream G200	054	Aspen Executive Air LLC. Aspen, Co.	N200GA
☐ N54BP	92	CitationJet	525-0002	SGE International P/L. Essendon, VIC. Australia.	N46JW
☐ N54CG	01	CitationJet CJ-1	525-0439	Craig Goess Inc/Greenville Toyota, Greenville, NC.	N395SD
☐ N54DC	00	Falcon 2000	117	Dow Chemical Co. Midland, Mi.	N2217
☐ N54DD	90	Citation V	560-0089	International Jet Aviation Inc. Van Nuys, Ca.	ZS-MPT
☐ N54FN	72	Learjet 25C	25C-083	L3 Communications Flight Capital LLC. Newport News, Va.	N200MH
☐ N54FT	79	Citation Eagle SP	501-0100	BitterBlue Inc. San Antonio, Tx.	C-GSUM
☐ N54HA	05	Challenger 300	20076	Wachovia Bank NA/Hawkaire, Charlotte, NC.	C-FGBY
☐ N54HC	96	CitationJet	525-0157	Capital Partners Advisory Co/AM AV Inc. Baltimore, Md.	N57HC
☐ N54HD	92	Beechjet 400A	RK-49	Colorado Timber Resources Inc. El Paso, Tx.	(N349HP)
☐ N54HG	04	Falcon 900EX EASY	140	American International Group Inc. Teterboro, NJ.	(N900EX)
☐ N54HP	97	Beechjet 400A	RK-160	AMPCO Inc. Riverhead, NY.	N2360F
☐ N54HT	96	Learjet 31A	31A-127	Parkland Development Management Corp. Boca Raton, Fl.	HB-VLR
☐ N54J	00	Falcon 2000	141	W W Grainger Inc. Palwaukee, Il.	N2000A
☐ N54JC	84	Challenger 601	3031	ISM Aviation Services Ltd. Humberside, UK.	(N181SM)
☐ N54JV	74	Citation	500-0163	Parrott Aviation Inc/Roth Law Firm, Marshall, Tx.	N8KH
☐ N54KB	00	Gulfstream V	627	Miranda International Aviation Inc. San Jose, Ca.	N627GA
☐ N54NW	82	Learjet 55	55-054	ATI Jet Sales West LLC. Reno, Nv.	(N54JZ)
☐ N54PA	74	Learjet 36	36-004	Phoenix Air Group Inc. Cartersville, Ga.	N180GC
☐ N54RM	87	Citation II	550-0562	Chapparal Boats Inc. Nashville, Ga.	N813A
☐ N54SL	06	Global Express	9187	Harpo Inc. Chicago-Midway, Il.	N540WY
☐ N54TG	98	Gulfstream V	523	Rochester Aviation Inc. Rochester, NY.	N790MC
☐ N54VS	95	Challenger 601-3R	5189	Challenger 5189 Leasing LLC. Fort Lauderdale, Fl.	XA-IMY
☐ N54YR	85	Falcon 50	158	Phifer Wire Products Inc. Tuscaloosa, Al.	N142FJ
☐ N55	93	Learjet 60	60-013	FAA, Oklahoma City, Ok.	N26011
☐ N55AR	84	Learjet 55	55-105	Fly Private LLC/OFM Inc. Holly Springs, NC.	C-GQBR
☐ N55BA	98	Hawker 800XP	258356	Basic American Property Management LLC. San Francisco, Ca.	N550H
☐ N55BH	84	Citation III	650-0041	International Industries Inc. Gilbert, WV.	
☐ N55CH	93	Citation V	560-0240	Family Video Movie Club Inc. Pal-Waukee, Il.	N966JM
☐ N55CJ	99	CitationJet	525-0298	Big Blue Express Inc. Omaha, Ne.	G-RSCJ
☐ N55DG	83	Falcon 100	207	Western Wings Corp. Roseburg, Or.	N456CM
☐ N55EA	90	Citation V	560-0055	Eagle Aviation Inc. West Columbia, SC.	N715PS
☐ N55F	78	Learjet 35A	35A-147	AirNet Systems Inc. Columbus, Oh.	N717W
☐ N55FG	79	Westwind-1124	267	Westwind Air LLC. Champaign, Il.	N241CT
☐ N55FN	78	Learjet 35A	35A-202	Med Air LLC. Lawrenceville, Ga.	D-CGPD
☐ N55FT	72	Citation Longwing SP	500-0009	Guilford Transportation Industries, Portsmouth, NH.	N147WS
☐ N55G	68	HS 125/731	NA709	Dr Paul Madison, Michigan City, In.	(N2G)
☐ N55GP	06	CitationJet CJ-3	525B-0113	Grat Planes Industries/Smalley Steel Ring Co. Wheeling, Il.	N5263U
Reg	Yr	Type	c/n	Owner/Operator	Prev Regn

Reg	Yr	Type	c/n	Owner/Operator	Prev Regn
☐ N55GR	74	Citation	500-0217	Educacion Tecnologica M R Q CA. Fort Lauderdale, Fl.	N217S
☐ N55GV	97	Gulfstream V	515	Starjet Ltd/Key Air, Oxford, Ct.	V8-001
☐ N55HA	06	Challenger 300	20090	Wachovia Bank NA/Hawkaire, Charlotte, NC.	C-FGWB
☐ N55HF	95	Challenger 601-3R	5183	HFP LLC/Hudson Foods Inc. Rogers, Ar.	N601HF
☐ N55KT	02	CitationJet CJ-2	525A-0065	ARS Air LLC. Lake Oswego, Or.	N225WW
☐ N55LC	01	Falcon 50EX	314	Lowe's Companies Inc. North Wilkesboro, NC.	N314EX
☐ N55MV	82	Citation II	550-0407	Max-Viz Inc. Portland, Or.	(N950FC)
☐ N55NG	06	Citation Excel XLS	560-5671	Nicewonder Group, Abingdon, Va.	N5296Z
☐ N55NY	82	Learjet 55	55-020	Air New York LLC/Northeastern Aviation Corp. Melville, NY.	N35PF
☐ N55PX	98	CitationJet	525-0285	Delco Overseas Inc. Wilmington, De.	N55PZ
☐ N55RF	86	BAe 125/800A	258066	National Aircraft Leasing LLC. Anchorage, Ak.	N75CS
☐ N55RG	66	Gulfstream II SP	1	R W Galvin/Motorola Inc. Wheeling, Il.	N801GA
☐ N55RZ	71	HS 125/400A	NA764	Safenet Security Services P/L. Pretoria, RSA.	XB-CUX
☐ N55SC	95	Citation VII	650-7060	Fifty Five LLC. Midland, Tx.	N5218T
☐ N55SK	94	CitationJet	525-0063	Skyline Corp. Elkhart, In.	N2649J
☐ N55SQ*	92	Beechjet 400A	RK-60	Jet Quest LLC. Cleveland, Oh.	N61SM
☐ N55TD	90	Gulfstream 4	1131	Threshold Ventures Inc. Scottsdale, Az.	N679RW
☐ N55UH	03	Gulfstream G550	5028	Patrick Defence Logistic P/L. Australia.	N928GA
☐ N55UJ	84	Learjet 55	55-090	Universal Jet Aviation Inc. Boca Raton, Fl.	N181EF
☐ N55VC	86	Learjet 55B	55B-130	R T Vanderbilt Co. White Plains, NY.	
☐ N55VR	95	Learjet 31	31-033C	Cool Corp Ltd. St Ann, Jamaica.	N555VR
☐ N55VY	91	Learjet 31A	31A-040	Viking Yacht Co. New Gretna, NJ.	N314MK
☐ N55WL	80	Citation II	550-0140	Jet Air Inc. Galesburg, Il.	N2646Z
☐ N56	94	Learjet 60	60-033	FAA, Oklahoma City, Ok.	N4031A
☐ N56BE	01	Hawker 800XP	258527	B-200 Corp. Farmingdale, NY.	N813TA
☐ N56BP	79	Westwind-1124	268	Bradley Flight LLC. Denver, Co.	N41WH
☐ N56D	96	Gulfstream 4SP	1309	White Cloud Aviation LLC. NYC.	N824CA
☐ N56EL	05	Falcon 2000EX EASY	71	Enterprise Rent-a-Car Co. St Louis, Mo.	N71EL
☐ N56EM	77	Learjet 35A	35A-144	AirNet Systems Inc. Columbus, Oh.	N56HF
☐ N56FE	02	Citation Excel	560-5250	FirstEnergy Solutions Corp. Akron-Canton, Oh.	N25NG
☐ N56GA	94	Citation V	560-0259	Dalton Aviation LLC. Eagle County, Co.	N37WP
☐ N56HA	06	Challenger 300	20105	Wachovia Bank NA/Hawkaire, Charlotte, NC.	C-FHNJ
☐ N56HX	99	Citation Excel	560-5063	H F Express GP. Ventura, Ca.	N56HA
☐ N56JA	80	Learjet 35A	35A-342	AirNet Systems Inc. Columbus, Oh.	YV-15CP
☐ N56KP	06	CitationJet CJ1+	525-0629	KTP Aviation LLC. Flint, Mi.	N.....
☐ N56L	93	Gulfstream 4SP	1213	NewsFlight Inc. Los Angeles, Ca.	N416GA
☐ N56LF	92	Learjet 31A	31A-056	Wal-Mart Stores Inc. Rogers, Ar.	N303WB
☐ N56LN	81	Falcon 50	79	Holly Corp/Navajo Refining Co. Dallas-Love, Tx.	(N79FJ)
☐ N56LP	99	Citation Excel	560-5068	LP Venture Group LLC. Teterboro, NJ.	N57HX
☐ N56LT	80	Falcon 50	21	BTE Equipment LLC. Broomfield, Co.	N770E
☐ N56LW	81	Citation 1/SP	501-0314	Larry Phillips, Fruitland Park, Fl.	N56MC
☐ N56MD	76	Learjet 25D	25D-214	H-F Aircraft LLC. Nederland, Tx.	N70TF
☐ N56MK	77	Citation 1/SP	501-0023	M L Kuhn Enterprises Inc. Whitesboro, Tx.	(N501FB)
☐ N56MM	76	Learjet 24F	24F-332	Northeastern Aviation Corp. Wilmington, De.	N13KL
☐ N56PA	77	Learjet 36A	36A-023	Phoenix Air Group Inc. Cartersville, Ga.	N6YY
☐ N56PB	81	Citation 1/SP	501-0219	Sound Container Inc. Renton, Wa.	N510GA
☐ N56PT	73	Learjet 24D	24D-276	LandAir Mapping Inc. Atlanta, Ga.	N25CV
☐ N56TE	06	Citation Encore+	560-0755	Thumb Energy Inc. Bad Axe, Mi.	N5218R
☐ N56UH	07	Gulfstream G500	5158	United Healthcare Services, St Paul, Mn.	N998GA
☐ N56WE	78	Citation 1/SP	501-0056	Port City Castings Corp. Muskegon, Mi.	CC-CTE
☐ N57	94	Learjet 60	60-039	FAA, Oklahoma City, Ok.	N8071J
☐ N57BE	85	Westwind-Two	428	Baldor Electric Co. Fort Smith, Ar.	N327SA
☐ N57BJ	85	Citation S/II	S550-0052	Plukair Delaware LLC. Wilmington, De.	N27GD
☐ N57CJ	85	Citation S/II	S550-0057	DSB Air LLC/Main Street Homes Inc. Austin, Tx.	N1UL
☐ N57EC	01	CitationJet CJ-1	525-0460	ECES Leasing LLC. Eastland, Tx.	D-IMMM
☐ N57EL	05	Falcon 2000EX EASY	69	Enterprise Rent-a-Car Co. St Louis, Mo.	N56EL
☐ N57FC	81	Citation 1/SP	501-0229	Bell Law Firm, Georgetown, SC.	N57MC
☐ N57FL	03	CitationJet CJ-2	525A-0198	Lill Air LLC/Frank Lill & Son Inc. Webster, NY.	N5162W
☐ N57HA	06	Challenger 300	20105	Wachovia Bank NA/Hawkaire, Charlotte, NC.	C-FIOB
☐ N57HC	02	CitationJet CJ-2	525A-0098	Bridgeport Associates Inc. Bedford, Ma.	N57HG
☐ N57HE	76	Gulfstream 2	194	EHR Investments, Ponte Vedra Beach, Fl.	N57HJ
☐ N57HJ	95	Gulfstream 4SP	1261	Heinz Family Foundation, Manassas, Va.	N399CB
☐ N57KW	02	Citation Excel	560-5214	Progress Energy Inc. Raleigh-Durham, NC.	N.....
☐ N57LL	72	Citation	500-0025	Skypro Enterprises Ltd. Salt Lake City, Ut.	N220W
☐ N57MC	03	Citation Bravo	550-1053	Massman Construction Co. Kansas City, Mo.	N.....
☐ N57MH	85	Learjet 55	55-113	Marriott International Inc. Manassas, Va.	N236HR

Reg	Yr	Type	c/n	Owner/Operator	Prev Regn
❏ N57MK	89	Falcon 50	197	Klein Tools Inc. Palwaukee, Il.	N404JF
❏ N57MN	04	Falcon 2000EX EASY	50	McClatchy Newspapers Inc. Sacramento, Ca.	F-WWGO
❏ N57MQ	79	Sabre-65	465-11	Coastal Corp. Houston, Tx.	N5739
❏ N57NP	82	Gulfstream 3	340	GAC 340 Inc. Stratford, Ct.	N2LY
❏ N57PT	77	Westwind-1124	208	Kingdom's Wings Inc. Wilmington, De.	N311DB
❏ N57SF	82	Citation II	550-0402	F M Howell & Co. Elmira, NY. (was 551-0057).	N717PC
❏ N57TP	02	Citation Excel	560-5261	Crimson Excel LLC. Tuscaloosa, Al.	N75TP
❏ N57TS	01	Learjet 31A	31A-236	Wareham Property Group, San Rafael, Ca.	N314DT
❏ N57TT	85	Gulfstream 3	471	Thompson Tractor Co. Birmingham, Al.	N583D
❏ N57UH	07	Gulfstream G550	5163	Gulfstream Aerospace Corp. Savannah, Ga.	N663GA
❏ N57WP	03	Citation Excel	560-5317	Weyerhaeuser Co. Tacoma, Wa.	N5269J
❏ N58	95	Learjet 60	60-057	FAA, Oklahoma City, Ok.	N50050
❏ N58AJ	85	Gulfstream 3	446	Air Sterling LLC/Richmor Aviation Inc. Columbia County, NY.	N446U
❏ N58BL	93	BAe 125/800A	258236	CDS Aviation LLC. Delray Beach, Fl.	(N39BL)
❏ N58CG	99	Falcon 900EX	47	Corning Inc. Hamilton, NY.	F-WWFO
❏ N58CW	77	Learjet 35A	35A-116	Worthington Ford of Alaska Inc. Anchorage, Ak.	N116AM
❏ N58EM	76	Learjet 35	35-046	N58EM LLC. West Columbia, SC. (status ?).	VH-LJL
❏ N58FN	69	Learjet 24B	24B-184	Hampton University, Newport News, Va.	(N58FN)
❏ N58HA	07	Challenger 300	20146	Wachovia Bank NA/Hawkaire, Charlotte, NC.	C-FLQH
❏ N58HC	81	Learjet 25D	25D-341	Bankair Inc. West Columbia, SC.	XA-SAE
❏ N58HT	81	Sabre-65	465-70	Summit Strategies Inc. St Louis, Mo.	N58CM
❏ N58HX	00	Citation Excel	560-5099	R W Hertel & Sons Inc. San Luis Obispo, Ca.	N58HA
❏ N58JF	69	Gulfstream 2	65	Government of Democratic Republic of Congo, Kinshasa.	(N300FN)
❏ N58LC	07	Challenger 300	20163	Atlantic Excel LLC/Lusardi Construction Co. San Marcos, Ca.	C-FMWG
❏ N58MM	79	Learjet 35A	35A-261	MFPI Partners LLC. Aspen, Co.	N63DH
❏ N58SR	82	Learjet 55	55-058	Chrysler Aviation Inc. Van Nuys, Ca.	N129SP
❏ N58ST	99	Learjet 60	60-186	Servicios Aereos Sateca CA. Caracas, Venezuela.	N186ST
❏ N58TC	75	Citation	500-0261	LBR Aviation Leasing LLC/Riley Aviation Inc. Sturgis, Mi.	N711SF
❏ N58TS	66	JetStar-731	5079	Faith Landmark Ministries, Richmond, Va.	XA-MAZ
❏ N59	96	Learjet 60	60-080	FAA, Oklahoma City, Ok.	N8080W
❏ N59AJ	83	Gulfstream 3	413	ACG3 LLC/Al Copeland Investments, Metairie, La.	N766WC
❏ N59AL	70	Learjet 24D	24D-236	Jets R Us Delaware LLC. Rutledge, Ga.	N47TK
❏ N59AP	01	Gulfstream 4SP	1476	Computer Sciences Corp. El Segundo, Ca.	N476GA
❏ N59BR	02	Hawker 800XP	258599	Spell Aviation Partners LLC. Minneapolis, Mn.	N51169
❏ N59CF	07	Gulfstream G450	4097	Kamis GmbH. Grunwald, Germany.	N397GA
❏ N59CJ	01	CitationJet CJ-2	525A-0059	DRDAN LLC/M & N Aviation Inc. San Juan, PR.	N.
❏ N59DF	91	Citation V	560-0098	Sierra Land Group Inc. Burbank, Ca.	(N18SK)
❏ N59DY	81	Citation II/SP	551-0059	Damon Young, Texarkana, Tx. (was 550-0397)	N59FY
❏ N59EC	01	Citation Excel	560-5123	JMZ LLC. Columbus, Oh.	N699BC
❏ N59FT	86	Citation III	650-0123	Hume & Johnson PA. Coral Springs, Fl.	(N491SS)
❏ N59GB	82	Citation II/SP	551-0060	Aircraft Leasing ApS. Ejsberg, Denmark.	(N60HW)
❏ N59HJ	82	Learjet 55	55-027	Hop-A-Jet Inc. Fort Lauderdale, Fl.	B-3980
❏ N59JN	05	CitationJet CJ1+	525-0607	CJ1 Plus LLC. Austin, Tx.	N5218T
❏ N59K	74	Sabre-60	306-82	Bill R Hay Trust, Albert Lea, Mn.	N60SL
❏ N59KC	96	Citation V Ultra	560-0363	KC LLC/AM AV Inc. Baltimore, Md.	N59KG
❏ N59KG	01	Citation Encore	560-0563	Krause Gentle Corp. Des Moines, Ia.	N51995
❏ N59MA	77	Citation 1/SP	501-0050	A & H Aircraft Sales Inc. Florence, Al.	N750LA
❏ N59NH	91	Citation V	560-0139	L35 LLC/The Sundance Co. Boise, Id.	(N75FV)
❏ N59TF	97	Citation V Ultra	560-0422	Teleflex Inc. Limerick, Pa.	N58RG
❏ N60AE*	01	Citation Encore	560-0561	LJ Associates Inc/LJ Aviation, Latrobe, Pa.	N511TH
❏ N60AG	01	Citation Excel	560-5255	Taylor Fresh Foods Inc. Salinas, Ca.	N52081
❏ N60AN	97	Learjet 60	60-099	Pinnacle Air Executive Jet, Springdale, Ar.	N212BX
❏ N60BT	87	Westwind-1124	432	E E Treadaway, Houston, Tx.	N282SM
❏ N60DK	83	Learjet 35A	35A-505	P & N Jets LLC. Stroudsburg, Pa.	N494PA
❏ N60EF	84	Diamond 1A	A070SA	Hooters of America Inc. Atlanta, Ga.	N84GA
❏ N60EW	82	Citation 1/SP	501-0319	Jet Star Inc/IPM E F Weisert GmbH. Nuremberg, Germany.	N124KC
❏ N60FE	92	Learjet 60	60-003	Lear 60003 LLC. Fort Lauderdale, Fl.	N808ML
❏ N60FJ	78	Citation II/SP	551-0007	Roadlink Transportation Inc. Livingston, Mt.	YV-05CP
❏ N60GF	96	Learjet 60	60-077	RocaWings LLC. NYC.	N227BX
❏ N60GH		Challenger 800	7274	Haas CNC Racing Inc. Kannapolis, NC.	N633BR
❏ N60GT	58	MS 760 Paris-1A	8	David Bennett/Executive Aero, Colorado Springs, Co.	G-APRU
❏ N60HD	97	Hawker 800XP2	258334	FS 800 LLC. Bellevue, Wa.	N80HD
❏ N60HM	95	Learjet 60	60-067	Harbert Aviation Inc. Birmingham, Al.	N118HC
❏ N60JC	70	Sabre-60	306-51	Airstream Aviation Inc. Delray Beach, Fl.	N141JA
❏ N60LJ	07	Learjet 60	60-337	Learjet Inc. Wichita, Ks.	
❏ N60LW	06	Citation Bravo	550-1129	Prestbury Two LLP. Luton, UK.	N52059

Reg	Yr	Type	c/n	Owner/Operator	Prev Regn
☐ N60MG	94	Learjet 60	60-042	Chantilly Air Inc. Silver Spring, Md.	N90AQ
☐ N60MN	97	Learjet 60	60-100	Morris Newspaper Corp. Savannah, Ga.	N6100
☐ N60ND	83	Learjet 55	55-088	Shamrock Charter LLC. Fort Lauderdale, Fl.	N522WK
☐ N60NF	00	Citation Encore	560-0562	OnFlight Inc. Cincinnati, Oh.	N5180K
☐ N60PC	07	Learjet 45	45-351	Learjet Inc. Wichita, Ks.	
☐ N60QB	90	Citation V	560-0087	Consolidated Transportation Services, McHenry, Il.	N600BW
☐ N60RL	04	Learjet 60	60-278	Lear 60 LLC/R & L Carriers Inc. Wilmington, Oh.	N5012K
☐ N60RU	98	Learjet 60	60-136	Aballi, Milne, Kalil & Escagedo PA. Miami, Fl.	N60RL
☐ N60SB	04	Challenger 300	20019	Richards Group Inc. Dallas, Tx.	N319RG
☐ N60SL	78	Sabre-75A	380-60	Centurion Investments Inc. St Louis, Mo.	XA-RDY
☐ N60SN	03	Learjet 60	60-267	SBE Entertainment Group LLC. Van Nuys, Ca.	N60YC
☐ N60SR	93	Learjet 60	60-023	Bandag Inc. Muscatine, Ia.	N60SB
☐ N60TC	98	Falcon 2000	80	Tristram Colket Jr/Tekloc Enterprises, N Philadelphia, Pa.	N2CW
☐ N60TL	89	Falcon 900	75	Capital Flight LLC. St Paul, Mn.	N60RE
☐ N60TX	97	Learjet 60	60-097	PA Exchange Corp. Nashville, Tn.	N897R
☐ N60VE	01	Learjet 60	60-222	Valero Energy/Valero Corporate Services Co. San Antonio, Tx.	N8088U
☐ N60WL	81	Learjet 35A	35A-382	Jet Sets Inc/Guardian Flight, Fairbanks, Ak.	OE-GAF
☐ N60XR	05	Learjet 60XR	60-294	Cloud Nine Aviation LLC. Van Nuys, Ca. (Ff 3 Apr 06).	N50163
☐ N61CK	87	Citation III	650-0150	E & M Aviation LLC. Venice Municipal, Fl.	N150F
☐ N61DF	04	Citation Sovereign	680-0012	Cintas Corp. Cincinnati, Oh.	N970RC
☐ N61DP	97	Learjet 60	60-122	Automatic Aviation LLC. Orlando, Fl.	N622LJ
☐ N61FB	74	Sabre-60	306-80	Fine Air Services Inc. Miami, Fl.	PT-KOT
☐ N61GB	02	Beechjet 400A	RK-341	N61GB LLC/Schneider National Inc. Green Bay, Wi.	N51241
☐ N61HT	80	Citation II	550-0157	Hi-Tech Construction Inc. Logan, WV.	N535PC
☐ N61KM	94	Citation V	560-0255	Faith Life Church Inc. Springfield, Mo.	N355EJ
☐ N61MA	80	Citation II	550-0176	Tropix Aviation Inc. San Juan, PR.	(N24TR)
☐ N61SH	95	CitationJet	525-0095	Acme Research LLC. Dover, De.	(N5153K)
☐ N61TL	98	Citation V Ultra	560-0461	Empress Entertainment Inc. Chicago-Romeoville, Il.	N461VP
☐ N61VC	05	Hawker 400XP	RK-450	International Veneer Co. South Hill, Va.	N650XP
☐ N61VE	00	Learjet 60	60-224	Valero Energy/Valero Corporate Services Co. San Antonio, Tx.	
☐ N61WH	88	Gulfstream 4	1075	HCG Leasing LLC. Fort Lauderdale, Fl.	N121JV
☐ N61YP	98	CitationJet	525-0237	FX Blue Holdings LLC. Melbourne, Fl.	N237CJ
☐ N62BR	73	Citation	500-0093	RA Air Inc. Wilmington, De.	G-OCPI
☐ N62CR	92	Citation V	560-0188	Rowe Aircraft Inc. Millington, Tn.	N395R
☐ N62DK	82	Learjet 25D	25D-356	DK Properties Inc. Newport Beach, Ca.	N251MD
☐ N62DM	72	Learjet 25B	25B-082	2nd Main Inc. Leesburg, Fl.	N700FC
☐ N62GB	07	Gulfstream G200	175	Graham Brothers Construction Co. Dublin, Ga.	N675GA
☐ N62GR	01	Citation Excel	560-5207	Chemtura Corp. Oxford, Ct.	N62GB
☐ N62GX	00	Gulfstream G200	031	RX Choice Inc/Rite Aid Corp. Harrisburg, Pa.	4X-CVH
☐ N62HM	95	Falcon 50	243	Hospital Managements Associates Inc. Naples, Fl.	N724R
☐ N62MB	80	Learjet 35A	35A-282	West Bend Air Inc. West Bend, Wi.	N444CM
☐ N62MS	03	Gulfstream G550	5017	Melvin Simon & Assocs Inc. Indianapolis, In.	N917GA
☐ N62MW	86	Gulfstream 3	484	Jet Place Inc. Dallas, Tx.	VP-BOR
☐ N62NS	85	Citation S/II	S550-0072	Longhorn Aviation Inc. Jupiter, Fl.	TC-NMC
☐ N62NW	96	Falcon 900B	157	Next Week LLC. Austin, Tx.	N626EK
☐ N62PG	77	Learjet 36A	36A-031	Phoenix Air Group Inc. Cartersville, Ga.	N20UG
☐ N62SH	03	CitationJet CJ-3	525B-0002	Stephen Hiller, Hayward, Ca. (First flight 6 Nov 03).	N763CJ
☐ N62TL	83	Citation II	550-0462	Aviation LLC/Cornett Homes Inc. Madison, Wi.	N550AL
☐ N62WA	06	Citation Encore+	560-0758	Muscatine Corp. Muscatine, Ia.	N.....
☐ N62WD	96	Citation V Ultra	560-0360	Hamra Management LLC. Springfield, Mo.	N62WA
☐ N63AX	82	Learjet 55	55-063	Averitt Aviation Group Inc. Nashville, Tn.	(N63TN)
☐ N63EM	73	HS 125/F400A	25272	Aviation Solutions LLC. Waterford, Mi.	N800JT
☐ N63FF	90	Citation V	560-0063	Radioactive LLC/Local TV LLC. Fort Wright, Ky.	N68CK
☐ N63GA	71	Learjet 24D	24D-241	Big Boys Toys Inc. Hialeah Gardens, Fl.	N363BC
☐ N63GB	98	Citation V Ultra	560-0454	Graham Brothers Construction Co. Dublin, Ga.	N454RT
☐ N63GC	89	Citation III	650-0179	CDWA LLC/Dupre Interests LLC. Houston, Tx.	N35FC
☐ N63HA	86	Citation S/II	S550-0119	Hawkins Aviation LLC. Carlsbad, Ca.	N11TS
☐ N63HS	02	Gulfstream G550	5013	Air Simon Inc. Indianapolis, In.	N913GA
☐ N63JG	92	Citation V	560-0189	Jay Gee Holdings Inc. Hazleton, Pa.	N62HA
☐ N63JT	88	Citation S/II	S550-0156	Raley's, West Sacramento, Ca.	N901PV
☐ N63LF	96	CitationJet	525-0127	Appleton Orchard LLC. Hood River, Or.	N63LB
☐ N63LX	06	Citation Sovereign	680-0084	Lennox Industries Inc. Dallas, Tx.	N4087B
☐ N63MU	90	Gulfstream 4	1152	International Group Inc/SCM Assocs Inc. Penn Yan, NY.	N63M
☐ N63PP	83	Westwind-Two	394	Arthur & Arthur LLC. Missoula, Mt.	N21RA
☐ N63TM	04	Citation Sovereign	680-0019	Ferdinand T Stent, Stone Mountain, Ga.	N5188N
☐ N63TS	75	Falcon 10	66	Centurion Investments Inc. St Louis, Mo.	YV-70CP

Reg	Yr	Type	c/n	Owner/Operator	Prev Regn
☐ N63WR	05	Learjet 45	45-278	Stallings Group Ltd/Four S's LLC. Greenville, NC.	
☐ N63XG	77	Falcon 10	103	X-Gen Pharmaceuticals Inc. Islip, NY.	N26TJ
☐ N64AH	67	Jet Commander	94	Linea Aerea Puertorriquena Inc. Carlina, PR.	N94WA
☐ N64BD	87	Falcon 900	16	Sky Aviation Corp. West Palm Beach, Fl.	VP-CBD
☐ N64BH	83	Citation 1/SP	501-0325	Pay & Save Inc. Littlefield, Tx.	N501LM
☐ N64CE	69	Learjet 24B	24B-205	Royal Air Freight Inc. Pontiac, Mi. (status ?).	(N721J)
☐ N64CF	82	Learjet 35A	35A-461	CF Industries Inc. Chicago, Il.	
☐ N64CP	79	Learjet 35A	35A-264	AirNet Systems Inc. Columbus, Oh.	VR-CDI
☐ N64DH	66	Sabre-40R	282-52	Sunshine Aero Industries Inc. Crestview, Fl.	N282MC
☐ N64HH	00	Learjet 45	45-087	TVPX Inc. Concord, Ma.	N645HJ
☐ N64LE	88	Challenger 601-3A	5031	Thomas Development Partners Inc. Van Nuys, Ca.	N721MD
☐ N64LV	96	Citation V Ultra	560-0345	Tulsa Aircraft LLC. Tulsa, Ok.	(N560NS)
☐ N64LX	06	Citation Excel XLS	560-5638	Lennox Industries Inc. Dallas, Tx.	N4086L
☐ N64MA	65	Sabre-40	282-44	Chadco Aviation Inc. Dalton, Ga.	N600JS
☐ N64NB	92	Learjet 31A	31A-065	North Coast Aviation Inc. Pontiac, Mi.	N44SU
☐ N64PM	06	390 Premier 1A	RB-168	Nowi LLC. Longboat Key, Fl.	N7268M
☐ N64RT	81	Citation 1/SP	501-0191	Rubaiyat Trading Co. Birmingham, Al.	N98ME
☐ N64SL	94	Learjet 60	60-029	Leche Inc. Key Biscayne, Fl.	N296TS
☐ N64TF	79	Citation II	550-0064	M & J Leisure Ltd. Ogden, Ut.	(N550TJ)
☐ N64UC	04	Challenger 604	5587	UC Challenger LLC/CMC Real Estate Group, Miami, Fl.	(N604UC)
☐ N64VM	85	Beechjet 400	RJ-1	Verco Manufacturing/Nektor Industries Inc. Phoenix, Az.	
☐ N65A	73	Learjet 25B	25B-134	World Heir Inc. College Park, Ga.	N26FN
☐ N65AK	80	Sabre-65	465-35	TVPX Inc. Concord, Ma.	N2590E
☐ N65BK	07	CitationJet CJ1+	525-0657	Beckley Flying Service/Mountaineer Structures, Mount Hope.	N52594
☐ N65BP	91	Citation VI	650-0202	Fly One Eighty Eight Ltd. Wilmington, De.	N202TJ
☐ N65BT	79	Sabre-65	465-3	Sabre 65 LLC/Master Realty Properties, KCI, Mo. (status ?).	N1CF
☐ N65CC	80	Sabre-65	465-46	Crown Controls Corp. New Bremen, Oh.	N65FF
☐ N65CE	92	BAe 125/800B	258234	900 Holdings LLC/Trafalet & Co. NYC.	VP-CDE
☐ N65CK	06	CitationJet CJ2+	525A-0323	Professional Flight Management LLC. Boca Raton, Fl.	N5132T
☐ N65CR	03	CitationJet CJ-2	525A-0185	HiFly Trading Inc. Cascais, Portugal.	N65CK
☐ N65DL	93	Hawker 800SP	258224	Chestnut Ridge Air Ltd. NYC.	N810V
☐ N65DV	89	Citation II	550-0624	Dole Fresh Vegetables Inc. Van Nuys, Ca.	N662AJ
☐ N65EM	05	CitationJet CJ1+	525-0615	Cessna Aircraft Co. Wichita, Ks.	N5095N
☐ N65FF	92	Challenger 601-3A	5122	Flying Fishawk LLC/FAF Manager Inc. Bedford, Ma.	N900CL
☐ N65HH	77	Sabre-65	465-1	Biardi Investments LLC. New Century, Ks.	(N117MN)
☐ N65HU	01	Learjet 60	60-228	Jacura Delaware Inc. Boca Raton, Fl.	N65HA
☐ N65JT	77	JetStar 2	5213	JWT Aircraft Holdings LLC. Phoenix, Az.	(N600JT)
☐ N65MC	80	Sabre-65	465-36	WKC Corp/Barry Wehmiller Companies Inc. St Louis, Mo.	N424JM
☐ N65ML	81	Sabre-65	465-69	AVSAT Inc. Benton Harbor, Mi.	N25KL
☐ N65PZ	01	CitationJet CJ-2	525A-0072	DAT-II LLC. Newark, De.	(N65PX)
☐ N65RA	85	Beechjet 400	RJ-9	Father & Son Aviation LLC. Georgetown, De.	N800FT
☐ N65RL	92	Citation V	560-0179	Levi, Ray & Shoup Inc. Springfield, Il.	N885M
☐ N65RZ	79	Learjet 35A	35A-236	Professional Air Services LLC. Fort Lauderdale, Fl.	EC-HLB
☐ N65SA	73	Citation	500-0114	Jet Air Inc. Galesburg, Il.	I-AMCT
☐ N65SR	81	Sabre-65	465-54	LDM Technologies Inc. Dearborn, Mi.	N1909R
☐ N65ST	02	Citation X	750-0211	Thomas Enterprises Inc. Smyrna, Ga.	N954Q
☐ N65T	80	Sabre-65	465-43	Marotta Scientific Controls Inc. Montville, NJ.	N955PR
☐ N65TC	80	Sabre-65	465-30	Whiteco Industries Inc. Merrillville, In.	N89MM
☐ N65VM	05	CitationJet CJ-3	525B-0034	Sierra Aviation Inc. Kansas City, Mo.	N52446
☐ N65WH	72	Learjet 25B	25B-086	Dolphin Aviation Inc. Sarasota, Fl.	N23DB
☐ N65WW	81	Citation 1/SP	501-0194	Stanley C Thomas, Fort Worth, Tx.	N28JG
☐ N66AM	96	CitationJet	525-0160	PCI LLC. Park Ridge, Il.	N5076J
☐ N66BE	97	CitationJet	525-0174	Apache Aviation LLC. Beaver Dam, Wi.	(N417Q)
☐ N66BK	82	Citation 1/SP	501-0254	Fisher Sand & Gravel Co. Glendive, Mt.	(N84GF)
☐ N66CF	75	Falcon 10	65	Key Equipment Finance Inc. Albany, NY. (dismantled ?).	(F-GJMA)
☐ N66DD	98	Gulfstream 4SP	1355	Duchossois Industries Inc. Palwaukee, Il.	N355GA
☐ N66ES	97	CitationJet	525-0244	Starjet Air Inc/Royal Street Corp. Salt Lake City, Ut.	
☐ N66GE	80	Sabre-65	465-28	C & K Leasing Co. St Louis, Mo.	(N129BA)
☐ N66KK	77	Learjet 35A	35A-095	Performance Aircraft Leasing Inc. Aspen, Co.	N68UW
☐ N66LE	74	Citation Eagle	500-0170	B A Holdings LLC/Blue Aviation LLC. Little Rock, Ar.	N818R
☐ N66LM	00	Citation Excel	560-5074	LMC Leasing Inc. Bartow, Fl.	N574AV
☐ N66MC	81	Citation II	550-0239	Horton Aviation LLC. Dallas-Love, Tx.	N4720T
☐ N66MS	81	Citation II	550-0399	R D Offut/Farmers Equipment Rental, Fargo, ND.(was 551-0053)	(N6890C)
☐ N66MT	00	Citation Bravo	550-0913	Manatts Inc. Grinnell, Ia.	N232BC
☐ N66NJ	80	Learjet 35A	35A-296	National Jets Inc. Fort Lauderdale, Fl.	N51JA
☐ N66SG	00	Learjet 45	45-073	Woolsington Wunderbus Inc. Luton, IK.	N65U

Reg	Yr	Type	c/n	Owner/Operator	Prev Regn
N66U	98	Citation V Ultra	560-0489	Spring Bay Aviation Inc. Ponte Vedra Beach, Fl.	
N66VA	83	Westwind-Two	375	SPB Vision LLC. Las Vegas, Nv.	N66LX
N66ZB	99	BBJ-74U	29233	Rank Services Ltd. Auckland, New Zealand.	N4AS
N67BE	79	Citation 1/SP	501-0142	Everair LLC. Sidney, Mt.	N15FJ
N67BK	01	Citation Bravo	550-0997	First Choice Equipment LLC. Ashland, Va.	N5192E
N67CC	04	CitationJet CJ-2	525A-0225	David Auth, Hobe Sound, Fl.	N67BC
N67DT	82	Westwind-Two	364	Richland LLC. Columbia, SC.	N944M
N67EL	95	Falcon 900B	153	Noble Drilling Services Inc. Houston, Tx.	N57EL
N67GH	04	CitationJet CJ-2	525A-0217	Hughes & Hughes Investments Corp. Salt Lake City, Ut.	N5211F
N67GW	03	Citation Encore	560-0641	Gary-Williams Energy Corp. Denver, Co.	N5270J
N67HB	75	Learjet 25B	25B-189	Water Soft Inc. Saxonburg, Pa.	N888DF
N67JB	01	Citation Bravo	550-0980	Burkhart Enterprises Inc. Lubbock, Tx.	N146CT
N67JF*	82	Falcon 50	73	Virginia Air Exchange Inc. Chicago, Il.	(N556LX)
N67JR	66	B 727-30W	18936	Bank of Utah, Salt Lake City, Ut. (trustor ?).	N18HH
N67LC	75	Falcon 10	49	Rainbow 7 LLC. Springdale Municipal, Ar.	PT-LMO
N67PA	78	Learjet 35A	35A-208	67PA LLC. West Columbia, SC.	(N39DJ)
N67PC	01	Citation Bravo	550-1007	Avent LLC/Prent Corp. Janesville, Wi.	N717CB
N67PW	95	Falcon 50	248	67PW LLC. Teterboro, NJ.	N25UB
N67RX	00	Global Express	9067	Wander Inc. Morristown, NJ.	N700BK
N67SF*	81	Citation II	550-0243	Seneca Foods Corp. Penn Yan, NY.	N214MD
N67TJ	80	Westwind-Two	299	Employee Benefit Management Services Inc. Billings, Mt.	(N288SJ)
N67TM	00	Gulfstream 4SP	1409	EMC Corp. Bedford-Hanscom Field, Ma.	N317GA
N67TW	00	Citation Excel	560-5122	Tom Wood Inc/TW Equipment Leasing Inc. Indianapolis, In.	N5211F
N67WB	97	Falcon 900EX	16	BDA/US Services Ltd & WRBC Transportation Inc. White Plains.	N916EX
N68BP	68	Falcon 20C	155	Vinson Group G111 LLC. Chesterfield, Mo.	N68BC
N68CB	99	Hawker 800XP	258453	Cracker Barrel Old Country Store Inc. Lebanon, Tn.	N802TA
N68ED	94	Citation VI	650-0239	Betteroads Asphalt Corp. San Juan, PR.	N17QC
N68ES	01	Learjet 31A	31A-221	Premier Aviation Leasing LLC. Boise, Id.	
N68GW	06	Citation Excel XLS	560-5626	Grady-White Boats Inc. Greenville, NC.	N5197M
N68HG	00	Citation Excel	560-5103	HCA Squared LLC. Nashville, Tn.	N68HC
N68JV	00	Beechjet 400A	RK-296	Johnsonville Foods, Milwaukee, Wi.	N311HS
N68PC	05	Learjet 45	45-289	Southern Company Services Inc. Atlanta, Ga.	N5013U
N68PT	81	Westwind-1124	325	Thomas Aircraft Sales Inc. Mulvane, Ks.	N467MW
N68QB	76	Learjet 35A	35A-079	American Jet International Corp. Houston, Tx.	N500DS
N68TS	83	Citation II	550-0479	D & R Maintenance LLC. Brentwood, Tn.	N45NS
N68VP	01	Learjet 31A	31A-232	Dycom Industries Inc. Stuart, Fl.	N668VP
N69BH	79	Learjet 35A	35A-276	Midlantic Jet Charters Inc. Atlantic City, NJ.	N613RR
N69EC	85	Falcon 200	498	CPRE LLC. Burr Ridge, Il.	N422L
N69FH	05	CitationJet CJ-3	525B-0042	CJ3 Inc. Norwood, Ma.	N5163K
N69GB	74	Falcon 10	24	Arnold & Arnold Real Estate Inc. Naples, Fl.	N230RS
N69LJ	94	Learjet 60	60-027	Federation International de l'Automobile, Biggin Hill, UK.	N12FU
N69PL	78	Learjet 25D	25D-253	Oil International Trading Group Inc. Fort Lauderdale, Fl.	YV-1049CP
N69VH	83	Learjet 55	55-062	Midlantic Jet Charters Inc. Atlantic City, NJ.	(N107MC)
N69WU	81	Sabre-65	465-51	40 Degrees North LLC. Drums, Pa.	N114LG
N69X	60	MS 760 Paris	90	AEI Fund Management Inc. St Paul, Mn.	(N5TA)
N69XW	74	Citation	500-0142	Pro-Trak Trailers Inc. Wills Point, Tx.	N200GM
N70AE	02	Learjet 45	45-227	Allegheny Energy Service Corp. Latrobe, Pa.	N903RL
N70AG	97	Gulfstream V	522	Chargers Football LLC. San Diego, Ca.	N20HN
N70AX	78	Learjet 35A	35A-155	AMTS Aircraft Holdings LLC. Sugar Grove, Il.	N110AE
N70AY	01	Learjet 31A	31A-188	Vamco International Inc. Allegheny County, Pa.	N70AE
N70BG	77	Citation Eagle	501-0024	Wheelock Law Firm LLC. Orlando, Fl.	N724EA
N70BJ	92	Beechjet 400A	RK-39	Corporate Jets Inc/Landmark Aviation LLC. Winston Salem, Ms.	(N97XP)
N70BR	02	390 Premier 1	RB-70	Independent Trustees Inc. Chapel Hill, NC.	ZS-ABG
N70CA	75	Citation	500-0234	Aero Sales Inc. Salem, Or.	PH-CTG
N70CG	80	Citation 1/SP	501-0187	SMW Aviation Inc/Saturn Machine & Welding Co. Sturgis, Ky.	(N614DD)
N70CK	68	Falcon 20C	128	Michigan Air Freight LLC. Ypsilanti, Mi.	N228CK
N70CR	05	Challenger 300	20048	NCR Corp. Dayton, Oh.	N348TS
N70DE	89	Beechjet 400	RJ-56	Omnipol A/S. Nekazanka, Czech Republic.	OK-UZI
N70EW	99	Global Express	9026	EWA Holdings LLC/East-West Air Inc.Teterboro, NJ.	C-GEWV
N70FL	07	Falcon 7X	7	Flight Levels Corp/LAPA SA. Buenos Aires, Argentina.	F-WWUD
N70HL	76	Sabre-60	306-102	Strata Aviation LLC. Taylor, Mi.	N265TJ
N70KW	02	CitationJet CJ-2	525A-0135	Wilair Inc. Memphis, Tn.	(N114RP)
N70LF	96	Falcon 900EX	9	G C I Aviation Inc/Gary Comer Inc. Chicago-O'Hare, Wi.	N909FJ
N70LJ	78	Learjet 36A	36A-044	Jet ICU Leasing Inc. Ozona, Fl.	N286AB
N70MG	73	Citation	500-0063	Billionaire Business Jets LLC. Van Nuys, Ca.	OO-RST
N70NB	81	Citation 1/SP	501-0209	McBurlow Leasing Corp. Laurel, Ms.	N98RG

Reg	Yr	Type	c/n	Owner/Operator	Prev Regn
☐ N70NE	87	BAe 125/800A	NA0407	Berkshire Leasing LLC. Pittsfield, Ma.	N552BA
☐ N70PC	01	Learjet 45	45-172	Southern Company Services Inc. Atlanta, Ga.	
☐ N70PL	80	Falcon 20F-5B	436	Pelican Leasing Inc. Little Rock, Ar.	N436RB
☐ N70PS	98	Global Express	9012	American International Group Inc. Teterboro, NJ.	C-GDGY
☐ N70QB	81	HS 125/700A	NA0289	River Run Projects LLC. Nashua, NH.	N802RC
☐ N70SK	70	Learjet 25	25-049	S K Logistics Inc. Jacksonville, Fl. (status ?).	N70HJ
☐ N70SW	74	Citation	500-0236	Sunburst Properties LLC. Summerville, SC.	N320RG
☐ N70TS	75	Citation	500-0281	Starbird Inc. Maitland, Fl.	N62TW
☐ N70TT	01	Gulfstream G200	045	CJE Inc. Fort Worth, Tx.	N107GX
☐ N70WA	76	Citation	500-0320	Wrangler Aviation Corp. Norman, Ok. (status ?).	(I-CARY)
☐ N70XL	05	Citation Excel XLS	560-5566	Delhaize America Inc. Salisbury, NC.	N52113
☐ N71AL	91	Learjet 31A	31A-039	Bastille Energy Corp. Oklahoma City, Ok.	N23AX
☐ N71BD	00	Gulfstream 4SP	1415	JJSA Aviation LLC. San Jose, Ca.	N415GA
☐ N71CC	73	Sabre-60A	306-71	Commercial Aviation Enterprises Inc. Delray Beach, Fl.	N1028Y
☐ N71CK	77	Learjet 36A	36A-035	Michigan Air Freight LLC. Ypsilanti, Mi.	VH-BIB
☐ N71FB	00	Learjet 31A	31A-205	Roxbury Technologies Inc. Zurich, Switzerland.	VP-CFB
☐ N71FE	03	Falcon 2000EX	13	FirstEnergy Solutions Corp. Akron-Canton, Oh.	N500FE
☐ N71FS	94	Astra-1125SP	071	SJA/Najafi Aviation LLC. Phoenix, Az.	N60AJ
☐ N71GH	83	Diamond 1A	A071SA	Fox Air Inc. Jacksonville, Fl.	N70GA
☐ N71GK	91	Falcon 900B	107	Fox Air Inc. Jacksonville, Fl.	N23BJ
☐ N71KV	03	390 Premier 1	RB-71	KVOG LLC/KV Oil & Gas Inc. Lexington, Ky.	N4471P
☐ N71L	82	Citation 1/SP	501-0242	Lindair Inc. Sarasota, Fl.	N500BK
☐ N71LP	79	Citation 1/SP	501-0120	M Kaplan Companies LLC. Houston, Tx.	OY-CPW
☐ N71LU	83	Citation III	650-0019	Liberty University Inc. Lynchburg, Va.	N707MS
☐ N71M	76	Falcon 10	88	Northern Illinois Flight Center Inc. Lake in the Hills, Il.	F-GHER
☐ N71NF	06	Learjet 40	45-2058	NFI Industries, Vineland, NJ.	
☐ N71NP	01	Challenger 604	5504	Nationwide Mutual Insurance Co. Columbus, Oh.	C-GLYH
☐ N71PG	75	Learjet 36	36-013	Phoenix Air Group Inc. Cartersville, Ga.	D-CBRD
☐ N71TV	00	Gulfstream 4SP	1430	The Direct TV Group Inc. Van Nuys, ca.	N913SQ
☐ N71WJ	79	Gulfstream II SP	248	W & J Air LLC/Bisso Marine, Houston, Tx.	(N70WG)
☐ N71ZZ	07	Global Express XRS	9239	Bombardier Aerospace Corp. Windsor Locks, Ct.	C-FLLO
☐ N72AX	81	Learjet 35A	35A-419	Omni Air International Inc. Tulsa, Ok.	N35SM
☐ N72BD	00	Gulfstream 4SP	1420	JJSA Aviation LLC. San Jose, Ca.	N420GA
☐ N72BP	79	Gulfstream 2TT	238	Charles Robert Palmer, Houston, Tx.	N335H
☐ N72CE	05	Learjet 60	60-285	Cimarex Energy Co. Denver, Co.	N5009T
☐ N72CK	78	Learjet 35A	35A-165	Kitty Hawk Charters Inc. Morristown, Tn.	N16BJ
☐ N72DA	77	Learjet 35A	35A-098	Duncan Aviation Inc. Lincoln, Ne.	(N998DJ)
☐ N72EL	86	Astra-1125	018	EDJCO Transit LLC. Bannockburn, Il.	N72FL
☐ N72EP*	84	Citation III	650-0058	Jeffy Jet LLC. Augusta, Ga.	N143PL
☐ N72FC	00	Hawker 800XP	258519	Best Aviation Inc. Baldwin, Ga.	N443M
☐ N72FD	99	Citation X	750-0072	D & F Partners LLC. Wilmington, De.	XA-VER
☐ N72GD	06	390 Premier 1A	RB-163	Stallion Enterprises LLC. Bournemouth-Hurn, UK.	N7163E
☐ N72GH	03	Hawker 400XP	RK-370	PCMT Aviation/The Palmer Team Inc. Sacramento, Ca.	(N470CW)
☐ N72GW	76	JetStar 2	5205	Hudson Leonard Drilling Co. Pampa, Tx.	N454JB
☐ N72HG	86	Beechjet 400	RJ-11	Ameriflight Aviation, Orlando, Fl. (was A1011SA).	N111BA
☐ N72JF	77	Learjet 35A	35A-088	AirNet Systems Inc. Columbus, Oh.	OE-GBR
☐ N72JW	00	CitationJet CJ-1	525-0406	Sims Wholesale Co/James Walker Aircraft LLC. Lynchburg, Va.	N5124F
☐ N72LL	79	Learjet 35A	35A-275	Jet Management Inc. Sanford, Fl.	N235SC
☐ N72NP	98	Challenger 604	5385	Nationwide Mutual Insurance Co. Columbus, Oh.	C-GLXD
☐ N72PS	07	Falcon 2000EX EASY	116	American International Group Inc. Teterboro, NJ.	N116EX
☐ N72PX	87	Falcon 900	18	American International Group Inc. Teterboro, NJ.	N72PS
☐ N72RK	94	Gulfstream 4SP	1248	Willowbend Golf Management Liberty LLC. Ma.	N244DS
☐ N72SG	04	Citation Excel XLS	560-5508	SIG Aviation LLC/Strickland Insurance Group, Goldsboro, NC.	N.....
☐ N72SJ	04	390 Premier 1	RB-115	Superstar Jet Corp. Portsmouth, NH.	N6015Y
☐ N72VJ	80	Citation 1/SP	501-0149	JVB LLC. San Diego, Ca.	N96FP
☐ N72WC	85	Learjet 25G	25G-371	Aircraft Guaranty Corp. Houston, Tx. (trustor ?).	N4ZB
☐ N72WS	97	Falcon 900EX	14	American International Group Inc. Teterboro, NJ.	F-WWFN
☐ N72WY	98	Challenger 604	5394	Fort Mitchell Construction LLC. Fort Mitchell, Ky.	N141DL
☐ N73CE	65	Learjet 23	23-068	Yanks Air Museum, Baldwin Park, Ca.	XB-GRR
☐ N73CK	77	Learjet 35A	35A-092	Kalitta Charters LLC. Detroit-Willow Run, Mi.	N39WA
☐ N73CL	82	Westwind-Two	365	Polar Bear Express LLC. Las Vegas, Nv.	N2BG
☐ N73DJ	79	Learjet 25D	25D-273	Water Street Aviation LLC. Olympia, Wa.	N321AS
☐ N73EM	06	CitationJet CJ-3	525B-0123	CJ2-123 LLC. Wilmington, DE.	N.....
☐ N73GH	97	Falcon 50EX	261	TCBY Ents/Hickinbotham Investments Inc. Little Rock, Ar.	(N97FJ)
☐ N73GP	86	Learjet 55B	55B-127	CADDO Investments Inc. Las Vegas, Nv.	HZ-AM2
☐ N73HM	88	Citation III	650-0169	Dash Services Inc/Conway Air Corp. Chesterfield, Mo.	N749DC

Reg	Yr	Type	c/n	Owner/Operator	Prev Regn
☐ N73KH	93	Citation V	560-0220	Killam & Hurd, San Antonio, Tx.	N23UB
☐ N73M	98	Gulfstream V	547	3M Co. St Paul, Mn.	N647GA
☐ N73ME	01	Citation X	750-0155	Mountain Enterprises Inc. Lexington, Ky.	N551AM
☐ N73MP	74	Citation	500-0164	Redd Realty Services, Atlanta, Ga.	(N164GJ)
☐ N73MR	81	Falcon 20F-5B	449	73 MR LLC. Dallas, Tx.	N39TT
☐ N73PJ	03	390 Premier 1	RB-101	Phillips & Jordan Inc. Knoxville, Tn.	N101PN
☐ N73RP	98	Gulfstream V	529	Warner Communications, Ronkonkoma, NY.	N529GA
☐ N73SK	84	Citation 1/SP	501-0679	H B D Inc. Missoula,	(N501HH)
☐ N73ST	79	Citation II	550-0376	S & T Marketing Services LLC. Brooklyn, Mn. (was 551-0022).	N30EJ
☐ N73TJ	79	Sabre-65	465-12	ABA Aviation Resources Inc. Doral, Fl.	N529SC
☐ N73UC*	95	Citation VII	650-7049	Desert Sky LLC/United Leasing Inc. Evansville, In.	N182PA
☐ N73UP	99	Hawker 800XP	258473	UnumProvident Corp. Chattanooga, Tn.	
☐ N73ZZ	07	Global Express	9251	Bombardier Aerospace Corp. Windsor Locks, Ct.	C-FMKW
☐ N74A	68	Gulfstream 2B	36	MDA-Missile Defence Agency, Tulsa-R L Jones, Ok.	N901KB
☐ N74BJ	80	Sabre-65	465-44	Rex Amini, San Antonio, Tx.	N7NR
☐ N74FH	79	Citation Eagle	501-0138	Flybylight LLC. Carlsbad, Ca.	N501CE
☐ N74FS	90	Falcon 900	85	35-55 Partnership LLC/Fayez Serofim & Co. Houston, Tx.	N461FJ
☐ N74GR	82	Challenger 601	3001	GAR Aviation Ltd. Houston, Tx.	N789DR
☐ N74GW	04	Hawker 800XP	258706	Air Blessing LLC/Stockamp & Assocs. Lake Oswego, Or.	N706XP
☐ N74HH	69	Gulfstream II SP	74	74HH LLC. Missoula, Mt.	N74TJ
☐ N74HR	84	Citation 1/SP	501-0677	GAR Aviation Ltd. Houston, Tx.	N54CG
☐ N74JA	82	Challenger 600S	1060	Pin Oak Stud LLC. Lexington, Ky.	N22AZ
☐ N74JE	85	Citation S/II	S550-0074	John Eaves Law Firm, Jackson, Ms.	N274PG
☐ N74LL	74	Citation Eagle	500-0212	Centurion American Aviation LLC. Bedford, Tx.	N92B
☐ N74LM	85	Citation S/II	S550-0041	Blessey Travel LLC. Big Sky, Mt.	N74BJ
☐ N74NP	03	Hawker 800XP	258631	Nationwide Mutual Insurance Co. Columbus, Oh.	N631XP
☐ N74PG	01	CitationJet CJ-1	525-0476	Computer Associates International Inc. Islip, NY.	N50ET
☐ N74PT	06	Learjet 45	45-314	The Palmer Team Inc. Sacramento, Ca.	
☐ N74RP	04	Gulfstream G550	5058	Time Warner Inc. Ronkonkoma, NY.	N958GA
☐ N74RQ	72	Gulfstream II SP	113	White Industries Inc. Bates City, Mo. (status ?).	N74RT
☐ N74RT	78	Gulfstream 2B	219	Visionaire 1 LLC. Wilmington, De.	(N575E)
☐ N74TS	82	Falcon 50	106	Aero Toy Store LLC. Fort Lauderdale, Fl.	N9300C
☐ N74VC	80	Sabre-65	465-17	Jett Aire Florida One Inc. West Palm Beach, Fl.	N32290
☐ N74VF	88	Citation III	650-0156	Vernon Faulconer Inc. Lafayette, La.	N209A
☐ N74ZC	04	Challenger 300	20018	Ziegler Inc. Minneapolis, Mn.	N84ZC
☐ N74ZZ	07	Global Express	9260	Bombardier Aerospace Corp. Windsor Locks, Ct.	C-FMND
☐ N75AX	79	Learjet 25D	25D-270	Anthony Aiello, DuPage, Il.	N123CG
☐ N75B	91	Citation V	560-0156	Hoar Construction LLC. Birmingham, Al.	N560L
☐ N75BC	86	Westwind-1124	426	James Higgins MD Inc. Tulsa, Ok.	N426WW
☐ N75BL	74	Learjet 25C	25C-156	Jet Makers LLC. Denison, Tx.	N613SZ
☐ N75BS	74	Sabre-75A	380-12	Centurion Investments Inc. St Louis, Mo.	(N4WJ)
☐ N75CC	92	Gulfstream 4	1182	Crown Controls Corp. New Bremen, Oh.	N202LS
☐ N75CK	78	Learjet 25D	25D-256	Michigan Air Freight LLC. Ypsilanti, Mi.	N6LL
☐ N75CT	06	Learjet 60	60-299	Coyne International Enterprises Corp. Syracuse, NY.	N50153
☐ N75GA	76	HS 125/F600A	256070	Duff Young Foundation Inc. West Palm Beach, Fl.	(N76TJ)
☐ N75HL	80	Sabre-65	465-16	My 3 Sons LLC. Charlottesville, Va.	N603MA
☐ N75HS	97	Citation X	750-0037	Rex Realty Co. St Louis, Mo.	N51160
☐ N75HU	00	Citation Excel	560-5119	Sherrohil LLC. Dover, De.	N357WC
☐ N75MC	86	Citation S/II	S550-0109	Leche Inc. Key Biscayne, Fl.	(N50SL)
☐ N75PP	02	CitationJet CJ-2	525A-0132	Von Housen Motors Inc. Carmichael, Ca.	N5211F
☐ N75RJ	91	Citation II	550-0692	Southeastern Freight Lines, Columbia Metro, SC.	N692TT
☐ N75RL	01	Beechjet 400A	RK-312	RLI Insurance Co. Peoria, Il.	N5012U
☐ N75RP	98	Gulfstream V	528	Warner Communications, Ronkonkoma, NY.	N80RP
☐ N75TP	07	Citation Excel XLS	560-5768	Cessna Aircraft Co. Wichita, Ks.	N5064Q
☐ N75VC	81	Sabre-65	465-71	NCI Operating Corp. Houston, Tx.	N75GL
☐ N75WE	84	Falcon 50	152	Fisher Scientific International Inc. Portsmouth, NH.	N75W
☐ N75WP	97	Citation V Ultra	560-0449	Salt River Project Ag/Power District, Phoenix, Az,	N555WK
☐ N75XL	05	Citation Excel XLS	560-5575	Delhaize America Inc. Salisbury, NC.	N5267J
☐ N76AM	79	Falcon 10	157	Moosehead Aviation Inc/Jet Maine Inc. Greenville, Me.	(N450CT)
☐ N76AS	82	Citation II	550-0432	T & S Aircraft, Huntersville, NC.	I-ASAZ
☐ N76AX	78	Learjet 25D	25D-254	Laredo Cardiovascular Consultants PA. Laredo, Tx.	I-AVJE
☐ N76CK	68	Learjet 25	25-020	Kalitta Charters LLC. Detroit-Willow Run, Mi.	N500JS
☐ N76CS	02	Hawker 800XP	258595	CSX Transportation Inc. Jacksonville, Fl.	N61495
☐ N76ER	87	Westwind-Two	369	Starwood Aviation Inc. Carson City, Nv.	N85WC
☐ N76FC	05	Hawker 850XP	258784	Ferro Corp. Cleveland, Oh.	N784XP
☐ N76FD	88	Falcon 900	41	Grindstone Aviation LLC. Lafayette Hill, Pa.	N404FF

Reg	Yr	Type	c/n	Owner/Operator	Prev Regn
N76HL	04	390 Premier 1	RB-112	Hixson Lumber Sales/Hixson Aviation LLC. Pine Bluff, Ar.	N60322
N76RP	00	Gulfstream 4SP	1440	Warner Communications, Ronkonkoma, NY.	N997AG
N76SF	05	Challenger 604	5603	State Farm Insurance Companies, Bloomington, Il.	C-GLXF
N76TF	97	Citation V Ultra	560-0431	Teleflex Inc. Limerick, Pa.	N560JP
N76UM	70	Learjet 25	25-051	Jet Makers Inc. Denison, Tx.	(N760A)
N76WR	98	Citation V Ultra	560-0459	Destinations LLC. Des Moines, Ia.	N79PM
N76ZZ	07	Global Express	9266	Bombardier Aerospace Corp. Windsor Locks, Ct.	C-FNDO
N77BT	84	Gulfstream 3	429	World Harvest Church Inc. Columbus-Rickenbacker, Oh.	N100HZ
N77C	79	JetStar 2	5232	Trenton Foods/Parn Aviation Corp. Dover, De.	N90QP
N77CP	98	Gulfstream V	565	Pfizer Inc. Mercer County Airport, NJ.	N460GA
N77CS	03	Hawker 800XP	258620	CSX Transportation Inc. Jacksonville, Fl.	N620XP
N77D	97	Gulfstream 4SP	1340	Luxury Delivery Service Inc. Allegheny County, Pa.	N800AL
N77DB	01	CitationJet CJ-1	525-0443	D'Arrigo Bros of California, Salinas, Ca.	N443CJ
N77FD	82	Citation 1/SP	501-0250	Ingles Markets Inc. Asheville, NC.	
N77FK	98	Gulfstream 4SP	1357	K Services Inc. Teterboro, NJ.	N357GA
N77HF	94	Citation VII	650-7036	Taft Sales & Leasing LLC. Dallas, Tx.	N95HF
N77HN	06	Learjet 40	45-2070	Harold W Nix, Addison, Tx.	
N77HW	66	JetStar-6	5080	Delta Omni Corp. Corona, Ca. (status ?)	N914P
N77JW	73	Falcon 10	6	N59CC LLC. Scottsdale, Az.	N59CC
N77LA	85	BAe 125/800A	258029	L2 Aviation Group/Aviation Charter Services, Indianapolis.	N600HS
N77LX	95	Citation VII	650-7051	Lexicon Inc. Little Rock, Ar.	N965JC
N77M	06	CitationJet CJ-3	525B-0100	J L Mark Inc. Chandler, Az.	N.....
N77MR	77	Learjet 24E	24E-351	Goldenwings Inc. Bloomington, Il.	(N94BD)
N77NJ	90	Learjet 35A	35A-658	National Jets Inc. Fort Lauderdale, Fl.	N162EM
N77NR	89	Citation V	560-0009	Nix, Patterson & Roach LLP. Longview-Gregg County, Tx.	N77HU
N77PR	81	Citation II	550-0211	PMP Air LLC/Peter Pan Bus Lines, Springfield, Ma.	N77PH
N77PY	94	Learjet 31A	31A-089	Wal-Mart Stores Inc. Rogers, Ar.	N77PH
N77SF	79	Falcon 10	141	Seneca Foods Corp. Penn Yan, NY.	N900D
N77TC	07	Hawker 900XP	HA-7	Timken Co. Akron-Canton, Oh.	N807HB
N77UW	98	Citation Excel	560-5005	Meisenbach LLC. Seattle, Wa.	N166MB
N77VR	05	CitationJet CJ-2	525A-0240	Georgia Air South Inc. Valdosta, Ga.	N5194B
N77VZ	99	CitationJet	525-0344	Fred J Smith Jr. Raleigh-Durham, NC.	N77VR
N77WL	90	Gulfstream 4	1140	Presley CMR Inc. Santa Ana, Ca.	N827JM
N78AP	84	Citation III	650-0056	Apothecas Aviation LLC. Ronkonkoma, NY.	N56JV
N78CK	81	Citation II	550-0319	Marks Aviation LLC. Mobile, Al.	N76CK
N78FJ	98	Falcon 2000	78	AM & JB Corp. Cuyahoga County, Oh.	N262PC
N78GJ	80	Westwind-1124	310	Mid Oaks Investments LLC. Buffalo Grove, Il.	D-CBBD
N78LF	81	Learjet 50	77	McDonough Leasing LLC. Scottsdale, Az.	N77NT
N78LT	81	Falcon 50	75	BTE Equipment LLC. Broomfield, Co.	N850CA
N78MC	77	Learjet 35A	35A-117	Westfield Group Services Inc. Allentown, Pa.	N3155B
N78MD	01	Citation Bravo	550-0970	MDU Resources Group Inc. Bismarck, ND.	N367BP
N78NT	00	Falcon 2000	121	Fans Air Ltd. Jacksonville, Fl.	VP-BNT
N78PR	94	Learjet 31A	31A-090	Wal-Mart Stores Inc. Rogers, Ar.	N78PH
N78PT	80	Westwind-Two	304	Westwind Services LLC. Little Rock, Ar.	N13NL
N78SD	00	Challenger 604	5469	Constructora Sambil CA. Caracas, Venezuela.	N469RC
N78SL	04	Citation X	750-0238	Schweizter Engineering Laboratories Inc. Pullman, Wa.	N238CX
N78TC	05	Challenger 300	20070	The Timken Co. Canton, Oh.	C-FGYU
N78ZZ	07	Global Express	9267	Echo Aircraft Holdings LLC. Beirut, Lebanon.	C-FNDQ
N79AD	00	Global Express	9058	Arthur S DeMoss Foundation Inc. West Palm Beach, Fl.	N700AD
N79AN	93	Challenger 601-3R	5140	AAR International Financial Services, Wood Dale, Il.	N79AD
N79BJ	94	Learjet 31A	31A-101	NASCAR Inc. Daytona Beach, Fl.	N900R
N79BK	79	Citation 1/SP	501-0111	Marine Oil Service of NYC LLC. Norfolk, Va.	N59WP
N79EH	78	HS 125/700A	NA0233	MKC Air Inc/Ker Inc. Largo, Fl.	N79TS
N79EL	98	Beechjet 400A	RK-214	G Kirkham/D F S Furniture Co. East Midlands, UK.	
N79EV*	73	Learjet 25C	25C-097	Marc Solomon, Wilmington, De.	(N220AR)
N79FT	78	Citation 1/SP	501-0079	WE Aviation LLC. Omaha, Ne.	N250GM
N79KF	86	Citation III	650-0118	Klaussner Corporate Services Inc. Asheboro, NC.	N770MR
N79LC	79	Westwind-1124	257	Wilmington Aero Ventures Inc. Wilmington, De.	N124UF
N79PF	00	Citation Excel	560-5151	Principal Life Insurance Co. Des Moines, Ia.	N5147B
N79PG	04	Citation Sovereign	680-0018	Principal Life Insurance Co. Des Moines, Ia.	N.....
N79RS	73	Citation	500-0107	Grover Sam Harben III, Gainesville, Ga.	N40RW
N79SE	00	Learjet 31A	31A-206	Southeast Air Transportation Inc. Montgomery, Al.	N5000E
N79SF	78	Learjet 36A	36A-041	Phoenix Air Group Inc. Cartersville, Ga.	
N79TJ	79	Falcon 10	148	Pannar P/L. Rand, RSA.	N103PJ
N80A	98	Gulfstream 4SP	1348	United States Steel Corp. Pittsburgh, Pa.	N348GA
N80AB	92	Citation V	560-0169	EMI-PA Inc/Express Marine Inc. Camden, NJ.	N6888C
Reg	Yr	Type	c/n	Owner/Operator	Prev Regn

Reg	Yr	Type	c/n	Owner/Operator	Prev Regn
☐ N80AJ	73	Citation	500-0100	Diamondback Torch LLC/Gulfport Energy, Oklahoma City, Ok.	(N58BT)
☐ N80AP	75	Learjet 24D	24D-312	Air Ambulance Professionals Inc. Fort Lauderdale, Fl.	N312NA
☐ N80AR	81	Learjet 35A	35A-454	Sarina Technologies, Pleasanton, Ca.	(N80KR)
☐ N80AT	00	Gulfstream 4SP	1410	Taubman Enterprises Inc. Waterford, Mi.	N318GA
☐ N80AW	80	Citation II	550-0186	Blue Heron Aviation Sales LLC. Melbourne, Fl.	YV-187CP
☐ N80C	02	CitationJet CJ-2	525A-0104	Eighty Charlie LLC. Avon, Co.	N.....
☐ N80CJ	80	Citation 1/SP	501-0159	Asian Ventures Co. Louisville, Ky.	N8189J
☐ N80CK	74	Learjet 24D	24D-309	TriCoastal Air Inc. Swanton, Oh.	N789AA
☐ N80DX*	93	Learjet 60	60-012	SSC Enterprises LLC/Data Exchange Corp. Camarillo, Ca.	N626KM
☐ N80E	04	Hawker 800XP	258680	United States Steel Corp. Pittsburgh, Pa.	N680XP
☐ N80EL	72	Learjet 25B	25B-092	Lanter Eye Care & Laser Surgery PC. Indianapolis, In.	N60DK
☐ N80F	00	Falcon 900EX	76	Anheuser Busch Companies Inc. St Louis, Mo.	F-WLJV
☐ N80GJ	88	BAe 125/800A	258136	Meurice Aviation Inc. Lawrenceville, Ga.	I-SDFG
☐ N80GM	80	Citation II	550-0147	WRI Aviation LLC/Western Roofing Inc. Nampa, Id.	(N155JK)
☐ N80GP	98	Falcon 50EX	274	Godwin Pumps of America Inc. Bridgeport, NJ.	(N904GP)
☐ N80GR	02	Citation Encore	560-0616	Allis-Chalmers Rental Services Inc. Patterson, La.	N616CE
☐ N80HB	07	CitationJet CJ-3	525B-0163	HBC Aviation Inc. Guernsey, C.I.	N5267K
☐ N80HD	02	Hawker 800XP	258609	Harley-Davidson Motor Co. Milwaukee, Wi.	N60159
☐ N80J	04	Hawker 800XP	258681	United States Steel Corp. Pittsburgh, Pa.	N681XP
☐ N80LP	02	Citation Excel	560-5249	JEP Leasing LLC/ASI Technology Corp. Henderson, Nv.	N5096S
☐ N80PG	76	Learjet 35	35-063	Phoenix Air Group Inc. Cartersville, Ga.	N663CA
☐ N80PJ	78	Learjet 25D	25D-260	Private Jets LLC. Oklahoma City, Ok.	N74RD
☐ N80PK	99	Hawker 800XP	258442	HEH Corp/HEH Nashville, Nashville, Tn.	N442XP
☐ N80Q	04	Gulfstream G450	4012	United States Steel Corp. Pittsburgh, Pa.	N812GA
☐ N80RP	97	Learjet 45	45-008	Eaton Corp. Cleveland, Oh.	N745E
☐ N80SL	79	Citation 1/SP	501-0294	James R Smith, Fort Scott, Ks. (was 500-0391).	N8EH
☐ N80TS	87	Beechjet 400	RJ-34	King Air 203 Leasing Inc. Caracas, Venezuela.	N7EY
☐ N80X	99	Citation Excel	560-5054	Capital City Press, Baton Rouge, La.	N1306V
☐ N81AX	79	Learjet 25D	25D-279	Med Air LLC. Lawrenceville, Ga.	N41ZP
☐ N81EB	77	Citation 1/SP	501-0003	T C Mueller Oil & Gas/TCM Air Inc. Fort Smith, Ar.	N781L
☐ N81ER	07	CitationJet CJ-3	525B-0190	Edward Rose Building Enterprises, Pontiac, Mi.	N5036Q
☐ N81FR	76	Learjet 35A	35A-081	AirNet Systems Inc. Columbus, Oh.	N118DA
☐ N81HR	07	390 Premier 1A	RB-200	Helderberg Aviation Inc/Hannay Reels Inc. Schenectady, NY.	
☐ N81KA	78	HS 125/700A	NA0227	South Aviation Inc. Fort Lauderdale, Fl.	N10CZ
☐ N81LR	02	Citation Bravo	550-1015	NKT Commercial LLC. San Luis Obispo, Ca.	N81ER
☐ N81MR	86	Learjet 35A	35A-622	N81MR LLC. Hollywood, Fl.	N610R
☐ N81P	81	Falcon 20F-5B	446	Pilot Corp. Knoxville, Tn.	N446P
☐ N81PJ	61	MS 760 Paris-1R	81	DFX LLC. Calhoun, Ga.	No 81
☐ N81RR	79	Gulfstream 2TT	246	New Hampshire Flight Procurement LLC. Pittsfield, NH.	N14LT
☐ N81SF	85	Citation III	650-0074	Broadway Air Corp/Stifel Financial Corp. St Louis, Mo.	N93CL
☐ N81SH	00	Citation Excel	560-5101	The Conair Group Inc. Pittsburgh, Pa.	N88845
☐ N81SN	98	Falcon 900EX	41	Amrash Aviation LLC. Greenville-Spartanburg, SC.	N5737
☐ N81SV	94	Falcon 900B	146	Mellon Bank NA. Allegheny County, Pa.	N4MB
☐ N81TJ	90	Beechjet 400A	RK-14	Trimfoot Aviation/Crown Diversified Industries Inc. St Louis	(N414RK)
☐ N81TX	76	Falcon 10	81	S R Forwarding Inc. Laredo, Tx.	N700BD
☐ N81ZZ	06	Global 5000	9222	Execujet Middle East Ltd. Dubai, UAE.	C-FJNJ
☐ N82A	89	Gulfstream 4	1068	Prudential Insurance Co. Newark, NJ.	N90AE
☐ N82AE	00	CitationJet CJ-1	525-0412	EDCO Products Inc. Hopkins, Mn.	N5161J
☐ N82AF	74	Sabre-80A	380-21	Electropac Co. Manchester, NH.	N647JP
☐ N82AJ	78	Citation 1/SP	501-0282	Freizeit Gastronomie,Vienna, Austria. (was 500-0376).	XA-SQX
☐ N82AX	80	Learjet 25D	25D-301	Tropical Jets of SRQ Inc. Sarasota, Fl.	N25CZ
☐ N82BE	99	Astra-1125SPX	113	BEF Aviation Co. Columbus, Oh.	(N297GA)
☐ N82CA	69	HS 125/731	NA730	Dean Coastal LLC. Tampa, Fl.	(N101HS)
☐ N82CR	70	Gulfstream II SP	80	Northrop Grumman Systems Corp. El Segundo, Ca.	N510RH
☐ N82CW	98	Challenger 604	5395	Costco Wholesale Inc. Seattle, Wa.	N606CC
☐ N82DT	78	Citation 1/SP	501-0289	C340 Ltd. North Royalton, Oh. (was 500-0375).	N501NZ
☐ N82GG	78	Learjet 36A	36A-040	Cornua Legis Inc. Honolulu, Hi.	N72RV
☐ N82GM	95	Citation VII	650-7064	Gander Mountain Co. Anoka County, Mn.	N5112
☐ N82KK	97	Learjet 60	60-095	Krispy Kreme Doughnut Corp. Winston-Salem, NC. 'Donut 1'	(N82KD)
☐ N82KW	01	Citation Excel	560-5202	Progress Energy Inc. Raleigh-Durham, NC.	(N467SA)
☐ N82P	81	Citation 1/SP	501-0208	Pink Jeep Tours Inc. Sedona, Az.	(N25M)
☐ N82PJ	68	Falcon 20D	177	Peaks Aviation Services Inc. Denison, Tx.	N41BP
☐ N82QD	93	Beechjet 400A	RK-72	Quality Dining Inc/Burger Management South Bend Inc. In.	N428WE
☐ N82RP	92	Falcon 900B	116	Rich Products/Rich Aviation Inc. Buffalo, NY.	N5VN
☐ N82SR	85	Hawker 800SP	258026	Silverleaf Resorts Inc. Dallas, Tx.	N826CW
☐ N82ST	81	Falcon 50	85	Pioneer Private Aviation of Delaware, Minneapolis, Mn.	N254DV

Reg	Yr	Type	c/n	Owner/Operator	Prev Regn
N82SV	96	Falcon 900B	163	Mellon Bank NA. Allegheny County, Pa.	N25MB
N82TS	74	Learjet 25B	25B-154	Royal Air Freight Inc. Pontiac, Mi.	N47DK
N83BG	82	Diamond 1	A018SA	JRS Aviation Inc. St Petersburg, Fl.	(N831TJ)
N83CG	83	Diamond 1A	A032SA	Advantage Jet Partners Inc. Albany, Ga.	(N996DR)
N83CK	74	Learjet 25B	25B-183	Michigan Air Freight LLC. Ypsilanti, Mi.	N5LL
N83CP	01	Gulfstream V	635	Pfizer Inc. Mercer County Airport, NJ.	N522GA
N83CW	01	Gulfstream V	649	Costco Wholesale Inc. Seattle, Wa.	N649GA
N83DM	81	Citation 1/SP	501-0227	DDM Holdings Inc. Wilmington, De.	N47CF
N83EP	89	Citation V	560-0021	Zuma Air LLC/Exploreco Pipe Ltd. Houston, Tx.	N410DW
N83FJ	81	Falcon 50	74	Civic Center Corp/Anheuser Busch, Chesterfield, Mo.	F-WZHA
N83FN	75	Learjet 36	36-007	Flight Capital LLC. Madison, Ms.	N83DM
N83JJ	06	Learjet 40	45-2072	Jimmy John's Franchise Inc. Champaign, Il.	N4003K
N83LJ	65	Learjet 23	23-076	AJM Airplane Co. Naples, Fl. (status ?).	N50PJ
N83M	98	Gulfstream V	557	3M Co. St Paul, Mn.	N657GA
N83MD	80	HS 125/700A	NA0286	Mad Dog Aviation Inc. Seattle, Wa.	(N501MD)
N83NW	76	Citation	500-0309	Colorado by Air LLC. Salida, Co.	N88NW
N83PP	85	Gulfstream 3	464	Exquisite Air LLC. Destin, Fl.	N83AG
N83RE	92	Citation V	560-0183	M & L Airways Inc. Jackson, Oh.	N83RR
N83SA	82	Diamond 1A	A030SA	Alatrade Foods, Guntersville, Al.	(N800GC)
N83SD	06	Citation Sovereign	680-0106	Hi Tail It LLC. Waukegan, Il.	N51869
N83SG	82	Westwind-Two	368	Arthur & Arthur LLC. Missoula, Mt.	N368MD
N83TF	06	CitationJet CJ-3	525B-0094	Tomco II LLC. Nashville, Tn.	N.....
N83TY	99	Falcon 50EX	288	Viper Aviation LLC. Englewood, Co.	N33TY
N83TZ	99	Learjet 45	45-057	WFBNW NA. Salt Lake City, Ut. (trustor ?).	N83TN
N83WM	82	Learjet 55	55-043	Norwalk Aircraft Corp. Hackensack, NJ.	(N455EC)
N84EA	04	390 Premier 1	RB-119	Eastham Enterprises, Houston, Tx.	N39DM
N84EC	84	Citation S/II	S550-0014	American Aviation LLC. Eugene, Or.	N777AM
N84FG	97	CitationJet	525-0192	McKenzie Aeronautics LLC. Cleveland, Tn.	N51444
N84FM	02	390 Premier 1	RB-30	Mach Schnell LLC. Wichita, Ks.	N84ML
N84FN	74	Learjet 36	36-002	Flight Capital LLC. Madison, Ms.	N84DM
N84GC	84	Citation II	550-0493	Aero Mark Aviation II LLC. San Bernardino, Ca.	N84AW
N84GV	99	Gulfstream V	584	EDS Information Services LLC. Dallas, Tx.	N584GA
N84LX	01	Citation Excel	560-5164	First Team Properties LLC. Orlando, Fl.	N64LX
N84MJ	87	Falcon 200	510	Execujet Inc. Eighty Four, Pa.	N36DA
N84NG	97	Citation VII	650-7078	Newport Group/Newport Leasing Inc. Sanford, Fl.	N78BR
N84NW	91	Falcon 50	216	Execujet Inc. Eighty-Four, Pa.	N56SN
N84PH	84	Citation III	650-0062	Harron Aircraft LLC. Wilmington, De.	N475M
N84PJ	98	Citation X	750-0048	Hampton Airways Inc. Sellersburg, In.	N5135A
N84TJ	81	Falcon 10	188	Hydro Aviation LLC/Keystone Energy Partners LP. Houston.	I-TFLY
N84TN	82	Falcon 50	110	Temple Inland Forest Products Corp. Austin, Tx.	N77TE
N84UP	99	Hawker 800XP	258484	UnumProvident Corp. Chattanooga, Tn.	
N84VA	05	390 Premier 1	RB-134	Ali-Gator Air LLC. Springfield, Oh.	N3734C
N84ZZ	06	Global 5000	9229	Bombardier Aerospace Corp. Windsor Locks, Ct.	C-FJOA
N85	93	Challenger 601-3R	5138	FAA, Oklahoma City, Ok.	N138CC
N85CC	96	Hawker 800XP	258307	New Bremen Investments Inc. Wapakoneta, Oh.	N307AD
N85CL	99	Falcon 900EX EASY	167	Cleveland Browns Transportation Ltd. Berea, Oh.	N167EX
N85D	00	Global Express	9078	Dole Foods Inc. Van Nuys, Ca.	N700AH
N85EB	98	Citation V Ultra	560-0492	Elkhart Brass Manufacturing Co. Elkhart, In.	N41VR
N85F	96	Falcon 50EX	253	Anheuser Busch Companies Inc. St Louis, Mo.	PT-WSC
N85HD	80	Citation II	550-0162	Cooke LLC. Alexandria, La.	N1UA
N85HH	06	Hawker 850XP	258817	Highlandview Inc. Dallas-Love, Tx.	(N826LX)
N85JV	02	CitationJet CJ-2	525A-0085	AMI LLC/Amama LLC. Allegheny County, Pa.	N5185J
N85JW	67	Jet Commander	95	Redstar Air Shows Inc. Discovery Bay, Ca.	CP-2259
N85KV	90	Gulfstream 4	1135	VK Services LLC/Khosla Ventures, Hayward, Ca.	N456BE
N85M	05	Falcon 2000EX EASY	73	Five Star Holding LLC. Cuyahoga County, Oh.	N85MQ
N85MG	85	BAe 125/800SP	258035	Apogee Medical Management Inc. Scottsdale, Az.	N835CW
N85MS	84	Citation III	650-0075	MS Advisors 1 LLC. Houston, Tx.	(N100MS)
N85NC*	96	Learjet 60	60-090	NRC Aviation LLC. NYC.	N460BG
N85PK	99	Hawker 800XP	258460	HEH Corp/HEH Nashville, Nashville, Tn.	C-FHRD
N85PL	01	390 Premier 1	RB-55	Lucky Dog Investments Inc. Newport Beach, Ca.	N390PL
N85PT	80	Westwind-1124	285	Westwind Air LLC. Oklahoma City, Ok.	XA-LIJ
N85SV	80	Learjet 35A	35A-347	Randall Aviation Inc. Fort Lauderdale, Fl.	OE-GNP
N85TN	93	Falcon 50	237	Temple Inland Forest Products Corp. Austin, Tx.	N89BM
N85TW	78	Learjet 25D	25D-251	Sierra American Corp. Addison, Tx.	TG-VOC
N85TZ*	78	Falcon 20F-5	381	Tuthill Corp. Chicago-Midway, Il.	N20T
N85V	99	Gulfstream V	595	Dart Container Corp. Sarasota, Fl.	(N595GV)

Reg	Yr	Type	c/n	Owner/Operator	Prev Regn
N85VP	90	Citation V	560-0085	PHC-Aviation/Province Healthcare Co. Brentwood, Tn.	N891M
N85WD	86	Gulfstream 4	1008	Week-Davies Aviation Inc. West Palm Beach, Fl.	N119R
N86	94	Challenger 601-3R	5167	FAA, Oklahoma City, Ok.	N151CC
N86BA	84	Citation S/II	S550-0001	Vase III Corp. Wilmington, De.	(N550VS)
N86BL	77	Learjet 36A	36A-026	Bruce Leven, Mercer Island, Wa.	N8UA
N86CP	74	Sabre-60	306-76	Halford R Price, Phoenix, Az.	(N760SA)
N86CV*	95	Citation V Ultra	560-0342	Price Co/Costco Wholesale Inc. Seattle, Wa.	(N82CW)
N86LA	93	CitationJet	525-0012	L O Aviation LLC. Little Rock, Ar.	N12PA
N86PC	99	Citation Bravo	550-0891	Swanaire LLC/C L Swanson Corp. Madison, Wi.	N82MA
N86RB	01	390 Premier 1	RB-40	Hawker Beechcraft Corp. Wichita, Ks.	PR-BER
N86SG	82	Citation II	550-0350	Seymour Grubman/Right Flight LLC. Beverly Hills, Ca.	
N86SK	00	Citation Encore	560-0551	86SK LLC. Wilmington, De.	N560RG
N86TN	95	Falcon 50	241	Inland Paperboard & Packaging Inc. Austin, Tx.	N233BC
N86TW	06	Global Express	9218	Tallwood Global Management LLC. Napa, Ca.	N96ZZ
N86VP	85	Citation III	650-0089	Jet One LLC. Waterford, Mi.	(N229J)
N87	95	Challenger 601-3R	5190	FAA, Oklahoma City, Ok.	N190EK
N87BA	87	Citation S/II	S550-0131	MTE Hydraulics, Rockford, Il.	D-CHJH
N87DY	84	Diamond 1A	A085SA	KSRJ LLC/Steve Rayman Chrysler Jeep Dodge, Union City, Ga.	N70VT
N87EB	94	Beechjet 400A	RK-87	J E Dunn Construction Co. Kansas City, Mo.	N702LP
N87GA	81	Learjet 35A	35A-370	Gulf Air Group Corp. Houston, Tx.	XA-CVD
N87GJ	85	Westwind-Two	422	Purcell Co. Diamonhead, Ms.	N87GS
N87JK	91	Citation V	560-0115	Allied Home Mortgage Corp. Christensted, USVI.	N91YC
N87NY	61	MS 760 Paris	87	Earl Small, Frederiksted, USVI.	87
N87PK	07	Hawker 900XP	HA-43	Hawker Beechcraft Corp. Wichita, Ks.	
N87PT	80	Citation II	550-0174	N731PC LLC/Treece Financial Service Corp. Toledo, Oh.	N666WW
N87SF	79	Citation II	550-0096	Seneca Foods Corp. Penn Yan, NY.	N30UC
N87SL	02	Citation X	750-0174	Schweitzer Engineering Laboratories Inc. Pullman, Wa.	N174CX
N87TH	81	Falcon 10	178	David Donnini/Flightstar Corp. Chicago-Midway, Il.	N79BP
N87TN	91	Falcon 50	224	Temple Inland Forest Products Corp. Austin, Tx.	N800BD
N87TR	82	Challenger 600S	1076	Harbortown Industries Inc. Waukegan, Il.	N601WW
N87VM	06	CitationJet CJ-3	525B-0098	Swift Properties LLC. Santa Ana, Ca.	N5270E
N87WU	98	Citation Excel	560-5039	Barristair LC/Provost & Umphrey Law Firm, Beaumont, Tx.	N88WU
N88	04	Challenger 604	5588	FAA, Oklahoma City, Ok.	C-GLXU
N88AD	00	CitationJet CJ-1	525-0174	Lincoln Park Leasing LLC. Salem, Or.	(N746JB)
N88AF	02	Learjet 45	45-205	Lakeview (CPC) Air LLC. Kenosha, Wi.	N5052K
N88AJ	99	Citation Bravo	550-0885	A & J Management Services Inc. Menomonee Falls, Wi.	N820JM
N88AY	06	Gulfstream G200	134	Metrojet Ltd. Hong Kong. 'Emperor Express'	N434GA
N88BF	81	Sabre-65	465-60	Western Jet LLC. Milton, Wa.	(N688WS)
N88BG	76	Learjet 35A	35A-090	AirNet Systems Inc. Columbus, Oh.	I-FIMI
N88BY	74	Learjet 25B	25B-168	Lear 25 LLC. West Columbia, SC.	N88BT
N88D	00	Gulfstream V	612	Intercontinental Air LLC/Everest Capital Inc. Miami, Fl.	N350C
N88DD	02	Falcon 2000	204	Duchossois Industries Inc. Palwaukee, Il.	N2317
N88DJ	89	Citation III	650-0167	Dale Jarrett Inc. Conover, NC.	N832CC
N88DU	67	HS 125/731	25153	Hawker 25153 Inc. Fort Lauderdale, Fl.	N88DJ
N88EJ	99	Citation X	750-0088	Qualcomm Inc. San Diego, Ca.	N5130J
N88EL	06	390 Premier 1A	RB-157	EL 88 Corp. Van Nuys, Ca.	N6178X
N88ER	01	390 Premier 1	RB-17	DP 64 LLC. Scottsdale, Az.	N88EL
N88HD	03	Hawker 800XP	258616	Harley-Davidson Motor Co. Milwaukee, Wi.	N61216
N88HP	99	Citation Excel	560-5050	NLP Leasing LLC. Boca Raton, Fl.	N184G
N88LC	03	Falcon 900EX EASY	137	Lowe's Companies Inc. North Wilkesboro, NC.	F-WWFO
N88LD	97	CitationJet	525-0181	Goldcup D 2987 AB. Solna, Sweden.	N181CJ
N88LJ	74	Learjet 24D	24D-290	Aviation Pioneers LLC. Charleston, WV.	N24TK
N88LN	68	Gulfstream 2	20	Segrave Aviation Inc. Kinston, NC.	N747NB
N88ME	06	Falcon 2000EX EASY	79	Harrah's Operating Co. Las Vegas, Nv.	F-WWGP
N88MF	90	Astra-1125SP	048	Mur-Fam Enterprises LLC. Rose Hill, NC.	N1125V
N88MM	02	390 Premier 1	RB-44	McMahans Furniture Co of Las Vegas, Carlsbad, Ca.	N5044X
N88ND	97	Falcon 900EX	19	PCMT Aviation LLC/DSU Aviation LLC. Seattle, Wa.	N900CX
N88NJ	78	Learjet 35A	35A-170	National Jets Inc. Fort Lauderdale, Fl.	N335AS
N88NW	87	Citation S/II	S550-0151	Peninsula Development Services Inc. Tumwater, Wa.	N550SP
N88SF	06	Citation Excel XLS	560-5645	Steiner Films Aviation Inc. Munich, Germany.	N5223X
N88TB	77	Citation 1/SP	501-0002	Gateway Aviation Inc. Carlsbad, Ca.	(N501WK)
N88UA	88	Beechjet 400	RJ-49	University of Arkansas, Fayetteville, Ar.	N1549J
N88V	99	Learjet 60	60-155	Jacura Delaware Inc. Boca Raton, Fl.	
N88WR	98	BBJ-79U	29441	Las Vegas Jet LLC.	N88WZ
N88WU	05	Gulfstream G200	111	Provost & Umphrey Law Firm LLP. Beaumont, Tx.	N995GA
N88WV	05	Learjet 45	45-276	WIV Air LLC. Calabasas, Ca.	N40084

Reg	Yr	Type	c/n	Owner/Operator	Prev Regn
N88ZL	65	B 707-330B	18928	Principal Air Services LLC. Huntington Valley, Pa.	N5381X
N89AM	83	Westwind-Two	389	Atherton & Murphy Investment Co. Tulsa-R L Jones, Ok.	N812G
N89CE	06	Falcon 2000EX EASY	81	Harrah's Operating Co. Las Vegas, Nv.	N81EX
N89D	79	Citation II	550-0056	Beechwood Enterprises LLC. Chino, Ca.	N444FJ
N89ES	69	Learjet 24B	24B-197	EBJ Aviation LLC. Veradale, Wa.	N24FU
N89GA	80	Citation II	550-0122	Southern Aircraft Leasing Inc. Port Orange, Fl.	C-GCUL
N89HB	89	Learjet 31	31-010	S L Air International LLC. Hinsdale, Il.	N311TS
N89HE	99	Gulfstream V	568	Harrah's Operating Co. Las Vegas, Nv.	N5HN
N89HS	97	Astra-1125SPX	089	560 Co Inc. Anchorage, Ak.	N918MK
N89LD	05	Embraer EMB-135LR	145648	McKee Foods Transportation LLC. Chattanooga, Tn.	PT-...
N89LS	89	Citation II	550-0623	Les Schwab Warehouse Center Inc. Prineville, Or.	(N1255L)
N89MD	02	Citation Encore	560-0612	MDU Resources Group Inc. Bismarck, ND.	N5260U
N89MF	80	Citation 1/SP	501-0193	DM Farms of Rose Hill LLC. Rose Hill, NC.	N45MK
N89NC	04	Falcon 50EX	337	National City Corp/NCC Services, Cleveland, Oh.	N50FJ
N89TC	75	Learjet 35	35-026	West Knob Air LLC. Wilmington, De.	N54754
N89TJ	71	Gulfstream II SP	103	Dodson International Parts Inc. Rantoul, Ks. (status ?).	(N103WJ)
N89ZZ	07	Global Express	9259	Bombardier Aerospace Corp. Windsor Locks, Ct.	C-FMMH
N90AH	75	Learjet 35	35-036	SMP Communications Corp. Scottsdale, Az.	N76GP
N90AJ	90	Astra-1125SP	052	Nie Planes LLC. Boise, Id.	
N90AM	99	Gulfstream V	592	ProFlite LLC/Really Quiet LLC. Teterboro, NJ.	N592GA
N90AR	93	Challenger 601-3R	5137	Elite Aviation LLC. Van Nuys, Ca.	N137CL
N90BA	90	Learjet 31	31-018	Blackfriars Aviation LLC/Venture Jets Inc. Lititz, Pa.	(N20LL)
N90BJ	92	Citation II	550-0710	Golden Shamrock Associates LLC. North Platte, Ne.	N510VP
N90BL*	05	Citation Excel XLS	560-5609	Bourland & Leverich Aviation, Pampa, Tx.	N442LU
N90BY	91	Citation II	550-0682	Bourland & Leverich Aviation Inc. Pampa, Tx.	N90BL
N90CF	00	Citation Excel	560-5080	Columbia Forest Products Aviation Inc. Portland, Or.	N52141
N90CJ	02	CitationJet CJ-2	525A-0149	Armstrong Aircraft LLC. Madison, Wi.	N.....
N90EW	99	Global Express	9039	EWA Holdings LLC/East-West Air Inc. San Jose, Ca.	N700GT
N90FB	02	Hawker 800XP	258613	Furniture Brands International. Tupelo, Ms.	
N90FJ	65	Citation S/II	S550-0065	Flying J Inc. Brigham City, Ut.	N995DC
N90GS	02	Learjet 45	45-225	G & S Holdings LLC. Richland, Ms.	N558GS
N90JJ	88	Citation II	550-0571	Aero Associates Inc. Pottsville, Pa.	(N12990)
N90LC	74	Falcon 10	23	Al-Morrell Development Inc. Latnarca, Cyprus.	N20WP
N90LJ	77	Learjet 25D	25D-226	Fast Walker LLC/Jet Investment Group Inc. Clearwater, Fl.	N234SV
N90MA	80	Citation II	550-0103	Windy City Air Services LLC. Holland, Il.	XA-JEZ
N90ML	80	Gulfstream 3	315	JetFirst/Flight Stream LLC. Van Nuys, Ca.	(N901JF)
N90NB	02	Citation Encore	560-0634	NBTY Inc. Bohemia, NY.	N5254Y
N90NF	01	Citation X	750-0170	OnFlight Inc. Cincinnati, Oh.	N5060K
N90PT	83	Citation II	550-0465	Berry Air LLC/Berry Nurseries, Tahlequah, Ok.	N551WJ
N90R	01	BBJ-7EL	32775	Swiflite Aircraft Corp. Burbank, Ca.	N376BJ
N90TH	99	Falcon 900C	180	Sony Aviation Inc. Teterboro, NJ. (status ?).	F-WWFX
N90WA	90	Learjet 31	31-028	Wal-Mart Stores Inc. Rogers, Ar.	
N90WR	75	Learjet 35	35-022	Bankair Inc. West Columbia, SC.	OY-BLG
N90XR	07	Learjet 40	45-2090	Northern Air Inc. Wichita, Ks.	N4003K
N90Z	82	Citation II	550-0336	Northern Jet, Iron Mountain, Mi.	N6830Z
N91A	02	CitationJet CJ-2	525A-0105	Spiral Inc. Chandler, Az.	N13M
N91AG	02	Citation Encore	560-0606	Monsanto Co. St Louis, Mo.	N606CE
N91AP	79	Citation 1/SP	501-0117	Smith Air Ltd. Hurst, Tx.	LV-MZG
N91B	80	Citation II	550-0194	Beckett Enterprises/Scott Fetzer Co. Lakewood, Oh.	N88723
N91BB	07	390 Premier 1A	RB-192	Interfoods of America, Tamiami, Fl.	N7192M
N91BZ	80	Sabre-65	465-19	General Foam Plastics Corp. Mount Gilead, NC.	N65RC
N91CH	85	BAe 125/800A	258030	CNC Aircraft Inc. Louisville, Ky.	N10WF
N91CW	98	Gulfstream V	543	Costco Wholesale Inc. Seattle, Wa.	N643GA
N91DP	93	Learjet 31A	31A-079	HS Equipment LLC. Westerville, Oh.	N41DP
N91HG	81	Citation 1/SP	501-0199	Marshall Oil & Gas Corp. Birmingham, Al.	N7SV
N91HK	01	Hawker 800XP	258578	Mueller East Inc. Palm Beach International, Fl.	N50378
N91KC	98	Citation VII	650-7082	WKC Corp/Barry Wehmiller Companies Inc. St Louis, Mo.	N2RF
N91KH	89	Challenger 601-3A	5038	Rhema Bible Church, Tulsa, Ok.	N78PP
N91KP	72	HS 125/600A	256003	Dr Paul Madison, Michigan City, In.	N91KH
N91LA	03	Gulfstream G550	5027	Leucadia Aviation Inc. Salt Lake City, Ut.	N927GA
N91LE	96	Learjet 60	60-091	HH & O Aviation LLC/Hartley & O'Brien, Wheeling, WV.	N896R
N91ML	87	Citation S/II	S550-0132	Cherokee Aviation LLC. Louisville, Ky.	N91ME
N91NA	77	Gulfstream 2B	198	Bopper Airways LLC/Indianapolis Colts Inc. Indianapolis, In.	N91LA
N91PB	82	Falcon 100	198	Gulf Aire II Inc. Gulfport, Ms.	N1PB
N91PE	77	Citation Eagle 400SP	501-0033	Arrow Leasing Ltd. Norwood, Ma.	C-GQJK
N91PN	72	Learjet 25B	25B-091	Aero Nash Inc. Tucson, Az.	VR-CCH

Reg	Yr	Type	c/n	Owner/Operator	Prev Regn
☐ N91TE	81	Citation 1/SP	501-0173	RD Aviation LP. NYC.	N91MS
☐ N91VB	79	Citation II	550-0068	KBS Realty Advisors, Newport Beach, Ca.	N1WB
☐ N92AE	96	Gulfstream 4SP	1301	American Express Co. Stewart, NY.	N433GA
☐ N92BE	78	Citation 1/SP	501-0098	Tumac Industries Inc. Grand Junction, Co.	HB-VIC
☐ N92BL	77	Citation 1/SP	501-0026	M & M Aircraft Investments LLC. Southaven, Ms.	N92CC
☐ N92DE	96	Citation V Ultra	560-0391	CSRB Properties Inc. El Paso, Tx.	N391CV
☐ N92FG	95	Learjet 60	60-056	Ellsworth Consulting LLC. Opa Locka, Fl.	(N556SA)
☐ N92FT	02	Hawker 800XP2	258598	Fidelity National Financial Corp. Jacksonville, Fl.	(N800JA)
☐ N92JC	86	Citation S/II	S550-0115	The First W D Co. Rockford, Il.	N92JT
☐ N92LA	02	Gulfstream G550	5002	Leucadia Aviation Inc/Baxter Investment LLC. NYC.	N550GA
☐ N92MA	05	CitationJet CJ-3	525B-0048	Mid-America Management Inc. Cleveland, Oh.	N853JL
☐ N92ME	85	Citation S/II	S550-0044	Old Dominion Freight Lines Inc. High Point, NC.	N92ME
☐ N92MG	82	Learjet 55	55-025	RDM Commerce Inc & Wilsonart International Inc. Temple, Tx.	N57FM
☐ N92MS	07	CitationJet CJ-3	525B-0214	Cessna Aircraft Co. Wichita, Ks.	N52433
☐ N92ND	97	CitationJet	525-0186	Atlantic Aero Inc. Greensboro, NC.	N186CJ
☐ N92RP	87	Citation III	650-0148	Lanmar Marine & Aviation/N3R LLC. Groton, Ct.	N7HF
☐ N92SM	73	Citation	500-0124	Thieman Enterprises Inc. Dayton, Oh.	N8FC
☐ N92SS	96	Citation V Ultra	560-0388	Southern States Co-operative Inc. Richmond, Va.	N5269A
☐ N92TE	91	Citation V	560-0123	TEC Equipment Inc. Aurora, Or.	N583CW
☐ N92TS	75	Learjet 35	35-035	Paca Air Inc. Caracas, Venezuela.	N350TS
☐ N92UP	97	Hawker 800XP	258309	Allyson Aviation LLC/Sun Air Jets LLC. Camarillo, Ca.	N5735
☐ N93AE	96	Gulfstream 4SP	1302	American Express Co. Stewart, NY.	(N98AE)
☐ N93AJ	82	Citation II	550-0337	Galyen Equipment Leasing LLC. Bedford, Tx.	N3FW
☐ N93AK	07	CitationJet CJ2+	525A-0368	Kennedy Rice Dryers Inc. Monroe, La.	N5032K
☐ N93AT	87	Gulfstream 4	1020	ASG/Tessler Aviation Leasing Corp. Teterboro, NJ.	N9300
☐ N93BA	81	Challenger 600S	1027	Somebody LLC/Comet Video Technologies, Cleveland, Oh.	N111FK
☐ N93CV	93	Citation V	560-0239	Rosebriar Transportation Inc. Dallas, Tx.	(N560RB)
☐ N93CW	06	CitationJet CJ-3	525B-0139	Will-Drill Production Co. Shreveport, La.	N52059
☐ N93EA	90	Citation V	560-0093	Aircraft Trust & Financing Corp. Fort Lauderdale, Fl.	F-GKJL
☐ N93FT	97	Beechjet 400A	RK-166	Fidelity National Financial Corp. Jacksonville, Fl.	N975CM
☐ N93JW	05	CitationJet CJ-3	525B-0035	Williams & Bailey LLC/W B Air Three LLC. Houston, Tx.	N51511
☐ N93KD	07	Falcon 900EX EASY	182	Pegasus VI LLC. Alamo, Ca.	F-WWFU
☐ N93LA	00	Citation X	750-0121	Williams Communications Aircraft LLC. Tulsa, Ok.	N358WC
☐ N93LE	84	Learjet 35A	35A-592	La Stella Corp. Pueblo, Co.	N45KK
☐ N93LS	05	CitationJet CJ-1	525-0556	Sweet Double S Ranch, Texhoma, Ok.	N.....
☐ N93M	99	Citation V	567	3M Co. St Paul, Mn.	N467GA
☐ N93MK	89	Gulfstream 4	1088	Pelican Development G-IV LLC. Rolling Hills, Ca.	N71JN
☐ N93PE	06	CitationJet CJ-3	525B-0093	Preco Electronics Inc. Boise, Id.	N5259Y
☐ N93S	01	Citation X	750-0189	U S Bank NA. St Paul, Mn.	N51984
☐ N93SK	91	Learjet 31	31-031	SK Logistics Inc. St Augustinee, Fl.	N878MA
☐ N93TX	99	Citation X	750-0099	Textron Inc. T F Green Airport, Rl.	N442WJ
☐ N93XP	93	Beechjet 400A	RK-74	Zephyr LLC/Becknell Development LLC. Champaign, Il.	N26JP
☐ N94AA	80	Learjet 35A	35A-295	AirNet Systems Inc. Columbus, Oh.	PT-LAA
☐ N94AE	96	Gulfstream 4SP	1307	American Express Co. Stewart, NY.	N443GA
☐ N94AF	77	Learjet 35A	35A-094	Ameriflight Inc. Burbank, Ca.	(N35PF)
☐ N94AJ	72	Citation	500-0024	Big Sky Aviation LLC. West Palm Beach, Fl.	VH-ICN
☐ N94AL	01	CitationJet CJ-1	525-0432	Business Aircraft Leasing Inc. Nashville, Tn.	N51342
☐ N94BA	98	Learjet 60	60-144	T & M Air LLC. Avon, Co.	D-CKKK
☐ N94FL	84	Gulfstream 3	424	Moncrief Oil International Inc. Fort Worth, Tx.	N228G
☐ N94GP	81	Learjet 35A	35A-411	Ridge Air LLC. Northbrook, Il.	PT-LBY
☐ N94HE	94	Beechjet 400A	RK-89	Hughes-Ergon Co. Jackson, Ms.	N1560G
☐ N94HL	07	CitationJet CJ1+	525-0654	Winfield Consumer Products Inc. Winfield, Ks.	N52691
☐ N94JT	86	BAe 125/800A	258071	LTJ LLC. Menlo Park, Ca.	N789LT
☐ N94LA	00	Citation Excel	560-5129	Leucadia Aviation Inc. Salt Lake City, Ut.	N359WC
☐ N94LD	83	Diamond 1A	A073SA	PAG Inc/Peter Cadillac, Little Rock, Ar.	N94LH
☐ N94LH	05	Hawker 400XP	RK-405	Cameron Communications LLC. Lake Charles, La.	N40ZH
☐ N94LT	96	Gulfstream 4SP	1313	Lucent Technologies Inc. Morristown, NJ.	N455GA
☐ N94MZ	95	CitationJet	525-0094	D & D Aircraft Inc. Portland, Me.	(N51522)
☐ N94PC	97	Falcon 50EX	254	Mountain Aviation Leasing LLC. Salt Lake City, Ut.	N345AP
☐ N94RL	77	Learjet 35A	35A-096	JetPlane LLC. Evanston, Wy.	N96FA
☐ N94TX	93	Citation V	560-0247	Granite Telecommunications, Quincy, Ma.	
☐ N94VP	90	Citation V	560-0094	West Bend Air Inc. West Bend, Wi.	N1827S
☐ N94ZZ	06	Global Express	9215	Nauthhiz P/L. Sydney, Australia.	C-FIPC
☐ N95AE	99	Gulfstream V	562	American Express Co. Stewart, NY.	N662GA
☐ N95AG	96	Learjet 60	60-079	Delta Airelite Business Jets Inc. Cincinnati, Oh.	N319LJ
☐ N95AN	01	Citation Bravo	550-0978	Alabama National Bancorp. Birmingham, Al.	N696CM

Reg	Yr	Type	c/n	Owner/Operator	Prev Regn
☐ N95BD	01	Learjet 60	60-232	Konfara LLC. Scottsdale, Az.	N232LJ
☐ N95BK	77	JetStar 2	5208	Denison Jet Sales Corp. Greer, SC.	N95BD
☐ N95BS	98	CitationJet	525-0283	Ferris Manufacturing Corp. Hinsdale, Il.	
☐ N95CC	02	Citation Excel	560-5278	Cessna Aircraft Co. Wichita, Ks.	N176GS
☐ N95CK	02	CitationJet CJ-1	525-0493	CJ Uno LLC. Broomfield, Co.	(N315N)
☐ N95CM	81	HS 125/700A	NA0309	Suncoast Aviation Services Corp. St Petersburg, Fl.	N309WM
☐ N95GK	90	Beechjet 400A	RK-27	GK Development Inc. Chicago-DuPage, Il.	(N405LX)
☐ N95HC	94	Falcon 50	244	Harsco Corp. New Cumberland, Pa.	N50FJ
☐ N95JK	80	Westwind-1124	283	McGriff, Seibels & Williams LLC. Birmingham, Al.	N17UC
☐ N95JN	84	Learjet 35A	35A-595	Flying Squirrel Productions LLC. Grand Junction, Co.	N414KL
☐ N95NB	03	Citation Encore	560-0644	National Beef Packing LLC. Kansas City, Mo.	N814QS
☐ N95RX	93	Citation VII	650-7035	Highland Leasing Corp - CVS Corp. Woonsocket, RI.	PT-WLC
☐ N95TD	91	Citation V	560-0110	Cozad Trailer Sales LLC. Madera, Ca.	N26DY
☐ N95TX	94	Citation VII	650-7037	Textron Inc. T F Green Airport, RI.	N737CC
☐ N95UP	03	Hawker 800XP	258639	Colonial Companies Inc. Chattanooga, Tn.	N639XP
☐ N95WK	84	Learjet 55	55-099	Bettis Leasing LLC. Memphis, Tn.	N17GL
☐ N95XL	00	Citation Excel	560-5095	Sikeston Financial Corp. Panama City, Panama.	N5135A
☐ N96	89	BAe 125/C-29A	258134	FAA, Oklahoma City, Ok.	88-0270
☐ N96AD	07	Gulfstream G150	246	Gulfstream Aerospace LP. Dallas-Love, Tx.	4X-C..
☐ N96CP	87	Citation III	650-0139	First American Corp. Santa Ana, Ca.	N4EG
☐ N96DA	81	Citation 1/SP	501-0176	MMI Hotel Management, Flowood, Ms.	VP-CFG
☐ N96DS	94	Challenger 601-3R	5146	SGI Air Holdings LLC/DLS Air LLC. Denver, Co.	N137MB
☐ N96FB	73	Citation	500-0094	Delta Wings Inc. Carson City, Nv.	N80GB
☐ N96FL	98	Astra-1125SPX	109	Frito Lay Inc/Pepsico Inc. Addison, Tx.	
☐ N96FN	78	Learjet 35A	35A-186	Flight Capital LLC. Madison, Ms.	N96DM
☐ N96FT	01	Hawker 800XP2	258568	Fidelity National Financial Corp. Jacksonville, Fl.	N4468K
☐ N96G	01	CitationJet CJ-2	525A-0018	Reading Bakery Systems, Robesonia, Pa.	N5148N
☐ N96GA	99	Beechjet 400A	RK-238	Messenger International Inc. Palmer Lake, Co.	XA-VRO
☐ N96GS	85	Learjet 35A	35A-606	Wings Service LP. Wilmington, De.	N3WP
☐ N96JA	93	Gulfstream 4SP	1226	Jordan Consulting Inc. Chicago-Midway, Il.	N415WW
☐ N96MR	05	CitationJet CJ-3	525B-0067	Martin Rowley, Bournemouth-Hurn, UK.	N51160
☐ N96MT	96	Citation VII	650-7065	Windway Capital Corp. Sheboygan, Wi.	N650W
☐ N96NA	02	CitationJet CJ-2	525A-0096	North American Jet LLC. Austin, Tx.	JA525G
☐ N96NB	04	Citation Encore	560-0673	National Beef Packing LLC. Kansas City, Mo.	N5245U
☐ N96NC	02	390 Premier 1	RB-86	Marks Hill Consulting LLC. Marshall, Tx.	(N390TA)
☐ N96NX	98	Falcon 900EX	35	Domestic USF Corp. Dulles, Va.	HB-IAQ
☐ N96PD	06	CitationJet CJ-3	525B-0111	David R Albin, Santa Fe, NM.	N5101J
☐ N96RE	81	Sabre-65	465-52	Denison Jet Sales Corp. Greer, SC.	N500E
☐ N96RX	98	Citation X	750-0044	Highland Leasing Corp - CVS Corp. Woonsocket, RI.	N5103J
☐ N96SG	65	HS 125/1A-522	25060	Gulf Air Group Corp. Houston, Tx.	XB-CXZ
☐ N96SK	07	Hawker 900XP	HA-6	SKF Aviation LLC/SK Foods Inc. Lemore, Ca.	N71956
☐ N96TM	79	Westwind-1124	275	Wings of West Virginia LLC. Parkersburg, WV.	N6TM
☐ N96TX	98	Citation X	750-0069	Textron Inc. T F Green Airport, RI.	N100FR
☐ N96UT	89	Falcon 50	192	MidAmerican Energy Co. Des Moines, Ia.	N96LT
☐ N97	89	BAe 125/C-29A	258154	FAA, Oklahoma City, Ok.	88-0272
☐ N97AL	88	Citation III	650-0155	Cardinal Aviation LC. Charlottesville, Va.	N788NB
☐ N97BH	95	Citation V Ultra	560-0290	Air Finance Corp. Van Nuys, Ca.	N5145P
☐ N97CC	85	Citation S/II	S550-0045	Cite Investments LLC. Raleigh, NC.	T9-BIH
☐ N97CE	78	Learjet 35A	35A-203	TRAM Aviation/Offshore Marine Contractors Inc. Cutoff, La.	N203RW
☐ N97CJ	02	CitationJet CJ-2	525A-0097	SLJ Holdings LLC/Stewart Title Co. Houston, Tx.	N.....
☐ N97DD	85	Citation III	650-0071	Bunker Aircraft Management Inc. Auburn, In.	N297DD
☐ N97DK	98	Citation X	750-0035	Emerald Air Co. Oak Brook, Il.	N5071M
☐ N97DQ	02	Global Express	9095	Egret Management LLC. White Plains, NY.	HB-IUJ
☐ N97EM	83	Citation II	550-0481	Express Messenger Systems Inc. Phoenix, Az. (was 551-0481)	N481VP
☐ N97FL	98	Astra-1125SPX	110	Frito Lay Inc/Pepsico Inc. Addison, Tx.	
☐ N97FN	67	Learjet 25	25-003	Hampton University, Newport News, Va.	N97DM
☐ N97FT	04	Gulfstream G450	4008	Fidelity National Financial Corp. Jacksonville, Fl.	N608GA
☐ N97GM	03	Falcon 2000EX	15	General Maritime Corp. Waterbury-Oxford, Ct.	N215EX
☐ N97JL*	92	Citation V	560-0163	LaPour Partners Inc. Las Vegas, Nv.	N953C
☐ N97LE	89	Learjet 35A	35A-648	La Stella Corp. Pueblo, Co.	N648J
☐ N97NX	98	Falcon 900EX	32	Sprint/United Management Co. Reston, Va.	N4425
☐ N97SG	86	Challenger 601	3051	Rocky Mountain Bingo (1995) LC. Edmonton, AB. Canada.	(N604LX)
☐ N97SJ	78	Falcon 20-5	378	J M Smucker Co. Akron-Canton, Oh.	N500JD
☐ N97TE	97	Citation V Ultra	560-0436	Centennial Management Inc. Aberdeen, SD.	N560BJ
☐ N97VF	96	CitationJet	525-0171	RAB Aviation LLC/GBR Properties Inc. Tulsa, Ok.	N5153Z
☐ N97WJ	67	Falcon 20C	101	J P Aviation Inc. Raleigh-Durham, NC.	N342F

Reg	Yr	Type	c/n	Owner/Operator	Prev Regn
N98	89	BAe 125/C-29A	258156	FAA, Oklahoma City, Ok.	88-0273
N98AC	02	Falcon 50EX	329	Allen Canning Co. Siloam Springs, Ar.	(N50FJ)
N98AV	81	Citation 1/SP	501-0177	Chelsea Communication Inc. Wilmington, De.	N457CS
N98BM	76	Westwind-1124	193	Corporate Aviation Services Inc. Pepper Pike, Oh.	N515LG
N98CG	74	Learjet 24D	24D-289	Memphis Aircraft Sales Inc. Memphis, Tn.	N289G
N98E	91	Citation V	560-0103	Cytex Plastics Inc. Houston, Tx.	(N67989)
N98FT	77	HS 125/700A	NA0216	Rocky Mountain Aviation Inc. Santa Barbara, Ca.	(N197FT)
N98JV	98	Learjet 60	60-135	Southern Plastics Inc/JVE Corp. Longview, Tx.	N135LJ
N98LC	76	Learjet 35A	35A-077	AirNet Systems Inc. Columbus, Oh.	ZS-NRZ
N98LT	95	Gulfstream 4SP	1278	Lucent Technologies Inc. Morristown, NJ.	VR-CTA
N98NX	93	Falcon 900B	128	Nextel Aviation Inc. Dulles, Va.	N11LK
N98Q	72	Citation	500-0040	Tri-State Care Flight LLC. Bullhead City, Az.	N600WM
N98RP	02	Falcon 2000	186	Radar Management LLC. Palo Alto, Ca.	N551SS
N98RS	74	Learjet 25XR	25XR-148	Stern Holdings Inc. Addison, Tx.	(N98JA)
N98WJ	70	Gulfstream II SP	89	Monarch Flight LLC/W B Johnson Properties LLC. Atlanta, Ga.	N36MW
N98XR	06	Learjet 45XR	45-292	Imperial Air LP. McAllen, Tx.	JA01GW
N98XS	95	Citation VII	650-7058	XSEED Aviation LLC. Chicago-Du Page, Il.	N625CC
N99BB	96	Citation X	750-0005	Harris Air Inc. Logan, Ut. (has winglets).	N5263S
N99CJ	99	CitationJet	525-0333	Acme Air Inc. Columbia, SC.	
N99CK	80	Citation 1/SP	501-0153	Sky Life Enterprises LLC. Long Beach, Ca.	(N484CS)
N99CN	81	Citation II	550-0396	Servicios Aeronauticos Sucre, Venezuela. (was 551-0065)	N99DE
N99GA	92	Gulfstream 4	1198	Moneygram Payment Systems Inc. Minneapolis, Mn.	N425GA
N99GK	03	Learjet 40	45-2008	Gold Key Aviation Inc. Woody Creek, Co.	N2408
N99KW	03	Challenger 604	5564	Florida Wings Inc. Boca Raton, Fl.	N564BA
N99MC	74	Learjet 25B	25B-182	Air Ambulance Aircraft Inc. Sarasota, Fl.	N225JL
N99NJ	82	Learjet 35A	35A-481	National Jets Inc. Fort Lauderdale, Fl.	OO-LFV
N99PD	80	Gulfstream 3	314	Hambrick Corp. Dallas, Tx.	(N99YD)
N99RS	78	Learjet 36A	36A-039	American Biomedical Group, Oklahoma City, Ok.	N25PK
N99TK	89	Citation II	550-0621	Pangel II LLC. Hailey, Id.	N102PA
N99UG	93	Challenger 601-3A	5126	UnitedGlobalCom Inc. Englewood, Co.	(N605LG)
N99WA	79	Falcon 10	150	Wheels of Africa, Rand Airport, South Africa.	N212NC
N99XR	06	Learjet 45XR	45-302	Saturn Jets LLC/Texas Aero Aircraft Sales Group, Waco, Tx.	JA02GW
N99ZB	02	Beechjet 400A	RK-344	Giles Nissan Volvo, Lafayette, La.	N6144S
N99ZC	99	Learjet 60	60-162	Plain Fish LLC. Memphis, Tn.	
N100A	06	Global Express	9205	Exxon Mobil Corp. Dallas-Love, Tx.	N205EX
N100AC	77	Falcon 20F-5	366	Smith, Vicars & Co LLC. Charlottesville, Va.	N300CT
N100AG	93	Hawker 800SP	258238	R S Allen Aviation Inc. San Diego, Ca.	N70PM
N100AM	76	Citation	500-0305	Aero-Auto Sales & Leasing Inc. Kent, Oh.	N137WC
N100AR	02	Citation Excel	560-5241	Independence Airlines Inc. Manchester, NH.	N.....
N100AS	73	Falcon 20F-5B	274	City Aviation Services Inc. Detroit, Mi.	N260MB
N100AT	81	Learjet 35A	35A-436	Betaco Inc. Indianapolis, In.	N436BL
N100AW	97	Beechjet 400A	RK-150	Concesionario MB de Venezuela SA. Caracas.	N100AG
N100BC	87	Westwind-1124	438	DHB Westwind LLC. Fort Worth, Tx.	(N438FS)
N100BL	96	Learjet 31A	31A-126	Bobby LaBonte Enterprises Inc. Greensboro, NC.	N18BL
N100CH	82	Citation II	550-0438	Choice Holdings LLC. Elkhart, In.	N643TD
N100CJ	00	Citation Excel	560-5100	Double Force Management LLC. Bowling Green, Ky.	N49MU
N100CU	77	Falcon 10	104	Jani King International Inc. Addison, Tx.	N800SB
N100DS	90	Citation II	550-0639	DBS Transit Inc. Harrisburg, Pa.	N62RG
N100EG	82	Falcon 50	105	Greenfield Aviation LLC/Volo Aviation Inc. Bridgeport, Ct.	(N881L)
N100EJ	73	Sabre-75A	380-1	N100EJ Corp. Sarasota, Fl.	N30GB
N100ES	01	Global Express	9108	Earth Star Inc. Burbank, Ca.	N700EK
N100G	97	Astra-1125SPX	092	Hawk Flight Inc. Coatsville, Pa.	N8MN
N100GN	94	Gulfstream 4SP	1236	Gannett Co. Dulles, Va.	N478GA
N100GV	99	Gulfstream V	600	New World Jet Corp. Ronkonkoma, NY.	N650GA
N100GY	99	Astra-1125SPX	120	The Loomis Co. Reading, Pa.	(N100LY)
N100HB	79	Citation II	550-0058	Dove Air Inc. Fletcher, NC.	N71CJ
N100HF	97	Gulfstream 4SP	1338	LHF Holdings Inc. Burlingame, Ca.	N401WT
N100HG	87	Gulfstream 4	1026	Harbour Group Industries Inc. St Louis, Mo.	(N277AG)
N100HW	05	Learjet 40	45-2036	Little Crow Airplane LLC. Fort Worth, Tx.	
N100JF	89	Gulfstream 4	1093	JHF LLC. Teterboro, NJ.	N624BP
N100JS	06	CitationJet CJ-3	525B-0095	JATO Aviation Ltd. Northolt, UK.	N5214K
N100KK	99	Learjet 45	45-065	Kohler Co. Kohler, Wi.	
N100KP	93	Falcon 50	232	King Pharmaceuticals Inc. Bristol, Tn.	N45NQ
N100KU	97	Citation Bravo	550-0813	University of Kansas, Lawrence, Ks.	N813GS
N100LR	82	Challenger 600S	1064	SynFuels Holdings Finance LLC. Birmingham, Al.	N75B
N100LX	81	Citation 1/SP	501-0220	Cash is King GP LLC, Seguin, Tx.	N100QH

Reg	Yr	Type	c/n	Owner/Operator	Prev Regn
N100MB	05	Falcon 2000EX EASY	60	M Bohlke Veneer Corp. Fairfield, Oh.	F-WWMI
N100NB	74	Learjet 25C	25C-181	High Altitude Mapping Missions Inc. Spokane, Wa.	N73TA
N100NG	01	Hawker 800XP2	258537	Aircierge LLC. Stevens Point, Wi.	
N100PF	00	CitationJet CJ-1	525-0390	Gottschalks Inc. Fresno, Ca.	N51396
N100QR	82	Challenger 600S	1043	Tara Louisiana Group Inc. Boca Raton, Fl.	N43NW
N100R	90	Citation III	650-0197	NASCAR Inc. Daytona Beach, Fl.	N840R
N100RC	05	CitationJet CJ-3	525B-0038	Rydell Co. Grand Forks, ND.	N51942
N100RS	82	Diamond 1A	A029SA	Great Escapes Aviation LLC. Fayetteville, NC.	(N22CX)
N100SC	99	Citation Excel	560-5065	100 SC Partners/560 Inc. Chattanooga, Tn.	N5204D
N100SR	89	Astra-1125	037	Steven Rayman, Big Rock, Il.	N589TB
N100SY	90	Citation V	560-0054	Aerotop Aviation LLC. Roswell, Ga.	(N748DC)
N100TM	02	Gulfstream V	692	Toyota Motor Sales USA Inc. Long Beach, Ca.	N692GA
N100U	91	BAe 1000A	NA1001	United Technologies Corp. Hartford, Ct.	G-BTTG
N100UP	88	Falcon 900B	44	Paget Holdings LLC. Westport, Ct.	HB-IBY
N100VR	01	Global Express	9098	DSC Enterprises Inc/Tisma Inc. Dulles, Va.	N149VB
N100WE	02	390 Premier 1	RB-45	Wiens Aviation LLC. Broomfield, Co.	N809RM
N100WN	79	Learjet 25D	25D-288	Columbus State Community College, Columbus, Oh. (status ?).	(N40BC)
N100WP	90	Citation V	560-0073	Thunderbird Air LLC. Tempe, Az.	
N100WT	98	Citation Bravo	550-0858	Charter Services Inc. Mobile, Al.	N1273Q
N100WY	01	Falcon 2000	178	WBY LLC. Carlsbad, Ca.	N884WY
N100Y	00	Citation Bravo	550-0919	Saratoga Inc. Lebanon, Or.	N52601
N100YB	00	Citation Excel	560-5136	Peach Aviation LLC/Yancey Brothers Co. De Kalb, GA.	N522RA
N100YP	88	Falcon 100	222	Villages Equipment Co. Leesburg, Fl.	N98VR
N101AJ	75	Learjet 36	36-008	Intermap Technologies Inc. Calgary, AB. Canada.	(N43A)
N101AR	06	Hawker 400XP	RK-461	A & R Aircraft LLC/Smith Pipe & Steel, Phoenix, Az.	N61XP
N101CC	00	Beechjet 400A	RK-277	Clark Distributing Co. Oakland, Ky.	(N566W)
N101CV	93	Gulfstream 4SP	1230	CSC Transport Inc. White Plains, NY.	9M-TRI
N101ET	82	Falcon 50	95	Morse Operations Inc. Fort Lauderdale Executive, Fl.	N95FJ
N101FC	98	Hawker 800XP2	258380	Field Container Aviation LLC. Elk Grove Village, Il.	N999JF
N101FG	98	Citation Bravo	550-0839	University Athletic Association Inc. Gainesville, Fl.	N839DW
N101HS	76	Falcon 10	82	Dassault Air LLC. Houston, Tx.	N602NC
N101HW	94	Learjet 60	60-037	RMSC West Palm Beach Inc. Fort Lauderdale, Fl.	N637LJ
N101JL	01	Citation Bravo	550-1002	Link Snacks Inc. Rice Lake Regional, Wi.	N52397
N101KP	99	Citation V Ultra	560-0520	King Pharmaceuticals Inc. Bristol, Tn.	N620AT
N101L	06	Gulfstream G200	156	Landow & Company Builders, Dulles, Va.	N656GA
N101MH	00	Gulfstream V	609	Standard & Poor's Securities Evaluations Inc. White Plains.	N418SM
N101PC	66	BAC 1-11/401AK	073	Sky King Inc. Sacramento, Ca.	N401SK
N101PG	86	Citation III	650-0126	The Pape' Group Inc. Coburg, Or.	N311MA
N101PV	03	Falcon 2000EX	23	Vegso Aviation Inc. Boca Raton, Fl.	N223EX
N101QS	06	Hawker 400XP	RK-484	NetJets/Marquis Jet Partners Inc. Port Columbus, Oh.	
N101RR	82	Citation 1/SP	501-0241	Crawford Products Co. Montebello, Ca.	C-GSTR
N101U	01	CitationJet CJ-1	525-0454	Varsity/Intropa Tours Inc. Southaven, Ms.	N541CJ
N101UD	04	Learjet 60	60-275	Unicorp National Development Inc. Orlando, Fl.	
N101VM	81	Falcon 10	177	MGM Time Machine LLC/BioMed Realty Trust, Berwyn, Pa.	F-GFGB
N101VS	70	Learjet 24B	24B-218	Calspan Corp. Buffalo, NY.	N682LJ
N101WY	02	Citation Encore	560-0620	Department of Transportation, Cheyenne, Wy.	N.....
N102BG	03	Gulfstream G550	5038	Berwind Corp. Philadelphia, Pa.	N372BG
N102BP	78	HS 125/700A	NA0226	Chocolate Chip Aviation LLC. Spring Branch, Tx.	N1776E
N102BQ	95	Gulfstream 4SP	1273	Invesco Group Services Inc. Atlanta, Ga.	N102BG
N102CE	95	Citation VII	650-7061	Centerpoint Energy Service Co. Houston, Tx.	N202CW
N102CL	06	390 Premier 1A	RB-178	Empire Companies Inc. Ontario, Ca.	N3378M
N102CX	71	Gulfstream 2B	102	Clorox Co/KaiserAir Inc. Oakland, Ca.	N400CC
N102DR	82	Citation II/SP	551-0436	D R Johnson Lumber Co/CO-GEN Co. Riddle, Or. (was 550-0437)	N11SS
N102FD	05	Gulfstream G200	128	Federated Mutual Insurance Co. Burbank, Ca.	4X-CVE
N102HB	82	Citation II	550-0409	Buzz-Air of Indiana Inc. East Chicago, In.	VR-CIT
N102KP	99	Citation V Ultra	560-0527	King Pharmaceuticals Inc. Bristol, Tn.	N627AT
N102LJ	97	Learjet 60	60-102	Williams International Air Inc. Rochester, NY.	LV-WXN
N102PT	01	CitationJet CJ-1	525-0433	Symons Living Trust. San Francisco, Ca.	N5223D
N102QS	04	Hawker 400XP	RK-380	NetJets, Port Columbus, Oh.	
N102TF	82	Falcon 50	125	VTEN Management LLC. Dallas, tx.	TS-JAM
N102VP	74	Citation	500-0200	K & KR Aircraft Inc. Taylorsville, Ut.	CS-DBM
N102VS	74	Learjet 25B	25B-180	Arvin Calspan Corp/Veridian Flight Research, Roswell, NM.	N266BS
N102WY	02	Citation Encore	560-0621	Department of Transportation, Cheyenne, Wy.	N.....
N103AL	06	Hawker 850XP	258822	KIRE Aviation LLC/Kiwah Development Partners, Charleston, SC	N822XP
N103BG	00	Citation V	560-0091	BG3 LLC/Sun Steel Co. Chicago, Il.	N32PB
N103CD	84	Gulfstream 3	418	World Heir Inc. College Park, Ga.	PT-ALK

Reg	Yr	Type	c/n	Owner/Operator	Prev Regn
❏ N103CX	98	Citation Bravo	550-0856	Clorox Services Co. Marietta, Ga.	N426JK
❏ N103F	66	HFB 320	1023	E O Ramonat, Murfresboro, Tn. (status ?).	N320AF
❏ N103HC	83	Diamond 1A	A068SA	SamCo Aviation LLC. Jacksonville, Fl.	(N68TK)
❏ N103HT	86	BAe 125/800A	258074	LKRD LLC/G4 Enterprises, Roslyn Heights, NY.	N850SM
❏ N103LS	05	Learjet 60	60-288	Turnberry Associates, Fort Lauderdale, Fl.	N40077
❏ N103PG	05	Citation Excel XLS	560-5590	The Pape' Group Inc. Coburg, Or.	N590XL
❏ N103SK	06	390 Premier 1A	RB-151	Aerospace Trust Management, Wilmington, De.	N102SK
❏ N103TA	69	Sabre-60	306-27	Ian Hassib Massry, Gainesville, Fl.	(N105SS)
❏ N103VF	85	Citation S/II	S550-0046	Geo M Martin Co. Emeryville, Ca.	N760NB
❏ N104AD	00	Gulfstream 4SP	1406	ACF Property Management Inc. Van Nuys, Ca.	N526EE
❏ N104AE	77	HS 125/700A	NA0203	L & C Aircraft Sales & Leasing LLC. Portland, Me.	N620M
❏ N104AG	07	Hawker 900XP	HA-52	Hawker Beechcraft Corp. Wichita, Ks.	
❏ N104AR	98	Gulfstream 4SP	1346	Greenaap Aviation Ltd.	N346GA
❏ N104CT*	07	Citation X	750-0275	Townsend Vision Inc. Des Moines, Ia.	N4119S
❏ N104FL	03	Citation Bravo	550-1071	State of Florida Aircraft Operations, Tallahassee, Fl.	N5090A
❏ N104GB	83	Diamond 1A	A041SA	Byram Aviation Ltd. Austin, Tx.	N300AR
❏ N104HW	87	Citation II	550-0555	White Flood LLC. San Jose, Ca. (was 551-0555).	N93BA
❏ N104LV	01	Citation Excel	560-5190	Pronto LLC/Love's Travel Shops & Country Store, OKC.	G-XLSB
❏ N104PC	04	CitationJet CJ-2	525A-0212	Caymus Vineyards, Rutherford, Ca.	N5226B
❏ N104RS	79	Westwind-1124	273	C 23 Ltd. Lewes, De.	(N566PG)
❏ N104VV	69	Gulfstream II SP	53	Sano Aviation, College Point, NY.	N104CD
❏ N104WJ	73	Learjet 25B	25B-104	Rodatz Financial Inc.	N35WJ
❏ N105AJ	77	Gulfstream 2TT	201	Gulfstream Parts LLC. Bradenton, Fl.	HZ-AFI
❏ N105AX	95	Beechjet 400A	RK-105	H A H A Air LLC/The Sembler Co. St Petersburg, Fl.	N127BV
❏ N105BA	74	Learjet 25XR	25XR-152	Flites Inc. Batavia, Il.	XA-JSC
❏ N105BG	86	Citation S/II	S550-0105	Republic Aviation LLC. Chattanooga, Tn.	(N12907)
❏ N105BK	89	Falcon 900	70	Springway,	(VH-VIW)
❏ N105CJ	04	CitationJet CJ-3	525B-0005	Noble Wings USA LLC. Strongsville, Oh.	N5270E
❏ N105FN	98	Astra-1125SPX	105	RAL Capital LLC. Scottsdale, Az.	HB-VMG
❏ N105GA	66	Learjet 24A	24A-116	Younkin Boreing Inc. Hot Springs, Ar.	(N1420)
❏ N105HD	75	Sabre-75A	380-39	Private Jet of Stuart Inc. Stuart, Fl. (status ?).	(N55HD)
❏ N105JA	73	Citation	500-0131	Jet Air Inc. Galesburg, Il.	PT-OJF
❏ N105P	99	CitationJet	525-0336	Oil Well Perforators Inc. Glendive, Mt.	N51564
❏ N105ST	07	Gulfstream G550	5170	Gulfstream Aerospace Corp. Savannah, Ga.	N770GA
❏ N105TB	68	Gulfstream 2	31	MIT Lincoln Labs/Air Force Material Command, Bedford, Ma.	N200CC
❏ N105TF	73	HFB 320	1055	Kalitta Flying Service Inc. Morristown, Tn.	N7865T
❏ N105UP	86	Challenger 601	3066	Millenium Aviation Inc. Kingstown, St Vincent, W.I.	VP-CLE
❏ N105VS	82	Gulfstream 3	370	Kaizen Aviation Inc. Jacksonville, Fl.	N463LM
❏ N105WC	81	Falcon 50	60	U S Leaseco Inc. Baltimore, Md.	CS-DFJ
❏ N106CG	88	Beechjet 400	RJ-12	Twin Springs Aviation, St Louis, Mo.	N3112K
❏ N106CJ	93	CitationJet	525-0006	Citation 525 Inc/Northwest Stamping Inc. Eugene, Or.	N1326P
❏ N106CX	99	Citation X	750-0106	Wilkes & McHugh PA/Mike's Airplane Rentals Inc. Tampa, Fl.	N52642
❏ N106FT	05	Citation Bravo	550-1123	Frac Tech Services Inc/Wilks Masonry Corp. Cisco, Tx.	N5212M
❏ N106JT	06	CitationJet CJ-3	525B-0106	CJ3 Charter LLC/Mountain Air Charter LLC. Taos, NM.	N5218T
❏ N106KC	96	Beechjet 400A	RK-132	Cambata Aviation inc. Roanoke, Va.	N1087Z
❏ N106KM	80	Gulfstream 3	305	Kingdom Aircraft IV LLC. Wilmington, De.	N553JT
❏ N106QS	04	Hawker 400XP	RK-381	NetJets, Port Columbus, Oh.	
❏ N106RW	02	Falcon 900EX EASY	120	MMRB/Global Transportation Systems Inc. Manassas, Va.	N900EX
❏ N106SP	95	Citation V Ultra	560-0347	Partee Aviation LLC/Partee Drilling Co. Big Spring, Tx.	N72FE
❏ N106SR	82	Citation II	550-0346	Wolper Aviation LLC. Salt Lake City, Ut.	N106SP
❏ N106TW	76	Falcon 10	84	Titan International Inc. Quincy, Il.	N192MC
❏ N107A	88	Gulfstream 4	1070	Airtime LLC. Kenosha, Wi.	N407GA
❏ N107CG	91	Citation VI	650-0207	Premier Communications Inc. Oklahoma City, Ok.	N334WC
❏ N107EE	91	Citation II	550-0667	E & J Aircraft Sales & Leasing Inc. Longwood, Fl.	N167EA
❏ N107EG	99	Citation Bravo	550-0894	Elmo Greer & Sons LLC. London-Corbin, Ky.	N550TE
❏ N107HF	69	Learjet 25XR	25XR-029	White Industries Inc. Bates City, Mo. (status ?).	N28LA
❏ N107J	67	Falcon 20C	107	Flying Investment LLC/Jones Motorcars Inc. Fayetteville, Ar.	N213LS
❏ N107LT	81	HS 125/700A	NA0301	Lifetouch Inc/LT Flight Services Inc. Minneapolis, Mn.	N421SZ
❏ N107PT	06	CitationJet CJ-3	525B-0127	Papa Tango LLC/Paul Financial LLC. Napa, Ca.	N5268A
❏ N107RC	87	Citation S/II	S550-0150	Esland Management LLC. Vista, Ca.	N150CJ
❏ N107RM	83	Learjet 25D	25D-362	Brian Pardo, Woodway, Tx.	(N107MS)
❏ N107WR	02	390 Premier 1	RB-73	Bank of Utah, Salt Lake City, Ut. (trustor ?).	(N107YR)
❏ N108AR	85	Gulfstream 3	461	Wilder Aviation Sales & Service Inc. Clearwater, Fl.	N104AR
❏ N108CG	98	Astra-1125SPX	108	Orne Equipment Leasing LLC. Portland, Me.	N302TS
❏ N108CJ	95	CitationJet	525-0108	Alta Absaroka LLC. Petaluma, Ca.	N5211Q
❏ N108DB	90	Gulfstream 4	1149	Blum Capital Partners LP. San Francisco, Ca.	N152KB

Reg	Yr	Type	c/n	Owner/Operator	Prev Regn
N108DD	04	Hawker 800XP2	258700	ADC Holdings LLC. Oakdale, Ca.	
N108EK	99	Citation Excel	560-5032	New Heights Aviation LLC. Minneapolis-Flying Cloud, Mn.	N165JB
N108FL	80	Learjet 25D	25D-300	Learjet 25D-300 LLC. Charleston, WV.	N659HX
N108JN	80	Learjet 35A	35A-358	Scholten Roofing Co. Mission Viego, Ca.	N358PG
N108KC	74	Falcon 10	8	Keller Companies Inc. Manchester, NH.	N88ME
N108LJ	95	Citation V Ultra	560-0337	Cessna Finance Corp. Wichita, Ks.	N5265N
N108MC	76	Citation	500-0322	Farmington Jet Center LLC. Tucson, Az.	N1AP
N108MS	02	BBJ-7BC	33102	Yona Aviation LLC. Needham, Ma.	N105QS
N108PJ	07	Hawker 900XP	HA-24	PinJet Aviation LLC/Preferred Care Partners, Plano, Tx.	N924XP
N108QS	04	Hawker 400XP	RK-382	NetJets, Port Columbus, Oh.	
N108R	67	Falcon 20DC	108	Kalitta Charters LLC. Detroit-Willow Run, Mi.	N101ZE
N108RB	77	Learjet 35A	35A-097	Turbo Commander Inc. Miami, Fl.	N135J
N108RF	97	Citation Bravo	550-0805	David Gifford, Weston, Ma.	(N4AT)
N108RL	73	Citation	500-0125	Edalpe Construcciones CA. Wilmington, De.	XA-SFE
N108WV	91	Citation VI	650-0204	Willamette Valley Co. Eugene, Or.	N811JT
N109BG	81	HS 125/700A	NA0310	GB Air Ltd/The Geis Companies, Streetsboro, Oh.	N128WU
N109CP	92	Beechjet 400A	RK-47	THV Seminars LLC/UCG Inc. Rockville, Md.	N408PC
N109CQ	04	Falcon 50EX	340	Richard Schaden PC. Broomfield, Co.	N340EX
N109DD	84	Gulfstream 3	415	TVPX Inc. Concord, Ma.	N21NR
N109GX	01	Gulfstream G100	142	Cook Inc. Bloomington, In.	4X-CVK
N109HV	95	Learjet 31A	31A-105	Travel Lear Charter Service Inc. Oklahoma City, Ok.	N109FX
N109JC	79	Citation II	550-0099	Stroud Aviation Inc. Stroud, Ok.	N2664L
N109NT	03	Hawker 400XP	RK-374	Perkins Transportation Co. Atlanta, Ga.	N374XP
N109SB	74	Sabre-75A	380-20	Sabre Direct, Raleigh, NC.	N773W
N109ST	04	Gulfstream G550	5049	ST Aviation LLC. Naples, Fl.	N949GA
N109WS	02	Citation Encore	560-0632	Southwestern Energy Co. Springdale, Ar.	N6521F
N110AJ	78	Sabre-75A	380-70	Amazon Aviation Corp. Pembroke Pines, Fl.	(N380RS)
N110BP	04	Challenger 604	5579	Popular Inc. San Juan, PR.	C-GLYC
N110DS	80	Diamond 1A	A005SA	Jet Charter Inc. Woodstock, Ga.	N30HD
N110ED	06	Gulfstream G550	5136	CandyBar Aviation LLC. Tampa, Fl.	N536GA
N110EJ	80	HS 125/700A	NA0273	Forest Air LLC. Chicago, Il.	(N4477X)
N110ET	82	Learjet 55	55-023	Perry Johnson Inc/Pontiac Aviation LLC. Mi. (status ?).	(N236PJ)
N110EX	00	Falcon 900EX	71	Sky River Consulting LLC. Las Vegas, Nv.	(N971EX)
N110FD	06	CitationJet CJ2+	525A-0308	Flournoy Development Co. Columbus, Oh.	N308CJ
N110FS	07	Gulfstream G150	247	Gulfstream Aerospace LP. Dallas-Love, Tx.	4X-C
N110GA	88	Beechjet 400	RJ-44	SRA Alliance LLC. Stillwater, Ok.	I-TOPJ
N110HA	01	Gulfstream G200	035	Ferehunt Investment Inc. Tortola, BVI.	N59GX
N110J	79	Falcon 10	139	Ian Air LLC. Troy, Mi.	(N610J)
N110JB	81	Citation 1/SP	501-0172	IMI Holdings LLC/Sky King Inc. Asheville, NC.	HI-581SP
N110LD	82	Citation II	550-0366	Warrington Development Corp. Gulf Shores, Al.	(N614GA)
N110MG	00	Astra-1125SPX	122	Teton Jet Inc. Bellegrade, Mt.	N419TK
N110PR	01	390 Premier 1	RB-29	John J Machado Inc. Modesto, Ca.	N747BK
N110RA	69	Learjet 25	25-025	Royal Air Freight Inc. Pontiac, Mi.	(N111LM)
N110SE	01	Learjet 31A	31A-217	Safety Supply Corp. Memphis, Tn.	N10SE
N110TP	06	Citation Bravo	550-1131	Kuala Lumpur Kepong Bhd. Ipoh, Perak, Malaysia.	N5227G
N110WA	82	Citation II	550-0408	Musco Sports Lighting Inc. Oskaloosa, Ia.	N400TX
N111AF	81	Citation II	550-0256	Cheyenne Distribution Inc. Tulsa, Ok.	N55TP
N111BB	75	Citation	500-0248	B & B Sales, Dallas, Tx.	(N70PB)
N111BF	96	CitationJet	525-0140	Home State County Mutual Insurance Co. Waco, Tx.	N725L
N111BP	67	Falcon 20C	111	Jones Motorcars Inc. Fayetteville, Ar.	N111AM
N111CQ	03	Gulfstream G450	4006	Professional Jet LLC/Qiznos Corp. Jeffco, Co.	N166GA
N111CX	95	Beechjet 400A	RK-210	Sabre Transportation Inc. Barboursville, WV.	
N111DT*	79	Citation II	550-0089	Shenandoah Petroleum Properties Inc. Midland, Tx.	N800RR
N111FA	80	Gulfstream 3	307	Quikrete International Inc. Atlanta-DeKalb, Ga.	C-GGPM
N111FK	92	Challenger 601-3A	5104	FK Air LLC/Kelley & Farraro LLP. Fort Lauderdale, Fl.	N720LM
N111FW	95	Beechjet 400A	RK-102	Acme Brick Co. Fort Worth, Tx.	N916GR
N111GD	75	Gulfstream 2	170	XTO Energy Corp. Fort Worth, Tx.	N202XT
N111GJ	02	CitationJet CJ-1	525-0500	PK Equipment Holding LLC. Tx.	N525CJ
N111GU	03	Citation Excel XLS	560-5504	Edinton Holdings USA Inc. Guatemala City, Guatemala.	N.....
N111HC	86	Gulfstream 3	482	Collins Brothers Corp. Las Vegas, Nv.	N268RJ
N111HZ	99	Falcon 2000	86	The Hertz Corp. Teterboro, NJ.	F-WWVF
N111JW	07	CitationJet CJ2+	525A-0387	Cessna Aircraft Co. Wichita, Ks.	N5268M
N111JX	70	BAC 1-11/414EG	163	Pearl Jam Touring Inc. Waukesha, Wi.	N123H
N111KK	99	Learjet 45	45-061	Kohler Co. Kohler, Wi.	
N111KR	82	Learjet 35A	35A-464	Cloud Travel LLC. Memphis, Tn.	VP-BJS
N111ME	74	Citation	500-0146	Westsky LLC. Schertz, Tx.	N194AT

Reg	Yr	Type	c/n	Owner/Operator	Prev Regn
N111MP	73	Learjet 25XR	25XR-139	223RS LLC. Dillon, Mt.	N605NE
N111NB	07	BBJ-7HE	36027		
N111QS	86	Citation S/II	S550-0111	Prestige Air LLC. Las Vegas, Nv.	(N777HN)
N111RZ	65	BAC 1-11/401AK	056	Rotec Industries Inc. Rockford, Il. (status ?).	N491ST
N111UN	76	HS 125/600A	256055	Arnoni Aviation Ltd. Houston, Tx.	(N600GP)
N111VG	99	Hawker 800XP	258403	VG Aircraft LLC-Viking Global Investors LP. Oxford, Ct.	N601RS
N111VM	07	BBJ2-7GV/W	36090	WFBNW NA. Salt Lake City, Ut. (trustor ?).	
N111WB	74	Learjet 35	35-003	Aero-Jet Aviation Inc. Fort Lauderdale, Fl.	N703MA
N111WW	80	Falcon 10	167	Joe Kirk Fulton, Lubbock, Tx.	N82CG
N111Y	06	Citation Sovereign	680-0127	Ingram Industries Inc. Nashville, Tn.	N51038
N111YW	92	Citation VI	650-0223	Summit Investments Aviation LLC. Smyrna, Tn.	N111Y
N111ZN	07	Hawker 850XP	258830	Zenith National Insurance Co. Van Nuys, Ca.	N72520
N111ZS	79	HS 125/700A	257076	Scozak Aviation LLC. Oakland Park, Fl.	(N776TS)
N112AB	04	Citation Excel	560-5361	ABF Aviation LLC/Arkansas Best Corp. Fort Smith, Ar.	G-CFGL
N112BJ	96	Beechjet 400A	RK-112	Corporate Jet Partners LLC. Atlanta, Ga.	N94LH
N112CF	01	Challenger 604	5509	First Data Corp. Englewood, Co.	N604BG
N112CM	04	390 Premier 1	RB-123	Odyssey Aviation LLC. Mosinee, Wi.	N3723A
N112CW	95	Citation V Ultra	560-0298	West Creek Aviation, Dallas, Tx.	N25CV
N112GS	02	CitationJet CJ-2	525A-0127	Blue Sky Inc. Coatesville, Pa.	N12GS
N112MV*	07	Citation Sovereign	680-0148	Metavante Corp. Milwaukee, Wi.	N515TB
N112PR	87	Astra-1125	013	Tevis Technology Partners LLC. Menlo Park, Ca.	(N77JW)
N112SH	79	Citation II	550-0043	Canary Aircraft Sales Corp. Fort Smith, Ar.	N801JP
N113	66	B 727-30	18935	Blue Falcon Corp. El Paso, Tx. (stored ?).	N18G
N113AR	87	Gulfstream 4	1018	Aviation Jets LLC. Opa Locka, Fl.	N418QA
N113BG	02	CitationJet CJ-2	525A-0078	7G's Aviation LLC. Bakersfield, Ca.	N5162W
N113CS	88	Gulfstream 4	1049	113CS LLC. Oxford, Ct.	N372CM
N113GH	80	Westwind-1124	286	Dexter Airways LLC/World Color Inc. Ormond Beach, Fl.	N110LP
N113SH	75	Citation	500-0285	SW Orthopaedic & Sports Medicine, Oklahoma City, Ok.	N86SS
N113US	06	Citation Encore	560-0701	Pamplemousse LLC/United Supermarkets Inc. Lubbock, Tx.	N.....
N113VP	91	Citation V	560-0113	Central Airlines LLC. Chesterfield, Mo.	N4
N113YS	82	Learjet 55	55-071	Stevens & Soldwisch Aircraft LLC. Denver, Co.	N155JC
N114BD	99	Learjet 60	60-166	Black Diamond Aviation Group LLC. White Plains, NY.	N60ZD
N114CJ	06	CitationJet CJ-3	525B-0114	TVPX Inc. Concord, Ma.	N52234
N114FW	98	CitationJet	525-0307	Fred Gibbons Separate Property Trust, Los Altos Hills, Ca.	(N114FG)
N114LJ	99	Learjet 60	60-157	Animus Aviation Support LLC.	N236FX
N114M	86	BAe 146-100	E1068	Moncrief Oil International, Fort Worth, Tx. 'Lucky Liz'	N861MC
N114QS	06	Hawker 400XP	RK-469	NetJets, Port Columbus, Oh.	(CS-DMM)
N114RA	75	Westwind-1123	179	Alberth Air Parts Inc. Cypress, Tx.	LV-WJU
N114SN	99	Astra-1125SPX	114	ROCK-TENN Co. Atlanta-DeKalb, Ga.	N114GA
N114VW	99	Citation X	750-0093	SELA Plane LLC. Houston, Tx.	N71RP
N114WD	67	HS 125/3A	25114	Ambient Aviation LLC. Fort Lauderdale, Fl.	XA-SGP
N115AN	06	Learjet 60	60-308	Anderson News Corp. Knoxville, Tn.	
N115BB	98	CitationJet	525-0325	SRM Developments, Spokane, Wa.	N764C
N115BR	98	Astra-1125SPX	099	Southstar 115 LLC. Boca Raton, Fl.	N838DB
N115BX	96	Learjet 31A	31A-129	Averitt Aviation Group Inc. Nashville, Tn.	N115FX
N115CJ	02	CitationJet CJ-2	525A-0115	Conquest Services Inc. Petaluma, Ca.	N.....
N115CR	69	Sabre-60	306-43	A S Aviation Inc. Wilmington, De.	N10UM
N115HK	97	Global Express	9004	Mezzanine Financing Ltd. Camas, Va.	(N11TK)
N115K	91	Citation V	560-0148	KaiserAir Inc. Oakland, Ca.	N560FB
N115QS	04	Hawker 400XP	RK-383	NetJets, Port Columbus, Oh.	
N115SK	02	Falcon 50EX	330	SAKS Inc. Memphis, Tn.	N330EX
N115TD	77	Falcon 10	96	Waterside Aircraft Marketing LLC. Old Saybrook, Ct.	N96TJ
N115WF	94	Challenger 601-3R	5153	Boards Aircraft LLC. Hillsboro, Or.	N653AC
N115WZ	07	390 Premier 1A	RB-197	Borisch Manufacturing Corp. Grand Rapids, Mi.	(LX-VAZ)
N116AD	02	Beechjet 400A	RK-338	West Cherry Sales LLC. Memphis, Tn.	(N726PG)
N116AP	98	Beechjet 400A	RK-192	Hawker Beechcraft Corp. Wichita, Ks.	N116AD
N116AS	99	Learjet 45	45-078	City Aviation Services Inc. Detroit, Mi.	N5016Z
N116DD	78	JetStar 2	5224	Charles Joekel, Houston, Tx.	N6QZ
N116GB	73	Falcon 20F	281	Greg Biffle Inc. Statesville, NC.	N341KA
N116JC	86	Astra-1125	014	CheckFree Services Corp. Norcross, Ga.	(N214TJ)
N116K	80	Citation II	550-0149	KaiserAir Inc. Oakland, Ca.	
N116LA	78	Citation II	550-0016	Tiger Jet Sales & Leasing LLC. Hollywood, Fl.	N204MC
N116LJ	05	CitationJet CJ1+	525-0617	Shamaley Pontiac Buick GMC, Santa Teresa, NM.	N1TG
N116LM*	98	Learjet 60	60-142	Lithia Motors Inc. Medford, Or.	(N940RL)
N116LS	87	Challenger 601-3A	5013	Moldex Leasing Inc. Burbank, Ca.	N950FB
N116MA	77	Learjet 36A	36A-029	Dutch Navy, Valkenburg, Holland.	N16MA

Reg	Yr	Type	c/n	Owner/Operator	Prev Regn
❏ N116PB	89	Astra-1125	032	Pelican Air LLC. Santa Ana, Ca.	N125MG
❏ N116QS	04	Hawker 400XP	RK-385	NetJets, Port Columbus, Oh.	
❏ N116RA	81	Challenger 600S	1011	Central Connecticut Aircraft LLC. Plainville, Ct.	N678ML
❏ N116SC	62	Sabre-40R	282-1	Sabreliner Corp. St Louis, Mo. 'Sabre One'	(N351JM)
❏ N117AH	81	Westwind-Two	352	Gabriel Investments LLC. Woodbury, Ct.	N117JW
❏ N117AJ*	85	Falcon 50	154	Real World Tours Inc. Brentwood, Tn.	N154PA
❏ N117DJ	79	Citation 1/SP	501-0127	Executive Travel Inc. Henderson, Nv.	N86SK
❏ N117FJ	78	Gulfstream 2	229	J T Aviation Corp. Ronkonkoma, NY.	N702H
❏ N117JJ	75	Gulfstream II SP	163	Gavilan Corp. Fort Lauderdale, Fl. 'El Condor'	N117JA
❏ N117JW	81	Sabre-65	465-61	AmQuip Sales & Leasing Inc. Bethlehem, Pa.	N23BX
❏ N117K	73	Learjet 24D	24D-272	Clay Lacy Aviation Inc. Van Nuys, Ca.	N51GL
❏ N117LR	83	Learjet 55	55-075	Paradiso Aviazione LLC/Inserra Supermarkets Inc. Teterboro.	N90NE
❏ N117MA	79	Citation 1/SP	501-0249	SabresAir Inc/Maguire Products Inc. Aston, Pa.	(N82MP)
❏ N117MS	94	Gulfstream 4SP	1241	Starwood Capital Group, White Plains, NY.	N843DF
❏ N117PK	84	Learjet C-21A	35A-513	Pert 35 Inc. Fenwick Island, De.	N35AQ
❏ N117QS	04	Hawker 400XP	RK-391	NetJets, Port Columbus, Oh.	
❏ N117RY	94	Challenger 601-3R	5162	Dependable Component Supply, Deerfield Beach, Fl.	N850FB
❏ N117SF	88	Falcon 900B	55	Constellation Leasing LLC. Fairport, NY.	C-GSMR
❏ N117TF	05	Global Express	9175	Tudor Investment Corp. White Plains, NY.	N771TF
❏ N117TW	73	Citation	500-0059	Zovinar Development LLC/Kutumian Construction, Fresno, Ca.	N913RC
❏ N117W	07	CitationJet CJ2+	525A-0350	Wallace Enterprises Inc. Atlanta-Fulton County, Ga.	N5260Y
❏ N117WR	04	Gulfstream G350	4015	Whisky Romeo Owner LLC. Las Vegas, Nv.	N915GA
❏ N118AD	78	Falcon 10	118	Curtis Air LLC. Connell, Wa.	(N97RJ)
❏ N118B	77	JetStar 2	5211	Four Star International Inc. Laredo, Tx.	N821MD
❏ N118CJ	07	CitationJet CJ2+	525A-0384	Cessna Aircraft Co. Wichita, Ks.	N5218R
❏ N118DA	66	HS 125/731	25118	Bluegrass Gas Sales Inc. Anchorage, Ky.	N14HH
❏ N118FN	77	Learjet 35A	35A-118	Aero-Jet Aviation Inc. Fort Lauderdale, Fl.	N88JA
❏ N118GA	87	BAe 125/800A	NA0408	Transnet/Garden Commercial Properties, Teterboro, NJ.	N703VZ
❏ N118K	92	BAe 125/800A	NA0471	KaiserAir Inc. Oakland, Ca.	N57PM
❏ N118MM	97	Citation VII	650-7105	Milgard Manufacturing Inc. Tacoma, Wa.	N715QS
❏ N118MT	90	Challenger 601-3A	5077	MTRM Realty LLC/Tennenbaum & Co. Santa Monica, Ca.	N64YP
❏ N118RH	01	Challenger 604	5516	Somerset Aviation LLC. Fort Lauderdale, Fl.	N516DG
❏ N118RJ	76	Westwind-1124	188	Gabriel Investments LLC. Woodbury, Ct.	C-GRDP
❏ N118RK	96	Citation V Ultra	560-0389	Telecommunications Financial Services, Baton Rouge, La.	N389JV
❏ N118ST	02	Citation Excel	560-5287	SunTrust Banks Inc. Atlanta, Ga.	N.....
❏ N119AC	67	Jet Commander	119	Aerocat SA. Catamarca, Argentina. (status ?).	C-FFBC
❏ N119AF	02	Gulfstream 4SP	1489	CDECRE Inc. Nashua, NH.	N212WZ
❏ N119AK	06	Hawker 4000	RC-9	Hawker Beechcraft Corp. Wichita, Ks.	(N809HH)
❏ N119BA	65	Learjet 23	23-084	House of Salt Inc. Calgary, AB. Canada.	N101JR
❏ N119EM*	07	Falcon 2000EX EASY	137	Dassault Falcon Jet Corp. Teterboro, NJ.	N137EM
❏ N119ES	91	Citation VI	650-0206	Elliott Sadler Enterprises Inc. Statesville, NC.	N610RP
❏ N119FM	00	Gulfstream 4SP	1464	KM Ventures 1 LLC. Latrobe, Pa.	N950HB
❏ N119QS	04	Hawker 400XP	RK-394	NetJets, Port Columbus, Oh.	
❏ N119RM	98	Citation X	750-0051	SA Wings of Texas LLC. San Antonio, Tx.	(N1419J)
❏ N119SJ	78	Falcon 10	119	Meregrass Inc. Dallas-Love, Tx.	N257V
❏ N119U	91	BAe 1000A	259007	Daniel Island Aviation LLC. Portsmouth, NH.	N119PW
❏ N120AK	04	Global Express	9153	Oak Management Corp. San Jose, Ca.	N454AJ
❏ N120AP	88	Hawker 800SP	258120	Airport Equipment Rentals Inc. Fairbanks, Ak.	G-POSN
❏ N120GS	07	Challenger 300	20165	Bombardier Aerospace Corp. Windsor Locks, Ct.	C-FOAE
❏ N120JC	79	HS 125/700A	NA0247	Southwestern Jet Charter Inc. Alton, Il.	N87AG
❏ N120JP	83	Citation II	550-0468	T & T Aviation Inc. Canonsburg, Pa.	N123FH
❏ N120NE	66	DC 9-15	45731	Genesis Aeronautics Inc. Van Nuys, Ca.	HB-IFA
❏ N120Q	82	Citation II	550-0332	Therm-O-Disc Inc. Mansfield, Oh.	N12CQ
❏ N120QS	05	Hawker 400XP	RK-409	NetJets, Port Columbus, Oh.	
❏ N120RA	67	Learjet 24	24-153	Royal Air Freight Inc. Pontiac, Mi.	N153BR
❏ N120YB	80	HS 125/700A	NA0282	Bemis Co Inc. Minneapolis, Mn.	N1982G
❏ N121AT	89	Falcon 100	226	Anthony Timberlands Inc. Phoenix, Az.	XA-RLX
❏ N121CG	86	Citation S/II	S550-0123	DJV Air Charters Inc. Tampa, Fl.	N1293A
❏ N121CK	65	Learjet 23	23-039	767070 Ontario Ltd. Niagara Falls, ON.	XA-...
❏ N121CN	01	Citation Bravo	550-1000	Chet Morrison Services LLC. Houma, La.	N5194B
❏ N121CP	00	CitationJet CJ-2	525A-0010	Sky Bank LLC/Pinnacle Bancorp Inc. Central City, Ne.	N5194J
❏ N121ET	04	Challenger 604	5583	E Trade Financial/BWL Aviation LLC. Menlo Park, Ca.	C-GLXK
❏ N121EZ	96	Beechjet 400A	RK-109	Roger Snellenberger Development Corp. Indio, Ca.	N3269A
❏ N121GF	06	Hawker 400XP	RK-503	San Crispin LLC/Viridian Management LLC.	XA-FLX
❏ N121GV	07	Gulfstream G200	094	Greenspun Corp/Starship Enterprise Leasing LLC. Las Vegas.	N394GA
❏ N121HL	80	Citation II	550-0121	Citation Air LLC/HSL Properties, Tucson, Az.	N899MA

Reg	Yr	Type	c/n	Owner/Operator	Prev Regn
N121JE	67	Sabre-60	306-4	JODA LLC. Chesterfield, Mo.	N1210
N121JJ	02	Gulfstream 4SP	1482	Liamaj Aviation Inc. Houston, Tx.	N13J
N121JM	99	Gulfstream 4SP	1399	SK Travel LLC/Emar Associates Inc. Livingston, NJ.	N499GA
N121KL	07	Citation Excel XLS	560-5720	KLC Transportation Ltd/Kwik Lok Corp. Seattle, Wa.	N.....
N121L	99	Citation Bravo	550-0896	SNI Bravo LLC/Southern Newspapers Inc. Houston, Tx.	
N121LJ	96	Learjet 31A	31A-121	Renfro Corp. Mount Airy, NC.	
N121LS	06	Citation Sovereign	680-0076	Frac Tech Services LLC. Cisco, Tx.	N.....
N121TL	05	Citation Sovereign	680-0058	Kirkwood Ventures LLC. Wilmington, De.	N5060K
N122BN	01	Global Express	9103	Barnes & Noble Inc. Teterboro, NJ.	C-GIXO
N122BX	97	Learjet 31A	31A-143	Priority Fulfillment Services Inc. Plano, Tx.	N122FX
N122DS	03	390 Premier 1	RB-100	American Air Charter Inc. Fort Lauderdale, Fl.	
N122EJ	86	Citation III	650-0122	Star XVI LLC. Jacksonville, Fl.	N65WL
N122GV	05	Gulfstream G450	4034	Greenspun Corp/Starship Enterprise Leasing LLC. Las Vegas.	N634GA
N122JW	79	Learjet 35A	35A-217	AirNet Systems Inc. Columbus, Oh.	N111RF
N122LM	05	CitationJet CJ1+	525-0604	Florida Flight LLC. Hazard, Ky.	N5183U
N122LX	82	Learjet 55	55-030	APLUX LLC. St Louis, Mo.	(N155CD)
N122MP	83	Westwind-1124	390	R & R Aircraft Inc. Delray Beach, Fl.	N59SM
N122NC	98	Citation Bravo	550-0836	North Carolina Department of Commerce, Raleigh, NC.	N51872
N122OS	05	Hawker 400XP	RK-467	NetJets, Port Columbus, Oh.	
N122SC	96	Falcon 2000	25	St Paul Aviation Inc. St Paul, Mn.	(N406ST)
N122SM	02	CitationJet CJ-2	525A-0151	Fegotila Ltd. Staverton, UK.	N.....
N122SP	82	Citation II/SP	551-0393	Erik Torbiorn Bjorck,	(N18CC)
N122ST	67	Jet Commander-B	122	Plain Old Plane LLC. Birmingham, Al.	XA-SCV
N122WS	86	Citation S/II	S550-0122	McDonald Investment Co/Watkins Air LLC. Birmingham, Al.	I-TALG
N122WW	82	Citation II	550-0365	Giddy Up N Go LLC. Dallas, Tx.	N129DV
N123CD	64	Sabre-40	282-23	National Bank of Commerce, Germantown, Tn. (status ?).	(N55ME)
N123CJ	07	CitationJet CJ-3	525B-0149	Cummings Air LLC/RAM Real Estate, Palm Beach Gardens, Fl.	N5261R
N123DG	76	Learjet 24F	24F-342	Commonwealth Aviation Corp. Port Orange, Fl.	N824GA
N123EB	77	Citation 1/SP	501-0020	Eagle Creek Aviation Services Inc. Indianapolis, In.	N32JJ
N123FT	98	Gulfstream V	549	Franklin Templeton Travel Inc. San Francisco, Ca.	N718MD
N123GF	97	Citation Bravo	550-0817	Rock Jet Inc. Burbank, Ca.	(YV-....)
N123GV	01	Gulfstream G200	043	Carabo Capital LLC. Greenville, Sc.	N122GV
N123HK	91	BAe 125/800A	258208	Hawk Aviation LLC. Houston, Tx.	N208BG
N123KD	81	Citation 1/SP	501-0195	Flight Solutions Inc. Gallatin, Tn.	N109DC
N123KH	95	Challenger 604	5301	Nag's Head Capital Management LLC. New Haven, Ct.	N608CC
N123M	01	Gulfstream V	667	Open Road Airways Inc. Palwaukee, Il.	N121BN
N123MJ	65	Learjet 23	23-036	Core One LLC. Boulder, Co.	YV-278CP
N123PL	82	Citation 1/SP	501-0234	MWBP Foundation LLC/Statsoft Inc. Tulsa, Ok.	N77PX
N123OS	06	Hawker 400XP	RK-486	NetJets/Marquis Jet Partners Inc. Port Columbus, Oh.	
N123RA	66	Falcon 20C	30	Royal Air Freight Inc. Pontiac, Mi.	N514SA
N123RC	81	Westwind-Two	349	Marck Aviation/Cambridge Industries Inc. Grosse Pointe, Mi.	N728L
N123S	03	CitationJet CJ-1	525-0525	RTS Consulting LLC. Far Hills, NJ.	N.....
N123SL	01	Citation X	750-0168	U S Bank NA. Milwaukee, Wi.	N1288B
N123VP	79	Citation II	550-0111	World Acceptance Corp. Greenville, SC.	(N3184Z)
N124BC	81	Westwind-Two	351	B Riley & Co. Los Angeles, Ca.	N111EL
N124BP	00	Learjet 45	45-113	Ben Carter Enterprises LLC. Atlanta-Fulton County, Ga.	N416FX
N124DC	74	Sabre-60	306-95	Drummond Company Inc. Birmingham, Al.	N999DC
N124DT	83	Gulfstream 3	390	Air Troxel LLC. Holualoa, Hi.	N102AQ
N124EP	84	Gulfstream 3	440	Maguire-Cushman Aviation LLC. Van Nuys, Ca.	N458BE
N124GR	81	Westwind-Two	315	Grupo Ruisanchez Corp. Fort Lauderdale, Fl.	(N89TJ)
N124HS	81	Westwind-1124	329	HSL LLC/McNichols Co. Tampa, Fl.	N7HM
N124JL	66	Learjet 24	24-127	Dolphin Aviation Inc. Sarasota, Fl.	(N6462)
N124LS	06	Embraer Legacy 600	14500948	L & G Management LLC. Palm City, Fl.	PT-SCT
N124NS	77	Citation	501-0278	Nolan's RV Center LLC. Jeffco, Co. (was 500-0368).	N124NB
N124PP	94	Beechjet 400A	RK-92	Bec-Faye LLC/Overton's Inc. Grimesland, NC.	N555KK
N124SD	79	Sabre-65	465-2	Healthy One Inc. Santa Monica, Ca.	N624DS
N124TF	86	Gulfstream 4	1004	Hume & Johnson PA. Coral Springs, Fl.	(N199LX)
N124WW	76	Westwind-1124	201	B & D Holdings Inc. Pembroke Pines, Fl.	C-FOIL
N124ZT	77	Learjet 35A	35A-138	55JS LC/Rehab Care Group, Salt Lake City, Ut.	N138NA
N125AW	92	BAe 125/800A	NA0472	J F Air Inc. Wilmington, De.	N58PM
N125BJ	03	CitationJet CJ-2	525A-0101	World Trade Enterprises Inc. Torrance, Ca.	(N533JF)
N125BW	06	Learjet 45	45-323	Celeste LLC/Cibolo Co. Fort Worth, Tx.	N50157
N125CH*	00	Global Express	9080	WFBNW NA. Salt Lake City, Ut. (trustor ?).	N283S
N125CK	71	HS 125/F400A	25266	Jet 4 You LLC. Missoula, Mt.	N135CK
N125CS	03	CitationJet CJ-1	525-0522	Vintage Air LLC/Barkley AG Enterprises LLP. Yuma, Az.	(N525BA)
N125DC	69	Gulfstream 2	55	Drummond Company Inc. Birmingham, Al.	N225SE

Reg	Yr	Type	c/n	Owner/Operator	Prev Regn
❏ N125DG	05	CitationJet CJ-3	525B-0060	Neils Fugal Sons Co. Pleasant Grove, Ut.	N5250P
❏ N125DH	71	HS 125/731	NA762	Bob's Aviation LLC/Westpac Properties Corp. Phoenix, Az.	N400GP
❏ N125DJ	00	CitationJet CJ-1	525-0422	Cimarron Av Corp. Dallas, Tx.	N51881
❏ N125DS	75	Citation	500-0258	FX Aviation LLC. Calhoun, Ga.	N886CA
❏ N125DT	74	TriStar 100	1079	Ultimate Air Corp/Donald Trump, NYC.	C-GIFE
❏ N125EA	80	Citation 1/SP	501-0125	Jackson-Shaw Co. Dallas, Tx.	N69EP
❏ N125FS	97	Learjet 31A	31A-125	Frontier Spinning Mills Inc. Sanford, NC.	N527JG
❏ N125GB	92	Hawker 800SP	NA0470	TCC Air Services Inc. Greenwich, Ct.	N60QJ
❏ N125HF	85	Westwind-1124	408	Henig Aviation LLC. Montgomery, Al.	N408MJ
❏ N125HH	85	BAe 125/800B	258034	Aero Toy Store LLC. Fort Lauderdale, Fl.	N85DW
❏ N125JG	93	Beechjet 400A	RK-75	Gettel Investments Inc. Sarasota, Fl.	N82400
❏ N125JR	65	HS 125/1A	25052	Aircraft R Us Corp. San Diego, Ca. (status ?).(wfu Toluca ?)	(N252MA)
❏ N125JW	81	Learjet 25G	25G-352	Bay Venture Management LLC. Atlanta, Ga.	N25FN
❏ N125LR	82	Learjet 55	55-032	DTA Charter LLC/Bari Management Inc. Van Nuys, Ca.	N255UJ
❏ N125NX	71	Sabre-75	370-3	Select Aviation Inc. Waukesha, Wi.	N125N
❏ N125PS	86	Challenger 601	3058	Omni Restaurant Consulting Co. Newport Beach, Ca.	C-GLXU
❏ N125PT	78	Learjet 25D	25D-244	Jet East Transportation LLC. Manhasset Hills, NY.	N831LH
❏ N125Q	86	Citation III	650-0128	Milliken & Co. Greenville, SC.	N628CC
❏ N125QA	86	Citation S/II	S550-0125	Capital City Aviation Inc. Madison, Wi.	(N552SM)
❏ N125QS	05	Hawker 400XP	RK-433	NetJets, Port Columbus, Oh.	
❏ N125RG	80	HS 125/700A	NA0263	Omnisure Consulting Group Inc. Love Field, Tx.	(N263TN)
❏ N125SB	85	BAe 125/800A	258046	McWhorter Properties Citation LLC. Anniston, Al.	N800BA
❏ N125ST	89	Challenger 601-3A	5052	Sterling Aviation Inc. Milwaukee, Wi.	(N615SA)
❏ N125TM	06	Challenger 300	20104	EMC Corp. Bedford-Hanscom Field, Ma.	C-FHNH
❏ N125XX	80	HS 125/700A	NA0254	Surewings Inc/Ambrion Aviation, Luton, UK.	N124AR
❏ N125ZZ	03	Hawker 800XP	258630	D & J Aviation Ltd. Luton, UK.	N630XP
❏ N126HY	06	Hawker 850XP	258782	Atlantic Paper & Foil LLC. Islip, NY.	(N260G)
❏ N126KC	95	Hawker 800SP	258276	Global Holding Corp. Hillsboro, Or.	N667H
❏ N126KD	03	Learjet 60	60-262	Kardan Inc. Northbrook, Il.	N5051A
❏ N126KL	84	Learjet 55	55-096	Williams Air Service Inc. St Augustine, Fl.	N126KD
❏ N126MT	84	Citation III	650-0044	Advent Aviation 1 LLC. Stewart, NY.	N129PJ
❏ N126TF	97	Citation Bravo	550-0815	Fox Lumber Sales Inc. Hamilton, Mt.	N51038
❏ N126ZZ	07	Hawker 4000	RC-10	Hawker Beechcraft Corp. Wichita, Ks.	(N810HH)
❏ N127BH	78	Learjet 25D	25D-250	BH Jr Motorsports Inc. White House, Tn.	N19JM
❏ N127BU	80	Citation II/SP	551-0179	Champagne Louis-Roederer, Biggin Hill, UK. (was 550-0134).	N203BE
❏ N127BW	05	Hawker 400XP	RK-449	B W Aviation LLC. Allegheny County, Pa.	N133QS
❏ N127GB	74	Learjet 25XR	25XR-175	Arredondo Ventures Inc. Bakersfield, Ca.	N75SJ
❏ N127GG	98	Gulfstream V	534	MGN Icarus LLC. Fort Lauderdale, Fl.	N920DC
❏ N127GK	80	Gulfstream 3	311	Cove Partners LLC. Van Nuys, Ca.	N127BK
❏ N127JJ	78	Citation II	550-0007	JJ's Jet LLC. Zanesville, Oh.	(N550TY)
❏ N127KC	94	Hawker 800	258255	AVX Corp/FlightWorks, Kennesaw, Ga.	N946H
❏ N127PM	78	Citation II	550-0027	Michael Crews Development II Inc. Carlsbad, Ca.	N222D
❏ N127QS	99	BBJ-7BC	30327	NetJets, Port Columbus, Oh.	N1786B
❏ N127RC	86	Citation S/II	S550-0088	TM1 LLC/Schenkel Shultz Architecture, Fort Wayne, In.	(N557TC)
❏ N127RP	93	BAe 1000A	259036	1489 LLC. Elmira-Corning, NY.	(N402FF)
❏ N127SF	97	Falcon 900EX	13	Constellation Brands Inc. Penn Yan, NY.	VP-BRO
❏ N127SG	93	CitationJet	525-0046	Airline Transport Professionals Corp. Jacksonville, Fl.	N123JN
❏ N127SR	97	Challenger 604	5358	P Dussman Inc. St Louis, Mo.	(C-GJQN)
❏ N127VL	91	Learjet 31A	31A-036	Konem Aviation LLC. Maimi, Fl.	(N127V)
❏ N127WL	74	Falcon 10	16	Westwood Lumber Co. Mahlon Sweet Field, Eugene, Or.	N416HC
❏ N128AB	02	Gulfstream G400	1501	Prime Jet LLC. Van Nuys, Ca.	(N402QS)
❏ N128CA	79	Learjet 35A	35A-248	Ameriflight Inc. Burbank, Ca.	C-GBFA
❏ N128CS	99	CitationJet CJ-1	525-0361	CitationShares Sales Inc. White Plains, NY.	N361RB
❏ N128GB	92	Challenger 601-3A	5113	BerryAir LLC. Orlando, Fl.	N733EX
❏ N128JL	02	390 Premier 1	RB-28	Premier 1 LLC. Wilmington, De.	N128RM
❏ N128JW	02	CitationJet CJ-2	525A-0152	Kolter Communities LLC. Boca Raton, Fl.	N123JW
❏ N128KG	69	Gulfstream 2	62	The Kipp Ginsburg Trust, Boca Raton, Fl.	N262PA
❏ N128LR	78	Learjet 28	28-001	Raven's Wing LLC. Allentown, Pa.	N3AS
❏ N128TS	95	Gulfstream 4SP	1263	DSA Aviation/Development Services of America, Seattle, Wa.	N263S
❏ N128V	01	Learjet 60	60-226	3 Air LLC. Chicago, Il.	N3011F
❏ N129BT	87	Beechjet 400	RJ-29	Beech Transportation Inc. Eden Prairie, Mn.	XA-OAC
❏ N129CK	07	CitationJet CJ2+	525A-0382	Cessna Aircraft Co. Wichita, Ks.	N5241Z
❏ N129ED	93	Citation II	550-0718	Enola Aviation & Development LLC. Chipley, Fl.	N142GA
❏ N129GB	83	Citation III	650-0006	BerryAir LLC. Orlando, Fl.	N128GB
❏ N129JD*	00	Learjet 31A	31A-193	Arizona LLC/Johnson Development Association, Spartanburg, SC	N44SZ
❏ N129JE	72	Falcon 20E	267	Sackett Corp. Oxford, Ct.	N267H

Reg	Yr	Type	c/n	Owner/Operator	Prev Regn
❏ N129KJ	00	Falcon 900C	184	Ohana Aircraft Ltd. Los Gatos, Ca.	F-WWFP
❏ N129MC	91	Citation V	560-0120	JLC Aviation LLC/Idle Air Technologies, Knoxville, Tn.	(N994CF)
❏ N129ME	79	Learjet 24F	24F-357	Kingswood Aviation Inc. Los Gatos, Ca.	N288J
❏ N129MH	03	Gulfstream G300	1517	Medco Health Solutions Inc. Franklin Lakes, NJ.	N517GA
❏ N129NS	96	Gulfstream 4SP	1281	National Air Service, Jeddah, Saudi Arabia.	N481QS
❏ N129PB	01	Citation Bravo	550-0973	Phoenix Bogo Inc. Wilmington, De.	N5245U
❏ N129QS	99	BBJ-7BC	30329	NetJets, Port Columbus, Oh.	N1787B
❏ N129RP	96	CitationJet	525-0173	Gage Aviation LLC/P & H Properties LLC. Tulsa, Ok.	N970SU
❏ N129SG	02	CitationJet CJ-2	525A-0129	Deer Horn Aviation LC. Midland, Tx.	N.....
❏ N129TS	79	Learjet 35A	35A-253	Development Services of America Inc. Seattle, Wa.	N611SH
❏ N129WA	67	Gulfstream 2B	9	John Wing Aviation Inc. Conroe, Tx.	N48EC
❏ N130CE	73	Citation Eagle	500-0130	Tumac Industries Inc. Grand Junction, Co.	N800AB
❏ N130CH	06	Challenger 300	20088	Empresas Puertoriquenes de Desarollo Inc. San Juan, PR.	C-FGVM
❏ N130CK	69	Learjet 25	25-038	Kalitta Charters LLC. Detroit-Willow Run, Mi.	N813JW
❏ N130CS	02	CitationJet CJ-1	525-0490	York House Real Estate KFT Inc. Wilmington, De.	(N130MH)
❏ N130DW	74	Citation	500-0187	Jet Thunder II LLC/Far West Capital Inc. Salt Lake City, Ut.	N5FW
❏ N130F	75	Learjet 35	35-044	AirNet Systems Inc. Columbus, Oh.	(N44VW)
❏ N130GA	07	Gulfstream G450	4130	Gulfstream Aerospace Corp. Savannah, Ga.	
❏ N130GV	00	Gulfstream V	630	EDS Information Services LLC. Dallas, Tx.	N630GA
❏ N130LC	92	BAe 125/800A	258228	Lakes Entertainment Inc. Minnetonka, Mn.	HB-VKV
❏ N130LM	97	CitationJet	525-0214	Capital Holdings 155 LLC. Naples, Fl.	N130NM
❏ N130RS	67	Learjet 24	24-138	Rocketplane Ltd Inc. Oklahoma City, Ok.	N94JJ
❏ N130TM	01	Gulfstream V	660	Toyota Motor Sales USA Inc. Long Beach, Ca.	N533GA
❏ N130WW	97	Beechjet 400A	RK-136	Widewaters Group, Syracuse, NY.	N397CA
❏ N130YB	80	HS 125/700A	NA0285	Curwood Inc. Oshkosh, Wi.	(N14WJ)
❏ N131AG	07	Falcon 2000EX EASY	131	Monsanto Co. St Louis, Mo.	F-WWGH
❏ N131AP	86	Beechjet 400	RJ-10	Cor Aviation Inc. Orlando, Fl. (was A1010SA).	I-ALSE
❏ N131BR	93	Learjet 31A	31A-074	DH Motorsports LLC. Mooresville, NC.	N174TS
❏ N131EP	95	Falcon 2000	10	Westshore Aviation/Prince Transportation Inc. Holland, Mi.	N652PC
❏ N131GG	95	Learjet 31A	31A-113	Hyena Air LLC. Atlanta, Ga.	(N642GG)
❏ N131GR	93	Learjet 31A	31A-068	GWR Aviation LLC. Houston, Tx.	N680AF
❏ N131LA	70	HS 125/400A	NA750	N131LA LLC. Salem, Or.	XA-RWN
❏ N131LJ	92	Learjet 31A	31A-063	Daniki LLC. Phoenix-Deer Valley, Az.	(N31AX)
❏ N131QS	05	Hawker 400XP	RK-431	NetJets, Port Columbus, Oh.	
❏ N131TR	00	Learjet 60	60-216	WFBNW NA. Salt Lake City, Ut. (trustor ?).	
❏ N131TT	91	Learjet 31A	31A-049	Learshares 31 Inc. Fort Lauderdale, Fl.	N107GM
❏ N132AH	96	CitationJet	525-0132	Air Prospect LLC. Louisville, Ky.	(N132RP)
❏ N132EP	82	Falcon 20F-5B	463	Westshore Aviation/Prince Transportation Inc. Holland, Mi.	N134JA
❏ N132FP	74	Gulfstream II SP	153	Crenshaw Christian Center Church, Van Nuys, Ca.	N110VW
❏ N132JC	01	Gulfstream G200	039	HM Aviation Inc. Wilmington, De.	(N302HM)
❏ N132LA	69	Jet Commander-B	133	Alberto Herreos, Miami, Fl. (status ?).	XB-GBZ
❏ N132MT	03	Citation Bravo	550-1080	Metal Technologies Inc. Auburn, In.	N.....
❏ N132QS	05	Hawker 400XP	RK-427	NetJets, Port Columbus, Oh.	
❏ N132SD	98	Gulfstream V	537	G5 OpCo Ltd. Hamilton, Bermuda.	8P-MAK
❏ N133B	02	390 Premier 1	RB-68	BravoAir LLC. Leesburg, Va.	N50648
❏ N133BA	00	Gulfstream G200	030	Sky G2300A Holding LLC.	B-HWB
❏ N133EJ	77	Learjet 35A	35A-133	Scott Smolen, N Tonawanda, NY.	N133GJ
❏ N133EP	78	Falcon 10	131	Westshore Aviation/Prince Transportation Inc. Holland, Mi.	HB-VME
❏ N133JM	72	Citation	500-0028	Turwel LLC/CRM Companies, Lexington, Ky.	(N9LV)
❏ N133SC	79	Citation 1/SP	501-0131	Patton, Tidwell & Schroeder LLP. Texarkana, Tx.	(N501NP)
❏ N133VP	87	Citation S/II	S550-0133	Morrow Aviation Inc. Ormond Beach, Fl.	N431WM
❏ N133WA	82	Citation II	550-0356	King Air E90 LLC. Apple Valley, Mn.	PT-OER
❏ N134AX	01	Gulfstream G200	034	Aspen Executive Air LLC. Aspen, Co.	(N200GA)
❏ N134BJ	97	Beechjet 400A	RK-134	Cabela's Wholesale Inc. Sidney, Ne.	N1094D
❏ N134BR	90	Gulfstream 4	1139	GSCP (NJ) Inc. Florham Park, NJ.	N331P
❏ N134CG	99	Learjet 31A	31A-195	Imperial Air LP. McAllen, Tx.	N134FX
❏ N134CM	97	Beechjet 400A	RK-144	Executive Charters Inc. Kinston, NC.	
❏ N134LJ	97	Learjet 31A	31A-134	My Jet LLC. Scottsdale, Az.	N977AR
❏ N134N	69	Jet Commander	134	N134N LLC. Wilmington, De.	N7638S
❏ N134NW	81	HS 125/700A	NA0295	Thompson Management LLC. NYC.	(N134RT)
❏ N134SW	04	390 Premier 1	RB-81	Sugar Woods Family Aviation LLC. Shreveport, La.	N390P
❏ N134VS	81	Challenger 600	1034	Challenger Aircraft Holdings Inc. NYC.	LV-YLB
❏ N134WE	77	Learjet 25XR	25XR-222	Air One Inc. Nashville, Tn.	N225TJ
❏ N135AG	77	Learjet 35A	35A-132	N135AG LLC. West Columbia, SC.	N37TJ
❏ N135BC	95	Challenger 800	7075	Burrell Professional Labs/Burrell Colour, Crown Point, In.	N877SE
❏ N135BJ	97	Beechjet 400A	RK-135	Corporate Jet Partners LLC. Atlanta, Ga.	N1135A

Reg	Yr	Type	c/n	Owner/Operator	Prev Regn
N135BP	00	Galaxy-1126	016	Cheetah Technologies/BP Group Inc. Sarasota, Fl.	N35BP
N135CG	07	Learjet 45	45-354	Learjet Inc. Wichita, Ks.	N40077
N135CS	03	CitationJet CJ-1	525-0520	CitationShares Sales Inc. White Plains, NY.	N.....
N135DA	81	Learjet 35A	35A-405	Delta Airelite Business Jets Inc. Cincinnati, Oh.	N442DM
N135DE	91	Learjet 35A	35A-667	U S Department of Energy, Albuquerque, NM.	N91566
N135FA	76	Learjet 35A	35A-067	American Jet International Corp. Houston, Tx.	(N52FL)
N135FT	06	Gulfstream G200	155	New Albertson's Inc. Boise, Id.	N136FT
N135HC	00	Citation VII	650-7117	Hood Industries Inc. Jackson, Ms.	N33D
N135LR	82	Learjet 55	55-068	Carborn Inc. Hinsdale, Il.	N38D
N135SG	03	Embraer Legacy 600	145706	United Aviation, Kuwait City, Kuwait.	PT-SAX
N135SK*	07	Embraer Legacy 600	14500989	Wilmington Trust Co. Wilmington, De. (trustor ?).	N556JT
N135SL	03	Embraer Legacy 600	145711	United Aviation, Kuwait City, Kuwait.	PT-SAY
N135WC	94	Citation V Ultra	560-0261	BATT Partners LLC. Shreveport, La.	N305QS
N135WE	79	Learjet 35A	35A-240	M & W Inc. Smyrna, Tn.	N249B
N136DH	78	Learjet 36A	36A-036	Intermap Technologies Inc. Englewood, Co.	N36MJ
N136JP	80	Learjet 35A	35A-359	ANGL Enterprises LLC. New Castle, De.	HB-VHB
N136MW	69	HFB 320	1036	Kalitta Flying Service Inc. Morristown, Tn.	(N92047)
N136QS	05	Hawker 400XP	RK-414	NetJets, Port Columbus, Oh.	
N136WE	78	Learjet 35A	35A-201	Air 1 Inc. Nashville, Tn.	N35AZ
N137BG	05	CitationJet CJ-3	525B-0032	C M Gatton, Bristol, Tn.	N52433
N137FA	83	Falcon 50	137	FA137 Inc/Avcorp Registrations Ltd. Gloucester, UK.	C-FJUH
N137JC	91	Citation V	560-0137	Isle of Capri Casinos Inc. Biloxi, Ms.	N193G
N137LA	94	Citation V Ultra	560-0274	TVPX Inc. Concord, Ma.	(N511DP)
N137PA	90	Citation II	550-0658	Petra Aviation, New Braunfels, Tx.	RP-C1180
N137TA	83	Falcon 200	487	Leon Air, Miami, Fl.	(N387FJ)
N137WB	06	Gulfstream G200	137	G137 LLC. Fort Lauderdale, Fl.	4X-CVH
N137WR	78	HS 125/700A	NA0225	Waddell & Reed Development Inc. Kansas City, Mo.	N995SA
N138AV	83	Falcon 50	138	Aerovertigo Inc/Aero Air LLC. Hillsboro, Or.	N380TJ
N138BG	07	Citation Sovereign	680-0135	EFI 1 LLC/Joseph Freed & Assocs LLC. Palwaukee, Il.	N229LC
N138CA	99	Citation Bravo	550-0900	Dowdle Aviation LLC/Dowdle Enterprises Inc. Columbus, Ms.	N214TJ
N138DM	81	Falcon 10	181	Jabil Circuit Inc. Page Field-Fort Myers, Fl.	F-GJHG
N138F	98	Falcon 900B	174	First International Aviation Inc. Caracas, Venezuela.	N138FA
N138FJ	77	Falcon 20F	369	Ethox Chemicals Inc. Greensboro-High Point, NC.	N420J
N138QS	06	Hawker 400XP	RK-492	NetJets/Marquis Jet Partners Inc. Port Columbus, Oh.	
N138SA	73	Citation	500-0138	Miller Management Group Inc. Erie, Pa.	N3056R
N138SP	00	Citation X	750-0138	Mirage Enterprises Inc. Van Nuys, Ca.	N5241Z
N138WE	82	Learjet 35A	35A-472	Air 1 Inc. Nashville, Tn.	N335MW
N139AL	88	Falcon 900	35	Magnitogorsk Iron & Steel Works, Moscow, Russia.	PH-OLI
N139CF	73	Gulfstream 2B	139	C A R LLC. Opa Locka, Fl.	N113AR
N139M	97	Hawker 800XP	258330	Brunswick Corp. Waukegan, Il.	N330XP
N139MY	85	Citation III	650-0072	MT Yack Aviation LLC. Wilmington, De.	N72ST
N139QS	06	Hawker 400XP	RK-483	NetJets, Port Columbus, Oh.	
N139SK	83	Learjet 55	55-082	SK Logistics Inc. St Augustine, Fl.	N817AM
N140CA	73	Learjet 25B	25-140	Cherry Air Inc. Addison, Tx.	N403AC
N140DA	02	CitationJet CJ-2	525A-0140	Dobber Aviation LLC. Tulsa-R L Jones, Ok.	N.....
N140HM	07	Learjet 40	45-2103	Learjet Inc. Wichita, Ks.	
N140JC	97	Learjet 60	60-106	Next Group LLC. Madison, Ms.	N106LJ
N140KR	01	Gulfstream G200	051	The Kor Group, Van Nuys, Ca.	LN-SUS
N140LF	68	HS 125/3B-RA	25140	Company Air, Thousand Oaks, Ca.	C6-MED
N140LJ	06	Learjet 40	45-2044	Distinctive Companies Ltd. Orland Park, Il.	N4004Q
N140QS	04	Hawker 400XP	RK-406	NetJets, Port Columbus, Oh.	
N140RF	66	Sabre-40A	282-67	Centurion Investments Inc. St Louis, Mo.	N711T
N140SC	74	TriStar 500	1067	Orbital Sciences Corp. Bakersfield, Ca.	C-FTNJ
N140TS	87	Citation III	650-0141	Crest Jet LLC/Crest Industries LLC. Pineville, La.	N21WJ
N140U	89	Citation V	560-0024	MacWig Holdings LLC. Dallas-Love, Tx.	N560FN
N140VJ	87	Westwind-1124	435	Carlisle Capital Corp. Portsmouth, NH.	N279JS
N140WH	90	Citation III	650-0195	Nita Jet LLC. Great Falls, Mt.	N800MC
N140WW	06	Learjet 40	45-2049	Waterway Plastics, Oxnard, Ca.	N5012K
N141AB	02	Citation Bravo	550-1044	R & L West Group LLC. Bend, Or.	N52369
N141AL	81	HS 125/700A	NA0306	ADESA Inc & ALLETE Inc. Duluth, Mn.	N800MP
N141AQ	91	Citation V	560-0141	The Rothbury Corp. Midlothian, Va.	N6876S
N141DR	98	Beechjet 400A	RK-184	Quad C Management Inc. Charlottesville, Va.	N2314F
N141FM	82	Learjet 55	55-041	Tactical Air LLC. Virginia Beach, Va.	HK-4016X
N141HL	97	Citation Bravo	550-0803	Hotel Lima LLC. New Orleans, La.	N550FB
N141JC	82	Citation II	550-0341	ALW Air LLC/Cypress Properties Inc. Little Rock, Ar.	(N367EA)
N141JF	71	Gulfstream 2	106	Aero Falcons LLC. Chino, Ca.	(N473JF)

Reg	Yr	Type	c/n	Owner/Operator	Prev Regn
N141M	77	Citation 1/SP	501-0039	Reef Investments LLC. Pontiac, Mi.	N507DS
N141MR	88	BAe 125/800A	NA0429	R-5 Holdings LLC/M F Ronca & Sons Inc. Bethlehem, Pa.	N73WF
N141QS	06	Hawker 400XP	RK-498	NetJets/Marquis Jet Partners Inc. Port Columbus, Oh.	
N141RD	82	Challenger 600S	1041	LVA Management & Consulting Inc. Lawrenceville, Ga.	
N141SL	78	Sabre-60	306-141	Greg Powe Ministries Inc. Tampa, Fl.	(N707GP)
N142AA	02	Citation Excel	560-5281	MYN Aviation Ltd. Riyadh, Saudi Arabia.	(N68AA)
N142DA	77	Citation 1/SP	501-0004	EKA Aviation LLC. Dover, De.	N86JJ
N142GA	90	Citation V	560-0042	Cloudscape Inc. Ruidoso, NM.	D-CAWU
N142HC	03	Gulfstream G450	4007	Delta Jet Ltd/Herb Chambers Real Estate, Oxford, Ct.	N185GA
N142QS	05	Hawker 400XP	RK-432	NetJets, Port Columbus, Oh.	
N143BP	03	Citation Bravo	550-1072	Cornerstone Aviation LLC. Aspen, Co.	N5148B
N143CK	73	Learjet 25B	25B-143	Cross & Kaufman Logging, Ashland, Or.	N113RF
N143CM	04	390 Premier 1	RB-114	Sand Castle Transport LLC. Morrisville, NC.	
N143DH	04	Citation Excel XLS	560-5514	Departures LLC. Daytona Beach, Fl.	N5086W
N143DZ	79	Sabre-60	306-142	CORE Projects Inc. Fresno, Ca.	(N700DA)
N143FA	98	Learjet 60	60-143	Four Aces Aviation LLC. Coral Gables, Fl.	N393TA
N143G	88	MD-87	49670	Otter Corp/422 Holdings Inc. Seattle, Wa.	N3H
N143GA	06	Gulfstream G200	143	Global Aviation Inc/Homelife Communities, Atlanta, Ga.	(N81TT)
N143HM	98	Beechjet 400A	RK-205	R2 Aviation LLC. Atlanta, Ga.	(N17CM)
N143JT	07	CitationJet CJ-3	525B-0181	Chinn Exploration Co. Longview, Tx.	N5239J
N143KS	98	Gulfstream 4SP	1364	Spectacor Inc & Kalco Corp. Raleigh, NC.	N364GA
N143LG	81	Learjet 35A	35A-426	Lifeguard Alaska/Aero Air LLC. Hillsboro, Or.	RP-C1426
N143RL	05	Hawker 850XP	258774	RDW Ventures LLC/Healthfield Inc. Atlanta, Ga.	N774XP
N144AL	05	CitationJet CJ-3	525B-0044	Conquest Holdings Inc. Santa Rosa, Ca.	N.....
N144AW	91	Beechjet 400A	RK-19	Waterton Property Management LLC. Chicago-Midway, Il.	(N405LX)
N144BS	89	Challenger 601-3A	5033	Monte Carlo Associates LLC. Carvallis, Or.	N397Q
N144FH	01	Falcon 900C	189	JBS Consulting LLC/Simpson Family Trust, San Jose, Ca.	C-GMND
N144GA	79	Citation II	550-0065	Boston Air Charter LLC. Norfolk, Ma.	ZS-RCS
N144HM	99	Hawker 800XP	258431	Hawker Beechcraft Corp. Wichita, Ks.	
N144LG	83	Learjet 35A	35A-500	Aero Air LLC. Hillsboro, Or.	N81QH
N144MH	95	Citation VII	650-7059	CDECRE Inc. Nashua, NH.	N76PR
N144PK	92	Gulfstream 4SP	1210	P K Aire Inc. Burbank, Ca.	N410QS
N144YD	02	CitationJet CJ-2	525A-0144	Air Shares LLC. Seekonk, Ma.	N.....
N144Z	00	Citation Bravo	550-0926	USDA Forest Service, Boise, Id.	N100Z
N145AM	76	Learjet 35A	35A-078	Trevor & Assocs Inc. Marion, Oh.	N45AW
N145AP	06	Learjet 45	45-300	United Agri Products Inc. Fort Collins, Co.	
N145AR	02	Learjet 45	45-203	Alan Ritchey Inc. Valley View, Tx.	
N145BL	05	Citation Sovereign	680-0045	Central Charter de Colombia SA. Bogota, Colombia.	N5203S
N145CM	06	Learjet 45	45-297	CTI of North Carolina Inc. Wilmington, NC.	(N145CG)
N145DF	84	Citation S/II	S550-0018	Star Diamond Co. Luton, UK.	N1AF
N145GL*	70	HS 125/400A	NA753	Lauther-Phillips LLC. Bradenton, Fl.	N345GL
N145GM	99	Learjet 45	45-081	Tiara Air LLC. Naples, Fl.	N76TE
N145HC	02	Learjet 45	45-231	United States Aviation Co. Tulsa, Ok.	N30PF
N145JF*	06	390 Premier 1A	RB-159	Hawker Beechcraft Corp. Wichita, Ks.	N146JF
N145K	05	Learjet 45	45-268	Koch Industries Inc. Wichita, Ks.	N5009V
N145KK	94	Citation V Ultra	560-0276	WFBNW NA. Salt Lake City, Ut. (trustor ?).	N376WC
N145QS	05	Hawker 400XP	RK-421	NetJets, Port Coulmbus, Oh.	
N145SB	02	Learjet 45	45-142	KAG Services LLC. Eugene, Or.	(N450DS)
N145SH	73	Learjet 25B	25B-145	Valdosta Mall Inc. Duluth, Ga.	N2127E
N145TA	74	Citation	500-0145	Sierra Foxtrot Charlie Inc. Kansas City, Mo.	(N415FC)
N145XL	01	Learjet 45	45-106	Xcel Energy Services Co. Minneapolis, Mn.	
N146AS	02	Falcon 50EX	325	SeeCon Builders Inc. Concord, Ca.	N325EX
N146BA	96	Challenger 604	5327	TPS LLC. Seattle, Wa.	D-AJAB
N146EX	04	Falcon 900EX EASY	146	Business Jet Ltd. Auckland, New Zealand.	F-WWFZ
N146XL	01	Learjet 45	45-187	Southwestern Public Service Co. Amarillo, Tx.	N5030J
N147A	80	Westwind-1124	294	Salter Labs, Arvin, Ca.	HK-3884X
N147BJ	97	Beechjet 400A	RK-147	Aircraft Leasing International Inc. Teterboro, NJ.	
N147CA	77	Learjet 25D	25D-221	Wing Financial LLC. Las Vegas, Nv.	YU-BKR
N147CK	67	Learjet 24	24-147	Kalitta Flying Service Inc. Morristown, Tn.	N147KH
N147CX	01	Citation X	750-0147	Swift Aviation Management Inc. Phoenix, Az.	(N787CW)
N147FM	05	390 Premier 1A	RB-147	Frank Air Leasing LLC/McKee Group, Coatesville, Pa.	N61678
N147G	07	Falcon 2000EX EASY	122	W W Grainger Inc. Palwaukee, Il.	F-WWGF
N147GX	87	Falcon 100	214	Cortez Transportation LLC. Little Rock, Ar.	N147G
N147HH	92	Challenger 601-3A	5123	D2 Aviation LLC/Harris Land Co. Concord, NC.	N601UP
N147QS	05	Hawker 400XP	RK-436	NetJets/Marquis Jet Partners Inc. Port Columbus, Oh.	
N147SB	96	Citation V Ultra	560-0380	Shields Bag & Printing/Shields Real Estate LLC. Yakima, Wa.	N190KL

Reg	Yr	Type	c/n	Owner/Operator	Prev Regn
❏ N147SW	02	Gulfstream G100	147	Sherwin-Williams Co. Cleveland, Oh.	N147GA
❏ N147TW	68	Learjet 25	25-023	Sierra American Corp. Addison, Tx.	N767SC
❏ N147X	81	Gulfstream 3	336	DX Service Co. Houston, Tx.	(N102PT)
❏ N148FB	02	CitationJet CJ-2	525A-0148	Hawker Aviation Services LLC. Nashville, Tn.	N5132T
❏ N148GB	98	Beechjet 400A	RK-185	Flight Capital LLC. Madison, Ms.	(N185FN)
❏ N148H	77	Westwind-1124	206	Jet Connect Inc. Oberlin, Ks.	N100ME
❏ N148J	83	Diamond 1A	A033SA	Air Charter & Sales LLC. Columbia, Mo.	N717DF
❏ N148MC	80	Falcon 20-5B	428	Mountaire Corp. Little Rock, Ar.	N98R
❏ N148TW	68	Falcon 20C	148	Sierra American Corp. Addison, Tx.	N148WC
❏ N148V	69	Gulfstream 2B	54	Bayoil (USA) Inc. Houston, Tx.	N955CC
❏ N149QS	06	Hawker 400XP	RK-473	NetJets, Port Columbus, Oh.	
❏ N149SB	03	Hawker 800XP	258654	Annett Holdings Inc. Des Moines, Ia.	N654XP
❏ N149VB	97	Falcon 2000	53	JVB Aviation Falcon LLC. Broomfield, Co.	N149V
❏ N149WW	07	CitationJet CJ-3	525B-0175	JHRD Investments LLC/Hayden Homes, Aurora, Or.	N.....
❏ N150BB	00	Challenger 604	5470	Dal-Briar Corp/Janice B Brittingham, Dallas, Tx.	N604AC
❏ N150BC	98	Falcon 2000	67	Holiday Retirement Corp. Salem, Or.	F-WWMK
❏ N150BV	98	CitationJet	525-0320	Dynamic Aviation LLC/Steel Dynamics Inc. Fort Wayne, In.	
❏ N150CA	82	Diamond 1	A023SA	Charlie Air LLC. Van Nuys, Ca.	N22BN
❏ N150CK	74	Learjet 25B	25B-150	Kalitta Charters LLC. Detroit-Willow Run, Mi.	N251JA
❏ N150CT	06	Gulfstream G150	208	Antelope Aviation LLC. Phoenix, Az.	N208GA
❏ N150EX	79	Westwind-1124	262	Boomerang Air Inc. Wiley Post, Ok.	N79KP
❏ N150GA	07	Gulfstream G150	238	Gulfstream Aerospace LP. Dallas-Love, Tx.	4X-C
❏ N150GD	06	Gulfstream G150	217	Gulfstream Aerospace Corp. Savannah, Ga.	N217GA
❏ N150JP	92	Citation VII	650-7010	SHP-Air Leasing LLC. Wilmington, NC.	(N403BL)
❏ N150K	82	Falcon 50	108	Koch Industries Inc. Wichita, Ks.	N350X
❏ N150LR	96	Hawker 1000	259050	Hawker Beechcraft Corp. Wichita, Ks.	N550QS
❏ N150MH	84	Challenger 601	3021	Coronado Nevada LLC. Las Vegas, Nv.	N966L
❏ N150MS	82	Learjet 55	55-049	Martin Sprocket & Gear Inc. Fort Worth, Tx.	D-CCHS
❏ N150NC	96	Hawker 800XP	258293	Circuit City Stores Inc. Richmond, Va.	N404CE
❏ N150PU	07	Gulfstream G150	225	Hume & Johnson PA. Valencia, Venezuela.	N399GA
❏ N150RJ	02	Falcon 50EX	324	Chief Exploration & Development LLC. Dallas, Tx.	LX-IRE
❏ N150RM	78	Citation 1/SP	501-0076	Cartrette LLC/AMC II LLC. Greenville, NC.	N315MP
❏ N150RS	74	Learjet 25XR	25XR-162	Rosemary Reja Winkler,	N97JJ
❏ N150RT	05	Gulfstream G150	201	GAC LP. Dallas-Love, Tx. (Ff 3 May 2005).	4X-TRA
❏ N150SB	91	BAe 125/800A	258197	Pecos Aircraft Sales & Leasing LLC. Irving, Tx.	G-OMGE
❏ N150TT	74	Citation	500-0176	Fostill West LLC. Chamblee, Ga.	G-TEFH
❏ N150TX	80	Falcon 50	13	DHM Aviation LLC. Dallas, Tx.	(N150NW)
❏ N151AG	66	Learjet 24	24-137	George Smith, Corona del Mar, Ca.	N72FP
❏ N151DR	87	Citation III	650-0147	B & K Citation SII LLC/LBJ Investments, San Antonio, Tx.	N94BJ
❏ N151EW*	04	CitationJet CJ-1	525-0529	Lou Holtz Foundation, Orlando, Fl.	N151CS
❏ N151FD	04	Citation Bravo	550-1087	Bravo Enterprises LLC. McKinney, Tx.	N.....
❏ N151GR	01	Falcon 2000	151	Guthy-Renker Corp. Palm Desert, Ca.	G-IBSF
❏ N151KV	02	Citation Excel	560-5320	Guthy-Renker Corp. Palm Desert, Ca.	N66W
❏ N151QS	05	Hawker 400XP	RK-422	NetJets, Port Columbus, Oh.	
❏ N151SD	94	Gulfstream 4SP	1249	NAJ/D S Advisors Inc. Palwaukee, Il.	N634S
❏ N151SG	65	HS 125/1A	25035	151SG LLC. Wilmington, De.	(N57TS)
❏ N151SP	77	Citation 1/SP	501-0021	Summa Peto LLC. Portola Valley, Ca.	ZS-MGL
❏ N151ST	90	Gulfstream 4	1151	S T Aviation LLC. Naples, Fl.	N109ST
❏ N151TM	03	Citation Bravo	550-1063	United American Insurance Co. McKinney, Tx.	N96TM
❏ N151WW	68	Learjet 24	24-170	Addison Aviation Services Inc. Addison, Tx.	N200DH
❏ N152CS	04	CitationJet CJ-1	525-0539	CitationShares Sales Inc. White Plains, NY.	N.....
❏ N152JH	02	Citation Encore	560-0615	Jack Henry & Associates Inc. Monett, Mo.	N5108G
❏ N152KV	96	CitationJet	525-0152	Plane House LLC. Indianapolis, In.	N152KC
❏ N152SV	07	Citation Sovereign	680-0152	Cessna Aircraft Co. Wichita, Ks.	N52113
❏ N152UT	08	Learjet 40	45-2101	Learjet Inc. Wichita, Ks.	
❏ N153AG	65	Learjet 23	23-058	Great Oaks Institute of Technology, Cincinnati, Oh.	N7FJ
❏ N153CS	04	CitationJet CJ-1	525-0548	CitationShares Sales Inc. White Plains, NY..	N5216A
❏ N153QS	06	Hawker 400XP	RK-490	NetJets/Marquis Jet Partners Inc. Port Columbus, Oh.	
❏ N153SG	04	Citation Bravo	550-1088	CC Industries Inc/Henry Crown & Co. Palwaukee, Il.	N.....
❏ N153TH	92	Citation II	550-0695	T Henry Properties LLC. Destin, Fl.	N77DD
❏ N154AK	97	Learjet 60	60-114	Aviation Properties Inc. Winnetka, Il.	N114PJ
❏ N154FJ	80	HS 125/700A	NA0271	F-Jets LLC/F-Jets Charters LLC. Tampa, Fl.	N177JW
❏ N154G	88	Gulfstream 4	1044	Timberland Aviation Inc. Manchester, NH.	N1540
❏ N154JH	01	Citation Encore	560-0555	Jack Henry & Associates Inc. Monett, Mo.	N5155G
❏ N154JS	00	Citation Encore	560-0540	J R Simplot Co. Boise, Id.	N540CV
❏ N154NS	94	Challenger 601-3R	5169	Norfolk Southern Railway Co. Norfolk, Va.	N773A

Reg	Yr	Type	c/n	Owner/Operator	Prev Regn
N154QS	06	Hawker 400XP	RK-509	NetJets, Port Columbus, Oh.	
N154RT	98	Learjet 31A	31A-154	Ruby Tuesday Inc. Knoxville, Tn.	N337RB
N154SC	80	Citation 1/SP	501-0154	Alan Aviation LLC. Santa Monica, Ca.	CC-CWW
N154VP	91	Citation V	560-0154	Panattoni Development Co. Atlanta, Ga.	N503T
N155AC	88	Citation II	550-0573	AC Aviation Inc. Dover, De.	PT-OKM
N155AM	77	Learjet 35A	35A-131	N155AM LLC. West Columbia, SC.	N26GD
N155AN	03	Gulfstream G550	5029	Nissan North America Inc. Smyrna, Tn.	(N550RN)
N155BC	85	Learjet 55	55-115	LJ Fifty-Five LLC. Largo, Fl.	N633AC
N155DB	90	Learjet 55C	55C-141	S T Wooten Corp. Wilson, NC.	
N155GM	82	Learjet 55	55-022	Fly 22 LLC. Livingston, NJ.	VP-BOL
N155JH	01	Citation Encore	560-0568	Jack Henry & Associates Inc. Monett, Mo.	N52369
N155MK	74	Citation	500-0155	Flying Moose LLC. Missoula, Mt.	(N188DR)
N155MM	81	Gulfstream 3	325	N15MM LLC/WLNY-TV Inc. Melville, NY.	N393U
N155MW		Challenger 800	7021	Michael Waltrip Racing, Sherrills Ford, NC.	C-FLHX
N155NS	01	Hawker 800XP	258549	Norfolk Southern Railway Co. Norfolk, Va.	N51149
N155PT	94	Citation V	560-0257	Rig Corp/P J Taggares Co. Othello, Wa.	N1293L
N155PX	81	Falcon 10	189	Trans-Equipment Services Inc. Greenville, SC.	N189JM
N155RJ	98	Gulfstream 4SP	1347	R E Jacobs Group, Cleveland, Oh.	N933JJ
N155RM	01	390 Premier 1	RB-6	Jake's Fireworks Inc. Nevada, Mo.	N390R
N155RW	05	Citation Excel XLS	560-5570	National Dental Development Inc. Effingham, Il.	N10VQ
N155SB	81	Learjet 55	55-013	Lencork LLC. Fort Lauderdale, Fl.	D-CUTE
N155SP	89	Learjet 55C	55C-137	Avigation Holdings LLC. Salt Lake City, Ut.	N95SC
N155VY	91	Citation V	560-0155	Meyer Chatfield Aviation Services Inc. N Philadelphia, Pa.	N40WP
N156BF	03	Learjet 60	60-266	Fuccillo Automotive Group Inc. Syracuse, NY.	N266LJ
N156DB	81	Falcon 50	40	AmeriCredit Corp. Fort Worth, Tx.	N150JT
N156DH	92	Beechjet 400A	RK-36	H & O Aviation LC. Wheeling, WV.	N57B
N156JH	01	Citation Encore	560-0575	Jack Henry & Associates Inc. Monett, Mo.	N5257C
N156ML	96	CitationJet	525-0156	Mark & Diana Levy, Paradise Valley, Az.	
N156NS	04	Hawker 800XP	258668	Norfolk Southern Railway Co. Norfolk, Va.	N668XP
N156PH	05	Citation Sovereign	680-0031	Parker Hannifin Corp. Cleveland, Oh.	N5223P
N157AG	72	Learjet 24D	24D-252	Wing Financial LLC. Las Vegas, Nv.	(C6-BGF)
N157DW	81	Citation II	550-0253	Moe Air LLC/Moretz Sportswear, Newton, NC. (was 551-0308).	N953FT
N157GA	86	Astra-1125	015	Avantair Inc. Clearwater, Fl.	N755PA
N157JH	01	Citation Encore	560-0581	Jack Henry & Associates Inc. Monett, Mo.	N5269Z
N157JL	06	CitationJet CJ-3	525B-0157	Opak LLC/Pzena Investment Management LLC. NYC.	N5096S
N157JS	95	Learjet 31	31-033D	AirMed Inc/Gold Cross EMS, Augusta, Ga.	N312LJ
N157PB	99	Learjet 45	45-030	Westlakes Aviation LLC. Coatesville, Pa.	N157PH
N157PH	05	Citation Sovereign	680-0035	Parker Hannifin Corp. Cleveland, Oh.	N5155G
N157QS	07	Hawker 400XP	RK-520	NetJets, Port Columbus, Oh.	
N157SP	91	Astra-1125SP	057	Cementario Promociones y Ventas CA. Caracas, Venezuela.	YV-785CP
N157TF	92	Citation V	560-0157	Mountain Solitude LLC. Big Sky, Mt.	N88WC
N157TW	68	Learjet 24	24-157	Sierra American Corp. Addison, Tx.	N659AT
N157WH	97	Beechjet 400A	RK-167	Next Higher Plane LLC. Manassas, Va.	N897AT
N158EC	01	Learjet 45	45-186	E C Aviation Services Inc. Holland-Tulip City, Mi.	
N158M	07	Falcon 50EX	351	Motorola Inc. Palwaukee, Il.	F-WWHH
N158PH	05	Citation Sovereign	680-0049	Parker Hannifin Corp. Cleveland, Oh.	N5058J
N158R	00	Learjet 31A	31A-189	Sea Horse Marine Inc. Houston, Tx.	N316RS
N158SV	07	Citation Sovereign	680-0158	Cessna Aircraft Co. Wichita, Ks.	N.....
N158TW	68	Falcon 20D	158	Sierra American Corp. Addison, Tx.	N450MA
N159AK	05	Hawker 400XP	RK-439	400A Air Charters LLC/Golden Eagle Air Inc. Farmingdale, NY.	N166QS
N159EC	02	Learjet 45	45-229	E C Aviation Services Inc. Holland-Tulip City, Mi.	
N159JA	04	Gulfstream G550	5062	eBay Inc. San Jose, Ca.	N962GA
N159KC	74	Citation	500-0159	M J Enterprises LLC. Springfield, Mo.	N97DD
N159NB	74	Gulfstream 2B	140	Tikchik LLC. Anchorage, Ak.	N730TK
N160AN	98	Learjet 60	60-126	Pinnacle Air Executive Jet, Springdale, Ar.	N224FX
N160CT	03	Gulfstream G100	152	Aero Jet Services Inc. Scottsdale, Az.	N150CT
N160EE	96	Learjet 60	60-093	G Edward Evans, Liberal, Ks.	N717JB
N160FJ	80	Falcon 10	160	OZ LLC/U S Foam Technologies Inc. Longview, Tx.	LX-JCG
N160GC	77	Learjet 36A	36A-030	Hudson Flight Ltd. Pampa, Tx.	(N36AX)
N160GG	97	Learjet 60	60-113	Gaines Aircraft LLC. Fort Lauderdale, Fl.	N702R
N160GH	98	Learjet 60	60-129	Hunt Corp/Lobo Aviation LLC. Scottsdale, Az.	N45US
N160JD	95	Learjet 60	60-068	Campbell Aircraft Holdings LLC. Coatesville, Pa.	N64LE
N160TM	03	Gulfstream G300	1526	Toyota Motor Sales USA Inc. Long Beach, Ca.	N526GA
N160W	72	Sabre-40A	282-101	Northrop Grumman Corp. Los Angeles, Ca.	N101RR
N160WC	86	Hawker 800SP	258069	Washington Corps. Missoula, Mt. 'The Future is on the Wing'	N364WC
N160WS	96	Falcon 2000	28	American International Group Inc. Houston, Tx.	N596A

Reg	Yr	Type	c/n	Owner/Operator	Prev Regn
☐ N161CM	67	Sabre-60	306-5	White Industries Inc. Bates City, Mo. (status ?).	(N477JM)
☐ N161MM	02	Gulfstream G400	1511	Aircraft Properties LLC. West Palm Beach, Fl.	N201GA
☐ N161NG	66	BAC 1-11/401AK	067	Northrop Grumman Aviation Inc. Baltimore, Md.	N765CF
☐ N161QS	05	Hawker 400XP	RK-435	NetJets/Marquis Jet Partners Inc. Port Columbus, Oh.	
☐ N161SM	99	CitationJet CJ-1	525-0369	Stowers Machinery Corp. Knoxville, Tn.	N629DM
☐ N161TM	98	Citation Bravo	550-0867	Step 2 Co. Dover, Oh.	
☐ N161WC	98	Global Express	9006	Washington Corps. Missoula, Mt.	N906GX
☐ N161X	79	Westwind-1124	234	Westwind Aircraft LLC. Bend, Or.	N1124Z
☐ N162DS	88	Citation III	650-0164	Dove Air Inc. Fletcher, NC.	N364CW
☐ N162EC	04	CitationJet CJ-3	525B-0026	The Entertainment Co. Sevierville, Tn.	N.....
☐ N162GB	05	Gulfstream G200	117	Graham Brothers Construction Co. Dublin, Ga.	N62GB
☐ N162JB	00	Hawker 800XP	258509	PNY Technologies Inc. Parsippany, NJ.	N983CE
☐ N162JC	98	Gulfstream V	539	Jim Carrey/Pit Bull Productions Inc. Van Nuys, Ca.	N1GC
☐ N162W	66	BAC 1-11/401AK	087	Northrop Grumman Corp. Los Angeles, Ca.	N173FE
☐ N163AG	69	HS 125/3A-RA	25169	AVMATS/Centurion Investments Inc. Chesterfield, Mo.	N122AW
☐ N163EB*	04	Falcon 2000EX EASY	36	Pacific Coast Steel Inc. San Diego, Ca.	N185G
☐ N163EG	81	Challenger 600S	1035	C DOT Aviation LLC. Metairie, La.	N187AP
☐ N163JM	88	Citation III	650-0163	The Tech Group, Scottsdale, Az.	N749CP
☐ N163PA	79	Citation 3	249	163PA LLC/Phoenix Air Group Inc. Cartersville, Ga.	F-249
☐ N163WC	77	Westwind-1124	217	Blue Water Aviation Inc. Allentown, Pa.	N217WC
☐ N163WG	86	Challenger 601	3057	Blue Water Aviation Inc. Allentown, Pa.	N747TS
☐ N164AS	01	Citation Excel	560-5192	Schwans Shared Services LLC. Marshall, Mn.	N192XL
☐ N164GB	86	Falcon 20	164	TVPX Inc. Concord, Ma.	N164MA
☐ N164NW	68	Falcon 20C	164	Indigo Air, Chicago, Il.	N654E
☐ N164RJ	99	BBJ-7BC	30328	Bausch & Lomb Inc. Rochester, NY.	N128QS
☐ N164SB	98	Learjet 31A	31A-164	Trans Oceano LLC. Miami, Fl.	N131GM
☐ N164TC	92	Citation V	560-0174	CDP Aviation/Great Ozarks Aviation Co. Sprigfield, Mo.	N563C
☐ N164W	66	BAC 1-11/401AK	090	Northrop Grumman Corp. Los Angeles, Ca.	G-AXCK
☐ N164WC	86	Hawker 800SP	258072	Washington Corps. Missoula, Mt.	N747UP
☐ N165CA	01	CitationJet CJ-1	525-0451	Captive Aire Systems Inc. Youngsville, NC.	N5135A
☐ N165CM	77	Learjet 24E	24E-355	Kevin Simmons, Narrows, Va.	N500NH
☐ N165G	83	Gulfstream 3	414	Harwinton Capital Corp/Key Air Inc. Oxford, Ct.	N165ST
☐ N165HB	94	Beechjet 400A	RK-90	Western Express Holdings Inc. Nashville, Tn.	N1570L
☐ N165JB	84	Citation S/II	S550-0009	Allegiance Aviation of Delaware LLC. Shreveport, La.	N550A
☐ N165JF	94	Gulfstream 4SP	1251	Jet Flight Corp. Mount Kisco, NY.	N60PE
☐ N165TW	66	Falcon 20C	65	Sierra American Corp. Addison, Tx.	C-GSKN
☐ N165W	68	B 737-247	19605	Northrop Grumman Corp. Los Angeles, Ca.	N4508W
☐ N166AN	07	390 Premier 1A	RB-227	Hawker Beechcraft Corp. Wichita, Ks.	
☐ N166DE	67	DC 9-15RC	47152	U S Department of Energy, Albuquerque, NM.	N66AF
☐ N166FA	80	Citation 1/SP	501-0166	Falcon Aviation LC. Durango, Co.	OY-INI
☐ N166FB	97	Falcon 900EX	18	Emergo Finance Inc/Bee Holdings LLC. Calgary, AB. Canada.	N18RF
☐ N166HL	94	Learjet 60	60-041	Schooner Inc/National Medical Care, Buffalo, NY.	N699SC
☐ N166MC	83	Citation III	650-0003	Groupe Valois/Valavia SNC. Paris-Le Bourget, France.	OY-CGG
☐ N166PC	74	Learjet 25B	25B-166	166PC LLC/Ocwen Inc. Dallas, Tx.	N918TD
☐ N166RD	07	Citation Excel XLS	560-5740	Island Park Aviation LLC. Fargo, ND.	N.....
☐ N166RM	90	Astra-1125SP	047	Cin-Air LLC/B & J Astra LLC. Cincinnati, Oh.	N30AJ
☐ N166WC	88	Hawker 800SP	NA0413	Washington Corps. Missoula, Mt.	N239R
☐ N167AA	89	Gulfstream 4	1096	American Assets Inc/AAI Aviation Inc. San Diego, Ca.	VP-CBW
☐ N167DD	86	BAe 125/800A	258068	Confort Vuela SA. Toluca, Mexico.	N68HR
☐ N167DP	03	390 Premier 1	RB-67	PCM Capital II LLC. Hayward, Ca.	ZS-MGK
☐ N168BF	98	Hawker 800XP	258373	Pearson Assets Group Ltd. Singapore.	N3270X
☐ N168BG	01	Citation Excel	560-5162	Cessna Aircraft Co. Wichita, Ks.	N51511
☐ N168CE	06	Falcon 2000EX EASY	95	Harrah's Operating Co. Las Vegas, Nv.	F-WWGJ
☐ N168CK	96	Challenger 800	7099	Clear Sky Holdings LLC. NYC.	N405CC
☐ N168DJ	69	Falcon 20-5B	168	Flynn-Gallagher Associates LLC. Las Vegas, Nv.	N514JJ
☐ N168EA	92	Citation V	560-0168	Hawkeye Group LLC. Cody, Wy.	N168CV
☐ N168NQ	02	Challenger 604	5531	Highfields Capital Management LP. Boston, Ma.	C-G...
☐ N168PK	88	Gulfstream 4	1053	PMC Global Inc. Van Nuys, Ca.	N17ND
☐ N168TR	76	Learjet 35A	35A-068	Career Aviation Co. Oakdale, Ca.	T-781
☐ N168VA	72	Gulfstream II SP	112	Mountain Jet Services LLC. Arden, NC.	N87AG
☐ N168W	65	Sabre-40	282-33	Northrop Grumman Corp. Los Angeles, Ca. (F-16 nose)	N903KB
☐ N168WM	86	Gulfstream 4	1002	Southlake Aviation LLC. Fort Worth, Tx.	N168WC
☐ N168WU	91	BAe 1000A	NA1002	Wu Aviation Corp. Portland, Me.	N229U
☐ N169HM	68	Gulfstream 2	13	Starwood Aviation Inc. Carson City, Nv.	N269HM
☐ N169JC	94	Gulfstream 4SP	1250	IT & Associates Inc. Chicago, Il.	XA-CHR
☐ N169KT	80	B 727-269	22359	WTC/Strong Aviation, Kuwait City, Kuwait.	9K-AFA

Reg	Yr	Type	c/n	Owner/Operator	Prev Regn
❏ N169LS	78	Falcon 10	115	SNF Inc/FW Aviation Management LLC. Fort Worth, Tx.	N636SC
❏ N169SM	07	Citation Excel XLS	560-5749	KVG Aviation Luftfahrt GmbH. Vienna, Austria.	N5076L
❏ N169TA	85	Challenger 601	3041	Truman Arnold Companies, Texarkana, Tx.	N600MS
❏ N169US	74	Learjet 24D	24D-298	Skycare Inc. Smyrna, Tn.	N470TR
❏ N170DC*	06	Hawker 900XP	HA-1	Joseph Jingoli & Son, Lawrenceville, NJ.	N90XP
❏ N170HL	99	Citation X	750-0100	Lichtin Corp. Raleigh, NC.	(N104UT)
❏ N170LS	99	Learjet 45	45-029	N170LS Holdings LLC. Fort Lauderdale, Fl.	N290LJ
❏ N170MK	92	Learjet 60	60-002	MK Aviation Inc. Statesville, NC.	(N602DM)
❏ N170MU	97	CitationJet	525-0170	Marshall Family Construction Inc. Lynn Haven, Fl.	N170BG
❏ N170SD	00	Citation Excel	560-5091	Wesdix Corp/DB Aviation Inc. Waukegan, Il.	N83SD
❏ N170SW	99	Global Express	9042	Wal-Mart Stores Inc. Rogers, Ar.	N700WL
❏ N170TM	02	CitationJet CJ-2	525A-0100	TitleMax Aviation Inc. Savannah, Ga.	N.....
❏ N171AM	84	Gulfstream 3	437	Florida Jet Service Inc. Fort Lauderdale, Fl.	N100AK
❏ N171JC	93	Gulfstream 4SP	1222	171JC LLC. Van Nuys, Ca.	N71RP
❏ N171JJ	06	Global 5000	9209	MBI International & Partners, Luton, UK.	C-FIIG
❏ N171TG	95	Falcon 50EX	251	Tudor Investment Corp. Waterbury-Oxford, Ct.	N565
❏ N171WH	78	Learjet 35A	35A-171	Hawk Communications.net LLC. Denver, Co.	N40DK
❏ N171WJ	81	Citation 1/SP	501-0171	Owen Woodward, Breckenridge, Tx.	VH-BNK
❏ N172DH	04	CitationJet CJ-3	525B-0012	Delaney Aviation LLC. New Windsor, NY.	N5093D
❏ N172EX	07	Gulfstream G200	172	Cowboy Aircraft Holdings Inc. Scottsdale, Az.	N672GA
❏ N173A	80	Sabre-65	465-20	PM Transportation LLC. Chicago, Il.	N2544E
❏ N173AA	80	Citation II	550-0234	Dove Air Inc. Fletcher, NC.	N65DA
❏ N173JM	05	Gulfstream G200	122	Miami Jet Professionals LLC. New Tamiami, Fl.	N200GA
❏ N173LC	98	Learjet 31A	31A-173	Seven KH Aviation LLC. Janesville, Wi.	
❏ N173PA	80	Gulfstream 3	313	173PA LLC/Phoenix Air Group Inc. Cartersville, Ga.	F-313
❏ N173TR	85	BAe 125/800A	258039	Dan Air LLC. Klamath Falls, Or.	N193TR
❏ N173VP	89	Citation III	650-0173	EPPS Air Service Inc. Atlanta-DeKalb, Ga.	N843G
❏ N173WF	00	Citation X	750-0112	Guidara Nordeste Participacoes Ltda. Maracanau, Brazil.	(N910RL)
❏ N174AB	98	Beechjet 400A	RK-174	Black Ink Solutions Inc. Denver, Co.	N2204J
❏ N174B	79	Falcon 10	142	Pinetimber Aero LLC. Austin, Tx.	N5LP
❏ N174DR	79	Citation II	550-0074	Robinson Industries Inc. Deland, Fl. (was 551-0109).	LX-THS
❏ N174JS	01	Citation Encore	560-0572	J R Simplot Co. Boise, Id.	N.....
❏ N174RD	75	Learjet 24XR	24XR-319	Reha 'Ray' Ekinci, Camden, NSW.	XC-SUP
❏ N174SJ	07	CitationJet CJ-3	525B-0174	SJ Aviation LLC. Novato, Ca.	N.....
❏ N174TM	04	Citation Sovereign	680-0021	Reyes Holding LLC. Des Plaines, Il.	N621SV
❏ N174VP	92	Citation VII	650-7004	Moran Foods Inc/Save-A-Lot Ltd. St Louis, Mo.	N913SQ
❏ N175BC	96	Falcon 2000	32	Barnard Construction Co. Bozeman, Mt.	N324CL
❏ N175BG	83	Gulfstream 3	396	Bentley Aviation LLC. Van Nuys, Ca.	N800MK
❏ N175BJ	97	Beechjet 400A	RK-175	WHW Transportation LLC. Jacksonville, Fl.	
❏ N175DP	00	Citation VII	650-7116	Marshall & Ilsley Bank/Milease LLC. Milwaukee, Wi.	N5268M
❏ N175FJ	77	Falcon 10	97	Marmac Corp. Parkersburg, WV.	F-WPXF
❏ N175FS	65	Learjet 24A	24A-031	Sally Aviation Inc. Wilmington, De.	N202BA
❏ N175J	89	Citation III	650-0168	BFB Aircraft LLC/Ben Barnes Group, Austin, Tx.	N1314H
❏ N175MC	82	HS 125/700A	257178	Horizon Flight LLC. McKinney, Tx.	N803BF
❏ N175MD	77	JetStar 2	5215	Dezer Development, Fort Lauderdale, Fl.	N808RP
❏ N175SR	88	Citation III	650-0175	Siepelia Interest Inc. Dallas, Tx.	N835KK
❏ N175WS	03	Citation Excel	560-5327	American International Group Inc. Teterboro, NJ.	N.....
❏ N176AK	71	Westwind-1124	154	Yucalpa Aviation Inc. Yucalpa, Ca.	N722AW
❏ N176CA	05	Learjet 40	45-2045	BS Twenty LLC/Barry Real Estate Companies, Atlanta, Ga.	
❏ N176CG	06	Falcon 2000EX EASY	92	CIGNA Corp. Bradley International, Ct.	F-WWGG
❏ N176CL	02	Falcon 900EX	110	CIGNA Corp. Bradley International, Ct.	F-WWFI
❏ N176KS	95	Learjet 60	60-066	F E R M Inc. Miami Lakes, Fl.	N8271
❏ N176WS	99	Learjet 31A	31A-176	Mid-America Aviation LLC. Lafayette, In.	
❏ N177AM	90	Learjet 55C	55C-147	Florida Jet Service Inc. Fort Lauderdale, Fl.	N160NE
❏ N177BB	88	Gulfstream 4	1073	Solar II Inc. Buffalo, NY.	N75PP
❏ N177EL	01	Citation X	750-0177	Rentair Inc/Ernst Langer, Hamburg, Germany.	N.....
❏ N177JB	98	Learjet 31A	31A-161	Classic Auto Campus LLC. Mentor, Oh.	N3016X
❏ N177JC	67	Jet Commander	77	Centennial Machine/Harrison Haynes, Gainesville, Ga.	N121JC
❏ N177JE	04	Citation Encore	560-0678	Dubois County Flight Services Inc/Air LLC. Huntingburg, In.	N399HS
❏ N177JF	96	CitationJet	525-0182	Rayco Industries Inc. Woooster, Oh.	N177JB
❏ N177KS	97	Learjet 60	60-109	C L Learjet LLC. Opa Locka, Fl.	N747SG
❏ N177RJ	87	Citation II	550-0550	RJ 1 LLC/Rinco of Delaware Inc. Canyon Lake, Tx.	N550FM
❏ N178AM	90	Learjet 55C	55C-144	Florida Jet Service Inc. Fort Lauderdale, Fl.	N40CR
❏ N178AX	90	BAe 125/800A	NA0449	Baron & Budd PC. Dallas, Tx.	N868WC
❏ N178B	73	Gulfstream 2B	125	MDA-Missile Defence Agency, Tulsa-R L Jones, Ok.	N92NA
❏ N178BR	03	Citation Excel	560-5354	HRL Ventures LLC. Chicago-Midway, Il.	(N71RL)

Reg	Yr	Type	c/n	Owner/Operator	Prev Regn
☐ N178CP	74	Learjet 35	35-005	EPPS Air Service Inc. Atlanta-DeKalb, Ga.	N175J
☐ N178DA*	84	Citation S/II	S550-0004	Dorf Air Leasing LLC. St Louis, Mo.	N72AM
☐ N178HL	86	Citation III	650-0125	Lichtin Corp. Raleigh-Durham, NC.	N170HL
☐ N178MM	99	Learjet 60	60-178	MAR Fun LLC/Jet Speed Aviation Inc. Latrobe, Pa.	N244FX
☐ N178NP	99	Learjet 31A	31A-178	Abarrotes Monterrey USA, San Antonio, Tx.	RP-C6178
☐ N178PC	71	HS 125/F400A	25264	Private Class Air LLC. Jeffco, Co.	N93TS
☐ N178SD	07	Gulfstream G350	4111	Gulfstream Aerospace Corp. Savannah, Ga.	N131GA
☐ N178WG	07	CitationJet CJ2+	525A-0342	T&A Aviation LLC/Gregg Orr Auto, Texarkana, Tx.	N18TD
☐ N179AE	02	Gulfstream G200	068	Darby Holdings LLC. Baltimore, Md.	N368GA
☐ N179CJ	07	CitationJet CJ-3	525B-0179	Cessna Aircraft Co. Wichita, Ks.	N5211A
☐ N179LF	97	Learjet 60	60-101	LF Essex House Corp/JetSmart Inc. Rochester, NY.	N215BX
☐ N179MR	01	Learjet 45	45-179	Butler Aviation LLC. Macon, Ga.	N45MR
☐ N179T	70	Gulfstream 2B	86	NMP Enterprises LLC. Dallas-Love, Tx.	(N179DE)
☐ N180AR	74	Gulfstream 2B	148	Yellow Tail G-1 LLC/Azar Mineral Ltd. San Antonio, Tx.	N2815
☐ N180CH	93	Gulfstream 4	1192	N180CH Inc/Crescent Heights Condominiums, Opa Locka, Fl.	N212K
☐ N180CP	96	Learjet 60	60-081	SFA of New Mexico Inc. Santa Fe, NM.	N60LJ
☐ N180FW	94	Citation V	560-0260	W Heywood Fralin, Roanoke, Va.	N883RT
☐ N180NE	87	BAe 125/800A	NA0401	Business Aircraft Leasing Inc. Nashville, Tn.	N815CC
☐ N181CA	81	Learjet 35A	35A-420	TWW Aviation Inc. Houston, Tx.	N100KZ
☐ N181CR	86	Gulfstream 4	1001	Corporate Wings LLC. Cuyahoga County, Oh.	N181CW
☐ N181EF	78	Learjet 35A	35A-190	Business Jets LLC/Executive Fliteways Inc. Ronkonkoma, NY.	(N208WR)
☐ N181FH	87	BAe 125/800A	258098	Barr Laboratories Inc. Pomona, NY.	N300LS
☐ N181G	84	Citation S/II	S550-0006	Mid-South Agricultural Products Inc. Lafayette, La.	N65DT
☐ N181GA	07	Gulfstream G550	5181	Gulfstream Aerospace Corp. Savannah, Ga.	
☐ N181J	99	Challenger 604	5433	Alta Enterprises Inc. Bedford, Ma.	N433FS
☐ N181MC	99	Falcon 50EX	279	MASCO Corp. Detroit-Metropolitan, Mi.	F-WWHE
☐ N181PA	98	Learjet 31A	31A-156	Schwyhart Holdings LLC. Carrollton, Tx.	N124FX
☐ N181RK	87	Falcon 200	515	Piccolo Aviation LLC. Scottsdale, Az.	XA-PFM
☐ N181SG	92	Citation V	560-0181	Garaventa Co. Concord, Ca.	N1280R
☐ N183CM	01	Learjet 45	45-133	D G Jenkins Development Corp. Suwanee, Ga.	N645KM
☐ N183JS	02	Citation Excel	560-5322	Ark-Air Flight Inc. Dallas, Tx.	N1838S
☐ N183PA	71	Gulfstream II SP	108	N183PA LLC. Norfolk, Va.	N900AK
☐ N183TS	05	Learjet 45	45-273	B & C Aviation/Columbus Bank & Trust Co. Columbus, Ga.	N4005Q
☐ N183TX	03	CitationJet CJ-2	525A-0183	Orkney Air LLC. Wilmington, De.	N283CJ
☐ N183WW	97	Falcon 900B	165	W & W 61/63 LLC. Boca Raton, Fl.	VP-BEC
☐ N184AR	92	Beechjet 400A	RK-34	HUSCO International Inc. Waukesha, Wi.	N134FA
☐ N184GP	94	Citation VI	650-0236	Contrarian Group Inc. Orange County, Ca.	N600UD
☐ N184NA	74	Citation	500-0184	Goldking Energy Corp. Houston, Tx.	N67BF
☐ N184PC	74	Sabre-80A	380-6	Sun Castle Aviation Inc. Las Vegas, Nv.	N711GD
☐ N184R	04	Challenger 300	20024	Rooney Brothers Co. Tulsa, Ok.	C-FAUZ
☐ N184TB	04	Hawker 800XP	258671	Thomas & Betts Corp. Memphis, Tn.	N671XP
☐ N184WW	76	Falcon 20F-5	352	Bazco LLC. West Palm Beach, Fl.	N920G
☐ N185GA	07	Gulfstream G550	5185	Gulfstream Aerospace Corp. Savannah, Ga.	
☐ N186CJ	07	CitationJet CJ-3	525B-0186	Jetaime LLC/Texakoma Operating LP. Addison, Tx.	N.....
☐ N186CP	74	Citation	500-0186	PriceFlight LLC/Charah Inc. Louisville, Ky.	(N510WL)
☐ N186DS	90	Gulfstream 4	1154	Alcatel USA Resources Inc. Addison, Tx.	N151GX
☐ N186PA	80	Gulfstream 3	317	C2D LLC/Phoenix Air Group Inc. Cartersville, Ga.	N90EP
☐ N186TW	00	CitationJet CJ-1	525-0416	Tallwood Management LLC. San Jose, Ca.	N8UC
☐ N186WS*	01	Citation Excel	560-5179	Beacon Eire Inc/Beacon Aviation Ltd. Weston, Ireland.	N188WS
☐ N186XL	00	Citation Excel	560-5186	Russell Corp. Alexander City, Al.	N.....
☐ N187CA	75	Learjet 25B	25B-187	Aviation Dynamics Inc. Henderson, Nv.	YU-BJG
☐ N187GA	07	Gulfstream G550	5187	Gulfstream Aerospace Corp. Savannah, Ga.	
☐ N187HF*	91	Astra-1125SP	054	Jersey Lincoln Inc. Stamford, Ct.	N198HF
☐ N187JN	82	Citation II	550-0335	Nemco Motor Sports Inc. Mooresville, NC.	N235TS
☐ N187MG	03	CitationJet CJ-2	525A-0187	Brooks Properties, Salem, NH.	N.....
☐ N187PN	76	Falcon 50	187	Paradise Aviation (Jersey) Ltd. Athens, Greece.	VH-PPF
☐ N187TJ	76	Westwind-1124	187	Jags of Sarasota Ltd. Sarasota, Fl. (status ?).	N241RH
☐ N188AK	99	Astra-1125SPX	121	Sallie Mae Inc. Dulles, Va.	N100AK
☐ N188CA	76	Learjet 25D	25D-208	N300SC Inc. Fort Lauderdale, Fl.	N300SC
☐ N188DC	76	Gulfstream 2	188	Avion LLC/Drummond Coal Inc. Birmingham, Al.	N555MU
☐ N188DM	02	Falcon 50EX	327	Archer Daniels Midland Co. Decatur, Il.	N327EX
☐ N188FJ	88	Falcon 50	188	Medill Co. Wilmington, De.	XA-ALA
☐ N188GA	07	Gulfstream G550	5188	Gulfstream Aerospace Corp. Savannah, Ga.	
☐ N188JF	05	Hawker 400XP	RK-446	Hawker Blue LLC/J F Shea Co. Santa Ana-Orange County, Ca.	N46XP
☐ N188JS	68	Gulfstream II SP	29	Bondstone Corp. Dallas-Love, Tx.	N941CW
☐ N188KA	81	HS 125/700A	NA0294	CDJD Transport LLC. Newtown Square, Pa.	N925DP

Reg	Yr	Type	c/n	Owner/Operator	Prev Regn
❏ N188ML	00	Gulfstream G200	024	BALA Aircraft Holdings LLC. Oxford, Ct.	N101LD
❏ N188MR	78	Gulfstream 2	218	R S Aircraft, Englewood, Co.	N187PH
❏ N188TG	96	Learjet 60	60-078	Drei T's LLC. O'Fallon, Mo.	N188TC
❏ N188TW	99	CitationJet	525-0326	Wheel-Air LLC. Mentor, Oh.	(N211LX)
❏ N189CM	97	CitationJet	525-0189	WPC Holdings LLC/Cole Automotive Group, Bluefield, WV.	
❏ N189GA	07	Gulfstream G550	5189	Gulfstream Aerospace Corp. Savannah, Ga.	
❏ N189H	89	Citation V	560-0004	Honeywell International Inc. Morristown, NJ.	
❏ N189K	90	Challenger 601-3A	5083	Swagelok Co/Crawford Fitting Co. Cleveland, Oh.	C-GLYA
❏ N189RB	72	Falcon 20F-5B	262	Middle East Jet Services, Beirut, Lebanon.	N795AB
❏ N189RR	71	HS 125/F400B	25248	Baypoit Holdings Ltd. Tortola, BVI.	(N119GH)
❏ N189TA	06	Hawker 850XP	258814	N189TA LLC/Tacala LLC. Birmingham, Al.	N70214
❏ N189WS	78	Gulfstream II SP	228	Osborne Aviation LLC. Little Rock, Ar.	N157LH
❏ N189WW	00	Citation Excel	560-5069	Window World Inc. Wilkesboro, NC.	N404SB
❏ N190AR	75	Learjet 25B	25B-190	World Jet of Delaware Inc. Fort Lauderdale, Fl.	XA-DAK
❏ N190CS	76	Gulfstream II SP	190	Air Pip Inc. Chicago, Il.	N914CF
❏ N190H	06	Global Express	9210	Realogy Corp. Parsippany, NJ.	C-FIOT
❏ N190JK	95	Citation V Ultra	560-0303	PCH Aviation LLC. Daytona Beach, Fl.	N190JH
❏ N190K	81	Citation 1/SP	501-0192	Klabzuba Oil & Gas Inc. Fort Worth, Tx.	(N6781G)
❏ N190MC	97	Falcon 2000	45	Masco Contractor Services, Daytona Beach, Fl.	N45SC
❏ N190MP	94	Challenger 601-3R	5161	MPI Transaction Management LLC. Atlanta, Ga.	(N997CT)
❏ N190MQ	80	Falcon 50	26	WPE 50 LLC. Dallas, Tx.	N190MC
❏ N191CP	07	Gulfstream G150	249	Gulfstream Aerospace LP. Dallas-Love, Tx.	4X-C..
❏ N191LJ	01	Learjet 45	45-191	Dean Foods Co. Dallas, Tx.	(N432FX)
❏ N191MC	98	Falcon 50EX	282	MASCO Corp. Detroit-Metropolitan, Mi.	F-WWHH
❏ N191PP	02	CitationJet CJ-1	525-0487	Matrix Sales & Service Inc. Lewes, De.	CC-CMS
❏ N191TD	06	Learjet 45	45-298	Richards Aviation Inc. Memphis, Tn.	N5000E
❏ N191VE	91	Citation V	560-0150	Spear Q Sub Inc/Spear Development Inc. Las Vegas, Nv.	N191VF
❏ N191VF	02	Citation Encore	560-0627	Primary Capital Management Inc. Las Vegas, Nv.	N191VB
❏ N192CK	69	Falcon 20D	192	Kalitta Charters LLC. Detroit-Willow Run, Mi.	N192R
❏ N192CN	07	Citation Sovereign	680-0137	Centcorp Investments Ltd. Miami, Fl.	N5093L
❏ N192DW	80	Citation II	550-0192	Fitch Aviation Inc. Reno, Nv.	YV-900CP
❏ N192F	98	Falcon 50EX	277	Freescale Semiconductor Inc. Austin, tx.	N198M
❏ N192FG	76	Gulfstream II SP	192	Stockwood Inc. Morristown, NJ.	N273LP
❏ N192NC	95	Gulfstream 4SP	1286	SCP Aviation LLC/Sun Capital Partners, Boca Raton, Fl.	N880G
❏ N192SJ	90	BAe 125/800A	258192	Hawker 192 Corp. San Juan, PR.	TR-LDB
❏ N192SW	06	Gulfstream G150	216	Sherwin-Williams Co. Cleveland, Oh.	N216GA
❏ N193DB	69	Learjet 24B	24B-193	Don Bessette Aviation Inc. Minot, ND.	N193JF
❏ N193F	05	Falcon 900EX EASY	147	Freescale Semiconductor Inc. Austin, Tx.	F-WWFE
❏ N193SB	93	Citation V	560-0229	Bradshaw & Co/B & C General Contractors Inc. Greensboro, NC.	N98GA
❏ N194JS	93	BAe 125/800A	258251	J R Simplot Co. Boise, Id.	N937H
❏ N194K	89	Falcon 50	194	Kendall-Jackson Wine Estates Ltd. Santa Rosa, Ca.	N95PH
❏ N194SA	93	Citation V	560-0238	William Hobby, Houston, Tx.	N46WB
❏ N194SJ	03	CitationJet CJ-2	525A-0194	BM Devco Inc/Menlo Oaks Corp. Larkspur, Ca.	N806MN
❏ N194WM	97	Challenger 604	5340	Challenger Administration LLC/Mente Corp. Seattle, Wa.	N606CC
❏ N195AR	76	Gulfstream 2	195	American Medical Products, Carson City, Nv. (status ?).	XA-ILV
❏ N195ME	95	CitationJet	525-0110	Methode Electronics Inc. Chicago, Il.	N5213S
❏ N195SV	99	Falcon 50EX	293	Silver Ventures Inc. San Antonio, Tx.	N293EX
❏ N195WS	87	Gulfstream 4	1050	ITT Flight Operations Inc. White Plains, NY.	N153RA
❏ N196CC	85	Gulfstream 3	463	CWIE Management Resources LLC. Tempe, Az.	N886DT
❏ N196CT	06	Learjet 45XR	45-318	Carry-On Trailer Corp. Spartanburg, SC.	(N45XR)
❏ N196EX	07	Falcon 900EX EASY	196	Dassault Falcon Jet Corp. Teterboro, NJ.	F-WWVA
❏ N196GA	07	Gulfstream G550	5196	Gulfstream Aerospace Corp. Savannah, Ga.	
❏ N196HA	98	CitationJet	525-0256	Papercone Aviation LLC. Louisville, Ky.	
❏ N196JS	80	Citation II	550-0196	Nesnah Aviation LLC. Holmen, Wi.	HB-VLS
❏ N196KC	02	Falcon 2000	195	Kansas City Life Insurance Co. Kansas City, Ks.	N297QS
❏ N196MG	87	BAe 125/800A	258081	Millbrook Properties Ltd. Manhasset, NY.	N196MC
❏ N196PH	99	Learjet 45	45-056	E I DuPont de Nemours & Co. Des Moines, Ia.	
❏ N196RG	00	Falcon 2000	135	RI-Relational Investors Aviation LLC. Carlsbad, Ca.	N222BN
❏ N196RJ	81	Citation II	550-0207	D & B Drilling Inc. Wheatridge, Co.	N207BA
❏ N196SB	04	Citation Excel XLS	560-5513	Kindred Healthcare Inc. Louisville, Ky.	N.....
❏ N196SD	85	Citation III	650-0093	Angel Air III Inc. Sunrise, Fl.	N196SG
❏ N196TB	69	Learjet 24B	24B-196	Brundage Management Co. San Antonio, Tx.	N196AF
❏ N196TS	69	Falcon 20D	196	A Nicole Entertainment, Chino, Ca.	(N142JF)
❏ N197BE	92	Beechjet 400A	RK-33	Bill Mullis Enterprises Inc. Sarasota, Fl.	N197PF
❏ N197CF	76	Learjet 25B	25B-197	Dodson Aviation Inc. Rantoul, Ks.	(N96DM)
❏ N197CJ	03	CitationJet CJ-2	525A-0197	Kilo Alpha Services LLC. Texarkana, Tx.	N.....

Reg	Yr	Type	c/n	Owner/Operator	Prev Regn
N197EX	07	Falcon 900EX EASY	197	Dassault Falcon Jet Corp. Teterboro, NJ.	F-WWFC
N197HF	07	Gulfstream G150	220	Hormel Foods Corp. Austin, Mn.	N220GA
N197LS	83	Learjet 25D	25D-363	La Stella Corp. Pueblo, Co.	XA-RSU
N197PH	99	Learjet 31A	31A-169	E I DuPont de Nemours & Co. Des Moines, Ia.	
N197PR	92	Citation II	550-0704	Golden Triangle Constructors Ltd. Beaumont, Tx.	(N187HF)
N197RJ	07	CitationJet CJ1+	525-0660	Tower Aviation of Reading Inc. Reading, Pa.	N5057F
N198CT	97	Beechjet 400A	RK-151	Eagle Construction of VA Inc. Richmond, Va.	N196CT
N198CV	92	Citation V	560-0198	DWC Aircraft LLC. Dayton, Oh.	N598CW
N198DC	01	Challenger 604	5481	Dow Corning Corp. Midland, Mi.	N481KW
N198DL	66	JetStar-731	5083	Woods Aviation Inc. Palm Beach, Fl.	N817BD
N198GJ	78	Learjet 35A	35A-198	Royal Air Freight Inc. Pontiac, Mi.	I-ALPT
N198GS	89	Gulfstream 4	1098	Maughold Ltd. Roadtown, BVI.	VP-BSF
N198GT	81	HS 125/700A	NA0288	LGT Aviation Inc. Van Nuys, Ca.	N700BW
N198HB	00	Learjet 60	60-198	United Furniture Equipment Rental Inc. Okolona, Ms.	
N198JA	75	Learjet 25B	25B-198	Royal Air Freight Inc. Pontiac, Mi.	N29TS
N198JH	97	CitationJet	525-0265	Enex Aviation Ltd. Barbados.	
N198M	98	Falcon 50EX	273	Kemper Ventures/TAG Aviation SA. Geneva, Switzerland.	N158M
N198MR	84	Falcon 50	149	Tampa Bay Airlines LLC. Dover, De.	N198M
N198ND	90	Citation II	550-0630	Dentressangle USA Inc. Lyon-Bron, France.	N198DF
N198NS	80	Citation II	550-0133	CFNS Inc. Encino, Ca.	N228CC
N198RG	97	CitationJet	525-0198	RJ Grad Aviation LLC. Van Nuys, Ca.	N315MR
N198SL	98	Citation Bravo	550-0835	Luminar Air/Zimmer Development LLC. Wilmington, NC.	(N835VP)
N199BB	99	Citation Bravo	550-0895	George Schreyer Revocable Trust, Newport Coast, Ca.	
N199BT	80	Learjet 25D	25D-311	Jet Makers Inc. Denison, Tx.	ZS-NJH
N199DF	04	Hawker 800XP	258713	Gore Creek Capital LLC. Eagle County, Co.	N713XP
N199FG	92	Falcon 50	231	Fremont Group/Bechtel Corp. Oakland, Ca.	N10PP
N199FJ	07	Falcon 900EX EASY	199	Dassault Falcon Jet Corp. Teterboro, NJ.	F-WWFJ
N199HE	88	Astra-1125	027	Lockton Enterprises Inc. Houston, Tx.	N199HF
N199HF	00	Gulfstream G200	028	Hormel Foods Corp. Austin Municipal, Mn.	N60GX
N199Q*	77	Citation II	550-0003	Nineteen Charlie Papa LLC. Sarasota, Fl. (was 551-0004)	N19CP
N199RM	03	390 Premier 1	RB-99	Robert Garriott, Austin, Tx.	N24YR
N199WT	96	Citation X	750-0018	PAFO-Premair Flight Options Inc. Indianapolis, In.	N5115
N199XP	97	Citation X	750-0019	Amini Innovation Corp. Pico Rivera, Ca.	N5116
N200A	05	Global Express	9203	Exxon Mobil Corp. Dallas-Love, Tx.	N203XX
N200AB	69	Gulfstream 2	71	7-N Aircorp. Dallas, Tx.	N47A
N200AP	95	Citation X	750-0003	Lifestyle Aviation Inc. Coburg, Or.	(N300VP)
N200AS	00	Citation Bravo	550-0934	Pacific Oak Development Inc. Carmel, Ca.	N5260Y
N200AX	99	Gulfstream G200	009	R & N Aviation Inc. Wilmington, De.	N83EJ
N200BA	02	Gulfstream G200	076	Bayou Helicopters Inc. Houston, Tx.	N376GA
N200BH	00	Gulfstream G200	013	R&R Transport/Richardson Operating Co. Greenwood Village, Co	HB-IGP
N200CG	75	Citation	500-0230	Illinois Data Mart Inc. DuPage, Il.	N299TB
N200CH	02	Falcon 2000EX	4	Cardal Inc. Columbus-OSU, Oh.	F-WWGD
N200CK	88	Astra-1125	021	DPMG Inc/Landmark Land Co. Upper Marlboro, Md.	N1125
N200CP	72	Falcon 20E-5	275	Trinity Industries Inc. Dallas, Tx.	(N999BG)
N200CQ	05	Citation X	750-0245	General Parts Inc. Raleigh, NC.	N5257C
N200CU	84	Falcon 200	499	Jani King International Inc. Addison, Tx.	N14CJ
N200DE	98	Challenger 604	5390	Dunavant Enterprises Inc. Memphis, Tn.	N541DE
N200DV	02	SJ 30-2	008	SJ30 Aircraft 1 LLC. Durand, Mi.	N80SJ
N200EE	66	BAC 1-11/212AR	083	Select Aviation Inc. Waukesha, Wi.	N490ST
N200EL	83	Gulfstream 3	393	JDL Aviation LLC/NRR Aviation LLC. Stuart, Fl.	N519AF
N200ES	07	Global 5000	9245	Earth Star Inc. Burbank, Ca.	C-FLTJ
N200FJ	84	Falcon 200	494	Whitesell Corp. Muscle Shoals, Al.	EC-HEG
N200GF	87	Citation II/SP	551-0556	Golden Flake Snack Foods Inc. Birmingham, Al.	(N12979)
N200GN	98	Falcon 2000	68	Gannett Co. Dulles, Va.	F-WWMN
N200GP	97	Beechjet 400A	RK-172	General Parts Inc. Raleigh, NC.	N615HP
N200GV	07	Gulfstream G200	167	TitleMax Aviation Inc. Savannah, Ga.	N367GA
N200JB	07	Gulfstream G200	164	JBI Inc/Flightworks Inc. Marietta, Ga.	N164GA
N200JP	78	HS 125/700A	NA0238	Flights Unlimited LLC/Millco Inc. Canonsburg, Pa.	N120MH
N200JR	05	Citation Excel XLS	560-5550	JRN Inc. Columbia, Tn.	N.....
N200JX	64	BAC 1-11/203AE	015	Select Aviation Inc. Waukesha, Wi.	N583CQ
N200KB	94	Learjet 31A	31A-098	Kurt Bush Inc/KB Aviation Inc. Concord, NC.	N797KB
N200LB	04	390 Premier 1	RB-116	Briar Hill Leasing Inc. Lexington, Ky.	N145ST
N200LC	88	Gulfstream 4	1067	Loral Space & Communications, NYC.	N145ST
N200LH	92	Citation VII	650-7005	Cypress Equities LLC. Addison, Tx.	N1259S
N200LJ	78	Learjet 35A	35A-200	World Jet Inc. Fort Lauderdale, Fl.	OO-LFY
N200LP	81	Diamond 1	A006SA	Central Flying Service Inc. Little Rock, Ar.	N750TJ

Reg	Yr	Type	c/n	Owner/Operator	Prev Regn
☐ N200LV	05	Gulfstream G200	115	ASNY Aviation LLC/Consolidated Realty Inc. Las Vegas, Nv.	N615GA
☐ N200MM	89	Citation V	560-0036	Exquisite Development LLC. Destin, Fl.	(N560EJ)
☐ N200MT	98	Learjet 60	60-150	Aerospace Leasing LLC/Meyer Tool Inc. Cincinnati, Oh.	N150BX
☐ N200NC	80	Citation II	550-0184	Thomas R Miller, Sartell, Mn.	(N20TV)
☐ N200QC	72	Citation Longwing SP	500-0023	AeroVision International LLC. Muskegon, Mi.	N50FT
☐ N200RT	82	Falcon 50	126	Pinnacle Air Exceutive Jet, Springdale, Ar.	(N986PA)
☐ N200SC	01	Citation Excel	560-5148	560 Inc/CBL & Associates Inc. Chattanooga, Tn.	N777FH
☐ N200SG	93	Falcon 50	239	Ingles Markets Inc. Asheville, NC.	N239FJ
☐ N200SK	80	Gulfstream 3	319	SK Travel LLC/Emar Associates Inc. Livingston, NJ.	N319Z
☐ N200SL	01	CitationJet CJ-1	525-0461	Sutherland Lumber & Home Centers Inc. Tulsa-R L Jones, Ok.	N5207A
☐ N200ST	92	Astra-1125SP	061	Constuctora Sambil CA. Caracas, Venezuela.	N550M
☐ N200TW	81	Learjet 35A	35A-397	Campbell Aircraft Holdings LLC. Coatesville, Pa.	(N335JD)
☐ N200UP	81	Falcon 50	55	United Pan-Europe Communications NV. Amsterdam, Holland.	N96UH
☐ N200VR*	06	Gulfstream G200	133	Vista Development LLC. Elmira, NY.	(N202GJ)
☐ N200VT	80	Citation II	550-0083	JFF Aviation LLC. Van Nuys, Ca.	N54CC
☐ N200WK	72	Falcon 20-5	261	TAG Aviation USA Inc. White Plains, NY.	N4368F
☐ N200YB	02	Gulfstream G200	075	KFC US Properties Inc/Yum! Brands Inc. Louisville, Ky.	N875GA
☐ N201BR	68	Falcon 20C-5	166	Carrington Capital Management LLC. Ithaca, NY.	N71TJ
☐ N201CP	03	Embraer EMB-135LR	145726	Pfizer Inc. Mercer County Airport, NJ.	PT-...
☐ N201CR	94	Falcon 2000	2	Romana Aircraft Inc. Santo Domingo, Dominican Republic.	F-GJHJ
☐ N201GA	04	Gulfstream G200	101	Tri-West Healthcare Alliance Corp. Fort Worth, Tx.	4X-CVJ
☐ N201GF	73	Falcon 20E	284	Jet Fleet International Corp. Van Nuys, Ca.	(N801MD)
☐ N201SU	01	Citation Encore	560-0586	Synthes (USA)LP/IMP Inc. Chester County, Pa.	N52691
☐ N201WR	02	Falcon 2000	201	Delaware Park LLC. Gaithersburg, Md.	F-WWFO
☐ N202AR	84	Falcon 200	496	Outback Steakhouse of Florida Inc. Tampa, Fl.	N256JC
☐ N202AV	99	Citation VII	650-7108	Avista Corp. Spokane, Wa.	
☐ N202BG	94	CitationJet	525-0089	Banco Espanol de Credito SA. Madrid, Spain.	N920MS
☐ N202CE	95	Falcon 2000	22	Clark Enterprises Inc. Easton, Md.	N609CH
☐ N202CP	03	Embraer EMB-135LR	145728	Pfizer Inc. Mercer County Airport, NJ.	PT-...
☐ N202DF	06	Citation Sovereign	680-0098	FlightWorks/Dupont Fabros Development LLC. Manassas, Va.	N52178
☐ N202EX	02	Falcon 2000EX	2	Watsco Holdings Inc. Miami, Fl.	F-WWGA
☐ N202HM	75	Citation	500-0260		A6-ESJ
☐ N202JK	85	Citation III	650-0100	A & S World Aircraft Inc. Las Vegas, Nv.	N200LL
☐ N202JS	73	Learjet 24D	24D-278	J R S Aviation Inc. St Petersburg, Fl.	N5695H
☐ N202N	02	Learjet 60	60-258	LJ60 LLC. Wilmington, De.	
☐ N202PX	68	Gulfstream II SP	17	Florida Aircraft Sales LLC. Lighthouse Point, Fl.	N143V
☐ N202RL	00	Citation Excel	560-5117	RBL LLC/DB Aviation Inc. Waukegan, Il.	N5233J
☐ N202SW	83	Citation II	550-0470	Huff Air LLC/Sierra Industries Inc. Uvalde, Tx.	N10RU
☐ N202TH	00	Falcon 2000	130	Mioplex Industries LLC/Global Equipment Leasing, Lewes, De.	N99TY
☐ N202TT	06	Hawker 400XP	RK-504	SSC Aviation 06 LLC/TVPX Inc. Denver, Co.	(N45LN)
☐ N202VZ	96	Gulfstream 4SP	1289	MCI Communications Services Inc. Dulles, Va.	N334MC
☐ N202WR	87	Falcon 900	24	Weichert Realtors/Dumont Associates Inc. Morristown, NJ.	N93GR
☐ N203	98	Challenger 604	5374	Jacura Delaware Inc. Boca Raton, Fl.	N97FJ
☐ N203A	07	Gulfstream G550	5169	APC Aviation Inc/Anadarko Petroleum Corp. Houston, Tx.	N569GA
☐ N203BA	85	Beechjet 400	RJ-3	P & I Inc/Cerner Corp. Kansas City, Mo.	N508DM
☐ N203BG	00	CitationJet CJ-1	525-0378	Brasfield & Gorrie LLC. Birmingham, Al.	N525CP
☐ N203BP	07	390 Premier 1A	RB-203	CW Aviation Holding Inc. Wilmington, De. (trustor ?).	
☐ N203DN	07	Citation Sovereign	680-0203	Cessna Aircraft Co. Wichita, Ks.	N.....
☐ N203GA	07	Gulfstream G550	5203	Gulfstream Aerospace Corp. Savannah, Ga.	
☐ N203JD	91	Challenger 601-3A	5099	Hume & Johnson PA. Coral Springs, Fl.	(N121GG)
☐ N203JE	99	Global Express	9019	9019 Holdings Inc. Wilmington, De.	HL7576
☐ N203JL	69	Learjet 24B	24B-203	Bruce Leven, Mercer Island, Wa.	N203CK
☐ N203NC	90	Falcon 50	203	Nova Chemicals Services Inc. Coraopolis, Pa.	C-GNCA
☐ N203PM	88	Citation II	550-0578	N203PM LLC. Davenport, Ia.	PT-LQJ
☐ N203QS	02	Falcon 2000	198	NetJets, Port Columbus, Oh.	F-WWVL
☐ N203R*	98	Challenger 604	5386	Raytheon Co. Waltham, Ma.	N119GA
☐ N203TA	96	Challenger 604	5316	Raytheon Travel Air Co. Wichita, Ks.	N200UL
☐ N203TM	03	Hawker 800XP	258653	Cerner Corp. Kansas City, Mo.	N653XP
☐ N203VS	81	Learjet 25D	25D-347	Calspan Corp. Buffalo, NY.	N347JV
☐ N203WB	01	Falcon 2000	144	W R Berkley Corp. White Plains, NY.	N317MR
☐ N203WS	07	Citation Encore+	560-0785	Cessna Aircraft Co. Wichita, Ks.	N.....
☐ N204AN	67	Falcon 20C	102	Nikki Air LLC. Las Vegas, Nv.	N403JW
☐ N204BG	99	Citation V Ultra	560-0503	Brasfield & Gorrie LLC. Birmingham, Al.	VP-BDB
☐ N204CA	78	Citation 1/SP	501-0283	James M Krueger, Newport Beach, Ca. (was 500-0377).	C-GPTC
☐ N204CF	81	Citation II	550-0238	Corporate Flight Inc. Detroit, Mi.	N97S
☐ N204CW	06	Falcon 2000EX EASY	101	A T & T Mobility Sales & Marketing, Fulton County, Ga.	F-WWMC

Reg	Yr	Type	c/n	Owner/Operator	Prev Regn
❏ N204DD	06	Gulfstream G200	139	Orange Crimson Aviation LLC. Dulles, Va.	N139GA
❏ N204DH	00	Beechjet 400A	RK-290	Drury Development Corp. St Louis, Mo.	N400QW
❏ N204J	96	CitationJet	525-0164	Betty MacGuire/MacGuire Aviation, Santa Teresa, NM.	D-ICGT
❏ N204JK	87	Challenger 601-3A	5015	Royal Oak Enterprises Inc. Atlanta-DeKalb, Ga.	N514RB
❏ N204PM	81	Citation II	550-0320	Prewett Hosiery Sales, Fort Payne-Isbell, Al.	N57MB
❏ N204QS	99	Falcon 2000	104	NetJets, Port Columbus, Oh.	F-WWVY
❏ N204RP	06	Citation Sovereign	680-0093	Pratte Development Co. Chandler, Az.	(N4RP)
❏ N204RT	00	Learjet 31A	31A-204	Ruby Tuesday Inc. Knoxville, Tn.	
❏ N204TM	81	Westwind-1124	320	International Air Services CA Inc. Fort Lauderdale, Fl.	N60JP
❏ N204TW	69	Falcon 20DC	204	Sierra American Corp. Addison, Tx.	EC-EGM
❏ N205BC	03	390 Premier 1	RB-69	Wheeler Trailer Inc. Chicago, Il.	
❏ N205BN	94	CitationJet	525-0050	Boone Newspapers Inc. Natchez, Ms.	N70KW
❏ N205CM	94	Citation V	560-0250	Charlotte-Macklenberg Hospital Authority, Charlotte, NC.	N1291Y
❏ N205CW	04	Falcon 2000EX EASY	45	Cingular Wireless Corp, Fulton County, Ga.	VP-BVP
❏ N205EE	97	Challenger 604	5347	Tuck Aviation LLC/Jim Click Automotive, Tucson, Az.	N205EL
❏ N205EL	06	Global 5000	9201	Invemed Associates Inc. Hudson, NY.	N95ZZ
❏ N205JC	81	Falcon 20F-5B	440	Pere Marquette Group LLC. Grand Rapids, Mi.	N7000G
❏ N205TW*	78	HS 125/700A	257025	Jet 205 TW LLC. Addison, Tx.	N886S
❏ N205WP	74	Falcon 20E-5	306	Wausau Paper Corp. Mosinee, Wi.	N205WM
❏ N205X	88	Gulfstream 4	1080	Occidental Petroleum Corp. Burbank, Ca.	N20XY
❏ N205YY	04	CitationJet CJ-2	525A-0205	Big Sky Aviation LLC. Portland, Or.	N5241Z
❏ N206AG	81	Citation II	550-0306	Austin Air LLC. Cleveland-Lakefront, Oh. (was 551-0341).	N296CW
❏ N206CK	99	Learjet 45	45-047	Cincinnati United Contractors Inc. Cincinnati, Oh.	N158PD
❏ N206HY	94	Learjet 60	60-028	Cottonwood Aviation LLC. Tulsa, Ok.	N206FX
❏ N207AH	07	390 Premier 1A	RB-207	American Speciality Insurance Services, Fort Wayne, In.	
❏ N207BC	97	Astra-1125SPX	093	R & S Airways Inc. Ocala, Ks.	N707BC
❏ N207BG	06	CitationJet CJ2+	525A-0326	Brasfield & Gorrie LLC. Birmingham, Al.	OE-FXX
❏ N207BS	01	CitationJet CJ-1	525-0445	Peco Air LLC/Phillips Edison & Co. Baltimore, Md.	N445CJ
❏ N207CA	68	Falcon 20D	153	Cherry Air Inc. Addison, Tx.	N70MD
❏ N207HF	77	Learjet 25D	25D-230	White Industries Inc. Bates City, Mo. (status ?).	N7RL
❏ N207JS	67	Falcon 20-5	117	Jet Fleet International Corp. Van Nuys, Ca.	F-GLMD
❏ N207MJ	58	MS 760 Paris-2	2	Tej Jet of Del LLC. Dover, De.	N1EP
❏ N207R	94	Hawker 1000	259045	Raytheon Co. Lexington, Ma.	(N545LR)
❏ N207RG	76	Learjet 24E	24E-339	Blue Sky Jets Corp. Sarasota, Fl.	N52DD
❏ N207TT	92	BAe 1000A	259008	Dill Aircraft II LLC. Delray Beach, Fl.	D-CADA
❏ N208BH	00	Learjet 60	60-208	V3 LLC. Hailey, Id.	(N112MT)
❏ N208BP	07	390 Premier 1A	RB-208	Permian Tank & Manufacturing Inc. Odessa, Tx,	
❏ N208HP	07	390 Premier 1A	RB-232	Hawker Beechcraft Corp. Wichita, Ks.	
❏ N208R	91	BAe 1000A	NA1003	Raytheon Co. Lexington, Ma.	N14GD
❏ N209CA	66	Falcon 20C	71	Source Investments LLC. Addison, Tx.	N195AS
❏ N209CV	93	Citation V	560-0209	209 Aircraft Co LLC. Columbia, Mo.	
❏ N209FJ	96	Falcon 900EX	2	Dassault Falcon Jet Corp. Teterboro, NJ.	N200L
❏ N209KM	02	Learjet 45	45-209	Executive Express Aviation SA. Zinacantepec, Mexico.	N300JC
❏ N209LS	00	Gulfstream 4SP	1449	Shaw International Inc. Baton Rouge, La. (status ?).	N200LS
❏ N209TM	03	Falcon 2000	209	Montalbano Enterprises LLC. DuPage, Il.	N209FS
❏ N209TS	77	HS 125/700A	NA0209	HS700 LLC. Danbury, Ct.	N843CP
❏ N210CM	96	Citation V Ultra	560-0369	Carolinas HealthCare Systems, Charlotte, NC.	N680GW
❏ N210QS	03	Falcon 2000	211	NetJets/Marquis Jet Partners Inc. Port Columbus, Oh.	F-WWVY
❏ N210RK	79	HS 125/700A	257073	Aspen Jet Inc. Blue Island, Il.	N701TA
❏ N211BC	90	Learjet 55C	55C-145	IBC Airways Inc. Miami, Fl.	N10CR
❏ N211BR	74	Sabre-60	306-85	Flight Research Inc. Starksville, Ms.	N855CD
❏ N211CC	91	Citation VI	650-0211	Crain Management Services Inc. Detroit, Mi.	N333WC
❏ N211DH	00	Gulfstream 4SP	1432	Hagadone Aviation LLC. Coeur d'Alene, Id.	N335GA
❏ N211DK	89	Gulfstream 4	1078	Urban Zen Air LLC/Donna Karan International, NYC.	G-DNVT
❏ N211EC	80	Falcon 10	166	East Coast Flight Services Inc. Easton, Md.	(N166SS)
❏ N211GA	81	Diamond 1A	A011SA	Lacerte Builders, Pompano Beach, Fl.	(N77GA)
❏ N211GM	97	CitationJet	525-0208	Spring House Inc. Alexandria, In.	N208JV
❏ N211JC	80	Learjet 25D	25D-310	Associations Inc. Dallas, Tx.	(N211JE)
❏ N211JL	81	Falcon 10	180	Ginju LLC. Arlington, Va.	N25MC
❏ N211JS	79	Citation II	550-0098	Scolari's Warehouse Markets Inc. Sparks, Nv. (was 551-0140).	N212H
❏ N211MA	94	Gulfstream 4SP	1247	Maguire Properties Inc. Van Nuys, Ca.	N477RP
❏ N211RN	93	Learjet 31A	31A-072	Blue Skies Aviation LLC. Washington, Pa.	(N14WT)
❏ N211ST	80	Westwind-Two	303	Western Airways Inc. Sugar Land, Tx.	N50QJ
❏ N211TB	06	Challenger 300	20117	Newcastle Aircraft LLC. Bedford, Ma.	C-FIOE
❏ N212BA	82	Gulfstream 3	353	Advance Flight Concepts Inc. Fort Lauderdale, Fl.	HZ-108
❏ N212BW	89	Citation V	560-0038	Warrior Energy Services Corp. Columbus, Oh.	N2296S

Reg	Yr	Type	c/n	Owner/Operator	Prev Regn
❏ N212FH	05	Hawker 400XP	RK-448	Andrews Lando & Assocs. Novato, Ca.	N146QS
❏ N212FJ	79	Falcon 10	147	Mobek Aviation LLC. Sioux City, Ia.	N125GA
❏ N212M	77	Citation	501-0280	Makaira Aircraft Sales LLC. Collierville, Tn. (was 500-0373)	T9-BKA
❏ N212MP	01	Gulfstream G200	033	Aerocentro de Servicios CA/Edificio Polar SA. Caracas.	N31SJ
❏ N212R	69	Falcon 20DC	212	Kalitta Charters LLC. Detroit-Willow Run, Mi.	N31FE
❏ N212RG	86	Hawker 800SP	258073	Onward & Upward LLC/Gilber Gagnon Howe LLC. Teterboro, NJ.	N2236
❏ N212RR	97	Challenger 604	5336	RoRo 212 LLC. Cincinnati-Lunken, Oh.	N310BX
❏ N212SL	01	Gulfstream G200	055	Aviones LLC. Dulles, Va.	N885RR
❏ N212VZ	03	Gulfstream G400	1531	Verizon Communications, Teterboro, NJ.	N531GA
❏ N213AR	95	Learjet 31A	31A-107	D A R M LLC/Aviation Jets LLC. Opa Locka, Fl.	N107LP
❏ N213BA	85	Gulfstream 3	453	Marquez Brothers Aviation LLC. San Jose, Ca.	HZ-103
❏ N213BK	98	Beechjet 400A	RK-216	B4A LLC/B A Karbank & Co. Kansas City, Mo.	N3050P
❏ N213CA	78	Learjet 25D	25D-241	Delaware DI Properties LLC. Addison, Tx.	N713LJ
❏ N213CC	81	Citation II	550-0213	RHA Air LLC. Little Rock, Ar.	N550HB
❏ N213GS	91	Challenger 601-3A	5101	Gamestop Inc/Barnes & Noble Inc. Teterboro, NJ.	(N108BN)
❏ N213HP	87	Citation III	650-0133	Jet 213HP LLC/Addison Jet Center, Addison, Tx.	N250CM
❏ N213JS	89	Citation II	550-0597	Idlewood Aviation Inc. DeKalb, Ga.	N400EX
❏ N213PC	06	390 Premier 1A	RB-173	Perryman Enterprises, Houston, Pa.	N73736
❏ N213PQ	02	390 Premier 1	RB-75	JSMGT LLC. Horseheads, NY.	N213PC
❏ N213QS	00	Falcon 2000	113	NetJets, Port Columbus, Oh.	F-WWVH
❏ N213TS	83	Challenger 601	3013	WFP Investments LLC. Snowmass Village, Co.	(N602LX)
❏ N213X	77	Gulfstream II SP	213	Two Thirteen Aviation LLC. Fort Myers, Fl.	(N96BK)
❏ N214AS	85	Falcon 200	501	Performance Investments Inc. Jacksonville, Fl.	N57TT
❏ N214DV*	06	Falcon 50EX	350	Maltese Falcon LLC/Sequoia Capital, Hayward, Ca.	N350DV
❏ N214JT	82	Citation II	550-0418	Moonlight Aviation LLC. Minneapolis, Mn.	N418CG
❏ N214PG	84	Diamond 1A	A082SA	Realty Predevelopment Inc. Amarillo, Tx.	N62CH
❏ N214RV	88	Falcon 100	217	Arch Air Ltd/Rafael Vinoly Architects PC. Teterboro, NJ.	N68GT
❏ N214RW	06	Challenger 300	20119	Midwest Onalaska Services LLC. La Crosse, Wi.	C-FIOH
❏ N214WY	84	Gulfstream 3	441	ES Aviation LLC. Ronkonkoma, NY.	N80J
❏ N215KH	02	Falcon 2000	197	Concord Jet Service Inc. Concord, Ca.	N2290
❏ N215NA	81	Citation 1/SP	501-0215	Spence & Associates Inc. The Woodlands, Tx.	ZS-LXT
❏ N215QS	03	Falcon 2000	214	NetJets, Port Columbus, Oh.	N214FJ
❏ N215RE	03	Falcon 2000	215	RE/MAX International Inc. Greenwood Village, Co.	F-WWVC
❏ N215RS	78	HS 125/700A	NA0215	Three Girls & A Dad LLC. Seattle, Wa.	N195XP
❏ N215RX	03	Citation X	750-0225	Highland Leasing Corp - CVS Corp. Woonsocket, RI.	N5223D
❏ N215TP	89	Beechjet 400	RJ-64	S2 Yachts Inc. Holland, Mi.	N195JH
❏ N215TT	93	Learjet 31A	31A-076	National City Commercial Capital Co. Cincinnati, Oh.	N518SA
❏ N215WC*	95	Citation V Ultra	560-0315	NetJets, Port Columbus, Oh.	N315QS
❏ N216CA	65	Falcon 20C	11	Delaware DI Properties LLC. Addison, Tx.	N983AJ
❏ N216GA	07	Gulfstream G450	4116	Gulfstream Aerospace Corp. Savannah, Ga.	
❏ N216RR	68	Gulfstream II SP	22	GS-II Holdings LLC/Skookum Air Inc. Irvine, Ca.	N217RR
❏ N216WD	82	Falcon 50	112	Woolbright Development Inc. Boca Raton, Fl.	N652AL
❏ N217AJ	68	Falcon 20D	171	Thunder Aviation Services Inc. Chesterfield, Mo.	F-GICB
❏ N217AL	03	Citation X	750-0217	AML Leasing LLC/TWC Aviation Inc. Burbank, Ca.	(N221AL)
❏ N217BA	06	Gulfstream G200	144	Max Aviation Group Inc. NYC.	4X-CVI
❏ N217BX	97	Learjet 60	60-105	B C Aviation LLC. Reno, Nv.	N217FX
❏ N217CA	67	Falcon 20C	75	Source Investments LLC. Addison, Tx.	UR-EFB
❏ N217EC	02	Hawker 400XP	RK-356	Wings Over Oregon LLC. Lodi, Ca.	N808HT
❏ N217FS	81	Citation II	550-0273	ORP Management LLC. Oak Hill, Fl.	N68637
❏ N217JS	76	Learjet 24E	24E-345	J & S Aviation Leasing LLC. Nashville, Tn.	(N99UP)
❏ N217MJ	02	Learjet 45	45-217	Meita LLC/Dairy Nutrition Service Inc. Chandler, Az.	(N977AR)
❏ N217RM	82	Challenger 600S	1054	Romeo Mike Aviation Inc. Fort Lauderdale, Fl.	N660RM
❏ N217RR	88	Gulfstream 4	1042	Rutter Aviation LLC. Irvine, Ca.	N68SL
❏ N217SA	81	Citation II	550-0217	MT Fluggesellschaft LLC. San Diego, Ca.	(D-IMME)
❏ N217TA	80	Learjet 35A	35A-289	Fox Aviation/Johnson Racing, Santa Monica, Ca.	N36TJ
❏ N217WC	95	Citation V Ultra	560-0317	NOM Aviation/Newton Oldacre McDonald LLC. Nashville, Tn.	N317QS
❏ N217WM	77	Learjet 25D	25D-217	M & V Airplane LLC. San Antonio, Tx.	N41H
❏ N218CA	69	Falcon 20DC	218	Delaware DI Properties LLC. Addison, Tx.	EC-EEU
❏ N218EC	00	Gulfstream V	656	Calpoint Funding LLC. Van Nuys, Ca.	(N218CP)
❏ N218G*	99	Citation Bravo	550-0888	Peddler LLC. Cedar Rapids, Ia.	N162TJ
❏ N218JG	81	Citation 1/SP	501-0218	N218JG Inc. Dover, De.	N218AM
❏ N218NB	98	Learjet 31A	31A-146	Well's Dairy Inc. Le Mars, Ia.	ZS-AGT
❏ N218PH	04	Falcon 2000	218	Pulte Homes Inc. Pontiac, Mi.	F-WWVF
❏ N218QS	00	Falcon 2000	118	NetJets, Port Columbus, Oh.	F-WWVN
❏ N218SE	72	Gulfstream 2	116	Pebble Air LLC. Van Nuys, Ca.	N716TE
❏ N218WW	06	Gulfstream G450	4058	1226 Enterprises LLC/Wassreman Media Group, Burbank, Ca.	N458GA

Reg	Yr	Type	c/n	Owner/Operator	Prev Regn
❏ N219AX	00	Galaxy-1126	019	BCOM Air LLC/Aspen Exceutive Air LLC. Aspen, Co.	N219GA
❏ N219CA	69	Falcon 20D	193	Delaware DI Properties LLC. Addison, Tx.	9Q-CTT
❏ N219CJ	97	CitationJet	525-0219	Dr F David Prentice, Houston, Tx.	N5197A
❏ N219L	06	CitationJet CJ-3	525B-0091	TC91 LLC. Chandler, Az.	N5214J
❏ N219LC	02	Citation Bravo	550-1020	Shilo Franchise International, Portland, Or.	N212BH
❏ N219MS	80	Citation II	550-0180	MDM Aviation LLC/Spoleta Construction Corp. Rochester, NY.	N3030T
❏ N219RB	78	Learjet 25D	25D-255	Pauli-Mar Investment Co. Centerline, Mi.	N717EP
❏ N220AB	01	Falcon 2000	170	Pacific Connection Inc. Phoenix, Az.	F-W...
❏ N220AU	71	DC 10-10ER	46501	Project Orbis International Inc. NYC.	G-GCAL
❏ N220BP*	85	Citation S/II	S550-0034	Toy Air Inc/Page Toyota Inc. Southfield, Mi.	N610GD
❏ N220CA	69	Falcon 20DC	220	Addison Aviation Services Inc. Addison, Tx.	EC-EDL
❏ N220CM	88	Citation III	650-0160	Charter Manufacturing Co. Milwaukee, Wi.	N650PT
❏ N220DF	98	Falcon 2000	69	Domino's Pizza LLC. Ann Arbor, Mi.	(N346SR)
❏ N220DH	86	Westwind-Two	440	Hughes Westwind Ltd. Beeville, Tx.	N127SA
❏ N220GS	79	Learjet 35A	35A-220	Two Twenty LLC. Teterboro, NJ.	N373LP
❏ N220HM	81	Citation 1/SP	501-0182	Blue Sky Aviation Group Inc. Lauderdale Lake, Fl.	VP-CAP
❏ N220JD	02	CitationJet CJ-2	525A-0120	Spirit Aviation Inc. Berwyn, Pa.	N144EM
❏ N220JR	69	Gulfstream 2	50	Air Tiger LLC/Key Air Inc. Oxford, Ct.	N220FL
❏ N220KS	77	Falcon 10	71	TMDF LLC/Belmont Plating Works, DuPage, Il.	N341DB
❏ N220LA	73	Falcon 20F-5	296	Lieblong Transport Delaware Inc. Little Rock, Ar.	N20TX
❏ N220LE	93	Citation II	550-0722	Raythom Aviation LLC. Addison, Tx.	N1886G
❏ N220NJ	75	Learjet 35A	35A-021	Amazon Aviation Corp. Fort Lauderdale, Fl.	N53FN
❏ N220PA	78	Falcon 10	113	Premier Air Center Inc. Alton/St Louis, Il.	VP-BGD
❏ N220SC	95	Citation V Ultra	560-0326	CBL & Assocs Inc/Tri-Par LLC. Dallas, Tx.	N200SC
❏ N220WE	76	Falcon 20F	349	Air One Inc. Nashville, Tn.	N287SA
❏ N221BR	67	Falcon 20-5	74	Carrington Capital Management LLC. Ithaca, NY.	N8TP
❏ N221CM	81	Gulfstream 3	343	Trans-Exec Air Service Inc. Van Nuys, Ca.	N400AL
❏ N221DA	74	Citation	500-0201	Dove Air Inc. Fletcher, NC.	C-GLAA
❏ N221DG	03	Gulfstream G550	5020	David Geffen Co. Long Beach, Ca.	N920GA
❏ N221H	81	Falcon 20F	461	Knoxville Aviation LLC. Knoxville, Tn.	OH-WIF
❏ N221LC	90	Challenger 601-3A	5066	Bailey Perrin Bailey LP. Houston, Tx.	N566TS
❏ N221PA	87	Astra-1125	016	Rancharrah Cutting Horses, Reno, Nv.	N221DT
❏ N221PB	03	Hawker 800XP	258623	Fortune Brands Inc. Lincolnshire, Il.	(N823CW)
❏ N221QS	04	Falcon 2000EX EASY	54	NetJets, Port Columbus, Oh.	F-WWMC
❏ N221SG	78	Learjet 35A	35A-182	Path Corp. Rehoboth Beach, De.	N3HA
❏ N221TR	79	Learjet 35A	35A-221	Pak West Airlines Inc. Oakdale, Ca.	VH-FSY
❏ N221TW	69	Falcon 20DC	221	Kitty Hawk Air Cargo Inc. Dallas, Tx.	EC-EIV
❏ N221VP	01	Citation Encore	560-0585	Citation Technology Partners LLC. Hayward, Ca.	N5254Y
❏ N221WR	83	Gulfstream 3	381	Westgate Aviation LLC. Orlando, Fl.	N621S
❏ N222B	69	Learjet 25	25-047	Michigan Air Freight LLC. Ypsilanti, Mi.	(N68CK)
❏ N222BE	82	Learjet 35A	35A-489	Mayo Aviation Inc. Englewood, Co.	
❏ N222BG	81	Learjet 35A	35A-448	Goody's Family Clothing Inc. McGhee-Tyson, Tn.	N48MJ
❏ N222BR	06	Learjet 60	60-310	Black Rock Development Inc. Coeur df'Alene, Id.	
❏ N222GY	90	Gulfstream 4	1142	Gypsy Two LLC. Seattle, Wa.	N222
❏ N222LH	82	Challenger 600S	1052	Lewis Hyman Inc. Van Nuys, Ca.	N152TS
❏ N222LX	01	Gulfstream V	633	Lexair Ltd/Trans-Exec Air Service Inc. Van Nuys, Ca.	N633GA
❏ N222MC	96	Challenger 604	5329	McCaw Communications Inc. Seattle, Wa.	(N222MZ)
❏ N222MS	88	BAe 125/800A	NA0422	Stavola Aviation Inc. Anthony, Fl.	N125TR
❏ N222MU	80	Falcon 10	164	Braggs & Herrington Inc. Little Rock, Ar.	N228FJ
❏ N222MW	00	Learjet 45	45-110	McWane Inc. Birmingham, Al.	N4002P
❏ N222NB	06	Gulfstream G450	4059	Triple Two Aviation Inc/Avjet Corp. Burbank, Ca.	N459GA
❏ N222NF	02	CitationJet CJ-2	525A-0074	Merak Aviation Inc. Opa Locka, Fl.	N5125J
❏ N222NG	65	HS 125/1A	25016	World Jet of Delaware Inc. Fort Lauderdale, Fl.	N4997E
❏ N222NP	79	Gulfstream 2B	245	222 Aviation LLC. Burbank, Ca.	N222NB
❏ N222QS	00	Falcon 2000	122	NetJets, Port Columbus, Oh.	F-WWVR
❏ N222TW	68	Learjet 24	24-161	Sierra American Corp. Addison, Tx.	N24KF
❏ N222VV	80	Citation II/SP	551-0180	BayAir GmbH. Germany. (was 550-0136).	(N729MJ)
❏ N222WA	77	Citation 1/SP	501-0007	Unitco Air/Ralph Kiewit Jr. Van Nuys, Ca.	N5360J
❏ N223BG	71	Falcon 20F	250	Jet Makers LLC. Denison, Tx.	XA-HEW
❏ N223F	01	390 Premier 1	RB-22	Center for Disease Detection LLC. San Antonio, Tx.	N45ND
❏ N223GA	01	Gulfstream G100	141	GAC LP. Dallas-Love, Tx.	CC-CWK
❏ N223HD	99	Falcon 50EX	283	The Home Depot Inc. Atlanta-Fulton County, Ga.	N283FJ
❏ N223JV	91	Citation V	560-0131	Daedalus Inc. Sioux Falls, SD.	PT-ORE
❏ N223LB	80	Sabre-65	465-23	Cody Ribera LLC. Laredo, Tx.	(N904KB)
❏ N223LC	78	Citation 1/SP	501-0055	Corus Hardware Corp. Catano, PR.	N145AJ
❏ N223MD	01	Gulfstream V	665	Open Road Airways Inc. Palwaukee, Il.	N845HS

Reg	Yr	Type	c/n	Owner/Operator	Prev Regn
☐ N223QS	06	Falcon 2000EX EASY	86	NetJets/Marquis Jet Partners Inc. Port Columbus, Oh.	F-WWGW
☐ N223TW	67	Falcon 20C	123	Sierra American Corp. Addison, Tx.	N45MR
☐ N224CJ	97	CitationJet	525-0224	Janabeck Aviation Inc. Cheltenham-Gloucester, UK.	
☐ N224CX	80	HS 125/700B	257088	Salem Communications/Atsinger Aviation LLC. Van Nuys, Ca.	N222HL
☐ N224F	94	Challenger 601-3R	5163	Freeman Air Charter Inc. Stowe, Vt.	N980HC
☐ N224GP	79	Citation 1/SP	501-0112	Ponder Investments LLC. Marshall, Tx.	N112EB
☐ N224GX	06	Global 5000	9224	J T Aviation Corp/Midtwon Equities, NYC.	C-FJNQ
☐ N224HD	04	Falcon 50EX	336	The Home Depot Inc. Atlanta-Fulton County, Ga.	F-WWHR
☐ N224KC	86	Citation S/II	S550-0104	Capital City Aviation Inc. Madison, Wi.	N12903
☐ N224MC	97	Beechjet 400A	RK-165	Midmark Corp. Versailles, Oh.	N2225Y
☐ N224N	06	Challenger 604	5661	NLC Inc/Nordstrom Inc. Seattle, Wa.	N224NS
☐ N224PA	84	Westwind-1124	411	Gulf States Health Services Inc. Baton Rouge, La.	HC-BVX
☐ N224QS	00	Falcon 2000	124	NetJets, Port Columbus, Oh.	F-WWVU
☐ N224WD	02	CitationJet CJ-2	525A-0122	Fall Line Equipment Co. Macon, Ga.	N5135A
☐ N224WE	72	Falcon 20F	272	Air 1 Inc/Western Express, Nashville, tn.	N770RR
☐ N225BJ	78	HS 125/700A	NA0231	World of Faith Christian Center Church, Southfield, Mi.	N125G
☐ N225CC	89	Falcon 100	225	Brunswick Aviation LLC. Brunswick, NJ.	(N814PJ)
☐ N225CF	79	Learjet 35A	35A-225	CF Air LLC/Aviation Jets LLC. Opa Locka, Fl.	(N225DG)
☐ N225CX	01	Gulfstream 4SP	1467	CXAir Holdings Inc. Princeton, NJ.	(N225BK)
☐ N225DC	94	Gulfstream 4SP	1253	Avion LLC/Drummond Coal Inc. Birmingham, Al.	N676RW
☐ N225EE	98	Gulfstream V	563	DI Management Co Ltd. Bermuda.	(N180CH)
☐ N225HD	01	Falcon 50EX	313	Homerlease Co. Atlanta-Fulton County, Ga.	N921EC
☐ N225KA	68	Learjet 25	25-004	SAP LLP. Las Cruces, NM.	N251AF
☐ N225LC	73	Learjet 25B	25B-127	Jetco Inc. Wilmington, De.	N425JL
☐ N225MD	83	Learjet 55	55-085	Orgar Aviation Holdings Inc. Wilmington, De.	(N146PA)
☐ N225MS	67	Gulfstream II SP	8	Dove Air Inc. Fletcher, NC.	N267PS
☐ N225N	06	Challenger 604	5652	JBW Reverse LLC/Reverse Exchange Corp. Seattle, Wa.	N604CM
☐ N225PB	01	Hawker 800XP	258558	Fortune Brands Inc. Lincolnshire, Il.	N51058
☐ N225RB	06	Hawker 850XP	258791	Regal Beloit Flight Services Inc. Janesville, Wi.	N70791
☐ N225RD	74	Citation	500-0194	Southeastern Aviation Group LLC. Clinton, Tn.	N501DG
☐ N225SB	06	Hawker 400XP	RK-510	KTA Corp/Sullivan Corp. Noblesville, In.	N510XP
☐ N225WT	97	Citation Bravo	550-0821	DBM Aviation Inc. Las Vegas, Nv.	N77797
☐ N226B	97	CitationJet	525-0200	Cardinal Aviation Co/Greer Industries Inc. Morgantown, WV.	N1276J
☐ N226CK*	70	Falcon 20DC	226	Kalitta Charters LLC. Detroit-Willow Run, Mi.	N226R
☐ N226CV	93	Citation V	560-0226	Penmor Aviation LLC. Boston, Ma.	N893CM
☐ N226EC	91	Challenger 601-3A	5090	Eagle Capital Management LLC. Chicago-Midway, Il.	N621CF
☐ N226HY	07	Embraer Legacy 600	14501014	Blue Skies EL 600/Executive Fliteways Inc. Ronkonkoma, NY.	PT-SVH
☐ N226JT	06	Citation Excel XLS	560-5652	Nucor Corp. Charlotte, NC.	N.....
☐ N226MP	96	Gulfstream 4SP	1300	MPM Financial LLC. Burbank, Ca.	(N500BL)
☐ N226QS	00	Falcon 2000	126	NetJets, Port Columbus, Oh.	F-WWVW
☐ N226RM	74	Gulfstream II SP	145	Starflite/Momentum BMW Ltd. Houston, Tx.	N339H
☐ N226RS	01	Gulfstream 4SP	1479	Harbor Island Management LLC. Santa Ana, Ca.	N1479G
☐ N226SF	96	Learjet 60	60-092	NuStar Logistics LP.	N907SK
☐ N227CK	70	Falcon 20DC	227	Kalitta Charters LLC. Detroit-Willow Run, Mi.	N227R
☐ N227CP	91	Challenger 601-3A	5097	Alesworth Inc. Panama City, Panama.	N120PA
☐ N227DH	06	Citation Sovereign	680-0086	Lakeside Air LLC. Erie, Pa.	N5090Y
☐ N227FH	03	390 Premier 1	RB-102	Deb Shops Inc/Flying Horse Garage LLC. Philadelphia, Pa.	N3901A
☐ N227FS*	05	CitationJet CJ-2	525A-0238	Assemblies of God Financial Services, Springfield, Mo.	N228FS
☐ N227HD	05	Falcon 900EX EASY	157	The Home Depot Inc. Atlanta-Fulton County, Ga.	F-WWFP
☐ N227KT	00	Learjet 31A	31A-208	1132 Investment Corp/U S Aviation Co. Tulsa, Ok.	N518JC
☐ N227LA	76	Gulfstream II SP	193	Resort Transportation GS LLC. Greenville, SC.	N54JJ
☐ N227LT	70	HS 125/731	NA754	World Jet Inc. Fort Lauderdale, Fl.	N711HL
☐ N227MC	99	Citation Excel	560-5064	Matsco Inc/FlightWorks, Kennesaw, Ga.	N386SF
☐ N227MK	73	Citation	500-0070	R & L Display Inc. Jupiter, Fl.	VP-CMO
☐ N227MM	79	HS 125/700A	NA0258	Betman Inc. Marlow Heights, MD.	N193RC
☐ N227PE	83	Challenger 601	3002	Petters Aviation LLC. Minnetonka, Mn.	N602CW
☐ N227QS	00	Falcon 2000	127	NetJets, Port Columbus, Oh.	F-WWVY
☐ N227RH	95	Challenger 601-3R	5177	Winnepeg LLC/Reyes Holding LLC. Waukegan, Il.	N601UC
☐ N227SV	91	Gulfstream 4	1172	Heritage Creations/Assembly Pointe Aviation Inc. Schenectady	N85VM
☐ N227TS	68	Gulfstream II SP	27	Highlands Group LLC. Monterey, Ca.	(N227TJ)
☐ N227WE	07	Embraer Legacy 600	14501018	7700 Properties LLC. Tulsa, Ok.	PT-SVV
☐ N227WL	77	Falcon 20F-5	344	7700 Properties LLC. Tulsa, Ok.	N227WE
☐ N228DB	04	Citation X	750-0228	Dudmaston Ltd. Milan, Italy.	N228BD
☐ N228FJ	92	Falcon 50	228	Samaritan's Purse Inc/Emmanuel Group. N Wilkesboro, NC.	C-GAZU
☐ N228H	99	Global Express	9040	CB Air LLC. Bellevue, WA.	N22BH
☐ N228KT*	06	Challenger 300	20142	Knight Oil Tools, Lafayette, La.	N605UK

Reg	Yr	Type	c/n	Owner/Operator	Prev Regn
N228MD	74	HS 125/600B	256037	Novanet Media, Torrance, Ca.	N63810
N228MH	80	Citation II/SP	551-0050	Jet II Aviation LLC. Wilmington, De. (was 550-0385).	N228AK
N228N	05	Challenger 300	20060	Nordstrom/NLC Inc. Seattle, Wa.	C-FGUT
N228PC	95	Citation V Ultra	560-0310	GTCR Golden Rauner LLC/Fremont Flights LLC. Midway, Il.	N868JT
N228PK	85	Challenger 601	3046	Arrowhead General Insurance Agency, San Diego, Ca.	N46SR
N228RE	00	Gulfstream 4SP	1438	Cape Clear LLC. Westborough, Ma.	N388GA
N228RH	06	Citation Sovereign	680-0128	Winnepeg LLC/Reyes Holding LLC. Waukegan, Il.	N5062S
N228TM	00	Hawker 800XP	258458	EMC Corp. Cork, Ireland.	N42685
N228Y	03	Citation Excel	560-5342	Anderson Equipment Co. Bridgeville, Pa.	N777JV
N229BP	06	Learjet 60XR	60-320	Clearwater Fine Foods Inc. Bedford, NS. Canada.	N60LJ
N229CE	04	Citation X	750-0229	Naples Citation LLC. Naples, Fl.	N5268A
N229CK	70	Falcon 20DC	229	Kalitta Charters LLC. Detroit-Willow Run, Mi.	N229R
N229D	85	Westwind-Two	427	Diamond Management/24E-340 Inc. Tucson, Az.	N229N
N229DE	67	DC 9-15F	45826	U S Department of Energy, Albuquerque, NM.	N29AF
N229KD	97	Learjet 31A	31A-139	Kevin Harvick Inc. Kernersville, NC.	N131AR
N229LJ	01	Learjet 31A	31A-229	W T B Financial Corp. Spokane, Wa.	(N11TK)
N229MC	81	Citation II	550-0229	NMC 550 LLC. Wilmington, De.	C-FGAT
N229QS	01	Falcon 2000	129	NetJets, Port Columbus, Oh.	F-WWVD
N229RB	07	390 Premier 1A	RB-229	Hawker Beechcraft Corp. Wichita, Ks.	
N230BT	81	Falcon 50	62	R A Bridgeford Inc. Napa County, Ca.	(CS-DFK)
N230JS	05	Citation Bravo	550-1119	J S Aviation LLC. Latrobe, Pa.	N630JS
N230LC	07	Citation Sovereign	680-0141	Southwestern Energy Co. Springdale, Ar.	N.....
N230LL	96	CitationJet	525-0169	The Lemak Group of Companies LLC. Birmingham, Al.	N68CJ
N230QS	05	Falcon 2000EX EASY	59	NetJets, Port Columbus, Oh.	F-WWMH
N230RA	70	Falcon 20DC	230	Kalitta Charters LLC. Detroit-Willow Run, Mi.	N26EV
N231JH	81	Falcon 10	176	Knoxville Aviation LLC. Knoxville, Tn.	N66HH
N231WJ	81	Gulfstream 3	331	World Jet Inc. Fort Lauderdale, Fl.	HZ-RC3
N232CE	84	Citation III	650-0067	Hinson Corporate Flight Services Inc. Baltimore, Md.	N232CF
N232CF	01	Citation X	750-0161	Hinson Corporate Flight Services Inc. Baltimore, Md.	N280DM
N232CL	87	Falcon 900A	9	Werner Enterprises Inc. Omaha, Ne.	N193TR
N232CW	78	Citation II	550-0032	High Sierra Inc. Wilmington, De.	N112JS
N232DM	79	Citation II	550-0079	Bruce Foods Corp. New Iberia, La.	N33RH
N232JR	98	Citation Bravo	550-0855	Texia Energy Management Inc. Houston, Tx.	N132LF
N232K	94	Gulfstream 4SP	1232	N232K LLC. San Rafael, Ca.	N471GA
N232PR	87	Falcon 50	179	CES Aviation IX LLC. Ronkonkoma, NY.	N212Q
N232QS	06	Falcon 2000EX EASY	115	NetJets, Port Columbus, Oh.	F-WWML
N232TN	78	HS 125/700A	NA0232	Blue Star Airlines SA de CV. (status ?).	(N331CG)
N232TW	66	Falcon 20C	32	Sierra American Corp. Addison, Tx.	F-GIVT
N233CA	73	Learjet 25B	25B-133	Addison Aviation Services Inc. Addison, Tx.	XA-RZY
N233CC	75	Learjet 35	35-031	CCI Corp. Tulsa, Ok.	N160AT
N233DB	74	Citation	500-0158	Southeastern Automotive Inc. Nashville, Tn.	OY-TAM
N233FJ	06	Global 5000	9233	Turnberry Associates, Opa Locka, Fl.	N233FJ
N233GA	90	Gulfstream 4	1144	Gulfstream Aerospace Corp. Savannah, Ga.	B-3999
N233JJ	74	Citation	500-0233	Blount Brothers Construction Inc. Shreveport, La.	N228S
N233KC	88	Falcon 900B	48	K Club Investments LLC/ACM Aviation Inc. San Jose, Ca.	N900MU
N233MM	06	CitationJet CJ-3	525B-0133	Convergent Wealth Advisors, Rockville, Md.	N5031E
N233MW	99	Beechjet 400A	RK-233	Industrial Realty Group LLC. Downey, Ca.	N2293V
N233QS	06	Falcon 2000EX EASY	91	NetJets, Port Columbus, Oh.	N91EX
N233TW	70	Learjet 24B	24B-221	Sierra American Corp. Addison, Tx.	N59JG
N233WC	08	390 Premier 1A	RB-233	Hawker Beechcraft Corp. Wichita, Ks.	
N233XL	01	Citation Excel	560-5233	Childish Creations International Inc. Norcross, Ga.	N.....
N234AQ	93	Citation V	560-0234	Midwest Air LLC/Fastener Equipment Corp. Homewood, Il.	
N234AT	74	Citation	500-0240	Mountain State University Inc. Beckley, WV.	N240CC
N234CA	65	Falcon 20C	17	Cherry Air Inc. Addison, Tx.	N55TH
N234DB	05	Gulfstream G550	5106	Skybird Aviation Inc. Santa Ana, Ca.	N986GA
N234DC	75	Sabre-60	306-103	Jet Works Inc. Fort Myers, Fl.	N40TL
N234DK	98	Beechjet 400A	RK-182	Nantucket Express LLC. Oakbrook Terrace, Il.	N2322B
N234FJ	96	Falcon 2000	34	U S Bancorp Equipment Finance Inc. St Paul, Mn.	HB-IAY
N234G	65	Jet Commander	28	Aviation Business Corp. St Louis, Mo.	N77NR
N234GF	87	Hawker 800SP	258096	Law Flight LLC. Waterford, Mi.	N311JX
N234GX	07	Global Express	9234	CPR Aviation Finance SA. Zug, Switzerland.	C-FLKZ
N235CA	68	Falcon 20C	139	Cherry Air Inc. Addison, Tx.	N900WB
N235CG	05	Gulfstream G450	4030	Easy Flight LLC. Opa Locka, Fl.	N630GA
N235DX	05	Gulfstream G550	5085	EWS LLC. Pittsburgh, Pa.	N585GA
N235EA	76	Learjet 35	35-061	Dickerson Associates Inc. West Columbia, SC.	N238RC
N235HR	84	Learjet 55	55-094	Newport Federal Corp. Newport Beach, Fl.	(N236HR)

Reg	Yr	Type	c/n	Owner/Operator	Prev Regn
☐ N235JS	78	Learjet 35A	35A-199	Management Co of South Carolina, Columbia, SC.	N444HC
☐ N235KK	00	Gulfstream 4SP	1458	Capital Airwings Two SA. Geneva, Switzerland.	N358GA
☐ N235KS	05	CitationJet CJ-2	525A-0235	Steel Holdings Inc/SPS Holdings LLC. Manhattan, Ks.	N.....
☐ N235LC	06	Gulfstream G200	142	HCE Leasing LLC. Chattanooga, Tn.	N842GA
☐ N235LP	97	Gulfstream 4SP	1336	Crest Aviation LLC. Van Nuys, Ca.	N41CP
☐ N235MC	80	Learjet 35A	35A-334	Kroger Co. Hutchinson, Ks.	(N334AB)
☐ N235SV	93	Citation VI	650-0235	First Cash Financial Services, Arlington, Tx.	N235CM
☐ N236CA	74	Learjet 25B	25B-161	Cherry Air Inc. Addison, Tx.	N61EW
☐ N236LB	98	Citation Excel	560-5023	Jacob Stern & Sons Inc. Santa Barbara, Ca.	N236LD
☐ N236LC	06	Gulfstream G200	154	Life Care Centers of America Inc. Chattanooga, Tn.	4X-CVG
☐ N236MJ*	92	Gulfstream 4	1177	MJ Air LLC. Dulles, Va.	N677RW
☐ N236N	92	Challenger 601-3A	5108	Winchester Air Inc/John Moriarty & Assocs. Winchester, Ma.	N224N
☐ N236QS	00	Falcon 2000	136	NetJets, Port Columbus, Oh.	F-WWVL
☐ N236TW	70	Falcon 20F	236	Sierra American Corp. Addison, Tx.	N936NW
☐ N237AF	79	Learjet 35A	35A-262	Ameriflight Inc. Burbank, Ca.	N237GA
☐ N237BG	07	Citation Encore+	560-0771	Bull Aviation Inc. Guatemala City, Guatemala.	N.....
☐ N237DM	99	Learjet 45	45-058	Griffin AG Inc. Tunica, Ms.	N660HC
☐ N237DX	81	HS 125/700A	NA0304	Dick's Sporting Goods Inc. Allegheny County, Pa.	N700NH
☐ N237GA	06	Gulfstream G450	4055	Arnel/Sunbird Aviation LLC-Orange County, Costa Mesa, Ca.	N455GA
☐ N237TW	71	Learjet 24D	24D-237	Sierra American Corp. Addison, Tx.	N825DM
☐ N237VP	93	Citation V	560-0237	SESI LLC/Superior Energy Services Inc. Harvey, La.	N893M
☐ N237WC	80	Citation II	550-0129	Collins Investment Corp. Eden, Mn.	(N550RD)
☐ N237WR	79	HS 125/700A	NA0252	Waddell & Reed Development Inc. Kansas City, Mo.	N895CC
☐ N238BG	82	Citation 1/SP	501-0240	Genesis 2001 Foundation, Princeton, Tx.	N501DY
☐ N238CA	69	Learjet 25	25-040	Source Investments LLC. Addison, Tx.	N23FN
☐ N238DB	77	Westwind-1124	215	LMDD Inc. Wilmington, De.	N946GM
☐ N238JA	77	Learjet 35A	35A-134	White Industries Inc. Bates City, Mo. (status ?).	N235DH
☐ N238PR	81	Learjet 35A	35A-394	Carpenter & Co. Cambridge, Ma.	N232PR
☐ N238SM	02	Citation Excel	560-5238	Continental Limited Inc. Detroit-Willow Run, Mi.	N5061P
☐ N238SW	06	CitationJet CJ-3	525B-0141	S & W Ready Mix Concrete Co. Clinton, NC.	N50756
☐ N239AX	87	Falcon 900B	39	Bank of Utah, Salt Lake City, Ut. (UK trustor ?).	N573J
☐ N239CA	74	Learjet 25B	25B-149	Cherry Air inc. Addison, Tx.	N149J
☐ N239CD	75	Falcon 20F-5B	339	FM Aircraft LLC. Aurora, Co.	N38TJ
☐ N239RT	05	390 Premier 1A	RB-139	Theken Aviation LLC. Akron-Canton, Oh.	N3039G
☐ N239WJ	79	Gulfstream 2TT	239	World Jet Inc. Fort Lauderdale, Fl.	HZ-AFK
☐ N240AK	92	Challenger 600S	1067	Amberwings Aviation Inc. Wilmington, De.	N205EL
☐ N240CJ	07	CitationJet CJ-3	525B-0240	Cessna Aircraft Co. Wichita, Ks.	N.....
☐ N240CK	66	Falcon 20C-5	24	Kalitta Charters LLC. Detroit-Willow Run, Mi.	(N240FJ)
☐ N240CM	90	Citation V	560-0048	JAS Investment Corp. Northbrook, Il.	N220CM
☐ N240CX	99	Gulfstream 4SP	1370	Skyaire Inc. Arlington, Tx.	N370GA
☐ N240JR	74	Sabre-40A	282-132	Robinson Air Crane Inc. Opa Locka, Fl.	N240CF
☐ N240RP	98	Learjet 40	45-2025	Global Aviation LLC. Lexington, Ky.	N225LJ
☐ N240TW	66	Falcon 20C	40	Sierra American Corp. Addison, Tx.	C-GSKQ
☐ N240V	99	Hawker 800XP	258417	Bluejet Ltd. Guernsey, C.I.	N246V
☐ N240Z	01	Hawker 800XP	258565	Nissan North America Inc. Smyrna, Tn.	N4465M
☐ N241BF	81	Citation 1/SP	501-0214	Barbladon Aircraft Leasing LLC. St Augustine, Fl.	N241MH
☐ N241BJ	88	Beechjet 400	RJ-41	River Capital, Atlanta, Ga.	(N270BJ)
☐ N241CJ*	07	CitationJet CJ-3	525B-0241	Cessna Aircraft Co. Wichita, Ks.	N241KA
☐ N241CT	81	Westwind-Two	355	Victory Outreach La Puente, San Diego, Ca.	N355JK
☐ N241DS	85	Citation S/II	S550-0042	Westair Leasing Corp. San Diego, Ca.	N250AF
☐ N241EP	98	CitationJet	525-0247	Diversified Interiors of El Paso Inc. Santa Teresa, NM.	(N208LX)
☐ N241FB	81	HS 125/700A	NA0292	Shelby Trading Co. Gardena, Ca.	N48FB
☐ N241FR	92	Challenger 601-3A	5102	LAFI Real Estate, Dubai, UAE.	N241FB
☐ N241FT	81	Citation II	550-0241	Poultney Ventures LLC. Incline Village, Nv.	XA-TQL
☐ N241JS	03	Hawker 800XP	258652	SkyLand Leasing Corp. Seffner, Fl.	N652XP
☐ N241KP*	96	Citation V Ultra	560-0383	SB Jets LLC. Santa Barbara, Ca.	N579BJ
☐ N241L	03	Learjet 45	45-241	KCC Contractor Inc/Killian Construction, Springfield, Mo.	
☐ N241N	91	Challenger 601-3A	5100	AK Resources LLC. Las Vegas, Nv.	N225N
☐ N241RT	79	HS 125/700A	NA0242	Patron Aviation Corp. Atlanta, Ga.	N418BA
☐ N241TR	88	Beechjet 400	RJ-45	Charles Bostater, Fayetteville, NC.	N218RG
☐ N242AC	02	Citation Encore	560-0609	AAA Cooper Transportation Inc. Dothan, Al.	N847HS
☐ N242DR	79	Learjet 35A	35A-242	Career Aviation Academy Inc. Oakdale, Ca.	VH-FSZ
☐ N242GB	96	CitationJet	525-0151	NPC International Inc. Pittsburg, Ks.	N28DM
☐ N242GS	78	Learjet 25D	25D-242	Outrageous Bluewater LP. McKinney, Tx.	(N242AF)
☐ N242LJ	98	CitationJet	525-0242	DBS Corp. Chattanooga, Tn.	(N27FB)
☐ N242ML	02	CitationJet CJ-1	525-0506	Brankstone Aviation Inc. Bournemouth-Hurn, UK.	N.....

Reg	Yr	Type	c/n	Owner/Operator	Prev Regn
N242PF	79	Learjet 25D	25D-298	Four Fox Air Inc. Dover, De.	N298DR
N242RB	87	Learjet 55B	55B-132	Pintail Aviation LLC/Rey Distributing Co. St Peters, Mo.	N122SU
N242SW	99	Citation Bravo	550-0908	Strongwell Corp. Bristol, Va.	N5264M
N243F	99	Learjet 60	60-175	Deseret Aviation LLC. Salt Lake City, Ut.	N243FX
N243FJ	80	Falcon 20F-5	430	RAL Capital Corp. NYC.	N660P
N243SH	75	Citation	500-0243	Interstate Leasing & Sales, Wheatridge, Co.	N53AJ
N244A	79	Falcon 10	145	Snap-Tite Inc. Erie. Pa.	N209FJ
N244AL	80	Challenger 600S	1005	ACP Aviation LLC/American Capital Partners, Opa Locka, Fl.	N180CH
N244CJ	99	CitationJet CJ-2	708	Cessna Aircraft Co. 525A CJ-2 prototype Ff 27 Apr 99.	N2CJ
N244DS	05	Gulfstream G450	4050	DS Aviation LLC/Melvin Simon & Assocs. Indianapolis, In.	N850GA
N244J*	00	Gulfstream 4SP	1451	J C Penney Co. Dallas, Tx.	N522BR
N244LJ	79	Learjet 35A	35A-244	Alton Corp. Nassau, Bahamas.	(N116KV)
N244RG	77	Learjet 35A	35A-154	Excelsior Air Express LLC. Wakefield, NH.	N117RB
N245BD	07	Gulfstream G550	5165	Gulfstream Aerospace Corp. Savannah, Ga.	N965GA
N245CC	81	Citation II	550-0212	SMP Aviation Inc. Bohemia, NY.	(N6801V)
N245J	02	Citation Excel	560-5245	Palisades Aircraft Inc. Austin, Tx.	N50820
N245K	05	Learjet 45	45-269	Koch Industries Inc. Wichita, Ks.	N4003W
N245MS	83	Learjet 55	55-077	N755JS Inc. Orlando, Fl.	(N99YB)
N245QS	01	Falcon 2000	145	NetJets, Port Columbus, Oh.	F-WWVZ
N245RA	07	CitationJet CJ2+	525A-0374	RAB Aviation Holdings Inc. Orlando, Fl.	N5108G
N245RS	74	HS 125/F600B	256027	World Jet Inc. Fort Lauderdale, Fl.	N800NM
N245SP	00	CitationJet CJ-2	525A-0006	Sierra Papa Inc. Bakersfield, Ca.	N800WC
N245TT	02	Gulfstream G550	5003	WOTAN America Inc. Fort Lauderdale, Fl.	N703GA
N246AG	03	Falcon 900EX EASY	135	Cableair LLC. Monticello, NY.	F-WWFM
N246DF	06	390 Premier 1A	RB-182	Fugate Aviation Inc. Wichita, Ks.	N7082V
N246FX	99	Learjet 60	60-183	BBJS/FlexJets, Addison, Tx.	
N246GS	01	CitationJet CJ-1	525-0446	Golden State Lumber/Advantage Flight Service Inc. Wilmington	N5211A
N246JL	82	Challenger 600S	1046	Fugate Aviation Inc. Wichita, Ks.	N46SR
N246V	01	Falcon 2000	152	New NGC Inc/National Gypsum Co. Charlotte, NC.	N317MQ
N247AB	77	Gulfstream II SP	208	Cutter Aviation Inc. Phoenix, Az.	N247AD
N247CJ	92	Falcon 900B	122	The Tashi Corp. Oakland, Ca.	N612BH
N247CK	82	Challenger 600S	1045	Merkur Invest Ltd. Roadtown, BVI.	C-GBKB
N247CN	92	Citation V	560-0173	Aerocentro de Servicios CA. Caracas, Venezuela.	N918BD
N247EM	88	Gulfstream 4	1045	Mariner Management LLC. Ronkonkoma, NY.	N227GH
N247FX	99	Learjet 60	60-187	Bombardier Aerospace Corp. Windsor Locks, Ct.	
N247KB	99	Gulfstream 4SP	1375	Pacific American Corp. NYC.	N375GA
N247MV	06	CitationJet CJ-3	525B-0105	Grocery Supply Co. Sulphur Springs, Tx.	N.....
N247PL	70	Falcon 20F	247	HRS Solutions, Davisburg, Mi.	N70PL
N247PS	93	Astra-1125SP	069	Gulfstream Aerospace Corp. Savannah, Ga.	N804JW
N247RG	79	Gulfstream 3	252	247RG LLC. Addison, Tx.	XA-MEY
N247VA	96	Vantage	001	VisionAire, Chesterfield, Mo. (Ff 16 Nov 96).	
N247WE	98	Challenger 604	5369	World Wrestling Federation Entertainment Inc. White Plains.	N247WF
N248CJ	98	CitationJet	525-0248	Oil Well Perforators Inc. Glendive, Mt.	
N248CK	78	Learjet 25D	25D-248	Kalitta Charters LLC. Detroit-Willow Run, Mi.	(N248LJ)
N248FX	99	Learjet 60	60-188	BBJS/FlexJets, Addison, Tx.	
N248HA	82	Citation II	550-0423	Health Systems Management Inc. Tifton, Ga.	C-FCCC
N248SL	06	Gulfstream G150	211	Stim-Air LLC/Stimson Lumber Co. Hillsboro, Or.	N757GA
N249AJ	82	Challenger 600S	1047	Mountain Eagle Aviation LLC. NYC.	N315MK
N249FX	00	Learjet 60	60-193	BBJS/FlexJets, Addison, Tx.	
N249HP	75	Learjet 24D	24D-301	RFS Aero Leasing Inc. Tucson, Az.	N31BG
N249RM	00	Beechjet 400A	RK-285	Roma Aviation Corp/Roma Realty, El Paso, Tx.	N249SB
N249SR	93	BAe 125/800A	258249	N800SR Aviation Inc/Kintore Ltd. Dublin, Ireland.	N500HF
N250AJ	91	Beechjet 400A	RK-23	U S Airports Air Charters Inc. Rochester, NY.	(N960AJ)
N250AL	02	Citation Encore	560-0605	Luhr Bros Inc. Columbia, Il.	N605CE
N250DH	69	HS 125/731	NA718	Arnoni Aviation Inc. Houston, Tx.	XA-SSV
N250DV	04	Gulfstream G550	5066	RDV Corp. Grand Rapids, Mi.	N966GA
N250FX	00	Learjet 60	60-194	BBJS/FlexJets, Addison, Tx.	
N250GP	83	Diamond 1A	A069SA	New Braunfels Aviation Inc. New Braunfels, Tx.	(N501EZ)
N250HP	99	Beechjet 400A	RK-250	Eagle Wings Inc. Lexington, Ky.	N2293V
N250KD*	82	Citation II	550-0454	U S Turbine Aircraft Sales Inc. Mason City, Ia.	N938D
N250LB	95	Gulfstream 4SP	1269	Lehman Brothers/Executive Fliteways Inc. Ronkonkoma, NY.	N677VU
N250MB	92	BAe 125/800A	258237	BJRK66 Inc/Blake Drilling & Workover Co. Houston, Tx.	N250JE
N250MS	69	Gulfstream II SP	45	Martin Sprocket & Gear Inc. Fort Worth, Tx.	N245GA
N250RJ	80	Falcon 50	31	Victor International/Vee Jay Equipment LLC. Pontiac, Mi	N987RC
N250SP	02	Hawker 800XP	258600	Sonoco Products Co. Darlington County, SC.	N61500
N250SR	93	Citation V	560-0211	BCBML LLP. Las Vegas, Nv.	N250SP

Reg	Yr	Type	c/n	Owner/Operator	Prev Regn
☐ N250VC	02	Gulfstream 4SP	1495	Dacion Corp. Teterboro, NJ.	N495GA
☐ N250VP	81	Citation II	550-0250	Overtime Aviation LLC/James A Lucas & Co. Raleigh, NC.	N33GK
☐ N251AL	80	Learjet 25D	25D-313	Milam International Inc. Englewood, Co.	N727CS
☐ N251CF	79	Citation 1/SP	501-0097	Lutz Aviation LLC/Morsani Foundation Inc. Brooksville, Fl.	N501RS
☐ N251DD	73	Citation	500-0088	DD251 LLC. Las Vegas, Nv.	N170MD
☐ N251DV	03	Gulfstream G400	1522	RDV Corp. Grand Rapids, Mi.	N522GA
☐ N251FX	00	Learjet 60	60-195	BBJS/FlexJets, Addison, Tx.	
☐ N251KD	02	CitationJet CJ-2	525A-0133	251KD LLC. Wilson, Wy.	N.....
☐ N251MG	75	Citation	500-0250	K-Air LLC/Terrebonne Wireline Service Inc. Houma, La.	N251P
☐ N251QS	02	Falcon 2000	202	NetJets, Port Columbus, Oh.	F-WWVP
☐ N251TS	75	Learjet 25B	25B-201	Yelvington Transport Inc. Daytona Beach, Fl.	N59BL
☐ N251VP	07	Gulfstream G450	4083	251 Finance Inc. Bonaire, Netherlands Antilles.	N383GA
☐ N252BK	73	Learjet 25B	25B-107	MCOCO Inc. Houston, Tx. (status ?).	N25NB
☐ N252CH	93	Gulfstream 4SP	1204	N252CH Inc. Opa Locka, Fl.	N212AT
☐ N252DH	99	Challenger 604	5419	Dafra Leasing LLC. Fort Lauderdale, Fl.	N500
☐ N252FX	00	Learjet 60	60-196	BBJS/FlexJets, Addison, Tx.	
☐ N252JK	96	CitationJet	525-0166	Kaney Citation LLC. Rockford, Il.	F-GRRM
☐ N252RP	01	Learjet 60	60-235	Electrolux Home Products Inc. Augusta, Ga.	N5013N
☐ N252RV	98	CitationJet	525-0252	Home Air Inc/Home Place Inc. Gainesville, Ga.	VP-CIS
☐ N252WJ	80	Learjet 35A	35A-349	Aero Toy Store LLC. Fort Lauderdale, Fl.	XA-TCI
☐ N253CM	00	Gulfstream V	610	Cargill Inc. Minneapolis, Mn.	(N610CM)
☐ N253CW	98	CitationJet	525-0253	Southaire Inc. Memphis, Tn.	(N209LX)
☐ N253CX	05	Citation X	750-0253	Waitt Media Inc. Omaha, Ne.	N.....
☐ N253DV	87	B 737-39A	23800	Magic Carpet Aviation Inc. Orlando, Fl.	N117DF
☐ N253FX	01	Learjet 60	60-241	BBJS/FlexJets, Addison, Tx.	N5026Q
☐ N253QS	01	Falcon 2000	153	NetJets, Port Columbus, Oh.	F-WWVK
☐ N254AD	05	Citation Encore	560-0688	The Shoe Show Inc. Concord, NC.	N52488
☐ N254AM	97	Challenger 604	5361	AKM Aviation LLC. Denver, Co.	N346BA
☐ N254CL	79	Learjet 25D	25D-275	Clay Lacy Aviation Inc. Van Nuys, Ca.	N211CD
☐ N254CX	06	Citation X	750-0254	Cessna Aircraft Co. Wichita, Ks.	N52627
☐ N254FX	01	Learjet 60	60-247	BBJS/FlexJets, Addison, Tx.	
☐ N254GA	87	Gulfstream 4	1032	NetJets Middle East, Jeddah, Saudi Arabia.	N432QS
☐ N254RK	99	Beechjet 400A	RK-254	Tripp Trademark Homes, Tampa, Fl.	TC-BYD
☐ N254SD	06	Gulfstream G550	5120	JMI Services Inc. Carlsbad, Ca.	N920GA
☐ N255AR	72	Learjet 24D	24D-255	World Jet of Delaware Inc. Fort Lauderdale, Fl.	XA-SMU
☐ N255BD	01	Learjet 60	60-221	Bill Heard Enterprises Inc. Columbus, Ga.	
☐ N255CC	95	Challenger 604	5302	Apollo Aviation LLC. Englewood, Co.	(N150SE)
☐ N255CM	97	Falcon 50EX	255	Cargill Inc. Minneapolis, Mn.	F-WWHC
☐ N255DG	83	Diamond 1A	A056SA	Richmor Aviation Inc. Garfield County, Rifle, Co.	I-FRTT
☐ N255DV	89	BAe 125/800A	258169	Aviation Inc. Grand Rapids, Mi.	N526AC
☐ N255DX	01	Hawker 800XP	258535	Quest Diagnostics Inc. Reading, Pa.	(N8530QS)
☐ N255FX	01	Learjet 60	60-220	BBJS/FlexJets, Addison, Tx.	N254FZ
☐ N255GA	88	Gulfstream 4	1055	NetJets Middle East, Jeddah, Saudi Arabia.	XB-OEM
☐ N255QS	01	Falcon 2000	155	NetJets, Port Columbus, Oh.	F-WWVM
☐ N255RM	92	Citation V	560-0201	Tower Aviation Reading Inc. Reading, Pa.	SU-EWA
☐ N255TC	90	Citation II	550-0638	B & J of Destin Inc. Destin, Fl.	N1717L
☐ N256A	86	Falcon 50	172	Ameritas Life Insurance Co/Bridgemark Assocs. Lincoln, Ne.	N9000F
☐ N256AH	05	Learjet 40	45-2042	Apple REIT Six Inc. Richmond, Va.	
☐ N256BC	94	Hawker 800	258256	Meridian Inc. Teterboro, NJ.	(N256FS)
☐ N256BM	82	Citation 1/SP	501-0256	Rick Mehrlich, Incline Village, Nv.	N256P
☐ N256CC	01	Citation Bravo	550-0965	Carlisle Aviation LLC. Olive Branch, Ms.	N741PP
☐ N256FX	02	Learjet 60	60-257	BBJS/FlexJets, Addison, Tx.	N50157
☐ N256JB	98	CitationJet	525-0284	John Bowen, Satellite Beach, Fl.	
☐ N256LK	97	Gulfstream V	514	Garthorpe Inc. Burbank, Ca.	N320K
☐ N256V	79	Falcon 10	151	Destin Airways LLC/Rush-Hal Properties, Conway, Ar.	N256W
☐ N256W	03	Citation X	750-0221	Wendy's International Inc. Columbus, Oh.	N51042
☐ N256WJ	73	HS 125/F600A	256008	Silverleaf Resorts Inc. Dallas, Tx.	XX508
☐ N257AL	04	Citation X	750-0226	AML Leasing LLC/TWC Aviation Inc. Burbank, Ca.	N226CX
☐ N257CB	98	Beechjet 400A	RK-207	Carlton-Bates Co. Little Rock, Ar.	N717DD
☐ N257DW	81	Citation II	550-0283	Woods & McCauley/Pier 57 Sales & Service, Olive Branch, Ms.	N225J
☐ N257H	93	Gulfstream 4SP	1223	H J Heinz Co. Pittsburgh, Pa.	N935SH
☐ N257SJ	85	Learjet 55	55-118	La Stella Corp. Pueblo, Co.	C-FCLJ
☐ N258A	81	Falcon 20F-5	438	HML Leasing LLC. Austin, Tx.	N256A
☐ N258MR	94	Hawker 800	258258	R-5 Holdings LLC/M F Ronca & Sons Inc. Bethlehem, Pa.	N258SP
☐ N258PE	68	Falcon 20D	163	Tricoastal Air Inc. Toledo, Oh.	N178GA
☐ N258QS	01	Falcon 2000	158	NetJets, Port Columbus, Oh.	F-WWVP

Reg	Yr	Type	c/n	Owner/Operator	Prev Regn
N259DB	65	Learjet 23	23-064	Jet Investment Group Inc. Springfield, Il. (for rebuild ?).	ZS-MBR
N259DH	75	Citation	500-0259	Amerivation LLC. Bend, Or.	RP-C1299
N259FX	05	Learjet 60	60-295	BBJS/FlexJets, Addison, Tx.	
N259QS	01	Falcon 2000	159	NetJets, Port Columbus, Oh.	F-W...
N259RH	00	Hawker 800XP	258529	AutoStar LLC. Pittsburgh, Pa.	N814TA
N259SK	81	Gulfstream 3	327	Lasher Investment Management Service, Tampa, Fl.	N829MG
N260AM	98	CitationJet	525-0260	Will-Flite Aviation Ltd. Longview, Tx.	D-IGZA
N260AN	98	Learjet 60	60-124	Pinnacle Air Executive Jet, Springdale, Ar.	(N223BX)
N260CH	89	Gulfstream 4	1072	Crescent Heights of America Inc. Stratford, Ct.	N500E
N260FX	07	Learjet 60XR	60-307	BBJS/FlexJets, Addison, Tx.	
N260LF	90	Learjet 31	31-015	Landscapes Unlimited LLC. Lincoln, Ne.	N111TT
N260V	81	Challenger 600S	1022	RCP's Lear LLC. Skillman, NJ.	144610
N261FX	07	Learjet 60XR	60-319	BBJS/FlexJets, Addison, Tx.	
N261JP	93	Beechjet 400A	RK-76	KAZ Aviation LLC. Nashville, Tn.	N8166A
N261PA	90	BAe 1000A	259003	Calla Airways LLC. Plymouth, Ma.	(N503LR)
N261PG	80	Learjet 35A	35A-329	Combs Aviation Corp. Denver, Co.	N261PC
N261SC	92	Learjet 31A	31A-061	Wal-Mart Stores Inc. Rogers, Ar.	N740F
N261WC	78	Learjet 25D	25D-261	Professional Air Services LLC. Fort Lauderdale, Fl.	N24JK
N261WR	97	Citation V Ultra	560-0447	W R Meadows Inc. Hampshire, Il.	N51246
N262BK	98	CitationJet	525-0262	Omicron Business Services Inc. Winter Park, Fl.	N52547
N262FX	07	Learjet 60XR	60-323	BBJS/FlexJets, Addison, Tx.	N50157
N262PA	98	Beechjet 400A	RK-203	Sloane Airways LLC. Plymouth, Ma.	N203RK
N262QS	01	Falcon 2000	162	NetJets, Port Columbus, Oh.	F-W...
N262Y	81	Citation II	550-0291	Colnan Inc. Tampa, Fl.	N40MA
N263CT	98	CitationJet	525-0263	JKZ Properties Ltd. Arlington, Wa.	
N263FX	07	Learjet 60XR	60-334	BBJS/FlexJets, Addison, Tx.	
N263MR	05	Learjet 45	45-263	Martin Resource Management, Longview, Tx.	N263RA
N263PA	05	Hawker 400XP	RK-429	Regis Funding II LLC. Boston, Ma.	N29XP
N264A	00	Global Express	9064	ALCOA Inc. Allegheny County, Pa.	N700PL
N264CL	78	Gulfstream II SP	227	Clay Lacy Aviation Inc. Van Nuys, Ca.	N200LS
N264FX	08	Learjet 60XR	60-340	BBJS/FlexJet, Addison, Tx.	
N264TW	77	Learjet 25D	25D-232	Chaparrel Inc. Lubbock, Tx.	N500LW
N265C	80	Sabre-65	465-33	GBP Management Inc. Greer, SC.	N465SR
N265CP	80	Sabre-65	465-48	Capitoline Products Inc/S & R Leasing LLC. Rome, Ga.	N265SP
N265DS	80	Sabre-65	465-45	GS Sabre 65 LLC. Pontiac, Mi.	N65DR
N265G	90	Falcon 50	214	CNL Group Services Inc. Orlando, Fl.	N55AS
N265GM	74	Sabre-60	306-84	Commercial Aviation Enterprises Inc. Delray Beach, Fl.	N55ZM
N265H	04	Falcon 900EX EASY	139	CNL Group Services Inc. Orlando, Fl.	N139EX
N265KC	76	Sabre-80A	380-49	Apache Peak Equestrian Center LLC. Scottsdale, Az.	(N480CF)
N265M	80	Sabre-65	465-31	Aero Charter Inc. St Louis, Mo.	N65FC
N265MK	74	Sabre-60	306-90	Jose J Perez, Laredo, Tx.	N123FG
N265MP	72	Falcon 20F	265	JNM Air Delaware LLC. St Louis, Mo.	N606RP
N265QS	01	Falcon 2000	165	NetJets, Port Columbus, Oh.	F-WWVE
N265RX*	05	Citation X	750-0249	CVS Pharmacy Inc/CVS Caremark, Providence, RI.	N49VE
N265SC	73	Sabre-40A	282-117	Sunshine Aero Industries Inc. Crestview, Fl.	(N298AS)
N265SJ	98	Gulfstream 4SP	1351	Mokulele LLC. Dulles, Va.	N451QS
N265TS	00	Citation Bravo	550-0942	Arcadia Companies, Atlanta, Ga.	N72SG
N265TW	78	Learjet 25D	25D-265	Chaparrel Inc. Lubbock, Tx.	N69GF
N265WS	81	Sabre-65	465-62	Whiteco Industries/Signco Transportation, Merrillville, In.	(N65BT)
N266CJ	98	CitationJet	525-0266	Baltimore Clipper Inc. Van Nuys, Ca.	
N266FX	07	Learjet 60XR	60-348	BBJS/FlexJets, Addison, Tx.	
N266GA	97	Challenger 604	5400	Zoom Zoom Zoom Aviation Inc. Wichita, Ks.	N237GA
N266TW	73	Learjet 24D	24D-266	Sierra American Corp. Addison, Tx.	N266BS
N267BB	79	Citation II	550-0067	Bohlke International Airways Inc. St Croix, USVI.	N267CW
N267BW	06	Falcon 2000EX EASY	107	United Healthcare Services, Minnetonka, Mn.	N367BW
N267DW	98	Challenger 604	5391	GSO Capital Partners LP. NYC.	N267BW
N267JE	80	HS 125/700A	NA0267	Pampa Aircraft Leasing LLC. Fort Lauderdale, Fl.	N36GS
N267WG	94	Citation V Ultra	560-0267	West Gaines Seed & Delinting Inc. Seminole, Tx.	N267VP
N268DM	07	Falcon 2000EX EASY	146	Dassault Falcon Jet Corp. Teterboro, NJ.	F-WWGH
N268PA	01	Beechjet 400A	RK-323	M M & S Airways LLC. Plymouth, Ma.	N5003G
N268QS	01	Falcon 2000	168	NetJets, Port Columbus, Oh.	(N2260)
N268WC	79	Learjet 25D	25D-268	Starwood Management LLC. Las Vegas, Nv.	(N829AA)
N268WS	03	Learjet 60	60-268	Wingedfoot Services LLC. West Palm Beach, Fl.	N5011L
N269HM	89	Gulfstream 4	1118	Flynt Aviation LLC. Beverly Hills, Ca.	N720CH
N269QS	01	Falcon 2000	169	NetJets, Port Columbus, Oh.	F-WWVJ
N269RC	73	Citation	500-0078	Magnetic Land Inc. Las Vegas, Nv.	N110CK

Reg	Yr	Type	c/n	Owner/Operator	Prev Regn
N269SW	78	Falcon 10	125	Dreamfields Aviation/Lynch Air LLC. Rancho Santa Fe, Ca.	XA-SAR
N269TA	99	Citation VII	650-7112	Truman Arnold Companies. Texarkana, Tx.	(N267W)
N270CW	88	Citation II	550-0570	TVPX Inc. Concord, Ma.	(N189WW)
N270HC	84	Hawker 800SP	258020	Corporate Oil & Gas Ltd. Stone Mountain, Ga.	(N251TJ)
N270KA	81	HS 125/700A	NA0307	Air Navigation Corp. Dover, De.	N270MC
N270LC	79	Westwind-1124	245	Moser, Patterson & Sheridan LLP. Houston, Tx.	N404CB
N270MC	83	Gulfstream 3	374	AWW Aircraft LLC/Santa Ana Homes Inc. Peoria, Az.	N24GA
N270PM	74	Citation	500-0196	Syed Faizullah, Decatur, Il.	(N711FW)
N270SC	93	Gulfstream 4SP	1229	Trans-Exec Air Service Inc. Van Nuys, Ca.	N830EC
N270V	81	Challenger 600S	1017	4KS Aviation III Inc. Dallas, Tx.	114609
N270WS	89	Learjet 55C	55C-138	Weather Shield Inc. Medford, Wi.	N338FP
N271AC	74	Citation	500-0218	Nolan's RV Center Inc. Jeffco, Co.	(N271MF)
N271AG	83	Citation II	550-0471	Austin Air LLC. Cleveland-Lakefront, Oh.	(N623KC)
N271CA	90	Citation V	560-0071	Chandler USA Inc. Chandler, Ok.	
N271CX	06	Citation X	750-0271	Cessna Aircraft Co. Wichita, Ks.	N.....
N271DV	00	Falcon 900EX	68	Poplar Glen LLC. Seattle, Wa.	N390DE
N271PS*	88	Gulfstream 4	1059	Levitical Equipment & Leasing LP. Houston-Hobby, Tx.	N612AC
N271RA	04	Gulfstream G200	104	Rite Aid Corp. Harrisburg, Pa.	N104GA
N271SC	93	Learjet 31A	31A-071	Wal-Mart Stores Inc. Rogers, Ar.	N742F
N272BC	04	Learjet 45	45-252	Bissell Inc. Grand Rapids, Mi.	N40076
N272DN	78	Falcon 10	135	American Equity Investment Properties LLC. Des Moines, Ia.	N707CX
N272MH	04	Citation Sovereign	680-0015	Sovereign 15 Holdings LLC. Fort Lauderdale, Fl.	N.....
N273CA	69	Learjet 25	25-039	Source Investments LLC. Addison, Tx.	(N25VJ)
N273JC	98	Falcon 2000	73	Cisco Systems Inc. San Jose, Ca.	(N97LT)
N273LJ	79	Learjet 35A	35A-273	Pinnacle Air Executive Jet, Springdale, Ar.	N103CL
N273LP	01	Learjet 45	45-185	Louisiana-Pacific Corp. Hillsboro, Or.	
N273LR	70	Learjet 25	25-058	Jet Components Aircraft Parts, Ovilla, Tx. (status ?).	N273LP
N273MC	00	Learjet 60	60-181	Meredith Corp. Des Moines, Ia.	
N273MG	85	Learjet 55	55-119	Spradling Oil Management LLC. Borger, Tx.	N273MC
N273S	98	Challenger 604	5396	Flight Management LLC. Kirkland, Wa.	N604SH
N274CA	68	Sabre-60	306-31	AVMATS/Centurion Investments Inc. Chesterfield, Mo.	N307D
N274CZ	05	Learjet 45	45-274	Sea Horse Marine Inc. Houston, Tx.	N40075
N274HM	81	Westwind-Two	342	CBA Flight Services Inc. Paramus, NJ.	N204AB
N274K	79	Westwind-1124	274	C L Frates & Co. Oklahoma City, Ok.	N701W
N274MA	66	Jet Commander	74	Constellation Airways Inc. Sugarland, Tx.	(N149SF)
N275E	71	Learjet 24D	24D-245	Rocket Air LLC. Olympia, Wa.	(N44KB)
N275HH	90	Falcon 50	207	RLG Test Flight Services LLC. Austin, Tx.	N369EG
N275QS	98	Falcon 2000	75	NetJets, Port Columbus, Oh.	F-WWMK
N275RA	97	Astra-1125SPX	098	Rite Aid Corp. Harrisburg, Pa.	
N276A	02	Citation Excel	560-5276	Alfa Mutual Insurance, Montgomery, Al.	N.....
N276GC	99	Challenger 604	5431	The Graham Companies, York, Pa.	C-GLWR
N276RS	07	390 Premier 1A	RB-194	Soinair LLC/Soin International LLC. Dayton, Oh.	N7294E
N277AL	84	Learjet 55	55-104	ATI Jet Sales LLC. El Paso, Tx.	N18CQ
N277CP*	99	Citation VII	650-7100	CITGO Petroleum Co. Tulsa, Ok.	N710VP
N277GA	02	Gulfstream G200	077	Business Aircraft Leasing Inc. Nashville, Tn.	4X-CVH
N277JM	81	Citation II/SP	551-0035	Air Cruise/John Myers, Long Beach, Ca.	N277HM
N277MG	67	Jet Commander-A	127	Dodson International Parts Inc. Rantoul, Ks.	N550K
N277QS	02	Falcon 2000	177	NetJets, Port Columbus, Oh.	F-WWMD
N277RA	65	Falcon 20C	8	Royal Air Freight Inc. Pontiac, Mi. (status ?).	N612GA
N277RC	93	Citation V	560-0210	Richard & Mary Cree, Jackson, Wy.	N420DM
N277SS	85	BAe 125/800A	258028	Covenant Limited USA LLC. Muskogee, Ok.	N85KH
N277TW	73	Learjet 24D	24D-277	Sierra American Corp. Addison, Tx.	N57BC
N278DM	77	Falcon 2000EX EASY	147	Dassault Falcon Jet Corp. Teterboro, NJ.	F-WWGU
N278GA	02	Gulfstream G200	078	LPC LLC. Silver Spring, Md.	(HB-IUS)
N278GS	02	Falcon 2000	193	Gilead Sciences Inc. San Jose, Ca.	N239QS
N278QS	98	Falcon 2000	77	NetJets/Marquis Jet Partners Inc. Port Columbus, Oh.	F-WWMM
N279AJ	05	Learjet 45XR	45-279	LJ279 LLC/Aero Jet Services Inc. Scottsdale, Az.	N45LJ
N279AK	05	Hawker 400XP	RK-419	Alt Energy LLC. Rowayton, Ct.	N619XP
N279DM	79	Learjet 35A	35A-214	AirNet Systems Inc. Columbus, Oh.	
N279DV	05	CitationJet CJ-3	525B-0070	DBD Properties LLC/R & H DeVos Foundation, Grand Rapids, Mi.	N51055
N279LE	73	Learjet 25B	25B-112	Tee Time Air LLC. Brookfield, Wi.	(YV-.....)
N280BC	03	Falcon 50EX	332	Liberty Mutual Insurance Co. Bedford, Ma.	N332EX
N280C	79	Learjet 25D	25D-280	Steve Sandlin, Las Vegas, Nv.	(N510L)
N280K	98	Challenger 604	5365	Eastman Kodak Co. Rochester, NY.	N618RP
N280PM	80	Citation II	550-0188	Planemasters Ltd. DuPage, Il.	N38NA
N280QS	02	Falcon 2000	181	NetJets, Port Columbus, Oh.	F-WWMH

Reg	Yr	Type	c/n	Owner/Operator	Prev Regn
N280R	69	Learjet 24B	24B-188	Spirit Wing Aviation Ltd. Guthrie, Ok.	N230R
N280TA	80	Citation II	550-0206	Catalina Leasing LLC. Atlanta, Ga.	XA-SQW
N281BT	80	HS 125/700A	NA0281	Three Leasing Inc/Gold King Energy Corp. Houston, Tx.	N403DP
N281QS	98	Falcon 2000	81	NetJets, Port Columbus, Oh.	F-WWVA
N282AC	67	Learjet 24	24-145	USA Jet Airlines Inc. Detroit-Willow Run, Mi.	(XA-LNA)
N282CX	07	Citation X	750-0282	Cessna Aircraft Co. Wichita, Ks.	N5064M
N282DR	06	Citation Sovereign	680-0111	Quad C Advisors LLC. Charlottesville, Va.	N.....
N282Q	05	Gulfstream G550	5090	Quintiles Transnational Corp. Raleigh-Durham, NC.	N590GA
N282T	75	Falcon 10	42	Abaco LLC. John C Tune, Nashville, Tn.	N100UB
N282WW	77	Sabre-60	306-134	IVEFA CA-Venezuela/Gadsden Holdings Inc. Miami, Fl.	N323EC
N283CW	92	Citation II	550-0713	Business Transportation Services Ltd. Columbus, Oh.	N95HE
N283DF	83	Citation II	550-0456	Tradewinds 12/21 Inc. Sherman, Tx.	C-GMPQ
N283SA	67	Falcon 20C	83	Sierra West Airlines, Oakdale, Ca.	(N82SR)
N283SL	06	Falcon 2000EX EASY	83	SL Management LLC. Morristown, NJ.	N83EX
N284CP	96	Citation V Ultra	560-0358	Cook Sales Inc. Carbondale, Il.	N30TV
N284DB	69	HS 125/731	NA715	284DB Inc. Newtown Square, Pa.	N824TJ
N284GA	07	Gulfstream G550	5184	Gulfstream Aerospace Corp. Savannah, Ga.	
N284L	05	Learjet 60	60-284	McLane Co. Temple, Tx.	EC-JIE
N284QS	02	Falcon 2000	185	NetJets, Port Columbus, Oh.	F-WWML
N284TJ	79	Learjet 25D	25D-284	Jets R Us Delaware LLC. Rutledge, Ca.	XC-CFM
N285CC	95	Citation V Ultra	560-0285	Ultra Management LLC. Tulsa, Ok.	N147VC
N285DH	82	Learjet 55	55-026	Insurance Investors Inc. Austin, Tx.	N1324B
N285GA	07	Gulfstream G200	185	Gulfstream Aerospace LP. Dallas-Love, Tx.	4X-C..
N285MC	86	Citation S/II	S550-0102	Bruce Oakley Inc. Little Rock, Ar.	N287MC
N285TW	73	Falcon 20E	285	Sierra American Corp. Addison, Tx.	N285AP
N285XP	95	Hawker 800XP	258285	Fremont Administrative Services Corp. Van Nuys, Ca.	N808H
N286CX*	99	Falcon 2000	102	Cros Inc. Niwot, Co.	N410AS
N286GA	07	Gulfstream G550	5186	Gulfstream Aerospace Corp. Savannah, Ga.	
N286MC	97	Citation VII	650-7076	Maytag Corp. Newton, Ia.	
N286MG	99	Falcon 2000	94	MLG LLC. Atherton, Ca.	N517PJ
N286PC	80	Citation 1/SP	501-0164	MSR Investment Properties LLC. Brentwood, Tn.	N170JS
N286SD	80	Learjet 35A	35A-286	DJB Air LLC. Sioux Falls, SD.	N286WL
N287DL	82	Challenger 600S	1065	K Aviation LLC. Sarasota, Fl.	N601WJ
N287KB	89	MD-87	49768	KEB Aircraft Sales Inc. Danville, Il.	D-ALLJ
N287MC	99	Citation VII	650-7096	Maytag Corp. Newton, Ia.	N5162W
N287Z	99	Global Express	9024	Chamarac Inc. White Plains, NY.	N288Z
N288AG	98	CitationJet	525-0288	How High Sir LLC. Albuquerque, NM.	
N288AS	07	Learjet 40	45-2088	Air Sierra Aviation Inc. Santa Ana, Ca.	
N288CB	05	Learjet 45	45-272	B & C Aviation/Columbus Bank & Trust Co. Columbus, Ga.	N40043
N288FF	95	Learjet 31A	31A-108	Bogey Free LLC. St Petersburg, Fl.	(N288BF)
N288G	01	CitationJet CJ-2	525A-0035	Airdine LLC. Novato, Ca.	N51564
N288HL	02	Citation Encore	560-0599	Mile High LLC/Pate Holdings Inc. Northport, Al.	N52690
N288JP	79	Learjet 35A	35A-288	AC Tech Holdings Inc. Kettleby, ON. Canada.	N288JE
N288KA	83	Gulfstream 3	391	Kookaburra Air/Dendrite International Inc. Morristown, NJ.	N14SY
N289CA	77	Falcon 10	111	Club Air Inc. Dallas-Redbird, Tx.	(N983MC)
N289K	93	Challenger 601-3A	5132	Swagelok Co/Crawford Fitting Co. Cleveland, Oh.	N610DB
N289Z	06	Global Express	9228	Bombardier Aerospace Corp. Windsor Locks, Ct.	N87ZZ
N290CA	78	Westwind-1124	216	Club Air Inc/Club Marketing Service, Dallas-Redbird, Tx.	(N65BK)
N290CP	77	Westwind-1124	219	Westwind Partners Inc/CP Investment Ltd. Caracas, Venezuela.	YV-190CP
N290GA	07	Gulfstream G550	5190	Gulfstream Aerospace Corp. Savannah, Ga.	
N290MX	89	Falcon 50	199	OfficeMax Inc. Itasca, Il.	N291BC
N290QS	02	Falcon 2000	190	NetJets, Port Columbus, Oh.	F-WWVA
N290VP	79	Citation II	550-0090	Heritage Food Service Equipment Inc. Fort Wayne, In.	N410NA
N291DV	00	Citation Excel	560-5146	Fall River Aviation LLC. Corvallis, Or.	N.....
N291GA	07	Gulfstream G550	5191	Gulfstream Aerospace Corp. Savannah, Ga.	
N292ME	80	Learjet 35A	35A-292	Aircraft Specialists Inc. Sellersburg, In.	N634H
N292PC	82	Falcon 50	99	Powers Construction Co/Rogers Aviation LLC. Florence, SC.	N816M
N292QS	99	Falcon 2000	93	NetJets, Port Columbus, Oh.	F-WWVM
N293BC	83	Falcon 50	135	Landia LLC. Northbrook, Il.	N125FJ
N293GA	07	Gulfstream G550	5193	Gulfstream Aerospace Corp. Savannah, Ga.	
N293MC	74	Learjet 24D	24D-293	Jack Air LLC. Morrison, Co.	N917BF
N293P	90	Astra-1125SP	049	Bigs Property LLC/FIMCO Inc. Sioux City, SD.	(N1TM)
N293RT	85	Citation S/II	S550-0023	SLAG Air LLC. Indianapolis, In.	N94RT
N293S	01	Hawker 800XP	258572	Shamrock Aviation Inc. Teterboro, NJ.	N80FB
N294AT	98	CitationJet	525-0294	U S Jet LLC. Rural Valley, Pa.	
N294CW	95	CitationJet	525-0114	Pride Air Inc/Reagan Clark Crop Insurance, Lake Village, Ar.	(N215LX)

Reg	Yr	Type	c/n	Owner/Operator	Prev Regn
☐ N294NW	69	Learjet 25	25-031	Miami Valley Aviation Inc. Middletown, Oh. (status ?).	(N294M)
☐ N294RT	94	Citation V Ultra	560-0264	ROCK-TENN Co. Atlanta-DeKalb, Ga.	N264U
☐ N294S	97	Astra-1125SPX	094	Sea Gate Enterprises X LLC. Sarasota, Fl.	
☐ N295DS	95	CitationJet	525-0091	DSW Development Corp. Cape Girardeau, Mo.	N5138F
☐ N295GA	07	Gulfstream G550	5195	Gulfstream Aerospace Corp. Savannah, Ga.	
☐ N295JR	89	BAe 125/800A	NA0440	Vincent Charters LLC. Horseheads, NY.	N74NP
☐ N295NW	74	Learjet 24XR	24XR-295	Universal Pacific Investments Corp. Bend, Or.	N590CH
☐ N295TW	65	Falcon 20C	5	Sierra American Corp. Addison, Tx.	F-GJPR
☐ N296DC	98	CitationJet	525-0296	Dement Construction Co. Jackson, Tn.	
☐ N296L	05	Learjet 60	60-296	LR60-296 Florida Holdings Inc. Miami, Fl.	EC-JPV
☐ N296QS	02	Falcon 2000	196	NetJets, Port Columbus, Oh.	F-WWVI
☐ N296RG	05	Falcon 2000	222	RI-Relational Investors Aviation LLC. Carlsbad, Ca.	N297RG
☐ N296SB	07	Challenger 300	20157	Ranger Corp. Everett, Wa.	C-FMXW
☐ N297AP	87	Falcon 900	13	Aspen Trading Corp. Miami, Fl.	N61TS
☐ N297GB	93	Gulfstream 4SP	1208	Great Buy Inc. Van Nuys, Ca.	VP-BNY
☐ N297MC	06	Challenger 300	20127	Frontliner Inc/Morris Creullo World Evangelism, Carlsbad, Ca	C-FJQP
☐ N297PF	75	Falcon 10	56	MCJM LLC/Pinnacle Data Services Inc. Houston, Tx.	N56WJ
☐ N297RJ	07	CitationJet CJ1+	525-0663	Cessna Aircraft Co. Wichita, Ks.	N5244W
☐ N297S	74	Citation	500-0197	Jet Air Inc. Galesburg, Il.	XA-SRB
☐ N298AG	84	BAe 125/800A	258014	Colava LLC. Boulder, Co.	N94WN
☐ N298DC	01	Challenger 604	5503	Dow Corning Corp. Midland, Mi.	C-GLYA
☐ N298EF	97	Learjet 60	60-103	Hegon LLC. San Juan, PR.	N216BX
☐ N298GA	07	Gulfstream G550	5198	Gulfstream Aerospace Corp. Savannah, Ga.	
☐ N298HM	78	Westwind-1124	240	JFB Aircraft Westwind Inc. Sarasota, Fl.	N72787
☐ N298NW	80	Learjet 35A	35A-298	Aeromed/Chipola Aviation Inc. Panama City, Fl.	I-FLYC
☐ N298QS	99	Falcon 2000	98	NetJets/Marquis Jet Partners Inc. Port Columbus, Oh.	F-WWVR
☐ N298W	88	Falcon 900	45	Fisher Scientific International Inc. Portsmouth, NH.	N64BE
☐ N299CW	97	CitationJet	525-0199	JBI Holding LLC. Madison, Wi.	(N205LX)
☐ N299DB	75	Falcon 10	50	Northern Aircraft Leasing LLC. Bozeman, Mt.	N411SC
☐ N299DH	03	Citation Encore	560-0645	Las Vegas Aviation III LLC. Bozeman, Mt.	N5269A
☐ N299GS	74	HS 125/F600A	256046	Marc Air Inc. San Antonio, Tx.	(N299DG)
☐ N299JC	73	Falcon 20F	299	Jones Motorcars Inc. Fayetteville, Ar.	(N669AC)
☐ N299MW	79	Learjet 25D	25D-299	DGF & Assocs Inc. Irving, Tx.	(N5B)
☐ N299RA	68	Falcon 20C	146	Royal Air Freight Inc. Pontiac, Mi.	N345FH
☐ N299SC	97	Learjet 60	60-112	Coyote Air LLC. Houston, Tx.	
☐ N299TW	74	Learjet 24D	24D-299	Chaparrel Inc. Lubbock, Tx.	XB-GJS
☐ N299WB	80	HS 125/700A	NA0265	Weisnell LLC/JDP EHP ET, Houston, Tx.	N91CM
☐ N300A	81	Falcon 50	64	Dunkin' Brands, Canton, Ma.	N418S
☐ N300AA	05	Learjet 45	45-285	Ewing Irrigation Products Inc. Albuquerque, NM.	N5012Z
☐ N300AK	01	Citation Encore	560-0593	Arizona-Kentucky LLC. Ashland, Ky.	N121LS
☐ N300AQ	02	Learjet 45	45-211	Boultbee Aviation 2 Inc/Hamlin Jet, Luton, UK.	N300AA
☐ N300BA	68	Falcon 20-5	142	Owners Jet Services Ltd. DuPage, Il.	XA-RNB
☐ N300BC	05	Challenger 300	20067	Ball Corp. Jeffco Airport, Co.	N304BC
☐ N300BP	77	Falcon 20F	239	Brazos Investment Partners 1 LP. Dallas, Tx.	N239BD
☐ N300BV	00	CitationJet CJ-1	525-0418	Hammill Manufacturing Co. Toledo, Oh.	N51444
☐ N300BZ	04	Challenger 300	20030	Bombardier Aerospace Corp. Windsor Locks, Ct.	C-FDIH
☐ N300CH	90	Citation V	560-0080	U S Helicopters Inc. Marshville, NC.	N5JU
☐ N300CQ	01	Hawker 800XP	258555	CEQUEL III Aviation LLC. St Louis, Mo.	N820TA
☐ N300CR	99	Gulfstream 4SP	1401	Crane Co. White Plains, NY.	N900LS
☐ N300CS	97	Citation Bravo	550-0818	CitationShares Sales Inc. White Plains, NY.	N818AJ
☐ N300CV	74	Falcon 20F	322	U S Auto Finance Leasing LLC. Lawrenceville, Ga.	N464M
☐ N300DA	02	Citation Excel	560-5270	Crete Carrier Corp. Lincoln, Ne.	N356WC
☐ N300DG	05	Challenger 300	20058	David Goldner/Plane Lucky LLC. Boca Raton, Fl.	C-FGJI
☐ N300DL	96	CitationJet	525-0148	LVNCS LLC/Great Wolf Resorts Inc. Madison, Wi.	XB-ATH
☐ N300ET	04	CitationJet CJ-3	525B-0014	SET Air LLC/Eagle Transport Corp. Rocky Mount, NC.	N114CJ
☐ N300FS	06	Challenger 300	20143	Aliquant Corp. Oxford, Ct.	C-FLEN
☐ N300GB	99	Beechjet 400A	RK-262	FAC Logistics LLC. Rocky Mount, NC.	
☐ N300GC	81	Citation II	550-0311	Guinn Construction Co. Bakersfield, Ca.	N211SP
☐ N300GF	02	Citation Bravo	550-1046	Gordon Food Service Inc. Grand Rapids, Mi.	N.....
☐ N300JC	07	Learjet 45	45-340	Ceco Enterprises LLC/Cashman Equipment Co. Las Vegas, Nv.	N300JQ
☐ N300JD	02	Citation X	750-0202	Deere & Co. Moline, Il.	N.....
☐ N300JZ	81	Gulfstream 3	875	UJZ LLC/Zimmerman & Partners Advertising, Boca Raton, Fl.	(N845FW)
☐ N300K	99	Gulfstream V	587	Ford Motor Co. Detroit, Mi.	N587GA
☐ N300KH	06	Challenger 300	20130	Seven KH Aviation LLC. Janesville, Wi.	C-FJQX
☐ N300L	95	Gulfstream V	507	Leonore Annenberg, Philadelphia, Pa.	N507GV
☐ N300PY	97	Citation Bravo	550-0806	Highland Homes, Lakeland, Fl.	N52141

Reg	Yr	Type	c/n	Owner/Operator	Prev Regn
☐ N300QS	07	Citation Sovereign	680-0164	NetJets, Port Columbus, Oh.	N52627
☐ N300RB	84	BAe 125/800B	258013	Virginia Properties Inc. Chicago, Il.	(N500RH)
☐ N300RD	67	Gulfstream 2	3	Rubloff 300 LLC. Brown Field, San Diego, Ca.	(N417RD)
☐ N300SC	81	Learjet 35A	35A-440	F Gerald Maples PA. New Orleans, La.	N917SC
☐ N300SF	76	Falcon 20F-5	258	Safe Flight Instrument Corp. White Plains, NY.	N20AE
☐ N300SJ	00	Citation Excel	560-5107	VF Finance Inc. Wilmington, De.	I-NYNY
☐ N300SL	03	390 Premier 1	RB-110	Roll International Corp. Van Nuys, Ca.	N701KB
☐ N300SM	04	Challenger 300	20015	U S Cable Corp. West Palm Beach, Fl.	A6-SMS
☐ N300TC	78	Westwind-1124	241	Orlando Financial Corp. Mount Dora, Fl.	N789TE
☐ N300TJ	74	Learjet 24XR	24XR-285	Magnolia River Development LLC. Summerdale, Al.	N430JW
☐ N300TK	82	Challenger 600S	1077	Three of a Kind XL LLC. Anchorage, Ak.	(N940DH)
☐ N300TS	80	Diamond 1	A003SA	ZHT Aviation LLC/ZMG Construction Inc. Longwood, Fl.	N300DM
☐ N300TW	83	Challenger 600S	1080	Flying M LLC. Irvine, Ca.	N3JL
☐ N300UJ	80	Gulfstream 3	316	Pontiac Aviation LLC. Wilmington, De.	(N69EH)
☐ N300WY	84	Gulfstream 3	427	C & S Aviation LLC. Dallas, Tx.	N87AC
☐ N300XL	80	Westwind-1124	276	TSTI LC. Houston, Tx.	N800XL
☐ N301DR	77	Citation 1/SP	501-0273	DCR Aviation Inc. Lakeland, Fl. (was 500-0363)	N110JA
☐ N301K	99	Gulfstream V	591	Ford Motor Co. Detroit, Mi.	N591GA
☐ N301PC	82	Westwind-Two	377	Dude Inc. Fort Smith, Ar.	4X-CUJ
☐ N301PE	92	BAe 1000A	259031	Peabody Energy Corp. St Louis, Mo.	N301PH
☐ N301PG	05	CitationJet CJ2+	525A-0301	Papa Golf Aviation LLC. Owasso, Ok.	N52609
☐ N301QS	04	Citation Sovereign	680-0010	NetJets, Port Columbus, Oh.	N5135A
☐ N301R	65	Falcon 20C	3	Kalitta Charters LLC. Detroit-Willow Run, Mi. (status ?)	N92MH
☐ N301RJ	95	Learjet 60	60-054	F1 Air Group LLC. Morristown, NJ.	VP-BMM
☐ N301TT	68	Falcon 20C	160	AVMATS/Centurion Investments Inc. Chesterfield, Mo.	N100UF
☐ N302AK	05	Global Express	9181	KP Holdings LLC. Chicago-Midway, Il.	C-FEAB
☐ N302CJ*	05	CitationJet CJ2+	525A-0302	Martin CJ2 Plus LLC. Greensboro, NC.	N6M
☐ N302CS	97	Citation Bravo	550-0820	CitationShares Sales Inc. White Plains, NY.	N820CB
☐ N302DP	79	Gulfstream 2B	237	N302DP LLC. Fort Lauderdale, Fl.	N237RF
☐ N302EM	05	Challenger 300	20054	Exxon Mobil Corp. Dallas-Love, Tx.	C-F-..
☐ N302GC	02	Embraer Legacy 600	145600	Embraer, Nashville, Tn.	PT-...
☐ N302JC	98	Falcon 2000	63	Aero Toy Store LLC. Fort Lauderdale, Fl.	N806JH
☐ N302MB	86	Citation S/II	S550-0097	Arizona Aviation LLC/Arizona Cardinals, Tempe, Az.	N551RF
☐ N302PC	82	Challenger 600S	1072	Lower Cross Corp. Stamford, Ct.	(N190SC)
☐ N302PE	04	Hawker 800XP	258693	Peabody Energy Corp. St Louis, Mo.	N693XP
☐ N302QS	97	Citation V Ultra	560-0402	NetJets, Port Columbus, Oh.	N5200U
☐ N302SE	94	Hawker 800	258269	Duke Energy Corp. Houston, Tx.	N380DE
☐ N302SG	81	Westwind-1124	379	Shaw Managed Services Inc. Baton Rouge, La.	N62ND
☐ N302SJ	79	Citation II	550-0052	P & S Air LLC. Frederiksted, USVI.	N550DR
☐ N302ST	80	Gulfstream 3	302	S T Aviation LLC. Naples, Fl.	N109ST
☐ N302TB	04	Hawker 400XP	RK-384	Moser Farms Inc. Casper, Wy.	N84XP
☐ N303A	79	Citation 1/SP	501-0092	Aardvark Aircraft Sales Corp. Wilmington, De.	N501X
☐ N303BC	96	Hawker 800XP	258324	Sam Holdings LLC. Hartford, Ct.	N324XP
☐ N303CJ	04	CitationJet CJ-3	525B-0031	CJ303 LLC/M & N Aviation Inc. San Juan, PR.	N.....
☐ N303CP	00	Citation Encore	560-0539	Center Charter LC. San Francisco, Ca.	N539CE
☐ N303CS	97	Citation Bravo	550-0814	CitationShares Sales Inc. White Plains, NY.	PT-WNH
☐ N303CZ	01	Challenger 300	20003	Horizon Americas Inc. Fort Lauderdale, Fl.	C-GIPX
☐ N303EM	05	Challenger 300	20068	Exxon Mobil Corp. Dallas-Love, Tx.	C-FGZE
☐ N303FZ	89	Falcon 100	218	Bogey Bird Inc. Indianapolis, In.	N130DS
☐ N303PC	86	Citation III	650-0110	J C Pace Holding Co & Kimball Inc. Fort Worth, Tx.	N76D
☐ N303QS	95	Citation V Ultra	560-0343	NetJets, Port Columbus, Oh.	N60AE
☐ N303RH	80	Citation 1/SP	501-0303	General Operations LLC. Kennedy, Tx.. (was 500-0397)	N370TP
☐ N303SE	86	BAe 125/800A	258060	Duke Energy Corp. Houston, Tx.	N330DE
☐ N303SG	83	Westwind-1124	391	Shaw Managed Services Inc. Baton Rouge, La.	N155ME
☐ N303TP	00	Gulfstream 4SP	1411	Big Dog Aviation LLC. Oxford, Ct.	N56D
☐ N304CS	98	Citation Bravo	550-0847	CitationShares Sales Inc. White Plains, NY.	N133AV
☐ N304EM	05	Challenger 300	20077	Exxon Mobil Corp. Dallas-Love, Tx.	C-FGCD
☐ N304JR	93	Beechjet 400A	RK-63	Lamair Aviation Corp. Wilmington, De.	N163RK
☐ N304QS	97	Citation V Ultra	560-0408	NetJets, Port Columbus, Oh.	N560NS
☐ N304RJ	95	Hawker 800XP	258286	F1 Air Group LLC. Morristown, NJ.	N501F
☐ N304SE	00	Beechjet 400A	RK-304	Hiwire Aviation LLC/American Wireless LLC. Jackson, Ms.	N5004Y
☐ N304TS	80	Gulfstream 3	304	Nomad Transportation LLC. Van Nuys, Ca.	VR-BSL
☐ N304TT	81	Challenger 600S	1033	Montelago Marketing Inc. Henderson, Nv.	(N518FS)
☐ N305AR	80	Learjet 25D	25D-314	Roger Woolstenhulme Jr. Orem, Ut.	N95BP
☐ N305CC	99	Global Express	9027	Carnival Corp. Fort Lauderdale, Fl.	C-GEZX
☐ N305CF	00	Gulfstream 4SP	1457	Homestead Management LLC. San Jose, Ca.	N234DN

Reg	Yr	Type	c/n	Owner/Operator	Prev Regn
N305CS	97	Citation Bravo	550-0825	CitationShares Sales Inc. White Plains, NY.	(N45HV)
N305EJ	06	Citation Sovereign	680-0105	WNC Air Services Inc. Chicago, Il.	N389QS
N305EM	06	Challenger 300	20098	Exxon Mobil Corp. Dallas-Love, Tx.	C-FHMQ
N305GA	96	Gulfstream 4SP	1305	Electronic Data Systems Corp. McKinney, Tx.	N888SQ
N305LM	00	Gulfstream 4SP	1443	HGA LLC. Dallas, Tx.	N443GA
N305MD	96	Beechjet 400A	RK-131	71 Leasing LLC. Cincinnati-Lunken., Oh.	N1083Z
N305PA	66	DC 9-15	45740	PharmAir Corp. Miami, Fl.	N911KM
N305QS	06	Citation Sovereign	680-0088	NetJets, Port Columbus, Oh.	N.....
N305S	76	Citation	500-0301	Odegaard Aviation Inc. Kindred, ND.	OE-FNG
N305SC	03	Hawker 800XP	258662	ADP Inc. Roseland, NJ.	N662XP
N305TC	89	Gulfstream 4	1116	TM Aviation Inc/Corporate Fleet Services, Charlotte, NC.	N971L
N306BP	07	390 Premier 1A	RB-206	JF Air Traffic Inc/Fikes Wholesale Inc. Temple, Tx.	
N306CJ	01	CitationJet CJ-2	525A-0016	Aqua Sun Investments LLC. Middleburg Heights, Oh.	(N547AC)
N306CS	99	Citation Bravo	550-0881	CitationShares Sales Inc. White Plains, NY.	(N312RD)
N306EM	06	Challenger 300	20101	Exxon Mobil Corp. Dallas-Love, Tx.	C-FHNC
N306JA	76	Learjet 24D	24D-306	Skyway Enterprises Inc. Kissimmee, Fl.	(N243RK)
N306JR	05	CitationJet CJ2+	525A-0306	N306JR LLC. Scottsdale, Az.	N5180K
N306PA	84	Citation III	650-0053	Jetcorp LLC/Edco Disposal Corp. Lemon Grove, Ca.	N367G
N306QS	94	Citation V Ultra	560-0266	NetJets, Port Columbus, Oh.	N288JR
N306TT	90	Gulfstream 4	1148	T Bird Aviation Inc. Du Page, Il.	HB-IEJ
N307BS	97	CitationJet	525-0241	JT Air LLC/Tim Marburger Dodge Inc. Concord, NC.	N110FD
N307D	77	Citation Eagle	501-0032	312D Leasing Inc. N Palm Beach County, Fl.	(N501SK)
N307HF	71	Learjet 25B	25B-075	White Industries Inc. Bates City, Mo. (status ?).	N82025
N307JW	00	Astra-1125SPX	123	Lawrence Finch, Concord, Ca.	N36GX
N307MS	01	Citation Bravo	550-0974	Michael Strasser GmbH. Salzburg, Austria.	N307CS
N307QS	06	Citation Sovereign	680-0130	NetJets, Port Columbus, Oh.	N52178
N307RM	97	Hawker 800XP2	258322	307 RM LLC. Fayetteville, Ar.	(N814LX)
N307SC	84	Challenger 601	3026	Admiral Beverage Corp. Worland, Wy.	(N810MB)
N308A	92	Citation II	550-0703	ARAMCO Associated Co. Dhahran, Saudi Arabia. 'Shabeen'	
N308AB	02	Gulfstream 4SP	1496	Prime Jet LLC. Van Nuys, Ca.	N496GA
N308BW	81	Learjet 35A	35A-438	William Walker Properties Inc. Tulsa, Ok.	N308R
N308CR	91	Challenger 601-3A	5092	Covington Aviation LLC. Hyannis, Ma.	N300CR
N308DD	79	HS 125/700A	NA0250	Summerwind Aviation Group Inc. Van Nuys, Ca.	(N900JG)
N308DM	02	Falcon 50EX	328	Archer Daniels Midland Co. Decatur, Il.	N328EX
N308DT	04	Citation Bravo	550-1094	Tippmann Aviation LLC. Fort Wayne, In.	N.....
N308GT	00	CitationJet CJ-2	525A-0004	Mark Solomon, Fort Lauderdale, Fl.	(N699JM)
N308HG	80	Gulfstream 3	308	The Glimcher Co. Columbus, Oh.	N308GA
N308MS	01	Citation Bravo	550-0976	Michael Strasser GmbH. Salzburg, Austria.	N308CS
N308QS	06	Citation Sovereign	680-0116	NetJets/Marquis Jet Partners Inc. Port Columbus, Oh.	N5225K
N308TW	79	Citation II	550-0044	Atlantic Northeast Aviation LLC. Farmingdale. (was 551-0092)	(N452AJ)
N308U	04	Falcon 2000EX EASY	37	UT Flight/United Technologies Corp. Windsor Locks, Ct.	F-WWGS
N309AK	02	Beechjet 400A	RK-348	Air Dishi LLC. Bethpage, NY.	N448CW
N309CJ	05	CitationJet CJ2+	525A-0309	CJ Airways Inc. Guernsey, C.I.	N.....
N309CS	01	Citation Bravo	550-0977	CitationShares Sales Inc. White Plains, NY.	N5172M
N309EL	79	Gulfstream 2TT	250	ABC Auto Wholesalers Inc. Orlando, Fl.	(N94SF)
N309ES	99	Global Express	9016	Earth Star Inc. Burbank, Ca.	N300ES
N309MG	01	Learjet 60	60-223	Western Service Contact Corp. Carsbad, Ca.	N109JZ
N309QS	99	Citation V Ultra	560-0509	NetJets, Port Columbus, Oh.	
N310EL	87	Gulfstream 4	1021	Eli Lilly & Co. Indianapolis, In.	EC-HGH
N310GJ	07	Gulfstream G450	4078	Londers Property SA. Moscow-Vnukovo, Russia.	N378GA
N310LJ	99	Learjet 45	45-031	Yamhill Finance Ltd. Ecuador.	9V-ATH
N310ME	80	Learjet 35A	35A-310	Aircraft Specialists Inc. Sellersburg, In.	N8280
N310TK	05	Challenger 604	5606	Alltech Inc. Lexington-Bluegrass, Ky.	N606CC
N310U	06	Falcon 2000EX EASY	100	United Technologies Corp. Hartford, Ct.	F-WWMB
N311AF	85	Citation S/II	S550-0051	Aero Film, Van Nuys, Ca.	N77PA
N311AG	71	B 727-17	20512	Vallejo Co. San Francisco, Ca.	N767RV
N311BD	79	Gulfstream 2TT	236	Newcastle Corp. Wichita Falls, Tx.	N311DH
N311BP	96	Learjet 45	45-010	Jet Plaid LLC. Nashville, Tn.	N903HC
N311CG	05	Gulfstream G550	5108	Crimson Group Inc. Tokyo, Japan.	N828GA
N311CS	01	Citation Bravo	550-0979	KTSC LLC. Madisonville, Tx.	N52475
N311EL	89	Gulfstream 4	1095	Eli Lilly & Co. Indianapolis, In.	N469GA
N311GL	01	Beechjet 400A	RK-311	Executive Charters Inc. Kinston, NC.	N711GL
N311JA	88	Falcon 900	63	CMS Energy Corp/Act Two Inc. Pontiac, Mi.	N75W
N311LJ	75	Learjet 24D	24D-311	Triplex Financing Corp. Carson City, Nv.	(N76PW)
N311MG	68	Gulfstream II SP	41	Goff Aviation Inc/Steelman Homes, Denton, Tx.	N365TC
N311RS	77	JetStar 2	5222	JetStar 5222 LLC. Fort Lauderdale, Fl.	N813P

Reg	Yr	Type	c/n	Owner/Operator	Prev Regn
❏ N311TP	81	Citation 1/SP	501-0196	MGKR Enterprises LLC. Lufkin, Tx.	(N311TT)
❏ N311VP	81	Citation 1/SP	501-0311	Aurora Aircraft Co. Asuncion, Paraguay. (was 500-0405).	(N501PY)
❏ N312AL	83	Learjet 55	55-089	LevAir Ltd. Palm Beach International, Fl.	N628PT
❏ N312AM	96	Challenger 604	5312	Marin Conveyancing Corp. Ronkonkoma, NY.	(N905SB)
❏ N312CC	98	Learjet 31A	31A-172	Downs Aircraft Inc. Van Nuys, Ca.	N130FX
❏ N312EL	89	Gulfstream 4	1105	Eli Lilly & Co. Indianapolis, In.	N408GA
❏ N312NC	81	Citation II	550-0290	Progress Aviation Corp. Dallas, Tx.	N217LG
❏ N312P	00	Falcon 900EX	67	Hyatt Corp. Chicago-Midway, Il.	N967EX
❏ N312QS	95	Citation V Ultra	560-0312	NetJets, Port Columbus, Oh.	(N52457)
❏ N312SB	99	CitationJet	525-0355	Lawson Airways LLC. Chattanooga, Tn.	N205FH
❏ N313BH	00	Learjet 45	45-108	Wal-Mart Stores Inc. Rogers, Ar.	N313BW
❏ N313BW	06	Learjet 45	45-322	AND Inc/Key Air Inc. Oxford, Ct.	N5011L
❏ N313CC	03	Falcon 2000EX	12	Comcast Cable Communication Holdings, N Philadelphia, Pa.	F-WWGK
❏ N313CR	04	CitationJet CJ-2	525A-0234	Super Fabrics/Crypton Air LLC. Pontiac, Mi.	N.....
❏ N313CV	95	Citation V Ultra	560-0313	Pacific Dental Services Inc. Irvine, Ca.	N5246Z
❏ N313HC	01	Citation Encore	560-0603	Hibernia Aviation Corp. Mobile, Al.	N603CV
❏ N313JS	66	JetStar-731	5086	Seagull Aircraft Corp. Fort Lauderdale, Fl.	(N65JW)
❏ N313K	79	Falcon 20F	404	F & S Air LLC. Dallas, Tx.	N28C
❏ N313QS	07	Citation Sovereign	680-0140	NetJets, Port Columbus, Oh.	N.....
❏ N313RF	06	Global Express	9194	Tudor Investment Corp. Oxford, Ct.	C-FEBH
❏ N313RG	95	Gulfstream V	504	Renco Group Inc. NYC.	N504GV
❏ N313TW	76	Westwind-1124	190	21st Century Air Inc/Mikal Watts, Corpus Christi, Tx.	N190WW
❏ N314AD	00	Astra-1125SPX	128	DPI Inc. Carson City, Nv.	N676TC
❏ N314CS	01	Citation Bravo	550-1004	CitationShares Sales Inc. White Plains, NY.	N.....
❏ N314ER	68	HS 125/3A-RA	NA710	Dodson International Parts Inc. Rantoul, Ks.	(N767LC)
❏ N314QS	97	Citation V Ultra	560-0441	NetJets, Port Columbus, Oh.	
❏ N314RW	90	Citation V	560-0051	Red Wing Shoe Co. Red Wing, Mn.	N599SG
❏ N314SG	97	Learjet 31A	31A-133	Bend Properties Inc. Santa Ana, Ca.	N331ZX
❏ N314SL	00	Citation VII	650-7115	Smurfit Stone Container Corp. St Louis, Mo.	N5267K
❏ N314TC	98	Hawker 800XP	258400	TNCD LLC. Chicago, Il.	N404JC
❏ N314TL	98	Beechjet 400A	RK-181	Eagle Gap LLC. Addison, Tx.	N2235V
❏ N314TW	74	Falcon 20E	314	Sierra American Corp. Addison, Tx.	F-GDLU
❏ N315CS	96	Citation V Ultra	560-0371	Pheasant Kay-Bee Toy Inc. Nashua, NH.	N371CV
❏ N315EJ	93	Citation V	560-0215	Intrepid Aviation LLC. Denver, Co.	N23NS
❏ N315JL	07	Hawker 850XP	258891	Jaindl Farms LLC. Orefield, Pa.	N31991
❏ N315MC	02	CitationJet CJ-2	525A-0068	Kestrel Inc/Madison Chemical Co. Madison, In.	N69AH
❏ N315MK	92	Gulfstream 4SP	1206	Athenian Air Link, Athens, Greece.	N162G
❏ N315R	90	Beechjet 400A	RK-9	Citation LLC. Evansville, In.	(N150TF)
❏ N315TS	00	BBJ-7CU	30772	Tutor-Saliba Corp. Van Nuys, Ca.	N1784B
❏ N316BG	90	Challenger 601-3A	5062	Goody's Family Clothing Inc. McGhee-Tyson, Tn.	N727S
❏ N316CS	02	Citation Bravo	550-1010	CitationShares Sales Inc. White Plains, NY.	N5228J
❏ N316EC	87	BAe 125/800A	NA0403	Cleveland Steel Container Corp. Twinsburg, Oh.	N89NC
❏ N316EQ	75	Sabre-75A	380-38	Jose Manuel Figueroa, McAllen, Tx.	N316EC
❏ N316GS	00	Global Express	9075	Citigroup Corporate Aviation, White Plains, NY.	C-GHEI
❏ N316LP	81	Diamond 1A	A012SA	L P M Air Inc. Pensacola, Fl.	N112GA
❏ N316MH	86	Citation S/II	S550-0108	Silverwood Inc. Athol, Id.	N108QS
❏ N316QS	99	Citation V Ultra	560-0516	NetJets, Port Columbus, Oh.	
❏ N316SS	86	Falcon 900	8	Guild Investments LLC. Northbrook, Il.	N5731
❏ N316TD*	00	Westwind-1124	312	NOA Group LLC. Wichita, Ks.	N24FJ
❏ N317BR	07	CitationJet CJ-3	525B-0150	RA Aviation LLC. Burbank, Ca.	N52626
❏ N317CC	01	Hawker 800XP	258532	Cozzens & Cudahy Air Inc. Milwaukee, Wi.	
❏ N317CS	02	Citation Bravo	550-1019	CitationShares Sales Inc. White Plains, NY.	N5231S
❏ N317HC	80	Citation II	550-0185	Tassa HN Inc. Wilmington, De.	N511DL
❏ N317JS	83	Westwind-Two	385	West Air LLC. Little Rock, Ar.	N962MV
❏ N317M	02	Falcon 2000	188	Lyondell Chemical Co. Houston, Tx.	N317MZ
❏ N317MJ	89	Gulfstream 4	1122	Lyon Aviation Inc/Majjec Jhett LLC. Pittsfield, Ma.	N317M
❏ N317PC	81	Hawker 400XP	RK-357	Airpak Financial Corp. Guatemala City, Guatemala.	N5057Z
❏ N317QS	07	Citation Sovereign	680-0160	NetJets, Port Columbus, Oh.	N51869
❏ N317TT	80	Learjet 35A	35A-317	Inter Island Yachts Inc. Zephyr Cove, Nv.	N98TE
❏ N318CS	02	Citation Bravo	550-1029	CitationShares Sales Inc. White Plains, NY.	N5270J
❏ N318CT	90	Citation V	560-0081	Century Tel Service Group LLC. Monroe, La.	N560HP
❏ N318DN	81	Citation 1/SP	501-0184	Reuland Electric Co. City of Industry, Ca.	N501VC
❏ N318MM	01	Citation Excel	560-5220	Schwans Shared Services LLC. Marshall, Mn.	N5112K
❏ N318NW	80	Learjet 35A	35A-318	SFG Commercial Aircraft Leasing Inc. South Bend, Or.	(N35WU)
❏ N318QS	97	Citation V Ultra	560-0418	NetJets, Port Columbus, Oh.	N5112K
❏ N318SA	00	Learjet 45	45-114	Symbolic Aviation Inc. La Jolla, Ca.	N417FX

Reg	Yr	Type	c/n	Owner/Operator	Prev Regn
N318SP	75	Gulfstream II SP	168	Jetvue LLC/Marathon Gulfstream LLC. Boca Raton, Fl.	N317AF
N319AJ	75	Gulfstream II SP	164	Gulfstream 164 Aviation Inc. Dover, De.	XA-ESC
N319CS	02	Citation Bravo	550-1036	CitationShares Sales Inc. White Plains, NY.	N.....
N319QS	99	Citation V Ultra	560-0519	NetJets, Port Columbus, Oh.	
N319SC	97	Learjet 31A	31A-131	Tradewind LLC. Sarasota, Fl.	N31LR
N320AF	76	HFB 320	1061	Kalitta Flying Service Inc. Morristown, Tn.	(D-CEDL)
N320BP	07	CitationJet CJ-3	525B-0143	Bass Pro Shops Inc. Springfield, Mo.	N5185V
N320GX	02	Global Express	9116	Texas Instruments Inc. McKinney, Tx.	N700EW
N320MD	82	Westwind-1124	366	M-D Building Products Inc. Oklahoma City, Ok.	N65TD
N320QS	07	Citation Sovereign	680-0169	NetJets, Port Columbus, Oh.	N5263D
N320TM	07	Citation Sovereign	680-0136	Bass Pro Shops Inc. Springfield, Mo.	N5093D.
N321AN	79	Learjet 35A	35A-272	Anderson News Corp .Knoxville, Tn.	N500EF
N321AR	87	Citation III	650-0151	Exodus Aviation LLC. Pineview, NY.	N660AF
N321GG	98	Citation V Ultra	560-0474	Edens & Avant Realty Inc. Columbia, SC.	N474VP
N321GL	93	Learjet 31A	31A-085	Starwood Industries Inc. Richmond, Va.	N531AT
N321MS	00	Hawker 800XP	258515	Ejent Group LLC. Gates Creek, Or.	N321EJ
N321SF	00	Galaxy-1126	021	Smithfield Foods Inc. Newport News, Va.	N41GX
N322AD	00	Gulfstream G200	022	ACF Property Management Inc. Van Nuys, Ca.	N200AX
N322AU	76	Learjet 24D	24D-326	MedJets LLC. Cedar Knolls, NJ.	N326KE
N322BC	85	HS 125/700A	NA0322	TCA Air LLC/Bratton Capital Inc. Wilmington, De.	C-FCHT
N322BJ	03	390 Premier 1	RB-93	RB93 LLC/Cole Inc. Three Lakes, Wi.	
N322CP	93	Falcon 900B	134	Gallagher Enterprises LLC. Pueblo, Co.	N88YF
N322CS	03	Citation Bravo	550-1052	CitationShares Sales Inc. White Plains, NY.	N.....
N322GC	81	Learjet 55	55-008	Caulkins Investment Co. Denver, Co.	N551SC
N322GT	02	Citation Bravo	550-1030	Throgmartin Leasing LLC. Murrells Inlet, SC.	N52397
N322K	94	Fokker 70	11521	Ford Motor Co. Detroit, MI.	PH-MKS
N322MA	82	Citation II/SP	551-0378	Mary-Ali 322 LLC. Wilmington, De.	(F-OGVA)
N322QS	97	Citation V Ultra	560-0421	NetJets, Port Columbus, Oh.	
N322RR	87	Falcon 200	514	Rogers Enterprises of Idaho LLC. Tyler, Tx.	N87AG
N322RS	76	Learjet 24D	24D-322	R & S Aircraft LLC. Melbourne, Fl.	(N322TJ)
N322TS	88	Learjet 31	31-002	Peake Motor Co. Kenner, La.	N350DS
N323G	03	CitationJet CJ-1	525-0532	West Cobb Building Supply Inc. Kennesaw, Ga.	N32BG
N323JA	95	CitationJet	525-0116	SRQ LLC. Boulder, Co.	(N202LX)
N323JH	84	Gulfstream 3	434	Z-Line Designs Inc. Livermore, Ca.	(N73ET)
N323JK	78	HS 125/700A	NA0234	Vista Aviation LLC. Atlanta, Ga.	N731DL
N323L	91	BAe 125/800B	258212	Jetcraft Corp. Raleigh-Durham, NC.	RP-C8008
N323MP	02	Hawker 800XP2	258594	Doane Pet Care Co. Nashville, Tn.	N140GB
N323NE*	97	Citation V Ultra	560-0442	Northwestern Energy, Sioux Falls, SD.	N778FW
N323P	97	Astra-1125SPX	096	Greene Group/Allease Inc. Tuscaloosa, Al.	N96AL
N323QS	07	Citation Sovereign	680-0134	NetJets, Port Columbus, Oh.	N5076K
N323SK	02	CitationJet CJ-2	525A-0134	Arvest Bank Group Inc. Bentonville, Ar.	N.....
N323SL	87	BAe 125/800A	258084	LCM 323 Inc. Tampa, Fl.	N124JG
N324AM	01	390 Premier 1	RB-42	Hawker Beechcraft Corp. Wichita, Ks.	N390CK
N324B	90	Challenger 601-3A	5069	Ripplewood Aviation LLC. NYC.	N655CN
N324BG	89	BAe 125/800A	258165	U S Construction Systems LLC. Birmingham, Al.	VT-RAY
N324CS	03	Citation Bravo	550-1059	CitationShares Sales Inc. White Plains, NY.	N.....
N324FP	01	Gulfstream 4SP	1475	Fox Paine & Co LLC. Stockton, Ca.	N67TH
N324JC	76	Citation	500-0324	Foxdale Aviation Inc. Ronaldsway, IOM.	(N721HW)
N324K	95	Fokker 70	11545	Ford Motor Co. Detroit, Mi.	PH-EZH
N324L	81	Citation 1/SP	501-0197	GLK Aviation LLC. Pearland, Tx.	N100SN
N324MM	88	Beechjet 400	RJ-52	Mazzei Pontiac-Cadillac Co. Concord, Ca.	N930MG
N324QS	97	Citation V Ultra	560-0423	NetJets, Port Columbus, Oh.	N5073G
N324SM	99	Global Express	9023	Busujima Trust, Wilmington, De.	C-GEZD
N324TW	76	Learjet 24D	24D-324	Chaparrel Inc. Lubbock, Tx.	XA-SCY
N325CS	03	Citation Bravo	550-1061	CitationShares Sales Inc. White Plains, NY.	N5267K
N325DM	01	CitationJet CJ-1	525-0438	WFBNW NA. salt Lake City, Ut. (trustor ?).	N103CS
N325FX	00	Challenger 604	5457	Bombardier Aerospace Corp. Windsor Locks, Ct.	C-GLXW
N325JF	01	Embraer Legacy 600	145499	Intel Corp/Executive Jet Management Inc. Cincinnati, Oh.	PT-...
N325LW	81	Westwind-Two	334	Floating Bulk Terminal LLC. Houston, Tx.	N40MP
N325NW	80	Learjet 35A	35A-325	The Zidd Agency Inc. Medina, Oh.	I-FFLY
N325QS	97	Citation V Ultra	560-0425	NetJets, Port Columbus, Oh.	
N325RC	05	CitationJet CJ-3	525B-0021	Riley Creek Lumber Co. Coeur d'Alene, Id.	N5073G
N325SJ	72	Learjet 25B	25B-102	Boston Fidelity Financial LLC. Wilmington, De.	N254SC
N325WP	00	Citation Bravo	550-0933	Blue Ridge King Inc. Martinsville, Va.	N417KW
N326B	98	CitationJet	525-0302	The Buckle Inc. Kearney, Ne.	N302CJ
N326DD	78	Learjet 35A	35A-173	326DD LLC. West Columbia, SC.	YU-BPY

130

Reg	Yr	Type	c/n	Owner/Operator	Prev Regn
❏ N326EW	05	Falcon 2000EX EASY	55	Leco Corp. South Bend, In.	N226EW
❏ N326FX	00	Challenger 604	5464	Assion Aircraft&Yachting Chartering Services Ltd. New Zealan	C-GLWR
❏ N326HG	99	Learjet 60	60-163	Chantilly Air Inc. Silver Spring, Md.	N238BX
❏ N326JD	01	Gulfstream 4SP	1460	57 Aviation Services LLC. White Plains, NY.	(N326LM)
❏ N326JK	03	CitationJet CJ-1	525-0511	Pioneer Inc. Oakley, Ks.	ZK-TBM
❏ N326MA	01	Citation Excel	560-5159	Michael Anderson, Victoria, Tx.	N336MA
❏ N326N	88	BAe 125/800A	NA0427	NLN Hawker Holdings LLC. Opa Locka, Fl.	N858XL
❏ N326QS	99	Citation V Ultra	560-0526	NetJets, Port Columbus, Oh.	
❏ N326VW	66	Falcon 20C-5	27	Tricoastal Air Inc. Toledo, Oh.	N174GA
❏ N327CB	82	Learjet 35A	35A-483	Eagle One Corp. San Juan, PR.	(N483TJ)
❏ N327FX	00	Challenger 604	5466	BBJS/FlexJets, Addison, Tx.	C-GLWV
❏ N327GA	05	Gulfstream G100	157	LMI LLC. Atlanta-DeKalb, Ga.	4X-CVK
❏ N327LJ	00	Hawker 800XP	258490	Cavallino Air LLC. Los Gatos, Ca.	N50490
❏ N327QS	95	Citation V Ultra	560-0327	NetJets, Port Columbus, Oh.	(N51038)
❏ N327TL	98	Gulfstream 4SP	1339	Thomas H Lee Co. Bedford, Ma.	N339GA
❏ N328AC	00	Dornier Do328JET	3132	ACA Private Shuttle, Dulles, Va.	D-C...
❏ N328CC	04	Challenger 300	20028	TXU Business Services Co. Dallas, Tx.	(N328RC)
❏ N328CJ	99	CitationJet	525-0328	BK Aviation LLC. Shellyville, Ky.	
❏ N328CR	01	Dornier Do328JET	3160	Comtran International Inc. San Antonio, Tx.	N408FJ
❏ N328CS	03	Citation Bravo	550-1074	JNF Aviation LLC. Pasadena, Ca.	N.....
❏ N328GT	01	Dornier Do328JET	3183	Ultimate Jetcharters Inc. Canton, Oh.	D-C...
❏ N328JK	69	Learjet 24B	24B-212	One Way Jet LLC. Wilmington, De.	N328TL
❏ N328NA	80	Citation 1/SP	501-0168	Citation Partners LLC. Signal Mountain, Tn.	N601WT
❏ N328PC	81	Westwind-Two	328	Jetmore Ventures LLC/Westport Homes, Stafford, Tx.	C-GPFC
❏ N328QS	97	Citation V Ultra	560-0428	NetJets, Port Columbus, Oh.	
❏ N328RC	07	CitationJet CJ-3	525B-0203	Ritz-Craft Corp. Mifflinburg, Pa.	N50776
❏ N328SA	84	Westwind-Two	425	Larry Reynolds, Valdez, Ak.	(N365QX)
❏ N329CJ	06	CitationJet CJ-3	525B-0130	L & S Aviation LLC. Wilmington, De.	(N910BH)
❏ N329CS	03	Citation Bravo	550-1077	CitationShares Sales Inc. White Plains, NY.	N.....
❏ N329FX	02	Challenger 604	5541	BBJS/FlexJets, Addison, Tx.	C-GLXO
❏ N329TJ	85	Learjet 55	55-120	BSI Holdings II LLC. Portland, Or.	N777YC
❏ N330AM	70	HS 125/F403A	25235	AmeriMark Direct LLC. Cleveland, Oh.	N101UR
❏ N330DK	81	Citation II	550-0266	Mach 1.0 Aviation LLC. Raleigh-Durham, NC.	N550TP
❏ N330FX	01	Challenger 604	5487	BBJS/FlexJets, Addison, Tx.	C-GLWT
❏ N330G	66	HS 125/731	25087	Kando Jet LLC. Wilmington, De.	N66AM
❏ N330K	02	Falcon 2000	189	Ford Motor Co. Detroit, Mi.	N2000A
❏ N330L	81	Learjet 25D	25D-330	Butler National Inc. Newton, Ks.	N330LJ
❏ N330MB	86	Citation III	650-0129	MB Aviation LLC/CS Construction Inc. Phoenix, Az.	N125N
❏ N330QS	95	Citation V Ultra	560-0329	NetJets, Port Columbus, Oh.	N5105F
❏ N330TS	01	Beechjet 400A	RK-330	Prometheus V LLC. Atlanta, Ga.	N33NL
❏ N330TW	76	Learjet 24E	24E-330	Sierra American Corp. Addison, Tx.	N511AT
❏ N330VP	95	Citation V Ultra	560-0330	J & N Leasing LLC. Spokane, Wa.	N851WC
❏ N330WR	81	Gulfstream 3	337	Orkin Inc. Atlanta-DeKalb, Ga.	N456SW
❏ N331AP	77	Westwind-1124	205	Luis Nunez/Westwindsouther LLC. Caracas, Venezuela.	(N775JC)
❏ N331BN	04	Gulfstream G200	095	Burlington Northern/Santa Fe Railway, Fort Worth, Tx.	N595GA
❏ N331DM	80	Falcon 20-5B	429	Busey Corp/Flightstar Corp. Chicago-Midway, Il.	N702CA
❏ N331EX	03	Falcon 50EX	331	SE Leasing LLC/Rooms To Go Inc. Seffner, Fl.	(N331SE)
❏ N331FX	01	Challenger 604	5491	Bombardier Aerospace Corp. Windsor Locks, Ct.	C-G...
❏ N331MC	97	Falcon 900EX	22	WISC Ltd. Greater Wilmington, De.	(N21HJ)
❏ N331MW	96	Citation V Ultra	560-0384	JJS Aviation LLC. Plano, Tx.	N950TC
❏ N331N	90	Learjet 31	31-022	Harbor Jet LLC. Alpena, Mi.	
❏ N331PR	97	Citation Bravo	550-0831	Eastern Aviation Fuels Inc. New Bern, NC.	N5145P
❏ N331QS	95	Citation V Ultra	560-0331	NetJets, Port Columbus, Oh.	N51072
❏ N331SK	92	Astra-1125SP	063	Winnebago Industries Inc. Forest City, Ia.	(N60RV)
❏ N331TP	97	Challenger 604	5350	Washington Times Aviation Inc. Washington-Dulles, Va.	C-GLXU
❏ N332CS	04	Citation Bravo	550-1081	CitationShares Sales Inc. White Plains, NY.	N.....
❏ N332FX	02	Challenger 604	5543	BBJS/FlexJets, Addison, Tx.	(N605BA)
❏ N332K	01	Learjet 45	45-169	Kiewit Engineering Co. Omaha, Ne.	N77HN
❏ N332LC	96	Citation V Ultra	560-0332	Cessna Finance Corp. Wichita, Ks.	(N5108G)
❏ N332MT	05	Citation Bravo	550-1105	Pine Tree Aircraft LLC. Longview, Tx.	N5117U
❏ N332QS	99	Citation V Ultra	560-0523	NetJets, Port Columbus, Oh.	
❏ N332SB	06	CitationJet CJ-3	525B-0145	Switchback Ranch LLC/Riverstone Holdings, NYC.	N.....
❏ N332SE	76	Citation	500-0332	Dialysis Clinic Inc. Nashville, Tn.	LV-LZR
❏ N333BD	05	CitationJet CJ-2	525A-0237	Sabine Aircraft LLC. Longview, Tx.	N5263U
❏ N333EB	99	Citation Bravo	550-0893	EBAA Iron Inc. Eastland, Tx.	N5073G
❏ N333EC	00	Gulfstream 4SP	1414	Flying Falcon Inc. Miami, Fl.	N505VS

Reg	Yr	Type	c/n	Owner/Operator	Prev Regn
N333FJ	73	Falcon 10	1	Delta Oil Inc. Wilmington, De.	F-BJLH
N333KC	75	Learjet 35	35-037	Aviation Applications LLC. Scottsdale, Az.	N45TK
N333KE	74	Falcon 10	14	Falconmitch Inc. Tyler Pounds, Tx.	N31TJ
N333KK	83	Challenger 600S	1082	Kohler Inc. Kohler, Wi.	N777KZ
N333MS	80	HS 125/700A	257115	King Air International LLC.	N125YY
N333MX	07	Falcon 2000EX EASY	120	M D C Holdings Inc. Denver, Co.	F-WWGG
N333NM	65	Sabre-40	282-45	Commercial Aviation Enterprises Inc. Delray Beach, Fl.	N333GM
N333PC*	04	Hawker 800XP	258669	Polco Inc. Washington, DC.	N520SP
N333PY	97	Gulfstream 4SP	1317	Perry Capital LLC. Teterboro, NJ.	N929WT
N333QS	95	Citation V Ultra	560-0333	NetJets, Port Columbus, Oh.	(N5109R)
N333RL	92	BAe 1000B	259027	Becker Aviation LLC. Troy, Mi.	N333RU
N333RY	69	Learjet 24B	24B-202	J 2 Partnership, San Antonio, Tx. (status ?)	N814JR
N333TW	68	Learjet 24	24-168	Sierra American Corp. Addison, Tx.	N155BT
N333VS	93	CitationJet	525-0034	Nowak Aviation Inc. Warwick, RI.	N9GU
N334AF	01	Learjet 45	45-143	Ashley Furniture Industries Inc. Arcadia, Wi.	N145GS
N334CS	04	Citation Bravo	550-1089	CitationShares Sales Inc. White Plains, NY.	N.....
N334ED	81	Citation II	550-0228	Wings LLC. Pelham, Al.	VH-EXM
N334FX	04	Challenger 604	5586	New York Life Insurance Co. NYC.	C-GLXQ
N334KC	83	Diamond 1A	A034SA	G W S Enterprises LLC. Coleman, Ok.	N303P
N334PS	74	HS 125/600A	256032	Canrose Air 1 LLC. Orem, Ut.	N801BC
N334QS	97	Citation V Ultra	560-0434	NetJets, Port Columbus, Oh.	
N334RC	73	Citation	500-0062	Eagle Air Services Inc. Wilmington, De.	N4KH
N334SR	96	Beechjet 400A	RK-129	TADR Investments LLC. Gary, In.	N129MC
N335AF	01	Learjet 60	60-244	Ashley Furniture Industries Inc. Arcadia, Wi.	N884TW
N335AT	74	Learjet 35	35-009	Quest Air Inc. Irving, Tx.	PT-LGR
N335CS	04	Citation Bravo	550-1091	CitationShares Sales Inc. White Plains, NY.	N.....
N335FX	05	Challenger 604	5619	BBJS/FlexJets, Addison, Tx.	C-GLWT
N335JJ	03	CitationJet CJ-2	525A-0162	Century Aviation of Colorado LLC. Telluride, Co.	N.....
N335MG	87	Learjet 35A	35A-626	Eagle Jet Aviation Inc/Milt's Eagle LLC. Las Vegas, Nv.	(N385MG)
N335MR	81	Learjet 35A	35A-443	Southern Jet Inc. Warner Robbins, Ga.	N258G
N335PR	89	Learjet 35A	35A-647	PIA LLC. Atlanta, Ga.	ZS-DJB
N335QS	95	Citation V Ultra	560-0335	NetJets, Port Columbus, Oh.	
N335RC	79	Learjet 35A	35A-256	Aircraft Management Assocs LLC. Sarasota, Fl.	(N66PJ)
N335RD	78	Learjet 35A	35A-216	RDC Marine Inc. Houston, Tx.	N142LG
N335TW	75	Falcon 20F	335	Chaparral Leasing Inc. Newton, Ks.	(N301FC)
N335VB	80	Westwind-1124	297	Pauls Operations Inc. Aurora, Co.	N801SM
N336CS	04	Citation Bravo	550-1095	CitationShares Sales Inc. White Plains, NY.	N.....
N336FX	05	Challenger 604	5634	BBJS/FlexJets, Addison, Tx.	C-GLXY
N336MA	78	Citation II	550-0036	Highlands Management Group, Scottsdale, Az.	N789BR
N336QS	95	Citation V Ultra	560-0336	NetJets, Port Columbus, Oh.	N5265B
N336RJ	79	Sabre-65	465-10	Six Star Inc. Winter Park, Fl.	N77TC
N336XL	03	Citation Excel	560-5336	CMH Aviation/Jim & Mike Leasing LLC. Columbus-Bolton, Oh.	(N336BC)
N337CS	04	Citation Bravo	550-1097	CitationShares Sales Inc. White Plains, NY.	N51488
N337FX	06	Challenger 604	5647	BBJS/FlexJets, Addison, Tx.	C-GLXF
N337QS	97	Citation V Ultra	560-0437	NetJets, Port Columbus, Oh.	
N337RE	84	BAe 125/800A	258024	Bar-Ned Aviation LLC. Tompkins County, NY.	N802D
N337WR	94	Hawker 800	258273	Waddell & Reed Development Inc. Kansas City, Mo.	N258RA
N338B	06	Citation Bravo	550-1132	Northern Air Inc. Grand Rapids, Mi.	N5165P
N338CL	77	Gulfstream 2B	199	Nashville Jet Charters Inc. Nashville, Tn.	N900TJ
N338CS	04	Citation Bravo	550-1084	CitationShares Sales Inc. White Plains, NY.	N52141
N338FX	06	Challenger 604	5656	BBJS/FlexJets, Addison, Tx.	C-FIXN
N338MC	04	Citation Encore	560-0662	Malphrus Construction Co. Ridgeland, SC.	N560CR
N338MM	88	Gulfstream 4	1076	Franklin Templeton Travel Inc. San Francisco, Ca.	HZ-MNC
N338PR	07	Learjet 60	60-338	Learjet Inc. Wichita, Ks.	N5016V
N338QS	04	Citation Sovereign	680-0011	NetJets, Port Columbus, Oh.	N5135K
N338R	95	Citation V Ultra	560-0338	Advanced Drainage Systems Inc. Columbus, Oh.	N592M
N338TM	07	Citation Sovereign	680-0177	Jadeline Network Sdn Bhd. Malaysia.	N52446
N338TP	00	Global Express	9073	Washington Times Aviation Inc. Washington-Dulles. Va.	N700XN
N339BC	82	Learjet 55	55-039	Trojan Air Services Inc. Paradise Valley, Az.	VR-BQF
N339CA	77	HS 125/700A	NA0213	Q-Jet Aviation LLC. Houston, Tx.	N370RR
N339CC	95	Hawker 800XP	258277	Cignal Development Corp. Timonium, Md.	(N339PC)
N339CS	04	Citation Bravo	550-1085	CitationShares Sales Inc. White Plains, NY.	N5068R
N339HP	79	Citation 1/SP	501-0292	DBL Inc. Palm Beach Gardens, Fl. (was 500-0383).	N456R
N339PM	65	Sabre-40	282-38	PM Transportation LLC. Chicago, Il.	N921JG
N339QS	95	Citation V Ultra	560-0339	NetJets, Port Columbus, Oh.	
N339RK	74	Falcon 20-5B	313	Planned Residential Communities Co. Belmar, NJ.	N184TS

Reg	Yr	Type	c/n	Owner/Operator	Prev Regn
N339SM	05	Hawker 400XP	RK-458	McNeils Pharmacy/McNeil Transportation LLC. Whiteville, NC.	N50858
N340AK	99	Challenger 604	5405	Oak Air Ltd. Akron, Oh.	N811BP
N340QS	99	Citation V Ultra	560-0514	NetJets, Port Columbus, Oh.	
N341AP	03	Falcon 2000EX	24	Air Products & Chemicals Inc. Allentown, Pa.	N224EX
N341AR	99	CitationJet	525-0341	Ahern Rentals Inc. Las Vegas, Nv.	
N341CS	04	Citation Bravo	550-1106	CitationShares Sales Inc. White Plains, NY.	N.....
N341K	01	Learjet 45	45-157	Kiewit Engineering Co. Omaha, Ne.	N545RA
N341QS	96	Citation V Ultra	560-0341	NetJets, Port Columbus, Oh.	
N342AJ	79	Citation II	550-0050	Holrob-Aircraft LLC. Knoxville, Tn.	F-GMCI
N342CS	04	Citation Bravo	550-1101	CitationShares Sales Inc. White Plains, NY.	N5264U
N342K	01	Learjet 45	45-171	Kiewit Engineering Co. Omaha, Ne.	N171DP
N342QS	95	Citation V Ultra	560-0324	NetJets, Port Columbus, Oh.	(N152WC)
N343CA	76	Learjet 25B	25B-202	Jim Donaldson/Cherry Air Inc. Dallas, Tx.	YU-BRA
N343CC	96	Citation V Ultra	560-0368	Westvaco Corp. NYC.	N5194J
N343CM	81	Citation II	550-0195	AirSouth Inc. Jonesboro, Ar.	N61CK
N343DF	06	Global 5000	9206	Parkview Holdings Inc. Farmingdale, NY.	N92ZZ
N343DP	86	Gulfstream 3	483	Meridian Equipment Co. Ronkonkoma, NY.	N343DF
N343MG	90	Falcon 900	95	M G Transportation Inc. West Palm Beach, Fl.	N478A
N343PR	01	390 Premier 1	RB-7	Town & Country Food Markets Inc. Wichita, Ks.	
N343QS	97	Citation V Ultra	560-0444	NetJets, Port Columbus, Oh.	
N344AA	93	Gulfstream 4SP	1207	7-11 Air Corp. Teterboro, NJ.	(N77VU)
N344CA	76	Learjet 25B	25B-203	Wilson Air LLC/Tim Wilson Investigations, Houston, Tx.	YU-BRB
N344CM	00	Falcon 50EX	300	Cargill Inc. Minneapolis, Mn.	F-WWHB
N344GW	81	Gulfstream 3	344	U S Department of Energy, Albuquerque, NM.	N344DD
N344KK	83	Citation II	550-0477	Legendary Air Inc. Destin, Fl.	(N846L)
N344QS	95	Citation V Ultra	560-0344	NetJets, Port Columbus, Oh.	N5268M
N344RJ	76	Citation	500-0340	Allegiance Health Management, Shreveport, La.	N26NS
N345AA	92	Gulfstream 4	1186	7-11 Air Corp. Teterboro, NJ.	8P-MAK
N345AW	01	Learjet 45	45-182	Saturn of Kansas City Inc. Kansas City, Mo.	N50248
N345BH	00	Learjet 45	45-100	Bowen Family Homes Inc. Lawrenceville, Ga.	RP-C1958
N345BS	75	Westwind-1124	181	Snider Industries LLP. Marshall, Tx.	N325LJ
N345CJ	02	CitationJet CJ-2	525A-0136	Brantigan Research, Santa Fe, NM.	N5141F
N345EX	07	Falcon 2000EX EASY	145	Dassault Falcon Jet Corp. Teterboro, NJ.	F-WWMB
N345FM	01	Learjet 45	45-151	Crenshaw Resources LLC. Houston, Tx.	N345K
N345GC	88	Astra-1125	023	Flying Wings LLC. Clearwater, Fl.	N23TJ
N345K	06	Learjet 45	45-310	Koch Industries Inc. Wichita, Ks.	
N345LC	07	Gulfstream G550	5145	Capelli Enterprises Inc. Farmingdale, NY.	N545GA
N345MA	99	Learjet 45	45-054	Richards Aviation Inc. Memphis, Tn.	
N345MC	69	Learjet 25	25-046	MCOCO Inc. Houston, Tx.	N33PT
N345MG	99	CitationJet CJ-1	525-0372	Anderson Aviation Inc. Lake Forest, Il.	N372CP
N345MP	05	Hawker 850XP	258757	Hawkeye Aviation Transportation Inc. Des Moines, Ia.	N757XP
N345PF	06	Citation Sovereign	680-0080	WAC Refining Co. El Paso, Tx.	OE-GLP
N345QS	97	Citation V Ultra	560-0445	NetJets, Port Columbus, Oh.	N5000R
N345RJ	83	Learjet 55	55-078	R J Corman Aviation Services LLC. Lexington, Ky.	N55VK
N345RL	01	Learjet 45	45-180	Knollwood LLC. Houston, Tx.	N880LJ
N345SV	01	Learjet 45	45-140	Blue Sky 45 LLC. Van Nuys, Ca.	XA-AED
N345TR	81	Westwind-Two	345	Chuck Latham Associates Inc. Parker, Co.	N534R
N345WB	99	Learjet 45	45-036	Air Four SpA. Milan, Italy.	
N346CM	00	Citation Bravo	550-0915	Massey Partners Ltd. Abilene, Tx.	N915BB
N346PC	05	Falcon 2000EX EASY	62	Global Pacific Aviation Inc. Hillsboro, Or.	(OH-FOX)
N346QS	04	Citation Sovereign	680-0013	NetJets, Port Columbus, Oh.	N5136J
N346XL	03	Citation Excel	560-5346	Florida Power & Light Co. Opa Locka, Fl.	N517CS
N347GA	81	Westwind-Two	347	Lane Co/Executive Time Management Inc/Lane Co. Atlanta, Ga.	N178HH
N347K	93	Falcon 50	236	Kiewit Engineering Co. Omaha, Ne.	N725PA
N347MH	80	Citation 1/SP	501-0155	Sky King Equipment Rental LLC. Cashiers, NC.	N321TS
N347QS	96	Citation V Ultra	560-0357	NetJets, Port Columbus, Oh.	N81SH
N347TC	79	HS 125/700A	257055	Centurion American Aviation LLC. Bedford, Tx.	N47PB
N348K	01	Learjet 45	45-150	Kiewit Engineering Co. Omaha, Ne.	N245KC
N348MC	95	Hawker 800XP	258290	Monsanto Co. St Louis, Mo.	N670H
N348QS	95	Citation V Ultra	560-0348	NetJets, Port Columbus, Oh.	N52682
N348W	76	Sabre-60	306-94	Platina Investment Corp. Wiley Post, Ok.	N217RN
N349AK	07	Hawker 850XP	258876	800 XPI Holdings LLC. Farmingdale, NY.	
N349BA	00	BBJ-73Q	30789	Boeing Executive Flight Operations, Seattle, Wa.	
N349H	87	Falcon 900	10	Beauty Central Inc/Conair Corp. Stamford, Ct.	N349K
N349HP*	98	Learjet 31A	31A-153	Home Properties Inc. Knoxville, Tn.	N153NP
N349JC	76	Falcon 10	70	Northern Jet Management Inc. Grand Rapids, Mi.	VP-BCH

Reg	Yr	Type	c/n	Owner/Operator	Prev Regn
N349JR	93	Challenger 601-3A	5130	L T Exchange Corp. Oklahoma City, Ok.	N601SR
N349K	02	Gulfstream G300	1510	Elk Mountain Ventures Inc. Omaha, Ne.	(N609RM)
N349MC	77	Westwind-1124	224	N349MC LLC. Houston, Tx.	N2756T
N349MR	77	Falcon 20F	360	Mitchell Ranch Aviation LLC. Scottsdale, Az.	N390AG
N349QS	05	Citation Sovereign	680-0029	NetJets, Port Columbus, Oh.	N5183V
N349RR	04	Citation X	750-0236	N349RR LLC/Midland Financial Co. Oklahoma City, Ok.	N53HF
N349SF	94	CitationJet	525-0049	Smithfield Foods Inc. Newport News, Va.	N49CJ
N350BN	07	Gulfstream G150	223	BNSF Railway Co. Fort Worth, Tx.	4X-CVK
N350BV	03	CitationJet CJ-2	525A-0186	Diane S Lake CA LLC. Bakersfield, Ca.	N5247U
N350EF	81	Learjet 35A	35A-385	Executive Flight Inc. Pangborn Memorial, Wa.	N535MC
N350FK	05	Gulfstream G350	4040	EJS-Executive Jet Shares Inc. Brazil.	N440GA
N350JS	80	Falcon 50	15	Jet Source Inc. Carlsbad, Ca.	(N595CW)
N350M	00	Falcon 2000	128	Murphy Oil Corp. El Dorado, Ar.	N628SA
N350PL	82	HS 125/700A	NA0338	Pelco Sales Inc. Clovis, Ca.	N797FA
N350QS	05	Citation Sovereign	680-0036	NetJets, Port Columbus, Oh.	N5108G
N350WB	50	Falcon 50	102	Wagner & Brown Inc. Midland, Tx.	(N50WB)
N351AC	92	Learjet 31A	31A-051	Alpha Charlie Inc. Mountville, Pa.	N1905H
N351AM	81	Learjet 35A	35A-409	Challenger One Holdings LLC. Wheeling, Il.	N35FE
N351AS	78	Learjet 35A	35A-146	Chipola Aviation Inc. Panama City, Fl.	N55AS
N351BC	96	CitationJet	525-0159	International Bank of Commerce, Laredo, Tx.	N131RG
N351CW	02	390 Premier 1	RB-53	Chandler Real Estate Inc. Helena, Mt.	N351CB
N351EF	77	Learjet 35A	35A-125	Executive Flight Inc. Pangborn Memorial, Wa.	N125GA
N351GL	73	Learjet 35	35-001	Learjet Inc. Wichita, Ks. (experimental).	N731GA
N351N	65	Learjet 23	23-054	LandAir Mapping Inc. Atlanta, Ga.	N351NR
N351PJ	76	Learjet 35A	35A-074	Premier Jets Inc. Hillsboro, Or.	N198T
N351QS	98	Citation V Ultra	560-0451	NetJets, Port Columbus, Oh.	N5124F
N351SB	95	Hawker 800XP	258280	Ruud Lighting Inc. Racine, Wi.	N351SP
N351SE	69	Gulfstream 2B	64	Gulfstream Aircraft Partners Inc. Wilmington, De.	N95SJ
N351SP*	07	Hawker 900XP	HA-4	Sonoco Products Co. Darlington County, SC.	N904XP
N351TC	04	Hawker 800XP	258675	Taylor Companies, Hagerstown, Md.	N675XP
N351TV	81	Learjet 35A	35A-368	Craig Air Center Inc. Jacksonville, Fl.	N450MC
N351WC	01	Citation Excel	560-5225	Cardinal Glass Industries Inc. Minnetonka, Mn.	(N351CG)
N352AF	98	Falcon 900B	172	Fayair Inc. Dover, De.	N177FJ
N352BH	99	Gulfstream 4SP	1393	World Healing Center Church Inc. Grapevine, Tx.	N297MC
N352DA	82	Citation II	550-0352	Millennium Realty Investment, Hallandale Beach, Fl.	VT-EUN
N352EF	91	Learjet 31A	31A-046	Executive Flight Inc. Pangborn Memorial, Wa.	N131PT
N352HS	85	Learjet 35A	35A-596	Ventures Acquisition LLC. McMinnville, Or.	N826CO
N352K	02	Learjet 45	45-215	Kiewit Engineering Co. Omaha, Ne.	N822CA
N352MD	77	Learjet 24F	24F-352	CPA Aviation Inc. Tulsa, Ok.	(N449JS)
N352QS	96	Citation V Ultra	560-0352	NetJets, Port Columbus, Oh.	N5153X
N352TV	81	Learjet 35A	35A-410	Craig Air Center Inc. Jacksonville, Fl.	N89RP
N352WB	81	Falcon 50	71	Wagner & Brown Inc. Midland, Tx.	J2-KBA
N353EF	81	Learjet 35A	35A-364	Harborview Medical Center, Seattle, Wa.	N490BC
N353FT	82	Citation II	550-0353	Superior Energy Services Inc. Harvey, La. (was 551-0398).	N477KM
N353MA	85	Gulfstream 3	472	Marshall Aviation LLC/MTM Enterprises Inc. Tampa, Fl.	(N454BE)
N353PC	05	Challenger 300	20053	PNC Finnacial Services Group LLC. Allegheny County, Pa.	C-FGBP
N353PJ	73	Citation	500-0104	All Altitude Aviation Inc. Edgewater, Fl.	(N3330)
N353QS	99	Citation V Ultra	560-0530	NetJets, Port Columbus, Oh.	
N353VA	83	Gulfstream 3	371	Venusair LLC. Burbank, Ca.	N681FM
N353WC	01	Citation X	750-0180	Williams Companies Inc. Tulsa, Ok.	N51511
N354AS	59	MS 760 Paris	54	Airborne Turbine LP. San Luis Obispo, Ca.	54
N354CL	83	Learjet 35A	35A-493	Clay Lacy Aviation Inc. Van Nuys, Ca.	N493CH
N354EF	81	Learjet 35A	35A-378	Executive Flight Inc. Pangborn Memorial, Wa.	N354ME
N354JC*	77	Learjet 35A	35A-112	Sky Wide Ventures LLC. Van Nuys, Ca.	(N120WH)
N354LQ	76	Learjet 35	35-055	ADEX-ASG LLC/Addison Express LLC. Addison, Tx.	C-GCJD
N354PM	75	Learjet 35	35-015	Griffin Aviation Holdings LLC. Addison, Tx.	(N335SS)
N354QS	96	Citation V Ultra	560-0356	NetJets, Port Columbus, Oh.	N5153Z
N354RB	02	390 Premier 1	RB-54	Elliott Aviation Aircraft Sales Inc. Des Moines, Ia.	ZS-MGK
N354TC	96	Challenger 601-3R	5192	Hilton Hotels Corp. Van Nuys, Ca.	C-GLYC
N354WC	02	Citation X	750-0191	Williams Companies Inc. Tulsa, Ok.	N5267G
N355CD	81	Sabre-65	465-57	Sound Trak Inc. Omaha, Ne.	N903K
N355PC*	81	Learjet 35A	35A-431	OneSource Aviation LLC. Southlake, Tx.	N431AS
N355RM	82	Learjet 55	55-033	Richmark Aircraft Leasing LLC. Boca Raton, Fl.	N355UJ
N355WC	06	Citation X	750-0266	Williams Companies Inc. Tulsa, Ok.	N5201M
N356BR	82	Gulfstream 3	356	Stephens Institute/Academy of Art College, San Francisco, Ca	N356TJ
N356JW	90	Learjet 35A	35A-656	Air Bear Inc. Amarillo, Tx.	N335SB

Reg	Yr	Type	c/n	Owner/Operator	Prev Regn
N356MR	06	CitationJet CJ-3	525B-0138	KRG Air LLC. Denver, Co.	N51942
N356SA	94	Citation V	560-0256	DXP Investments LLC. Houston, Tx.	N356EJ
N356SR	82	HS 125/700A	NA0318	Schumacher Aircraft LLC/DB Aviation Inc. Waukegan, Il.	N114BA
N356WA	97	Learjet 60	60-123	Wilsonart International Inc. Temple, Tx.	
N357BE	04	Citation Encore	560-0663	Basin Electric Power Co-operative, Bismark, ND.	N5266F
N357EC	04	Citation Excel XLS	560-5510	Entergy Services Inc. New Orleans, La.	N41118
N357EF	80	Learjet 35A	35A-323	Executive Flight Inc. Pangborn Memorial, Wa.	N735A
N357EJ	03	CitationJet CJ-2	525A-0184	InComm Leasing LC. Atlanta, Ga.	N.....
N357JV	99	CitationJet	525-0357	MGA Services LLC/Myrick Gurosky & Assocs. Alabaster, Al.	
N357KM	85	Gulfstream 3	435	Komar Aviation LLC. Long Beach, Ca.	N32KA
N357LJ	80	Learjet 35A	35A-357	Pinnacle Air Executive Jet, Springdale, Ar.	N104SB
N357PR	82	Gulfstream 3	348	From the Heart Minisitries Inc. Temple Hills, Md.	N756S
N357PS	76	Falcon 20F-5	357	Pangulf Aviation Ltd. Farnborough, UK.	N342KF
N357QS	07	Citation Sovereign	680-0155	NetJets, Port Columbus, Oh.	N5040E
N357RM	75	Learjet 35	35-007	Richmark Aircraft Leasing LLC. Boca Raton, Fl.	N35UJ
N358BJ	02	BBJ-7ES	33542	Boeing Business Jets, Seattle, Wa.	
N358CY*	82	Gulfstream 3	358	Conrad Yelvington, Daytona Beach, Fl.	N475DJ
N358MH	90	Falcon 50	209	Intervest Construction Inc. Daytona Beach, Fl.	VP-BSL
N358P	00	Learjet 60	60-205	PPL Aviation LLC/Pizzagalli Properties LLC. Burlington, Vt.	(N64HX)
N358QS	97	Citation V Ultra	560-0455	NetJets, Port Columbus, Oh.	N51396
N359CW	88	Citation III	650-0159	CSC Trust Co of Delaware, Wilmington, De. (trustor ?).	N267TG
N359EC	00	Citation Encore	560-0559	UCC Washington Park Inc. Trenton, NJ.	(N659SA)
N359EF	78	Learjet 35A	35A-193	Harborview Medical Center, Seattle, Wa.	N9EE
N359K	02	Learjet 45	45-216	Kiewit Engineering Co. Omaha, Ne.	C-GHCY
N359QS	06	Citation Sovereign	680-0126	NetJets, Port Columbus, Oh.	N5270M
N359V	97	Challenger 604	5349	Valmont Industries Inc. Omaha, Ne.	N5349
N359WJ	67	Sabre-60	306-1	Commercial Aviation Enterprises Inc. Delray Beach.(status ?)	XA-REC
N360AN	98	Learjet 60	60-137	Pinnacle Air Executive Jet, Springdale, Ar.	N229FX
N360AV	07	Gulfstream G150	240	Gulfstream Aerospace LP. Dallas-Love, Tx.	4X-C..
N360AX	81	Learjet 35A	35A-367	Omni Air International Inc. Tulsa, Ok.	N232CC
N360CA	81	Diamond 1A	A009SA	Charlie Air LLC. West Columbia, SC.	N318RS
N360CK	07	CitationJet CJ-3	525B-0180	Crawler LLC/Extreme Crafts VI LLC. Boca Raton, Fl.	N5185J
N360HS	99	Citation Bravo	550-0889	Auctionair LLC. Cottonwood, Az.	N619JM
N360JG	83	Learjet 25D	25D-360	Pegasus Aviation LLC. Nashville, Tn.	N618P
N360LA	00	Global Express	9087	Luft Aviation Charter P/L. Melbourne, VIC. Australia.	N700BQ
N360LJ	80	Learjet 35A	35A-360	Meridian Silver LLC. Naples, Fl.	(N987DK)
N360MB	80	Gulfstream 3	306	FKA Distributing Co/Homedics Inc. Pontiac, Mi.	N104BK
N360MC	77	Citation 1/SP	501-0036	P C & S LLC/C H Yarber Construction LLC. Bozeman, Mt.	HI-493
N360QS	98	Citation V Ultra	560-0460	NetJets, Port Columbus, Oh.	N5157E
N360RP	79	Citation II	550-0066	Republic Aviation LLC. Boerne, Tx.	N19HU
N360SL	91	Challenger 601-3A	5089	Luft Aviation Charter P/L. Melbourne, VIC. Australia.	N516SM
N361AS	00	Beechjet 400A	RK-287	Munn River LLC. Barnes Municipal, Westfield, Ma.	N4467E
N361DE	85	Citation 1/SP	501-0687	RockStar Aire LLC/Brent Coon & Assocs. Beaumont, Tx.	N361DB
N361EC	03	Citation Excel	560-5515	Entergy Services Inc. Jackson, Ms.	N4118K
N361JR	07	CitationJet CJ2+	525A-0361	Juan Gerardo Rodriguez Garcia,	N5157E
N361K	89	Falcon 900	83	A Joy Aviation LLC. Coral Gables, Fl.	N900NE
N361PJ	74	Learjet 36	36-003	Premier Jets Inc. Hillsboro, Or.	N55CJ
N361QS	95	Citation V Ultra	560-0361	NetJets, Port Columbus, Oh.	N5156B
N361TL	05	CitationJet CJ-3	525B-0061	Talon Capital LLC. Oxford, Ct.	N5262Z
N362FL	99	CitationJet CJ-1	525-0362	National Energy Resorces Inc. Knoxville, Tn.	N362PE
N362FW	80	Learjet 35A	35A-362	Eric Stirling/Guardian Flight, Fairbanks, Ak.	N633DS
N362PT	76	Falcon 10	73	N378C LLC/Falcon Flight Group LLC. Lakewood, Co.	N378C
N362QS	05	Citation Sovereign	680-0051	NetJets, Port Columbus, Oh.	N.....
N362TW	83	Citation III	650-0011	Citation N362TW LLC. Amarillo, Tx.	N311CW
N363CL	05	Challenger 300	20063	The Devonwood Company LLC. Durham, NC.	C-GZET
N363GA	02	Gulfstream G200	063	Gates Group Air LLC/Taga Corp. Salt Lake City, Ut	N20PL
N363NH	97	Astra-1125SPX	097	Pacific Coast Feather Co/BSLCC II LLC. Seattle, Wa.	N273RA
N363QS	02	Citation V Ultra	560-0536	NetJets, Port Columbus, Oh.	
N363TD	78	Citation 1/SP	501-0068	North West Air Travel LLC. Albany, Or.	N68EA
N364CL	81	Learjet 35A	35A-383	Clay Lacy Aviation Inc. Van Nuys, Ca.	N66FE
N364QS	05	Citation Sovereign	680-0062	NetJets, Port Columbus, Oh.	N.....
N365AT	99	Hawker 800XP	258449	Draupnir Services LLC. Sanford, Fl.	N41431
N365EA	91	Citation V	560-0107	Quest II LLC. Moline, Il.	N560RJ
N365GA	94	Astra-1125SP	072	Gulfstream Aerospace Corp. Savannah, Ga.	N32TM
N365GL	96	Learjet 31A	31A-128	Gurley-Leep Oldsmobile Cadillac Inc. Mishawaka, In.	(N469)
N365N	81	Learjet 35A	35A-300	LA Pair LLC. Omaha, Ne.	

Reg	Yr	Type	c/n	Owner/Operator	Prev Regn
☐ N365QS	05	Citation Sovereign	680-0057	NetJets, Port Columbus, Oh.	N51872
☐ N365WA	81	Citation II	550-0333	Wrenair Ltd. Weston Airport, Ireland.	N123GM
☐ N366CJ	07	CitationJet CJ2+	525A-0366	Carson Wealth Management Group Inc. Omaha, Ne.	N.....
☐ N366F	88	Gulfstream 4	1041	Connell Industries Inc. Beverly, Ma.	N433GA
☐ N366JA	82	Gulfstream 3	366	Air Castle Worldwide Jet Charter Inc. Millville, NJ.	N333LX
☐ N366QS	98	Citation V Ultra	560-0466	NetJets, Port Columbus, Oh.	N.....
☐ N366TT	79	Learjet 35A	35A-227	My Jet LLC/Amerimade Technology, Hayward, Ca.	N902JC
☐ N367CJ	07	CitationJet CJ2+	525A-0367	Cessna Aircraft Co. Wichita, Ks.	N.....
☐ N367DA	85	Learjet 35A	35A-599	Global Holding Corp. Hillsboro, Or.	N58GL
☐ N367G	98	BBJ-75V	28579	General Electric Co. Stewart, NY.	
☐ N367HB	81	Citation 1/SP	501-0204	Butler Properties Aviation LLC. Georgetown, SC.	(N345HB)
☐ N367JC	90	Citation V	560-0069	Walter Air Corp. Houston, Tx.	N857WC
☐ N367QS	96	Citation V Ultra	560-0367	NetJets, Port Columbus, Oh.	N5161J
☐ N367WW	82	Westwind-1124	367	Fred Hallmark, Warrior, Al.	N455S
☐ N368AG	89	Gulfstream 4	1087	Blue Sky Group Inc. Van Nuys, Ca.	N110TM
☐ N368BE	00	Citation Encore	560-0546	Basin Electric Power Co-operative, Bismark, ND.	N5151D
☐ N368CE	95	B 737-33A	27456	Club Excellence Inc/Finova Capital Corp. Paramus, NJ.	9M-CHG
☐ N368CS	06	390 Premier 1A	RB-184	PTJ Assocs LLC/Cogent Systems, Burbank, Ca.	
☐ N368D	84	Learjet 25D	25D-368	K & R Enterprises LLC. Shelbyville, Tn.	N8567J
☐ N368EA	92	Beechjet 400A	RK-57	Godfrey Conveyor Co. Elkhart, In.	(N416LX)
☐ N368QS	06	Citation Sovereign	680-0073	NetJets, Port Columbus, Oh.	N5264S
☐ N369B	97	Citation X	750-0030	The Buckle Inc. Kearney, Ne.	(N855WC)
☐ N369BA	80	Learjet 35A	35A-312	369BA LLC. West Columbia, SC.	LV-OFV
☐ N369EA	85	Beechjet 400	RJ-2	Charter Express Inc. Little Rock, Ar.	N402FB
☐ N369QS	06	Citation Sovereign	680-0081	NetJets, Port Columbus, Oh.	N.....
☐ N370BA	04	Citation Excel XLS	560-5525	Credomatic of Florida Inc. Miami, Fl.	N5264A
☐ N370BC	86	B 737-205	23468	BCM Majestic Corp. Dallas, Tx.	HZ-TBA
☐ N370DE	99	Hawker 800XP	258441	Duke Energy Corp. Houston, Tx.	N800PB
☐ N370EK	01	Citation X	750-0185	EWK LLC/Torco Racing Fuels Inc. Kalamazoo, Mi.	N185CX
☐ N370FC	03	Hawker 400XP	RK-378	Franklin Corp. Starkville, Ms.	
☐ N370JJ	07	CitationJet CJ2+	525A-0370	N370JJ LLC/Joe Jackson, Lee's Summit, Mo.	N51993
☐ N370JL	83	Gulfstream 3	401	JGL Aviation LLC/Leprino Aviation Co. Broomfield, Co.	N97AG
☐ N370KP	82	Falcon 50	103	Southern Cross Ranch LLC. Monroe, NC.	N83MP
☐ N370M	05	Citation Excel XLS	560-5565	Murphy Oil Corp. El Dorado, Ar.	N5196U
☐ N370QS	06	Citation Sovereign	680-0099	NetJets, Port Columbus, Oh.	N.....
☐ N370SC	93	Learjet 31A	31A-070	Wal-Mart Stores Inc. Rogers, Ar.	(N270SC)
☐ N370TC	05	Citation Encore	560-0684	Varistar Corp. Fargo, ND.	(N827TV)
☐ N370TP	84	Citation III	650-0059	TP Aviation LLC/American Door Co. DeLand, Fl.	N660AA
☐ N371AS	59	MS 760 Paris	34	Your Aircraft Source LLC. Calhoun, Ga.	34
☐ N371BC	01	BBJ2-8EF	32971	Mideast Jet, Jeddah, Saudi Arabia.	
☐ N371CF	02	Beechjet 400A	RK-351	International Coffee & Fertilizer Trading Co. Guatemala City	N6051C
☐ N371FP	99	Gulfstream 4SP	1371	Fox Paine & Co LLC. Sacramento, Ca.	VP-CIP
☐ N371JC	96	Gulfstream V	505	Sky Beyond Holdings Ltd. Road Town, BVI.	N505AX
☐ N371QS	98	Citation V Ultra	560-0471	NetJets, Port Columbus, Oh.	N5188A
☐ N372BG*	07	Gulfstream G550	5164	Berwind Corp. Philadelphia, Pa.	N764GA
☐ N372BJ	07	BBJ2-7HI	36108	Boeing Co. Seattle, Wa.	
☐ N372G	97	Challenger 604	5351	General Electric Co. Stewart, NY.	N374G
☐ N372QS	07	Citation Sovereign	680-0201	NetJets, Port Columbus, Oh.	N.....
☐ N372WC	96	Citation V Ultra	560-0372	Malone Air Holding LLC. Jacksonville, Fl.	N372QS
☐ N373AB	05	Citation X	750-0243	Salem Aviation, Jeddah, Saudi Arabia.	N5214J
☐ N373AF	98	CitationJet	525-0308	TVPX Inc. Concord, Ma.	N525DR
☐ N373AS	59	MS 760 Paris	36	Your Aircraft Source LLC. Calhoun, Ga.	36
☐ N373DJ	84	Citation III	650-0038	Billion-Air Ltd. Dublin, Ireland.	N366GE
☐ N373DN	75	Falcon 20F-5	324	American Equity Investment Properties LLC. Des Moines, Ia.	N312K
☐ N373G	03	Challenger 604	5556	General Electric Co. Stewart, NY.	C-GLWZ
☐ N373ML	06	Gulfstream G150	204	Mary Rose Aviation Services LLC. Houston, Tx.	4X-WID
☐ N373QS	96	Citation V Ultra	560-0373	NetJets, Port Columbus, Oh.	
☐ N373RB	06	Embraer Legacy 600	14500957	RBGT LLC. Dover, De.	PT-SFF
☐ N373RR	83	Gulfstream 3	373	Roberts Aviation LLC. St Louis, Mo.	N373GS
☐ N373RS	97	Falcon 50EX	259	Kalamazoo Group LLC. Mattawan, Mi.	VP-CHG
☐ N374AS	59	MS 760 Paris	38	Your Aircraft Source LLC. Calhoun, Ga.	38
☐ N374G	98	Challenger 604	5368	General Electric Co. Stewart, NY.	N368G
☐ N374PS	70	Gulfstream II SP	92	Without Walls International Church, Tampa, Fl.	N629TD
☐ N374QS	98	Citation V Ultra	560-0475	NetJets, Port Columbus, Oh.	
☐ N375AS	59	MS 760 Paris	44	Your Aircraft Source LLC. Calhoun, Ga.	44
☐ N375DT	03	Hawker 400XP	RK-372	CarDan Air Inc/Towbin Management Inc. Las Vegas, Nv.	N6172V

Reg	Yr	Type	c/n	Owner/Operator	Prev Regn
❏ N375E	92	Citation VII	650-7014	Cessna Aircraft Co. Wichita, Ks.	(N714VP)
❏ N375G	07	Global Express	9242	General Electric Co. Stewart, NY.	(OH-PPS)
❏ N375LT	83	Gulfstream 3	375	Pacific Institute Aviation Corp. Seattle, Wa.	(N75GJ)
❏ N375MD	78	JetStar 2	5227	GLE Aircraft LLC. Fort Lauderdale, Fl.	N117AJ
❏ N375QS	96	Citation V Ultra	560-0375	NetJets, Port Columbus, Oh.	
❏ N375WB	04	Challenger 300	20025	White Birch Aviation LLC. Oxford, Ct.	EC-JEG
❏ N376D	81	Sabre-65	465-76	Salyer Farms Airport, Corcoran, Ca.	N65L
❏ N376G	05	Global 5000	9164	General Electric Co. Stewart, NY.	C-FCSF
❏ N376HA	82	Learjet 35A	35A-477	Bluegrass Aviation Partners LLC. Bardstown, Ky.	N608GF
❏ N376MB	01	Learjet 31A	31A-234	MB Aviation Corp. Fairfield, Oh.	N5028E
❏ N376PJ	83	Gulfstream 3	376	Asjet Aviation Inc. Chino, Ca.	N376EJ
❏ N376QS	07	Citation Sovereign	680-0180	NetJets, Port Columbus, Oh.	N5124F
❏ N376SC	05	Falcon 2000EX EASY	57	Steelcase Inc. Grand Rapids, Mi.	F-WWMF
❏ N377GM	04	Falcon 2000EX EASY	32	Propinvest Asset Management LLP. London, UK.	N999BE
❏ N377GS	01	CitationJet CJ-2	525A-0077	Grand Sport Leasing LLC. Cincinnati-Lunken, Oh.	N5148N
❏ N377JC	98	Hawker 800XP2	258349	KForce Professional Staffing, Tampa, Fl.	C-FEPC
❏ N377QS	07	Citation Sovereign	680-0187	NetJets, Port Columbus, Oh.	N5135A
❏ N377RX	83	Gulfstream 3	377	Sea-Ya Enterprises LLC. Long Beach, Ca.	N760AC
❏ N377SC	00	Falcon 900EX	66	Steelcase Inc. Grand Rapids, Mi.	F-WWFA
❏ N377SF	98	Citation X	750-0068	Mandan LLC. Chicago, Il.	N5100J
❏ N378AS	59	MS 760 Paris	45	Your Aircraft Source LLC. Calhoun, Ga.	45
❏ N378BC	02	BBJ-7ES	33474	Boeing Co. Seattle, Wa.	
❏ N378D	75	Sabre-60A	306-101	L'Avoion Inc. Mojave, Ca.	N376D
❏ N378L	02	Gulfstream G550	5008	Abraxis Bioscience Inc. Van Nuys, Ca.	XA-EOF
❏ N378QS	06	Citation Sovereign	680-0103	NetJets, Port Columbus, Oh.	N.....
❏ N378SE*	83	Gulfstream 3	378	N378SE LLC. Boise, Id.	N444KM
❏ N379DB	07	CitationJet CJ-3	525B-0191	DRW Aviation LLC. Zelienople, Pa.	N52626
❏ N379G	06	Global Express	9199	General Electric Co. Stewart, NY.	(N799TS)
❏ N379QS	98	Citation V Ultra	560-0479	NetJets, Port Columbus, Oh.	N5125J
❏ N379XX	83	Gulfstream 3	394	Nexxus Products Inc. Santa Barbara, Ca. 'Jheri Reading'	N311GA
❏ N380AK	97	Citation Bravo	550-0809	Smith Management Corp. Dallas, Tx.	N300AK
❏ N380BA	05	Learjet 60	60-292	Credomatic Air Services LLC. Miami, Fl.	N5011L
❏ N380CF	77	Sabre-75A	380-51	Habari Inc. Rancho Cucamonga, Ca.	N382LS
❏ N380CR	07	CitationJet CJ1+	525-0643	50 North Aviation Inc. Leeds-Bradford, UK.	N5228Z
❏ N380FP	77	Sabre-75A	380-54	Fowler Marketing Express LLC. Fresno, Ca.	N910BH
❏ N380GA	07	Gulfstream G450	4080	Everbest Technology Enterprise Co. Hong Kong.	
❏ N380GK	76	Sabre-75A	380-44	Jet Harbor Inc. Fort Lauderdale, Fl.	N2440G
❏ N380GP	02	Hawker 800XP2	258591	Titan Aviation LLC/Godwin Pappas LLP. Dallas-Love, Tx.	N380GG
❏ N380JR	04	Hawker 400XP	RK-411	AJR Development Inc. Pontiac, Mi.	N611XP
❏ N380M	00	Citation Excel	560-5111	Charles H Murphy Family Investments, El Dorado, Ar.	N522CC
❏ N380QS	06	Citation Sovereign	680-0089	NetJets, Port Columbus, Oh.	N.....
❏ N380RD	89	Citation V	560-0026	Aviation Charter Inc. Eden Prairie, Mn.	N350RD
❏ N381BJ	78	Citation	501-0286	Private Travel LLC. Owensboro, Ky. (was 500-0381).	(N789AA)
❏ N381CW	86	Citation III	650-0111	N650RJ LLC. Marshall, Mn.	(N381EM)
❏ N381QS	06	Citation Sovereign	680-0097	NetJets/Marquis Jet Partners Inc. Port Columbus, Oh.	N.....
❏ N381VP	80	Citation II	550-0381	Gon LLC. Wilmington, De. (was 551-0049).	N391KC
❏ N382AA	66	Jet Commander	56	Mach Aero International Corp. Tulsa, Ok.	(N53AA)
❏ N382EM	02	CitationJet CJ-1	525-0496	Rotorwing LLC/The Klein Group, Coldwater, Mi.	N5223P
❏ N382G	02	Gulfstream G200	079	General Dynamics Corp. Pontiac, Mi.	N379GA
❏ N382QS	96	Citation V Ultra	560-0382	NetJets, Port Columbus, Oh.	
❏ N382TC	75	Learjet 35	35-039	Tulsair Beechcraft Inc. Tulsa, Ok.	N1HP
❏ N383LS	98	Gulfstream V	544	Las Vegas Sands Inc. Las Vegas, Nv.	N910DC
❏ N383MB	03	Challenger 604	5568	Zulu Equipment LLC. Seattle, Wa.	N604JC
❏ N383QS	98	Citation V Ultra	560-0483	NetJets, Port Columbus, Oh.	
❏ N383SF	96	Astra-1125SPX	083	Smithfield Foods Inc. Newport News, Va.	
❏ N384BB	86	Gulfstream 3	496	384BB Aviation LLC. Dallas, Tx.	VP-CNP
❏ N384CF	81	Learjet 35A	35A-384	CF Palwaukee LLC. Palwaukee, Il.	N811DD
❏ N384EM	87	Citation III	650-0144	WWF Air LLC. Newport Beach, Ca.	N384CW
❏ N384GA	07	Gulfstream G200	184	Gulfstream Aerospace LP. Dallas-Love, Tx.	4X-C..
❏ N384JW*	98	Learjet 60	60-130	Winner Aviation Corp. Vienna, Oh.	N90MC
❏ N384K	78	Falcon 20F-5B	387	Quality Shipyards Inc/Tidewater Inc. New Orleans, La.	N676DW
❏ N384MP	89	Challenger 601-3A	5047	CR Holdings LLC. Chicago-Midway, Il.	N900SS
❏ N384PS	78	Falcon 20F-5	384	N384PS LLC/Lynxxjet International Inc. Georgetown, Tx.	N82TN
❏ N384QS	06	Citation Sovereign	680-0110	NetJets, Port Columbus, Oh.	N.....
❏ N384TC*	88	BAe 125/800A	NA0428	Tulsair Beechcraft Inc. Tulsa, Ok.	N244JM
❏ N385CT	04	Challenger 604	5592	Caterpillar Inc. Peoria, Il.	C-GLYH

Reg   Yr   Type   c/n   Owner/Operator   Prev Regn

Reg	Yr	Type	c/n	Owner/Operator	Prev Regn
N385EM	87	Citation III	650-0145	WFBNW NA. Salt Lake City, Ut. (trustor ?).	N385CW
N385MG	05	Citation Excel XLS	560-5556	M/G Transport Services/The Midland Co. Amelia, Oh.	N.....
N385PB	98	Beechjet 400A	RK-217	Moen Inc. Cleveland, Oh.	N217MB
N385QS	06	Citation Sovereign	680-0115	NetJets, Port Columbus, Oh.	N5250P
N385RC	85	Learjet 55	55-117	Tulsair Beechcraft Inc. Tulsa, Ok.	N155RB
N386AM	80	Citation II/SP	551-0191	S F Aircraft Inc. St Thomas, USVI.	N127KR
N386CH	01	Embraer EMB-135ER	145467	Intel Corp/Executive Jet Management Inc. Cincinnati, Oh.	PT-...
N386CM	80	Learjet 35A	35A-283	Indiana Aircraft Charter LLC. Scherville, In.	N205FL
N386QS	98	Citation V Ultra	560-0486	NetJets, Port Columbus, Oh.	
N386RF	00	CitationJet CJ-1	525-0386	Lariat Ranch LLC. Tulsa, Ok.	N45MH
N386RL	83	Westwind-1124	386	Jet Ex Inc/R W Lynch Co. Concord, Ca.	N348DH
N387HA	79	Learjet 35A	35A-251	CL Air LLC/Clay Lacy Aviation Inc. Van Nuys, Ca.	N251CT
N387PA	01	Gulfstream G100	145	Dayco Holding Corp. Fort Lauderdale, Fl.	N264GA
N387PC	05	Challenger 300	20087	PNC Financial Services Group LLC. Allegheny County, Pa.	C-FGVK
N387QS	06	Citation Sovereign	680-0119	NetJets, Port Columbus, Oh.	N5260M
N387RE	88	Citation II	550-0575	McNeill & Assocs Inc. Germantown, Tn.	N337RE
N387SC	80	Citation II	550-0142	Cavalear LLC. Boca Raton, Fl.	PT-LCR
N387SV	06	Citation Encore+	560-0759	BTI Aviation LLC/Central Bancorp. Jeffco, Co.	N.....
N388AC	06	Gulfstream G550	5125	A C Travel LLC/Franklin Templeton Investments, San Mateo.	N550GD
N388BS	99	Hawker 800XP	258423	Tanara Inc. Dallas-Love Field, Tx.	N925JF
N388CA	88	Gulfstream 4	1034	S/A Holdings LLC. Oxford, Ct.	N841PA
N388CW	86	Gulfstream 3	489	Sierra Madre Inc. Dover, De.	N888CW
N388DB	83	Challenger 601	3016	Barnes Aviation LLC. Dallas, Tx.	VP-BIE
N388FW	07	CitationJet CJ1+	525-0656	Gilardi Aviation Ltd. Sidney, Oh.	N5069E
N388GM	76	Citation	500-0323	Thomas Pacific Construction Inc. San Rafael, Ca.	(N268GM)
N388GS	99	Falcon 900EX	55	Citigroup Corporate Aviation, White Plains, NY.	(N399CG)
N388LS	83	TriStar 500	1249	Las Vegas Sands Inc. Las Vegas, Nv.	HZ-HM6
N388MM	86	Gulfstream 3	490	AC Travel LLC. San Mateo, Ca.	N28R
N388PD	87	Learjet 35A	35A-630	Dooney & Bourke PR Inc. Yabucoa, PR.	N742P
N388PS	02	CitationJet CJ-1	525-0492	P & S Aerowest Inc. Forney, Tx.	N492CJ
N388QS	06	Citation Sovereign	680-0113	NetJets/Marquis Jet Partners Inc. Port Columbus, Oh.	N.....
N388SB	81	Citation II	550-0245	Kollsman Inc. Merrimack, NH.	N505GP
N388TC	89	Falcon 50	196	Tulsair Beechcraft Inc. Tulsa, Ok.	VP-BSA
N388WS	06	Challenger 300	20108	Marvell Semiconductor Inc. Santa Clara, Ca.	C-FIDU
N388WW	83	Westwind-1124	388	KLSF LLC. Cherry Hills, Co.	N900H
N389AT	79	Learjet 25D	25D-297	Spirit Wing Aviation Ltd. Guthrie, Ok.	N24KW
N389KA	81	Learjet 35A	35A-389	L F S T LLC. Las Cruces, NM.	N79AX
N389LS	83	TriStar 500	1250	Las Vegas Sands Inc. Las Vegas, Nv.	HZ-HM5
N389QS	07	Citation Sovereign	680-0149	NetJets, Port Columbus, Oh.	N5030U
N390AJ	81	Citation II	550-0326	Arstar Inc. Fort Lauderdale, Fl.	(N390JP)
N390BR	04	390 Premier 1	RB-118	Hawker Beechcraft Corp. Wichita, Ks.	B-8018
N390DB	06	Challenger 300	20131	DB Challenger Inc/Vektra Corp. Podgorica, Montenegro.	C-FJQZ
N390DP	02	390 Premier 1	RB-34	Davison Transport Inc. Ruston, La.	
N390GG	07	Learjet 45	45-325	AG Aviation LLC. Oak Brook, Il.	N40085
N390GS	07	390 Premier 1A	RB-231	Hawker Beechcraft Corp. Wichita, Ks.	
N390JK	01	390 Premier 1	RB-39	Kelley Aviation Associates Inc. Amarillo, Tx.	N39KT
N390JV	05	390 Premier 1	RB-129	Jon Vesely, Du Page, Il.	N6129U
N390JW	01	390 Premier 1	RB-78	A & G Coal Co. Lonesome Pine, Va.	
N390PR	04	390 Premier 1	RB-113	Pride Companies, Abilene, Tx.	N113BR
N390PT	05	390 Premier 1A	RB-135	XOJET Inc. Sacramento, Ca.	N3735V
N390QS	98	Citation V Ultra	560-0490	NetJets, Port Columbus, Oh.	
N390RA	98	390 Premier 1	RB-1	Hawker Beechcraft Corp. Wichita, Ks. (Ff 23 Dec 98).	
N390TC	99	390 Premier 1	RB-3	Hawker Beechcraft Corp. Wichita, Ks. (Ff 17 Sep 99).	
N391AN	79	Citation II	550-0084	Prebul Chrysler Jeep Dodge Kia, Nashville. (was 551-0129).	(N467MW)
N391BC	99	Citation Bravo	550-0909	Dorado Aviation LLC. Guyano, PR.	N44KW
N391DT	89	Citation II	550-0620	DWL Holding Co. Oklahoma City, Ok.	(N391DH)
N391KK	05	Citation Sovereign	680-0074	Kojaian Management Corp. Pontiac, Mi.	N5105F
N391QS	98	Citation V Ultra	560-0493	NetJets, Port Columbus, Oh.	
N391SH	83	Gulfstream 3	392	Flyjock LLC/Reach Media Inc. Irving, Tx.	N801WC
N391TC	86	BAe 125/800A	258063	Tulsair Beechcraft Inc. Tulsa, Ok.	N74ND
N391W	01	Challenger 300	20091	Worthington Industries Inc. Columbus, Oh.	C-FGWF
N392FV	84	Challenger 601	3032	Sugar Pine Aviation LLC. Medford, Or.	N111GX
N392QS	97	Citation V Ultra	560-0429	NetJets, Port Columbus, Oh.	
N392RG	99	CitationJet	525-0340	Whitt Family Interests Inc. Slinger, Wi.	
N392SM	00	CitationJet CJ-1	525-0392	Pacific Flight Services LLC. Santa Barbara, Ca.	N5165T
N393BB	07	Hawker 400XP	RK-542	Brown & Brown Inc. Daytona Beach, Fl.	N542XP

Reg	Yr	Type	c/n	Owner/Operator	Prev Regn
☐ N393BZ	99	Global Express	9022	IAC Falcon Holdings LLC & T16 Holdings LLC. New York, NY.	N226HD
☐ N393E	85	Citation S/II	S550-0053	Tarp-It Inc. Ellensburg, Wa.	N1223N
☐ N393GH	99	Beechjet 400A	RK-240	Jet Linx/Riverton Management Resources LLC. Ralston, Ne.	N150TF
☐ N393JC	86	Citation III	650-0113	Phoenix Air LLC. Columbia, SC.	N393CW
☐ N393QS	96	Citation V Ultra	560-0393	NetJets, Port Columbus, Oh.	N5156V
☐ N393S	83	Falcon 20F	473	Sunoco Inc. Philadelphia, Pa.	N473SH
☐ N398BB	88	Beechjet 400	RJ-39	Hawker Beechcraft Corp. Wichita, Ks.	N393BB
☐ N394AJ	93	Citation V	560-0230	Copart Inc. Benicia, Ca.	N169CP
☐ N394AK	01	Gulfstream 4SP	1470	Roxann Management Corp. Farmingdale, NY.	N34UH
☐ N394BB	03	Hawker 400XP	RK-364	Brown & Brown Inc. Daytona Beach, Fl.	
☐ N394CK	94	Citation V Ultra	560-0270	Lone Wolf Aviation LLC. Brighton, Mi.	N4FC
☐ N394GA	07	Gulfstream G550	5194	Gulfstream Aerospace Corp. Savannah, Ga.	
☐ N394PA	82	Learjet 35A	35A-462	Schwyhart Holdings LLC. Carrollton, Tx.	N135TP
☐ N394QS	96	Citation V Ultra	560-0394	NetJets, Port Columbus, Oh.	N5093Y
☐ N394TR	94	Gulfstream 4SP	1252	Triarc Companies Inc. Stewart, NY.	N252C
☐ N395BC	04	Learjet 45	45-258	Teknon LLC. Carlsbad, Ca.	N45LJ
☐ N395EJ	76	HS 125/600B	256060	T-Bird Aviation Inc Tampa, Fl.	N422TR
☐ N395GA	81	Sabre-65	465-65	Christopher's Jet World LLC. Golden, Co.	(N600WE)
☐ N395HE	91	BAe 125/800A	NA0466	Sewanee Investments LLC/Houston Energy Inc. Houston, tx.	N466AE
☐ N395LJ	94	Learjet 31A	31A-095	Wal-Mart Stores Inc. Rogers, Ar.	OK-AJD
☐ N395MY	81	Learjet 35A	35A-395	Young Properties LLC. Vail, Co.	N246CM
☐ N395QS	98	Citation V Ultra	560-0496	NetJets, Port Columbus, Oh.	
☐ N395TJ	83	Westwind-Two	395	Alaska Flight Services LLC. Tuscaloosa, Al.	N395SR
☐ N395WB	83	Diamond 1A	A045SA	Watts Brothers Cable Construction, Owensboro, Ky.	N545TP
☐ N395WJ	03	Citation Excel	560-5330	Agile Aviation LLC. San Jose, Ca.	(N638Q)
☐ N396BB	06	Citation Sovereign	680-0123	Brown & Brown Inc. Daytona Beach, Fl.	N52582
☐ N396CF	70	Gulfstream II SP	96	Hollywood Realty Inc. Van Nuys, Ca.	XA-EYA
☐ N396CJ	07	CitationJet CJ-3	525B-0196	Cessna Aircraft Co. Wichita, Ks.	N.....
☐ N396M	82	Citation II	550-0362	Peter Sturdivant LLC. Hailey, Id.	(N440PJ)
☐ N396NS	99	Gulfstream 4SP	1395	National Air Services, Jeddah, Saudi Arabia.	N961SV
☐ N396QS	96	Citation V Ultra	560-0396	NetJets, Port Columbus, Oh.	N50938
☐ N396U	98	Gulfstream 4SP	1350	Unisys Corp. Trenton, NJ.	N330GA
☐ N396V	80	Challenger 600S	1009	4KS Aviation III Inc. Dallas, Tx.	144606
☐ N397AT	00	Learjet 45	45-105	ITC Service Co. Valley, Al.	N105LJ
☐ N397BC	02	Citation Excel	560-5291	Best Air Inc/Best Chairs Inc. Huntingburg, In.	N829JQ
☐ N397DR	86	Citation III	650-0107	Raab Air LLC. Santa Barbara, Ca.	N397CW
☐ N397JJ	98	Gulfstream 4SP	1354	ACE INA/Recovery Services International Inc. Philadelphia..	N397J
☐ N397QS	07	Citation Sovereign	680-0144	Marquis Jet Partners Inc. Port Columbus, Oh.	N.....
☐ N397SC	72	Citation Eagle	500-0019	B&B Leasing LLC/Independent Stave Co. Lebanon, Mo.	OB-1280
☐ N398AC	93	Falcon 50	240	Iowa Land & Building Co. Cedar Rapids, Ia.	(N200BN)
☐ N398DL	85	Citation III	650-0098	Transporte Citation CA. Venezuela.	N398CW
☐ N398LS	98	Citation Bravo	550-0853	Les Schwab Warehouse Center Inc. Prineville, Or.	N5086W
☐ N398QS	99	Citation V Ultra	560-0522	NetJets, Port Columbus, Oh.	
☐ N398RS	98	Citation Excel	560-5009	Roaring Springs Ranch Inc. Portland, Or.	N52113
☐ N399AP	83	Gulfstream 3	399	Arrow Plane LLC. Salt Lake City, Ut.	N528AP
☐ N399BA	81	Learjet 35A	35A-371	Bankair Inc. West Columbia, SC.	LV-ALF
☐ N399DM	81	Diamond 1A	A008SA	Diamond Jet Aviation,	(N56SK)
☐ N399FG	77	Falcon 20F-5	373	EPC Aircraft Sales LLC. Bellevue, Wa.	N620CC
☐ N399FL	83	Challenger 600S	1083	Challenger 600 LLC/The Air Group, Chesterfield, Mo.	N471SB
☐ N399G	96	CitationJet	525-0183	Dineair Corp. Red Bank, NJ.	N97CJ
☐ N399GA	07	Gulfstream G550	5199	Gulfstream Aerospace Corp. Savannah, Ga.	
☐ N399GS	00	Global Express	9074	Citigroup Corporate Aviation, White Plains, NY.	C-GHEA
☐ N399MM	82	Diamond 1A	A017SA	H2 Enterprises LLC. Sarasota, Fl.	(N33MM)
☐ N399QS	99	Citation V Ultra	560-0510	NetJets, Port Columbus, Oh.	
☐ N399RA	98	Beechjet 400A	RK-200	MaLeCo, Salem, Or.	VP-CKK
☐ N399RW	99	Learjet 31A	31A-182	Sky Lodge LLC. Newport, RI.	N527GP
☐ N399SF	07	Citation Excel XLS	560-5718	MEU Holdings WI LLC. Appleton, Wi.	N.....
☐ N399W	01	Citation X	750-0171	Williams International LLC. Waterford, Mi.	N51160
☐ N399WB	81	Challenger 600S	1025	JDP CM & E LLC. Houston, Tx.	N711GA
☐ N400AJ	97	Beechjet 400A	RK-137	Schuele German Technologies GmbH. Bad Radolfszell, Germany	N1117Z
☐ N400CC	88	Gulfstream 4	1046	KaiserAir Inc. Oakland, Ca.	N119K
☐ N400CP	00	Gulfstream G100	131	Promociones RH CA. Caracas, Venezuela.	N57GX
☐ N400CT	98	Beechjet 400A	RK-179	Forest River Inc. Elkhart, In.	N75GK
☐ N400CV	07	CitationJet CJ2+	525A-0396	Cessna Aircraft Co. Wichita, Ks.	N.....
☐ N400D	70	Gulfstream II SP	100	Gulfstream 2 100 Holding Co. Wilmington, De.	XB-FVL
☐ N400DW	88	Beechjet 400	RJ-40	RSP Air LLC. Manhasset, NY.	N3240M

Reg	Yr	Type	c/n	Owner/Operator	Prev Regn
☐ N400EP	70	Learjet 24XR	24XR-215	Abofamalom Inc. Palm Harbor, Fl.	(N57JR)
☐ N400ES*	07	Challenger 605	5727	Bombardier Aerospace Corp. Windsor Locks, Ct.	C-FOXV
☐ N400FJ	02	Gulfstream 4SP	1494	Fletcher Jones Management Group Inc. Las Vegas, Nv.	N494GA
☐ N400FR	70	HS 125/400A	NA751	Romair Inc. Fort Lauderdale Executive, Fl.	HC-BTT
☐ N400FT	95	Beechjet 400A	RK-101	Featherlite Aviation Co. Cresco, Ia.	ZS-JRO
☐ N400GG	07	CitationJet CJ-3	525B-0195	Cessna Aircraft Co. Wichita, Ks.	N5202D
☐ N400GJ	87	Beechjet 400	RJ-23	C C Medflight Inc. Lawrenceville, Ga.	N3123T
☐ N400GK	82	Diamond 1	A019SA	BLB Construction Inc. Baton Rouge, La.	N319DM
☐ N400GR	01	Beechjet 400A	RK-335	Texas State Bank, McAllen, Tx.	N5015B
☐ N400GX	99	Global Express	9037	Spitfire Aviation/MicroStrategy Inc. Dulles, Va.	N777VU
☐ N400HD	98	Beechjet 400A	RK-191	Two Rivers Aviation LLC. Sioux City, SD.	N367EA
☐ N400HH	82	Diamond 1	A025SA	400HH Inc. Lebanon, NJ.	N1843A
☐ N400HS	01	Beechjet 400A	RK-314	H S Aero Services LLC/Condor Express Corp. Danbury, Ct.	N5014G
☐ N400HT	04	CitationJet CJ-2	525A-0208	Hudson Thompson Development LLC. Georgetown, De.	N.....
☐ N400J	97	Gulfstream 4SP	1330	Johnson & Johnson, Mercer County Airport, NJ.	N324GA
☐ N400JD	04	Citation X	750-0235	Deere & Co. Moline, Il.	N.....
☐ N400JE	77	Learjet 35A	35A-120	AirNet Systems Inc. Columbus, Oh.	(N400RV)
☐ N400JH	93	Citation VI	650-0226	Hans Management Corp/FlightWorks, Kennesaw, Ga.	N1302A
☐ N400KE	81	Falcon 50	54	Top Ride LLC/McKinley Capital Management, Anchorage, Ak.	N51MJ
☐ N400KP	01	Beechjet 400A	RK-308	Kingston Aviation LLC. Idaho Falls, Id.	N51008
☐ N400KS	89	Citation V	560-0041	4KS Aviation III Inc. Dallas, Tx.	VH-NTH
☐ N400LX	97	Citation V Ultra	560-0453	L J Associates Inc. Latrobe, Pa.	N453CV
☐ N400M	73	Gulfstream II SP	132	Lorien Aviation Inc. Van Nuys, Ca.	N873GA
☐ N400MC	97	Citation V Ultra	560-0440	Clayton Aviation/RCM Industries Inc. Il. (was 560-0424).	PT-WSN
☐ N400MP	99	Gulfstream 4SP	1369	Tisma Inc. Dulles, Va.	N469G
☐ N400MR	07	Hawker 4000	RC-12	Martin Rowley, Bournemouth-Hurn, UK.	
☐ N400MS	72	Learjet 24D	24D-246	Butler National Inc. Newton, Ks.	N500MS
☐ N400MV	00	Beechjet 400A	RK-286	Michigan Veneer Ltd. Pewamo, Mi.	
☐ N400NF	84	Diamond 1A	A091SA	Heartland Management Co. Topeka, Ks.	N400HG
☐ N400NR	76	Sabre-75A	380-41	JHM Leasing Corp. Pittsfield, Ma.	N400N
☐ N400NS	91	Beechjet 400A	RK-28	Nextant Aerospace LLC. Mayfield Heights, Oh.	(N902PC)
☐ N400PR	69	HS 125/400A	NA732	Aircraft Aloft II LLC. Spring, Tx.	N732TS
☐ N400PU	97	Beechjet 400A	RK-156	Purdue Research Foundation, West Lafayette, In.	N2056E
☐ N400RE	90	Citation III	650-0199	Evernham Motorsports LLC. Statesville, NC.	N527CP
☐ N400RG	67	B 727-22	19149	MBI Aviation Inc. Wilmington, De. 'Al Bashaer'	N7085U
☐ N400RM	75	Citation Longwing SP	500-0290	ICSA Labs/Paris Jet Inc. Mechanicsburg, Pa.	N896MB
☐ N400RS	74	Sabre-75A	380-25	R2D2 LLC. Stuart, Fl.	N13NH
☐ N400RY	02	Beechjet 400A	RK-355	Robert Yates Racing Inc. Concord, NC.	N767SB
☐ N400SF	98	Beechjet 400A	RK-221	400A LLC. Wilmington, De.	N400KG
☐ N400SH	95	Beechjet 400A	RK-100	Davisco Foods International Inc. Le Sueur, Mn.	N1570B
☐ N400TB	92	Challenger 601-3A	5120	Taco Bell Corp. Santa Ana, Ca.	(N500TB)
☐ N400TE	98	Beechjet 400A	RK-187	MRSA Jets LLC/Excel Aviation Inc. Braintree, Ma.	N2298S
☐ N400TL	01	Beechjet 400A	RK-339	LGI Training LLC/Lipar Group Development, Conroe, Tx.	N439CW
☐ N400UF	82	Diamond 1A	A022SA	Shamrock Capital Corp LLC. San Angelo, Tx.	(N397SL)
☐ N400VC	78	Learjet 25XR	25XR-235	Newell Recycling/N W Aircraft LLC. San Antonio, Tx.	N400JS
☐ N400VP	96	Beechjet 400A	RK-110	Skytravel LLC. Atlanta, Ga.	(N400A)
☐ N400WD	00	CitationJet CJ-2	525A-0002	WD Forty Something LLC. Hillsboro, Or.	N765CT
☐ N400WK	93	Citation VI	650-0231	Truck Body Aviation Inc. Lynchburg, Va.	(N650FA)
☐ N400WY	85	Gulfstream 3	467	C & S Aviation LLC. Dallas, Tx.	N551AC
☐ N401AB	70	HS 125/731	NA747	Catex LLC. Oak Hill, Va.	P4-AOB
☐ N401AJ	74	Learjet 25B	25B-171	Travel Lear Charter Service Inc. Oklahoma City, Ok.	N888LR
☐ N401CS	05	CitationJet CJ-3	525B-0030	CitationShares Sales Inc. White Plains, NY.	N5145P
☐ N401DP	81	Learjet 25D	25D-329	Moana Management LLC. Sacramento, Ca.	N83TE
☐ N401EG	04	Learjet 40	45-2021	A Lakin & Sons Inc. Chicago, Il.	N5013U
☐ N401FF	92	BAe 1000A	259021	Interjet Inc. Addison, Tx.	N137RP
☐ N401FT	03	Gulfstream G400	1523	EJS-Executive Jet Shares Inc. Brazil.	N423GA
☐ N401GJ	87	Beechjet 400	RJ-26	Desert Aviation LLC. Salt Lake City, Ut.	N91MT
☐ N401HB	07	Gulfstream G550	5173	Gulfstream Aerospace Corp. Savannah, Ga.	N673GA
☐ N401HF	03	Gulfstream G550	5039	Central Management Services Inc. Camarillo, Ca.	N939GA
☐ N401JW	75	Falcon 10	46	Hudson Flight Ltd. Pampa, Tx.	N908RF
☐ N401KC	01	Citation Bravo	550-0969	LynCo Trust, Rapid City, SD.	N5228J
☐ N401KH	95	Citation V Ultra	560-0304	Elliott Aviation Aircraft Sales Inc. Des Moines, Ia.	N47VC
☐ N401LG	01	CitationJet CJ-2	525A-0037	FB Aire LLC/Fletcher Bright Co. Chattanooga, Tn..	N5221Y
☐ N401LJ	02	Learjet 40	45-2001	Wall Design Inc. Irvine, Ca. (Ff 5 Sep 02).	N40LJ
☐ N401MC	89	Citation V	560-0034	Moyer Aviation Inc. Ulysses, Ks.	N895LD
☐ N401NK	99	Challenger 604	5409	PACPAL LLC. Seattle, Wa.	C-GETU

Reg	Yr	Type	c/n	Owner/Operator	Prev Regn
N401PG	08	Citation Sovereign	680-0221	Cessna Aircraft Co. Wichita, Ks.	N.....
N401PP	05	390 Premier 1	RB-130	Brinkman Constructors, Spirit of St Louis, Mo.	N5030V
N401QS	00	Gulfstream 4SP	1408	NetJets, Port Columbus, Oh.	(N448QS)
N401RJ	94	Challenger 601-3R	5155	RJJ Aviation LLC. Las Vegas, Nv.	N342TC
N401SR	03	Gulfstream G450	4001	Gulfstream Aerospace Corp. Savannah, Ga (Ff 30 Apr 03)	
N401WT	93	Astra-1125SP	068	MESH LLC. Hillsboro, Or.	N1125Z
N402AC	66	HS 125/1A-522	25103	Lomax International Inc. Miami, Fl.	N60HU
N402FB	99	Beechjet 400A	RK-255	Farm Bureau Life Insurance Co. Des Moines, Ia.	N960JJ
N402FG	90	Falcon 900B	87	Flex Air Ltd/Flightstar Corp. Chicago-Midway, Il.	N33GG
N402FT	03	Gulfstream G400	1527	EJS-Executive Jet Shares Inc. Brazil.	N327GA
N402GS	93	Beechjet 400A	RK-71	Commonwealth Aviation Services Inc. Richmond, Va.	N73BL
N402JP	95	Gulfstream 4SP	1283	Colleen Corp. Philadelphia, Pa.	N401JL
N402LM	03	Gulfstream G200	082	Lockheed Martin Corp. Baltimore, Md.	N282GA
N403BG	77	HS 125/700A	NA0202	BG3 LLC/Sun Steel Co. Chicago, Il.	N727TA
N403CT	06	Hawker 850XP	258818	Forest River Inc. Elkhart, In.	(N827LX)
N403DP	81	Learjet 35A	35A-446	Palm Air, Memphis, Tn.	N794GC
N403ET	99	Citation V Ultra	560-0535	Yardelle Investment Management LLC. Fort Worth, Tx.	(N57ML)
N403FF	93	BAe 1000A	259038	1489 LLC. Elmira-Corning, NY.	N107RP
N403FW	81	Learjet 35A	35A-403	Alliance Air Parts Inc. Oklahoma City, Ok.	N100HW
N403GA	07	Gulfstream G200	173	Gulfstream Aerospace LP. Dallas-Love, Tx.	4X-CVI
N403JP	85	Beechjet 400	RJ-7	Patterson Capital Corp. Van Nuys, Ca. (was A1007SA).	N85BN
N403LM	03	Gulfstream G200	083	Lockheed Martin Corp. Baltimore, Md.	N283GA
N403QS	99	Gulfstream 4SP	1403	NetJets, Port Columbus, Oh.	N403GA
N403TB	93	Gulfstream 4	1191	Knickerbocker Aviation LLC. Hollis, NH.	N317MB
N403W	84	Westwind-1124	403	NIBCO Inc. Elkhart, In.	4X-CUH
N403WY	82	Challenger 600S	1059	K-N Partners LLC. Houston, Tx.	N103HB
N404AC	99	Gulfstream 4SP	1384	Apache Corp/Apache Aviation Inc. Houston, Tx.	(HZ-KS3)
N404BL	03	Hawker 400XP	RK-367	Bausch & Lomb Inc. Rochester, NY.	
N404BS	82	Citation II	550-0403	Barry Real Estate Co. DeKalb, Ga. (was 551-0058).	N362CP
N404BT	99	Citation Excel	560-5038	BellSouth Corp. Atlanta-Fulton County, Ga.	N5214K
N404CS	05	CitationJet CJ-3	525B-0033	CitationShares Sales Inc. White Plains, NY.	N5243K
N404EL	05	Learjet 40	45-2033	Aerodynamics LLC/Dynamic Industries Inc. Lafayette, La.	
N404F	99	Falcon 900EX	49	WCF-William C Ford Aircraft Corp. Detroit, Mi.	N949EX
N404G	90	Citation V	560-0095	Cushing Stone Co. Amsterdam, NY.	N707CV
N404HG	88	Challenger 601-3A	5017	Kimberly-Clark Corp. Atlanta-DeKalb, Ga.	N77058
N404HR	81	Westwind-Two	324	Campus Crest Group, Greensboro, NC.	(N884MT)
N404HS	99	Gulfstream 4SP	1404	H & S Ventures LLC. Newport Beach, Ca.	N404HA
N404JM	06	390 Premier 1A	RB-167	Premier Real Estate Management LLC. Brookfield, Wi.	N71167
N404JW	74	Falcon 10	29	Safari Air LLC. Easton, Md.	N999F
N404LN	92	Citation V	560-0190	HASBRO LLC. Pontiac, Mi.	(N214LS)
N404M	00	Gulfstream V	654	Bristol-Myers Squibb Co. White Plains, NY.	VP-BLA
N404MM	07	Citation Excel XLS	560-5737	Martin Marietta Materials Inc. Raleigh-Durham, NC.	N.....
N404MS	00	Beechjet 400A	RK-283	Mississippi State University Foundation, Starkville, Ms.	N600SB
N404PG	81	Westwind-Two	358	The Powell Lumber Co. Baton Rouge, La.	N720MC
N404PX	05	Gulfstream G450	4033	Plains Exploration & Production Co. Houston, Tx.	N989WS
N404QS	96	Gulfstream 4SP	1304	NetJets, Port Columbus, Oh.	N436GA
N404RK	00	Citation Bravo	550-0958	Iron Cloud Aviation LLC. Mesa, Az.	N833BD
N404RP	78	Citation II	550-0024	Blue Horizon LLC. Kalamazoo, Mi.	N413CK
N404SJ	03	SJ 30-2	004	Sino Swearingen Aircraft Co. San Antonio, Tx.	N709JB
N404ST	03	Falcon 900C	200	The Travelers Indemnity Co. Windsor Locks, Ct.	N207FJ
N404UK	04	Falcon 2000EX EASY	47	Acme International Services Inc/ProLogis, Denver, Co.	(N707LX)
N404VL	00	Global Express	9085	The Von Liebig Office Inc. Naples, Fl.	N700GQ
N404WC	68	Jet Commander-A	128	Aquarius Air LLC. Roanoke, Va.	(N386JM)
N404XT	99	Gulfstream 4SP	1366	XTO Energy Corp. Fort Worth, Tx.	N404M
N405CJ	08	CitationJet CJ2+	525A-0405	Cessna Aircraft Co. Wichita, Ks.	N.....
N405CS	05	CitationJet CJ-3	525B-0036	CitationShares Sales Inc. White Plains, NY.	N5244F
N405CT	06	Hawker 850XP	258819	Essar Steel Ltd. Mumbai, India.	
N405DC	81	Falcon 50	42	Tower Operating LLC. Oklahoma City, Ok.	N185BA
N405DW	81	HS 125/700A	257130	Leaseco Aviation 405DW Inc. Orangevale, Ca.	N405TP
N405GJ	82	Learjet 35A	35A-354	CPA Land Co. Tulsa, Ok.	N212GA
N405HG	01	Gulfstream V	661	Kimberly-Clark Corp. Dallas-Love, Tx.	N561GA
N405LA	05	Hawker 800XP2	258726	Western Asset Management Co. Van Nuys, Ca.	N726XP
N405LM	98	Gulfstream V	541	Lockheed Martin Corp. Baltimore, Md.	N641GA
N405MM	82	Diamond 1	A021SA	General Aviation Services LLC. Lake Zurich, Il.	N678PC
N405MM	00	Citation Excel	560-5161	Martin Marietta Materials Inc. Raleigh-Durham, NC.	N404MM
N405PC	89	Learjet 35A	35A-651	Ventures Acquisition LLC. McMinnville, Or.	HB-VJK

Reg   Yr   Type   c/n   Owner/Operator   Prev Regn

Reg	Yr	Type	c/n	Owner/Operator	Prev Regn
N405QS	06	Gulfstream G450	4054	NetJets, Port Columbus, Oh.	N454GA
N405ST	95	Falcon 2000	20	Weiss Special Operations LLC. Hartford, Ct.	N822TP
N406CS	05	CitationJet CJ-3	525B-0043	CitationShares Sales Inc. White Plains, NY.	N5183V
N406CT	85	Citation S/II	S550-0038	Forest River Inc. Elkhart, In.	N214PN
N406FA	83	Gulfstream 3	406	Matrix Trading Inc. Wilmington, De.	N80L
N406J	81	HS 125/700A	NA0293	Jimsair Aviation Services Inc. San Diego, Ca.	N296RG
N406TS	85	Beechjet 400	RJ-6	Teton Aviation Inc. Teton Village, Wy. (was A1006SA).	YV-838CP
N406VJ	90	Citation V	560-0056	Montana Jet LLC. Bozeman, Mt.	N560AE
N407BS	91	Learjet 31	31-033	Jet One LLC/Sterett Crane & Rigging, Owensboro, Ky.	(N638PB)
N407CJ	08	CitationJet CJ2+	525A-0407	Cessna Aircraft Co. Wichita, Ks.	N.....
N407CW	00	Beechjet 400A	RK-307	Anglin Aircraft Recovery Services, Clayton, De.	(N467LX)
N407GC	94	Gulfstream 4SP	1242	Brokerage & Management Corp. NYC.	N982HC
N407NS	00	Gulfstream 4SP	1407	National Air Services, Jeddah, Saudi Arabia.	N40HB
N407RA	95	Learjet 31A	31A-103	Renar Charter Services LLC. Stuart, Fl.	N766AJ
N407W	84	Westwind-Two	407	Cross Creek Aviation Inc. Dallas, Tx.	4X-CUK
N408CS	05	CitationJet CJ-3	525B-0045	CitationShares Sales Inc. White Plains, NY.	N5221Y
N408CT	85	Citation S/II	S550-0055	Forest River Inc. Elkhart, In.	N417RC
N408CW	96	Beechjet 400A	RK-108	Flight Options LLC. Cuyahoga County, Oh.	(N424LX)
N408J	07	390 Premier 1A	RB-193	Jimsair Aviation Services Inc. San Diego, Ca.	N7193W
N408JD	84	Citation III	650-0035	Eagle Jets LLC. Jonesboro, Ga.	N400JD
N408MG	80	Learjet 35A	35A-328	Millenium Air Xpress, Van Nuys, Ca.	N392JP
N408PC	01	Beechjet 400A	RK-325	Pridgeon & Clay Inc. Grand Rapids, Mi.	N275BC
N408QS	96	Gulfstream 4SP	1308	NetJets, Port Columbus, Oh.	N446GA
N408RT	99	Hawker 800XP	258440	Aikman Enterprises Inc. Addison, Tx.	N801MB
N409AV	98	Hawker 800XP	258347	Avjet Corp. Burbank, Ca.	N40PL
N409CC	06	Gulfstream G450	4035	Sextant Holdings LLC. Boston, Ma.	(N119AD)
N409CS	05	CitationJet CJ-3	525B-0050	CitationShares Sales Inc. White Plains, NY.	N.....
N409CT	86	Citation S/II	S550-0095	Forest River Inc. Elkhart, In.	N345CC
N409GB	03	Citation Sovereign	680-0006	Green Bay Packaging Inc. Green Bay, Wi.	N5264U
N409GL	73	Sabre-40A	282-122	AVMATS/Centurion Investments Inc. Chesterfield, Mo.	N188PS
N409LM	02	Gulfstream G200	059	Lockheed Martin Corp. Baltimore, Md.	(OY-RAK)
N409S	75	Citation Eagle	500-0238	NMJ Group LLC/Atlas Resources, Albuquerque, NM.	VP-CON
N409SF	84	Citation III	650-0029	Aircraft Resource Center Inc. Lakeville, Mn.	N89AC
N409ST	87	Citation II	550-0559	Gantt Aviation Inc. Georgetown, Tx. (was 551-0559)	OO-MMP
N409WT	63	Jet Commander	3	GeoCom Enterprises Inc. Fort Lauderdale, Fl.	N400WT
N410AZ	79	Falcon 20-5B	410	Stone Air Aviation LLC. Scottsdale, Az.	N410SB
N410CT	06	Hawker 400XP	RK-495	Forest River Inc. Elkhart, In.	N495XP
N410DM	92	Citation V	560-0184	Dibrell Brothers Tobacco Co. Lanseria, South Africa.	N873DB
N410FJ*	69	Falcon 20D	206	Aviation Team Inc. Fort Lauderdale, Fl	N28RK
N410GS	00	Falcon 2000	112	Gilead Sciences Inc. San Jose, Ca.	(N378GS)
N410KC	01	Falcon 50EX	318	SpenAero Inc. Salt Lake City, Ut.	N416KC
N410KD	06	Hawker 400XP	RK-496	816 Charter LLC. Houston, Tx.	N496XP
N410LM	99	Gulfstream V	578	Lockheed Martin Corp. Baltimore, Md.	N21GN
N410LX*	98	Beechjet 400A	RK-195	Flight Options LLC. Cuyahoga County, Oh.	(N435LX)
N410M	99	Gulfstream V	575	Bristol-Myers Squibb Co. White Plains, NY.	N475GA
N410MT	99	Citation Excel	560-5018	Biomet Orthopaedics Inc. Warsaw, In.	N223AM
N410WW	99	Global Express	9047	William Wrigley/Zeno Air Inc. Chicago, Il.	C-GFLU
N411AJ	04	Learjet 40	45-2011	My Jet LLC/Aero Jet Services, Scottsdale, Az.	N51001
N411AL	99	Gulfstream 4SP	1368	AML Leasing LLC/TWC Aviation Inc. Burbank, Ca.	N610MC
N411BA	75	Learjet 35	35-024	Divine Aviation LLC. Van Nuys, Ca.	N241RT
N411BE*	05	CitationJet CJ-2	525A-0116	Guaranty Development Co. Bozeman, Mt.	N711BE
N411DJ	01	Learjet 31A	31A-224	Disaster Flight Services LLC. Auburn, Al.	N224LJ
N411EC	07	Citation Excel XLS	560-5734	Chouest Air Inc. Galliano, La.	(N711EC)
N411FB	66	HS 125/1A-522	25074	North American Tactical Aviation Inc. Lincoln Park, NJ.	N300GB
N411GA	73	HS 125/600A	256024	Arnoni Aviation Ltd. Houston, Tx. (status ?). (wfu ?).	N669SC
N411GC	90	Falcon 50	210	Guitar Center Inc. Van Nuys, Ca.	XA-TXB
N411HC	05	Learjet 40	45-2056	Hytrol Conveyor Co. Jonesboro, Ar.	
N411LL*	98	Gulfstream 4SP	1344	Alberto-Culver USA Inc. Wheeling, Il.	N18AC
N411MM	96	Astra-1125SPX	080	Meisner Aircraft Inc. Lake in the Hills, Il.	C-GSSS
N411MY	03	CitationJet CJ-1	525-0512	1031 Services Corp. Amarillo, Tx.	N.....
N411PA	77	HS 125/700A	NA0211	Boca Airplane Leasing Corp/PAS Inc. Boca Raton, Fl.	(N602JJ)
N411QS	96	Gulfstream 4SP	1311	NetJets, Port Columbus, Oh.	N449GA
N411RE	82	Diamond 1A	A016SA	A La Jet LLC. Oklahoma City, Ok.	N706JH
N411SP	83	Diamond 1A	A049SA	KC Flight LLC/Gyrocam Systems, Sarasota, Fl.	XA-SOD
N411ST	04	Challenger 300	20031	Benson Football Inc. Metairie, La.	N131LJ
N411TJ	83	Challenger 601	3010	Idaho Rivers LLC. Mountain View, Ca.	N601BD

Reg	Yr	Type	c/n	Owner/Operator	Prev Regn
N411TN	75	Citation	500-0275	Maxfly Aviation Inc. Fort Lauderdale, Fl.	(N275BH)
N411VZ	97	Hawker 800XP	258313	Verizon Communications, Teterboro, NJ.	N908VZ
N411WW	04	Gulfstream G550	5063	Zeno Air Inc. Kenosha, Wi.	N759WR
N412AB	07	Citation Excel XLS	560-5752	ABF Aviation LLC/Arkansas Best Corp. Fort Smith, Ar.	N5096S
N412BT	06	Citation Bravo	550-1134	Northern Air Inc. Grand Rapids, Mi.	N412ET
N412CS	05	CitationJet CJ-3	525B-0059	CitationShares Sales Inc. White Plains, NY.	N.....
N412DA	86	BAe 125/800A	258061	Dan Development Ltd. Janesville, Wi.	(N805LX)
N412GJ	04	Hawker 400XP	RK-412	La Paloma Verde Inc. Lawrenceville, Ga.	N37312
N412JT	71	Gulfstream II SP	101	Aero-Marine LLC. Draper, Ut.	N512JT
N412PG	82	Falcon 50	97	BPG 412 LLC/Berwind Group, Philadelphia, Pa.	N850MC
N412SE	81	Citation 1/SP	501-0225	Richard Carroll, Newport Beach, Ca.	TG-KIT
N412WW	92	Gulfstream 4SP	1203	PremAir Properties USA Inc. Indianapolis, In.	(N199PZ)
N413CK	99	Citation Excel	560-5042	American Proteins Inc/Ampro Aviation LLC. Gainesville, Ga.	N418CK
N413CS	06	CitationJet CJ-3	525B-0082	CitationShares Sales Inc. White Plains, NY.	N.....
N413CT	85	Citation S/II	S550-0017	Aircraft Holding Co 1 LLC. Elkhart, In.	N86PC
N413HB	07	Hawker 4000	RC-13	Hawker Beechcraft Corp. Wichita, Ks.	
N413LC	89	Citation V	560-0003	CP Transportation Inc. Minneapolis Flying Cloud, Mn.	N560ER
N413LX	98	Beechjet 400A	RK-209	Flight Options LLC. Cuyahoga County, Oh.	(N439LX)
N413QS	03	Gulfstream G400	1521	NetJets, Port Columbus, Oh.	N221GA
N414AA	07	Citation Excel XLS	560-5701	Gulf Jet LLC. Dubai, UAE.	(A6-GJC)
N414DH	03	Gulfstream G200	081	AirBill Inc. Portsmouth, NH.	N881GA
N414FW	02	CitationJet CJ-2	525A-0081	Berdan Holdings LLC/BLT Enterprises, Oxnard, Ca.	N51342
N414KD	07	CitationJet CJ-3	525B-0208	Oakmont Corp. Van Nuys, Ca.	N5180K
N414PE	87	Hawker 800SP	258090	Palikea Eheu LLC. Laguna Beach, Ca.	N901RP
N414RF	79	HS 125/700A	NA0244	Summerwind Aviation Group Inc. Van Nuys, Ca.	N230DP
N414TE	01	390 Premier 1	RB-4	TyRose Investments Inc. Wilmington, De.	N842PM
N414TR	07	Falcon 2000EX EASY	135	Dassault Falcon Jet Corp. Teterboro, NJ.	F-WWGE
N415AJ	89	Citation II	550-0600	Video Professor Inc. Lakewood, Co.	PT-LSR
N415BJ	94	Hawker 800	258257	Piney Branch Motors Inc. Savaga, Md.	N802DC
N415CS	99	CitationJet CJ-1	525-0373	Wilson Construction Co. Canby, Or.	
N415CT	86	Beechjet 400	RJ-15	Forest River Inc. Elkhart, In.	N902P
N415FW	99	Citation X	750-0095	Citation General Inc. Wilmington, De.	
N415LJ	66	Learjet 23	23-092	Skycare Inc. Smyrna, Tn.	N344WC
N415NP	93	Learjet 60	60-024	Nie Planes LLC. Boise, Id.	LV-WFM
N415P*	95	Gulfstream 4SP	1260	1260 LLC. San Francisco, Ca.	N810LP
N415QS	05	Gulfstream G450	4014	NetJets, Port Columbus, Oh.	N314GA
N415SL	01	CitationJet CJ-2	525A-0051	Southern Equity LLC. Nashville, Tn.	N6JR
N415TH	84	Westwind-Two	415	Frynati LLC. Chicago, Il.	N415EL
N416BA	96	Citation V Ultra	560-0359	Business Air LLC. Cleveland, Oh.	ZS-SMB
N416BD	99	Global Express	9043	Outpost International (US) LLC. Nashua, NH.	N700ML
N416CC	82	Citation II	550-0416	Span Construction & Engineering Inc. Madera, Ca.	N12167
N416CG	76	Gulfstream II SP	180	Kingsway Aviation Inc. Chino, Ca.	N702JA
N416CT	88	Beechjet 400	RJ-43	Forest River Inc. Elkhart, In.	N500DG
N416HF	90	Citation V	560-0037	Pacific Real Estate Consulting LLC. Larkspur, Ca.	N17LK
N416KC	07	Falcon 900DX	618	Dassault Falcon Jet Corp. Teterboro, NJ.	F-WWFO
N416KD	78	Gulfstream 2	231	KDF Corp. Dallas-Love, Tx.	N47EC
N416QS	97	Gulfstream 4SP	1316	NetJets, Port Columbus, Oh.	N427GA
N416RX	06	Hawker 400XP	RK-514	21st Century Oncology Management Services, Fort Myers, Fl.	N514XP
N416SJ	72	JetStar-731	5153	World Jet Inc. Fort Lauderdale, Fl.	N416KD
N416WM	86	Gulfstream 3	487	ADI/Hi Flite Inc. Rochester Hills, Mi.	N618KM
N417BA	79	Learjet 35A	35A-257	MCA-Midwest Corporate Aviation Lear 24 LP. Wichita, Ks.	N275DJ
N417C	04	CitationJet CJ-3	525B-0006	P B Simon/The Wing Trust, Santa Monica, Ca.	N1278D
N417CS	06	CitationJet CJ-3	525B-0090	CitationShares Sales Inc. White Plains, NY.	N5197A
N417EK	72	Gulfstream II SP	110	Starflite/Dr Eric Scheffey, Houston, Tx.	N92AG
N417GA	07	Gulfstream G450	4117	Gulfstream Aerospace Corp. Savannah, Ga.	
N417JD	06	Citation Bravo	550-1124	TRMSI Inc. Wings Field, Pa.	N5076K
N417KM	06	CitationJet CJ-3	525B-0103	Pilatus Leasing LLC. Willoughby, Oh.	N103CJ
N417KT	84	Diamond 1A	A083SA	Jet Linx Aviation Corp. Omaha, Ne.	N83TK
N417LX	99	Beechjet 400A	RK-230	Flight Options LLC. Cuyahoga County, Oh.	(N441LX)
N417Q	00	CitationJet CJ-1	525-0385	KM Aviation LLC/Kimco Staffing Services Inc. Irvine, Ca.	N417C
N417WW	68	Learjet 24	24-171	Artemis Aviation Group LLC. Wilmington, De.	N737FN
N418CA	75	Learjet 36A	36A-018	(status ?).	PT-ACC
N418CS	06	CitationJet CJ-3	525B-0108	CitationShares Sales Inc. White Plains, NY.	N.....
N418CT*	88	Beechjet 400	RJ-42	Forest River Inc. Elkhart, In.	N40MA
N418DL	99	Learjet 31A	31A-181	DL Charter LLC/Douglas Labs, Allegheny County, Pa.	N526GP
N418FX	00	Learjet 45	45-120	Bombardier Aerospace Corp. Windsor Locks, Ct.	

Reg	Yr	Type	c/n	Owner/Operator	Prev Regn
N418GA	07	Gulfstream G450	4118	Gulfstream Aerospace Corp. Savannah, Ga.	
N418GJ	05	Hawker 400XP	RK-418	C C Medflight Inc. Lawrenceville, Ga.	N618XP
N418KC	96	CitationJet	525-0130	First Interstate Bancsystem Inc. Billings, Mt.	N416KC
N418MG	88	Beechjet 400	RJ-54	Florida Air LLC. Jacksonville, Fl.	XB-FDH
N418MN	01	Learjet 45	45-130	Aerometro LLC. Houston, Tx.	N4001G
N418RD	77	HS 125/700A	NA0210	Rubloff Development Group Inc. Rockford, Il.	P4-AOF
N418RM	87	Beechjet 400	RJ-18	Image Air LLC. Warsaw, In.	N824SS
N418WA	79	Westwind-1124	250	Websta's Aviation Services Inc. St Croix, USVI.	N914MM
N419ET	07	Learjet 40	45-2083	E T MacKenzie LLC. Grand Rapids, Mi.	N51054
N419FX	00	Learjet 45	45-125	BBJS/FlexJets, Addison, Tx.	
N419MB	94	Beechjet 400A	RK-85	Boesen RK 85 LLC. Des Moines, Ia.	N419MS
N419MS	70	Gulfstream II SP	81	Newton Oldacre McDonald, Nashville, Tn.	N151SD
N419WC	74	Falcon 10	11	Willow Creek Association, Barrington, Il.	(N11WC)
N420BG	85	Learjet 55	55-123	Medical Air Services Association, Fort Lauderdale, Fl.	N417AM
N420CC	91	Gulfstream 4	1164	KaiserAir Inc. Oakland, Ca.	N300GX
N420CE	01	Gulfstream G100	139	Ceridian Corp. Minneapolis, Mn.	N100GA
N420CH	07	CitationJet CJ-3	525B-0151	Four Twenty Charlie Hotel LLC. Seattle, Wa.	N52086
N420CL	79	Falcon 50	10	Channelock Inc. Franklin-Venango Regional, Pa.	N65B
N420CS	06	CitationJet CJ-3	525B-0115	CitationShares Sales Inc. White Plains, NY.	N5207A
N420CT	06	Hawker 400XP	RK-517	Forest River Inc. Elkhart, In.	N517XP
N420DH	01	Beechjet 400A	RK-326	Duc Housing Partners Inc. Los Gatos, Ca.	N749RH
N420EH	01	CitationJet CJ-2	525A-0027	Foxtrot Partners LLC. Watsonville, Ca.	N420CH
N420GA	07	Gulfstream G550	4120	Gulfstream Aerospace Corp. Savannah, Ga.	
N420GT	83	Citation III	650-0020	GAT II Inc. North Mankato, Mn.	N650WB
N420JC	81	Gulfstream 3	326	James McMahan, Van Nuys, Ca.	(N326DD)
N420JM	81	Westwind-1124	363	River East Transportation Inc. Chicago, Il.	(N723JM)
N420JP	98	Learjet 60	60-147	Monty Motorsport LLC. Miami, Fl.	(N158JP)
N420LJ	95	Learjet 31A	31A-111	N420LJ Inc. Scottsdale, Az.	N111AF
N420PC	81	Citation 1/SP	501-0237	Leisuretime Services Inc. Green Bay, Wi.	(N712VE)
N420PD	00	Falcon 900EX	84	PPD-Pharmaceutical Product Development, Wilmington, NC.	N420KK
N420QS	97	Gulfstream 4SP	1320	NetJets, Port Columbus, Oh.	N437GA
N420SS	83	Citation II	550-0469	K3C Inc/Sierra Industries Inc. Uvalde, Tx.	(I-....)
N421AL	00	Global Express	9051	Eagle Flight Services Inc. Chicago-Midway, Il.	N700DZ
N421FX	01	Learjet 45	45-145	BBJS/FlexJets, Addison, Tx.	N50145
N421SV	90	Learjet 35A	35A-660	Sovereign Air LLC/Brian Vickers LLC. Thomasville, NC.	C-GLJQ
N421SZ	00	Global Express	9056	Eagle Flight Services Inc. Chicago-Midway, Il.	N700DU
N422AB	02	Citation Excel	560-5285	ABF Aviation LLC/Arkansas Best Corp. Fort Smith, Ar.	N285XL
N422BC	84	Citation III	650-0024	Bradley Fixtures Corp. Menomonee Falls, Wi.	N650SL
N422CP	05	Challenger 300	20061	Pohlad Companies, Minneapolis, Mn.	C-FGUD
N422DA	77	Citation 1/SP	501-0051	Dominion Citation Group LC. Richmond, Va.	N303CB
N422FX	01	Learjet 45	45-135	BBJS/FlexJets, Addison, Tx.	N4004Y
N422GA	07	Gulfstream G450	4122	Gulfstream Aerospace Corp. Savannah, Ga.	
N422JT	07	Citation Encore+	560-0774	Strongwell Corp. Abingdon, Va.	N774CC
N422QS	97	Gulfstream 4SP	1322	NetJets, Port Columbus, Oh.	N445GA
N422TK	83	Gulfstream 3	395	T-Bird Aviation Inc. Tampa, Fl.	N395EJ
N422X	79	HS 125/700A	NA0253	Blackberry Aviation LLC. Boalsburg, Pa.	(N831QJ)
N423CS	06	CitationJet CJ-3	525B-0121	CitationShares Sales Inc. White Plains, NY.	N52229
N423FX	01	Learjet 45	45-134	BBJS/FlexJets, Addison, Tx.	N4004Q
N423GA	07	Gulfstream G450	4123	Gulfstream Aerospace Corp. Savannah, Ga.	
N423HB	07	Hawker 4000	RC-23	Hawker Beechcraft Corp. Wichita, Ks.	
N423SJ	88	BAe 125/800A	NA0423	American Seafoods Group LLC. Seattle, Wa.	N204SM
N423TT	89	Gulfstream 4	1085	TRT Leasing LLC. West Palm Beach, Fl.	N677RP
N424BT	89	Beechjet 400	RJ-62	B J Tidwell Industries Inc. San Antonio, Tx.	N333RS
N424CS	79	Westwind-1124	255	Sam Susser, Corpus Christi, Tx.	N202MW
N424DA	72	Citation	500-0029	Dove Air Inc. Asheville, NC.	C-GDWN
N424FX	01	Learjet 45	45-146	BBJS/FlexJets, Addison, Tx.	
N424GA	07	Gulfstream G450	4124	Gulfstream Aerospace Corp. Savannah, Ga.	
N424GC	72	Gulfstream II SP	115	Bluegrass Gulfstream Investments LLC. Lexington, Ky.	N42PP
N424HH	04	Citation Excel XLS	560-5534	National Real Estate Information Service, Pittsburgh, Pa.	N5165P
N424JR	84	Westwind-Two	405	Allan Kanner & Assocs LLC. New Orleans, La.	N420CE
N424KW	99	Learjet 60	60-153	Kennard Warfield Jr. Dulles, Va.	(N235BX)
N424MP	00	Astra-1125SPX	129	424MP Financial Corp. Fort Lauderdale, Fl.	N52GX
N424MW	99	Learjet 60	60-171	Kennard Warfield Jr. Dulles, Va.	N422CR
N424PX	07	Gulfstream G450	4101	Gulfstream Aerospace Corp. Savannah, Ga.	N401GA
N424QS	98	Gulfstream 4SP	1324	NetJets, Port Columbus, Oh.	N457GA
N424R	74	Sabre-75A	380-15	Roblene Enterprises Inc. Daytona Beach, Fl.	N22JW

Reg	Yr	Type	c/n	Owner/Operator	Prev Regn
❏ N424RS	72	Learjet 24D	24D-258	Aloha Jet Inc. Bear, De.	(N24DZ)
❏ N424TM	05	Challenger 300	20051	EMC Corp. Bedford-Hanscom Field, Ma.	C-FFLJ
❏ N424TV	96	CitationJet	525-0145	Darrold Cannan Jr. Wichita Falls, Tx.	N145CJ
❏ N424XT	74	Falcon 20-5B	316	Aircorp Inc. Dallas, Tx.	N242CT
❏ N425AS	80	Learjet 35A	35A-281	Jetlease LLC. Fargo, ND.	N425M
❏ N425BJ	87	Beechjet 400	RJ-25	Southeast Air Charter Inc. Carthage, NC.	ZS-OUU
❏ N425CS	06	CitationJet CJ-3	525B-0132	CitationShares Sales Inc. White Plains, NY.	N5058J
❏ N425CT	07	Hawker 400XP	RK-523	Forest River Inc. Elkhart, In.	N523XP
❏ N425CW	01	Beechjet 400A	RK-345	Flight Options LLC. Cuyahoga County, Oh.	(N474LX)
❏ N425FX	01	Learjet 45	45-147	BBJS/FlexJets, Addison, Tx.	
❏ N425G	05	Learjet 45	45-307	GEICO Corp. Washington, DC.	
❏ N425GA	07	Gulfstream G450	4125	Gulfstream Aerospace Corp. Savannah, Ga.	
❏ N425JF	66	Falcon 20C	64	Elite Yacht Brokers/Bluegrass Gas Sales, Anchorage, Ky.	N513AG
❏ N425JR	80	Falcon 10	162	Fant Aircraft Enterprises LLC. Houston, Tx.	N602DM
❏ N425KG	76	HS 125/700A	257001	South Aviation Inc. Fort Lauderdale, Fl.	(N807CW)
❏ N425M	92	Learjet 31A	31A-055	GEICO Corp. Washington, DC.	N666RE
❏ N425QS	04	Gulfstream G450	4010	NetJets, Port Columbus, Oh.	N910GA
❏ N425RJ	83	Falcon 200	484	Fant Aircraft Enterprises LLC. Houston, Tx.	N24JG
❏ N425SA	81	Learjet 35A	35A-425	Jedami Aircraft Charter LLC. Fort Lauderdale, Fl.	N111KZ
❏ N425SD	77	HS 125/700A	NA0212	Saona Holding LLC. Miami, Fl.	(N125MJ)
❏ N425SV	82	Gulfstream 3	360	N425SV LLC.Boise, Id.	N705JA
❏ N425WN	86	Challenger 601	3052	Navellier Management Ltd. Reno, Nv.	VP-CRX
❏ N426CF	97	Challenger 604	5338	Montgomery Capital of Delaware LLC. Fort Washington, Pa.	N78RP
❏ N426CH	03	Citation Excel	560-5222	Heers Management Co. Las Vegas, Nv.	N560JP
❏ N426CM	00	Citation X	750-0117	VMD Aviation LLC/Flannery Properties, Van Nuys, Ca.	N50612
❏ N426EA	00	Beechjet 400A	RK-275	Heartland Air LLC. Bismarck, ND.	N4275K
❏ N426ED	00	CitationJet CJ-1	525-0426	Sunseeker Air Inc. Bend, Or.	N5197A
❏ N426FX	01	Learjet 45	45-162	BBJS/FlexJets, Addison, Tx.	
❏ N426GA	07	Gulfstream G450	4126	Gulfstream Aerospace Corp. Savannah, Ga.	
❏ N426JK	07	Learjet 40	45-2092	Learjet Inc. Wichita, Ks.	
❏ N426MJ	05	Hawker 850XP	258759	Mi-Jack Products Inc. Chicago-Romeoville, Il.	N801RR
❏ N426PE	89	Challenger 601-3A	5046	Sterling Aviation Inc. Milwaukee, Wi.	N426PF
❏ N426PF	02	Challenger 604	5547	Sagitta LLC/DB Aviation LLC. Waukegan, Il.	N350ZE
❏ N426QS	00	Gulfstream 4SP	1426	NetJets, Port Columbus, Oh.	N426GA
❏ N426RJ	77	Westwind-1124	218	WWW LLC/Petroleum Development Corp. Bridgeport, WV.	N425RJ
❏ N426TA	69	Learjet 24B	24B-181	Windwalker Aero Corp. Naperville, Il.	N254JT
❏ N427CJ	75	Falcon 10	67	Rockbridge Consulting Inc. Santa Barbara, Ca.	D-COME
❏ N427CS	07	CitationJet CJ-3	525B-0152	CitationShares Sales Inc. White Plains, NY.	N5262B
❏ N427DB*	07	390 Premier 1A	RB-223	Charolais Corp. Madisonville, Ky.	N3203L
❏ N427GA	07	Gulfstream G450	4127	Gulfstream Aerospace Corp. Savannah, Ga.	
❏ N427SS	84	Citation 1/SP	501-0681	Grayling, Trout & Co LLC. Newport Beach, Ca.	N82LS
❏ N427TL	81	Learjet 55	55-006	Home Solutions of Aventura LLC. Hollywood, Fl.	N228PK
❏ N428AS	02	Gulfstream 4SP	1487	Market Air LLC. Virginia Beach, Va.	N487GA
❏ N428BB	00	Learjet 31A	31A-209	Laredo National Bank, Laredo, Tx.	N209HR
❏ N428BR	07	CitationJet CJ-3	525B-0205	VBG Aviation LLC. Omaha, Ne.	N52682
❏ N428CC	91	Falcon 50	225	Colony Capital LLC. Van Nuys, Ca.	N32TC
❏ N428CS	07	CitationJet CJ-3	525B-0165	CitationShares Sales Inc. White Plains, NY.	N5267T
❏ N428DA	64	JetStar-6	5048	814K LLC. Pleasant View, Tn. (status ? for museum ?).	(N130LW)
❏ N428FX	01	Learjet 45	45-164	BBJS/FlexJets, Addison, Tx.	
❏ N428JD	86	Beechjet 400	RJ-13	Dewberry Air LLC. Dover, De.	(N400TN)
❏ N428M	99	Gulfstream 4SP	1382	Swiftlite Aircraft Corp. Burbank, Ca.	N1GC
❏ N428QS	97	Gulfstream 4SP	1328	NetJets, Port Columbus, Oh.	N328GA
❏ N428SJ	01	Citation Encore	560-0584	Arlie Air LLC. Eugene, Or.	N90HB
❏ N428WT	99	Gulfstream V	599	Avalon Capital Group Inc. La Jolla, Ca.	N401WJ
❏ N429CS	07	CitationJet CJ-3	525B-0177	CitationShares Sales Inc. White Plains, NY.	N5037F
❏ N429DA	66	HS 125/1B-S522	25090	American Aircraft Sales International Inc. Fl. (status ?).	N102TW
❏ N429DD	82	Gulfstream 3	354	MTF Corp. Coral Gables, Fl.	N420RC
❏ N429FX	01	Learjet 45	45-165	BBJS/FlexJets, Addison, Tx.	
❏ N429GA	07	Gulfstream G450	4129	Gulfstream Aerospace Corp. Savannah, Ga.	
❏ N429SA	96	Gulfstream 4SP	1314	USAA, San Antonio, Tx.	N461GA
❏ N429SJ	98	Falcon 2000	66	TSTC LLC/Steve Tisch Co. Van Nuys, Ca.	N30TH
❏ N429WG	87	Challenger 601-3A	5010	Exploration Air LLC/Bois d'Arc Energy Inc. Houston, Tx.	N181AP
❏ N430CS	07	CitationJet CJ-3	525B-0185	CitationShares Sales Inc. White Plains, NY.	N5076K
❏ N430FX	01	Learjet 45	45-166	BBJS/FlexJets, Addison, Tx.	
❏ N430GR	01	CitationJet CJ-1	525-0430	Tindle Aviation LLC. Freeport, Fl.	N52081
❏ N430JH	04	CitationJet CJ-1	525-0530	Harvey Aircraft LLC/Harvey Farms, Flora, Ms.	N5244F

Reg	Yr	Type	c/n	Owner/Operator	Prev Regn
N430MP	73	Sabre-40A	282-113	ABA Aviation Resources Inc. Doral, Fl.	N430MB
N430PT	85	Westwind-1124	430	P T Air LLC. Seattle, Wa.	N430BJ
N430QS	05	Gulfstream G450	4021	NetJets, Port Columbus, Oh.	N621GA
N430SA	94	Citation VII	650-7041	Lakeside Air LLC. Erie, Pa.	(N449SA)
N431CB	94	Challenger 601-3R	5164	C R Bard Inc. Morristown, NJ.	N164CC
N431CS	08	CitationJet CJ-3	525B-0228	CitationShares Sales Inc. White Plains, NY.	N.....
N431DA	98	Learjet 31A	31A-163	Bombardier Aerospace Corp. Windsor Locks, Ct.	N128FX
N431FX	01	Learjet 45	45-177	BBJS/FlexJets, Addison, Tx.	
N431JT	84	Gulfstream 3	417	Hunters Glen Inc/TTG Enterprises Ltd. Dallas, Tx.	N300M
N431LC	74	Citation	500-0177	Cimarron Aviation LLC/My Lucky Candy Inc. Wilmington, De.	N883XL
N431MS	87	Citation S/II	S550-0127	Sky Hop LLC/Romulus Inc. Scottsdale, Az.	N97SK
N431WA	87	Westwind-1124	431	Whiskey Alpha LLC. Baton Rouge, Fl.	C-FGGH
N432AC	04	Citation X	750-0231	Apache Corp/Apache Aviation Inc. Houston, Tx.	N5190R
N432AQ	89	BAe 125/800A	NA0434	PSP Aviation LLC. Englewood, Co.	N432AC
N432CC	79	Sabre-65	465-6	Michigan Aircraft Sales LLC. Freeland, Mi.	N2CC
N432CJ	01	CitationJet CJ-2	525A-0043	PT Air LLC. Murrels Inlet, SC.	N52002
N432CS	08	CitationJet CJ-3	525B-0244	CitationShares Sales Inc. White Plains, NY.	N.....
N432FX	01	Learjet 45	45-197	BBJS/FlexJets, Addison, Tx.	
N432LW	04	CitationJet CJ-3	525B-0003	Breslow Enterprises LLC. Las Vegas, Nv.	(N627BB)
N432MA	05	CitationJet CJ2+	525A-0300	Flight Level LLC. Madison, Wi (Ff 2 Apr 05), (was 525A-0232)	N5245D
N432NM	79	Citation II	550-0078	Lea King LLC/Lasco Construction, Hobbs, NM.	N533MA
N432RJ	01	Citation Bravo	550-0967	Directors Air Corp. Abilene, Tx.	N967CB
N433CS	08	CitationJet CJ-3	525B-0257	CitationShares Sales Inc. White Plains, NY.	N.....
N433DD	78	Learjet 35A	35A-161	WFBNW NA. Salt Lake City, Ut. (trustor ?).	YV-65CP
N433FX	01	Learjet 45	45-192	BBJS/FlexJets, Addison, Tx.	
N433GA	07	Gulfstream G450	4133	Gulfstream Aerospace Corp. Savannah, Ga.	
N433GM	85	Westwind-Two	433	Fried Companies Inc. Crozet, Va.	N433WR
N434CS	08	CitationJet CJ-3	525B-0268	CitationShares Sales Inc. White Plains, NY.	N.....
N434FX	02	Learjet 45	45-212	BBJS/FlexJets, Addison, Tx.	N50111
N434GA	07	Gulfstream G450	4134	Gulfstream Aerospace Corp. Savannah, Ga.	
N434LX	00	Beechjet 400A	RK-274	Flight Options LLC. Cuyahoga County, Oh.	(N456LX)
N434SB	82	Citation II	550-0426	Air Century Inc. Tampa, Fl.	(N426VP)
N434UM	74	Citation	500-0190	Aero Vision International LLC. Muskegon, Mi. (status ?)	N602BC
N435CT	07	Hawker 400XP	RK-531	Forest River Inc. Elkhart, In.	
N435CW	92	Beechjet 400A	RK-35	ICON Corporate LLC. Las Vegas, Nv.	(N409LX)
N435FX	05	Learjet 45	45-271	BBJS/FlexJets, Addison, Tx.	N45XR
N435HC	00	Gulfstream 4SP	1450	Hood Industries Inc. Jackson, Ms.	N809C
N435HH	07	Learjet 45	45-335	American Industries Inc. Hillsboro, Or.	
N435JF	97	Falcon 2000	47	JF Aircraft Corp. Dearborn, Mi.	N800BL
N435MS	76	Learjet 35	35-054	Allene LaPides, Santa Fe, NM.	N109MC
N435QS	06	Gulfstream G450	4068	NetJets, Port Columbus, Oh.	N468GA
N435T	00	Falcon 900EX	63	The Marmon Group Inc. Chicago-Midway, Il.	N900EX
N435UJ	75	Learjet 35	35-025	Dodson International Parts Inc. Rantoul, Ks.	(N188JA)
N435UM	82	Citation II	550-0424	Marlin Air Inc. Belleview, Mi.	N551BP
N436CS	08	CitationJet CJ-3	525B-0274	CitationShares Sales Inc. White Plains, NY.	N.....
N436FX	06	Learjet 45	45-309	BBJS/FlexJets, Addison, Tx.	
N436JW	69	Gulfstream 2B	73	David Topokh, Pietersburg, RSA.	7P-TCB
N436LX	00	Beechjet 400A	RK-279	Flight Options LLC. Cuyahoga County, Oh.	(N458LX)
N436QS	00	Gulfstream 4SP	1436	NetJets, Port Columbus, Oh.	N436GA
N437CS	08	CitationJet CJ-3	525B-0282	CitationShares Sales Inc. White Plains, NY.	N.....
N437FX	06	Learjet 45	45-315	BBJS/FlexJets, Addison, Tx.	
N437GA	00	Gulfstream 4SP	1437	National Air Services, Jeddah, Saudi Arabia.	
N437JD	06	CitationJet CJ2+	525A-0325	Iowa Select Farms, Des Moines, Ia.	N.....
N437MC	02	Challenger 604	5537	United of Omaha Life Insurance Co. Omaha, Ne.	N537DR
N437SJ	86	Westwind-Two	437	Louisiana Aircraft/Davison Transport Inc. Ruston, La.	N437WW
N438BC	05	Hawker 400XP	RK-438	PBM Products LLC. Gordonsville, Va.	N162QS
N438FX	07	Learjet 45	45-333	BBJS/FlexJets, Addison, Tx.	
N438LX	98	Beechjet 400A	RK-202	Flight Options LLC. Cuyahoga County, Oh.	N742TA
N438MC	97	Citation V Ultra	560-0438	American Air Travelers Inc. Stuart, Fl.	(PT-WQE)
N438SP	02	Citation Bravo	550-1026	Southern Pipe & Supply Co. Meridian, Ms.	N552CB
N439FX	07	Learjet 45	45-341	BBJS/FlexJets, Addison, Tx.	
N439LX	00	Beechjet 400A	RK-284	Flight Options LLC. Cuyahoga County, Oh.	(N460LX)
N439WW	86	Westwind-Two	439	American Jet SA. Buenos Aires, Argentina.	4X-CUG
N440AS	07	Gulfstream G450	4075	Trane Aviation LLC/American Standad Inc. Allentown, Pa.	N375GA
N440CE	00	Citation Bravo	550-0937	Elizabeth Prothro, Wichita Falls, Tx.	N51666
N440CT	07	Hawker 400XP	RK-534	Forest River Inc. Elkhart, In.	

Reg	Yr	Type	c/n	Owner/Operator	Prev Regn
❏ N440CW	92	Beechjet 400A	RK-40	JLL Aviation Inc. Wilmington, De.	(N410LX)
❏ N440DM	81	Learjet 55	55-005	MBK Aviation Services LLC. Fort Lauderdale Executive, Fl.	(N94TJ)
❏ N440DS	90	Beechjet 400A	RK-8	Motors Flight LLC/Sansone Motor Group, Ocean, NJ.	
❏ N440FX	07	Learjet 45	45-346	BBJS/FlexJets, Addison, Tx.	
❏ N440KT	72	Learjet 24D	24D-249	Spirit Wing Aviation Ltd. Guthrie, Ok.	N249RA
❏ N440MC	83	Learjet 35A	35A-495	McClane Company Inc. Temple, Tx.	
❏ N440PC	84	Citation III	650-0061	Refreshment Services Inc. Green Bay, Wi.	N450RS
❏ N440QS	05	Gulfstream G450	4025	NetJets, Port Columbus, Oh.	N998GA
❏ N440RC	00	Beechjet 400A	RK-269	Rineco Chemical Industries Inc. Little Rock, Ar.	N400MR
❏ N440RD	72	HS 125/F403B	25270	RD Air LLC/Rubloff Development Group Inc. Rockford, Il.	N400GP
❏ N440SC	02	Learjet 31A	31A-240	SCC of Tennessee LLC. Chattanooga, Tn.	N990AE
❏ N440TC	89	Gulfstream 4	1115	Meridian Services Inc. Teterboro, NY.	N410MY
❏ N440WF	05	Hawker 400XP	RK-440	Cabela's Wholesale Inc. Sidney, Ne.	N152QS
❏ N441BC	89	Astra-1125	033	JB Holdings LLC. Anchorage, Ak.	N52KS
❏ N441BP	05	Citation Excel XLS	560-5612	Dom Alive SA. Santo Domingo, Dominican Republic.	N926DR
❏ N441FX	07	Learjet 45	45-357	BBJS/FlexJets, Addison, Tx.	
❏ N441LX	00	Beechjet 400A	RK-292	Flight Options LLC. Cuyahoga County, Oh.	(N462LX)
❏ N441PC	92	Learjet 35A	35A-668	Allmetal Inc. Wheeling, Il.	N9168Q
❏ N441QS	98	Gulfstream 4SP	1341	NetJets, Port Columbus, Oh.	N341GA
❏ N442EA	83	Diamond 1A	A058SA	Sourek Trail Co. Barberton, Oh.	N7050V
❏ N442GA	07	Gulfstream G150	242	Gulfstream Aerospace LP. Dallas-Love, Tx.	4X-C..
❏ N442GJ	05	Hawker 400XP	RK-442	C C Medflight Inc. Lawrenceville, Ga.	N124QS
❏ N442JB	73	Citation	500-0117	Invest-Air, Fresno, Ca.	N161WC
❏ N442KM	85	Citation S/II	S550-0060	N/S One LLC/Aero Film, Santa Monica, Ca.	N260QS
❏ N442LW	07	Citation Sovereign	680-0168	Wachob Industries Inc. Sapulpa, Ok.	N5094D
❏ N442MA	98	Hawker 800XP	258378	Energy Equipment Resources Inc. Dallas, Tx.	N494RG
❏ N442NR	04	Citation Bravo	550-1078	Refuse Equipment Manufacturing, Riyadh, Saudi Arabia.	N.....
❏ N442RM	74	Sabre-60	306-73	BAe Systems Information & Electronic Systems Integration Inc	XA-TNW
❏ N442WT	04	Citation X	750-0233	Wilson Trailer Co. Sioux City, Ia.	N51612
❏ N443C	92	Beechjet 400A	RK-42	WFBNW NA. Salt Lake City, Ut. (trustor ?).	(N411LX)
❏ N443GA	07	Gulfstream G150	243	Gulfstream Aerospace LP. Dallas-Love, Tx.	4X-C..
❏ N443LX	99	Beechjet 400A	RK-237	Flight Options LLC. Cuyahoga County, Oh.	N437CW
❏ N443RK	75	Learjet 35	35-023	Florida Jet Center, Fort Lauderdale, Fl. (status ?).	N886CS
❏ N444CW	84	Citation III	650-0064	Aviation Enterprises LLC. Longwood, Fl.	N650TC
❏ N444EA	04	Citation Bravo	550-1079	Edgar Aviation LLC. Kansas City, Ks.	N1271B
❏ N444EP	85	Westwind-Two	436	Brothers Equipment Leasing LLC. Charlotte, NC.	N100AK
❏ N444ET	82	Challenger 600	1062	DayStar TV Network/Word of God Fellowship, Fort Worth, Tx.	N95EB
❏ N444EX	95	Citation VII	650-7056	Bohemian Breweries Inc. Jeffco, Co.	N60PL
❏ N444G	81	Citation II	550-0209	Thomas F Mitts MD Inc/Wadwelle Inc. Visalia, Ca.	(N877DB)
❏ N444GG	94	Citation V Ultra	560-0262	Elias-Savion-Fox LLC. Allegheny County, Pa.	N262CV
❏ N444HC	93	Learjet 31A	31A-064	John Sessa, Fort Lauderdale, Fl.	N142GT
❏ N444KE	94	Citation VII	650-7029	Rhine River Investments Inc. Annapolis, Md.	N650RL
❏ N444MK	78	Learjet 25D	25D-252	Vail Jet Inc. Vail, Co.	N44FH
❏ N444MW	01	Learjet 45	45-131	McWane Inc. Birmingham, Al.	
❏ N444PE	84	Falcon 50	143	P & E Properties Inc. Teterboro, NJ.	N77CP
❏ N444QG	00	Gulfstream 4SP	1453	Quad/Graphics Inc. Waukesha, Wi.	N453GA
❏ N444TG	81	Learjet 25D	25D-327	Gaines Motor Lines Inc. Hickory, NC.	(N327BC)
❏ N444WB	77	Learjet 35A	35A-105	Aero-Jet Aviation Inc. Fort Lauderdale, Fl.	(D-CHRC)
❏ N444WW	79	Learjet 25D	25D-283	Domingo Olivares, Caracas, Venezuela.	N312GK
❏ N445AK	05	Gulfstream G100	155	AK Steel Corp. Middletown, Oh.	4X-CVJ
❏ N445BL	82	Westwind-1124	382	Jet Services Enterprises Inc. Bethany, Ok.	N999BL
❏ N445CT	07	Hawker 400XP	RK-535	Forest River Inc. Elkhart, In.	
❏ N445LX	00	Beechjet 400A	RK-298	Flight Options LLC. Cuyahoga County, Oh.	N698TA
❏ N445N	02	Learjet 45	45-202	NIBCO Inc. Elkhart, In.	N5048Q
❏ N445PK	93	Beechjet 400A	RK-45	Four Twenty One Inc/Veenker Resources, Oklahoma City, Ok.	(N412LX)
❏ N445QS	05	Gulfstream G450	4037	NetJets, Port Columbus, Oh.	N537GA
❏ N445SB	99	Learjet 45	45-027	MCCKC LLC/Trilogy International Partners LLC. Bellevue, Wa.	N156PB
❏ N445SE	07	Learjet 45	45-334	Southeastern Freight Lines Inc. Columbia Metro, SC.	N4003Q
❏ N446CW	02	Beechjet 400A	RK-346	Flight Options LLC. Cuyahoga County, Oh.	(N475LX)
❏ N446LX	00	Beechjet 400A	RK-299	Flight Options LLC. Cuyahoga County, Oh.	N697TA
❏ N446M	98	Beechjet 400A	RK-199	Motion Industries Inc. Atlanta, Ga.	N739TA
❏ N446RT	03	Citation Sovereign	680-0017	CUNA Mutual Life Insurance Co. Madison, Wi.	(N121LS)
❏ N447LX	99	Beechjet 400A	RK-248	Flight Options LLC. Cuyahoga County, Oh.	N786TA
❏ N448AS	04	Challenger 300	20027	American Seafoods Group LLC. Seattle, Wa.	C-GZEH
❏ N448CC	92	BAe 1000A	NA1007	Continental Carrier Inc. Columbus, Oh.	N600LS
❏ N448GR	93	Astra-1125SP	070	GLP Aviation Inc. Miami, Fl.	(N149LP)

Reg   Yr   Type   c/n   Owner/Operator   Prev Regn

Reg	Yr	Type	c/n	Owner/Operator	Prev Regn
❏ N448JM	99	Hawker 800XP	258404	Valutech Outsourcing LLC. Capistrano Beach, Ca.	N404DB
❏ N448LX	00	Beechjet 400A	RK-305	Flight Options LLC. Cuyahoga County, Oh.	(N466LX)
❏ N448QS	07	Gulfstream G450	4100	NetJets, Port Columbus, Oh.	N120GA
❏ N448RL	01	Citation Bravo	550-0990	JRD Investments LLC. Lafayette, La.	N990JM
❏ N448TB	81	Guardian HU-25B	439	USAF, Electronic Systems Command, Hanscom AFB. Ma.	N523NA
❏ N448W	78	Sabre-75A	380-63	Platina Investment Corp. Wiley Post, Ok.	N75RS
❏ N449DT	77	Citation Eagle II	501-0012	Par Three LLC. Orem, Ut. (Ff FJ44 Eagle II 30 Sep 00).	N15FJ
❏ N449EB	77	HS 125/700A	NA0208	Catex LLC. Oak Hill, Va.	N41HF
❏ N449LX	99	Beechjet 400A	RK-257	Flight Options LLC. Cuyahoga County, Oh.	N739TA
❏ N449ML	00	Global Express	9055	WFC Air Inc. Teterboro, NJ.	C-GFWZ
❏ N450AB	05	Gulfstream G450	4043	West Teton LLC. Santa Ana, Ca.	N443GA
❏ N450AJ	82	Challenger 600S	1075	Jones Airways LLC. Cleveland, Tn.	N751DB
❏ N450AR*	88	Gulfstream 4	1069	Al Rushaid Aviation Ltd. Wilmington, De.	(N646AR)
❏ N450BC	99	Learjet 45	45-075	Cunningham Charter Corp. Anna, Il.	
❏ N450BF	87	Gulfstream 4	1015	Kona Coast LLC/Knudson Management Co. Council Bluffs, Ia.	VP-BRF
❏ N450BK	00	Learjet 45	45-104	Elite Air Inc. St Petersburg, Fl.	OH-IPJ
❏ N450BV	07	CitationJet CJ-3	525B-0167	Canine Aviation LLC/Banjo Corp. Crawfordsville, In.	N.....
❏ N450CB	81	Gulfstream 3	324	Forsythe Delaware Investments LLC. Vero Beach, Fl.	N96MR
❏ N450CL	81	Falcon 50	76	Werner Enterprises Inc. Omaha, Ne.	N411WW
❏ N450CP	73	Falcon 20F-5	289	Carolina Blue Air Corp. Greensboro, NC.	N75TJ
❏ N450CW	92	Beechjet 400A	RK-50	Flight Options LLC. Cuyahoga County, Oh.	(N413LX)
❏ N450DR	82	Falcon 50	113	HM LLC. Armonk, NY.	N75RZ
❏ N450EJ	07	Gulfstream G450	4088	Kerry Group, Hong Kong.	N388GA
❏ N450GA	07	Gulfstream G450	4091	Gulfstream Aerospace Corp. Savannah, Ga.	N391GA
❏ N450JC	00	Learjet 45	45-070	A & H Aviation SA. San Jose, Costa Rica.	LX-IMS
❏ N450JE	94	Gulfstream 4SP	1233	N450JE LLC. Windsor Locks, Ct.	A6-OME
❏ N450KD*	82	Citation II	550-0412	U S Turbine Aircraft Sales Inc. Mason City, Ia.	N223J
❏ N450LV	06	Gulfstream G450	4061	ASNY Aviation LLC/Consolidated Realty Inc. Las Vegas, Nv.	N461GA
❏ N450MH	78	Gulfstream II SP	225	Jenson Aviation LLC. Holladay, Ut.	N225TR
❏ N450MM	91	Citation V	560-0119	Triple F Management LLC. Baltimore, Md.	N119CV
❏ N450MQ	04	Citation Encore	560-0657	Encore 560-0657 LLC. Denver, Co.	N778BC
❏ N450NS	07	Gulfstream G450	4079	National Air Services, Jeddah, Saudi Arabia.	N379GA
❏ N450PG	06	Gulfstream G450	4072	CA Research Inc. Farmingdale, NY.	N372GA
❏ N450PU	07	Gulfstream G450	4095	Astra Holdings Inc. Wilmington, De.	N495GA
❏ N450QS	05	Gulfstream G450	4046	NetJets, Port Columbus, Oh.	N446GA
❏ N450RG	05	Gulfstream G350	4038	G350 Leasing LLC/Kingsley Management, Provo, Ut.	N538GA
❏ N450T	07	Gulfstream G450	4105	Gulfstream Aerospace Corp. Savannah, Ga.	N405GA
❏ N450TJ	98	Learjet 45	45-012	JACO Oil Co. Bakersfield, Ca.	D-CMLP
❏ N450WB	07	Gulfstream G450	4110	Gulfstream Aerospace Corp. Savannah, Ga.	N610GA
❏ N450XX	06	Gulfstream G450	4062	Stephenson Air Services LLC. San Jose, Ca.	N462GA
❏ N451AJ	02	CitationJet CJ-2	525A-0110	Velox Aircraft LLC. Port Hueneme, Ca.	N.....
❏ N451BW	04	Learjet 45	45-261	Integrated Management Services LLC. Venice, Fl.	(LX-IMS)
❏ N451C*	95	Gulfstream 4SP	1279	J C Penney Corp. Dallas, Tx.	N2002P
❏ N451CL	91	Falcon 50	223	Werner Enterprises Inc. Omaha, Ne.	N840FJ
❏ N451CM	05	Gulfstream G450	4024	L & L Leasing LLC. White Plains, NY.	(N927EM)
❏ N451CS	02	Global Express	9134	Saban Capital Group Inc/Avjet Corp. Burbank, Ca.	N452CS
❏ N451DC	05	Gulfstream G450	4041	Dow Chemical Co. Midland, Mi.	N401GA
❏ N451DJ	04	Embraer Legacy 600	145789	DJT LLC. Pompano Beach, Fl.	N456MT
❏ N451DP	71	Falcon 20F	249	Dad's Products Inc. Meadville, Pa.	N777JF
❏ N451GA	93	Gulfstream 4SP	1221	Amgen Inc. Camarillo, Ca.	
❏ N451GP	06	CitationJet CJ-3	525B-0080	Gregory Poole Equipment Co. Raleigh-Durham, NC.	N380CJ
❏ N451HC	05	Learjet 45	45-267	United States Aviation Co. Tulsa, Ok.	N4002P
❏ N451LX	01	Beechjet 400A	RK-310	Flight Options LLC. Cuyahoga County, Oh.	(N468LX)
❏ N451MM	05	390 Premier 1A	RB-137	RP20 P/L-GoJet P/L. Gold Coast Airport, Australia.	N6137U
❏ N451N	03	Learjet 45	45-230	Newell Rubbermaid Inc. Rockford, Il.	N4008G
❏ N451NS	07	Gulfstream G450	4082	National Air Services, Jeddah, Saudi Arabia.	N382GA
❏ N451R	07	Gulfstream G150	227	Integral Resources LLC. Modesto, Ca.	4X-C..
❏ N451ST	01	Learjet 45	45-200	JM Family Enterprises Inc. Fort Lauderdale, Fl.	
❏ N451WM	99	Learjet 45	45-091	Wal-Mart Stores Inc. Rogers, Ar.	(N408BX)
❏ N452A	06	Learjet 45	45-320	Averitt Aviation Group Inc. Nashville, Tn.	
❏ N452AC	83	Learjet 35A	35A-508	Avex Corp. Fort Lauderdale, Fl.	N508TF
❏ N452AJ	98	Citation V Ultra	560-0494	Jones Airways LLC. Cleveland, Tn.	N86GR
❏ N452CJ	99	Learjet 45	45-090	Wal-Mart Stores Inc. Rogers, Ar.	N407FX
❏ N452DA	81	Learjet 35A	35A-452	Duncan Aviation Inc. Lincoln, Ne.	N279SP
❏ N452LJ	96	Learjet 45	45-002	Learjet Inc. Wichita, Ks. (Ff 6 Apr 96).	N45LJ
❏ N452LX	01	Beechjet 400A	RK-317	Flight Options LLC. Cuyahoga County, Oh.	(N469LX)

Reg	Yr	Type	c/n	Owner/Operator	Prev Regn
N452NS	07	Gulfstream G450	4094	National Air Service, Jeddah, Saudi Arabia.	N494GA
N452QS	98	Gulfstream 4SP	1352	NetJets, Port Columbus, Oh.	N352GA
N452ST	02	Learjet 45	45-201	JM Family Enterprises Inc. Fort Lauderdale, Fl.	N473LP
N453A	07	Learjet 45	45-363	Learjet Inc. Wichita, Ks.	
N453AM	82	Learjet 35A	35A-453	Anderson News Corp. Knoxville, Tn.	(N802EC)
N453DP	74	HS 125/600A	256044	Arnoni Aviation Inc. Houston, Tx.	N454DP
N453GS	83	Challenger 601	3011	The Bistate Oil Co/Aero Ways Inc. Wilmington, De.	N202PH
N453JS	06	Falcon 900DX	605	J B Scott, Boise, Id.	N605FJ
N453MA	79	Learjet 25D	25D-291	3M Aviation LLC/McCar Development Corp. Alpharetta, Ga.	(N477MM)
N453S	82	Citation II	550-0445	Selman Hangar, Monroe, La. (was 551-0445).	N1248K
N453SB	78	Falcon 20F-5B	382	Sierra Bravo Graco/Sinclair Broadcast Group, Baltimore, Md.	N10AZ
N453ST	05	Learjet 45	45-299	JM Family Enterprises Inc. Fort Lauderdale, Fl.	
N454AC	77	Citation 1/SP	501-0015	McClain Enterprises Inc. Mountain Home, Ar.	N4446P
N454CG	00	Learjet 45	45-085	George's Enterprises LLC. Springdale, Ar.	
N454DP	81	Falcon 10	130	ARC Aviation 1 Inc. Englewood, Co.	N432EZ
N454JB	82	Gulfstream 3	345	Shaw Managed Services Inc. Baton Rouge, La.	N76TJ
N454LC	06	Learjet 45	45-296	Lamar Advertising Co. Baton Rouge, La.	N4003K
N454LX	01	Beechjet 400A	RK-327	Flight Options LLC. Cuyahoga County, Oh.	(N471LX)
N454N	07	Learjet 45	45-339	Newell Rubbermaid Inc. Rockford, Il.	
N454QS	00	Gulfstream 4SP	1454	NetJets, Port Columbus, Oh.	N454GA
N455BK	79	HS 125/700A	NA0256	Oral Roberts Evangelistic Association, Tulsa, Ok.	(N830LR)
N455DW	87	Beechjet 400	RJ-20	Dudley Walker, Martinsville, Va.	N901P
N455DX	01	Falcon 2000	146	Quest Diagnostics Inc. Reading, Pa.	N317MN
N455FD	77	Citation 1/SP	501-0005	Frank Branson PC. Dallas-Love Field, Tx.	N284RJ
N455JD	84	Citation III	650-0069	STG Realty Ventures Inc. Santa Rosa, Ca.	XB-GRN
N455QS	07	Gulfstream G450	4074	NetJets, Port Columbus, Oh.	N374GA
N455RH	85	Learjet 55	55-110	Hunt Aviation Inc. Indianapolis, In.	N55GY
N455SH	87	Astra-1125	017	DDMR LLC. Tampa, Fl.	(N800JS)
N456AL	83	Gulfstream 3	405	BDJ Aircraft Inc. Oklahoma City, Ok.	N789TR
N456BE	81	Gulfstream 3	335	Billionaire Inc/Mortgage Investors Corp. St Petersburg, Fl.	N717MS
N456CG	81	Learjet 25D	25D-343	LDL Aircraft Leasing LLC. Pittsfield, Ma.	N3797L
N456CL	81	Learjet 35A	35A-456	Suburban Propreties LLC. Elgin, Il.	N711CD
N456JG	96	Beechjet 400A	RK-119	Rymeg LLC/Tricam Industries, Minneapolis-Flying Cloud, Mn.	(N7981M)
N456MS	04	Global 5000	9149	Echo Aircraft Holdings LLC/TAG Aviation UK Ltd. Farnborough.	N356MS
N456Q	05	Learjet 45	45-282	Quinn Group Inc. Long Beach, Ca.	
N456SM	05	Citation Sovereign	680-0038	On Time Aviation Corp. Riyadh, Saudi Arabia.	N.....
N456SW	93	Citation V	560-0222	DBF/Sky High Aviation LLC. Stockton, Ca.	N1286C
N456TX	80	Citation II	550-0249	Bell Helicopter Textron Inc. Fort Worth, Tx. (was 551-0236).	N456AB
N457DS	88	Gulfstream 4	1077	Dankjold Reed Aviation LLC. Palm Beach, Fl.	N477TS
N457H	01	Gulfstream 4SP	1462	H J Heinz Co. Pittsburgh, Pa.	N462CK
N457HL	82	Challenger 600S	1063	Henry IV LLC/Dankjold Reed Aviation LLC. Palm Beach, Fl.	N409CC
N457JC	85	Gulfstream 3	457	Corporate Air LLC/Titleserv Inc. Fort Lauderdale, Fl.	N972G
N458CK	92	Citation V	560-0160	Strasser Construction Co. Ormond Beach, Fl.	ZS-NDT
N458DA	98	Citation V Ultra	560-0458	Domair Aviation LLC. Dover, De.	LV-YMA
N458F	01	Citation Bravo	550-0986	Terra Management Co. Grand Rapids, Mi.	N45NF
N458HC	89	Beechjet 400	RJ-58	K & P Aviation LLC. Tampa, Fl.	(N750KP)
N458LC	00	Citation Excel	560-5109	FCAL Aviation LLC/JenMar Inc. Latrobe, Pa.	N58LC
N458MT	98	CitationJet	525-0316	J M Thomas Forest Products Co. Ogden, Ut.	N316EJ
N458N	79	Citation II	550-0061	On Eagles Wings 1 LLC. Salem, Or.	N456N
N458NC	98	Citation V Ultra	560-0478	Naphcare Inc. Birmingham, Al.	N111JW
N458PE	87	Citation S/II	S550-0143	Cardal AG. Vaduz, Liechestenstein.	N1VA
N458SB	74	Falcon 20F	308	Jet Fleet International Corp. Van Nuys, Ca.	N453B
N459A	97	Learjet 31A	31A-137	Averitt Aviation Group Inc. Nashville, Tn.	N120RV
N459BN	02	Gulfstream G200	071	Burlington Northern/Santa Fe Railway, Fort Worth, Tx.	(N706QS)
N459CS	02	Challenger 604	5546	KP Flyers LLC. Glyndon, Md.	N604BA
N459LC	99	Learjet 45	45-060	Krueger International Inc. Green Bay, Wi.	N1MG
N459LX	03	Hawker 400XP	RK-365	Flight Options LLC. Cuyahoga County, Oh.	N455CW
N459NA	01	CitationJet CJ-1	525-0459	Nephrology Associates PC. Cape Girardeau, Mo.	N.....
N459SF	94	Learjet 60	60-049	Phillips Aviation Co LLC. Wilmington, De.	N126CX
N460AN	98	Learjet 60	60-127	Pinnacle Air Executive Jet, Springdale, Ar.	(N225BX)
N460AS	01	390 Premier 1	RB-8	Diversified Equipment Leasing LLC. Houma, La.	
N460CP	83	Citation III	650-0021	Zalina LLC/T F Hendricks LLC. Downers Grove, Il.	N650SS
N460D	07	Falcon 900EX EASY	188	OD Aviation Inc. Boca Raton, Fl.	F-WWFW
N460F	89	Challenger 601-3A	5055	Bon Voyage Holdings LLC. NYC.	N46F
N460JD	99	Learjet 60	60-158	Spirit Aviation Inc. Berwyn, Pa.	N50EL
N460KG	06	Hawker 400XP	RK-460	Lee Cole Advisors LLC. Novato, Ca.	(N460JW)

Reg	Yr	Type	c/n	Owner/Operator	Prev Regn
N460L	02	390 Premier 1	RB-46	Jetflight Aviation Inc. Salzburg, Austria.	
N460M	84	Citation S/II	S550-0022	ILD Communications Inc. Ponte Vedra Beach, Fl.	N360M
N460MC	05	Learjet 60	60-309	McLane Co. Temple, Tx.	
N460QS	98	Gulfstream 4SP	1360	NetJets, Port Columbus, Oh.	N360GA
N460SB	91	Learjet 35A	35A-670	Brickman Aviation LLC. Wilmington, De.	N987LP
N461EA	89	Beechjet 400	RJ-61	B D Aire LLC/Remington Admin Service Inc. Little Rock, Ar.	N701LP
N461GA	06	Gulfstream G200	181	Gulfstream Aerospace LP. Dallas-Love, Tx.	4X-C..
N461GT	83	Gulfstream 3	411	Airmont Ltd-Deeside Trading Co. Reno, Nv.	N966H
N461LX	03	Hawker 400XP	RK-368	Flight Options LLC. Cuyahoga County, Oh.	N448CW
N462B	89	Citation V	560-0016	James Koehler, Aberdeen, SD.	N68HQ
N462CB	05	390 Premier 1A	RB-136	C&B LLC/Charles Cusumano Corp. Burbank, Ca.	N36636
N462CW	92	Beechjet 400A	RK-62	Ward/Kraft Inc. Fort Scott, Ks.	(N418LX)
N462LX	05	Hawker 400XP	RK-423	Flight Options LLC. Cuyahoga County, Oh.	N223XP
N462QS	95	Gulfstream 4SP	1262	NetJets, Port Columbus, Oh.	N496GA
N463LX	05	Hawker 400XP	RK-426	Flight Options LLC. Cuyahoga County, Oh.	N26XP
N463MA	89	Gulfstream 4	1108	Marshall Aviation LLC/MTM Enterprises Inc. Tampa, Fl.	N778MT
N464AM	83	Diamond 1A	A090SA	Executive Jet LLC. Rogers, Ar.	C-GLIG
N464CL	66	Learjet 24A	24A-096	Clay Lacy Aviation Inc. Van Nuys, Ca.	N1972L
N464LX	05	Hawker 400XP	RK-453	Flight Options LLC. Cuyahoga County, Oh.	
N464QS	95	Gulfstream 4SP	1264	NetJets, Port Columbus, Oh.	N499GA
N464ST	05	Gulfstream G450	4022	JM Family Enterprises Inc. Fort Lauderdale, Fl.	N622GA
N464TF	99	Learjet 60	60-185	Hawkeye Airplane Inc. Kirkland, Wa.	
N465BC	81	Sabre-65	465-53	BFA Leasing LLC/Bryce Corp. Memphis, Tn.	N80RN
N465LX	05	Hawker 400XP	RK-454	Flight Options LLC. Cuyahoga County, Oh.	
N465NW	82	Learjet 35A	35A-465	465NW LLC. West Columbia, SC.	
N465QS	01	Gulfstream 4SP	1463	NetJets, Port Columbus, Oh.	N463GA
N465SP	81	Sabre-65	465-72	Bolthouse Properties LLC. Bakersfield, Ca.	OO-RSE
N466AE	07	CitationJet CJ1+	525-0642	Sasset AG/Lions Air AG. Zurich, Switzerland.	N5151D
N466CW	03	Hawker 400XP	RK-366	Flight Options LLC. Cuyahoga County, Oh.	
N466F	95	CitationJet	525-0119	Fagen Inc. Granite Falls, Mn.	N47TH
N466JB	69	Gulfstream II SP	57	Dream Toy LLC. Van Nuys, Ca.	N33PJ
N466SS	89	Citation II	550-0626	Capital Buyers of Delaware Inc. Conway, Ar.	LV-WOZ
N467AM	75	Gulfstream II SP	169	The Videotape Center, Burbank, Ca.	N169EA
N467F	99	CitationJet	525-0335	Fagen Inc. Granite Falls, Mn.	N335CT
N467H	63	Sabre-40	282-3	AVMATS/Centurion Investments Inc. Chesterfield, Mo.	(N57QR)
N467LX	05	Hawker 400XP	RK-447	Flight Options LLC. Cuyahoga County, Oh.	
N467MW	00	Gulfstream G200	014	Sunstate Aviation & Leasing LLC. Phoenix, Az.	N121GX
N467QS	04	Gulfstream G400	1533	NetJets, Port Columbus, Oh.	N533GA
N468AB	01	Gulfstream 4SP	1477	Prime Jet LLC. Van Nuys, Ca.	N284DS
N468GH	01	Falcon 900C	190	Highland Alternative LLC. Waukegan, Il.	N906NB
N468HW	75	Gulfstream 2	157	Night Flight LLC. Las Vegas, Nv.	N683EC
N468KL	89	Challenger 601-3A	5036	LK Air Inc. Menlo Park, Ca.	N225N
N468LX	05	Hawker 400XP	RK-468	Flight Options LLC. Cuyahoga County, Oh.	
N468RB	77	Sabre-60	306-133	Taylor's Aviation Services LLC. Marion, Oh.	N400JH
N468RW	01	CitationJet CJ-1	525-0468	Warren Inc. Collins, Ms.	N.....
N468SA	06	Citation Sovereign	680-0122	Cessna Aircraft Co. Wichita, Ks.	N122SV
N469AL	86	BAe 125/800B	258067	American Laser Center, Pontiac, Mi.	(N807LX)
N469BB	81	Learjet 35A	35A-434	469BB LLC. Scottsdale, Az.	N4401
N469BT	84	Gulfstream 3	432	G3 Tampa LLC. Tampa, Fl.	N704JA
N469DE	99	Citation Bravo	550-0883	Indy Bravo LLC. Indianapolis-Metropolitan, In.	
N469DN	98	Citation V Ultra	560-0469	Air Land Leasing LLC. Madera, Ca.	N7010R
N469LX	05	Hawker 400XP	RK-463	Flight Options LLC. Cuyahoga County, Oh.	
N469RS	00	Citation Excel	560-5082	MDX Leasing LLC/Middlesex Corp. Orlando, Fl.	N145SM
N469TB	85	Gulfstream 3	469	River West Investments/Falcon West LLC. Sacramento, Ca.	N1956M
N469WC	76	Westwind-1124	202	Business Limo LLC. Denton, Tx.	N59PT
N470BC	03	Hawker 800XP	258651	Architectural LLC. Washington-Dulles, Va.	N651XP
N470CT	07	Hawker 400XP	RK-536	Forest River Inc. Elkhart, In.	
N470D	07	Falcon 2000EX EASY	139	Dassault Falcon Jet Corp. Teterboro, NJ.	F-WWGZ
N470DP	95	Citation V Ultra	560-0291	Executive Air Taxi Corp. Bismarck, ND.	N744R
N470LX	05	Hawker 400XP	RK-478	Flight Options LLC. Cuyahoga County, Oh.	
N470QS	07	Gulfstream G450	4084	NetJets, Port Columbus, Oh.	N384GA
N470SK	03	Citation Excel	560-5348	Sugar Creek Inc. Olathe, Ks.	N.....
N471LX	06	Hawker 400XP	RK-506	Flight Options LLC. Cuyahoga County, Oh.	
N471XP	05	Hawker 400XP	RK-347	BC Air LLC. Albuquerque, NM.	N471LX
N472LX	06	Hawker 400XP	RK-481	Target Corp. Minneapolis, Mn.	
N472QS	99	Gulfstream 4SP	1372	NetJets, Port Columbus, Oh.	N372GA

Reg	Yr	Type	c/n	Owner/Operator	Prev Regn
☐ N473CW	92	Gulfstream 4	1194	ALII Aviation LLC. Menlo Park, Ca.	N77QR
☐ N473JE	96	Beechjet 400A	RK-121	Jet Ex LLC. Wayzata, Mn.	N419MS
☐ N473KT	84	Gulfstream 3	438	Aero Jet Services Inc. Scottsdale, Az.	N911KT
☐ N473LP	01	Learjet 45	45-196	Louisiana-Pacific Corp. Hillsboro, Or.	N50353
☐ N473LX	07	Hawker 400XP	RK-518	Flight Options LLC. Cuyahoga County, Oh.	N518XP
☐ N474D	00	Gulfstream 4SP	1445	Millard Drexler Inc. San Francisco, Ca.	N445QS
☐ N474LX*	07	Hawker 400XP	RK-541	Flight Options LLC. Cuyahoga County, Oh.	N32051
☐ N474M	06	Gulfstream G450	4073	Motorola Inc. Palwaukee, Il.	N373GA
☐ N474ME	05	Hawker 400XP	RK-474	Corporacion Pipasa SA. Belen, Costa Rica.	N474XP
☐ N474PC	02	CitationJet CJ-2	525A-0087	Pio-Trans Inc. Cleveland, Tn.	N.....
☐ N475DH	02	CitationJet CJ-2	525A-0090	Design Homes Inc. Prairie du Chien, Wi.	N.....
☐ N475HC	83	Citation II	550-0475	Potomac Street Partners LLP. Englewood, Co.	N475WA
☐ N475HM	99	Hawker 800XP	258451	General American Enterprises Inc. Little Rock, Ar.	N41534
☐ N475LC	01	Gulfstream 4SP	1472	L-3 IS LLC. Great Falls, Mt.	N4DA
☐ N475LX	07	Hawker 400XP	RK-554	Flight Options LLC. Cuyahoga County, Oh.	
☐ N475M	06	Gulfstream G450	4067	Motorola Inc. Palwaukee, Il.	N467GA
☐ N475MD	68	JetStar-731	5112	Paxson Communications Management Co. Fort Lauderdale, Fl.	N728PX
☐ N475QS	95	Gulfstream 4SP	1275	NetJets, Port Columbus, Oh.	N459GA
☐ N476BJ	97	Beechjet 400A	RK-176	MG Aviation LLC. Richmond, Va.	
☐ N476GA	07	Gulfstream G550	5176	Gulfstream Aerospace Corp. Savannah, Ga.	
☐ N476JD*	00	CitationJet CJ-1	525-0381	Qualico Steel Co. Webb, Al.	N855BB
☐ N476LC	86	Citation S/II	S550-0091	Braxton Management Services LLC. Great Falls, Mt.	N241LA
☐ N476LX	04	Hawker 400XP	RK-376	Flight Options LLC. Cuyahoga County, Oh.	N476CW
☐ N476MK	00	Falcon 50EX	301	Merck & Co. Mercer County, NJ.	N301EX
☐ N477A	79	Citation II	550-0374	M & B Holdings of Delaware LLC. Gulf Shores. (was 551-0020).	(N999LL)
☐ N477DM	98	Challenger 604	5398	Delta Airelite Business Jets Inc. Cincinnati, Oh.	N597DM
☐ N477GG	74	Gulfstream 2B	155	477 Aviation LLC/Fashion Resources Inc. Van Nuys, Ca.	XA-GAC
☐ N477GJ	06	Hawker 400XP	RK-477	Edmunds Investment LLP-GHE & Assocs. Scottsdale, Az.	(N2944M)
☐ N477JB	93	Gulfstream 4SP	1214	Jerry Bruckheimer Inc. Burbank, Ca.	N2615B
☐ N477LC	87	Citation S/II	S550-0153	Braxton Management Services LLC. Great Falls, Mt.	N242LA
☐ N477LX	04	Hawker 400XP	RK-377	Flight Options LLC. Cuyahoga County, Oh.	N477CW
☐ N477QS	99	Gulfstream 4SP	1377	NetJets, Port Columbus, Oh.	N377GA
☐ N477SA	03	Gulfstream G400	1529	USAA, San Antonio, Tx.	N529GA
☐ N477SJ	85	Gulfstream 3	477	Gulfstream Aerospace Corp. Savannah, Ga.	01 USCG
☐ N477X	74	Sabre-60	306-78	AVMATS/Centurion Investments Inc. Chesterfield, Mo.	N140JA
☐ N478DR	93	Beechjet 400A	RK-61	Data Recognition Corp-DRC Transportation, Mankato, Mn.	(N417LX)
☐ N478GS	01	Gulfstream 4SP	1478	Braxton Management Services LLC. Great Falls, Mt.	N378GA
☐ N478LX	04	Hawker 400XP	RK-387	Flight Options LLC. Cuyahoga County, Oh.	
☐ N478PM	97	Citation X	750-0014	Air Reese LLC/Reese International Ltd. Austin, Tx.	(N14VP)
☐ N479LX	04	Hawker 400XP	RK-397	Flight Options LLC. Cuyahoga County, Oh.	N36997
☐ N479PR	99	Galaxy-1126	008	HWK LLC. DuPage, Il.	VP-CRS
☐ N480CB	07	Challenger 300	20147	Comerica Leasing Corp. Pontiac, Mi.	(N600LS)
☐ N480CC	87	Citation S/II	S550-0129	Crounse Corp. Paducah, Ky.	N87TH
☐ N480CT	07	Hawker 400XP	RK-544	Forest River Inc. Elkhart, In.	
☐ N480DG	89	Citation V	560-0015	Genter Airways LLC. Van Nuys, Ca.	N580MR
☐ N480GA	07	Gulfstream G200	180	Gulfstream Aerospace LP. Dallas-Love, Tx.	4X-C..
☐ N480JJ*	07	Gulfstream G150	241	Jimmie Johnson Racing II Inc. Charlotte, NC.	N631GA
☐ N480LX	04	Hawker 400XP	RK-398	Flight Options LLC. Cuyahoga County, Oh.	(N483LX)
☐ N480M	90	Beechjet 400A	RK-6	MBC Air LLC/McLaughlin Body Co. Moline, Il.	(N406ML)
☐ N480QS	99	Gulfstream 4SP	1380	NetJets, Port Columbus, Oh.	N380GA
☐ N480RL	91	Citation V	560-0109	Rand Consulting Inc. Napa, Ca.	N109VP
☐ N481CW	89	Beechjet 400A	RK-1	Angel Food Ministries, Monroe, Ga.	(N401CW)
☐ N481JJ	00	Learjet 31A	31A-212	Fontana Aviation Inc. Concord, NC.	N480JJ
☐ N481MC	75	Westwind-1123	184	Deer Horn Aviation LC. Midland, Tx.	CC-CRK
☐ N481NS	82	Westwind-1124	378	HL Aviation LLC. Palm Coast, Fl.	C-GXKF
☐ N482DM	84	Diamond 1A	A088SA	Avis Aviation LLC. St Louis, Mo.	
☐ N482GA	07	Gulfstream G200	182	Gulfstream Aerospace LP. Dallas-Love, Tx.	4X-C..
☐ N482GS*	06	Hawker 400XP	RK-482	Catawba Management Corp. Middleburg, Va.	N482XP
☐ N482LX	05	Hawker 400XP	RK-413	Flight Options LLC. Cuyahoga County, Oh.	
☐ N483BA	01	Challenger 604	5483	Boeing Executive Flight Operations, Seattle, Wa.	C-GLYK
☐ N483DM	74	Learjet 24D	24D-291	Jets R Us Delaware LLC. Rutledge, Ga.	N488DM
☐ N483FG	80	HS 125/700A	257094	Plane 1 LLC. Oakbrook Terrace, Il.	N415RD
☐ N483LX	08	Hawker 400XP	RK-563	Flight Options LLC. Cuyahoga County, Oh.	
☐ N484AT	05	390 Premier 1A	RB-141	The Langston Law Firm PA. Booneville, Ms.	N3481V
☐ N484CH	07	Learjet 40XR	45-2075	CLICO Holdings (Barbados) Ltd.	N75XR
☐ N484CW	01	Beechjet 400A	RK-334	Flight Options LLC. Cuyahoga County, Oh.	(N473LX)

Reg	Yr	Type	c/n	Owner/Operator	Prev Regn
☐ N484J	94	CitationJet	525-0048	Jackson Food Stores Inc. Boise, Id.	N525NA
☐ N484JC	03	Hawker 850XP	258644	Johnson Controls Inc. Milwaukee, Wi.	N644XP
☐ N484LC	01	Learjet 45	45-123	Circuit City Stores Inc. Richmond, Va.	N454LC
☐ N484LX	08	Hawker 400XP	RK-570	Flight Options LLC. Cuyahoga County, Oh.	
☐ N484MM	98	Citation V Ultra	560-0491	Phantom Sales Inc. Plantation, Fl.	N404MM
☐ N484T	02	Citation X	750-0199	Target Corp. Minneapolis, Mn. 'Speed is Life'	N5245L
☐ N485AC	82	Learjet 35A	35A-485	Sunward Corp. Billings, Mt.	N710WL
☐ N485AK	81	Citation II	550-0193	AKSM Equipment LLC. Columbus, Oh.	N260J
☐ N485AS	88	Falcon 100	219	Astec Industries Inc. Chattanooga, Tn.	N219JW
☐ N485CT	07	Hawker 400XP	RK-545	Forest River Inc. Elkhart, In.	
☐ N485GM	83	Gulfstream 3	387	Glen W Morgan, Beaumont, Tx.	N620JA
☐ N485LT	00	Hawker 800XP	258485	Surewings Ltd/Ambrion Aviation, Luton, UK.	N44515
☐ N485LX	08	Hawker 400XP	RK-573	Flight Options LLC. Cuyahoga County, Oh.	
☐ N485XP	06	Hawker 400XP	RK-485	Hawker Beechcraft Corp. Wichita, ks.	
☐ N486BG	93	Challenger 601-3A	5133	Berkley Aviation Inc. Fort Lauderdale, Fl.	N121FF
☐ N486CW	82	Diamond 1	A026SA	South Aviation Inc. Fort Lauderdale, Fl.	(N26FA)
☐ N486GA	07	Gulfstream G200	186	Gulfstream Aerospace LP. Dallas-Love, Tx.	4X-C..
☐ N486LX	08	Hawker 400XP	RK-580	Flight Options LLC. Cuyahoga County, Oh.	
☐ N486QS	99	Gulfstream 4SP	1386	NetJets, Port Columbus, Oh.	N486GA
☐ N486TM	00	EMB-135ER	145364	Intel Corp/Executive Jet Management Inc. Cincinnati, Oh.	PT-...
☐ N487DT	03	390 Premier 1	RB-85	D/T Carson Enterprises Inc. Murrieta, Ca.	N4485B
☐ N487F	07	Challenger 300	20152	Venture 487 LLC. Raleigh-Durham, NC.	C-FLQY
☐ N487LX	08	Hawker 400XP	RK-583		
☐ N487QS	95	Gulfstream 4SP	1287	NetJets, Port Columbus, Oh.	N484GA
☐ N488CH	04	Global Express	9150	Charles Schwab, San Francisco, Ca.	C-FAIV
☐ N488CP	99	Citation Excel	560-5055	Reverse Exchange Corp. Seattle, Wa.	(N560KN)
☐ N488GR	64	JetStar-6	5051	Avion Jet Center LLC. Sanford, Fl. (stored Orlando SFB).	N488JS
☐ N488HP	00	Hawker 800XP	258488	Hantz Group Inc. Southfield, Mi.	N50788
☐ N488KF	84	Falcon 200	488	JetSmart Inc. Rochester, NY.	N200NP
☐ N488SR	02	CitationJet CJ-1	525-0488	Chaparral Aviation Inc. San Jose, Ca.	N525WH
☐ N488VC	01	Hawker 800XP	258546	OAKIR LLC/Vestar Capital Partners, NYC.	N108BP
☐ N489B	06	Hawker 400XP	RK-489	BancorpSouth Bank, Tupelo, Ms.	N489XP
☐ N489CB	01	CitationJet CJ-1	525-0489	Cimarron Aviation Inc/Baney Corp. Bend, Or.	N489ED
☐ N489GM	86	Citation S/II	S550-0092	Golden Class Jet LLC. Fort Lauderdale, Fl.	N723S
☐ N489QS	99	Gulfstream 4SP	1389	NetJets, Port Columbus, Oh.	N389GA
☐ N489SA	85	BAe 125/800A	258053	HSH Hawker Inc. Las Vegas, Nv.	N484RA
☐ N489SS	84	Citation II	550-0489	Sierra Sierra Enterprises Inc. Minden, Nv.	(N801TA)
☐ N489VC	99	Hawker 800XP	258443	OAKIR LLC/Vestar Capital Partners, NYC.	N310AS
☐ N490CC	84	Citation II	550-0490	Canouan Resorts Development, Nassau. (was 551-0490)	(N490CD)
☐ N490CT	07	Hawker 400XP	RK-546	Forest River Inc. Elkhart, In.	
☐ N490DC	80	Citation II	550-0117	Dixie Capital Corp. Richmond, Va.	N550RB
☐ N490JC	03	Hawker 400XP	RK-373	Freight Handlers Inc. Raleigh-Durham, NC.	N373XP
☐ N490QS	02	Gulfstream 4SP	1488	NetJets, Port Columbus, Oh.	N488GA
☐ N490SJ	83	Falcon 200	490	Aircraft Guaranty Title LLC. Houston, Tx. (trustor ?).	PH-APV
☐ N491AN	83	Westwind-1124	393	Aircraft Guaranty Title LLC. Houston, Tx. (trustor ?)	N53WW
☐ N491BT	83	Diamond 1A	A054SA	IBT Inc. Merriam, Ks.	N141H
☐ N491CW	94	Beechjet 400A	RK-91	Flight Options LLC. Cuyahoga County, Oh.	(N420LX)
☐ N491EC	02	Gulfstream 4SP	1491	Eastman Chemical Co. Bristol-Tri Cities Regional, Tn.	N491GA
☐ N491HR	06	Hawker 400XP	RK-491	RJS LLC/Hawkeye Renewables, Iowa Falls, Ia.	N491XP
☐ N491JB	89	Citation III	650-0182	MAG Air LLC/Tim Marburger Dodge Inc. Concord, NC.	N682CC
☐ N491N	04	Citation Excel XLS	560-5530	Indium Corp of America Inc. Utica, NY.	N4107W
☐ N491PT	73	Citation	500-0102	Sunflower Air LLC. Wilmington, De.	N491BF
☐ N492A	84	Gulfstream 3	425	Sonic Financial Corp. Charlotte, NC.	N425SP
☐ N492CC	84	Falcon 200	492	Aviation Consultants of Aspen Inc. Nashua, NH.	N412AB
☐ N492GA	07	Gulfstream G550	5192	Gulfstream Aerospace Corp. Savannah, Ga.	
☐ N492JT	70	Gulfstream II SP	82	John Travolta/Atlo Inc. Jumbolair Aviation Community, Ocala.	N728T
☐ N492QS	99	Gulfstream 4SP	1392	NetJets, Port Columbus, Oh.	N392GA
☐ N492RM	82	Learjet 35A	35A-492	N492RM LLC. Hollywood, Fl.	N994CR
☐ N493AG	07	BBJ2-7FY/W	36493	WFBNW NA. Salt Lake City, Ut. (trustor ?).	
☐ N493CW	94	Beechjet 400A	RK-93	Flight Options LLC. Cuyahoga County, Oh.	(N421LX)
☐ N493QS	96	Gulfstream 4SP	1293	NetJets, Port Columbus, Oh.	N415GA
☐ N493S	05	Falcon 2000EX EASY	64	Sammina-SCI Corp. San Jose, Ca.	N493SF
☐ N494CC	91	Beechjet 400A	RK-30	CareCore National LLC. Poughkeepsie, NY.	(N406LX)
☐ N494CW	90	Beechjet 400A	RK-4	Higher Cause LLC/NETech Corp. Grand Rapids, Mi.	N771EL
☐ N494PA	96	Learjet 60	60-076	Pinnacle Group, Rogers, Ar.	N211BX
☐ N494TG	03	Embraer Legacy 600	145678	Answer Group Inc. Fort Lauderdale, Fl.	PT-SAS

Reg	Yr	Type	c/n	Owner/Operator	Prev Regn
N495BA	01	Challenger 604	5495	Boeing Executive Flight Operations, Seattle, Wa.	C-GLXK
N495CM	80	Citation II	550-0151	Powersource Transportation Inc. Griffith, In.	N35HC
N495CT	07	Hawker 400XP	RK-547	Forest River Inc. Elkhart, In.	
N495QS	96	Gulfstream 4SP	1295	NetJets, Port Columbus, Oh.	N417GA
N495RS	91	Gulfstream 4	1161	Sugar Pine Aviation LLC. Medford, Or.	N461TS
N496AS	96	Beechjet 400A	RK-117	Executive AirShare Corp. Wichita, Ks.	N12MQ
N497CW	00	Beechjet 400A	RK-297	Redi-Carpet Inc. Stafford, Tx.	(N464LX)
N497DM	97	Challenger 604	5359	Delta Airelite Business Jets Inc. Cincinnati, Oh.	C-GLWR
N497XP	06	Hawker 400XP	RK-497	V & P Midlands Ltd. East Midlands, UK.	
N498AB	00	Citation Excel	560-5116	Romeo Delta Enterprises LLC. Bedford, Ma.	N5246Z
N498AS*	02	Beechjet 400A	RK-347	Executive AirShare Corp. Wichita, Ks.	N168PJ
N498CS	90	Citation III	650-0180	Pheasant Kay-Bee Toy Inc. Nashua, NH.	N768NB
N498QS	99	Gulfstream 4SP	1398	NetJets, Port Columbus, Oh.	N398GA
N498SW*	93	Learjet 60	60-017	Sunway Hotel Group, Overland Park, Ks.	N864PA
N499AS	98	Beechjet 400A	RK-220	Executive AirShare Corp. Wichita, Ks.	N799SM
N499EH	78	Learjet 25D	25D-239	Gerald T Knox, Missoula, Mt.	N45H
N499HS	05	Citation Excel XLS	560-5602	Marathon Holdings LLC. Raleigh, NC.	N52235
N499NH	81	Sabre-65	465-56	Newman Racing, Lincolnshire, Il.	N65TL
N499P	87	Beechjet 400	RJ-31	Middlebury Equity Partners LLC. Hinsdale, NH.	N114AP
N499PA	05	Hawker 800XPi	258739	Aaron Rents Inc. Atlanta-DeKalb, Ga.	N739XP
N499QS	96	Gulfstream 4SP	1299	NetJets, Port Columbus, Oh.	N423GA
N499RC	86	Citation S/II	S550-0090	Racing Champions Corp/T-Bird Aviation Inc. Chicago-DuPage.	N113VP
N499WM	98	Citation Bravo	550-0869	Weis Markets Inc. Sunbury, Pa.	N98RX
N500AD	73	Citation	500-0091	Investment Leasing LLC. St Charles, Mo.	(N1899)
N500AF	01	Falcon 50EX	320	AFLAC Inc. Columbus, Ga.	N662P
N500AL	06	Challenger 300	20092	Abbott Laboratories Inc. Waukegan, Il.	C-FGWL
N500AS	07	CitationJet CJ-3	525B-0164	Newair Inc/Sandals Resorts, Fl.	N1314V
N500BJ	78	Westwind-1124	242	Air Metro Leasing Inc. Wilmington, De.	N140DR
N500CG	98	Learjet 45	45-009	Tessa Two Inc/Chip Ganassi Racing, Indianapolis, In.	N459LJ
N500CW	04	CitationJet CJ-1	525-0542	ATC Freightliner Group Inc.	N5125J
N500CZ	03	390 Premier 1	RB-98	CZZC Aviation LLC/HSL Properties Inc. Tucson, Az.	N61998
N500DW	92	Citation V	560-0199	DarWal Inc. Harrisburg, NC.	N4895Q
N500E	01	Global Express	9105	Mobil Corp. Dallas-Love, Tx.	N100A
N500ED	79	Learjet 35A	35A-241	500ED LLC. West Columbia, SC.	N500EX
N500EF	83	Gulfstream 3	400	WFBNW NA. Salt Lake City, Ut. (trustor ?).	(N990ML)
N500ET	74	Citation	500-0180	Sunshine Air Inc. Double Springs, Al.	N772C
N500FA	86	Astra-1125	011	Astra II LLC. Las Vegas, Nv.	N991RV
N500FM	80	HS 125/700A	NA0280	First Magnus Financial Corp. Tucson, Az.	N280VC
N500FR	91	Citation VI	650-0208	Cope Enterprises, Hobbs, NM.	I-TALW
N500FZ	90	Citation V	560-0018	Waverly Investors LLC. Highland Park, Il.	N114CP
N500GF	86	Gulfstream 3	488	Waffle House Inc. Norcross, Ga.	(N45PG)
N500GR	73	Citation	500-0098	G J R Leasing Inc/Reebaire Aircraft Inc. Hot Springs, Ar.	PH-CTC
N500GV	96	Gulfstream V	506	Aerolinx LLC. NYC.	(N110LE)
N500HY	97	Beechjet 400A	RK-153	NACCO Materials Handling Group Inc. Greenville, SC.	N153BJ
N500J	06	Gulfstream G450	4052	Johnson & Johnson, Mercer County Airport, NJ.	N452GA
N500JD	82	Falcon 50	84	JHD Aircraft Sales LLC. Memphis, Tn.	N503EZ
N500JE	94	Learjet 31A	31A-088	RP Sales & Leasing Inc. Sandford, Fl.	N508J
N500JW	78	Gulfstream 2TT	234	Jet-A-Way Charters LLC. Willimantic, Ct.	(N956MJ)
N500KE	81	Westwind-1124	360	The Ride Inc. Anchorage, Ak.	N816S
N500LG	79	Learjet 28	28-005	Jet Manager Inc. Hanford, Ca.	N8LL
N500LJ	02	Beechjet 400A	RK-340	Curry Stone Family LLC. Salem, Or.	N51540
N500LR	87	Challenger 601-3A	5012	Circuit City Stores Inc. Richmond, Va.	N1868M
N500LS	98	BBJ-73T	29054	Limited Inc. Columbus, Oh.	N6067E
N500M	01	Challenger 604	5480	Cook Inc. Bloomington, In.	N121DF
N500MG	02	Citation Encore	560-0624	Pacific Monarch Resorts Inc. Santa Ana, Ca.	N1242K
N500ML	73	Citation	500-0074	M & L Aviation LLC/Bethlehem Construction, Cashmere, Wa.	PT-OOF
N500MP	99	Learjet 31A	31A-198	N500MP LLC. Grand Rapids, Mi.	
N500N	06	Gulfstream G450	4056	Twin Oaks LLC. New Haven, Ct.	(N450PG)
N500NB	06	CitationJet CJ2+	525A-0339	Omni Leasing Corp. Atlanta, Ga.	N.....
N500ND	80	Learjet 35A	35A-351	World Jet Inc. Fort Lauderdale, Fl. (status ?).	N500DD
N500NH	82	Falcon 20F-5B	470	Haas Enterprises LLC. Lincolnshire, Il.	N470G
N500NJ	73	Citation	500-0113	Northern Air Inc. Grand Rapids, Mi.	N684H
N500PC	02	Gulfstream 4SP	1492	Noble Leasing LLC. White Plains, NY.	N123MR
N500PE	99	Challenger 604	5440	Applera Corp. White Plains, NY.	C-GLXU
N500PG	85	Challenger 601	3039	Air Kelso LLC. Teterboro, NJ.	N639CL
N500PP	83	Diamond 1A	A061SA	Diamond Aviation of Jackson LLC. Jackson, Mi.	N18T

Reg	Yr	Type	c/n	Owner/Operator	Prev Regn
❏ N500PR	02	Challenger 800	7846	Penske Jet Inc. Pontiac, Mi.	N846PR
❏ N500PX	05	Citation Encore	560-0691	Phoenix Construction Services Inc. Panama City, Fl.	N300PX
❏ N500R	02	Falcon 50EX	323	NASCAR Inc. Daytona Beach, Fl.	N50QN
❏ N500RD	05	Gulfstream G550	5105	Oakmont Corp. Van Nuys, Ca.	N935GA
❏ N500RE	85	Falcon 50	156	Regal Cinemas Inc. Knoxville, tn.	N377HW
❏ N500RH	98	Gulfstream V	558	Hendrick Motorsports Inc. Concord, NC.	N600RH
❏ N500RL	73	Gulfstream 2	122	R Lacy Inc Oil & Gas Production, Longview, Tx.	N84A
❏ N500RP	06	Gulfstream G450	4057	Penske Jet Inc. Pontiac, Mi.	N457GA
❏ N500RR	83	Falcon 200	491	Sonic Financial Corp. Charlotte, NC.	N843MG
❏ N500SK	73	Citation	500-0129	M H Aviation LLC. Cleveland, Tn.	N8114G
❏ N500SV	03	CitationJet CJ-2	525A-0153	Peoples Management of South Texas Inc. Laredo, Tx.	N5223P
❏ N500SW	76	Learjet 24D	24D-325	Performance Aircraft Leasing Inc. Aspen, Co.	(N117CC)
❏ N500TH	99	Beechjet 400A	RK-246	Lin R Rogers Electrical Contractors, Winston Salem, NC.	
❏ N500TM	73	Citation Eagle	500-0112	Heizer Aviation Inc. St Louis, Mo.	N515DC
❏ N500TS	99	Citation Bravo	550-0886	True Speed Enterprises II Inc. Indianapolis, In.	N550KH
❏ N500UB	90	Citation V	560-0052	Pomeroy Transport Inc. Stamford, Ct.	N500LE
❏ N500UJ	90	Citation V	560-0062	Harris Air Inc. Logan, Ut.	(N405RH)
❏ N500VA	01	Citation Bravo	550-0987	Martinsville Speedway, Martinsville, Va.	N471WR
❏ N500VC	91	Citation V	560-0144	Van Creb LLC. Corvallis, Or.	N2000X
❏ N500WN	69	F 28-1000	11016	Wayne Newton/Desert Eagle LLC. Las Vegas, Nv.	N43AE
❏ N500WR	91	Learjet 31A	31A-038	Diamond Aviation II Inc. Concord, NC.	N131NA
❏ N500XY	66	HS 125/731	25119	Dove Air Inc. Asheville, NC.	N213H
❏ N500ZA	77	Learjet 24F	24F-350	Onager Co. Odessa, Tx.	N741GL
❏ N501AD	78	Citation 1/SP	501-0093	Ace Aviation Service LLC. Carlsbad, Ca.	N501RM
❏ N501AF	80	Citation 1/SP	501-0139	Newport Aeronaut LLC. Bellevue, Wa.	N888BH
❏ N501AT	77	Citation 1/SP	501-0017	Matthew Spitzer, Hayward, Ca.	N100WJ
❏ N501BB	79	Citation 1/SP	501-0087	HBC Aviation LLC. Fargo, ND.	N501SJ
❏ N501BE	77	Citation 1/SP	501-0263	501BE LLC. Alexandria, La.	(N501BF)
❏ N501BP	81	Citation 1/SP	501-0231	Central Virginia Aircraft Sales Inc. Lynchburg, Va.	N29HE
❏ N501BW	97	Beechjet 400A	RK-167	Romero Leasing Inc. Stuttgart, Ar.	N711EC
❏ N501CB	78	Citation 1/SP	501-0281	501CB LLC. Reno, Nv. (was 500-0372).	N501SJ
❏ N501CD	78	Citation 1/SP	501-0066	David MacHugh, Pasco, Wa.	VP-CTB
❏ N501CF	79	Citation 1/SP	501-0128	WL Aircraft Inc. Richmond, Va.	N900MM
❏ N501CG	98	Learjet 45	45-040	Spitfire Aviation Parts Inc. Concord, NC.	N68PQ
❏ N501CP	77	Citation 1/SP	501-0034	VonJet LLC. Las Cruces, NM.	N444MV
❏ N501CT	00	Hawker 800XP	258512	Century Tel Service Group LLC. Monroe, La.	
❏ N501CV	01	Gulfstream V	639	CSC Transport Inc. White Plains, NY.	N639GA
❏ N501CW	90	Citation V	560-0050	Asheville Aviation LLC. Asheville, NC.	N208BC
❏ N501D	79	Citation 1/SP	501-0298	S Aviation LLC. Las Vegas, Nv.	VR-CMS
❏ N501DA	77	Citation Eagle	500-0349	Dove Air Inc. Fletcher, NC.	VH-HVH
❏ N501DB	02	Falcon 900C	196	Konfara LLC. Scottsdale, Az.	N196FJ
❏ N501DD	77	Citation 1/SP	501-0035	Dukes Deux Leasing Co. Scottsdale, Az.	N35JF
❏ N501DP	80	Citation 1/SP	501-0162	Dunn Equipment Leasing LLC. Daytona Beach, Fl.	N446V
❏ N501DR	79	Citation 1/SP	501-0141	Eagle Aviation LLC. Wilmington, De.	N501GG
❏ N501EA	77	Citation 1/SP	501-0054	Sierra Tel Business Systems/S T Air Services, Oakhurst, Ca.	N2BT
❏ N501EJ	73	Citation	500-0119	Citation Montana Inc. Buffalo, Wy.	N95Q
❏ N501FJ	80	Citation 1/SP	501-0167	Southern Counties Oil Co. Orange, Ca.	N723JM
❏ N501FP	80	Citation 1/SP	501-0161	Flying Services NV. Antwerp, Belgium.	XB-FXO
❏ N501G	81	Citation 1/SP	501-0202	DWT Inc. Oklahoma City, Ok.	N477KM
❏ N501GB	74	Citation	500-0231	Guiffre Organization Ltd. Watertown, Wi.	N500SJ
❏ N501GF	83	HS 125/700B	257208	Waffle House Inc. Norcross, Ga.	G-BLSM
❏ N501GG	83	Citation II	550-0484	North American Jet Charter Inc. Banning, Ca.	N84EA
❏ N501HG	82	Citation 1/SP	501-0221	State of Georgia DoT, Atlanta, Ga.	(N643VP)
❏ N501HS	79	Citation 1/SP	501-0096	Garry Lewis, Baton Rouge, La.	N660KC
❏ N501JD	79	Citation 1/SP	501-0129	Margar Industries Inc. Greeley, Co.	PT-LQQ
❏ N501JE	83	Citation 1/SP	501-0253	Asset Backed Enterprises LLC. Atlanta, Ga.	N2650Y
❏ N501JF	76	Citation	500-0343	WB Aviation LLC. Atlanta, Ga.	C-FOSM
❏ N501JG	77	Citation 1/SP	501-0038	Challenger Aircraft Charters LLC. Newport, RI.	N315S
❏ N501JJ	77	Citation 1/SP	501-0269	Josef Eoff, Salem, Or. (was 500-0357).	XB-GVY
❏ N501JM	81	Citation 1/SP	501-0226	R & R Aviation LLC. Wilmington, De.	N226VP
❏ N501JP	94	Citation II	550-0730	WWG Citation Air LLC. Tucson, Az.	(N650JP)
❏ N501JS	90	Citation V	560-0066	Chrysler Aviation Inc. Van Nuys, Ca.	N60S
❏ N501KC	79	Falcon 200	401	Los Ruisenores SPR de RL. Leon, Guanajuato, Mexico.	N699GA
❏ N501KG	75	Citation	500-0279	Eagle Mountain International Church, Fort Worth, Tx.	N120S
❏ N501KK	81	Citation 1/SP	501-0181	Barnhill & Associates LLC. Amarillo, Tx.	N250SR
❏ N501KM	79	Citation 1/SP	501-0101	Mahaney Air LLC. Portland, Me.	(N323JB)

Reg	Yr	Type	c/n	Owner/Operator	Prev Regn
N501KR	93	CitationJet	525-0033	King Ranch Inc. Houston, Tx.	N116AP
N501LC	80	Citation II	550-0146	ILC Interests Ltd. San Antonio, Tx.	(N611RR)
N501LH	76	Citation	500-0342	Americraft Carton Inc. Kansas City, Mo.	N501DR
N501LR	92	BAe 1000A	259025	Hawker Beechcraft Corp. Wichita, Ks.	N525QS
N501LS	03	Regional Jet	7584	The Limited Inc. Columbus, Oh.	C-G...
N501MB	79	Citation 1/SP	501-0122	Chardan Aero/Wistar Management Corp. West Palm Beach, Fl.	(N501MD)
N501PC	97	Falcon 50EX	265	PepsiCo Inc. White Plains, NY.	N9550A
N501PV	77	Citation 1/SP	501-0028	C1NV LLC. Las Vegas, Nv.	N1234X
N501Q	82	Citation 1/SP	501-0233	SMDA LLC/Ozark Management Inc. Jefferson City, Mo.	N18860
N501RC	80	Citation 1/SP	501-0165	New Hampshire Jet Holdings Inc. Nashua, NH.	N165NA
N501RG	81	Citation 1/SP	501-0260	PAMA Ventures LLC. Seattle, Wa.	N41LE
N501RL	88	Citation II	550-0601	Arkansas Wholesale Lumber Co. Searcy, Ar.	N42NA
N501RP	06	Gulfstream G150	209	Penske Jet Inc. Pontiac, Mi.	N409GA
N501RS	01	Learjet 31A	31A-223	RS1 LLC. Mooresville, NC.	N800CH
N501SP	77	Citation 1/SP	501-0019	Premier Air Management LLC. Lake Oswego, Or. (status ?).	(N5EM)
N501SS	78	Citation	500-0374	Dove Air Inc. Fletcher, NC.	(N505BB)
N501ST	77	Citation 1/SP	501-0270	Apple Air LLC. Minot, ND.	N105JM
N501T	82	Citation 1/SP	501-0244	H & D Aviation/Hudak & Dawson Construction, Charlotte, NC.	(N501HD)
N501TJ	77	Citation 1/SP	501-0013	VoiceNet Air Inc. Ivyland, Pa.	VR-BJK
N501TL	74	Citation	500-0207	Fran Inc. Wilmington, De.	(N107SE)
N501TP	84	Citation 1/SP	501-0684	Stage Aviation Inc. Carmel, Ca.	N3683G
N501U	77	Citation 1/SP	501-0037	Gualjaina LLC. Miami, Fl.	N234JW
N501VP	77	Citation 1/SP	501-0261	Aberrone LLC. Wilmington, De. (was 500-0351).	N7NE
N501WB	80	Citation 1/SP	501-0158	Bannen Enterprises/Davric Corp. Medford, Or.	N1MX
N501WD	83	Citation 1/SP	501-0251	TOH Aircraft Partners LLC. Birmingham, Al.	N501RG
N501WJ*	80	Citation 1/SP	501-0143	SNA Aircraft Sales Ltd. Santa Ana, Ca.	N520BH
N501WL	79	Citation 1/SP	501-0135	W L Paris Enterprises Inc. Louisville, Ky.	N63CG
N501WX*	82	Citation 1/SP	501-0257	Westwind Aviation Inc. Fort Worth, Tx.	N570D
N501X	82	Citation 1/SP	501-0255	Firstlook Properties Inc/Private Sky Aviation, Marietta, Ga.	N901NB
N501ZK	02	Gulfstream G550	5001	Atlas Tube Inc. Harrow, ON. Canada.	N621KD
N502BC	00	Citation Excel	560-5098	Wellmark Inc/Blue Cross & Blue Shield, Des Moines, Ia.	N200PF
N502BE	74	Citation	500-0195	Grosso Aviation LLC. Cottage Grove, Wi.	N500LJ
N502BG	78	Falcon 20F-5	388	Cobalt Resources LLC. Jackson, Wy.	N756
N502CA	07	Hawker 400XP	RK-525	Aerolineas Ejecutivas SA. Toluca, Mexico.	
N502CC	79	Citation 1/SP	501-0113	Sewell Brothers Inc. Cordell, Ok.	N200ES
N502CL	78	Citation II/SP	551-0002	Tudor Oak Farms, Lake in the Hills, Il.	N39ML
N502E	93	Citation V	560-0232	Emerson Electric Co. St Louis, Mo.	
N502EG	04	Citation Excel XLS	560-5502	Distribution Air & Transportation Service LLC. Lebanon, Mo.	N502XL
N502GF	83	HS 125/700B	257210	Waffle House Inc. Norcross, Ga.	G-BLTP
N502GM	04	Gulfstream G350	4011	GM Aviation/Multi Inversiones, Guatemala City, Guatemala.	N121GA
N502HE	92	Challenger 601-3A	5111	Heckmann Enterprises Inc. Palm Springs, Ca.	N502F
N502HR	00	Hawker 800XP	258502	Hawker Beechcraft Corp. Wichita, Ks.	XA-AET
N502JF	82	Learjet 35A	35A-490	Floyd Aviation LLC. Destin, Fl.	N64MP
N502JL	00	Global Express	9050	Hanover Aviation Inc. Orlando, Fl.	VP-COP
N502JM	04	Learjet 40	45-2017	MALCO Aircraft Sales & Leasing LLC. Las Vegas, Nv.	N5009T
N502KA	96	Gulfstream V	502	Kataiba Al Ghanim, Oxford, Ct.	N502GV
N502N	04	Hawker 400XP	RK-386	Twin Palms LLC. Charlotte, NC.	N524LP
N502PG	79	Falcon 10	144	WWC Golf Ventures LLC. Murrieta, Ca.	N502BG
N502PM	00	390 Premier 1A	RB-185	Premier Equity LLC. St Paul, Mn.	N7085V
N502QS	00	Gulfstream V	601	NetJets, Port Columbus, Oh.	N536GA
N502RP	06	Gulfstream G150	212	Penske Jet Inc. Pontiac, Mi.	N412GA
N502TN	02	CitationJet CJ-1	525-0505	Modern Aero Inc. Eden Prairie, Mn.	N.....
N502XL	08	Citation Excel XLS+	560-6002	Cessna Aircraft Co. Wichita, Ks.	N.....
N503BC	01	Learjet 60	60-239	The Brinks Co. Richmond, Va.	(ZS-SCT)
N503CC	72	Citation	500-0003	JetPlus LLC. Little Rock, Ar.	
N503CS	01	Citation Excel	560-5205	CitationShares Sales Inc. White Plains, NY.	N5100J
N503LC	07	CitationJet CJ-3	525B-0162	Loren Cook Co. Springfield, Mo.	N.....
N503MG	66	B 727-191	19392	Roush Racing Inc. Livonia, Mi.	N503RA
N503PC	97	Falcon 50EX	263	PepsiCo Inc. White Plains, NY.	N8550A
N503RE	01	Learjet 60	60-227	West Air LLC/Pet Supermarkets Inc. Fort Lauderdale, Fl.	N503RP
N503RP	06	Gulfstream G150	215	Omicron Transportation Inc. Reading, Pa.	N615GA
N503RV	68	Falcon 20C-5	161	AGI Holding Corp/Affinity Group Inc. Ventura, Ca.	N10RZ
N504BW	91	Citation V	560-0128	BorgWarner Inc. Chicago, Il.	N85KC
N504CC	99	Citation V Ultra	560-0504	Casto Plane LLC. Columbus, Oh.	
N504CS	02	Citation Excel	560-5229	CitationShares Sales Inc. White Plains, NY.	N5105F
N504CX	81	Falcon 50-4	81	ACXIOM Corp. Conway, Ar.	N718DW

Reg	Yr	Type	c/n	Owner/Operator	Prev Regn
N504D	79	Citation Eagle	500-0387	Capital City Bank, Topeka, Ks.	N484KA
N504F	80	Learjet 35A	35A-340	ExpressJet Airlines Inc. Houston, Tx.	N11YM
N504FJ	85	Falcon 200	504	Aerocraft International Inc. Coconut Grove, Fl.	N504CL
N504MK	90	Falcon 50	205	Keller Uchida Realty Resources LLC. Portland, Or.	(N848K)
N504PK	04	Citation Excel	560-5369	Pike Electric Inc. Mount Airy, NC.	N678QS
N504RP	88	Citation III	650-0176	Penske Jet Inc. Pontiac, Mi.	N176AF
N504T	94	Citation VII	650-7040	PDT Aviation LLC. Barrington, Il.	N1265B
N504YP	86	Falcon 50-4	170	Premier Air Center Inc. Alton/St Louis, Il.	N508AF
N505AG	99	Citation Bravo	550-0905	Mike Rutherford, Houston, Tx.	N5101J
N505AZ	74	Citation	500-0188	The Painters Store USA Inc. Miami, Fl.	PT-KPB
N505BB	83	Citation 1/SP	501-0323	T & T Ball Corp. Wilmington, De.	(N142AL)
N505BG	80	Citation 1/SP	501-0185	Gunn Oil Co. Wichita Falls, Tx.	N501LL
N505CF	79	Citation 1/SP	501-0130	Coburn's Inc. St Cloud, Mn.	N102HS
N505CL	80	Falcon 50	38	Stephenson Aviation LP. Schaumburg, Il.	N993
N505CS	02	Citation Excel	560-5252	CitationShares Sales Inc. White Plains, NY.	N5145V
N505EH	83	Learjet 55	55-067	TVPX Inc. Concord, Ma.	N127GT
N505FX	03	Challenger 300	20006	BBJS/FlexJets, Addison, Tx.	N5014F
N505GA	98	Galaxy-1126	005	Bay Jet LLC. Concord, Ca.	4X-IGB
N505HG	75	Learjet 36	36-009	General Transervice Inc. New Castle, De.	N505RA
N505JH	79	Citation 1/SP	501-0126	Jackson Hole Air Charter Inc. Jackson, Wy.	N505SP
N505LR	91	BAe 1000A	259005	Executive Charters Inc. Kinston, NC. (was NA1000).	N505QS
N505MA	98	Citation X	750-0057	Precision Jet Management Inc. Syracuse, NY.	
N505PM	82	Challenger 600S	1051	Lexion Medical LLC. St Paul, Mn.	N27BH
N505RJ	77	Citation 1/SP	501-0009	Richard J Rico Revocable Trust, Vacaville, Ca.	N505BC
N505RP	83	Citation II	550-0450	Boston Air Charter LLC. Norfolk, Ma.	N15EA
N505RR	97	Falcon 2000	46	Sonic Financial Corp. Charlotte, NC.	CS-DCM
N505TC	81	Falcon 50	57	Thornton Corp. Van Nuys, Ca.	N138E
N505XP	06	Hawker 400XP	RK-505	Harbor Air LC. Vero Beach, Fl.	
N506BA	96	Falcon 900B	160	Mill-Max Manufacturing Corp. Islip, NY.	N176CF
N506CS	02	Citation Excel	560-5267	CitationShares Sales Inc. White Plains, NY.	N5246Z
N506E	93	Citation V	560-0236	Emerson Electric Co. St Louis, Mo.	
N506FX	03	Challenger 300	20007	BBJS/FlexJets, Addison, Tx.	C-G...
N506KS	06	Learjet 40	45-2055	Wal-Mart Stores Inc. Rogers, Ar.	N55XR
N506QS	00	Gulfstream V	623	NetJets, Port Columbus, Oh.	N623GA
N506TF	77	Citation Stallion	501-0001	Sierra Industries Inc. Uvalde, Tx.	N51CJ
N506TS	87	Challenger 601-3A	5006	Aero Toy Store LLC. Fort Lauderdale, Fl.	C-GENA
N507CS	02	Citation Excel	560-5282	CitationShares Sales Inc. White Plains, NY.	N5094D
N507FG	06	Learjet 45	45-326	Flex Air Ltd/FlightStar Corp. Chicago-Midway, Il.	
N507FX	03	Challenger 300	20008	BBJS/FlexJets, Addison, Tx.	C-GZDV
N507HB	05	Hawker 400XP	RK-507	Executive Charters Inc. Kinston, NC.	N466LX
N507HF	70	Learjet 25	25-057	White Industries Inc. Bates City, Mo. (status ?).	(N225EA)
N507HP	00	CitationJet CJ-1	525-0395	R T Moore Mechanical Contractors, Indianapolis, In.	N525AR
N507QS	01	Gulfstream V	625	NetJets, Port Columbus, Oh.	N625GA
N507SA	00	Gulfstream 4SP	1456	AMB Group LLC. Atlanta, Ga.	N396GA
N508BP	99	Hawker 800XP	258419	Pilgrim's Pride Corp. Pittsburgh, Tx.	N419XP
N508CS	02	Citation Excel	560-5294	CitationShares Sales Inc. White Plains, NY.	N5068R
N508FX	03	Challenger 300	20009	BBJS/FlexJets, Addison, Tx.	C-GZDY
N508KD*	91	Citation V	560-0147	Woundenburg Executive Offices, Scottsdale, Az.	(N880EF)
N508P	02	Gulfstream V	693	Hewlett Packard Co. San Jose, Ca.	N693GA
N508PC	02	Falcon 900EX	111	PepsiCo Inc. White Plains, NY.	N57EL
N508QS	01	Gulfstream V	631	NetJets, Port Columbus, Oh.	N631GA
N508SR	77	Learjet 24E	24E-347	Falcon Air LLC/Merex Inc. Camarillo, Ca.	N500SR
N508VM	75	HS 125/F600B	256045	VIP World Jet Charter, Pompano, Fl.	G-BGYR
N509CS	02	Citation Excel	560-5310	CitationShares Sales Inc. White Plains, NY.	N.....
N509FX	03	Challenger 300	20012	BBJS/FlexJets, Addison, Tx.	C-GZEH
N509QS	00	Gulfstream V	637	NetJets, Port Columbus, Oh.	N637GA
N510BC	83	Diamond 1A	A057SA	Happy Trails LLC. Birmingham, Al.	N334WM
N510CL	73	Falcon 10	9	Tudor Oak Farms, Lake in the Hills, Il.	N149TJ
N510FX	04	Challenger 300	20017	BBJS/FlexJets, Addison, Tx.	C-GZEP
N510GP	82	Citation II	550-0421	Dry Cleaning Information Systems Inc. Van Nuys, Ca.	(N801TA)
N510HF	03	Citation Excel	560-5331	ElanAir Inc/Heritage Flight, Burlington, Vt.	N946TC
N510JC	80	Citation II	550-0197	Renda Aviation LLC. Grapevine, Tx.	HB-VIT
N510MG	98	Gulfstream 4SP	1349	OM Group Inc. Cleveland, Oh.	N616DG
N510NJ	81	Citation 1/SP	501-0180	Southern Cross Aircraft LLC. Fort Lauderdale, Fl.	LV-BHJ
N510RR	00	Falcon 2000	137	Sonic Financial Corp. Charlotte, NC.	N61KW
N510SD	88	Citation III	650-0161	Freudenberg-NOK/Marlin Air Inc. Detroit, Mi.	N500AE

Reg	Yr	Type	c/n	Owner/Operator	Prev Regn
N510SR	93	Gulfstream 4	1183	Related Gulfstream LLC. NYC.	N510ST
N510US	78	Gulfstream II SP	223	AIP Jets LLC. Salt Lake City, Ut.	N257H
N511AB	81	Citation II	550-0299	Elizabeth Cardide Die Co. Allegheny County. (was 551-0339).	HB-VIR
N511AC	95	CitationJet	525-0098	Avis Industrial Corp. Upland, In.	N5156D
N511AT	74	Citation	500-0166	Air Ambulance by Air Trek Inc. Punta Gorda, Fl. (status ?).	N8DE
N511BA	69	Gulfstream 2	49	Wing Financial LLC. Las Vegas, Nv.	(N49JS)
N511BP	99	CitationJet	525-0332	Alabama Farmers Cooperative, Decatur, Al.	(N332VP)
N511CS	03	Citation Excel	560-5324	CitationShares Sales Inc. White Plains, NY.	N.....
N511CT	07	Gulfstream G150	234	Advance America Cash Advance Centers, Spartanburg, SC.	4X-C..
N511DN	01	Citation Excel	560-5231	Ultra Capital LLC. Jackson, Ms.	N417JD
N511FL	67	Falcon 20C-5	122	IFL Group Inc. Pontiac Mi.	N302TT
N511FX	04	Challenger 300	20021	BBJS/FlexJets, Addison, Tx.	C-GZDQ
N511HC	79	Citation 1/SP	501-0136	Triple Seven LLC. Modesto, Ca.	N800TW
N511JP	00	Citation Bravo	550-0959	Northshore Air LLC. Baton Rouge, La.	N418KW
N511KA	78	HS 125/700A	NA0237	Habari Inc. Rancho Cucamonga, Ca.	N511GP
N511LD	82	HS 125/700A	NA0333	Power Design Inc. St Petersburg, Fl.	N125AS
N511PA	89	Gulfstream 4	1111	Apex Oil Co. St Louis, Mo.	N111ZT
N511QS	01	Gulfstream V	647	NetJets, Port Columbus, Oh.	N647GA
N511RG	83	HS 125/700A	NA0344	Ben Hill Griffin Inc. Frostproof, Fl.	XA-GIC
N511TC	94	CitationJet	525-0074	Semitool Inc. Cambridge, UK.	N26581
N511WV	91	Citation V	560-0138	Cin-Jet Inc. Cincinnati, Oh.	OY-FFV
N512CC	72	Citation	500-0012	K3C Inc/Sierra Industries Inc. Uvalde, Tx.	XC-FIU
N512CS	03	Citation Excel	560-5326	CitationShares Sales Inc. White Plains, NY.	N.....
N512FX	04	Challenger 300	20022	BBJS/FlexJets, Addison, Tx.	C-GZDS
N512JB	90	Falcon 50	202	Hunt Lindsey LLC. Fayetteville, Ar.	N750MC
N512JT	03	Gulfstream G450	4005	Kilmer Management LP. Toronto-Pearson, Canada.	N165GA
N512JY	94	Falcon 900B	144	Dassault Falcon Jet Corp. Teterboro, NJ.	N453JS
N513AC	70	Falcon 20D	242	IAL Corp/Dodson International Inc. Rantoul, Ks.	(N242MA)
N513HS	06	Falcon 900EX EASY	175	Contran Corp. Dallas, Tx.	F-WWFV
N513LR	91	BAe 1000A	NA1004	Executive Charters Inc. Kinston, NC.	(N513RA)
N513ML	03	Hawker 800XP	258641	M P Air Inc/Mylan Pharmaceuticals Inc. Morgantown, WV.	N641XP
N513MW	97	Gulfstream V	510	BMW GmbH. Munich, Germany.	N598GA
N513RV	03	CitationJet CJ-1	525-0513	La Mesa RV Center Inc. San Diego, Ca.	N52591
N513XP	06	Hawker 400XP	RK-513	Buck Management Corp. Charleston, SC.	
N514AJ	74	HS 125/600B	256033	A J Foyt Enterprises Inc. Waller, Tx.	N600HS
N514BC	00	Citation Bravo	550-0947	J Oliver Cunningham, Phoenix, Az.	N947CB
N514CS	03	Citation Excel	560-5328	CitationShares Sales Inc. White Plains, NY.	N.....
N514DS	97	CitationJet	525-0255	D S Aviation Inc. Irving, Tx.	
N514FX	04	Challenger 300	20023	BBJS/FlexJets, Addison, Tx.	N513FX
N514HB	07	Hawker 4000	RC-14	Hawker Beechcraft Corp. Wichita, Ks.	
N514LR	91	BAe 1000A	NA1005	Sovereign Air Sdn Bhd.	N514QS
N514MB	86	Falcon 50	168	Virginia Air Exchange Inc. Chicago, Il.	(N420JP)
N514MM	99	Astra-1125SPX	115	Wilmax International NC. Curacao, Netherlands Antilles.	OE-GPG
N514TS	87	Challenger 601-3A	5014	Aero Toy Store LLC. Fort Lauderdale, Fl.	(N714TS)
N515BP	80	Challenger 600S	1006	Tami's Jet LLC. Dallas, Tx.	(N6972Z)
N515CS	03	Citation Excel	560-5335	CitationShares Sales Inc. White Plains, NY.	N.....
N515EV	03	CitationJet CJ-2	525A-0211	Everair LLC. Niagara Falls, NY.	N.....
N515FX	04	Challenger 300	20032	BBJS/FlexJets, Addison, Tx.	C-FDIJ
N515HB	07	Hawker 4000	RC-15	Hawker Beechcraft Corp. Wichita, Ks.	
N515JT	06	Embraer Legacy 600	14500950	J T Aviation Corp. Ronkonkoma, NY.	PT-SCX
N515KK	84	Diamond 1A	A086SA	Kent Kelly/Diamond Aircraft Leasing Corp. Montgomery, Al.	N486DM
N515LP	76	Falcon 10	87	Ashley Development Corp. Bethlehem, Pa.	N156BE
N515LR	91	BAe 1000A	NA1006	Executive Charters Inc. Kinston, NC.	N515QS
N515MW	92	Beechjet 400A	RK-38	RK-38 Leasing LLC. Wilmington, De.	N522EF
N515PL	07	Gulfstream G500	5144	NBL LLC. Columbia, Mo.	N644GA
N515PV	02	Falcon 2000	192	Sentry Aviation Services LLC. Stevens Point, Wi.	N2000A
N515RW	93	Citation V	560-0219	CSC Trust Co of Delaware, Wilmington, De. (trustor ?).	N229VP
N515RY	92	Beechjet 400A	RK-46	Nulife Aviation LLC. Sarasota, Fl.	N8239E
N515TC	81	Learjet 25D	25D-354	Calspan Corp. Buffalo, NY.	N3795U
N515TJ	99	Beechjet 400A	RK-229	Drake Aviation Inc. Bloomfield Hills, Mi.	N3129X
N515WA	98	Beechjet 400A	RK-215	Aalfs Manufacturing Inc. Sioux City, SD.	N3038W
N516CC	00	Galaxy-1126	020	Morgan Flight LLC. Naples, Fl.	N46GX
N516FX	04	Challenger 300	20036	BBJS/FlexJets, Addison, Tx.	C-GZDQ
N516GH	98	Gulfstream V	553	MDL Consulting Associates LLC. Nashua, NH.	N653GA
N516QS	01	Gulfstream V	658	NetJets, Port Columbus, Oh.	N532GA
N516TH	99	Hawker 800XP	258418	Key Air Inc. Oxford, Ct.	(N516TM)

Reg	Yr	Type	c/n	Owner/Operator	Prev Regn
N517AF	98	Citation Bravo	550-0846	N517AF Inc. Wilmington, De.	N5101J
N517CC	96	Learjet 31A	31A-117	Carmike Cinemas Inc. Columbus, Ga.	N317LJ
N517FX	04	Challenger 300	20038	BBJS/FlexJets, Addison, Tx.	(ZS-ACT)
N517GP	98	Learjet 31A	31A-152	Smail Automotive/Smail Aviation Inc. Latrobe, Pa.	
N517LR	92	BAe 1000A	259017	Executive Charters Inc. Kinston, NC.	A6-ELA
N517MD	05	Hawker 400XP	RK-459	Old Dominion Aviation LLC. Winter Park, Fl.	N459XP
N518CL	95	Challenger 601-3R	5180	Applera Corp. White Plains, NY.	C-GLYO
N518FX	05	Challenger 300	20046	BBJS/FlexJets, Addison, Tx.	C-FDAH
N518GS	06	Challenger 300	20132	George Strait Productions Inc. San Antonio, Tx.	C-FJRE
N518JG	00	Learjet 31A	31A-219	Joe Gibbs Racing Inc. Concord, NC.	N214PW
N518M	05	Hawker 800XPi	258737	Marathon Oil Co. Houston, Tx.	
N518MV	81	Citation II/SP	551-0046	JFM Development LLC. Modesto, Ca.	N81GD
N518N	87	Citation II	550-0563	L & R Investment Partners LLC. Lafayette, La.	G-THCL
N518QS	05	Gulfstream G550	5075	NetJets, Port Columbus, Oh.	N967GA
N518RR	80	HS 125/700A	NA0278	Midas Air Corp. Groton, Ct.	N770CC
N518SB	79	Learjet 55C	55C-139A	La Stella Corp. Pueblo, Co. (was 55-002)	N518SA
N518WA	78	Westwind-1124	223	Websta's Aviation Services Inc. St Croix, USVI.	N20KH
N519AA	79	Citation II	550-0053	Security Aviation Inc. Anchorage, Ak.	N550EC
N519EM	80	Falcon 50	19	Avion Sales LLC. Sanford, Fl.	(N551LX)
N519FX	05	Challenger 300	20055	BBJS/FlexJets, Addison, Tx.	C-FFZE
N519M	05	Hawker 800XPi	258747	Marathon Oil Co. Houston, Tx.	
N519RW	90	Beechjet 400A	RK-3	Rusty Wallis Honda, Addison, Tx.	N400VK
N520AF	94	Falcon 50	247	AFLAC Inc. Columbus, Ga.	N740R
N520AW	81	Falcon 20F-5B	453	Armstrong World Industries Inc. Lancaster, Pa.	N189MM
N520CH	02	390 Premier 1	RB-121	Concord Hospitality Enterprises Co. Raleigh-Durham, NC.	N602DV
N520CM	99	Citation X	750-0107	Caremark RX Inc. Birmingham, Al.	N107CX
N520DB	63	MS 760 Paris-2	101	R S Fox LP, Calhoun, Ga.	N444ET
N520DF	96	CitationJet	525-0154	K Transit LLC. Branson, Mo.	(N204LX)
N520E	00	Global Express	9077	Mobil Corp. Dallas-Love, Va.	N200A
N520EP	90	Gulfstream 4	1138	Adams Office LLC. Roxbury, Ct.	N520E
N520FX	05	Challenger 300	20056	BBJS/FlexJets, Addison, Tx.	C-FGMR
N520G	00	Citation Excel	560-5083	Oldenburg Aviation Inc. Milwaukee, Wi.	N52144
N520GB	00	CitationJet CJ-1	525-0388	OGB JET LLC. Pittsburgh-Atkinson, Ks.	N525LB
N520JF	97	Hawker 800XP	258317	Scott Reichelm/TAG Aviation Inc. White Plains, NY.	N520BA
N520LR	92	BAe 1000A	NA1008	Wachtel & Masyr LLP. Corning, NY.	N520QS
N520MP	85	Westwind-1124	421	Interselect Inc. Dallas, Tx.	N317MQ
N520RM	01	CitationJet CJ-1	525-0469	Dream Aviation LLC. Pompano Beach, Fl.	N122CS
N520SC	01	Learjet 60	60-233	Stryker Corp. Kalamazoo, Mi.	N33DC
N520SR	79	Learjet 25D	25D-272	Conrad Yelvington, Daytona Beach, Fl.	N717AN
N520WS	88	Beechjet 400	RJ-53	CADDO Investments Inc. Las Vegas, Nv.	N53EB
N521BH	90	Citation III	650-0185	JetCom LLC/Edco Disposal Corp. Lemon Grove, Ca.	4X-CMR
N521CH	05	Learjet 40	45-2023	Davidson Hotel Co. Memphis, Tn.	N50163
N521CS	04	Citation Excel	560-5362	CitationShares Sales Inc. White Plains, NY.	N.....
N521DC	86	Falcon 50	163	St Jude Medical Inc. St Paul, Mn.	(N854W)
N521FL	66	Falcon 20-5	68	IFL Group Inc. Pontiac, Mi.	N458SW
N521FP	97	Citation X	750-0016	Universal Forest Products Inc. Grand Rapids, Mi.	N206PC
N521FX	05	Challenger 300	20057	BBJS/FlexJets, Addison, Tx.	C-FGGF
N521HN	99	Gulfstream V	570	The Air Group Inc. Van Nuys, Ca.	N451CS
N521JK	94	Hawker 800	258262	Spankie Inc. Van Nuys, Ca.	N959H
N521LF	91	Citation V	560-0132	Interlease Aviation Corp. Van Nuys, Ca.	N226JV
N521LL	94	Citation V Ultra	560-0273	Lewis Training LLC/Lee Lewis Construction Inc. Lubbock, Tx.	(N861CF)
N521PF	93	CitationJet	525-0005	Riester Corp. Phoenix, Az.	N58KJ
N521RA	99	Citation Excel	560-5076	Shea Aviation Inc. Newton, NC.	
N521TM	92	Citation II	550-0705	Idaho Power Co. Boise, Id.	
N521XP	07	Hawker 400XP	RK-521	Executive Charters Inc. Kinston, NC.	EI-ICE
N522AC	03	Gulfstream G400	1524	RDV Corp. Grand Rapids, Mi.	N524GA
N522AG*	87	Learjet C-21A	35A-625	King Air FA-63 Leasing Corp. Fort Lauderdale, Fl.	N625BL
N522BD	06	Falcon 2000EX EASY	84	Becton-Dickinson & Co. Teterboro, NJ.	F-WWGU
N522BP	06	Gulfstream G550	5135	TBP Management LLC. Pampa, Tx.	N535GA
N522CS	04	Citation Excel	560-5364	CitationShares Sales Inc. White Plains, NY.	N.....
N522EE	05	Hawker 850XP	258764	Energy Education of Montana Inc. Dallas-Love, Tx.	N764XP
N522EF	03	Hawker 800XP	258621	Capital Management LLC. Windsor Locks, Ct.	N522EE
N522EL	02	Beechjet 400A	RK-342	TT Transport LLC. Memphis, Tn.	N522EE
N522FX	05	Challenger 300	20064	BBJS/FlexJets, Addison, Tx.	C-FGXW
N522JA	95	Citation V Ultra	560-0288	C&D Aviation LLC/JCM Engineering Corp. Ontario, Ca.	N5141F
N522MB	07	Hawker 400XP	RK-522	MasterBrand Cabinets Inc. Huntingburg, In.	(N385PB)

Reg	Yr	Type	c/n	Owner/Operator	Prev Regn
N523AM	82	Gulfstream 3	372	TVPX Inc. Concord, Ma.	N724DD
N523BT	02	CitationJet CJ-2	525A-0124	Beall Corp. Portland, Or.	N27CJ
N523CC	01	Citation Excel	560-5201	Knowlton Aviation LLC. Philadelphia, Pa.	N533CC
N523CS	04	Citation Excel XLS	560-5507	CitationShares Sales Inc. White Plains, NY.	N.....
N523DG	01	CitationJet CJ-2	525A-0084	National City Commercial Capital Corp. Dallas, Tx.	N525DG
N523FX	06	Challenger 300	20074	BBJS/FlexJets, Addison, Tx.	C-FHDE
N523JM	92	Challenger 601-3A	5106	Worthington Industries/McAir Inc. Columbus, Oh.	(N601PR)
N523KW	98	Citation Excel	560-5015	Capital Excel Inc. Wichita, Ks.	N5223D
N523LR	92	BAe 1000A	NA1010	Executive Charters Inc. Kinston, NC.	N523QS
N523PB	80	Falcon 50	23	Renar Development Co. Stuart, Fl.	(N553LX)
N523TS	00	CitationJet CJ-1	525-0363	T&S Aviation LLC/Todd & Sargent Inc. Ames, Ia.	N525AS
N523WC	03	Falcon 2000	212	N523WC LLC/Marion Plaza Inc. Youngstown, Oh.	N523W
N523WG	87	BAe 125/800A	258086	Jen-Air LLC. DuPage, Il.	(N523W)
N524AC	02	Gulfstream V	686	Alticor Inc. Grand Rapids, Mi.	N686GA
N524AN	89	Gulfstream 4	1119	Harrinford Ltd. Tortola, BVI.	N768J
N524DW	71	Learjet 25B	25B-081	Charter Airlines Inc. Las Vegas, Nv.	N66TJ
N524FX	06	Challenger 300	20095	BBJS/FlexJets, Addison, Tx.	C-FGWZ
N524HC	95	Learjet 31A	31A-114	Prebul Chrysler Jeed Dodge Kia, Chattanooga, Tn.	
N524MA	78	Citation II	550-0029	Lakeshore RV Supercenters, Muskegon, Mi.	N550TJ
N524PA	75	Learjet 35	35-033	Phoenix Air Group Inc. Cartersville, Ga.	N31FN
N524S	81	Falcon 50	51	Meregrass Inc. Dallas-Love, Tx.	(N551S)
N524SF	98	CitationJet	525-0240	CPL Aviation/C P Lockyer Inc. Coventry, UK.	N525GM
N524XP	07	Hawker 400XP	RK-524	WFBNW NA. Salt Lake City, Ut. (trustor ?).	(N425CT)
N525AC	02	Gulfstream V	691	Alticor Inc. Grand Rapids, Mi.	N250DV
N525AK	79	Westwind-1124	260	Crown Air LLC. Bend, Or.	N80FD
N525AL	93	CitationJet	525-0011	Signature Aviation LLC. Monroe, NC.	(N1327N)
N525AM	04	CitationJet CJ-1	525-0538	Managed Air Inc. Greenwood Village, Co.	N51564
N525BP	01	CitationJet CJ-1	525-0479	Pinnacle Country Club Inc. Rockland, Il.	N5200R
N525BR	01	CitationJet CJ-1	525-0444	WS Aviation LLC/Voters News Network, Birmingham, Al.	(N525WS)
N525BT	96	CitationJet	525-0161	Vichon Nevelle (Nevada) Inc. Las Vegas, Nv.	N5076K
N525BW*	00	CitationJet CJ-1	525-0409	Whitaker Oil Co. Atlanta, Ga.	N530AQ
N525CC	00	CitationJet CJ-2	525A-0007	Cessna Aircraft Co. Wichita, Ks.	(N8CQ)
N525CD	99	CitationJet CJ-1	525-0360	Giacomo LLC. Fort Mohave, Az.	N31CJ
N525CE	03	CitationJet CJ-2	525A-0181	PDX VFR LLC. Aurora, Or.	N93AQ
N525CF	07	CitationJet CJ-3	525B-0189	CFA Holdings LLC. Knoxville, Tn.	N5197A
N525CH	94	CitationJet	525-0078	Cooper Hosiery Mills Inc. Fort Payne, Al.	N5085E
N525CK	02	CitationJet CJ-2	525A-0128	Dr Charles Key MD. Dallas, Tx.	N5204D
N525CM	95	CitationJet	525-0093	HAALO Ltd. Las Vegas, Nv.	I-IDAG
N525DC	97	CitationJet	525-0195	Harris Land Co. Charlotte, NC.	(N525ST)
N525DG	05	CitationJet CJ-3	525B-0039	Direct Jet Charter LLC. Greensboro, NC.	N526DG
N525DL	02	CitationJet CJ-2	525A-0050	Briar Development LLP. Bellingham, Wa.	N.....
N525DM	99	CitationJet	525-0314	Marco Opthalmic Inc. Jacksonville, Fl.	N428PC
N525DP	99	CitationJet	525-0318	Means to Go LLC. Altoona, Pa.	
N525DT	00	CitationJet CJ-2	525A-0003	Leonard Green & Partners LP. Van Nuys, Ca.	N132CJ
N525DU	01	CitationJet	525-0205	North Palm Aviation LLC. Mount Clemens, Mi.	(N205NP)
N525DV	02	CitationJet CJ-2	525A-0119	Pacific Cataract & Laser Institute, Chehalis-Centralia, Wa.	N.....
N525DY	98	CitationJet	525-0306	ExecuFlight LLC. Monroeville, Al.	N4RH
N525EP	07	CitationJet CJ2+	525A-0346	Ethanol Products LLC. Wichita, Ks.	N.....
N525EZ	06	CitationJet CJ-3	525B-0089	Eli's Bread (Eli Zabar) Inc. Danbury, Ct.	N5076J
N525F	94	CitationJet	525-0058	Semitool Europe, Salzburg, Austria.	N526CK
N525FC	04	CitationJet CJ-1	525-0531	Frank's Casing Crew & Rental Tools, Lafayette, La.	N333J
N525FD	93	CitationJet	525-0008	Donaldson Aircraft Leasing LLC. Dade City, Fl.	C-GDKI
N525FF	03	CitationJet CJ-2	525A-0161	Santas Ltd. Turks & Caicos Islands.	N28NH
N525FN	99	CitationJet CJ-1	525-0368	Valentine Aviation LLC. Wilmington, De.	N820CE
N525FT	99	CitationJet CJ-1	525-0367	PP & JJ LLC. Gillette, Wy.	N51872
N525FX	06	Challenger 300	20112	BBJS/FlexJets, Addison, Tx.	C-FIEE
N525GB	97	CitationJet	525-0232	Day Trip Aviation LLC. Salt Lake City, Ut.	N525PB
N525GM	05	CitationJet CJ-3	525B-0024	IntegriCare Inc. Wallingford, Ct.	N5221Y
N525GV	91	CitationJet	525-0001	Guardian Enterprises Inc. Portland, Or.	N525VP
N525HA	94	CitationJet	525-0081	Anciliary Services LLC. Madisonville, Ky.	N181JT
N525HB	01	CitationJet CJ-2	525A-0040	Bagwell Aviation LLC. Smithfield, NC.	N.....
N525HC	98	CitationJet	525-0270	Springfield Flying Service Inc. Springfield, Mo.	N5194J
N525HG	07	CitationJet CJ2+	525A-0352	Bagwell Aviation LLC. Smithfield, NC.	N51896
N525HS	93	CitationJet	525-0035	ABA Energy Corp. Bakersfield, Ca.	N1779L
N525HV	97	CitationJet	525-0201	Blue Sky Jet Inc. Spring Valley, Ca.	N5156D
N525J	97	CitationJet	525-0184	National Pacific Fund Inc. Beckeley, Ca.	N5185V

Reg	Yr	Type	c/n	Owner/Operator	Prev Regn
❏ N525JA	81	Citation II	550-0252	Jetz Service Co. Topeka, Ks.	N6JU
❏ N525JJ	02	CitationJet CJ-1	525-0497	Ahern Rentals Inc. Las Vegas, Nv.	N132CS
❏ N525JL	00	CitationJet CJ-1	525-0407	Lewis Investment Co. Birmingham, Al.	N51872
❏ N525JM	96	CitationJet	525-0134	Granberry Supply Corp. Phoenix, Az.	(N525KT)
❏ N525JV	93	CitationJet	525-0010	Flying B's LLC. Rogers, Ar.	ZS-MVX
❏ N525JW	96	CitationJet	525-0162	Honey B LLC/Honey Buckets, Puyallup, Wa.	(N39GA)
❏ N525KA	92	CitationJet	525-0019	Physical Systems Inc. Carson City, Nv.	(N525SP)
❏ N525KM	01	CitationJet CJ-1	525-0472	Kice Industries Inc. Wichita-Jabara, Ks.	N124CS
❏ N525KN	93	CitationJet	525-0007	R & B Air LLC. Cary, NC.	(N1327E)
❏ N525KR	03	CitationJet CJ-2	525A-0160	R A Bridgeford Inc. Napa County, Ca.	N.....
❏ N525KT*	02	CitationJet CJ-2	525A-0058	Keen Transport Inc. Carlisle, Pa.	N811RC
❏ N525L	05	CitationJet CJ-3	525B-0051	Metro Corral Partners/Lemoine Investments, Maitland, Fl.	N5148N
❏ N525LC	82	Citation II	550-0349	United Builders Service Inc. Jeffco Airport, Co.	N600SZ
❏ N525LD	06	CitationJet CJ2+	525A-0335	Lewco Air LLC/Lewco Speciality Products, Baton Rouge, La.	N.....
❏ N525LF	00	CitationJet CJ-1	525-0382	Mallard Air LLC. El Cerrito, Ca.	N5124F
❏ N525LM	00	CitationJet CJ-1	525-0427	MML Investments LLC. Medford, Or.	N128GW
❏ N525LP	97	CitationJet	525-0196	LP Adventures Inc/Scottsdale Flyers LLC. Scottsdale, Az.	N250GM
❏ N525LR	93	BAe 1000A	259035	Hawker Beechcraft Corp. Wichita, Ks.	N535QS
❏ N525LW	94	CitationJet	525-0082	Tita Air SRL. Verona, Italy.	D-IHHS
❏ N525M	99	CitationJet	525-0334	Baron Partners LLC/Dobbs Management Service, Memphis, Tn.	(N44FE)
❏ N525MA	01	CitationJet CJ-2	525A-0012	Commodity Logistics LLC. Missoula, Mt.	N525MP
❏ N525MB	93	CitationJet	525-0036	Falcon Aviation Inc. Columbus, Oh.	N1782E
❏ N525MC	93	CitationJet	525-0018	McCoy Corp. San Marcos, Tx.	(N1328X)
❏ N525MF	98	CitationJet	525-0313	Baron Exploration Co. Edmond, Ok.	N525MR
❏ N525MH	92	Falcon 900B	113	HM LLC. Manassas, Va.	N612NL
❏ N525ML	00	CitationJet CJ-1	525-0402	N525ML LLC. Las Vegas, Nv.	N.....
❏ N525MP	06	CitationJet CJ-3	525B-0088	Petersen Holdings LLC. Orange County, Ca.	N5264U
❏ N525MR	03	CitationJet CJ-2	525A-0173	Philips Holding LLC. Minneapolis-Flying Cloud, Mn.	N.....
❏ N525MW	00	CitationJet CJ-1	525-0370	P D Gaus, Duessseldorf, Germany.	N5145P
❏ N525NP	01	CitationJet CJ-1	525-0458	Deanna Enterprises LLC. Baton Rouge, La.	LX-MSP
❏ N525NT	01	CitationJet CJ-1	525-0440	221 Eclipse LLC. Las Vegas, Nv.	(N440CJ)
❏ N525P	96	CitationJet	525-0165	Augusta Aviation LLC. Augusta, Ga.	D-IHCW
❏ N525PB	03	CitationJet CJ-2	525A-0172	JCL Aviation LLC. Jackson Hole, Wy.	N706TF
❏ N525PE	02	Citation Bravo	550-1031	Plastic Engineering Co. Sheboygan, Wi.	N.....
❏ N525PF	01	CitationJet CJ-2	525A-0023	Fenske Media Corp. Rapid City, SD.	N5135K
❏ N525PH	06	CitationJet CJ2+	525A-0329	Paul M Hunter Trust, Everett, Wa.	N5147B
❏ N525PL	93	CitationJet	525-0043	Chandelle Investment Corp. Portland, Or.	N2616L
❏ N525PM	02	CitationJet CJ-2	525A-0067	Continental Management Co. Oxford-Kidlington, UK.	N5141F
❏ N525PS	94	CitationJet	525-0061	SMI Air LLC. Carrollton, Ga.	N61CJ
❏ N525PT	95	CitationJet	525-0125	Eric Travel Inc. Stewart, Mn.	N525PE
❏ N525PV	80	Citation 1/SP	501-0188	Rio Grande Chemical (GP) LLC. Addison, Tx.	N251CT
❏ N525RA	96	CitationJet	525-0167	Jet Lease Finance, Luxembourg.	N1EF
❏ N525RC	97	CitationJet	525-0178	Mansfield Oil Co. Gainesville, Ga.	N.....
❏ N525RD	91	Citation V	560-0106	Phillips Plastics Corp. Phillips, Wi.	N60SH
❏ N525RF	06	CitationJet CJ2+	525A-0327	Riverdale Plaza Properties, Newport News, Va.	N5226B
❏ N525RK	00	CitationJet CJ-1	525-0413	Napa Aviation LLC. Napa, Ca.	N5185J
❏ N525RM	97	CitationJet	525-0225	B & H Air LLC. Victoria, Tx.	N.....
❏ N525RP	93	CitationJet	525-0023	Fly Rite LLC/TypeHaus Inc. Laconia, NH.	N525RF
❏ N525RW	02	CitationJet CJ-2	525A-0060	Warren Inc. Collins, Ms.	N57HC
❏ N525RZ	05	CitationJet CJ1+	525-0612	Aviarent SARL. Monaco.	N.....
❏ N525SD	89	Challenger 601-3A	5056	Skye Gryphon LLC. Hooksatt, NH.	N153NS
❏ N525SM	03	CitationJet CJ-2	525A-0175	Safe Aviation Leasing Inc. Fort Lauderdale, Fl.	N.....
❏ N525TF	94	CitationJet	525-0067	TFP Corp. Medina, Oh.	N594JB
❏ N525TG	01	CitationJet CJ-2	525A-0021	Means to Go LLC. Altoona, Pa.	N.....
❏ N525TW	68	Learjet 25	25-011	Sierra American Corp. Addison, Tx.	N108GA
❏ N525TX*	99	CitationJet	525-0304	Saturn Jets LLC. Waco, Tx.	N154RA
❏ N525VG	98	CitationJet	525-0239	Omni Leasing Corp. Atlanta, Ga.	PT-XJS
❏ N525WB	94	CitationJet	525-0079	Barnet Vistas LLC. Spartanburg, SC.	N179CJ
❏ N525WC	95	CitationJet	525-0107	Option Air LLC. Boston, Ma.	N5211F
❏ N525WD	02	CitationJet CJ-2	525A-0107	WD Aviation Inc. Louisville, Ky.	N.....
❏ N525WF	98	CitationJet	525-0246	CJ Partners LLC. North Wilkesboro, NC.	N525EC
❏ N525WH*	93	CitationJet	525-0028	WTH Aviation LLC/Hiller Group Inc. Tampa, Fl.	N7RL
❏ N525WL	08	CitationJet CJ-3	525B-0237	Cessna Aircraft Co. Wichita, Ks.	N.....
❏ N525WM	97	CitationJet	525-0213	Thompson Tractor Co. Birmingham, Al.	
❏ N525WW	94	CitationJet	525-0060	Walters & Wolff, Fremont, Ca.	XA-TRI
❏ N525XD	06	CitationJet CJ2+	525A-0337	Capital Holdings 170 LLC. Fort Worth, Tx.	N5063P

Reg	Yr	Type	c/n	Owner/Operator	Prev Regn
☐ N525XL	73	Gulfstream II SP	135	J J J Aviation Inc. Brooklyn, NY.	N552JT
☐ N525XX	81	Westwind-1124	336	Trans Alliance Inc. Plainfield, Il.	N255RB
☐ N525ZZ	01	CitationJet CJ-2	525A-0055	The Des Moines Co. Des Moines, Ia.	N207BS
☐ N526CP	95	CitationJet	525-0099	HawgWild Air LLC. Springdale, Ar.	N525CP
☐ N526DV	04	CitationJet CJ-2	525A-0226	Pacific Cataract & Laser Institute, Chehalis-Centralia, Wa.	N5266F
☐ N526EE	97	Gulfstream V	519	E Els/Grass Green II LLC.	VP-CMG
☐ N526EL	07	Learjet 45	45-327	Aircraft Trust & Financing Corp. Fort Lauderdale, Fl.	N816LP
☐ N526FX	06	Challenger 300	20118	BBJS/FlexJets, Addison, Tx.	C-FIOG
☐ N526HV	03	CitationJet CJ-2	525A-0139	Hy-Vee Inc. Des Moines, Ia.	N5228Z
☐ N527AC	87	BAe 125/800A	NA0405	Alticor Inc. Grand Rapids, Mi.	N542BA
☐ N527CC	83	Gulfstream 3	412	Kaslik LLC. Torrance, Ca.	N105Y
☐ N527DS	81	Citation II	550-0287	Fernando Dominguez, Puerto Ordaz, Venezuela.	(N221JS)
☐ N527EW	83	Citation 1/SP	501-0322	Rockville Investments (Jersey) Ltd. Jersey, C.I. (AVB 5EW).	(N769EW)
☐ N527FX	06	Challenger 300	20124	BBJS/FlexJets, Addison, Tx.	C-FIOP
☐ N527HV	07	CitationJet CJ-3	525B-0213	Cessna Aircraft Co. Wichita, Ks.	N5188A
☐ N527JA	90	Rockwell 601-3A	5058	Endeavour Partners LLC. Matthews, NC.	N101SK
☐ N527JC	91	Gulfstream 4	1179	G-IV Exec-Jet LLC/United Refining Inc. Warren, Pa.	N265ST
☐ N527JG	03	Gulfstream G400	1519	Gibbs International Inc. Spartanburg, SC.	N519GA
☐ N527M	86	BAe 125/800A	258054	CAT Marketing LLC/Dick Broadcasting Co. Greensboro, NC.	G-5-15
☐ N527PA	76	Learjet 36A	36A-019	Phoenix Air Group Inc. Cartersville, Ga. (status ?).	N540PA
☐ N527XP	07	Hawker 400XP	RK-527	Executive Charters Inc. Kinston, NC.	(N527DF)
☐ N528AP*	07	Gulfstream G550	5168	Gulfstream Aerospace Corp. Savannah, Ga.	N668GA
☐ N528BP	03	Hawker 800XP	258646	Pilgrims Pride Corp. Pittsburgh, Tx.	N646XP
☐ N528CE	05	CitationJet CJ-3	525B-0022	Commercial Envelope Manufacturing Co. Deer Park, NY.	N5109W
☐ N528CJ	04	CitationJet CJ-1	525-0528	Hi Fli Aviation Too LLC. Charleston, SC.	N.....
☐ N528DS	81	Citation 1/SP	501-0206	Danny Ray Smith Realty & Construction Co. Tuscaloosa, Al.	N943RC
☐ N528FX	06	Challenger 300	20125	BBJS/FlexJets, Addison, Tx.	C-FJQD
☐ N528GA	07	Gulfstream G450	4128	Gulfstream Aerospace Corp. Savannah, Ga.	
☐ N528GP	99	Challenger 604	5401	Jet Finance Group LLC. Nashville, Tn.	(N604GJ)
☐ N528JD	76	Falcon 10	76	Jax Jets LLC. Easton, Md.	N727TS
☐ N528JR	05	Global Express	9177	Joluk Air LLC/J E Robert Co. Dulles, Va.	N528J
☐ N528KW	92	Citation V	560-0224	Five in Five LLC. Dallas, Tx.	N523KW
☐ N528LG	83	Diamond 1A	A050SA	Guardian Angel Nursing Inc. Batesville, Ms.	N826JH
☐ N528QS	04	Gulfstream G550	5042	NetJets, Port Columbus, Oh.	N942GA
☐ N528RM	81	Citation 1/SP	501-0205	Kinnaird Air Oregon Inc. Portland, Or.	(N501DL)
☐ N528RR	90	Astra-1125SP	042	RFP Aeronautical Corp. Irving, Tx.	N588R
☐ N529BC	82	Learjet 35A	35A-471	Milam International Inc. Englewood, Co.	N110FT
☐ N529DB	97	Challenger 800	7152	Hardwicke Properties LLC. Wilmington, De.	N655CC
☐ N529DM*	07	Challenger 605	5711	Bombardier Aerospace Corp. Windsor Locks, Ct.	N529D
☐ N529FX	06	Challenger 300	20128	BBJS/FlexJets, Addison, Tx.	C-FJQR
☐ N529KF	95	Learjet 60	60-064	EL Holdings LLC. Chicago, Il.	N210HV
☐ N529PC	99	CitationJet CJ-2	525A-0001	Edward Rose Building Enterprises, Farmington Hills, Mi.	N525AZ
☐ N529PP	07	BBJ-7HJC	36756	WFBNW NA. Salt Lake City, Ut. (trustor ?).	
☐ N529QS	07	Gulfstream G550	5156	NetJets, Port Columbus, Oh.	N936GA
☐ N530DL	80	Westwind-1124	287	Leprino Foods/Leprino Aviation Co. Broomfield, Co.	N146BF
☐ N530FX	07	Challenger 300	20148	BBJS/FlexJets, Addison, Tx.	C-FLQO
☐ N530GA	79	Gulfstream II SP	247	EG Air LLC. Detroit, Mi/MG-75 Inc. Waterford, Mi.	N75MG
☐ N530GP	06	Gulfstream G150	203	Georgia Pacific Corp. Atlanta-Fulton County, Ga.	N528GA
☐ N530P	81	Citation II	550-0310	Business Aircraft Group Inc. Cleveland, Oh.	N7798D
☐ N530PT	02	390 Premier 1	RB-51	RGP Enterprises LLC. Tulsa, Ok.	LX-LCG
☐ N530SM	04	Hawker 800XP	258697	Loretto Aviation LLC. San Jose, Ca.	N697XP
☐ N531AB	75	Sabre-60	306-98	Hubert Jet LLC. Pontiac, Mi.	N169AC
☐ N531AF	98	Gulfstream V	531	Vulcan Northwest Inc. Seattle-Tacoma, Wa.	(N8CA)
☐ N531AJ	75	Learjet 35	35-011	Western Aviation Services Inc. Englewood, Co.	N408RB
☐ N531CM	06	CitationJet CJ-3	525B-0071	Myers Group V Inc. Omaha, Ne.	N51511
☐ N531CW	77	Learjet 25D	25D-231	DZT Inc. Lawrenceville, Ga.	N225HW
☐ N531FL	67	Falcon 20-5B	113	IFL Group Inc. Pontiac, Mi.	N22WJ
☐ N531FX	07	Challenger 300	20150	BBJS/FlexJets, Addison, Tx.	C-FLQR
☐ N531GA	07	Gulfstream G450	4131	Gulfstream Aerospace Corp. Savannah, Ga.	
☐ N531GP	06	Gulfstream G150	207	Georgia Pacific Corp. Atlanta-Fulton County, Ga.	N807GA
☐ N531K	83	Learjet 55	55-053	I J Knight Inc. New Tripoli, Pa.	N253S
☐ N531MB	89	Citation V	560-0027	R B Baker Construction Inc. Savannah, Ga.	N560JR
☐ N531PM	85	Citation S/II	S550-0059	Imaginary Images Inc. Richmond, Va.	(N904VA)
☐ N531QS	06	Gulfstream G550	5133	NetJets, Port Columbus, Oh.	N533GA
☐ N531RA	00	Learjet 31A	31A-192	R A Aviation LLC. Chattanooga, Tn.	N50088
☐ N531RC	06	Citation Sovereign	680-0107	Great Dane Financial LLC. Palwaukee, Il.	N5235G

Reg	Yr	Type	c/n	Owner/Operator	Prev Regn
❏ N531RQ	01	Citation Excel	560-5184	P & M Leasing Inc. Green Bay, Wi.	N531RC
❏ N531SK	92	Learjet 31A	31A-043	SK Logistics Inc. St Augustine, Fl.	N43LJ
❏ N531TS	95	Learjet 31A	31A-106	Lear N89TC LLC/N A Degerstrom Inc. Spokane, Wa.	N581RA
❏ N531VP*	95	Citation V Ultra	560-0311	Cessna Aircraft Co. Wichita, Ks.	(N211WC)
❏ N532CC	06	Falcon 2000	230	Charlotte Pipe & Foundry Co. Charlotte, NC.	N230FJ
❏ N532FX	07	Challenger 300	20154	BBJS/FlexJets, Addison, Tx.	C-FMYA
❏ N532GA	07	Gulfstream G450	4132	Gulfstream Aerospace Corp. Savannah, Ga.	
❏ N532GP	07	Gulfstream G150	221	Georgia-Pacific Corp. Atlanta-Fulton County, Ga.	4X-WID
❏ N532SP	00	Gulfstream V-SP	632	Gulfstream Aerospace Corp. Savannah, Ga. (Ff 31 Aug 01).	N5SP
❏ N533CC	07	Citation Excel XLS	560-5687	Ruddick Corp. Charlotte, NC.	N5068F
❏ N533FX	07	Challenger 300	20160	BBJS/FlexJets, Addison, Tx.	C-FMXK
❏ N533LR	92	BAe 1000A	259033	Executive Charters Inc. Kinston, NC.	N533QS
❏ N534CC	07	Citation Excel XLS	560-5707	Ruddick Corp. Charlotte, NC.	N52535
❏ N534FX	07	Challenger 300	20161	BBJS/FlexJets, Addison, Tx.	C-FMXH
❏ N534H	90	Citation III	650-0196	Hillenbrand Industries Inc. Batesville, In.	N896EC
❏ N534NA	04	CitationJet CJ-1	525-0534	CPJR LLC/Dean Delaware LLC. Chantilly, Va.	JA100C
❏ N534QS	05	Gulfstream G550	5103	NetJets, Port Columbus, Oh.	N923GA
❏ N534TX	95	CitationJet	525-0092	Golondrina Air Inc. Sandia, Tx.	N523AS
❏ N535AF	78	Learjet 35A	35A-191	Ameriflight Inc. Burbank, Ca.	N35SE
❏ N535BC	06	Hawker 850XP	258776	AvPro Inc. Annapolis, Md.	N36726
❏ N535BP	03	Citation Encore	560-0646	Beef Products Inc. Sioux City, Ia.	N846QS
❏ N535CD	03	390 Premier 1	RB-96	Wave Equity Partners LLC. Santa Ana, Ca.	
❏ N535CE	02	Citation Encore	560-0635	Latium Jet Services Inc. Staverton, UK.	N5257C
❏ N535CM	07	CitationJet CJ-3	525B-0182	Carlmax Aviation LLC. Nashville, Tn.	N5243K
❏ N535DL	07	CitationJet CJ-3	525B-0172	North Central Group Aviation, Madison, Wi.	N.....
❏ N535DT	05	CitationJet CJ-3	525B-0069	Apex Alarm Management Inc. Provo, Ut.	N3UD
❏ N535FX	07	Challenger 300	20167	BBJS/FlexJets, Addison, Tx.	C-FOAJ
❏ N535GA	07	Gulfstream G450	4135	Gulfstream Aerospace Corp. Savannah, Ga.	
❏ N535GH	05	CitationJet CJ-3	525B-0054	Haas Automation Inc. Camarillo, Ca.	N5200U
❏ N535JM	81	Learjet 35A	35A-401	Green Chair Productions Inc. Van Nuys, Ca.	N771SB
❏ N535LR	95	CitationJet	525-0128	Blackstar Aviation LLC/Ervin Equipment Inc. Toledo, Il.	N5092D
❏ N535PS	93	Learjet 31A	31A-087	Dulcich Jet LLC. Troutdale, Or.	N167BA
❏ N535SW	99	Citation Bravo	550-0899	Setzer Wood LLC. Georgetown, Ky.	N899DC
❏ N535TA	75	Learjet 35	35-013	Kalitta Charters LLC. Detroit-Willow Run, Mi.	(N913CK)
❏ N535TV	07	CitationJet CJ2+	525A-0349	Vance & Hines, Long Beach, Ca.	N52609
❏ N535V	98	Gulfstream V	535	GVX Inc/Dart Container Corp. Sarasota, Fl.	N775US
❏ N536FX	07	Challenger 300	20171	BBJS/FlexJets, Addison, Tx.	C-FPMQ
❏ N536KN	76	Learjet 35A	35A-073	Kalitta Charters LLC. Detroit-Willow Run, Mi.	N610GA
❏ N536TS	07	Challenger 605	5736	Aero Toy Store LLC. Fort Lauderdale, Fl.	C-FPSJ
❏ N536V	05	Hawker 400XP	RK-445	Florida Health Plan Administrators LLC. Boca Raton, Fl.	N45XP
❏ N537RB	07	390 Premier 1A	RB-190	Vandalia Aviation Partners LLC. Charleston, WV.	N70890
❏ N537VP*	96	Citation V Ultra	560-0377	Cessna Aircraft Co. Wichita, Ks.	N377WC
❏ N537XP	07	Hawker 400XP	RK-537	Trinity Lighting Co. Jonesboro, Ar.	
❏ N539LB	93	Learjet 31A	31A-078	Bettcher Industries Inc. Birmingham, Oh.	N112CM
❏ N539LR	93	BAe 1000A	259039	Executive Charters Inc. Kinston, NC.	N539QS
❏ N539PG	74	Sabre-60	306-79	Cobra Gold Inc. Carson City, Nv.	N43JG
❏ N539VE*	05	Gulfstream G450	4039	Valero Energy Corp. San Antonio, Tx.	N760G
❏ N539WA	00	Citation Encore	560-0556	Westchester Air Inc. Jonesville, Tx.	N5165P
❏ N539XP	07	Hawker 400XP	RK-539	JPT Associates Inc. Minneapolis, Mn.	
❏ N540BA	07	Challenger 605	5729	Boeing Executive Flight Operations, Seattle, Wa.	C-FOBF
❏ N540CS	04	Citation Excel XLS	560-5516	CitationShares Sales Inc. White Plains, NY.	N.....
❏ N540EA	75	Gulfstream II SP	174	Jetmark Aviation LLC/Richmor Aviation Inc. Waterbury-Oxford.	N900ES
❏ N540LR	93	BAe 1000A	259040	Triumphal Industries Supply Sdn Bhd. Malaysia.	N540QS
❏ N540M	00	Gulfstream V	597	Marathon Oil Co. Houston, Tx.	N302K
❏ N541CS	04	Citation Excel XLS	560-5521	CitationShares Sales Inc. White Plains, NY.	N.....
❏ N541FL	66	Falcon 20C-5	48	IFL Group Inc. Pontiac, Mi.	N23ND
❏ N541LR	93	BAe 1000A	259041	Executive Charters Inc. Kinston, NC.	N541QS
❏ N541PA	76	Learjet 35	35-053	Phoenix Air Group Inc. Cartersville, Ga.	N53FN
❏ N541RL	89	Astra-1125	034	Transcendent Investments LLC. Tualatin, Or.	N511WA
❏ N541RS	05	390 Premier 1A	RB-144	White Oak Holdings LLC. Rutherfordton, NC.	
❏ N541S	86	Citation III	650-0115	CGW Southeast Management LLC. Atlanta, Ga.	N1419J
❏ N541WG	07	CitationJet CJ-3	525B-0188	Woodland Eagle/Merit Energy Co. Dallas, Tx.	N.....
❏ N542BA	07	Challenger 605	5737	Boeing Executive Flight Operations, Seattle, Wa.	C-FPSQ
❏ N542CS	04	Citation Excel XLS	560-5523	CitationShares Sales Inc. White Plains, NY.	N.....
❏ N542LR	93	BAe 1000A	259042	Executive Charters Inc. Kinston, NC.	(G-TAGM)
❏ N542M	05	Hawker 850XP	258766	Marathon Oil Co. Houston, Tx.	

Reg	Yr	Type	c/n	Owner/Operator	Prev Regn
N542PA	75	Learjet 35	35-030	CFF Air Inc/Phoenix Air, Cartersville, Ga.	C-GKPE
N542SA	83	Learjet 35A	35A-503	Exxel Pacific Inc. Bellingham, Wa.	N77NR
N542TW	68	JetStar-731	5113	White Industries Inc. Bates City, Mo. (status ?).	N77BT
N543CM	99	Learjet 45	45-062	MM Air Inc/Kirkland Construction LLP. Pueblo, Co.	N512RB
N543H	02	Gulfstream V	688	Hewlett-Packard Co. San Jose, Ca.	(N254W)
N543LE	00	Citation Encore	560-0543	Code Aviation LLC. La Jolla, Ca.	N51995
N543SC	87	Citation S/II	S550-0144	Town & Country Chevrolet, Ashland, Or.	N6516V
N544CM	86	Falcon 50	173	Carpau Corp. St Petersburg, Fl.	PT-LJI
N544KB	05	Citation Sovereign	680-0047	On Time Aviation Corp. Riyadh, Saudi Arabia.	N737KB
N544LR	94	Hawker 1000	259044	Executive Charters Inc. Kinston, NC.	N544QS
N544PA	79	Learjet 35A	35A-247	Phoenix Air Group Inc. Cartersville, Ga.	N523PA
N544RA	84	Falcon 50	144	Four Directions Air Inc. Syracuse, NY.	(LX-FTJ)
N544TS	02	Challenger 604	5544	General Electric Co. Stewart, NY.	N50DS
N544XL	99	Citation Excel	560-5044	Armstrong Group/437 North Main Partners LP. Butler, Pa.	N5218T
N545BP	07	Citation Encore+	560-0756	Beef Products Inc. Sioux City, SD.	N52645
N545CS	98	Gulfstream 4SP	1361	Campbell Soup Co. Camden, NJ.	N361GA
N545GM	78	HS 125/700A	NA0228	GR Corp. Albuquerque, NM.	N555CR
N545K	04	Learjet 45	45-244	Koch Industries Inc. Wichita, Ks.	N5009V
N545PA	77	Learjet 36A	36A-028	Phoenix Air Group Inc. Cartersville, Ga.	N75TD
N545PL	93	Citation V	560-0225	N545PL LLC. Jeffco, Co.	N225CV
N545RW	96	CitationJet	525-0141	Wooldridge Organization/BHR Air Service, Pleasant Hill, Ca.	N725CF
N545SH*	77	HS 125/700A	257007	World Jet Inc. Fort Lauderdale, Fl.	N54WH
N545TC	98	Beechjet 400A	RK-213	MHS Aviation LLC/THF Realty Inc. St Louis, Mo.	N175PS
N545TG	04	CitationJet CJ-1	525-0545	Interstate Warehousing Inc. Auburn, In.	N.....
N546BZ	92	Beechjet 400A	RK-41	Brazeway Inc. Adrian, Mi.	N920SA
N546CS	04	Citation Excel XLS	560-5524	CitationShares Sales Inc. White Plains, NY.	N5267G
N546LR	94	Hawker 1000	259046	Executive Charters Inc. Kinston, NC.	N546QS
N547CS	04	Citation Excel XLS	560-5542	CitationShares Sales Inc. White Plains, NY.	N5267K
N547JG	78	Learjet 25D	25D-264	Executive Jet Group 1 LLC. Kansas City, Ks.	N502JC
N547LR	94	Hawker 1000	259047	Executive Charters Inc. Kinston, NC.	N547QS
N547PA	75	Learjet 36	36-012	Phoenix Air Group Inc. Cartersville, Ga.	N712JE
N547TW	05	CitationJet CJ-1	525-0547	Truck World Inc/JGB Aviation LLC. Hubbard, Oh.	N547ST
N548LR	94	Hawker 1000	259048	Executive Charters Inc. Kinston, NC.	N548QS
N548XP	07	Hawker 400XP	RK-548	Hawker Beechcraft Corp. Wichita, Ks.	
N549CS	04	Citation Excel XLS	560-5546	CitationShares Sales Inc. White Plains, NY.	N51881
N549LR	96	Hawker 1000	259049	J F Aviation LLC. Van Nuys, Ca.	N549QS
N549PA	77	Learjet 35A	35A-119	Phoenix Air Group Inc. Cartersville, Ga.	(N64DH)
N550AB	90	Citation II	550-0633	LPOD Inc. Bakersfield, Ca.	N7AB
N550AJ	87	Citation S/II	S550-0141	Gainesville Aircraft Sales Inc. Gainesville, Fl.	N26JJ
N550AS	82	Learjet 55	55-045	Jet Shares LLC. Lexington-Bluegrass, Ky.	(N123LC)
N550AS	85	Citation S/II	S550-0020	Norsan Financial & Leasing Inc. Pittsburg, Ca.	(N1259R)
N550BB	95	Citation Bravo	550-0734	Cessna Aircraft Co. Wichita, Ks. (Ff 19 Apr 95).	(N1214J)
N550BC	97	Citation Bravo	550-0804	Elijah Reed Corp. Monroe, Wi.	(N41VY)
N550BG	88	Citation S/II	S550-0148	Grafair Inc. Vero Beach, Fl.	(SE-RCY)
N550BJ	81	Citation II	550-0277	Inversiones 1902 CA Trust. Coral Gables, Fl.	N550WJ
N550BM	07	Gulfstream G550	5171	Gulfstream Aerospace Corp. Savannah, Ga.	N971GA
N550BT	86	Citation S/II	S550-0085	Browning Brothers LLC. Ogden, Ut.	N143BP
N550CA	80	Citation II	550-0152	National Computer Protection Inc. Charlottesville, Va.	N88840
N550CG	79	Citation II	550-0095	Aerovida SA. Buenos Aires, Argentina.	N100UF
N550CK*	83	Learjet 55	55-083	Hammer Holdings LLC. Van Nuys, Ca.	N550HG
N550CL	79	Falcon 50	8	International Aviation LLC. Palwaukee, Il.	N508EJ
N550CS	04	Citation Excel XLS	560-5551	CitationShares Sales Inc. White Plains, NY.	N.....
N550CU	80	Citation II	550-0175	CAAIR Corp. Wilmington, De.	C-GHWW
N550CW	83	Challenger 600S	1084	Cleveland Peak LLC/Chinati Peak Ltd. Anchorage, Ak.	N175ST
N550CY	05	Citation Bravo	550-1118	ISBRA Enterprises LLC. Copenhagen, Denmark.	N.....
N550CZ	87	Citation S/II	S550-0128	Boxer Property Management Corp. Houston, Tx.	N370M
N550DA	80	Citation II	550-0170	Jet U S Inc. New Castle, De.	N508CV
N550DL	88	Citation S/II	S550-0155	Tour America Inc. Wilmington, De.	N155GB
N550DS	88	Citation S/II	S550-0154	Mount Ida LLC. Meredith, NH.	N660AJ
N550DW	84	Citation II	550-0487	The Charles Machine Works Inc. Perry, Ok.	N444BL
N550EZ*	88	Citation S/II	S550-0158	E-Z Mart Stores Inc. Texarkana, Tx.	N889RP
N550F	84	Citation S/II	S550-0010	Eagle Creek Aviation Services Inc. Indianapolis, In.	N422MJ
N550FP	02	Citation Bravo	550-1024	Flying Services NV. Antwerp, Belgium.	N5254Y
N550GA	07	Gulfstream G550	5155	Air Luther AG. Zug, Switzerland.	N935GA
N550GH	99	Citation Bravo	550-0898	B R M Management LLC. Carlsbad, Ca.	
N550GW	02	Gulfstream G550	5006	Grand Warehouse Inc. Tokyo, Japan.	N906GA

Reg	Yr	Type	c/n	Owner/Operator	Prev Regn
N550GX	87	Citation II	550-0560	Incline Aviation Inc. Incline Village, Nv. (was 551-0560).	D-IMMF
N550HB	84	Westwind-Two	414	The KBH Corp. Clarksdale, Ms.	N524RH
N550HC	86	Citation S/II	S550-0116	First Financial Resources Inc. Denton, Tx.	N125CG
N550HH	96	Citation Bravo	550-0802	Continental Resources Inc. Enid, Ok.	N802CB
N550HW	90	Citation II	550-0635	McGriff, Siebels & Williams Inc. Birmingham, Al.	N277JE
N550J	98	Citation Bravo	550-0848	John Mayes, Palo Alto, Ca.	N997HT
N550JC	78	Citation II	550-0038	Ryan Aerospace Corp. Belmar, NJ.	(N842CC)
N550KA	80	Citation II	550-0279	CVG Logistics LLC/Commercial Vehicle Group Inc. New Albany.	N566CC
N550KD	79	Citation II	550-0113	Low Tide LLC. Riverside, Ia.	N90DA
N550KF	05	Gulfstream G550	5095	Kraft Foods Inc. Milwaukee, Wi.	N595GA
N550KL	98	Citation Bravo	550-0844	Trinity Lighting Inc. Jonesboro, Ar.	
N550KR	02	CitationJet CJ-2	525A-0130	Two G's Aviation LLC. Memphis, Tn.	N525JD
N550KT	82	Citation II	550-0401	Knight Aviation LLC. Lafayette, La. (was 551-0066).	(N551GC)
N550KW	82	Citation II	550-0411	TVPX Inc. Concord, Ma.	C-FMPP
N550LA	78	Citation II	550-0006	Direct Air Charters LLC. Medford, NJ.	N725RH
N550LD	82	Citation II	550-0323	Maine Aviation Corp. Portland, Me.	VP-CLD
N550LH	79	Citation II	550-0105	Heartland Aviation Inc, Eau Claire, Wi.	N105BA
N550LS	79	Citation II	550-0371	Mixed Wing LLC. Addison, Tx.	N585DM
N550M	05	Gulfstream G550	5101	Motorola Inc. Palwaukee, Il.	N821GA
N550MJ	81	Citation II	550-0215	Midwest Jet LLC. Marshall, Mn.	N40MT
N550MT	03	Gulfstream G550	5026	Cleopatra Group/Abou El Enein LLC. Cairo, Egypt.	N926GA
N550MW	93	Citation II	550-0720	McGriff, Seibels & Williams LLC. Birmingham, Al.	N260TB
N550MX	06	CitationJet CJ-3	525B-0137	CJ3 Holdings LLC. Scottsdale, Az.	N51042
N550PA	80	Citation II	550-0191	Rocamar Group LLC. Dover, De.	C-GWCJ
N550PD	01	Citation Bravo	550-0995	Ravenheat Aviation Ltd. Leeds-Bradford, UK.	N.....
N550PF	82	Citation II	550-0428	Chancellor Services LLC. Redding, Ca.	N97BG
N550PG	81	Citation II	550-0216	FSA Aviation LLC. Oklahoma City, Ok.	(N911NJ)
N550PR	06	Gulfstream G550	5121	Prem Rawat/Priyan Foundation, Oxnard, Ca.	N921GA
N550PW	80	Citation II	550-0159	Plato Woodwork/Wood I Fly LLC. St Louis, Mn.	N444GB
N550RS	74	Citation Longwing SP	500-0202	Santiago Communities Inc. Orange, Ca.	(N108WT)
N550SA	81	Citation II	550-0248	Security Aviation Inc. Anchorage, Ak.	N6804C
N550SF	79	Citation II	550-0110	National Marketing & Management Services, Livingston, Mt.	N122G
N550SJ	86	Citation S/II	S550-0100	Bed Rock Inc/Tri State Motor Transit Co. Joplin, Mo.	N300QW
N550T	05	CitationJet CJ-3	525B-0040	Taft Broadcasting Co. Charlotte, NC.	N52369
N550TB	01	CitationJet CJ-2	525A-0025	Molded Fiber Glass Companies, Ashtabula, Oh.	N550T
N550TC	82	Learjet 55	55-034	Continental Jet LLC/Blackhawk Construction Co. Wilmington.	N123LC
N550TF	93	CitationJet	525-0013	Dixie Chopper Bravo LLC. Coatesville, In.	N550T
N550TH	01	Falcon 900EX	100	Aviation Newco Inc. Wilmington, De.	JA55TH
N550TL	92	Citation II	550-0716	Amboseli LLC. Fort Worth, Tx.	VP-CTF
N550TM	00	Citation Bravo	550-0936	Smooth Route Sdn Bhd. Malaysia.	N5101J
N550TT	04	Citation Bravo	550-1076	Airmid Aviation Services P/L. New Delhi, India.	N359GW
N550TW	89	Citation II	550-0603	Conquest Air Corp. Shreveport, La.	N560AB
N550U	77	Citation Eagle	501-0047	Valcom Services LLC. Roanoke, Va.	N550T
N550VW	81	Citation II	550-0307	Saratoga Aircraft Holdings LLC. Ballston Spa, NY.	N37BM
N550WB	81	Citation II	550-0230	Southeast Equipment Co. Cambridge, Oh.	N550EK
N550WG	01	Citation Bravo	550-0953	Aeromil Pacific P/L. Sunshine Coast, QLD. Australia.	C-GZEK
N550WL	81	Citation II	550-0223	W L Paris Enterprises Inc. Louisville, Ky.	N239CD
N550WM	92	Falcon 50	229	Jabil Circuit Inc. Page Field-Fort Myers, Fl.	C-GMID
N550WS	98	Citation Bravo	550-0845	Spence Enterprises 1 Inc. Crystal Lake, Il.	N51817
N550WW	92	Citation V	560-0180	Wasser & Winters Co. West Linn, Or.	N1280K
N551BC	79	Citation II	550-0242	Boulder Capital Inc. La Jolla, Ca. (was 551-0012).	N1955E
N551BD	95	Learjet 60	60-062	Fortune Fashions Industries LLC. Van Nuys, Ca.	N62BX
N551CL	80	Citation II/SP	551-0215	W M Cramer Lumber Co. Hickory, NC.	N500PX
N551CZ	78	Citation II	550-0028	Clifford Group LLC. Toledo, Oh.	(N370CD)
N551DA	78	Citation II	550-0025	Millennium Development Enterprise, Weston, Fl.	OY-GMC
N551EA	81	Citation II/SP	551-0360	Ernesto Ancira Jr. Wilmington, De. (was 550-0328).	N24CJ
N551FP*	03	CitationJet CJ-1	525-0515	IFP Air LLC/Brakes Plus Inc. Centennial, Co.	N132CS
N551G	01	Citation Bravo	550-0968	Auto Glass Center of Kansas Inc. Cedar Rapids, Ia.	N51612
N551GA	00	Gulfstream V	606	Amgen Inc. Camarillo, Ca.	N53HS
N551GF	81	Citation II/SP	551-0039	CCM Aviation LLC/Great Floors LLC. Coeur d'Alene. (status ?)	N550TA
N551GS	82	Citation II/SP	551-0431	Triple SSS Aviation Ltd/Shelltech Ltd. Muskegon, Mi.	N4NM
N551HH	78	Citation II/SP	551-0071	GEM Air LLC/Golden Encore Mortgage, Bakersfield, Ca.	N551DS
N551KF	07	Gulfstream G500	5148	Kraft Foods Inc. Milwaukee, Wi.	N648GA
N551MF	81	Learjet 55	55-015	Quality Aircraft Sales Inc. Boca Raton, Fl.	N27DD
N551MS	80	Citation Eagle	501-0147	Michael Simpson, Bridgeport, Tx.	N27TS
N551PS	84	Citation S/II	S550-0013	Louisiana Gas Development Corp. Shreveport, La.	N561PS

Reg	Yr	Type	c/n	Owner/Operator	Prev Regn
N551V	98	Citation Bravo	550-0850	N551V LLC. Mission Viejo, Ca.	N551G
N551WL	81	Citation II	550-0261	W L Paris Enterprises Inc. Louisville, Ky.	N50AZ
N551WM	05	CitationJet CJ-2	525A-0243	0243 LLC. Seattle, Wa.	N5165T
N551XP	07	Hawker 400XP	RK-551	Hawker Beechcraft Corp. Wichita, Ks.	
N552AJ	78	Citation 1/SP	501-0074	Cellular Partner's Inc. Hilton Head, SC.	N28GC
N552CN	04	Citation Encore	560-0674	Choctaw Nation of Oklahoma, Durant, Ok.	N552TC
N552HV	00	Citation Encore	560-0552	Maren Aviation/Corundum Partners Inc. Colorado Springs, Co.	N55HV
N552SD	87	Citation S/II	S550-0130	Sand Ridge Operating Co. Bethany, Ok.	N550PL
N552SK	00	Learjet 60	60-219	Red River Resources Inc. Belgrade, Mt.	N660KS
N552SM	00	Citation Bravo	550-0929	Focal Point Lighting LLC. Chicago, Il.	N5086W
N552TL	89	Learjet 55C	55C-139	Caledon Aviation LLC. Houston, Tx.	N139ST
N552XP	07	Hawker 400XP	RK-552	Hawker Beechcraft Corp. Wichita, Ks.	
N553M	89	Falcon 50	201	Koosharem Corp. Santa Barbara, Ca.	N54DA
N553MC	79	Westwind-1124	252	PMB Aviation Inc. Van Nuys, Ca.	(N9WW)
N553MJ	87	Citation II	550-0553	Rat Pack LLC/WB Aviation Inc. Panama City Beach, Fl.	N5XR
N553SD	86	Citation S/II	S550-0107	Sandridge Operating Co. Bethany, Ok.	C-GBGC
N553V	78	Learjet 35A	35A-141	Mayo Aviation Inc. Englewood, Co.	N553M
N553XP	07	Hawker 400XP	RK-553	Hawker Beechcraft Corp. Wichita, Ks.	
N554CL	82	Learjet 55	55-040	Clay Lacy Aviation Inc. Van Nuys, Ca.	N55HK
N554CS	05	Citation Excel XLS	560-5572	CitationShares Sales Inc. White Plains, NY.	N5194B
N554MB	78	Citation II	550-0040	James D Nelson, Newport Beach, Ca. (was 551-0085).	N545GA
N554T	86	Citation S/II	S550-0124	T & T Enterprises LLC. Santa Clara, Ca.	N52CK
N555BK	00	Citation Bravo	550-0916	Koop Aviation BV. Groningen-Eelde, Holland.	N5265N
N555DS	81	Citation II	550-0275	Gable S Corp. Broussard, La.	N550CP
N555DW	85	Gulfstream 3	459	Leaseco Aviation 405DW Inc. Reno, Nv.	N54HF
N555DZ	81	Falcon 10	186	Desert Skies of Arizona LLC. Scottsdale, Az.	N555DH
N555EF	04	Global 5000	9154	Hualalai LLC/Young America Homes, Petaluma, Ca.	C-FBPL
N555GL	83	Gulfstream 3	403	GSL Aviation Inc. Fort Lauderdale, Fl.	N403WJ
N555HD	84	Gulfstream 3	444	Colonial Acquisitions Ltd. Hanover, Ma.	N110MT
N555HM	00	Citation Bravo	550-0950	S & D Coffee Inc. Concord, NC.	
N555KT	82	Citation II	550-0420	Sweetwater Sound Inc. Fort Wayne, In. (was 551-0419)	I-AGSM
N555KW	78	Citation 1/SP	501-0063	Mountain Jet Services LLC. Asheville, NC. (was 500-0476).	N501BA
N555LG	93	Challenger 601-3A	5127	Leonard Green & Partners LP. Van Nuys, Ca.	N718R
N555LJ	69	Learjet 24B	24B-195	Butler National Inc. Newton, Ks.	(N46LM)
N555LR*	06	Gulfstream G450	4065	Beauty Central Inc/Conair Corp. Stamford, Ct.	N450GD
N555PG	90	Citation V	560-0102	BTM Enterprises Inc. Frisco, Tx.	N560BA
N555RE	83	Gulfstream 3	409	Raleigh Holdings LLC. Van Nuys, Ca.	N828MG
N555RT	81	Citation II/SP	551-0323	Ret Butler Communications Corp. Steamboat Springs, Co.	N819Y
N555SD	81	Learjet 25D	25D-333	Diamond Shamrock/Joe Brand Inc. Laredo, Tx.	N34MJ
N555SR	83	Falcon 20F-5	455	Brunswick Boat Group, Ashua, Tn.	F-GKAL
N555TF	06	Challenger 300	20102	Master Four LLC/Town Fair Tire Center, Oxford, Ct.	C-FHND
N555VR	04	Learjet 45	45-257	Victory Racing LLC. City of Industry, Ca.	N5012H
N555WD	97	Challenger 604	5355	WDW Aviation Inc/Executive Flight Service, Jacksonville, Fl.	C-GLWV
N555WL	98	Citation V Ultra	560-0488	Golf Air Ltd. Bloomfield Hills, Mi.	N555WF
N555WZ	04	Citation Excel	560-5366	Atlanta Jet Inc. Lawrenceville, Ga.	N555WF
N556AF	86	Gulfstream 3	479	Alfa Fox LLC. NYC.	N50RL
N556BG	98	Citation V Ultra	560-0499	High Flight Leasing LLC. Leawood, Ks.	
N556CS	05	Citation Excel XLS	560-5577	CitationShares Sales Inc. White Plains, NY.	N5267K
N556HD	01	Learjet 31A	31A-230	DKH Services LLC. Salt Lake City, Ut.	N295PS
N556HJ	82	Learjet 55	55-028	Hop-A-Jet Inc. Fort Lauderdale, Fl.	N556GA
N557CS	85	Citation S/II	S550-0016	Rabbit Hill Industries Inc. White Plains, NY.	N85MP
N557GA	07	Gulfstream G550	5154	Goxxy Inc. Vaduz, Liechtenstein.	N654GA
N557HP	07	CitationJet CJ-1	525-0668	Cessna Aircraft Co. Wichita, Ks.	N.....
N557PG	01	Citation Encore	560-0557	National Aircraft Leasing Corp. Greenville, De.	N221CE
N557WY*	95	Gulfstream 4SP	1276	ES Aviation LLC. Ronkonkoma, NY.	N856AF
N557XP	07	Hawker 400XP	RK-557	Hawker Beechcraft Corp. Wichita, Ks.	(N481LX)
N558AK	01	Citation Encore	560-0558	Amy's Kitchen Inc. Santa Rosa, Ca.	N558GG
N558HJ	82	Learjet 55	55-048	JODA LLC/Worldwide Jet Charter Inc. Fort Lauderdale, Fl.	N558AC
N558R	99	Citation Excel	560-5075	Rogers Group Inc. Nashville, Tn.	
N558XP	07	Hawker 400XP	RK-558	Hawker Beechcraft Corp. Wichita, Ks.	
N559AM	99	Citation VII	650-7107	TXU Business Services Co. Dallas, Tx.	
N559GV	98	Gulfstream V	559	WFBNW NA. Salt Lake City, Ut. (trustor ?).	N659GA
N559LC	74	Gulfstream 2	152	Little Caesar Enterprises Inc. Pontiac, Mi.	N62WB
N560AF	90	Citation V	560-0100	Falcon LLC. Dallas, Tx.	N560WE
N560AN	98	Learjet 60	60-138	Pinnacle Air Executive Jet, Springdale, Ar.	(N230BX)
N560AV	95	Citation V Ultra	560-0321	Teton Leasing LLC. Pocatello, Id.	N220WC

165

Reg	Yr	Type	c/n	Owner/Operator	Prev Regn
☐ N560AW	03	Citation Excel	560-5351	Aurora Ventures LLC. St Paul, Mn.	N71HS
☐ N560BA	05	Citation Excel XLS	560-5585	Ball Homes Inc. Lexington, Ky.	N558CS
☐ N560BC	89	Citation V	560-0032	N560BC & N148H Exchange LLC/TVPX Inc. Concord, Ma.	N96MY
☐ N560BD*	92	Citation V	560-0172	Big Dog Demolition NC Inc. Marietta, Ga.	N560BP
☐ N560BG	94	Citation V Ultra	560-0277	The Brickman Group Ltd. Frederick, Md.	N130WC
☐ N560BT	99	Citation Excel	560-5031	Dorand Aviation LLC. Portland, Or.	N531BJ
☐ N560CE	98	Citation Excel	560-5012	Hesco Parts Corp. Louisville, Ky.	I-JETS
☐ N560CF	89	Citation V	560-0040	Max Air Group LLC/Corporate Flight Inc. Detroit, Mi.	N91NL
☐ N560CG	00	Citation Excel	560-5121	Cardinal Glass Industries Inc. Minnetonka, Mn.	N5223Y
☐ N560CH	01	Citation Encore	560-0611	CMH Homes Inc. Knoxville, Tn.	N98AQ
☐ N560CJ	90	Citation V	560-0086	Trans-Exec Air Service Inc. Van Nuys, Ca.	N218SE
☐ N560CK	93	Citation V	560-0207	Koury Aviation Inc. Liberty, NC.	N780BF
☐ N560CM	02	Citation Excel	560-5277	Hensley & Co. Phoenix, Az.	N5076K
☐ N560CR	05	Citation Excel XLS	560-5560	Cumberland Resources Corp. Abingdon, Va.	N264SC
☐ N560CX	01	Citation Encore	560-0582	Schoonover Enterprises LLC. Shreveport, La.	N843HS
☐ N560CZ	89	Citation V	560-0002	Central Connecticut Aircraft LLC. Plainville, Ct.	N560VP
☐ N560DL	07	Citation Encore+	560-0761	Landmark Communications Inc. Norfolk, Va.	N5036Q
☐ N560DM	04	Gulfstream G550	5045	McDonald Aviation LLC. Fresno, Ca.	N789RR
☐ N560DP	01	Citation Excel	560-5212	Union Underwear Co. Bowling Green, Ky.	N5090Y
☐ N560DR	00	Citation Excel	560-5073	TD Air LLC. Allegheny County, Pa.	N121TE
☐ N560EL	90	Citation V	560-0049	McLang Aircraft Charter LLC. Ronkonkoma, NY.	(N2672X)
☐ N560EM	94	Citation V Ultra	560-0278	OIA Air Corp. Nashua, NH.	VH-FHJ
☐ N560EP	91	Citation V	560-0101	Eastway Aviation Inc. Ronkonkoma, NY.	N560DM
☐ N560FP	01	Citation Encore	560-0566	Inner Harbor LLC. Baltimore, Md.	C-FAMI
☐ N560G	91	Citation V	560-0112	WMB 560G LLC. Chester Springs, Pa.	N145MK
☐ N560GB	99	Citation Excel	560-5027	Accent Stripe Inc. Orchard Park, NY.	N5202D
☐ N560GC*	00	Citation Excel	560-5089	Devcon Construction Inc. Tualatin, Or.	N21MA
☐ N560GL	90	Citation V	560-0079	Solair LLC. Santa Fe, NM.	(N2746C)
☐ N560GS	94	Citation V Ultra	560-0263	Cochran, Cherry, Givens & Smith PC. Albany, Ga.	N979C
☐ N560GT	91	Citation V	560-0142	Georges Tranchant/Techni Airplane LLC. Paris-Le Bourget.	N560FA
☐ N560HC	02	Citation Encore	560-0631	Collins Brothers Corp. Las Vegas, Nv.	N8130S
☐ N560HG	89	Citation V	560-0020	Collins Brothers Corp. Las Vegas, Nv.	N560HC
☐ N560HJ	00	Citation Excel	560-5078	Kinnarps AB. Falkoping, Sweden.	C-FPWC
☐ N560HM	05	Citation Encore	560-0699	CAM Investments Inc. Allegheny County, Pa.	N52462
☐ N560JC	94	Citation V Ultra	560-0283	CMH Homes Inc. Knoxville, Tn.	N1CH
☐ N560JF	00	Citation Excel	560-5173	Dee-Jay Aviation LLC/Layton Construction Co. Sandy, Ut.	N5173F
☐ N560JG	04	Citation Excel XLS	560-5531	Aero Leasing LLC/Gregory Management Co. Bristol, Tn.	N52229
☐ N560JL	89	Citation V	560-0044	PDQ Business Travel LLC. Duncan, Ok.	N331CC
☐ N560JM	89	Citation V	560-0010	Apex Aviation Corp. Napa, Ca.	N643RT
☐ N560JT	04	Citation Encore	560-0670	Mobile Crane Services Inc. Ottumwa, Ia.	N611CS
☐ N560JW	01	Citation Encore	560-0560	Scion LLC. Allen, Ky.	N5180C
☐ N560KL	02	Citation Encore	560-0622	C Kevin Landry. Bedford-Hanscom, Ma.	N5197A
☐ N560KT	02	Citation Excel	560-5127	RK560 Citation Leasing LLC. Scottsdale, Az.	N.....
☐ N560KW*	05	Citation Encore+	560-0751	Cessna Aircraft Co. Wichita, Ks. (Ff 22 Mar 06).	N560CC
☐ N560L	98	Citation Excel	560-5011	Lozier Corp. Omaha, Ne.	N52141
☐ N560LC	95	Citation V Ultra	560-0296	Landmark Communications Inc. Norfolk, Va.	(N5163C)
☐ N560LM	90	Citation V	560-0068	MS Management Services Inc. Hartford, Ct.	N246NW
☐ N560MG	93	Citation V	560-0223	Apogee Medical Management Inc. Scottsdale, Az.	N223CV
☐ N560MH	91	Citation V	560-0105	Bell Aviation Inc. West Columbia, SC.	N147VG
☐ N560MM	93	Citation V	560-0228	SureFlight LLC/McCauley Management, Phoenix, Az.	N87GA
☐ N560MR	01	Citation Encore	560-0594	Citation Associates Inc. Roanoke, Va.	N52446
☐ N560NY	01	Citation Excel	560-5198	Trans-Marine Management Corp. Tampa, Fl.	N552MA
☐ N560PA	91	Citation V	560-0136	Performance Air LLC. Gaithersburg, Md.	N999AD
☐ N560PD	02	Citation Excel	560-5311	Patterson-UTI Management Services LLC. Snyder, Tx.	N560JP
☐ N560PK	91	Citation V	560-0133	Solaire LLC. Corvallis, Or.	N93DW
☐ N560PL	05	Citation Excel XLS	560-5600	Flying Services NV. Antwerp, Belgium.	N51780
☐ N560RF	96	Citation V Ultra	560-0379	N560RF LLC. Ontario, Ca.	C-GWCR
☐ N560RK	96	Citation V Ultra	560-0407	LigonAir LLC. Allegheny County, Pa.	F-OHRU
☐ N560RM	04	Citation Encore	560-0658	Moore Air LLC.MIV Assocs LLC. Oklahoma City, Ok.	N52234
☐ N560RN	95	Citation V Ultra	560-0309	Rocking N Air Inc. Camarillo, Ca.	N212BD
☐ N560RP	91	Citation V	560-0158	RDD Leasing Inc/Plote Inc. Lake in the Hills, Il.	N801AB
☐ N560RR	89	Citation V	560-0012	McBride Properties of Chapin LLC. Chapin, SC.	N560ME
☐ N560RS	03	Citation Excel	560-5323	Eastway Aviation LLC & Group Outcome LLC. Islip, NY.	(N561RW)
☐ N560RV	97	Citation V Ultra	560-0417	Guaranty RV. Junction City, Or.	N525BA
☐ N560RW	92	Citation V	560-0196	RBW Enterprises Inc. West Conshohocken, Pa.	N357AZ
☐ N560SB	80	HS 125/700A	NA0274	Grafair Inc. Vero Beach, Fl.	(OY-VIA)

Reg	Yr	Type	c/n	Owner/Operator	Prev Regn
N560SH	83	Gulfstream 3	404	Safari Aero/Safari Charters Ltd. Fort Pierce, Fl.	(N24TJ)
N560TA	97	Citation V Ultra	560-0430	Concrete Systems Inc. Portsmouth, NH.	C-GLIM
N560TD	07	Citation Excel XLS	560-5711	Teradata Operations Inc. Dayton, Oh.	N1315D
N560TE	01	Citation Encore	560-0595	B & B Aircraft LC/E C Barton & Co. Jonesboro, Ar.	N.....
N560TH	01	Citation Excel	560-5215	N560TH Inc. Wilmington, De.	VP-CPC
N560TS	00	Citation Excel	560-5144	A R Sanchez Holdings Inc. Laredo, Tx.	N52MW
N560TV	04	Citation Excel XLS	560-5545	Daryl R Verdoorn, St Paul, Mn.	N45XL
N560VR	99	Citation Excel	560-5049	Viking Aircraft LLC/Viking Range Corp. Greenwood, Ms.	N680VR
N560VU	97	Citation Encore	707	Cessna Aircraft Co. Wichita, Ks. (was 560-0424).	N5079V
N560WH	89	Citation V	560-0013	Exchange Air Partners LLC. Oakhurst, NJ.	(N1217P)
N560WW	90	Citation V	560-0047	Petro Wings LC. Pampa, Tx.	N500FK
N560XL	96	Citation Excel	706	Cessna Aircraft Co. Wichita, Ks. (Ff 29 Feb 96).	
N561AC	93	Citation V	560-0218	JW & JA Inc/Aire Corr LLC. Indianapolis, In.	N5GE
N561AS	80	Citation II	550-0383	Spitfire Aviation Services LLC. Fayetteville, Ar.	N551AB
N561B	89	Citation V	560-0008	J G Boswell Co. Burbank, Ca.	
N561BC	98	CitationJet	525-0257	International Bank of Commerce, Laredo, Tx.	N26DK
N561BP	00	Citation Excel	560-5134	Beneto Inc/Beneto Jet Sales Inc. Sacramento, ca.	N52352
N561CC	97	Citation V Ultra	560-0416	Air Land Leasing LLC. Madera, Ca.	N416VP
N561CE	01	Citation Excel	560-5206	Excel Air Charter LLC. Louisville, Ky.	N206CX
N561CM	97	Citation V Ultra	560-0443	Kaliper Sales & Leasing Corp. Panama City, Panama.	N568RL
N561DA	95	Citation V Ultra	560-0314	Dove Air Inc. Fletcher, NC.	C-FYMT
N561EJ	89	Citation V	560-0035	WE Enterprises LLC. Franklin Lakes, NJ.	N36H
N561JS	96	Citation V Ultra	560-0413	Enhancement of Illinois Inc. Springfield, Il.	N8041R
N561MK	06	Citation Excel XLS	560-5622	Lark Wine LLC. Redding, Ct.	N52691
N561MT	91	Citation V	560-0122	Warren Transportation/Energy Transfer Equity LP. Addison, Tx	(N710MT)
N561PA	91	Citation V	560-0116	Preferred Airparts LLC. Kidron, Oh. (status ?).	N49NS
N561PS	80	HS 125/700A	NA0262	PBI Air LLC/Paul Broadhead Interests, Meridian, Ms.	N396RC
N561TS	90	Citation V	560-0057	Southern Aircraft & Transportation, Laredo, Tx.	N561BC
N561VP	87	Citation V	560-0001	Tradition Aviation LLC. Bermuda Dunes, Ca.(was S550-0136).	N1217V
N561XL	96	Citation Excel	560-5001	Cessna Aircraft Co. Wichita, Ks.	
N562DB	05	Citation Excel XLS	560-5604	Berge Group/BCB Air LLC. Phoenix, Az.	N.....
N562DD	00	Citation Excel	560-5108	Zoe Aviation & Charter Service Inc. Euless, Tx.	N562DB
N562LD	04	Citation Excel XLS	560-5532	Casey Co. Long Beach, Ca.	N562DB
N562ME	03	Challenger 604	5562	Mercury Engineering Executive Travel Ltd. Dublin, Ireland.	N562BA
N562MS	70	Sabre-60	306-44	Jet Air LLC. Dublin, Oh.	HC-BQU
N562RM	90	Citation II	550-0646	Moran Enterprises LLC. Long Beach, Ca.	N9VF
N562TS	02	Citation Excel	560-5178	Turquoise Sky LLC/Turquoise Delaware Inc. San Antonio, Tx.	
N562WD	01	Citation Excel	560-5226	CWD Jr Exploration Inc. Houston, Tx.	N350WC
N563BA	01	Citation X	750-0169	Best Friends Air LLC. Kerrville, Tx.	N68LP
N563CH	01	Citation Excel	560-5182	CHR Aviation LLC. Minneapolis-Flying Cloud, Mn.	N98RX
N563XP	05	Citation Excel XLS+	560-5617	Cessna Aircraft Co. Wichita, Ks. (Ff 7 Aug 07).	N5201J
N564BR	81	HS 125/700A	NA0287	Kaleidoscope Aviation Corp. Kansas City, Mo.	(N731GA)
N564CL	70	Learjet 25	25-060	Clay Lacy Aviation Inc. Van Nuys, Ca.	N695LJ
N564RM	85	Westwind-Two	434	Mystic Systems Technology Corp. Scottsdale, Az.	(N102AK)
N564TJ	97	Citation V Ultra	560-0432	Branch Aircraft Leasing Inc/Seminole Feed, Ocala, Fl.	N856WC
N565A	04	Citation Sovereign	680-0024	APC Aviation Inc/Anadarko Petroleum Corp. Houston, Tx.	N5241R
N565AB	99	Citation Excel	560-5072	CCA Industries Inc. Richmond, Va.	N52178
N565CC	73	Citation	500-0065	Trendway Corp. Holland, Mi.	(N565TW)
N565EJ	90	Citation V	560-0099	Edwards Jet Center, Logan Field, Mt.	N560GM
N565GB	06	Gulfstream G200	130	Trans Jet Equipment Inc. Naples, Fl.	N330GA
N565GG	83	Learjet 35A	35A-501	Chantilly Crushed Stone Inc. Chantilly, Va.	N326HG
N565JF	93	CitationJet	525-0041	BioTek Instruments Inc. Winooski, Vt.	N565JP
N565JP	07	CitationJet CJ-3	525B-0159	JP Aviation LLC/Epoch Properties Inc. Orlando, Fl.	N50275
N565JW	91	Citation V	560-0149	S C Johnson & Son Inc/Johnson's Wax, Racine, Wi.	(N68786)
N565NC	87	Citation II	550-0565	Idaho Potato Packers Corp. Blackfoot, Id.	N565JS
N565QS	08	Citation Excel XLS	560-5818	NetJets, Port Columbus, Oh.	N.....
N565RV	97	Gulfstream 4SP	1323	Xamex Investments Inc. Champlain, NY.	N503PC
N565ST	02	Gulfstream G550	5015	JM Family Enterprises Inc. Fort Lauderdale, Fl.	N915GA
N565V	77	Citation 1/SP	501-0267	Pikes Peak Flyers LLP. Colorado Springs, Co. (was 500-0355).	N565VV
N566F	05	Citation Excel XLS	560-5606	Fagen Inc. Granite Falls, Mn.	N.....
N566KB	95	Citation V Ultra	560-0325	Bravo Transportation Inc. Ocala, Fl.	N140WC
N566QS	08	Citation Excel XLS	560-5825	NetJets, Port Columbus, Oh.	N.....
N566VR	98	Citation V Ultra	560-0480	Dove Aviation LLC/Grand Peaks Properties, Denver, Co.	N560VR
N566YT	67	Falcon 20C	94	Tricoastal Air Inc. Toledo, Oh.	N614GA
N567CA	79	Citation II	550-0092	Accessories Inc. Allison Park, Pa.	F-GNLF
N567DK	97	Beechjet 400A	RK-155	Ivory Aviation LLC/Rader Automobiles Inc. Aiken, SC.	N631PP

Reg	Yr	Type	c/n	Owner/Operator	Prev Regn
N567EA	73	Citation	500-0067	Eastern Fishing & Rental Tools Inc. Laurel, Ms.	(N949SA)
N567F	92	Citation V	560-0171	Federated Department Stores Inc. Cincinnati, Oh.	N573F
N567JK	81	Diamond 1A	A007SA	NLK LLC. Milwaukee, Wi.	N24HD
N567MC	03	Citation Excel	560-5357	Maurice McAlister, Bullhead, Az.	N5161J
N567RA	76	Falcon 10	80	Air Bob Inc/Danro Corp. Fort Worth, Tx.	(N803RA)
N567T	01	390 Premier 1	RB-37	Puckett Machinery Co. Jackson, Ms.	N452A
N567WB	79	Citation 1/SP	501-0109	Millennium Aviation Group LLC. Wallace, NC.	N30RE
N568CS	06	Citation Excel XLS	560-5637	CitationShares Sales Inc. White Plains, NY.	N5225K
N568DM	02	Citation Excel	560-5325	ADM Milling Co/Archer Daniels Midland Co. Decatur, Il.	N52397
N568PA	78	Learjet 35A	35A-205	CFF Air Inc/Phoenix Air, Cartersville, Ga.	N59FN
N568QS	08	Citation Excel XLS	560-5829	NetJets, Port Columbus, Oh.	N.....
N568WC	90	Citation V	560-0083	Werco Manufacturing Inc. Broken Arrow, Ok.	N22LP
N569BW	81	Falcon 50	45	Quality Jet LLC. Chattanooga, Tn.	N9BX
N569CW	90	Gulfstream 4	1145	Countrywide Home Loans Inc. Van Nuys, Ca.	N797CD
N569D	72	Falcon 20F	259	Mass Development LLC. Oklahoma City, Ok.	N569DW
N569DM	02	CitationJet CJ-2	525A-0088	Euro Exec Aviation Inc. Cranfield, UK.	N.....
N569DW	88	Falcon 100	220	Quality Jet LLC. Chattanooga, Tn.	N702NC
N569SC	99	Learjet 31A	31A-177	Swiss Colony Inc. Janesville, Wi.	N132FX
N569TA	89	Citation V	560-0006	Philmar LLC. Winneconne, Wi.	(N917PK)
N570AM	03	Learjet 45	45-238	National Dairy Holdings LP. Dallas, Tx.	
N570BJ	89	Citation V	560-0030	King Aviation LLC. Dallas, Tx.	XB-MTS
N570DC	92	Gulfstream 4SP	1185	JAS Enterprises/David Cutter Group, Atlantic City, NJ.	N635AV
N570DM	94	CitationJet	525-0055	MH Aviation LLC/Meridian Development Corp. Lawrenceville, Ga	N923AR
N570EJ	92	Citation V	560-0164	Lynch Flying Service Inc. Logan Field, Mt.	N392BS
N570PT	06	Citation X	750-0270	XOJET Inc. Sacramento, Ca.	N270CX
N570R	81	Sabre-65	465-75	Frontenac Properties Inc/Aero Charter Inc. Chesterfield, Mo.	N2581E
N571BA	03	Challenger 604	5571	Boeing Co. Chicago, Il.	N604BA
N571BC	88	Citation II	550-0599	International Bank of Commerce, Laredo, Tx.	VR-BYE
N571CH	79	HS 125/700A	NA0251	Roto-Rooter Inc. Cincinnati, Oh.	M810CR
N571CS	06	Citation Excel XLS	560-5680	CitationShares Sales Inc. White Plains, NY.	N52960
N571P	60	MS 760 Paris	71	JSI Holdings Inc. Calhoun, Ga.	71
N572EC	05	Gulfstream G550	5072	East Coast Brokerage Services LLC. Ocala, Fl.	(N25GV)
N573AB	06	Citation Excel XLS	560-5635	Black Magic Flightops LLC. San Juan, PR.	N1312T
N573BA	03	Challenger 604	5573	The Boeing Co. Chicago, Il.	C-GLXB
N573BP*	91	Citation V	560-0108	BBI-Blue Beacon International Inc. Salina, Ks.	N573BB
N573LR	78	Learjet 35A	35A-153	Image Air, Bloomington, Il.	N573LP
N573M	03	Citation Bravo	550-1066	Menard Inc. Eau Claire, Wi.	N.....
N573QS	08	Citation Excel XLS	560-5827	NetJets, Port Columbus, Oh.	N.....
N573TR	91	Falcon 50	217	Trident Seafoods Corp. Sand Point, Ak.	N573AC
N574BB	07	CitationJet CJ2+	525A-0371	BBI Inc/Blue Beacon International, Salina, Ks.	N51160
N574BP	89	Citation V	560-0022	Waterside Aircraft Marketing LLC. Old Saybrook, Ct.	N574BB
N574CS	07	Citation Excel XLS	560-5705	CitationShares Sales Inc. White Plains, NY.	N50736
N574DA	95	Learjet 60	60-055	Fielding Aviation LLC. St Louis, Mo.	N660CB
N574M	99	Citation Bravo	550-0910	Menard Inc. Eau Claire, Wi.	N5207V
N574QS	08	Citation Excel XLS	560-5820	NetJets, Port Columbus, Oh.	N.....
N575AG	06	Learjet 45XR	45-312	L45XR Leasing Corp. Santo Domingo, DR.	
N575BW	80	Citation II	550-0116	Lighting Science Group Corp. Dallas, Tx.	N669MA
N575CT	95	Gulfstream 4SP	1284	Chevron USA Inc. Oakland, Ca.	N90AM
N575E	86	Gulfstream 4	1007	Inter Travel & Services Inc. Irvine, Ca.	N59JR
N575EW	87	Citation S/II	S550-0140	Gulf Atlantic Airways/University Air Center, Gainesville, Fl	C-GLCR
N575GH	82	Learjet 55	55-042	American Jet International Corp. Houston, Tx.	D-CMTM
N575JR	05	Hawker 850XP	258755	John Eagle Motors, Dallas, Tx.	
N575M	99	Citation Bravo	550-0911	Menard Inc. Eau Claire, Wi.	N52655
N575MA	07	Hawker 900XP	HA-16	Annessi Corp. Colon, Panama.	
N575NR	07	Citation Excel XLS	560-5759	Cessna Aircraft Co. Wichita, Ks.	N50484
N575QS	07	Citation Excel XLS	560-5730	NetJets, Port Columbus, Oh.	N.....
N575RB	95	Beechjet 400A	RK-99	BC Aviation LLC/Bruno Capital Management Corp. Birmingham.	N95FA
N575SG	85	Citation S/II	S550-0064	TM1 LLC. Fort Wayne, In.	(N557MG)
N575WB	06	Challenger 300	20075	Boich Companies, Port Columbus, Oh.	C-FHCY
N575WW	76	Learjet 35	35-043	Executive Jet Services Inc. Carlsbad, Tx.	C-GVCA
N576CS	07	Citation Excel XLS	560-5794	CitationShares Sales Inc. White Plains, NY.	N.....
N576QS	07	Citation Excel XLS	560-5708	NetJets, Port Columbus, Oh.	N.....
N576SC	04	CitationJet CJ-2	525A-0224	Sharpline Converting Inc. Wichita, Ks.	N424CJ
N577CS	07	Citation Excel XLS	560-5726	CitationShares Sales Inc. White Plains, NY.	N50054
N577JC	00	Citation X	750-0122	Dragon Leasing Corp. DuPage, Il.	N800W
N577JT	78	Citation 1/SP	501-0057	Citation Aviation LLC. Birmingham, Al.	N577VM

Reg	Yr	Type	c/n	Owner/Operator	Prev Regn
❏ N577PS	05	Citation Excel XLS	560-5581	Wilderness Investment Co. Silver Springs, Md.	N5153K
❏ N577QS	07	Citation Excel XLS	560-5735	NetJets, Port Columbus, Oh.	N.....
❏ N577T	89	BAe 125/800B	258149	612 Corp. Miami, Fl.	N155T
❏ N577VM	98	Citation Bravo	550-0863	Walls Aircraft LLC/Cleveland Newspapers Inc. Birmingham, Al.	N709JW
❏ N578BB	85	Citation S/II	S550-0037	Bermuda Air Medivac Services Ltd. Hamilton, Bermuda.	N573BB
❏ N578CS	07	Citation Excel XLS	560-5800	CitationShares Sales Inc. White Plains, NY.	N.....
❏ N578M	89	Citation II	550-0612	GO Interests LLC. Manvel, Tx.	(N534M)
❏ N579CE	01	Citation Encore	560-0579	Next Century Aviation Inc. Sausalito, Ca.	N5259Y
❏ N579CS	08	Citation Excel XLS	560-5807	CitationShares Sales Inc. White Plains, NY.	N.....
❏ N579M	06	Citation Bravo	550-1133	Menard Inc. Eau Claire, Wi.	N5201M
❏ N579QS	07	Citation Excel XLS	560-5773	NetJets, Port Columbus, Oh.	N.....
❏ N580AW	98	Citation Excel	560-5017	American Woodmark Corp. Winchester, Va.	N865CE
❏ N580BC	99	Citation Excel	560-5059	Broin & Assocs Inc. Sioux Falls, SD.	N55HX
❏ N580CS	08	Citation Excel XLS	560-5815	CitationShares Sales Inc. White Plains, NY.	N.....
❏ N580JT	92	Citation V	560-0167	Sand Hills Holdings LLC/Sligo Investments LLC. Denver, Co.	N560JT
❏ N580ML	07	Embraer Legacy 600	14500990	Stone Tower Air LLC.	PT-SKK
❏ N580QS	07	Citation Excel XLS	560-5741	NetJets, Port Columbus, Oh.	N.....
❏ N580R	73	Citation	500-0127	Mid Continent Corp. Sunset Hills, Mo.	N500R
❏ N580RC	01	Citation Excel	560-5166	Rosewood Resources Inc. Dallas, Tx.	N5068R
❏ N580RJ	07	Hawker 900XP	HA-39	HincoJet LLC/The Hinman Co. Grand Rapids, Mi.	
❏ N580RK	02	Beechjet 400A	RK-329	Hincojet LLC/Hinman Co. Grand Rapids, Mi.	N580RJ
❏ N581CM	85	Citation S/II	S550-0033	Doc Harley LLC. Baton Rouge, La.	N531CM
❏ N581CS	08	Citation Excel XLS	560-5817	CitationShares Sales Inc. White Plains, NY.	N.....
❏ N581MB	72	Gulfstream II SP	109	Marquez Brothers Aviation LLC. Las Vegas, Nv.	N73AW
❏ N581PH	76	Learjet 35A	35A-083	Impact Fulfillment Services Inc. Burlington, NC.	N581CC
❏ N581SF	02	390 Premier 1	RB-47	FKM Enterprises LLC. Minneapolis, Mn.	(N145SD)
❏ N581TS	01	Challenger 604	5482	The Bendini Group Inc. Tupelo, Ms.	N322LA
❏ N582EJ	81	Falcon 50	82	Luxury Motors Inc. Downers Grove, Il.	N150BP
❏ N583AJ	92	Gulfstream 4	1184	Jerome Moss, Van Nuys, Ca.	(N805JM)
❏ N583BS	79	Learjet 35A	35A-258	Horsham Valley Airways Inc. Horsham, Pa.	(N17UF)
❏ N583CC	75	B 737-291	21069	Cavalier Sports Marketing LLC. Cleveland, Oh.	N15255
❏ N583CE	01	Citation Encore	560-0583	Lakeside Industries Inc. Issaquah, Wa.	N52591
❏ N583PS	07	Learjet 45	45-331	PSS World Medical Inc. Jacksonville, Fl.	N40084
❏ N583QS	08	Citation Excel XLS	560-5812	NetJets, Port Columbus, Oh.	N.....
❏ N585A	05	Gulfstream G550	5110	ARAMCO Associated Co. Dhahran, Saudi Arabia.	N940GA
❏ N585BP	06	Falcon 900EX EASY	170	BPI Aviation LLC/Beef Products Inc. Sioux City, SD.	F-WWFJ
❏ N585D	94	Gulfstream 4SP	1258	E I DuPont de Nemours & Co. New Castle, De.	N400UP
❏ N585DG	94	CitationJet	525-0057	Seward L Schreder Construction Inc. Chico, Ca.	(N525FM)
❏ N585JC	00	Gulfstream V	618	Hilton Hotels Corp. Van Nuys, Ca.	(N123H)
❏ N585KS	00	Citation Bravo	550-0945	Panda Restaurant Group Inc. Van Nuys, Ca.	N5109R
❏ N585M	99	Citation X	750-0096	Menard Inc. Eau Claire, Wi.	
❏ N585MC	01	CitationJet CJ-1	525-0452	Montana Cowboy LLC. Lake Geneva, Wi.	N585PK
❏ N585PK	04	CitationJet CJ-3	525B-0011	Pegasus Starflight LLC. Scotts Valley, Ca.	N110MG
❏ N585PS	88	Citation II	550-0585	Parminter Investments Ltd. Georgetown, Grand Cayman.	N65AR
❏ N585T	01	Citation X	750-0197	Target Corp. Minneapolis, Mn.	N.....
❏ N585TC	83	Diamond 1A	A060SA	White Industries Inc. Bates City, Mo. (status ?).	(N300SJ)
❏ N585TH	02	Citation Bravo	550-1035	Jaguar Aviation Inc/Blazer Resources Inc. Mount Vernon, Tx.	N.....
❏ N585VC	02	Hawker 800XP2	258585	Vitesse Corp. Greenfield, In.	(N885VC)
❏ N586CS	97	Falcon 50EX	260	Valkyrie Aviation Corp. Seattle, Wa.	F-WWHK
❏ N586D	00	Gulfstream 4SP	1439	E I DuPont de Nemours & Co. New Castle, De.	N439GA
❏ N586ED	06	CitationJet CJ2+	525A-0324	Paragon Industries Inc. Santa Ana, Ca.	N5228Z
❏ N586RE	80	Citation II	550-0199	U S Customs Service, Oklahoma City, Ok.	N67983
❏ N586SF	05	Citation Excel XLS	560-5592	Carolina First Bank, Greenville, SC.	N52639
❏ N587QS	08	Citation Excel XLS	560-5805	NetJets, Port Columbus, Oh.	N.....
❏ N588AC	00	Citation Bravo	550-0912	Cloverleaf Cold Storage Co. Sioux City, Ia.	N5117U
❏ N588AT	05	Gulfstream G450	4020	Hillwood Development LLC. Dallas, Tx.	(N450GA)
❏ N588GS	01	Falcon 900EX	104	Citigroup Corporate Aviation, White Plains, NY.	F-WWFA
❏ N588LS	94	Gulfstream 4SP	1245	Las Vegas Sands Inc. Las Vegas, Nv.	N459PE
❏ N588QS	07	Citation Excel XLS	560-5721	NetJets, Port Columbus, Oh.	N.....
❏ N588SS	74	Gulfstream 2	142	KKSM Aircraft Holdings LLC. Hollywood, Fl.	N742TS
❏ N589DC	66	Falcon 20C	45	Career Aviation Co. Oakdale, Ca.	N175GA
❏ N589FJ*	99	Falcon 50EX	289	Dassault Falcon Jet Corp. Teterboro, NJ.	N315DV
❏ N589HM	90	Gulfstream 4	1153	Cirrus Gas LLC. Dallas-Love, Tx.	N590HM
❏ N589QS	08	Citation Excel XLS	560-5810	NetJets, Port Columbus, Oh.	N.....
❏ N589SJ	88	Citation II	550-0589	Sky Access Jet LLC/Carroll Properties, Fort Myers, Fl.	N787JD
❏ N590A	89	Citation V	560-0029	Alascom Inc. Anchorage, Ak.	(N1229C)

Reg	Yr	Type	c/n	Owner/Operator	Prev Regn
N590F	90	Falcon 900B	98	Compass Foods Inc. Montvale, NJ.	N59CF
N590FA	07	Gulfstream G150	224	Iron Gate Finance Corp. Wilmington, De.	N424GA
N590PJ	06	CitationJet CJ-3	525B-0104	PWS Air LLC. Portland, Or.	N5216A
N590QS	07	Citation Excel XLS	560-5738	NetJets/Marquis Jet Partners Inc. Port Columbus, Oh.	N.....
N590RA	80	Falcon 50	20	Avion Sales LLC. Sanford, Fl.	(N552LX)
N591CF	04	Citation Encore	560-0661	Growmark Inc/CC Services Inc. Bloomington, Il.	N5162W
N591DK	02	Citation Encore	560-0591	Iron Ring Aviation/David Kashtan, La Selva Beach, Ca.	N.....
N591M	99	Citation V Ultra	560-0533	Modine Manufacturing Co. Racine, Wi.	
N591MA	01	Citation Excel	560-5163	N591MA LLC. Jacksonville, Fl.	N68LX
N592DR	01	CitationJet CJ-2	525A-0028	Western Oilfields Supply Co. Bakersfield, Ca.	D-IBBB
N592HC	02	390 Premier 1	RB-92	Bozeman 592 LLC. Bozeman, Mt.	N62LW
N592QS	07	Citation Excel XLS	560-5706	NetJets, Port Columbus, Oh.	N.....
N592SP	06	Challenger 300	20123	Century Air LLC/Century Homebuilders, Opa Locka, Fl.	C-FIOO
N592VP	90	Citation V	560-0092A	Rockman Rocketeers LC. Austin, Tx.	(N713HH)
N592WP	75	Citation	500-0253	Miyasaka & Soilfume Inc. Watsonville, Ca.	N8TG
N593BW	83	Citation 1/SP	501-0675	Jetcraft Corp. Raleigh-Durham, NC.	N501MT
N593HR	87	BAe 125/800A	258089	593HR Inc. Nashville, Tn.	N862CE
N593M	99	Citation V Ultra	560-0525	U S Energy Corp. Riverton, Wy.	N5093Y
N594CA	05	Challenger 300	20082	NAC 300 LLC/National Air Cargo Inc. Farmingdale, NY.	C-FGCV
N594G	83	Citation II	550-0482	Aircraft Resource Center Inc. Lakeville, Mn.	N62WG
N594M	94	Citation V Ultra	560-0279	Croghan & Assocs LLC. Boulder, Co.	N361EC
N594QS	07	Citation Excel XLS	560-5697	NetJets, Port Columbus, Oh.	N5136J
N594RJ	88	Challenger 601-3A	5029	R J Corman Aviation Services LLC. Lexington, Ky.	N83LC
N594WP	91	Citation II	550-0693	S & M Brands Inc. Keysville, Va.	VP-BTR
N595A	05	Gulfstream G550	5117	ARAMCO Associated Co. Dhahran, Saudi Arabia.	N967GA
N595BA	79	Learjet 35A	35A-230	Jets of the Atlantic LLC. Orlando, Fl.	N37HJ
N595DC	75	Citation	500-0265	Davis Companies Air LLC. Newberry, Fl.	N501SC
N595E*	87	Gulfstream 4	1025	E I Aviation LLC. Miami, Fl.	N900GB
N595G*	01	Citation Excel	560-5224	Growmark Inc. Bloomington, Il.	N146EP
N595MA	04	Citation Encore	560-0680	R L Campbell Roofing Co. Jacksonville, Fl.	N5245L
N595PA	97	Learjet 31A	31A-150	PA Lear 31A-150 LLC. Springdale, Ar.	N316AS
N595PC	97	Citation Bravo	550-0826	Rite Flite Aviation Ltd. Cleveland, Oh.	N51072
N595PE	98	Gulfstream 4SP	1373	Platinum Equity LLC. Van Nuys, Ca.	N106KA
N595QS	07	Citation Excel XLS	560-5712	NetJets, Port Columbus, Oh.	N.....
N595SY	06	Citation Sovereign	680-0091	Mega International Commercial Bank, Taipei, Taiwan.	N5200R
N596GA	99	Gulfstream V	596	Aero Graphics Inc. Manassas, Va.	N596GA
N597CS	79	Citation 1/SP	501-0293	Banker Steel LLC. Lynchburg, Va. (was 500-0389).	N850MA
N597GA	07	Gulfstream G550	5197	Gulfstream Aerospace Corp. Savannah, Ga.	
N598AW	86	Citation III	650-0112	Aurora Ventures LLC. St Paul, Mn.	N598C
N598CA	80	Citation II	550-0187	Staff Air System Inc. Wilmington, De.	C-GHOM
N598GS	70	Gulfstream II SP	85	Centralise Leasing Corp. Irvine, Ca.	N524MM
N598JL	87	Beechjet 400	RJ-19	Jet Linx Aviation Corp. Omaha, Ne.	N101CC
N598JM	78	Westwind-1124	222	Weisbrod & Weisbrod LLP. Dallas, Tx.	N3RC
N598KW	86	Citation S/II	S550-0098	K Air Leasing Inc. Fort Wayne, In.	N598WC
N599BR	82	Citation 1/SP	501-0258	Jack Wall Aircraft Sales Inc. Memphis, Tn.	N16KW
N599CB	85	Citation S/II	S550-0054	Kentucky Aviation Partners LLC. Bardstown, Ky.	(N599HA)
N599CT	00	Learjet 31A	31A-200	Lestralaur LLC. Friday Harbor, Wa.	N797WB
N599DA	01	Challenger 604	5498	Delphi Automotive Systems LLC. Troy, Mi.	N598DA
N599GB	07	Citation Sovereign	680-0146	Green Bay Packaging Inc. Green Bay, Wi.	N.....
N599JL	86	Beechjet 400	RJ-14	Jet Linx Aviation Corp. Omaha, Ne.	(N770TB)
N599QS	07	Citation Excel XLS	560-5714	NetJets, Port Columbus, Oh.	N.....
N599ZM	84	Falcon 20F-5	481	Sabre Internacional SA. Panama City, Panama.	OH-WIN
N600AE	76	HS 125/F600A	256068	Air Eagle LLC. Detroit, Mi.	N501R
N600AJ	00	Learjet 60	60-199	R J Gullo Properties 3 LLC. Rochester, NY.	(N912MM)
N600AK	99	Global Express	9033	Colwend LLC/Dallah Al Baraka, Jeddah, Saudi Arabia.	C-GFAN
N600AL	00	CitationJet CJ-1	525-0383	Means to Go LLC. Altoona, Pa.	N5231S
N600AM	97	Challenger 604	5345	Media Consulting Services, New Windsor, NY.	N345BA
N600AR	00	Gulfstream 4SP	1419	Atlantic Investment Management, NYC.	(N419GA)
N600AT	87	Citation II	550-0551	C J Mahan Construction Co. Grove City, Oh. (was 551-0551).	N487LD
N600AW	01	Citation X	750-0181	CBX Aviation LLC. Mineral Wells, Tx.	N181BR
N600BW	04	Citation Encore	560-0671	BorgWarner Inc. Chicago, Il.	N52457
N600C	82	Learjet 55	55-047	35-55 Partnership/Fayez Sarofim & Co. Houston, Tx.	
N600CD	78	Falcon 20F-5	377	Rapid Leasing Inc. Cedar Rapids, Ia.	N377RP
N600CK	91	Gulfstream 4	1169	CRK Studio LLC. Waterbury, Ct.	N600DW
N600CN	94	Learjet 60	60-040	Chickasaw Nation, Ada, Ok.	N600AS
N600DR	98	Gulfstream 4SP	1356	Dominion Resources Inc. Richmond, Va.	(JY-TWO)

Reg	Yr	Type	c/n	Owner/Operator	Prev Regn
N600DT	75	Learjet 35	35-017	MartinAir Inc. Richmond, Va.	N456MS
N600EA	85	Citation S/II	S550-0015	Estancia Aviation LLC. Gresham, Or.	C-GMTV
N600EF	96	Citation V Ultra	560-0376	Kennedy Aviation LLC. Los Altos, Ca.	N600LF
N600ES	99	Challenger 604	5439	Earth Star Inc. Burbank, Ca.	C-GLXQ
N600G	76	HS 125/F600A	256066	TK Aero Inc. Edmond, Ok.	N800JP
N600GA	93	Learjet 60	60-021	Larry Hansel Aircraft/Rampage Clothing Co. Commerce, Ca.	(N732LH)
N600GG	97	Learjet 60	60-115	North American Jet Charter Inc. Banning, Ca.	N500ZH
N600GL	68	Sabre-60A	306-24	OTW Farms LLC. Hollister, Ca.	(N600GE)
N600GM	79	Learjet 25D	25D-290	Milam International Inc. Englewood, Co.	N321RB
N600GW	83	Diamond 1A	A044SA	Baer Air, Merritt Island, Fl.	N606JM
N600HA	82	Challenger 600S	1071	CL600 Holdings LLC. St Louis, Mo.	N220LC
N600HL	74	Falcon 10	19	Falcon Flyers Inc. New Castle, De.	LX-TRG
N600HR	93	CitationJet	525-0038	J & K Aviation Co. Wilmington, De.	N135MM
N600J	06	Gulfstream G550	5138	Johnson & Johnson, Mercer County Airport, NJ.	N638GA
N600JB	91	Citation II	550-0691	Twin Lakes Development Corp. Hinsdale, Il.	C-GAPV
N600JD	01	Gulfstream V	640	Deere & Co. Moline, Il.	N752BA
N600JM	96	Falcon 900EX	5	Otari LLC. Boeing Field, Seattle, Wa.	N500VM
N600KE	85	Westwind-1124	416	Fastest 1124 LLC/Wolf Creek Industries Inc. Summerdale, Al.	N815RK
N600KM	84	Citation S/II	S550-0008	Kreuter Engineering Inc. New Paris, In.	(N40KM)
N600L	02	Learjet 60	60-259	Lincoln National Life Insurance Co. Fort Wayne, In.	N40075
N600LC	03	Learjet 60	60-265	Lincoln National Life Insurance Co. Fort Wayne, In.	N40086
N600LG	01	Learjet 60	60-230	Lincoln National Life Insurance Co. Fort Wayne, In.	N356CG
N600LN	96	Learjet 60	60-082	Lincoln National Life Insurance Co. Fort Wayne, In.	N682LJ
N600LS	06	Challenger 300	20134	Midwest Visions LLC/Retail Transport Co. Las Vegas, Nv.	C-FLCY
N600MK	72	HS 125/600A	256004	Boyington Capital Group LLC. Plano, Tx.	N5AH
N600N	97	Falcon 50EX	256	Civic Center Corp/Anheuser Busch, Chesterfield, Mo.	VP-CBT
N600NM*	99	Learjet 60	60-182	Me Salve Inc. Catana, PR.	N245FX
N600NY	78	Westwind-1124	231	Clueless Aviation LLC/Belle Tire, Allen Park, Mi.	N331GW
N600PH*	95	Learjet 60	60-074	Huizenga Capital Management, Oak Brook, Il.	N674BP
N600QS	06	Citation Excel XLS	560-5664	NetJets/Marquis Jet Partners Inc. Port Columbus, Oh.	N.....
N600RH	85	Gulfstream 3	451	Sky View Aviation Inc. Orlando, Fl.	N5159Y
N600RM	78	Citation 1/SP	501-0044	Capital City Aviation Inc. Madison, Wi.	N50US
N600ST	03	Citation Bravo	550-1054	Sandair LLC. Redmond, Or.	N254CB
N600SV	68	HS 125/731	25159	Dove Air Inc. Fletcher, NC.	(N17GG)
N600TW	79	Falcon 10	153	Titan International Inc. Quincy, Il.	N81PX
N600VC	93	Gulfstream 4SP	1227	VC Aviation Services LLC. Pontiac, Mi.	N626TC
N600WD	74	Falcon 20E-5	300	WRRCO Inc. Beaumont, Tx.	N300FJ
N600WG	82	Falcon 50	98	Greenleaf Corp. Saegertown, Pa.	N50MK
N600XJ	69	Learjet 24B	24B-190	Pavair Inc. Santa Monica, Ca.	N190BP
N600XL	06	Embraer Legacy 600	14500965	Excelaire LLC. Islip, NY.	PT-SFN
N600YB	04	Gulfstream G200	096	Yum Restaurant Services Group, Louisville, Ky.	N196GA
N601AA	86	Challenger 601	3061	Integral Partners LLC. Santa Ana, Ca.	N597FJ
N601AB	01	Gulfstream G200	047	Aircraft Trust & Financing Corp. Fort Lauderdale, Fl.	N110GX
N601AD	95	Challenger 601-3R	5186	Cameron-Henkind Corp. White Plains, NY.	N9700X
N601AF	89	Challenger 601-3A	5045	Airgas Inc. New Castle, De.	N500GS
N601BC	79	Citation II	550-0091	Hickory Springs Manufacturing Co. Hickory, NC.	N527AG
N601BE	92	Challenger 601-3A	5103	BE Aerospace Inc. Wellington, Fl.	N76CS
N601BW	94	Challenger 601-3R	5150	Bindley Western Industries Inc. Indianapolis, In.	N602CC
N601CM	83	Challenger 600	1079	Waste Connections Transportation Co. Portland, Or.	N601SA
N601CN	96	Learjet 60	60-087	Chickasaw Nation, Ada, Ok.	N787LP
N601CT	82	Challenger 600S	1049	International Consolidated Technologies LLC. Las Vegas, Nv.	N600CF
N601CV	94	Challenger 601-3R	5144	Summit Seafood Supply Inc. Houston, Tx.	N347BA
N601DR	96	Hawker 800XP	258299	Dominion Resources Inc. Richmond, Va.	(N32BC)
N601DT	88	Challenger 601-3A	5024	Arizona Diamondbacks, Phoenix, Az.	N601NB
N601DV	04	Gulfstream G200	102	L A Fitness International LLC. Orange County, Ca.	N702GA
N601EC	90	Challenger 601-3A	5064	Virginia Air Corp. Richmond, Va.	N564TS
N601FR	87	Challenger 601-3A	5003	Furniture Row Leasing LLC. Lakewood, Co.	HB-IKT
N601GB	85	Challenger 601	3044	Challenger Leasing LLC. Bellevue, Wa.	(N801PA)
N601GG	06	Learjet 60	60-192	North American Jet Charter Inc. Banning, Ca.	
N601GL	70	Sabre-60A	306-50	Sabre Fifty Inc. Opa Locka, Fl. (status ?).	XB-FSZ
N601GN	74	Citation	500-0214	Roby Auto Group, Marysville, Oh.	N709TB
N601GT	01	Challenger 604	5524	IGT-International Game Technology, Reno, Nv.	N251CP
N601HW	94	Challenger 601-3R	5154	Wal-Mart Stores Inc. Rogers, Ar.	C-FJLA
N601JE	91	Challenger 601-3A	5086	Omni Group of Companies, Vancouver, BC. Canada.	N343KA
N601JG	83	Challenger 601	3006	Glidewell Laboratories, Newport Beach, Ca.	N256SD
N601JM	85	Challenger 601	3048	Airborne Charter Inc. Santa Monica, Ca.	(N628WC)

Reg	Yr	Type	c/n	Owner/Operator	Prev Regn
N601JP	93	Challenger 601-3R	5141	Golden Gate Capital Management, San Francisco, Ca.	(N613LX)
N601KJ	95	Challenger 601-3R	5187	Veinte-Siete LLC & Charlies Wings LLC. NYC.	C-GLXK
N601KK	82	Challenger 600S	1061	Kamilla Aircraft Holdings Inc. Fort Lauderdale, Fl.	(N661TS)
N601LJ	92	Learjet 60	60-001	Learjet Inc. Wichita, Ks.	
N601LS	93	Challenger 800	7008	Limited Inc. Columbus, Oh.	N501LS
N601PR	85	Challenger 601	3045	Ravello Enterprises LLC. London, UK.	N998JR
N601QS	02	Citation Excel	560-5301	NetJets, Port Columbus, Oh.	N.....
N601RC	86	Challenger 601	3055	Rockwell Collins Inc. Cedar Rapids, Ia.	N608RP
N601RL	88	Challenger 601-3A	5028	A T Massey Coal Co/Massey Energy Co. Richmond, Va.	(N601EA)
N601S	86	Challenger 601	3060	The Bistate Oil Co/Aero Ways Inc. Wilmington, De.	C-GLXY
N601ST	90	Challenger 601-3A	5081	John & June Rogers/Sky Trek Aviation, Modesto, Ca.	HL7202
N601TP	94	Challenger 601-3R	5156	The Pyle Group LLC. Madison, Wi.	N255CC
N601TX	83	Challenger 601	3005	Crow Family Inc/Crow Holdings, Dallas, Tx.	C-FAAL
N601VH	89	Challenger 601-3A	5043	Vector Research Ltd. Durham, NC.	N601BH
N601WM	88	Challenger 601-3A	5026	Tower LLC. Chicago, Il.	C-GLWT
N602AB	01	Gulfstream G200	048	Gulfstream Aerospace LP. Dallas-Love, Tx.	N112GX
N602AJ	81	Challenger 600S	1020	Kastlemar Inc. Boca Raton, Fl.	N600BD
N602AT	89	Citation II	550-0606	State of Alabama, Birmingham, Al.	N770BB
N602CA	93	CitationJet	525-0026	First Washington Management Group, Elkridge, Md.	(N214LX)
N602CS	03	Citation Sovereign	680-0003	CitationShares Sales Inc. White Plains, NY.	N103SV
N602JR	70	HS 125/731	NA752	Vernon Sorenson MD. Santa Barbara, Ca.	N700FA
N602MJ	05	CitationJet CJ-3	525B-0066	Uniroy Air Corp. San Juan, PR.	N6243M
N602QS	04	Citation Excel XLS	560-5518	NetJets, Port Columbus, Oh.	N52699
N602RF	06	Gulfstream G200	146	Regions Financial Corp. Birmingham, Al.	N138GA
N602TS	87	Challenger 601-3A	5002	Aero Toy Store LLC. Fort Lauderdale, Fl.	N43PR
N602VC	01	Gulfstream G200	038	VC Aviation Services LLC. Pontiac, Mi.	N168EC
N603CS	95	Gulfstream 4SP	1257	Indycar Aviation LLC. Indianapolis, In.	(N99PD)
N603GA	07	Gulfstream G450	4103	Gulfstream Aerospace Corp. Savannah, Ga.	
N603HC*	97	Citation VII	650-7077	A G Hauck Co. Cincinnati, Oh.	N603HD
N603KE	00	Gulfstream 4SP	1452	WFBNW NA. Salt Lake City, Ut. (trustor ?).	N603KF
N603QS	01	Citation Excel	560-5203	NetJets, Port Columbus, Oh.	N.....
N603RF	06	Gulfstream G200	147	Regions Financial Corp. Birmingham, Al.	4X-CVF
N603SC	97	Learjet 60	60-096	Flextronics Photonics PPT Inc. Hillsboro, Or.	N8086L
N603TS	75	HS 125/600A	256041	Corp Industrial Delta SA. Toluca, Mexico.	N808RP
N604AC	81	Challenger 600S	1012	Chanel Air LLC. Van Nuys, Ca.	N310PE
N604AF	00	Challenger 604	5444	Ashley Furniture Industries Inc. Arcadia, Wi.	N604VF
N604AS	79	Learjet 25D	25D-292	Royal Air Freight Inc. Pontiac, Mi.	N711VK
N604AU	99	Challenger 604	5434	AGG Learjet P/L. Sydney, QLD. Australia.	N322BX
N604AX	97	Challenger 604	5342	Apex Babcock & Brown LLC. San Francisco, Ca.	N371JC
N604B	97	Challenger 604	5335	Stream Enterprises LLC. Punta Gorda, Fl.	N801P
N604BB	04	Challenger 604	5582	MA Aviation LLC/MidAmerica Charters Ltd. Fargo, ND.	C-GLXH
N604BC	03	Challenger 604	5563	Ball Corp. Jeffco Airport, Co.	N300BC
N604BS	03	Challenger 604	5560	Boston Scientific Corp. Natick, Ma.	(N560TS)
N604CA	96	Challenger 604	5304	Fresh Mountains Inc. Panama City, Panama.	(N604TS)
N604CB	01	Challenger 604	5526	Colonial Bank, Montgomery, Al.	N804CB
N604CC	05	Challenger 604	5633	Cresair Inc. Northvale, NJ.	C-GLXW
N604CE	00	Challenger 604	5446	Reynolds DeWitt & Co. Cincinnati, Oh.	C-GLWZ
N604CL	03	Challenger 604	5570	Hershey Foods Corp. Middletown, Pa.	C-GLYH
N604CP	96	Challenger 604	5321	C Cary Patterson, Addison, Tx.	C-FZPG
N604CR	99	Challenger 604	5418	Grande Aviation LLC. Columbia, Md.	(N609CR)
N604CS	04	Citation Sovereign	680-0007	CitationShares Sales Inc. White Plains, NY.	N52081
N604CW	00	Challenger 604	5455	Jayhawk Inc. Dallas, Tx.	C-GCDF
N604D	07	Challenger 605	5713	Bombardier Aerospace Corp. Windsor Locks, Ct.	C-FMVQ
N604DE	00	Challenger 604	5471	Duke Energy Corp. Charlotte, NC.	N604WS
N604DH	97	Challenger 604	5344	Advance PCS/Caris Air Services Ltd. Irving, Tx.	N344BA
N604DS	90	Citation II	550-0647	Dartswift Inc. N Philadelphia, Pa.	N800MT
N604DT	05	Challenger 604	5627	Verde Capital Corp. Phoenix, Az.	C-GLXK
N604EF	82	Challenger 600S	1068	Royal Pacific Aviation/Executive Flight, Pangborn Memorial.	N160LC
N604EG	05	Challenger 604	5635	South Seas Helicopter Co. Carlsbad, Ca.	N604SL
N604FJ	86	Challenger 601-3A	5001	Carco Leasing/Carco Training Inc. Addison, Tx.	(N59FJ)
N604FK	84	Learjet 55	55-102	FK Air LLC. Cleveland, Oh.	N112FK
N604FS	00	Challenger 604	5465	JDC Support Services Inc. Mobile, Al.	N465AV
N604GM	98	Challenger 604	5399	Plum Creek Timber Co. Seattle, Wa.	C-GLXB
N604GR	00	Challenger 604	5478	Goodrich Corp. Richfield, Oh.	N478BA
N604GS	85	Learjet 35A	35A-604	Six Hundred Four Corp/ASAP Jets Inc. Teterboro, NJ.	N73LP
N604GW	99	Challenger 604	5424	Cook Inc. Bloomington, In.	G-DAAC

Reg	Yr	Type	c/n	Owner/Operator	Prev Regn
N604HC	02	Challenger 604	5555	Harbert Fund Advisors/Harbert Aviation Inc. Birmingham, Al.	N555VV
N604HF	03	Challenger 604	5575	Samtex (USA) Inc. Manchester, NH.	N529DM
N604HJ	98	Challenger 604	5382	Brunner & Lay Inc. Franklin Park, Il.	C-GLXS
N604HT	05	Challenger 604	5638	RCM Management Services GP Inc. Rutherfordton, NC.	N604MG
N604JS	96	Challenger 604	5311	Great Point Advisors LLC. Boston, Ma.	(N989DH)
N604JW	96	Challenger 604	5325	Red Desert Holdings LLC. White Plains, NY.	N331TH
N604KJ	02	Challenger 604	5554	Kevin Jaffe/Marine Charter Enterprises, Hillsboro, Or.	C-GLWV
N604KS	03	Challenger 604	5558	K & S Aircraft LLC. Scottsdale, Az.	N604SR
N604KT	06	Learjet 60	60-315	KTI Inc. Rialto, Ca.	
N604LC	98	Challenger 604	5373	L & L Leasing LLC. White Plains, NY.	HB-ILL
N604LJ	03	CitationJet CJ-2	525A-0180	Lan Jet LLC. Gadsden, Al.	N.....
N604LL	02	Challenger 604	5548	Legatum Aviation Ltd. Dubai, UAE.	N410BD
N604MC	04	Challenger 604	5581	Dean Foods Co. Dallas, Tx.	C-GLXF
N604ME	92	Challenger 601-3A	5112	Victor Tango LLC/MacFarlane Partners, San Francisco, Ca.	N404AB
N604MH	82	Challenger 600S	1042	Jetsons LLC/The Goodman Foundation, Seattle, Wa.	(N939CG)
N604MM	98	Challenger 604	5381	WJM Aviation LLC. Romeoville, Il.	PR-TUB
N604MU	99	Challenger 604	5406	Suiza Foods Corp. Dallas, Tx.	C-GLXS
N604PA	03	Challenger 604	5566	Prime Aire Inc. Springfield, Mo.	C-GLXU
N604PJ	83	Citation II	550-0459	P J Leasing LLC. Fort Myers, Fl.	N315ES
N604QS	01	Citation Excel	560-5204	NetJets, Port Columbus, Oh.	N.....
N604RB	98	Challenger 604	5377	RB Aviation LLC. Kalispell, Mt.	N315BX
N604RF	04	Challenger 300	20026	Regions Financial Corp. Birmingham, Al.	N26FA
N604RP	00	Challenger 604	5473	Nestle Purina PetCare Co. St Louis, Mo.	C-GLXK
N604RS	02	Challenger 604	5551	M/I Schottenstein Homes Inc. Columbus, Oh.	N551BT
N604RT	01	Challenger 604	5497	Sonic Aviation LLC. Scottsdale, Az.	C-GLXO
N604S	85	Learjet 35A	35A-597	Sandler Management Group LLC. Norfolk, Va.	N355CA
N604SA	97	Challenger 604	5341	Sandler Management Group LLC. Norfolk, Va.	C-GJBA
N604SB	03	Challenger 604	5569	Polear Inc. Camarillo, Ca.	C-GZVZ
N604SH	80	Challenger 600S	1008	Mountain Aviation LC. Cheyenne, Wy.	(D-C...)
N604ST	00	Challenger 604	5479	SMC Aviation-Seatankers Management Co. Oslo, Norway.	ZS-CMB
N604SX	01	Challenger 604	5492	Intralot Inc/Aircraft N604SX, Pleasant Valley, NY.	N711SX
N604TB	06	Challenger 604	5663	D3T LLC. White Plains, NY.	N664JC
N604TC	96	Challenger 604	5323	Tharaldson Executive Management Inc. Fargo, ND.	N623TS
N604TF	06	Challenger 604	5655	Chubb Corp. Morristown, NJ.	C-GLXW
N604TH	01	Challenger 604	5496	Glaceair Ltd.	N604UP
N604W	99	Challenger 604	5421	Commander Airways Inc. Tampa, Fl.	N604JP
N604WB	96	Challenger 604	5306	California Choice Benefit Administration, Orange County, Ca.	N604AB
N604ZH	98	Challenger 604	5376	Zimmer Inc. Warsaw, In.	N604CD
N605AG	07	Challenger 605	5739	Bombardier Aerospace Corp. Windsor Locks, Ct.	C-FQQE
N605BA	06	Challenger 605	5707	Kirin GmbH. Austria.	C-FLSJ
N605CB	06	Challenger 605	5708	Colonial Bank, Montgomery, Al.	C-GLXK
N605CC	06	Challenger 605	5702	Russell Aviation Leasing LLC. Hyannis, Ma.	(N225AR)
N605CH	00	Gulfstream V	621	Chase Manhattan Bank, White Plains, NY.	(N605M)
N605CS	02	Citation Sovereign	680-0001	CitationShares Sales Inc. White Plains, NY. (Ff 27 Jun 02).	N681CS
N605DS	89	Citation III	650-0178	TVPX Inc. Concord, Ma.	N57CE
N605DX	07	Challenger 605	5735	Aero Toy Store LLC. Fort Lauderdale, Fl.	C-FPQZ
N605FX	03	Learjet 40	45-2004	BBJS/FlexJets, Addison, Tx.	N40082
N605HC	07	Challenger 605	5720	Bombardier Aerospace Corp. Windsor Locks, Ct.	N720HG
N605HG	07	Challenger 605	5721	Bombardier Aerospace Corp. Windsor Locks, Ct.	C-FNTP
N605JM	07	Challenger 605	5716	GE Capital Solutions GmbH. Cologne, Germany.	C-FNIN
N605JP	07	Challenger 605	5726	Bombardier Aerospace Corp. Windsor Locks, Ct.	C-FOXU
N605LD	07	Challenger 605	5730	Bombardier Aerospace Corp. Windsor Locks, Ct.	C-FPWI
N605NA	66	Learjet 23	23-049	NASA Glenn Research Center, Cleveland, Oh.	(N933N)
N605QS	03	Citation Excel	560-5321	NetJets, Port Columbus, Oh.	N.....
N605RF	06	Challenger 300	20089	Regions Financial Corp. Birmingham, Al.	N71FA
N605SA	87	Citation III	650-0152	Sterling Aviation Inc. Milwaukee, Wi.	(N260VP)
N605SB	99	Learjet 60	60-156	World Class Automotive Operations, Dallas, Tx.	N76QF
N605SE	06	Learjet 45	45-317	Saracen Energy Advisors LP. Houston, Tx.	N438FX
N605T	96	Challenger 601-3R	5191	Avion LLC/Airmax LLC. Englewood, Co.	N191BE
N605TC	02	390 Premier 1	RB-52	Tomcat Air LLP. Redington Beach, Fl.	N60152
N605VF	04	Global 5000	9152	Dwight Management LLC. Minneapolis. (150th Global Express).	C-FBPK
N605WG	06	Embraer Legacy 600	14500980	Northeastern Aviation Corp. Wilmington, De.	PT-SHS
N606AM	83	Falcon 100	205	Flight Management Corp/Dart Container Corp. Sarasota, Fl.	N700DW
N606AT	93	Citation VI	650-0225	S'Porter Management Ltd/City West Hotels, Weston, Ireland.	N1301Z
N606CH	07	Gulfstream G350	4089	J P Morgan Chase Bank, White Plains, NY.	N389GA
N606CS	05	Citation Sovereign	680-0061	CitationShares Sales Inc. White Plains, NY.	N51575

Reg	Yr	Type	c/n	Owner/Operator	Prev Regn
☐ N606DH	84	Gulfstream 3	445	Pirue Consultancy Inc. Nassau, Bahamas.	N590DA
☐ N606FX	03	Learjet 40	45-2005	BBJS/FlexJets, Addison, Tx.	N40083
☐ N606GA	07	Gulfstream G450	4106	Gulfstream Aerospace Corp. Savannah, Ga.	
☐ N606GB	78	Learjet 25D	25D-245	Mobile Beverage Systems Inc. Newnan, Ga.	(N531GC)
☐ N606GG	01	Challenger 604	5500	TD Airways LLC/Development Group of S Florida, Opa Locka.	N225AR
☐ N606HC	94	CitationJet	525-0087	Hudson Co/Hudson Air LLC. Fort Payne, Al.	N100CQ
☐ N606JL	97	Challenger 604	5332	N606JL LLC. Jacksonville, Fl.	C-FNYU
☐ N606KK	76	Citation	500-0306	Karl Klement, West Hartford, Ct.	N36SJ
☐ N606L	93	Learjet 60	60-020	Curves International Inc. Waco, Tx.	N600L
☐ N606MA	76	Westwind-1124	196	Eastern Fishing & Rental Tools Inc. Laurel, Ms.	N863AB
☐ N606MG	97	CitationJet	525-0231	Scotts Miracle-Gro/Hagedorn Aviation Inc. Columbus, Oh.	N606JR
☐ N606PM	02	Gulfstream G300	1512	Altria Corporate Services Inc. Richmond, Va.	(N606KF)
☐ N606QS	03	Citation Excel	560-5338	NetJets, Port Columbus, Oh.	N5094D
☐ N606RP	04	Challenger 604	5578	Nestle Purina PetCare Co. St Louis, Mo.	C-GLWZ
☐ N606SB	00	Learjet 60	60-184	World Class Automotive Operations, Dallas, Tx.	N752BP
☐ N606SM	74	Learjet 25B	25B-185	Southern Jet Inc. Raleigh, NC.	N988AC
☐ N606SV	07	Citation Sovereign	680-0206	Cessna Aircraft Co. Wichita, Ks.	N.....
☐ N606XT	05	Challenger 300	20052	XTO Energy Corp. Fort Worth, Tx.	C-FCZV
☐ N607AX	90	Challenger 601-3A	5075	REL Services LLC/Avion Services Inc. Manassas, Va.	N409KC
☐ N607BF	83	Learjet 55	55-056	607BF Inc/Flynn Enterprises Inc. Chicago, Il.	N156JC
☐ N607BH*	80	Challenger 600S	1007	HRS Solutions LLC. Allentown, Pa.	(N799HF)
☐ N607CF	76	Sabre-60	306-118	W R Fry/CC2B Trust, San Jose, Ca.	N607SR
☐ N607CH	07	Gulfstream G550	5159	J P Morgan Chase Bank NA. NYC.	N659GA
☐ N607CV	97	Falcon 900EX	25	Tyco International Ltd. Portsmouth, NH.	N55TY
☐ N607DB	98	CitationJet	525-0269	Corporate Jets Inc/Landmark Aviation, Winston Salem, NC.	N5219T
☐ N607FG	07	Learjet 45	45-344	Flex Air Ltd. Champaign, Il.	
☐ N607FX	04	Learjet 40	45-2012	BBJS/FlexJets, Addison, Tx.	
☐ N607GA	07	Gulfstream G450	4107	Gulfstream Aerospace Corp. Savannah, Ga.	
☐ N607HB*	06	Hawker 4000	RC-6	Hawker Beechcraft Corp. Wichita, Ks.	N15QS
☐ N607HM	95	Citation V Ultra	560-0322	Hale-Mills Construction Ltd. Houston, Tx.	N300WC
☐ N607PM	07	Gulfstream G550	5146	Altria Corporate Services Inc. White Plains, NY.	N646GA
☐ N607QS	03	Citation Excel	560-5340	NetJets, Port Columbus, Oh.	N50820
☐ N607RP	95	Challenger 601-3R	5184	Nestle Purina PetCare Co. St Louis, Mo.	N605RP
☐ N607SG*	01	Falcon 50EX	317	Stephens Group Inc. Little Rock, Ar.	N1839S
☐ N607TC	76	Falcon 10	77	Third Coast Aviation LLC. Nashville, Tn.	N107TB
☐ N607TN	07	CitationJet CJ1+	525-0662	Midwest Transplant Network, Westwood, Ks.	N5267G
☐ N607X	06	Falcon 7X	6	Aero Rio Taxi Aereo Ltda. Rio de Janeiro, RJ. Brazil.	F-WWUC
☐ N608BG	84	Gulfstream 3	430	BSI Holdings Inc. Paradise Valley, Az.	N600BG
☐ N608CE	01	Citation Encore	560-0608	Belk Inc. Charlotte, NC.	N52059
☐ N608CH	07	Gulfstream G450	4098	J P Morgan Chase Bank NA. White Plains, NY.	N398GA
☐ N608CL	92	Gulfstream 4	1193	Cassandra Lee Flight Operations LLC. Carmel, Ca.	N620KA
☐ N608CS	05	Citation Sovereign	680-0063	CitationShares Sales Inc. White Plains, NY.	N5148B
☐ N608CT	90	Citation V	560-0065	Century Tel Service Group LLC. Monroe, La.	N560JV
☐ N608CW	06	390 Premier 1A	RB-162	Avco Partners LLC. Van Nuys, Ca.	
☐ N608DB	97	CitationJet	525-0179	R R Dawson Bridge Co. Lexington, Ky.	N877GS
☐ N608FX	04	Learjet 40	45-2014	BBJS/FlexJets, Addison, Tx.	
☐ N608GA	07	Gulfstream G450	4108	Gulfstream Aerospace Corp. Savannah, Ga.	
☐ N608JR	88	Citation II/SP	551-0591	Rosfam Airplane Co/National Lumber, Warren. (was 550-0591).	N1AT
☐ N608MD	77	Gulfstream 2	197	Starflite/Senterra Consulting LLC. Houston, Tx.	(N217AH)
☐ N608MM	95	CitationJet	525-0104	Allegis Corp. Minneapolis, Mn.	N606MM
☐ N608PM	02	Gulfstream 4SP	1486	Altria Corporate Services Inc. White Plains, NY.	(N608KF)
☐ N608QS	02	Citation Excel	560-5308	NetJets, Port Columbus, Oh.	N.....
☐ N608WB*	00	Gulfstream V	608	Hewlett-Packard Co. San Jose, Ca.	N111LX
☐ N609CC	99	Challenger 604	5438	Rhine River Investments Inc. Annapolis, Md.	C-GLXM
☐ N609FX	04	Learjet 40	45-2022	BBJS/FlexJets, Addison, Tx.	N5013Y
☐ N609GA	07	Gulfstream G450	4109	Gulfstream Aerospace Corp. Savannah, Ga.	
☐ N609PM	05	Gulfstream G550	5086	Altria Corporate Services Inc. White Plains, NY.	N586GA
☐ N609QS	04	Citation Excel XLS	560-5522	NetJets, Port Columbus, Oh.	N51872
☐ N609SG	93	Falcon 900B	136	Stephens Group Inc. Little Rock, Ar.	(N1836S)
☐ N610AB	83	Gulfstream 3	398	Air Lake Lines Inc. Brooklyn Center, Mn.	N777RZ
☐ N610CB	02	Citation Bravo	550-1014	Ocotillo Partners LLC. Scottsdale, Az.	N52475
☐ N610CS	06	Citation Sovereign	680-0092	CitationShares Sales Inc. White Plains, NY.	N51444
☐ N610ED	75	Citation	500-0241	Dufresne Inc. Murrieta, Ca.	N288SP
☐ N610EG	91	Beechjet 400A	RK-13	RMN Group LLC. Coatesville, Pa.	N13GB
☐ N610FX	05	Learjet 40	45-2027	BBJS/FlexJets, Addison, Tx.	N40LJ
☐ N610GR	01	Citation X	750-0163	B F Goodrich Co. Akron, Oh.	N5253S

Reg	Yr	Type	c/n	Owner/Operator	Prev Regn
N610HC	98	Citation X	750-0054	Holt Company of Texas/HC Aviation Co. San Antonio, Tx.	N450T
N610JB	89	Citation II	550-0610	Eastern Jet LLC. Wilmington, NC.	N610BL
N610JR	86	Learjet 55	55-125	Tele/Com Air Inc. Sugar Grove, Il.	
N610LJ	86	Learjet 35A	35A-610	EPC Transport Inc. Denver, Co.	(N354GE)
N610LS	06	Challenger 300	20139	North Port Enterprises LLC. Las Vegas, Nv.	C-FLDX
N610PR	05	Hawker 400XP	RK-466	Loco Denim LLC. Wilmington, De.	N466XP
N610QS	01	Citation Excel	560-5210	NetJets, Port Columbus, Oh.	N.....
N610RA	70	Sabre-60	306-54	Golden Aviation de Mexico SA. Naulcalpan.	N97SC
N610SE	81	Westwind-Two	346	Jetco Inc. Wilmington, De.	N610HC
N610SM	98	Astra-1125SPX	101	Sallie Mae Inc. Dulles, Va.	(N291WK)
N610TT	80	Citation 1/SP	501-0170	2141 Corp. Atlanta, Ga.	N170EA
N611CS*	05	CitationJet CJ-3	525B-0063	Acrylic Encore Inc/Cal Spas, Ontario, Ca.	N128CJ
N611DB	75	Learjet 24D	24D-318	Air Center Helicopters Inc. St Thomas, USVI.	N114JT
N611FX	05	Learjet 40XR	45-2037	BBJS/FlexJets, Addison, Tx.	N237LJ
N611GA	65	Falcon 20C	9	Grand Aire Express Inc. Toledo, Oh. (status ?).	LV-WMF
N611JM	92	Gulfstream 4	1178	JFM Inc. Chicago-Du Page, Il.	N909LS
N611JW	96	Falcon 900B	162	Tristram Inc/Florida Marlins, Boca Raton, Fl.	N162FJ
N611MC	79	HS 125/700A	NA0257	Life Time Fitness Inc. Eden Prairie, Mn.	(N611EL)
N611QS	05	Citation Excel XLS	560-5548	General Electric Co. Stewart, NY.	N5168Y
N611TA*	81	Learjet 35A	35A-439	Air Med Services LLC. Lafayette, La.	N911WX
N611TG	87	Beechjet 400	RJ-27	Swing Plane Aviation LLC.	(N427CW)
N611VT	06	Global 5000	9219	Bombardier Aerospace Corp. Windsor Locks, Ct.	N80ZZ
N611WM	99	Beechjet 400A	RK-249	Wilkes & McHugh PA/Mike's Airplane Rentals Inc. Tampa, Fl.	N4249K
N612AF	06	Gulfstream G450	4069	Ameriprise Financial Inc. Stewart, NY.	N469GA
N612EQ	81	Learjet 55	55-003	B & E Aircraft Sales LLC. Coral Gables, Fl.	(N553GJ)
N612FX	05	Learjet 40XR	45-2039	BBJS/FlexJets, Addison, Tx.	
N612GA	07	Gulfstream G450	4112	Gulfstream Aerospace Corp. Savannah, Ga.	
N612MC	82	HS 125/700A	NA0317	May Department Stores Co. St. Louis, Mo.	(N612EL)
N612QS	02	Citation Excel	560-5312	NetJets, Port Columbus, Oh.	N.....
N612VR	79	Citation II/SP	551-0026	JWR Enterprises Inc. Dover, De. (was 550-0377).	N32PB
N612XP*	03	Hawker 800XP	258612	Sunflower Aircraft Inc/Halls Food Mart, Joplin, Mo.	N711GD
N613AL	07	CitationJet CJ1+	525-0661	Jetcraft Corp. Raleigh-Durham, NC.	N5244F
N613BS	83	Falcon 200	489	489BB LLC/Palm Beach Grading, Fort Lauderdale, Fl.	N489BB
N613H	06	Learjet 60	60-313	Begel Air Ltd. Farnborough, UK.	(G-HOIL)
N613KS	02	Citation Excel	560-5300	Horizon Aviation Leasing LLC/Sutton Co. Naples, Fl.	N613GY
N613QS	05	Citation Excel XLS	560-5599	NetJets, Port Columbus, Oh.	N.....
N613SB	91	Challenger 601-3A	5088	BACJET LLC. Broken Arrow, Ok.	C-GPCS
N614AF	95	Challenger 601-3R	5171	CDECRE Inc. Nashua, NH.	N213MC
N614AP	86	BAe 125/800A	258057	GW Enterprises/Wingate Healthcare Holdings Inc. Needham, Ma	N614AF
N614B	04	CitationJet CJ-3	525B-0017	Ross Devlopment Corp. Cortland, Oh.	N.....
N614BA	05	Challenger 604	5614	The Boeing Co. Seattle, Wa.	N614JA
N614BG	04	Hawker 800XP	258704	Bear Aviation Inc. Guatemala City, Guatemala.	
N614CM	00	Gulfstream V	614	CYMI Investments Sub Inc. Dayton, Oh.	N571GA
N614EP	07	Citation Excel XLS	560-5713	Complejo Educativo Parra Diaz, Caracas, Venezuela.	N51881
N614FX	05	Learjet 40XR	45-2041	BBJS/FlexJets, Addison, Tx.	
N614GA	07	Gulfstream G450	4114	Gulfstream Aerospace Corp. Savannah, Ga.	
N614JH	00	Learjet 60	60-201	Winner 614JH LLC. Wilmington, De.	N411SK
N614QS	05	Citation Excel XLS	560-5580	NetJets, Port Columbus, Oh.	N.....
N614RD	86	Gulfstream 4	1006	Cor Aviation LLC/Liberty Woods International, Carlsbad, Ca.	N3338
N614SJ*	81	Citation II	550-0220	Bates Engineers/Contractors Inc. Bainbridge, Ga.	N123RF
N614TS	97	Learjet 60	60-104	Mayberry Aviation LLC/Young Oil Corp. Knob Lick, Ky.	N903AM
N615EC	01	Citation Excel	560-5158	Emerald Coast Aviation LLC. Birmingham, Al.	N917EE
N615FX	05	Learjet 40	45-2051	BBJS/FlexJets, Addison, Tx.	
N615HB	81	Learjet 35A	35A-444	G A Robinson III, Memphis, Tn.	N615HP
N615HP	99	Beechjet 400A	RK-231	General Parts Inc. Raleigh, NC.	N781TP
N615MS	87	Falcon 900B	25	MSS Falcon 900 LLC. New Nuys, Ca.	N660BD
N615PG	07	Embraer Legacy 600	14501004	Pacific Gas & Electric Co. Oakland, Ca.	PT-SKV
N615QS	04	Citation Excel	560-5360	NetJets, Port Columbus, Oh.	N5079V
N615RG	98	Citation Excel	560-5016	Aircraft Leasing & Sales Inc. Wichita, Ks.	
N615SR	00	Falcon 50EX	298	Cooper Industries Inc. Houston, Tx.	F-WWHZ
N615TL	98	Challenger 604	5393	CP Management LLC. Baltimore, Md.	N355CC
N616BM	98	CitationJet	525-0251	CBC Financial Corp. North Las Vegas, Nv.	N86JB
N616CC	00	Gulfstream 4SP	1455	AMFM Air Services Inc. San Antonio, Tx.	N455GA
N616DC	99	Global Express	9025	Network Appliance, San Jose, Ca.	N700AQ
N616FX	06	Learjet 40	45-2057	BBJS/FlexJets, Addison, Tx.	
N616KG	03	Gulfstream G400	1534	International Forest Products Corp/Kraft Group, Foxboro, Ma.	(N616KF)
Reg	Yr	Type	c/n	Owner/Operator	Prev Regn

Reg	Yr	Type	c/n	Owner/Operator	Prev Regn
☐ N616NA	69	Learjet 25	25-035	National Aeronautics, Cleveland, Oh.	N33TR
☐ N616QS	03	Citation Excel	560-5345	NetJets, Port Columbus, Oh.	N.....
☐ N616TR*	69	Sabre-60	306-23	Anthony Romero, Tucson, Az.	N85HS
☐ N617CB	07	CitationJet CJ2+	525A-0356	Concordia Resources LLC. Fairfield, Ia.	N5197A
☐ N617CS	06	Citation Sovereign	680-0102	CitationShares Sales Inc. White Plains, NY.	N.....
☐ N617FX	06	Learjet 40	45-2065	BBJS/FlexJets, Addison, Tx.	
☐ N617PD	02	Citation Excel	560-5273	Cobalt Aviation II LLC. N Philadelphia, Pa.	N1268D
☐ N617QS	04	Citation Excel XLS	560-5509	NetJets, Port Columbus, Oh.	N.....
☐ N617TM	99	Hawker 800XP2	258411	JetSet LLC. Las Vegas, Nv.	
☐ N617WA	05	Embraer Legacy 600	14500884	John Wing Aviation Inc. Conroe, Tx.	PT-SIU
☐ N618BR	65	Learjet 23	23-082A	Robert West Jr. Orinda, Ca.	(N118LS)
☐ N618CF	86	Learjet 35A	35A-618	Time Flies LLC. Pal Waukee, Il.	N618DM
☐ N618FX	07	Learjet 40	45-2076	BBJS/FlexJets, Addison, Tx.	
☐ N618GH	87	Falcon 200	513	Voyager Charters LLC. Rancho Cucamonga, Ca.	N5UQ
☐ N618KA	05	CitationJet CJ1+	525-0618	Empire Properties LLC. Kennesaw, Ga.	N.....
☐ N618KR	77	HS 125/700A	NA0205	BDK Aircraft Inc. Tulsa, Ok.	N700FW
☐ N618QS	04	Citation Excel XLS	560-5506	NetJets, Port Columbus, Oh.	N.....
☐ N618R	05	Challenger 300	20045	Contessa Premium Foods Inc. Van Nuys, Ca.	N145LJ
☐ N618RL	81	Challenger 600S	1018	N618AJ LLC/Empire Companies, Ontario, Ca.	N618AJ
☐ N618WF*	97	Global Express	9005	N613WF Inc/Meadow Park Estates Ltd. Tortola, BVI.	N613WF
☐ N619A	90	Gulfstream 4	1123	Willliam Aldinger, Lake Forest, Il.	N529AL
☐ N619FX	07	Learjet 40	45-2082	BBJS/FlexJets, Addison, Tx.	
☐ N619GA	98	Beechjet 400A	RK-196	C C Medflight Inc. Lawrenceville, Ga.	XA-MEX
☐ N619KK	88	Gulfstream 4	1062	Virtucon LLC/First Commercial Corp. San Diego, Ca.	N104JG
☐ N619KS	06	Gulfstream G200	151	SoarAir Leasing LLC. Salt Lake City, Ut.	N200GA
☐ N619MC	76	Gulfstream 2	196	Lags Air LLC/Hooters of South Florida, Fort Myers, Fl.	N610MC
☐ N619MJ	82	Learjet 55	55-021	ASAP Jets Inc. Teterboro, NJ.	I-LOOK
☐ N619QS	05	Citation Excel XLS	560-5562	NetJets, Port Columbus, Oh.	N5109R
☐ N619SM	06	Falcon 2000EX EASY	112	Quality Shipyards Inc/Tidewater Inc. New Orleans, La.	F-WWMI
☐ N620A	79	Falcon 20F-5	412	Armstrong World Industries Inc. Lancaster, Pa.	N12FU
☐ N620BA	05	Falcon 2000	220	Bank of America NA. Charlotte, NC.	F-WWVH
☐ N620BB	01	CitationJet CJ-1	525-0467	B & B Shore Associates, Oyster Bay, NY.	N5157E
☐ N620DS	88	Gulfstream 4	1040	GR1040 Inc. Los Angeles, Ca.	N74RP
☐ N620DX	07	Falcon 900DX	620	Dassault Falcon Jet Corp. Teterboro, NJ.	F-WWFI
☐ N620EM	86	Learjet 35A	35A-620	South Aviation Inc. Fort Lauderdale, Fl.	XA-COI
☐ N620FX	07	Learjet 40	45-2085	BBJS/FlexJets, Addison, Tx.	
☐ N620JF	05	Challenger 300	20059	Shearwater Air LLC. San Jose, Ca.	C-FGNO
☐ N620JH	95	Gulfstream 4SP	1272	AirStar Corp. Salt Lake City, Ut	N621JA
☐ N620K	00	Global Express	9052	Eastman Kodak Co. Rochester, NY.	N752DS
☐ N620KE	01	Gulfstream G100	137	PPD Aeronautics LLC. Wilmington, NC.	N75GX
☐ N620M	01	Gulfstream 4SP	1473	Americo Services Inc. Kansas City, Mo.	XA-EOF
☐ N620MJ	92	Learjet 35A	35A-676	M-S Air Inc/Aviation Charter Services, Indianapolis, In.	N235AC
☐ N620MS	04	Falcon 2000EX EASY	31	Air Kaitar LLC/Kaitar Resources LLC. Tallahassee, Fl.	N31EX
☐ N620RM	88	BAe 125/800A	NA0417	Finley Aviation LLC. Hobbs, NM.	N67JF
☐ N620S	81	Challenger 600S	1031	LTMC Inc/Mulberry Street Investment Corp. Macon, Ga.	C-GLXS
☐ N620TC	93	CitationJet	525-0014	Golden Eagle Aviation Inc. Southfield, Mi.	N70TR
☐ N621AD	06	CitationJet CJ1+	525-0621	Air Direct LLC. Paris, Tx.	N52475
☐ N621CS	06	Citation Sovereign	680-0120	McLean Aviation/A J Dwoskin & Assoc Realty, Fairfax, Va.	N52038
☐ N621FX	07	Learjet 40	45-2089	BBJS/FlexJets, Addison, Tx.	
☐ N621GA	06	CitationJet CJ-3	525B-0126	Granite Development LLC. Greensboro, NC.	N5030U
☐ N621HB	07	Hawker 4000	RC-21	Hawker Beechcraft Corp. Wichita, Ks.	
☐ N621JH	00	Gulfstream 4SP	1423	Huntsman Chemical Corp/Airstar Corp. Salt Lake City, Ut.	N423GA
☐ N621JS	76	Falcon 20F	356	Fun Times Boat Inc/Slidell Landfill LLC. New Orleans, La.	N69SW
☐ N621QS	02	Citation Excel	560-5280	NetJets, Port Columbus, Oh.	N.....
☐ N621RB	78	Learjet 35A	35A-211	Jets R Us Delaware LLC. Rutledge, Ga.	N44TT
☐ N621SC	01	Gulfstream 4SP	1481	SCS Services LLC. San Jose, Ca.	N281GA
☐ N621WP	85	Hawker 800SP	258033	PRV Transportation LLC/Petrie Ross Ventures, Easton, Md.	N408MM
☐ N622AT	75	Citation	500-0252	Air Ambulance by Air Trek Inc. Punta Gorda, Fl.	N501JC
☐ N622CS	06	Citation Sovereign	680-0124	CitationShares Sales Inc. White Plains, NY.	N5233J
☐ N622FX	07	Learjet 40	45-2095	BBJS/FlexJets, Addison, Tx.	
☐ N622JK	02	390 Premier 1	RB-59	JIK Mission Lakes Manager Inc. Opa Locka, Fl.	N701DF
☐ N622PC	99	Citation Excel	560-5024	PNB Aero Services Inc. Love Field, Tx.	N654EL
☐ N622PG	78	Citation II	550-0037	PGC Services Inc. Amarillo, Tx.	(N37GA)
☐ N622PM	93	Citation VII	650-7027	MNI Equipment Inc/Nicholas Homes, Scottsdale, Az.	N900MN
☐ N622QS	02	Citation Excel	560-5286	NetJets, Port Columbus, Oh.	N.....
☐ N622QW	00	Falcon 2000	134	QWest Services Corp. Denver, Co.	(N493SV)
Reg	Yr	Type	c/n	Owner/Operator	Prev Regn

Reg	Yr	Type	c/n	Owner/Operator	Prev Regn
☐ N622RB*	76	Learjet 35	35-064	Jets R Us Delaware LLC. Rutledge, Ca.	N257SD
☐ N622RR	68	Gulfstream II SP	12	ECTC Aviation LLC/Anchor Management LLC. Tempe, Az.	N794SB
☐ N622SL	06	CitationJet CJ1+	525-0622	Commander Properties Inc. Kenner, La.	N5270K
☐ N622SV	00	Galaxy-1126	015	Simon Ventures Inc/NIC Air Inc. Naples, Fl.	N38GX
☐ N622VL	01	Hawker 800XP	258531	Canary Enterprises LLC. San Jose, Ca.	N259SP
☐ N622WM	90	Challenger 601-3A	5084	AirBill Inc. Newark, NJ.	N399CF
☐ N623BM	77	Gulfstream 2	205	MJG JetCorp LLC. Bradenton, Fl.	N205BL
☐ N623FX	07	Learjet 40	45-2099	BBJS/FlexJets, Addison, Tx.	
☐ N623JL	90	Citation II	550-0662	Llamex SA & Inthiers SA. Mexico.	N623DS
☐ N623KC	90	Citation V	560-0076	Austin Air LLC. Cleveland-Lakefront, Oh.	N94NB
☐ N623KM	80	Learjet 35A	35A-307	K & M Equipment Co. Van Nuys, Ca.	N677CT
☐ N623MS	82	Gulfstream 3	351	Yona Aviation LLC. Needham, Ma	N18TM
☐ N623N	98	Citation Bravo	550-0849	C & C Jetting LLC. Lynchburg, Va.	N315N
☐ N623NP	82	Gulfstream 3	357	Barrier Beach LLC/N V Perricone M D Ltd. New Haven, Ct.	N723MM
☐ N623PM	92	Citation VII	650-7018	Berry & Berry Inc. Madera, Ca.	N119RM
☐ N623QS	02	Citation Excel	560-5299	NetJets, Port Columbus, Oh.	N.....
☐ N623QW	97	Falcon 2000	44	QWest Corp. Denver, Co.	N37TH
☐ N624AT	01	Citation Excel	560-5174	ALLTEL Corp. Little Rock, Ar.	N5223X
☐ N624B	03	Hawker 400XP	RK-369	Bunn-O-Matic Corp. Springfield, Il.	N369XP
☐ N624CS	07	Citation Sovereign	680-0131	CitationShares Sales Inc. White Plains, NY.	N5000R
☐ N624GJ	95	Gulfstream 4SP	1267	Peregrine Aviation LLC. Seattle, Wa.	N301K
☐ N624KM	78	Westwind-1124	227	K & M Equipment Co. Van Nuys, Ca.	N64FG
☐ N624N	02	Gulfstream V	681	ITT Flight Operations Inc. White Plains, NY.	(N519QS)
☐ N624PD	70	HS 125/731	NA756	Bristol Capital Advisors LLC. Winter Park, Fl.	N400JK
☐ N624PL	07	CitationJet CJ2+	525A-0357	OA LLC/Montco Offshore Inc. Houma, La.	N50820
☐ N624PP	81	Gulfstream 3	320	FM Holding Group LLC. Boca Raton, Fl.	N624BP
☐ N624QS	02	Citation Excel	560-5302	NetJets, Port Columbus, Oh.	(N118ST)
☐ N625AC	94	Citation V	560-0251	CHULEE Inc. Newark, De.	(N621AC)
☐ N625AT	01	Citation Excel	560-5175	ALLTEL Corp. Little Rock, Ar.	N52114
☐ N625MM	00	Astra-1125SPX	125	Coos & Deschutes LLC. Sunriver, Or.	N2488L
☐ N625PG	98	CitationJet	525-0282	BGM Inc. Fort Worth, Tx.	
☐ N625QS	03	Citation Excel	560-5319	NetJets, Port Columbus, Oh.	N.....
☐ N625W	95	Beechjet 400A	RK-106	Apache Ranch/Stuart Family Land & Cattle Inc. Lincoln, Ne.	N1HS
☐ N626AT	01	Citation Excel	560-5239	Windstream Corp. Little Rock, Ar.	N239XL
☐ N626BM	88	Learjet 35ZR	35A-634	Jet Air Holdings Inc. Wilmington, De.	I-EAMM
☐ N626CG	85	BAe 125/800A	258041	Keystone Aviation LLC/Million Air, Salt Lake City, Ut.	N71NP
☐ N626CS	07	Citation Sovereign	680-0188	CitationShares Sales Inc. White Plains, NY.	N51881
☐ N626CV	06	CitationJet CJ1+	525-0626	Coldwater Veneer Inc. Coldwater, Mi.	N5117U
☐ N626JP*	85	Challenger 601	3050	Frontier Homes, Ontario, Ca.	N802PA
☐ N626JS	97	Gulfstream 4SP	1334	JWC Huntington LLC. Bedford, Ma.	N434QS
☐ N626QS	01	Citation Excel	560-5126	NetJets, Port Columbus, Oh.	
☐ N626RB	93	Citation V	560-0221	Robert Millard, Stratford, Ct.	N701DK
☐ N626TN	02	Citation Excel	560-5254	St Simons Aviation LLC. Atlanta-Fulton County, Ga.	N681RP
☐ N627AK	05	Hawker 800XPi	258723	LJJP Aviation LLC.	N723XP
☐ N627BC	98	Citation Bravo	550-0868	A T Massey Coal Co/Massey Energy Co. Richmond, Va.	N5117U
☐ N627E	79	Citation 1/SP	501-0123	Air Hardware LLC. Springfield, Mo.	N627L
☐ N627JJ	76	Learjet 24E	24E-340	JSAP LLC. Wilmington, De.	N825AM
☐ N627MW	06	CitationJet CJ1+	525-0627	627MW LLC. Wilmington, De.	N5264N
☐ N627QS	02	Citation Excel	560-5227	NetJets, Port Columbus, Oh.	N5197M
☐ N627R	00	Citation X	750-0132	WEHCO Media/Camden News Publishing Co. Little Rock, Ar.	N51055
☐ N627XL	01	Citation Excel	560-5149	Lord Leasing Inc. Cary, NC.	N.....
☐ N628BD*	00	Gulfstream V	628	Hewlett-Packard Co. San Jose, Ca.	N42GX
☐ N628BS	72	Citation	500-0045	Chippewa Aerospace Inc. Myrtle Beach, SC.	(N628FS)
☐ N628CB	05	CitationJet CJ-3	525B-0049	Cimarron Aviation Inc/Baney Corp. Bend, Or.	N.....
☐ N628CC	99	Falcon 2000	95	Comcast Cable Communication Holdings, N Philadelphia, Pa.	F-WWVO
☐ N628CK	92	Citation V	560-0194	Knowlton Aviation LLC. Philadelphia, Pa.	N413GK
☐ N628CM	86	Challenger 601	3062	International Game Technology/CNM Gulf Air LLC. Reno, Nv.	N2183N
☐ N628DB	79	Learjet 35A	35A-246	Ameriplan USA Corp. Dallas, Tx.	N1DC
☐ N628GB	01	Citation Bravo	550-0991	Sunwest Management Inc. Salem, Or.	N628CB
☐ N628HC	73	Gulfstream 2	134	Electronic Instrument Co/EICO II Corp. NYC.	(N810MY)
☐ N628QS	02	Citation Excel	560-5305	NetJets, Port Columbus, Oh.	N.....
☐ N629CS	07	Citation Sovereign	680-0165	CitationShares Sales Inc. White Plains, NY.	N5268A
☐ N629DR	07	CitationJet CJ-1	525-0627	Cessna Aircraft Co. Wichita, Ks.	N.....
☐ N629EE	06	CitationJet CJ-3	525B-0129	Eduardo Elberg Simi, Vina del Mar, Chile.	N.....
☐ N629GB	07	Challenger 300	20144	Canyon Creek Development Inc. Salem, Or.	C-FLQF
☐ N629MD	85	Citation III	650-0096	RDM Enterprises LLC. Denver, Co.	N629RM

Reg	Yr	Type	c/n	Owner/Operator	Prev Regn
N629PA	01	CitationJet CJ-2	525A-0015	Pearl Aviation LLC/Pearl Development Co. Sheridan, Wy.	N606XG
N629QS	02	Citation Excel	560-5306	NetJets, Port Columbus, Oh.	N.....
N629RA	86	Citation S/II	S550-0093	Stevenson&Ammons/Advocate Travel LLC. Houston, Tx.	N400RE
N629TS	84	Challenger 601	3029	Societe Hellin SA. Caracas, Venezuela.	N773JC
N630CC	80	Citation II	550-0130	Lawful Air Genpar LLC/Rose, Walker Law Firm, Dallas, Tx.	N778C
N630CS	07	Citation Sovereign	680-0170	Scott Charters LLC. Boca Raton, Fl.	N5268E
N630JS	07	Hawker 900XP	HA-30	J S Aviation LLC. McMurray, Pa.	N930XP
N630QS	00	Citation Excel	560-5130	NetJets, Port Columbus, Oh.	N52113
N630S	90	Astra-1125SP	046	Fountainhead Sales & Leasing Corp. Braselton, Ga.	N140DR
N630SJ	80	Learjet 35A	35A-344	Atlas Settlement Group GA Inc. Atlanta, Ga.	(N111BJ)
N630TF	01	CitationJet CJ-2	525A-0022	Horizon Aviation LLC. Smyrna, Ga.	(N117W)
N631CC	95	Learjet 31A	31A-104	Cleveland Construction Inc. Cleveland, Oh.	N104BX
N631CS	08	Citation Sovereign	680-0197	CitationShares Sales Inc. White Plains, NY.	N5061F
N631DV	07	Gulfstream G200	166	Leonilda Rodrigues da Silva, Venezuela.	N566GA
N631QS	01	Citation Excel	560-5131	NetJets, Port Columbus, Oh.	N52136
N631RP	05	Citation Sovereign	680-0037	Ring Air LLC/Ring Power Corp. Jacksonville, Fl.	N5130J
N631SF	93	Learjet 31A	31A-075	Sanderson Farms Inc. Laurel, Ms.	(N418RT)
N631TS	90	Citation II	550-0631	Tristar Risk Management, Long Beach, Ca.	N631EA
N632BL	01	Citation Excel	560-5171	Pacific Simon LLC. Scottsdale, Az.	SU-EWB
N632CS	08	Citation Sovereign	680-0222	CitationShares Sales Inc. White Plains, NY.	N.....
N632FW	96	Hawker 800XP2	258294	Marine R Corp. Naples, Fl.	N404BS
N632PB*	76	Falcon 20F-5B	355	Modern Welding Co. Owensboro, Ky.	N803WC
N632QS	01	Citation Excel	560-5132	NetJets, Port Columbus, Oh.	N5225K
N632XL	06	Citation Excel XLS	560-5632	Night Eagle Aviation LLC. Pittsburgh, Pa.	N5262W
N633AT	73	Citation	500-0087	Air Ambulance by Air Trek Inc. Punta Gorda, Fl.	(N911CJ)
N633CS	08	Citation Sovereign	680-0236	CitationShares Sales Inc. White Plains, NY.	N.....
N633EE	85	Citation S/II	S550-0058	A K Guthrie, Big Spring, Tx.	N1271E
N633QS	04	Citation Excel XLS	560-5526	NetJets, Port Columbus, Oh.	N5194B
N633RP	07	Citation Sovereign	680-0172	Ring Power Corp. St Augustine, Fl.	N5045W
N633RT	88	Citation II	550-0588	5670 Partners LLC/Legacy Capital Partners Inc. Jeffco, Co.	(N747RT)
N633SA	93	Citation V	560-0235	Sumlin Group/Sumlin Aviation LLC. Hickory, NC.	N92BF
N633SF	02	Learjet 31A	31A-241	Sanderson Farms Inc. Laurel, Ms.	N335AF
N633W	87	Falcon 50	184	Pinnacle Air Executive Jet, Springdale, Ar.	N25ME
N634CS	08	Citation Sovereign	680-0244	CitationShares Sales Inc. White Plains, NY.	N.....
N634H	87	Falcon 50	178	Hillenbrand Industries Inc. Batesville, In.	N59PM
N634QS	05	Citation Excel XLS	560-5558	NetJets, Port Columbus, Oh.	N52609
N635E	99	Falcon 2000	106	PLA Aircraft Corp. Dearborn, Mi.	F-W...
N635QS	03	Citation Excel	560-5358	NetJets, Port Columbus, Oh.	N5235G
N636BC	89	Astra-1125	039	British Creek Air LLC. Denver, Co.	XA-JRM
N636GA	07	Gulfstream G200	183	Gulfstream Aerospace LP. Dallas-Love, Tx.	4X-C..
N636MA*	79	Citation II/SP	551-0141	Dove Air Inc. Fletcher, NC. (was 550-0093).	N451DA
N636MF	05	Gulfstream G550	5112	ROP Aviation Inc. Teterboro, NJ.	N832GA
N636N	78	Citation 1/SP	501-0069	Carbontec Energy Corp. McMinnville, Or.	N501EF
N636QS	02	Citation Excel	560-5304	NetJets, Port Columbus, Oh.	N.....
N637QS	01	Citation Excel	560-5137	NetJets, Port Columbus, Oh.	N.....
N637RP	06	Citation Excel XLS	560-5669	Star International Transportation Inc. St Augustine, Fl.	N633RP
N637SF	07	Gulfstream G150	248	Gulfstream Aerospace LP. Dallas-Love, Tx.	4X-C..
N637TF	05	Challenger 604	5637	EAC Air LLC/East-West Air Inc. NYC.	C-GLYK
N638QS	04	Citation Excel	560-5363	NetJets, Port Columbus, Oh.	N.....
N639AT	80	Westwind-Two	308	Air Ambulance by Air Trek Inc. Punta Gorda, Fl.	N628KM
N639QS	01	Citation Excel	560-5139	NetJets, Port Columbus, Oh.	N.....
N639TS	93	Challenger 601-3R	5139	Aero Toy Store LLC. Fort Lauderdale, Fl.	(N612LX)
N640BA	90	Learjet 35A	35A-664	Beta Aire Ltd. Toledo, Oh.	C-GRMJ
N640CH	99	Challenger 604	5428	Wilson Air LLC. Montgomery, Al.	C-GLYO
N640QS	02	Citation Excel	560-5240	NetJets, Port Columbus, Oh.	N51055
N641QS	02	Citation Excel	560-5295	NetJets/Marquis Jet Partners Inc. Port Columbus, Oh.	N50820
N642AC	99	Beechjet 400A	RK-224	SK Logistics Inc/AC Expeditions LLC. St Augustine, Fl.	N51NP
N642AG	02	Embraer Legacy 600	145642	Apollo Group, Scottsdale, Az.	PT-SAQ
N642JC	89	Falcon 900B	71	Remember Glencar LLC. Bedford-Hansom, Ma.	N280BQ
N642LF	03	Citation Encore	560-0642	Lufkin Industries Inc. Lufkin, Tx.	N.....
N642QS	05	Citation Excel XLS	560-5561	NetJets, Port Columbus, Oh.	N5296X
N642RP	69	Sabre-60	306-46	AVMATS/Centurion Investments Inc. Chesterfield, Mo.	N100FN
N643CR	82	Challenger 600	1055	Monfort Aviation LLC. Denver, Co.	N217MB
N643QS	05	Citation Excel XLS	560-5588	NetJets, Port Columbus, Oh.	N.....
N643RT	89	Citation V	560-0019	W D Larson Companies Ltd. Bloomington, Mn.	N61TW
N644QS	05	Citation Excel XLS	560-5582	NetJets, Port Columbus, Oh.	N.....

Reg	Yr	Type	c/n	Owner/Operator	Prev Regn
☐ N645AM	88	Learjet 35A	35A-645	Samanta SpA. Naples, Italy.	N43TR
☐ N645G	76	Learjet 35	35-056	Harry O Barr, Raymond, Ne.	N106GL
☐ N645QS	00	Citation Excel	560-5145	NetJets, Port Columbus, Oh.	N52645
☐ N646QS	01	Citation Excel	560-5246	NetJets, Port Columbus, Oh.	N.....
☐ N647EF	94	Learjet 60	60-047	Royal Pacific Aviation LR60 LLC. Wenatchee, Wa.	(N225LC)
☐ N647JP	67	Falcon 20-5	120	Luiginos Inc. Duluth, Mn.	N20AF
☐ N647QS	05	Citation Excel XLS	560-5547	NetJets, Port Columbus, Oh.	N5156D
☐ N648JW	81	Learjet 25D	25D-350	Kodiak Jet LLC. Anchorage, Ak.	(N428CH)
☐ N648QS	05	Citation Excel XLS	560-5574	NetJets, Port Columbus, Oh.	N5090A
☐ N649TT	05	Falcon 50EX	342	Townes Telecommunications Inc. Paris, Tx.	N342EX
☐ N650AL	81	Falcon 50	49	Marigot LLC. Chicago-Midway, Il.	N978W
☐ N650AS	83	Citation III	650-0002	650-0002 Inc/Jet 1 Inc. Naples, Fl.	(N650BG)
☐ N650AT	94	Citation VII	650-7053	Teletech Services Corp. Englewood, Co.	N128SL
☐ N650BP	80	Citation II	550-0118	Apple Restaurants Management Co. Marietta, Ga.	N138J
☐ N650BW	84	Citation III	650-0028	Mid Florida Jet Sales & Leasing Inc. Orlando, Fl.	N38ED
☐ N650CB	85	Citation III	650-0084	Dolan, Pollack, Schram Development Co. Bluffton, SC.	(N431CQ)
☐ N650CD	84	Citation III	650-0066	TRT Leasing LLC. West Palm Beach, Fl.	N138V
☐ N650CE	86	Citation III	650-0106	HBO Holdings LLC/WRH Properties, Memphis, Tn.	N106CC
☐ N650CG	84	Citation III	650-0023	C G Bretting Manufacturing Inc. Ashland, Wi.	N38DD
☐ N650CH	88	Citation III	650-0154	Bohns Point Leasing LLC. Wilmington, De.	N696HC
☐ N650CJ	94	Citation VII	650-7044	Tailwind East LLC. Turkey, NC.	N7005
☐ N650CM	92	Citation V	560-0177	CM Aviation LLC. Santa Barbara, Ca.	N242AC
☐ N650CP	92	Citation VII	650-7016	CFP Leasing LLC. Wheeling, Il.	N650RP
☐ N650CZ	95	Citation VII	650-7050	Air Waukegan Management Inc. Waukegan, Il.	N83GK
☐ N650DA	86	Citation III	650-0114	Duncan Aviation Inc. Lincoln, Ne.	N651AF
☐ N650DD	94	Citation VII	650-7047	N650DD LLC. Fort Myers, Fl.	N198TX
☐ N650DR	89	Citation III	650-0181	Management Services Inc. Buffalo, NY.	N743CC
☐ N650FC	87	Citation III	650-0146	Frank's Casing Crew & Rental Tools, Lafayette, La.	XA-PIP
☐ N650FP	90	Citation III	650-0188	DeJarnette Enterprises Inc. Lee's Summit, Mo.	N587S
☐ N650GC	92	Citation VI	650-0215	Aero Toy Store LLC. Fort Lauderdale, Fl.	N650KC
☐ N650GE	06	Gulfstream G150	210	Gaylord Entertainment Co. Nashville, Tn.	N510GA
☐ N650GF	93	Astra-1125SP	064	Empire LLC. Ontario, Or.	N650GE
☐ N650GH	84	Citation III	650-0034	Chattern Inc. Chattanooga, Tn.	(N45US)
☐ N650HC	86	Citation III	650-0124	KGC Aviation LLC/Fairway Chevrolet, Las Vegas, Nv.	N7HV
☐ N650HG	85	Citation III	650-0083	Starlight Aviation LLC. Harvey, La.	N677LM
☐ N650HM	86	Citation III	650-0119	Contran Corp. Dallas-Love, Tx.	N147TA
☐ N650J	83	Citation III	650-0022	Hines Interests LP. Houston, Tx.	
☐ N650JL	98	Citation VII	650-7101	Littlefield 2000 Trust, Hayward, Ca.	N612AB
☐ N650K	93	Citation III	650-7034	Taft Sales & Leasing LLC. Dallas, Tx.	VP-CDW
☐ N650KB	85	Citation III	650-0078	John R Sebo Revocable Trust, Salem, Oh.	N650WL
☐ N650LA	83	Citation III	650-0004	KWA Air LLC/William Lynch Associates, Boston, Ma.	N650GT
☐ N650LR	89	Learjet 35A	35A-650	SC Aviation Inc/Swiss Colony Inc. Monroe, Wi.	N135MW
☐ N650LW	83	Citation III	650-0010	DeBordieu/Dallas II Inc. Dallas, Tx.	OK-NKN
☐ N650MG	83	Citation III	650-0007	Odyssey Air LLC. Aurora, Il.	N719HG
☐ N650PW	03	Gulfstream G400	1530	Bohemian Breweries Inc. Jeffco, Co.	N330GA
☐ N650QS	01	Citation Excel	560-5150	NetJets, Port Columbus, Oh.	N5100J
☐ N650RB	85	Citation III	650-0079	Clayton Mountain Energy LLC. Fort Worth, Tx.	N217RJ
☐ N650RP	88	Citation III	650-0157	Trillium Staffing Inc. Kalamazoo, Mi.	N10JP
☐ N650SB	83	Citation III	650-0018	Hogs Fly LLC/WJR Enterprises, Winnetka, Il.	N275WN
☐ N650SG	90	Citation III	650-0191	Thomas Schweizer Jr. Baltimore, Md.	N650TJ
☐ N650TA	85	Citation III	650-0088	SOB Inc. Sioux Falls, SD.	(N590AQ)
☐ N650TS	92	Citation VI	650-0219	RCZS LLC/Devcon Enterprises Inc. Hartford, Ct.	(N211MA)
☐ N650VW	90	Citation III	650-0184	MI Home Products Inc. Middletown, Pa.	N11288
☐ N650W	94	Citation VI	650-0237	Brindlee Air Travel LLC. Union Grove, Al.	(N656LE)
☐ N650WE	84	Citation III	650-0040	533MA LLC. Vancouver, Wa.	HB-VIY
☐ N650Z	86	Citation III	650-0108	Bohemian Breweries Inc. Jeffco, Co.	(N1302U)
☐ N651AR	91	Citation VI	650-0212	Idearc Media Corp. DFW Airport, Tx.	N972VZ
☐ N651AT	84	Citation III	650-0063	MBO Internet/MBO Aviation LLC. Earlsboro, Ok.	N650AT
☐ N651BP	83	Citation III	650-0017	MMR West LLC. Portland, Or.	(N650BP)
☐ N651CC	00	Citation VII	650-7119	Pictsweet Co/United Foods Inc. Bells, Tn.	N5152X
☐ N651CG	82	Citation III	650-0001	SBK Capital LLC. Atlanta, Ga.	N651CC
☐ N651CJ	99	CitationJet CJ-1	525-0365	MAC Aviation LLC. Prior Lake, Mn.	N5130J
☐ N651CV	84	Citation III	650-0036	Summit Seafood Supply Inc. Houston, Tx.	N650BS
☐ N651EJ	95	Citation VI	650-0241	Lomax Stern Development Co. West Bloomfield, Mi.	N651JM
☐ N651LJ	66	Learjet 24A	24A-125	Steven Lysdale, Bellevue, Wa.	
☐ N651MK	81	Sabre-65	465-73	Stempre Listo LLC/Energy Services Inc. Dover, De.	N64MQ

Reg	Yr	Type	c/n	Owner/Operator	Prev Regn
❏ N651PW	85	Citation III	650-0090	Bohemian Breweries Inc. Jeffco, Co.	N555DH
❏ N651QS	02	Citation Excel	560-5251	NetJets, Port Columbus, Oh.	N.....
❏ N652CV	84	Citation III	650-0055	Jet Set Aviation LLC. Irving, Tx.	N16AS
❏ N652GA	07	Gulfstream G550	5152	Gulfstream Aerospace Corp. Savannah, Ga.	
❏ N652KZ	89	Learjet 35A	35A-652	CPA Land Co. Tulsa, Ok.	N2KZ
❏ N652NR	03	Citation Encore	560-0652	Cross Jet Inc. Farranfoe, Ireland.	N.....
❏ N652QS	01	Citation Excel	560-5152	NetJets, Port Columbus, Oh.	
❏ N653CW	89	Challenger 601-3A	5053	K&M One LLC/EPC Exchange Corp. Bellevue, Wa.	(N440KM)
❏ N653FJ	77	Falcon 10	110	Community Financial Services Inc. Marietta, Ga.	N43US
❏ N653MF	69	Falcon 20-5B	185	Community Financial Services Inc. Marietta, Ga.	N818LS
❏ N654AN	95	Learjet 60	60-065	Anderson & Anderson LLC. Muscle Shoals, Al.	N718AN
❏ N654AP	94	Beechjet 400A	RK-88	Food Service Sales & Marketing Assoc. Tampa, Fl.	N654AT
❏ N654AT	00	Learjet 45	45-136	RBJ Industries Inc/Anderson Trucking Service, St Cloud, Mn.	N883BS
❏ N654CE	04	Citation Encore	560-0654	Assemblies of God Financial Services, Springfield, Mo.	N52653
❏ N654CM	87	Challenger 601-3A	5009	Crossmark Aviation, McKinney, Tx.	(N610LX)
❏ N654QS	05	Citation Excel XLS	560-5611	NetJets, Port Columbus, Oh.	N.....
❏ N655AL	86	Learjet 55B	55B-129	TAL Enterprises/Cornerstone Granite & Marble, Boca Raton.	N75GP
❏ N655CM	86	Beechjet 400	RJ-17	CH Aircraft LLC. St Louis, Mo.	N455FD
❏ N655PE	82	Falcon 100	199	Dunbar Aviation LLC. Groton-New London, Ct.	N60HM
❏ N655QS	06	Citation Excel XLS	560-5655	NetJets/Marquis Jet Partners Inc. Port Columbus, Oh.	N5161J
❏ N655TH	88	Challenger 601-3A	5022	Great Bay Aviation LLC. Portsmouth, NH.	VP-CJP
❏ N656PS	78	Citation II	550-0009	California Oregon Broadcasting, Medford, Or.	N744DC
❏ N656QS	07	Citation Excel XLS	560-5732	NetJets, Port Columbus, Oh.	N.....
❏ N656Z	04	Citation Encore	560-0656	Rainier Fruit Co. Yakima, Wa.	N.....
❏ N657BM	81	Learjet 25D	25D-331	WHM Plumbing & Heating Contractors, E Setauket, NY.	N482CP
❏ N657CT	06	Challenger 604	5665	Caterpillar Inc. Peoria, Il.	N665CT
❏ N657P	59	MS 760 Paris	57	Airborne Turbine LP. San Luis Obispo, Ca.	57
❏ N657QS	06	Citation Excel XLS	560-5636	NetJets, Port Columbus, Oh.	N5225K
❏ N657T	94	Citation VII	650-7042	Hershey Foods Corp. Middletown, Pa.	N1265K
❏ N658CF	82	Challenger 600S	1058	Freeman Jet LLC. Forbes Field, Ks.	N60HJ
❏ N658KS	95	Learjet 60	60-071	BD Ventures LLC. St Louis, Mo.	N940P
❏ N658QS	06	Citation Excel XLS	560-5665	NetJets, Port Columbus, Oh.	N.....
❏ N659FM	95	Falcon 2000	17	Thayer Services LLC. Manassas, Va.	N89TY
❏ N659QS	04	Citation Excel	560-5359	NetJets, Port Columbus, Oh.	N.....
❏ N659WL	77	Gulfstream II SP	204	Global Estate & Aviation Ltd. Burr Ridge, Il.	VP-CPA
❏ N660AF	69	Gulfstream 2B	70	Island Management Services LLC. NYC.	N510SE
❏ N660AL	06	Challenger 300	20129	Abbott Laboratories Inc. Waukegan, Il.	C-FJQT
❏ N660BC	95	Learjet 60	60-063	BC Air LLC/Prestige Builders Group Corp. Miami, Fl.	N8270
❏ N660CC	01	Beechjet 400A	RK-319	Burt Aviation Corp. Rochester Hills, Mi.	N689TA
❏ N660HC	03	Hawker 800XP	258624	DEC LLC/District Equipment Co. Atlanta, Ga.	N866RR
❏ N660PA	93	Citation VI	650-0230	Mutual Assurance Agency Inc. Birmingham, Al.	N616AT
❏ N660Q	88	Citation III	650-0162	Excellent Aviation Rentals Inc. Houston, Tx.	N275GC
❏ N660QS	06	Citation Excel XLS	560-5647	NetJets, Port Columbus, Oh.	N.....
❏ N660S	05	CitationJet CJ2+	525A-0305	Lario Oil & Gas Co. Denver, Co.	N5213S
❏ N661AC	74	Citation	500-0121	N661AC Inc. Wilmington, De.	N3QE
❏ N661AJ	92	Citation V	560-0176	Shepherd's Chapel Inc. Gravette, Ar.	PT-WOM
❏ N661CP	05	Gulfstream G550	5104	CONOCO-Phillips Co. Houston, Tx.	N824GA
❏ N661GA	98	Gulfstream V	561	Lear Investment LLC/Lear Corp. Pontiac, Mi.	
❏ N661QS	06	Citation Excel XLS	560-5677	NetJets, Port Columbus, Oh.	N5180K
❏ N661WD	94	Beechjet 400A	RK-94	WayneWorks Aviation LLC. Aiken, SC.	N681WD
❏ N662CB	03	Citation Bravo	550-1062	Information Technology Inc. Lincoln, Ne.	N.....
❏ N662CC	75	Citation	500-0277	Heritage Aviation LLC. Oxford, Ms.	N652ND
❏ N662CP	05	Gulfstream G550	5107	CONOCO-Phillips Co. Houston, Tx.	N937GA
❏ N662JN	06	Hawker 850XP	258837	Jackson National Life Insurance Co. Lansing, Mi.	
❏ N662QS	02	Citation Excel	560-5262	NetJets, Port Columbus, Oh.	N.....
❏ N663CP	05	Gulfstream G450	4044	CONOCO-Phillips Co. Houston, Tx.	N644GA
❏ N663MK	01	Falcon 900EX	94	Merck & Co. Mercer County, NJ.	N994EX
❏ N663P	00	Gulfstream 4SP	1434	Nabors Equipment Leasing LLC. Houston, Tx.	N434GA
❏ N663PD	87	Gulfstream 4	1022	HMS Air LLC. Los Angeles, Ca.	N23MU
❏ N663QS	02	Citation Excel	560-5263	NetJets, Port Columbus, Oh.	N.....
❏ N664AC	01	Hawker 800XP	258566	A C Corp. Washington-Dulles, DC.	N4466Z
❏ N664AJ	89	Citation II	550-0613	Southlake Aviation LLC. Fort Worth, Tx.	PT-OAC
❏ N664CE	04	Citation Encore	560-0664	Active Organics, Lewisville, Tx.	N5151D
❏ N664CJ	07	CitationJet CJ1+	525-0664	Cessna Aircraft Co. Wichita, Ks.	N.....
❏ N664CL	68	Learjet 24	24-167	Clay Lacy Aviation Inc. Van Nuys, Ca.	N888RL
❏ N664CP	06	Gulfstream G450	4047	CONOCO-Phillips Co. Houston, Tx.	N447GA

Reg	Yr	Type	c/n	Owner/Operator	Prev Regn
❏ N664CW	86	Challenger 601	3064	Flight Options LLC. Cuyahoga County, Oh.	(N606LX)
❏ N664QS	02	Citation Excel	560-5264	NetJets, Port Columbus, Oh.	N5066U
❏ N665CH	02	CitationJet CJ-1	525-0504	Volante Aviation Inc. Coventry, UK.	N52081
❏ N665CP	05	Gulfstream G450	4049	CONOCO-Phillips Co. Houston, Tx.	N449GA
❏ N665MM	81	Citation 1/SP	501-0228	West Palm Air LLC. Cuyahoga Falls, Oh.	XA-SEY
❏ N665QS	01	Citation Excel	560-5165	NetJets, Port Columbus, Oh.	N5109W
❏ N666AG	73	Citation	500-0101	Luis Nunez, Caracas, Venezuela.	C-GKCZ
❏ N666CT	87	Challenger 601-3A	5007	Polygon Air Corp. White Plains, NY.	N17TZ
❏ N666FH	06	Citation Sovereign	680-0125	Dr Schenk Flugbetrieb GmbH. Munich.	N5053R
❏ N666K	90	Astra-1125	040	Aerojet Inc. Gaithersburg, Md.	N279DS
❏ N666LN	84	Citation S/II	S550-0005	Sky Eagle Corp. Reno, Nv.	(N1256G)
❏ N666MX	02	Citation Excel	560-5292	ComJet BV. Rotterdam, Holland.	N5101J
❏ N666SA	73	Gulfstream II SP	130	SG Air Leasing Ltd. Singapore.	A6-PHY
❏ N666TF	96	Challenger 604	5309	Med 4 Home Inc. Clearwater, Fl.	(N509TS)
❏ N666TK	82	Learjet 55	55-038	Polygon Air Corp. White Plains, NY.	N50AF
❏ N666TR	01	Falcon 900C	195	Janus Transair Corp. Windsor Locks, Ct.	(N100EQ)
❏ N666TS	78	Citation 1/SP	501-0071	Aero Toy Store LLC. Fort Lauderdale, Fl.	YV232T
❏ N666TV	81	Learjet 55	55-012	R Television Services LLC. San Antonio, Tx.	N85XL
❏ N667LC	96	Challenger 604	5324	Loews Corp/Clinton Court Corp. Teterboro, NJ.	N601CC
❏ N667MB	83	Learjet 55	55-073	Jedami Jet LLC. Fort Lauderdale, Fl.	N155V
❏ N667QS	04	Citation Excel	560-5365	NetJets, Port Columbus, Oh.	N.....
❏ N668AJ	82	Citation II	550-0442	DAC Aviation LLC/Douglas Asphalt Co. Douglas, Ga.	N442ME
❏ N668CB	03	Citation Bravo	550-1068	Information Technology Inc. Lincoln, Ne.	N.....
❏ N668JT	75	Gulfstream 2	162	Plan 15 Aviation LLC. Elmira-Corning, NY.	N666JT
❏ N668QS	02	Citation Excel	560-5268	NetJets, Port Columbus, Oh.	N.....
❏ N668RC	94	Learjet 60	60-044	Tri-Marine International Inc. Seattle, Wa.	N613R
❏ N668S	76	Citation	500-0314	K L Process Design Group LLC. Rapid City, SD.	N66ES
❏ N669B	03	Citation Bravo	550-1060	Northern Air Inc. Grand Rapids, Mi.	N.....
❏ N669BJ	99	Gulfstream 4SP	1397	S & H Automotive Products Inc. Fort Lauderdale, Fl.	N397GA
❏ N669DB	97	CitationJet	525-0228	Cyprus Management LLC. San Marcos, Tx.	N668VB
❏ N669QS	07	Citation Excel XLS	560-5689	NetJets, Port Columbus, Oh.	N50275
❏ N669TT	06	Citation Excel XLS	560-5684	TTI Aviation LLC/One World Technologies Inc. Anderson, SC.	N5061P
❏ N669W	96	Citation VII	650-7066	David Smith Farms Inc. Jonesboro, Ar.	N766CG
❏ N670C	72	Sabre-75A	370-7	Independent Air Inc. North Miami Beach, Fl.	XA-...
❏ N670CM	01	Challenger 604	5488	Cephalon Inc. Frazer, Pa.	(N8570)
❏ N670H	81	Sabre-65	465-58	Honeywell International Inc. Phoenix, Az.	N670AS
❏ N670JD	84	Citation S/II	S550-0019	Amber Services Inc. Chicago, Il.	N550TB
❏ N670MW	04	Citation Excel XLS	560-5350	Marvin Lumber & Cedar Co. Warroad, Mn.	N52609
❏ N670QS	01	Citation Excel	560-5170	NetJets, Port Columbus, Oh.	
❏ N670RW	07	Gulfstream G200	160	Coca Cola Co. Atlanta-Fulton County, Ga.	4X-CVG
❏ N671AF	93	Gulfstream 4SP	1205	Ameriprise Financial Inc. Stewart, NY.	N393BD
❏ N671LE	06	Gulfstream G550	5130	Access Industries, NYC.	N130GA
❏ N671LW	70	Gulfstream 2	90	Scott Aviation Inc. DuPage, Il.	N20GP
❏ N671QS	00	Citation Excel	560-5071	NetJets, Port Columbus, Oh.	N51881
❏ N671RW	06	Gulfstream G550	5131	Coca-Cola Co. Atlanta-Fulton County, Ga.	N531GA
❏ N671TS	92	Learjet 35A	35A-671	Aero Toy Store LLC. Fort Lauderdale, Fl.	N671BX
❏ N671WM	02	Falcon 2000	194	Waste Management Inc. Andrau Airpark-Houston, Tx.	F-WWVF
❏ N672PS	99	Galaxy-1126	010	GC International LLC. Lawrenceville, Ga.	N121LS
❏ N672QS	06	Citation Excel XLS	560-5663	NetJets/Marquis Jet Partners Inc. Port Columbus, Oh.	N.....
❏ N673BA	01	Falcon 2000	173	Bank of America NA. Charlotte, NC.	F-WWVR
❏ N673BH*	82	Challenger 600S	1073	M & B Holdings LLC. Allentown, Pa.	N673YS
❏ N673LR	80	Citation II	550-0179	BDMP LLC. Tulsa, Ok.	N673LP
❏ N673P	01	Gulfstream V	673	Hewlett-Packard Co. San Jose, Ca.	N282QT
❏ N673QS	06	Citation Excel XLS	560-5651	NetJets, Port Columbus, Oh.	N5228J
❏ N674AC	82	Diamond 1A	A024SA	S L K Family LLC. Blanco, Tx.	N450PC
❏ N674AS	06	CitationJet CJ2+	525A-0307	All-State Industries Inc. Des Moines, Ia.	N5239J
❏ N674G	82	Citation II	550-0435	Findlay Industries Inc. Findlay, Oh. (was 551-0434).	N390DA
❏ N674JM	01	CitationJet CJ-1	525-0485	Evan Morgan Massey, Richmond-Chesterfield County, Va.	N52136
❏ N674SF	99	Beechjet 400A	RK-232	Dakota-Jet LLP. Grand Forks, ND.	N2355N
❏ N675BP	07	Learjet 60	60-321	Tafel Motors Inc. Louisville, Ky.	N5010U
❏ N675QS	02	Citation Excel	560-5275	NetJets, Port Columbus, Oh.	N.....
❏ N675RW	98	Gulfstream V	526	Coca-Cola Co. Atlanta, Ga.	N526GA
❏ N675SS	88	Citation II	550-0576	Structural Steel Services Inc. Meridian-Key Field, Ms.	N438SP
❏ N676AH	07	Hawker 850XP	258831	Andover Healthcare Inc. Salisbury, Ma.	
❏ N676BA	01	Falcon 2000	176	Bank of America NA. Charlotte, NC.	F-WWMC
❏ N676BB	03	Citation Excel	560-5349	Becker Trading Co. Vero Beach, Fl.	N.....

Reg	Yr	Type	c/n	Owner/Operator	Prev Regn
☐ N676CC	84	Citation 1/SP	501-0676	Lud Corrao Revocable Family Trust, Reno, Nv.	N76JY
☐ N676DG	75	Citation	500-0256	G & G Group LLC. Parsons, Tn.	N131SB
☐ N676GH	04	Hawker 800XP	258676	Guardian Holdings Ltd. Port of Spain, Trinidad.	N676XP
☐ N676JB	03	Hawker 800XP	258619	LRB LLC. Burbank, Ca.	N61719
☐ N676QS	01	Citation Excel	560-5176	NetJets, Port Columbus, Oh.	
☐ N676RW	06	Gulfstream G550	5126	Coca-Cola Co. Atlanta-Fulton County, Ga.	N526GA
☐ N676TC	03	Embraer Legacy 600	145699	Alpine Cascade Corp. Santa Barbara, Ca.	N691AN
☐ N677AS	02	390 Premier 1	RB-33	Skin Consultants LLC/The Skin Institute, Greenville, Ms.	N50843
☐ N677F	02	Gulfstream V	677	National Science Foundation, Washington, DC.	N677GA
☐ N677GA	07	Gulfstream G200	177	Gulfstream Aerospace LP. Dallas-Love, Tx.	4X-C..
☐ N677GS	91	Citation II	550-0669	Gantt Aviation Inc. Georgetown, Tx.	N846HS
☐ N677JM	78	Citation 1/SP	501-0052	Godwin Aviation LLC. Dunn, NC.	N900MC
☐ N677QS	04	Citation Excel	560-5367	NetJets, Port Columbus, Oh.	N.....
☐ N678CH	88	Falcon 900	47	CH Flyers LLC. Scottsdale, Az.	F-WQBK
☐ N678EQ	92	Citation VII	650-7008	Equity Marketing Services Inc. Chicago, Il.	N16KB
☐ N678MA	82	Falcon 50	116	FA116 Inc. Wilmington, De. (trustor ?).	XB-SOL
☐ N678QS	06	Citation Excel XLS	560-5616	NetJets, Port Columbus, Oh.	N.....
☐ N678RF	04	CitationJet CJ-1	525-0537	Rick's Custom Fencing & Decking Inc. Portland, Or.	N839AC
☐ N679QS	02	Citation Excel	560-5279	NetJets, Port Columbus, Oh.	N.....
☐ N680AR	04	Citation Sovereign	680-0025	Perpetual Air LLC. Dulles, Va.	N5247S
☐ N680CG	05	Citation Sovereign	680-0044	Blue Cross & Blue Shield of SC, Columbia, SC.	N680SW
☐ N680CJ	69	Learjet 24B	24B-211	Diplomat Aviation Inc. Tulsa, Ok.	N413WF
☐ N680CM	07	Citation Sovereign	680-0194	Cessna Aircraft Co. Wichita, Ks.	N52526
☐ N680CS	02	Citation Sovereign	709	Cessna Aircraft Co. Wichita, Ks. (Ff 27 Feb 02).	
☐ N680DF	01	Falcon 2000	180	International Paper Co. White Plains, NY.	(N203DD)
☐ N680FA*	83	Challenger 601	3003	ALG Transportation/Aviation Leasing Group, Kansas City, Mo.	N601CL
☐ N680GA	01	Gulfstream V	680	BMA Charter s r o, Prague, Czech Republic.	
☐ N680GG	06	Citation Sovereign	680-0104	Countrywide Coventry Ltd. East Midlands, UK.	N51872
☐ N680HC	06	Citation Sovereign	680-0079	Hamkar Ltd. Cairo, Egypt.	N5172M
☐ N680ME	86	Westwind-1124	423	Meridian Leasing LLC. Georgetown, De.	N223WA
☐ N680RC	07	Citation Sovereign	680-0192	Cessna Aircraft Co. Wichita, Ks.	N.....
☐ N680SE	05	Citation Sovereign	680-0078	NV Sea-Invest International Services, Antwerp, Belgium.	(OO-SIN)
☐ N680SW*	03	Learjet 31	31A-242	SSI Land & Cattle, Baker City, Or.	N600AN
☐ N680VR	06	Citation Sovereign	680-0108	Viking Range Corp. Greenwood, Ms.	N.....
☐ N681CE	04	Citation Encore	560-0681	Sierra Pacific Industries Inc. Anderson, Ca.	N5265B
☐ N681LF	07	Citation Sovereign	680-0151	International Lease Finance Co. Van Nuys, Ca.	N5204D
☐ N681QS	01	Citation Excel	560-5181	NetJets, Port Columbus, Oh.	
☐ N681WD	98	Citation X	750-0052	Fortune Jet Group Inc. Boca Raton, Fl.	N712JC
☐ N682B	89	BAe 125/800A	NA0431	E I DuPont de Nemours & Co. New Castle, De.	N585BA
☐ N682BF	84	Citation 1/SP	501-0682	BGT Minerals LLC. Aledo, Tx.	(N602HC)
☐ N682DB	03	Citation Sovereign	680-0009	Adler Group Inc. Miami, Fl.	N.....
☐ N682QS	06	Citation Excel XLS	560-5654	NetJets/Marquis Jet Partners Inc. Port Columbus, Oh.	N5264S
☐ N683E	87	BAe 125/800A	NA0410	E I DuPont de Nemours & Co. New Castle, De.	N555BA
☐ N683EF	86	Learjet 35A	35A-614	Executive Flight Inc. Pangborn Memorial, Wa.	N683EL
☐ N683PF	86	Citation S/II	S550-0083	BKMS BigSky LLC. San Jose, Ca.	N883PF
☐ N683QS	06	Citation Excel XLS	560-5643	NetJets, Port Columbus, Oh.	N.....
☐ N684DK	04	Hawker 800XP	258684	Monsanto Co. St Louis, Mo.	
☐ N684HA	77	Learjet 35A	35A-113	AirNet Systems Inc. Columbus, Oh.	(N113AN)
☐ N684KF	03	Falcon 2000	213	JCG Aviation LLC/Koch Meat Co. Park Ridge, Il.	N212QS
☐ N684QS	00	Citation Excel	560-5084	NetJets, Port Columbus, Oh.	N5211A
☐ N684SW	88	Challenger 601-3A	5032	Safeway Inc. Oakland, Ca.	N950SW
☐ N684TS	98	Challenger 604	5384	TVPX Inc. Concord, Ma.	VP-BNS
☐ N685CS	07	Citation Sovereign	680-0142	CitationShares Sales Inc. White Plains, NY.	N51817
☐ N685QS	06	Citation Excel XLS	560-5650	NetJets/Marquis Jet Partners Inc. Port Columbus, Oh.	N.....
☐ N685RC	98	Learjet 31A	31A-149	Luis Eusebio Barquin Gomez, Vera Cruz, Mexico.	N1904S
☐ N685SF	70	Gulfstream II SP	94	Spirit of Faith Christian Center, Temple Hills, Md.	N18AQ
☐ N685TA	02	Gulfstream V	685	G IV Corp/American Home Products, Morristown, NJ.	N585GA
☐ N686AB	02	Learjet 31A	31A-239	AirBrock LLC. Waccabuc, NY.	
☐ N686CP	86	Hawker 800SP	258059	CP Air LLC. White Plains, NY.	N355RB
☐ N686QS	06	Citation Excel XLS	560-5661	NetJets, Port Columbus, Oh.	N.....
☐ N686SC	98	Beechjet 400A	RK-211	KA Corp/Webb Road Development Inc. Whitefish, Mt.	N3028U
☐ N686TA	01	Beechjet 400A	RK-328	Flight Options LLC. Cuyahoga County, Oh.	(N472LX)
☐ N686TR	96	Beechjet 400A	RK-127	U-Haul International Inc. Portland, Or.	N696TR
☐ N687DS	05	CitationJet CJ-3	525B-0087	Duralake LLC. Minneapolis-Anoka, Mn.	N.....
☐ N687QS	01	Citation Excel	560-5187	NetJets, Port Columbus, Oh.	
☐ N688CF	74	Citation	500-0147	Big Chief Aviation Inc. Goshen, In.	N494G

Reg	Yr	Type	c/n	Owner/Operator	Prev Regn
N688DB	03	CitationJet CJ-2	525A-0192	Paradise Companies LLC. Natchez, Ms.	N.....
N688G	04	Hawker 850XP	258688	Giant Industries Inc. Scottsdale, Az.	
N688GS	73	Learjet 25B	25B-123	Royal Air Freight Inc. Pontiac, Mi.	N906SU
N688JD	99	Citation Bravo	550-0902	Conex International Corp. Jasper, Tx.	N770UM
N688LS	95	Gulfstream 4SP	1280	Yona Venetian LLC/Las Vegas Sands Inc. Las Vegas, Nv.	N531MD
N688QS	02	Citation Excel	560-5188	NetJets, Port Columbus, Oh.	N.....
N688TT	93	Gulfstream 4SP	1220	T-Jet Dream Aviation Ltd/Tsuchiya Gumi Co Ltd. Dgeki, Japan.	N79RP
N688TY	98	Gulfstream V	536	TY Jet Aviation LLC/Scott Fesler, Castaic, Ca.	N5UH
N689AK	05	Hawker 400XP	RK-462	400A Air Charters LLC/Golden Eagle Air Inc. Farmingdale, NY.	N462XP
N689AM	03	Hawker 800XP	258665	Alpha Mike Aviation Inc. Winnetka, Il.	N665XP
N689JE	79	Gulfstream II SP	258	Lacy-Landon Aviation LLC. Oxford, Ct.	N87GS
N689QS	06	Citation Excel XLS	560-5659	NetJets/Marquis Jet Partners Inc. Port Columbus, Oh.	N.....
N689VP	91	Citation II	550-0689	HNB Investments LLC. San Diego, Ca.	XA-JYO
N689W	84	Citation III	650-0045	Liz Air LLC. Las Vegas, Nv.	N669W
N689WC	78	Falcon 10	123	Chi Air 1-Wes Air LLC/Westcor Construction, Las Vegas, Nv.	N110TP
N690AN	91	Citation II	550-0674	B/F 674 LLC. Wilmington, De.	N918HM
N690EW	79	Citation II	550-0108	Boyd Air Corp. Dallas, Tx.	N36NA
N690JC	80	Learjet 25D	25D-320	N690JC LLC/Jet Fleet Inc. Lewes, De.	OO-LFR
N690QS	00	Citation Excel	560-5090	NetJets, Port Columbus, Oh.	N51246
N690WY	81	Gulfstream 1/SP	501-0222	Young Revocable Trust, Concord, Ca.	N690DM
N691QS	02	Citation Excel	560-5290	NetJets, Port Columbus, Oh.	N.....
N691RC	00	Gulfstream V	605	Hudson Group, Teterboro, NJ.	N62ML
N692BE	85	Citation III	650-0092	Alliance Continental Leasing LLC. Canfield, Oh.	N692CC
N692EB	69	Gulfstream 2B	775	Motor Air LLC. San Bernardino, Ca.	N4PC
N692FG	70	Learjet 25	25-052	Lear 25-052 Inc. Chula Vista, Ca. (status ?).	N692FC
N692PC	93	Learjet 60	60-010	Peter Capone Design LLC. Santa Barbara, Ca.	N610TS
N692QS	00	Citation Excel	560-5092	NetJets, Port Columbus, Oh.	N5125J
N692US	76	Falcon 10	79	FIT LLC. Danbury, Ct.	N73B
N693QS	06	Citation Excel XLS	560-5657	NetJets, Port Columbus, Oh.	N.....
N693SH	88	Falcon 900B	43	Dittmer Trading LLC. Chicago, Il.	N388Z
N694JP	99	Falcon 900EX	59	Liberty Mutual Insurance Co. Bedford, Ma.	N959EX
N694LM	77	Citation	500-0354	Dodson Aviation Inc. Rantoul, Ks.	N354RC
N694PG	81	Challenger 600S	1026	IDM Aviation Services LLC. Austin, Tx.	N694JC
N694QS	01	Citation Excel	560-5194	NetJets, Port Columbus, Oh.	N.....
N695BK	99	Beechjet 400A	RK-235	Big Country Air LLC. Fargo, ND.	
N695QS	02	Citation Excel	560-5293	NetJets, Port Columbus, Oh.	N.....
N695V	05	Citation Encore	560-0695	Steel Stadiums Ltd. Graham, Tx.	N5172M
N696HC	06	Citation Sovereign	680-0101	CC Industries Inc/Henry Crown & Co. Palwaukee, Il.	N51072
N696HQ	01	Falcon 50EX	316	Stephens Group Inc. Little Rock, Ar.	N696HC
N696MJ	75	Gulfstream 2B	165	Rellet Services Inc. Vero Beach, Fl.	N183V
N696QS	02	Citation Excel	560-5296	NetJets, Port Columbus, Oh.	N.....
N696RV	67	Jet Commander	118	Aeronaval Inc. Carson City, Nv.	N381DA
N696ST	97	CitationJet	525-0187	Dr Robert Knollenberg, Boulder, Co.	N5130J
N696TA	00	Beechjet 400A	RK-301	Flight Options LLC. Cuyahoga County, Oh.	(N465LX)
N696US	01	Sabre-65	465-18	United Space Alliance LLC. Houston, Tx.	N4M
N696VP	92	Citation II	550-0696	RLH Enterprises LLC. Chicago, Il.	(N74EH)
N697A	01	Gulfstream V	662	ALCOA Inc. Allegheny County, Pa.	N662GA
N697CE	05	Citation Encore	560-0697	LC Corp SA. Wroclaw, Poland.	N.....
N697MC	85	Citation III	650-0097	Century Building Materials, Lindenhurst, NY. (status ?).	N725WH
N697QS	01	Citation Excel	560-5197	NetJets, Port Columbus, Oh.	N.....
N697US	80	Sabre-65	465-49	United Space Alliance LLC. Houston, Tx.	N82CR
N698DC	94	Hawker 1000	259043	Lear 006 Holding Ltd. Fort Lauderdale, Fl.	(N117CP)
N698MM	97	Learjet 31A	31A-142	MM Air Inc/Kirkland Construction, Wilmington, De.	ZS-EAG
N698QS	06	Citation Excel XLS	560-5653	NetJets, Port Columbus, Oh.	N5257C
N698RS	00	Challenger 604	5460	Miami Dolphins/Ariana LLC. Fort Lauderdale, Fl.	VP-BMG
N699BA	82	Learjet 35A	35A-463	32HJ LLC. West Columbia, SC.	N32HJ
N699BG	90	Falcon 900	82	Ginn Development LLC. Bunnell-Flagler County, Fl.	N649TT
N699CP	92	Learjet 31A	31A-060	Consolidated Pipe & Supply Co. Birmingham, Al.	N696PA
N699DA	01	Learjet 60	60-237	Delphi Automotive Systems LLC. Troy, Mi.	
N699HH	94	Gulfstream 4SP	1239	Cirrus Gas LLC. Dallas-Love, Tx.	(N105TR)
N699MC	03	Falcon 2000EX	25	Mazama Capital Management Inc. Hillsboro, Or.	N225EX
N699MG	85	Citation III	650-0094	Maund Automotive Group LP. Austin, Tx.	N926HC
N699QS	01	Citation Excel	560-5199	NetJets, Port Columbus, Oh.	N.....
N699SA	81	Learjet 35A	35A-441	Sterling Aviation LLC/Terranova Corp. Miami, Fl.	RP-C1404
N699TS	72	HS 125/F600A	256001	Aviation Solutions LLC. Waterford, Mi.	N773JC
N699TW	66	Falcon 20DC	50	Kitty Hawk Air Cargo Inc. Dallas, Tx.	EC-EDO

Reg	Yr	Type	c/n	Owner/Operator	Prev Regn
N699XP	04	Hawker 800XPi	258699	New Country Motor Group Inc. Oxford, Ct.	(5N-...)
N700AL	75	Falcon 10	55	SBM Aviation Inc. Jackson-Thompson, Ms.	(N700PD)
N700BX	00	Global Express	9068	Wilmington Trust Co. Wilmington, De. (trustor ?).	(N889JC)
N700CE	84	HS 125/700A	257213	Codale Electric Supply Inc. Salt Lake City, Ut.	(N703MJ)
N700CH	01	Falcon 2000	147	Cardal Inc. Columbus-OSU, Oh.	N777MN
N700CJ	93	CitationJet	525-0027	Bruun Aircraft LLC. Hillsboro, Or.	N816RD
N700CN	90	Gulfstream 4	1133	Copley Press Inc. Carlsbad, Ca.	N443GA
N700FA	04	Hawker 400XP	RK-399	F & F Aviation Inc. Fort Lauderdale, Fl.	
N700FH	79	Falcon 10	158	Flex Air Ltd/Flightstar Corp. Chicago-Midway, Il.	N790FH
N700FL	96	Falcon 2000	29	FL Aircraft LLC. Little Rock, Ar.	XA-TDU
N700FS	99	Gulfstream 4SP	1400	Agro-Industrial Management, West Palm Beach, Fl.	N215TM
N700GB	02	Global Express	9124	Bombardier Aerospace Corp. Windsor Locks, Ct.	C-FZVN
N700GG	78	Learjet 36A	36A-038	North American Jet Charter Inc. Banning, Ca.	N548PA
N700GW	98	CitationJet	525-0275	Joe Morten & Son Inc. South Sioux City, Ne.	
N700JC	81	Sabre-65	465-74	Oxley Petroleum Co. Tulsa, Ok.	
N700JR	04	Citation Encore	560-0666	Johnny Ribeiro Builder Air LLC. Las Vegas, Nv.	N51160
N700KS	01	Global Express	9109	Amblin Entertainment Inc/Dreamworks LLC. Burbank, Ca.	N700DU
N700LH	01	Citation X	750-0148	Limerick Holdings LLC/The Broe Companies Inc. Denver, Co.	N.....
N700LK	06	Global 5000	9192	Trey Aviation LLC/API Group Inc. Naples, Fl.	C-FECY
N700LS	06	Global 5000	9217	Southern Key Properties LLC. Las Vegas, Nv.	C-FIPP
N700LX	98	Citation X	750-0038	Flight Options LLC. Cuyahoga County, Oh.	(N788CW)
N700MD	77	Westwind-1124	212	Kal Kustom NW Inc. Salem, Or.	N900CS
N700MG	01	Hawker 800XP	258540	Abbott Laboratories Inc. Waukegan, Il.	(XA-...)
N700MH	86	Citation III	650-0127	James Hammond, Minneapolis, Mn.	(N95UJ)
N700MP	81	Falcon 50	70	HOP Air One GP Inc. Frisco, Tx.	N306ES
N700NK	05	Citation Encore	560-0700	EnKay Corp. Shreveport, La.	N5268E
N700NP	83	HS 125/700A	NA0345	Sage-Popovich Inc. Valparaiso, In.	(N313VR)
N700NW	79	HS 125/700A	NA0246	Howe Electric Inc. Fresno, Ca.	N79HC
N700NY	00	Gulfstream 4SP	1468	DLJ Partners LLC. Teterboro, NJ.	N468GA
N700QS	01	Gulfstream G200	052	NetJets, Port Columbus, Oh.	N294GA
N700R	04	Hawker 800XP	258692	NASCAR Inc. Daytona Beach, Fl.	N37092
N700RR	78	HS 125/700A	NA0217	Roberts Aviation LLC. St Louis, Mo.	(N6960)
N700RY	83	Citation III	650-0005	Aircraft Guaranty Title LLC. Houston, Tx. (trustor ?).	N693BA
N700SA	81	HS 125/700A	NA0339	American Food Grain Inc. Wilmington, De.	PT-ORJ
N700SJ	76	Learjet 35A	35A-082	AirNet Systems Inc. Columbus, Oh.	N700GB
N700SP	80	Citation 1/SP	501-0133	Gateway Design, Van Nuys, Ca.	N51WP
N700SR	83	Learjet 55	55-079	Chrysler Aviation Inc. Van Nuys, Ca.	N1983Y
N700SW	00	Citation X	750-0142	Safeway Insurance Co. Westmont, Il.	N5172M
N700TR	70	HS 125/731	NA745	Career Aviation Academy Inc/NA745 LLC. Las Vegas, Nv.	N400XJ
N700VC	72	Citation Eagle	500-0011	Agape Church Inc. Little Rock, Ar.	C-GJEM
N700WC	78	HS 125/700A	257022	Jet Capital LLC. Tulsa, Ok.	N109AF
N700WH*	89	Beechjet 400	RJ-60	Haines Capital Group LLC. Oklahoma City, Ok.	N95RT
N700WY	07	Hawker 900XP	HA-29	Hawker Beechcraft Corp. Wichita, Ks.	
N700XF	80	HS 125/700A	NA0272	Bitz Aviation Inc. Allegheny County, Pa.	N89GN
N701AS	76	Learjet 35A	35A-047	AirNet Systems Inc. Columbus, Oh.	N13MJ
N701BG	87	Citation S/II	S550-0142	Black Gold Potato Sales Inc. Grand Forks, ND.	C-GCRG
N701CP	00	Beechjet 400A	RK-272	Central Plains Steel Co/Richard Owen LLC. Kansas City, Ks.	N3237H
N701CR	07	Citation Sovereign	680-0176	Cessna Aircraft Co. Wichita, Ks.	N5072X
N701DA	78	Learjet 35A	35A-180	CKU Aviation LLC. Dothan, Al.	N44HG
N701FW	80	Sabre-65	465-21	Heartland Airways LLC. Overland Park, Ks.	(N265CA)
N701HA	92	Citation VII	650-7001	Blue Pacific Aviation Inc. Carlsbad, Ca.	N404JF
N701JH	78	JetStar 2	5230	Trump International Sonesta Resort, Sunny Isles Beach, Fl.	(N275MD)
N701KB	07	390 Premier 1A	RB-211	K W Brock Directories Inc. Pittsburg, Ks.	
N701LX	00	Citation X	750-0114	Flight Options LLC. Cuyahoga County, Oh.	N114CX
N701MS	76	HS 125/F600A	256061	NOVI Kids Inc. San Diego, Ca.	N331DC
N701NB	93	Citation V	560-0244	First National Bank, McAllen, Tx.	N60RD
N701QS	06	Gulfstream G200	141	NetJets, Port Columbus, Oh.	N641GA
N701SC	71	Learjet 24XR	24XR-235	MCA-Taylor Lear 24 LLC. Wichita, Ks.	N51VL
N701SF	02	CitationJet CJ-2	525A-0071	Air Frantz Inc. White Plains, NY.	N34RF
N701TF	02	CitationJet CJ-2	525A-0112	TVPX Inc. Concord, Ma.	N525U
N701TP	97	CitationJet	525-0190	Smooth Air LLC. Helena, Mt.	N708TF
N701TS	77	HS 125/700A	NA0201	South Aviation Inc. Fort Lauderdale, Fl.	(N828SA)
N701VV	02	Citation Bravo	550-1033	Miller Container Aviation Inc. Moline-Quad City, Il.	N933BB
N701WC	03	Falcon 50EX	333	Liberty Mutual Insurance Co. Bedford, Ma.	N334EX
N701WH	98	Global Express	9010	N2T Inc/Oakley Inc. Bellingham, Wa.	C-GDGQ
N702AC	07	Citation Excel XLS	560-5678	Garwin Holdings Ltd. Santo Domingo, Dominican Republic.	N52613

Reg	Yr	Type	c/n	Owner/Operator	Prev Regn
☐ N702AM	05	Citation Encore	560-0702	Charter Services Inc. Mobile, Al.	N.....
☐ N702DM	84	Gulfstream 3	428	D Q Automobiles/Papa Grande Management Co. Irving, Tx.	N760G
☐ N702DR	05	Embraer Legacy 600	14500925	SCSM Aviation LLC. Las Vegas, Nv.	N702CM
☐ N702GH	02	Gulfstream 4SP	1497	GEH Air Transportation LLC. White Plains, NY.	(N497QS)
☐ N702LP	05	Hawker 400XP	RK-444	Leggett & Platt Inc. Joplin, Mo.	N144XP
☐ N702LX	99	Citation X	750-0076	Flight Options LLC. Cuyahoga County, Oh.	N400RB
☐ N702NV	96	Beechjet 400A	RK-120	Investment Equity Development, Las Vegas, Nv.	N159AK
☐ N702QS	02	Gulfstream G200	070	NetJets, Port Columbus, Oh.	N268GA
☐ N702RT	84	Citation 1/SP	501-0683	Innovative Communities/RJ Crook Corp. Carlsbad, Ca.	N96LC
☐ N702RV	90	Challenger 601-3A	5078	RV Aviation LLC. Columbia, Mo.	N578FP
☐ N703HA	05	Gulfstream G150	202	Horton Aviation LLC. Dallas-Love, Tx. (Ff 2 Sep 05)	N150GA
☐ N703JN	78	HS 125/700A	257031	South Aviation Inc. Fort Lauderdale, Fl.	N703TS
☐ N703LP	91	Beechjet 400A	RK-20	Celero Energy LP. Midland, Tx.	N870P
☐ N703LX	99	Citation X	750-0074	Flight Options LLC. Cuyahoga County, Oh.	N7418F
☐ N703QS	02	Gulfstream G200	060	NetJets, Port Columbus, Oh.	N270GA
☐ N703RB	94	Citation VII	650-7046	ETC Flight LLC. Nashville, Tn.	(N328BT)
☐ N703RK	01	Gulfstream V	671	Molinaro Koger Inc. Dulles, Va.	(N703MK)
☐ N703SM*	90	BAe 125/800A	NA0464	East Coast Jets Inc. Allentown, Pa.	N57LN
☐ N703TM	91	Falcon 50	218	Carlisle Holdings LLC. Bedford, Ma.	N750FJ
☐ N704DA	81	Citation II	550-0202	D + A Investments LLC. Albuquerque, NM.	N550NE
☐ N704GA	07	Gulfstream G450	4104	Gulfstream Aerospace Corp. Savannah, Ga.	
☐ N704JM	98	Hawker 800XP	258367	Media Aviation Associates LLC. Montgomery, Al.	OY-GIP
☐ N704JW	03	Gulfstream G200	088	Moon, Sun & Stars Inc. Coral Gables, Fl.	N200GA
☐ N704LX	99	Citation X	750-0091	Flight Options LLC. Cuyahoga County, Oh.	(N791CW)
☐ N704MF	00	Global Express	9065	MC Group, Hillsboro, Or.	N711SW
☐ N704T	99	390 Premier 1	RB-2	Hawker Beechcraft Corp. Wichita, Ks.	
☐ N705AC	77	Westwind-1124	209	SMA LLC. Clearwater, Fl.	N222LH
☐ N705BB	84	BAe 125/800A	258015	Co-Mo LLC. St Louis, Mo.	C-GWEM
☐ N705LP	99	Beechjet 400A	RK-251	Leggett & Platt Inc. Joplin, Mo.	N3106Y
☐ N705LX	99	Citation X	750-0082	Flight Options LLC. Cuyahoga County, Oh.	(N242LT)
☐ N705PC	94	Gulfstream 4SP	1240	Phanstiel Enterprises LLC. Los Angeles, Ca.	N212AW
☐ N705QS	02	Gulfstream G200	061	NetJets, Port Columbus, Oh.	N271GA
☐ N705SG	00	Citation Excel	560-5142	Union of Operating Engineers, Van Nuys, Ca.	N5093D
☐ N705SP	85	Citation S/II	S550-0045	Sportsmans Market Inc. Batavia, Oh.	N999TJ
☐ N706AM	77	HS 125/700A	NA0206	Laguna Landmark Inc. Laguna Beach, Ca.	N828KC
☐ N706CJ	00	Learjet 60	60-207	King Aircraft Ltd. White Plains, NY.	N777VQ
☐ N706CR	99	Learjet 60	60-168	Jupiter Aviation LLC. Darby, Pa.	N706CJ
☐ N706HB	84	Citation III	650-0047	Southern Wind Aviation LLC. New Orleans, La.	N711VZ
☐ N706JA	81	Gulfstream 3	322	N706JA LLC. Salt Lake City, Ut.	N606ES
☐ N706JP	67	B 727-35	19835	Petters Aviation LLC. Lantana, Fl.	N727HC
☐ N706LP	01	Beechjet 400A	RK-336	Leggatt & Platt Inc. Joplin, Mo.	(N706PL)
☐ N706LX	99	Citation X	750-0073	Flight Options LLC. Cuyahoga County, Oh.	N269JR
☐ N706NA	92	Citation II	550-0706	Gale Aviation LLC. Ormond Beach, Fl.	7Q-YLF
☐ N706QS	06	Gulfstream G200	131	NetJets, Port Columbus, Oh.	N771GA
☐ N706RM	97	Beechjet 400A	RK-161	6RM LLC/RVR Air Charter, Fort Worth, Tx.	(N428LX)
☐ N706SA	90	Learjet 31	31-026	RGM LLC. Charleston, WV.	(N184RM)
☐ N706VA	03	Gulfstream G400	1528	Van Andel Institute, Grand Rapids, Mi.	N523AC
☐ N706VP	96	Citation X	750-0006	Precision Jet Management Inc. Syracuse, NY.	N484H
☐ N707AM	80	Falcon 10	159	D-10 Falcon LLC/Tensor Engineering, Melbourne, Fl.	N707DC
☐ N707BC	04	Gulfstream G200	107	Westwind Acquisition LLC. Dulles, Va.	N107GA
☐ N707CS	07	Learjet 60	60-324	CommScope Inc of NC. Hickory, NC.	N50126
☐ N707GG	79	Citation 1/SP	501-0108	Day Air LLC. Brunswick, Ga.	N777GG
☐ N707GW	01	Gulfstream V	629	Sea Pioneer Shipping Corp. Athens, Greece.	N711RQ
☐ N707HD	92	BAe 1000A	259016	Gray & Co. New Orleans, La.	N678SB
☐ N707HP	04	Citation Bravo	550-1096	Blue Neon LLC. Fort Lauderdale, Fl.	(N877B)
☐ N707JC	04	Hawker 800XP	258703	Carney Management Co. Oxford, Ct.	N50553
☐ N707JT	64	B 707-138B	18740	John Travolta/Jet Clipper Johnny LLC. Encino, Ca.	N707XX
☐ N707JU	79	B 707-3W6C	21956	Omega Air Inc. Washington, DC.	CN-CCC
☐ N707KD	78	Gulfstream II SP	214	Alchemist Jet Air LLC. Nashua, NH.	N914KB
☐ N707KN	74	B 707-366C	20919	Omega Air Inc. San Antonio, Tx. (stored ?).	SU-AXJ
☐ N707LM	81	Citation II	550-0398	Electromatic International Inc. Hollywood, Fl.	N610ED
☐ N707LX	99	Citation X	750-0078	Flight Options LLC. Cuyahoga County, Oh.	N711HQ
☐ N707MM	00	Falcon 2000	131	Massachusetts Mutual Life Insurance Co. Bedford, Ma.	F-WWVG
☐ N707PF	82	Citation II	550-0452	Eagle Creek Aviation Inc. Longview, Tx.	N707PE
☐ N707QJ	76	B 707-368C	21261	Thomas Vaughan, Hartford, Ct.	A20-261
☐ N707QS	02	Gulfstream G200	066	NetJets, Port Columbus, Oh.	N276GA

Reg	Yr	Type	c/n	Owner/Operator	Prev Regn
☐ N707RG	78	Learjet 35A	35A-169	Robby Gordon Motorsports, Concord, NC.	N500JS
☐ N707SC	65	Learjet 24	24-065	RM Property Service Inc. Fort Lauderdale, Fl.	(XA-...)
☐ N707SG	03	Gulfstream G200	087	Grossman Company Properties Inc. Santa Monica, Ca.	(N747SG)
☐ N707TE	99	Gulfstream 4SP	1383	Tyco Electronics Corp. Harrisburg, Pa.	(N507TE)
☐ N707TF	71	Westwind-1123	155	Ferrante Aviation Inc. Vandergrift, Pa.	N707TE
☐ N707W	79	Citation 1/SP	501-0085	Wellons Inc. Sherwood, Or.	N25DD
☐ N707WB	93	Falcon 900B	132	The Home Depot Inc. Atlanta-Fulton County, Ga.	N132FJ
☐ N708GP	03	CitationJet CJ-2	525A-0154	RSF Jet LLC. Carlsbad, Ca.	N5091J
☐ N708LX	99	Citation X	750-0109	Flight Options LLC. Cuyahoga County, Oh.	N750PT
☐ N708QS	02	Gulfstream G200	069	NetJets, Port Columbus, Oh.	N279GA
☐ N708SP	97	Learjet 45	45-014	Tappetto Magico Inc. Biggin Hill, UK.	
☐ N708TA	98	Beechjet 400A	RK-178	Flight Options LLC. Cuyahoga County, Oh.	(N430LX)
☐ N709DW	05	Gulfstream G550	5082	Dubai World Aviation Inc. Dubai, UAE.	N550FG
☐ N709EL	92	Beechjet 400A	RK-52	Gal Air Inc. Atlanta, Ga.	(N709EW)
☐ N709LS	00	Gulfstream 4SP	1412	Dubai World Aviation Inc. Dubai, UAE.	N700LS
☐ N709LX	00	Citation X	750-0145	Flight Options LLC. Cuyahoga County, Oh.	(N745CW)
☐ N709TA	98	Beechjet 400A	RK-180	Flight Options LLC. Cuyahoga County, Oh.	(N480CW)
☐ N710A	88	BAe 125/800B	258110	ARAMCO Associated Co. Dhahran, Saudi Arabia.	D-CMIR
☐ N710AF	81	HS 125/700A	NA0290	Air4 Aviation LLC/Tri C Aviation Inc. Houston, Tx.	N17WG
☐ N710AW	97	Citation X	750-0033	Quicksilver Jet Sales Inc. Waco, Tx.	N5093D
☐ N710BG	00	Falcon 50EX	305	Contrail Aviation LLC/Berwind Group, Philadelphia, Pa.	N102BQ
☐ N710CF	84	Gulfstream 3	448	Addington Aviation LLC. Ashland, Ky.	N178HH
☐ N710DC	67	Jet Commander	112	SkyPro Enterprises Ltd. Las Vegas, Nv. (status ?).	(C-G...)
☐ N710EC	02	Gulfstream G400	1502	Chouest Air Inc. Houma, La.	N202GA
☐ N710ET	96	Falcon 2000	38	Wilshire Rental Corp. Dallas, Tx.	(N800BG)
☐ N710GA	83	Challenger 601	3008	Green Aviation V Corp. White Plains, NY.	(N600LX)
☐ N710GS	75	Learjet 35	35-032	Maritime Sales & Leasing Inc. Newnan, Ga.	N711MA
☐ N710HL	82	Challenger 600S	1050	Caesh Air LLC. St Charles, Il.	N82CN
☐ N710JC	78	Falcon 10	120	Minnesota Choice Aviation LLC. St Paul, Mn.	N402JW
☐ N710LC	90	Citation V	560-0058	Rockies West LLC/Lanz Cabinet Shop Inc. Eugene, Or.	N62GA
☐ N710LM	89	Challenger 601-3A	5037	Liberty Media Group. Englewood, Co.	N212LM
☐ N710ML	94	Citation V	560-0254	Biomet Inc/Air Warsaw Inc. Warsaw, In.	N710MT
☐ N710MT	03	Citation Excel	560-5332	Biomet Inc/Air Warsaw Inc. Warsaw, In.	N727YB
☐ N710R	07	Learjet 45	45-359	Learjet Inc. Wichita, Ks.	
☐ N710SA	80	Westwind-1124	296	Sun Air Inc. Laredo, Tx.	N89TJ
☐ N710SG*	00	Learjet 60	60-191	Hot Doggie Air Services/Scott Ginsburg Law Firm, Irving, Tx.	N660AS
☐ N710TA	98	Beechjet 400A	RK-183	Flight Options LLC. Cuyahoga County, Oh.	(N432LX)
☐ N710TF*	94	Learjet 60	60-046	Thomas Development Partners Inc. Van Nuys, Ca.	N710TP
☐ N710TS	07	Challenger 605	5710	Aero Toy Store LLC. Fort Lauderdale, Fl.	C-GSAP
☐ N710TV	68	Learjet 24	24-159	Royal Air Freight Inc. Pontiac, Mi.	(N269AL)
☐ N710VF	89	Challenger 601-3A	5050	VILLCo Aviation LLC. Pontiac, Mi.	(N25GG)
☐ N710VL	76	Citation	500-0302	Jefferson County Racing Association, Montgomery, Al.	(N777QE)
☐ N711BX	98	CitationJet	525-0299	Donald Baker, Tucson, Az.	N711BE
☐ N711C	06	CitationJet CJ1+	525-0630	525-0630 LLC. Tupelo, Ms.	N50054
☐ N711CC	82	Citation II	550-0427	Central Bank, Lebanon, Mo.	N840MQ
☐ N711CW	65	Learjet 24	24-055	Premier Jets Inc. Hillsboro, Or.	N511WH
☐ N711EC	80	Learjet 35A	35A-311	East Coast Jets Inc. Allentown, Pa.	N581AS
☐ N711EG	82	Gulfstream 3	349	Entrepreneurial Asset Management LLC. Long Beach, Ca.	N6458
☐ N711EJ	79	Falcon 10	149	Embee Inc. Santa Ana, Ca.	(N830SR)
☐ N711FG	94	Learjet 31A	31A-092	Frontier Hotel & Gambling Hall, Las Vegas, Nv.	N50302
☐ N711FJ	76	Falcon 20F-5	347	Embee Inc. Santa Ana, Ca.	N20VF
☐ N711FW	88	Gulfstream 4	1033	EB Phoenix LLC. Rancho Mirage, ca.	N711SW
☐ N711GF	96	Citation VII	650-7075	IPO-Indeck Power Overseas LLC. Wheeling, Il.	N52613
☐ N711GL	90	Gulfstream 4	1130	G & L Aviation Inc. Van Nuys, Ca.	N404LM
☐ N711HA	06	Citation Excel XLS	560-5648	Hoyt Air Inc/Arizona Industrial Properties, Phoenix, Az.	N1320P
☐ N711HF	87	Falcon 100	213	Hartford Financial Corp. Naples, Fl.	F-WKAE
☐ N711JC	75	Falcon 10	69	Diamonte Air LLC. Long Beach, Ca.	N7TJ
☐ N711KE	80	Westwind-1124	288	Independent Cuss LLC. Suawnee, Ga.	N48AH
☐ N711LS	04	Global 5000	9155	The Whitewind Co. Windsor Locks, Ct.	C-FBPT
☐ N711LV	93	Citation VI	650-0232	National Education Loan Network Inc. Lincoln, Ne.	(N512MT)
☐ N711MC	02	Global Express	9121	N & M D Investment Corp. Fort Lauderdale, Fl.	N700FN
☐ N711MD	85	Citation S/II	S550-0066	Cabot Air LLC. Boston, Ma.	N1272P
☐ N711MN	97	Global Express	9002	Qualcomm Inc. San Diego, Ca.	N711MC
☐ N711MQ	76	Gulfstream 2B	189	ABCO Aviation Inc. Houston, Tx.	N404AC
☐ N711MT	76	Citation	500-0316	January Transport Inc. Oklahoma City, Ok.	(N127CJ)
☐ N711NB	92	Citation VII	650-7009	First National Bank, McAllen, Tx.	N709VP

Reg	Yr	Type	c/n	Owner/Operator	Prev Regn
N711NL*	06	Citation Sovereign	680-0095	Spartan Organization Inc. Wings Field, Pa.	N711NK
N711NR	04	Citation Excel XLS	560-5533	Nadir Industries Ltd. Geneva, Switzerland.	N711NK
N711NV	87	Citation II/SP	551-0557	Nevada Department of Transport, Carson City. (was 550-0557).	N1298C
N711PC	76	Learjet 24D	24D-327	World of Faith Christian Center Church, Southfield, Mi.	N327GJ
N711PE	99	Falcon 2000	105	Pinnacle Entertainment Inc. Las Vegas, Nv.	N105LF
N711QS	05	Gulfstream G200	129	NetJets, Port Columbus, Oh.	N229GA
N711R	99	Learjet 45	45-049	Cockrell Resources Inc. Houston, Tx.	
N711RL	03	Gulfstream G550	5010	Ralph & Ricky Lauren/RL Wings LLC. NYC.	N910GA
N711SW	07	Gulfstream G450	4085	Wynn Las Vegas, Las Vegas, Nv.	N385GA
N711SX	02	Global Express	9125	Acme Operating Co. Cleveland, Oh.	N700FR
N711T	96	Falcon 900EX	6	Grey Falcon LLC/Toll Brothers Inc. Northeast Philadelphia.	N900FH
N711TF	75	Falcon 10	52	Contemporary Industries Leasing Corp. Omaha, Ne.	N860E
N711UF	84	Gulfstream 3	421	Frank Fertitta Enterprises Inc. Las Vegas, Nv.	N921FF
N711VH	02	Citation Excel	560-5260	Trio Air Holdings LLC. Hackensack, NJ.	N711HA
N711VJ	99	Citation X	750-0101	Aerohead Aviation Inc. Scottsdale, Az.	N711VT
N711VL	72	Gulfstream II SP	120	Macon Co Greyhound Park Inc. Montgomery, Al.	C-GTEW
N711VT	07	Citation X	750-0283	Cessna Aircraft Co. Wichita, Ks.	N5221Y
N711WG	00	CitationJet CJ-1	525-0424	Midwest Transport LLC. St Joseph, Mo.	N28SW
N711WM	96	Challenger 800	7140	Gaughan Flying/Coast Hotels & Casinos Inc. Las Vegas, Nv.	N140WC
N711WV	78	Falcon 20F-5	396	SBR Inc. Parkersburg, WV.	N711GL
N711XR	86	Citation S/II	S550-0121	Fortuna Aviation LLC.	(N20NM)
N712AS	84	Gulfstream 3	423	The Andalex Group INC. NYC.	N399RV
N712CC	87	Gulfstream 4	1028	SAH Enterprises Inc. Santa Monica, Ca. 'Camille'.	N712CW
N712DP	80	Learjet 25D	25D-319	Don Prudhomme Leasing Inc. Carlsbad, Ca.	N680JC
N712EJ	01	Learjet 31A	31A-231	R H Bluestein & Co. Birmingham, Mi.	XA-VTR
N712GK	92	Beechjet 400A	RK-44	KS Air 3-7-12 III LLC. Charlotte, NC.	N908R
N712KC	06	Citation X	750-0255	JRC Citation LLC/James Crane, Houston, Tx.	N51666
N712KM	77	Citation	500-0348	Klotz Aviation LLC. Garden City, Ks.	C-GCLQ
N712KT	06	Gulfstream G550	5134	Wilmington Trust Co. Wilmington, De. (trustor ?).	N534GA
N712MB	73	Citation	500-0120	RSF Jet LLC. Carlsbad, Ca.	N127BJ
N712MQ	71	Gulfstream 2	104	ABCO Aviation Inc. Houston, Tx.	C-FHPM
N712PD	79	Citation II	550-0069	Bennett Law Office PC. Missoula, Mt.	C-FFCL
N712PR	96	Challenger 604	5313	RM Aviation LLC. San Juan, PR.	N3HB
N712QS	02	Gulfstream G200	073	NetJets, Port Columbus, Oh.	N673GA
N712TA	98	Beechjet 400A	RK-186	Flight Options LLC. Cuyahoga County, Oh.	(N433LX)
N712VP*	96	Citation X	750-0012	Cessna Aircraft Co. Wichita, Ks.	N912QS
N713AZ	04	390 Premier 1	RB-111	Charlie Air Inc/Azzar Store Equipment Inc. Grand Rapids	N6111F
N713DH	04	Citation Excel XLS	560-5527	HMC Aviation Inc. New Smyrna Beach, Fl.	N5254Y
N713HC	96	Challenger 604	5308	5308 Acquisition LLC/HCC Insurance Holdings Inc. Belgrade, Mt	(N713HG)
N713JD	78	Citation 1/SP	501-0075	Jordan Foster Aviation Inc. Jacksonville, Fl.	N51ET
N713MC	79	Falcon 20F-5B	392	Stephen Haight Construction, Sioux Falls, SD..	(N392FJ)
N713SA	73	Citation	500-0132	Aeromedevac Inc. San Diego, Ca.	(N992MG)
N713SD	97	CitationJet	525-0218	SDI Leasing LLC. Houston, Tx.	(N207LX)
N713SN	87	Falcon 50	182	Alaska Eastern Inc. Eureka, Ca.	N250AS
N713VP	99	Citation VII	650-7103	Pinnacle Trading LLC. Fresno, Ca.	N713QS
N713WD	07	Citation Encore+	560-0765	Winds Away 07 LLC. Houston, Tx.	N5245U
N713WH	05	CitationJet CJ1+	525-0606	Collect Air LLC. Denver, Co.	N51896
N714RM	03	Citation Bravo	550-1057	Raj Consulting LLC. Santa Ana, Ca.	N5245U
N715CG	02	Learjet 45	45-208	CG Cars LLC/Carl Gregory Cars Inc. Fort Payne, Al.	N5050G
N715JS	72	Citation	500-0001	Jerry Savelle Ministries International, Crowley, Tx.	N501KG
N715PH	05	Hawker 800XP	258715	Pulte Homes Inc. Pontiac, Mi.	N715XP
N715TA	98	Beechjet 400A	RK-189	Flight Options LLC. Cuyahoga County, Oh.	(N434LX)
N715WG	06	Gulfstream G150	205	La Costa Village Inc. Carlsbad, Ca.	N405GA
N715WS	74	Falcon 20F-5B	305	Regency Aircraft Leasing LLC. Carson City, Nv.	N34EW
N715WT	98	Hawker 800XP2	258386	Plise Equipment/Aquila Management LLC. Las Vegas, Nv.	N715WG
N716BD	94	Learjet 31A	31A-093	Bolavi Aviation/Ambulatory Surgical Centers, Westfield, Ma.	N916BD
N716CB	72	Citation	500-0055	AeroVision International LLC. Muskegon, Mi.	N999SF
N716DB	85	BAe 125/800A	258048	Western Leasing Co. Green Bay, Wi.	C-GCIB
N716DD	86	Citation S/II	S550-0120	J Bar B Aviation LLC/J & B Sausage Co. Waelder, Tx.	N716DB
N716GS	07	390 Premier 1A	RB-199	SRS Aviation LLC. Atlanta-Fulton County, Ga.	N133CM
N716LT	72	Citation	500-0034	LeBeouf Bros Towing LLC. Bourg, La.	N11HJ
N716QS	06	Gulfstream G200	148	NetJets, Port Columbus, Oh.	N844GA
N716SX	94	Citation V Ultra	560-0281	Saxon Business Systems Inc. Fort Lauderdale, Fl.	N281VP
N717AF	79	HS 125/700A-2	NA0243	Air 4 Aviation LLC/Tri-C Aviation Inc. Houston, Tx.	N9395Y
N717AJ	78	Learjet 35A	35A-183	Neptune Aviation Services Inc. Missoula, Mt.	N183FD
N717AM	84	Learjet 55	55-100	Florida Jet Service Inc. Fort Lauderdale, Fl.	(N500NB)

Reg	Yr	Type	c/n	Owner/Operator	Prev Regn
☐ N717CB	98	Citation Bravo	550-0830	NC Aviation Corp/Timberline Land Co. Greenville, NC.	N830KE
☐ N717CF	98	Beechjet 400A	RK-177	Red Barn Farms LLC. Sanford, NC.	N2277G
☐ N717CH*	98	Beechjet 400A	RK-164	Cloudhopper LLC. Middleburg, Va.	N280AJ
☐ N717CP	91	Astra-1125SP	053	Cousins Properties Inc. Atlanta-DeKalb, Ga.	N121SG
☐ N717D	94	Citation V Ultra	560-0275	Seven D Industries LP/Degol Aviation Inc. Huntingdon, Pa.	N560LT
☐ N717DD	04	Hawker 400XP	RK-389	Pluck Air LLC/Tony Downs Food Co. St James, Mn.	N50727
☐ N717DM	82	Citation II	550-0436	GRM Aviation Inc. Novato, Ca.	N711Z
☐ N717DT	80	Citation II	550-0167	Daystar TV Network/Word of God Fellowship, Fort Worth, Tx.	N100CJ
☐ N717DX	02	Gulfstream 4SP	1493	Dick's Sporting Goods Inc. Allegheny County, Pa.	N235DX
☐ N717EA	02	Beechjet 400A	RK-354	Earnhardt Aviation LLC. Scottsdale, Az.	N5084U
☐ N717EB	82	Learjet 55	55-016	Glo LLC. Engelewood, Co.	N717EP
☐ N717EP	07	Gulfstream G150	222	Ossian Airways III Inc/JetSmart Inc. Rochester, NY.	N422GA
☐ N717FF	01	Learjet 60	60-213	Duty Free Aviation LLC. Fort Lauderdale, Fl.	N14T
☐ N717GK	01	Citation Bravo	550-0971	Gould Investment Management LLC. Bellevue, Wa.	N717KQ
☐ N717HA	02	CitationJet CJ-2	525A-0079	Reliant Air Charter Inc. Danbury, Ct.	N117W
☐ N717HB	83	Learjet 55	55-066	HBE Corp. Chesterfield, Mo.	N50DD
☐ N717JM	86	Citation III	650-0138	Premier Jet Services LLC. Coral Gables, Fl.	N35PN
☐ N717LA	80	Falcon 50	32	Papalote Aviation LLP/Miller of Dallas, Dallas, Tx.	N80TR
☐ N717LC	81	Citation II	550-0390	Lockard Development Inc. Waterloo, Ia.	N14RZ
☐ N717MB	00	Citation Excel	560-5114	MPW Industrial Services Group, Newark-Heath, Oh.	N20SB
☐ N717MT	89	BAe 125/800A	NA0443	TTG Enterprises LLC. White Plains, NY.	N360DE
☐ N717NA	01	CitationJet CJ-1	525-0437	Omega Industries Inc. Las Vegas, Nv.	N5185V
☐ N717NB	07	Citation Excel XLS	560-5694	Bolthouse Properties LLC. Bakersfield, Ca.	N5072X
☐ N717TG	01	Beechjet 400A	RK-320	PrivatAir Ltd. Bahamas.	N4469E
☐ N717VB	02	CitationJet CJ-2	525A-0137	Starlight Air LLC. Tacoma Narrows, Wa.	N.....
☐ N717VL	04	Citation Bravo	550-1108	Mustang Interests LLC. Odessa, Tx.	N5181U
☐ N718CK	82	Citation II	550-0368	Excel Credit Inc. Longwood, Fl.	N94MF
☐ N718DW	00	Gulfstream 4SP	1442	Colleen Corp. Philadelphia, Pa.	N345LC
☐ N718GM	96	Gulfstream 4SP	1294	Triangle Air Services Inc. Oxford, Ct.	HZ-KAA
☐ N718HC	85	BAe 125/800B	258040	Noblestar Consulting Inc. Dallas, Tx.	N713HC
☐ N718JS	69	Gulfstream 2	66	SEI-Sykes Enterprises Inc. Tampa, Fl.	N165U
☐ N718KS	04	Falcon 2000	216	KSI Services Inc. Dulles, Va.	F-WWVD
☐ N718MC	05	Gulfstream G550	5061	Radical Ventures LLC. Dallas, Tx.	N961GA
☐ N718MN	05	Citation Sovereign	680-0043	Foxy Air LLC/Nami Resources LLC. London, Ky.	N5233J
☐ N718QS	06	Gulfstream G200	136	NetJets, Port Columbus, Oh.	N436GA
☐ N718SA	81	Citation 1/SP	501-0179	DeNova Homes, Pleasant Hill, Ca.	(N406RH)
☐ N718SJ	05	Hawker 800XP	258718	Guatemala City, Guatemala.	N718XP
☐ N719CC	80	Westwind-1124	290	Bears Aviation LLC. Wilmington, De.	N800JJ
☐ N719D	94	CitationJet	525-0075	Sturgis Iron & Metal Co. Sturgis, Mi.	N719L
☐ N719EL	06	Hawker 400XP	RK-488	Edra Lauren Leasing/Donington Aviation, East Midlands, UK.	
☐ N719L	01	390 Premier 1	RB-25	North American Air Charter Corp. Marlborough, Ma.	(N713L)
☐ N719QS	07	Gulfstream G200	162	NetJets, Port Columbus, Oh.	N562GA
☐ N719RM	90	Citation V	560-0092	Friedman, Fleischer & Lowe LLC. Novato, Ca.	XB-RTT
☐ N719SQ*	74	Gulfstream 2B	154	SA Holding LLC. Allentown, Pa.	N719SA
☐ N720AS	06	Challenger 604	5653	Hawkjet Ltd. Hamilton, Bermuda.	C-FIMF
☐ N720C	73	Citation	500-0073	M Mirage Inc. Rockford, Il.	C-FKMC
☐ N720CC	00	Learjet 45	45-072	Carlisle Flight Services Inc. Syracuse, NY.	I-ERJC
☐ N720CH	99	BBJ-7AK	29866	N720CH Inc. Dover, De.	HB-IIP
☐ N720DF	74	Falcon 10	26	Saturn Aviation Inc. Fort Wayne, In.	N707AM
☐ N720DR	77	Gulfstream II SP	209	E R Aviation LLC. Salt Lake City, Ut.	N277T
☐ N720GM	99	CitationJet	525-0350	GEM Property Management Inc. Scottsdale, Az.	N1848T
☐ N720JC	72	Falcon 20F-5	273	Minnesota Choice Aviation LLC. St Paul, Mn.	N596DA
☐ N720JW	76	Gulfstream II SP	178	Lone Star Land & Cattle Co. Conroe, Tx..	N42LC
☐ N720LH	78	Gulfstream 2TT	233	Foxfire Aviation LLC. Henderson, Nv.	N233RS
☐ N720MC	00	Learjet 45	45-103	MKC Consolidated LLC. Addison, Tx.	(N412F)
☐ N720ML	02	Falcon 900EX	115	Northwestern Mutual Life Insurance Co. Milwaukee, Wi.	F-WWFN
☐ N720MM	02	BBJ-7BC	33010	MGM Mirage Inc. Las Vegas, Nv.	N4476S
☐ N720PT	78	HS 125/700A	NA0223	Pinnacle Trading LLC. Fresno, Ca.	N154JD
☐ N720PW	60	B 720-023B	18021	Pratt & Whitney Canada Inc. Montreal, PQ. Canada.	C-FWXI
☐ N720QS	03	Gulfstream G200	085	NetJets, Port Columbus, Oh.	N285GA
☐ N720TA	97	Hawker 800XP	258320	Flight Options LLC. Cuyahoga County, Oh.	(N813LX)
☐ N720WS	03	Global 5000	9176	American International Group Inc. Teterboro, NJ.	C-FCUK
☐ N720WW	79	Learjet 35A	35A-254	WPW Aircraft LLC. Scottsdale, Az.	N254US
☐ N721BS	04	Gulfstream G400	1516	Golden Gaming Inc. Las Vegas, Nv.	N400GA
☐ N721CC	93	Citation II	550-0721	Munoco LC. El Dorado, Ar.	N1207B
☐ N721CN	77	Gulfstream II SP	206	J I Aviation LLC/Apex Oil Co. St Louis, Mo.	N900BF

Reg	Yr	Type	c/n	Owner/Operator	Prev Regn
N721CP	97	Learjet 45	45-006	Lear 006 Holding Ltd. Fort Lauderdale, Fl.	N456LM
N721CX	69	DC 8-72CF	46013	Air Transport International LLC.	F-RAFG
N721DR	80	Citation II	550-0164	Citation Partners Inc. Fort Lauderdale, Fl.	N916RC
N721EC	80	Learjet 35A	35A-355	East Coast Jets Inc. Allentown, Pa.	N351WB
N721FA	87	Beechjet 400	RJ-21	Fish Fly LLC. Nashville, Tn.	N3121B
N721FF	01	Gulfstream 4SP	1484	Frank Fertitta Enterprises Inc. Las Vegas, Nv.	N484GA
N721G	92	Challenger 601-3A	5109	Abbey Challenger LLC. Bedford, Ma.	N721S
N721HM	96	Falcon 900B	158	Quantitative Financial Strategies, Stamford, Ct.	N404VC
N721J	04	Challenger 604	5590	Starbucks Coffee Co. Seattle, Wa.	C-GLXY
N721LH	73	HS 125/600A	256025	NAT Aviation USA Inc. Miami, Fl.	C-GTPC
N721LR	86	Citation S/II	S550-0118	Patch Air Inc. Titusville, Fl.	N100LH
N721MC	89	Gulfstream 4	1110	MCA Capital Corp. Missoula, Mt.	N888MX
N721MF	81	B 727-2X8	22687	Wedge Group Europe, Paris, France.	N4523N
N721MJ	99	Learjet 60	60-159	Maui Jim Inc. Peoria, Il.	N43QF
N721MM	00	Gulfstream V	613	MGM Mirage Inc. Las Vegas, Nv.	N504QS
N721NB	04	Citation Encore	560-0659	First National Bank Group Inc. McAllen, Tx.	N191KL
N721PA	65	JetStar-731	5054	Trump International Sonesta Resort, Sunny Isles Beach, Fl.	N354CA
N721QS	04	Gulfstream G200	092	NetJets, Port Columbus, Oh.	N492GA
N721RL	99	Gulfstream 4SP	1394	High Tech Aircraft Corp. Portsmouth, NH.	N394GA
N721RM	75	HS 125/600B	256053	Servicios Aereos Profesionales Inc. Carolina, PR.	N5NR
N721S	01	Gulfstream V	668	Starbucks Coffee Co. Seattle, Wa.	N568GA
N721ST	81	Challenger 600S	1030	Cusick Aviation LLC/Benefit Planners Ltd. Boerne, Tx.	N630BB
N721T	01	Citation Bravo	550-0993	Sadler/Chauncey LLC. Scottsdale, Az.	N5244W
N721VT	01	Citation X	750-0167	V T Inc. Kansas City, Mo.	N4165Y
N722A	90	BAe 125/800A	NA0461	ARAMCO Associated Co. Dhahran, Saudi Arabia.	N461W
N722AZ	00	Gulfstream G100	132	Sentinel Air LLC. Rutherford, Ca.	N775DF
N722CC	84	Hawker 800SP	258008	Victorair Corp. Fort Lauderdale, Fl.	G-5-11
N722DJ	81	Challenger 600S	1029	Djurin Aviation Inc/DB Aviation Inc. Waukegan, Il.	N600TN
N722EM	85	Learjet 25D	25D-372	SBS & DH Aviation LLC. Salt lake City, Ut.	N5NC
N722HP	86	Challenger 601	3054	HSPT LLC/HSP Group Carlsbad, Ca.	N50TG
N722JB	95	Falcon 2000	13	Clos de Berry Management Ltd. Dayton, Oh.	N2004
N722MM	07	Gulfstream G350	4086	Mandalay Base Hotel/MGM Mirage Inc. Las Vegas, Nv.	N486GA
N722Q	58	MS 760 Paris	9	David Bennett/Executive Aero, Colorado Springs, Co.	N334RK
N722QS	04	Gulfstream G200	093	NetJets, Port Columbus, Oh.	N393GA
N722SG	94	CitationJet	525-0088	Southwest Gas Corp. Las Vegas, Nv.	N188CJ
N722SM	06	CitationJet CJ2+	525A-0338	Granite Aviation Inc. Tamiami, Fl.	N.....
N722SW	07	Gulfstream G150	230	Stedman West Interests Inc. Houston, Tx.	N630GA
N722TS	02	CitationJet CJ-2	525A-0138	Harden Aviation LLC. Haleyville-Posey Field, Al.	N.....
N723AB	06	Global 5000	9207	NAB LLC/Braman Automotive Management, Opa Locka, Fl.	C-FIIC
N723CC	82	Learjet 55	55-036	Valor Management Corp. Chicago, Il.	N155HM
N723HA	07	Challenger 605	5718	Hawker 723 Holdings Inc. Fort Lauderdale, Fl.	C-FNTM
N723HH	94	Challenger 601-3R	5165	Hawker 723 Holdings Inc. Fort Lauderdale, Fl.	N723HA
N723JR	81	Citation 1/SP	501-0190	Allsup's Convenience Stores Inc. Clovis, NM.	N40AW
N723JW	67	Learjet 24	24-142	Charter Airlines Inc. Las Vegas, Nv.	N777MR
N723LK*	89	Hawker 800SP	258155	Pinnacle Entertainment Inc. Las Vegas, Nv.	N702PE
N723MM	07	Gulfstream G350	4077	Mandalay Base Hotel/MGM Mirage Inc. Las Vegas, Nv.	N377GA
N723QS	04	Gulfstream G200	099	NetJets, Port Columbus, Oh.	N499GA
N723RE	00	Citation Bravo	550-0944	Edinton Holdings USA Inc. Guatemala City, Guatemala.	N5267J
N724AF	99	Global Express	9031	Vulcan Northwest Inc. Seattle-Tacoma, Wa.	N700FN
N724AS	76	Falcon 10	83	Union Air LLC/Jetway Flight Corp. Camp Douglas, Wi.	N76MB
N724B	77	HS 125/700A	NA0204	BOY-CEN Air LLC. Traverse City, Mi.	G-BERX
N724CC	98	Citation X	750-0062	Clear Channel Communications Inc. San Antonio, Tx.	
N724CL	66	B 727-21	19121	Clay Lacy Aviation Inc. Van Nuys, Ca.	N299LA
N724CP	74	Falcon 20F-5B	319	Centra Properties LLC. Las Vegas, Nv.	N205K
N724DB	93	Gulfstream 4SP	1209	N724DB LLC/Ginader Jones & Co LLP. Philadelphia, Pa.	N157H
N724DS	69	Falcon 20D-5B	198	Amjet Aviation Co. Atlanta, Ga.	N339TG
N724EA	80	HS 125/700A	NA0264	Ace Boca Aviation LLC. Wilmington, De.	N161WC
N724EH	05	Citation Bravo	550-1113	Holm Improvement Inc. Maitland, Fl.	N5218R
N724FS	00	CitationJet CJ-1	525-0387	Frank Ford Smith Jr. Austin, Tx.	N7715Y
N724HB	89	Beechjet 400	RJ-55	AirLouie LLC. Tampa, Fl.	N780GT
N724JC	74	Falcon 20E-5B	310	Cardinal LLC. Naples, Fl.	N31FJ
N724KW	99	Beechjet 400A	RK-263	MidAmerican Holding Co. Kansas City, Mo.	N724MH
N724MF	05	Challenger 604	5631	MBF Healthcare Management LLC. Fort Lauderdale, Fl.	C-GLXS
N724QS	04	Gulfstream G200	100	NetJets, Port Columbus, Oh.	N500GA
N724SC	05	Challenger 300	20072	SunCal Management LLC. Santa Ana, Ca.	C-G...
N724TS	69	HS 125/731	NA724	New Light Church World Outreach Centre, Houston, Tx.	C-FSDH

Reg	Yr	Type	c/n	Owner/Operator	Prev Regn
☐ N725CC	93	Citation II	550-0725	Air Fred LLC. Fresno, Ca.	N222FA
☐ N725CF	07	Challenger 300	20186	Moreno Energy Services, Lafayette, La.	C-FQEI
☐ N725CS	05	Hawker 850XP	258758	C & S Wholesale Grocers Inc. Keene, NH.	N37158
☐ N725DM	81	Falcon 10	184	Roppe Corp. Columbus, Oh.	N4AC
☐ N725DS	97	Citation Bravo	550-0822	Data Sales Financial Co. Burnsville, Mn.	N2029E
☐ N725FL	82	Citation II	550-0369	Aircraft Management Holdings Inc. Wilmington, De.	N725BF
☐ N725JG	79	Falcon 20F-5B	416	25 Hitman JG LLC. Henderson, Nv.	N416F
☐ N725LB	02	Global Express	9129	Moore Capital Management LLC. New York, NY.	N700FZ
☐ N725MK	02	JetStar-731	5123	Ken Sale Resources Inc. Hillsborough, Ca.	(N425MK)
☐ N725MM	07	Gulfstream G550	5161	Mandalay Resort Group, Las Vegas, Nv.	N261GA
☐ N725PA	90	Falcon 50	204	Peregrine Aviation Services Inc. Teterboro, NJ.	EC-HHS
☐ N725QS	04	Gulfstream G200	105	NetJets, Port Columbus, Oh.	N305GA
☐ N725SC	96	Learjet 60	60-083	SunCal Management LLC. Santa Ana, Ca.	N255RK
☐ N725ST	80	Learjet 35A	35A-285	Sontan Investments LLC. Kenansville, NC.	(N528VP)
☐ N725TA	96	Hawker 800XP	258297	Flight Options LLC. Cuyahoga County, Oh.	(N843LX)
☐ N725XL	07	Citation Excel XLS	560-5725	Derek Stimson Holdings Ltd. Lethbridge, AB. Canada.	N5260U
☐ N726AG	05	CitationJet CJ-3	525B-0029	Infinity Aviation Inc. St Augustine, Fl.	N......
☐ N726AM	93	Citation II	550-0726	AM Aircraft LLC. Las Vegas, Nv.	N726BM
☐ N726CL	00	CitationJet CJ-1	525-0420	Createc Lewis Flight Services Inc. Indianapolis, In.	N86SK
☐ N726DC	02	Gulfstream G200	058	DC Aviation LLC/Hexagon Investments Inc. Denver, Co.	N272MW
☐ N726JR	71	Sabre-75	370-4	Jet Lease Corp. Bradenton, Fl. (status ?).	(N404DB)
☐ N726PG	02	Beechjet 400A	RK-337	Wheless Industries Inc. New Orleans, La.	N5037L
☐ N726QS	04	Gulfstream G200	108	NetJets, Port Columbus, Oh.	N508GA
☐ N726RP	02	CitationJet CJ-2	525A-0114	SabrAir LLC/Capitva Corp. Denver, Co.	N......
☐ N726RW	88	Gulfstream 4	1039	N444SS LLC. Manhattan Beach, Ca.	N1901M
☐ N726SC	94	CitationJet	525-0051	Arkansas Air Venture LLC/U S Renal Care, Jonesboro, Ar.	N808HS
☐ N726WR	68	Learjet 25	25-007	Aviation Equipment Resources Inc. Van Nuys, Ca.	(N58JA)
☐ N727AH	67	B 727-21	19261	Paxson Communications Management Co. West Palm Beach, Fl.	N727PX
☐ N727AT	80	Westwind-1124	284	RHF Ventures, Stockton, Ca.	N217BL
☐ N727AW	87	Citation III	650-0132	Alpha Whiskey LLC. Topeka-Forbes Field, Ks.	N49SM
☐ N727BT	93	Learjet 31A	31A-082	Wal-Mart Stores Inc. Rogers, Ar.	PT-MVI
☐ N727C	84	Citation II	550-0485	Sunset Aviation LLC. Lebanon, Ms.	PT-WBV
☐ N727EC	64	B 727-30	18365	Aircraft Guaranty Corp. Houston, Tx. (trustor ?).	N700TE
☐ N727EF	85	Citation S/II	S550-0043	Amici 727EF LLC. Horseheads, NY.	N727NA
☐ N727GG	66	B 727-95	19252	Trans Gulf Corp. Clearwater, Fl.	HZ-WBT2
☐ N727KG	05	390 Premier 1A	RB-143	Stony Point Group, Asheville, NC.	N61948
☐ N727LJ	69	Learjet 25	25-028	Anthony Aviation Center Inc. Pompano Beach, Fl.	N33PF
☐ N727LM	80	Learjet 25D	25D-308	L & M Forwarding Inc. Laredo, Tx.	N102RR
☐ N727MG	80	Learjet 35A	35A-320	Air Center Helicopters Inc. St Thomas, USVI.	N32PJ
☐ N727MH	06	390 Premier 1	RB-158	Mango Air Inc/Mangano Homes Inc. San Luis Obispo, Ca.	N36758
☐ N727NY	73	B 727-232	20646	727 Exec-Jet LLC. Wilmington, De.	N59792
☐ N727PN	70	B 727-17	20327	WFBNW NA. Salt Lake City, Ut. (trustor ?).	N624VA
☐ N727QS	05	Gulfstream G200	113	NetJets, Port Columbus, Oh.	N413GA
☐ N727TK	74	Citation Eagle SP	500-0141	GE Engine Services, Tempe, Az. (status ?).	XB-EWQ
☐ N727VJ	67	B 727-44	19318	N727VJ Inc. Wilmington, De.	N44MD
☐ N727YB	07	CitationJet CJ-3	525B-0171	Yellowdog Aviation LLC. Hartford, Ct.	N5172M
☐ N728A	69	DC 8-72	46081	ARAMCO Associated Co. Houston, Tx.	N8971U
☐ N728CL*	95	Learjet 31A	31A-109	Mile High Executive Group LLC. Centreville, De.	N882JD
☐ N728GH	86	Falcon 900B	3	GMH Communities, Coatsville, Pa.	N991RF
☐ N728JC	78	Falcon 20-5	399	Jet Choice Inc. St Paul, Mn.	N21FE
☐ N728LB	96	Gulfstream 4SP	1296	Jetstream Ventures LLC. Wilmington, De.	N725LB
☐ N728LW	78	Falcon 50	3	Laurence Carr, Anchorage, Ak.	N8805
☐ N728MB	85	Westwind-Two	419	Air Justice LLC/Lundy & Davis LLP. Lake Charles, La.	N411HB
☐ N728MC	79	Citation 1/SP	501-0115	Polymer Compounds Inc. Coral Gables, Fl.	N95RE
☐ N728MG	81	Learjet 55	55-004	Jet Partners LLC. Teterboro, NJ.	N155PJ
☐ N728PH	06	Embraer Legacy 600	14500985	BHM-SCM Services LLC. Ronkonkoma, NY.	PT-SKB
☐ N728QS	05	Gulfstream G200	116	NetJets, Port Columbus, Oh.	N216GA
☐ N728TA	98	Hawker 800XP	258364	Flight Options LLC. Cuyahoga County, Oh.	(N817LX)
☐ N728TG	84	Westwind-Two	420	Geneva Woods Pharmacy Inc. Anchorage, Ak.	N91SA
☐ N729AG	05	Hawker 850XP	258729	Monsanto Co. St Louis, Mo.	N729XP
☐ N729AT	99	Hawker 800XP	258402	Sinercon SA. Santo Domingo, Dominican Republic.	N23550
☐ N729EZ	89	BAe 125/800A	NA0442	Samuel Zell, Chicago-Midway, Il.	N729HZ
☐ N729HZ	92	Challenger 601-3A	5107	Samuel Zell, Chicago-Midway, Il.	N417CL
☐ N729KF	05	Global 5000	9172	THF Realty/KW Flight LLC. Bozeman, Mt.	C-FCTK
☐ N729KP	01	Challenger 604	5513	Tapaj Inc. Morristown, NJ.	N729KF
☐ N729LJ	06	Learjet 60	60-298	Wijaya Baru Aviation Sdn Bhd. Malaysia.	

Reg	Yr	Type	c/n	Owner/Operator	Prev Regn
N729QS	05	Gulfstream G200	118	NetJets, Port Columbus, Oh.	N118GA
N729SB	04	Learjet 45	45-254	Sky Blue Aviation LLC. Santa Ana, Ca.	
N729TY	90	Gulfstream 4	1141	Tyco International Ltd. Portsmouth, NH.	N115FL
N730BH	03	Embraer Legacy 600	145730	Briad Restaurant Group, Florham Park, NJ.	PT-SHG
N730CA	80	Westwind-Two	295	Byram Asgar Aviation LLC. Austin, Tx.	N555CW
N730DF	93	Astra-1125SP	067	Dunn Diehl Farms LLC. St Petersburg, Fl.	N46386
N730LM	01	Falcon 900EX	101	Liberty Media Group. Englewood, Co.	(N875F)
N730M	94	Learjet 60	60-048	Monomy Investments LLC. Shaker Heights, Oh.	N648LJ
N730MM	08	BBJ-75G/W	36852	MGM Mirage Inc. Las Vegas, Nv.	
N730QS	05	Gulfstream G200	120	NetJets, Port Columbus, Oh.	N220GA
N731DC	05	Challenger 300	20073	Corus Estates & Vineyards, Seattle, Wa.	(N731BF)
N731GA	90	Learjet 31	31-024	Global Aviation 1 Inc. Dover, De.	XA-MRS
N731PS	07	Hawker 400XP	RK-543	PLS Properties LLC. Las Vegas, Nv.	
N731QS	05	Gulfstream G200	123	NetJets, Port Columbus, Oh.	N223GA
N731TA	00	Beechjet 400A	RK-273	Flight Options LLC. Cuyahoga County, Oh.	(N433LX)
N731WH	06	CitationJet CJ-3	525B-0112	Whittier Health Network, Lawrence, Ma.	N.....
N732JR	04	Citation Excel XLS	560-5503	FJL Leasing Corp. Cincinnati, Oh.	N503XS
N733A	04	Hawker 800XP	258687	Humana Inc. Louisville, Ky.	N61987
N733CF	90	Challenger 601-3A	5057	C R Bard Inc. Morristown, NJ.	N830CD
N733E	82	Learjet 55	55-057	Fisher Aviation LLC/IJA, Denver, Co.	N733EY
N733H	02	Hawker 800XP	258590	Humana Inc. Louisville, Ky.	(N590VC)
N733K	93	Falcon 50	242	Humana Inc. Louisville, Ky.	N733N
N733M	05	Falcon 50EX	343	JAPC Inc. Louisville, Ky.	N343EX
N733PA	86	B 737-205	23466	CONOCO-Phillips Alaska, Anchorage, Ak.	N733AR
N733SW	92	Learjet 60	60-007	Sunway Hotel Group, Olathe, Ks.	N760CF
N733TA	97	Hawker 800XP	258337	Flight Options LLC. Cuyahoga County, Oh.	(N815LX)
N734DB	84	Falcon 200	500	DHB Consulting Group Inc. Brookfield, Wi.	C-GRPM
N736BP	86	B 737-205	23465	CONOCO-Phillips Alaska, Anchorage, Ak.	LN-SUU
N736LE	69	HS 125/731	NA736	Lady Edith Hawker Flight LLC/Wittsend Aviation, Wittman, Md.	N800AF
N737A	00	B 737-7AX	30181	ARAMCO Associated Co. Dhahran, Saudi Arabia.	
N737AG	99	BBJ-7BF	30496	Funair Corp. Miami, Fl.	N180AD
N737CC	99	BBJ-74Q	29135	Mideast Jet, Jeddah, Saudi Arabia.	N60436
N737DB	06	BBJ-7EG/W	35990	Samsung Techwin Co. Seoul, South Korea.	
N737DX	90	B 737-408	24804	Sports Jet LLC/BancBoston Transport Leasing Inc. Boston, Ma.	TF-FIC
N737ER	00	BBJ-7CJ	30754	Boetti Air Inc. Jeddah, Saudi Arabia.	N61MJ
N737GG	99	BBJ-74Q	29136	Mideast Jet, Jeddah, Saudi Arabia. (stored at Geneva).	N1779B
N737M	03	BBJ2-8EQ	33361	EIE Eagle Inc Estab. Luton, UK.	N737SP
N737MM	00	Citation VII	650-7113	737MM LLC. Tacoma, Wa.	N560JB
N737QS	05	Gulfstream G200	127	NetJets, Port Columbus, Oh.	N424GA
N737RJ	82	Citation Eagle II	501-0238	Aviation Equipment Leasing Ltd. Douglas, IOM.	N995PA
N737WH	98	BBJ-75T	29142	Southern Aircraft Services Inc. Fort Lauderdale, Fl.	N700WH
N738A	00	B 737-7AX	30182	ARAMCO Associated Co. Dhahran, Saudi Arabia.	N1785B
N739A	00	B 737-7AX	30183	ARAMCO Associated Co. Dhahran, Saudi Arabia.	N1786B
N739LN*	04	CitationJet CJ-1	525-0541	Monticello Air LLC/AUL Administrators, Napa, Ca.	N458SM
N740BA	97	Gulfstream V	516	Qualcomm Inc. San Diego, Ca.	N555CS
N740E	98	Learjet 45	45-023	Eaton Corp. Cuyahoga County, Oh.	
N740JB*	81	Citation II/SP	551-0359	Ballard Aviation Inc. Wichita, Ks.	N142TJ
N740K	89	Gulfstream 4	1094	Air PC LLC. Littleton, Co.	(N628NP)
N740KG	06	Learjet 40	45-2063	DRG Star Management LLC. Sonoma, Ca.	N240WG
N740SS	98	Gulfstream V	532	Shorenstein Management Inc. San Francisco, Ca.	N282QA
N740TA	96	Beechjet 400A	RK-123	Flight Options LLC. Cuyahoga County, Oh.	N110TG
N740TF	00	Learjet 45	45-074	Clarcor Inc. Rockford, Il.	N815A
N741C	80	Westwind-1124	292	ECP Westwind LLC. Fort Wayne, In.	N292JC
N741CC	97	CitationJet	525-0227	Bell Aviation Enterprises Inc. Anchorage, Ak.	
N741F*	97	Learjet 45	45-011	Eaton Corp. Cuyahoga County, Oh.	N741E
N741MR	74	Falcon 20F	312	BCBG Max Azria Group Inc. Vernon, Ca.	N132AP
N741PC	02	CitationJet CJ-2	525A-0066	Corporacion Mariposa SA. Guatemala City, Guatemala.	N51396
N741TA	98	Beechjet 400A	RK-201	Flight Options LLC. Cuyahoga County, Oh.	(N437LX)
N741TS	07	Challenger 605	5741	Bombardier Aerospace Corp. Windsor Locks, Ct.	C-FQQH
N742AR	06	CitationJet CJ-3	525B-0074	Ahern Rentals Inc. Las Vegas, Nv.	N5221Y
N742E	98	Learjet 45	45-025	Eaton Corp. Cuyahoga County, Oh.	
N742PB	99	BBJ-73U	29200	Chartwell Partners LLC. Burbank, Ca.	
N743A	01	B 737-7AXC	30184	ARAMCO Associated Co. Dhahran, Saudi Arabia.	
N743E	97	Learjet 45	45-016	Eaton Corp. Cuyahoga County, Oh.	
N743JG	02	CitationJet CJ-2	525A-0056	King Air 90B LLC. Chicago-DuPage, Il.	N5202D
N743TA	00	Beechjet 400A	RK-271	Flight Options LLC. Cuyahoga County, Oh.	(N454LX)

Reg	Yr	Type	c/n	Owner/Operator	Prev Regn
N744AT	78	Citation II	550-0017	Air Ambulance by Air Trek Inc. Punta Gorda, Fl.	N771ST
N744DB	95	Learjet 60	60-053	RSJ Industries LLC/Perfect World Air Inc. Westbury, NY.	N360UJ
N744E	07	Learjet 45	45-348	Eaton Corp. Cuyahoga County, Oh.	N4005Q
N744GA	07	Gulfstream G150	244	Gulfstream Aerospace LP. Dallas-Love, Tx.	4X-C..
N744N	93	Learjet 31A	31A-069	Prior Aviation Service Inc. Buffalo, NY.	(N169SC)
N744TA	99	Beechjet 400A	RK-245	Flight Options LLC. Cuyahoga County, Oh.	(N446LX)
N744XP	05	Hawker 800XPi	258744	Universal Health Management LLC. Detroit, Mi.	
N745A	01	B 737-7AXC	30185	ARAMCO Associated Co. Dhahran, Saudi Arabia.	
N745CC	03	Citation Bravo	550-1051	Fred Beans Ford Inc. Doylestown, Pa.	N251CB
N745GA	07	Gulfstream G150	245	Gulfstream Aerospace LP. Dallas-Love, Tx.	4X-C..
N745K	04	Learjet 45	45-245	Koch Industries Inc. Wichita, Ks.	N5010U
N745QS	07	Gulfstream G200	170	NetJets, Port Columbus, Oh.	N370GA
N745RS	88	Gulfstream 4	1063	M Ventures LLC/Wenner Media LLC. Islip, NY.	N720LH
N745SA	99	Learjet 45	45-052	Safe Boats International, Port Orchard, Wa.	ZS-DCT
N745TA	97	Beechjet 400A	RK-145	Flight Options LLC. Cuyahoga County, Oh.	(N425LX)
N745TC	04	Learjet 45	45-260	TennThom Aviation Corp. Smyrna, Tn.	
N745UP	97	Hawker 800XP	258336	Rance King Properties Inc. Long Beach, Ca.	N2286U
N746TA	97	Beechjet 400A	RK-146	Flight Options LLC. Cuyahoga County, Oh.	(N426LX)
N746UP	00	Hawker 800XP	258522	MPM Financial LLC. Burbank, Ca.	N812TA
N747AC	97	CitationJet	525-0202	Going Going Gone LLC. Las Vegas, Nv.	N202CJ
N747AE	24	Gulfstream G550	5065	Servicios Aereos Sudamericanos SA. Buenos Aires, Argentina.	N965GA
N747AN	86	Learjet 55	55-121	Worrell Investment Co. Charlottesville, Va.	N155SC
N747BW	84	Learjet 35A	35A-594	Oxford LLC. Easton, Md.	N410BD
N747CP	83	Learjet 35A	35A-502	Kress Enterprises Inc. Brimfield, Il.	N8565X
N747CX	81	Falcon 20F-5B	442	MorAir Inc/ACXIOM Inc. Little Rock, Ar.	I-SREG
N747DP	02	Learjet 60	60-251	Bretford Manufacturing Inc. Waukegan, Il.	N50458
N747FU	80	B 747SP-27	21992	Sabre Cats, San Jose, Ca.	A40-SP
N747GM	80	Learjet 35A	35A-308	Addison Jet Management Inc. Addison, Tx.	(N7LA)
N747KR	05	CitationJet CJ-3	525B-0015	Lewis Aeronautical LLC. San Antonio, Tx.	N4RH
N747NB	68	Gulfstream II SP	33	New Birth Design Group LLC. Atlanta-Fulton County, Ga.	N926NY
N747RL	04	Citation Sovereign	680-0002	Lewis Energy Group/Lewis Aeronautical LLC. San Antonio, Tx.	(N682CS)
N747RR	94	Beechjet 400A	RK-95	Danny's Aviation LLC. Scottsdale, Az.	HS-UCM
N747RY	79	Learjet 35A	35A-243	Platinum 23 Leasing Co. Fort Lauderdale, Fl.	XA-THD
N747SC	66	Learjet 24	24-019	Dolphin Aviation Inc. Sarasota, Fl.	N100EA
N748MN	78	Gulfstream II SP	215	Merle Norman Cosmetics Inc. Van Nuys, Ca.	N816GA
N748QS	06	Gulfstream G200	157	NetJets, Port Columbus, Oh.	N557GA
N748RE	04	CitationJet CJ-2	525A-0215	Hawk Air LLC. Waukegan, Il.	N.....
N748RM	05	CitationJet CJ-3	525B-0056	Romac Gas Co. Throckmorton, Tx.	N156TW
N748TS	70	HS 125/731	NA748	Mark Soloman, Fort Lauderdale, Fl.	N77WD
N749CP	89	Falcon 50	200	SLMF LLC. Minneapolis-Anoka, Mn.	N595JS
N749DC	96	Citation V Ultra	560-0370	R S & I Inc/Recreational Sports & Imports, Idaho Falls, Id.	N607RJ
N749DX	02	Citation X	750-0173	Dobson Communications Corp. Oklahoma City, Ok.	N173CX
N749GA	03	Gulfstream G100	149	Gulfstream Aerospace LP. Dallas-Love, Tx.	4X-C..
N749GP	97	Falcon 2000	52	Center Air LLC/Center Oil Co. St Louis, Mo.	N212T
N749P	98	Citation X	750-0046	Foster Poultry Farms, Eugene, Or.	N749DX
N749QS	07	Gulfstream G200	165	NetJets, Port Columbus, Oh.	N565GA
N749SS	02	Learjet 60	60-252	Smith Aircraft Leasing LLC. Talledega, Al.	N5051X
N749TA	97	Beechjet 400A	RK-149	Flight Options LLC. Cuyahoga County, Oh.	(N427LX)
N750AJ	00	Beechjet 400A	RK-278	CBS Air LLC/Anthony J Costello & Son Management, Rochester.	N823TT
N750BL	02	Citation X	750-0178	Badger Liquor Co. Fond du Lac, Wi.	N275NM
N750BP	99	Citation X	750-0111	BLR Leasing LLC/Beeler Properties Inc. Sugar Land, Tx.	N5264A
N750BR	82	Falcon 50	131	Carrington Capital Management LLC. Ithaca, NY.	F-GOAL
N750CC	80	Sabre-65	465-37	Marathon Aviation Inc. Georgetown, De.	N750CS
N750CK	92	Citation VII	650-7015	Teena Koury, Burlington, NC.	N817MQ
N750CR*	05	Citation X	750-0248	Hawker Aviation LLC. Bridgewater, Ma.	N48VE
N750CW	96	Citation X	750-0008	Sierra Stellar Inc. Encinatas, Ca.	N708VP
N750CX	93	Citation X	703	Model 750 Citation X with winglets, first flight 25 Sep 07.	
N750DF	84	Falcon 50	140	DF Industries LLC/DFE Partners, Springfield, Ma.	N303JW
N750DM	01	Citation X	750-0146	Morgan's Mach One Machine LLC. Aspen, Co.	N5152X
N750DX	06	Citation X	750-0263	Dick's Sporting Goods Inc. Allegheny County, Pa.	N52609
N750EC	96	Citation X	750-0007	RNW Enterprises LLC. Reno, Nv.	N52655
N750FL	94	Citation V Ultra	560-0268	W I Aviation LLC/Western International, Dallas-Redbird, Tx.	N269CM
N750GF	05	Citation X	750-0244	S'porter Air Inc. Gloucester-Staverton, UK.	N52655
N750GM	98	Citation X	750-0066	General Mills Inc. Minneapolis, Mn.	
N750H	86	Falcon 50-40	171	White Lodging Services, Gypsum, Co.	(N650AS)
N750HS	99	Citation X	750-0103	HealthSouth Aviation Inc. Birmingham, Al.	N96TX

Reg	Yr	Type	c/n	Owner/Operator	Prev Regn
❏ N750JB	98	Citation X	750-0063	Sweatmore Air LLC/DMB Associates Inc. Scottsdale, Az.	N51038
❏ N750JC	86	Falcon 50	162	Jet Choice/Minnesota Choice Aviation LLC. St Paul, Mn.	N244AD
❏ N750JJ	98	Citation X	750-0065	J J Gumberg Co. Pittsburgh, Pa.	(N965QS)
❏ N750NS	01	Citation X	750-0172	Flying Group NV. Antwerp, Belgium.	N5066U
❏ N750PP	84	Citation 1/SP	501-0686	Michael Woods, Petaluma, Ca.	N6763M
❏ N750PT	03	Citation X	750-0222	The Related Companies, NYC.	(N850PT)
❏ N750RA	72	Gulfstream II SP	117	Reliance Aviation Management LLC. Fort Lauderdale, Fl.	N7500
❏ N750RL	97	Citation X	750-0025	Rosebud Air LLC/Westcor Aviation, (2500th Citation built).	N50612
❏ N750RM	75	Learjet 35	35-019	Montis Jets LLC. Coral Gables, Fl.	N157AK
❏ N750SL	87	Citation II	550-0554	Kern Global Service LLC. Bakersfield, Ca.	(N705JT)
❏ N750SP	76	Westwind-1124	198	Watertower Surgicenter, Chicago, Il.	(N750SB)
❏ N750SW	81	Gulfstream 3	338	Safeway Inc. Oakland, Ca.	(N338RJ)
❏ N750TA	99	Beechjet 400A	RK-226	Flight Options LLC. Cuyahoga County, Oh.	N59BP
❏ N750TB	88	Citation II	550-0579	Connector Manufacturing Co. Hamilton, Oh.	N579L
❏ N750TX	01	Citation X	750-0150	Textron Inc. T F Green Airport, RI.	N750MD
❏ N750VP	96	Citation X	750-0022	CKE Restaurants Inc. Santa Barbara, Ca.	(N750AG)
❏ N750WM	04	Citation X	750-0230	WM Aviation LLC/Southland Aviation Corp. Maitland, Fl.	N......
❏ N750XX	99	Citation X	750-0094	Marlis Aviation Inc/Old Orchard Brands, Sparta, Mi.	N51038
❏ N751AC	77	Learjet 35A	35A-101	Golden Flight Enterprises LLC. Wadsworth, Oh.	N721AS
❏ N751BC	06	Gulfstream G200	132	International Bank of Commerce, Laredo, Tx.	N732GA
❏ N751BG	07	Citation Sovereign	680-0181	Melrose Inc. Guatemala City, Guatemala.	N5174W
❏ N751BH	98	Citation X	750-0059	Bob Herd/Ty-Tex Exploration Inc. Tyler, Tx.	(N570BH)
❏ N751GM	02	Citation X	750-0207	General Mills Inc. Minneapolis, Mn.	N5152X
❏ N751JC	82	Falcon 50	129	Minnesota Choice Aviation LLC. St Paul, Mn.	N99JD
❏ N751MT	05	Hawker 800XPi	258751	Michelin North America Inc. Greenville, SC.	
❏ N751NS*	07	Hawker 750	HB-1	National Air Service, Jeddah, Saudi Arabia.	N750HB
❏ N751PJ	60	MS 760 Paris-1R	51	Alexandair Inc. de Kooy/Den Helder, Holland.	No 51
❏ N751PL	02	Citation Excel	560-5237	Preformed Line Products Co. Cleveland, Oh.	N5061W
❏ N751PT	05	Citation X	750-0247	PCMT Aviation LLC. Monterey, Ca.	N5257C
❏ N751TA	99	Beechjet 400A	RK-225	Flight Options LLC. Cuyahoga County, Oh.	
❏ N752AC	77	Learjet 35A	35A-121	Golden Flight Enterprises LLC/Zidd Agency, Medina, Oh.	N43TJ
❏ N752CC	79	Citation II	550-0018	U S Customs Service, Oklahoma City, Ok.	(N3225M)
❏ N752CE	06	Citation Encore+	560-0752	HCW Development Co. Branson, Mo.	N5112K
❏ N752CK	75	Citation	500-0255	Hi-Way Paving Inc. Zanesville, Oh.	N907RT
❏ N752CM	80	HS 125/700A	257082	Foxone 77 LLC. Tulsa, Ok.	N70HF
❏ N752CS	96	Hawker 800XP	258323	Seabury Equipment LLC. Van Nuys, Ca.	N877SL
❏ N752EA	73	Learjet 25B	25B-137	Mike Naughton Ford Inc. Aurora, Co.	N752CA
❏ N752GS	81	Citation II	550-0258	GS Air LLC. Allegheny County, Pa.	N424TG
❏ N752MT	05	Hawker 800XPi	258752	Michelin North America Inc. Greenville, SC.	
❏ N752NS*	07	Hawker 750	HB-2	National Air Service, Jeddah, Saudi Arabia.	N752HB
❏ N752PT	05	Citation X	750-0250	PCMT Aviation LLC. Monterey, Ca.	N52526
❏ N752QS	06	Gulfstream G200	152	NetJets, Port Columbus, Oh.	N152GA
❏ N752S	99	Falcon 2000	82	Shell Aviation Corp. Houston, Tx.	F-WWVB
❏ N753BC	01	Gulfstream G200	049	Wild Wings LLC. Lahaina, Hi.	N751BC
❏ N753BP	01	Learjet 60	60-238	Three Valleys Ranch LLC. Bridgeport, Or.	(N140CT)
❏ N753CC	80	Citation II	550-0109	U S Customs Service, Oklahoma City, Ok.	N2665N
❏ N753CE	06	Citation Encore+	560-0753	Beneto Jet Sales Inc. Sacramento, Ca.	N5095N
❏ N753GJ*	95	Citation V Ultra	560-0306	Amedisys Air LLC. Baton Rouge, La.	(N753GL)
❏ N753JC	80	Falcon 50	25	Jet Choice/Minnesota Choice Aviation LLC. St Paul, Mn.	N502EZ
❏ N753PT	06	Citation X	750-0256	Irongate Capital Partners, Los Angeles, Ca.	N5268A
❏ N754AE	05	Hawker 800XPi	258754	American Electric Power Co. Columbus, Oh.	N37054
❏ N754BA	02	Gulfstream G550	5007	Bank of America NA. Charlotte, NC.	N907GA
❏ N754JB	71	Gulfstream II SP	105	Starwood Aviation Inc. Carson City, Nv.	N711TE
❏ N754PT	06	Citation X	750-0257	XOJET Inc. Sacramento, Ca.	N5090A
❏ N754TS	07	Global Express	9254	Aero Toy Store LLC. Fort Lauderdale, Fl.	C-FMLE
❏ N754WS	78	Learjet 35A	35A-197	Ameriflight Inc. Burbank, Ca.	N754GL
❏ N755A	98	Astra-1125SPX	103	Astra 103 Holdings Inc. Wilmington, De.	
❏ N755BP	81	Citation II	550-0334	Bentley Aviation LLC. Columbia, SC.	N404KS
❏ N755FL	99	Falcon 2000	96	IMG Worldwide Inc. Morristwn, NJ.	N53TG
❏ N755PA	01	Gulfstream G200	042	SanMar Corp. Issaquah, Wa.	N701HB
❏ N755PT	06	Citation X	750-0258	JMP Citation LLC. Miami, Fl.	N5264N
❏ N755QS	07	Gulfstream G200	168	NetJets, Port Columbus, Oh.	N368GA
❏ N755TA	01	Beechjet 400A	RK-324	Flight Options LLC. Cuyahoga County, Oh.	(N470LX)
❏ N755VE	04	Gulfstream G550	5055	Valero Energy Corp. San Antonio, Tx.	N144KK
❏ N755VT	89	Learjet 55C	55C-142	Aerohead Aviation Inc. Scottsdale, Az.	N555MX
❏ N756AF	91	B 757-23A	24923	Bank of Utah, Salt Lake City, Ut. (trustor ?).	N680FM

Reg	Yr	Type	c/n	Owner/Operator	Prev Regn
❏ N757AF	91	B 757-2J4	25155	Vulcan Northwest Inc. Seattle-Tacoma, Wa.	N115FS
❏ N757AL	77	Learjet 35A	35A-130	Mark McDonald, Nashville, Tn.	(N116PR)
❏ N757BD	89	Astra-1125	036	DePonte Investments Inc. Albuquerque, NM.	N230AJ
❏ N757BJ	83	B 757-236	22176	Luxury Air LLC. Charlotte, NC.	N267PW
❏ N757BL	87	BAe 125/800B	258088	Worldwide Aircraft Group LLC. Atlanta-Fulton County, Ga.	G-BTAB
❏ N757CK	89	Citation V	560-0028	Koury Aviation Inc. Liberty, NC.	N6FZ
❏ N757CP	02	CitationJet CJ-2	525A-0069	Falcon LLC. Indianapolis, In.	N51564
❏ N757CX	79	Falcon 20F-5	408	Helms Briscow, Scottsdale, Az.	N408PA
❏ N757M	87	BAe 125/800A	NA0402	Dan Air LLC. Klamath Falls, Or.	N1125
❏ N757MA	97	B 757-24Q	28463	Mideast Jet, Jeddah, Saudi Arabia.	
❏ N757WS	98	Beechjet 400A	RK-169	Williams Marketing Services Inc. Joplin, Mo.	N2329N
❏ N758CC	97	Challenger 604	5353	Challenger Management LLC. Beckley, WV.	VH-LAM
❏ N758CX	98	Citation X	750-0058	Alliance Energy New York, Ogdensburg, NY.	(N87N)
❏ N758PM*	93	Citation V	560-0208	Martin International Resorts & Aviation LLC. Gulf Shores, Al	N208VP
❏ N758QS	07	Gulfstream G200	178	NetJets, Port Columbus, Oh.	N678GA
❏ N758XL	07	Citation Excel XLS	560-5758	Cessna Aircraft Co. Wichita, Ks.	N5214R
❏ N759R	02	CitationJet CJ-2	525A-0086	WCAO Aviation/World Class Automotive Operations, Houston, Tx	N520JM
❏ N760	96	Falcon 900EX	3	Anheuser Busch Companies Inc. St Louis, Mo.	JA50TH
❏ N760AR	61	MS 760 Paris-2B	108	Kevin K Knutsen, Phoenix, Az.	PH-MSX
❏ N760F	59	MS 760 Paris	58	Airborne Turbine LP. San Luis Obispo, Ca.	58
❏ N760FM	62	MS 760 Paris-2	111	FM Aero Inc. Calhoun, Ga.	C6-BEV
❏ N760FR	61	MS 760 Paris-1A	72	National Test Pilots School, Mojave, Ca.	F-BJLV
❏ N760JS	61	MS 760 Paris	88	Your Aircraft Source LLC. Calhoun, Ga.	N626TC
❏ N760PJ	59	MS 760 Paris	27	Relentless Air Racing Inc. San Luis Obispo, Ca.	27
❏ N760PT	06	Citation X	750-0260	XOJET Inc. Sacramento, Ca.	N260CX
❏ N760R	61	MS 760 Paris-2B	104	Upper Limits Sales & Leasing Inc.	N760P
❏ N760S	59	MS 760 Paris	43	B Air Inc. Alexandria, Va.	N760C
❏ N760X	59	MS 760 Paris	28	John Snedden, Sandpoint, Id.	I-SNAI
❏ N761JS	61	MS 760 Paris-1R	82	JSI Holdings Inc. Calhoun, Ga.	No 82
❏ N761KG	05	CitationJet CJ-2	525A-0227	Lake Flyers LLC/Triad Surgical Associates, Winston-Salem, NC	N5174W
❏ N761QS	07	Gulfstream G200	176	NetJets, Port Columbus, Oh.	N276GA
❏ N761X	59	MS 760 Paris	30	N9164Z LLC. Salt Lake City, Ut.	N370AS
❏ N761XP	05	Hawker 850XP	258761	Euston Property Management Ltd. Moscow-Vnukovo, Russia.	
❏ N762EL	01	Learjet 45	45-107	Gainey Transportation Services, Grand Rapids, Mi.	(N145CM)
❏ N763D	89	Citation V	560-0007	B E Richardson Investments, Denver, Co.	N717MB
❏ N763JS	61	MS 760 Paris-1R	92	JSI Holdings Inc. Calhoun, Ga.	No 92
❏ N764JS	61	MS 760 Paris-1R	93	JSI Holdings Inc. Calhoun, Ga.	No 93
❏ N764KF	78	Learjet 25D	25D-234	Temm LLC. Tampa, Fl.	N18BL
❏ N764LA	69	Falcon 20D	211	Royal Air Freight Inc. Pontiac, Mi.	N618GA
❏ N764PT	06	Citation X	750-0264	XOJet Inc. Sacramento, Ca.	N52462
❏ N764RH	76	Learjet 25D	25D-210	Plane Fun Sales LLC. Memphis, Tn.	N75TJ
❏ N765JS	61	MS 760 Paris-1R	94	JSI Holdings Inc. Calhoun, Ga.	No 94
❏ N765KC	84	Diamond 1A	A079SA	Kings Bay Airmotive Inc. Tampa, Fl.	N213LG
❏ N765M	05	Gulfstream G200	124	Federated Department Stores Inc. Cincinnati, Oh.	4X-CVF
❏ N765PT	06	Citation X	750-0265	Related Citation LLC. NYC.	N5262Z
❏ N765TS	71	HS 125/731	NA765	Diversified Speciality Institues, Nashville, Tn.	N68CB
❏ N765WT	89	Challenger 601-3A	5039	W W Tichenor & Co/Stargazer Aviation, San Antonio, Tx.	N811BR
❏ N766CE	06	Citation Encore+	560-0766	Cessna Aircraft Co. Wichita, Ks.	N.....
❏ N766HK	85	Falcon 50	161	K H Aviation LLC/H Katz Capital Group, Southampton, Pa.	N770MP
❏ N766JS	67	B 727-27	19535	Aircraft Guaranty LLC. Las Vegas, Nv. (stored SAT).	N60FM
❏ N766MH	83	Citation III	650-0015	Marketing Management Inc. Fort Worth, Tx.	N15QS
❏ N767A	03	B 767-2AXER	33685	ARAMCO Associated Co. Houston, Tx.	
❏ N767BS	01	Citation Excel	560-5191	Briggs & Stratton Corp. Milwaukee, Wi.	N5090A
❏ N767CB	83	Gulfstream 3	397	Tyco Electronics Corp. Harrisburg, Pa.	N692TV
❏ N767CS	05	390 Premier 1A	RB-142	Yosemite Water Co. Long Beach, Ca.	N646S
❏ N767FL	96	Gulfstream V	503	FL Aviation Inc. Morristown, NJ.	N503GV
❏ N767JH	72	Sabre-40A	282-98	Robinson Air Crane Inc. Opa Locka, Fl.	N516LW
❏ N767KS	98	B 767-29N	28270	Mideast Jet, Jeddah, Saudi Arabia.	
❏ N768JJ	06	Gulfstream G250	4064	Julio Inglesias/International Concerts Ltd. Opa Locka, Ca.	N464GA
❏ N768TA	98	Beechjet 400A	RK-168	Flight Options LLC. Cuyahoga County, Oh.	(N429LX)
❏ N769BH	75	Falcon 10	60	Gabriel Investments LLC. Woodbury, Ct.	N69WJ
❏ N769CS	07	Citation Encore+	560-0769	Cessna Finance Corp. Wichita, Ks.	N5241Z
❏ N769H	80	Citation II	550-0158	Honeywell International Inc. Phoenix, Az.	N258CW
❏ N769JW	98	Falcon 2000	72	Devon Energy Management LLC. Wiley Post, Ok.	N96LT
❏ N769MS	81	Westwind-Two	344	Sitrick & Co. Burbank, Ca.	N379AV
❏ N769PT	07	Citation X	750-0269	XOJET Inc. Sacramento, Ca.	N5066F

Reg   Yr   Type   c/n   Owner/Operator   Prev Regn

Reg	Yr	Type	c/n	Owner/Operator	Prev Regn
☐ N769SC	74	Falcon 10	7	Home Solutions of Aventura LLC. Hollywood, Fl.	HB-VKE
☐ N770AF	74	Citation	500-0208	Southern Air Services Inc. Tuscaloosa, Al.	N515WE
☐ N770AZ	78	HS 125/700A	257046	AT Investments & Management LLC. Scottsdale, Az.	N257AM
☐ N770BB	91	B 757-2J4	25220	Yucaipa Management Co. Burbank, Ca.	VP-CAU
☐ N770BC	97	Challenger 604	5352	Franke & Co. Phoenix, Az.	N5352J
☐ N770BM	89	Learjet 35A	35A-654	Heights Aviation, Tucson, Az.	N8189
☐ N770BX	03	CitationJet CJ-1	525-0524	TBMCO Development LLC. Manteo, NC.	N759R
☐ N770CC	02	Hawker 800XP	258587	Newco Management Group LLC. Binghampton, NY.	(N703RE)
☐ N770FG	67	Falcon 20-5B	116	Flynn-Gallagher Associates LLC. Las Vegas, Nv.	F-GLMM
☐ N770GF	83	Citation III	650-0013	Free Green Aviation LLC. Du Page, Il.	N377JE
☐ N770HS	82	HS 125/700A	NA0336	644HH Exchange LLC/Harsch Investment Corp. Portland, Or.	(N778HS)
☐ N770JB*	01	Learjet 60	60-225	Flying G LLC. Atlanta-De Kalb, Ga.	N60TG
☐ N770JD	84	Falcon 50	148	Jesse Duplantis Ministries, New Orleans, La.	N50JQ
☐ N770JM	04	Citation Excel	560-5370	McDonough Capital LLC. Deerfield, Il.	N5270P
☐ N770JP	78	Learjet 35A	35A-210	JEP Development Corp. Dallas, Tx.	N210WL
☐ N770MC	75	Falcon 20F	330	ITTAG LLC/Tensor Engineering, Indian Harbour Beach, Fl.	(N227LA)
☐ N770MD	80	Sabre-65	465-26	Mardal Properties LLC. Islip, NY.	N488DM
☐ N770MP	99	Falcon 2000	99	Air Travel Inc. Islip, NY.	N111VW
☐ N770SC	88	Gulfstream 4	1056	Station Casinos Inc/STN Aviation Inc. Las Vegas, Nv.	N33MX
☐ N771B	79	Westwind-1124	258	Living World International Inc. Saginaw-Tri City, Mi.	N58FB
☐ N771DE	05	Citation Excel XLS	560-5591	DE Executive Aviation LLC. Wilmington, De.	N.....
☐ N771DV	06	Falcon 2000EX EASY	106	Devon Energy Management LLC. Wiley Post, Ok.	F-WWGU
☐ N771JT	05	Gulfstream G550	5089	Windsor Media Inc. Van Nuys, Ca.	N589GA
☐ N771PM	07	Citation Excel XLS	560-5799	Cessna Aircraft Co. Wichita, Ks.	N.....
☐ N771WY*	81	Citation II	550-0264	U S Energy Corp & Crested Corp. Riverton, Wy.	N777WY
☐ N772BC	98	BBJ-73Q	29102	NetJets Large Aircraft Sales LLC. Hartford, Ct.	VT-HSS
☐ N772CS	07	Citation Encore+	560-0772	RGB Enterprises LLC. Locust Grove, Ga.	N5244F
☐ N772JS	07	Challenger 300	20153	HIP Air LLC/Harsch Investment Corp. Portland, Or.	C-FLQZ
☐ N772PP	05	Learjet 60	60-293	Pre-Paid Legal Services Inc. Oklahoma City, Ok.	N60SE
☐ N772PT	07	Citation X	750-0272	XOJET Inc. Sacramento, Ca.	N5200R
☐ N772SB	84	Citation II	550-0498	Bridgeway Enterprises Inc. Spicewood, Tx.	N78FK
☐ N772WH	69	B 737-112	19772	Savannah Aviation LLC. San Antonio, Tx. (stored Tucson ?).	XC-UJL
☐ N773CA	98	Citation Bravo	550-0840	DeJarnette Enterprises Inc. Lee's Summit, Mo.	(N442SW)
☐ N773DL	78	Learjet 35A	35A-174	ICI Realty Inc. Dallas-Love, Tx.	N38AM
☐ N773HR	07	Hawker 850XP	258836	Cipla Enterprises Ltd. Moscow, Russia.	N7236L
☐ N773JC	88	Gulfstream 4	1066	Aero Toy Store LLC. Fort Lauderdale, Fl.	N466TS
☐ N773MJ	93	Gulfstream 4SP	1225	Silver Stream Aviation LLC. NYC.	N816GS
☐ N773RS	06	Learjet 40	45-2046	AirLink LLC/Concord Enterprises Inc. Lincoln, Ne.	N40LJ
☐ N773SW	02	Learjet 60	60-254	Sportsman's Warehouse, St Paul, Mn.	RP-C6003
☐ N774AK	81	Gulfstream 3	339	Mill Creek Systems LLC. Oakland, Ca.	N684AT
☐ N774GE	07	CitationJet CJ-1	525-0457	TX OK Air LLC. Denton, Tx.	N118CS
☐ N774PC	91	Challenger 601-3A	5094	Atlanta Jet Inc. Lawrenceville, Ga.	5B-CKK
☐ N774TS	71	HS 125/731	NA774	North American Air LLC. Hudson, Fl.	G-5-821
☐ N775M	92	Citation VII	650-7017	M & I Marshall & Ilsley Bank, Milwaukee, Wi.	
☐ N775SM	06	Embraer Legacy 600	14500971	Encore 684 LLC. Lewes, De.	PT-SFY
☐ N775ST	97	Falcon 2000	43	Storm Aviation BV. Curacao, Netherlands Antilles.	N86TW
☐ N775TA	00	Beechjet 400A	RK-276	Flight Options LLC. Cuyahoga County, Oh.	(N457LX)
☐ N775TF	07	CitationJet CJ2+	525A-0393	Cessna Aircraft Co. Wichita, Ks.	N.....
☐ N776BG	90	Learjet 35A	35A-659	Rosedale Leasing LLC. Olympia, Wa.	N413LC
☐ N776DF	95	CitationJet	525-0111	Songbird LLC. Bloomfield Hills, Mi.	N52136
☐ N776JB	05	Gulfstream G450	4042	Wilderness Point Associates LLC. Cambridge, Ma.	N442GA
☐ N776JS	82	Learjet 35A	35A-476	Airspeed Holdings LLC. Boca Raton, Fl.	N777LB
☐ N776MA	85	Gulfstream 3	447	Auto Properties II/Atlantic Automotive Corp. Baltimore, Md.	N707JA
☐ N776PT	07	Citation X	750-0276	XOJET Inc. Sacramento, Ca.	N51743
☐ N777AM	89	Astra-1125	038	American Aviation LLC. Eugene, Or.	N930UC
☐ N777AS	98	B 777-24Q	29271	Mideast Jet, Jeddah, Saudi Arabia.	
☐ N777AX	87	Citation S/II	S550-0149	Southeastern Asset Management LLC. Pocohantas, Ar.	N43RC
☐ N777AY	76	JetStar 2	5201	Dezer Properties, NYC.	N745DM
☐ N777CJ	03	CitationJet CJ-2	525A-0182	Bramac LLC/Nuclear Filter Technology, Jeffco, Co.	N.....
☐ N777DB	01	Challenger 604	5502	Cosmos Air LLC/Bigelow Aerospace, Las Vegas, Nv.	N598MT
☐ N777DC	84	Westwind-Two	410	Skyliner Inc/Precision Industries, Omaha, Ne.	N26VB
☐ N777DM	80	Learjet 35A	35A-297	Business Jet Leasing Inc. Salt Lake City, Ut.	N38US
☐ N777DY	03	CitationJet CJ-2	525A-0189	Oregon Flight Services LLC. Portland, Or.	N5124F
☐ N777EH	75	HS 125/700B	257020	Charter Equipment Leasing LLC. Bellevue, Wa.	N311JD
☐ N777EN	07	Citation Encore+	560-0777	Cessna Aircraft Co. Wichita, Ks.	N5216A
☐ N777FC	86	Falcon 200	508	Junisa Inc. Georgetown, Tx.	XA-RKE

Reg	Yr	Type	c/n	Owner/Operator	Prev Regn
☐ N777FD	86	Citation S/II	S550-0099	Lacetos y Camicos San Simon CA. Maracaibo, Venezuela.	N777FD
☐ N777FE	87	Beechjet 400	RJ-30	R Prince Realtors Inc. Discovery Bay, Ca.	N468MJ
☐ N777FL	06	Gulfstream G150	214	Agnes LLC. Ashland, Or.	N314GA
☐ N777FZ	00	Astra-1125SPX	124	Lauren Engineers & Constructors Inc. Abilene, Tx.	N777FL
☐ N777G	07	Hawker 400XP	RK-540	Northwestern Aviation Inc. Des Moines, Ia.	N540RK
☐ N777GA	82	Challenger 600S	1056	Eagle Canyon Leasing Inc. Las Vegas, Nv.	N2HZ
☐ N777GD	81	Challenger 600S	1023	Apollo Aviation LP. Lincoln, Ne.	(N333TS)
☐ N777GG	84	Citation S/II	S550-0012	M G Aviation Inc. Catlettsburg, Ky.	N550RV
☐ N777HD	83	Westwind-1124	397	White Dove Fellowship Inc. Harvey, La.	N11CS
☐ N777HN	02	CitationJet CJ-2	525A-0099	Aeronaves Internacionales SA. Tegucigalpa, Honduras.	N444RH
☐ N777JE	93	Citation II	550-0723	Air Plane LLC. Huntingburg, In.	(N888NA)
☐ N777JF	04	390 Premier 1	RB-105	Kensington Transcom Inc. Gaithersburg, Md.	N5105
☐ N777JJ	72	Citation Eagle	500-0056	Jag Aviation LLC/Panther Helicopters Inc. Belle Chasse, La.	N52ET
☐ N777KK	00	Gulfstream 4SP	1429	Kohler Co. Kohler, Wi.	N429GA
☐ N777KY	75	B 727-2B6	21068	Team Aviation LLC. Charlotte, NC.	N119GA
☐ N777LD	80	Learjet 35A	35A-314	Lowell Dunn Co. Hialeah, Fl.	(N118GM)
☐ N777LX	07	Citation Excel XLS	560-5736	Kean Aviation LLC/Triad Resources Inc. Marietta, Oh..	N52229
☐ N777MC	00	Learjet 60	60-180	Meredith Corp. Des Moines, Ia.	
☐ N777MW	86	Gulfstream 3	485	McWane Inc. Birmingham, Al.	N721CW
☐ N777MX	84	Citation III	650-0051	Duke Woody Aviation LLC. Denver, Co.	N651BH
☐ N777NJ	06	CitationJet CJ-3	525B-0099	Arcon Development Inc/NorthJet Lease LLC. Edina, Mn.	N.....
☐ N777QP	05	CitationJet CJ-2	525A-0241	Airlease Inc. Panama City, Panama.	N52081
☐ N777RN	65	HS 125/1A	25027	Triton Ranch & Cattle Co. Henderson, Nv.	N125BH
☐ N777RW	76	Gulfstream 2	184	Big Play Flight Services LLC. New Orleans, La.	N254CR
☐ N777SL	76	Citation	500-0307	NKC Inc. & WCS Inc. Troy, Al.	N2613
☐ N777TC	90	Gulfstream 4	1137	Luna Entertainment Inc. Pontiac, Mi.	N37RX
☐ N777TX	72	Learjet 25C	25C-084	Z Line Designs Inc. Livermore, Ca.	F-BYAL
☐ N777UT	05	Citation Sovereign	680-0048	ShoDeen Inc. Chicago-Aurora, Il.	N52601
☐ N777VC	06	Learjet 60	60-318	CMK Air LLC/Vencom Group Inc. Vernon Hills, Il.	
☐ N777XS	83	Citation III	650-0008	AJL Leasing LLC. Lakeland, Fl.	N926CR
☐ N777XY	87	Falcon 50	176	Kroll Zolfo Cooper, NYC.	(N711T)
☐ N777YG	95	Challenger 601-3R	5172	GY Challenger 1 LLC. Las Vegas, Nv.	C-FUND
☐ N777ZL	81	Falcon 50	46	Z-Line Designs Inc. Livermore, Ca.	N547K
☐ N778BC	04	Citation Excel XLS	560-5517	Justice Aviation LLC. Beckley, WV.	PR-RAV
☐ N778GM	72	Learjet 25B	25B-078	G M Miller & Co. Suwanee, Ga.	N778JC
☐ N778JA	72	HS 125/731	NA778	BIC Aviation Services LLC. Tulsa, Ok.	N88AF
☐ N778JC	81	Citation II/SP	551-0369	West Star Construction Inc. Kingsburg, Ca.	N68BK
☐ N778PT	07	Citation X	750-0278	XOJET Inc. Sacramento, Ca.	N5203J
☐ N779AZ	95	Challenger 601-3R	5176	Pittco Inc. Memphis, Tn.	N600DH
☐ N779CS	07	Gulfstream G450	4076	Copper Station Holdings LLC. Walterboro, SC.	N376GA
☐ N779DC	84	Diamond 1A	A072SA	Hawkins Air LLC. Omaha, Ne.	N777DC
☐ N779LC	70	Gulfstream 2B	88	Letica Corp. Pontiac, Mi.	N80WD
☐ N780CC	05	Citation Excel XLS	560-5597	Galena Air Services Co. Englewood, Co.	N562CS
☐ N780CE	07	Citation Encore+	560-0780	Cessna Aircraft Co. Wichita, Ks.	N.....
☐ N780CF	78	Citation II	550-0014	CarFaye Inc. Eugene, Or.	N780GT
☐ N780CS	01	Citation Excel	560-5168	Pegasus Air LLC. Scottsdale, Az.	N565DR
☐ N780E	91	Gulfstream 4	1165	IBM Corp. Dutchess County Airport, NY.	N460GA
☐ N780F	97	Gulfstream V	530	IBM Corp. Dutchess County Airport, NY.	N530GA
☐ N780GT	93	Citation VI	650-0222	Air GTI Inc/Gordon Trucking Inc. Tacoma, Wa.	N738K
☐ N780PT	07	Citation X	750-0280	XOJET Inc. Sacramento, Ca.	N5163C
☐ N780RH	02	Gulfstream 4SP	1498	Huffco Group LLC. Houston, Tx.	N398GA
☐ N780SP	91	Falcon 900B	93	Riverside Aviation LLC/Volo Aviation Inc. Bridgeport, Ct.	N900Q
☐ N780TA	99	Hawker 800XP	258437	Flight Options LLC. Cuyahoga County, Oh.	(N825LX)
☐ N781CE	07	Citation Encore+	560-0781	Cessna Aircraft Co. Wichita, Ks.	N.....
☐ N781JR	72	HS 125/731	NA779	Air Bob LLC/The Brossier Co. Winter Park, Fl.	(N989AB)
☐ N781KB	03	390 Premier 1	RB-103	Southeast Kansas Leasing LLC. Pittsburg, Ks.	N701KB
☐ N782BJ	07	Challenger 300	20164	Jerbo Holdings VIII Inc. Waukegan, Il.	C-FNUH
☐ N782CC	93	Citation VII	650-7030	Centcorp Investments Ltd. Miami, Fl.	N95CC
☐ N782GA	07	Gulfstream G550	5182	Gulfstream Aerospace Corp. Savannah, Ga.	
☐ N782ST	91	Citation II	550-0679	Silver Eagle Air Ents/Smith Transport Inc. Rolling Springs.	N622EX
☐ N782TP	99	Beechjet 400A	RK-243	York Aviation Inc. York, Pa.	
☐ N783FS	95	Falcon 2000	9	Farspo LLC/Thornton Aircraft, Van Nuys, Ca.	N209FJ
☐ N783H	91	Citation VI	650-0210	AAN Leasing Inc. Dallas, Tx.	(N650RA)
☐ N783TA	99	Beechjet 400A	RK-234	Flight Options LLC. Cuyahoga County, Oh.	(N418LX)
☐ N783XL	08	Citation Excel XLS	560-5783	Cessna Aircraft Co. Wichita, Ks.	N.....
☐ N784BX	98	Falcon 2000	56	Cockrell Resources Inc. Houston, Tx.	TC-CYL

Reg	Yr	Type	c/n	Owner/Operator	Prev Regn
N784CC	05	Learjet 40	45-2052	Culver Franchising System Inc. Madison, Wi.	
N785QS	07	Gulfstream G550	5157	NetJets, Port Columbus, Oh.	N657GA
N785RC	05	Citation Sovereign	680-0040	C-Jay Aviation LLC. Cartersville, Ga.	N5241R
N785TA	99	Beechjet 400A	RK-239	Flight Options LLC. Cuyahoga County, Oh.	(N444LX)
N785VC	06	Hawker 850XP	258785	Vitesse Charter Management Inc. Greenfield, In.	N785XP
N786AC	06	CitationJet CJ2+	525A-0312	Dr Bernd Schottdorf, Augsburg, Germany.	N5000R
N786CC	99	Learjet 45	45-095	786CC LLC/Dukes Inc. Northridge, Ca.	N409F
N786JB	89	Gulfstream 4	1092	JB Mining Holdings Ltd. Hong Kong.	N515PE
N786YA	00	Learjet 31A	31A-215	Lima Bravo LLC. Sparta, Mi.	(N784LB)
N787CM	94	Hawker 800	258271	Millennium Seismic Ltd. Houston, Tx.	N803CE
N787GT	86	Learjet 55B	55B-128	Greenpoint Air Leasing LLC. Seattle, Wa.	N655GP
N787JC	05	Hawker 800XPi	258727	Johnson Controls Inc. Milwaukee, Wi.	
N787LP	01	Learjet 60	60-248	Southeastern Asset Management Inc. Memphis, Tn.	N248L
N787PR	06	Gulfstream G200	138	Portland Aviation Management Services, Valencia, Venezuela.	4X-C..
N787TA	99	Beechjet 400A	RK-260	Flight Options LLC. Cuyahoga County, Oh.	(N450LX)
N787WH	81	B 737-2V6	22431	Perpetual Motion Inc. Indianapolis, In.	N737WH
N788CG	00	Falcon 900EX	79	Corning Inc. Hamilton, NY.	F-WWFS
N788FS	81	Westwind-Two	319	KAP Aviation LLC/Kessler Schneider & Co. Van Nuys, Ca.	N783FS
N788LS		B 737-3L9	24220	Las Vegas Sands Inc. Las Vegas, Nv.	N232DZ
N788MM	93	Learjet 60	60-016	Aircraft Guaranty Title LLC. Houston, Tx. (trustor ?).	TC-MEK
N789CA	94	Astra-1125SP	074	California Pizza Kitchen Inc. Van Nuys, Ca.	N500AJ
N789CF	66	BAC 1-11/422EQ	119	Kori Air Inc. Reno, Nv.	(N114MX)
N789CN	00	Citation Excel	560-5070	CN Aviation LLC. Santa Ana, Ca.	N507VP
N789DD*	80	Citation II	550-0124	Jim Clark & Assocs Inc. Oklahoma City, Ok.	N109GA
N789DJ	82	Diamond 1A	A015SA	BLB Construction Inc. Baton Rouge, La.	N789DD
N789H	05	Citation Sovereign	680-0041	Honeywell International Inc. Phoenix, Az.	N5200U
N789JC	81	Falcon 50	66	Aviation Partners Inc. Seattle, Wa.	9U-BTB
N789LB	93	BAe 125/800A	258248	Air Group/Superior Industries International Inc. Van Nuys.	N388H
N789MB	04	Challenger 300	20020	Mathis Brothers Furniture Co. Oklahoma City, Ok.	C-GZET
N789ME	98	Falcon 50EX	276	Mid American Energy Holdings Co. Omaha, Ne.	N128M
N789RR*	03	Gulfstream G300	1509	Black Diamond Aviation Inc. Tampa, Fl.	N607KF
N789SG	76	Sabre-60	306-121	Model Transportation LLC. Van Nuys, Ca.	XA-SYS
N789SR	93	Learjet 31A	31A-083	North Slope Borough Search & Rescue, Barrow, Ak.	N40363
N789TA	00	Beechjet 400A	RK-268	Flight Options LLC. Cuyahoga County, Oh.	(N453LX)
N789TT	82	Citation II	550-0343	Tahoe-Teton Associates Inc. Menlo Park, Ca.	G-ORCE
N790AL	85	Citation S/II	S550-0024	Mahon Investments LLC. Columbia, Tn.	N34NS
N790FH	91	Astra-1125SP	056	Frontier Resources LLC. Veneta, Or.	N3175T
N790JC	87	Falcon 900	17	Link Aviation LLC. Wethersfield, Ct.	N944AD
N790JR	84	Westwind-Two	424	Journal Register Co. Trenton, NJ.	N424W
N790L	95	Falcon 2000	15	IBM Corp. White Plains, NY.	F-WWMO
N790M	95	Falcon 2000	19	IBM Corp. White Plains, NY.	F-WWMC
N790PS	94	Citation V Ultra	560-0272	N700PS LLC. San Luis Obispo, Ca.	N700PS
N790SS	03	Hawker 400XP	RK-363	E F Edwards LLC. Orange County-Santa Ana, Ca.	(N363XP)
N790TA	99	Beechjet 400A	RK-252	Flight Options LLC. Cuyahoga County, Oh.	
N790Z	96	Falcon 2000	31	IBM Corp. White Plains, NY.	N2032
N791CP*	75	Falcon 10	54	Applied N America Insurance Brokerage, Atlanta, Ga.	N110LA
N791DM	06	CitationJet CJ2+	525A-0314	MacNeil Automotive Products, Downers Grove, Il.	N1DM
N791TA	95	Hawker 800XP	258291	Flight Options LLC. Cuyahoga County, Oh.	N291SJ
N792CT	94	Challenger 601-3R	5148	Dartswift Inc. Philadelphia, Pa.	N793CT
N792TA	99	Beechjet 400A	RK-264	Flight Options LLC. Cuyahoga County, Oh.	(N428LX)
N793AA	79	Citation 1/SP	501-0106	Citation One LLC. Corolla, NC.	(D-ISKY)
N793BG	83	Westwind-Two	392	SynFuels Holdings Finance LLC. Birmingham, Al.	N95WC
N793CJ	93	CitationJet	525-0021	SelectJet Lease LLC. Mora, Mn.	(N1329G)
N793CS	07	Citation Encore+	560-0793	Cessna Aircraft Co. Wichita, Ks.	N.....
N793CT	06	Challenger 604	5643	Caterpillar Inc. Peoria, Il.	N643CT
N793RC	01	Hawker 800XP	258550	Raymond Transportation Corp. Binghampton, NY.	
N793TA	99	Beechjet 400A	RK-244	Flight Options LLC. Cuyahoga County, Oh.	(N445LX)
N794MH	89	Gulfstream 4	1079	Cinema Aircraft Executive Transport, Hillsboro, Or.	N691RC
N794PF	07	CitationJet CJ1+	525-0649	Prestage Farms of South Carolina LLC. Camden, SC.	N51806
N794SB	90	Challenger 601-3A	5082	SPG Management LLC/Monarch Capital, Dallas-Love, Tx.	N82FJ
N794SC	76	Gulfstream II SP	176	Octagon Properties LLC. Pontiac, Mi.	N794SB
N794TA	00	Beechjet 400A	RK-282	Flight Options LLC. Cuyahoga County, Oh.	(N459LX)
N794TK	82	Westwind-Two	373	Lifestyle Aviation Inc. Coburg, Or.	N555DH
N794VP*	98	Citation VII	650-7094	Cessna Aircraft Co. Wichita, Ks.	N794QS
N795A	81	HS 125/700B	257127	WW Aircraft LLC/Arnweld Building Products, Garrettsville, Oh	HB-VLC
N795BA	04	Gulfstream G550	5031	Bank of America NA. Charlotte, NC.	N931GA

Reg	Yr	Type	c/n	Owner/Operator	Prev Regn
❏ N795BM	01	CitationJet CJ-1	525-0481	Bill Miller Equipment Sales Inc. Eckhart Mines, Md.	N4DF
❏ N795FM	78	Westwind-1124	228	Aero Toy Store LLC. Fort Lauderdale, Fl.	N305BB
❏ N795HG	98	Citation X	750-0053	PGA Tour Air Inc. Ponte Vedra, Fl.	(N795HC)
❏ N795VP	99	Citation VII	650-7095	Cessna Aircraft Co. Wichita, Ks.	N795QS
❏ N796CH	85	BAe 125/800A	258049	White Oak Aviation LLC. Northbrook, Il.	N93CT
❏ N796HR	96	Astra-1125SPX	085	CPX Charter Inc. Covington, Ky.	N796HP
❏ N796TA	00	Beechjet 400A	RK-289	Flight Options LLC. Cuyahoga County, Oh.	
❏ N797BD	83	Gulfstream 3	388	DePonte Investments Inc. Albuquerque, NM.	N8JL
❏ N797CB	07	Challenger 300	20158	H E Butt Grocery Co. San Antonio, Tx.	C-FMXU
❏ N797CC	99	Citation VII	650-7097	On Time Aviation Corp. Riyadh, Saudi Arabia.	N797QS
❏ N797CP	96	Learjet 60	60-086	World Class Automotive Operations, Dallas, Tx.	N797CB
❏ N797CW	81	Citation II	550-0232	U S Customs Service, Oklahoma City, Ok.	N929DS
❏ N797EP	88	BAe 125/800A	NA0426	Cooper/T Smith Stevedoring Co. Mobile, Al.	N726EP
❏ N797HT	02	Falcon 2000	171	HTT Group Ltd. Schaan, Liechstenstein.	F-ORAV
❏ N797M	07	Gulfstream G200	179	Gulfstream Aerospace LP. Dallas-Love, Tx.	N479GA
❏ N797PA	97	Learjet 60	60-098	Schwyhart Holdings LLC. Carrollton, Tx.	N218BX
❏ N797SE	80	Citation 1/SP	501-0151	CMC Aviation LLC. Denver, Co.	N797SF
❏ N797SF	80	Citation II	550-0200	Hilltex Properties Inc/Elite Flight LLC. Addison, Tx.	(N810MG)
❏ N797TA	99	Beechjet 400A	RK-265	Flight Options LLC. Cuyahoga County, Oh.	(N429LX)
❏ N797TE	01	Citation Bravo	550-0962	Tampa Electric/Peoples Gas System Inc. Tampa, Fl.	N5212M
❏ N797WC	00	Falcon 2000	140	Land Sea Air Leasing Corp. Van Nuys, Ca.	N797SM
❏ N797WQ	77	JetStar 2	5216	Pacific Exchange Corp. Van Nuys, Ca.	N797WC
❏ N798PA*	86	BAe 125/800A	258070	Phaeton Aviation Inc. Raleigh-Durham, NC.	N998PA
❏ N798TA	98	Beechjet 400A	RK-198	Flight Options LLC. Cuyahoga County, Oh.	(N436LX)
❏ N799AG*	07	Hawker 900XP	HA-27	Hawker Beechcraft Corp. Wichita, Ks.	N33527
❏ N799JC	01	Hawker 800XP	258544	Xenel Aviation/Xenel Industries Ltd. Jeddah, Saudi Arabia.	
❏ N799RM	04	Hawker 800XP	258708	Red Wings Inc. Panama City, Panama.	
❏ N799S	02	Hawker 800XP	258588	CYMI Investments Sub Inc. Dayton, Oh.	N44888
❏ N799WW	01	Global Express	9092	Wideworld Services Ltd.	N15FX
❏ N800AB*	00	Learjet 45	45-137	Check Clearing House Aviation LLC. Glenwood Springs, Co.	(N45MU)
❏ N800AF	89	Hawker 800SP	258158	Air 4 Aviation LLC/Tri-C Aviation Inc. Houston, Tx.	N158TN
❏ N800AK	68	B 727-23	20045	ARABASCO-Arabian Aircraft Services Co Ltd. Jeddah.	N727WF
❏ N800AL	07	Gulfstream G450	4087	Abbott Laboratories Inc. Waukegan, Il.	N387GA
❏ N800AR	82	Gulfstream 3	362	Perpetual Corp & Lazy Lane Farms, Dulles, Va.	N408M
❏ N800BF	78	Citation 1/SP	501-0080	Bravo-Fox LLC.	N37LA
❏ N800BN	04	Challenger 604	5600	JM Aircraft Ltd/Twinjet Aircraft Sales Ltd. Luton, UK.	C-GLWZ
❏ N800BT	82	Challenger 600S	1044	Direct Jet Services LLC. Kansas City, Mo.	N55AR
❏ N800BV	87	BAe 125/800B	258097	Daybreak Properties Inc/Van Stavern Development, Lebanon, M	N170BA
❏ N800BW	02	Citation Encore	560-0640	Borg Warner Air/Fluid System, Pontiac, Mi.	N640CE
❏ N800CC	94	Hawker 800XP	258266	Charter Communications Inc. St Louis, Mo. (status ?).	N414XP
❏ N800CD	74	Sabre-75A	380-23	Kastlemar Inc/Compson Development Co. Boca Raton, Fl.	N102RD
❏ N800CJ	76	Citation	500-0330	SK Jets Inc. Fort Lauderdale, Fl.	N141SG
❏ N800CK	98	Learjet 31A	31A-157	AXA LLC/South Hill AXA Corp. Klamath Falls, Or.	N125FX
❏ N800CQ	03	Hawker 800XP	258636	Carpau Corp. St Petersburg, Fl.	(N775RB)
❏ N800CS	02	390 Premier 1	RB-62	CAT Scale Co/CS Flight Services Inc. Moline, Il.	N6162Z
❏ N800DA	66	HS 125/1A-522	25047	Dabia Corp. Wilmington, De.	(N717GF)
❏ N800DR	00	Hawker 800XP	258478	Dominion Resources Inc. Richmond, Va.	N806TA
❏ N800DT	81	Citation 1/SP	501-0198	Liberty Press Group, Ardmore, New Zealand.	N198VP
❏ N800DW	68	Falcon 20-5	135	MFB Aircraft LLC. St Louis, Mo.	N194MC
❏ N800E	78	HS 125/700A	NA0240	ExecuFlite LLC. Nassau, Bahamas.	N700HH
❏ N800EC	87	Hawker 800SP	NA0411	Energy Corp of America, Denver, Co.	N600LS
❏ N800EH	01	Beechjet 400A	RK-322	Agri Beef Co. Boise, Id.	N800EL
❏ N800EL	03	Hawker 800XP	258622	American Bizjet Corp. Panama City, Panama.	N622XP
❏ N800EM	03	Hawker 800XP	258649	Killer Creek LLC. St Thomas, USVI.	N649XP
❏ N800FD	98	Hawker 800XP	258390	Federated Investors Inc. Pittsburgh, Pa.	(N800SG)
❏ N800FF	79	Falcon 20F	406	Sutterfield Financial Group Inc. Bartlesville, Ok.	G-BGOP
❏ N800FH	84	BAe 125/800A	258006	G Howard & Assocs Inc. Ronkonkoma, NY.	(N886GW)
❏ N800FL	84	BAe 125/800A	258005	Bir Aviation Corp. Indianapolis, In.	N601UU
❏ N800FM	80	Falcon 50	28	Walker Aircraft LLC/JLT Group Inc. St Paul, Mn.	N47UF
❏ N800FR	06	390 Premier 1A	RB-165	White & Cope Aviation LLP. Luton, UK.	N7165X
❏ N800GA	79	Learjet 28	28-003	Gorilla Aviation LLC/Sullivan Hayes Brokerage, Denver, Co.	N28GW
❏ N800GD	77	JetStar 2	5219	Call Plane Solutions Inc. Waukesha, Wi.	(N5VN)
❏ N800GE	69	HS 125/400A	NA735	Gan Eden Air Inc. Santa Fe, NM.	N165AG
❏ N800GF	94	Beechjet 400A	RK-96	Aero Gat Inc. St Louis, Mo.	N824JM
❏ N800GH	99	Falcon 2000	89	Leading Edge LLC/CSM Corp. St Paul, Mn.	N2000A
❏ N800GJ	80	Learjet 35	35A-352	S P Aviation Inc/Silverado Partners, Hayward, Ca.	N35CZ

Reg	Yr	Type	c/n	Owner/Operator	Prev Regn
N800GM	85	Citation III	650-0077	John Hagee Ministries, San Antonio, Tx.	N701AG
N800GN	98	Hawker 800XP	258372	MS Multiservicios del Sur SA. San Jose, Costa Rica.	LV-ZHY
N800GP	78	Learjet 35A	35A-158	AGA Aviation LLC. Wheeling, Il.	N158NE
N800GW	98	CitationJet	525-0276	Joe Morten & Son Inc. South Sioux City, Ne.	
N800HH	82	Challenger 600S	1074	Aircraft No 1074 LLC. St Paul, Mn.	HZ-RFM
N800HT	05	Hawker 400XP	RK-455	Holliday Companies LLC. Charleston, SC.	N466LX
N800J	97	Gulfstream 4SP	1333	Johnson & Johnson, Mercer County Airport, NJ.	N333GA
N800JH	05	Gulfstream G550	5073	J & J Aviation LLC. Eagle, Co.	N673GA
N800KS	00	BBJ-7BC	30782	Classic Limited Air Inc. Van Nuys, Ca.	N515GM
N800LA	04	Hawker 800XP2	258679	BAe Systems Inc. Dulles, Va.	N800AH
N800LF	00	Hawker 800XP	258492	NADA Airline Inc. Ocala, Fl.	N800FJ
N800LJ	81	Learjet 55	55-009	N800LJ Inc. Coconut Grove, Fl.	N559BC
N800LL	86	BAe 125/800B	258079	Q Air LLC/Executive Fliteways Inc. Ronkonkoma, NY.	9M-DDW
N800LM	81	HS 125/700A	NA0299	Renda Aviation LLC. Grapevine, Tx.	N700NY
N800LQ*	01	Hawker 850XP	258551	Liquid Aviation Inc. San Diego, Ca.	N85594
N800LR	99	Hawker 800XP	258415	Morgan Aviation Group Inc. Luton, UK.	TC-STR
N800LX*	95	Hawker 800XP	258282	Flight Options LLC. Cuyahoga County, Oh.	(N811LX)
N800M	80	Sabre-65	465-41	Fitness Management Corp. West Bloomfield, Mi.	N2556E
N800MJ	92	BAe 125/800A	258226	Gulf Hawk LLC/Panattoni Development Co. Dallas-Love, Tx.	N709EA
N800MT	01	Citation Bravo	550-0981	Maverick Transportation Inc. North Little Rock, Ar.	N313CS
N800NB	97	CitationJet	525-0212	National By-Products LLC. Des Moines, Ia.	N67VW
N800NJ	96	Hawker 800XP	258314	N90BJ Inc. Warsaw, In.	OM-SKY
N800NP	70	HS 125/731	NA758	Air Navigation Corp. Dover, De.	N731MS
N800PA	89	BAe 125/800A	NA0438	O & G Industries Inc. Torrington, Ct.	N753G
N800PC	98	Hawker 800XP	258369	Taughannock Aviation Corp. Tompkins County, NY.	
N800PE	00	Hawker 800XP	258508	PandaAir Corp/Panda Energy Corp. Dallas, Tx.	N5008S
N800PF	05	CitationJet CJ1+	525-0605	PSF Associates LLC. South Hadley, Ma.	N5188A
N800PJ	00	Gulfstream G200	026	Asset Management Co. Palo Alto, Ca.	N56GX
N800PL	04	Hawker 800XP	258696	Computer Associates International Inc. Islip, NY.	N36896
N800PM	78	Gulfstream 2TT	224	PAM Aviation LLC/Phil Mickelson, Scottsdale, Az.	N90CP
N800PP	66	Falcon 20C	44	Company Air, Thousand Oaks, Ca.	(N773HS)
N800PW	96	Astra-1125SPX	079	Au Revoir Ltd. Santa Fe, NM.	C-FCFP
N800QC	89	BAe 125/800A	NA0445	Quikrete International Inc. Atlanta-DeKalb, Ga.	N174NW
N800QS	02	Citation Encore	560-0598	NetJets, Port Columbus, Oh.	N5250P
N800R	04	Hawker 800XP	258694	NASCAR Inc. Daytona Beach, Fl.	N36894
N800RC	04	Hawker 800XP	258660	Rockwell Collins Inc. Cedar Rapids, Ia.	N660XP
N800RF	79	Learjet 25D	25D-281	L25-281 LLC. Fort Lauderdale, Fl.	N555PG
N800RG	92	BAe 125/800A	258230	Glimcher Group Inc. Allegheny County, Pa.	N71MT
N800RK	96	CitationJet	525-0158	VTC Inc/Triple-T Foods Inc. Springdale, Ar.	N800RL
N800RL	04	CitationJet CJ-2	525A-0220	Rice Lake Weighing Systems Inc. Rice Lake, Wi.	N.....
N800RM	83	BAe 125/800B	258001	Romeo Mike Aviation Inc. Fort Lauderdale, Fl.	N801CR
N800RT	69	Gulfstream II SP	47	Robert E Torray & Co. Bethesda, Md.	N800FL
N800S	87	BAe 125/800A	258082	MSI Aviation LLC/Massey Services Inc. Maitland, Fl.	(N601BX)
N800SD	00	Beechjet 400A	RK-270	Burkland Distributors Inc/Bur-Con LLC. Peoria, Il.	N3231H
N800SE	88	BAe 125/800A	NA0425	Shasta Enterprises, Red Bluff, Ca.	N110MH
N800TD	85	Gulfstream 3	452	Oslo Express Inc. Bridgeport, Ct.	N123TL
N800TG	72	HS 125/731	NA780	Dodson Services Inc. Rantoul, Ks.	N265DL
N800TL	99	Hawker 800XP	258394	Air Excellence LLC/The Cedarwood Compnaies, Akron, Oh.	N800ER
N800UK	01	Hawker 800XP	258577	Liberty Aviation Co, Leeds-Bradford, UK.	N51027
N800VA	00	Citation Bravo	550-0956	University of Virginia Foundation, Charlotteville, Va.	N572PB
N800VL*	77	Learjet 35A	35A-127	Aviation Team Inc. Fort Lauderdale, Fl.	N351TX
N800VR	84	Hawker 800SP	258016	Four Twenty One Inc/Veenker Resources, Oklahoma City, Ok.	N816CW
N800VT	02	CitationJet CJ-2	525A-0103	Clausen Investments Inc/V-T Industries Inc. Storm Lake, Ia.	N5218R
N800WA	88	BAe 125/800A	NA0414	Avalon Air Leasing LLC. Nashua, NH.	N4361Q
N800WC	99	Learjet 45	45-094	Air Wolff III LLC. Aurora, Or.	N300JE
N800WD	97	Hawker 1000	259052	Westlake Realty Group, Camarillo, Ca.	N552LR
N800WH	86	BAe 125/800A	258080	G Howard & Assocs Inc. Ronkonkoma, NY.	N800BP
N800WP	00	Hawker 800XP	258459	Aviation Partners of America, Miami, Fl.	N800WW
N800WS	98	Astra-1125SPX	106	SPX Leasing LLC. Cincinnati, Oh.	N800MK
N800WV	87	Beechjet 400	RJ-24	XXtreme Pipe Services LLC. Houston, Tx.	N800WW
N800WW	03	Hawker 800XP	258661	KTW & PNW Transport LLC. Tucson, Az.	N661XP
N800WY	01	Hawker 800XP2	258556	M & N Aviation, Casper, Wy.	N51556
N800XM	99	Hawker 800XP	258414	AEA Services LLC. Saddle River, NJ.	EI-RNJ
N800XP	01	Hawker 800XP2	258541	M & N Aviation, Casper, Wy.	N50441
N800YB	95	Challenger 601-3R	5175	Kentucky Fried Chicken Corp/Yum! Brands Inc. Louisville, Ky.	N601KF
N800ZZ	89	Astra-1125	028	Palm Coast Leasing Inc. Fort Lauderdale, Fl.	N816HB

Reg	Yr	Type	c/n	Owner/Operator	Prev Regn
N801BB	96	Citation Bravo	550-0801	Bandyco LLC. Stanford, Ky.	N5135K
N801CF	90	BAe 125/800A	NA0452	Shuert Industries LLC/Corporate Flight Inc. Detroit, Mi.	XA-SIV
N801CT	90	Learjet 31	31-017	Inter-Tel Technologies Inc. Reno, Nv.	N600AW
N801DL	90	Falcon 50	206	Indefensible Corp. Miami, Fl.	VP-BMF
N801DM	93	B 757-256	26240	Dallas Mavericks/MLW Aviation LLC. Dallas, Tx.	N286CD
N801FT	74	Sabre-75A	380-16	Flight Test Associates Inc. Mojave, Ca.	N12659
N801G	96	Astra-1125SPX	081	Pulice Construction Inc. Phoenix, Az.	N800AJ
N801HB	96	Hawker 800XP2	258327	Dolan Enterprises LLC. Trenton, NJ.	(N219DC)
N801LM	87	Hawker 800SP	NA0409	Livemercial Inc. Valparaiso, In.	N870CA
N801P	90	BAe 125/800A	NA0456	BG Aircraft Leasing LLC. Lyndhurst, Oh.	(N730BG)
N801PN	00	Global Express	9062	Sabrina Aviation Corp. Punta Gorda, Fl.	N700CJ
N801QS	01	Citation Encore	560-0601	NetJets, Port Columbus, Oh.	N5239J
N801RM	84	BAe 125/800A	258011	Image Air LLC. Warsaw, In.	N820GA
N801RS	96	Astra-1125SPX	084	Xtreme Ltd/Agencia Vehiculos Especiales Rurales,	N795HB
N801SA	07	390 Premier 1A	RB-205	Sargeant Marine Inc. Boca Raton, Fl.	N205GY
N801SS	80	Sabre-65	465-40	Stephen Susman PC. Houston, Tx.	N465PM
N801WM	00	Hawker 800XP	258503	Waste Management Inc. Andrau Airpark-Houston, Tx.	N802WM
N801WW	03	Falcon 2000EX	21	Cendant Corp. Teterboro, NY.	N521CD
N802AB	93	Citation V	560-0217	Acorn Leasing LLC. Savannah, Ga.	N602AB
N802CC	76	Gulfstream 2	187	Rubloff Development Group Inc. Rockford, Il.	N202GA
N802CF	99	Hawker 800XP2	258425	MCM Management Aviation LLC. Pontiac, Mi.	N438PM
N802DC	02	Hawker 800XP	258562	Gresham & Assocs Inc. Stockbridge, Ga.	(N877S)
N802DR	04	Hawker 800XP	258667	Dominion Resources Inc. Richmond, Va.	N667XP
N802FT	75	Sabre-75A	380-33	Flight Test Associates Inc. Mojave, Ca.	N7148J
N802HH	02	Hawker 4000	RC-2	Hawker Beechcraft Corp. Wichita, Ks. (Ff 10 May 02).	
N802Q	88	Citation S/II	S550-0157	The Rivett Group LLC. Aberdeen, SD.	N157BM
N802QS	06	Citation Encore	560-0706	NetJets, Port Columbus, Oh.	N.....
N802SA*	05	BAe 125/800A	258045	IOTC Aviation LLC. Boca Raton, Fl.	(N803LX)
N802TA	99	Hawker 800XP	258454	Flight Options LLC. Cuyahoga County, Oh.	(N826LX)
N803E	86	Beechjet 400	RJ-16	Professional Air Services Inc. Bend, Or.	(N440MP)
N803GE	84	Hawker 800SP	258003	Blue Sky Properties II LLC. Miami, Fl.	N583VC
N803HH	02	Hawker 4000	RC-3	Meir Aviation Inc. Luton, UK.	
N803JL	89	BAe 125/800A	NA0436	Access Aviation LLC. Omaha, Ne.	N160NW
N803QS	07	Citation Encore+	560-0775	NetJets, Port Columbus, Oh.	N5211Q
N803RR	90	Challenger 601-3A	5073	Alsco Inc. Salt Lake City, Ut.	N5073
N803SA	07	Hawker 4000	RC-8	Hawker Beechcraft Corp. Wichita, Ks.	(N808HH)
N803SC	89	Citation II	550-0615	STB Aviation LLC. Columbia Metropolitan, SC.	N577VN
N803TA	00	Hawker 800XP	258455	Flight Options LLC. Cuyahoga County, Oh.	(N827LX)
N804AC	98	Hawker 800XP	258368	Albemarle Corp. Richmond, Va.	
N804BC	90	Citation II	550-0627	Clary Aviation LLC/Bud Clary Auto Dealerships, Kelso, Wa.	N650WC
N804BH	02	Hawker 800XP	258596	Mahaska Bottling Co. Oskaloosa, Ia.	N596XP
N804CC	80	Westwind-Two	305	Charles Campbell, Corpus Christi, Tx.	N629WH
N804CE	01	Dornier Do328JET	3184	Cummins Inc. Columbus, In.	N328PM
N804CS	80	HS 125/700A	NA0266	Alpen LLC. Kettering, Oh.	N497PT
N804HH	04	Hawker 4000	RC-4	Hawker Beechcraft Corp. Wichita, Ks. (Ff 29 Apr 04).	
N804JJ	77	Falcon 10	105	Biokine Inc. Lawrenceville, Ga.	N16WJ
N804MR	84	Hawker 800SP	258012	G Howard & Assocs Inc. Ronkonkoma, NY.	(N801LX)
N804MS	93	B 767-3P6ER	27255	Interface Operations LLC. Las Vegas, Nv.	HZ-WBT6
N804PA	79	Sabre-65	465-4	Studer Group Travel LLC. Gulf Breeze, Fl.	N800TW
N804QS	02	Citation Encore	560-0610	NetJets, Port Columbus, Oh.	N52699
N804TF	81	Learjet 35A	35A-404	Lion Aviation LLC. Richmond, Va.	N404DP
N805CJ	05	CitationJet CJ1+	525-0603	Aqua Sun Investments LLC. Ormond Beach, Fl.	N51143
N805HH	04	Hawker 4000	RC-5	Wichita Air Services Inc. Wichita, Ks.	(N974JD)
N805JL	90	BAe 125/800A	258203	CRD Air LLC/Tapalian & Tadros PC. Providence, RI.	N453TM
N805LC	88	Citation II	550-0581	Loraine LLC. Easley, SC.	N905LC
N805LX	98	Hawker 800XP	258374	Flight Options LLC. Cuyahoga County, Oh.	(N818LX)
N805M	05	Hawker 800XPi	258753	Pomeroy Computer Resources Inc. Hebron, Ky.	
N805SM	69	Jet Commander-B	145	RAA Enterprises Inc. Wilmington, De.	N145AJ
N805VC	94	CitationJet	525-0076	Baker Street Air LLC. Albuquerque, NM.	N4TF
N805VZ	99	Challenger 604	5410	Verizon Aviation Corp. Teterboro, NJ.	N199BA
N805WD	71	HS 125/731	NA770	W D Aviation Group Inc. DeKalb, Ga.	N38LB
N806AC	05	Gulfstream G550	5097	Casden Aircraft Leasing LLC. Burbank, Ca.	N550GA
N806AD	07	Citation Excel XLS	560-5743	Advanced Drainage Systems Inc. Columbus, Oh.	N53613
N806CB	65	HS 125/731	25038	CBG Aviation Inc. Miami, Fl.	N42CK
N806LJ	65	Learjet 23	23-073	A Liner 8 Aviation, Livonia, Mi.	
N806LX	98	Hawker 800XP	258383	Lead Eagle Airways LLC. Mullins, SC.	(N819LX)

Reg	Yr	Type	c/n	Owner/Operator	Prev Regn
☐ N806QS	02	Citation Encore	560-0614	NetJets, Port Columbus, Oh.	N5296X
☐ N807BF	76	Westwind-1124	194	BSDF LLC. La Mesa, Ca.	N40TA
☐ N807CC	77	Gulfstream 2TT	212	Lear 35 LLC. Van Nuys, Ca.	N551MD
☐ N807MB	92	Citation II	550-0694	Burford's Tree Surgeons Inc. Birmingham, Al.	N550KE
☐ N807QS	02	Citation Encore	560-0617	NetJets, Port Columbus, Oh.	N5207A
☐ N808AC	95	Citation V Ultra	560-0323	Interwings Aircharter Corp. South Africa.	N323QS
☐ N808BL	03	Hawker 800XP	258634	Bausch & Lomb Inc. Rochester, NY.	
☐ N808CZ	96	Citation X	750-0010	Arrow Trading Inc. Fort Lauderdale, Fl.	N5112S
☐ N808G	91	Challenger 601-3A	5098	Fortune Jet Group, Fort Lauderdale, Fl.	N812GS
☐ N808HG	94	Challenger 601-3R	5157	Kimberly-Clark Integrated Services Inc. Roswell, Ga.	N800KC
☐ N808KS	06	Learjet 45XR	45-305	Barbedos Group, Kaduna, Nigeria.	N45XR
☐ N808MN*	05	Citation Excel XLS	560-5587	Hepar LLC/Mobren Transport Inc. Jefferson, SD.	N806MN
☐ N808QS	02	Citation Encore	560-0619	NetJets, Port Columbus, Oh.	N52135
☐ N808SK	93	Learjet 60	60-008	SK Logistics Inc. St Augustine, Fl.	(N359RM)
☐ N808T	98	Gulfstream 4SP	1342	Odin Aviation Inc. Burbank, Ca.	N555KC
☐ N808TA	01	Hawker 800XP	258548	Flight Options LLC. Cuyahoga County, Oh.	(N835LX)
☐ N808TH	96	Citation V Ultra	560-0378	Royal Traval SA. Panama City, Panama.	(N378VP)
☐ N808V	01	390 Premier 1	RB-5	Frank Fletcher Premier One Inc. Little Rock, Ar.	N155GD
☐ N808VA*	96	Citation VII	650-7057	Vinnair LLC/Thunderbird Airways Inc. Houston, Tx.	N361EE
☐ N808W	98	Learjet 31A	31A-165	Danny Souders, Denver-Jeffco, Co.	N885TW
☐ N808WA	98	CitationJet	525-0290	SGP Land LLC. Tulsa, Ok.	
☐ N808WC	04	Citation Sovereign	680-0030	Developers Management Services Inc. Santa Monica, Ca.	N86LF
☐ N809BA	98	Hawker 800XP	258388	OD Aviation Inc. Delray Beach, Fl.	(N809TP)
☐ N809JC	80	Westwind-1124	298	American Premier Inc. Las Vegas, Nv.	N298CM
☐ N809JW	00	Gulfstream G100	135	Jeld-Wen Inc. Klamath Falls, Or.	N58GX
☐ N809LX	99	Hawker 800XP	258432	Flight Options LLC. Cuyahoga County, Oh.	(N824LX)
☐ N809QS	05	Citation Encore	560-0698	NetJets, Port Columbus, Oh.	N.....
☐ N809R	98	Learjet 60	60-146	Riata Management LLC. Liberal, Ks.	N800R
☐ N809SG	04	Embraer Legacy 600	14500809	Meadow Lane Air Partners LLC. Southampton, NY.	(N809TD)
☐ N809VC	79	Westwind-1124	264	Dundon Management LLC. Dallas, Tx.	N351C
☐ N810BA	84	BAe 125/800A	258010	Bloomfield Air LLC. West Palm Beach, Fl.	(N800LX)
☐ N810D	97	Challenger 604	5331	Jet Express Transit Corp. Morristown, NJ.	C-GLYH
☐ N810HS	72	HS 125/400A	25271	Centurion Investments Inc. St Louis, Mo.	N70AP
☐ N810JW	01	Gulfstream G100	138	Jeld-Wen Inc. Klamath Falls, Or.	N80GX
☐ N810KB	80	HS 125/700A	257118	KBA/Bridges & Shields LLC. East Point, Ga.	N619TD
☐ N810PF	07	CitationJet CJ2+	525A-0399	Cessna Aircraft Co. Wichita, Ks.	N.....
☐ N810QS	02	Citation Encore	560-0625	NetJets, Port Columbus, Oh.	N
☐ N810RA	67	Falcon 20C	81	Kalitta Charters LLC. Detroit-Willow Run, Mi.	N93RS
☐ N810SS	96	CitationJet	525-0137	Viaticus LLC. Park City, Ut.	(N525SE)
☐ N810TM	02	Gulfstream 4SP	1483	Toyota Motor Sales USA Inc. Long Beach, Ca.	N483GA
☐ N810VC	81	Westwind-1124	321	Westwood Air Partners II LP. Irving, Tx.	N217F
☐ N811AG	98	Falcon 2000	71	CIT Group, Tempe, Az.	N811TY
☐ N811AM	89	Hawker 800SP	NA0444	AirMed International LLC. Birmingham, Al.	N290EC
☐ N811DE	79	Gulfstream II SP	244	Flynn Financial Corp. San Francisco, Ca.	N811DF
☐ N811DF*	96	Gulfstream 4SP	1306	Flynn Financial Corp. Boca Raton, Fl.	N540CH
☐ N811JW	01	Gulfstream G100	140	Jeld-Wen Inc. Klamath Falls, Or.	4X-CVK
☐ N811MT	81	Challenger 600S	1024	CPH Aircraft LLC/Capital Pacific Holdings Inc. Newport Beach	N810MT
☐ N811QS	03	Hawker 800XP	258614	NetJets, Port Columbus, Oh.	
☐ N811RA	02	Learjet 60	60-264	AR Aircraft Leasing LLC. Rochester, NY.	N214PW
☐ N811RG	85	Citation S/II	S550-0061	EBITDA LLC. Louisville, Ky.	N200LX
☐ N811ST	01	Citation Excel	560-5193	SunTrust Banks Inc. Atlanta, Ga.	N.....
☐ N811VC	81	Westwind-1124	331	Westwind Partner 1 LP. Irving, Tx.	N228L
☐ N811VG	79	Citation II/SP	551-0017	Pacific Coast Aviation Inc. Sacramento, Ca.	N811VC
☐ N812AA	66	Falcon 20C	57	USA Jet Airlines Inc. Detroit-Willow Run, Mi.	N711KG
☐ N812DC	00	Citation Encore	560-0541	Tribute Aviation LLC. Thermal, Ca.	(N486BG)
☐ N812G	97	Challenger 604	5330	The GAP Inc/TAG Aviation USA, San Francisco, Ca.	C-GLYO
☐ N812GJ	88	BAe 125/800A	258112	La Paloma Verde Inc. Lawrenceville, Ga.	N831DC
☐ N812QS	02	Citation Encore	560-0628	NetJets, Port Columbus, Oh.	N.....
☐ N813AS	78	Learjet 35A	35A-167	AirNet Systems Inc. Columbus, Oh.	N725P
☐ N813CW	95	Hawker 800XP	258413	Flight Options LLC. Cuyahoga County, Oh.	(N822LX)
☐ N813JD	98	Citation Bravo	550-0838	Silvertip Peak Development LLC. Yakima, Wa.	N49KW
☐ N813LS	84	Gulfstream 3	443	Irish Air LLC. Cincinnati, Oh.	N21AM
☐ N813QS	07	Gulfstream G550	5160	Globe Trust & Earth Trust,	N660GA
☐ N813TL	66	DC 9-15	45732	Robinson Air Crane Inc. Opa Locka, Fl.	N29
☐ N813VZ	94	Challenger 601-3R	5160	Verizon Communications, Teterboro, NJ.	N94BA
☐ N814AM	82	Citation II	550-0414	AirMed International LLC. Birmingham, Al.	(N414VP)

Reg	Yr	Type	c/n	Owner/Operator	Prev Regn
N814BP	07	390 Premier 1A	RB-214	Clark 1207 Inc. Wilmington, De. (trustor ?).	
N814CM	92	Citation V	560-0170	HNI Corp. Muscatine, Ia.	(N417H)
N814D	71	HS 125/400A	NA761	Flight Associates LLC. Vero Beach, Fl.	XA-RIL
N814DM	00	CitationJet CJ-1	525-0376	Sail Rock Systems Inc. Carmel, Ca.	C-GTRG
N814ER	66	Falcon 20C	66	Flite Services Inc/Electric Mantenance & Construction, Tampa	N830RA
N814GF	96	Learjet 60	60-085	Papy LLC. Coral Gables, Fl.	N89KW
N814K	76	JetStar 2	5204	618BR LLC. Pleasant View, Tx.	N202ES
N814PS	94	Challenger 601-3R	5159	Aero Toy Store LLC. Fort Lauderdale, Fl.	(N659TS)
N814QS	07	Citation Encore+	560-0776	NetJets, Port Columbus, Oh.	N5223D
N814RW	67	DC 9-15F	47011	U S Marshals Service, Oklahoma City, Ok.	N179DE
N814T	67	Jet Commander	106	Barron Thomas Scottsdale LLC. Dallas, Tx.	N814K
N815CE	81	Citation II	550-0204	Blue Yonder LLC/Vitex Inc. Mooresville, NC.	(N300PR)
N815CM	91	Citation V	560-0104	KFB LLC/American Waste Control Inc. Tulsa, Ok.	(N907EA)
N815DD	81	Learjet 35A	35A-414	TCL Air Inc/Douglas Communications, Midland Park, NJ.	N196SP
N815E	96	Learjet 31A	31A-118	Wal-Mart Stores Inc. Rogers, Ar.	N815A
N815GA	07	Gulfstream G450	4115	Gulfstream Aerospace Corp. Savannah, Ga.	
N815H	87	Citation S/II	S550-0146	Aircraft Trust & Financing Corp. Fort Lauderdale, Fl.	N81SH
N815JW	01	Gulfstream G200	053	Jeld-Wen Inc. Klamath Falls, Or.	(N601AV)
N815L	77	Learjet 35A	35A-142	EPPS Air Service Inc. Atlanta-DeKalb, Ga.	N815A
N815MA	82	Citation II	550-0406	Caribair SA. Santo Domingo, Dominican Republic.	HH-JPD
N815MC	96	CitationJet	525-0142	L & L Aviation LLC/Hardware Resources, Bossier City, La.	N5068R
N815PA	01	Challenger 604	5511	PepsiAmericas Inc. Minneapolis, Mn.	C-GLWX
N815QS	04	Hawker 800XP	258705	NetJets, Port Columbus, Oh.	
N815TA	01	Hawker 800XP	258534	Flight Options LLC. Cuyahoga County, Oh.	(N833LX)
N816CS	00	Citation Excel	560-5153	CHF Express LLC. Ventura, Ca.	N916CS
N816DK	00	Beechjet 400A	RK-291	Hendricks & Partners Aviation LLC. Phoenix, Az.	N3191L
N816FC	94	CitationJet	525-0059	Fortney Companies Inc. La Crosse, Wi.	N71GW
N816JM	77	HS 125/700A	NA0207	JMN LLC. Austin, Tx.	N7UV
N816JW	04	Gulfstream G200	097	Jeld-Wen Inc. Klamath Falls, Or.	N397GA
N816LX	98	Hawker 800XP	258363	Odyssey Properties LLC. Orland Park, Il.	N726TA
N816MC	82	Learjet 55	55-035	Macon USA Corp. Wilmington, De.	VP-CUC
N816QS	99	Hawker 800XP	258416	NetJets, Port Columbus, Oh.	
N817AM	83	Learjet 55	55-069	Raven's Wing LLC. Allentown, Pa.	N102ST
N817BT	06	CitationJet CJ1+	525-0635	525-0635 LLC. Chandler, Az.	(N525JN)
N817CK	82	Challenger 600S	1069	Net Charter Inc/BLT-Building & Land Technology, Norwalk, Ct.	N455BE
N817GR	83	Diamond 1A	A062SA	Betony Enterprises LLC & AN Ryder LLC. Tiburon, Ca.	N616MM
N817LX	00	Hawker 800XP	258516	Flight Options LLC. Cuyahoga County, Oh.	(N832LX)
N817MB	92	Citation VII	650-7012	Koury Aviation Inc. Liberty, NC.	N317MB
N817ME	00	Gulfstream 4SP	1446	ME Leasing LLC. Las Vegas, Nv.	N317ML
N817MF	85	Gulfstream 3	466	Monroe Business Ventures LLC. Farmingdale, NY.	N102AK
N817PD	90	Citation V	560-0075	Henderson Leasing LLC. Bryn Mawr, Pa.	(N619PD)
N817QS	01	Hawker 800XP	258517	NetJets, Port Columbus, Oh.	
N818BA	87	Gulfstream 4	1017	Belair Aviation/NJL Enterprises LLC. Greenwich, Ct.	N402KC
N818CK	73	Learjet 25B	25B-118	Kalitta Charters LLC. Detroit-Willow Run, Mi.	N118MB
N818DA	97	Gulfstream V	520	Aspen 1 LLC. Van Nuys, Ca.	N450AR
N818DD	85	Gulfstream 3	455	Falcon Seaboard Services, Houston, Tx.	N28YC
N818DE	86	Citation III	650-0121	Word of Life Christian Center, Baton Rouge, La.	N24VB
N818FH	05	Global 5000	9180	Ivanhoe Mines, Vancouver, Canada.	C-FCFD
N818G	06	Gulfstream G450	4070	General Dynamics Corp. Dulles, Va.	N470GA
N818JH	81	Westwind-Two	341	Westwind Aviation Services LLC.	N52KS
N818JW	05	Gulfstream G200	121	Jeld-Wen Inc. Klamath Falls, Or.	N223GA
N818KC	05	Challenger 300	20043	Helpern Continental LLC. Farmingdale, NY.	N143LJ
N818LD	82	HS 125/700A	NA0337	L D Holdings LLC. Sussex, NJ.	N300TK
N818ME	00	Gulfstream 4SP	1431	Cape Clear LLC. Westborough, Ma.	(N818RM)
N818MV	90	BAe 125/800A	258186	MVA Aircraft Leasing Inc. Greenwich, Ct.	N818G
N818QS	07	Citation Encore+	560-0778	NetJets, Port Columbus, Oh.	N5185V
N818RF	03	Gulfstream G550	5018	Global Jet Luxembourg SA. Moscow, Russia.	N518GA
N818SS	81	Gulfstream 3	342	Hilcorp Energy Co. Houston, Tx.	N1JK
N818TH	96	Challenger 604	5315	Tommy Hilfeger USA Inc. NYC.	N818LS
N818TJ	83	Gulfstream 3	384	GKW Unified Holdings LLC. Van Nuys, Ca.	N112GS
N818WF	97	Astra-1125SPX	091	Steel Air LLC/Triple S Steel Supply Co. Houston, Tx.	N91GX
N818WM	88	Hawker 800SP	NA0419	McMahon Development Group, Solana Beach, Ca.	N196GA
N819AB	01	Hawker 800XP	258559	Red Eagle Air Corp. San Francisco, Ca.	N819AP
N819AP	05	Gulfstream G200	109	Matadoro Management Investments LLC. San Jose, Ca.	N409GA
N819DM	81	HS 125/700A	NA0326	TBC LLC/Jayco Associates Inc. Tampa, Fl.	N194WC
N819GA	07	Gulfstream G450	4119	Gulfstream Aerospace Corp. Savannah, Ga.	

Reg	Yr	Type	c/n	Owner/Operator	Prev Regn
N819GY	78	Sabre-75A	380-66	Centurion Investments Inc. St Louis, Mo.	N943CC
N819KR	79	Citation II	550-0114	KR Aviation LLC/Starcraft Corp. Elkhart, In.	N991BM
N819QS	08	Citation Encore+	560-0786	NetJets, Port Columbus, Oh.	N.....
N819RC	76	Westwind-1124	192	N682KA LLC. Palm Harbor, Fl.	N319BG
N819WG	77	HS 125/700A	257010	Banks Holdings LLC. Atlanta-Fulton County, Ga.	N424RJ
N820AV	03	Gulfstream G450	4002	Avaya Inc. Morristown, NJ.	N442SR
N820BA	84	Gulfstream 3	422	Bloomfield Air LLC. West Palm Beach, Fl.	(N903GL)
N820FJ	90	Citation III	650-0183	Mac-Air LLC. Plymouth, Ma.	(N820F)
N820HB	87	Gulfstream 4	1024	Howard & Brett LLC. NYC.	N116HM
N820L	65	Learjet 23	23-020	Butler National Inc. Newton, Ks.	N388R
N820MC	79	Citation II	550-0106	RGRB Aircraft Leasing LLC. Fargo, ND.	(N820MQ)
N820MG	69	HS 125/731	NA739	Mediacom Communications Corp. Middletown, NY.	N820MC
N820MS	90	Gulfstream 4	1147	Koloa Aviation Inc. Honolulu, Hi.	N200PM
N820QS	03	Citation Encore	560-0650	NetJets, Port Columbus, Oh.	N5260Y
N820TM	02	Gulfstream G300	1508	Toyota Motor Sales USA Inc. Long Beach, Ca.	N508GA
N821AM	05	Global Express	9183	Joust Capital II LLC. Richardson, Tx.	C-FEAD
N821AV	03	Gulfstream G450	4003	Avaya Inc. Morristown, NJ.	N403SR
N821GA	07	Gulfstream G450	4121	Gulfstream Aerospace Corp. Savannah, Ga.	
N821LX	99	Hawker 800XP	258406	Flight Options LLC. Cuyahoga County, Oh.	N754TA
N821PA	76	Gulfstream II SP	183	Chrysler Aviation Inc. Van Nuys, Ca.	N400PJ
N821QS	89	Hawker 800XP	258709	NetJets, Port Columbus, Oh.	(N709XP)
N822A	00	Gulfstream 4SP	1447	Anardarko Petroleum Corp. The Woodlands, Tx.	N667P
N822AA	69	Falcon 20D	195	USA Jet Airlines Inc. Detroit-Willow Run, Mi.	N195MP
N822BL	85	BAe 125/800B	258022	Branch Law Firm Aviation Ltd. Albuquerque, NM.	N4257R
N822DS	06	Citation Sovereign	680-0121	I DES Inc. Rio Vista, Ca.	N5188N
N822HA	83	Citation II	550-0464	Hill Aircraft & Leasing Corp. Atlanta-Fulton County, Ga.	N117TA
N822MC	82	Learjet 55	55-018	AAA Flight Inc/Hy-Wing Aviation Inc. Rancho Sante Fe, Ca.	N797CS
N822QS	08	Citation Encore+	560-0789	NetJets, Port Columbus, Oh.	N.....
N822ST	05	Falcon 2000EX EASY	66	U S Smokeless Tobacco Brands Inc. White Plains, NY.	F-WWMO
N823AA	70	Falcon 20D	228	USA Jet Airlines Inc. Detroit-Willow Run, Mi.	OE-GRU
N823CA	02	Learjet 45	45-221	ConAgra Foods Inc. Omaha, Ne.	N40078
N823DF	00	Global Express	9066	DDF Y2K Family Trust, Hillsboro, Or.	N708SC
N823ET	03	Hawker 400XP	RK-360	Aquila Air LLC/Finelight Communications, Bloomington, In.	N6200D
N823GA	86	Gulfstream 4	1005	Guardian Services Inc. Ontario, Ca.	VR-BJZ
N823L*	01	CitationJet CJ-2	525A-0020	Thunder Aviation Acquisitions Inc. Spirit of St Louis, Mo.	N323LM
N823NA	81	Citation II	550-0236	Privatair Inc. Stratford, Ct.	LN-AAD
N823PM	03	Citation Bravo	550-1064	TBN Group. Reno, Nv.	N.....
N823QS	08	Citation Encore+	560-0794	NetJets, Port Columbus, Oh.	N.....
N823WB	91	Citation V	560-0124	TIC Properties LLC. Greenville, SC.	N7513D
N823XP	06	Hawker 850XP	258823	Greenhawk Aviation LLC.	(N150GF)
N824CB	97	Citation Bravo	550-0824	LJ Associates Inc/LJ Aviation, Latrobe, Pa.	N5121N
N824CC	82	Learjet 55	55-024	Indiana Aircraft Charter LLC. Scherville, In.	N900FA
N824DH	85	Challenger 601	3047	Promotional Researchers of Delaware, Charlottesville, Va.	OE-HLE
N824DS	76	Falcon 10	92	Limousin Air LLC. Nashville, Tn.	N724DS
N824DW	84	Diamond 1A	A075SA	Access Aviation LLC. Omaha, Ne.	N11WF
N824ES	94	CitationJet	525-0066	Scope Leasing Inc. Columbus, Oh.	(N823ES)
N824GB	03	Hawker 400XP	RK-371	Executive Charters Inc. Kinston, NC.	N401CW
N824HG	97	Beechjet 400A	RK-143	Hantz Financial Services Inc. Willow Run, Mi.	N191NQ
N824LA	75	Falcon 10	53	Fly 2 Fuse 1 LLC/Spinal Solutions LLC. Murrieta, Ca.	HI-836SP
N824LX	05	Hawker 800XPi	258740	Flight Options LLC. Cuyahoga County, Oh.	N740XP
N824MG	84	Learjet 55	55-106	ATI Jet Sales West LLC. Reno, Nv.	(N850PA)
N824QS	00	Hawker 800XP	258523	NetJets, Port Columbus, Oh.	N5023J
N825AC	92	Learjet 31A	31A-058	Southern Cross Aircraft LLC. Fort Lauderdale, Fl.	N298CH
N825CA	02	Learjet 45	45-220	ConAgra Foods Inc. Omaha, Ne.	N40077
N825CP*	97	Hawker 800XP2	258329	Civil Air Patrol, Maxwell AFB. Al.	N903K
N825CT	00	Hawker 800XP	258497	Cooper Tire & Rubber Co. Findlay, Oh.	N51197
N825GA	00	Citation X	750-0143	Galt Aviation LLC. San Jose, Ca.	N51744
N825JW	85	Citation III	650-0082	LNW Consulting/Wolff Urban Management Inc. Van Nuys, Ca.	N4VY
N825LJ	83	Learjet 35A	35A-496	Skyways Inc. Pottsville, Pa.	N496SW
N825LM	01	Gulfstream V	655	Penobscot Properties LLC. New Castle, De.	N529GA
N825LX	05	Hawker 800XPi	258767	Flight Options LLC. Cuyahoga County, Oh.	(N143RL)
N825MS	81	HS 125/700A	257151	Stead Auto Group, Walnut Creek, Ca.	(N613EL)
N825PS	81	Citation 1/SP	501-0224	Dawson Oil Co. LaCrosse, Wi.	N456CE
N825QS	04	Citation Encore	560-0655	NetJets, Port Columbus, Oh.	N.....
N825SB	68	Sabre-40	282-92	Tulsa Technology Center, Tulsa, Ok.	158382
N825T	03	Gulfstream G300	1535	Toyota Industries of N America Inc. NYC.	N435GA

Reg	Yr	Type	c/n	Owner/Operator	Prev Regn
❏ N826AA	67	Falcon 20C	67	USA Jet Airlines Inc. Detroit-Willow Run, Mi.	N821AA
❏ N826AC	93	Citation V	560-0242	Investors Warranty of America Inc. Cedar Rapids, Ia.	N605AT
❏ N826CA	02	Learjet 45	45-222	ConAgra Foods Inc. Santa Ana, Ca.	N673LB
❏ N826EW	98	Falcon 2000	58	Vanguard Health Management Inc. Nashville, Tn.	N326EW
❏ N826GA	94	Hawker 800	258263	PPG Industries Inc. Allegheny County, Pa.	N961H
❏ N826GW	77	Gulfstream II SP	210	PF Air LLC/W Polisseni Inc. Fairport, NY.	N30FW
❏ N826HS	98	CitationJet	525-0305	Overall Management 1 LLC. Palm Beach, Fl.	
❏ N826JH	93	Beechjet 400A	RK-70	Triple C Development Inc. Centre, AL.	N79HM
❏ N826K	98	Falcon 900EX	36	Alten Consulting LLC. St Louis, Mo.	N326K
❏ N826KR	02	Falcon 2000	182	K A Equipment Leasing LLC. Houston, Tx.	N329K
❏ N826LX	06	Hawker 850XP	258826	Flight Options LLC. Cuyahoga County, Oh.	
❏ N826QS	07	Citation Encore+	560-0782	NetJets, Port Columbus, Oh.	N.....
❏ N826RP	03	Gulfstream G300	1507	United Group Aviation LLC. Miami, Fl.	N91KL
❏ N826RT	81	Citation II/SP	551-0056	Ron Adkison, Henderson, Tx.	N36WJ
❏ N827AA	74	Falcon 20E	298	USA Jet Airlines Inc. Detroit-Willow Run, Mi.	OE-GNN
❏ N827CR	80	Learjet 35A	35A-332	Inter Continental Express LLC. Hosford, Fl.	N543WW
❏ N827CT	94	Falcon 50	245	Comstock Homebuilding Companies, Dulles, Va.	N530DG
❏ N827DC	05	Citation Sovereign	680-0027	TFA LLC. Las Vegas, Nv.	VH-EXA
❏ N827DP	90	Citation II	550-0660	Drug Plastics & Glass Co. Boyertown, Pa.	N160SP
❏ N827GA	99	Gulfstream 4SP	1391	PPG Industries Inc. Allegheny County, Pa.	N391GA
❏ N827LX	07	Hawker 850XP	258848	Flight Options LLC. Cuyahoga County, Oh.	
❏ N827NS	99	Hawker 800XP	258409	National Air Services, Jeddah, Saudi Arabia.	VP-BSK
❏ N827QS	08	Citation Encore+	560-0801	NetJets, Port Columbus, Oh.	N.....
❏ N827SA	99	Hawker 800XP	258438	WEKEL SA. Bogota, Colombia.	VP-BHZ
❏ N827SB	90	Beechjet 400A	RK-2	Tri-State Aero Inc. Evansville, In.	N402CW
❏ N828AF	85	Citation S/II	S550-0067	Summit Group Inc/ARTC, Columbia, SC.	N900DM
❏ N828CA	02	Learjet 45	45-159	ConAgra Foods Inc. Omaha, Ne.	N5001J
❏ N828CW	99	Hawker 800XP	258428	Flight Options LLC. Cuyahoga County, Oh.	(N823LX)
❏ N828KD	04	Challenger 604	5584	Suzuki del Caribe Inc. San Juan, PR.	C-FAWU
❏ N828LX	99	Hawker 800XP	258461	Flight Options LLC. Cuyahoga County, Oh.	N881CW
❏ N828NS	00	Hawker 800XP	258464	National Air Services, Jeddah, Saudi Arabia.	HZ-KRSA
❏ N828QS	01	Hawker 800XP	258528	NetJets, Port Columbus, Oh.	
❏ N828SK	88	Challenger 601-3A	5018	JCI Transportation LLC. Chattanooga, Tn.	N893AC
❏ N828SS	80	Citation II/SP	551-0205	Sierra Stone Co. Dallas, Tx. (was 550-0161)	HB-VIO
❏ N829AA	72	Learjet 25B	25B-100	USA Jet Airlines Inc. Detroit-Willow Run, Mi.	N25TK
❏ N829CB	98	Citation Bravo	550-0829	Infinity King Air LLC. Litchfield, Ct.	N5096S
❏ N829JC	06	Citation Sovereign	680-0112	CC Industries Inc/Henry Crown & Co. Palwaukee, Il.	N52446
❏ N829LX	99	Hawker 800XP	258466	Flight Options LLC. Cuyahoga County, Oh.	N866CW
❏ N829NL	73	Gulfstream 2	128	New Light Church World Outreach Centre, Houston, Tx.	N128TS
❏ N829NS	00	Hawker 800XP	258475	National Air Services, Jeddah, Saudi Arabia.	HZ-KRSB
❏ N829QS	08	Citation Encore+	560-0796	NetJets, Port Columbus, Oh.	N.....
❏ N829RN	00	EMB-135ER	145361	Intel Corp/Executive Jet Management Inc. Cincinnati, Oh.	PT-...
❏ N830	84	Westwind-1124	406	Triumph Aviation Inc. Wayne, Pa.	N100CH
❏ N830BA*	88	BAe 125/800A	NA0415	Bloomfield Air II LLC. West Palm Beach, Fl.	N800VC
❏ N830C	87	Westwind-Two	442	Air Travel Services Inc. Nashville, Tn.	N71WF
❏ N830DB	06	Gulfstream G150	206	Aledo Sub LLC/Fairfield Residential LLC. Fort Worth, Tx.	N806GA
❏ N830EF	87	Gulfstream 4	1023	EFB Aviation LLC. Arlington, Va.	(N830FB)
❏ N830LX	00	Hawker 800XP	258483	Flight Options LLC. Cuyahoga County, Oh.	N807TA
❏ N830NS	00	Hawker 800XP	258476	National Air Services, Jeddah, Saudi Arabia.	N192NC
❏ N830QS	07	Citation Encore+	560-0784	NetJets, Port Columbus, Oh.	N.....
❏ N831ET	00	Challenger 604	5451	BWL Aviation LLC/E*Trade Group Inc. Arlington, Va.	(N120MT)
❏ N831FC	07	CitationJet CJ-3	525B-0155	Kloshe Aviation LLC/Investor Financial Corp. Seattle, Wa.	N.....
❏ N831GA	90	Citation III	650-0194	TP Air LLC/Timber Products Co. Eugene, Or.	N2606
❏ N831LX	01	Hawker 800XP	258510	Flight Options LLC. Cuyahoga County, Oh.	N890CW
❏ N831QS	08	Citation Encore+	560-0792	NetJets, Port Columbus, Oh.	N.....
❏ N831S	93	CitationJet	525-0031	Golden Eagle Aviation/Regal Marine Industries Inc. Orlando.	N31CJ
❏ N832CB	92	Citation VII	650-7020	Mount Hood Transport Inc. Klamath Falls, Or.	N700RR
❏ N832LX	95	Hawker 800XP	258281	Flight Options LLC. Cuyahoga County, Oh.	N781TA
❏ N832QS	04	Hawker 800XP	258683	NetJets, Port Columbus, Oh.	N61343
❏ N832SC	00	Challenger 604	5461	Delta Airelite Business Jets Inc. Lexington-Bluegrass, Ky.	C-GLYK
❏ N832UJ	98	Citation Bravo	550-0832	Great River Energy, Elk River, Mn.	PT-WSO
❏ N833QS	99	Hawker 800XP	258433	NetJets, Port Columbus, Oh.	
❏ N833WM*	96	Citation V Ultra	560-0385	Morris Communications Corp. Augusta, Ga.	N333WM
❏ N834AF	01	Learjet 31A	31A-225	Wal-Mart Stores Inc. Rogers, Ar.	N334AF
❏ N834DC	85	Citation S/II	S550-0035	Young Family Trust, Portola Valley, Ca.	XA-THO
❏ N834H	89	Citation III	650-0177	Hillenbrand Industries Inc. Batesville, In.	N707HJ

Reg   Yr   Type   c/n   Owner/Operator   Prev Regn

Reg	Yr	Type	c/n	Owner/Operator	Prev Regn
☐ N834LX	01	Hawker 800XP	258552	Flight Options LLC. Cuyahoga County, Oh.	(N836LX)
☐ N834QS	04	Citation Encore	560-0669	NetJets, Port Columbus, Oh.	N5216A
☐ N835BA	99	BBJ-7BC	30572	Boeing Executive Flight Operations, Seattle, Wa.	N339BA
☐ N835DM	06	CitationJet CJ-3	525B-0079	COR Group Inc. Strathmore, AB. Canada.	N52081
☐ N835MC	92	Learjet 35A	35A-673	Air Affairs Australia P/L. Nowra, NSW, Australia.	C-GPDO
☐ N835QS	00	Hawker 800XP	258505	NetJets, Port Columbus, Oh.	N8050S
☐ N835TB	04	Hawker 400XP	RK-393	Traylor Bros Inc. Evansville, In.	N1118QS
☐ N835ZT	06	390 Premier 1A	RB-180	Zotec Solutions Inc. Indianapolis, In.	N133CQ
☐ N836BA	00	BBJ-7BC	30756	WFBNW NA. Salt Lake City, Ut. (trustor ?).	N156QS
☐ N836MF	87	Gulfstream 4	1012	AM General LLC. South Bend, In.	N636GD
☐ N836QS	99	Hawker 800XP	258436	NetJets, Port Columbus, Oh.	
☐ N837AC	03	CitationJet CJ-2	525A-0188	Aho Construction 1 Inc. Portland, Or.	N188JR
☐ N837BA	06	Gulfstream G550	5122	Bank of America NA. Charlotte, NC.	N522GA
☐ N837JM	06	390 Premier 1A	RB-169	Family Air LLC/Mudd Group, Waterloo, Ia.	N7269Z
☐ N837MA	73	Citation	500-0096	C & M Aero Inc. Fort Worth, Tx.	(N187AP)
☐ N837QS	05	Citation Encore	560-0685	NetJets, Port Columbus, Oh.	N5086W
☐ N837RE	01	Hawker 800XP	258526	United Dominion Realty Trust Inc. Denver-Centennial, Co.	N525XP
☐ N838BA	06	Gulfstream G550	5140	Bank of America NA. Charlotte, NC.	N740GA
☐ N838JL	94	Hawker 800	258270	AirMed International LLC. Birmingham, Al.	N802CE
☐ N838MF	97	Gulfstream V	512	Ropa Two Corp. Teterboro, NJ.	N636MF
☐ N838QS	97	Hawker 800XP	258338	NetJets, Port Columbus, Oh.	
☐ N838RT	99	Citation Excel	560-5047	Astec Industries Inc. Chattanooga, Tn.	N888RT
☐ N838SC	99	Global Express	9035	Falcon International Inc. Cleveland, Oh.	N818LS
☐ N839LX	03	Hawker 800XP	258657	Flight Options LLC. Cuyahoga County, Oh.	(N857CW)
☐ N839QS	05	Citation Encore	560-0690	NetJets, Port Columbus, Oh.	N5218T
☐ N839RM	85	Falcon 50	159	Moody National Realty Co LP. Houston, Tx.	HB-ISD
☐ N840CC	99	Citation Excel	560-5040	Blue Cross & Blue Shield Inc. Jacksonville, Fl.	N54HA
☐ N840GL	77	Falcon 10	109	GLCC/SMC Aircraft Services LLC. Port Meadville, Pa.	N89EC
☐ N840LX	04	Hawker 800XP	258666	Flight Options LLC. Cuyahoga County, Oh.	(N866LX)
☐ N840QS	97	Hawker 800XP	258340	NetJets, Port Columbus, Oh.	
☐ N840RG	79	Gulfstream 2TT	235	R & G Aviation LLC. Huntsville, Al.	N430RG
☐ N840SW	93	Learjet 31A	31A-084	Quattro Air Ventures LLC. Houston, Tx.	N196HA
☐ N841AM	06	CitationJet CJ-3	525B-0084	Rancho Pacific Holdings LLC. Ontario, Ca.	N.....
☐ N841CW	79	Citation 1/SP	501-0134	Commonwealth Aircraft Leasing Inc. Wilmington, De.	N501EM
☐ N841DW	01	Citation Excel	560-5177	Micron Technology Inc. Boise, Id.	N5061P
☐ N841QS	08	Citation Encore+	560-0799	NetJets, Port Columbus, Oh.	N.....
☐ N841TC*	99	CitationJet	525-0339	TEDA Holding Corp. Minneapolis, Mn.	(N212LX)
☐ N841TF	81	Learjet 35A	35A-416	Dreamstream Aviation LLC. Prescott, Az.	N841TT
☐ N841TT	94	Learjet 60	60-031	Salem Leasing Corp. Winston-Salem, NC.	N228N
☐ N841WS	07	Gulfstream G450	4099	Walter Scott International Ltd. Edinburgh, Scotland.	N199GA
☐ N842CB	98	Citation Bravo	550-0842	Louisiana Aircraft LLC. Oklahoma City, Ok.	N86AJ
☐ N842DW	05	Citation Excel XLS	560-5589	Wm Victor Aviation/Davis & Weight Motorsports, Jacksonville.	N5262W
☐ N842PA	88	Gulfstream 4	1057	Presidential Aviation Leasing Inc. Fort Lauderdale, Fl.	N226AL
☐ N842QS	01	Hawker 800XP	258542	NetJets, Port Columbus, Oh.	
☐ N843B	70	HS 125/731	NA742	Phaeton LLC. East Haven, Ct.	N74RT
☐ N843CP	93	Learjet 60	60-011	N74B LLC. Salem, Or.	N611TS
☐ N843CW	01	Hawker 800XP	258543	Flight Options LLC. Cuyahoga County, Oh.	(N834LX)
☐ N843DW	08	Citation Sovereign	680-0219	Cessna Aircraft Co. Wichita, Ks.	N.....
☐ N843QS	08	Citation Encore+	560-0790	NetJets, Port Columbus, Oh.	N.....
☐ N844DR	98	Citation Bravo	550-0860	Marine Terminals Air Inc. Isle of Palms, SC.	(N860J)
☐ N844F	82	Falcon 100	201	Semitool Inc. Kalispell, Mt.	N100NW
☐ N844GF	89	Gulfstream 4	1107	Madison Financial Inc. Dallas, Tx.	N844GS
☐ N844HS	01	Citation Encore	560-0596	HealthSouth Aviation Inc. Birmingham, Al.	N52235
☐ N844L	75	Learjet 35	35-014	Nevada Jet Aviation Inc. Las Vegas, Nv.	N190GC
☐ N844NX	85	Falcon 50	147	Western Stone & Metal Corp/Shane Co. Denver, Co.	N526CC
☐ N844QS	02	Citation Encore	560-0629	NetJets, Port Columbus, Oh.	N.....
☐ N844TM	04	Citation Encore	560-0660	Encore 1944 LLC/Munoz Bermudez Inc. Santurce, PR.	N5264M
☐ N844UP	01	Falcon 2000	156	Union Pacific Railroad, Omaha, Ne.	F-WWVN
☐ N845FW	88	Citation III	650-0153	FW Oil Interests Inc. Thermal, Ca.	N2DH
☐ N845G	06	Gulfstream G450	4053	General Dynamics Corp. Dulles, Va.	N453GA
☐ N845QS	01	Hawker 800XP	258545	NetJets, Port Columbus, Oh.	N50445
☐ N845UP	05	Challenger 300	20081	Union Pacific Railroad, Omaha, Ne.	C-FGCN
☐ N846MA	90	Citation V	560-0046	Pan Maritime Inc. Bristol-Filton, UK.	(G-OURD)
☐ N846QM	00	Gulfstream V	626	Kenneth Ambrose, Orinda, Ca.	(N5JR)
☐ N846QS	08	Citation Encore+	560-0797	NetJets, Port Columbus, Oh.	N.....
☐ N846UP	05	Challenger 300	20086	Union Pacific Railroad, Omaha, Ne.	C-FGVJ

Reg	Yr	Type	c/n	Owner/Operator	Prev Regn
☐ N847C	84	Citation S/II	S550-0003	Transit Air Services Inc. Morristown, NJ.	(N847G)
☐ N847CW	03	Hawker 800XP	258647	Flight Options LLC. Cuyahoga County, Oh.	(N837LX)
☐ N847NG	07	CitationJet CJ-3	525B-0144	Milford Investments II LLC/Northland Group Inc. Edina, Mn.	(C-FXFJ)
☐ N847RP	03	EMB-135LR Legacy	145608	WFBNW NA. Salt Lake City, Ut. (trustor ?).	N303GC
☐ N848C	89	Beechjet 400	RJ-63	F&S LLC/Triple S Hauling Inc. Columbia, Mo.	
☐ N848CC	06	Challenger 604	5660	Centene Corp/MHS Consulting Corp. St Louis, Mo.	N650KS
☐ N848C	03	Hawker 800XP	258648	Flight Options LLC. Cuyahoga County, Oh.	
☐ N848D	78	Citation II	550-0039	Carter County Bank/Summers-Taylor Inc. Tn. (was 551-0084).	ZP-TYO
☐ N848DM	02	Citation Excel	560-5329	Archer Daniels Midland Co. Decatur, Il.	N.....
☐ N848G	97	Citation V Ultra	560-0465	Waylock Overseas Ltd. Moscow, Russia.	N465CV
☐ N848N	98	Hawker 800XP	258371	ITT Flight Operations Inc. Allentown, Pa.	
☐ N848PF	00	Beechjet 400A	RK-288	Peoples First Courier Inc. Panama City, Fl.	N51VC
☐ N848QS	07	Hawker 900XP	HA-31	NetJets, Port Columbus, Oh.	
☐ N850BA	82	Falcon 50	115	Penrose Group, Fort Worth, Tx.	N950S
☐ N850C	91	Beechjet 400A	RK-31	BC Air LLC. Phoenix, Az.	(N407LX)
☐ N850CC	80	Sabre-65	465-38	Corporate Aviation LLC. Lafayette, La.	(N4LQ)
☐ N850CT	04	Hawker 800XP2	258677	Copeland Corp. Dayton, Oh.	N677XP
☐ N850DG	98	CitationJet	525-0268	Delta Health Group Inc. Pensacola, Fl.	
☐ N850EP	81	Falcon 50	39	Fisher Controls International LLC. St Louis, Mo.	N326FB
☐ N850HB	07	Hawker 850XP	258900	Hawker Beechcraft Corp. Wichita, Ks.	
☐ N850J	97	Hawker 800XP	258311	DePuy Orthopaedics Inc. Warsaw, In.	N800RD
☐ N850K	03	Falcon 2000	210	Koch Industries Inc. Wichita, Ks.	N2325
☐ N850KE	06	Hawker 850XP	258796	Oneok Inc. Tulsa, Ok.	N796XP
☐ N850ME	07	Hawker 850XP	258861	Grupo Unipharm SA. Guatemala City, Guatemala.	N861ME
☐ N850NS	06	Hawker 850XP	258789	Novamerica Steel Inc. Norwood, Ma.	N789XP
☐ N850PM	81	Citation II	550-0210	Risk Strategies LLC/Great Metro Autogroup, Montclair, Ca.	XA-KMX
☐ N850TC	92	BAe 1000A	259032	Taubman Enterprises Inc. Waterford, Mi.	N300LS
☐ N850TS	07	Challenger 850	8056	WFBNW NA. Salt Lake City, Ut. (trustor ?).	C-....
☐ N850VP	05	Hawker 850XP	258768	Childress Klein Management Services LLC. Charlotte, NC.	N768XP
☐ N850ZH	06	Hawker 850XP	258798	Zimmer Inc. Warsaw, In.	N798XP
☐ N851C	84	Diamond 1A	A077SA	Cutter Aviation Inc. Phoenix, Az.	N975GR
☐ N851CC	06	Hawker 850XP	258787	Cummins Inc. Columbus, In.	N72617
☐ N851DB	94	CitationJet	525-0054	American Aviation Inc. Henderson, NC.	N54CJ
☐ N851EL	03	Gulfstream G300	1515	Pleasant Travel Service, Van Nuys, Ca.	N415GA
☐ N851LE	04	Gulfstream G200	106	Pleasant Travel Service, Van Nuys, Ca.	(N200GA)
☐ N852A	87	BAe 125/800A	258083	Win Win Aviation Inc. Long Meadow, Ma.	(N805AF)
☐ N852CC	07	Hawker 900XP	HA-12	Cummins Inc. Columbus, In.	
☐ N852GA	75	HS 125/600A	256048	Arnoni Aviation Ltd. Houston, Tx.	TC-COS
☐ N852LX*	99	Hawker 800XP	258397	Flight Options LLC. Cuyahoga County, Oh.	(N752LX)
☐ N852QS	99	Hawker 800XP	258452	NetJets, Port Columbus, Oh.	
☐ N852SB	80	Citation II	550-0382	BHC Financial LLC. Wilmington, De. (was 551-0032).	N852SP
☐ N852SP	06	CitationJet CJ-3	525B-0092	Stephen Pipe & Steel LLC. Jamestown, Ky.	N52653
☐ N853CC	06	Hawker 850XP	258803	Cummins Inc. Columbus, In.	
☐ N854JA	00	Citation Bravo	550-0920	Juliett Alpha Aircraft Leasing LLC. Naples, Fl.	N63LB
☐ N854SD	99	Gulfstream 4SP	1387	Halliburton Energy Services, Houston, Tx.	N254SD
☐ N854SM	71	HS 125/731	NA766	Melissa Aviation Ltd. Wilmington, De.	N150SA
☐ N855DG	80	Falcon 20-5	432	Dollar General Corp. Nashville-Berry Field, Tn.	N237PT
☐ N855FC	97	Beechjet 400A	RK-141	Flow Companies Inc. Winston-Salem, NC.	N874JD
☐ N855G	05	Gulfstream G550	5118	General Dynamics Corp. Dulles, Va.	N838GA
☐ N855GA	92	BAe 125/800A	258211	Guardian/Garden Commercial Properties, Teterboro, NJ.	N151TC
☐ N855JB	04	390 Premier 1	RB-104	George Inc. Wilmington, De.	N5104G
☐ N855PT	82	Learjet 55	55-046	Jet 55 LLC/Prestige Properties & Development Co. NYC.	N55HL
☐ N855QS	98	Hawker 800XP	258355	NetJets, Port Columbus, Oh.	
☐ N855RA*	96	Beechjet 400A	RK-114	RA Aviation Corp. Gulfport, Ms.	N698PW
☐ N855RB	97	Gulfstream V	509	EMAX LLC. Charlottesville, Va.	N509GV
☐ N855RM	06	390 Premier 1A	RB-174	ExteNet Systems Inc. Aurora, Il.	N71874
☐ N855SA	82	Gulfstream 3	363	Sun Air Jets LLC. Camarillo, Ca.	N77EK
☐ N855TJ	03	Falcon 2000EX	19	Lark Aviation LLC. Manchester, NH.	N528BD
☐ N856BB	07	CitationJet CJ-3	525B-0207	Boyd Brothers Transportation Inc. Clayton, Al.	N5262W
☐ N856F	01	Falcon 2000	138	M & K Premier Air LLC. St Louis, Mo.	N799BC
☐ N856JB	65	Learjet 23	23-052	John Kowal/Skyway Enterprises Inc. Kissimmee, Fl.	N360EJ
☐ N857AA	99	Citation Bravo	550-0901	JV Jet Services LLC. Norfolk, Va.	N5058J
☐ N857C	91	Beechjet 400A	RK-17	Sun Development & Management Corp. Indianapolis, In.	(N401LX)
☐ N857ST	98	Gulfstream 4SP	1345	Seminole Tribe of Florida, Hollywood, Fl.	N457ST
☐ N858ME	94	Citation V	560-0253	858ME LLC. Fort Worth, Tx.	N553CW
☐ N858MK	00	Learjet 45	45-141	KMI Management LLC. Indianapolis, In.	N142HQ

Reg	Yr	Type	c/n	Owner/Operator	Prev Regn
N858PJ	81	Challenger 600S	1028	Challenger 1 Inc. Wilmington, De.	YV-1111CP
N858QS	04	Hawker 800XP	258691	NetJets, Port Columbus, Oh.	
N860AA	05	Gulfstream G550	5079	ALA Services LLC/Allen Systems Group Inc. Naples, Fl.	N579GA
N860BA	84	Falcon 50	142	Outback Steakhouse of Florida Inc. Tampa, Fl.	N4350M
N860CR	98	Citation V Ultra	560-0500	Pratt Aviation P/L. Melbourne, VIC. Australia.	N960CR
N860DB	01	CitationJet CJ-1	525-0434	OKM LLC. Madison, Ms.	N860DD
N860DD	05	CitationJet CJ-3	525B-0046	Shelburne Limestone Corp. Burlington, Vt.	N5124F
N860FJ	97	Falcon 900EX	30	SemGroup LP. Tulsa, Ok.	N662P
N860JB	88	Gulfstream 4	1054	JBNB Falcon LLC/Sky Communications Inc. Newport Beach, Ca.	(N1DC)
N860PD	95	Learjet 60	60-073	Parker Drilling Co. Tulsa, Ok.	N256M
N860QS	04	Hawker 800XP	258698	NetJets, Port Columbus, Oh.	
N860S	76	Learjet 35A	35A-086	Houck Leasing Inc. Fort Pierce, Fl.	N86CS
N860W	97	Citation VII	650-7086	H & E Equipment Services Inc. Baton Rouge, La.	N5134Z
N861CE	90	Hawker 800SP	NA0450	Coca-Cola Enterprises Inc. Atlanta-Fulton County, Ga.	C-GAGQ
N861PA	93	Learjet 60	60-015	Presidential Air LLC. Fort Lauderdale, Fl.	N826SS
N861QS	98	Hawker 800XP	258361	NetJets, Port Columbus, Oh.	
N862CE	93	Hawker 800SP	258244	Coca-Cola Enterprises Inc. Atlanta-Fulton County, Ga.	N252DT
N862CF	99	Citation Excel	560-5021	CHF Express LLC/R W Hertel & Sons Inc. San Luis Obispo, Ca.	N862CE
N862CW	86	BAe 125/800A	258062	Dan Air LLC. Klamath Falls, Or.	(N806LX)
N862KM	99	Beechjet 400A	RK-227	Executive Airshare Corp. Wichita, Ks.	N362KM
N862PA	93	Learjet 60	60-014	Pointe Aviation LLC/Cap Estate Corp. Bradley, Il.	(N827SS)
N862QS	98	Hawker 800XP	258362	NetJets, Port Columbus, Oh	
N863CA	01	Learjet 45	45-160	ConAgra Foods Inc. Omaha, Ne.	N455DE
N863CE	95	Hawker 800XP2	258289	Coca-Cola Enterprises Inc. Atlanta-Fulton County, Ga.	N515GP
N863PA	92	Learjet 60	60-004	JSH Properties Inc/L60 Jet Partners LLC. Fort Lauderdale, Fl	N600PJ
N863QS	99	Hawker 800XP	258463	NetJets, Port Columbus, Oh.	
N863RD	95	Citation V Ultra	560-0287	Premier Electric Aviation LLC. Naples, Fl.	N117MR
N864CC	99	Citation Excel	560-5067	Cliffs Real Estate Inc. Greenville, SC.	OE-GPZ
N864CE	97	Hawker 800XP2	258331	Coca-Cola Enterprises Inc. Atlanta-Fulton County, Ga.	N160CT
N864KB	91	Learjet 31A	31A-048	KBLA LLC. Van Nuys, Ca.	N314XS
N864QS	01	Hawker 800XP	258564	NetJets, Port Columbus, Oh.	
N864YC	86	Gulfstream 4	1003	Western Aviation & Marine LLC. Bozeman, Mt.	N885TA
N864YD	75	Gulfstream 2B	156	Western Aviation & Marine LLC. Palm Springs, Ca.	N83TE
N865AA	69	Gulfstream 2B	48	Washington Penn Plastic Co. Washington, Pa.	N61WE
N865AM	03	Hawker 400XP	RK-358	AMFI LLC/Accurate Metal Fabricators Inc. Orange County, Ca.	N5158D
N865CA	01	Learjet 45	45-193	ConAgra Foods Inc. Omaha, Ne.	N434FX
N865EC	05	Citation Sovereign	680-0028	Entergy Services Inc. New Orleans, La.	N5264E
N865JT	06	Hawker 850XP	258800	Jewelry Television, Knoxville, Tn.	N880XP
N865LS	07	Hawker 900XP	HA-37	Hawker Beechcraft Corp. Wichita, Ks.	
N865M	00	Citation Encore	560-0550	Central Trust Bank, Jefferson City, Mo.	N51072
N865SM	98	Hawker 800XP2	258365	SummitJets Inc. Newport Beach, Ca.	
N866CA	01	Learjet 45	45-184	ConAgra Foods Inc. Omaha, Ne.	N45VP
N866G	00	Gulfstream G200	025	General Dynamics Network Systems, Needham, Ma.	N302MC
N866TM	05	Challenger 300	20066	EMC Corp. Cork, Ireland.	C-FGXK
N867JC	80	Citation II	550-0166	Masthead Hose & Supply, Orange Park, Fl.	N367JC
N867QS	02	Hawker 800XP	258576	NetJets, Port Columbus, Oh.	
N867W	05	Citation Excel XLS	560-5601	Westmark Enterprises Inc. Dubuque, Ia.	N563XL
N868BT	82	Falcon 50	93	Sirius Inc. Corvallis, Or.	N844X
N868CC	06	Challenger 604	5662	MHS Conculting Corp. St Louis, Mo.	N652MC
N868DS	73	Gulfstream 2B	123	World Jet Inc. Ontario, Ca.	N368DS
N868EM	06	CitationJet CJ-3	525B-0081	DCCO Aviation LLC/Victory Management Leasing Inc. Detroit.	N52457
N868J	01	Citation Excel	560-5180	HealthTrust Inc/HCA Squared LLC. Nashville, Tn.	N868JB
N868SM	79	Gulfstream 2B	254	Tricycle Aviation LLC. Van Nuys, Ca.	N706TS
N868XL	05	Citation Excel XLS	560-5603	Florida Power & Light Co. Opa Locka, Fl.	N5244W
N869CB	01	CitationJet CJ-1	525-0453	CJ1 Partners LLC. Augusta, SC.	N928VC
N869GR	01	CitationJet CJ-1	525-0478	Fun Bike Center Inc. San Diego, Ca.	N5233J
N870BA	84	Westwind-Two	412	Trimex Medical Management Inc. Macon, Ga.	N999MC
N870BB	91	Beechjet 400A	RK-22	BYB Southwest LLC. Jonesboro, Ar.	(N522KJ)
N870CM	05	Gulfstream G550	5076	Caremark RX Inc. Birmingham, Al.	N576GA
N870QS	05	Hawker 800XPi	258732	NetJets, Port Columbus, Oh.	
N871QS	05	Hawker 800XPi	258763	NetJets, Port Columbus, Oh.	
N872AT	95	Hawker 800XP	258278	Hawker Beechcraft Corp. Wichita, Ks.	G-BVZK
N872BC	01	Hawker 800XP	258524	BCC Aviation LLC, DuPage, Il.	(N666BC)
N872EC	01	Falcon 2000	143	Entergy Services Inc. New Orleans, La.	N2230
N872QS	00	Hawker 800XP	258472	NetJets, Port Columbus, Oh.	N44722
N872RD	81	Citation II	550-0226	Cobell Air LLC. Boca Raton, Fl.	N872RT

Reg Yr Type c/n Owner/Operator Prev Regn

Reg	Yr	Type	c/n	Owner/Operator	Prev Regn
☐ N873G	83	Challenger 601	3009	Air Castle Corp. Santa Monica, Ca.	(N651AC)
☐ N873QS	02	Hawker 800XP	258573	NetJets, Port Columbus, Oh.	
☐ N874C	93	Gulfstream 4SP	1219	Hewlett-Packard Co. San Jose, Ca.	N87HP
☐ N874PT	07	Citation X	750-0274	XOJET Inc. Sacramento, Ca.	N5109W
☐ N874QS	99	Hawker 800XP	258474	NetJets, Port Columbus, Oh.	
☐ N874RA	82	Gulfstream 3	361	Private Jet Inc. New Canaan, Ct.	(N874RR)
☐ N874WD	92	Astra-1125SP	062	Williamson-Dickie Manufacturing Co. Fort Worth, Tx.	N866Q
☐ N875CA	80	Sabre-65	465-42	MA Inc. Oshkosh, Wi.	N45NP
☐ N875LP	96	Hawker 800XP	258308	Thomas H Lee Co. Bedford, Ma.	N345BR
☐ N875P	82	Westwind-1124	370	International Jet Management Inc. Dulles, Va.	N875HS
☐ N875QS	98	Hawker 800XP	258375	NetJets, Port Columbus, Oh.	
☐ N876CS	02	Learjet 60	60-263	CommScope Inc of NC. Hickory, NC.	N258FX
☐ N876G	95	Citation VII	650-7062	Bath Iron Works, Bath, Me.	N5262Z
☐ N876H	02	Challenger 604	5542	Household International Inc. Palwaukee, Il.	C-GLXQ
☐ N876MA	75	Falcon 10	63	Deniston Enterprises Inc. Baltimore, Md.	N70TS
☐ N876MC	70	Learjet 24B	24B-217	Royal Air Freight Inc. Pontiac, Mi.	C-FZHT
☐ N876QS	02	Hawker 800XP	258586	NetJets, Port Columbus, Oh.	
☐ N876WB	77	Citation	500-0347	Schaefer Ambulance Service Inc. Van Nuys, Ca.	N500XY
☐ N877A	01	Gulfstream 4SP	1461	APC Aviation Inc/Anadarko Petroleum Corp. Houston, Tx.	(N874RA)
☐ N877B	04	Citation Bravo	550-1110	Northern Air Inc. Grand Rapids, Mi.	N.....
☐ N877D	98	Astra-1125SPX	102	Sevens Aviation LLC/Mercury Exploration Co. Fort Worth, Tx.	N359D
☐ N877DM	95	Hawker 800XP	258279	Dan Air V LLC. Chicago, Il.	N817H
☐ N877FL	99	Beechjet 400A	RK-223	LandAmerica Financial Group Inc. Richmond, Va.	N777FL
☐ N877G	95	Citation VII	650-7063	General Dynamics Land Systems, Sterling Heights, Mi.	N95CC
☐ N877H	00	Challenger 604	5445	Household International Inc. Palwaukee, Il.	N604HD
☐ N877J	93	Beechjet 400A	RK-69	Asset Real Estate & Investment Co. Redding, Ca.	N877S
☐ N877JG	75	Falcon 20F	325	GHS Liner LLC. Belleville, Mi.	(N325MC)
☐ N877RF	01	Citation Excel	560-5219	Reinhart Real Estate Group Inc. La Crosse, Wi.	N5079H
☐ N877S	04	Hawker 400XP	RK-420	NHS Management LLC. Tuscaloosa, Al.	N620XP
☐ N877SD	99	Citation Bravo	550-0875	MKPL1 LLC. Scottsdale, Az.	N800AB
☐ N877W	04	390 Premier 1	RB-107	Georgia Crown Distributing Co. Columbus, Ga.	N61717
☐ N878SM	97	Gulfstream 4SP	1319	Symax Aviation Inc. West Palm Beach, Fl.	N429GA
☐ N879PT	07	Citation X	750-0279	CBC Companies, Columbus, Oh.	N5031E
☐ N879WC	98	Hawker 800XP	258379	Alliance Air Parts Inc. Oklahoma City, Ok. (status ?).	N879QS
☐ N880CR	97	Challenger 604	5356	Omnicare Management Co. Covington, Ky.	(N605AG)
☐ N880DP	74	DC 9-32	47635	Detroit Pistons/Round Ball One Corp. Detroit, Mi.	N880RB
☐ N880ET	01	Challenger 604	5514	Delek Group, Tel Aviv, Israel.	C-GJOE
☐ N880GC	87	Gulfstream 4	1016	Guardian Industries Corp. Detroit, Mi.	N29GY
☐ N880LT	96	Hawker 1000	259051	Life Time Fitness Inc. Minneapolis, Mn.	N551LR
☐ N880M	85	BAe 125/800A	258027	Algot Aviation LLC. Manhasset, NY.	N80CC
☐ N880MR	07	CitationJet CJ-3	525B-0226	Cessna Aircraft Co. Wichita, Ks.	N.....
☐ N880QS	02	Hawker 800XP	258570	NetJets, Port Columbus, Oh.	(N873QS)
☐ N880RG	80	HS 125/700A	257107	RG Aviation LLC. Fort Lauderdale, Fl.	N900MD
☐ N880RJ	75	Gulfstream II SP	159	Bentley Autojet LLC. New Castle, De.	(N397JT)
☐ N880SP	96	Hawker 800XP	258298	NiSource Corporate Services, Merrillville, In.	N298XP
☐ N880WD	91	Gulfstream 4	1170	J Porter Enterprises Inc. Romulus, Mi.	N997BC
☐ N880WE	78	Gulfstream 2	217	HBJ Leasing LLC. Waterford, Mi.	N880WD
☐ N880WW	84	BAe 125/800A	258019	Amweld Building Products Inc/W W Aircraft LLC. Garrettsville	N7996
☐ N880Z	84	Learjet 35A	35A-591	Potomac Corp. Wheeling, Il.	N9ZB
☐ N881A	87	Citation S/II	S550-0139	Nevell Group Inc. Brea, Ca.	N39TF
☐ N881KS	98	CitationJet	525-0300	Kansas State University, Salina, Ks.	N300CQ
☐ N881P	80	Learjet 25D	25D-302	Image Aircraft LLC. Wilmington, NC.	N25CY
☐ N881Q	00	Falcon 900EX	80	International Paper Co. White Plains, NY.	F-WWFV
☐ N881SA	89	Citation II/SP	551-0617	Esper Petersen, Camarillo, Ca.	N747GB
☐ N881TW	97	Challenger 604	5348	881TW LLC. Dallas, Tx.	C-GLWR
☐ N882C	90	Challenger 601-3A	5065	Transit Air Services Inc. Morristown, NJ.	N601BF
☐ N882CA	01	Learjet 45	45-155	ConAgra Foods Inc. Omaha, Ne.	N145MC
☐ N882GA	96	Astra-1125SPX	082	GEP Air LLC/Gary E Primm Family Trust, Las Vegas, Nv.	N121GV
☐ N882KB	03	Citation X	750-0216	F Korbel & Brothers Inc. Guerneville, Ca.	N1268F
☐ N882LT	01	Gulfstream G200	044	Eve II LLC. Newark, NJ.	N621KB
☐ N882QS	00	Hawker 800XP	258482	NetJets, Port Columbus, Oh.	N43182
☐ N882RB	85	Citation S/II	S550-0075	David Hutton, Killen, Al.	N882KB
☐ N882SC	04	Learjet 35A	35A-590	ATI Jet Sales LLC. El Paso, Tx.	(N822SF)
☐ N882WF	99	Citation Bravo	550-0882	Everest Development LLC. Denver, Co.	VH-VFP
☐ N883PF	00	Citation Excel	560-5085	Prestage Farms Inc. Clinton, NC.	N85XL
☐ N883QS	05	Hawker 800XPi	258773	NetJets, Port Columbus, Oh.	

Reg	Yr	Type	c/n	Owner/Operator	Prev Regn
☐ N883RA	04	Falcon 50EX	338	GHK Company LLC/The Glebe Group Inc. Oklahoma City, Ok.	N338FJ
☐ N883RP	02	Citation Excel XLS	560-5501	BostonPost Technology Inc. Nashua, NH. (was 560-5313)	N683RP
☐ N884B	00	Citation Excel	560-5140	ElanAir Inc/Heritage Flight, Burlington, Vt.	N52655
☐ N884BB	99	Citation Excel	560-5036	Olympus Aviation Inc. Minneapolis, Mn.	N36XL
☐ N884JW	80	Learjet 35A	35A-316	Winner Aviation Corp. Youngstown, Oh.	N384JW
☐ N884L	93	Gulfstream 4SP	1212	Hewlett-Packard Co. San Jose, Ca.	N88HP
☐ N884QS	05	Hawker 800XPi	258734	NetJets, Port Columbus, Oh.	
☐ N884VC	02	Hawker 800XP2	258584	Vitesse Corp. Greenfield, In.	N51384
☐ N885	86	Falcon 900	6	Anheuser-Busch Companies Inc. St Louis, Mo.	N80F
☐ N885AR	04	Gulfstream G450	4009	Rabbit Run LLC. Washington, DC.	N909GA
☐ N885BB	00	Citation Excel	560-5135	Olympus Aviation Inc. Minneapolis, Mn.	LV-ZXW
☐ N885BT	05	CitationJet CJ-3	525B-0058	Collier Family Office Inc. Naples, Fl.	N5066U
☐ N885G	97	Gulfstream V	518	Jetaway Air Service LLC. Muskegon, Mi.	(N917ND)
☐ N885KT	01	Gulfstream V	699	Troutt LLC. Tulsa, Ok. (was s/n 666).	N699GA
☐ N885M	99	Hawker 800XP2	258410	Jimbob Aviation Inc. Westfield, Ma.	N315BK
☐ N885QS	05	Hawker 800XPi	258743	NetJets, Port Columbus, Oh.	
☐ N885TW	04	Challenger 300	20037	Trans West Air Service Inc. Salt Lake City, Ut.	C-GZDS
☐ N886DC	98	Falcon 900B	177	FJ 900 Inc/Danaher Corp. Washington, DC.	F-WWFY
☐ N886G	02	Gulfstream G200	057	Electric Boat Corp. Groton, Ct.	N299GA
☐ N886QS	00	Hawker 800XP	258486	NetJets, Port Columbus, Oh.	
☐ N886R	79	Learjet 35A	35A-269	CSLJ LLC. Colorado Springs, Co.	N211WH
☐ N887CS	08	Citation Encore+	560-0787	Cessna Aircraft Co. Wichita, Ks.	N.....
☐ N887DT	78	JetStar 2	5223	Flight Source International Inc. Sarasota, Fl.	N886DT
☐ N887QS	99	Hawker 800XP	258387	NetJets, Port Columbus, Oh.	
☐ N887WM	99	Global Express	9041	Challenger Administration LLC/Mente Corp. Seattle, Wa.	N195WM
☐ N887WS	02	Global Express	9120	Williams-Sonoma Inc. Oakland Metropolitan, Ca.	N700FG
☐ N888AQ	06	BBJ-7HF/W	35977	White Sapphire LLC. NYC.	VP-CLL
☐ N888AZ	84	Challenger 601	3024	C & C Enterprises Inc. Tompkins County, NY.	N93CR
☐ N888CE*	07	Falcon 2000EX EASY	124	Magic Carpet Management Ltd. Ithaca, NY.	N124EX
☐ N888CJ	66	HS 125/1A	25084	Hawker Holdings Inc. Fort Lauderdale, Fl.	N890RC
☐ N888CN	05	Challenger 300	20062	Premier One Corp. Taipei, Taiwan.	C-GZER
☐ N888CP	88	Learjet 31	31-003	Ten Air Aircraft Corp. Minneapolis, Mn.	N331CC
☐ N888CW	98	Gulfstream V	545	Countrywide Home Loans Inc. Van Nuys, Ca.	N5GV
☐ N888CX	99	Learjet 45	45-044	Compar Foundation, Belgrade, Serbia.	D-CLUB
☐ N888DH	96	Challenger 604	5305	R D Hubbard Enterprises Inc. Palm Springs, Ca.	N747Y
☐ N888ES	90	Gulfstream 4	1120	C&S Aviation LLC/Executive Software International , Burbank.	N20H
☐ N888FA	72	Learjet 24D	24D-257	Intermountain Fixed Wing LC. Salt Lake City, Ut.	C-GHDP
☐ N888FG	81	Citation II	550-0298	Gold Key Aviation Inc/Johnson International, Scottsdale, Az.	D-ILCC
☐ N888FJ	73	Falcon 10	4	Falcon 10 Aviation LLC. Scottsdale, Az.	XA-SYY
☐ N888FL	77	Citation 1/SP	501-0014	Sky Blue Aviation Sales LLC/Cyber Operations, Pelham, Al.	N22TP
☐ N888GL	03	CitationJet CJ-2	525A-0201	Garmin International Inc. Olathe, Ks.	N.....
☐ N888HE	00	Gulfstream V	638	N888HE Inc/Meadow Poppy Ltd. Tortola, BVI.	(N888HK)
☐ N888HH	05	Gulfstream G450	4029	Haworth Inc. Holland, Mi.	N629GA
☐ N888JL	75	Citation	500-0242	Triple Eight LLC/Dialysis Laboratories Inc. Deland, Fl.	(N884DR)
☐ N888KL	98	Learjet 60	60-141	Great Bay Aviation LLC. Portsmouth, NH.	N655TH
☐ N888KU	94	CitationJet	525-0068	Sencon International Inc. Miami, Fl.	N303LC
☐ N888LK	02	Gulfstream G550	5012	Mojo Aviation Inc. Oxford-Kidlington, UK.	N812GA
☐ N888LV	82	Gulfstream 3	347	GC Asset Management LLC/Midtown Equities, Islip, NY.	N545JT
☐ N888ME	81	Falcon 50	41	Virginia Properties LLC. Chicago, Il.	N888MF
☐ N888MF	95	Gulfstream 4SP	1268	Sleep Air LLC. Teterboro, NJ.	N600BG
☐ N888ML	04	Embraer Legacy 600	14500818	Jet Asia Ltd/New Macau Landmark Management Ltd. Macau.	PT-SIM
☐ N888MN	06	390 Premier 1A	RB-153	MCM Associates LLC. Los Angeles, Ca.	(N321DC)
☐ N888NY	99	BBJ-7CG	30751	Hualalai II LLC. NYC.	VP-BMC
☐ N888PM	92	Gulfstream 4	1195	Red, White & Blue Pictures Inc. Van Nuys, Ca.	N867CE
☐ N888QS	07	Hawker 900XP	HA-42	NetJets, Port Columbus, Oh.	
☐ N888RA	96	CitationJet	525-0135	Richard Auhll, Santa Barbara, Ca.	N5207A
☐ N888RK	06	CitationJet CJ-3	525B-0097	Kom Activity BV. Rotterdam, Holland.	N5216A
☐ N888RL	81	Citation II	550-0254	Bozeman Jet Services LLC/Sunbird Aviation Inc. Bozeman, Mt.	N888RT
☐ N888RT	07	Challenger 300	20162	R T Oliver Investments Inc. Oklahoma City, Ok.	C-FMWX
☐ N888SF	07	Citation Sovereign	680-0154	Steiner Films Aviation Inc. Munich, Germany.	N52234
☐ N888TJ	71	HS 125/731	25250	Crusader Aero Inc. Bata, Equatorial Guinea.	N7SJ
☐ N888TW	74	Learjet 24D	24D-292	Sierra American Corp. Addison, Tx.	N800PC
☐ N888TX	92	Citation VII	650-7003	A & C Business Services Inc. Orlando, Fl.	(N650RJ)
☐ N888TY	99	BBJ-7AH	29749	TY Air Inc. Westmont, Il.	N134AR
☐ N888UP	81	Sabre-65	465-68	Agilis Management Inc. Palm Beach, Fl.	N6NR
☐ N888WS	94	Challenger 601-3R	5170	Williams-Sonoma Inc. Oakland-Metropolitan, Ca.	N166A

Reg	Yr	Type	c/n	Owner/Operator	Prev Regn
N888XL	89	Citation II	550-0598	Citation II LLC. Richardson, Tx.	N7WY
N888YF	02	BBJ-7BC	33036	Eva Air, Taipei, Taiwan.	N110QS
N888ZF	01	Gulfstream 4SP	1466	Ponderosa Asset LLC. Oxford, Ct.	VP-BSH
N888ZZ	84	BAe 125/800A	258017	Current Aviation Group Inc.	N217RM
N889B	02	Citation Bravo	550-1047	JenMar Corp. Pittsburgh, Pa.	N5231S
N889CA	00	Learjet 45	45-132	MD45 Transport LLC. Omaha, Ne.	N132LJ
N889CP	01	Global Express	9104	Kirra Aircraft Leasing Partnership 1, Melbourne, Australia	N190WP
N889DW	97	Learjet 60	60-117	New Vistas LLC. Seattle, Wa.	
N889FA	80	Citation II/SP	551-0036	First American Title Insurance Co. Santa Ana, Ca.	N3170B
N889G	01	Gulfstream G200	046	General Dynamics Information Technology, Needham, Ma.	PR-MEN
N889JA	04	Global Express	9148	Jet Asia Ltd. Taipa, Macau.	C-FAIO
N889JC	75	Gulfstream II SP	158	Amador LLC/Capital Royalty LP. Houston, Tx.	N2S
N889MR	02	Gulfstream G200	074	Majestic Realty Co. Van Nuys, Ca.	N80R
N889NC	99	BBJ-7AV	30070	NewsFlight Inc. Los Angeles, Ca.	N18NC
N889QS	07	Hawker 900XP	HA-21	NetJets/Marquis Jet Partners Inc. Port Columbus, Oh.	N899QS
N890A	99	Gulfstream 4SP	1396	Jackson National Life Insurance Co. Lansing, Mi.	N396GA
N890BA	80	Westwind-Two	301	Outback Steakhouse of Florida Inc. Tampa, Fl.	N301KF
N890BB	06	Falcon 900DX	611	New Heights LLC/Varde Partners, Minneapolis, Mn.	N886BB
N890BJ	77	Learjet 25D	25D-229	2nd Main Inc. Leesburg, Fl.	N229WJ
N890LE	06	Citation Excel XLS	560-5628	Lee Enterprises Inc. Davenport, Ia.	N51038
N890LR*	82	Learjet 35A	35A-487	Stevens Aviation Inc. Greenville, SC.	N487FW
N890QS	07	Hawker 900XP	HA-10	NetJets/Marquis Jet Partners Inc. Port Columbus, Oh.	
N890SP	01	Hawker 800XP	258530	SoarAir Leasing LLC/Sorenson Companies, Salt Lake City, Ut.	
N890TJ	68	Gulfstream 2	23	Bizjet International Sales & Support Inc. Tulsa, Ok.	N7TJ
N891CA	74	Citation	500-0168	Gulf Atlantic Airways/University Air Center, Gainesville, Fl	(N46JA)
N891FV	97	Citation V Ultra	560-0427	Investors Warranty of America Inc. Cedar Rapids, Ia.	(N427EA)
N891P	81	Learjet 25D	25D-340	Image Products LLC. Wilmington, NC.	N625AU
N891QS	06	Hawker 850XPi	258788	NetJets/Marquis Jet Partners Inc. Port Columbus, Oh.	
N892BP*	90	BAe 125/800A	NA0454	Monroe LLC. Dulles, Va.	N180EG
N892PB	79	Citation II	550-0070	Tansoar Inc. Rogers, Ar.	N550KA
N892QS	03	Hawker 800XP	258592	RenaissanceRe Holdings Ltd. Hamilton, Bermuda.	
N892S	78	Falcon 20F-5B	379	Scruggs Law Firm PA. Oxford, Ms.	(N724JS)
N892SB	02	Gulfstream G200	072	Security Benefit Corp. Topeka, Ks.	N679RW
N892TM	72	Gulfstream II SP	121	Trayton Aviation LLC. Fort Lauderdale, Fl.	N721PL
N893CW	02	Hawker 800XP	258603	Flight Options LLC. Cuyahoga County, Oh.	(N803CW)
N893QS	99	Hawker 800XP	258393	NetJets, Port Columbus, Oh.	
N894C	01	CitationJet CJ-2	525A-0013	N177RE LLC. Milwaukie, Or.	(N177RE)
N894CA	98	Hawker 800XP	258366	Avwest P/L. Perth, WA. Australia.	(CS-MAI)
N894QS	07	Hawker 900XP	HA-5	NetJets, Port Columbus, Oh.	
N894TW	81	Westwind-1124	354	Bulard Air Services LLC. NYC.	N124LS
N895BB	07	Challenger 300	20156	HF LLC/Olympus Aviation LLC. Minneapolis, Mn.	C-FMXX
N895HE	90	Citation II	550-0641	Schwarz Partners LP. Indianapolis, In.	(N391DT)
N895QS	03	Hawker 800XP	258606	NetJets, Port Columbus, Oh.	N60506
N896C	92	Beechjet 400A	RK-53	CONOCO Flight Support, San Angelo, Tx.	(N414LX)
N896CG	03	Citation Bravo	550-1055	Gallo Air Inc. Guatemala City, Guatemala.	N.....
N896DA	83	Falcon 50	117	Dura Automotive Systems Inc. Pontiac, Mi.	N50J
N896MA	03	Citation Bravo	550-1065	Joe H Anderson Jr & Sons Inc. Lake City, Fl.	N175CW
N896P	07	CitationJet CJ2+	525A-0379	EJP Air LLC. Boise, Id.	N5270J
N896QS	03	Hawker 800XP	258640	NetJets, Port Columbus, Oh.	N640XP
N897A	97	Hawker 800XP2	258326	House of Raeford Farms Inc. Rose Hill, NC.	N1897A
N897CW	86	BAe 125/800A	258077	Private Fliers LLC. Boise, Id.	(N808LX)
N897MC	99	Citation Bravo	550-0914	Manitowoc Co. Manitowoc, Wi.	N5105F
N897QS	07	Hawker 900XP	HA-14	NetJets, Port Columbus, Oh.	
N898AK*	89	Challenger 601-3A	5040	Poppa Air LLC. Boston, Ma.	N807Z
N898AN	99	Challenger 604	5408	Resources Aviation Inc. Fort Lauderdale, Fl.	N898R
N898CB	91	Citation V	560-0097	Robert L Kimball & Assocs Inc. Westfield, Ma.	(N6790L)
N898CT	98	Falcon 2000	60	Nortom Corp. Concord, Ca.	N524SA
N898EW	93	Challenger 601-3A	5134	Tango Jet SA/Tango Sur, Buenos Aires, Argentina.	N511WN
N898MC	02	Citation Excel	560-5244	Manitowoc Co. Manitowoc, Wi.	N244XL
N898PA	97	Learjet 60	60-111	PA Lear 60-111 LLC. Carrollton, Tx.	N221FX
N898QS	02	Hawker 800XP	258593	NetJets, Port Columbus, Oh.	
N898TA	00	Beechjet 400A	RK-295	Flight Options LLC. Cuyahoga County, Oh.	(N463LX)
N899AB	78	HS 125/700A	NA0230	Allen Transport LLC. Anchorage, Ak.	N881S
N899B	03	Citation Bravo	550-1073	Wilbur & Orville Inc/Northern Air Inc. Grand Rapids, Mi.	N.....
N899MA	06	CitationJet CJ-3	525B-0073	Braun Corp. Winamac, In.	N.....
N899QS	07	Hawker 900XP	HA-19	NetJets/Marquis Jet Partners, Port Columbus, Oh.	N889QS

Reg	Yr	Type	c/n	Owner/Operator	Prev Regn
N899RR	05	CitationJet CJ-3	525B-0020	Raven Air LLC. Oklahoma City, Ok.	N52038
N899SC	02	Hawker 800XP2	258602	SCI Texas Funeral Services Inc. Houston, Tx.	N61702
N899U	02	Falcon 2000	199	International Paper Co. White Plains, NY.	N2295
N900AD	71	HS 125/400A	NA769	MBNA Corp. Greater Wilmington, De. (status ?).	N369JH
N900AL	05	Gulfstream G450	4048	Abbott Laboratories Inc. Waukegan, Il.	N448GA
N900AP	89	Gulfstream 4	1097	Frontier Oil Corp. Houston, Tx.	N900AL
N900BJ	77	Learjet 35A	35A-123	N900BJ LLC. West Columbia, SC.	N900JE
N900BT	00	CitationJet CJ-1	525-0377	Techni Airplane LLC. Armonk, NY.	N15C
N900BZ	98	Falcon 900EX	37	ZG Aircraft Leasing LLC/Boulder Aviation LLC. Tampa, Fl.	N327K
N900CC	76	Citation	500-0310	Construcciones Atina 2000 CA. Caracas, Venezuela.	N941JC
N900CE	68	Gulfstream II SP	10	Cashman Equipment Corp. Boston, Ma.	HR-AUJ
N900CH	01	Falcon 2000EX	1	Cardinal Health Inc/Cardal Inc. Dublin, Oh. (Ff 25 Oct 01).	VP-BMJ
N900CM	01	Falcon 50EX	321	Cargill Meat Solutions Corp. Wichita, Ks.	N321EX
N900CP	79	HS 125/700A	NA0248	Allied Services Inc. Norfolk, Va.	N900CQ
N900CS	91	Falcon 900B	104	Pilot Partners LLC/Macklowe Properties Inc. NYC.	N881G
N900D	93	Falcon 900B	131	Oakmont Corp. Van Nuys, Ca.	N900KD
N900DB	78	JetStar 2	5225	5161 Romeo LLC. Chicago, Il.	(N5161R)
N900DH	72	Gulfstream 2	111	Sagem Avionics Inc. Grand Prairie, Tx.	N900BR
N900DL	89	Astra-1125	030	Duro-Last Inc/Duro-Last Roofing Inc. Sigourney, Ia.	N902G
N900DP	05	Embraer Legacy 600	14500903	BusAv/Del Inc. Aiken, SC.	PT-SIW
N900DS	93	CitationJet	525-0032	Great Southern Bank, Springfield, Mo.	N32VP
N900DW	99	Falcon 900B	179	Whiteco Industries Inc. Merrillville, In.	N900FJ
N900E	93	Citation V	560-0206	N900E LLC. Stuart, Fl.	N560TX
N900EB	04	Citation Sovereign	680-0008	Subaru of New England Inc. Norwood, Ma.	N.....
N900EF	93	Beechjet 400A	RK-68	WFBNW NA. Salt Lake City, Ut. (trustor ?).	XA-PYN
N900EG	89	Gulfstream 4	1101	Greenfield Aviation LLC. Bridgeport, Ct.	N365G
N900EM	06	Embraer Legacy 600	14500976	EWM Investments LLC. Las Vegas, Nv.	PT-SHI
N900FN	92	Challenger 601-3A	5118	Pivotal Group Inc. Scottsdale, Az.	N24JK
N900FS	76	Westwind-1124	191	Franks Petroleum Inc. Shreveport, La.	(N900RR)
N900G	75	Citation	500-0268	The Wisdom Center Inc. Fort Worth, Tx.	A6-RKH
N900GC	76	Citation	500-0298	Granite Construction Co. Watsonville, Ca.	N5298J
N900GG	70	Learjet 24B	24B-216	Foster & Hendricks LLC. Tomball, Tx.	N777LB
N900GW	99	CitationJet	525-0323	Joe Morten & Son Inc. South Sioux City, Ne.	
N900H	90	Challenger 601-3A	5080	Hoak Travel Inc. Dallas, Tx.	N903TA
N900HA	01	CitationJet CJ-2	525A-0039	Auberach Aeronautic Associates Inc. East Hampton, NY.	(N525L)
N900HC	03	Falcon 900EX EASY	127	Group Falcon EX Holdings LLC. Portland, Or.	F-WWFD
N900HD	01	Falcon 900EX	103	NII Aviation Inc. Dulles, Va.	N103FJ
N900HE	89	Falcon 900	68	Group Holdings EG Inc. Fort Worth, Tx.	N900HC
N900HG	95	Falcon 900EX	1	Jetflight Aviation Inc. Lugano-Agno, Switzerland.	PH-ERP
N900JC	78	Learjet 35A	35A-178	AirNet Systems Inc. Columbus, Oh.	(N104AA)
N900JD	06	Citation Sovereign	680-0109	Deere & Co. Moline, Il.	N.....
N900JG	06	Falcon 900EX EASY	168	Elmet Air 900 Inc. Miami, Fl.	(N900JF)
N900JT	81	HS 125/700A	NA0303	J T Inc. Southfield, Mi.	N678W
N900KE	81	Falcon 50	52	Arctic Rides/McKinley Capital Management Inc. Anchorage, Ak.	N163WW
N900KJ	02	Falcon 900C	199	Kendall-Jackson Wine Estates Ltd. Santa Rosa, Ca.	N199FJ
N900KK	95	Learjet 60	60-052	Rubicon Leasing LLC. Boca Raton, Fl.	N247CP
N900KX	01	Falcon 900EX	98	Juniper Networks/Adventair LLC-VC Jets LLC. San Jose, Ca.	N998EX
N900LA	83	Gulfstream 3	379	Sonoran Charters LLC. Scottsdale, Az.	N28QQ
N900LC	00	Falcon 900C	186	DB Aviation Inc. Waukegan, Il.	F-WWFJ
N900LD	07	Hawker 900XP	HA-8	ICI Development Co. Santa Ana, Ca.	
N900LG	81	Challenger 600S	1036	Bramblebush Training LLC/Cheniere Energy Inc. Houston, Tx.	N900DP
N900LM	87	Citation S/II	S550-0145	CB Capital Aviation LLC. Centerville, Oh.	4X-CPT
N900LS	06	Global 5000	9216	Eastern Key Properties LLC. Las Vegas, Nv.	C-FIPN
N900MC	06	Falcon 2000	228	Deer Horn Aviation Ltd. Midland, Tx.	F-WWVP
N900MF	02	Falcon 900EX	112	Jarden Corp. Oxford, Ct.	G-JJMX
N900MG	88	Falcon 900B	67	Scotts Miracle-Gro/The Scotts Co. Columbus, Oh.	N900MA
N900MJ	99	Falcon 900EX	57	ACM Aviation Inc. San Jose, Ca.	N900MT
N900MV	03	Falcon 900EX EASY	131	Bloomberg Services LLC. Morristown, NJ.	VP-BFM
N900NB	06	Falcon 900EX EASY	169	900NB Corp/JMB Realty Corp. Chicago, Il.	N900NF
N900NH	02	Falcon 2000	206	BSLCC III LLC/Second Avenue Partners, Seattle, Wa.	N831DC
N900NS	05	Falcon 900EX EASY	150	Aviamax Aviation Ltd. Farnborough, UK.	F-WWFI
N900P	01	Learjet 45	45-173	Riverside Financial LLC. Wisconsin Dells, Wi.	
N900PF	07	Hawker 900XP	HA-22	Pigeon Air One LLC. New Castle, De.	N922XP
N900PS	91	Citation V	560-0118	Papa Sierra LLC. San Luis Obsipo, Ca.	N626SL
N900Q	96	Falcon 900EX	10	TP Aviation LLC/Tarrant Partners LP. Fort Worth, Tx.	N22CS
N900QS	00	Citation X	750-0123	NetJets, Port Columbus, Oh.	(N51038)

Reg	Yr	Type	c/n	Owner/Operator	Prev Regn
N900R	07	Hawker 900XP	HA-13	NASCAR Inc. Daytona Beach, Fl.	N113XP
N900RA	67	Falcon 20C	59	Royal Air Freight Inc. Pontiac, Mi.	N159MV
N900RL	90	Gulfstream 4	1150	Elite Aviation LLC. Van Nuys, Ca.	N386AG
N900RX	99	Falcon 900C	183	Roux Investment Management LLC. Hayward, Ca.	(N900WP)
N900SA	66	DC 9-15	45775	HW Aviation LLC. Chicago, Il.	N40SH
N900SB	97	Falcon 900EX	26	SBC Management Services Inc. San Antonio, Tx.	F-WWFX
N900SJ	87	Falcon 900	19	Sid R Bass Inc. Fort Worth, Tx.	N414FJ
N900SM	89	Citation V	560-0014	ServiceMaster Holding Corp. Downers Grove, Il.	(N650ST)
N900SN	02	Falcon 900EX	117	First Quality Enterprises Inc. Farmingdale, NY.	(N900EX)
N900ST	06	Hawker 850XP	258777	Southern Tire Aviation LLC. Hattiesburg, Ms.	N877XP
N900SX	94	Falcon 900B	139	Space Exploration Technologies/Elon Musk, Van Nuys, Ca.	(N523AG)
N900TG	95	Falcon 900B	155	CSIM Air LLC. Portland, Or.	N155FJ
N900TN	83	Westwind-Two	400	AirCorp Inc. Anchorage, Ak.	N900PA
N900TR	97	Falcon 900B	170	Crusader Acquisitions Inc. Rockland, Ma.	N900DA
N900UD	91	Citation VI	650-0213	UAML Corp. Jacksonville, Fl.	N900JD
N900VG	94	Falcon 900B	148	Vecellio Management Services Inc. West Palm Beach, Fl.	N900DV
N900VL	88	Falcon 900B	60	Outfitter Aviation LLC. Medford, Or.	N91TH
N900VP	80	Westwind-1124	289	Venture Air LLC. Newark, De.	VR-CIL
N900WF	92	Falcon 900B	117	BentleyForbes Group Inc. Van Nuys, Ca.	N70TH
N900WK	88	Falcon 900B	57	Kellogg Co. Battle Creek, Mi.	N441FJ
N900WR	00	Gulfstream 4SP	1416	Wayne Reaud, Beaumont, Tx.	N416GA
N900WY	04	Challenger 300	20035	M & N Aviation, Casper, Wy.	C-GZET
N900YP	02	Falcon 900EX	114	Villages Equipment Co. Leesburg, Fl.	(N114EX)
N901AB	95	Citation V Ultra	560-0302	Angel Brothers Enterprises Ltd. Baytown, Tx.	N302EJ
N901CD	80	Sabre-65	465-39	Kastlemar Inc/Compson Development Co. Boca Raton, Fl.	N41LV
N901CJ	98	CitationJet	525-0278	Helicopter Express Inc. Lawrenceville, Ga.	N100SM
N901CR	00	Citation Excel	560-5141	AON Corp/Globe Leasing Inc. Chicago-Midway, Il.	N701CR
N901DK	04	Citation Excel XLS	560-5505	Keffer Management Co. Charlotte, NC.	N.....
N901EB	00	CitationJet CJ-2	525A-0008	Elite Jets LLC. Charleston, SC.	N900EB
N901EH	81	Gulfstream 3	333	MH Aviation Inc. Cheyenne, Wy.	N901FH
N901FH	01	Citation Excel	560-5160	CCBCC Operations LLC. Charlotte, NC.	N903FH
N901G	06	Citation Sovereign	680-0065	Owens-Illinois General Inc. Toledo, Oh.	N.....
N901GW	01	CitationJet CJ-1	525-0470	Joe Morten & Son Inc. South Sioux City, Ne.	N.....
N901GX	96	Global Express	9001	Learjet Inc. Wichita, Ks. (ASTOR prototype. Ff 3 Aug 01).	C-FBGX
N901HB	05	SJ 30-2	006	Jetran LLC. Austin, Tx.	N60SJ
N901K	07	Hawker 900XP	HA-9	Rosetree Aviation LLC. Allegheny County, Pa.	N809HB
N901MD	98	Falcon 900EX	38	MacDermid Inc. Arapahoe, Co.	N68CG
N901MM	97	Falcon 900EX	21	Marcus & Millichap Co. San Jose, Ca.	(N331MC)
N901P	00	Learjet 31A	31A-199	Camlu Retirement Centers, Wenatchee, Wa.	N900P
N901QS	99	Citation X	750-0102	NetJets, Port Columbus, Oh.	N51995
N901RD	07	Hawker 900XP	HA-18	R R Donnelley & Sons Co. Chicago, Il.	
N901SB	02	Falcon 900EX EASY	122	SBC Management Services Inc. San Antonio, Tx.	F-WWFX
N901SG	05	Hawker 850XP	258762	Blanca Paloma LLC/Sergio Garcia, Valencia, Spain.	N762XP
N901SS	00	Falcon 900C	187	EOS Aviation LLC. San Jose, Ca.	N181FJ
N901TF	99	Falcon 50EX	285	Tyson Foods Inc. Fayetteville, Ar.	F-WWHM
N901WG	73	Gulfstream 2	126	Gary Aircraft, Stuart, Fl. 'Wings of Justice'	N416K
N902	96	Gulfstream 4SP	1310	Owens-Illinois General Inc. Toledo, Oh.	(N2425)
N902AG	02	Challenger 604	5512	AGCO Corp. DeKalb-Peachtree, Ga.	N512SH
N902AU	88	Astra-1125	025	S Hawk Holdings Inc. Indianapolis-Terry, In.	N887PA
N902BW	87	Challenger 601-3A	5005	Goodfriend Aviation/Goody's Family Clothing, McGhee-Tyson.	N64FE
N902DD	73	Citation	500-0126	Del Mar Citation LLC/Dyson Development, Solana Beach, Ca.	N404MA
N902DK	94	Citation II	550-0732	Equipment Leasing LLC/DRC Inc. Mobile, Al.	N101AF
N902DP	07	CitationJet CJ1+	525-0644	Nucor Corp. Charlotte, NC.	N50321
N902F	93	Citation VII	650-7022	TF Aircraft LLC/TGF Investments LP. Palatine, Il.	N902RM
N902GW	04	CitationJet CJ-1	525-0553	Joe Morton & Son Inc. South Sioux City, Ne.	N51612
N902L	02	Gulfstream G400	1504	Pinehurst Timber LLC. Carslbad, Ca.	(N402QS)
N902MM	02	Global Express	9097	MP Air Inc/Mylan Pharmaceuticals Inc. Morgantown, WV.	N908TE
N902MP	03	Challenger 604	5559	MP Air Inc/Mylan Pharmaceuticals Inc. Morgantown, WV.	N559JA
N902NC	90	Falcon 900	97	Newell Co. Rockford, Il.	(N900UU)
N902SB	00	Falcon 50EX	308	SBC Management Services Inc. San Antonio, Tx.	F-WWHL
N902TF	00	Falcon 50EX	303	Tyson Foods Inc. Fayetteville, Ar.	F-WWHE
N902WG	81	B 737-2H6	22620	Gary 737 LLC/Gary Aircraft, Stuart, Fl.	N22620
N903AG	94	Learjet 60	60-045	Books-a-Million Inc. Birmingham, Al.	N711VJ
N903AL	76	Learjet 35A	35A-084	ALCO Holdings Inc/Agnew Co. Portland, Or.	(N696JH)
N903AM	03	Learjet 60	60-269	Lincare Holdings Inc/Med 4 Home Inc. Clearwater, Fl.	N100NR
N903BH	95	Citation V Ultra	560-0295	Matlock Aviation LLC. Pocatello, Id.	N295BM

Reg	Yr	Type	c/n	Owner/Operator	Prev Regn
N903BT	07	Learjet 45	45-353	Learjet Inc. Wichita, Ks.	
N903CG	01	Beechjet 400A	RK-333	Sims Enterprises Inc. Norfolk, Va.	(N72FL)
N903DD	82	Challenger 600S	1038	Sky View Aviation Inc. Orlando, Fl.	N616DF
N903DK	00	Citation Excel	560-5093	Keffer Management Co. Charlotte, NC.	N19MZ
N903GS*	02	Falcon 2000	183	Gilead Sciences Inc. Foster City, Ca.	N88MX
N903JC	83	Learjet 55	55-081	Coin Acceptors Inc. St Louis, Mo.	N777MQ
N903MM	78	Westwind-1124	235	Professional Air Leasing LLC. Miami, Fl.	N30AB
N903MT	01	390 Premier 1	RB-24	MT Air LLC/McVean Trading & Investments, Memphis, Tn.	N124BR
N903QS	01	Citation X	750-0162	NetJets, Port Columbus, Oh.	
N903SB	00	Falcon 50EX	309	SBC Management Services Inc. San Antonio, Tx.	F-WWHM
N903SC	77	HS 125/700A	NA0218	Caribbean Skies Aviation LLC. St Thomas, USVI.	N804FF
N903TC	85	Gulfstream 3	454	Tesoro Corp. San Antonio, Tx.	N111GX
N903XP	07	Hawker 900XP	HA-3	Specialised Aircraft Services Inc. Wichita, Ks.	
N904BB	99	Citation Bravo	550-0904	Nunes Co. Salinas, Ca.	N5093Y
N904BW	85	BAe 125/800A	258042	Robert Mondavi Corp. Oakland, Ca.	N804RM
N904DS	02	Global Express	9118	DSWA Communications LP. Dulles, Va.	N700EZ
N904GR	89	BAe 125/800A	NA0448	Schwarz Partners LP. Indianapolis, In.	N904GP
N904HD	01	Learjet 45	45-149	HDR Construction Control Corp. Omaha, Ne.	N451GL
N904JK	05	Challenger 604	5615	Hamilton Aviation Inc. Lake Oswego, Or.	N604SG
N904JR	84	BAe 125/800A	258018	Black Creek Partners Inc. Dallas-Love, Tx.	N525CF
N904JY	07	Falcon 900EX EASY	187	B & D Aviation LLC. Hillsboro, Or.	F-WWFA
N904LX	04	Embraer Legacy 600	145780	Flight Options LLC. Cuyahoga County, Oh.	N780SG
N904QS	03	Citation X	750-0210	NetJets, Port Columbus, Oh.	N51666
N904SB	99	Falcon 50EX	284	SBC Management Services Inc. San Antonio, Tx.	F-WWHL
N904SJ	89	Citation II	550-0604	SJ Aire Aviation Co. Laredo, Tx.	N887SA
N904TC	00	Gulfstream 4SP	1444	Tesoro Corp. San Antonio, Tx.	N400HF
N905B	00	Falcon 2000	132	JRB Air LLC. Bellevue, Wa.	N97NX
N905CK	75	Learjet 36	36-005	Kalitta Charters LLC. Detroit-Willow Run, Mi.	N9108Z
N905CW	79	Citation II	550-0072	Premier Aviation LLC/Colman Funding, Napa County, Ca.	N778JM
N905LC	95	Citation V Ultra	560-0334	Flight 2006 Inc/Special Services Corp. Greenville, SC.	N4TL
N905LP	97	Gulfstream 4SP	1321	Thomas H Lee Co. Bedford, Ma.	N500CD
N905LX	04	Embraer Legacy 600	145775	Southwest Homes Ltd/Flight Options LLC. Cuyahoga County.	PT-SIC
N905MP	82	Challenger 600S	1039	Univex Aviation LLC. Houston, Tx.	N895CC
N905QS	99	Citation X	750-0105	NetJets, Port Columbus, Oh.	
N905RL	83	Learjet 55	55-074	RL Aviation LLC. Van Nuys, Ca.	N155LR
N905SB	06	Falcon 50EX	348	SBC Management Services Inc. San Antonio, Tx.	F-WWHD
N906AS	01	Hawker 800XP	258569	A T Shaw Co. Concord, Ca.	N244LS
N906BL	06	Hawker 850XP	258806	Flyaway Inc. Fort Worth, Tx.	N36826
N906FM	06	390 Premier 1A	RB-176	Foresight Management/Cline Resource & Development Co. WV.	N7176J
N906JW	01	Global Express	9110	JW Asset Management Ltd. UK.	N14R
N906LX	04	Embraer Legacy 600	14500825	Flight Options LLC. Cuyahoga County, Oh.	N825SG
N906QS	03	Citation X	750-0206	NetJets, Port Columbus, Oh.	
N906SB	06	Falcon 50EX	349	SBC Management Services Inc. San Antonio, Tx.	F-WWHE
N906TC	05	Challenger 300	20083	Tesoro Corp. San Antonio, Tx.	N1DH
N906TF	98	Challenger 604	5366	Tyson Foods Inc. Fayetteville, Ar.	C-GJFC
N906WK	91	Falcon 900	102	Kellogg Co. Battle Creek, Mi.	N467FJ
N907DF	86	Citation III	650-0120	Duraflame Inc. Stockton, Ca.	N30NM
N907DK	99	CitationJet	525-0338	Keffer Management Co. Charlotte, NC.	N977DM
N907DP	98	Astra-1125SPX	100	Alaska Flight Services LLC. Anchorage, Ak.	N807JW
N907JE	95	Beechjet 400A	RK-107	Bleka Aviation LLC. Romeoville, Il.	N733MK
N907QS	02	Citation X	750-0201	NetJets, Port Columbus, Oh.	
N907SB*	07	Falcon 7X	13	Dassault Falcon Jet Corp. Teterboro, NJ.	F-WWUJ
N907TF	77	Falcon 10	107	Tyson Foods Inc. Fayetteville, Ar.	N91BP
N907WL	07	CitationJet CJ1+	525-0658	RSC Equity LLC. Orlando, Fl.	N.....
N907WS	89	Challenger 601-3A	5048	Shidler Investment Corp. Honolulu, Hi.	N716RD
N908AS	00	Citation Encore	560-0547	June Tenth LLC/Island Lincoln Mercury, Merritt Island, Fl.	N906AS
N908CA	95	Falcon 900B	151	CMI Aviation Inc/Atkins Group, Chicago-Midway, Il.	EC-HHK
N908CH	78	Falcon 20F-5	383	Lear 55 LLC/Bestjets of Million Air St Louis LLC. Mo.	N900CH
N908JB	91	Falcon 900B	112	Strange Bird Inc. Tallahassee, Fl.	N248AG
N908JE	69	B 727-31	20115	JEGE Inc. Wilmington, De.	N505LS
N908QS	99	Citation X	750-0108	NetJets, Port Columbus, Oh.	N51744
N908SB	00	Falcon 900EX	81	SBC Management Services Inc. San Antonio, Tx.	N404R
N908TF	77	Falcon 10	102	Tyson Foods Inc. Fayetteville, Ar.	N61BP
N908VZ	05	Gulfstream G450	4051	Verizon Communications, White Plains, NY.	N351GA
N909DP	02	CitationJet CJ-1	525-0503	NuMark Industries LLC. Fort Lauderdale, Fl.	N904DP
N909F*	98	CitationJet	525-0249	Marseille-Kliniken AG/VDSE GmbH. Hamburg, Germany.	N909M

Reg	Yr	Type	c/n	Owner/Operator	Prev Regn
❏ N909FK	79	Gulfstream II SP	241	Warrington Aviation/Kenwal Steel Corp. Pontiac, Mi.	N909MK
❏ N909JE	74	Gulfstream 2B	151	Hyperion Air Inc. Wilmington, De.	(N988JE)
❏ N909JS	00	Learjet 60	60-206	Spear Q Sub Inc/Spear Development Inc. Las Vegas, Nv.	N916BG
❏ N909LX	05	Embraer Legacy 600	14500942	Flight Options LLC. Cuyahoga County, Oh.	PT-SCN
❏ N909MM	01	Falcon 900EX	88	Massachusetts Mutual Life Insurance Co. Bedford, Ma.	F-W...
❏ N909MN	07	CitationJet CJ2+	525A-0351	Services Sozialer GmbH. Hamburg, Germany.	N.....
❏ N909PM	98	Falcon 900B	176	FJ 900 Inc/Danaher Corp. Washington, DC.	(N900SM)
❏ N909PS	77	Citation 1/SP	501-0008	Mill Properties Ltd/Aviation Beauport Ltd. Jersey, C.I.	N900PS
❏ N909RR	81	Gulfstream 3	332	Ramsey Asset Management LLC. McLean, Va.	N921AS
❏ N909SB	99	Falcon 900EX	56	SBC Management Services Inc. San Antonio, Tx.	N404A
❏ N909SK	95	Learjet 60	60-060	SK Logistics Inc. St Augustine, Fl.	N175BA
❏ N909ST	98	Beechjet 400A	RK-194	Star Transport Inc. Morton, Il.	N194BJ
❏ N909TF	75	Falcon 10	51	Tyson Foods Inc. Fayetteville, Ar.	N51BP
❏ N909VJ	81	Falcon 50	69	WC Aviation LLC. Eagle, Co.	(N69VJ)
❏ N910CN	81	Falcon 50	59	Skyfarm LLC. Carlsbad, Ca.	N900JB
❏ N910DF	85	Citation III	650-0081	Barrett Business Services Inc. Vancouver, Wa.	N910DP
❏ N910DP	04	Citation X	750-0239	Westair Corp. Duluth, Ga.	N50QN
❏ N910G	78	Citation 1/SP	501-0083	AeroJet LLC. Gardner, Il.	N101LD
❏ N910HM	95	Citation V Ultra	560-0318	Markflite LLC. Manassas, Va.	N877RB
❏ N910J	05	Challenger 604	5640	Penn National Gaming Inc. Wyomissing, Pa.	N640PN
❏ N910JB	76	Learjet 25D	25D-213	Ocean Air Aviation, North Bend, Or.	N925DW
❏ N910JD	99	Hawker 800XP2	258420	Dawson Montana LLC. Big Fork, Mt.	N31340
❏ N910JW	87	Falcon 900	31	S C Johnson & Son Inc/Johnson's Wax, Racine, Wi.	N900FJ
❏ N910KB	83	Challenger 601	3007	Kayne Anderson Capital Advisors, Van Nuys, Ca.	N711SZ
❏ N910LX	06	Embraer Legacy 600	14500952	Flight Options LLC. Cuyahoga County, Oh.	PT-SFB
❏ N910MT	79	Citation II	550-0075	Corporate Properties Air Charter LLC. Lockport, Il.	N710MT
❏ N910MW	01	Falcon 900EX	85	Wilson Aviation LLC. Glacier International, Mt.	(N410MW)
❏ N910N	02	Citation Bravo	550-1032	Screaming Eagle Air/Ion Health Care, Pittsburgh, Pa.	N880CM
❏ N910Q	95	Falcon 900B	156	Tarrant Partners LP. Fort Worth, Tx.	HL7301
❏ N910QS	00	Citation X	750-0110	NetJets, Port Columbus, Oh.	
❏ N910RB	81	Citation II	550-0267	New York Central Mutual Fire Insurance Co. Edmeston, NY.	XA-AOC
❏ N910S	90	Gulfstream 4	1155	OAC Air LLC. Little Rock, Ar.	N1761B
❏ N910VP*	87	BAe 125/800A	258085	V-P Aviation LLC/First Florida Companies Inc. Tampa, Fl.	N285AL
❏ N911AJ	74	Learjet 25B	25B-163	Mordtair Corp. Harare, Zimbabwe.	(N65RC)
❏ N911CB	01	Citation Encore	560-0604	Commerce Bank NA. Kansas City, Mo.	N.....
❏ N911CR	71	JetStar-731	5150	JetStar Aviation Services LLC. Sunny Isles Beach, Fl.	N721CR
❏ N911CU	78	Westwind-1124	246	Security Aviation Inc. Anchorage, Ak.	N101SV
❏ N911DG	69	Falcon 20C	162	Aero Taxi Rockford Inc. Rockford, Il. (status ?).	(N389AC)
❏ N911DT	82	Falcon 20F-5B	471	Alpha Charlie Aviation LLC. Addison, Tx.	N44JQ
❏ N911DX	83	Learjet 35A	35A-499	Sales Operating Control Services, Littleton, Co.	N1TS
❏ N911EK	07	Citation Excel XLS	560-5742	CCXLS LLC. Ann Arbor, Mi.	N5221Y
❏ N911FC	83	Learjet 55	55-091	This Thing of Ours LLC. San Juan Capistrano, Ca.	N30TK
❏ N911GM	72	Citation	500-0048	JetSet International, Wilmington, De.	N67JR
❏ N911GU*	81	Westwind-Two	343	Jet Care Inc. Barrigada, Guam.	N999AZ
❏ N911MM	77	Citation Eagle	501-0030	MercMed LLC/Mercury Air Group Inc. Burbank, Ca.	(N911MU)
❏ N911NP	98	CitationJet	525-0273	Kingfisher Aviation LC. Waterloo, Ia.	(N525HC)
❏ N911RD	72	HS 125/F400A	25253	Nevada Air Transport LLC. Carson City, Nv.	(N253CC)
❏ N911SH	00	Falcon 2000	125	The Anschutz Corp. Englewood, Co.	N813GH
❏ N911SP	78	Westwind-1124	244	FlightStar Inc. Van Nuys, Ca.	N124PA
❏ N911UN	78	Falcon 10	122	AeroVision International LLC. Muskegon, Mi.	(N104KW)
❏ N912DA	69	Jet Commander-B	147	Agro Air Associates Inc. Miami, Fl.	(N888MP)
❏ N912GW	05	CitationJet CJ2+	525A-0304	MT Training LLC. Tyler, Tx.	N52699
❏ N912JC	07	Embraer Legacy 600	14501015	Dalcam LLC. Dallas, Tx. 'Dream Chaser'	PT-S..
❏ N912LX	07	Embraer Legacy 600	14500993	Flight Options LLC. Cuyahoga County, Oh.	PT-SKM
❏ N912MM	82	Learjet 55	55-064	M A R Fun LLC. Latrobe, Pa.	N900PJ
❏ N912MT	06	Falcon 2000EX EASY	94	B2 Flight LLC. Hillsboro, Or.	F-WWGI
❏ N912SH	96	Beechjet 400A	RK-128	Beartooth Aviation LLC. Minneapolis, Mn.	N1108Y
❏ N913BJ	89	Citation V	560-0011	Walco Air LLC/Walters Management LLC. Greenville, SC.	N700TF
❏ N913DC	03	CitationJet CJ-2	525-0157	Rico Aviation LLC/Sanford Texas Ranch Inc. Amarillo, Tx.	N88KC
❏ N913GA	07	Gulfstream G450	4113	Gulfstream Aerospace Corp. Savannah, Ga.	
❏ N913LX	07	Embraer Legacy 600	14501007	Flight Options LLC. Cuyahoga County, Oh.	PT-SKX
❏ N913MC	87	Beechjet 400	RJ-22	Fairway Aviation LLC. Stockbridge, Ga.	(N315SA)
❏ N913MK	84	Gulfstream 3	407	Mary Kay Inc. Dallas, Tx.	N407GA
❏ N913QS	99	Citation X	750-0113	NetJets, Port Columbus, Oh.	
❏ N913SC	88	BAe 125/800A	NA0418	SMC LLC. Cincinnati, OH.	(N99DA)
❏ N914BD	02	Gulfstream V	690	J B Ivey & Co. Salisbury, NC.	N690GA

Reg	Yr	Type	c/n	Owner/Operator	Prev Regn
N914CD	74	Citation	500-0150	James Lee Sr. Portland, Or.	N9V
N914DD	89	Falcon 900	80	Koosharem Corp. Santa Barbara, Ca. (status ?).	N914BD
N914DM	81	Westwind-1124	357	MCL Transportation Inc. Chicago, Il.	N357BC
N914EG	91	Gulfstream 4	1174	Krystal Air LLC. Van Nuys, Ca.	N10ZK
N914FF	07	CitationJet CJ-3	525B-0184	Rowser Funk Aviation LLC. Portland, Or.	(N914BC)
N914J	00	Gulfstream V	615	Metromedia Aircraft Co. Teterboro, NJ.	N572GA
N914QS	08	Citation X	750-0296	NetJets, Port Columbus, Oh.	N.....
N914SH	98	Beechjet 400A	RK-193	HSI Air Travel LLC. Boulder, Co.	N13US
N914SP	04	Citation Sovereign	680-0020	Space Shuttle Aircraft Leasing Co. Salem, Or.	N5245U
N914X	95	Challenger 601-3R	5185	Xerox Corp. White Plains, NY.	N611CC
N915AM	01	Hawker 800XP	258574	WFBNW NA. Salt Lake City, Ut. (trustor ?).	N51274
N915BD	05	Gulfstream G450	4028	Dillard's Inc. Little Rock, Ar.	N628GA
N915C	79	Gulfstream II SP	253	CONSOL Inc. Allegheny County, Pa.	N154C
N915LX	07	Embraer Legacy 600	14501021	Flight Options LLC. Cuyahoga County, Oh.	PT-SVX
N915MP	01	CitationJet CJ-2	525A-0024	Finnegan Air Inc/Multi-Plastics Inc. Port Columbus, Oh.	N525TJ
N915QS	97	Citation X	750-0015	NetJets, Port Columbus, Oh.	N326SU
N915RB	98	Citation X	750-0042	FHC Flight Services Inc. Norfolk, Va.	N95CM
N915RP	05	CitationJet CJ1+	525-0608	Romeo Papa Holdings Inc/El Paso Honda, Santa Teresa, NM.	N4017L
N915ST	98	CitationJet	525-0301	Desert Aircraft Leasing LLC. Pontiac, Mi.	N291CW
N916BD	05	Learjet 45	45-264	Dillard's Inc. Little Rock, Ar.	N910BD
N916BG*	01	Learjet 60	60-236	Spear Q Sub Inc. Las Vegas, Nv.	N716BG
N916CG	90	Astra-1125SP	045	Wilson & Assocs of Delaware LLC. Little Rock, Ar.	N916BG
N916CS	06	Citation Excel XLS	560-5625	Avlease LLC/CRS Acquisition Corp. Ann Arbor, Mi.	N.....
N916GB	02	Gulfstream G200	067	Rite Aid Corp. Harrisburg, Pa.	N916GR
N916GR	05	Gulfstream G200	126	Gene Reed Enterprises Inc. Charleston, SC.	N126GA
N916QS	00	Citation X	750-0116	NetJets, Port Columbus, Oh.	
N917BD	05	Learjet 45	45-281	Dillard's Inc. Little Rock, Ar.	N617BD
N917BE	80	Westwind-1124	291	Basler Electric Co. Highland, Il.	N124WK
N917GL	02	Global Express	9117	Texas Instruments Inc. McKinney, Tx.	N700EY
N917JC	94	Falcon 50	250	Corbantrade Cia Ltda. Quito, Ecuador.	N277JW
N917R	98	Global Express	9008	Navair LLC. Ronkonkoma, NY.	(N90005)
N917RG	04	CitationJet CJ-3	525B-0010	Realmark Ovation LLC. Cape Coral, Fl.	N5097H
N917SB	80	Falcon 50	14	SKA Consulting LLC. Santa Maria, Ca.	N955E
N917SC	87	Astra-1125	020	917SC Ltd/Creston & True North Inc. Fort Lauderdale, Fl.	N212LD
N917TF	81	HS 125/700A	NA0298	Bayshore Logistics Inc. Tampa, Fl.	N298BP
N917VZ	96	Gulfstream 4SP	1292	Verizon Communications, Teterboro, NJ.	N1GT
N917W	91	Gulfstream 4	1158	Evergreen International Aviation Inc. McMinnville, Or.	N17582
N918BD	05	Learjet 45	45-277	Dillard's Inc. Little Rock, Ar.	N912BD
N918BG	80	Gulfstream 3	300	BHG Flights LLC/ECFS Inc. Easton, Md.	N71TJ
N918BH	86	Citation III	650-0130	HBO Holdings LLC/Rusco Co. Memphis, Tn.	N603HP
N918CC	97	Gulfstream 4SP	1335	Astor Street Asset Management Inc. Chicago, Il.	N720BA
N918CW	99	CitationJet	525-0342	Saturn Jets LLC. Waco, Tx.	N9180K
N918EG	01	Learjet 45	45-154	Ameristar Fence Products Inc. Tulsa, Ok.	N886CA
N918JM	00	Falcon 50EX	304	999 Aviation LLC/DB Aviation Inc. Waukegan, Il.	F-WWHF
N918MJ	94	Astra-1125SPX	073	T-Bird Aviation Inc/MJB Tri-Motor LLC. DuPage, Il.	N173W
N918QS	03	Citation X	750-0223	NetJets, Port Columbus, Oh.	N.....
N918SS	79	Westwind-1124	263	Jetstream Enterprises LLC. Chicago, Il.	N29PC
N918TB	02	Gulfstream 4SP	1499	Atticus Capital LLC. Westhampton Beach, NY.	N941AM
N918TT	07	Hawker 400XP	RK-529	TT Aviation LLC/Triple Net Properties LLC. Santa Ana, Ca.	N167QS
N919CT	88	Gulfstream 4	1051	TWB LLC/Pegasus Consulting Group Inc. Ithaca, NY.	(N903KP)
N919DS	00	Astra-1125SPX	127	General Dynamics Decision Systems Inc. Scottsdale, Az.	N247PS
N919GA*	92	Falcon 50	233	Garden Air LLC/Garden Commercial Properties, Morristown, NJ.	N318GA
N919MC	04	CitationJet CJ1+	525-0600	Hanson Flight LLC. Roswell, NM. (was 525-0536)	(N55KT)
N919QS	03	Citation X	750-0224	NetJets, Port Columbus, Oh.	N.....
N919RS	94	Learjet 60	60-025	Ceebraid-Signal Corp/Aero Zap III LLC. West Palm Beach, Fl.	N299SG
N919RT	02	Hawker 800XP	258607	CJC Equipment LLC. Teterboro, NJ.	N60507
N919SA	03	Falcon 900EX EASY	124	Synthes (USA) LP/IMP Inc. Chester County, Pa.	F-WWFZ
N919SF	03	Hawker 800XP	258635	Swift & Co International Sales Corp. Greeley, Co.	N635XP
N919SS	92	BAe 125/800A	NA0473	Avola LLC. Bellevue, Wa.	VP-BHB
N920DB	87	Falcon 900B	20	Conanicut Aviation LLC/Walcott Partners LP. Danbury, Ct.	N256DV
N920QS	00	Citation X	750-0120	NetJets, Port Columbus, Oh.	
N920RV	81	Challenger 600S	1016	J & V Aircraft Leasing Inc. San Antonio, Tx.	(N812XL)
N921BE	81	Citation 1/SP	501-0174	921BE LLC/Luckett Tyner Law Firm PA. Clarksdale, Ms.	N1AG
N921CC	81	Sabre-65	465-67	U S Europe Africa Trade Inc. Ljamsville, Md.	N65AR
N921CH	79	Learjet 35A	35A-228	DJL LLC/Pruhs Corp. Anchorage, Ak.	N72LG
N921MB	78	Sabre-60	306-135	Eagle Investments International Inc. Miami, Fl.	N60AM
Reg	Yr	Type	c/n	Owner/Operator	Prev Regn

Reg	Yr	Type	c/n	Owner/Operator	Prev Regn
N921ML	67	Falcon 20C	99	AMI/Marion Merrell Dow-Marion Laboratories Inc. Kansas City.	N982F
N921MW	06	Citation Excel XLS	560-5646	Whitefish Investments Partners LLC. Edina, Mn.	(N562MP)
N921QS	05	Citation X	750-0241	NetJets, Port Columbus, Oh.	N5197M
N922AC	92	Citation V	560-0187	Autocam Corp. Kentwood, Mi.	N80GE
N922GK	69	HS 125/400A	NA726	Ken-Gil Aviation Inc. Palm Beach, Fl.	N922RR
N922H	05	Gulfstream G450	4036	Honeywell International Inc. Morristown, NJ.	N936GA
N922JW	87	Falcon 900	36	S C Johnson & Son Inc/Johnson's Wax, Racine, Wi.	N91MK
N922MR	70	Gulfstream II SP	93	White Hills Group, Las Vegas, Nv.	N396BC
N922MS	67	JetStar-731	5097	Dodson International Parts Inc. Rantoul, Ks.	N1BL
N922QS	07	Citation X	750-0293	NetJets, Port Columbus, Oh.	N.....
N922SL	78	Citation II	550-0034	Summerland LLC. Summerland, Fl.	N60CC
N923CL	01	Gulfstream 4SP	1471	Avenue Capital Management II LP. Oxford, Ct.	N471CR
N923HB	77	Falcon 10	99	MB Aviation LLC/CS Construction Inc. Phoenix, Az.	N63BA
N923JH	92	Citation II	550-0708	Harper Excavating Inc. Salt Lake City, Ut.	N720WC
N923QS	97	Citation X	750-0023	NetJets, Port Columbus, Oh.	N5000R
N923SK	95	Learjet 60	60-050	CPA Land Co. Tulsa, Ok.	N207BX
N924AM	78	Learjet 35A	35A-188	SGIII LLC/Sachs Group Inc. Wheeling, Il.	N999JF
N924BW	74	Learjet 25B	25B-158	Butler National Inc. Newton, Ks.	N71RB
N924JE	00	Citation Excel	560-5138	AEE Holdings Inc. Atlanta, Ga.	N704JW
N924JM	96	Hawker 800XP2	258312	Empire Aviation Group FZCO. Dubai, UAE.	N251X
N924QS	00	Citation X	750-0124	NetJets, Port Columbus, Oh.	N.....
N924S	87	Falcon 900B	40	Meregrass Inc. Dallas-Love, Tx.	(N940SJ)
N924WJ	83	Falcon 50	141	LCG Enterprises LLC. Waterbury-Oxford, Ct.	N96NX
N925AJ	94	Falcon 2000	4	Seneca Livestock Co. Eugene, Or.	F-WWMA
N925BC	97	Falcon 50EX	257	BASF Corp. Morristown, NJ..	F-OKSY
N925CA	85	Learjet 35A	35A-605	Sacks Consulting LLC. Jenkinton, Pa.	N825CA
N925DM	82	Learjet 35A	35A-486	Milam International Inc. Englewood, Co.	N810CC
N925GS	82	Falcon 50	90	AIW Inc/American Ironworks Inc. Baltimore, Md.	N4351M
N925MJ	83	Diamond 1	A065SA	Power Design Inc. St Petersburg, Fl.	N16MF
N925QS	08	Citation X	750-0299	NetJets, Port Columbus, Oh.	N.....
N925WC	80	HS 125/700A	257100	WCA Management LP. Houston, Tx.	N801RA
N926CB	00	Citation VII	650-7114	CB Transport Inc/Compass Bank, Birmingham, Al.	N68BR
N926CC	01	CitationJet CJ-1	525-0491	Le Tourneau Inc. Longview, Tx.	N491LT
N926CE	07	Citation Encore+	560-0763	Grouper LLC. Bozeman, Mt.	N50612
N926FM	01	Embraer EMB-135ER	145466	Intel Corp. Folsom, Ca.	PT-...
N926JJ	06	CitationJet CJ2+	525A-0310	Ruan Inc. Des Moines, Ia.	N5267G
N926JR	06	Challenger 300	20103	Ruan Inc. Des Moines, Ia.	C-FHNF
N926MC	78	HS 125/700A	NA0214	MC Aviation Corp. Van Nuys, Ca.	N926TC
N926NC	95	Citation V Ultra	560-0328	Cantu Enterprises LLC. McAllen, Tx.	N984GA
N926QS	97	Citation X	750-0026	NetJets, Port Columbus, Oh.	N5066U
N926RM	87	Citation II	550-0567	CB of Gainesville LLC. Gainesville, Fl.. (was 551-0567.)	N41BH
N926RR	07	Gulfstream G450	4081	TRT Juniper Holdings Inc. Dallas-Love, Tx.	N381GA
N926SS	99	Challenger 604	5436	JCPE LLC. Boston, Ma.	(N955CE)
N926TF	03	CitationJet CJ-1	525-0519	TFF LLC. Nashville, Tn.	N.....
N927DJ	00	Learjet 31A	31A-210	Schwab Industries Inc. Dover, Oh.	
N927LL	81	HS 125/700A	NA0296	Lifestyle Lift Holding Inc. Troy, Mi.	N10QJ
N927LT	05	Citation Sovereign	680-0070	Cooper Beech Capital LLC. Addison, Tx.	N51869
N927QS	07	Citation X	750-0290	NetJets, Port Columbus, Oh.	N.....
N927SK	99	Learjet 45	45-051	Kesler Enterprises LLC/Bodor Corp. Warsaw, In.	N145KC
N928CD	97	Learjet 60	60-110	A L Inc. Omaha, Ne.	N60LJ
N928GC	03	Gulfstream G400	1513	Graham Capital Management LP. Bridgeport, Ct.	N4UC
N928JA	95	Astra-1125SP	075	JMAK Air LLC. White Plains, NY.	N225AL
N928PS	86	Citation III	650-0116	Vatring Aviation LLC/Wythe Therapeutics, Wytheville, Va.	C-FJJG
N928QS	07	Citation X	750-0288	NetJets, Port Columbus, Oh.	N.....
N928RD	74	Citation	500-0204	103BL LLC. Quakertown, Pa.	N204Y
N928ST	07	Gulfstream G150	232	Flying Bar B LLC/Nu Skin Enterprises, Salt Lake City, Ut.	4X-C..
N929AK	03	Hawker 850XP	258627	RJ Air LLC. NYC.	N627XP
N929BC	06	CitationJet CJ2+	525A-0333	B Gentry Acquisitions LLC. Houston, Tx.	N.....
N929CG	77	Sabre-75A	380-52	N929CG LLC. St Thomas, USVI.	(N929GC)
N929GA	00	Gulfstream G200	029	Gulfstream Aerospace LP. Dallas-Love, Tx.	D-BAIR
N929GW	99	Learjet 60	60-165	Publix Supermarkets Inc. Lakeland, Fl.	
N929HG	98	Falcon 2000	79	M C Aviation LLC. Tulsa, Ok.	(N772MC)
N929JH	97	Learjet 31A	31A-132	Bunch of Birdies LLC. St Petersburg, Fl.	N116BX
N929MC	72	Learjet 24XR	24XR-243	Church for All Nations, Colorado Springs, Co.	N929HF
N929ML	82	Falcon 50	92	Flightstar Inc/Executive Fliteways Inc. Ronkonkoma, NY.	(N881J)
N929QS	00	Citation X	750-0129	NetJets, Port Columbus, Oh.	

Reg	Yr	Type	c/n	Owner/Operator	Prev Regn
N929SL	80	Learjet 35A	35A-287	Business Aircraft Group Inc. Cleveland, Oh.	N929SR
N929SS	01	390 Premier 1	RB-15	T S Aviation Inc. Phoenix-Sky Harbor, Az.	(N153SW)
N929T	80	Falcon 50	24	Eagle II LLC/Semitool Inc. Kalispell, Mt.	N280RT
N929VC	07	CitationJet CJ2+	525A-0353	HCH Inc. Fort Myers, Fl.	N.....
N929WG	01	Gulfstream G200	056	Fort Calumet Corp. Chicago-Midway, Il.	N298GA
N929WQ	90	BAe 125/800A	NA0459	Fort Calumet Corp. Chicago-Midway, Il.	N929WG
N930DC	06	Gulfstream G450	4063	DaimlerChrysler Corp. Pontiac, Mi.	N463GA
N930JG	93	Falcon 50	230	Frapair Ltd. Jersey, Channel Islands.	N506BA
N930LS	73	Gulfstream 2	133	Lester Smith Management Co. Houston, Tx.	N442QG
N930MG	91	Citation VI	650-0209	Gonsalves & Santucci Inc. Concord, Ca.	(N830MG)
N930PJ	75	Learjet 24D	24D-305	F & SA LLC. Merritt Island, Fl.	N666MW
N930QS	00	Citation X	750-0130	NetJets, Port Columbus, Oh.	
N931FD	96	Learjet 31A	31A-124	Family Dollar Inc. Charlotte, NC.	
N931MA	81	Diamond 1A	A010SA	Diamond 703 LLC. Owensboro, Ky.	N703JH
N931QS	98	Citation X	750-0064	NetJets, Port Columbus, Oh.	N964EJ
N931RS	99	Learjet 31A	31A-184	Russell Stover Candies Inc. Kansas City, Mo.	
N932BC	07	Hawker 900XP	HA-32	WAC Charter Inc. Aurora, Or.	
N932EA	91	Beechjet 400A	RK-32	Elliott Aviation Aircraft Sales Inc. Des Moines, Ia.	(N408LX)
N932FD	99	Learjet 31A	31A-187	Family Dollar Inc. Charlotte, NC.	
N932QS	97	Citation X	750-0032	NetJets, Port Columbus, Oh.	
N933AC	85	Beechjet 400	RJ-5	Air Chestler LLC. Racine, Wi. (was A1005SA)	N54TK
N933EY	00	Global Express	9063	CB Applications LLC. White Plains, NY.	B-HMA
N933H	05	Gulfstream G550	5077	Honeywell International Inc. Morristown, NJ.	N577GA
N933JC	79	Sabre-75A	380-72	Flight 180 LLC/Bingham Financial, Detroit-Willow Run, Mi.	N555JR
N933ML	06	Challenger 605	5705	Pacific Islander P/L. Singapore.	C-FLNZ
N933PA	82	Gulfstream 3	367	Executive Investment Properties, Opa Locka, Fl.	N300FS
N933PB	02	Citation Encore	560-0618	Jackson & Wade Services/Full Throttle Air LLC. Jabara, Ks.	N51995
N933QS	00	Citation X	750-0133	NetJets, Port Columbus, Oh.	
N933RD	79	Gulfstream 2	251	RD Air LLC/Rubloff Development Group Inc. Rockford, Il.	N251JS
N933SH	83	Citation III	650-0009	HCT Air LLC. Seekonk, Ma.	N933DB
N933TS*	74	Falcon 10	33	Aero Toy Store LLC. Fort Lauderdale, Fl.	N33BV
N934AM	97	CitationJet	525-0230	LAS Aviation LLC/LASCO Development Corp. Houston, Tx.	(N904AM)
N934BD	01	Citation X	750-0152	Nighthawk Ventures LLC. San Jose, Ca.	OH-PPJ
N934H	89	Citation III	650-0172	Hillenbrand Industries Inc. Batesville, In.	N672CC
N934QS	98	Citation X	750-0034	NetJets, Port Columbus, Oh.	
N934RD	96	Hawker 800XP2	258296	Dividend Capital Group, Denver, Co.	(N812LX)
N934ST	05	Falcon 2000EX EASY	68	U S Smokeless Tobacco Brands Inc. White Plains, NY.	F-WWGC
N935H	92	BAe 125/800A	NA0475	Rent-A-Center Addison LLC. Plano, Tx.	N800CJ
N935QS	99	Citation X	750-0135	NetJets, Port Columbus, Oh.	
N936QS	98	Citation X	750-0036	NetJets, Port Columbus, Oh.	
N937BC	85	Hawker 800SP	258043	Bradford G Corbett Sr. Fort Worth, Tx.	N5085E
N937QS	00	Citation X	750-0137	NetJets, Port Columbus, Oh.	N313CQ
N938QS	02	Citation X	750-0183	NetJets, Port Columbus, Oh.	
N939AJ	05	Embraer Legacy 600	14500939	WTC/Orfro LLC. Van Nuys, Ca.	PT-SCK
N939CK	74	Falcon 20E	317	Air Century Inc. Miami, Fl.	HB-VEV
N939GP	96	Beechjet 400A	RK-125	The Polisseni Family LP/PF Air LLC. Rochester, NY.	N400KL
N939KM	86	Gulfstream 3	492	Double X LLC. Palo Alto, Ca.	N848RJ
N939MC	86	Astra-1125	012	Multi-Chem Group, San Angelo, Tx.	N618HC
N939QS	02	Citation X	750-0193	NetJets, Port Columbus, Oh.	N.....
N939TT	91	BAe 125/800A	NA0465	Tito Tiberti/T Aereo LLC. Las Vegas, Nv.	N805X
N939TW	92	Citation V	560-0185	Rodney Robertson, Albuquerque, NM.	N989TW
N940CC	65	Sabre-40	282-34	Coastal Corp/ANR Coal Co. Roanoke, Va.	N400CS
N940DC	06	Gulfstream G550	5128	Chrysler Pentastar Aviation, Waterford, Mi.	N928GA
N940QS	02	Citation X	750-0285	NetJets, Port Columbus, Oh.	N5060K
N940SW	94	CitationJet	525-0071	IMA Holdings Inc. Fishers, In.	N26509
N940VA	98	Beechjet 400A	RK-197	Gear to Go LLC. Sarasota, Fl.	N214WM
N941CE	80	HS 125/700A	NA0259	Corporate Eagle Capital LLC. Pontiac, Mi.	N128CS
N941KA	85	Citation III	650-0095	Beneto Jet Sales Inc. Sacramento, Ca.	N883KB
N941QS	01	Citation X	750-0141	NetJets, Port Columbus, Oh.	N5068R
N941RM	98	Citation V Ultra	560-0476	CAVU Inc. Saratoga, Ca.	N150S
N941TS	07	Global 5000	9241	Aero Toy Store LLC. Fort Lauderdale, Fl.	(G-LLGC)
N942DS	95	HS 125/731	25032	Bluegrass Gas Sales Inc. Anchorage, Ak.	(N16GG)
N942EB	82	Westwind-1124	372	Ernie Ball Inc. San Luis Obispo, Ca.	N224GP
N942QS	97	Citation X	750-0024	NetJets, Port Columbus, Oh.	N504SU
N942WC	82	Westwind-1124	383	HMV Aviation LLC. Bristol, Tn.	N84VV
N943CE	81	HS 125/700A	NA0300	Corporate Eagle Capital LLC. Pontiac, Mi.	N700SA

Reg	Yr	Type	c/n	Owner/Operator	Prev Regn
☐ N943JB	03	Falcon 2000EX	18	TS Servicing Co/Joseph Bank Clothiers Inc. Baltimore, Md.	F-GUHB
☐ N943QS	98	Citation X	750-0043	NetJets, Port Columbus, Oh.	N5090Y
☐ N943RL	82	Falcon 50	88	Premier Air Center Inc. Alton/St Louis, Il.	(D-CHIC)
☐ N944AH	98	Citation Excel	560-5008	DDAC LLC/Pacific Assembly Inc. Wheeling, Il.	SE-RBC
☐ N944BB	03	Hawker 800XP	258611	Zargeo Inc. Santa Teresa, NM.	(N944PP)
☐ N944H	03	Gulfstream G550	5016	Honeywell International Inc. Morristown, NJ.	N916GA
☐ N944KM	76	Learjet 24E	24E-334	Southern Turbines LLC. Cartersville, Ga.	N66MJ
☐ N944NA	74	Gulfstream 2	144	NASA Johnson Space Center, Houston, Tx.	HB-ITR
☐ N944QS	01	Citation X	750-0144	NetJets, Port Columbus, Oh.	
☐ N944XP	07	Hawker 900XP	HA-44	Hawker Beechcraft Corp. Wichita, Ks.	
☐ N945CC	79	Sabre-65	465-13	Air Medical Partners II Inc. San Diego, Ca.	(N950CS)
☐ N945CE	81	HS 125/700A	NA0297	Corporate Eagle Capital LLC. Pontiac, Mi.	N589UC
☐ N945ER	85	Citation S/II	S550-0021	PLKA Management Inc. Fort Lauderdale, Fl.	N320DG
☐ N945FD	01	Learjet 45	45-122	Family Dollar Inc. Charlotte, NC.	
☐ N945HC*	00	Learjet 45	45-109	Sterling Aviation Inc. Milwaukee, Wi.	N451CF
☐ N945MA	88	MD-87	49725	Miami Air International, Miami, Fl.	VP-BPO
☐ N945NA	72	Gulfstream 2	118	NASA Johnson Space Center, Houston, Tx. (NASA 650).	(N651NA)
☐ N945QS	97	Citation X	750-0029	NetJets, Port Columbus, Oh.	N929EJ
☐ N945W	80	Learjet 35A	35A-301	Walthall Asset Management Corp. Dallas, Tx.	N98AC
☐ N946NA	74	Gulfstream 2	146	NASA Johnson Space Center, Houston, Tx.	N897GA
☐ N946PC	07	Citation Excel XLS	560-5728	Pacific Coast Building Products Inc. Sacramento, Ca.	N5264A
☐ N946QS	02	Citation X	750-0195	NetJets, Port Columbus, Oh.	N5241R
☐ N946RM	04	CitationJet CJ-3	525B-0008	Robins & Morton Group, Birmingham, Al.	N51HF
☐ N946TC	82	Falcon 50-4	94	CFA Aviation LLC/Chick-Fil-A Inc. Atlanta, Ga.	N504PA
☐ N947CE	81	HS 125/700A	NA0291	Corporate Eagle Capital LLC. Pontiac, Mi.	N45AF
☐ N947GA	04	Gulfstream G550	5047	White Lotus LLC/Aviation Legal Group PA. Fort Lauderdale, Fl	(N550YM)
☐ N947GS	79	Learjet 35A	35A-250	Saldana Air LLC. Chicago, Il.	N63LF
☐ N947ML	71	DC 9-32	47514	Homfeld II LLC. Eastpointe, Mi.	PH-MAX
☐ N947NA	74	Gulfstream 2	147	NASA Johnson Space Center, Houston, Tx.	N898GA
☐ N947QS	98	Citation X	750-0047	NetJets, Port Columbus, Oh.	N5091J
☐ N947TC	78	Learjet 25D	25D-233	Jets R Us Delaware LLC. Rutledge, Ca.	N75LM
☐ N948AL	01	Embraer EMB-135ER	145450	Intel Corp. Folsom, Ca.	PT-...
☐ N948DC	80	Citation II	550-0123	Nashville Air Inc. Wilmington, De.	N748DC
☐ N948MA	89	MD-87	49778	U S Marshals Service, Oklahoma City, Ok.	VP-BOO
☐ N948QS	01	Citation X	750-0149	NetJets, Port Columbus, Oh.	N52601
☐ N949CC	80	Westwind-1124	280	Solid Axle Management II LLC. Marshall, Tx.	N508R
☐ N949CE	83	HS 125/700A	NA0343	Corporate Eagle Capital LLC. Pontiac, Mi.	N524M
☐ N949GP	99	Global Express	9049	Aviation Concepts Inc.	N471DG
☐ N949L	66	DC 9-14	45844	International Airline Support Group, Miami, Fl.	N8963
☐ N949NA	78	Gulfstream II SP	221	NASA Johnson Space Center, Houston, Tx.	N827K
☐ N949QS	98	Citation X	750-0049	NetJets, Port Columbus, Oh.	N5153K
☐ N949SA	81	Citation II	550-0329	P & L Aviation II Inc. Ridgeland, Ms.	N491N
☐ N950CM	96	Gulfstream 4SP	1315	Oaktree Capital Management, Van Nuys, Ca.	N315GA
☐ N950DB	07	CitationJet CJ2+	525A-0377	Century Air Conditioning Transportation, Houston, Tx.	N5211F
☐ N950DM	86	Gulfstream 4	1010	Fairmont Aviation Inc/Key Air Inc. Oxford, Ct.	N824CA
☐ N950F	88	Falcon 50	191	Russell Stover Candies Inc. Kansas City, Mo.	N282FJ
☐ N950H	00	Falcon 50EX	307	Hines Interests LP. Farnborough, UK.	F-WWHK
☐ N950HB	05	Falcon 900DX	602	Sweatmore Air LLC/DMB Associates Inc. Scottsdale, Az.	F-WWFB
☐ N950NA	76	Gulfstream II SP	185	NASA Johnson Space Center, Houston, Tx.	N297GB
☐ N950P	97	CitationJet	525-0234	Intrepid Aviation Acquisition Service, Germantown, Tn.	(N91GH)
☐ N950PC	96	Hawker 800XP	258300	Noble Energy Inc. Houston, Tx.	(N800NE)
☐ N950QS	98	Citation X	750-0050	NetJets, Port Columbus, Oh.	N5156D
☐ N950RL	05	Falcon 2000	221	R & L Carriers Inc. Wilmington, Oh.	N1MG
☐ N950SF	88	Falcon 900B	50	Bechtel Equipment Operations, Louisville, Ky.	(N711WK)
☐ N950SP	81	Learjet 35A	35A-450	Jet Air Inc. Lexington-Bluegrass, Ky.	N450KK
☐ N951DB	76	Westwind-1124	195	South Aviation Inc. Fort Lauderdale, Fl.	N195ML
☐ N951QS	01	Citation X	750-0151	NetJets, Port Columbus, Oh.	
☐ N951RK	76	Gulfstream II SP	191	Kenair Inc. West Palm Beach, Fl.	N675RW
☐ N951RM	85	Challenger 601	3042	Rail Management Corp. Panama City Beach, Fl.	N333GJ
☐ N951XP	07	Hawker 900XP	HA-51	Hawker Beechcraft Corp. Wichita, Ks.	
☐ N952CH	00	Citation Bravo	550-0952	Big Dog Aviation Inc. Elmhurst, Il.	N5268V
☐ N952GL	07	390 Premier 1A	RB-213	Rio Bravo Helicopters Corp. Laredo, Tx.	N213BP
☐ N952GM	03	390 Premier 1	RB-87	T&K Equipment Leasing 1 Inc. Lexington, Ky.	N952GL
☐ N952QS	02	Citation X	750-0200	NetJets, Port Columbus, Oh.	N.....
☐ N952SP	01	CitationJet CJ-1	525-0447	Scannell Citation LLC. Indianapolis, In.	N116CS
☐ N953F	89	Citation V	560-0005	Affordable Equity Partners Inc. Columbia, Mo.	

Reg	Yr	Type	c/n	Owner/Operator	Prev Regn
N953FA	89	Challenger 601-3A	5041	Mondoil Enterprises LLC. Mora, NM.	(N541TS)
N953HC	81	Citation 1/SP	501-0201	Southwind Air Inc. Olive Branch, Ms.	(XA-...)
N953JF	84	Citation III	650-0043	Frontier Refining & Marketing, Denver, Co.	N643CC
N953QS	01	Citation X	750-0153	NetJets, Port Columbus, Oh.	
N954FJ	88	Falcon 900	54	Dassault Falcon Jet Corp. Teterboro, NJ.	F-GKAY
N954H	94	Hawker 800	258259	BRBF Inc. Ithaca, NY.	(N966L)
N954L	05	Challenger 604	5607	Lennar Corp. Fort Lauderdale Excecutive, Fl.	N607LC
N954RM	02	CitationJet CJ-2	525A-0093	Mayes Air LLC. Austin, Tx.	N98PE
N954SP	05	Falcon 2000EX EASY	56	Stephens Group Inc. Little Rock, Ar.	N56EX
N954WS	04	Learjet 60	60-271	Jet Advantage LLC. Fort Lauderdale, Fl.	N271L
N955EA	73	Learjet 24D	24D-279	Exec Air Montana Inc. Helena, Mt.	N101AR
N955H	06	Challenger 300	20109	Honeywell International Inc. Morristown, NJ.	C-FIDV
N955HG*	84	Citation III	650-0057	Spree LLC/Rivergate Farms, Tualatin, Or.	N400PC
N955JS	01	Learjet 31A	31A-228	Jesus Silva, Houston, Tx.	N3018P
N955QS	98	Citation X	750-0055	NetJets, Port Columbus, Oh.	N5068R
N956P	59	MS 760 Paris	56	Airborne Turbine LP. San Luis Obispo, Ca.	56
N956PP	89	Astra-1125	029	PrintPack Inc. Atlanta, Ga.	N131DA
N956QS	01	Citation X	750-0156	NetJets, Port Columbus, Oh.	
N957BJ	00	Citation Excel	560-5086	The O'Leary Group Inc. Charlotte, NC.	N394WJ
N957F	98	Astra-1125SPX	104	Navesink Corp. Wilmington, De.	(N104GA)
N957H	94	Hawker 800	258260	Mr Excitement LLC/Able Body Labor, Clearwater, Fl.	G-5-800
N957MB	73	HS 125/F600A	256015	Marquez Brothers Aviation LLC. Las Vegas, Nv.	N700XJ
N957P	02	Gulfstream G200	062	Marmon Group/Navigator Investments LLC. Chicago, Il.	N362GA
N958DM	02	Falcon 900EX	119	Archer Danield Midland Co. Decatur, Il.	N119EX
N958GC	01	Citation Bravo	550-1016	GILC Inc/Granite Construction Inc. Watsonville, Ca.	N926EC
N958PP	83	Diamond 1A	A031SA	ROM Corp. Belton, Mo.	N956PP
N958QS	01	Citation X	750-0158	NetJets, Port Columbus, Oh.	
N959P	05	MS 760 Paris	59	JSI Holdings Inc. Calhoun, Ga.	59
N959RP	07	Learjet 40	45-2100	Learjet Inc. Wichita, Ks.	
N959SA	76	Learjet 35A	35A-076	AirNet Systems Inc. Columbus, Oh.	
N960AA	68	Falcon 20C	144	Falcon Leasing Inc. Argyle, Tx.	N385AC
N960CD	91	Citation V	560-0121	RT-TTO Aviation LLC. Little Rock, Ar.	N821VP
N960CR	05	Challenger 300	20080	Village Transport Corp/PCI Co. Cuyahoga County, Oh.	C-FGCL
N960FA	81	Westwind-Two	348	Westwoods Aviation II Inc. Sharon, Ct.	N348SJ
N960JH	03	Citation Encore	560-0643	RJM Aviation Associates Inc. Berlin, Ct.	(N990JH)
N960KC	96	Citation X	750-0011	Honeywell Inc. Minneapolis, Mn.	N944D
N960QS	01	Citation X	750-0160	NetJets/Marquis Jet Partners Inc. Port Columbus, Oh.	
N960S	82	Falcon 50	86	Outback Steakhouse of Florida Inc. Tampa, Fl.	N86JC
N960SF	00	Falcon 900EX	62	Bechtel Corp. Oakland, Ca.	EC-HNU
N960TX	79	Falcon 20F-5B	403	MMB Aircraft Leasing LLC. Fair Lawn, NJ.	(N175BC)
N961AA	69	Falcon 20D	205	Falcon Leasing Inc. Argyle, Tx.	N585AC
N961EX	99	Falcon 900EX	61	Liberty Media Group. Englewood, Co.	F-WWFL
N961P	59	MS 760 Paris	61	JSI Holdings Inc. Calhoun, Ga.	61
N961QS	98	Citation X	750-0061	NetJets, Port Columbus, Oh.	N5109R
N961TC	05	Citation Sovereign	680-0077	Teojama Comercial SA. Quito, Ecuador.	N.....
N961V	96	Gulfstream 4SP	1298	Swiflite Aircraft Corp. Burbank, Ca.	N501PC
N962A*	89	Astra-1125	031	Jackson Ridge MT LLC. Jackson, Wy.	N987G
N962J	82	Citation II	550-0453	D & D Aviation, Grandview, Mo.	N962JC
N962QS	00	Citation X	750-0126	NetJets, Port Columbus, Oh.	N5076K
N962SS	89	Gulfstream 4	1121	Henn Leasing LLC. Fort Lauderdale Excecutive, Fl.	N178MH
N963JF	80	Falcon 50	18	John Fabick Tractor Co. Spirit of St Louis, Mo.	(N10UG)
N963RB	06	Challenger 300	20121	FTI Consulting Inc/Summit Jet, Farmingdale, NY.	N963RS
N963RS*	93	Falcon 900B	127	RHJ Advisory LLC. NYC.	N909AS
N964C	81	Sabre-65	465-66	Saint Gobain Containers, Muncie, In.	
N964H	98	Challenger 604	5363	Harris Corp. Melbourne, Fl.	C-GLXF
N964JD	05	Hawker 400XP	RK-451	Wichita Air Services Inc. Wichita, Ks.	N51XP
N964QS	01	Citation X	750-0164	NetJets, Port Columbus, Oh.	
N965LC	01	CitationJet CJ-1	525-0462	Lane Construction Corp. Meriden, Ct.	N5197A
N965M	00	Falcon 900EX	65	Volkswagen of America Inc. Auburn Hills, Mi.	N965EX
N966H	03	Falcon 900EX EASY	126	Honeywell International Inc. Morristown, NJ.	F-WWFC
N966JM	00	Citation Excel	560-5143	Johnson Machinery Co. Riverside, Ca.	N1836S
N966JS*	06	Embraer Legacy 600	14500966	Winner 614JH LLC. Wilmington, De.	N907LX
N966QS	01	Citation X	750-0166	NetJets, Port Columbus, Oh.	
N966SW	94	Citation V Ultra	560-0284	Old Dominion Freight Lines Inc. High Point, NC.	(N369TC)
N967F	05	390 Premier 1	RB-133	Fastenal Co/Fastenal Air Fleet LLC. Winona, Mn.	N575PT
N967PC	05	Gulfstream G200	110	Polo Ralph Lauren Corp. White Plains, NY.	N221BS

Reg	Yr	Type	c/n	Owner/Operator	Prev Regn
N967QS	98	Citation X	750-0067	NetJets, Port Columbus, Oh.	
N967TC	05	CitationJet CJ2+	525A-0319	Chick-Fil-A Inc. Atlanta, Ga.	N.....
N969AR	77	Learjet 25XR	25XR-220	Amazon Aviation Corp. Fort Lauderdale, Fl.	N99NJ
N969DW	97	Citation V Ultra	560-0399	Double D Farms/Cal-West Land & Livestock, Coalinga, Ca.	(N560DW)
N969JD	99	Learjet 60	60-154	Northern Flights LLC/Trakair, Burlington, Vt.	N233FX
N969RE	01	390 Premier 1	RB-14	390 LLC. North Las Vegas, Nv.	
N969WR	06	Gulfstream G150	218	W A Richardson Builders, Las Vegas, Nv.	N218GA
N970DM	07	CitationJet CJ-3	525B-0168	Bluegrass Aero Inc. Verona, Ky.	N.....
N970QS	98	Citation X	750-0070	NetJets, Port Columbus, Oh.	
N970RP	75	Citation	500-0270	B & M Aviation LLC. Fairhope, Al.	N915RP
N970S	93	Falcon 50	238	Outback Steakhouse of Florida Inc. Tampa, Fl.	SE-DVL
N970SJ	90	Gulfstream 4	1146	New World Aircraft LLC. Allentown, Pa.	N776US
N970SK	02	Citation X	750-0186	Oshkosh Truck Corp. Appleton, Wi.	N5188N
N970WJ	80	Learjet 25D	25D-324	SalJet LLC/Diaz-Verson Capital, Columbus, Ga.	XA-POP
N971EC	85	Gulfstream 4	1000	Emmis Communications Corp. Indianapolis, In.	N404DB
N971EQ	68	Gulfstream 2B	32	Red Barn Farms LLC. Sanford, NC.	N971EC
N971QS	99	Citation X	750-0071	NetJets, Port Columbus, Oh.	
N971TB	03	CitationJet CJ-2	525A-0118	TBAC LLC/Waterfront Realty Corp. NYC.	N464C
N972AB	74	Citation	500-0140	Homeland Companies LLC. Marion, Oh.	N441TC
N972GA	07	Gulfstream G550	5172	Gulfstream Aerospace Corp. Savannah, Ga.	
N972MS	96	Citation 4SP	1285	Interface Operations LLC. Las Vegas, Nv.	N874A
N972NR	78	Sabre-75A	380-65	Compass Acquisition & Development, Addison, Tx.	N69JN
N972PF	01	390 Premier 1	RB-38	Plastic Ingenuity Inc. Cross Plains, Wi.	
N972W	80	HS 125/700A	NA0277	WRS Air LLC/W R Starkey Mortgage LLP. Plano, Tx.	N509QC
N973HR	02	Learjet 60	60-260	Hoffman-LaRoche Inc. Teterboro, NJ.	N257FX
N973M	00	Falcon 900EX	73	Volkswagen of America Inc. Auburn Hills, Mi.	F-WWFI
N973MW*	80	Gulfstream 3	301	MW Sky LLC/Men's Wearhouse LLC. Houston, Tx.	N444GA
N974BK	91	Falcon 900B	105	Oxbow Group LLC. West Palm Beach, Fl.	N225KS
N974JD	06	Hawker 4000	RC-11	Wichita Air Services Inc. Wichita, Ks.	
N975DM	07	Learjet 40	45-2073	Dynamic International of Wisconsin Inc. Waukesha, Wi.	N40083
N975GA	07	Gulfstream G550	5175	Gulfstream Aerospace Corp. Savannah, Ga.	
N975P	60	MS 760 Paris	75	Airborne Turbine LP. San Luis Obispo, Co.	75
N975QS	02	Citation X	750-0175	NetJets, Port Columbus, Oh.	
N975RD	04	Hawker 400XP	RK-390	Colson-Colson General Contractor Inc. Salem, Or.	N480LX
N975RR	02	Beechjet 400A	RK-349	Flexible Foam Products Inc. Lima-Allen County, Oh.	N449CW
N976GA	80	Citation II	550-0165	Perryton Service Co. Perryton, Tx.	ZS-LHU
N976SR	80	Sabre-65	465-29	Copper Station Holdings LLC. Columbia, SC.	N6NR
N977AE	00	Citation X	750-0125	Bitz Aviation Inc. Allegheny County, Pa.	N444CX
N977CP	03	Falcon 2000EX	17	CITGO Petroleum Corp. Tulsa, Ok.	N217EX
N977GA	07	Gulfstream G550	5177	Gulfstream Aerospace Corp. Savannah, Ga.	
N977JP	97	Learjet 31A	31A-140	Azure Air LLC. Auburn, Ca.	N95HG
N977LP	00	Falcon 900EX	77	Lima Papa LLC. Farmingdale, NY.	F-WWFQ
N977MR	02	Citation Encore	560-0623	TDMC LLC. Incline Village, Nv.	N51993
N977QS	99	Citation X	750-0077	NetJets, Port Columbus, Oh.	
N977TW	65	Falcon 20C	13	Sierra American Corp. Addison, Tx.	F-BTCY
N978DB	96	Citation X	750-0009	BoAir LLC/Denver Broncos Football Club, Englewood, Co.	(N109VP)
N978GA	07	Gulfstream G550	5178	Gulfstream Aerospace Corp. Savannah, Ga.	
N978PW	94	Falcon 900B	125	TAS LLC/Welsh, Carson, Anderson & Stowe, NYC.	RP-C7808
N978QS	02	Citation X	750-0187	NetJets, Port Columbus, Oh.	N.....
N979CB	93	Gulfstream 4SP	1217	Design Professionals LLC/Cohen Bros Realty Corp. NYC.	(N711PE)
N979GA	07	Gulfstream G550	5179	Gulfstream Aerospace Corp. Savannah, Ga.	
N979QS	99	Citation X	750-0079	NetJets, Port Columbus, Oh.	
N979RF	97	Learjet 35A	35A-376	Jedami Jet LLC. Fort Lauderdale, Fl.	XA-SBF
N979WC	88	Citation II	550-0584	Steven Anderson, Bakersfield, Ca. (was 551-0584).	N25QF
N980DM	77	Citation 1/SP	501-0062	PAS Flight Systems LLC. Scottsdale, Az.	N900DM
N980GA	07	Gulfstream G550	5180	Gulfstream Aerospace Corp. Savannah, Ga.	
N980GG	98	Global Express	9009	Lucky Fives LLC. Concord, Ma.	N998AM
N980S	94	Falcon 50	249	Outback Steakhouse of Florida Inc. Tampa, Fl.	N247CJ
N980SK	06	Challenger 605	5701	Bombardier Aerospace Corp. Windsor Locks. (Ff 22 Jan 06).	N605KS
N981CE	01	Hawker 800XP	258563	Corporate Eagle Capital LLC. Pontiac, Mi.	N4469M
N981LB	04	CitationJet CJ-1	525-0546	Beyond Aviation LLC/Labov & Beyond Inc. Fort Wayne, In.	N5188N
N982AR	98	Beechjet 400A	RK-206	Bob Jones University Inc. Greenville, SC.	N30046
N982B	71	Gulfstream 2B	98	Falcon West LLC. Sacramento, Ca.	N883ES
N982MC	77	Falcon 10	114	Club Air Inc. Dallas-Redbird, Tx.	N108TG
N982NA	82	Citation II	550-0345	304 MC LLC. Syracuse, NY.	N267TC
N982QS	02	Citation X	750-0182	NetJets, Port Columbus, Oh.	

Reg	Yr	Type	c/n	Owner/Operator	Prev Regn
N982RK	80	Gulfstream 3	310	Gulfstream Acquisition LLC. Englewood Cliffs, NJ.	(N373LP)
N983EC*	99	Hawker 800XP	258446	Corporate Eagle Jet LLC. Waterford, Mi.	N529M
N983GA	07	Gulfstream G550	5183	Gulfstream Aerospace Corp. Savannah, Ga.	
N983J	00	Global Express	9072	Jacobs Family Trust, Central Point, Or.	N700LN
N983JC	06	Embraer Legacy 600	14500977	St Thomas Energy Exports Inc. St Croix, USVI.	PT-SHK
N983QS	99	Citation X	750-0083	NetJets, Port Columbus, Oh.	
N984BK	98	Citation Bravo	550-0857	Farm B Leasing Inc. Atlanta, Ga.	VP-CCP
N984GB	05	Citation Bravo	550-1122	ACBC Inc. Panama City, Panama.	N5211Q
N984HM	92	Hawker 800SP	258229	Nevada N674LJ LLC. San Antonio, Tx.	TC-TEK
N984JW	89	Gulfstream 4	1091	InterOP Technologies, Fort Myers, Fl.	N364G
N984QS	99	Citation X	750-0084	NetJets, Port Columbus, Oh.	
N984SA	83	Diamond 1A	A063SA	Media Aviation Associates LLC. Montgomery, Al.	N51BE
N985FM	06	Challenger 300	20113	Riverbend Enterprises Inc. Idaho Falls, Id.	C-FIEM
N985JC	05	Gulfstream G550	5083	St Thomas Energy Exports Inc. St Croix, USVI.	N583GA
N986DS	83	Citation 1/SP	501-0321	Oncourse Charter LLC. Rogers, Ar.	N510SJ
N986MA	93	Learjet 31A	31A-080	Mescalero Apache Tribe, Mescalero, NM.	N80LJ
N986QS	99	Citation X	750-0086	NetJets, Port Columbus, Oh.	N888CN
N986SA	85	Learjet 35A	35A-609	RSB Investments Inc/Skyward Aviation, Washington, Pa.	N609TF
N987AL	07	Falcon 900EX EASY	194	Dassault Falcon Jet Corp. Teterboro, NJ.	F-WWFK
N987CJ	88	Citation S/II	S550-0152	Southwest Wings GmbH. Thalmaessing, Germany.	N843G
N987F	82	Falcon 50	124	Peekey Lumbus LLC. Del Mar, Ca.	N50MV
N987GK	90	Falcon 900B	88	Shadowfax LLC. Carlsbad, Ca.	N987QK
N987HP	05	Challenger 300	20069	Aero Timber Partners/HAP Investment Group LLC. Atlanta, Ga.	C-FGZD
N987QS	99	Citation X	750-0087	NetJets, Port Columbus, Oh.	
N988AA	81	Learjet 25D	25D-348	Butler National Inc. Newton, Ks.	N522JS
N988AS	78	Learjet 25D	25D-257	Flite Services Inc. Tampa, Fl.	N377Q
N988DV	98	Falcon 2000	74	Devon Energy Management LLC. Wiley Post, Ok.	OO-VMB
N988H	03	Falcon 900EX EASY	125	Honeywell International Inc. Morristwon, NJ.	F-WWFB
N988LS	96	Gulfstream 4SP	1290	Yona Venetian LLC/Las Vegas Sands Inc. Las Vegas, Nv.	N71VR
N988MC	07	Learjet 45	45-352	Michigan Tractor & Machinery Co. Pontiac, Mi.	
N988PA	99	Learjet 45	45-076	Schwyhart Holdings LLC. Carrollton, Tx.	N2451Y
N988QC	81	Learjet 35A	35A-455	Moyle Petroleum Co. Rapid City, SD.	N455NE
N988SB	88	Falcon 50	174	Sembler Investments/Ojos Verdes Aviation LLC. St Petersburg.	N8KG
N988T	88	Falcon 900B	65	Semitool Inc. Kalispell, Mt.	(N990MQ)
N989AL	78	Learjet 35A	35A-212	Air Ambulance Professionals Inc. Fort Lauderdale, Fl.	N291A
N989BC	88	Challenger 601-3A	5021	Boulder U S LLC. Bedford-Hanscom, Ma.	N620HF
N989PA	99	Learjet 45	45-071	Schwyhart Holdings LLC. Carrollton, Tx.	N145KL
N989QS	99	Citation X	750-0089	NetJets, Port Columbus, Oh.	
N989SC	74	Citation	500-0148	Genesis Air LLC. Columbus, Ms.	LV-WXJ
N989TL	68	Learjet 24	24-160	Booth Ranches/F Otis Booth Jr. Van Nuys, Ca.	N4791C
N989TW	98	Citation Excel	560-5014	Wamburg Financial Corp. Barrington, Il.	(N16SN)
N990AK	97	Challenger 604	5337	Oak Management Corp. San Jose, Ca.	N270RA
N990AL	72	Citation	500-0033	N990AL LLC. Mesa, Ak.	(N130AL)
N990BB	88	Falcon 900B	42	Bresnan Aviation LLC. Greenwich, Ct.	N901BB
N990DF	05	Hawker 400XP	RK-430	Dickinson Financial Corp. Kansas City, Mo.	N30XP
N990DK	98	Citation Excel	560-5019	CottonAire LLC/Parkdale Mills Inc. Gastonia, NC.	N980DK
N990GA	07	Gulfstream G550	5200	Gulfstream Aerospace Corp. Savannah, Ga.	
N990GC	93	Learjet 31	31-033A	AirMed Inc/Gold Cross EMS, Augusta, Ga.	N156JS
N990HC	99	Hawker 800XP2	258412	Harsco Corp. New Cumberland, Pa.	N30682
N990JH	06	Citation Encore+	560-0754	JetEx LLC/Medallion Exploration, Salt Lake City, Ut.	(N960JH)
N990M	89	Citation II	550-0608	Menzil Enterprises Inc. Allegheny County, Pa.	N608AM
N990MC	03	Falcon 900EX EASY	123	MASCO Corp. Detroit-Metropolitan, Mi.	N990ML
N990MF	99	Citation Excel	560-5052	Caledonia Leasing LLC/MacLean-Fogg Co. Wheeling, Il.	N5228Z
N990MR	83	Citation II	550-0488	MRS Leasing LLC. Lakeland, Fl.	N990MM
N990NB	00	Gulfstream 4SP	1428	Jet Shoe LLC. Boston, Ma.	N512C
N990PA	75	Sabre-65	306-114	Taylor Energy LLC. New Orleans, La.	N990PT
N990PT	90	Gulfstream 4	1134	Taylor Energy LLC. New Orleans, La.	N8796J
N990QS	02	Citation X	750-0190	NetJets, Port Columbus, Oh.	N.....
N990S	81	Westwind-Two	322	PJC Equipment Leasing LLC. Hewitt, Tx.	N2AV
N990TC	01	Citation Bravo	550-0963	Seven Bar Flying Service Inc. Dallas-Love, Ttx.	N24QF
N990WM	98	Falcon 900EX	40	Jabil Circuit Inc. Page Field-Fort Myers, Fl.	N606DR
N991DB	99	Learjet 60	60-177	Riverhorse Investments Inc. Van Nuys, Ca.	N60LR
N991GA	07	Gulfstream G550	5201	Gulfstream Aerospace Corp. Savannah, Ga.	
N991GS	06	Challenger 300	20099	Newair Inc. NYC.	
N991LF	99	Gulfstream V	576	International Lease Finance Co. Van Nuys, Ca.	C-FHMS
N991TD	66	Learjet 24	24-124	Envoy Air Services LLC. Leipsic, Oh.	N476GA
					XA-RTV

Reg	Yr	Type	c/n	Owner/Operator	Prev Regn
N991TW	97	Challenger 604	5333	Ross Investments Inc. Oakland, Ca.	N600MS
N992AS	79	Citation II	550-0338	Global Aviation Partners Inc. Las Vegas, Nv. (was 551-0016).	N900MF
N992GA	07	Gulfstream G550	5202	Gulfstream Aerospace Corp. Savannah, Ga.	
N992HE	01	Citation Bravo	550-1006	Whayne Supply Co. Louisville, Ky.	N106BB
N992SC	07	390 Premier 1A	RB-191	Barclays North Inc. Everett, Wa.	N7191K
N992TD	65	Learjet 23	23-035	Envoy Air Services LLC. Leipsic, Oh.	(N10QX)
N993DS	81	Westwind-Two	356	Second Bridge LLC/Thornton Construction, Norman, Ok.	N38TJ
N993EX	01	Falcon 900EX	93	KAD Aviation LLC. San Jose, Ca.	F-WWFL
N993GH	06	Falcon 2000EX EASY	85	Allstate Insurance Co. Palwaukee, Il.	F-WWGV
N993GL	02	CitationJet CJ-1	525-0509	Cresair Inc. Northvale, NJ.	(N904DP)
N993H	99	Beechjet 400A	RK-241	Horton Transportation Inc. Minneapolis, Mn.	N3241Q
N993LC	84	Citation III	650-0027	D & R Ventures LLC/Spiegel Development, Sherman Oaks, Ca.	N433LF
N993SA	98	Hawker 800XP2	258377	TSA Stores/Sports Authority, Denver, Co.	N984GC
N993TD	68	Learjet 24	24-166	Bob Rhue Agriculture Service, Leipsic, Oh.	N124HF
N994CF	82	Citation II	550-0448	City Furniture Inc. Tamarac, Fl.	N938W
N994GC	00	Gulfstream 4SP	1435	Noble Leasing LLC. White Plains, NY.	N435GA
N994GG	69	Gulfstream 2	77	Berger-Dean Marketing LLC. Long Beach, Ca.	N994GC
N994GP	06	Falcon 2000EX EASY	105	Avtorita Holdings Ltd/PIK Group, Moscow, Russia.	F-WWGR
N994JR	06	390 Premier 1A	RB-183	JRC Investments LLC. Wilkesboro, NC.	
N994U	85	Citation III	650-0099	Francisco Bulnes Malo,	XA-PYN
N995CK	67	Falcon 20C	95	Kalitta Charters LLC. Detroit-Willow Run, Mi.	N950RA
N995CR	80	Learjet 35A	35A-304	A First Class Air Charter Inc. Boca Raton, Fl.	(N97QA)
N995DP	85	Learjet 35A	35A-600	A Duie Pyle Inc. Coatesville, Pa.	N823CP
N995GG	88	Gulfstream 4	1074	Rayfield Investment Co. Chapel Hill, NC.	N740JA
N995GH	05	Falcon 2000EX EASY	72	Allstate Insurance Co. Palwaukee, Il.	(N431GH)
N995RD	74	Sabre-80A	380-9	Jet Harbor Inc. Fort Lauderdale, Fl.	N383CF
N995SK	97	Falcon 900B	166	Tiburon Transportation Ltd. Santa Rosa, Ca.	F-GLHI
N996AG	98	Falcon 2000	64	American General Corp. Houston, Tx.	F-WWMH
N996BP	06	Learjet 45	45-301	NV707 LLC/O'Shaughnessy Real Estate Winery, Angwin, Ca.	N45KJ
N996CR	83	Learjet 55	55-060	Champion Racing Aviation LLC. Boca Raton, Fl.	N255TS
N996JR	96	CitationJet	525-0147	Charles Hutter, Carson City, Nv.(status ?).(w/o 22 Jul 03?)	N52178
N996JS	96	Learjet 31A	31A-119	MRK LLC. Dallas-Love, Tx.	N114HY
N996PE	07	CitationJet CJ-3	525B-0170	KRG Capital LLC. Denver, Co.	N50543
N996QS	02	Citation X	750-0196	NetJets, Port Columbus, Oh.	S5-BAB
N996TD	75	Learjet 24D	24D-320	Ruhe Sales Inc. Leipsic, Oh.	N5135K
N997CB	00	Citation Excel	560-5102	H E Butt Grocery Co. San Antonio, Tx.	N500PX
N997EA	92	Citation V	560-0178	Ernie Elliott Aviation Inc. Dawsonville, Ga.	N363CR
N997GC*	84	Challenger 601	3025	Northeastern Aviation Corp. Farmingdale, NY.	N18AA
N997MX	83	Diamond 1	A036SA	Metal Exchange Corp. Matthews, NC.	
N997QS	03	Citation X	750-0208	NetJets, Port Columbus, Oh.	(N45LN)
N997RS	04	Hawker 400XP	RK-388	Columbia Collier Properties LLC. Naples, Fl.	N996AL
N998AL	05	Learjet 40	45-2029	Alex Lyon & Son, Syracuse, NY.	N665MC
N998BC	90	Citation II	550-0665	Professional Office Services Inc. Waterloo, Ia.	N980R
N998CK	67	Falcon 20C	98	Kalitta Charters LLC. Detroit-Willow Run, Mi.	(N798CW)
N998CX	99	Citation X	750-0098	Swift Aviation Management Inc. Phoenix, Az.	N33HC
N998EA	79	Citation 1/SP	501-0104	Nationwide 501SP LLC. Gallatin, Tn.	
N998QS	02	Citation X	750-0198	NetJets, Port Columbus, Oh.	
N998SA	98	Citation V Ultra	560-0485	Synthes (USA) LP/IMP Inc. Chester County, Pa.	N51743
N998SR	06	Citation Bravo	550-1136	Base Skypower Sdn Bhd. Lahat, Malaysia.	N831MM
N998TW	96	Citation V Ultra	560-0362	Ponderosa Farms LLC. Lake in the Hills, Il.	(N971AB)
N999AM	74	Citation	500-0232	K3C Inc/Sierra Industries Inc. Uvalde, Tx.	F-WWUE
N999BE*	07	Falcon 7X	8	Formula One Management Ltd. Biggin Hill, UK.	N300JJ
N999BL	86	Astra-1125	024	N501KB Inc. Fort Lauderdale, Fl.	N87BL
N999BW	67	BAC 1-11/419EP	120	Business Jet Services Ltd. Dallas-Love, Tx.	N40166
N999CB	05	Citation Encore	560-0692	Charles M Brewer Ltd. Scottsdale, Az.	N841W
N999CX	98	Citation Bravo	550-0841	Big Sky LLC. Oklahoma City, Ok.	N983GT
N999CY	80	HS 125/700A	NA0261	Advanced Air LLC. Ocala, Fl.	N.....
N999EB	05	CitationJet CJ1+	525-0616	Southern Sky Inc. Miami, Fl.	(N115FJ)
N999EH	87	Falcon 900	15	999EH LLC/East Hampton Airlines, Farmingdale, NY.	
N999EK	06	Learjet 40	45-2060	Frontera Produce Ltd. McAllen, Tx.	N40077
N999GN	00	Learjet 31A	31A-216	Chimney Creek Ranch, Goldsboro, NC.	HB-IWZ
N999GP	88	Gulfstream 4	1061	Gary Primm/GEP Air LLC. Las Vegas, Nv.	N202CE
N999GR	79	Citation S Super II	550-0097	K3C Inc/Sierra Industries Inc. Uvalde, Tx.	(N999GL)
N999HC	85	Citation S/II	S550-0030	Ameriflight Aviation, Orlando, Fl.	N2WQ
N999JS	79	Learjet 35A	35A-277	Jetset Airlines LLC. Long Beach, Ca.	N5239J
N999LB	05	CitationJet CJ-3	525B-0397	Speedbird Inc. Cincinnati, Oh.	

Reg	Yr	Type	c/n	Owner/Operator	Prev Regn
N999LJ	06	Learjet 60	60-314	Inter Travel & Services Inc. Irvine, Ca.	
N999LL	80	Falcon 10	152	Golen Wings Inc/Owen Nursery & Florist, Bloomington, Il.	(N999AH)
N999LX	89	Gulfstream 4	1099	CKE Associates LLC. Van Nuys, Ca.	N1199QS
N999MF	69	Learjet 25	25-050	LandAir Mapping Inc. Atlanta, Ga.	N55FN
N999MK	81	Citation II/SP	551-0304	Meisner Aircraft Inc. Lake in the Hills, Il.	N304KT
N999MS	81	Citation 1/SP	501-0230	Gaven Industries Inc. Pittsburgh, Pa.	9A-DVR
N999PJ	61	MS 760 Paris-2	89	Tej Jet of Del LLC. Dover, De.	F-BJLY
N999PM	00	Falcon 900EX	70	Pacific Marine Leasing Inc. Phoenix, Az.	N970EX
N999PW	80	Citation 1/SP	501-0160	2141 Corp. Atlanta, Ga. (status ?).	C-GAAA
N999PX	98	Challenger 604	5387	Lima Delta Co. Wilmington, De. (trustor ?).	N387CL
N999QH	85	Citation S/II	S550-0077	Seaport Aviation Inc. Norwood, Ma.	N999EA
N999QS	02	Citation X	750-0203	NetJets, Port Columbus, Oh.	
N999SM	05	CitationJet CJ-3	525B-0052	SGP Land LLC/Alliance Resource Partners LP. Tulsa, Ok.	N51995
N999TH	87	Falcon 200	512	Journal Publishing Co. Albuquerque, NM.	N45WH
N999VK	01	Challenger 604	5499	VKRM Aviation LLC. Los Altos Hills, Ca.	N499KR
N999WA	71	Learjet 24D	24D-242	JetSet Airlines LLC. Long Beach, Ca.	N1972G
N999WE	02	CitationJet CJ-2	525A-0126	Business Aircraft Leasing Inc. Nashville, Tn.	N534CJ
N999WS	81	Citation 1/SP	501-0186	Airflite Inc. Shawnee, Ok.	N37HW
N999YB*	95	Beechjet 400A	RK-98	Teton Aviation Inc. Teton Village, Wy.	N999JF
N999YY	02	Global Express	9114	JAY Aviation LLC. Hillsboro, Or.	N1SL
N1000E	94	CitationJet	525-0077	W E Hess Co/WRHC LLC. Chickasha, Ok.	N50820
N1000W	92	Citation V	560-0204	Ashland Inc. Ashland-Boyd, Ky.	N1283Y
N1023C	01	EMB-135LR	145550	CONOCO-Phillips Co. Houston, Tx.	PT-...
N1040	00	Gulfstream V	650	Cox Enterprises Inc. Atlanta, Ga.	N520GA
N1086	88	Gulfstream 4	1086	Stockwood Inc. Morristown, NJ.	N23SY
N1090X	04	Challenger 300	5576	Xerox Corp. White Plains, NY.	C-GLWV
N1094L	00	Citation Excel	560-5094	MCMI-Mission City Management Inc. San Antonio, Tx.	
N1116R	96	Beechjet 400A	RK-116	CTB Inc. Milford, In.	
N1121R	69	Jet Commander-A	125	Albert Lea Airport Inc. Albert Lea, Mn.	N30LS
N1123G	75	Gulfstream II SP	160	Leonard Green & Partners LP. Van Nuys, Ca.	N919TG
N1125A	90	Astra-1125SP	051	Parsons & Whittemore Inc. Rye Brook, NY.	
N1125J	98	Astra-1125SPX	078	Kroger Co. Cincinnati, Oh.	
N1125K	89	Astra-1125	035	BauAir II LLC. Wilton, Ma.	
N1125M	82	Learjet 55	55-065	JKB Jet Holdings LLC. Palm Harbor, Fl.	(N565B)
N1125S	00	Gulfstream G100	134	PGA Tour Air Inc. Ponte Vedra, Fl.	N64GX
N1127K	98	CitationJet	525-0293	Charles Hutter, Carson City, Nv.	
N1127M	02	Learjet 60	60-253	Bayer Corp. Pittsburgh, Pa.	C-FBLU
N1128B	99	Falcon 2000	83	Florida Power & Light Co. Opa Locka, Fl.	F-WWVC
N1129E	00	Citation Excel	560-5112	Air 1 Aviation Services LLC. Baltimore, Md.	N52547
N1129L	99	Citation V Ultra	560-0507	Speciality Air LLP. Austin, Tx.	N5059N
N1129M	84	Learjet 55	55-101	Bayer Corp. Pittsburgh, Pa.	C-FNRG
N1140A	76	Learjet 35	35-045	AirNet Systems Inc. Columbus, Oh.	(N40AN)
N1200N	92	Citation II	550-0681	U S Customs Service, Oklahoma City, Ok. (XC-LHA as required)	(N6776Y)
N1218C	71	Gulfstream II SP	99	FBX Aviation LLC/FlightWorks, Kennesaw, Ga.	N900MP
N1220W	02	CitationJet CJ-2	525A-0146	Overland West Investments Inc. Ogden, Ut.	N.....
N1221J	00	Learjet 60	60-209	Turner Holdings LLC. Dallas, Tx.	N40085
N1230F	06	Citation Excel XLS	560-5679	Gulf Jet LLC. Dubai, UAE.	(A6-GJB)
N1249P	82	Citation II	550-0451	Hummer 1 LLC/JSI Realty Group, Greenville, SC.	
N1250V	82	Citation II	550-0439	Aquila Air LLC/Air Bavarta Ltd. Cincinnati, Oh.	N511WS
N1252D	83	Citation II	550-0476	Esto Logistics LLC. Jeffersonville, In.	
N1254C	99	Citation VII	650-7098	CB Transport Inc/Compass Bank, Birmingham, Al.	N621AB
N1254X	84	Citation II	550-0494	U S Customs Service, Phoenix, Az.	XC-JBR
N1255J	06	CitationJet CJ-3	525B-0109	Davis Leasing LLC. Vero Beach, Fl.	N5145V
N1255K	84	Citation II	550-0505	U S Customs Service, Oklahoma City, Ok.	XC-JAY
N1257D	84	Citation II	550-0497	U S Customs Service, Oklahoma City, Ok.	(XC-JBQ)
N1258B	02	Citation Bravo	550-1037	Air 10/Midwest Jet Center LLC. Cincinnati, Oh.	N5180C
N1277E	02	CitationJet CJ-2	525A-0076	Heaven Express LLC. Watsonville, CA.	N5156D
N1312V	06	Citation Sovereign	680-0075	Gulf Jet LLC. Dubai, UAE.	(A6-GJA)
N1315G	07	Citation Sovereign	680-0173	Cessna Aircraft Co. Wichita, Ks.	N52475
N1324P	84	Learjet 55	55-098	ARK Interests LLC. Wilmington, De.	(N134TP)
N1326A	02	Citation Excel	560-5272	Airplane International Holdings Inc. Wilmington, De.	N5079V
N1327J	93	CitationJet	525-0009	ZellAir LLC. Akron, Oh.	
N1329G	96	CitationJet	525-0146	Radomir Zivanic/Novabank SA. Attica, Greece.	(OE-FGG)
N1400M	87	Citation III	650-0140	Mustang Fuel Corp. Oklahoma City, Ok.	N4FC
N1414P	06	CitationJet CJ2+	525A-0315	West Texas PCS LLC. Albuquerque, NM.	N5094D
N1419J	90	Citation VI	650-0201	Kenneth Anderson, Memphis, Tn.	N347BG

Reg	Yr	Type	c/n	Owner/Operator	Prev Regn
☐ N1454	82	Gulfstream 3	350	Pinnacle Air Executive Jet, Springdale, Ar.	N1454H
☐ N1454H	00	Gulfstream V	619	Amerada Hess Corp. Trenton, NJ.	N608GA
☐ N1504*	83	Challenger 600S	1078	Wegmans Food Markets Inc. Rochester, NY.	N1500
☐ N1540	99	Gulfstream V	580	Cox Enterprises Inc. Atlanta, Ga.	N580GA
☐ N1547B	88	Beechjet 400	RJ-47	Beall Ltd. Hollywood, Fl.	(N900EF)
☐ N1620	07	Hawker 850XP	258893	Cox Enterprises Inc. Atlanta, Ga.	
☐ N1624	97	Gulfstream 4SP	1318	Chevron USA Inc. New Orleans, La.	N418GA
☐ N1625	98	Gulfstream 4SP	1358	Chevron USA Inc. New Orleans, La.	N358GA
☐ N1630	01	Hawker 800XP	258557	Cox Enterprises Inc. Atlanta, Ga.	N51457
☐ N1640	98	Hawker 800XP	258376	Cox Enterprises Inc. Atlanta, Ga.	
☐ N1776A	05	Hawker 850XP	258750	Voyager LM Aviation LLC/Montana Jet Leasing LLC. Pittsburgh.	N950XP
☐ N1776C	07	Hawker 900XP	HA-2	Montana TW Aviation LLC. Bozeman, Mt.	
☐ N1776H	87	BAe 125/800A	258091	320 LLC. Helena, Mt.	N165BA
☐ N1818C	99	Gulfstream 4SP	1385	Ab Initio Software Corp. Bedford, Ma.	N577VU
☐ N1818S	05	Falcon 900EX EASY	153	Stephens Group Inc. Little Rock, Ar.	N7818S
☐ N1823D	69	Gulfstream II SP	59	The Air Group Inc. Van Nuys, Ca.	N879GA
☐ N1829S	98	Falcon 50EX	280	Stephens Group Inc. Little Rock, Ar.	N50FJ
☐ N1836S	07	Falcon 50EX	352	Dassault Falcon Jet Corp. Teterboro, NJ.	F-WWHK
☐ N1837S	98	Citation Excel	560-5155	KM & Z Aviation LLC. Henderson, Nv.	N5095N
☐ N1848T	05	Learjet 40	45-2035	Air Quincy LLC. Pittsfield, Il.	N40050
☐ N1852	83	Learjet 55	55-087	Hastens Sangar AB. Vasteras, Sweden.	SE-RGU
☐ N1865M	85	Citation S/II	S550-0071	Milliken & Co. Greenville, SC.	N571CC
☐ N1867M	02	Citation Excel	560-5303	Mericos Aviation Ltd. Van Nuys, Ca.	N.....
☐ N1868M	00	Global Express	9069	Metropolitan Life Insurance Co. NYC.	N700LD
☐ N1871R	02	Citation Excel	560-5297	CFG Service Corp. Windsor Locks, Ct.	(N721DG)
☐ N1873	01	Citation X	750-0128	George Koch Sons Inc. Evansville, In.	N67CX
☐ N1881Q	79	Falcon 20F-5B	414	Emerson Power Transmissions Inc. Tomkins County, NY.	N412F
☐ N1884	81	Challenger 600S	1032	Spectrum Air Services Inc. Atlanta-DeKalb, Ga.	(N31DC)
☐ N1892	97	Gulfstream V	524	DFZ LLC. New Albany, Oh.	N674RW
☐ N1895C	06	CitationJet CJ1+	525-0647	Goettemoeller Corp/Continental Express Inc. Sidney, Oh.	N.....
☐ N1896T	97	Falcon 50EX	262	New York Times Co. Bradley, Ct.	N262EX
☐ N1897A	05	Citation Excel XLS	560-5629	1897 Corp. Chicago-Midway, Il.	N560VH
☐ N1897S	77	Falcon 20-5	376	J M Smucker Co. Akron-Canton, Oh.	N1892S
☐ N1900W	90	Gulfstream 4	1124	Whirlpool Corp. Benton Harbor, Mi.	N420GA
☐ N1901	05	Citation Sovereign	680-0022	Flag Air LLC. Birmingham, Al.	N.....
☐ N1902P	93	Challenger 601-3R	5135	Nashoba Inc. Dallas, Tx.	N1902J
☐ N1903G	96	Challenger 604	5326	Tri C Inc/Gaylord Broadcasting, Oklahoma City, Ok.	N908G
☐ N1904P	92	Challenger 601-3A	5116	J C Penney Corp. Dallas, Tx.	N841PC
☐ N1904S	99	Learjet 45	45-053	1904 LLC/Spitzer Management Inc. Elyria, Oh.	N3211Q
☐ N1904W	05	Gulfstream 4SP	1237	Whirlpool Corp. Benton Harbor, Mi.	N480GA
☐ N1910A	04	Hawker 800XP	258711	Hallmark Cards Inc. Kansas City, Mo.	N37211
☐ N1910H	96	Hawker 800XP	258318	Hallmark Cards Inc. Kansas City, Mo.	N318XP
☐ N1920	91	Beechjet 400A	RK-21	Perdue Farms Inc. Salisbury, Md.	N717VA
☐ N1925M	96	Gulfstream 4SP	1282	Mannco LLC. Sylmar, Ca.	N9KN
☐ N1925P*	01	Learjet 45	45-199	Pella Corp. Pella, Ia.	N545EC
☐ N1926S	99	Learjet 31A	31A-180	Ararat Rock Products Co. Mount Airy, NC.	
☐ N1927G	96	Falcon 2000	35	W W Grainger Inc. Palwaukee, Il.	N27WP
☐ N1929Y	99	Falcon 2000	84	Oak Spring Farms LLC. Dulles, Va.	F-WWVD
☐ N1932K	94	Learjet 31A	31A-099	Advance America Cash Advance Centers, Spartanburg, SC.	N1932P
☐ N1932P	02	Gulfstream G400	1514	Mozart Investments Inc. Roanoke, Va.	N314GA
☐ N1944P	69	Jet Commander-C	142	Pittsburgh Institute of Aeronautics, Pittsburgh, Pa.	N51038
☐ N1955M	05	Global Express	9185	McDonalds Corp. DuPage, Il.	C-FEAG
☐ N1956M	01	Gulfstream V	675	Perot Management GP LLC. Plano, Tx.	N505RX
☐ N1958N	85	Citation S/II	S550-0073	Milliken & Co. Greenville, SC.	(N1273E)
☐ N1961S	99	Citation Bravo	550-0890	Union Air LLC. Camp Douglas, Wi.	
☐ N1962J	05	Citation X	750-0240	Eagle Mountain International Church, Fort Worth, Tx.	N40CX
☐ N1965L	65	Learjet 24A	24A-012	Clay Lacy Aviation Inc. Van Nuys, Ca.	N1969L
☐ N1967J	98	Citation Bravo	550-0862	Eagle Mountain International Church, Fort Worth, Tx.	N888HS
☐ N1967M	04	Challenger 300	20040	McDonalds Corp. DuPage, Il.	C-GZEB
☐ N1980Z	05	Challenger 300	20049	Aevergreen LLC. Englewood, Co.	C-FFZI
☐ N1987	02	Challenger 604	5550	Petsmart Inc. Scottsdale, Az.	N250CC
☐ N1989D	02	Hawker 800XP	258580	Hensel Phelps Construction Co. Leesburg, Va.	(N880QS)
☐ N1990C	05	Global 5000	9166	Voyage International Ltd. Hamilton, Bermuda.	N166J
☐ N1993	82	Falcon 100	195	TCC Air Services Inc. Oxford, Ct.	TS-IAM
☐ N1999	04	Falcon 2000	219	Petsmart Inc. Scottsdale, Az.	N219FJ
☐ N2000	69	Gulfstream II SP	56	Model Transportation LLC. Van Nuys, Ca.	N690PC

Reg	Yr	Type	c/n	Owner/Operator	Prev Regn
N2000A	07	Falcon 2000EX EASY	119	Dassault Falcon Jet Corp. Teterboro, NJ.	F-WWGD
N2000L	99	Falcon 2000	92	Millard Refrigerated Services Inc/MPS Inc. Omaha, Ne.	N2191
N2000X	94	Citation V	560-0249	P & S LLC. Denver, Co.	N733M
N2006	74	Sabre-40A	282-135	Air Camis Inc. Canton, Oh.	(N67BK)
N2015M	94	BAe 125/800A	258254	Liberty Aviation Corp. Maitland, Fl.	N943H
N2032	89	BAe 125/800A	258175	U S Marshals Service, Oklahoma City, Ok.	N175U
N2033	87	BAe 125/800A	258093	U S Marshals Service, Oklahoma City, Ok.	N317CQ
N2040E	07	CitationJet CJ2+	525A-0386	Cessna Aircraft Co. Wichita, Ks.	N5270P
N2057H	81	Citation II	550-0274	USA Logistics Carriers LLC. McAllen, Tx.	XB-JLJ
N2060V	07	Citation Excel XLS	560-5761	Cessna Aircraft Co. Wichita, Ks.	N5156D
N2065X	07	Citation Excel XLS	560-5766	Cessna Aircraft Co. Wichita, Ks.	N5155G
N2093A	69	Learjet 24B	24B-194	Butler National Inc. Newton, Ks.	(N62FN)
N2094L	72	Learjet 25B	25B-095	Royal Air Freight Inc. Pontiac, Mi.	G-GRCO
N2105	80	Challenger 600S	1010	Suncrest Farms/Peacock Cheese Co. Ontario, Ca.	N7JM
N2107Z	93	Gulfstream 4SP	1211	Air Prestigio LLC. Van Nuys, Ca.	N447GA
N2121	06	BBJ-7E1	34683	Shangri La Entertainment LLC. Burbank, Ca.	
N2150H	77	Westwind-1124	210	Jet Flight LLC. Shreveport, La.	N428JF
N2158U	79	Citation 1/SP	501-0091	RBK Aviation Inc. Wilson, NY.	N2158U
N2243	81	Citation 1/SP	501-0212	Smiley Investment Co. Little Rock, Ar.	N70AA
N2250G	01	CitationJet CJ-2	525A-0047	Hickory Aviation LLC. Adel, Ia.	N5148N
N2273Z	97	Beechjet 400A	RK-173	Tox Inc. San Juan, PR.	
N2411A	85	Citation III	650-0103	R M Excel LLC/Massie & Co. Sacramento, Ca.	(N907RM)
N2425	05	Citation Sovereign	680-0054	Owens Corning, Swanton, Oh.	N5168Y
N2426	05	Citation Sovereign	680-0034	Crain Management Services Inc. Detroit, Mi.	N5260U
N2428	05	Citation Sovereign	680-0046	Owens Corning, Swanton, Oh.	N5260M
N2500B	96	Citation OT-47B	560-0386	U S Dept of State, Oklahoma City, Ok.	N615L
N2531K	89	Citation II	550-0594	U S Customs Service, Oklahoma City, Ok.	N1302X
N2617U	82	Citation 1/SP	501-0235	Corporate Consulting & Financial Inc/ACM, San Jose, Ca.	(N31CF)
N2648X	79	Citation 1/SP	501-0105	Eagle Jet LLC/Outrigger Funds, Holladay, Ut.	(N231LC)
N2663Y	89	Citation II	550-0602	U S Customs Service, Oklahoma City, Ok.	XC-JAZ
N2700	79	Sabre-65	465-7	R-Plane Inc. Houston, Tx.	N2000
N2734K	89	Citation II	550-0595	U S Customs Service, New Orleans NAS, La.	XC-JCV
N2758W	06	Learjet 40	45-2066	Sunrise Aviation Inc. Fayetteville, Ar.	
N2929	04	Gulfstream G550	5053	Roma 550 LLC/TRW Building Management, Dallas, Tx.	N953GA
N3007	00	Hawker 800XP	258487	Empire Airlines Inc. Lebanon, Mo.	N51387
N3008	87	BAe 125/800A	258092	Angair LLC/Pristine Corp. Colorado Springs, Co.	N3007
N3050	05	Gulfstream G550	5096	Lexair Ltd/Trans-Exec Air Service Inc. Van Nuys, Ca.	N696GA
N3170B	86	Citation III	650-0136	Spring Mountain Enterprises Inc. Santa Ana, Ca.	N650DF
N3195F	07	Hawker 850XP	258895	Hawker Beechcraft Corp. Wichita, Ks.	
N3201T	07	Hawker 850XP	258901	Hawker Beechcraft Corp. Wichita, Ks.	
N3204P	07	390 Premier 1A	RB-224	WFBNW NA. Salt Lake City, Ut. (trustor ?).	
N3204T	07	Hawker 850XP	258904	Hawker Beechcraft Corp. Wichita, Ks.	
N3205W	07	390 Premier 1A	RB-225	Hawker Beechcraft Corp. Wichita, Ks.	
N3207T	07	Hawker 850XP	258907	Hawker Beechcraft Corp. Wichita, Ks.	
N3216G	07	390 Premier 1	RB-216	WFBNW NA. Salt Lake City, Ut. (trustor ?).	
N3217P	07	390 Premier 1	RB-217	Hawker Beechcraft Corp. Wichita, Ks.	
N3228M	07	390 Premier 1A	RB-228	Hawker Beechcraft Corp. Wichita, Ks.	
N3262M	91	Citation II	550-0652	U S Customs Service, Oklahoma City, Ok. (XC-HJF as required)	(N1311P)
N3280G	66	Sabre-40	282-70	United CCM Corp. San Antonio, Tx. (status ?).	N34LP
N3285N	07	Hawker 900XP	HA-45	Hawker Beechcraft Corp. Wichita, Ks.	
N3289N	07	Hawker 850XP	258909	Hawker Beechcraft Corp. Wichita, Ks.	
N3330S	07	390 Premier 1A	RB-230	Hawker Beechcraft Corp. Wichita, Ks.	
N3337J	97	Beechjet 400A	RK-159	Woodbridge Logistics LLC. Brattleboro, Vt.	N2159P
N3444B	92	Citation V	560-0192	Figg Transportation Inc. Tallahassee, Fl.	N238JC
N3546	02	Gulfstream V	672	Nike Inc/Aero Air LLC. Hillsboro, Or.	N225GV
N3616	01	Citation Encore	560-0571	Carter Machinery Co. Salem, Va.	N5244W
N3618F	06	Airbus A319-115XCJ	2748	PharmAir Corp. Miami, Fl.	D-AVWB
N3725L	06	390 Premier 1A	RB-155	Empire Companies Inc. Ontario, Ca.	
N3726T	06	390 Premier 1A	RB-156	Empire Companies Inc. Ontario, Ca.	(VT-ANF)
N4000K	00	Citation Excel	560-5081	Kimball International Transit Inc. Huntingburg, In.	
N4000R	01	Hawker 4000	RC-1	Hawker Beechcraft Corp. Wichita, Ks. (Ff 11 Aug 01).	
N4004Y	07	Learjet 60	60-336	Learjet Inc. Wichita, Ks.	
N4009	06	Learjet 45	45-304	RedZone Aviation LLC/NVR Inc. Dulles, Va.	N400
N4053T	99	Beechjet 400A	RK-253	Florida Rock Industries Inc. Jacksonville, Fl.	(N395HB)
N4108E	00	CitationJet CJ-1	525-0410	Commercial Aviation Inc. Kerrville, Tx.	(N292SG)
N4115H	07	CitationJet CJ-3	525B-0183	City World Enterprises Ltd. Road Town, Tortola, BVI.	N5062S

Reg	Yr	Type	c/n	Owner/Operator	Prev Regn
☐ N4200	99	Falcon 2000	87	Key Corp Aviation Co. Cleveland, Oh.	N287QS
☐ N4200K	96	Citation V Ultra	560-0354	Kimball International Transit Inc. Huntingburg, In.	N5157E
☐ N4242	90	Hawker 800SP	NA0453	Two Trees Holdings LLC. Jeffco, Co.	(N242JG)
☐ N4358N	76	Learjet 35	35-065	AirNet Systems Inc. Columbus, Oh.	N425DN
☐ N4402	90	BAe 125/800A	NA0460	MV Flight Service LLC. Weslaco, Tx.	N632BA
☐ N4403	00	Hawker 800XP	258480	GMRI Leasing Inc/Darden Restaurants, Orlando, Fl.	
☐ N4415S	79	Learjet 35A	35A-232	Zoom Zoom Zoom Aviation Inc. Wichita, Ks.	N8281
☐ N4415W	79	Learjet 35A	35A-229	L S Management Inc. Wichita, Ks.	N415LS
☐ N4426	94	Hawker 800	258272	Douglas Allred Co. San Diego, Ca.	N2426
☐ N4447P	81	Learjet 25D	25D-338	Houck Leasing Inc. Fort Pierce, Fl.	XA-LOF
☐ N4467X	00	Beechjet 400A	RK-267	MarBry Charters LLC. Naples, Fl.	
☐ N4483W	01	Beechjet 400A	RK-313	Tulip Air BV. Rotterdam, Holland.	(PH-BBC)
☐ N4488W	83	Learjet 25D	25D-367	Ompir Avir Inc. Orlando, Fl.	VT-SWP
☐ N4500X	84	Gulfstream 3	416	Platinum Dunes Productions, Van Nuys, Ca.	(N500XB)
☐ N4545	98	Learjet 45	45-045	Rancho del Sol LLC. Byron, Ca.	
☐ N4614N	90	Citation II	550-0659	U S Customs Service, Oklahoma City, Ok.	XC-HGZ
☐ N4753	92	Gulfstream 4	1197	Bank of Utah, Salt Lake City, Ut. (trustor ?).	N969SG
☐ N5000X	00	Gulfstream V	611	Teratorn LLC. Seattle, Wa.	N568GA
☐ N5009	06	Learjet 60	60-306	Indycar Aviation LLC. Indianapolis, In.	N500
☐ N5010X	01	390 Premier 1	RB-10	Raytheon Aircraft Co. Wichita, Ks. (status ?).	
☐ N5014E	07	Learjet 60	60-335	Learjet Inc. Wichita, Ks.	
☐ N5016Z	07	Learjet 40	45-2093	Learjet Inc. Wichita, Ks.	
☐ N5026	03	CitationJet CJ-2	525A-0159	Overseas Transcom Corp. Jacksonville, Fl.	N.....
☐ N5037F	07	CitationJet CJ1+	525-0665	Cessna Aircraft Co. Wichita, Ks.	
☐ N5059X	07	Citation Excel XLS	560-5767	Cessna Aircraft Co. Wichita, Ks.	
☐ N5066U	07	Citation Excel XLS	560-5769	Cessna Aircraft Co. Wichita, Ks.	
☐ N5076K	07	CitationJet CJ-1	525-0666	Cessna Aircraft Co. Wichita, Ks.	
☐ N5095N	07	Citation Excel XLS	560-5750	Cessna Aircraft Co. Wichita, Ks.	
☐ N5098F	69	Falcon 20D	197	Air Cargo Carriers Inc. Milwaukee, Wi.	C-GTAK
☐ N5101	98	Gulfstream V	550	General Motors Corp. Detroit, Mi.	N650GA
☐ N5102	98	Gulfstream V	551	General Motors Corp. Detroit, Mi.	N651GA
☐ N5107	82	Falcon 50	109	N280BG LLC/Beanstalk Group, Troy, Mi.	N280BG
☐ N5113	04	Gulfstream G350	4013	General Motors Corp. Detroit, Mi.	N913GA
☐ N5113S	97	Citation X	750-0013	Inter Air Leasing LLC. Wilmington, De.	N5113
☐ N5114	04	Gulfstream G350	4016	General Motors Corp. Detroit, Mi.	N816GA
☐ N5115	05	Gulfstream G350	4019	General Motors Corp. Detroit, Mi.	N989GA
☐ N5116	05	Gulfstream G350	4023	General Motors Corp. Detroit, Mi.	N623GA
☐ N5117	05	Gulfstream G350	4026	General Motors Corp. Detroit, Mi.	N626GA
☐ N5119	90	BAe 125/800A	258177	NSI Leasing LLC/National System Inc. St Louis, Mo.	N217AL
☐ N5135K	07	Citation Sovereign	680-0186	Cessna Aircraft Co. Wichita, Ks.	
☐ N5136J	07	Citation Sovereign	680-0191	Cessna Aircraft Co. Wichita, Ks.	
☐ N5144	97	Citation X	750-0017	GR Aviation Corp. Fort Lauderdale, Fl.	N5114
☐ N5153K	07	CitationJet CJ2+	525A-0389	Cessna Aircraft Co. Wichita, Ks.	
☐ N5175U	73	B 737/T-43A	20689	EG&G/Department of the Air Force, McCarran, Nv.	72-0282
☐ N5176Y	74	B 737/T-43A	20692	EG&G/Department of the Air Force, McCarran, Nv.	72-0285
☐ N5177C	74	B 737/T-43A	20693	EG&G/Department of the Air Force, McCarran, Nv.	72-0286
☐ N5185V	07	Citation Encore+	560-0779	Cessna Aircraft Co. Wichita, Ks.	N5223X
☐ N5188A	05	Citation Encore	560-0686	Cessna Aircraft Co. Wichita, Ks.	
☐ N5200	99	Falcon 2000	90	KeyCorp Aviation Co. Cleveland, Oh.	N930SD
☐ N5201J	07	CitationJet CJ-3	525B-0215	Cessna Aircraft Co. Wichita, Ks.	
☐ N5203S	07	Citation Sovereign	680-0196	Cessna Aircraft Co. Wichita, Ks.	
☐ N5207V	07	Citation Sovereign	680-0195	Cessna Aircraft Co. Wichita, Ks.	
☐ N5225G	68	Falcon 20D	181	LVA Management & Consulting Inc. Lawrenceville, Ga.	N817JS
☐ N5231S	07	Citation Sovereign	680-0184	Cessna Aircraft Co. Wichita, Ks.	
☐ N5243K	07	CitationJet CJ-3	525B-0219	Cessna Aircraft Co. Wichita, Ks.	
☐ N5245D	07	Citation Sovereign	680-0189	Cessna Aircraft Co. Wichita, Ks.	
☐ N5245L	07	Citation X	750-0286	Cessna Aircraft Co. Wichita, Ks.	
☐ N5250E	07	CitationJet CJ-3	525B-0216	Cessna Aircraft Co. Wichita, Ks.	
☐ N5257V	07	Citation Sovereign	680-0193	Cessna Aircraft Co. Wichita, Ks.	
☐ N5262	06	Challenger 300	20122	State Street Corp. Sikorsky, Ct.	C-FION
☐ N5263	97	Citation V Ultra	560-0435	Orchard Management/Pinefield Consulting Inc. Portsmouth, NH.	N410NA
☐ N5265B	07	Citation Excel XLS	560-5756	Cessna Aircraft Co. Wichita, Ks.	
☐ N5267T	07	CitationJet CJ2+	525A-0388	Cessna Aircraft Co. Wichita, Ks.	
☐ N5294E	74	B 737/T-43A	20691	EG&G/Department of the Air Force, McCarran, Nv.	72-0284
☐ N5294M	74	B 737/T-43A	20694	EG&G/Department of the Air Force, McCarran, Nv.	72-0287
☐ N5314J	91	Citation II	550-0663	U S Customs Service, New Orleans NAS, La.	(XC-JCX)

Reg	Yr	Type	c/n	Owner/Operator	Prev Regn
N5322	02	Falcon 50EX	322	Vulcan Aggregates LLC. Birmingham, Al.	F-WWHB
N5408G	91	Citation II	550-0666	U S Customs Service, Oklahoma City, Ok. (XC-JBS as required)	XC-JBS
N5572	83	Learjet 55	55-072	Milam International Inc. Englewood, Co.	SX-BNS
N5601T	01	Citation Encore	560-0564	Tennyson Enterprises Inc. Ottumwa, Ia.	N660LT
N5616	00	Gulfstream V	616	Halliburton Energy Services Inc. Houston, Tx.	N141HC
N5734	97	Hawker 800XP	258304	Air Time Aviation LLC. Bethesda, Md.	N802JT
N5736	00	Hawker 800XP2	258471	The Hawker Partnership, Luton, UK.	N43642
N5879	61	MS 760 Paris-2B	107	CJT Holdings LLC. Dallas, Tx.	PH-MSW
N5950C	06	Gulfstream G150	213	Milloaks LLC/Okland Construction Co. Salt Lake City, Ut.	N613GA
N5956B	00	Gulfstream 4SP	1469	Oakmont Holdings LLC. Van Nuys, Ca.	N269GA
N6001L	80	Citation II	550-0169	U S Customs Service, New Orleans NAS, La.	(XC-JDA)
N6110	93	Citation VII	650-7023	AESR LLC. Minneapolis, Mn.	N1262G
N6117G	04	390 Premier 1	RB-117	RichSmith Development LLC. Little Rock, Ar.	
N6150Y	05	390 Premier 1A	RB-150	Barclays North Inc. Everett, Wa.	(N575PT)
N6177Y	67	Learjet 24	24-151	Adventure Capital Group Expedition, Fort Lauderdale, Fl.	N53GH
N6453	03	Falcon 2000EX	26	Nike Inc/Aero Air LLC. Hillsboro, Or.	N226EX
N6525B	04	CitationJet CJ-3	525B-0004	C3SP LLC. Fort Worth, Tx.	N1308L
N6555L	67	Falcon 20C	85	Aircraft Holdings LLC. Scottsdale, Az.	VH-JSY
N6637G	91	Citation II	550-0670	U S Customs Service, New Orleans NAS. (uses XC-JEG).	(XC-JCZ)
N6666R	01	Falcon 900EX	102	Burnett Aviation Co. Fort Worth, Tx.	N6666P
N6757M	02	Challenger 604	5545	McCormick & Co. Baltimore-Martin County, Md.	N334FX
N6763L	91	Citation II	550-0673	U S Customs Service, Oklahoma City, Ok. (XC-HHA as required)	XC-HHA
N6775C	91	Citation II	550-0677	U S Customs Service, Oklahoma City, Ok. (XC-HJC as required)	
N6776T	92	Citation II	550-0680	U S Customs Service, Oklahoma City, Ok. (XC-HJE as required)	
N7007Q	06	Hawker 4000	RC-7	Hawker Beechcraft Corp. Wichita, Ks.	(N807HH)
N7070A	85	Citation S/II	S550-0068	Omega Air Inc. Sligo-Starndhill, Ireland.	N4049
N7074X	70	Learjet 24B	24B-223	Interlease Aviation Corp. Northfield, Il. (status ?).	D-CFVG
N7088S	06	390 Premier 1A	RB-188	Jetgroup, Sydney, NSW. Australia.	
N7092C	78	Learjet 35A	35A-184	Cefaratti International Inc. Coronado, Ca.	HB-VFO
N7170Y	06	390 Premier 1A	RB-170	CJ 181JT LLC/Empire Companies, Ontario, Ca.	(N181JT)
N7270B	73	B 727-232	20641	Museum of Flight Foundation, Tukwila, Wa.	N18786
N7402	05	Citation Sovereign	680-0082	GMRI Leasing Inc/Darden Restaurants, Orlando, Fl.	N.....
N7490A	82	HS 125/700A	NA0320	Oehmig Aviation LLC. Houston, Tx.	N700HW
N7513H	86	Gulfstream 3	493	Frigorifco Yacambu CA. Miami, Fl.	G-540
N7600	04	Hawker 400XP	RK-395	SAS Institute Inc. Raleigh-Durham, NC.	
N7600G	01	Citation X	750-0159	State Jet Services LLC/SAS Institute Inc. Cary, NC.	N1128V
N7600K	02	BBJ-7BC	32628	SAS Institute Inc. Raleigh-Durham, NC.	N102QS
N7600S	06	Falcon 900EX EASY	173	SAS Institute Inc. Cary, NC.	F-WWFE
N7601R	60	MS 760 Paris-1R	60	William Spriggs, Santa Paula, Ca.	No 60
N7700T	82	Citation 1/SP	501-0248	Big Tex Trailers Inc. Mount Pleasant, Tx.	(N711EG)
N7701L	74	Learjet 24D	24D-288	Spradling Oil Development LLC. Borger, Tx.	N288DF
N7715X	07	CitationJet CJ1+	525-0653	B H Aviation Inc. Sherman Oaks, Ca.	N52526
N7725D	07	CitationJet CJ-3	525B-0218	Cessna Aircraft Co. Wichita, Ks.	N5201M
N7734T	98	Learjet 60	60-139	Tejas Aviation Management, Fort Worth, Tx.	(N77511)
N7765D	02	Citation Bravo	550-1041	Blanco One LLC. San Antonio, Tx.	N7725D
N7777B	91	Citation VI	650-0214	Bergstrom Pioneer Auto & Truck Leasing, Neenah, Wi.	N771JB
N7799T	01	Gulfstream 4SP	1474	Western Air Charter Inc/Jet Edge, Malaysia.	N248AB
N7814	07	CitationJet CJ-3	525B-0166	Westgate Aviation LLC. Angel Fire, NM.	N5061W
N7877T	06	CitationJet CJ-3	525B-0077	Jet Duluth LLC. Duluth, Mn.	N.....
N7895Q	00	CitationJet CJ-1	525-0405	Corporate Aviation Inc. Raleigh-Durham, NC.	N121EB
N8000U	07	Citation Excel XLS	560-5746	Ashland Inc. Covington, Ky.	N50715
N8005	98	Citation Excel	560-5006	RAW Inc. Raleigh, NC.	N5141F
N8005Y	73	Learjet 25B	25B-121	Source Investments LLC. Addison, Tx.	XA-SAL
N8030F	89	BAe 125/800A	258131	Bay Aviation LLC. Boca Raton, Fl.	N95
N8040A	76	Learjet 35	35-048	AirNet Systems Inc. Columbus, Oh.	F-GHMP
N8073R	91	Beechjet 400A	RK-24	Hawker Beechcraft Corp. Wichita, Ks.	
N8085T	92	Beechjet 400A	RK-51	KD Construction of Florida Inc. Pompano Beach, Fl.	
N8100E	96	Falcon 900EX	4	Emerson Electric Co. St Louis, Mo.	N204FJ
N8106V	06	CitationJet CJ-3	525B-0072	CCMP Capital Advisors LLC. Oxford, Ct.	N107CQ
N8167Y	93	Beechjet 400A	RK-67	Coastal Aviation LLC. Oklahoma City, Ok.	
N8186	02	Hawker 800XP	258604	CYMI Investments Sub Inc. Dayton, Oh.	N60664
N8200E	87	Falcon 900B	34	Emerson Electric Co. St Louis, Mo.	N8100E
N8279G	93	Beechjet 400A	RK-79	MPJ Jet LLC. Vail, Co.	OH-RIF
N8283C	94	Beechjet 400A	RK-83	Stark Airways LLC. Canton, Oh.	XA-MII
N8288R	99	CitationJet	525-0348	Gillco Energy Air LLC. Tradewind, Tx.	(N213LX)
N8300E	80	Falcon 50	33	Emerson Electric Co. St Louis, Mo.	N8100E

Reg	Yr	Type	c/n	Owner/Operator	Prev Regn
N8341C	96	CitationJet	525-0150	Air Commander LLC. St Paul, Mn.	ZS-NUW
N8344M	88	Citation II	550-0577	JWG Inc. Winston-Salem, NC.	N827JB
N8400E	84	Falcon 50	150	Emerson Electric Co. St Louis, Mo.	N8200E
N8486	00	Citation Encore	560-0554	Encore Aircraft Ventures LLC. Burlington, Vt.	N749RL
N8500	72	Sabre-40A	282-108	Haws Aviation LLC. Huntsville, Al.	N85CC
N8701L	07	Citation Excel XLS	560-5751	Citation Oil & Gas Corp. Houston, Tx.	N5100J
N8762M	02	Global Express	9113	University of Pittsburgh Medical Center, Allegheny County, P	N920DS
N8778	01	Hawker 800XP	258560	Ligon Industries LLC. Birmingham, Al.	N877S
N8783	92	Learjet 60	60-006	Truman Aviation Holdings LLC. Lexington, Ky.	N606BR
N8811A*	97	Learjet 60	60-119	Aspire Holdings LLC. Boca Raton, Fl.	N626LJ
N8821C	04	Gulfstream G150	226	Chevron USA Inc. Houston, Tx.	4X-C...
N8841C	07	Gulfstream G150	229	Chevron USA Inc. Houston, Tx.	4X-C...
N8860	66	DC 9-15	45797	Richard Mellon Scaife, Latrobe, Pa.	(EC-BAX)
N8881J	92	BAe 125/800A	258219	Gatlin Development Co. San Diego, Ca.	9M-AZZ
N8888	98	Learjet 60	60-128	Zulu Air Services LLC. White Plains, NY.	N61ZZ
N8940	02	CitationJet CJ-2	525-0091	Mac-Tech Inc. Wellington, Ks.	N.....
N9035Y	61	MS 760 Paris-1A	86	North Pacific Aircraft Development Co. Helena, Mt.	F-BJLX
N9072U	86	Citation S/II	S550-0106	Harper Cattle Aviation LLC. Arlington, Tx.	N666TR
N9180K	07	CitationJet CJ2+	525A-0345	Caruso LLC/OK Industries, Fort Smith, Ar.	N5153K
N9200M	98	Learjet 60	60-132	Risk Strategies LLC. Montclair, Ca.	N228FX
N9292X	97	Hawker 800XP	258315	Warner Road Aviation Inc. Steamboat Springs, Co.	N2169X
N9611Z	07	Gulfstream G150	231	The Geo Group Inc. Boca Raton, Fl.	4X-C..
N9700T	92	Citation V	560-0203	Hutchens Industries inc/Tandem Air LLC. Springfield, Mo.	N7700L
N9707X*	07	Falcon 7X	9	Dassault Falcon Jet Corp. Teterboro, NJ.	F-WWUF
N9867	04	Hawker 800XP	258678	CYMI Investments Sub Inc. Dayton, Oh.	N678XP
N9871R	04	Falcon 2000EX EASY	43	CFG Service Corp. Windsor Locks, Ct.	F-WWGY
N9990S	91	BAe 125/800A	NA0468	OliverStone LLC/Oliver McMillan LLC. Carlsbad, Ca.	N661JN
N9999M	89	Gulfstream 4	1090	Star Plane Inc. NYC.	VP-CYM
N9999V	81	HS 125/700A	NA0308	Columbus Capital Partners LLC. Chesterfield, Mo.	N10CN
N10123	71	Gulfstream 2TT	107	EarthData International Inc. Van Nuys, Ca.	N5113H
N11887	73	Sabre-75A	380-4	Jose Manuel Figueroa, McAllen, Tx.	XA-RLP
N12068	93	Citation II	550-0719	Translatin SA. Guatemala City, Guatemala.	(N550BG)
N12549	84	Citation II	550-0501	U S Customs Service, Oklahoma City, Ok.	
N13092	06	Citation Encore	560-0707	NXT Inc. Oklahoma City, Ok.	N.....
N24237	85	Citation III	650-0102	Lake Air Inc. Fort Lauderdale, Fl.	N406LM
N26494	89	Citation II	550-0605	Department of Homeland Security,	(N1304B)
N26496	89	Citation II	550-0607	U S Customs Service, New Orleans NAS. La.	(XC-JCW)
N26621	89	Citation II	550-0593	U S Customs Service, Oklahoma City, Ok.	(XC-JBT)
N30156	73	Westwind-1123	165	RAA Enterprises Inc. Wilmington, De.	N22RD
N30501	83	Gulfstream 3	383	U S Army Corp of Engineers/Mississippi Valley Division.	N65CE
N31946	07	Hawker 900XP	HA-46	Hawker Beechcraft Corp. Wichita, Ks.	
N31959	08	Hawker 900XP	HA-49	Hawker Beechcraft Corp. Wichita, Ks.	
N32012	07	Hawker 850XP	258912	Hawker Beechcraft Corp. Wichita, Ks.	
N32022	07	390 Premier 1A	RB-222	Lider Taxi Aereo SA. Belo Horizonte, MG. Brazil.	
N34441	07	Hawker 900XP	HA-41	Hawker Beechcraft Corp. Wichita, Ks.	
N34548	07	Hawker 900XP	HA-48	Hawker Beechcraft Corp. Wichita, Ks.	
N34838	07	Hawker 900XP	HA-38	Hawker Beechcraft Corp. Wichita, Ks.	
N35004	07	Hawker 4000	RC-24	Hawker Beechcraft Corp. Wichita, Ks.	
N36866	06	390 Premier 1A	RB-166	Empire Companies Inc. Ontario, Ca.	
N37201	91	Citation II	550-0655	U S Customs Service, New Orleans NAS, La. (uses XC-LHH).	
N37971	82	Learjet 25D	25D-358	Trust of the American West, Las Vegas, Nv.	
N40079	07	Learjet 40	45-2094	Learjet Inc. Wichita, Ks.	
N42799	75	Sabre-75A	380-30	Centurion Investments Inc. St Louis, Mo.	N818LD
N45678	03	Citation Bravo	550-1056	Department of Justice, Fort Worth, Tx.	N52601
N46452	66	Learjet 23	23-095	Royal Air Freight Inc. Pontiac, Mi. (status ?).	N9RA
N50153	07	Learjet 45	45-350	Learjet Inc. Wichita, Ks.	
N50446	66	Falcon 20C	21	Sierra American Corp. Addison, Tx. (status ?)	C-FTUT
N50756	07	Citation Excel XLS	560-5760	Cessna Aircraft Co. Wichita, Ks.	
N50820	07	CitationJet CJ2+	525A-0385	Cessna Aircraft Co. Wichita, Ks.	
N51099	74	Citation	500-0203	International Turbine Service Inc. Grapevine, Tx.	CC-PZM
N51666	07	Citation Excel XLS	560-5764	Cessna Aircraft Co. Wichita, Ks.	
N51869	07	Citation Excel XLS	560-5763	Cessna Aircraft Co. Wichita, Ks.	
N52114	07	CitationJet CJ-3	525B-0210	Cessna Aircraft Co. Wichita, Ks.	
N52136	07	CitationJet CJ-3	525B-0220	Cessna Aircraft Co. Wichita, Ks.	
N52178	07	Citation X	750-0284	Cessna Aircraft Co. Wichita, Ks.	
N52235	07	CitationJet CJ-3	525B-0212	Cessna Aircraft Co. Wichita, Ks.	

Reg	Yr	Type	c/n	Owner/Operator	Prev Regn
❏ N52352	07	Citation Sovereign	680-0190	Cessna Aircraft Co. Wichita, Ks.	
❏ N52690	07	CitationJet CJ-3	525B-0217	Cessna Aircraft Co. Wichita, Ks.	
❏ N61442*	80	Citation II/SP	551-0181	565VV Ltd/Van Voorst Lumber Co. Union Hill, Il.	N565VV
❏ N61908	04	390 Premier 1	RB-108	RCS Holdings LLC. Yeager, WV.	
❏ N63357	67	Jet Commander	99	N22RD Inc. Corpus Christi, Tx.	N22RD
❏ N77702	02	Learjet 45	45-224	O'Gara Aviation LLC. Atlanta, Ga.	N822GA
❏ N77709	07	Gulfstream G150	236	Miller's Inc. Pittsburg, Ks.	4X-C..
❏ N77794	94	CitationJet	525-0073	Executive Wings Inc. Wexford, Pa.	N2656G
❏ N79711	00	BBJ-7BQ	30547	Dallah Al Baraka, Jeddah, Saudi Arabia.	(HZ-DG5)
❏ N80364	76	Citation Eagle	500-0299	Farnley Investments Ltd. Weston, Ireland.	OY-TKI
❏ N87011	04	Citation Bravo	550-1075	B E & K Inc. Birmingham, Al.	N8701L
Military					
❏ 00-1051	01	Citation UC-35C	560-0565	U S Army, B-2/228th AVN,	(00-0002)
❏ 00-1052	01	Citation UC-35C	560-0574	U S Army, PATD,	N52526
❏ 00-1053	01	Citation UC-35C	560-0577	U S Army, PATD,	N5207V
❏ 01	00	Gulfstream C-37A	653	USCG, Washington, DC.	N527GA
❏ 01-0015	01	BBJ-7DM (C-40B)	32916	USAF, 65th AS, 15ABW, Hickam AFB. Hi.	N378BJ
❏ 01-0028	00	Gulfstream C-37A	620	USAF, 310 Airlift Squadron, MacDill AFB. Fl.	N535GA
❏ 01-0029	00	Gulfstream C-37A	624	USAF, 310 Airlift Squadron, MacDill AFB. Fl.	N624GA
❏ 01-0030	01	Gulfstream C-37A	663	USAF, 310 Airlift Squadron, MacDill AFB. Fl.	N663GA
❏ 01-0040	00	BBJ-7DM (C-40B)	29971	USAF, 1st AS/89th AW, Andrews AFB. Md.	N371BJ
❏ 01-0041	02	BBJ-7CP (C-40B)	33080	USAF, 1st AS/89th AW, Andrews AFB. Md.	(01-0005)
❏ 01-0065	00	Gulfstream C-37A	652	USAF, Hickam AFB. Hi.	N582GA
❏ 01-0076	01	Gulfstream V	645	USAF,	N645GA
❏ 01-0301	01	Citation UC-35C	560-0589	U S Army, PATD,	N5151D
❏ 02	99	Challenger 604	5427	C-143A, USCG, Washington, DC.	N321FX
❏ 02-0042	02	BBJ-7FD (C-40B)	33500	USAF,	N237BA
❏ 02-0201	00	BBJ-7CPS (C-40C)	30755	D C ANG, 201st Airlift Squadron, Andrews AFB. Md.	N752BC
❏ 02-0202	99	BBJ-7CPS (C-40C)	30753	D C ANG, 201st Airlift Squadron, Andrews AFB. Md.	N754BC
❏ 02-0203	02	BBJ-7CPS (C-40C)	33434	D C ANG, 201st Airlift Squadron, Andrews AFB. Md.	N236BA
❏ 02-1863	01	Gulfstream C-37A	670	U S Army. 'Gettysburg'	N670GA
❏ 03-0016	03	Citation UC-35D	560-0649	U S Army,	N5267T
❏ 03-0726	04	Citation UC-35C	560-0667	U S Army,	N52462
❏ 04-1778	03	Gulfstream C-37B	5034	U S Army, Andrews AFB. Md.	N934GA
❏ 05-0730	06	BBJ-7DM (C-40B)	34807	USAF, 932AW, Scott AFB. Il.	N365BJ
❏ 05-0932	06	BBJ-7DM (C-40B)	34808	USAF, 932AW, Scott AFB. Il.	N366BJ
❏ 05-4613	06	BBJ-7DM (C-40B)	34809	USAF, 932AW, Scott AFB. Il.	N368BJ
❏ 150972	60	Sabreliner T-39D	285-4	U. S. Navy, Pensacola NAS, Fl.	
❏ 150977	60	Sabreliner T-39D	285-9	U. S. Navy, Pensacola NAS, Fl.	
❏ 150992	61	Sabreliner T-39D	285-24	U. S. Navy, Naval Weapons Center, China Lake, Ca.	
❏ 151337	61	Sabreliner T-39D	285-26	U. S. Navy, Pensacola NAS, Fl.	
❏ 158380	68	Sabreliner CT-39E	282-95	U. S. Navy, Pensacola NAS, Fl.	N425NA
❏ 158381	68	Sabreliner CT-39E	282-93	U. S. Navy, VRC-50, Cubi Point, Philippines. (status ?).	N4701N
❏ 158844	71	Sabreliner CT-39G	306-55	U. S. Navy,	N5419
❏ 159361	73	Sabreliner CT-39G	306-65	U. S. Navy, Code 30, VR-24, NAF Sigonella, Italy.	N8364N
❏ 159364	74	Sabreliner CT-39G	306-69	25. U S Navy, NAS Pensacola, Fl.	
❏ 159365	74	Sabreliner CT-39G	306-70	U. S. Marine Corps, El Toro MCAS, Ca.	
❏ 160053	75	Sabreliner CT-39G	306-104	U. S. Navy,	N65795
❏ 160054	75	Sabreliner CT-39G	306-105	22. U S Navy, NAS Pensacola, Fl.	N65796
❏ 160055	75	Sabreliner CT-39G	306-106	Station Operations & Engineering Sqn. Cherry Point MCAS, NC.	N65797
❏ 160056	75	Sabreliner CT-39G	306-107	Station Operations & Engineering Sqn. Cherry Point MCAS, NC.	N65798
❏ 163691	86	Gulfstream C-20D	480	USN, VR-1, CFLSW, Andrews AFB. Md.	N302GA
❏ 163692	86	Gulfstream C-20D	481	USMC/USN, VR-1, CFLSW, Andrews AFB. Md.	N304GA
❏ 165093	92	Gulfstream C-20G	1187	USN, VR-48, Andrews AFB. Md. 'City of Annapolis'	N481GA
❏ 165094	92	Gulfstream C-20G	1189	USN, VR-48, Andrews AFB. Md. 'City of Baltimore'	N402GA
❏ 165151	92	Gulfstream C-20G	1199	USN, VR-51, Code RG, Kaneohe, Hi.	N428GA
❏ 165152	92	Gulfstream C-20G	1201	USN, VR-51, Code RG, Kaneohe. 'Spirit of Wake Island'	N431GA
❏ 165153	92	Gulfstream C-20G	1200	USMC, MASD, NAF Washington, Andrews AFB. Md.	N430GA
❏ 165509	64	Sabre T-39N	282-9	01. U S Navy, Pensacola NAS, Fl.	N301NT
❏ 165510	66	Sabre T-39N	282-81	02. U S Navy, Pensacola NAS, Fl.	N302NT
❏ 165511	65	Sabre T-39N	282-29	03. U S Navy, Pensacola NAS, Fl.	N303NT
❏ 165512	63	Sabre T-39N	282-2	04. U S Navy, Pensacola NAS, Fl.	N304NT
❏ 165513	66	Sabre T-39N	282-66	05. U S Navy, Pensacola NAS, Fl.	N305NT
❏ 165514	65	Sabre T-39N	282-30	06. U S Navy, Pensacola NAS, Fl.	N306NT
❏ 165515	66	Sabre T-39N	282-72	07. U S Navy, Pensacola NAS, Fl.	N307NT
❏ 165516	67	Sabre T-39N	282-90	08. U S Navy, Pensacola NAS, Fl.	N308NT

Reg	Yr	Type	c/n	Owner/Operator	Prev Regn
165517	66	Sabre T-39N	282-61	09. U S Navy, Pensacola NAS, Fl.	N309NT
165518	66	Sabre T-39N	282-77	10. U S Navy, Pensacola NAS, Fl.	N310NT
165519	64	Sabre T-39N	282-19	11. U S Navy, Pensacola NAS, Fl.	N311NT
165520	65	Sabre T-39N	282-32	12. U S Navy, Pensacola NAS, Fl.	N312NT
165521	68	Sabre T-39N	282-94	13. U S Navy, Pensacola NAS, Fl.	N313NT
165523	64	Sabre T-39N	282-20	14. U S Navy, Pensacola NAS, Fl.	N315NT
165740	99	Citation UC-35C	560-0524	USMC, MWHS-4/EZ, New Orleans NAS, La.	N5091J
165741	99	Citation UC-35C	560-0529	USMC, MWHS-4/EZ, New Orleans NAS, La.	N5097H
165829	00	B 737-7AF (C-40A)	29979	U S Navy, VR-59/RY, NAS Fort Worth JRB, Tx.	N1003N
165830	00	B 737-7AF (C-40A)	29980	U S Navy, VR-59/RY, NAS Fort Worth JRB, Tx.	N1003M
165831	00	B 737-7AF (C-40A)	30200	U S Navy, VR-59/RY, NAS Fort Worth JRB, Tx.	N1786B
165832	01	B 737-7AF (C-40A)	30781	U S Marine Corp, VR-58/JV, 'City of St Augustine'	
165833	01	B 737-7AF (C-40A)	32597	U S Navy, VR-58/JV, 'City of Dallas'	
165834	02	B 737-7AF (C-40A)	32598	U S Navy, VR-58/JV,	
165835	04	B 737-7AF (C-40A)	33826	U S Navy, VR-57,	N543BA
165939	01	Citation UC-35D	560-0570	U S Marine Corps. MWHS-1,	N5262W
166374	02	Citation UC-35D	560-0592	U S Marine Corps, 4 MAW, Andrews AFB. Md.	N5180C
166375	00	Gulfstream V	657	U S Navy, 'Spirit of Midway Island'	N587GA
166376	03	Gulfstream G550	5041	U S Navy,	N841GA
166377	05	Gulfstream G550	5087	U S Navy,	N587GA
166378	05	Gulfstream G550	5098	U S Navy,	N598GA
166474	02	Citation UC-35D	560-0630	USMC, 4 MAW, Andrews AFB. Md.	N5180K
166500	04	Citation UC-35D	560-0651	USMC, MCAS Miramar, Ca.	N5156D
166693	06	B 737-7AF (C-40A)	34304	U S Navy,	
166712	04	Citation UC-35D	560-0672	U S Navy,	N5253G
166713	04	Citation UC-35D	560-0677	U S Navy,	N5079V
166714	05	Citation UC-35D	560-0679	MCAS, Cherry Point, NC.	N.....
166715	05	Citation UC-35D	560-0682	U S Navy,	N5204D
166766	05	Citation UC-35D	560-0693	U S Marine Corps.	N5076K
166767	05	Citation UC-35D	560-0696	U S Marine Corps.	N50715
2101	77	Guardian HU-25B	374	USCG, ARSC, CGAS Elizabeth City, NC. (as at 11/04).	N1045F
2102	78	Guardian HU-25A	386	USCG, CGAS Miami, Fl. (as at 9/05).	N149F
2103	78	Guardian HU-25B	394	FAA, Sandia National Laboratory, Albuquerque, NM. (stored).	N178F
2104	78	Guardian HU-25C	390	USCG, CGAS Corpus Christi, Tx. (as at 4/06).	N173F
2105	78	Guardian HU-25D	398	USCG, CGAS Miami, Fl. (as at 4/06).	N183F
2109	79	Guardian HU-25A	407	USCG, CGAS Cape Cod, Ma. (as at 4/06).	N406F
2110	79	Guardian HU-25A	411	USCG, CGAS Elizabeth City, NC. (as at 9/05).	N408F
2112	79	Guardian HU-25C	415	USCG, CGAS Miami, Fl. (as at 4/06).	N413F
2113	79	Guardian HU-25A	417	USCG, CGAS Miami, Fl. (as at 4/06).	N416FJ
2114	79	Guardian HU-25A	418	USCG, CGAS Miami, Fl. (as at 4/06).	N417F
2117	80	Guardian HU-25A	421	USCG, CGAS Miami, Fl. (as at 4/06).	N422F
2118	80	Guardian HU-25B	423	USCG, ATC, Mobile, Al. (as at 4/06).	N423F
2120	80	Guardian HU-25A	425	USCG, CGAS Cape Cod, Ma. (as at 4/06).	N425F
2121	80	Guardian HU-25A	431	USCG, ATC, Mobile, Al. (as at 4/06).	N429F
2127	81	Guardian HU-25A	443	USCG, ATC, Mobile, Al. (as at 4/06).	N447F
2128	81	Guardian HU-25A	445	USCG, CGAS Miami, Fl. (as at 4/06).	N449F
2129	81	Guardian HU-25C	447	USCG, CGAS Miami, Fl. (as at 4/06).	N455F
2131	81	Guardian HU-25C	452	USCG, CGAS Miami, Fl. (as at 4/06).	N459F
2133	81	Guardian HU-25C	456	USCG, CGAS Cape Cod, Ma. (as at 10/05).	N462F
2134	81	Guardian HU-25A	458	USCG, ATC, Mobile, Al. (as at 4/06).	N465F
2135	81	Guardian HU-25C	459	USCG, CGAS Corpus Christi, Tx. (as at 4/06).	N466F
2136	81	Guardian HU-25A	460	USCG, ATC, Mobile, Al. (as at 4/06).	N467F
2139	82	Guardian HU-25C	466	USCG, CGAS Cape Cod, Ma. (as at 4/06).	N473F
2140	82	Guardian HU-25C	467	USCG, CGAS Cape Cod, Ma. (as at 4/06).	N474F
2141	77	Guardian HU-25C	371	USCG, CGAS Cape Cod, Ma. (as at 4/06).	N1039F
59-2873	59	Sabreliner CT-39B	270-1	USAF/4950th Test Wing-ASD, Edwards AFB. Ca.	
60-3474	60	Sabreliner CT-39B	270-3	USAF/4950th Test Wing-ASD, Edwards AFB. Ca.	
62-4125	62	C-135B	18465	USAF, 58th MAS, Ramstein AB. Germany.	
62-4126	62	C-135B	18466	USAF, 89th MAW, Andrews AFB. Md.	
62-4127	62	C-135B	18467	USAF, 89th MAW, Andrews AFB. Md.	
62-4129	62	C-135B	18469	USAF, 89th MAW, Andrews AFB. Md.	
62-4130	62	C-135B	18470	USAF, 89th MAW, Andrews AFB. Md.	
62-4488	62	Sabreliner CT-39A	276-41	USAF, ANG, Andrews AFB. Md.	
72-3025	05	Hawker U-125A	258735	JASDF,	N6135H
73-1681	75	C-9C	47668	USAF, SAM, 1st MAS/89th MAW, Andrews AFB. Md.	
73-1682	75	C-9C	47670	USAF, SAM, 1st MAS/89th MAW, Andrews AFB. Md.	

Reg	Yr	Type	c/n	Owner/Operator	Prev Regn
☐ 73-1683	75	C-9C	47671	USAF, SAM, 99th AS, Andrews AFB. Md.	
☐ 82-8000	87	B 747-2G4B (VC-25A)	23824	Presidential aircraft, 89th MAW, Andrews AFB. Md.	
☐ 830500	83	Gulfstream C-20A	382	U S Navy, C-in-C USNE, Sigonella, Italy.	83-0500
☐ 83-0502	83	Gulfstream C-20A	389	NASA, Edwards AFB. Ca.	N310GA
☐ 84-0064	84	Learjet C-21A	35A-510	USAF, 375th AW/458th AS/84th ALF,	N7263D
☐ 84-0065	84	Learjet C-21A	35A-511	USAF, 375th AW/458th AS/332nd ALF,	N7263E
☐ 84-0069	84	Learjet C-21A	35A-515	USAF, KS/314th AW/45th AS, Keesler AFB. Ms.	N7263L
☐ 84-0070	84	Learjet C-21A	35A-516	USAF, KS/314th AW/45th AS, Keesler AFB. Ms.	N7263N
☐ 84-0071	84	Learjet C-21A	35A-517	USAF, KS/314th AW/45th AS, Keesler AFB. Ms.	N7263R
☐ 84-0072	84	Learjet C-21A	35A-518	USAF, KS/314th AW/45th AS, Keesler AFB. Ms.	N7263X
☐ 84-0075	84	Learjet C-21A	35A-521	USAF, 375th AW/457th AS, Andrews AFB. Md.	N400AN
☐ 84-0076	84	Learjet C-21A	35A-522	USAF, 375th AW/457th AS, Andrews AFB. Md.	N400AP
☐ 84-0077	84	Learjet C-21A	35A-523	USAF, 375th AW/457th AS, Andrews AFB. Md.	N400AQ
☐ 84-0079	84	Learjet C-21A	35A-525	USAF, 375th AW/457th AS, Andrews AFB. Md.	N400AT
☐ 84-0081	84	Learjet C-21A	35A-527	USAF, 76th AS/86th AW, (USAFE), Stuttgart AB. Germany.	N400AX
☐ 84-0082	84	Learjet C-21A	35A-528	USAF, 76th AS/86th AW, (USAFE), Stuttgart AB. Germany.	N400AY
☐ 84-0083	84	Learjet C-21A	35A-529	USAF, 76th AS/86th AW, (USAFE), Stuttgart AB. Germany.	N400AZ
☐ 84-0084	84	Learjet C-21A	35A-530	USAF, 76th AS/86th AW, (USAFE), Ramstein AB. Germany.	N400BA
☐ 84-0085	84	Learjet C-21A	35A-531	USAF, 76th AS/86th AW, (USAFE), Ramstein AB. Germany.	N400FY
☐ 84-0087	84	Learjet C-21A	35A-533	USAF, 76th AS/86th AW, (USAFE), Ramstein AB. Germany.	N400BQ
☐ 84-0090	84	Learjet C-21A	35A-536	USAF, 375th AW/456th AS/311th ALF,	N400BZ
☐ 84-0091	84	Learjet C-21A	35A-537	USAF, 375th AW/458th AS/311th ALF,	N400CD
☐ 84-0092	85	Learjet C-21A	35A-538	USAF, 375th AW/458th AS/311th ALF,	N400CG
☐ 84-0093	85	Learjet C-21A	35A-539	USAF, 375th AW/458th AS/311th ALF,	N400CJ
☐ 84-0094	85	Learjet C-21A	35A-540	USAF, 375th AW/457th AS/47th ALF,	N400CK
☐ 84-0095	85	Learjet C-21A	35A-541	USAF, 375th AW/457th AS/47th ALF,	N400CQ
☐ 84-0096	85	Learjet C-21A	35A-542	USAF, 375th AW/457th AS/47th ALF,	N400CR
☐ 84-0098	85	Learjet C-21A	35A-544	USAF, 475th AW/457th AS/47th ALF,	N400CV
☐ 84-0099	85	Learjet C-21A	35A-545	USAF, 475th AW/457th AS/47th ALF,	N400CX
☐ 84-0100	85	Learjet C-21A	35A-546	USAF, 475th AW/457th AS/47th ALF,	N400CY
☐ 84-0101	85	Learjet C-21A	35A-547	USAF, 374th AW/459th AS, (PACAF), Yokota AB. Japan.	N400CZ
☐ 84-0102	85	Learjet C-21A	35A-548	USAF, 374th AW/459th AS, (PACAF), Yokota AB. Japan.	N400DD
☐ 84-0103	85	Learjet C-21A	35A-549	USAF, 375th AW/458th AS/84th ALF,	N400DJ
☐ 84-0106	85	Learjet C-21A	35A-552	USAF, 314th AW/45th AS,	N400DQ
☐ 84-0107	85	Learjet C-21A	35A-553	USAF, 375th AW/458th AS/84th ALF,	N400DR
☐ 84-0109	85	Learjet C-21A	35A-555	USAF, 76th AS/86th AW, (USAFE), Ramstein AB. Germany.	N400DV
☐ 84-0110	85	Learjet C-21A	35A-556	USAF, 76th AS/86th AW, (USAFE), Ramstein AB. Germany.	N400DX
☐ 84-0111	85	Learjet C-21A	35A-557	USAF, 76th AS/86th AW, (USAFE), Ramstein AB. Germany.	N400DY
☐ 84-0112	85	Learjet C-21A	35A-558	USAF, 76th AS/86th AW, (USAFE), Ramstein AB. Germany.	N400DZ
☐ 84-0114	85	Learjet C-21A	35A-560	USAF, 375th AW/457th AS/12th ALF,	N400EE
☐ 84-0118	85	Learjet C-21A	35A-564	USAF, 375th AW/458th AS, Scott AFB. Il.	N400EK
☐ 84-0119	85	Learjet C-21A	35A-565	USAF, 375th AW/458th AS, Scott AFB. Il.	N400EL
☐ 84-0120	85	Learjet C-21A	35A-566	USAF, 375th AW/458th AS, Scott AFB. Il.	N400EM
☐ 84-0123	85	Learjet C-21A	35A-569	USAF, 119th FW,	N400ER
☐ 84-0124	85	Learjet C-21A	35A-570	USAF, 375th AW/457th AS,	N400ES
☐ 84-0125	85	Learjet C-21A	35A-571	USAF, 375th AW/457th AS,	N400ET
☐ 84-0126	85	Learjet C-21A	35A-572	USAF, 375th AW/458th AS/332nd ALF	N400EU
☐ 84-0127	85	Learjet C-21A	35A-573	USAF, 375th AW/458th AS,	N400EV
☐ 84-0128	85	Learjet C-21A	35A-575	USAF, 375th AW/458th AS,	N400EY
☐ 84-0129	85	Learjet C-21A	35A-576	USAF, 375th AW/458th AS,	N400EZ
☐ 84-0130	85	Learjet C-21A	35A-577	USAF, 374th AW/459th AS,	N400FE
☐ 84-0131	85	Learjet C-21A	35A-578	USAF, 374th AW/459th AS,	N400FG
☐ 84-0134	85	Learjet C-21A	35A-581	USAF, RA/12th FTW (ABTC), Randolph AFB. Tx.	N400FM
☐ 84-0135	85	Learjet C-21A	35A-582	USAF, RA/12th FTW (ABTC), Randolph AFB. Tx.	N400FN
☐ 84-0137	85	Learjet C-21A	35A-585	USAF, 375th AW/458th AS/332nd ALF,	N400FR
☐ 84-0139	85	Learjet C-21A	35A-587	USAF, 375th AW/457th AS/12th ALF,	N400FU
☐ 84-0140	85	Learjet C-21A	35A-588	USAF, 375th AW/458th AS,	N400FV
☐ 84-0142	85	Learjet C-21A	35A-586	USAF, 375th AW/458th AS,	N400FT
☐ 85-0049	85	Gulfstream C-20C	456	U S Army, 99th AS/89th AW, Andrews AFB. Md.	N336GA
☐ 85-0050	85	Gulfstream C-20C	458	U S Army, 99th AS/89th AW, Andrews AFB. Md.	N338GA
☐ 86-0201	85	Gulfstream C-20B	470	USAF, 99th AS/89th AW, Andrews AFB. Md.	N344GA
☐ 86-0202	85	Gulfstream C-20B	468	USAF, 99th AS/89th AW, Andrews AFB. Md.	N342GA
☐ 86-0203	85	Gulfstream C-20B	475	USAF, 99th AS/89th AW, Andrews AFB. Md.	N312GA
☐ 86-0204	85	Gulfstream C-20B	476	USAF, 99th AS/89th AW, Andrews AFB. Md.	N314GA
☐ 86-0206	85	Gulfstream C-20B	478	USAF, 99th AS/89th AW, Andrews AFB. Md.	N318GA
☐ 86-0374	87	Learjet C-21A	35A-624	USAF, Peterson AFB. Co.	

Reg	Yr	Type	c/n	Owner/Operator	Prev Regn
☐ 86-0377	87	Learjet C-21A	35A-629	USAF, Peterson AFB. Co.	
☐ 86-0403	85	Gulfstream C-20D	473	USAF, 99th AS/89th AW, Andrews AFB. Md.	N326GA
☐ 87-0139	86	Gulfstream C-20E	497	U S Army, PATFD, Hickam AFB. Hi.	N7096G
☐ 87-0140	86	Gulfstream C-20E	498	U S Army, OSACOM PAT Flight Det. Andrews AFB. Md.	N7096E
☐ 89-0284	92	Jayhawk T-1A	TT-5	USAF, VN/71 FTW 26 FTS, Vance AFB. Ok.	N2876B
☐ 90-0300	92	Gulfstream C-20G	1181	USAF, 99th AS, Andrews AFB. Md.	N473GA
☐ 90-0400	91	Jayhawk T-1A	TT-3	USAF, XL/47 FTW 86 FTS, Laughlin AFB. Tx.	N2892B
☐ 90-0401	92	Jayhawk T-1A	TT-7	USAF, XL/47 FTW 86 FTS, Laughlin AFB. Tx.	N2869B
☐ 90-0402	92	Jayhawk T-1A	TT-8	USAF, XL/47 FTW 86 FTS, Laughlin AFB. Tx.	N2868B
☐ 90-0403	92	Jayhawk T-1A	TT-9	USAF, VN/71 FTW 26 FTS, Vance AFB. Ok.	
☐ 90-0404	92	Jayhawk T-1A	TT-6	USAF, RA/12 FTW 99 FTS, Randolph AFB. Tx.	N2872B
☐ 90-0405	92	Jayhawk T-1A	TT-4	USAF, RA/12 FTW 99 FTS, Randolph AFB. Tx.	
☐ 90-0406	92	Jayhawk T-1A	TT-11	USAF, XL/47 FTW 86 FTS, Laughlin AFB. Tx.	
☐ 90-0407	92	Jayhawk T-1A	TT-10	USAF, CB/14 FTW, Columbus AFB. Ms.	
☐ 90-0408	92	Jayhawk T-1A	TT-12	USAF, CB/14 FTW, Columbus AFB. Ms.	
☐ 90-0409	92	Jayhawk T-1A	TT-13	USAF, CB/14 FTW, Columbus AFB. Ms.	
☐ 90-0410	92	Jayhawk T-1A	TT-14	USAF, VN/71 FTW 26 FTS, Vance AFB. Ok.	
☐ 90-0411	92	Jayhawk T-1A	TT-15	USAF, VN/71 FTW 26 FTS, Vance AFB. Ok.	
☐ 90-0412	91	Jayhawk T-1A	TT-2	USAF, CB/14 FTW, Columbus AFB. Ms. (was RK-15).	N2887B
☐ 90-0413	92	Jayhawk T-1A	TT-16	USAF, CB/14 FTW, Columbus AFB. Ms.	
☐ 91-0075	92	Jayhawk T-1A	TT-18	USAF, XL/47 FTW 86 FTS, Laughlin AFB. Tx.	
☐ 91-0076	92	Jayhawk T-1A	TT-17	USAF, XL/47 FTW 86 FTS, Laughlin AFB. Tx.	
☐ 91-0077	91	Jayhawk T-1A	TT-1	USAF, VN/71 FTW 26 FTS, Vance AFB. Ok. (was RK-12).	N2886B
☐ 91-0078	92	Jayhawk T-1A	TT-19	USAF, XL/47 FTW 86 FTS, Laughlin AFB. Tx.	
☐ 91-0079	92	Jayhawk T-1A	TT-20	USAF, XL/47 FTW 86 FTS, Laughlin AFB. Tx.	
☐ 91-0080	92	Jayhawk T-1A	TT-21	USAF, VN/71 FTW 26 FTS, Vance AFB. Ok.	
☐ 91-0081	92	Jayhawk T-1A	TT-22	USAF, XL/47 FTW 86 FTS, Laughlin AFB. Tx.	
☐ 91-0082	92	Jayhawk T-1A	TT-23	USAF, XL/47 FTW 86 FTS, Laughlin AFB. Tx.	
☐ 91-0083	92	Jayhawk T-1A	TT-24	USAF, XL/47 FTW 86 FTS, Laughlin AFB. Tx.	
☐ 91-0084	92	Jayhawk T-1A	TT-25	USAF, VN/71 FTW 26 FTS, Vance AFB. Ok.	
☐ 91-0085	92	Jayhawk T-1A	TT-26	USAF, XL/47 FTW 86 FTS, Laughlin AFB. Tx.	
☐ 91-0086	92	Jayhawk T-1A	TT-27	USAF, XL/47 FTW 86 FTS, Laughlin AFB. Tx.	
☐ 91-0087	92	Jayhawk T-1A	TT-28	USAF, XL/47 FTW 86 FTS, Laughlin AFB. Tx. 'Rio Lobos'	
☐ 91-0088	92	Jayhawk T-1A	TT-29	USAF, VN/71 FTW 26 FTS, Vance AFB. Ok.	
☐ 91-0089	92	Jayhawk T-1A	TT-30	USAF, XL/47 FTW 86 FTS, Laughlin AFB. Tx.	
☐ 91-0090	93	Jayhawk T-1A	TT-31	USAF, XL/47 FTW 86 FTS, Laughlin AFB. Tx.	
☐ 91-0091	93	Jayhawk T-1A	TT-32	USAF, XL/47 FTW 86 FTS, Laughlin AFB. Tx.	
☐ 91-0092	93	Jayhawk T-1A	TT-33	USAF, XL/47 FTW 86 FTS, Laughlin AFB. Tx.	
☐ 91-0094	93	Jayhawk T-1A	TT-35	USAF, XL/47 FTW 86 FTS, Laughlin AFB. Tx.	
☐ 91-0095	93	Jayhawk T-1A	TT-36	USAF, VN/71 FTW 26 FTS, Vance AFB. Ok.	
☐ 91-0096	93	Jayhawk T-1A	TT-37	USAF, RA/12 FTW 99 FTS, Randolph AFB. Tx.	
☐ 91-0097	93	Jayhawk T-1A	TT-38	USAF, RA/12 FTW 99 FTS, Randolph AFB. Tx.	
☐ 91-0098	93	Jayhawk T-1A	TT-39	USAF, VN/71 FTW 26 FTS, Vance AFB. Ok.	
☐ 91-0099	93	Jayhawk T-1A	TT-40	USAF, RA/12 FTW 99 FTS, Randolph AFB. Tx.	
☐ 91-0100	93	Jayhawk T-1A	TT-41	USAF, CB/14 FTW, Columbus AFB. Ms.	
☐ 91-0101	93	Jayhawk T-1A	TT-42	USAF, RA/12 FTW 99 FTS, Randolph AFB. Tx.	
☐ 91-0102	93	Jayhawk T-1A	TT-43	USAF, RA/12 FTW 99 FTS, Randolph AFB. Tx.	
☐ 91-0108	91	Gulfstream C-20F	1162	U S Army, OSACOM PAT Flight Det. Andrews AFB. Md.	N7096B
☐ 92-0330	93	Jayhawk T-1A	TT-44	USAF, RA/12 FTW 99 FTS, Randolph AFB. Tx.	
☐ 92-0331	93	Jayhawk T-1A	TT-45	USAF, RA/12 FTW 99 FTS, Randolph AFB. Tx.	
☐ 92-0332	93	Jayhawk T-1A	TT-46	USAF, RA/12 FTW 99 FTS, Randolph AFB. Tx.	
☐ 92-0333	93	Jayhawk T-1A	TT-47	USAF, RA/12 FTW 99 FTS, Randolph AFB. Tx.	
☐ 92-0334	93	Jayhawk T-1A	TT-48	USAF, RA/12 FTW 99 FTS, Randolph AFB. Tx.	
☐ 92-0335	93	Jayhawk T-1A	TT-49	USAF, RA/12 FTW 99 FTS, Randolph AFB. Tx.	
☐ 92-0336	93	Jayhawk T-1A	TT-50	USAF, RA/12 FTW 99 FTS, Randolph AFB. Tx.	
☐ 92-0337	93	Jayhawk T-1A	TT-51	USAF, RA/12 FTW 99 FTS, Randolph AFB. Tx.	
☐ 92-0338	93	Jayhawk T-1A	TT-52	USAF, RA/12 FTW 99 FTS, Randolph AFB. Tx.	
☐ 92-0339	93	Jayhawk T-1A	TT-53	USAF, RA/12 FTW 99 FTS, Randolph AFB. Tx.	
☐ 92-0340	93	Jayhawk T-1A	TT-54	USAF, RA/12 FTW 99 FTS, Randolph AFB. Tx.	
☐ 92-0341	93	Jayhawk T-1A	TT-55	USAF, VN/71 FTW 26 FTS, Vance AFB. Ok.	
☐ 92-0342	93	Jayhawk T-1A	TT-56	USAF, XL/47 FTW 86 FTS, Laughlin AFB. Tx.	
☐ 92-0343	93	Jayhawk T-1A	TT-57	USAF, VN/71 FTW 26 FTS, Vance AFB. Ok.	
☐ 92-0344	93	Jayhawk T-1A	TT-58	USAF, XL/47 FTW 86 FTS, Laughlin AFB. Tx.	
☐ 92-0345	93	Jayhawk T-1A	TT-59	USAF, XL/47 FTW 86 FTS, Laughlin AFB. Tx.	
☐ 92-0346	93	Jayhawk T-1A	TT-60	USAF, XL/47 FTW 86 FTS, Laughlin AFB. Tx.	
☐ 92-0347	93	Jayhawk T-1A	TT-61	USAF, XL/47 FTW 86 FTS, Laughlin AFB. Tx.	

Reg	Yr	Type	c/n	Owner/Operator	Prev Regn
❏ 92-0348	93	Jayhawk T-1A	TT-62	USAF, XL/47 FTW 86 FTS, Laughlin AFB. Tx.	
❏ 92-0349	93	Jayhawk T-1A	TT-63	USAF, XL/47 FTW 86 FTS, Laughlin AFB. Tx.	
❏ 92-0350	93	Jayhawk T-1A	TT-64	USAF, XL/47 FTW 86 FTS, Laughlin AFB. Tx.	
❏ 92-0351	93	Jayhawk T-1A	TT-65	USAF, VN/71 FTW 26 FTS, Vance AFB. Ok.	
❏ 92-0352	93	Jayhawk T-1A	TT-66	USAF, XL/47 FTW 86 FTS, Laughlin AFB. Tx.	
❏ 92-0353	93	Jayhawk T-1A	TT-67	USAF, RA/12 FTW 99 FTS, Randolph AFB. Tx.	
❏ 92-0354	93	Jayhawk T-1A	TT-68	USAF, XL/47 FTW 86 FTS, Laughlin AFB. Tx.	
❏ 92-0355	93	Jayhawk T-1A	TT-69	USAF, XL/47 FTW 86 FTS, Laughlin AFB. Tx.	
❏ 92-0356	94	Jayhawk T-1A	TT-70	USAF, XL/47 FTW 86 FTS, Laughlin AFB. Tx.	
❏ 92-0357	94	Jayhawk T-1A	TT-71	USAF, XL/47 FTW 86 FTS, Laughlin AFB. Tx.	
❏ 92-0358	94	Jayhawk T-1A	TT-72	USAF, XL/47 FTW 86 FTS, Laughlin AFB. Tx.	
❏ 92-0359	94	Jayhawk T-1A	TT-73	USAF, RA/12 FTW 99 FTS, Randolph AFB. Tx.	
❏ 92-0360	94	Jayhawk T-1A	TT-74	USAF, XL/47 FTW 86 FTS, Laughlin AFB. Tx.	
❏ 92-0361	94	Jayhawk T-1A	TT-75	USAF, XL/47 FTW 86 FTS, Laughlin AFB. Tx.	
❏ 92-0362	94	Jayhawk T-1A	TT-76	USAF, XL/47 FTW 86 FTS, Laughlin AFB. Tx.	
❏ 92-0363	94	Jayhawk T-1A	TT-77	USAF, CB/14 FTW, Columbus AFB. Ms.	
❏ 92-0375	94	Gulfstream 4SP	1256	C-20H, USAF, 76th AS,	N438GA
❏ 92-9000	87	B 747-2G4B (VC-25A)	23825	Presidential aircraft, 89th MAW, Andrews AFB. Md.	
❏ 93-0621	94	Jayhawk T-1A	TT-78	USAF, XL/47 FTW 86 FTS, Laughlin AFB. Tx.	
❏ 93-0622	94	Jayhawk T-1A	TT-79	USAF, XL/47 FTW 86 FTS, Laughlin AFB. Tx.	
❏ 93-0623	94	Jayhawk T-1A	TT-80	USAF, XL/47 FTW 86 FTS, Laughlin AFB. Tx.	
❏ 93-0624	94	Jayhawk T-1A	TT-81	USAF, XL/47 FTW 86 FTS, Laughlin AFB. Tx.	
❏ 93-0625	94	Jayhawk T-1A	TT-82	USAF, XL/47 FTW 86 FTS, Laughlin AFB. Tx.	
❏ 93-0626	94	Jayhawk T-1A	TT-83	USAF, XL/47 FTW 86 FTS, Laughlin AFB. Tx.	
❏ 93-0627	94	Jayhawk T-1A	TT-84	USAF, XL/47 FTW 86 FTS, Laughlin AFB. Tx.	
❏ 93-0628	94	Jayhawk T-1A	TT-85	USAF, XL/47 FTW 86 FTS, Laughlin AFB. Tx.	
❏ 93-0629	94	Jayhawk T-1A	TT-86	USAF, XL/47 FTW 86 FTS, Laughlin AFB. Tx.	
❏ 93-0630	94	Jayhawk T-1A	TT-87	USAF, RA/12 FTW 99 FTS, Randolph AFB. Tx.	
❏ 93-0631	94	Jayhawk T-1A	TT-88	USAF, RA/12 FTW 99 FTS, Randolph AFB. Tx.	
❏ 93-0632	94	Jayhawk T-1A	TT-89	USAF, XL/47 FTW 86 FTS, Laughlin AFB. Tx.	
❏ 93-0633	94	Jayhawk T-1A	TT-90	USAF, XL/47 FTW 86 FTS, Laughlin AFB. Tx.	
❏ 93-0634	94	Jayhawk T-1A	TT-91	USAF, XL/47 FTW 86 FTS, Laughlin AFB. Tx.	
❏ 93-0635	94	Jayhawk T-1A	TT-92	USAF, XL/47 FTW 86 FTS, Laughlin AFB. Tx.	
❏ 93-0636	94	Jayhawk T-1A	TT-93	USAF, XL/47 FTW 86 FTS, Laughlin AFB. Tx.	
❏ 93-0637	94	Jayhawk T-1A	TT-94	USAF, XL/47 FTW 86 FTS, Laughlin AFB. Tx.	
❏ 93-0638	94	Jayhawk T-1A	TT-95	USAF, VN/71 FTW 26 FTS, Vance AFB. Ok.	
❏ 93-0639	94	Jayhawk T-1A	TT-96	USAF, VN/71 FTW 26 FTS, Vance AFB. Ok.	
❏ 93-0640	94	Jayhawk T-1A	TT-97	USAF, XL/47 FTW 86 FTS, Laughlin AFB. Tx.	
❏ 93-0641	94	Jayhawk T-1A	TT-98	USAF, VN/71 FTW 26 FTS, Vance AFB. Ok.	
❏ 93-0642	94	Jayhawk T-1A	TT-99	USAF, VN/71 FTW 26 FTS, Vance AFB. Ok.	
❏ 93-0643	94	Jayhawk T-1A	TT-100	USAF, VN/71 FTW 26 FTS, Vance AFB. Ok.	
❏ 93-0644	95	Jayhawk T-1A	TT-101	USAF, VN/71 FTW 26 FTS, Vance AFB. Ok.	
❏ 93-0645	95	Jayhawk T-1A	TT-102	USAF, VN/71 FTW 26 FTS, Vance AFB. Ok.	
❏ 93-0646	95	Jayhawk T-1A	TT-103	USAF, VN/71 FTW 26 FTS, Vance AFB. Ok.	
❏ 93-0647	95	Jayhawk T-1A	TT-104	USAF, VN/71 FTW 26 FTS, Vance AFB. Ok.	
❏ 93-0648	95	Jayhawk T-1A	TT-105	USAF, VN/71 FTW 26 FTS, Vance AFB. Ok.	
❏ 93-0649	95	Jayhawk T-1A	TT-106	USAF, VN/71 FTW 26 FTS, Vance AFB. Ok.	
❏ 93-0650	95	Jayhawk T-1A	TT-107	USAF, VN/71 FTW 26 FTS, Vance AFB. Ok.	
❏ 93-0651	95	Jayhawk T-1A	TT-108	USAF, XL/47 FTW 86 FTS, Laughlin AFB. Tx.	
❏ 93-0652	95	Jayhawk T-1A	TT-109	USAF, XL/47 FTW 86 FTS, Laughlin AFB. Tx.	
❏ 93-0653	95	Jayhawk T-1A	TT-110	USAF, VN/71 FTW 26 FTS, Vance AFB. Ok.	
❏ 93-0654	95	Jayhawk T-1A	TT-111	USAF, VN/71 FTW 26 FTS, Vance AFB. Ok.	
❏ 93-0655	95	Jayhawk T-1A	TT-112	USAF, VN/71 FTW 26 FTS, Vance AFB. Ok.	
❏ 93-0656	95	Jayhawk T-1A	TT-113	USAF, VN/71 FTW 26 FTS, Vance AFB. Ok.	
❏ 94-0114	95	Jayhawk T-1A	TT-114	USAF, CB/14 FTW, Columbus AFB. Ms.	
❏ 94-0115	95	Jayhawk T-1A	TT-115	USAF, VN/71 FTW 26 FTS, Vance AFB. Ok.	
❏ 94-0116	95	Jayhawk T-1A	TT-116	USAF, VN/71 FTW 26 FTS, Vance AFB. Ok.	
❏ 94-0117	95	Jayhawk T-1A	TT-117	USAF, VN/71 FTW 26 FTS, Vance AFB. Ok.	
❏ 94-0118	95	Jayhawk T-1A	TT-118	USAF, VN/71 FTW 26 FTS, Vance AFB. Ok.	
❏ 94-0119	95	Jayhawk T-1A	TT-119	USAF, VN/71 FTW 26 FTS, Vance AFB. Ok.	
❏ 94-0120	95	Jayhawk T-1A	TT-120	USAF, VN/71 FTW 26 FTS, Vance AFB. Ok.	
❏ 94-0121	95	Jayhawk T-1A	TT-121	USAF, VN/71 FTW 26 FTS, Vance AFB. Ok.	
❏ 94-0122	95	Jayhawk T-1A	TT-122	USAF, VN/71 FTW 26 FTS, Vance AFB. Ok.	
❏ 94-0123	95	Jayhawk T-1A	TT-123	USAF, VN/71 FTW 26 FTS, Vance AFB. Ok.	
❏ 94-0124	95	Jayhawk T-1A	TT-124	USAF, VN/71 FTW 26 FTS, Vance AFB. Ok.	
❏ 94-0125	95	Jayhawk T-1A	TT-125	USAF, VN/71 FTW 26 FTS, Vance AFB. Ok.	

Reg	Yr	Type	c/n	Owner/Operator	Prev Regn
❏ 94-0126	95	Jayhawk T-1A	TT-126	USAF, VN/71 FTW 26 FTS, Vance AFB. Ok.	
❏ 94-0127	95	Jayhawk T-1A	TT-127	USAF, VN/71 FTW 26 FTS, Vance AFB. Ok.	
❏ 94-0128	95	Jayhawk T-1A	TT-128	USAF, VN/71 FTW 26 FTS, Vance AFB. Ok.	
❏ 94-0129	95	Jayhawk T-1A	TT-129	USAF, VN/71 FTW 26 FTS, Vance AFB. Ok.	
❏ 94-0130	95	Jayhawk T-1A	TT-130	USAF, VN/71 FTW 26 FTS, Vance AFB. Ok.	
❏ 94-0131	96	Jayhawk T-1A	TT-131	USAF, CB/14 FTW, Columbus AFB. Ms.	
❏ 94-0132	96	Jayhawk T-1A	TT-132	USAF, VN/71 FTW 26 FTS, Vance AFB. Ok.	
❏ 94-0133	96	Jayhawk T-1A	TT-133	USAF, VN/71 FTW 26 FTS, Vance AFB. Ok.	
❏ 94-0134	96	Jayhawk T-1A	TT-134	USAF, CB/14 FTW, Columbus AFB. Ms.	
❏ 94-0135	96	Jayhawk T-1A	TT-135	USAF, CB/14 FTW, Columbus AFB. Ms.	
❏ 94-0136	96	Jayhawk T-1A	TT-136	USAF, CB/14 FTW, Columbus AFB. Ms.	
❏ 94-0137	96	Jayhawk T-1A	TT-137	USAF, CB/14 FTW, Columbus AFB. Ms.	
❏ 94-0138	96	Jayhawk T-1A	TT-138	USAF, CB/14 FTW, Columbus AFB. Ms.	
❏ 94-0139	96	Jayhawk T-1A	TT-139	USAF, CB/14 FTW, Columbus AFB. Ms.	
❏ 94-0140	96	Jayhawk T-1A	TT-140	USAF, CB/14 FTW, Columbus AFB. Ms.	
❏ 94-0141	96	Jayhawk T-1A	TT-141	USAF, CB/14 FTW, Columbus AFB. Ms.	
❏ 94-0142	96	Jayhawk T-1A	TT-142	USAF, CB/14 FTW, Columbus AFB. Ms.	
❏ 94-0143	96	Jayhawk T-1A	TT-143	USAF, CB/14 FTW, Columbus AFB. Ms.	
❏ 94-0144	96	Jayhawk T-1A	TT-144	USAF, CB/14 FTW, Columbus AFB. Ms.	
❏ 94-0145	96	Jayhawk T-1A	TT-145	USAF, CB/14 FTW, Columbus AFB. Ms.	
❏ 94-0146	96	Jayhawk T-1A	TT-146	USAF, CB/14 FTW, Columbus AFB. Ms.	
❏ 94-0147	96	Jayhawk T-1A	TT-147	USAF, CB/14 FTW, Columbus AFB. Ms.	
❏ 94-0148	96	Jayhawk T-1A	TT-148	USAF, CB/14 FTW, Columbus AFB. Ms.	
❏ 94-1569	97	Astra C-38A	088	USAF, 201st Airlift Wing, Maryland ANG, Andrews AFB. Md.	N398AG
❏ 94-1570	97	Astra C-38A	090	USAF, 201st Airlift Wing, Maryland ANG. Andrews AFB. Md.	N399AG
❏ 95-0040	96	Jayhawk T-1A	TT-149	USAF, CB/14 FTW, Columbus AFB. Ms.	
❏ 95-0041	96	Jayhawk T-1A	TT-150	USAF, CB/14 FTW, Columbus AFB. Ms.	
❏ 95-0042	96	Jayhawk T-1A	TT-151	USAF, CB/14 FTW, Columbus AFB. Ms.	
❏ 95-0043	96	Jayhawk T-1A	TT-152	USAF, CB/14 FTW, Columbus AFB. Ms.	
❏ 95-0044	96	Jayhawk T-1A	TT-153	USAF, CB/14 FTW, Columbus AFB. Ms.	
❏ 95-0045	96	Jayhawk T-1A	TT-154	USAF, CB/14 FTW, Columbus AFB. Ms.	
❏ 95-0046	96	Jayhawk T-1A	TT-155	USAF, CB/14 FTW, Columbus AFB. Ms.	
❏ 95-0047	96	Jayhawk T-1A	TT-156	USAF, XL/47 FTW 86 FTS, Laughlin AFB. Tx.	
❏ 95-0048	96	Jayhawk T-1A	TT-157	USAF, CB/14 FTW, Columbus AFB. Ms.	
❏ 95-0049	96	Jayhawk T-1A	TT-158	USAF, CB/14 FTW, Columbus AFB. Ms.	
❏ 95-0050	96	Jayhawk T-1A	TT-159	USAF, CB/14 FTW, Columbus AFB. Ms.	
❏ 95-0051	96	Jayhawk T-1A	TT-160	USAF, CB/14 FTW, Columbus AFB. Ms.	
❏ 95-0052	96	Jayhawk T-1A	TT-161	USAF, CB/14 FTW, Columbus AFB. Ms.	
❏ 95-0053	96	Jayhawk T-1A	TT-162	USAF, CB/14 FTW, Columbus AFB. Ms.	
❏ 95-0054	96	Jayhawk T-1A	TT-163	USAF, CB/14 FTW, Columbus AFB. Ms.	
❏ 95-0055	96	Jayhawk T-1A	TT-164	USAF, CB/14 FTW, Columbus AFB. Ms.	
❏ 95-0056	96	Jayhawk T-1A	TT-165	USAF, CB/14 FTW, Columbus AFB. Ms.	
❏ 95-0057	96	Jayhawk T-1A	TT-166	USAF, CB/14 FTW, Columbus AFB. Ms.	
❏ 95-0058	96	Jayhawk T-1A	TT-167	USAF, CB/14 FTW, Columbus AFB. Ms.	
❏ 95-0059	97	Jayhawk T-1A	TT-168	USAF, CB/14 FTW, Columbus AFB. Ms.	
❏ 95-0060	97	Jayhawk T-1A	TT-169	USAF, CB/14 FTW, Columbus AFB. Ms.	
❏ 95-0061	97	Jayhawk T-1A	TT-170	USAF, CB/14 FTW, Columbus AFB. Ms.	
❏ 95-0062	97	Jayhawk T-1A	TT-171	USAF, CB/14 FTW, Columbus AFB. Ms.	
❏ 95-0063	97	Jayhawk T-1A	TT-172	USAF, RA/12 FTW 99FTS, Randolph AFB. Tx.	
❏ 95-0064	97	Jayhawk T-1A	TT-173	USAF, CB/14 FTW, Columbus AFB. Ms.	
❏ 95-0065	97	Jayhawk T-1A	TT-174	USAF, CB/14 FTW, Columbus AFB. Ms.	
❏ 95-0066	97	Jayhawk T-1A	TT-175	USAF, XL/47 FTW 86 FTS, Laughlin AFB. Tx.	
❏ 95-0067	97	Jayhawk T-1A	TT-176	USAF, XL/47 FTW 86 FTS, Laughlin AFB. Tx.	
❏ 95-0068	97	Jayhawk T-1A	TT-177	USAF, CB/14 FTW, Columbus AFB. Ms.	
❏ 95-0069	97	Jayhawk T-1A	TT-178	USAF, VN/71 FTW 26 FTS, Vance AFB. Ok.	
❏ 95-0070	97	Jayhawk T-1A	TT-179	USAF, VN/71 FTW 26 FTS, Vance AFB. Ok.	
❏ 95-0071	97	Jayhawk T-1A	TT-180	USAF, VN/71 FTW 26 FTS, Vance AFB. Ok.	
❏ 95-0123	96	Citation UC-35A	560-0387	U S Army, B-1/214th AVN, Wiesbaden, Germany.	N5108G
❏ 95-0124	96	Citation UC-35A	560-0392	U S Army, B-1/214th AVN, Wiesbaden, Germany.	N5124F
❏ 96-0107	97	Citation UC-35A	560-0404	U S Army, C/2-228th AVN,.	N5201M
❏ 96-0108	97	Citation UC-35A	560-0410	U S Army, Puerto Rico RFC,	N5211A
❏ 96-0109	97	Citation UC-35A	560-0415	U S Army, A/6 52nd Aviation, Kastner AAF, NAF Atsugi, Japan.	N52457
❏ 96-0110	97	Citation UC-35A	560-0420	U S Army, A/6 52nd Aviation, Kastner AAF, NAS Atsugi, Japan.	N51942
❏ 96-0111	98	Citation UC-35A	560-0426	U S Army, C/6-52nd AVN,	N5101J
❏ 97-0101	98	Citation UC-35A	560-0452	U S Army, B-1/214th AVN, Wiesbaden, Germany.	N5130J
❏ 97-0102	98	Citation UC-35A	560-0456	U S Army, B-1/214th AVN, Wiesbaden, Germany.	N51444

| Reg | Yr | Type | c/n | Owner/Operator | Prev Regn |

☐ 97-0103	98	Citation UC-35A	560-0462	U S Army, B6/52nd Aviation, Dobbins ARB. Ga.	N5183U
☐ 97-0104	98	Citation UC-35A	560-0468	U S Army, Puerto Rico RFC,	N51042
☐ 97-0105	98	Citation UC-35A	560-0472	U S Army, B-1/214th AVN, Wiesbaden, Germany.	N5079H
☐ 97-0400	98	Gulfstream C-37A	521	USAF, 99th AS, Andrews AFB. Md.	
☐ 97-0401	98	Gulfstream C-37A	542	USAF, 99th AS, Andrews AFB. Md.	N642GA
☐ 97-1944	98	Gulfstream C-37A	566	U S Army, Wright Patterson, Oh. 'Normandy'	N8VQ
☐ 98-0001	98	B 757-2G4 (VC-32A)	29025	USAF, 99th AS, Andrews AFB. Md.	N3519L
☐ 98-0002	98	B 757-2G4 (VC-32A)	29026	USAF, 99th AS, Andrews AFB. Md.	N3519M
☐ 98-0006	99	Citation UC-35A	560-0495	U S Army, A Det.1/6-52nd AVN.	
☐ 98-0007	99	Citation UC-35A	560-0501	U S Army, Alaska RFC,	N51896
☐ 98-0008	99	Citation UC-35A	560-0505	U S Army, Alaska RFC,	N52229
☐ 98-0009	99	Citation UC-35A	560-0508	U S Army, Puerto Rico RFC,	N5085E
☐ 98-0010	99	Citation UC-35A	560-0513	U S Army, B-6/52nd AVN,	N5061W
☐ 99-0003	98	B 757-2G4 (VC-32A)	29027	USAF, 89th MAW, Andrews AFB. Md.	
☐ 99-0004	98	B 757-2G4 (VC-32A)	29028	USAF, 89th MAW, Andrews AFB. Md.	
☐ 99-0100	99	Citation UC-35A	560-0532	U S Army, B-6/52nd AVN,	N5268V
☐ 99-0101	99	Citation UC-35A	560-0534	U S Army, B-6/52nd AVN,	N5112K
☐ 99-0102	00	Citation UC-35A	560-0538	U S Army, B-1/214th AVN, Wiesbaden, Germany.	N51143
☐ 99-0103	00	Citation UC-35B	560-0545	U S Army, B-2/228th AVN,	N5091J
☐ 99-0104	00	Citation UC-35B	560-0548	U S Army, Puerto Rico RFC,	N5097H
☐ 99-0402	99	Gulfstream C-37A	571	USAF, SHAPE, Chievres, Belgium.	N671GA
☐ 99-0404	99	Gulfstream C-37A	590	USAF, 99th AS, Andrews AFB. Md.	N590GA

OB = PERU *Total 9*
Civil

☐ OB-1396	75	F 28-1000	11100	Government of Peru, Lima.	FAP-390
☐ OB-1703	85	Astra-1125	004	Aero Transporte SA. Lima.	N425TS
☐ OB-1824	05	Citation Excel XLS	560-5605	Southern Peru Copper Corp. Lima.	N5101J

Military

☐ FAP 300	80	Falcon 20F	434	FAP, Grupo Aereo 8, Las Palmas-Lima.	OB-1433
☐ FAP 356	95	B 737-528	27426	FAP, Grupo Aereo 8, Las Palmas-Lima.	PRP-001
☐ FAP 370	69	DC 8-62CF	46078	FAP, Grupo Aereo 8, Las Palmas-Lima.	HB-IDK
☐ FAP 371		DC 8-62CF	45984	FAP, Grupo Aereo 8, Las Palmas-Lima.	HB-IDH
☐ FAP 524	83	Learjet 36A	36A-051	Peruvian Air Force, Lima-Las Palmas. (status ?).	OB-1431
☐ FAP 525	83	Learjet 36A	36A-052	Peruvian Air Force, Lima-Las Palmas.	OB-1432

OD = LEBANON *Total 5*
Civil

☐ OD-FNF	81	HS 125/700B	257124	Fahed Fadel, Jeddah, Saudi Arabia.	HZ-DA4
☐ OD-HHF	79	HS 125/700B	257054	R Antonios & Assoc/M E Aviation Services, Beirut.	G-OURB
☐ OD-MHA	07	Learjet 60	60-326		N80172
☐ OD-PWC	00	Learjet 31A	31A-203	PWC Logistics Aviation, Kuwait.	VP-BAW
☐ OD-SAS	74	Citation	500-0165	ASAS Airtaxi, Beirut.	(N501FF)

OE = AUSTRIA *Total 187*
Civil

☐ OE-...	98	CitationJet	525-0331		PH-KOM
☐ OE-...	07	Falcon 2000EX EASY	189		F-WWFZ
☐ OE-FAD	84	Citation II/SP	551-0496	GLS/Airlink Luftverkehrs GmbH. Salzburg. (was 550-0496).	LN-ACX
☐ OE-FAP	07	390 Premier 1A	RB-215	MAP Management + Planning GmbH. Vienna.	N215BR
☐ OE-FBS	87	Citation II/SP	551-0574	Airlink Luftverkehrs GmbH. Salzburg.	N60GF
☐ OE-FCM	76	Citation	500-0294	Beckerton Ltd. Manston, UK.	OY-VIP
☐ OE-FCU	04	CitationJet CJ-2	525A-0210	Business Express Luftfahrt GmbH. Graz.	N28DM
☐ OE-FCW	98	CitationJet	525-0292	Daedalos Flugbetriebs GmbH. Graz.	N525CU
☐ OE-FCY	04	CitationJet CJ-2	525A-0204	Jetalliance Flugbetriebs AG. Vienna.	N.....
☐ OE-FDM	79	Citation 1/SP	501-0140	Goldeck-Flug GmbH. Klagenfurt.	N96CF
☐ OE-FET	01	CitationJet CJ-1	525-0421	Braunegg Lufttaxi GmbH. Vienna.	D-ILME
☐ OE-FGB	07	CitationJet CJ2+	525A-0362	Jetalliance Flugbetriebs AG. Oberswaltersdorf.	N51564
☐ OE-FGD	93	CitationJet	525-0020	Glock GmbH. Klagenfurt.	(OO-LFU)
☐ OE-FGI	98	CitationJet	525-0254	ABC Bedarfsflug GmbH. Innsbruck.	N5193V
☐ OE-FGL	02	CitationJet CJ-2	525A-0082	Alpla Air Charter GmbH. Hard.	N282CJ
☐ OE-FGN	75	Citation	500-0291	Airlink Luftverkehrs GmbH. Salzburg.	N291DS
☐ OE-FHB	02	CitationJet CJ-2	525A-0049	Bertsch Aviation GmbH. Bludenz.	D-IEFD
☐ OE-FHH	82	Citation 1/SP	501-0246	Daedalos Flugbetriebs GmbH. Graz.	N26LC
☐ OE-FHW	79	Citation 1/SP	501-0121	Daedalos Flugbetriebs GmbH. Graz.	D-IANO
☐ OE-FII	06	CitationJet CJ2+	525A-0321	Jetalliance Flugbetriebs AG. Vienna.	N13195
☐ OE-FIN	05	CitationJet CJ-2	525A-0239	Avcon Jet AG. Vienna.	(OE-FEB)
☐ OE-FIX	02	CitationJet CJ-1	525-0480	Hasi-Air GmbH. Zirl.	N103SK
Reg	*Yr*	*Type*	*c/n*	*Owner/Operator*	*Prev Regn*

Reg	Yr	Type	c/n	Owner/Operator	Prev Regn
OE-FJU	98	CitationJet	525-0295	Jetalliance Flugbetriebs AG. Vienna.	N5209E
OE-FKW	03	390 Premier 1	RB-77	Europ Star Aircraft GmbH. Klagenfurt.	N32BR
OE-FLA	07	CitationJet CJ2+	525A-0365	Avcon Jet AG. Vienna.	N50736
OE-FLB	07	CitationJet CJ2+	525A-0369	Jetalliance Flugbetriebs AG. Vienna.	N5181U
OE-FLG	95	CitationJet	525-0103	VIF Luftfahrt GmbH. Vienna.	D-IVHA
OE-FLP	00	CitationJet CJ-2	525A-0011	ABC Bedarfsflug GmbH. Salzburg.	N567JP
OE-FMA	97	CitationJet	525-0188	Airlink Luftverkehrs GmbH. Salzburg.	D-IVIN
OE-FMC	01	390 Premier 1	RB-41	International jet Management GmbH. Vienna.	N43HJ
OE-FMD	05	CitationJet CJ1+	525-0614	Austin Jet Holding GmbH. Vienna.	D-IMMG
OE-FMI	99	CitationJet	525-0315	ABC Bedarfsflug GmbH. Salzburg.	S5-BAY
OE-FMK	80	Citation 1/SP	501-0144	Mali Air Luftverkehr GmbH. Graz.	N270NF
OE-FMS	79	Citation 1/SP	501-0239	BFS-Business Flight Salzburg, Salzburg.	N164CB
OE-FMT	97	CitationJet	525-0217	VIF Luftfahrt GmbH. Vienna.	D-IEWS
OE-FMU	93	CitationJet	525-0040	Salzburg Jet Aviation GmbH. Salzburg.	N525AJ
OE-FNA	07	CitationJet CJ1+	525-0659	Avcon Jet AG. Vienna.	N659CJ
OE-FOA	07	CitationJet CJ2+	525A-0354	Vienna Jet Bedarfsluftfahrt GmbH. Vienna.	N5101J
OE-FOE	07	CitationJet CJ2+	525A-0375	Avcon Jet AG. Vienna.	N51055
OE-FOI	02	CitationJet CJ-1	525-0477	ABC Bedarfsflug GmbH. Innsbruck.	D-IDIG
OE-FPA	87	Citation II/SP	551-0552	Airlink Luftverkehrs GmbH. Salzburg.	
OE-FPO	07	CitationJet CJ1+	525-0645	Porsche Konstruktionen KG. Salzburg.	N......
OE-FPS	03	CitationJet CJ-2	525A-0142	DJT Aviation GmbH. Graz.	N5207A
OE-FRA	02	CitationJet CJ-2	525A-0150	ABC Bedarfsflug GmbH. Salzburg.	N525GM
OE-FRC	02	390 Premier 1	RB-57	Europ Star Aircraft GmbH. Klagenfurt.	VP-CRD
OE-FRJ	01	390 Premier 1	RB-12	International Jet Management GmbH. Vienna.	N390BW
OE-FRR	95	CitationJet	525-0124	Salzburg Jet Aviation GmbH. Salzburg.	(ZS-BSS)
OE-FSG	04	CitationJet CJ-2	525A-0203	Tyrolean Jet Service GmbH. Innsbruck.	N736LB
OE-FSR	06	CitationJet CJ1+	525-0634	JAG/Austro Control GmbH. Vienna.	N634CJ
OE-FSS	97	CitationJet	525-0226	Aero-Charter Krifka GmbH. Wels.	TC-LIM
OE-FUX	02	CitationJet CJ-2	525A-0106	Vienna Jet Bedarfsluftfahrt GmbH. Vienna.	D-IUAC
OE-FVB	05	CitationJet CJ-2	525A-0229	Vienna Jet Bedarfsluftfahrt GmbH. Vienna.	SX-SMH
OE-FYH	03	CitationJet CJ-2	525A-0176	Kingfisher Aviation Inc/Ing Christian Koenig, Feldkirchen.	N319R
OE-GAA	91	Citation V	560-0111	Tyrol Air Ambulance GmbH. Innsbruck.	(N6802T)
OE-GAD	79	Citation II	550-0071	GLS/Airlink Luftverkehrs GmbH. Vienna.	(D-CIRR)
OE-GAH	00	Citation Bravo	550-0922	Airlink Luftverkehrs GmBH. Linz.	I-FJTB
OE-GAR	01	Learjet 45	45-148	MAP Management + Planning GmbH. Vienna.	D-CDEN
OE-GBA	79	Citation II	550-0085	Bannert Air GmbH. Vienna.	N57AJ
OE-GBC	93	Citation II	550-0717	Bannert Air GmbH. Vienna.	SE-RBM
OE-GBD	00	Gulfstream G100	133	Bannert Air GmbH. Vienna.	D-CGMA
OE-GBE	04	Gulfstream G100	153	Bannert Air GmbH. Vienna.	N353GA
OE-GCA	00	Citation Excel	560-5157	Goldeck-Flug GmbH. Klagenfurt.	OH-ONE
OE-GCB	99	Citation V Ultra	560-0517	Goldeck-Flug GmbH. Klagenfurt.	N424HH
OE-GCC	91	Citation V	560-0125	International Jet Management GmbH. Vienna.	N6809V
OE-GCE	01	Hawker 800XP	258536	Goldeck-Flug GmbH. Klagenfurt.	N102PA
OE-GCF	88	Learjet 55C	55C-136	Schaffer GmbH. Vienna.	N155PS
OE-GCG	04	Citation Excel	560-5316	Goldeck-Flug GmbH. Klagenfurt.	D-CWWW
OE-GCH	92	Citation VII	650-7006	COMTEL Air Luftverkehrs GmbH. Vienna.	TC-KOC
OE-GCI	78	Citation II	550-0041	WWW Bedarfsluftfahrt GmbH. Vienna.	N177HH
OE-GCO	83	Citation III	650-0012	COMTEL Air Luftverkehrs GmbH. Vienna.	N15VF
OE-GCP	93	Citation V	560-0214	Krono Air GmbH. Salzburg.	N1285D
OE-GDA	92	Citation V	560-0200	JAG/Austro Control GmbH. Vienna.	
OE-GDF	04	Learjet 60	60-276	Ocean Sky GmbH. Salzburg.	N838RC
OE-GDI	99	Learjet 45	45-037	MAP Executive Flight Service GmbH. Vienna.	N50145
OE-GEG	04	Citation Excel XLS	560-5529	Jetalliance Flugbetriebs AG. Vienna.	N5262X
OE-GEH	07	Citation Excel XLS	560-5755	Avcon Jet AG. Vienna.	N51038
OE-GFA	01	Learjet 60	60-214	Jetalliance Flugbetriebs AG. Vienna.	D-CIMM
OE-GGL	05	Learjet 60	60-287	International Jet Management GmbH. Vienna.	N4003L
OE-GHM	97	Beechjet 400A	RK-148	International Jet Management GmbH. Vienna.	N663AJ
OE-GHP	01	Citation Bravo	550-0998	MAP Management + Planning GmbH. Vienna.	N5165P
OE-GHU	97	Hawker 800XP	258335	Goldeck-Flug GmbH. Klagenfurt.	OY-RAC
OE-GII	99	Learjet 60	60-169	Cirrus Middle East SAL. Beirut, Lebanon.	N5014F
OE-GIL	79	Citation II	550-0060	Air-Styria Luftfahrtunternehmen GmbH. Graz.	N315CK
OE-GKK	99	Citation Bravo	550-0872	Jetfly Airline GmbH. Linz.	N5093L
OE-GLL	03	Citation Bravo	550-1069	Jetfly Airline GmbH. Linz.	N5093Y
OE-GLS	00	Citation VII	650-7110	Tyrolean Jet Service GmbH. Innsbruck.	N657JW
OE-GLX	07	Learjet 60	60-332		N5013U
OE-GLY	07	Learjet 60	60-333	Vistajet Luftfahrt GmbH. Salzburg.	N4003L
Reg	Yr	Type	c/n	Owner/Operator	Prev Regn

Reg	Yr	Type	c/n	Owner/Operator	Prev Regn
OE-GMC	97	Beechjet 400A	RK-162	International Jet Management GmbH. Vienna.	N520CH
OE-GME	00	Citation Excel	560-5113	Air Styria GmbH. Thalerhof.	N52178
OE-GMJ	83	Learjet 35A	35A-504	WWW Bedarfsluftfahrt GmbH. Vienna.	N505DH
OE-GMM	03	Citation Sovereign	680-0005	Magna Air Luftfahrt GmbH. Vienna.	N105SV
OE-GMS	80	Learjet 35A	35A-341	WWW Bedarfsluftfahrt GmbH. Vienna.	P4-KIS
OE-GNB	05	Citation Sovereign	680-0055	MAP Management + Planning GmbH. Vienna.	N5147B
OE-GNF	06	Learjet 60	60-304	Vistajet Luftfahrt GmbH. Salzburg.	N40076
OE-GNW	03	Citation Excel	560-5339	Jetalliance Flugbetriebs AG & Zenith Airways GmbH. Vienna.	N51143
OE-GNY	07	Hawker 850XP	258859	Global Jet Austria GmbH. Vienna.	N859XP
OE-GPA	02	Citation Excel	560-5265	AVAG Air GmbH fuer Luftfahrt, Salzburg.	N5100J
OE-GPH	01	Citation Encore	560-0590	Jetfly Airline GmbH. Linz.	N5166T
OE-GPN	01	Citation Excel	560-5169	ABC Bedarfsflug GmbH. Salzburg.	N923PC
OE-GPO	06	CitationJet CJ-3	525B-0125	Porsche Konstruktionen KG. Salzburg.	N5194J
OE-GPS	98	Citation Bravo	550-0837	Tyrol Air Ambulance GmbH. Innsbruck.	N5185J
OE-GRA	06	CitationJet CJ-3	525B-0135	Rath Aviation GmbH. Salzburg.	N5059X
OE-GRB	02	Citation Bravo	550-1039	The Flying Bulls GmbH. Salzburg.	N511HA
OE-GRF	06	Hawker 850XP	258813	Global Jet Austria GmbH. Vienna.	N73793
OE-GRR	82	Learjet 55	55-059	Goldeck-Flug GmbH. Klagenfurt.	N59LJ
OE-GRS	06	Hawker 850XP	258804	Global Jet Austria GmbH. Vienna.	N71904
OE-GSG	04	Hawker 400XP	RK-402	Jetalliance Flugbetriebs AG. Vienna.	N61CP
OE-GSR	07	Citation Excel XLS	560-5695	Rath Aviation GmbH. Salzburg.	N5166T
OE-GSU	07	Learjet 60	60-317	International Jet Management GmbH. Vienna.	(OH-GVI)
OE-GTA	99	Learjet 31A	31A-191	ABC Bedarfslug GmbH. Innsbruck.	N631AT
OE-GTI	99	Citation Excel	560-5037	MAP Management + Planning GmbH. Vienna.	D-CIII
OE-GTK	98	Citation Excel	560-5007	International Jet Management GmbH. Vienna.	N97VN
OE-GTM	02	Beechjet 400A	RK-343	SLAM Lavori Aerei SRL. Naples, Italy.	N106DD
OE-GTO	06	Learjet 60	60-303	MAP Management + Planning GmbH. Vienna.	(OH-GVI)
OE-GTT	07	Citation Sovereign	680-0153	Comfort Air GmbH. Munich. Germany.	N5223P
OE-GVO	07	Citation Sovereign	680-0145	Jetalliance Flugbetriebs AG. Vienna.	N5117U
OE-GYG	00	Learjet 60	60-197	Transair GmbH. Vienna.	P4-AVM
OE-GZK	06	Citation Excel XLS	560-5668	Jetalliance Flugbetriebs AG. Vienna.	(I-AGLS)
OE-HAC	04	Citation X	750-0232	Jetalliance Flugbetriebs AG. Vienna.	N232CX
OE-HAF	05	Falcon 2000	223	Jetalliance Flugbetriebs AG. Vienna.	F-WWVK
OE-HAL	06	Citation X	750-0259	Jetalliance Flugbetriebs AG. Vienna.	N52114
OE-HEC*	07	Citation X	750-0277		N52178
OE-HEM	03	Falcon 2000	207	Business Express Luftfahrt GmbH. Graz.	N207EM
OE-HFC	01	Gulfstream G200	050	Jetalliance Flugbetriebs AG. Vienna.	N789PR
OE-HGG	03	Citation X	750-0214	Glock GmbH. Klagenfurt.	N5154J
OE-HHH	00	Falcon 50EX	297	Global Jet Austria GmbH. Vienna.	F-WQBJ
OE-HII	06	Challenger 300	20111	Amira Air GmbH. Vienna.	C-FIED
OE-HIT	91	Falcon 50	222	Ingrid Flick, Vienna.	D-BELL
OE-HJA	06	Citation X	750-0261	Jetalliance Flugbetriebs AG. Vienna.	N5079V
OE-HKY	05	Falcon 2000	226	Jetalliance Flugbetriebs AG. Vienna.	F-WWVN
OE-HMS	99	Dornier Do328JET	3121	Tyrolean Jet Service GmbH. Innsbruck.	D-BDXI
OE-HNL	05	Challenger 300	20039	International Jet Management GmbH. Vienna.	HB-JEU
OE-HOT	06	Falcon 2000EX EASY	88	Schaffer GmbH. Vienna.	F-WWGY
OE-HPK	02	Challenger 300	20004	Amira Air GmbH. Vienna.	C-GJCV
OE-HPS	03	Falcon 50EX	334	DJT Aviation GmbH. Graz.	N335EX
OE-HPZ	05	Challenger 300	20047	International Jet Management GmbH. Vienna.	(N147LJ)
OE-HRR	04	Challenger 300	20033	TUPACK Verpackungen GmbH. Vienna.	C-FCMG
OE-HTG	01	Dornier Do328JET	3162	Grossmann Air Service GmbH. Vienna.	D-B...
OE-HTJ	99	Dornier Do328JET	3114	Tyrolean Jet Service GmbH. Innsbruck.	D-BDXA
OE-HUB	07	Citation X	750-0273	Vienna Jet Bedarfsluftfahrt GmbH. Vienna.	N5132T
OE-HVA	04	Falcon 2000	217	COMTEL Air Luftverkehrs GmbH. Vienna.	N863TM
OE-IAC	07	A 319-115CJ	3260	Jetalliance Flugbetriebs AG/Government of Ukraine, Kiev.	D-AVXN
OE-ICF	87	Falcon 900B	22	COMTEL Air Luftverkehrs GmbH. Vienna.	N54DC
OE-IDB	07	Embraer Legacy 600	14500999	Jetalliance Flugbetriebs AG. Vienna.	PT-SKR
OE-IDG	06	Challenger 604	5654	Global Jet Austria GmbH. Vienna.	N604MG
OE-IDM	99	Falcon 900EX	51	The Flying Bulls GmbH. Salzburg.	F-GVDP
OE-IDX	05	Falcon 900DX	604	Global Jet Austria GmbH. Vienna.	F-WWFD
OE-IEL	07	Global Express	9099	Tyrolean Jet Service GmbH. Innsbruck.	C-GZKL
OE-IFB	06	Challenger 605	5704	Vistajet Luftfahrt GmbH. Oxford, UK.	(D-AFIB)
OE-IFG	05	Global Express	9182	Global Jet Austria GmbH. Vienna.	N182GX
OE-IGJ	04	Challenger 604	5598	Global Jet Austria GmbH. Vienna.	C-FDJN
OE-IGR	06	Embraer Legacy 600	14500967	Luxe Aviation GmbH. Vienna.	G-RLGG
OE-IGS	99	Global Express	9044	Triple Alpha Luftfahrt GmbH. Vienna..	I-MOVE

Reg	Yr	Type	c/n	Owner/Operator	Prev Regn
☐ OE-IIA	01	Gulfstream V	641	International Jet Management GmbH. Vienna.	HB-IIZ
☐ OE-IIB	92	Fokker 100	11403	MJ Aviation GmbH. Vienna.	C-GKZA
☐ OE-IIC	92	Fokker 100	11406	International Jet Management GmbH. Vienna.	C-GKZP
☐ OE-IID	91	Fokker 100	11368	MJet Aviation GmbH. Vienna.	C-GKZL
☐ OE-IKP	04	Challenger 604	5599	Amira Air GmbH. Vienna.	C-G...
☐ OE-ILI	06	Challenger 850	8048	Vistajet Luftfahrt GmbH. Salzburg.	C-FFVE
☐ OE-ILX	01	BBJ2-8DR	32777	Global Jet Austria GmbH. Vienna.	P4-BBJ
☐ OE-ILY	07	Challenger 850	8076	Vistajet Luftfahrt GmbH. Salzburg.	C-G...
☐ OE-IMA	07	Global 5000	9243	Global Jet Austria GmbH. Vienna.	C-FLTH
☐ OE-IMC	06	Falcon 900EX EASY	165	Pacelli Beteiligungs GmbH. Munich, Germany.	(F-GUDA)
☐ OE-IMK	06	Challenger 604	5664	MAP Management + Planning GmbH. Vienna.	C-FKDV
☐ OE-INB	07	Falcon 900EX EASY	189	Global Jet Austria GmbH. Vienna.	F-WWFZ
☐ OE-INC	05	Global 5000	9168	Global Jet Austria GmbH. Vienna.	C-FCSP
☐ OE-INF	96	Challenger 604	5303	Jetair Flug GmbH. Zweibruecken, Germany.	(D-ARWE)
☐ OE-INI	04	Challenger 604	5595	Vistajet Luftfahrt GmbH. Salzburg.	C-FCOE
☐ OE-INJ	99	Challenger 604	5435	Amira Air GmbH. Vienna.	OE-IYA
☐ OE-INX	05	Challenger 604	5629	Vistajet Luftfahrt GmbH. Salzburg.	C-FBGE
☐ OE-INY	06	Challenger 604	5644	Vistajet Luftfahrt GmbH. Salzburg.	C-FHCM
☐ OE-IPH	06	Hawker 850XP	258778	Global Jet Austria GmbH. Vienna.	N36578
☐ OE-IPK	05	Challenger 604	5612	Global Jet Austria GmbH. Vienna.	C-FEPN
☐ OE-IRG	06	Gulfstream G550	5139	Jetalliance Flugbetriebs AG. Vienna.	N539GA
☐ OE-IRK	05	Embraer Legacy 600	14500916	Jetalliance Flugbetriebs AG. Vienna.	PT-SOM
☐ OE-IRP	01	Global Express	9106	Amira Air GmbH. Vienna.	N10E
☐ OE-ISA	06	Challenger 850	8043	Jetalliance Flugbetriebs AG. Vienna.	C-FFHA
☐ OE-ISM*	07	Falcon 900DX	617		F-WWFH
☐ OE-ISN	04	Embraer Legacy 600	14500851	Jetalliance Flugbetriebs AG. Vienna.	PT-SIO
☐ OE-ISS	03	Gulfstream G550	5022	Jetalliance Flugbetriebs AG. Vienna.	N550GV
☐ OE-ITA	95	B 737-3L9	27924	Ion Tiriac Air SA/Jetalliance Flugbetriebs AG. Vienna.	N730PA
☐ OE-ITH	05	Challenger 604	5636	MAP Management + Planning GmbH. Vienna.	(N636TS)
☐ OE-IVK	04	Falcon 900EX EASY	138	MAP Executive Flight Service GmbH. Linz.	F-WWFP
☐ OE-IVV	04	Gulfstream G550	5054	Jetalliance Flugbetriebs AG. Vienna.	N954GA
☐ OE-IVY	02	Gulfstream V	687	International Jet Management GmbH. Vienna.	N687GA
☐ OE-LGS	07	Airbus A319-115XCJ	3046	Triple Alpha Luftfahrt GmbH. Vienna.	D-AVYF

OH = FINLAND Total 18
Civil

Reg	Yr	Type	c/n	Owner/Operator	Prev Regn
☐ OH-BZM	05	Challenger 604	5626	Bichos Ltd. Nicosia/Jetflite OY. Helsinki.	VP-BZM
☐ OH-FEX	03	Falcon 2000EX	27	Cedok Air Ltd. Nicosia/Airfix Aviation OY. Helsinki-Vantaa.	F-WWGZ
☐ OH-FFC	97	Falcon 900EX	23	Airfix Aviation OY. Helsinki-Vantaa.	SE-DVE
☐ OH-FIX	02	Falcon 2000	179	Jetflite OY. Helsinki.	F-WWMF
☐ OH-FLM	07	Challenger 300	20155	Jetflite OY. Helsinki.	C-FMYB
☐ OH-FOX	05	Falcon 2000EX EASY	67	ZGG Trading GmbH.Vienna/Airfix Aviation OY. Helsinki-Vantaa.	F-WWGA
☐ OH-KNE	81	Diamond 1	A014SA	River Aviation Avoin Yhtio, Pojanluoma.	N339DM
☐ OH-MOL	06	Challenger 604	5658	Jetflite OY. Helsinki.	(OH-NEM)
☐ OH-PPI	00	Citation X	750-0115	Merropoint OY/Airfix Aviation OY. Helsinki-Vantaa.	N5085E
☐ OH-PPR	02	Falcon 900EX	118	Airfix Aviation OY. Helsinki-Vantaa.	F-WWFS
☐ OH-PPS	07	Global Express XRS	9237	Airfix Aviation OY. Helsinki-Vantaa.	(OE-LNY)
☐ OH-VMF	07	Learjet 60	60-312	Jetflite OY. Helsinki.	N5013U
☐ OH-WIC	00	Challenger 604	5452	Jetflite OY. Helsinki.	N452WU
☐ OH-WII	06	Challenger 604	5642	Jetflite OY. Helsinki.	N642JA
☐ OH-WIP	77	Falcon 20F-5B	359	Jetflite OY. Helsinki.	N369CE

Military

Reg	Yr	Type	c/n	Owner/Operator	Prev Regn
☐ LJ-1	81	Learjet 35A	35A-430	Finnish Air Force, Air Support Squadron, Jyvaskyla.	N10870
☐ LJ-2	82	Learjet 35A	35A-451	Finnish Air Force, Air Support Squadron, Jyvaskyla.	N1462B
☐ LJ-3	82	Learjet 35A	35A-470	Finnish Air Force, Air Support Squadron, Jyvaskyla.	N3810G

OK = CZECH REPUBLIC / CZECHIA Total 17
Civil

Reg	Yr	Type	c/n	Owner/Operator	Prev Regn
☐ OK-...	99	CitationJet	525-0351		F-HGOL
☐ OK-ACH	05	Citation Bravo	550-1111	ABS Jets a.s. Prague.	N5165P
☐ OK-CAA	01	Citation Excel	560-5183	Directorate of Civil Aviation, Prague.	G-IAMS
☐ OK-GGG	06	Embraer Legacy 600	14500986	ABS Jets a.s. Prague. (100th Legacy).	PT-SKC
☐ OK-JDM	07	Learjet 60XR	60-330	ABS Jets a.s. Prague.	N5012G
☐ OK-KAZ	07	Hawker 900XP	HA-34	Grossmann Jet Service s.r.o. Prague.	N31624
☐ OK-KKG	05	Embraer Legacy 600	14500873	ABS Jets a.s. Prague.	PT-SIS
☐ OK-SLA	99	CitationJet	525-0310	Silesia Air, Ostrava.	D-IIJS
☐ OK-SLN	04	Embraer Legacy 600	145796	ABS Jets a.s. Prague.	PT-SIF

Reg	Yr	Type	c/n	Owner/Operator	Prev Regn
☐ OK-SLS	90	Citation V	560-0088	Silesia Air, Ostrava.	D-CMCM
☐ OK-SLX	01	Citation Excel	560-5243	Silesia Air, Ostrava.	(D-CSLX)
☐ OK-SUN	06	Embraer Legacy 600	14500963	ABS Jets a.s. Prague.	PT-SFK
☐ OK-UNI	07	Citation Sovereign	680-0139	Travel Service a.s. Prague.	N52081
☐ OK-VSZ	02	Citation Bravo	550-1040	ABS Jets a.s. Prague.	N12378

Military

Reg	Yr	Type	c/n	Owner/Operator	Prev Regn
☐ 2801	06	Airbus A319-115XCJ	2801	Government of Czech Republic, Prague.'Gen. Janousek'	D-AIFR
☐ 3085	07	Airbus A319-115XCJ	3085	Government of Czech Republic, Prague.	D-AICY
☐ 5105	92	Challenger 601-3A	5105	Czech Government, Prague.	OK-BYA

OM = SLOVAKIA   Total   4

Civil

Reg	Yr	Type	c/n	Owner/Operator	Prev Regn
☐ OM-HLY	00	CitationJet CJ-1	525-0393	Seagle Air Sro. Bratislava.	D-IBIT
☐ OM-HLZ	97	CitationJet	525-0223	Seagle Jet Sro. Bratislava.	OY-INV
☐ OM-OPR	95	CitationJet	525-0101	Air Carpatia sro, Bratislava.	F-GPFC
☐ OM-USS	05	Hawker 800XP	258720	U S Steel Kosice sro. Kosice.	N36820

OO = BELGIUM   Total   43

Civil

Reg	Yr	Type	c/n	Owner/Operator	Prev Regn
☐ OO-ACT	02	Falcon 900C	194	Flying Group NV. Antwerp.	F-WWFZ
☐ OO-AIE	07	Citation Excel XLS	560-5733	Flying Group NV. Antwerp.	N51143
☐ OO-CEJ	97	CitationJet	525-0172	ASL-Air Service Liege NV. Antwerp.	D-IFUP
☐ OO-CIV	04	CitationJet CJ-2	525A-0206	ASL-Air Service Liege NV. Antwerp.	N29MR
☐ OO-CLX	99	Citation V Ultra	560-0537	Celox SA. Luxembourg/Sky Service BV. Brussels.	G-TTFN
☐ OO-DDA	02	CitationJet CJ-2	525A-0164	Sky-Service BV. Wevelgem.	N164CJ
☐ OO-DFG*	07	Falcon 2000EX EASY	140	Groupe Bruxelles Lambert, Brussels.	F-WWMA
☐ OO-EDV	07	CitationJet CJ-3	525B-0200	ASL-Air Service Liege NV. Antwerp.	N5073G
☐ OO-EPU	06	Learjet 45	45-291	Abelag Aviation, Brussels.	N4002P
☐ OO-FLN	03	CitationJet CJ-2	525A-0179	Flying Group NV. Antwerp.	N179FZ
☐ OO-FOI	03	Falcon 900EX EASY	121	Siadora, Netherlands/Flying Group NV, Antwerp.	F-GSEF
☐ OO-FPA	02	Citation Excel	560-5248	Flying Group NV. Cannes-Mandelieu, France.	HB-VNR
☐ OO-FPB	05	Citation Bravo	550-1117	Flying Group NV. Antwerp.	N52591
☐ OO-FPC	07	CitationJet CJ-3	525B-0147	Flying Group NV. Antwerp.	(OO-DRM)
☐ OO-FPE	07	CitationJet CJ-3	525B-0158	Flying Group NV. Antwerp.	(OO-FPD)
☐ OO-FTS	02	Citation Excel	560-5318	Fortis Brussels SA/Flying Group NV. Antwerp.	N102FS
☐ OO-FYG	02	Citation Bravo	550-1027	Flying Group NV. Antwerp.	N52691
☐ OO-GFD	99	Falcon 2000	101	Abelag Aviation, Brussels.	N399FA
☐ OO-GML	05	Falcon 2000EX EASY	75	Abelag Aviation, Brussels.	F-GUPH
☐ OO-IDE	93	CitationJet	525-0037	ASL-Air Service Liege NV. Antwerp.	(N87319)
☐ OO-IIG	02	Citation Bravo	550-1018	Sky-Service BV. Wevelgem.	(D-CEFM)
☐ OO-KRC	04	Challenger 604	5577	Flying Group/ComJet BV. Rotterdam, Holland.	C-FEUR
☐ OO-LFN	04	Learjet 45	45-250	Abelag Aviation, Brussels.	N40050
☐ OO-LFS	98	Learjet 45	45-018	Abelag Aviation, Brussels.	N418LJ
☐ OO-LIE	07	CitationJet CJ-3	525B-0173	Sky-Service BV. Wevelgem.	N5228J
☐ OO-MLG	99	Citation Excel	560-5028	Abelag Aviation, Brussels.	CS-DDB
☐ OO-PAP	07	Falcon 2000EX EASY	123	Flying Group NV. Antwerp.	F-WWGJ
☐ OO-PGG	02	Citation Excel	560-5230	Abelag Aviation, Brussels.	G-NETA
☐ OO-PHI	95	CitationJet	525-0115	Flying Group NV. Antwerp.	N52141
☐ OO-SAV	01	Citation Excel	560-5189	Flying Group NV. Antwerp.	OY-GKC
☐ OO-SKP	84	Citation S/II	S550-0007	Sky-Service BV. Wevelgem.	CS-DCE
☐ OO-SKV	91	Citation V	560-0153	Sky-Service BV. Wevelgem.	SE-DYZ
☐ OO-TME	02	Learjet 60	60-255	Toyota Motor Marketing Europe, Brussels.	N5013U
☐ OO-VMI	05	Falcon 900DX	603	Flying Group NV. Antwerp.	F-WWFC

Military

Reg	Yr	Type	c/n	Owner/Operator	Prev Regn
☐ CA-01	85	Airbus A310-222	372	Belgian Defence, 21 Sqn. 15TW, Melsbroek.	9V-STN
☐ CA-02	85	Airbus A310-222	367	Belgian Defence, 21 Sqn. 15TW, Melsbroek.	9V-STM
☐ CD-01	91	Falcon 900B	109	Belgian Defence, 21 Sqn. 15TW, Melsbroek.	G-BTIB
☐ CE-01	01	EMB-135LR	145449	Belgian Defence, 21 Sqn. 15TW, Melsbroek.	PT-SUU
☐ CE-02	01	EMB-135LR	145480	Belgian Defence, 21 Sqn. 15TW, Melsbroek.	
☐ CE-03	01	EMB-145LR	145526	Belgian Defence, 21 Sqn. 15TW, Melsbroek.	PT-STR
☐ CE-04	01	EMB-145LR	145548	Belgian Defence, 21 Sqn. 15TW, Melsbroek.	PT-...
☐ CM-01	73	Falcon 20E	276	BAF 31, Belgian Defence, 21 Sqn. Melsbroek.	F-WNGL
☐ CM-02	73	Falcon 20E-5	278	BAF 32, Belgian Defence, 21 Sqn. Melsbroek.	F-WQBN

OY = DENMARK   Total   61

Civil

Reg	Yr	Type	c/n	Owner/Operator	Prev Regn
☐ OY-BZT	81	Citation II	550-0259	Benair A/S. Stauning.	N810JT
☐ OY-CCJ	82	Learjet 35A	35A-468	North Flying A/S. Aalborg.	N486LM

Reg	Yr	Type	c/n	Owner/Operator	Prev Regn
☐ OY-CEV	75	Citation	500-0329	North Flying A/S. Aalborg.	N4999H
☐ OY-CJN	07	Hawker 400XP	RK-530	Airon Air ApS. Roskilde.	N530XP
☐ OY-CKE	95	Citation VII	650-7070	Danfoss Aviation/Air Alsie A/S. Sonderborg.	N654EJ
☐ OY-CKF	01	Falcon 2000	163	Air Alsie A/S. Sonderborg.	N163J
☐ OY-CKI	01	Falcon 2000	154	Air Alsie A/S. Sonderborg.	F-WWVL
☐ OY-CKK	07	Citation Excel XLS	560-5757		N51246
☐ OY-CKN	98	Falcon 2000	76	Grundfos Management A/S. Bjerringbro.	F-WQBN
☐ OY-CKW	01	Falcon 2000	166	Air Alsie A/S. Sonderborg.	TC-DGC
☐ OY-CLN	04	Falcon 2000EX EASY	35	Danfoss Aviation/Air Alsie A/S. Sonderborg.	F-WWGQ
☐ OY-CLP	98	Citation VII	650-7093	K/S Clipper Air Transport,	CS-DNE
☐ OY-CVS	04	Global Express	9139	Blue Aviation/Air Four SpA. Milan, Italy.	C-FYZP
☐ OY-CYV	82	Citation II	550-0440	North Flying A/S. Aalborg.	N120TC
☐ OY-EDP	83	Citation III	650-0014	VIP Partnerfly K/S. Aarup.	(N855DH)
☐ OY-EJD	05	Falcon 2000EX EASY	63	Armada Shipping A/S. Fredsborg.	F-WWML
☐ OY-ELY	80	Citation II	550-0139	Jet Plane Corp ApS. Bolzano, Italy.	(PT-WQG)
☐ OY-FFB	81	Citation	500-0406	Karlog Air A/S. Sonderborg.	SE-DET
☐ OY-FIT	05	Global 5000	9186	Execujet Scandinavia A/S. Moscow-Vnukovo.	P4-HER
☐ OY-GLO	05	CitationJet CJ2+	525A-0303	Gloria Aviation-Amicorp Denmark A/S. Copenhagen.	N85JE
☐ OY-GVG	06	Gulfstream G250	4066	Delia A/S. Roskilde.	N466GA
☐ OY-ICE	96	Falcon 2000	26	Air Alsie A/S. Sonderborg.	HB-ISF
☐ OY-ILG	04	Global Express	9163	GRAFF/Execujet Scandinavia A/S. Luton, UK.	C-FCPH
☐ OY-JAI	74	Citation	500-0193	FlexJet Operation A/S.	N293S
☐ OY-JBJ	98	Hawker 800XP	258358	Sun Air of Scandinavia A/S. Billund.	D-CJET
☐ OY-JEV	81	Citation II	550-0284	Weibel Scientific A/S. Copenhagen.	I-ARIB
☐ OY-JMC	98	CitationJet	525-0277	Linak A/S. Nordborg.	N277CJ
☐ OY-JPJ	84	Citation III	650-0060	Dantax A/S-North Flying A/S. Aalborg.	N220TV
☐ OY-KVP*	06	Learjet 40	45-2064	Scanomat Airlines Systems,	(OY-KPV)
☐ OY-LJJ	00	Learjet 45	45-116	Execujet Europe A/S. Zurich, Switzerland.	A6-MED
☐ OY-LKG	97	Hawker 800XP	258345	Air Alsie A/S. Sonderborg.	(G-VONI)
☐ OY-LKS	03	Citation X	750-0212	North Flying A/S. Aalborg.	N69SB
☐ OY-MFL	80	HS 125/700B	257103	Paragon Air ApS/Air Alsie A/S. Sonderborg.	G-GIRA
☐ OY-MIR	07	Learjet 60	60-322	Execujet Scandinavia A/S. Copenhagen.	N5014F
☐ OY-MMM	99	Challenger 604	5430	Maersk Air A/S. Copenhagen.	C-GFOE
☐ OY-MSI	99	Global Express	9032	Execujet Scandinavia A/S. Stansted, UK.	G-CBNP
☐ OY-NAD	06	Challenger 850	8052	Execujet Scandinavia A/S. Copenhagen.	C-FGQS
☐ OY-NCO	04	Do 328-310 ENVOY	3210	Sun Air of Scandinavia A/S. Billund.	OE-HAB
☐ OY-NDP	07	CitationJet CJ2+	525A-0372	Damson A/S.	(OY-PDN)
☐ OY-NLA	84	Citation III	650-0070	Nordic Air A/S. Nooerresundby.	N38ED
☐ OY-NUD	90	Citation V	560-0064	Air Alpha A/S. Odense.	OE-GPC
☐ OY-OAA	03	Hawker 800XP	258645	European Beverage Co. Moscow, Russia.	N618AR
☐ OY-OCV	06	Learjet 45	45-306	Airlink Airways Ltd. Dublin, Ireland.	N5009T
☐ OY-OKK	03	Falcon 900EX EASY	128	Air Alsie A/S. Sonderborg.	F-WWFE
☐ OY-PHN	84	Falcon 100	209	Pharma Nord ApS. Billund.	HB-VKR
☐ OY-PNO	06	Falcon 2000EX EASY	103	Pharma Nord ApS/Air Alsie A/S. Vejle.	F-WWME
☐ OY-RAA	92	BAe 125/800B	258235	Air Alsie A/S. Sonderborg.	(PH-WOL)
☐ OY-REN	06	CitationJet CJ2+	525A-0331	FlyJet A/S. Copenhagen.	N5148B
☐ OY-RGG	02	CitationJet CJ-1	525-0495	FlyJet A/S. Copenhagen.	N5246Z
☐ OY-SBT	76	Corvette	33	North Flying A/S. Aalborg. (status ?).	F-BTTT
☐ OY-SGM	04	Challenger 604	5596	Execujet Scandinavia A/S. Cherepovets, Russia.	C-FCSD
☐ OY-SML	98	CitationJet	525-0258	Skan Service ApS. Billund.	N108CR
☐ OY-TMA	83	Citation II	550-0457	Nilan A/S. Hedensted.	N63TM
☐ OY-UCA	04	CitationJet CJ-2	525A-0209	Air Alsie A/S. Sonderborg.	N5085E
☐ OY-VIS	91	Citation II	550-0672	DRT/Dansk Radio Teknik A/S. Billund.	(N394MA)
☐ OY-WET	06	Citation Sovereign	680-0067	Weibel Scientific A/S. Copenhagen.	(OY-JET)
☐ OY-WWW	07	CitationJet CJ-3	525B-0194	Weibel Scientific A/S. Copenhagen.	N52645
☐ OY-ZAN	07	Learjet 40	45-2071	Execujet Scandinavia AS. Copenhagen.	N40077
Military					
☐ C-080	98	Challenger 604	5380	RDAF, ESK.721, Aalborg.	C-GEGM
☐ C-168	00	Challenger 604	5468	RDAF, ESK.721, Aalborg.	C-GHRJ
☐ C-172	00	Challenger 604	5472	RDAF, ESK.721, Aalborg.	C-GHRZ

PH = NETHERLANDS

Total 34

Civil

Reg	Yr	Type	c/n	Owner/Operator	Prev Regn
☐ PH-ANO	07	Citation Excel XLS	560-5745	Jet Netherlands BV. Amsterdam.	N5067U
☐ PH-BPS	74	Falcon 20F-5B	321	Jet Netherlands BV. Amsterdam.	N104SB
☐ PH-CHT	04	Falcon 2000EX EASY	40	Jet Netherlands BV. Amsterdam.	N888NX
☐ PH-CJI	00	Citation Excel	560-5128	Cartier Europe BV. Amsterdam.	N5228Z

Reg	Yr	Type	c/n	Owner/Operator	Prev Regn
❏ PH-CMW	05	CitationJet CJ1+	525-0613	Uniwest Group BV. Teuge.	N1309V
❏ PH-DEZ	77	Citation 1/SP	501-0279	Stella Aviation Charter BV. Teuge. (was 500-0371)	SE-DEZ
❏ PH-DRK	02	Citation Excel	560-5258	Jet Netherlands BV. Amsterdam.	C-GWII
❏ PH-DYE	00	Citation Bravo	550-0927	Jet Management Europe BV. Amsterdam.	N5061P
❏ PH-DYN	00	Citation Bravo	550-0928	Dynamic Air BV. Rotterdam.	(N928DA)
❏ PH-ECI	99	CitationJet	525-0321	Exact Nederland BV. Rotterdam.	D-IAAS
❏ PH-ECL	01	CitationJet CJ-2	525A-0054	Exact Nederland BV. Rotterdam.	D-IAAS
❏ PH-EDM	01	Falcon 900C	188	EDM Air BV/Jet Management Europe BV. Amsterdam.	F-WWFZ
❏ PH-EZF	96	Fokker 70	11576	PT Caltex Pacific Indonesia/Pelita, Jakarta. 'Rokan'	
❏ PH-FIS	03	CitationJet CJ-1	525-0514	KNSF Vastgoed Management BV. Amsterdam.	N514RV
❏ PH-HMA	01	Citation Bravo	550-0972	Heerema Engineering BV. Rotterdam.	N52462
❏ PH-ILA	90	Citation V	560-0078	Solid Air BV. Eindhoven.	D-CSUN
❏ PH-ILC	96	Falcon 900B	161	Jet Management Europe BV. Amsterdam.	G-GSEB
❏ PH-ILI	91	Citation V	560-0114	Solid Air BV. Eindhoven.	D-CZAR
❏ PH-ILZ	91	Citation V	560-0145	Solid Air BV. Eindhoven.	D-CFLY
❏ PH-JNE	05	CitationJet CJ-2	525A-0242	Jet Netherlands BV. Amsterdam.	N5073G
❏ PH-JNX	06	Citation Excel XLS	560-5641	Jet Netherlands BV. Amsterdam.	N51342
❏ PH-KBX	94	Fokker 70	11547	Dutch Royal Flight, Amsterdam.	PH-...
❏ PH-LAB	92	Citation II	550-0712	NLR-National Aerospace Laboratory, Amsterdam.	N12030
❏ PH-LCG	94	Falcon 900B	143	Jet Management Europe BV. Amsterdam.	CS-DDI
❏ PH-LSV	01	Falcon 50EX	315	Solid Air BV. Eindhoven.	N668P
❏ PH-MEX	92	Citation VI	650-0217	Solid Air BV. Eindhoven.	N217CM
❏ PH-MFX	94	Citation VI	650-0240	Solid Air BV. Eindhoven.	D-CAKE
❏ PH-MGT	93	CitationJet	525-0042	Jet Netherlands BV. Amsterdam.	N96GD
❏ PH-MSX	86	Citation III	650-0134	Solid Air BV. Eindhoven.	(PH-EVY)
❏ PH-NDK	98	Falcon 900B	175	Solid Air BV. Eindhoven.	CS-TMQ
❏ PH-RSA	00	Citation Excel	560-5110	Cartier Europe BV. Amsterdam.	N5200Z
❏ PH-SOL	01	CitationJet CJ-1	525-0417	Solid Air BV. Eindhoven.	(PH-SLD)
❏ PH-VBG	02	Falcon 2000EX	5	Jet Netherlands BV. Amsterdam.	F-GUDN

Military

❏ V-11	86	Gulfstream 4	1009	RNAF, 334 Squadron, Eindhoven.	VR-BOY

PK = INDONESIA Total 25

Civil

Reg	Yr	Type	c/n	Owner/Operator	Prev Regn
❏ PK-...	02	390 Premier 1	RB-56		N390RC
❏ PK-CAH	92	Learjet 31A	31A-066	Directorate of Civil Aviation, Jakarta.	N26006
❏ PK-CAJ	93	Learjet 31A	31A-077	Directorate of Civil Aviation, Jakarta.	N26002
❏ PK-ILA	05	Citation Excel XLS	560-5598	PT Sampoerna Air Nusantara, Surabaya.	N12990
❏ PK-OCF	68	B 737-247	19601	(stored KUL).	N466AC
❏ PK-OCG	70	B 737-293	20335	(stored KUL).	N469AC
❏ PK-OME	02	Embraer Legacy 600	145516	Airfast Service Indonesia PT. Jakarta.	(N254AL)
❏ PK-OSP	89	BAe 146/CC2	E1124	Government of Indonesia, Jakarta.	G-CBXY
❏ PK-PFZ	95	Fokker 100	11486	Pelita Air Service, Jakarta.	PH-ZFA
❏ PK-PJF	66	BAC 1-11/401AK	065	Citra Aviation PT. Jakarta.	N117MR
❏ PK-PJJ	93	BAe 146/RJ-85	E2239	Pelita Air Service/Government of Indonesia, Jakarta.'Wamema'	G-5-239
❏ PK-PJK	83	F 28-4000	11192	Caltex/Pelita Air Service, Jakarta. 'Lengguru'	PH-EXW
❏ PK-PJL	76	F 28-4000	11111	Pelita Air Service, Jakarta. 'Kurau'	PH-EXA
❏ PK-PJM	81	F 28-4000	11178	Pelita Air Service, Jakarta. 'Matak'	PH-EXW
❏ PK-PJY	79	F 28-4000	11146	Pelita Air Service, Jakarta. 'Arun'	PH-EXN
❏ PK-RJG	06	Embraer Legacy 600	14500969	Premiair/Ekspres Transportasi Antarbenua, Jakarta.	PT-SF.
❏ PK-RJW	71	F 28-1000	11045	Post Ekspres Prima, Jakarta. 'Anugerah'	PH-PBX
❏ PK-TRI	68	Falcon 20F	173	Indonesian Air Transport, Jakarta.	N729S
❏ PK-TRU	80	BAC 1-11/492GM	262	Indonesian Air Transport, Jakarta.	G-BLDH
❏ PK-TST	68	BAC 1-11/423ET	118	Indonesian Air Transport, Jakarta.	G-BEJM
❏ PK-TVO	01	Hawker 800XP	258579	Travira Air, Jakarta.	N50309
❏ PK-VBA	66	B 727-25	18970	PENAS/Bakrie Aviation, Jakarta.	N680AM
❏ PK-YRL	96	Citation VII	650-7073		XA-UAM

Military

❏ A-2801	71	F 28-1000	11042	TNI-AU, SkU 17, Jakarta.	PK-PJT
❏ P-2034	03	Hawker 400XP	RK-362	Indonesian Police, Jakarta.	N362XP

PP = BRAZIL Total 342

Civil

Reg	Yr	Type	c/n	Owner/Operator	Prev Regn
❏ PP-AAA	04	Citation X	750-0234	COTEMINAS, Montes Clares, MG.	N52526
❏ PP-AAF	03	Falcon 2000EX	16	Metro Taxi Aereo Ltda. Sao Paulo, SP.	F-WWGO
❏ PP-AIO	85	Citation III	650-0087	State Government of the Amazonas, Manaus, AM.	N37VP
❏ PP-ANA	03	Hawker 800XP	258637	Centro de Ensino Unificado do Maranhao Ltda. Sao Luis, MA.	N637XP

| Reg | Yr | Type | c/n | Owner/Operator | Prev Regn |

Reg	Yr	Type	c/n	Owner/Operator	Prev Regn
☐ PP-BMG	03	Citation Bravo	550-1045	Banco BMG SA. Belo Horizonte, MG.	N52690
☐ PP-BRS	05	Citation Excel XLS	560-5544	TAM Jatos Executivos Marilia SA. Sao Paulo, SP.	N5268M
☐ PP-CFF	00	Falcon 2000	110	Iguatemi Shopping Centers SA. Sao Paulo, SP.	N2194
☐ PP-CRS	99	CitationJet	525-0346	Taxi Aereo Piracicaba Ltda. Sao Paulo, SP.	N5136J
☐ PP-CTA	98	Learjet 31A	31A-168	Colt Taxi Aereo SA. Sao Paulo, SP.	N952VS
☐ PP-EIF	84	Citation 1/SP	501-0680	State Government of Parana, Curitiba, PR.	PT-LFR
☐ PP-ERR	75	Learjet 35	35-008	State Government of Roraima, Boa Vista, RR.	PT-LFS
☐ PP-ESC	89	Citation II	550-0618	Sec. Est. Casa Civil S Catarina, Florianopolis, SC.	PT-LXG
☐ PP-FMW	06	Learjet 40	45-2068		N5012G
☐ PP-ISJ	94	Citation V	560-0258	LinkNet Informatica Ltda. Brasilia, DF.	N60NS
☐ PP-JAA	84	Learjet 36A	36A-055	Lider Taxi Aereo SA. Belo Horizonte, MG.	N365AS
☐ PP-JBS	00	CitationJet CJ-1	525-0408	JCPM Investimentos Ltda.	N408GR
☐ PP-JCF	06	Hawker 400XP	RK-479	Claudino SA. Lojas de Departamentos, Teresina, PI.	N479XP
☐ PP-JET	00	CitationJet CJ-1	525-0384	Reali Taxi Aereo Ltda. Sao Paulo, SP.	N5148B
☐ PP-JFM	99	Citation Excel	560-5045	Martins Com e Servicios de Distribuica SA. Uberlandia, MG.	N5221Y
☐ PP-JGV	00	Citation Excel	560-5105	Interavia Taxi Aereo Ltda. Sao Paulo, SP.	PR-RAA
☐ PP-JQM	98	Citation X	750-0056	Caiua Servicos de Electricidade SA. Sao Paulo, SP.	N5105F
☐ PP-MDB	05	Citation Excel XLS	560-5552	M Dias Blanco SA.	N5231S
☐ PP-MJC	06	Falcon 2000EX EASY	99	Alliance Jet Taxi Aereo Ltda.	F-WWMA
☐ PP-OAA	00	Citation Bravo	550-0954	Usina Alto Alegre SA. Presidente Prudente, SP.	N5079V
☐ PP-ORM	00	Citation Bravo	550-0930	Localiza Rent a Car,	N5086U
☐ PP-PMV	00	Falcon 50EX	299	Morro Vermelho Taxi Aerea Ltda. Sao Paulo, SP.	N299EX
☐ PP-RAA	99	Citation Excel	560-5034	TAM Jatos Executivos Marilia SA. Sao Paulo, SP.	N52113
☐ PP-UQF	04	Hawker 400XP	RK-379	Uniao Quimica Farmaceutica Nacional SA.	N979XP
☐ PP-WRV	00	Beechjet 400A	RK-258	WRV Empreendimentos e Participacoes Ltda.	(PP-LUA)
☐ PP-XOL	07	Embraer Lineage 1000	19000109	Embraer SA. Sao Jose dos Campos, SP.	PT-SQD
☐ PP-XTE	07	Embraer Lineage 1000	19000140	Embraer SA. Sao Jose dos Campos, SP.	PT-...
☐ PP-XUM	62	MS 760 Paris-1R	97		N97PJ
☐ PP-YOF	99	CitationJet	525-0356	Curtume Tropical Ltda. Franca, SP.	N5213S
☐ PR-...	07	Challenger 605	5714		C-FMVN
☐ PR-...	07	Citation Sovereign	680-0182		N5194B
☐ PR-AAA	00	Citation Excel	560-5120	ICAL Energia SA.	N5211Q
☐ PR-ABP	86	Learjet 35A	35A-621		N242MT
☐ PR-ABV	01	CitationJet CJ-1	525-0428	Cia Cervejaria Brahma, Sao Paulo, SP.	N5203J
☐ PR-ACC	02	Citation Excel	560-5274	Morro Vermelho Taxi Aereo Ltda. Sao Paulo, SP.	N5060K
☐ PR-AJG	99	Citation VII	650-7111	Primo Schincariol Industria de Cerveja e Refrigerantes SA.	N226W
☐ PR-ALC	06	CitationJet CJ-3	525B-0124	AIC Ltda. Contagem,	N5203S
☐ PR-ALL*	03	Citation Encore	560-0637		CS-DIG
☐ PR-AMA	01	390 Premier 1	RB-21	ESAT Aerotaxi Ltda. Brasilia, DF.	N390MB
☐ PR-ARA	01	CitationJet CJ-1	525-0441	Alphaville Urbanismo SA. Alphaville, SP.	N5200R
☐ PR-AUR	06	Gulfstream G200	140	Passaro Azul Taxi Aereo Ltda. Brasilia, DF.	N640GA
☐ PR-AVM	89	Learjet 31	31-005	Colt Taxi Aereo Ltda. Sao Paulo, SP.	N431BC
☐ PR-BBS	02	BBJ-7BC	32575	Banco Safra SA. Sao Paulo, SP.	N182QS
☐ PR-CAN	97	CitationJet	525-0233	Canopus Empreendimentos Incorp. Ltda. Belo Horizonre, MG.	N53CG
☐ PR-CCC	05	Falcon 900EX EASY	162	Sucocitrico Cutrale Ltda. Sao Paulo, SP.	N962EX
☐ PR-CCV	91	Citation V	560-0130	Reali Taxi Aereo SA. Sao Paulo, SP.	N14VF
☐ PR-CIM	01	390 Premier 1	RB-32	Expand Group do Brasil SA.	N5132D
☐ PR-CON	05	Citation Excel XLS	560-5583	Passaro Azul Taxi Aereo Ltda. Brasilia, DF.	N5076J
☐ PR-CSM	07	Learjet 45	45-329	VZ Flights LLC.	N454JF
☐ PR-CTB	07	Citation Encore+	560-0760		N5245L
☐ PR-CVC*	07	CitationJet CJ-3	525B-0199		N51817
☐ PR-DBB	95	Hawker 800XP	258284	Enguia Electrica Gen Ce Ltda.	(N919H)
☐ PR-DOT	95	Beechjet 400A	RK-104	Deib Otoch & Cia Ltda.	N704SC
☐ PR-EBD	05	CitationJet CJ-3	525B-0047	Empresa Brasileira de Distribuicao Ltda. Belem, Pa.	N50820
☐ PR-EGB	75	Falcon 10	45	ENGEBRA-Empresa de Energia Eletrica do Brasil Ltda.	N444CR
☐ PR-EMS	02	Citation Excel	560-5223	EMS Industria Farmaceutica Ltda. S B de Campo, SP.	N5086R
☐ PR-EOB	01	CitationJet CJ-1	525-0483	Aerofar Taxi Aereo Ltda. Campo de Marte, SP.	N5250E
☐ PR-ERP	99	Citation Bravo	550-0903	Real Engenharia Ltda. Brasilia, DF.	N903VP
☐ PR-EXP	01	CitationJet CJ-1	525-0482	Armazens Gerais Agricolas Ltda.	N5211Q
☐ PR-FEP	98	Citation Bravo	550-0833	Empresa de Onibus Nossa Senhora da Penha,	N833PA
☐ PR-FJA	07	Citation Excel XLS	560-5739		N52623
☐ PR-FNP	97	Citation X	750-0028	N Piquet/TAM Jatos Executivos Marilia SA. Sao Paulo, SP.	N100FF
☐ PR-FRU	07	Falcon 900EX EASY	181	Avenue Distribuidora de Veiculos Ltda. Sao Paulo, SP.	N181EX
☐ PR-GAM	02	Citation Excel	560-5256	Andre Maggi Export Import Ltda.	N4107V
☐ PR-GBN	98	Learjet 31A	31A-166		N366TS
☐ PR-GCA	02	390 Premier 1	RB-65	Lider Taxi Aereo SA. Belo Horizonte, MG.	N4395D

Reg	Yr	Type	c/n	Owner/Operator	Prev Regn
☐ PR-GCL	04	Learjet 60	60-283	SOTAN-Soc de Taxi Aereo do Nordeste Ltda. Maceio, AL.	N5009T
☐ PR-GPA	00	Falcon 900EX	82	Grupo Pao de Acucar SA. Sao Paulo, SP.	N982EX
☐ PR-GQG	06	Citation Encore	560-0704	Constructora Queiroz Galvao SA. Rio de Janeiro, RJ.	N5248V
☐ PR-IND	06	Hawker 400XP	RK-470	Independencia Alimentos Ltda. Sao Paulo, SP. Brazil.	N470XP
☐ PR-ITN	89	Citation III	650-0171	Construfert Ambiental Ltda.	PT-LVF
☐ PR-JAP	94	Citation VII	650-7038	Transportes Aereo de Fortaleza SA.	N398W
☐ PR-JAQ	98	Citation X	750-0060	Monte Cristalina SA.	N98CX
☐ PR-JBS	06	Learjet 40	45-2048	Friboli Ltda. Sao Paulo, SP.	N80169
☐ PR-JET	01	CitationJet CJ-2	525A-0042	Global Taxi Aereo Ltda. Sao Paulo, SP.	N52342
☐ PR-JRR	03	390 Premier 1	RB-84	Lider Taxi Aereo SA. Belo Horizonte, MG.	N61784
☐ PR-JST	02	CitationJet CJ-2	525A-0044	Transportadora Julio Simoes Ltda.	N5241Z
☐ PR-JTS	83	Diamond 1A	A066SA	Jet Sul Taxi Aereo Ltda. Curitiba, PR.	N88ME
☐ PR-JVF	07	CitationJet CJ2+	525A-0376		N51444
☐ PR-LAM	01	Citation Encore	560-0600	Lojas Americanas SA. Rio de Janeiro, RJ.	N52369
☐ PR-LFT	06	Citation Excel XLS	560-5619	TAM Jatos Executivos Marilia SA. Sao Paulo, SP.	N5246Z
☐ PR-LJM	01	CitationJet CJ-1	525-0456	Kissama Co. Loc. Equip. Elet. Ltda.	N5185J
☐ PR-LRJ	98	Learjet 31A	31A-158	Aguia Sistemas de Armazenegem SA.	N126BX
☐ PR-LTA	84	BAe 125/800B	258025	Lider Taxi Aereo SA. Belo Horizonte, MG.	C-GGYT
☐ PR-LUG	01	Hawker 800XP	258553	LUG Taxi Aereo Ltda. Maceio, AL.	N51453
☐ PR-LUZ	96	Citation X	750-0004	Luciano Antonio Zogbi,	N62VE
☐ PR-MCN	85	Citation S/II	S550-0081	Tropic Air Taxi Aereo Ltda.	N550KM
☐ PR-MJC	04	Citation X	750-0237	TAM/Igreja Universal do Reino de Deus,	N5197M
☐ PR-MLA	76	Learjet 35A	35A-072	Colt Taxi Aereo SA. Sao Paulo, SP.	N4415M
☐ PR-MMS	05	Hawker 400XP	RK-457	Marfrig Frigorficoes Comercio de Alimentos, Bataguassa, MG.	N6137Y
☐ PR-MMV*	07	Citation Excel XLS	560-5744	Morro Vermelho Taxi Aereo Ltda. Sao Paulo, SP.	N2003J
☐ PR-MRG*	07	CitationJet CJ-3	525B-0187		N5076P
☐ PR-MVB	02	Beechjet 400A	RK-350	Megaforte Distribuidora Importacao e Exportacao Ltda.	N61850
☐ PR-NBR	02	Citation Excel	560-5289	CBMM-Cia Brasileiros de Metal e Mineracao, Sao Paulo, SP.	N5105F
☐ PR-NIO	07	Embraer Legacy 600	14501012	Cia Brasileira de Metalurgia e Mineracao,	PT-SVG
☐ PR-NNP	06	CitationJet CJ2+	525A-0316	Banco Pine SA. Sao Paulo, SP.	N5165T
☐ PR-NTX	05	CitationJet CJ-2	525A-0228	Nortox SA. Arapongas, PR.	N5154J
☐ PR-OFT	00	Gulfstream G200	027	Andrade Gutierrez SA. Belo Horizonte, MG.	N878CS
☐ PR-ONE	04	Learjet 40	45-2020	Bertin Ltda.	(N720JP)
☐ PR-OPP	01	Hawker 800XP	258547	Braskem SA.	N4469N
☐ PR-ORE	03	Embraer Legacy 600	145625	Companhia Vale Do Rio Doce, Rio de Janeiro, RJ.	PT-SDN
☐ PR-OTA	04	Learjet 45	45-242	OceanAir Taxi Aereo Ltda.	N45SY
☐ PR-OUR	03	Citation Excel	560-5371	Global Taxi Aereo Ltda. Sao Paulo, SP.	N371P
☐ PR-PJD	01	Learjet 31A	31A-214	Magazine Luiza Ltda. Franca.	N125DF
☐ PR-PTR	07	Learjet 40	45-2086		N4003W
☐ PR-RCB	06	Citation Sovereign	680-0090	Casa Bahia Comercio Ltda. Sao Paulo, SP.	(N84LF)
☐ PR-RIO	03	Embraer Legacy 600	145717	Consorcio Unibanco BW. Rio de Janeiro.	PT-SAZ
☐ PR-SCB	94	Learjet 31A	31A-100	Braulino Basilio Maia Filho, Aracatuba, SP.	N31LK
☐ PR-SCR	04	Citation Encore	560-0653	Banco Rural SA. Belo Horizonte, MG.	N5265N
☐ PR-SFA	90	Learjet 31	31-023	PH Transportes e Construccoes SA.	N111VV
☐ PR-SMT	86	Falcon 200	509	Santana Textil Mato Grosso SA.	(N277AT)
☐ PR-SOL	88	BAe 125/800B	258133	EMSA-Empresa Sul Americana de Montagens SA. Goiania.	N800FK
☐ PR-SOV	06	Citation Sovereign	680-0069	Global Taxi Aereo Ltda. Sao Paulo, SP.	N1315Y
☐ PR-SPO	05	CitationJet CJ-3	525B-0028	HRO Empreendimentos e Agropecuaria Ltda.	N5085E
☐ PR-SPR	07	Citation Sovereign	680-0132	Global Taxi Aereo Ltda. Sao Paulo, SP.	N5090A
☐ PR-STJ*	80	Westwind-Two	300		(PR-ESR)
☐ PR-SUN	05	Citation Sovereign	680-0060	Reali Taxi Aereo Ltda. Sao Paulo, SP.	N5207A
☐ PR-TOP	01	CitationJet CJ-2	525A-0061	TAM Jatos Executivos Marilia SA. Sao Paulo, SP.	N5214J
☐ PR-TRJ	06	Citation Excel XLS	560-5644	Jereissati Centros Comerciais Ltda.	N52626
☐ PR-VDR	99	Global Express	9018		C-FOXA
☐ PR-VGD	95	CitationJet	525-0120	Intertel Comerco e Construcao Ltda. Sao Paulo, SP.	N525CZ
☐ PR-VOT*	07	Embraer Legacy 600	14501006	Sao Conrado Taxi Aereo Ltda. Rio de Janeiro, RJ.	PT-SKW
☐ PR-VRD	01	Citation Excel	560-5211	Seguranca Taxi Aereo Ltda. Sao Jose do Rio, SP.	N5076K
☐ PR-WOB	02	CitationJet CJ-2	525A-0089	EHL-Elettro Hidro Ltda. Palmas,	N525SA
☐ PR-WRI	99	Falcon 900EX	44	Globo TV Ltda/Aero Rio Taxi Aereo Ltda. Rio de Janeiro, RJ.	N947LF
☐ PR-WSM	04	Falcon 2000	6	Globo TV Ltda/Aero Rio Taxi Aereo Ltda. Rio de Janeiro, RJ.	N93GT
☐ PR-WTR	98	Gulfstream G200	004	Cotia Trading SA. Vitoria, ES.	N789AT
☐ PR-WYW	93	Falcon 50	234	Walduck Wanderley/Wanair Taxi Aereo Ltda. Belo Horizonte.	PT-AAF
☐ PR-XDN	06	Global Express	9190		N99XN
☐ PR-XDY	00	Citation X	750-0118	Conforto Empreendimentos e Particapacoes SA. Campinas, SP.	N753BD
☐ PR-XJS	00	Learjet 60	60-189	Transporte Julio Simoes SA/Taxi Aereo Weston Ltda. Recife.	N189LJ
☐ PT-FJA	99	CitationJet	525-0337	Laboratorio Neo Quimica SA. Anapolis, GO.	

Reg	Yr	Type	c/n	Owner/Operator	Prev Regn
PT-FNP	99	CitationJet	525-0319	AUTOCRAC. Brasilia, DF.	
PT-FPP	98	Citation Excel	560-5003	Distribuidor Farmaceutica Panarello Ltda. Sao Paulo, SP.	(PT-WZO)
PT-FTB	90	Citation V	560-0060	TAM Jatos Exceutivos Marilia SA. Sao Paulo, SP.	N60MF
PT-FTC	01	CitationJet CJ-2	525A-0048	Alliance Jet Taxi Aereo Ltda.	N5183U
PT-FTE	02	CitationJet CJ-2	525A-0053	Sococos SA Industrias Alimenticias,	N5194J
PT-FTG	02	CitationJet CJ-2	525A-0117	TAM Jatos Executivos Marilia SA. Sao Paulo, SP.	N5214K
PT-GAF	94	Hawker 800	258261	Banjet Taxi Aereo Ltda. Belo Horizonte, MG.	N958H
PT-GAP	84	Learjet 35A	35A-589	Cervejara Petropolis SA.	(N3215K)
PT-IIQ	72	Learjet 25C	25C-089	Delmar Taxi Aereo Ltda. Tatui, SP.	(N890K)
PT-ISO	73	Learjet 25C	25C-115	Golden Key Participacoes Ltda. Camboriu, SC.	
PT-JAA	90	BAe 125/800B	258190	Lider Taxi Aereo SA. Belo Horizonte, MG.	PT-OHB
PT-JKQ	74	Learjet 24D	24D-284	Proserc Proc. Dados SDVA Ltda. Curitiba, PR.	
PT-JMJ	73	Citation	500-0134	TAMIG-Mendes Junior Engenharia SA. Belo Horizonte, MG.	N134CC
PT-KBR	74	Citation	500-0156	DS Air Taxi Aereo Ltda. Rio de Janeiro, RJ.	
PT-KPA	74	Citation	500-0181	Taxi Aereo Weston Ltda. Recife, PE.	N181CC
PT-KZR	79	Learjet 35A	35A-252	Lider Taxi Aereo SA. Belo Horizonte, MG.	N28CR
PT-LBN	73	Citation	500-0079	Mario Celso Lopes, Andradina, SP.	N40JF
PT-LBW	70	Learjet 25XR	25XR-056	Eucatur Emp Uniao Casc Tur Ltda. Cascavel, PR.	N780A
PT-LCC	81	Citation Eagle	500-0413	Banco Rural SA. Belo Horizonte, MG.	(PT-LBZ)
PT-LCD	77	Learjet 35A	35A-103	Premier Taxi Aereo Ltda. Sao Paulo, SP.	N50MJ
PT-LDI	77	Citation	500-0335	Safra Leasing SA. Arrend Mercantil, S C do Sul, SP.	N2937L
PT-LDM	82	Learjet 35A	35A-494	ELO Particip e Administracao Ltda.	
PT-LDR	88	Learjet 55B	55B-134	BRATA-Brasilia Taxi Aereo Ltda. Brasilia, DF.	N7261D
PT-LDY	79	Westwind-1124	251	TAMIG-Mendes Junior Engenharia SA. Belo Horizonte, MG.	CX-CMJ
PT-LEA	74	Learjet 25B	25B-155	Christos Argyrios Mitropoulos,	N24TA
PT-LEB	82	Learjet 35A	35A-474	Soc. de Taxi Aereo Weston Ltda. Recife, PE.	N37975
PT-LEN	72	Learjet 25B	25B-093	Pires do Rio CITEP C I F Aco Ltda. S Caet do Sul, SP.	N33NM
PT-LET	83	Learjet 55	55-080	LUG Taxi Aereo Ltda. Maceio, AL.	N85632
PT-LGW	85	Learjet 35A	35A-598	State Government of Minas Gerais, Belo Horizonte, MG.	N8567T
PT-LHB	85	BAe 125/800B	258031	CTEEP-Cia Transm Energ Elet Paulista,	PT-ZAA
PT-LHC	85	Citation III	650-0086	IBIS Participacoes e Servicos,	(N1317X)
PT-LHK	69	HS 125/400B	25197	Jet Sul Taxi Aereo Ltda. Curitiba, PR.	PP-EEM
PT-LHR	82	Learjet 55	55-044	SOTAN-Soc de Taxi Aereo do Nordeste Ltda. Maceio, AL.	N3797C
PT-LHT	82	Learjet 35A	35A-479	Constructora Queiroz Galvao SA. Rio de Janeiro, RJ.	N30SA
PT-LIV	84	Citation II	550-0499	Celso Paulino Rigo/Pirahy Alimentos Ltda. Sao Borja, RS.	N550PT
PT-LIX	74	Citation	500-0171	ATA-Aerotaxi Abaeta Ltda. Salvador, BA.	PP-LEM
PT-LJF	81	Citation II/SP	551-0289	Hyram G Delado Garcete, Dourados, MS. (was 550-0244).	N551BW
PT-LJJ	81	Citation II	550-0247	Renda Partiipacoes,	(N85NA)
PT-LJK	81	Learjet 35A	35A-372	Lider Taxi Aereo SA. Belo Horizonte, MG.	N372AS
PT-LJL	86	Citation S/II	S550-0084	Caco de Telha Producoes e Eventos Ltda.	N1274N
PT-LJQ	86	Citation S/II	S550-0113	SOIECOM-Soc. Empr. Ind. Com. Mineracao SA.	N553CC
PT-LKD	78	Learjet 24F	24F-356	LMS/Intersul Aviacao Executiva Ltda. Sao Paulo, SP.	N113JS
PT-LKS	86	Citation S/II	S550-0114	Aeromil Taxi Aereo Ltda. Sao Paulo, SP.	N1292A
PT-LLN	74	Learjet 25C	25C-176	BCN Leasing SA. Barueri, SP.	N28KV
PT-LLS	80	Learjet 35A	35A-303	Viacao Araguarina Ltda. Goiania, GO.	N771A
PT-LLT	81	Citation II	550-0327	Banorte Leasing SA. Barueri, SP.	N74JN
PT-LLU	80	Citation II	550-0132	Taxi Aereo Piracicaba Ltda. Sao Paulo, SP.	(N330MG)
PT-LMM	80	Learjet 25D	25D-323	NTA-Nacional Taxi Aereo Ltda. Goiania, GO.	N6YY
PT-LMS	74	Learjet 24D	24D-296	Sul America Taxi Aereo Ltda. Sao Paulo, SP.	N500DJ
PT-LMY	87	Learjet 35A	35A-627	D F Patrimonial Ltda.	N7260T
PT-LNC	81	Citation II	550-0222	Wellborn Participacoes Societarias Ltda.	N17RG
PT-LOE	81	Learjet 35A	35A-393	Jet Sul Taxi Aereo Ltda. Curitiba, PR.	N700WJ
PT-LOG	75	Citation	500-0284	Adriano Coselli SA. Riberao Preto, SP.	N37DW
PT-LOT	77	Learjet 35A	35A-093	Antena um Radiodifusao Ltda. Rio de Janeiro, RJ.	N44PT
PT-LPH	73	Learjet 24D	24D-275	Nova Prospera Mineracao SA. Belo Horizonte, MG.	N216HB
PT-LPK	78	Citation II	550-0010	ATA-Aerotaxi Abaete Ltda. Salvador, BA.	N806C
PT-LPN	81	Citation II	550-0294	Constructora Barbosa Mello SA. Belo Horizonte, MG.	N323CJ
PT-LPP	80	Citation II	550-0218	EMS Industria Farmaceutica Ltda. S B de Campo, SP.	(N250DR)
PT-LPZ	72	Citation	500-0015	Anicuns SA Alccol e Derivados SA. Anicuns, GO.	N14JL
PT-LQK	76	Learjet 24E	24E-333	Rubens de Carvalho,	N75GR
PT-LQP	88	BAe 125/800B	258116	Sergio Maggiore,	G-5-592
PT-LQR	75	Citation	500-0246	Reali Taxi Aereo Ltda. Sao Paulo, SP.	N227VG
PT-LSJ	78	Learjet 35A	35A-181	Lider Taxi Aereo SA. Belo Horizonte, MG.	N5114G
PT-LTB	89	Citation III	650-0166	PONTAX-Ponta Grossa Taxi Aereo Ltda. Sao Paulo, SP.	N1313J
PT-LTI	75	Citation	500-0226	Cervejaria Belco SA. Sao Manuel, SP.	N100AD
PT-LTJ	81	Citation II	550-0225	Produtos Electricos Corona Ltda. Sao Paulo, SP.	N258CC

Reg	Yr	Type	c/n	Owner/Operator	Prev Regn
PT-LUA	77	Citation	500-0346	Silvio Name Jr, Curitiba, PR.	N56DV
PT-LUE	85	Citation III	650-0091	TAM Jatos Executivos Marilia SA. Sao Paulo, SP.	N58HC
PT-LUG	80	Learjet 35A	35A-356	JK Taxi Aereo Ltda. Brasilia, DF.	N800WJ
PT-LUK	83	Learjet 55	55-086	Soc. de Taxi Aereo Weston Ltda. Recife, PE.	N8227P
PT-LUZ	81	Learjet 25D	25D-335	Transportadora Rio Itaipu Ltda. Rio de Janeiro, RJ.	N27KG
PT-LVD	88	Falcon 100	223	Patrimonial Mira Boa Ltda.	N126FJ
PT-LXH	73	Citation	500-0133	Nacional Expresso Ltda. Uberlandia, MG.	N1270K
PT-LXO	88	Learjet 55C	55C-135	Manaca Taxi Aereo Ltda. Sao Paulo, SP.	N1055C
PT-LXX	89	Learjet 31	31-007	Cia Brasileira de Cartuchos, Sao Paulo, SP.	N3819G
PT-LZP	80	Learjet 35A	35A-339	Anicuns SA Alcool e Derivados SA. Anicuns, GO.	N1500
PT-LZQ	89	Citation V	560-0045	TAM Jatos Executivos Marilia SA. Sao Paulo, SP.	N2665Y
PT-MBZ	88	Astra-1125	022	Serv-Jet Servicos e Pecos Para Avioes Ltda. Brasilia, DF.	4X-CUT
PT-MGS	92	Citation VII	650-7021	State Government of Minas Gerais, Belo Horizonte, MG.	N1262B
PT-MIL	95	CitationJet	525-0086	TAM Jatos Executivos Marilia SA. Sao Paulo, SP.	N5093L
PT-MJC	94	CitationJet	525-0085	Radio Record SA. Sao Paulo.	VR-CDN
PT-MMO	83	Citation II	550-0455	Nor-Jet Particip. e Serv. Ltda. Bauru, SP.	N90SF
PT-MMV	97	Citation Bravo	550-0811	Morro Vermelho Taxi Aereo Ltda. Sao Paulo, SP.	N5221Y
PT-MPE	93	CitationJet	525-0015	TAM Jatos Executivos Marilia SA. Sao Paulo, SP.	N115CJ
PT-MPL	97	Beechjet 400A	RK-158	MPE Montagens e Projetos Especiais, Rio de Janeiro, RJ.	N2358X
PT-MSK	00	Citation Excel	560-5087	Richard Paul Matheson,	N5165T
PT-MSP	98	CitationJet	525-0259	Flexiveix Diadema Ltda.	N5235G
PT-OAG	82	Citation II	550-0357	ZLC Intermed. de Negocios SC Ltda. Goiania, GO.	N29FA
PT-OCZ	80	Learjet 35A	35A-361	BRATA-Brasilia Taxi Aereo Ltda. Brasilia, DF.	PT-FAT
PT-ODC	84	Citation 1/SP	501-0678	MRV Servicos de Engenharia Ltda.	(N26AA)
PT-ODL	90	Citation II	550-0640	Primo Schincariol Industria de Cerveja e Regrigerantes SA.	N1308V
PT-ODZ	90	Citation II	550-0645	Antonio Wagner Da C Henriques, Belo Horizonte, MG.	N1310C
PT-OEX	90	Falcon 900	92	Banco Safra SA. Sao Paulo, SP.	N463FJ
PT-OHD	79	Learjet 25D	25D-296	Superjet Aerotaxi Ltda. Florianapolis, SC.	N55MJ
PT-OIG	72	Citation	500-0005	Luiz Carlos Sella e Outro, Curitiba, PR.	N815HC
PT-OJG	91	Citation II	550-0676	EMS Industria Farmaceutica Ltda. S B de Campo, SP.	N67741
PT-OKP	83	Citation II	550-0460	Parana Jet Taxi Aereo Ltda. Curitiba, PR. (was 551-0460).	N6523A
PT-OMS	75	Citation	500-0251	ATA-Aerotaxi Abaete Ltda. Salvador, BA.	N790EA
PT-OMT	74	Citation	500-0179	ATA-Aerotaxi Abaete Ltda. Salvador, BA.	N179EA
PT-OMU	91	Citation VI	650-0205	TAM Jatos Executivos Marilia SA. Sao Paulo, SP.	N2630N
PT-OOI	91	BAe 125/800B	258214	Grupo OK Benefica Cia Nacional de Pneus Ltda. Brasilia, DF.	VR-CCX
PT-OOL	73	Citation	500-0060	Nort Jet Taxi Aereo Ltda. Belem, PA.	N712G
PT-OPJ	81	Learjet 35A	35A-396	ABC Taxi Aereo Ltda. Uberlandia, MG.	N74JL
PT-OQD	75	Citation	500-0244	Superjet Taxi Aereo Ltda. Florianopolis, SC.	N516AB
PT-ORA	90	Learjet 55C	55C-146	Soc. de Taxi Aereo Weston Ltda. Recife, PE.	N9125M
PT-ORC	92	Citation V	560-0195	Vetorial Siderurgia Ltda.	N1282N
PT-ORM	04	Citation Excel XLS	560-5535	ORM Air Taxi Aereo SA.	N5141F
PT-OSD	75	Citation	500-0325	Anicuns SA Alcool e Derivados SA. Anicuns, GO.	N60MP
PT-OSM	88	Citation S/II	S550-0160	EBTA-Empresa Baiana de Taxi Aereo Ltda. Salvador, BA.	N550GT
PT-OSW	90	BAe 125/800B	258184	Schmidt Irmis Calacdos Ltda.	G-5-678
PT-OTC	90	BAe 125/800B	258194	Lider Taxi Aereo SA. Belo Horizonte, MG.	G-5-692
PT-OTQ	72	Citation	500-0046	Diogenes Setti Sobreira, Rio de Janeiro, RJ.	N929RW
PT-OTS	93	Citation V	560-0213	Guaxupe Taxi Aereo Ltda. Guaxupe, MG.	N12845
PT-OVK	72	Citation	500-0027	Douglas Aldred, Sao Paulo, SP.	N777AN
PT-OVU	93	Citation VII	650-7033	MMX Siderugia Brasil Ltda.	N1264B
PT-OVV	89	Citation II	550-0616	Delta National Bank Trust Co. NYC. USA.	(D-IAFA)
PT-OVZ	91	Learjet 31A	31A-037	Frigorifico Margem Ltda.	N31TF
PT-OXT	83	Diamond 1A	A039SA	Himaco Hidraulicos e Maquinas Ltda. Porto Alegre, RS.	N399MJ
PT-POK	86	Learjet 35A	35A-619	Partpar Administ e Particip Ltda. Rio de Janeiro, RJ.	N8568V
PT-PRR	00	CitationJet CJ-1	525-0403	Remar Admin e Comercio SA.	N51817
PT-PTL	99	Citation X	750-0080	Seven Taxi Aereo Ltda.	(N178AT)
PT-SAA	00	Embraer Legacy 600	145363	Embraer SA. Sao Jose dos Campos, SP.	PP-XJO
PT-SBF*	07	390 Premier 1A	RB-210	SBF Comercio de Productos Esportivos Ltda. Belo Horizonte.	N210KP
PT-SCR	06	Embraer Legacy 600	14500946	Sao Conrado Taxi Aereo Ltda. Rio de Janeiro, RJ.	
PT-SKF	06	Embraer 145LR	14500987	Embraer SA. Sao Jose dos Campos, SP.	
PT-SKP	07	Embraer Legacy 600	14500997	Embraer SA. Sao Jose dos Campos, SP.	
PT-TJS	06	CitationJet CJ-3	525B-0136	Transportes Julio Simoes Ltda. Sao Paulo, SP.	N5073G
PT-WAL	90	BAe 125/800B	258198	Ayrton Senna Empreendimentos Ltda. Sao Paulo, SP.	G-5-694
PT-WBC	96	Astra-1125SPX	086	Cia de Bebidas das Americas,	N793A
PT-WBY	72	Citation	500-0008	Clipper Agencia de Viagens Ltda. Aracaju, SE.	ZP-TYP
PT-WEW	68	Learjet 24	24-158	Pedro Muffato e Cia Ltda. Cascavel, PR.	N220PM
PT-WFD	95	Citation V Ultra	560-0308	Serveng Civilsan SA Emp Assoc Eng. Brasilia, DF.	N5235G

Reg	Yr	Type	c/n	Owner/Operator	Prev Regn
☐ PT-WGF	80	Learjet 35A	35A-322	Lider Taxi Aereo SA. Belo Horizonte, MG.	N305SC
☐ PT-WHB	93	Beechjet 400A	RK-73	Berneck Aglomerados SA. Curitiba, PR.	N8070Q
☐ PT-WHC	93	Beechjet 400A	RK-58	Lider Taxi Aereo SA. Belo Horizonte, MG.	(N76MC)
☐ PT-WHD	93	Beechjet 400A	RK-77	Lider Taxi Aereo SA. Belo Horizonte, MG.	N8277Y
☐ PT-WHE	93	Beechjet 400A	RK-81	Lider Taxi Aereo SA. Belo Horizonte, MG.	N8167G
☐ PT-WHF	93	Beechjet 400A	RK-82	Lider Taxi Aereo SA. Belo Horizonte, MG.	N8282E
☐ PT-WHG	92	Beechjet 400A	RK-54	Lider Taxi Aereo SA. Belo Horizonte, MG.	N80938
☐ PT-WIB	87	Citation S/II	S550-0137	Bertol Aerotaxi Ltda. Porte Alegre, RS.	N100TB
☐ PT-WIV	95	Learjet 31A	31A-110	Joao Carlos de Castro Cavalcanti, Caetite, BA.	N40130
☐ PT-WJS	96	Beechjet 400A	RK-122	Frigorifico Bertin Ltda. Sao Paulo. SP.	N1102B
☐ PT-WJZ	81	Citation II	550-0318	TAM Jetos Executivos Marilia SA. Rio de Janeiro, RJ.	PT-LJT
☐ PT-WKL	74	Learjet 24D	24D-294	Isaias Santos de Carvalho, Curitiba, PR. (status ?).	PP-EIW
☐ PT-WKQ	91	Citation II	550-0675	TAM Jatos Exceutivos Marilia SA. Sao Paulo, SP.	N275BD
☐ PT-WLO	97	Learjet 31A	31A-122	Helimed Aerotaxi Ltda. Belo Horizonte, MG.	N122LJ
☐ PT-WLY	96	Citation VII	650-7074	Companhia Muller de Bebidas,	N5183V
☐ PT-WMA	96	Hawker 800XP	258301	Casa Bahia Comercial Ltda. Sao Paulo, SP.	N1105Z
☐ PT-WMZ	97	Citation V Ultra	560-0406	UNIMAR-Associacao de Ensino de Marilia,	N5203S
☐ PT-WQH	98	Citation VII	650-7083	Banco Bradesco SA. Rio de Janeiro, RJ.	
☐ PT-WQI	98	CitationJet	525-0238	Saturno Taxi Aereo Ltda.	N5203S
☐ PT-WSB	97	Learjet 31A	31A-135	VIP Jet Aero Taxi Ltda. Curitiba, PR.	N80645
☐ PT-WSF	80	Falcon 10	169	Florida Agrocitros Ltda. Ribeirao Preto.	(N107AF)
☐ PT-WUM	99	Citation X	750-0092	TAM Jatos Executivos Marilia SA. Sao Paulo, SP.	N5066U
☐ PT-WVG	99	Hawker 800XP	258395	Interavia Taxi Aereo Ltda. Sao Paulo, SP.	N23577
☐ PT-WYC	98	Falcon 2000	59	Unica Industria de Moveis SA.	N2146
☐ PT-WYU	98	Citation Excel	560-5060	Citrosuco Paulista SA. Matao, SP.	N5201J
☐ PT-XAC	98	CitationJet	525-0280	Andriano Coselli SA. Ribeirao Preto, SP.	N5151D
☐ PT-XCF	98	Citation V Ultra	560-0450	Equip Taxi Aereo Ltda. Sao Jose dos Pinhais, PR.	N51246
☐ PT-XCL	99	Citation Excel	560-5020	Global Taxi Aereo Ltda. Sao Paulo, SP.	N61850
☐ PT-XDB	98	CitationJet	525-0274	Empresa Brasileira de Distribuicao Ltda. Belem, Pa.	
☐ PT-XDN	06	Learjet 40	45-2062	Medley SA. Ind. Farmaceutica SA.	N4005Q
☐ PT-XFG	99	Citation VII	650-7099	Casa Bahia Comercial Ltda. Sao Paulo, SP.	N5141F
☐ PT-XFS	97	Learjet 60	60-121	Soc. de Taxi Aereo Weston Ltda. Recife, PE.	N621LJ
☐ PT-XGS	99	Learjet 60	60-164	Soc. de Taxi Aereo Weston Ltda. Recife, PE.	N60LJ
☐ PT-XIB	99	Citation Excel	560-5043	Jose Wellington de Oliveira Jereissat Centro Comercial SA	N5218R
☐ PT-XLI	80	Learjet 35A	35A-299	Lider Taxi Aereo SA. Belo Horizonte, MG.	(PT-PMV)
☐ PT-XLR	99	Learjet 45	45-048	Lojas Riachuelo SA. Sao Paulo, SP.	
☐ PT-XMM	98	CitationJet	525-0267	EMCCamp Edifiacacoes & Taxi Aeroes,	N5201J
☐ PT-XPP	97	Learjet 31A	31A-148	Fast Flight Taxi Aereo Ltda.	(PT-XIT)
☐ PT-XSX	99	Citation Bravo	550-0873	Frigorifico Quatro Marcos Ltda.	N5109R
☐ PT-XTA	89	Learjet 31	31-013	ESAT Aerotaxi Ltda. Brasilia, DF.	N213PA

Military

Reg	Yr	Type	c/n	Owner/Operator	Prev Regn
☐ 2101	04	Airbus A319-133XCJ	2263	FAB/Republica Federativa do Brasil. 'Santos Dumont'	D-AICY
☐ 2401	68	B 707-345C	19840	FAB=Forca Aerea Brasileira.	PP-VJY
☐ 2580	01	Embraer Legacy 600	145412	VC-99C. Brazilian Air Force,	(N903LX)
☐ 2581	01	Embraer Legacy 600	145462	VC-99C. Brazilian Air Force,	N962CW
☐ 2582	01	Embraer Legacy 600	145495	VC-99C. Brazilian Air Force.	N902LX
☐ 2583	02	Embraer Legacy 600	145528	VC-99C. Brazilian Air Force.	N908LX
☐ 2710	87	Learjet 35A	35A-631	Brazilian Air Force,	N3818G
☐ 2711	87	Learjet 35A	35A-632	Brazilian Air Force,	N1461B
☐ 2712	87	Learjet 35A	35A-633	Brazilian Air Force,	N39416
☐ 2713	88	Learjet 35A	35A-636	Brazilian Air Force,	
☐ 2714	88	Learjet 35A	35A-638	Brazilian Air Force,	
☐ 2715	88	Learjet 35A	35A-639	Brazilian Air Force,	
☐ 2716	88	Learjet 35A	35A-640	Brazilian Air Force.	N8568Y
☐ 2717	88	Learjet 35A	35A-641	Brazilian Air Force,	N7261H
☐ 2718	88	Learjet 35A	35A-642	Brazilian Air Force,	N7262X
☐ 6700	01	EMB-145RS	145257	Brazilian Air Force,	PP-XRU
☐ EC93-2125	68	HS 125/3B-RC	25164	FAB, Experimental at CTA, Sao Jose dos Campos.	
☐ EU93-6050	99	BAe U-125A	258401	FAB, G.E.I.V., Rio-Santos Dumont. (flight calibration).	N23592
☐ EU93-6051	99	BAe U-125A	258421	FAB, G.E.I.V., Rio-Santos Dumont. (flight calibration).	N31820
☐ EU93-6052	99	BAe U-125A	258434	FAB, G.E.I.V., Rio-Santos Dumont. (flight calibration).	N40027
☐ EU93-6053	99	BAe U-125A	258447	FAB, G.E.I.V., Rio-Santos Dumont. (flight calibration).	N40310
☐ FAB6000	86	Learjet 35A	35A-613	FAB=Forca Aerea Brasileira.	N4289X
☐ FAB6001	86	Learjet 35A	35A-615	FAB=Forca Aerea Brasileira.	N7260E
☐ FAB6002	86	Learjet 35A	35A-617	FAB=Forca Aerea Brasileira.	N4289Z
☐ FAB6100	89	Learjet 55C	55C-140	FAB=Forca Aerea Brasileira.	PT-OCA

Reg	Yr	Type	c/n	Owner/Operator	Prev Regn
☐ VC93-2120	68	HS 125/3B-RC	25162	FAB, GTE=Grupo do Transporte Especiale, Brasilia.	
☐ VC96-2115	76	B 737-2N3	21165	FAB, GTE=Grupo do Transporte Especiale, Brasilia.	
☐ VC96-2116	76	B 737-2N5	21166	FAB, GTE=Grupo do Transporte Especiale, Brasilia.	
☐ VU93-2113	67	HS 125/3A-RA	NA701	FAB, GTE=Grupo do Transporte Especiale, Brasilia. (status ?)	N125HS
☐ VU93-2118	69	HS 125/400A	NA729	FAB, GTE=Grupo do Transporte Especiale, Brasilia.	N702SS
☐ VU93-2123	68	HS 125/3B-RC	25167	FAB, GTE=Grupo do Transporte Especiale, Brasilia.	VC93-2123
☐ VU93-2126	73	HS 125/403B	25277	FAB, GTE=Grupo do Transporte Especiale, Brasilia.	
☐ VU93-2127	73	HS 125/403B	25288	FAB, GTE=Grupo do Transporte Especiale, Brasilia.	
☐ VU93-2128	73	HS 125/403B	25289	FAB, GTE=Grupo do Transporte Especiale, Brasilia.	G-5-16

P2 = PAPUA NEW GUINEA   Total   1
Civil

Reg	Yr	Type	c/n	Owner/Operator	Prev Regn
☐ P2-TAA	80	Citation II	550-0145	Trans Air P/L. Port Moresby.	P2-MBN

P4 = ARUBA   Total   53
Civil

Reg	Yr	Type	c/n	Owner/Operator	Prev Regn
☐ P4-AAA	04	Global Express	9136	Xiamen Aviation AVV/Global Jet Luxembourg SA.	C-GPZV
☐ P4-ABC	05	Challenger 604	5628	Conoma Ltd AVV/Global Jet Luxemburg SA.	C-FFZP
☐ P4-ALE	98	Hawker 800XP	258359	Flash Jet Aviation AVV/Premier Avia, Moscow, Russia.	N25WX
☐ P4-ALM	01	Citation Excel	560-5218	Fayco International AVV. Riyadh, Saudi Arabia.	N218AM
☐ P4-AMF	91	BAe 125/800B	258201	Eurex Trading Ltd-Orion X, Moscow-Vnukovo, Russia.	G-BWSY
☐ P4-AMH	79	HS 125/700B	257070	Simon Air AVV-Petroff Air, Moscow-Vnukovo, Russia.	G-DEZC
☐ P4-AND	99	Citation X	750-0075	Avangard Aviation AVV. Moscow, Russia.	N21HQ
☐ P4-ANG	07	Hawker 900XP	HA-25	Altair AVV. Donetsk, Ukraine.	N33055
☐ P4-AOC	66	HS 125/731	25079	AVCOM/Evolga AVV. Moscow-Vnukovo, Russia.	N942WN
☐ P4-ARL	04	Airbus A319-133XCJ	2192	SCM-Systems Capital Management Ltd. Donetsk, Ukraine.	D-AIJO
☐ P4-AVJ	01	Challenger 604	5519	Agamo AVV/Execujet Middle East, Amman, Jordan.	N519MZ
☐ P4-AVN	79	Falcon 10	128	Avangard Aviation AVV. Moscow, Russia.	N228SJ
☐ P4-BAK	82	Falcon 50	130	TAK Service Ltd AVV. Amman, Jordan.	C-GSRS
☐ P4-BAZ	04	Learjet 60	60-272	Vertical Investments AVV/Prime Aviation, Almaty, Kazakhstan..	N60KH
☐ P4-BOB	88	BAe 125/800B	258115	Beaver Jet (Aruba) AVV/Orion X, Moscow-Vnukovo, Russia.	G-TCAP
☐ P4-BTA	06	Challenger 604	5649	Challenger Alliance AVV/Excellent Glide, Almaty, Kazakhstan.	N649JA
☐ P4-CBA	06	Global Express	9220	White Wings Ltd/Global Jet Luxembourg SA.	C-FIPG
☐ P4-CHV	04	Challenger 604	5580	Advent Flight AVV/Prime Aviation, Almaty, Kazakhstan.	XA-IGE
☐ P4-EPI	93	Challenger 601-3A	5125	V-S Aviation AVV/Vizavi Avia, Moscow, Russia.	(N14DP)
☐ P4-FLY	67	B 727-22	19148	MPJ-My Personal Jets AVV/Aviation Connections, Dubai, UAE.	P4-ONE
☐ P4-FSH	80	B 747SP-31	21963	Crestwind Aviation AVV/Grace Cathedral Inc. Akron, Oh. USA.	A6-SMM
☐ P4-GJL	07	Challenger 850	8053	Olpon AVV/Global Jet Luxembourg SA.	N854SA
☐ P4-IKF	08	Falcon 2000	227	Ikaros Aviation AVV. Kiev, Ukraine.	F-WWVO
☐ P4-IVM	03	Embraer Legacy 600	145686	Pacific Information Technology Inc/Rusjet, Moscow, Russia.	N686SG
☐ P4-JET	00	Falcon 50EX	295	Sunwood Aviation/Global Jet Luxembourg SA.	I-FJDN
☐ P4-JLD	67	B 727-193	19620	Joylud Dist International. (status ?).	VP-CWC
☐ P4-KAZ	02	BBJ-7EJ	32774	Mint Juleps Investments AVV/Prime Aviation, Almaty.	(N774EC)
☐ P4-LJG	04	Citation X	750-0227	Ven Air Ltd. Dublin, Ireland.	N5267J
☐ P4-LVF	78	HS 125/700B	257040	Eurex Trading Ltd-Orion X, Moscow-Vnukovo, Russia.	G-OWDB
☐ P4-MAF	92	BAe 1000B	259026	Eurex Trading Ltd-Orion X, Moscow-Vnukovo, Russia.	G-GDEZ
☐ P4-MED	74	TriStar 100	1064	Eagle Jet Aviation Inc. Tucson, Az. USA.	N787M
☐ P4-MES	02	B 767-33AER	33425	Crocus Corp AVV/Global Jet Luxembourg SA.	N595HA
☐ P4-MIS	07	Airbus A319-115XCJ	3133	Select Transport AVV/Global Jet Luxembourg SA.	D-AVXC
☐ P4-MMG	65	B 727-30	18368	Cx P4- (status ?).	VP-CMM
☐ P4-MSG	05	Embraer Legacy 600	14500913	High Winds Corp AVV/Premier Avia, Moscow, Russia.	(N590RB)
☐ P4-NRA	06	Embraer Legacy 600	14500960	OrgJet Aviation AVV/NR Air Ltd-Petroff Air, Moscow, Russia.	PT-SFH
☐ P4-NVB	07	Embraer Legacy 600	14501002	Planet Aviation Group Ltd. Moscow, Russia. 'Saint Nicholas'	PT-SKT
☐ P4-OMC	79	B 737-268	22050	Mercury Limited AVV. Saudi Arabia.	N5WM
☐ P4-PET	07	Hawker 900XP	HA-35	Cygnus Holdings AVV/Global Jet Luxembourg SA.	N33235
☐ P4-RUS	05	BBJ-7GC/W	34622	Jet Harbor AVV/Global Jet Luxembourg SA. Moscow, Russia.	
☐ P4-SAI	02	Challenger 604	5553	Darley Aviation AVV/Aviation Assocs. Almaty, Kazakhstan.	HB-JRZ
☐ P4-SCM	05	Falcon 900EX EASY	152	SCM-Systems Capital Management Ltd. Donetsk, Ukraine.	F-WWFK
☐ P4-SEN	02	Hawker 800XP	258617	Daidalos Aviation AVV. Dnepropetrovsk, Ukraine.	N557VB
☐ P4-SIS	03	Embraer Legacy 600	145586	K A B Holding AVV/Premier Avia, Moscow.	PT-...
☐ P4-SKY	77	HS 125/700A	257013	Jet Support Group AVV/BDJ Aircraft Inc. Moscow, Russia.	P4-AOH
☐ P4-SNT	01	Hawker 800XP	258538	Daidalos Aviation AVV. Dnepropetrovsk, Ukraine.	N538LD
☐ P4-SSV	07	Learjet 60	60-325	SVV Inc. Nice, France.	N5013Y
☐ P4-TAK	00	Gulfstream 4SP	1425	Mint Juleps Investment AVV/Prime Aviation, Almaty	XA-ABA
☐ P4-TBN	99	BBJ-7BH	29791	TBN Aviation AVV/ARABASCO, Jeddah, Saudi Arabia.	N348BA
☐ P4-VNL	06	Airbus A319-115XCJ	2921	Caesarair AVV/Global Jet Luxembourg,	P4-VML
☐ P4-VVF	04	Global Express	9147	Wachuta Consultancy/Global Jet Luxembourg SA. Geneva.	C-FAHX

Reg	Yr	Type	c/n	Owner/Operator	Prev Regn
☐ P4-VVP	02	Embraer Legacy 600	145549	Orex Aviation AVV/Petroff Air, Moscow-Vnukovo, Russia.	PT-SAJ
☐ P4-XZX	81	HS 125/700B	257136	AllJets Capital AVV/GreenEx Airlink, Moscow-Vnukovo, Russia.	P4-AOE

RA = RUSSIA / RUSSIAN FEDERATION Total 17
Civil

Reg	Yr	Type	c/n	Owner/Operator	Prev Regn
☐ RA-.....	07	CitationJet CJ1+	525-0652	Elara/OAO, Cheboksary, Russia.	N41159
☐ RA-.....	82	HS 125/700B	257175		G-MKSS
☐ RA-02801	80	HS 125/700B	257097	S-Air JSC. Moscow-Vnukovo.	G-5-810
☐ RA-02802	81	HS 125/700B	257142	S-Air JSC. Moscow-Vnukovo.	P4-OBE
☐ RA-02803	81	HS 125/700B	257139	Jet 2000 Business Jets, Moscow-Vnukovo.	G-5-875
☐ RA-02807	86	BAe 125/800B	258076	Aero Rent/Master Group, Moscow.	G-5-535
☐ RA-02850	80	HS 125/700B	257112	S-Air JSC. Moscow-Vnukovo.	G-SVLB
☐ RA-09000	92	Falcon 900B	118	Gazpromavia Ltd. Moscow-Vnukovo.	F-GNFI
☐ RA-09001	94	Falcon 900B	123	Gazpromavia Ltd. Moscow-Vnukovo.	F-WWFL
☐ RA-09003	68	Falcon 20D	183	AVCOM, Moscow-Vnukovo. (status ?).	EC-EFR
☐ RA-09006	06	Falcon 900EX EASY	164	Gazpromavia Ltd. Moscow-Vnukovo.	F-WWFY
☐ RA-09008	04	Falcon 900EX EASY	142	Gazpromavia Ltd. Moscow-Vnukovo.	N142EX
☐ RA-10201	00	Gulfstream 4SP	1465	UTAir Aviation/Surguneftegaz, Khanty-Mansisk.	N465GA
☐ RA-10202	06	Gulfstream G550	5119	UTAir Aviation/Surguneftegaz, Khanty-Mansisk.	N519GA
☐ RA-67216	03	Challenger 604	5567	Tartarstan Ait, Kazan, Tartarstan.	P4-TAT
☐ RA-73000		B 737-76N	28630	Gazpromavia Ltd. Moscow.	VT-JNP
☐ RF-14423	67	Sabre-60	306-13	Aeroclub KVS, Moscow.	RA-3077K

RP = PHILIPPINES Total 18
Civil

Reg	Yr	Type	c/n	Owner/Operator	Prev Regn
☐ RP-1250	79	F 28-3000	11153	Government of Philippines, Manila.	PH-ZBV
☐ RP-C....	78	Learjet 35A	35A-185		ZS-SES
☐ RP-C....	79	Westwind-1124	254	LionAir Inc. Manila.	N60AV
☐ RP-C125	65	HS 125/1A-522	25033	Makar Properties Development Inc. Cebu.	N125LL
☐ RP-C1747	73	Learjet 24XR	24XR-264	Subic International Air Charter Inc. Subic Bay.	PI-C1747
☐ RP-C1911	80	Falcon 10	174	Jet Eagle International Ltd/Far Horizons Inc.	N402ES
☐ RP-C2324	69	Learjet 24B	24B-182	Jans Helicopter Services Inc. Guam.	N155J
☐ RP-C2424	70	Learjet 24B	24B-226	Marlin Bay Helicopters, Port Vila, Vanuatu. (status ?).	N335RY
☐ RP-C2956	04	Learjet 60	60-273	Aerovision Corp. Cebu City.	VH-OCV
☐ RP-C3110	05	Learjet 40	45-2031	Subic International Air Charter Inc. Subic Bay.	N40085
☐ RP-C390	07	390 Premier 1A	RB-204	AEV Aviation Inc. Manila.	N204BP
☐ RP-C3958	77	Citation	500-0327		N399PA
☐ RP-C4007	92	B 737-332	25996	Government of Philippines, Manila.	RP-C2000
☐ RP-C610	80	Learjet 35A	35A-338	Subic International Air Charter Inc. Subic Bay.	N610GE
☐ RP-C848	65	Learjet 23	23-072	Air Ads Inc. Manila.	N2SN
☐ RP-C8576	02	Hawker 800XP	258571	Challenger Aero Corp. Subic Bay.	N4471N
☐ RP-C8822	92	Learjet 31A	31A-041	Asia Pacific Helicopters, Manila.	N319CH
☐ RP-C9808	83	HS 125/700A	257209	Aerospeed Inc. Subic Bay.	N805CD

SE = SWEDEN Total 46
Civil

Reg	Yr	Type	c/n	Owner/Operator	Prev Regn
☐ SE-DDY	80	Citation II	550-0115	Scandinavian Airleasing AB.	OY-CCU
☐ SE-DEG	75	Citation	500-0276	HYPO Bautrager GmbH.	N29EB
☐ SE-DEY	77	Citation	500-0370	Holland Alcomix BV. Amsterdam, Holland.	N36897
☐ SE-DHO	78	Learjet 35A	35A-195	SAAB Nyge-Aero AB. Skavsta. (Target 01).	N555JE
☐ SE-DHP	76	Learjet 35A	35A-075	SAAB Nyge-Aero AB. Skavsta. (Target 02)	N30FN
☐ SE-DJA	06	Falcon 900EX EASY	171	Volvo AB/Blue Chip Jet AB. Goeteborg-Saeve.	F-WWFK
☐ SE-DJB	07	Falcon 900EX EASY	179	Blue Chip Jet, Save.	F-WWFC
☐ SE-DJM	02	Falcon 900EX	106	Andersson Business Jet AB. Stockholm-Bromma.	LX-ZAK
☐ SE-DLB	81	Falcon 100	183	Andersson Business Jet AB. Stockholm-Bromma.	N183SR
☐ SE-DLZ	82	Citation	500-0411	Jiv Air AB. Goeteborg-Saeve.	G-NCMT
☐ SE-DRS	91	Beechjet 400A	RK-37	PA Flyg AB. Lagan.	N8014Q
☐ SE-DRZ	76	Citation	500-0315	ETM/West Air Sweden AB. Lidkoeping-Hovby.	(OY-TCP)
☐ SE-DUZ	74	Citation	500-0143	Polvere di Stelle SRL. Ancona, Italy.	N767BA
☐ SE-DVP	89	Falcon 100	224	Andersson Business Jet AB. Stockholm-Bromma.	F-WWZN
☐ SE-DYB	87	Falcon 100	216	Andersson Business Jet AB. Stockholm-Bromma.	(N71M)
☐ SE-DYO	87	Citation S/II	S550-0134	Harley Davidson Sweden AB/East Air KB. Stockholm.	N66HD
☐ SE-DYR	79	Citation II/SP	551-0132	Dafgards AB. Lidkoeping-Hovby. (was 550-0087).	C-GTBR
☐ SE-DYV	98	Hawker 800XP	258385	Volvo AB/Blue Chip Jet AB. Goeteborg-Saeve.	G-05-02
☐ SE-DYX	99	Citation Excel	560-5029	EFS-European Flight Service AB. Goeteborg-Saeve.	N5203S
☐ SE-DZZ	81	Learjet 35A	35A-415	East Air KB. Stockholm-Bromma.	D-COSY
☐ SE-RBD	82	Citation II	550-0354	QuickNet Air AB. Stockholm.	VP-CJR
☐ SE-RBK	81	Citation II	550-0315	Waltair Europe AB. Noerrkoping.	N59GU

Reg Yr Type c/n Owner/Operator Prev Regn

Reg	Yr	Type	c/n	Owner/Operator	Prev Regn
☐ SE-RBO	00	Beechjet 400A	RK-303	Stralfors AB/PA-Flyg AB. Ljunbgby-Feringe.	N400HD
☐ SE-RBX	99	Citation Excel	560-5056	Next Jet AB. Stockholm-Bromma.	N688AG
☐ SE-RBY	02	Citation Bravo	550-1038	Benders Air AB/Next Jet AB. Stockholm-Bromma.	(N551VP)
☐ SE-RCA	78	Learjet 35A	35A-175	SAAB Nyge-Aero AB. Skavsta. (Target 03).	D-CDWN
☐ SE-RCL	01	Citation Excel	560-5217	EFS-European Flight Service AB. Goeteborg-Saeve.	OY-EKC
☐ SE-RCM	06	Citation Excel XLS	560-5624	EFS-European Flight Service AB. Goeteborg-Saeve.	(SE-RCN)
☐ SE-RCY	81	Citation II	550-0302	Grafair AB. Stockholm-Bromma.	(SE-RCX)
☐ SE-RCZ	80	Citation II	550-0172	Grafair AB. Stockholm-Bromma.	N800TV
☐ SE-RDY	05	Gulfstream G550	5080	EFS-European Flight Service AB. Goeteborg-Saeve.	N580GA
☐ SE-RDZ	07	Gulfstream G550	5153	EFS-European Flight Service AB. Goeteborg-Saeve.	N923GA
☐ SE-RFH	05	Citation Sovereign	680-0059	EFS-European Flight Service AB. Goeteborg-Saeve.	N4017X
☐ SE-RFI	06	Citation Sovereign	680-0114	EFS-European Flight Service AB. Goeteborg-Saeve.	N11084
☐ SE-RGN	77	Citation	500-0364	Waltair Europe AB. Norrkoepping.	N501E
☐ SE-RGX	02	CitationJet CJ-1	525-0502	Mariebo Aviation AB. Jonkoping.	N133CS
☐ SE-RGY	97	Citation V Ultra	560-0414	Procent i Torsby AB/PS Aviation AB.	ZS-CDS
☐ SE-RGZ	02	Citation Encore	560-0607	Petter Solberg/P S Aviation AB. Torsby.	ZS-UCH
☐ SE-RIK	80	Citation II	550-0378	Grafair AB. Stockholm-Bromma.	D-CIFA
☐ SE-RIT	07	Citation Encore+	560-0773	Ittur AB/Waltair Europe AB. Norrkoepping.	M-ANSL
☐ SE-RIX*	07	CitationJet CJ1+	525-0671	Roplan Aircraft AB.	N.....
Military					
☐ 102001	87	Gulfstream 4/Tp 102	1014	Swedish Air Force, Bromma. (Code 021 of F16).	N779SW
☐ 102002	93	Gulfstream 4/Tp 102B	1215	Swedish Air Force, Linkoeping-Malmen. (Code 022 of F16).	N426GA
☐ 102003	93	Gulfstream 4/Tp 102B	1216	Swedish Air Force, Linkoeping-Malmen. (Code 023 of F16).	N440GA
☐ 102004	95	Gulfstream 4/Tp 102C	1274	Swedish Air Force, Uppsala. (Code 024 of F16).	LV-WOM
☐ 86001	65	Sabre-40/Tp 86	282-49	Defense Material Administration, Linkoeping.	N905KB

SP = POLAND Total 5
Civil

Reg	Yr	Type	c/n	Owner/Operator	Prev Regn
☐ SP-KBM	75	Citation	500-0269	Kuba Olejniczak,	(PH-CTW)
☐ SP-KCK	03	CitationJet CJ-2	525A-0158	Zygmunt Solorz-Zak, Warsaw, Poland.	N158CJ
☐ SP-KCS	05	Citation Excel XLS	560-5649	Jet Service SP Zoo. Warsaw.	N5155G
☐ SP-KKA	05	CitationJet CJ-1	525-0550	Columbus Pro Equity Fund II SP. Kielce.	N1288P
☐ SP-ZSZ	05	Challenger 300	20044	Jet Service SP Zoo. Warsaw.	N74WL

ST = SUDAN Total 4
Civil

Reg	Yr	Type	c/n	Owner/Operator	Prev Regn
☐ ST-FSA	79	JetStar 2	5236	Government of Sudan, Khartoum.	N741AM
☐ ST-PRS	77	Falcon 20F	372	Government of Sudan, Khartoum.	F-WRQV
☐ ST-PSA	90	Falcon 900	84	Government of Sudan, Khartoum.	F-WQBM
☐ ST-PSR	82	Falcon 50	114	Government of Sudan, Khartoum.	F-WPXM

SU = EGYPT Total 19
Civil

Reg	Yr	Type	c/n	Owner/Operator	Prev Regn
☐ SU-AXN	73	Falcon 20-5B	294	Government of Egypt, Cairo.	F-BVPM
☐ SU-AYD	77	Falcon 20-5B	361	Government of Egypt, Cairo.	F-WMKF
☐ SU-AZJ	76	Falcon 20-5B	358	Government of Egypt, Cairo.	F-WRQY
☐ SU-BNC	97	Gulfstream 4SP	1329	Government of Egypt, Cairo.	N329GA
☐ SU-BND	97	Gulfstream 4SP	1332	Government of Egypt, Cairo.	N332GA
☐ SU-BNO	01	Gulfstream 4SP	1424	Government of Egypt, Cairo.	N328GA
☐ SU-BNP	00	Gulfstream 4SP	1427	Government of Egypt, Cairo.	N427GA
☐ SU-BPE	03	Gulfstream G400	1506	Government of Egypt, Cairo.	N306GA
☐ SU-BPF	03	Gulfstream G400	1518	Government of Egypt, Cairo.	N218GA
☐ SU-EWD	04	Citation Sovereign	680-0026	Executive Wings Aviation, Cairo.	N5260Y
☐ SU-GGG	94	Airbus A340-211	061	Government of Egypt, Cairo.	F-W...
☐ SU-MAN	07	Hawker 850XP	258832	Alkan Air, Cairo.	N74142
☐ SU-PIX	82	HS 125/700B	257184	National Aviation Co. Cairo.	G-36-2
☐ SU-SMA	06	Citation Sovereign	680-0118	Smart Aviation, Cairo.	(N2UJ)
☐ SU-SMB	07	Citation Sovereign	680-0167	Smart Aviation, Cairo.	N5180C
☐ SU-ZBB	06	Hawker 800XP	RK-480	Orscom Tourist Installation Co.	N36880
Military					
☐ SU-BGM	88	Gulfstream 4	1048	Egyptian Air Force/Arab Republic of Egypt, Cairo.	N448GA
☐ SU-BGU	85	Gulfstream 3	439	Egyptian Air Force/Arab Republic of Egypt, Cairo.	N17586
☐ SU-BGV	85	Gulfstream 3	442	Egyptian Air Force/Arab Republic of Egypt, Cairo.	N17587

SX = GREECE Total 21
Civil

Reg	Yr	Type	c/n	Owner/Operator	Prev Regn
☐ SX-BMK	99	Citation Bravo	550-0907	Hellados Hotels/Mitsis SA. Athens.	HB-VMM
☐ SX-BNR	01	Learjet 60	60-231	Aegean Aviation Ltd. Athens.	D-CDNX

Reg	Yr	Type	c/n	Owner/Operator	Prev Regn
☐ SX-BTX	75	Gulfstream 2	171	GeeBee Air, Athens. (stored at Geneva).	HZ-AFH
☐ SX-CDK	07	Embraer Legacy 600	14500998	K2 SmartJets, Athens.	PT-SKQ
☐ SX-DCA	04	Falcon 2000EX	29	Interjet SA. Athens.	F-WWGD
☐ SX-DCD	06	Citation Excel XLS	560-5662	Interjet SA. Athens.	N5211Q
☐ SX-DCE	02	Citation Excel	560-5288	Interjet SA. Athens.	N5117U
☐ SX-DCI	96	Citation V Ultra	560-0366	Interjet SA. Athens.	N52352
☐ SX-DCM	99	Citation Excel	560-5051	Interjet SA. Athens.	N1324B
☐ SX-DGM	07	Embraer Legacy 600	14501023	Interjet SA. Athens.	PT-SVY
☐ SX-ECI	07	Citation X	750-0262	Government of Greece, CAA, Athens.	N262CX
☐ SX-EDP	07	CitationJet CJ-3	525B-0193		N1382N
☐ SX-IDA	06	Gulfstream G200	149	Gainjet Aviation SA. Athens.	(SX-IFB)
☐ SX-ONE	02	Gulfstream G200	065	Gainjet Aviation SA. Athens.	(SX-MAD)
☐ SX-SEA	07	Gulfstream G200	163	Gainjet Aviation SA. Athens.	N35BP
☐ SX-SMG	07	Gulfstream G200	159	Gainjet Aviation SA. Athens.	(VP-CSG)
☐ SX-SMR	06	Citation Excel XLS	560-5631	Interjet SA. Athens.	N51042
Military					
☐ 209	99	EMB-135LR	145209	Greek Air Force/Government, Athens.	PT-SFX
☐ 374	01	EMB-135EW	145374	Greek Air Force/Government, Athens.	PP-XHL
☐ 484	02	Embraer Legacy 600	145484	Greek Air Force/Government, Athens.	PT-...
☐ 678	02	Gulfstream V	678	MoD/Government of Greece, Elefis.	N678GA

S5 = SLOVENIA Total 10

Civil

Reg	Yr	Type	c/n	Owner/Operator	Prev Regn
☐ S5-ABL	07	Embraer Legacy 600	14501008	Linx Air Business Airline, Ljubljana.	PT-SKY
☐ S5-ADA	07	Challenger 605	5712	Elit'Avia, Ljubljana.	(OE-IPR)
☐ S5-ADB	07	Challenger 605	5715	Elit'Avia, Ljubljana.	(OE-IVB)
☐ S5-BAJ	00	CitationJet CJ-1	525-0394	Ganaam Co/Linx Air doo. Ljubliana.	N64PZ
☐ S5-BAS	07	CitationJet CJ2+	525A-0348	Linx Air doo. Ljubljana.	N5076J
☐ S5-BAV	06	Citation Excel XLS	560-5660	Linx Air doo. Ljubljana.	N602MA
☐ S5-BAW	05	CitationJet CJ-3	525B-0016	Linx Air doo. Ljubljana.	(D-CORA)
☐ S5-BAX	85	Citation S/II	S550-0028	Smelt Air/GIO Business Aviation, Ljubljana.	HB-VHH
☐ S5-BAZ	02	Citation Excel	560-5236	Linx Air doo. Ljubljana.	N236LD
☐ S5-BBD	99	Citation Excel	560-5058	GIO Business Aviation, Ljubljana.	HB-VNC

S9 = SAO TOME & PRINCIPE Total 3

Civil

Reg	Yr	Type	c/n	Owner/Operator	Prev Regn
☐ S9-PDG	73	HS 125/600A	256021	Hewa Bora Airways, Gombe, DRC.	S9-DBG
☐ S9-PDH	67	HS 125/3B	25132		G-OCBA
☐ S9-SVE	64	B 727-30	18366		5V-TPX

TC = TURKEY Total 56

Civil

Reg	Yr	Type	c/n	Owner/Operator	Prev Regn
☐ TC-...	98	Citation VII	650-7091	AK Finansal Kiralama AS. Istanbul.	N791VP
☐ TC-...	07	Hawker 900XP	HA-20	Capital Energy SA.	N920XP
☐ TC-ADO	05	Hawker 800XPi	258738	Adopen, Istanbul.	N138XP
☐ TC-AHE	05	Citation Bravo	550-1107	TAHE/Menekse Havacilik, Ankara.	N51744
☐ TC-AHS	00	Hawker 800XP	258504	Ahsel Air Transportation Co. Ankara.	N5004B
☐ TC-AKK	97	Falcon 900B	171	AK Aviation, Istanbul.	F-WWFW
☐ TC-ANA	07	Airbus A319-115XCJ	1002	Government of Turkey, Istanbul.	TC-TCB
☐ TC-ANT	93	Citation VI	650-0229	Emair-Emelki Ticaret Havacilik Ithalat-Ihraca, Ankara.	N1302X
☐ TC-ARC	97	Learjet 60	60-094	ArkasAir AS. Izmir.	N93BA
☐ TC-ARD	05	Challenger 604	5611	ArkasAir AS. Izmir.	C-FEIH
☐ TC-ASE	07	Beechjet 400A	RK-18	Sindel Havacilik AS. Ankara.	(N402LX)
☐ TC-ATC	07	Falcon 2000LX EASY	136	Park Havacilik Tasimacilik Ve Ticaret/Park Group,	F-WWGF
☐ TC-CLK	06	Hawker 850XP	258808	Servis Air Hava Isletmesi AS. Istanbul.	N70708
☐ TC-CMB	96	Learjet 45	45-007	Airancyra, Istanbul.	(ZS-ITT)
☐ TC-DGN	06	Falcon 2000EX EASY	104	DOGAN Havacilik AS. Istanbul.	F-WWGE
☐ TC-DOY	06	Hawker 850XP	258801	Doysa VIP Havacilik AS. Istanbul.	(N906BL)
☐ TC-FIN	05	Hawker 850XP	258742	FIBA Air, Istanbul.	N742XP
☐ TC-GGG	75	Falcon 20E	326	Form Air, Istanbul.	TC-CEN
☐ TC-IST	07	Citation Sovereign	680-0159	Veyen Air, Istanbul.	N51872
☐ TC-KAR	07	Challenger 300	20149	Cukurova Air AS. Istanbul.	C-FLQP
☐ TC-KON	98	Citation VII	650-7084	Super Air Hava AS. Gaziantep.	N1127G
☐ TC-LAA	93	Citation V	560-0212	DHMI Hava Taksi, Ankara.	N1284X
☐ TC-LAB	93	Citation V	560-0216	DHMI Hava Taksi, Ankara.	N1285N
☐ TC-LEY	69	HFB 320	1043	Genel Air AS. Istanbul.	16+03
☐ TC-LNS	07	Citation Excel XLS	560-5693	Limak Ins AS. Ankara.	N5069E
☐ TC-MDG	92	Challenger 601-3A	5110	MNG Airlines, Istanbul.	N308BX

Reg	Yr	Type	c/n	Owner/Operator	Prev Regn
☐ TC-MKA	01	Citation Bravo	550-0960	Bon Air AS. Istanbul.	N960CB
☐ TC-MMG	05	Falcon 900EX EASY	161	Palmali Shipping Group, Istanbul.	F-WWFU
☐ TC-MSB	97	Beechjet 400A	RK-170	Airenka Hava Tasimaciligi AS. Istanbul.	TC-MCX
☐ TC-NEO	97	Beechjet 400A	RK-130	Nurol Aviation, Ankara.	N1130B
☐ TC-NOA	77	JetStar 2	5220	Genel Air AS. Istanbul.	A6-KAH
☐ TC-NUB	07	Hawker 850XP	258874	Sindel Havacilik AS/Gozen Air Services, Istanbul.	N874XP
☐ TC-RKS	05	Learjet 60	60-282	Riksos Turizm Yatcilik Havacilik, Antalya.	N5013Y
☐ TC-RMK	01	Falcon 2000	157	Set Air, Istanbul.	(F-GZAK)
☐ TC-SCR	06	Challenger 300	20136	SOCAR/Palmali Shipping Group, Istanbul.	C-FLDK
☐ TC-SHE	07	Hawker 850XP	258872	Erben Havacilik A/S. Istanbul.	N872XP
☐ TC-SNK	06	Falcon 2000	229	Sanko Group/Super Air Hava AS. Gaziantep.	F-GXDA
☐ TC-SSS	78	JetStar 2	5226	Genel Air AS. Istanbul.	N308SG
☐ TC-STA	06	Hawker 400XP	RK-476	Sertur Havacilik AS. Istanburl.	N36846
☐ TC-STB	06	Hawker 850XP	258793	Sertur Havacilik AS. Istanbul.	N793XP
☐ TC-STD	07	Hawker 850XP	258845	Sertur Havacilik AS. Istanbul.	N72645
☐ TC-TAN	00	Challenger 604	5459	DOGUS Air. Istanbul.	N459MT
☐ TC-TAV	05	Hawker 800XPi	258736	TAV-Tepe Akfen Ventures Aviation Co.	N136XP
☐ TC-TKC	06	Hawker 850XP	258790	Cukurova Air AS. Istanbul.	N790XP
☐ TC-TKN	07	Citation Sovereign	680-0174	Turkon Holding AS.	N5212M
☐ TC-TMO		Citation Excel	...	Sindel Havacilik AS. Ankara.	
☐ TC-VSC	99	Hawker 800XP	258398	Bon Air AS. Istanbul.	N168HH
☐ TC-VYN	05	CitationJet CJ-2	525A-0236		N5259Y
Military					
☐ 001	87	Gulfstream 4	1027	TC-GAP. Government of Turkey, Istanbul.	TC-GAP
☐ 002	88	Gulfstream 4	1043	TC-ATA. Government of Turkey, Istanbul.	TC-ATA
☐ 06-001	04	BBJ-7ES	33962	Turkish Air Force, 224 Filo, Etimesgut-Ankara.	N356BJ
☐ 12-003	91	Gulfstream 4	1163	Turkish Air Force, 224 Filo, Etimesgut-Ankara.	N458GA
☐ 84-007	84	Citation II	550-0502	Turkish Air Force, 224 Filo, Etimesgut. (flight calibration)	12-001
☐ 84-008	84	Citation II	550-0503	Turkish Air Force, 224 Filo, Etimesgut. (flight calibration)	12-002
☐ 93-004	93	Citation VII	650-7024	Turkish Air Force, 224 Filo, Etimesgut-Ankara.	93-7024
☐ 93-005	93	Citation VII	650-7026	Turkish Air Force, 224 Filo, Etimesgut-Ankara.	93-7026

TG = GUATEMALA   Total   5
Civil

Reg	Yr	Type	c/n	Owner/Operator	Prev Regn
☐ TG-ABY	05	Learjet 45	45-293	Aldan SA/Textiles del Lagos SA. Guatemala City.	(N694SC)
☐ TG-AIR	93	Learjet 31A	31A-067	Aceros de Guatemala SA. Guatemala City.	N9173M
☐ TG-RIE	81	Citation 1/SP	501-0216	Trans RIF SA. Guatemala City.	TG-RIF
☐ TG-RIF	94	CitationJet	525-0072	Trans RIF SA. Guatemala City.	N2651R
☐ TG-TJF	66	BAC 1-11/401AK	089	Tikal Jets, Guatemala City. 'Quirigua'	N97JF

TI = COSTA RICA   Total   1
Civil

Reg	Yr	Type	c/n	Owner/Operator	Prev Regn
☐ TI-AZX	75	Citation Eagle	500-0227	Mapoli Aviation, San Jose.	N227GM

TJ = CAMEROON   Total   4
Civil

Reg	Yr	Type	c/n	Owner/Operator	Prev Regn
☐ TJ-...	74	HS 125/600A	256040		(N287DM)
☐ TJ-AAM	78	B 727-2R1	21636	Government of Cameroon, Yaounde.	
☐ TJ-AAW	86	Gulfstream 3	486	Government of Cameroon, Yaounde.	N316GA
☐ TJ-ALG		F 28-4000	11227	Commercial Bank of Cameroun, Douala.	N159AD

TR = GABON   Total   9
Civil

Reg	Yr	Type	c/n	Owner/Operator	Prev Regn
☐ TR-AAG	90	Challenger 601-3A	5071	Air Affaires Gabon, Libreville.	(N5032H)
☐ TR-AFJ	88	Falcon 900B	46	Afrijet, Libreville.	N46FJ
☐ TR-KSP	97	Gulfstream 4SP	1327	Government of Gabon, Libreville.	(TR-KHD)
☐ TR-LEX	97	Falcon 900EX	24	Government of Gabon, Libreville.	F-WWFU
☐ TR-LFB	67	HS 125/3B	25130	Avirex SA. Libreville.	F-BSIM
☐ TR-LGV	82	Falcon 50	89	Afrijet, Libreville.	N156WC
☐ TR-LGY	80	Falcon 50	9	Afrijet, Libreville.	F-GGCP
☐ TR-LGZ	78	Falcon 20F	391	Afrijet, Libreville.	N420GL
☐ TR-LTZ	69	DC 8-73CF	46053	Government of Gabon, Libreville.	N8638

TS = TUNISIA   Total   3
Civil

Reg	Yr	Type	c/n	Owner/Operator	Prev Regn
☐ TS-IAM	99	Challenger 604	5412	Fly International Airways, Tunis.	N529GP
☐ TS-IAY	84	Airbus A300B4-620	354	Government of Libya, Tripoli, Libya.	A6-SHZ
☐ TS-IOO	99	BBJ-7H3	29149	Government of Tunisia, Tunis.	N5573L

Reg	Yr	Type	c/n	Owner/Operator	Prev Regn
TT = CHAD				Total	**1**
Civil					
☐ TT-AAI	79	Gulfstream 2	240	Government of Tchad, N'Djamena.	5A-DDR
TU = IVORY COAST				Total	**4**
Civil					
☐ TU-TIZ	76	F 28-1000C	11099	Air Ivoire, Abidjan.	PH-VAB
Military					
☐ TU-VAD	87	Gulfstream 4	1019	Government of Ivory Coast, Abidjan.	N17584
☐ TU-VAF	85	Gulfstream 3	462	Government of Ivory Coast, Abidjan.	N303GA
☐ TU-VAJ		F 28-4000VIP	11124	Government of Ivory Coast, Abidjan.	TU-VAZ
TY = BENIN				Total	**2**
Civil					
☐ TY-AOM	87	Falcon 900	33	Comfort Jet Aviation Ltd. Cotonou.	N203CW
☐ TY-SAM	83	HS 125/700A	NA0334	Comfort Jet Aviation Ltd/Alafia Jet, Cotonou.	N46WQ
TZ = MALI				Total	**3**
Civil					
☐ TZ-BSB	66	BAC 1-11/401AK	086	Government of Mali, Bamako.	YR-CJL
☐ TZ-NBA	80	B 727-2K5	21853	Mali Air Transport, Bamako.	P4-JLI
☐ TZ-TAC	74	B 707-3L6B	21049	Government of Mali, Bamako.	5V-TGE
T7 = SAN MARINO				Total	**2**
Civil					
☐ T7-FRA	06	CitationJet CJ1+	525-0628	Nikair,	N52433
☐ T7-VII	98	Citation VII	650-7090	Air Wing SpA. San Marino.	D-CVII
T9 = BOSNIA-HERZEGOVINA				Total	**1**
Civil					
☐ T9-SBA	80	Citation	500-0399	Air Service R.S/Republic of Srpska,	YU-BML
UK = UZBEKISTAN				Total	**1**
Civil					
☐ UK-80001	97	BAe 146/RJ-85	E2312	Government of Uzbekistan, Tashkent.	G-6-312
UN = KAZAKHSTAN				Total	**6**
Civil					
☐ UN-A1901	05	Airbus A319-115XCJ	2592	Government of Kazakhstan, Almaty.	HB-IPO
☐ UN-B5701	86	B 757-2M6	23454	Government of Kazakhstan, Almaty.	P4-NSN
☐ UN-B6701		B 767-2DXER	32954	Government of Kazakhstan, Almaty.	
☐ UN-C8501	07	Challenger 850	8054	Khozu Avia JSC, Almaty.	C-FHTO
☐ UN-C8502	06	Challenger 850	8049	Khozu Avia, JSC. Almaty.	C-FHGK
☐ UN-P1001	04	390 Premier 1	RB-120	SAT Airlines,	N311SL
UR = UKRAINE				Total	**9**
Civil					
☐ UR-CCB	68	Falcon 20-5	141	ISD Avia Aircompany Ltd. Donetzk.	(UR-BCA)
☐ UR-CCC	93	Falcon 50	235	CABI Airlines Ltd/KABI Avia, Donetzk.	(UR-ACA)
☐ UR-CCF	90	Falcon 50	212	CABI Airlines Ltd/KABI Avia, Donetzk.	LX-APG
☐ UR-CLE	73	Falcon 20E	279	Challenge Aero, Kiev.	D-CLBE
☐ UR-CLF	73	Falcon 20E-5	293	Challenge Aero, Kiev.	RA-09005
☐ UR-KKA	79	Falcon 20F	389	Aerostar Airlines, Kiev.	I-CMUT
☐ UR-MOA	70	Falcon 20E-5	237	ISD Avia Aircompany Ltd. Donetsk.	EC-JDV
☐ UR-NOA	76	Falcon 20F	345	Aerostar Airlines, Kiev.	OH-FPC
☐ UR-WOG	00	Dornier Do328JET	3118	Aerostar Ltd. Kiev.	N873JC
VH = AUSTRALIA				Total	**108**
Civil					
☐ VH-...	77	Learjet 36A	36A-032	Jet City P/L. Melbourne, VIC. Australia.	(N16AJ)
☐ VH-ACE	87	Falcon 900	37	Remorex P/L. Perth, WA.	VH-FCP
☐ VH-AJG	80	Westwind-1124	281	Pel-Air Aviation P/L. Sydney, NSW.	(N200XJ)
☐ VH-AJJ	79	Westwind-1124	248	Pel-Air Aviation P/L. Sydney, NSW.	N25RE
☐ VH-AJK	79	Westwind-1124	256	Pel-Air Aviation P/L. Sydney, NSW.	4X-CNB
☐ VH-AJP	78	Westwind-1124	238	Pel-Air Aviation P/L. Sydney, NSW.	4X-CMJ
☐ VH-AJV	80	Westwind-1124	282	Pel-Air Aviation P/L. Sydney, NSW.	N186G
☐ VH-APJ	98	CitationJet	525-0281	Southern Air Services P/L.	N508TL
☐ VH-BZL	97	Beechjet 400A	RK-139	Buzz Aviation P/L. Sydney, NSW.	VH-MZL
☐ VH-CCC	99	Gulfstream V	581	Crown Melbourne Ltd. Melbourne, VIC.	N126CH
☐ VH-CGF	89	Gulfstream 4	1083	Crown Melbourne Ltd. Melbourne, VIC.	VH-CCC

Reg	Yr	Type	c/n	Owner/Operator	Prev Regn
☐ VH-CRW	05	Falcon 2000EX EASY	58	Brenzil P/L-Sydney Jet Charter P/L. Brisbane, QLD.	VH-CRQ
☐ VH-CXJ	01	Learjet 45	45-152	Dramatic Investments P/L. Mascot, NSW.	N5014E
☐ VH-DAA	96	CitationJet	525-0138	GoJet P/L-Pacific Media Corp P/L. Wollongong, NSW.	VH-MOJ
☐ VH-DBT	98	Gulfstream 4SP	1363	Mahaya Aviation P/L. Melbourne, VIC.	N48CC
☐ VH-DHN	92	Citation VII	650-7011	Orkdale P/L. Oxenford, QLD.	SE-DVY
☐ VH-EGK	72	Citation	500-0051	Orkdale P/L. Oxenford, QLD.	VH-EMM
☐ VH-EJY	80	Citation II	550-0141	Executive Jet Charter P/L. Aitkenvale, QLD.	VH-INX
☐ VH-EMO	85	Citation S/II	S550-0063	Adams (UK) Corp P/L. Hawthorne, VIC.	(N12717)
☐ VH-ESM	86	Learjet 35A	35A-611	Raytheon Australia P/L. RANAS, Nowra, NSW.	N611TW
☐ VH-ESW	76	Learjet 35A	35A-071	Raytheon Australia P/L. RANAS, Nowra, NSW.	N99FN
☐ VH-EXB	97	Beechjet 400A	RK-154	Executive Airlines P/L. Essendon, VIC.	VH-BJC
☐ VH-EXG	05	Citation Sovereign	680-0072	Executive Airlines P/L. Essendon, VIC.	N5254Y
☐ VH-EXQ	06	Citation Sovereign	680-0129	Executive Airlines P/L. Essendon, VIC.	N1314T
☐ VH-FCS	79	Citation Eagle II	501-0102	Fox Aviation P/L. Brighton, VIC.	N45FS
☐ VH-FGK	98	Citation Bravo	550-0852	Executive Airlines P/L. Essendon, VIC.	N5076J
☐ VH-FUM	81	Citation 1/SP	501-0189	NetJets P/L-General Flying Services P/L. Melbourne, VIC.	(N500SS)
☐ VH-HKX	72	Citation Eagle	500-0050	Metropolis City Promotions P/L. Essendon, VIC.	N333PP
☐ VH-HVM	01	Citation Bravo	550-0984	Heathgate Resources P/L. Adelaide, SA.	(N984VP)
☐ VH-ING	99	Citation VII	650-7104	Inghams Enterprises P/L. Bankstown, NSW.	N5148B
☐ VH-INT	79	Citation II	550-0102	Revesco Aviation P/L. Perth, WA.	VH-OYC
☐ VH-JCR	79	Learjet 35A	35A-231	Jet City P/L. Melbourne, VIC.	N62DK
☐ VH-JCX	86	Learjet 36A	36A-057	Careflight Queensland Ltd. Gold Coast, QLD.	HB-VIF
☐ VH-JMK	81	Citation II	550-0289	J M Kelly (Project Builders) P/L. Rockhampton, QLD.	C-FTMS
☐ VH-KEF	96	Hawker 800XP	258295	Prime Aviation P/L/Kefford Corp P/L. Essendon, VIC.	VH-LAT
☐ VH-KNR	81	Westwind-Two	340	Pel-Air Aviation P/L. Sydney, NSW.	N118MP
☐ VH-KNS	81	Westwind-1124	323	Pel-Air Aviation P/L. Sydney, NSW.	N816H
☐ VH-KNU	81	Westwind-1124	317	Pel-Air Aviation P/L. Sydney, NSW.	VH-UUZ
☐ VH-KXL	95	CitationJet	525-0100	Edwards Coaches P/L. Armidale, NSW.	VH-CIT
☐ VH-LAL	01	Falcon 900C	192	PAL Aviation P/L. Melbourne, VIC.	VH-LAW
☐ VH-LEF	07	Challenger 850	8060	Linfox Aviation P/L. Melbourne, VIC.	C-FGTV
☐ VH-LJJ	80	Learjet 35A	35A-324	Turbojet Holdings P/L-Jet City P/L. Melbourne, VIC.	N8064A
☐ VH-LMP	92	BAe 1000B	259022	Boston LHF P/L-Santos Ltd. Adelaide, SA.	G-5-734
☐ VH-LPJ	84	Learjet 35A	35A-593	Linfox Aircraft Charter/Air National Australia, Melbourne.	VH-PPF
☐ VH-MBP	05	Hawker 800XP	258712	Marcplan P/L. Essendon, VIC.	N18AQ
☐ VH-MGC	95	Beechjet 400A	RK-97	Aarton No 001 P/L-Sydney Jet Charter P/L. Bankstown, NSW.	N3197Q
☐ VH-MIF	06	CitationJet CJ-3	525B-0078	Dick Smith Adventure P/L. Bankstown, NSW.	N525DR
☐ VH-MMC	79	Citation 1/SP	501-0089	Redbank Engineering/Silver Cross Aviation P/L. Milton, QLD.	VH-CCJ
☐ VH-MOR	02	CitationJet CJ-2	525A-0063	Airborne Imaging P/L. Archerfield, QLD.	N5208F
☐ VH-MQY	06	Hawker 850XP	258807	Government of Western Australia, Perth, WA.	N36878
☐ VH-MXJ	95	Citation V Ultra	560-0320	Maxem Aviation P/L. Perth, WA.	VH-SMF
☐ VH-MYE	07	CitationJet CJ1+	525-0638	Andrew Norbury Aircraft P/L. Richmond, VIC.	N51342
☐ VH-MZL	03	Challenger 604	5561	Wellard Aviation P/L-AvWest P/L. Perth, WA.	N604WF
☐ VH-NGA	83	Westwind-Two	387	Pel-Air Aviation P/L. Sydney, NSW.	N97AL
☐ VH-NGH	07	Citation Excel XLS	560-5727	SJMF/Sunshine Express Airlines P/L. Sunshine Coast, QLD.	N5192E
☐ VH-OCV	05	Challenger 604	5625	Execujet Australia P/L. Sydney, NSW.	C-FFQQ
☐ VH-OSW	00	Gulfstream 4SP	1441	Garuda Aviation P/L-AvWest P/L. Perth, WA.	N123LC
☐ VH-OVB	81	Learjet 35A	35A-400	GCM/Shortstop Jet Charter P/L. Melbourne, VIC. 'Angel One'	VH-RHQ
☐ VH-PFA	90	Learjet 35A	35A-661	ST Aerospace Engineering P/L. Seletar, Singapore.	N1268G
☐ VH-PFS	01	Learjet 45	45-168	ST Aerospace Engineering P/L. Seletar, Singapore.	N50088
☐ VH-PPD	00	Falcon 900C	185	Paspaley Pearling Co P/L-Lloyd Aviation Jet Charter, Darwin.	HB-IGT
☐ VH-PSM	79	Citation II	550-0054	Melbourne Jets P/L-Shortstop Jet Charter P/L. Essendon, VIC.	VH-OYW
☐ VH-PSU	99	Citation V Ultra	560-0515	Queensland Police Service, Brisbane, QLD.	N51042
☐ VH-QQZ	79	Citation II	550-0076	Skytrans Regional P/L. Cairns, QLD.	P2-BMD
☐ VH-RAM	07	Hawker 850XP	258844	Ramsay Air Charter P/L. Sydney.	N71944
☐ VH-RJB	02	CitationJet CJ-2	525A-0094	Airlux P/L-Edwards Coaches P/L. Armidale, NSW.	N942CJ
☐ VH-SBU	86	Citation III	650-0109	Shazo Holdings P/L/Professional Jet Aviation P/L.	N106ST
☐ VH-SCC	03	Citation Bravo	550-1058	Falcon 50 P/L-MacArthur Jet Charter, Bankstown, NSW.	N52691
☐ VH-SCD	82	Citation II	550-0339	DHM Aircraft Sales P/L-Dream Aviation, Bankstown, NSW.	VH-KTK
☐ VH-SGY	06	Hawker 850XP	258780	Queensland Government Air Wing, Brisbane, QLD.	N37070
☐ VH-SLD	78	Learjet 35A	35A-145	Pel Air Aviation P/L-RANAS, Nowra, NSW.	(N166AG)
☐ VH-SLE	81	Learjet 35A	35A-428	Pel Air Aviation P/L-RANAS, Nowra, NSW.	N17LH
☐ VH-SLF	81	Learjet 36A	36A-049	Pel Air Aviation P/L-RANAS, Nowra, NSW.	N136ST
☐ VH-SLJ	75	Learjet 36	36-014	Pel Air Aviation P/L-RANAS, Nowra, NSW.	N200Y
☐ VH-SOU	76	Citation	500-0333	Sydney Jet Charter P/L. Sydney, NSW.	N275AL
☐ VH-SPJ	85	Citation III	650-0101	Private Air P/L. Wangi Wangi, NSW.	N9NL
☐ VH-SQD	99	Learjet 45	45-033	Singapore Airlines Flying College P/L. Maroochydore, QLD.	9V-ATI

Reg	Yr	Type	c/n	Owner/Operator	Prev Regn
VH-SQM	99	Learjet 45	45-035	Singapore Airlines Flying College P/L. Maroochydore, QLD.	9V-ATJ
VH-SQR	01	Learjet 45	45-195	Singapore Airlines Flying College P/L. Maroochydore, QLD.	N5040Y
VH-SQV	02	Learjet 45	45-207	Singapore Airlines Flying College P/L. Maroochydore, QLD.	N5000E
VH-SSZ	88	Citation III	650-0158	Flightpath Aviation P/L. West End, QLD.	N721ST
VH-TEN	03	Citation X	750-0215	Balmoral Air P/L. Artarmon, NSW.	N215CX
VH-TGG	04	Global Express	9143	Gandel Investments P/L. Melbourne.	C-FAGU
VH-VGX	00	Global Express	9079	Pratt Aviation P/L. Melbourne, VIC.	(N217JC)
VH-VHD	03	Airbus A319-155	1999	Skytraders P/L-Government of Australia Antarctic Division,	F-GYAS
VH-VHP	06	390 Premier 1A	RB-175	Sydney Jet Charter P/L. Sydney, NSW.	N71865
VH-VLJ	81	Learjet 35A	35A-432	Australasian Jet P/L. Essendon, VIC.	G-HUGG
VH-VLZ	91	Citation II	550-0690	Professional Jet Aviation P/L. Georges Hall, NSW.	OE-GLZ
VH-VPL	06	Citation Encore	560-0703	SCT Logistics P/L. Melbourne, VIC.	N52144
VH-VRC	98	Citation VII	650-7089	Christie Aviation P/L-Private Air P/L. Wangi Wangi, NSW.	N789VP
VH-WJW	78	Falcon 10	134	Wagner Aviation P/L-Careflight Medical Services, Gold Coast.	VH-MCX
VH-WNZ	79	Citation II	550-0057	Kendell/Tasman Australia Airlines P/L. Paradise Point, QLD.	(N2661N)
VH-XBP	97	Citation Bravo	550-0810	Buildex Aviation P/L. Newcastle, NSW.	VH-XCJ
VH-XCJ	06	Citation Excel XLS	560-5673	Mount Craigie Holdings P/L-Jet City P/L. Melbourne, VIC.	N5269J
VH-YNE	03	CitationJet CJ-1	525-0521	Celijet Charter P/L. Leeton, NSW.	VH-ANE
VH-YRC	99	Beechjet 400A	RK-222	International Publishing Group P/L-Private Air P/L. Sydney.	N482RK
VH-YXY	06	Citation Bravo	550-1125	Bydand Aviation P/L. Brisbane, QLD.	N5262X
VH-ZLE	82	Citation II	550-0347	China Southern WA Flying College P/L. Jandakot, WA.	ZS-LEE
VH-ZLT	99	Citation Bravo	550-0878	China Southern WA Flying College P/L. Jandakot, WA.	N5135K
VH-ZMD	75	Citation	500-0263	Australasian Jet P/L. Essendon, VIC.	VH-AQS
VH-ZYH	83	Westwind-Two	376	Westwind II P/L-Kestrel Aviation College P/L.Managalore, VIC	N376BE
VH-ZZH	00	Challenger 604	5456	Avwest P/L. Perth, WA.	VH-MXK

Military

Reg	Yr	Type	c/n	Owner/Operator	Prev Regn
A20-624	68	B 707-338C	19624	RAAF, 33 Squadron, Richmond, NSW. 'Richmond Town'	VH-EAD
A36-001	00	BBJ-7DT	30829	RAAF, 34 Squadron, Fairbairn, Canberra, ACT.	N372BJ
A36-002	00	BBJ-7DF	30790	RAAF, 34 Squadron, Fairbairn, Canberra, ACT.	N10040
A37-001	02	Challenger 604	5521	RAAF, 34 Squadron, Fairbairn, Canberra, ACT.	N521RF
A37-002	02	Challenger 604	5534	RAAF, 34 Squadron, Fairbairn, Canberra, ACT.	N534RF
A37-003	01	Challenger 604	5538	RAAF, 34 Squadron, Fairbairn, Canberra, ACT.	N538RF

VP-B = BERMUDA   Total 149

Civil

Reg	Yr	Type	c/n	Owner/Operator	Prev Regn
VP-BAA	66	B 727-51	19123	Marbyia Investments Ltd/KAK Aviation Ltd. Malaga, Spain.	N727AK
VP-BAB	66	B 727-76	19254	Marbyia Investments Ltd/KAK Aviation Ltd. Malaga, Spain.	N682G
VP-BAC	99	Gulfstream V	588	Fairmont Aviation/TAG Aviation SA. Geneva, Switzerland.	N588GA
VP-BAF	84	Falcon 100	210	Laret Aviation Ltd. Basle, Switzerland.	N210EM
VP-BAH	06	Global Express	9223	Deerborn Bermuda Ltd/Execujet Middle East Ltd. Dubai, UAE.	N83ZZ
VP-BAK	06	Falcon 2000EX EASY	110	STCO/Shaher Trading Co. Sana'a, Republic of Yemen.	F-WWMG
VP-BAM	04	Global 5000	9157	Dobro Ltd. Farnborough, UK.	C-FBQD
VP-BAP	67	B 727-21	19260	Malibu Consulting Corp. Van Nuys, Ca. USA.	N727GP
VP-BAR	07	Falcon 7X	11	Ali Ghandour/Jana Co.	F-WWUH
VP-BAS	04	Hawker 800XP	258702	Nordex Air Ltd. Moscow, Russia.	N966K
VP-BAT	79	B 747SP-21	21648	Worldwide Aircraft Holding Co. Bournemouth-Hurn, UK.	VR-BAT
VP-BBD	92	Falcon 50	226	Blue Heron Aviation Ltd/Chagoury Brothers, Lagos, Nigeria.	F-WQBN
VP-BBF	84	Challenger 601	3033	Vacuna Jets Ltd/Evolga AVV. Moscow, Russia.	HB-ILK
VP-BBJ	98	BBJ-72U/W	29273	JABJ/Picton II Ltd. Geneva, Switzerland.	(N1GN)
VP-BBO	06	Gulfstream G550	5123	Varbra SA. Sao Paulo, SP. Brazil.	N523GA
VP-BBP	01	Falcon 2000	160	Albinati Aeronautics SA. Moscow, Russia.	F-WQBL
VP-BBQ	06	390 Premier 1A	RB-181	Asia Universal Aircraft Ltd. Moscow, Russia.	N7081V
VP-BBV	74	Falcon 10	22	Bourgogne Aero Services, Paris-Le Bourget, France.	F-GJLL
VP-BBW	98	BBJ-78J	30076	Altitude 41 Ltd/GAMA Aviation Ltd. Farnborough, UK.	P4-CZT
VP-BBX	00	Gulfstream V	622	GAMA Aviation Ltd. Farnborough, UK.	N806AC
VP-BBY	06	Embraer Legacy 600	14500970	AKK Co Ltd. Beirut, Lebanon.	PT-SFX
VP-BBZ	07	Learjet 60	60-328	Learjet Inc. Wichita, Ks. USA.	N5000E
VP-BCC	02	Regional Jet	7717	Consolidated Contractors Co. Athens, Greece.	C-GZSQ
VP-BCI	00	Challenger 800	7351	Consolidated Contractors Co. Athens, Greece.	N351BA
VP-BCL	06	Challenger 700	10247	Consolidated Contractors Co. Farnborough, UK.	N710TS
VP-BCV	02	Falcon 2000	187	Vitesse Corp. Greenfield, In. USA.	N87FJ
VP-BCW	05	Hawker 800XP	258719	Jadayel Aviation, Jeddah, Saudi Arabia.	N19XP
VP-BCX	01	Falcon 900C	193	S K M Ltd. Moscow, Russia.	F-WQBL
VP-BCY	01	Learjet 60	60-215	ACASS Canada Ltd. Moscow-Vnukovo, Russia.	N44QF
VP-BDJ	68	B 727-23	20046	Donald Trump/D J Aerospace (Bermuda) Ltd. NYC.	VR-BDJ
VP-BDL	00	Falcon 2000	111	Sioux Co. Luton, UK.	F-WWVF
VP-BDS	97	CitationJet	525-0180	Ekron Ltd/AVCON AG. Zurich, Switzerland.	(N133AV)

Reg	Yr	Type	c/n	Owner/Operator	Prev Regn
☐ VP-BDU	00	Global Express	9057	Bonidea/TAG Aviation Charter UK Ltd. Farnborough, UK.	N18WY
☐ VP-BDV	03	Falcon 2000EX	22	Squadron Aviation Services Ltd. Hamilton.	N218EX
☐ VP-BDX	99	Challenger 604	5402	J & S Service & Investment Ltd. Warsaw, Poland.	N98AG
☐ VP-BDZ	99	Falcon 900EX	53	Squadron Aviation Services, Sao Paulo, SP. Brazil.	N900XE
☐ VP-BEA	99	Falcon 50EX	286	Petroff Air, Moscow, Russia.	N286ZT
☐ VP-BEB	02	Global Express	9115	Rus-Jet Air Co. Moscow, Russia.	C-FNDF
☐ VP-BEE	02	Falcon 900EX	109	Sonair SA. Luanda, Angola.	F-WWFG
☐ VP-BEF	04	Falcon 900EX EASY	130	China Sonangol International,	F-WWFH
☐ VP-BEG	97	Falcon 900EX	17	Sonair SA/China SONANGOL International, Luanda, Angola.	N990H
☐ VP-BEH	00	Falcon 900EX	75	GT Services Ltd. Malaga, Spain.	(F-GYDP)
☐ VP-BEJ	90	Challenger 601-3A	5061	Eurojet Holdings Ltd. Stansted, UK.	(N575MA)
☐ VP-BEK	08	Challenger 300	…	Vulcan Aviation Ltd.	
☐ VP-BEL	99	BBJ-74T	29139	Ventura Aviation/Execujet Air Charter AG. Zurich.	N21KR
☐ VP-BEM	99	Global Express	9036	Symphony Millenium Ltd. Kuala Lumpur, Malaysia.	HB-ITG
☐ VP-BEN	99	Global Express	9020	Symphony Millenium Ltd. Kuala Lumpur, Malaysia.	N700GK
☐ VP-BEP	01	Gulfstream V	636	Global Aviation Services Ltd/NetJets Europe,	N910V
☐ VP-BER	03	Falcon 2000EX	10	Birgma Sweden AB. Stockholm, Sweden.	(SE-RBV)
☐ VP-BEX	06	Airbus A319-115XCJ	2706	Sonair SA/China SONANGOL International, Luanda, Angola.	D-AVIP
☐ VP-BEY	06	Airbus A319-115XCJ	2675	Sonair SA/China SONANGOL International, Luanda, Angola.	D-AIJO
☐ VP-BEZ	01	Falcon 900EX	86	Al Ezz Group, Cairo, Egypt.	HB-IGX
☐ VP-BFF	76	Gulfstream II SP	186	Shukra Nigeria Ltd.	VP-BJV
☐ VP-BFH	98	Falcon 900B	173	Al Hokair Aviation Ltd. Riyadh, Saudi Arabia.	PH-LBA
☐ VP-BFS	94	Challenger 601-3R	5149	ACASS Canada/2060352 Ontario Ltd. Toronto, ON, Canada.	N63ST
☐ VP-BFT	07	BBJ-7JB	36714	Boeing Business Jets, Seattle, Wa. USA.	F-WWDA
☐ VP-BFU	07	390 Premier 1A	RB-220	JSC RusJet, Moscow-Vnukovo, Russia.	N34820
☐ VP-BGB	93	Learjet 60	60-005	Lemco Holdings Ltd. Hamilton.	N60KJ
☐ VP-BGE	75	Citation	500-0287	Ross Aviation Ltd. Bristol-Filton, UK.	(VP-CAW)
☐ VP-BGG	06	Falcon 7X	5	Parc Aviation Ltd/Chagoury Brothers, Lagos, Nigeria.	F-WWUB
☐ VP-BGI	07	Falcon 2000EX EASY	126	Elmet Aviation/Banco de Bogota, Colombia.	N669PG
☐ VP-BGL	04	Gulfstream G550	5043	PT BUMI Resources Tbk. Jakarta, Indonesia.	(N88NB)
☐ VP-BGN	02	Gulfstream G550	5011	Rockfield Holdings Ltd/Jetclub AG. Farnborough, UK.	(N522QS)
☐ VP-BGO	99	Challenger 604	5404	Sun International Management Ltd. Nassau, Bahamas.	C-GLYO
☐ VP-BGS	05	Learjet 60	60-289	Gulf Global Services Ltd. Farnborough, UK.	N785DR
☐ VP-BHH	00	Challenger 604	5448	Mouawad SA. Jeddah, Saudi Arabia.	TC-DHH
☐ VP-BHM	69	DC 8-62	46111	Brisair Ltd/Sheikh El Khreiji, Saudi Arabia.	VR-BHM
☐ VP-BHN	01	BBJ2-8AN	32438	Saudi Oger Ltd. Riyadh, Saudi Arabia.	N1786B
☐ VP-BHO	81	Citation 1/SP	501-0207	Cardinal Aviation Ltd.	OE-FYC
☐ VP-BHR	82	Gulfstream 3	346	Saudi Oger Ltd. Riyadh, Saudi Arabia.	(N126AH)
☐ VP-BHT	06	Learjet 40	45-2050	A55 Co LLC.	N5015U
☐ VP-BHX	98	Challenger 800	7176	Carre Aviation, Moscow, Russia.	P4-CRJ
☐ VP-BIF	71	B 727-1H2	20533	Next Century Aviation Inc. Sausalito, Ca. USA.	N727XL
☐ VP-BIP	06	Gulfstream G550	5109	Blue Sapphire Services Ltd. Jakarta, Indonesia.	N829GA
☐ VP-BIV	07	Gulfstream G450	4092	Government of Jordan, Amman, Jordan.	N392GA
☐ VP-BJA	05	Challenger 604	5639	WJE Associates Ltd. Biggin Hill, UK.	C-FGYI
☐ VP-BJD	04	Gulfstream G550	5064	Transworld Oil America Inc. Newark, NJ. USA.	N964GA
☐ VP-BJE	05	Challenger 604	5605	TAG Asia/Johnson Electric Holdings Ltd. Hong Kong.	N605CL
☐ VP-BJH	98	Challenger 604	5397	Prestige Jet, Abu Dhabi, United Arab Emirates.	A6-PJA
☐ VP-BJM	04	Challenger 604	5593	Globacom Ltd. Lagos, Nigeria. 'Mistys'	N604SC
☐ VP-BKI	94	Gulfstream 4SP	1255	Stella Air Services, Hamilton.	N934DF
☐ VP-BKK	70	HS 125/731	25238	WJE Associates Ltd. Bournemouth-Hurn, UK.	G-36-1
☐ VP-BKS	93	B 767-3P6ER	27254	Kalair USA Corp/Mideast Jet, Jeddah, Saudi Arabia.	A40-GW
☐ VP-BKZ	99	Gulfstream V	602	Dennis Vanguard International Ltd. Birmingham, UK.	N602GV
☐ VP-BLA	03	Gulfstream G550	5024	ISPAT Group Ltd. Luton, UK.	N924GA
☐ VP-BLB	89	Falcon 900B	49	Maritime Investment & Shipping/Stavros Niarchos, Athens.	VR-BLB
☐ VP-BLC	06	Learjet 60	60-311	Quantex Financial Ltd. Caracas, Venezuela.	N202SJ
☐ VP-BLK	79	B 747SP-31	21961	Interface Operations LLC. Las Vegas, Nv. USA.	N992MS
☐ VP-BLM	90	Falcon 900B	72	Globus Travel/Aileron/Sen Montegazza, Lugano, Switzerland.	VR-BLM
☐ VP-BLR	04	Gulfstream G550	5059	International Jet Club Ltd. Farnborough, UK.	N959GA
☐ VP-BLT	81	Westwind-Two	337	Island Aviation Ltd/Longtail Aviation Ltd. McKinley.	N2518M
☐ VP-BLV	76	Citation	500-0344	Santom Ltd	VR-BLV
☐ VP-BLW	06	Gulfstream G550	5129	Specialised Transportation Ltd. Farnborough, UK.	N529GA
☐ VP-BMA	07	Gulfstream G150	228	Micron Leasing Inc.	(VP-BMT)
☐ VP-BMB	88	Falcon 900	51	Longtail Aviation Ltd. McKinley.	N328JR
☐ VP-BMD	83	HS 125/700B	257200	Air VIP Ltd. Athens, Greece.	VR-BMD
☐ VP-BMH	90	BAe 125/800B	258180	Air VIP, Riga, Latvia.	G-BZNR
☐ VP-BML	06	Challenger 605	5703		C-FLGN

Reg	Yr	Type	c/n	Owner/Operator	Prev Regn
❏ VP-BMM	07	Hawker 850XP	258841	TAG Aviation Charter UK Ltd. Farnborough, UK.	N70431
❏ VP-BMP	05	Falcon 50EX	345	Tower House Consultants Ltd. Jersey, C.I.	F-WWHA
❏ VP-BMS	99	Falcon 900EX	42	Flying Lion/Stork Ltd. Boca Raton, Fl. USA.	N942EX
❏ VP-BMT	01	Gulfstream G100	144	Omyaviation Inc/Execujet Charter AG. Zurich, Switzerland.	N262GA
❏ VP-BMU	84	HS 125/700A	257212	Air VIP Ltd. Moscow-Vnukovo, Russia.	LY-BSK
❏ VP-BMV	04	Falcon 900C	202	OMYA International, Switzerland.	F-WWFF
❏ VP-BMW	02	Gulfstream G100	146	Omyaviation Inc/Execujet Charter AG. Zurich, Switzerland.	N646GA
❏ VP-BMY	07	Gulfstream G450	4096	Orient Wonder International Ltd. Hamilton.	N496GA
❏ VP-BNA	67	B 727-21	19262	Skyways International Inc. Houston, Tx. USA.	VR-BNA
❏ VP-BNB	94	Gulfstream 4SP	1234	BH Aviation Ltd/JABJ AG. Zurich, Switzerland.	I-LXGR
❏ VP-BNE	04	Gulfstream G550	5051	Natasha Estab/Jet Aviation AG. Zurich, Switzerland.	N851GA
❏ VP-BNK	03	Hawker 800XP	258625	Challenge Aero, Kiev, Ukraine.	N305JA
❏ VP-BNL	00	Gulfstream V	607	Nebula Ltd/GAMA Aviation Ltd. Farnborough, UK.	N303K
❏ VP-BNO	04	Gulfstream G550	5050	Nebula Ltd/GAMA Aviation Ltd. Farnborough, UK.	N950GA
❏ VP-BNP	06	Challenger 604	5657	XClusive Jet Charter Ltd. Bournemouth-Hurn, UK.	C-FIYA
❏ VP-BNR	03	Gulfstream G550	5033	Saudi Oger Ltd/Eiger Jet Ltd, Riyadh, Saudi Arabia.	N933GA
❏ VP-BNS	06	Falcon 900DX	609	NS Aviation Ltd. Cairo, Egypt.	F-WWFO
❏ VP-BNX	07	Global 5000	9246		C-FMFK
❏ VP-BNZ	06	BBJ-7H9	35959	Dennis Vanguard International Ltd. Birmingham, UK.	
❏ VP-BOA	92	Challenger 601-3A	5114	SAMCO Aviation, Riyadh, Saudi Arabia.	VR-BOA
❏ VP-BOK	02	Global Express	9101	Falconair/Rembrandt Tobacco Group, Capetown, RSA.	C-GIXJ
❏ VP-BOL	95	Gulfstream 4SP	1266	Rida Aviation Ltd. Hamilton.	N77D
❏ VP-BON	92	Astra-1125SP	060	Aerocentro de Servicios CA. Caracas, Venezuela.	VR-BON
❏ VP-BOO	00	Hawker 800XP	258477	XClusive Jet Charter Ltd. Bournemouth-Hurn, UK.	OE-GEO
❏ VP-BOS	05	Global Express XRS	9165	YYA Aviation Ltd. Cairo, Egypt.	C-FCSH
❏ VP-BOW	04	Global Express	9141	International Jet Club Ltd. Luton, UK.	C-GAGS
❏ VP-BOY	80	HS 125/700B	257109	B-Jet Ltd. Beirut, Lebanon.	VP-BTZ
❏ VP-BPO	05	390 Premier 1A	RB-138	Asia Universal Aircraft Ltd. Moscow, Russia.	N5118J
❏ VP-BRA	07	Falcon 2000EX EASY	133	E F Education, Stockholm, Sweden.	F-WWGP
❏ VP-BRH	99	B 777-2ANER	29953	R B Hariri/Saudi Oger Ltd. Riyadh, Saudi Arabia.	
❏ VP-BRJ	07	CitationJet CJ-3	525B-0198		(VP-BJR)
❏ VP-BRM	98	BBJ-75U	28976	Dobro Ltd. Stansted, UK.	(VP-BOC)
❏ VP-BRT	02	BBJ-7BC	32970	E & A Aviation Ltd/JABJ AG. Zurich, Switzerland.	N707BZ
❏ VP-BSC	04	Global Express	9142	Execujet Middle East Ltd. Dubai, UAE.	N700EW
❏ VP-BSD	06	Challenger 850	8051	Alpha 55 LLC.	(A6-DSK)
❏ VP-BSE	99	Global Express	9028	Tradanta Ltd. Hamilton.	N717TF
❏ VP-BSI	05	Gulfstream G550	5084	SEA Aviation Ltd. Athens, Greece.	N584GA
❏ VP-BSJ	98	Gulfstream V	555	JABJ AG. Zurich, Switzerland.	VP-BSM
❏ VP-BSN	01	Gulfstream V	648	Shell Aircraft Ltd. Rotterdam, Holland.	N85ML
❏ VP-BSO	04	Falcon 900EX EASY	144	Shell Aircraft Ltd. Rotterdam, Holland.	N144EX
❏ VP-BSP	05	Falcon 900EX EASY	151	Shell Aircraft Ltd. Rotterdam, Holland.	F-WWFJ
❏ VP-BST	05	Challenger 604	5620	Springway Ltd. Hamilton.	OE-IVE
❏ VP-BUG	07	CitationJet CJ-3	525B-0160		N5201J
❏ VP-BUS	90	Gulfstream 4	1127	JABJ AG/Urs Schwarzenbach, Farnborough, UK.	VR-BUS
❏ VP-BVG	06	Global Express	9193	MVA Aviation, Farnborough, UK.	C-FEBG
❏ VP-BVS	06	Embraer Legacy 600	14500979	International Jet Club Ltd. Luton, UK.	PT-SHQ
❏ VP-BWB	04	Global 5000	9161	Westbury Jet Ltd. Naples, Fl. USA.	(N944AM)
❏ VP-BWR	99	BBJ-79T	29317	USAL Ltd. Stansted, UK.	N1787B
❏ VP-BYA	01	BBJ-7AN	29972	Saudi Oger Ltd. Riyadh, Saudi Arabia.	N1786B
❏ VP-BYY	99	Global Express	9030	Executive Jets Ltd/Mideast Jet, Jeddah, Saudi Arabia.	C-GFAD
❏ VP-BZL	01	BBJ2-8DV	32915	LOWA London-Washington Ltd. Boston, Ma. USA.	D-ABZL

VP-C = CAYMAN ISLANDS
Total 115

Civil

Reg	Yr	Type	c/n	Owner/Operator	Prev Regn
❏ VP-CAB	91	Falcon 900B	101	ASW Airservice Werkflugdienst GmbH. Hamburg, Germany.	D-ALME
❏ VP-CAD	98	CitationJet	525-0297	Reynard Motor Sport, Bremen, Germany.	N316MJ
❏ VP-CAE	05	Gulfstream G450	4031	FTC/Crocus Group, Moscow, Russia.	N1JK
❏ VP-CAF	94	Hawker 800	258267	WAF United,	I-SIRF
❏ VP-CAI	99	Citation Excel	560-5048	Chester Holding Ltd. Georgetown.	N548XL
❏ VP-CAM	06	Falcon 2000EX EASY	89	Delta Technical Services Ltd/Allianz AG. Munich, Germany.	F-WWGZ
❏ VP-CAN	03	Airbus A319-112	1886	National Air Services, Jeddah, Saudi Arabia.	C-GKOC
❏ VP-CAO	06	Challenger 300	20100	Gutmen Investment Corp. Brazil.	(N928MC)
❏ VP-CAP	99	Challenger 604	5415	Thunder Air Ltd. Reykjavik, Iceland.	N318FX
❏ VP-CAR	86	Citation III	650-0135	Wheels Aviation Industries Ltd.	N135AF
❏ VP-CAS	93	Falcon 2000	1	Layan International Trading Ltd. Jeddah, Saudi Arabia.	F-GMOE
❏ VP-CAT	81	Citation 1/SP	501-0232	Tubetime Ltd. Biggin Hill, UK.	VR-CAT
❏ VP-CAU	06	Global 5000	9231		C-FJOK

The Registry of Aruba
International Air Safety Office, Inc.

The Aircraft Registry of Choice

8750 NW 36 St, Suite #210 • Miami, Florida 33178 • Tel: +1.305.471.9889 • Fax: +1.305.471.8122 • admin@airsafetyfirst.com • www.airsafetyfirst.com

Ministry of Transport & Tourism

DEPARTMENT OF CIVIL AVIATION
SABANA BERDE 73-B
ORANJESTAD, ARUBA

ARE YOU CONSIDERING REGISTERING YOUR AIRCRAFT IN A CREDIBLE **CATEGORY 1** ASSESSED COUNTRY, FOR POLITICAL FISCAL, ECONOMIC, COMMERCIAL OR ANY OTHER REASON?

Worldwide Private Aircraft Owners and Operators, Commercial Jet and Regional Airlines, International Leasing Companies, Banks, Financial Groups, value our services for high safety oversight standards, superior customer service, efficiency, cost containment, financial benefits, premier tax advantages, reliability, maintenance conformity, regulations compliance to **EASA & FAA** standards, quickness and much more... **Call us today.**

For more information and a Brochure, please contact:

International Air Safety Office
8750 NW 36th Street, Suite 210
Miami, Florida 33178 USA
Tel: +1305- 471-9889
Fax: +1305- 471-8122 or 8561
E-mail: admin@airsafetyfirst.com
Website: www.airsafetyfirst.com

ONE STEP FOR SAFETY, QUALITY AND DEPENDABILITY

Aruba Registry welcomes all Aircraft Owners and Operators, because we have the know how and the know who!

Member of

NBAA   ISTAT   EBAA

P4-BAK   Falcon 50   photo: Barry Ambrose BIZAV

P4-LJG   Citation X   photo: Barry Ambrose BIZAV

P4-BOB   BAe 125/800B   photo: Jean-Luc Altherr

Reg	Yr	Type	c/n	Owner/Operator	Prev Regn
VP-CAZ	07	390 Premier 1A	RB-202	Global Jet Luxembourg SA. Luxembourg.	N202BP
VP-CBA	81	B 737-2W8	22628	Casbah AG.	VP-CSA
VP-CBB	01	BBJ2-8AW	32806	Bosco Aviation Ltd. Riyadh, Saudi Arabia. 'Al Halkiah'	N757BC
VP-CBC	05	Falcon 2000EX EASY	61	TAG Aviation Charter UK Ltd. Farnborough.	LX-NLK
VP-CBF	00	Falcon 50EX	311	Global Jet Luxembourg, Luxembourg.	N507AS
VP-CBN	07	Airbus A319-115XCJ	3243	Airbus Industrie, Hamburg, Germany.	D-AVWD
VP-CBS	89	Challenger 601-3A	5044	Aprilia Holdings Inc. Tel Aviv, Israel.	VP-CMC
VP-CBX	97	Gulfstream V	511	Tag Aviation Charter UK Ltd. Farnborough, UK.	N511GA
VP-CCC	06	Airbus A340-642X	779	National Air Services, Jeddah, Saudi Arabia.	F-WWCS
VP-CCH	87	BAe 125/800A	NA0404	Jetclub AG. Zurich, Switzerland.	N494AT
VP-CCJ	05	Airbus A319-133XCJ	2421	AL SALAM 319 Ltd.	
VP-CCL	84	Falcon 200	482	SHK Jeans Co. Braunschweig, Germany.	(N94TJ)
VP-CCP	00	Challenger 604	5449	Cleavant Participation Corp. Moscow-Vnukovo, Russia.	N604JR
VP-CCR	90	Challenger 601-3A	5079	Shoreditch Investments Ltd. Jeddah, Saudi Arabia.	VR-CCR
VP-CDF	07	Global Express	9093	Spirit of Spices/Fuchs Gewurze GmbH. Paderborn.	C-GZVZ
VP-CDH	07	Embraer Legacy 600	14501026	Baltic Jet Air Co Ltd. Moscow, Russia.	PT-SZA
VP-CDV	06	Challenger 300	20140	Arven Ltd.	C-FLEC
VP-CEB	01	Global Express	9083	Silver Arrows SA. Luton, UK.	C-GKLF
VP-CEC	99	BBJ-7AW	30031	JABJ AG/Bugshan Construction Co. Jeddah, Saudi Arabia.	N73715
VP-CED	99	Citation Bravo	550-0870	Iceland Frozen Foods plc. Manchester, UK.	N50612
VP-CEO	02	Challenger 604	5539	Spring Air Ltd. Farnborough, UK.	VP-BDY
VP-CES	01	Gulfstream V	669	Ebony Shine International Ltd/JABJ AG. Zurich.	N1UB
VP-CFA	02	Embraer Legacy 600	145637	Alfal/Sheikh Fahad Al Athel, Riyadh, Saudi Arabia.	PT-SAP
VP-CFD	05	Challenger 604	5616	TAG Aviation Charter UK Ltd. Farnborough, UK.	C-FEXH
VP-CFF	95	Gulfstream 4SP	1265	Meral Holdings Ltd/International Jet Club, Farnborough, UK.	N540W
VP-CFL	96	Falcon 900B	164	Proair Charter Transport GmbH. Frankfurt, Germany.	F-WQBM
VP-CFP	05	Citation Sovereign	680-0039	Weber Management GmbH. Stuttgart, Germany.	N680SB
VP-CFR	03	Falcon 900EX EASY	134	Norilsk Nickel, Moscow.	VP-CEZ
VP-CFS	02	Hawker 800XP	258582	Fountain Air/Avijet, Farnborough, UK.	XA-JMS
VP-CFT	90	Challenger 601-3A	5067	Meral Holdings Ltd. Farnborough, UK.	HB-IUF
VP-CFW	07	390 Premier 1A	RB-189	AvCorp Holdings Inc. Wilmington, De. (trustor ?).	N7189J
VP-CFZ	05	Citation X	750-0251	Flying Services NV. Antwerp, Belgium.	N251CX
VP-CGA	99	Falcon 2000	100	Volkswagenwerke AG. Braunschweig, Germany.	F-WWVT
VP-CGB	94	Falcon 900B	145	Volkswagenwerke AG. Braunschweig, Germany.	VR-CGB
VP-CGC	99	Falcon 2000	107	Volkswagenwerke AG. Braunschweig, Germany.	F-WWVB
VP-CGN	06	Gulfstream G550	5149	TAG Aviation Charter UK Ltd. Farnborough, UK.	N649GA
VP-CGO	05	Global Express	9171	Anggarda Paramita, Jakarta, Indonesia.	C-FCTE
VP-CGS	01	Global Express	9102	Jet Aviation Business Jets AG. Zurich, Switzerland.	HB-IGS
VP-CHA	07	Falcon 900DX	614	Twin Rivers Capital Corp.	F-WWFS
VP-CHK	79	B 737-2S9	21957	Executive Air Transport AG. Zurich, Switzerland.	PK-HHS
VP-CHP	05	Embraer Legacy 600	14500802	JABJ AG. Zurich. Switzerland.	HB-JEO
VP-CHU	01	Challenger 604	5510	Avijet, Farnborough, UK.	N610SA
VP-CIC	87	Challenger 601-3A	5011	TAG Aviation Inc. Stansted, UK.	VR-CIC
VP-CIE	01	Airbus A319-133XCJ	1589	Wadi Aviation/Bugshan Construction Co. Jeddah, Saudi Arabia.	D-AVYF
VP-CIP	04	Gulfstream G550	5048	TAG Aviation SA. Geneva, Switzerland.	VP-CIF
VP-CIT	06	Falcon 900DX	610	Corporate Jet Ltd. Beirut, Lebanon.	F-WWFI
VP-CJA	96	Falcon 2000	18	Concoff Trading Corp.	EI-LJR
VP-CJI	04	CitationJet CJ-1	525-0526	LC Corp.	SP-KCL
VP-CJN	70	B 727-76	20371	Starling Aviation (Cayman) Ltd. Grand Cayman.	5X-AMM
VP-CKA	71	B 727-82	20489	SAMCO Aviation, Riyadh, Saudi Arabia.	VR-CKA
VP-CKN	02	Hawker 800XP	258615	Westdeutsche Gipswerke Baldwin & Nikolaus Knauf, Nuremberg	N61515
VP-CKR	04	Challenger 604	5597	JABJ AG. Zurich, Switzerland.	N597JA
VP-CKS	07	Airbus A318 Elite	3238	National Air Services, Jeddah, Saudi Arabia.	D-AUAJ
VP-CLA	99	Gulfstream 4SP	1402	International Jet Club Ltd. Farnborough, UK.	N602PL
VP-CLB	98	Falcon 900EX	34	Volkswagenwerke AG. Braunschweig, Germany.	F-WWF.
VP-CLI	07	Embraer Legacy 600	14501003	Execujet Europe GmbH. Zurich. Switzerland.	HB-JGZ
VP-CLM	66	BAC 1-11/401AK	072	Aeroleasing SA. Grand Cayman. (status ?).	N119DA
VP-CLO	01	Falcon 900EX	90	LUKOIL-Avia Inc. Moscow, Russia.	F-WWFG
VP-CLR	06	BBJ-7EB	34865	FTC/LUKOIL-Avia Inc. Moscow, Russia.	N786BA
VP-CLT	75	Learjet 35	35-016	Lion Tropical Wings, Grand Cayman.	N18CV
VP-CLU	79	HS 125/700A	NA0245	LUKOIL-Avia Inc. Moscow, Russia.	N81QV
VP-CLV	05	Challenger 300	20041	Interdean London/Interdean AG. Munich, Germany.	N141LJ
VP-CLX	80	HS 125/700B	257091	LUKOIL-Avia Inc. Moscow, Russia.	G-OCAA
VP-CMA	07	Hawker 850XP	258835	Mundra Aviation Ltd/Adani Group P/L. India.	N7235R
VP-CMB	05	Challenger 604	5618	Baltic Jet Ltd. Riga, Latvia.	C-FEYZ
VP-CMD	06	Falcon 2000EX EASY	82	FIA, Cannes/Easy Aviation Ltd. Farnborough, UK.	F-WWGS

Reg	Yr	Type	c/n	Owner/Operator	Prev Regn
☐ VP-CME		B 767-231	22567	Dursh Ltd.	(N515DL)
☐ VP-CMG	07	Gulfstream G450	4093	Walkers SPV Ltd/MAG II Aviation Inc. Georgetown.	N393GA
☐ VP-CMH	07	Citation Sovereign	680-0171	Herrenknecht AG. Schwanau, Germany.	(D-CLLS)
☐ VP-CMI	07	Falcon 2000EX EASY	113	Mascair Ltd. Jeddah, Saudi Arabia.	F-WWMJ
☐ VP-CMN	67	B 727-46	19282	IDG (Cayman) Ltd.	VR-CMN
☐ VP-CMP	84	HS 125/700B	257214	Costair Ltd/Viamax, Athens, Greece.	P4-CMP
☐ VP-CMR	90	Gulfstream 4	1117	Fitzwilton plc. Dublin, Ireland.	N105BH
☐ VP-CMS	05	Airbus A320-232	2403	Saad Air (320) Ltd/National Air Services, Jeddah.	(ZK-OJJ)
☐ VP-CNI	89	MD-87	49767	MGM Mirage Inc. Las Vegas, Nv. USA.	N721MM
☐ VP-CNJ	07	Embraer Legacy 600	14501025	International Jet Club Ltd. Farnborough, UK.	PT-SVZ
☐ VP-CNK	05	Challenger 604	5621	Twinjet Aircraft Sales Ltd. Luton, UK.	C-FFHX
☐ VP-CNR	06	Gulfstream G550	5113	Saudi Oger Ltd/Eiger Jet Ltd. Riyadh, Saudi Arabia.	N833GA
☐ VP-CNZ	00	Falcon 900EX	74	NewJetCo (Europe) Ltd. Douglas, IOM.	(G-HNJC)
☐ VP-COD	06	Hawker 850XP	258816	Iceland Frozen Foods plc. Hawarden, UK.	(N850ZH)
☐ VP-COK	78	HS 125/700A	257028	Joli Ltd. Moscow, Russia.	N899DM
☐ VP-COM	76	Citation	500-0318	Rapid 3864 Ltd/Colin McGill, Biggin Hill, UK.	VR-COM
☐ VP-COP	02	Challenger 604	5552	Avijet, Farnborough, UK.	N552TS
☐ VP-CPH	98	Beechjet 400A	RK-188	Pelican Securities Ltd.	N2298W
☐ VP-CPT	91	BAe 1000B	259004	Remo Investments, Biggin Hill, UK.	VR-CPT
☐ VP-CRB	97	Learjet 60	60-125	Lisanne Ltd. Guernsey, Channel Islands. 'La Petite Souris'	N60LR
☐ VP-CRC	06	Global Express	9196	Hamlin Jet, Luton.	C-FEBQ
☐ VP-CRF	81	Falcon 50	61	Ocean Waves Ltd/Aircraft Portfolio Management Ltd. Amman.	HB-IES
☐ VP-CRR	93	Challenger 601-3A	5129	Baltic Jet Ltd. Riga, Latvia.	N129TF
☐ VP-CSF	99	Gulfstream 4SP	1390	Mohammed Fakhry/MSF Aviation, Luton, UK.	N1874M
☐ VP-CSK	05	BBJ2-8GG/W	34620	Nola Ltd.	N852AK
☐ VP-CSN	97	Citation V Ultra	560-0401	Scottish & Newcastle Breweries plc. Edinburgh, Scotland.	N401CV
☐ VP-CSP	91	BAe 125/800B	258210	Springline, Moscow-Vnukovo, Russia.	HB-VMI
☐ VP-CUP	02	Embraer Legacy 600	145555	Reatex Invest SA. Moscow, Russia.	HB-JEA
☐ VP-CVI	05	Gulfstream G550	5092	JABJ/SAP AG Systems, Frankfurt, Germany.	N592GA
☐ VP-CVP	00	Beechjet 400A	RK-300	Sky Jet Flugservice GmbH. Baden-Baden, Germany.	N4001M
☐ VP-CVT	05	Gulfstream G550	5102	Jet Aviation Hong Kong, Lantau, Hong Kong.	(B-HVT)
☐ VP-CVX	00	Airbus A319-133XCJ	1212	Volkswagenwerke AG. Braunschweig, Germany.	(D-AIKA)
☐ VP-CWW	03	390 Premier 1	RB-74	Weber Management GmbH. Stuttgart, Germany.	(N9011P)
☐ VP-CXP	05	Hawker 800XPi	258728	Scottish & Newcastle Breweries plc. Edinburgh, Scotland.	N110DD
☐ VP-CZY	79	B 727-2P1/W	21595	Dunview Ltd-Zarki Yamani/JABJ AG. Zurich, Switzerland.	N727MJ
☐ VR-CKO	68	DC 9-15	47151	K A K Aviation Ltd. Malaga, Spain. (status ?).	VR-CKE

VT = INDIA Total 81

Civil

Reg	Yr	Type	c/n	Owner/Operator	Prev Regn
☐ VT-...	06	Falcon 900EX EASY	177	Reliance Transport & Travel Ltd. Mumbai.	F-WQBM
☐ VT-...	07	390 Premier 1A	RB-219		N34859
☐ VT-...	07	CitationJet CJ2+	525A-0373		N41174
☐ VT-AAA	82	HS 125/700A	NA0323	Reliance Transport & Travel Ltd. Mumbai.	N2830
☐ VT-AAT	05	Falcon 2000	225	Reliance Transport & Travel Ltd. Mumbai.	F-WWVM
☐ VT-AMA	88	Gulfstream 4	1060	Reliance Transport & Travel Ltd. Mumbai.	N1SF
☐ VT-ANF	05	390 Premier 1	RB-128	M/S Force Motors Ltd.	N6128Y
☐ VT-ARA	00	Citation Excel	560-5115	Uflex Ltd/AR Airways P/L. New Delhi.	N20WE
☐ VT-ARV	04	Gulfstream G200	098	Futura Travels Ltd. Mumbai.	ZS-PKD
☐ VT-BAV	01	Gulfstream G100	143	Aditya Birla Technologies, Mumbai.	N261GA
☐ VT-BSF	05	Embraer Legacy 600	14500901	Border Security Force, New Delhi.	PT-SIX
☐ VT-CLA	98	Citation Excel	560-5010	M/S Air Airways P/L. New Delhi.	N27XL
☐ VT-CLB	90	Citation II	550-0661	Club One Air/AR Airways Pte Ltd.	N550AR
☐ VT-CLC	92	Citation II	550-0698	AR Airways Pte Ltd. New Delhi.	N550RM
☐ VT-CLD	93	Citation II	550-0727	AR Airways Pte Ltd. New Delhi.	N550KR
☐ VT-COT	96	Falcon 2000	36	Tata Steel Ltd. New Delhi.	F-GNBL
☐ VT-CSP	04	Citation Excel	560-5368	Poonawalla Group, Pune.	N12686
☐ VT-DHA	01	Global Express	9111	Reliance Transport & Travel Ltd. Mumbai.	C-GJTK
☐ VT-DLF	93	Gulfstream 4SP	1231	DLF Universal Ltd. New Delhi.	N255TS
☐ VT-DOV	04	CitationJet CJ-2	525A-0222	Dove Airlines P/L. Calcutta.	N778MA
☐ VT-EHS	82	Learjet 29	29-003	Aviation Research Centre/Government of India Agency, Delhi.	N289CA
☐ VT-EIH	84	Learjet 29	29-004	Aviation Research Centre/Government of India Agency, Delhi.	N294CA
☐ VT-EQZ	67	HS 125/3B	25133	Flytech Aviation Ltd.	G-ILLS
☐ VT-ETG	86	Citation S/II	S550-0089	Rusi H Modi/Tata Engineering Services Ltd. Calcutta.	VT-RHM
☐ VT-EUX	95	Citation V Ultra	560-0299	State Government of Tamil Nadu, Madras.	N5168F
☐ VT-FAF	05	Hawker 800XPi	258745	Hero Group/Forum 1 Aviation P/L. New Delhi.	N745XP
☐ VT-HGL	06	Falcon 2000	231	Hinduja Group Ltd/Ashok Leyland Ltd. Chennai.	F-WWVS
☐ VT-IAH	06	Airbus A319-115XCJ	2837	Reliance Transport & Travel Ltd. Mumbai.	D-AIMM

Reg	Yr	Type	c/n	Owner/Operator	Prev Regn
☐ VT-IBR	99	Challenger 604	5425	Airmid Aviation Services P/L. New Delhi.	N604PC
☐ VT-IPA	91	Citation VI	650-0203	Universal Airways P/L. New Delhi.	N350MQ
☐ VT-ISH	06	Falcon 900EX EASY	166	Reliance Transport & Travel Ltd. Mumbai.	F-WWFM
☐ VT-JHP	06	Hawker 850XP	258794	Jaiprakash Associates Ltd. New Delhi.	N71794
☐ VT-JSK	06	Global 5000	9214	Reliance Transport & Travel Ltd. Mumbai.	N93ZZ
☐ VT-JSP	04	CitationJet CJ-2	525A-0207	Jindal Group, New Delhi.	N1267B
☐ VT-JSS	05	Citation Excel XLS	560-5594	JSW Steel Ltd. New Delhi.	(VT-XLS)
☐ VT-KAV	98	Challenger 604	5370	Sun TV Network Ltd. Tamil Nadu.	N755RV
☐ VT-KMB	87	Citation S/II	S550-0135	AR Airways Pte Ltd. New Delhi.	N2235
☐ VT-KNB	06	Hawker 850XP	258815	Span Air P/L. New Delhi.	N74155
☐ VT-MST	99	Gulfstream 4SP	1379	Asia Aviation Ltd. New Delhi.	N60PT
☐ VT-NAB	06	CitationJet CJ1+	525-0619	MSPL Ltd. Karnataka.	N1317Y
☐ VT-NGS	96	Challenger 604	5314	Raymond Ltd. Mumbai.	N604CT
☐ VT-NID	07	CitationJet CJ2+	525A-0378		N41184
☐ VT-NJB	03	CitationJet CJ-2	525A-0163	Hindalco Industries Ltd. Mumbai.	ZS-CJT
☐ VT-OBE	84	HS 125/700B	257215	Shaw Wallace & Co. Calcutta.	VH-HSP
☐ VT-OBR	07	Hawker 850XP	258838	EIH Ltd. Delhi.	N71938
☐ VT-OPJ	95	CitationJet	525-0112	Jindal Group, Mumbai.	N1006F
☐ VT-PLL	94	Gulfstream 4SP	1254	M S Indopacific Aviation/Punj Llyod Ltd. New Delhi.	N920TB
☐ VT-RAL	01	390 Premier 1	RB-23	Ran Air Services Ltd. New Delhi.	N488RC
☐ VT-RAN	00	Hawker 800XP	258521	RAN Air Services Ltd. New Delhi.	N58521
☐ VT-RBK	05	Hawker 800XP	258716	Bajaj Auto Ltd. New Delhi.	N716XP
☐ VT-RPG	98	Beechjet 400A	RK-190	Spencer Travel Services Ltd. Bangalore.	N325JG
☐ VT-RPL	00	Hawker 800XP	258465	Reliance Transport & Travel Ltd. Mumbai.	ZS-DDT
☐ VT-SBK	01	Falcon 900EX	89	Bharat Forge Co Ltd. Pune.	N802CJ
☐ VT-SGT	92	Citation II	550-0709	Asia Aviation Ltd. New Delhi.	N709RS
☐ VT-SMI	97	Gulfstream V	525	Essar Shipping Ltd. Mumbai.	N40SR
☐ VT-SRS	05	BBJ-7AU	34477	Sahara Group of Companies, New Delhi.	N746BA
☐ VT-TAT	98	Falcon 2000	65	Taj Air Ltd. Mumbai.	(F-OIBA)
☐ VT-TBT	97	Falcon 2000	49	Taj Air Ltd. Mumbai.	F-WQBK
☐ VT-TEL	88	Beechjet 400	RJ-46	Spencer Travel Services Ltd. Bangalore.	N146JB
☐ VT-TVR	06	Hawker 400XP	RK-511	Deccan Chronicle Holdings Ltd. Bangalore.	N511XP
☐ VT-UBG	71	HS 125/F400B	25254	United Breweries Holdings Ltd/UB Ltd. Bangalore. 'Leana'	G-5-624
☐ VT-VED	05	Citation Sovereign	680-0056	Vedanta Alumina Ltd. Mumbai.	N680SV
☐ VT-VJM	06	Airbus A319-133XCJ	2650	Kingfisher Airlines Ltd. Mumbai.	D-AICY
☐ VT-VLM	95	Falcon 2000	8	GMR Industries Ltd. Hyderabad.	F-WQBK
☐ VT-VLN	07	Falcon 2000EX EASY	117	GMR Industries Ltd. Bangalore.	F-WWMO

Military

Reg	Yr	Type	c/n	Owner/Operator	Prev Regn
☐ K....	06	BBJ2-7HI/W	36106	Indian Air Force, Delhi.	N370BJ
☐ K-....	07	BBJ2-7HI/W	36107	Indian Air Force, Delhi.	N719BA
☐ K2412	83	B 737-2A8	23036	Indian Air Force, Delhi.	VT-EHW
☐ K2413	83	B 737-2A8	23037	Indian Air Force, Delhi.	VT-EHX
☐ K2899	68	B 707-337C	19988	Indian Air Force, Delhi.	VT-DXT
☐ K2960	84	Gulfstream SRA-1	420	Indian Air Force, Delhi. (used VT-ENR 1987-2007).	N47449
☐ K2961	86	Gulfstream SRA-1	494	Indian Air Force, Delhi.	N370GA
☐ K2962	86	Gulfstream SRA-1	495	Indian Air Force, Delhi.	N371GA
☐ K3186	71	B 737-2A8	20484	Indian Air Force, Delhi.	VT-EAK
☐ K3187	70	B 737-2A8	20483	Indian Air Force, Delhi.	VT-EAJ
☐ K3601	05	Embraer Legacy 600	14500867	Indian Air Force, Delhi. 'Megadoot'	PT-SIR
☐ K3602	05	Embraer Legacy 600	14500880	Indian Air Force, Delhi. 'Vayudoot'	PT-SIT
☐ K3603	05	Embraer Legacy 600	14500910	Indian Air Force, Delhi.	PT-SIY
☐ K3604	05	Embraer Legacy 600	14500919	Indian Air Force, Delhi.	PT-SON
☐ L3458	00	Astra-1125SPX	126	Indian Air Force R & D,	4X-CVJ
☐ L3467	02	Gulfstream G100	148	Indian Air Force R & D,	4X-CVI

V5 = NAMIBIA   Total   5

Civil

Reg	Yr	Type	c/n	Owner/Operator	Prev Regn
☐ V5-CDM	91	Citation V	560-0151	Consolidated Diamond Mines,	ZS-NDU
☐ V5-NAG	94	Learjet 31A	31A-091	Government of Namibia, Windhoek.	N5019Y
☐ V5-NAM	91	Falcon 900B	103	Government of Namibia, Windhoek.	F-WWFJ
☐ V5-NPC	97	Learjet 31A	31A-138	NamPower, Windhoek.	N138LJ
☐ V5-OGL	73	Citation	500-0080	NCA-Namibia Commercial Aviation P/L. Windhoek.	ZS-NGR

V8 = BRUNEI   Total   3

Civil

Reg	Yr	Type	c/n	Owner/Operator	Prev Regn
☐ V8-ALI	91	B 747-430	26426	Government of Brunei, Bandar Seri Begawan.	(D-ABVM)
☐ V8-BKH	94	Airbus A340-212	046	Government of Brunei, Bandar Seri Begawan.	V8-PJB

☐ V8-MHB	93	B 767-27GER	25537	Government of Brunei, Bandar Seri Begawan.		V8-MJB

XA = MEXICO   Total   614
Civil

☐ XA-...	07	Falcon 7X	10	Aero Personal SA. Toluca.		F-WWUG
☐ XA-...	70	Learjet 24B	24B-213			N24JZ
☐ XA-...	69	HS 125/400A	NA722			(N280CH)
☐ XA-...	78	HS 125/700A	NA0229	VIP Empresarial SA. Monterrey, NL.		N820CT
☐ XA-...	82	Citation II	550-0348			C-GSCX
☐ XA-...	65	Sabre-40	282-41			N240AC
☐ XA-...	81	Learjet 25G	25G-337	AeroJL SA.		N14CK
☐ XA-...	73	HS 125/F600A	256026			N450TB
☐ XA-...	77	Sabre-75A	380-53			N827SL
☐ XA-...	69	Gulfstream 2	43	Aero Fox SA. Toluca.		(N247LG)
☐ XA-...	77	Learjet 25D	25D-216			N77FN
☐ XA-...	73	Learjet 25B	25B-122			N751CA
☐ XA-...	65	HS 125/1A	25053			N25JT
☐ XA-...	77	JetStar 2	5214			N50127
☐ XA-...	66	Falcon 20C	31			N131MV
☐ XA-...	70	HS 125/F403B	25227			N355AC
☐ XA-...	72	Learjet 25B	25B-096			N20NW
☐ XA-...	79	HS 125/700A	NA0241			N84GA
☐ XA-...	81	HS 125/700A	257158	Aries Coil Coatings SA. Cienega de Flores, NL.		N700VT
☐ XA-...	76	Sabre-75A	380-48	PAFCAR Arrendado,		N100BP
☐ XA-...	79	Falcon 10	146	Aero Servicios Regiomontanos SA.		N110GF
☐ XA-...	72	Gulfstream 2B	119	Javia Garcia Sanchez, Mexico City.		N500MA
☐ XA-...	71	JetStar-8	5148			XA-OLI
☐ XA-...	07	CitationJet CJ-3	525B-0192			N5214L
☐ XA-...	80	Citation 1/SP	501-0148	Campestre de la Paz SA.		N148ED
☐ XA-...	70	Gulfstream II SP	91			N914MH
☐ XA-...	68	Gulfstream 2	24	Five Star Airplane Services SA. Naucalpan.		(N800XC)
☐ XA-...	81	Citation II	550-0227			N227DR
☐ XA-...	68	Learjet 25	25-006			N44CP
☐ XA-...	68	Falcon 20C	159			N67AX
☐ XA-...	66	HS 125/731	25075			N600EG
☐ XA-...	88	Gulfstream 4	1081			N797SA
☐ XA-...	68	HS 125/731	NA713			N773AA
☐ XA-...	78	Learjet 36A	36A-043			(N521JW)
☐ XA-...	00	Learjet 45	45-102	Executive Express Aviation SA. Zinacantepec.		N810YS
☐ XA-...	04	Learjet 45	45-256			N97XR
☐ XA-...	62	Sabreliner CT-39A	276-25	Jett Paqueteria SA. San Luis Potosi.		N39RG
☐ XA-...	92	Beechjet 400A	RK-56	Worldwide Aviation Group LLC. Scottsdale, Az.		N56FF
☐ XA-...	98	Citation Bravo	550-0854	Agricola Pony SA. Culiacan, SIN.		N550KJ
☐ XA-...	86	BAe 125/800A	258055			N508MM
☐ XA-...	79	Learjet 25D	25D-282			N711WD
☐ XA-...	60	Sabreliner CT-39A	265-15	Jett Paqueteria SA. San Luis Potosi.		N510TD
☐ XA-...	90	Learjet 31	31-020	Lineas Aereas Comerciales SA. Saltillo, Coahuila.		N337FP
☐ XA-...	90	Citation III	650-0186			N386CW
☐ XA-...	89	BAe 125/800A	258152			N800WG
☐ XA-...	02	Beechjet 400A	RK-352	Transportes Castores de Baja California, Leon, GTO.		N6052U
☐ XA-...	97	Citation V Ultra	560-0433			N88EX
☐ XA-...	95	Hawker 800	258275	GE Capital CEF Mexico SA. Mexico City. (trustor ?).		N7775
☐ XA-...	99	Learjet 31A	31A-179			N133BG
☐ XA-AAA	69	Learjet 24B	24B-208	Aerofreight SA.		N14PT
☐ XA-AAK	84	Citation II	550-0486	Fiesta Inn/Sky Aeronautical Services SA. Puebla La Noria.		(N35PN)
☐ XA-AAW*	67	Sabreliner CT-39E	282-85	Jett Paqueteria SA. San Luis Potosi. (status ?).		N958M
☐ XA-AAY	75	Falcon 10	27	Aerotaxis y Servicios Alfe SA. Tampico.		N38DA
☐ XA-ABA	84	Gulfstream 3	426	Aeromundo Ejecutivo SA. Toluca.		N703JA
☐ XA-ABE	99	Citation Bravo	550-0887	Aero Roca SA. Celaya.		N887BB
☐ XA-ACA	68	Falcon 20D	179	Sirvair SA. Toluca.		(N669JL)
☐ XA-ACD	76	Sabre-80A	380-50	Aero Jets Corporativos SA. Torreon.		XA-TDQ
☐ XA-ACH	92	Citation VI	650-0218	Servicios Aeronauticos del Oriente SA.		XA-MTZ
☐ XA-ACN	74	HS 125/600A	256038	Aero Central SA. Jurica, Quintana Roo.		N199SG
☐ XA-ACX	85	Learjet 25D	25D-373	AITSA-Aerotransportes Internacionales de Torreon SA.		EC-EGY
☐ XA-ADJ	65	Learjet 24	24-060	Aeronaves TSM SA. Saltillo.		N90J
☐ XA-AEI	74	Citation	500-0213	Almaver SA.		(N213CE)
☐ XA-AEJ		Gulfstream G550	...	noted Long Beach 7/06.		
Reg	Yr	Type	c/n	Owner/Operator		Prev Regn

Reg	Yr	Type	c/n	Owner/Operator	Prev Regn
XA-AEX	88	Gulfstream 4	1064	Omni Flys SA. Zapopan, JAL.	N797CM
XA-AFA	01	Beechjet 400A	RK-316	Aero Safin SA.	N3216X
XA-AFG	77	Sabre-60	306-130	Aerolineas Sol SA. Toluca.	XB-JMM
XA-AFH	81	Learjet 25D	25D-332	PRI, Toluca. (status ?).	XB-DZQ
XA-AFP	73	Gulfstream II SP	136	Aeromundo Ejecutivo SA. Toluca.	XA-ABA
XA-AFS	99	Beechjet 400A	RK-259	Aerolineas Ejecutivas SA. Toluca.	N3259Z
XA-AFX	98	Learjet 31A	31A-159	Servicios Aereos Estrella SA. Toluca.	N127BX
XA-AGA	79	Citation 1/SP	501-0095	Puerto Vallarta Taxi Aereo SA. Puerto Vallarta.	N612DS
XA-AGL	70	HS 125/731	NA757	Aeroservicios Sipse SA. Merida, Yucatan.	N900WG
XA-AGN	79	Citation II	550-0077	Antair SA. Toluca.	XA-PIJ
XA-AGT	70	Sabre-60	306-58	Golden Aviation de Mexico SA. Naulcalpan.	N529CF
XA-AHM	75	Gulfstream 2	161	Antair SA/Grupo Acerero del Norte SA. Toluca.	XA-RUS
XA-AIM	00	Learjet 45	45-077	Transportes Aereos de Xalapa SA. Vera Cruz.	N770DS
XA-AJL	73	Learjet 25B	25B-120	Aero J L SA. Toluca.	N120SL
XA-ALA	02	Learjet 45	45-210		N29ZE
XA-ALF	00	Learjet 45	45-127	El Caminante Taxi Aereo SA. Guadalajara, JAL.	N421FY
XA-ALV	73	Learjet 25B	25B-124	Airlink US-MX SA. Guadalajara.	N33TW
XA-AMI	80	HS 125/700A	NA0269	Servicios Privados de Aviacion SA. Toluca.	(N61GF)
XA-AOC	88	Beechjet 400	RJ-36	Corporacion Aerea Cencor SA. Chihuahua.	N52GA
XA-APE	99	Falcon 900B	178	Aero Personal SA. Toluca.	N179FJ
XA-ARB	05	Learjet 45	45-284	Taxi Aereos del Noroeste SA.	N40078
XA-ARQ	97	Learjet 31A	31A-141	GE Capital CEF Mexico SA. Toluca. (trustor ?).	N121PX
XA-ASI	92	Gulfstream 4	1180	Antair SA. Toluca.	N827K
XA-ASP	80	Learjet 25D	25D-315	Aero Servicios Platinum SA.	N315FW
XA-ASR	74	Citation	500-0199	Aero Servicios Regiomontanas SA. Monterrey, NL.	C-FGAT
XA-AST	97	Challenger 604	5357	AeroVena SA.	N604FS
XA-ATC		Hawker	...	noted Austin 11/07.	
XA-ATE	77	Sabre-60	306-123	Aero Transportes Empresariales SA. Toluca.	N97SC
XA-ATL	04	Gulfstream G550	5052	Aerofrisco SA. Toluca.	N952GA
XA-AVE	01	Falcon 2000	175	Aerolineas Ejecutivas SA. Toluca.	N2258
XA-AVV	71	Learjet 25XR	25XR-079	Golden Aviation de Mexico SA. Naulcalpan.	XA-SVG
XA-BAE	00	Citation X	750-0136	Taxi Aereo BAE SA.	N8TU
XA-BAL	98	Gulfstream V	546	Aerovics SA. Toluca.	N646GA
XA-BEB	69	JetStar-731	5132	TAESA. Toluca. 'Ishtar - Goddess of Luck'	XA-PSD
XA-BEG	98	Falcon 900EX	33	Servicios Ejecutivos Continental SA. Tampico.	XA-TMH
XA-BET	75	Citation	500-0296	Aerodinamica de Monterrey SA. Monterrey, NL.	N269BF
XA-BFX	00	Learjet 45	45-111	Executive Express Aviation SA.	N414BX
XA-BLZ		Citation	...	noted Houston 10/05.	
XA-BNG	87	Beechjet 400	RJ-33	Servicios Aereos Gana SA. San Luis Potosi.	XA-JJA
XA-BNO	80	Learjet 35A	35A-336	TAESA-Transportes Aereos Ejecutivos SA. Toulca.	(N336EA)
XA-BRE	95	Learjet 60	60-058	XABRE Aerolineas SA. Toluca.	N92BL
XA-BRG	91	Learjet 31	31-032	Aerolineas Commerciales SA. Morelia.	XA-AAP
XA-BUX	78	Learjet 35A	35A-176	Transportes Aereos Tecnico Ejecutivo SA. Monterrey, NL.	(N67GA)
XA-BVG	87	Gulfstream 4	1013	BVG Viajes SA.	N64AL
XA-BYP		HS 125/700A	...	VIP Empresarial SA.	
XA-CAP	03	Citation Bravo	550-1070	Air Palace SA.	N327CS
XA-CEN	68	Sabre-60	306-26	Aerologic SA. Toluca.	(N377EM)
XA-CGF	05	Learjet 40	45-2040	Aerolineas Ejecutivas SA. Toluca.	(XA-GPE)
XA-CHA	93	Hawker 800XP	258241	Transportes Aereos Sierra Madre SA. Monterrey, NL.	N540BA
XA-CHP	68	Sabre-60	306-22	Aerotrans Privados SA/Seguros Chapultepec SA. (status ?)..	(N450CE)
XA-CMM	07	Falcon 2000EX EASY	121	Aviacion Comercial de America SA. Monterrey, NL.	N121EX
XA-COI	99	Learjet 60	60-174		N242ZX
XA-CON	78	JetStar 2	5228	Servicios Aereos SAAR SA. Veracruz, VER.	N400MR
XA-CPQ	98	Gulfstream V	533	Commander Mexicana SA. Toluca.	N533GA
XA-CVS	75	Gulfstream II SP	167	Aereo Dorado SA. Toluca.	XA-UEC
XA-CYA	90	Learjet 31	31-021	Aeroservicios Corporativos de San Luis SA.	XA-RNK
XA-CYS	66	Sabre-40	282-79		N111AC
XA-CZG	78	Learjet 35A	35A-162	Aerojobeni SA. Toluca.	N222SL
XA-DAN	68	HS 125/3A-RA	25158	Aero Dan SA. Saltillo.	(N702GA)
XA-DCS	66	HS 125/3A	25078	Aero Dan SA. Saltillo.	(N16PJ)
XA-DCX		Learjet 35	...	noted Toluca 1/07.	
XA-DET	76	Learjet 24F	24F-337	AEMSA/Gutsa Construcciones SA.	XA-GEO
XA-DGO	99	Learjet 60	60-172	Corporativo Durango SA. Durango.	N241BX
XA-DIJ	73	Learjet 24D	24D-269	Jet Rent SA. Toluca.	XA-MOV
XA-DRM	03	Citation Excel	560-5307	Transportes Aereos Excel SA.	N.....
XA-DSC	71	Sabre-60	306-56	TAESA-Transportes Aereos Ejecutivos SA. Toluca.	XA-RXP

Reg	Yr	Type	c/n	Owner/Operator	Prev Regn
☐ XA-DUC	72	Falcon 20F	269	Aerolineas Ejecutivas SA. Toluca.	XA-NAY
☐ XA-DUQ	84	Falcon 50	146	Duque Jet SA. Toluca.	N7228K
☐ XA-EAJ	99	Gulfstream V	604	Desarollo Milaz SA/Aero Personal SA. Toluca.	N551GA
☐ XA-EFM	00	Learjet 45	45-089		N406BX
☐ XA-EKT	79	JetStar 2	5234	Aerotaxis Metropolitanos SA. Toluca.	(N234TS)
☐ XA-ELM	86	BAe 125/800A	258051	Aerotransportes Empresariales SA. Toluca.	(N804LX)
☐ XA-EMA	72	HS 125/731	NA775	Servicios Privados de Aviacion SA. Toluca.	N333DP
☐ XA-ERH	81	Gulfstream 3	323	Sirvair SA. Toluca.	N323G
☐ XA-ESX	70	Sabre-60A	306-47	Grupo Corporativo Cever SA. Toluca.	XA-ZOM
☐ XA-EYA	99	Gulfstream 4SP	1388	Ronso SA. Toluca.	N4SP
☐ XA-FEX	99	Falcon 900EX	46	Execujet Mexico SA. Monterrey, NL.	N946EX
☐ XA-FFF	75	Learjet 35	35-042	Aero Rentas de Coahulia SA. Saltillo.	N270CS
☐ XA-FGS	85	BAe 125/800A	258047	Comercializacion de Aviacion Ejecutiva SA.	N324SA
☐ XA-FLY	02	Learjet 60	60-250	Servicios Integrales de Aviacion SA. Toluca.	N50433
☐ XA-FMK	79	HS 125/700A	NA0249	Juan R Brittingham SA. Monterrey, NL..	XB-FMK
☐ XA-FMR	79	Learjet 25D	25D-274	Aero Copter SA. Toluca.	XA-RZE
☐ XA-FMT	92	Learjet 35A	35A-672	Servicios Aereos Regiomontanos SA. Monterrey, NL.	N45KK
☐ XA-FMX	00	Citation X	750-0119	Servicios Aereos Regiomontanos SA. Monterrey, NL.	N5223X
☐ XA-FNY	77	Gulfstream II SP	211	Naviera Mexicana SA. Toluca.	N7079N
☐ XA-FRD	05	Challenger 300	20078	Aviacion Comercial de America SA. Monterrey, NL.	C-FGCE
☐ XA-FRI	97	Citation VII	650-7081	Frisa Industries SA/Aero Servicios Regiomontanos SA.	N8VX
☐ XA-FUD	05	Citation Sovereign	680-0053	Transportacion Aerea del Norte SA. Monterrey, NL.	N53HS
☐ XA-FVK	80	Falcon 50	35	Aerolineas Ejecutivas SA. Toluca.	N350AF
☐ XA-GAO	02	Beechjet 400A	RK-353	Aerolineas Ejecutivas SA. Toluca.	N353AE
☐ XA-GAP	79	Sabre-65	465-8	Commander Mexicana SA/El Heraldo de Mexico SA. Toluca.	N10581
☐ XA-GBM	94	Citation VI	650-0234	Aero Servicios Regiomontanos SA. Monterrey, NL.	(N735A)
☐ XA-GCD	92	Challenger 601-3A	5121	Viajes Ejecutivos Mexicanos SA. Toluca.	N702PC
☐ XA-GCH	81	Falcon 50	50	Comercial Aerea SA. Chihuahua.	(N247BV)
☐ XA-GDO	81	Learjet 35A	35A-449	Guja SA. Mexico City.	N449QS
☐ XA-GDW	61	Sabreliner CT-39A	265-86	Jett Paqueteria SA. Quetzalcoatl.	XB-GDW
☐ XA-GGG	73	Learjet 25B	25B-147	Aero Rentas de Coahuila SA. Saltillo.	N147BP
☐ XA-GIC	90	BAe 125/800A	NA0451	Viajes Ejecutivos Mexicanos SA. Toluca.	N731JR
☐ XA-GIE	96	Hawker 800XP	258302	Aerolineas Ejecutivas SA. Toluca.	XA-RUY
☐ XA-GLG	02	Hawker 800XP	258583	Servicios Aereos Regiomontanos SA. Monterrey, NL.	N50983
☐ XA-GMD	01	Falcon 900EX	99	Aeromodelo SA/Grup Modelo SA. Toluca.	N890FH
☐ XA-GME	93	Challenger 601-3A	5128	Mexico Transportes Aereos SA. Toluca.	C-FPOX
☐ XA-GMO	03	Citation Sovereign	680-0004	Gof-Air SA.	N5233J
☐ XA-GMX	07	Gulfstream G450	4102		N702GA
☐ XA-GNI	03	Falcon 2000EX	20	Transportes Aereos Mexiquenses SA. Toluca.	N219EX
☐ XA-GPR	05	Challenger 300	20084	Aerolineas Centrales SA.	C-FGCX
☐ XA-GRB	98	Challenger 604	5375	Aerolineas de Tuhuacan SA. Tehuacan, Puebla.	N604HP
☐ XA-GRR	04	Learjet 40	45-2013	Vuelos Corporativos de Tehuacan SA.	N5018G
☐ XA-GTC	69	HS 125/731	NA734	Aeronaves del Nordeste SA.	(N38TS)
☐ XA-GTE	01	Hawker 800XP	258554	Aerolineas Ejecutivas SA. Toluca.	(5B-CKG)
☐ XA-GUA	90	Challenger 601-3A	5076	Apoyo Aereo SA.	N5TM
☐ XA-GUR	76	Sabre-60A	306-122	Servicios Aereos Milenio SA. Toluca.	N56RN
☐ XA-GYA	81	Citation II	550-0251	Coapa Air SA. Toluca.	N20FB
☐ XA-HDL	67	Sabre-60	306-7	Aerovias Ejecutivas SA. Toluca.	XB-HDL
☐ XA-HHF	99	Falcon 2000	85	Aerotaxi Grupo Tampico SA. Tampico.	N344GC
☐ XA-HIT	04	Citation Sovereign	680-0014	Aero Transportes Corporativos SA.	N5270K
☐ XA-HNY	73	JetStar-8	5162	Naviera Mexicana SA. Toluca.	N10JJ
☐ XA-HOM	83	HS 125/700A	NA0340	Aero Homex SA. Culiacan.	N242AL
☐ XA-HVP	84	Citation III	650-0032	Aerotron, Puerto Vallarta, Guadalajara.	N332FW
☐ XA-HXM	80	HS 125/700A	NA0260	Aero Homex SA. Culiacan.	N184TB
☐ XA-ICK	74	Sabre-60	306-86	Servicios Aereos del Centro SA. Toluca.	N60TG
☐ XA-ICO	01	Citation Excel	560-5196	AVEMEX SA/Ingenerios Civiles Associados SA. Toluca.	N51038
☐ XA-IKE	01	Learjet 45	45-176	GE Capital CEF Mexico SA. Mexico City. (trustor ?).	N176TK
☐ XA-ISR	94	Falcon 900B	147	Aeroxtra SA. Toluca.	N147FJ
☐ XA-IZA	89	BAe 125/C-29A	258129	Servicios Privados de Aviacion SA. Toluca.	N8029Z
☐ XA-JAI	82	HS 125/700A	NA0319	Viajes Ejecutivos Mexicanos SA. Toluca.	N319NW
☐ XA-JAM		Hawker 400XP	...	noted Teterboro 9/07.	
☐ XA-JCP	04	Challenger 300	20014	Commander Mexicana SA. Toluca.	N27MX
☐ XA-JCT	02	Hawker 800XP	258581	Servicios Aereos Premier SA.	N581GE
☐ XA-JET	03	Hawker 800XP	258628	Aerolineas Ejecutivas SA. Toluca.	N628XP
☐ XA-JFE	01	Challenger 604	5525	Transporte Ejecutivo Aereo SA. Toluca.	N525E
☐ XA-JHE	03	Gulfstream G200	086	Servicios Ejecutivos Gosa SA.	N286GA

Reg	Yr	Type	c/n	Owner/Operator	Prev Regn
☐ XA-JIQ	75	Learjet 24D	24D-317	Servicios de Alquiler Aereo SA. Toluca.	N45AJ
☐ XA-JJJ	82	Learjet 35A	35A-460	Servicios Aereos del Centro SA. Toluca.	XA-MPS
☐ XA-JJS	89	Gulfstream 4	1113	Aero Lider SA/Arrendadora Banamex SA. Toluca.	N169TT
☐ XA-JMF	01	Learjet 45	45-178	Aerobona SA. Toluca.	N50207
☐ XA-JML	77	Sabre-60	306-125	Organizacion de Transportes Aereos SA. Toluca.	XA-AEV
☐ XA-JOC	80	Learjet 25D	25D-303	Jet Rent SA. Toluca.	
☐ XA-JRF	75	Sabre-80A	380-32	Aerotaxis de Aguascalientes SA. Aguascalientes.	N198GB
☐ XA-JRV	74	Citation	500-0136	Sistemas Aeronauticas 2000 SA. Naucalpan.	N136SA
☐ XA-JSC	74	Learjet 25XR	25XR-173	Aeroejecutivos de Baja California SA. Tijuana, BC.	N104BW
☐ XA-JYC	90	Learjet 31	31-030	Jomar Taxi Aereo SA.	N255DY
☐ XA-JYL	81	Learjet 25D	25D-336	El Caminante Taxi Aereo SA. Guadalajara, JAL.	XA-VYA
☐ XA-JYQ		Learjet		noted Toluca 1/07.	
☐ XA-JZL	94	Challenger 601-3R	5158	Servicios Aeronauticos Zeta SA. Juarez, Chihuahua.	XA-MKI
☐ XA-KCM	05	Learjet 60	60-291	Taxi Aereo de Mexico SA/Kimberly Clark SA. Toluca.	N4003Q
☐ XA-KIM	83	Challenger 601	3015	Taxi Aereo de Mexico SA/Kimberly Clark SA. Toluca.	N374G
☐ XA-KKK	74	Learjet 25B	25B-169	Aerotaxis Dos Mil SA. Toluca.	N59FL
☐ XA-KLZ	05	Learjet 60	60-297	Aero Kaluz SA.	N5012G
☐ XA-KMX	84	Citation III	650-0039	AVEMEX SA/PACCAR Mexico Logistics Inc. Mexicali, BC.	N171L
☐ XA-KOF	65	HS 125/1A	25065	Aerovias del Golfo SA. Veracruz.	N1YE
☐ XA-LDV		HS 125/	...	noted Toluca 9/05.	
☐ XA-LEG	98	Beechjet 400A	RK-171	Corporacion Aerea Cencor SA. Chihuahua.	N287CD
☐ XA-LEY	85	Citation III	650-0073	Aero Transportes de Humaya SA.	N85DA
☐ XA-LFA	05	Falcon 2000EX EASY	77	Transportacion Aerea del Norte SA. Monterrey, NL.	N377EX
☐ XA-LIO	75	Falcon 10	40	Transpais Aereo SA. Monterrey, NL.	N15SJ
☐ XA-LLL	68	Learjet 25	25-015	Rajet Aeroservicios SA. Ramos Arizpe, Coah.	N125U
☐ XA-LMA	74	Sabre-40A	282-137	Alejandro Malenado, Mexico City.	(N666VC)
☐ XA-LMG	04	Hawker 400XP	RK-416	Aerolineas Ejecutivas SA. Toluca.	N900SQ
☐ XA-LML	73	Sabre-40A	282-115	Aerotron, Puerto Vallarta, Guadalajara.	XA-GCH
☐ XA-LMS		Learjet 31	...	noted San Diego 10/07.	
☐ XA-LNK	68	Learjet 24	24-174	Personas y Paqueetees Por Aire SA.	N77GJ
☐ XA-LOF	01	Citation Bravo	550-0989	AeroVirel SA.	N5270E
☐ XA-LOV	72	HS 125/403A	NA776	Desarollo Inmobiliario SA. Monterrey, NL.	XB-GNF
☐ XA-LRJ	82	Learjet 25D	25D-359	Albisa SA.	N116JR
☐ XA-LRL	89	Citation II	550-0619	Transportes Ejecutiva del Golfo SA.	N550BD
☐ XA-MAM	85	Falcon 200	506	International Charter Services SA. Tampico.	N147TA
☐ XA-MAR		HS 125/	...	noted Toluca 3/06.	
☐ XA-MAV	01	Falcon 2000	149	Aviacion Ejecutiva Mexicana SA. Toluca.	N2235
☐ XA-MBM	66	HS 125/731	25101	Grupo Salinas y Rochas SA.	N78AG
☐ XA-MCC	77	Learjet 25XR	25XR-219	Aerotaxis Dos Mil SA. Toluca.	XA-CCC
☐ XA-MDK	02	Gulfstream G200	080	Aerolineas Marcos SA. Toluca.	N380GA
☐ XA-MDM	97	Learjet 60	60-089	Aeroservicios Dinamicos SA. Toluca.	N8089Y
☐ XA-MEG	04	Gulfstream G100	154	Antair SA. Toluca.	N221AL
☐ XA-MEX	04	Hawker 400XP	RK-396	Aerolineas Ejecutivas SA. Toluca.	N31496
☐ XA-MGM	77	Falcon 10	100	Transporte Aereo MGM SA. Guadalajara, JAL.	N100FJ
☐ XA-MIK	65	JetStar-731	5066	TAESA-Transportes Aereos Ejecutivos SA. Toluca. (status ?).	XA-SAE
☐ XA-MJE	66	Sabre-40	282-65	Aerojet Corporativo SA.	XA-GGR
☐ XA-MKI	01	Gulfstream V	664	Servicios Aeronauticos Zeta SA. Juarez, Chihuahua.	(N564QS)
☐ XA-MKY	77	HS 125/600A	256064		N125HF
☐ XA-MMM	75	Falcon 10	36	Aerodiplomatic SA.	N76AF
☐ XA-MMX	06	Citation Excel XLS	560-5639		N5152X
☐ XA-MSA	74	Falcon 20F	327	Aereo Saba SA. Monterrey, NL.	N327BC
☐ XA-MUU	68	Learjet 25	25-008	Global Life Flight, Guadalajara.	N800GG
☐ XA-MVG	04	Learjet 45	45-251	Aceros San Luis SA. San Luis Potosi.	N145XR
☐ XA-MYN	94	Challenger 601-3R	5142	Hoteles Dinamicos SA. Guadalajara, JAL.	N22AQ
☐ XA-NCC	72	Falcon 20F	264	Aerotaxis Dos Mil SA. Toluca.	XA-III
☐ XA-NEM		Hawker	...	Aero Rey SA. Monterrey, NL.	
☐ XA-NGS	98	Global Express	9014	Aero Vitro SA/Aeroempresarial SA. Monterrey, NL.	C-FRGX
☐ XA-NJM	06	Learjet 40	45-2067	Jetpro SA.	(N618FX)
☐ XA-NLA	69	Learjet 24	24-180	Aerolineas Amanecer SA. Toluca.	XA-SBR
☐ XA-NLK	66	Learjet 24	24-109	Aerolineas Amanecer SA. Toluca.	N900DL
☐ XA-NTE	03	Hawker 800XP	258638	Grupo Maseca SA. Toluca.	N638XP
☐ XA-OCU	05	HS 125/	...	noted Houston 10/05.	
☐ XA-OEM	98	Gulfstream V	540	Aerolineas Sol SA. Toluca.	N640GA
☐ XA-OLE	91	Learjet 31A	31A-044	Operadora de Lineas Ejecutivas SA.	XA-MJG
☐ XA-ORA	01	Learjet 60	60-245	AVEMEX SA. Toluca.	N50330
☐ XA-ORO	80	Learjet 35A	35A-290	Aero J L SA. Toluca.	XA-RAV

Reg	Yr	Type	c/n	Owner/Operator	Prev Regn
XA-OVR	02	Global Express	9119	Corporacion Aero Angeles SA. Toluca.	C-GZOW
XA-PAZ	80	Learjet 25D	25D-309	Transportes La PAZ SA. Matehuala.	XB-DKS
XA-PIU	80	Learjet 25D	25D-293	Servicios Aereos Estrella SA. Toluca.	N97JP
XA-PRO	74	Sabre-60	306-72	Transportes Aereos de Xalapa SA. Vera Cruz.	XA-GIH
XA-PRR	01	Falcon 50EX	319	Aerolineas Sol SA. Toluca.	N85DN
XA-PVR	85	Citation III	650-0076	Servicios Aereos Corporativos SA. Puerto Vallarta, JAL.	N424LB
XA-PYN	98	Citation VII	650-7088	Aero Cabo SA.	XA-UGX
XA-QUE	00	Learjet 45	45-067	Aviacion Comercial de America SA. Monterrey, NL.	XA-LRX
XA-RAB	05	Learjet 40	45-2047		N473BD
XA-RAP	74	Sabre-60	306-88	Servicios Privados de Aviacion SA. Toluca.	N22CG
XA-RAR	87	Beechjet 400	RJ-32	Servicios Aereos Interestatales SA. Monterrey, NL.	N31432
XA-RBP	68	Gulfstream II SP	14	Servicios Aereos Noticiosos SA.	XA-RBS
XA-RBS	89	Gulfstream 4	1102	Aerotaxis Metropolitanos SA. Toluca.	N910B
XA-RDD	65	HS 125/1A	25030	Aerotaxis Metropolitanos SA. Toluca.	XA-MBM
XA-RED	65	Sabre-40	282-26	Aereo Centro SA. Quintana Roo.	N300CH
XA-RFB	74	Sabre-60	306-87	Aero Quimmco SA. Monterrey.	N200CE
XA-RFH		Sabre-	...	noted Pontiac 4/05.	
XA-RGB	03	Falcon 900EX EASY	129	GRUMA-Grupo Maseca SA/TATESA, Toluca.	N129EX
XA-RGH	81	Learjet 35A	35A-412	Sistemas Aeronauticos 2000 SA. Toluca.	N314C
XA-RGS	90	Citation III	650-0189	Aero Servicios Regiomontanos SA. Monterrey, NL.	N26174
XA-RHK		Hawker 800XP	...	noted Orlando 10/06.	
XA-RIE	89	Citation III	650-0170	GE Capital Leasing SA. Mexico City. (lessor ?).	(N650BA)
XA-RIZ	72	Westwind-1123	160	Servicios Aereos del Mar SA. Acapulco.	XA-MUI
XA-RLH	73	Sabre-40A	282-129	Aerotaxis Latino Americanos SA. Culiacan. (status ?).	(N99FF)
XA-RLL	74	Sabre-60	306-83	Servindustria Aeronautica SA. Celaya.	N99FF
XA-RLS	70	Sabre-60	306-57	Organizacion de Servicios Ejecutivos Aereos SA. (status ?).	N465JH
XA-RMT	99	Learjet 45	45-046		XB-RMT
XA-ROM		Gulfstream 4	...	noted Los Angeles 3/06.	
XA-RPM		Citation	...	noted Toluca 3/06.	
XA-RPS	66	Sabre-40	282-56	Servicios Aereos de Los Angeles SA. Puebla.	N85DA
XA-RPT	68	HS 125/3A-RA	NA708	AeroDan SA. Saltillo.	N75GN
XA-RRG	06	390 Premier 1A	RB-154	Aerolineas Ejecutivas SA. Toluca.	(G-CJAJ)
XA-RRQ	93	Citation VII	650-7025	Servicios Aereos Regiomontanos SA. Monterrey, NL.	XA-RTS
XA-RSP	66	HS 125/1A	25091	Aerotaxi Monse SA. Morelos. (stored at FXE since 1993).	N65FC
XA-RSR	65	HS 125/1A-522	25017	Aerotaxi Monse SA. Morelos. (stored at FXE since 1993).	N333M
XA-RTS	04	Citation Sovereign	680-0016	Servicios Aereos Textra SA.	(N21FR)
XA-RUY	95	Falcon 50EX	252	Aerolineas Ejecutivas SA. Toluca.	N52FJ
XA-RVT	78	Sabre-60	306-138	Aero Danta SA. Mexico City.	N702JR
XA-RVV	90	Falcon 50	213	Taxi Aereo de Vera Cruz SA. Vera Cruz, JAL.	N295FJ
XA-RYJ	71	Sabre-75	370-5	Servicios Aereos Corporativos SA. Puerto Vallarta.	N250BC
XA-RYM	86	BAe 125/800A	258075	Monterrey Air Taxi SA. Monterrey, NL.	N3GU
XA-RYR	01	Gulfstream 4SP	1417	GE Capital Leasing SA. Mexico City. (lessor ?).	N122RS
XA-RZD	91	Challenger 601-3A	5087	Aerotransportes Privados SA. Toluca.	N601CC
XA-SAD	05	Challenger 604	5630	Grupo Denim SA.	C-FGBD
XA-SAH	78	Sabre-60	306-137	Aviones Ejecutivos JFA SA. Tuxtla Gutierrez Militar.	N18X
XA-SAP	04	Learjet 45	45-246	Potosina Del Aire SA.	N1019K
XA-SAU	78	HS 125/700A	NA0220	Aero Gisa SA/Grupo Industrial Saltillo SA. Saltillo.	N725CC
XA-SBV	75	Sabre-60A	306-109	Aero Rey SA. Monterrey, NL.	N602KB
XA-SCA	81	Learjet 35A	35A-418	SCALA SA.	XA-KCM
XA-SCE	73	Learjet 24D	24D-271	Aerovias Castillo SA. Guadalajara.	N4305U
XA-SDI	01	Citation Bravo	550-0983	Hoteles Dinamicos SA. Guadalajara, JAL.	N51055
XA-SDT	92	Citation V	560-0162	Stars de Mexico SA. Toluca.	N68864
XA-SDU	84	Citation III	650-0052	Servicios Aeronauticos Zeta SA. Juarez, Chihuahua.	N20MW
XA-SEN	79	HS 125/700A	NA0255	Aero Sami SA. Monterrey, NL.	N540B
XA-SFQ	72	HS 125/400A	NA768	Aero Cheyenne SA. Monterrey. (status ?).	N2155P
XA-SIM	91	Falcon 900B	114	Aerolineas Mexicanos JS SA. Toluca.	N474FJ
XA-SJM	77	Sabre-60	306-128	Servicios Aereos Denim SA. Durango.	(N24TK)
XA-SJN	83	Learjet 25D	25D-365	DGO-JET SA. Durango.	N365CM
XA-SJS	71	Learjet 25B	25B-076	SACSA, Toluca.	N77KW
XA-SLB	93	Citation VI	650-0228	Taxis Aereos de Valle de Toluca SA. Toluca.	N228CM
XA-SLP	72	HS 125/600A	256002	Aero Magar SA. Guadalajara.	N602MM
XA-SLR	66	HS 125/3A	25112	Maria del Pilar Oliver Gaya Vd. Toluca.	XB-FFV
XA-SMF	67	Sabre-60A	306-6	Aerotaxi Monse SA. Morelos.	XA-ADC
XA-SMR	66	Sabre-40	282-71	Aerodan SA. Saltillo, Coah. (status ?).	N957CC
XA-SMS	84	Challenger 601	3019	Aero Rey SA. Monterrey, NL.	N875G
XA-SNI	05	Learjet 40	45-2030	Soni Aviones SA.	N40076

Reg	Yr	Type	c/n	Owner/Operator	Prev Regn
☐ XA-SOH	83	Learjet 25D	25D-366		XB-IFW
☐ XA-SOL	01	Challenger 604	5501	Aerolineas Ejecutivas SA. Toluca.	N501AJ
☐ XA-SON	79	HS 125/700A	NA0268	Aero Sami SA. Monterrey, NL.	N501MM
☐ XA-SOR	94	Challenger 601-3R	5147	Aeropycsa SA. Toluca.	C-FRJX
☐ XA-SPM	80	Sabre-65	465-14	Aero Toluca International SA. Toluca.	N25SR
☐ XA-SPQ	93	Citation VII	650-7028	Aero Transportes Corporativos SA.	N728CM
☐ XA-SQA	73	Sabre-40A	282-125	Jett Paqueteria SA. Quetzalcoatl.	XB-NIB
☐ XA-SQV	80	Citation II	550-0198	Servicios Aereos Especializados Mexicanos SA. Del Norte.	XC-DOK
☐ XA-SSS	82	Falcon 50	119	Transportes Aereos Tauro SA	N57DC
☐ XA-SSU	70	Learjet 24D	24D-230	Aero-Jet Express SA/Arrendadora Union SA. Guadalajara.	N32287
☐ XA-SSV	78	Sabre-60	306-140	Golden Aviation de Mexico SA. Naulcalpan.	N26SQ
☐ XA-SVG	75	Sabre-60	306-97	Golden Aviation de Mexico SA. Naulcalpan.	N15DJ
☐ XA-SVX	75	Learjet 35	35-012	Aerotransportes de Toluca SA. (status ?).	N97TJ
☐ XA-TAB	88	Falcon 50	177	Aerovics SA. Toluca.	XA-UCN
☐ XA-TAQ	80	Learjet 25D	25D-305	Aerocentral SA.	XA-TAK
☐ XA-TCA	70	Learjet 24B	24B-224	Servicios Aereos SAAR SA. Veracruz, VER.	(N51GJ)
☐ XA-TCN	78	JetStar 2	5229		N222MF
☐ XA-TDQ	00	Beechjet 400A	RK-281	Aero Jets Corporativos SA. Torreon.	N4081L
☐ XA-TDX	62	Sabreliner CT-39A	276-27	Jett Paqueteria SA. Quetzalcoatl.	XB-GDV
☐ XA-TEI	07	Falcon 900EX EASY	186	Aero Frisco SA. Toluca.	XA-SCO
☐ XA-TEL	97	Falcon 900B	168	TELMEX/Aero Frisco SA. Mexico City.	N167FJ
☐ XA-TFD	60	Sabreliner CT-39A	265-10	Jett Paqueteria SA. San Luis Potosi. (status ?).	N510TA
☐ XA-TGA	77	Sabre-60	306-126	Coapa Air SA. Toluca.	N111F
☐ XA-TGM	92	Learjet 31A	31A-052	Hoteles Dinamicos SA.	N899CS
☐ XA-TGO	62	Sabreliner T-39A	276-6	Jett Paqueteria SA. San Luis Potosi.	N6552R
☐ XA-TGS*		Sabre-	...	noted Fort Lauderdale 11/05.	
☐ XA-THF	67	Jet Commander	109	Millenium Air Servicios Aereos Integrados SA. Guadalajara.	TG-VWA
☐ XA-TIE	83	Learjet 25D	25D-364	Aero Silza SA. Chihuahua.	N25TZ
☐ XA-TIW	62	Sabreliner CT-39A	276-44	Jett Paqueteria SA. San Luis Potosi.	N63811
☐ XA-TIX	62	Sabreliner CT-39A	276-21	Jett Paqueteria SA. San Luis Potosi.	N63611
☐ XA-TIY	60	Sabreliner CT-39A	265-14	Jett Paqueteria SA. Quetzalcoatl.	60-3486
☐ XA-TJY	62	Sabreliner CT-39A	276-39	Jett Paqueteria SA. San Luis Potosi.	N265WB
☐ XA-TJZ	61	Sabreliner CT-39A	265-76	Jett Paqueteria SA. San Luis Potosi.	N4313V
☐ XA-TKW	64	Sabre-40	282-13	Jett Paqueteria SA. San Luis Potosi.	N502RR
☐ XA-TKY	77	Citation 1/SP	501-0029	Aerotaxi Paba SA.	(N45AQ)
☐ XA-TKZ	01	Citation Excel	560-5208	AVEMEX SA. Toluca.	N5109W
☐ XA-TMF	75	Sabre-60	306-100	Hunter's del Valle SA. Monterrey, NL.	XB-LAW
☐ XA-TMX	96	Citation VII	650-7069	Aero Frisco SA. Toluca.	N5117U
☐ XA-TMZ	85	Citation III	650-0068	Servicios Aeronauticos del Oriente SA.	N650AJ
☐ XA-TNY	69	HS 125/731	NA727	Aeroservicio Azteca SA.	N100RH
☐ XA-TPB	89	BAe 125/800A	258176	Aero Sami SA. Monterrey, NL.	N176WA
☐ XA-TPU	79	Sabre-60	306-143	Horizontes Aereos SA.	XA-SUN
☐ XA-TQA	84	Citation II	550-0504	Aerotaxi del Potosi SA. San Luis Potosi.	N72SL
☐ XA-TQR	62	Sabreliner CT-39A	276-4	Jett Paqueteria SA. San Luis Potosi.	N31403
☐ XA-TRE	92	Citation VII	650-7019	AVEMEX SA. Toluca.	XA-TCZ
☐ XA-TRQ	66	Learjet 24	24-112	Aeronaves TSM SA. Saltillo.	N104GA
☐ XA-TSA	01	Learjet 60	60-202	Verataxis SA. Vera Cruz.	N202LJ
☐ XA-TSS	70	Sabre-60	306-63	TAESA-Transportes Aereos Ejecutivos SA. Toluca.	XB-ZNP
☐ XA-TSZ	79	Sabre-75A	380-71	Aero Util SA. Toluca.	N80HK
☐ XA-TTG	01	CitationJet CJ-1	525-0475	Aero Barloz SA. Monterrey, NL.	N475CJ
☐ XA-TTH	67	HS 125/3A-R	25148	Intervuelos Nacionales SA.	(N819P)
☐ XA-TTS	00	Beechjet 400A	RK-302	Aerolineas Ejecutivas SA. Toluca.	N5002G
☐ XA-TTT	69	Learjet 24B	24B-199	Aerotaxis Dos Mil SA. Toluca.	N70TJ
☐ XA-TUD	74	Sabre-75A	380-5	First Sabre SA.	N71460
☐ XA-TUL	89	Learjet 31	31-012	Verataxis SA. Vera Cruz.	XA-RUU
☐ XA-TVH	91	Citation II	550-0668	Aeronautica La Esperanza SA.	(N866VP)
☐ XA-TVI	84	BAe 125/800A	258004	Transportes Aerea del Mar de Cortes SA.	XA-RET
☐ XA-TVK	67	JetStar-731	5098		(N963Y)
☐ XA-TVZ	76	Sabre-60	306-113	Servicios Aeronauticos de Oriente SA.	N113T
☐ XA-TWH	80	Learjet 25D	25D-289	Grupo Desarrollador Mares del Pacifico SA.	N321GE
☐ XA-TWW	01	Beechjet 400A	RK-332	Aerolineas Ejecutivas SA. Toluca.	N5032N
☐ XA-TYD	01	Beechjet 400A	RK-321	Servicios Aereos Interestatales SA. Monterrey, NL.	N379DR
☐ XA-TYH	00	Hawker 800XP	258491	Crelam SA.	N51191
☐ XA-TYK	02	Hawker 800XP	258597	Aerolineas Ejecutivas SA. Toluca.	N597XP
☐ XA-TYW	83	Learjet 25D	25D-361	Personas y Paquetes Por Aire SA. Guadalajara.	N804RH
☐ XA-TYZ	73	Sabre-40A	282-124		N70ES

Reg	Yr	Type	c/n	Owner/Operator	Prev Regn
XA-TZF	01	Challenger 604	5527	Aero Tomza SA.	N554SC
XA-TZI	96	Learjet 60	60-088	Aero Silza SA. Chihuahua.	XA-TZF
XA-UAF	03	Citation Excel	560-5356	AVEMEX SA. Toluca.	N519CS
XA-UAG	01	Learjet 45	45-139	Servicios Aereos Universitarios SA.	N45VL
XA-UAW	03	Hawker 400XP	RK-359	Aerolineas Ejecutivas SA. Toluca.	N61959
XA-UBI	01	Learjet 31A	31A-235	Servicios Aereos Ilsa SA.	N317K
XA-UBK	66	HS 125/1A-522	25107	Aeromedica SA. Toluca.	XA-HFM
XA-UCV	03	Hawker 400XP	RK-375	Aerolineas Ejecutivas SA. Toluca.	N375XP
XA-UDW	99	Falcon 50EX	291	Grupo Chedraui,	XA-GMD
XA-UEA	79	HS 125/700A	257061	Aero Rey SA, Monterrey, NL.	N810GS
XA-UEC		Gulfstream 2	...	noted Newark 6/05.	
XA-UEF	05	Citation Encore	560-0687		N5207V
XA-UEH	85	BAe 125/800A	258044	Aero Servicios Azteca SA. Santa Catarina, NL.	N833JP
XA-UEK	75	Sabre-75A	380-40	Aereo Taxi Paraza SA. Toluca.	XA-UBH
XA-UEQ	78	Sabre-75A	380-58		N8267D
XA-UEV	05	Hawker 400XP	RK-434	Aerolineas Ejecutivas SA. Toluca.	(N464LX)
XA-UEW	90	Challenger 601-3A	5063		N563TS
XA-UEX	65	HS 125/731	25066	MID Taxi Aereo SA.	N372RS
XA-UEY	73	Sabre-40A	282-112	Aereo Taxi Paraza SA. Toluca.	XA-UBG
XA-UFB	06	Learjet 45	45-295	Aereo Transportes Los Angeles de America SA.	N4004Y
XA-UFK	95	Hawker 800XP2	258287	GE Capital CEF Mexico SA. Toluca. (trustor ?).	N801WB
XA-UFQ		Sabre-	...	noted Toluca 1/07.	
XA-UFR	05	Hawker 400XP	RK-452	Aerolineas Ejecutivas SA. Toluca.	N36752
XA-UFS	04	Hawker 400XP	RK-415	Aerolineas Ejecutivas SA. Toluca.	N37115
XA-UGG	88	Citation II	550-0590		N88NM
XA-UGK	82	Learjet 35A	35A-488	Servicios Estatales Aeroportuarias SA. Guadalupe..	N61SJ
XA-UGO	05	Hawker 800XPi	258731	Aerolineas Ejecutivas SA. Toluca.	N37061
XA-UGQ	06	Citation Excel XLS	560-5667		N5192E
XA-UHI		Hawker	...	Aero Ermes SA. Apodaca, NL.	
XA-UHJ	74	Westwind-1124	174	Servicios Aereos Corporativos, Puerto Vallarta, Guadalajara.	XA-PVR
XA-UHQ	07	Citation Excel XLS	560-5709		N5227G
XA-UHT	74	Learjet 24XR	24XR-283	Scala Aviation SA. Toluca.	N24XR
XA-UIC	83	Diamond 1A	A055SA		N600CG
XA-UIS		Citation VI	...	noted Opa Locka 12/07.	
XA-UUU	79	Learjet 25D	25D-276		N188TA
XA-UVA	99	Citation Excel	560-5033	Taxi Aereo Del Norte SA. Monterrey, NL.	N456JW
XA-UVH		Hawker 800	...	noted Houston 8/07.	
XA-VDG	87	Challenger 601-3A	5004	GE Capital CEF Mexico SA. Mexico City. (trustor ?).	N504TS
XA-VEL	69	Sabre-60	306-42	Arrendadora Financiera Dina SA. Merida.	N128JC
XA-VFV	07	Learjet 40	45-2077		N5015U
XA-VGF	86	Citation S/II	S550-0080		N260BS
XA-VIG	97	Learjet 60	60-116	Servicios Aereos Interestatales SA. Monterrey, NL.	N166LJ
XA-VLA	01	Learjet 60	60-217	Aerotaxis y Servicios Alfe SA. Tampico.	N600ML
XA-VMC	73	Learjet 25B	25B-114	Aeroejecutivos de Baja California SA. Tijuana, BC.	N114HC
XA-VMX		Learjet	...	noted Fort Lauderdale 1/06.	
XA-VTO	93	Falcon 900B	129	Aero Vitro SA/Vitro Corporativo SA. Monterrey, NL.	N483FJ
XA-VYC	99	Learjet 45	45-034	El Caminante Taxi Aereo SA. Guadalajara, JAL.	N454LP
XA-WIN	78	Learjet 35A	35A-152	Aero J L SA. Toluca.	XA-RIN
XA-WWW	75	Learjet 25B	25B-193	Universal Jet Rental de Mexico SA.	N125TN
XA-XGX	90	Citation III	650-0198	Aeroservicios de Nuevo Leon SA.	N650BC
XA-YSM	69	HS 125/400A	NA737	Salvador Gaxiola Espinoza, Gudalajara, JAL.	N400KD
XA-YUR	83	Falcon 20F	475	Servicios Aereos Milenio SA. Toluca.	N475EZ
XA-YYY	79	Learjet 25D	25D-263	Rajet Aeroservicios SA. Ramos Arizpe, Coah.	N825D
XA-ZAP	77	Learjet 35A	35A-129	Aerolineas Ejecutivas SA. Toluca.	N229X
XA-ZTA	98	Learjet 60	60-134	Servicios Aeronauticos Zeta SA. Juarez, Chihuahua.	N134LJ
XA-ZTH	89	Learjet 31	31-004	Servicios Especiales del Pacifico Jalisco, Silao	
XA-ZYZ	93	Learjet 31A	31A-073	Transportes Aereos Pegaso SA. Toluca.	N46UF
XA-ZZZ	81	Learjet 25D	25D-346	Aero Rentas de Coahuila SA. Saltillo.	N71AX
XB-ADR	66	Learjet 24	24-103	Aeronaves TSM SA. Saltillo.	N105EC
XB-ADZ	73	HS 125/600A	256018	Aero Continental SA.	XA-TNX
XB-AGV	82	Citation II	550-0430	Arrendadora y Commercial Industrial del Golfo SA.	N56FT
XB-AJS	76	Sabre-60	306-110	Alfonso Celis Romero, Tehuacan, Puebla.	XB-HJS
XB-AMO	74	Citation	500-0152	Ricardo Garza Laguera,	N2782D
XB-AYJ		Sabre-	...	impounded Panama City 12/01-3/05.	
XB-AZD	77	Learjet 25D	25D-224	Grupo Discovery/GDD Cancun SA.	XB-OZA
XB-BON	90	Citation II	550-0654	Agricola BON S de R de CV. (now XC-BON ?).	XA-RZB

Reg	Yr	Type	c/n	Owner/Operator	Prev Regn
☐ XB-CSI	76	Citation	500-0345	Aeronaves del Nordeste SA.	XA-TOF
☐ XB-DBS	73	JetStar-8	5159	Sindicato Petrolero Mexicano SA. Mexico City. (status ?).	N520M
☐ XB-DGA	99	CitationJet	525-0329	Pablo Villareal Guajardo,	XA-DGP
☐ XB-DVF	81	Citation	500-0408	Manuel Ramon Saldana Garza,	XA-LUD
☐ XB-DZD	77	Learjet 24F	24F-349	Impulsora Azucarera del Noroes, Culiacan.	XA-CAP
☐ XB-DZR	73	Learjet 24D	24D-273	Sindicato Nacional de Trabaja Education, Toluca.	XC-DOP
☐ XB-EEP	85	Citation S/II	S550-0070	Marca-Tel International SA. Monterrey, NL.	N570RC
☐ XB-ESG	76	Citation Eagle	500-0292	Medicina y Movimiento SA.	N333JH
☐ XB-ESS	73	Sabre-40A	282-123	Cafe Descafeinado de Chis. Cordoba.	XA-APD
☐ XB-ETV	75	Sabre-60	306-96	Aceros San Luis SA. San Luis Potosi.	N315JM
☐ XB-FKT	90	Learjet 31	31-029	Zeferino Romero Bringas, Tehuacan.	N9173L
☐ XB-GBF	75	Citation	500-0273	Jaime M Benavides Pompa, Monterrey, NL.	XA-RUR
☐ XB-GCC	93	BAe 125/800A	258252	Cementos de Chihuahua SA. Chihuahua.	N938H
☐ XB-GCP	81	Learjet 25D	25D-325	Grupo Constructor Plata SA.	XB-HGE
☐ XB-GDJ	81	Citation	500-0412	Constructora y Pavimentadora SA. Leon, Guanjuato.	XA-LUV
☐ XB-GLZ	81	Citation II	550-0303	Lineas de Producciones SA y Perforadora Central SA. Toluca.	N450CC
☐ XB-GSP	77	Sabre-75A	380-55	Treviso Ballesteros Lillia, Del Norte, NL.	XB-RDB
☐ XB-HRA	67	Falcon 20C	127	Transpais Aereo SA. Monterrey, NL.	XB-GCR
☐ XB-IHB	66	Sabre-40	282-63	Aviones de Sonora SA. Hermosillo.	XA-AFW
☐ XB-IKS	72	Citation	500-0010		XC-DGA
☐ XB-IKY	90	Citation II	550-0642	Antonio Velazquez Cruz,	XA-SEX
☐ XB-ILD		HS 125/400	...		
☐ XB-INI	96	Beechjet 400A	RK-126	Servicios Aereos de Chihuahua SA.	N197SD
☐ XB-IPX	69	HS 125/731	NA719	Moises Cherem Smeke,	N545S
☐ XB-IRH	76	Learjet 24D	24D-308	Jose Fernandez,	N89AA
☐ XB-IRZ		HS 125/	...	noted Las Vegas 3/06.	
☐ XB-IUW	74	Citation	500-0198		XB-IJW
☐ XB-IVR		Learjet	...	noted Las Vegas 7/05.	
☐ XB-IWL	81	Learjet 35A	35A-379	Todo Para La Aeronautica SA. Jalsico.	N217RT
☐ XB-IXE	76	Citation	500-0328	Constructora Textor SA.	N168AS
☐ XB-IXJ	74	Sabre-60	306-93		XA-JCE
☐ XB-IXT	84	Citation 1/SP	501-0685		N501EG
☐ XB-IYS		Sabre-	...	noted Monterrey 3/06.	
☐ XB-IZK	83	Citation II	550-0473	Aviones Regios SA. General Escobedo, Monterrey, NL.	N70224
☐ XB-JCG	98	Learjet 60	60-131	Javier Canedo Gonzalez,	XA-JJS
☐ XB-JDG	79	Citation	500-0110		N172MA
☐ XB-JFV	79	Citation	500-0395	Transportes Internacionales Tamaulipecos SA.	XA-JEX
☐ XB-JGI	66	Sabre-40	282-80	Francisco Torres Nieto,	XA-FTN
☐ XB-JHD	91	Citation V	560-0127	Miguel Carlos Barragan Villareal,	N127VP
☐ XB-JHV	79	Learjet 29	29-002		XC-HIE
☐ XB-JJS	84	Learjet 25D	25D-369	Fabrica de Sulfato el Aguila SA.	N369D
☐ XB-JKB		Sabre-	...	noted Toluca 12/05.	
☐ XB-JKG	68	HS 125/3A-RA	NA706	Aerolineas Inter SA.	XA-ADR
☐ XB-JKK	81	Learjet 25D	25D-334		N23W
☐ XB-JKV	72	Sabre-40A	282-102		XA-PIH
☐ XB-JLP		Gulfstream 2	...	noted Honduras 3/06.	
☐ XB-JLU	81	Learjet 25D	25D-328	Arrendadora y Comercial Immobiliaria de Sol SA.	N518JG
☐ XB-JLY	68	HS 125/3A-RA	NA703	Aeronautica Condor SA. Toluca.	XA-AEE
☐ XB-JMR	68	Sabre-60	306-35	Cia J M Romo SA. Aguascalientes.	N3456B
☐ XB-JND	80	HS 125/700A	NA0275	Inmobiliara Archov SA.	(N550JP)
☐ XB-JPS	73	Sabre-40A	282-128	Juan Jose Munoz Flores, Monterrey, NL.	N99114
☐ XB-JTG	77	Sabre-60	306-127	Peninter Aerea SA. Merida.	XA-CUR
☐ XB-JTN	82	HS 125/700A	NA0331	Jamil Textil SA. Toluca.	N900BL
☐ XB-JTO		Learjet 25	...	noted Toluca 1/07.	
☐ XB-JVK		Citation	...	noted Houston 9/06.	
☐ XB-JVL		HS 125/400A	...	noted Toluca 1/07	
☐ XB-JXG	77	Citation 1/SP	501-0018		N228ES
☐ XB-JXZ	76	Learjet 24E	24E-346	Juan Jose Sanchez, Naucalpan,	XC-LJE
☐ XB-JYS	78	HS 125/700A	NA0224	Grupo Inmobiliario JY SA.	N336AC
☐ XB-JYZ		Sabre-	...	noted Toluca 3/07.	
☐ XB-JZX	69	BAC 1-11/212AR	183		XB-JSC
☐ XB-KBW	77	Falcon 20F	364	Transportaciones y Servicios Aereo SA.	N134PA
☐ XB-KCV	73	JetStar-731	5161		N5161R
☐ XB-KCW	72	Gulfstream 2	114		XB-KBE
☐ XB-KCX	68	Gulfstream 2B	30	Procurad General de la Republica SA. Mexico City.	XB-KBO
☐ XB-KFR		JetStar	...	Sol y Aire SA. (5161 ?).	

Reg	Yr	Type	c/n	Owner/Operator	Prev Regn
☐ XB-KKS	70	HS 125/731	NA749	Fernando Lopez Salinas,	N498RS
☐ XB-LYG		Learjet 25	...	noted Toluca 11/07.	
☐ XB-MAR	69	HS 125/400A	NA731	Taxi Aereo Nacional SA. Sotelo.	XA-MAR
☐ XB-MDG	73	Sabre-40A	282-114	AeroDan SA. Saltillo.	XB-RGO
☐ XB-MGM		Hawker 1000	...	Maria Elena Hampshire Sabntibanez Torres,	
☐ XB-MMW	77	Sabre-60	306-132		N265U
☐ XB-MSV	69	HS 125/400A	NA720	Productos Rolmex SA. Monterrey, NL.	XB-FRP
☐ XB-MYE	65	Learjet 23	23-066	Maclovio Hernandez, Vera Cruz.	N211TS
☐ XB-MYG	80	Learjet 25D	25D-295		N25HF
☐ XB-MYP	81	Sabre-65	465-50	Armando Alanis Rodriguez,	(N920DG)
☐ XB-PBT	72	Citation	500-0054		(N54FT)
☐ XB-RSC	81	Sabre-65	465-55	Reynaldo Santos, Toluca.	XA-TOM
☐ XB-RSH	80	Sabre-65	465-22	Roberto Santos de Hoyos, Garza Garcia, NL.	N889RA
☐ XB-TMG	79	Citation 1/SP	501-0118	Javier Lucio Barragan Villareal,	N311ME
☐ XB-TRY	74	Citation Eagle SP	500-0210	Juan Gerardo Rodriguez Garcia,	N501TK
☐ XB-ULF	77	Sabre-60	306-129	Moldes y Plasticos de Monterrey SA. Monterrey, NL.	N60ML
☐ XB-USD	79	Learjet 35A	35A-255	Adame Barocio Alfonso, Toluca.	XB-FNW
☐ XB-UVA	01	Citation Bravo	550-0999	Maria Elena Rangel Espinosa,	XA-UVA
☐ XB-VGT	73	Citation	500-0068	Leader Aerocraft de Mexico FM PM SA. Toluca.	XA-RYE
☐ XB-ZZZ	92	Citation II	550-0711		N58LC
☐ XC-AA70	68	Gulfstream 2	18	Procurad General de la Republica, Mexico City.	XA-LZZ
☐ XC-AA89	76	Sabre-75A	380-46	Procurad General de la Republica, Mexico City.	XC-HFY
☐ XC-AAC	68	Sabre-60	306-21	Procurad General de la Republica, Mexico City.	XB-QND
☐ XC-AAJ	68	Sabre-60	306-20		XA-TLL
☐ XC-AGH		Learjet 25	...	noted Houston 10/07.	
☐ XC-AGU	72	Learjet 24D	24D-260	Secretaria de Gobernacion, Mexico City.	XC-PFP
☐ XC-CUZ	79	Learjet 35A	35A-213	Fonseca Alvarez Guillermo, San Luis Potosi.	(N935NA)
☐ XC-DDA	75	Sabre-75A	380-34	DGAC, Mexico City.	N97SC
☐ XC-DIP	73	Falcon 20E	282	Transporte Aereo Federal, Mexico City. (status ?).	N282C
☐ XC-FEZ	81	Citation	500-0409	SCT/DGAC Verificaciones, Mexico City.	N67815
☐ XC-FIV	72	Citation	500-0013	SCT/DGAC Verificaciones, Mexico City.	N513CC
☐ XC-GAW	81	Citation	500-0410	State Government of Tamaulipas, Victoria.	N6780Z
☐ XC-GDC	05	CitationJet CJ-3	525B-0062	Governor of the State of Chihuahua, Chihuahua.	N5269A
☐ XC-GDT	05	Citation Encore	560-0689	State Government of Tamaulipas, Victoria.	N52059
☐ XC-GTO	80	Citation	500-0396	State Government of Guanajuato, Guanajuato.	(XA-JEW)
☐ XC-GUB	80	Learjet 25D	25D-306	SARH/Ministry of Agriculture, Mexico City.	XA-DUB
☐ XC-HGY	69	Sabre-60	306-38	Aerotaxis del Golfo SA. Acapulco, Guerrero.	XA-DCO
☐ XC-HHJ	81	Learjet 35A	35A-435	State Government of Chiapas, Tuxtla Gutierrez.	N435N
☐ XC-HID		Falcon 20	...	noted Toluca 4/06.	
☐ XC-HIE	99	Learjet 45	45-026	Secretaria de Seguridad Publica, Mexico City.	N405BX
☐ XC-HIS	80	Learjet 25D	25D-312	State Government of Chiapas, Tuxtla Gutierrez.	N94MJ
☐ XC-HIX	71	Falcon 20E	248	Governor of the State of Sinalao, Bachigualato.	XB-VRM
☐ XC-IST	79	Learjet 29	29-001	ISSSTE/Institute of Security Social Services, Mexico City.	N929GL
☐ XC-JCC	65	JetStar-731	5053	noted at Topeka Forbes Field since 6/07. (status ?).	XA-BCE
☐ XC-JDC	79	Sabre-60	306-145	Governor of the State of Campeche.	XA-LOQ
☐ XC-LAH		Citation	...	noted Davis Monthan 10/05.	
☐ XC-LGD	65	Learjet 23	23-037	Comision Nacional del Agua, Mexico City.	XC-AA28
☐ XC-LHB		Citation	...	Procurad General/Mexican Customs Service.	
☐ XC-LJS	89	Beechjet 400	RJ-48	Gobierno of the State of Jalisco.	XB-JHE
☐ XC-LKA	69	Gulfstream II SP	69	Procurad General de la Republica, Mexico City.	XA-MEM
☐ XC-LKB		Sabre-75A	...	Procurad General de la Republica, Mexico City.	
☐ XC-MIC	68	Falcon 20C	169	Governor of the State of Michoacan.	XC-SEY
☐ XC-MMM	72	Citation	500-0035	State Government of Michoacan,	XA-JOV
☐ XC-NSP	75	Learjet 25B	25B-194	CONASUPO, Toluca.	XB-GPJ
☐ XC-OAH		Learjet	...	Servicios Estatales Aeropuertuarios,	
☐ XC-PFT	75	Gulfstream II SP	175	PF-210, Policia Federal Preventiva, Mexico City.	XA-FNY
☐ XC-PGM	90	Citation II	550-0644	PGR/PJF-Policia Judicial Federal, Mexico City.	(N1310B)
☐ XC-PGN	89	Citation III	650-0165	Procurad General de la Republica, Mexico City.	(N650GJ)
☐ XC-PGP	91	Citation II	550-0648	Procurad General de la Republica, Mexico City.	N1260G
☐ XC-PJN		Citation III	...	noted Miami 9/05.	
☐ XC-QER	73	Falcon 20E	287	State Government of Queretaro, Queretaro.	XC-PFJ
☐ XC-RJS		Hawker 400XP	...	noted Toluca 3/06.	
☐ XC-RPP	78	Learjet 25D	25D-236	Secretaria de Hacienda y Credito Publico, Aguascalientes.	N1466B
☐ XC-SCT	80	Citation II	550-0138	SCT, Mexico City. 'Mexico es Primero'.	N2646X
☐ XC-SKI	68	JetStar-8	5124	Secretaria de la Reforma Agraria, Toluca.	XA-SKI
☐ XC-SON	78	Falcon 20F-5	393	State Government of Sonora, Bachigualato.	XC-FVH

Reg	Yr	Type	c/n	Owner/Operator	Prev Regn
☐ XC-SST	94	Citation II	550-0731	DGAC, Mexico City.	N550BP
☐ XC-VMC	00	Learjet 45	45-028	Secretaria de Gobernacion, Mexico City.	HB-VMC
☐ XC-VSA	79	Learjet 28	28-002	State Government of Tabasco, Villahermosa. 'El Chontal'	N511DB

Military

Reg	Yr	Type	c/n	Owner/Operator	Prev Regn
☐ 3501	65	B 727-64	18912	EA302, Santa Lucia.	(XB-DLM)
☐ 3503	65	B 727-14	18908	EA302, Santa Lucia.	10503/XC-F
☐ 3504	65	B 727-14	18909	EA302, Santa Lucia.	10504/XC-F
☐ 3505		B 727-264	22661	EA302, Santa Lucia.	XA-MXA
☐ 3506		B 727-264	22662	EA302, Santa Lucia.	XA-MXB
☐ 3908	69	JetStar-8	5144	Ministry of Defence, Mexico City.	10201
☐ 3909	80	Learjet 35A	35A-321	Ministry of Defence, Mexico City.	TP-106
☐ 3929	73	Citation	500-0090	EA501, Santa Lucia.	ETE-1329
☐ AMT-200	98	Learjet 60	60-152	Marina Transporte, Mexico City.	MTX-01
☐ AMT-201	99	Learjet 31A	31A-174	Marina Transporte, Mexico City.	MTX-02
☐ AMT-202	81	Learjet 25D	25D-339	Marina Transporte, Mexico City.	MTX-03
☐ AMT-203	69	Sabre-60	306-34	Marina Transporte, Mexico City.	MTX-04
☐ AMT-204		Sabre-	...	Marina Transporte, Mexico City.	
☐ TP-01	87	B 757-225	22690	XC-UJM, Estado Mayor Presidencial, Mexico City.	XC-UJM/TP
☐ TP-02	89	B 737-33A	24095	XC-UJB, Estado Mayor Presidencial, Mexico City.	N731XL
☐ TP-104	75	Learjet 35	35-028	CGATP, Mexico City.	XC-IPP
☐ TP-105	81	Learjet 36A	36A-050	CGATP, Mexico City.	XC-AA24
☐ XC-UJF	78	Sabre-60	306-144	Aeropuertos y Servicios Auxiliares, Mexico City.	XC-AA51
☐ XC-UJN	82	Gulfstream 3	352	TP-06, Presidencia de la Republica, Chiapas.	HB-ITM
☐ XC-UJO	83	Gulfstream 3	386	TP-07, Estado Mayor Presidencial, Mexico City.	N902KB

XT = BURKINA FASO   Total   2
Civil

Reg	Yr	Type	c/n	Owner/Operator	Prev Regn
☐ XT-BBE	66	B 727-14	18990	Government of Burkina Faso, Ouagadougou.	N21UC
☐ XT-BFA	81	B 727-282	22430	Government of Burkina Faso, Ouagadougou.	N727RE

XU = CAMBODIA   Total   2
Civil

Reg	Yr	Type	c/n	Owner/Operator	Prev Regn
☐ XU-008	75	Falcon 20E	323	Government of Cambodia, Phnom Penh.	OE-GLF
☐ XU-888	69	F 28-1000	11012	President Airlines, Phnom Penh.	XU-001

XY = MYANMAR   Total   1
Military

Reg	Yr	Type	c/n	Owner/Operator	Prev Regn
☐ 4400	82	Citation II	550-0358	MoD/Myanmar Air Force, Mingaladon.	N6801Q

YI = IRAQ   Total   7
Civil

Reg	Yr	Type	c/n	Owner/Operator	Prev Regn
☐ YI-AHH	76	Falcon 20F	337	Ministry of Defence, Muthana.	F-WRQR
☐ YI-AHJ	76	Falcon 20F	343	Ministry of Defence, Muthana.	F-WRQR
☐ YI-AKB	79	JetStar 2	5235	Government/Iraqi Airways, Baghdad. (status ?).	N4055M
☐ YI-AKC	79	JetStar 2	5237	Government/Iraqi Airways, Baghdad. (status ?).	N4058M
☐ YI-AKD	79	JetStar 2	5238	Government/Iraqi Airways, Baghdad. (status ?).	N4062M
☐ YI-AKE	79	JetStar 2	5239	Government/Iraqi Airways, Baghdad. (status ?).	N4063M
☐ YI-AKF	79	JetStar 2	5240	Government/Iraqi Airways, Baghdad. (status ?).	N4065M

YK = SYRIA   Total   3
Military

Reg	Yr	Type	c/n	Owner/Operator	Prev Regn
☐ YK-ASA	75	Falcon 20F	328	Government of Syria, Damascus.	(N4459F)
☐ YK-ASB	75	Falcon 20F	331	Government of Syria, Damascus.	F-WRQS
☐ YK-ASC	91	Falcon 900	100	Government of Syria, Damascus.	F-WWFB

YL = LATVIA   Total   5
Civil

Reg	Yr	Type	c/n	Owner/Operator	Prev Regn
☐ YL-KSC	01	390 Premier 1	RB-20	K S Avia Ltd. Riga.	(N390BP)
☐ YL-MAR	99	Hawker 800XP	258389	PAREX/VIP Avia Ltd. Riga.	YR-VPA
☐ YL-NST	99	Hawker 800XP	258424	VIP Avia Ltd. Riga.	N1899K
☐ YL-SKY	02	Challenger 604	5532	VIP Avia Ltd. Riga.	N432MC
☐ YL-VIP	87	BAe 125/800B	258078	PAREX/VIP Avia Ltd. Riga.	G-88-01

YR = ROMANIA   Total   9
Civil

Reg	Yr	Type	c/n	Owner/Operator	Prev Regn
☐ YR-BRE	86	BAC 1-11/561RC	405	Romavia/Government of Romania, Bucharest.	
☐ YR-CJF	87	Falcon 900B	26	MIA Airlines, Bucharest.	VP-CJF
☐ YR-HRS	78	BAC 1-11/488GH	259	MIA Airlines, Bucharest.	G-MAAH
☐ YR-MIA	80	BAC 1-11/492GM	260	MIA Airlines, Bucharest. 'Mirjane'	HR-ATS
☐ YR-RPB	94	Learjet 60	60-030	Eurojet Romania SA. Bucharest.	TC-ELL

Reg	Yr	Type	c/n	Owner/Operator	Prev Regn
☐ YR-RPG	04	Citation Encore	560-0665	Eurojet Romania SA. Bucharest.	OE-GEJ
☐ YR-RPR	03	Citation Excel	560-5337	Eurojet Romania SA. Bucharest.	N79BC
☐ YR-TIG	99	Galaxy-1126	012	Ion Tiriac Air SA. Bucharest.	(HB-IGK)
☐ YR-TII	03	Gulfstream G200	089	Ion Tiriac Air SA. Bucharest.	OE-HTI

YU = SERBIA *Total* 10

Civil

Reg	Yr	Type	c/n	Owner/Operator	Prev Regn
☐ YU-BNA	81	Falcon 50	43	Government of Serbia & Montenegro, Belgrade.	72102
☐ YU-BRZ	91	Learjet 31A	31A-045	Avio Service, Belgrade.	N67SB
☐ YU-BSG	03	Citation Bravo	550-1049	Prince Aviation, Belgrade.	N299HS
☐ YU-BSM	97	Citation Bravo	550-0808	Prince Aviation, Belgrade.	SE-DVZ
☐ YU-BTM	97	Citation VII	650-7080	Pelikan Airways,	S5-BBA
☐ YU-BTT	81	Citation II/SP	551-0038	Air Pink, Belgrade.	N551BB
☐ YU-BVA	96	Beechjet 400A	RK-124	Vektra Corp. Podgorica.	OE-GUK
☐ YU-BVV	81	Citation II	550-0272	Air Pink, Belgrade.	SE-DVV
☐ YU-BZZ	00	Citation Bravo	550-0924	Air Pink, Belgrade.	N550VC
☐ YU-FCS	81	Citation II	550-0321		VP-CCO

YV = VENEZUELA *Total* 83

Civil

Reg	Yr	Type	c/n	Owner/Operator	Prev Regn
☐ YV....	71	HS 125/400A	NA760	Luiz Alberto Castilo Melendez, Caracas.	N456WH
☐ YV....	72	Citation	500-0047	Jorge Lopez, Caracas.	N7281Z
☐ YV....	79	Citation II	550-0112	Antonio Korol, Caracas.	N213CF
☐ YV....	81	Citation II	550-0203	Conjunto Dapsany SA.	(N857BT)
☐ YV....	70	HS 125/400A	NA759		(N400MR)
☐ YV-03CP	67	JetStar-731	5106	Servicios Aerofacility SA. Caracas.	N1329K
☐ YV1022	91	Citation V	560-0134	Inversiones Lunfa CA. Caracas.	YV-811CP
☐ YV1083	80	Falcon 50	22	PDVSA Petroleo SA. Caracas.	FAV-0018
☐ YV1128	81	Falcon 50	53	SATA, Caracas.	N53FJ
☐ YV1129	81	Falcon 50	63	SATA, Caracas.	N63FJ
☐ YV-1133CP	76	Citation	500-0317		N317VP
☐ YV113T	70	HS 125/731	25231	Rainbow Air,	N831DF
☐ YV1152	72	Citation	500-0043	Servicios Aereos Permagas CA.. Caracas.	N502RD
☐ YV1192	91	Citation II	550-0683	Luis Mendoza, Caracas.	YV-701CP
☐ YV120T	72	Sabre-40A	282-106	Super Autos Carabobo CA. Valencia.	YV-1144CP
☐ YV-122CP		Hawker 800XP	...	noted Fort Lauderdale 9/04.	
☐ YV1316	72	Citation	500-0052	Command Air SA. Caracas.	YV-881CP
☐ YV1401	01	Gulfstream G200	041	Corporacion Grucat CA. Caracas.	YV-772CP
☐ YV1432	74	Citation Longwing SP	500-0167	Seven Clouds CA. Caracas.	YV-2821P
☐ YV1495	83	Falcon 50	136	PDVSA Petroleo SA. Caracas.	YV-455CP
☐ YV1496	91	Falcon 50	219	PDVSA Petroleo SA. Caracas.	YV-450CP
☐ YV1563	83	Citation II	550-0463	Promociones Orizaba CA.. Caracas. (was 551-0463).	YV-713CP
☐ YV1677	73	Citation	500-0109	Aereomedid 2005 CA. Caracas.	N221AM
☐ YV1681	68	Gulfstream 2	25	Transhipment Petroleum Global Co. Caracas.	N711RZ
☐ YV1685	81	Westwind-Two	330	Transporte 330 SA/Cia Tamesis SA. Caracas.	YV-332CP
☐ YV1686	74	Citation	500-0216	Construcciones e Inversiones Vesubio, Valencia.	N199CK
☐ YV1687	69	HS 125/731	NA723	Inversiones Alfamaq CA. Caracas.	YV-1145CP
☐ YV1771	95	Astra-1125SP	077	Transporte Polar CA. Caracas.	YV-771CP
☐ YV1776	80	Citation II/SP	551-0223	Inversiones 2567 CA. Caracas.	(N28GZ)
☐ YV1794	82	Learjet 55	55-031	Coca-Cola OCAAT C.A. Caracas.	YV-12CP
☐ YV1813	82	Citation II	550-0405	Aviacion Ciyunia CA. Caracas.	YV-778CP
☐ YV1820	81	Citation II/SP	551-0313	Multinacional de Seguros CA.(was 550-0270).	YV-2426P
☐ YV195T	83	Diamond 1A	A064SA		N400ML
☐ YV198T	01	Beechjet 400A	RK-306	Automotriz Los Llanos CA.	YV-968CP
☐ YV2030	74	Citation	500-0215	Coin Inspectra CA.	YV-55CP
☐ YV2039	91	Falcon 900B	108	PDVSA Petroleo SA. Caracas.	(N108FJ)
☐ YV-203CP	70	Learjet 25C	25C-061	Tranarg C.A. Caracas.	N9CN
☐ YV2040	94	Falcon 900B	133	PDVSA Petroleo SA. Caracas.	N813TS
☐ YV2044	81	Learjet 35A	35A-437	Constructora Pedeca CA. La Carlota.	YV-432CP
☐ YV2053	99	Falcon 900EX	60	SATA, Caracas.	N60EX
☐ YV2073	79	Citation II	550-0370	Inversiones Lunfa CA. Caracas. (was 551-0015).	YV-2671P
☐ YV2103	81	Citation II	550-0135	Inversiones Brancom SA. Caracas.	YV-888CP
☐ YV2110	99	Citation V Ultra	560-0511	Cerveceria Polar CA. Caracas.	N200NK
☐ YV213T	97	Beechjet 400A	RK-152		YV-754CP
☐ YV2165	79	Falcon 50	4	Petroleos de Venezuela SA. Caracas.	YV-462CP
☐ YV2166	83	Citation II	550-0467	Venezolana de Coberturas CA. Caracas.	YV-810CP
☐ YV2246	81	Citation II	550-0300	Aero Servicios ALAS C.A. Caracas.	YV-162CP

Reg	Yr	Type	c/n	Owner/Operator	Prev Regn
YV2254		Citation	...		N73DR
YV225T	73	Sabre-40A	282-120	Super Autos Carabobo CA. Valencia.	
YV2286	90	Citation II	550-0637	Miralta CA. Caracas.	YV-376CP
YV2331	06	CitationJet CJ1+	525-0631		N5206T
YV2346	81	Falcon 50	44	Petroleos de Venezuela SA. Caracas.	N285CP
YV2389	06	Citation Encore+	560-0757		N52141
YV238T	73	Citation	500-0072	Ludotech Aviation Inc/Hotel Maruma, Maracaibo.	N72DJ
YV2416		Hawker 1000	...	noted Fort Lauderdale 10/07.	
YV2443	81	Citation II	550-0214	Hotel Tampa, Caracas.	YV205T
YV-2482P	74	Westwind-1123	172	West Wind Air C.A. Caracas.	YV-58CP
YV251T	81	Westwind-1124	362		N445A
YV255T	81	Citation II	550-0312		YV-1055CP
YV265T	74	Sabre-75A	380-2	(status ?).	N406PW
YV266T	00	Citation Bravo	550-0943	Inversiones SCL 12 SA. Caracas.	YV-2711P
YV289T	06	CitationJet CJ2+	525A-0318		N525TA
YV305T	04	CitationJet CJ-2	525A-0221	Gadget Intervest Ltd. Barquismeto.	N27VQ
YV-388CP	71	HFB 320	1057	Inversiones Guraica CA. Caracas.	VR-CYR
YV-52CP	77	Citation	500-0367	Construcciones CADE. Barquisimeto.	N36906
YV-572CP	75	Corvette	17	Aerocolon S.A. Caracas. (status ?).	F-ODTM
YV-697CP		Citation	...	noted Aruba 8/05.	
YV-815CP	66	HS 125/731	25098	Inversiones Desirio CA.	N29CR
YV-901CP	72	Citation	500-0058	Corporacion 385 CA. Caracas.	N6145Q
YV-939CP	72	Citation	500-0031	Executive Air C.A. Caracas.	YV-646CP

Military

Reg	Yr	Type	c/n	Owner/Operator	Prev Regn
0001	01	Airbus A319-133XCJ	1468	Government of Venezuela, Caracas.	D-AVYQ
0002	78	Citation II	550-0011	FAV, MoD, Caracas.	(N98876)
0006	72	Learjet 24D	24D-250	FAV, MoD, Caracas. (status ?).	N85CD
0207	76	B 737-2N1	21167	Republica Bolivariana de Venezuela, Caracas.	0001
0222	73	Citation	500-0092	FAV, MoD, Caracas.	N592CC
0442	70	Falcon 20D	235	FAV, Palo Negro AB. Maracau.	(N442)
1060	00	Citation X	750-0134	FAV, MoD, Caracas.	YV1969
1650	83	Falcon 20F	476	FAV, MoD, Caracas.	F-ZJTD
1967	78	Citation II/SP	551-0006	FAV, MoD, Caracas.	YV-O-CVG2
2222	81	Citation II	550-0224	FAV, MoD, Caracas.	YV-O-MTC-
5761	66	Falcon 20C	23	FAV, Palo Negro AB. Maracau.	(N582G)
5840	69	Falcon 20D	216	FAV, Palo Negro AB. Maracau.	N9FE
YV-2338P	82	Citation II	550-0449	FAV, MoD, Caracas.	(FAV1107)

Z = ZIMBABWE   Total 1

Civil

Reg	Yr	Type	c/n	Owner/Operator	Prev Regn
Z-WPD	87	BAe 146 Statesman	E2065	Air Zimbabwe/Government of Zimbabwe,	G-5-065

ZK = NEW ZEALAND   Total 7

Civil

Reg	Yr	Type	c/n	Owner/Operator	Prev Regn
ZK-KFB	98	Gulfstream 4SP	1362	Air National Corporate Ltd. Auckland.	(N888LF)
ZK-RGB	07	Gulfstream G200	158	ZKR Aviation Ltd/Air National Ltd. Auckland.	N658GA
ZK-RML	81	Westwind-Two	339	Air National Corporate Ltd. Auckland.	N90KC
ZK-TBM	05	CitationJet CJ-3	525B-0027	Pacific Jets, Christchurch.	N1287D
ZK-XVL	89	Learjet 35A	35A-649	Auckland Air Charter Ltd. Auckland.	N35QB

Military

Reg	Yr	Type	c/n	Owner/Operator	Prev Regn
NZ7571		B 757-2K2	26633	RNZAF, Ohakea.	PH-TKA
NZ7572		B 757-2K2	26634	RNZAF, Ohakea.	PH-TKB

ZP = PARAGUAY   Total 3

Civil

Reg	Yr	Type	c/n	Owner/Operator	Prev Regn
ZP-AGD	71	Westwind-1123	151	Humberto Dominguez Dibb, Asuncion.	N88WP
ZP-TKO	68	HS 125/400A	NA711	TSAVO Co. Asuncion.	ZP-TDF
ZP-TZH	74	Citation	500-0185	L C Santi, Asuncion.	N500AZ

ZS = SOUTH AFRICA   Total 126

Civil

Reg	Yr	Type	c/n	Owner/Operator	Prev Regn
ZS-...	07	CitationJet CJ-3	525B-0211		N51396
ZS-...	04	Hawker 800XP	258670		N1776N
ZS-ABG	92	BAe 1000A	259024	Abalengani Aviation P/L. Lanseria.	(G-WWDB)
ZS-ACE	82	Citation 1/SP	501-0245	ACE P/L-ZS-KMO P/L. Lanseria.	A2-AGM
ZS-ACT	04	Challenger 300	20034	Searay BD100 Charters Partners, Capetown.	C-FCXJ
ZS-AFG	05	Hawker 800XPi	258724	Air Affaires Gabon, Libreville, Gabon.	N724XP
ZS-AJD	00	Learjet 31A	31A-202	Ramblite P/L. Lanseria.	ZS-PNP

Reg	Yr	Type	c/n	Owner/Operator	Prev Regn
ZS-AOL	01	Gulfstream V	634	Anglo Operations Ltd. Johannesburg.	N534GA
ZS-ARG	80	Citation II/SP	551-0163	Bevrick P/L. Kimberley.	D-IGRC
ZS-AVM	02	390 Premier 1	RB-31	Cape Air Charter Partnership P/L. Capetown.	N3231K
ZS-BAR	02	Learjet 45	45-219	Barloworld Capital P/L. Lanseria.	N4003K
ZS-BBB	08	Global Express	...		
ZS-BFS	75	Citation	500-0262	Blue Employee Benefits P/L. Lynwood Ridge.	N110AB
ZS-BTC	74	Citation	500-0161	Universal Pulse Trading 199 P/L. Lanseria.	N161CC
ZS-BXR	73	Learjet 25XR	25XR-141	King Air Services Partnership, Lanseria.	N25HA
ZS-CAG	82	HS 125/700B	257172	King Air Services Partnership, Lanseria.	N355WJ
ZS-CAL	69	HS 125/F3B-RA	25172	King Air Services Partnership, Lanseria.	(G-5-506)
ZS-CAR	86	Citation S/II	S550-0078	Civil Aviation Authority, Johannesburg.	N1273X
ZS-CJT	06	CitationJet CJ-3	525B-0116	ZS-CJT Partnership P/L.	N5244W
ZS-CWD	78	Citation 1/SP	501-0049	Containerworld P/L. Durban.	OY-SVL
ZS-DAV	95	Falcon 900B	149	Hawker Air Services P/L. Lanseria.	VP-BPI
ZS-DBS	73	Citation	500-0061	Pcubed Aviation P/L. Lanseria.	N916RC
ZS-DCA	00	Learjet 45	45-117	Skystream Air Charters P/L. Capetown.	N40081
ZS-DDA	03	Hawker 800XP	258601	Beechjet Charter Partnership P/L. Pinegowrie.	N61101
ZS-DDM	02	390 Premier 1	RB-63	Fourie's Poultry Farm P/L. Potchefstrom.	N6163T
ZS-DGW	75	Gulfstream 2B	166	MCC Aviation P/L. Lanseria.	N776MA
ZS-DSA	72	Citation	500-0044	D S Avnit, Lanseria.	N501VH
ZS-EDA	87	Citation S/II	S550-0126	Netcare 911 Aeromedical Services P/L. Edenvale.	(N127RC)
ZS-ESA	00	Global Express	9061	Government of Rwanda, Kigali.	ZS-ESA
ZS-FOX	76	Falcon 10	72	Awesome Flight Services P/L. Lanseria.	N50TY
ZS-FUN	77	Learjet 24F	24F-354	Nelair Aviation Services P/L. Nelspruit.	PT-LYE
ZS-GJB	02	Global Express	9122	Kangra Group P/L. Lanseria.	N700FW
ZS-GSG	06	Learjet 60	60-301	Skyros Properties P/L. Lanseria.	N50157
ZS-ICU	80	HS 125/700A	NA0279	Netcare 911 Aeromedical Services P/L. Edenvale.	N90FF
ZS-IDC	03	Citation Excel	560-5352	IDC/Kindoc Airways P/L. Lanseria.	N5245D
ZS-IGP	85	Learjet 35A	35A-608	Aeronautic Solutions Investments P/L. Lanseria.	N96AX
ZS-IOC	04	Dornier Do328JET	3219	Sishen Iron Ore Co. Centurion.	OY-NCP
ZS-IPE	83	HS 125/700A	NA0342	Landonia Trust CC. Lanseria.	(ZS-IPI)
ZS-ISA	74	Citation	500-0224	Phomella Property Investments P/L. Lanseria.	N697MB
ZS-JDL	05	Citation Sovereign	680-0033	Newshelf 783 P/L. Lanseria.	N52114
ZS-JGC	80	Gulfstream 3	312	Midnight Storm Investments 264 P/L. Lanseria.	N116AR
ZS-KBS	07	Hawker 900XP	HA-17	NAC P/L. Lanseria.	N917XP
ZS-KGS	78	Falcon 20F-5B	385	Gough Aviation P/L. Lanseria.	N385FJ
ZS-KJY	68	Learjet 24	24-165	MCC Aviation P/L. Lanseria.	V5-KJY
ZS-LAH	81	Gulfstream 3	328	Norse Air Charter P/L. Lanseria.	N97AG
ZS-LDV	82	Citation	500-0418	Pabair Trust, Lanseria.	N2628B
ZS-LME	70	HS 125/403B	25242	King Air Services Partnership, Lanseria.	3D-ABZ
ZS-LOG	68	Gulfstream II SP	19	PLC Logistics Corp P/L. Lanseria.	(N213DC)
ZS-LOW	02	Learjet 45	45-228	Barloworld Equipment P/L. Lanseria.	N5012Z
ZS-LPE	69	HS 125/400B	25184	TCT Leisure P/L. Lanseria.	SAAF04
ZS-LWU	69	Learjet 24B	24B-209	Air Quarius Contracts P/L. Lanseria.	N14BC
ZS-LXH	76	Learjet 25D	25D-206	Nelair Aviation Services P/L. Nelspruit.	N206EQ
ZS-MAN	66	HS 125/1B	25067	Sabre Pharmaceuticals P/L. Lanseria.	Z-TBX
ZS-MCU	73	Citation	500-0137	Moraine Freight P/L. Lanseria.	(N922BA)
ZS-MDA	91	Astra-1125SP	055	Global Equities Aviation P/L. Benmore.	N120GA
ZS-MEG	70	HS 125/400A	NA755	Multimedia Entertainment Group, Honeydew.	(N871MA)
ZS-MGD	05	Falcon 2000EX EASY	51	South African Breweries P/L. Lanseria.	F-WWGP
ZS-MGJ	69	Learjet 24XR	24XR-207	Nelair Aviation Services P/L. Nelspruit.	N457JA
ZS-MHN	89	Beechjet 400	RJ-59	South African Police Services, Pretoria.	N1559U
ZS-MTD	74	Learjet 25B	25B-160	M R Barnes/MCC Aviation, Halfway House.	3D-AEZ
ZS-NDX	91	Citation V	560-0152	De Beers Consolidated Mines Ltd. Johannesburg.	N6882R
ZS-NGL	92	Citation V	560-0202	Sappi Manufacturing P/L. Lanseria.	N1283V
ZS-NGS	93	Citation V	560-0241	De Beers Consolidated Mines Ltd. Johannesburg.	N241CV
ZS-NII	80	Citation II	550-0168	Bersdale Farm P/L. Capetown.	N68GA
ZS-NUZ	96	Citation V Ultra	560-0398	Paerstan P/L. Capetown.	N5061W
ZS-NYG	73	Learjet 25C	25C-098	The Core Computer Business P/L. Morningside.	N502MH
ZS-NYV	95	Learjet 31A	31A-115	Government of Kwazulu-Natal, Ulundi.	N31NR
ZS-OEA	73	Learjet 24XR	24XR-267	Nelair Aviation Services P/L. Nelspruit.	N267MP
ZS-OHZ	00	Citation Excel	560-5079	Anglo Operations Ltd. Johannesburg.	N5218T
ZS-OIE	83	Citation II	550-0480	Sukramark P/L. Malelane.	N380MS
ZS-OIF	70	HS 125/731	NA746	Landonia Trust CC. Upington.	N103RR
ZS-OML	99	Learjet 31A	31A-170	Professional Flight Training P/L. Lanseria.	(OY-LJN)
ZS-ONE	71	Citation Eagle	500-0002	Golden Dividend 502 P/L. Pretoria.	C-FCPW

Reg	Yr	Type	c/n	Owner/Operator	Prev Regn
ZS-ONG	99	Falcon 50EX	287	Perstan P/L. Capetown.	F-WWHO
ZS-OPM	06	Learjet 45	45-308	De Beers Consolidated Mines Ltd. Johannesburg.	N415CL
ZS-OPN	06	Learjet 45	45-321	De Beers Consolidated Mines Ltd. Johannesburg.	N4002P
ZS-OPO	07	Learjet 45	45-342	De Beers Consolidated Mines Ltd. Johannesburg.	N5011L
ZS-OPY	02	Learjet 45	45-218	Nungu Private Game Reserve P/L. Johannesburg.	N451JC
ZS-ORW	88	Beechjet 400	RJ-37	Skyinvest Administration P/L-Skyfalcon, Tokai.	N31437
ZS-PCY	02	Hawker 850XP	258589	NAC P/L. Lanseria.	N874JD
ZS-PDG	00	Learjet 45	45-092	Friedshelf 366 P/L. Capetown.	(ZS-PPR)
ZS-PFE	03	390 Premier 1	RB-94	Waste Product Utilisation P/L. Lanseria.	N6194N
ZS-PFG	73	Citation Eagle	500-0122	Changing Tides 142 P/L. Menlo Park.	N122AP
ZS-PHP	79	Citation 1/SP	501-0103	Manetrade 120 P/L. Lanseria.	(N906EA)
ZS-PKR	00	Falcon 2000	114	Pepkor Group P/L-Flicape P/L. Capetown.	F-WWVI
ZS-PKY	99	Hawker 800XP	258429	Ovlas Trading P/L. Johannesburg.	N68HD
ZS-PLC	69	HS 125/731	NA733	Landonia Trust Co. Upington.	N243JB
ZS-PMA	73	Citation Eagle	500-0123	Inter African Investments CC. Erasmuskloof.	VH-ECD
ZS-PNP	00	Learjet 45	45-059	Pick N'Pay Gabriel Road P/L. Lanseria.	N590JC
ZS-POT	04	Hawker 400XP	RK-400	Sahara Computers P/L. Halfway House.	N400XP
ZS-PPH	05	Hawker 800XPi	258717	Pinnacle Point Resorts P/L. Capetown.	N717XP
ZS-PSE	92	BAe 125/800A	258231	NAC P/L. Lanseria.	N75MT
ZS-PSG	86	Citation S/II	S550-0112	Access Freight International P/L. Bluff.	A2-MCB
ZS-PTL	01	Learjet 45	45-181	Rodo Investments P/L. Lanseria.	(ZS-FUL)
ZS-PTP	03	Hawker 800XP	258633	NAC P/L. Lanseria.	N800NS
ZS-PWT	73	Citation	500-0076	Philken Aviation CC. Westgate.	N65WS
ZS-PWU	01	CitationJet CJ-1	525-0431	Venture Otto South Africa P/L. Menlo Park.	N431YD
ZS-PXD	75	Citation	500-0257	Graham Family Trust, Somerset West.	N75GW
ZS-PYY	68	Gulfstream II SP	26	Fastjet Aviation Holdings P/L. Lanseria.	N4RT
ZS-PZA	03	Hawker 800XP	258632	Pezula Private Estate P/L-Crucial Trade 101 P/L. Knysa.	N632XP
ZS-RCC	73	Citation	500-0106	Jet Air Charter P/L. Lanseria	N606CC
ZS-RKV	79	Citation II	550-0051	Mouritzen Family Trust, Randburg.	N678CA
ZS-RSA	01	BBJ-7ED	32627	Government of South Africa. Waterkloof AFB. 'Inkwazi'	N373BJ
ZS-SAH	07	Hawker 900XP	HA-26	NAC P/L. Lanseria.	N32926
ZS-SEA	79	Falcon 10	156	ESCOM/Sapphire Executive Air, Grand Central.	SE-DEK
ZS-SEB	80	Falcon 10	127	ESCOM/Sapphire Executive Air, Grand Central.	(N7RZ)
ZS-SGC	90	Challenger 601-3A	5070	Midnight Storm Investments 264 P/L. Houghton.	OY-CLD
ZS-SGS	03	390 Premier 1	RB-72	Bee Line Aviation P/L. Capetown.	N535BR
ZS-SMT	67	HS 125/3B	25128	Interlink Airlines P/L. Gardenview.	F-GECR
ZS-SOS	84	Falcon 200	493	International SOS Assistance P/L. Lanseria.	VH-ECG
ZS-SSM	68	Learjet 25XR	25XR-022	Swift Flite P/L. Lanseria.	N111WB
ZS-TBN	65	HS 125/731	25023	Trinity Broadcasting Investments, East London.	ZS-PJE
ZS-TEX	82	Gulfstream 3	355	Diamond Air Charters P/L. Lanseria.	N355TS
ZS-TJS	00	Learjet 45	45-083	Tokyo Sexwale, Lanseria.	OY-LJG
ZS-TMG	74	Citation	500-0149	COMAV, Menlo Park.	N149PJ
ZS-TOW	82	Learjet 35A	35A-475	NAC P/L. Lanseria.	(N42AJ)
ZS-TOY	70	Learjet 24B	24B-219	Landonia Trust CC. Upington.	N977GA
ZS-TPG	74	Gulfstream II SP	150	TPG Aviation P/L. Lanseria.	N60GU
ZS-ULT	01	Learjet 45	45-194	Intra International Trading P/L. Steenberg.	ZS-YES
ZS-WHG	69	Gulfstream II SP	67	O W Hennig, Cape Town.	N568TN
ZS-WJW	81	HS 125/700A	NA0311	Baranza Air Services CC. Durban.	N700LP

Military

Reg	Yr	Type	c/n	Owner/Operator	Prev Regn
ZS-CAQ	83	Falcon 50	133	South African Air Force, Pretoria.	HB-IEA
ZS-CAS	82	Falcon 50	91	South African Air Force, Pretoria.	ZS-BMB
ZS-LIG	83	Citation II	550-0474	South African Air Force, Pretoria.	N12514
ZS-MLN	81	Citation II/SP	551-0285	South African Air Force, Waterkloof AFB.	VDF-030
ZS-NAN	91	Falcon 900B	99	South African Air Force, Waterkloof AFB.	F-WWFE

Z3 = MACEDONIA   Total 2

Civil

Reg	Yr	Type	c/n	Owner/Operator	Prev Regn
Z3-BAA	76	Learjet 25B	25B-205	Government of Macedonia, Skopje.	YU-BKJ
Z3-MKD	05	Learjet 60	60-279	Government of Macedonia, Skopje.	N50145

3A = MONACO   Total 3

Civil

Reg	Yr	Type	c/n	Owner/Operator	Prev Regn
3A-...	07	Falcon 900EX EASY	195		F-WWFL
3A-MGA	01	Falcon 2000	167	Prince Albert, Nice, France.	3A-MGR
3A-MRG		CitationJet CJ-3	525B-0096	Roberto Giori, Lausanne, Switzerland.	LX-GAP

3B = MAURITIUS   Total   4
Civil

☐ 3B-GFI	81	Challenger 600S	1019	Generale Aviation et Finance Internationale Ltd. Lumbumbashi	ZS-NER
☐ 3B-NGT	06	Challenger 300	20133		C-FJRG
☐ 3B-SSD	06	Challenger 300	20126		C-FJQH
☐ 3B-TSL	07	Airbus A330-2	863	Midroc Aviation,	F-W...

3C = EQUATORIAL GUINEA   Total   4
Civil

☐ 3C-EGE	02	BBJ-7FB/W	33367	Government of Equatorial Guinea, Malabo.	N377JC
☐ 3C-LGE	95	Falcon 50	246	GEASA-Guinea Ecuatorial Aire Lines SA. Malabo.	F-GTJF
☐ 3C-ONM	97	Falcon 900B	167	Government of Equatorial Guinea, Malabo.	F-GUEQ
☐ 3C-QQU	66	JetStar-731	5082	MIA Airlines, Bucharest, Romania.	(P4-CBJ)

3D = SWAZILAND   Total   5
Civil

☐ 3D-...	66	B 727-61	19176		N530KF
☐ 3D-BOE	65	B 727-30	18933	Government of Democratic Republic of Congo, Kinshasa.	N7271P
☐ 3D-IER	79	Citation	500-0392	Di Air, Podgorica, Montenegro.	D-ISSS
☐ 3D-JNM	66	B 727-89	19139	Global Airways,	N511DB
☐ 3D-KMJ	68	B 727-22C	19892		NZ7271

4K = AZERBAIJAN   Total   3
Civil

☐ 4K-8888		B 727-251W	22543	Government of Azerbaijan, Baku.	4K-AZ9
☐ 4K-AZ01	05	Airbus A319-115XCJ	2487	Government of Azerbaijan, Baku.	
☐ 4K-AZ888	05	Gulfstream G450	4045	Silk Way Airlines, Baku.	N445GA

4L = GEORGIA   Total   1
Civil

| ☐ 4L-GAF | 06 | Challenger 850 | 8046 | Government of Georgia, Tbilisi. | OY-YVI |

4X = ISRAEL   Total   31
Civil

☐ 4X-...	00	Citation Bravo	550-0941		N878AG
☐ 4X-CLL	01	Gulfstream G200	040	Memorand Management (1998) Ltd. Tel Aviv.	N90GX
☐ 4X-CMF	01	Challenger 604	5522	Fishman Properties Ltd/Noy Aviation Ltd. Tel Aviv.	C-GKCB
☐ 4X-CMY	98	Challenger 604	5388	Merhav MNF Ltd/Noy Aviation Ltd. Tel Aviv.	C-GDVM
☐ 4X-CMZ	00	Challenger 604	5450	Jet Link, Tel Aviv.	N450DK
☐ 4X-COG	00	Gulfstream G200	018	Chim-Nir Aviation, Tel Aviv.	N18GZ
☐ 4X-COI	04	Global 5000	9130	Iscar Ltd/Arkia Airlines Ltd. Tel Aviv.	C-GLRM
☐ 4X-CPS	98	Hawker 800XP	258391	D S Airline Ltd. Tel Aviv.	N771SV
☐ 4X-CPV	05	Challenger 300	20065	Arkia Airlines Ltd. Tel Aviv.	C-FFNT
☐ 4X-CPY	98	Beechjet 400A	RK-219	Nanyah Ltd. Tel Aviv.	N219SJ
☐ 4X-CUR	06	Challenger 604	5645	Ray Aviation Ltd. Tel Aviv.	C-FHCL
☐ 4X-CYH	07	Learjet 45	45-336	Yoav Harlap, Tel Aviv Sde-Dov.	N45YH
☐ 4X-CZD	79	Citation II/SP	551-0117	Gesher Aviri Co/Aviation Bridge Israel Ltd. (was 550-0063).	N551AD
☐ 4X-WIA	84	Astra-1125	002	Israel Aircraft Industries Ltd. Tel Aviv. (status ?).	

Military

☐ 4X-...	06	Gulfstream G550	5132	Israel Air & Space Force, CAEW, Tel Aviv. (532?)	N432GA
☐ 4X-...	06	Gulfstream G550	5143	Israel Air & Space Force, CAEW, Tel Aviv. (543?)	N643GA
☐ 4X-JY.	77	B 707-3PIC	21334	275, ISDAF, Tel Aviv.	A7-AAA
☐ 4X-JYB	72	B 707-3H7C	20629	255, ISDAF, Tel Aviv.	4X-BYR
☐ 4X-JYH	65	B 707-3J6B	20721	264, ISDAF, Tel Aviv.	B-2416
☐ 4X-JYJ	76	Westwind-1124N	185	927, ISDAF/195 Squadron, Tel Aviv.	N1123U
☐ 4X-JYO	76	Westwind-1124N	186	931, ISDAF/195 Squadron, Tel Aviv.	N1123R
☐ 4X-JYQ	69	B 707-344C	20110	242, ISDAF, Tel Aviv.	4X-BYQ
☐ 4X-JYR	71	Westwind-1124N	152	929, ISDAF/195 Squadron, Tel Aviv.	4X-CJC
☐ 4X-JYV	75	B 707-3L6C	21096	272, ISDAF, Tel Aviv.	P4-MDJ
☐ 514	02	Gulfstream G550	5014	Israel Air & Space Force, CAEW, Tel Aviv.	N914GA
☐ 537	03	Gulfstream G550	5037	Israel Air & Space Force, CAEW, Tel Aviv.	N637GA
☐ 544	04	Gulfstream G550	5044	Israel Air & Space Force, CAEW, Tel Aviv.	N944GA
☐ 569	04	Gulfstream G550	5069	Israel Air & Space Force, CAEW, Tel Aviv.	N969GA
☐ 676	02	Gulfstream V	676	Israel Defence Force, Tel Aviv.	N676GA
☐ 679	02	Gulfstream V	679	Israel Defence Force, Tel Aviv.	N679GA
☐ 684	02	Gulfstream V	684	Israel Defence Force, Tel Aviv.	N684GA

Reg   Yr   Type   c/n   Owner/Operator   Prev Regn

5A = LIBYA   Total 13
Civil

Reg	Yr	Type	c/n	Owner/Operator	Prev Regn
☐ 5A-DAG	68	Falcon 20C	143	Air Jamahiriya, Tripoli.	F-WMKH
☐ 5A-DAJ	69	JetStar-8	5136	Libyan Air Ambulance/Ministry of Health, Tripoli.	LAAF001
☐ 5A-DAK	76	B 707-3L5C	21228	Government of Libya, Tripoli.	
☐ 5A-DCK	78	Corvette	38	Libyan Air Ambulance/Ministry of Health, Tripoli.	F-ODIF
☐ 5A-DCM	81	Falcon 50	68	Government of Libya, Tripoli.	F-WZHQ
☐ 5A-DCN	04	Falcon 900EX EASY	148	Libyan Arab Airlines, Tripoli.	F-WWFG
☐ 5A-DCO	70	Falcon 20C	190	Air Jamahiriya, Tripoli.	LAAF002
☐ 5A-DDQ	70	BAC 1-11/414EG	158	Libyan Arab Airlines, Tripoli.	C5-LKI
☐ 5A-DDS	79	Gulfstream 2	242	Libyan Arab Airlines, Tripoli.	
☐ 5A-DKO	67	BAC 1-11/422EQ	126	Libavia Aviation,	VP-BBA
☐ 5A-DKQ	68	Falcon 20D-5B	175	Medi Avia, Luqa, Malta.	SU-AOE
☐ 5A-DRK	07	Citation Excel XLS	560-5710		N1312T
☐ 5A-ONE	96	Airbus A340-213	151	Afrigiyah Airways, Tripoli.	HZ-WBT4

5B = CYPRUS   Total 3
Civil

Reg	Yr	Type	c/n	Owner/Operator	Prev Regn
☐ 5B-...	66	HS 125/1A	25088	J A T Overseas Ltd. Nicosia. (status ?).	N1230B
☐ 5B-CKL	00	Hawker 800XP	258495	Lexata Aviation Ltd. Athens, Greece.	C-GGCH
☐ 5B-CKO	06	Falcon 2000EX EASY	96	CSM Aviation Co. Limassol.	F-WWGN

5H = TANZANIA   Total 2
Civil

Reg	Yr	Type	c/n	Owner/Operator	Prev Regn
☐ 5H-CCM	78	F 28-3000	11137	Government of Tanzania, Dar es Salaam. 'Uhuru na Umoja'	PH-ZBS
☐ 5H-ONE	03	Gulfstream G550	5030	Government of Tanzania, Dar es Salaam.	N830GA

5N = NIGERIA   Total 33
Civil

Reg	Yr	Type	c/n	Owner/Operator	Prev Regn
☐ 5N-AGV	76	Gulfstream 2	177	Federal Government of Nigeria, Lagos.	N17587
☐ 5N-AGZ	89	BAe 125/800B	258143	Central Bank of Nigeria, Lagos.	5N-NPF
☐ 5N-AOC	81	Learjet 25D	25D-322	AIC Co Ltd. Ibadan.	
☐ 5N-AVK	82	HS 125/700B	257160	(status ?).	G-5-19
☐ 5N-BEL	85	Citation S/II	S550-0079	Air Logistics International Ltd.	N97LB
☐ 5N-BEX	83	HS 125/700A	257197	Associated Aviation Ltd. Lagos.	(N2QL)
☐ 5N-BFC	81	HS 125/700A	NA0305	Associated Aviation Ltd. Lagos.	N305TH
☐ 5N-BGR	01	Learjet 45	45-163	Capital Aviation Services BV. Kaduna.	N427BX
☐ 5N-BJM	06	Embraer 145LR	14500984	State Government of Bauchi, Nigeria.	PT-SKE
☐ 5N-BJS	07	Citation Excel XLS	560-5703		N560MF
☐ 5N-DAO	82	HS 125/700A	NA0329	Associated Aviation Ltd. Lagos.	N190WC
☐ 5N-DGN	92	BAe 1000B	259018	Executive Jets Service Ltd.	5N-FGR
☐ 5N-DOT	76	HS 125/600B	256062	EAS Airlines Ltd.	5N-MAY
☐ 5N-EAS	70	HS 125/403B	25217	Executive Airline Services Ltd. Lagos. (stored FXE).	G-OLFR
☐ 5N-EMA	76	HS 125/600A	256069	Southern Airlines Ltd. Lagos.	N369TS
☐ 5N-FGE	90	Falcon 900	96	Federal Government of Nigeria, Lagos.	5N-OIL
☐ 5N-FGN	82	B 727-2N5	22825	Federal Government of Nigeria, Lagos.	5N-AGY
☐ 5N-FGO	88	Falcon 900	52	Federal Government of Nigeria, Lagos.	F-WWFC
☐ 5N-FGP	90	Gulfstream 4	1126	Federal Government of Nigeria, Lagos. (status ?).	N426GA
☐ 5N-FGT	05	BBJ-7N6/W	34260	Federal Government of Nigeria, Lagos.	N1781B
☐ 5N-JMA	03	Hawker 800XP	258658	Arik Air Ltd. Lagos.	(ZS-ARK)
☐ 5N-JMB	03	Hawker 800XP	258659	Arik Air Ltd. Lagos.	N659XP
☐ 5N-MAO	82	HS 125/700A	NA0332	King Airlines & Travel Ltd. Lagos.	N332WE
☐ 5N-MAZ	82	HS 125/700B	257169	King Airlines & Travel Ltd. Lagos.	B-HSS
☐ 5N-NPC	88	BAe 125/800B	258109	Aero Contractors Ltd/Nigerian National Petroleum Co. Lagos.	G-5-581
☐ 5N-RSG	05	Embraer Legacy 600	14500891	Government of Rivers State, Port Harcourt.	PT-S..
☐ 5N-SPE	01	Dornier Do328JET	3151	Shell Petroleum Development Co. Lagos.	D-BDXT
☐ 5N-SPM	01	Dornier Do328JET	3141	Shell Petroleum Development Co. Lagos.	D-BDXR
☐ 5N-SPN	99	Dornier Do328JET	3120	Shell Petroleum Development Co. Lagos.	D-BABA
☐ 5N-YET	73	HS 125/600A	256013	Associated Aviation Ltd. Lagos.	VR-CDG
☐ ZS-PTT	73	Citation	500-0085	Retail Marketing Services P/L. Lanseria.	5N-BCI

Military

Reg	Yr	Type	c/n	Owner/Operator	Prev Regn
☐ 5N-AYA	90	Citation II	550-0632	Nigerian Air Force, Lagos.	N12570
☐ 5N-FGS	01	Gulfstream V	643	Nigerian Air Force, Lagos.	N523GA

5R = MADAGASCAR   Total 4
Civil

Reg	Yr	Type	c/n	Owner/Operator	Prev Regn
☐ 5R-MBR	75	Corvette	16	Aeromarine, Antananarivo-Ivato.	5R-MVN
☐ 5R-MHF	80	Citation II/SP	551-0171	Ste Henri Fraise Fils et Cie, Tananarive-Ivato.	ZS-PMC

Reg	Yr	Type	c/n	Owner/Operator	Prev Regn
☐ 5R-MHK *Military*	76	Corvette	34	Trimeta SA. Ivato. (status ?).	CN-TCS
☐ 5R-MRM		B 737-3Z9	24081	Government of Madagascar, Ivato.	OE-ILG

5T = MAURITANIA   Total 1
Civil

☐ 5T-CJP	79	B 727-294	22044	Government of Mauritania, Nouakchott.	ZS-OBM

5U = NIGER   Total 1
Military

☐ 5U-BAG	78	B 737-2N9C	21499	Government of Niger Republic, Niamey. 'Monts Baghezan'	(5U-MAF)

5V = TOGO   Total 3
Civil

☐ 5V-TAI	74	F 28-1000	11079	Government of Togo, Lome.	5V-MAB
☐ 5V-TGF	69	DC 8-62H	46071	Government of Togo, Lome.	P4-DCE
☐ 5V-TTP	75	HS 125/600B	256049	JPM Aviation, Gnassingbe-Eyadema.	P4-PJR

5X = UGANDA   Total 1
Civil

☐ 5X-UEF	00	Gulfstream 4SP	1413	Government of Uganda, Kampala.	N413GA

5Y = KENYA   Total 4
Civil

☐ 5Y-MNG	99	Citation Bravo	550-0876	Phoenix Aviation Ltd. Nairobi.	N876CB
☐ 5Y-MSR	01	Citation Bravo	550-0975	AMREF-African Medical & Research Foundation, Nairobi.	N975HM
☐ 5Y-TWE	88	Citation II	550-0569	Transworld Safaris (K) Ltd. Nairobi.	G-OSNB

Military

☐ KAF308	95	Fokker 70	11557	Government of Kenya, Nairobi.	PH-MXM

6V = SENEGAL   Total 1
Civil

☐ 6V-AEF	75	B 727-2M1	21091	Government of Senegal, Dakar. 'Pointe de Sangomar'	N40104

7O = YEMEN   Total 1
Civil

☐ 7O-YMN	79	B 747SP-27	21786	Government of Yemen, Sana'a.	A7-AHM

7Q = MALAWI   Total 1
Military

☐ MAAW-J1	86	BAe 125/800B	258064	Government of Malawi, Zomba.	G-5-514

7T = ALGERIA   Total 7
Civil

☐ 7T-VCW	82	HS 125/700B	257163	E.N. pour l'Exploitation Meteorlogique et Aeronautique.	G-5-12
☐ 7T-VVL	68	HS 125/3B	25131	Sahara Airlines, Algiers.	3A-MDE

Military

☐ 7T-VPC	00	Gulfstream 4SP	1418	Government of Algeria, Algiers.	N418GA
☐ 7T-VPG	00	Gulfstream V	617	Government of Algeria, Algiers.	N5G
☐ 7T-VPM	00	Gulfstream 4SP	1421	Government of Algeria, Algiers.	N421GA
☐ 7T-VPR	96	Gulfstream 4SP	1288	Government of Algeria, Algiers.	N403GA
☐ 7T-VPS	96	Gulfstream 4SP	1291	Government of Algeria, Algiers.	N412GA

8P = BARBADOS   Total 1
Civil

☐ 8P-MSD	06	Gulfstream G550	5137	Augusto Lopez/Helicol SA. Bogota, Colombia.	N287GA

9A = CROATIA   Total 1
Civil

☐ 9A-CRO	96	Challenger 604	5322	Government of Croatia/Republika Hrvatska, Zagreb.	N604CL

9G = GHANA   Total 1
Military

☐ G-530	77	F 28-3000	11125	Government/Ghana Air Force, Accra.	PH-ZBP

9H = MALTA   Total 2
Civil

☐ 9H-AEE	99	Learjet 60	60-170	Eurojet Ltd. Luqa.	D-COWS
☐ 9H-AFB	07	Learjet 60XR	60-327	Europe Executive Jet Services.	N5016Z

9J = ZAMBIA   Total 1
Civil

☐ 9J-...	01	Challenger 604	5486	Government of Zambia, Lusaka.	ZS-OSG

9K = KUWAIT   Total 6
Civil

☐ 9K-AHI	84	Airbus A300C-620	344	Government of Kuwait, Kuwait City. 'Al Sabahiya'	PK-MAY
☐ 9K-AJD	98	Gulfstream V	560	Kuwait Airways Corp. Kuwait City.	N660GA
☐ 9K-AJE	99	Gulfstream V	569	Kuwait Airways Corp. Kuwait City.	N469GA
☐ 9K-AJF	99	Gulfstream V	573	Kuwait Airways Corp. Kuwait City.	N673GA
☐ 9K-AKD	03	Airbus A320-212	2046	Government of Kuwait, Kuwait City. 'Al-Mobarakiya'	F-WWBG
☐ 9K-ALD	93	Airbus A310-308	648	Government of Kuwait, Kuwait City. 'Al-Salmiya'	F-WWCR

9M = MALAYSIA   Total 14
Civil

☐ 9M-...	73	Falcon 20-5B	292	Maxland Sdn Bhd. Sabah.	N510WS
☐ 9M-ABC	96	Gulfstream 4SP	1312	Flightplan Jet Club Ltd/T Ananda Krishnan, Kuala Lumpur.	N453GA
☐ 9M-ATM	05	Citation X	750-0242	Hornbill Skyways. Kuching, Sarawak.	N1289G
☐ 9M-CAL	94	Learjet 60	60-034	Civil Aviation Directorate, Kuala Lumpur.	N5034Z
☐ 9M-FCL	95	Learjet 60	60-072	Civil Aviation Directorate, Kuala Lumpur.	N5072L
☐ 9M-FRA	70	Falcon 20EW	224	Falcon Special Air Services Sdn Bhd. Subang.	G-FRAM
☐ 9M-ISJ	89	Gulfstream 4	1106	Government of Johore, Johore Bahru.	N17608
☐ 9M-NAA	06	Airbus A319-115XCJ	2949	Government of Malaysia, Kuala Lumpur.	D-AIDR
☐ 9M-TAN	06	Challenger 300	20135	Berjaya Air Sdn Bhd. Kuala Lumpur.	C-FLDD
☐ 9M-ZAB	05	Citation Bravo	550-1121	Pan Northern Air Services Sdn Bhd. Halim.	N1309B

Military

☐ M28-01	75	F 28-1000	11088	9M-EBE, TUDM, 2 Sku, Subang.	FM2101
☐ M37-01	88	Falcon 900	64	9M-..., TUDM, 2 Sku, Subang.	N446FJ
☐ M48-02	02	Global Express	9096	TUDM, 2 Sku, Subang.	M52-01
☐ M53-01	99	BBJ-7H6	29274	TUDM, 2 Sku, Subang.	9M-BBJ

9Q = CONGO KINSHASA   Total 8
Civil

☐ 9Q-CAI	75	HS 125/600A	256047	ITAB, Lubumbashi.	9Q-CYA
☐ 9Q-CBC	71	HS 125/F600B	25258	SCIBE Airlift, Kinshasa.	TL-ADK
☐ 9Q-CDC	66	B 727-30	18934	Democratic Republic of Congo, Kinshasa. 'Hewa Bora'	9Q-RDZ
☐ 9Q-CFJ	75	HS 125/600A	256051	Bionic Aviation,	N601JA
☐ 9Q-CGF	74	HS 125/600B	256031	Forrest Industries, Lumbumbashi.	9Q-CFW
☐ 9Q-CLK	59	B 707-138B	17702	Government of Democratic Republic of Congo, Kinshasa.	N707SK
☐ 9Q-CMC	65	B 727-30	18371	Government of Democratic Republic of Congo, Kinshasa.	N134AS
☐ 9Q-CPR	71	HS 125/403B	25247	Shabair SPRL. Lumbumbashi.	9Q-CSN

9XR = RWANDA   Total 1
Civil

☐ 9XR-CH		Caravelle 3	209	Government of Rwanda, Kigali.	F-BUFM

* *Denotes reserved registration*

Total Bizjets   16410

Reg   Yr   Type   c/n   Owner/Operator   Prev Regn

Business Jets - Written Off /Withdrawn From Use

A4O = OMAN
Civil

Reg	Yr	Type	c/n	Owner/Operator	Prev Regn
❏ A4O-AB		VC 10-1103	820	Wfu. Displayed at Brooklands Museum, Weybridge, UK.	G-ASIX

A6 = UNITED ARAB EMIRATES
Civil

Reg	Yr	Type	c/n	Owner/Operator	Prev Regn
❏ A6-SHK	1987	BAe 146 Statesman	E1091	Wfu. Last located Bournemouth-Hurn UK.	G-BOMA

B = CHINA
Civil

Reg	Yr	Type	c/n	Owner/Operator	Prev Regn
❏ B-7023	1992	Citation VI	650-0221	W/o Xichang, China. 2 Sep 02.	B-4107

B = CHINA - TAIWAN
Civil

Reg	Yr	Type	c/n	Owner/Operator	Prev Regn
❏ B-98181	1993	Learjet 35A	35A-675	W/o target towing Eastern Taiwan. 17 Sep 94.	N2602M

Military

Reg	Yr	Type	c/n	Owner/Operator	Prev Regn
❏ 18351	1961	B 720-051B	18351	Wfu. Preserved at Kangshan AB Museum, Taiwan.	N721US
❏ 2721	1967	B 727-109	19399	Wfu.	B-1818
❏ 2722	1967	B 727-109	19520	Wfu. Located Taiching, Taiwan.	B-1820
❏ 2723	1969	B 727-109C	20111	Wfu. Located Nankang, Taiwan.	B-1822
❏ 2724	1967	B 727-121C	19818	Wfu.	B-188

C = CANADA
Civil

Reg	Yr	Type	c/n	Owner/Operator	Prev Regn
❏ C-FBCL	1972	Citation	500-0042	Wfu. Cx C- 6/97. Last located at Addison, Tx. USA.	N542CC
❏ CF-BRL	1972	Sabre-40A	282-107	W/o Frobisher Bay, NT. Canada. 27 Feb 74.	N40NR
❏ C-FCFL	1970	HS 125/400A	NA741	W/o Labrador, NF. Canada. 9 Dec 77.	G-AXTT
❏ CF-CFL	1969	HS 125/400A	NA725	W/o Labrador, NF. Canada. 11 Nov 69.	
❏ C-FDTF	1966	JetStar-6	5088	Wfu. Located Atlantic Canada Museum, Halifax, NS.	N9244R
❏ C-FDTX	1961	JetStar-6	5018	Wfu. Located Rockcliffe Museum, Ottawa, ON. Canada.	N9287R
❏ C-FEYG	1966	Jet Commander	81	W/o Winnipeg, MT. Canada. 26 May 78.	CF-KBI
❏ C-FHLL	1965	HS 125/1A	25034	Wfu. Accident 4/83. Wing fitted to s/n 25027. YHU 10/95.	
❏ C-FMTC	1966	HS 125/1A-522	25104	Wfu. Last located at Lakeland, Fl. USA.	N140AK
❏ C-FMWW	1982	Westwind-Two	380	W/o Meadowlake, SK. Canada. 27 Jan 94.	N380DA
❏ C-FRBC	1973	JetStar-8	5160	Wfu. Last located Memphis, Tn. USA. Parted out 1988.	(N60EE)
❏ C-FSKC	1972	Citation	500-0018	W/o Rawlins, Wy. USA. 25 Jul 98.	N70841
❏ C-FTBZ	1994	Challenger 604	5991	W/o Wichita, Ks. USA. 10 Oct 00. (prototype Ff 18 Sep 94).	C-GLYA
❏ C-GBNE	1978	Citation	500-0378	Wfu. Located Stephenson Technical School, Winnipeg, Canada.	N3156M
❏ C-GBRW	1973	Learjet 36	36-001	Wfu. Cx C- 4/97. College of Aeronautics, Montreal St Hubert.	N26GL
❏ C-GBWA	1973	Learjet 24D	24D-261	Wfu. Last located Detroit-Willow Run, Mi. USA.	D-COOL
❏ C-GCGR-X	1978	Challenger 600	1001	W/o Mojave, Ca. USA. 3 Apr 80.	
❏ C-GCGT	1979	Challenger 601	1003	Wfu. Located National Aviation Museum, Rockcliffe, Canada.	
❏ C-GESZ	1972	Citation	500-0022	Wfu. Last located St Hubert-Montreal, Canada.	N800JD
❏ C-GJCF	2001	Challenger 300	20002	Wfu. Cx C- 8/06.	
❏ C-GKHA	1965	Falcon 20C	19	Wfu. Last located Ottawa-Rockcliffe, Canada. Cx C- 4/04.	(N41PD)
❏ C-GMAJ	1975	Citation	500-0247	Wfu. Last located at Addison, Tx. USA.	XA-JUA
❏ C-GMEA	1968	HS 125/3A-RA	NA702	Wfu. Located Arnoni Aviation Inc. Houston, Tx. USA.	N813PR
❏ C-GNSA	1974	Citation	500-0160	Wfu. Parts at White Industries Inc. Bates City, Mo. USA.	N59TS
❏ C-GNVT	1979	Falcon 10	138	W/o Kuujjuaq, PQ. Canada. 14 Aug 01.	N236DJ
❏ C-GPUN	1976	Learjet 35	35-058	W/o Queen Charlotte Island, BC. Canada. 11 Jan 95.	
❏ C-GQCC	1973	Citation	500-0066	Wfu. CoR Cx 4/05.	N66CC
❏ C-GWPB	1967	Falcon 20C	92	Wfu. Located B C Institute of Technology, Vancouver, Canada.	117503
❏ C-GXFZ	1972	Citation	500-0032	W/o Orillia, ON. Canada. 26 Sep 84.	(N5364U)
❏ C-GYCJ	1987	Citation II	550-0561	W/o Sandspit, BC. Canada. 12 Nov 02. (parts at Rantoul, Ks.)	N234RA

Military

Reg	Yr	Type	c/n	Owner/Operator	Prev Regn
❏ 144612	1979	Challenger 600S	1002	Wfu. Last located at Heritage Park, Winnipeg, MT. Canada.	C-GCGS-X
❏ 144613	1984	Challenger 601	3035	W/o Shearwater, NS. Canada. 24 Apr 95.	C-GCUN

CC = CHILE
Military

Reg	Yr	Type	c/n	Owner/Operator	Prev Regn
❏ E-302	1984	Citation III	650-0033	W/o Concepcion, Chile. 9 Jul 92.	CC-ECE

D = GERMANY
Civil

Reg	Yr	Type	c/n	Owner/Operator	Prev Regn
❏ D-ARWE	2000	Challenger 604	5454	W/o Almaty, Kazakhstan. 26 Dec 07.	N324FX
❏ D-ASDB	1977	VFW 614	G19	Wfu. Located RAF St Athan, UK.	OY-RRW
❏ D-AXDB	1977	VFW 614	G18	Wfu. Located Nordholtz, Germany.	(OY-RGT)
❏ D-CARA	1966	HFB 320	1021	Wfu. Cx D- 3 Jul 84. Displayed at Finkenwerder, Germany.	

Reg Yr Type c/n Owner/Operator Prev Regn

Reg	Yr	Type	c/n	Owner/Operator	Prev Regn
☐ D-CARE	1966	HFB 320	1022	Wfu. Located at Finow Museum, Germany.	
☐ D-CARY	1967	HFB 320	1026	Wfu. Located Laatzen Museum, Hanover, Germany.	TC-FNS
☐ D-CASH	1987	Citation II	550-0564	W/o Salzburg, Austria. 19 Feb 96.	N674CA
☐ D-CASY	1968	HFB 320	1029	W/o Blackpool, UK. 29 Jun 72.	
☐ D-CATY	1977	Learjet 35A	35A-114	W/o Moscow, Russia. 15 Dec 94. (Parts at Dodsons).	(N851L)
☐ D-CBNA	1967	Falcon 20C	63	W/o Narsarsuaq, Greenland. 4 Aug 01.	PH-LPS
☐ D-CBUR	1977	Falcon 10	98	W/o Friesenheim, Germany. 8 Aug 96.	F-WPXG
☐ D-CDFA	1975	Learjet 36	36-006	W/o Libya. 26 Mar 80.	D-CAFO
☐ D-CDPD	1974	Learjet 25B	25B-177	W/o North Atlantic. 18 May 83.	N74SW
☐ D-CGSP	2006	Grob G-180 SPn	90002	W/o Tussenhausen-Mattsies, Germany. 29 November 06.	
☐ D-CHFB	1964	HFB 320	V1	W/o Torrejon, Spain. 12 May 65.	
☐ D-CHVB	1989	Citation II	550-0629	W/o Allendorf, Germany 25 Jan 95.	N1256T
☐ D-CIRO	1969	HFB 320	1044	W/o Texel Island, Netherlands. 18 Dec 70.	
☐ D-CLOU	1964	HFB 320	V2	Wfu. Located at Deutsches Museum, Munich, Germany.	
☐ D-CMMM	1976	Learjet 24D	24D-328	Wfu. Located Fliegernuseum, Altenrhein, Germany.	D-IMMM
☐ D-COCO	1982	Learjet 35A	35A-466	W/o Cologne-Bonn, Germany. 7 Jun 93.	N600WJ
☐ D-COSA	1971	HFB 320	1056	Wfu. Located Niederaltaich, Germany.	
☐ D-IAEC	1981	Citation 1/SP	501-0203	W/o Blankensee Airport, Lubeck, Germany. 31 May 87.	N67830
☐ D-IEVX	2001	CitationJet CJ-2	525A-0036	W/o Milan, Italy. 8 Oct 01.	N5246Z
☐ D-IHAQ	1965	Learjet 23	23-007	W/o Zurich, Switzerland. 12 Dec 65.	N826L
☐ D-IHLZ	1970	Learjet 24B	24B-225	W/o Mariensiel, Germany. 18 Jun 73.	N618R
☐ D-IJHM	1980	Citation II/SP	551-0033	W/o Kassel, Germany. 19 May 82.	N88692
☐ D-IMRX	1985	Citation 1/SP	501-0688	W/o Nr Bushin, N.Iraq. 16 Feb 06.	

Military

Reg	Yr	Type	c/n	Owner/Operator	Prev Regn
☐ 10+01	1968	B 707-307C	19997	Wfu. to NATO as LX-N19997.	(68-11071)
☐ 10+02	1968	B 707-307C	19998	Wfu. to USAF for E-8C J-STARS.	(68-11072)
☐ 10+04	1968	B 707-307C	20000	Wfu. to NATO as LX-N20000.	(68-11074)
☐ 16+06	1969	HFB 320	1048	Wfu. Located Luftwaffe Museum Gatow-Berlin, Germany.	D-CISI
☐ 16+08	1966	HFB 320	1025	Wfu. Located Hamburg, Germany. (for restoration).	D-9537
☐ 16+22	1976	HFB 320	1059	W/o Schwabmuenchen, Germany. 27 Nov 76.	98+25
☐ 16+26	1979	HFB 320ECM	1063	Wfu. Located Luftwaffe Museum Gatow-Berlin, Germany.	D-CANU
☐ CA+102	1962	JetStar-6	5035	W/o Bremen, Germany. 16 Jan 68.	(62-12167)

EC = SPAIN

Civil

Reg	Yr	Type	c/n	Owner/Operator	Prev Regn
☐ EC-CGG	1973	Citation	500-0108	W/o Barcelona, Spain. 22 Nov 74.	N108CC
☐ EC-CKR	1975	Learjet 25B	25B-184	W/o Northolt, UK. 13 Aug 96. (parts at Bates City, Mo.).	
☐ EC-DFA	1978	Learjet 35A	35A-196	W/o Palma, Spain. 13 Aug 80.	HB-VFU
☐ EC-DQC	1976	Corvette	24	Wfu. Sold as spares 2/91.	F-BVPI
☐ EC-DQE	1976	Corvette	26	Wfu. Cx EC- 8/97, Fuselage at Dieupentale, France.	F-GDAY
☐ EC-DQG	1976	Corvette	27	W/o Cordoba, Spain. 25 Nov 00.	F-BVPH
☐ EC-ECB	1969	Falcon 20DC	210	W/o Las Palmas, Canary Islands. 30 Sep 87.	N66VG
☐ EC-EFI	1968	Falcon 20D	189	W/o Nr Keflavik, Iceland. 11 Oct 87.	N444BF
☐ EC-EGS	1974	HS 125/600A	256034	Wfu. Parts at Spirit of St Louis, Mo. USA.	EC-115
☐ EC-EGT	1966	HS 125/1A-522	25080	Wfu. Parts at Dodsons, Rantoul, Ks. USA.	N23KL
☐ EC-EHF	1973	HS 125/600A	256011	Wfu. Parts at Dodsons, Rantoul, Ks. USA.	N81D
☐ EC-EKK	1967	Falcon 20C	106	Wfu. Located Madrid-Barajas, Spain.	N31V
☐ EC-EQP	1968	Falcon 20C	149	Wfu. Located Madrid-Barajas, Spain.	EC-263
☐ EC-FGX	1965	JetStar-731	5062	Wfu. Cx USA 5/97.	EC-697
☐ EC-GXX	1979	Learjet 35A	35A-263	Wfu.	(ZS-PBA)
☐ EC-HFA	1974	Citation	500-0209	Wfu. Last located at Griffin, Ga. USA.	N800AV
☐ EC-HHZ	1975	Corvette	15	Wfu. Located Toulouse-Blagnac, France.	F-GNAF

EI = EIRE

Military

Reg	Yr	Type	c/n	Owner/Operator	Prev Regn
☐ 236	1971	HS 125/F600B	25256	W/o Casement-Dublin, Ireland. 27 Nov 79.	G-AYBH

EL = LIBERIA

Civil

Reg	Yr	Type	c/n	Owner/Operator	Prev Regn
☐ EL-VDY	1971	Falcon 20E	245	Wfu. Parts at Dodsons, Rantoul, Ks. USA.	HB-VDY

EP = IRAN

Civil

Reg	Yr	Type	c/n	Owner/Operator	Prev Regn
☐ EP-AGX	1973	Falcon 20E	283	W/o Kermanshah, Iran. 21 Nov 74.	F-WRQS
☐ EP-PLN	1964	B 727-30	18363	Wfu. Last located Tehran, Iran.	EP-SHP

Military

Reg	Yr	Type	c/n	Owner/Operator	Prev Regn
☐ 15-2233	1975	Falcon 20E	333	W/o Orumiyeh, Iran. 9 Jan 06.	5-2801
☐ 5-2802	1975	Falcon 20E	336	Wfu. Last located Tehran, Iran.	F-WRQP
☐ 5-2803	1976	Falcon 20E	340	Wfu. Last located Tehran, Iran.	F-WRQX

Reg	Yr	Type	c/n	Owner/Operator	Prev Regn
☐ 5-2804	1976	Falcon 20E	346	Wfu. Last located Tehran, Iran.	F-WRQP
☐ 5-3020	1976	Falcon 20E	348	W/o Ardebil, Iran. 3 March 97.	5-4039
☐ 5-9001	1976	Falcon 20F	351	W/o Iran. 15 Feb 91.	F-WMKJ
☐ 5-9002	1976	Falcon 20F	353	W/o Iran. 31 Jan 91.	F-WRQP

F = FRANCE

Civil

Reg	Yr	Type	c/n	Owner/Operator	Prev Regn
☐ F-BKMF	1964	HS 125/1	25007	W/o Nice, France. 5 Jun 66.	HB-VAH
☐ F-BMSS	1965	Falcon 20F	2	Wfu. Located Musee de l'Air, Paris-Le Bourget.	F-WMSS
☐ F-BRNL	1969	Learjet 24B	24B-183	W/o Toulouse, France. 18 Dec 85.	OY-AGZ
☐ F-BSQN	1972	Falcon 10	03	Wfu. CoA expiry 4/81.	F-WSQN
☐ F-BSRL	1969	Learjet 24B	24B-210	W/o Provins Nr Paris, France. 10 Jun 85.	ZS-LLG
☐ F-BSTM	1965	AC 680V-TU	1540-6	Wfu. Cx F- 18 Nov 91. Museum exhibit Pelegry-Perpignan.	F-WSTM
☐ F-BTTU	1977	Corvette	37	W/o St Yan, France. 31 Jul 90.	
☐ F-BUQP	1974	Corvette	4	Wfu. Located Toulouse-Blagnac, France.	F-WUQP
☐ F-BVPB	1974	Corvette	6	Wfu. Cx F- 26 Nov 99. Located Paris-Le Bourget, France.	F-OGJL
☐ F-BVPG	1976	Corvette	25	Wfu. CoA expiry 20 May 02. Cx F- 10/06.	F-OBZV
☐ F-BXPT	1965	Learjet 23	23-014	Wfu. CoA expiry 11 Mar 93. Located Limoges, France.	(HB-VEL)
☐ F-GAMA	1965	Learjet 23	23-023	Wfu. Located Perigeux-Bassillac Technical school, France.	HB-VEL
☐ F-GAPY	1965	Learjet 23	23-027	Wfu. at White Industries, Bates City, Mo. USA.	(N108TW)
☐ F-GBTC	1978	Falcon 10	124	W/o Chalons-Vatry Nr Paris, France. 15 Jan 86.	F-WPUY
☐ F-GDAE	1966	Learjet 24	24-105	Wfu. Last located Allibaudiere, Troyes, France.	TR-LYB
☐ F-GDAV	1965	Learjet 23	23-017	W/o Lisbon, Portugal. 30 Jan 89.	F-GBTA
☐ F-GDHR	1982	Learjet 55	55-070	W/o Nr Jakiri, Cameroun. 5 Feb 87.	
☐ F-GHLN	1972	Falcon 20E	255	W/o Paris-Le Bourget, France. 20 Jan 95.	VH-MIQ
☐ F-GJCC	1967	Falcon 20C	72	Wfu. Last located Middletown Hook, Oh, USA.	(N172MV)
☐ F-GJGB	1975	Falcon 10	47	W/o Besancon, France. 30 Sep 93.	N79PB
☐ F-GJHK	1977	Falcon 10	108	W/o Brest, France. 26 Mar 92.	(F-GFJK)
☐ F-GJMA	1978	Falcon 10	116	W/o Madrid, Spain. 27 Sep 96.	N525RC
☐ F-GKDB	1973	Falcon 20E	271	Wfu. Located at Flight Safety International, Paris-LeBourget	F-GHPO
☐ F-GKPP	1961	MS 760 Paris-2	98	W/o Calvi, Corsica. Oct 91.	3A-MPP
☐ F-ODSR	1976	Corvette	35	Wfu. Cx F- 14 Jun 07.	5R-MVD
☐ F-OVJR	1970	Falcon 20C-5B	180	W/o Kiel, Germany. 15 Feb 06.	(F-GVJR)
☐ F-WAMD		Falcon 30	01	Wfu. Last located CAEA, Bordeaux, France.	
☐ F-WDFJ	1977	Falcon 20G	362	Wfu. Conservatoire de l'Air et de l'Espace d'Aquitaine.	F-WATF
☐ F-WFAL	1970	Falcon 10	01	W/o Romorantin-Loire Valley, France. 31 Oct 72.	
☐ F-WLKB	1963	Falcon 20C	01	Wfu. Located Musee de l'Air, Paris-Le Bourget.	F-BLKB
☐ F-WMSH	1965	Falcon 20C	1	Wfu. Conservatoire de l'Air et de l'Espace d'Aquitaine.	F-ZACV
☐ F-WNDB	1976	Falcon 50	1	Wfu. Conservatoire de l'Air et de l'Espace d'Aquitaine.	F-BNDB
☐ F-WRSN	1970	Corvette	01	W/o Marseilles, France. 23 Mar 71.	(F-WSSE)
☐ F-WUQN	1973	Corvette	3	Wfu. Gate Guardian at St Nazaire Airbus factory.	F-WUQN
☐ F-WZIH	1966	HFB 320	1024	Wfu. at Musee de l'Air, Paris-Le Bourget, France.	16+07

Military

Reg	Yr	Type	c/n	Owner/Operator	Prev Regn
☐ 141	1963	Caravelle 3	141	Wfu. Located at Musee de l'Air, Paris-Le Bourget, France.	F-BJTK
☐ 154	1968	Falcon 20C	154	W/o Rambouillet, France. 22 Jan 76.	F-WLCV
☐ 39	1975	Falcon 10MER	39	W/o Toul-Rosieres, France. 30 Jan 80.	F-WPUX
☐ F-RAED	1967	Falcon 20C	93	Wfu. Located Chateaudun, France.	F-RAEC
☐ F-RAEE	1971	Falcon 20C	238	Wfu. Located Vigenis, France.	F-RAFM
☐ F-RAEG	1974	Falcon 20E	291	Wfu. Last located Chateaudun, France.	F-RAEC
☐ F-RAEH	1980	Falcon 20F	422	Wfu. Located Vilgenis, France.	F-RCAL
☐ F-RHFA	1966	Falcon 20C	49	Wfu. Located at Villacoublay, Paris, France.	F-TEOA
☐ F-UGWP	1975	Falcon 20E	309	W/o Nr Villacoublay-Paris, France. 2 Dec 91.	F-RAFU
☐ F-UKJE/463	1970	Falcon 20SNA	186	Wfu. Last located Chateaudun, France..	F-UGWM/463
☐ F-UKJG	1967	Falcon 20SNA	115	Wfu. Last located at Chateaudun, France.	F-UGWL/115
☐ F-UKJI	1983	Falcon 20F	483	Wfu.	F-UGWO
☐ F-ZACB	1971	Falcon 10	02	Wfu. Located ENSAE at Lespinet near Toulouse, France.	F-ZJTA
☐ F-ZACS	1966	Falcon 20C	22	Wfu. Located with Thales mechanics N of Le Bourget, Paris.	F-BMKK
☐ F-ZACU	1968	Falcon 20C	145	Wfu. Conservatoire de l'Air et de l'Espace d'Aquitaine.	F-GCGY
☐ F-ZACW	1967	Falcon 20C	104	Wfu. Located Vilgenis, France.	F-BOXV
☐ F-ZVMV	1972	Corvette	1	Wfu. Located Istres, France.	F-BUAS
☐ F-ZVMW	1973	Corvette	2	Wfu. Located P Mendes-France Technical College, Vitrolles.	F-BNRZ
☐ F-ZVMX	1974	Corvette	10	Wfu. Located Toulouse-Blagnac, France.	F-GFEJ

G = GREAT BRITAIN

Civil

Reg	Yr	Type	c/n	Owner/Operator	Prev Regn
☐ G-ARVF		VC 10-1101	808	Wfu. Located Hermeskiel collection Nr Trier, Germany	
☐ G-ARYA	1962	HS 125/1	25001	Wfu. De Havilland Aircraft Heritage Centre. (bare nose only)	

| Reg | Yr | Type | c/n | Owner/Operator | Prev Regn |

Reg	Yr	Type	c/n	Owner/Operator	Prev Regn
G-ARYB	1962	HS 125/1	25002	Wfu. Located Midlands Air Museum, Coventry, UK.	
G-ARYC	1963	HS 125/1	25003	Wfu. Located De Havilland Aircraft Heritage Centre, Colney.	
G-ASNU	1964	HS 125/1	25005	Wfu. Cx G- 18 Nov 91. Last located Lagos, Nigeria .	D-COMA
G-ASSM	1965	HS 125/1-522	25010	Wfu. Located Kensington Science Museum, London, UK.	G-ASSM
G-ATPD	1966	HS 125/1B-522	25085	Wfu. Located Bournemouth-Hurn, UK.	5N-AGU
G-ATPE	1966	HS 125/1B-522	25092	Wfu. Cx G- 14 Mar 90.	
G-AVGW	1967	HS 125/3B	25120	W/o Luton, UK. 23 Dec 67.	
G-AXDM	1969	HS 125/403B	25194	Wfu. Located Farnborough, UK. Cx G- 11/03.	
G-AXPS	1967	HS 125/3B	25135	W/o Edinburgh, Scotland. 20 Jul 70.	HB-VAY
G-AZCH	1969	HS 125/3B-RA	25154	Wfu. Central fuselage in use as a mobile display, Luton, UK.	EP-AHK
G-BBRT	1974	HS 125/600B	256036	Wfu. Fuselage divided to Bristows-Redhill & Rolls Royce.	
G-BCUX	1974	HS 125/600B	256043	W/o Dunsfold, UK. 20 Nov 75.	
G-BKBH	1975	HS 125/600B	256052	Wfu. Cx G- 15 Jul 99. Located Southampton, UK.	5N-DNL
G-BKRL	1988	Leopard	001	Wfu. Cx G- 1/99. Parts at Bournemouth Aviation Museum, UK.	
G-BOCB	1966	HS 125/1B-522	25106	Wfu. Cx G- 22 Feb 95.	G-OMCA
G-BPCP	1980	Citation	500-0403	W/o Jersey, Channel Islands. 1 Oct 80.	N1710E
G-BRNM	1997	Leopard	002	Wfu. Located Bournemouth Aviation Museum, Hurn, UK.	
G-DBAL	1966	HS 125/3B	25117	Wfu. Cx G- 4/93.	G-BSAA
G-EXLR	1990	BAe 1000B	258151	Wfu. Instructional airframe at Raytheon, Wichita, Ks. USA.	
G-FIVE	1963	HS 125/1	25004	Wfu. Wings used in rebuild of s/n 25008, but not finalised.	G-ASEC
G-GMAC	1988	Gulfstream 4	1058	W/o Teterboro, NJ. USA. 1 Dec 04.	VP-BME
G-JETB	1981	Citation II	550-0288	W/o Southampton, UK. 26 May 1993.	G-MAMA
G-JSAX	1969	HS 125/3B-RA	25157	Wfu. Broken up 4/86 at Southampton, UK.	G-GGAE
G-LORI	1971	HS 125/403B	25246	Wfu. at Lagos, Nigeria.	G-AYOJ
G-MURI	1988	Learjet 35A	35A-646	W/o Lyon-Satolas, France. 2 May 00.	N712JB
G-OBOB	1966	HS 125/3B	25069	W/o Columbia, Mo. USA. 30 Jan 89. (parts at White Inds.).	G-BAXL
G-OHEA	1967	HS 125/3B-RA	25144	Wfu. Cx G- 6/94. Last located Cranfield, UK.	G-AVRG
G-OMGB	1974	HS 125/600B	256039	Wfu. at Luton, UK. TT 6944. Parts at Hooks Airport, Tx. USA.	EC-EAO
G-OMGC	1975	HS 125/600B	256056	Wfu. at Luton, UK. TT 6404. Parts at Hooks Airport, Tx. USA.	G-BKCD
G-TACE	1970	HS 125/403B	25223	Wfu. Cx G-1 /90. Last located Dunsfold, UK.	G-AYIZ
G-UESS	1976	Citation	500-0326	W/o Stornaway, Scotland. 8 Dec 83.	N45LC
G-YUGO	1966	HS 125/1B-522	25094	Wfu. Cx G- 3/93. Last located Biggin Hill, UK.	G-ATWH

Military

Reg	Yr	Type	c/n	Owner/Operator	Prev Regn
XS710/O	1965	Dominie T1	25012	Wfu. Instructional airframe as 9259M, RAF Cosford, UK.	XS710
XS714/P	1966	Dominie T1	25054	Wfu. Fire school RAF Manston, UK.	
XS726/T	1965	Dominie T1	25044	Wfu. Instructional airframe as 9273M, RAF Cosford, UK.	
XS729/G	1966	Dominie T1	25049	Wfu. Instructional airframe as 9275M, RAF Cosford, UK.	
XS732/B	1966	Dominie T1	25056	Wfu.	
XS733/Q	1966	Dominie T1	25059	Wfu. Instructional airframe as 9276M, RAF Cosford, UK.	
XS734/N	1966	Dominie T1	25061	Wfu. Instructional airframe as 9260M, RAF Cosford, UK.	
XS735/R	1966	Dominie T2	25071	Wfu. Instructional airframe at RAF St Athan, UK.	
XS736/S	1966	Dominie T2	25072	Wfu. Last located Cranwell, UK.	
XS738/U	1966	Dominie T1	25077	Wfu. Located RNAS Predannack, UK..	
XW930	1966	HS 125/1	25009	Wfu. Located Jordan's scrapyard Portsmouth, UK.	G-ATPC
ZF130	1976	HS 125/600B	256059	Wfu. Located Elektrowerkz Nightclub, Islington, UK.	(9M-DMF)

HB = SWITZERLAND

Civil

Reg	Yr	Type	c/n	Owner/Operator	Prev Regn
HB-PAA	1960	MS 760 Paris	69	Wfu. Cx HB- 25 Jun 84. Located Montelimar-Ancone.	J-4117
HB-VAM	1965	Learjet 23	23-044	W/o Innsbruck, Austria. 28 Aug 72.	N22B
HB-VAP	1966	Falcon 20C	37	W/o Goose Bay, NF, Canada. 1 Oct 67.	(N11WA)
HB-VCG	1970	Falcon 20D	231	W/o St Moritz, Switzerland. 20 Feb 72.	F-WPXE
HB-VFS	1978	Learjet 36A	36A-042	W/o Zarzaitine, Algeria. 23 Sep 95.	N39391
HB-VLV	1990	Citation V	560-0077	W/o Zurich, Switzerland. 20 Dec 01.	N42NA

HC = ECUADOR

Military

Reg	Yr	Type	c/n	Owner/Operator	Prev Regn
AEE-402	1976	Sabre-75A	380-45	W/o Quito, Ecuador. 10 Dec 92.	FAE-045
FAE-068	1966	Sabre-40R	282-68	W/o Quito, Ecuador. 3 Jun 88.	N4469N

HK = COLOMBIA

Civil

Reg	Yr	Type	c/n	Owner/Operator	Prev Regn
HK-3885	1973	Citation	500-0135	W/o Pereira, Colombia. 7 Mar 97.	YV-717CP

HP = PANAMA

Military

Reg	Yr	Type	c/n	Owner/Operator	Prev Regn
HP-500A	1965	B 727-44C	18894	Wfu. (to N61944 and bu). Located Opa Locka, Fl. USA.	FAP 400

HS = THAILAND
Military

Reg	Yr	Type	c/n	Owner/Operator	Prev Regn
☐ 33-333	1990	B 737-3Z6	24480	W/o Nr Khon Kaen, Thailand. 30 Mar 93.	
☐ 40207	1987	Learjet 35A	35A-623	W/o Nakhon Sawan, Thailand. 11 Nov 06.(B.TL 12-1/30)	60504

HZ = SAUDI ARABIA
Civil

Reg	Yr	Type	c/n	Owner/Operator	Prev Regn
☐ HZ-AA1	1973	HS 125/600B	256019	Wfu. Cx G- 3/93. Last located Dunsfold, UK.	(G-FANN)
☐ HZ-ABM2	1966	BAC 1-11/401AK	060	Wfu. Last located Jeddah, Saudi Arabia.	HZ-MAA
☐ HZ-AFJ	1977	Gulfstream 2TT	203	Wfu.	N17587
☐ HZ-FMA	1966	HS 125/1B	25105	Wfu. Located Jeddah, Saudi Arabia.	G-AYRY
☐ HZ-FNA	1965	JetStar-8	5056	Wfu. Last located Spirit of St Louis, Mo. USA.	HZ-FK1
☐ HZ-GP5	1975	Learjet 25XR	25XR-199	W/o Narsarsuaq, Greenland. 11 Jan 82.	HZ-RI1
☐ HZ-HM2	1975	B 707-368C	21081	Wfu. Cx HZ- 8/03.	HZ-HM1
☐ HZ-MA1	1967	JetStar-8	5105	Wfu. Located Lycee de Blagnac, Toulouse, France.	N17005
☐ HZ-TAS	1962	B 707-321B	18338	Wfu. Last located Manston, UK.	N98WS
☐ HZ-TNA	1968	JetStar-731	5120	Wfu. Last located at Geneva, Switzerland.	N40DC
☐ SA-R-7		DH Comet 4C	6461	W/o Cuneo, Italy. 20 Mar 63.	

I = ITALY
Civil

Reg	Yr	Type	c/n	Owner/Operator	Prev Regn
☐ I-AIFA	1976	Learjet 36A	36A-021	W/o Forli, Italy. 10 Dec 79.	N3524F
☐ I-ALSU	1990	Beechjet 400A	RK-11	W/o Parma, Italy. 27 Nov 91. (parts at Dodsons, Ks. USA).	N5680Z
☐ I-AMME	1975	Learjet 24D	24D-310	W/o Bari, Italy. 6 Feb 76.	HB-VDU
☐ I-AROM	1977	Citation 1/SP	501-0042	W/o Roma-Ciampino, Italy. 9 Sep 05.	N420AM
☐ I-AVJG	1978	Learjet 35A	35A-189	W/o Portofino, Italy. 24 Oct 99.	N727JP
☐ I-CIST	1985	Citation III	650-0085	W/o Roma-Ciampino, Italy. 4 Nov 00. (parts at Bates City).	N650DA
☐ I-COTO	1979	Learjet 25D	25D-285	Wfu. Broken up 10/86 at Paris-Le Bourget, France.	N422G
☐ I-DRIB	1969	Falcon 20D	201	Wfu. CoA expiry 13 Apr 93.	D-CELL
☐ I-ERJC	2000	Learjet 45	45-093	W/o Milan, Italy. 1 Jun 03.	(PT-XLF)
☐ I-KILO	1981	Learjet 55	55-007	W/o Seville, Spain 4 Apr 94. (parts at Griffin, Ga. USA).	N41ES
☐ I-LIAB	1968	Falcon 20C	172	Wfu. CoA expiry 2001.	F-BRHB
☐ I-LIAC	1970	Falcon 20D	234	Wfu. CoA expiry 9 Sep 02.	D-COLL
☐ I-MCSA	1977	Learjet 35A	35A-099	W/o Palermo, Sicily. 22 Feb 78.	HB-VFC
☐ I-MOCO	1981	Learjet 35A	35A-445	W/o Nuremberg, Germany. 7 Feb 01.	HB-VHG
☐ I-NICK	1964	Sabre-40	282-25	Wfu. Parts at White Industries, Bates City, Mo. USA.	N40SJ
☐ I-NLAE	1968	Falcon 20C	134	W/o Kiel-Holtenau, Germany. 25 Sep 91.	N897D
☐ I-PIAI	1968	PD 808	503	W/o San Sebastian, Spain. 18 Jun 68.	
☐ I-RACE	1964	HS 125/1	25006	Wfu.	HB-VAG
☐ I-SNAF	1968	HS 125/3B	25145	Wfu.	G-AVXL
☐ I-SNAP	1961	MS 760 Paris	99	W/o Milan, Italy. 27 Oct 62.	
☐ I-VIGI	1981	Diamond 1	A013SA	W/o Parma, Italy. 15 Oct 99.	N81HH

Military

Reg	Yr	Type	c/n	Owner/Operator	Prev Regn
☐ MM577	1968	PD 808-TA	501	Wfu. RS-48. Located Pratica di Mare, Italy.	
☐ MM578	1968	PD 808-TA	502	Wfu. RS-49, Located Pratica di Mare, Italy.	
☐ MM61948	1969	PD 808-VIP	506	Wfu. at Pratica di Mare, Italy.	
☐ MM61949	1969	PD 808-VIP	507	Wfu. at Pratica di Mare, Italy.	
☐ MM61951	1969	PD 808-VIP	509	Wfu. Located Pratica di Mare, Italy.	
☐ MM61952	1969	PD 808-GE2	510	Wfu. Located Pratica di Mare, Italy.	
☐ MM61953	1969	PD 808-TP	511	W/o Venice, Italy. 15 Sep 93.	
☐ MM61955	1969	PD 808-GE2	513	Wfu. Located Parma, Italy.	
☐ MM61956	1969	PD 808-TP	514	Wfu. Located Pratica di Mare, Italy.	
☐ MM61957	1969	PD 808-TP	515	Wfu. Located Pratica di Mare, Italy.	
☐ MM61958	1970	PD 808-GE1	505	Wfu. Located Pratica di Mare, Italy.	
☐ MM61959	1970	PD 808-GE1	516	Wfu. Located Pratica di Mare, Italy.	
☐ MM61960	1970	PD 808-GE1	517	Wfu. Located Pratica di Mare, Italy.	
☐ MM61961	1970	PD 808-GE1	518	Wfu. Last flight 17 May 03.	
☐ MM61962	1970	PD 808-GE1	519	Wfu. Located Pratica di Mare, Italy.	
☐ MM61963	1970	PD 808-GE1	520	Wfu. Located Ditallandia, Castel Volturno, Italy.	
☐ MM62013	1974	DC 9-32	47600	W/o ground collision Moscow-Vnukovo, Russia. 8 Feb 99.	
☐ MM62014	1970	PD 808-RM	521	Wfu. Located Pratica di Mare, Italy.	
☐ MM62015	1970	PD 808-RM	522	Wfu. Located Pratica di Mare, Italy.	I-PIAY
☐ MM62016	1970	PD 808-RM	523	Wfu. Located Pratica di Mare, Italy.	
☐ MM62017	1970	PD 808-RM	524	Wfu. Located Pratica di Mare, Italy.	

JA = JAPAN
Civil

Reg	Yr	Type	c/n	Owner/Operator	Prev Regn
☐ JA8246	1984	Diamond 1A	A092SA	W/o Sado Island, Japan. 23 Jul 86.	

Reg	Yr	Type	c/n	Owner/Operator	Prev Regn
☐ JA8438	1976	Citation	500-0321	Wfu. Cx JA 17 Sep 96. Located Yokohama, Japan.	N5321J
Military					
☐ 9202	1986	Learjet U36A	36A-056	W/o Iwakuni AB. Japan. 21 May 03.	N3802G
☐ 9203	1990	Learjet U36A	36A-058	W/o Shikoku Island, Japan. 28 Feb 91.	N4290J

JY = JORDAN
Civil

Reg	Yr	Type	c/n	Owner/Operator	Prev Regn
☐ JY-AEW	1976	Learjet 35	35-052	W/o Riyadh, Saudi Arabia. 28 Apr 77.	
☐ JY-AFC	1976	Learjet 36A	36A-020	W/o Amman, Jordan. 21 Sep 77.	
☐ JY-HS1	1969	B 727-76/W	20228	Wfu. Last located Amman, Jordan.	VR-CHS
☐ JY-HS2	1975	B 727-2L4	21010	Wfu. Last located Fort Worth-Meacham, Tx. USA.	VR-CCA

LN = NORWAY
Civil

Reg	Yr	Type	c/n	Owner/Operator	Prev Regn
☐ LN-AAA	1967	Falcon 20CC	73	Wfu. Parted out at Memphis, Tn. USA.	LX-AAA
☐ LN-AAB	1965	Falcon 20C	12	Wfu. Parted out at Memphis, Tn. USA.	N51SF
☐ LN-AAE	1980	Citation II/SP	551-0285	W/o Bardufoss, Norway. 15 Nov 89.	N224CC
☐ LN-FOE	1967	Falcon 20C	62	W/o Norwich, England. 12 Dec 73.	(N17401)

LV = ARGENTINA
Civil

Reg	Yr	Type	c/n	Owner/Operator	Prev Regn
☐ LV-ALW	1981	HS 125/700B	257133	W/o Salta, Argentina. 11 Apr 85.	LV-PMM
☐ LV-JXA	1971	Learjet 24D	24D-240	Wfu. Located at Olathe Johnson/Century Airport, Ks. USA.	LV-PRB
☐ LV-MMV	1978	Learjet 25D	25D-259	W/o Posadas, Argentina. 23 Sep 89. (parts at Moron).	LV-PAW
☐ LV-RDB	1965	Jet Commander	12	W/o Moron, Argentina. 1991.	N344DA
☐ LV-TDF	1982	Learjet 35A	35A-478	W/o Ushula, Argentina. 15 May 84.	N3815G
☐ LV-WEN	1969	Jet Commander-B	126	W/o Cordoba, Argentina. 29 Sep 94.	N87DL
☐ LV-WHZ	1967	Jet Commander	108	Wfu. Located Aeroparque Buenos Aires, Argentina.	N77ST
☐ LV-WLH	1966	Falcon 20C	34	W/o Nr Salta, Argentina 7 Feb 97.	LV-PHV
☐ LV-WMR	1966	Learjet 24	24-135	W/o Pasadas. Argentina. 28 Aug 95.	N77LB
☐ LV-WOF	1968	Sabre-60	306-25	Wfu. Located San Fernando, Argentina.	(OB-1550)
☐ LV-WPO	1967	Sabre-60	306-3	W/o Cordoba, Argentina. 16 Jul 98.	N160CF
Military					
☐ 5-T-10-074		F 28-3000M	11147	Wfu. Located Ezeiza, Argentina.	PH-EXW
☐ T-11	1974	Sabre-75A	380-3	Wfu. Last located Moron, Argentina.	T-10
☐ T-21	1977	Learjet 35A	35A-115	W/o Nr La Paz, Bolivia. 9 Mar 06.	
☐ T-24	1980	Learjet 35A	35A-333	W/o Pebble Island, Falklands, South Atlantic. 7 Jun 82.	

N = USA
Civil

Reg	Yr	Type	c/n	Owner/Operator	Prev Regn
☐ N.....	1991	Learjet 35A	35-666	Wfu. Aircraft not built because of '666' connotation.	
☐ N1AH	1981	Learjet 35A	35A-398	W/o Great Falls, Mt. USA. 16 May 97. (parts at Bates City.)	N3797A
☐ N1DC	1994	Learjet 60	60-035	W/o Troy, Al. USA. 14 Jan 01.	N116AS
☐ N1DK	1974	Citation	500-0175	W/o Allegheny County, Pa. USA. 6 Jan 98.	N175CC
☐ N1EC	1966	Jet Commander	51	Wfu. Cx USA 8/94. Parts at Dodsons, Rantoul, Ks. USA.	N18JL
☐ N1EM	1966	JetStar-6	5077	W/o Chicago-Midway, Il. USA. 25 Mar 76.	N1924V
☐ N1JR	1975	Learjet 25B	25B-188	W/o Waterville, Me. USA. 28 Jul 84. (parts at Bates City.).	A4O-AJ
☐ N1JS	1979	Westwind-1124	249	Wfu. Accident Mexico in /85.	4X-CMU
☐ N1JU	1965	Jet Commander	13	Wfu. Parts at White Industries, Bates City, Mo. USA.	N1JU
☐ N1JX	1970	Sabre-60	306-61	Wfu. Last located Battle Creek, Mi. USA.	N1JN
☐ N1PT	1967	Jet Commander	93	Wfu. Cx USA 11/94.	(N999RA)
☐ N1R	1960	B 720-023B	18022	Wfu. To USAF 4/83 for KC-135E spares.	N7536A
☐ N1SJ	1962	Sabreliner CT-39A	276-45	Wfu. Located San Jose University, San Jose, Ca. USA.	62-4492
☐ N2CA	1979	Citation II/SP	551-0024	W/o Mountain View, Mo. USA. 18 Dec 82.	N26628
☐ N2TE	1958	MS 760 Paris	5	W/o Nr John Wayne Airport, Ca. USA. 30 Nov 96.	(N760LB)
☐ N2WU	1966	Jet Commander	72	Wfu. Located at Don Torcuato, Argentina.	VR-CAU
☐ N3MF	1966	HS 125/1A-522	25093	Wfu. Used in repair of s/n 25271.	N306L
☐ N3QL	1965	JetStar-731	5064	Wfu. Parts at Dodsons, Rantoul, Ks. USA.	N3QS
☐ N3VL	1975	Westwind-1123	180	Wfu. Cx USA 4/01.	N192LH
☐ N3ZA	1965	Learjet 23	23-024	Wfu. Cx USA 5/91. Parts at White Industries, Mo. USA.	N3ZA
☐ N4LG	1967	Sabre-60	306-9	Wfu. Located Greenville Tech Foundation Inc. SC. USA.	N5071L
☐ N4SX	1966	JetStar-8	5081	Wfu. Cx USA 11/87.	N4SP
☐ N5JR	1966	Jet Commander	49	Wfu. Parts at White Industries, Bates City, Mo. USA.	N430C
☐ N5NG	1973	HS 125/600A	256020	Wfu. Last located at Monterrey-Mexico as XA-NTE.	XA-NTE
☐ N5UJ	1972	Learjet 25B	25B-088	W/o Pittsburgh, Pa. USA. 23 Nov 01. (parts at Rantoul, Ks.).	N125JL
☐ N6CD	1974	Citation	500-0151	Wfu. Cx USA 11/91. Parts at White Industries, Mo. USA.	N151CC
☐ N6ES	1961	JetStar-6	5023	Wfu. Parts at White Industries, Bates City, Mo. USA. (3/88).	N2ES
☐ N6NE	1961	JetStar-731	5006	Wfu. Last located 2/97 on fire dump Southampton, UK.	(VR-CCC)
☐ N6NF	1968	Learjet 25	25-021	Wfu. Displayed at Ozark Municipal Airport, Dothan, Al. USA.	N40SN

Reg	Yr	Type	c/n	Owner/Operator	Prev Regn
☐ N7ES	1969	HFB 320	1045	Wfu. Located Opa Locka, Fl. USA.	N4ZA
☐ N7GP	1965	Learjet 23	23-082	Wfu. Located at Tara Field, Ga. USA.	(N216SA)
☐ N7RC	1978	Citation II	550-0019	W/o Walker's Cay, Bahamas. 26 Apr 95. (parts at Dodsons).	N900AF
☐ N8FE	1969	Falcon 20DC	199	Wfu. Located Steven F Udvar-Hazy Center, Dulles, Va. USA.	N4388F
☐ N8GE	1966	Jet Commander	63	Wfu. Parts at White Industries, Bates City, Mo. USA.	N8GA
☐ N8MQ	1972	Learjet 25B	25B-085	Wfu. Cx USA 3/98. Located Nr Lake City Airport, Fl. USA.	N8MA
☐ N8RA	1967	Jet Commander	104	Wfu. Last lLocated Walker's Aviation, Fort Lauderdale, USA.	N87B
☐ N9FE	1967	Falcon 20DC	84	Wfu. Exhibited at FEDEX Corporate HQ. Memphis, Tn. USA.	(N150FE)
☐ N9QM	1979	Learjet 25D	25D-286	Wfu. Cx USA 3/07.	N850MX
☐ N10BD	1983	Learjet 35A	35A-506	Wfu. Cx USA 3/03. Located Denver International, Co. USA.	N317BG
☐ N10D	1965	HS 125/1A-522	25029	Wfu. Parts at White Industries, Bates City, Mo. USA.	N391DA
☐ N10EA	1965	Jet Commander	39	Wfu. Located at Copenhagen, Denmark.	N16FP
☐ N10GE	1977	Citation 1/SP	501-0022	W/o Nr Harrison Airport, Ar. USA. 21 May 85.	(N800WC)
☐ N10LN	1968	HS 125/3A-RA	25156	Wfu. Last located Lakeland, Fl. USA.	N522M
☐ N10M	1971	Sabre-75	370-2	Wfu. Cx USA 7/05.	N80K
☐ N10MB	1972	Westwind-1123	157	Wfu. Parts at OK Aircraft, Gilroy, Ca. USA.	(N820RT)
☐ N10SL	1964	Sabre-40	282-11	Wfu. Located at Fort Lauderdale Executive, Fl. USA.	XA-...
☐ N10UH	1976	Citation	500-0304	Wfu. Cx USA 6/05. Last located San Antonio, Tx. USA.	N70U
☐ N10UJ	1977	Westwind-1124	204	Wfu. Cx USA 5/03.	(N100XJ)
☐ N10YJ	1975	Falcon 10	57	W/o White Plains, NY. USA 30 Jun 97. (parts at Bates City)	(N50YJ)
☐ N11AQ	1968	Learjet 24	24-178	Wfu. Cx USA 8/05. Last located Addison, Tx. USA.	N723JW
☐ N11QM	1966	Learjet 23	23-091	Wfu. Cx USA 12/89.	N110M
☐ N11UE	1962	JetStar-6	5038	Wfu. Last located at El Mirage, Ca. USA.	(N44KF)
☐ N12AR	1969	Falcon 20D	200	Wfu. Located Ontario, Ca. USA. Cx USA 5/03.	YV-876P
☐ N12MK	1969	Learjet 24B	24B-192	W/o Palm Springs, Ca. USA. 6 Jan 77.	N1919W
☐ N12TX	1976	Falcon 10	90	Wfu. Parts at White Industries, Bates City, Mo. USA.	N14U
☐ N13MJ	1975	Learjet 24D	24D-314	W/o Elizabeth City, NC. USA. 6 Nov 82.	N501MH
☐ N14TX	1977	Learjet 36A	36A-033	W/o Stephenville, NF.Canada. 6 Dec 96. (parts at Bates City)	N762L
☐ N15EC	1962	Sabreliner CT-39A	276-22	Wfu. East Coast Technical School, Hanscom, Ma. USA.	62-4469
☐ N15NY	1979	Citation 1/SP	501-0110	W/o Akron, Oh. USA. 2 Aug 79.	(N26481)
☐ N15TW	1977	Learjet 35A	35A-106	W/o Minneapolis, Mn. USA. 8 Dec 85. (parts at Taylorville).	N101BG
☐ N15TX	1974	Falcon 10	13	Wfu. Cx USA 2/93.	N777SN
☐ N16AZ	1972	JetStar-8	5156	Wfu.	XB-DBT
☐ N16SK	1967	Jet Commander	101	Wfu. Cx USA 5/88. Located Bodo Aviation Museum, Norway.	N16MA
☐ N17FN	1970	Learjet 24B	24B-220	Wfu. Parts at Dodsons, Rantoul, Ks. USA.	N248J
☐ N17SL	1966	HS 125/1A-522	25082	Wfu. Parts at White Industries, Bates City, Mo. USA.	N1MY
☐ N18CA	1965	Jet Commander	5	Wfu. Cx USA 10/86. Parts at Dodsons, Rantoul, Ks. USA.	C-GKFT
☐ N19BG	1973	Sabre-40A	282-118	Wfu. Cx USA 8/95. Parts at AVMATS Paynesville, Mo. USA.	PT-JNJ
☐ N19LH	1979	Learjet 35A	35A-279	W/o Avon Park, Fl. USA. 15 Jul 97.	
☐ N20EP	1965	Learjet 23	23-008	Wfu. Displayed at White Industries, Bates City, Mo. USA.	N20BD
☐ N20K	1969	Jet Commander-C	144	Wfu. Parts at White Industries, Bates City, Mo. USA.	(N920KP)
☐ N20M	1966	Learjet 23	23-094	W/o Detroit, Mi. USA. 15 Dec 72.	N417LJ
☐ N21AK	1966	Jet Commander	59	Wfu.	N59JC
☐ N21CC	1973	Citation	500-0099	Wfu. Last located Addison, Tx. USA.	N599CC
☐ N21SA	1973	HS 125/F600A	256006	W/o Bromont, Canada, 21 Feb 05.	N606TS
☐ N22FM	1974	Citation	500-0229	W/o Wichita, Ks. USA. 26 Apr 83.	
☐ N22HP	1986	Citation S/II	S550-0103	W/o Dillon, Mt. USA. 3 May 07.	N103QS
☐ N22RB	1967	JetStar-8	5093	Wfu. Cx USA 10/90.	N76EB
☐ N23AC	1988	Gulfstream 4	1047	W/o Pal-Waukee Chicago, Il. USA. 30 Oct 96.	N461GA
☐ N23AJ	1965	Learjet 23	23-053	Wfu. Cx USA 9/92.	F-BTQK
☐ N23ST	1959	MS 760 Paris	50	W/o New Mexico, USA. 11 Sep 90.	N42BL
☐ N23TJ	1965	Learjet 23	23-033	Wfu. See www.airzoo.org	N60DH
☐ N24RZ	1974	Learjet 25B	25B-159	W/o Fort Lauderdale, Fl. USA. 22 Feb 04. (parts at Rantoul)	OB-1429
☐ N24SA	1965	Learjet 23	23-025	Wfu. Cx USA 6/89.	N508M
☐ N24VM	1965	Learjet 24	24-051	Wfu. Cx USA 8/88. Parts at White Industries, Mo. USA.	N70JC
☐ N24YE	1965	Learjet 24	24-087	Wfu. Cx USA 1/03. Parts at Dodsons, Rantoul, Ks. USA.	N24YA
☐ N25AG	1976	JetStar 2	5202	Wfu. Last located Kemble, UK.	3C-QRK
☐ N25BR	1989	Beechjet 400	RJ-57	W/o Rome, Ga. USA. 11 Dec 91.	
☐ N25TA	1975	Learjet 25B	25B-196	W/o New Mexico. USA. 11 Apr 80.	N711WD
☐ N25TE	1972	Learjet 25C	25C-087	Wfu. Parts at White Industries Inc. Bates City, Mo. USA.	N99XZ
☐ N26BA	1967	Learjet 24	24-134	Wfu. Parts at Dodsons, Rantoul, Ks. USA.	N911TR
☐ N26TL	1965	HS 125/1A	25037	Wfu. Cx USA 8/92.	(N389DA)
☐ N27AX	1976	Learjet 24D	24D-323	Wfu. Cx USA 11/05.	N453
☐ N27BD	1966	Jet Commander	53	Wfu. Cx USA 1/95. Parts at White Industries, Mo. USA.	N925HB
☐ N27MD	1967	Jet Commander	102	Wfu. Parts at White Industries, Bates City, Mo. USA.	
☐ N27R	1974	Falcon 20E	303	W/o Naples, Fl. USA. 12 Nov 76.	N4445F

Reg	Yr	Type	c/n	Owner/Operator	Prev Regn
N28CK	1969	Learjet 25	25-045	Wfu. Located Montgomery, Al. USA.	N24FN
N28ST	1965	Learjet 23	23-013	W/o Nr Guatemala City, Guatemala. 31 Jul 87.	N37BL
N29FN	1968	Learjet 25	25-018	Wfu. Parts at Brandis Aviation, Taylorville, Il. USA.	(N23FN)
N29LB	1966	Jet Commander	61	W/o Many Airport, La. USA. 19 Dec 80.	N29LP
N30AD	1969	Jet Commander-C	143	Wfu. Cx USA 4/99. Located Boeing Field, Wa. USA.	N41
N30AN	1974	Westwind-1123	173	Wfu. Parts at El Mirage, Ca. USA.	N30JM
N30BE	1964	Sabre-40	282-14	Wfu. Parts at AVMATS Paynesville, Mo. USA.	(N30PN)
N30CC	1974	Sabre-60A	306-81	Wfu. Cx USA 12/95. Parts at AVMATS Paynesville, Mo. USA.	N6ND
N30DK	1980	Learjet 35A	35A-345	Wfu. W/o San Diego, Ca. USA. 24 Oct 04.	N345LJ
N30EM	1976	Learjet 24E	24E-338	Wfu. Cx USA 12/89. Parts at Taylorville, Il. USA.	N30LM
N30SJ	1991	SJ 30-2	001	Wfu. Cx USA 10/99.	
N30W	1964	Sabre-40	282-5	W/o Perryville, Mo. USA. 21 Dec 67.	
N31BP	1968	JetStar-731	5125	Wfu. Last located Fort Lauderdale Executive, Fl. USA.	N48UC
N31CK	1965	Learjet 23	23-079	Wfu. Last located El Mirage, Ca. USA.	N240AQ
N31LT	1966	Falcon 20C	69	Wfu. Last located March Aviation Inc. Naples, Fl. USA.	N176BN
N31SK	1966	Learjet 24	24-118	W/o Vail, Co. USA. 27 Mar 87.	N1919W
N32CA	1966	Learjet 24	24-132	Wfu. Cx USA 9/01.	N238R
N32WE	1973	Westwind-1123	164	Wfu. Parts at White Industries, Bates City, Mo. USA.	N9114S
N34NW	1967	Jet Commander	117	Wfu. Parts at White Industries, Bates City, Mo. USA.	N54WC
N34SW	1967	Jet Commander	97	Wfu. Parts at Hollister, Ca. USA. Cx USA 5/06,	N3082B
N34W	1965	Sabre-40	282-47	W/o Midland, Tx. USA. 4 Jan 74.	N740R
N36HJ	1981	Learjet 35A	35A-427	Wfu. Cx USA 3/07.	N358AC
N36MK	1966	HS 125/1A	25073	W/o Boise, Id. USA. 28 Dec 70.	N372GM
N36PT	1966	Jet Commander	79	Wfu. Cx USA 1/97.	N100LL
N37BL	1965	Learjet 23	23-069	W/o Oakdale, Ca. USA. 4 Mar 98. (parts at Bates City, Mo.).	(N34TR)
N37CP	1965	Learjet 23	23-028	Wfu. Parts at White Industries Inc. Bates City, Mo. USA.	N5QY
N37SJ	1965	Jet Commander	38	Wfu. Parts at White Industries, Bates City, Mo. USA.	N106CJ
N38B	1971	King Air 200	BB-1	Wfu. Project shelved 1978.	
N38DJ	1975	Learjet 25B	25B-191	W/o Sheboygan, Wi. USA. 12 Jun 92. (parts at Hampton, Ga.).	N78BT
N39DM	1975	Learjet 35	35-040	W/o San Clemente Island, Ca. USA. 5 Mar 86.	C-GGYV
N39LH	1973	Citation	500-0089	Wfu. Cx USA 12/04.	EC-EBR
N39Q	1968	JetStar-8	5126	Wfu. Parted out 1983.	N39E
N40BC	1973	Learjet 25B	25B-128	W/o Pueblo, Co. USA. 6 Jul 79. (parts at White Industries).	N1MX
N40BP	1965	Sabre-40	282-40	Wfu. Parts at Clarksville, Mo. USA.	N40BP
N40LB	1965	Sabre-40	282-36	Wfu. Located Fort Lauderdale Executive, Fl. USA.	N200MP
N40LB	1968	Learjet 25	25-009	W/o Omaha, Ne. USA. 25 Sep 73.	9Q-CHC
N40PC	1973	HS 125/600A	256010	W/o McLean, Va. USA. 28 Apr 77.	N23BH
N40UA	1966	Jet Commander	40	Wfu. Parts at White Industries, Bates City, Mo. USA.	N40AJ
N41GS	1964	Sabre-40	282-16	Wfu. Last located 10/88 Miami International, Fl. USA.	N40GP
N42		Convair 880	55	Wfu.	N112
N42QB	1965	Jet Commander	6	Wfu. Parts at White Industries, Bates City, Mo. USA.	N420P
N43AR	1972	JetStar-8	5154	Wfu. Located Fort Lauderdale Executive, Fl. USA.	XC-SRH
N43CF	1966	Sabre-40	282-59	Wfu. Cx USA 8/95.	N40SE
N44	1969	Jet Commander-A	130	W/o Latrobe, Pa. USA. 2 Nov 88.	N84
N44CJ	1967	Learjet 24	24-146	W/o Felt, Ok. USA. 1 Oct 81.	N235Z
N44GA	1966	Learjet 24	24-129	W/o Santa Catalina, Ca. USA. 30 Jan 84.	C-GSAX
N44PA	1973	Learjet 25B	25B-144	W/o Carlsbad, Ca. USA. 23 Dec 91.	N10NT
N45BP	1978	HS 125/700A	NA0219	W/o Beaumont, Tx. USA. 20 Sep 03.	N219TS
N45CP	1972	Learjet 25XR	25XR-073	W/o Lexington, Ky. USA. 30 Aug 02.	N888DB
N46	1964	B 727-30	18360	Wfu. Cx USA 8/94.	N97
N46TE	1979	Gulfstream 2	243	W/o Little Rock, Ar. USA. 19 Jan 90.	N119RC
N47BA	1976	Learjet 35	35-060	W/o Aberdeen, SD. USA. 25 Oct 99.	(N590CH)
N47CE	1969	Jet Commander-B	137	Wfu. Parts at White Industries, Bates City, Mo. USA.	XB-FKV
N48AJ	1968	Learjet 24	24-172	Wfu. Parts at White Industries Inc. Bates City, Mo. USA.	N234WR
N48BA	1967	Learjet 24	24-152	Wfu. Parts at Dodsons, Rantoul, Ks. USA.	N9LM
N48CG	1966	Sabre-40	282-75	Wfu. Cx USA 12/83. Parts at Clarksville, Mo. USA.	(N48CE)
N48CQ	1976	Gulfstream 2	181	Wfu. Cx USA 11/05. Last located Tulsa, Ok. USA.	N48CC
N49RJ	1966	Sabre-40	282-69	Wfu. Last located at Fort Lauderdale Executive, Fl. USA.	N777VZ
N49UC	1967	JetStar-731	5110	Wfu. Parted out 1991.	N788S
N50AS	1966	HS 125/1A-522	25083	Wfu. Cx USA 9/92.	N538
N50BA	1965	Learjet 24	24-043	Wfu. Cx USA 8/89 as N43AC.	(N43AC)
N50BK	1985	Citation S/II	S550-0031	W/o Big Bear, Ca. USA. 13 Aug 02.	N54WJ
N50CD	1965	Sabre-40	282-42	Wfu. Cx USA 10/91. Parts at Paynesville, Mo. USA.	N500RK
N50DG	1968	Sabre-60	306-19	Wfu. Cx USA 10/98.	N8000U
N50HH	1965	HS 125/1A-522	25022	W/o Bedford, In. USA. 2 Aug 86. (parts at O K Aircraft, Ca.)	N100GB
N50JP	1966	Jet Commander	69	Wfu. Cx USA 10/97. Parts at Dodsons, Rantoul, Ks. USA.	N10SN

Reg	Yr	Type	c/n	Owner/Operator	Prev Regn
N50MM	1973	Citation	500-0118	Wfu. Display fuselage for Aviation Fabrications Inc. Mo. USA	N972GW
N50PA	1979	Challenger 600S	1004	Wfu. Cx USA 11/06.	N640TS
N50PL	1981	Westwind-Two	338	W/o Pocono Mountains, Nr Scranton, Pa. USA. 12 Dec 99.	N114WL
N50SK	1980	Westwind-Two	309	W/o Bowie County, Tx. USA. 4 Apr 86.	N240S
N50TE	1976	Falcon 10	86	Wfu. Parts at White Industries, Bates City, Mo. USA.	N411WW
N50UD	1961	JetStar-6	5019	Wfu. Parts noted 1990 at N Perry & Fort Lauderdale, Fl. USA.	N50UD
N51CA	1969	Learjet 25	25-030	W/o Newark, NJ. USA. 30 Mar 83.	N45DM
N51DB	1978	Learjet 25XR	25XR-246	W/o Nr Medina, Saudi Arabia. 24 Oct 86.	N40162
N51FN	1976	Learjet 35	35-059	W/o Carlsbad, Ca. USA. 2 Apr 90. (parts at White Industries)	N221Z
N52	1974	Sabre-75A	380-10	Wfu. Cx USA 9/95. Located Burlington, Vt. USA.	
N52AN	1972	Citation	500-0030	Wfu.	N530CC
N52NW	1969	Gulfstream 2	52	Wfu. Parts at Dodsons, Rantoul, Ks. USA.	N211MT
N52TJ	1973	Falcon 10	3	Wfu.	(N149DG)
N53CC	1981	Citation II	550-0400	W/o Roxboro, NC. USA. 1 Oct 89.	N888EB
N55FJ	1976	Falcon 10	74	Wfu. Located Aerospace Museum, McClelland AFB. Ca. USA.	N5JY
N55LF	1985	Learjet 55	55-112	W/o Fort Lauderdale, Fl. USA. 19 Jul 04.	EC-HAI
N55NC	1965	JetStar-6	5060	Wfu. Last located Fort Lauderdale, Fl. USA. Cx USA 7/88.	N31F
N55NJ	1968	Learjet 24	24-162	Wfu. Parts at Guthrie, Ok. USA.	N835AG
N55RF	1965	HS 125/731	25020	Wfu. Cx USA 8/03.	N125TJ
N56B	1965	BAC 1-11/401AK	055	Wfu. Cx USA 8/91.	N1JR
N57EJ	2001	CitationJet CJ-2	525A-0057	W/o Dexter, Me. USA. 7 Oct 02.	N.....
N57TA	1981	Learjet 55	55-010	W/o Waterkloof AFB. Pretoria, South Africa. 13 Nov 81.	
N59RD	1963	B 707-441	17905	Wfu. Cx USA 7/89.	PP-VJA
N60	1975	Sabre-75A	380-28	Wfu. Cx USA 6/96.	
N60BC	1968	JetStar-8	5116	Wfu. Parts at Spirit of St Louis, Mo. USA.	N3HB
N60CD	1965	Jet Commander	44	Wfu. Parts at Dodsons, Rantoul, Ks. USA.	N69GT
N60JN	1967	Sabre-60	306-14	Wfu. Parts at Perryville, Mo. USA.	N43GB
N60MB	1974	Falcon 10	15	W/o Stapleton-Denver, Co. USA. 3 Apr 77.	N109FJ
N60XL	1987	Learjet 60	55C-001	Wfu. Cx USA 9/96.	N551DF
N61RH	1965	Sabre-40	282-27	Wfu. Located College of Technology, Tulsa, Ok. USA.	N111EA
N61RS	1983	Westwind-Two	384	W/o Taos, NM. USA. 8 Nov 02.	(N50MF)
N61TJ	1979	Gulfstream 2	256	Wfu. Parts at Dodsons, Rantoul, Ks. USA.	(N135WJ)
N61TS	1965	Learjet 23	23-029	Wfu. Parted out 10/85.	N66AS
N63CK	1967	Learjet 24	24-119	Wfu. Parts at Dodsons, Rantoul, Ks. USA.	N61CK
N63HJ	1981	Challenger 600S	1021	Wfu. Cx USA 10/04.	N914XA
N64	1975	Sabre-75A	380-35	W/o Liberal, Ks. USA. 29 Sep 86.	
N65DU	1982	HS 125/700A	NA0321	Wfu. Cx USA 9/07.	N65DL
N65TS	1965	HS 125/1A-522	25043	Wfu. Parts at Dodsons, Rantoul, Ks. USA	N522ME
N66GZ	1975	Sabre-60	306-99	Wfu. Cx USA 7/06.	N66GE
N66HA	1967	HS 125/3A	25126	W/o Houston, Tx. USA. 13 Aug 89.	N510X
N66JE	1981	Westwind-1124	326	W/o ground fire Denver, Co. USA. 21 Feb 95.	(N88JE)
N66MP	1961	JetStar-6	5015	Wfu. Last located at S Seattle Community College, Wa. USA.	N9064F
N67KM	1974	Sabre-75A	380-7	W/o Watertown, SD. USA. 14 Jun 75.	
N67TS	1966	HS 125/1A-522	25097	Wfu. Cx USA 11/01.	N89HB
N68LU	1968	Learjet 24	24-163	Wfu. Located Lewis University, Romeoville, Il. USA.	N65WM
N69KB	1965	Learjet 23	23-042	Wfu. Cx USA 12/91. Parts at White Industries, Mo. USA.	N701RZ
N69MT	1967	JetStar-8	5107	Wfu. Last located at Hollister, Ca. USA.	N69MT
N70FJ	1978	Citation 1/SP	501-0073	W/o Nr Hailey, Id. USA. 15 Mar 03.	(N840MC)
N70HC	1972	Sabre-75	370-8	Wfu. Cx USA 4/96. Parts at AVMATS Paynesville, Mo. USA.	N3TE
N70JF	1979	Learjet 25D	25D-278	Wfu. Parts at White Industries Inc. Bates City, Mo. USA.	
N70XX	1983	Diamond 1	A052SA	Wfu. Parts at White Industries Inc.Bates City, Mo. USA.	I-FRAB
N71JC	1989	Learjet 31	31-008	W/o Amory, Ms. USA. 2 Sep 97. (parts at Griffin, Ga.).	
N71TS	1976	Falcon 10	75	Wfu. Cx USA 2/06.	N97DX
N72TQ	1964	Jet Commander	4	Wfu.	N72TC
N74AG	1966	JetStar-731	5072	Wfu. Cx USA 11/99.	N74AG
N74BS	1973	Sabre-60	306-64	Wfu. Located AVMATS Spirit of St Louis, Mo. USA.	N96CP
N75CN	1975	Sabre-75A	380-31	Wfu. Parts at Dodsons, Rantoul, Ks. USA.	N62
N76HG	1966	JetStar-731	5076	Wfu. Last located Rockford, Il. USA.	N69ME
N77AP	1965	Sabre-40	282-37	W/o New Orleans, La. USA. 7 Nov 77.	N265W
N77BT	1967	HS 125/3A-RA	25155	Wfu. Last located Montgomery, Al. USA.	(N158AG)
N77FV	1965	Jet Commander	26	Wfu. Cx USA 10/88.	N10MC
N77JL	1974	Learjet 24XR	24XR-286	W/o Bellevile, Il. USA. 12 Nov 03.	N57DB
N77ND	1978	Citation II	550-0005	Wfu. Cx USA 9/06.	OE-GKP
N77NJ	1969	Learjet 25	25-033	Wfu. Cx USA 7/03.	YV-88CP
N77NT	1965	Jet Commander	7	Wfu. Cx USA 11/91.	N77NT
N77RS	1973	Learjet 25C	25C-094	W/o Anchorage, Ak. USA. 4 Dec 78. (parts at White Inds.).	N97J

Reg	Yr	Type	c/n	Owner/Operator	Prev Regn
N77VJ	1965	Learjet 23	23-041	Wfu. Located MTW Aerospace Inc. Montgomery, Al. USA.	C-GDDB
N77VK	1965	HS 125/731	25051	Wfu. Cx USA 1/87.	C6-BEY
N78JR	1966	Falcon 20C	70	Wfu. Parted out 3/89. Last located El Mirage, Ca. USA.	(N400NL)
N79DD	1975	Citation	500-0254	W/o San Luis Obispo, Ca. USA. 24 Sep 90.	N29991
N80DH	1969	Learjet 24B	24B-191	Wfu. Cx USA 3/89. Parts at Dodsons, Rantoul, Ks. USA.	(N44TL)
N80TN	1974	Sabre-75A	380-19	Wfu. Cx USA 6/02.	N80HG
N81MC	1977	Learjet 24F	24F-344	W/o St Thomas, USVI. 10 Nov 84.	
N82ML	1967	Sabre-40	282-83	Wfu. Cx USA 3/95. Parts at AVMATS Paynesville, Mo. USA.	N160TC
N83CE	1965	Learjet 23	23-074	Wfu. Located Gilbert Community College, Chandler, Az.	XB-GRQ
N84GP	1983	Peregrine	551	Wfu. Located Oklahoma Air & Space Museum Exhibit, USA.	N9881S
N85	1968	Sabre-40	282-97	W/o Nr Recife, Brazil. 14 Jan 76.	N4706N
N85DW	1975	Sabre-75A	380-27	W/o Ironwood, Mi. USA. 14 Aug 00.	N90GW
N85JM	1976	Falcon 10	85	W/o Aurillac, France. 17 Feb 93. (parts at White Industries)	(N95DW)
N85VT	1985	Gulfstream 3	449	W/o Houston, Tx. USA. 22 Nov 04.	N85V
N86	1967	Sabre-40	282-86	Wfu. Cx USA 9/92.	N2255C
N86BE	1978	Learjet 35A	35A-194	W/o Marianna, Fl. USA. 5 Apr 00.	N86BL
N86CC	1966	Learjet 24	24-115	Wfu. Parts at Brandis Aviation, Taylorville, Il. USA.	N591DL
N86CE	1994	Citation V Ultra	560-0265	W/o Carlsbad, Ca. USA. 24 Jan 06.	LV-WIJ
N87CM	1964	Sabre-40	282-21	Wfu. Parts at AVMATS Paynesville, Mo. USA.	N168D
N87DG	1965	Jet Commander	14	Wfu. Cx USA 7/94. Parts at White Industries, Mo. USA.	N87DC
N87TD	1968	Gulfstream II SP	39	Wfu. Last located Chino, Ca. USA.	N87HB
N88	1967	Sabre-40	282-88	Wfu. Located Hampton University, Newport News, Va. USA.	N2237C
N88B	1965	Learjet 24	24-015	Wfu. Located Pima County Museum, Tucson, Az. USA.	
N88CH	1961	Convair 880	58	Wfu. Located Bonza Bay, East London, RSA.	VR-HGF
N88HA	1990	Challenger 601-3A	5072	W/o Nr Bassett-Rock County Airport, Ne. USA. 20 Mar 94.	N609K
N88JF	1966	Learjet 24A	24A-110	W/o Detroit, Mi. USA. Oct 86. (parts at Taylorville, Il.).	N35JF
N88JM	1961	JetStar-731	5011	Wfu. Fuselage noted 1988 at Lincoln, Ne. USA.	N159B
N88MR	1964	HS 125/1A	25013	Wfu. Cx USA 6/86. Parts at White Industries, Mo. USA.	N4646S
N88NB	1963	BAC 1-11/201AC	005	Wfu. Cx USA 8/89.	N97KR
N89	1967	Sabre-40	282-89	Wfu. Parted out 10/91.	N2276C
N89AJ	1975	Citation	500-0272	Wfu. Parts at White Industries Inc. Bates City, Mo. USA.	N30JN
N89MR	1965	Jet Commander	9	Wfu. Parts at OK Aircraft, Gilroy, Ca. USA.	(N98KK)
N89XL	1974	Westwind-1123	171	Wfu. Located Lanseria, RSA.	(ZS-ODP)
N90AG	1999	Challenger 604	5414	W/o Birmingham, UK. 4 Jan 02.	N604AG
N90HM	1973	Westwind-1123	170	Wfu. Cx USA 5/94.	N150HR
N90ME	1965	JetStar-6	5057	Wfu. Last located 5/88 at Memphis, Tn. USA.	N90ME
N91MJ	1979	Citation II	550-0101	W/o Marco Island, Fl. USA. 31 Dec 95.	(N42BM)
N92GS	1962	B 720-047B	18452	Wfu. Last located Miami, Fl. USA.	N93146
N93BE	1965	Jet Commander	27	Wfu. Parts at White Industries, Bates City, Mo. USA.	N93B
N93BP	1968	Learjet 24	24-169	Wfu. Parts at Dodsons, Rantoul, Ks. USA.	N927AA
N93BR	1970	Learjet 24D	24D-231	Wfu. Parts at Brandis Aviation, Taylorville, Il. USA.	N37DH
N93SC	1967	Jet Commander	90	Wfu. Parts at Dodsons, Rantoul, Ks. USA.	N1121E
N95B	1965	Jet Commander	19	Wfu. Instructional airframe Norway 5/88.	
N95GS	1961	JetStar-6	5014	Wfu. Parted out in 1989 at Miami, Fl. USA.	N54BW
N95TC	1975	Learjet 35	35-020	W/o Waco, Tx. USA. 20 Dec 84. (parts at Bates City, Mo.).	XA-BUK
N96AA	1967	Learjet 24	24-139	Wfu. Parts at Dodsons, Rantoul, Ks. USA.	N481EZ
N96BB	1964	JetStar-6	5049	Wfu. Located at S Seattle Community College, Wa. USA.	N96B
N96CK	1965	Learjet 23	23-016	Wfu. Last located El Mirage, Ca. USA.	N7GF
N96GS	1965	JetStar-731	5068	W/o Miami, Fl. USA. 6 Jan 90.	N9231R
N96TS	1973	Westwind-1123	159	Wfu. Parts were at Hollister, Ca. USA. Cx USA 3/05.	N344CK
N97DM	1972	Learjet 24D	24D-253	W/o San Clemente Island, Ca. USA. 5 Mar 86.	N417JD
N98KT	1961	Caravelle 6R	102	Wfu. Located at Van Nuys, Ca. USA.	N2296N
N98SC	1965	Jet Commander	32	Wfu. Last located Washington County, Pa. USA.	N101BU
N99FT	1965	JetStar-731	5055	Wfu. Last located scrapyard Long Beach, Ca. USA.	N707EZ
N99GS	1965	Jet Commander	31	Wfu.	N399D
N99S	1981	Sabre-65	465-64	W/o Toronto, Canada. 11 Jan 83.	
N99TC	1966	Learjet 23	23-098	Wfu. Parts at Brandis Aviation, Taylorville, Il. USA.	N711AE
N99W	1965	Jet Commander	46	Wfu. Cx USA 2/95.	N202ST
N100DL	1969	Learjet 24B	24B-201	Wfu. Parts at White Industries Inc. Bates City, Mo. USA.	C-GTFA
N100EP	1977	Learjet 35A	35A-150	W/o Allegheny County Airport, Pa. USA. 11 May 67.	
N100MK	1968	Learjet 25	25-019	W/o Sandusky, Oh. USA. 21 Oct 78.	N88FP
N100RC	1966	Jet Commander	60	W/o Lexington, Ky. USA. 14 Nov 70.	N6545V
N100SQ	1966	Learjet 24	24-113	Wfu. Cx USA 10/81.	N204Y
N100TA	1965	Learjet 23	23-045	W/o Savannah, Ga. USA. 6 May 82.	N711MR
N100TR	1966	Jet Commander	76	Wfu. Parts at Hollister, Ca. USA.	N100DR
N100VQ	1967	Learjet 24	24-140	Wfu. Located St Petersburg-Clearwater, Fl. USA.	N100VC

Reg	Yr	Type	c/n	Owner/Operator	Prev Regn
N100WM	1966	Jet Commander	73	Wfu. Located at Sarasota, Fl. USA.	N100W
N101AD	1972	HS 125/731	NA777	Wfu. Parted out 10/91. (fuselage at Tulsa, Ok. USA.).	(N425JF)
N101LB	1965	Jet Commander	8	Wfu. Parts at Tucson, Az. USA.	(N1MM)
N101PP	1966	Learjet 23	23-085	W/o Windsor Locks, Ct. USA. 4 Jun 84.	N385J
N102AR	1968	Learjet 25	25-012	Wfu. Parts at White Industries Inc. Bates City, Mo. USA.	N846YC
N102CJ	1966	Jet Commander	78	Wfu. Located at Opa Locka, Fl. USA.	N866DH
N104CE	1967	JetStar-8	5108	Wfu. Located at MTW Aerospace, Montgomery, Al. USA.	XA-SWD
N104SL	1972	Sabre-40A	282-104	Wfu. Cx USA 1/01.	XA-SEU
N104SS	1968	Sabre-60	306-30	Wfu. Parts at White Industries, Bates City, Mo. USA.	N1116A
N105HS	1965	HS 125/1A	25031	Wfu. Last located Oklahoma City, Ok. USA.	N79AE
N106TF	1969	HFB 320	1042	Wfu. Located Louisville, Ky. USA.	(N603GA)
N107CJ	1964	Sabre-40	282-12	Wfu. Cx USA 1/97.	N368DA
N108PA	1975	Learjet 25B	25B-195	Wfu. Cx USA 5/06.	OB-M-1004
N110FS	1966	Sabre-40	282-58	Wfu. Parts at Spirit of St Louis, Mo. USA.	N1101G
N111DC	1968	HFB 320	1030	Wfu. Located at Monroe, Mi. USA.	(N247GW)
N111LR	1997	CitationJet	525-0222	W/o Atlanta, Ga. USA. 4 Apr 98.	
N111M	1965	Falcon 20C	10	Wfu. Cx USA 8/87. Parts at AVMATS Paynesville, Mo. USA.	N810F
N111NF	1973	Westwind-1123	168	Wfu. Located at Dallas-Love Field, Tx. USA.	N66SM
N111TD	1965	Jet Commander	11	Wfu. Last located St Simons Island, Ga. USA.	(N55CM)
N111YL	1965	Jet Commander	42	Wfu. Cx USA 7/94.	N111Y
N112TJ	1961	JetStar-731	5029	Wfu. Last located El Mirage, Ca. USA.	(N1406)
N114GB	1966	Learjet 23	23-022	Wfu. Parts at White Industries Inc. Bates City, Mo. USA.	N456SC
N115DX	1968	JetStar-8	5111	Wfu. Parted out 8/91.	N115MR
N116DD	1972	JetStar-731	5155	Wfu. Cx USA 11/06.	N84GA
N116KX	1966	Jet Commander	87	Wfu. Parts were at Hollister, Ca. USA.	N430DC
N117GL	1978	Gulfstream 2	220	Wfu. Cx USA 5/05. Last located at Van Nuys, Ca. USA.	N315TS
N118AF	1974	Westwind-1123	177	Wfu. Cx USA 10/91.	(N114ED)
N118BA	1966	JetStar-6	5091	Wfu. Cx USA 5/93. Parts at White Industries Inc. Mo. USA.	N118B
N118LA	1972	Citation	500-0039	Wfu. Parts at White Industries, Bates City, Mo. USA.	PT-OOK
N119MA	1969	Learjet 24B	24B-200	Wfu. Parts at White Industries Inc. Bates City, Mo. USA.	N246CM
N120AR	1966	JetStar-8	5089	Wfu.	(N85DL)
N120ES	1977	Citation 1/SP	501-0041	W/o San Salvador, El Salvador 24 Apr 95. (parts at Dodsons).	N173SK
N120TA		BAC 1-11/520FN	236	Wfu. Last located Mojave, Ca. USA.	PP-SDS
N121AJ	1966	Jet Commander	57	Wfu. Cx USA 4/82.	N770WL
N121DJ	1967	Falcon 20C	121	Wfu. Parts at at Dodsons, Rantoul, Ks. USA.	N500BG
N121EL	1968	Learjet 25	25-010	Wfu. Located Kingston University, UK.	(N82UH)
N121FJ	1981	Falcon 100	192	W/o Rancho Murieta Airport, Ca. USA. 15 Oct 87.	N100FJ
N121GW	1965	Falcon 20C	4	W/o Memphis, Tn. USA. 18 May 78.	N116JD
N121HM	1965	Jet Commander	18	Wfu. Instructional airframe at Copenhagen, Denmark.	N1166Z
N121PA	1969	Jet Commander-A	129	Wfu. Parts at Dodsons, Rantoul, Ks. USA.	N102CE
N122DU	1967	Gulfstream 2	6	Wfu. Parts at Air Salvage International, Alton, UK.	N122DJ
N122M	1965	Learjet 23	23-065A	Wfu. Last located El Mirage, Ca. USA.	(N156AG)
N123AC	1966	HS 125/3A	25122	Wfu. Parts at OK Aircraft, Gilroy, Ca. USA.	N255CB
N123CB	1970	Learjet 24D	24D-232	W/o Butte, Mt. USA. 17 Apr 71.	
N123CV	1974	Westwind-1123	178	Wfu. Cx USA 8/04.	N999U
N123DR	1973	Westwind-1123	158	Wfu. Located Aeroparque Buenos Aires, Argentina.	N1123G
N123RE	1967	Learjet 24	24-154	W/o Lancaster, Ca. USA. 17 Oct 78.	N11AK
N124RM	1966	JetStar-731	5078	Wfu. Located Westwood College of Aeronautics, Tx. USA.	N515AJ
N124TV	1973	Gulfstream 2	124	Wfu. Last located Long Beach, Ca. USA.	(N980EF)
N124VS	1966	Jet Commander	64	Wfu. Located Manila, Philippines.	N124JB
N125AW	1965	HS 125/1A	25057	Wfu. American Flight&Technology Center, Pontiac, Mi. USA.	N188K
N125CA	1967	Falcon 20DC	208	W/o Catersville, Al. USA. 29 Jun 89.	N300JJ
N125CM	1971	HS 125/400A	NA767	Wfu. Cx USA 6/95. Parts at AVMATS Paynesville, Mo. USA.	N28GE
N125E	1966	HS 125/1A-522	25110	Wfu. Hobby-Houston, Tx. USA. 29 Jun 83.	N3125B
N125F	1967	HS 125/3A-RA	25151	Wfu. Last located Collique, Peru.	G-AVTY
N125FD	1966	HS 125/3A	25123	Wfu. Parts at Dodsons, Rantoul, Ks. USA.	N44PW
N125GK	1967	HS 125/F3B	25127	W/o Barcelona, Venezuela. 26 Jun 06.	G-KASS
N125NE	1979	Learjet 25D	25D-271	W/o Gulf of Mexico. 21 May 80.	(N183AP)
N126R	1968	Falcon 20C	126	W/o El Paso, Tx. USA. 28 Aug 98.	N102ZE
N127MS	1974	Sabre-75A	380-18	Wfu. Cx USA 6/95. Parts at Perryville, Mo. USA.	N55
N127MW	1967	HFB 320	1027	W/o Aberdeen, SD. USA. 5 Oct 84.	N905MW
N128GA	1966	BAC 1-11/401AK	058	Wfu.	N128TA
N128SD	1969	HFB 320	1035	Wfu. Located Monroe, Mi. USA.	PH-HFC
N128YT	1974	HS 125/600A	256035	Wfu. Parts at White Industries, Bates City, Mo. USA.	(N635PA)
N129DM	1969	Learjet 24B	24B-187	Wfu.	N5WJ
N129K	1966	Jet Commander	70	Wfu. Parts at White Industries, Bates City, Mo. USA.	N1194Z

Reg	Yr	Type	c/n	Owner/Operator	Prev Regn
N130MR	1995	CitationJet	525-0097	W/o Buda, Tx. USA. 26 Mar 00.	N234WS
N130MW	1968	HFB 320	1033	Wfu. Located Monterey, Ca. USA.	N132MW
N131BH	1964	Sabre-40	282-18	Wfu. Cx USA 5/07.	N15TS
N131MS	1975	Sabre-75A	380-22	Wfu. Cx USA 6/95. Parts at Perryville, Mo. USA.	N132MS
N132MW	1968	HFB 320	1032	Wfu. Located Monterey, Ca. USA.	N130MW
N132RL	1967	HS 125/3A-RA	NA704	Wfu. Parts at White Industries, Bates City, Mo. USA.	C-GSKV
N133BL	1965	Learjet 24	24-133	Wfu. Cx USA 3/04.	N133DF
N133ME	1966	Jet Commander	50	Wfu.	N612JC
N133W	1965	Learjet 23	23-021	W/o Burbank, Ca. USA. 1 Apr 78.	N427NJ
N134RG	1983	Diamond 1A	A037SA	Wfu. Parts at White Industries Inc. Bates City, Mo. USA.	N109TW
N135PT	1984	Learjet C-21A	35A-509	W/o Groton, Ct. USA. 4 Aug 03.	N826RD
N136DH	1965	HS 125/1A	25036	Wfu. Cx USA 7/95.	C-FPQG
N137GL	1978	Learjet 25D	25D-237	W/o Detroit, Mi. USA. 19 Jan 79.	(N28BP)
N138BF	2000	SJ 30-2	002	W/o N of Del Rio, Tx. USA. 26 Apr 03.	
N138SR	1959	B 707-138B	17697	W/o Hangar fire Port Harcourt, Nigeria. 28 Aug 98.	(N138MJ)
N140GC	1977	Learjet 25D	25D-225	Wfu,. Parts at Dodsons, Rantoul, Ks. USA.	N808DS
N140MM	1964	Sabre-40	282-8	Wfu. Cx USA 9/96.	N369N
N140RC	1965	Learjet 23	23-048	Wfu. Last located Montgomery, Al. USA.	N48MW
N144CP	1969	Learjet 24B	24B-185	Wfu. Parts at Dodsons, Rantoul, Ks. USA.	N44CP
N148E	1965	Jet Commander	22	W/o Burbank, Ca. USA. 13 Sep 68.	N200M
N148PE	1960	JetStar-6	5002	Wfu. Parted out at Minneapolis, Mn. USA. (during 1987).	N81JJ
N149HP	1979	Falcon 10	154	Wfu. Parts at White Industries, Bates City, Mo. USA.	N777FJ
N149SF	1969	Jet Commander-B	149	Wfu. Cx USA 11/03.	(N803AU)
N151AS	1974	Citation	500-0183	Wfu. Cx USA 8/07.	N112CP
N151TB	1974	Sabre-80A	380-11	Wfu. Cx USA 11/04. Parts at White Industries, Mo. USA.	N265SR
N153TW	1970	Learjet 25	25-053	W/o Lansing, NY. USA. 24 Aug 01.	N37GB
N155AG	1969	Learjet 25	25-037	Wfu. Fuselage used for display by Best Aeronet Ltd.	N28AA
N155TJ	1967	JetStar-731	5104	Wfu. Last located Fort Lauderdale Executive, Fl. USA.	N155AV
N158DP	1961	JetStar-8	5013	Wfu. Parts at White Industries, Bates City, Mo. USA. (3/88).	(N5AX)
N159DP	1966	Jet Commander	52	Wfu. Located Aviation Museum, Darwin, Australia.	N159MP
N160AG	1968	HS 125/3A-RA	NA707	Wfu. Parts at Dodsons, Rantoul, Ks. USA.	SE-DHH
N162JB	1970	Sabre-60	306-62	Wfu. Cx USA 8/01.	N62CF
N163DC	1967	Jet Commander	89	Wfu. Located New Orleans Lakefront, La. USA.	N10BK
N163DL	1973	Westwind-1123	163	Wfu. Cx USA 10/97. Parts at Dodsons, Rantoul, Ks. USA.	N47DC
N163WS	1969	Jet Commander-B	141	Wfu. Cx USA 12/03.	5N-EZE
N165WC	1968	Falcon 20C-PW300	140	Wfu. Located Detroit Willow Run, Mi. USA.	N314AE
N167G	1977	JetStar 2	5212	Wfu. Cx USA 7/03. Parts at Conroe, Tx. USA.	(N95SR)
N169RF	1969	Sabre-60	306-45	W/o Phoenix, Az. USA. 7 Nov 92.	N742K
N170CS	1975	Falcon 10	58	Wfu. Parts at Dodsons, Rantoul, Ks. USA.	(F-GHJL)
N171CC	1968	JetStar-8	5127	Wfu. Located El Mirage, Ca. USA. (as N171SG).	N636
N171GA	1969	HFB 320	1039	Wfu. Located Portage Quarry, Bowling Green, Ky.(underwater)	N208MM
N171JL	1966	JetStar-731	5074	Wfu. Cx USA 10/01.	N171JL
N171MC	1974	Falcon 10	30	Wfu. Parts at White Industries, Bates City, Mo. USA.	N191MC
N171TS	1976	HS 125/600A	256071	Wfu. Cx USA 5/04.	(XA-...)
N172AC	1968	Jet Commander	1	Wfu.	N112AC
N173EL	1975	Gulfstream 2TT	173	Wfu. Last located Van Nuys, Ca. USA.	(N444ML)
N173GA	1971	HFB 320	1052	Wfu. Located Jefferson Technical College, Louisville, Ky.	PT-IDW
N174BD	1969	Falcon 20C	174	Wfu. Last located Fayetteville, Ar. USA.	(D-CFAI)
N176GA	1971	HFB 320	1053	Wfu. Last located at Toledo, Oh. USA.	PT-IOB
N179GA	1967	Falcon 20C	100	W/o St Louis, Mo. USA. 8 Apr 03. (at Rantoul, Ks).	I-VEPA
N181MA	1979	Diamond-Two	A001SA	Wfu. Located Wichita-Beech Field, USA.	JQ2001
N182K	1980	Learjet 35A	35A-293	W/o Long Island Sound, Ct. USA. 2 Jun 06.	
N183GA	1968	Falcon 20C	147	W/o Swanton, Oh. USA. 8 Apr 03.	N41154
N184GA	1972	Falcon 20E	266	Wfu. Parts at White Industries, Bates City, Mo. USA.	N4115B
N196CF	1969	Learjet 24B	24B-186	Wfu. Last located Montgomery, Al. USA.	N73PS
N196KC	1966	Jet Commander	68	W/o Fayetteville, Ar. USA. 1 Jul 68.	N619JC
N197JS	1966	JetStar-731	5069	Wfu. Cx USA 2/99.	XA-PGO
N200CK	1962	JetStar-6	5039	Wfu. Last located 7/90 at Spirit of St Louis, Mo. USA.	N200CK
N200GT	1968	Falcon 20C	137	Wfu. Cx USA 2/07.	N777PV
N200JE	1968	Falcon 20C	133	Wfu. Parts at Dodsons, Rantoul, Ks. USA.	N133FJ
N200LF	1966	Jet Commander	47	Wfu. Parts at White Industries, Bates City, Mo. USA.	N222HM
N200PR	2003	390 Premier 1	RB-79	W/o Blackbushe, UK. 7 Apr 04.	
N200RC	1969	Jet Commander-B	140	W/o Tampa, Fl. USA. 25 Sep 73.	4X-CPG
N202DN	1983	Falcon 100	202	W/o Lawrence, Ks. USA. 9 Dec 01.	N80WJ
N203M	1970	Falcon 20C	120	Wfu. Cx USA 1/85.	N200M
N204C	1974	Gulfstream 2	143	W/o Kota Kinabalu, Borneo. 4 Sep 91.	N334

Reg	Yr	Type	c/n	Owner/Operator	Prev Regn
N204RC	1968	Gulfstream 2	34	W/o Caracas, Venezuela. 17 Jun 91.	N500JR
N207JC	1976	Learjet 25D	25D-207	Wfu. Parts at White Industries Inc. Bates City, Mo. USA.	I-LEAR
N210RS	1965	Falcon 20C	18	Wfu. Cx USA 8/96.	N9DM
N211MB	1970	Learjet 25	25-059	W/o Port au Prince, Haiti. 3 Aug 80.	N425JX
N212AP	1972	JetStar-8	5147	Wfu. Located Greenwood, Ms. USA.	N718R
N212CW	1966	Jet Commander	75	Wfu. Parts at White Industries, Bates City, Mo. USA.	N1121R
N212NE	1976	Learjet 25D	25D-212	Wfu. Parted out 1989.	N911MG
N213AP	1968	JetStar-8	5122	Wfu. Cx USA 3/89.	N1107M
N216SA	1965	Falcon 20DC	16	Wfu. Parts at Dodsons, Rantoul, Ks. USA.	N216TW
N217A	1974	HS 125/600B	256030	Wfu.	G-TOMI
N219TT	1975	Sabre-75A	380-24	Wfu. Cx USA 2/95. Located Tulsa Technology Center, Ok. USA.	N58
N220JC	1983	Learjet 55	55-050	W/o Boca Raton, Fl. USA. 23 Jun 00.	(N55UJ)
N220MT	1978	Corvette	40	Wfu. Last located at Griffin, Ga. USA.	N200MT
N220RB	1960	DC 8-21	45280	Wfu. Located Datang Shan Museum, Beijing, China.	N8003U
N221PH	1966	Sabre-40	282-55	Wfu. Cx USA 8/86, Parts at AVMATS, Mo. USA.	(N221PX)
N222FJ	1997	Williams V-Jet II	001	Wfu. Located EAA Museum Oshkosh, Wi. USA.	
N222KN	1968	JetStar-8	5118	Wfu. Last located Memphis, Tn. USA.	N333KN
N222WL	1981	Citation II	550-0208	Wfu. Cx USA 3/91.	N54RC
N224SC	1966	Learjet 24A	24A-100	W/o Gainesville, Ga. USA. 26 Sep 99. (parts at Rantoul, Ks)	N427LJ
N225HR	1973	HS 125/600B	256017	Wfu. Parts at White Industries, Bates City, Mo. USA.	(N415BA)
N225LS	1965	Sabre-40	282-51	Wfu. Parts at Paynesville, Mo. USA.	(N51MN)
N227GA	1969	Gulfstream II SP	76	Wfu. Cx USA 4/04. Last located Van Nys, Ca. USA.	N227G
N228SW	1977	Learjet 25D	25D-228	Wfu. Parts at Dodsons, Ottawa, Ks. USA.	
N230TS	1968	HS 125/3A-RA	NA700	Wfu. Parts at Dodsons, Rantoul, Ks. USA.	N946FS
N232RA	1970	Falcon 20DC	232	W/o Binghampton, NY. USA. 15 Feb 89.	N27EV
N234CM	1970	Learjet 24B	24B-214	W/o Nr Monclova, Mexico. 16 Dec 88.	N42NF
N234F	1965	Learjet 23	23-063	W/o Palm Springs, Ca. USA. 14 Nov 65.	
N234MR	1966	Learjet 24	24-130	Wfu. Cx USA 10/87.	N330J
N234UM	1973	Citation	500-0105	Wfu. Last located at Montgomery, Al. USA.	N32W
N235KC	1966	HS 125/1A	25096	W/o Grand Bahama, Bahamas. 21 Nov 66.	G-ATNR
N235R	1965	Learjet 23	23-032	W/o Clarendon, Tx. USA. 23 Apr 66.	
N236BN	1979	HS 125/700A	NA0236	W/o Jackson, Wy. USA. 20 Dec 00.	N64HA
N236JP	1967	Jet Commander	116	W/o Marion, Va. USA. 31 Oct 69.	N4743E
N240AA	1966	Jet Commander	82	Wfu. Cx USA 9/03.	N103BW
N241H	1979	Sabre-65	465-5	W/o Molokai-Hoolehua, Hi. USA. 11 May 00.	(N60CR)
N241JA	1966	Learjet 24	24-131	Wfu. Displayed at Wings Over the Rockies Museum, Jeffco, Co.	N11FH
N241JC	1971	Falcon 20E	241	Wfu. Cx USA 6/07.	I-FLYK
N241RS	1974	Falcon 10	18	Wfu. Parts at Dodsons, Rantoul, Ks. USA.	N1TJ
N250EC	1972	Sabre-40A	282-110	Wfu. Cx USA 4/04. Last located Entebbe, Uganda.	N477A
N250UA	1967	Jet Commander-A	121	W/o Flatwood, La. USA. 27 Apr 78.	N1121R
N251DS	1977	Learjet 25D	25D-218	Wfu. Parts at Dodsons, Rantoul, Ks. USA.	N14NA
N253K	1974	Falcon 10	10	W/o Meigs-Chicago, Il. USA. 30 Jan 80. (at Bates City, Mo.)	N105FJ
N256WM	1972	Learjet 24D	24D-256	Wfu. Cx USA 2/06.	N256MJ
N257TM	1966	Sabre-40	282-76	Wfu. Cx USA 6/02.	N256CM
N265DC	1965	Learjet 23	23-081	Wfu. Last located Rifle, Co. USA.	ZS-MDN
N267L	1965	JetStar-6	5067	W/o Luton, UK. 29 Mar 81.	(N267AD)
N280AT	1978	Westwind-1124	247	W/o Panama City, Panama. 2 Jul 04.	N280AZ
N281FP	1973	Learjet 24D	24D-281	Wfu. Located at Frontiers of Flight Museum, Love Field, Tx.	N23MJ
N287W	1969	Falcon 20D	194	Wfu. Parts at AVMATS Paynesville, Mo. USA.	N297W
N300HW	1965	HS 125/1A	25021	Wfu. Parts at White Industries, Bates City, Mo. USA.	N711WJ
N300JA	1974	Learjet 24D	24D-282	W/o Dutch Harbour, Ak. USA. 2 Dec 79.	D-INKA
N300PL	1978	Learjet 25D	25D-247	Wfu. Parted out following accident 12/83.	
N301AJ	1966	Jet Commander	48	W/o Cozumel, Mexico. 13 Aug 90.	N502U
N302EJ	1975	Learjet 24D	24D-302	W/o Puerta Vallarta, Mexico. 14 Apr 83.	N39DM
N303AF	1967	Learjet 24	24-144	Wfu. Parts at White Industries Inc. Bates City, Mo. USA.	N700C
N303EJ	1975	Learjet 24D	24D-303	Wfu. Parts at White Industries Inc. Bates City, Mo. USA.	PT-LOJ
N303GA	1980	Gulfstream 3	303	W/o Aspen, Co. USA. 29 Mar 01.	N1761W
N305AJ	1967	Jet Commander	100	Wfu. Parts at OK Aircraft, Gilroy, Ca. USA.	N11WP
N306SA	1969	Sabre-60	306-40	Wfu. Cx USA 8/06.	XA-SBX
N308WC	1961	JetStar-6	5020	Wfu. Cx USA 8/88.	(N777NN)
N309CK	1981	Westwind-Two	350	W/o Irvine, Ca. USA. 15 Dec 93.	N777LU
N309LJ	1970	Learjet 25	25-034	Wfu. Located Gloucester-Staverton, UK.	N309AJ
N315AJ	1966	Learjet 24	24-108	Wfu. Parts at White Industries Inc. Bates City, Mo. USA.	N900JA
N316M	1965	Learjet 23	23-061	W/o Lake Michigan, USA. 19 Mar 66.	
N317TC	1972	HS 125/600B	256007	Wfu. Cx USA 9/07.	N3007
N320MC	1968	HFB 320	1034	W/o Phoenix, Az. USA. 9 Mar 73.	N320J

Reg	Yr	Type	c/n	Owner/Operator	Prev Regn
N320MJ	1969	B 707-321B	20028	W/o Marana, Az. USA. 20 Sep 90.	VR-CBN
N320W	1965	Jet Commander	15	Wfu. Parts at White Industries, Bates City, Mo. USA.	N125K
N321AF	1976	HFB 320	1060	Wfu. at Hollister, Ca. USA.	(D-CCCH)
N322AF	1975	HFB 320	1058	Wfu. at Hollister, Ca. USA.	16+21
N323AF	1979	HFB 320	1062	Wfu. at Hollister, Ca. USA.	N323AF
N324AF	1980	HFB 320	1064	Wfu. at Hollister, Ca. USA.	16+27
N325AF	1980	HFB 320	1065	Wfu. at Hollister, Ca. USA.	16+28
N326CB	1969	JetStar-8	5143	Wfu. Cx USA 1/00.	N326CB
N329J	1957	JetStar	1001	Wfu. Located Museum of Flight, Seattle, Wa. USA..	
N329JS	1977	JetStar 2	5206	Wfu. Parts at White Industries Inc. Bates City, Mo. USA.	XA-JML
N331DP	1965	Learjet 23	23-067	W/o Dayton, Oh. USA. 18 Jan 90.	N720UA
N331DP	1965	Learjet 23	23-059	Wfu. Located at Detroit, Mi. (N331DP transferred to 23-067).	N31DP
N332PC	1965	Learjet 23	23-056	W/o Flint, Mi. USA. 6 Jan 77. (parts at White Inds.).	N362EJ
N333AV	1966	Falcon 20C	28	Wfu. College of Aeronautics, Montreal St Hubert, Canada.	C-GEAQ
N333BG	1967	Jet Commander	98	Wfu. Cx USA 6/97.	N301L
N333CG	1978	Learjet 25D	25D-262	W/o Salina, Ks. USA. 12 Jun 01.	N440F
N333GB	1966	BAC 1-11/401AK	076	Wfu. Last located San Antonio, Tx. USA.	VR-BHS
N333GZ	1965	HS 125/1A-522	25070	Wfu. Parts at White Industries Inc. Bates City, Mo. USA.	N470TS
N333SV	1968	Jet Commander	114	Wfu. Cx USA 1/98. Parts at Hollister, Ca. USA.	N85MR
N334JC	1976	Citation	500-0334	Wfu. Cx USA 3/98.	ZS-MPI
N338EC	1965	JetStar-731	5061	Wfu. Last located Palm Beach International, Fl. USA.	N333EC
N349M	1965	Jet Commander	23	Wfu. Parts at White Industries, Bates City, Mo. USA.	N2100X
N350JF	1979	Learjet 35A	35A-219	W/o over Adwa, Ethiopia. 29 Aug 99.	N502G
N350JH	1975	Learjet 25B	25B-200	Wfu. Parts at White Industries Inc. Bates City, Mo. USA.	N680BC
N353CA	1969	Sabre-60	306-28	Wfu. Last located Fort Lauderdale Executive, Fl. USA.	N741RL
N360HK	1973	Westwind-1123	166	Wfu.	C-GDOC
N366AA	1974	Learjet 25B	25B-151	W/o Briggsdale, Co. USA. 31 Aug 74.	
N370V	1980	Challenger 600S	1014	W/o Teterboro, NJ. USA. 2 Feb 05.	144607
N374FD	1985	Airbus A300C4-620	374	Wfu. Cx USA 7/04.	A6-PFD
N375MD	1977	JetStar 2	5209	Wfu. Cx USA 12/05. Parts at Dodsons, Rantoul, Ks. USA.	N529TS
N377HS	1975	Sabre-75A	380-36	Wfu. Cx USA 1/05.	XB-MCB
N380AA	1969	JetStar-8	5131	Wfu. Last located at Van Nuys, Ca. USA. Cx USA 3/92.	N212JW
N380BC	1974	Sabre-80A	380-17	Wfu. Cx USA 1/07.	N1115
N384AT	1974	Westwind-1123	175	Wfu. Parts at Dodsons, Rantoul, Ks. USA.	(N571MC)
N386G	1965	Jet Commander	43	Wfu. Parted out 1989.	N121CS
N388LS	1981	Learjet 35A	35A-388	W/o Lebanon, NH. USA. 24 Dec 96.	N388PD
N390RB	2001	390 Premier 1	RB-26	W/o Herrera Santo Domingo, Dominican Republic. 7 Jan 03.	(N390HR)
N395BB	1979	Falcon 20F	395	Wfu. Parts at White Industries, Mo. USA. (as OD-PAL).	OD-PAL
N397F	1969	Gulfstream 2	72	W/o Burlington, Vt. USA. 22 Feb 76.	
N397QS	1999	Citation V Ultra	560-0531	W/o Leakey, Tx. USA. 2 May 02.	
N397RD	1968	Gulfstream 2	37	Wfu. Cx USA 11/02. Last located El Mirage, Ca. USA.	N994JD
N399P	1967	Sabre-40	282-87	Wfu. Donated Pittsburgh Institute of Aeronautics, Pa. USA.	N36P
N399RP	1982	Diamond 1A	A020SA	Wfu. Parts at White Industries Inc. Bates City, Mo. USA.	(N911JJ)
N400CP	1965	Jet Commander	30	W/o Burlington, Vt. USA. 21 Jan 71.	N401V
N400M	1961	JetStar-6	5008	W/o Saranac Lake, NY. USA. 27 Dec 72.	N9233R
N400PH	1968	HS 125/400A	NA716	W/o Lexington, Ky. USA. 5 Dec 87.	N888CR
N400VG	1996	Beechjet 400A	RK-113	W/o Beckley, WV. USA. 17 Apr 99.	N3263N
N401DE	1967	Jet Commander	92	Wfu. Cx USA 3/89.	N33PS
N401MS	1968	Sabre-60	306-17	Wfu. Cx USA 8/01.	N13SL
N401RD	1975	Citation Longwing	500-0267	Wfu. Parts at Dodsons, Rantoul, Ks. USA.	(N4090P)
N403M	1969	Jet Commander	132	W/o Salt Lake City, Ut. USA. 16 Dec 69.	N200M
N405PC	1980	Citation 1/SP	501-0150	W/o Depere, Wi. USA. 3 Apr 01.	N73FW
N407V	1965	Learjet 23	23-034	Wfu. Located Everett PAE, Seattle, Wa. USA.	N154AG
N408TR	1964	Sabre-40	282-4	Wfu. Last located Tech College, Toledo, Oh. USA.	N111MS
N409MA	1970	Gulfstream 2	83	W/o Quito, Ecuador. 4 May 95.	(N48MS)
N411BW	1985	Diamond-Two	A1008SA	Wfu. Parts at Dodsons, Rantoul, Ks. USA.	
N418MA	1980	Citation II	550-0144	Wfu. Mineral Wells, Tx. USA. 18 Nov 03.	RP-C689
N422BC	1980	Westwind-Two	302	W/o Milwaukee, Wi. USA. 26 Dec 99.	N100AK
N425JA	1966	Falcon 20C	51	Wfu. Cx USA 10/94.	N425JF
N428JX	1973	Learjet 25B	25B-103	W/o Richmond, In. USA. 3 Jul 75.	
N431NA	1968	Sabreliner T-39D	285-2	Wfu. Cx USA 12/91.	USN 150970
N431NA	1960	Sabreliner CT-39A	265-16	Wfu. Located Des Moines Educational Resources, Ia. USA.	USAF 60-348
N432EJ	1965	Learjet 23	23-028A	W/o Muskegon, Mi. USA. 25 Oct 67.	N803LJ
N434AN	1964	JetStar-731	5050	Wfu. Last located at Griffin, Ga. USA.	HZ-THZ
N434EJ	1965	Learjet 23	23-046	W/o Pellston, Mi. USA. 9 May 70.	(N822LJ)
N435GM	1973	Gulfstream II SP	137	Wfu. Last located Beaumont-Port Arthur, Tx. USA.	N485GM

Reg	Yr	Type	c/n	Owner/Operator	Prev Regn
N435JL	1975	Learjet 35	35-018	Wfu. Parts at White Industries Inc. Bates City, Mo. USA.	(N435EC)
N440BC	1970	HS 125/400A	NA744	Wfu. Georgia Aviation Technical College, Eastman, Ga. USA.	N711BP
N440HM	1980	Learjet 35A	35A-294	W/o Greenville, SC. USA. 27 Feb 97. (parts at Bates City.).	N35VP
N440RM	1961	JetStar-6	5016	Wfu. Last located Roswell, NM. USA.	N712GW
N442NE	1981	Learjet 35A	35A-442	W/o Morristown, NJ. USA. 26 Jul 88. (parts at Bates City.).	N35BK
N444TJ	1969	Jet Commander-B	146	Wfu. Parts at Griffin, Ga. USA.	N926JM
N444TW	1977	Learjet 24F	24F-348	W/o Nr Guadalajara, Mexico. 9 Jan 07.	N8BG
N444WC	1965	Learjet 23	23-047	Wfu. Parts at Dodsons, Rantoul, Ks. USA.	(N2503L)
N444WJ	1975	Falcon 10	64	Wfu. Parts at White Industries, Bates City, Mo. USA.	N718CA
N445	1965	Jet Commander	37	Wfu. Last located scrapyard near Wiley Post, Ok. USA.	N723JB
N448GG	1965	Learjet 23	23-057	Wfu. Parts at Dodsons, Rantoul, Ks. USA.	N448GC
N453LJ	1996	Learjet 45	45-003	Wfu. Located Pima Community College,Tuscon, Az. USA.	
N454LJ	1996	Learjet 45	45-004	W/o Wallops Island, Va. USA. 27 Oct 98.	
N454RN	1966	Learjet 24	24-121	W/o Atlanta, Ga. USA. 26 Feb 73.	N454GL
N455JA	1974	Learjet 24XR	24XR-300	W/o Gulkana, Ak. USA. 20 Aug 85.	N300EJ
N456JA	1973	Learjet 24XR	24XR-265	W/o Nr Juneau, Ak. USA. 24 Oct 85.	N32WL
N458J	1973	Learjet 25XR	25XR-106	W/o Columbus, Oh. USA. 1 Jul 91.	N458JA
N460MC	1967	Falcon 20C	105	Wfu. Parts at Spirit of St Louis, Mo. USA.	N97FJ
N463HK	1968	Gulfstream 2	11	Wfu. Nose section located Banyan Pilot Shop, Ft Lauderdale.	N611TJ
N463LJ		Learjet 25	25-001	Wfu. Used in construction of s/n 25-002.	
N473TC	1969	Learjet 25	25-043	Wfu. Parts at Dodsons, Rantoul, Ks. USA.	N234ND
N475AT	1979	Westwind-1124	270	W/o Georgetown, Bahamas. 24 May 06.	N501DT
N480LR	1972	HFB 320	1054	Wfu. Cx USA 1/87. GTCC Aviation Center, Greensboro, NC.	N896HJ
N481DH	1969	Jet Commander-B	139	Wfu. Parts at White Industries, Bates City, Mo. USA.	N188G
N486SB	2001	Citation Encore	560-0580	W/o Upland, Ca. USA. 24 Jun 06.	N1871R
N487GS	1968	B 737-247	19600	Wfu.	N307VA
N492AT	1983	Citation II	550-0472	W/o Butler, Pa. USA. 24 Jan 07.	N492MA
N498YY	2002	CitationJet CJ-1	525-0498	Wfu. Last located Paris-Le Bourget, France.	N5201J
N500AD	1972	Citation	500-0006	Wfu. Cx USA 5/91.	(N500AH)
N500AT	1991	Citation V	560-0146	W/o Pueblo, Co. USA. 16 Feb 05.	N2000M
N500BF	1965	Learjet 23	23-010	Wfu. Located Detroit-Willow Run, Mi. USA.	N400BF
N500CC	1969	Citation	669	Wfu. Cx USA 1/78.	
N500EL	1974	Citation	500-0173	Wfu. Parts at White Industries Inc. Bates City, Mo. USA.	N59CL
N500ES	1966	JetStar-731	5075	Wfu. Last located Rockford, Il. USA.	N1DB
N500FM	1966	Learjet 23	23-088	W/o Columbia, Tn. USA. 2 Jul 91. (parts at Detroit).	(N500LH)
N500HH	1974	Citation	500-0189	Wfu. Cx USA 5/01. Located Addison, Tx. USA.	N189CC
N500J	1969	Gulfstream 2	60	W/o Hot Springs, Va. USA. 26 Sep 76.	N892GA
N500JJ	1959	B 707-138B	17699	Wfu.	G-AVZZ
N500JR	1966	Jet Commander	65	W/o North Platte, SD. USA. 26 Sep 66.	
N500JW	1964	Learjet 23	23-005	Wfu. Cx USA 8/87. Parts at Willow Run Detroit, Mi. USA.	N15BE
N500MA	1962	JetStar-731	5033	Wfu. Cx USA 9/02. Last located Conroe, Tx. USA.	N50EC
N500MF	1965	Jet Commander	34	Wfu. Parts at White Industries, Bates City, Mo. USA.	TG-OMF
N500NL	1974	Sabre-75A	380-8	W/o 23 Feb 75.	N5107
N500RW	1978	Learjet 35A	35A-148	W/o Teterboro, NJ. USA. 24 May 88.	N333RP
N500WN	1969	JetStar-8	5135	Wfu. Located AVMATS Spirit of St Louis, Mo. USA.	(N500FG)
N501AL	1961	JetStar-6	5012	Wfu. Derelict by 3/94 at Opa Locka, Fl. USA.	N500SJ
N501CC	1970	Citation	701	Wfu. Smithsonian 'Business Wings' exhibit, DC (was s/n 670).	
N501EZ	1978	Citation 1/SP	501-0058	W/o Grannis, Ar. USA. 2 Dec 98.	N211X
N501GP	1972	Citation	500-0026	W/o Bluefield, WV. USA. 21 Jan 81.	N526CC
N501PS	1974	Learjet 25B	25B-153	W/o Detroit, Mi. USA. 26 May 77.	
N503U	1966	Jet Commander	83	W/o nr Guatamala City, Guatamala. 19 Dec 95.	C-GHPR
N505AJ	1967	Falcon 20C	89	Wfu. Last located Detroit YIP, Mi. USA.	N71CP
N505K	1972	Citation	500-0004	W/o Houston, Tx. USA. 5 Nov 2005.	N5005
N505PF	1965	Learjet 23	23-006	Wfu. Exhibit Kansas Aviation Museum, Mo. USA.	N111JD
N510BM	1969	Falcon 20D	215	Wfu. Last located Pontiac, Mi. USA.	N619GA
N510MS	1969	Learjet 24B	24B-204	Wfu. Last located Hollister, Ca. USA.	N510ND
N511AJ	1970	Learjet 25	25-055	Wfu. Parts at White Industries, Bates City, Mo. USA.	N65RC
N511TD	1969	JetStar-8	5145	Wfu. Cx USA 6/06. Located Great St Louis Air & Space Museum.	XA-JFE
N511TS	1967	JetStar-731	5101	Wfu. Last located at Guthrie, Ok. USA.	N800AF
N515VW	1968	Learjet 25	25-013	W/o Delemont, Switzerland. 17 Apr 69.	
N520S	1966	JetStar-731	5084	W/o Westchester, NY. USA. 11 Feb 81.	N901E
N521M	1967	HS 125/3A	25129	W/o Findlay, Oh. USA. 12 Dec 72.	G-AVDM
N521PA	1979	Learjet 35A	35A-239	W/o Fresno, Ca. USA. 14 Dec 94. Cx USA 5/95.	N239GJ
N525CJ	1991	CitationJet	702	Wfu. Modified to CJ-2 prototype with s/n 708.	
N525KL	1996	CitationJet	525-0136	W/o Point Lookout, Mo. USA. 10 Dec 99.	N52081
N530G	1967	JetStar-731	5096	Wfu. Cx USA 6/04. Last located Conroe, Tx. USA.	N9252R

Reg	Yr	Type	c/n	Owner/Operator	Prev Regn
N535PC	1980	Learjet 35A	35A-291	W/o Aspen, Co. USA. 13 Feb 91.	N7US
N540CL	1965	Learjet 23	23-026	Wfu. Parts at Hollister, Ca. USA. Cx USA 5/06.	N404DB
N541CW	1980	Diamond 1	A004SA	Wfu. Parts at White Industries, Bates City, Mo. USA.	(N541TM)
N545BF	1970	JetStar-8	5146	Wfu. Cx USA 2/97.	N499AS
N546PA	1980	Learjet 36A	36A-045	W/o Astoria, Or. USA. 3 Dec 02.	N13FN
N547JL	1979	Sabre-75A	380-69	W/o Marion, Ks. USA. 20 Jul 98.	N111VX
N550BP	1981	Citation II	550-0246	W/o Lake Michigan, USA. 4 Jun 07. (was 551-0296).	N551TK
N550CC	1977	Citation	686	Wfu. (wef 14 Apr 91).	
N555AJ	1971	Citation	500-0007	W/o Denver, Co. USA. 19 Nov 79.	N500LF
N555DM	1965	Jet Commander	25	Wfu. Parts at Dodsons, Rantoul, Ks. USA.	
N555LB	1968	Learjet 24	24-177	Wfu. Last located El Mirage, Ca. USA.	(N524DW)
N555PB	1964	JetStar-6	5047	Wfu. Last located Rockland, Me. USA. Cx USA 10/90.	N409MA
N555PT	1966	Sabre-40	282-53	Wfu. Cx USA 2/91. Parts at AVMATS, Mo. USA.	N600BP
N555SG	1966	JetStar-8	5090	Wfu. Last located Fort Lauderdale, Fl. USA.	N55CJ
N556AT	1972	Citation	500-0020	Wfu. Cx USA 2/93.	C-FBAX
N560CC	1977	Citation V	550-0001	Wfu. Located Wichita Area Technical College, Ks. USA.	N5050J
N560MC	1965	Jet Commander	24	Wfu.	(N7GW)
N560RA	1966	Falcon 20C	56	Wfu. Last located Detroit-Willow Run, Mi. USA.	N388AJ
N562R	1969	Sabre-60	306-37	Wfu. Cx USA 5/05.	N4SE
N564MG	1961	JetStar-6	5021	Wfu. Fuselage only 5/88 at Memphis, Tn. USA.	C-FETN
N565KC	1969	Gulfstream 2TT	46	Wfu. Last located Islip, NY. USA.	N505JT
N565SS	1972	Citation	500-0017	Wfu. Last located Griffin, Ga. USA.	N49EA
N566NA	1972	Learjet 25	25-064	Wfu. Located John C Stennis Space Center, Ms. USA.	N266GL
N567DW	1965	Sabre-40	282-35	Wfu. Parts at AVMATS Paynesville, Mo. USA.	N341AR
N571BJ	1968	Gulfstream 2	15	Wfu. Cx USA 11/07.	N125JJ
N575RD	1973	Citation	500-0075	Wfu. Parts at White Industries, Bates City, Mo. USA.	(N600TT)
N580NJ	1966	Jet Commander	58	Wfu. Cx USA 12/00.	CP-2263
N580WE	1968	Jet Commander-A	123	Wfu. Cx USA 7/02. Parts at Dodsons, Rantoul, Ks. USA.	N1121A
N588CG	1975	Learjet 24D	24D-304	Wfu. Last Located Detroit-Willow Run, Mi. USA.	N500CG
N598JC	1977	Falcon 10	112	Wfu. Located White Industries, Bates City, Mo. USA.	N12MB
N600K	1969	Jet Commander-B	148	Wfu. Cx USA 6/99. Parts at Hollister, Ca. USA.	(N22LL)
N600RA	1977	Corvette	36	Wfu. Last located at Griffin, Ga. USA.	N601RC
N600SJ	1968	Sabre-60	306-15	Wfu. Last located PBI, Fl. USA. Cx USA 7/05.	N604MK
N601JJ	1967	JetStar-8	5102	Wfu. Cx USA 2/00.	N601JJ
N602GA	1969	HFB 320	1041	Wfu. Last located Toledo, Oh. USA.	N92045
N604AN	1975	Corvette	18	Wfu. Cx USA 12/90. To Spain for spares.	F-BTTO
N604GA	1969	HFB 320	1037	W/o Howell Island, Chesterfield, Mo. USA. 30 Nov 04.	YV-999P
N605GA	1969	HFB 320	1038	Wfu. Located Jefferson Technical College, Louisville, Ky.	N301AT
N611JC	1963	Jet Commander	2	Wfu. Test airframe for static fatigue.	
N611PA	1994	Beechjet 400A	RK-78	Wfu. Parts at Dodsons, Rantoul, Ks. USA.	N8278Z
N614GB	1977	VFW 614	G14	Wfu. Located Oldenburg, Germany.	(OY-RGB)
N617BG	1983	Diamond 1A	A067SA	Wfu. Parts at White Industries, Bates City, Mo. USA.	N63DR
N617CC	1981	Citation 1/SP	501-0211	Wfu. Cx USA 6/96.	N6785C
N617GA	1967	Falcon 20C	88	Wfu. Last located at White Industries, Bates City, Mo. USA.	N41CD
N620JM	1978	Learjet 35A	35A-207	W/o Eagle County, Co. USA. 15 Jul 05.	N3PW
N621ST	1964	HS 125/1A	25014	Wfu. Broken up for spares 3/85. Cx USA 6/02.	XA-JUZ
N626CC	1984	Citation III	650-0026	Wfu. Damaged on production line 1984, now test airframe.	
N627WS	1974	Learjet 25B	25B-170	W/o Houston, Tx. USA. 13 Jan 98.	N98796
N630N	1966	Sabre-40	282-73	Wfu. Cx USA 6/85. Parts at Spirit of St Louis, Mo. USA.	N630M
N632PE	1968	HS 125/1A	25058	Wfu. Cx USA 10/05.	(EC-...)
N633SL	1969	Sabre-60	306-33	Wfu. Cx USA 7/05.	CC-CGT
N636SE	2002	Citation Encore	560-0636	W/o Cresco, Ia. USA. 19 Jul 06.	N83TK
N650	1980	Citation VII	697	Wfu. Located Wichita-Mid Continent, Ks. USA.	
N650CC	1979	Citation	696	Wfu. Cx USA 11/89.	
N650DH	1966	BAC 1-11/2400	059	Wfu. Cx USA 12/92.	N700JA
N658TC	1969	Learjet 25	25-044	W/o Victoria, Tx. USA. 18 Jan 72.	N962GA
N660A	1968	Learjet 24	24-155	Wfu. Parts at El Mirage, Ca. USA. (as N464CL).	N210FP
N661LJ		Learjet 25	25-002	Wfu. AiResearch engine tests.	
N666BT	1965	Falcon 20C	7	Wfu. Last located at Oklahoma City, Ok. USA.	XA-ACI
N666TW	1973	Learjet 25B	25B-116	W/o Del Rio, Tx. USA. 19 Sep 03.	(N818GY)
N678BC	1967	JetStar-731	5109	Wfu. Cx USA 11/92.	N968BN
N685FF	1966	HS 125/731	25121	Wfu. Cx USA 9/07.	N125LK
N690LJ	1965	Learjet 23	23-078	W/o Orlando, Fl. USA. 30 Nov 67.	
N699RD	1970	Sabre-60	306-53	Wfu. Cx USA 7/05.	(N999LG)
N700CW	1974	Citation	500-0205	W/o Eagle Pass, Tx. USA. 1 Apr 83.	(N541NC)
N700DK	1981	Falcon 10	191	W/o Pal-Waukee, Il. USA. 23 Sep 85.	N256FJ

Reg	Yr	Type	c/n	Owner/Operator	Prev Regn
❏ N701JA	1967	Gulfstream II SP	7	Wfu. Cx USA 11/03. Last located 12/04 at Van Nuys, Ca. USA.	N118NP
❏ N702HC	1973	HS 125/600A	256023	Wfu. Parts at White Industries, Bates City, Mo. USA.	N523MA
❏ N705EA	1968	HS 125/731	NA705	Wfu. Parts at White Industries, Bates City, Mo. USA.	N25MJ
❏ N706A	1964	Sabre-40	282-7	Wfu. Last located Opa Locka, Fl. USA.	XA-STU
❏ N707CA	1963	B 707-351C	18586	Wfu.	P4-FDH
❏ N707CG	1980	Falcon 10	165	Wfu. Cx USA 10/05. Parts at Dodsons, Rantoul, Ks. USA.	N56LP
❏ N707FH	1966	Sabre-40	282-74	Wfu. Cx USA 10/02.	N707TG
❏ N707RZ	1972	B 707-328	18375	Wfu. Broken up at Fort Lauderdale, Fl. USA.	F-BHSU
❏ N710JW	1965	Jet Commander	35	Wfu. Cx USA 11/92.	N7HL
❏ N710K	1962	MS 760 Paris	112	Wfu. Located Mojave, Ca. USA.	N7277X
❏ N710MB	1984	Diamond 1A	A078SA	W/o Nr Goodland, Ks. USA. 15 Dec 93. (parts at Bates City).	N378DM
❏ N711AF	1975	Learjet 35	35-029	W/o 100km South of Katab, Egypt. 11 Aug 79.	
❏ N711EV	1973	Gulfstream II SP	129	Wfu. Cx USA 10/03.	N626TC
❏ N711JT	1967	Jet Commander	91	W/o Tullahoma, Tn. USA. 13 Mar 75.	N73535
❏ N711WM	1982	Citation II/SP	551-0388	W/o 6 Nov 86.	
❏ N711Z	1960	JetStar	1002	Wfu. Displayed as USAF 89001 at Andrews AFB, Md. USA.	N711Z
❏ N713SS	1968	HS 125/400A	NA712	Wfu. Parts at White Industries, Bates City, Mo. USA.	N712VS
❏ N715MH	1973	Learjet 25B	25B-132	W/o Ciudad Victoria, Mexico. 26 Oct 01. (parts at Rantoul).	N715JF
❏ N717JM	1961	JetStar-6	5009	Wfu. Cx USA 8/84.	(HB-VET)
❏ N720DC	1966	B 727-77	19253	Wfu.	N448DR
❏ N720JR	1962	B 720-047B	18451	Wfu. Last located Malta.	N720JR
❏ N720Q	1969	Gulfstream 2	58	W/o Kline, SC. USA. 24 Jun 74.	N878GA
❏ N722KS	1968	Falcon 20C	130	Wfu. Last located Ontario, Ca,. USA. Cx USA 3/04.	(N130TJ)
❏ N723GL	1977	Learjet 35A	35A-107	W/o College Station-Easterwood, Tx. USA. 12 Dec 85.	
❏ N724LG	1967	Learjet 24	24-143	Wfu. Last located El Mirage, Ca. USA.	(N24WF)
❏ N725WH	1965	HS 125/731	25042	Wfu. Parts at White Industries, Bates City, Mo. USA.	(N42FD)
❏ N727RL	1964	B 727-25	18253	Wfu. Cx USA 11/06.	EL-GOL
❏ N727US	1978	Sabre-75A	380-61	Wfu. Cx USA 10/99. Parts at AVMATS St Louis, Mo. USA.	9L-LAW
❏ N730CP	1972	Sabre-40A	282-103	Wfu. Last located Toledo, Oh. USA.	N730CA
❏ N731L	1966	JetStar-731	5095	Wfu. Cx USA 11/03.	N780RH
❏ N731WL	1965	JetStar-731	5070	Wfu. Cx USA 1/05.	N712TE
❏ N739R	1966	Sabre-40	282-78	W/o Ventura, Ca. USA. 16 May 67.	
❏ N740EJ	1970	Learjet 24B	24B-222	Wfu. Last located Montgomery, Al. USA.	N740F
❏ N741MT	1962	Sabreliner CT-39A	276-34	Wfu. Located University of Tennessee, Tullahoma, Tn. USA.	N33UT
❏ N743R	1968	Sabre-60	306-11	W/o Montrose, Ca. USA. 13 Apr 73.	N723R
❏ N745F	1965	Learjet 23	23-077	W/o Perris, Ca. USA. 30 Jul 88.	(N611CA)
❏ N747E	1964	Sabre-40	282-22	W/o Buenos Aires, Argentina. 22 Dec 94.	N747
❏ N747GB	1969	JetStar-8	5141	Wfu. Last located Lagos, Nigeria.	N3982A
❏ N747LB	1966	Jet Commander-B	55	Wfu. Cx USA 11/03.	N11MC
❏ N750SB	1968	HFB 320	1031	Wfu. Located Opa Locka, Fl. USA.	N300SB
❏ N751CR	1966	Jet Commander	88	Wfu. Located at OK Aircraft, Gilroy, Ca. USA.	N70CS
❏ N754DB	1968	Learjet 25	25-014	Wfu. Cx USA 5/04.	N14LJ
❏ N760J	1958	MS 760 Paris	6	Wfu.	N84J
❏ N760M	1959	MS 760 Paris	49	W/o Evadale, Tx. USA. 3 May 69.	
❏ N760T	1961	MS 760 Paris-2B	103	Wfu. Located Mojave, Ca. USA.	N760N
❏ N769K	1974	Citation	500-0228	Wfu. Parts at White Industries, Bates City, Mo. USA.	N6365C
❏ N770JR	1962	JetStar-731	5037	Wfu. Last located West Palm Beach, Fl. USA.	N552JH
❏ N771HR	1974	Citation	500-0206	W/o Conway, Ar. USA. 30 Jun 07.	VH-LGL
❏ N771WB	1969	Sabre-60	306-29	Wfu. Destroyed by fire as N771WW. (parts at Bates City).	N771WW
❏ N774W	1975	Sabre-75A	380-37	Wfu. Cx USA 9/03.	N65
❏ N777EP	1960	JetStar-6	5004	Wfu. Located at Gracelands, Memphis, Tn. USA.	N69HM
❏ N777PQ	1970	HFB 320	1050	Wfu. Last located Monroe, Mi. USA.	N777PZ
❏ N777PY	1997	Gulfstream V	508	Wfu. Last located Savannah, Ga. USA.	N777TY
❏ N777PZ	1968	JetStar-731	5128	Wfu. Last located Houston-Hobby, Tx. USA.	N128BP
❏ N779XX	1983	Challenger 601	3018	W/o Milan, Italy. 7 Feb 85.	C-GBXW
❏ N780PV	1965	Jet Commander	36	Wfu. Cx USA 5/88. Was instructional airframe Norway.	N730PV
❏ N781RS	1979	Learjet 35A	35A-218	W/o Truckee, Ca. USA. 28 Dec 05.	(N83TE)
❏ N784B	1982	Falcon 50	118	W/o Teterboro, NJ. USA. 10 Nov 85.	(N183B)
❏ N787R	1974	Sabre-60	306-77	Wfu. Parts at AVMATS Spirit of St Louis, Mo. USA.	N180AR
❏ N787WB	1977	JetStar 2	5210	W/o Austin, Tx. USA 27 Nov 98. (parts at Conroe, Tx.).	N707WB
❏ N793NA	1959	B 707-138B	17700	Wfu. Located, Tucson, Az.	VP-BDE
❏ N797SC	1969	Learjet 25	25-042	Wfu. Located Deland, Fl. USA.	(N125WD)
❏ N800AW	1978	Learjet 35A	35A-149	W/o Utica, NY. USA. 19 Mar 04.	(N40AN)
❏ N800CS	1966	Sabre-40	282-64	Wfu. Cx USA 2/90.	N9000S
❏ N800GD	1967	JetStar-731	5100	Wfu. Cx USA 5/06. Last located Conroe, Tx. USA.	N510TS
❏ N801	1969	JetStar-8	5138	Wfu. Located Greenville Technical College, SC. USA.	N31DK

Reg	Yr	Type	c/n	Owner/Operator	Prev Regn
N801L	1963	Learjet 23	23-001	W/o Wichita, Ks. USA. 4 Jun 64.	
N802L	1964	Learjet 23	23-002	Wfu. Located Steven F Udar-Hazy Center, Dulles, Va.	
N804LJ	1964	Learjet 23	23-004	Wfu. Re-certlificated s/n 23-015A. Subsequently W/o 21 Oct 65	
N804LJ	1965	Learjet 23	23-015A	W/o Jackson, Mi. USA. 21 Oct 65.	
N805C	1981	Challenger 600	1037	W/o Sun Valley, Id. USA. 3 Jan 83.	C-GLYE
N805F	1966	Falcon 20C	60	W/o Boca Raton, Fl. USA. 5 Jul 71.	N885F
N805NA	1966	Learjet 24A	24A-102	W/o Victorville, Ca. USA. 7 Jun 01.	N705NA
N808JA	1965	Learjet 23	23-050A	W/o in ground fire 23 May 82.	N808LJ
N811AA	1968	Falcon 20D	187	Wfu. Last located Detroit YIP, Mi. USA.	N750R
N811HL	1979	Citation 1/SP	501-0114	Wfu. Parts at White Industries, Bates City, Mo. USA.	(N725RH)
N813AA	1966	Falcon 20C	25	Wfu. Last located Detroit-Willow Run, Mi. USA.	TG-GGA
N813BR	1967	Sabre-60	306-8	Wfu. Cx USA 7/06.	N613BR
N813M	1978	Learjet 35A	35A-151	Wfu. Stolen ex Wichita 13 Apr 84. Cx USA 6/86.	N711L
N814ER	1975	Citation	500-0280	W/o Greensboro, NC. USA. 1 Feb 06.	N102AD
N814NA	1960	JetStar-6	5003	Wfu. Last located Plant 42 Heritage Park, Palmdale, Ca. USA.	NASA14
N816AA	1973	Falcon 20E	290	Wfu. Last located Detroit YIP, Mi. USA.	I-TIAL
N817AA	1970	Falcon 20DC	233	Wfu. Parts at Dodsons, Rantoul, Ks. USA.	I-TIAG
N818AA	1966	Falcon 20C	36	Wfu. Last located Detroit YIP, Mi. USA.	OE-GUS
N819AA	1966	Falcon 20C	26	Wfu. Last located Detroit YIP, Mi. USA.	N11827
N820AA	1967	Falcon 20C	118	Wfu. Last located Detroit YIP, Mi. USA.	F-GGKE
N821AA	1969	Falcon 20D	203	W/o Lorrain County Airport, Elyria, USA. 2 Sep 05.	N36P
N821LG	1980	Falcon 10	170	W/o Nr West Chester, Pa. USA. 2 Feb 86.	N236FJ
N822LJ	1965	Learjet 23	23-080	W/o Detroit, Mi. USA. 9 Dec 67.	
N824LJ	1966	Learjet 23	23-083	Wfu. Located Kalamazoo Air Zoo, Kalamazoo, Mi. USA.	
N829CA	1982	Learjet 35A	35A-459	W/o St Kitts. 21 Jul 04. (at Rantoul, Ks.).	N969MT
N830AA	1966	Falcon 20C	55	Wfu. Last located Detroit YIP, Mi. USA.	N520FD
N830G	1968	Gulfstream 2	44	Wfu. Cx USA 1/02.	N585A
N831LC	1966	HS 125/1A-522	25095	W/o Nr San Diego, Ca. USA. 16 Mar 91.	N25AW
N831RA	1968	Learjet 24	24-164	Wfu. Last located Dodsons, Rantoul, Ks.	(XA-TKC)
N833NA	1961	B 720-061	18066	W/o Edwards AFB. Ca. USA. 1 Dec 84.	N2697V
N837F	1978	Falcon 10	137	Wfu.	C-GTVO
N844SL	1967	Falcon 20C	77	Wfu. Last located Pontiac, Mi. USA.	N613GA
N848C	1966	Jet Commander	54	Wfu. Cx USA 8/88.	N6534V
N856MA	1969	Sabre-60	306-41	W/o Democratic Republic of Congo in 2003.	(N62DW)
N860MX	1973	Learjet 25B	25B-109	Wfu. Parts at Dodsons, Rantoul, Ks. USA.	C-GSAS
N864CL	1970	Learjet 24B	24B-229	W/o San Francisco, Ca. USA. 9 Oct 84.	N551AS
N866JS	1965	Learjet 23	23-018	W/o Richmond, Va. USA. 6 May 80. (parts at White Inds.).	N866DB
N873LP	1977	Learjet 35A	35A-104	W/o Auburn, Al. USA. 22 Sep 85.	N87W
N880A	1968	Gulfstream 2	38	Wfu. Cx USA 4/95. Located Detroit Willow Run, Mi. USA.	N80A
N880EP	1960	Convair 880	38	Wfu. Located at Elvis Presley's Graceland Estate, Memphis.	N8809E
N881FC	1968	Learjet 24	24-175	Wfu. Last located FXE, USA. Cx USA 3/93.	N28BK
N881J	1979	Learjet 25D	25D-294	Wfu. Cx USA 3/06. Parts at Dodsons, Rantoul, Ks. USA.	N88NJ
N888AR	1966	Falcon 20C	33	W/o Acapulco, Mexico. 7 Aug 76.	N369EJ
N888DL	1971	HFB 320	1051	Wfu. Cx USA 8/90.	N6ZA
N888DV	1985	Learjet 25G	25G-370	Wfu. Parts at Dodsons, Rantoul, Ks. USA.	N972H
N888RW	1962	JetStar-6	5040	Wfu. Cx USA 6/88.	(N88892)
N897WA	1962	B 707-321B	18339	Wfu.	OE-IEB
N900AJ	1969	Learjet 25	25-027	Wfu. Cx USA 11/06.	N500DL
N900CD	1966	HS 125/3A	25111	Wfu. Cx USA 7/99. Parts at White Industries, Mo. USA.	N177GP
N900CR	1962	JetStar-731	5036	Wfu. Last located 10/99 at Griffin, Ga. USA.	N90KR
N900NA	1966	Learjet 24A	24A-111	Wfu. Last located at MTW Aerospace, Montgomery, Al. USA.	N44WD
N900TA	1974	Citation	500-0182	Wfu. Parts at White Industries Inc. Bates City, Mo. USA.	N23W
N900WJ	1982	Diamond 1A	A028SA	W/o Dallas, Tx. USA. 27 Jan 00. (at Rantoul, Ks.).	N331DC
N901C	1977	JetStar 2	5218	Wfu. Cx USA 12/05.	N816RD
N902GT	1967	Gulfstream II SP	2	Wfu. Located Chicago-Aurora, Il. USA.	N434JW
N902WC	1968	B 737-247	19613	Wfu.	N308VA
N910MH	1965	Jet Commander	45	Wfu. Located College of Aeronautics, La Guardia, NY. USA.	N121PG
N911AE	1977	Learjet 35A	35A-109	Wfu. Parts at White Industries Inc. Bates City, Mo. USA.	N506GP
N911AS	1965	HS 125/1A	25039	Wfu. Last located Montgomery, Al. USA.	N125TB
N911LM	1971	Learjet 25C	25C-070	Wfu. Last located Griffin, Ga. USA.	C-FHZU
N911RF	1973	Learjet 25B	25B-138	Wfu. Last located at Griffin, Ga. USA.	N73LJ
N912AS	1977	HS 125/3A	25124	Wfu. Last located Montgomery, Al. USA.	N552N
N915US	1976	Learjet 24B	24B-189	Wfu. Last located at Montgomery, Al. USA.	N711DX
N920G	1974	Sabre-60	306-74	W/o Lancaster, Pa. USA. 27 Dec 74.	
N921FP	1984	Learjet 55	55-103	W/o Rutland, Vt. USA. 6 Aug 86.	
N925BE	1967	Falcon 20C	80	Wfu. Last located Pontiac, Mi. USA.	N24TW

Reg	Yr	Type	c/n	Owner/Operator	Prev Regn
N925R	1966	Jet Commander	80	Wfu.	N173AR
N930GL	1980	Learjet 35A	35A-330	Wfu. Cx USA 7/91.	
N945MC	1975	Falcon 10	37	Wfu. Cx USA 1/04. Last located at Griffin, Ga. USA.	N72GW
N946JR	1968	Sabre-60	306-10	Wfu. Parts at AVMATS Paynesville, Mo. USA.	N125MC
N948NA	1978	Gulfstream 2	222	Wfu. Displayed at Pima Air & Space Museum, Az. USA.	N5253A
N957TH	1966	Falcon 20C	38	Wfu. Parts at Elsberry, Mo. USA.	N1107M
N959SC	1965	Learjet 23	23-045A	W/o Detroit City, Mi. USA. 23 Jul 91.	F-BSUX
N960CC	1959	B 707-123B	17634	Wfu. Last located Amarillo, Tx. USA.	N707AR
N970GA	1971	Falcon 20F	246	Wfu. Parts at White Industries Inc. Bates City, Mo. USA.	(F-GLMT)
N971AS	1961	JetStar-731	5007	Wfu. Last located Atlanta-Peachtree, USA..	N72CT
N971TB	2003	CitationJet CJ-2	525A-0111	W/o Danbury, Ct. USA. 12 Sep 07.	N219FL
N972TF	1969	Jet Commander-B	138	Wfu. Last located Lagos, Nigeria.	N5BA
N976BS	1968	Learjet 25	25-016	Wfu. Cx USA 9/05.	(N35WE)
N984HF	1969	HS 125/731	NA717	W/o Sparta, Tn. USA. 7 Nov 85.	N100HF
N984JD	1987	Learjet 31	31-001	Wfu. Cx USA 4/99. Parts at Dodsons, Rantoul, Ks. USA.	N311DF
N987SA	1975	Gulfstream II SP	172	W/o Nr Merida, Mexico. 24 Sep 07.	N903AG
N988MT	1962	Sabreliner CT-39A	276-32	Wfu. Located Metro Aviation Tech Career Center, OKC. USA.	62-4479
N990L	1966	Falcon 20C	43	W/o Dallas NAS, Tx. USA. 8 Mar 75.	N872F
N991PC	1989	Citation V	560-0043	W/o Eagle River, Wi. USA. 30 Dec 95.	(N2665F)
N994TD	1968	Learjet 24	24-179	Wfu. Last located at Fort Wayne, In. USA.	XA-RQP
N995TD	1967	Learjet 24	24-149	Wfu. Located Pulaski Technical College, Little Rock, Ar.	N64HB
N997TD	1972	Learjet 24D	24D-247	W/o Sierra Blanca, Tx. USA. 10 Dec 01.	N247DB
N998RD	1967	Jet Commander	103	Wfu. at Dodsons, Rantoul, Ks. USA.	N77HH
N999BH	1980	Learjet 25D	25D-318	W/o nr Santa Fe, NM. USA. 5 Sep 93.	N522TA
N999CV	1974	Citation	500-0211	Wfu. Parts at White Industries, Bates City, Mo. USA.	N999CB
N999HG	1974	Learjet 25B	25B-178	W/o Sanford, NC. USA. 8 Sep 77.	N999MV
N1001U		Caravelle 6R	86	Wfu. Located Pima Air Museum, Tucson, Az. USA.	PT-DUW
N1021B	1966	Learjet 23	23-086	W/o Racine, Wi. USA. 6 Nov 69.	
N1121E	1965	Jet Commander	20	Wfu. Parts at Hollister, Ca. USA.	N334LP
N1121F	1969	Jet Commander-B	150	W/o La Carbonera, Zacatecas, Mexico. 21 May 97.	N121FM
N1121G	1966	Jet Commander	67	Wfu. Parts at Dodsons, Rantoul, Ks. USA.	N650M
N1121M	1967	Jet Commander	111	Wfu. Parts at Long Beach, Ca. USA.	C-GDJW
N1121N	1967	Jet Commander	110	Wfu. Parts were at Hollister, Ca. USA.	N16GH
N1123H	1973	Westwind-1123	167	Wfu. Parts at White Industries, Bates City, Mo. USA.	N873EJ
N1125E	1967	HS 125/3A-R	25149	Wfu. MIAT at Salak Tinggi, Selangor, Malysia.	N99KR
N1135K	1965	HS 125/1A	25019	W/o Des Moines, Ia. USA. 24 Feb 66.	N1125G
N1151K	1968	JetStar-731	5115	Wfu. Cx USA 9/96.	N8300E
N1181G	1981	Falcon 50	72	W/o Lake Geneva, Wi. USA. 12 May 85. (parts at Paynesville).	N82FJ
N1218S	1982	Citation II/SP	551-0428	W/o Cordele, Ga. USA. 22 Dec 99.	(N147RP)
N1501	1965	Falcon 20C	15	Wfu. Last located Detroit-Willow Run, Mi. USA.	N151CG
N1777T	1966	Jet Commander	62	Wfu. Last located at Tucson, Az. USA.	C-GKFS
N1846	1966	Falcon 20C	47	W/o Parkersburg, WV. USA. 13 Mar 68.	N875F
N1863T	1966	Sabre-40	282-62	Wfu. Cx USA 8/87.	
N1909D	1966	Sabre-40	282-57	Wfu. Cx USA 4/97. Parts at AVMATS St Louis, Mo. USA.	N1909R
N1929P	1962	Sabreliner CT-39A	276-48	Wfu. Pittsburgh Institute of Aeronautics. USA. (or Taiwan ?)	N6612S
N1963A	1966	Learjet 23	23-097	Wfu. Parts at Tara Field, Hampton, Ga. USA. .	N1968A
N1965W	1962	Sabreliner CT-39A	276-9	Wfu. Located Westwood College of Aviation Technology, Ca.	62-4456
N1966J	1966	Jet Commander	66	Wfu. Parts at White Industries, Bates City, Mo. USA.	
N1968W	1966	Learjet 23	23-089	Wfu. Cx USA 4/01. Parts at Dodsons, Rantoul, Ks. USA.	N969B
N2114E	1973	HS 125/600A	256022	Wfu. Located Hooks Airport, Tx. USA.	XA-XET
N2120Q	1967	Westwind-1123	107	Wfu. Cx USA 12/90.	CA-01
N2143H	1959	B 707-123B	17644	Wfu.	HZ-DAT
N2200A	1975	Sabre-75A	380-26	Wfu. Last located Spirit of St Louis, Mo. USA.	N128MS
N2265Z	1976	Sabre-75A	380-43	Wfu. Parts at Clarksville, Mo. USA.	N6NR
N2286D	1982	Learjet 35A	35A-482	W/o Straits of Malacca, Malaysia. 14 Feb 93.	N482U
N2579E	1965	Jet Commander	21	Wfu. Parts at White Industries, Bates City, Mo. USA.	CF-WOA
N2627U	1982	Citation I/SP	501-0247	W/o Wichita, Ks. USA. 12 Nov 82.	(N24CH)
N2954T	1966	Falcon 20C	58	Wfu. Parted out 1987.	HB-VDG
N3034B	1968	Learjet 24	24-176	Wfu. Last located Montgomery, Al. USA.	PT-CXJ
N3080	1966	JetStar-6	5094	Wfu. Last located Opa Locka, Fl. USA.	N3030
N3118M	1969	HS 125/400A	25199	Wfu. Parts Dodsons, Rantoul, Ks. USA.	(N905Y)
N3274Q	1966	HS 125/1A	25102	Wfu. Cx USA 12/95.	XB-AKW
N3278	1969	Sabre-60	306-32	Wfu. Parts at AVMATS Spirit of St Louis, Mo. USA.	N4743N
N3490L	1974	Citation	500-0128	Wfu. Cx USA 8/07.	N501AR
N3504	1960	Sabreliner CT-39A	265-32	Wfu. Located Parks College Aviation School, St Louis. USA.	60-3504
N3507W	1960	Sabreliner CT-39A	265-35	Wfu. Located West Los Angeles College, Ca. USA.	60-3507

Reg	Yr	Type	c/n	Owner/Operator	Prev Regn
N3833L	1967	B 720-047B	19523	Wfu. To USAF for KC-135E spares 9/83.	5V-TAD
N4060K		Sabre-UTX	246-1	Wfu. Mock up until 1967, and subsequently broken up.	
N4253A	1973	HS 125/600B	256005	Wfu. Cx USA 6/95. Parts at White Industries, Mo. USA.	EC-EAC
N4400E	1965	HS 125/1A	25026	Wfu. Parts at Spirit of St Louis, Mo. USA.	(XA-...)
N4550T	1968	BAC 1-11/204AF	135	Wfu. Cx USA 12/93.	HZ-MO1
N5027Q	2001	Learjet 60	60-242	W/o Santa Cruz do Sul, Brazil. 7 Oct 02.	(PR-LDF)
N5038	1959	B 707-123B	17652	Wfu.	N7525A
N5075L	1968	Sabre-60A	306-16	Wfu. Cx USA 5/95. Parts at AVMATS Paynesville, Mo. USA.	N38UT
N5094B	1968	Jet Commander	105	Wfu. Parts at White Industries, Bates City, Mo. USA.	C-GWPV
N5096F	1968	Falcon 20C	157	Wfu. Last located Denton, Tx. USA.	C-GRSD
N5098H	1970	Falcon 20D	225	Wfu. Last located Denton, Tx. USA.	C-FONX
N5269A	1998	Citation VII	650-7109	W/o ground accident Wichita, Ks. USA. Dec 99.	(N709QS)
N5565	1973	Sabre-40A	282-119	W/o Oklahoma City, Ok. USA. 15 Jan 74.	N8341N
N5863		Convair 880	48	Wfu. Cx USA 10/86.	N58RD
N5878	1961	MS 760 Paris-2B	106	Wfu.	PH-MSV
N6555C	1967	Falcon 20C	78	Wfu. Located Greenville/Donaldson Center, SC. USA.	VH-JSX
N6581E	1961	Sabreliner CT-39A	265-82	Wfu. Located Spokane Community College, Wa. USA.	61-0679
N6887Y	1981	Citation II	550-0293	W/o Billings, Mt. USA. 19 Dec 92.	
N7028F	1969	Jet Commander-A	131	Wfu. Located Fairmont State College, Fairmont, WV. USA.	N43
N7143N	1961	Sabreliner CT-39A	265-70	Wfu. Last located Fujairah, UAE.	61-0667
N7145V	1960	JetStar-731	5001	Wfu. Parts at White Industries, Bates City, Mo. USA. (4/98).	N11
N7158Q	1969	HFB 320	1040	Wfu. Cx USA 3/99. Last located El Mirage, Ca. (as I-ITAL)	I-ITAL
N7200K	1966	Learjet 23	23-099	Wfu. Last located at MTW Aerospace, Montgomery, Al. USA.	
N7201U	1959	B 720-022	17907	Wfu. Scrapped at Luton, UK. 13 Jul 82.	
N7224U	1962	B 720-022	18077	Wfu. Cx USA 2/87.	
N7381	1965	B 720-060B	18977	Wfu.	N440DS
N7572N	1971	Sabre-75	370-1	Wfu. Used as parts in other test aircraft.	
N7775	1966	JetStar-6	5073	Wfu. Cx USA 12/86.	
N7810W	1973	Learjet 25B	25B-117	Wfu. Parts at White Industries, Bates City, Mo. USA.	N731CW
N7842M	1966	Falcon 20C	42	W/o Fort Worth, Tx. USA. 16 Jan 74.	N1503
N8000Z	1973	HS 125/600A	256012	Wfu. Cx USA 12/95. Parts at Hooks Airport,Tx. USA.	EC-EOQ
N8052V	1960	Sabreliner CT-39A	265-18	Wfu. Located S Seattle Community College, Wa. USA.	60-3490
N8070U	1967	Jet Commander-B	124	Wfu. Parts at OK Aviation Inc. Monterey, Ca. USA.	XA-RQT
N8221M	1984	Diamond 1A	A076SA	W/o Jasper Hinton, Alberta, Canada as C-GLIG. 1 Mar 95.	C-GLIG
N8534	1968	Jet Commander	113	Wfu. Last located Deland, Fl. USA.	4X-CPB
N8733	1969	B 707-331B	20062	Wfu. To USAF for KC-135E spares 5/86.	
N9023W	1965	Jet Commander	10	Wfu. Instructional airframe Norwegian Mechanics School.	N5BP
N9166Y	1961	Sabreliner CT-39A	265-80	Wfu. Located Helena VoTec Center, Helena, Mt. USA.	61-0677
N9258U	1978	Falcon 10	132	Wfu. Parts at White Industries, Bates City, Mo. USA.	TC-ATI
N9503Z	1964	Sabre-40	282-10	W/o Blaine, Mn. USA. 7 Mar 73.	N525N
N9739B	1964	JetStar-6	5052	Wfu. Last located Bi-States Park, St Louis, Mo. USA.	C-FDTM
N10855	1990	BAe 1000B	258159	Wfu. Cx USA 7/03.	G-OPFC
N10857	1991	BAe 125/800A	258213	Wfu. Cx USA 7/05.	G-BURV
N12058	1984	Citation T-47A	552-0004	W/o hangar fire Forbes Field, Topeka, Ks. USA. 20 Jul 93.	(162758)
N12065	1985	Citation T-47A	552-0011	W/o hangar fire Forbes Field, Topeka, Ks. USA. 20 Jul 93.	(162765)
N12269	1985	Citation T-47A	552-0015	W/o hangar fire Forbes Field, Topeka, Ks. USA. 20 Jul 93.	(162769)
N12557	1984	Citation T-47A	552-0003	W/o hangar fire Forbes Field, Topeka, Ks. USA. 20 Jul 93.	(162757)
N12564	1985	Citation T-47A	552-0010	W/o hangar fire Forbes Field, Topeka, Ks. USA. 20 Jul 93.	(162764)
N12566	1985	Citation T-47A	552-0012	Wfu. Located Technical School, Columbus-Bolton, Oh.	(162766)
N12568	1985	Citation T-47A	552-0014	Wfu. Located at Cessna Experimental, Wichita, Ks. USA.	(162768)
N12660	1985	Citation T-47A	552-0006	W/o hangar fire Forbes Field, Topeka, Ks. USA. 20 Jul 93.	(162760)
N12756	1984	Citation T-47A	552-0002	W/o hangar fire Forbes Field, Topeka, Ks. USA. 20 Jul 93.	(162756)
N12761	1984	Citation T-47A	552-0007	W/o hangar fire Forbes Field, Topeka, Ks. USA. 20 Jul 93.	(162761)
N12762	1985	Citation T-47A	552-0008	W/o hangar fire Forbes Field, Topeka, Ks. USA. 20 Jul 93.	(162762)
N12763	1985	Citation T-47A	552-0009	W/o hangar fire Forbes Field, Topeka, Ks. USA. 20 Jul 93.	(162763)
N12855	1984	Citation T-47A	552-0001	W/o hangar fire Forbes Field, Topeka, Ks. USA. 20 Jul 93.	(167255)
N12859	1984	Citation T-47A	552-0005	W/o hangar fire Forbes Field, Topeka, Ks. USA. 20 Jul 93.	(162759)
N12967	1985	Citation T-47A	552-0013	W/o hangar fire Forbes Field, Topeka, Ks. USA. 20 Jul 93.	(162767)
N21092	1961	Sabreliner CT-39A	265-42	Wfu. Blackhawk Technical College, Janesville, Wi. USA.	61-0639
N29019	1970	Sabre-75	370-6	Wfu. Cx USA 10/91. Parts at AVMATS Paynesville, Mo. USA.	(N30EV)
N29977	1966	HS 125/1A	25028	Wfu. Cx USA 4/91. Parts at White Industries, Mo. USA.	XA-ESQ
N32010	1961	Sabreliner CT-39A	265-83	Wfu. University of Central Missouri, Warrensburg, Mo. USA.	61-0680
N32508	1961	Sabreliner T-39D	285-17	Wfu. National Museum of Naval Aviation, Pensacola, Fl. USA.	150985
N35403	1980	Citation II/SP	551-0029	W/o Ainsworth, Ne. USA. 1 Jan 05. (was 550-0379).	N450GM
N40180	1976	Falcon 10	93	Wfu. Parts at White Industries, Bates City, Mo. USA.	F-BYCV
N40593	1965	Jet Commander	41	Wfu. Cx USA 3/06.	(N499TR)

Reg	Yr	Type	c/n	Owner/Operator	Prev Regn
☐ N41953	1971	HS 125/F400A	25268	Wfu. Located Arnoni Aviation Inc. Houston, Tx. USA.	(N268TS)
☐ N46190	1966	HS 125/731	25108	Wfu. Parts at Bates City, Mo. USA. (as C-GTTS).	C-GTTS
☐ N46253	1978	Citation	500-0369	Wfu. Parts at White Industries, Bates City, Mo. (as C-GVER)	C-GVER
☐ N50812	1972	Citation	500-0036	Wfu. Located Brussels, Belgium (as OO-LCM).	OO-LCM
☐ N65618	1962	Sabreliner CT-39A	276-42	Wfu. Northwestern Community College, Rangely, Co. USA.	62-4489
☐ N71543	1975	Sabre-75A	380-29	Wfu. Last Located University of Illinois.	N132MS
☐ N72028	1974	Sabre-75A	380-14	Wfu. Parts at Dodsons, Rantoul, Ks. USA.	N53
☐ N77215	1996	CitationJet	525-0149	W/o Nr Van Nuys, Ca. USA. 12 Jan 07.	(N67GU)
☐ N91669	1965	Jet Commander	17	Wfu. Parts at OK Aircraft, Gilroy, Ca. USA.	C-FSUA
☐ N98386	1965	Learjet 23	23-040	Wfu. Cx USA 8/82.	(N12HJ)

Military

Reg	Yr	Type	c/n	Owner/Operator	Prev Regn
☐ 150542		Sabreliner T-39D	277-1	Wfu. Stored China Lake, Ca. USA.	
☐ 150543		Sabreliner T-39D	277-2	Wfu. at AMARC 9/90 as 7T-027. (still there 5/06)..	(XA-AAG)
☐ 150544		Sabreliner T-39D	277-3	Wfu. at AMARC 3/85 as 7T-006. Tt 5872. (still there 5/06).	
☐ 150545		Sabreliner T-39D	277-4	Wfu.	
☐ 150546		Sabreliner T-39D	277-5	Wfu. at AMARC 7/85 as 7T-014. Tt 9124. (still there 5/06).	
☐ 150547		Sabreliner T-39D	277-6	Wfu. at AMARC 1/86 as 7T-021. (still there 5/06).	(XA-AAI)
☐ 150548		Sabreliner T-39D	277-7	Wfu. at AMARC 3/85 as 7T-008. (still there 5/06).	(XA-AAF)
☐ 150549		Sabreliner T-39D	277-8	Wfu. at AMARC 3/85 as 7T-011. Tt 7886. (still there 5/06).	
☐ 150550		Sabreliner T-39D	277-9	Wfu. at AMARC.	
☐ 150551		Sabreliner T-39D	277-10	Wfu. at AMARC 10/81 as 7T-002.	
☐ 150969	1960	Sabreliner T-39D	285-1	Wfu. at AMARC 9/90 as 7T-026. (still there 5/06).	(XA-AAJ)
☐ 150971	1960	Sabreliner T-39D	285-3	Wfu. at AMARC as 7T-001.	
☐ 150973	1960	Sabreliner T-39D	285-5	Wfu. at AMARC 4/85 as 7T-013. Tt 7155. (still there 5/06).	
☐ 150974	1960	Sabreliner T-39D	285-6	Wfu. at AMARC 7/85 as 7T-015. Tt 8737. (still there 5/06).	
☐ 150975	1960	Sabreliner T-39D	285-7	Wfu. at AMARC 3/85 as 7T-007. Tt 9524. (still there 5/06).	
☐ 150976	1960	Sabreliner T-39D	285-8	Wfu. at AMARC 7/85 as 7T-016. Tt 7943. (still there 5/06).	
☐ 150978	1961	Sabreliner T-39D	285-10	Wfu. at AMARC 8/03 as TG0104. (still there 5/06).	
☐ 150979	1961	Sabreliner T-39D	285-11	Wfu. at AMARC 7/85 as 7T-017. Tt 8631. (still there 5/06).	
☐ 150980	1961	Sabreliner T-39D	285-12	Wfu. at AMARC 3/85 as 7T-004. (still there 5/06).	
☐ 150981	1961	Sabreliner T-39D	285-13	Wfu. at AMARC 3/85 as 7T-012. Tt 8184. (still there 5/06).	
☐ 150982	1961	Sabreliner T-39D	285-14	Wfu. at AMARC 2/86 as 7T-022. Tt 8188. (still there 5/06).	
☐ 150983	1961	Sabreliner T-39D	285-15	Wfu. at AMARC 2/86 as 7T-023. Tt 9833. (still there 5/06).	
☐ 150984	1961	Sabreliner T-39D	285-16	Wfu. at AMARC 3/85 as 7T-010. Tt 8552. (still there 5/06).	
☐ 150986	1961	Sabreliner T-39D	285-18	Wfu. Preserved Robins AFB. Ga. USA.	
☐ 150987	1961	Sabreliner T-39D	285-19	Wfu. Preserved at NAS Patuxent River, Md. USA.	
☐ 150988	1961	Sabreliner T-39D	285-20	Wfu. at AMARC 3/85 as 7T-005. Tt 9208. (still there 5/06).	
☐ 150989	1961	Sabreliner T-39D	285-21	Wfu. Stored China Lake, Ca. USA.	
☐ 150990	1961	Sabreliner T-39D	285-22	Wfu. at AMARC 2/86 as 7T-024. Tt 9804. (still there 5/06).	
☐ 150991	1961	Sabreliner T-39D	285-23	Wfu. at AMARC 7/84 as 7T-003. Tt 8677. (still there 5/06).	
☐ 151336	1961	Sabreliner T-39D	285-25	Wfu. at AMARC 2/86 as 7T-025. (still there 5/06).	(XA-AAH)
☐ 151338	1961	Sabreliner T-39D	285-27	Wfu. Southern Museum of Flight, Birmingham, Al. USA.	
☐ 151339	1961	Sabreliner T-39D	285-28	Wfu. Preserved NAS Pensacola, Fl. USA.	
☐ 151340	1961	Sabreliner T-39D	285-29	Wfu. at AMARC 1/86 as 7T-018. Tt 8563.	
☐ 151341	1961	Sabreliner T-39D	285-30	Wfu. at AMARC 1/86 as 7T-019. Tt 10118. (still there 5/06).	
☐ 151342	1961	Sabreliner T-39D	285-31	Wfu. Milwaukee Technical College, Milwaukee, Wi. USA.	
☐ 151343	1961	Sabreliner T-39D	285-32	Wfu. NAS Pensacola, Fl. USA.	
☐ 157352	1965	Sabreliner CT-39E	282-46	W/o Alameda AFB. Ca. USA. 21 Dec 75.	test
☐ 157353	1967	Sabreliner CT-39E	282-84	Wfu. at AMARC 11/90 as ND0001. (still there 5/06).	N2254B
☐ 158383	1968	Sabreliner CT-39E	282-96	Wfu. Parts at Dodsons, Rantoul, Ks. USA.	N4705N
☐ 158843	1971	Sabreliner CT-39G	306-52	Wfu. at AMARC 5/04 as 7T-035. (still there 5/06).	N955R
☐ 159362	1973	Sabreliner CT-39G	306-66	Wfu. at AMARC 5/04 as 7T-036. (still there 5/06).	N8365N
☐ 159363	1973	Sabreliner CT-39G	306-67	Wfu. Located AFFTC Museum store Edwards AFB. Ca. USA.	
☐ 160057	1975	Sabreliner CT-39G	306-108	W/o Glenview NAS, USA. 3 Mar 91.	N65799
☐ 165522	1965	Sabreliner T-39N	282-28	W/o Nr Pensacola NAS, Fl. USA. 8 May 02.	N314NT
☐ 165524	1966	Sabre T-39N	282-60	W/o in N W Georgia, USA. 10 Jan 06.	N316NT
☐ 165525	1972	Sabreliner T-39N	282-100	W/o Nr Pensacola NAS, Fl. USA. 8 May 02.	N317NT
☐ 165938	2001	Citation UC-35D	560-0567	W/o Miramar, Ca. USA. 10 Mar 04.	N5268A
☐ 2106	1978	Guardian HU-25A	402	Wfu. at AMARC 4/95 as 410007. (still there 5/06).	N187F
☐ 2107	1979	Guardian HU-25D	409	Wfu. at AMARC 9/01 as 410018. (still there 5/06).	N407F
☐ 2108	1979	Guardian HU-25A	405	Wfu. at AMARC 8/01 as 410016. (still there 5/06).	N405F
☐ 2111	1979	Guardian HU-25B	413	Wfu. Located 10km off N Carolina coast (habitat enhancer).	N410F
☐ 2115	1979	Guardian HU-25A	419	Wfu. at AMARC 4/01 as 410017. (still there 5/06).	N419F
☐ 2116	1980	Guardian HU-25A	420	Wfu. at AMARC 4/94 as 410005. (still there 5/06).	N420F
☐ 2119	1980	Guardian HU-25A	424	Wfu. at AMARC Davis Monthan as 410002 /94. (not noted 11/03)	N424F
☐ 2122	1980	Guardian HU-25B	433	Wfu. at AMARC 9/01 as 410020. (still there 5/06).	N432F

Reg	Yr	Type	c/n	Owner/Operator	Prev Regn
2123	1980	Guardian HU-25A	435	Wfu. Last located Alton-St Louis, Mo. USA.	N433F
2124	1980	Guardian HU-25A	437	Wfu. at AMARC 9/01 as 410022. (still there 5/06).	N435F
2126	1981	Guardian HU-25B	441	Wfu. at AMARC 9/01 as 410021. (still there 5/06).	N445F
2130	1981	Guardian HU-25C	450	Wfu. at AMARC 4/94 as 410004. (still there 5/06).	N458F
2132	1981	Guardian HU-25B	454	Wfu. at AMARC 9/01 as 410019. (still there 5/06).	N461F
2137	1981	Guardian HU-25A	462	Wfu. at AMARC 4/95 as 410008. (still there 5/06).	N470F
2138	1982	Guardian HU-25A	464	Wfu. at AMARC 4/95 as 410009. (still there 5/06).	N472F
58-6970	1959	C-137B	17925	Wfu. Located Boeing Museum of Flight, Seattle, Wa. USA.	
58-6971	1959	C-137B	17926	Wfu. Located Pima County Museum, Tuscon, Az. USA.	
58-6972	1959	C-137B	17927	Wfu.	
59-2868	1959	Sabreliner CT-39A	265-1	Wfu. Located Albuquerque, NM. USA.	(N2259V)
59-2869	1959	Sabreliner CT-39A	265-2	Wfu. Dept of General Services, Memphis, Tn. USA.	(N4999G)
59-2870	1959	Sabreliner T-39A	265-3	Wfu. at AMARC 8/03 as TG0105. (still there 5/06).	
59-2871	1959	Sabreliner T-39A	265-4	W/o Eglin AFB. Fl. USA. 13 Nov 69.	
59-2872	1959	Sabreliner CT-39A	265-5	Wfu. at AMARC 7/84 as TG015. Tt 12728. (still there 5/06).	(N2296C)
59-2874	1959	Sabreliner NT-39B	270-2	Wfu. at AMARC 3/95 as TG0103. (still there 5/06).	
59-5958	1961	JetStar-6	5010	Wfu. Displayed Travis AFB Museum, Ca. USA.	(N161L)
59-5959	1962	JetStar-6	5026	Wfu. C-140A, USAF located at Scott AFB. Il. USA.	
59-5960	1962	JetStar-6	5028	Wfu. Last located Greenville, Tx. USA.	
59-5961	1962	JetStar-6	5030	W/o Robins AFB. Ga. USA. 7 Nov 62.	
59-5962	1962	JetStar-6	5032	Wfu. Last located at Edwards AFB. Ca. USA.	
60-3475	1960	Sabreliner CT-39B	270-4	Wfu. at AMARC 6/93 as TG098. (still there 5/06).	
60-3476	1960	Sabreliner NT-39B	270-5	Wfu. at AMARC 2/95 as TG0102.	
60-3477	1960	Sabreliner CT-39B	270-6	Wfu. at AMARC 1/95 as TG0101. (still there 5/06).	
60-3478	1959	Sabreliner CT-39A	265-6	Wfu. at AMARC 8/03 as TG0106. (still there 5/06).	
60-3479	1959	Sabreliner CT-39A	265-7	Wfu. at AMARC 8/85 as TG082. Tt 22494. (still there 5/06).	
60-3480	1960	Sabreliner CT-39A	265-8	Wfu. at AMARC 6/84 as TG013. (still there 5/06).	
60-3481	1960	Sabreliner CT-39A	265-9	Wfu. Lane Community College, Eugene, Or. USA.	
60-3483	1960	Sabreliner CT-39A	265-11	Wfu. Preserved at Travis AFB. Ca. USA.	
60-3485	1960	Sabreliner CT-39A	265-13	Wfu. Western International Aviation, Tucson, Az. USA.	
60-3489	1960	Sabreliner CT-39A	265-17	Wfu. Houston Community College, Houston, Tx. USA.	
60-3491	1960	Sabreliner CT-39A	265-19	Wfu. at AMARC 5/84 as TG009. Tt 20372. (still there 5/06).	
60-3492	1960	Sabreliner CT-39A	265-20	Wfu. Thief River Falls Technical Institute, Mn. USA.	
60-3493	1960	Sabreliner CT-39A	265-21	Wfu. Instructional airframe at Moses Lake, Wa. USA.	
60-3494	1960	Sabreliner CT-39A	265-22	Wfu. at AMARC 12/85 as TG094. Tt 18375. (still there 5/06).	
60-3495	1960	Sabreliner CT-39A	265-23	Wfu. Preserved at Scott AFB. Il. USA.	
60-3496	1960	Sabreliner CT-39A	265-24	Wfu. Cochise Community College, Douglas, Az. USA.	
60-3497	1960	Sabreliner CT-39A	265-25	Wfu. R J Daley College, Chicago, Il. USA.	
60-3498	1960	Sabreliner CT-39A	265-26	Wfu. Williams Gateway, Chandler Municipal, Az. USA.	
60-3499	1960	Sabreliner CT-39A	265-27	Wfu. at AMARC 10/84 as TG037. Tt 20506. (still there 5/06).	
60-3500	1960	Sabreliner CT-39A	265-28	Wfu. Located Le Tourneau College, Longview, Tx. USA.	
60-3501	1960	Sabreliner CT-39A	265-29	Wfu. at AMARC 12/85 as TG093. Tt 15817. (still there 5/06).	
60-3502	1960	Sabreliner CT-39A	265-30	Wfu. Dr R Smirnow, NYC. USA.	
60-3503	1960	Sabreliner GCT-39A	265-31	Wfu. Located Museum at Aurora Municipal, Il. USA.	
60-3505	1960	Sabreliner CT-39A	265-33	Wfu. Preserved at Edwards Flight Test Museum, Ca. USA.	
60-3506	1960	Sabreliner T-39A	265-34	W/o Colorado Springs, Co. USA. 9 Feb 74.	
60-3508	1960	Sabreliner CT-39A	265-36	Wfu. Lake Area Vocational Technical College, Waterstown, SD.	
61-0634	1961	Sabreliner CT-39A	265-37	Wfu. Preserved at Dyess AFB. Tx. USA.	
61-0635	1961	Sabreliner CT-39A	265-38	Wfu. Regional Vocational Technical Institute, Lafayette, La.	
61-0636	1961	Sabreliner CT-39A	265-39	Wfu. at AMARC 9/85 as TG089. Tt 19841. (still there 5/06).	
61-0637	1961	Sabreliner CT-39A	265-40	Wfu. at AMARC 10/84 as TG035. Tt 21729. (still there 5/06).	
61-0638	1961	Sabreliner CT-39A	265-41	Wfu. Last located Laredo, Tx. USA.	
61-0640	1961	Sabreliner T-39A	265-43	W/o Halifax County Airport, NC. USA. 16 Apr 70.	
61-0641	1961	Sabreliner CT-39A	265-44	Wfu. Rock Valley College, Rockford, Il. USA.	
61-0642	1961	Sabreliner CT-39A	265-45	Wfu. at AMARC 12/84 as TG045. Tt 17270. (still there 5/06).	
61-0643	1961	Sabreliner CT-39A	265-46	Wfu. at AMARC 9/84 as TG022. Tt 20288. (still there 5/06).	
61-0644	1961	Sabreliner T-39A	265-47	W/o Andrews AFB. Md. USA. 7 May 63.	
61-0646	1961	Sabreliner T-39A	265-49	W/o. Richmond, Va. USA. 14 May 75.	
61-0647	1961	Sabreliner CT-39A	265-50	Wfu. Community College, Costa Mesa, Ca. USA.	
61-0648	1961	Sabreliner CT-39A	265-51	Wfu. DMI Aviation, Tucson, Az. USA.	
61-0649	1961	Sabreliner T-39A	265-52	Wfu. Portland Airport Museum, Portland, Or. USA.	(N1064)
61-0650	1961	Sabreliner CT-39A	265-53	Wfu. Everett Community College, Seattle, Wa. USA.	
61-0651	1961	Sabreliner CT-39A	265-54	Wfu. Florence Technical College, Florence, SC. USA.	
61-0652	1961	Sabreliner CT-39A	265-55	Wfu. at AMARC 9/85 as TG087. Tt 16815. (still there 5/06).	(N4999H)
61-0653	1961	Sabreliner CT-39A	265-56	Wfu. Community College, San Francisco, Ca. USA.	
61-0654	1961	Sabreliner CT-39A	265-57	Wfu. Last located Laredo, Tx. USA.	

Reg	Yr	Type	c/n	Owner/Operator	Prev Regn
61-0655	1961	Sabreliner CT-39A	265-58	Wfu. P Regina, Granada Hills, Ca. USA.	
61-0656	1961	Sabreliner CT-39A	265-59	Wfu. at AMARC 5/84 as TG010. Tt 21617. (still there 5/06).	
61-0657	1961	Sabreliner CT-39A	265-60	Wfu. Located Westwood College of Aeronautics yard, Houston.	
61-0658	1961	Sabreliner CT-39A	265-61	Wfu.	
61-0660	1961	Sabreliner CT-39A	265-63	Wfu. Preserved at McClellan AFB. Ca. USA.	
61-0661	1961	Sabreliner T-39A	265-64	W/o Paine Field, Wa. USA. 29 Jul 62.	
61-0662	1961	Sabreliner CT-39A	265-65	Wfu. Parts at AVMATS Paynesville, Mo. USA.	
61-0663	1961	Sabreliner CT-39A	265-66	Wfu.	
61-0664	1961	Sabreliner CT-39A	265-67	Wfu. Duel Vocational Institute, Tracy, Ca. USA.	
61-0665	1961	Sabreliner CT-39A	265-68	Wfu. at AMARC 10/84 as TG028. Tt 19423. (still there 5/06).	
61-0666	1961	Sabreliner CT-39A	265-69	Wfu. at AMARC 6/84 as TG014. Tt 20336. (still there 5/06).	
61-0668	1961	Sabreliner CT-39A	265-71	Wfu. Thief River Falls Technical Institute, Mn. USA.	
61-0669	1961	Sabreliner CT-39A	265-72	Wfu. Metro Aviation Center, Oklahoma City, Ok. USA.	
61-0670	1961	Sabreliner T-39A	265-73	Wfu. Parts at Dodsons, Rantoul, Ks. USA.	
61-0671	1961	Sabreliner CT-39A	265-74	Wfu. Keesler AFB. Ms. USA.	
61-0672	1961	Sabreliner T-39A	265-75	W/o Kunsong, Korea. 13 Mar 79.	
61-0674	1961	Sabreliner T-39A	265-77	Wfu. Displayed at Hill AFB. Ut. USA. USA.	
61-0675	1961	Sabreliner T-39A	265-78	Wfu.	
61-0676	1961	Sabreliner CT-39A	265-79	Wfu. at AMARC 12/84 as TG049. Tt 21692. (still there 5/06).	
61-0678	1961	Sabreliner CT-39A	265-81	Wfu. at AMARC 5/84 as TG012. Tt 14666. (still there 5/06).	
61-0681	1961	Sabreliner CT-39A	265-84	Wfu. Located Tech School, Detroit City Airport, Mi.	
61-0682	1961	Sabreliner CT-39A	265-85	Wfu. Dross Metals, Tucson, Az. USA.	
61-0684	1961	Sabreliner T-39A	265-87	Wfu.	
61-0685	1961	Sabreliner CT-39A	265-88	Wfu. at U S Army Aviation Museum, Fort Rucker, Al. USA.	61-0685
61-2488	1961	JetStar-6	5017	Wfu. VC-140B, USAF/preserved Warner Robins AFB. Ga. USA.	N9286R
61-2489	1961	JetStar-6	5022	Wfu. Located Pima County Museum, Tucson, Az. USA..	
61-2490	1961	JetStar-6	5024	Wfu. at AMARC as CL-009. (wef 4/98). (still there 5/06).	
61-2491	1962	JetStar-6	5027	Wfu. Located Rhein-Main AFB. Frankfurt, Germany.	
61-2492	1962	JetStar-6	5031	Wfu. Located Wright-Patterson Museum, Oh. USA.	
61-2493	1962	JetStar-6	5034	Wfu. at AMARC as CL003 2/84.	
62-4197	1962	JetStar-6	5041	Wfu. at AMARC as CL007 7/87.	
62-4198	1962	JetStar-6	5042	Wfu. Broken up at Mildenhall, UK. 1/92.	
62-4199	1962	JetStar-6	5043	Wfu. at AMARC as CL002 2/84.	
62-4200	1963	JetStar-6	5044	Wfu. at AMARC as CL005 6/87.	
62-4201	1963	JetStar-6	5045	Wfu. Located at Hill AFB. Ut. USA.	
62-4448	1962	Sabreliner T-39A	276-1	W/o Erfurt, East Germany. 28 Jan 64.	
62-4449	1962	Sabreliner CT-39A	276-2	Wfu. Located Pima County Museum, Tucson, Az. USA.	
62-4450	1962	Sabreliner CT-39A	276-3	Wfu. Last located Laredo, Tx. USA.	
62-4452	1962	Sabreliner CT-39A	276-5	Wfu. Located at Travis AFB. Ca. USA.	
62-4454	1962	Sabreliner CT-39A	276-7	Wfu. at AMARC 8/84 as TG018. Tt 20878. (still there 5/06).	
62-4457	1962	Sabreliner CT-39A	276-10	Wfu. at AMARC 11/83 as TG002. Tt 19944. (still there 5/06).	
62-4458	1962	Sabreliner T-39A	276-11	W/o Clark AFB. Philippines. 25 Mar 65.	
62-4459	1962	Sabreliner CT-39A	276-12	Wfu. Located Clover Park VoTec College, Tacoma, Wa.	
62-4460	1962	Sabreliner T-39A	276-13	W/o Torrejon AB. Spain. 28 Feb 70.	
62-4461	1962	Sabreliner CT-39A	276-14	Wfu. at Robins AFB. Ga. USA.	
62-4462	1962	Sabreliner CT-39A	276-15	Wfu. Trident Technical College, Charleston, SC.	
62-4463	1962	Sabreliner CT-39A	276-16	Wfu. at AMARC 8/94 as TG0100. (still there 5/06).	
62-4464	1962	Sabreliner CT-39A	276-17	Wfu. Utah State University, Salt Lake City, Ut.	
62-4465	1962	Sabreliner T-39A	276-18	Wfu. at March AFB. Ca.	
62-4466	1962	Sabreliner CT-39A	276-19	Wfu. Tech School, Battle Creek, Wi.	
62-4467	1962	Sabreliner CT-39A	276-20	Wfu. Guilford TCC Aviation Center, Greensboro, NC. USA.	
62-4470	1962	Sabreliner T-39A	276-23	Wfu. at Maxwell AFB. Al. USA.	
62-4471	1962	Sabreliner CT-39A	276-24	Wfu. at Ramstein AB. Germany.	
62-4473	1962	Sabreliner CT-39A	276-26	Wfu. to Dr R Smirnow, NYC. USA.	62-4473
62-4475	1962	Sabreliner CT-39A	276-28	Wfu. Milwaukee Technical College, Milwaukee, Wi. USA.	
62-4476	1962	Sabreliner T-39A	276-29	Wfu. at AMARC 8/94 as TG099. (still there 5/06).	
62-4477	1962	Sabreliner CT-39A	276-30	Wfu. Milwaukee Technical College, Milwaukee, Wi. USA.	
62-4478	1962	Sabreliner T-39A	276-31	Wfu. Located Wright-Patterson Museum, Oh. USA.	
62-4482	1962	Sabreliner T-39A	276-35	Wfu. at AMARC 1/04 as TG0107. (still there 5/06).	
62-4483	1962	Sabreliner CT-39A	276-36	Wfu. Indian Hills Community College, Ottumwa, Ia. USA.	
62-4484	1962	Sabreliner T-39A	276-37	Wfu. at Kadena AB. Okinawa, Japan.	
62-4485	1962	Sabreliner T-39A	276-38	Wfu. fire dump Yokota AB. Japan.	
62-4487	1962	Sabreliner T-39A	276-40	Wfu. Displayed at SAC Museum, Ne. USA.	
62-4490	1962	Sabreliner CT-39A	276-43	Wfu. Last located at Laredo, Tx. USA.	
62-4493	1962	Sabreliner CT-39A	276-46	Wfu. College of Technology, Williamsport, Pa. USA.	
62-4494	1962	Sabreliner CT-39A	276-47	Wfu. at Chanute AFB. Il. USA.	

Reg	Yr	Type	c/n	Owner/Operator	Prev Regn
☐ 62-4496	1962	Sabreliner T-39A	276-49	W/o Scranton, Pa. USA. 20 Apr 85.	
☐ 62-4497	1962	Sabreliner CT-39A	276-50	Wfu. East Coast Technical College, Bedford-Hanscom, Ma. USA.	
☐ 62-4498	1962	Sabreliner CT-39A	276-51	Wfu. Salt Lake City Community College, Ut. USA.	
☐ 62-4499	1962	Sabreliner T-39A	276-52	W/o 24 Jun 69.	
☐ 62-4500	1962	Sabreliner CT-39A	276-53	Wfu. Milwaukee Technical College, Milwukee, Wi. USA.	
☐ 62-4501	1962	Sabreliner CT-39A	276-54	Wfu. O'Fallon Technical College, St Louis, Mo. USA.	
☐ 62-4502	1962	Sabreliner T-39A	276-55	W/o Langley AFB. Va. USA 31 Dec 68.	
☐ 62-6000	1962	C-137C	18461	Wfu. Located USAF Museum, nr Wright-Patterson AFB.	
☐ 72-0283	1972	B 737-253 (CT-43A)	20690	Wfu. TH0003 at AMARC 1/03.	
☐ 72-7000	1972	C-137C	20630	Wfu. Located Presidential Library, Simi Valley, Santa Monica	N8459
☐ 84-0066	1984	Learjet C-21A	35A-512	W/o Decatur, Il. USA. 2 Oct 06.	N7263F
☐ 84-0068	1984	Learjet C-21A	35A-514	Wfu. At AMARC as AACJ0020 1/07.	N7263K
☐ 84-0073	1984	Learjet C-21A	35A-519	Wfu. At AMARC as AACJ0011 1/07.	N400AD
☐ 84-0074	1984	Learjet C-21A	35A-520	Wfu. At AMARC as AACJ0005 1/07.	N400AK
☐ 84-0078	1984	Learjet C-21A	35A-524	Wfu. At AMARC as AACJ0006 1/07.	N400AS
☐ 84-0080	1984	Learjet C-21A	35A-526	Wfu. At AMARC as AACJ0007 1/07.	N400AU
☐ 84-0086	1984	Learjet C-21A	35A-532	Wfu. At AMARC as AACJ0013 1/07.	N400BN
☐ 84-0088	1984	Learjet C-21A	35A-534	Wfu. At AMARC as AACJ0015 1/07.	N400BU
☐ 84-0089	1984	Learjet C-21A	35A-535	Wfu. At AMARC as AACJ0008 1/07.	(N61905)
☐ 84-0097	1985	Learjet C-21A	35A-543	W/o Ellsworth AFB. SD. USA. 2 Feb 02.	N400CU
☐ 84-0104	1985	Learjet C-21A	35A-550	Wfu. At AMARC as AACJ0012 1/07.	N400DL
☐ 84-0105	1985	Learjet C-21A	35A-551	Wfu. At AMARC as AACJ0004 1/07.	N400DN
☐ 84-0108	1985	Learjet C-21A	35A-554	Wfu. At AMARC as AACJ0010 1/07.	N400DU
☐ 84-0113	1985	Learjet C-21A	35A-559	Wfu. At AMARC as AACJ0018 1/07.	N400EC
☐ 84-0115	1985	Learjet C-21A	35A-561	Wfu. At AMARC as AACJ0009 1/07.	N400EF
☐ 84-0116	1985	Learjet C-21A	35A-562	Wfu. At AMARC as AACJ0017 1/07.	N400EG
☐ 84-0117	1985	Learjet C-21A	35A-563	Wfu. At AMARC as AACJ0016 1/07.	N400EJ
☐ 84-0121	1985	Learjet C-21A	35A-567	W/o Alabama, USA. 15 Jan 87.	N400EN
☐ 84-0122	1985	Learjet C-21A	35A-568	Wfu. At AMARC as AACJ0014 1/07.	N400EQ
☐ 84-0132	1985	Learjet C-21A	35A-579	Wfu. At AMARC as AACJ0019 1/07.	N400FH
☐ 84-0133	1985	Learjet C-21A	35A-580	Wfu. At AMARCas AACJ0002 1/07.	N400FK
☐ 84-0136	1985	Learjet C-21A	35A-583	W/o Thomas Russell Field, Alexander City, Al. USA. 17 Apr 95	N400FP
☐ 84-0138	1985	Learjet C-21A	35A-574	Wfu. at AMARC CJ0001 10/02.	N400EX
☐ 84-0141	1985	Learjet C-21A	35A-584	Wfu. At AMARC AACJ0003 1/07.	N400FQ
☐ 84-0193	1974	B 727-30	18362	Wfu. Located Davis Monthan AFB. USA.	N78
☐ 91-0093	1993	Jayhawk T-1A	TT-34	Wfu. Located at Wright-Patterson AFB. USA.	

OB = PERU
Civil

Reg	Yr	Type	c/n	Owner/Operator	Prev Regn
☐ OB-1319	1973	Sabre-40A	282-127	W/o Buenos Aires, Argentina. 3 Sep 93.	OB-T-1919

OE = AUSTRIA
Civil

Reg	Yr	Type	c/n	Owner/Operator	Prev Regn
☐ OE-FAN	1976	Citation	500-0289	W/o Mount Creisa, Sardinia. 24 Feb 04.	N939KS
☐ OE-FAP	1975	Citation	500-0300	W/o as OE-FAP Greece 6 Oct 84. (parts at Dodsons, Ks.).	(N500CX)
☐ OE-FFK	1979	Citation 1/SP	501-0124	W/o Nr Salzburg, Austria. 26 Oct 88.	N95RE

OH = FINLAND
Civil

Reg	Yr	Type	c/n	Owner/Operator	Prev Regn
☐ OH-CAR	1974	Citation	500-0144	W/o Nr Helsinki, Finland. 19 Nov 87.	N332H
☐ OH-FFW	1970	Falcon 20F	243	W/o Montreal, Canada. 1 Mar 72.	F-WMKH
☐ OH-GLB	1973	Learjet 24D	24D-262	Wfu. Located Rovaniemi, Finland.	N110PS

OY = DENMARK
Civil

Reg	Yr	Type	c/n	Owner/Operator	Prev Regn
☐ OY-SBR	1975	Corvette	23	Wfu. Last located Aalborg, Denmark.	F-BVPF
☐ OY-SBS	1975	Corvette	21	W/o Nice, France. 3 Sep 79.	F-BVPE

Military

Reg	Yr	Type	c/n	Owner/Operator	Prev Regn
☐ F-330	1981	Gulfstream 3	330	W/o Vagar, Faroe Islands. 3 Aug 96.	

PK = INDONESIA
Civil

Reg	Yr	Type	c/n	Owner/Operator	Prev Regn
☐ PK-CIR	1967	Falcon 20C	90	Wfu. Located at Jakarta International, Indonesia.	VH-CIR
☐ PK-DJW	1968	HS 125/3B-RA	25147	Wfu. Located near Halim-Jakarta airport, Indonesia.	PK-PJR

Military

Reg	Yr	Type	c/n	Owner/Operator	Prev Regn
☐ A-1645	1965	JetStar-6	5059	Wfu. Exhibit at Yogjakarta-Adisutjipto. (became A-9446 /05).	T-1645
☐ A-9446	1964	JetStar-6	5046	Wfu. Last located Kushadasi nr Jakarta, Indonesia.	T-9446

PP = BRAZIL
Civil

Reg	Yr	Type	c/n	Owner/Operator	Prev Regn
PP-FMX	1966	Learjet 23	23-090	W/o Rio de Janeiro, Brazil. 30 Aug 69.	
PP-SED	1973	Sabre-40A	282-121	Wfu. Cx USA 8/97.	N8349N
PR-SUL	1967	Falcon 20C	129	Wfu. Last located at Aruba, Netherlands Antilles.	N119LA
PT-ASJ	1976	Falcon 10	95	W/o Rio de Janeiro, Brazil. 17 Feb 89.	N173FJ
PT-CMY	1974	Learjet 25C	25C-108	W/o Juiz de Fora, Brazil. 6 Apr 90.	
PT-CXK	1966	Learjet 24	24-122	W/o Rio-Galeon, Brazil. 4 May 73.	N461LJ
PT-DVL	1971	Learjet 25B	25B-077	W/o Sao Paulo, Brazil. 12 Nov 76.	
PT-DZU	1971	Learjet 24D	24D-244	W/o Sao Paulo, Brazil. 23 Aug 79.	
PT-IBR	1972	Learjet 25C	25C-072	W/o Sao Paulo, Brazil. 26 Sep 76.	N256GL
PT-ILJ	1973	Citation	500-0057	W/o Rio, Brazil. 3 Jul 97. (parts at Dodsons, Ks. USA).	N557CC
PT-ISN	1973	Learjet 25C	25C-113	W/o Belo Horizonte, Brazil. 4 Nov 89. Cx PT- 1/90.	
PT-JBQ	1973	Learjet 25B	25B-119	W/o Rio Branco, Brazil. 4 Sep 82.	N3810G
PT-JDX	1973	Learjet 25C	25C-131	W/o Congonhas, Brazil. 26 Dec 78.	N3803G
PT-JXS	1974	Citation	500-0162	W/o Belem, Brazil. 16 Mar 75.	
PT-KBC	1974	Learjet 25C	25C-165	W/o Riberao Preto, Brazil. 4 Jun 96.	
PT-KIU	1974	Citation	500-0172	W/o Aracatuba, Brazil. 12 Nov 76.	N172CC
PT-KKV	1974	Learjet 25C	25C-172	W/o Macre, Brazil. 20 Feb 88, rebuilt, W/o again 11 Jan 91.	
PT-KPE	1975	Learjet 24D	24D-315	Wfu. Located at Sao Paulo-Congonhas, Brazil.	
PT-KYR	1979	Learjet 25D	25D-266	W/o 23 Aug 86.	
PT-KZY	1976	Learjet 25B	25B-204	W/o Uberaba, Brazil. 16 May 82.	N472J
PT-LAU	1971	Learjet 24D	24D-239	W/o Brasilia, Brazil. 10 Sep 94.	N83MJ
PT-LCN	1974	Learjet 24D	24D-287	W/o Florianapolis, Brazil. 4 Apr 84.	N92565
PT-LCV	1972	Learjet 24D	24D-254	Wfu.	N13606
PT-LEM	1973	Learjet 24D	24D-270	W/o Riberao Preto, Brazil. 7 Apr 99.	N3979P
PT-LGJ	1985	Citation S/II	S550-0025	W/o Rio de Janeiro, Brazil. 6 Sep 88.	(N12596)
PT-LHU	1973	Learjet 25C	25C-099	W/o Icuape, Brazil. 28 Jul 92. Cx PT- 10/94.	PT-FAF
PT-LIG	1985	Learjet 55	55-111	W/o Guanabara Bay, Brazil. 9 Nov 94. (at Rantoul, Ks.)	N7260G
PT-LIH	1981	Learjet 35A	35A-433	W/o Uberlandia, Brazil. 15 Mar 91.	(N93RC)
PT-LIY	1975	Citation	500-0219	W/o Marilia, Brazil. 1 Dec 02.	N408CA
PT-LKQ	1965	Learjet 23	23-038	Wfu. Bu at Michigan Institute of Aeronautics,Detroit, USA.	N175BA
PT-LKT	1986	Citation S/II	S550-0117	W/o Sao Paulo-Congonhas, Brazil. 1 Dec 92. Cx PT- 10/94.	N1292N
PT-LLL	1978	Learjet 25D	25D-258	W/o Nr Brasilia, Brazil. 18 Mar 91.	N258MD
PT-LMA	1977	Learjet 24F	24F-353	W/o Macre, Brazil. 24 Feb 88.	N63BW
PT-LME	1980	Citation II/SP	551-0023	W/o Soracaba, Brazil. 23 Jul 03.	N34DL
PT-LMF	1966	Learjet 24	24-120	Wfu. Parts at Dodsons, Rantoul, Ks. USA.	(N244RD)
PT-LML	1978	Citation II	550-0013	W/o Criciuma, Santa Catarina, Brazil. 15 Aug 97.	N21SV
PT-LNE	1966	Learjet 24	24-114	Wfu. Last located at Belo Horizonte, Brazil.	N99DM
PT-LNN	1983	Diamond 1A	A048SA	W/o Santos AFB. Brazil. 23 Mar 03. (at Rantoul, Ks.).	N335DM
PT-LOS	1974	Citation	500-0239	Wfu. Last located at Dodsons, Rantoul, Ks. USA.	N6034F
PT-LQG	1975	Citation	500-0271	W/o Canelo, Rio Sul, Brazil. 31 Oct 97.	N53FB
PT-LSD	1978	Learjet 25D	25D-243	W/o Sierra de Cantareira, Sao Paulo, Brazil. 2 Mar 96.	N711JT
PT-OBD	1971	Learjet 24B	24B-228	Wfu. Last located at Belo Horizonte, Brazil.	N150AB
PT-OEF	1977	Learjet 35A	35A-102	W/o Morelia, Mexico. 2 May 92. (parts at Dodsons).	N232R
PT-OMV	1990	Citation VI	650-0200	W/o Nr Bogota, Colombia. 23 Mar 94.	N650CM
PT-OVC	1981	Learjet 35A	35A-399	W/o Sao Paulo-Campo de Marte, Brazil. 4 Nov 07.	(N399AZ)
PT-WLX	1997	CitationJet	525-0176	W/o Rio de Janeiro, Brazil. 16 Sep 05.	N5161J

Military

Reg	Yr	Type	c/n	Owner/Operator	Prev Regn
EU93-2119	1973	HS 125/403B	25274	Wfu. Located EEAR, Guaratingueta, Brazil.	G-5-20
EU93-2121	1968	HS 125/3B-RC	25165	Wfu. Located EEAR, Guaratingueta, Brazil.	VC93-2121
VC93-2122	1968	HS 125/3B-RC	25166	W/o Brasilia, Brazil. 18 Jun 79.	
VU93-2114	1970	HS 125/400A	NA740	Wfu.	N702P
VU93-2124	1968	HS 125/3B-RC	25168	Wfu. Last located PAMA Recife, Brazil.	VC93-2124
VU93-2129	1973	HS 125/403B	25290	W/o Carajas, Brazil. 9 Sep 87.	
XU93-2117	1969	HS 125/400A	NA738	Wfu. Last located at EEAR, Guaratingueta, Brazil.	VU93-2117

P4 = ARUBA
Civil

Reg	Yr	Type	c/n	Owner/Operator	Prev Regn
P4-AFE	1980	B 747SP-31	21962	Wfu.	TF-ABN
P4-AMB	1972	HS 125/400B	25252	Wfu.	N48US
P4-AOD	1981	HS 125/700A	NA0313	W/o Kharkov, Ukraine. 2 Jan 06.	N419RD
P4-CBH	1966	BAC 1-11/401AK	088	Wfu. Last located Bucharest, Romania.	HZ-MAJ
P4-DRS	1975	B 707-368C	21104	Wfu. Located San Antonio, Tx. USA.	ST-DRS

RA = RUSSIA / RUSSIAN FEDERATION
Civil

Reg	Yr	Type	c/n	Owner/Operator	Prev Regn
☐ RA-09004	1969	Falcon 20C	170	Wfu. Dismantled at Geneva, Switzerland 3/06.	F-GHPA
☐ RA-09007	1968	Falcon 20C	136	W/o Moscow-SVO, Russia. 20 May 05.	N20MY

RP = PHILIPPINES
Civil

Reg	Yr	Type	c/n	Owner/Operator	Prev Regn
☐ RP-C1500	1975	Citation	500-0225	W/o between Cagayan & Butuan, Philippines. 1 Feb 97.	VH-OIL
☐ RP-C1980	1979	Falcon 20F	400	W/o Davao City, Philippines. 24 Apr 96.	F-WRQR
☐ RP-C911	1960	B 707-321	17606	Wfu. Located at Manila as 'Club 707' restaurant.	N728PA

SE = SWEDEN
Civil

Reg	Yr	Type	c/n	Owner/Operator	Prev Regn
☐ SE-DCY	1969	Jet Commander	136	W/o Stockholm, Sweden. 4 Dec 69.	N5044E
☐ SE-DLK	1976	Westwind-1124	197	W/o Umeaa, Sweden. 21 Sep 92.	N29CL

Military

Reg	Yr	Type	c/n	Owner/Operator	Prev Regn
☐ 86002	1967	Sabre-40/Tp 86	282-91	Wfu. Instructional airframe Linkoping-Malmen, Sweden.	N40NR

SP = POLAND
Civil

Reg	Yr	Type	c/n	Owner/Operator	Prev Regn
☐ SP-FOA	1975	Corvette	14	Wfu. Last located at Aero Stock, Paris-Le Bourget, France.	(F-GIRH)

ST = SUDAN
Civil

Reg	Yr	Type	c/n	Owner/Operator	Prev Regn
☐ ST-PRE	1965	JetStar-6	5071	Wfu. Last located at Khartoum, Sudan.	SU-DAH

SU = EGYPT
Civil

Reg	Yr	Type	c/n	Owner/Operator	Prev Regn
☐ SU-DAF	1962	JetStar-6	5025	Wfu.	(ST-JRM)
☐ SU-DAG	1968	JetStar-8	5121	Wfu. Located Cairo, Egypt.	(ST-PRM)

SX = GREECE
Civil

Reg	Yr	Type	c/n	Owner/Operator	Prev Regn
☐ SX-ASO	1971	Learjet 25B	25B-074	W/o Antibes, France. 18 Feb 72.	N251GL
☐ SX-BSS	1966	HS 125/3A	25116	Wfu. Located Thessaloniki, Greece.	N726CC

S9 = SAO TOME & PRINCIPE
Civil

Reg	Yr	Type	c/n	Owner/Operator	Prev Regn
☐ S9-NAD	1965	JetStar-6	5065	Wfu. Spares for s/n 5085 in 1989.	N1966G
☐ S9-NAE	1966	JetStar-6	5085	Wfu. Located Abu Dhabi Mens College, UAE.	VR-CCY

TC = TURKEY
Civil

Reg	Yr	Type	c/n	Owner/Operator	Prev Regn
☐ TC-NSU	1969	HFB 320	1046	Wfu.	16+04
☐ TC-OMR	1969	HFB 320	1047	Wfu.	16+05
☐ TC-YIB	1983	Diamond 1A	A051SA	Wfu. Parts at Dodsons, Rantoul, Ks. USA.	D-CFGV

TL = CENTRAL AFRICAN REPUBLIC
Civil

Reg	Yr	Type	c/n	Owner/Operator	Prev Regn
☐ TL-AAI		Caravelle 3	10	Wfu. Broken up at Paris-Orly 2/83.	F-BNGE
☐ TL-FCA	1960	Caravelle 3	42	Wfu.	TL-KAB

TN = CONGO BRAZZAVILLE
Civil

Reg	Yr	Type	c/n	Owner/Operator	Prev Regn
☐ TN-ADB	1975	Corvette	22	W/o Nkayi, Congo Republic. 30 Mar 79.	F-ODFE
☐ TN-ADI	1975	Corvette	9	Wfu.	F-OCRN

TR = GABON
Civil

Reg	Yr	Type	c/n	Owner/Operator	Prev Regn
☐ TR-KHB	1973	Gulfstream 2	127	W/o Ngaoundere, Cameroun. 6 Feb 80.	N17581
☐ TR-LZT	1975	Corvette	20	Wfu. Located Toulouse-Blagnac, France.	(F-GKJB)

TT = CHAD
Civil

Reg	Yr	Type	c/n	Owner/Operator	Prev Regn
☐ TT-AAM		Caravelle 6R	100	Wfu. Cx TT- 5/80. Last located N'Djamena, Chad.	(TT-AAD)

TU = IVORY COAST
Military

Reg	Yr	Type	c/n	Owner/Operator	Prev Regn
☐ TU-VAA	1987	Fokker 100	11245	W/o Bouake, Ivory Coast. 29 Jun 07.	PH-CDI

TY = BENIN
Civil

Reg	Yr	Type	c/n	Owner/Operator	Prev Regn
☐ TY-BBK	1976	Corvette	29	W/o Lagos, Nigeria. 16 Nov 81.	F-OBZP
☐ TY-BBR	1971	B 707-336B	20457	W/o Sebha, Libya. 13 Jun 85.	9G-ADB
☐ TY-BBW	1962	B 707-321	18084	Wfu.	TY-AAM

UR = UKRAINE
Civil

Reg	Yr	Type	c/n	Owner/Operator	Prev Regn
☐ UR-NIK	1967	Falcon 20C	112	Wfu. Last located Basle, Switzerland.	UR-CCD

VH = AUSTRALIA
Civil

Reg	Yr	Type	c/n	Owner/Operator	Prev Regn
☐ VH-AJS	1977	Westwind-1124	221	W/o Alice Springs, Australia. 27 Apr 95.	(N969EG)
☐ VH-ANQ	1975	Citation Eagle	500-0283	W/o Cairns, Australia. 11 May 90.	N18AF
☐ VH-CAO	1965	HS 125/3B	25015	Wfu. Located The Oaks, Nr Camden, NSW, Australia.	(N750D)
☐ VH-ECE	1966	HS 125/3B	25062	Wfu. Located The Oaks, Nr Camden, NSW, Australia.	
☐ VH-FSA	1974	Citation	500-0237	W/o Prosperine, Queensland, Australia. 20 Feb 84.	N14TT
☐ VH-FWO	1967	Falcon 20C	110	Wfu. Parts at Springfield, Il. USA.	C-FWRA
☐ VH-IWJ	1982	Westwind-1124	371	W/o Botany Bay, Australia. 10 Oct 85.	4X-CUH
☐ VH-LCL	1980	Citation 1/SP	501-0145	W/o Lord Howe Island. 22 Apr 90. (parts at Dodsons, Ks.).	(N2652Z)
☐ VH-LLW	1979	Westwind Sea Scan	253	Wfu. Last located Jandakot, WA. Australia.	N253MD
☐ VH-LLX	1979	Westwind Sea Scan	259	Wfu. Last located Jandakot, WA. Australia.	N315JM
☐ VH-LLY	1979	Westwind Sea Scan	272	Wfu. Last located Jandakot, WA. Australia.	N723R
☐ VH-XBA	1959	B 707-138B	17696	Wfu. QANTAS Founders Outback Museum, Longreach, QLD.	HZ-123

Military

Reg	Yr	Type	c/n	Owner/Operator	Prev Regn
☐ A20-103	1975	B 707-368C	21103	W/o Nr RAAF E Sale, VIC. Australia. 29 Oct 91.	HZ-ACG
☐ A20-623	1968	B 707-338C	19623	Wfu. Last located, Richmond, NSW. Australia.	C-GRYN
☐ A20-627	1968	B 707-338C	19627	Wfu! located Richmond, NSW. Australia.	VH-EAG
☐ A20-629	1968	B 707-338C	19629	Wfu. Last located Richmond, NSW. Australia.	C-GGAB

VP-B = BERMUDA
Civil

Reg	Yr	Type	c/n	Owner/Operator	Prev Regn
☐ VP-BIA	1963	DC 8-52	45658	Wfu. Last located Lasham, UK.	VR-BIA
☐ VP-BLD	1968	JetStar-731	5117	Wfu. Last located Toulouse, France.	(N858SH)
☐ VP-BLN	1983	Gulfstream 3	402	W/o Lac du Bourget, Chambery, France. 6 Feb 98.	VR-BLN
☐ VR-BJB	1970	Falcon 20F	244	W/o Lugano, Switzerland. 15 Jan 88. (at Rantoul, Ks.)	(OE-GCS)
☐ VR-BJI	1971	JetStar-731	5149	Wfu. Cx VR-B 7/91.	N110MZ
☐ VR-BLJ	1968	Gulfstream 2	40	W/o Jos, Nigeria. 20 Jun 96.	N1039
☐ VR-BMB	1970	HS 125/400B	25240	Wfu. Last located Stansted, UK.	VR-BKN
☐ VR-BZA	1970	B 707-336C	20375	Wfu. Located Lake Charles, La. USA.	VR-BZA

VP-C = CAYMAN ISLANDS
Civil

Reg	Yr	Type	c/n	Owner/Operator	Prev Regn
☐ VP-CCG	1966	BAC 1-11/401AK	081	Wfu. Last located Bucharest, Romania.	VR-CCG
☐ VP-CSM	1966	JetStar-731	5092	Wfu. Last located Toulouse, France.	VR-CSM
☐ VR-CAN	1961	B 707-138B	18067	Wfu.	9Y-TDC

VT = INDIA
Civil

Reg	Yr	Type	c/n	Owner/Operator	Prev Regn
☐ VT-ERO	1965	Jet Commander	33	Wfu. Parts at Hollister, Ca. USA.	N104CJ

Military

Reg	Yr	Type	c/n	Owner/Operator	Prev Regn
☐ K2900	1967	B 707-337C	19248	Wfu. Last located at Delhi, India.	VT-DVB

XA = MEXICO
Civil

Reg	Yr	Type	c/n	Owner/Operator	Prev Regn
☐ XA-...	1970	HS 125/400A	NA743	Wfu.	N400LC
☐ XA-...	1965	HS 125/731	25018	Wfu. Last located Toluca, Mexico.	(P4-ZAW)
☐ XA-AAL	1979	JetStar 2	5231	Wfu. Last located Toluca, Mexico.	XA-TPJ
☐ XA-ADC	1966	BAC 1-11/211AH	084	Wfu. Last located San Antonio, Tx. USA.	S9-TAE
☐ XA-ARA	1970	Gulfstream II SP	79	Wfu. Last located Houston, Tx. USA.	XA-STO
☐ XA-BBA	1977	Learjet 25D	25D-223	W/o Washington-Dulles, USA. 18 Jun 94.	XA-RWH
☐ XA-COL	1966	HS 125/1A	25086	W/o Acalpulco, Mexico. 12 Oct 73.	N3699T
☐ XA-CUZ	1972	HS 125/400A	NA772	W/o Cancun, Mexico. 26 Dec 80.	N69BH
☐ XA-EEU	1966	Sabre-40	282-54	W/o ground accident Mexico 1980.	N256CT
☐ XA-EMO	1969	JetStar-8	5140	Wfu. Last located at Toluca, Mexico.	XA-JCG
☐ XA-GBP	1963	B 727-25	18252	Wfu.	XB-GBP
☐ XA-GUR	1977	Sabre-60	306-131	Wfu. Last located Toluca, Mexico.	(N131SE)
☐ XA-HOK	1964	Sabre-40	282-41	Wfu. Parts at AVMATS Paynesville, Mo. USA.	N900CS
☐ XA-ISH	1985	BAe 125/800A	258036	W/o Nr Tampico, Mexico. 27 Oct 03.	N621MT
☐ XA-JLV	1967	Learjet 24	24-136	Wfu.	N24LW
☐ XA-KEW	1980	HS 125/700A	NA0276	W/o Norte-Monterrey, Mexico. 2 May 81.	G-5-14
☐ XA-KUT	1974	HS 125/600A	256028	W/o Houston, Tx. USA. 18 Jan 88. (parts at Dodsons, Ks)	C-GDHW
☐ XA-LAN	1979	Learjet 35A	35A-267	W/o Hermosillo, Mexico. 8 Jan 93.	N39418
☐ XA-NOG	1981	Learjet 25D	25D-349	W/o Tijuana, Mexico. 2 Sep 93.	N20GT
☐ XA-PES	1969	JetStar-8	5130	Wfu. Last located Toluca, Mexico.	XA-TZV

Reg	Yr	Type	c/n	Owner/Operator	Prev Regn
☐ XA-PIC	1965	Sabre-40R	282-39	Wfu. Last located Toluca, Mexico.	XA-RTM
☐ XA-POG	1972	Learjet 25B	25B-080	Wfu. Last located Toluca, Mexico.	N30AP
☐ XA-POJ	1972	Westwind-1123	161	Wfu. Parts at Dodsons, Rantoul, Ks. USA.	N33WD
☐ XA-PUF	1972	Westwind-1123	153	Wfu. Parts were at Hollister, Ca. USA.	N223WW
☐ XA-PUL	1972	JetStar-8	5151	Wfu.	N45K
☐ XA-RIR	1969	Sabre-60	306-36	Wfu. Located at Azteca, Toluca, Mexico.	N436CC
☐ XA-RMA	1966	Falcon 20C	39	Wfu. Last located Toluca, Mexico.	XB-EDU
☐ XA-RNR	1970	Sabre-60	306-49	Wfu.	XA-POR
☐ XA-ROK	1969	JetStar-8	5133	Wfu.	HZ-FK1
☐ XA-RQB	1967	Learjet 24XR	24XR-150	Wfu. Last located at Dodsons, Rantoul, Ks. USA.	N24XR
☐ XA-RQI	1969	Learjet 25	25-032	Wfu. Exhibit main terminal Mexico City 1994.	XA-ZYZ
☐ XA-RRC	1972	Learjet 24D	24D-259	Wfu. Parts at White Industries Inc. Bates City, Mo. USA.	N22MH
☐ XA-RRK	1976	Learjet 24D	24D-307	W/o Tampico, Mexico. 2 Jan 98. (Parts at Dodsons).	N307BJ
☐ XA-RVG	1969	JetStar-731	5139	Wfu. Parts at Griffin, Ga. USA. Cx USA 2/97.	(N1189A)
☐ XA-RZC	1965	Learjet 23	23-071	Wfu. Parts at Dodsons, Rantoul, Ks. USA.	(N6262T)
☐ XA-SAI	1974	HS 125/600A	256016	Wfu. Parts at White Industries, Bates City, Mo. USA.	N99SC
☐ XA-SBC	1966	HS 125/1A-522	25068	Wfu. Parts at Dodsons, Rantoul, Ks. USA.	(N5274U)
☐ XA-SHA	1966	Jet Commander	86	Wfu. Parts at Dodsons, Rantoul, Ks. USA.	XA-RIW
☐ XA-SLH	1969	Sabre-60	306-39	Wfu. Cx USA 4/00. Parts at AVMATS SUS, Mo. USA.	(N82197)
☐ XA-SLQ	1973	Citation	500-0111	W/o Ensenada, Mexico. 6 Feb 96.	XA-SHO
☐ XA-SMH	1973	Citation	500-0084	W/o Aleman, Veracruz, Mexico. 25 March 94.	XB-FPK
☐ XA-SMQ	1965	Sabre-40	282-50	Wfu. Parts at AVMATS Spririt of St Louis, Mo. USA.	(N282CA)
☐ XA-SOC	1972	JetStar-8	5152	Wfu. Last located Toluca, Mexico.	N113KH
☐ XA-SOY	1969	JetStar-8	5142	Wfu. Last located Toluca, Mexico.	N23FE
☐ XA-STI	1974	Sabre-60	306-89	Wfu. Last located Toluca, Mexico.	N86RM
☐ XA-SWF	1981	Learjet 35A	35A-391	W/o Nr Tepic Airport, Mexico. 23 Jun 95.	N888PT
☐ XA-TAL	1966	HS 125/1A-522	25064	W/o Toluca, Mexico. 9 Jul 99.	XB-GGK
☐ XA-TAV	1967	JetStar-8	5103	Wfu. Located Aruba, Netherlands Antilles.	XA-TAZ
☐ XA-TDG	1973	JetStar-8	5158	Wfu. Located Mexico City, Mexico.	XA-FHR
☐ XA-TDP	1966	Learjet 24	24-128	Wfu. Parts at Dodsons, Rantoul, Ks. USA.	(N128WD)
☐ XA-TFC	1960	Sabreliner CT-39A	265-12	W/o Monterrey, Mexico. 16 May 97. USA.	XB-GDU
☐ XA-TFL	1961	Sabreliner CT-39A	265-48	W/o Culiacan, Sinalao. Mexico. 5 Jul 07.	N6CF
☐ XA-TJU	1962	Sabreliner CT-39A	276-8	W/o Monterrey, Mexico. 19 Dec 06.	N4314B
☐ XA-TNP	1961	Sabreliner CT-39A	265-29	W/o Culiacan, Mexico. 30 Dec 06.	(N6581K)
☐ XA-TPD	1969	JetStar-731	5134	Wfu. Last located Addison, Tx. USA.	XA-JMN
☐ XA-TZW	1969	JetStar-8	5129	Wfu. Located Toluca, Mexico.	XA-TJW
☐ XA-UCS	1964	Sabre-40	282-6	W/o Mexico City, Mexico. 5 Jul 06.	XA-GYR
☐ XA-ZZZ	1979	Learjet 25D	25D-287	Wfu. Parts at White Industries Inc. Bates City, Mo. USA.	N20AD
☐ XB-BBL	1973	Sabre-40A	282-116	Wfu. Located Toluca, Mexico.	N4PH
☐ XB-DLV	1961	JetStar-8	5005	Wfu. Cx USA as N22265 6/02.	(N22265)
☐ XB-DUH	1972	JetStar-8	5157	Wfu. Displayed as N001DI at Dodsons,Rantoul, Ks. USA.	N29WP
☐ XB-FJI	1967	Jet Commander	115	Wfu. Located Monterrey, Mexico.	N500VF
☐ XB-GHO	1967	Learjet 24	24-141	Wfu. Located Addison, Tx. USA.	XB-FJW
☐ XB-GJO	1973	Sabre-75	370-9	Wfu. Parts at Spirit of St Louis, Mo. USA.	(N370SL)
☐ XB-JIZ	1965	JetStar-731	5058	Wfu. Last located Toluca, Mexico.	XA-TTE
☐ XB-JOY	1973	Learjet 24D	24D-263	W/o Mexico City, Mexico. 29 Jun 76.	N3812G
☐ XB-KKU	1969	Gulfstream 2B	75	W/o Santo Domingo, Venezuela. 7 Oct 07.	N211SJ
☐ XC-AA26	1968	Sabre-60A	306-12	Wfu.	XC-HHL
☐ XC-AA73	1972	Sabre-40A	282-105	Wfu. Located Mexico City, Mexico.	XA-SCN
☐ XC-COL	1980	Westwind-1124	279	W/o Sapotita, Mexico. 24 Feb 2005.	N400TF
☐ XC-COL	1969	Jet Commander-B	135	Wfu. Last located at Wiley Post, Ok, USA.	N1121N
☐ XC-HAD	1966	Jet Commander	85	Wfu.	N201S
☐ XC-JDX	1965	Learjet 23	23-070	Wfu. Last located Mexico City.	XC-AA104
☐ XC-LIT	1965	JetStar-6	5063	Wfu.	N499PB
☐ XC-PFN	1975	Sabre-60	306-111	W/o Mexacali, Mexico 28 Jul 04.	XA-SKB
☐ XC-PGE	1974	Sabre-40A	282-130	Wfu. Located Mexico City, Mexico.	XC-PGE
☐ XC-TIJ	1970	HFB 320	1049	W/o San Diego, Ca. USA. 6 Jun 84.	XC-DGA
Military					
☐ MTX-02	1975	Learjet 24D	24D-313	W/o Mexico City, Mexico. 20 Nov 98. (at Bates City, Mo.).	MTX-01
☐ XC-UJC	1978	Sabre-75A	380-67	W/o Saltillo, Mexico. 26 Oct 89. (parts at AVMATS, Mo.).	TP-103
☐ XC-UJI	1969	B 737-247	20127	W/o Lomar, Bonita, Mexico. 14 May 99.	B-12001
☐ XC-UJS	1978	Sabre-60	306-139	Wfu. Last located Mexico City.	XC-UJE
☐ XC-UJU	1978	Sabre-75A	380-68	Wfu. Last located Mexico City.	XC-UJD

YI = IRAQ
Civil

Reg	Yr	Type	c/n	Owner/Operator	Prev Regn
☐ YI-AKH	1982	HS 125/700B	257187	W/o as destroyed during Gulf War 2/91,	YI-AKH
☐ YI-AKI	1983	Gulfstream 3	408	W/o as destroyed during Gulf War 2/91.	9K-AEG
☐ YI-AKJ	1984	Gulfstream 3	419	W/o as destroyed during Gulf War 2/91.	9K-AEH

YU = SERBIA
Civil

Reg	Yr	Type	c/n	Owner/Operator	Prev Regn
☐ YU-BJH	1975	Learjet 25B	25B-186	W/o Sarajevo, Yugoslavia. 18 Jan 77.	

YV = VENEZUELA
Civil

Reg	Yr	Type	c/n	Owner/Operator	Prev Regn
☐ YV1079	1968	Learjet 24	24-173		YV-824CP
☐ YV-123CP	1965	Jet Commander	16	Wfu.	N177A
☐ YV-160CP	1977	Westwind-1124	211	W/o La Aurora, Guatemala City, Guatemala. 19 Feb 97.	4X-CLI
☐ YV-21CP	1973	Citation	500-0115	W/o Charallave, Venezuela. 8 Mar 05.	YV-TAFA
☐ YV-2454P	1967	Jet Commander	96	Wfu. Last located at Caracas-Charallave, Venezuela.	(N2ES)
☐ YV-O-MAC-	1976	Citation	500-0336	W/o Caracas, Venezuela. Jun 79.	N336CC

ZK = NEW ZEALAND
Military

Reg	Yr	Type	c/n	Owner/Operator	Prev Regn
☐ NZ7272	1968	B 727-22C	19895	Wfu. Located RNZAF Ground Training Wing Woodbourne..	N7438U
☐ NZ7273	1968	B 727-22C	19893	Wfu. Last located Blenheim, New Zealand.	N7436U

ZS = SOUTH AFRICA
Civil

Reg	Yr	Type	c/n	Owner/Operator	Prev Regn
☐ ZS-JBA	1971	HS 125/400B	25259	Wfu. Cx ZS- 3/03. Last located Lanseria, RSA.	SAAF05
☐ ZS-JWC	1965	Learjet 23	23-030	Wfu. Located Aviation Warehouse, El Mirage, Ca. USA.	N431CA
☐ ZS-NGG	1973	Learjet 24XR	24XR-280	Wfu. Last located Lanseria, RSA.	N79RS
☐ ZS-NNM	1967	BAC 1-11/409AY	108	Wfu.	G-BGTU

Military

Reg	Yr	Type	c/n	Owner/Operator	Prev Regn
☐ SAAF01	1969	HS 125/400B	25177	W/o Devil's Peak, South Africa. 26 May 71.	G-AWXN
☐ SAAF02	1969	HS 125/400B	25181	W/o Devil's Peak, South Africa. 26 May 71.	G-AXLU
☐ SAAF03	1969	HS 125/400B	25182	W/o Devil's Peak, South Africa. 26 May 71.	G-AXLV

3C = EQUATORIAL GUINEA
Civil

Reg	Yr	Type	c/n	Owner/Operator	Prev Regn
☐ 3C-QRF	1966	BAC 1-11/401AK	061	Wfu. Last located Bucharest, Romania.	P4-CBI

3D = SWAZILAND
Civil

Reg	Yr	Type	c/n	Owner/Operator	Prev Regn
☐ 3D-ART	1975	Falcon 10	61	W/o Magoebaskloof, Transvaal, RSA. 3 Oct 86.	F-BFDG

4X = ISRAEL
Civil

Reg	Yr	Type	c/n	Owner/Operator	Prev Regn
☐ 4X-...	1985	Astra-1125	003	Wfu. static and fatigue test airframe.	
☐ 4X-AIP	1978	Westwind-1124	243	W/o Rosh-Pina, Israel. 23 Jul 96.	N215SC
☐ 4X-COA	1966	Jet Commander	71	Wfu. Located at Hatzerim Air Force Museum, Israel.	N721GB
☐ 4X-COJ	1965	Jet Commodore	29	W/o Tel Aviv, Israel. 21 Jan 70.	N615JC
☐ 4X-IGA	1997	Galaxy-1126	003	Wfu. Located Tel Aviv, Israel.	
☐ 4X-WIN	1984	Astra-1125	001	Wfu. Broken up by 31 Aug 86.	

5A = LIBYA
Civil

Reg	Yr	Type	c/n	Owner/Operator	Prev Regn
☐ 5A-DAD	1965	Learjet 23	23-075	W/o Damascus, Syria. 5 Jun 67.	
☐ 5A-DAR	1977	JetStar 2	5221	W/o en route Tripoli-Algeria, North Africa. 16 Jan 83.	N5547L

5B = CYPRUS
Civil

Reg	Yr	Type	c/n	Owner/Operator	Prev Regn
☐ 5B-CHE	1968	JetStar-731	5114	Wfu. Cx 5B- 2/03.	N26GL

5N = NIGERIA
Civil

Reg	Yr	Type	c/n	Owner/Operator	Prev Regn
☐ 5N-AAN	1967	HS 125/3B	25125	Wfu. Located Kingston University, Newcastle, UK.	F-GFMP
☐ 5N-AER	1968	HS 125/1B-522	25099	Wfu. Located Zaria, Nigeria.	(N2246)
☐ 5N-ALH	1966	HS 125/1B	25089	Wfu. CoA expiry by 3/01.	OO-SKJ
☐ 5N-AMF	1967	HFB 320	1028	W/o Abidjan, Ivory Coast. 25 Jul 77.	D-CASU
☐ 5N-AMR	1978	Citation II	550-0045	W/o Bauchi, Nigeria. 21 May 91.	N4CR
☐ 5N-AOG	1967	HS 125/3B-RA	25143	Wfu.	G-AVXK
☐ 5N-AOL	1975	HS 125/600B	256050	Wfu. Located Lagos, Nigeria.	G-BLOI
☐ 5N-APN	1975	Citation	500-0286	Wfu. CoA expiry by 3/01.	N286CC
☐ 5N-ASQ	1981	Learjet 25D	25D-344	W/o Lagos, Nigeria. 22 Jul 83.	N37943
☐ 5N-ASZ	1966	HS 125/1B	25063	Wfu. Broken up at Southampton-UK 11/86.	G-ONPN

Reg	Yr	Type	c/n	Owner/Operator	Prev Regn
☐ 5N-AVV	1967	HS 125/3B	25138	Wfu.	I-BOGI
☐ 5N-AVZ	1967	HS 125/3B-RA	25113	Wfu. Located Lagos, Nigeria.	G-AVDX
☐ 5N-AWB	1966	HS 125/1B	25025	Wfu.	(F-OCGK)
☐ 5N-AWD	1964	HS 125/1	25008	Wfu.	G-ASSI
☐ 5N-AWS	1975	HS 125/600B	256042	W/o Casablanca, Morocco. 31 Dec 86.	(G-5-505)
☐ 5N-AXO	1983	HS 125/700B	257196	W/o Kano, Nigeria. 17 Jan 96.	G-5-766
☐ 5N-AXP	1983	HS 125/700B	257203	W/o Kaduna, Nigeria. 31 Dec 85.	G-5-14
☐ 5N-BDC	1967	BAC 1-11/412EB	111	W/o Libreville, Gabon. 28 Aug 01.	EL-LIB
☐ 5N-HHH	1966	BAC 1-11/401AK	064	Wfu. Last located Southend, UK.	HZ-NB2
☐ 5N-MBM	1966	BAC 1-11/401AK	068	Wfu.	N263PC
☐ 5N-NPF	1980	Citation II	550-0125	Wfu. CoA expiry by 3/01.	N125RR
☐ 5N-RNO	1975	HS 125/600B	256054	W/o Lagos, Nigeria. May 01.	5N-YFS
☐ 5N-VVV	1966	BAC 1-11/401AK	080	Wfu. CoA expiry by 3/01.	HZ-BL1
☐ 5N-WMA	1968	HS 125/400B	25178	Wfu. CoA expiry by 3/01.	G-OOSP

5T = MAURITANIA
Civil

Reg	Yr	Type	c/n	Owner/Operator	Prev Regn
☐ 5T-RIM	1961	Caravelle 6R	91	Wfu.	5T-MAL

5V = TOGO
Civil

Reg	Yr	Type	c/n	Owner/Operator	Prev Regn
☐ 5V-TAA	1974	Gulfstream 2	149	W/o Lome, Togo. 26 Dec 74.	N17586
☐ 5V-TAG	1968	B 707-312B	19739	W/o Niamey, Niger. 21 Sep 00.	N600CS

5Y = KENYA
Civil

Reg	Yr	Type	c/n	Owner/Operator	Prev Regn
☐ 5Y-BNJ	1967	B 707-336C	19498	Wfu.	N14AZ

6V = SENEGAL
Civil

Reg	Yr	Type	c/n	Owner/Operator	Prev Regn
☐ 6V-AAR	1959	Caravelle 3	5	Wfu. Last located Dakar, Senegal.	6V-ACP

7T = ALGERIA
Civil

Reg	Yr	Type	c/n	Owner/Operator	Prev Regn
☐ 7T-VHB	1978	Gulfstream 2	230	W/o Nr Qotur, NW Iranian Border. 3 May 82.	N17586
☐ 7T-VRE	1969	Falcon 20C	156	W/o 30 May 81.	F-WMKI

9K = KUWAIT
Military

Reg	Yr	Type	c/n	Owner/Operator	Prev Regn
☐ KAF 320		DC 9-32	47691	W/o during Gulf War 2/91.	160749

9M = MALAYSIA
Civil

Reg	Yr	Type	c/n	Owner/Operator	Prev Regn
☐ 9M-BCR	1966	Falcon 20C	35	Wfu. Located Everett Aero, Sproughton, Ipswich. UK.	N809P
☐ 9M-HLG	1972	HS 125/400B	25257	Wfu.	G-BATA

Military

Reg	Yr	Type	c/n	Owner/Operator	Prev Regn
☐ M24-01	1969	HS 125/400B	25189	Wfu. Stored RMAF Subang, Malaysia.	FM1801
☐ M24-02	1969	HS 125/400B	25209	Wfu. Stored RMAF Subang, Malaysia.	FM1802

9Q = CONGO KINSHASA
Civil

Reg	Yr	Type	c/n	Owner/Operator	Prev Regn
☐ 9Q-CBC	1972	Learjet 24D	24D-248	W/o Kinshasa, Zaire. 18 Jan 94.	OO-LFA

Military

Reg	Yr	Type	c/n	Owner/Operator	Prev Regn
☐ 9T-MSS	1968	B 707-382B	19969	Wfu. Located Lisbon, Portugal.	CS-TBD

9V = SINGAPORE
Civil

Reg	Yr	Type	c/n	Owner/Operator	Prev Regn
☐ 9V-ATD	1993	Learjet 31	31-033B	W/o between Phuket & Ranong, Thailand. 21 Jul 97.	N2600S

9XR = RWANDA
Civil

Reg	Yr	Type	c/n	Owner/Operator	Prev Regn
☐ 9XR-NN	1979	Falcon 50	6	W/o Kigali, Rwanda. 6 Apr 94.	N815CA
☐ 9XR-RA	1964	BAC 1-11/201AC	011	Wfu. Last located Lanseria, RSA.	EL-ALD

Business Jets and VLJ's
Cross-Reference by Construction Number

Aerospatiale		1002	TC-ANA	18928	N88ZL	19262	VP-BNA	22600	HZ-MIS
Corvette		1053	D-ADNA	19000	904	19282	VP-CMN	22620	N902WG
01	wo	1086	F-OHJX	19248	wfu	19318	N727VJ	22628	VP-CBA
1	wfu	1124	F-OHJY	19443	902	19392	N503MG	23036	K2412
2	wfu	1157	MM62174	19498	wfu	19394	J2-KBA	23037	K2413
3	wfu	1202	EP-AGB	19623	wfu	19399	wfu	23059	60201
4	wfu	1212	VP-CVX	19624	A20-624	19402	D2-EVG	23152	85101
5	CN-TDE	1256	CS-TLU	19627	wfu	19403	D2-EVD	23465	N736BP
6	wfu	1335	A7-HHJ	19629	wfu	19520	wfu	23466	N733PA
7	F-BVPK	1468	0001	19635	68-19635	19535	N766JS	23468	N370BC
8	F-GJAS	1485	F-RBFA	19716	FAC-1201	19620	P4-JLD	23800	N253DV
9	wfu	1556	F-RBFB	19739	wo	19818	wfu	23976	N37NY
10	wfu	1589	VP-CIE	19840	2401	19835	N706JP	24081	5R-MRM
11	F-GKGA	1656	A7-CJA	19866	68-19866	19854	N40	24095	TP-02
12	F-GMOF	1727	D-APAC	19969	wfu	19859	C-FPXD	24220	N788LS
13	F-GFDH	1795	MM62209	19988	K2899	19892	3D-KMJ	24480	wo
14	wfu	1880	D-APAD	19997	wfu	19893	wfu	24804	N737DX
15	wfu	1886	VP-CAN	19998	wfu	19895	wfu	24866	HS-HRH
16	5R-MBR	1908	60221	20000	wfu	20045	N800AK	24970	C-FPHS
17	YV-572CP	1947	D-APAA	20025	D2-MAN	20046	VP-BDJ	25502	B-4018
18	wfu	1955	D-APAB	20028	wo	20111	wfu	25503	B-4019
19	EC-HIA	1999	VH-VHD	20060	T 17-1	20115	N908JE	25504	AP-BEH
20	wfu	2046	9K-AKD	20062	wfu	20228	wfu	25996	RP-C4007
21	wo	2165	HZ-XY7	20110	4X-JYQ	20327	N727PN	27426	FAP 356
22	wo	2192	P4-ARL	20375	wfu	20371	VP-CJN	27456	N368CE
23	wfu	2263	2101	20457	wo	20489	VP-CKA	27906	HS-CMV
24	wfu	2341	A7-CJB	20629	4X-JYB	20512	N311AG	27924	OE-ITA
25	wfu	2403	VP-CMS	20715	D2-TPR	20523	LV-JTD	28081	B-4020
26	wfu	2421	VP-CCJ	20721	4X-JYH	20533	VP-BIF	28082	B-4021
27	wo	2440	I-ECJA	20919	N707KN	20641	N7270B	28630	RA-73000
28	F-GPLA	2487	4K-AZ01	21049	TZ-TAC	20646	N727NY	28866	921
29	wo	2507	MM62243	21081	wfu	21010	wfu	29979	165829
30	F-GLEC	2550	G-NMAK	21096	4X-JYV	21068	N777KY	29980	165830
31	F-GJAP	2566	A40-AA	21103	wo	21091	6V-AEF	30181	N737A
32	F-GILM	2592	UN-A1901	21104	wfu	21460	HZ-SKI	30182	N738A
33	OY-SBT	2650	VT-VJM	21228	5A-DAK	21595	VP-CZY	30183	N739A
34	5R-MHK	2675	VP-BEY	21261	N707QJ	21636	TJ-AAM	30184	N743A
35	wfu	2706	VP-BEX	21334	4X-JY.	21824	A9C-BA	30185	N745A
36	wfu	2748	N3618F	21367	T 17-3	21853	TZ-NBA	30200	165831
37	wo	2801	2801	21396	1001	21948	N31TR	30781	165832
38	5A-DCK	2837	VT-IAH	21956	N707JU	22044	5T-CJP	32597	165833
39	CN-THL	2910	HB-IPP	727		22359	N169KT	32598	165834
40	wfu	2921	P4-VNL	18252	wfu	22362	HZ-AB3	33826	165835
Airbus		2935	B-6165	18253	wfu	22430	XT-BFA	34303	HB-JJA
Airbus ACJ		2949	9M-NAA	18360	wfu	22543	4K-8888	34304	166693
004	HZ-124	3046	OE-LGS	18362	wfu	22661	3505	*747*	
009	JY-ABH	3073	D-AIFR	18363	wfu	22662	3506	21648	VP-BAT
026	A7-HHK	3085	3085	18365	N727EC	22687	N721MF	21649	A9C-HMH
046	V8-BKH	3133	P4-MIS	18366	S9-SVE	22825	5N-FGN	21652	HZ-HM1B
061	SU-GGG	3238	VP-CKS	18368	P4-MMG	22968	HZ-HR3	21785	A40-SO
151	5A-ONE	3243	VP-CBN	18370	N25AZ	*737*		21786	70-YMN
204	HZ-HMS	3260	OE-IAC	18371	9Q-CMC	19600	wfu	21961	VP-BLK
344	9K-AHI	3333	D-AIMM	18894	wfu	19601	PK-OCF	21962	wfu
354	TS-IAY	**Boeing**		18908	3503	19605	N165W	21963	P4-FSH
367	CA-02	*707*		18909	3504	19613	wfu	21992	N747FU
372	CA-01	17606	wfu	18912	3501	19772	N772WH	22750	HZ-AIJ
374	wfu	17634	wfu	18933	3D-BOE	20127	wo	23070	HZ-HM1A
431	HZ-NSA	17644	wfu	18934	9Q-CDC	20335	PK-OCG	23610	A9C-HAK
446	15001	17652	wfu	18935	N113	20483	K3187	23824	82-8000
473	A7-AAF	17696	wfu	18936	N67JR	20484	K3186	23825	92-9000
487	A7-HJJ	17697	wo	18970	PK-VBA	20689	N5175U	24730	20-1101
495	A7-HHH	17699	wfu	18990	XT-BBE	20690	wfu	24731	20-1102
498	10+21	17700	wfu	18998	N30MP	20691	N5294E	25880	HZ-WBT3
499	10+22	17702	90-CLK	19006	HZ-MBA	20692	N5176Y	26426	V8-ALI
550	T 22-1	17905	wfu	19121	N724CL	20693	N5177C	26903	A6-HRM
551	T 22-2	18067	wfu	19123	VP-BAA	20694	N5294M	26906	A6-MMM
591	60202	18084	wfu	19139	3D-JNM	21069	N583CC	28551	A6-UAE
605	A7-HHM	18334	CN-ANS	19148	P4-FLY	21165	VC96-2115	28961	A6-YAS
648	9K-ALD	18338	wfu	19149	N400RG	21166	VC96-2116	32445	A40-OMN
667	A7-AFE	18339	wfu	19176	3D-...	21167	0207	33684	A9C-HMK
779	VP-CCC	18375	wfu	19252	N727GG	21317	EP-AGA	*757*	
863	3B-TSL	18586	wfu	19253	wfu	21499	5U-BAG	22176	N757BJ
910	A6-ESH	18740	N707JT	19254	VP-BAB	21957	VP-CHK	22690	TP-01
927	A7-AAG	18757	T 17-2	19260	VP-BAP	22050	P4-OMC	23454	UN-B5701
		18926	903	19261	N727AH	22431	N787WH	24527	HB-IEE

24923	N756AF	30884	A6-DFR	45844	N949L	9060	EC-IBD	9141	VP-BOW
25155	N757AF	32438	VP-BHN	47011	N814RW	9061	ZS-ESA	9142	VP-BSC
25220	N770BB	32450	A6-MRM	47151	VR-CKO	9062	N801PN	9143	VH-TGG
25487	T-01	32451	HZ-102	47152	N166DE	9063	N933EY	9144	N6VB
25495	HZ-HMED	32575	PR-BBS	47514	N947ML	9064	N264A	9145	HB-JEX
26240	N801DM	32627	ZS-RSA	47595	MM62012	9065	N704MF	9146	EC-JIL
26633	NZ7571	32628	N7600K	47600	wo	9066	N823DF	9147	P4-VVF
26634	NZ7572	32774	P4-KAZ	47635	N880DP	9067	N67RX	9148	N889JA
28463	N757MA	32775	N90R	47691	wo	9068	N700BX	9149	N456MS
29025	98-0001	32777	OE-ILX	49670	N143G	9069	N1868M	9150	N488CH
29026	98-0002	32805	HZ-101	49725	N945MA	9070	N34U	9151	C-FBOC
29027	99-0003	32806	VP-CBB	49767	VP-CNI	9071	D-ADNB	9152	N605VF
29028	99-0004	32807	HL7770	49768	N287KB	9072	N983J	9153	N120AK
767		32825	A6-HEH	49778	N948MA	9073	N338TP	9154	N555EF
22567	VP-CME	32915	VP-BZL	**DC-10**		9074	N399GS	9155	N711LS
25537	V8-MHB	32916	01-0015	46501	N220AU	9075	N316GS	9156	N1DG
27254	VP-BKS	32970	VP-BRT	**MD-11**		9076	LX-VIP	9157	VP-BAM
27255	N804MS	32971	N371BC	48532	HZ-HM7	9077	N520E	9158	C-GPPI
28270	N767KS	33010	N720MM	48533	HZ-AFAS	9078	N85D	9159	D-ATNR
32954	UN-B6701	33036	N888YF	**Bombardier**		9079	VH-VGX	9160	N47
33425	P4-MES	33079	EW-001PA	*Gl-Ex/5000/Sentinel*		9080	N125CH*	9161	VP-BWB
33685	N767A	33080	01-0041	9001	N901GX	9081	F-GVML	9162	N2T
777		33102	N108MS	9002	N711MN	9082	JA006G	9163	OY-ILG
29271	N777AS	33361	N737M	9003	C-FBDR	9083	VP-CEB	9164	N376G
29953	VP-BRH	33367	3C-EGE	9004	N115HK	9084	EC-KKN	9165	VP-BOS
BBJ/BBJ2		33405	HZ-MF1	9005	N618WF*	9085	N404VL	9166	N1990C
28579	N367G	33434	02-0203	9006	N161WC	9086	HB-INJ	9167	HB-JGY
28581	N43PR*	33473	A6-AUH	9007	EC-IUQ	9087	N360LA	9168	OE-INC
28976	VP-BRM	33474	N378BC	9008	N917R	9088	C-GNCB	9169	M-XXRS*
29024	N50TC	33499	HZ-MF2	9009	N980GG	9089	EC-IFS	9170	D-AAAZ
29054	N500LS	33500	02-0042	9010	N701WH	9090	N18TM	9171	VP-CGO
29102	N772BC	33542	N358BJ	9011	HB-IHQ	9091	N1FE	9172	N729KF
29135	N737CC	33962	06-001	9012	N70PS	9092	N799WW	9173	HB-JEY
29136	N737GG	34260	5N-FGT	9013	LX-GEX	9093	VP-CDF	9174	HB-JRS
29139	VP-BEL	34477	VT-SRS	9014	XA-NGS	9094	EC-KJH	9175	N117TF
29142	N737WH	34620	VP-CSK	9015	HB-JEN	9095	N97DQ	9176	N720WS
29149	TS-IOO	34622	P4-RUS	9016	N309ES	9096	M48-02	9177	N528JR
29188	HZ-TAA	34683	N2121	9017	HB-JER	9097	N902MM	9178	C-GDPG
29200	N742PB	34807	05-0730	9018	PR-VDR	9098	N100VR	9179	HL7748
29233	N66ZB	34808	05-0932	9019	N203JE	9099	OE-IEL	9180	N818FH
29251	A6-HRS	34809	05-4613	9020	VP-BEN	9100	N1SA	9181	N302AK
29268	A6-AIN	34865	VP-CLR	9021	N8VB	9101	VP-BOK	9182	OE-IFG
29269	A6-RJZ	35238	A6-MRS	9022	N393BZ	9102	VP-CGS	9183	N821AM
29272	FAC-0001	35478	55-555	9023	N324SM	9103	N122BN	9184	HL7749
29273	VP-BBJ	35959	VP-BNZ	9024	N287Z	9104	N889CP	9185	N1955M
29274	M53-01	35977	N888AQ	9025	N616DC	9105	N500E	9186	OY-FIT
29317	VP-BWR	35990	N737DB	9026	N70EW	9106	OE-IRP	9187	N54SL
29441	N88WR	36027	N111NB	9027	N305CC	9107	ZJ690	9188	F-HFBY
29749	N888TY	36090	N111VM	9028	VP-BSE	9108	N100ES	9189	LX-GJM
29791	P4-TBN	36106	K....	9029	N5UU	9109	N700KS	9190	PR-XDN
29857	A6-RJY	36107	K....	9030	VP-BYY	9110	N906JW	9191	N6D
29858	A6-DAS	36108	N372BJ	9031	N724AF	9111	VT-DHA	9192	N700LK
29865	A6-RJX	36493	N493AG	9032	OY-MSI	9112	C-GBLX	9193	VP-BVG
29866	N720CH	36714	VP-BFT	9033	N600AK	9113	N8762M	9194	N313RF
29971	01-0040	36756	N529PP	9034	JA005G	9114	N999YY	9195	N4T
29972	VP-BYA	36852	N730MM	9035	N838SC	9115	VP-BEB	9196	VP-CRC
30031	VP-CEC	**DC-8**		9036	VP-BEM	9116	N320GX	9197	LX-PAK
30070	N889NC	45280	wfu	9037	N400GX	9117	N917GL	9198	HB-JRR
30076	VP-BBW	45570	F-RAFE	9038	N20EG	9118	N904DS	9199	N379G
30139	3701	45658	wfu	9039	N90EW	9119	XA-OVR	9200	G-LXRS
30295	HB-IIR	45819	F-RAFC	9040	N228H	9120	N887WS	9201	N205EL
30327	N127QS	45984	FAP 371	9041	N887WM	9121	N711MC	9202	F-GVMV
30328	N164RJ	46013	N721CX	9042	N170SW	9122	ZS-GJB	9203	N200A
30329	N129QS	46043	F-ZVMT	9043	N416BD	9123	ZJ691	9204	LX-ZAK
30330	HB-JGV	46053	TR-LTZ	9044	OE-IGS	9124	N700GB	9205	N100A
30496	N737AG	46067	HB-IGH	9045	N17GX	9125	N711SX	9206	N343DF
30547	N79711	46071	5V-TGF	9046	N1TS	9126	A7-AAM	9207	N723AB
30572	N835BA	46078	FAP 370	9047	N410WW	9127	C-GERS	9208	EC-KFS
30751	N888NY	46081	N728A	9048	N4GX	9128	N38WF*	9209	N171JJ
30752	HB-IIQ	46084	HZ-HM11	9049	N949GP	9129	N725LB	9210	N190H
30753	02-0202	46111	VP-BHM	9050	N502JL	9130	4X-COI	9211	C-GXPR
30754	N737ER	46130	F-RAFF	9051	N421AL	9131	ZJ692	9212	N13JS
30755	02-0201	**DC-9/MD80 Series**		9052	N620K	9132	ZJ693	9213	D-AEKT
30756	N836BA	45706	N13FE	9053	N53GX	9133	LX-AAA	9214	VT-JSK
30772	N315TS	45731	N120NE	9054	HB-IKZ	9134	N451CS	9215	N94ZZ
30782	N800KS	45732	N813TL	9055	N449ML	9135	ZJ694	9216	N900LS
30789	N349BA	45740	N305PA	9056	N421SZ	9136	P4-AAA	9217	N700LS
30790	A36-002	45775	N900SA	9057	VP-BDU	9137	C-GCDS	9218	N86TW
30791	LX-GVV	45797	N8860	9058	N79AD	9138	N51SE	9219	N611VT
30829	A36-001	45826	N229DE	9059	N18WZ	9139	OY-CVS	9220	P4-CBA
						9140	N50DS	9221	N10SL

9222	N81ZZ	23-026	wfu	24-060	XA-ADJ	24-177	wfu	24D-258	N424RS
9223	VP-BAH	23-027	wfu	24-065	N707SC	24-178	wfu	24D-259	wfu
9224	N224GX	23-028	wfu	24-087	wfu	24-179	wfu	24D-260	XC-AGU
9225	N36LG	23-028A	wo	24A-096	N464CL	24-180	XA-NLA	24D-261	wfu
9226	A6-DHG	23-029	wfu	24A-100	wo	24B-181	N426TA	24D-262	wfu
9227	M-LLGC	23-030	wfu	24-101	N24WX	24B-182	RP-C2324	24D-263	wo
9228	N289Z	23-032	wo	24A-102	wo	24B-183	wfu	24XR-264	RP-C1747
9229	N84ZZ	23-033	wfu	24-103	XB-ADR	24B-184	N58FN	24XR-265	wo
9230	A7-GEY	23-034	wfu	24-104	N45ED	24B-185	wfu	24D-266	N266TW
9231	VP-CAU	23-035	N992TD	24-105	wfu	24B-186	wfu	24XR-267	ZS-OEA
9232	C-FJMX	23-036	N123MJ	24-106	C-FNMC	24B-187	wfu	24D-268	N24TK
9233	N233FJ	23-037	XC-LGD	24A-107	N48L	24B-188	N280R	24D-269	XA-DIJ
9234	N234GX	23-038	wfu	24-108	wfu	24B-189	wfu	24D-270	wo
9235	C-FLLA	23-039	N121CK	24-109	XA-NLK	24B-190	N600XJ	24D-271	XA-SCE
9236	C-FLLF	23-040	wfu	24A-110	wo	24B-191	wfu	24D-272	N117K
9237	OH-PPS	23-041	wfu	24A-111	wfu	24B-192	wo	24D-273	XB-DZR
9238	C-FLLN	23-042	wfu	24-112	XA-TRQ	24B-193	N193DB	24XR-274	N48CT
9239	N71ZZ	23-044	wo	24-113	wfu	24B-194	N2093A	24D-275	PT-LPH
9240	C-FLLV	23-045	wfu	24-114	wfu	24B-195	N555LJ	24D-276	N56PT
9241	N941TS	23-045A	wo	24-115	wfu	24B-196	N196TB	24D-277	N277TW
9242	N375G	23-046	wo	24A-116	N105GA	24B-197	N89ES	24D-278	N202JS
9243	OE-IMA	23-047	wfu	24XR-117	N24SA	24B-198	N39KM	24D-279	N955EA
9244	C-FLTI	23-048	wfu	24-118	wo	24B-199	XA-TTT	24XR-280	wfu
9245	N200ES	23-049	N605NA	24-119	wfu	24B-200	wfu	24D-281	wfu
9246	VP-BNX	23-050A	wo	24-120	wfu	24B-201	wfu	24D-282	wo
9247	C-FMFN	23-052	N856JB	24-121	wo	24B-202	N333RY	24XR-283	XA-UHT
9248	C-FMFO	23-053	wfu	24-122	wo	24B-203	N203JL	24D-284	PT-JKQ
9249	C-FMGE	23-054	N351N	24-123	N25LJ	24B-204	wfu	24XR-285	N300TJ
9250	C-FMGK	23-056	wo	24-124	N991TD	24B-205	N64CE	24XR-286	wo
9251	N73ZZ	23-057	wfu	24A-125	N651LJ	24B-206	N24YA	24D-287	wo
9252	C-FMKZ	23-058	N153AG	24-126	N16HC	24XR-207	ZS-MGJ	24D-288	N7701L
9253	C-FMLB	23-059	wfu	24-127	N124JL	24B-208	XA-AAA	24D-289	N98CG
9254	N754TS	23-061	wo	24-128	wfu	24B-209	ZS-LWU	24D-290	N88LJ
9255	C-FMLI	23-062	N20TA	24-129	wo	24B-210	wo	24D-291	N483DM
9256	C-FMLQ	23-063	wo	24-130	wfu	24B-211	N680CJ	24D-292	N888TW
9257	C-FMLT	23-064	N259DB	24-131	wfu	24B-212	N328JK	24D-293	N293MC
9258	C-FMLV	23-065A	wfu	24-132	wfu	24B-213	XA-...	24D-294	PT-WKL
9259	N89ZZ	23-066	XB-MYE	24-133	wfu	24B-214	wo	24XR-295	N295NW
9260	N74ZZ	23-067	wo	24-134	wfu	24XR-215	N400EP	24D-296	PT-LMS
9261	C-FMUI	23-068	N73CE	24-135	wo	24B-216	N900GG	24D-297	N24S
9262	C-FMUN	23-069	wo	24-136	wfu	24B-217	N876MC	24D-298	N169US
9264	C-FNDN	23-070	wfu	24-137	N151AG	24B-218	N101VS	24D-299	N299TW
9265	C-FNDK	23-071	wfu	24-138	N130RS	24B-219	ZS-TOY	24XR-300	wo
9266	N76ZZ	23-072	RP-C848	24-139	wfu	24B-220	wfu	24D-301	N249HP
9267	N78ZZ	23-073	N806LJ	24-140	wfu	24B-221	N233TW	24D-302	wo
9268	C-FNDT	23-074	wfu	24-141	wfu	24B-222	wfu	24D-303	wfu
9269	C-FNRP	23-075	wo	24-142	N723JW	24B-223	N7074X	24D-304	wfu
9270	C-FNRR	23-076	N83LJ	24-143	wfu	24B-224	XA-TCA	24D-305	N930PJ
9271	C-FNSN	23-077	wo	24-144	wo	24B-225	wo	24D-306	N306JA
9272	C-FNSV	23-078	wo	24-145	N282AC	24B-226	RP-C2424	24D-307	wo
9273	C-FNZZ	23-079	wfu	24-146	wo	24B-227	N27BJ	24D-308	XB-IRH
9274	C-FOAB	23-080	wo	24-147	N147CK	24B-228	wfu	24D-309	N80CK
9275	C-FOAD	23-081	wfu	24-148	N24ET	24B-229	wo	24D-310	wo
9276	C-FOKD	23-082	wfu			24B-230	XA-SSU	24D-311	N311LJ
9277	C-FOKF	23-082A	N618BR	24XR-150	wfu	24B-231	wfu	24D-312	N80AP
9278	C-FOKH	23-083	wfu	24-151	N6177Y	24D-232	wo	24D-313	wo
9279	C-FOKJ	23-084	N119BA	24-152	wfu	24XR-233	N19LJ	24D-314	wo
Learjet 23		23-085	wo	24-153	N120RA	24D-234	LV-JTZ	24D-315	wfu
23-001	wo	23-086	wo	24-154	wo	24XR-235	N701SC	24D-316	LV-LRC
23-002	wfu	23-088	wo	24-155	wfu	24D-236	N59AL	24D-317	XA-JIQ
23-003	N3BL	23-089	wfu	24-156	LZ-VTS	24D-237	N237TW	24D-318	N611DB
23-004	wfu	23-090	wo	24-157	N157TW	24D-238	N48FN	24XR-319	N174RD
23-005	wfu	23-091	wfu	24-158	PT-WEW	24D-239	wo	24D-320	N996TD
23-006	wfu	23-092	N415LJ	24-159	N710TV	24D-240	wfu	24D-321	N33TP
23-007	wo	23-093	N7GF	24-160	N989TL	24D-241	N63GA	24D-322	N322RS
23-008	wfu	23-094	wo	24-161	N222TW	24D-242	N999WA	24D-323	wfu
23-009	N23BY	23-095	N46452	24-162	wfu	24XR-243	N929MC	24D-324	N324TW
23-010	wfu	23-097	wfu	24-163	wfu	24D-244	wo	24D-325	N500SW
23-013	wo	23-098	wfu	24-164	wfu	24D-245	N275E	24D-326	N322AU
23-014	wfu	23-099	wfu	24-165	ZS-KJY	24D-246	N400MS	24D-327	N711PC
23-015A	wo	**Learjet 24**		24-166	N993TD	24D-247	wfu	24D-328	wfu
23-016	wfu	24A-011	N24LG	24-167	N664CL	24D-248	wo	24E-329	N24FW
23-017	wo	24A-012	N1965L	24-168	N333TW	24D-249	N440KT	24E-330	N330TW
23-018	wo	24-015	wfu	24-169	wfu	24D-250	0006	24E-331	N32DD
23-020	N820L	24-019	N747SC	24-170	N151WW	24D-251	N39EL	24F-332	N56MM
23-021	wo	24A-031	N175FS	24-171	N417WW	24D-252	N157AG	24E-333	PT-LQK
23-022	wfu	24-043	wfu	24-172	wfu	24D-253	wo	24E-334	N944KM
23-023	wfu	24-050	N24NJ	24-173	wfu	24D-254	wfu	24E-335	N2DD
23-024	wfu	24-051	wfu	24-174	XA-LNK	24D-255	N255AR	24F-336	N49GS
23-025	wfu	24-055	N711CW	24-175	wfu	24D-256	wfu	24F-337	XA-DET
				24-176	wfu	24D-257	N888FA	24E-338	wfu

24E-339	N207RG	25C-061	YV-203CP	25B-147	XA-GGG	25D-228	wfu	25D-309	XA-PAZ
24E-340	N627JJ	25-062	N21FN	25XR-148	N98RS	25D-229	N890BJ	25D-310	N211JC
24E-341	N14DM	25-063	N25FM	25B-149	N239CA	25D-230	N207HF	25D-311	N199BT
24F-342	N123DG	25-064	wfu	25B-150	N150CK	25D-231	N531CW	25D-312	XC-HIS
24E-343	N7EJ	25C-070	wfu	25B-151	wo	25D-232	N264TW	25D-313	N251AL
24F-344	wo	25C-071	LV-ZTH	25XR-152	N105BA	25D-233	N947TC	25D-314	N305AR
24E-345	N217JS	25C-072	wo	25B-153	wo	25D-234	N764KF	25D-315	XA-ASP
24E-346	XB-JXZ	25XR-073	wo	25B-154	N82TS	25XR-235	N400VC	25D-316	N17AH
24E-347	N508SR	25B-074	wo	25B-155	PT-LEA	25D-236	XC-RPP	25D-317	N35DL
24E-348	wo	25B-075	N307HF	25C-156	N75BL	25D-237	wo	25D-318	wo
24F-349	XB-DZD	25B-076	XA-SJS	25B-157	N50CK	25D-238	N41NK	25D-319	N712DP
24F-350	N500ZA	25B-077	wo	25B-158	N924BW	25D-239	N499EH	25D-320	N690JC
24E-351	N77MR	25B-078	N778GM	25B-159	wo	25D-240	N33PT	25D-321	N25AM
24F-352	N352MD	25XR-079	XA-AVV	25B-160	ZS-MTD	25D-241	N213CA	25D-322	5N-AOC
24F-353	wo	25B-080	wfu	25B-161	N236CA	25D-242	N242GS	25D-323	PT-LMM
24F-354	ZS-FUN	25B-081	N524DW	25XR-162	N150RS	25D-243	wo	25D-324	N970WJ
24E-355	N165CM	25B-082	N62DM	25B-163	N911AJ	25D-244	N125PT	25D-325	XB-GCP
24F-356	PT-LKD	25C-083	N54FN	25B-164	N23RZ	25D-245	N606GB	25D-326	N25NB
24F-357	N129ME	25C-084	N777TX	25C-165	wo	25XR-246	wo	25D-327	N444TG
Learjet 25		25B-085	wfu	25B-166	N166PC	25D-247	wfu	25D-328	XB-JLU
25-001	wfu	25B-086	N65WH	25B-167	C-GBFP	25D-248	N248CK	25D-329	N401DP
25-002	wfu	25C-087	wfu	25B-168	N88BY	25D-249	N34TN	25D-330	N330L
25-003	N97FN	25B-088	wo	25B-169	XA-KKK	25D-250	N127BH	25D-331	N657BM
25-004	N225KA	25C-089	PT-IIQ	25B-170	wo	25D-251	N85TW	25D-332	XA-AFH
25-005	N39CK	25B-090	C-FPUB	25B-171	N401AJ	25D-252	N444MK	25D-333	N555SD
25-006	XA-...	25B-091	N91PN	25C-172	wo	25D-253	N69PL	25D-334	XB-JKK
25-007	N726WR	25B-092	N80EL	25XR-173	XA-JSC	25D-254	N76AX	25D-335	PT-LUZ
25-008	XA-MUU	25B-093	PT-LEN	25B-174	N16KK	25D-255	N219RB	25D-336	XA-JYL
25-009	wo	25C-094	wo	25XR-175	N127GB	25D-256	N75CK	25G-337	XA-...
25-010	wfu	25B-095	N2094L	25C-176	PT-LLN	25D-257	N988AS	25D-338	N4447P
25-011	N525TW	25B-096	XA-...	25B-177	wo	25D-258	wo	25D-339	AMT-202
25-012	wfu	25C-097	N79EV*	25B-178	wo	25D-259	wo	25D-340	N891P
25-013	wo	25C-098	ZS-NYG	25B-179	C-GSKL	25D-260	N80PJ	25D-341	N58HC
25-014	wfu	25C-099	wo	25B-180	N102VS	25D-261	N261WC	25D-342	N25PW
25-015	XA-LLL	25B-100	N829AA	25C-181	N100NB	25D-262	wo	25D-343	N456CG
25-016	wfu	25B-101	N47MR	25B-182	N99MC	25D-263	XA-YYY	25D-344	wo
25-017	N53FL	25B-102	N325SJ	25B-183	N83CK	25D-264	N547JG	25D-345	LV-WLG
25-018	wfu	25B-103	wo	25B-184	wo	25D-265	N265TW	25D-346	XA-ZZZ
25-019	wo	25B-104	N104WJ	25B-185	N606SM	25D-266	wo	25D-347	N203VS
25-020	N76CK	25B-105	N25WJ	25B-186	wo	25D-267	N15ER	25D-348	N988AA
25-021	wfu	25XR-106	wo	25B-187	N187CA	25D-268	N268WC	25D-349	wo
25XR-022	ZS-SSM	25B-107	N252BK	25B-188	wo	25D-269	LV-WOC	25D-350	N648JW
25-023	N147TW	25C-108	wo	25B-189	N67HB	25D-270	N75AX	25D-351	N21NW
25-024	N20RZ	25B-109	wfu	25B-190	N190AR	25D-271	wo	25G-352	N125JW
25-025	N110RA	25B-110	LV-...	25B-191	wo	25D-272	N520SR	25D-353	N43DR
25-026	N25EC	25B-111	N45BS	25B-192	FAB 008	25D-273	N73DJ	25D-354	N515TC
25-027	wfu	25B-112	N279LE	25B-193	XA-WWW	25D-274	XA-FMR	25D-355	LV-WRE
25-028	N727LJ	25C-113	wo	25B-194	XC-NSP	25D-275	N254CL	25D-356	N62DK
25XR-029	N107HF	25B-114	XA-VMC	25B-195	wfu	25D-276	XA-UUU	25D-357	LV-WXY
25-030	wo	25C-115	PT-ISO	25B-196	wo	25D-277	N9RA	25D-358	N37971
25-031	N294NW	25B-116	wo	25B-197	N197CF	25D-278	wfu	25D-359	XA-LRJ
25-032	wfu	25B-117	wfu	25B-198	N198JA	25D-279	N81AX	25D-360	N360JG
25-033	wfu	25B-118	N818CK	25XR-199	wo	25D-280	N280C	25D-361	XA-TYW
25-034	wfu	25B-119	wo	25B-200	wfu	25D-281	N800RF	25D-362	N107RM
25-035	N616NA	25B-120	XA-AJL	25B-201	N251TS	25D-282	XA-...	25D-363	N197LS
25-036	N45BK	25B-121	N8005Y	25B-202	N343CA	25D-283	N444WW	25D-364	XA-TIE
25-037	wfu	25B-122	XA-...	25B-203	N344CA	25D-284	N284TJ	25D-365	XA-SJN
25-038	N130CK	25B-123	N688GS	25B-204	wo	25D-285	wfu	25D-366	XA-SOH
25-039	N273CA	25B-124	XA-ALV	25D-205	Z3-BAA	25D-286	wfu	25D-367	N4488W
25-040	N238CA	25B-125	N10VG	25D-206	ZS-LXH	25D-287	wfu	25D-368	N368D
25-041	N31AA	25C-126	N14FN	25D-207	wfu	25D-288	N100WN	25D-369	XB-JJS
25-042	wfu	25B-127	N225LC	25D-208	N188CA	25D-289	XA-TWH	25G-370	wfu
25-043	wfu	25B-128	wo	25D-209	N30LJ	25D-290	N600GM	25G-371	N72WC
25-044	wo	25C-129	N25MT	25D-210	N764RH	25D-291	N453MA	25D-372	N722EM
25-045	wfu	25B-130	N26AT	25D-211	FAB 010	25D-292	N604AS	25D-373	XA-ACX
25-046	N345MC	25C-131	wo	25D-212	wfu	25D-293	XA-PIU	Learjet 28	
25-047	N222B	25B-132	wo	25D-213	N910JB	25D-294	wfu	28-001	N128LR
25-048	N48GR	25B-133	N233CA	25D-214	N56MD	25D-295	XB-MYG	28-002	XC-VSA
25-049	N70SK	25B-134	N65A	25D-215	N25UJ	25D-296	PT-OHD	28-003	N800GA
25-050	N999MF	25B-135	N50RW	25D-216	XA-...	25D-297	N389AT	28-004	N43PJ
25-051	N76UM	25B-136	N48WA	25D-217	N217WM	25D-298	N242PF	28-005	N500LG
25-052	N692FG	25B-137	N752EA	25D-218	wfu	25D-299	N299MW	Learjet 29	
25-053	wo	25B-138	wfu	25XR-219	XA-MCC	25D-300	N108FL	29-001	XC-IST
25-054	N25MD	25XR-139	N111MP	25XR-220	N969AR	25D-301	N82AX	29-002	XB-JHV
25-055	wfu	25B-140	N140CA	25D-221	N147CA	25D-302	N881P	29-003	VT-EHS
25XR-056	PT-LBW	25XR-141	ZS-BXR	25XR-222	N134WE	25D-303	XA-JOC	29-004	VT-EIH
25-057	N507HF	25B-142	N49WA	25D-223	wo	25D-304	N25NY	Learjet 31	
25-058	N273LR	25B-143	N143CK	25D-224	XB-AZD	25D-305	XA-TAQ	31-001	wfu
25-059	wo	25B-144	wo	25D-225	wfu	25D-306	XC-GUB	31-002	N322TS
25-060	N564CL	25B-145	N145SH	25D-226	N90LJ	25D-307	LV-OEL	31-003	N888CP
		25C-146	I-BMFE	25D-227	N25RE	25D-308	N727LM		

31-004	XA-ZTH	31A-081	LV-YMB	31A-162	ES-PVH	**Learjet 35**		35A-080	N17AZ
31-005	PR-AVM	31A-082	N727BT	31A-163	N431DA	35-001	N351GL	35A-081	N81FR
31-006	C-GKMS	31A-083	N789SR	31A-164	N164SB	35-002	C-GVVA	35A-082	N700SJ
31-007	PT-LXX	31A-084	N840SW	31A-165	N808W	35-003	N111WB	35A-083	N581PH
31-008	wo	31A-085	N321GL	31A-166	PR-GBN	35-004	C-GIRE	35A-084	N903AL
31-009	N38MG	31A-086	N1BR	31A-167	I-CFLY	35-005	N178CP	35A-085	N15WH
31-010	N89HB	31A-087	N535PS	31A-168	PP-CTA	35-006	N39FN	35A-086	N860S
31-011	D-CTWO	31A-088	N500JE	31A-169	N197PH	35-007	N357RM	35A-087	N18AX
31-012	XA-TUL	31A-089	N77PY	31A-170	ZS-OML	35-008	PP-ERR	35A-088	N72JF
31-013	PT-XTA	31A-090	N78PR	31A-171	N31MW	35-009	N335AT	35A-089	D-CCHB
31-014	N5VG	31A-091	V5-NAG	31A-172	N312CC	35-010	N35AJ	35A-090	N88BG
31-015	N260LF	31A-092	N711FG	31A-173	N173LC	35-011	N531AJ	35A-091	N37FA
31-016	N1DE	31A-093	N716BD	31A-174	AMT-201	35-012	XA-SVX	35A-092	N73CK
31-017	N801CT	31A-094	N36BL	31A-175	N31WU	35-013	N535TA	35A-093	PT-LOT
31-018	N90BA	31A-095	N395LJ	31A-176	N176WS	35-014	N844L	35A-094	N94AF
31-019	N19LT	31A-096	N37BM	31A-177	N569SC	35-015	N354PM	35A-095	N66KK
31-020	XA-...	31A-097	N31LJ	31A-178	N178NP	35-016	VP-CLT	35A-096	N94RL
31-021	XA-CYA	31A-098	N200KB	31A-179	XA-...	35-017	N600DT	35A-097	N108RB
31-022	N331N	31A-099	N1932K	31A-180	N1926S	35-018	wfu	35A-098	N72DA
31-023	PR-SFA	31A-100	PR-SCB	31A-181	N418DL	35-019	N750RM	35A-099	wo
31-024	N731GA	31A-101	N79BJ	31A-182	N399RW	35-020	wo	35A-100	C-GRFO
31-025	I-AIRW	31A-102	C-GHJJ	31A-183	LV-BFE	35A-021	N220NJ	35A-101	N751AC
31-026	N706SA	31A-103	N407RA	31A-184	N931RS	35-022	N90WR	35A-102	wo
31-027	N2FU	31A-104	N631CC	31A-185	N31MJ	35-023	N443RK	35A-103	PT-LCD
31-028	N90WA	31A-105	N109HV	31A-186	N45PD	35-024	N411BA	35A-104	wo
31-029	XB-FKT	31A-106	N531TS	31A-187	N932FD	35-025	N435UJ	35A-105	N444WB
31-030	XA-JYC	31A-107	N213AR	31A-188	N70AY	35-026	N89TC	35A-106	wo
31-031	N93SK	31A-108	N288FF	31A-189	N158R	35-027	N31WS	35A-107	wo
31-032	XA-BRG	31A-109	N728CL*	31A-190	N8TG	35-028	TP-104	35A-108	D-CJPG
31-033	N407BS	31A-110	PT-WIV	31A-191	OE-GTA	35-029	wo	35A-109	wfu
31-033A	N990GC	31A-111	N420LJ	31A-192	N531RA	35-030	N542PA	35A-110	N4J
31-033B	wo	31A-112	LX-PCT	31A-193	N129JD*	35-031	N233CC	35A-111	D-CONE
31-033C	N55VR	31A-113	N131GG	31A-194	N29SN	35-032	N710GS	35A-112	N354JC*
31-033D	N157JS	31A-114	N524HC	31A-195	N134CG	35-033	N524PA	35A-113	N684HA
31-034	CS-DDZ	31A-115	ZS-NYV	31A-196	N1JM	35-034	N37TA	35A-114	wo
31A-035	N3VJ	31A-116	N31UJ	31A-197	N20XP	35-035	N92TS	35A-115	wo
31A-036	N127VL	31A-117	N517CC	31A-198	N500MP	35-036	N90AH	35A-116	N58CW
31A-037	PT-OVZ	31A-118	N815E	31A-199	N901P	35-037	N333KC	35A-117	N78MC
31A-038	N500WR	31A-119	N996JS	31A-200	N599CT	35-038	C-FBFP	35A-118	N118FN
31A-039	N71AL	31A-120	C-GHJU	31A-201	N32HH	35-039	N382TC	35A-119	N549PA
31A-040	N55VY	31A-121	N121LJ	31A-202	ZS-AJD	35-040	wo	35A-120	N400JE
31A-041	RP-C8822	31A-122	PT-WLO	31A-203	OD-PWC	35-041	N41NW	35A-121	N752AC
31A-042	D-CURT	31A-123	N23VG	31A-204	N204RT	35-042	XA-FFF	35A-122	N27TT
31A-043	N531SK	31A-124	N931FD	31A-205	N71FB	35-043	N575WW	35A-123	N900BJ
31A-044	XA-OLE	31A-125	N125FS	31A-206	N79SE	35-044	N130F	35A-124	C-GTJL
31A-045	YU-BRZ	31A-126	N100BL	31A-207	D-CSIE	35-045	N1140A	35A-125	N351EF
31A-046	N352EF	31A-127	N54HT	31A-208	N227KT	35-046	N58EM	35A-126	N15EH
31A-047	N39TW	31A-128	N365GL	31A-209	N428BB	35A-047	N701AS	35A-127	N800VL*
31A-048	N864KB	31A-129	N115BX	31A-210	N927DJ	35-048	N8040A	35A-128	N39PJ
31A-049	N131TT	31A-130	N31PV	31A-211	N5NC	35-049	LV-ZZF	35A-129	XA-ZAP
31A-050	N38SK	31A-131	N319SC	31A-212	N481JJ	35-050	351	35A-130	N757AL
31A-051	N351AC	31A-132	N929JH	31A-213	D-CMRM	35-051	N2BA	35A-131	N155AM
31A-052	XA-TGM	31A-133	N314SG	31A-214	PR-PJD	35-052	wo	35A-132	N135AG
31A-053	N31FF	31A-134	N134LJ	31A-215	N786YA	35-053	N541PA	35A-133	N133EJ
31A-054	LV-BFG	31A-135	PT-WSB	31A-216	N999GH	35-054	N435MS	35A-134	N238JA
31A-055	N425M	31A-136	N47TR	31A-217	N110SE	35-055	N354LQ	35A-135	D-CFAX
31A-056	N56LF	31A-137	N459A	31A-218	N1ED	35-056	N645G	35A-136	T-22
31A-057	D-CSAP	31A-138	V5-NPC	31A-219	N518JG	35-057	C-GTDE	35A-137	N35TJ
31A-058	N825AC	31A-139	N229KD	31A-220	N54AP	35-058	wo	35A-138	N124ZT
31A-059	N31TK	31A-140	N977JP	31A-221	N68ES	35-059	wo	35A-139	D-CGFD
31A-060	N699CP	31A-141	XA-ARQ	31A-222	N14T	35-060	wo	35A-140	N40BD
31A-061	N261SC	31A-142	N698MM	31A-223	N501RS	35-061	N235EA	35A-141	N553V
31A-062	AP-BEK	31A-143	N122BX	31A-224	N411DJ	35-062	N31DP	35A-142	N815L
31A-063	N131LJ	31A-144	JA01CP	31A-225	N834AF	35-063	N80PG	35A-143	N20DK
31A-064	N444HC	31A-145	LV-BDM	31A-226	N7SN	35-064	N622RB*	35A-144	N56EM
31A-065	N64NB	31A-146	N218NB	31A-227	D-CGGG	35-065	N4358N	35A-145	VH-SLD
31A-066	PK-CAH	31A-147	N31GQ	31A-228	N955JS	35-066	352	35A-146	N351AS
31A-067	TG-AIR	31A-148	PT-XPP	31A-229	N229LJ	35A-067	N135FA	35A-147	N55F
31A-068	N131GR	31A-149	N685RC	31A-230	N556HD	35-068	N168TR	35A-148	wo
31A-069	N744N	31A-150	N595PA	31A-231	N712EJ	35-069	N48GP	35A-149	wo
31A-070	N370SC	31A-151	N31NF	31A-232	N68VP	35A-070	N50FN	35A-150	wo
31A-071	N271SC	31A-152	N517GC	31A-233	EI-MAX	35A-071	VH-ESW	35A-151	wfu
31A-072	N211RN	31A-153	N349HP*	31A-234	N376MB	35A-072	PR-MLA	35A-152	XA-WIN
31A-073	XA-ZYZ	31A-154	N154RT	31A-235	XA-UBI	35A-073	N536KN	35A-153	N573LR
31A-074	N131BR	31A-155	D-CPRO	31A-236	N57TS	35A-074	N351PJ	35A-154	N244RG
31A-075	N631SF	31A-156	N181PA	31a-237	N44LG	35A-075	SE-DHP	35A-155	N70AX
31A-076	N215TT	31A-157	N800CK	31A-238	N36UP	35A-076	N959SA	35A-156	N35WE
31A-077	PK-CAJ	31A-158	PR-LRJ	31A-239	N686AB	35A-077	N98LC	35A-157	N26GP
31A-078	N539LB	31A-159	XA-AFX	31A-240	N440SC	35A-078	N145AM	35A-158	N800GP
31A-079	N91DP	31A-160	LX-EAR	31A-241	N633SF	35A-079	N68QB	35A-159	D-CAPO
31A-080	N986MA	31A-161	N177JB	31A-242	N680SW*			35A-160	D-CCCA

35A-161	N433DD	35A-242	N242DR	35A-323	N357EF	35A-404	N804TF	35A-485	N485AC
35A-162	XA-CZG	35A-243	N747RY	35A-324	VH-LJJ	35A-405	N135DA	35A-486	N925DM
35A-163	N27BL	35A-244	N244LJ	35A-325	N325NW	35A-406	ER-LGA	35A-487	N890LR*
35A-164	N50MJ	35A-245	N30PA	35A-326	N35SA	35A-407	C-GIWO	35A-488	XA-UGK
35A-165	N72CK	35A-246	N628DB	35A-327	N32PE	35A-408	LV-AIT	35A-489	N222BE
35A-166	N10UF	35A-247	N544PA	35A-328	N408MG	35A-409	N351AM	35A-490	N502JF
35A-167	N813AS	35A-248	N128CA	35A-329	N261PG	35A-410	N352TV	35A-491	N35NK
35A-168	C-FZQP	35A-249	C-FICU	35A-330	wfu	35A-411	N94GP	35A-492	N492RM
35A-169	N707RG	35A-250	N947GS	35A-331	D-CGFC	35A-412	XA-RGH	35A-493	N354CL
35A-170	N88NJ	35A-251	N387HA	35A-332	N827CR	35A-413	D-CFCF	35A-494	PT-LDM
35A-171	N171WH	35A-252	PT-KZR	35A-333	wo	35A-414	N815DD	35A-495	N440MC
35A-172	N50AK	35A-253	N129TS	35A-334	N235MC	35A-415	SE-DZZ	35A-496	N825LJ
35A-173	N326DD	35A-254	N720WW	35A-335	N3MB	35A-416	N841TF	35A-497	N15RH
35A-174	N773DL	35A-255	XB-USD	35A-336	XA-BNO	35A-417	LX-ONE	35A-498	C-GTDM
35A-175	SE-RCA	35A-256	N335RC	35A-337	N39HJ	35A-418	XA-SCA	35A-499	N911DX
35A-176	XA-BUX	35A-257	N417BA	35A-338	RP-C610	35A-419	N72AX	35A-500	N144LG
35A-177	D-CITY	35A-258	N583BS	35A-339	PT-LZP	35A-420	N181CA	35A-501	N55GG
35A-178	N900JC	35A-259	N25AN	35A-340	N504F	35A-421	D-CDSF	35A-502	N747CP
35A-179	D-CGFA	35A-260	N40PK	35A-341	OE-GMS	35A-422	N45AE	35A-503	N542SA
35A-180	N701DA	35A-261	N58MM	35A-342	N56JA	35A-423	D-CAVE	35A-504	OE-GMJ
35A-181	PT-LSJ	35A-262	N237AF	35A-343	LV-...	35A-424	N52FN	35A-505	N60DK
35A-182	N221SG	35A-263	wfu	35A-344	N630SJ	35A-425	N425SA	35A-506	wfu
35A-183	N717AJ	35A-264	N64CP	35A-345	wo	35A-426	N143LG	35A-507	N42HN
35A-184	N7092C	35A-265	A6-RJI	35A-346	D-CTRI	35A-427	wfu	35A-508	N452AC
35A-185	RP-C....	35A-266	N35GC	35A-347	N85SV	35A-428	VH-SLE	35A-509	wo
35A-186	N96FN	35A-267	wo	35A-348	N7ZH	35A-429	A6-RJH	35A-510	84-0064
35A-187	N32HM	35A-268	D-CGFB	35A-349	N252WJ	35A-430	LJ-1	35A-511	84-0065
35A-188	N924AM	35A-269	N886R	35A-350	N35WB	35A-431	N355PC*	35A-512	wo
35A-189	wo	35A-270	N31MC	35A-351	N500ND	35A-432	VH-VLJ	35A-513	N117PK
35A-190	N181EF	35A-271	N40AN	35A-352	N800GJ	35A-433	wo	35A-514	wfu
35A-191	N535AF	35A-272	N321AN	35A-353	C-GDJH	35A-434	N469BB	35A-515	84-0069
35A-192	N49BE	35A-273	N273LJ	35A-354	N405GJ	35A-435	XC-HHJ	35A-516	84-0070
35A-193	N359EF	35A-274	N53G	35A-355	N721EC	35A-436	N100AT	35A-517	84-0071
35A-194	wo	35A-275	N72LL	35A-356	PT-LUG	35A-437	YV2044	35A-518	84-0072
35A-195	SE-DHO	35A-276	N69BH	35A-357	N357LJ	35A-438	N308BW	35A-519	wfu
35A-196	wo	35A-277	N999JS	35A-358	N108JN	35A-439	N611TA*	35A-520	wfu
35A-197	N754WS	35A-278	N12RP	35A-359	N136JP	35A-440	N300SC	35A-521	84-0075
35A-198	N198GJ	35A-279	wo	35A-360	N360LJ	35A-441	N699ST	35A-522	84-0076
35A-199	N235JS	35A-280	N35AX	35A-361	PT-OCZ	35A-442	wo	35A-523	84-0077
35A-200	N200LJ	35A-281	N425AS	35A-362	N362FW	35A-443	N335MR	35A-524	wfu
35A-201	N136WE	35A-282	N62MB	35A-363	N19RP	35A-444	N615HB	35A-525	84-0079
35A-202	N55FN	35A-283	N386CM	35A-364	N353EF	35A-445	wo	35A-526	wfu
35A-203	N97CE	35A-284	N43MF	35A-365	D-CFAI	35A-446	N403DP	35A-527	84-0081
35A-204	D-CFTG	35A-285	N725ST	35A-366	HS-CFS	35A-447	D-COKE	35A-528	84-0082
35A-205	N568PA	35A-286	N286SD	35A-367	N360AX	35A-448	N222BG	35A-529	84-0083
35A-206	N38PS	35A-287	N929SL	35A-368	N351TV	35A-449	XA-GOO	35A-530	84-0084
35A-207	wo	35A-288	N288JP	35A-369	T-26	35A-450	N950SP	35A-531	84-0085
35A-208	N67PA	35A-289	N217TA	35A-370	N87GA	35A-451	LJ-2	35A-532	wfu
35A-209	N22MS	35A-290	XA-ORO	35A-371	N399BA	35A-452	N452DA	35A-533	84-0087
35A-210	N770JP	35A-291	wo	35A-372	PT-LJK	35A-453	N453AM	35A-534	wfu
35A-211	N621RB	35A-292	N292ME	35A-373	LV-B..	35A-454	N80AR	35A-535	wfu
35A-212	N989AL	35A-293	wo	35A-374	HZ-106	35A-455	N988QC	35A-536	84-0090
35A-213	XC-CUZ	35A-294	wo	35A-375	HZ-107	35A-456	N456CL	35A-537	84-0091
35A-214	N279DM	35A-295	N94AA	35A-376	N979RF	35A-457	N49WL	35A-538	84-0092
35A-215	N35ED	35A-296	N66NJ	35A-377	N46MF	35A-458	N4EA	35A-539	84-0093
35A-216	N335RD	35A-297	N777DM	35A-378	N354EF	35A-459	wo	35A-540	84-0094
35A-217	N122JW	35A-298	N298NW	35A-379	XB-IWL	35A-460	XA-JJJ	35A-541	84-0095
35A-218	wo	35A-299	PT-XLI	35A-380	C-GAJS	35A-461	N64CF	35A-542	84-0096
35A-219	wo	35A-300	N365N	35A-381	N35NA	35A-462	N394PA	35A-543	wo
35A-220	N220GS	35A-301	N945W	35A-382	N60WL	35A-463	N699BA	35A-544	84-0098
35A-221	N221TR	35A-302	N51LC	35A-383	N364CL	35A-464	N111KR	35A-545	84-0099
35A-222	D-CGFG	35A-303	PT-LLS	35A-384	N384CF	35A-465	N465NW	35A-546	84-0100
35A-223	D-CGRC	35A-304	N995CR	35A-385	N350EF	35A-466	wo	35A-547	84-0101
35A-224	N28MJ	35A-305	N33NJ	35A-386	LV-BAW	35A-467	HZ-MS1C	35A-548	84-0102
35A-225	N225CF	35A-306	N9ZD	35A-387	D-CARL	35A-468	OY-CCJ	35A-549	84-0103
35A-226	N30HJ	35A-307	N623KM	35A-388	wo	35A-469	N35JN	35A-550	wfu
35A-227	N366TT	35A-308	N747GM	35A-389	N389KA	35A-470	LJ-3	35A-551	wfu
35A-228	N921CH	35A-309	C-GUAC	35A-390	C-FPRP	35A-471	N529BC	35A-552	84-0106
35A-229	N4415W	35A-310	N310ME	35A-391	wo	35A-472	N138WE	35A-553	84-0107
35A-230	N595BA	35A-311	N711EC	35A-392	N1XL	35A-473	N35CY	35A-554	wfu
35A-231	VH-JCR	35A-312	N369BA	35A-393	PT-LOE	35A-474	PT-LEB	35A-555	84-0109
35A-232	N4415S	35A-313	N31WR	35A-394	N238PR	35A-475	ZS-TOW	35A-556	84-0110
35A-233	N23A	35A-314	N777LD	35A-395	N395MY	35A-476	N776JS	35A-557	84-0111
35A-234	N35WR	35A-315	D-CCAA	35A-396	PT-OPJ	35A-477	N376HA	35A-558	84-0112
35A-235	LV-ZSZ	35A-316	N884JW	35A-397	N200TW	35A-478	wo	35A-559	wfu
35A-236	N65RZ	35A-317	N317TT	35A-398	wo	35A-479	PT-LHT	35A-560	84-0114
35A-237	N11UF	35A-318	N318NW	35A-399	wo	35A-480	N39DK	35A-561	wfu
35A-238	N32RZ	35A-319	T-23	35A-400	VH-OVB	35A-481	N99NJ	35A-562	wfu
35A-239	wo	35A-320	N727MG	35A-401	N535JM	35A-482	wo	35A-563	wfu
35A-240	N135WE	35A-321	3909	35A-402	N35BG	35A-483	N327CB	35A-564	84-0118
35A-241	N500ED	35A-322	PT-WGF	35A-403	N403FW	35A-484	T-25	35A-565	84-0119

35A-566	84-0120	35A-648	N97LE	36A-051	FAP 524	45-068	I-ERJD	45-149	N904HD
35A-567	wo	35A-649	ZK-XVL	36A-052	FAP 525	45-069	D2-EBN	45-150	N348K
35A-568	wfu	35A-650	N650LR	36A-053	HY-984	45-070	N450JC	45-151	N345FM
35A-569	84-0123	35A-651	N405PC	36A-054	9201	45-071	N989PA	45-152	VH-CXJ
35A-570	84-0124	35A-652	N652KZ	36A-055	PP-JAA	45-072	N720CC	45-153	C-GCMP
35A-571	84-0125	35A-653	LX-LAR	36A-056	wo	45-073	N66SG	45-154	N918EG
35A-572	84-0126	35A-654	N770BM	36A-057	VH-JCX	45-074	N740TF	45-155	N882CA
35A-573	84-0127	35A-655	C-GMMA	36A-058	wo	45-075	N450BC	45-156	C-FLRJ
35A-574	wfu	35A-656	N356JW	36A-059	9204	45-076	N988PA	45-157	N341K
35A-575	84-0128	35A-657	N10AH	36A-060	9205	45-077	XA-AIM	45-158	I-DFSL
35A-576	84-0129	35A-658	N77NJ	36A-061	9206	45-078	N116AS	45-159	N828CA
35A-577	84-0130	35A-659	N776BG	36A-062	D-CGFE	45-079	N5FE	45-160	N863CA
35A-578	84-0131	35A-660	N421SV	36A-063	D-CGFF	45-080	N45EJ	45-161	G-SOVC
35A-579	wfu	35A-661	VH-PFA	Learjet 45/45XR		45-081	N145GM	45-162	N426FX
35A-580	wfu	35A-662	N27AX	45-002	N452LJ	45-082	N1HP	45-163	5N-BGR
35A-581	84-0134	35A-663	D-CCCB	45-003	wfu	45-083	ZS-TJS	45-164	N428FX
35A-582	84-0135	35A-664	N640BA	45-004	wo	45-084	HB-VML	45-165	N429FX
35A-583	wo	35A-665	N35UA	45-005	G-ZXZX	45-085	N454CG	45-166	N430FX
35A-584	wfu	35A-666	wfu	45-006	N721CP	45-086	C-GMRO	45-167	G-GMAA
35A-585	84-0137	35A-667	N135DE	45-007	TC-CMB	45-087	N64HH	45-168	VH-PFS
35A-586	84-0142	35A-668	N441PC	45-008	N80RP	45-088	C-FMGL	45-169	N332K
35A-587	84-0139	35A-669	C-GWFG	45-009	N500CG	45-089	XA-EFM	45-170	N45VS
35A-588	84-0140	35A-670	N460SB	45-010	N311BP	45-090	N452CJ	45-171	N342K
35A-589	PT-GAP	35A-671	N671TS	45-011	N741F*	45-091	N451WM	45-172	N70PC
35A-590	N882SC	35A-672	XA-FMT	45-012	N450TJ	45-092	ZS-PDG	45-173	N900P
35A-591	N880Z	35A-673	N835MC	45-013	N45LR	45-093	wo	45-174	N45HC
35A-592	N93LE	35A-674	LV-BIE	45-014	N708SP	45-094	N800WC	45-175	N41TF
35A-593	VH-LPJ	35A-675	wo	45-015	N31V	45-095	N786CC	45-176	XA-IKE
35A-594	N747BW	35A-676	N620MJ	45-016	N743E	45-096	C-GDMI	45-177	N431FX
35A-595	N95JN	Learjet 36		45-017	D-CSMS	45-097	D-CMSC	45-178	XA-JMF
35A-596	N352HS	36-001	wfu	45-018	OO-LFS	45-098	N6FE	45-179	N179MR
35A-597	N604S	36-002	N84FN	45-019	C-GLRJ	45-099	N7FE	45-180	N345RL
35A-598	PT-LGW	36-003	N361PJ	45-020	C-GVVZ	45-100	N345BH	45-181	ZS-PTL
35A-599	N367DA	36-004	N54PA	45-021	CS-TFI	45-101	N22AX	45-182	N345AW
35A-600	N995DP	36-005	N905CK	45-022	C-GSWQ	45-102	XA-...	45-183	C-GHMP
35A-601	HY-986	36-006	wo	45-023	N740E	45-103	N720MC	45-184	N866CA
35A-602	HY-987	36-007	N83FN	45-024	C-FVSL	45-104	N450BK	45-185	N273LP
35A-603	HY-988	36-008	N101AJ	45-025	N742E	45-105	N397AT	45-186	N158EC
35A-604	N604GS	36-009	N505HG	45-026	XC-HIE	45-106	N145XL	45-187	N146XL
35A-605	N925CA	36-010	N45FG	45-027	N445SB	45-107	N762EL	45-188	N21BD
35A-606	N96GS	36-011	N26FN	45-028	XC-VMC	45-108	N313BH	45-189	D-CSUL
35A-607	D-CGFH	36-012	N547PA	45-029	N170LS	45-109	N945HC*	45-190	N41PC
35A-608	ZS-IGP	36-013	N71PG	45-030	N157PB	45-110	N222MW	45-191	N191LJ
35A-609	N986SA	36-014	VH-SLJ	45-031	N310LJ	45-111	XA-BFX	45-192	N433FX
35A-610	N610LJ	36-015	N10FN	45-032	N4FE	45-112	CN-TJB	45-193	N865CA
35A-611	VH-ESM	36-016	N12FN	45-033	VH-SQD	45-113	N124BP	45-194	ZS-ULT
35A-612	D-CGFI	36-017	N17LJ	45-034	XA-VYC	45-114	N318SA	45-195	VH-SQR
35A-613	FAB6000	36A-018	N418CA	45-035	VH-SQM	45-115	N45MW	45-196	N473LP
35A-614	N683EF	36A-019	N527PA	45-036	N345WB	45-116	OY-LJJ	45-197	N432FX
35A-615	FAB6001	36A-020	wo	45-037	OE-GDI	45-117	ZS-DCA	45-198	N45UG
35A-616	D-CEXP	36A-021	wo	45-038	N14FE	45-118	N5XP	45-199	N1925P*
35A-617	FAB6002	36A-022	N44EV	45-039	N15FE	45-119	N1RB	45-200	N451ST
35A-618	N618CF	36A-023	N56PA	45-040	N501CG	45-120	N418FX	45-201	N452ST
35A-619	PT-POK	36A-024	C-FEMT	45-041	C-GPDQ	45-121	N45HF	45-202	N445N
35A-620	N620EM	36A-025	N32PA	45-042	N10R	45-122	N945FD	45-203	N145AR
35A-621	PR-ABP	36A-026	N86BL	45-043	N45VB	45-123	N484LC	45-204	N45NP
35A-622	N81MR	36A-027	N27MJ	45-044	N888CA	45-124	G-JANV	45-205	N88AF
35A-623	wo	36A-028	N545PA	45-045	N4545	45-125	N419FX	45-206	N45AX
35A-624	86-0374	36A-029	N116MA	45-046	XA-RMT	45-126	C-FXHN	45-207	VH-SQV
35A-625	N522AG*	36A-030	N160GC	45-047	N206CK	45-127	XA-ALF	45-208	N715CG
35A-626	N335MG	36A-031	N62PG	45-048	PT-XLR	45-128	N10NL	45-209	N209KM
35A-627	PT-LMY	36A-032	VH-...	45-049	N711R	45-129	N9CH	45-210	XA-ALA
35A-628	LX-TWO	36A-033	wo	45-050	N16PQ	45-130	N418MN	45-211	N300AQ
35A-629	86-0377	36A-034	B-4599	45-051	N927SK	45-131	N444MW	45-212	N434FX
35A-630	N388PD	36A-035	N71CK	45-052	N745SA	45-132	N889CA	45-213	G-RWGW
35A-631	2710	36A-036	N136DH	45-053	N1904S	45-133	N183CM	45-214	N29SM
35A-632	2711	36A-037	C-FCLJ	45-054	N345MA	45-134	N423FX	45-215	N352K
35A-633	2712	36A-038	N700GG	45-055	G-GOMO	45-135	N422FX	45-216	N359K
35A-634	N626BM	36A-039	N99RS	45-056	N196PH	45-136	N654AT	45-217	N217MJ
35A-635	40208	36A-040	N82GG	45-057	N83TZ	45-137	N800AB*	45-218	ZS-OPY
35A-636	2713	36A-041	N79SF	45-058	N237DM	45-138	G-SOVB	45-219	ZS-BAR
35A-638	2714	36A-042	wo	45-059	ZS-PNP	45-139	XA-UAG	45-220	N825CA
35A-639	2715	36A-043	XA-...	45-060	N459LC	45-140	N345SV	45-221	N823CA
35A-640	2716	36A-044	N70LJ	45-061	N111KK	45-141	N858MK	45-222	N826CA
35A-641	2717	36A-045	wo	45-062	N543COM	45-142	N145SB	45-223	C-FNRG
35A-642	2718	36A-046	N17A	45-063	N10JY	45-143	N334AF	45-224	N77702
35A-643	D-CGFJ	36A-047	N36PJ	45-064	EC-ILK	45-144	CS-TLW	45-225	N90GS
35A-644	C-GMMY	36A-048	D-CFGG	45-065	N100KK	45-145	N421FX	45-226	I-ERJE
35A-645	N645AM	36A-049	VH-SLF	45-066	D2-...	45-146	N424FX	45-227	N70AE
35A-646	wo	36A-050	TP-105	45-067	XA-QUE	45-147	N425FX	45-228	ZS-LOW
35A-647	N335PR					45-148	OE-GAR	45-229	N159EC

45-230	N451N	45-311	G-OLDK	45-2030	XA-SNI	55-012	N666TV	55-093	N32KJ
45-231	N145HC	45-312	N575AG	45-2031	RP-C3110	55-013	N155SB	55-094	N235HR
45-232	LV-ARD	45-313	N45KH	45-2032	N10SE	55-014	N1CG	55-095	D-CAAE
45-233	N45KX	45-314	N74PT	45-2033	N404EL	55-015	N551MF	55-096	N126KL
45-234	258	45-315	N437FX	45-2034	I-PARS	55-016	N717EB	55-097	N20CR
45-235	N30PC	45-316	AP-BHY	45-2035	N1848T	55-017	D-CCGN	55-098	N1324P
45-236	G-LLOD	45-317	N605SE	45-2036	N100HW	55-018	N822MC	55-099	N95WK
45-237	N44QG	45-318	N196CT	45-2037	N611FX	55-019	C-GSWP	55-100	N717AM
45-238	N570AM	45-319	N16PC	45-2038	N22GM	55-020	N55NY	55-101	N1129M
45-239	C-GJCY	45-320	N452A	45-2039	N612FX	55-021	N619MJ	55-102	N604FK
45-240	N9FE	45-321	ZS-OPN	45-2040	XA-CGF	55-022	N155GM	55-103	wo
45-241	N241LJ	45-322	N313BW	45-2041	N614FX	55-023	N110ET	55-104	N277AL
45-242	PR-OTA	45-323	N125BW	45-2042	N256AH	55-024	N824CC	55-105	N55AR
45-243	G-IOOX	45-324	N12VU	45-2043	C-FMHA	55-025	N92MG	55-106	N824MG
45-244	N545K	45-325	N390GG	45-2044	N140LJ	55-026	N285DH	55-107	D-CWAY
45-245	N745K	45-326	N507FG	45-2045	N176CA	55-027	N59HJ	55-108	D-CUNO
45-246	XA-SAP	45-327	N526EL	45-2046	N773RS	55-028	N556HJ	55-109	D-CVIP
45-247	N3AS	45-328	F-HCGD	45-2047	XA-RAB	55-029	N29NW	55-110	N455RH
45-248	N48TF	45-329	PR-CSM	45-2048	PR-JBS	55-030	N122LX	55-111	wo
45-249	C-GLRS	45-330	N2HP	45-2049	N140WW	55-031	YV1794	55-112	wo
45-250	OO-LFN	45-331	N583PS	45-2050	VP-BHT	55-032	N125LR	55-113	N57MH
45-251	XA-MVG	45-332	N45XR	45-2051	N615FX	55-033	N355RM	55-114	N34GB
45-252	N272BC	45-333	N438FX	45-2052	N784CC	55-034	N550TC	55-115	N155BC
45-253	N45NM	45-334	N445SE	45-2053	I-ERJJ	55-035	N816MC	55-116	N51VL
45-254	N729SB	45-335	N435HH	45-2054	G-MEET	55-036	N723CC	55-117	N385RC
45-255	C-FSDL	45-336	4X-CYH	45-2055	N506KS	55-037	N53HJ	55-118	N257SJ
45-256	XA-...	45-337	N10J	45-2056	N411HC	55-038	N666TK	55-119	N273MG
45-257	N555VR	45-338	N45TK	45-2057	N616FX	55-039	N339BC	55-120	N329TJ
45-258	N395BC	45-339	N454N	45-2058	N71NF	55-040	N554CL	55-121	N747AN
45-259	N40PC	45-340	N300JC	45-2059	I-GURU	55-041	N141FM	55-122	D-CGBR
45-260	N745TC	45-341	N439FX	45-2060	N999EK	55-042	N575GH	55-123	N420BG
45-261	N451BW	45-342	ZS-OPO	45-2061	D-CLUX	55-043	N83WM	55-124	D-CONU
45-262	N45AU	45-343	N45HG	45-2062	PT-XDN	55-044	PT-LHR	55-125	N610JR
45-263	N263MR	45-344	N607FG	45-2063	N740KG	55-045	N550AK	55-126	N16LJ
45-264	N916BD	45-345	N45MR	45-2064	OY-KVP*	55-046	N855PT	55B-127	N73GP
45-265	G-OLDT	45-346	N440FX	45-2065	N617FX	55-047	N600C	55B-128	N787GT
45-266	LX-IMZ	45-347	D-CINS	45-2066	N2758W	55-048	N558HJ	55B-129	N655AL
45-267	N451HC	45-348	N744E	45-2067	XA-NJM	55-049	N150MS	55B-130	N55VC
45-268	N145K	45-349	N45HK	45-2068	PP-FMW	55-050	wo	55B-131	N52CT
45-269	N245K	45-350	N50153	45-2069	N29RE	55-051	D-CATL	55B-132	N242RB
45-270	C-FBLJ	45-351	N60PC	45-2070	N77HN	55-052	D-COOL	55B-133	EC-INS
45-271	N435FX	45-352	N988MC	45-2071	OY-ZAN	55-053	N531K	55B-134	PT-LDR
45-272	N288CB	45-353	N903BT	45-2072	N83JJ	55-054	N54NW	55C-135	PT-LXO
45-273	N183TS	45-354	N135CG	45-2073	N975DM	55-055	N1JG	55C-136	OE-GCF
45-274	N274CZ	45-355	N45XP	45-2074	G-STUF	55-056	N607BF	55C-137	N155SP
45-275	C-FRYS	45-357	N441FX	45-2075	N484CH	55-057	N733E	55C-138	N270WS
45-276	N88WV	45-359	N710R	45-2076	N618FX	55-058	N58SR	55C-139	N552TL
45-277	N918BD	45-361	N45LJ	45-2077	XA-VFV	55-059	OE-GRR	55C-139A	N155VT
45-278	N63WR	45-363	N453A	45-2078	I-GOCO	55-060	N996CR	55C-140	FAB6100
45-279	N279AJ	Learjet 40		45-2079	D-CVJP	55-061	ES-PVT	55C-141	N155DB
45-280	G-CDNK	45-001	N40LX	45-2080	D-CPDR	55-062	N69VH	55C-142	N755VT
45-281	N917BD	45-2001	N401LJ	45-2081	N24VP	55-063	N63AX	55C-143	ES-PVD
45-282	N456Q	45-2002	N40KJ	45-2082	N619FX	55-064	N912MM	55C-144	N178AM
45-283	N4DA	45-2003	LQ-BFS	45-2083	N419ET	55-065	N1125M	55C-145	N211BC
45-284	XA-ARB	45-2004	N605FX	45-2084	N40LJ	55-066	N717HB	55C-146	PT-ORA
45-285	N300AA	45-2005	N606FX	45-2085	N620FX	55-067	N505EH	55C-147	N177AM
45-286	G-CDSR	45-2006	D-CNIK	45-2086	PR-PTR	55-068	N135LR	Learjet 60/60XR	
45-287	F-HACP	45-2007	G-MOOO	45-2087	N40NB	55-069	N817AM	55C-001	wfu
45-288	C-FBCL	45-2008	N99GK	45-2088	N288AS	55-070	wo	60-001	N601LJ
45-289	N68PC	45-2009	CC-CMS	45-2089	N621FX	55-071	N113YS	60-002	N170MK
45-290	N45BZ	45-2010	N46E	45-2090	N90XR	55-072	N5572	60-003	N60FE
45-291	OO-EPU	45-2011	N411AJ	45-2091	D-CVJN	55-073	N667MB	60-004	N863PA
45-292	N98XR	45-2012	N607FX	45-2092	N426JK	55-074	N905RL	60-005	VP-BGB
45-293	TG-ABY	45-2013	XA-GRR	45-2093	N5016Z	55-075	N117LR	60-006	N8783
45-294	G-OLDW	45-2014	N608FX	45-2094	N40079	55-076	C-GKTM	60-007	N733SW
45-295	XA-UFB	45-2015	I-ERJG	45-2095	N622FX	55-077	N245MS	60-008	N808SK
45-296	N454LC	45-2016	I-ELYS	45-2099	N623FX	55-078	N345RJ	60-009	N54
45-297	N145CM	45-2017	N502JM	45-2100	N959RP	55-079	N700SR	60-010	N692PC
45-298	N191TD	45-2018	D-CGGB	45-2101	N152UT	55-080	PT-LET	60-011	N843CP
45-299	N453ST	45-2019	I-FORR	45-2103	N140HM	55-081	N903JC	60-012	N80DX*
45-300	N145AP	45-2020	PR-ONE	Learjet 55		55-082	N139SK	60-013	N55
45-301	N996BP	45-2021	N401EG	55-003	N612EQ	55-083	N550CK*	60-014	N862PA
45-302	N99XR	45-2022	N609FX	55-004	N728MG	55-084	D-CWDL	60-015	N861PA
45-303	C-FANS	45-2023	N521CH	55-005	N440DM	55-085	N225MD	60-016	N788MM
45-304	N4009	45-2024	N40ML	55-006	N427TL	55-086	PT-LUN	60-017	N498SW*
45-305	N808KS	45-2025	N240RP	55-007	wo	55-087	N1852	60-018	N24G
45-306	OY-OCV	45-2026	EC-JYY	55-008	N322GC	55-088	N60ND	60-019	D-CRAN
45-307	N425G	45-2027	N610FX	55-009	N800LJ	55-089	N312AL	60-020	N606L
45-308	ZS-OPM	45-2028	N40XR	55-010	wo	55-090	N55UJ	60-021	N600GA
45-309	N436FX	45-2029	N998AL	55-011	D-CMAX	55-091	N911FC	60-022	N22G
45-310	N345KL					55-092	N40DK		

60-023	N60SR	60-104	N614TS	60-185	N464TF	60-266	N156BF	1006	N515BP
60-024	N415NP	60-105	N217BX	60-186	N58ST	60-267	N60SN	1007	N607BH*
60-025	N919RS	60-106	N140JC	60-187	N247FX	60-268	N268WS	1008	N604SH
60-026	N14TU	60-107	D-CFFB	60-188	N248FX	60-269	N903AM	1009	N396V
60-027	N69LJ	60-108	N38CP	60-189	PR-XJS	60-270	A6-MAJ	1010	N2105
60-028	N206HY	60-109	N177KS	60-190	ES-PVS	60-271	N954WS	1011	N116RA
60-029	N64SL	60-110	N928CD	60-191	N710SG*	60-272	P4-BAZ	1012	N604AC
60-030	YR-RPB	60-111	N898PA	60-192	N601GG	60-273	RP-C2956	1013	N16RW
60-031	N841TT	60-112	N299SC	60-193	N249FX	60-274	D-CSIM	1014	wo
60-032	D-CPMU	60-113	N160GG	60-194	N250FX	60-275	N101UD	1015	N25V
60-033	N56	60-114	N154AK	60-195	N251FX	60-276	OE-GDF	1016	N920RV
60-034	9M-CAL	60-115	N600GG	60-196	N252FX	60-277	LX-LOU	1017	N270V
60-035	wo	60-116	XA-VIG	60-197	OE-GYG	60-278	N60RL	1018	N618RL
60-036	N44EL	60-117	N889DW	60-198	N198HB	60-279	Z3-MKD	1019	3B-GFI
60-037	N101HW	60-118	N11AM	60-199	N600AJ	60-280	G-SXTY	1020	N602AJ
60-038	C-FJGG	60-119	N8811A*	60-200	A6-EJA	60-281	D-CGTF	1021	wfu
60-039	N57	60-120	D-CSIX	60-201	N614JH	60-282	TC-RKS	1022	N260V
60-040	N600CN	60-121	PT-XFS	60-202	XA-TSA	60-283	PR-GCL	1023	N777GD
60-041	N166HL	60-122	N61DP	60-203	LZ-BVV	60-284	N284L	1024	N811MT
60-042	N60MG	60-123	N356WA	60-204	N30GJ	60-285	N72CE	1025	N399WB
60-043	N43NR	60-124	N260AN	60-205	N358P	60-286	G-LGAR	1026	N694PG
60-044	N668RC	60-125	VP-CRB	60-206	N909JS	60-287	OE-GGL	1027	N93BA
60-045	N903AG	60-126	N160AN	60-207	N706CJ	60-288	N103LS	1028	N858PJ
60-046	N710TF*	60-127	N460AN	60-208	N208BH	60-289	VP-BGS	1029	N722DJ
60-047	N647EF	60-128	N8888	60-209	N1221J	60-290	D-CFLG	1030	N721ST
60-048	N730M	60-129	N160GH	60-210	C-FGJC	60-291	XA-KCM	1031	N620S
60-049	N459SF	60-130	N384JW*	60-211	D-CHLE	60-292	N380BA	1032	N1884
60-050	N923SK	60-131	XB-JCG	60-212	I-RPLY	60-293	N772PP	1033	N304TT
60-051	ES-PVC	60-132	N9200M	60-213	N717FF	60-294	N60XR	1034	N134VS
60-052	N900KK	60-133	C-FCMG	60-214	OE-GFA	60-295	N259FX	1035	N163EG
60-053	N744DB	60-134	XA-ZTA	60-215	VP-BCY	60-296	N296L	1036	N900LG
60-054	N301RJ	60-135	N98JV	60-216	N131TR	60-297	XA-KLZ	1037	wo
60-055	N574DA	60-136	N60RU	60-217	XA-VLA	60-298	N729LJ	1038	N903DD
60-056	N92FG	60-137	N360AN	60-218	EI-IAW	60-299	N75CT	1039	N905MP
60-057	N58	60-138	N560AN	60-219	N552SK	60-300	EI-DXW	1040	144601
60-058	XA-BRE	60-139	N7734T	60-220	N255FX	60-301	ZS-GSG	1041	N141RD
60-059	LV-BFR	60-140	T-10	60-221	N255BD	60-302	ES-PVP	1042	N604MH
60-060	N909SK	60-141	N888KL	60-222	N60VE	60-303	OE-GTO	1043	N1000R
60-061	C-FRGY	60-142	N116LM*	60-223	N309MG	60-304	OE-GNF	1044	N800BT
60-062	N551BD	60-143	N143FA	60-224	N61VE	60-305	EI-VIV	1045	N247CK
60-063	N660BC	60-144	N94BA	60-225	N770JB*	60-306	N5009	1046	N246JL
60-064	N529KF	60-145	I-PRAD	60-226	N128V	60-307	N260FX	1047	N249AJ
60-065	N654AN	60-146	N809R	60-227	N503RE	60-308	N115AN	1048	C-GDDR
60-066	N176KS	60-147	N420JP	60-228	N65HU	60-309	N460MC	1049	N601CT
60-067	N60HM	60-148	HB-VOZ	60-229	N23SR	60-310	N222BR	1050	N710HL
60-068	N160JD	60-149	EI-REX	60-230	N600LG	60-311	VP-BLC	1051	N505PM
60-069	D-CITA	60-150	N200MT	60-231	SX-BNR	60-312	OH-VMF	1052	N222LH
60-070	N21AC	60-151	N11TS	60-232	N95BD	60-313	N613H	1053	LV-BAS
60-071	N658KS	60-152	AMT-200	60-233	N520SC	60-314	N999LJ	1054	N217RM
60-072	9M-FCL	60-153	N424KW	60-234	N24SR	60-315	N604KT	1055	N643CR
60-073	N860PD	60-154	N969JD	60-235	N252RP	60-316	N50LK	1056	N777GA
60-074	N600PH*	60-155	N88V	60-236	N916BG*	60-317	OE-GSU	1057	N6MW
60-075	N9CU	60-156	N605SB	60-237	N699DA	60-318	N777VC	1058	N658CF
60-076	N494PA	60-157	N114LJ	60-238	N753BP	60-319	N261FX	1059	N403WY
60-077	N60GF	60-158	N460JD	60-239	N503BC	60-320	N229BP	1060	N74JA
60-078	N188TG	60-159	N721MJ	60-240	N29LJ	60-321	N675BP	1061	N601KK
60-079	N95AG	60-160	D-CGEO	60-241	N253FX	60-322	OY-MIR	1062	N444ET
60-080	N59	60-161	EC-JVM	60-242	wo	60-323	N262FX	1063	N457HL
60-081	N180CP	60-162	N99ZC	60-243	EC-JVB	60-324	N707CS	1064	N100LR
60-082	N600LN	60-163	N326HG	60-244	N335AF	60-325	P4-SSV	1065	N287DL
60-083	N725SC	60-164	PT-XGS	60-245	XA-ORA	60-326	OD-MHA	1066	D-BSNA
60-084	N8JR	60-165	N929GW	60-246	D-CWHS	60-327	9H-AFB	1067	N240AK
60-085	N814GF	60-166	N114BD	60-247	N254FX	60-328	VP-BBZ	1068	N604EF
60-086	N797CP	60-167	LZ-...	60-248	N787LP	60-329	LZ-BVE	1069	N817CK
60-087	N601CN	60-168	N706CR	60-249	EC-JYQ	60-330	OK-JOM	1070	D-BUSY
60-088	XA-TZI	60-169	OE-GII	60-250	XA-FLY	60-331	D-CDEF	1071	N600HA
60-089	XA-MDM	60-170	9H-AEE	60-251	N747DP	60-332	OE-GLX	1072	N302PC
60-090	N85NC*	60-171	N424MW	60-252	N749SS	60-333	OE-GLY	1073	N673BH*
60-091	N91LE	60-172	XA-DGO	60-253	N1127M	60-334	N263FX	1074	N800HH
60-092	N226SF	60-173	D-CEJA	60-254	N773SW	60-335	N5014E	1075	N450AJ
60-093	N160EE	60-174	XA-COI	60-255	OO-TME	60-336	N4004Y	1076	N87TR
60-094	TC-ARC	60-175	N243F	60-256	D-CCGG	60-337	N60LJ	1077	N300TK
60-095	N82KK	60-176	N10MB	60-257	N256FX	60-338	N338PR	1078	N1504*
60-096	N603SC	60-177	N991DB	60-258	N202N	60-340	N264FX	1079	N601CM
60-097	N60TX	60-178	N178MM	60-259	N600L	60-348	N266FX	1080	N300TW
60-098	N797PA	60-179	HB-VNV	60-260	N973HR	Challenger 600		1081	N19DD
60-099	N60AN	60-180	N777MC	60-261	D-CROB	1001	wo	1082	N333KK
60-100	N60MN	60-181	N273MC	60-262	N126KD	1002	wfu	1083	N399FL
60-101	N179LF	60-182	N600NM*	60-263	N876CS	1004	wfu	1084	N550CW
60-102	N102LJ	60-183	N246FX	60-264	N811RA	1005	N244AL	1085	LZ-YUM
60-103	N298EF	60-184	N606SB	60-265	N600LC			10004	N1RL

Challenger 601

#	Reg	#	Reg	#	Reg	#	Reg	#	Reg
1003	wfu	5012	N500LR	5093	C-GMGB	5175	N800YB	5360	C-GHML
3001	N74GR	5013	N116LS	5094	N774PC	5176	N779AZ	5361	N254AM
3002	N227PE	5014	N514TS	5095	N2FE	5177	N227RH	5362	JY-AW3
3003	N680FA*	5015	N204JK	5096	C-FJJC	5178	B-MAC	5363	N964H
3004	N45PH	5016	C-GQWI	5097	N227CP	5179	C-GDLI	5364	C-FBNS
3005	N601TX	5017	N404HG	5098	N808G	5180	N518CL	5365	N280K
3006	N601JG	5018	N828SK	5099	N203JD	5181	C-FCIB	5366	N906TF
3007	N910KB	5019	C-GHGC	5100	N241N	5182	HL7577	5367	N16YD*
3008	N710GA	5020	N39RE	5101	N213GS	5183	N55HF	5368	N374G
3009	N873G	5021	N989BC	5102	N241FR	5184	N607RP	5369	N247WE
3010	N411TJ	5022	N655TH	5103	N601BE	5185	N914X	5370	VT-KAV
3011	N453GS	5023	D-AAMA	5104	N111FK	5186	N601AD	5371	C-GGWH
3012	C-FKJM	5024	N601DT	5105	5105	5187	N601KJ	5372	G-LVLV
3013	N213TS	5025	N1DW	5106	N523JM	5188	N10FE	5373	N604LC
3014	C-GDBF	5026	N601WM	5107	N729HZ	5189	N54VS	5374	N203
3015	XA-KIM	5027	N7PS*	5108	N236N	5190	N87	5375	XA-GRB
3016	N388DB	5028	N601RL	5109	N721G	5191	N605T	5376	N604ZH
3017	JY-RY1	5029	N594RJ	5110	TC-MDG	5192	N354TC	5377	N604RB
3018	wo	5030	N1HZ	5111	N502HE	5193	N11LK	5378	D-ASTS
3019	XA-SMS	5031	N64LE	5112	N604ME	5194	A9C-BXD	5379	C-GQPA
3020	C-GCFI	5032	N684SW	5113	N128GB			5380	C-080
3021	N150MH	5033	N144BS	5114	VP-BOA	**Challenger 604**		5381	N604MM
3022	C-GCFG	5034	C-GIOH	5115	N25SB	5301	N123KH	5382	N604HJ
3023	AP-MIR	5035	HB-JRV	5116	N1904P	5302	N255CC	5383	G-EMLI
3024	N888AZ	5036	N468KL	5117	C-FBCR	5303	OE-INF	5384	N684TS
3025	N997GC*	5037	N710LM	5118	N900FN	5304	N604CA	5385	N72NP
3026	N307SC	5038	N91KH	5119	C-FNEU	5305	N888DH	5386	N203R*
3027	C-GPSI	5039	N765WT	5120	N400TB	5306	N604WB	5387	N999PX
3028	C-FBEL	5040	N898AK*	5121	XA-GCD	5307	LX-FAZ	5388	4X-CMY
3029	N629TS	5041	N953FA	5122	N65FF	5308	N713HC	5389	D-AUKE
3030	N39CD	5042	HB-IKS	5123	N147HH	5309	N666TF	5390	N200DE
3031	N54JC	5043	N601VH	5124	C-FBOM	5310	C-GPFC	5391	N267DW
3032	N392FV	5044	VP-CBS	5125	P4-EPI	5311	N604JS	5392	C-FCDE
3033	VP-BBF	5045	N601AF	5126	N99UG	5312	N312AM	5393	N615TL
3034	C-GLOJ	5046	N426PE	5127	N555LG	5313	N712PR	5394	N72WY
3035	wo	5047	N384MP	5128	XA-GME	5314	VT-NGS	5395	N82CW
3036	144614	5048	N907WS	5129	VP-CRR	5315	N818TH	5396	N273S
3037	144615	5049	B-MAI	5130	N349JR	5316	N203TA	5397	VP-BJH
3038	144616	5050	N710VF	5131	N6JB	5317	C-FNNT	5398	N477DM
3039	N500PG	5051	C-GQBQ	5132	N289K	5318	HB-IVR	5399	N604GM
3040	12+02	5052	N125ST	5133	N486BG	5319	N27X	5400	N266GA
3041	N169TA	5053	N653CW	5134	N898EW	5320	HZ-AFA2	5401	N528GP
3042	N951RM	5054	N3FE	5135	N1902P	5321	N604CP	5402	VP-BDX
3043	12+03	5055	N460F	5136	N20G	5322	9A-CRO	5403	D-ADND
3044	N601GB	5056	N525SD	5137	N90AR	5323	N604TC	5404	VP-BGO
3045	N601PR	5057	N733CF	5138	N85	5324	N667LC	5405	N340AK
3046	N228PK	5058	N527JA	5139	N639TS	5325	N604JW	5406	N604MU
3047	N824DH	5059	C-FJNS	5140	N79AN	5326	N1903G	5407	LV-...
3048	N601JM	5060	D-ARTE	5141	N601JP	5327	N146BA	5408	N898AN
3049	12+04	5061	VP-BEJ	5142	XA-MYN	5328	LN-BWG	5409	N401NK
3050	N626JP*	5062	N316BG	5143	N601CV	5329	N222MC	5410	N805VZ
3051	N97SG	5063	XA-UEW	5144	N1DH	5330	N812G	5411	N3PC
3052	N425WN	5064	N601EC	5145	N96DS	5331	N810D	5412	TS-IAM
3053	12+05	5065	N882C	5146	XA-SOR	5332	N606JL	5413	C-FSJR
3054	N722HP	5066	N221LC	5147	N792CT	5333	N991TW	5414	wo
3055	N601RC	5067	VP-CFT	5148	VP-BFS	5334	N43R	5415	VP-CAP
3056	12+06	5068	C-FNNS	5149	N601BW	5335	N604B	5416	G-FTSL
3057	N163WG	5069	N324B	5150	C-GMMI	5336	N212RR	5417	D-AETV
3058	N125PS	5070	ZS-SGC	5151	G-CHAI	5337	N990AK	5418	N604CR
3059	12+07	5071	TR-AAG	5152	N115WF	5338	N426CF	5419	N252DH
3060	N601S	5072	wo	5153	N601HW	5339	C-GCNR	5420	C-GBKB
3061	N601AA	5073	N803RR	5154	N401RJ	5340	N194WM	5421	N604W
3062	N628CM	5074	N23SB	5155	N601TP	5341	N604SA	5422	D-ADNE
3063	C-FURG	5075	N607AX	5156	N808HG	5342	N604AX	5423	N38SW
3064	N664CW	5076	XA-GUA	5157	XA-JZL	5343	C-GHKY	5424	N604GW
3065	G-IMAC	5077	N118MT	5158	N814PS	5344	N604DH	5425	VT-IBR
3066	N105UP	5078	N702RV	5159	N813VZ	5345	N600AM	5426	N51VR
		5079	VP-CCR	5160	N190MP	5346	HZ-SJP3	5427	02
Challenger 601-3A		5080	N900H	5161	N117RY	5347	N205EE	5428	N640CH
5001	N604FJ	5081	N601ST	5162	N224F	5348	N881TW	5429	701
5002	N602TS	5082	N794SB	5163	N431CB	5349	N359V	5430	OY-MMM
5003	N601FR	5083	N189K	5164	N723HH	5350	N331TP	5431	N276GC
5004	XA-VDG	5084	N622WM	5165	HB-IVS	5351	N372G	5432	C-GPGD
5005	N902BW	5085	I-DAGS	5166	N86	5352	N770BC	5433	N181J
5006	N506TS	5086	N601JE	5167	C-GRPF	5353	N758CC	5434	N604AU
5007	N666CT	5087	XA-RZD	5168	N154NS	5354	N11A	5435	OE-INJ
5008	N1M	5088	N613SB	5169	N888WS	5355	N555WD	5436	N926SS
5009	N654CM	5089	N360SL	5170	N614AF	5356	N880CR	5437	N17TZ
5010	N429WG	5090	N226EC	5171	N777YG	5357	XA-AST	5438	N609CC
5011	VP-CIC	5091	C-FTFC	5172	D-AKUE	5358	N127SR	5439	N600ES
		5092	N308CR	5173	N28KA	5359	N497DM	5440	N500PE

5441	N36HA	5522	4X-CMF	5603	N76SF	5716	N605JM	20050	A6-KNH
5442	HB-JRT	5523	LX-ZAV	5604	B-LBL	5717	C-FSCI	20051	N424TM
5443	JY-TWO	5524	N601GT	5605	VP-BJE	5718	N723HA	20052	N606XT
5444	N604AF	5525	XA-JFE	5606	N310TK	5719	C-FOBK	20053	N353PC
5445	N877H	5526	N604CB	5607	N954L	5720	N605HC	20054	N302EM
5446	N604CE	5527	XA-TZF	5608	G-DGET	5721	N605HG	20055	N519FX
5447	N1NA	5528	D-AJAG	5609	D-ATTT	5722	M-BIGG*	20056	N520FX
5448	VP-BHH	5529	HB-JRA	5610	G-LGKO	5723	C-FOGI	20057	N521FX
5449	VP-CCP	5530	HB-JRB	5611	TC-ARD	5724	N17TE	20058	N300DG
5450	4X-CMZ	5531	N168NQ	5612	OE-IPK	5725	C-FOMU	20059	N620JF
5451	N831ET	5532	YL-SKY	5613	HB-JEM	5726	N605JP	20060	N228N
5452	OH-WIC	5533	144617	5614	N614BA	5727	N400ES*	20061	N422CP
5453	C-FHGC	5534	A37-002	5615	N904JK	5728	C-FOYE	20062	N888CN
5454	wo	5535	144618	5616	VP-CFD	5729	N540BA	20063	N363CL
5455	N604CW	5536	N25GG	5617	G-PRKR	5730	N605LD	20064	N522FX
5456	VH-ZZH	5537	N437MC	5618	VP-CMB	5731	C-FPQT	20065	4X-CPV
5457	N325FX	5538	A37-003	5619	N335FX	5732	C-FPQV	20066	N866TM
5458	C-GZPX	5539	VP-CEO	5620	VP-BST	5733	C-FPQW	20067	N300BC
5459	TC-TAN	5540	HB-JRC	5621	VP-CNK	5734	C-FPQY	20068	N303EM
5460	N698RS	5541	N329FX	5622	B-LLL	5735	N605DX	20069	N987HP
5461	N832SC	5542	N876H	5623	G-STCC	5736	N536TS	20070	N78TC
5462	D-AHLE	5543	N332FX	5624	HB-JGR	5737	N542BA	20071	D-BSMI
5463	D-AHEI	5544	N544TS	5625	VH-OCV	5738	C-FPSV	20072	N724SC
5464	N326FX	5545	N6757M	5626	OH-BZM	5739	N605AG	20073	N731DC
5465	N604FS	5546	N459CS	5627	N604DT	5740	C-FQQG	20074	N523FX
5466	N327FX	5547	N426PF	5628	P4-ABC	5741	N741TS	20075	N575WB
5467	G-REYS	5548	N604LL	5629	OE-INS	5742	C-FQQK	20076	N54HA
5468	C-168	5549	N2JW	5630	XA-SAD	5743	C-FQQO	20077	N304EM
5469	N78SD	5550	N1987	5631	N724MF	5744	C-F...	20078	XA-FRD
5470	N150BB	5551	N604RS	5632	D-AEUK	5745	C-FQQW	20079	D-BETA
5471	N604DE	5552	VP-COP	5633	N604CC	Challenger 300		20080	N960CR
5472	C-172	5553	P4-SAI	5634	N336FX	20001	C-GJCJ	20081	N845UP
5473	N604RP	5554	N604KJ	5635	N604EG	20002	wfu	20082	N594CA
5474	C-FXCN	5555	N604HC	5636	OE-ITH	20003	N303CZ	20083	N906TC
5475	D-ASIE	5556	N373G	5637	N637TF	20004	OE-HPK	20084	XA-GPR
5476	A9C-BXH	5557	C-GAWH	5638	N604HT	20005	C-GIPZ	20085	N42GJ
5477	A9C-BXB	5558	N604KS	5639	VP-BJA	20006	N505FX	20086	N846UP
5478	N604GR	5559	N902MP	5640	N910J	20007	N506FX	20087	N387PC
5479	N604ST	5560	N604BS	5641	A6-IFA	20008	N507FX	20088	N130CH
5480	N500M	5561	VH-MZL	5642	OH-WII	20009	N508FX	20089	N605RF
5481	N198DC	5562	N562ME	5643	N793CT	20010	N41DP	20090	N55HA
5482	N581TS	5563	N604BC	5644	OE-INY	20011	N17UC	20091	N391W
5483	N483BA	5564	N99KW	5645	4X-CUR	20012	N509FX	20092	N500AL
5484	C-GWLL	5565	D-ABCD	5646	G-HARK	20013	I-SDFC	20093	C-FDOL
5485	A9C-BXG	5566	N604PA	5647	N337FX	20014	XA-JCP	20094	I-CCCH
5486	9J-...	5567	RA-67216	5648	EC-JYT	20015	N300SM	20095	N524FX
5487	N330FX	5568	N383MB	5649	P4-BTA	20016	C-GFHR	20096	C-GPCZ
5488	N670CM	5569	N604SB	5650	C-FRCI	20017	N510FX	20097	LX-PMA
5489	C-GGBL	5570	N604CL	5651	HB-JRQ	20018	N74ZC	20098	N305EM
5490	N14GD	5571	N571BA	5652	N225N	20019	N60SB	20099	N991GS
5491	N331FX	5572	D-AIND	5653	N720AS	20020	N789MB	20100	VP-CAO
5492	N604SX	5573	N573BA	5654	OE-IDG	20021	N511FX	20101	N306EM
5493	LV-BHP	5574	N46F	5655	N604TF	20022	N512FX	20102	N555TF
5494	D-ANKE	5575	N604HF	5656	N338FX	20023	N514FX	20103	N926JR
5495	N495BA	5576	N1090X	5657	VP-BNP	20024	N184R	20104	N125TM
5496	N604TH	5577	OO-KRC	5658	OH-MOL	20025	N375WB	20105	N56HA
5497	N604RT	5578	N606RP	5659	G-TAGA	20026	N604RF	20106	G-KALS
5498	N599DA	5579	N110BP	5660	N848CC	20027	N448AS	20107	C-GFIL
5499	N999VK	5580	P4-CHV	5661	N224N	20028	N328CC	20108	N388WS
5500	N606GG	5581	N604MC	5662	N868CC	20029	HB-JEC	20109	N955H
5501	XA-SOL	5582	N604BB	5663	N604TB	20030	N300BZ	20110	C-GESO
5502	N777DB	5583	N121ET	5664	OE-IMK	20031	N411ST	20111	OE-HII
5503	N298DC	5584	N828KD	5665	N657CT	20032	N515FX	20112	N525FX
5504	N71NP	5585	D-AAOK	5991	wo	20033	OE-HRR	20113	N985FM
5505	G-OCSC	5586	N334FX	Challenger 605		20034	ZS-ACT	20114	C-FCSI
5506	C-FHYL	5587	N64UC	5701	N980SK	20035	N900WY	20115	N57HA
5507	N53DF	5588	N88	5702	N605CC	20036	N516FX	20116	D-BADO
5508	LZ-YUN	5589	N22SF	5703	VP-BML	20037	N885TW	20117	N211TB
5509	N112CF	5590	N721J	5704	OE-IFB	20038	N517FX	20118	N526FX
5510	VP-CHU	5591	G-OCSD	5705	N933ML	20039	OE-HNL	20119	N214RW
5511	N815PA	5592	N385CT	5706	C-FLSF	20040	N1967M	20120	N15GT
5512	N902AG	5593	VP-BJM	5707	N605BA	20041	VP-CLV	20121	N963RB
5513	N729KP	5594	N43SF	5708	N605CB	20042	A7-AAN	20122	N5262
5514	N880ET	5595	OE-INI	5709	HB-JRP	20043	N818KC	20123	N592SP
5515	EI-IRE	5596	OY-SGM	5710	N710TS	20044	SP-ZSZ	20124	N527FX
5516	N118RH	5597	VP-CKR	5711	N529DM*	20045	N618R	20125	N528FX
5517	LN-SUN	5598	OE-IGJ	5712	S5-ADA	20046	N518FX	20126	3B-SSD
5518	N8SP	5599	OE-IKP	5713	N604D	20047	OE-HPZ	20127	N297MC
5519	P4-AVJ	5600	N800BN	5714	PR-...	20048	N70CR	20128	N529FX
5520	A6-MBH	5601	N44SF	5715	S5-ADB	20049	N1980Z	20129	N660AL
5521	A37-001	5602	LZ-YUP					20130	N300KH

319

20131	N390DB	7189	B-4010	E2018	G-TBAE	500-0069	C-FTMI	500-0151	wfu
20132	N518GS	7193	B-4011	E2065	Z-WPD	500-0070	N227MK	500-0152	XB-AMO
20133	3B-NGT	7274	N60GH	E2239	PK-PJJ	500-0071	D2-EDC	500-0153	N2RM
20134	N600LS	7351	VP-BCI	E2306	A9C-HWR	500-0072	YV238T	500-0154	C-GRFT
20135	9M-TAN	7846	N500PR	E2312	UK-80001	500-0073	N720C	500-0155	N155MK
20136	TC-SCR	*Challenger 850*		E2390	A9C-BDF	500-0074	N500ML	500-0156	PT-KBR
20137	HB-JFO	8043	OE-ISA	**Cessna**		500-0075	wfu	500-0157	EC-HPQ
20138	N12SS	8046	4L-GAF	*500 Citation I*		500-0076	ZS-PWT	500-0158	N233DB
20139	N610LS	8047	C-GSUW	669	wfu	500-0077	N28WL	500-0159	N159KC
20140	VP-CDV	8048	OE-ILI	686	wfu	500-0078	N269RC	500-0160	wfu
20141	LN-AIR	8049	UN-C8502	696	wfu	500-0079	PT-LBN	500-0161	ZS-BTC
20142	N228KT*	8051	VP-BSD	701	wfu	500-0080	V5-OGL	500-0162	wo
20143	N300FS	8052	OY-NAD	500-0001	N715JS	500-0081	D-IEGA	500-0163	N54JV
20144	N629GB	8053	P4-GJL	500-0002	ZS-ONE	500-0082	C-GREK	500-0164	N73MP
20145	D-BUBI	8054	UN-C8501	500-0003	N503CC	500-0083	N31LW	500-0165	OD-SAS
20146	N58HA	8055	G-CJMB	500-0004	wo	500-0084	wo	500-0166	N511AT
20147	N480CB	8056	N850TS	500-0005	PT-OIG	500-0085	ZS-PTT	500-0167	YV1432
20148	N530FX	8057	C-GWWW	500-0006	wfu	500-0086	D-ICIA	500-0168	N891CA
20149	TC-KAR	8060	VH-LEF	500-0007	wo	500-0087	N633AT	500-0169	C-GTNG
20150	N531FX	8069	C-FMGV	500-0008	PT-WBY	500-0088	N251DD	500-0170	N66LE
20151	M-NEWT	8076	OE-ILY	500-0009	N55FT	500-0089	wfu	500-0171	PT-LIX
20152	N487F	*Regional Jet*		500-0010	XB-IKS	500-0090	3929	500-0172	wo
20153	N772JS	7508	G-ELNX	500-0011	N700VC	500-0091	N500AD	500-0173	wfu
20154	N532FX	7584	N501LS	500-0012	N512CC	500-0092	0222	500-0174	N15JH
20155	OH-FLM	7717	VP-BCC	500-0013	XC-FIV	500-0093	N62BR	500-0175	wo
20156	N895BB	*British Aerospace*		500-0014	N18FM	500-0094	N96FB	500-0176	N150TT
20157	N296SB	*BAC 1-11*		500-0015	PT-LPZ	500-0095	I-ARON	500-0177	N431LC
20158	N797CB			500-0016	C-GPLN	500-0096	N837MA	500-0178	EC-IBA
20159	LX-TQJ	005	wfu	500-0017	wfu	500-0097	N500GR	500-0179	PT-OMT
20160	N533FX	011	wfu	500-0018	wo	500-0099	wfu	500-0180	N500ET
20161	N534FX	015	N200JX	500-0019	N397SC	500-0100	N80AJ	500-0181	PT-KPA
20162	N888RT	054	N17MK	500-0020	wfu	500-0101	N666AG	500-0182	wfu
20163	N58LC	055	wfu	500-0021	N7GJ	500-0102	N491PT	500-0183	wfu
20164	N782BJ	056	N111RZ	500-0022	wfu	500-0103	C-GJVK	500-0184	N184NA
20165	N120GS	058	wfu	500-0023	N200QC	500-0104	N353PJ	500-0185	ZP-TZH
20166	C-FOAI	059	wfu	500-0024	N94AJ	500-0105	wfu	500-0186	N186CP
20167	N535FX	060	wfu	500-0025	N57LL	500-0106	ZS-RCC	500-0187	N130DW
20168	C-FOAQ	061	wfu	500-0026	wo	500-0107	N79RS	500-0188	N505AZ
20169	G-UYGB	064	wfu	500-0027	PT-OVK	500-0108	wo	500-0189	wfu
20170	C-FOAU	065	PK-PJF	500-0028	N133JM	500-0109	YV1677	500-0190	N434UM
20171	N536FX	067	N161NG	500-0029	N424DA	500-0110	XB-JDG	500-0191	LV-YRB
20172	M-TAGB*	068	wfu	500-0030	wfu	500-0111	wo	500-0192	I-AMCY
20173	C-FOBJ	072	VP-CLM	500-0031	YV-939CP	500-0112	N500TM	500-0193	OY-JAI
20174	C-FOQR	073	N101PC	500-0032	wo	500-0113	N500NJ	500-0194	N225RD
20175	C-FOQW	076	wfu	500-0033	N990AL	500-0114	N65SA	500-0195	N502BE
20176	C-FORB	080	wfu	500-0034	N716LT	500-0115	wo	500-0196	N270PM
20177	C-FOSB	081	wfu	500-0035	XC-MMM	500-0116	EC-HRH	500-0197	N297S
20178	C-FOSG	083	N200EE	500-0036	wfu	500-0117	N442JB	500-0198	XB-IUW
20179	C-FOSM	084	wfu	500-0037	EC-GTS	500-0118	wfu	500-0199	XA-ASR
20180	C-FOSQ	086	TZ-BSB	500-0038	N27L	500-0119	N501EJ	500-0200	N102VP
20181	C-FOSW	087	N162W	500-0039	wfu	500-0120	N712MB	500-0201	N221DA
20182	C-FOSX	088	wfu	500-0040	N98Q	500-0121	N661AC	500-0202	N550RS
20183	C-FOTF	089	TG-TJF	500-0041	N50AM	500-0122	ZS-PFG	500-0203	N51099
20184	C-FPZZ	090	N164W	500-0042	wfu	500-0123	ZS-PMA	500-0204	N928RD
20185	C-FQCF	108	wfu	500-0043	YV1152	500-0124	N92SM	500-0205	wo
20186	N725CF	111	wo	500-0044	ZS-DSA	500-0125	N108RL	500-0206	wo
20187	C-FQOA	118	PK-TST	500-0045	N628BS	500-0126	N902DD	500-0207	N501TL
20188	C-FQOF	119	N789CF	500-0046	PT-OTQ	500-0127	N580R	500-0208	N770AF
20189	C-FQOI	120	N999BW	500-0047	YV-....	500-0128	wfu	500-0209	wfu
20190	C-FQOK	126	5A-DKO	500-0048	N911GM	500-0129	N500SK	500-0210	XB-TRY
20191	C-FQOL	135	wfu	500-0049	N25UT	500-0130	N130CE	500-0211	wfu
20192	C-FQOM	158	5A-DDQ	500-0050	VH-HKX	500-0131	N105JA	500-0212	N74LL
20193	C-FQOQ	163	N111JX	500-0051	VH-EGK	500-0132	N713SA	500-0213	XA-AEI
20194	C-FRQA	183	XB-JZX	500-0052	YV1316	500-0133	PT-LXH	500-0214	N601GN
20195	C-FRQC	236	wfu	500-0053	I-AEAL	500-0134	PT-JMJ	500-0215	YV2030
20196	C-FRQH	259	YR-HRS	500-0054	XB-PBT	500-0135	wo	500-0216	YV1686
20197	C-FRQK	260	YR-MIA	500-0055	N716CB	500-0136	XA-JRV	500-0217	N55GR
20198	C-FRQM	262	PK-TRU	500-0056	N777JJ	500-0137	ZS-MCU	500-0218	N271AC
Challenger 800		263	ZH763	500-0057	wo	500-0138	N138SA	500-0219	wo
7008	N601LS	405	YR-BRE	500-0058	YV-901CP	500-0139	N15AW	500-0220	G-ORHE
7021	N155MW	*BAe 146*		500-0059	N117TW	500-0140	N972AB	500-0221	N24AJ
7075	N135BC	E1006	G-OFOA	500-0060	PT-OOL	500-0141	N727TK	500-0222	N52PM
7099	N168CK	E1017	G-BLRA	500-0061	ZS-DBS	500-0142	N69XW	500-0223	I-CLAD
7136	HB-IDJ	E1021	ZE700	500-0062	N334RC	500-0143	SE-DUZ	500-0224	ZS-ISA
7138	B-4005	E1029	ZE701	500-0063	N70MG	500-0144	wo	500-0225	wo
7140	N711WM	E1068	N114M	500-0064	N27SF	500-0145	N145TA	500-0226	PT-LTI
7149	B-4006	E1076	FAB 098	500-0065	N565CC	500-0146	N111ME	500-0227	TI-AZX
7152	N529DB	E1091	wfu	500-0066	wfu	500-0147	N688CF	500-0228	wfu
7176	VP-BHX	E1124	PK-OSP	500-0067	N567EA	500-0148	N989SC	500-0229	wo
7180	B-4007	E1144	G-OFOM	500-0068	XB-VGT	500-0149	ZS-TMG	500-0230	N200CG
						500-0150	N914CD	500-0231	N501GB

500-0232	N999AM	500-0314	N668F	501-0013	N501TJ	501-0094	C-FBDS	501-0175	N23VK
500-0233	N233JJ	500-0315	SE-DRZ	501-0014	N888FL	501-0095	XA-AGA	501-0176	N96DA
500-0234	N70CA	500-0316	N711MT	501-0015	N454AC	501-0096	N501HS	501-0177	N98AV
500-0235	N12AM	500-0317	YV-1133CP	501-0016	N45TL	501-0097	N251CF	501-0178	G-VUEM
500-0236	N70SW	500-0318	VP-COM	501-0017	N501AT	501-0098	N92BE	501-0179	N718SA
500-0237	wo	500-0319	F-GKID	501-0018	XB-JXG	501-0099	I-FLYA	501-0180	N510NJ
500-0238	N409S	500-0320	N70WA	501-0019	N501SP	501-0100	N54FT	501-0181	N501KK
500-0239	wfu	500-0321	wfu	501-0020	N123EB	501-0101	N501KM	501-0182	N220HM
500-0240	N234AT	500-0322	N108MC	501-0021	N151SP	501-0102	VH-FCS	501-0183	CS-AYY
500-0241	N610ED	500-0323	N388GM	501-0022	wo	501-0103	ZS-PHP	501-0184	N318DN
500-0242	N888JL	500-0324	N324JC	501-0023	N56MK	501-0104	N998EA	501-0185	N505BG
500-0243	N243SH	500-0325	PT-OSD	501-0024	N70BG	501-0105	N2648X	501-0186	N999WS
500-0244	PT-OQD	500-0326	wo	501-0025	N20RM	501-0106	N793AA	501-0187	N70CG
500-0245	D-IAJJ	500-0327	RP-C3958	501-0026	N92BL	501-0107	EC-GJF	501-0188	N525PV
500-0246	PT-LQR	500-0328	XB-IXE	501-0027	JA8380	501-0108	N707GG	501-0189	VH-FUM
500-0247	wfu	500-0329	OY-CEV	501-0028	N501PV	501-0109	N567WB	501-0190	N723JR
500-0248	N111BB	500-0330	N800CJ	501-0029	XA-TKY	501-0110	wo	501-0191	N64RT
500-0249	HA-JET	500-0331	G-LOFT	501-0030	N911MM	501-0111	N79BK	501-0192	N190K
500-0250	N251MG	500-0332	N332SE	501-0031	LV-BFM	501-0112	N224GP	501-0193	N89MF
500-0251	PT-OMS	500-0333	VH-SOU	501-0032	N307D	501-0113	N502CC	501-0194	N65WW
500-0252	N622AT	500-0334	wfu	501-0033	N91PE	501-0114	wfu	501-0195	N123KD
500-0253	N592WP	500-0335	PT-LDI	501-0034	N501CP	501-0115	N728MC	501-0196	N311TP
500-0254	wo	500-0336	wo	501-0035	N501DD	501-0116	N7TK	501-0197	N324L
500-0255	N752CK	500-0337	N17KD	501-0036	N360MC	501-0117	N91AP	501-0198	N800DT
500-0256	N676DG	500-0338	N41HL	501-0037	N501U	501-0118	XB-TMG	501-0199	N91HG
500-0257	ZS-PXD	500-0339	G-DJAE	501-0038	N501JG	501-0119	N13KD	501-0200	N47TL
500-0258	N125DS	500-0340	N344RJ	501-0039	N141M	501-0120	N71LP	501-0201	N953HC
500-0259	N259DH	500-0341	C-FDMB	501-0040	N21EP	501-0121	OE-FHW	501-0202	N501G
500-0260	N202HM	500-0342	N501LN	501-0041	wo	501-0122	N501MB	501-0203	wo
500-0261	N58TC	500-0343	N501JF	501-0042	wo	501-0123	N627E	501-0204	N367HB
500-0262	ZS-BFS	500-0344	VP-BLV	501-0043	N16NL	501-0124	wo	501-0205	N528RM
500-0263	VH-ZMD	500-0345	XB-CSI	501-0044	N600RM	501-0125	N125EA	501-0206	N528DS
500-0264	G-JTNC	500-0346	PT-LUA	501-0045	N22EL	501-0126	N505JH	501-0207	VP-BHO
500-0265	N595DC	500-0347	N876WB	501-0046	N5VP	501-0127	N117DJ	501-0208	N82P
500-0266	N11MN	500-0348	N712KM	501-0047	N550U	501-0128	N501CF	501-0209	N70NB
500-0267	wfu	500-0349	N501DA	501-0048	I-OTEL	501-0129	N501JD	501-0210	N32FM
500-0268	N900G	500-0354	N694LM	501-0049	ZS-CWD	501-0130	N505CF	501-0211	wfu
500-0269	SP-KBM	500-0356	AE-185	501-0050	N59MA	501-0131	N133SC	501-0212	N2243
500-0270	N970RP	500-0358	I-UUNY	501-0051	N422DA	501-0132	N39HH	501-0213	I-AUNY
500-0271	wo	500-0361	F-GKIR	501-0052	N677JM	501-0133	N700SP	501-0214	N241BF
500-0272	wfu	500-0364	SE-RGN	501-0053	N52TL	501-0134	N841CW	501-0215	N215NA
500-0273	XB-GBF	500-0367	YV-52CP	501-0054	N501EA	501-0135	N501WL	501-0216	TG-RIE
500-0274	N5LK	500-0369	wfu	501-0055	N223LC	501-0136	N511HC	501-0217	N7MZ
500-0275	N411TN	500-0370	SE-DEY	501-0056	N56WE	501-0137	N14VA	501-0218	N218JG
500-0276	SE-DEG	500-0374	N501SS	501-0057	N577JT	501-0138	N74FH	501-0219	N56PB
500-0277	N662CC	500-0378	wfu	501-0058	wo	501-0139	N501AF	501-0220	N100LX
500-0278	EC-JXC	500-0386	LQ-MRM	501-0059	N16HL	501-0140	OE-FDM	501-0221	N501HG
500-0279	N501KG	500-0387	N504D	501-0060	N11TM	501-0141	N501DR	501-0222	N690WY
500-0280	wo	500-0392	3D-IER	501-0061	EC-KGX	501-0142	N67BE	501-0223	N18HC
500-0281	N70TS	500-0395	XB-JFV	501-0062	N980DM	501-0143	N501WJ*	501-0224	N825PS
500-0282	HB-VNU	500-0396	XC-GTO	501-0063	N555KW	501-0144	OE-FMK	501-0225	N412SE
500-0283	wo	500-0399	T9-SBA	501-0064	N12WH	501-0145	wo	501-0226	N501JM
500-0284	PT-LOG	500-0401	I-FARN	501-0065	N33WW	501-0146	N53BB	501-0227	N83DM
500-0285	N113SH	500-0403	wo	501-0066	N501CD	501-0147	N551MS	501-0228	N665MM
500-0286	wfu	500-0404	LV-BID	501-0067	HB-VJB	501-0148	XA-...	501-0229	N57FC
500-0287	VP-BGE	500-0406	OY-FFB	501-0068	N363TD	501-0149	N72VJ	501-0230	N999MS
500-0288	N1DA	500-0408	XB-DVF	501-0069	N636N	501-0150	wo	501-0231	N501BP
500-0289	wo	500-0409	XC-FEZ	501-0070	N45MM	501-0151	N797SE	501-0232	VP-CAT
500-0290	N400RM	500-0410	XC-GAW	501-0071	N666TS	501-0152	N15CY	501-0233	N501Q
500-0291	OE-FGN	500-0411	SE-DLZ	501-0072	N17HA	501-0153	N99CK	501-0234	N123PL
500-0292	XB-ESG	500-0412	XB-GDJ	501-0073	wo	501-0154	N154SC	501-0235	N2617U
500-0294	OE-FCM	500-0413	PT-LCC	501-0074	N552AJ	501-0155	N347MH	501-0236	C-GQJJ
500-0295	N10FG	500-0415	N53RD	501-0075	N713JD	501-0156	N44FM	501-0237	N420PC
500-0296	XA-BET	500-0418	ZS-LDV	501-0076	N150RM	501-0157	N16VG	501-0238	N737RJ
500-0297	N38SA	501-0278	N124NS	501-0077	I-FRAI	501-0158	N501WB	501-0239	OE-FMS
500-0298	N900GC	501-0280	N212M	501-0078	N25MB	501-0159	N80CJ	501-0240	N238BG
500-0299	N80364	501-0286	N381BJ	501-0079	N79FT	501-0160	N999PW	501-0241	N101RR
500-0300	wo	500 Citation I/SP		501-0080	N800BF	501-0161	N501FP	501-0242	N71L
500-0301	N305S	501-0001	N506TF	501-0081	N12CV	501-0162	N501DP	501-0243	N43SP
500-0302	N710VL	501-0002	N88TB	501-0082	N5WF	501-0163	I-CIGB	501-0244	N501T
500-0303	N8DX	501-0003	N81EB	501-0083	N910G	501-0164	N286PC	501-0245	ZS-ACE
500-0304	wfu	501-0004	N142DA	501-0084	EC-ISP	501-0165	N501RC	501-0246	OE-FHH
500-0305	N100AM	501-0005	N455FD	501-0085	N707W	501-0166	N166FA	501-0247	wo
500-0306	N606KK	501-0006	I-ERJA	501-0086	EC-INJ	501-0167	N501FJ	501-0248	N7700T
500-0307	N777SL	501-0007	N222WA	501-0087	N501BB	501-0168	N328NA	501-0249	N117MA
500-0308	F-GSMC	501-0008	N909PS	501-0088	N3WT	501-0169	C-GFEE	501-0250	N77FD
500-0309	N83NW	501-0009	N505RJ	501-0089	VH-MMC	501-0170	N610TT	501-0251	N501WD
500-0310	N900CC	501-0010	EC-EDN	501-0090	N3GN	501-0171	N171WJ	501-0252	I-TOIO
500-0311	I-RAGW	501-0011	N1UM	501-0091	N2158U	501-0172	N110JB	501-0253	N501JE
500-0312	EC-KGE	501-0012	N449DT	501-0092	N303A	501-0173	N91TE	501-0254	N66BK
500-0313	D-ISKM			501-0093	N501AD	501-0174	N921BE	501-0255	N501X

501-0256	N256BM	525-0023	N525RP	525-0104	N608MM	525-0185	N13FH	525-0266	N266CJ
501-0257	N501WX*	525-0024	D-IAOA	525-0105	G-EDCJ	525-0186	N92ND	525-0267	PT-XMM
501-0258	N599BR	525-0025	D-IBBA	525-0106	N21VC	525-0187	N696ST	525-0268	N850DG
501-0259	D-IEIR	525-0026	N602CA	525-0107	N525WC	525-0188	OE-FMA	525-0269	N607DB
501-0260	N501RG	525-0027	N700CJ	525-0108	N108CJ	525-0189	N189CM	525-0270	N525HC
501-0261	N501VP	525-0028	N525WH*	525-0109	C-GDWS	525-0190	N701TP	525-0271	HB-VNK
501-0262	N20CZ	525-0029	D-IWHL	525-0110	N195ME	525-0191	N15LV	525-0272	N4QP
501-0263	N501BE	525-0030	N53KV	525-0111	N776DF	525-0192	N84FG	525-0273	N911NP
501-0264	N27WW	525-0031	N831S	525-0112	VT-OPJ	525-0193	HB-VOZ	525-0274	PT-XDB
501-0267	N565V	525-0032	N900DS	525-0113	G-SEAJ*	525-0194	I-DEAC	525-0275	N700GW
501-0269	N501JJ	525-0033	N501KR	525-0114	N294CW	525-0195	N525DC	525-0276	N800GW
501-0270	N501ST	525-0034	N333VS	525-0115	OO-PHI	525-0196	N525LP	525-0277	OY-JMC
501-0272	N44MK	525-0035	N525HS	525-0116	N323JA	525-0197	EC-HIN	525-0278	N901CJ
501-0273	N301DR	525-0036	N525MB	525-0117	N26QB	525-0198	N198RG	525-0279	D-IGME
501-0275	N40AJ	525-0037	OO-IDE	525-0118	D-IRWR	525-0199	N299CW	525-0280	PT-XAC
501-0279	PH-DEZ	525-0038	N600HR	525-0119	N466F	525-0200	N226B	525-0281	VH-APJ
501-0281	N501CB	525-0039	N39CJ	525-0120	PR-VGD	525-0201	N525HV	525-0282	N625PG
501-0282	N82AJ	525-0040	OE-FMU	525-0121	D-ICSS	525-0202	N747AC	525-0283	N95BS
501-0283	N204CA	525-0041	N565JF	525-0122	N41YP	525-0203	N33FW	525-0284	N256JB
501-0284	N45AF	525-0042	PH-MGT	525-0123	D-IRKE	525-0204	B-4108	525-0285	N55PX
501-0285	N13ST	525-0043	N525PL	525-0124	OE-FRR	525-0205	N525DU	525-0286	D-INFS
501-0289	N82DT	525-0044	EC-KKE	525-0125	N525PT	525-0206	N45PF*	525-0287	C-GBPM
501-0292	N339HP	525-0045	LV-AMB	525-0126	D-IAHG	525-0207	N26RL	525-0288	N288AG
501-0293	N597CS	525-0046	N127SG	525-0127	N63LF	525-0208	N211GM	525-0289	D-ISHW
501-0294	N80SL	525-0047	N47FH	525-0128	N535LR	525-0209	D-ILAT	525-0290	N808WA
501-0297	N41GT	525-0048	N484J	525-0129	C-GPOS	525-0210	N28CK	525-0291	F-GPLF
501-0298	N501D	525-0049	N349SF	525-0130	N418KC	525-0211	D-IMMD	525-0292	OE-FCW
501-0302	N7EN	525-0050	N205BN	525-0131	N41EA	525-0212	N800NB	525-0293	N1127K
501-0303	N303RH	525-0051	N726SC	525-0132	N132AH	525-0213	N525WM	525-0294	N294AT
501-0311	N311VP	525-0052	N52PK	525-0133	EC-GIE	525-0214	N130LM	525-0295	OE-FJU
501-0314	N56LW	525-0053	N3WB	525-0134	N525JM	525-0215	N28GA	525-0296	N296DC
501-0317	N51FT	525-0054	N851DB	525-0135	N888RA	525-0216	N18GA	525-0297	VP-CAD
501-0319	N60EW	525-0055	N570DM	525-0136	wo	525-0217	OE-FMT	525-0298	N55CJ
501-0320	C-GTOL	525-0056	JA8420	525-0137	N810SS	525-0218	N713SD	525-0299	N711BX
501-0321	N986DS	525-0057	N585DG	525-0138	VH-DAA	525-0219	N219CJ	525-0300	N881KS
501-0322	N527EW	525-0058	N525F	525-0139	N36RG	525-0220	N25MX	525-0301	N915ST
501-0323	N505BB	525-0059	N816FC	525-0140	N111BF	525-0221	D-IWIL	525-0302	N326B
501-0324	JA8493	525-0060	N525WW	525-0141	N545RW	525-0222	wo	525-0303	D-IMMI
501-0325	N64BH	525-0061	N525PS	525-0142	N815MC	525-0223	OM-HLZ	525-0304	N525TX*
501-0446	A7-ASA	525-0062	C-FPWB	525-0143	EC-KJV	525-0224	N224CJ	525-0305	N826HS
501-0643	C-GQPJ	525-0063	N55SK	525-0144	D-IDAG	525-0225	N525RM	525-0306	N525DY
501-0675	N593BW	525-0064	D-IHEB	525-0145	N424TV	525-0226	OE-FSS	525-0307	N114FW
501-0676	N676CC	525-0065	EC-FZP	525-0146	N1329G	525-0227	N741CC	525-0308	N373AF
501-0677	N74HR	525-0066	N824ES	525-0147	N996JR	525-0228	N669DB	525-0309	D-IBMS
501-0678	PT-ODC	525-0067	N525TF	525-0148	N300DL	525-0229	F-GXRK	525-0310	OK-SLA
501-0679	N73SK	525-0068	N888KU	525-0149	wo	525-0230	N934AM	525-0311	N27CJ
501-0680	PP-EIF	525-0069	N20VL	525-0150	N8341C	525-0231	N606MG	525-0312	CN-TLB
501-0681	N427SS	525-0070	D-ISGW	525-0151	N242GB	525-0232	N525GB	525-0313	N525MF
501-0682	N682BF	525-0071	N940SW	525-0152	N152KV	525-0233	PR-CAN	525-0314	N525DM
501-0683	N702RT	525-0072	TG-RIF	525-0153	G-PWNS	525-0234	N950P	525-0315	OE-FMI
501-0684	N501TP	525-0073	N77794	525-0154	N520DF	525-0235	LX-GCA	525-0316	N458MT
501-0685	XB-IXT	525-0074	N511TC	525-0155	I-EDEM	525-0236	D-ISWA	525-0317	N51GS
501-0686	N750PP	525-0075	N719D	525-0156	N156ML	525-0237	N61YP	525-0318	N525DP
501-0687	N361DE	525-0076	N805VC	525-0157	N54HC	525-0238	PT-WQI	525-0319	PT-FNP
501-0688	wo	525-0077	N1000E	525-0158	N800RK	525-0239	N525VG	525-0320	N150BV
501-0689	C-FNHZ	525-0078	N525CH	525-0159	N351BC	525-0240	N524SF	525-0321	PH-ECI
525 CitationJet		525-0079	N525WB	525-0160	N66AM	525-0241	N307BS	525-0322	LX-YSL
702	wfu	525-0080	N33DT	525-0161	N525BT	525-0242	N242LJ	525-0323	N900GW
525-0001	N525GV	525-0081	N525HA	525-0162	N525JW	525-0243	CC-CVO	525-0324	G-IUAN
525-0002	N54BP	525-0082	N525LW	525-0163	N51CD	525-0244	N66ES	525-0325	N115BB
525-0003	N45FJ	525-0083	N50PL*	525-0164	N204J	525-0245	G-SFCJ	525-0326	N188TW
525-0004	N7CQ	525-0084	G-CITJ	525-0165	N525P	525-0246	N525WF	525-0327	LV-AXN
525-0005	N521PF	525-0085	PT-MJC	525-0166	N252JK	525-0247	N241EP	525-0328	N328CJ
525-0006	N106CJ	525-0086	PT-MIL	525-0167	N525RA	525-0248	N248CJ	525-0329	XB-DGA
525-0007	N525KN	525-0087	N606HC	525-0168	D-IRON	525-0249	N909F*	525-0330	N38SC
525-0008	N525FD	525-0088	N722SG	525-0169	N230LL	525-0250	F-HMJC	525-0331	OE-...
525-0009	N1327J	525-0089	N202BG	525-0170	N170MU	525-0251	N616BM	525-0332	N511BP
525-0010	N525JV	525-0090	LZ-DIN	525-0171	N97VF	525-0252	N252RV	525-0333	N99CJ
525-0011	N525AL	525-0091	N295DS	525-0172	OO-CEJ	525-0253	N253CW	525-0334	N525M
525-0012	N86LA	525-0092	N534TX	525-0173	N129RP	525-0254	OE-FGI	525-0335	N467F
525-0013	N550TF	525-0093	N525CM	525-0174	N66BE	525-0255	N514DS	525-0336	N105P
525-0014	N620TC	525-0094	N94MZ	525-0175	N41PG	525-0256	N196HA	525-0337	PT-FJA
525-0015	PT-MPE	525-0095	N61SH	525-0176	wo	525-0257	N561BC	525-0338	N907DK
525-0016	D-IKOP	525-0096	D-ICEE	525-0177	F-HASC	525-0258	OY-SML	525-0339	N841TC*
525-0017	N28PT	525-0097	wo	525-0178	N525RC	525-0259	PT-MSP	525-0340	N392RG
525-0018	N525MC	525-0098	N511AC	525-0179	N608DB	525-0260	N260AM	525-0341	N341AR
525-0019	N525KA	525-0099	N526CP	525-0180	VP-BDS	525-0261	N31HD	525-0342	N918CW
525-0020	OE-FGD	525-0100	VH-KXL	525-0181	N88LD	525-0262	N262BK	525-0343	D-IURS
525-0021	N793CJ	525-0101	OM-OPR	525-0182	N177JF	525-0263	N263CT	525-0344	N77VZ
525-0022	G-BVCM	525-0102	LX-LOV	525-0183	N399G	525-0264	D-IPCS	525-0345	G-ZIZI
		525-0103	OE-FLG	525-0184	N525J	525-0265	N198JH	525-0346	PP-CRS

525-0347	I-DAGF	525-0426	N426ED	525-0507	364	525-0630	N711C	525A-0039	N900HA
525-0348	N8288R	525-0427	N525LM	525-0508	EC-JSH	525-0631	YV2331	525A-0040	N525HB
525-0349	D-ICWB	525-0428	PR-ABV	525-0509	N993GL	525-0632	CC-PGK	525A-0041	D-IHHN
525-0350	N720GM	525-0429	EC-IVJ	525-0510	G-EDCK	525-0633	N43BH	525A-0042	PR-JET
525-0351	OK-...	525-0430	N430GR	525-0511	N326JK	525-0634	OE-FSR	525A-0043	N432CJ
525-0352	N31JB	525-0431	ZS-PWU	525-0512	N411MY	525-0635	N817BT	525A-0044	PR-JST
525-0353	D-ICOL	525-0432	N94AL	525-0513	N513RV	525-0636	C-GTRG	525A-0045	N3ST
525-0354	I-CABD	525-0433	N102PT	525-0514	PH-FIS	525-0637	C-G...	525A-0046	N46NT
525-0355	N312SB	525-0434	N860DB	525-0515	N551FP*	525-0638	VH-MYE	525A-0047	N2250G
525-0356	PP-YOF	525-0435	G-CJAD	525-0516	D-INER	525-0639	D-IMPC	525A-0048	PT-FTC
525-0357	N357JV	525-0436	EC-HVQ	525-0517	D-IFDH	525-0640	N34DZ	525A-0049	OE-FHB
525-0358	G-HMMV	525-0437	N717NA	525-0518	F-HAGH	525-0641	C-GIRL	525A-0050	N525DL
525-0359	F-GTRY	525-0438	N325DM	525-0519	N926TF	525-0642	N466AE	525A-0051	N415SL
525 CitationJet CJ-1/+		525-0439	N54CG	525-0520	N135CS	525-0643	N380CR	525A-0052	D-ISCH
525-0360	N525CD	525-0440	N525NT	525-0521	VH-YNE	525-0644	N902DP	525A-0053	PT-FTE
525-0361	N128CS	525-0441	PR-ARA	525-0522	N125CS	525-0645	OE-FPO	525A-0054	PH-ECL
525-0362	N362FL	525-0442	D-ILLY	525-0523	F-HAJD	525-0646	A7-CJI	525A-0055	N525ZZ
525-0363	N523TS	525-0443	N77DB	525-0524	N770BX	525-0647	N1895C	525A-0056	N743JG
525-0364	C-FTKX	525-0444	N525BR	525-0525	N123S	525-0648	G-CJDB	525A-0057	wo
525-0365	N651CJ	525-0445	N207BS	525-0526	VP-CJI	525-0649	N794PF	525A-0058	N525KT*
525-0366	D-....	525-0446	N246GS	525-0527	N15BV	525-0650	HB-VWF	525A-0059	N59CJ
525-0367	N525FT	525-0447	N952SP	525-0528	N528CJ	525-0651	N24BC	525A-0060	N525RW
525-0368	N525FN	525-0448	EC-JFD	525-0529	N151EW*	525-0652	RA-.....	525A-0061	PR-TOP
525-0369	N161SM	525-0449	JA525A	525-0530	N430JH	525-0653	N7715X	525A-0062	N30HD
525-0370	N525MW	525-0450	I-BOAT	525-0531	N525FC	525-0654	N94HL	525A-0063	VH-MOR
525-0371	HZ-BL1	525-0451	N165CA	525-0532	N323G	525-0655	B-7777	525A-0064	EC-IEB
525-0372	N345MG	525-0452	N585MC	525-0533	D-IPMI	525-0656	N388FW	525A-0065	N55KT
525-0373	N415CS	525-0453	N869CB	525-0534	N534NA	525-0657	N65BK	525A-0066	N741PC
525-0374	N12GY	525-0454	N101U	525-0535	JA525Y	525-0658	N907WL	525A-0067	N525PM
525-0375	HB-VNL	525-0455	N15SS*	525-0537	N678RF	525-0659	OE-FNA	525A-0068	N315MC
525-0376	N814DM	525-0456	PR-LJM	525-0538	N525AM	525-0660	N197RJ	525A-0069	N757CP
525-0377	N900BT	525-0457	N774GE	525-0539	N152CS	525-0661	N613AL	525A-0070	D-ILAM
525-0378	N203BG	525-0458	N525NP	525-0540	N40CJ	525-0662	N607TN	525A-0071	N701SF
525-0379	I-IMMI	525-0459	N459NA	525-0541	N739LN*	525-0663	N297RJ	525A-0072	N65PZ
525-0380	B-3669	525-0460	N57EC	525-0542	N500CW	525-0664	N664CJ	525A-0073	I-LVNB
525-0381	N476JD*	525-0461	N200SL	525-0543	N43NW	525-0665	N5037F	525A-0074	N222NF
525-0382	N525LF	525-0462	N965LC	525-0544	HB-VOG	525-0666	N5076K	525A-0075	N52AG
525-0383	N600AL	525-0463	361	525-0545	N545TG	525-0667	N629DR	525A-0076	N1277E
525-0384	PP-JET	525-0464	362	525-0546	N981LB	525-0668	N557HP	525A-0077	N377GS
525-0385	N417Q	525-0465	363	525-0547	N547TW	525-0671	SE-RIX*	525A-0078	N113BG
525-0386	N386RF	525-0466	D-INCS	525-0548	N153CS	*525A CitationJet CJ-2/+*		525A-0079	N77HA
525-0387	N724FS	525-0467	N620BB	525-0549	JA525J	708	N244CJ	525A-0080	F-HEKO
525-0388	N520GB	525-0468	N468RW	525-0550	SP-KKA	525A-0001	N529PC	525A-0081	N414FW
525-0389	D-IDAS	525-0469	N520RM	525-0551	B-3644	525A-0002	N400WD	525A-0082	OE-FGL
525-0390	N100PF	525-0470	N901GW	525-0552	B-3645	525A-0003	N525DT	525A-0083	G-EDCL
525-0391	LX-IIH	525-0471	B-3668	525-0553	N902GW	525A-0004	N308GT	525A-0084	N523DG
525-0392	N392SM	525-0472	N525KM	525-0554	B-3647	525A-0005	I-LALL	525A-0085	N85JV
525-0393	OM-HLY	525-0473	HB-VOR	525-0555	B-3648	525A-0006	N245SP	525A-0086	N759R
525-0394	S5-BAJ	525-0474	N31CJ	525-0556	N93LS	525A-0007	N525CC	525A-0087	N474PC
525-0395	N507HP	525-0475	XA-TTG	525-0557	B-3649	525A-0008	N901EB	525A-0088	N569DM
525-0396	D-IMAC	525-0476	N74PG	525-0558	B-3650	525A-0009	F-HAPP	525A-0089	PR-WOB
525-0397	I-RVRP	525-0477	OE-FOI	525-0600	N919MC	525A-0010	N121CP	525A-0090	N475DH
525-0398	C-GMTI	525-0478	N869GR	525-0601	N29ET	525A-0011	OE-FLP	525A-0091	N8940
525-0399	D-ITAN	525-0479	N525BP	525-0602	D-ISJM	525A-0012	N525MA	525A-0092	N21RA
525-0400	F-GMDL	525-0480	OE-FIX	525-0603	N805CJ	525A-0013	N894C	525A-0093	N954RM
525-0401	N44CK	525-0481	N795BM	525-0604	N122LM	525A-0014	N18TF	525A-0094	VH-RJB
525-0402	N525ML	525-0482	PR-EXP	525-0605	N800PF	525A-0015	N629PA	525A-0095	I-DEUM
525-0403	PT-PRR	525-0483	PR-EOB	525-0606	N713WH	525A-0016	N306CJ	525A-0096	N96NA
525-0404	N88AD	525-0484	F-HALO	525-0607	N59JN	525A-0017	HB-VOE	525A-0097	N97CJ
525-0405	N7895Q	525-0485	N674JM	525-0608	N915RP	525A-0018	N96G	525A-0098	N57HC
525-0406	N72JW	525-0486	EC-JIU	525-0609	N50VC	525A-0019	F-GXRL	525A-0099	N777HN
525-0407	N525JL	525-0487	N191PP	525-0610	N35TK	525A-0020	N823L*	525A-0100	N170TM
525-0408	PP-JBS	525-0488	N488SR	525-0611	D-ICEY	525A-0021	N525TG	525A-0101	N125BJ
525-0409	N525BW*	525-0489	N489CB	525-0612	N525RZ	525A-0022	N630TF	525A-0102	D-IWIR
525-0410	N4108E	525-0490	N130CS	525-0613	PH-CMW	525A-0023	N525PF	525A-0103	N800VT
525-0411	D-ILIF	525-0491	N926CC	525-0614	OE-FMD	525A-0024	N915MP	525A-0104	N80C
525-0412	N82AE	525-0492	N388PS	525-0615	N65EM	525A-0025	N550TB	525A-0105	N91A
525-0413	N525RK	525-0493	N95CK	525-0616	N999EB	525A-0026	EK-52526	525A-0106	OE-FUX
525-0414	N26DV*	525-0494	D-ITIP	525-0617	N116LJ	525A-0027	N420EH	525A-0107	N525WD
525-0415	HB-VOD	525-0495	OY-RGG	525-0618	N618KA	525A-0028	N592DR	525A-0108	D-ICMS
525-0416	N186TW	525-0496	N382EM	525-0619	VT-NAB	525A-0029	D-IKJS	525A-0109	N22LX
525-0417	PH-SOL	525-0497	N525JJ	525-0620	N5UD	525A-0030	D-ISJP	525A-0110	N451AJ
525-0418	N300BV	525-0498	wfu	525-0621	N621AD	525A-0031	M-XONE	525A-0111	wo
525-0419	N7XE	525-0499	HB-VNP	525-0622	N622SL	525A-0032	D-IGIT	525A-0112	N701TF
525-0420	N726CL	525-0500	N111LQ	525-0623	HB-VOF	525A-0033	EC-JJU	525A-0113	G-OCJT
525-0421	OE-FET	525-0501	N41LF	525-0624	D-IOWA	525A-0034	D-IJOA	525A-0114	N726RP
525-0422	N125DJ	525-0502	SE-RGX	525-0625	D-IEPR	525A-0035	N288G	525A-0115	N115CJ
525-0423	G-OEBJ	525-0503	N909DP	525-0626	N626CV	525A-0036	wo	525A-0116	N411BE*
525-0424	N711WG	525-0504	N665CH	525-0627	N627MW	525A-0037	N401LG	525A-0117	PT-FTG
525-0425	C-FWBK	525-0505	N502TN	525-0628	T7-FRA	525A-0038	I-IMMG	525A-0118	N971TB
		525-0506	N242ML	525-0629	N56KP			525A-0119	N525DV

Serial	Reg	Serial	Reg	Serial	Reg	Serial	Reg	Serial	Reg
525A-0120	N220JD	525A-0201	N888GL	525A-0339	N500NB	525B-0023	N15C	525B-0105	N247MV
525A-0121	N5YD	525A-0202	G-EEBJ	525A-0340	D-IFIS	525B-0024	N525GM	525B-0106	N106JT
525A-0122	N224WD	525A-0203	OE-FSG	525A-0341	HB-VOL	525B-0025	N7NE	525B-0107	D-COBO
525A-0123	N37BG	525A-0204	OE-FCY	525A-0342	N178WG	525B-0026	N162EC	525B-0108	N418CS
525A-0124	N523BT	525A-0205	N205YY	525A-0343	D-IFDN	525B-0027	ZK-TBM	525B-0109	N1255J
525A-0125	D-IBJJ	525A-0206	OO-CIV	525A-0344	N45MH	525B-0028	PR-SPO	525B-0110	N28MH
525A-0126	N999WE	525A-0207	VT-JSP	525A-0345	N9180K	525B-0029	N726AG	525B-0111	N96PD
525A-0127	N112GS	525A-0208	N400HT	525A-0346	N525EP	525B-0030	N401CS	525B-0112	N731WH
525A-0128	N525CK	525A-0209	OY-UCA	525A-0347	M-ICRO	525B-0031	N303CJ	525B-0113	N55GP
525A-0129	N129SG	525A-0210	OE-FCU	525A-0348	S5-BAS	525B-0032	N137BG	525B-0114	N114CJ
525A-0130	N550KR	525A-0211	N515EV	525A-0349	N535TV	525B-0033	N404CS	525B-0115	N420CS
525A-0131	N20GP	525A-0212	N104PC	525A-0350	N117W	525B-0034	N65VM	525B-0116	ZS-CJT
525A-0132	N75PP	525A-0213	ES-LUX	525A-0351	N909MN	525B-0035	N93JW	525B-0117	F-GRUJ
525A-0133	N251KD	525A-0214	N7QM	525A-0352	N525HG	525B-0036	N405CS	525B-0118	C-GSSC
525A-0134	N323SK	525A-0215	N748RE	525A-0353	N929VC	525B-0037	C-FXTC	525B-0119	D-CNOB
525A-0135	N70KW	525A-0216	EC-JMS	525A-0354	OE-FOA	525B-0038	N100RC	525B-0120	D-CEFD
525A-0136	N345CJ	525A-0217	N67GH	525A-0355	D-IWBL	525B-0039	N525DG	525B-0121	N423CS
525A-0137	N717VB	525A-0218	D-IPVD	525A-0356	N617CB	525B-0040	N550T	525B-0122	N12GS
525A-0138	N722TS	525A-0219	F-HEOL	525A-0357	N624PL	525B-0041	N3CT	525B-0123	N73EM
525A-0139	N526HV	525A-0220	N800RL	525A-0358	D-IEFA	525B-0042	N69FH	525B-0124	PR-ALC
525A-0140	N140DA	525A-0221	YV305T	525A-0359	JA359C	525B-0043	N406CS	525B-0125	OE-GPO
525A-0141	N6ZE	525A-0222	VT-DOV	525A-0360	G-HGRC	525B-0044	N144AL	525B-0126	N621GA
525A-0142	OE-FPS	525A-0223	D-IWAN	525A-0361	N361JR	525B-0045	N408CS	525B-0127	N107PT
525A-0143	D-ISUN	525A-0224	N576SC	525A-0362	OE-FGB	525B-0046	N860DD	525B-0128	N17CN
525A-0144	N144YD	525A-0225	N67CC	525A-0363	D-IETZ	525B-0047	PR-EBD	525B-0129	N629EE
525A-0145	N7GZ	525A-0226	N526DV	525A-0364	D-ITOR	525B-0048	N92MA	525B-0130	N329CJ
525A-0146	N1220W	525A-0227	N761KG	525A-0365	OE-FLA	525B-0049	N628CB	525B-0131	N30UD
525A-0147	D-IVVA	525A-0228	PR-NTX	525A-0366	N366CJ	525B-0050	N409CS	525B-0132	N425CS
525A-0148	N148FB	525A-0229	OE-FVB	525A-0367	N367CJ	525B-0051	N525L	525B-0133	N233MM
525A-0149	N90CJ	525A-0230	D-IGRO	525A-0368	N93AK	525B-0052	N999SM	525B-0134	N41ND
525A-0150	OE-FRA	525A-0231	D-IWIN	525A-0369	OE-FLB	525B-0053	N53NW	525B-0135	OE-GRA
525A-0151	N122SM	525A-0233	D-IOHL	525A-0370	N370JJ	525B-0054	N535GH	525B-0136	PT-TJS
525A-0152	N128JW	525A-0234	N313CR	525A-0371	N574BB	525B-0055	N4GA	525B-0137	N550MX
525A-0153	N500SV	525A-0235	N235KS	525A-0372	OY-NDP	525B-0056	N748RM	525B-0138	N356MR
525A-0154	N708GP	525A-0236	TC-VYN	525A-0373	VT-...	525B-0057	N999LB	525B-0139	N93CW
525A-0155	EC-KES	525A-0237	N333BD	525A-0374	N245RA	525B-0058	N885BT	525B-0140	N42AA
525A-0156	JA525B	525A-0238	N227FS*	525A-0375	OE-FOE	525B-0059	N412CS	525B-0141	N238SW
525A-0157	N913DC	525A-0239	OE-FIN	525A-0376	PR-JVF	525B-0060	N125DG	525B-0142	N28DM
525A-0158	SP-KCK	525A-0240	N77VR	525A-0377	N950DB	525B-0061	N361TL	525B-0143	N320BP
525A-0159	N5026	525A-0241	N777QP	525A-0378	VT-NID	525B-0062	XC-GDC	525B-0144	N847NG
525A-0160	N525KR	525A-0242	PH-JNE	525A-0379	N896P	525B-0063	N611CS*	525B-0145	N332SB
525A-0161	N525FF	525A-0243	N551WM	525A-0380	JA....	525B-0064	N1CH	525B-0146	CS-DIY
525A-0162	N335JJ	525A-0244	JA525C	525A-0381	EC-K..	525B-0065	LN-HOT	525B-0147	OO-FPC
525A-0163	VT-NJB	525A-0300	N432MA	525A-0382	N129CK	525B-0066	N602MJ	525B-0148	M-ELON
525A-0164	OO-DDA	525A-0301	N301PG	525A-0383	HB-VWA	525B-0067	N96MR	525B-0149	N123CJ
525A-0165	N30AD	525A-0302	N302CJ*	525A-0384	N118CJ	525B-0068	N51JJ	525B-0150	N317BR
525A-0166	D-IAMO	525A-0303	OY-GLO	525A-0385	N50820	525B-0069	N535DT	525B-0151	N420CH
525A-0167	D-ILDL	525A-0304	N912GW	525A-0386	N2040E	525B-0070	N279DV	525B-0152	N427CS
525A-0168	D-IHRA	525A-0305	N660S	525A-0387	N111JW	525B-0071	N531CM	525B-0153	N28FR
525A-0169	F-GPUJ	525A-0306	N306JR	525A-0388	N5267T	525B-0072	N8106V	525B-0154	D-CRAH
525A-0170	C6-LVU	525A-0307	N674AS	525A-0389	N5153K	525B-0073	N899MA	525B-0155	N831FC
525A-0171	CC-CHE	525A-0308	N110FD	525A-0393	N775TF	525B-0074	N742AR	525B-0156	F-GVUJ
525A-0172	N525PB	525A-0309	N309CJ	525A-0399	N810PF	525B-0075	D-CJAK	525B-0157	N157JL
525A-0173	N525CM	525A-0310	N926JJ	525A-0405	N405CJ	525B-0076	N1KA	525B-0158	OO-FPE
525A-0174	D-IDMH	525A-0311	JA001T	525A-0407	N407CJ	525B-0077	N7877T	525B-0159	N565JP
525A-0175	N525SM	525A-0312	N786AC	*525B CitationJet CJ-3*		525B-0078	VH-MIF	525B-0160	VP-BUG
525A-0176	OE-FYH	525A-0313	D-IBBS	525B-0096	3A-MRG	525B-0079	N835DM	525B-0161	D-CMHS
525A-0177	N25LZ	525A-0314	N791DM	711	N3CJ	525B-0080	N451GP	525B-0162	N503LC
525A-0178	N44FJ	525A-0315	N1414P	525B-0001	N53SF	525B-0081	N868EM	525B-0163	N80HB
525A-0179	OO-FLN	525A-0316	PR-NNP	525B-0002	N62SH	525B-0082	N413CS	525B-0164	N500AS
525A-0180	N604LJ	525A-0317	N9UD	525B-0003	N432LW	525B-0083	HS-MCL	525B-0165	N428CS
525A-0181	N525CE	525A-0318	YV289T	525B-0004	N6525B	525B-0084	N841AM	525B-0166	N7814
525A-0182	N777CJ	525A-0319	N967TC	525B-0005	N105CJ	525B-0085	D-CLAT	525B-0167	N450BV
525A-0183	N183TX	525A-0320	F-ONYY	525B-0006	N417C	525B-0086	D-CKJS	525B-0168	N970DM
525A-0184	N357J	525A-0321	OE-FII	525B-0007	N7CC	525B-0087	N687DS	525B-0169	D-CUBA
525A-0185	N65CR	525A-0322	F-GMIR	525B-0008	N946RM	525B-0088	N525MP	525B-0170	N996PE
525A-0186	N350BV	525A-0323	N65CK	525B-0009	N5GU	525B-0089	N525EZ	525B-0171	N727YB
525A-0187	N187MG	525A-0324	N586ED	525B-0010	N917RG	525B-0090	N417CS	525B-0172	N535DL
525A-0188	N837AC	525A-0325	N437JD	525B-0011	N585PK	525B-0091	N219L	525B-0173	OO-LIE
525A-0189	N777DY	525A-0326	N207BG	525B-0012	N172DH	525B-0092	N852SP	525B-0174	N174SJ
525A-0190	G-OODM	525A-0327	N525RF	525B-0013	F-HBPP	525B-0093	N93PE	525B-0175	N149WW
525A-0191	G-TBEA	525A-0328	D-IBCT	525B-0014	N300ET	525B-0094	N83TF	525B-0176	F-GYFC
525A-0192	N688DB	525A-0329	N525PH	525B-0015	N747KR	525B-0095	N100JS	525B-0177	N429CS
525A-0193	F-HAMG	525A-0331	OY-REN	525B-0016	S5-BAW	525B-0097	N888RK	525B-0178	F-GSGL
525A-0194	N194SJ	525A-0332	D-IOBO	525B-0017	N614B	525B-0098	N87VM	525B-0179	N179CJ
525A-0195	D-IMAX	525A-0333	N929BC	525B-0018	N52ET	525B-0099	N777NJ	525B-0180	N360CK
525A-0196	D-INOB	525A-0334	G-HCSA	525B-0019	N11LB	525B-0100	N77M	525B-0181	N143JT
525A-0197	N197CJ	525A-0335	N525LD	525B-0020	N899RR	525B-0101	D-CTEC	525B-0182	N535CM
525A-0198	N57FL	525A-0336	N15YD	525B-0021	N325RC	525B-0102	N3JM	525B-0183	N4115H
525A-0199	LN-AVA	525A-0337	N525XD	525B-0022	N528CE	525B-0103	N417KM	525B-0184	N914FF
525A-0200	CS-DGQ	525A-0338	N722SM			525B-0104	N590PJ	525B-0185	N430CS

525B-0186	N186CJ	550-0036	N336MA	550-0127	G-ESTA	550-0220	N614SJ*	550-0307	N550VW
525B-0187	PR-MRG*	550-0037	N622PG	550-0129	N237WC	550-0221	N31GA	550-0308	N15XM
525B-0188	N541WG	550-0038	N550JC	550-0130	N630CC	550-0222	PT-LNC	550-0310	N530P
525B-0189	N525CF	550-0039	N848D	550-0132	PT-LLU	550-0223	N550WL	550-0311	N300GC
525B-0190	N81ER	550-0040	N554MB	550-0133	N198NS	550-0224	2222	550-0312	YV255T
525B-0191	N379DB	550-0041	OE-GCI	550-0135	YV2103	550-0225	PT-LTJ	550-0313	N32TK
525B-0192	XA-...	550-0042	N41GA	550-0138	XC-SCT	550-0226	N872RD	550-0315	SE-RBK
525B-0193	SX-EDP	550-0043	N112SH	550-0139	OY-ELY	550-0227	XA-...	550-0316	N26HH
525B-0194	OY-WWW	550-0044	N308TW	550-0140	N55WL	550-0228	N334ED	550-0318	PT-WJZ
525B-0195	N400GG	550-0045	wo	550-0141	VH-EJY	550-0229	N229MC	550-0319	N78CK
525B-0196	N396CJ	550-0046	C-GRHC	550-0142	N387SC	550-0230	N550WB	550-0320	N204PM
525B-0197	D-CUUU	550-0047	N44AS	550-0143	N50JP	550-0231	N41SM	550-0321	YU-FCS
525B-0198	VP-BRJ	550-0048	N19ER	550-0144	wo	550-0232	N797CW	550-0323	N550LD
525B-0199	PR-CVC*	550-0050	N342AJ	550-0145	P2-TAA	550-0234	N173AA	550-0324	F-HBMB
525B-0200	OO-EDV	550-0051	ZS-RKV	550-0146	N501LC	550-0235	I-PNCA	550-0326	N390AJ
525B-0201	C-FANJ	550-0052	N302SJ	550-0147	N80GM	550-0236	N823NA	550-0327	PT-LLT
525B-0202	N7CH	550-0053	N519AA	550-0149	N116K	550-0237	N41WJ	550-0329	N949SA
525B-0203	N328RC	550-0054	VH-PSM	550-0150	N1SV	550-0238	N204CF	550-0332	N120Q
525B-0204	N5WN	550-0055	N10EG	550-0151	N495CM	550-0239	N66MC	550-0333	N365WA
525B-0205	N428BR	550-0056	N89D	550-0152	N550CA	550-0241	N241FT	550-0334	N755BP
525B-0206	C-GPMW	550-0057	VH-WNZ	550-0153	N37MH	550-0242	N551BC	550-0335	N187JN
525B-0207	N856BB	550-0058	N100HB	550-0154	G-JETJ	550-0243	N67SF*	550-0336	N90Z
525B-0208	N414KD	550-0060	OE-GIL	550-0155	C-FNCT	550-0245	N388SB	550-0337	N93AJ
525B-0209	HB-VOW*	550-0061	N458N	550-0156	EC-IAX	550-0246	wo	550-0338	N992AS
525B-0210	N52114	550-0062	C-GDLR	550-0157	N61HT	550-0247	PT-LJJ	550-0339	VH-SCD
525B-0211	ZS-...	550-0064	N64TF	550-0158	N769H	550-0248	N550SA	550-0340	N38DD
525B-0212	N52235	550-0065	N144GA	550-0159	N550PW	550-0249	N456TX	550-0341	N141JC
525B-0213	N527HV	550-0066	N360RP	550-0162	N85HD	550-0250	N120M	550-0343	N789TT
525B-0214	N92MS	550-0067	N267BB	550-0164	N721DR	550-0251	XA-GYA	550-0344	C-GVGM
525B-0215	N5201J	550-0068	N91VB	550-0165	N976GA	550-0252	N525JA	550-0345	N982NA
525B-0216	N5250E	550-0069	N712PD	550-0166	N867JC	550-0253	N157DW	550-0346	N106SR
525B-0217	N52690	550-0070	N892PB	550-0167	N717DT	550-0254	N888RL	550-0347	VH-ZLE
525B-0218	N7725D	550-0071	OE-GAD	550-0168	ZS-NII	550-0255	D-CIAO	550-0348	XA-...
525B-0219	N5243K	550-0072	N905CW	550-0169	N6001L	550-0256	N111AF	550-0349	N525LC
525B-0220	N52136	550-0073	G-JBIZ	550-0170	N550DA	550-0257	N53RG	550-0350	N86SG
525B-0221	N15ZZ	550-0074	N174DR	550-0171	N1TY	550-0258	N752GS	550-0351	I-ALKA
525B-0224	F-HCIC*	550-0075	N910MT	550-0172	SE-RCZ	550-0259	OY-BZT	550-0352	N352DA
525B-0226	N880MR	550-0076	VH-QQZ	550-0174	N87PT	550-0260	N6HF	550-0353	N353FT
525B-0228	N431CS	550-0077	XA-AGN	550-0175	N550CU	550-0261	N551WL	550-0354	SE-RBD
525B-0237	N525WL	550-0078	N432NM	550-0176	N61MA	550-0263	N13VP	550-0355	N52LT
525B-0240	N240CJ	550-0079	N232DM	550-0179	N673LR	550-0264	N771WY*	550-0356	N133WA
525B-0241	N241CJ*	550-0080	N45ME	550-0180	N219MS	550-0265	N16PL	550-0357	PT-OAG
525B-0244	N432CS	550-0081	I-AROO	550-0181	N50US	550-0266	N330DK	550-0358	4400
525B-0253	N38M	550-0082	N49U	550-0182	F-HACA	550-0267	N910RB	550-0362	N396M
525B-0257	N433CS	550-0083	N200VT	550-0183	G-JMDW	550-0268	N38TT	550-0363	N46NR*
525B-0268	N434CS	550-0084	N391AN	550-0184	N200NC	550-0269	N1MM	550-0364	N10VT
525B-0274	N436CS	550-0085	OE-GBA	550-0185	N317HC	550-0271	N1NL	550-0365	N122WW
525B-0282	N437DS	550-0086	N43SA	550-0186	N80AW	550-0272	YU-BVV	550-0366	N110LD
525A-0330	D-IFLY	550-0089	N111DT*	550-0187	N598CA	550-0273	N217FS	550-0367	N45ML
525A-0396	N400CV	550-0090	N290VP	550-0188	N280PM	550-0274	N2057H	550-0368	N718CK
550 Citation II		550-0091	N601BC	550-0189	D-CCCF	550-0275	N555DS	550-0369	N725FL
550-0003	N199Q*	550-0092	N567CA	550-0190	EC-JON	550-0276	N53FT	550-0370	YV2073
550-0004	F-GNCP	550-0094	G-JETA	550-0191	N550PA	550-0277	N550BJ	550-0371	N550LS
550-0005	wfu	550-0095	N550CG	550-0192	N192DW	550-0279	N550KA	550-0374	N477A
550-0006	N550LA	550-0096	N87SF	550-0193	N485AK	550-0280	C-GKAU	550-0376	N73ST
550-0007	N127JJ	550-0097	N999GR	550-0194	N91B	550-0281	N33EK	550-0378	SE-RIK
550-0008	G-VUEZ	550-0098	N211JS	550-0195	N343CM	550-0282	G-JETC	550-0381	N381VP
550-0009	N656PS	550-0099	N109JC	550-0196	N196JS	550-0283	N257DW	550-0382	N852SB
550-0010	PT-LPK	550-0100	C-GLMK	550-0197	N510JC	550-0284	OY-JEV	550-0383	N561AS
550-0011	0002	550-0101	wo	550-0198	XA-SQV	550-0285	C-GQCC	550-0390	N717LC
550-0012	N11FH	550-0102	VH-INT	550-0199	N586RE	550-0286	N2GG	550-0393	I-FLYD
550-0013	wo	550-0103	N90MA	550-0200	N797SF	550-0287	N527DS	550-0396	N99CN
550-0014	N780CF	550-0104	CC-CLC	550-0201	N1GH	550-0288	wo	550-0398	N707LM
550-0016	N116LA	550-0105	N550LH	550-0202	N704DA	550-0289	VH-JMK	550-0399	N66MS
550-0017	N744AT	550-0106	N820MC	550-0203	YV....	550-0290	N312NC	550-0400	wo
550-0018	N752CC	550-0108	N690EW	550-0204	N815CE	550-0291	N262Y	550-0401	N550KT
550-0019	wo	550-0109	N753CC	550-0205	N30JD	550-0292	C-GTDK	550-0402	N57SF
550-0021	N52RF	550-0110	N550SF	550-0206	N280TA	550-0293	wo	550-0403	N404BS
550-0024	N404RP	550-0111	N123VP	550-0207	N196RJ	550-0294	PT-LPN	550-0405	YV1813
550-0025	N551DA	550-0112	YV-....	550-0208	wfu	550-0295	N48KH	550-0406	N815MA
550-0026	N30AV	550-0113	N550KD	550-0209	N444G	550-0296	G-DWJM	550-0407	N55MV
550-0027	N127PM	550-0114	N819KR	550-0210	N850PM	550-0297	B-7025	550-0408	N110WA
550-0028	N551CZ	550-0115	SE-DDY	550-0211	N77PR	550-0298	N888FG	550-0409	N102HB
550-0029	N524MA	550-0116	N575BW	550-0212	N245CC	550-0299	N511AB	550-0410	C-GNWM
550-0030	N16TS	550-0117	N490DC	550-0213	N213CC	550-0300	YV2246	550-0411	N550KW
550-0031	N9DC	550-0118	N650BP	550-0214	YV2443	550-0301	B-7024	550-0412	N450KD*
550-0032	N232CW	550-0121	N121HL	550-0215	N550MJ	550-0302	SE-RCY	550-0414	N814AM
550-0033	G-CEUO	550-0122	N89GA	550-0216	N550PG	550-0303	XB-GLZ	550-0415	EC-KJJ
550-0034	N922SL	550-0123	N948DC	550-0217	N217SA	550-0304	N42PH	550-0416	N416CC
550-0035	N15JA	550-0124	N789DD*	550-0218	PT-LPP	550-0305	B-7026	550-0417	N17DM
		550-0125	wfu	550-0219	N10JA	550-0306	N206AG	550-0418	N214JT

325

550-0419	G-FJET	550-0550	N177RJ	550-0639	N100DS	550-0720	N550MW	550-0863	N577VM
550-0420	N555KT	550-0551	N600AT	550-0640	PT-ODL	550-0721	N721CC	550-0864	HB-VOH
550-0421	N510GP	550-0553	N553MJ	550-0641	N895HE	550-0722	N220LE	550-0865	D-CPPP
550-0423	N248HA	550-0554	N750SL	550-0642	XB-IKY	550-0723	N777JE	550-0866	D-CHZF
550-0424	N435UM	550-0555	N104HW	550-0643	G-EJEL	550-0724	LV-WEJ	550-0867	N161TM
550-0425	U 20-1	550-0558	LV-WJN	550-0644	XC-PGM	550-0725	N725CC	550-0868	N627BC
550-0426	N434SB	550-0559	N409ST	550-0645	PT-ODZ	550-0726	N726AM	550-0869	N499WM
550-0427	N711CC	550-0560	N550GX	550-0646	N562RM	550-0727	VT-CLD	550-0870	VP-CED
550-0428	N550PF	550-0561	wo	550-0647	N604DS	550-0728	LV-WJO	550-0871	I-GIWW
550-0430	XB-AGV	550-0562	N54RM	550-0648	XC-PGP	550-0729	N38NA	550-0872	OE-GKK
550-0432	N76AS	550-0563	N518N	550-0649	G-SOVA	550-0730	N501JP	550-0873	PT-XSX
550-0433	N7ZU	550-0564	wo	550-0650	C-GBBX	550-0731	XC-SST	550-0874	D-CHMC
550-0434	N53FP	550-0565	N565NC	550-0651	N24E	550-0732	N902DK	550-0875	N877SD
550-0435	N674G	550-0566	N15SN	550-0652	N3262M	550-0733	N44SW	550-0876	5Y-MNG
550-0436	N717DM	550-0567	N926RM	550-0653	N30RL	551-0351	N5TR	550-0877	N21SL
550-0438	N100CH	550-0568	N47SM	550-0654	XB-BON	551-0572	D-IRUP	550-0878	VH-ZLT
550-0439	N1250V	550-0569	5Y-TWE	550-0655	N37201	*Citation Bravo*		550-0879	N35ET
550-0440	OY-CYV	550-0570	N270CW	550-0656	N30GR	550-0734	N550BB	550-0880	N7YA
550-0441	G-JETO	550-0571	N90JJ	550-0657	CC-DGA	550-0801	N801BB	550-0881	N306CS
550-0442	N668AJ	550-0573	N155AC	550-0658	N137PA	550-0802	N550HH	550-0882	N882WF
550-0443	EC-IMF	550-0575	N387RE	550-0659	N4614N	550-0803	N141HL	550-0883	N469DE
550-0444	C-FMJM	550-0576	N675SS	550-0660	N827DP	550-0804	N550BC	550-0884	D-CSWM
550-0445	N453S	550-0577	N8344M	550-0661	VT-CLB	550-0805	N108RF	550-0885	N88AJ
550-0446	U 20-2	550-0578	N203PM	550-0662	N623JL	550-0806	N300PY	550-0886	N500TS
550-0447	G-JBIS	550-0579	N750TB	550-0663	N5314J	550-0807	C-GPGA	550-0887	XA-ABE
550-0448	N994CF	550-0580	N18NA	550-0664	N45BE	550-0808	YU-BSM	550-0888	N218G*
550-0449	YV-2338P	550-0581	N805LC	550-0665	N998BC	550-0809	N380AK	550-0889	N360HS
550-0450	N505RP	550-0582	FAC-1211	550-0666	N5408G	550-0810	VH-XBP	550-0890	N1961S
550-0451	N1249P	550-0583	N22PC	550-0667	N107EE	550-0811	PT-MMV	550-0891	N86PC
550-0452	N707PF	550-0584	N979WC	550-0668	XA-TVH	550-0812	C-FJBO	550-0892	N22GR
550-0453	N962J	550-0585	N585PS	550-0669	N677GS	550-0813	N100KU	550-0893	N333EB
550-0454	N250KD*	550-0586	F-GGGA	550-0670	N6637G	550-0814	N303CS	550-0894	N107EG
550-0455	PT-MMO	550-0587	N18HJ	550-0671	G-VUEA	550-0815	N126TF	550-0895	N199BB
550-0456	N283DF	550-0588	N633RT	550-0672	OY-VIS	550-0816	C-FMCI	550-0896	N121L
550-0457	OY-TMA	550-0589	N589SJ	550-0673	N6763L	550-0817	N123GF	550-0897	G-GHPG
550-0458	LV-BCO	550-0590	XA-UGG	550-0674	N690AN	550-0818	N300CS	550-0898	N550GH
550-0459	N604PJ	550-0592	U 20-3	550-0675	PT-WKQ	550-0819	N15CV	550-0899	N535SW
550-0460	PT-OKP	550-0593	N32002	550-0676	PT-OJG	550-0820	N302CS	550-0900	N138CA
550-0461	N22FM	550-0594	N2531K	550-0677	N6775C	550-0821	N225WT	550-0901	N857AA
550-0462	N62TL	550-0595	N2734K	550-0678	EC-KBZ	550-0822	N725DS	550-0902	N688JD
550-0463	YV1563	550-0596	EC-HGI	550-0679	N782ST	550-0823	N25FS	550-0903	PR-ERP
550-0464	N822HA	550-0597	N213JS	550-0680	N6776T	550-0824	N824CB	550-0904	N904BB
550-0465	N90PT	550-0598	N888XL	550-0681	N1200N	550-0825	N305CS	550-0905	N505AG
550-0466	N10LY	550-0599	N571BC	550-0682	N90BY	550-0826	N595PC	550-0906	HB-VNZ
550-0467	YV2166	550-0600	N415AJ	550-0683	YV1192	550-0827	D-CCAB	550-0907	SX-BMK
550-0468	N120JP	550-0601	N501RL	550-0684	C-FJXN	550-0828	N6FR	550-0908	N242SW
550-0469	N420SS	550-0602	N2663Y	550-0685	C-FJWZ	550-0829	N829CB	550-0909	N391BC
550-0470	N202SW	550-0603	N550TW	550-0686	C-FKCE	550-0830	N717CB	550-0910	N574M
550-0471	N271AG	550-0604	N904SJ	550-0687	C-FKDX	550-0831	N331PR	550-0911	N575M
550-0472	wo	550-0605	N26494	550-0688	C-FKEB	550-0832	N832UJ	550-0912	N588AC
550-0473	XB-IZK	550-0606	N602AT	550-0689	N689VP	550-0833	PR-FEP	550-0913	N66MT
550-0474	ZS-LIG	550-0607	N26496	550-0690	VH-VLZ	550-0834	D-CALL	550-0914	N897MC
550-0475	N475HC	550-0608	N990M	550-0691	N600JB	550-0835	N198SL	550-0915	N346CM
550-0476	N1252D	550-0609	F-GLTK	550-0692	N75RJ	550-0836	N122NC	550-0916	N555BK
550-0477	N344KK	550-0610	N610JB	550-0693	N594WP	550-0837	OE-GPS	550-0917	G-IDAB
550-0478	N32SM	550-0611	F-GGGT	550-0694	N807MB	550-0838	N813JD	550-0918	N45VM
550-0479	N68TS	550-0612	N578M	550-0695	N153TH	550-0839	N101FG	550-0919	N100Y
550-0480	ZS-OIE	550-0613	N664AJ	550-0696	N696VP	550-0840	N773CA	550-0920	N854JA
550-0481	N97EM	550-0615	N803SC	550-0697	D-CHEP	550-0841	N999CX	550-0921	N40MF
550-0482	N594G	550-0616	PT-OVV	550-0698	VT-CLC	550-0842	N842CB	550-0922	OE-GAH
550-0483	N17VP	550-0618	PP-ESC	550-0699	C-FKLB	550-0843	AP-BHE	550-0923	N23YC
550-0484	N501GG	550-0619	XA-LRL	550-0700	C-FJCZ	550-0844	N550KL	550-0924	YU-BZZ
550-0485	N727C	550-0620	N391DT	550-0701	C-FLZA	550-0845	N550WS	550-0925	N10UH
550-0486	XA-AAK	550-0621	N99TK	550-0702	C-FMFM	550-0846	N517AF	550-0926	N144Z
550-0487	N550DW	550-0622	F-HAJV	550-0703	N308A	550-0847	N304CS	550-0927	PH-DYE
550-0488	N990MR	550-0623	N89LS	550-0704	N197PR	550-0848	N550J	550-0928	PH-DYN
550-0489	N489SS	550-0624	N65DV	550-0705	N521TM	550-0849	N623N	550-0929	N552SM
550-0490	N490CC	550-0625	F-....	550-0706	N706NA	550-0850	N551V	550-0930	PP-ORM
550-0491	I-AVRM	550-0626	N466SS	550-0707	HS-RBL	550-0851	N7NN	550-0931	C-FAMJ
550-0492	I-AVGM	550-0627	N804BC	550-0708	N923JH	550-0852	VH-FGK	550-0932	I-MTVB
550-0493	N84GC	550-0628	IGM-628	550-0709	VT-SGT	550-0853	N398LS	550-0933	N325WP
550-0494	N1254X	550-0629	wo	550-0710	N90BJ	550-0854	XA-...	550-0934	N200AS
550-0495	N10TC	550-0630	N198ND	550-0711	XB-ZZZ	550-0855	N232JR	550-0935	G-IPAL
550-0497	N1257B	550-0631	N631TS	550-0712	PH-LAB	550-0856	N103CX	550-0936	N550TM
550-0498	N772SB	550-0632	5N-AYA	550-0713	N283CW	550-0857	N984BK	550-0937	N440CE
550-0499	PT-LIV	550-0633	N550AB	550-0714	G-SPUR	550-0858	N100WT	550-0938	EC-HRO
550-0501	N12549	550-0634	F-HDGT	550-0715	LV-YHC	550-0859	I-BENN	550-0939	N48NS
550-0502	84-007	550-0635	N550HW	550-0716	N550TL	550-0860	N844DR	550-0940	G-FIRM
550-0503	84-008	550-0636	N50NF	550-0717	OE-GBC	550-0861	N26CV	550-0941	4X-...
550-0504	XA-TQA	550-0637	YV2286	550-0718	N129ED	550-0862	N1967J	550-0942	N265TS
550-0505	N1255K	550-0638	N255TC	550-0719	N12068			550-0943	YV266T

550-0944	N723RE	550-1025	CS-DHF	550-1106	N341CS	S550-0049	B-4101	S550-0130	N552SD
550-0945	N585KS	550-1026	N438SP	550-1107	TC-AHE	S550-0050	B-4102	S550-0131	N87BA
550-0946	HB-VMX	550-1027	OO-FYG	550-1108	N717VL	S550-0051	N311AF	S550-0132	N91ML
550-0947	N514BC	550-1028	C-FYUL	550-1109	CS-DHQ	S550-0052	N57BJ	S550-0133	N133VP
550-0948	N48FW	550-1029	N318CS	550-1110	N877B	S550-0053	N393E	S550-0134	SE-DYO
550-0949	N45NS*	550-1030	N322GT	550-1111	OK-ACH	S550-0054	N599CB	S550-0135	VT-KMB
550-0950	N555HM	550-1031	N525PE	550-1112	N47NM	S550-0055	N408CT	S550-0137	PT-WIB
550-0951	LN-SUV	550-1032	N910N	550-1113	N724EH	S550-0056	N52FT	S550-0138	N20CS
550-0952	N952CH	550-1033	N701VV	550-1114	CS-DHR	S550-0057	N57CJ	S550-0139	N881A
550-0953	N550WG	550-1034	CS-DHG	550-1115	HZ-133	S550-0058	N633EE	S550-0140	N575EW
550-0954	PP-OAA	550-1035	N585TH	550-1116	HZ-134	S550-0059	N531PM	S550-0141	N550AJ
550-0955	EC-KHP	550-1036	N319CS	550-1117	OO-FPB	S550-0060	N442KM	S550-0142	N701BG
550-0956	N800VA	550-1037	N1258B	550-1118	N550CY	S550-0061	N811RG	S550-0143	N458PE
550-0957	G-IKOS	550-1038	SE-RBY	550-1119	N230JS	S550-0062	I-AVVM	S550-0144	N543SC
550-0958	N404RK	550-1039	OE-GRB	550-1120	LV-BEU	S550-0063	VH-EMO	S550-0145	N900LM
550-0959	N511JP	550-1040	OK-VSZ	550-1121	9M-ZAB	S550-0064	N575SG	S550-0146	N815H
550-0960	TC-MKA	550-1041	N7765D	550-1122	N984GB	S550-0065	N90FJ	S550-0147	CS-DDV
550-0961	HK-4250X	550-1042	G-OJMW	550-1123	N106FT	S550-0066	N711MD	S550-0148	N550BG
550-0962	N797TE	550-1043	CS-DHH	550-1124	N417JD	S550-0067	N828AF	S550-0149	N777AX
550-0963	N990TC	550-1044	N141AB	550-1125	VH-YXY	S550-0068	N7070A	S550-0150	N107RC
550-0964	HB-VMY	550-1045	PP-BMG	550-1126	HZ-135	S550-0069	N43VS	S550-0151	N88NW
550-0965	N256CC	550-1046	N300GF	550-1127	HZ-136	S550-0070	XB-EEP	S550-0152	N987CJ
550-0966	N36PT	550-1047	N889B	550-1128	N23AJ	S550-0071	N1865M	S550-0153	N477LC
550-0967	N432RJ	550-1048	CS-DHI	550-1129	N60LW	S550-0072	N62NS	S550-0154	N550DS
550-0968	N551G	550-1049	YU-BSG	550-1130	D-CSMB	S550-0073	N1958N	S550-0155	N550DL
550-0969	N401KC	550-1050	D-CMIX	550-1131	N110TP	S550-0074	N74JE	S550-0156	N63JT
550-0970	N78MD	550-1051	N745CC	550-1132	N338B	S550-0075	N882RB	S550-0157	N802Q
550-0971	N717GK	550-1052	N322CS	550-1133	N579M	S550-0076	N52CK	S550-0158	N550EZ*
550-0972	PH-HMA	550-1053	N57MC	550-1134	N412BT	S550-0077	N999OH	S550-0159	N9GY
550-0973	N129PB	550-1054	N600ST	550-1135	D2-GES	S550-0078	ZS-CAR	S550-0160	PT-OSM
550-0974	N307MS	550-1055	N896CG	550-1136	N998SR	S550-0079	5N-BEL	551 Citation II/SP	
550-0975	5Y-MSR	550-1056	N45678	S550 Citation II		S550-0080	XA-VGF	551-0002	N502CL
550-0976	N308MS	550-1057	N714RM	S550-0001	N86BA	S550-0081	PR-MCN	551-0003	I-MESK
550-0977	N309CS	550-1058	VH-SCC	S550-0002	CC-CWW	S550-0082	N27TB	551-0006	1967
550-0978	N95AN	550-1059	N324CS	S550-0003	N847C	S550-0083	N683PF	551-0007	N60FJ
550-0979	N311CS	550-1060	N669B	S550-0004	N178DA*	S550-0084	PT-LJL	551-0010	D-ICAC
550-0980	N67JB	550-1061	N325CS	S550-0005	N666LN	S550-0085	N550BT	551-0017	N811VG
550-0981	N800MT	550-1062	N662CB	S550-0006	N181G	S550-0086	D-CJJJ	551-0018	D-IEAR
550-0982	C-FMOS	550-1063	N151TM	S550-0007	OO-SKP	S550-0087	N21EG	551-0021	N1HA
550-0983	XA-SDI	550-1064	N823PM	S550-0008	N600KM	S550-0088	N127RC	551-0023	wo
550-0984	VH-HVM	550-1065	N896MA	S550-0009	N165JB	S550-0089	VT-ETG	551-0024	wo
550-0985	G-FCDB	550-1066	N573M	S550-0010	N550F	S550-0090	N499RC	551-0026	N612VR
550-0986	N458F	550-1067	N6TM	S550-0011	N25GZ	S550-0091	N476LC	551-0027	N46PJ
550-0987	N500VA	550-1068	N668CB	S550-0012	N777GG	S550-0092	N489GM	551-0029	wo
550-0988	I-FJTC	550-1069	OE-GLL	S550-0013	N551PS	S550-0093	N629RA	551-0031	EC-JTH
550-0989	XA-LOF	550-1070	XA-CAP	S550-0014	N84EC	S550-0094	N19ZA	551-0033	wo
550-0990	N448RL	550-1071	N104FL	S550-0015	N600EA	S550-0095	N409CT	551-0035	N277JM
550-0991	N628GB	550-1072	N143BP	S550-0016	N557CS	S550-0096	N29XA	551-0036	N889FA
550-0992	EC-KKO	550-1073	N899B	S550-0017	N413CT	S550-0097	N302MB	551-0038	YU-BTT
550-0993	N721T	550-1074	N328CS	S550-0018	N145DF	S550-0098	N598KW	551-0039	N551GF
550-0994	C-GLGB	550-1075	N87011	S550-0019	N670JD	S550-0099	N777FD	551-0046	N518MV
550-0995	N550PD	550-1076	N550TT	S550-0020	N550AS	S550-0100	N550SJ	551-0050	N228MH
550-0996	CC-LLM	550-1077	N329CS	S550-0021	N945ER	S550-0101	C-FABF	551-0051	D-ICTA
550-0997	N67BK	550-1078	N442NR	S550-0022	N460M	S550-0102	N285MC	551-0056	N826RT
550-0998	OE-GHP	550-1079	N444EA	S550-0023	N293RT	S550-0103	wo	551-0059	N59DY
550-0999	XB-UVA	550-1080	N132MT	S550-0024	N790AL	S550-0104	N224KC	551-0060	N59GB
550-1000	N121CN	550-1081	N332CS	S550-0025	wo	S550-0105	N105BG	551-0071	N551HH
550-1001	N26CB	550-1082	CS-DHJ	S550-0026	N32TX	S550-0106	N9072U	551-0095	N48DK
550-1002	N101JL	550-1083	I-PABL	S550-0027	C-GSSK	S550-0107	N553SD	551-0117	4X-CZD
550-1003	1003	550-1084	N338CS	S550-0028	S5-BAX	S550-0108	N316MH	551-0122	N10LR
550-1004	N314CS	550-1085	N339CS	S550-0029	HB-VMJ	S550-0109	N75MC	551-0132	SE-DYR
550-1005	CS-DHA	550-1086	G-OMRH	S550-0030	N999HC	S550-0110	N45GP	551-0133	HB-VDO
550-1006	N992HE	550-1087	N151FD	S550-0031	wo	S550-0111	N111OS	551-0141	N636MA*
550-1007	N67PC	550-1088	N153SG	S550-0032	N48BV	S550-0112	ZS-PSG	551-0149	N5WT
550-1008	D2-ECE	550-1089	N334CS	S550-0033	N581CM	S550-0113	PT-LJO	551-0163	ZS-ARG
550-1009	CS-DHB	550-1090	CS-DHK	S550-0034	N220BP*	S550-0114	PT-LKS	551-0169	N14RM
550-1010	N316CS	550-1091	N335CS	S550-0035	N834DC	S550-0115	N92JC	551-0171	5R-MHF
550-1011	C-FRST	550-1092	CS-DHL	S550-0036	C-FOBQ	S550-0116	N550HC	551-0174	EI-CIR
550-1012	N20AU	550-1093	CS-DHM	S550-0037	N578BB	S550-0117	wo	551-0179	N127BU
550-1013	CS-DHC	550-1094	N308DT	S550-0038	N406CT	S550-0118	N721LR	551-0180	N222VV
550-1014	N610CB	550-1095	N336CS	S550-0039	N22UL	S550-0119	N63HA	551-0181	N61442*
550-1015	N81LR	550-1096	N707HP	S550-0040	C-FEMA	S550-0120	N716DD	551-0191	N386AM
550-1016	N958GC	550-1097	N337CS	S550-0041	N74LM	S550-0121	N711XR	551-0201	D-ISEC
550-1017	CS-DHD	550-1098	CS-DHN	S550-0042	N241DS	S550-0122	N122WS	551-0205	N828SS
550-1018	OO-IIG	550-1099	CS-DHO	S550-0043	N727EF	S550-0123	N121CG	551-0214	N9SS
550-1019	N317CS	550-1100	G-WAIN	S550-0044	N92ME	S550-0124	N554T	551-0215	N551CL
550-1020	N219LC	550-1101	N342CS	S550-0045	N97CC	S550-0125	N125QA	551-0223	YV1776
550-1021	N49KW	550-1102	AP-BHD	S550-0046	N103VF	S550-0126	ZS-EDA	551-0245	wo
550-1022	CS-DHE	550-1103	LZ-ABV	S550-0047	N16RP	S550-0127	N431MS	551-0285	ZS-MLN
550-1023	C-FEVC	550-1104	CS-DHP	S550-0048	N705SP	S550-0128	N550CZ	551-0289	PT-LJF
550-1024	N550FP	550-1105	N332MT			S550-0129	N480CC		

327

551-0304	N999MK	560-0052	N500UB	560-0130	PR-CCV	560-0211	N250SR	560-0292	HL7501
551-0313	YV1820	560-0053	C-FACO	560-0131	N223JV	560-0212	TC-LAA	560-0293	N50CV
551-0323	N555RT	560-0054	N100SY	560-0132	N521LF	560-0213	PT-OTS	560-0294	HL7502
551-0355	I-ALPG	560-0055	N55EA	560-0133	N560PK	560-0214	OE-GCP	560-0295	N903BH
551-0359	N740JB*	560-0056	N406VJ	560-0134	YV1022	560-0215	N315EJ	560-0296	N560LC
551-0360	N551EA	560-0057	N561TS	560-0135	N19HU	560-0216	TC-LAB	560-0297	HL7503
551-0361	LV-APL	560-0058	N710LC	560-0136	N560PA	560-0217	N802AB	560-0298	N112CW
551-0369	N778JC	560-0059	G-PPLC	560-0137	N137JC	560-0218	N561AC	560-0299	VT-EUX
551-0378	N322MA	560-0060	PT-FTB	560-0138	N511WV	560-0219	N515RW	560-0300	HL7504
551-0388	wo	560-0061	N46GA	560-0139	N59NH	560-0220	N73KH	560-0301	HB-VOC
551-0393	N122SP	560-0062	N500UJ	560-0140	N24JD	560-0221	N626RB	560-0302	N901AB
551-0396	LV-WXD	560-0063	N63FF	560-0141	N141AQ	560-0222	N456SW	560-0303	N190JK
551-0400	D-IMME	560-0064	OY-NUD	560-0142	N560GT	560-0223	N560MG	560-0304	N401KH
551-0412	EC-KJR	560-0065	N608CT	560-0143	N10TB	560-0224	N528KW	560-0305	LV-WMT
551-0421	G-LUXY	560-0066	N501JS	560-0144	N500VC	560-0225	N545PL	560-0306	N753GJ*
551-0428	wo	560-0067	JA119N	560-0145	PH-ILZ	560-0226	N226CV	560-0307	N51FK
551-0431	N551GS	560-0068	N560LM	560-0146	wo	560-0227	LV-WDR	560-0308	PT-WFD
551-0436	N102DR	560-0069	N367JC	560-0147	N508KD*	560-0228	N560MM	560-0309	N560RN
551-0496	OE-FAD	560-0070	F-GJXX	560-0148	N115K	560-0229	N193SB	560-0310	N228PC
551-0500	N9CR	560-0071	N271CA	560-0149	N565JW	560-0230	N394AJ	560-0311	N531VP*
551-0552	OE-FPA	560-0071A	N45RC	560-0150	N191VE	560-0231	N12CQ	560-0312	N312QS
551-0556	N200GF	560-0072	JA120N	560-0151	V5-CDM	560-0232	N502E	560-0313	N313CV
551-0557	N711NV	560-0073	N100WP	560-0152	ZS-NDX	560-0233	0233	560-0314	N561DA
551-0574	OE-FBS	560-0074	C-GBNX	560-0153	OO-SKV	560-0234	N234AQ	560-0315	N215WC*
551-0591	N608JR	560-0075	N817PD	560-0154	N154VP	560-0235	N633SA	560-0316	N12RN
551-0614	N26HG	560-0076	N623KC	560-0155	N155VP	560-0236	N506E	560-0317	N217WC
551-0617	N881SA	560-0077	wo	560-0156	N75B	560-0237	N237VP	560-0318	N910HM
560 Citation V/Ultra		560-0078	PH-ILA	560-0157	N157TF	560-0238	N194SA	560-0319	N2RC
550-0001	wfu	560-0079	N560GL	560-0158	N560RP	560-0239	N93CV	560-0320	VH-MXJ
560-0001	N561VP	560-0080	N300CH	560-0159	G-JOPT	560-0240	N55CH	560-0321	N560AV
560-0002	N560CZ	560-0081	N318CT	560-0160	N458CK	560-0241	ZS-NGS	560-0322	N607HM
560-0003	N413LC	560-0082	C-FETJ	560-0161	TR 20-01	560-0242	N826AC	560-0323	N808AC
560-0004	N189H	560-0083	N568WC	560-0162	XA-SDT	560-0243	D-CAMS	560-0324	N342QS
560-0005	N953F	560-0084	N51C	560-0163	N97JL*	560-0244	N701NB	560-0325	N566KB
560-0006	N569TA	560-0085	N85VP	560-0164	N570EJ	560-0245	N43RC	560-0326	N220SC
560-0007	N763D	560-0086	N560CJ	560-0165	N24HX	560-0246	LV-WGY	560-0327	N327QS
560-0008	N561B	560-0087	N60QB	560-0166	HB-VMV	560-0247	N94TX	560-0328	N926NC
560-0009	N77NR	560-0088	OK-SLS	560-0167	N580JT	560-0248	N50DR	560-0329	N330QS
560-0010	N560JM	560-0089	N54DD	560-0168	N168EA	560-0249	N2000X	560-0330	N330VP
560-0011	N913BJ	560-0090	LV-AHX	560-0169	N80AB	560-0250	N205CM	560-0331	N331QS
560-0012	N560RR	560-0091	N103BG	560-0170	N814CM	560-0251	N625AC	560-0332	N332LC
560-0013	N560WH	560-0092	N719RM	560-0171	N567F	560-0252	N44GT	560-0333	N333QS
560-0014	N900SM	560-0092A	N592VP	560-0172	N560BD*	560-0253	N858ME	560-0334	N905LC
560-0015	N480DG	560-0093	N93EA	560-0173	N247CN	560-0254	N710ML	560-0335	N335QS
560-0016	N462B	560-0094	N94VP	560-0174	N164TC	560-0255	N61KM	560-0336	N336QS
560-0017	C-FPJT	560-0095	N404G	560-0175	N49LD	560-0256	N356SA	560-0337	N108LJ
560-0018	N500FZ	560-0096	N10TD	560-0176	N661AJ	560-0257	N155PT	560-0338	N338R
560-0019	N643RT	560-0097	N898CB	560-0177	N650CM	560-0258	PP-ISJ	560-0339	N339QS
560-0020	N560HG	560-0098	N59DF	560-0178	N997EA	560-0259	N56GA	560-0340	N21CV
560-0021	N83EP	560-0099	N565EJ	560-0179	N65RL	560-0260	N180FW	560-0341	N341QS
560-0022	N574BP	560-0100	N560AF	560-0180	N550WW	560-0261	N135WC	560-0342	N86CV*
560-0023	N3FA	560-0101	N560EP	560-0181	N181SG	560-0262	N444GG	560-0343	N303QS
560-0024	N140U	560-0102	N555PG	560-0182	C-FEPG	560-0263	N560GS	560-0344	N344QS
560-0025	CN-ANV	560-0103	N98E	560-0183	N83RE	560-0264	N294RT	560-0345	N64LV
560-0026	N380RD	560-0104	N815CM	560-0184	N410DM	560-0265	wo	560-0346	C-GFCL
560-0027	N531MB	560-0105	N560MH	560-0185	N939TW	560-0266	N306QS	560-0347	N106SP
560-0028	N757CK	560-0106	N525RD	560-0186	N47PW	560-0267	N267WG	560-0348	N348QS
560-0029	N590A	560-0107	N365EA	560-0187	N922AC	560-0268	N750FL	560-0349	JA001A
560-0030	N570BJ	560-0108	N573BP*	560-0188	N62CR	560-0269	C-GRCC	560-0351	C-GAWU
560-0031	D-CHDE	560-0109	N480RL	560-0189	N63JG	560-0270	N394CK	560-0352	N352QS
560-0032	N560BC	560-0109A	N4MM	560-0190	N404LN	560-0271	HB-VNB	560-0353	N20SM
560-0033	C-GAPC	560-0110	N95TD	560-0191	N45KB	560-0272	N790PS	560-0354	N4200K
560-0034	N401MC	560-0111	OE-GAA	560-0192	N3444B	560-0273	N521LL	560-0355	HK-4304
560-0035	N561EJ	560-0112	N560G	560-0193	TR 20-02	560-0274	N137LA	560-0356	N354QS
560-0036	N200MM	560-0113	N113VP	560-0194	N628CK	560-0275	N717D	560-0357	N347QS
560-0037	N416HF	560-0114	PH-ILI	560-0195	PT-ORC	560-0276	N145KK	560-0358	N284CP
560-0038	N212BW	560-0115	N87JK	560-0196	N560RW	560-0277	N560BG	560-0359	N416BA
560-0039	CN-ANW	560-0116	N561PA	560-0197	N21LG	560-0278	N560EM	560-0360	N62WD
560-0040	N560CF	560-0117	D-CMEI	560-0198	N198CV	560-0279	N594M	560-0361	N361QS
560-0041	N400KS	560-0118	N900PS	560-0199	N500DW	560-0280	HB-VNA	560-0362	N998TW
560-0042	N142GA	560-0119	N450MM	560-0200	OE-GDA	560-0281	N716SX	560-0363	N59KC
560-0043	wo	560-0120	N129MC	560-0201	N255RM	560-0282	D-CBEN	560-0364	N51ND
560-0044	N560JL	560-0121	N960CD	560-0202	ZS-NGL	560-0283	N560JC	560-0366	SX-DCI
560-0045	PT-LZQ	560-0122	N561MT	560-0203	N9700T	560-0284	N966SW	560-0367	N367QS
560-0046	N846MA	560-0123	N92TE	560-0204	N1000W	560-0285	N285CC	560-0368	N343CC
560-0047	N560WW	560-0124	N823WB	560-0205	N1AK*	560-0286	N31NS	560-0369	N210CM
560-0048	N240CM	560-0125	OE-GCC	560-0206	N900E	560-0287	N863RD	560-0370	N749DC
560-0049	N560EL	560-0126	LV-RED	560-0207	N560CK	560-0288	N522JA	560-0371	N315CS
560-0050	N501CW	560-0127	XB-JHD	560-0208	N758PM*	560-0289	LV-WLS	560-0372	N372WC
560-0051	N314RW	560-0128	N504BW	560-0209	N209CV	560-0290	N97BH	560-0373	N373QS
		560-0129	N22AF	560-0210	N277RC	560-0291	N470DP	560-0375	N375QS

560-0376	N600EF	560-0460	N360QS	560-0565	00-1051	560-0609	N242AC	560-0700	N700NK
560-0377	N537VP*	560-0461	N61TL	560-0567	wo	560-0610	N804QS	560-0701	N113US
560-0378	N808TH	560-0462	97-0103	560-0570	165939	560-0611	N560CH	560-0702	N702AM
560-0379	N560RF	560-0463	D-CEMG	560-0574	00-1052	560-0612	N89MD	560-0703	VH-VPL
560-0380	N147SB	560-0464	N53PE	560-0577	00-1053	560-0613	N25QT	560-0704	PR-GQG
560-0382	N382QS	560-0465	N848G	560-0589	01-0301	560-0614	N806QS	560-0705	C-FYMM
560-0383	N241KP*	560-0466	N366QS	560-0592	166374	560-0615	N152JH	560-0706	N802QS
560-0384	N331MW	560-0467	N20CC	560-0630	166474	560-0616	N80GR	560-0707	N13092
560-0385	N833WM*	560-0468	97-0104	560-0649	03-0016	560-0617	N807QS	560-0751	N560KW*
560-0387	95-0123	560-0469	N469DN	560-0651	166500	560-0618	N933PB	560-0752	N752CE
560-0388	N92SS	560-0470	N44FG	560-0667	03-0726	560-0619	N808QS	560-0753	N753CE
560-0389	N118RK	560-0471	N371QS	560-0672	166712	560-0620	N101WY	560-0754	N990JH
560-0390	C-GNLQ	560-0472	97-0105	560-0677	166713	560-0621	N102WY	560-0755	N56TE
560-0391	N92DE	560-0473	N1CF	560-0679	166714	560-0622	N560KL	560-0756	N545BP
560-0392	95-0124	560-0474	N321GG	560-0682	166715	560-0623	N977MR	560-0757	YV2389
560-0393	N393QS	560-0475	N374QS	560-0693	166766	560-0624	N500MG	560-0758	N62WA
560-0394	N394QS	560-0476	N941RM	560-0696	166767	560-0625	N810QS	560-0759	N387SV
560-0395	N15SK	560-0477	N50GP	*Citation Encore/+*		560-0626	N41VP	560-0760	PR-CTB
560-0396	N396QS	560-0478	N458NC	707	N560VU	560-0627	N191VF	560-0761	N560DL
560-0397	N44LV	560-0479	N379QS	560-0539	N303CP	560-0628	N812QS	560-0762	N24QT
560-0398	ZS-NUZ	560-0480	N566VR	560-0540	N154JS	560-0629	N844QS	560-0763	N926CE
560-0399	N969DW	560-0481	C-GXCG	560-0541	N812DC	560-0631	N560HC	560-0764	LN-AKA*
560-0400	N42ND	560-0482	N44LQ	560-0542	I-CMCC	560-0632	N109WS	560-0765	N713WD
560-0401	VP-CSN	560-0483	N383QS	560-0543	N543LE	560-0633	C-FTOM	560-0766	N766CE
560-0402	N302QS	560-0484	C-GYMM	560-0544	D-CASA	560-0634	N90NB	560-0767	I-ZACK
560-0403	JA01TM	560-0485	N998SA	560-0546	N368BE	560-0635	N535CE	560-0768	EC-KKB
560-0404	96-0107	560-0486	N386QS	560-0547	N908AS	560-0636	wo	560-0769	N769CS
560-0405	N45TE	560-0487	N51EF	560-0549	N33TS	560-0637	PR-ALL*	560-0770	EC-KKK
560-0406	PT-WMZ	560-0488	N555WL	560-0550	N865M	560-0638	N23YZ	560-0771	N237BG
560-0407	N560RK	560-0489	N66U	560-0551	N86SK	560-0639	N24GF	560-0772	N772CS
560-0408	N304QS	560-0490	N390QS	560-0552	N552HV	560-0640	N800BW	560-0773	SE-RIT
560-0409	C-FKBC	560-0491	N484MM	560-0553	G-KDMA	560-0641	N67GW	560-0774	N422JT
560-0410	96-0108	560-0492	N85EB	560-0554	N8486	560-0642	N642LF	560-0775	N803QS
560-0411	N38NS	560-0493	N391QS	560-0555	N154JH	560-0643	N960JH	560-0776	N814QS
560-0412	N17PL	560-0494	N452AJ	560-0556	N539WA	560-0644	N95NB	560-0777	N777EN
560-0413	N561JS	560-0495	98-0006	560-0557	N557PG	560-0645	N299DH	560-0778	N818QS
560-0414	SE-RGY	560-0496	N395QS	560-0558	N558AK	560-0646	N535BP	560-0779	N5185V
560-0415	96-0109	560-0497	G-OBCC	560-0559	N359EC	560-0647	C-GDSH	560-0780	N780CE
560-0416	N561CC	560-0498	N26QT	560-0560	N560JW	560-0648	C-GTOG	560-0781	N781CE
560-0417	N560RV	560-0499	N556BG	560-0561	N60AE*	560-0650	N820QS	560-0782	N826QS
560-0418	N318QS	560-0500	N860CR	560-0562	N60NF	560-0652	N652NR	560-0784	N830QS
560-0419	EC-GOV	560-0501	98-0007	560-0563	N59KG	560-0653	PR-SCR	560-0785	N203WS
560-0420	96-0110	560-0502	D2-EBA	560-0564	N5601T	560-0654	N654CE	560-0786	N8190S
560-0421	N322QS	560-0503	N204BG	560-0566	N560FP	560-0655	N825QS	560-0787	N887CS
560-0422	N59TF	560-0504	N504CC	560-0568	N155JH	560-0656	N656Z	560-0789	N822QS
560-0423	N324QS	560-0505	98-0008	560-0569	D-CEBM	560-0657	N450MQ	560-0790	N843QS
560-0425	N325QS	560-0506	EC-JFT	560-0571	N3616	560-0658	N560RM	560-0792	N831QS
560-0426	96-0111	560-0507	N1129L	560-0572	N174JS	560-0659	N721NB	560-0793	N793CS
560-0427	N891FV	560-0508	98-0009	560-0573	C-FALI	560-0660	N844TM	560-0794	N823QS
560-0428	N328QS	560-0509	N309QS	560-0575	N156JH	560-0661	N591CF	560-0796	N829QS
560-0429	N392QS	560-0510	N399QS	560-0576	C-GTGO	560-0662	N338MC	560-0797	N846QS
560-0430	N560TA	560-0511	YV2110	560-0578	D-CAUW	560-0663	N357BE	560-0799	N841QS
560-0431	N76TF	560-0512	N10AU	560-0579	N579CE	560-0664	N664CE	560-0801	N827QS
560-0432	N564TJ	560-0513	98-0010	560-0580	wo	560-0665	YR-RPG	*Citation Excel/XLS*	
560-0433	XA-...	560-0514	N340QS	560-0581	N157JH	560-0666	N700JR	706	N560XL
560-0434	N334QS	560-0515	VH-PSU	560-0582	N560CX	560-0668	N45TP	560-5001	N561XL
560-0435	N5263	560-0516	N316QS	560-0583	N353CE	560-0669	N834QS	560-5002	N12L
560-0436	N97TE	560-0517	OE-GCB	560-0584	N428SJ	560-0670	N560JT	560-5003	PT-FPP
560-0437	N337QS	560-0518	JA02AA	560-0585	N221VP	560-0671	N600BW	560-5004	J 754
560-0438	N438MC	560-0519	N319QS	560-0586	N201SU	560-0673	N96NB	560-5005	N77UW
560-0439	N6NY	560-0520	N101KP	560-0587	N4TL	560-0674	N552CN	560-5006	N8005
560-0440	N400MC	560-0521	N22LQ	560-0588	C-GJEI	560-0675	N29QC	560-5007	OE-GTK
560-0441	N314QS	560-0522	N398QS	560-0590	OE-GPH	560-0676	C-FSNC	560-5008	N944AH
560-0442	N323NE*	560-0523	N332QS	560-0591	N591DK	560-0678	N177JE	560-5009	N398RS
560-0443	N561CM	560-0524	165740	560-0593	N300AK	560-0680	N595MA	560-5010	VT-CLA
560-0444	N343QS	560-0525	N593M	560-0594	N560MR	560-0681	N681CE	560-5011	N560L
560-0445	N345QS	560-0526	N326QS	560-0595	N560TE	560-0683	F-HLIM	560-5012	N560CE
560-0446	HB-VLZ	560-0527	N102KP	560-0596	N844HS	560-0684	N370TC	560-5013	N1PB
560-0447	N261WR	560-0528	N52WF	560-0597	JA002A	560-0685	N837QS	560-5014	N989TW
560-0448	N4ZL	560-0529	165741	560-0598	N800QS	560-0686	N5188A	560-5015	N523KW
560-0449	N75WP	560-0530	N353QS	560-0599	N288HL	560-0687	XA-UEF	560-5016	N615RG
560-0450	PT-XCF	560-0531	wo	560-0600	PR-LAM	560-0688	N254AD	560-5017	N580AW
560-0451	N351QS	560-0532	99-0100	560-0601	N801QS	560-0689	XC-GDT	560-5018	N410MT
560-0452	97-0101	560-0533	N591M	560-0602	N9CN	560-0690	N839QS	560-5019	N990DK
560-0453	N400LX	560-0534	99-0101	560-0603	N313HC	560-0691	N500PX	560-5020	PT-XCL
560-0454	N63GB	560-0535	N403ET	560-0604	N911CB	560-0692	N999CB	560-5021	N862CF
560-0455	N358QS	560-0536	N363QS	560-0605	N250AL	560-0694	JA560Y	560-5022	D-CSFD
560-0456	97-0102	560-0537	OO-CLX	560-0606	N91AG	560-0695	N695V	560-5023	N236LB
560-0457	HB-VNW	560-0538	99-0102	560-0607	SE-RGZ	560-0697	N697CE	560-5024	N622PC
560-0458	N458DA	560-0545	99-0103	560-0608	N608CE	560-0698	N809QS	560-5025	LV-...
560-0459	N76WR	560-0548	99-0104			560-0699	N560HM		

560-5026	C-GJRB	560-5107	N300SJ	560-5188	N688QS	560-5269	T-784	560-5351	N560AW
560-5027	N560GB	560-5108	N562DD	560-5189	OO-SAV	560-5270	N300DA	560-5352	ZS-IDC
560-5028	OO-MLG	560-5109	N458LC	560-5190	N104LV	560-5271	LN-SUX	560-5353	EC-ISQ
560-5029	SE-DYX	560-5110	PH-RSA	560-5191	N767BS	560-5272	N1326A	560-5354	N178BR
560-5030	N17AN	560-5111	N380M	560-5192	N164AS	560-5273	N617PD	560-5355	CS-DFR
560-5031	N560BT	560-5112	N1129E	560-5193	N811ST	560-5274	PR-ACC	560-5356	XA-UAF
560-5032	N108EK	560-5113	OE-GME	560-5194	N694QS	560-5275	N675QS	560-5357	N567MC
560-5033	XA-UVA	560-5114	N717MB	560-5195	D-CVHI	560-5276	N276A	560-5358	N635QS
560-5034	PP-RAA	560-5115	VT-ARA	560-5196	XA-ICO	560-5277	N560CM	560-5359	N659QS
560-5035	N4JS	560-5116	N498AB	560-5197	N697QS	560-5278	N95CC	560-5360	N615QS
560-5036	N884BB	560-5117	N202RL	560-5198	N560NY	560-5279	N679QS	560-5361	N112AB
560-5037	OE-GTI	560-5118	B-7019	560-5199	N699QS	560-5280	N621QS	560-5362	N521CS
560-5038	N404BT	560-5119	N75HU	560-5200	C-GXCO	560-5281	N142AA	560-5363	N638QS
560-5039	N87WU	560-5120	PR-AAA	560-5201	N523CC	560-5282	N507CS	560-5364	N522CS
560-5040	N840CC	560-5121	N560CG	560-5202	N82KW	560-5283	CS-DFN	560-5365	N667QS
560-5041	N39RC	560-5122	N67TW	560-5203	N603QS	560-5284	C-GUPC	560-5366	N555WZ
560-5042	N413CK	560-5123	N59EC	560-5204	N604QS	560-5285	N422AB	560-5367	N677QS
560-5043	PT-XIB	560-5124	N24NG	560-5205	N503CS	560-5286	N622QS	560-5368	VT-CSP
560-5044	N544XL	560-5125	N4JB	560-5206	N561CE	560-5287	N118ST	560-5369	N504PK
560-5045	PP-JFM	560-5126	N626QS	560-5207	N62GR	560-5288	SX-DCE	560-5370	N770JM
560-5046	A9C-BXA	560-5127	N560KT	560-5208	XA-TKZ	560-5289	PR-NBR	560-5371	PR-OUR
560-5047	N838RT	560-5128	PH-CJI	560-5209	HB-VNS	560-5290	N691QS	560-5372	CS-DFS
560-5048	VP-CAI	560-5129	N94LA	560-5210	N610QS	560-5291	N397BC	560-5501	N883RP
560-5049	N560VR	560-5130	N630QS	560-5211	PR-VRD	560-5292	N666MX	560-5502	N502EG
560-5050	N88HP	560-5131	N631QS	560-5212	N560DP	560-5293	N695QS	560-5503	N732JR
560-5051	SX-DCM	560-5132	N632QS	560-5213	N24EP	560-5294	N508CS	560-5504	N111GU
560-5052	N990MF	560-5133	N23NG	560-5214	N57KW	560-5295	N641QS	560-5505	N901DK
560-5053	I-BENT	560-5134	N561BP	560-5215	N560TH	560-5296	N696QS	560-5506	N618QS
560-5054	N80X	560-5135	N885BB	560-5216	CS-DNY	560-5297	N1871R	560-5507	N523CS
560-5055	N488CP	560-5136	N100YB	560-5217	SE-RCL	560-5298	C-FBXL	560-5508	N72SG
560-5056	SE-RBX	560-5137	N637QS	560-5218	P4-ALM	560-5299	N623QS	560-5509	N617QS
560-5057	N53WF	560-5138	N924JE	560-5219	N877RF	560-5300	N613KS	560-5510	N357EC
560-5058	S5-BBD	560-5139	N639QS	560-5220	N318MM	560-5301	N601QS	560-5511	N670MW
560-5059	N580BC	560-5140	N884B	560-5221	CS-DNW	560-5302	N624QS	560-5512	CS-DFT
560-5060	PT-WYU	560-5141	N901CR	560-5222	N426CH	560-5303	N1867M	560-5513	N196SB
560-5061	HB-VMO	560-5142	N705SG	560-5223	PR-EMS	560-5304	N636QS	560-5514	N143DH
560-5062	N23LM	560-5143	N966JM	560-5224	N595G*	560-5305	N628QS	560-5515	N361EC
560-5063	N56HX	560-5144	N560TS	560-5225	N351WC	560-5306	N629QS	560-5516	N540CS
560-5064	N227MC	560-5145	N645QS	560-5226	N562WD	560-5307	XA-DRM	560-5517	N778BC
560-5065	N100SC	560-5146	N291DV	560-5227	N627QS	560-5308	N608QS	560-5518	N602QS
560-5066	HB-VMU	560-5147	N24UD	560-5228	G-IPAX	560-5309	C-GMKZ	560-5519	N43HF
560-5067	N864CC	560-5148	N200SC	560-5229	N504CS	560-5310	N509CS	560-5520	CS-DFU
560-5068	N56LP	560-5149	N627XL	560-5230	OO-PGG	560-5311	N560PD	560-5521	N541CS
560-5069	N189WW	560-5150	N650QS	560-5231	N511DN	560-5312	N612QS	560-5522	N609QS
560-5070	N789CN	560-5151	N79PF	560-5232	N34WP	560-5314	CS-DFO	560-5523	N542CS
560-5071	N671QS	560-5152	N652QS	560-5233	N233XL	560-5315	CS-DFP	560-5524	N546CS
560-5072	N565AB	560-5153	N816CS	560-5234	C-FCXL	560-5316	OE-GCG	560-5525	N370BA
560-5073	N560DR	560-5154	HB-VNI	560-5235	CS-DNZ	560-5317	N57WP	560-5526	N633QS
560-5074	N66LM	560-5155	N1837S	560-5236	S5-BAZ	560-5318	OO-FTS	560-5527	N713DH
560-5075	N558R	560-5156	N2ZC	560-5237	N751PL	560-5319	N625QS	560-5528	HB-VON
560-5076	N521RA	560-5157	OE-GCA	560-5238	N238SM	560-5320	N151KV	560-5529	OE-GEG
560-5077	N46VE	560-5158	N615EC	560-5239	N626AT	560-5321	N605QS	560-5530	N491N
560-5078	N560HJ	560-5159	N326MA	560-5240	N640QS	560-5322	N183JS	560-5531	N560JG
560-5079	ZS-OHZ	560-5160	N901FH	560-5241	N100AR	560-5323	N560RS	560-5532	N562LD
560-5080	N90CF	560-5161	N405MM	560-5242	G-LDFM	560-5324	N511CS	560-5533	N711NR
560-5081	N4000K	560-5162	N168BG	560-5243	OK-SLX	560-5325	N568DM	560-5534	N424HH
560-5082	N469RS	560-5163	N591MA	560-5244	N898MC	560-5326	N512CS	560-5535	PT-ORM
560-5083	N520G	560-5164	N84LX	560-5245	N245J	560-5327	N175WS	560-5536	D-CHSP
560-5084	N684QS	560-5165	N665QS	560-5246	N646QS	560-5328	N514CS	560-5537	I-TAKA
560-5085	N883PF	560-5166	N580RC	560-5247	G-CIEL	560-5329	N848DM	560-5538	D-CMMI
560-5086	N957BJ	560-5167	G-REDS	560-5248	OO-FPA	560-5330	N395WJ	560-5539	B-3642
560-5087	PT-MSK	560-5168	N780CS	560-5249	N80LP	560-5331	N510HF	560-5540	B-3643
560-5088	G-WCIN	560-5169	OE-GPN	560-5250	N56FE	560-5332	N710MT	560-5541	LV-BCS
560-5089	N560GC*	560-5170	N670QS	560-5251	N651QS	560-5333	N2	560-5542	N547CS
560-5090	N690QS	560-5171	N632BL	560-5252	N560CS	560-5334	CS-DFQ	560-5543	CS-DFV
560-5091	N170SD	560-5172	HB-VNH	560-5253	C-FTIL	560-5335	N515CS	560-5544	PP-BRS
560-5092	N692QS	560-5173	N560JF	560-5254	N626TN	560-5336	N336XL	560-5545	N560TV
560-5093	N903DK	560-5174	N624AT	560-5255	N60AG	560-5337	YR-RPR	560-5546	N549CS
560-5094	N1094L	560-5175	N625AT	560-5256	PR-GAM	560-5338	N606QS	560-5547	N647QS
560-5095	N95XL	560-5176	N676QS	560-5257	CS-DFM	560-5339	OE-GNW	560-5548	N611QS
560-5096	C-GCXL	560-5177	N841DW	560-5258	PH-DRK	560-5340	N607QS	560-5549	N39GA
560-5097	C-GLMI	560-5178	N562TS	560-5259	G-XLMB	560-5341	N3	560-5550	N200JR
560-5098	N502BC	560-5179	N186WS*	560-5260	N711VH	560-5342	N228Y	560-5551	N550CS
560-5099	N58HX	560-5180	N868J	560-5261	N57TP	560-5343	G-WINA	560-5552	PP-MDB
560-5100	N100CJ	560-5181	N681QS	560-5262	N662QS	560-5344	I-CMAL	560-5553	CS-DXB
560-5101	N81SH	560-5182	N563CH	560-5263	N663QS	560-5345	N616QS	560-5554	EC-JZK
560-5102	N997CB	560-5183	OK-CAA	560-5264	N664QS	560-5346	N346XL	560-5555	D-CAAA
560-5103	N68HG	560-5184	N531RQ	560-5265	OE-GPA	560-5347	N47HF	560-5556	N385MG
560-5104	LX-JCD	560-5185	G-SIRS	560-5266	G-CBRG	560-5348	N470SK	560-5557	N5NR
560-5105	PP-JGV	560-5186	N186XL	560-5267	N506CS	560-5349	N676BB	560-5558	N634QS
560-5106	G-ELOA	560-5187	N687QS	560-5268	N668QS	560-5350	LV-AIW	560-5559	CS-DXC

560-5560	N560CR	560-5641	PH-JNX	560-5722	D-CLLL	650-0008	N777XS	650-0089	N86VP
560-5561	N642QS	560-5642	HB-VOM	560-5723	D-CVVV	650-0009	N933SH	650-0090	N651PW
560-5562	N619QS	560-5643	N683QS	560-5724	G-OROO	650-0010	N650LW	650-0091	PT-LUE
560-5563	N45NF	560-5644	PR-TRJ	560-5725	N725XL	650-0011	N362TW	650-0092	N692BE
560-5564	EC-JVF	560-5645	N88SF	560-5726	N577CS	650-0012	OE-GCO	650-0093	N196SD
560-5565	N370M	560-5646	N921MW	560-5727	VH-NGH	650-0013	N770GF	650-0094	N699MG
560-5566	N70XL	560-5647	N660QS	560-5728	N946PC	650-0014	OY-EDP	650-0095	N941KA
560-5567	D-CBBB	560-5648	N711HA	560-5729	C-GKEG	650-0015	N766MH	650-0096	N629MD
560-5568	CS-DXD	560-5649	SP-KCS	560-5730	N575QS	650-0016	N21LL	650-0097	N697MC
560-5569	D-CTLX	560-5650	N685QS	560-5731	I-CMAB	650-0017	N651BP	650-0098	N398DL
560-5570	N155RW	560-5651	N673QS	560-5732	N656QS	650-0018	N650SB	650-0099	N994U
560-5571	N24PH	560-5652	N226JT	560-5733	OO-AIE	650-0019	N71LU	650-0100	N202JK
560-5572	N554CS	560-5653	N698QS	560-5734	N411EC	650-0020	N420GT	650-0101	VH-SPJ
560-5573	D-CTTT	560-5654	N682QS	560-5735	N577QS	650-0021	N460CP	650-0102	N24237
560-5574	N648QS	560-5655	N655QS	560-5736	N777LX	650-0022	N650J	650-0103	N2411A
560-5575	N75XL	560-5656	N35SE	560-5737	N404MM	650-0023	N650CG	650-0104	C-FORJ
560-5576	HB-VNY	560-5657	N693QS	560-5738	N590QS	650-0024	N422BC	650-0105	I-FEEV
560-5577	N556CS	560-5658	A9C-BXI	560-5739	PR-FJA	650-0025	N16SU	650-0106	N650CE
560-5578	CS-DXE	560-5659	N689QS	560-5740	N166RD	650-0026	wfu	650-0107	N397DR
560-5579	N2HB	560-5660	S5-BAV	560-5741	N580QS	650-0027	N993LC	650-0108	N650Z
560-5580	N614QS	560-5661	N686QS	560-5742	N911EK	650-0028	N650BW	650-0109	VH-SBU
560-5581	N577PS	560-5662	SX-DCD	560-5743	N806AD	650-0029	N409SF	650-0110	N303PC
560-5582	N644QS	560-5663	N672QS	560-5744	PR-MMV*	650-0030	N51EM	650-0111	N381CW
560-5583	PR-CON	560-5664	N600QS	560-5745	PH-ANO	650-0031	N7ZG	650-0112	N598AW
560-5584	I-CDOL	560-5665	N658QS	560-5746	N8000U	650-0032	XA-HVP	650-0113	N393JC
560-5585	N560BA	560-5666	LN-EXL	560-5747	N47XL	650-0033	wo	650-0114	N650DA
560-5586	CS-DXF	560-5667	XA-UGQ	560-5748	CS-DXR	650-0034	N650GH	650-0115	N541S
560-5587	N808MN*	560-5668	OE-GZK	560-5749	N169SM	650-0035	N408JD	650-0116	N928PS
560-5588	N643QS	560-5669	N637RP	560-5750	N5095N	650-0036	N651CV	650-0117	F-GGAL
560-5589	N842DW	560-5670	D-CAJK	560-5751	N8701L	650-0037	D-C...	650-0118	N79KF
560-5590	N103PG	560-5671	N55NG	560-5752	N412AB	650-0038	N373DJ	650-0119	N650HM
560-5591	N771DE	560-5672	C-FTXL	560-5753	EC-K..	650-0039	XA-KMX	650-0120	N907DF
560-5592	N586SF	560-5673	VH-XCJ	560-5754	CS-DXS*	650-0040	N650WE	650-0121	N818DE
560-5593	EC-JXI	560-5674	D-CHHH	560-5755	OE-GEH	650-0041	N55BH	650-0122	N122EJ
560-5594	VT-JSS	560-5675	G-OXLS	560-5756	N5265B	650-0042	C-GPOP	650-0123	N59FT
560-5595	CS-DXG	560-5676	A9C-BXJ	560-5757	OY-CKK	650-0043	N953JF	650-0124	N650HC
560-5596	N1HS	560-5677	N661QS	560-5758	N758XL	650-0044	N126MT	650-0125	N178HL
560-5597	N780CC	560-5678	N702AC	560-5759	N575NR	650-0045	N689W	650-0126	N101PG
560-5598	PK-ILA	560-5679	N1230F	560-5760	N50756	650-0046	C-FBNA	650-0127	N700MH
560-5599	N613QS	560-5680	N571CS	560-5761	N2060V	650-0047	N706HB	650-0128	N125Q
560-5600	N560PL	560-5681	C-GPAW	560-5762	D-CRON*	650-0048	A6-CGK	650-0129	N330MB
560-5601	N867W	560-5682	F-GVYC	560-5763	N51869	650-0049	N30AF	650-0130	N918BH
560-5602	N499HS	560-5683	CS-DXM	560-5764	N51666	650-0050	N51JV	650-0131	303
560-5603	N868XL	560-5684	N669TT	560-5765	CS-DXT*	650-0051	N777MX	650-0132	N727AW
560-5604	N562DB	560-5685	CS-DXN	560-5766	N2065X	650-0052	XA-SDU	650-0133	N213HP
560-5605	OB-1824	560-5686	C-FNXL	560-5767	N5059X	650-0053	N306PA	650-0134	PH-MSX
560-5606	N566F	560-5687	N533CC	560-5768	N75TP	650-0054	N47AN	650-0135	VP-CAR
560-5607	N7HB	560-5688	D-CVHB	560-5769	N5066U	650-0055	N652CV	650-0136	N3170B
560-5608	LN-XLS	560-5689	N669QS	560-5773	N579QS	650-0056	N78AP	650-0137	N4Y
560-5609	N90BL*	560-5690	M-BWFC	560-5775	CS-DXU*	650-0057	N955HG*	650-0138	N717JM
560-5610	G-OMEA	560-5691	C-FWXL	560-5782	CS-DXV*	650-0058	N72EP*	650-0139	N96CP
560-5611	N654QS	560-5692	CS-DXO	560-5783	N783XL	650-0059	N370TP	650-0140	N1400M
560-5612	N441BP	560-5693	TC-LNS	560-5787	CS-DXW*	650-0060	OY-JPJ	650-0141	N140TS
560-5613	G-PKRG	560-5694	N717NB	560-5788	D-CWWW*	650-0061	N440PC	650-0142	D-CRHR
560-5614	N45PK	560-5695	OE-GSR	560-5789	CS-DXX*	650-0062	N84PH	650-0143	N40FC
560-5615	CS-DXH	560-5696	LV-BIB	560-5791	CS-DXY*	650-0063	N651AT	650-0144	N384EM
560-5616	N678QS	560-5697	N594QS	560-5794	N576CS	650-0064	N444CW	650-0145	N385EM
560-5617	N563XP	560-5698	G-XBEL	560-5796	CS-DXZ*	650-0065	C-FIMO	650-0146	N650FC
560-5618	C-GRPB	560-5699	G-RSXL	560-5799	N771PM	650-0066	N650CD	650-0147	N151DR
560-5619	PR-LFT	560-5700	ES-SKY	560-5800	N578CS	650-0067	N232CE	650-0148	N92RP
560-5620	D-CAIR	560-5701	N414AA	560-5805	N587QS	650-0068	XA-TMZ	650-0149	D-CBPL
560-5621	CS-DXI	560-5702	CS-DXP	560-5807	N579CS	650-0069	N455JD	650-0150	N61CK
560-5622	N561MK	560-5703	5N-BJS	560-5810	N589QS	650-0070	OY-NLA	650-0151	N321AR
560-5623	D-CDDD	560-5704	CS-DXQ	560-5812	N583QS	650-0071	N97DD	650-0152	N605SA
560-5624	SE-RCM	560-5705	N574CS	560-5815	N580CS	650-0072	N139MY	650-0153	N845FW
560-5625	N916CS	560-5706	N592QS	560-5817	N581CS	650-0073	XA-LEY	650-0154	N650CH
560-5626	N68GW	560-5707	N534CC	560-5818	N565QS	650-0074	N81SF	650-0155	N97AL
560-5627	CS-DXJ	560-5708	N576QS	560-5820	N574QS	650-0075	N85MS	650-0156	N74VF
560-5628	N890LE	560-5709	XA-UHQ	560-5825	N566QS	650-0076	XA-PVR	650-0157	N650RP
560-5629	N1897A	560-5710	5A-DRK	560-5827	N573QS	650-0077	N800GM	650-0158	VH-SSZ
560-5630	D-CEEE	560-5711	N560TD	560-5829	N568QS	650-0078	N650KB	650-0159	N359CW
560-5631	SX-SMR	560-5712	N595QS	560-5832XL	N502XL	650-0079	N650RB	650-0160	N220CM
560-5632	N632XL	560-5713	N614EP	**650 Citation III**		650-0080	C-FDJC	650-0161	N510SD
560-5633	CS-DXK	560-5714	N599QS	650-0001	N651CG	650-0081	N910DF	650-0162	N660Q
560-5634	D-CFFF	560-5715	N32KM	650-0002	N650AS	650-0082	N825JW	650-0163	N163JM
560-5635	N573AB	560-5716	N38KW	650-0003	N166MC	650-0083	N650HG	650-0164	N162DS
560-5636	N657QS	560-5717	C-GAWR	650-0004	N650LA	650-0084	N650CB	650-0165	XC-PGN
560-5637	N568CS	560-5718	N399SF	650-0005	N700RY	650-0085	wo	650-0166	PT-LTB
560-5638	N64LX	560-5719	D-CMMP	650-0006	N129GB	650-0086	PT-LHC	650-0167	N88DJ
560-5639	XA-MMX	560-5720	N121KL	650-0007	N650MG	650-0087	PP-AIO	650-0168	N175J
560-5640	CS-DXL	560-5721	N588QS			650-0088	N650TA	650-0169	N73HM

650-0170	XA-RIE	650-7006	OE-GCH	650-7087	N43FC	680-0046	N2428	680-0127	N111Y
650-0171	PR-ITN	650-7007	N28TX	650-7088	XA-PYN	680-0047	N544KB	680-0128	N228RH
650-0172	N934H	650-7008	N678EQ	650-7089	VH-VRC	680-0048	N777UT	680-0129	VH-EXQ
650-0173	N173VP	650-7009	N711NB	650-7090	T7-VII	680-0049	N158PH	680-0130	N307QS
650-0174	D-CLUE	650-7010	N150JP	650-7091	TC-...	680-0050	D-CVHA	680-0131	N624CS
650-0175	N175SR	650-7011	VH-DHN	650-7092	C-GCIX	680-0051	N362QS	680-0132	PR-SPR
650-0176	N504RP	650-7012	N817MB	650-7093	OY-CLP	680-0052	N19MK	680-0133	LN-SSS
650-0177	N834H	650-7013	N15LN	650-7094	N794VP*	680-0053	XA-FUD	680-0134	N323QS
650-0178	N605DS	650-7014	N375E	650-7095	N795VP	680-0054	N2425	680-0135	N138BG
650-0179	N63GC	650-7015	N750CK	650-7096	N287MC	680-0055	OE-GNB	680-0136	N320TM
650-0180	N498CS	650-7016	N650CP	650-7097	N797CC	680-0056	VT-VED	680-0137	N192CN
650-0181	N650DR	650-7017	N775M	650-7098	N1254C	680-0057	N365QS	680-0138	M-AGIC
650-0182	N491JB	650-7018	N623PM	650-7099	PT-XFG	680-0058	N121TL	680-0139	OK-UNI
650-0183	N820FJ	650-7019	XA-TRE	650-7100	N277CP*	680-0059	SE-RFH	680-0140	N313QS
650-0184	N650VW	650-7020	N832CB	650-7101	N650JL	680-0060	PR-SUN	680-0141	N230LC
650-0185	N521BH	650-7021	PT-MGS	650-7102	D-CNCJ	680-0061	N606CS	680-0142	N685CS
650-0186	XA-...	650-7022	N902F	650-7103	N713VP	680-0062	N364QS	680-0143	G-XBLU
650-0187	D-CRRR	650-7023	N6110	650-7104	VH-ING	680-0063	N608CS	680-0144	N397QS
650-0188	N650FP	650-7024	93-004	650-7105	N118MM	680-0064	C-GNEQ	680-0145	OE-GVO
650-0189	XA-RGS	650-7025	XA-RRQ	650-7106	N33RL	680-0065	N901G	680-0146	N599GB
650-0190	D-CCEU	650-7026	93-005	650-7107	N559AM	680-0066	D-CUPI	680-0147	N1TG
650-0191	N650SG	650-7027	N622PM	650-7108	N202AV	680-0067	OY-WET	680-0148	N112MV*
650-0192	D-CREY	650-7028	XA-SPQ	650-7109	wo	680-0068	C-GSUN	680-0149	N389QS
650-0193	N2DH	650-7029	N444KE	650-7110	OE-GLS	680-0069	PR-SOV	680-0150	D-CHDC
650-0194	N831GA	650-7030	N782CC	650-7111	PR-AJG	680-0070	N927LT	680-0151	N681LF
650-0195	N140WH	650-7031	N4QN	650-7112	N269TA	680-0071	C-GJKI	680-0152	N152SV
650-0196	N534H	650-7032	N32FJ	650-7113	N737MM	680-0072	VH-EXG	680-0153	OE-GTT
650-0197	N100R	650-7033	PT-OVU	650-7114	N926CB	680-0073	N368QS	680-0154	N888SF
650-0198	XA-XGX	650-7034	N650K	650-7115	N314SL	680-0074	N391KK	680-0155	N357QS
650-0199	N400RE	650-7035	N95RX	650-7116	N175DP	680-0075	N1312V	680-0156	D-CHIP
650 Citation VI		650-7036	N77HF	650-7117	N135HC	680-0076	N121LS	680-0157	C-FCPR
650-0200	wo	650-7037	N95TX	650-7118	N33L	680-0077	N961TC	680-0158	N158SV
650-0201	N1419J	650-7038	PR-JAP	650-7119	N651CC	680-0078	N680SE	680-0159	TC-IST
650-0202	N65BP	650-7039	D-CBIZ	680 Sovereign		680-0079	N680HC	680-0160	N317QS
650-0203	VT-IPA	650-7040	N504T	709	N680CS	680-0080	N345PF	680-0161	G-NSJS
650-0204	N108WV	650-7041	N430SA	680-0001	N605CS	680-0081	N369QS	680-0162	D-CMES
650-0205	PT-OMU	650-7042	N657T	680-0002	N747RL	680-0082	N7402	680-0163	N1RF
650-0206	N119ES	650-7043	N44MQ	680-0003	N602CS	680-0083	N44M	680-0164	N300QS
650-0207	N107CG	650-7044	N650CJ	680-0004	XA-GMO	680-0084	N63LX	680-0165	N629CS
650-0208	N500FR	650-7045	CS-DGR	680-0005	OE-GMM	680-0085	N1ZC	680-0166	N1FJ
650-0209	N930MG	650-7046	N703RB	680-0006	N409GB	680-0086	N227DH	680-0167	SU-SMB
650-0210	N783H	650-7047	N650DD	680-0007	N604CS	680-0087	EC-JYG	680-0168	N442LW
650-0211	N211CC	650-7048	N18GB	680-0008	N900EB	680-0088	N305QS	680-0169	N320QS
650-0212	N651AR	650-7049	N73UC*	680-0009	N682DB	680-0089	N380QS	680-0170	N630CS
650-0213	N900UD	650-7050	N650CZ	680-0010	N301QS	680-0090	PR-RCB	680-0171	VP-CMH
650-0214	N7777B	650-7051	N77LX	680-0011	N338QS	680-0091	N595SY	680-0172	N633RP
650-0215	N650GC	650-7052	N24KT	680-0012	N61DF	680-0092	N610CS	680-0173	N1315G
650-0216	I-BLUB	650-7053	N650AT	680-0013	N346QS	680-0093	N204RP	680-0174	TC-TKN
650-0217	PH-MEX	650-7054	LV-WTN	680-0014	XA-HIT	680-0094	G-SVSB	680-0175	D-CCJS
650-0218	XA-ACH	650-7055	D-CMPI	680-0015	N272MH	680-0095	N711NL*	680-0176	N701CR
650-0219	N650TS	650-7056	N444EX	680-0016	XA-RTS	680-0096	N16GS	680-0177	N338TM
650-0220	B-7022	650-7057	N808VA*	680-0017	N446RT	680-0097	N381QS	680-0178	EC-KMK
650-0221	wo	650-7058	N98XS	680-0018	N79PG	680-0098	N202DF	680-0179	N2UJ
650-0222	N780GT	650-7059	N144MH	680-0019	N63TM	680-0099	N370QS	680-0180	N376QS
650-0223	N111YW	650-7060	N55SC	680-0020	N914SP	680-0100	C-GAGU	680-0181	N751BG
650-0224	N1UP	650-7061	N102CE	680-0021	N174TM	680-0101	N696HC	680-0182	PR-...
650-0225	N606AT	650-7062	N876G	680-0022	N1901	680-0102	N617CS	680-0183	LN-...
650-0226	N400JH	650-7063	N877G	680-0023	N44SH	680-0103	N378QS	680-0184	N5231S
650-0227	N2UP	650-7064	N82GM	680-0024	N565A	680-0104	N680GG	680-0186	N5135K
650-0228	XA-SLB	650-7065	N96MT	680-0025	N680AR	680-0105	N305EJ	680-0187	N377QS
650-0229	TC-ANT	650-7066	N669W	680-0026	SU-EWD	680-0106	N83SD	680-0188	N626CS
650-0230	N660PA	650-7067	C-FTOR	680-0027	N827DC	680-0107	N531RC	680-0189	N5245D
650-0231	N400WK	650-7068	N7AB	680-0028	N865EC	680-0108	N680VR	680-0190	N52352
650-0232	N711LV	650-7069	XA-TMX	680-0029	N349QS	680-0109	N900JD	680-0191	N5136J
650-0233	CC-DAC	650-7070	OY-CKE	680-0030	N808WC	680-0110	N384QS	680-0192	N680RC
650-0234	XA-GBM	650-7071	HS-DCG	680-0031	N156PH	680-0111	N282DR	680-0193	N5257V
650-0235	N235SV	650-7072	N35HS	680-0032	C-FDHD	680-0112	N829JC	680-0194	N680CM
650-0236	N184GP	650-7073	PK-YRL	680-0033	ZS-JDL	680-0113	N388QS	680-0195	N5207V
650-0237	N650W	650-7074	PT-WLY	680-0034	N2426	680-0114	SE-RFI	680-0196	N5203S
650-0238	N19QC	650-7075	N711GF	680-0035	N157PH	680-0115	N385QS	680-0197	N631CS
650-0239	N68ED	650-7076	N286MC	680-0036	N350QS	680-0116	N308QS	680-0201	N372QS
650-0240	PH-MFX	650-7077	N603HC*	680-0037	N631RP	680-0117	EC-KKC	680-0203	N203DN
650-0241	N651EJ	650-7078	N84NG	680-0038	N456SM	680-0118	SU-SMA	680-0206	N606SV
650 Citation VII		650-7079	U 21-01	680-0039	VP-CFP	680-0119	N387QS	680-0219	N843DW
697	wfu	650-7080	YU-BTM	680-0040	N785RC	680-0120	N621CS	680-0221	N401PG
650-7001	N701HA	650-7081	XA-FRI	680-0041	N789H	680-0121	N822DS	680-0222	N632CS
650-7002	N19SV	650-7082	N91KC	680-0042	N29WE	680-0122	N468SA	680-0236	N633CS
650-7003	N888TX	650-7083	PT-WQH	680-0043	N718MN	680-0123	N396BB	680-0244	N634CS
650-7004	N174VP	650-7084	TC-KON	680-0044	N680CG	680-0124	N622CS	750 Citation X	
650-7005	N200LH	650-7085	D-CLDF	680-0045	N145BL	680-0125	N666FH	703	N750CX
		650-7086	N860W			680-0126	N359QS		

750-0001	HB-JGU	750-0082	N705LX	750-0163	N610GR	750-0244	N750GF	6	N77JW
750-0002	C-FPUI	750-0083	N983QS	750-0164	N964QS	750-0245	N200CQ	7	N769SC
750-0003	N200AP	750-0084	N984QS	750-0165	N15RL	750-0246	C-GSEC	8	N108KC
750-0004	PR-LUZ	750-0085	D-BTEN	750-0166	N966QS	750-0247	N751PT	9	N510CL
750-0005	N99BB	750-0086	N986QS	750-0167	N721VT	750-0248	N750CR*	10	wo
750-0006	N706VP	750-0087	N987QS	750-0168	N123SL	750-0249	N265RX*	11	N419WC
750-0007	N750EC	750-0088	N88EJ	750-0169	N563BA	750-0250	N752PT	12	N10F
750-0008	N750CW	750-0089	N989QS	750-0170	N90NF	750-0251	VP-CFZ	13	wfu
750-0009	N978DB	750-0090	C-GCUL	750-0171	N399W	750-0252	G-CEDK	14	N333KE
750-0010	N808CZ	750-0091	N704LX	750-0172	N750NS	750-0253	N253CX	15	wo
750-0011	N960KC	750-0092	PT-WUM	750-0173	N749DX	750-0254	N254CX	16	N127WL
750-0012	N712VP*	750-0093	N114VW	750-0174	N87SL	750-0255	N712KC	17	F-GNDZ
750-0013	N5113S	750-0094	N750XX	750-0175	N975QS	750-0256	N753PT	18	wfu
750-0014	N478PM	750-0095	N415FW	750-0176	N1AP	750-0257	N754PT	19	N600HL
750-0015	N915QS	750-0096	N585M	750-0177	N177EL	750-0258	N755PT	20	N42G
750-0016	N521FP	750-0097	C-GMNC	750-0178	N750BL	750-0259	OE-HAL	21	N40ND
750-0017	N5144	750-0098	N998CX	750-0179	HB-JEZ	750-0260	N760PT	22	VP-BBV
750-0018	N199WT	750-0099	N93TX	750-0180	N353WC	750-0261	OE-HJA	23	N90LC
750-0019	N199XP	750-0100	N170HL	750-0181	N600AW	750-0262	SX-ECI	24	N69GB
750-0020	N8JQ	750-0101	N711VJ	750-0182	N982QS	750-0263	N750DX	25	C-GJET
750-0021	N49FW	750-0102	N901QS	750-0183	N938QS	750-0264	N764PT	26	N720DF
750-0022	N750VP	750-0103	N750HS	750-0184	HS-CDY	750-0265	N765PT	27	XA-AAY
750-0023	N923QS	750-0104	N5T	750-0185	N370EK	750-0266	N355WC	28	N42EH
750-0024	N942QS	750-0105	N905QS	750-0186	N970SK	750-0267	N17CX	29	N404JW
750-0025	N750RL	750-0106	N106CX	750-0187	N978QS	750-0268	CC-CPS	30	wfu
750-0026	N926QS	750-0107	N520CM	750-0188	C-FTEN	750-0269	N769PT	31	N27AJ
750-0027	N27VP	750-0108	N908QS	750-0189	N93S	750-0270	N570PT	32	32
750-0028	PR-FNP	750-0109	N708LX	750-0190	N990QS	750-0271	N271CX	33	N933TS*
750-0029	N945QS	750-0110	N910QS	750-0191	N354WC	750-0272	N772PT	34	N18SK
750-0030	N369B	750-0111	N750BP	750-0192	N5FF	750-0273	OE-HUB	35	N17WG
750-0031	N22RG	750-0112	N173WF	750-0193	N939QS	750-0274	N874PT	36	XA-MMM
750-0032	N932QS	750-0113	N913QS	750-0194	G-CDCX	750-0275	N104CT*	37	wfu
750-0033	N710AW	750-0114	N701LX	750-0195	N946QS	750-0276	N776PT	38	F-GBRF
750-0034	N934QS	750-0115	OH-PPI	750-0196	N996QS	750-0277	OE-HEC*	39	wo
750-0035	N97DK	750-0116	N916QS	750-0197	N585T	750-0278	N778PT	40	XA-LIO
750-0036	N936QS	750-0117	N426CM	750-0198	N998QS	750-0279	N879PT	41	N34TJ
750-0037	N75HS	750-0118	PR-XDY	750-0199	N484T	750-0280	N780PT	42	N282T
750-0038	N700LX	750-0119	XA-FMX	750-0200	N952QS	750-0281	G-CTEN	43	N17TJ
750-0039	N32NG	750-0120	N920QS	750-0201	N907QS	750-0282	N282CX	44	C-FZOP
750-0040	N40KW	750-0121	N93LA	750-0202	N300JD	750-0283	N711VT	45	PR-EGB
750-0041	C-GIWZ	750-0122	N577JC	750-0203	N999QS	750-0284	N52178	46	N401JW
750-0042	N915RB	750-0123	N900QS	750-0204	N22NG	750-0285	N940QS	47	wo
750-0043	N943QS	750-0124	N924QS	750-0205	C-GSUX	750-0286	N5245L	48	N20LW
750-0044	N96RX	750-0125	N977AE	750-0206	N906QS	750-0288	N928QS	49	N67LC
750-0045	N45BR	750-0126	N962QS	750-0207	N751GM	750-0290	N927QS	50	N299DB
750-0046	N749P	750-0127	N15TT	750-0208	N997QS	750-0293	N922QS	51	N909TF
750-0047	N947QS	750-0128	N1873	750-0209	N7SB	750-0296	N914QS	52	N711TF
750-0048	N84PJ	750-0129	N929QS	750-0210	N904QS	750-0299	N925QS	53	N824LA
750-0049	N949QS	750-0130	N930QS	750-0211	N65ST	Citation T-47A		54	N791CP*
750-0050	N950QS	750-0131	C-GAPT	750-0212	OY-LKS	552-0001	wo	55	N700AL
750-0051	N119RM	750-0132	N627R	750-0213	N9NG	552-0002	wo	56	N297PF
750-0052	N681WD	750-0133	N933QS	750-0214	OE-HGG	552-0003	wo	57	wo
750-0053	N795HG	750-0134	1060	750-0215	VH-TEN	552-0004	wo	58	wfu
750-0054	N610HC	750-0135	N935QS	750-0216	N882KB	552-0005	wo	59	N52JA
750-0055	N955QS	750-0136	XA-BAE	750-0217	N217AL	552-0006	wo	60	N769BH
750-0056	PP-JQM	750-0137	N937QS	750-0218	D-BLDI	552-0007	wo	61	wo
750-0057	N505MA	750-0138	N138SP	750-0219	D-BKLI	552-0008	wo	62	N6VG
750-0058	N758CX	750-0139	N26MJ	750-0220	N48HF	552-0009	wo	63	N876MA
750-0059	N751BH	750-0140	CS-DGO	750-0221	N256W	552-0010	wo	64	wfu
750-0060	PR-JAQ	750-0141	N941QS	750-0222	N750PT	552-0011	wo	65	N66CF
750-0061	N961QS	750-0142	N700SW	750-0223	N918QS	552-0012	wfu	66	N63TS
750-0062	N724CC	750-0143	N825GA	750-0224	N919QS	552-0013	wo	67	N427CJ
750-0063	N750JB	750-0144	N944QS	750-0225	N215RX	552-0014	wfu	68	F-GFPF
750-0064	N931QS	750-0145	N709LX	750-0226	N257AL	552-0015	wo	69	N711JC
750-0065	N750JJ	750-0146	N750DM	750-0227	P4-LJG	Citation OT-47B		70	N349JC
750-0066	N750GM	750-0147	N147CX	750-0228	N228DB	560-0350	FAC-5760	71	N220KS
750-0067	N967QS	750-0148	N700LH	750-0229	N229CE	560-0365	FAC-5763	72	ZS-FOX
750-0068	N377SF	750-0149	N948QS	750-0230	N750WM	560-0374	FAC-5761	73	N362PT
750-0069	N96TX	750-0150	N750TX	750-0231	N432AC	560-0381	FAC-5764	74	wfu
750-0070	N970QS	750-0151	N951QS	750-0232	OE-HAC	560-0386	N2500B	75	wfu
750-0071	N971QS	750-0152	N934BD	750-0233	N442WT	**Dassault**		76	N528JD
750-0072	N72FD	750-0153	N953QS	750-0234	PP-AAA	*Falcon 10/100*		77	N607TC
750-0073	N706LX	750-0154	N8JC	750-0235	N400JD			78	C-FEXD
750-0074	N703LX	750-0155	N73ME	750-0236	N349RR	01	wo	79	N692US
750-0075	P4-AND	750-0156	N956QS	750-0237	PR-MJC	02	wfu	80	N567RA
750-0076	N702LX	750-0157	B-7021	750-0238	N78SL	03	wfu	81	N81TX
750-0077	N770S	750-0158	N958QS	750-0239	N910DP	1	N333FJ	82	N101HS
750-0078	N707LX	750-0159	N7600G	750-0240	N1962J	2	C-GRIS	83	N724AS
750-0079	N979QS	750-0160	N960QS	750-0241	N921QS	3	wfu	84	N106TW
750-0080	PT-PTL	750-0161	N232CF	750-0242	9M-ATM	4	N888FJ	85	wo
750-0081	N1BS	750-0162	N903QS	750-0243	N373AB	5	F-BVPR	86	wfu

87	N515LP	168	N43EC	20	G-FRAJ	101	N97WJ	182	F-UKJA
88	N71M	169	PT-WSF	21	N50446	102	N204AN	183	RA-09003
89	N23TJ	170	wo	22	wfu	103	F-GPAA	184	EC-HCX
90	wfu	171	N42US	23	5761	104	wfu	185	N653MF
91	N23VP	172	N10NC	24	N240CK	105	wfu	186	wfu
92	N824DS	173	N8LT	25	wfu	106	wo	187	wfu
93	wfu	174	RP-C1911	26	wfu	107	N107J	188	F-ZACX
94	N13BK	175	N12EP	27	N326VW	108	N108R	189	wo
95	wo	176	N231JH	28	wfu	109	C-FIGD	190	5A-DCO
96	N115TD	177	N101VJ	29	LV-WMM	110	wfu	191	N20HF
97	N175FJ	178	N87TH	30	N123RA	111	N111BP	192	N192CK
98	wo	179	N3PW	31	XA-...	112	wfu	193	N219CA
99	N923HB	180	N211JL	32	N232TW	113	N531FL	194	wfu
100	XA-MGM	181	N138DM	33	wo	114	G-FRAW	195	N822AA
101	101	182	C-GOJC	34	wo	115	wfu	196	N196TS
102	N908TF	183	SE-DLB	35	wfu	116	N770FG	197	N5098F
103	N63XG	184	N725DM	36	wfu	117	N207JS	198	N724DS
104	N100CU	185	185	37	wo	118	wfu	199	wfu
105	N804JJ	186	N555DZ	38	wfu	119	N20FJ	200	wfu
106	N20CF	187	N5CA	39	wfu	120	N647JP	201	wfu
107	N907TF	188	N84TJ	40	N240TW	121	wfu	202	N29TE
108	wo	189	N155PX	41	041	122	N511FL	203	wo
109	N840GL	190	C-FBNW	42	wo	123	N223TW	204	N204TW
110	N653FJ	191	wo	43	wo	124	F-ZACC	205	N961AA
111	N289CA	192	wo	44	N800PP	125	0125	206	N410FJ*
112	wfu	193	EC-HVV	45	N589DC	126	wo	207	G-FRAP
113	N220PA	194	F-GIPH	46	EC-EHC	127	XB-HRA	208	wo
114	N982MC	195	N1993	47	wo	128	N70CK	209	G-FRAR
115	N169LS	196	C-FICA	48	N541FL	129	wfu	210	wo
116	wo	197	N52N	49	wfu	130	wfu	211	N764LA
117	N18MX	198	N91PB	50	N699TW	131	F-ZACD	212	N212R
118	N118AD	199	N655PE	51	wfu	132	G-FFRA	213	G-FRAK
119	N119SJ	200	N1JW	52	D-CLBR	133	wfu	214	G-FRAO
120	N710JC	201	N844F	53	053	134	wo	215	wfu
121	F-GDLR	202	wo	54	D2-JMM	135	N800DW	216	5840
122	N911UN	203	F-GPGL	55	wfu	136	wo	217	17103
123	N689WC	204	C-FFEV	56	wfu	137	wfu	218	N218CA
124	wo	205	N606AM	57	N812AA	138	F-ZACR	219	TM 11-3
125	N269SW	206	N46MK	58	wfu	139	N235CA	220	N220CA
126	N36WJ	207	N55DG	59	N900RA	140	wfu	221	N221TW
127	ZS-SEB	208	F-GSLZ	60	wo	141	UR-CCB	222	TM 11-2
128	P4-AVN	209	OY-PHN	61	N20NY	142	N300BA	223	G-FRAH
129	129	210	VP-BAF	62	wo	143	5A-DAG	224	9M-FRA
130	N454DP	211	F-GELT	63	wo	144	N960AA	225	wfu
131	N133EP	212	CN-ANZ	64	N425JF	145	wfu	226	N226CK*
132	wfu	213	N711HF	65	N165TW	146	N299RA	227	N227CK
133	133	214	N147GX	66	N814ER	147	wo	228	N823AA
134	VH-WJW	215	F-GHPB	67	N826AA	148	N148TW	229	N229CK
135	N272DN	216	SE-DYB	68	N521FL	149	wfu	230	N230RA
136	F-GFMD	217	N214RV	69	wfu	150	HC-BSS	231	wo
137	wfu	218	N303FZ	70	wfu	151	G-FRAL	232	wo
138	wo	219	N485AS	71	N209CA	152	CN-ANN	233	wfu
139	N110J	220	N569DW	72	wfu	153	N207CA	234	wfu
140	F-GHDX	221	F-GPFD	73	wfu	154	wo	235	0442
141	N77SF	222	N100YP	74	N221BR	155	N68BP	236	N236TW
142	N174B	223	PT-LVD	75	N217CA	156	wo	237	UR-MOA
143	143	224	SE-DVP	76	F-GJDB	157	wfu	238	wfu
144	N502PG	225	N225CC	77	wfu	158	N158TW	239	N300BP
145	N244A	226	N121AT	78	wfu	159	XA-...	240	F-GYCA
146	XA-...	*Falcon 20/200 Guardian*		79	F-ZACT	160	N301TT	241	wfu
147	N212FJ	01	wfu	80	wfu	161	N503RV	242	N513AC
148	N79TJ	1	wfu	81	N810AA	162	N911DG	243	wo
149	N711EJ	2	wfu	82	G-FRAS	163	N258PE	244	wo
150	N99WA	3	N301R	83	N283SA	164	N164NW	245	wfu
151	N256V	4	wo	84	wfu	165	CN-ANM	246	wfu
152	N999LL	5	N295TW	85	N6555L	166	N201BR	247	N247PL
153	N600TW	6	EC-EDC	86	F-ZACG	167	F-RAEB	248	XC-HIX
154	wfu	7	wfu	87	G-FRAT	168	N168DJ	249	N451DP
155	F-GTOD	8	N277RA	88	wfu	169	XC-MIC	250	N223BG
156	ZS-SEA	9	N611GA	89	wfu	170	wfu	251	EP-IPA
157	N76AM	10	wfu	90	wfu	171	N217AJ	252	F-ZACA
158	N700FH	11	N216CA	91	N20UA	172	wfu	253	TM 11-1
159	N707AM	12	wfu	92	wfu	173	PK-TRI	254	F-GPAB
160	N160FJ	13	N977TW	93	wfu	174	wfu	255	wo
161	G-ECJI	14	N41MH	94	N566YT	175	5A-DKQ	256	N15SL
162	N425JR	15	wfu	95	N995CK	176	EC-JJH	257	N18HN
163	N50HT	16	wfu	96	F-ZACB	177	N82PJ	258	N300SF
164	N222MU	17	N234CA	97	G-FRAU	178	G-FRBA	259	N569D
165	wfu	18	wfu	98	N998CK	179	XA-ACA	260	F-RAEA
166	N211EC	19	wfu	99	N921ML	180	wo	261	N200WK
167	N111WW			100	wo	181	N5225G	262	N189RB

263	F-ZACY	344	N227WL	425	2120	506	XA-MAM	70	N700MP
264	XA-NCC	345	UR-NOA	426	HB-VNM	507	N22HS	71	N352WB
265	N265MP	346	wfu	427	N42WJ	508	N777FC	72	wo
266	wfu	347	N711FJ	428	N148MC	509	PR-SMT	73	N67JF*
267	N129JE	348	wo	429	N331DM	510	N84MJ	74	N83FJ
268	F-RAEF	349	N220WE	430	N243FJ	511	EC-JBH	75	N78LT
269	XA-DUC	350	5-3021	431	2121	512	N999TH	76	N450CL
270	G-FRAI	351	wo	432	N855DG	513	N618GH	77	N78LF
271	wfu	352	N184WW	433	wfu	514	N322RR	78	F-RAFJ
272	N224WE	353	wo	434	FAP 300	515	N181RK	79	N56LN
273	N720JC	354	5-9003	435	wfu	**Falcon 50/50EX**		80	N50XJ
274	N100AS	355	N632PB*	436	N70PL	1	wfu	81	N504CX
275	N200CP	356	N621JS	437	wfu	2	N50BL	82	N582EJ
276	CM-01	357	N357PS	438	N258A	3	N728LW	83	N50HD
277	J 753	358	SU-AZJ	439	N448TB	4	YV2165	84	N500JD
278	CM-02	359	OH-WIP	440	N205JC	5	F-RAFI	85	N82ST
279	UR-CLE	360	N349MR	441	wfu	6	wo	86	N960S
280	F-GPAD	361	SU-AYD	442	N747CX	7	7	87	C-GOIL
281	N116GB	362	wfu	443	2127	8	N550CL	88	N943RL
282	XC-DIP	363	N3VF	444	LV-BIY	9	TR-LGY	89	TR-LGV
283	wo	364	XB-KBW	445	2128	10	N420CL	90	N925GS
284	N201GF	365	N50BV	446	N81P	11	F-GGVB	91	ZS-CAS
285	N285TW	366	N100AC	447	2129	12	CN-ANO	92	N929ML
286	EP-AGY	367	EP-SEA	448	48	13	N150TX	93	N868BT
287	XC-QER	368	N15H	449	N73MR	14	N917SB	94	N946TC
288	F-ZACV	369	N138FJ	450	wfu	15	N350JS	95	N101ET
289	N450CP	370	N20WN	451	F-UKJC	16	F-HBBM	96	C-FMFL
290	wfu	371	2141	452	2131	17	N9TE	97	N412PG
291	wfu	372	ST-PRS	453	N520AW	18	N963JF	98	N600WG
292	9M-...	373	N399FG	454	wfu	19	N519EM	99	N292PC
293	UR-CLF	374	2101	455	N555SR	20	N590RA	100	N14CG
294	SU-AXN	375	F-ZACZ	456	2133	21	N56LT	101	EP-TFA
295	G-FRAF	376	N1897S	457	N47LP	22	YV1083	102	N350WB
296	N220LA	377	N600CD	458	2134	23	N523PB	103	N370KP
297	CS-DCK	378	N97SJ	459	2135	24	N929T	104	N49KR
298	N827AA	379	N892S	460	2136	25	N753JC	105	N100EG
299	N299JC	380	I-ULJA	461	N221H	26	N190MQ	106	N74TS
300	N600WD	381	N85TZ*	462	wfu	27	F-RAFK	107	F-GLSJ
301	EP-AKC	382	N453SB	463	N132EP	28	N800FM	108	N150K
302	F-GOPM	383	N908CH	464	wfu	29	C-GRGE	109	N5107
303	wo	384	N384PS	465	65	30	30/F-ZVMB	110	N84TN
304	G-FRAD	385	ZS-KGS	466	2139	31	N250RJ	111	F-GMOT
305	N715WS	386	2102	467	2140	32	N717LA	112	N216WD
306	N205WP	387	N384K	468	J 468	33	N8300E	113	N450DR
307	F-GYMC	388	N502BG	469	J 469	34	F-RAFL	114	ST-PSR
308	N458SB	389	UR-KKA	470	N500NH	35	XA-FVK	115	N850BA
309	wo	390	2104	471	N911DT	36	36	116	N678MA
310	N724JC	391	TR-LGZ	472	72	37	F-HAIR	117	N896DA
311	F-BVPN	392	N713MC	473	N393S	38	N505CL	118	wo
312	N741MR	393	XC-SON	474	N1HF	39	N850EP	119	XA-SSS
313	N339RK	394	2103	475	XA-YUR	40	N156DB	120	EP-TFI
314	N314TW	395	wfu	476	1650	41	N888ME	121	N51FE
315	D-CLBB	396	N711WV	477	77	42	N405DC	122	5-9013
316	N424XT	397	F-GBTM	478	C-GBCI	43	YU-BNA	123	F-GPSA
317	N939CK	398	2105	479	N7KC	44	YV2346	124	N987F
318	15-2235	399	N728JC	480	80	45	N569BW	125	N102TF
319	N724CP	400	wo	481	N599ZM	46	N777ZL	126	N200RT
320	EP-FIF	401	N501KC	482	VP-CCL	47	N37ER	127	N48KR
321	PH-BPS	402	wfu	483	wfu	48	C-FBVF	128	N42NA
322	N300CV	403	N960TX	484	N425RJ	49	N650AL	129	N751JC
323	XU-008	404	N313K	485	N22FW	50	XA-GCH	130	P4-BAK
324	N373DN	405	wfu	486	N6VF	51	N524S	131	N750BR
325	N877JG	406	N800FF	487	N137TA	52	N900KE	132	132
326	TC-GGG	407	2109	488	N488KF	53	YV1128	133	ZS-CAQ
327	XA-MSA	408	N757CX	489	N613BS	54	N400KE	134	F-HALM
328	YK-ASA	409	wfu	490	N490SJ	55	N200UP	135	N293BC
329	D-CMET	410	N410AZ	491	N500RR	56	C-FCRH	136	YV1495
330	N770MC	411	2110	492	N492CC	57	N505TC	137	N137FA
331	YK-ASB	412	N620A	493	ZS-SOS	58	N50KR	138	N138AV
332	TM 11-4	413	wfu	494	N200FJ	59	N910CN	139	N7GX
333	wo	414	N1881Q	495	N1D*	60	N105WC	140	N750DF
334	EP-FIC	415	2112	496	N202AR	61	VP-CRF	141	N924WJ
335	N335TW	416	N725JG	497	N20CL	62	N230BT	142	N860BA
336	wfu	417	2113	498	N69EC	63	YV1129	143	N444PE
337	YI-AHH	418	2114	499	N200CU	64	N300A	144	N544RA
338	EP-FID	419	wfu	500	N734DB	65	F-GPPF	145	N50KD
339	N239CD	420	wfu	501	N214AS	66	N789JC	146	XA-DUQ
340	wfu	421	2117	502	HB-VNG	67	T-783	147	N844NX
341	F-GYSL	422	wfu	503	N50MW	68	5A-DCM	148	N770JD
342	F-RAEC	423	2118	504	N504FJ	69	N909VJ	149	N198MR
343	YI-AHJ	424	wfu	505	N45JB			150	N8400E

151	I-DARK	232	N100KP	313	N225HD	40	N924S	121	HB-IFQ
152	N75WE	233	N919GA*	314	N55LC	41	N76FD	122	N247CJ
153	N50HM	234	PR-WYW	315	PH-LSV	42	N990BB	123	RA-09001
154	N117AJ*	235	UR-CCC	316	N696HQ	43	N693SH	124	N14NA
155	I-RODJ	236	N347K	317	N607SG*	44	N100UP	125	N978PW
156	N500RE	237	N85TN	318	N410KC	45	N298W	126	N3HB
157	N15FX*	238	N970S	319	XA-PRR	46	TR-AFJ	127	N963RS*
158	N54YR	239	N200SG	320	N500AF	47	N678CH	128	N98NX
159	N839RM	240	N398AC	321	N900CM	48	N233KC	129	XA-VTO
160	N4VF	241	N86TN	322	N5322	49	VP-BLB	130	HB-JSR
161	N766HK	242	N733K	323	N500R	50	N950SF	131	N900D
162	N750JC	243	N62HM	324	N150RJ	51	VP-BMB	132	N707WB
163	N521DC	244	N95HC	325	N146AS	52	5N-FGO	133	YV2040
164	N164GB	245	N827CT	326	N33LC	53	JA8570	134	N322CP
165	LX-FMR	246	3C-LGE	327	N188DM	54	N954FJ	135	F-GYCP
166	N5VF	247	N520AF	328	N308DM	55	N117ST	136	N609SG
167	N2FQ	248	N67PW	329	N98AC	56	JA8571	137	N35RZ
168	N514MB	249	N980S	330	N115SK	57	N900WK	138	C-FGFI
169	F-GUAJ	250	N917JC	331	N331EX	58	HB-IGL	139	N900SX
170	N504YP	251	N171TG	332	N280BC	59	N32B	140	M-RURU
171	N750H	252	XA-RUY	333	N701WC	60	N900VL	141	M-SAIR
172	N256A	253	N85F	334	OE-HPS	61	HZ-AFZ	142	F-GXRM
173	N544CM	254	N94PC	335	C-GMII	62	LX-LFB	143	PH-LCG
174	N988SB	255	N255CM	336	N224HD	63	N311JA	144	N512JY
175	N50FX	256	N600N	337	N89NC	64	M37-01	145	VP-CGB
176	N777XY	257	N925BC	338	N883RA	65	N988T	146	N81SV
177	XA-TAB	258	N48G	339	I-PBRA	66	CS-TFN	147	XA-ISR
178	N634H	259	N373RS	340	N109CQ	67	N900MG	148	N900VG
179	N232PR	260	N586CS	341	I-ZUGR	68	N900HE	149	ZS-DAV
180	N50SF	261	N73GH	342	N649TT	69	I-SNAX	150	HB-IUW
181	N26WJ	262	N1896T	343	N733M	70	N105BK	151	N908CA
182	N713SN	263	N503PC	344	N50YP	71	N642JC	152	N18FX*
183	I-CAFD	264	C-GWFM	345	VP-BMP	72	VP-BLM	153	N67EL
184	N633W	265	N501PC	346	F-HAPM	73	T 18-5	154	I-TCGR
185	LX-THS	266	N50NM	347	F-HAPN	74	T 18-4	155	N900TG
186	N25SJ	267	F-OHFO	348	N905SB	75	N60TL	156	N910Q
187	N187PN	268	M-DASO	349	N906SB	76	HZ-DME	157	N62NW
188	N188FJ	269	F-GJBZ	350	N214DV*	77	T 18-3	158	N721HM
189	N51V	270	C-GJLB	351	N158M	78	LX-GES	159	LX-COS
190	F-GXMC	271	N30FT	352	N1836S	79	N6BX	160	N506BA
191	N950F	272	C-GKCI	*Falcon 900 A/B/C*		80	N914DD	161	PH-ILC
192	N96UT	273	N198M	1	G-HMEI	81	I-TLCM	162	N611JW
193	MM62026	274	N80GP	2	F-RAFP	82	N699BG	163	N82SV
194	N194K	275	N44LC	3	N728GH	83	N361K	164	VP-CFL
195	17401	276	N789ME	4	F-RAFQ	84	ST-PSA	165	N183WW
196	N388TC	277	N192F	5	G-HMEV	85	N74FS	166	N995SK
197	N57MK	278	C-GXBB	6	N885	86	HB-JEI	167	3C-ONM
198	17402	279	N181MC	7	F-GMOH	87	N402FG	168	XA-TEL
199	N290MX	280	N1829S	8	N316SS	88	N987GK	169	EC-KFA
200	N749CP	281	C-GNET	9	N232CL	89	I-NUMI	170	N900TR
201	N553M	282	N191MC	10	N349H	90	T 18-2	171	TC-AKK
202	N512JB	283	N223HD	11	F-GKHJ	91	CS-DFH	172	N352AF
203	N203NC	284	N904SB	12	N8VF	92	PT-OEX	173	VP-BFH
204	N725PA	285	N901TF	13	N297AP	93	N780SP	174	N138F
205	N504MK	286	VP-BEA	14	N44EG	94	CS-DFB	175	PH-NDK
206	N801DL	287	ZS-ONG	15	N999EH	95	N343MG	176	N909PM
207	N275HH	288	N83TY	16	N64BD	96	5N-FGE	177	N886DC
208	N50HC	289	N589FJ*	17	N790JC	97	N902NC	178	XA-APE
209	N358MH	290	N42SK	18	N72PX	98	N590F	179	N900DW
210	N411GC	291	XA-UDW	19	N900SJ	99	ZS-NAN	180	N90TH
211	MM62029	292	N38WP	20	N920DB	100	YK-ASC	181	EC-JNZ
212	UR-CCF	293	N195SV	21	HZ-AFT	101	VP-CAB	182	EC-JBB
213	XA-RVV	294	N39WP	22	OE-ICF	102	N906WK	183	N900RX
214	N265G	295	P4-JET	23	I-BEAU	103	V5-NAM	184	N129KJ
215	HB-JSV	296	N23FM	24	N202WR	104	N900CS	185	VH-PPD
216	N84NW	297	OE-HHH	25	N615MS	105	N974BK	186	N900LC
217	N573TH	298	N615SR	26	YR-CJF	106	EC-JXV	187	N901SS
218	N703TM	299	PP-PMV	27	N5VJ	107	N71GK	188	PH-EDM
219	YV1496	300	N344CM	28	N1S	108	YV2039	189	N144FH
220	N50FF	301	N476MK	29	N19VF	109	CD-01	190	N468GH
221	17403	302	N45NC	30	I-DIES	110	C-GJPG	191	N31D
222	OE-HIT	303	N902TF	31	N910JW	111	N8BX	192	VH-LAL
223	N451CL	304	N918JM	32	N18MZ	112	N908JB	193	VP-BCX
224	N87TN	305	N710BG	33	TY-AOM	113	N525MH	194	OO-ACT
225	N428CC	306	LX-AKI	34	N8200E	114	XA-SIM	195	N666TR
226	VP-BBD	307	N950H	35	N139AL	115	I-FLYS	196	N501DB
227	C-GGFP	308	N902SB	36	N922JW	116	N82RP	197	LX-GJL
228	N228FJ	309	N903SB	37	VH-ACE	117	N900WF	198	C-GAZU
229	N550WM	310	N50SN	38	T 18-1	118	RA-09000	199	N900KJ
230	N930JG	311	VP-CBF	39	N239AX	119	N22T	200	N404ST
231	N199FG	312	N26WP			120	CS-DLA	201	LX-FTA

202 VP-BMV
Falcon 900EX

#	Reg	#	Reg	#	Reg	#	Reg	#	Reg
1	N900HG	79	N788CG	158	N18DF	15	N790L	96	N755FL
2	N209FJ	80	N881Q	159	G-FNES	16	HB-IAW	97	N12MW
3	N760	81	N908SB	160	I-DAKO	17	N659FM	98	N298QS
4	N8100E	82	PR-GPA	161	TC-MMG	18	VP-CJA	99	N770MP
5	N600JM	83	HB-IGI	162	PR-CCC	19	N790M	100	VP-CGA
6	N711T	84	N420PD	163	G-GALX	20	N405ST	101	OO-GFD
7	N45SJ	85	N910MW	164	RA-09006	21	N11BV	102	N286CX*
8	N30LB	86	VP-BEZ	165	OE-IMC	22	N202CE	103	I-FLYP
9	N70LF	87	C-GGMI	166	VT-ISH	23	N10JP	104	N204QS
10	N900Q	88	N909MM	167	N85CL	24	N18MV	105	N711PE
11	F-GOYA	89	VT-SBK	168	N900JG	25	N122SC	106	N635E
12	F-HAXA	90	VP-CLO	169	N900NB	26	OY-ICE	107	VP-CGC
13	N127SF	91	I-CAEX	170	N585BP	27	B-8020	108	I-FLYV
14	N72WS	92	HB-IFJ	171	SE-DJA	28	N160WS	109	CS-DNP
15	C-GOAG	93	N993EX	172	G-SIRO	29	N700FL	110	PP-CFF
16	N67WB	94	N663MK	173	N7600S	30	HB-IAZ	111	VP-BDL
17	VP-BEG	95	HB-IGY	174	F-HCBM	31	N790Z	112	N410GS
18	N166FB	96	HB-JSY	175	N513HS	32	N175BC	113	N213QS
19	N88ND	98	N900KX	176	D-AMBI	33	HB-IAX	114	ZS-PKR
20	D-AWKG	99	XA-GMD	177	VT-...	34	N234FJ	115	CS-DNQ
21	N901MM	100	N550TH	178	D-....	35	N1927G	116	N52DC
22	N331MC	101	N730LM	179	SE-DJB	36	VT-COT	117	N54DC
23	OH-FFC	102	N6666R	180	HZ-OFC5	37	EC-GNK	118	N218QS
24	TR-LEX	103	N900HD	181	PR-FRU	38	N710ET	119	F-GESP
25	N607CV	104	N588GS	182	N93KD	39	N42ST	120	CS-DNR
26	N900SB	105	G-LCYA	183	A6-MAF	40	N1C	121	N78NT
27	I-FLYW	106	SE-DJM	184	G-JJMX	41	N48CG	122	N222QS
28	HB-IAH	107	F-HBOL	185	LN-AKR	42	HB-IBH	123	LZ-OOI
29	N17FX*	108	N9WV	186	XA-TEI	43	N775ST	124	N224QS
30	N860FJ	109	VP-BEE	187	N904JY	44	N623QW	125	N911SH
31	M-FALC	110	N176CL	188	N460D	45	N190MC	126	N226QS
32	N97NX	111	N508PC	189	OE-INB	46	N505RR	127	N227QS
33	XA-BEG	112	N900MF	190	C-GLXC	47	N435JF	128	N350M
34	VP-CLB	113	F-GYRB	191	F-WWFP	48	N48WK	129	N229QS
35	N96NX	114	N900YP	192	I-SEAS	49	VT-TBT	130	N202TH
36	N826K	115	N720ML	193	G-REYG*	50	D-BEST	131	N707MM
37	N900BZ	116	MM62210	194	N987AL	51	N2AT	132	N905B
38	N901MD	117	N900SN	195	3A-...	52	N749GP	133	LX-SVW
39	N39NP	118	OH-PPR	196	N196EX	53	N149VB	134	N622QW
40	N990WM	119	N958DM	197	N197EX	54	I-JAMY	135	N196RG
41	N81SN		*Falcon 900EX EASY*	198	F-WWFF	55	EC-JXR	136	N236QS
42	VP-BMS	97	CS-DFL	199	N199FJ	56	N784BX	136	TC-ATC
43	EC-HOB	120	N106RW	200	F-WWFW	57	N18CG	137	N510RR
44	PR-WRI	121	OO-FOI	**201**	**F-WWFY**	58	N826EW	138	N856F
45	MM62171	122	N901SB		**Falcon 900DX**	59	PT-WYC	139	CS-DNS
46	XA-FEX	123	N990MC	601	HB-JSW	60	N898CT	140	N797WC
47	N58CG	124	N919SA	602	N950JB	61	EC-JVI	141	N54J
48	G-CBHT	125	N988H	603	OO-VMI	62	HB-IVO	141	G-WVLS*
49	N404F	126	N966H	604	OE-IDX	63	N302JC	142	HZ-KSDC
50	F-GPNJ	127	N900HC	605	N453JS	64	N996AG	143	N872EC
51	OE-IDM	128	OY-OKK	606	D-AUCR	65	VT-TAT	143	F-WWGR
52	MM62172	129	XA-RGB	607	C-GPOT	66	N429SJ	144	N203WB
53	VP-BDZ	130	VP-BEF	608	N50LB	67	N150BC	145	N245QS
54	HB-IUX	131	N900MV	609	VP-BNS	68	N200GN	146	N455DX
55	N388GS	132	G-JPSX	610	VP-CIT	69	N220DF	147	N700CH
56	N909SB	133	D-AZEM	611	N890BB	70	D-BAMA	148	CS-DFC
57	N900MJ	134	VP-CFR	612	HB-JSU	71	N811AG	149	XA-MAV
58	N11WM	135	N246AG	613	B-8021	72	N769JW	150	EC-HYI
59	N694JP	136	N22LC	614	VP-CHA	73	N273JC	151	N151GR
60	YV2053	137	N88LC	615	LX-AFD	74	N988DV	152	N246V
61	N961EX	138	OE-IVK	616	A6-SMS	75	N275QS	153	N253QS
62	N960SF	139	N265H	617	OE-ISM*	76	OY-CKN	154	OY-CKI
63	N435T	140	N54HG	618	N416KC	77	N278QS	155	N255QS
64	D-AJAD	141	HB-JSX	619	F-WWVB	78	N78FJ	156	N844UP
65	N965M	142	RA-09008	**620**	**N620DX**	79	N929HG	157	TC-RMK
66	N377SC	143	HA-LKN		*Falcon 2000*	80	N60TC	158	N258QS
67	N312P	144	VP-BSO	1	VP-CAS	81	N2810S	159	N259QS
68	N271DV	145	F-GSNA	2	N201CR	82	N752S	160	VP-BBP
69	C-FJOI	146	N146EX	3	N15AS	83	N1128B	161	I-DDVF
70	N999PM	147	N193F	4	N925AJ	84	N1929Y	162	N262QS
71	N110EX	148	5A-DCN	5	N27R	85	XA-HHF	163	OY-CKF
72	N2BD	149	MM62244	6	PR-WSM	86	N111HZ	164	N44JC
73	N973M	150	N900NS	7	N28R	87	N4200	165	N265QS
74	VP-CNZ	151	VP-BSP	8	VT-VLM	88	C-GSMR	166	OY-CKW
75	VP-BEH	152	P4-SCM	9	N783FS	89	N800GH	167	3A-MGA
76	N80F	153	N1818S	10	N131EP	90	N5200	168	N268QS
77	N977LP	154	N47EG	11	N48FB	91	N46HA	169	N269QS
78	D-AGSI	155	LN-AOC	12	I-SNAW	92	N2000L	170	N220AB
		156	MM62245	13	N722JB	93	N292QS	171	N797HT
		157	N227HD	14	N51MN	94	N286MG	172	N36EP
						95	N628CC	173	N673BA

174	CS-DFD	20	XA-GNI	101	N204CW	3120	5N-SPN	14500901	VT-BSF
175	XA-AVE	21	N801WW	102	G-ITIG	3121	OE-HMS	14500903	N900DP
176	N676BA	22	VP-BDV	103	OY-PNO	3132	N328AC	14500910	K3603
177	N277QS	23	N101PV	104	TC-DGN	3141	5N-SPM	14500913	P4-MSG
178	N100WY	24	N341AP	105	N994GP	3151	5N-SPE	14500916	OE-IRK
179	OH-FIX	25	N699MC	106	N771DV	3160	N328CR	14500919	K3604
180	N680DF	26	N6453	107	N267BW	3162	OE-HTG	14500925	N702DR
181	N280QS	27	OH-FEX	108	I-JAMJ	3183	N328QS	14500933	HB-JEL
182	N826KR	28	N4QG	109	CS-DLD	3184	N804CE	14500937	G-SYLJ
183	N903GS*	29	SX-DCA	110	VP-BAK	3199	HB-AEU	14500939	N939AJ
184	G-MDBA	30	D-BERT	111	D-BASE	3200	G-CJAB	14500941	D-ARTN
185	N284QS	31	N620MS	112	N619SM	3207	D-BJET	14500942	N909LX
186	N98RP	32	N377GM	113	VP-CMI	3216	D-BADC	14500944	A6-NKL
187	VP-BCV	33	D-BOSS	114	F-GVNG	3219	ZS-IOC	14500946	PT-SCR
188	N317M	34	HB-JEG	115	N232QS	3220	G-CJA.	14500948	N124LS
189	N330K	35	OY-CLN	116	N72PS	3224	D-BADA	14500950	N515JT
190	N290QS	36	N163EB*	117	VT-VLN	**Embraer**		14500952	N910LX
191	I-BNTN	37	N308U	118	D-BONN	*135/145/Legacy 600*		14500954	G-RRAZ
192	N515PV	38	N3BM	119	N2000A			14500955	A6-DPW
193	N278GS	39	CS-TLP	120	N333MX	145209	209	14500957	N373RB
194	N671WM	40	PH-CHT	121	XA-CMM	145257	6700	14500960	P4-NRA
195	N196KC	41	CS-DFF	122	N147G	145361	N829RN	14500961	M-YNJC
196	N296QS	42	D-BMVV	123	OO-PAP	145363	PT-SAA	14500963	OK-SUN
197	N215KH	43	N9871R	124	N888CE*	145364	N486TM	14500965	N600XL
198	N203QS	44	CS-DFG	125	F-WWGM	145374	374	14500966	N966JS*
199	N899U	45	N205CW	126	VP-BGI	145412	2580	14500967	OE-IGR
200	I-SEAE	46	N10EU	127	CS-DLE	145431	G-CDFS	14500969	PK-RJG
201	N201WR	47	N404UK	128	M-CHEM	145449	CE-01	14500970	VP-BBY
202	N251QS	48	N1NC	129	C-GENW	145450	N948AL	14500971	N775SM
203	I-ARIF	49	N1JK	130	N1JK	145462	2581	14500972	G-MGYB
204	N88DD	50	N57MN	131	N131AG	145466	N926FM	14500973	A6-KWT
205	CS-DFE	51	ZS-MGD	132	G-OJAJ	145467	N386CH	14500974	N10SV
206	N900NH	52	G-KWIN	133	VP-BRA	145480	CE-02	14500975	A9C-MTC
207	OE-HEM	53	N36TH	134	CS-DLF	145484	484	14500976	N900EM
208	G-GEDY	54	N221QS	135	N414TR	145495	2582	14500977	N983JC
209	N209TM	55	N326EW	137	N119EM*	145499	N325JF	14500978	A9C-MAN
210	N850K	56	N954SP	138	F-WWGI	145505	G-WCCI	14500979	VP-BVS
211	N210QS	57	N376SC	139	N470D	145516	PK-OME	14500980	N605WG
212	N523WC	58	VH-CRW	140	OO-DFG*	145526	CE-03	14500981	T-501
213	N684KF	59	N230QS	142	F-WWGO	145528	2583	14500982	G-RBRO
214	N215QS	60	N100MB	144	CS-DLG	145540	EC-IIR	14500983	N6GD*
215	N215RE	61	VP-CBC	145	N345EX	145548	CE-04	14500984	5N-BJM
216	N718KS	62	N346PC	146	N268DM	145549	P4-VVP	14500985	N728PH
217	OE-HVA	63	OY-EJD	147	N278DM	145550	N1023C	14500986	OK-GGG
218	N218PH	64	N493S	148	F-WWGE	145555	VP-CUP	14500987	PT-SKF
219	N1999	65	CS-DFK	149	F-WWGJ	145586	P4-SIS	14500988	D-AONE
220	N620BA	66	N822ST	150	F-WWGL	145600	N302GC	14500989	N135SK*
221	N950RL	67	OH-FOX	151	F-WWMD	145608	N847RP	14500990	N580ML
222	N296RG	68	N934ST	152	F-WWGA	145625	PR-ORE	14500991	D-AAAI
223	OE-HAF	69	N57EL	189	OE-...	145637	VP-CFA	14500993	N912LX
224	N33D	70	D-BOOK	*Falcon 7X*		145642	N642AG	14500994	G-CJMD
225	VT-AAT	71	N56EL			145644	HB-JED	14500995	EC-KFQ
226	OE-HKY	72	N995GH	01	F-WFBW	145648	N89LD	14500997	PT-SKP
227	P4-IKF	73	N85M	2	F-WTDA	145678	N494TG	14500998	SX-CDK
228	N900MC	74	D-BAMM	3	F-WSKY	145686	P4-IVM	14500999	OE-IDB
229	TC-SNK	75	OO-GML	4	HB-JSZ	145699	N676TC	14501001	A6-SUN
230	N532CC	76	F-WQBL	5	VP-BGG	145706	N135SG	14501002	P4-NVB
231	VT-HGL	77	XA-LFA	6	N607X	145711	N135SL	14501003	VP-CLI
601	F-WWGY	78	G-JETF	7	N70FL	145717	PR-RIO	14501004	N615PG
602	N30LF	79	N88ME	8	N999BE*	145726	N201CP	14501006	PR-VOT*
Falcon 2000EX EASY		80	CS-DLB	9	N9707X*	145728	N202CP	14501007	N913LX
1	N900CH	81	N89CE	10	XA-...	145730	N730BH	14501008	S5-ABL
2	N202EX	82	VP-CMD	11	VP-BAR	145770	N53NA	14501010	D-ATWO
3	HB-IAJ	83	N283SL	12	HB-JSO*	145775	N905LX	14501011	G-CMAF
4	N200CH	84	N522BD	13	N907SB*	145780	N904LX	14501013	PR-NIO
5	PH-VBG	85	N993GH	14	F-WWUK	145787	N451DJ	14501014	N226HY
6	F-WXEY	86	N223QS	15	F-WWUL	145796	OK-SLN	14501015	N912JC
7	N40TH	87	C-GTPL	15	CS-TLY	14500802	VP-CHP	14501016	D-ACBG
8	LX-AAM	88	OE-HOT	16	HB-JSS*	14500809	N809SG	14501017	D-ATON
9	HB-IGQ	89	VP-CAM	17	F-WWUN	14500818	N888ML	14501018	N227WE
10	VP-BER	90	C-GOHB	18	F-WWUO	14500825	N906LX	14501020	G-FECR
11	I-NATS	91	N233QS	19	F-WWUP	14500832	G-SIRA	14501021	N915LX
12	N313CC	92	N176CG	20	F-WWUQ	14500841	HB-IWX	14501024	SX-DGM
13	N71FE	93	D-BFFB	21	F-WWUR	14500851	OE-ISN	14501025	VP-CNJ
14	HB-IAU	94	N912MT	22	F-WWUS	14500854	HB-JGS	14501026	VP-CDH
15	N97GM	95	N168CE	30	CS-DSA*	14500863	EC-KHT	19000109	PP-XOL
16	PP-AAF	96	5B-CKO	34	F-GVRB*	14500867	K3601	19000140	PP-XTE
17	N977CP	97	N12AR	*Dornier*		14500873	OK-KKG	**Fokker**	
18	N943JB	98	CS-DLC	*328JET*		14500880	K3602	*F 28*	
19	N855TJ	99	PP-MJC	3114	OE-HTJ	14500883	N617WA		
		100	N310U	3118	UR-WOG	14500891	5N-RSG	11012	XU-888

11016	N500WN	43	XA-...	125	N178B	206	N721CN	325	N155MM
11028	T-03	44	wfu	126	N901WG	207	N4UB	326	N420JC
11042	A-2801	45	N250MS	127	wo	208	N247AB	327	N259SK
11045	PK-RJW	46	wfu	128	N829NL	209	N720DR	328	ZS-LAH
11048	T-50	47	N800RT	129	wfu	210	N826GW	329	N1LW
11079	5V-TAI	48	N865AA	130	N666SA	211	XA-FNY	330	wo
11088	M28-01	49	N511BA	131	N2JR	212	N807CC	331	N231WJ
11099	TU-TIZ	50	N220JR	132	N400M	213	N213X	332	N909RR
11100	OB-1396	51	N20H	133	N930LS	214	N707KD	333	N901EH
11104	EP-PAZ	52	wfu	134	N628HC	215	N748MN	334	N3DP
11111	PK-PJL	53	N104VV	135	N525XL	216	HZ-HA1	335	N456BE
11124	TU-VAJ	54	N148V	136	XA-AFP	217	N880WE	336	N147X
11125	G-530	55	N125DC	137	wfu	218	N188MR	337	N330WR
11137	5H-CCM	56	N2000	138	N6JW	219	N74RT	338	N750SW
11145	5-P-20-074	57	N466JB	139	N139CF	220	wfu	339	N774AK
11146	PK-PJY	58	wo	140	N159NB	221	N949NA	340	N57NP
11147	wfu	59	N1823D	141	JA8431	222	wfu	341	N1PR
11150	5-T-21-074	60	wo	142	N588SS	223	N510US	342	N818SS
11153	RP-1250	61	N41AV	143	wo	224	N800PM	343	N221CM
11178	PK-PJM	62	N128KG	144	N944NA	225	N450MH	344	N344GW
11192	PK-PJK	63	N12GP	145	N226RM	226	N5DL	345	N454JB
11203	T-02	64	N351SE	146	N946NA	227	N264CL	346	VP-BHR
11227	TJ-ALG	65	N58JF	147	N947NA	228	N189WS	347	N888LV
11992	FAC-0002	66	N718JS	148	N180AR	229	N117FJ	348	N357PR
Fokker 100		67	ZS-WHG	149	wo	230	wo	349	N711EG
11245	wo	68	HP-....	150	ZS-TPG	231	N416KD	350	N1454
11368	OE-IID	69	XC-LKA	151	N909JE	232	N10RQ	351	N623MS
11403	OE-IIB	70	N660AF	152	N559LC	233	N720LH	352	XC-UJN
11406	OE-IIC	71	N200AB	153	N132FP	234	N500JW	353	N212BA
11486	PK-PFZ	72	wo	154	N719SQ*	235	N840RG	354	N429DD
Fokker 70		73	N436JW	155	N477GG	236	N311BD	355	ZS-TEX
11521	N322K	74	N74HH	156	N864YD	237	N302DP	356	N356BR
11545	N324K	75	wo	157	N468HW	238	N72BP	357	N623NP
11547	PH-KBX	76	wfu	158	N889JC	239	N239WJ	358	N358CY*
11557	KAF308	77	N994GG	159	N880RJ	240	TT-AAI	359	N50BH
11576	PH-EFZ	78	HP-1A	160	N1123G	241	N909FK	360	N425SV
Gulfstream		79	wfu	161	XA-AHM	242	5A-DDS	361	N874RA
		80	N82CR	162	N668JT	243	wo	362	N800AR
Gulfstream 2		81	N419MS	163	N117JJ	244	N811DE	363	N855SA
1	N55RG	82	N492JT	164	N319AJ	245	N222NP	364	HZ-AFN
2	wfu	83	wo	165	N696MJ	246	N81RR	365	CN-ANU
3	N300RD	84	N27SL	166	ZS-DGW	247	N530GA	366	N366JA
4	N36RR	85	N598GS	167	XA-CVS	248	N71WJ	367	N933PA
5	N34S	86	N179T	168	N318SP	250	N309EL	368	C-GBBB
6	wfu	88	N779LC	169	N467AM	251	N933RD	369	N15HE
7	wfu	89	N98WJ	170	N111GD	253	N915C	370	N105VS
8	N225MS	90	N671LW	171	SX-BTX	254	N868SM	371	N353VA
9	N129WA	91	XA-...	172	wo	255	N4NR	372	N523AM
10	N900CE	92	N374PS	173	wfu	256	wfu	373	N373RR
11	wfu	93	N922MR	174	N540EA	257	N1CC	374	N270MC
12	N622RR	94	N685SF	175	XC-PFT	258	N689JE	375	N375LT
13	N169HM	95	N2DF	176	N794SC	775	N692EB	376	N376PJ
14	XA-RBP	96	N396CF	177	5N-AGV	Gulfstream 3		377	N377RX
15	wfu	97	N25GJ	178	N720JW	249	N163PA	378	N378SE*
16	N24YS	98	N982B	179	HZ-PCA	252	N247RG	379	N900LA
17	N202PX	99	N1218C	180	N416CG	300	N918BG	380	N30WR
18	XC-AA70	100	N400D	181	wfu	301	N973MW*	381	N221WR
19	ZS-LOG	101	N412JT	182	CN-ANL	302	N302ST	382	830500
20	N88LN	102	N102CX	183	N821PA	303	wo	383	N30501
21	HP-....	103	N89TJ	184	N777RW	304	N304TS	384	N818TJ
22	N216RR	104	N712MQ	185	N950NA	305	N106KM	385	HZ-MS3
23	N890TJ	105	N754JB	186	VP-BFF	306	N360MB	386	XC-UJO
24	XA-...	106	N141JF	187	N802CC	307	N111FA	387	N485GM
25	YV1681	107	N10123	188	N188DC	308	N308HG	388	N797BD
26	ZS-PYY	108	N183PA	189	N711MQ	309	N2NA	389	83-0502
27	N227TS	109	N581MB	190	N190CS	310	N982RK	390	N124DT
28	N17KW	110	N417EK	191	N951RK	311	N127GK	391	N288KA
29	N188JS	111	N900DH	192	N192FG	312	ZS-JGC	392	N391SH
30	XB-KCX	112	N168VA	193	N227LA	313	N173PA	393	N200EL
31	N105TB	113	N74RQ	194	N57HE	314	N99PD	394	N379XX
32	N971EQ	114	XB-KCW	195	N195AR	315	N90ML	395	N422TK
33	N747NB	115	N424GC	196	N619MC	316	N300UJ	396	N175BG
34	wo	116	N218SE	197	N608MD	317	N186PA	397	N767CB
35	N30PR	117	N750RA	198	N91NA	318	N17NC	398	N610AB
36	N74A	118	N945NA	199	N338CL	319	N200SK	399	N399AP
37	wfu	119	XA-...	200	N17KJ	320	N624PP	400	N500EF
38	wfu	120	N711VL	201	N105AJ	321	N9KL	401	N370JL
39	wfu	121	N892TM	202	A9C-BG	322	N706JA	402	wo
40	wo	122	N500RL	203	wfu	323	XA-ERH	403	N555GL
41	N311MG	123	N868DS	204	N659WL	324	N450CB	404	N560SH
42	N36PN	124	wfu	205	N623BM			405	N456AL

406	N406FA	487	N416WM	1066	N773JC	1147	N820MS	1228	N18AN
407	N913MK	488	N500GF	1067	N200LC	1148	N306TT	1229	N2708C
408	wo	489	N388CW	1068	N82A	1149	N108DB	1230	N101CV
409	N555RE	490	N388MM	1069	N450AR*	1150	N900RL	1231	VT-DLF
410	HZ-AFR	491	A6-INF	1070	N107A	1151	N151ST	1232	N232K
411	N461GT	492	N939KM	1071	N1	1152	N63MU	1233	N450JE
412	N527CC	493	N7513H	1072	N260CH	1153	N589HM	1234	VP-BNB
413	N59AJ	494	K2961	1073	N177BB	1154	N186DS	1235	N17JK
414	N165G	495	K2962	1074	N995GG	1155	N910S	1236	N100GN
415	N109DD	496	N384BB	1075	N61WH	1156	N5RD	1237	N1904W
416	N4500X	497	87-0139	1076	N338MM	1157	B-8082	1238	C-GCPM
417	N431JT	498	87-0140	1077	N457DS	1158	N917W	1239	N699HH
418	N103CD	875	N300JZ	1078	N211DK	1159	HB-IKR	1240	N705PC
419	wo		*Gulfstream 4/G300/400*	1079	N794MH	1160	251	1241	N117MS
420	K2960	1000	N971EC	1080	N205X	1161	N495RS	1242	N407GC
421	N711FD	1001	N181CR	1081	XA-...	1162	91-0108	1243	N37WN
422	N820BA	1002	N168WM	1082	M-GULF	1163	12-003	1244	JA002G
423	N712AS	1003	N864YC	1083	VH-CGF	1164	N420CC	1245	N588LS
424	N94FL	1004	N124TF	1084	HB-IMY	1165	N780E	1246	N49RF
425	N492A	1005	N823GA	1085	N423TT	1166	HZ-AFY	1247	N211MA
426	XA-ABA	1006	N614RD	1086	N1086	1167	N1SL	1248	N72RK
427	N300WY	1007	N575E	1087	N368AG	1168	A40-AB	1249	N151SD
428	N702DM	1008	N85WD	1088	N93MK	1169	N600CK	1250	N169JC
429	N77BT	1009	V-11	1089	911	1170	N880WD	1251	N165JF
430	N608BG	1010	N950DM	1090	N9999M	1171	N3SA	1252	N394TR
431	N17LK	1011	A6-HHH	1091	N984JW	1172	N227SV	1253	N225DC
432	N469BT	1012	N836MF	1092	N786JB	1173	OK1	1254	VT-PLL
433	N45KR	1013	XA-BVG	1093	N100JF	1174	N914EG	1255	VP-BKI
434	N323JH	1014	102001	1094	N740K	1175	G-EVLN	1256	92-0375
435	N357KM	1015	N450BF	1095	N311EL	1176	HB-IWY	1257	N603CS
436	N10EH	1016	N880GC	1096	N167AA	1177	N236MJ*	1258	N585D
437	N171AM	1017	N818BA	1097	N900AP	1178	N611JM	1259	N4PG
438	N473KT	1018	N113AR	1098	N198GS	1179	N527JC	1260	N415P*
439	SU-BGU	1019	TU-VAD	1099	N999LX	1180	XA-ASI	1261	N57HJ
440	N124EP	1020	N93AT	1100	B-8080	1181	90-0300	1262	N462QS
441	N214WY	1021	N310EL	1101	N900EG	1182	N75CC	1263	N128TS
442	SU-BGV	1022	N663PD	1102	XA-RBS	1183	N510SR	1264	N464QS
443	N813LS	1023	N830EF	1103	C-FHPM	1184	N583AJ	1265	VP-CFF
444	N555HD	1024	N820HB	1104	N2SA	1185	N570DC	1266	VP-BOL
445	N606DH	1025	N595E*	1105	N312EL	1186	N345AA	1267	N624GJ
446	N58AJ	1026	N100HG	1106	9M-ISJ	1187	165093	1268	N888MF
447	N776MA	1027	001	1107	N844GF	1188	HL7222	1269	N250LB
448	N710CF	1028	N712CC	1108	N463MA	1189	165094	1270	75-3251
449	wo	1029	N44ZF	1109	G-MATF	1190	JA001G	1271	75-3252
450	N36DA	1030	N1WP	1110	N721MC	1191	N403TB	1272	N620JH
451	N600RH	1031	HZ-AFU	1111	N511PA	1192	N180CH	1273	N102BQ
452	N800TD	1032	N254GA	1112	N12U	1193	N608CL	1274	102004
453	N213BA	1033	N711FW	1113	XA-JJS	1194	N473CW	1275	N475QS
454	N903TC	1034	N388CA	1114	N44LX	1195	N888PM	1276	N557WY*
455	N818DD	1035	HZ-AFV	1115	N440TC	1196	A40-AC	1277	N5GF
456	85-0049	1036	N45AC	1116	N305TC	1197	N4753	1278	N98LT
457	N457JC	1037	HZ-103	1117	VP-CMR	1198	N99GA	1279	N451C*
458	85-0050	1038	HZ-AFW	1118	N269HM	1199	165151	1280	N688LS
459	N555DW	1039	N726RW	1119	N524AN	1200	165153	1281	N129NS
460	N32MJ	1040	N620DS	1120	N888ES	1201	165152	1282	N1925M
461	N108AR	1041	N366F	1121	N962SS	1202	HB-ITF	1283	N402JP
462	TU-VAF	1042	N217RR	1122	N317MJ	1203	N412WW	1284	N575CT
463	N196CC	1043	002	1123	N619A	1204	N252CH	1285	N972MS
464	N83PP	1044	N154G	1124	N1900W	1205	N671AF	1286	N192NC
465	N35GZ	1045	N247EM	1125	N44CE	1206	N315MK	1287	N487QS
466	N817MF	1046	N400CC	1126	5N-FGP	1207	N344AA	1288	7T-VPR
467	N400WY	1047	wo	1127	VP-BUS	1208	N297GB	1289	N202VZ
468	86-0202	1048	SU-BGM	1128	HZ-MFL	1209	N724DB	1290	N988LS
469	N469TB	1049	N113CS	1129	N8MC	1210	N144PK	1291	7T-VPS
470	86-0201	1050	N195WS	1130	N711GL	1211	N2107Z	1292	N917VZ
471	N57TT	1051	N919CT	1131	N55TD	1212	N884L	1293	N493QS
472	N353MA	1052	N48GL	1132	N7JM	1213	N56L	1294	N718GM
473	86-0403	1053	N168PK	1133	N700CN	1214	N477JB	1295	N495QS
474	D2-ECB	1054	N860JB	1134	N990PT	1215	102002	1296	N728LB
475	86-0203	1055	N255GA	1135	N85KV	1216	102003	1297	LV-WSS
476	86-0204	1056	N770SC	1136	N27CD	1217	N979CB	1298	N961V
477	N477SJ	1057	N842PA	1137	N777TC	1218	N5MC	1299	N497QS
478	86-0206	1058	wo	1138	N520EP	1219	N874C	1300	N226MP
479	N556AF	1059	N271PS*	1139	N134BR	1220	N688TT	1301	N92AE
480	163691	1060	VT-AMA	1140	N77WL	1221	N451GA	1302	N93AE
481	163692	1061	N999GP	1141	N729TY	1222	N171JC	1303	85-3253
482	N111HC	1062	N619KK	1142	N222GY	1223	N257H	1304	N404QS
483	N343DP	1063	N745RS	1143	HZ-AFX	1224	C-GEIV	1305	N305GA
484	N62MW	1064	XA-AEX	1144	N233GA	1225	N773MJ	1306	N811DF*
485	N777MW	1065	C-FCNR	1145	N569CW	1226	N96JA	1307	N94AE
486	TJ-AAW			1146	N970SJ	1227	N600VC	1308	N408QS

1309	N56D	1390	VP-CSF	1471	N923CL	4015	N117WR	4096	VP-BMY
1310	N902	1391	N827GA	1472	N475LC	4016	N5114	4097	N59CF
1311	N411QS	1392	N492QS	1473	N620M	4017	N7RX	4098	N608CH
1312	9M-ABC	1393	N352BH	1474	N7799T	4018	B-KHK	4099	N841WS
1313	N94LT	1394	N721RL	1475	N324FP	4019	N5115	4100	N448QS
1314	N429SA	1395	N396NS	1476	N59AP	4020	N588AT	4101	N424PX
1315	N950CM	1396	N890A	1477	N468AB	4021	N430QS	4102	XA-GMX
1316	N416QS	1397	N669BJ	1478	N478GS	4022	N464ST	4103	N603GA
1317	N333PY	1398	N498QS	1479	N226RS	4023	N5116	4104	N704GA
1318	N1624	1399	N121JM	1480	CS-DKA	4024	N451CM	4105	N450T
1319	N878SM	1400	N700FS	1481	N621SC	4025	N440QS	4106	N606GA
1320	N420QS	1401	N300CR	1482	N121JJ	4026	N5117	4107	N607GA
1321	N905LP	1402	VP-CLA	1483	N810TM	4027	HB-JEQ	4108	N608GA
1322	N422QS	1403	N403QS	1484	N721FF	4028	N915BD	4109	N609GA
1323	N565RV	1404	N404HS	1485	N5NG	4029	N888HH	4110	N450WB
1324	N424QS	1405	N45ET	1486	N608PM	4030	N235CG	4111	N178SD
1325	J 755	1406	N104AD	1487	N428AS	4031	VP-CAE	4112	N612GA
1326	95-3254	1407	N407NS	1488	N490QS	4032	N24XC	4113	N913GA
1327	TR-KSP	1408	N401QS	1489	N119AF	4033	N404PX	4114	N614GA
1328	N428QS	1409	N67TM	1490	N1TM	4034	N122GV	4115	N815GA
1329	SU-BNC	1410	N80AT	1491	N491EC	4035	N409CC	4116	N216GA
1330	N400J	1411	N303TP	1492	N500PC	4036	N922H	4117	N417GA
1331	EC-KEY	1412	N709LS	1493	N717DX	4037	N445QS	4118	N418GA
1332	SU-BND	1413	5X-UEF	1494	N400FJ	4038	N450RG	4119	N819GA
1333	N800J	1414	N333EC	1495	N250VC	4039	N539VE*	4121	N821GA
1334	N626JS	1415	N71BD	1496	N308AB	4040	N350FK	4122	N422GA
1335	N918CC	1416	N900WR	1497	N702GH	4041	N451DC	4123	N423GA
1336	N235LP	1417	XA-RYR	1498	N780RH	4042	N776JB	4124	N424GA
1337	N52MK	1418	7T-VPC	1499	N918TB	4043	N450AB	4125	N425GA
1338	N100HF	1419	N600AR	1500	N50EE	4044	N663CP	4126	N426GA
1339	N327TL	1420	N72BD	1501	N128AB	4045	4K-AZ888	4127	N427GA
1340	N77D	1421	7T-VPM	1502	N710EC	4046	N450QS	4128	N528GA
1341	N441QS	1422	N7UF	1503	A6-RJA	4047	N664CP	4129	N429GA
1342	N808T	1423	N621JH	1504	N902L	4048	N900AL	4130	N130GA
1343	N2CC	1424	SU-BNO	1505	A6-RJB	4049	N665CP	4131	N531GA
1344	N411LL*	1425	P4-TAK	1506	SU-BPE	4050	N244DS	4132	N532GA
1345	N857ST	1426	N426QS	1507	N826RP	4051	N908VZ	4133	N433GA
1346	N104AR	1427	SU-BNP	1508	N820TM	4052	N500J	4134	N434GA
1347	N155RJ	1428	N990NB	1509	N789RR*	4053	N845G	4135	N535GA
1348	N80A	1429	N777KK	1510	N349K	4054	N405QS	Gulfstream V/G500/550	
1349	N510MG	1430	N71TV	1511	N161MM	4055	N237GA	501	N22
1350	N396U	1431	N818ME	1512	N606PM	4056	N500N	502	N502KA
1351	N265SJ	1432	N211DH	1513	N928GC	4057	N500RP	503	N767FL
1352	N452QS	1433	N1SN	1514	N1932P	4058	N218WW	504	N313RG
1353	A9C-BAH	1434	N663P	1515	N851EL	4059	N222NB	505	N371JC
1354	N397JJ	1435	N994GC	1516	N721BS	4060	G-TAYC	506	N500GV
1355	N66DD	1436	N436QS	1517	N129MH	4061	N450LV	507	N300L
1356	N600DR	1437	N437GA	1518	SU-BPF	4062	N450XX	508	wfu
1357	N77FK	1438	N228RE	1519	N527JG	4063	N930DC	509	N855RB
1358	N1625	1439	N586D	1520	HZ-MF3	4064	N768JJ	510	N513MW
1359	05-3255	1440	N76RP	1521	N413QS	4065	N555LR*	511	VP-CBX
1360	N460QS	1441	VH-OSW	1522	N251DV	4066	OY-GVG	512	N838MF
1361	N545CS	1442	N718DW	1523	N401FT	4067	N475M	513	HB-IVL
1362	ZK-KFB	1443	N305LM	1524	N522AC	4068	N435QS	514	N256LK
1363	VH-DBT	1444	N904TC	1525	HZ-MF4	4069	N612AF	515	N55GV
1364	N143KS	1445	N474D	1526	N160TM	4070	N818G	516	N740BA
1365	HZ-MS4	1446	N817ME	1527	N402FT	4071	N24TH	517	HB-IMJ
1366	N404XT	1447	N822A	1528	N706VA	4072	N450PG	518	N885G
1367	N1EB	1448	N1LB	1529	N477SA	4073	N474M	519	N526EE
1368	N411AL	1449	N209LS	1530	N650PW	4074	N455QS	520	N818DA
1369	N400MP	1450	N435HC	1531	N212VZ	4075	N440AS	521	97-0400
1370	N240CX	1451	N244J*	1532	HZ-MF5	4076	N779CS	522	N70AG
1371	N371FP	1452	N603KE	1533	N467QS	4077	N723MM	523	N54TG
1372	N472QS	1453	N444QG	1534	N616KG	4078	N310GJ	524	N1892
1373	N595PE	1454	N454QS	1535	N825T	4079	N450NS	525	VT-SMI
1374	N1PG	1455	N616CC	Gulfstream G350/G450		4080	N380GA	526	N675RW
1375	N247KB	1456	N507SA	4001	N401SR	4081	N926RR	527	N5SA
1376	N12NZ	1457	N305CF	4002	N820AV	4082	N451NS	528	N75RP
1377	N477QS	1458	N235KK	4003	N821AV	4083	N251VP	529	N73RP
1378	N2PG	1459	D-AJGK	4004	D-ARKK	4084	N470QS	530	N780T
1379	VT-MST	1460	N326JD	4005	N512JT	4085	N711SW	531	N531AF
1380	N480QS	1461	N877A	4006	N111CQ	4086	N722MM	532	N740SS
1381	A6-NMA	1462	N457H	4007	N142HC	4087	N800AL	533	XA-CPQ
1382	N428M	1463	N465QS	4008	N97FT	4088	N450EJ	534	N127GG
1383	N707TE	1464	N119FM	4009	N885AR	4089	N606CH	535	N535V
1384	N404AC	1465	RA-10201	4010	N425QS	4090	J 756	536	N688TY
1385	N1818C	1466	N888ZF	4011	N502GM	4091	N450GA	537	N132SD
1386	N486QS	1467	N225CX	4012	N80Q	4092	VP-BIV	538	N1JN
1387	N854SD	1468	N700NY	4013	N5113	4093	VP-CMG	539	N162JC
1388	XA-EYA	1469	N5956B	4014	N415QS	4094	N452NS	540	XA-OEM
1389	N489QS	1470	N394AK			4095	N450PU		

541	N405LM	622	VP-BBX	5009	N1HC	5090	N282Q	5171	N550BM
542	97-0401	623	N506QS	5010	N711RL	5091	N3PG	5172	N972GA
543	N91CW	624	01-0029	5011	VP-BGN	5092	VP-CVI	5173	N401HB
544	N383LS	625	N507QS	5012	N888LK	5093	D-ADLR*	5174	CS-DKJ
545	N888CW	626	N846QM	5013	N63HS	5094	CS-DKE	5175	N975GA
546	XA-BAL	627	N54EE	5014	514	5095	N550KF	5176	N476GA
547	N73M	628	N628BD*	5015	N565ST	5096	N3050	5177	N977GA
548	N32BD	629	N707GW	5016	N944H	5097	N806AC	5178	N978GA
549	N123FT	630	N130GV	5017	N62MS	5098	166378	5179	N979GA
550	N5101	631	N508QS	5018	N818RF	5099	CS-DKF	5180	N980GA
551	N5102	632	N532SP	5019	G-GSSO	5100	N51MF	5181	N181GA
552	N9SC	633	N222LX	5020	N221DG	5101	N550M	5182	N782GA
553	N516GH	634	ZS-AOL	5021	N5DA	5102	VP-CVT	5183	N983GA
554	HB-JKA	635	N83CP	5022	OE-ISS	5103	N534QS	5184	N284GA
555	VP-BSJ	636	VP-BEP	5023	N1GN	5104	N661CP	5185	N185GA
556	HB-JES	637	N509QS	5024	VP-BLA	5105	N500RD	5186	N286GA
557	N83M	638	N888HE	5025	HB-JEE	5106	N234DB	5187	N187GA
558	N500RH	639	N501CV	5026	N550MT	5107	N662CP	5188	N188GA
559	N559GV	640	N600JD	5027	N91LA	5108	N311CG	5189	N189GA
560	9K-AJD	641	OE-IIA	5028	N55UH	5109	VP-BIP	5190	N290GA
561	N661GA	642	CS-DKB	5029	N155AN	5110	N585A	5191	N291GA
562	N95AE	643	5N-FGS	5030	5H-ONE	5111	B-KGV	5192	N492GA
563	N225EE	644	HZ-MS5A	5031	N795BA	5112	N636MF	5193	N293GA
564	A6-DEJ	645	01-0076	5032	G-HRDS	5113	VP-CNR	5194	N394GA
565	N77CP	646	N51FL	5033	VP-BNR	5114	D-ADCA	5195	N295GA
566	97-1944	647	N511QS	5034	04-1778	5115	B-KID	5196	N196GA
567	N93M	648	VP-BSN	5035	N1TF	5116	EC-JYR	5197	N597GA
568	N89HE	649	N83CW	5036	N1BN	5117	N595A	5198	N298GA
569	9K-AJE	650	N1040	5037	537	5118	N855G	5199	N399GA
570	N521HN	651	N1DC	5038	N102BG	5119	RA-10202	5200	N990GA
571	99-0402	652	01-0065	5039	N401HF	5120	N254SD	5201	N991GA
572	HB-IIS	653	01	5040	HB-JEV	5121	N550PR	5202	N992GA
573	9K-AJF	654	N404M	5041	166376	5122	N837BA	5203	N203GA
574	N1KE	655	N825LM	5042	N528QS	5123	VP-BBO	**Hawker Beechcraft**	
575	N410M	656	N218EC	5043	VP-BGL	5124	EC-KBR	*Diamond*	
576	N991LF	657	166375	5044	544	5125	N388AC	A001SA	wfu
577	HB-IVZ	658	N516QS	5045	N560DM	5126	N676RW	A002SA	JA8248
578	N410LM	659	N50KC	5046	N5PG	5127	CS-DKG	A003SA	N300TS
579	N23M	660	N130TM	5047	N947GA	5128	N940DC	A004SA	wfu
580	N1540	661	N405HG	5048	VP-CIP	5129	VP-BLW	A005SA	N110DS
581	VH-CCC	662	N697A	5049	N109ST	5130	N671LE	A006SA	N200LP
582	EC-IRZ	663	01-0030	5050	VP-BNO	5131	N671RW	A007SA	N567JK
583	HZ-MS5B	664	XA-MKI	5051	VP-BNE	5132	4X-...	A008SA	N399DM
584	N84GV	665	N223MD	5052	XA-ATL	5133	N531QS	A009SA	N360CA
585	N16NK	666	N123M	5053	N2929	5134	N712KT	A010SA	N931MA
586	N2N	667	N721S	5054	OE-IVV	5135	N522BP	A011SA	N211GA
587	N300K	668	VP-CES	5055	N755VE	5136	N110ED	A012SA	N316LP
588	VP-BAC	669	02-1863	5056	N45ST	5137	8P-MSD	A013SA	wo
589	N15UC	670	N703RK	5057	CS-DKC	5138	N600J	A014SA	OH-KNE
590	99-0404	671	N3546	5058	N74RP	5139	OE-IRG	A015SA	N789DJ
591	N301K	672	N673P	5059	VP-BLR	5140	N838BA	A016SA	N411RE
592	N90AM	673	N36GV	5060	G-JCBC	5141	N10MZ	A017SA	N399MM
593	I-DEAS	674	N1956M	5061	N718MC	5142	D-ADCB	A018SA	N83BG
594	N33M	675	676	5062	N159JA	5143	4X-...	A019SA	N400GK
595	N85V	676	N677F	5063	N411WW	5144	N515PL	A020SA	wfu
596	N596GA	677	678	5064	VP-BJD	5145	N345LC	A021SA	N405MG
597	N540M	678	679	5065	N747AE	5146	N607PM	A022SA	N400UF
598	N1SF	679	N680GA	5066	N250DV	5147	B-LUE	A023SA	N150CA
599	N428WT	680	N624N	5067	N50HA	5148	N551KF	A024SA	N674AC
600	N100GV	681	N38BA	5068	EI-GDL	5149	VP-CGN	A025SA	N400HH
601	N502QS	682	JA500A	5069	569	5150	CS-DKH	A026SA	N486CW
602	VP-BKZ	683	684	5070	HB-JEP	5151	EC-KJS	A027SA	N7PW
603	N35CD	684	N685TA	5071	I-LUXO	5152	N652GA	A028SA	wo
604	XA-EAJ	685	N524AC	5072	N572EC	5153	SE-RDZ	A029SA	N100RS
605	N691RC	686	OE-IVY	5073	N800JH	5154	N557GA	A030SA	N83SA
606	N551GA	687	N543H	5074	HZ-ARK	5155	N550GA	A031SA	N958PP
607	VP-BNL	688	JA501A	5075	N518QS	5156	N529QS	A032SA	N83CG
608	N608WB*	689	N914BD	5076	N870CM	5157	N785QS	A033SA	N148J
609	N101MH	690	N525AC	5077	N933H	5158	N56UH	A034SA	N334KC
610	N253CM	691	N100TM	5078	EC-JPK	5159	N607CH	A035SA	N37CB
611	N5000X	692	N508P	5079	N860AA	5160	N813QS	A036SA	N997MX
612	N88D	693	N885KT	5080	SE-RDY	5161	N725MM	A037SA	wfu
613	N721MM	699	N420GA	5081	CS-DKD	5162	EC-KLS	A038SA	N42SR
614	N614CM	4120	N501ZK	5082	N709DW	5163	N57UH	A039SA	PT-OXT
615	N914J	5001	N92LA	5083	N985JC	5164	N372BG*	A040SA	N40GA
616	N5616	5002	N245TT	5084	VP-BSI	5165	N245BD	A041SA	N104GB
617	7T-VPG	5003	HB-IGM	5085	N235DX	5166	CS-DKI	A042SA	N8LE
618	N585JC	5004	N4CP	5086	N609PM	5167	G-EGNS*	A043SA	N19R
619	N1454H	5005	N550GW	5087	166377	5168	N528AP*	A044SA	N600GW
620	01-0028	5006	N754BA	5088	N5VS	5169	N203Z	A045SA	N395WB
621	N605CH	5007	N378L	5089	N771JT	5170	N105ST		

A046SA	HA-YFE	RJ-33	XA-BNG	RK-50	N450CW	RK-131	N305MD	RK-212	N11UB
A047SA	N2WC	RJ-34	N80TS	RK-51	N8085T	RK-132	N106KC	RK-213	N545TC
A048SA	wo	RJ-35	N1AG	RK-52	N709EL	RK-133	I-TOPB	RK-214	N79EL
A049SA	N411SP	RJ-36	XA-AOC	RK-53	N896C	RK-134	N134BJ	RK-215	N515WA
A050SA	N528LG	RJ-37	ZS-ORW	RK-54	PT-WHG	RK-135	N135BJ	RK-216	N213BK
A051SA	wfu	RJ-38	N52AL	RK-55	N42AJ	RK-136	N130WW	RK-217	N385PB
A052SA	wfu	RJ-39	N398BB	RK-56	XA-...	RK-137	N400AJ	RK-218	N48MF
A053SA	JA30DA	RJ-40	N400DW	RK-57	N368EA	RK-138	N48PL	RK-219	4X-CPY
A054SA	N491BT	RJ-41	N241BJ	RK-58	PT-WHC	RK-139	VH-BZL	RK-220	N499AS
A055SA	XA-UIC	RJ-42	N418CT*	RK-59	N27JJ	RK-140	A2-MCG	RK-221	N400SF
A056SA	N255DG	RJ-43	N416CT	RK-60	N55SQ*	RK-141	N855FC	RK-222	VH-YRC
A057SA	N510BC	RJ-44	N110GA	RK-61	N478DR	RK-142	N9WW	RK-223	N877FL
A058SA	N442EA	RJ-45	N241TR	RK-62	N462CW	RK-143	N824HG	RK-224	N642AC
A059SA	N1JC	RJ-46	VT-TEL	RK-63	N304JR	RK-144	N134CM	RK-225	N751TA
A060SA	N585TC	RJ-47	N1547B	RK-64	N53MS	RK-145	N745TA	RK-226	N750TA
A061SA	N500PP	RJ-48	XC-LJS	RK-65	N39HF	RK-146	N746TA	RK-227	N862KM
A062SA	N817GR	RJ-49	N88UA	RK-66	I-AVSS	RK-147	N147BJ	RK-228	N12WF
A063SA	N984SA	RJ-50	N8HQ	RK-67	N8167Y	RK-148	OE-GHM	RK-229	N515TJ
A064SA	YV195T	RJ-52	N324MM	RK-68	N900EF	RK-149	N749TA	RK-230	N417LX
A065SA	N925MJ	RJ-53	N520WS	RK-69	N877J	RK-150	N100AW	RK-231	N615HP
A066SA	PR-JTS	RJ-54	N418MG	RK-70	N826JH	RK-151	N198CT	RK-232	N674SF
A067SA	wfu	RJ-55	N724HB	RK-71	N402GS	RK-152	YV213T	RK-233	N233MW
A068SA	N103HC	RJ-56	N70DE	RK-72	N82QD	RK-153	N500HY	RK-234	N783TA
A069SA	N250GP	RJ-57	wo	RK-73	PT-WHB	RK-154	VH-EXB	RK-235	N695BK
A070SA	N60EF	RJ-58	N458HC	RK-74	N93XP	RK-155	N567DK	RK-236	N11WF
A071SA	N71GH	RJ-59	ZS-MHN	RK-75	N125JG	RK-156	N400PU	RK-237	N443LX
A072SA	N779DC	RJ-60	N700WH*	RK-76	N261JP	RK-157	N157WH	RK-238	N96GA
A073SA	N94LD	RJ-61	N461EA	RK-77	PT-WHD	RK-158	PT-MPL	RK-239	N785TA
A074SA	N32HP	RJ-62	N424BT	RK-78	wfu	RK-159	N3337J	RK-240	N393GH
A075SA	N824DW	RJ-63	N848C	RK-79	N8279G	RK-160	N54HP	RK-241	N993H
A076SA	wo	RJ-64	N215TP	RK-80	AP-BEX	RK-161	N706RM	RK-242	N32AA
A077SA	N851C	RJ-65	N16MF	RK-81	PT-WHE	RK-162	OE-GMC	RK-243	N782TP
A078SA	wo	400A/Hawker 400XP		RK-82	PT-WHF	RK-163	I-TOPD	RK-244	N793TA
A079SA	N765KC	RK-1	N481CW	RK-83	N8283C	RK-164	N717CH*	RK-245	N744TA
A080SA	N44MM	RK-2	N827SB	RK-84	D-CHSW	RK-165	N224MC	RK-246	N500TH
A081SA	N50EF	RK-3	N519RW	RK-85	N419MB	RK-166	N93FT	RK-247	N25XP
A082SA	N214PG	RK-4	N494CW	RK-86	N20ZC	RK-167	N501BW	RK-248	N447LX
A083SA	N417KT	RK-5	N30XL	RK-87	N87EB	RK-168	N768TA	RK-249	N611WM
A084SA	EC-JKL	RK-6	N480M	RK-88	N654AP	RK-169	N757WS	RK-250	N250HP
A085SA	N87DY	RK-7	N9PW	RK-89	N94HE	RK-170	TC-MSB	RK-251	N705LP
A086SA	N515KK	RK-8	N440DS	RK-90	N165HB	RK-171	XA-LEG	RK-252	N790TA
A087SA	I-AVEB	RK-9	N315R	RK-91	N491CW	RK-172	N200GP	RK-253	N4053T
A088SA	N482DM	RK-10	D-CEIS	RK-92	N124PP	RK-173	N2273Z	RK-254	N254RK
A089SA	N20PA	RK-11	wo	RK-93	N493CW	RK-174	N174AB	RK-255	N402FB
A090SA	N464AM	RK-13	N610EG	RK-94	N661WD	RK-175	N175BJ	RK-256	N26PA
A091SA	N400NF	RK-14	N81TJ	RK-95	N747RR	RK-176	N476BJ	RK-257	N449LX
A092SA	wo	RK-16	N16HD	RK-96	N800GF	RK-177	N717CF	RK-258	PP-WRV
A1008SA	wfu	RK-17	N857C	RK-97	VH-MGC	RK-178	N708TA	RK-259	XA-AFS
Beechjet 400		RK-18	TC-ASE	RK-98	N999YB*	RK-179	N400CT	RK-260	N787TA
RJ-1	N64VM	RK-19	N144AW	RK-99	N575RB	RK-180	N709TA	RK-261	N51B
RJ-2	N369EA	RK-20	N703LP	RK-100	N400SH	RK-181	N314TL	RK-262	N300GB
RJ-3	N203BA	RK-21	N1920	RK-101	N400FT	RK-182	N234DK	RK-263	N724KW
RJ-4	N8YM	RK-22	N870BB	RK-102	N111FW	RK-183	N710TA	RK-264	N792TA
RJ-5	N933AC	RK-23	N250AJ	RK-103	N12NV	RK-184	N141DR	RK-265	N797TA
RJ-6	N406TS	RK-24	N8073R	RK-104	PR-DOT	RK-185	N148GB	RK-266	N27XP
RJ-7	N403JP	RK-25	D-CLBA	RK-105	N105AX	RK-186	N712TA	RK-267	N4467X
RJ-9	N65RA	RK-26	HK-4446W	RK-106	N625W	RK-187	N400TE	RK-268	N789TA
RJ-10	N131AP	RK-27	N95GK	RK-107	N907JE	RK-188	VP-CPH	RK-269	N440RC
RJ-11	N72HG	RK-28	N400NS	RK-108	N408CW	RK-189	N715TA	RK-270	N800SD
RJ-12	N106CG	RK-29	I-IPIZ	RK-109	N121EZ	RK-190	VT-RPG	RK-271	N743TA
RJ-13	N428JD	RK-30	N494CC	RK-110	N400VP	RK-191	N400HD	RK-272	N701CP
RJ-14	N599JL	RK-31	N850C	RK-111	N13SY	RK-192	N116AP	RK-273	N731TA
RJ-15	N415CT	RK-32	N932EA	RK-112	N112BJ	RK-193	N914SH	RK-274	N434LX
RJ-16	N803E	RK-33	N197BE	RK-113	wo	RK-194	N909ST	RK-275	N426EA
RJ-17	N655CM	RK-34	N184AR	RK-114	N855RA*	RK-195	N410LX*	RK-276	N775TA
RJ-18	N418RM	RK-35	N435CW	RK-115	N52AW	RK-196	N619GA	RK-277	N101CC
RJ-19	N598JL	RK-36	N156DH	RK-116	N1116R	RK-197	N940VA	RK-278	N750AJ
RJ-20	N455GW	RK-37	SE-DRS	RK-117	N496AS	RK-198	N798TA	RK-279	N436LX
RJ-21	N721FA	RK-38	N515MW	RK-118	LV-WTP	RK-199	N446M	RK-280	N26XP
RJ-22	N913MC	RK-39	N70BJ	RK-119	N456JG	RK-200	N399RA	RK-281	XA-TDQ
RJ-23	N400GJ	RK-40	N440CW	RK-120	N702NV	RK-201	N741TA	RK-282	N794TA
RJ-24	N800WV	RK-41	N546BZ	RK-121	N473JE	RK-202	N438LX	RK-283	N404MS
RJ-25	N425BJ	RK-42	N443C	RK-122	PT-WJS	RK-203	N262PA	RK-284	N439LX
RJ-26	N401GJ	RK-43	N45RK	RK-123	N740TA	RK-204	I-ASER	RK-285	N249RM
RJ-27	N611TG	RK-44	N712GK	RK-124	YU-BVA	RK-205	N143HM	RK-286	N400MV
RJ-28	N51EB	RK-45	N445PK	RK-125	N939GP	RK-206	N982AR	RK-287	N361AS
RJ-29	N129BT	RK-46	N515RY	RK-126	XB-INI	RK-207	N257CB	RK-288	N848PF
RJ-30	N777FE	RK-47	N109CP	RK-127	N686TR	RK-208	HI-766SP	RK-289	N796TA
RJ-31	N499P	RK-48	N48SE	RK-128	N912SH	RK-209	N413LX	RK-290	N204DH
RJ-32	XA-RAR	RK-49	N54HD	RK-129	N334SR	RK-210	N111CX	RK-291	N816DK
				RK-130	TC-NEO	RK-211	N686SC	RK-292	N441LX

RK-293	EC-HTR	RK-374	N109NT	RK-455	N800HT	RK-537	N537XP	TT-37	91-0096
RK-294	HS-TPD	RK-375	XA-UCV	RK-456	LV-BEM	RK-538	CS-DMU	TT-38	91-0097
RK-295	N898TA	RK-376	N476LX	RK-457	PR-MMS	RK-539	N539XP	TT-39	91-0098
RK-296	N68JV	RK-377	N477LX	RK-458	N339SM	RK-540	N777G	TT-40	91-0099
RK-297	N497CW	RK-378	N370FC	RK-459	N517MD	RK-541	N474LX*	TT-41	91-0100
RK-298	N445LX	RK-379	PP-UQF	RK-460	N460KG	RK-542	N393BB	TT-42	91-0101
RK-299	N446LX	RK-380	N102QS	RK-461	N101AR	RK-543	N731PS	TT-43	91-0102
RK-300	VP-CVP	RK-381	N106QS	RK-462	N689AK	RK-544	N480CT	TT-44	92-0330
RK-301	N696TA	RK-382	N108QS	RK-463	N469LX	RK-545	N485CT	TT-45	92-0331
RK-302	XA-TTS	RK-383	N115QS	RK-464	CS-DMK	RK-546	N490CT	TT-46	92-0332
RK-303	SE-RBO	RK-384	N302TB	RK-465	CS-DML	RK-547	N495CT	TT-47	92-0333
RK-304	N304SE	RK-385	N116QS	RK-466	N610PR	RK-548	N548XP	TT-48	92-0334
RK-305	N448LX	RK-386	N502N	RK-467	N122QS	RK-549	CS-DMV*	TT-49	92-0335
RK-306	YV198T	RK-387	N478LX	RK-468	N468LX	RK-550	CS-DMW*	TT-50	92-0336
RK-307	N407CW	RK-388	N997RS	RK-469	N114QS	RK-551	N551XP	TT-51	92-0337
RK-308	N400KP	RK-389	N717DD	RK-470	PR-IND	RK-552	N552XP	TT-52	92-0338
RK-309	I-VITH	RK-390	N975RD	RK-471	N471XP	RK-553	N553XP	TT-53	92-0339
RK-310	N451LX	RK-391	N117QS	RK-472	CS-DMM	RK-554	N475LX	TT-54	92-0340
RK-311	N311GL	RK-392	AP-BHQ	RK-473	N149QS	RK-555	CS-DMX*	TT-55	92-0341
RK-312	N75RL	RK-393	N835TB	RK-474	N474ME	RK-556	CS-DMY*	TT-56	92-0342
RK-313	N4483W	RK-394	N119QS	RK-475	CS-DMN	RK-557	N557XP	TT-57	92-0343
RK-314	N400HS	RK-395	N7600	RK-476	TC-STA	RK-558	N558XP	TT-58	92-0344
RK-315	N6MF	RK-396	XA-MEX	RK-477	N477GJ	RK-559	CS-DMZ*	TT-59	92-0345
RK-316	XA-AFA	RK-397	N479LX	RK-478	N470LX	RK-561	CS-DOA*	TT-60	92-0346
RK-317	N452LX	RK-398	N480LX	RK-479	PP-JCF	RK-563	N483LX	TT-61	92-0347
RK-318	HB-VNE	RK-399	N700FA	RK-481	N472LX	RK-570	N484LX	TT-62	92-0348
RK-319	N660CC	RK-400	ZS-POT	RK-482	N482GS*	RK-573	N485LX	TT-63	92-0349
RK-320	N717TG	RK-401	CS-DMA	RK-483	N139QS	RK-580	N486LX	TT-64	92-0350
RK-321	XA-TYD	RK-402	OE-GSG	RK-484	N101QS	RK-583	N487LX	TT-65	92-0351
RK-322	N800EH	RK-403	CS-DMB	RK-485	N485XP	Beechjet 400T		TT-66	92-0352
RK-323	N268PA	RK-404	CS-DMC	RK-486	N123QS	TX-1	41-5051	TT-67	92-0353
RK-324	N755TA	RK-405	N94LH	RK-487	G-EDCS	TX-2	41-5052	TT-68	92-0354
RK-325	N408PC	RK-406	N140QS	RK-488	N719EL	TX-3	41-5053	TT-69	92-0355
RK-326	N420DH	RK-407	CS-DMD	RK-489	N489B	TX-4	41-5054	TT-70	92-0356
RK-327	N454LX	RK-408	CS-DME	RK-490	N153QS	TX-5	41-5055	TT-71	92-0357
RK-328	N686TA	RK-409	N120QS	RK-491	N491HR	TX-6	51-5056	TT-72	92-0358
RK-329	N580RK	RK-410	CS-DMF	RK-492	N138QS	TX-7	51-5057	TT-73	92-0359
RK-330	N330TS	RK-411	N380JR	RK-493	CC-CRT	TX-8	51-5058	TT-74	92-0360
RK-331	N12MG	RK-412	N412GJ	RK-494	CS-DMO	TX-9	71-5059	TT-75	92-0361
RK-332	XA-TWW	RK-413	N482LX	RK-495	N410CT	TX-10	01-5060	TT-76	92-0362
RK-333	N903CG	RK-414	N136QS	RK-496	N410KD	TX-11	21-5011	TT-77	92-0363
RK-334	N484CW	RK-415	XA-UFS	RK-497	N497XP	TX-12	21-5012	TT-78	93-0621
RK-335	N400GR	RK-416	XA-LMG	RK-498	N141QS	TX-13	41-5063	TT-79	93-0622
RK-336	N706LP	RK-417	CS-DMG	RK-499	I-GFVF	Jayhawk		TT-80	93-0623
RK-337	N726PG	RK-418	N418GJ	RK-500	I-FDED	TT-1	91-0077	TT-81	93-0624
RK-338	N116AD	RK-419	N279AK	RK-501	F-HITM	TT-2	90-0412	TT-82	93-0625
RK-339	N400TL	RK-420	N877S	RK-502	G-STOB	TT-3	90-0400	TT-83	93-0626
RK-340	N500LJ	RK-421	N145QS	RK-503	N121GF	TT-4	90-0405	TT-84	93-0627
RK-341	N61GB	RK-422	N151QS	RK-504	N202TT	TT-5	89-0284	TT-85	93-0628
RK-342	N522EL	RK-423	N462LX	RK-505	N505XP	TT-6	90-0404	TT-86	93-0629
RK-343	OE-GTM	RK-424	N1JB	RK-506	N471LX	TT-7	90-0401	TT-87	93-0630
RK-344	N99ZB	RK-425	CS-DMH	RK-507	N507HB	TT-8	90-0402	TT-88	93-0631
RK-345	N425CW	RK-426	N463LX	RK-508	CS-DMP	TT-9	90-0403	TT-89	93-0632
RK-346	N446CW	RK-427	N132QS	RK-509	N154QS	TT-10	90-0407	TT-90	93-0633
RK-347	N498AS*	RK-428	EC-JPN	RK-510	N225SB	TT-11	90-0406	TT-91	93-0634
RK-348	N309AK	RK-429	N263PA	RK-511	VT-TVR	TT-12	90-0408	TT-92	93-0635
RK-349	N975RR	RK-430	N990DF	RK-512	CS-DMQ	TT-13	90-0409	TT-93	93-0636
RK-350	PR-MVB	RK-431	N131QS	RK-513	N513XP	TT-14	90-0410	TT-94	93-0637
RK-351	N371CF	RK-432	N142QS	RK-514	N416RX	TT-15	90-0411	TT-95	93-0638
RK-352	XA-...	RK-433	N125QS	RK-515	I-ALVC	TT-16	90-0413	TT-96	93-0639
RK-353	XA-GAO	RK-434	XA-UEV	RK-516	CS-DMR	TT-17	91-0076	TT-97	93-0640
RK-354	N717EA	RK-435	N161QS	RK-517	N420CT	TT-18	91-0075	TT-98	93-0641
RK-355	N400RY	RK-436	N147QS	RK-518	N473LX	TT-19	91-0078	TT-99	93-0642
RK-356	N217EC	RK-437	CS-DMI	RK-519	CS-DMS	TT-20	91-0079	TT-100	93-0643
RK-357	N317PC	RK-438	N438BC	RK-520	N157QS	TT-21	91-0080	TT-101	93-0644
RK-358	N865AM	RK-439	N159AK	RK-521	N521XP	TT-22	91-0081	TT-102	93-0645
RK-359	XA-UAW	RK-440	N440WF	RK-522	N522MB	TT-23	91-0082	TT-103	93-0646
RK-360	N823ET	RK-441	N43BD	RK-523	N425CT	TT-24	91-0083	TT-104	93-0647
RK-361	N25CU	RK-442	N442GJ	RK-524	N524XP	TT-25	91-0084	TT-105	93-0648
RK-362	P-2034	RK-443	CS-DMJ	RK-525	N502CA	TT-26	91-0085	TT-106	93-0649
RK-363	N790SS	RK-444	N702LP	RK-526	AP-PAL	TT-27	91-0086	TT-107	93-0650
RK-364	N394BB	RK-445	N536V	RK-527	N527XP	TT-28	91-0087	TT-108	93-0651
RK-365	N459LX	RK-446	N188JF	RK-528	HA-YFH	TT-29	91-0088	TT-109	93-0652
RK-366	N466CW	RK-447	N467LX	RK-529	N918TT	TT-30	91-0089	TT-110	93-0653
RK-367	N4404BL	RK-448	N212FH	RK-530	OY-CJN	TT-31	91-0090	TT-111	93-0654
RK-368	N461LX	RK-449	N127BW	RK-531	N435CT	TT-32	91-0091	TT-112	93-0655
RK-369	N624B	RK-450	N61VC	RK-532	CS-DMT	TT-33	91-0092	TT-113	93-0656
RK-370	N72GH	RK-451	N964JD	RK-533	EC-KKD	TT-34	wfu	TT-114	94-0114
RK-371	N824GB	RK-452	XA-UFR	RK-534	N440CT	TT-35	91-0094	TT-115	94-0115
RK-372	N375DT	RK-453	N464LX	RK-535	N445CT	TT-36	91-0095	TT-116	94-0116
RK-373	N490JC	RK-454	N465LX	RK-536	N470CT			TT-117	94-0117

TT-118	94-0118	NA716	wo	25017	XA-RSR	25098	YV-815CP	25238	VP-BKK
TT-119	94-0119	NA717	wo	25018	wfu	25099	wfu	25240	wfu
TT-120	94-0120	NA718	N250DH	25019	wo	25100	N6SS	25242	ZS-LME
TT-121	94-0121	NA719	XB-IPX	25020	wfu	25101	XA-MBM	25243	N4ES
TT-122	94-0122	NA720	XB-MSV	25021	wfu	25102	wfu	25246	wfu
TT-123	94-0123	NA721	N43TS	25022	wo	25103	N402AC	25247	9Q-CPR
TT-124	94-0124	NA722	XA-...	25023	ZS-TBN	25104	wfu	25248	N189RR
TT-125	94-0125	NA723	YV1687	25024	XS711/L	25105	wfu	25249	N27UM
TT-126	94-0126	NA724	N724TS	25025	wfu	25106	wfu	25250	N888TJ
TT-127	94-0127	NA725	wo	25026	wfu	25107	XA-UBK	25251	LV-AXZ
TT-128	94-0128	NA726	N922GK	25027	N777RN	25108	wfu	25252	wfu
TT-129	94-0129	NA727	XA-TNY	25028	wfu	25109	N4CR	25253	N911RD
TT-130	94-0130	NA728	N32GM	25029	wfu	25110	wo	25254	VT-UBG
TT-131	94-0131	NA729	VU93-2118	25030	XA-RDD	25111	wfu	25255	N4QB
TT-132	94-0132	NA730	N82CA	25031	wfu	25112	XA-SLR	25257	wfu
TT-133	94-0133	NA731	XB-MAR	25032	N942DS	25113	wfu	25259	wfu
TT-134	94-0134	NA732	N400PR	25033	RP-C125	25114	N114WD	25260	D2-EFM
TT-135	94-0135	NA733	ZS-PLC	25034	wfu	25115	N48DD	25264	N178PC
TT-136	94-0136	NA734	XA-GTC	25035	N151SG	25116	wfu	25266	N125CK
TT-137	94-0137	NA735	N800GE	25036	wfu	25117	wfu	25268	wfu
TT-138	94-0138	NA736	N736LE	25037	wfu	25118	N118DA	25269	AP-BGI
TT-139	94-0139	NA737	XA-YSM	25038	N806CB	25119	N500XY	25270	N440RD
TT-140	94-0140	NA738	wfu	25039	wfu	25120	wo	25271	N810HS
TT-141	94-0141	NA739	N820MG	25040	XS712/A	25121	wfu	25272	N63EM
TT-142	94-0142	NA740	wfu	25041	XS713/C	25122	wfu	25274	wfu
TT-143	94-0143	NA741	wo	25042	wfu	25123	wfu	25277	VU93-2126
TT-144	94-0144	NA742	N843B	25043	wfu	25124	wfu	25288	VU93-2127
TT-145	94-0145	NA743	wfu	25044	wfu	25125	wfu	25289	VU93-2128
TT-146	94-0146	NA744	wfu	25045	XS727/D	25126	wo	25290	wo
TT-147	94-0147	NA745	N700TR	25046	LV-YGC	25127	wo	*125-600*	
TT-148	94-0148	NA746	ZS-OIF	25047	N800DA	25128	ZS-SMT	25256	wo
TT-149	95-0040	NA747	N401AB	25048	XS728/E	25129	wo	25258	9Q-CBC
TT-150	95-0041	NA748	N748TS	25049	wfu	25130	TR-LFB	256001	N699TS
TT-151	95-0042	NA749	XB-KKS	25050	XS730/H	25131	7T-VVL	256002	XA-SLP
TT-152	95-0043	NA750	N131LA	25051	wfu	25132	S9-PDH	256003	N91KP
TT-153	95-0044	NA751	N400FR	25052	N125JR	25133	VT-EQZ	256004	N600MK
TT-154	95-0045	NA752	N602JR	25053	XA-...	25135	wo	256005	wfu
TT-155	95-0046	NA753	N145GL*	25054	wfu	25138	wfu	256006	wo
TT-156	95-0047	NA754	N227LT	25055	XS731/J	25140	N140LF	256007	wfu
TT-157	95-0048	NA755	ZS-MEG	25056	wfu	25143	wfu	256008	N256WJ
TT-158	95-0049	NA756	N624PD	25057	wfu	25144	wfu	256009	N28TS
TT-159	95-0050	NA757	XA-AGL	25058	wfu	25145	wfu	256010	wo
TT-160	95-0051	NA758	N800NP	25059	wfu	25147	wfu	256011	wfu
TT-161	95-0052	NA759	YV-....	25060	N96SG	25148	XA-TTH	256012	wfu
TT-162	95-0053	NA760	YV-....	25061	wfu	25149	wfu	256013	5N-YET
TT-163	95-0054	NA761	N814D	25062	wfu	25150	N42AS	256014	N47HV
TT-164	95-0055	NA762	N125DH	25063	wfu	25151	wfu	256015	N957MB
TT-165	95-0056	NA763	N1QH	25064	wo	25152	N23CJ	256016	wfu
TT-166	95-0057	NA764	N55RZ	25065	XA-KOF	25153	N88DU	256017	wfu
TT-167	95-0058	NA765	N765TS	25066	XA-UEX	25154	wfu	256018	XB-ADZ
TT-168	95-0059	NA766	N854SM	25067	ZS-MAN	25155	wfu	256019	wfu
TT-169	95-0060	NA767	wfu	25068	wfu	25156	wfu	256020	wfu
TT-170	95-0061	NA768	XA-SFQ	25069	wo	25157	wfu	256021	S9-PDG
TT-171	95-0062	NA769	N900AD	25070	wfu	25158	XA-DAN	256022	wfu
TT-172	95-0063	NA770	N805WD	25071	wfu	25159	N600SV	256023	wfu
TT-173	95-0064	NA771	N4WC	25072	wfu	25162	VC93-2120	256024	N411GA
TT-174	95-0065	NA772	wo	25073	wo	25164	EC93-2125	256025	N721LH
TT-175	95-0066	NA773	N32KB	25074	N411FB	25165	wfu	256026	XA-...
TT-176	95-0067	NA774	N774TS	25075	XA-...	25166	wo	256027	N245RS
TT-177	95-0068	NA775	XA-EMA	25076	XS737/K	25167	VU93-2123	256028	wo
TT-178	95-0069	NA776	XA-LOV	25077	wfu	25168	wfu	256029	N35WP
TT-179	95-0070	NA777	wfu	25078	XA-DCS	25169	N163AG	256030	wfu
TT-180	95-0071	NA778	N778JA	25079	P4-AOC	25171	D2-FEZ	256031	9Q-CGF
HS/BAe125/Dominie		NA779	N781JR	25080	wfu	25172	ZS-CAL	256032	N334PS
NA700	wfu	NA780	N800TG	25081	XS739/F	25177	wo	256033	N514AJ
NA701	VU93-2113	25001	wfu	25082	wfu	25178	wfu	256034	wfu
NA702	wfu	25002	wfu	25083	wfu	25181	wo	256035	wfu
NA703	XB-JLY	25003	wfu	25084	N888CJ	25182	wo	256036	wfu
NA704	wfu	25004	wfu	25085	wfu	25184	ZS-LPE	256037	N228MD
NA705	wfu	25005	wfu	25086	wo	25189	wfu	256038	XA-ACN
NA706	XB-JKG	25006	wfu	25087	N330G	25194	wfu	256039	wfu
NA707	wfu	25007	wo	25088	5B-...	25197	PT-LHK	256040	TJ-...
NA708	XA-RPT	25008	wfu	25089	wfu	25199	wfu	256041	N603TS
NA709	N55G	25009	wfu	25090	N429DA	25209	wfu	256042	wo
NA710	N314ER	25010	wfu	25091	XA-RSP	25215	D2-EXR	256043	wo
NA711	ZP-TKO	25011	XS709/M	25092	wfu	25217	5N-EAS	256044	N453DP
NA712	wfu	25012	wfu	25093	wfu	25219	D2-FFH	256045	N508VM
NA713	XA-...	25013	wfu	25094	wfu	25223	wfu	256046	N299GS
NA714	N31EP	25014	wfu	25095	wo	25227	XA-...	256047	9Q-CAI
NA715	N284DB	25015	wfu	25096	wo	25231	YV113T	256048	N852GA
		25016	N222NG	25097	wfu	25235	N330AM		

256049	5V-TTP	NA0257	N611MC	NA0339	N700SA	NA0402	N757M	258011	N801RM
256050	wfu	NA0258	N227MM	NA0340	XA-HOM	NA0403	N316EC	258012	N804MR
256051	9Q-CFJ	NA0259	N941CE	NA0341	I-AZFB	NA0404	VP-CCH	258013	N300RB
256052	wfu	NA0260	XA-HXM	NA0342	ZS-IPE	NA0405	N527AC	258014	N298AG
256053	N721RM	NA0261	N999CY	NA0343	N949CE	NA0406	C-GCCU	258015	N705BB
256054	wo	NA0262	N561PS	NA0344	N511RG	NA0407	N70NE	258016	N800VR
256055	N111UN	NA0263	N125RG	NA0345	N700NP	NA0408	N118GA	258017	N888ZZ
256056	wfu	NA0264	N724EA	257001	N425KG	NA0409	N801LM	258018	N904JR
256057	N11AF	NA0265	N299WB	257007	N545SH*	NA0410	N683E	258019	N880WW
256058	N20FM	NA0266	N804CS	257010	N819WG	NA0411	N800EC	258020	N270HC
256059	wfu	NA0267	N267JE	257013	P4-SKY	NA0413	N166WC	258021	G-RCEJ
256060	N395EJ	NA0268	XA-SON	257020	N777EH	NA0414	N800WA	258022	N822BL
256061	N701MS	NA0269	XA-AMI	257022	N700WC	NA0415	N830BA*	258023	N47HW
256062	5N-DOT	NA0270	N52GA	257025	N205TW*	NA0416	C-GCGS	258024	N337RE
256063	N9AZ	NA0271	N154FJ	257028	VP-COK	NA0417	N620RM	258025	PR-LTA
256064	XA-MKY	NA0272	N700XF	257031	N703JN	NA0418	N913SC	258026	N82SR
256065	N10SA	NA0273	N110EJ	257034	N34GG	NA0419	N818WM	258027	N880M
256066	N600G	NA0274	N560SB	257037	G-IFTE	NA0420	N3QG	258028	N277SS
256067	CX-CBS	NA0275	XB-JND	257040	P4-LVF	NA0421	N40GS	258029	N77LA
256068	N600AE	NA0276	wo	257046	N770AZ	NA0422	N222MS	258030	N91CH
256069	5N-EMA	NA0277	N972W	257054	OD-HHF	NA0423	N423SJ	258031	PT-LHB
256070	N75GA	NA0278	N518RR	257055	N347TC	NA0425	N800SE	258032	HZ-WBT5
256071	*wfu*	NA0279	ZS-ICU	257061	XA-UEA	NA0426	N797EP	258033	N621WP
125-700		NA0280	N500FM	257062	EI-WJN	NA0427	N326N	258034	N125HH
NA0201	N701TS	NA0281	N281BT	257064	N48LB	NA0428	N384TC*	258035	N85MG
NA0202	N403BG	NA0282	N120YB	257067	N42TS	NA0429	N141MR	258036	wo
NA0203	N104AE	NA0283	N26SC	257070	P4-AMH	NA0430	N45GD	258037	M-HDAM
NA0204	N724B	NA0284	N10UC	257073	N210RK	NA0431	N682R	258038	C-FDDD
NA0205	N618KR	NA0285	N130YB	257076	N111ZS	NA0432	N22NF	258039	N173TR
NA0206	N706AM	NA0286	N83MD	257082	N752CM	NA0433	N9UP	258040	N718HC
NA0207	N816JM	NA0287	N564BR	257085	N10TN	NA0434	N432AQ	258041	N626CG
NA0208	N449EB	NA0288	N198GT	257088	N224EA	NA0435	C-GMTR	258042	N904BW
NA0209	N209TS	NA0289	N70QB	257091	VP-CLX	NA0436	N803JL	258043	N937BC
NA0210	N418RD	NA0290	N710AF	257094	N483FG	NA0437	N17DD	258044	XA-UEH
NA0211	N411PA	NA0291	N947CE	257097	RA-02801	NA0438	N800PA	258045	N802SA*
NA0212	N425SD	NA0292	N241FB	257100	N925WC	NA0439	C-GKPP	258046	N125SB
NA0213	N339CA	NA0293	N406J	257103	OY-MFL	NA0440	N295JR	258047	XA-FGS
NA0214	N926MC	NA0294	N188KA	257107	N880RG	NA0441	N24JG	258048	N716DB
NA0215	N215RS	NA0295	N134NW	257109	VP-BOY	NA0442	N729EZ	258049	N796CH
NA0216	N98FT	NA0296	N927LL	257112	RA-02850	NA0443	N717MT	258050	D-CLBC
NA0217	N700RR	NA0297	N945CE	257115	N333MS	NA0444	N811AM	258051	XA-ELM
NA0218	N903SC	NA0298	N917TF	257118	N810KB	NA0445	N800QC	258052	C-FKGN
NA0219	wo	NA0299	N800LM	257124	OD-FNF	NA0447	C-FCRF	258053	N489SA
NA0220	XA-SAU	NA0300	N943CE	257127	N795A	NA0448	N904GR	258054	N527M
NA0221	C-GTOR	NA0301	N107LT	257130	N405DW	NA0449	N178AX	258055	XA-...
NA0222	N18CC	NA0302	C-GLIG	257133	wo	NA0450	N861CE	258056	G-JETI
NA0223	N720PT	NA0303	N900JT	257136	P4-XZX	NA0451	XA-GIC	258057	N614AP
NA0224	XB-JYS	NA0304	N237DX	257139	RA-02803	NA0452	N801CF	258058	G-JJSI
NA0225	N137WR	NA0305	5N-BFC	257142	RA-02802	NA0453	N4242	258059	N686CP
NA0226	N102BP	NA0306	N141AL	257151	N825MS	NA0454	N892BP*	258060	N303SE
NA0227	N81KA	NA0307	N270KA	257158	XA-...	NA0455	N25BB	258061	N412DA
NA0228	N545GM	NA0308	N9999V	257160	5N-AVK	NA0456	N801P	258062	N862CW
NA0229	XA-...	NA0309	N95CM	257163	7T-VCW	NA0457	C-GDBC	258063	N391TC
NA0230	N899AB	NA0310	N109BG	257166	EC-HRQ	NA0458	N28ZF*	258064	MAAW-J1
NA0231	N225BJ	NA0311	ZS-WJW	257169	5N-MAZ	NA0459	N929WQ	258065	N16GH
NA0232	N232TN	NA0312	C-GLBJ	257172	ZS-CAG	NA0460	N4402	258066	N55RF
NA0233	N79EH	NA0313	wo	257175	RA-......	NA0461	N722A	258067	N469AL
NA0234	N323JK	NA0314	N53GH	257178	N175MC	NA0462	A6-MAA	258068	N167DD
NA0235	N10C	NA0315	N26ME	257181	ZD620	NA0464	N703SM*	258069	N160WC
NA0236	wo	NA0316	N18BA	257183	ZD703	NA0465	N939TT	258070	N798PA*
NA0237	N511KA	NA0317	N612MC	257184	SU-PIX	NA0466	N395HE	258071	N94JT
NA0238	N200JP	NA0318	N356SR	257187	wo	NA0467	N2QG	258072	N164WC
NA0239	C-GOHJ	NA0319	XA-JAI	257189	N45KG	NA0468	N9990S	258073	N212RG
NA0240	N800E	NA0320	N7490A	257190	ZD621	NA0469	N50OJ	258074	N103HT
NA0241	XA-...	NA0321	wfu	257194	ZD704	NA0470	N125GB	258075	XA-RYM
NA0242	N241RT	NA0322	N322BC	257196	wo	NA0471	N118K	258076	RA-02807
NA0243	N717AF	NA0323	VT-AAA	257197	5N-BEX	NA0472	N125AW	258077	N897CW
NA0244	N414RF	NA0324	N2KZ	257200	VP-BMD	NA0473	N919SS	258078	YL-VIP
NA0245	VP-CLU	NA0325	C-FCSS	257203	wo	NA0474	N44HH	258079	N800LL
NA0246	N700NW	NA0326	N819DM	257205	ZE395	NA0475	N935H	258080	N800WH
NA0247	N120JC	NA0327	C-GAAA	257208	N501GF	RK-480	SU-ZBB	258081	N196MG
NA0248	N900CP	NA0328	C-FEAE	257209	RP-C9808	258001	N800RM	258082	N800S
NA0249	XA-FMK	NA0329	5N-DAO	257210	N502GF	258002	N15AX	258083	N852A
NA0250	N308DD	NA0331	XB-JTN	257211	ZE396	258003	N803GE	258084	N323SL
NA0251	N571CH	NA0332	5N-MAO	257212	VP-BMU	258004	XA-TVI	258085	N910VP*
NA0252	N237WR	NA0333	N511LD	257213	N700CE	258005	N800FL	258086	N523WG
NA0253	N422X	NA0334	TY-SAM	257214	VP-CMP	258006	N800FH	258087	C-FIGO
NA0254	N125XX	NA0335	C-GJBJ	*257215*	*VT-OBE*	258007	C-GWLE	258088	N757BL
NA0255	XA-SEN	NA0336	N770HS	*125-800/Hawker 800XP*		258008	N722CC	258089	N593HR
NA0256	N455BK	NA0337	N818LD	NA0401	N180NE	258009	N48Y	258090	N414PE
		NA0338	N350PL			258010	N810BA	258091	N1776H

258092	N3008	258246	HB-VKW	258327	N801HB	258408	B-3990	258489	N28GP
258093	N2033	258247	52-3002	258328	A6-MAH	258409	N827NS	258490	N327LJ
258094	LN-ESA	258248	N789LB	258329	N825CP*	258410	N885M	258491	XA-TYH
258095	AP-BJL	258249	N249SR	258330	N139M	258411	N617TM	258492	N800LF
258096	N234GF	258250	52-3003	258331	N864CE	258412	N990HC	258493	12-3018
258097	N800BV	258251	N194JS	258332	N53LB	258413	N813CW	258494	M-HAWK
258098	N181FH	258252	XB-GCC	258333	92-3009	258414	N800XM	258495	5B-CKL
258099	N10YJ	258253	N3RC	258334	N60HD	258415	N800LR	258496	G-RDMV
258106	G-OLDD	258254	N2015M	258335	OE-GHU	258416	N816QS	258497	N825CT
258109	5N-NPC	258255	N127KC	258336	N745UP	258417	N240V	258498	N11UL
258110	N710A	258256	N256BC	258337	N733TA	258418	N516TH	258499	CS-DNV
258112	N812GJ	258257	N415BJ	258338	N838QS	258419	N508BP	258500	C-FPCE
258115	P4-BOB	258258	N258MR	258339	N14SA	258420	N910JD	258501	B-3992
258116	PT-LQP	258259	N954H	258340	N840QS	258421	EU93-6051	258502	N502HR
258117	C-GBIS	258260	N957H	258341	92-3010	258422	CS-DNM	258503	N801WM
258118	HZ-105	258261	PT-GAF	258342	258-342	258423	N388BS	258504	TC-AHS
258120	N120AP	258262	N521JK	258343	258-343	258424	YL-NST	258505	N835QS
258129	XA-IZA	258263	N826GA	258344	N29GP	258425	N802CF	258506	I-RONY
258130	G-DCTA	258264	HB-VLF	258345	OY-LKG	258426	N27FL	258507	C-GIBU
258131	N8030F	258265	HB-VLG	258346	258-346	258427	12-3016	258508	N800PE
258133	PR-SOL	258266	N800CC	258347	N409AV	258428	N828CW	258509	N162JB
258134	N96	258267	VP-CAF	258348	92-3011	258429	ZS-PKY	258510	N831LX
258136	N80GJ	258268	62-3004	258349	N377JC	258430	CS-DNK	258511	CS-DNX
258143	5N-AGZ	258269	N302SE	258350	258-350	258431	N144HM	258512	N501CT
258146	HZ-109	258270	N838JL	258351	258-351	258432	N809LX	258513	22-3020
258148	HZ-110	258271	N787CM	258352	258-352	258433	N833QS	258514	D-CHEF
258149	N577T	258272	N4426	258353	258-353	258434	EU93-6052	258515	N321MS
258152	XA-...	258273	N337WR	258354	N2G	258435	CS-DNN	258516	N817LX
258153	HB-VHV	258274	N41HF	258355	N855QS	258436	N836QS	258517	N817QS
258154	N97	258275	XA-...	258356	N55BA	258437	N780TA	258518	N29B
258155	N723LK*	258276	N126KC	258357	258-357	258438	N827SA	258519	N72FC
258156	N98	258277	N339CC	258358	OY-JBJ	258439	CS-DNL	258520	JY-AW4
258158	N800AF	258278	N872AT	258359	P4-ALE	258440	N408RT	258521	VT-RAN
258164	HZ-130	258279	N877DM	258360	92-3012	258441	N370DE	258522	N746UP
258165	N324BG	258280	N351SB	258361	N861QS	258442	N80PK	258523	N824QS
258167	N48AL	258281	N832LX	258362	N862QS	258443	N489VC	258524	N872BC
258169	N255DV	258282	N800LX*	258363	N816LX	258444	C-GBAP	258525	B-3993
258175	N2032	258283	C-FJHS	258364	N728TA	258445	12-3017	258526	N837RE
258176	XA-TPB	258284	PR-DBB	258365	N865SM	258446	N983EC*	258527	N56BE
258177	N5119	258285	N285XP	258366	N894CA	258447	EU93-6053	258528	N828QS
258180	VP-BMH	258286	N304RJ	258367	N704JM	258448	N19DU	258529	N259RH
258182	N12F	258287	XA-UFK	258368	N804AC	258449	N365AT	258530	N890SP
258184	PT-OSW	258288	72-3005	258369	N800PC	258450	I-DLOH	258531	N622VL
258186	N818MV	258289	N863CE	258370	02-3013	258451	N475HM	258532	N317CC
258190	PT-JAA	258290	N348MC	258371	N848N	258452	N852QS	258533	32-3021
258192	N192SJ	258291	N791TA	258372	N800GN	258453	N68CB	258534	N815TA
258194	PT-OTC	258292	N33BC	258373	N168BF	258454	N802TA	258535	N255DX
258197	N150SB	258293	N150NC	258374	N805LX	258455	N803TA	258536	OE-GCE
258198	PT-WAL	258294	N632FW	258375	N875QS	258456	G-JMAX	258537	N100NG
258201	P4-AMF	258295	VH-KEF	258376	N1640	258457	CS-DNO	258538	P4-SNT
258203	N805JL	258296	N934RD	258377	N993SA	258458	N228TM	258539	JY-AW5
258208	N123HK	258297	N725TA	258378	N442MA	258459	N800WP	258540	N700MG
258210	VP-CSP	258298	N880SP	258379	N879WC	258460	N85PK	258541	N800XP
258211	N855GA	258299	N601DR	258380	N101FC	258461	N828LX	258542	N842QS
258212	N323L	258300	N950PC	258381	02-3014	258462	LV-ZTR	258543	N843CW
258213	wfu	258301	PT-WMA	258382	EI-WXP	258463	N863QS	258544	N799JC
258214	PT-OOI	258302	XA-GIE	258383	N806LX	258464	N828NS	258545	N845QS
258215	29-3041	258303	N4SA	258384	G-LAOR	258465	VT-RPL	258546	N488VC
258219	N8881J	258304	N5734	258385	SE-DYV	258466	N829LX	258547	PR-OPP
258222	G-VIPI	258305	72-3006	258386	N715WT	258467	N42FB	258548	N808TA
258224	N65DL	258306	82-3007	258387	N887QS	258468	CS-DNT	258549	N155NS
258226	N800MJ	258307	N85CC	258388	N809BA	258469	22-3019	258550	N793RC
258227	39-3042	258308	N875LP	258389	YL-MAR	258470	B-3991	258552	N834LX
258228	N130LC	258309	N92UP	258390	N800FD	258471	N5736	258553	PR-LUG
258229	N984HM	258310	N33VC	258391	4X-CPS	258472	N872QS	258554	XA-GTE
258230	N800RG	258311	N850J	258392	LX-GBY	258473	N73UP	258555	N300CQ
258231	ZS-PSE	258312	N924JM	258393	N893QS	258474	N874QS	258556	N800WY
258232	C-FBUR	258313	N411VZ	258394	N800TL	258475	N829NS	258557	N1630
258233	G-BYHM	258314	N800NJ	258395	PT-WVG	258476	N830NS	258558	N225PB
258234	N65CE	258315	N9292X	258396	N21EL	258477	VP-BOO	258559	N819AB
258235	OY-RAA	258316	C-GDII	258397	N852LX*	258478	N800DR	258560	N8778
258236	N58BL	258317	N520JF	258398	TC-VSC	258479	CS-DNU	258561	I-ALHO
258237	N250MB	258318	N1910H	258399	CS-DNJ	258480	N4403	258562	N802DC
258238	N100AG	258319	C-FIPE	258400	N314TC	258481	HZ-KSRC	258563	N981CE
258239	C-GMLR	258320	N720TA	258401	EU93-6050	258482	N882QS	258564	N864QS
258240	G-WYNE	258321	N32BC	258402	N729AT	258483	N830LX	258565	N240Z
258241	XA-CHA	258322	N307RM	258403	N111VG	258484	N84UP	258566	N664AC
258242	49-3043	258323	N752CS	258404	N448JM	258485	N485LT	258567	N24SM
258243	C-FTVC	258324	N303BC	258405	D-CLBD	258486	N886QS	258568	N96FT
258244	N862CE	258325	82-3008	258406	N821LX	258487	N3007	258569	N906AS
258245	52-3001	258326	N897A	258407	12-3015	258488	N488HP	258570	N880QS

258571	RP-C8576	258655	N22SM	258729	N729AG	258812	D-CLBH	HA-25	P4-ANG
258572	N293S	258656	CS-DFX	258730	CS-DRF	258813	OE-GRF	HA-26	ZS-SAH
258573	N873QS	258657	N839LX	258731	XA-UGO	258814	N189TA	HA-27	N799AG*
258574	N915AM	258658	5N-JMA	258732	N870QS	258815	VT-KNB	HA-28	B-M..
258575	B-3997	258659	5N-JMB	258733	HB-VOB	258816	VP-COD	HA-29	N700WY
258576	N867QS	258660	N800RC	258734	N884QS	258817	N85HH	HA-30	N630JS
258577	N800UK	258661	N800WW	258735	TC-TAV	258818	N403CT	HA-31	N848QS
258578	N91HK	258662	N305SC	258737	N518M	258819	N405CT	HA-32	N932BC
258579	PK-TVO	258663	CS-DFY	258738	TC-ADO	258821	CS-DRU	HA-33	EC-KMT
258580	N1989D	258664	CS-DFW	258739	N499PA	258822	N103AL	HA-34	OK-KAZ
258581	XA-JCT	258665	N689AM	258740	N824LX	258823	N823XP	HA-35	P4-PET
258582	VP-CFS	258666	N840LX	258741	CS-DRG	258825	CS-DRV	HA-36	B-M..
258583	XA-GLG	258667	N802DR	258742	TC-FIN	258826	N826LX	HA-37	N865LS
258584	N884VC	258668	N156NS	258743	N885QS	258827	G-HSXP	HA-38	N34838
258585	N585VC	258669	N333PC*	258744	N744XP	258828	C-GCGT	HA-39	N580RJ
258586	N876QS	258670	ZS-...	258745	VT-FAF	258829	CS-DRW	HA-40	N16SM
258587	N770CC	258671	N184TB	258746	CS-DRH	258830	N111ZN	HA-41	N34441
258588	N799S	258672	N1CA	258747	N519M	258831	N676AH	HA-42	N888QS
258590	N733H	258673	CS-DFZ	258748	EC-JNY	258832	SU-MAN	HA-43	N87PK
258591	N380GP	258674	G-OJWB	258749	N50UG	258833	HS-CPG	HA-44	N944XP
258592	N892QS	258675	N351TC	258750	N1776A	258834	CS-DRX	HA-45	N3285N
258593	N898QS	258676	N676GH	258751	N751MT	258835	VP-CMA	HA-46	N31946
258594	N323MP	258677	N850CT	258752	N752MT	258836	N773HR	HA-47	N22VS
258595	N76CS	258678	N9867	258753	N805M	258837	N662JN	HA-48	N34548
258596	N804BH	258679	N800LA	258754	N754AE	258838	VT-OBR	HA-49	N31959
258597	XA-TYK	258680	N80E	258755	N575JR	258840	CS-DRY	HA-51	N951XP
258598	N92FT	258681	N80J	258756	CS-DRI	258841	VP-BMM	HA-52	N104AG
258599	N59BR	258682	D-CLBG	258757	N345MP	258844	VH-RAM	*125-1000*	
258600	N250SP	258683	N832QS	258758	N725CS	258845	TC-STD	NA1001	N100U
258601	ZS-DDA	258684	N684DK	258759	N426MJ	258847	CS-DRZ	NA1002	N168WU
258602	N899SC	258685	62-3024	258760	CS-DRJ	258848	N827LX	NA1003	N208R
258603	N893CW	258686	CS-DRA	258761	N761XP	258852	C-GROG	NA1004	N513LR
258604	N8186	258687	N733A	258762	N901SG	258855	LX-OKR	NA1005	N514LR
258605	C-GJKK	258689	F-HBFP	258763	N871QS	258856	B-3901	NA1006	N515LR
258606	N895QS	258690	CS-DRB	258764	N522EE	258858	B-3902	NA1007	N448CC
258607	N919RT	258691	N858QS	258765	CS-DRK	258859	OE-GNY	NA1008	N520LR
258608	I-KREM	258692	N700R	258766	N542M	258861	N850ME	NA1009	N52SM
258609	N80HD	258693	N302PE	258767	N825LX	258872	TC-SHE	NA1010	N523LR
258610	42-3022	258694	N800R	258768	N850VP	258874	TC-NUB	258151	wfu
258611	N944BB	258695	N39H	258769	CC-CAB	258876	N349AK	258159	wfu
258612	N612XP*	258696	N800PL	258770	CS-DRL	258891	N315JL	259003	N261PA
258613	N90FB	258697	N530SM	258771	CS-DRM	258893	N1620	259004	VP-CPT
258614	N811QS	258698	N860QS	258772	CS-DRN	258895	N3195F	259005	N505LR
258615	VP-CKN	258700	N108DD	258773	N883QS	258900	N850HB	259007	N119U
258616	N88HD	258701	N6NR	258774	N143RL	258901	N3201T	259008	N207TT
258617	P4-SEN	258702	VP-BAS	258775	CS-DRO	258904	N3204T	259012	I-SRAF
258618	G-IWDB	258703	N707JC	258776	N535BC	258907	N3207T	259016	N707HD
258619	N676JB	258704	N614BG	258777	N900ST	258909	N3289N	259017	N517LR
258620	N77CS	258705	N815QS	258778	OE-IPH	258912	N32012	259018	5N-DGN
258621	N522EF	258706	N74GW	258779	CS-DRP	*Hawker 750/900XP*		259021	N401FF
258622	N800EL	258707	LV-BBG	258780	VH-SGY	HA-1	N170DC*	259022	VH-LMP
258623	N221PB	258708	N799RM	258781	A6-ELC	HB-1	N751NS*	259024	ZS-ABG
258624	N660HC	258709	N821QS	258782	N126HY	HA-2	N1776C	259025	N501LR
258625	VP-BNK	258710	G-CDLT	258783	CS-DRQ	HB-2	N752NS*	259026	P4-MAF
258626	N25W	258711	N1910A	258784	N76FC	HA-3	N903XP	259027	N333RL
258628	XA-JET	258712	VH-MBP	258785	N785VC	HA-4	N351SP*	259028	N46WC
258629	52-3023	258713	N199DF	258786	CS-DRR	HA-5	N894QS	259029	EZ-B021
258630	N125ZZ	258714	CS-DRC	258787	N851CC	HA-6	N96SK	259030	HB-VOO
258631	N74NP	258715	N715PH	258788	N891QS	HB-6	CS-DUA*	259031	N301PE
258632	ZS-PZA	258716	VT-RBK	258789	N850NS	HA-7	N77TC	259032	N850TC
258633	ZS-PTP	258718	N718SJ	258790	TC-TKC	HB-7	CS-DUB*	259033	N533LR
258634	N808BL	258719	VP-BCW	258791	N225RB	HA-8	N900LD	259034	G-GMAB
258635	N919SF	258720	OM-USS	258792	A6-TBF	HB-8	CS-DUC*	259035	N525LR
258636	N800CQ	258721	CS-DRD	258793	TC-STB	HA-9	N901K	259036	N127RP
258637	PP-ANA	258722	I-PZZR	258794	VT-JHP	HA-10	N890QS	259037	G-FINK
258638	XA-NTE	258726	N405LA	258795	CS-DRS	HA-11	C-GGMP	259038	N403FF
258639	N95UP	258797	N71907	258796	N850KE	HB-11	CS-DUD*	259039	N539LR
258640	N896QS	*Hawker 800XPi/850XP*		258798	N850ZH	HA-12	N852CC	259040	N540LR
258641	N513ML	258551	N800LQ*	258799	HB-VOJ	HA-13	N900R	259041	N541LR
258642	N12PA	258589	ZS-PCY	258800	N865JT	HA-14	N897QS	259042	N542LR
258643	N33NL	258627	N929AK	258801	TC-DOY	HA-15	C-GVMP	259043	N698DC
258645	OY-OAA	258644	N484JC	258802	CS-DRT	HA-16	N575MA	259044	N544LR
258646	N528BP	258688	N688G	258803	N853CC	HA-17	ZS-KBS	259045	N207R
258647	N847CW	258699	N699XP	258804	OE-GRS	HA-18	N901RD	259046	N546LR
258648	N848CW	258717	ZS-PPH	258805	EI-KJC	HA-19	N899QS	259047	N547LR
258649	N800EM	258723	N627AH	258806	N906BL	HA-20	TC-...	259048	N548LR
258650	N50AE	258724	ZS-AFG	258807	VH-MQY	HA-21	N889QS	259049	N549LR
258651	N470BC	258725	CS-DRE	258808	TC-CLK	HA-22	N900PF	259050	N150LR
258652	N241JS	258727	N787JC	258809	I-TOPH	HA-23	HZ-BIN	259051	N880LT
258653	N203TM	258728	VP-CXP	258810	G-CERX	HA-24	N108PJ	259052	N800WD
258654	N149SB			258811	LY-DSK				

348

Hawker 4000

RC-1	N4000R
RC-2	N802HH
RC-3	N803HH
RC-4	N804HH
RC-5	N805HH
RC-6	N607HB*
RC-7	N7007Q
RC-8	N803SA
RC-9	N119AK
RC-10	N126ZZ
RC-11	N974JD
RC-12	N400MR
RC-13	N413HB
RC-14	N514HB
RC-15	N515HB
RC-20	N500S
RC-21	N621HB
RC-22	N100QS
RC-23	N423HB
RC-24	N35004

Premier 1/1A

RB-1	N390RA
RB-2	N704T
RB-3	N390TC
RB-4	N414TE
RB-5	N808V
RB-6	N155RM
RB-7	N343PR
RB-8	N460AS
RB-9	N21XP
RB-10	N5010X
RB-11	N50PN
RB-12	OE-FRJ
RB-13	N48TC
RB-14	N969RE
RB-15	N929SS
RB-16	C-GYPV
RB-17	N88ER
RB-18	N23WA
RB-19	N16DK
RB-20	YL-KSC
RB-21	PR-AMA
RB-22	N223F
RB-23	VT-RAL
RB-24	N903MT
RB-25	N719L
RB-26	wo
RB-27	D-IFMC
RB-28	N128JL
RB-29	N110PR
RB-30	N84FM
RB-31	ZS-AVM
RB-32	PR-CIM
RB-33	N677AS
RB-34	N390DP
RB-35	D-IAGG
RB-36	N1XT
RB-37	N567T
RB-38	N972PF
RB-39	N390JK
RB-40	N86RB
RB-41	OE-FMC
RB-42	N324AM
RB-43	N1EG
RB-44	N88MM
RB-45	N100WE
RB-46	N460L
RB-47	N581SF
RB-48	D-IATT
RB-49	N25MC
RB-50	D-ISXT
RB-51	N530PT
RB-52	N605TC
RB-53	N351CW
RB-54	N354RB
RB-55	N85PL
RB-56	PK-...
RB-57	OE-FRC
RB-58	N34GN
RB-59	N622JK
RB-60	G-PREI
RB-61	EC-IOZ
RB-62	N800CS
RB-63	ZS-DDM
RB-64	LX-PMR
RB-65	PR-GCA
RB-66	G-VONJ
RB-67	N167DP
RB-68	N133B
RB-69	N205BC
RB-70	N70BR
RB-71	N71KV
RB-72	ZS-SGS
RB-73	N107WR
RB-74	VP-CWW
RB-75	N213PQ
RB-76	N1XH
RB-77	OE-FKW
RB-78	N390JW
RB-79	wo
RB-80	N50PM
RB-81	N134SW
RB-82	D-IBBB
RB-83	LY-HER
RB-84	PR-JRR
RB-85	N487DT
RB-86	N96NC
RB-87	N952GM
RB-88	G-OMJC
RB-89	D-IWWW
RB-90	N32SG
RB-91	N45NB
RB-92	N592HC
RB-93	N322BJ
RB-94	ZS-PFE
RB-95	N24YP
RB-96	N535CD
RB-97	G-FRYL
RB-98	N500CZ
RB-99	N199RM
RB-100	N122DS
RB-101	N73PJ
RB-102	N227FH
RB-103	N781KB
RB-104	N855JB
RB-105	N777JF
RB-106	N20NL
RB-107	N877W
RB-108	N61908
RB-109	D-IFMG
RB-110	N300SL
RB-111	N713AZ
RB-112	N76HL
RB-113	N390PR
RB-114	N143CM
RB-115	N72SJ
RB-116	N200LB
RB-117	N6117G
RB-118	N390BR
RB-119	N84EA
RB-120	UN-P1001
RB-121	N520CH
RB-122	G-CJAG
RB-123	N112CM
RB-124	N23SP
RB-125	G-PHTO
RB-126	G-OEWD
RB-127	N18RF
RB-128	VT-ANF
RB-129	N390JV
RB-130	N401PP
RB-131	G-CJAH
RB-132	N48VC*
RB-133	N967F
RB-134	N84VA
RB-135	N390PT
RB-136	N462CB
RB-137	N451MM
RB-138	VP-BPO
RB-139	N239RT
RB-140	N22VK
RB-141	N484AT
RB-142	N767CS
RB-143	N727KG
RB-144	N541RS
RB-145	N42EL
RB-146	N1CR
RB-147	N147FM
RB-148	D-ISAR
RB-149	F-HAST
RB-150	N6150Y
RB-151	N103SK
RB-152	HB-VOI
RB-153	N888MN
RB-154	XA-RRG
RB-155	N3725L
RB-156	N3726T
RB-157	N88EL
RB-158	N727MH
RB-159	N145JF*
RB-160	EC-KHH
RB-161	N6JR
RB-162	N608CW
RB-163	N72GD
RB-164	D-IDBA
RB-165	N800FR
RB-166	N36866
RB-167	N404JM
RB-168	N64PM
RB-169	N837JM
RB-170	N7170Y
RB-171	N17CJ
RB-172	G-EVRD
RB-173	N213PC
RB-174	N855RM
RB-175	VH-VHP
RB-176	N906FM
RB-177	A6-RZJ
RB-178	N102CL
RB-179	N33PJ
RB-180	N835ZT
RB-181	VP-BBQ
RB-182	N246DF
RB-183	N994JR
RB-184	N368CS
RB-185	N502PM
RB-186	N2HZ
RB-187	HB-VOS
RB-188	N7088S
RB-189	VP-CFW
RB-190	N537RB
RB-191	N992SC
RB-192	N91BB
RB-193	N408J
RB-194	N276RS
RB-195	A9C-RJA
RB-196	D-IIMC
RB-197	N115WZ
RB-198	C-FDMM
RB-199	N716GS
RB-200	N81HR
RB-201	I-DMSA
RB-202	VP-CAZ
RB-203	N203BP
RB-204	RP-C390
RB-205	N801SA
RB-206	N306BP
RB-207	N207AH
RB-208	N208BP
RB-209	M-YSKY
RB-210	PT-SBF*
RB-211	N701KB
RB-212	N42SC
RB-213	N952GL
RB-214	N814BP
RB-215	OE-FAP
RB-216	N3216G
RB-217	N3217P
RB-218	N3K
RB-219	VT-...
RB-220	VP-BFU
RB-221	D-ISAG
RB-222	N32022
RB-223	N427DB*
RB-224	N3204P
RB-225	N3205W
RB-227	N166AN
RB-228	N3228M
RB-229	N229RB
RB-230	N3330S
RB-231	N390GS
RB-232	N208HP
RB-233	N233WC

Israeli Aircraft Ind
Astra-1125 SPX

001	wfu
002	4X-WIA
003	wfu
004	OB-1703
011	N500FA
012	N939MC
013	N112PR
014	N116JC
015	N157GA
016	N221PA
017	N455SH
018	N72EL
019	N49MN
020	N917SC
021	N200CK
022	PT-MBZ
023	N345GC
024	N999BL
025	N902AU
026	N24PR
027	N199HE
028	N800ZZ
029	N956PP
030	N900DL
031	N962A*
032	N116PB
033	N441BC
034	N541RL
035	N1125K
036	N757BD
037	N100SR
038	N777AM
039	N636BC
040	N666K
041	N41AU
042	N528RR
043	N43MH
044	N1UA
045	N916CG
046	N630S
047	N166RM
048	N88MF
049	N293P
050	N45H
051	N1125A
052	N90AJ
053	N717CP
054	N187HF*
055	ZS-MDA
056	N790FH
057	N157SP
058	C-FDAX
059	pass
060	VP-BON
061	N200ST
062	N874WD
063	N331SK
064	N650GF
065	N50TQ
066	C-FMHL
067	N730DF
068	N401WT
069	N247PS
070	N448GR
071	N71FS
072	N365GA
073	N918MJ
074	N789CA
075	N928JA
076	N20YL
077	YV1771
078	N1125J
079	N800PW
080	N411MM
081	N801G
082	N882GA
083	N383SF
084	N801RS
085	N796HR
086	PT-WBC
087	C-FRJZ
088	94-1569
089	N89HS
090	94-1570
091	N818WF
092	N100G
093	N207BC
094	N294S
095	C6-JET
096	N323P
097	N363NH
098	N275RA
099	N115BR
100	N907DP
101	N610SM
102	N877D
103	N755A
104	N957F
105	N105FN
106	N800WS
107	D-CRIS
108	N108CG
109	N96FL
110	N97FL
111	HB-VOA
112	N1MC
113	N82BE
114	N114SN
115	N514MM
116	N12ND
117	C-GGHZ
118	N28NP
119	B-20001
120	N100GY
121	N188AK
122	N110MG
123	N307JW
124	N777FZ
125	N625MM
126	L3458
127	N919DS
128	N314AD
129	N424MP
130	C-GBSW

G100

059	D-CABB
131	N400CP
132	N722AZ
133	OE-GBD
134	N1125S
135	N809JW
136	N43RJ
137	N620KE
138	N810JW
139	N420CE
140	N811JW
141	N223GA
142	N109GX
143	VT-BAV
144	VP-BMT
145	N387PA
146	VP-BMW
147	N147SW
148	L3467
149	N749GA
150	C-FHRL
151	C-GTDO

349

152	N160CT	074	N889MR	155	N135FT	248	N637SF	78	wfu
153	OE-GBE	075	N200YB	156	N101L	249	N191CP	79	wfu
154	XA-MEG	076	N200BA	157	N748QS		Commander/Westwind	80	wfu
155	N445AK	077	N277GA	158	ZK-RGB	1	wfu	81	wo
156	C-FHNS	078	N278GA	159	SX-SMG	2	wfu	82	wfu
157	N327GA	079	N382G	160	N670RW	3	N409WT	83	wo
158	EC-JXE	080	XA-MDK	161	N49VC	4	wfu	84	N16MK

Galaxy

003	wfu	081	N414DH	162	N719QS	5	wfu	85	wfu
005	N505GA	082	N402LM	163	SX-SEA	6	wfu	86	wfu
006	N8MF	083	N403LM	164	N200JB	7	wfu	87	wfu
007	HB-IUT	084	N1Z	165	N749QS	8	wfu	88	wfu
008	N479PR	085	N720QS	166	N631DV	9	wfu	89	wfu
010	N672PS	086	XA-JHE	167	N200GV	10	wfu	90	wfu
011	LZ-FIB	087	N707SG	168	N755QS	11	wfu	91	wo
012	YR-TIG	088	N704JW	169	N10XQ	12	wo	92	wfu
015	N622SV	089	YR-TII	170	N745QS	13	wfu	93	wfu
016	N135BP	090	B-KMJ	171	EC-KLL	14	wfu	94	N64AH
017	N48GX	091	N2HL	172	N172EX	15	wfu	95	N85JW
019	N219AX	092	N721QS	173	N403GA	16	wfu	96	wfu
020	N516CC	093	N722QS	174	B-8087	17	wfu	97	wfu
021	N321SF	094	N121GV	175	N62GB	18	wfu	98	wfu

G200

		095	N331BN	176	N761QS	19	wfu	99	N63357
004	PR-WTR	096	N600YB	177	N677GA	20	wfu	100	wfu
009	N200AX	097	N816JW	178	N758QS	21	wfu	101	wfu
013	N200BH	098	VT-ARV	179	N797M	22	wo	102	wfu
014	N467MW	099	N723QS	180	N480GA	23	wfu	103	wfu
018	4X-COG	100	N724QS	181	N461GA	24	wfu	104	wfu
022	N322AD	101	N201GA	182	N482GA	25	wfu	105	wfu
023	N32TM	102	N601DV	183	N636GA	26	wfu	106	N814T
024	N188ML	103	EC-JGN	184	N384GA	27	wfu	107	wfu
025	N866G	104	N271RA	185	N285GA	28	N234G	108	wfu
026	N800PJ	105	N725QS	186	N486GA	29	wo	109	XA-THF
027	PR-OFT	106	N851LE		G150	30	wo	110	wfu
028	N199HF	107	N707BC	201	N150RT	31	wfu	111	wfu
029	N929GA	108	N726QS	202	N703HA	32	wfu	112	N710DC
030	N133BA	109	N819AP	203	N530GP	33	wfu	113	wfu
031	N62GX	110	N967PC	204	N373ML	34	wfu	114	wfu
032	HB-JEB	111	N88WU	205	N715WG	35	wfu	115	wfu
033	N212MP	112	C-GTRL	206	N830DB	36	wfu	116	wo
034	N134AX	113	N727QS	207	N531GP	37	wfu	117	wfu
035	N110HA	114	B-8085	208	N150CT	38	wfu	118	N696RV
036	B-KSJ	115	N200LV	209	N501RP	39	wfu	119	N119AC
037	B-8083	116	N728QS	210	N650GE	40	wfu	120	wfu
038	N602VC	117	N162GB	211	N248SL	41	wfu	121	wo
039	N132JC	118	N729QS	212	N502RP	42	wfu	122	N122ST
040	4X-CLL	119	C-GWPB	213	N5950C	43	wfu	123	wfu
041	YV1401	120	N730QS	214	N777FL	44	wfu	124	wfu
042	N755PA	121	N818JW	215	N503RP	45	wfu	125	N1121R
043	N123GV	122	N173JM	216	N192SW	46	wfu	126	wo
044	N882LT	123	N731QS	217	N150GD	47	wfu	127	N277MG
045	N70TT	124	N765M	218	N969WR	48	wo	128	N404WC
046	N889G	125	EC-JQE	219	CC-CWK	49	wfu	129	wfu
047	N601AB	126	N916GR	220	N197HF	50	wfu	130	wo
048	N602AB	127	N737QS	221	N532GP	51	wfu	131	wfu
049	N753BC	128	N102FD	222	N717EP	52	wfu	132	wo
050	OE-HFC	129	N711QS	223	N350BN	53	wfu	133	N132LA
051	N140KR	130	N565GB	224	N590FA	54	wfu	134	N134N
052	N700QS	131	N706QS	225	N150PU	55	wfu	135	wfu
053	N815JW	132	N751BC	226	N8821C	56	N382AA	136	wo
054	N54AX	133	N200VR*	227	N451R	57	wfu	137	wfu
055	N212SL	134	N88AY	228	VP-BMA	58	wfu	138	wfu
056	N929WG	135	B-8081	229	N8841C	59	wfu	139	wfu
057	N886G	136	N718QS	230	N722SW	60	wo	140	wo
058	N726DC	137	N137WB	231	N9611Z	61	wo	141	wfu
059	N409LM	138	N787PR	232	N928ST	62	wfu	142	N1944P
060	N703QS	139	N204DD	233	EC-KMF	63	wfu	143	wfu
061	N705QS	140	PR-AUR	234	N511CT	64	wfu	144	wfu
062	N957P	141	N701QS	235	D-CKDM	65	wo	145	N805SM
063	N363GA	142	N235LC	236	N77709	66	wfu	146	wfu
064	N2BG	143	N143GA	237	EC-KMS	67	wfu	147	N912DA
065	SX-ONE	144	N217BA	238	N150GA	68	wo	148	wfu
066	N707QS	145	EC-KBC	239	AP-MMM	69	wfu	149	wfu
067	N916GB	146	N602RF	240	N360AV	70	wfu	150	wo
068	N179AE	147	N603RF	241	N480JJ*	71	wfu	151	ZP-AGD
069	N708QS	148	N716QS	242	N442GA	72	wfu	152	4X-JYR
070	N702QS	149	SX-IDA	243	N443GA	73	wfu	153	wfu
071	N459BN	150	EC-KCA	244	N744GA	74	N274MA	154	N176AK
072	N892SB	151	N619KS	245	N745GA	75	wfu	155	N707TF
073	N712QS	152	N752QS	246	N96AD	76	wfu	156	N35D
		153	B-LMJ	247	N110FS	77	N177JC	157	wfu
		154	N236LC					158	wfu

159	wfu	240	N298HM	321	N810VC	402	N51TV	5036	wfu
160	XA-RIZ	241	N300TC	322	N990S	403	N403W	5037	wfu
161	wfu	242	N500BJ	323	VH-KNS	404	N29CL	5038	wfu
162	N13GW	243	wo	324	N404HR	405	N424JR	5039	wfu
163	wfu	244	N911SP	325	N68PT	406	N830	5040	wfu
164	wfu	245	N270LC	326	wo	407	N407W	5041	wfu
165	N30156	246	N911CU	327	N50M	408	N125HF	5042	wfu
166	wfu	247	wo	328	N328PC	409	N26KL	5043	wfu
167	wfu	248	VH-AJJ	329	N124HS	410	N777DC	5044	wfu
168	wfu	249	wfu	330	YV1685	411	N224PA	5045	wfu
169	N44PR	250	N418WA	331	N811VC	412	N870BA	5046	wfu
170	wfu	251	PT-LDY	332	N43RP	413	N35LH	5047	wfu
171	wfu	252	N553MC	333	HR-PHO	414	N550HB	5048	N428DA
172	YV-2482P	253	wfu	334	N325LW	415	N415TH	5049	wfu
173	wfu	254	RP-C....	335	N21HR	416	N600KE	5050	wfu
174	XA-UHJ	255	N424CS	336	N525XX	417	N34FS	5051	N488GR
175	wfu	256	VH-AJK	337	VP-BLT	418	N26TN	5052	wfu
176	N35CR	257	N79LC	338	wo	419	N728MB	5053	XC-JCC
177	wfu	258	N771B	339	ZK-RML	420	N728TG	5054	N721PA
178	wfu	259	wfu	340	VH-KNR	421	N520MP	5055	wfu
179	N114RA	260	N525AK	341	N818JH	422	N87GJ	5056	wfu
180	wfu	261	N11LN	342	N274HM	423	N680ME	5057	wfu
181	N345BS	262	N150EX	343	N911GU*	424	N790JR	5058	wfu
182	LV-WYL	263	N918SS	344	N769MS	425	N328SA	5059	wfu
183	LV-WLR	264	N809VC	345	N345TR	426	N75BC	5060	wfu
184	N481MC	265	N7DJ	346	N610SE	427	N229D	5061	wfu
185	4X-JYJ	266	N5HQ	347	N347GA	428	N57BE	5062	wfu
186	4X-JYO	267	N55FG	348	N960FA	429	N42FL	5063	wfu
187	N187TJ	268	N56BP	349	N123RC	430	N430PT	5064	wfu
188	N118RJ	269	N21DX	350	wo	431	N431WA	5065	wfu
189	N42CM	270	wo	351	N124BC	432	N60BT	5066	XA-MIK
190	N313TW	271	C-FJOJ	352	N117AH	433	N433GM	5067	wo
191	N900FS	272	wfu	353	EC-GSL	434	N564RM	5068	wo
192	N819RC	273	N104RS	354	N894TW	435	N140VJ	5069	wfu
193	N98BM	274	N274K	355	N241CT	436	N444EP	5070	wfu
194	N807BF	275	N96TM	356	N993DS	437	N437SJ	5071	wfu
195	N951DB	276	N300XL	357	N914DM	438	N100BC	5072	wfu
196	N606MA	277	C-GAWJ	358	N404PG	439	N439WW	5073	wfu
197	wo	278	C-GHYD	359	N14CN	440	N220DH	5074	wfu
198	N750SP	279	wo	360	N500KE	441	C-FPEP	5075	wfu
199	C-FTWO	280	N949CC	361	N3AV	442	N830C	5076	wfu
200	N4WG	281	VH-AJG	362	YV251T	**Lockheed**		5077	wo
201	N124WW	282	VH-AJV	363	N420JM			5078	wfu
202	N469WC	283	N95JK	364	N67DT	*JetStar*		5079	N58TS
203	N22RD	284	N727AT	365	N73CL	1001	wfu	5080	N77HW
204	wfu	285	N85PT	366	N320MD	1002	wfu	5081	wfu
205	N331AP	286	N113GH	367	N367WW	5001	wfu	5082	3C-QQU
206	N148H	287	N530DL	368	N83SG	5002	wfu	5083	N198DL
207	C-FTWR	288	N711KE	369	N76ER	5003	wfu	5084	wo
208	N57PT	289	N900VP	370	N875P	5004	wfu	5085	wfu
209	N705AC	290	N719CC	371	wo	5005	wfu	5086	N313JS
210	N2150H	291	N917BE	372	N942EB	5006	wfu	5087	N33SJ
211	wo	292	N741C	373	N794TK	5007	wfu	5088	wfu
212	N700MD	293	N26TZ	374	N43W	5008	wo	5089	wfu
213	N27TZ	294	N147A	375	N66VA	5009	wfu	5090	wfu
214	N21SF	295	N730CA	376	VH-ZYH	5010	wfu	5091	wfu
215	N238DB	296	N710SA	377	N301PC	5011	wfu	5092	wfu
216	N290CA	297	N335VB	378	N481NS	5012	wfu	5093	wfu
217	N163WC	298	N809JC	379	N302SG	5013	wfu	5094	wfu
218	N426RJ	299	N67TJ	380	wo	5014	wfu	5095	wfu
219	N290CP	300	PR-STJ*	381	N50FD	5015	wfu	5096	wfu
220	N9RD	301	N890BA	382	N445BL	5016	wfu	5097	N922MS
221	wo	302	wo	383	N942WC	5017	wfu	5098	XA-TVK
222	N598JM	303	N211ST	384	wo	5018	wfu	5099	N18BH
223	N518WA	304	N78PT	385	N317JS	5019	wfu	5100	wfu
224	N349MC	305	N804CC	386	N386RL	5020	wfu	5101	wfu
225	N30MR	306	HK-4204	387	VH-NGA	5021	wfu	5102	wfu
226	C-GTWV	307	N4SQ	388	N388WW	5022	wfu	5103	wfu
227	N624KM	308	N639AT	389	N89AM	5023	wfu	5104	wfu
228	N795FM	309	wo	390	N122MP	5024	wfu	5105	wfu
229	N40GG	310	N78GJ	391	N303SG	5025	wfu	5106	YV-03CP
230	N1KT	311	N53LM	392	N793BG	5026	wfu	5107	wfu
231	N600NY	312	N316TD*	393	N491AN	5027	wfu	5108	wfu
232	N4MH	313	C-GDSR	394	N63PP	5028	wfu	5109	wfu
233	N36SF	314	N49CT	395	N395TJ	5029	wfu	5110	wfu
234	N161A	315	N124GR	396	N37BE	5030	wo	5111	wfu
235	N903MM	316	N33TW	397	N777HD	5031	wfu	5112	N475MD
236	N22LZ	317	VH-KNU	398	N41C	5032	wfu	5113	N542TW
237	N24KL	318	N38AE	399	N48SD	5033	wfu	5114	wfu
238	VH-AJP	319	N788FS	400	N900TN	5034	wfu	5115	wfu
239	HK-2485W	320	N204TM	401	N30GF	5035	wo	5116	wfu

5117	wfu	5236	ST-FSA	282-9	165509	282-97	wo	306-38	XC-HGY
5118	wfu	5237	YI-AKC	282-10	wo	282-98	N767JH	306-39	wfu
5119	N9GU	5238	YI-AKD	282-11	wfu	282-99	N12BW	306-40	wfu
5120	wfu	5239	YI-AKE	282-12	wfu	282-101	N160W	306-41	wo
5121	wfu	5240	YI-AKF	282-13	XA-TKW	282-102	XB-JKV	306-42	XA-VEL
5122	wfu	Tristar		282-14	wfu	282-103	wfu	306-43	N115CR
5123	N725MK	1064	P4-MED	282-15	N43WL	282-104	wfu	306-44	N562MS
5124	XC-SKI	1067	N140SC	282-16	wfu	282-105	wfu	306-45	wo
5125	wfu	1079	N125DT	282-17	wfu	282-106	YV120T	306-46	N642RP
5126	wfu	1247	HZ-AB1	282-18	wfu	282-107	wo	306-47	XA-ESX
5127	wfu	1249	N388LS	282-19	165519	282-108	N8500	306-48	N4NT
5128	wfu	1250	N389LS	282-20	165523	282-109	FAE-047	306-49	wfu
5129	wfu	Morane Saulnier		282-21	wfu	282-110	wfu	306-50	N601GL
5130	wfu	MS760 Paris		282-22	wo	282-111	N7KG	306-51	N60JC
5131	wfu			282-23	N123CD	282-112	XA-UEY	306-52	wfu
5132	XA-BEB	01	F-BLKL	282-24	N8AF	282-113	N430MP	306-53	wfu
5133	wfu	2	N207MJ	282-25	wfu	282-114	XB-MDG	306-54	N610RA
5134	wfu	5	wo	282-26	XA-RED	282-115	XA-LML	306-55	158844
5135	wfu	6	wfu	282-27	wfu	282-116	wfu	306-56	XA-DSC
5136	5A-DAJ	8	N60GT	282-29	165511	282-117	N265SC	306-57	XA-RLS
5137	5-9001	9	N722Q	282-30	165514	282-118	wfu	306-58	XA-AGT
5138	wfu	27	N760PJ	282-31	N34AM	282-119	wo	306-59	N10LX
5139	wfu	28	N760X	282-32	165520	282-120	YV225T	306-60	N15HF
5140	wfu	30	N761X	282-33	N168W	282-121	wfu	306-61	wfu
5141	wfu	34	N371AS	282-34	N940CC	282-122	N409GL	306-62	wfu
5142	wfu	36	N373AS	282-35	wfu	282-123	XB-ESS	306-63	XA-TSS
5143	wfu	38	N374AS	282-36	wfu	282-124	XA-TYZ	306-64	wfu
5144	3908	39	F-BJET	282-37	wo	282-125	XA-SQA	306-65	159361
5145	wfu	41	N41NY	282-38	N339PM	282-126	N40GT	306-66	wfu
5146	wfu	43	N760S	282-39	wfu	282-127	wo	306-67	wfu
5147	wfu	44	N375AS	282-40	wfu	282-128	XB-JPS	306-68	FAE-049
5148	XA-…	45	N378AS	282-41	XA-…	282-129	XA-RLH	306-69	159364
5149	wfu	49	wo	282-42	wfu	282-130	wfu	306-70	159365
5150	N911CR	50	wo	282-43	FAE-043	282-131	LV-WND	306-71	N71CC
5151	wfu	51	N751PJ	282-44	N64MA	282-132	N240JR	306-72	XA-PRO
5152	wfu	53	N53PJ	282-45	N333NM	282-133	I-RELT	306-73	N442RM
5153	N416SJ	54	N354AS	282-47	wo	282-134	N40NJ	306-74	wo
5154	wfu	56	N956P	282-48	N47VL	282-135	N2006	306-75	N11LX
5155	wfu	57	N657P	282-49	86001	282-136	CP-2317	306-76	N86CP
5156	wfu	58	N760F	282-50	wfu	282-137	XA-LMA	306-77	wfu
5157	wfu	59	N959P	282-51	wfu	Sabre 50		306-78	N477X
5158	wfu	60	N7601R	282-52	N64DH	287-1	N50CR	306-79	N539PG
5159	XB-DBS	61	N961P	282-53	wfu	Sabre 60		306-80	N61FB
5160	wfu	69	wfu	282-54	wo	306-1	N359WJ	306-81	wfu
5161	XB-KCV	71	N571PJ	282-55	wfu	306-2	N36RZ	306-82	N59K
5162	XA-HNY	72	N760FR	282-56	XA-RPS	306-3	wo	306-83	XA-RLL
5201	N777AY	75	N975P	282-57	wfu	306-4	N121JE	306-84	N265GM
5202	wfu	81	N81PJ	282-58	wfu	306-5	N161CM	306-85	N211BR
5203	1003	82	N761JS	282-59	wfu	306-6	XA-SMF	306-86	XA-ICK
5204	N814K	86	N9035Y	282-60	wo	306-7	XA-HDL	306-87	XA-RFB
5205	N72GW	87	N87NY	282-61	165517	306-8	wfu	306-88	XA-RAP
5206	wfu	88	N760JS	282-62	wfu	306-9	wfu	306-89	wfu
5207	N34WR	89	N999PJ	282-63	XB-IHB	306-10	wfu	306-90	N265MK
5208	N95BK	90	N69X	282-64	wfu	306-11	wo	306-91	LV-WXX
5209	wfu	92	N763JS	282-65	XA-MJE	306-12	wfu	306-92	N33JW
5210	wo	93	N764JS	282-66	165513	306-13	RF-14423	306-93	XB-IXJ
5211	N118B	94	N765JS	282-67	N140RF	306-14	wfu	306-94	N348W
5212	wfu	97	PP-XUM	282-68	wo	306-15	wfu	306-95	N124DC
5213	N65JT	98	wo	282-69	wfu	306-16	wfu	306-96	XB-ETV
5214	XA-…	99	wo	282-70	N3280G	306-17	wfu	306-97	XA-SVG
5215	N175MD	101	N520DB	282-71	XA-SMR	306-18	N29PB	306-98	N531AB
5216	N797WQ	102	N20DA	282-72	165515	306-19	wfu	306-99	wfu
5217	N1MJ	103	wfu	282-73	wfu	306-20	XC-AAJ	306-100	XA-TMF
5218	wfu	104	N760R	282-74	wfu	306-21	XC-AAC	306-101	N378D
5219	N800GD	105	F-BXQL	282-75	wfu	306-22	XA-CHP	306-102	N70HL
5220	TC-NOA	106	wfu	282-76	wfu	306-23	N616TR*	306-103	N234DC
5221	wo	107	N5879	282-77	165518	306-24	N600GL	306-104	160053
5222	N311RS	108	N760AR	282-78	wo	306-25	wfu	306-105	160054
5223	N887DT	111	N760FM	282-79	XA-CYS	306-26	XA-CEN	306-106	160055
5224	N116DD	112	wfu	282-80	XB-JGI	306-27	N103TA	306-107	160056
5225	N900DB	Sabre		282-81	165510	306-28	wfu	306-108	wo
5226	TC-SSS	Sabre 40		282-82	N39RG	306-29	wfu	306-109	XA-SBV
5227	N375MD	282-1	N116SC	282-83	wfu	306-30	wfu	306-110	XB-AJS
5228	XA-CON	282-2	165512	282-86	wfu	306-31	N274CA	306-111	wo
5229	XA-TCN	282-3	N467H	282-87	wfu	306-32	wfu	306-112	CC-CTC
5230	N701JH	282-4	wfu	282-88	wfu	306-33	wfu	306-113	XA-TVZ
5231	wfu	282-5	wo	282-89	wfu	306-34	AMT-203	306-115	FAB 001
5232	N77C	282-6	wo	282-90	165516	306-35	XB-JMR	306-116	N39CB
5233	HB-JGK	282-7	wfu	282-91	wfu	306-36	wfu	306-117	FAE-001A
5234	XA-EKT	282-8	wfu	282-92	N825SB	306-37	wfu	306-118	N607CF
5235	YI-AKB			282-94	165521			306-119	N41RG

306-120	N1GM	465-54	N65SR	380-54	N380FP	265-53	wfu	276-44	XA-TIW
306-121	N789SG	465-55	XB-RSC	380-55	XB-GSP	265-54	wfu	276-45	wfu
306-122	XA-GUR	465-56	N499NH	380-56	N22NB	265-55	wfu	276-46	wfu
306-123	XA-ATE	465-57	N355CD	380-57	JY-AFH	265-56	wfu	276-47	wfu
306-124	N48WS	465-58	N670H	380-58	XA-UEQ	265-57	wfu	276-48	wfu
306-125	XA-JML	465-59	N35CC	380-59	N1LT	265-58	wfu	276-49	wo
306-126	XA-TGA	465-60	N88BF	380-60	N60SL	265-59	wfu	276-50	wfu
306-127	XB-JTG	465-61	N117JW	380-61	wfu	265-60	wfu	276-51	wfu
306-128	XA-SJM	465-62	N265WS	380-62	JY-AFP	265-61	wfu	276-52	wo
306-129	XB-ULF	465-63	N2NL	380-63	N448W	265-62	wo	276-53	wfu
306-130	XA-AFG	465-64	wo	380-64	JY-JAS	265-63	wfu	276-54	wfu
306-131	wfu	465-65	N395GA	380-65	N972NR	265-64	wo	276-55	wo
306-132	XB-MMW	465-66	N964C	380-66	N819GY	265-65	wfu	Sabreliner T-39B	
306-133	N468RB	465-67	N921CC	380-67	wo	265-66	wfu	265-6	wfu
306-134	N282WW	465-68	N888UP	380-68	wfu	265-67	wfu	270-1	59-2873
306-135	N921MB	465-69	N65ML	380-69	wo	265-68	wfu	270-2	wfu
306-137	XA-SAH	465-70	N58HT	380-70	N110AJ	265-69	wfu	270-3	60-3474
306-138	XA-RVT	465-71	N75VC	380-71	XA-TSZ	265-70	wfu	270-4	wfu
306-139	wfu	465-72	N465SP	380-72	N933JC	265-71	wfu	270-5	wfu
306-140	XA-SSV	465-73	N651MK	Sabre 80		265-72	wfu	270-6	wfu
306-141	N141SL	465-74	N700JC	380-6	N184PC	265-73	wfu	Sabreliner T-39D	
306-142	N143DZ	465-75	N570R	380-9	N995RD	265-74	wfu	277-1	wfu
306-143	XA-TPU	465-76	N376D	380-11	wfu	265-75	wo	277-2	wfu
306-144	XC-UJF	306-114	N990PA	380-17	wfu	265-76	XA-TJZ	277-3	wfu
306-145	XC-JDC	Sabre 75		380-21	N82AF	265-77	wfu	277-4	wfu
306-146	N44DD	370-1	wfu	380-32	XA-JRF	265-78	wfu	277-5	wfu
Sabre 65		370-2	wfu	380-49	N265KC	265-79	wfu	277-6	wfu
465-1	N65HH	370-3	N125NX	380-50	XA-ACD	265-80	wfu	277-7	wfu
465-2	N124SD	370-4	N726JR	Sabreliner T-39A(265)		265-81	wfu	277-8	wfu
465-3	N65BT	370-5	XA-RYJ	265-1	wfu	265-82	wfu	277-9	wfu
465-4	N804PA	370-6	wfu	265-2	wfu	265-83	wfu	285-1	wfu
465-5	wo	370-8	wfu	265-3	wfu	265-84	wfu	285-2	wfu
465-6	N432CC	370-9	wfu	265-4	wo	265-85	wfu	285-3	wfu
465-7	N2700	Sabre 75A		265-5	wfu	265-86	XA-GDW	285-4	150972
465-8	XA-GAP	370-7	N670C	265-7	wfu	265-87	wfu	285-5	wfu
465-9	N6GV	380-1	N100EJ	265-8	wfu	265-88	wfu	285-6	wfu
465-10	N336RJ	380-2	YV265T	265-9	wfu	Sabreliner T-39A(276)		285-7	wfu
465-11	N57MQ	380-3	wfu	265-10	XA-TFD	276-1	wo	285-8	wfu
465-12	N73TJ	380-4	N11887	265-11	wfu	276-2	wfu	285-9	150977
465-13	N945CC	380-5	XA-TUD	265-12	wo	276-3	wfu	277-10	wfu
465-14	XA-SPM	380-7	wo	265-13	wfu	276-4	XA-TQR	285-10	wfu
465-15	N25VC	380-8	wo	265-14	XA-TIY	276-5	wfu	285-11	wfu
465-16	N75HL	380-10	wfu	265-15	XA-...	276-6	XA-TGO	285-12	wfu
465-17	N74VC	380-12	N75BS	265-16	wfu	276-7	wfu	285-13	wfu
465-18	N696US	380-13	AE-175	265-17	wfu	276-8	wo	285-14	wfu
465-19	N91BZ	380-14	wfu	265-18	wfu	276-9	wfu	285-15	wfu
465-20	N173A	380-15	N424R	265-19	wfu	276-10	wfu	285-16	wfu
465-21	N701FW	380-16	N801FT	265-20	wfu	276-11	wo	285-17	wfu
465-22	XB-RSH	380-18	wfu	265-21	wfu	276-12	wfu	285-18	wfu
465-23	N223LB	380-19	wfu	265-22	wfu	276-13	wo	285-19	wfu
465-24	N22CS	380-20	N109SB	265-23	wfu	276-14	wfu	285-20	wfu
465-25	N42DC	380-22	wfu	265-24	wfu	276-15	wfu	285-21	wfu
465-26	N770MD	380-23	N800CD	265-25	wfu	276-16	wfu	285-22	wfu
465-27	N4CS	380-24	wfu	265-26	wfu	276-17	wfu	285-23	wfu
465-28	N66GE	380-25	N400RS	265-27	wfu	276-18	wfu	285-24	150992
465-29	N976SR	380-26	wfu	265-28	wfu	276-19	wfu	285-25	wfu
465-30	N65TC	380-27	wo	265-29	wfu	276-20	wfu	285-26	151337
465-31	N265M	380-28	wfu	265-30	wfu	276-21	XA-TIX	285-27	wfu
465-32	HB-VCN	380-29	wfu	265-31	wfu	276-22	wfu	285-28	wfu
465-33	N265C	380-30	N42799	265-32	wfu	276-23	wfu	285-29	wfu
465-34	N47SE	380-31	wfu	265-33	wfu	276-24	wfu	285-30	wfu
465-35	N65AK	380-33	N802FT	265-34	wo	276-25	XA-...	285-31	wfu
465-36	N65MC	380-34	XC-DDA	265-35	wfu	276-26	wfu	285-32	wfu
465-37	N750CC	380-35	wo	265-36	wfu	276-27	XA-TDX	Sabreliner T-39E	
465-38	N850CC	380-36	wfu	265-37	wfu	276-28	wfu	282-46	wo
465-39	N901CD	380-37	wfu	265-38	wfu	276-29	wfu	282-84	wfu
465-40	N801SS	380-38	N316EQ	265-39	wfu	276-30	wfu	282-85	XA-AAW*
465-41	N800M	380-39	N105HD	265-40	wfu	276-31	wfu	282-93	158381
465-42	N875CA	380-40	XA-UEK	265-41	wfu	276-32	wfu	282-95	158380
465-43	N65T	380-41	N400NR	265-42	wfu	276-33	N39FS	282-96	wfu
465-44	N74BJ	380-42	N3RP	265-43	wo	276-34	wfu	**Swearingen**	
465-45	N265DS	380-43	wfu	265-44	wfu	276-35	wfu	SJ 30	
465-46	N65CC	380-44	N380GK	265-45	wfu	276-36	wfu	001	wfu
465-47	N33TR	380-45	wo	265-46	wfu	276-37	wfu	002	wo
465-48	N265CP	380-46	XC-AA89	265-47	wo	276-38	wfu	003	N30SJ
465-49	N697US	380-47	N33RZ	265-48	wo	276-39	XA-TJY	004	N404SJ
465-50	XB-MYP	380-48	XA-...	265-49	wo	276-40	wfu	005	N50SJ
465-51	N69WU	380-51	N380CF	265-50	wfu	276-41	62-4488	006	N901HB
465-52	N96RE	380-52	N929CG	265-51	wfu	276-42	wfu	007	N7SJ
465-53	N465BC	380-53	XA-...	265-52	wfu	276-43	wfu		

008	N200DV

VFW

VFW614

G14	wfu
G17	D-ADAM
G18	wfu
G19	wfu

BIZTURBOPROPS 2007

BizProps - Country Index

Country	Code	Page
ALGERIA	7T	528
ANGOLA	D2	370
ARGENTINA	LV	385
ARUBA	P4	503
AUSTRALIA	VH	507
AUSTRIA	OE	495
BAHAMAS	C6	367
BAHRAIN	A9C	357
BANGLADESH	S2	505
BELGIUM	OO	495
BERMUDA	VP-B	511
BOLIVIA	CP	366
BOTSWANA	A2	357
BRAZIL	PP	497
BULGARIA	LZ	387
BURKINA FASO	XT	517
CAMBODIA	XU	517
CAMEROON	TJ	507
CANADA	C	358
CAYMAN ISLANDS	VP-C	511
CENTRAL AFRICAN REPUBLIC	TL	507
CHAD	TT	507
CHILE	CC	366
CHINA	B	357
CHINA - HONG KONG	B-H	358
CHINA - TAIWAN	B	358
COLOMBIA	HK	378
CONGO BRAZZAVILLE	TN	507
CONGO KINSHASA	9Q	529
COSTA RICA	TI	506
CROATIA	9A	528
CYPRUS	5B	527
CZECH REPUBLIC / CZECHIA	OK	495
DENMARK	OY	496
DOMINICAN REPUBLIC	HI	378
ECUADOR	HC	377
EGYPT	SU	505
EIRE	EI	371
EL SALVADOR	YS	517
ERITREA	E3	371
FINLAND	OH	495
FRANCE	F	371
GABON	TR	507
GERMANY	D	367
GREAT BRITAIN	G	375
GREECE	SX	505
GUATEMALA	TG	506
HONDURAS	HR	382
HUNGARY	HA	376
ICELAND	TF	506
INDIA	VT	511
INDONESIA	PK	497
IRAN	EP	371
ISLE OF MAN	M	388
ISRAEL	4X	526
ITALY	I	382
IVORY COAST	TU	507
JAMAICA	6Y	528
JAPAN	JA	383
JORDAN	JY	385
KAZAKHSTAN	UN	507
KENYA	5Y	527
KOREA	HL	381
LATVIA	YL	517
LIBYA	5A	527
LITHUANIA	LY	387
LUXEMBOURG	LX	387
MADAGASCAR	5R	527
MALAWI	7Q	528
MALAYSIA	9M	529
MALI	TZ	507
MAURITANIA	5T	527
MAURITIUS	3B	526
MEXICO	XA	512
MONACO	3A	526
MOROCCO	CN	366
MOZAMBIQUE	C9	367
NAMIBIA	V5	512
NETHERLANDS	PH	496
NETHERLANDS ANTILLES	PJ	497
NEW ZEALAND	ZK	522
NICARAGUA	YN	517
NIGERIA	5N	527
NORWAY	LN	385
OMAN	A4O	357
PAKISTAN	AP	357
PANAMA	HP	381
PAPUA NEW GUINEA	P2	503
PARAGUAY	ZP	522
PERU	OB	494
PHILIPPINES	RP	504
POLAND	SP	505
PORTUGAL	CS	367
ROMANIA	YR	517
RUSSIA / RUSSIAN FEDERATION	RA	503
SAO TOME & PRINCIPE	S9	505
SAUDI ARABIA	HZ	382
SENEGAL	6V	528
SERBIA	YU	517
SEYCHELLES	S7	505
SLOVAKIA	OM	495
SLOVENIA	S5	505
SOUTH AFRICA	ZS	523
SPAIN	EC	370
SRI LANKA	4R	526
SUDAN	ST	505
SWEDEN	SE	504
SWITZERLAND	HB	376
TANZANIA	5H	527
THAILAND	HS	382
TOGO	5V	527
TURKEY	TC	506
TURKS & CAICOS ISLANDS	VQ-T	511
UGANDA	5X	527
UKRAINE	UR	507
UNITED ARAB EMIRATES	A6	357
URUGUAY	CX	367
USA	N	388
VENEZUELA	YV	517
VIETNAM	VN	510
ZAMBIA	9J	529
ZIMBABWE	Z	522

Business TurboProps - By Country

AP = PAKISTAN   Total 11

Civil
Reg	Yr	Type	c/n	Owner/Operator	Prev Regn
☐ AP-BBR	90	DHC 6-300	782	Oil & Gas Development Corp.	C-GEVP
☐ AP-BCQ	85	Conquest II	441-0352	Government of Punjab, Lahore.	N1213N
☐ AP-BCY	85	Conquest II	441-0350	Government of Sind, Karachi.	N12127
☐ AP-BFK	91	Reims/Cessna F406	F406-0059	M Nawaz, Karachi.	N3122E
☐ AP-CAA	77	King Air 200	BB-278	Directorate of Civil Aviation, Karachi.	AP-CAD

Military
☐ 11667	81	Gulfstream 840	11667	Pakistan Army,	N5919K
☐ 11733	84	Gulfstream 840	11733	Pakistan Army,	N56GA
☐ 927	82	King Air B200	BB-927	Pakistan Air Force, Rawalpindi.	N18262
☐ AP-...	04	King Air 350	FL-419	Pakistan MoD, Rawalpindi.	N810N
☐ AP-...	05	King Air 350	FL-444	Pakistan MoD, Rawalpindi.	N36744
☐ J 752	65	Fokker F 27-200	10281	Pakistan Air Force, 12 Squadron Chakala, Islamabad.	AP-ATW

A2 = BOTSWANA   Total 12

Civil
☐ A2-	79	King Air C90	LJ-842	Flying Mission, Gaborone	N90CE
☐ A2-AEZ	79	King Air 200	BB-421	Kalahari Air Services & Charter, Gaborone.	N4488L
☐ A2-AGO	90	King Air B200	BB-1353	De Beers Botswana Mining Co P/L. Orapa.	N15599
☐ A2-AHT	80	Conquest 1	425-0011	B L C Aviation Ltd.	N6161P
☐ A2-AHV	83	King Air F90-1	LA-212	Sladden International P/L. Gaborone.	N6726P
☐ A2-AHZ	76	King Air 200	BB-95	Air Charter Botswana P/L. Gaborone.	ZS-JPD
☐ A2-AJK	80	King Air 200	BB-704	Botswana Ash,	ZS-KLO
☐ A2-DBH	81	King Air C90	LJ-988	Air Charter Botswana P/L. Gaborone.	ZS-LUU
☐ A2-KAS	80	King Air 200	BB-614	Air Charter Botswana P/L. Gaborone.	ZS-LKA
☐ A2-MXI	79	King Air 200T	BT-5	Maxi Save, (was BB-469).	N205EC
☐ A2-OLM	01	Beech 1900D	UE-423	Debswana Diamond Co P/L. Gaborone.	N3241X

Military
☐ OB-2	90	King Air B200	BB-1352	Government/Botswana Defence Force, Gaborone.	N5568V

A4O = OMAN   Total 1

Civil
☐ A4O-CQ	84	Dornier 228-100	7028	Royal Oman Police, Seeb.	D-IBLN

A6 = UNITED ARAB EMIRATES   Total 6

Civil
☐ A6-	89	King Air 300LW	FA-204		N65LW
☐ A6-MAR	89	DHC 6-300	841	Mohammed Abdul Rahim Al Ali, Dubai	N9045S
☐ A6-SKY	68	King Air B90	LJ-397	UAQ Aeroclub, Um Al Quwain.	ZS-OYS
☐ A6-YST	98	Beech 1900D	UE-324	Dubai Air Wing, Dubai.	ZS-OYL

Military
☐ 801	96	King Air 350	FL-131	United Arab Emirates Air Force.	A6-MHH
☐ 825	96	King Air 350	FL-132	United Arab Emirates Air Force.	A6-KHZ

A9C = BAHRAIN   Total 1

Civil
☐ A9C-...	67	King Air A90	LJ-301		N11FL

B = CHINA   Total 11

Civil
☐ B-3551	85	King Air B200	BB-1204	CAAC Special Services Division, Beijing.	N6927C
☐ B-3552	85	King Air B200	BB-1205	CAAC Special Services Division, Beijing.	N6927D
☐ B-3553	85	King Air B200	BB-1206	CAAC Special Services Division, Beijing.	N6927G
☐ B-3581	94	King Air 350	FL-111	CAAC Special Services Division, Beijing.	N8139K
☐ B-3582	94	King Air 350	FL-113	CAAC Special Services Division, Beijing.	N8291Y
☐ B-3583	00	King Air 350	FL-318	CAAC Special Services Division, Beijing.	N3218Z
☐ B-3621	90	PA-42 Cheyenne IIIA	5501051	CAAC Flying College, Guanghan.	(D-IOSF)
☐ B-3622	90	PA-42 Cheyenne IIIA	5501052	CAAC Flying College, Guanghan.	(D-IOSG)
☐ B-3624	90	PA-42 Cheyenne IIIA	5501056	CAAC Flying College, Guanghan.	N9241D
☐ B-3625	92	PA-42 Cheyenne IIIA	5501059	CAAC Flying College, Guanghan.	(OE-FAB)
☐ B-3626	94	PA-42 Cheyenne IIIA	5501060	CAAC Flying College, Guanghan.	N9115X

B-H = CHINA - HONG KONG   Total   2
Civil

| ☐ B-HRS | 98 BAe Jetstream 41 | 41102 | Government Flying Service, Chek Lap Kok. | G-4-102 |
| ☐ B-HRT | 98 BAe Jetstream 41 | 41104 | Government Flying Service, Chek Lap Kok. | G-BXWN |

B = CHINA - TAIWAN   Total   3
Civil

☐ B-00135	91 King Air 350	FL-52	Civil Aeronautical Administration, Taipei.	B-135
☐ B-13152	79 King Air 200	BB-449	Government of Taiwan, Taipei.	N2068L
☐ B-13153	93 King Air 350	FL-108	Department of Forests/Council of Agriculture, Taipei.	(VH-...)

C = CANADA   Total   506
Civil

☐ C-	77 PA-31T Cheyenne II	7720017	Westcan Aircraft Sales & Salvage Ltd, Kamloops BC	N12TW
☐ C-	73 SA-226AT Merlin 4	AT-011		N750AA
☐ C-	76 King Air A100	B-227	Sky North Air Ltd, St Andrews	N227BC
☐ C-FAFD	70 King Air 100	B-42	Kenn Borek Air Ltd. Calgary, AB.	LN-VIP
☐ C-FAFE	79 King Air B100	BE-72	Alta Flights (Charters) Inc. Edmonton, AB.	ZS-MZS
☐ C-FAFS	77 King Air B100	BE-31	Alta Flights (Charters) Inc. Edmonton, AB.	N80DB
☐ C-FAFT	75 King Air/Catpass 250	BB-57	Keystone Air Service Ltd. St Andrews, MT.	N121DA
☐ C-FAIO	70 King Air A100	B-132	Air Inuit Ltd. Kuujjuaq, PQ.	C-GXHP
☐ C-FAIP	74 King Air A100	B-193	Air Inuit Ltd. Kuujjuaq, PQ.	F-GXAB
☐ C-FAJV	98 Pilatus PC-12/45	234	Air Bravo Corp. Thunder Bay, ON.	HB-FRE
☐ C-FAKN	77 King Air 200	BB-216	Alkan Air Ltd. Whitehorse, Yukon, NT.	LN-VIU
☐ C-FAKP	72 Rockwell 690	11040	Air Spray (1967) Ltd. Edmonton, AB.	N690DC
☐ C-FAKW	89 King Air 300	FA-183	Alkan Air Ltd. Whitehorse, Yukon, NT.	N19NC
☐ C-FALQ	74 King Air 200	BB-10	Sky Jet M.G. Inc, Quebec, PQ.	N660M
☐ C-FAMB	87 King Air B200	BB-1281	Air Mikisew Ltd. Fort McMurray, AB.	N856TC
☐ C-FAMF	76 SA-226T Merlin 3A	T-274	Perimeter Aviation Ltd. Winnipeg, MT.	I-SWAA
☐ C-FAMO	69 BAe HS 748-2A	1669	Aerial Recon Surveys Ltd. Whitecourt, AB.	
☐ C-FAMU	73 King Air A100	B-166	Voyageur Airways Ltd. North Bay, ON.	N221SS
☐ C-FAPP	73 King Air A100	B-169	Voyageur Airways Ltd. North Bay, ON.	N305TZ
☐ C-FASB	73 King Air A100	B-163	Thunder Airlines Ltd. Thunder Bay, ON.	SE-ING
☐ C-FASF	01 Pilatus PC-12/45	416	RJM Aviation Ltd/Airsprint, Ottawa, ON.	N416PC
☐ C-FASN	77 King Air B100	BE-17	Arctic Sunwest Charters, Yellowknife, NT.	(N1981B)
☐ C-FASP	00 Pilatus PC-12/45	331	Airsprint Inc. Calgary, AB.	HB-FRP
☐ C-FASR	00 Pilatus PC-12/45	353	RJM Aviation Ltd/Airsprint, Edmonton, AB.	N353PC
☐ C-FATA	77 King Air 200	BB-283	Air Tindi Ltd. Yellowknife, NT.	N283JP
☐ C-FAWE	68 Gulfstream 1	188	Propair Inc. Rouyn-Noranda, PQ.	HB-LDT
☐ C-FAXE	70 King Air 100	B-41	Integra Operations Ltd., Richmond, BC	N1100A
☐ C-FAXN	66 680V Turbo Commander	1546-9	Aero Aviation Centre (1981) Ltd. Edmonton, AB.	N2549E
☐ C-FBCN	74 King Air 200	BB-7	Kenn Borek Air Ltd. Calgary, AB.	
☐ C-FBGS	74 King Air A100	B-204	Voyageur Airways Ltd. North Bay, ON.	N108JL
☐ C-FBPT	65 King Air 90	LJ-13	Toranda Leasing Inc. Calgary, AB.	N99W
☐ C-FCAK	72 King Air U-21J	B-96	Courtesy Air, Buffalo Narrows, SK.	N116RJ
☐ C-FCAW	70 SA-26AT Merlin 2B	T26-172E	Carson Air Ltd. Williams Lake, BC.	N135SR
☐ C-FCDF	80 King Air F90	LA-81	Dan Anderson, Calgary, AB.	N444MF
☐ C-FCEC	81 Cheyenne II-XL	8166030	Craig Evan Corp/CEC Flightexec, London, ON.	N76TW
☐ C-FCEF	79 PA-31T Cheyenne II	7920069	Craig Evan Corp/CEC Flightexec, London, ON.	N250KA
☐ C-FCGB	75 King Air/Catpass 250	BB-24	Bar XH Air Inc. Medicine Hat, AB.	N183MC
☐ C-FCGC	77 King Air/Catpass 250	BB-236	North Cariboo Flying Service Ltd. Fort St John, BC.	N46KA
☐ C-FCGE	66 King Air A90	LJ-118	Buffalo Airways Ltd. Hay River, NT.	
☐ C-FCGH	67 King Air A90	LJ-203	Buffalo Airways Ltd. Hay River, NT.	
☐ C-FCGI	67 King Air A90	LJ-220	Northwestern Air, Fort Smith, Nt.	
☐ C-FCGL	77 King Air/Catpass 250	BB-190	Central Mountain Air Ltd. Smithers, BC.	N190MD
☐ C-FCGM	77 King Air 200	BB-217	North Cariboo Flying Service Ltd. Fort St John, BC.	N200CD
☐ C-FCGN	68 King Air A90	LJ-313	AeroPro, Ste Foy, PQ.	
☐ C-FCGT	76 King Air/Catpass 250	BB-159	Keewatin Air Ltd. Winnipeg, MT.	N47FH
☐ C-FCGU	78 King Air/Catpass 250	BB-301	Air Tindi Ltd. Yellowknife, NT.	N611SW
☐ C-FCGW	77 King Air/Catpass 250	BB-207	Air Nunavut Ltd. Iqaluit, NT.	N111WH
☐ C-FCJV	98 Pilatus PC-12/45	240	North Ameroican Charters Ltd. Thunder Bay, ON.	N240PD
☐ C-FCLH	83 King Air F90	LA-184	Falcon Air Services, Saskatoon, SK.	OY-CCC
☐ C-FCMJ	71 681B Turbo Commander	6054	Perimeter Aviation Ltd. Winnipeg, MT.	N21HC
☐ C-FCZZ	73 Rockwell 690A	11106	Conair Group Inc. Abbotsford, BC.	N57106
☐ C-FDAM	69 King Air/Catpass 250	B-8	North Cariboo Flying Service Ltd. Fort St John, BC.	N59T

Reg   Yr   Type   c/n   Owner/Operator   Prev Regn

Reg	Yr	Type	c/n	Owner/Operator	Prev Regn
☐ C-FDEB	75	King Air 200	BB-55	Fast Air Ltd. Winnipeg, MT.	N200BC
☐ C-FDJX	73	King Air A100	B-165	Propair Inc. Rouyn-Noranda, PQ.	N811CU
☐ C-FDOR	72	King Air A100	B-103	Maritime Air Charter Ltd. Halifax, NS.	
☐ C-FDOS	72	King Air A100	B-106	Exact Air Inc., Baie-Comeau, PQ.	
☐ C-FDOU	72	King Air A100	B-112	Propair Inc. Rouyn-Noranda, PQ.	
☐ C-FDOV	72	King Air A100	B-117	5H Management Co/National Aviation Centre, Prince Albert, SK	
☐ C-FDOY	72	King Air A100	B-120	164061 BC Ltd. Moosonee, ON.	
☐ C-FDTC	99	King Air 350	FL-234	Execaire Inc., Dorval, PQ.	N3234K
☐ C-FEKB	79	King Air 1300	BB-468	Kenn Borek Air Ltd. Calgary, AB.	N9UT
☐ C-FEYP	75	King Air A100	B-206	Transwest Air Ltd., Prince Albert, SK.	N86BM
☐ C-FEYT	75	King Air A100	B-210	Northern Thunderbird Air Ltd. Vancouver, BC.	N75GR
☐ C-FFAR	77	King Air 200	BB-281	Fast Air Ltd. Winnipeg, MT.	N4AT
☐ C-FFFG	75	Mitsubishi MU-2L	662	Thunder Airlines Ltd. Thunder Bay, ON.	N5191B
☐ C-FFNV	77	PA-31T Cheyenne II	7720058	Integra Air Inc. Lethbridge, AB.	N167DA
☐ C-FFSS	80	MU-2 Marquise	783SA	IMP Group Ltd/Execaire Inc. Ottawa, ON.	N81604
☐ C-FGEM	80	MU-2 Solitaire	434SA	886875 Ontario Inc. St Catherines, ON.	N24MW
☐ C-FGFL	00	Pilatus PC-12/45	339	Airsprint Inc. Calgary, AB.	HB-FRU
☐ C-FGFZ	78	King Air 200	BB-403	Provincial Airlines Ltd. St Johns, NF.	N147K
☐ C-FGIN	73	King Air A100	B-164	AeroPro, Ste Foy, PQ.	N164RA
☐ C-FGMG	03	King Air B200	BB-1841	Shoreland Transport Inc., Quispamsis, NB.	N69LS
☐ C-FGNL	74	King Air A100	B-184	Province of Newfoundland, St Johns, NF.	
☐ C-FGSX	83	Cheyenne II-XL	8166048	Aviation Commercial Aviation, Hearst, ON.	N600XL
☐ C-FGWA	79	PA-31T Cheyenne II	7920045	Craig Evan Corp/CEC Flightexec, London, ON.	N52LS
☐ C-FGWR	97	King Air B200	BB-1599	Nor-Alta Aviation Leasing Inc., Lacrete, AB.	C-FGWD
☐ C-FGWT	85	Gulfstream 900	15042	Labrador Grenfell Regional Health Authority, St Anthony, NF.	N71GA
☐ C-FGXE	88	King Air C90A	LJ-1179	Dept of Transport, Ottawa, ON.	N179RC
☐ C-FGXG	86	King Air C90A	LJ-1139	Dept of Transport, Ottawa, ON.	N121RL
☐ C-FGXH	88	King Air C90A	LJ-1162	Dept of Transport, Ottawa, ON.	N477JA
☐ C-FGXJ	88	King Air C90A	LJ-1178	Dept of Transport, Ottawa, ON.	N357CY
☐ C-FGXL	88	King Air C90A	LJ-1189	Dept of Transport, Ottawa, ON.	(N203SL)
☐ C-FGXO	89	King Air C90A	LJ-1200	Dept of Transport, Ottawa, ON.	N68TW
☐ C-FGXQ	89	King Air C90A	LJ-1192	Dept of Transport, Hamilton, ON.	N616SC
☐ C-FGXS	89	King Air C90A	LJ-1207	Dept of Transport, Ottawa, ON.	N207RC
☐ C-FGXT	90	King Air C90A	LJ-1230	Dept of Transport, Ottawa, ON.	N1564P
☐ C-FGXU	86	King Air C90A	LJ-1140	Dept of Transport, Winnipeg, MT.	N8841
☐ C-FGXX	87	King Air C90A	LJ-1151	Dept of Transport, Winnipeg, MT.	N126RL
☐ C-FGXZ	88	King Air C90A	LJ-1177	Dept of Transport, Edmonton, AB.	(N357CA)
☐ C-FHBO	63	Gulfstream 1	104	Southern Alberta Institute of Technology, Calgary, AB.	N719G
☐ C-FHGG	75	King Air A100	B-207	Air Crebeec Inc. Timmins, ON.	N727LE
☐ C-FHKB	70	King Air 100	B-63	Kenn Borek Air Ltd. Calgary, AB.	N20880
☐ C-FHLP	76	King Air C90	LJ-685	1332666 Alberta Ltd., Grande Prairie, AB.	C-FATW
☐ C-FHMA	81	MU-2 Marquise	1523SA	Jetstream Capital Corp. Springbank, AB.	N65JG
☐ C-FHSC	81	King Air B100	BE-105	Pascan Aviation Inc. Ste Hubert, PQ.	N87XX
☐ C-FHSP	82	Conquest II	441-0265	Pacific Sky Aviation Inc., Victoria, BC.	N441E
☐ C-FHVM	01	PA-46-500TP Meridian	4697091	Voortman Cookies Ltd. Burlington, ON.	
☐ C-FHWI	67	King Air A90	LJ-309	Grondair/Grondin Transport Inc. St Frederic, PQ.	N329H
☐ C-FIAS	01	Pilatus PC-12/45	361	Airsprint Inc. Calgary, AB.	N717PT
☐ C-FIDC	77	King Air B100	BE-27	Pascan Aviation Inc. St Hubert, PQ.	(N297SL)
☐ C-FIDN	69	King Air 100	B-3	North Cariboo Flying Service Ltd. Fort St John, BC.	N128RC
☐ C-FIFE	76	Mitsubishi MU-2L	683	Nav Air Charter Inc. Victoria, BC.	OY-CEF
☐ C-FIFO	79	King Air 200	BB-527	Provincial Airlines Ltd. St Johns, NF.	N662L
☐ C-FIIL	74	Rockwell 690A	11167	Air Spray (1967) Ltd. Red Deer, AB.	N85AB
☐ C-FIJV	98	Pilatus PC-12/45	222	North American Charters 2000 Ltd. Thunder Bay, ON.	C-FKEN
☐ C-FIME	81	King Air B100	BE-115	Coopair-Cooperative Transport Aerien, Victoriaville, PQ.	C-FXRJ
☐ C-FIPO	01	PA-46-500TP Meridian	4697060	Invicta Research Inc. Niagara District Airport, ON.	
☐ C-FJAK	81	Cheyenne II-XL	8166028	Centerline (Windsor) Ltd. Windsor, ON.	N355SS
☐ C-FJDF	87	Beech 1900C	UB-68	Fowler Financial Holdings Inc., Buffalo Narrows, SK.	N68GH
☐ C-FJDQ	70	King Air B100	BE-16	Diamond Jet Charter Inc., Calgary, AB.	C-GDFZ
☐ C-FJEL	78	Mitsubishi MU-2N	706SA	Thunder Airlines Ltd. Thunder Bay, ON.	N866MA
☐ C-FJHP	68	King Air B90	LJ-325	Air Roberval Ltd. Roberval, PQ.	N900LD
☐ C-FJTN	06	King Air C90GT	LJ-1814	AirExpress Ontario Inc., Oshawa, ON.	N70944
☐ C-FJVB	81	PA-31T Cheyenne II	8120012	Lochhead-Haggerty Engineering & Manufacturing, Vancouver.	C-FZIH
☐ C-FJVR	79	Conquest II	441-0096	Sunwest Aviation Ltd. Calgary, AB.	N451WS
☐ C-FJWU	80	King Air E90	LW-332	Alberta Central Airways Ltd. Lac La Biche, AB.	N636GW
☐ C-FKBU	77	King Air 200	BB-285	Kenn Borek Air Ltd. Calgary, AB.	C-GQXF

Reg	Yr	Type	c/n	Owner/Operator	Prev Regn
☐ C-FKCW	82	King Air B200	BB-973	Can-West Corporate Air Charters Ltd. Edmonton, AB.	C-FEVC
☐ C-FKJI	76	King Air 200	BB-105	Hicks & Lawrence Limited, Dryden, ON.	N71TZ
☐ C-FKPA	99	Pilatus PC-12/45	275	Air Bravo Corp. Thunder Bay, ON.	N275PC
☐ C-FKPI	99	Pilatus PC-12/45	250	Wasaya Airways Ltd. Thunder Bay, ON.	N250PB
☐ C-FKPX	02	Pilatus PC-12/45	451	Pascan Aviation Inc. Ste Hubert, PQ.	HB-FSJ
☐ C-FKRB	98	Pilatus PC-12/45	233	Wasaya Airways LP. Thunder Bay, ON.	HB-FRD
☐ C-FKSL	00	Pilatus PC-12/45	324	North American Charters 2000 Ltd. Thunder Bay, ON.	N324PC
☐ C-FKTL	80	Conquest 1	425-0008	Kal Air Ltd. Vernon, BC.	N811NA
☐ C-FKTN	83	Conquest 1	425-0190	Kal Air Ltd. Vernon, BC.	N444RU
☐ C-FKUL	98	Pilatus PC-12/45	204	Wasaya Airways Ltd. Thunder Bay, ON.	ZS-PAY
☐ C-FKVL	00	Pilatus PC-12/45	307	Air Bravo Corp., Blind River, ON.	N307PB
☐ C-FLRB	72	King Air A100	B-131	Nor-Alta Aviation Leasing Inc., Lacrete, AB.	N102FG
☐ C-FLRD	79	King Air A100	B-243	Nor-Alta Aviation Leasing Inc., Lacrete, AB.	N63SJ
☐ C-FLRM	83	King Air B200	BB-1115	C-K Air Service Ltd. Toronto-Pearson, ON.	N764NB
☐ C-FLTC	74	King Air C90	LJ-631	The Moncton Flight College, Dieppe, NB.	N103FG
☐ C-FLTS	73	King Air A100	B-149	Exact Air Inc., Baie-Comeau, PQ.	N883CA
☐ C-FMCX	78	Rockwell 690B	11446	Air Spray (1967) Ltd. Edmonton, AB.	N137BW
☐ C-FMDF	06	Pilatus PC-12/47	800	Execaire Inc., Dorval, PQ.	HB-FQW
☐ C-FMFP	76	Rockwell 690A	11307	Province of Saskatchewan, La Ronge, SK.	N690TD
☐ C-FMFQ	05	King Air C90B	LJ-1740	Allied Wings LP. Kelowna, BC.	N36640
☐ C-FMFR	05	King Air C90B	LJ-1744	Allied Wings LP. Kelowna, BC.	N60724
☐ C-FMFS	05	King Air C90B	LJ-1745	Allied Wings LP. Kelowna, BC.	N36745
☐ C-FMFU	05	King Air C90B	LJ-1746	Allied Wings LP. Kelowna, BC.	N30246
☐ C-FMFX	05	King Air C90B	LJ-1747	Allied Wings LP. Kelowna, BC.	N36667
☐ C-FMFY	05	King Air C90B	LJ-1749	Allied Wings LP. Kelowna, BC.	N37149
☐ C-FMFZ	05	King Air C90B	LJ-1750	Allied Wings LP. Kelowna, BC.	N36850
☐ C-FMHD	92	King Air 350	FL-87	Aviation CMP Inc. St Georges, PQ.	C-GSCL
☐ C-FMKD	68	King Air B90	LJ-376	North Cariboo Flying Service Ltd. Fort St John, BC.	N300RV
☐ C-FMKK	06	PA-46-500TP Meridian	4697268	Lorenzo Girones, Timmins, OT	
☐ C-FMPA	96	Pilatus PC-12	164	RCMP-GRC Air Services, Winnipeg, MT.	HB-FRZ
☐ C-FMPB	99	Pilatus PC-12/45	283	RCMP-GRC Air Services, Ottawa, ON.	N1983R
☐ C-FMPE	00	Pilatus PC-12/45	314	RCMP-GRC Air Services, Edmonton, AB.	HB-FQZ
☐ C-FMPF	06	Pilatus PC-12/47	768	RCMP-GRC Air Services, Ottawa, ON.	HB-FSY
☐ C-FMPN	99	Pilatus PC-12/45	296	RCMP-GRC Air Services, Ottawa, ON.	HB-FQK
☐ C-FMPO	98	Pilatus PC-12/45	229	RCMP-GRC Air Services, Edmonton, AB.	HB-FRA
☐ C-FMPW	00	Pilatus PC-12/45	315	RCMP-GRC Air Services, Prince Albert, SK.	HB-FRA
☐ C-FMWM	70	King Air 100	B-59	Kenn Borek Air Ltd. Calgary, AB.	N702JL
☐ C-FMXY	70	King Air 100	B-40	North Cariboo Flying Service Ltd. Fort St John, BC.	N923K
☐ C-FNAO	83	Gulfstream 840	11731	Province of Saskatchewan, Regina, SK.	N815BC
☐ C-FNCB	78	King Air E90	LW-287	Pentastar Transportation Ltd. Edmonton, AB.	N23660
☐ C-FNCN	69	King Air B90	LJ-468	Grondair/Grondin Transport inc. St Frederic, PQ.	N1FC
☐ C-FNED	76	King Air C90	LJ-680	Alberta Central Airways Ltd. Lac La Biche, AB.	N928RD
☐ C-FNGA	90	P-180 Avanti	1007	Cascades Inc. St Hubert, PQ.	I-RAII
☐ C-FNIF	74	King Air A100	B-178	Air Creebec Inc., Timmins, Ontario	N764K
☐ C-FNIL	02	King Air 350	FL-354	North Cariboo Flying Service Ltd. Fort St John, BC.	N354H
☐ C-FNRM	81	Gulfstream 840	11692	Morgan Air Services Co. Calgary, AB.	N152X
☐ C-FNWC	81	Conquest II	441-0216	The North West Co. Winnipeg, MT.	N441DM
☐ C-FNWD	78	Rockwell 690B	11497	Conair Aviation Ltd., Abbotsford, BC.	N81831
☐ C-FNYM	76	PA-31T Cheyenne II	7620033	Northern Youth Programs Foundation, Dryden, BC.	N44TC
☐ C-FODC	79	King Air B100	BE-59	Pascan Aviation Inc. Ste Hubert, PQ.	(N47KS)
☐ C-FOGP	83	King Air B100	BE-134	Max Aviation Inc. St Hubert, PQ.	N363EA
☐ C-FOGY	76	King Air 200	BB-168	Propair Inc. Rouyn-Noranda, PQ.	N10VW
☐ C-FONY	73	King Air A100	B-154	Grondin Transport Inc. St Frederic, PQ.	N46JK
☐ C-FOPD	97	Pilatus PC-12/45	182	Province of Ontario Provincial Police, Sault Ste Marie, ON.	C-FKAC
☐ C-FOUR	73	Mitsubishi MU-2J	606	Shooter Aircourier Corp. Saskatoon, SK.	N338MA
☐ C-FPAJ	73	King Air A100	B-151	Propair Inc. Rouyn-Noranda, PQ.	N324B
☐ C-FPAW	86	120ER Brasilia	120018	Pratt & Whitney Canada, Montreal, PQ.	N516P
☐ C-FPBC	78	King Air B100	BE-44	1514592 Ontario Inc. Ontario	N300MP
☐ C-FPBL	01	TBM 700B	178	Lakeview Aviation, Lloydminster, AB.	N888TF
☐ C-FPCI	01	Pilatus PC-12/45	399	NAC Air LP. Thunder Bay, ON.	N399PB
☐ C-FPCL	99	Pilatus PC-12/45	276	North American Charters 2000 Ltd. Thunder Bay, ON.	N276CN
☐ C-FPCN	99	Pilatus PC-12/45	258	Air Bravo Corp. Thunder Bay, ON.	N258WC
☐ C-FPCP	00	King Air 350	FL-317	Sunwest Aviation Ltd. Calgary, AB.	(XA-...)
☐ C-FPCZ	01	Pilatus PC-12/45	433	Airsprint Inc. Calgary, AB.	HB-FRU
☐ C-FPLG	75	King Air A100	B-224	AeroPro, Ste Foy, PQ.	N16SM

Reg	Yr	Type	c/n	Owner/Operator	Prev Regn
C-FPLZ	06	King Air C90GT	LJ-1812	Plaza Atlantic Limited, Fredericton, NB.	N73712
C-FPQQ	88	King Air B200	BB-1304	Nor-Alta Aviation Leasing Inc., Lacrete, AB.	(VT-...)
C-FPWR	91	King Air 350	FL-62	Churchill Falls (Labrador) Corp. Churchill Falls, NF.	N82882
C-FQMM	05	Pilatus PC-12/45	612	Airsprint Inc. Calgary, AB.	N120CJ
C-FQOV	70	King Air 100	B-38	Ashe Aircraft Enterprises Ltd. Calgary, AB. (status ?).	N931M
C-FRJE	78	PA-31T Cheyenne II	7820002	Westair Aviation Inc. Kamloops,BC.	C-GCUL
C-FRKB	70	King Air 100	B-72	Kenn Borek Air Ltd. Calgary, AB.	C-GTLF
C-FRLD	90	King Air 350	FL-33	Carson Air Ltd. Kelowna, BC.	N15WS
C-FRMV	82	King Air B200	BB-979	Keewatin Air Ltd. Rankin Inlet, MT.	N22TP
C-FROM	73	Mitsubishi MU-2J	601	Nav Air Charter Inc. Victoria, BC.	N308MA
C-FROW	74	Mitsubishi MU-2J	628	Nav Air Charter Inc. Victoria, BC.	N4202M
C-FRWK	81	MU-2 Marquise	1521SA	Thunder Airlines Ltd. Thunder Bay, ON.	N437MA
C-FSAO	98	King Air B200	BB-1610	Can-West Corporate Air Charters Ltd. Edmonton, AB.	N713TA
C-FSAT	96	King Air B200	BB-1526	Can-West Corporate Air Charters Ltd. Edmonton, AB.	N417MC
C-FSCO	01	Dornier 328-130	3109	Shell Canada Ltd. Calgary, AB.	D-CDXV
C-FSEA	84	Conquest 1	425-0192	Sunlite Electric (St Paul) Ltd. St Paul, AB.	N1221T
C-FSFI	83	Conquest II	441-0316	Sunwest Aviation Ltd.,Calgary, AB.	N800SR
C-FSIK	78	King Air B100	BE-39	Max Aviation Inc. St Hubert, PQ.	N129CP
C-FSKA	78	King Air A100	B-239	North Cariboo Flying Service Ltd. Calgary, AB.	N154TC
C-FSKG	80	Conquest II	441-0120	2080061 Ontario Inc. Sudbury, ON.	N544AL
C-FSKN	83	King Air B200	BB-1109	Keewatin Air Ltd. Winnipeg, MT.	F-GLLH
C-FSKO	82	King Air B200	BB-1007	Keewatin Air Ltd. Winnipeg, MT.	N514MA
C-FSKQ	76	King Air 200	BB-99	La Loge Mecatina Inc. Lac Ste Marie, PQ.	5Y-SEL
C-FSPM	82	Gulfstream 900	15002	Province of Saskatchewan, La Ronge, SK.	N721ML
C-FSRK	97	Pilatus PC-12/45	202	Wasaya Airways LP. Thunder Bay, ON.	ZS-SRK
C-FSTP	02	P-180 Avanti	1055	Corpac Canada Ltd., Calgary, AB.	N925GS
C-FSVC	68	SA-26T Merlin 2A	T26-19	Keewatin Air Ltd. Rankin Inlet, NT.	N2JE
C-FTMA	73	King Air A100	B-174	Alpha Aviation Inc. Boundary Bay, BC.	N151A
C-FTML	70	Mitsubishi MU-2G	525	Kitts Aviation, Lloydminster, AB.	N360JK
C-FTOO	72	Mitsubishi MU-2J	549	Nav Air Charter Inc. Victoria, BC.	N65198
C-FTPE	93	King Air C90B	LJ-1342	Tatham Process Engineering Inc. Toronto, ON.	
C-FUFW	66	King Air 90	LJ-84	College d'Enseignement General et Professionel, Longueil, PQ	N619GS
C-FVAX	83	Conquest 1	425-0178	North Cariboo Flying Service Ltd. Calgary, AB.	(N90GM)
C-FVKC	00	King Air 350	FL-273	Carson Air Ltd. Kelowna, BC.	OY-JVL
C-FVPC	00	Pilatus PC-12/45	358	North Star Air Ltd., Pickle Lake, ON.	HB-FSK
C-FVPK	98	Pilatus PC-12/45	211	Airsprint Inc. Calgary, AB.	ZS-OEW
C-FWAV	99	Pilatus PC-12/45	280	Wasaya Airways LP. Thunder Bay, ON.	HB-FSY
C-FWCP	81	Cheyenne II-XL	8166018	1358938 Alberta Ltd, Alberta	N22VF
C-FWPG	71	King Air 100	B-67	Airco Aircraft Charters Ltd. Edmonton, AB.	N26KW
C-FWPN	70	King Air 100	B-51	Alberta Central Airways Ltd. Lac La Biche, AB.	N16SW
C-FWPR	95	King Air 350	FL-125	Carson Air Ltd. Kelowna, BC.	N32KC
C-FWPT	83	Cheyenne II-XL	8166066	Sawridge Energy Ltd. Edmonton, AB.	N9170C
C-FWRL	78	Conquest II	441-0079	9519 Investments Ltd. Prince George, BC.	N441KR
C-FWRM	72	King Air A100	B-125	Propair Inc. Rouyn-Noranda, PQ.	N89JM
C-FWUT	76	PA-31T Cheyenne II	7620039	Ashe Aircraft Enterprises Ltd. Calgary, AB..	N82031
C-FWWK	89	King Air 300	FA-182	Carrier Lumber Ltd. Prince George, BC.	N8840A
C-FWWQ	80	King Air 200	BB-667	West Wind Aviation LP. Saskatoon, SK.	N667NA
C-FWXI	85	King Air B200	BB-1224	Beaver Air Services LP. The Pas, MT.	C-GTLA
C-FWYF	71	King Air 100	B-89	Airco Aircraft Charters Ltd. Edmonton, AB.	N169RA
C-FWYN	70	King Air 100	B-47	Airco Aircraft Charters Ltd. Edmonton, AB.	C-GNAX
C-FWYO	70	King Air 100	B-28	Airco Aircraft Charters Ltd. Edmonton, AB.	N27JJ
C-FXAJ	72	King Air A100	B-122	NAC Air LP. Thunder Bay, ON.	N8181Z
C-FYBV	75	PA-31T Cheyenne II	7520015	Ashe Aircraft Enterprises Ltd. Calgary, AB.	N11232
C-FYUT	99	Pilatus PC-12/45	254	Pascan Aviation Inc. Ste Hubert, PQ.	N254PC
C-FYZS	98	Pilatus PC-12/45	227	Wasaya Airways LP. Thunder Bay, ON.	HB-FQY
C-FZNQ	77	King Air/Catpass 250	BB-264	Air Nunavut Ltd. Iqaluit, NT.	N456CJ
C-FZPW	81	King Air B200	BB-940	Keewatin Air Ltd. Winnipeg, MT.	N519SA
C-FZRQ	72	Rockwell 690	11025	Air Spray (1967) Ltd. Red Deer, AB.	N100LS
C-FZVW	81	King Air 200	BB-787	Voyageur Airways Ltd. North Bay, ON.	N26G
C-FZVX	77	King Air 200	BB-231	Voyageur Airways Ltd. North Bay, ON.	N200FH
C-GAAL	73	Rockwell 690A	11104	Conair Group Inc. Abbotsford, BC.	N690AZ
C-GACA	88	King Air 1300	BB-1309	Alberta Central Airways Ltd. Lac La Biche, AB.	N4277C
C-GACN	90	King Air 1300	BB-1384	Alberta Central Airways Ltd. Lac La Biche, AB.	N575T
C-GADI	81	King Air B200	BB-853	West Wind Aviation LP. Saskatoon, SK.	N44SR
C-GAEO	06	King Air 350	FL-479	Airborne Energy Solutions Ltd. Whitecourt, AB.	N3179V

Reg	Yr Type	c/n	Owner/Operator	Prev Regn
☐ C-GAGE	81 Conquest II	441-0214	126700 Aircraft Canada Inc/Lake Central Airways, Toronto, ON	N792KC
☐ C-GAIK	72 King Air A100	B-104	Air Inuit Ltd. Kuujjuaq, PQ.	C-GCFD
☐ C-GAMC	80 MU-2 Marquise	785SA	Thunder Airlines Ltd. Thunder Bay, ON.	N273MA
☐ C-GASI	72 King Air A100	B-126	Thunder Airlines Ltd. Thunder Bay, ON.	N23BW
☐ C-GAVI	74 King Air A100	B-201	Kenn Borek Air Ltd. Calgary, AB.	G-BBVM
☐ C-GAWA	82 King Air C90	LJ-1002	President Air Charter, Peterborough, ON.	N900VA
☐ C-GAWP	97 Pilatus PC-12/45	187	102662 Canada Inc/ExpressAir, Ottawa, ON.	HB-FSV
☐ C-GBBG	95 King Air B200	BB-1507	Newfoundland Labrador Air Transport Ltd. Deer Lake, NF.	N232JS
☐ C-GBBS	81 King Air 200	BB-757	Air Express Ontario Inc. Oshawa, ON.(Damaged)	N948MB
☐ C-GBCE	06 King Air 350	FL-502	Northern Thunderbird Air Inc. Prince George, BC.	N7102Y
☐ C-GBCO	02 TBM 700B	238	034449 NB Ltd/Atlantic Flight Centre, St John, NB.	(N700EF)
☐ C-GBFO	81 Cheyenne II-XL	8166069	Aviation Commercial Aviation, Hearst, ON.	N511SC
☐ C-GBJV	98 Pilatus PC-12/45	237	Wasaya Airways LP. Thunder Bay, ON.	HB-FRH
☐ C-GBMF	06 Pilatus PC-12/47	727	843420 Alberta Ltd. Edmonton, AB.	HB-FRM
☐ C-GBOT	81 PA-42 Cheyenne III	8001063	BOT Construction (Canada) Ltd. Hamilton, ON.	C-FCEH
☐ C-GBTL	96 Pilatus PC-12/45	159	Pascan Aviation Inc. Ste Hubert, PQ.	N159PB
☐ C-GBTS	91 TBM 700	19	Brucelandair International, Kitchener, ON.	N635DS
☐ C-GBVX	80 King Air B100	BE-99	North Cariboo Flying Service Ltd. Fort St John, BC.	N524BA
☐ C-GBXW	97 Pilatus PC-12	170	Wasaya Airways LP. Thunder Bay, ON.	N170PD
☐ C-GBYN	85 King Air B200	BB-1232	Adlair Aviation (1983) Ltd. Yellowknife, NT.	N209CM
☐ C-GBZM	69 SA-26AT Merlin 2B	T26-122	Air Dorval Ltee. Dorval, PQ.	N63SC
☐ C-GCET	76 King Air 200	BB-124	Craig Evan Corp/CEC Flightexec, London, ON.	N109TM
☐ C-GCFB	81 King Air C90	LJ-929	NAV Canada, Vancouver, BC.	N81DD
☐ C-GCFF	79 King Air 200	BB-474	Image Air Charter Inc., Mississauga, Ont.	
☐ C-GCFL	70 King Air B90	LJ-500	Hutch Air Inc., Edmonton, AB.	N20WC
☐ C-GCFM	80 King Air C90	LJ-886	North Cariboo Flying Service Ltd. Calgary, AB.	N15SL
☐ C-GCFZ	79 King Air C90	LJ-849	NAV Canada, Vancouver, BC.	N6647P
☐ C-GCGB	05 King Air 350	FL-450	Omega Air Corp. Richmond, BC.	N6150U
☐ C-GCIL	83 Conquest II	441-0314	Sunwest Aviation Ltd. Calgary, AB.	XB-CSB
☐ C-GCLQ	79 King Air 200	BB-519	Sky Jet M.G. Inc., Quebec, PQ	N721SW
☐ C-GCOL	06 PA-46-500TP Meridian	4697287	1277101 Alberta Inc. Calgary, AB.	N.....
☐ C-GCOM	06 P-180 Avanti II	1117	Bell Aliant regional Communications Halifx NS.	N179S
☐ C-GCYB	83 Conquest II	441-0298	Image Air Charter Inc. Toronto-Buttonville, ON.	N245DL
☐ C-GCYN	80 King Air 200	BB-710	Adlair Aviation (1983) Ltd. Yellowknife, NT.	C-GXHW
☐ C-GDCL	74 Rockwell 690A	11192	Conair Group Inc. Abbotsford, BC.	N57192
☐ C-GDFJ	76 King Air B100	BE-15	North Cariboo Flying Service Ltd, Calgary AB.	N300DG
☐ C-GDFN	78 King Air 200	BB-359	North Cariboo Flying Service Ltd Calgary AB.	N351MA
☐ C-GDFT	78 King Air 200	BB-354	Dynamic Flight Services Inc. Calgary, AB.	N221BG
☐ C-GDGD	97 Pilatus PC-12/45	193	North American Charters 2000 Ltd. Thunder Bay, ON.	N193PC
☐ C-GDHF	83 King Air/Catpass 250	BB-1129	Fast Air Ltd. Winnipeg, MT.	CS-DDF
☐ C-GDPB	82 King Air B200C	BL-44	Air Tindi Ltd. Yellowknife, NT.	N18379
☐ C-GDPI	73 King Air A100	B-156	Voyageur Airways Ltd. North Bay, ON.	N21RX
☐ C-GDVF	06 King Air B200	BB-1940	Interforest Ltd. Hanover Saugeen Municipal, ON.	N999DZ
☐ C-GEAS	90 King Air 350	FL-17	Province of Saskatchewan, Regina, SK.	N56872
☐ C-GEHS	80 MU-2 Marquise	763SA	Thunder Airlines Ltd. Thunder Bay, ON.	N26AP
☐ C-GEJE	03 King Air 350	FL-385	Grant Executive Jets Inc. Earlton, ON.	N5085T
☐ C-GEOS	76 Rockwell 690A	11279	Geographic Air Survey Ltd. Edmonton, AB.	N57180
☐ C-GEOW	98 Pilatus PC-12/45	244	Nakina Outpost Camps & Air Service Ltd. Nakina, ON.	HB-FRO
☐ C-GFAB	66 680V Turbo Commander	1601-43	Province of New Brunswick, Fredericton, NB.	N577RH
☐ C-GFAD	93 King Air/Catpass 250	BB-1428	Fast Air Ltd.,Winnipeg, MT.	N660MW
☐ C-GFIL	99 Pilatus PC-12/45	268	Air Bravo Corp., Blind River, ON.	N268PC
☐ C-GFLA	99 Pilatus PC-12/45	293	RCMP-GRC Air Services, Ottawa, ON.	N293PC
☐ C-GFLN	06 Pilatus PC-12/47	789	Les Chantiers De Chibougamau Ltee., Chibougamau, PQ	HB-FQK
☐ C-GFOL	75 King Air 200	BB-27	Keystone Air Service Ltd. St Andrews, MT.	N120DP
☐ C-GFOX	03 P-180 Avanti	1065	RCMP-GRC Air Services, Ottawa, ON.	N126PA
☐ C-GFPP	72 Rockwell 690	11032	Air Spray (1967) Ltd. Red Deer, AB.	N349AC
☐ C-GFSA	97 King Air 350	FL-174	Province of Alberta, Edmonton, AB.	
☐ C-GFSB	75 King Air 200	BB-84	Fast Air Ltd. Winnipeg, MT.	
☐ C-GFSD	06 King Air B200	BB-1962	Province of Alberta, Edmonton, AB.	N7162V
☐ C-GFSE	06 King Air B200	BB-1963	Province of Alberta, Edmonton, AB.	N7063F
☐ C-GFSG	75 King Air 200	BB-671	Transwest Air Ltd., Prince Albert, SK.	
☐ C-GFSH	81 King Air B200	BB-912	Province of Alberta, Edmonton, AB.	
☐ C-GGAO	78 King Air 200	BB-659	Provincial Airlines Ltd. St Johns, NF.	N77QX
☐ C-GGDC	80 MU-2 Marquise	796SA	IMP Group Ltd/Execaire Inc. Toronto-Pearson, ON.	N700MA
☐ C-GGGQ	83 King Air B200	BB-1128	Bell Aliant Regional Communications Ltd. Halifax, NS.	

Reg	Yr Type	c/n	Owner/Operator	Prev Regn
☐ C-GGJF	81 King Air B200	BB-939	Provincial Airlines Ltd. St Johns, NF.	N125KW
☐ C-GGKJ	78 King Air B100	BE-49	Alta Flights (Charters) Inc. Edmonton, AB.	N400RK
☐ C-GGOO	73 Rockwell 690	11068	Air Spray (1967) Ltd. Edmonton, AB.	N9168N
☐ C-GGPS	78 PA-31T Cheyenne II	7820023	Craig Evan Corp/CEC Flightexec. London, ON.	
☐ C-GHDP	81 King Air B200	BB-891	Keewatin Air Ltd. Winnipeg, MT.	N888HG
☐ C-GHJF	95 King Air B200	BB-1493	Nor-Alta Aviation Leasing Inc., Lacrete, AB.	N3015Q
☐ C-GHOC	74 King Air A100	B-194	Kenn Borek Air Ltd. Calgary, AB.	N57237
☐ C-GHOP	76 King Air 200	BB-120	Sunwest Aviation Ltd. Calgary, AB.	N6773S
☐ C-GHQG	85 King Air 300	FA-39	Government of Canada, Ottawa, ON.	N339WD
☐ C-GHVM	07 PA-46-500TP Meridian	4697339	Voortman Cookies Ltd, Ontario	
☐ C-GHVR	68 King Air B90	LJ-337	Northern Lights College, Dawson Creek, BC.	
☐ C-GHWF	73 Rockwell 690A	11134	Conair Group Inc. Abbotsford, BC.	N45VT
☐ C-GHYT	72 King Air U-21J	B-98	L & A Aviation Ltd/Landa Aviation, Hay River, NT.	N998RC
☐ C-GIND	81 King Air B200C	BL-42	Voyageur Airways Ltd. North Bay, ON.	N819CD
☐ C-GISH	73 King Air A100	B-152	Voyageur Airways Ltd. North Bay, ON.	(N67LG)
☐ C-GITC	01 TBM 700B	223	1087485 Alberta Ltd. Calgary, AB.	N700BY
☐ C-GIZX	73 King Air A100	B-172	Air Creebec Inc. Val D'Or, PQ.	N735DB
☐ C-GJBQ	74 King Air A100	B-191	AeroPro, Ste Foy, PQ.	N214CK
☐ C-GJBV	72 King Air A100	B-100	Voyageur Airways Ltd. North Bay, ON.	N100S
☐ C-GJFO	72 Rockwell 690	11035	Air Spray (1967) Ltd. Edmonton, AB.	N15VZ
☐ C-GJFY	81 King Air 200	BB-812	Sunwest Aviation Ltd. Calgary, AB.	C-GYUI
☐ C-GJHF	81 Conquest 1	425-0080	618232 Alberta Ltd. Edmonton, AB.	N880EA
☐ C-GJHW	73 King Air A100	B-175	Transwest Air LP. Prince Albert, SK.	N92DL
☐ C-GJJF	72 King Air A100	B-123	Voyageur Airways Ltd. North Bay, ON.	N741EB
☐ C-GJJT	81 King Air 200	BB-828	Voyageur Airways Ltd. North Bay, ON.	N62GA
☐ C-GJKS	70 King Air 100	B-14	North American Charters 2000 Ltd. Thunder Bay, ON.	N402G
☐ C-GJLI	78 King Air 200	BB-347	Hicks & Lawrence Limited, Dryden, ON.	N424CR
☐ C-GJLJ	77 King Air A100	B-235	Propair Inc. Rouyn-Noranda, PQ.	N23517
☐ C-GJLK	90 King Air 350	FL-13	Carson Air Ltd. Kelowna, BC.	C-FWXR
☐ C-GJLP	73 King Air A100	B-148	Propair Inc. Rouyn-Noranda, PQ.	N67V
☐ C-GJMM	01 P-180 Avanti	1037	Skyservice Aviation Inc., Dorval, PQ.	(N180UJ)
☐ C-GJOL	03 P-180 Avanti	1069	Hazlet Oils Ltd., Calgary, AB.	N320CA
☐ C-GJPT	75 PA-31T Cheyenne II	7520039	Province of Saskatchewan, Regina, SK.	
☐ C-GJSU	71 King Air 100	B-88	Northern Thunderbird Air Ltd., Prince George, BC.	N100ZM
☐ C-GKAJ	77 King Air A100	B-232	Skynorth Air Ltd., St. Andrews, Man.	N400WH
☐ C-GKAY	97 Pilatus PC-12	178	1401277 Ontario Ltd. Thunder Bay, ON.	N178PC
☐ C-GKBB	73 King Air C90	LJ-607	Kenn Borek Air Ltd. Calgary, AB.	N48DA
☐ C-GKBN	75 King Air 200	BB-29	Kenn Borek Air Ltd. Calgary, AB.	LN-ASG
☐ C-GKBP	79 King Air 200	BB-505	Kenn Borek Air Ltd. Calgary, AB.	C-GKBP
☐ C-GKBQ	70 King Air 100	B-62	Kenn Borek Air Ltd. Calgary, AB.	LN-NLB
☐ C-GKBZ	71 King Air 100	B-85	Kenn Borek Air Ltd. Calgary, AB.	LN-PAJ
☐ C-GKDZ	72 Rockwell 690	11016	Air Spray (1967) Ltd. Edmonton, AB.	N428SJ
☐ C-GKNR	00 Pilatus PC-12/45	308	V Kelner Pilatus Centre Inc.. Thunder Bay, ON.	HB-FQV
☐ C-GKOS	06 King Air 350	FL-511	Kos Air Ltd. Drayton Valley, AB.	N7011Y
☐ C-GKOX	78 King Air 200	BB-389	Can-West Corporate Air Charters Ltd, Edmonton AB.	C-GKOS
☐ C-GKPC	75 PA-31T Cheyenne II	7520021	Kelly Panteluk Construction Ltd. Salmon Arm, SK.	C-GZQD
☐ C-GKPL	98 Pilatus PC-12/45	245	Wasaya Airways Ltd. Thunder Bay, ON.	ZS-DET
☐ C-GKSC	81 King Air F90	LA-113	Sanjel Corp. Calgary, AB.	N890CA
☐ C-GKWQ	05 P-180 Avanti	1095	Corpac Canada Ltd., Calgary, AB.	N143PA
☐ C-GLCE	02 Pilatus PC-12/45	475	Road Trailer Rentals Inc. Buttonville, ON.	N475PC
☐ C-GLEM	91 P-180 Avanti	1009	Cascades Inc. St Hubert, PQ.	D-IHMO
☐ C-GLER	04 PA-46-500TP Meridian	4697185	DFM Aviation LP. Ste Julie, PQ.	N556MP
☐ C-GLFN	00 King Air B200	BB-1738	Caravan Airlines Ltd. Lloydminster, AB.	N5075C
☐ C-GLKA	68 SA-26T Merlin 2A	T26-20	Keewatin Air Ltd. Rankin Inlet, NT.	N77WF
☐ C-GLLS	98 King Air B200	BB-1601	Province of Saskatchewan, Regina, SK.	N2303F
☐ C-GLOX	94 King Air 350	FL-106	Jet Share Aviation Inc. Toronto, ON.	N223P
☐ C-GLPG	73 King Air A100	B-159	AeroPro, Ste Foy, PQ.	N110KF
☐ C-GLRR	66 King Air A90	LJ-134	Little Red Air Service Ltd. Fort Vermilion, AB.	N38LA
☐ C-GMAG	74 King Air A100	B-229	West Wind Aviation LP. Saskatoon, SK.	N100HC
☐ C-GMDF	76 PA-31T Cheyenne II	7620019	Bar XH Air Inc. Medicine Hat, AB.	
☐ C-GMEH	02 King Air 350	FL-353	Clearwater Fine Foods Inc. Upper Tantallon, NS.	N6153V
☐ C-GMEJ	75 PA-31T Cheyenne II	7620008	The Driving Force Inc., Edmonton, Ab.	N584PS
☐ C-GMET	06 TBM 850	355	Met Inc. Edmonton, AB.	N850HM
☐ C-GMLF	07 Pilatus PC-12/47	849	V Kelner Pilatus Center Inc. Thunder Bay, ON.	HB-FSE
☐ C-GMOC	79 King Air/Catpass 250	BB-513	Alkan Air Ltd. Whitehorse, Yukon, NT.	N513SA
Reg	Yr Type	c/n	Owner/Operator	Prev Regn

Reg	Yr	Type	c/n	Owner/Operator	Prev Regn
☐ C-GMPE	98	Pilatus PC-12/45	184	Wasaya Airways Ltd. Thunder Bay, ON.	HB-FSS
☐ C-GMPI	99	Pilatus PC-12/45	239	RCMP-GRC Air Services, Ottawa, ON.	HB-FRJ
☐ C-GMPP	01	Pilatus PC-12/45	374	RCMP-GRC Air Services, Winnipeg, MT.	N374PC
☐ C-GMPW	99	Pilatus PC-12/45	274	RCMP-GRC Air Services, Ottawa, ON.	N274PC
☐ C-GMPY	00	Pilatus PC-12/45	311	RCMP-GRC Air Services, Edmonton, AB.	N311PB
☐ C-GMPZ	99	Pilatus PC-12/45	272	RCMP-GRC Air Services, Montreal, PQ.	HB-FSQ
☐ C-GMRS	76	King Air 200	BB-187	Provincial Airlines Ltd. St John's, NF.	N630DB
☐ C-GMVP	74	King Air C90	LJ-616	1260465 Alberta Ltd. Grand Prairie, AB.	I-LIPO
☐ C-GMWR	75	King Air 200	BB-68	Provincial Airlines Ltd. St Johns, NF.	N844N
☐ C-GMYM	01	PA-46-500TP Meridian	4697114	Mackenzie Capital Corp. Bracebridge,	
☐ C-GNAA	70	King Air 100	B-24	NAC Air LP. Thunder Bay, ON.	N382WC
☐ C-GNAJ	72	King Air A100	B-107	Northern Air Charter (PR) Inc. Peace River, AB.	LN-AAH
☐ C-GNAK	90	King Air 1300	BB-1376	Northern Air Charter (PR) Inc. Peace River, AB.	HK-3990X
☐ C-GNAM	89	King Air 1300	BB-1339	Northern Air Charter (PR) Inc. Peace River, AB.	(N131AZ)
☐ C-GNAX	92	King Air B200	BB-1419	Northern Air Charter (PR) Inc. Peace River, AB.	N146SB
☐ C-GNBB	79	King Air 200	BB-479	La Loge Mecatina Inc. La Romaine, PQ.	N200UQ
☐ C-GNCV	70	King Air 100	B-23	North Cariboo Flying Service Ltd. Fort St John, BC.	N701RJ
☐ C-GNDI	76	PA-31T Cheyenne II	7620036	Fast Air Ltd. Winnipeg, MT.	N73TB
☐ C-GNDR	88	King Air B200	BB-1290	Storm Aviation Flight Academy Inc., Sherwood Park, AB.	N788JB
☐ C-GNEP	84	Conquest 1	425-0221	Conquest Air Ltd. Prince George, BC.	N904RM
☐ C-GNEX	75	King Air A100	B-211	Thunder Airlines Ltd. Thunder Bay, ON.	
☐ C-GNGI	87	BAe Jetstream 31	739	Infinity Flight Services Ltd. Edmonton, AB.	N855JS
☐ C-GNKP	75	PA-31T Cheyenne II	7520008	Province of Saskatchewan, Regina, SK.	
☐ C-GNLA	90	King Air 350	FL-26	Government of Newfoundland & Labrador, St Johns, NF.	N59TF
☐ C-GNSC	80	King Air B100	BE-102	Pascan Aviation Inc. Ste Hubert, PQ.	N57TJ
☐ C-GNSS	05	PA-46-500TP Meridian	4697200	Aviation Unlimited (1990) Inc., Markham, Ont.	N.....
☐ C-GNWD	76	PA-31T Cheyenne II	7620029	Northway Aviation Ltd. St Andrews, MT.	C-GEBA
☐ C-GODE	06	Pilatus PC-12/47	707	V Kelner Pilatus Center Inc. Thunder Bay, ON.	HB-F..
☐ C-GOGS	99	King Air 350	FL-269	Province of Ontario, Sault Ste Marie, ON.	N3169N
☐ C-GOGT	79	King Air 200	BB-535	Beaver Air Services LP. The Pas, MT.	
☐ C-GOIC	99	King Air 350	FL-272	Province of Ontario, Sault Ste Marie, ON.	N3172N
☐ C-GOVT	83	Gulfstream 900	15020	Province of Saskatchewan, Regina, SK.	N600CM
☐ C-GPAI	03	Pilatus PC-12/45	491	Wasaya Airways LP. Thunder Bay, ON.	N491VA
☐ C-GPBA	75	King Air A100	B-215	Exact Air Inc. St Honore, PQ.	N552GA
☐ C-GPCB	70	King Air 100	B-45	North Cariboo Flying Service Ltd. Fort St John, BC.	N704S
☐ C-GPCL	74	SA-226AT Merlin 4	AT-017	Perimeter Aviation Ltd. Winnipeg, MT.	N5RT
☐ C-GPCO	04	Pilatus PC-12/45	603	Airsprint Inc. Calgary, AB.	HB-FRC
☐ C-GPCP	76	King Air 200	BB-140	Pacific Coastal Airlines Ltd. Richmond, BC.	
☐ C-GPDJ	02	P-180 Avanti	1057	Road Trailer Rentals Inc., Unionville, ON.	C-GBCI
☐ C-GPEA	76	King Air/Catpass 250	BB-170	Prince Edward Air Ltd. Moncton, NB.	N869MA
☐ C-GPIA	04	P-180 Avanti	1072	Execaire Inc., Dorval, PQ.	N157PA
☐ C-GPJL	81	King Air B100	BE-107	Max Aviation Inc. St Hubert, PQ.	N3699B
☐ C-GPII	07	P-180 Avanti II	1133	Corpac Canada Ltd Calgary AB.	N139PA
☐ C-GPLT	04	Pilatus PC-12/45	566	Martini Aviation Ltd. Fort Langley, BC.	HB-FPX
☐ C-GPNB	92	King Air C90B	LJ-1305	Province of New Brunswick, Fredericton, NB.	N488JR
☐ C-GPNC	07	King Air B300C	FM-15	Heli-Max Ltd., Trois Rivieres, PQ.	N415KA
☐ C-GPNP	75	PA-31T Cheyenne II	7520024	Fast Air Ltd, Winnipeg, Manitoba	N431AC
☐ C-GPRU	77	King Air B100	BE-26	Max Aviation Inc. St Hubert, PQ.	N36WH
☐ C-GPSB	81	PA-42 Cheyenne III	8001030	Swanberg Air Inc. Grand Prairie, AB.	N855GA
☐ C-GPSP	78	Conquest II	441-0058	Hauts-Monts Inc. Beauport, PQ.	OY-BHM
☐ C-GPSQ	78	Conquest II	441-0076	Hauts-Monts Inc. Beauport, PQ.	N441RC
☐ C-GPSR	80	Conquest II	441-0143	Hauts-Monts Inc. Beauport, PQ.	N26PK
☐ C-GPTA	65	Gulfstream 1	162	Ptarmigan Airways Ltd. Yellowknife, NT.	N300GP
☐ C-GQJG	77	King Air 200	BB-249	Aviation Starlink Inc. Dorval, PQ.	
☐ C-GQNJ	77	King Air 200	BB-275	Hicks & Lawrence Limited, Dryden, ON.	
☐ C-GRBA	98	Pilatus PC-12/45	238	1222196 Alberta Ltd. Grand Prairie, AB.	N238PC
☐ C-GRBF	70	SA-26AT Merlin 2B	T26-171E	Peace Air/Roberts Brothers Farming Ltd. Falher, AB.	N50AK
☐ C-GRBV	01	TBM 700B	191	Breadner Trailer Sales Amalgamated Limited, Kitchener, ON.	N706AV
☐ C-GRCN	05	Pilatus PC-12/45	675	Airsprint Inc. Calgary, AB.	HB-FQH
☐ C-GRDC	98	Pilatus PC-12/45	214	Pascan Aviation Inc. Ste Hubert, PQ.	PT-XTG
☐ C-GRHD	83	Conquest 1	425-0167	Gary L Redhead Holdings Ltd. Regina, SK.	N6872L
☐ C-GRJP	98	Pilatus PC-12/45	196	RJM Aviation Ltd/Airsprint, Calgary, AB.	N196PC
☐ C-GRJZ	00	King Air 350	FL-285	Jetport Inc. Hamilton, ON.	N3185J
☐ C-GRMS	97	Pilatus PC-12/45	200	Road Trailer Rentals Inc. Buttonville, ON.	N200PD
☐ C-GRRO	74	Rockwell 690A	11166	Orr Air Inc. Vancouver, BC.	N78BA

Reg	Yr	Type	c/n	Owner/Operator	Prev Regn
☐ C-GRSL	74	King Air C90	LJ-609	Montair Aviation Inc, BC	N38BA
☐ C-GSAA	91	PA-42 Cheyenne IIIA	5501057	Province of Saskatchewan, Regina, SK.	N120GA
☐ C-GSAE	00	King Air B200	BB-1748	Province of Saskatchewan, Regina, SK.	N50848
☐ C-GSAH	06	King Air B200	BB-1972	Province of Saskatchewan, Regina, SK.	N7022F
☐ C-GSAU	07	King Air B200	BB-1974	Province of Saskatchewan, Regina, SK.	N7074N
☐ C-GSAV	01	King Air B200	BB-1790	Province of Saskatchewan, Regina, SK.	N4470T
☐ C-GSBC	01	King Air B200	BB-1780	Sunwest Aviation Ltd. Calgary, AB.	N46TF
☐ C-GSFF	83	Conquest 1	425-0177	PGS Holdings Ltd. Kamloops, BC.	C-GSFI
☐ C-GSFM	68	King Air B90	LJ-422	Kenn Borek Air Ltd. Calgary, AB.	N513SC
☐ C-GSLC	01	Pilatus PC-12/45	365	IMP Group Ltd/Execaire Inc. Halifax, NS.	C-FMDF
☐ C-GSVQ	66	680V Turbo Commander	1544-8	Northern Lights College, Dawson Creek, BC.	N146E
☐ C-GSWF	82	King Air B100	BE-129	Infinity Flight Services Ltd. Edmonton, AB.	N2074M
☐ C-GSWG	82	King Air B100	BE-131	Max Aviation Inc. St Hubert, PQ.	N6354H
☐ C-GSWX	93	Beech 1900D	UE-63	Sunwest Aviation Ltd. Calgary, AB.	N166K
☐ C-GSYN	70	King Air 100	B-61	Adlair Aviation (1983) Ltd. Yellowknife, NT.	N418LA
☐ C-GTBM	92	TBM 700	53	Gautmain s.e.c., Ste Foy, PQ.	N700BF
☐ C-GTDB	91	King Air 300	FA-215	Pentastar Transportation Ltd. Acheson, AB.	OE-FSO
☐ C-GTDF	96	King Air B200	BB-1546	Sunwest Aviation Ltd. Calgary, AB.	N770U
☐ C-GTEM	99	King Air 350	FL-236	Skyservice Aviation Inc. Dorval, PQ.	N2346S
☐ C-GTFP	76	PA-31T Cheyenne II	7620016	491549 Alberta Ltd. Calgary, AB.	N57524
☐ C-GTJZ	79	King Air 200	BB-499	Provincial Airlines Ltd. St Johns, NF.	N6051C
☐ C-GTLS	70	King Air 100	B-35	North Cariboo Flying Service Ltd. Fort St John, BC.	N178WM
☐ C-GTMA	68	King Air B90	LJ-348	Province of Alberta, Edmonton, AB.	N805K
☐ C-GTMM	79	PA-31T Cheyenne 1	7904008	Marivent Corp. St Bruno, PQ.	N528DS
☐ C-GTMW	70	SA-226AT Merlin 4	AT-002	Provincial Airlines Ltd. St Johns, NF.	N39RD
☐ C-GTTS	80	PA-31T Cheyenne II	8020053	Centura 2005 Inc. Buttonville, ON.	N39K
☐ C-GTUC	77	King Air 200	BB-268	Air Tindi Ltd. Yellowknife, NT.	N565RA
☐ C-GTWW	75	King Air C90	LJ-657	Hicks & Lawrence Limited, Dryden, ON.	N9030R
☐ C-GUPP	73	King Air A100	B-157	Thunder Airlines Ltd. Thunder Bay, ON.	N123CS
☐ C-GUXL	07	PA-46-500TP Meridian	4697292	National Socket Screw Manufacturing Ltd., Delta, BC.	
☐ C-GVIK	76	King Air B100	BE-7	Max Aviation Inc. St Hubert, PQ.	N57HT
☐ C-GVJV	06	PA-46-500TP Meridian	4697261	Jamie Vins, Buttonville, ON.	
☐ C-GVKA	78	PA-31T Cheyenne II	7920008	Westair Aviation Inc. Kamloops, BC.	
☐ C-GVKC	98	Pilatus PC-12/45	207	V Kelner Pilatus Center Inc. Thunder Bay, ON.	ZS-OEV
☐ C-GVKK	78	PA-31T Cheyenne II	7820038	The Craig Evan Corp/Flight Exec, London, ON.	N679MM
☐ C-GVLH	81	King Air F90	LA-105	Heck Transworld Inc., Red Deer, Alberta	N188BF
☐ C-GWEW	73	Rockwell 690	11057	Conair Group Inc. Abbotsford, BC.	N376TC
☐ C-GWGI	82	King Air B200	BB-1022	Fast Air Ltd. Winnipeg, MT.	C-FDGP
☐ C-GWII	04	P-180 Avanti	1074	1102734 Ontario Inc. Brantford, ON.	N72EE
☐ C-GWRK	02	P-180 Avanti	1061	Corpac Canada Ltd /Corporate Express, Calgary, AB.	N129PA
☐ C-GWUY	75	King Air 200	BB-77	North-Wright Airways Ltd. Norman Wells, NT.	N300CP
☐ C-GWWA	70	King Air 100	B-27	Kenn Borek Air Ltd. Calgary, AB.	G-BOFN
☐ C-GWWN	74	King Air 200	BB-14	West Wind Aviation LP. Saskatoon, SK.	N418CS
☐ C-GWWQ	71	King Air 100	B-76	West Wind Aviation LP. Saskatoon, SK.	N300DA
☐ C-GXBF	76	PA-31T Cheyenne II	7620010	Canlynx Airways Inc. Mississauga, ON.	N54988
☐ C-GXCD	76	PA-31T Cheyenne II	7620026	Ashe Aircraft Enterprises Ltd. Calgary, AB. (status ?).	
☐ C-GXHD	89	King Air 1300	BB-1338	Bar XH Air Inc. Medicine Hat, AB.	(OY-...)
☐ C-GXHF	89	King Air 1300	BB-1343	Bar XH Air Inc. Medicine Hat, AB.	5Y-ECO
☐ C-GXHG	90	King Air 1300	BB-1383	Bar XH Air Inc. Medicine Hat, AB.	N913YW
☐ C-GXHN	80	King Air 200	BB-693	Bar XH Air Inc. Medicine Hat, AB.	N245JS
☐ C-GXHR	88	King Air 1300	BB-1305	Bar XH Air Inc. Medicine Hat, AB.	5Y-EOB
☐ C-GXHS	88	King Air 1300	BB-1302	Bar XH Air Inc. Medicine Hat, AB.	PT-WYY
☐ C-GXRX	70	King Air 100	B-36	Northern Thunderbird Air Inc. Vancouver, BC.	N600CB
☐ C-GXTC	77	PA-31T Cheyenne II	7720052	Walsten Aircraft Parts & Lasing Inc. Ontario.	(N82165)
☐ C-GYDQ	79	King Air 200	BB-455	Diamond Jet Charter Inc., Calgary, AB.	N900DG
☐ C-GYQK	73	King Air A100	B-153	Skynorth Air Ltd. St Andrews, MT.	N120AS
☐ C-GYSC	97	King Air B200	BB-1579	Sanjel Corp. Calgary, AB.	(N886AT)
☐ C-GZGZ	00	Pilatus PC-12/45	357	Road Trailer Rentals Inc., Unionville, ON.	N7725X
☐ C-GZNS	82	MU-2 Marquise	1550SA	Thunder Airlines Ltd. Thunder Bay, ON.	N64WB
☐ C-GZON	72	Rockwell 690	11020	Air Spray (1967) Ltd. Edmonton, AB.	N14CV
☐ C-GZRX	80	King Air 200	BB-574	North Cariboo Flying Service Ltd. Fort St John, BC.	N75WL
☐ C-GZUZ	73	King Air A100	B-143	Exploits Valley Air Services Ltd. Gander, NF.	C-GNVB
☐ C-GZYO	78	King Air 200	BB-383	Air Nunavut Ltd. Iqaluit, NT.	N384DB
☐ N318CB	00	King Air B200	BB-1730	Brown Flight Properties, Midland Tx.	N204C

CC = CHILE   Total   33
Civil

☐ CC-CAO	79 PA-31T Cheyenne II	7920058	Servicios Aereos Romeomike Limitada, Chile	CC-PJG
☐ CC-CBD	83 PA-31T Cheyenne 1	8104070	Aerobenic SA. Santiago.	(D-IIHW)
☐ CC-CFP	81 PA-31T Cheyenne II	8120058	Servicios Aereos San Esteban Ltda. Santiago.	OE-FMO
☐ CC-CGS	07 King Air C90GT	LJ-1835	Aeroservicios Conimex Ltda.	N7185C
☐ CC-CIW	78 PA-31T Cheyenne II	7820018	Transportes Aereos Corporativos Ltda. Santiago.	N35RT
☐ CC-CLY	71 King Air 100	B-79	Maquinarias Pivcevic E Hijos Ltda/Aerovias DAP. Punta Arenas	CC-PIE
☐ CC-CMH	78 PA-31T Cheyenne II	7820035	Regais Airlines, Tobalaba.	N5MQ
☐ CC-COT	67 King Air A90	LJ-217		F-GJRD
☐ CC-CPB	01 King Air B200	BB-1796	Transportes y Servicios Aereos SA. Santiago.	N4126T
☐ CC-CPR	81 Cheyenne II-XL	8166070	Transportes A.S.	N333X
☐ CC-CVT	99 King Air C90B	LJ-1556	Bonir Ltda. Santiago.	N3156F
☐ CC-CVZ	69 King Air B90	LJ-441	Turismo Aereo Chile Ltda. Santiago.	CC-PBZ
☐ CC-CWD	81 PA-31T Cheyenne 1	8104071	Aero Cardal Ltda. Tobalaba.	CC-CRU
☐ CC-CYB	81 PA-31T Cheyenne II	8120028	Aeroantilco S.A.	CC-PCY
☐ CC-CYT	79 PA-31T Cheyenne II	7920053	Avionek S.A.	N27GD
☐ CC-CZC	79 PA-31T Cheyenne II	7920072	Servicios Aereos El Loa SA. Chuquicamata.	N620P
☐ CC-DIV	81 King Air B200CT	BN-1	D.G.A.C. Santiago. (was BL-24)	CC-EAA
☐ CC-DSN	75 King Air E90	LW-153	D.G.A.C. Santiago.	CC-EAB
☐ CC-PBT	81 PA-31T Cheyenne 1	8104063	Metalurgica Ducasse Ltda. Santiago.	N2568Y
☐ CC-PHM	79 PA-31T Cheyenne 1	7904054	Industria Metalurgica del Norte, Santiago.	CC-CPV
☐ CC-PJH	81 PA-31T Cheyenne II	8120049	Inversiones Cerro Negrao Ltda. Quillota.	CC-CNT
☐ CC-PLL	79 PA-31T Cheyenne II	7920005	Compania Chilena de Fosforos SA. Santiago.	N817CJ
☐ CC-PML	84 Cheyenne II-XL	1166002	Banco O Higgins/Rimac SA. Santiago. (was 8166074).	N2580Z
☐ CC-PNA	79 PA-31T Cheyenne II	7920082	Comercial US Prodexport Ltda. San felipe.	N109TT
☐ CC-PNS	81 PA-31T Cheyenne 1	8104022	Constructora Raul del Rio SA. Santiago.	N780CA
☐ CC-PVE	81 Cheyenne II-XL	8166038	Soc de Servicios Latinoamericana Ltda. Santiago.	N161TC
☐ CC-PWA	92 King Air 300LW	FA-225	Ducasse Comercial Ltda.	D-IBAB
☐ CC-PWH	81 PA-31T Cheyenne 1	8104023	Transportes Modern Air SA. Tobalaba.	CC-CWK
☐ CC-PZB	78 PA-31T Cheyenne II	7820020	San Andreas Ltda. Santiago.	CC-CZB
☐ CC-PZX	80 PA-31T Cheyenne II	8020069	Elalba SA & Westfield Business, Los Cerillos.	CC-CNH

Military

☐ 331	75 King Air A100	B-219	Fuerza Aerea de Chile, Gr 10, Santiago.	CC-ESA
☐ 336	96 King Air B200	BB-1530	Fuerza Aerea de Chile, Gr 10, Santiago.	
☐ C-51	80 PA-31T Cheyenne II	8020090	Carabineros de Chile, Tobalaba.	CC-PMZ

CN = MOROCCO   Total   18
Civil

☐ CN-...	03 King Air 350	FL-374		CN-ANJ
☐ CN-CDF	80 King Air 200	BB-577	Royal Air Maroc, Casablanca.	
☐ CN-CDN	80 King Air 200	BB-713	Royal Air Maroc, Casablanca.	N36741
☐ CN-RLE	97 King Air 350	FL-170	Regional Air Lines, Casablanca.	N2015G
☐ CN-RLL	05 King Air 350	FL-452	Regional Air Lines, Casablanca	N36932
☐ CN-TAX	80 King Air C90	LJ-922	Omnium Nord Africain, Casablanca.	F-GCPN
☐ CN-TPH	82 King Air B200	BB-1006	Ste de Production Agricole, Anfa.	N680CB

Military

☐ CNA-NB	74 King Air A100	B-181	Government of Morocco, Rabat.	
☐ CNA-NC	74 King Air A100	B-182	Government of Morocco, Rabat.	
☐ CNA-ND	74 King Air A100	B-183	Government of Morocco, Rabat.	
☐ CNA-NE	74 King Air A100	B-186	Government of Morocco, Rabat.	
☐ CNA-NF	74 King Air A100	B-187	Government of Morocco, Rabat.	
☐ CNA-NG	82 King Air B200	BB-1072	Government of Morocco, Rabat.	
☐ CNA-NH	82 King Air B200	BB-1073	Government of Morocco, Rabat.	
☐ CNA-NI	82 King Air B200C	BL-57	Government of Morocco, Rabat.	
☐ CNA-NJ	06 King Air 350	FL-494	Government of Morocco, Rabat.	N37094
☐ CNA-NX	89 King Air 300	FA-207	Government of Morocco, Rabat.	
☐ CNA-NY	89 King Air 300	FA-208	Government of Morocco, Rabat.	

CP = BOLIVIA   Total   13
Civil

☐ CP-	79 King Air E90	LW-314		N20564
☐ CP-1678	81 PA-31T Cheyenne II	8120017	Luis A Gomez,	EB-004
☐ CP-1934	69 680W Turbo Commander	1835-40		N81LC
☐ CP-2042	70 681 Turbo Commander	6025		N10HG

Reg	Yr Type	c/n	Owner/Operator	Prev Regn

Reg	Yr	Type	c/n	Owner/Operator	Prev Regn
☐ CP-2224	79	Rockwell 690B	11564	Aero Inca Ltda. La Paz.	N401SP
☐ CP-2266	77	Rockwell 690B	11395	Aeroeste Ltda/Dr. Jorge Velasco Monasterio, Santa Cruz.	N816PC
☐ CP-2467	73	Rockwell 690A	11107	Apex Silver Mines Corp. Denver, Co. USA.	N69010
Military					
☐ EB-50		CASA 212-300	369	Ejercito de Bolivia, La Paz.	
☐ FAB 002	74	King Air 200	BB-11	Fuerza Aerea Boliviana, La Paz.	FAB 001
☐ FAB 018	81	King Air 200C	BL-28	Fuerza Aerea Boliviana, Esc 810, La Paz.	
☐ FAB 028	73	Rockwell 690	11067	Fuerza Aerea Boliviana, La Paz.	CP-1076
☐ FAB 030	80	Gulfstream 980	95004	Fuerza Aerea Boliviana, La Paz.	CP-2078
☐ FAB 042	73	King Air E90	LW-28	Fuerza Aerea Boliviana, La Paz.	CP-...

CS = PORTUGAL   Total 3
Civil

Reg	Yr	Type	c/n	Owner/Operator	Prev Regn
☐ CS-DDU	80	King Air 200	BB-640	OMNI Aviacao & Tecnologia Ltda. Cascais-Tires.	N47CF
☐ CS-DIQ	05	Pilatus PC-12/45	625	Helibravo Aviacao Lda. Cascais.	HB-FPU
☐ CS-DOC	00	Beech 1900D	UE-371	NTA/European NetJets, Northolt, UK.	N371UE

CX = URUGUAY   Total 4
Civil

Reg	Yr	Type	c/n	Owner/Operator	Prev Regn
☐ CX-...	85	Gulfstream 1000	96093		C-FALI
☐ CX-FCS	06	Pilatus PC-12/47	765	Mr. Correa, Melilla	HB-FST
Military					
☐ 550	88	120ER Brasilia	120089	Government of Uruguay/Fuerza Aerea Uruguayo, Montevideo	N12705
☐ AU-871	78	King Air 200T	BT-4	Uruguayan Navy. (was BB-408). (status ?).	N2067D

C6 = BAHAMAS   Total 2
Civil

Reg	Yr	Type	c/n	Owner/Operator	Prev Regn
☐ C6-MIP	04	King Air B200	BB-1851		N6151C
Military					
☐ DF-103/C	93	King Air 350	FL-95	Bahamas Defence Force, Nassau.	N8145E

C9 = MOZAMBIQUE   Total 4
Civil

Reg	Yr	Type	c/n	Owner/Operator	Prev Regn
☐ C9-ASK	81	King Air C90	LJ-954	Airplus SARL, Maputo.	F-GDCC
☐ C9-ASV	81	King Air 200C	BL-21	LAM-Linhas Aereas de Mocambique, Maputo.	N3831T
☐ C9-ENH	80	King Air 200	BB-626	ENH-Nacional Hidrocarbonetos de Mocambique, Maputo.	C9-ASS
☐ C9-JTP	76	PA-31T Cheyenne II	7620012	Reliable Fork Lift & Truck Services, Alrode.	ZS-JTP

D = GERMANY   Total 159
Civil

Reg	Yr	Type	c/n	Owner/Operator	Prev Regn
☐ D-	82	King Air B200	BB-944		G-FPLA
☐ D-	99	King Air 350	FL-256		N350WD
☐ D-	84	Conquest 1	425-0222	Aerowest GmbH, Hanover	N1777X
☐ D-	07	PA-46-500TP Meridian	4697325		
☐ D-	00	King Air C90B	LJ-1606		D-ITOP
☐ D-....	70	SA-226T Merlin 3	T-202	Aircraft Guaranty Title LLC. (trustor ?).	N103PA
☐ D-C	07	King Air 350	FL-557		N557KA
☐ D-C...	89	King Air 300	FA-192	Beechcraft Vertrieb & Service GmbH. Augsburg.	N900RB
☐ D-CACB	83	King Air B200T	BT-27	German Flight Inspection, Braunschweig. (was BB-1105).	N7244R
☐ D-CADN	93	King Air 350	FL-101	ADAC/R+R Flugzeughandels u Vermietungs GmbH. Kamenz.	N82311
☐ D-CBIN	82	SA-227AT Merlin 4C	AT-440B	BinairAero Service GmbH. Munich.	I-FSAD
☐ D-CCCC	82	SA-227AT Merlin 4C	AT-511	Northern Air Freight GmbH. Flensburg./Binair GmbH	N600N
☐ D-CFMA	92	King Air 350	FL-76	FCS-Flight Calibration Services GmbH. Braunschweig.	N8274U
☐ D-CFMB	93	King Air 350	FL-97	FCS-Flight Calibration Services GmbH. Braunschweig.	N8297L
☐ D-CFMD	06	King Air 350	FL-473	FCS-Flight Calibration Services GmbH. Braunschweig.	N37173
☐ D-CLOG	00	King Air 350	FL-276	Kronotrans Speditions GmbH.	N3176T
☐ D-CNAY	81	SA-227AT Merlin 4C	AT-493	Hahn Airlines GmbH. Hahn.	PH-RAX
☐ D-COEB	99	King Air 350	FL-255	exported	N3205M
☐ D-CRAO	06	King Air 350	FL-515		N70155
☐ D-CSKY	96	King Air 350	FL-130	ADAC/Intro Verwaltungs GmbH/Aero-Dienst GmbH. Templehof.	
☐ D-CWKM	04	King Air 350	FL-410	WEKA Firmengruppe GmbH. Kissing.	N61740
☐ D-EALL	01	PA-46-500TP Meridian	4697050		LX-FUN
☐ D-ECBE	01	PA-46-500TP Meridian	4697063		N253MM
☐ D-ECRB	01	PA-46-500TP Meridian	4697061	OPS-Europe GmbH, Schoenefeld	N633RB
☐ D-EICO	01	PA-46-500TP Meridian	4697125	Schrage Rohrkettensystem GmbH. Wilhelmshaven.	N5361C
☐ D-EPKD	00	PA-46-500TP Meridian	4697019	Kraemer Marktforschung GmbH. Muenster.	OY-GPT
☐ D-EPUS	01	PA-46-500TP Meridian	4697079		(D-EARG)

Reg	Yr	Type	c/n	Owner/Operator	Prev Regn
D-ERAH	06	PA-46-500TP Meridian	4697276		
D-ESSS	01	PA-46-500TP Meridian	4697070		D-FOXI
D-EVER	01	PA-46-500TP Meridian	4697105	Milan, Italy.	N429MM
D-FALF	99	TBM 700B	157	J Herz, Hamburg.	F-WWRN
D-FAPC	04	Pilatus PC-12/45	579	Busche GmbH	
D-FATN	06	Pilatus PC-12/47	788	ATON GmbH., Fulda	HB-FVV
D-FBFS	06	TBM 850	387	Brose Fahrzeugteile GmbH., Coburg	F-WWRR
D-FCGH	05	Pilatus PC-12/45	633	Rhein-Mosel-Flug KG. Koblenz.	HB-FSL
D-FFHZ	07	Pilatus PC-12/47	847	Pilatus Flugzeugwerke	
D-FGPE	07	TBM 850	413		N50KK
D-FGYY	00	TBM 700B	162	Bega GmbH. Hannover.	
D-FHGN	05	Pilatus PC-12/47	684	Eichsfeldair GmbH	HB-F..
D-FIBI	06	Pilatus PC-12/47	773		HB-FSX
D-FINE	06	Pilatus PC-12/47	761	Natenco, Leinfelden-Echterdingen	HB-F..
D-FIRE	99	TBM 700B	137	Ulrich Brunner Ofen und Heiztechnik GmbH. Eggenfelden.	
D-FIVE	01	TBM 700B	186	Atremed Aviation GmbH.	
D-FKAI	04	TBM 700C2	288	Kaiser Bekleidungs GmbH. Mainbullau.	
D-FMOR	07	PA-46-500TP Meridian	4697299		
D-FNRE	99	TBM 700A	142	Richard Engstler Elastometall GmbH. Ottersweier.	
D-FOOO	92	TBM 700	24	Tan Siekmann, Hamburg.	D-FTAN
D-FSJP	98	TBM 700	130	Diamond Aircraft GmbH. Siegerland.	N38KJ
D-FTBG	05	Grob G160 Ranger	87001	Grob Aerospace, Allgaeu.	
D-IAAC	78	Conquest II	441-0073	Ruediger Kueckelhaus/CCF Manager Airline GmbH. Cologne.	N88834
D-IAAE	87	PA-42 Cheyenne IIIA	5501047	Air Alliance GmbH., Siegerland	I-TRER
D-IAAH	90	King Air C90A	LJ-1247	Dipl. Kfm. Steuerberater Dietmar Volkmann, Nuremberg.	N5651J
D-IABA	81	PA-42 Cheyenne III	8001011	Grosstischlerei Aldershot GmbH.	N247WW
D-IABC	67	680V Turbo Commander	1684-65	Air Tempelhof Flug GmbH. Tempelhof-Berlin.	EC-HDE
D-IAHT	77	Mitsubishi MU-2P	352SA	Fly Point, Eisenach	N41AD
D-IANA	95	King Air B200	BB-1517	KLW Mietflug/Dix Aviation, Paderborn-Lippstadt.	N3217V
D-IAVI	99	King Air C90B	LJ-1583		F-HADR
D-IAWB	90	PA-42 Cheyenne IIIA	5501054	Aerowest GmbH. Hanover.	B-3623
D-IBAD	85	King Air B200	BB-1229	PTL-Pilot Training GmbH. Landshut.	
D-IBAG	74	Rockwell 690A	11211	Vorgebirgs-Residenz Bonn-Edenich GmbH. Saarbruecken.	
D-IBAR	87	King Air B200	BB-1280	Lindner Hotels AG. Dusseldorf/ACH Hamburg Flug, Hamburg.	
D-IBBP	04	King Air C90B	LJ-1716	Comair Reise u Charter GmbH. Vilshofen.	N61716
D-IBCB	00	King Air B200	BB-1729	Work Aviation Services Ltd.	5B-CJK
D-IBER	89	King Air 300LW	FA-184	DSF Flugdienst AG.Air Alliance, Siegerland.	
D-IBFE	00	King Air B200	BB-1716	Beechcraft Berlin Aviation GmbH. Tempelhof.	N3216G
D-IBFT	96	King Air B200	BB-1535	Brose Fahrzeugteile GmbH/BFS Flugservice GmbH. Coburg.	N1135Z
D-IBHL	84	SA-227TT Merlin 3C	TT-512A	Reederei und Schiffmakler Egon Oldendorf oHG. Luebeck.	N123GM
D-IBMC	81	King Air C90	LJ-931	Garant Import und Export GmbH. Hamm.	HB-GIE
D-IBMP	87	King Air B200	BB-1284	B200 Flug Charter Leer GmbH/ACH Hamburg Flug GmbH. Hamburg.	N6321V
D-IBSA	81	PA-31T Cheyenne II	8120033	Frau Amalie-Barbara Fuchs/Fuchs Mineraloelwerke, Mannheim.	N42TW
D-IBSG	06	King Air C90GT	LJ-1760		N23HF
D-ICCC	90	Reims/Cessna F406	F406-0050	C 406 N50 Eigentums GmbH & Co KG,Braunschweig, Germany	N406P
D-ICHG	91	King Air B200	BB-1400	Avanti Air GmbH. Siegerland.	N8085D
D-ICHS	85	Conquest 1	425-0233	A W Aerowest GmbH. Hannover.	N80938
D-ICKM	82	King Air B200	BB-1005		OE-FKW
D-ICMF	81	Conquest 1	425-0102	IMCON Immobilienentwicklungs und Betriebs GmbH. Herne.	N151GA
D-IDAK	75	King Air C90	LJ-647	Transavia GmbH. Speyer.	LX-DAK
D-IDAX	84	Conquest 1	425-0209		D-IMPC
D-IDBU	84	PA-42 Cheyenne IIIA	5501029	DSF Flugdienst AG.Air Alliance, Siegerland.	N700CC
D-IDCV	00	King Air C90B	LJ-1622	Christine Volkmann, Gelsenkirchen.	N4172Q
D-IDEA	80	SA-226T Merlin 3B	T-322	Gerhard Schmid, Koeln-Bonn.	(N330JP)
D-IDIA	90	PA-42 Cheyenne IIIA	5501055	ACH Hamburg Flug GmbH. Hamburg.	N955TA
D-IDIX	99	King Air C90B	LJ-1571	Dix Aviation, Paderborn.	N90KA
D-IDPL	77	King Air B100	BE-29	Zell Air GmbH. Muehlheim.	D-IZAC
D-IDRF	81	King Air B200	BB-933	German Air Rescue, Karlsruhe.	OE-FRF
D-IEAH	89	King Air C90A	LJ-1216	Fischerwerke Artur Fischer GmbH. Donaueschingen.	N1562Z
D-IEDI	98	King Air B200	BB-1633	Flyer SA AG. Weiterstadt.	N2345M
D-IEFB	81	King Air B200	BB-897	Flugbereitschaft GmbH. Karlsruhe.	N200TM
D-IEMR	84	PA-31T Cheyenne 1A	1104015		D-IHJL
D-IEXP	85	PA-42 Cheyenne 400LS	5527030	Dr Bernt Schottdorf	N41198
D-IFFB	93	King Air 300LW	FA-224	Strathmann AG/FLM Aviation KG. Hamburg.	N56449
D-IFGN	81	PA-31T Cheyenne II	8120052	Hans-Juergen Guido, Regensburg.	(D-IEJG)

Reg	Yr Type	c/n	Owner/Operator	Prev Regn
D-IFHI	81 King Air C90	LJ-977	Ailana Vermoegens und Grundstuecksverwaltungs GmbH. Munich.	N1813P
D-IFHZ	84 PA-31T Cheyenne 1A	1104016	Zollern Flugdienste GmbH. Mengen.	N91201
D-IFMI	85 King Air C90A	LJ-1101	Fritz Mueller, Ingelfingen.	N17EL
D-IFSH	84 PA-42 Cheyenne IIIA	5501014	FSH Schul u Charter GmbH. Leipzig.	N45SL
D-IFTC	71 King Air C90	LJ-513	Peak Air GmbH	4X-DZT
D-IGKN	84 King Air C90A	LJ-1077	Lufttaxi Flug GmbH. Dortmund.	N4111U
D-IGOB	92 P-180 Avanti	1016	MFS-Manager Flug Service GmbH. Zweibruecken.	I-PJAT
D-IHAH	94 King Air C90B	LJ-1370	EFD Eisele Flugdienst GmbH, Stuttgart	N1570C
D-IHHE	93 King Air C90B	LJ-1327	FVG-Flugzeugvermietungs GmbH. Saarbruecken.	N8227P
D-IHJK	81 PA-31T Cheyenne 1	8104057	H J Kuepper/Avanti Air GmbH. Siegerland.	N62BW
D-IHKM	87 King Air C90A	LJ-1158	Porta Flug GmbH. Porta Westfalica.	N38H
D-IHLA	83 PA-42 Cheyenne IIIA	8301001	Aerowest Flugcharter GmbH. Hanover.	C-GNRD
D-IHMV	93 King Air C90B	LJ-1325	SFD Stuttgarter Flugdienst GmbH, Stuttgart	N8135M
D-IHRG	07 King Air C90GT	LJ-1845		N845KA
D-IHSI	80 Gulfstream 980	95039	Air Evertz GmbH. Herdorf.	N9790S
D-IHSW	92 King Air C90B	LJ-1315	Kapp Werkzeugmaschinenfabrik GmbH. Coburg.	N8103E
D-IICE	77 King Air 200	BB-269	Excellent Air GmbH. Amsterdam, Holland.	N269D
D-IIHA	72 King Air C90	LJ-562	Dr Joachim von Meister, Bad Homburg.	(N333FJ)
D-IIKM	85 King Air C90A	LJ-1120	Kurt Jaeger, Berlin.	N7237K
D-IIVA	06 P-180 Avanti II	1125	Air Go Flugservice GmbH. Hahn	
D-IIWB	93 King Air C90B	LJ-1340	ACH Hamburg Flug GmbH. Hamburg.	N10799
D-IJAH	05 King Air B200	BB-1917	A Haering, Donaueschingen.	N37097
D-IJET	02 P-180 Avanti	1056	Vibrogruppe Air Flugservice GmbH. Moenchengladbach.	
D-IKET	80 PA-31T Cheyenne II	8020017	Karosserie Entwicklung Thurner, Landshut.	N154CA
D-IKEW	78 PA-31T Cheyenne II	7820066	Kress Elektrik GmbH. Bisingen.	N6108A
D-IKIM	93 King Air C90B	LJ-1324	Rudolf Kimmerle Gewerbebau, Augsburg.	N82430
D-IKKY	80 MU-2 Solitaire	420SA	Karl George Theruer, Stuttgart.	I-SOLT
D-IKOB	81 King Air B200	BB-921	MediAir GmbH. Munich.	N244JB
D-ILCE	80 PA-31T Cheyenne 1	8004053	DSF Flugdienst AG./Air Alliance, Siegerland.	
D-ILGA	84 PA-31T Cheyenne 1A	1104014	ElektroMstr. Willy Stuecker, Brokdorf.	N9382T
D-ILGI	85 King Air C90A	LJ-1090	Georg Wissler, Aschaffenburg-Grossostheim.	N7210H
D-ILIN	79 King Air 200	BB-545	EAS-Executive Air Service Flug GmbH. Mannheim.	OY-CBY
D-ILYS	85 Conquest II	441-0355	Lufttaxi Flug GmbH. Dortmund.	N355VB
D-IMAG	07 King Air C90GT	LJ-1833		N37064
D-IMWK	84 SA-227TT Merlin 300	TT-529	LTO-Lufttransport Muenster-Osnabrueck GmbH. Munster.	N3109S
D-INAS	99 King Air C90B	LJ-1551	NAS Nordwest Service	XA-GSA
D-INNN	81 PA-31T Cheyenne II	8120102	Raiffeisenbank Vilshofener Land eG. Vilshofen.(was 8120067).	N822SW
D-IONE	80 PA-42 Cheyenne III	8001002	DSF Flugdienst AG. Siegerland.	C-GIDC
D-IOSA	87 PA-42 Cheyenne IIIA	5501041	Lufthansa Flight Training GmbH. Bremen.	N9578N
D-IOSB	87 PA-42 Cheyenne IIIA	5501042	Lufthansa Flight Training GmbH. Bremen.	
D-IOSC	87 PA-42 Cheyenne IIIA	5501043	Lufthansa Flight Training GmbH. Bremen.	D-IOKP
D-IOSD	87 PA-42 Cheyenne IIIA	5501044	Lufthansa Flight Training GmbH. Bremen.	
D-IOTT	79 PA-31T Cheyenne II	7920010	Dr Bernd Koenes, Erkelenz.	N6196A
D-IPOS	82 Conquest 1	425-0120	Dr Peters GmbH/MSR-Flug Charter GmbH. M-Osnabrueck.	N425R
D-IPSY	97 King Air B200	BB-1591	Winter & Kamp GmbH/ACM Air Charter Minninger, Baden-Baden.	N1819H
D-IQAS	84 PA-42 Cheyenne 400LS	5527022	Quick Air Service GmbH. Cologne.	N322KW
D-IRAR	06 King Air B200	BB-1957	Rettenmeier Holding AG., Wilburgstetten	N957BA
D-IRIS	85 King Air F90-1	LA-229	Frau Uta Ackermans-Meynen, Kerken.	N7209Z
D-IRVK	80 PA-31T Cheyenne 1	8004052	VK Aviation & Trading GmbH. Egelsbach	I-LIAT
D-ISIG	81 PA-31T Cheyenne 1	8104055	Schindler Ingenieur GmbH. Aschaffenburg.	N123AT
D-ISIX	94 King Air C90B	LJ-1355	Brinkmann Maschinenfabrik GmbH. Schloss Holte.	N995PA
D-ISTB	85 King Air F90-1	LA-227	A & G Bumueller Grossbaeckerei u Konditorei, Stuttgart.	N330VP
D-ITCH	86 King Air C90A	LJ-1138	Roland & Meckbach GmbH. Kassel-Calden.	N17KA
D-ITDK	07 King Air C90GT	LJ-1865		N34975
D-ITFC	06 King Air B200	BB-1973	Pea Air GmbH	N74753
D-ITLL	82 King Air F90	LA-192	Tamsen Ferrari, RR & Bentley Import & Export GmbH. Stuhr.	N17TS
D-ITRI	87 PA-42 Cheyenne IIIA	5501045	Air Alliance GmbH. Burbach.	N56MV
D-ITWO	87 PA-42 Cheyenne IIIA	5501046	Air Alliance GmbH., Siegerland	I-TREQ
D-IUDE	93 King Air C90B	LJ-1323	Wolfgang Preinfalk Werkzeug & Machinenbau GmbH. Sulzbach.	N90KA
D-IUTA	80 Gulfstream 840	11639	Wilhelm Huelpert, Dortmund.	HB-LOL
D-IVAN	99 King Air B200	BB-1662	CMAC-City Marketing Advertising & Communications GmbH	S5-CEC
D-IVIP	99 King Air B200	BB-1672	VHM Schul und Charterflug GmbH. Essen.	
D-IWID	96 King Air C90B	LJ-1450	Widerker Aircraft GmbH. Stuttgart.	N3265K
D-IWKB	98 King Air B200	...	Wittgensteiner Rehakliniken GmbH/Avanti Air GmbH. Frankfurt.	
D-IXXX	84 PA-42 Cheyenne IIIA	5501007	FSH Schul u Charter GmbH., Leipzig	D-ICGB

Reg	Yr Type	c/n	Owner/Operator	Prev Regn
☐ D-IYYY	84 PA-42 Cheyenne 400LS	5527018	Air Alliance Express, Siegerland	EC-IIP
☐ D-IZZY	99 P-180 Avanti	1034	Air Go Flugservice GmbH. Hahn.	N680JP

D2 = ANGOLA   Total 31
Civil

Reg	Yr Type	c/n	Owner/Operator	Prev Regn
☐ D2-	99 King Air B200	BB-1654	Escom Espirito Santo Comercial Ltda., Luanda, Angola	N771JH
☐ D2-	07 King Air 350	FL-548		N548KA
☐ D2-ALS	66 King Air 90	LJ-80	Intertransit, Luanda.	ZS-NED
☐ D2-EAA	73 Rockwell 690A	11132	Directorate of Civil Aviation, Luanda.	CR-LAA
☐ D2-EBF	81 King Air 200	BB-836	Tropicana. Luanda.	S9-NAQ
☐ D2-EBG	78 King Air 200	BB-334	Manewa Taxi Aereo Ltda. Luanda.	ZS-NRT
☐ D2-ECN	85 Reims/Cessna F406	F406-0002	SAL-Sociedade de Aviacao Ligeira SA. Luanda.	PH-MNS
☐ D2-ECO	86 Reims/Cessna F406	F406-0011	SAL-Sociedade de Aviacao Ligeira SA. Luanda.	D-IDAA
☐ D2-ECP	87 Reims/Cessna F406	F406-0016	SAL-Sociedade de Aviacao Ligeira SA. Luanda.	PH-LAS
☐ D2-ECQ	87 Reims/Cessna F406	F406-0019	SAL-Sociedade de Aviacao Ligeira SA. Luanda.	G-CVAN
☐ D2-ECW	93 King Air 350	FL-102	SAL-Sociedade de Aviacao Ligeira SA. Luanda.	S9-TAP
☐ D2-ECX	90 King Air B200	BB-1362	SAL-Sociedade de Aviacao Ligeira SA. Luanda.	N1565F
☐ D2-ECY	89 King Air B200C	BL-135	SAL-Sociedade de Aviacao Ligeira SA. Luanda.	S9-NAP
☐ D2-EDD	95 King Air B200	BB-1512	Harlow Resources Ltd. Roadtown, Tortola, BVI.	N700FT
☐ D2-EMX	79 King Air 200	BB-480	Intertransit, Luanda. 'Rita Yara'	ZS-MJH
☐ D2-EOJ	90 King Air B200	BB-1371	Equator Leasing 14 Ltd. Luanda.	N56616
☐ D2-EQC	68 King Air B90	LJ-324	SONANGOL Aeronautica - Helipetrol, Luanda.	N892DF
☐ D2-ERK	81 King Air B200	BB-937	U N WFP-World Food Programme - Skylink Canada,	C9-ATW
☐ D2-ERO	79 King Air 200T	BT-8	Turismo e Viagem, (was BB-530).	ZS-OPR
☐ D2-ESP	90 King Air B200	BB-1391	SONANGOL Aeronautica - Helipetrol, Luanda.	N8048W
☐ D2-EXB	65 Gulfstream 1	166	Intertransit/GMX-Grupo Mello Xavier, Luanda. (stored)	4X-ARG
☐ D2-EXC	61 Gulfstream 1	80	Intertransit, Luanda.	F-GGGY
☐ D2-EXD	64 Gulfstream 1	124	Intertransit, Luanda.	ZS-NKT
☐ D2-EXW	76 King Air 200	BB-101	Government of Angola, Luanda.	ZS-MGR
☐ D2-FEG	82 King Air B200	BB-1060	Tropicana, Luanda.	ZS-TON
☐ D2-FEI	80 King Air 200	BB-620	Transteco, Luanda.	ZS-OGV
☐ D2-FFK	82 King Air B200	BB-1026	Aeronautica	N153D
☐ D2-FFL	76 King Air 200	BB-126	Gira Globo Ltda Aeronautica, Luanda. 'Capembe'	ZS-PBB
☐ D2-FFO	90 King Air 350	FL-10	Diexim Expresso, Luanda.	N350FH
☐ D2-FFT	80 King Air 200	BB-607		ZS-LTE
☐ D2-FMD	80 King Air/Catpass 250	BT-18	Capricorn Systems Ltd. Lanseria, RSA. (was BB-695).	N123PW

EC = SPAIN   Total 41
Civil

Reg	Yr Type	c/n	Owner/Operator	Prev Regn
☐ EC-	07 PA-46-500TP Meridian	4697291		D-EAVK
☐ EC-CHE	74 King Air A100	B-195	FAASA Aviacion, Palma del Rio.	E23-2
☐ EC-DHF	79 PA-31T Cheyenne II	7920073	Dominguez Toledo SA/Mayoral, Malaga.	N23699
☐ EC-DSA	66 680T Turbo Commander	1564-20	Ambulancias Insulares SA. Palma de Mallorca. (status ?).	I-ARBO
☐ EC-DXA	76 Rockwell 690A	11328	Tur Air SA. Madrid. 'Don Mendo'	D-IHVB
☐ EC-EVJ	60 Gulfstream 1	39	Stellair, Madrid. (status ?).(stored Madrid).	EC-376
☐ EC-FPF	91 TBM 700	12	Arturo Beltran SA. Zaragoza.	F-OHBD
☐ EC-GBB	76 King Air 200	BB-182	Policia, Madrid-Cuatro Vientos.	EC-727
☐ EC-GBI	75 SA-226AT Merlin 4A	AT-041	Medit Air SA. Valencia.	EC-867
☐ EC-GFK	77 SA-226AT Merlin 4A	AT-062	Flightline SL/Ibertrans Aerea SL. Barcelona-El Prat.	EC-125
☐ EC-GHZ	79 King Air 200	BB-555	Urgemer Canarias SL. Las Palmas.	D-IFOR
☐ EC-GIJ	68 King Air B90	LJ-382	Aqua Air, Barcelona.	F-WQCC
☐ EC-GJZ	69 SA-26AT Merlin 2B	T26-149	Air Business SL. Madrid.	EC-202
☐ EC-GOK	74 Mitsubishi MU-2J	635	Airnor - Aeronaves del Noroeste SL. Ponteareas.	OY-ARV
☐ EC-GOY	71 King Air C90	LJ-527	SOKO Aviation SL. Ibiza.	N55SG
☐ EC-GSQ	95 King Air 350	FL-128	TAS-Transportes Aereos del Sur SA. Seville.	N128FL
☐ EC-HBF	80 SA-226AT Merlin 4A	AT-074	Flightline SL/MRW Worldwide Courier, Barcelona-El Prat.	EC-GDR
☐ EC-HHO	77 King Air 200	BB-262	SOKO Aviation SL. Ibiza.	N92V
☐ EC-HMA	73 King Air C90	LJ-577	Rivafleca SL/BKS Air, Bilbao.	N57KA
☐ EC-HNH	73 Rockwell 690	11058	Trabajos Aereos SA. Cuatro Vientos.	N690PJ
☐ EC-IBK	01 King Air 350	FL-328	Gestair Executive Jet SA. Madrid-Torrejon.	N4328W
☐ EC-ILE	01 King Air B200	BB-1792	Helisureste SA. Palma. 'Mutxamel'.	N5092K
☐ EC-IPZ	81 Cheyenne II-XL	8166056	Mayoral Executive Jet, Malaga.	D-ICGA
☐ EC-ISH	03 Pilatus PC-12/45	498	NorestAir SL.Barcelona-El Prat.	HB-FPG
☐ EC-IUV	78 King Air 200	BB-366	Wondair on Demand Aviation SL. Valencia.	D-IBHK
☐ EC-IUX	03 King Air B200	BB-1840	Transportes Aereos del Sur SA. Seville.	N816LD
☐ EC-IVZ	03 PA-46-500TP Meridian	4697170	Gavina, Sabadell.	N3046P

Reg	Yr Type	c/n	Owner/Operator	Prev Regn
☐ EC-JCV	75 SA-226AT Merlin 4A	AT-038	Swift Air SA. Madrid.	SX-BGT
☐ EC-JFO	04 Pilatus PC-12/45	549	NorestAir SL Barcelona-El Prat.	G-CCPU
☐ EC-JGB	94 King Air B200	BB-1478	BKS Air/Inversiones Aeronauticas Baleares, Mahon.	D-IHAN
☐ EC-JJP	81 King Air 200	BB-845	Urgemer Canarias SL. Las Palmas.	OY-GRB
☐ EC-JQC	78 SA-226AT Merlin 4A	AT-066	Canarias Aeronautica, Las Palmas	N5FY
☐ EC-JRF	84 Cheyenne II-XL	1166003	Mayoral Aviacion SL. Malaga.	D-IXXX
☐ EC-JXM	97 Pilatus PC-12	177	Norestair SL, Biscarri	D-FCJA
☐ EC-KFK	03 Pilatus PC-12/45	513	Aerodynamics Malaga S.L., Malaga	HB-FPK
☐ EC-KHR	97 King Air B200	BB-1564	Euroairlines, Barcelona	G-IMGL

Military

☐ E 22-..	73 King Air C90	LJ-608	Grupo 42, Getafe.	EC-CDK
☐ E 22-01	75 King Air C90	LJ-666	Grupo 42, Getafe.	EC-COL
☐ E 22-03	73 King Air C90	LJ-605	Grupo 42, Getafe.	EC-CDJ
☐ E 22-04	73 King Air C90	LJ-603	Grupo 42, Getafe.	EC-CDI
☐ E 22-05	74 King Air C90	LJ-624	Grupo 42, Getafe.	EC-CHC

EI = EIRE   Total 3

Civil

☐ EI-DMG	80 Conquest II	441-0165	Dawn Meats Group Ltd. Waterford.	N140MP
☐ EI-TBM	02 TBM 700B	232	Folens Management Services Ltd. Weston.	F-OIKH

Military

☐ 240	80 King Air 200	BB-672	Irish Air Corps. Casement-Dublin.	

EP = IRAN   Total 24

Civil

☐ EP-AGU	70 681 Turbo Commander	6012	Government of Iran, Tehran.	N9061N
☐ EP-AGV	72 Rockwell 690	11045	Government of Iran, Tehran.	
☐ EP-AGW	72 Rockwell 690	11047	Government of Iran, Tehran.	
☐ EP-AHL	74 Rockwell 690A	11143	Sazemane Sanoye Nazami, Tehran.	N57142
☐ EP-AHM	74 Rockwell 690A	11182	State Television Company of Iran, Tehran.	
☐ EP-AKI	73 Rockwell 690	11075	Department of Forest Protection, Tehran.	
☐ EP-FIA	69 680W Turbo Commander	1849-45	Directorate of Civil Aviation, Tehran.	
☐ EP-FIB	69 680W Turbo Commander	1850-46	Directorate of Civil Aviation, Tehran.	
☐ EP-FSS	69 680W Turbo Commander	1848-44	Directorate of Civil Aviation, Tehran.	
☐ EP-KCD	75 Rockwell 690A	11256	Iran Asseman Airlines, Tehran.	

Military

☐ 4-901	73 Rockwell 690	11077	Iranian Army, Mehrabad.	
☐ 4-902	73 Rockwell 690	11078	Iranian Army, Mehrabad.	
☐ 4-903	73 Rockwell 690	11079	Iranian Army, Mehrabad.	
☐ 5-2501	73 Rockwell 690	11076	Iranian Navy, Mehrabad.	
☐ 5-2505	74 Rockwell 690A	11183	Iranian Navy, Mehrabad.	
☐ 5-280	71 681B Turbo Commander	6062	Iranian Air Force, Tehran.	
☐ 5-281	72 681B Turbo Commander	6068	Iranian Air Force, Tehran.	
☐ 5-282	72 681B Turbo Commander	6072	Iranian Air Force, Tehran.	
☐ 5-4035	76 Rockwell 690A	11294	Iranian Navy, Mehrabad.	N9187N
☐ 5-4036	76 Rockwell 690A	11295	Iranian Navy, Mehrabad.	N81427
☐ 5-4037	76 Rockwell 690A	11333	Iranian Navy, Mehrabad.	N57196
☐ 5-4038	76 Rockwell 690A	11334	Iranian Navy, Mehrabad.	N81467
☐ 6-3201	74 Rockwell 690A	11181	Iranian Police Wing, Tehran.	N57196
☐ 6-3202	76 Rockwell 690A	11293	Iranian Police Wing, Tehran.	N81467

E3 = ERITREA   Total 1

Military

☐ E3-AAJ	93 King Air B200	BB-1475	Eritrean Air Force,	ZS-NKE

F = FRANCE   Total 212

Civil

☐ F-	77 SA-226T Merlin 3B	T-276		N188SC
☐ F-	84 King Air C90A	LJ-1066	Aero Capital SAS, Paris	N300FN
☐ F-....	93 Reims/Cessna F406	F406-0072		
☐ F-ASFA	73 King Air E90	LW-47	SEFA, Muret. (status ?)	
☐ F-BOSY	66 King Air A90	LJ-128	Crepusculo Getao e Participacoes Ltda., Funchal, Portugal	D-IMTW
☐ F-BRNO	69 King Air B90	LJ-482	Oceanis Promotion SAS. Montpellier.	HB-GEE
☐ F-BTQP	65 King Air 90	LJ-40	Air Bor SARL. Dijon-Longvic.	I-GNIS
☐ F-BVTB	73 King Air C90	LJ-579	Ste FFM/Twin Jet, Marseille.	D-INAF
☐ F-BXAP	71 King Air C90	LJ-522	Air Normandie, Le Havre-Octeville.	D-IHVB
☐ F-BXAS	75 Rockwell 690AT	11240	Ste Turbomeca, Pau.	F-WXAS

Reg	Yr	Type	c/n	Owner/Operator	Prev Regn
❏ F-BXON	75	King Air E90	LW-161	Aero Stock, Paris-Le Bourget.	
❏ F-BXPY	76	King Air C90	LJ-684	Atlantic-Ste Francaise de Developpement Thermique, La Roche	
❏ F-BXSK	76	PA-31T Cheyenne II	7620020	Jack Simonet & Virginie Avril, St. Barthelemy	
❏ F-BXSL	75	King Air C90	LJ-648	Herve Coral, Le Landin.	
❏ F-GALD	76	PA-31T Cheyenne II	7620032	Ste SITRAM Inox, St Benoit du Sault.	
❏ F-GALN	76	King Air 200T	BT-1	IGN France, Creil. (was BB-186).	
❏ F-GALP	77	King Air 200T	BT-2	IGN France, Creil. (was BB-203).	
❏ F-GALZ	76	King Air E90	LW-199	Ste Transport Air Centre, Roanne-Renaison.	
❏ F-GBLU	79	King Air C90	LJ-822	Icare Franche Comte, Montbeliard.	(F-GNCY)
❏ F-GBPB	66	King Air 90	LJ-98	France Aviation Support SAS, Paris Le-Bourget.	OY-ANP
❏ F-GBPZ	79	King Air C90	LJ-860	AVDEF-Aviation Defence Service, Nimes-Garons.	
❏ F-GCGA	80	King Air C90	LJ-894	Aelia Assurance SARL. Pontoise.	
❏ F-GCLD	74	King Air C90	LJ-637	Crepusculo Getao e Participacoes Ltda., Funchal, Portugal	N95DD
❏ F-GCLH	80	PA-31T Cheyenne II	8020044	Thomas Kruse, Bielefeld, Germany.	N2330V
❏ F-GCTR	81	King Air F90	LA-115	Starcraft, Toussus Le Noble.	
❏ F-GDAK	81	King Air F90	LA-141	Aero Liaisons 5 SARL, Toussus Le Noble.	
❏ F-GDJS	83	King Air B200	BB-1116	Aero Entreprise, Toussus le Noble.	(D-ILOC)
❏ F-GEFZ	81	Conquest 1	425-0059	Les Ailes Roussillonnaises, Montpellier.	LN-AFB
❏ F-GEOU	81	King Air C90	LJ-941	Yankee Romeo Aviation SARL. Strasbourg-Entzheim.	N3804C
❏ F-GERP	73	SA-226AT Merlin 4	AT-012	CEGEBAIL, Marcq en Baroeul.	N111MV
❏ F-GERS	80	King Air 200	BB-753	Air Taxi SAT, Blois le Breuil.	N3705B
❏ F-GESJ	74	King Air E90	LW-97	Aerostock?	F-GESJ
❏ F-GETI	80	King Air F90	LA-19	Alpha Tango EURL, Toussus Le Noble.	N90NS
❏ F-GETJ	78	King Air E90	LW-296	Aero Saint Exupery Co. Toussus Le Noble.	(F-GZZB)
❏ F-GEXK	68	King Air B90	LJ-331	Air Provence International, Marseille.	N886BD
❏ F-GEXV	74	King Air A100	B-199	Phenix Aviation, Le Havre.	N110TD
❏ F-GFDJ	74	King Air E90	LW-86	Aria/Melba Invest SARL. Toussus-le-Noble.	(N505N)
❏ F-GFEA	76	PA-31T Cheyenne II	7620011	France Europe Aviajet, Paris-Le Bourget.	N76PT
❏ F-GFEF	63	Gulfstream 1	122	DIWAN, Rennes-St Jacques.	N707MP
❏ F-GFHC	77	King Air C90	LJ-717	Locavia France, Nantes-Atlantique.	N200BX
❏ F-GFHQ	68	King Air B90	LJ-347	Y P Aviation, Pointoise-Cormeilles.	N777SB
❏ F-GFIR	68	King Air B90	LJ-434	Air Chateaux SARL. Sarlat la Caneda.	C-GRCN
❏ F-GFLE	75	PA-31T Cheyenne II	7520002	Ste Prestavia SA. Coulommiers.	N90589
❏ F-GFVN	82	King Air F90	LA-166	Electronique Mecanique et Conseil SARL. Toussus Le Noble.	HB-GHM
❏ F-GGLA	80	King Air 200	BB-744	Global Air Invest, Montpellier	F-GGPJ
❏ F-GGLN	79	King Air 200	BB-439	Air Net GIE. Montpellier.	N500JA
❏ F-GGLV	73	King Air A100	B-150	Air Bretagne, Noyal-Pontivy.	N51BL
❏ F-GGMS	75	King Air 200	BB-80	ASE/Ste Aeronautique Auboise, Troyes.	N444TW
❏ F-GGMV	80	King Air 200	BB-616	Trans Helicoptere Service, Lyon-Bron.	SE-IUN
❏ F-GGPR	80	King Air 200	BB-681	Aero Services France, Paris-Le Bourget.	LN-AXA
❏ F-GGRV	77	PA-31T Cheyenne II	7720036	Airlec Air Espace SA. Bordeaux-Merignac.	N41RC
❏ F-GGVG	78	SA-226T Merlin 3B	T-293	Airlec Air Espace SA. Bordeaux-Merignac.	D-IBBB
❏ F-GHBD	72	King Air C90	LJ-545	Henri Semin, Mohammedia, Morocco.	D-ILHD
❏ F-GHDO	67	King Air A90	LJ-206	Ste Aero Stock, Toussus-le-Noble. (status ?)	F-BTAK
❏ F-GHFE	72	King Air C90	LJ-544	Lux Aero SA. Pointoise.	(F-GHFC)
❏ F-GHHV	72	King Air A100	B-91	Air Bretagne, Noyal-Pontivy.	N9050V
❏ F-GHIV	80	King Air F90	LA-22	Air Poitiers/Iso Air, Vouille.	(N444EM)
❏ F-GHJV	77	PA-31T Cheyenne II	7720067	G F R, Annemasse.	N900SF
❏ F-GHLB	78	King Air 200	BB-349	RM Holdings, Lome, Togo.	(N349JW)
❏ F-GHOC	78	King Air 200	BB-466	DARTA Aero Charter, Paris-Le Bourget.	G-OEMS
❏ F-GHRR	86	PA-46-500TP Meridian	4608058		
❏ F-GHSV	80	King Air 200	BB-622	Phenix Aviation, Le Havre.	N212BF
❏ F-GHTA	78	PA-31T Cheyenne II	7820015	Yankee Delta, Montpellier.	N107BK
❏ F-GHUV	78	King Air E90	LW-278	Avialim, Limoges.	N700MA
❏ F-GHVF	82	SA-227AT Merlin 4C	AT-423	Compagnie Aeronautique Europeenne, Marseille. (status ?).	9Q-CFK
❏ F-GHVV	80	King Air 200	BB-676	Seine Aviation/Chalair, Caen-Carpiquet.	N970AA
❏ F-GICA	88	King Air 300	FA-146	Soframa Holding & Sacha Boileau, Noumea, New Caledonia.	N2650C
❏ F-GICE	68	King Air B90	LJ-363	Michel Bidoux/Air Transport Pyrenees SA. Pau.	N303WJ
❏ F-GIDL	89	King Air C90A	LJ-1224	Bleu Horizon GIE., Rouen	N123AT
❏ F-GIFC	69	King Air B90	LJ-456	EAL-Europe Air Lines, Montpellier.	D-ILTY
❏ F-GIFK	80	King Air F90	LA-62	Loc Air SA. Perpignan.	(F-HAAG)
❏ F-GIII	80	PA-31T Cheyenne II	8020037	SAS Weishardt International, Agen-La Garenne.	N805SW
❏ F-GIJB	74	King Air 200	BB-13	Seine Aviation/Chalair, Caen-Carpiquet.	N83MA
❏ F-GIZB	81	King Air C90	LJ-955	Atlantique Air Assistance, Nantes-Atlantique.	N768SB
❏ F-GJAD	72	King Air E90	LW-3	Ste Grenobloise d'Electronique et d'Automatisme, Grenoble.	N888BH

Reg	Yr	Type	c/n	Owner/Operator	Prev Regn
☐ F-GJBS	83	King Air B200	BB-1181	Aerophoto Europe Investigation, Moulins-Montbeuguy.	N6725Y
☐ F-GJCR	78	King Air E90	LW-251	Dassault Aviation, Istres.	N7ZU
☐ F-GJFA	87	King Air B200	BB-1270	SEFA, Muret.	N30391
☐ F-GJFC	89	King Air B200	BB-1347	SEFA, Muret.	
☐ F-GJFE	91	King Air B200	BB-1399	SEFA, Muret.	
☐ F-GJFG	99	Pilatus PC-12/45	256	Fortis Lease France/GDP Vendome, Geneva	N141VY
☐ F-GJPD	80	King Air E90	LW-328	Trans Helicoptere Service, Lyon-Bron.	N551M
☐ F-GJPE	77	PA-31T Cheyenne II	7720042	Ste Air Mont Blanc, Sallanches.	YU-BKT
☐ F-GJRK	77	King Air C90	LJ-710	Icare Enterprises, Funchal, Madeira.	3A-MON
☐ F-GKCV	77	King Air 200	BB-251	Global Air Invest/EAL, Montpellier.	I-BMPE
☐ F-GKEL	76	King Air A100	B-228	Locavia France, Nantes-Atlantique.	ZS-LVL
☐ F-GKII	79	King Air 200	BB-515	Sogelease France SA/THS, Lyon-Bron.	(F-HADA)
☐ F-GKSP	95	King Air C90B	LJ-1409	Transport'Air, Avignon.	(F-GKDG)
☐ F-GKYY	02	King Air 350	FL-357	SOFIM, Orleans St Denis de l'Hotel.	N61907
☐ F-GLBZ	91	TBM 700	32	Aero Services SARL, Issy Les Moulineaux	N356M
☐ F-GLIF	77	King Air 200	BB-192	Trans Helicoptere Service, Lyon-Bron.	F-OGPQ
☐ F-GLPT	79	SA-226T Merlin 3B	T-298	Airlec Air Espace SA. Bordeaux-Merignac.	VH-AWU
☐ F-GLRF	98	King Air B200	BB-1607	L & F Airways SAS, Agen.	(F-HBTX)
☐ F-GLRP	81	PA-31T Cheyenne II	8120064	SNC Helijet, Chambery.	F-ZBFZ
☐ F-GLRZ	91	King Air C90A	LJ-1296	Oyonnair SARL. Lyon-Bron.	(F-GJDK)
☐ F-GMGB	90	King Air B200	BB-1390	IGN France, Creil.	(F-GLOP)
☐ F-GMLT	92	King Air B200T	BT-34	IGN France, Creil. (was BB-1426)	N56361
☐ F-GMLV	01	TBM 700B	219	Stephex Stables Wolverton	
☐ F-GMPM	92	King Air C90B	LJ-1303	SARL Evasair, Grenoble.	(F-GIAO)
☐ F-GMRN	78	King Air E90	LW-304	Global Air Invest, Montpellier.	N113SB
☐ F-GMTO	74	SA-226AT Merlin 4A	AT-031	Etat Francais Meteo France, Bretigny.	N22KW
☐ F-GNEE	93	King Air C90B	LJ-1328	G I E Avion Ecco, Lyon-Bron.	N90HB
☐ F-GNMA	92	King Air C90A	LJ-1299	Franciscair SAS. Lyon-Bron.	N8253D
☐ F-GNMP	79	King Air C90	LJ-828	Carry Air, Lyon-Bron.	(F-GPJC)
☐ F-GNOE	97	King Air 350	FL-183	GCE Bail SA, Paris	HB-GJL
☐ F-GNPD	77	King Air 200	BB-199	AVDEF-Aviation Defence Service, Nimes-Garons.	LN-PAD
☐ F-GOBK		ATR 42-320	264	France Telecom, Lannion-Servel.	F-SEBK
☐ F-GOCF	78	King Air 200	BB-397	TGB SARL. La Rochelle.	LX-GDB
☐ F-GOSB	00	King Air 350	FL-301	S. A. ACCOR, Toussus Le Noble.	N4211V
☐ F-GPAC	81	King Air B200	BB-920	AVDEF-Aviation Defense Service, Nimes-Garons.	SE-LMM
☐ F-GPAS	77	King Air 200	BB-209	SARL West Aero/Ocean Airlines, La Rochelle.	D-IACS
☐ F-GPBF	79	PA-31T Cheyenne II	7920094	Fabio Michienzi, Elstree, UK.	OH-PYE
☐ F-GPGH	94	King Air 350	FL-120	PGA Motors Holding et Joseph Landreau, Poitiers-Biard.	D-CBBB
☐ F-GPKN	07	P-180 Avanti II	1123	CIPM International SA.Transport Air, Avignon	
☐ F-GPKO	07	P-180 Avanti II	1132	CIPM International SA/Transport'Air SA, Avignon	
☐ F-GPLK	95	King Air C90B	LJ-1391	SNC Airco, Brive.	3A-MRL
☐ F-GPRH	93	King Air 300LW	FA-226	SNC CAVOK, Paris-Le Bourget.	F-OHRT
☐ F-GQJD	75	King Air C90	LJ-667	Avialim, Limoges.	N888GN
☐ F-GRAJ	01	Pilatus PC-12/45	406	Nicodis/SA Lavel Distribution, Lavel-Entrammes.	
☐ F-GRAZ	86	Reims/Cessna F406	F406-0013	Reims Aviation, Reims	V5-MAD
☐ F-GRNT	80	SA-226T Merlin 3B	T-312	Airlec Air Espace SA. Bordeaux-Merignac.	(F-WRNT)
☐ F-GRPS	78	PA-31T Cheyenne II	7820010	Pastej SARL. Annemasse.	(LX-GPP)
☐ F-GRSO	80	King Air 200C	BL-11	Manag'Air, Amiens-Gilsy.	(F-GYMD)
☐ F-GSCF	06	TBM 850	383	Voyag'Air, Strasbourg	
☐ F-GSEB	83	King Air B200	BB-1110	J M Communication, Paris-Le Bourget.	TR-LDU
☐ F-GSIN	77	King Air 200	BB-239	Chalair, Caen-Carpiquet.	N517JM
☐ F-GTCR	01	King Air C90B	LJ-1660	Bel Air Provence SAS, Marseille	N4470M
☐ F-GTEF	79	King Air 200	BB-560	PG Air, Paris-Le Bourget.	LN-MAA
☐ F-GTEM	93	King Air 350	FL-80	Oyonnair SARL. Lyon-Bron.	PH-BRN
☐ F-GTJM	99	TBM 700B	145	Ouest Participations, Paris-Le Bourget.	
☐ F-GUFP	00	King Air B200	BB-1698	NYCO SA. Paris-Le Bourget.	N32287
☐ F-GULJ	79	King Air 200	BB-561	Air Taxi SAT, Blois Le Breuil.	(F-GZAT)
☐ F-GULM	89	King Air C90A	LJ-1226	Rapido SA. Laval.	N369B
☐ F-GVJB	00	Pilatus PC-12/45	359	Transaltis, Charlerois, Belgium.	HB-FSN
☐ F-GVLB	00	King Air 350	FL-300	JDP France SARL. Paris-Le Bourget.	LX-MLB
☐ F-GXES	81	PA-42 Cheyenne III	8001043	Air Bor SARL. Dijon-Longvic.	D-IYES
☐ F-GZJM	76	SA-226T Merlin 3A	T-264	Air Mana SARL. Dijon.	N422AG
☐ F-GZPE	03	P-180 Avanti	1064	Bio Merieux & Pan Europeenne Air Service, Chambery.	
☐ F-HAAA	76	King Air E90	LW-175	Thierry Miallier, Tchad	F-BXSN
☐ F-HALF	06	P-180 Avanti II	1112	Landesbank Baden Wurtenberg, Dijon.	

Reg	Yr Type	c/n	Owner/Operator	Prev Regn
F-HAMI	04 King Air B200	BB-1874	Air Ailes SARL, Colmar-Houssen.	N6194V
F-HARR	04 King Air B200	BB-1898	Lorraine Aviation SARL. Nancy-Essey.	N6198P
F-HBAI	06 P-180 Avanti II	1110	Bretagne Angleterre Irlande SA. Rennes St Jacques.	
F-HBCF	04 TBM 700C2	321	Landesbank Baden-Wurtemberg, Stuttgart	(N700ZB)
F-HBRU	97 King Air B200	BB-1561	Air 5P.F SARL, Blois Le Breuil.	N200HW
F-HHAM	94 King Air C90B	LJ-1361	DARTA Aero Charter, Paris-Le Bourget.	N5521T
F-HJCM	85 King Air C90A	LJ-1098	Formula 1 Ltda. Coimbra, Portugal.	N294TT
F-HJPD	97 King Air 350	FL-173	Air Vendee Investissements, La Roche sur Yon.	SU-BMW
F-HJPM	04 King Air B200	BB-1887	OCIM Location et Cie SNC. Toussus Le Noble.	N36987
F-ODGS	77 PA-31T Cheyenne II	7720041	Franck Jean Gallo, Noumea, New Caledonia.	TS-LAZ
F-ODMM	80 PA-31T Cheyenne II	8020084	Ste Pacific Perles, Papeete, Tahiti.	F-WFLQ
F-OGOG	88 Reims/Cessna F406	F406-0026	Air Guyane, Cayenne-Rochambeau.	
F-OHCP	81 King Air 200	BB-831	Capsud Tahiti SARL, Faaa	F-ODUA
F-OHJK	96 King Air B200	BB-1544	Air Archipels, Faaa-Tahiti.	N1094S
F-OIAN	85 King Air B200	BB-1220	SNC Noumea Renting, Noumea, New Caledonia.	TR-LDM
F-OIKM	06 King Air B200	BB-1934	Air Archipels, Faaa, Tahiti.	N37134
F-OIQK	04 King Air B200C	BL-149	Air Archipels, Faaa-Tahiti.	N36949
F-OIQL	04 King Air B200C	BL-148	Air Archipels, Faaa-Tahiti.	N36948
F-OITQ	03 ATR 42-500	622	High Commissioner of French Polynesia, Papeete, Tahiti.	F-WQMT
F-OSPJ	03 Reims/Cessna F406	F406-0091	Air St Pierre SA. St Pierre et Miquelon Islands.	
F-WKDL	91 TBM 700	03	SOCATA/TBM SA. Tarbes.	
F-WKPG	91 TBM 700	02	SOCATA/TBM SA. Tarbes.	
F-WQAY	86 Reims/Cessna F406	F406-0010	Reims Aviation, Reims	0010
F-WQUD	87 Reims/Cessna F406	F406-0008	Reims Aviation, Reims	0008
F-WTBM	83 TBM 700	01	SOCATA/TBM SA. Tarbes.	
F-WWRI	05 TBM 700C2	269	EADS Socata, Tarbes.	
F-ZBGD	02 Reims/Cessna F406	F406-0090	French Customs, Paris-Dugny.	F-WWNP
F-ZBGE	91 Reims/Cessna F406	F406-0061	French Customs, Paris-Dugny.	F-GRAI

Military

Reg	Yr Type	c/n	Owner/Operator	Prev Regn
35	92 TBM 700	35	35/ABW, EAAT, Rennes	
70	93 TBM 700	70	70/ABX, EAAT, Rennes	
80	93 TBM 700	80	80/ABY, EAAT, Rennes.	
94	92 TBM 700	94	94/ABZ, EAAT, Rennes.	
F-MABO	94 TBM 700	99	99/ABO, EAAT, Rennes-St Jacques.	
F-MABP	94 TBM 700	100	100/ABP, EAAT, Rennes-St Jacques.	
F-MABQ	96 TBM 700	115	115/ABQ, EAAT, Rennes-St Jacques.	
F-MABR	98 TBM 700	136	136/ABR, EAAT, Rennes-St Jacques.	
F-MABS	99 TBM 700	139	139/ABS, EAAT, Rennes-St Jacques.	
F-MABT	99 TBM 700B	156	156/ABT, EAAT, Rennes-St Jacques.	
F-MABU	99 TBM 700B	159	159/ABU, EAAT, Rennes-St Jacques.	
F-MABV	99 TBM 700B	160	160/ABV, EAAT, Rennes-St Jacques.	
F-RAXA	92 TBM 700	33	33/43-XA, ETE.043, Bordeaux-Merignac.	F-..ID
F-RAXD	93 TBM 700	77	77/65-XD, COTAM, ETEC.065, Villacoublay.	
F-RAXE	93 TBM 700	78	78/44-XE, ETE.044, Aix-Les-Milles.	
F-RAXH	92 TBM 700	95	95/65-XH, COTAM, ETEC.065 Villacoublay.	
F-RAXI	94 TBM 700	103	103/41-XI, ETE.041 Metz-Frescarty.	
F-RAXJ	94 TBM 700	104	104/41-XJ, ETE.041 Metz-Frescarty.	
F-RAXK	94 TBM 700	105	105/65-XK, COTAM, ETEC.065 Villacoublay.	
F-RAXL	92 TBM 700	93	93/43-XL, ETE.043, Bordeaux-Merignac.	
F-RAXM	95 TBM 700	111	111/65-XM, COTAM, ETEC.065 Villacoublay.	
F-RAXN	96 TBM 700	117	117/44-XN, ETE.044, Aix-Les-Milles.	
F-RAXO	97 TBM 700	125	125/65-XO, COTAM, ETEC.065, Villacoublay.	
F-RAXP	95 TBM 700	110	110/41-XP, ETE.041 Metz-Frescarty.	
F-RAXQ	98 TBM 700	131	131/65-XQ, COTAM, ETE.065, Villacoublay.	
F-RAXR	99 TBM 700B	146	146/65-XR, COTAM, ETE.065, Villacoublay.	
F-RAXS	99 TBM 700B	147	147/65-XS, COTAM, ETE.065, Villacoublay.	
F-ZBAB	88 Reims/Cessna F406	F406-0025	French Customs, Paris-Dugny.	
F-ZBBB	89 Reims/Cessna F406	F406-0039	French Customs, Paris-Dugny.	F-WZDS
F-ZBBF	71 King Air C90	LJ-518	Securite Civile, Paris.	F-BTCA
F-ZBCE	89 Reims/Cessna F406	F406-0042	French Customs, Paris-Dugny.	F-WKRA
F-ZBCF	95 Reims/Cessna F406	F406-0077	French Customs, Paris-Dugny.	F-WZDZ
F-ZBCG	93 Reims/Cessna F406	F406-0066	French Customs, Paris-Dugny.	F-WZDT
F-ZBCH	94 Reims/Cessna F406	F406-0075	French Customs, Paris-Dugny.	
F-ZBCI	93 Reims/Cessna F406	F406-0070	French Customs, Paris-Dugny.	
F-ZBCJ	94 Reims/Cessna F406	F406-0074	French Customs, Paris-Dugny.	
Reg	Yr Type	c/n	Owner/Operator	Prev Regn

Reg	Yr	Type	c/n	Owner/Operator	Prev Regn
☐ F-ZBEP	85	Reims/Cessna F406	F406-0006	French Customs, Paris-Dugny.	
☐ F-ZBES	85	Reims/Cessna F406	F406-0017	French Customs, Paris-Dugny.	
☐ F-ZBFA	83	Reims/Cessna F406	F406-01	French Customs, Paris-Dugny.	F-GGRA
☐ F-ZBFJ/98	83	King Air B200	BB-1102	GMA/Ministry of the Interior, Marseille-Marignane.	(F-GKDO)
☐ F-ZBFK/96	81	King Air B200	BB-876	GMA/Ministry of the Interior, Marseille-Marignane.	F-GHSC
☐ F-ZBGA	99	Reims/Cessna F406	F406-0086	French Customs, Paris-Dugny.	F-WWSR
☐ F-ZBMB/97	90	King Air B200	BB-1379	GMA/Ministry of the Interior, Marseille-Marignane.	F-GJFD
☐ F-ZVMN	94	TBM 700	106	106/MN, CEV-Centre d'Essais en Vol, Bretigny.	

G = GREAT BRITAIN   Total   85

Civil

Reg	Yr	Type	c/n	Owner/Operator	Prev Regn
☐ G-BGRE	79	King Air 200	BB-568	Martin Baker (Engineering) Ltd. Chalgrove.	
☐ G-BMKD	84	King Air C90A	LJ-1069	Alan Bristow, Cranleigh.	N223CG
☐ G-BRGN	84	BAe Jetstream 31	637	Cranfield University, Cranfield.	G-BLHC
☐ G-BVJT	94	Reims/Cessna F406	F406-0073	NOR Leasing, Surbiton UK	G-BVJT
☐ G-BVMA	81	King Air 200	BB-797	Dragonfly Aviation Services LP. Cardiff.	G-VPLC
☐ G-BYCP	82	King Air B200	BB-966	London Executive Aviation, London City.	F-GDCS
☐ G-BZNE	00	King Air 350	FL-286	Skyhopper LLP. London.	N4486V
☐ G-CCWY	04	Pilatus PC-12/45	568	Harpin Ltd. Leeds-Bradford.	HB-F..
☐ G-CDFY	00	King Air B200	BB-1715	BAe Systems Marine Ltd. Walney.	N607TA
☐ G-CDZT	98	King Air B200	BB-1619	BAe Systems Marine Ltd. Walney.	N240AJ
☐ G-CECN	78	Rockwell 690B	11482	FM-International OY., Helsinki, Finland	HS-TFG
☐ G-CEGP	80	King Air 200	BB-726	CEGA Aviation Ltd. Goodwood.	N50AJ
☐ G-CEGR	78	King Air 200	BB-351	Henfield Lodge Aviation Ltd/CEGA Aviation Ltd. Goodwood.	N68CP
☐ G-CEJB	06	PA-46-500TP Meridian	4697240	The Van Meeuwen Flying Company Ltd., Kingston upon Thames	OY-PHO
☐ G-CGAW	80	King Air 200	BB-700	George Anthony Warburton, Guernsey	N440WA
☐ G-CHEY	81	Cheyenne II-XL	8166033	Air Medical Fleet Ltd. Oxford-Kidlington.	N67PD
☐ G-CLOW	81	King Air 200	BB-821	Clowes Estates Ltd/Eastern Air Executive, Sturgate.	N821RC
☐ G-DERI	01	PA-46-500TP Meridian	4697078	Intesa Leasing SpA. Milan, Italy.	N51151
☐ G-DERK	02	PA-46-500TP Meridian	4697152	Derek Priestley, Jersey, Cl.	N165MA
☐ G-FCED	81	Cheyenne II-XL	8166010	Air Medical Fleet Ltd. Oxford-Kidlington.	C-FCED
☐ G-FIND	89	Reims/Cessna F406	F406-0045	Reconnaisance Ventures Ltd., Coventry	OY-PEU
☐ G-FPLB	82	King Air B200	BB-1048	Flight Precision Ltd. Durham Tees Valley.	N739MG
☐ G-FPLD	92	King Air B200	BB-1433	Flight Precision Ltd. Durham Tees Valley.	N43CE
☐ G-FPLE	86	King Air B200	BB-1256	Flight Precision Ltd. Durham Tees Valley.	N230DC
☐ G-FRYI	76	King Air 200	BB-210	London Executive Aviation, London City.	G-OAVX
☐ G-FSEU	78	King Air 200	BB-331	Air Mercia Ltd. Wolverhampton.	N87LP
☐ G-GBMR	99	King Air B200	BB-1693	M & R Aviation LLP. Leicester.	N773TP
☐ G-GZRP	84	PA-42 Cheyenne IIIA	5501011	Air Medical Fleet Ltd. Oxford-Kidlington.	C-GZRP
☐ G-IJYS	86	BAe Jetstream 31	715	Air Kilroe Ltd /Eastern Airways Ltd. Humberside.	G-BTZT
☐ G-ILMD	01	Pilatus PC-12/45	412	Nicholas J Vetch, Petersfield.	N10778
☐ G-IMEA	78	King Air 200	BB-302	Airtime Ltd. Bournemouth-Hurn.	G-OWAX
☐ G-INTO	05	Pilatus PC-12/45	609	Skydrift / A.Colin t/a Into Air, Norwich	HS-SMC
☐ G-JENC	07	King Air B300C	FM-14	Raytheon Systems Ltd., Harlow	N814KA
☐ G-JOAL	83	King Air B200	BB-1158	Southcoast Air Charter LLP. Southampton.	N66LM
☐ G-KLYN	06	King Air B200	BB-1931	Klyne Air Ltd., Lowestoft	N37101
☐ G-KRMA	80	Conquest 1	425-0003	Speedstar Holdings, London	D-INGA
☐ G-KVIP	79	King Air 200	BB-487	Capital Trading Aviation Ltd. Filton.	G-CBFS
☐ G-LEAF	87	Reims/Cessna F406	F406-0018	Highland Airways Ltd, Inverness	EI-CKY
☐ G-MAFA	89	Reims/Cessna F406	F406-0036	Directflight Ltd. Prestwick.	G-DFLT
☐ G-MAFB	96	Reims/Cessna F406	F406-0080	Directflight Ltd. Prestwick.	F-WWSR
☐ G-MAMD	97	King Air B200	BB-1549	Forest Aviation Ltd. Doncaster.	N1069S
☐ G-MATX	05	Pilatus PC-12/45	682	Matrix Group Ltd.	HB-F..
☐ G-MCMC	03	TBM 700C2	261	Sogestao Administraca Gerencia SA. Cascais, Portugal.	N181PC
☐ G-MEGN	96	King Air B200	BB-1518	Dragonfly Aviation Services LLP. Cardiff, Wales.	N65LA
☐ G-MOUN	00	King Air B200	BB-1734	Real Aeroclub de Valencia, Valencia, Spain	N123NA
☐ G-NICY	07	King Air B300C	FM-16	Raytheon Systems Ltd	N816KA
☐ G-OCEG	79	King Air 200	BB-588	Cega Aviation Ltd., Chichester	N578BM
☐ G-OCLE	07	Pilatus PC-12/47	867	Pilatus PC-12 Centre UK Ltd, Bournemouth	HB-FSY
☐ G-OJRO	68	King Air B90	LJ-327	Fly (CI) Ltd., Alderney	OY-JRO
☐ G-OLTT	05	Pilatus PC-12/45	648	Hilton Nathanson, London.	HB-FSU
☐ G-OMGI	86	King Air B200	BB-1259	MGI Aviation Ltd. Kidlington-Oxford, UK.	N800MG
☐ G-ONAL	75	King Air 200	BB-30	Northern Aviation Ltd. Durham Tees Valley.	G-HAMA
☐ G-ORJA	97	King Air B200	BB-1570	Air West Ltd/Centerline Air Charter Ltd. Bristol-Lulsgate.	N1120Z
☐ G-ORTH	75	King Air E90	LW-136	Caroline & Paul Crowther, Shoreham.	G-DEXY

Reg	Yr Type	c/n	Owner/Operator	Prev Regn
☐ G-PCOP	04 King Air B200	BB-1860	Albert Bartlett & Sons, Cambridge.	N6200G
☐ G-PFFN	79 King Air 200	BB-456	The Puffin Club Ltd. Leicester.	N456CD
☐ G-POWB	06 King Air 350	FL-506	NAC Aviation Ltd., Kidlington, Oxford	N7106L
☐ G-PVPC	05 Pilatus PC-12/45	632	GECC/Pilatus PC-12 Centre UK Ltd. Bournemouth-Hurn.	HB-FPV
☐ G-RACI	79 King Air C90	LJ-819	E Flight Srl.Milan	G-SHAM
☐ G-SASC	05 King Air B200C	BL-150	Scottish Ambulance Service, Aberdeen.	N6178D
☐ G-SASD	05 King Air B200C	BL-151	Scottish Ambulance Service, Aberdeen.	N6178F
☐ G-SAXN	76 King Air 200	BB-108	Saxonair Ltd. Ipswich.	G-OMNH
☐ G-SERC	05 King Air 350	FL-438	Bridgtown Plant Ltd. Halfpenny Green.	N61638
☐ G-SFP.	06 Reims/Cessna F406	F406-0095	Fisheries Protection Agency, Edinburgh.	
☐ G-SFPA	91 Reims/Cessna F406	F406-0064	Fisheries Protection Agency, Edinburgh.	
☐ G-SFPB	91 Reims/Cessna F406	F406-0065	Fisheries Protection Agency, Edinburgh.	
☐ G-SGEC	00 King Air B200	BB-1747	Keypoint Aviation LLP. Gamston.	N214FW
☐ G-SPOR	97 King Air B200	BB-1557	Select Plant Hire Co/Platinum Air Charter Ltd. Southend.	N57TL
☐ G-SYGA	82 King Air B200	BB-1044	Synergy Aircraft Leasing, 12/07	G-BPPM
☐ G-TAGH	00 King Air B200	BB-1720	Taggart Aviation Ltd. Bristol-Lulsgate.	N208CW
☐ G-TRAT	06 Pilatus PC-12/47	710	D J Trathen, Plymouth.	HB-FQX
☐ G-TURF	87 Reims/Cessna F406	F406-0020	Reconnaisance Ventures Ltd., Coventry	EI-CND
☐ G-WATJ	07 King Air B200GT	BY-14	Saxonhenge Ltd, Bangor	N34004
☐ G-WCCP	88 King Air B200	BB-1295	William Cook Aviation Ltd. Sheffield.	N295CP
☐ G-WINT	07 Pilatus PC-12/47	830	Air Winton Ltd., London	HB-F
☐ G-WVIP	80 King Air 200	BB-625	Capital Trading Aviation Ltd. Filton.	N869AM
☐ G-ZUMO	06 Pilatus PC-12/47	732	Breckenridge Ltd. Jersey, Channel Islands.	HB-FRQ

Military

Reg	Yr Type	c/n	Owner/Operator	Prev Regn
☐ ZK450/J	03 King Air B200S	BB-1829	RAF, 45(R) Squadron, Cranwell.	G-RAFJ
☐ ZK451/K	03 King Air B200S	BB-1830	RAF, 45(R) Squadron, Cranwell.	G-RAFK
☐ ZK452/L	03 King Air B200S	BB-1832	RAF, 45(R) Squadron, Cranwell.	G-RAFL
☐ ZK453/M	03 King Air B200S	BB-1833	RAF, 45(R) Squadron, Cranwell.	G-RAFM
☐ ZK454/N	03 King Air B200S	BB-1835	RAF, 45(R) Squadron, Cranwell.	G-RAFN
☐ ZK455/O	03 King Air B200S	BB-1836	RAF, 45(R) Squadron, Cranwell.	G-RAFO
☐ ZK456/P	03 King Air B200S	BB-1837	RAF, 45(R) Squadron, Cranwell.	G-RAFP
☐ ZK457	80 King Air 200	BB-684	RAF, 45(R) Squadron, Cranwell.	G-BHLC

HA = HUNGARY   Total   3
Civil

Reg	Yr Type	c/n	Owner/Operator	Prev Regn
☐ HA-ACE	05 King Air B200	BB-1902	Jet Stream 2004 KfT. Toekoel.	N36872
☐ HA-SIP	69 SA-26AT Merlin 2B	T26-132	Bailer Barna EV. Budapest.	N72CF
☐ HA-SIT	78 PA-31T Cheyenne II	7820011	Pannon Air Service KfT, Tokol	N250CT

HB = SWITZERLAND   Total   75
Civil

Reg	Yr Type	c/n	Owner/Operator	Prev Regn
☐ HB-FOB	93 Pilatus PC-12M Eagle	P-02	Pilatus Flugzeugwerke AG., Stans.	
☐ HB-FOG	96 Pilatus PC-12/45	134	Armasuisse, Geschäftseinheit Luftfahrtsysteme, Berne.	
☐ HB-FOI	96 Pilatus PC-12	157	Air Engiadina AG. Samedan.	
☐ HB-FOP	99 Pilatus PC-12/45	291	Translem SA. Sion.	
☐ HB-FOQ	00 Pilatus PC-12/45	349	Aero Gear AG/Lions Air AG. Zurich.	(ZS-SRO)
☐ HB-FOS	00 Pilatus PC-12/45	366	Sasset AG/Lions Air AG. Zurich.	
☐ HB-FOT	95 Pilatus PC-12/45	121	Pilatus Flugzeugwerke AG,. Stans.	ZS-PVT
☐ HB-FOW	01 Pilatus PC-12/45	411	Future Wings AG. Zug.	
☐ HB-FOX	00 Pilatus PC-12/45	334	Lions Air AG. Zurich.	
☐ HB-FOY	01 Pilatus PC-12/45	386	Central Aviation AG/Aviswiss GmbH. Zurich.	
☐ HB-FPC	01 Pilatus PC-12/45	422	Moliair AG. Altenrhein.	HB-FRK
☐ HB-FPE	02 Pilatus PC-12/45	479	Griffin Privatair Ltd. Vaduz, Liechtenstein.	A6-GAK
☐ HB-FPI	04 Pilatus PC-12/45	551	Cemex Investments SA. Schaan, Liechtenstein.	VH-PCE
☐ HB-FPL	99 Pilatus PC-12/45	247	Lions Air AG. Zurich.	(PH-CVA)
☐ HB-FPR	05 Pilatus PC-12/45	544	Rosen Swiss AG. Stans.	
☐ HB-FPS	05 Pilatus PC-12/45	608	Redexair AG. Cham.	
☐ HB-FPT	04 Pilatus PC-12/45	545	Pilatus Aircraft	
☐ HB-FPW	01 Pilatus PC-12/45	407	Aron Finanz AG. Stansstad.	VP-BBB
☐ HB-FPY	05 Pilatus PC-12/47	685	Momentum Value Management SA. Lausanne.	
☐ HB-FPZ	06 Pilatus PC-12/47	702	Air Sarina GmbH. Saanen.	
☐ HB-FQH	07 Pilatus PC-12/47	876	Pilatus Flugzeugwerke AG., Stans	
☐ HB-FQI	07 Pilatus PC-12/47	877	Pilatus Flugzeugwerke AG., Stans	
☐ HB-FQJ	07 Pilatus PC-12/47	878	Pilatus Flugzeugwerke AG., Stans	
☐ HB-FQK	07 Pilatus PC-12/47	879	Pilatus Flugzeugwerke AG., Stans	
☐ HB-FQL	07 Pilatus PC-12/47	880	Pilatus Flugzeugwerke AG., Stans	

Reg	Yr Type	c/n	Owner/Operator	Prev Regn
☐ HB-FQN	07 Pilatus PC-12/47	882	Pilatus Flugzeugwerke AG., Stans	
☐ HB-FQO	07 Pilatus PC-12/47	883	Pilatus Flugzeugwerke AG., Stans	
☐ HB-FQP	07 Pilatus PC-12/47	884	Pilatus Flugzeugwerke AG., Stans	
☐ HB-FQR	07 Pilatus PC-12/47	885	Pilatus Flugzeugwerke AG., Stans	
☐ HB-FRJ	06 Pilatus PC-12/47	723	Pilatus Flugzeugwerke AG., Stans.	
☐ HB-FSO	07 Pilatus PC-12/47	864	Pilatus Flugzeugwerke AG., Stans	
☐ HB-FSP	07 Pilatus PC-12/47	841	Pilatus Flugzeugwerke AG., Stans	
☐ HB-FSU	07 Pilatus PC-12/47	862	Pilatus Flugzeugwerke AG., Stans	
☐ HB-FSW	07 Pilatus PC-12/47	865	Pilatus Flugzeugwerke AG., Stans	
☐ HB-FVA	07 Pilatus PC-12/47	833	Explorair AG. Lausanne	
☐ HB-FVB	07 Pilatus PC-12/47E	1001	Pilatus Flugzeugwerke AG., Stans	
☐ HB-FVC	07 Pilatus PC-12/47	1002	Pilatus Flugzeugwerke AG., Stans	
☐ HB-FVV	06 Pilatus PC-12/47	778	Pilatus Flugzeugwerke AG., Stans.	
☐ HB-FVZ	00 Pilatus PC-12/45	343	Happy Lines SA., Lausanne	N31DX
☐ HB-GHD	80 King Air F90	LA-50	Air Evasion SA. Lausanne.	F-GCLS
☐ HB-GHK	81 Gulfstream 1000	96023	Gofir SA Aerotaxi, Lugano.	ZS-KZV
☐ HB-GHV	88 King Air 300	FA-170	ATG Swiss First GmbH. Zug.	
☐ HB-GIL	77 King Air 200	BB-194	Air Glaciers SA. Sion.	N300PH
☐ HB-GJD	80 King Air 200C	BL-7	Zimex Business Aviation AG. Zurich.	F-GJBJ
☐ HB-GJH	81 King Air C90	LJ-972	Flying Devil SA. Lausanne.	N18080
☐ HB-GJI	79 King Air 200	BB-451	Air Glaciers SA. Sion.	D-IBOW
☐ HB-GJM	77 King Air 200	BB-255	Air Glaciers SA. Sion.	N32KD
☐ HB-GJP	06 King Air 350	FL-477	BergAir SA. Lausanne.	N71837
☐ HB-GJQ	79 King Air F90	LA-4	Rotorflug Anstalt, Altenrhein.	N502SP
☐ HB-GJT	07 King Air 350	FL-535	Breitling SA., Grenchen	N7035V
☐ HB-GJW	95 King Air B200	BB-1505	Family Airlines SA. Lausanne.	VH-HPX
☐ HB-GJX	81 King Air B200	BB-932	Zimex Business Aviation AG. Zurich.	SE-KKM
☐ HB-GPG	78 King Air 200	BB-307	Preferencial SA. La Chaux de Fonds.	N703HT
☐ HB-GPH	97 King Air B200	BB-1569	Pinkerton AG. Baar.	EI-WHE
☐ HB-GPI	91 King Air 300LW	FA-220	Technomag AG. Berne.	N41GA
☐ HB-KFR	01 TBM 700B	195	Olivier Rochat, Lausanne.	(N700EN)
☐ HB-KHC	05 TBM 700C2	342	Olivier Rochat, Lausanne.	F-.....
☐ HB-KHP	07 TBM 850	426	Chiari Gaggia Anne Et Alvise, Sion .	N850WC
☐ HB-KOL	01 TBM 700B	218	Aerolift AG. Zurich.	N700NE
☐ HB-KOR	06 TBM 850	349	Contaco Establishment Vaduz, Altenrhein.	F-HBGA
☐ HB-LLK	79 PA-31T Cheyenne 1	7904014	Kogno Anstalt, Vaduz. Liechstenstein.	N401PT
☐ HB-LNL	80 PA-31T Cheyenne II	8020083	Daniel Knutti, Magglingen-Macolin.	N54JB
☐ HB-LNX	81 Cheyenne II-XL	8166050	Transwing AG. Grenchen.	N700XL
☐ HB-LOE	81 Conquest 1	425-0016	Mecaplex AG. Grenchen.	ZS-KST
☐ HB-LQP	80 PA-31T Cheyenne 1	8004044	Ursella Holding AG. Berne.	OO-JMR
☐ HB-LRV	78 PA-31T Cheyenne II	7820017	Thomke AG. Stans.	N82222
☐ HB-LTE	01 P-180 Avanti	1042	Ovala AG. Lugano.	
☐ HB-LTI	80 PA-31T Cheyenne II	8020091	Symbios Orthopedie SA. Yverdon.	F-GIPL
☐ HB-LTM	85 PA-42 Cheyenne 400LS	5527028	Thomke Management AG. Grenchen.	N4119X
☐ HB-LTN	03 P-180 Avanti	1066	Hara International AG. Altenrhein.	
☐ HB-LTZ	05 P-180 Avanti II	1105	Fly Wings SA/Gofir SA. Lugano-Agno.	I-RAIL
☐ HB-LUF	81 PA-31T Cheyenne II	8120015	Hans-Ulrich Wurgler/Intra Invest SA., Greng	N107TT
☐ HB-PQX	04 PA-46-500TP Meridian	4697194	Herve Andre Schick, Gorgier	D-EXTP
☐ N866PE	07 Pilatus PC-12/47	866	Pilatus Business Aircraft Ltd Bloomfield, Co.	HB-FSX

Military

☐ T-729	97 Beech 1900D	UE-288	Swiss Air Force, Dubendorf	D-CBIG

HC = ECUADOR   Total 18

Civil

Reg	Yr Type	c/n	Owner/Operator	Prev Regn
☐ HC-...	80 Gulfstream 980	95026		N903L
☐ HC-...	80 King Air 200	BB-703		N703KH
☐ HC-...	81 King Air C90-1	LJ-986	San Sierra Aero Servicios, Quito.	N18300
☐ HC-...	83 Gulfstream 900	15023		N88RC
☐ HC-BHU	80 Gulfstream 840	11634	TAESA. Quito. (stolen).	N5886K
☐ HC-BIF	81 PA-31T Cheyenne II	8120019	Ecuavia SA. Guayaquil.	N2425X
☐ HC-BUD	81 Gulfstream 840	11669	SAEREO SA. Quito.	N844MA
☐ HC-BXH	82 Conquest II	441-0268	Union de Bananeros Ecuatorianos, Quito.	VP-BPH
☐ HC-BYO	98 Beech 1900D	UE-317	ICARO-Instituto Civil Aeronautico SA. Quito.	N2290B
☐ HC-DAC	76 King Air E90	LW-178	Directorate of Civil Aviation, Quito.	

Military

Reg	Yr Type	c/n	Owner/Operator	Prev Regn
☐ AEE-101	81 King Air 200	BB-811	Ministry of National Defence, Quito.	AEE-001
☐ ANE-231	81 King Air 200	BB-771	Aviacion Naval Ecuatoriana, Guayaquil.	N3831Q
☐ ANE-232	85 King Air 300	FA-75	Aviacion Naval Ecuatoriana, Guayaquil.	N7247A
☐ ANE-233	80 King Air 200	BB-580	Aviacion Naval Ecuatoriana, Guayaquil.	N48450
☐ ANE-234	79 King Air 200	BB-458	Aviacion Naval Ecuatoriana, Guayaquil.	N169DB
☐ ANE-235	92 King Air 350	FL-85	Aviacion Naval Ecuatoriana, Guayaquil.	N8080C
☐ FAE-001	70 BAe HS 748-2A	1684	Government of Ecuador, Quito.	HC-AUK
☐ IGM-240	78 King Air A100	B-242	Instituto Geografico Militar, Ejercito-army photo survey.	

HI = DOMINICAN REPUBLIC   Total   4

Civil

Reg	Yr Type	c/n	Owner/Operator	Prev Regn
☐ HI-	71 Mitsubishi MU-2F	194	Agroaplica Corp. Santo Domingo, Dominican Republic.	N440EZ
☐ HI-678CT	69 Gulfstream 1	323	Caribe SA. Santo Domingo. (status?)	HI-678CA
☐ HI-701SP	82 King Air B200	BB-984	Corp Aeroportuaria del Este,	N9RU
☐ HI-776SP	88 King Air C90A	LJ-1163	Juliano Chiozzoli,	N777J

HK = COLOMBIA   Total   179

Civil

Reg	Yr Type	c/n	Owner/Operator	Prev Regn
☐ HK-	79 King Air/Catpass 250	BB-512		N512KA
☐ HK-...	84 King Air 300	FA-22		N72069
☐ HK-...	80 Gulfstream 980	95001	Gustavo Durango, Cali.	N980AA
☐ HK-....	81 King Air F90	LA-84		N122GA
☐ HK-....	79 Conquest II	441-0110		HP-....
☐ HK-....	74 King Air E90	LW-90		N114AT
☐ HK-....	79 PA-31T Cheyenne II	7920088		N171DA
☐ HK-....	77 Rockwell 690B	11386		N568H
☐ HK-....	78 King Air 200	BB-310	Transpaton SA. Bogota. (status ?).	N988SC
☐ HK-....	86 King Air 300	FA-99	Amazonian Investment Inc. Bogota.	N6293V
☐ HK-....	67 King Air A90	LJ-248	Elias Valera Morales, Bogota.	N562P
☐ HK-....	81 PA-31T Cheyenne 1	8104007		N914CR
☐ HK-....	70 681 Turbo Commander	6014	David Quinones, Medellin.	N681SM
☐ HK-....	69 King Air B90	LJ-469	David F Q Younges, Medellin.	N90GB
☐ HK-....	80 Gulfstream 840	11604	Carlos Alberto Cortez, Bogota.	N5855K
☐ HK-....	67 King Air A90	LJ-210	David Quinones, Medellin.	N43TT
☐ HK-....	80 Gulfstream 840	11602	ALICOL-Aerolineas Intercolombianos Ltda. Bogota.	N2647C
☐ HK-....	75 SA-226T Merlin 3A	T-253		N959M
☐ HK-1770G	74 Rockwell 690A	11216	Instituto Geografico Agustin Codazzi, Bogota.	N57216
☐ HK-1977	70 681 Turbo Commander	6035	SEARCA-Servicio Aereo de Capurgana Ltda.	HK-1977W
☐ HK-1982	72 Rockwell 690	11014	TAS-Transporte Aereo de Santander,	HK-1982W
☐ HK-2055	72 Rockwell 690	11005	ARPA-Aerolineas Regionales de Paz de Ariporo Ltda.	HK-2055W
☐ HK-2120	74 Mitsubishi MU-2J	621	Carlos Alberto Aragon Orozco,	HK-2120
☐ HK-2218W	78 Rockwell 690B	11453	Fabrica de Dulces Colombina Ltda.	N81736
☐ HK-2281	72 Rockwell 690	11033	AVIEL-Aviones Ejecutivos Ltda. Bogota.	HK-2281P
☐ HK-2282P	73 Rockwell 690	11128	Gabriel Antonio Valencia Rendon,	HK-2282W
☐ HK-2285P	67 680T Turbo Commander	1632-57	Jimenez Alfonso Mejia,	HK-2285
☐ HK-2291X	77 Rockwell 690B	11364	Mineros de Antioquia SA.	HK-2291
☐ HK-2347	79 PA-31T Cheyenne II	7920076	HELICONDOR-Helicopteros El Condor Ltda/Helicafe Ltda.	HK-2347P
☐ HK-2376P	71 681 Turbo Commander	6043	Martha Lucy Hernandez de Dominguez,	HK-2376
☐ HK-2390W	77 Conquest II	441-0016	Norman Gonzalez y Asociados Ltda.	N36938
☐ HK-2414P	76 Rockwell 690A	11296	Nestor Manuel Gutierrez Sanchez,	HK-2414
☐ HK-2455	80 PA-31T Cheyenne II	8020047	LIRA-Lineas Aereas de Uraba Ltda.	HK-2455
☐ HK-2479W	80 SA-226T Merlin 3B	T-320	AGROCASA Ltda/Inversiones Agropecuarias Casanare,	HK-2479
☐ HK-2491	76 King Air E90	LW-183	Interamericana de Aviacion SA. Bogota.	YV-940P
☐ HK-2495P	80 Gulfstream 840	11633	Dario Maja Velasquez,	N5885K
☐ HK-2538P	80 Conquest II	441-0114	Pozo Hernando Buitrago,	HK-2538X
☐ HK-2551P	78 Rockwell 690B	11489	Francisco Antonio Molina Laverde,	N7701L
☐ HK-2585P	80 PA-31T Cheyenne II	8020077	Giraldo Eliecer Giraldo,	(N2519V)
☐ HK-2596	81 King Air C90	LJ-957	AEROTACA SA-Aerotransportes Casanare/Aerotaxi Casanare	HK-2596G
☐ HK-2601	81 Gulfstream 840	11651	Lopez Montoya Cia S C S.	N840JP
☐ HK-2631G	81 PA-31T Cheyenne II	8120032	Ministerio de Obras Publicas y Transporte, Bogota.	HK-2631X
☐ HK-2642P	81 PA-31T Cheyenne II	8120037	Hector Gomez Alvarez,	
☐ HK-2684X	81 PA-42 Cheyenne III	8001068		N4099Y
☐ HK-2749P	81 Cheyenne II-XL	8166019	Adriana Gomez Larroche,	HK-2749X
☐ HK-2772P	81 PA-42 Cheyenne III	8001059	Fernando Rafael Llanos Avila,	HK-2772X
☐ HK-2909P	82 Gulfstream 1000	96045	Jorge Arturo Buelvas Marchena,	HK-2909

Reg	Yr	Type	c/n	Owner/Operator	Prev Regn
HK-2926P	82	Cheyenne T-1040	8275015	Felipe Sandoval Rincon,	HK-2926
HK-2951	82	Gulfstream 1000	96049	Aerotayrona Ltda.	HK-2951P
HK-2963	81	Cheyenne II-XL	8166053	Supertiendas y Droguerias Olimpicas SA/Char Hermanos Ltda.	N174CC
HK-3009	83	Conquest II	441-0273	Helicopteros El Condor-Helicondor Ltda/Helicafe Ltda.	HK-3009P
HK-3043P	81	PA-31T Cheyenne II	8120051	Juan Climaco Prieto Cabrera,	(N2525Y)
HK-3060	82	Gulfstream 1000	96039	ATTA-Asociacion Tolimense de Transporte Aereo Ltda.	HK-3060W
HK-3074P	81	Cheyenne II-XL	8166035	Giraldo Arteaga Salvador Dario,	HK-3074
HK-3117W	81	Cheyenne II-XL	8166073	Carvajal SA.	HK-3117X
HK-3147X	73	Rockwell 690A	11122		N9229Y
HK-3193	85	Gulfstream 1000	96086	AEROES-Aerolineas Especiales/Taxi Aereo Aereos Ltda.	HK-3193X
HK-3214	81	King Air B200	BB-854	Servialas de Colombia Ltda	HK-3214X
HK-3218	83	Gulfstream 1000	96061	AVIEL-Aviones Ejecutivos Ltda. Bogota.	N184BB
HK-3239W	82	Gulfstream 1000	96010	Aero Antigua Ltda.	HK-3239X
HK-3253P	85	Gulfstream 1000	96074	Mario Montoya Gomez,	HK-3253X
HK-3275	85	Gulfstream 1000	96076	Hector Fabio Gonzalez Martinez,	HK-3275X
HK-3277P	80	King Air C90	LJ-892	Lazaro Estrada Ospina,	HK-3277W
HK-3279	84	Gulfstream 1000	96072	Aerocarbones del Cesar Ltda/Aerocarbon,	HK-3279W
HK-3283W	85	Gulfstream 1000	96099	Compania Exploradora del Pacifico Ltda.	HK-3293
HK-3290P	81	Gulfstream 840	11653	Irene Leonor Clamote Lagnoro,	HK-3290
HK-3291P	85	Gulfstream 1000	96088	Diamar Ltda.	HK-3291W
HK-3314W	75	Rockwell 690A	11255	SIRVE-Sociedad Importadora de Repuestos y Vehiculos Ltda.	HK-3314
HK-3324P	85	Gulfstream 1000	96100	Adriana Lopez Cardona,	N111VP
HK-3366X	82	Gulfstream 1000	96033	LAPAZ Colombia, Paz de Ariporo.	G-IOOO
HK-3367	82	Gulfstream 1000	96018	SERPA-Servicios Aereos del Pacifico,	YV-416CP
HK-3379P	79	Rockwell 690B	11525	Velez y Valencia Compania S en C.	HK-3379
HK-3385P	82	Gulfstream 840	11728	Hector Eduardo Tautna Cinturia,	HK-3385X
HK-3389P	82	Gulfstream 1000	96037	Oscar Alberto Morales Salazar,	HK-3389
HK-3390	82	Gulfstream 1000	96047	Air Caribe Ltda. Cartagena.	HK-3390X
HK-3391W	82	Gulfstream 1000	96059	Aerominas de Colombia Ltda.	HK-3391
HK-3401	78	Conquest II	441-0059	VIANA-Vias Aereas Nacionales Ltda. Arauca.	N441MS
HK-3406	81	Gulfstream 980	95062	JET-Jet Express Ltda/Cia Sinuana de Transp. Aer Costa Ltda.	N92MT
HK-3407	81	Gulfstream 980	95075	LIRA-Lineas Aereas de Uraba Ltda.	HK-3407X
HK-3408	81	Gulfstream 980	95050	Servicios Aereos de la Capital Ltda. Bogota.	HK-3408X
HK-3418	84	Conquest II	441-0333	SADA-Sociedad Aeronautica de Armenia Ltda.	HK-3418P
HK-3424	80	Gulfstream 840	11611	APEL Express SA/Aerolineas Petroleros del Llano,	N35DR
HK-3429W	79	King Air C90	LJ-831	NADAL Ltda/Asesores de Seguros y Servicios Generales,	HK-3429X
HK-3432	85	King Air B200	BB-1227	SAVA-Servicios Aereos del Valle/Aviaco Ltda. Bogota.	N7237A
HK-3439	82	Gulfstream 1000	96021	Aeroejecutivos Colombia SA. Bogota.	N132PR
HK-3444	81	Gulfstream 980	95057	Servicios Aereos de la Capital Ltda. Bogota.	HK-3444X
HK-3447P	82	Gulfstream 840	11722	Alvaro Jose Salgado Calle,	HK-3447
HK-3450	81	Gulfstream 980	95083	RAA-Rutas Aereas Araucanas Ltda. Arauca.	HK-3450W
HK-3451	86	PA-42 Cheyenne 400LS	5527033	SATURNO-Servicio Aereo Turistico del Nororiente Ltda.	N827PC
HK-3455	81	Gulfstream 980	95065	RAA-Rutas Aereas Aruacanas Ltda. Arauca.	HK-3455X
HK-3456W	83	Conquest II	441-0271	Aero Antigua Ltda.	HK-3456
HK-3461	81	Gulfstream 980	95043	ALICOL-Aerolineas Intercolombianos Ltda. Bogota.	HK-3461X
HK-3465P	73	Rockwell 690	11059	Sergio Jose Cardona Jimenez,	HK-3465X
HK-3466	74	Rockwell 690A	11165	Helitaxi Ltda. Bogota.	N690LP
HK-3472X	80	PA-31T Cheyenne II	8020043	F de Jesus Ocampo de Sepulveda. (status ?).	
HK-3474	80	Gulfstream 980	95016	RAA-Rutas Aereas Aruacanas Ltda. Arauca.	N7050S
HK-3481	81	Gulfstream 980	95079	Alfuturo Aereo Ltda/Aerocali Luego Alfuturo Air Ltda.	N9831S
HK-3484	80	Gulfstream 980	95022	LAR-Lineas Aereas de Rionegro Ltda.	N20HG
HK-3497	84	Conquest II	441-0335	LAR-Lineas Aereas de Rionegro Ltda.	HK-3497X
HK-3505	84	King Air F90-1	LA-221	Aeropei Ltda.	HK-3505W
HK-3507	82	King Air B200	BB-974	Lineas Aereas de Los Libertadores/Lineas Aereas Petroleras,	N1861B
HK-3512	82	Conquest II	441-0261	AEROLLANO Ltda/Aerovias del Llano, Villavicencio (Meta).	N261DW
HK-3514	74	Rockwell 690A	11221	Julio Cesar Gerena Diaz,	N132RD
HK-3529	85	Conquest II	441-0348	VIANA-Vias Aereas Nacionales Ltda. Arauca.	HK-3529X
HK-3534	86	King Air 300	FA-96	SAETA-Servicios Aereos del Metay Territorios Nacionales Ltda	N2586E
HK-3540E	83	Conquest II	441-0287	ARO-Aerovias Regionales del Oriente,	HK-3540
HK-3547	85	King Air 300	FA-86	AEROATLANTICO-Aerovias del Atlantico Ltda.	N955AA
HK-3550	83	Conquest II	441-0320	SARPA-Servicios Aereos Panamericanos Ltda. Puerto Asis.	N189WS
HK-3554	82	King Air B200	BB-1068	TAG-Trans Aereo de Girardot/Taxi Aereo Girardot Ltda.	N2157L
HK-3556P	85	King Air 300	FA-47	Martha Lucia Obando Pena,	N961AA
HK-3561	77	Rockwell 690B	11365	Helitaxi Ltda. Bogota.	LV-LZS
HK-3568	83	Conquest II	441-0309	LARCO-Lineas Aereas de Corozal Ltda.	N441MT

Reg	Yr	Type	c/n	Owner/Operator	Prev Regn
HK-3573	82	Conquest II	441-0251	SARPA-Servicios Aereos Panamericanos Ltda. Puerto Asis.	N711GF
HK-3580W	64	Gulfstream 1	145	Compania Rural de Occidente Ltda.	HK-3329X
HK-3596	82	Conquest II	441-0276	Aerotaxi de Valledupar Ltda. Bogota.	HK-3596X
HK-3597	73	Rockwell 690A	11110	Aerotaxi de Valledupar Ltda. Bogota.	HK-3597X
HK-3611	84	Conquest II	441-0324	Taxi Aereo de Caldas Ltda.	N1209P
HK-3613	81	Conquest II	441-0206	Aero Antigua Ltda.	N7049Y
HK-3615	82	Conquest II	441-0239	Cx HK- 7/95 to ?	N45TF
HK-3620X	80	Conquest II	441-0152	Aerotaxi de Valledupar Ltda. Bogota.	N2628X
HK-3648	86	King Air 300	FA-100	Aerolimosina Ltda. (status ?).	N2614C
HK-3654	86	King Air 300LW	FA-101	Aerotaxi del Quindio Ltda.	G-BSTF
HK-3656	76	Rockwell 690A	11314	SERCU-Servicios Aereos de Cucuta Ltda. (status ?).	N14AD
HK-3680	80	Gulfstream 840	11620	Air Tropical Ltda. Bahia Solano.	G-BXYZ
HK-3681	61	Gulfstream 1	78	Aerotaxi de Valledupar Ltda. Bogota.	N33CP
HK-3693X	82	PA-42 Cheyenne III	8001075	HELIVALLE/Helicopteros del Valle Ltda.	N4998M
HK-3700	82	Gulfstream 840	11721	APEL Express SA/Aerolineas Petroleras del Llano.	XA-...
HK-3704	90	King Air/Catpass 250	BB-1392	BPX Colombia SA. Bogota.	HK-3704W
HK-3705	75	King Air 200	BB-63	Aerotaxi del Quindio Ltda.	HK-3705X
HK-3819	81	Gulfstream 980	95059	SAHO-Servicios Aereos Horizonte Ltda.	N9811S
HK-3822	77	King Air 200	BB-248	AERUBA-Aerotaxi de Uraba Ltda. (status ?).	N123PM
HK-3828	84	King Air 300	FA-10	Aerotaxi del Quindio Ltda.	N13PD
HK-3860	88	King Air 300	FA-169	SADA-Sociedad Aeronautica de Armenia Ltda.	XA-PUD
HK-3907	73	King Air E90	LW-39	AERVAL-Aereos y Valores Ltda. Bogota.	OB-1466
HK-3912	81	Gulfstream 840	11668	Taxi Aereo del Uraba Ltda.	YV-2413P
HK-3922P	78	King Air 200	BB-352	Oscar Alberto Monsalve Arbelaez,	YV-...
HK-3923X	79	King Air 200	BB-450	JET-Jet Express Ltda/Cia Sinuana de Transp. Aer Costa Ltda.	C-GJCM
HK-3935W	81	King Air F90	LA-151	Air Charter Ltda.	YV-445CP
HK-3936	75	King Air 200	BB-75	TAXOR-Taxi Aereo de la Orinoquia Ltda.	N70LA
HK-3941W	78	King Air 200	BB-333	Air Charter Ltda. (status ?).	TC-AUY
HK-3961X	84	Gulfstream 1000	96069	Danilo Botero Bustos, Bogota.	N6151T
HK-3965X		King Air E90	...		
HK-3995X	77	King Air 200	BB-196		LN-FKF
HK-3997W	95	DHC 8-202	391	BPX Colombia SA. Bogota.	C-GFBW
HK-4...	82	King Air F90	LA-191		N822BA
HK-4...	76	King Air 200	BB-180		PH-SBK
HK-4065W	81	Gulfstream 840	11673	Servicios Aereos y Terrestres Ltda.	YV-779CP
HK-4108X	75	King Air 200	BB-60	S A de Capurgana Ltda.	N530JA
HK-4179X	81	PA-31T Cheyenne II	8120062	Jardines de Paz SA.	HK-3025
HK-4278		King Air	...	noted Bogota 3/06.	
HK-4282X	82	King Air B200	BB-1049	Helicargo SA. Medellin.	HK-4256
HK-4323	77	Rockwell 690B	11354	Heliservice Ltda.	HP-1415
HK-4343	82	King Air B200	BB-1024	Servicios Aero de Capurgana	N83RZ
HK-4357	75	King Air C90	LJ-668		N668WJ
HK-4370X	85	Gulfstream 1000	96080		N960AC
HK-44..	77	King Air C90	LJ-733	Baru Air SA. Panama City, Panama.	N977FC
HK-853W	69	King Air B90	LJ-458	Jorge Hernando Carvajal Administradores Ltda y Cia S En C.	HK-353P

Military

Reg	Yr	Type	c/n	Owner/Operator	Prev Regn
EJC-111	83	Gulfstream 900	15024	Colombian Army, Bogata.	N5911N
EJC-114	85	Gulfstream 1000	96083	Colombian Army, Bogota.	HK-3376
EJC-115	81	Gulfstream 980	95066	Colombian Army, Bogota.	HK-2682P
EJC-116	77	King Air C90	LJ-739	Colombian Army, Bogota.	YV-152CP
EJC-117	80	King Air 200	BB-694	Colombian Army, Bogota.	PT-OTO
EJC-118	98	King Air/Catpass 250	BB-1615	Colombian Army, Bogota.	N170L
EJC-119	93	King Air B200	BB-1452	Ejercito de Colombia	N15HV
FAC-5198	82	Gulfstream 1000	96030	Fuerza Aerea Colombiana, Bogota-El Dorado.	HK-...
FAC-542	66	680V Turbo Commander	1563-19	Fuerza Aerea Colombiana, Bogota-El Dorado.	HK-2539G
FAC-5454	82	Gulfstream 900	15010		N900BE
FAC-5553	81	Gulfstream 980	95055	Fuerza Aerea Colombiana, Bogota-El Dorado.	FAC-553
FAC-5570	78	King Air C90	LJ-752	Fuerza Aerea Colombiana, Bogota-El Dorado.	FAC-570
FAC-5739	75	PA-31T Cheyenne II	7520014	Fuerza Aerea Colombiana, Bogota-El Dorado.	N8TK
FAC-5743	87	PA-42 Cheyenne IIIA	5501039	Fuerza Aerea Colombiana, Bogota-El Dorado.	HK-3381G
FAC-5744	81	PA-42 Cheyenne III	8001062	Fuerza Aerea Colombiana, Bogota-El Dorado.	HK-3000G
FAC-5746	00	King Air 350	FL-282	Colombia Defence Ministry	N350WP
FAC-5750		King Air 200	...	Fuerza Aerea Colombiana, Bogota-El Dorado.	
PNC-...	85	King Air 300	FA-69	Policia Nacional de Colombia, Bogota.	N531ML
PNC-204	77	Conquest II	441-0031	Policia Nacional de Colombia, Bogota.	N918FE

Reg	Yr	Type	c/n	Owner/Operator	Prev Regn
☐ PNC-208	88	King Air 300	FA-159	Policia Nacional de Colombia, Bogota.	HK-3433X
☐ PNC-209	77	King Air 200	BB-212	Policia Nacional de Colombia, Bogota.	N910P
☐ PNC-225	99	King Air B200	BB-1644	Policia Nacional de Colombia, Bogota.	N3055K

HL = KOREA Total 7
Civil
Reg	Yr	Type	c/n	Owner/Operator	Prev Regn
☐ HL5200	06	King Air C90GT	LJ-1801	Hangseo Univesity, Choongnam.	N73991

Military
Reg	Yr	Type	c/n	Owner/Operator	Prev Regn
☐ 98-1001	98	Reims/Cessna F406	F406-0081	Republic of Korea Navy, Seoul.	F-WWSR
☐ 98-1002	98	Reims/Cessna F406	F406-0082	Republic of Korea Navy, Seoul.	F-WWSS
☐ 98-1003	98	Reims/Cessna F406	F406-0083	Republic of Korea Navy, Seoul.	F-W...
☐ 98-1004	99	Reims/Cessna F406	F406-00..	Republic of Korea Navy, Seoul.	F-W...
☐ 98-1005	99	Reims/Cessna F406	F406-0084	Republic of Korea Navy, Seoul.	F-WSSU
☐ 98-1006	99	Reims/Cessna F406	F406-0085	Republic of Korea Navy, Seoul.	F-W...

HP = PANAMA Total 53
Civil
Reg	Yr	Type	c/n	Owner/Operator	Prev Regn
☐ HP-	67	King Air A90	LJ-184		N566CA
☐ HP-	01	King Air C90B	LJ-1663	Avionx International Inc., Panama City	N588SD
☐ HP-	79	King Air 200	BB-569	Baru Air SA. Panama City, Panama.	N40HE
☐ HP-	69	King Air B90	LJ-455		PT-OYD
☐ HP-	93	King Air 350	FL-98	Creekland Holding Corporaton, Panama City	N8302N
☐ HP-...	79	Rockwell 690B	11565	TRANSPASA, Panama-Paitilla.	N81HK
☐ HP-...	82	Conquest II	441-0277	Revise SA.	N441HT
☐ HP-...	76	King Air 200	BB-164	Air Anstro Services SA. Panama City.	N70PQ
☐ HP-...	82	Gulfstream 900	15004		N5838N
☐ HP-...	85	Gulfstream 1000	96081		N600BM
☐ HP-...	82	Gulfstream 900	15003		N900RH
☐ HP-...	84	Conquest II	441-0328	City Investments Ltd. Panama City.	N12093
☐ HP-...	78	King Air 200	BB-329		N587DR
☐ HP-...	85	Gulfstream 1000	96082		N89GA
☐ HP-....	76	King Air 200	BB-330		N127TT
☐ HP-....	77	King Air 200	BB-237	Blue Water Reef International Research, Panama City.	N114JF
☐ HP-....	68	King Air B90	LJ-384	Hugo Belaverdi, Panama City.	N563MC
☐ HP-....	65	King Air 90	LJ-5		N357JR
☐ HP-....	73	Rockwell 690	11073	Heliatlantic SA. El Dorado.	N680AD
☐ HP-....	78	King Air 200	BB-362	Baru Air SA. Panama City, Panama.	N506AB
☐ HP-....	77	King Air 200	BB-300	Transportes Aereos de Maracay, Panama City.	F-GHLV
☐ HP-....	71	King Air C90	LJ-520		N1869
☐ HP-....	80	Gulfstream 840	11621		N920WJ
☐ HP-....	65	King Air 90	LJ-55	Air Anstro Services SA. Panama City.	N711BP
☐ HP-....	75	King Air 200	BB-33	Transportes Aereos de Maracay, Panama City.	N90806
☐ HP-....	81	King Air 200C	BL-26	Parts & Pieces, Panama City.	N326AA
☐ HP-....	80	King Air 200	BB-644	Rio Soul Air SA. Panama City.	N750HG
☐ HP-....	67	King Air A90	LJ-296		N30EH
☐ HP-....	73	Rockwell 690A	11102	TAMCA SA.	N697JM
☐ HP-....	78	King Air C-12C	BC-63	Eduardo Finol de Leon, Caracas, Venezuela.	N712GA
☐ HP-1069	77	SA-226T Merlin 3A	T-288	Inversiones Humbolt SA. Panama City.	HP-1069P
☐ HP-1136AP	68	SA-26AT Merlin 2B	T26-113	Raul Arias/Apair SA. Paitilla.	N878SC
☐ HP-1149P	82	Gulfstream 1000	96031	World Interstate Corp.	C-FDGD
☐ HP-1182	90	King Air 300	FA-209	Motta Internacional SA. Panama City.	N148M
☐ HP-1189	84	Conquest II	441-0332	Marucci Holdings SA.	N888FL
☐ HP-1316	88	King Air B200T	BT-33	Bocas Fruit Co. Panama City. (was BB-1301).	N600RD
☐ HP-1336APP	73	King Air A100	B-173	Aeroperlas SA/Apair SA. El Dorado.	C-GAST
☐ HP-1433	68	680W Turbo Commander	1820-34	Cx HP- to ?	HK-3975X
☐ HP-1457	87	King Air 300	FA-123	Airleasing International Corp.	HK-3670
☐ HP-1500	01	King Air C90B	LJ-1648	Aeronaves del Atlantico SA. El Dorado.	N3178H
☐ HP-1512	77	King Air 200	BB-311	Transportes Aereos del Toro SA.	N370TC
☐ HP-1544	82	Conquest 1	425-0118	Cosmo Air Support SA. Albrook.	HK-3036P
☐ HP-1555	04	King Air 350	FL-395		N61185
☐ HP-1588	04	King Air 350	FL-429	Cressida International Investment Corp. Panama City.	N6129Q
☐ HP-1591	76	King Air 200	BB-128	San Francisco Air Cargo Leasing,	N110TA
☐ HP-1595	85	King Air 300	FA-60	Trans Aero Partes SA. Panama City.	HK-3659
☐ HP-1598	76	King Air 200	BB-135	Tiuna Air Leasing SA., M.A.Gelabert	HK-4236
☐ HP-1607	74	Rockwell 690A	11209		N107JJ
☐ HP-1608	97	King Air C90B	LJ-1500	Executive Wings Corp., M.A.Gelabert	(N290JS)

☐ HP-2888	91 King Air B300C	FM-2	Blue Cascade Inc.		N749RH
☐ HP-77PE	77 Rockwell 690B	11368	Aviacion Panamena SA. Panama City.		N77PE
☐ HP-809	80 PA-31T Cheyenne II	8020015	Colony Trading SA.		N2353W
☐ HP-960P	80 King Air 200	BB-617	Stowage SA. (status ?).		HP-960
				Total	5

HR = HONDURAS
Civil

☐ HR-...	67 Mitsubishi MU-2B	021			N22JZ
☐ HR-CEM	76 Rockwell 690A	11302	Tassa HN Inc. Tegucigalpa.		N302BA
☐ HR-IAH	66 King Air A90	LJ-122	Islena Airlines, La Ceiba.		N860K
☐ HR-JFA	81 PA-42 Cheyenne III	8001056	AVE SA.		

Military

☐ FAH-006	83 Gulfstream 1000	96060	Fuerza Aerea Honduras, Tegucigalpa.		HK-3194X
				Total	26

HS = THAILAND
Civil

☐ HS-ATS	07 King Air B200	BB-1988	Aeronautical Radio of Thailand		N988KA
☐ HS-CNS	05 King Air B200	BB-1923	Aerothai, Bangkok.		N3123J
☐ HS-DCB	76 King Air 200	BB-132	Aerothai, Bangkok.		HS-FFI
☐ HS-DCF	88 King Air B200	BB-1315	Aerothai, Bangkok.		HS-AFI
☐ HS-ITD	96 King Air 350	FL-151	Italian/Thai Development Co. Bangkok.		N10817
☐ HS-KCH	83 King Air B200	BB-1125	Siam Land Flying Co. Don Muang.		VH-KCH
☐ HS-SLA	91 King Air 350	FL-53	Siam Land Flying Co. Don Muang.		HS-TFI
☐ HS-SLC	98 King Air 350	FL-194			VH-KJD

Military

☐ 00923	73 King Air E90	LW-26	Royal Thai Army, Don Muang.		01769
☐ 0169	Beech 1900C-1	UC-169	Royal Thai Army, Don Muang.		N.....
☐ 0170	Beech 1900C-1	UC-170	Royal Thai Army, Don Muang.		N.....
☐ 0342	78 King Air 200	BB-342	Royal Thai Army, Don Muang.		794
☐ 1112	95 Dornier 228-212	8226	Royal Thai Navy,		D-CBDF
☐ 1113	95 Dornier 228-212	8227	Royal Thai Navy,		D-CCCP
☐ 1114	96 Dornier 228-212	8228	Royal Thai Navy,		D-C...
☐ 1165	83 King Air B200	BB-1165	Royal Thai Army, Don Muang.		N6922P
☐ 2011	96 King Air 350	FL-146	KASET, Bangkok.		N3268Z
☐ 2012	96 King Air 350	FL-147	KASET, Bangkok.		N3269W
☐ 41060	95 BAe Jetstream 41	41060	Royal Thai Army, Don Muang.		G-BWGW
☐ 41094	96 BAe Jetstream 41	41094	Royal Thai Army, Don Muang.		G-BWTZ
☐ 60501	79 SA-226AT Merlin 4A	AT-071	Royal Thai Air Force, Bangkok. (status ?).		60301
☐ 60502	79 SA-226AT Merlin 4A	AT-072	Royal Thai Air Force, Bangkok.		60302
☐ 60503	79 SA-226AT Merlin 4A	AT-073	Royal Thai Air Force, Bangkok.		60303
☐ 93303	92 King Air B200	BB-1436	Royal Thai Survey Dept. Bangkok.		N1564M
☐ 93304	92 King Air B200	BB-1441	Royal Thai Survey Dept. Bangkok.		56385
☐ 93305	92 King Air B200	BB-1443	Royal Thai Survey Dept. Bangkok.		56379
				Total	3

HZ = SAUDI ARABIA
Civil

☐ HZ-PC2	87 Beech 1900C-1	UC-4	Directorate of Civil Aviation,		N3078C
☐ HZ-SN6	72 SA-226AT Merlin 4	AT-007	DHL/SNAS WorldWide Express, Bahrain.		N2610
☐ HZ-SN8	82 SA-227AT Merlin 4C	AT-434	DHL/SNAS WorldWide Express, Bahrain.		N3110F
				Total	56

I = ITALY
Civil

☐ I-ASMI	83 King Air B200	BB-1124	Assicuratrice Milanese, Parma.		LX-DUC
☐ I-BCOM	00 P-180 Avanti	1040	Air Walser SRL. Milan.		
☐ I-BPAE	04 P-180 Avanti	1081	Blue Panorama Airlines SpA. Roma-Fiumicino.		
☐ I-CFPA	05 P-180 Avanti	1094	Ministry of Agriculture & Forests, Ciampino.		
☐ I-CGAT	75 PA-31T Cheyenne II	7520033	Compagnia Generale Aeronautica, Genoa.		N54964
☐ I-CGTT	78 PA-31T Cheyenne II	7820045	Soc. New Bristol SRL. Milan.		N82288
☐ I-CNDB	06 Pilatus PC-12/47	728	Blue Mercury, Milan.		HB-FRN
☐ I-DPCR	95 P-180 Avanti	1032	Protezione Civile, Genoa.		(D-IMLP)
☐ I-DPCS	99 P-180 Avanti	1033	Protezione Civile, Genoa.		
☐ I-FXRB	00 P-180 Avanti	1035	Fox Air SRL. Bologna.		
☐ I-FXRC	00 P-180 Avanti	1045	Fox Air SRL. Bologna.		
☐ I-FXRD	03 P-180 Avanti	1067	Fox Air SRL. Bologna.		
☐ I-FXRE	02 P-180 Avanti	1049	Loop SpA/Fox Air SRL. Bologna.		
☐ I-HYDR	75 PA-31T Cheyenne II	7520034	Compagnia Generale Aeronautica, Genoa.		N54966
☐ I-LOAN	02 Pilatus PC-12/45	381	LAL Air 2003 SRL. Parma.		HB-FPB
Reg	*Yr Type*	*c/n*	*Owner/Operator*		*Prev Regn*

Reg	Yr Type	c/n	Owner/Operator	Prev Regn
☐ I-MAGJ	75 Rockwell 690A	11265	Aviomar SRL. Roma-Urbe.	N81540
☐ I-MCAP	07 King Air B200	BB-1975	Modena Capitale Aviation, Reggio Emilia	N7075V
☐ I-MTOP	03 King Air B200	BB-1825	Toscana Jet, Florence.	N4485Z
☐ I-NARB	74 SA-226AT Merlin 4	AT-020	BESIT SNC. Servizi Aerei, Olbia. 'Cises'	N747BD
☐ I-NARC	75 SA-226AT Merlin 4A	AT-035	BESIT SNC. Servizi Aerei, Olbia.	N90090
☐ I-NARW	77 SA-226AT Merlin 4A	AT-058	BESIT SNC. Servizi Aerei, Olbia.	D-ICFB
☐ I-PALS	75 PA-31T Cheyenne II	7620005	Soc. PAL SRL. Pollone (BI).	N54979
☐ I-PIAH	81 King Air 200	BB-777	Interfly SRL. Brescia, Italy. (At Van Nuys, Ca., USA)	
☐ I-PREE	07 P-180 Avanti II	1138	Air Walser SRL., Trontano	
☐ I-REEF	05 King Air B200	BB-1905	Interfly SRL. Brescia.	N36705
☐ I-SASA	80 PA-31T Cheyenne 1	8004024	Soc. Alibrixia Nord SRL. Brescia.	N2321V
☐ I-TICO	06 TBM 700C2	345	Luca Barilla, Parma.	F-OIKM
☐ I-TOPS	00 Pilatus PC-12/45	352	Topjet Executive SRL., Milan	HB-FOZ

Military

Reg	Yr Type	c/n	Owner/Operator	Prev Regn
☐ I-DVFM	04 P-180 Avanti	1078	Code VF-181, Vigili del Fuoco, Roma-Ciampino.	
☐ MM62159	94 P-180 Avanti	1023	AMI, 36 Stormo, Giola del Colle.	
☐ MM62160	94 P-180 Avanti	1024	AMI, 14 Stormo, Pratica di Mare.	
☐ MM62161	94 P-180 Avanti	1025	AMI, Sq Coll e Soccorso, Milan.	
☐ MM62162	94 P-180 Avanti	1028	AMI, 14 Stormo, Pratica di Mare.	
☐ MM62163	94 P-180 Avanti	1029	AMI, 14 Stormo, Pratica di Mare.	
☐ MM62164	94 P-180 Avanti	1030	AMI, Centro Sperimentale, Pratica di Mare.	
☐ MM62165	96 ATR 42-400MP	500	GF-13. AMI/Guardia di Finanza,	F-WWEW
☐ MM62166	96 ATR 42-400MP	502	GF-14. AMI/Guardia di Finanza,	F-WWEM
☐ MM62167	94 P-180 Avanti	1026	Cavelleria dell'Aria, ACTL 28 Gr Sqd 'Tucano', Roma-Ciampino	(D-IMED)
☐ MM62168	92 P-180 Avanti	1027	Cavelleria dell'Aria, ACTL 28 Gr Sqd 'Tucano', Roma-Ciampino	F-GMRM
☐ MM62169	95 P-180 Avanti	1031	Cavelleria dell'Aria, ACTL 28 Gr Sqd 'Tucano', Roma-Ciampino	
☐ MM62199	01 P-180 Avanti	1041	AMI, 14 Stormo, Pratica di Mare.	
☐ MM62200	01 P-180 Avanti	1047	AMI, 14 Stormo, Pratica di Mare.	
☐ MM62201	01 P-180 Avanti	1053	AMI, 14 Stormo, Pratica di Mare.	
☐ MM62202	02 P-180 Avanti	1058	AMI, 14 Stormo, Pratica di Mare.	
☐ MM62203	02 P-180 Avanti	1071	AMI, 14 Stormo, Pratica di Mare.	I-RAII
☐ MM62204	03 P-180 Avanti	1082	Code 9-02, Italian Navy,	
☐ MM62205	03 P-180 Avanti	1075	AMI,	
☐ MM62206	04 P-180 Avanti	1087	AMI,	
☐ MM62207	05 P-180 Avanti	1096	AMI,	
☐ MM62211	04 P-180 Avanti	1085	Italian Navy,	
☐ MM62212	04 P-180 Avanti	1076	Code 9-01, Italian Navy,	
☐ MM62213	04 P-180 Avanti	1090	Italian Navy,	
☐ MM62246	06 P-180 Avanti II	1114	Carabinieri. Coded CC-112	
☐ MM62247	06 P-180 Avanti II	1113	Polizia. Coded PS-B15	
☐ MM62248	07 P-180 Avanti II	1118	G di F	
☐ MM62249	07 P-180 Avanti II	1126	G di F	

JA = JAPAN   Total   100

Civil

Reg	Yr Type	c/n	Owner/Operator	Prev Regn
☐ JA	89 King Air C90A	LJ-1198		N611CF
☐ JA....	02 King Air C90B	LJ-1690		N61669
☐ JA003G	98 SAAB 2000	051	JCAB, Tokyo.	SE-051
☐ JA004G	98 SAAB 2000	054	JCAB, Tokyo.	SE-054
☐ JA01EP	98 King Air B200	BB-1604	Seiko Epson Corp. Kagoshima-Makarazaki.	N1017V
☐ JA01KA	99 King Air C90B	LJ-1567	Kawasaki Heavy Industries, Gifu.	N31279
☐ JA02EP	04 King Air 350	FL-425	Seiko Epson Corp. Kagoshima-Makarazaki.	N37025
☐ JA121N	97 King Air B200	BB-1577	Mitsui Lease Jigyo,	N33AR
☐ JA377N	05 King Air 350	FL-451	Noevir Co. Tokyo.	N36851
☐ JA8600	81 Gulfstream 980	95070	Asia Air Survey Ltd. Chofu.	N38AA
☐ JA8705	92 King Air B200	BB-1431	Naka Nihon Air Service Co. Nagoya.	N82696
☐ JA870A	00 King Air 350	FL-297	JCG-Japanese Coast Guard, Hiroshima.	N3197N
☐ JA8737	70 Mitsubishi MU-2G	501	Diamond Air Service, Nagoya	
☐ JA8824	81 King Air 200T	BT-17	Diamond Air Service, Nagoya	N37180
☐ JA8828	74 SA-226AT Merlin 4	AT-016	Showa Aviation Co. Osaka-Yao.	N76MX
☐ JA8833	83 King Air B200T	BT-28	JCG-Japanese Coast Guard, Kagoshima. (was BB-1117).	N1846M
☐ JA8844	86 King Air C90A	LJ-1141	Nishi Nihon Iryo Service, Oita.	N2736D
☐ JA8845	87 King Air C90A	LJ-1142	Flying Training, Sendai.	N2860A
☐ JA8846	87 King Air C90A	LJ-1143	Taian Kensetsu, Nagoya.	N7239S
☐ JA8847	87 King Air C90A	LJ-1144	Flying Training, Sendai.	N7239U

Reg   Yr Type   c/n   Owner/Operator   Prev Regn

Reg	Yr	Type	c/n	Owner/Operator	Prev Regn
JA8848	87	King Air C90A	LJ-1145	Flying Training, Sendai.	N7239Y
JA8850	87	King Air C90A	LJ-1149	Flying Training, Sendai.	N7240E
JA8851	87	King Air C90A	LJ-1150	Flying Training, Sendai.	N7240K
JA8853	85	PA-42 Cheyenne 400LS	5527026	Bell Hand Club Co. Chofu.	(N429BX)
JA8854	87	King Air B200T	BT-31	JCG-Japanese Coast Guard, Yao. (was BB-1264).	N72392
JA8855	85	Conquest 1	425-0235	Konan Co. Tokunoshima.	N1262P
JA8860	88	King Air B200T	BT-32	JCG-Japanese Coast Guard, Fukuoka. (was BB-1289).	N3184A
JA8867	87	PA-42 Cheyenne 400LS	5527035	Mainichi Shimbun, Tokyo.	N9295A
JA8881	91	King Air 300	FA-219	Japan Digital Laboratories, Honda.	N6080W
JA8882	91	King Air C90A	LJ-1290	JAL Capital,	N81763
JA8883	91	King Air C90A	LJ-1291	JAL Capital,	N8178W
JA8884	91	King Air C90A	LJ-1292	JAL Capital,	N81826
JA8894	92	TBM 700	38	Auto Panther Company	F-OHBG
JA8951	96	SAAB 340B-SAR	385	JCG-Japanese Coast Guard, Tokyo-Haneda.	SE-C85
JA8952	97	SAAB 340B-SAR	405	JCG-Japanese Coast Guard, Tokyo-Haneda.	SE-C...

Military

Reg	Yr	Type	c/n	Owner/Operator	Prev Regn
22003	72	Mitsubishi LR-1	803	JG-2003, JGSDF, Tachikawa. (was s/n 230).	
22007	76	Mitsubishi LR-1	807	JG-2007, JGSDF, Osaka-Yao. (was s/n 334).	
22008	77	Mitsubishi LR-1	808	JG-2008, JGSDF, Kasuminome. (was s/n 359).	
22009	78	Mitsubishi LR-1	809	JG-2009, JGSDF, Osaka-Yao. (was s/n 376).	
22010	78	Mitsubishi LR-1	810	JG-2010, JGSDF, Sapporo-Okadama. (was s/n 394).	
22013	81	Mitsubishi LR-1	813	JG-2013, JGSDF, Sapporo-Okadama. (was s/n 442).	
22014	81	Mitsubishi LR-1	814	JG-2014, JGSDF, Takayubaru. (was s/n 443).	
22015	81	Mitsubishi LR-1	815	JG-2015, JGSDF, Osaka-Yao. (was s/n 444).	
22016	83	Mitsubishi LR-1	816	JG-8016, JGSDF, Utsonimiya. (was s/n 456).	
22017	83	Mitsubishi LR-1	817	JG-8017, JGSDF, Sapporo-Okadama. (was s/n 457).	
22018	85	Mitsubishi LR-1	818	JG-2018, JGSDF, Kisarazu. (was s/n 465).	
22019	85	Mitsubishi LR-1	819	JG-2019, JGSDF, Naha. (was s/n 463).	
22020	85	Mitsubishi LR-1	820	JG-2020, JGSDF, Kasuminome. (was s/n 466).	
23051	98	King Air 350 (LR-2)	FL-176	JG-3051, JGSDF, Utsunomiya.	N11309
23052	98	King Air 350 (LR-2)	FL-186	JG-3052, JGSDF, Kisarazu.	N11310
23053	00	King Air 350 (LR-2)	FL-266	JG-3053, JGSDF, Naha.	N31379
23054	00	King Air 350 (LR-2)	FL-307	JG-3054, JGSDF, Takayubaru.	N5007H
23055	01	King Air 350 (LR-2)	FL-331	JG-3055, JGSDF,	N350KD
23056	03	King Air 350	FL-382	JG-3056, JGSDF,	N61942
23-3226	81	Mitsubishi MU-2E	926	JASDF. (was s/n 455).	
23-3227	85	Mitsubishi MU-2E	927	JASDF. (was s/n 464).	
6808	80	King Air TC90	LJ-916	JMSDF, 202nd Air Training Squadron, Tokushima AB.	N67233
6809	80	King Air TC90	LJ-917	JMSDF, 202nd Air Training Squadron, Tokushima AB.	N6724D
6810	81	King Air TC90	LJ-976	JMSDF, 202nd Air Training Squadron, Tokushima AB.	N3832G
6811	81	King Air TC90	LJ-980	JMSDF, 202nd Air Training Squadron, Tokushima AB.	N3832K
6812	82	King Air TC90	LJ-1042	JMSDF, 202nd Air Training Squadron, Tokushima AB.	N18460
6813	82	King Air TC90	LJ-1043	JMSDF, 202nd Air Training Squadron, Tokushima AB.	N1846B
6814	82	King Air TC90	LJ-1044	JMSDF, 202nd Air Training Squadron, Tokushima AB.	N1846D
6815	82	King Air TC90	LJ-1047	JMSDF, 202nd Air Training Squadron, Tokushima AB.	N1846F
6816	83	King Air TC90	LJ-1060	JMSDF, 202nd Air Training Squadron, Tokushima AB.	N1875Z
6817	83	King Air TC90	LJ-1061	JMSDF, 202nd Air Training Squadron, Tokushima AB.	N1876Z
6818	83	King Air TC90	LJ-1062	JMSDF, 202nd Air Training Squadron, Tokushima AB.	N6886S
6819	84	King Air TC90	LJ-1083	JMSDF, 202nd Air Training Squadron, Tokushima AB.	N6923Z
6820	84	King Air TC90	LJ-1084	JMSDF, 202nd Air Training Squadron, Tokushima AB.	N69237
6821	85	King Air TC90	LJ-1110	JMSDF, 202nd Air Training Squadron, Tokushima AB.	N7238J
6822	87	King Air TC90	LJ-1146	JMSDF, 202nd Air Training Squadron, Tokushima AB.	N72400
6823	93	King Air TC90	LJ-1335	JMSDF, 202nd Air Training Squadron, Tokushima AB.	N82323
6824	93	King Air TC90	LJ-1336	JMSDF, 202nd Air Training Squadron, Tokushima AB.	N82326
6825	93	King Air TC90	LJ-1337	JMSDF, 202nd Air Training Squadron, Tokushima AB.	N82349
6826	93	King Air TC90	LJ-1338	JMSDF, 202nd Air Training Squadron, Tokushima AB.	N82366
6827	93	King Air TC90	LJ-1339	JMSDF, 202nd Air Training Squadron, Tokushima AB.	N82376
6828	00	King Air TC90	LJ-1584	JMSDF, 202nd Air Training Squadron, Tokushima AB.	N3184F
6829	00	King Air TC90	LJ-1592	JMSDF, 202nd Air Training Squadron, Tokushima AB.	N40490
6830	00	King Air TC90	LJ-1596	JMSDF, 202nd Air Training Squadron, Tokushima AB.	N43046
6831	00	King Air TC90	LJ-1634	JMSDF, 202nd Air Training Squadron, Tokushima AB.	N50344
6832	00	King Air TC90	LJ-1636	JMSDF, 202nd Air Training Squadron, Tokushima AB.	N50785
6833	00	King Air TC90	LJ-1638	JMSDF, 202nd Air Training Squadron, Tokushima AB.	N50778
83-3223	78	Mitsubishi MU-2E	923	JASDF. (was s/n 377).	
83-3224	78	Mitsubishi MU-2E	924	JASDF. (was s/n 378).	

Reg	Yr Type	c/n	Owner/Operator	Prev Regn
☐ 9102	82 King Air UC-90	LJ-1038	JMSDF-Japanese Maritime Self Defence Force.	N1839D
☐ 9301	88 King Air LC-90	LJ-1182	JMSDF-Japanese Maritime Self Defence Force.	
☐ 9302	90 King Air LC-90	LJ-1248	JMSDF-Japanese Maritime Self Defence Force.	N56633
☐ 9303	90 King Air LC-90	LJ-1249	JMSDF-Japanese Maritime Self Defence Force, Atsugi.	N56638
☐ 9304	91 King Air LC-90	LJ-1281	JMSDF-Japanese Maritime Self Defence Force, Atsugi.	N81538
☐ 9305	91 King Air LC-90	LJ-1282	JMSDF-Japanese Maritime Self Defence Force.	N8154G
☐ 93-3225	81 Mitsubishi MU-2E	925	JASDF. (was s/n 445).	
☐ JA861A	97 King Air 350	FL-180	JCG-Japanese Coast Guard, Kagoshima.	N18327
☐ JA862A	97 King Air 350	FL-188	JCG-Japanese Coast Guard, Naha.	N18297
☐ JA863A	98 King Air 350	FL-191	JCG-Japanese Coast Guard, Yonago.	N11191
☐ JA864A	98 King Air 350	FL-193	JCG-Japanese Coast Guard, Yonago.	N11250
☐ JA865A	98 King Air 350	FL-195	JCG-Japanese Coast Guard, Ishigaki.	N11278
☐ JA866A	98 King Air 350	FL-218	JCG-Japanese Coast Guard, Fukuoka.	N2352N
☐ JA867A	98 King Air 350	FL-222	JCG-Japanese Coast Guard, Niigata.	N23272
☐ JA868A	00 King Air 350	FL-292	JCG-Japanese Coast Guard, Shin-Chitose.	N3192N
☐ JA869A	00 King Air 350	FL-295	JCG-Japanese Coast Guard, Sendai.	N3195T

JY = JORDAN Total 1

Civil

Reg	Yr Type	c/n	Owner/Operator	Prev Regn
☐ JY-AW2	99 King Air B200	BB-1701	Arab Wings Ltd. Amman.	N85GP

LN = NORWAY Total 25

Civil

Reg	Yr Type	c/n	Owner/Operator	Prev Regn
☐ LN-ACV	85 PA-42 Cheyenne 400LS	5527023	Guard Systems ASA. Larvik.	N722ER
☐ LN-ACY	79 King Air E90	LW-309	Trovald Klaveness & Co AS. Gardermoen.	N160TT
☐ LN-AWA	75 King Air A100	B-213	AirWing A/S. Oslo.	SE-LDL
☐ LN-AWB	75 King Air A100	B-217	AirWing A/S. Oslo.	N730EJ
☐ LN-BAA	89 King Air B200	BB-1327	Bergen Air Transport A/S. Bergen.	N67SD
☐ LN-HTD	78 SA-226T Merlin 3B	T-294	Helitrans A/S. Trondheim	PH-DYB
☐ LN-IDA	01 King Air B200C	BL-141	Hesnes Flyinvest A/S. Sandjeford-Torp.	G-ZAPT
☐ LN-LTA	04 King Air B200	BB-1868	Lufttransport A/S. Tromso.	N954RM
☐ LN-LYY	84 PA-42 Cheyenne 400LS	5527010	Guard Systems ASA. Oslo, Norway.	SE-LYY
☐ LN-MMM	07 King Air B200	BB-1994	Sundt Air A/S., Gardemoen	N994KA
☐ LN-MOB	80 King Air 200	BB-584	Lufttransport A/S. Tromso.	N400WP
☐ LN-MOC	93 King Air B200	BB-1449	Lufttransport A/S. Tromso.	N200KA
☐ LN-MOD	93 King Air B200	BB-1459	Lufttransport A/S. Tromso.	N8163R
☐ LN-MOE	93 King Air B200	BB-1460	Lufttransport A/S. Tromso.	N8164G
☐ LN-MOF	93 King Air B200	BB-1461	Lufttransport A/S. Tromso.	N8261E
☐ LN-MOG	93 King Air B200	BB-1465	Lufttransport A/S. Tromso.	N8214T
☐ LN-MOH	93 King Air B200	BB-1466	Lufttransport A/S. Tromso.	N8216Z
☐ LN-MOI	93 King Air B200	BB-1470	Lufttransport A/S. Tromso.	N8225Z
☐ LN-MOJ	89 King Air B200	BB-1334	Lufttransport A/S. Tromso.	TC-SKO
☐ LN-MOT	97 King Air B200	BB-1590	Lufttransport A/S. Tromso.	D-IHUT
☐ LN-NOA	81 King Air B200	BB-829	Sundt Air A/S. Oslo.	N829AJ
☐ LN-SFT	80 SA-226T Merlin 3B	T-342	Helitrans A/S. Trondheim.	N342NX
☐ LN-SUZ	96 King Air B200	BB-1547	Sundt Air A/S. Oslo.	N780CA
☐ LN-TRG	06 King Air B200	BB-1936	The Resource Group TRG A/S. Oslo-Gardermoen.	N36566
☐ LN-TWL	83 King Air B200	BB-1144	Bergen Air Transport A/S. Bergen.	N120AJ

LV = ARGENTINA Total 107

Civil

Reg	Yr Type	c/n	Owner/Operator	Prev Regn
☐ LQ-BLU	88 PA-42 Cheyenne 400LS	5527037	Corte Suprema de Justica Nacional, Buenos Aires.	HK-3397W
☐ LQ-PIE	King Air C90B	...		
☐ LQ-ZRB	99 King Air C90B	LJ-1552	Gobierno Santiago del Estero, Santiago del Estero.	N3132D
☐ LQ-ZRG	99 King Air B200	BB-1652	Gobierno Provincia del Chaco, Chaco.	N3152K
☐ LV-	82 King Air C90A	LJ-1028		G-BKFY
☐ LV-	07 King Air B200GT	BY-1	Aero Baires SACI, Buenos Aires	
☐ LV-	07 King Air B200GT	BY-12	Aero Baires SACI, Buenos Aires	N34712
☐ LV-	79 King Air 200	BB-447		N356GA
☐ LV-	92 King Air B200	BB-1417	For Export to Argentina	N230TW
☐ LV-AIY	83 King Air B200	BB-1131	Finca de la Represa SA.	HP-1180
☐ LV-APF	81 PA-42 Cheyenne III	8001026	Government Province of Catamarca, Catamarca. (status ?)	LQ-APF
☐ LV-ARU	00 King Air C90B	LJ-1617	Aero B S A,	N363K
☐ LV-AXO	04 King Air B200	BB-1877	Facchini Servicios Aereos SA. San Isidro.	N61767
☐ LV-AYG	75 King Air E90	LW-135		N74VR
☐ LV-BAN	04 King Air 350	FL-420	Aero Baires SACI. Buenos Aires.	N36620

Reg	Yr	Type	c/n	Owner/Operator	Prev Regn
LV-BCJ	72	Rockwell 690	11022		N184RL
LV-BCP	78	PA-31T Cheyenne II	7820006		N14EA
LV-BCR	76	PA-31T Cheyenne II	7620022		N57MR
LV-BCT	76	PA-31T Cheyenne II	7620035		N199ND
LV-BCU	77	PA-31T Cheyenne II	7720044		N23MV
LV-BDG	05	King Air C90B	LJ-1730	Ingeneria Sima SA. Neuquen.	N36720
LV-BDU	70	King Air B90	LJ-489	La Delicia Felipe Fort, Buenos Aires.	LV-ZXZ
LV-BEI	81	PA-42 Cheyenne III	8001009		D-IDSF
LV-BIC	06	King Air C90GT	LJ-1819	Ameriflight SA	N70689
LV-BNA	77	Rockwell 690B	11419	Government Province of Cordoba.	LV-PYH
LV-JJW	69	King Air B90	LJ-449	Jose Luis Colombero, Cordoba. (status ?).	LV-PIZ
LV-LEY	72	Rockwell 690	11019	CATA Linea Aerea S A C I F I., Buenos Aires.	LQ-LEY
LV-LRH	75	Rockwell 690A	11236	Odol SA. (status ?).	LV-PTT
LV-LTB	75	Rockwell 690A	11238	Government Province of Jujuy, San Salvador.	LV-PUA
LV-LTC	75	Rockwell 690A	11241	SAPSE-Servicios Aereos Patagonicas, Viedma. (status ?).	LV-PUB
LV-LTU	75	Rockwell 690A	11261	SASA-Sudamericana de Aviacion SA. Buenos Aires.	LV-PUI
LV-LTV	75	PA-31T Cheyenne II	7520022	Government Province of Corrientes.	LV-PTS
LV-LTX	75	Rockwell 690A	11258	SASA-Sudamericana de Aviacion SA. Buenos Aires.	LV-PUH
LV-LTY	74	Rockwell 690A	11230	Government Province of Tucuman.	LV-PTY
LV-LZL	75	Rockwell 690A	11246	Emepa SA. Buenos Aires.	LV-PUW
LV-LZM	75	Rockwell 690A	11268	Banco Mercantil Argentino SA. Buenos Aires.	LV-PUX
LV-LZO	75	PA-31T Cheyenne II	7620003	Esco SA. Buenos Aires.	LV-LZO
LV-MAW	77	Rockwell 690B	11398	TAN-Transportes Aereos Neuquen, Neuquen. `Collon Cora'	LV-PVN
LV-MBY	77	Rockwell 690B	11412	Government Province of Chaco, Resistencia.	LV-PXN
LV-MCV	77	Mitsubishi MU-2P	361SA	Industrias Metalurgica Pescarmona, Buenos Aires.	LV-PYI
LV-MDG	77	PA-31T Cheyenne II	7720065	Ver Part. Vinelli,	LV-PYD
LV-MDN	78	Rockwell 690B	11442	Government Province of Cordoba.	LV-PYT
LV-MGC	77	Mitsubishi MU-2N	704SA	T A F T SRL. Buenos Aires.	LV-PZT
LV-MMY	78	Conquest II	441-0075	Government Province of Buenos Aires.	LV-PBA
LV-MNR	79	PA-31T Cheyenne II	7920017	Meldorek SA.	LV-P..
LV-MOE	79	PA-31T Cheyenne II	7920050	Government Province of Catamarca, Catamarca.	LV-P..
LV-MRT	78	Conquest II	441-0082	Government Province of Buenos Aires.	LV-PAZ
LV-MRU	78	Conquest II	441-0077	Government Province of Buenos Aires.	LV-PBB
LV-MTU	79	PA-31T Cheyenne II	7920080	Inst. Argentina de Sanidad y Calidad, Buenos Aires.	LV-P..
LV-MYA	79	Rockwell 690B	11558	Government Province of Santa Fe.	LV-PDH
LV-MYX	79	PA-31T Cheyenne 1	7904045	Aviacenter SA.	LV-P..
LV-OAP	79	PA-31T Cheyenne II	7920065	Inst. Argentina de Sanidad y Calidad, Buenos Aires.	LV-PCJ
LV-OBB	80	King Air E90	LW-330	Aerorutas S A T A, Buenos Aires.	LV-PFJ
LV-OEI	80	Gulfstream 840	11612	Government Province of La Pampa, Santa Rosa.	LV-PGD
LV-OFT	80	King Air 200	BB-699	Don Roberto S A A C I., Buenos Aires.	LV-PIF
LV-OFX	67	680V Turbo Commander	1682-63	Empesur SA. Rio Gallegos, Santa Cruz.	AE-129
LV-OGF	80	PA-31T Cheyenne II	8020013	Santa Monica SA.	LV-P..
LV-ROC	88	King Air C90A	LJ-1180	Petrel Aereos Servicios SRL. Buenos Aires.	LV-PAJ
LV-RZB	69	SA-26AT Merlin 2B	T26-143	Coronaire SA. Quimes.	LV-PFR
LV-VHO	68	King Air B90	LJ-428	Orion Aviacion SA. Buenos Aires.	N74GR
LV-VHR	68	King Air B90	LJ-323	Aviajet SA. San Fernando.	N90SM
LV-WDO	71	King Air 100	B-82	Navy Jet SA.	AE-100
LV-WEW	81	King Air 200	BB-870	Tenil SA. Buenos Aires.	N200EL
LV-WFP	75	King Air E90	LW-129	Servicio Aerocomercial Essair, Venado Tuerto, Santa Fe.	N423JD
LV-WGP	79	King Air 200	BB-558	Minera del Altoplano SA. Don Torcuato.	N58JR
LV-WHV	78	King Air E90	LW-259	Starman SA. Buenos Aires.	N269JB
LV-WIO	80	King Air 200	BB-606	Cheyenne SA. Buenos Aires.	N29AJ
LV-WIP	93	King Air 300LW	FA-229	G & M S A, Buenos Aires.	LV-PHI
LV-WIR	73	SA-226T Merlin 3	T-232	Hawk Air SA. Don Torcuato.	N56TA
LV-WJE	94	King Air C90B	LJ-1354	Granbril SACIFIA, Lanus, Buenos Aires.	N8294Z
LV-WJY	74	Mitsubishi MU-2J	644	Parala SRL. Buenos Aires.	N494WC
LV-WLT	92	King Air 300	FA-221	TIA SA. Don Torcuato.	N70FL
LV-WMA	93	King Air 300	FA-222	Banco Mercantil Argentino SA. Buenos Aires.	N8273L
LV-WMG	95	King Air C90B	LJ-1395	Aero Federal SA. Don Torcuato.	LV-PHZ
LV-WNC	75	SA-226AT Merlin 4A	AT-036	Hawk Air SA. Don Torcuato.	N642TS
LV-WOR	96	King Air B200	BB-1521	Heli-Air SA. Don Torcuato.	N3241N
LV-WOS	80	King Air 200	BB-639	Promas SA. La Rioja.	N550E
LV-WPB	95	King Air C90B	LJ-1416	Government Province of Chubut, Rawson, Chubut.	N3254E
LV-WPM	80	King Air/Catpass 250	BB-729	Government Province of La Pampa, Santa Rosa.	N743P
LV-WRM	68	King Air B90	LJ-333	Urbantop SA., Buenos Aires	OB-1495

Reg	Yr Type	c/n	Owner/Operator	Prev Regn
☐ LV-WXC	97 King Air C90B	LJ-1466		N466SC
☐ LV-WXG	81 PA-42 Cheyenne III	8001044	Sancor SA. Sunchales Oeste, Santa Fe.	ZP-TYZ
☐ LV-WZR	73 King Air E90	LW-70	VIP Air SA. Buenos Aires.	N5911P
☐ LV-YBP	97 King Air C90B	LJ-1489	Olmedo Agropecuaria Rosario de la Frontera,	N1069F
☐ LV-YCS	97 King Air B200	BB-1588	Per Trans SA. Buenos Aires.	N3247Q
☐ LV-YLC	98 King Air 350	FL-190	Aero Baires SACI. Buenos Aires.	N2290V
☐ LV-YTB	98 King Air B200	BB-1616	Petrel Aereos Servicios SRL. Buenos Aires.	N2294B
☐ LV-ZPY	81 King Air F90	LA-89	Bravo Foxtrot SRL. Buenos Aires.	N77PA
☐ LV-ZSX	95 Pilatus PC-12	133	Horizon Americas Inc. San Fernando.	N133CZ
☐ LV-ZTV	99 King Air B200	BB-1703		N3203Z
☐ LV-ZXX	00 King Air 350	FL-310	Gobierno Provincia de Santa Cruz, Santa Cruz.	N5010R
☐ LV-ZYB	99 King Air B200	BB-1690	Tandil Air SA. Buenos Aires.	N600DF
☐ LV-ZZH	03 King Air B200	BB-1817	Las Matildes Flights SA.	N5117M

Military

Reg	Yr Type	c/n	Owner/Operator	Prev Regn
☐ 4-F-43/0743	79 King Air 200	BB-460	FA1-EAN4/EAR4, Argentine Naval Base, Punta Indio.	4-G-43/074
☐ 4-G-41/0697	75 King Air 200	BB-54	FA1/EAN4/EA4R, Argentine Naval Base, Punta Indio.	5-T-31/069
☐ 4-G-42/0698	75 King Air 200	BB-71	FA1-EAN4-EA4R, Argentine Naval Base, Punta Indio.	5-T-32/069
☐ 4-G-45/0745	79 King Air 200	BB-488	FA1-EAN4/EAR4, Argentine Naval Base, Punta Indio.	
☐ 4-G-47/0747	79 King Air 200	BB-546	FA1-EAN4/EAR4, Argentine Naval Base, Punta Indio.	
☐ 4-G-48/0748	79 King Air 200	BB-549	FA1-EAN4/EAR4, Argentine Naval Base, Punta Indio.	
☐ AE-176	77 SA-226T Merlin 3A	T-275	Argentine Army,	N5393M
☐ AE-178	77 SA-226T Merlin 3A	T-280	Argentine Army,	N5397M
☐ AE-179	77 SA-226T Merlin 3A	T-281	Argentine Army,	N5399M
☐ AE-180	79 SA-226AT Merlin 4A	AT-071E	Argentine Army. (was TC-286).	N5656M
☐ AE-181	77 SA-226AT Merlin 4A	AT-063	Argentine Army,	TS-01
☐ AE-182	78 SA-226T Merlin 4A	AT-064	Argentine Army,	TS-02
☐ GN-810	00 Pilatus PC-12/45	294	Gendamerie Nacional, Campo de Mayo.	HB-FQI
☐ LV-RTC	79 King Air 200	BB-471	Argentine Navy, Buenos Aires.	4-G-44/074

LX = LUXEMBOURG Total 24

Civil

Reg	Yr Type	c/n	Owner/Operator	Prev Regn
☐ LX-ACR	81 PA-31T Cheyenne 1	8104067	Leander Reichle Stassenbau GmbH. Gerolstein, Germany.	D-IACR
☐ LX-APB	79 King Air C90	LJ-867		3A-MKB
☐ LX-DNI	06 Pilatus PC-12/47	751	Odyssee Jet SA/JetCruising SA	HB-FSN
☐ LX-JDP	77 King Air/Catpass 250	BB-303	JDP Lux SA/JDP & Financiere de Rosario, Paris, France.	F-GHCS
☐ LX-JFA	92 TBM 700	63	Jetfly Aviation SA. Luxembourg.	F-GLJS
☐ LX-JFD	01 TBM 700B	199	Jetfly Aviation SA. Luxembourg.	F-OIKC
☐ LX-JFE	01 TBM 700B	208	Jetfly Aviation SA. Luxembourg.	F-OIKE
☐ LX-JFF	01 TBM 700B	212	Jetfly Aviation SA. Luxembourg.	F-OIKF
☐ LX-JFH	03 Pilatus PC-12/45	522	Jetfly Aviation SA. Luxembourg.	HB-...
☐ LX-JFI	04 Pilatus PC-12/45	574	Jetfly Aviation SA. Luxembourg.	HB-...
☐ LX-JFJ	05 Pilatus PC-12/45	678	Jetfly Aviation SA. Luxembourg.	HB-F..
☐ LX-JFK	05 Pilatus PC-12/45	683	Jetfly Aviation SA. Luxembourg.	HB-F..
☐ LX-JFL	01 TBM 700B	185	EADS Socata, Tarbes.	N700AU
☐ LX-JFL	06 TBM 850	391	Jetfly Aviation SA. Luxembourg.	
☐ LX-JFM	07 Pilatus PC-12/47	812	Jetfly Aviation SA.,Luxembourg	
☐ LX-JFN	07 Pilatus PC-12/47	855	Jetfly Aviation SA. Luxembourg	HB-FSQ
☐ LX-JFO	07 TBM 850	422	EADS SOCATA	F-OIKQ
☐ LX-LAB	03 Pilatus PC-12/45	531	Dublet et Cie/Jetfly Aviation SA. Luxemborg.	(LX-DOG)
☐ LX-NRJ	76 SA-226T Merlin 3A	T-265	Aeroservice, Luxembourg.	CF-05
☐ LX-PBL	98 King Air C90B	LJ-1539	Locadis SA. Orleans, France.	D-IGAH
☐ LX-PRG	98 King Air C90B	LJ-1526	Europe Air Service, Nantes, France.	(F-GPRG)
☐ LX-RST	78 PA-31T Cheyenne II	7820027	Luxembourg Air Rescue as. Luxembourg.	F-GGPJ
☐ LX-SEA	86 King Air 300	FA-94	Aeroservice Amtec Corp/Fly Air SA. Annemasse, France.	F-GVPE
☐ LX-SKY	95 Pilatus PC-12	108	Luxembird S.C.	D-FANS

LY = LITHUANIA Total 1

Civil

Reg	Yr Type	c/n	Owner/Operator	Prev Regn
☐ LY-ZDV	81 MU-2 Marquise	1515SA	Joana Airlines, Vilnius	OH-STA

LZ = BULGARIA Total 5

Civil

Reg	Yr Type	c/n	Owner/Operator	Prev Regn
☐ LZ-BIZ	97 King Air B200	BB-1595	Inter Air JSC. Sofia.	D-IATM
☐ LZ-ITV	90 King Air B200	BB-1369	Inter Air JSC. Sofia.	D-IKLN
☐ LZ-TBM	07 TBM 850	421	Intersky, Sofia	
☐ LZ-YUK	75 King Air 200	BB-82	Petrol Holding Aviation/Air Lazur, Sofia.	LZ-FEO

Military
☐ 020 | 03 Pilatus PC-12M | 518 | Bulgarian Air Force, 16 Transport AB, Sofia-Vrazhdebna. | HB-FPH

M = ISLE OF MAN   Total   4
Civil

Reg	Yr Type	c/n	Owner/Operator	Prev Regn
☐ M-ICKY	03 Pilatus PC-12/45	508	Saxon Logistics, London	N508DL
☐ M-MANX	81 Conquest 1	425-0044	Offshore Marine Inc/MasterCraft Ltd. Douglas	N425HS
☐ M-OORE	07 King Air 350	FL-569	Byecross (IOM) Ltd, Ronaldsway	N569KA
☐ M-OTOR	05 King Air C90B	LJ-1733	Pekton Group Ltd, Derby	N590PS

N = USA   Total 6911
Civil

Reg	Yr Type	c/n	Owner/Operator	Prev Regn
☐ C-FSPN	80 King Air 200	BB-745	Keystone Air Service Ltd, St Andrews	N428P
☐ N874AF	07 Pilatus PC-12/47	874	Pilatus Business Aircraft Ltd, Broomfield, Co.	HB-FQF
☐ SE-LOG	95 SAAB 2000	031		SE-LOG
☐ N1BK	85 King Air 300	FA-76	RMX Acquisitions LLC., Dover, De.	N404SD
☐ N1BM	81 Conquest 1	425-0042	Acme Aviation Inc. Idabell, Ok.	N67735
☐ N1CW	06 Pilatus PC-12/47	705	Howco Inc. Charlotte, NC.	N569AB
☐ N1GF	82 King Air C90-1	LJ-1031	Sawtooth Inc. Dothan, Al.	N397CA
☐ N1HX	78 King Air 200	BB-361	Leisure Hotels & Resorts, Leawood, Ks.	N334RR
☐ N1LF	01 King Air B200	BB-1778	Sizewise Rentals Inc. Ellis, Ks.	N4368X
☐ N1MA	79 King Air F90	LA-3	Alan & Diane Gaudenti, Rancho Palos Verde, Ca.	(N87AG)
☐ N1MN	84 SA-227TT Merlin 3C	TT-486A	Devcon Construction Inc/Ceka Aviation, San Jose, Ca.	N86SH
☐ N1MT	79 King Air C90	LJ-824	Delta State University, Cleveland, Ms.	N724TD
☐ N1MU	86 King Air B200	BB-1245	S J & K Aviation LLC. Clive, Ia.	N776RM
☐ N1MW	88 King Air 300	FA-151	Dog Leg Transportation LLC. Sherrill's Ford, NC.	C-FMHD
☐ N1NP	03 King Air B200	BB-1834	Nebraska Public Power District, Columbus, NE.	N399AE
☐ N1PD	94 King Air 350	FL-121	JLJ Equipment Leasing Corp. Pottersville, NJ.	N351EB
☐ N1RH	05 Pilatus PC-12/45	627	Heiniger Leasing LLC. Hiawatha, Ks.	HB-FRU
☐ N1RQ	01 PA-46-500TP Meridian	4697112	Quast Aviation LLC. Maple Plain, Mn.	N53415
☐ N1SC	90 King Air 350	FL-9	South Carolina Department of Commerce, Columbia, SC.	N2SC
☐ N1SP	77 King Air C-12C	BC-42	Delaware State Police, Dover, De.	N6SP
☐ N1TC	95 Pilatus PC-12	130	Marcare Air LLC. San Luis Obispo, Ca.	HB-FQU
☐ N1TR	78 King Air A100	B-238	Trinity River Authority, Arlington, Tx.	N9100S
☐ N1TX	81 King Air 200	BB-800	State of Texas, Austin, Tx.	N200GA
☐ N1UC	75 King Air E90	LW-140	K&K Aircraft Sales, Fort Dodge, Ia.	N8069S
☐ N1VA	07 King Air 350	FL-549	Virginia Department of Aviation, Richmond, Va.	N21VA
☐ N1VQ	77 Rockwell 690B	11369	First Star Inc. Hollister, Ca.	N369GM
☐ N1WJ	65 King Air 90	LJ-60	RidgeAire Inc., Jacksonville, Tx.	N763K
☐ N1WV	07 King Air 350	FL-527	West Virginia Dept of Aviation Div., Charleston, WV.	N7017C
☐ N2DB	85 King Air 300	FA-37	KA300 LLC., Englewood, Co.	N600LP
☐ N2DS	78 PA-31T Cheyenne II	7820081	Alpine Aviation Inc. White Lake, Mi.	N34CA
☐ N2FJ	76 PA-31T Cheyenne II	7620050	JP2 LLC. Willoughby, Oh.	(N39RP)
☐ N2GL	82 SA-227TT Merlin 3C	TT-426A	Finair LLC. Ponte Vedra Beach, Fl.	N4491E
☐ N2GZ	67 Mitsubishi MU-2B	025	Tarrant County Junior College, Fort Worth, Tx.	N2GT
☐ N2JB	00 Pilatus PC-12/45	342	Breco International,	(ZS-SRJ)
☐ N2MP	76 King Air C-12C	BC-32	Bellco Inc., Lewes, De.	76-22556
☐ N2NC	83 Conquest II	441-0307	North Carolina Dept of Transportation, Raleigh, NC.	N8617K
☐ N2PY	77 King Air 200	BB-200	Ameris Health Systems LLC. Nashville, Tn.	N2PX
☐ N2QE	06 PA-46-500TP Meridian	4697247	QE Air Inc. Naples, Fl.	
☐ N2RA	77 Mitsubishi MU-2P	366SA	Michael Sydow, Mount Crested Butte, Co.	N66UP
☐ N2SM	97 King Air 350	FL-185	Oso Rio LLC. Houston, Tx.	N18269
☐ N2TS	85 Beech 1900C	UB-39	SABCO Racing Inc. Mooresville, NC.	N404SS
☐ N2TX	81 King Air B100	BE-103	Robert Schumacher/Texland Aviation Co. Abilene, Tx.	N3699T
☐ N2U	77 King Air 200	BB-263	Helicopters Inc. Cahokia, Il.	N48Q
☐ N2UV	69 King Air B90	LJ-480	Charles Greene, Fort Lauderdale, Fl.	N92BA
☐ N2UW	77 King Air 200T	BT-3	University of Wyoming, Laramie, Wy. (was BB-270)	
☐ N2VA	07 King Air 350	FL-537	Virginia Department of Aviation, Richmond, Va.	N71970
☐ N2WF	02 TBM 700B	220	Leasing Systems LLC. Sewalls Point, Fl.	VH-TBO
☐ N2YF	96 Pilatus PC-12	140	Tactair Fluid Controls Inc. Liverpool, NY.	N129DH
☐ N3AH	87 King Air 300	FA-130	American Aviation Charters LLC. Lafayette, La.	N9UP
☐ N3AT	81 King Air C90	LJ-933	Appalachian Tire Products Inc. Charleston, WV.	N3709S
☐ N3AW	06 King Air 350	FL-491	Arrowhead Co. Burbank, Ok.	
☐ N3CR	81 King Air 200	BB-850	Richard Childress Racing Enterprises Inc. Welcome, NC.	N2UH
☐ N3DE	81 King Air 200	BB-849	Champion Air LLC. Mooresville, NC.	N711MZ
☐ N3DF	65 King Air 90	LJ-36	Donald Bush, Warner Robins, Ga.	(N312DS)

Reg	Yr	Type	c/n	Owner/Operator	Prev Regn
N3GC	73	King Air C90	LJ-576	AlliedSignal Avionics Inc. Everett, Wa.	
N3GT	73	Mitsubishi MU-2K	277	Donald & Gail Taylor Trust, Albuquerque, NM.	N390K
N3KF	71	King Air C90	LJ-530	Ohio Medical Transportation Inc. Columbus, Oh.	N404VW
N3LS	67	King Air E90	LW-245	DZM Inc. Houston, Tx.	N18DV
N3MA	81	MU-2 Marquise	1511SA	Kirkendoll Management LLC. Telluride, Co.	N27TJ
N3PX	84	King Air B200	BB-1173	King Air LLC./Eclipse Contractors Inc., Houma, La.	N2842B
N3RK	81	Cheyenne II-XL	8166022	Superior Distributing Co. Fostoria, Oh.	N81502
N3TK	80	Conquest II	441-0158	Centaur Corp. Irvine, Ca.	N36EF
N3UN	78	Mitsubishi MU-2N	720SA	Turbine Aircraft Marketing Inc. San Angelo, Tx.	VH-MIT
N3WM	78	Conquest II	441-0068	R & S Consulting LLC., Avon, Ct.	N88827
N3WU	76	Rockwell 690A	11336	Aero Air LLC. Hillsboro, Or.	N16GL
N3ZC	85	King Air B200	BB-1207	Zachary Construction Corp. San Antonio, Tx.	(N321SF)
N4DF	07	Pilatus PC-12/47	831	Gulf States Toyota Inc, Houston, Tx.	HB-FRT
N4FB	67	680V Turbo Commander	1688-68	Fernando Rodrigo, Miami, Fl.	N4F
N4KU	89	King Air B200	BB-1323	N4KU LLC/First Management Inc. New Country, Ks.	(N769WT)
N4MD	99	TBM 700B	153	Airborne Inc. Wilmington, De.	(N40DN)
N4NF	88	King Air 300LW	FA-165	Nash Finch Co. Rapid City, SD.	N886CA
N4NU	01	King Air B200	BB-1782	University of Nebraska Foundation, Lincoln, Ne.	N4482Z
N4PT	81	King Air B200	BB-879	Ironwood Resort Development, Park City, Ut.	
N4PZ	75	Rockwell 690A	11269	Phillip Zeeck Inc. Odessa, Tx.	N690DM
N4QL	81	King Air B200	BB-942	Quarry Lane LLC. Moorpark, Ca.	N707NV
N4R	82	MU-2 Marquise	1542SA	Rough Ryder Aircraft Corp. Wilmington, De.	N88HL
N4RX	79	PA-31T Cheyenne 1	7904012	IMFESA/Ernesto S Botello, Santo Domingo, Dominican Republic.	(N204MB)
N4RY	65	King Air 90	LJ-8	Magic Carpet Ride Leasing LLC. Daytona Beach, Fl.	(N16CG)
N4TF	04	Pilatus PC-12/45	557	Gulf States Toyota Inc. Houston, Tx.	(N557DF)
N4TJ	75	King Air 200	BB-40	Jaco Oil Co. Bakersfield, SC.	N35TT
N4TS	03	Pilatus PC-12/45	509	First Virtual Air LLC. Wolf Creek, Mt.	N509PB
N4WE	87	PA-42 Cheyenne 400LS	5527041	Portofino Air Corp. Elgin, SC.	N9518N
N4WF	80	PA-31T Cheyenne II	8020025	Ralphnal Inc., Gold Canyon, Az.	N135MA
N4YF	01	King Air C90B	LJ-1658	Globe Aero Ltd Inc. Lakeland Fl.	
N4YS	92	King Air 350	FL-82	W R Fry/CC2B Trust, San Jose, Ca.	N8182C
N5AE	04	King Air B200	BB-1891	L J Associates Inc. LaTrobe, Pa.	N6191H
N5AH	80	King Air F90	LA-53	Empire Air LLC. Torrance, Ca.	N514LM
N5BR	93	TBM 700	89	Lloyd Rasner, Corona del Mar, Ca.	D-FEIN
N5CE	83	Conquest 1	425-0135	Avion Capital Corp. Anchorage, Ak.	N6884D
N5D	78	PA-31T Cheyenne II	7820080	William Packer, Orchard, Mi.	N6097A
N5DM	00	Pilatus PC-12/45	355	News Flight Inc. NYC.	HB-FSG
N5HG	82	Conquest II	441-0247	HRL Ventures LLC. Chicago Ridge, Il.	N6857T
N5HT	91	TBM 700	9	Quik-Cook Inc/Q C Aviation LLC. Rochester, NY.	N969RF
N5LC	80	MU-2 Solitaire	433SA	Manitoba Leasing Corp. Lancaster, NY.	N209MA
N5MK	79	King Air 200	BB-537	LHI Air Corp. West Palm Beach, Fl.	N700BX
N5NV	85	King Air B200	BB-1202	IAL Leasing Ltd. Hamilton, Bermuda. (Based Sion,Switzerland)	VP-BYR
N5PA	81	PA-42 Cheyenne III	8001051	Saperston Asset Management, Buffalo, NY.	N810L
N5PP	02	PA-46-500TP Meridian	4697145	Rixmann Aireamerica LLC. Burnsville, Mn.	
N5PX	79	King Air 200	BB-554	Dunagan Joint Property LLC. Huntsville, Al.	N204BR
N5RB	81	PA-31T Cheyenne 1	8104042	Equity Management Inc. Columbus, Oh.	N12WZ
N5RE	68	680W Turbo Commander	1818-32	Pennsylvania College of Technology, Williamsport, Pa.	N3RA
N5RF	04	King Air 350	FL-423	Avalon Laboratories Inc. Rancho Dominguez, Ca.	N3723Q
N5ST	77	King Air 200	BB-289	Mayo Aviation Inc. Englewood, Co.	N7MB
N5SY	81	PA-42 Cheyenne III	8001069	Dialysis Clinic Inc. Nashville, Tn.	N5SS
N5TA	77	King Air C90	LJ-724	MacDonald Enterprises Inc. Kentwood, Mi.	N5TW
N5TW	93	King Air B200	BB-1471	Backe Aviation Inc. Bonita Springs, Fl.	
N5UN	80	King Air 200	BB-697	Western Skies Aviation LLC. Arnold, Ca.	N5ON
N5WG	67	King Air A90	LJ-289	G M B Aviation Inc. Fort Worth, Tx.	N35P
N5XM	94	King Air 350	FL-115	C & C Aviation LLC. Worcester, Ma.	N35DT
N5Y	67	King Air A90	LJ-272	Carrier Enterprises Corp. Wilmington, De.	
N6BZ	82	Gulfstream 900	15008	Nebraska Aero LLC., Cascade, Mt.	ZS-KZT
N6DM	03	PA-46-500TP Meridian	4697154	Strategic Organizational Management Ltd. Denver, Co.	N3055C
N6E	70	681 Turbo Commander	6002	Cardozo Technologies Inc. Manor, Tx.	N9052N
N6FZ	97	Pilatus PC-12/45	290	Bravo Delta Management LLC. Wilmington, De.	N565EZ
N6HU	78	King Air 200	BB-319	Harding University Inc. Searcy, Ar.	N300WJ
N6JL	99	King Air 350	FL-247	Champair Aviation/Permian Mud Services Inc. Houston, Tx.	N516BA
N6KE	80	MU-2 Marquise	766SA	William Denniston Jr. Lake Forest, Il.	(N6KU)
N6KF	75	Mitsubishi MU-2L	659	Flight Line Inc. Denver, Co.	N5JE
N6KZ	67	King Air A90	LJ-238	Gregg Aviation Inc. Wilmington, De.	N190RF

Reg	Yr Type	c/n	Owner/Operator	Prev Regn
☐ N6PX	77 King Air 200	BB-205	OKC Rig Builders, Oklahoma City, Ok.	N6PW
☐ N6UD	82 King Air B200	BB-1055	Braun Racing LLC. Winamac, In.	N6LD
☐ N6UP	82 SA-227TT Merlin 3C	TT-441	Plane Folk LLC. Las Vegas, Nv.	N125RG
☐ N6VJ	81 King Air F90	LA-88	Hansen Group A/S. Stauning, Denmark.	F-GVJV
☐ N7BF	68 King Air B90	LJ-350	Rainbow International Airlines Inc. St Thomas, USVI.	(N579B)
☐ N7DD	74 Mitsubishi MU-2K	297	Business Air Inc. Bennington, Vt.	N106GB
☐ N7FL	78 PA-31T Cheyenne II	7820082	Liberty Charter Inc. Wilmington, De.	N6100A
☐ N7HN	84 MU-2 Marquise	1563SA	Soft Computer Consultants Inc. Palm Harbor, Fl.	(D-IOMX)
☐ N7KS	79 Rockwell 690B	11521	California Architectural Lighting, Portland, Or.	N81746
☐ N7NA	82 King Air/Catpass 250	BB-997	NASA HQ/OSSA, Washington, DC.	
☐ N7NW	80 Conquest II	441-0186	Aztlan Corp. Ashland, Or.	N2724S
☐ N7PA	92 King Air B200	BB-1444	Warren Spieker Jr. Soledad, Ca.	N663CS
☐ N7RC	85 King Air 300	FA-58	Ring Container Technologies, Olive Branch, Ms.	N555WF
☐ N7SL	59 Gulfstream 1	11	Tropical Air Trading Co. Tierra Verde, Fl.	N100EL
☐ N7TD	78 King Air E90	LW-276	Ascension Aviation LLC. Gaylord, Mi.	N125L
☐ N7TW	69 King Air B90	LJ-478	Airspeed Aviation of Oklahoma LLC. Bethany, Ok.	N40WS
☐ N7VR	78 PA-31T Cheyenne 1	7804010	Woftam Inc. Lock Haven, Pa.	N93TW
☐ N7WF	82 Conquest 1	425-0119	Foxtrot Inc. Wichita Falls, Tx.	N17RC
☐ N7WU	75 King Air E90	LW-142	BuzzEd LLC/Suburban Plastics Co. Elgin, Il.	N7WS
☐ N7YR	03 Pilatus PC-12/45	532	Shikari Capital LLC. Portland, Or.	N532WA
☐ N7ZT	01 Pilatus PC-12/45	385	Zia Air LLC. San Luis Obispo, Ca.	HB-FQD
☐ N8AM	77 King Air 200	BB-274	MRAF LLC. Grand Blanc, Mi.	N1MM
☐ N8BG	77 King Air 200	BB-267	Colonel Science LLC. Santa Ynez, Ca.	N267TT
☐ N8CF	80 PA-31T Cheyenne II	8020062	Copto Inc. Jacksonville, Fl.	N5452J
☐ N8E	62 Gulfstream 1	94	N8E LLC. Newton, Ga.	N794G
☐ N8EF	80 King Air 200	BB-721	M-Air of Delaware LLC. Wilmington, De.	N610HG
☐ N8EG	92 TBM 700	34	Doug Carlson, Aspen, Co.	
☐ N8FR	81 Conquest 1	425-0095	Frank Rhodes Jr. Newport Beach, Ca.	N68481
☐ N8GU	85 King Air C90A	LJ-1103	McCall Aircraft Leasing LLC. Lebanon, Tn.	N8GT
☐ N8KF	04 TBM 700C2	304	Key City Leasing Co., Sioux City, Ia.	N700EK
☐ N8KT	69 SA-26AT Merlin 2B	T26-158E	Davidson Air Inc. Little Rock, Ar.	N256WC
☐ N8MG	78 King Air C90	LJ-747	Netfly LLC, Lexington Ky.	N529JH
☐ N8NA	82 King Air B200	BB-950	NASA/OSSA, Wallops Island, Va.	
☐ N8NX	81 King Air 200	BB-774	Spitfire Aviation Parts Inc., Concord, NC.	N3738B
☐ N8PC	71 Mitsubishi MU-2F	193	A Lamas, Buenos Aires, Argentina.	N1210W
☐ N8RW	82 MU-2 Marquise	1548SA	Titan Aviation LC. West Palm Beach, Fl.	N47RW
☐ N8RY	81 PA-42 Cheyenne III	8001036	Cheyenne Transportation LLC. Boise, Id.	N3JQ
☐ N8SV	79 King Air 200	BB-506	King Air IV Inc. Seattle, Wa.	N945BV
☐ N8UM	01 PA-46-500TP Meridian	4697067	N8UM Corp. Wilmington, De.	N44SK
☐ N8VL	83 Gulfstream 840	11732	Brays Air LLC. Sheldon,SC.	N29DS
☐ N8YN	04 King Air 350	FL-417	MMA Investments LLC. Winnetka, Il.	N6117C
☐ N9DA	82 King Air C90	LJ-944	Tampa Aircraft Holding Inc. Tampa, Fl.	N944TT
☐ N9EE	03 TBM 700C2	286	Poet Research Inc. Sioux Falls, SD.	N386MA
☐ N9HW	69 King Air B90	LJ-459	Michael Mullins, Germantown, Tn.	N2JR
☐ N9KG	77 Rockwell 690B	11426	Catlan Company LLC/Beef Northwest Feeders, North Powder, Or.	(N690DM)
☐ N9NB	78 Mitsubishi MU-2N	728SA	SDS Project LLC. Austin, Tx.	N9NC
☐ N9NZ	75 SA-226T Merlin 3A	T-255	Jet Venture Inc. Bear, De.	D-INWK
☐ N9UZ	78 King Air C90	LJ-641	Airline Leasing International Ltd., Wilmington, De.	D-IKIW
☐ N9VC	78 King Air C90	LJ-763	Dakota King Air LLC/Executive Air Taxi Corp. Bismark, ND.	N78JD
☐ N9WR	81 King Air B200	BB-913	JPW Investments Inc., Frederick, Md.	(N501E)
☐ N10AG	80 King Air B100	BE-100	Pacific Cycle Inc. Madison, Wi.	N3688F
☐ N10BQ	74 PA-31T Cheyenne II	7400005	West Tenessee Aviation Inc. Union City, Tn.	(N80BC)
☐ N10CS	80 PA-31T Cheyenne 1	8004001	Legendary Air Services Inc. Deston Fl..	N118BW
☐ N10CW	03 King Air B200	BB-1846	South Holland Trust & Savings Bank, South Holland, Il.	
☐ N10EC	85 King Air B200	BB-1215	State of Tennessee, Nashville, Tn.	N7220C
☐ N10FB	82 Conquest 1	425-0117	Western Farm Bureau Service Co. Laramie, Wy.	N123SC
☐ N10HT	80 MU-2 Marquise	778SA	MU-2 LLC./Dickerson Associates, West Columbia, SC.	N264MA
☐ N10JE	65 King Air 90	LJ-10	APA Enterprises Inc. Poughskeepsie, NY.	N10J
☐ N10K	90 King Air 350	FL-4	Department of Public Safety, Oklahoma City, Ok.	N97DL
☐ N10MR	77 Mitsubishi MU-2P	351SA	Agri-Systems, Hardin, Mt.	N10FR
☐ N10PF	97 Pilatus PC-12	165	Air Opportunities LLC. Sacramento, Ca.	N65KW
☐ N10RM	81 Conquest 1	425-0074	Conquest 1 N10RM LLC. Jacksonville, Fl.	N146GA
☐ N10ST	05 PA-46-500TP Meridian	4697220	Buena Vista Air LLC	
☐ N10TQ	90 2000 Starship	NC-8	Raytheon Aircraft Co. Wichita, Ks.	N10TX
☐ N10TX	89 King Air 350	FL-1	Bryan Hardeman, Albuquerque, NM.	N552TR

Reg	Yr	Type	c/n	Owner/Operator	Prev Regn
☐ N10UN	97	King Air 350	FL-158	Universal Avionics Systems Corp. Tucson, Az.	N1095Q
☐ N10UT	76	Mitsubishi MU-2M	346	NFM Inc. Henderson, Nv.	(N45PD)
☐ N10VU	81	MU-2 Solitaire	438SA	Chester Upham Jr. Mineral Wells, Tx.	N99LC
☐ N10WG	79	King Air E90	LW-310	Wings to Go Leasing Co. Doylestown, Pa.	LV-MRN
☐ N10XJ	74	King Air E90	LW-117	Reynolds Texas Properties LC. Dallas, Tx.	N76PW
☐ N10YP	67	King Air A90	LJ-265	Gary Yost, Sherman, Tx.	(N126AT)
☐ N11	73	King Air C-12C	BD-1	FAA, Oklahoma City, Ok.	73-1205
☐ N11AB	78	King Air 200	BB-305	JJJ Aviation LLC/M S Walker & Assocs. Bakersfield, Ca.	N30XY
☐ N11CT	68	680W Turbo Commander	1773-11	Bob Jones University Inc. Greenville, SC.	N4852E
☐ N11DT	72	King Air E90	LW-11	Marjet Inc. Honolulu, Hi.	N241B
☐ N11FT	81	King Air C90	LJ-958	SKS Management Inc. Cocoa, Fl.	N505MT
☐ N11HM	66	680V Turbo Commander	1620-51	Christopher M. Oldenburg, Golden, Co.	N680MH
☐ N11MM	79	Conquest II	441-0105	Abbott Air Inc., Hydro, Ok.	(N11MM)
☐ N11SJ	74	Mitsubishi MU-2K	285	Air 1st Aviation Companies Inc. Aiken, SC.	N111JE
☐ N11SN	82	King Air C90-1	LJ-1036	Sierra Process Systems Inc. Bakersfield, Ca.	(N59WP)
☐ N11TE	98	King Air 350	FL-211	Tractor & Equipment Co. Birmingham, Al.	N715CG
☐ N11TN	68	King Air B90	LJ-419	M & C Aviation Inc. Bronx, NY.	N11TE
☐ N11UN	63	Gulfstream 1	102	Advanced Aviation Sales Inc. Naples, Fl.	C6-UNO
☐ N12	73	King Air C-12C	BD-8	FAA, Oklahoma City, Ok.	73-1212
☐ N12AG	07	Pilatus PC-12/47	854	Aircraft Guaranty Management LLC, Houston Tx.	HB-FSK
☐ N12AX	78	King Air E90	LW-293	Corporate Aircraft Leasing LLC. Winston-Salem, NC.	N12AU
☐ N12CF	79	King Air 200	BB-534	N12CF LLC/Bremer Family Trust, Corona, Ca.	
☐ N12DE	78	Rockwell 690B	11501	Gimlet Aviation LLC., Mercer Island, Wa.	N25CL
☐ N12DZ	01	Pilatus PC-12/45	390	PC-12 LLC. York Springs, Pa.	N46CE
☐ N12FA	95	Pilatus PC-12	117	Fisher Auto Parts Inc. Staunton, Va.	N117WF
☐ N12GJ	72	King Air E90	LW-12	Building Ideas Inc. Palo Alto, Ca.	RP-C289
☐ N12JD	98	Pilatus PC-12/45	228	Mariposa Group LLC. Salina, Ks.	HB-FQZ
☐ N12KR	98	King Air B200	BB-1632	N12KR LLC., Advance, NC.	N500VA
☐ N12LA	73	King Air E90	LW-49	JJMW LLC, Franklin Tn.	N777AJ
☐ N12MA	04	TBM 700C2	318	R B J Ranch LLC. Elroy, Wi.	F-WWRL
☐ N12MF	81	SA-226T Merlin 3B	T-417	5-T Aviation LLC. Eunice, La.	N89RP
☐ N12NG	80	King Air 200	BB-581	Northrop Grumman Aviation Inc. Melbourne, Fl.	N14NA
☐ N12NL	81	Conquest 1	425-0069	Dapcon Consulting Inc. Chicago, Il.	N634M
☐ N12RA	69	Mitsubishi MU-2F	177	BH Jr Motorsports Inc. White House, Tn.	N177SA
☐ N12RW	61	Gulfstream 1	82	Air Cess/CCET Aviation Enterprise, Ras Al Khaimah, UAE.	SE-LFV
☐ N12VA	83	Gulfstream 1000	96062	GRD Contractors Inc./Day Construction, Costa Mesa, Ca.	N2VA
☐ N12WC	69	SA-26AT Merlin 2B	T26-118	RKC Properties LLC. Tampa, Fl.	N1224S
☐ N13GZ	99	King Air C90B	LJ-1590	Eagle Air Med Corp. Blanding, Ut.	PT-WXH
☐ N13K	72	King Air A100	B-101	Dynamic AvLease Inc. Bridgewater, Va.	N921SA
☐ N13LY	00	King Air B200	BB-1718	Harris Air LLC. Chowchilla, Ca.	N3018C
☐ N13NW	79	Conquest II	441-0090	North West Group Inc/North West Geomatics Canada Inc Calgary	N4061K
☐ N13YS	77	Mitsubishi MU-2L	694	TRE Aviation Corp. Globe, Az.	N800PC
☐ N14BM	81	Conquest 1	425-0076	Albert Sickinger, Bloomfield Hills, Mi.	N67735
☐ N14CP	73	King Air C90	LJ-585	Dynamic Aviation Group Inc. Bridgewater, Va.	
☐ N14FJ	79	Conquest II	441-0118	Land Safely LLC. Monmouth Beach, NJ.	5N-DOV
☐ N14GV	01	PA-46-500TP Meridian	4697092	Number One for Great Veneers LLC. Wilmington, De.	
☐ N14HG	82	King Air B200	BB-1071	Steady Compass LLC. Minden, Nv.	N82BS
☐ N14NG	87	King Air B200	BB-1276	Northrop Grumman Aviation Inc. Montgomery-San Diego, Ca.	N40TD
☐ N14NM	73	King Air E90	LW-35	N14NM LLC. Hailey, Id.	N811JB
☐ N14NW	80	Conquest II	441-0171	North West Group Inc. Denver, Co.	C-GKMA
☐ N14PX	81	PA-31T Cheyenne 1	8104060	Nor Con Limited Inc. Fargo, ND.	N74ML
☐ N14RD	01	Pilatus PC-12/45	384	RDC Marine Inc. Houston, Tx.	HB-FQC
☐ N14SB	77	King Air E90	LW-214	Clayton Motors Inc. Knoxville, Tn.	N17603
☐ N14TF	81	King Air 200	BB-810	Jetstream Air LLC. Colfax, NC.	N711AE
☐ N14V	68	King Air B90	LJ-411	Donald Warren, Clinton, Ar.	N807K
☐ N14VL	81	MU-2 Marquise	1514SA	JPW Aviation LLC. Clarksdale, Ms.	YV-108CP
☐ N14YS	74	Mitsubishi MU-2K	290	Ross Trucking LLC., Goldendale, Wa.	N4186Y
☐ N15	81	King Air F90	LA-138	FAA, Oklahoma City, Ok.	
☐ N15CD	74	Rockwell 690A	11177	Philip Sellers Co. Montgomery, Al.	N16TB
☐ N15CT	67	King Air A90	LJ-192	Charles Thomas, Loves Park, Il.	N792K
☐ N15DB	82	Conquest II	441-0278	Apothe-Care Inc/Owens Healthcare, Redding, Ca.	N98718
☐ N15EK	95	Pilatus PC-12	120	Quest Diagnostics Inc. Reading, Pa.	N112AF
☐ N15ET	79	MU-2 Marquise	733SA	Intercontinental Jet Inc., Tulsa, Ok.	N142BK
☐ N15EW	03	King Air 350	FL-388	EWC Aviation Corp. McKinney, Tx.	N4488H
☐ N15KA	79	King Air 200	BB-457	Flight Tech LLC. Virginia Beach, Va.	(N825AA)

Reg	Yr	Type	c/n	Owner/Operator	Prev Regn
N15KW	81	Cheyenne II-XL	8166014	Alfons Ribitsch, Torrance, Ca.	(N31KP)
N15L	75	King Air A100	B-212	Dynamic AvLease Inc. Bridgewater, Va.	(N29N)
N15PX	85	King Air 300	FA-82	D & S Industries of Louisiana LLC. New Orleans, La.	(N317BC)
N15SB	02	TBM 700C2	247	N15SB LLC. Chatham, NJ.	F-WWRN
N15SF	79	Rockwell 690B	11528	EMS Air Services of NY Inc. Canandaiga, NY.	N690SH
N15ST	83	Conquest 1	425-0140	Nicholas Street/The United Co. Blountville, Tn.	N5829J
N15TR	81	MU-2 Solitaire	446SA	Northwest Aviation LLC. Fargo, ND.	N81MW
N15UB	06	King Air C90GT	LJ-1776	Jimmy John's Franchise Inc. Champaign, Il.	N774EA
N15UE	80	PA-31T Cheyenne II	8020049	REMC Leasing LLC. Bismarck, ND.	N2338V
N15WN	73	King Air E90	LW-78	G L Wilson Building Co. Statesville, NC.	N4378W
N15WS	04	King Air 350	FL-411	Peconic Aviation LLC. Vero Beach, Fl.	N953PC
N15YS	73	Mitsubishi MU-2J	598	Flight Line Inc., Watkins, Co.	C-FMBL
N16	80	King Air C90	LJ-893	FAA, Oklahoma City, Ok.	
N16BM	80	King Air F90	LA-23	Malibu Partners LLC. Ocala, Fl.	N27WH
N16GF	96	King Air B200	BB-1531	G F Air LLC. Charleston, SC.	N1081F
N16KM	81	King Air C90	LJ-961	Cox-Flanders Air LLC. Evansville, In.	XA-ISL
N16KW	96	King Air C90B	LJ-1435	F C Stone Group Inc. Des Moines, Ia.	N1095M
N16LH	77	King Air E90	LW-217	Antlers Natural Gas Enterprises, Colorado Springs, Co.	
N16NG	78	DHC 6-300	596	Northrop Grumman Aviation Inc. Hawthorne, Ca.	N16NA
N16VK	06	Pilatus PC-12/47	763	Aircraft Guaranty Title & Trust, Houston, Tx.	HB-FSR
N16WG	85	King Air F90-1	LA-226	Rialto Riverside Corp. Corona, Ca.	N6690L
N17	80	King Air C90	LJ-896	FAA, Oklahoma City, Ok.	
N17CE	78	PA-31T Cheyenne 1	7804007	Capital Equity LLC. Piney Flats Tn.	N22UC
N17CK	85	Reims/Cessna F406	F406-0001	Clint Aero Inc. St Thomas, USVI.	PH-ALO
N17CP	83	Conquest 1	425-0156	V2 Air LLC. Monterey, Ca.	(N156CC)
N17HF	73	Rockwell 690A	11127	Meyer Co. Garfield Heights, Oh.	N199WP
N17HG	81	MU-2 Marquise	1510SA	Castlehill Aviation LLC. Ashburn, Va.	N417MA
N17HM	76	King Air 200	BB-94	Sun Western Flyers Inc., Yuma, Az.	N28AH
N17JG	68	680W Turbo Commander	1802-24	Tulsa County Area Vo-Tec School, Tulsa, Ok.	N102US
N17KK	93	King Air C90B	LJ-1318	Av Advantage LLC. Bloomfield Hills, Mi.	N131SA
N17LH	01	PA-46-500TP Meridian	4697007	Paul Sciarra, Montclair, NJ.	
N17NM	77	King Air E90	LW-237	Seven Bar Flying Service Inc. Albuquerque, NM.	N5NM
N17PA	92	P-180 Avanti	1017	Aurora Aviation Inc. Batavia, Il.	D-IJCL
N17SA	66	King Air A90	LJ-164	Flanagan Enterprises (Nevada) Inc. Carson City, Nv.	N8GF
N17TU	75	PA-31T Cheyenne II	7520035	Midwest Flying Service Inc. Sheldon, Ia.	N66LD
N17VA	80	King Air 200	BB-670	C S & A Aircraft LLC, Franklin Tn.	N7VA
N17VV	84	SA-227TT Merlin 300	TT-536	ABM Air LLC. Wilmington, De.	N72WC
N17WC	97	King Air 350	FL-168	West Coast Charters LLC, Santa Ana, Ca.	N108NT
N17WT	66	King Air 90	LJ-86	Jeffair LLC. Fayetteville, Ga.	N6ORJ
N17ZD	82	Gulfstream 1000	96017	International Air Service Inc. Opa Locka, Fl. (status ?).	(N17QC)
N18	81	King Air F90	LA-145	FAA, Oklahoma City, Ok.	
N18AF	95	King Air B200	BB-1497	N220PB LLC. Mesa, Az.	(N220PB)
N18AH	72	King Air A100	B-118	Joe Dan Manis, Laurinburg, NC.	N100MX
N18BF	69	Mitsubishi MU-2F	173	AMCAP Leasing LLC. Houston, Tx.	N887Q
N18CJ	77	King Air 200	BB-260	ZZ Leasing Inc. Memphis, Tn.	N1SC
N18CM	84	King Air F90-1	LA-219	MMI Air LLC/MMI Services Inc. Bakersfield, Ca.	N8YK
N18KA	78	King Air 200	BB-360	Flight King LLC. Spencer, Ia.	N210PH
N18KK	71	681B Turbo Commander	6055	Karl Koster, Fremont, Ca.	N9127N
N18KW	81	PA-31T Cheyenne II	8120059	Windsock Aviation LLC., Bridgeport, WV.	N20WE
N18SR	00	TBM 700B	161	Tuthill Corp. Burr Ridge, Il.	I-AESR
N18ZX	78	PA-31T Cheyenne II	7820014	Pace Aviation Corp. Norfolk, Va.	C-GSBC
N19	80	King Air C90	LJ-909	FAA, Oklahoma City, Ok.	
N19BX	65	Gulfstream 1	153	19th Hole Corp, Bath, UK	EC-EXB
N19CX	01	PA-46-500TP Meridian	4697077	Jack McClelland, Edinburg, Tx.	N797BG
N19DA	80	King Air B100	BE-87	Alliance Air Parts Inc., Oklahoma City, Ok.	N980KA
N19FF	72	Gulfstream 1	20	Executive Jet Support Ltd. Aston Abbotts, UK.	TU-TDM
N19GA	81	Mitsubishi MU-2P	454SA	Solitaire Hawk LLC. Alva, Ok.	I-FRTL
N19GR	04	King Air 350	FL-414	Gorman-Rupp Co. Mansfield, Oh.	N36814
N19GU	73	Mitsubishi MU-2J	574	Bush Field Aircraft Co. Augusta, Ga.	N243MA
N19LW	73	King Air C90	LJ-991	Carlock Air LLC. Jackson, Tn.	N504AB
N19MC	88	King Air 300	FA-167	Orta Vez Inc., Dover, De.	N1517K
N19MU	71	681B Turbo Commander	6051	Guaranty 1031A LLC, Fond du Lac, Wi.	N12MU
N19RK	80	King Air F90	LA-12	Ring Container Technologies, Olive Branch, Ms.	N200E
N19SG	00	TBM 700B	194	UTS Beteiligungs GmbH. Germany.	
N19TZ	60	Gulfstream 1	40	19th Hole Corp, Bath, UK	EC-FIO

Reg	Yr	Type	c/n	Owner/Operator	Prev Regn
N19UM	71	King Air C90	LJ-524	SKET Maschinen u Anlagenbau GmbH. Memmingen, Germany.	N19CM
N20	80	King Air C90	LJ-912	FAA, Oklahoma City, Ok. (status ?).	
N20AE	81	King Air 200	BB-827	GO Interests LLC., Manvel, Tx.	D-IFES
N20BL	66	King Air A90	LJ-163	Business Aircraft Sales Corp. Chattanooga, Tn.	N2RR
N20BM	67	680V Turbo Commander	1698-75	Swanson Air LLC. Fort Wayne, In.	N420J
N20DH	87	King Air B200	BB-1263	Los Medio Corp., Corpus Christi, Tx.	N263SW
N20EB	76	Rockwell 690A	11282	Texas Aerospace Services Inc. Abilene, Tx.	N429K
N20EF	69	SA-26AT Merlin 2B	T26-157	North Star Air Cargo Inc. Milwaukee, Wi.	N20ER
N20FD	98	King Air C90B	LJ-1528	LegendAir LLC. Nashville, Tn.	N2273A
N20KV	69	SA-26AT Merlin 2B	T26-154	Alti International Inc, Miami Shores, Fl.	N71SF
N20KW	85	King Air 300	FA-44	K & W Restaurants Inc. Winston Salem, NC.	N48EB
N20LB	96	King Air B200	BB-1541	Silver Dollar City Inc. Branson, Mo.	N1003W
N20LH	07	King Air B200	BB-1996	LH Air LLC./Clark, Depew & Tracey LLP., Houston, Tx.	N996KA
N20MA	78	Rockwell 690B	11514	Aviation Enterprises LLC., Longwood, Fl.	N14BU
N20ME	78	Rockwell 690B	11440	Wrangler Aviation Corp. Norman, Ok.	N47CF
N20RA	85	Beech 1900C	UB-42	EG&G, Las Vegas, Nv.	(N272HK)
N20RE	81	King Air 200	BB-758	Rodney Mitchell, Granite Bay, Ca.	
N20S	78	King Air E90	LW-267	Helicopter Express Inc. Lawrenceville, Ga.	N23726
N20TN	79	PA-31T Cheyenne II	7920019	Sierra Aviation Inc. Bishop, Ca.	N20TV
N20WL	77	PA-31T Cheyenne II	7720011	Hamblen Aero Inc. Morristown, Tn.	N51BJ
N20WP	77	King Air C90	LJ-738	LA Aviation LLC. Sorrento, Fl.	N239C
N20WS	73	King Air E90	LW-30	Southeast Airmotive Corp. Charlotte, NC.	(N24TF)
N21	80	King Air C90	LJ-902	FAA, Oklahoma City, Ok.	N5
N21AU	04	Pilatus PC-12/45	606	Aurora Flight Sciences Corp. Manassas, Va.	HB-FQP
N21CJ	80	MU-2 Marquise	789SA	Bankair Inc. West Columbia, SC.	N278MA
N21DE	76	King Air 200	BB-117	Silverton Air LLC. Bardstown, Ky.	(N410SH)
N21FG	81	King Air 200	BB-839	Department of Fish & Game, Sacramento, Ca.	N3849B
N21HP	77	Mitsubishi MU-2P	357SA	Richland Aviation, Sidney, Mt.	N2HP
N21JA	74	Mitsubishi MU-2J	614	Bankair Inc. West Columbia, SC.	N998CA
N21LE	02	King Air C90B	LJ-1682	UL-ECO Inc. Tampa, Fl.	N6082A
N21NM	80	King Air E90	LW-336	Seven Bar Flying Service Inc. Albuquerque, NM.	N675J
N21SP	74	King Air C90	LJ-630	Southwest Aviation Specialities LLC. Tulsa, Ok.	N22BM
N22BB	67	King Air A90	LJ-241	Robert Spillman, Elyria, Oh.	N27UU
N22BJ	72	King Air A100	B-133	Albatros Aviation Group, Sacramento, Ca.	N1200Z
N22CG	80	Conquest II	441-0119	Jubilee Airways Inc. Glasgow, Scotland.	N26231
N22CK	79	Rockwell 690B	11524	Acme Aviation LLC. Swanson, Il.	N81773
N22CR	06	King Air C90GT	LJ-1811	Christopher Ranch LLC., Gilroy, Ca.	
N22DT	80	PA-31T Cheyenne II	8020057	Conyan Aviation Inc. Boise, Id.	N806CM
N22EQ	72	SA-226T Merlin 3	T-221	Professional Aviation Group LLC,Ft Lauderdale, Fl.	(N18BQ)
N22ER	72	King Air E90	LW-18	Ascension Aviation LLC. Gaylord, Mi.	N22EH
N22ET	68	680W Turbo Commander	1793-23	R Con Aviation Inc. Billings, Mt.	N22RT
N22F	82	King Air B200	BB-1025	Timmerman Land & Cattle Co. Springfield, Ne.	(N2227F)
N22FS	96	King Air C90B	LJ-1452	Frank & Rona Singer Living Trust, Huntington Beach, Ca.	N548JG
N22HD	04	King Air C90B	LJ-1720	The Lyden Company/Truenorthair LLC., Toledo, Oh.	
N22LP	01	Pilatus PC-12/45	402	DTI/Oldham Associates LLC. Springville, Ut.	N9DC
N22MY	07	TBM 850	443	EADS SOCATA North America, Pembroke Pines, Fl.	
N22MZ	69	Mitsubishi MU-2F	158	Africano Aircraft Management LLC. Peoria, Il.	PT-BPY
N22N	73	King Air E90	LW-48	Dynamic AvLease Inc. Bridgewater, Va.	N70MV
N22NR	70	SA-26AT Merlin 2B	T26-173	Chandler Air LLC, Bossier, La.	N99RK
N22RT	70	681 Turbo Commander	6001	J & J Service, Tulsa, Ok.	N66CP
N22ST		PA-46 Turbo Malibu	4636122	Sijben, Maastricht, Holland.	
N22TL	80	King Air E90	LW-334	Peake Motor Co. Kenner, La.	
N22UP	82	PA-42 Cheyenne III	8001079	L G Brooker Equipment Sales & Leasing, Odessa, Tx.	N515M
N22WF	79	PA-31T Cheyenne II	7920007	Worsley Companies Inc. Wilmington, NC.	(N53TR)
N22XY	73	Mitsubishi MU-2J	599	Air Flight Enterprises Inc. Port Orange, Fl.	N121BA
N22YC	81	Cheyenne II-XL	8166020	Northeast Air Charter LLC. Greenwich, Ct.	N11YC
N23AE	73	SA-226T Merlin 3	T-241	Explosive Professionals Inc. Worthington, Ky.	N73542
N23BD	86	Beech 1900C	UB-64	Bill Davis Racing, Greensboro, NC.	N93BD
N23EA	80	Conquest II	441-0183	Jackson Air Inc. Jackson, Oh.	N120EA
N23EW	76	King Air E90	LW-168	Wiseman Aviation Inc. Flagstaff, Az.	(N616DD)
N23HD	06	King Air B200	BB-1960	Windward Aviation LLC, Olympia, Wa.	N7260R
N23NW	78	Conquest II	441-0066	North West Geomatics Ltd., Calgary, AB, Canada	N385GH
N23RF	04	P-180 Avanti	1080	Trek Ventures LLC. Annapolis, Md.	G-OESL
N23ST	78	King Air 200	BB-375	Dept of Natural Resources, Olympia, Wa.	N89FC
N23TC	79	King Air 200	BB-453	DIHE Inc. Van Nuys, Ca.	N1284

Reg	Yr	Type	c/n	Owner/Operator	Prev Regn
N23W	77	King Air E90	LW-230	Dynamic AvLease Inc. Bridgewater, Va.	N48TE
N23WJ	88	King Air B200	BB-1297	Peter, Scott & Palmer LLC. Cashiers, NC.	N55FJ
N23WP	80	PA-31T Cheyenne II	8020004	PFC Inc/Stingray Boat Co. Hartsville, SC.	N51RL
N23WS	83	King Air B200	BB-1143	Dovey Air Inc. Birmingham, Mi.	(N330BH)
N23YR	06	King Air B200	BB-1976	Rushton Air Inc., Auburn, Al.	N124AR
N24BL	88	King Air 300	FA-153	Bennett Lumber Products Inc. Princeton, Id.	N21CY
N24CC	74	Rockwell 690A	11201	JWS Inc. Bozeman, Mt.	N50ST
N24DD	79	PA-31T Cheyenne II	7920074	Summit Helicopters Inc. Cloverdale, Va.	N204EF
N24DS	00	King Air C90B	LJ-1616	Whiskey Tango LLC. Midland, Tx.	N342P
N24EM	76	King Air B100	BE-6	ERM Charters Inc. Irving, Tx.	N8514B
N24GJ	78	King Air C90	LJ-769	C C Medflight Inc. Lawrenceville, Ga.	N911UM
N24GN	82	King Air B200	BB-953	Flat Creek Development Co. Jackson, Wy.	N953L
N24GT	75	Rockwell 690A	11254	Rogers Helicopters Inc. Clovis, Ca.	XA-RMZ
N24HD	07	King Air B200GT	BY-18	Harley Davidson of Valparaisos, Valparaso, In..	
N24PE	78	Mitsubishi MU-2P	369SA	Anaconda Aviation Corp. Boca Raton, Fl.	N202MC
N24PT	77	Conquest II	441-0015	Donald Aircraft LLC. Wilmington, De.	N441TJ
N24SP	74	King Air C-12L	BB-3	Kentucky State Police, Frankfort, Ky.	71-21058
N24TW	83	Conquest 1	425-0132	Tri-Went Inc. Knoxville, Tn.	N83GF
N24WC	78	Mitsubishi MU-2N	705SA	Mobile Instrument Service & Repair Inc. Bellefontaine, Oh.	N865MA
N24XJ	07	P-180 Avanti II	1149	Aspect Aviation III LLC, Denver Co.	
N24YC	97	King Air C90B	LJ-1484	W G Yates & Sons Construction Co. Philadelphia, Ms.	N1134D
N25BD	72	Rockwell 690	11009	Haas Chemical Co. Melrose, Fl.	N9209N
N25BE	70	681 Turbo Commander	6041	Midwestern Jet Sales & Service Inc. Oklahoma City, Ok.	N9101N
N25CE	77	Rockwell 690B	11400	Milton Koy, Portland, Or.	(N3TJ)
N25CS	82	King Air B200	BB-948	Mastriana & Christiansen PA., Ft Lauderdale, Fl.	N150RH
N25DL	77	King Air C90	LJ-716	Sunmor Aviation Ltd. Dayton, Tx.	N25KW
N25EN	77	King Air E90	LW-239	Farbman Group, Southfield, Mi.	G-SFSG
N25EP	98	Pilatus PC-12/45	217	25EP Corp. Wilmington, De.	N124PC
N25GM	79	MU-2 Solitaire	412SA	Rod Aero Aircraft Brokerage, Fort Lauderdale, Fl.	N814HH
N25HB	96	King Air C90B	LJ-1453	Hempt Brothers Inc. Camp Hill, Pa.	N1092G
N25KA	81	King Air 200	BB-783	Eric & Theresa Stirling, Fairbanks, Ak.	N3714P
N25MG	79	PA-31T Cheyenne II	7920059	Gypsum Aviation Services LLC., Fulton, NY.	N63SC
N25ND	80	PA-31T Cheyenne II	8020005	Chieftain Development Enterprises, Newport Beach, Ca.	N25AS
N25RZ	79	Rockwell 690B	11518	EAL Inc/Executive Aviation Logistics, Chino, Ca.	(N91AV)
N25TN	80	Gulfstream 980	95013	Truly Nolen of America Inc. Orlando, Fl.	N519HB
N25WC	98	King Air B200	BB-1640	FreshAir LLC/Fresh Beginnings Inc. Valdosta, Ga.	N351SC
N26BE	78	King Air 200	BB-388	Manchester Plastics Ltd. Troy, Mi.	N388MC
N26E	73	King Air E90	LW-62	Dynamic Aviation Group Inc. Bridgewater, Va.	N14C
N26JB	81	PA-31T Cheyenne 1	8104020	Gilmanton Associates LLC. Incline Village, Nv.	N31WM
N26KC	01	PA-46-500TP Meridian	4697113	Aircraft Guaranty Title & Trust LLC., Houston, Tx.	N6DM
N26KH	04	Pilatus PC-12/45	592	Concord Jet Service Inc. Portland, Or.	HB-FRD
N26KR	06	Pilatus PC-12/47	764	Aviation 26 LLC., Hayden, Id.	HB-FSS
N26RE	76	King Air C90	LJ-676	Group 2 Inc., Hilton Head, SC.	N1DK
N26SL	79	PA-31T Cheyenne II	7920091	Sierra Lima LLC. Bozeman, Mt.	N19GA
N26UT	81	King Air B200	BB-901	PRE Management Inc/King Air Leasing Portland Or.	
N26VW	02	Pilatus PC-12/45	478	Canvasback Enterprises LP. Kerrville, Tx.	N478PC
N27BF	81	PA-31T Cheyenne 1	8104038	27 Bravo Foxtrot Inc. Columbia, SC.	N130CC
N27BM	91	King Air C90B	LJ-1288	Sevron Ent./Sterling Boiler & Mechanical, Evansville, In.	N90KB
N27CS	79	King Air B100	BE-63	King Air 27CS LLC. Hickory, NC.	N924RM
N27CV	83	King Air B200	BB-1161	Valley International Properties, Stuart, Fl.	N77CV
N27DK	04	PA-46-500TP Meridian	4697196	TJD Corp. Wilmington, De.	
N27GE	92	King Air 350	FL-86	Sarina Aviation Inc. Pleasanton Ca.	(N60CC)
N27GH	86	King Air B200	BB-1260	Centennial American Real Estate Ltd. Greenville, SC.	N2PX
N27HK	90	King Air B200	BB-1350	Airelock Holdings Ltd., Tortola, British Virgin Isles.	A7-AHK
N27KG	85	King Air 300LW	FA-79	Keith D Graham Jr. Austin, Tx.	N873CA
N27NG	99	Beech 1900D	UE-382	Northrop Grumman Systems Corp. El Segundo, Ca.	N.....
N27RC	83	King Air B200	BB-1134	U R Flying LLC. Eutah, Al.	N98LP
N27SE	82	King Air F90	LA-194	RF Aviation LLC. Wheeling, Il.	N6685P
N27VE	85	Gulfstream 1000B	96202	Edelbrock Corp. Torrance, Ca.	N695P
N28BG	77	PA-31T Cheyenne II	7720005	GRL Investments LLC. Kalispell, Mt.	N444ET
N28C	75	King Air A100	B-216	Dynamic Aviation Group Inc. Bridgewater, Va.	JDFT-3
N28CA	79	PA-31T Cheyenne II	7920042	Westlog Inc./CAL-ORE Life Flight, Brookings, Or.	C-GFAM
N28CG	94	Dornier 328-100	3024	Corning Inc. Corning, NY.	N95CG
N28DA	82	PA-42 Cheyenne III	8001078	Hortman Aviation Services Inc. New Hope Pa.	N22HD
N28DC	68	Mitsubishi MU-2D	106	Eastern New Mexico University, Roswell, NM.	N518TQ

Reg	Yr	Type	c/n	Owner/Operator	Prev Regn
N28GC	89	King Air 300	FA-172	AFS Services Inc. Tampa, Fl.	N34BS
N28J	78	King Air 200	BB-348	Sierra Pacific Industries Inc. Redding, Ca.	
N28KP	79	King Air C90	LJ-845	State of Montana, Helena, Mt.	N28KC
N28M	75	King Air E90	LW-147	K & K Aircraft Inc. Bridgewater, Va.	N553MA
N28MS	74	King Air E90	LW-100	Rocky Mountain Holdings LLC. Provo, Ut.	N31FN
N28NG	96	Beech 1900D	UE-258	Management West LLC, Aurora, Or.	N10936
N28NK	04	PA-46-500TP Meridian	4697191	MMS Services Inc. Wilmington, De.	
N28PH	99	King Air 350	FL-248	Prime Lines LLC/Prime Home Builders, Boca Raton, Fl.	N3078W
N28TC	78	Rockwell 690B	11449	Jets Of The Atlantic LLC, Orlando Fl.	D-ICSM
N28TM	82	King Air C90-1	LJ-1029	Luke Ready Air LLC. Hypoluxo, Fl.	N6567C
N28VM	01	King Air B200	BB-1772	Van Metre Air LLC. Burke, Va.	N4472C
N28VU	80	King Air 200	BB-743	Shiver Security Systems Inc. Cincinnati, Oh.	N111LP
N28WN	81	Cheyenne II-XL	8166026	Malco Leasing Corp. Danbury, Ct.	N77UH
N29DE	67	680V Turbo Commander	1699-76	World Wide Wings, Duncan, Ok.	N7029P
N29GA	83	Gulfstream 900	15025	David A Miller, Palmer, Tx.	
N29HF	80	King Air 200	BB-685	Sherwood McGuigan, Midland, Tx.	N29CH
N29JS	01	P-180 Avanti	1046	Pelham Air LLC. Wilmington, De.	N124PA
N29LA	80	PA-31T Cheyenne II	8020076	Exeat Aviation Inc. Marco Island, Fl.	F-GNAC
N29LH	04	PA-46-500TP Meridian	4697179	H & M Bay Inc. Federalsburg, Md.	
N29M	74	King Air E90	LW-88	Dynamic Aviation Group Inc. Bridgewater, Va.	F-GELL
N29NG	97	Beech 1900D	UE-303	Northrop Grumman Systems Corp. El Segundo, Ca.	N.....
N29PE	05	King Air B200	BB-1913	Patrick Engineering Inc. DuPage, Il.	
N29PR	70	681 Turbo Commander	6018	AC Air Inc., Chino, Ca.	PT-DQX
N29TB	79	King Air C90	LJ-846	Weir Capital Management LLC. Simpsonville, SC.	OY-MBA
N29TF	84	PA-42 Cheyenne IIIA	5501003	Cheyenne Partners LLC. Darien, Ct.	(N340BH)
N29TV	83	King Air B200	BB-1138	Big Creek Aviation LLC. Jacksonville, Fl.	N138AJ
N29WD	77	Mitsubishi MU-2P	355SA	Whiskey Delta LLC. Stuart, Fl.	N741MA
N30BG	71	681B Turbo Commander	6059	Vvoortech Inc. Council Bluffs, Ia.	N333RK
N30CN	95	King Air C90B	LJ-1415	Streamline Air LLC. Santa Barbara, Ca.	
N30CV	78	King Air E90	LW-252	CVA Aviation LLC. Atlanta, Ga.	N969CL
N30DU	77	PA-31T Cheyenne II	7720054	Scheufler Inc. Valley City, Oh.	(N98AS)
N30FE	88	King Air 300	FA-148	Fresh Express Inc. Salinas, Ca.	N3086D
N30GT	80	King Air F90	LA-37	Hodge Law Firm, Spartanburg, SC.	
N30HS	69	SA-26AT Merlin 2B	T26-156	David Uthoff, Wickenburg, Az.	N112A
N30HV	89	King Air 300	FA-173	Central Cooling Co. Fremont, Ca.	(N177GA)
N30KC	77	King Air E90	LW-241	Clorox Services Co. Oakland, Ca.	N17844
N30MA	78	Mitsubishi MU-2P	371SA	Wilson Construction Delaware Corp. Wilmington, De.	ZK-ECR
N30MC	06	King Air 350	FL-493	Madden Contracting Co. Minden, La.	
N30NH	80	King Air F90	LA-48	SQH Air Corp. Menlo Park, Ca.	C-FOMH
N30PH	80	King Air 200	BB-635	GECC, Danbury, Ct.	N30PM
N30RR	73	Mitsubishi MU-2K	263	Tony Equipment Leasing Corp. Lewes, De.	N10VU
N30SE	78	King Air 200	BB-313	A & M Holdings LLC. Stuttgart, Ar. (status ?).	N23313
N30SM	93	King Air 350	FL-99	State of Mississippi, Jackson, Ms.	N850MS
N30W	78	King Air C-12C	BC-72	Dynamic Aviation Group Inc. Bridgewater, Va.	N200EJ
N31A	78	King Air E90	LW-281	DavisAir Inc. Allegheny County, Pa.	N502SC
N31CG	06	King Air B200	BB-1946	Clark-Griffin Air LLC/Bradshaw & Co. Banner Elk, NC.	N37046
N31DV	74	Rockwell 690A	11154	Dunn Vineyards LLC. Angwin, Ca.	N102JK
N31ET	78	PA-31T Cheyenne II	7820019	SJ Aero Corp./Broad Peak LLC, Wilmington, De	N727SM
N31FM	81	King Air 200	BB-869	3M Aviation LLC./Arnold Crushed Stone Inc., Burleson, Tx.	N2135J
N31HL	81	PA-31T Cheyenne II	8120060	Navionics LLC. Sussex, De.	N816JA
N31JN	06	King Air C90GT	LJ-1774	Nance Air Inc. Melbourne, Fl.	N730EB
N31JV	82	SA-227TT Merlin 3C	TT-453	JV Air LLC. La Porte, Tx.	N944KR
N31MB	80	PA-31T Cheyenne 1	8004013	Bison Air LLC/Real Estate of Jackson Hole, Missoula, Mt.	
N31SN	68	King Air B90	LJ-362	Professional Air Services LLC. Fort Lauderdale, Fl.	N31SV
N31SV	95	King Air B200	BB-1514	Sanford Medical Center, Sioux Falls, SD.	N214SE
N31TL	81	King Air F90	LA-133	Southern Lady Inc. Lakeland, Fl.	N1803P
N31WC	79	King Air 200	BB-465	Ocean Aviation LLC/Gulf Fleet Management LLC. Lafayette, La.	(N113MH)
N31WD	77	Rockwell 690B	11353	Teton Leasing LLC. Pocatello, Id.	N690JT
N31WM	67	Mitsubishi MU-2B	031	Robert F Moon, Phenix City, Al.	(N631BA)
N31WP	74	King Air E90	LW-99	N31WP King Air E90 LP. Houston, Tx.	N31JJ
N31ZS	79	PA-31T Cheyenne II	7920027	Southern Aircraft Consultancy Inc. St Mawgan, UK.	C-GLAG
N32BA	69	King Air B90	LJ-475	Sky's The Limit Inc. Hutchinson, Mn.	N500RK
N32BW	79	Rockwell 690B	11545	Ehrenfeld Air LLC. River Edge, NJ.	N25LS
N32CA	05	PA-46-500TP Meridian	4697216	Bruce Feldstein DDS PC. West Lebanon, NH.	
N32CC	71	King Air C90	LJ-506	City College Inc. Fort Lauderdale, Fl.	N30HF

Reg	Yr	Type	c/n	Owner/Operator	Prev Regn
N32CK	01	PA-46-500TP Meridian	4697123	Southern Aircraft Consultancy Ltd., St. Just, UK	N633P
N32CM	80	King Air C90	LJ-881	Red Spot Paint & Varnish Co. Evansville, In.	N32SJ
N32EC	77	Mitsubishi MU-2N	699SA	Security Air Service LLC. Murrels Inlet, SC.	N859MA
N32FH	65	King Air 90	LJ-74	Special Ops Aviation Inc. Norfolk, Va.	XA-RMH
N32GA	74	Rockwell 690A	11215	Petroleum Helicopters Inc. Lafayette, La.	N215BA
N32JP	88	King Air C90A	LJ-1172	Price Services Inc. Monticello, Ar.	N904TD
N32KE	01	PA-46-500TP Meridian	4697048	Group Growth Services Inc. Richmond, In.	
N32KW	78	PA-31T Cheyenne II	7820090	Exec Air Montana Inc. Helena, Mt.	D-IJPG
N32LJ	82	King Air B200	BB-993	Larry Collins, Portland, Tn.	N32TJ
N32MT	87	King Air C90A	LJ-1155	Management Specialities LLC/Dunham Price Inc. Westlake, La.	N3077Y
N32P	66	King Air A90	LM-31	Dynamic AvLease Inc. Bridgewater, Va.	N7040J
N32PH	81	Gulfstream 840	11691	Petroleum Helicopters Inc. Lafayette, La.	N800BM
N32PR	76	Rockwell 690A	11332	David Miller, Palmer, Tx.	(N216PL)
N32SV	81	King Air 200	BB-865	Sanford Medical Center, Sioux Falls, SD.	N531BB
N32WC	87	King Air B200	BB-1285	West Coast Charters LLC. Santa Ana, Ca.	N280JR
N32WS	76	Rockwell 690A	11339	R & S Aviation LLC. Neenah, Wi.	ZS-JRL
N32WZ	07	TBM 850	400	Jerry Fussell, Wilson, Wy.	
N33DE	83	Conquest II	441-0308	PMI Aviation LLC., Beverly Hills, Ca.	N87494
N33EW	81	MU-2 Marquise	1519SA	Florida Express Corp. Wilmington, De.	N331W
N33JA	99	Pilatus PC-12/45	261	Jet Capital Inc. Edwards, Co.	N654CA
N33LA	01	King Air B200	BB-1777	NPP Inc./Landis International, Valdosta, Ga.	N4347X
N33MC	81	PA-31T Cheyenne II	8120050	James Costello, Bend, Or.	N194MA
N33MS	81	PA-31T Cheyenne II	8120036	Maurice Shacket, West Bloomfield, Mi.	N25WA
N33SB	67	King Air A90	LJ-252	David Harden, Washington, Pa.	N728K
N33WG	72	Rockwell 690	11038	Big Eye Helicopters, Agana, Guam.	(N38PR)
N34AL	80	MU-2 Marquise	792SA	Flight Line Inc. Salt Lake City, Ut.	N66LA
N34CE	81	King Air C90	LJ-932	Trans Oceano LLC. San Jose, Costa Rica.	(N90CE)
N34ER	88	PA-42 Cheyenne 400LS	5527036	Starwood Air LLC. Missoula, Mt.	D-IONE
N34GA	82	Gulfstream 1000	96057	Franklin Realty Group Inc. Blue Bell, Pa.	(N9977S)
N34HA	67	King Air A90	LJ-315	Hawk Aviation Inc. Hanahan, SC.	XB-FJM
N34HM	77	PA-31T Cheyenne II	7720003	Pace Aviation Ltd. Reno, Nv.	N28FM
N34LT	92	King Air B200	BB-1437	Corporate Airways Inc. Thomasville, Ga.	N8059Y
N34MF	76	King Air E90	LW-163	Home Buyers Marketing Inc. Excelsior, Mn.	(N112CM)
N34RF	94	King Air C90B	LJ-1371	Roflec Inc/R Forests Ltd. Guernsey, Channel Islands.	VT-PPC
N34UP	73	King Air C-12C	BC-6	Eagles Quest LLC. Wayne, Pa.	N530SP
N35	75	King Air 200	BB-88	FAA, Oklahoma City, Ok.	N4
N35GR	85	King Air B200	BB-1167	JNG Services Inc. Lexington, Ky.	N18CM
N35HC	94	King Air C90B	LJ-1375	Bruce Barclay, Mechanicsburg, Pa.	XA-TDW
N35HD	05	King Air C90B	LJ-1731	Harvest Moon Aviation Corp. Fort Worth, Tx.	N851CM
N35JL	71	Mitsubishi MU-2F	209	JTL Enterprises Inc. Lexington, NC.	(N34LC)
N35LW	85	King Air 300LW	FA-63	King Air FA-63 Leasing Corp. Fort Lauderdale, Fl.	D-IILG
N35RR	81	MU-2 Marquise	1525SA	Flight Line Inc. Denver, Co.	N442MA
N35TV	73	King Air C90	LJ-572	TFC Equipment LLC/Bank of Utah, Salt Lake City, Ut.	N46RF
N35TY	81	Conquest 1	425-0088	SouthAir LLC/Augusta Fiberglass Coatings Inc. Blackville, SC	N35TK
N35VP	05	King Air 350	FL-466	Valley Proteins Inc. Winchester, Va.	
N35WA	06	Pilatus PC-12/47	770	Aircraft Guaranty Title & Trust LLC. Houston, Tx. (trustor?)	HB-FSW
N36AG	83	Gulfstream 1000	96058	L C Leasing Co. Annapolis, Md.	HP-11GT
N36AT	80	MU-2 Solitaire	426SA	JS Holdings LLC. Indianapolis, In.	N181RS
N36CP	76	King Air 200	BB-178	IFL Group Inc. Waterford, Mi.	N355AF
N36EG	07	Pilatus PC-12/47	809	NAG Leasing LLC., Ada, Mi.	HB-FRA
N36FR	86	Conquest II	441-0362	N4272C LLC. Wilmington, De.	C-GSSK
N36G	67	Mitsubishi MU-2B	035	Buckeye Holding Ltd. Newark, De.	N601CT
N36GS	88	King Air B200	BB-1298	Andrew Heller, Austin, Tx.	N734A
N36JF	78	Rockwell 690B	11478	MMDEX LLC. Carlisle, Pa.	N81797
N36JT	80	Gulfstream 980	95024	K Banett & Sons Inc. NM	N66FP
N36LC	81	SA-226T Merlin 3B	T-387	Max Sam Venture LLC., Gibson, La.	N777JE
N36SW	78	Rockwell 690B	11505	Eagle Leasing Inc. Midland City, Al.	N28WR
N36TW	80	PA-31T Cheyenne II	8020075	Esposita Aviation Inc.Albroek, Panama.	
N37BW	73	Rockwell 690A	11129	Damin Sir Paul Inc. Boca Raton, Fl.	(N500AL)
N37CN	78	King Air C90	LJ-745	Business & Pleasure Air Charter LC. Schulenberg, Tx.	N384H
N37GA	87	King Air B200	BB-1272	Legacy Air II LLC/Crossland Construction Company, Rogers,Ar.	VT-EQD
N37GP	65	King Air 90	LJ-15	APA Enterprises Inc. Poughskepsie, NY.	N733KL
N37H	67	King Air A90	LM-48	Dynamic AvLease Inc. Bridgewater, Va.	N7059H
N37HB	77	PA-31T Cheyenne II	7720020	R L Riemenschneider Enterprises Co. Redmond, Or.	N37RT
N37HC	74	King Air E90	LW-108	DRL Air LLC. Hendersonville, NC.	N37X

Reg	Yr	Type	c/n	Owner/Operator	Prev Regn
N37KK	73	Mitsubishi MU-2J	588	Bar Aircraft Leasing Co. Clarkston, Mi.	N32CK
N37KW	89	PA-42 Cheyenne 400LS	5527039	Broco VIII LLC. Sheridan, In.	C-FPQA
N37PC	79	King Air B100	BE-66	Jim & Mike Leasing II LLC. Dublin, Oh.	N6032E
N37PJ	79	PA-31T Cheyenne 1	7904003	Rock Creek Corp. Henderson, Nv.	N800CM
N37PS	81	Conquest 1	425-0050	Grand Junction Aircraft Sales Inc., Grand Junction, Co.	N425FB
N37RR	79	Rockwell 690B	11552	Aircraft Mergers Inc., Wilmington, De.	N888SL
N37SB	82	Gulfstream 840	11724	ZB Investments Intd. Dallas, Tx.	N5962K
N37SV	06	TBM 850	358	SV Leasing Co of Florida, Miami, Fl.	N850SL
N37TD	90	King Air 350	FL-25	Twin Disc Inc. Racine, Wi.	N768WT
N37TW	81	PA-31T Cheyenne 1	8104006	Virga Corp/Virga Enviromental Corp. Loveland, Co.	(N816CM)
N37XX	85	King Air C90A	LJ-1112	Winslow Acquisitions LLC/N37XX LLC. Aromas, Ca.	N66LM
N38AF	73	Mitsubishi MU-2K	264	Air 1st Aviation Companies Inc. Aiken, SC.	N261KW
N38BE	71	Mitsubishi MU-2F	210	Avmanco 1 Ltd/Steven Bernstein, Dickens, Tx.	N34DD
N38CG	95	Dornier 328-100	3034	Corning Inc. Corning, NY.	D-CDXA
N38H	92	King Air 350	FL-71	Starlight Pines Realty/S & K Aviation LLC., Phoenix, Az.	N56456
N38JV	92	King Air B200	BB-1439	KA 300AJ LLC. Dallas, Tx.	N423PC
N38LM	77	Rockwell 690B	11424	Multi-International Supply LLC. San Juan, Tx.	CP-2299
N38RE	81	PA-31T Cheyenne 1	8104028	Javelin Air Inc. Blakely, Ga.	N241AC
N38RP	77	King Air C90	LJ-722	The Card Plane LLC. Birmingham, Al.	N35HP
N38RY	87	King Air 300	FA-134	Samet Corporation , Greensboro NC.	N28RY
N38TA	81	SA-226T Merlin 3B	T-397	Hospital Management Systems Inc. Lewes, De.	
N38TJ	79	King Air 200	BB-501	Island Flight Aviation LLC, De.	N175GM
N38TR	80	King Air C90	LJ-908	TRC Aviation LLC. Signal Mountain, Tn.	N1078
N38TW	81	PA-31T Cheyenne 1	8104008	Tango Whiskey Inc. Wilmington, De.	
N38V	68	King Air A90	LM-105	Dynamic AvLease Inc. Bridgewater, Va.	N7148A
N38VT	80	PA-31T Cheyenne II	8020022	Cavalier Motor Co. Mechanicsville, Va.	N38V
N38VV	91	King Air B200	BB-1412	JHAMR LLC/MartinAir Inc. Richmond, Va.	N38V
N38WA	74	Rockwell 690A	11169	Airborne Support Inc. Houma, La.	XB-FLF
N38WV	96	King Air B200	BB-1554	Caribbean Trading & Shipping SA. Barranquilla, Colombia.	N88WV
N38XJ	98	King Air C90B	LJ-1512	United Interstate Financial Services, Van Nuys, Ca.	
N39A	83	Conquest 1	425-0138	Tailwind Airline LLC. Farmington, NM.	N6884Q
N39AS	68	680W Turbo Commander	1721-1	Southern Turbines Inc. Vero Beach, Fl. (was 1721-92).	N954HE
N39EH	79	PA-31T Cheyenne II	7920020	Deanco Auction Co Philadelphia, Ms.	N224EC
N39FB	88	King Air C90A	LJ-1165	TA Capital LLC Minneapolis, Mn.	(N325A)
N39GK	00	P-180 Avanti	1039	Meyer Tool Inc. Cincinnati, Oh.	N120PA
N39MS	75	SA-226T Merlin 3A	T-257	Khan Aviation Inc. Elkhart, In.	N45BB
N39PH	79	King Air 200C	BL-3	TriState CareFlight LLC., Bullhead City, Az.	N141GS
N39Q	68	King Air A90	LM-106	Dynamic AvLease Inc. Bridgewater, Va.	N7154W
N39TE	67	King Air A90	LJ-281	Constellation Aircraft Services Inc. Wilmington, De.	C-FFRZ
N39TL	81	PA-31T Cheyenne 1	8104012	Panhandle Telecommunications & Systems Inc. Guymon, Ok.	N39TW
N40AM	80	MU-2 Solitaire	427SA	Scope Leasing Inc. Columbus, Oh.	N166MA
N40BA	69	King Air B90	LJ-444	San Juan 55 Inc. San Juan Pr.	(HI-...)
N40BC	84	King Air B200	BB-1169	MOCI Leasing Inc. Dover, De.	N90LP
N40FK	84	PA-42 Cheyenne 400LS	5527003	Destinations LLC/KFS Property Co. LLC, West Des Moines, Ia.	(N42AJ)
N40GZ	04	King Air 350	FL-400	Jorge C Zamora-Quezada, Mission, Tx.	N40TH
N40JJ	78	Mitsubishi MU-2P	383SA	PLSR LLC. Plano, Tx.	N10JJ
N40KC	75	Mitsubishi MU-2M	322	Keller Companies Inc. Manchester, NH.	N20KC
N40MV	85	PA-42 Cheyenne 400LS	5527029	The Vorbs Group LLC. Sarasota, Fl.	N689CA
N40PT	88	King Air B200	BB-1291	N40PT LLC. Fort Myers, Fl.	D-CIRA
N40R	73	King Air C-12C	BC-7	Dynamic Aviation Group Inc. Bridgewater, Va.	N380SA
N40RA	76	King Air 200	BB-104	Georgetown Aviation Services LLC., San Antonio, Tx.	
N40SM	79	Rockwell 690B	11559	First Windsor Inc. Mendota Heights, De.	
N40TT	75	PA-31T Cheyenne II	7520023	Ocean Aircraft Ltd. Chesapeake, Va.	N314GA
N40WG	78	Rockwell 690B	11459	Envision Homes, Merced, Ca.	N333KD
N40XJ	00	King Air C90B	LJ-1640	WFBNW NA. Salt Lake City, Ut. (trustor ?).	
N41AK	82	King Air F90	LA-188	I & S Graham Aviation, Glasgow, Scotland.	(N46BA)
N41HH	75	King Air E90	LW-146	Sundancer Enterprises LLC. Norman, Ok.	N141DA
N41J	67	King Air A90	LM-89	Dynamic AvLease Inc. Bridgewater, Va.	N7113Z
N41R	76	King Air C-12C	BC-31	Dynamic Aviation Group Inc. Bridgewater, Va.	76-22555
N41T	70	Rockwell 690	11001	Turbo Commander Inc. Miami, Fl. (was s/n 6031).	N700CB
N41WC	68	King Air B90	LJ-430	Beech Transportation Inc/Aviation Charter, Eden Prairie, Mn.	N551SS
N42AF	81	MU-2 Marquise	1539SA	EPPS Air Service Inc. Atlanta, Ga.	ZS-MRJ
N42CQ	67	King Air A90	LJ-245	Oklahoma State Department Vo-Tech, Stillwater, Ok.	(N221ML)
N42CV	80	PA-31T Cheyenne II	8020067	South Georgia Motor Sports LLC. Cecil, Ga.	N42CV
N42ED	00	King Air 350	FL-302	Eldorado Resorts LLC. Reno, Nv.	N42EL

Reg	Yr	Type	c/n	Owner/Operator	Prev Regn
☐ N42FC	96	King Air B200	BB-1553	Frank's Casing Crew & Rental Tools, Lafayette, La.	N200ZK
☐ N42LJ	79	King Air 200	BB-564	Smith Newspapers Inc. Fort Payne, Al.	ZS-KHK
☐ N42LW	99	King Air B200	BB-1688	Air Hobbs LLC. Paradise Valley, Az.	
☐ N42PC	74	King Air E90	LW-85	Krohn Aviation LLC, Springfield Oh.	N20RF
☐ N42QB	84	PA-42 Cheyenne 400LS	5527015	Kladstrup-Wetzel Associates Ltd. Engelwood, Co.	ZK-RUR
☐ N42SQ	96	King Air B200	BB-1550	Aurora Aviation Inc. Waco, Tx.	N42SC
☐ N42Z	76	King Air C-12C	BC-28	Dynamic AvLease Inc. Bridgewater, Va.	N213UV
☐ N43AJ	77	King Air 200	BB-243	American Aviation Inc Brooksville Fl.	N300US
☐ N43BG	94	King Air 350	FL-117	Boyd Central Region Inc. Memphis, Tn.	N1553V
☐ N43CB	74	SA-226T Merlin 3	T-246	Bahamas Red Bird Inc. North Miami, Fl.	N43FG
☐ N43GT	78	Conquest II	441-0043	Physicians Aviation Inc. Wichita, Ks.	N445AE
☐ N43JT	67	King Air A90	LJ-286	Alexander Consutling Services Inc. Griffin, Ga.	(N67PT)
☐ N43KM	93	King Air C90B	LJ-1345	KenMor Properties LLC/Kenmor Aviation LLC., Desdemona, Tx.	VH-ZGQ
☐ N43MB	69	King Air B90	LJ-463	Abrotec GmbH. Magdeburg, Germany.	(N300A)
☐ N43MN	05	PA-46-500TP Meridian	4697205	Wells Fargo Bank NW NA., Salt Lake City, Ut.	
☐ N43PC	78	King Air E90	LW-253	N43PC LLC/Goodman Packaging Equipment, Waukegan, Il.	N709DB
☐ N43TA	92	King Air B200	BB-1432	Banyan Aircraft Sales LLC, Fort Lauderdale Fl.	N8037J
☐ N43TL	97	King Air B200	BB-1582	T-L Irrigation Co. Hastings, Ne.	N1130R
☐ N43VM	00	PA-46-500TP Meridian	4697005	Borealis Investments, Washington, DC.	
☐ N43WA	70	King Air B90	LJ-501	Todd Robinson, Tumwater, Wa.	N865MA
☐ N43WH	81	PA-31T Cheyenne II	8120068	Big Timber Ltd. Clovis, NM.	D-IJOE
☐ N43WS	72	King Air E90	LW-16	Colemill Enterprises Inc. Nashville, Tn.	N80NC
☐ N44AX	80	MU-2 Solitaire	416SA	Downs Aircraft Inc. Wilmington, De.	(N613CF)
☐ N44DT	78	PA-31T Cheyenne II	7820043	Enchantment Aviation Inc. Elephant Butte, NM.	(N82267)
☐ N44GK	78	King Air E90	LW-298	Seven Bar Flying Service Inc. Albuquerque, NM.	(N118SB)
☐ N44GP	89	King Air C90A	LJ-1208	Capital Holdings 183 LLC., Sebring, Fl.	N427RB
☐ N44HP	77	King Air C90	LJ-702	Belk Farms, Bermuda Dunes, Ca.	
☐ N44HT	79	PA-31T Cheyenne II	7920061	Billings Flying Service Inc., Billings, Mt.	N117FN
☐ N44KA	00	King Air B200	BB-1711	No Free Lunch LLC, Marshall Mn.	N606TA
☐ N44KS	86	SAAB 340A	050	JMJ Flight Services,	N340SA
☐ N44KT	76	King Air 200	BB-154	Orval Yarger, Normal, Il.	N44KA
☐ N44KU	74	Mitsubishi MU-2J	647	Bankair Inc. West Columbia, SC.	(N110SS)
☐ N44MR	81	King Air 200C	BL-27	Delta Life Insurance Co. Thomasville, Ga.	N3827Z
☐ N44MV	74	King Air E90	LW-107	CDD LLC. Gold Beach, Or.	N96TB
☐ N44MX	81	MU-2 Marquise	1526SA	Agri-Systems, Billings, Mt.	N44MM
☐ N44NC	77	Rockwell 690B	11387	Abaco LLC. Nashville, Tn.	(N790CB)
☐ N44NL	94	King Air B200	BB-1492	Pronto Enterprises Trust, Pittsburgh, Pa.	
☐ N44PA	81	King Air F90	LA-149	Sassafras Aviation LLC. Knoxville, Tn.	(N10DR)
☐ N44RG	68	King Air B90	LJ-417	Southern Stars Aviation LLC. Montgomery, Al.	N29TC
☐ N44U	80	King Air 200T	BT-14	Dynamic AvLease Inc. Bridgewater, Va.	JA8818
☐ N44UF	75	King Air 200	BB-36	Maxair Inc. Appleton, Wi.	N816RB
☐ N44US	75	King Air 200	BB-56	Eagle Creek Aviation Services Inc. Indianapolis, In.	N55BN
☐ N44VR	80	MU-2 Solitaire	432SA	SamaritanAir Inc. Anchorage, Ak.	N15WF
☐ N45A	77	King Air C-12C	BC-48	Dynamic Aviation Group Inc. Bridgewater, Va.	77-22937
☐ N45AR	92	Beech 1900D	UE-12	CSC Applied Technologies LLC. West Palm Beach, Fl.	N138MA
☐ N45AZ	77	Rockwell 690B	11383	State of Arizona, Phoenix, Az.	YV-149CP
☐ N45E	80	King Air 200T	BT-13	Dynamic AvLease Inc. Bridgewater, Va. (was BB-609).	JA8817
☐ N45FF	05	PA-46-500TP Meridian	4697241	Crystal Clear Aviation LLC. Clearwater, Fl.	
☐ N45FL	94	2000A Starship	NC-45	Renaissance Enegy LLC. Tulsa, Ok.	N8215Q
☐ N45LU	76	King Air B100	BE-8	Creo Capital Partners, Pacific Palisades, Ca.	N688DS
☐ N45MW	82	SA-227AT Merlin 4C	AT-452	Crescent Equipment LLC. Wilmington, De.	N3010Q
☐ N45N	80	King Air 200T	BT-15	Dynamic AvLease Inc. Bridgewater, Va. (was BB-647).	N41R
☐ N45PJ	01	PA-46-500TP Meridian	4697031	Billings Flying Service Inc., Billings, Mt.	
☐ N45PM	00	Pilatus PC-12/45	367	Time Tool Inc. Hillsboro, Or.	HB-FSR
☐ N45PR	66	King Air A90	LJ-145	Al's Aerial Spraying, Ovid, Mi.	N89991
☐ N45RF	85	Gulfstream 1000	96089	U S Dept of Commerce/NOAA, MacDill AFB. Fl.	N7912
☐ N45RL	72	King Air C90	LJ-565	Aviapana SA. Panama City, Panama.	N711MP
☐ N45RR	05	King Air B200	BB-1909	American Golden Pt/Great American Capital, Agoura Hills, Ca.	N909RA
☐ N45SA	80	King Air C90	LJ-903	SAF Ltd/Safari Aviation, Lihue, Hi.	N1UM
☐ N45SQ	00	King Air B200	BB-1719	N37XX LLC, Oxnard Ca.	N45RR
☐ N46AE	99	King Air C90B	LJ-1582	Stafford Development Company, Charlotte, NC.	
☐ N46AK	79	MU-2 Marquise	754SA	EPPS Air Service Inc. Atlanta, Ga.	XB-FBY
☐ N46AR	92	Beech 1900D	UE-27	CSC Applied Technologies LLC. West Palm Beach, Fl.	
☐ N46AX	67	King Air A90	LJ-317	Golden Valley Aviation, Clinton, Mo.	N46A
☐ N46BM	76	King Air E90	LW-198	Sherbourne Aviation Inc.	G-WELL

Reg	Yr	Type	c/n	Owner/Operator	Prev Regn
☐ N46BR	81	King Air 200	BB-852	South Coast Lumber Co. Brookings, Or.	
☐ N46CE	89	King Air B200	BB-1349	Century Equipment Co Inc.. Salt Lake City, Ut.	D-IBFS
☐ N46FD	85	PA-42 Cheyenne 400LS	5527027	Zibby Flight Service LLC., St. George, Ut.	HP-1341
☐ N46HL	84	PA-42 Cheyenne 400LS	5527017	Metro Corp/Peregrine Air Charters LLC, Philadelphia, Pa.	N410TW
☐ N46JX	82	King Air F90	LA-171	Alyair LLC. Terrell, Tx.	N46JW
☐ N46KC	80	SA-226T Merlin 3B	T-332	BBEG Ltd./First Merlin Corporation, Midland, Tx.	(N46KM)
☐ N46L	77	King Air C-12C	BC-56	Dynamic Aviation Group Inc. Bridgewater, Va.	N771AK
☐ N46ME	05	PA-46-500TP Meridian	4697207	Eugene Pope, Sammamish, Wa.	
☐ N46MJ	07	King Air C90GT	LJ-1860	Hawker Beechcraft Corporation,Wichita,Ks.	
☐ N46NA	70	SA-226T Merlin 3	T-206	Avtrend Inc. Miami, Fl.	N11RM
☐ N46PL	01	PA-46-500TP Meridian	4697054	Avco Leasing Inc. Wilmington, De.	D-FKAI
☐ N46PV	01	PA-46-500TP Meridian	4697046	Flying Machines LLC. Seattle, Wa.	
☐ N46RP	76	King Air E90	LW-193	Branch Leasing LLC. Paris, Tn.	(N6410X)
☐ N46SA	73	SA-226T Merlin 3	T-231	Automation Support Inc., Midlothian, Tx.	N20QN
☐ N46WE	02	PA-46-500TP Meridian	4697134	Piper Aircraft Corp. Vero Beach, Fl.	
☐ N46WK	01	PA-46-500TP Meridian	4697090	Skypark Holding Inc., Wilmington, De.	SE-LTM
☐ N46X	77	King Air C-12C	BC-47	Dynamic Aviation Group Inc. Bridgewater, Va.	N103BN
☐ N47AW	75	King Air E90	LW-130	M&V Airplane LLC. Roswell, NM.	N75KC
☐ N47BH	78	King Air E90	LW-275	Trans Services Inc. NYC.	N4725M
☐ N47CA	79	PA-31T Cheyenne II	7920043	Westlog Inc./CAL-ORE Life Flight, Brookings, Or.	
☐ N47DG	82	King Air B200	BB-1040	Auro King Air LLC. Greenville, SC.	N27LJ
☐ N47EP	79	Rockwell 690B	11520	Rum Bum Distributors Inc., Miami, Fl.	(N471HP)
☐ N47GW	81	PA-31T Cheyenne 1	8104030	T-210 Holdings LLC., Dover, De.	N917F
☐ N47HM	67	680V Turbo Commander	1691-70	Cochise Community College, Douglas, Az.	N4585E
☐ N47JF	80	PA-31T Cheyenne II	8020031	Minnetrista Corp. Muncie, In.	N102AR
☐ N47JR	80	Conquest II	441-0160	Rusk Cattle Co. Austin, Tx.	D-IAAV
☐ N47RM	03	King Air B200	BB-1820	V A Resources LLC. Casper, Wy.	N6020Z
☐ N47SW	83	King Air C90-1	LJ-1057	Interstate Mechanical Corp. Phoenix, Az.	N424TV
☐ N47TE	81	King Air F90	LA-96	European Investments Leasing LLC. Hialeah, Fl.	D-IXIE
☐ N47TT	80	Gulfstream 840	11600	Leslie Farming, Miles City, Mt.	N840RC
☐ N48A	73	King Air C-12C	BC-12	K & K Aircraft Inc. Bridgewater, Va.	(N9TW)
☐ N48AM	84	PA-31T Cheyenne 1A	1104013	New Braunfels Aviation Inc. New Braunfels, Tx.	N65EZ
☐ N48BA	81	Gulfstream 840	11665	Pioneer Health Services of Simpson, Magee Ms.	D-IWKW
☐ N48BS	80	Conquest II	441-0125	The Brothers Signal Co. Leesburg, Va.	N375K
☐ N48CS	86	King Air B200	BB-1247	General Equipment & Manufacturing Co. Louisville, Ky.	N392DF
☐ N48GA	06	Pilatus PC-12/47	780	Grafe Auction Co., Spring Valley, Mn.	HB-FQC
☐ N48NP	81	MU-2 Solitaire	447SA	Niles Chemical Paint Co. Niles, Mi.	(N348CP)
☐ N48PA	82	King Air B200	BB-996	Pollard Aircraft Sales Inc., Southlake, Tx.	N247JM
☐ N48PG	97	Pilatus PC-12/45	191	Devnick LLC. Oklahoma City, Ok.	(N242PM)
☐ N48RA	78	PA-42 Cheyenne III	7801004	David Whitt, Texarkana, Tx.	XA-RLW
☐ N48TA	78	King Air E90	LW-283	Tidewater Aero LLC & Stanton Aviation LLC. Norfolk, Va.	N845MC
☐ N48VZ	77	King Air E90	LW-221	Vane-Zane LLC/Precision Jet Service Inc. Stuart, Fl.	N429DW
☐ N48W	78	King Air E90	LW-254	Platina Investment Corp. Wiley Post, Ok.	N22654
☐ N48XP	66	King Air 90	LJ-109	K & K Aircraft Inc. Bridgewater, Va.	N48N
☐ N49AC	80	PA-31T Cheyenne 1	8004021	James Cook III & Jana Cook, Panama City, Fl.	N2317V
☐ N49B	81	PA-31T Cheyenne II	8120055	Grimans Air LLC. Wilmington, De.	N19BG
☐ N49CH	79	King Air F90	LA-2	Quality Lease Air Services LLC., El Campo, Tx.	N58AB
☐ N49CL	99	King Air 350	FL-268	The Jones Co. Waycross, Ga.	
☐ N49E	78	King Air B100	BE-47	Southern Homes Rentals/McCoy Leasing LLC., Chattanooga, Tn.	N4996M
☐ N49GM	83	Conquest 1	425-0165	Hans Kuen GmbH. Hard, Austria.	D-IRGW
☐ N49GN	68	King Air B90	LJ-381	Gemair Inc., Fort Lauderdale, Fl.	N48A
☐ N49H	80	SA-226T Merlin 3B	T-310	Howell Instruments Inc. Fort Worth, Tx.	N400FF
☐ N49JG	81	King Air B200	BB-884	James Taylor, Albany, Ga.	C-FLOR
☐ N49K	76	King Air C-12C	BD-26	Dynamic Aviation Group Inc. Bridgewater, Va.	76-0169
☐ N49KC	78	King Air 200	BB-318	Beech Transportation Inc/Aviation Charter, Eden Prairie, Mn.	
☐ N49LG	05	PA-46-500TP Meridian	4697212	Schloenleben Aero Inc. St Marys, Oh.	N812MA
☐ N49LM	96	Pilatus PC-12	163	M L Morse LLC/Mikalix Aviation Group, Great Falls, Va.	HB-FRY
☐ N49NM	93	PA-31T Cheyenne II	7520006	IVO Inc. Ontario, Or.	N19NM
☐ N49PH	80	King Air F90	LA-33	King Aero LLC. Santa Rosa, Ca.	N90FL
☐ N49R	73	King Air C-12C	BD-2	Dynamic Aviation Group Inc. Bridgewater, Va.	N390SA
☐ N49SK	82	King Air B200	BB-1090	J & B Wood Enterprises LLC. Wilmington, De.	N54SK
☐ N49WC	96	King Air 350	FL-144	West Coast Charters LLC. Santa Ana, Ca.	N397S
☐ N50AJ	79	King Air 200	BB-434	Communications International Inc., Vero Beach, Fl.	N68AA
☐ N50AW	81	King Air F90	LA-142	Thoroughbred Aviation Ltd. Newark, De.	N1815T
☐ N50DX	74	Rockwell 690A	11227	Christopher Zupsic, Clovis, Or.	N131JN

Reg	Yr	Type	c/n	Owner/Operator	Prev Regn
☐ N50EB	75	King Air E90	LW-128	FNB Investments LLC/Fly N Buy Aircraft Sales, Mesa, Az.	N1CB
☐ N50ET	73	Mitsubishi MU-2K	260	Eumundi Trading Co., Aiken, SC.	N444FF
☐ N50K	74	Mitsubishi MU-2K	305	Astrid Contract Technical Services, New Ellenton, SC.	N465MA
☐ N50KG	82	King Air B200	BB-1066	Kenco Group, Chattanooga, Tn.	N356WG
☐ N50LG	80	SA-226T Merlin 3B	T-315	WildAir LLC/WildLands Inc. Rocklin, Ca.	N315DB
☐ N50MF	82	Conquest II	441-0262	CS Systems Inc. Irvine, Ca.	N489WC
☐ N50MT	79	SA-226T Merlin 3B	T-308	Corporate Air LLC. Madison, Wi.	N900TX
☐ N50NA	95	King Air B200	BB-1504	Stratix Corp. Norcross, Ga.	N60383
☐ N50PD	04	King Air C90B	LJ-1704	Pee Dee Electricom Inc. Darlington, SC.	N794P
☐ N50ST	91	TBM 700	20	J & H Equipment Leasing LLC. Anthony, NM.	N95BM
☐ N50VM	06	King Air B200	BB-1964	N50VM Inc., Puerto Nuevo, Pr.	
☐ N50VP	88	King Air C90A	LJ-1225	Comm-Craft Inc. Winfield, La.	N44GP
☐ N50WG	01	P-180 Avanti	1050	Crossbow 50 LLC. Carlsbad, Ca.	N134PA
☐ N51CT	06	King Air C90GT	LJ-1780	Chapter 2 Leasing LLC. Brentwood, Tn.	N6180P
☐ N51DM	82	Gulfstream 1000	96014	Donald & E L Mashburn, Oklahoma City, Ok.	N9934S
☐ N51DN	72	King Air E90	LW-7	D-W Corp. Des Moines, Ia.	N51SG
☐ N51EE	80	King Air 200	BB-674	Desert Aviation LLC., Kingman, Az.	N851MK
☐ N51JK	81	PA-31T Cheyenne II	8120025	Blue Sky Aviation LLC. St Croix, VI.	D-ICPA
☐ N51KC	80	PA-42 Cheyenne III	8001001	S A Comunale Co. Barbertown, Oh.	C-FWCC
☐ N51RM	80	PA-31T Cheyenne 1	8004054	Carlos Cordoba/Carlos Pastrana Trust, Houston, Tx.	N176CS
☐ N51WF	81	Gulfstream 840	11684	MBH Services Ltd. Southend, UK.	N5936K
☐ N51WN	94	Pilatus PC-12	104	Priority Aircraft Exchange LLC, Harrisonburg, Va.	N5WN
☐ N52BG	04	King Air C90B	LJ-1732	Mason Building Group/Blue Gander LLC. Newark, De.	N501P
☐ N52C	85	King Air 300	FA-40	Eagle Support Corporation, Doral Fl.	N1MC
☐ N52CD	69	Mitsubishi MU-2F	174	Hayes Landing LLC. Edenton, NC.	C-FCCD
☐ N52EL	67	King Air A90	LJ-204	Allied Signal Corp. Fort Lauderdale, Fl.	N165U
☐ N52GP	81	King Air 200	BB-766	N52GP-05 LLC. Birmingham, Al.	N510H
☐ N52HL	80	PA-31T Cheyenne 1	8004023	JH Leasing Inc. Wilmington, De.	N4QG
☐ N52KA	73	King Air E90	LW-42	Kenneth Rogers, Oklahoma City, Ok.	
☐ N52LP	84	King Air 300	FA-8	Line Power Manufacturing Co. Bristol, Va..	N826MA
☐ N52MA	80	MU-2 Solitaire	419SA	James Paige Jr. Port Orange, Fl.	N322GB
☐ N52NK	06	Pilatus PC-12/47	737	Maxamillion LLC. Delray Beach, Fl.	HB-FRV
☐ N52PF	79	PA-31T Cheyenne 1	7904023	Papa Fox LLC. Yuma, Az.	N52PC
☐ N52PY	74	Rockwell 690A	11196	Economy Transport Inc. Central Point, Or.	N52PB
☐ N52SF	75	King Air 200	BB-106	SAK Aviation Inc. Pittsburgh, Pa.	N383AS
☐ N52SZ	99	King Air B200	BB-1686	Sheetz Aviation Inc. Altoona, Pa.	
☐ N52TT	79	PA-31T Cheyenne II	7920057	Minuteman Aviation Inc. Missoula, Mt.	N102E
☐ N52WM	78	Mitsubishi MU-2P	385SA	EM Transport LLC/Employers Mutual Inc. Stuart, Fl.	N808PK
☐ N53AM	79	PA-31T Cheyenne II	7920037	Collen Clark, Dallas, Tx.	N610MW
☐ N53CE	76	King Air E90	LW-160	Engineering & Manufacturing Services Inc. Huntsville, Al.	N251SR
☐ N53DA	82	SA-227TT Merlin 3C	TT-438	Nimbus Corp. Shaw Island, Wa.	(N312ST)
☐ N53EC	72	King Air C90	LJ-552	Leo Naeger, Fair Oaks Ranch, Tx.	VH-WNT
☐ N53GA	85	King Air B200	BB-1201	Selge Leasing Inc./Selge Construction Co. Niles, Mi.	D-IMMM
☐ N53KA	81	King Air B200	BB-880	Red Barn Farms LLC. Sanford, Fl.	YV-1006CP
☐ N53KB	05	PA-46-500TP Meridian	4697231	GT Leasing LLC., Coconut Grove, Fl.	
☐ N53MD	71	King Air 100	B-86	Lynch Flying Service Inc. Logan Field, Mt.	N500Y
☐ N53PK	01	PA-46-500TP Meridian	4697093	One Charlie Victor Ltd., Cincinnati, Oh.	N249C
☐ N53SP	80	King Air 200	BB-576	Gibbs Test Flight Services LLC. Houston, Tx.	N802CA
☐ N53TA	78	PA-31T Cheyenne II	7820083	Indiana Paging Network Inc. Michigan City, In.	N53TM
☐ N53TD	78	King Air B100	BE-53	Howe Nice Inc. Bozeman, Mt.	N2037C
☐ N53TJ	89	King Air C90A	LJ-1209	K K S Aviation Inc/Sky Trek Aviation, Modesto, Ca.	N3030C
☐ N53TM	97	King Air 350	FL-165	Katherine Meredith, Des Moines, Ia.	(N393CF)
☐ N54AM	97	King Air C90B	LJ-1506	Alice Manufacturing Co. Greenville, SC.	N988P
☐ N54CK	68	Mitsubishi MU-2F	135	Caltherm Corporation, Winfield, Mi.	N66CL
☐ N54EC	71	King Air C90	LJ-526	Seven Lamb LLC./Kilo Alpha Holdings Inc. Hopewell, Va.	ZS-MLO
☐ N54FB	85	King Air B200	BB-1212	Farm Bureau Life Insurance Co. Des Moines, Ia.	N7221Y
☐ N54GA	83	Gulfstream 1000	96066	Air-Glo LLC, Golden Meadow, La.	
☐ N54GP	75	SA-226AT Merlin 4A	AT-034	Milestone Partners Inc. Dover De.	N717CC
☐ N54JW	70	King Air 100	B-60	Dodson Aviation Inc. Ottawa, Ks.	N2FA
☐ N54PC	75	Mitsubishi MU-2M	319	Saxton Leasing Inc. Plymouth, Mi.	N475CA
☐ N54PT	80	King Air E90	LW-331	PT Pope Ranch Inc. Portland, Or.	RP-C319
☐ N54TK	80	King Air 200	BB-686	Shamrock Equipment Co./United Fuel & Energy, Midland, Tx.	N3663M
☐ N54UM	80	Gulfstream 980	95025	Trust Aviation Inc. Miami, Fl.	N9779S
☐ N54US	81	King Air B100	BE-122	HR Developers LLC. Columbia, SC.	N74RR
☐ N54WW	67	King Air A90	LJ-209	Concrete Structures of the Midwest, Chicago, Il.	N90BE

Reg	Yr	Type	c/n	Owner/Operator	Prev Regn
☐ N54YC	90	King Air 300	FA-212	AirColor LLC. Wilmington, De.	N5070W
☐ N55AC	81	Conquest 1	425-0020	King Aviation Dallas Inc., Addison, Tx.	N200MT
☐ N55BK	96	Pilatus PC-12/45	160	JK Moving & Storage Inc. Sterling, Va.	N160PC
☐ N55FY	67	King Air A90	LJ-194	Dodson International Parts Inc. Rantoul, Ks.	N55FW
☐ N55GD	78	PA-31 Cheyenne II	7820003	Pro Air LLC. Manhattan, Ks.	N547TA
☐ N55HC	75	King Air E90	LW-134	NEQ Air LLC. Baytown, Tx.	N663LS
☐ N55JP	80	PA-31 Cheyenne 1	8004048	Dakota Aircraft Inc. Pierre, SD.	N169DC
☐ N55KW	81	PA-31 Cheyenne II	8120007	WTM Transport Management BV. Amstelveen, Holland.	N2369X
☐ N55MG	68	King Air B90	LJ-391	T & T Delaware Aviation LLC. Wilmington, De.	N22JJ
☐ N55MN	85	King Air C90	LJ-974	State of Minnesota DoT, St Paul, Mn.	N555RA
☐ N55MP	99	King Air B200	BB-1679	Maxon Corp. Muncie, In.	
☐ N55PC	84	King Air B200	BB-1170	Center for Toxicology & Environmental Health, Little Rock.	N6930P
☐ N55R	76	PA-31 Cheyenne II	7620055	Grani Installation Inc. Las Vegas, Nv.	N85KA
☐ N55SR	79	King Air 200	BB-445	ENS Aviation LLC/Smith Energy Corp. Marshall, Tx.	(N790NA)
☐ N55WF	85	King Air C90A	LJ-1114	Perry Park Investments Inc. Larkspur, Co.	N808W
☐ N55WJ	77	Rockwell 690B	11427	Kingdom Management Group, Thomasville, Ga.	N46802
☐ N55ZG	01	PA-46-500TP Meridian	4697082	Upper Cumberland Aircraft Services Inc. Cookeville, Tn.	N262TL
☐ N56AY	95	King Air B200	BB-1511	A Y McDonald Industries Inc. Dubuque, Ia.	N507EF
☐ N56CC	77	King Air 200	BB-189	AGEV Air Inc. Lafayette, La.	N392K
☐ N56CD	75	King Air 200	BB-64	Commander Inc. Lyon, Ms.	N608DK
☐ N56DL	77	King Air C90	LJ-732	Vintage Air II LLC/TVPX Inc. Concord, Ma.	N473LP
☐ N56EZ	03	Pilatus PC-12/45	488	Sierra Nevada Corp., Sparks, Nv.	(SP-KEZ)
☐ N56HT	77	King Air E90	LW-215	Mark Seaman, San Antonio, Tx.	I-MCCC
☐ N56KA	85	King Air 200	BB-763	Vigil Aviation LLC. Concord, NC.	N50PM
☐ N56RJ	06	Pilatus PC-12/47	758	Flying Fish Aviation LLC. San Francisco, Ca.	HB-FSM
☐ N56RT	81	King Air 200	BB-817	Rust Family LLC. Albuquerque, NM.	
☐ N56WF	91	TBM 700	8	Doc Savage Enterprises Inc. Springboro Oh.	JA8892
☐ N57AG	68	King Air B90	LJ-343	Batenfield Air LLC, Dover De.	N880X
☐ N57EG	74	Rockwell 690A	11178	Joe Walraven/Eagle Construction & Environment, Eastland, Tx.	N57EC
☐ N57EM	67	King Air A90	LJ-295	Trim-Aire Aviation Inc. Mexia, Tx.	N57FM
☐ N57FT	76	King Air 200	BB-136	Sandpoint Aviation LLC. San Antonio, Tx.	N277JB
☐ N57GA	79	King Air 200	BB-477	G & A Aviation LLC. Greenwood, SC.	F-GILB
☐ N57HQ	92	TBM 700	90	B H Sports Marketing & Aviation Inc. Bear, De.	N57HC
☐ N57KC	83	Cheyenne II-XL	8166076	KC Leasing LLC/Micro Industries Inc. Salt Lake City, Ut.	N516S
☐ N57KE	91	King Air 350	FL-61	Eberl's Management LLC. Lakewood, Co.	N350CS
☐ N57LT	02	Pilatus PC-12/45	474	Lexington Turbo LLC. Lexington, Ma.	HB-FQE
☐ N57MA	68	King Air B90	LJ-414	Thomas Howell Kiewit (USA) Inc. Miami, Fl.	C-GVCC
☐ N57RS	74	Rockwell 690A	11149	International Steel & Tube SA. Santo Domingo, D R.	N5KW
☐ N57SC	90	King Air 350	FL-34	HRB Systems Inc. State College, Pa.	N987HT
☐ N57SL	92	TBM 700	57	U S Financial Services Inc. Wilmington, De.	
☐ N57TM	80	King Air F90	LA-34	A T T Aviation Inc. Lafayette, La.	N43WS
☐ N57TX	98	King Air 350	FL-225	Carl E Gungoll Exploration LLC., Oklahoma City, Ok.	N57TS
☐ N57VA	96	King Air 350	FL-154	FAMSA Inc., Santa Fe Springs, Ca.	N160AR
☐ N57WR	02	King Air C90B	LJ-1678	Blue Sky Airways Inc. Dallas, Ga.	N53PB
☐ N58AC	65	King Air 90	LJ-77	Sunny South Inc. Gainesville, Fl.	N56SQ
☐ N58AM	84	PA-31 Cheyenne 1A	1104005	Air Medical Ltd, New Braunfels, Tx.	N2427W
☐ N58BT	07	PA-46-500TP Meridian	4697289	San B Air Ltd., Wilmington, De.	N760C
☐ N58CA	69	Mitsubishi MU-2F	170	F J Grieser Co. Miami, Fl.	N239MA
☐ N58ES	84	King Air 300	FA-17	Forest Hill Management LLC. Forest Hill, Md.	N71FA
☐ N58GA	82	King Air B200	BB-1003	Pollard Aircraft Sales Inc., Southlake, Tx.	I-MEPE
☐ N58GG	04	King Air C90B	LJ-1728	Wilks Masonry Corp/Frac Tech Services LLC. Cisco, Tx.	N6028Y
☐ N58HP	00	TBM 700B	170	Hartzell Propeller Inc. Piqua, Oh.	
☐ N58KA	65	King Air 90	LJ-58	Leonard Sallustro, Throgg Station, NY.	C-GXHD
☐ N58PL	81	Cheyenne II-XL	8166024	Exec Air Montana Inc. Helena, Mt.	N2586Y
☐ N58VS	00	Pilatus PC-12/45	341	DMH Inc. Forest Grove, Or.	HB-FRW
☐ N59EK	80	King Air F90	LA-58	Jet Enterprises Inc., Macon, Ga.	N67TM
☐ N59EZ	81	SA-226T Merlin 3B	T-394	Financial Southern Corp. Wilmington, De.	N1QL
☐ N59GG	05	King Air C90B	LJ-1734	Glasdon Group Ltd. Blackpool, UK.	N36634
☐ N59KA	73	King Air C90	LJ-589	American Furniture Inc. Albuquerque, NM.	
☐ N59KS	75	Mitsubishi MU-2L	664	O'Connell Meares Investments Ltd. Tampa, Fl.	N555BC
☐ N59MS	95	King Air C90B	LJ-1405	Snijder Air Service Inc. Antwerp, Belgium.	
☐ N59RT	79	Conquest II	441-0111	WFBNW NA. Salt Lake City, Ut. (trustor ?).	N462AC
☐ N59RW	73	Mitsubishi MU-2K	267	D O Aviation Inc. Indianapolis, In.	N313MA
☐ N59WF	01	PA-46-500TP Meridian	4697042	Klotz Aviation LLC, Holcomb Ks.	
☐ N60AR	00	King Air B200	BB-1743	MRJJ Aviation LLC/Norwich Ventures Wyomissing Pa.	N4443V

Reg	Yr Type	c/n	Owner/Operator	Prev Regn
N60BA	74 King Air E90	LW-79	Bemidji Aviation Services Inc. Bemidji, Mn.	N12AK
N60BM	74 Rockwell 690A	11172	GetMapping Plc., Hartley Wintney, Hants, UK.	(D-IIGI)
N60CM	96 King Air 350	FL-139	Mewbourne Oil Co. Tyler, Tx.	
N60DB	77 Rockwell 690B	11420	CSC Trust Company of Delaware, Wilmington, De.	N813AW
N60DL	05 King Air 350	FL-446	Adams Homes of NW Florida Inc. Gulf Breeze, Fl.	N37246
N60FL	81 MU-2 Marquise	1512SA	Flight Line Inc. Denver, Co.	HB-LQB
N60HT	68 King Air B90	LJ-358	King Aire Inc. Charleston, WV.	N61HT
N60JW	80 PA-31T Cheyenne 1	8004031	Cortez Aviation LLC. Las Vegas, Nv.	N2349V
N60KA	73 King Air C90	LJ-586	Biscayne Capital LLC, Wilmington De.	
N60KC	80 MU-2 Marquise	781SA	Keller Companies Inc. Manchester, NH.	N7045X
N60KV	79 PA-31T Cheyenne 1	7904032	Concept Management Corp. Inman, SC.	(N188EC)
N60KW	78 King Air C90	LJ-800	Robert James, Fallbrook, Ca.	N2032N
N60MH	78 King Air E90	LW-290	Commercial Aviation Services Inc. Miami, Fl.	N79NS
N60NH	80 SA-226T Merlin 3B	T-309	Orion Air LLC, Sacramento Ca.	N999MM
N60PD	75 King Air 200	BB-58	CWW Inc. Englewood, Co.	N60PC
N60SM	75 King Air 200	BB-50	SSTKA LLC. Gulfport, Ms.	N888TR
N60TJ	77 King Air B100	BE-21	ARK Leasing Inc. Newport Beach, Ca.	N17821
N60VP	97 King Air C90B	LJ-1516	SmytheAir LLC. Newburgh, In.	
N60WC	93 King Air 350	FL-96	West Coast Charters LLC. Santa Ana, Ca.	N19GD
N60YP	00 King Air 350	FL-304	Yates Petroleum Corp. Artesia, NM.	N44866
N61AP	84 King Air B200	BB-1192	James McMahan, Van Nuys, Ca.	N6743D
N61BA	78 Mitsubishi MU-2N	729SA	B & H Air LLC. Victoria, Tx.	C-FHXZ
N61GJ	79 MU-2 Solitaire	398SA	Craig Sjoberg & Assocs Inc. Pleasanton, Ca.	N61DP
N61GN	95 King Air C90B	LJ-1421	AIS Construction Equipt/Michigan Corp Svs, Grand Rapids,Mt.	N3252B
N61GT	01 P-180 Avanti	1051	IGT-International Game Technology, Reno, Nv.	N129PA
N61JB	80 MU-2 Solitaire	417SA	Pro Flight LLC. Greenville, SC.	N29JS
N61KA	89 King Air 300LW	FA-200	SDT Leasing LLC. The Woodlands, Tx.	OY-CCZ
N61Q	66 King Air A90	LM-92	Dynamic Aviation Group Inc. Bridgewater, Va.	N7123C
N61SB	63 Gulfstream 1	115	Apex Aviation Group Inc. Southlake, Tx.	C-FASC
N61TS	78 Rockwell 690B	11510	Courr-Torr Inc. Wilmington, De.	N1JG
N62AZ	05 King Air 350	FL-453	DC Interests LLC/Geneva Holdings LLC. Phoenix, Az.	N36953
N62CN	81 MU-2 Solitaire	436SA	Air 1st Aviation Companies Inc. Aiken, SC.	D-ISTC
N62DL	77 King Air 200	BB-208	ZMM Services LLC. Tampa, Fl.	N188WG
N62E	80 PA-31T Cheyenne II	8020074	Star Air LLC/AGT Enterprises Inc. Prairie du Chien, Wi.	(N47DR)
N62FB	94 King Air B200	BB-1482	Texas Farm Bureau Building Corp. Waco, Tx.	N77CX
N62GA	99 Pilatus PC-12/45	259	Guardian Air/Flagstaff Medical Centre, Flagstaff, Az.	N259WA
N62LM	92 TBM 700	67	Primus Leasing Corp. Wilmington, De.	
N62LT	01 PA-46-500TP Meridian	4697027	Dana Hunter, Lake Havasu City, Az.	
N62V	67 King Air A90	LM-74	Dynamic Aviation Group Inc. Bridgewater, Va.	N7087U
N62WC	89 King Air B200	BB-1326	West Coast Charters LLC. Santa Ana, Ca.	N38LA
N62WM	04 PA-46-500TP Meridian	4697177	H & M Bay Inc. Federalsburg, Md.	
N63BV	78 King Air E90	LW-256	Mayo Aviation Inc. Englewood, Co.	N63BW
N63CA	78 PA-31T Cheyenne II	7820033	Speciality Industries, Red Lion, Pa.	OO-DGS
N63CM	80 PA-31T Cheyenne II	8020039	Cheyenne Transportation LLC. Boise, Id.	N2584W
N63DL	07 TBM 850	409	Larry Lehmkuhl, Naples, Fl.	N850EE
N63DU	08 Gulfstream 840	11601	Green Aircraft Leasing Inc/Green Chevrolet Hummer,Peoria,Il.	N63DL
N63LB	04 King Air B200	BB-1894	Lee Beverage Co. Oshkosh, Wi.	N6194X
N63SE	07 PA-46-500TP Meridian	4697333	Piper Aircraft Inc. Vero Beach, Fl.	
N63SK	80 King Air 200	BB-747	IED-Innovative Electronic Designs, Louisville, Ky.	N117CM
N63TP	97 TBM 700	128	Hot Air LLC. Cambridge, Ma.	N128PC
N64C	66 King Air A90	LM-32	Dynamic Aviation Group Inc. Bridgewater, Va.	N7040V
N64DC	79 King Air 200	BB-492	Pontiac Flight Service Inc. Waterford, Mi.	N200PD
N64FB	00 King Air 350	FL-308	Fremont Bank, Fremont, Ca.	N825TS
N64GG	99 King Air 350	FL-274	Specsavers Aviation Ltd. Guernsey, C.I.	(N350GL)
N64GT	06 King Air C90GT	LJ-1765	Kite Realty Group, Indianapolis, In.	
N64KA	73 King Air C90	LJ-606	St Simons Executive LLC. St Simons Island, Ga.	
N64LG	72 Mitsubishi MU-2K	240	Air 1st Aviation Companies Inc. Aiken, SC.	N222HL
N64MD	82 MU-2 Marquise	1561SA	Marquise Investments LLC. Memphis, Tn.	N486MA
N64PS	81 Gulfstream 840	11702	Peter Schiff, Cookeville, Tn.	N5954K
N64TR	07 King Air 350	FL-544	TR Flight Inc., Lufkin, Tx.	N544KA
N64WF	99 Pilatus PC-12/45	298	DDH Enterprises LLC. Ruidoso, NM.	HB-FQM
N65AF	04 Pilatus PC-12/45	565	Angel Fire Express LLC. Angel Fire, NM.	HB-FSM
N65CL	92 King Air C90B	LJ-1306	Coastal Lumber Co. Weldon, NC.	N422RJ
N65EB	78 King Air 200	BB-325	Clement Aviation Inc. Fort Dodge, Ia.	F-GGAK
N65GP	04 King Air B200	BB-1869	FF Aviation Investments LLC, Ventura Ca.	N5109V

Reg	Yr Type	c/n	Owner/Operator	Prev Regn
N65JA	67 King Air A90	LM-34	JAARS Inc. Waxhaw, NC.	N7042R
N65KA	74 King Air C90	LJ-611	Christie F. Johnson, Zebulon, NC.	
N65KG	81 King Air 200	BB-841	Law Offices of Kevin Glasheen, Lubbock, Tx.	N366EA
N65MS	77 King Air E90	LW-202	Summey Aviation LLC. Asheville, NC.	N934DC
N65MT	80 King Air F90	LA-38	Starship Holdings Inc/Taft-Vineyard Properties, Orlando, Fl.	D-IAGB
N65RT	76 King Air 200	BB-97	Professional Travel Inc. La Porte, In.	N7EG
N65TA	72 King Air C90	LJ-538	Esco Transportation LLC., Brownsville, Tx.	VH-LLS
N65TB	99 Pilatus PC-12/45	263	Dalks Leasing Inc. Wilmington, De.	N329PA
N65TW	81 King Air B200	BB-902	Word Aviation LLC, Austin Tx.	N5TW
N65U	67 King Air A90	LM-87	Dynamic Aviation Group Inc. Bridgewater, Va.	N7112M
N65V	69 King Air A90	LM-113	Dynamic Aviation Group Inc. Bridgewater, Va.	N7156J
N66	87 King Air 300	FF-1	FAA, Oklahoma City, Ok. (was FA-126).	
N66AD	68 King Air B90	LJ-380	Freefall Express Inc. Keene, NH.	C-GHLA
N66BS	80 King Air F90	LA-40	Spitfire Aviation Parts Inc., Concord, NC.	N6748P
N66CK	98 King Air C90B	LJ-1529	Carson & Co. Bon Secour, Al.	
N66CY	72 Mitsubishi MU-2J	562	AJM Airplane Co. Naples, Fl.	N29CY
N66FF	80 MU-2 Solitaire	430SA	Noremak Corporation, Wilmington, De.	N856JC
N66FV	67 680V Turbo Commander	1676-59	Valley International Airport, Harlingen, Tx.	N580M
N66GS	67 King Air A90	LJ-237	Mile-Hi Skydivers Inc. Longmont, Co.	N232A
N66GW	74 Rockwell 690A	11174	Kolob Canyons Air Services Wilmington De.	N6B
N66JC	81 Cheyenne II-XL	8166029	G & T Partners LLC. Gainesville, Ga.	N346JC
N66KA	73 King Air C90	LJ-582	Panthers Inc., Wilmington, De.	
N66LP	80 King Air F90	LA-21	Peterson Farms Inc. Decatur, Il.	
N66MD	69 SA-26AT Merlin 2B	T26-159	Donald Paolucci/Mohican Air Service Inc. Fairview Park, Oh.	N14JK
N66RE	67 King Air A90	LJ-307	Stefan Joseph Leer, Manteca, Ca.	N966CY
N66TG	88 King Air 300	FA-155	Tom Growney Equipment Inc. Albuquerque, NM.	N408C
N66TJ	75 King Air 200	BB-42	Tyler Jet LLC. Tyler, Tx.	N3GY
N66TL	74 King Air C90	LJ-636	Barclays North Inc./Sky Jet IV LLC., Everett, Wa.	N222BJ
N66TW	80 PA-31T Cheyenne 1	8004030	N66TW LLC. Panama City, Fl.	N2347V
N66W	67 King Air A90	LM-68	K & K Aircraft Inc. Bridgewater, Va.	(N73Q)
N67	87 King Air 300	FF-2	FAA, Oklahoma City, Ok. (was FA-129).	
N67B	66 King Air A90	LM-59	Dynamic AvLease Inc. Bridgewater, Va.	N7071N
N67BA	81 Conquest 1	425-0007	Triple H & J LLC, Kenosha Wi.	C-GJEB
N67BS	81 King Air B100	BE-104	Team Health Inc. Knoxville, Tn.	N67KA
N67BW	01 PA-46-500TP Meridian	4697011	Piper Aircraft Inc. Vero Beach, Fl.	
N67CG	79 Rockwell 690B	11540	ESI Inc of Tennessee, Kennesaw, Ga.	N81697
N67CL	87 King Air C90A	LJ-1154	Moree Enterprises Inc. Society Hill, SC.	N3076U
N67CQ	00 King Air C90	LJ-1619	53 PM LLC/Roy Carver, Muscatine, Ia.	N67CC
N67DW	76 PA-31T Cheyenne II	7620041	Donald & Trevor Williams, Haddonfield, NJ.	N27856
N67FE	82 Gulfstream 840	11729	Furnas Electric Co. Sugar Grove, Il.	N5967K
N67GA	76 King Air 200	BB-176	Aviation Advisors International Inc. Sarasota, Fl.	F-GFMJ
N67JE	81 Conquest 1	425-0058	John & Colleen Gerken, Sandpoint, Id.	N67CA
N67K	67 King Air A90	LM-24	Dynamic Aviation Group Inc. Bridgewater, Va.	N7035B
N67PS	74 King Air E90	LW-112	Timberland Aviation Inc. Eufaula, Al.	N3034W
N67V	79 King Air 100	LW-306	Modern Tool Inc. Minneapolis, Mn.	N90SR
N67X	66 King Air A90	LM-14	Dynamic AvLease Inc. Bridgewater, Va.	N70224
N68	87 King Air 300	FF-3	FAA, Oklahoma City, Ok.	
N68AJ	84 King Air C90A	LJ-1071	W Hampton Pitts, Nashville, Tn.	ZS-LOK
N68BJ	79 PA-31T Cheyenne II	7920029	Arrow Leasing Ltd. Norwood, Ma.	TG-VDG
N68CD	68 King Air B90	LJ-366	Pleasure Leasing Ltd Calverton NY.	N66CD
N68CL	81 MU-2 Solitaire	448SA	Robert & Cynthia Peterson Living Trust, Harrodsburg, Ky.	N231LC
N68DA	76 King Air B100	BE-14	Augusta Aviation Inc/Synovus Capital Finance, Murphy, NC.	N86FD
N68DK	80 King Air F90	LA-56	Rogue Aviation LLC. Grants Pass, Or.	N777AQ
N68FA	82 King Air B200	BB-1088	Hoar Construction LLC. Birmingham, Al.	N868HC
N68FB	00 King Air B200	BB-1710	FBL Leasing Services Inc. Des Moines, Ia.	C6-MIP
N68HS	84 Conquest II	441-0331	Hastings Books, Music & Video, Amarillo, Tx.	N1210D
N68MN	00 King Air B200	BB-1704	East Coast Jet Center Inc., Stuart Fl.	N3204W
N68MU	78 King Air 100	BE-37	All Planes Inc. Wilmington, De.	N49SS
N68MY	83 King Air B200	BB-1142	Myco Industries Inc. Artesia, NM.	N23YP
N68PK	99 Pilatus PC-12/45	265	Knight Flight LLC. Wilmington, De.	HB-FSJ
N68RF	07 King Air B300C	FM-21	Hawker Beechcraft Corp., Wichita, Ks.	
N68TD	73 Rockwell 690	11066	Aviation 2000 C.A., La Guaira, Venezuela	N36WR
N68TN	75 Mitsubishi MU-2L	675	Air 1st Aviation Companies Inc, Aiken,SC.	N835MA
N68VH	70 681 Turbo Commander	6007	Forte Management Corp. Cincinnati, Oh.	LV-JOJ
N69	88 King Air 300	FF-4	FAA, Oklahoma City, Ok.	
Reg	Yr Type	c/n	Owner/Operator	Prev Regn

Reg	Yr Type	c/n	Owner/Operator	Prev Regn
☐ N69AD	81 King Air F90	LA-143	Zulu Golf Aviation LLC. Aspen, Co.	N624LF
☐ N69CD	76 King Air 200	BB-156	Glady's Enterprises Inc. El Paso, Tx.	N69LD
☐ N69FG	98 Pilatus PC-12/45	225	R J Aviation Equipment Inc. Wilmington, De.	HB-FQW
☐ N69GA	84 Gulfstream 1000	96071	DS Transportation LLC. Costa Mesa, Ca.	
☐ N69PC	81 PA-42 Cheyenne III	8001023	Cheyenne III Inc. Gainesville, Ga.	N5PF
☐ N69ST	74 SA-226AT Merlin 4A	AT-030	OM Enterprise Inc. Michigan City, In.	N5440F
☐ N70	88 King Air 300	FF-5	FAA, Oklahoma City, Ok.	
☐ N70AJ	77 King Air 200	BB-206	Suburban Properties LLC., Elgin, Il.	(N30AJ)
☐ N70CM	01 King Air C90B	LJ-1670	TPW Aviation LLC. Cedartown, Ga.	N4470K
☐ N70CU	81 King Air B200	BB-888	Corair of Delaware LLC. Louisville, Ky.	N700U
☐ N70FC	73 SA-226T Merlin 3	T-226	Gospel Ministries International, Ooltewah, Tn. (status ?).	N41BA
☐ N70FE	78 King Air C90	LJ-750	Three LZ LLC., Htree LZ LLC., Valparaiso, In.	N10MD
☐ N70GM	82 Conquest 1	425-0108	Yingling Aircraft Inc.,Wichita, Ks.	D-IAAX
☐ N70GW	81 PA-31T Cheyenne 1	8104004	Minion Morgans Inc. Oxford, Mi.	N4WP
☐ N70JL	71 King Air 100	B-87	Southern Air Charter, Nassau, Bahamas.	N125DB
☐ N70KC	80 MU-2 Marquise	775SA	MU2 LLC/McDevitt Trucks Inc. Manchester, NH.	N93GN
☐ N70LG	83 King Air B200C	BL-67	Northwestern Arctic Air Inc. Anchorage, Ak.	TR-LBP
☐ N70LR	02 TBM 700B	225	Caterer's Leasing Inc. Downey, Ca.	I-AESW
☐ N70LT	99 TBM 700B	151	Dreams1 LLC., Mt Sterling, Il.	(N950WA)
☐ N70MD	74 Rockwell 690A	11210	Aero Air LLC. Hillsboro, Or.	N1SS
☐ N70MN	93 King Air B200	BB-1447	State of Minnesota DoT, St Paul, Mn.	N8138V
☐ N70PH	00 TBM 700B	172	Peter Huff, McKinney, Tx.	N700WS
☐ N70RD	79 King Air 200	BB-426	DonteJet II LLC, Snellville, Ga.	N220CB
☐ N70RF	70 681 Turbo Commander	6013	E M Travels & Sales Inc. Opa Locka, Fl.	N60BC
☐ N70TJ	79 PA-31T Cheyenne 1	7904019	Laurel Marketing & Management Group, Venice, Fl.	N506TQ
☐ N70TW	79 PA-31T Cheyenne 1	7904043	Bronco Boring LLC. Center, Tx.	
☐ N70U	68 King Air A90	LM-51	Dynamic AvLease Inc. Bridgewater, Va.	N7063W
☐ N70VM	67 King Air A90	LJ-300	Texas Biz Jet, Fort Worth, Tx.	N222MB
☐ N70VR	01 King Air C90B	LJ-1651	B A Jacobs Flight Services LLC, Winfield Il.	
☐ N71	88 King Air 300	FF-6	FAA, Oklahoma City, Ok.	
☐ N71DP	81 MU-2 Marquise	1502SA	Jaax Flying Service/Marquise Investments LLC. Calexico, Ca.	VH-MVU
☐ N71EE	05 TBM 700C2	343	Lincoln Aviation Inc. Dover, De.	N2UX
☐ N71EN	74 King Air C90	LJ-632	Premier West Bancorp. Medford, Or.	N71FN
☐ N71HE	81 Conquest 1	425-0085	Codding Investments Inc. Santa Rosa, Ca.	N5HE
☐ N71KA	73 King Air C90	LJ-578	David & Catherine Paine, Templeton, Ca.	N84JH
☐ N71MR	83 Gulfstream 1000	96054	Boomerang Financial Corp. Wilmington, De.	N8LB
☐ N71RG	79 King Air 200	BB-443	New Vision Air LLC. Louisville, Ky.	N700Z
☐ N71SE	07 PA-46-500TP Meridian	4697327	Piper Aircraft Inc. Vero Beach, Fl.	
☐ N71TP	00 Pilatus PC-12/45	371	Timesaver LLC., Wilmington, De.	HBFSU
☐ N71VE	72 Rockwell 690	11043	Cooper Aerial Surveys Ltd. Sandtoft, UK.	N71VT
☐ N71VT	80 King Air 200	BB-709	Apple AB Enterprises Inc. Medford, Or.	(N202VT)
☐ N71WB	75 King Air E90	LW-127	Brown Suburu/Panhandle Trinity Equipt., Amarillo, Tx.	N711RQ
☐ N72	88 King Air 300	FF-7	FAA, Oklahoma City, Ok.	
☐ N72DZ	06 Pilatus PC-12/47	777	Zipp Express Inc., Fort Myers, Fl.	HB-FQJ
☐ N72EA	06 Pilatus PC-12/47	736	Sierra Nevada Corp., Sparks, Nv.	HB-FRU
☐ N72GL	91 King Air C90A	LJ-1261	Newmaster Associates SA. Luxembourg.	LX-LLM
☐ N72L	66 King Air A90	LM-19	Dynamic Aviation Group Inc. Bridgewater, Va.	N7031F
☐ N72MM	79 King Air 200	BB-497	Northeastern Aviation Corp. Wilmington, De.	N73CA
☐ N72RE	02 King Air 350	FL-344	Aero Coastal LLC. Newport Beach, Ca.	N5044B
☐ N72RL	79 King Air 200	BB-509	R J Allen Inc. Garden Grove, Ca.	N72DD
☐ N72SE	80 King Air 200	BB-596	Southern Energy Homes Inc. Addison, Al.	N918JN
☐ N72TB	80 Gulfstream 840	11619	WFBNW NA. Salt Lake City, Ut. (trustor ?).	N16TG
☐ N72TG	90 King Air C90A	LJ-1252	D & J Oil Co/Rite-Way Construction Inc. Enid, Ok.	N92CD
☐ N73	88 King Air 300	FF-8	FAA, Oklahoma City, Ok.	
☐ N73BG	80 PA-31T Cheyenne 1	8004027	R W Air Services Inc. Hatfield, Pa.	(N701GP)
☐ N73DW	81 Conquest 1	425-0089	Automotive Consultants Inc. Columbia, SC.	N74JW
☐ N73EF	80 Gulfstream 840	11617	Executive Flight Inc. Pangborn Memorial, Wa.	N840LC
☐ N73HC	69 SA-26AT Merlin 2B	T26-138	Yaw Nix LLC., Shreveport, La.	N52L
☐ N73MA	79 MU-2 Solitaire	414SA	RA Aircraft Management Inc., Kenosha, Wi.	N72TJ
☐ N73MC	73 King Air C90	LJ-600	Silver King LLC. St Simons Island, Ga.	N3PR
☐ N73MH	73 King Air C90	LJ-570	Final Draw LLC. Lookout Mountain, Tn.	N240RE
☐ N73PG	00 King Air C90B	LJ-1607	BR Aircraft LLC. Sacramento, Ca.	N782P
☐ N73PH	80 King Air C90	LJ-875	Provine Flying Service, Greenwood Ms.	N6672N
☐ N73WC	96 King Air 350	FL-135	West Coast Charters LLC. Santa Ana, Ca.	N283CB
☐ N73WW	05 King Air 350	FL-449	K350 LLC/PDX Inc. Charlottesville, Va.	N6179X

Reg	Yr Type	c/n	Owner/Operator	Prev Regn
N73YP	01 PA-46-500TP Meridian	4697080	Mid-America Freightways Inc. Evergreen, Co.	
N74	88 King Air 300	FF-9	FAA, Oklahoma City, Ok.	
N74AW	85 King Air B200	BB-1233	Spectrum Laboratory Network, Greensboro, NC.	N887T
N74AX	96 Pilatus PC-12	149	Concepts Aviation Inc. Wilmington, De.	N15TP
N74B	06 King Air C90GT	LJ-1766	Centennial Air Transport LLC. Newport News, Va.	N753P
N74BY	77 Conquest II	441-0039	Aspen Flight Holding LLC. Aspen, Co.	N36972
N74EF	80 Gulfstream 840	11614	Harborview Medical Center, Seattle, Wa.	N74RF
N74GB	74 Rockwell 690A	11206	A.C. Express Inc., Fairmont, WV.	N75RR
N74GL	81 Conquest II	441-0203	Aviation Services LLC. Chicago, Il.	N60TR
N74GS	83 King Air B200	BB-1135	Penn-Aire Aviation Inc., Franklin, Pa.	N399LA
N74JV	71 King Air 100	B-74	Vernon Sorenson MD./Whitehawk Enterprises, Bakersfield, Ca.	N3500E
N74KS	00 King Air 350	FL-299	Ken Small Construction Inc. Bakersfield, Ca.	N3128K
N74MA	06 TBM 850	385	AAA Roofing Co. Inc., Indianapolis, In.	F-WWRM
N74ML	83 King Air B200	BB-1123	Miller Livestock Co. Bakersfield, Ca.	(N282TA)
N74RG	99 King Air B200	BB-1651	Kansas City Royals Baseball Corp. Kansas City, Mo.	N32434
N74RR	93 King Air 350	FL-104	R & R Charters LLC. San Juan Capistran, Ca.	N8207D
N74TC	74 Mitsubishi MU-2J	642	Air 1st Aviation Companies Inc	N680CA
N74TF	03 King Air 350	FL-370	Tripifoods Inc. Buffalo, NY.	N6170D
N74TW	79 PA-31T Cheyenne II	7920067	John Williams, Aurora, Il.	(N4301L)
N75	88 King Air 300	FF-10	FAA, Oklahoma City, Ok.	
N75AP	79 King Air B100	BE-57	4D Aviation Ltd/W Central Enviromental Corp. Watervliet, NY.	N57AK
N75AW	81 PA-42 Cheyenne III	8001046	Clearwater Aircraft Inc.Clearwater Fl.	N148CA
N75FL	83 PA-42 Cheyenne IIIA	8301002	Mustang Enterprises Co. Santa Fe, NM.	(N830AM)
N75HW	85 Conquest 1	425-0232	G & W Air Inc. Middletown, De.	N50JN
N75JP	76 King Air E90	LW-158	Prior Aviation Service Inc. Buffalo, NY.	N940SR
N75LA	71 King Air 100	B-75	Infra Limited SE, San Juan, PR.	C-FCSD
N75LS	84 PA-42 Cheyenne IIIA	5501017	Barnett Investments Inc. La Verne, Ca.	N4118H
N75LV	82 King Air B200	BB-1075	Cook-Fort Worth Children's Medical Center, Fort Worth, Tx.	C-GTDY
N75LW	74 King Air E90	LW-75	GMJ Co. Topeka, Ks.	XB-AEU
N75ME	85 King Air 300	FA-57	Golden Rule Financial Corp. Indianapolis, In.	N75MC
N75MS	83 King Air F90-1	LA-204	Dodson International Parts Inc. Rantoul, Ks.	XA-PEM
N75MX	71 SA-226T Merlin 3	T-218	Flight Research, Mojave, Ca.	N990M
N75N	67 King Air A90	LM-57	Dynamic Aviation Group Inc. Bridgewater, Va.	66-18056
N75PG	95 King Air C90B	LJ-1390	Dasch Air LLC. Walnut Creek, Ca.	N3237K
N75PX	04 King Air 350	FL-431	Publix Super Markets Inc. Lakeland, Fl.	N6131Q
N75RS	71 King Air C90	LJ-533	JRS Aviation Inc. St Petersburg, Fl.	N739K
N75SR	95 King Air B200	BB-1506	Alabama Electric Cooperative Inc., Andalusia, Al.	N95AN
N75TF	78 PA-31T Cheyenne II	7820075	Bank of Utah Trustee, Salt Lake City, Ut.	N781CW
N75TW	80 PA-31T Cheyenne 1	8004016	NCMC Inc. Greeley, Co.	
N75U	74 Rockwell 690A	11218	Alan Huggins, Gilroy, Ca.	N690TP
N75V	68 King Air A90	LM-103	Dynamic Aviation Group Inc. Bridgewater, Va.	N7143Y
N75WA	81 PA-31T Cheyenne 1	8104101	Robinette Aviation LLC. Bristol, Tn.	D-IASW
N75WD	91 King Air 350	FL-51	Carolina Turbine Sales Inc. Tyler Tx.	N8055J
N75WZ	98 King Air 350	FL-228	Carolina Tractor & Equipment Co. Charlotte, NC.	N124DA
N75X	82 SA-227TT Merlin 3C	TT-421	Blackwater USA, McLean, Va.	N1014B
N75ZT	82 King Air B200	BB-967	Behlen Manufacturing Co. Columbus, Ne.	N75Z
N76	88 King Air 300	FF-11	FAA, Oklahoma City, Ok.	
N76CC	79 SA-226T Merlin 3B	T-304	Ameri-Air One Leasing Corp., Sunny Isles, Fl.	N48HH
N76EC	74 Rockwell 690A	11208	North American Financial Inc. Hayward, Ca.	N74RR
N76HH	81 Gulfstream 980	95076	Eagle Air Inc. Memphis, Tn.	N9828S
N76MG	01 PA-46-500TP Meridian	4697056	JGF Aviation LLC. Vail, Co.	
N76PM	98 King Air 350	FL-200	Pinon Air LLC. Monroe, La.	N2122M
N76Q	66 King Air A90	LM-15	Dynamic AvLease Inc. Bridgewater, Va.	N7026H
N76SJ	84 Conquest 1	425-0204	N76SJ LLC. Houston, Tx.	N1223P
N76SK	74 King Air E90	LW-195	Malouf Aero LLC. Greenwood, Ms.	N37MC
N76WA	76 Rockwell 690A	11342	Aspen Aerocommander LLC., Aspen, Co.	XA-RPD
N77	88 King Air 300	FF-12	FAA, Oklahoma City, Ok.	
N77CA	80 King Air 200	BB-717	Frances Christmann, Pinedale, NY.	
N77CE	78 King Air E90	LW-257	JRMC Inc. Chesterton, In.	N355JS
N77CV	98 King Air B200	BB-1625	Pennsylvania State University, University Park, Pa.	
N77HD	91 King Air B200	BB-1397	Arkansas State Highway & Transportation Dept. Little Rock.	N8062J
N77HE	81 King Air C90	LJ-969	Air MD LLC., Wichita, Ks.	9Q-CHE
N77HS	85 Gulfstream 900	15041	Harrison Steel Castings Co. Attica, In.	N82BA
N77JX	73 King Air E90	LW-54	Barry Richardson, Marston, Mo.	N771HM
N77ML	81 Conquest II	441-0202	Martin & Evelyn Lutin Family Trust, Van Nys, Ca.	N449DR

Reg	Yr Type	c/n	Owner/Operator	Prev Regn
N77NB	79 King Air C90	LJ-818	Phyxsius Air LLC., Ada, Ok.	N97SF
N77NL	77 PA-31T Cheyenne II	7720038	New South Inc. Charleston, SC.	N82136
N77PF	70 King Air 100	B-70	Air Charter Service Inc. Washington, Pa.	N25JL
N77PV	80 King Air F90	LA-68	Matthew Shieman, Moraga, Ca.	N99LM
N77R	83 Conquest II	441-0288	Barker Homes Inc. Sparks, Nv.	N352RT
N77SS	67 King Air A90	LJ-230	K & K Aircraft Inc. Bridgewater, Va.	N93BA
N77WF	72 King Air E90	LW-4	Thomas Stanton, McAllen, Tx.	N44EC
N77WM	86 King Air C90A	LJ-1133	Cobb Aviation Services Inc. Macomb, Il.	N300HH
N77WW	85 King Air F90-1	LA-235	NWI Aero LLC., Nashville, Tn.	N722PT
N77YP	82 Conquest 1	425-0111	Chapin Services LLC. West Columbia, SC.	N50FS
N77ZA	00 Pilatus PC-12/45	300	PMC Distribution Inc. Orange, Va.	C-FNAS
N78	88 King Air 300	FF-13	FAA, Oklahoma City, Ok.	
N78CA	79 PA-31T Cheyenne II	7920062	TMC210 LLC. Hampton, Va.	F-GIYV
N78CC	03 PA-46-500TP Meridian	4697163	Carl Conti, Melbourne, Fl.	
N78CH	70 681 Turbo Commander	6038	Wrangler Aviation Corp. Norman, Ok.	N46JC
N78CT	81 King Air 200	BB-761	Springfield Aviation LLC. Santa Cruz, Ca.	N107TM
N78D	67 King Air F90	LM-78	Dynamic Aviation Group Inc. Bridgewater, Va.	N7089D
N78DA	76 King Air B100	BE-11	CW Aviation LLC. Richmond, Va.	N1911L
N78FB	85 King Air F90-1	LA-231	Landmark Dodge Chrysler/SGA Aviation Inc.Morrow Ga	N129JS
N78NA	77 Rockwell 690B	11401	Wings Unlimited Inc. Costa Mesa Ca.	N28SE
N78PG	01 Pilatus PC-12/45	370	Lance Toland Ltd. Wilmington, De.	N373KM
N78PK	81 MU-2 Marquise	1522SA	Zwana LLC. Fairhaven, Ma.	C-GFFH
N78TT	78 Rockwell 690B	11509	Going South LLC., Iredell, Tx.	(N269PK)
N78WD	78 Mitsubishi MU-2P	368SA	Pleasure Craft Marine Engines, Canal Winchester, Oh.	N16TQ
N79	88 King Air 300	FF-14	FAA, Oklahoma City, Ok.	
N79BE	77 Rockwell 690B	11408	Elcor Corp. St Louis, Mo.	(N690SA)
N79CB	91 King Air 300	FA-217	Clint Bowyer Racing Inc., Clemmons, NC.	N507P
N79CF	79 King Air/Catpass 250	BB-441	Bering Air Inc. Nome, Ak.	
N79CT	79 King Air E90	LW-303	RR Enterprises Inc/Randall Stores Inc. Mitchell, SD.	N20351
N79EC	80 King Air F90	LA-74	MAH Aviation LLC Grand Prairie Tx.	N81PS
N79JS	90 King Air B200	BB-1370	JDS Aviation Inc/Scully Co. Jenkintown, Pa.	N200BM
N79PE	04 King Air C90B	LJ-1724	Patrick Engineering Inc. DuPage, Il.	
N79PH	82 Gulfstream 1000	96029	Anodyne Corp. Nashua, NH.	N282AC
N79RR	78 King Air 200	BB-356	BR Equipment Leasing LLC. Palm Beach, Fl.	N28KC
N79TE	85 King Air 300	FA-67	Eagle Support Corporation, Miami, Fl.	N55SC
N80	88 King Air 300	FF-15	FAA, Oklahoma City, Ok.	
N80BC	97 King Air B200	BB-1571	Carter's Shooting Center Inc. Spring, Tx.	
N80BT	75 King Air E90	LW-148	Boggs Transport Inc. Monroe, NC.	N300CH
N80BZ	87 King Air 300	FA-117	Tucker Inc. Ellicott City, Md.	N80X
N80CP	79 PA-31T Cheyenne II	7920040	Cheyenne Shares LLC. Willoughby, Oh.	
N80DG	66 King Air A90	LJ-131	John Judice, Shreveport, La.	N700S
N80HH	79 MU-2 Marquise	732SA	Mitts Corp. Gainesville, Fl.	(N30MA)
N80KA	07 King Air C90GT	LJ-1862	Hawker Beechcraft Corp., Wichita, Ks.	
N80M	81 King Air F90	LA-150	GHK Aviation LLC. Naples, Fl.	N700RL
N80MA	77 PA-31T Cheyenne II	7720043	Sims Enterprises, Kaysville, Ut.	(F-GJDK)
N80PM	84 Conquest 1	425-0181	GTA Containers Inc./Yatish Air LLC., South Bend, In.	N24QF
N80R	67 King Air A90	LM-21	Dynamic AvLease Inc. Bridgewater, Va.	N7031L
N80RT	78 King Air 200	BB-370	Ed Boesen, Des Moines, Ia.	N117WD
N80TB	76 Rockwell 690A	11300	Eagle Creek Aviation Services Inc. Indianapolis, In.	N471SC
N80VP	01 King Air B200	BB-1769	Avstar Inc./Aviation Partners Inc., Seattle, Wa.	N520GM
N80WM	81 King Air 200	BB-863	South Florida Water Management Division, West Palm Beach.	N44919
N80Y	67 King Air A90	LM-79	Dynamic AvLease Inc. Bridgewater, Va.	N65U
N81	88 King Air 300	FF-16	FAA, Oklahoma City, Ok.	
N81AT	70 King Air B90	LJ-490	Miles A Gamage LLC. Dover, De.	N881LT
N81BL	03 PA-46-500TP Meridian	4697160	Scott Manufacturing LLC. Henderson, Ky.	
N81DC	90 King Air B200	BB-1361	Liberte Air Corporation, Asheville, NC.	N5552U
N81GC	80 King Air F90	LA-73	6646K Inc. Tulsa, Ok.	N369BR
N81HP	73 King Air E90	LW-72	Pegasus Aviation Inc. Cleveland, Oh.	N102MC
N81LT	81 King Air B200	BB-892	Vermdeco Aviation LPC. Wilmington, De.	(SE-IIS)
N81MF	78 Mitsubishi MU-2P	375SA	Itinerant Airways Inc. Great Neck, NY.	N17JQ
N81NA	81 King Air C90	LJ-993	M & H International Spedition u Logistik GmbH. Neuensalz.	RP-C...
N81PA	99 King Air 350	FL-250	Pennsylvania DoT Bureau of Aviation, New Cumberland, Pa.	N3092K
N81PF	76 King Air 200	BB-158	North Bay Charter LLC. Reno, Nv.	N81PA
N81PN	77 Conquest II	441-0037	Conquest Aviation Inc. Redding, Ca.	N441TH
N81RZ	80 King Air 200	BB-739	Vacuum Industrial Pollution International Inc. Baton Rouge.	VT-ESR

Reg	Yr	Type	c/n	Owner/Operator	Prev Regn
N81TF	81	King Air 200	BB-750	JD Air LLC., New Kensington, Pa.	(N750TT)
N81TL	82	King Air B200	BB-959	Chemical Seal & Packing Co. Houston, Tx.	N469TA
N81WE	79	PA-31T Cheyenne II	7920060	Gerald Holmes & Assocs. Chattanooga, Tn.	N31WE
N81WS	84	SA-227TT Merlin 3C	TT-480	Blackwater USA, McLean, Va.	N500DB
N82HR	01	Pilatus PC-12/45	408	Harris Farms Inc., Coalinga, Ca.	N408LB
N82LP	85	King Air 300	FA-72	Line Power Manufacturing Co. Bristol, Va.	N72GA
N82PC	80	PA-31T Cheyenne II	8020082	Jet Finance Group LLC, Nashvlle Tn.	N2580V
N82PG	82	PA-42 Cheyenne III	8001070	Mitch Probasco, Floydata, Tx.	N721CA
N82PK	97	King Air B200	BB-1596	HEH Corp. Brentwood, Tn.	
N82TW	80	PA-31T Cheyenne 1	8004034	Dugan Funeral Services Inc. Fremont, Ne.	(N81TW)
N82WC	78	Mitsubishi MU-2P	393SA	Scott Dann, Libertyville, Il.	N9SR
N82WU	98	King Air 350	FL-197	Flying High Inc/Provost & Umphrey Law Firm, Beaumont, Tx.	
N82XL	81	Cheyenne II-XL	8166034	Fast Fly Inc./Rigney Friedman Bsiness Management LA Ca.	HK-3603X
N83	88	King Air 300	FF-18	FAA, Oklahoma City, Ok.	
N83A	78	Conquest II	441-0050	Peacock Aviation Inc. Omaha, Ne.	N55FC
N83AJ	03	Pilatus PC-12/45	495	Beach Aviation Inc. Palisades Verdes Est, Ca.	N495PC
N83CA	80	PA-31T Cheyenne II	8020072	Southern Bracing Systems Inc., Armuchee, Ga.	C-FEVC
N83CH	81	Conquest 1	425-0025	Waste Industries Dev Corp.Birmingham Al.	N53MS
N83FE	77	King Air E90	LW-219	Aviation Holdings Ltd. Houston, Tx.	N77AG
N83FT	98	King Air B200	BB-1621	Red Dog Aviation LLC. Destin, Fl.	N698P
N83G	73	Rockwell 690	11064	Don McCormack, Oklahoma City, Ok. (status ?).	N830
N83GA	79	King Air 200	BB-518	Guardian Eagle Co. Eden Prairie, Mn.	VH-MKR
N83KA	83	King Air B200	BB-1111	RCBK Equipment LLC., Las Vegas, Nv.	ZS-LVK
N83KB	05	King Air 350	FL-436	3 KB Investments LLC, Wilmington De.	N253P
N83MG	81	PA-31T Cheyenne 1	8104047	J & B Watkins 1997 Family Trust, San Marcos, Ca.	N2420Y
N83P	82	King Air C90-1	LJ-1027	Kyanite Mining Corp. Dillwyn, Va.	
N83PH	82	King Air B200	BB-976	Eagle Support Corporation, Miami, Fl.	N83RH
N83TC	70	King Air B90	LJ-483	Dynamic AvLease Inc. Bridgewater, Va.	N210K
N83WA	83	Gulfstream 1000	96063	R & C Aviation LLC. Portland, Or.	N61508
N83WE	78	King Air E90	LW-289	Miner's Inc. Hermantown, Mn.	N222MC
N83XL	81	Cheyenne II-XL	8166075	North Shore Properties, Erie, Pa.	N2325W
N84	88	King Air 300	FF-19	FAA, Oklahoma City, Ok.	
N84CA	76	King Air 200	BB-166	Buffalo Air LLC. Waterford, Mi.	N89MP
N84CF	83	PA-31T Cheyenne 1A	8304003	Insync Investments LLC. Dothan, Al.	N26DV
N84CQ	80	King Air 200	BB-691	Navacorp III LLC. NYC.	N84CC
N84G	67	King Air A90	LM-33	Dynamic Aviation Group Inc. Bridgewater, Va.	N7041M
N84GU	79	Rockwell 690B	11522	Aircraft Investments Inc. Batesville, Ar.	N691TP
N84HS	92	TBM 700	50	Skycare LLC. Port Orange, Fl.	(N67LF)
N84JL	80	King Air F90	LA-18	J-L Chieftain Inc. Longview, Tx.	N65SF
N84LG	84	Gulfstream 900	15035	Jet Prop Air Services Corp.Wilmington De.	N84LG
N84LJ	79	Conquest II	441-0084	Lovejoy Industries/L J Aircraft Inc. Oak Brook, Il.	N441GN
N84P	83	King Air C90	LJ-1045	Divine Aviation LLC. El Dorado Hills, Ca.	
N84PA	81	King Air 200	BB-835	Pennsylvania DoT Bureau of Aviation, New Cumberland, Pa.	N81CT
N84PC	81	King Air B200	BB-860	Triss Corp. Melvindale, Mi.	N488AD
N84TP	80	King Air C90	LJ-911	Berryman Investments Inc. Boerne, Tx.	N107K
N84XP	81	King Air 200	BB-481	Griffin Aviation Holdings LLC, Addison Tx.	TG-KAD
N85DR	78	King Air C90	LJ-767	J & D Aircraft Sales LLC., Pasco, Wa.	(N85PR)
N85EM	81	Cheyenne II-XL	8166055	Cheyenne Sales & Leasing LLC/Tiffin Aire Inc. Tiffin, Oh.	(CP-1699)
N85FC	81	King Air 200	BB-785	Woodway Aero Holdings Co. Houston, Tx.	RP-C582
N85GC	81	PA-31T Cheyenne II	8120009	Gerard Comboul Aviation Inc. Nice, France.	D-IHMS
N85GW	77	King Air C90	LJ-712	Wolfe Transportation Inc. Boise, Id.	N70AB
N85HB	81	PA-31T Cheyenne II	8120021	Michael Spear, Columbia, Md.	N80WA
N85JE	06	TBM 850	396	Victor Charlie Partners LLC., Naples, Fl.	N85JE
N85KG	84	PA-31T Cheyenne 1A	1104017	Universal Asset Management Inc., Memphis, Tn.	N65KG
N85PH	87	King Air C90A	LJ-1157	Provine Helicopter Service Inc. Greenwood, Ms.	N388MT
N85PJ	82	King Air F90	LA-163	Evergreen Forest Products Inc., Roseburg, Or.	N154AJ
N85SL	84	PA-42 Cheyenne 400LS	5527002	Sierra Aviation Inc. Bishop, Ca.	HP-2001
N85TB	79	King Air C90	LJ-833	Hillsboro Aviation Inc., Hillsboro, Or.	(N45AW)
N85TK	02	PA-46-500TP Meridian	4697128	Meridian Air LLC. Dover, De.	
N85Z	66	King Air A90	LM-9	Dynamic AvLease Inc. Bridgewater, Va.	N70135
N86GA	93	King Air 350	FL-100	Falcon Gas Storage Co. Houston, Tx.	C-FABR
N86JG	84	King Air C90A	LJ-1076	Evan Enterprises Inc., Wichita, Ks.	N69275
N86LD	00	King Air C90B	LJ-1631	Dion Aircraft Sales Inc. Key West, Fl.	N4031K
N86MG	67	King Air A90	LJ-264	Aviation Parts Exchange Inc. Southlake, Tx.	N86JR
N87BT	67	680V Turbo Commander	1705-81	City of New York, Long Island City, NY.	N87D
Reg	Yr	Type	c/n	Owner/Operator	Prev Regn

Reg	Yr Type	c/n	Owner/Operator	Prev Regn
☐ N87CA	78 King Air A100	B-240	Midwest Regional Airlines Inc. Eldon, Mo.	(N112CM)
☐ N87CF	83 King Air B200	BB-1122	Feltus Aviation LLC. Little Rock, Ar.	N6606R
☐ N87CH	72 King Air E90	LW-20	Dionisio Arriola, Moses Lake, Wa.	N84LS
☐ N87E	66 King Air A90	LM-5	Dynamic AvLease Inc. Bridgewater, Va.	N7007Q
☐ N87HB	90 King Air C90A	LJ-1251	Mountain Air Cargo Inc. Denver, NC.	N5607X
☐ N87LN	06 King Air B200	BB-1952	Lamar Aviation LLC. Windermere, Fl.	
☐ N87MM	68 King Air B90	LJ-415	Engines Inc. Weiner, Ar.	N210X
☐ N87NW	78 King Air B100	BE-42	LA Aviation Inc. Houston, Tx.	N700SB
☐ N87Q	67 King Air A90	LM-60	Dynamic Aviation Group Inc. Bridgewater, Va.	N7076X
☐ N87SA	82 King Air B200	BB-1089	James F Humphreys & Assocs LLC. Charleston, WV.	(N69JH)
☐ N87V	70 King Air A90	LM-130	Dynamic AvLease Inc. Bridgewater, Va.	N71764
☐ N87WS	77 Conquest II	441-0009	Alliance Travel LLC. Kansas City, Mo.	N777ED
☐ N87WZ	78 Rockwell 690B	11511	Kentucky Aircraft Leasing LLC. Anchorage, Ky.	N81795
☐ N87YP	81 PA-31T Cheyenne II	8120053	Ridge Finance Corp. Cranford, NJ.	N53TW
☐ N88B	81 Cheyenne II-XL	8166023	F McLeskey, Virginia Beach, Va.	N2577Y
☐ N88BC	79 PA-31T Cheyenne II	7920032	Mark Miracle, Tazewell, Tn.	(N814LM)
☐ N88BJ	80 Gulfstream 840	11627	MAX 1 LLC. Aspen, Co.	N24A
☐ N88DW	07 King Air C90GT	LJ-1855	W Aviation Inc. Wilmington De.	
☐ N88FA	79 King Air B100	BE-74	Crow Executive Air Inc. Toledo-Metcalf, Oh.	N56FL
☐ N88GL	81 King Air C90	LJ-945	Austin Lopez, St John, USVI.	N979C
☐ N88GW	81 Conquest II	441-0187	Hamburg Aero Leasing LP. Hamburg, NY.	N405JB
☐ N88HM	71 King Air C90	LJ-502	Western Flyers Air Service, McAllen, Tx.	N881K
☐ N88JH	89 King Air B200	BB-1331	Teton Aviation LLC. Jackson, Wy.	N5530H
☐ N88KE	88 King Air B200	BB-1313	Accipiter Air LLC. Wellesley, Ma.	N312SB
☐ N88MT	81 King Air 200	BB-830	Flight LLC. Chattanooga, Tn.	N88P
☐ N88NT	99 Pilatus PC-12/45	285	The Newtron Group Inc. Baton Rouge, La.	N285PS
☐ N88PD	90 King Air C90A	LJ-1242	Pipe Distributors Inc. Houston, Tx.	N15696
☐ N88QM	81 PA-31T Cheyenne 1	8104025	RB LLC. Tequesta, Fl.	N2476X
☐ N88QT	82 Conquest II	441-0228	Start Renting Inc/SRI Sky LLC. Madison, Wi.	(N363PD)
☐ N88RP	70 King Air B90	LJ-491	Air Share Holdings Inc. Petersburg, Va.	N88RB
☐ N88RY	81 King Air 300	FA-122	Corporate Jets Inc/Landmark Aviation, Winston-Salem NC.	N112HF
☐ N88SP	66 King Air A90	LJ-116A	Air Reldan Inc. New Orleans, La.	N885K
☐ N88TL	81 King Air B100	BE-113	BWOC Air Services Inc. Columbus, Ga.	N1888M
☐ N88TR	73 King Air E90	LW-57	JTB Aviation LLC/Microbac Laboratories Inc. Hampton, Va.	N86TR
☐ N88U	98 TBM 700	135	SOCATA Aircraft, Pembroke Pines, Fl.	
☐ N88VN	86 King Air B200	BB-1250	Van Ness Management LLC. Lubbock, Tx.	(N383CA)
☐ N88XJ	98 King Air C90B	LJ-1525	James Frost, Avon, Co.	
☐ N89CA	81 King Air F90	LA-152	C A Transportation LLC. Birmingham, Al.	N152WE
☐ N89DR	78 Mitsubishi MU-2N	713SA	R & M Foods Inc. Hattiesburg, Ms.	N874MA
☐ N89F	69 King Air A90	LM-124	Dynamic AvLease Inc. Bridgewater, Va.	N72014
☐ N89FF	75 King Air C90	LJ-671	Dodson Services Inc. Rantoul, Ks.	ZS-MNC
☐ N89JA	79 PA-31T Cheyenne II	7920030	Teak International Co SA. Panama City, Panama.	4X-CIE
☐ N89SC	81 MU-2 Marquise	1516SA	Nashville Air Flights Inc. Nashville, Tn.	N4SY
☐ N89ST	01 PA-46-500TP Meridian	4697008	Johanneson Properties (N D) LLC., Bemidji, Mn.	N62WM
☐ N89TM	73 King Air C90	LJ-610	Garmin AT Inc. Salem, Or.	(N169WD)
☐ N89UA	89 King Air B200	BB-1336	University of Arkansas, Fayetteville, Ar.	N131BP
☐ N89WA	96 King Air B200	BB-1540	DeBruce Grain Inc. Kansas City, Mo.	
☐ N90AT	76 Rockwell 690A	11272	Kolob Canyons Air Services Inc. Cedar City, Ut.	N888PB
☐ N90AW	76 King Air C90	LJ-697	Krider Construction Inc. Pineville, Or.	C-GSAX
☐ N90BD	81 King Air F90	LA-134	Robert DeLong, San Clemente, Ca.	N993M
☐ N90BF	75 King Air E90	LW-124	First Air Leasing Inc. Greenville, SC.	N90GK
☐ N90CB	69 King Air B90	LJ-473	Sale reported	N9390C
☐ N90CH	96 King Air C90B	LJ-1445	Chartco LLC. Salisbury, NC.	N209P
☐ N90CN	95 King Air C90B	LJ-1410	Nogle & Black Aviation Inc. Tuscola, Il.	N771SG
☐ N90CP	03 TBM 700C2	285	Century Enterprises Group LLC. Fort Lauderdale, Fl.	N706CA
☐ N90CT	75 King Air C90	LJ-645	Robert Schroeder, Kaukauna, Wi.	(N999MJ)
☐ N90DN	68 King Air B90	LJ-437	Aircraft Investment Co. Casselton, ND.	N12JG
☐ N90EJ	78 King Air C90	LJ-749	Edwards Jet Center, Billings, Mt.	N552R
☐ N90EL	73 King Air C90	LJ-592	Hathaway Aviation LLC. Atlanta, Ga.	N383DA
☐ N90FA	66 King Air A90	LJ-133	Fox Valley Technical College, Appleton, Wi.	N90SA
☐ N90FS	80 PA-31T Cheyenne II	8020011	James Beasley/JEB PAY 2 LLC. Philadelphia, Pa.	N73CA
☐ N90GA	90 King Air B200	BB-1359	Stark Truss Co. Canton, Oh.	RP-C4188
☐ N90GN	66 King Air A90	LJ-157	TVC Marketing/C & F Ranch LC. Oklahoma City, Ok.	N288HH
☐ N90GP	06 King Air C90GT	LJ-1795	Reliable Management LLC. Greenbriar, Tn.	N7295T
☐ N90GT	84 SA-227TT Merlin 3C	TT-534	E C Menzies Electrical Inc. Essendon, VIC. Australia.	N139F

Reg	Yr	Type	c/n	Owner/Operator	Prev Regn
☐ N90KS	98	King Air C90B	LJ-1517	The Way Inc., Picayune, Ms.	N90KA
☐ N90LB	73	King Air C90	LJ-573	Front Page Corp. Douglas, Ga.	N707RW
☐ N90LF	79	King Air C90	LJ-852	Wyoming Med Center Life Flight, Casper, Wy.	YV-250CP
☐ N90LG	68	King Air B90	LJ-351	Dodson International Parts Inc. Rantoul, Ks.	N62BW
☐ N90ME	75	King Air C90	LJ-661	BHA Leasing Inc. Standish, Me.	N88SD
☐ N90MU	76	King Air C90	LJ-679	J & D Aircraft Sales LLC., Pasco, Wa.	N90ML
☐ N90MV	77	King Air C90	LJ-701	Big Kahuna Aviation LLC. Cleveland, Al.	N90LJ
☐ N90NA	81	King Air F90	LA-104	Imperial Airlines LLC. Seeley, Ca.	(N900BK)
☐ N90NH	75	SA-226AT Merlin 4A	AT-032	Alpha Tango Zero Inc/Jimbo Corp. Miami, Fl.	N44GL
☐ N90NM	68	King Air B90	LJ-404	John Antunes/J A Air LLC. Hilton Head, SC.	N90NM
☐ N90PB	76	King Air 200	BB-125	Grant Aviation Inc. Anchorage, Ak.	TG-UGA
☐ N90PH	73	King Air E90	LW-60	Omni Air Transport LLC/10 Tanker Lead LLC., Tulsa, Ok.	N999TB
☐ N90PR	96	King Air C90B	LJ-1437	Palmetto Construction Group, Wilmington, De.	N1067L
☐ N90PW	76	King Air C90	LJ-681	Longin Consultants Inc. Burlington, Wi.	N1581L
☐ N90RK	99	King Air C90B	LJ-1554	Diamond Coach Corp. Oswego, Ks.	(N90ND)
☐ N90RT	81	King Air F90	LA-146	Save Mart Supermarkets/Sky Trek Aviation, Modesto, Ca.	N90TX
☐ N90SB	81	King Air F90	LA-154	Red River Cellular Telephone Co. Texarkana, Tx.	(C-GFFY)
☐ N90TD	82	King Air F90	LA-183	Voice of Evangelism Inc. Cleveland, Oh.	N82WC
☐ N90TP	80	King Air F90	LA-66	Triton Air Inc. Wilmington, De.	(YV-373CP)
☐ N90TW	84	PA-42 Cheyenne IIIA	5501013	La Stella Corp. Pueblo, Co.	N40833
☐ N90VM	81	PA-31T Cheyenne 1	8104031	Monaghan Management Corp. Commerce City, Co.	(N90FJ)
☐ N90VP	67	King Air A90	LJ-276	APA Enterprises Inc. Deland, Fl.	N574M
☐ N90WE	88	King Air 300LW	FA-164	Warren Equipment Co. Midland, Tx.	N42AJ
☐ N90WG	79	PA-31T Cheyenne II	7920044	C W Aviation Inc. Bryan, Tx.	PT-OTF
☐ N90WJ	71	King Air C90	LJ-525	Blackhawk Technical College, Janesville, Wi.	N70MT
☐ N90WL	69	King Air B90	LJ-461	W L Paris Enterprises Inc. Louisville, Ky.	N453SR
☐ N90WT	73	King Air E90	LW-31	Aviacion Lider SA. Lima, Peru.	N17GD
☐ N90WW	84	PA-31T Cheyenne 1A	1104004	Phy-Leon LLC., Shalimar, Fl.	N15AT
☐ N90XS	81	King Air E90	LW-342	Flying King LLC. Chanhassen, Mn.	N3741M
☐ N90YA	81	Conquest 1	425-0090	Tower Fish Co. Donegal, Ireland.	N90GA
☐ N90ZH	73	King Air C90	LJ-594	Edward Craig Sasser Family Trust, Whiteville, NC.	N3094W
☐ N91CT	78	Rockwell 690B	11428	Clemson University, Clemson, SC.	N91CS
☐ N91HT	85	King Air B200	BB-1183	Hawkeye Aviation LLC. Pikeville, Ky.	N44MH
☐ N91KA	90	King Air C90A	LJ-1232	4BK Cattle LLC. Haskell, Ks.	XA-RGL
☐ N91KM	02	PA-46-500TP Meridian	4697120	Standiford Bluffs LLC. Chapel Hill, NC.	(N402PS)
☐ N91LW	82	King Air C90	LJ-1001	Air MD LLC., Wichita, Ks.	N88EL
☐ N91MF	80	King Air 200	BB-657	Med Flight Air Ambulance Inc. Albuquerque, NM.	N301PS
☐ N91MM	71	Mitsubishi MU-2F	198	Anderson Aerial Spraying Service, Canby, Mn.	N71MF
☐ N91RK	76	King Air A100	B-226	Piper East Inc. Manchester, NH.	N9126S
☐ N91S	70	King Air A90	LU-15	Dynamic AvLease Inc. Bridgewater, Va.	N71998
☐ N91TJ	78	King Air C90	LJ-744	Cannon Air LLC. Scottsdale, Az.	N771PS
☐ N91TS	80	PA-31T Cheyenne II	8020050	Lowe Aviation Co. Macon, Ga.	C-FSRW
☐ N92AG	99	Pilatus PC-12/45	257	Aircraft Guaranty Management LLC., Houston, Tx.	HB-FOR
☐ N92BK	94	King Air C90B	LJ-1381	F & F Aviation Inc. Fort Lauderdale, Fl.	N381SC
☐ N92CA	06	Pilatus PC-12/47	753	Century Aircraft LLC., Wilmington, De.	HB-FSI
☐ N92DV	78	King Air E90	LW-292	Air Methods Corp/KMRC Guardian Air Inc. Flagstaff, Az.	N7MA
☐ N92FC	90	King Air C90A	LJ-1235	Longleaf AIF LLC. Hilton Head, SC.	D-IABB
☐ N92JQ	81	Conquest II	441-0223	TasAir LLC/T A Solberg Co. Minocqua, Wi.	N92JC
☐ N92JR	81	King Air 200	BB-751	Tennair LLC. Clarksville, Tn.	N751EB
☐ N92S	70	King Air A90	LU-5	Dynamic AvLease Inc. Bridgewater, Va.	N7199B
☐ N92TH	06	King Air 350	FL-509	Fluid Aviation LLC. Seattle, Wa.	
☐ N92TW	90	King Air 350	FL-3	Noel Aviation Interests Ltd. Odessa, Tx.	(N350PC)
☐ N92TX	87	King Air 300	FA-121	Spencer Youngblood, Rockport, Tx.	N268CB
☐ N92WC	89	King Air B200	BB-1330	Aircraft Guaranty Management LLC, Houston, Tx.	N681PC
☐ N92WG	66	King Air A90	LJ-182	Five Star Aircraft Inc. Wilmington, De.	N92W
☐ N93A	73	King Air E90	LW-63	Alpha Horizon LLC/Fairway Ford Isuzu Inc. Greenville, SC.	N808GA
☐ N93AH	73	Mitsubishi MU-2J	581	Trans Check Inc. Carlsbad, Ca.	N161WC
☐ N93BN	92	TBM 700A	74	Brose North America, Auburn Hills, Mi.	D-FBFS
☐ N93CN	80	PA-31T Cheyenne 1	8004029	Jerry & Corrine Nothman, Portland, Or.	N49GG
☐ N93D	77	King Air B100	BE-23	A & Q LLC. Ada, Mi.	N13KA
☐ N93GA	86	King Air 300	FA-93	CC Aviation LLC/Dulany Aviation Inc. Wilmington, De.	(N92CC)
☐ N93HC	77	Conquest II	441-0011	Wells Fargo Bank NW NA, Salt Lake City ,Ut.	N900JT
☐ N93J	69	King Air A90	LM-128	Dynamic Aviation Group Inc. Bridgewater, Va.	N7173Y
☐ N93KA	80	King Air F90	LA-24	John Braly, Boerne, Tx.	
☐ N93LL	01	PA-46-500TP Meridian	4697045	Dynamic Industrial Supply, Calexico, Ca.	

Reg	Yr Type	c/n	Owner/Operator	Prev Regn
N93LP	80 King Air C90	LJ-901	Wings of Faith LLC., St Louis, Mo.	N23LF
N93MA	82 Gulfstream 1000	96035	Eagle Air Inc. Memphis, Tn. (now XC-HFZ ?).	D-IBER
N93ME	77 Rockwell 690B	11414	JCO Sandlapper LLC., Union, SC.	VH-PCD
N93NP	84 King Air B200	BB-1184	N Philadelphia Aviation Corp/Summit Aviation, Middletown, De	N27SE
N93RA	68 680W Turbo Commander	1722-2	American Aviation Ground Services, Miami, Fl. (was 1722-93).	N93D
N93RR	04 King Air B200	BB-1853	MJP Aviation LLC. Winthrop Harbor, Il.	N45RR
N93RY	66 King Air A90	LJ-174	Air Capital Insurance LLC. Wichita, Ks.	(N193SF)
N93SF	76 King Air B100	BE-13	Life Guard International Inc., Las Vegas, Nv.	N4213S
N93SH	79 PA-31T Cheyenne 1	7904029	Basin Air LLC Pasco, Wa.	N29CA
N93WT	80 King Air B100	BE-80	Wes-Tex Drilling Co. Abilene, Tx.	N13DR
N94AC	78 Rockwell 690B	11486	Apollo Aviation II LLC. Glastonbury, Ct.	N34EF
N94CD	81 King Air C90	LJ-939	The Penn Warranty Corporation, Wilkes Barre, Pa.	N26803
N94CE	71 SA-226AT Merlin 4	AT-004	U S Army Corps of Engineers, Omaha, Ne.	N55CE
N94EA	85 Gulfstream 1000	96094	Midtex Investments Inc. Austin, Tx.	N131GA
N94EG	81 PA-31T Cheyenne 1	8104033	Boston Air Charter LLC. Norfolk, Ma.	N881SW
N94EW	81 PA-42 Cheyenne III	8001054	Derby Air LLC. Willoughby, Oh.	N29HS
N94FE	96 Pilatus PC-12	150	Air Falcon LLC. Pinellas Park, Fl.	N950GC
N94FG	79 King Air 200	BB-433	Pollard Aircraft Sales Inc., Southlake, Tx.	N133GA
N94HB	80 King Air C90	LJ-904	Central Flying Service Inc. Little Rock, Ar.	N90HB
N94JD	81 King Air F90	LA-139	Gap Air Inc. Johnstown, Pa.	N333EB
N94KC	76 King Air 200	BB-172	Louisville Medical Center STATCARE, Bowman Field, Ky.	N68RR
N94MG	90 King Air C90A	LJ-1229	Charles N White Construction Co. Ridgeland, Ms.	D-IAFF
N94N	70 King Air A90	LU-4	Dynamic AvLease Inc. Bridgewater, Va.	N71984
N94PA	82 Gulfstream 1000	96005	Quasar Aviation, Dover, De.	N815S
N94S	69 King Air A90	LM-133	Dynamic Aviation Group Inc. Bridgewater, Va.	N7202D
N94SA	65 Gulfstream 1	157	World Sales & Turbine Co. El Dorado, Panama.	N741G
N94TK	94 King Air C90B	LJ-1358	Tem-Kil Co. Macogdoches, Tx.	N80927
N95AB	81 Gulfstream 1000	96012	Talon Erectors Inc. Hagerstown, Md.	N695BA
N95CT	85 King Air B200	BB-1235	Bison Investments, Tampa, Fl.	N43CE
N95GA	93 King Air B200	BB-1467	Pride Mobility Products Corp. Exeter, Pa.	(N929AK)
N95JM	76 Rockwell 690A	11289	Valley Oil/Pond LLC. Salem, Or.	(N27JT)
N95KW	07 PA-46-500TP Meridian	4697301	Wilson Family Funeral Chapel Inc., Atwater, Ca.	N490CA
N95LB	73 King Air E90	LW-24	James Tate, Christiansted, USVI.	N95RB
N95LM	06 King Air B200	BB-1956	Lauren International Inc. New Philadelphia, Oh.	N37156
N95NW	94 Pilatus PC-12	105	DIRT MAN LLC/M & W Tucson LLC. Tucson, Az.	(N91MT)
N95PC	85 King Air B200	LJ-1109	Chieftain Aircraft LLC. Bend, Or.	
N95S	69 King Air A90	LM-125	Dynamic Aviation Group Inc. Bridgewater, Va.	N7170A
N95SA	89 PA-42 Cheyenne IIIA	5501040	Blackhawk Modifications/Aurora Aviation Inc. Waco, Tx.	N556BR
N95TT	81 King Air B200	BB-917	M B Aviation LLC. Pawleys Island, SC.	(N115SB)
N95UT	00 King Air B200	BB-1759	Pacificorp, Portland, Or.	N1Z
N95VR	81 PA-42 Cheyenne III	8001049	Golden Eagle Aviation Inc/Henry Luken, Bradenton, Fl.	C-FIZG
N96AG	67 King Air A90	LJ-260	Aviation Group LLC. Concord, NC.	N303NH
N96AH	75 King Air C90	LJ-643	Schmueser & Associates Inc./Two L Leasing LLC., Rifle, Co.	N909HC
N96AM	00 King Air B200	BB-1713	Texas A & M University, College Station, Tx.	N3053Q
N96CE	96 King Air B200	BB-1536	CAIAIR Inc. Beaumont, Tx.	N10436
N96DQ	79 King Air C90	LJ-814	Tres Hombres South LLC. Wilmington, De.	N96DC
N96FA	85 King Air C90A	LJ-1111	Flad & Assocs Inc. Madison, Wi.	N240EA
N96JF	96 King Air C90B	LJ-1429	Aero Harbor LLC/Fabiano Brothers Inc. Mount Pleasant, Mi.	N3251Q
N96KA	90 King Air 350	FL-36	Louis Beecherl LLC. Wanut Springs, Tx.	(N825G)
N96MA	78 PA-31T Cheyenne 1	7804005	Headstrong Inc. Lyon, Ms.	N6095A
N96MV	06 Pilatus PC-12/47	793	Ryan Capital Management Inc., San Diego, Ca.	HB-FQN
N96RL	68 SA-26AT Merlin 2B	T26-116	Sky Way Intnl LLC/CariLink Intnl Inc, Bay Harbor Island, Fl.	N100AW
N96S	70 King Air A90	LU-13	Dynamic AvLease Inc. Bridgewater, Va.	N71996
N96TH	94 King Air C90B	LJ-1382	Harding Road Boring Inc., Bryan, Tx.	N3120U
N96TT	80 King Air F90	LA-26	ROMCO Inc. Dallas, Tx.	N6668C
N96VC	79 SA-226T Merlin 3B	T-303	National Childrens Leukemia Foundation, NYC.	N5654M
N96WC*	82 King Air B200	BB-969	West Coast Charters LLC. Santa Ana, Ca.	N969WB
N97D	69 King Air A90	LM-137	Dynamic Aviation Group Inc. Bridgewater, Va.	N7182H
N97DA	05 King Air C90B	LJ-1755	Jack Anglin Civil Constructors Ltd. Novi, Mi.	N896P
N97DR	96 King Air 350	FL-133	Danchar Inc/Sun Aviation Inc. Vero Beach, Fl.	
N97EB	86 King Air 300	FA-97	MAACO Enterprises Inc. King of Prussia, Pa.	N50NL
N97KA	97 King Air C90B	LJ-1469	Crutchfield Corp. Charlottesville, Va.	
N97LL	01 PA-46-500TP Meridian	4697058	Enginair LLC. Avon, Co.	
N97PC	80 PA-31T Cheyenne II	8020034	DR Holdings LLC. Franklin, NC.	N4241Y
N97SZ	83 King Air B200	BB-1166	Zimmerman Development Inc. Los Angeles, Ca.	D-ITAB

Reg	Yr	Type	c/n	Owner/Operator	Prev Regn
❏ N97TW	79	PA-31T Cheyenne II	7920051	Roger Mellon, Lakeland, Fl.	
❏ N97WC	90	King Air B200	BB-1382	West Coast Charters LLC. Santa Ana, Ca.	N678RM
❏ N97WD	80	King Air B100	BE-97	KA South Inc. Hilton Head Island, SC.	N43RJ
❏ N97WE	97	King Air B200	BB-1586	Wagner Equipment Co. Englewood, Co.	N3181Q
❏ N97WT	81	Gulfstream 840	11709	Coop Air LLC. Kansas City, Mo.	N690BA
❏ N98AJ	78	Rockwell 690B	11458	Cascadian Aviation LLC. Bellevue, Wa.	ZS-KEF
❏ N98AR	79	King Air C90	LJ-829	BizAir LLC./Accutech Data Supplies, Ventura, Ca.	(N11FX)
❏ N98AT	76	PA-31T Cheyenne II	7620014	Custom Fabric & Repair Inc. Marshfield, Wi.	(N460LC)
❏ N98B	66	King Air 90	LJ-87	Aerosports Inc/Bay Area Skydiving, Byron, Ca.	
❏ N98BK	98	King Air C90B	LJ-1522	Brinn Enterprises Inc., Chapel Hill, NC.	N58XJ
❏ N98EP	85	Conquest 1	425-0230	Ernest Pestana Inc. Incline Village, Nv.	N1227V
❏ N98GF	80	PA-31T Cheyenne 1	8004009	Great Southwest Aviation Inc. Roswell, NM.	N2412W
❏ N98HB	67	King Air A90	LJ-285	Hermann Bodmer & Co. Zurich, Switzerland.	PH-IND
❏ N98HF	74	King Air E90	LW-89	T & R Aircraft LLC. Memphis, Tn.	N77PA
❏ N98KS	97	King Air C90B	LJ-1502	Eagle Air Med Corp.,Blanding, Ut.	N5UL
❏ N98NF	98	TBM 700	133	Baker Air LLC. San Francisco, Ca.	F-WWRP
❏ N98PJ	76	Rockwell 690A	11320	Kolob Canyons Air Services Inc. Cedar City, Ut.	N220HC
❏ N98PM	75	King Air E90	LW-131	Pollard Aircraft Sales Inc., Southlake, Tx.	N98PC
❏ N98TA	79	King Air B100	BE-56	Tower Aviation Management LLC., Porter, Tx.	N9933S
❏ N98TB	78	PA-31T Cheyenne II	7820040	Schrepfer Industries, Trinidad, Co.	N68MB
❏ N98TG	79	PA-31T Cheyenne 1	7904027	NCMC Inc. Greeley, Co.	N98TW
❏ N98UC	81	SA-226T Merlin 3B	T-378	Universal Associates Inc., Highlands, NC.	N1011P
❏ N98WP	97	King Air C90B	LJ-1493	Aven Williamson Construction, Texarkana, Tx.	(N98WS)
❏ N99AC	75	King Air E90	LW-120	Air-Estess LLC., New Albany, Ms.	(N870BB)
❏ N99BT	73	Mitsubishi MU-2J	591	S & W Aircraft Sales Inc. Wilmington, De.	N295MA
❏ N99EL	59	Gulfstream 1	7	Range 1 Corp. Wilmington, De.	N5VX
❏ N99G	69	King Air A90	LM-129	Dynamic Aviation Group Inc. Bridgewater, Va.	N7174J
❏ N99JW	82	SA-227TT Merlin 3C	TT-450	GDE Aviation LLC. Destin, Fl.	N53PC
❏ N99KF	79	PA-31T Cheyenne II	7920093	SST Corp. Klamath Falls, Or.	N2416R
❏ N99LL	82	King Air B200	BB-994	Alabama River Pulp Co. Purdue Hill, Al.	N25CN
❏ N99ML	07	King Air B200GT	BY-25	Hawker Beechcraft Corp., Wichita, Ks.	
❏ N99SR	74	Mitsubishi MU-2K	315	Jetset Ltd. Lanseria, RSA.	N505MA
❏ N99U	90	King Air 350	FL-20	Helicopters Inc. Cahokia, Il.	N350NJ
❏ N99VA	77	PA-31T Cheyenne II	7720007	Avro Ltd. Las Vegas, Nv.	N721RP
❏ N100AQ	89	King Air 300	FA-190	1st Source Leasing Inc. South Bend, In.	N17TW
❏ N100BE	04	King Air 350	FL-403	Bemis Manufacturing Co. Sheboygan Falls, Mi.	N6113X
❏ N100BY	84	MU-2 Marquise	1565SA	TAG Air LLC., Houston, Tx.	N530DP
❏ N100BZ	85	King Air 300	FA-32	M & S Aviation LLC/Echo Aviation LC. Tempe, Az.	N100BE
❏ N100CC	83	Conquest 1	425-0170	Honey B LLC/Honey Buckets, Puyallup, Wa.	N68721
❏ N100CE	80	SA-226T Merlin 3B	T-325	SMMS 2 LLC. Sacramento, Ca.	HC-BUA
❏ N100CF	72	Mitsubishi MU-2F	229	Tabrizi Inc. Huntington Beach, Ca.	N217MA
❏ N100CM	80	PA-31T Cheyenne II	8020073	Langdale Industries, Valdosta, Ga.	N2474V
❏ N100EC	75	King Air E90	LW-150	Sunburst Aviation LLC. Summerville, SC.	N23AE
❏ N100FL	85	King Air 300	FA-34	Dept of Management Services, Tallahassee, Fl.	N865M
❏ N100GL	70	681 Turbo Commander	6028	Ecological Services International, Los Fresnos, Tx.	N9028N
❏ N100JD	97	King Air C90B	LJ-1472	N21WY Aviation LLC/Nielson & Assocs Inc. Cody, Wy.	N1099L
❏ N100KA	70	King Air 100	B-11	On-Air LLC. Sewickley, Pa.	
❏ N100KB	79	King Air C90	LJ-820	Lyndale Farms/Johnny Reb Avn LC/Tate Air LLC. Senatobia, Ms.	
❏ N100KE	74	Mitsubishi MU-2P	313SA	Putnam County National Bank, Carmel, NY.	N100KP
❏ N100MS	07	Pilatus PC-12/47	835	Calliope Investment Company LLC., Seattle, Wa.	HB-FRW
❏ N100MW	72	King Air E90	LW-2	Market West Properties Inc. Visalia, Ca.	N412SR
❏ N100NP	80	MU-2 Solitaire	423SA	Fountainbleau Management Services, New Orleans, La.	N156MA
❏ N100PY	81	King Air B200	BB-890	TBM Flying LC/Terry Holding Co of Nevada, Pampa, Tx.	N100PX
❏ N100QT	76	King Air C90	LJ-689	Quality Trailer Sales Inc. Milan, Il.	(N45FE)
❏ N100SM	99	King Air C90	LJ-1561	Missouri State Highway Patrol, Jefferson City, Mo.	N3171A
❏ N100TW	78	King Air B100	BE-51	New Horizons LLC., Lee's Summit, Mo.	N1DA
❏ N100UE	66	King Air A90	LJ-138	CAB Air Inc. Cedartown, Ga.	N100UF
❏ N100V	78	King Air C90	LJ-796	RHW Metals Inc., Longview, Tx.	
❏ N100WB	66	King Air A90	LJ-139	Brown Boy Aviation, Royal City, Wa.	N1515T
❏ N100WQ	78	PA-31T Cheyenne II	7820084	JS Aircraft LLC. Eden, NC.	N450DA
❏ N100YC	99	Pilatus PC-12/45	281	Passport Leasing Corp. Fort Lauderdale, Fl.	HB-FSZ
❏ N101BS	68	King Air B90	LJ-375	Bruce Scheffer/Valparaiso International, Valparaiso, In.	N110BS
❏ N101BU	85	King Air C90A	LJ-1107	Bigg Aviation LLC., Hixon, Tn.	N72260
❏ N101CA	82	Conquest 1	425-0142	State of Texas, Austin, Tx.	OH-CIK
❏ N101CS	76	King Air C-12C	BC-41	Profile Aviation Services Inc. Hickory, NC.	N257AG

Reg	Yr	Type	c/n	Owner/Operator	Prev Regn
N101MC	73	SA-226T Merlin 3A	T-234	Cappaert Air Planes LLC. Vicksburg, Ms.	N531LP
N101NX	04	TBM 700C2	309	Steven & Julie Castle, South Hamilton, Ma.	N930CA
N101SG	01	King Air B200	BB-1785	Andair Inc. McAllen, Tx.	N4455U
N101SN	81	King Air B100	BE-118	Trace Air Inc. Fort Worth, Tx.	N4700K
N101SS	67	King Air C90	LJ-537	Russell Smith, Pensacola, Fl.	N133LA
N101WR	81	King Air C90	LJ-934	Wiginton Rumley LP. Corpus Christi, Tx.	N369GA
N102AD	83	Conquest II	441-0311	Donald & Alice Fehrenbach, Naples, Fl.	N823AD
N102AE	90	PA-42 Cheyenne IIIA	5501053	Cobalt Aviation III LLC. Philadelphia, Pa.	PT-WQA
N102BX	79	MU-2 Marquise	748SA	Bankair Inc. West Columbia, SC.	N102BG
N102DY	70	SA-26AT Merlin 2B	T26-169	Avco Holdings LLC, Murfreesboro Tn.	N22GW
N102FG	02	King Air B200	BB-1799	University Athletic Association Inc. Gainesville, Fl.	N211HV
N102FK	81	King Air C90	LJ-982	Florida Aircraft Enterprises Inc. Gulf Breeze, Fl.	N102FL
N102FL	99	King Air 350	FL-263	Florida Dept of Management Services, Tallahassee, Fl.	N823SE
N102LF	70	King Air 100	B-65	Lynch Flying Service Inc. Logan Field, Mt.	N102RS
N102NA	80	Conquest II	441-0159	Fly-4-You Inc. Anchorage, Ak.	ZS-TMA
N102SL	02	P-180 Avanti	1052	AvantAir Inc. Clearwater, Fl.	N139PA
N102WK	80	King Air F90	LA-36	Willis Knighton Medical Center, Shreveport, La.	N6736C
N103AD	85	King Air 300	FA-62	Liberty University, Lynchburg, Va.	N103AL
N103AP	75	King Air C90	LW-126	Pamplemousse Corp. Key Biscayne, Fl.	RP-C201
N103BL	75	King Air C90	LJ-650	Twin County Aviation LLC, Galax Va.	N103FL
N103CB	81	King Air F90	LA-98	Consort Transportation LLC., Chesterfield, Mo.	N77JT
N103CW	85	King Air 300	FA-64	Flying Pigs LLC. Greensboro, NC.	(N64HF)
N103RN	98	King Air 350	FL-231	Noel Corp. Yakima, Wa.	N231PK
N103SL	02	P-180 Avanti	1059	AvantAir Inc. Clearwater, Fl.	N128PA
N104AJ	88	King Air C90A	LJ-1164	Luwe Flug Inc. Lux & Weigl, Bayreuth, Germany.	ZS-MIL
N104BH	01	PA-46-500TP Meridian	4697104	French Onion LLC. Langhorne, Pa.	
N104CX	82	King Air B200	BB-1004	Crux Subsurface Inc. Spokane, Wa.	N104AK
N104EM	74	SA-226T Merlin 3	T-248	White Industries Inc. Bates City, Mo. (status ?).	OH-ADA
N104JB	80	MU-2 Solitaire	435SA	John Broome Ranches, Oxnard, Ca.	N213MA
N104LC	78	King Air C90	LJ-757	Pax Dei LLC. Hot Springs, Ar.	N23675
N104TA	77	SA-226T Merlin 3A	T-289	Aero-Inter Corp. Fayetteville, Ga.	(F-GBBD)
N105FC	81	Conquest 1	425-0094	105 LLC/F Carroll, San Francisco, Ca.	N104HW
N105GP	01	P-180 Avanti	1048	P-1048 LLC, Grand Rapids Mi.	N629GT
N105K	66	King Air 90	LJ-113	Airlift California Inc. Hollister, Ca.	N16CS
N105MA	81	King Air C90A	8104015	Antonio Gonzalez-Ruiz MD PC. Maumee, Oh.	N381SW
N105MW	98	Pilatus PC-12/45	235	Management West LLC. Aurora, Or.	N235AH
N105RG	69	King Air B90	LJ-454	W L Barefoot LLC. Four Oaks, NC.	N105RJ
N105SL	03	P-180 Avanti	1068	AvantAir Inc. Clearwater, Fl.	
N105TC	84	King Air C90A	LJ-1086	Take Off Time LLC/Sunshine House, Greenwood, Ms.	N18182
N105VY	81	King Air B100	BE-109	Midlantic Jet Charters Inc. Egg Harbour, NJ	N3811F
N105WM	78	Mitsubishi MU-2N	709SA	Richland LLC. Columbia, SC.	N105NM
N106DD	05	King Air C90B	LJ-1738	HLP Aviation LLC/Hand Construction LLC, Heeveport La.	XA-EAM
N106ER	04	King Air 350ER	FL-424	Hawker Beechcraft Corp., Wichita, Ks.	N3724Q
N106GB	86	King Air 200	BB-1249	University of Georgia Athletic Association, Athens, Ga.	N879C
N106ML	05	King Air C90GT	LJ-1757	Zoe Aviation Inc. Chiacgo, Il.	N157EA
N106PA	07	King Air B200GT	BY-11	Wells Fargo Bank NW NA, Salt Lake City Ut.	N3311N
N106RH	79	King Air 200	BB-428	Renaissance Air LLC. Raleigh, NC.	N106PA
N106SL	03	P-180 Avanti	1070	AvantAir Inc. Fairfield NJ	
N106TT	80	Gulfstream 840	11630	Skytel Inc. Fort Lauderdale, Fl.	D-INRO
N107FL	76	King Air 200	BB-150	Selverne, Mandelbaum & Mintz LLP. NYC.	N203SF
N107GL	79	Rockwell 690B	11554	Western Eagle Express LLC. Brawley, Ca.	N84WA
N107PC	83	Cheyenne II-XL	8166046	Maca Inc. Wilmington, DE.	(N18KW)
N107SB	72	Mitsubishi MU-2F	226	Hilgy's LP Gas Inc. Tomahawk, Wi.	N187SB
N107SC	78	King Air C90	LJ-788	Golden Eagle Prtnrshp LC./T&TB Invstmnts, San Antonio, Tx.	N2030W
N107SL	03	P-180 Avanti	1073	AvantAir Inc. Fairfield NJ.	
N108AL	80	King Air 200	BB-730	High Flyin LLC. Daytona Beach, Fl.	N103AL
N108EB	81	King Air B100	BE-108	Andrie Inc. Muskegon, Mi.	N38005
N108JC	98	Pilatus PC-12/45	209	J W Connolly of Sewickley, Pa.	N209PB
N108JD	80	King Air C90	LJ-923	Procoil Aviation LLC. Marshall, Tx.	N30GK
N108KU	73	King Air C90	LJ-568	Magic Express Airlines Inc. Birmingham, Al.	N100KU
N108NL	79	PA-31T Cheyenne II	7920092	Plantation Holdings Ltd. Wilmington, De.	N78TW
N108SA	77	Rockwell 690B	11416	Top Wing LLC/Lund Assocs Inc. Rapid City, SD.	N81658
N108SL	06	P-180 Avanti II	1108	AvantAir Inc. Clearwater, Fl.	
N108TJ	79	Conquest II	441-0108	Martin's Super Markets Inc. South Bend, In.	N104RD
N108UC	80	PA-31T Cheyenne II	8020018	Inductotherm Industries Inc. Rancocas, NJ.	N802HC

Reg	Yr	Type	c/n	Owner/Operator	Prev Regn
☐ N109DT	85	King Air C90A	LJ-1102	HMS Aviation LLC. Jonesboro, Ar.	N682TA
☐ N109EM	90	120ER Brasilia	120195	Gillett Evernham Motorsports, Statesville, NC.	N15732
☐ N109MD	85	King Air B200	BB-1213	Mike Duncan/MBD Inc. Dover, De.	N74AL
☐ N109MS	90	P-180 Avanti	1008	Daymon Worldwide Inc/Draceana Corp. Stamford, Ct.	N1LY
☐ N109SL	04	P-180 Avanti	1092	AvantAir Inc. Clearwater, Fl.	N136PA
☐ N110BM	76	King Air 200	BB-110	Robert Hayes, Concord, NC.	OE-FIM
☐ N110CE	81	King Air B100	BE-120	Clark Services Consulting Corp. Bethesda, Md.	N2OE
☐ N110EL	65	King Air 90	LJ-71	Tradewinds Air Delaware LLC. Stockbridge, Ga.	N1100X
☐ N110G	81	King Air 200	BB-792	Gared Graphics Inc. Van Nuys, Ca.	
☐ N110GC	77	Mitsubishi MU-2P	363SA	Engineered Products Co. San Juan, PR.	(N178GV)
☐ N110HC	92	King Air 350	FL-69	BFL Aviation LLC., San Antonio, Tx.	N293TA
☐ N110MA	74	Mitsubishi MU-2J	616	AIC Aviation Inc. Sullivan, In.	SE-IUB
☐ N110PM	97	King Air C90B	LJ-1481	Mueller Transportation inc. Springfield, Mo.	N1101U
☐ N110RB	64	Gulfstream 1	126	Intermediaries International Inc. Del Mar, Ca.	N63AU
☐ N111AA	79	King Air F90	LA-6	Blue Water Aviation LLC. Oakman, Al.	C-GSSA
☐ N111CT	76	PA-31T Cheyenne II	7620047	Millennium Realty, Weston, Fl.	N82039
☐ N111EL	88	King Air 300	FA-144	C & E Holdings Inc., Madison, Md.	N333DV
☐ N111EN	85	King Air F90	LA-230	Pecos Air Inc./Read & Stevens Inc., Roswell, NM.	N111EL
☐ N111FV	74	King Air E90	LW-105	T & H Logistics LLC., Mt. Pleasant, SC.	N111FW
☐ N111HF	71	Mitsubishi MU-2F	208	DBH Attachments Inc. Adamsville, Tn.	N288MA
☐ N111JA	74	King Air E90	LW-84	Executive Air Charter of New Orleans, New Orleans, La.	TF-DCA
☐ N111KA	83	King Air C90-1	LJ-1051	PP & J LLC/Cyclone Drilling Inc. Gillette, Wy.	HP-976P
☐ N111KC	90	King Air C90A	LJ-1258	Shermore LLC. Dover, De.	N40MH
☐ N111KU	86	Conquest 1	425-0226	Herbert Baskin, Berkley, Ca.	(N264HB)
☐ N111KV	79	PA-31T Cheyenne II	7920035	American Medflight Inc. Reno, Nv.	N110MP
☐ N111LP	05	King Air B200	BB-1900	Lightnin' Production Rentals Inc. Lawrenceville, Ga.	N323JG
☐ N111M	98	King Air 350	FL-210	Ingram Industries Inc. Nashville, Tn.	N350WH
☐ N111MD	07	King Air 350	FL-547	Argosy Aircraft Inc., Reno, Nv.	
☐ N111MQ	99	King Air B200	BB-1665	Execumed Corp., Guaynabo, PR.	N111MD
☐ N111NS	81	King Air 200C	BL-36	Columbia Helicopters Inc. Aurora, Or.	
☐ N111PV	81	King Air 200	BB-772	Tarbert Aviation/MacAllister Machinery Co. Indianapolis, In.	(N917GP)
☐ N111RC	07	PA-46-500TP Meridian	4697330	Piper Aircraft Inc. Vero Beach, Fl.	
☐ N111SF	91	King Air 350	FL-45	Furrow Services LLC. Knoxville, Tn.	(N350FT)
☐ N111SK	67	680V Turbo Commander	1710-85	Bergman Photographic Services Inc. Portland, Or.	N111ST
☐ N111SS	84	King Air 300	FA-4	Robert Buhrmaster, Diamond Point, NY.	(N788SC)
☐ N111SU	84	Conquest 1	425-0205	Pilgrims Holdings Ltd. Hickory Corners, Mi.	N105TC
☐ N111TC	79	King Air E90	LW-305	Echo Rental/DeArtley Crushing Co. Lewiston, Id.	N942RM
☐ N111UT	78	King Air 200	BB-374	University of Tennessee, Alcoa, Tn.	N7QR
☐ N111VR	91	P-180 Avanti	1006	Neal Hawks/NNH Air LLC. Omaha, Ne.	N34S
☐ N111WA	73	King Air E90	LW-73	William Arrington, Pampa, Tx.	(N743EC)
☐ N111YF	77	King Air B200	BE-30	David Hawkins/Mission Aviation Group LLC. Odessa, Mo.	N110EC
☐ N112BB	81	PA-31T Cheyenne 1	8104021	Neil Whitesell, Muscle Shoals, Al.	N633AB
☐ N112BC	81	PA-42 Cheyenne III	8001027	Covington Aviation Inc. Covington, Ga.	
☐ N112BL	77	PA-31T Cheyenne II	7720037	North Dakota Department of Transport, Bismarck, ND.	
☐ N112CE	85	Gulfstream 1000	96097	Clark Transportation Co. Bethesda, Md.	N134GA
☐ N112CS	84	SA-227TT Merlin 3C	TT-541	Cal-Ark Inc. Little Rock, Ar.	N348KN
☐ N112ED	80	PA-31T Cheyenne II	8020060	E H Derby & Co/Alpha Jet Interrnational, Muscle Shoals, Al.	N703CJ
☐ N112EF	73	Rockwell 690A	11123	E F W Aircraft Sales Corp. Dover, De.	N122PG
☐ N112EM	76	Rockwell 690A	11330	E Micah Aviation Inc. Cincinnati, Oh.	N567H
☐ N112MA	77	Mitsubishi MU-2N	689SA	Somerset Spring & Alighment Inc. Raritan, NJ.	C-FTAD
☐ N113CT	70	681 Turbo Commander	6006	John Migliaccio MD PC. Idabel, Ok.	N2725B
☐ N113GF	93	King Air 350	FL-103	Grimmway Enterprises Inc. Bakersfield, Ca.	N6103K
☐ N113GS	80	SA-226T Merlin 3B	T-330	S & H Aircraft LLC., Portland, Or.	YV-788CP
☐ N113RC	75	PA-31T Cheyenne II	7520009	Air-Midsouth LLC. Jonesboro, Ar.	(N117BL)
☐ N113SD	73	Mitsubishi MU-2J	600	Air Flight Enterprises Inc. Port Orange, Fl.	N707TT
☐ N113SL	92	P-180 Avanti	1020	AvantAir Inc. Clearwater, Fl.	D-ITCN
☐ N113T	07	PA-46-500TP Meridian	4697312	Bill White Transportation Inc., Fort Smith, Ar.	
☐ N113UL	87	King Air B200	BB-1283	Aluminum Saloon LLC. Fort Worth, Tx.	N113US
☐ N113WC	80	PA-42 Cheyenne III	8001005	C & D Investments Inc. Fort Smith, Ar.	N13TT
☐ N114CW	81	King Air F90	LA-97	Louisiana Crane LLC. Sulphur, La.	N58EZ
☐ N114DB	85	King Air C90A	LJ-1097	Sump Ltd. Wilmington, De.	OY-JAJ
☐ N114HB	96	King Air B200	BB-1533	Mattic/Navajo Inc. Onalaska, Wi.	N14HB
☐ N114HL	82	Conquest 1	425-0110	K & D Aviation LLC. Johannesburg, Mi.	N555TP
☐ N114JR	80	PA-31T Cheyenne 1	8004037	Aysen Aviation Inc., Miami, Fl.	N900PC
☐ N114RG	06	King Air 350	FL-512	Royal Charter Inc/Royal Oil & Gas Corp. Indiana, Pa.	N7212S

Reg	Yr Type	c/n	Owner/Operator	Prev Regn
N114SB	76 King Air 200	BB-161	Seven Bar Flying Service Inc. Albuquerque, NM.	N131PA
N114WA	81 King Air E90	LW-346	Sawyer Air LLC., Columbia, SC.	N3821S
N115AB	74 Rockwell 690A	11231	Daedalus Enterprises LLC. Great Falls, Mt.	N115BH
N115AP	68 Mitsubishi MU-2F	136	Lagonia Holdings LLC/MAL Aircraft Sales, Cordova, Tn.	N75RJ
N115CT	99 King Air B200	BB-1669	Kavak Enterprises Ltd. Roadtown , Tortola, BVI.	
N115GA	85 Gulfstream 1000B	96201	Horizon Aircraft Sales Inc. Miami, Fl.	
N115KC	02 TBM 700B	239	Pegasus 115 LLC. Miami, Fl.	
N115PA	66 King Air A90	LJ-117	APA Enterprises Inc. Poughskeepsie, NY.	N10430
N115PC	78 PA-31T Cheyenne II	7820001	Eagles WingsAviation LLC. Monroeville, Al.	(N300PR)
N115TT	92 King Air 350	FL-74	Proressive Pipeline Inc. Livingston Al.	N317P
N116AF	96 Pilatus PC-12	137	Sanford Group LLC., Papillon, Ne.	(N316WF)
N116DG	81 King Air B100	BE-116	Structures Inc. Gilbert, Az.	N116AC
N116JP	81 PA-42 Cheyenne III	8001050	Turbines Inc. Terre Haute, In.	N4098K
N116SK	95 Pilatus PC-12	116	Kane Aviation LLC. Trenton, NJ.	N1JW
N116TH	07 Pilatus PC-12/47	860	Pilatus Business Aircraft Ltd, Broomfield Co.	HB-FSN
N117FH	76 King Air E90	LW-194	Uhrig Vournas Ventures Inc. New York NY.	N194KA
N117H	79 MU-2 Marquise	751SA	GoBuyAir LLC. Flint, Mi.	N948MA
N117MF	78 King Air C90	LJ-779	Mercy Flights Inc. Medford, Or.	(N107RE)
N117PW	01 PA-46-500TP Meridian	4697030	Johnson Potato Co. Walhalla, ND.	
N117TJ	80 King Air F90	LA-17	RaCon Inc. Tuscaloosa, Al.	N19EG
N118AF	97 Pilatus PC-12	175	CED Management Services Inc. Northbrook, Il.	HB-FSK
N118CR	76 Rockwell 690A	11276	Hokie Airco Inc. Roanoke, Va.	N57172
N118GW	87 King Air 300	FA-119	Majestic Aviation Inc. Bakersfield, Ca.	N688RL
N118JV	05 PA-46-500TP Meridian	4697235	Wells Fargo Bank NW NA.Salt Lake City, Ut	
N118MF	94 King Air C90B	LJ-1383	Mercy Flights Inc., Medford, Or.	N90WP
N118MJ	82 King Air F90	LA-199	Coshocton Air Ltd., Coshocton, Oh.	N5NW
N118NL	81 King Air B100	BE-111	Lambert's Cafe/Bo-Lamb Corp., Sikeston, Mo.	N400TJ
N118P	74 Mitsubishi MU-2J	646	Newair LLC. Newport, Ar.	N113P
N118WC	80 PA-31T Cheyenne II	8020020	Halair Inc. Wilmington, De.	N113WC
N119AR	04 King Air B200	BB-1867	AR Equipment/Armstrong Transfer & Storage Co. Morrisville.	N6167R
N119EB	77 PA-31T Cheyenne II	7720012	Michael Harper, Duncanville, Tx.	N79ML
N119FJ	80 King Air F90	LA-70	Floyd Johnston Construction, Clovis, Ca.	N990BM
N119MC	85 King Air B200	BB-1225	B200 LLC/Downing Co. Zanesville, Oh.	N848PF
N119RL	79 PA-31T Cheyenne 1	7904002	VP 410 LLC/Virginia Air Exchange Inc., Chicago, Il.	D-IEIS
N119SA	89 King Air C90A	LJ-1196	Sara Air LLC/Ledford Medical Electronics Inc. Greensboro, NC	N484JA
N120FA	82 SA-227AT Merlin 4C	AT-461	Transair America Inc. Buffalo Grove, Il. (status ?).	F-GGLF
N120FS	03 King Air B200	BB-1843	Dubois County Flight Services Inc., Huntingburg, In.	N356CC
N120JM	84 SA-227AT Merlin 4C	AT-577	Worldwide Aircraft Services Inc., Springfield, Mo.	N31136
N120MG	79 King Air B100	BE-70	Eagle Creek Aviation Services Inc. Indianapolis, In.	N926HS
N120NA	83 King Air B200	BB-1120	Washington State Patrol, Olympia, Wa.	N6609K
N120P	81 King Air 200	BB-786	Air Shares Inc., Grand Island, Ne.	
N120PR	83 King Air B200T	BT-29	Commonwealth of Puerto Rico, San Juan, PR.(was BB-1097).	N150BA
N120RC	81 King Air F90	LA-117	R R Cassidy Inc. Baton Rouge, La.	N7775
N120RL	79 King Air 200T	BT-9	Global Aircraft Leasing Inc. Griffin, Ga. (was BB-551).	JA8814
N120RP	84 King Air C90A	LJ-1075	Mallory & Evans Aviation LLC., Scottdale, Ga.	N129RP
N120SC	78 SA-226AT Merlin 4A	AT-067	McNeely Charter Service Inc. West Memphis, Az.	C-FJTL
N120SK	81 Cheyenne II-XL	8166039	Kingland Systems/SK Air LLC., Clear Lake, Ia.	N121EH
N120SL	01 PA-46-500TP Meridian	4697057	VIP Flight US Corp. Wilmington, De.	C-FGDM
N120TM	81 SA-226T Merlin 3B	T-405	OG LLC. Birmingham, Al.	N189CC
N120TT	84 King Air C90A	LJ-1073	ASM Air LLC. Apopka, Fl.	HP-1152
N120WW	01 PA-46-500TP Meridian	4697047	Aircraft Guaranty Title LLC. Houston, Tx. (trustor ?).	LX-ILE
N121B	72 King Air E90	LW-21	Goodland Regional Medical Center, Goodland, Ks.	
N121CA	73 King Air C-12C	BD-9	California Department of Justice, Sacramento, Ca.	73-1213
N121EG	73 King Air E90	LW-71	Falcon Executive Inc. Mesa, Az.	
N121FM	75 Rockwell 690A	11257	ELG Holdings & Mngmt/Aircraft Guaranty Title, Houston, Tx.	XB-HGG
N121JW	76 Rockwell 690A	11299	K Investments Ltd. Montoursville, Pa.	(N121DK)
N121KB	68 SA-26T Merlin 2A	T26-33	Eastern Aviation & Marine Underwriters, Towson, Md.	N1215S
N121LB	79 King Air 200	BB-475	Berry Air LLC. Tahlequah, Ok.	
N121LH	90 PA-42 Cheyenne IIIA	5501049	Wells Fargo Bank NW NA/Banco de Machaia S.A., Ecuador	N949TA
N121P	81 King Air C90	LJ-970	Lane Aviation Corp. Columbus, Oh.	
N121PH	97 Pilatus PC-12	186	Patrick McCall, Orange, Ca.	(N186PH)
N121RF	95 Pilatus PC-12	114	Richard A Foreman Associates Inc. Wilmington, De.	N114SV
N121TD	78 King Air C-12C	BC-74	Idaho Department of Law Enforcement, Boise, Id.	78-23138
N121WH	92 P-180 Avanti	1019	N Idaho Air/Tomlinson Black Real Estate, Coeur d'Alene, Id.	D-IHRA
N122AV	75 Rockwell 690A	11235	Willowbrook Ford Inc. Willowbrook, Il.	N1KG

Reg	Yr Type	c/n	Owner/Operator	Prev Regn
N122CK	78 Mitsubishi MU-2P	374SA	Lycoming Aviation Inc. Williamsport, Pa.	N9HA
N122K	77 King Air C90	LJ-707	Dycom Aviation LLC. Greensboro, NC.	(N32HF)
N122MA	71 Mitsubishi MU-2F	207	Jovan Aircraft Services Inc.	
N122PA	00 P-180 Avanti	1038	AvantAir Inc. Fairfield Nj.	
N122RG	05 King Air 350	FL-448	Riversville Aircraft Corp. White Plains, NY.	I-FXRD
N122TP	88 King Air B200	BB-1293	Tango Papa Aviation LLC. Telluride, Co.	N3127K
N122U	70 King Air 100	B-32	Coastal Wings Inc. Nantucket, Ma.	C-GSAM
N122ZZ	69 King Air 100	B-6	Pelican Aircraft LLC. Naples, Fl.	N169MM
N123AC	98 King Air B200	BB-1605	ACS Air LLC. Oklahoma City, Ok.	N923FP
N123AF	85 King Air 300	FA-46	Tecnicard Inc. Miami, Fl.	N7222U
N123AG	81 PA-42 Cheyenne III	8001031	Cheyenne III Inc. Gainesville, Ga.	N123CN
N123BL	80 King Air B100	BE-83	Skyway K West LLC. Clarksville, Tn.	N412FC
N123CF	99 Pilatus PC-12/45	286	Hud-Four LLC. Sanford, Fl.	ZS-SDP
N123CH	80 King Air F90	LA-32	Adobe Airways LLC/Adobe Oilfield Services Odesa Tx.	N969MC
N123EA	79 PA-31T Cheyenne II	7920028	Beech Group Inc. Carnegie, Pa.	N10MC
N123LH	82 SA-227TT Merlin 3C	TT-433	Blackwater USA, McLean, Va.	C-GFCE
N123LL	80 King Air C90	LJ-885	Page Air Inc. Midlothian, Va.	N1WB
N123ME	86 Conquest II	441-0359	Time Quest LLC/Hilliard Construction, Midland, Tx.	N40FJ
N123MH	74 King Air E90	LW-104	Findlay LLC. McCall, Id.	N133PL
N123ML	97 King Air B200	BB-1587	ML Wings LLC. Chappaqua, NY.	N3270Q
N123SK	72 King Air C90	LJ-540	Metair LLC/Met Games LLC Tulsa, Ok.	(N690CA)
N123TS	05 PA-46-500TP Meridian	4697219	T Stacy & Assocs Inc. Austin, Tx.	
N123V	67 King Air A90	LJ-258	Milwaukee Area Technical College, Milwaukee, Wi.	N915BD
N123ZC	02 TBM 700B	229	Jasper Industries Ltd. Wilmington, De.	F-HELO
N124BK	80 King Air F90	LA-15	MTB Investments LLC. Idaho Falls, Id.	N237JS
N124CM	84 King Air 300	FA-24	Snow Peak Ventures LLC. Spanish Fork, Ut.	N300KA
N124EB	94 King Air 350	FL-126	Natural Selection Foods, San Juan Baitista, Ca.	N102CS
N124EK	07 King Air B200	BB-1993	Franed Corp., Akron, Oh.	
N124GA	82 King Air B200	BB-1039	SBP Aviation LLC. Richmond, Tx.	HB-GHS
N124LL	03 King Air C90B	LJ-1695	Longleaf Aviation LLC. Newton, Ga.	
N124PA	06 P-180 Avanti II	1122	Robert J Pond Living Trust, Palm Springs, Ca.	
N124PS	03 Pilatus PC-12/45	502	Duck Pond Aviation II LLC. San Jose, Ca.	HB-FRH
N124SA	67 King Air A90	LJ-306	Smyrna Air Center Inc. Smyrna, Tn.	YV-2683P
N124UV	95 Pilatus PC-12	124	Kiowa Aircraft Leasing LLC. Colorado Springs, Co.	N124PB
N125A	68 King Air B90	LJ-360	Kijivu Aviation LLC., Charlottesville, Va.	N1250B
N125AR	06 King Air C90GT	LJ-1790	Rushton Air Inc., Auburn, Al.	N42MJ
N125BK	82 King Air B200	BB-977	KLM Oil Properties LLC. Amarillo, Tx.	N607KW
N125D	81 King Air B100	BE-114	James Naples/New Boston General Hospital Inc. New Boston, Tx	
N125MM	80 Gulfstream 840	11605	Xentrapharm Ltd. Dublin, Ireland.	HB-GPB
N125NC	82 King Air B200	BB-1023	N Carolina Department of Commerce, Raleigh, NC.	N62546
N125PG	82 Conquest 1	425-0125	Douglas Barkdull, Scottsdale, Az.	N125VE
N125SC	83 Conquest 1	425-0136	James E Simon Co. Cheyenne, Wy.	N6884G
N125TS	92 King Air B200	BB-1422	Tri-State Generation & Transmission Inc. Broomfield, Co.	N422BW
N125VH	77 King Air B100	BE-25	Valley Hope Association, Norton, Ks.	N125U
N125WG	75 SA-226T Merlin 3A	T-250	Century Turbines of Nevada Inc., Georgetown, Tx.	N85DB
N125WZ	01 PA-46-500TP Meridian	4697032	Miniter Resources Partners Inc. Norwell, Ma.	
N126BK	06 Pilatus PC-12/47	696	Aircraft Guaranty Title LLC. Houston, Tx. (trustor ?).	HB-FQZ
N126DS	90 King Air 350	FL-31	CanDo Air LLC. Martinez, Ga.	(N331JH)
N126KA	85 King Air B200	BB-1222	Integrity Aero LLC., San Antonio, Tx.	(N50FC)
N126M	80 Gulfstream 980	95033	Barbee's Freeway Ford Inc. Denver, Co.	N8774P
N126MM	01 King Air C90B	LJ-1669	Technical Film Systems Inc. Van Nuys, Ca.	N4469Z
N126SP	85 King Air B200	BB-1209	Aero Care Services LLC. Mendham, NJ.	(N53GA)
N126WA	85 King Air C90A	LJ-1093	Sea & Air Inc/Atlantic Shellfish Inc. Cape May, NJ.	F-GLLA
N127AA	77 Rockwell 690B	11403	Atlantic Aviation Group Inc. Miami Fl.	N11HY
N127BB	80 Conquest 1	425-0012	Sound Security Inc. Portland, Or.	N127DC
N127DC	82 King Air F90	LA-177	King Air F90 Charter LLC. Zanesville, Oh.	N418DY
N127EC	78 King Air E90	LW-299	Fridge & Associates LLP, Houston Tx.	N127BB
N127GA	77 King Air 200	BB-312	Beech Transportation Inc/Aviation Charter, Eden Prairie, Mn.	F-GEBC
N127MC	85 Conquest 1	425-0231	McCoy Corp. San Marcos, Tx.	N12270
N127MJ	83 King Air B200	BB-1132	King Air Charter LLC. Zanesville, Oh.	N152C
N127TA	80 King Air 200	BB-636	Pacific International Marketing, Salinas, Ca.	N806TC
N127WD	79 SA-226T Merlin 3B	T-297	Nassau Aircraft Holdings LLC. Garden City, Ga.	N111CZ
N127Z	74 King Air A100	B-179	USDA Forest Service, Boise, Id.	N20EG
N128AS	06 King Air B200	BB-1950	A Schulman Inc. Akron, Oh.	N70150
N128CM	01 Pilatus PC-12/45	403	Eagle Cap Leasing Inc. Enterprises, Or.	HB-FQT

Reg	Yr Type	c/n	Owner/Operator	Prev Regn
N128EZ	80 Conquest II	441-0128	D & D Enterprises LLC. Anchorage, Ak.	N441TM
N128GH	01 Pilatus PC-12/45	369	Grimme Aviation LLC. Fort Lauderdale, Fl.	VP-BKD
N128JP	80 King Air F90	LA-25	Oklahoma Steel & Wire Co. Madill, Ok.	N616CP
N128SB	97 King Air C90B	LJ-1503	Digger Pine Enterprises LLC. Saratoga, Ca.	N9MU
N128SL	91 P-180 Avanti	1011	AvantAir Inc. Clearwater, Fl.	N301SL
N128VT	92 King Air B200	BB-1442	Missouri Dept of Conservation, Jefferson City, Mo.	N128V
N129AG	00 TBM 700B	171	Aircraft Guaranty Management LLC/Allan Thomsen N.V.	D-FBOY
N129AG	97 Pilatus PC-12	171	Aircraft Guaranty Management LLC, Houston Tx.	N171PD
N129C	79 King Air E90	LW-61	Eagle Aviation LLC/Eagle Resort Properties, Avon, Co.	N120GR
N129DW	74 Mitsubishi MU-2J	653	Bill Austin Aircraft & Yacht Sales, Sparta, Tn.	N45CE
N129EJ	01 PA-46-500TP Meridian	4697065	Ventana Enterprises LLC. Tulsa, Ok.	
N129JW	96 Pilatus PC-12	129	AirCorp Inc. Dallas, Tx.	N412KC
N129LA	66 King Air A90	LJ-129	Aviones Inc. Wilmington, De.	N7202L
N129LC	79 PA-31T Cheyenne 1	7904042	129LC LLC/High Air Inc. Plano, Tx.	N247R
N129TB	81 Gulfstream 840	11676	Semitool Inc. Kalispell, Mt.	N5928K
N129TT	82 King Air B200	BB-1078	MN King Air LLC. White Bear, Mn.	(N781HM)
N130CT	79 King Air 200	BB-578	Southeast Airmotive Corp. Charlotte, NC.	N303DK
N130DM	68 King Air B90	LJ-385	FMCO Promotions, Little Rock, Ar.	N33AS
N130EM	03 P-180 Avanti	1063	Eagle Materials Aviation LLC. Dallas, Tx.	C-FFST
N130MS	79 MU-2 Marquise	750SA	International Aviation Inc. Hydes, Md.	N947MA
N130RL	80 King Air 200T	BT-16	Airtec Inc./Oscar Charlie II LLC., California, Md.	JA8820
N130SC	88 King Air B200C	BL-130	LLM Air LLC/Coral Industries, Tuscaloosa, Al.	C-GWXM
N130SL	04 P-180 Avanti	1084	AvantAir Inc. Clearwater, Fl.	N306SL
N130TT	78 Rockwell 690B	11495	T & T Machine Shop Inc. Kingmont, WV.	N76EC
N131DF	79 PA-31T Cheyenne 1	7904015	Great Bear Aviation Co. Wheeling, Il.	N23235
N131JN	02 Pilatus PC-12/45	446	Arizona Aircraft Inc Prescott Valley,Az.	N446PC
N131PC	78 PA-31T Cheyenne II	7820009	N131PC LLC. Springfield, Mo.	
N131SJ	76 King Air 200	BB-131	Dominion Gas LLC. Dallas, Tx.	TC-TAB
N131SL	05 P-180 Avanti	1097	AvantAir Inc. Clearwater, Fl.	
N131SP	83 King Air F90-1	LA-206	Kaufmann Land & Development LLC. Denver, Co.	(N4UC)
N131TC	77 King Air 200	BB-271	Trical Inc. Hollister, Ca.	N69BK
N132AS	81 King Air C90	LJ-928	ASI Holdings Inc. Albany, Ga.	N5095K
N132BK	81 MU-2 Marquise	1529SA	Flight Line Inc. Salt Lake City, Ut.	N818R
N132CC	84 King Air 300	FA-11	Club Car Inc. Augusta, Ga.	N732P
N132DD	79 King Air E90	LW-308	Innovative Aviators LLC. Norman, Ok.	N2DD
N132HS	72 King Air E90	LW-8	TNT Air LLC	N132B
N132JH	73 Rockwell 690A	11126	C & F Aviation, Norman, Ok.	(N345SP)
N132MC	92 King Air B200	BB-1395	Louisiana Aircraft LLC. Oklahoma City, Ok.	N8049H
N132N	82 King Air B200	BB-1053	David & Diane Miller, Bandon, Or.	(N212DM)
N132SL	05 P-180 Avanti	1098	AvantAir Inc. Fairield, NJ	
N133DL	80 Gulfstream 840	11616	Safeguards International Inc. Charlotte, NC.	D-IGEL
N133FM	81 PA-42 Cheyenne III	8001010	Plane 1 Leasing Co. Naples, Fl.	YV-O-ICA-1
N133GA	89 King Air B200	BB-1321	Mid-America Apartments LP. Memphis, Tn.	F-GILI
N133K	94 King Air B200	BB-1487	Super King Partners LLC. Fayetteville, NC.	(D-IAJK)
N133NL	01 King Air 350	FL-332	Executive Airshare Corp. Wichita Ks.	N4332U
N133PA	02 P-180 Avanti	1062	Copo Aviation LLC., Salem, Or.	
N133US	90 King Air B200C	BL-133	Universal Sales & Leasing LLC, Prattville, Al.	VQ-TRS
N134G	01 PA-46-500TP Meridian	4697041	Imperial Air LP, McAllen, Tx.	
N134M	03 PA-46-500TP Meridian	4697169	Cos Aircraft LLC. Colorado Springs, Co.	
N134SL	05 P-180 Avanti	1100	AvantAir Inc. Clearwater, Fl.	
N134W	65 King Air A90	LJ-52	Lucaya Air Enterprise Inc. Opa Locka, Fl.	N90BL
N134WJ	89 King Air B200C	BL-134	Evergreen Helicopters Inc. McMinnville, Or.	SE-LMP
N135CL	77 PA-31T Cheyenne II	7720019	Blue Sky of Arizona LLC., Scottsdale, Az.	N75465
N135FL	02 PA-46-500TP Meridian	4697135	Pearl Runway Inc. Irvine, Ca.	
N135JM	01 PA-46-500TP Meridian	4697072	P & M Land Ventures LLC. Oceanside, Ca.	C-GNSS
N135MK	84 King Air 300	FA-3	McDonald Oil Company, La Grange, Ga.	N67683
N136AJ	90 King Air B200C	BL-136	Balmoral Central Contracts Inc.	ZS-SON
N136JH	70 King Air 100	B-25	Sky Med Inc. Haleiwa, Hi.	N352NR
N136MB	78 King Air B100	BE-50	AirStar Aviation LLC. Athens, Ga.	N955FC
N136PA	75 King Air C90	LJ-662	Cactus Feeders Inc/Amstad Aviation. Amarillo Tx.	RP-C3650
N136SL	05 P-180 Avanti	1101	AvantAir Inc. Clearwater, Fl.	
N137CD	84 Conquest 1	425-0220	Emerald Eagle LLC. Claremont, NH.	N425AD
N137CP	69 SA-26AT Merlin 2B	T26-136	Air Jordan LLC. Newport News, Va.	N51LF
N137CW	79 PA-31T Cheyenne 1	7904052	Airvest LLC. Bristol, Va.	N72TW
N137JE	80 PA-31T Cheyenne II	8020014	J & T Implements LLC. Lenexa, Ks.	N137JT

Reg   Yr Type   c/n   Owner/Operator   Prev Regn

Reg	Yr	Type	c/n	Owner/Operator	Prev Regn
N137SL	05	P-180 Avanti	1102	AvantAir Inc. Fairfield NJ.	
N138JM	91	TBM 700	7	Howard J Gross, Linwood, NJ.	D-FGYY
N138RB	81	King Air F90	LA-111	Matrix Development Corp/Red Baron Air LLC., Portland, Or.	N10DH
N138SL	05	P-180 Avanti	1103	AvantAir Inc. Fairfield Nj.	
N139B	72	King Air C90	LJ-563	Rocky Mountain Air PMG LLC. Hamilton, Mt.	
N139CS	81	PA-31T Cheyenne II	8120004	Chandler Systems Inc. Ashland, Oh.	C-GSSC
N139SC	79	King Air C90	LJ-868	Southwest Aviation dba Midwest Aviation,Marshall, Mn.	F-GERL
N139SL	05	P-180 Avanti	1104	AvantAir Inc. Clearwater, Fl.	
N140CM	70	Mitsubishi MU-2F	190	Marlin Crane Inc. Greenwood, In.	N111MA
N140CP	77	Mitsubishi MU-2P	362SA	Kozarksy Aviation Inc. Atlanta, Ga.	N801L
N140PA	67	King Air A90	LJ-297	Prime Aviation LLC. Brookfield, Wi.	N839K
N140RL	82	King Air 200T	BT-22	Global Aircraft Leasing Inc. Griffin, Ga.	JA8829
N140SL	06	P-180 Avanti II	1107	AvantAir Inc. Clearwater, Fl.	
N140WT	96	King Air 350	FL-140	Plane Crackers LLC. Avon Park, Fl. (5000th King Air).	(N806JN)
N141CE	03	King Air 350	FL-387	Request Air Services LLC, Piney Flats Tn.	N5117S
N141CT	80	King Air 200	BB-651	CG Aviation LLC., Pittsburgh, Pa.	N132GA
N141DA	93	King Air 350	FL-92	L & K Inc. Omaha, Ne.	(N141DB)
N141GA	80	PA-31T Cheyenne 1	8004022	Stratford Aviation Co. Lincoln, Ne.	G-BHTP
N141K	97	King Air 350	FL-161	Victor One Four One LLC. Lincoln, Ma.	OY-LEL
N141L	06	King Air 350	FL-524	Cooper-Healey/Victor One Four One LLC., Lincoln, Ma.	
N141RR	65	King Air 90	LJ-38	APA Enterprises Inc. Poughskeepsie, NY.	C-GGGL
N141SM	84	King Air 300	FA-23	Smith Air LLC/Le Bleu Corp. Advance, NC.	N313MP
N141TC	84	PA-42 Cheyenne IIIA	5501021	Joseph Meyer, Edwardsville, Il.	N200JH
N142CE	04	King Air 350	FL-391	Request Air Services LLC, Piney Flats, Tn.	N5091G
N142EB	82	King Air B200	BB-1042	MITC Aviation LLC. Prairie Village, Ks.	N447AC
N142EE	05	PA-46-500TP Meridian	4697217	Hartley/Derenzo LLC., Ocala, Fl.	
N142JC	80	King Air B100	BE-93	The Quintin Little Company LLC,Ardmore, Ok.	XC-IMC
N142LT	00	Pilatus PC-12/45	312	Turner Lyle C	N142LT
N143CE	92	King Air 350	FL-91	Request Air Svs LLC/Total Land Exploration Inc, Baltimore,Md	N227KM
N143DE	80	King Air 200	BB-585	PTC Aviation LLC. Wilmington, De.	N43PE
N143DK	00	King Air 350	FL-309	Caliber Capital Group LLC., Anaheim, Ca.	C-GKMS
N143JA	75	Mitsubishi MU-2M	324	BAR Realty Corp. San Juan, PR.	N512MA
N143SL	06	P-180 Avanti II	1109	AvantAir Inc. Clearwater, Fl./R & E Enterprises	
N143Z		DHC 6-300	437	USDA Forest Service, Boise, Id.	
N144AB	89	King Air 300	FA-176	BAL Metals International Inc.Stamford, Ct.	XA-ALT
N144JB	85	Gulfstream 900	15039	Skytel Inc. Fort Lauderdale, Fl.	N61GA
N144JT	98	TBM 700B	144	Hallick Aviation Services LLC, Madison Wi.	
N144MF	07	Pilatus PC-12/47	828	Pilatus 144MF LLC., Ketchum, Id.	HB-FRQ
N144PL	84	PA-42 Cheyenne 400LS	5527014	Four-Four Inc., Farmington, NM.	N400SN
N145AF	04	King Air C90B	LJ-1721	Downwind Aviation Sales Inc. Gorham Me.	N6196S
N145DC	92	King Air 350	FL-89	DC & Assocs of SC Inc/Dublin Construction Co., Columbia,SC.	N490TN
N145DP	03	PA-46-500TP Meridian	4697166	Duratek LLC. Brooksville, Fl.	N166PM
N145FS	81	MU-2 Solitaire	437SA	Professional Aviation Sales & Service, Millington, Tn.	N666AM
N145GS	07	P-180 Avanti II	1145	Starboard Aviation LLC, Addison, Tx.	
N145JP	81	King Air 200	BB-818	Flynt Inc. Wilmington De.	N80QB
N145LG	82	King Air B200	BB-1069	Aero Air LLC. Hillsboro, Or.	N828FM
N145MJ	76	King Air C-12C	BC-24	My Jet Inc. Cary, NC.	N716GA
N145MR	81	King Air F90	LA-125	Aviation M R LLC. Wilmington, De.	N65MM
N145SL	04	P-180 Avanti	1093	AvantAir Inc. Clearwater, Fl.	N308SL
N146FL	80	King Air F90	LA-59	Keep Holdings Inc. Wilmington, De.	G-FLTI
N146GW	83	Conquest 1	425-0146	C & E Cattle Co. Yuma, Az.	N146FW
N146MH	81	King Air B200	BB-885	MHG Leasing Inc. Greenville, SC.	N146BC
N146PC	96	PC-12 Spectre	146	LMCO, Las Vegas, Nv.	N777JF
N146SL	04	P-180 Avanti	1091	AvantAir Inc. Clearwater, Fl.	N307SL
N147AA	91	King Air B200	BB-1403	Arcadia Aviation/Chesapeake Bay Partners LLC, New York, NY.	N33BK
N147NA	82	King Air B200	BB-1047	C C Medflight Inc. Lawrenceville, Ga.	ZS-LIL
N147SL	04	P-180 Avanti	1083	AvantAir Inc. Clearwater, Fl.	N305SL
N147TA	99	King Air C90B	LJ-1553	Flag Air LLC/Buffalo Rock Company, Birmingham, Al.	N394B
N148AA	05	King Air B300C	FM-12	Arcadia Aviation/Chesapeake Bay Partners I LLC., New York,	N132TJ
N148Z	69	King Air B90	LJ-472	USDA Forest Service, Washington, DC.	(N204FW)
N149CC	88	King Air 300	FA-145	Cianbro Corp. Baltimore, Md.	N145NA
N149CF	80	King Air C90	LJ-925	Careflite/LaSalle Natl Leasing Corp, Grand Prairie, Tx.	N925MM
N149CM	88	King Air C90A	LJ-1184	KBC Air LLC/Cogswell Motors Inc. Russellville, Ar.	N483JA
N149SL	04	P-180 Avanti	1077	AvantAir Inc. Clearwater, Fl.	N304SL
N149Z	82	King Air B200C	BL-124	USDA Forest Service, Washington, DC.	N107Z

Reg	Yr	Type	c/n	Owner/Operator	Prev Regn
N150GW	98	King Air C90B	LJ-1531	Southwest Tape & Label Inc. El Paso, Tx.	N2309J
N150RL	82	King Air B200C	BL-50	Global Aircraft Leasing Inc.,Griffin, Ca.	N58AS
N150SL	06	P-180 Avanti II	1111	AvantAir Inc. Bedfod Ma.	
N150TJ	76	King Air B100	BE-3	Pennington Seed Inc. Madison, Ga.	N9103S
N150TK	84	Cheyenne II-XL	1166008	Tiffin Aire Inc. Tiffin,/Wilcox Aviation LLC Oh.	N150RC
N150TW	73	King Air E90	LW-50	Chaparral Inc/Ameristar Jet Charter Inc. Dallas, Tx.	N88GC
N150VE	76	King Air C90	LJ-678	Eagle Oil & Gas Co. Wichita Falls, Ks.	N9091S
N150YA	82	King Air B100	BE-124	Hospital Investors Management Corp. Englewood Cliffs, NJ.	(N150YR)
N150YR	82	King Air B100	BE-132	Central Control Inc. Alexandria, La.	
N151BG	90	King Air B200	BB-1381	Blossman Gas of N Carolina Inc. Asheville, NC.	N800ET
N151CF	96	King Air B200	BB-1551	Weather Modification Inc./Aerolease LLC., Fargo, ND.	N969TS
N151E	00	King Air 350	FL-298	Waterloo Industries Inc. Waterloo, Ia.	N4298H
N151EL	78	King Air 200	BB-371	Di Ma Corp. Alnbert Lea, Mn.	N151E
N151GS	80	PA-31T Cheyenne II	8020024	Strausser Enterprises Inc. Easton, Pa.	N103SP
N151MP	81	Cheyenne II-XL	8166063	Minnkota Power Co-Operative, Grand Forks, ND.	N776AK
N151WT	83	King Air B200	BB-1151	KO Aviation LLC./Coach Quarters LLC., Cleves, Oh.	XA-MCB
N152AL	04	PA-46-500TP Meridian	4697182	Aeromed Equipment Leasing LLC. Minnetonka, Mn.	
N152D	75	King Air E90	LW-119	Stone Land Co. Startford, Ca.	N102CU
N152PC	04	Pilatus PC-12/45	552	Aircraft Guaranty Title LLC. Houston, Tx. (trustor ?).	HB-FSU
N152RP	86	King Air B200	BB-1255	Sendero Energy Inc. Dallas, Tx.	(N86KA)
N152SL	92	P-180 Avanti	1014	JMMS LLC/River East Transportation Inc. Chicago, Il.	N330DM
N152TW	76	King Air 200	BB-152	Chapparal Inc/Ameristar Jet Charter Inc. Dallas, Tx.	N1223C
N152WW	75	King Air C90	LJ-654	Excell Aviation LLC/Jetflite Inc. Gulf Stream, Fl.	N917K
N153JA	70	King Air 100	B-53	King Air N153JA LLC., Hopewell, Va.	N153JW
N153JM	83	Conquest 1	425-0153	231 Inc. Nashville, Tn.	C-GAGE
N153ML	75	King Air 200	BB-23	L & G Equipment Company/Lindsey Contractors Inc.Waco Tx.	N814KA
N153PB	96	Pilatus PC-12/45	153	E L Thompson & Son Inc. St Croix, USVI.	HB-FRO
N153PE	87	King Air 300	FA-133	Platt Electric Supply Inc. Beaverton, Or.	N53PE
N153SL	02	P-180 Avanti	1054	AvantAir Inc. Clearwater, Fl.	N701GT
N153TC	07	PA-46-500TP Meridian	4697307	Croley Equipment Leasing LLC., Ocala, Fl.	
N154BA	80	King Air 200	BB-599	Hydro Aviation LLC. Houston, Tx.	N48CR
N154CA	80	PA-31T Cheyenne II	8020085	Fedair Inc. Wilmington, De.	D-IIPA
N154DF	04	Pilatus PC-12/45	601	DMF Equipment Leasing LLC. Eau Claire, Wi.	N1983R
N154DR	01	PA-46-500TP Meridian	4697034	Jessee Kent, Big Sky, Mt.	N4189N
N154L	77	SA-226T Merlin 3A	T-284	RGOI LLC., Tehachapi, Ca.	(N28TA)
N154WC	70	Mitsubishi MU-2G	509	Schuybroeck Aviation Inc. Dover, De.	C-GBOX
N155A	91	King Air C90A	LJ-1257	Air Partners N155A Co. Youngstown, Oh.	N8255A
N155AV	85	King Air B200	BB-1216	Avcenter Inc./Teton Aviation LLC. Pocatello, Id.	(N210AC)
N155CA	78	PA-31T Cheyenne II	7820024	Reno Flying Service Inc. Reno, Nv.	YV-...
N155LS	78	King Air E90	LW-286	Wallingford Corp. Blowing Rock, NC.	N18754
N155MC	78	PA-31T Cheyenne II	7820069	BG Aviation Inc/B-G Machine Inc. New Haven, Ky.	N168DA
N155QS	75	King Air 200	BB-79	R & J Aviation Inc. Sugar Grove, Il.	N155RJ
N155RG	06	King Air C90GT	LJ-1782	Rasmussen Group Inc. Des Moines, Ia.	N782EA
N155SL	91	P-180 Avanti	1013	ComVest Group Holdings LLC. West Palm Beach, Fl.	N128PA
N156CH	89	King Air 300	FA-188	Family Video Movie Club Inc. Glenview, Il.	N815D
N156GA	83	Conquest 1	425-0134	M-W Air LC. Lubbock, Tx.	HB-LNT
N156MG	00	King Air C90B	LJ-1615	Pinehill Capital Partners Inc. Tampa, Fl.	N700KB
N156SB	96	Pilatus PC-12	156	Yoyo LLC. Bremerton, Wa.	HB-FRR
N156SL	06	P-180 Avanti II	1115	AvantAir Inc. Clearwater, Fl.	(N140SL)
N156SW	03	Pilatus PC-12/45	514	Classic Flight Corp. Forney, Tx.	HB-FRQ
N157A	82	King Air B200C	BL-53	Aviation Specialities Inc. Washington, DC.	N320JS
N157CA	82	MU-2 Marquise	1558SA	Flight Line Inc. Denver, Co.	N5PQ
N157CB	78	King Air C90	LJ-758	Prairie Investments LLC. Crossett, Ar.	N900SC
N157JB	91	TBM 700	6	Milton Holcombe, Dallas, Tx.	N700ZL
N157LL	81	PA-42 Cheyenne III	8001058	Lima/Lima Aviation Services LLC. Lakeland, Fl.	N4098T
N157MA	80	MU-2 Solitaire	424SA	Sabre Investments Inc. Rapid City, SD.	
N157PA	86	Beech 1900C	UB-56	Joda LLC., Chesterfield, Mo.	N505RH
N157SL	06	P-180 Avanti II	1116	AvantAir Inc. Bedford Ma.	
N158CA	68	SA-26AT Merlin 2B	T26-107	S & J Enterprises Inc. Fort Lauderdale, Fl.	C-GMOU
N158J	07	King Air C90GT	LJ-1859	Stevens Aviation Inc. Greenville, SC	
N158SL	06	P-180 Avanti II	1119	AvantAir Inc. Fairfield NJ.	
N158TJ	81	PA-42 Cheyenne III	8001057	Northeast Skywagon LLC/Frank L Woodworth, Pittsfield, Me.	(N821TB)
N159DG	79	PA-31T Cheyenne II	7920024	Garbo Lobster Co. Groton, Ct.	N111HT
N159GS	69	Gulfstream 1	200	Aircraft Sales Corp. Crystal Lake, Il.	N255TK
N159JB	91	King Air 350	FL-57	Byram Properties/By-Car Inc. Austin, Tx.	N15WD

Reg	Yr Type	c/n	Owner/Operator	Prev Regn
❏ N159SL	06 P-180 Avanti II	1121	AvantAir Inc. Fairfield, Nj.	
❏ N160AC	03 King Air 350	FL-367	Elkhorn Aviation LLC./Andreini & Company, San Mateo, Ca.	N6167K
❏ N160EA	69 SA-26AT Merlin 2B	T26-165	JBI Holdings Inc. Wilmington, De.	C-GMZG
❏ N160MW	04 King Air 350	FL-407	Cenac Towing Company Inc., Houma, La.	
❏ N160SF	75 King Air 200	BB-32	LVAC LLC. Henderson, Nv.	N100SF
❏ N160SL	06 P-180 Avanti II	1127	AvantAir Inc.,Fairfield, NJ./Seven Sugar Whiskey LLC	
❏ N160SM	98 King Air 350	FL-215	Stowers Machinery Corp. Knoxville, Tn.	N160AC
❏ N160SP	81 MU-2 Marquise	1506SA	Jerry Woolf DDS Inc. Bakersfield, Ca.	N15MV
❏ N160WJ	76 King Air 200	BB-160	World Jet of Delaware Inc Wilmington De..	XB-KCQ
❏ N161AJ	96 Pilatus PC-12	161	Garrett Gruener, Berkeley, Ca.	VH-FAM
❏ N161GC	83 King Air B200	BB-1160	ERG Aviation Inc. Palm Coast, Fl.	N444KA
❏ N161RC	90 King Air B200	BB-1356	JW KKA Holdings LLC./Greenway Capital, Dallas, Tx.	N5598N
❏ N161SL	06 P-180 Avanti II	1128	AvantAir Inc. Bedford, Ma.	
❏ N161XX*	79 PA-31T Cheyenne II	7920016	Cheyenne II Aircraft LLC. Carlsbad, Ca.	N79FB
❏ N162GC	85 King Air B200	BB-1238	Ginn Development Co. Celebration, Fl.	N212JB
❏ N162PA	77 King Air 200	BB-232	Aero Lima/John Air Services Inc. Miami, Fl. (status ?).	YV-112CP
❏ N162PB	96 Pilatus PC-12/45	162	Pyxis LLC., Edmond, Ok.	(N377AC)
❏ N162Q	83 King Air B200	BB-1104	EZ Flight LLC. Chatsworth, Ga.	N1628
❏ N162SL	07 P-180 Avanti II	1130	AvantAir Inc. Fairfield, Nj.	
❏ N163BA	84 King Air 300	FA-18	Aviation Management & Construction, Franklin, Tn.	(N398W)
❏ N163SL	07 P-180 Avanti II	1131	AvantAir Inc. Bedford, Ma.	
❏ N164BT	69 SA-26AT Merlin 2B	T26-164	Ted Noble, Big Bear Lake, Ca.	N36PE
❏ N164GP	80 Conquest II	441-0164	Maritime Sales & Leasing Inc., Newnan, Ga.	ZS-SMA
❏ N164PA	60 Gulfstream 1	54	Phoenix Air Group Inc. Cartersville, Ga.	N26AJ
❏ N164SL	07 P-180 Avanti II	1134	AvantAir Inc. Fairfield NJ.	
❏ N164ST	01 PA-46-500TP Meridian	4697064	Ball Air LLC. Cheyenne, Wy.	
❏ N164WS	05 King Air C90B	LJ-1736	Pacific Marine Leasing Inc. Lakewood, Wa.	N35436
❏ N165BC	80 Gulfstream 840	11646	Ian Herzog A Professional Corp. Santa Monica, Ca.	N65Y
❏ N165KC	79 PA-31T Cheyenne 1	7904022	Reeves Commercial Properties LLC, Lake Charles, La.	N46CR
❏ N165MA	75 Mitsubishi MU-2M	326	Bill Terrell, Thayne, Wy.	N401JC
❏ N165SL	07 P-180 Avanti II	1135	AvantAir Inc. Bedford, Ma.	
❏ N165SW	79 PA-31T Cheyenne 1	7904051	Mihada Inc. Auburn, Al.	N49RM
❏ N166GC	95 SAAB 2000	034	ERG Aviation III Inc. / Ginn Development LLC., Celebration,Fl	N512RH
❏ N166SA	88 King Air 300	FA-166	Clear Skies Ltd/Ford Development Corp. Cincinnati, Oh.	9J-AFI
❏ N166SB	00 Pilatus PC-12/45	310	Edge Wireless LLC. Mukilteo, Wa.	HB-FQW
❏ N166WT	80 PA-31T Cheyenne 1	8004020	H & M Properties Inc. Jacksonville, NC.	N700BS
❏ N167AR	99 Pilatus PC-12/45	279	Edgemont Aviation LLC, Wilmington De.	HB-FSX
❏ N167BB	83 King Air C90-1	LJ-1054	Million Miles Aviation LLC. Granite Bay, Ca.	N10AV
❏ N167PA	69 Gulfstream 1	199	Phoenix Air Group Inc. Cartersville, Ga.	N183CP
❏ N167R	78 Rockwell 690B	11437	Central Bank & Trust Co. Lexington, Ky.	HL5261
❏ N167SL	07 P-180 Avanti II	1136	AvantAir Inc. Fairfield Nj.	
❏ N168CA	07 PA-46-500TP Meridian	4697314	Columbia Aircraft Sales Inc., Groton, Ct.	
❏ N168MA	83 Conquest 1	425-0155	Paloma Packing Inc/Paloma Air LLC. Santa Maria, Ca.	YV-266CP
❏ N168RV	06 PA-46-500TP Meridian	4697252	Piper Aircraft Inc. Vero Beach, Fl.	N566HP
❏ N168SL	07 P-180 Avanti II	1139	AvantAir Inc, Bedford Ma.	
❏ N169CA	07 PA-46-500TP Meridian	4697300	PD Leasing LLC., San Antonio, Tx.	N336P
❏ N169DR	89 King Air C90A	LJ-1205	W W McCook LLC. Shreveport, La.	N1552F
❏ N169SL	07 P-180 Avanti II	1140	Midsouth Services Inc. Clearwater, Fl.	
❏ N170S	04 King Air C90B	LJ-1708	Shanair LLC. Visalia, Ca.	N974C
❏ N170SE	00 King Air B200	BB-1740	ERS Aviation LLC. Ligonier, In.	N170S
❏ N171AF	79 PA-31T Cheyenne II	7920089	Aero Oro LLC. Colorado Springs, Co.	N101AF
❏ N171AT	66 680V Turbo Commander	1616-49	Harold Wright, Anchorage, Ak.	N311PD
❏ N171CP	99 King Air 350	FL-244	InterCity Investments Properties Inc. Dallas, Tx.	N2344N
❏ N171JP	77 PA-31T Cheyenne II	7720028	Frost Flying Inc. Marianna, Ar.	N29JM
❏ N171PA	68 Gulfstream 1	192	Phoenix Air Group Inc. Cartersville, Ga.	YV-76CP
❏ N172MA	06 PA-46-500TP Meridian	4697263	Chandler Aviation Corp, Ashland, Oh.	
❏ N172PB	97 Pilatus PC-12	172	Locker Inc. Texico, NM.	HB-FSH
❏ N172SL	07 P-180 Avanti II	1141	Avantair Inc. Fairfield, NJ.	
❏ N173DB	78 Rockwell 690B	11485	DMB Packing Corp. Newman, Ca.	N46NH
❏ N173PL	81 King Air F90	LA-106	C340 LLC/GHH Real Estate Services LLC. Texarkana, Ar.	C-GQGA
❏ N173RC	76 King Air 200	BB-173	Access Investments LLC. Oxford, Ms.	N55FG
❏ N173S	92 King Air B300C	FM-4	Stevens Express Leasing Inc. Memphis, Tn.	N8275P
❏ N173SL	07 P-180 Avanti II	1146	Avantair Inc. Fairfield NJ.	
❏ N173TC	04 King Air B200	BB-1893	Tidwell Carruth Properties LLC. Dallas, Ga.	N36893
❏ N174MA	79 MU-2 Marquise	753SA	Bankair Inc. West Columbia, SC.	N100BY

Reg	Yr	Type	c/n	Owner/Operator	Prev Regn
N174WB	81	King Air 200	BB-804	TJM Air LLC., St Petersburg, Fl.	N3824P
N175AA	81	PA-42 Cheyenne III	8001017	Trial Support Services Inc. Mesquite, Tx.	XA-SEK
N175AZ	82	King Air C90	LJ-1006	Kirkland's Inc. Jackson, Tn.	N123NA
N175CA	79	MU-2 Marquise	736SA	Intercontinental Jet Inc., Tulsa, Ok.	N711PD
N175DB	63	680V Turbo Commander	1519-95	Richard Rohrman, Shawnee Mission, Ks. (status ?).	N1161Z
N175PL	07	King Air B200GT	BY-2	EPL Laredo Inc. Palenque Air LLC Laredo Tx.	
N175SA	76	King Air 200	BB-183	General Atomics Inc. San Diego, Ca.	N418GA
N175SL	07	P-180 Avanti II	1147	Piaggio America Inc. West Palm Beach, Fl.	
N175WB	04	PA-46-500TP Meridian	4697181	Perkin Holding Co. Lake Ozark, Mo.	
N176FB	81	PA-42 Cheyenne III	8001041	P R Transportation LLC. Washington, NC.	G-BWTX
N176M	82	King Air B200	BB-1029	APACO Inc./Miller Industries Inc., Ooltewah, Tn.	N95BD
N176TW	74	King Air E90	LW-76	Ameristar Jet Charter Inc. Dallas, Tx.	ZS-LJF
N176XL	07	P-180 Avanti II	1150	Piaggio America Inc. West Palm Beach, Fl.	
N177CN	84	King Air B200	BB-1191	Pine Telephone Co. Broken Bow, Ok.	(YV-....)
N177GA	97	King Air 350	FL-160	Clouscape Inc/Gantt Aviation inc Georgetown Tx.	VT-JNK
N177LA	85	King Air B200	BB-1203	WCF XX LLC. Houston, Tx.	N177JE
N177MK	75	King Air E90	LW-149	Trans-Equipment Services Inc. Greenville, SC.	N177KA
N178CD	81	PA-31T Cheyenne II	8120046	Mathew Emmens, Durham, NC.	N101DH
N178EJ	06	King Air C90GT	LJ-1818	Home Acres Building Supply/Blue Skies Lsg, Grand Rapids, Mi.	(N7218Y)
N178LA	82	King Air E90	LA-178	Blackhorse LLC. Fresno, Ca.	N53G
N178MH	07	Pilatus PC-12/47	875	Pilatus Business Aircraft Ltd, Broomfield, Co.	HB-FQG
N178SL	07	P-180 Avanti II	1151	Piaggio America Inc. West Palm Beach, Fl.	
N179MD	85	King Air C90A	LJ-1091	Gem City Properties LLC. Laramie, Wy.	N179D
N180AV	92	P-180 Avanti	1018	Din Aero Inc. Troy, Mi.	N220TW
N180BP	90	P-180 Avanti	1004	Eenhoorn Inc./Rapid Capital LLC., Grandville, Mi.	I-RAIH
N180HM	01	P-180 Avanti	1043	Clear Aviation Inc. Clearwater Fl.	N122PA
N181CG	77	King Air E90	LW-225	Classic Aviation Inc., San Luis Obispo, Ca.	(N419HM)
N181DC	75	PA-31T Cheyenne II	7520026	Industrial Products Co. Lynchburg, Va.	N180JS
N181MD	83	Conquest II	441-0295	Birchwood Lumber & Veneer Co. Birchwood, Wi.	N6837R
N181NK	66	King Air A90	LJ-142	Jack Wall Aircraft Sales Inc. Memphis, Tn.	N101NK
N181SW	81	PA-31T Cheyenne 1	8104001	MacFarlane Co USA LLC. El Dorado, Ar.	
N181Z	73	King Air E90	LW-52	USDA/Forest Service Fire & Aviation, Boise, Id.	N74171
N182CA	81	King Air F90	LA-174	Price Construction Inc. Big Spring, Tx.	N82DD
N182ME	78	PA-31T Cheyenne II	7820021	Universal Turbine Parts Inc. Prattville, Al.	N102FL
N182Z	78	King Air 200	BB-402	USDA Forest Service, Boise, Id.	N318W
N183PC	97	Pilatus PC-12	183	Hughes Unlimited Inc. Port Bolivar, Tx.	HB-FSR
N183SA	73	King Air C90	LJ-571	Signature Air Inc. Canonsburg, Pa.	D-ILKB
N184AE	01	PA-46-500TP Meridian	4697026	Airmann LLC. Shelbyville, Tn.	N184AL
N184D	87	King Air 300	FA-132	Cross County Carriers Ltd. Knoxville, Tn.	N1845
N184K	85	SAAB 340A	029	Indiana University Foundation, Bloomington, In.	N98AL
N184PA	62	Gulfstream 1	97	Phoenix Air Group Inc. Cartersville, Ga.	YV-85CP
N184RB	01	PA-46-500TP Meridian	4697087	Clear Air Aviation LLC. Jacksonville, Fl.	
N184TH	07	Pilatus PC-12/47	810	Aircraft Guaranty Trust LLC., Houston,. Tx.	HB-FRO
N184VB	80	Conquest II	441-0184	Diplomat Freight Services Inc. Annapolis, Md.	(N184DF)
N185MA	72	Mitsubishi MU-2F	219	Lloyd Burson, Canutillo, Tx.	
N185MV	82	King Air B200	BB-1034	Midwest Aviation, Marshall, Mn.	N185MC
N185PA	59	Gulfstream 1	26	Phoenix Air Group Inc. Cartersville, Ga.	YV-82CP
N185PB	97	Pilatus PC-12	185	Roger & Gayle Block, Gardnerville, Nv.	HB-FST
N185XP	82	King Air B200	BB-952	U S Department of Energy, Las Vegas, Nv.	N1852B
N186E	79	Rockwell 690B	11566	The O'Meara Family Trust, Newport Beach, Ca.	N186EC
N186EB	84	King Air B200	BB-1186	Executive Business Aviation Inc. Nashville, Tn.	ZS-NBA
N186GA	78	PA-31T Cheyenne II	7820086	W & V LLC. Macon, Ga.	N44CS
N186PS	05	PA-46-500TP Meridian	4697228	Clipper LLC. Rancho Cucamonga, Ca.	
N187CP	79	PA-31T Cheyenne II	7920054	Jochl Sports Inc. Banner Elk, NC.	(N690CA)
N187JD	03	PA-46-500TP Meridian	4697180	Jeff Dinklage Agri-Business Inc. Wisner, Ne.	
N187JP	04	King Air B200	BB-1888	Bennett Law Office PC. Missoula, Mt.	N6188N
N187SB	77	Mitsubishi MU-2N	698SA	Keystone Advertising Inc. East Freedom, Pa.	N263ND
N187SC	79	PA-31T Cheyenne 1	7904020	Aviation Parts Exchange Inc. Southlake, Tx.	N800MP
N187Z	68	SA-26T Merlin 2A	T26-29	U S Department of Agriculture, Washington, DC.	N22CE
N188CE	05	PA-46-500TP Meridian	4697239	STC Acquisitions Inc. Wilmington, De.	N439KC
N188DF	84	Conquest 1	425-0188	J P Air Charter Inc. Ontario, Ca.	N188CP
N188LL	81	King Air B100	BE-119	6088P Inc. Dallas, Tx.	N1807H
N188MC	93	King Air 350	FL-93	MASCO Corp. Taylor, Mi.	N82678
N188PC	97	Pilatus PC-12	188	Strata Equity Group Inc. La Jolla, Ca.	HB-FSW
N188RM	74	Mitsubishi MU-2K	298	Kelly Green Seeds Inc. Farwell, Tx.	PT-OFV

Reg	Yr	Type	c/n	Owner/Operator	Prev Regn
N188TC	83	King Air B200C	BL-64	Era Helicopters LLC. Lake Charles, La.	N1240S
N189CB	06	King Air 350	FL-513	Corundum Partners Inc. Colorado Springs Co.	N7193K
N189JR	80	King Air F90	LA-61	Viper Air LLC. Springfield, Il.	N444RS
N189MC	96	King Air 350	FL-136	MASCO Corp. Taylor, Mi.	N35017
N190BT	65	King Air 90	LJ-59	Tiger Pass Properties Inc. Gretna, La.	N1909R
N190CA	81	PA-42 Cheyenne III	8001028	Coastal Aviation Group LLC. Panama City, Fl.	N48GS
N190EF	85	King Air C90	LJ-1122	Easterday Farms, Pasco, Wa.	N992C
N190FD	80	King Air F90	LA-42	Alfred Tria Jr. Princeton, NJ.	(D-ILIM)
N190JL	65	King Air 90	LJ-69	APA Enterprises Inc. Poughkeepsie, NY.	N120DP
N190PA	68	Gulfstream 1	195	Phoenix Air Group Inc. Cartersville, Ga.	N1900W
N190PE	97	Pilatus PC-12/45	190	Pilatus Business Aircraft Ltd. Jeffco Airport, Co.	HB-FOV
N190RM	72	King Air E90	LW-1	Cloudscape Inc, Ruidoso Nm./Gantt Aviation Inc.Tx.	N64RJ
N190SS	92	King Air C90A	LJ-1298	J & H Kramer Inc. Redwood City, Ca.	N170AJ
N191CS	00	Beech 1900D	UE-392	Phelps Dodge Corp. Phoenix, Az.	N855CA
N191MA	81	PA-31T Cheyenne 1	8104019	B & E Leasing LLC. Dubuque, Ia.	N817QT
N191SP	99	Pilatus PC-12/45	284	PBCB LLC. Bellevue, Wa.	N284LK
N191TP	89	King Air C90A	LJ-1223	We Fly LLC/McNeil Development LLC. Idaho Falls, Id.	N8CA
N191WB	91	King Air C90B	LJ-1295	Wild Blue Yonder of Oklahoma LLC. Goldsby, Ok.	N91LY
N192PA	65	Gulfstream 1	149	Phoenix Air Group Inc. Cartersville, Ga.	N684FM
N192TB	81	Cheyenne II-XL	8166015	Cheyenne Leasing LLC. West Palm Beach, Fl.	N131XL
N193AA	79	MU-2 Marquise	741SA	AEF LC VII, Pensacola, Fl.	(N98CF)
N193FS	91	King Air 300	FA-218	Flexsteel Industries Inc. Dubuque, Ia.	N770GX
N193JC	84	King Air B200	BB-1177	Impact Air LLC. Henderson, Nv.	N608JR
N193PA	64	Gulfstream 1	125	Phoenix Air Group Inc. Cartersville, Ga.	N5NA
N193RA	94	King Air 350	FL-105	Barnett Investments Inc.La Verne Ca.	VT-BHL
N194JL	07	PA-46-500TP Meridian	4697337	Piper Aircraft Inc. Vero Beach, Fl.	
N194TR	83	King Air B200	BB-1146	Tony Green & Assocs Inc. Boone, NC.	N60FC
N195AA	79	PA-31T Cheyenne 1	7904001	Bondy's Air Inc. Dover, De.	D-ILOR
N195AE	89	King Air 300	FA-155	Air Eagle LLC. Detroit, Mi.	N1554U
N195AL	86	King Air 300	FA-102	Red Stripe Air LLC. Odessa, Tx.	(N886DT)
N195CA	94	King Air B200	BB-1488	KB Aircraft LLC. Dayton, Oh.	N1568E
N195DP	66	King Air 90	LJ-89	Skydive Alabama Inc. Decatur, Il.	N195DR
N195MA	70	King Air 100	B-20	W L Paris Enterprises Inc. Louisville, Ky. (status ?).	(N28WL)
N195PA	62	Gulfstream 1C	88	Phoenix Air Group Inc. Cartersville, Ga.	C-GPTN
N196MA	80	MU-2 Marquise	764SA	Cebolla Inc. Pharr, Tx.	
N196PA	64	Gulfstream 1	139	Phoenix Air Group Inc. Cartersville, Ga.	C-FRTU
N196SC	96	King Air B200	BB-1525	Oracle Charter LLC. Baton Rouge, La.	N260G
N197AS	81	King Air F90	LA-116	Asset Sales Inc. Indian Trail, NC.	N3825E
N197CC	78	King Air C90	LJ-783	Carl Carr, Destin, Fl.	N197SC
N197SC	87	King Air C90B	LJ-1490	Union Air LLC., Searcy, Ar.	(N520AM)
N198DM	85	King Air B200	BB-1198	Bomac Air Inc. Wayne, Il.	VT-JKC
N198FM	83	King Air F90	LA-198	IMTEC Aviation LLC. Ardmore, Ok.	HK-....
N198KA	66	King Air A90	LJ-162	Assure Aviation LLC. Memphis, Tn.	N198T
N198PA	59	Gulfstream 1C	27	Phoenix Air Group Inc. Cartersville, Ga.	N415CA
N198PP	92	King Air C90B	LJ-1314	Peterson Toyota Inc. Lumberton, NC.	N8022Q
N199BC	80	King Air F90	LA-30	Airco King LLC. Wichita Falls, Tx.	(N483JM)
N199CE	89	King Air 300	FA-199	Cypress KA 1 LLC., Fort Lauderdale, Fl.	N169MC
N199CG	01	King Air C90B	LJ-1661	CG Aviation LLC. Asheboro, NC.	N5061X
N199CM	99	Pilatus PC-12/45	262	K & A Aero LLC. Eureka, Ca.	HB-FSG
N199CP	01	PA-46-500TP Meridian	4697099	Bluebonnets Inc. Charlotte, NC.	C-GPDP
N199DW	80	King Air E90	LW-338	D W Davies Co. Racine, Wi.	N50RV
N199MA	81	PA-31T Cheyenne 1	8104005	We-Lease LC. Johnston, Ia.	N944JG
N199MH	81	King Air/Catpass 250	BB-855	ITC Equipment LLC, Novi, Mi.	N223HC
N199PL	76	King Air E90	LW-167	Polaris Industries Inc. Minneapolis, Mn.	N213RW
N199TT	76	King Air E90	LW-157	Magic Aviation LLC. Ankeny, Ia.	N81AS
N199WF	98	Pilatus PC-12/45	199	CCLM LLC. Greensboro, NC.	HB-FQH
N199Y	91	King Air 350	FL-66	Task Aviation LLC. Richmond, Va.	VP-CRI
N200AE	66	Gulfstream 1	169	Termnet Merchant Services Inc. Atlanta, Ga.	N400WF
N200AF	75	King Air 200	BB-102	Quebec Enterprises Inc. Burbank, Ca.	N997MA
N200AJ	73	King Air A100	B-146	Royal Air Freight Inc. Waterford, Mi.	N410SB
N200AU	79	King Air 200	BB-432	Business Aircraft Group Inc., Cleveland, Oh.	N33KM
N200BM	83	King Air B200	BB-1147	Softshell Aviation Inc. Middletown, De.	N647JM
N200BR	80	King Air 200	BB-600	B & R Motorsports LLC. Greenwich, Ct.	N500W
N200BT	77	King Air 200	BB-293	Crystal Aviation LLC. Atlantic Beach, NC.	(N202QS)
N200CJ	76	King Air 200	BB-143	Four Kings Air LLC. Montello, Wi.	N1PC

Reg	Yr Type	c/n	Owner/Operator	Prev Regn
N200CY	98 King Air B200	BB-1617	Cyclone Land Development, Atlanta, Ga.	N550DC
N200DA	83 King Air B200	BB-1095	Tradewinds Air Communities. Stockbridge, Ga.	N170L
N200DK	82 Gulfstream 1000	96019	Coast Aircraft Brokerage Inc. Tarzana, Ca.	(N9939S)
N200DT	68 680W Turbo Commander	1763-9	Commander Services Inc. Hayward, Ca.	N97011
N200EA	90 King Air B200	BB-1368	EPPS Air Service Inc. Atlanta, Ga.	CC-CDN
N200EC	76 King Air 200	BB-134	Chouest Air Inc. Houma, La.	D-IAAK
N200EG	95 King Air B200	BB-1501	Greenfield Partners LLC/Volo Aviation Inc. Bridgeport, Ct.	N145AJ
N200EJ	97 King Air B200	BB-1585	Executive Jet Management Inc. Cincinnati, Oh.	N200QS
N200ET	78 King Air C-12C	BC-73	Mission Aviation Fellowship, Nampa, Id.	78-23137
N200EZ	74 King Air 200	BB-9	Air Atlapa Ltd S.A., Panama City, Panama	N5PC
N200FB	79 PA-31T Cheyenne 1	7904037	E-Z Mart Stores Inc. Texarkana, Ar.	N2332R
N200FE	78 King Air 200	BB-373	Vero Executive Flyers Inc. Vero Beach, Fl.	N4799W
N200FM	75 King Air 200	BB-81	Citation Ventures Inc. Long Beach, Ca.	N18DN
N200FV	77 King Air 200	BB-299	ZZ Leasing Inc. Memphis, Tn.	N6111
N200GS	85 King Air B200	BB-1214	Navajo Nation, Window Rock, Az.	N7225D
N200HD	82 King Air B200	BB-987	Oahu Properties LLC. Tuscaloosa, Al.	N358ST
N200HF	04 King Air B200	BB-1858	Hunt Aviation LLC. Ruston, La.	N6158Q
N200HK	99 King Air B200	BB-1677	Mississippi Dept of Public Safety, Jackson, Ms.	N200HF
N200HV	97 King Air C90B	LJ-1478	Hy-Vee Food Stores Inc. West Des Moines, Ia.	N1108M
N200HX	86 King Air B200	BB-1243	DD Construction Inc., Alpharetta, Ga.	N84CC
N200JC	98 Jetcruzer 500	002	AASI Aircraft, Long Beach, Ca.	
N200JL	76 King Air 200	BB-127	John Lyddon, Las Vegas, Nv.	N2127L
N200JQ	74 Rockwell 690A	11224	Corona Aircraft Inc. Corona, Ca.	N200JN
N200KP	85 King Air B200	BB-1215	Grayback Forestry Inc. Merlin, Or.	PH-ACZ
N200MH	69 SA-26AT Merlin 2B	T26-148	Lionel Nerwich, Farmersville, Tx.	N540MC
N200MJ	82 King Air B200	BB-1012	Prior Aviation Service Inc. Buffalo, NY.	N14BW
N200NA	82 King Air B200	BB-1079	Trueb Emulsions Chemie AG. Switzerland.	HB-GDL
N200NB	77 PA-31T Cheyenne II	7720035	Medical Imaging Consultants PC. Lavista, Ne.	
N200ND	98 King Air B200	BB-1612	North Dakota Department of Transport, Bismarck, ND.	
N200NR	91 King Air B200	BB-1380	Skinner Management Company, Jacksonville, Fl.	(N884VP)
N200NW	99 King Air B200	BB-1691	Viking Transport/Northland Aluminum Products, St Louis Park.	
N200NY	76 King Air C-12C	BC-25	New York State Police, Latham, NY.	N1172J
N200PG	79 PA-31T Cheyenne II	7920015	Road Builders Inc. Lincoln, Ne.	N200GH
N200PH	77 King Air 200	BB-238	Prairie Ventures Aviation LLC. Worthington, Mn.	N891MA
N200PL	78 King Air 200	BB-410	Polaris Industries Inc. Minneapolis, Mn.	N275Z
N200PU	94 King Air B200	BB-1477	Purdue University, Lafayette, In.	N8301D
N200QN	79 King Air 200	BB-521	Quincy Newspapers Inc. Quincy, Il.	N355TW
N200RE	76 King Air E90	LW-164	Jorge Fernando Villon, London, UK	
N200RM	73 King Air E90	LW-45	Phoenix Partners Leasing LLC. University Place, Wa.	N777SS
N200RR	87 King Air B200	BB-1282	Texas Dept of Criminal Justice, Huntsville, Tx.	N3082C
N200RS	94 King Air B200	BB-1481	Patterson Aviation LLC. Omaha, Ne.	N1559W
N200RW	77 King Air 200	BB-242	Dodson International Parts Inc. Rantoul, Ks. (status ?)	N24201
N200RX	72 Mitsubishi MU-2J	548	National Seating & Mobility Inc. Franklin, Tn.	N68DA
N200SE	85 King Air B200	BB-1208	King Flyers Partners LP. Magnolia, Tx.	N7213K
N200SN	80 SA-226T Merlin 3B	T-354	Wizrd Aviation LLC/Barr & Mudford LLP. Redding, Ca.	N656PS
N200SV	84 King Air B200	BB-1187	MPR Consultants Inc. Augusta, Ga.	N610SW
N200TB	67 680V Turbo Commander	1708-83	East Coast Aero Technical School, Holden, Ma.	N500HY
N200TG	73 King Air C90	LJ-583	Skyline Construction Services Inc.. Eatonton, Ga.	N21WB
N200TK	85 King Air B200	BB-1240	Flight Line Holdings LLC. Harahan, La.	N90BL
N200TN	77 King Air 200	BB-191	3 Lone Stars LLC. Arlington, Tx.	N1PC
N200TR	84 King Air C90A	LJ-1067	Taylor Ramsey Enterprises Inc. Lynchburg, Va.	N224P
N200TS	78 PA-31T Cheyenne 1	7804002	Hayes LLC. Wilmington, De.	N94TB
N200TT	81 Gulfstream 980	95073	Aero Executive International Inc. (FAA status in question).	N9825S
N200U	95 King Air C90B	LJ-1389	Ohio University, Athens, Oh.	CC-CTW
N200UW	83 King Air B200	BB-1155	University of Wyoming, Laramie, Wy.	N155NA
N200VA	77 King Air 200	BB-246	TJ3 Air LLC., Allentown, Pa.	(N138CC)
N200VC	00 King Air 350	FL-316	Vectren Aero Inc. Evansville, In.	N3216L
N200VE	76 PA-31T Cheyenne II	7620057	Alliance Air Parts Inc.	TJ-TAC
N200VJ	06 King Air 350	FL-489	Sky Flight Services LLC, St Louis Mo.	
N200VU	90 King Air B200	BB-1393	Bridgeway Enterprises Inc. Marble Falls, Tx.	N200ZT
N200WB	01 King Air B200	BB-1754	West Bay Builders LLC., Novato, Ca.	N618TA
N200WX	80 King Air 200	BB-680	Reliance Health Care Management Inc., Conway, Ar.	N919WM
N200WZ	76 King Air 200	BB-89	Holmes Aviation Inc. Des Moines, Ia.	N16BF
N200XC	82 King Air B200	BB-1061	Stiles Corp. Fort Lauderdale, Fl.	N200JM
N200XL	81 Cheyenne II-XL	8166010	J Jeffrey Brausch & Co. Medina, Oh.	

Reg	Yr Type	c/n	Owner/Operator	Prev Regn
❏ N200ZC	75 King Air 200	BB-41	Honeywell International Inc. Morristown, NJ.	
❏ N201CH	76 King Air 200	BB-103	Marcraft LLC. Mesquite, Nv.	
❏ N201KA	79 King Air 200	BB-417	N720JS Inc., Orlando, Fl.	HB-GHF
❏ N201NY	88 King Air B200	BB-1308	New York State Police, Latham, NY.	N1509G
❏ N201SM	67 SA-26T Merlin 2A	T26-5	J Sills, Lakeland, Fl.	N400P
❏ N201UV	76 Mitsubishi MU-2L	680	Royal Air Freight Inc. Waterford, Mi.	N201U
❏ N202AJ	79 King Air 200	BB-511	Yaris Air Transport Inc. Panama City, Panama.	N200LW
❏ N202FF	02 King Air B200	BB-1786	D&B Truck & Trailer Service LLC/Fleetco Corp. Nashville, Tn.	(N716GS)
❏ N202FG	98 King Air C90B	LJ-1507	Val Ward Cadillac Inc., Fort Myers, Fl.	N2097W
❏ N202HC	78 PA-31T Cheyenne II	7820036	Mr Brad Heard Jr. Newton Ga.	N82251
❏ N202WS	75 SA-226AT Merlin 4A	AT-037	Harvest Two Outreach Inc. Merced, Ca.	N216GA
❏ N203BS	79 King Air 200	BB-476	Bill Smith, Oklahoma City, Ok.	N6040T
❏ N203HQ	98 King Air B200	BB-1602	Executive Jet Center LLC. Broken Arrow, Ok.	N203HC
❏ N203LG	81 King Air B200	BB-926	CWW Inc. Englewood, Co.	N68GK
❏ N203PC	78 King Air E90	LW-258	Flying Swan Inc. Wilmington, De.	N20316
❏ N203PT	05 King Air B200	BB-1903	Beri 210	N521RS
❏ N203RC	03 King Air B200	BB-1822	Warren Manufacturing Inc. Birmingham, Al.	N6022Q
❏ N203RD	77 King Air E90	LW-203	PBSA Aviation Corp. Fort Lauderdale, Fl.	YV-O-SAS-
❏ N203RR	84 King Air 300	FA-27	Fly With Us LLC./Greer Law Firm, Tupelo, Ms.	N300PE
❏ N204JS	81 King Air 200	BB-842	Eric Stirling/Guardian Flight, Fairbanks, Ak.	N38473
❏ N204PT	05 King Air B200	BB-1908	Allied Aircraft LLC., Anaheim, Ca.	N37308
❏ N204RA	04 King Air B200	BB-1885	Gillis Holdings Inc., Sulphur Springs, Tx.	ZS-DEV
❏ N204W	98 King Air 350	FL-204	State of Wisconsin, Madison, Wi.	N2301Q
❏ N204WB	84 King Air B200	BB-1179	Helicopters of Northwest Florida Inc. Navarre, Fl.	N444WB
❏ N205MS	81 King Air C90	LJ-948	Instant Air of NC Corporation, Winterville, NC.	N4495U
❏ N205RA	06 King Air B200	BB-1959	Beechcraft de Guatemala SA. Guatemala City, Guatemala.	
❏ N205RA	05 King Air B200	BB-1919	Roquette America Inc. Keokuk, Ia.	
❏ N205SM	83 King Air F90-1	LA-205	Air Aero LLC/Aero Automatic Sprinkler Co. Phoenix, Az.	N6690R
❏ N205SP	03 King Air B200	BB-1826	Colorado State Patrol, Denver, Co.	N200KA
❏ N205ST	81 King Air C90	LJ-965	Pate & Pate Air LLC. Andalusia, Al.	N205SP
❏ N205TM	07 King Air B200	BB-1991	Smitty's Supply Inc. Roseland La.	N991HB
❏ N206K	85 King Air 300	FA-36	Diamond 1A Inc. Divide, Co.	
❏ N206P	79 King Air 200	BB-466	WBJ Aviation LLC. Elm City, NC.	N200TW
❏ N207BA	75 Mitsubishi MU-2L	666	AJM Airplane Co. Naples, Fl.	EC-IJA
❏ N207CM	86 King Air B200	BB-1246	Carolinas Medical Center, Charlotte, NC.	(N210CM)
❏ N207DB	81 King Air 200	BB-862	Hermes Aviation LLC/Sky Trek Aviation, Modesto, Ca.	N260F
❏ N207HB	95 King Air B200	BB-1516	Washington State Patrol, Olympia, Wa.	N1CQ
❏ N207P	95 King Air C90B	LJ-1406	S & B Equipment Leasing Inc. Broadview Heights, Oh.	
❏ N207RS	83 Conquest 1	425-0195	207RS LLC., Kerrville, Tx.	(N316LR)
❏ N207SB	71 King Air 100	B-69	Ken Schrader Racing Inc. Concord, NC.	(N501KS)
❏ N207SS	80 Conquest II	441-0136	TM Aero LLC/ProSolutions International Inc. Tampa, Fl.	N441HC
❏ N208AJ	94 King Air B200	BB-1490	Fowler Foods of Delaware LLC, Wilmington De.	VH-SMZ
❏ N208CL	76 Rockwell 690A	11297	HWW Commander LLC. Houston, Tx.	N514GP
❏ N208F	81 King Air 200	BB-851	Two Shay Inc./Shay Financial Services Inc., Miami, Fl.	N200E
❏ N208RC	80 King Air F90	LA-46	King Air Corp. Miami, Fl.	ZP-TZF
❏ N208SR	75 King Air A100	B-208	Urias L Bardoo, Layou, St. Vincent	9Y-TJA
❏ N208TC	82 King Air B200	BB-990	Coble Crane & Equipment Company, Greensboro, NC.	N990JC
❏ N209CM	98 King Air B200	BB-1613	Chalotte Mecklenburg Hospital Authority, Charlotte, NC.	N299RJ
❏ N209KC	01 PA-46-500TP Meridian	4697009	Air Dover Corp. Wilmington, De.	
❏ N209ST	04 PA-46-500TP Meridian	4697209	Bell Air Management Services LLC. Rockville, Md.	
❏ N209WC	83 King Air B200	BB-1130	The Zaken Corporation, Chatsworth, Ca.	N200QS
❏ N210AJ	81 King Air F90	LA-131	Tailplane Corp. Wilmington, De.	N42SY
❏ N210CL	04 TBM 700C2	303	Goldeneye Aviation LLC., Wilmington, De.	
❏ N210EC	84 King Air C90A	LJ-1070	State of Tennessee, Nashville, Tn.	N67554
❏ N210PT	98 Pilatus PC-12/45	210	Raging River Management Corp. Wilmington, De.	HB-FQR
❏ N210YS	78 King Air E90	LW-268	Mr Marco Baldocchi Tyler Tx.	TI-GEV
❏ N211AD	85 Gulfstream 1000	96092	Allison Development Corp. Charlotte, NC.	N127GA
❏ N211AE	77 PA-31T Cheyenne II	7720064	Hap's Aerial Enterprises Inc. Sellersburg, In.	N60DR
❏ N211BE	74 Mitsubishi MU-2J	641	Intercontinental Jet Inc., Tulsa, Ok.	N114MA
❏ N211CG	74 King Air E90	LW-101	Precious Air LLC. Wilmington, De.	N70SW
❏ N211CP	81 King Air 200	BB-843	Suncore Aviation LLC., Wilmington, De.	N3850K
❏ N211EZ	01 PA-46-500TP Meridian	4697117	Brand New Entertainment LLC. Sausalito, Ca.	N53353
❏ N211PC	80 King Air C90	LJ-910	R & J Associates Inc. Colorado Springs, Co.	TC-FRT
❏ N211RV	70 Mitsubishi MU-2G	502	Mits 502 LLC. Lansing, Il. (was s/n 153).	C-FAXP
❏ N211VP	69 King Air 100	B-2	Vintage Props & Jets Inc. New Smyrna Beach, Fl.	N11JJ

Reg	Yr	Type	c/n	Owner/Operator	Prev Regn
☐ N212D	67	King Air A90	LJ-234	Central Missouri State University, Warrenburg, Mo.	N800BP
☐ N212EJ	81	King Air B200	BB-898	Lynch Flying Service Inc. Logan Field, Mt.	N911SR
☐ N212GA	91	King Air B200	BB-1406	Madix Inc. Goodwater, Al.	5B-CJM
☐ N212HH	79	PA-31T Cheyenne 1	7904010	L P & F Inc. Joplin, Mo.	N25BF
☐ N212LT	04	Pilatus PC-12/45	595	Plane Holdings Inc. Maastricht, Holland.	HB-FRG
☐ N212LW	92	King Air B200	BB-1420	Power Flame Inc. Parsons, Ks.	N210SA
☐ N212PB	98	Pilatus PC-12/45	212	Arbor Financial Corp. Glenbrook, Nv.	HB-FQT
☐ N212PK	05	Pilatus PC-12/45	668	Ponderosa Technology Ventures LLC. San Martin, Ca.	HB-FQB
☐ N212WP	65	King Air 90	LJ-62	Volunteer Machinery Sales Co. Portland, Tn.	N512WP
☐ N213DB	93	King Air B200	BB-1450	Marshall Air Systems Inc. Charlotte, NC.	N8059Q
☐ N213PA	84	SA-227TT Merlin 3C	TT-518	Delaris Inc. St Thomas, USVI.	N861CG
☐ N213PH	79	King Air 200	BB-486	Holland Management Inc., Sharon Centre, Oh.	N56DA
☐ N213RJ*	77	King Air B100	BE-22	JRT Group Properties LLC/Brentwood Healthcare, Atlanta, Ga.	N86TR
☐ N213SC	69	SA-26AT Merlin 2B	T26-135	Baskidball Equipment Leasing LLC. Dallas, Tx.	N124PS
☐ N213UV	75	King Air 200	BB-35	N213UV Inc/Three Cities Research Inc. NYC.	N35KD
☐ N214CS	06	Pilatus PC-12/47	766	CC Air LLC., Eagle, Id.	HB-FSU
☐ N214EC	85	King Air 300	FA-50	Shamrock Aviation Inc. Warren, Mi.	N85GA
☐ N214GB	99	King Air B200	BB-1668	Thyssen Aviation LLC, Dallas Tx.	N6WU
☐ N214P	91	King Air C90A	LJ-1293	Navajo Nation, Window Rock, Az.	
☐ N214PH	84	King Air B200	BB-1182	Petroleum Helicopters Inc. Lafayette, La.	N416CS
☐ N214SC	74	King Air E90	LW-96	Aviacion Lider SA. Lima, Peru.	N35KA
☐ N214TP	03	King Air B200	BB-1855	Platinum Aviation LLC/TAG Manufacturing, Monte Sereno, Ca.	N6155T
☐ N214WL	07	King Air 350	FL-529	Hartman Oil Company Inc./Hartmoor Avn LLC., Wichita, Ks.	
☐ N215HC	03	King Air B200	BB-1848	Plane Lease Co. Minneapolis, Mn.	N5148Q
☐ N215HP	77	King Air C-12C	BC-57	San Bernardino County Sheriffs Department, Rialto, Ca.	N7308B
☐ N215MH	82	MU-2 Marquise	1544SA	W & O Leasing LLC. Wilmington, De.	N202DT
☐ N215ML	06	King Air B200	BB-1955	M D Lung Inc. Elkhart, In.	N7055T
☐ N215SD	01	PA-46-500TP Meridian	4697049	Loolol LLC. Redington Beach, Fl.	
☐ N216CD	75	Mitsubishi MU-2K	323	Camile Landry, Baton Rouge, La.	N511MA
☐ N216KC	98	Pilatus PC-12/45	216	Chulee Inc. Newark, De.	N4PC
☐ N216LJ	67	King Air A90	LJ-190	CNS Ventures LLC. Houston, Tx.	N216AJ
☐ N216RP	82	King Air B200	BB-1015	Primore Inc. Adrian, Mi.	N901EB
☐ N216TM	02	Pilatus PC-12/45	441	Stephan Kruse, Amelia Island, Fl.	N216TM
☐ N217CM	80	King Air 200	BB-621	Eze Trucking Inc., Rialto, Ca.	N210CM
☐ N217CS	82	Cheyenne T-1040	8275014	Frontier Flying Service Inc. Fairbanks, Ak.	C-FYPL
☐ N217DC	92	TBM 700	88	Skyshoe LLC, Boston Ma.	N700KL
☐ N217EB	96	Pilatus PC-12	154	PPC12 LLC, Mt Pleasant SC	N144PC
☐ N218MS	81	Gulfstream 980	95041	Say-Air LLC. Nashua, NH.	N3U
☐ N218WA	98	Pilatus PC-12/45	218	Air Plane Holdings LLC., Detroit, Mi.	HB-FQK
☐ N219CS	82	Cheyenne T-1040	8275005	Universal Turbine Parts Inc. Prattville, Al. (status ?).	C-GPBC
☐ N219GR	05	PA-46-500TP Meridian	4697244	Roberts Pipeline Inc. Sulphur Springs, In.	N210MA
☐ N219MA	81	MU-2 Solitaire	440SA	River City Aviation Inc., West Memphis, Ar.	
☐ N219PC	98	Pilatus PC-12/45	219	SB Meridian LLC. Heber, Ca.	HB-FQL
☐ N219SC	80	PA-31T Cheyenne 1	8004040	Wyman Consulting Associates Inc. Hanover, NH.	N744WP
☐ N219WC	81	King Air 200	BB-768	Wittwer Construction Co. Stillwater, OK.	N413DM
☐ N220AA	76	King Air B100	BE-5	Abilene Aero Charter/Lubbock Aero Charter, Abilene, Tx.	N577RW
☐ N220AJ	98	King Air B200	BB-1539	Going Coastal LLC/CJRE Investments Family LP. Stillwater, Ok	N1089S
☐ N220CG	04	King Air 350	FL-397	Offshore Energy Services Inc. Lafayette, La.	
☐ N220CL	00	Pilatus PC-12/45	364	Bozeman Technology Incubator, Bozeman, Mt.	HB-FSP
☐ N220FS	76	PA-31T Cheyenne II	7620052	Honker Air LLC/Styline Industries Inc. Huntingburg, In.	N577JE
☐ N220JB	80	King Air 200	BB-638	Memphis Aereo Co SA. Memphis, Tn.	N8DX
☐ N220JL	07	PA-46-500TP Meridian	4697336	Piper Aircraft Inc. Vero Beach, Fl.	
☐ N220JM	06	TBM 850	388	BD & GD LLC., Tucson, Az.	N850TM
☐ N220JP	06	Pilatus PC-12/47	787	Pantheon Energy Resources LLC., Belle Chasse, La.	N787PB
☐ N220KW	73	King Air A100	B-185	N220KW LLC. Wenatchee, Wa.	N818AS
☐ N220MA	02	TBM 700C2	248	Angel Peralta, El Paso, Tx.	N220MA
☐ N220N	81	MU-2 Solitaire	450SA	Racing Designs LLC. Missoula, Mt.	N220W
☐ N220TB	82	King Air B200	BB-1057	Rocky Mountain Holdings LLC. Provo, Ut.	F-GILY
☐ N220TT	79	King Air 200	BB-462	Shann Air Inc/Shannahan Crane & Hoist Inc. St Louis, Mo.	G-MOAT
☐ N220UM	04	PA-46-500TP Meridian	4697343	VLIHP Investments LLC., Rocklin, Ca.	(N220JN)
☐ N221CR	90	120ER Brasilia	120171	RCR Air Inc.,Lexington, NC.	N16724
☐ N221G	98	King Air 350	FL-198	Gage Marketing Group LLC. Minneapolis, Mn.	(N64GG)
☐ N221K	81	Gulfstream 980	95077	Nayko Inc. Portland, Or.	N9829S
☐ N221MM	88	King Air 300	FA-161	Franklin/Templeton Travel Inc. San Mateo, Ca.	N3113A
☐ N221PC	98	Pilatus PC-12/45	221	Stephen Scherer, St Louis, Mo.	HB-FQM

Reg	Yr	Type	c/n	Owner/Operator	Prev Regn
N221RC	81	PA-31T Cheyenne 1	8104046	Four-O Management LLC. Lubbock, Tx.	N478PC
N221TC	83	King Air B100	BE-136	Texas Christian University, Fort Worth, Tx.	N18348
N222AG	82	King Air F90	LA-159	Cutting Tools & Trilogy Air Inc. Louisville, Ky.	N76HC
N222CM	95	Pilatus PC-12	111	Briar Lakes Productions Inc. Athens, Tx.	HB-FQE
N222DM	73	King Air C-12C	BC-15	Los Angeles Police Department, Van Nuys, Ca.	N382PD
N222FA	78	Mitsubishi MU-2N	714SA	Helitech Inc. Hampton, Va.	N994PE
N222GW	79	PA-31T Cheyenne 1	7904050	Dodson International Parts Inc. Rantoul, Ks.	N2512R
N222HH	85	MU-2 Marquise	1569SA	Vulcan Drywall & Acoustical Inc., Birmingham, Al.	N502MA
N222LA	78	King Air 200	BB-409	Abilene Aero Charter/Lubbock Aero Charter, Abilene, Tx.	N220TA
N222LP	80	King Air B100	BE-85	Land O'Frost Inc. Lansing, Il.	N6723T
N222ME	76	Rockwell 690A	11338	AK Air LLC., Cheney, Wa.	N46906
N222MV	71	SA-226T Merlin 3	T-212	Denny Hastings Family LP. Las Vegas, Nv.	VR-BHQ
N222PV	97	King Air 350	FL-167	Peavey Electronics Corp. Meridian, Ms.	OY-GIG
N222SL	79	PA-31T Cheyenne 1	7904046	Dr James Langley MD. Golden, Co.	N23658
N222WJ	85	King Air C90A	LJ-1106	Lock Haven Aircraft Sales Inc. Lock Haven, Pa.	N6690C
N223BD	91	120ER Brasilia	120260	Bill Davis Racing, Greensboro, NC.	N205SW
N223CH	68	King Air B90	LJ-321	International Airline Training Academy Inc. Tucson, Az.	N269RR
N223CS	82	Cheyenne T-1040	8275008	Cape Smythe Air Service Inc. Barrow, Ak.	N315SC
N223EA	05	TBM 700C2	323	N223EA LLC. Tallahassee, Fl.	
N223JB	78	Mitsubishi MU-2N	724SA	Burton Air Corp. Fairfax, Va.	N300GM
N223JG	07	TBM 850	406	JAG Aviation Inc., Wilmington, De.	
N223JR	85	King Air 300	FA-45	Delta Coals Inc. Nashville, Tn.	N7220L
N223LH	76	King Air A100	B-223	LELAH Holdings LP. Reno, Nv.	N233AL
N224CC	89	King Air C90A	LJ-1218	James Harris, Houston, Tx.	N15628
N224CR	91	King Air 350	FL-60	Dartswift Inc. Rosemont, Pa.	(N65GR)
N224EZ	85	Gulfstream 1000B	96206	Marjo Ventures Inc. Lake Geneva, Wi.	N97315
N224HR	71	SA-226T Merlin 3	T-217	Farney Aviation One LP, Georgetown, Tx.	N224HR
N224JD	98	Pilatus PC-12/45	220	Conway Aviation Sales & Leasing LLC., Austin, Tx	N220ED
N224JV	00	King Air C90B	LJ-1629	James R Vannoy & Sons Construction, Jefferson, NC.	(N229J)
N224LB	73	King Air A100	B-162	Allison Aviation LLC. Wilmington, De.	N96AL
N224LM	05	King Air B200	BB-1921	Carpe Diem Montana Inc., Columbus, Mt.	(N225LM)
N224P	85	King Air B200	BB-1230	King Airways LLC, Austin Tx.	
N225CA	81	PA-31T Cheyenne 1	8104024	Windward Aviation Corp. Katonah, NY.	SE-IUG
N225CM	03	King Air 350	FL-378	San Diego Diversified Builder Services, El Cajon, Ca.	N4478H
N225DF	85	Conquest 1	425-0225	Peregrine Aviation LLC. Naples, Fl.	(N425KK)
N225LH	76	King Air C-12C	BC-33	Department of Public Safety, Montgomery, Al.	76-22557
N225MA	01	PA-46-500TP Meridian	4697106	Coppergate LLC. Carmel, In.	N2HD
N225MM	78	Rockwell 690B	11462	SABAW Trading LLC. Seabroo, Tx.	N81764
N225PT	82	Cheyenne II-XL	8166032	Perair Corp. New Hyde Park, NY.	(N107MQ)
N225TL	99	King Air B200	BB-1689	CSC Trust Company/Embla Holdings, Wilmington De.	N203TS
N225WC	04	King Air B200	BB-1862	Flightstream LLC. Seattle, Wa.	N6162X
N225WL	85	King Air B200	BB-1226	Floyd's Equipment Inc. Sikeston, Mo.	(N346EA)
N225WW	79	PA-31T Cheyenne II	7920003	Win Win Aviation Inc., Franklinton, NC.	LV-MNU
N226DL	01	PA-46-500TP Meridian	4697039	Fly Grado LLC. St Louis, Mo.	N139KC
N226JW	68	King Air B90	LJ-406	Win Win Aviation Inc., Franklinton, NC.	N438
N226K	98	King Air 350	FL-226	RSE Aviation Sales & Leasing LLC. Lawrenceville, Ga.	
N226N	01	Pilatus PC-12/45	414	JD Plane LLC. Bellevue, Wa.	N905B
N226PB	02	TBM 700B	226	Thai Flying Club/Johor Flying Club. Singapore.	N226GS
N226RA	06	TBM 850	364	Norm Air LLC. New Orleans, La.	
N226SR	76	SA-226T Merlin 3A	T-270	Falcon Flight, Telluride, Co.	N953AE
N227DC	80	King Air C90	LJ-876	David Connor/Air King LLC. Tucson, Az.	N153PM
N227JT	83	SA-227TT Merlin 3C	TT-477	Fleming Aircraft Sales, St Paul, Mn.	60-SBV
N227NS	06	Pilatus PC-12/47	715	Nextflight LLC. Phoenix, Az.	HB-FRD
N227TM	74	PA-31T Cheyenne II	7400008	Anafair LLC. Green Bay, Wi.	N66837
N227TT	82	SA-227TT Merlin 3C	TT-444	Tarrant Aviation LLC. Dover, De.	VH-UZA
N228CX	93	TBM 700	84	Bernard Holmes, Southend, UK.	
N228RC	04	King Air B200	BB-1910	Reike Leasing Co.Inc./Reike Packaging Ststems Auburn In.	
N228WP	72	Mitsubishi MU-2F	228	Wayne Perry Construction Inc. Buena Park, Ca.	N963MA
N229CR	88	120ER Brasilia	120111	RCR Air Inc.,Lexington, NC.	N34712
N230CS	78	King Air 200	BB-306	Benjamin Nemser, North Miami, Fl.	4X-DZK
N230PG	98	Pilatus PC-12/45	230	U-Haul Co of Oregon, Portland, Or.	OY-TUS
N231CM	02	PA-46-500TP Meridian	4697146	PB One Aviation LLC. Austin, Tx.	
N231PT	74	PA-31T Cheyenne II	7400003	Premark Realty LC. Ashburn, Va.	(N177PT)
N231SW	79	PA-31T Cheyenne 1	7904007	Hummer 1 LLC. Camden, SC.	
N232AL	75	King Air A100	B-222	Para Drop, Elroy, Az.	(N304TC)

Reg	Yr Type	c/n	Owner/Operator	Prev Regn
N232DH	79 PA-31T Cheyenne 1	7904021	Yamato Inc. Beaufort, SC.	N23263
N232GM	84 Conquest 1	425-0219	Mook Enterprises LLC. Scottsdale, Az.	N242GB
N232JS	79 King Air 200	BB-446	Biddulph Oldsmobile Inc. Peoria, Az.	(N727KB)
N233PS	78 PA-31T Cheyenne II	7820039	Aerolease LLC. Fargo, ND.	SX-BFQ
N233RC	81 Conquest II	441-0263	Rico Marketing Corp. Flint, Mi.	N815MC
N234K	84 PA-31T Cheyenne II	7520001	Weather Modification Inc. Fargo, ND.	N668DH
N234KK	90 King Air 350	FL-29	St Andrews Aircraft LLC. Tequesta, Fl.	N67DW
N234KW	82 King Air B200	BB-1065	General Atomics Inc. San Diego, Ca.	D-ICOA
N234RG	03 Pilatus PC-12/45	520	WFBNW NA. Salt Lake City, Ut. (trustor ?).	HB-FRV
N234TK	77 King Air B100	BE-24	Mr Gary Ray Hickman, Placide Fl.	N187J
N235GA	85 Gulfstream 1000B	96209	GAC/U S Government,	
N235KT	58 Fairchild F-27F	16	Jeppesen Development Inc. Howey on the Hills, Fl.	N101FG
N235PB	94 King Air 350	FL-124	Orbit Construction Corp. Wilmington, De.	D-CKWM
N235TW	03 PA-46-500TP Meridian	4697157	Subscriberbase Holdings Inc., Columbia, SC.	
N236CP	76 King Air B100	BE-9	Wharf Place/Glenmark Holdings LLC. Morgantown, WV.	(N360BA)
N236JS	81 King Air F90	LA-90	David Schlosser, Phoenix, Az.	N290DK
N236PC	84 PA-42 Cheyenne IIIA	5501006	Aero Transport Professionals Inc. Hot Springs, Ar.	N809E
N236WR	07 Pilatus PC-12/47	804	236WR LLC., Sacramento, Ca.	HB-FQV
N237PC	81 Cheyenne II-XL	8166045	Aero Transport Professionals Inc. Hot Springs, Ar.	N600BS
N237ST	05 PA-46-500TP Meridian	4697237	Kubitz Meridian LLC. Santa Fe, NM.	
N238GA	85 Gulfstream 1000B	96210	GAC/U S Government,	
N238PC	81 PA-42 Cheyenne III	8001029	Aero Transport Professionals Inc. Hot Springs, Ar.	N811DA
N239DR	73 SA-226T Merlin 3	T-239	Dr Johnson Lumber Aviation Inc. Riddle, Or.	C-GPRO
N239JV	82 King Air B200	BB-1014	MMH Aviation LLC/Pete Martin Drilling Inc., Vernal, Ut.	N6308F
N239PF	79 King Air 200	BB-565	TM Ventures LLC / Helm Builders LLC, ApexNC.	N6630C
N239TT	87 King Air 300	FA-114	T2 Holdings LLP. Lewes, De.	N976EA
N240CT	82 King Air B200	BB-1063	Case Leasing LLC. White Plains, NY.	HR-ASY
N240DH	85 SA-227AT Merlin 4C	AT-602B	Ameriflight Inc/DHL Airways Inc. Cincinnati, Oh.	N3117P
N240K	68 King Air B90	LJ-340	Merlin Associates Inc. Princeton, NJ.	N925B
N241CK	77 King Air 200	BB-272	Kalitta Charters LLC. Ypsilanti, Mi.	N302MB
N241CW	78 King Air B100	BE-54	Blossom Valley Aviation LLC. El Cajon, Ca.	N2025S
N241DH	85 SA-227AT Merlin 4C	AT-607B	Ameriflight Inc/DHL Airways Inc. Cincinnati, Oh.	N3118A
N241PM	03 PA-46-500TP Meridian	4697150	Rearden Aviation LLC. Helena, Mt.	C-GMCM
N242DH	85 SA-227AT Merlin 4C	AT-608B	Ameriflight Inc/DHL Airways Inc. Cincinnati, Oh.	N3118G
N242JH	98 Pilatus PC-12/45	232	Center Charter LLC. San Francisco, Ca.	HB-FRC
N242LF	81 King Air F90	LA-86	Metro Aviation Inc. Shreveport, La.	N249RC
N242NA	85 King Air B200	BB-1242	Global Aviation Partners Inc. Moscow, Russia.	LV-ZFC
N242NS	91 King Air C90A	LJ-1271	Plan B Ventures LLC. College Station, Tx.	N80904
N242RA	80 PA-42 Cheyenne III	8001003	Shirley Flyin LLC. Rantoul, Il.	N8EA
N243DH	85 SA-227AT Merlin 4C	AT-609B	Ameriflight Inc/DHL Airways Inc. Cincinnati, Oh.	N3118H
N243JB	90 King Air C90	LJ-1243	TBC Aviation LLC., Mobile, Al.	HS-SKT
N244AB	80 PA-31T Cheyenne 1	8004015	The Parton Companies, Rutherfordton, NC.	N2442W
N244CH	81 King Air 200	BB-801	CEH Inc. Drummond Island, Mi.	N123WN
N244DH	85 SA-227AT Merlin 4C	AT-618B	Ameriflight Inc/DHL Airways Inc. Cincinnati, Oh.	N242DM
N244JS	81 King Air 200	BB-754	San Fernando Air LP. Harlingen, Tx.	
N244MP	79 Rockwell 690B	11531	GOR Commercial Enterprises Inc. Miami, Fl.	N101RF
N244SA	74 SA-226T Merlin 3	T-244	Land Coast Insulation LLC., New Iberia, La.	RP-C203
N245CF	76 Rockwell 690A	11313	MWJ Industries LLC. Fort Smith, Ar.	N245CT
N245DH	85 SA-227AT Merlin 4C	AT-624B	Ameriflight Inc/DHL Airways Inc. Cincinnati, Oh.	
N246CA	80 King Air F90	LA-27	PLDC Aviation Group LLC., Houston, Tx.	N40BR
N246CK	76 King Air C90	LJ-694	421DK LLC. Pasco, Wa.	N901JA
N246DH	85 SA-227AT Merlin 4C	AT-625B	Ameriflight Inc/DHL Airways Inc. Cincinnati, Oh.	
N246PH	90 King Air B200	BB-1373	Petroleum Helicopters Inc. Lafayette, La.	N25GK
N246SD	05 King Air 350	FL-441	Spring Valley Ranch LLC. Dublin, Ca.	N36941
N246W	82 MU-2 Marquise	1552SA	Pamida Inc. Omaha, Ne.	N478MA
N247AF	80 King Air 200	BB-587	Trans World Health Services Inc. Reno, Nv.	N30AB
N247B	73 King Air A100	B-139	Aviation Charter Services, Indianapolis, In.	
N247C	05 King Air C90B	LJ-1754	Crowley Management Services Inc. City of Industry, Ca.	N24FH
N247DH	85 SA-227AT Merlin 4C	AT-626B	Ameriflight Inc/DHL Airways Inc. Cincinnati, Oh.	
N247LM	81 PA-31T Cheyenne 1	8104043	Mystair Inc. Dover, De.	N527JC
N247MD	90 King Air C90A	LJ-1244	Alan A Binette, Medford, Or.	N5644E
N248DA	03 PA-46-500TP Meridian	4697156	Home Builders Marketing Services Inc. Encinitas, Ca.	N156SE
N248DH	85 SA-227AT Merlin 4C	AT-630B	Ameriflight Inc/DHL Airways Inc. Cincinnati, Oh.	
N248J	81 Cheyenne II-XL	8166009	Jomax Construction Co. Great Bend, Ks.	N2488Y
N248JH	82 King Air B100	BE-126	Executive King Air Transportation,	(N512DS)

Reg	Yr	Type	c/n	Owner/Operator	Prev Regn
N249CP	79	King Air C90	LJ-841	Guardian Aircraft Leasing LLC. Albuquerque, NM.	YV-249CP
N249DH	85	SA-227AT Merlin 4C	AT-631B	Ameriflight Inc/DHL Airways Inc. Cincinnati, Oh.	
N249PA	65	King Air 90	LJ-21	Loan Guarantee Insurance Agency Inc. Irvine, Ca.	N5Y
N249WM	75	King Air E90	LW-139	Meadspeak LLC. Ormond Beach, Fl.	N345KA
N250AF	72	Mitsubishi MU-2K	243	Air 1st Aviation Companies Inc. Aiken, SC.	HK-2060W
N250GM	83	Conquest 1	425-0131	Lindow Aircraft Corp. Springboat Springs, Co.	D-ILPC
N250PW	82	King Air B200	BB-1058	Westgrove Holdings LLC., Carson City, Nv.	C-FWXB
N250SA	00	PA-46-500TP Meridian	4697004	Smith Air LLC. Walnut Creek, Ca.	(N711HQ)
N250TM	81	King Air 200	BB-822	Trafficmaster plc. Cranfield, UK.	F-GIND
N250TT	78	PA-31T Cheyenne II	7820050	Smith & Chambers LLC. Fort Scott, Ks.	F-GGPV
N250U	67	King Air A90	LJ-213	Midland College, Midland, Tx.	N417CS
N251ES	75	Rockwell 690A	11251	Schwertner Farms Inc. Schwertner, Tx.	N690RC
N251LL	84	King Air 300	FA-2	BCBML LLP. Las Vegas, Nv.	C-GFES
N252CP	01	King Air B200	BB-1791	Osage Air LLC. Baton Rouge, La.	N4471C
N252RC	87	King Air C90A	LJ-1152	Ivey Mechanical LLC. Kosciusko, Ms.	C-FGXA
N253AS	97	King Air 350	FL-155	Executive AirShare Corp. Wichita, Ks.	N253MS
N253JM	79	Rockwell 690B	11551	Montgomery Aviation LLC. St Louis, Mo.	N358HF
N253PC	99	Pilatus PC-12/45	253	Ascendant Partners LLC. Carefree, Az.	HB-FRM
N255DW	01	PA-46-500TP Meridian	4697020	Bonair Inc. Boulder, Co.	
N256DD	82	Conquest II	441-0256	Berry Construction, Madera, Ca.	N256DP
N256TA	67	King Air A90	LJ-256	Flanagan Enterprises (Nevada) Inc. Carson City, Nv.	C-FOLR
N257CQ	95	King Air C90B	LJ-1419	Absher Air Inc. Somerset, Ky.	N257CG
N257JM	06	TBM 850	356	Blackbrook Aviation Inc. Wilmington, De.	N850XX
N257NA	77	King Air 200	BB-257	Dihe Inc. New Orleans, La.	(N257BH)
N257YA	98	King Air B200	BB-1622	Pruitt Tran Inc/Pruitt Corp. Toccoa, Ga.	N30365
N258AG	77	King Air C-12C	BC-44	Profile Aviation Services/Eagle Aviation LLC. Hickory, NC.	77-22933
N258JC	76	King Air E90	LW-191	Blackjack Air LLC. Waco, Tx.	N63EC
N258VB	82	Conquest II	441-0258	High Plains Pizza Inc. Great Falls, Mt.	(N6859Y)
N259SC	72	King Air E90	LW-17	Aircraft Guaranty Title LLC. Houston, Tx. (trustor ?).	(N906BB)
N260CB	73	Mitsubishi MU-2J	573	Clyde Barton, Lake Jackson, Tx.	N203GA
N260GF	06	PA-46-500TP Meridian	4697260	Geo-Flo Products Corp. Bedford, In.	N444RR
N260HS	99	Pilatus PC-12/45	260	Jen-Linz Ltd. Oklahoma City, Ok.	(N472SW)
N260WE	79	Rockwell 690B	11536	EMS Air Services of NY Inc. Canandaiga, NY.	N81707
N261AC	78	King Air 200	BB-321	DFB Pharmaceuticals Inc. Fort Worth, Tx.	N38JL
N261GB	85	King Air C90A	LJ-1119	Magic Leasing LLC. Orland Park, Il.	N386CP
N261MA	80	MU-2 Marquise	758SA	Robert & Cynthia Peterson Living Trust, Harrodsburg, Ky.	N777FL
N261WB	75	Mitsubishi MU-2M	330	Roy Kinsey Jr. Pensacola, Fl.	N261WR
N262J	03	TBM 700C2	292	Sales Force Management Inc. Wilmington, De.	
N262MM	01	PA-46-500TP Meridian	4697040	Cx USA 9/06 to ?	
N262SP	85	King Air 300	FA-33	Samaritan's Purse Inc. Boone, NC.	N311RF
N263CM	72	SA-226T Merlin 3	T-223	Damax Inc. Las Vegas, Nv.	N2630M
N263CW	03	TBM 700C2	263	Cuprum Aviation LLC. Angola, In.	N700BU
N263RS	95	Pilatus PC-12	112	Stuart Enterprises LLC., Kearneysville, WV.	N263AL
N264B	01	PA-46-500TP Meridian	4697028	Comfly Corp. Middleburn, Ct.	
N264KW	79	MU-2 Solitaire	403SA	Dr Kenneth Wolf MD. Lewiston, Me.	N12LE
N264PA	80	King Air B100	BE-86	Papa Alpha LLC/Time Saver Aviation/Southen Pines, NC.	N85KA
N264SP	00	King Air B200	BB-1756	Indiana State Police, Indianapolis, In.	N5056U
N264WF	99	Pilatus PC-12/45	264	Tim Williams/Williams Aviation, Knoxville, Tn.	HB-FSI
N265EJ	81	King Air B200	BB-911	Lynch Flying Service Inc. Logan Field, Mt.	N411CC
N265EX	80	Gulfstream 980	95032	Benchmark Ventures Ltd. Wilmington, De.	N9785S
N265PA	86	King Air 300	FA-106	Cohassett Associates Inc./RLR Flying LLC Cohasset Ma.	N156BA
N266M	82	SA-227TT Merlin 3C	TT-424	Jan Kovacic, Lafayette, In.	N900AK
N266RD	01	King Air C90A	LJ-1633	Windy City Express LLC/Condor Express Corp. Danbury, Ct.	N4473M
N267CB	04	King Air B200	BB-1873	DeltaCore Charter Services LLC. Seattle, Wa.	N6113P
N267RD	78	Rockwell 690B	11456	R A Daffer Inc. Fulton, Md.	N267R
N267WF	99	Pilatus PC-12/45	267	Emerging Growth Advisors Inc. Baltimore, Md.	HB-FSL
N268LB	07	King Air 350	FL-570	Lark Builders, Vidalia Ga.	
N269AB	99	Pilatus PC-12/45	297	Bear Creek Aviation LLC. Baltimore, Md.	N269AF
N269DE	71	SA-226T Merlin 3	T-208	A Z Aviation, Berryville, Ar. (status ?).	N429LC
N269JG	81	King Air C90	LJ-949	J & G Aviation LLC. Mountain View, Ar.	N100HS
N269LS	81	King Air 200	BB-799	Chetcam LLC. Northridge, Ca.	N250DL
N269ML	81	King Air 200	BB-760	MidSouth Air LLC. Russellville, Ar.	N3710A
N269PB	99	Pilatus PC-12/45	269	Rocky Mountain Group Technologies LLC. Evergreen, Co.	HB-FSN
N269PM	68	SA-26T Merlin 2A	T26-26	Perris Air LLC, Perris Ca.	C-GWKA
N269SC	76	King Air C90	LJ-683	Community Health Associates Inc. Nashville, Tn.	(F-GVEP)

Reg	Yr Type	c/n	Owner/Operator	Prev Regn
☐ N270AB	02 King Air 350	FL-362	Baker Commander LLC., Birmingham, Al.	N300R
☐ N270DP	79 Rockwell 690B	11541	Commander Aviation LLC. Raleigh, NC.	N690BD
☐ N270M	67 King Air A90	LJ-288	Clark Brothers Felt, Waco, Tx.	
☐ N271AK	07 King Air C90GT	LJ-1856	Roxann Management Corporation,Great Neck, NY	
☐ N271BC	85 King Air 300	FA-48	Victorair Corp., Fort Lauderdale, Fl.	N7221N
☐ N271SS	00 Pilatus PC-12/45	306	I S & S Aviation LLC. Wilmington, De.	HB-FQT
☐ N271TW	79 MU-2 Marquise	734SA	MooToo 1 Inc. Newark, De.	(N331J)
☐ N271WN	67 King Air B90	LJ-226	Carole Broderick, Pinellas Park, Fl.	N14TG
☐ N272EA	02 King Air C90B	LJ-1686	HBC Aviation LLC/Haydon Building Corporation, Phoenix, Az.	
☐ N272MA	03 TBM 700C2	272	TBM 272 LLC. Jackson, Ms.	
☐ N272MC	73 Mitsubishi MU-2K	272	RLSPP LLC. Plano, Tx.	N10BK
☐ N273AF	99 Pilatus PC-12/45	273	Alpha Flying Inc. Manchester, NH.	HB-FSR
☐ N273AZ	79 Conquest II	441-0104	Amberhill Development Ltd./Songbird LLC., Costa Mesa, Ca.	N8194Z
☐ N273NA	78 King Air E90	LW-273	Nebrig & Assocs Inc. Denton, Tx.	N10SA
☐ N273TA	06 King Air 350	FL-518	Tanimura & Antle Inc., Salinas, Ca.	
☐ N274GC	85 Conquest II	441-0349	Pro Aviation II LLC. Ogden, Ut.	N12125
☐ N274KA	78 King Air E90	LW-274	Air Transportation of South Texas, Edinburg, Tx.	C-GTIO
☐ N274SB	78 PA-31T Cheyenne II	7820074	Lyddon Aero Center Inc. Liberal, Ks.	N787SW
☐ N275BT	00 King Air 350	FL-275	Executive AirShare Corp. Wichita, Ks.	(N350RC)
☐ N275CA	01 TBM 700B	200	Spirit of St. Louis Inc., Waite Park, Mn.	
☐ N275LA	91 King Air C90A	LJ-1275	Davis Petroleum Products LLC. Glasgow, UK.	TC-AEM
☐ N275LE	68 King Air B90	LJ-373	Take-Off LLC. Santa Rosa Beach, Fl.	N99KA
☐ N275X	79 King Air 200	BB-502	Western Airways Inc. Sugar Land, Tx.	N77PA
☐ N276JB	98 King Air 350	FL-219	Allen Concrete & Masonry Inc. Raleigh, NC.	
☐ N276VM	66 King Air 90	LJ-81	DC Engineering & Development Ltd., London, Oh.	N950K
☐ N277DG	81 PA-31T Cheyenne 1	8104058	Ideal Aviation LLC. Meridian, Ms.	(N130A)
☐ N277GE	90 King Air B200	BB-1389	Abilene Aero Inc., Abilene, Tx.	N389SA
☐ N277JJ	82 King Air B200	BB-1043	Full Gospel Baptist Church, New Orlaeans, La.	(N666JJ)
☐ N277PC	99 Pilatus PC-12/45	277	C & R Aviation LLC. Incline Village, Nv.	HB-FSV
☐ N277SP	80 King Air F90	LA-77	All Systems Satellite Distributors, Newark, NJ.	N827DP
☐ N277SW	81 King Air C90	LJ-968	Cowboy Aviation Services LP., Poolville, Tx.	VH-FOP
☐ N277WC	03 King Air B200	BB-1824	Legal Aire Services Inc. Jacksonville, Fl.	N6124A
☐ N278AB	82 King Air C90-1	LJ-1012	Alton Blakely Aviation Inc. Somerset, Ky.	N617LM
☐ N278SW	82 King Air C90-1	LJ-1011	Citation Ventures Inc. Long Beach, Ca.	VH-FDW
☐ N278WC	99 Pilatus PC-12/45	278	NLT LLC. Santa Barbara, Ca.	HB-FSW
☐ N279DD	77 Rockwell 690B	11373	Robert Perkins/Romara Airplane LLC. Carmel, Ca.	N911AC
☐ N279M	77 SA-226T Merlin 3A	T-279	Century Turbines of Nevada Inc., Georgetown, Tx.	N34SM
☐ N279ST	06 PA-46-500TP Meridian	4697279	Masser Farming Inc., Sacramento, Pa.	
☐ N280RA	75 King Air 200	BB-53	P & S Transport LLC. Shreveport, La.	N6ES
☐ N280SC	80 King Air 200	BB-664	PEC Aviation LLC. Troutman, NC.	(N364EA)
☐ N280TT	77 King Air 200	BB-280	Sunquest Executive Air Charter Inc. Van Nuys, Ca.	F-GJPD
☐ N280YR	82 King Air B200	BB-943	B & H Aviation LLC. Butler, Pa.	N250YR
☐ N281DD	06 PA-46-500TP Meridian	4697262	PD Leasing LLC. Bonsall, Ca.	N704C
☐ N281MA	73 Mitsubishi MU-2K	261	North Hughes Flying Service Inc. Brickeys, Ar.	
☐ N281SE	06 PA-46-500TP Meridian	4697281	Flightline Group Inc., Tallahassee, Fl.	
☐ N281WB	03 Pilatus PC-12/45	483	Worden Brothers Inc/Right Rudder Inc. Fort Lauderdale, Fl.	N483PC
☐ N282CT	82 King Air B200	BB-1002	Windsor/Aughtry Company/AHG Hotels LLC. Greenville, SC.	N6169S
☐ N282DB	77 King Air E90	LW-209	Custom Air Charter Inc. Greenville, Ms.	N32NS
☐ N282JD	01 King Air B200	BB-1779	Corporate Jets Inc.Winston Salem, NC	N624TA
☐ N282PC	81 Cheyenne II-XL	8166006	Powers Construction/Mini Max Warehouses Inc. Florence, SC.	N38WA
☐ N282SJ	81 King Air 200	BB-925	Big Air LLC. Stockton, Ca.	N115D
☐ N282SW	01 PA-46-500TP Meridian	4697073	Williams Enterprises Inc. Carmi, Il.	
☐ N282TC	79 King Air E90	LW-311	BLR Aerospace LLC Everett Wa.	N505RP
☐ N283B	76 King Air C-12C	BC-35	A H Charters Inc. Belle Chasse, La.	N7067B
☐ N283BS	91 TBM 700	16	Seymour Transport Inc. Grammer, In.	N700CT
☐ N283KA	75 King Air 200	BB-83	Med Air LLC. Lawrenceville, Ga.	RP-C711
☐ N284K	80 King Air 200	BB-608	Indiana University Foundation, Bloomington, In.	N16AS
☐ N284PM	77 King Air C90	LJ-734	Kijivu Aviation LLC., Charlottesville, Va.	(N700BN)
☐ N286AF	76 Rockwell 690A	11286	Mojoe LLC. Wilmington, De.	ZS-NXK
☐ N287CB	82 Cheyenne II-XL	8166051	Cottingham & Butler Insurance Service Inc. Dubuque, Ia.	N30VB
☐ N287MA	07 PA-46-500TP Meridian	4697319	Piper Aircraft Inc. Vero Beach, Fl.	
☐ N287PC	99 Pilatus PC-12/45	287	DGM Leasing, Oceanside, Ca.	HB-FQD
☐ N288CC	06 TBM 850	369	Falcon Aviation LLC. McComb, Ms.	N850LA
☐ N288CR	78 King Air E90	LW-269	Home Aviation LLC/Horne Ford Inc. Pinetop, Az.	N288CB
☐ N288GS	97 King Air B200	BB-1555	Avtrade Limited, Hove, UK	N98DA

Reg	Yr	Type	c/n	Owner/Operator	Prev Regn
N288KM	95	King Air B200	BB-1508	Garmin International Inc. Olathe Ks.	N3208T
N288RA	69	King Air 100	B-5	Southern Star Aviation Corp. Trujillo Alto, PR.	N280RA
N289PB	99	Pilatus PC-12/45	289	Philip Rosenbaum, Austin, Tx.	N289PB
N289RP	01	King Air C90B	LJ-1665	Snoopy LLC/Parrish Group Inc., Tallassasee, Fl.	N4465F
N290AJ	80	King Air C90	LJ-871	King Leasing Inc. Asheville, NC.	N29EB
N290AS	00	King Air 350	FL-296	Executive AirShare Corp. Wichita, Ks.	N877SA
N290CC	66	King Air A90	LJ-132	Devonshire Aviation LLC., Richmond, Va.	ZP-TYF
N290DP	71	King Air C90	LJ-529	Dodson International/Nion LLC, Rantoul, Ks.	LV-WJP
N290K	80	King Air E90	LW-337	Projects Plus Ltd. Mason City, Ia.	
N290KA	73	King Air E90	LW-59	Robil LLC., Orangeburg, SC.	N992MA
N290MC	77	King Air E90	LW-206	Maconix Ltd. Minster, Oh.	N6406S
N290PA	71	King Air C90	LJ-519	Simply Living Ltd. Liege-Bierset, Belgium.	N82307
N290PF	76	Rockwell 690A	11290	Aero Air LLC. Hillsboro, Or.	N100JJ
N290RS	79	PA-31T Cheyenne 1	7904033	JSA Aviation LLC. Pineville, La.	N627NB
N290SJ	77	King Air 200	BB-290	Citation Ventures Inc. Long Beach, Ca.	YV-161CP
N290TA	73	SA-226T Merlin 3	T-228	Helibase 99 Inc. Wilmington, Oh.	N610ED
N291B	07	King Air 350	FL-559	Battelle Memorial Institute Columbus Oh.	
N291CC	77	King Air C90	LJ-728	D L Morgan Aviation Inc. Charleston, SC.	N275L
N291DF	98	King Air C90B	LJ-1534	Davis & Floyd Inc. Greenwood, SC.	N268P
N291MB	74	Mitsubishi MU-2K	291	Interncontinental Jet Inc. Tulsa, Ok.	CP-1147
N291MM	73	King Air E90	LW-32	KA73 LLC Little Rock Ar.	N123PP
N291PA	77	King Air 200	BB-291	Jay Bird Air LLC. Dublin, Oh.	N769
N292A	66	King Air 90	LJ-99	Placebo Air LLC. Ridgecrest, Ca.	N73679
N292P	05	Pilatus PC-12/45	630	Steelman Aviation Inc. Las Vegas, Nv.	HB-FRX
N292Z	66	680T Turbo Commander	1566-22	Pegasus Force, Homestead, Fl.	OB-T-924
N294DR	04	PA-46-500TP Meridian	4697184	Oak Island Air Orlando Fl.	
N294PJ	07	TBM 850	438	EADS SOCATA North America, Pembroke Pines, Fl.	
N295CE	81	Conquest II	441-0205	Cessna Conquest LLC. Brasstown, NC.	N3330S
N296AS	77	King Air C90	LJ-704	JSW Investments Inc/Aero-Smith Inc. Martinsburg, WV.	N1565L
N296ST	07	PA-46-500TP Meridian	4697296	Coastal Instrument & Electronics Company, Burgaw, NC.	
N298D	00	King Air C90B	LJ-1603	Laursen Aviation Inc. Auburn, Ca.	N445D
N299AK	03	King Air B200	BB-1850	B200 Air Charters LLC. Farmingdale, NY.	N6150Q
N299AL	03	King Air B200	BB-1823	Aviation Specialities Inc. Washington, DC.	N299AK
N299AM	98	Pilatus PC-12/45	236	Wilmington Trust Co Trustee, Wilmington, De.	HB-FRG
N299AS	99	King Air 350	FL-243	Executive AirShare Corp. Wichita, Ks.	N333M
N299AV	99	King Air B200	BB-1680	Teton Leasing LLC. Pocatello, Id.	N604TA
N299D	67	King Air A90	LJ-257	Sun Charter LLC. St Petersburg, Fl.	C-FXNB
N299EC	81	SA-226T Merlin 3B	T-410	Richard Gasser, Midland, Tx.	(D-IFLY)
N299K	79	King Air C90	LJ-839	OK Consultants Inc. Monterey, Ca.	9G-SAM
N299KP	84	King Air F90-1	LA-218	King Air 200 Partners LLC. Palo Alto, Ca.	N218BA
N299MA	07	PA-46-500TP Meridian	4697294	Interactive Aviation LLC., Indianapolis, In.	
N299MK	90	King Air B200	BB-1357	Boman & Kemp Manufacturing Inc. Ogden, Ut.	D-IBSY
N299MS	69	King Air B90	LJ-457	Dynamic Aviation Group Inc.,Bridgewater, Va.	N405BC
N299RP	98	King Air C90B	LJ-1537	Utility Air Inc. Moberly, Mo.	N99ML
N299VM	85	King Air C90A	LJ-1125	Skyline Crest Enterprises LLC. Antioch, Ca.	N299KA
N300AE	94	TBM 700	97	Yankee Bravo Inc. Ponte Verde, Fl.	
N300AJ	82	King Air B200	BB-965	Mooreland Aviation LLC., Santa Fe, NM.	N184MQ
N300AL	80	SA-226T Merlin 3B	T-326	M & C Leasing Inc. Hammond, In.	N19J
N300AW	99	King Air C90	LJ-1570	Air Warsaw LLC/Henrietta Building Supplies, W Henrietta, NY.	N214KF
N300AZ	04	TBM 700C2	300	AVA Leasing LLC., Bay Harbor Island, Fl.	
N300CE	80	PA-31T Cheyenne 1	8004028	Cheyenne 1 Ltd. Dover, De.	C-GTOL
N300CW	87	King Air 300	FA-115	TumiAir Inc. Woodside, Ca.	XC-AA20
N300CX	05	TBM 700C2	327	Socata Ventures LLC. Lenexa, Ks.	N732C
N300DM	82	King Air F90	LA-165	Las Montanas Aviation LLC. Tucson, Az.	N686LD
N300FL	98	King Air B200	BB-1629	Alaro Inc. Giddings, Tx.	N2221Z
N300HB	79	King Air 200	BB-566	Whiting Wings/Whiting Systems Inc. Alexander, Ar.	N200ER
N300HH	85	King Air 300	FA-80	Air Charters Europe, Eelde, Netherlands	N300HH
N300KA	90	King Air 350	FL-28	Malone Aero Sales LLC. Atlanta, Ga.	N220CL
N300LS	95	King Air 350	FL-127	Osprey Flight Management Inc. Houston, Tx.	C-GPPC
N300MC	86	King Air 300	FA-91	Ridgeway Enterprises Inc/Rose Packing Co. Barrington, Il.	N990PT
N300MT	75	King Air E90	LW-143	Air Evac EMS Inc., West Plains, Mo.	N300BA
N300PP	88	King Air 300LW	FA-171	B V Handel en Exploitatienmaatschappij Ruygrok, Rotterdam.	D-COIL
N300PR	84	King Air 300	FA-13	Burst Brothers Properties LLC. Kenner, La.	(N500GC)
N300PU	99	King Air B200	BB-1657	Purdue University, Lafayette, In.	
N300PW	76	King Air 200	BB-114	AirCorp Inc.Dallas Tx.	XA-PMX

Reg	Yr	Type	c/n	Owner/Operator	Prev Regn
N300RC	89 King Air 300	FA-177	Elliot Aviation Aircraft Sales Inc., Des Moines Ia.	(N350CD)
N300SE	85 King Air 300	FA-68	Georgia Theatre Co. St Simons Island, Ga.	N10QY
N300SR	81 PA-31T Cheyenne 1	8104022	Seastar Inc. Carmel, In.	N77NH
N300SV	87 King Air 300	FA-112	Performance Aviation LLC. Farmington, NM.	F-GJHH
N300TA	80 King Air F90	LA-9	Michael Williams, LaPorte, In.	N200FA
N300TE	84 King Air 300	FA-19	Alice Enviromental Services LP. Alice, Tx.	N888BR
N300TM	91 King Air 350	FL-50	Taylor & Martin/T & M Enterprises Inc. Fremont, Ne.	N202PV
N300TN	88 King Air 300	FA-168	Conquest Charter Inc. Carson City, Nv.	N300TM
N300TP	87 King Air B200	BB-1279	Otter Tail Power Co. Fergus Falls, Mn.	N58AB
N300VA	80 King Air C90	LJ-877	Shammach. Shreveport, La.	N66877
N300WP	79 PA-31T Cheyenne 1	7904002	Philips Oil Inc./GP Air LLC., Crestview, Fl.	N6182
N301CG	85 King Air 300	FA-87	John Lister, Hondo, Tx. (status ?).	N899EA
N301D	01 PA-46-500TP Meridian	4697043	EZ Jet LLC., Plantation, Fl.	N5077Y
N301GM	77 Mitsubishi MU-2L	696	JEC3 LLC., Spanish Fort, Al.	N856MA
N301HC	85 King Air B200	BB-1219	Intermountain Health Care Services, Salt Lake City, Ut.	N200YB
N301PT	82 King Air C-12D	BP-28	PACTEC, Redlands, Ca.	82-23780
N301TA	79 PA-31T Cheyenne 1	7904041	Mikal Watts, Corpus Christi, Tx.	N65CK
N301TS	79 King Air B100	BE-76	Energy Aviation LLC. Atlanta, Ga.	N812WJ
N302NC	84 King Air 300	FA-9	Middle Coast Enterprises LLC. Austin, Tx.	N930G
N302PB	00 Pilatus PC-12/45	302	Muntley Air LLC. Seaside, Ca.	HB-FQO
N302PT	82 King Air C-12D	BP-30	PACTEC, Redlands, Ca.	82-23782
N302RJ	07 TBM 850	425	F1 Air Group Two LLC, Wilmngton De.	
N302TA	80 PA-31T Cheyenne II	8020046	Avsim LLC. Wilmington, De.	N1879D
N303CA	86 King Air C90A	LJ-1134	Dunlap & Kyle Co. Batesville, Ms.	D-IEVO
N303G	77 Rockwell 690B	11355	Clemson University, Clemson, SC.	N303G
N303GM	82 Gulfstream 1000	96042	South Pacific Air Transport, Houston, Tx.	N9962S
N303JD	00 Pilatus PC-12/45	343	Lisgar II LLC. Lincoln, Ca.	N912RP
N303JW	02 PA-46-500TP Meridian	4697149	Champ Leasing I LLC, Wilmington De.	N5348S
N303MA	77 SA-226T Merlin 3A	T-278	Pioneer Aircraft LLC. Sheridan, Wy.	N475MG
N303TS	81 Cheyenne II-XL	8166007	Travel Services LLC/Specchio Farms, Rantoul, Il.	N491MB
N304BP	07 King Air 350	FL-542	Penkhus Motor Co., Colorado Springs, Co.	
N304JS	88 King Air 300	FA-142	Johnson River LLC. Sherman, Tx.	N27TB
N304LG	77 King Air E90	LW-231	Seven Bar Flying Service Inc. Albuquerque, NM.	N4954S
N304PT	00 Pilatus PC-12/45	304	Ruby Air LLC., Pleasanton, Ca.	(N304PR)
N304SC	92 Cheyenne T-1040	8275017	SouthCentral Air Inc. Kenai, Ak.	N9096C
N304TC	04 King Air C90B	LJ-1719	The H Truman Chafin Law Firm LLC. Williamson, WV.	N36719
N305CW	75 Mitsubishi MU-2L	667	Murray Aviation Inc. Ypsilanti, Mi.	N300CW
N305DG	07 PA-46-500TP Meridian	4697305	Daniel L George, Bonita Springs, Fl.	
N305DS	75 Mitsubishi MU-2M	328	Florida Fast Flight Corp. Miami Lakes, Fl.	N5PC
N305JS	79 King Air 200	BB-472	Aegis Jet LLC., Carlsbad, Ca.	G-WRCF
N305PC	97 Beech 1900D	UE-299	BCC Equipment Leasing Corp. Long Beach, Ca.	
N305SA	86 King Air 300	FA-111	SteakAir Inc. Little Rock, Ar.	N391MT
N305TT	81 King Air C90	LJ-992	Sky One LLC. Wilmer, Al.	HB-GJA
N306M	86 King Air 300	FA-98	CKM Leasing LLC/Merlin Law Group PA., Tampa, Fl.	N30SM
N307DM	78 King Air 200	BB-332	JETSS LLC /Jet Sales of Stuart LLC., Stuart, Fl.	N58DE
N307PA	79 SA-226T Merlin 3B	T-307	James Mason, DeKalb, Il.	N606PS
N308MD	90 King Air C90A	LJ-1246	Gem City Proprties/Gem City Bone & Joint, Laramie, Wy.	XA-RFN
N308RH	76 King Air 200	BB-109	CSSJ Aviation LLC. Conway, Ar .	N244JP
N308ST	07 PA-46-500TP Meridian	4697308	Piper Aircraft Inc. Vero Beach, Fl.	
N308TC	81 MU-2 Marquise	1507SA	Turbine Aircraft Holdings, Wilmington, De	N888FS
N310JM	01 PA-46-500TP Meridian	4697069	William Trimble III, Washington, DC.	
N310MA	69 Mitsubishi MU-2F	167	Jackson Tennessee Leasing Co. Jackson, Tn.	N549LK
N311AC	81 PA-31T Cheyenne II	8120016	AJH Enterprises LLC./Hoar Construction LLC., Birmingham, Al.	N241PS
N311AV	78 King Air 200	BB-336	Colemill Enterprises Inc. Nashville, Tn.	N50TW
N311CM	80 King Air B100	BE-101	Luxury Butler LLC., Raleigh, NC.	N3695A
N311GC	80 King Air F90	LA-55	RTE Enterprises Inc. Van Nuys, Ca.	N300GC
N311GM	96 King Air 350	FL-138	Garan Manufacturing Corp. Starkville, Ms.	N350P
N311KB	73 King Air C-12C	BD-3	Conch Cruiser LLC. Orlando, Fl.	N140MT
N311MP	83 King Air B200	BB-1112	Med-Pro Leasing, Oklahoma City, Ok.	(N7090U)
N311RN	74 Mitsubishi MU-2K	311	Raju Leasing LLC. Jackson, Ms.	N311JB
N311SC	82 Cheyenne T-1040	8275006	SouthCentral Air Inc. Kenai, Ak.	N9176Y
N311SR	66 King Air 90	LJ-107	International Airline Training Academy Inc. Tucson, Az.	N7BQ
N312AR	91 King Air 300	FA-216	Aaron Rents Inc. Atlanta, Ga.	N160AB
N312BC	94 Pilatus PC-12	101	CPG Leasing LLC. Wayzata, Mn. (was s/n P-03).	HB-FOC
N312DB	85 King Air 300	FA-35	Drone Aviation LLC./Scenic Homes, Snellville, Ga.	N26JP

Reg	Yr	Type	c/n	Owner/Operator	Prev Regn
❏ N312DE	85 King Air 300	FA-49		Atlantic Coast Carriers Inc. Fayetteville, NC.	N984SW
❏ N312JC	88 King Air B200	BB-1312		Sterling Custom Homes Inc. Lakeway, Tx.	N506EB
❏ N312ME	82 King Air B200C	BL-46		Aviation Specialities Inc. Washington, DC.	N3125J
❏ N312MT	81 Cheyenne II-XL	8166062		Opechee Construction Corp., Belmont, NH.	N31JZ
❏ N312PC	96 Pilatus PC-12	144		James Aviation Inc. Erie, Pa.	HB-FRF
❏ N312RL	97 King Air 350	FL-164		Belk Simpson Co. Greenville, SC.	C-FOIL
❏ N312VF	67 King Air A90	LJ-299		B & S Aviation LLC. Wilmington, De.	(N312MH)
❏ N313BA	89 King Air 300	FA-178		Beta Aire Ltd/Heidtman Steel Products Inc. Toledo, Oh.	ZS-MNG
❏ N313BB	84 PA-42 Cheyenne IIIA	5501016		Southern Tank Leasing Inc. Demopolis, Al.	N94CS
❏ N313CT	79 King Air 200	BB-461		Corporate Trading Inc., St. Petersburg, Fl.	N277RS
❏ N313D	82 SA-227AT Merlin 4C	AT-464		Mana-Igreja Crista Inc. Tulsa, Ok.	N30364
❏ N313DW	96 King Air C90B	LJ-1434		Durair Inc. Sedona, Az.	
❏ N313EE	80 King Air 200	BB-708		Mirax Aviation Inc. Carmel, In.	N313EL
❏ N313HS	88 King Air B200	BB-1300		Reeves Ditching & Contracting Co. Sugar Hill Ga.	(N43GJ)
❏ N313KY	86 King Air 300	FA-110		Yellow Iron LLC/Reese Air LLP. Las Vegas, Nv.	ZS-NPL
❏ N313PC	91 PA-42 Cheyenne 400LS	5527044		Aircraft Guaranty Title LLC, Houston, Tx.	N495CA
❏ N313SA	84 King Air 300	FA-5		Spud Air LLC/Alford Farms Inc. Pasco, Wa.	N200WB
❏ N314DD	80 PA-31T Cheyenne 1	8004025		Walker Evans Enterprises, Riverside Ca.	N2323V
❏ N314GK	80 PA-31T Cheyenne 1	8004026		N314GK LLC., Angola, NY.	N76CP
❏ N314MR	76 King Air E90	LW-184		840 LLC, Knoxville Tn.	N4MR
❏ N314P	82 King Air F90	LA-170		Aurignac Realty/VP Air LLC. San Luis Obispo, Ca.	N605CC
❏ N314TD	80 PA-31T Cheyenne II	8020056		PL Flight LLC. Kirkland, Wa.	N144RL
❏ N315MS	78 King Air 200	BB-404		INHS Leasing LLC. Spokane, Wa.	N777PR
❏ N316EN	77 Mitsubishi MU-2M	349SA		Land Design Inc. Southern Pines, NC.	N734MA
❏ N316GC	79 King Air 200	BB-430		Gospel Carrier International Inc. Gaithersburg, Md.	N1YS
❏ N316JP	81 King Air B200	BB-923		Tonic Air Inc. Sharpsburg, Ga.	N200MG
❏ N316MS	78 King Air 200	BB-412		INHS Leasing LLC. Spokane, Wa.	N2030P
❏ N316PM	98 Pilatus PC-12/45	241		Liberty Aviation Corp. Altamonte Springs, Fl.	C-FGRE
❏ N316RS	88 King Air 300	FA-139		Triple Rainbow LLC., Gary, In.	N797P
❏ N316W	05 King Air 350	FL-456		WAH LLC/Wellborn Cabinet Inc. Ashland, Al.	
❏ N316WB	80 PA-31T Cheyenne 1	8004057		American Bilk Carriers LLC. Houston, Tx.	N316JP
❏ N317NA	98 Pilatus PC-12/45	223		Native Air Services Inc. Mesa, Az.	N223PD
❏ N317RT	99 King Air B200	BB-1694		O'Reilly II Aviation, Springfield, Mo.	(ZS-...)
❏ N318AK	78 Conquest II	441-0070		Roadlink Transportation inc. Livingston Mt.	N621SC
❏ N318F	73 King Air C90	LJ-574		Fayard Enterprises Inc. Louisburg, NC.	(N1097S)
❏ N318MT	00 Pilatus PC-12/45	318		Micron Technology Inc. Boise, Id.	HB-FRB
❏ N318TK	73 Rockwell 690A	11136		AED Aviation Inc. Wilmington, De.	N333CA
❏ N318WA	77 Rockwell 690B	11444		Websta's Aviation Services Inc. St Croix, USVI.	N690TG
❏ N319BF	81 Gulfstream 840	11675		Jose Manuel Gardilla,	N39SA
❏ N319EE	04 King Air 350	FL-401		Energy East Corp. New Gloucester, Me.	
❏ N319MB	85 King Air C90A	LJ-1126		391MB LLC. El Segundo, Ca.	N497P
❏ N319TB	04 TBM 700C2	319		Fairway Aviation LLC, Charlotte, NC.	
❏ N320PW	05 Pilatus PC-12/45	647		Felicity Aviation LLC. Newark, De.	HB-F..
❏ N321AV	81 King Air C90	LJ-942		Southern Aircraft Consultancy Inc.Tr. St Just UK	D-IKES
❏ N321CW	99 TBM 700B	155		Carson Wealth Management Group Inc. Omaha, Ne.	N345HB
❏ N321DZ	68 King Air B90	LJ-367		R W Aircraft Inc. Missoula, Mt.	N9711B
❏ N321F	78 King Air C-12C	BC-70		Dynamic Aviation Group Inc. Bridgewater, Va.	78-23134
❏ N321FJ	79 King Air C90	LJ-862		Jet Aviation LLC. Fort Lauderdale, Fl.	N380SC
❏ N321GC	06 King Air B200	BB-1942		Citrus One Inc/Glen Curtis Inc. Yuma, Az.	
❏ N321GM	81 MU-2 Marquise	1505SA		Modular Devices Inc. Carmel, In.	N999ET
❏ N321LB	81 Cheyenne II-XL	8166012		Strategic Technology Resources LLC. Roswell, NM.	N888PT
❏ N321LH	84 PA-42 Cheyenne 400LS	5527012		JANA Aviation Inc. Wilmington, De.	C-GRGE
❏ N321MX	98 Pilatus PC-12/45	215		Peter Pathe, Kirkland, Wa.	N119AF
❏ N321P	78 King Air RC-12C	GR-10		Dynamic Aviation Group Inc. Bridgewater, Va. (was BP-6)	78-23145
❏ N321PH	69 SA-26AT Merlin 2B	T26-140		Mr James V Parran FPO, Ap.	N718GL
❏ N321PL	00 Pilatus PC-12/45	321		Bell Aviation Inc. West Columbia,SC.	HB-FRD
❏ N322BR	89 King Air C90A	LJ-1222		AMTS Aircraft Holdings LLC. Sugar Grove, Il.	OM-VKE
❏ N322BS	80 King Air F90	LA-64		Milford Bostik, Waco, Tx.	N3698H
❏ N322MR	00 King Air C90B	LJ-1611		LSR LLC. Hattiesburg, Ms.	N530AC
❏ N322P	83 Conquest II	441-0274		Herbert & Marigrace Boyer, Novato, Ca.	N98468
❏ N322R	78 King Air C90	LJ-746		B G Transport LLC. Phoenix, Az.	(N122RG)
❏ N322TA	80 MU-2 Marquise	760SA		Indiana State Medical Association, Indianapolis, In.	N321RC
❏ N322TC	92 King Air C90B	LJ-1302		KJV Aviation Inc. Petersburg, WV.	N5670D
❏ N323DB	90 King Air 350	FL-23		B-Air Inc/Castle Partners, Sikeston, Mo.	N391RR
❏ N323HA	79 King Air E90	LW-323		Dale Aviation Inc. Rapid City, SD.	N323KA

Reg	Yr	Type	c/n	Owner/Operator	Prev Regn
N323RR	78 King Air 200	BB-380	Crandall Bowles & Company Lancaster,SC.	N59GS
N324BK	06 Pilatus PC-12/47	718	Blue Water Express LLC. Coral Gables, Fl.	HB-FRG
N324EC	72 King Air U-21J	B-99	C & M Aviation LLC., Dewey, Ok.	N100GJ
N324GM	74 Mitsubishi MU-2K	310	Modular Devices Inc. Carmel, In.	N290GC
N324JS	02 TBM 700B	230	Sunlit Beacon Inc, Wilmington De.	N242CA
N324SC	03 Pilatus PC-12/45	490	International Skychase Corp. Wilmington, De.	G-IJIM
N325FS	06 Pilatus PC-12/47	746	FLIR Systems Aviation LLC. Wilsonville, Or.	HB-FSD
N325JM	99 King Air 350	FL-235	H & S Production Inc/Piano Oil Doc. Piano Tx.	
N325MA	75 Mitsubishi MU-2M	325	Hahn Transportation Ltd. Decatur, Il.	N440RB
N325MW	00 Pilatus PC-12/45	325	325MW Inc. Los Altos Hills, Ca.	(ZS-SRI)
N325WR	80 King Air F90	LA-10	Apple Sauce Inc. Crestview Hills, Il.	N325WP
N326AJ	78 King Air 200	BB-396	Packers Sanitation Services Inc Ltd., Mt. Pleasant, Ia.	(N98HH)
N326KW	90 King Air/Catpass 250	BB-1360	Bering Air Inc. Nome, Ak.	HK-3703X
N326PA	00 Pilatus PC-12/45	362	CC Aviation LLC., Omaha, Ne.	HB-FSM
N326PT	99 King Air C90B	LJ-1581	Southern Kansas Telephone Company, Clearwater Ks.	N32211
N326RS	83 Conquest II	441-0326	IAS Air LLC. Shelley, Id.	N171SP
N326RT	79 King Air 200	BB-553	Perfect Agreements Leasing Inc., Las Vegas, Nv.	N83JN
N326V	06 Pilatus PC-12/47	733	Victor Bravo Aviation LLC. Danbury, Ct.	HB-FRR
N327JZ	00 Pilatus PC-12/45	327	DHZ Inc. Cincinnati, Oh.	N767JT
N327R	99 King Air 350	FL-259	Healthcare Capital Consolidated Inc. Charlotte, NC.	C-GDKI
N327RB	78 King Air 200	BB-335	RDD Real Estate Holdings Two LLC,Overland Park, Ks.	N327RK
N327SE	99 King Air B200	BB-1670	CB Aviation Inc. Gainesville, Fl.	N3117N
N327YR	02 Pilatus PC-12/45	457	Yellow Rose Aviation LLC. Golden, Co.	N457PC
N328AJ	99 King Air 350	FL-245	Aries Aviation LLC. Columbus, Oh.	N350G
N328DC	94 Dornier 328-100	3019	Pacific Gas & Electric Co. San Francisco, Ca.	
N328JP	00 Pilatus PC-12/45	328	Pezold Air Charter LLC. Columbus, Ga.	N328AF
N328KK	81 Cheyenne II-XL	8166068	Kent Kelly/Bristol Aircraft Leasing LLC. Montgomery, Al.	N612BB
N329HS	80 SA-226T Merlin 3B	T-323	Cypress Aviation Inc. Marks, Ms.	(N329HP)
N329KK	81 PA-31T Cheyenne 1	8104011	Kent Kelly/Bristol Aircraft Leasing LLC. Montgomery, Al.	(N839CH)
N329NG	00 Pilatus PC-12/45	329	Grewal Narotam, Gilford, NH.	(ZS-SRJ)
N330CS	89 King Air B200	BB-1337	Worldwide Insurance Network Inc.Greensboro NC.	N1550U
N330DB	99 King Air C90B	LJ-1542	Bennett Air LLC. Hayden Lake, Id.	N2178A
N330ES	78 Rockwell 690B	11476	Earth Search Sciences Inc. McCall, Id.	N690SC
N330V	79 King Air C90	LJ-811	Tucson AeroService Center Corp., Marana, Az.	
N331CR	89 120ER Brasilia	120121	RCR Air Inc.,Lexington, NC.	PH-XLG
N331GM	80 SA-226T Merlin 3B	T-331	Spinal Solutions LLC. Murrieta, Ca.	N331TB
N331KB	78 PA-31T Cheyenne 1	7804009	Kelbrach Aviation LLC. Overland Park, Ks.	N6125A
N331MP	83 Conquest II	441-0312	Martin's Famous Pastry Shoppe Inc. Chambersburg, Pa.	N514MC
N331RC	73 Rockwell 690A	11137	Ace Air Inc. Lafayette, La.	N876MC
N332DE	76 King Air C90	LJ-674	Delta Echo LLC. Sioux Falls, SD.	N9074S
N332DM	80 Conquest II	441-0167	Fury Management of Delaware Inc. Wilmington, De.	N312KJ
N332MS	82 King Air C90	LJ-1023	McRight-Smith Capital LP. McInney, Tx.	N32MA
N332SA	85 PA-42 Cheyenne 400LS	5527025	Golden Air Inc. Dothan, Al.	N325KW
N332SM	81 PA-42 Cheyenne III	8001020	Rok-Mor Inc, Murrells InletSC.	N332SA
N333AP	83 King Air B200	BB-1137	Carrefour Air LLC., Muskogee, Ok.	N133LJ
N333BM	97 King Air C90B	LJ-1504	Atkin Air LLC, Lincoln Ca.	
N333F	68 SA-26AT Merlin 2B	T26-100	Century Turbines, Georgetown, Tx.	(N500SN)
N333G	66 King Air 90	LJ-101	Bramco Aircraft Leasing, Miami, Fl.	N42B
N333HC	74 Rockwell 690A	11150	Robert Holt, Midland, Tx.	N47150
N333LE	77 King Air E90	LW-223	Standridge Color Corp. Social Circle, Ga.	N7UM
N333MM	00 PA-46-500TP Meridian	4697010	Piper Meridian LLC. Mesa, Az.	(N113WE)
N333P	80 PA-31T Cheyenne II	8020002	Genesis Flight LLC. Macon, Ga.	(N4LH)
N333RK	78 Mitsubishi MU-2P	380SA	Orison B Curpier Co. Cooperstown, NY.	ZS-NIY
N333TK	06 King Air C90GT	LJ-1783	Mount View Farming LLC/Sundale Vineyards, Tulare, Ca.	
N333TL	82 King Air C90	LJ-999	Scope Leasing Inc. Columbus, Oh.	N333TP
N333TN	80 PA-31T Cheyenne II	8020089	Betnr Engineering & Construction Corp. Pittsfield, Ma.	D-IGEM
N333TP	88 King Air B200	BB-1292	Azalea Aviation Inc/Mobile Air Center, Mobile, Al.	N3109Y
N333TX	76 Mitsubishi MU-2M	332	Thomas J Bond, Austin, Tx.	(N4DM)
N333UJ	83 Conquest 1	425-0179	Ugly John's Aircraft LLC. Afton, Ok.	N918CK
N333UP	82 Gulfstream 1000	96015	Anderson Fought, Portland, Or.	N325MM
N333WC	85 King Air 300	FA-55	Fisher Aviation Services LLC., Pleasant Grove, Ut.	N321EC
N333WT	81 King Air F90	LA-91	SumTranz LLC/Sumter Petroleum Co. Sumter, SC.	N641PE
N333XX	79 PA-31T Cheyenne II	7920038	Robert Arnot, South Newbury, NH.	N333CE
N334CA	79 PA-31T Cheyenne 1	7904034	Quik Flight LLC. Scotia, NY.	C9-ENT
N334EB	73 Mitsubishi MU-2J	568	Bankair inc. West Columbia, SC.	N99SL

Reg	Yr	Type	c/n	Owner/Operator	Prev Regn
N334JR	05	TBM 700C2	334	High Calling LLC. Golden, Co.	
N334ST	07	PA-46-500TP Meridian	4697334	Piper Aircraft Inc. Vero Beach, Fl.	
N335KW	89	King Air B200	BB-1335	McKnight LLC. Virginia Beach, Va.	(N10SA)
N335MA	02	TBM 700B	235	Foxy Air LLC. London, Ky.	
N335S	77	King Air 200	BB-227	Skyways Ltd. Huron, SD.	N90BR
N335TA	79	King Air 200	BB-514	Scott Air LLC/Ravin Homes Inc. Fayetteville, Ga.	(N435TA)
N335WH	00	Pilatus PC-12/45	335	Presco Inc. Lafayette, La.	N335PB
N336JM	81	King Air E90	LW-345	ASI Holdings Inc. Albany, Ga.	N173AS
N337C	80	Conquest II	441-0126	Chapman Corp. Washington, Pa.	N98630
N337DR	82	Gulfstream 900	15007	Dodson International Parts Inc. Rantoul, Ks.	N695LD
N337KC	84	Conquest II	441-0337	Kinsley Construction, York, Pa.	XA-PEH
N337TB	07	King Air B200	BB-1979	RB Aviation LLC., Menominee Falls, Wi.	N71089
N337TF	01	PA-46-500TP Meridian	4697094	Aero Equipment Leasing Inc. Indianapolis, In.	N221FP
N337TP	00	Pilatus PC-12/45	326	A & M Pilatus LLC., Cheshire, Ct.	PT-TPU
N338CM	77	Mitsubishi MU-2N	703SA	Summer Breeze Sales LLC., LaVergne, Tn.	N333GM
N338DB	03	PA-46-500TP Meridian	4697155	Oakfield Aviation Inc. Wilmington, De.	N53677
N338PC	00	Pilatus PC-12/45	338	338PC LLC/Columbus Bank & Trust Co. Columbus, Ga.	HB-FRT
N339JG	82	King Air B100	BE-130	Country Air Services LLC. Ballwin, Mo.	C-GTCL
N339KA	80	King Air E90	LW-339	Old Glory Inc. Tulsa, Ok.	LV-VFC
N339RW	80	SA-226T Merlin 3B	T-339	Dr. Richard L. Weiner M.D., Dallas, Tx.	N15CN
N340SS	85	SAAB 340A	022	Overland Airways,	N804CE
N341MH	80	King Air E90	LW-341	Clement Auto & Truck Inc., Fort Dodge, Ia.	RP-C1990
N343CP	74	King Air 200	BB-8	Ferry Flight Corp. Wilmington, De.	N343CL
N343CW	00	Pilatus PC-12/45	340	Roney Leasing LLC, Naples Fl.	HB-FRV
N343RR	04	PA-46-500TP Meridian	4697197	Herb Aviation Inc. Wilmington, De.	N46KH
N344DP	95	King Air C90B	LJ-1414	AMTS Aircraft Holdings LLC. Sugar Grove, Il.	N523P
N344KL	73	Mitsubishi MU-2K	257	Flight Service Co. Munhall, Pa.	N344K
N344L	94	King Air 350	FL-107	Synergy International LLC. Grand Haven, Mi.	N4S
N345CM	77	Rockwell 690B	11402	Smith Aircraft Management LLC. Shreveport, La.	N81638
N345DG	04	King Air 350	FL-427	GAF Holdings Inc. Visalia, Ca.	(N246DF)
N345RF	00	Pilatus PC-12/45	345	Claire Air LLC. Addison, Il.	N1983R
N345T	68	SA-26AT Merlin 2B	T26-105	Commercial Concrete Systems, Naples, Fl.	
N345TP	80	Conquest 1	425-0005	Allen W Smith, Austin, Tx.	N6SK
N345TT	68	680W Turbo Commander	1791-21	Thunder Commander Ltd. Van Nuys, Ca.	N77JL
N345V	72	King Air E90	LW-23	Rich Jones Aviation, Alexandria, NM.	
N345WK	97	King Air B200	BB-1580	Phoenix Equipment Leasing LLC., Tempe, Az.	N200KA
N345WT	06	PA-46-500TP Meridian	4697267	McElwee Firm PLLC. N Wilkesboro, NC.	N267ST
N346BA	98	King Air B200	BB-1653	Clara City Telephone Co. Clara City, Mn.	N345DG
N346VL	72	Mitsubishi MU-2F	231	Diamond, Lakee & Pearson Resources, Austin, Tx.	N666MA
N347D	85	King Air B200	BB-1197	Bill Putnam, Mills, Wy.	
N347KC	00	Pilatus PC-12/45	347	Task Force Tips Inc. Valparaiso, In.	HB-FSA
N348AC	67	King Air A90	LJ-196	St Louis Public Schools Gateway Institute of Technology, Mo.	N300DD
N348PC	00	Pilatus PC-12/45	348	J Luis Franco, McAllen, Tx.	HB-FSB
N350AB	98	King Air 350	FL-212	Rolling Plains Well Service Inc. Midland, Tx.	N2341F
N350AG	06	King Air 350	FL-546	Peninsula Assets Inc. Wilmington De.	N350AG
N350AJ	90	King Air 350	FL-22	Land Trends Inc. Joliet, Il.	ZS-NGI
N350BD	94	King Air 350	FL-123	Southlake Aviation Management LLC. Fort Worth, Tx.	N30YR
N350BF	89	King Air 300	FA-187	Bassett Furniture Industries Inc. Bassett, Va.	N89GC
N350BG	98	King Air 350	FL-217	American Bridge Company, Coraopolis, Pa.	N350FC
N350BS	90	King Air 350	FL-6	Raytan LLC. Joliet, Il.	N100BG
N350BW	00	King Air 350	FL-278	C & D Air LLC/Century Steel Inc., Las Vegas, Nv.	
N350CB	04	King Air 350	FL-392	Aviara LLP./Brock Enterprises Inc., Beaumont, Tx.	N6192C
N350CS	98	King Air 350	FL-214	LANCO Well Servicing Inc. Corpus Christi, Tx.	N350WG
N350D	01	King Air 350	FL-334	Deep South Avn/Southlake Aviation Mngmnt LLC. Ft Worth, Tx.	N5034F
N350DK	90	King Air 350	FL-30	Tex-Sin Aircorp LLC/LB Ventures, Wilmington, De.	N448BC
N350DR	91	King Air 350	FL-63	DeRoyal Industries Inc. Powell, Tn.	(N10DR)
N350DW	88	King Air 300	FA-157	L&K Consulting/Fairplay Electric Cars, Grand Junction, Co.	YV-1077CP
N350EB	07	King Air 350	FL-561	Goldwing Aircraft Trust	
N350FW	04	King Air 350	FL-421	Air Excursions LLC. Chicago, Il.	
N350GA	90	King Air 350	FL-16	Gasser Air Co. Youngstown, Oh.	N48HP
N350GL	99	King Air 350	FL-253	G & L Aviation, Van Nuys, Ca.	N88WV
N350HA	04	King Air 350	FL-393	Hawks Transportation LLC. Omaha, Ne.	N6193S
N350J	00	King Air 350	FL-314	DePuy Orthopaedics Inc. Warsaw, In.	N4314X
N350JB	98	King Air 350	FL-213	Land Rover Denver East Inc. Aurora, Co.	
N350JR	00	King Air 350	FL-312	Integral Resources LLC/J C Williams Co. Modesto, Ca.	HB-GJN

Reg	Yr Type	c/n	Owner/Operator	Prev Regn
☐ N350JW	98 King Air 350	FL-208	350 Partners LLC, Anchorage Ak.	C-FJOL
☐ N350K	04 King Air 350	FL-422	ETS Laboratories, St Helena, Ca.	N3722Y
☐ N350KS	04 King Air 350	FL-323	State of Kansas, Topeka, Ks.	N4323W
☐ N350LL	97 King Air 350	FL-157	A/K Service LLC. Friendswood, Tx.	N1093Q
☐ N350LM	06 King Air 350	FL-514	Jerry C Wardlaw Construction Inc. Savannah, Ga.	N7014X
☐ N350MC	81 SA-226T Merlin 3B	T-400	GoldAire LLC/Marlin Capital Corp. Wellesley, Ma..	N10126
☐ N350MG	07 King Air 350	FL-528	Martin Management Group/Ashley St Hldgs., Bowling Green, Ky.	N7418L
☐ N350MR	04 King Air 350	FL-408	Southern Sky Aviation Inc/Manti Group, Corpus Christi, Tx.	N929BG
☐ N350MS	06 King Air 350	FL-470	Southern Cross Aircraft LLC, Ft. Lauderdale Fl.	N3070R
☐ N350NY	07 King Air 350	FL-539	New York Power Authority, White Plains, NY.	
☐ N350P	91 King Air 350	FL-47	Sara Air LLC/Ledford Medical Electronics Inc. Greensboro, NC	N326MX
☐ N350PJ	03 King Air 350	FL-384	AS Aspen LLC., Aspen, Co.	N465SC
☐ N350PT	05 King Air 350	FL-467	FL467 LLC. Del Ray Oaks, Ca.	N36767
☐ N350PX	07 King Air 350	FL-560	Plains Exploration & Production Co, Houston, Tx.	
☐ N350Q	90 King Air 350	FL-14	Milton Partners LLC/Roswell Capital Partners, Alpharetta, Ga	N355MR
☐ N350RG	80 MU-2 Marquise	773SA	International Amusement Ltd. Durand, Mi.	N259MA
☐ N350RK	06 King Air 350	FL-516	Midwest Jet Inc/Rural King Supply, Mattoon, Il.	
☐ N350RR	03 King Air 350	FL-365	Gulf & Ohio Railways Inc./422W Cumberland LLC Knoxville, Tn.	N6165J
☐ N350RV	07 King Air B300	FL-575	Hawker Beechcraft Corp., Wichita, Ks.	N3215G
☐ N350RV	07 King Air B300	FL-585	Hawker Beechcraft Corp., Wichita, Ks.	
☐ N350S	97 King Air 350	FL-179	Fenway Acquisitions LLC/TVPX, Concord, Ma.	N744W
☐ N350SM	06 King Air 350	FL-474	Scott-McRae Automotive Group Inc. Jacksonville, Fl.	N37174
☐ N350ST	80 PA-31T Cheyenne II	8020068	Ivory Air LLC. Tallahassee, Fl.	N2467V
☐ N350TC	79 King Air B100	BE-62	King Airways LLC., Odessa, Tx.	N991DM
☐ N350TF	79 King Air 350	FL-202	Apple Aviation LLC. McDonough, Ga.	N2217C
☐ N350TJ	82 King Air B100	BE-125	Home Health Holdings Inc. Silsbee, Tx.	N314EB
☐ N350TT	04 King Air 350	FL-413	Luther Aircraft LLC. Brookfield, Wi.	N36813
☐ N350TV	00 King Air 350	FL-319	Tennessee Valley Authority, Muscle Shoals, Al.	N4319T
☐ N350VM	91 King Air 350	FL-41	Hawk Aviation LLC. Farmington Hills, Mi.	N25CU
☐ N350WA	78 King Air C90	LJ-762	BW & KW LLC. Wilmington, De.	N178RC
☐ N351CB	04 King Air B200	BB-1889	Hawker Beechcraft Corporation, Wichita, Ks.	N36739
☐ N351CK	06 TBM 850	351	Aircraft Guaranty Holdings & Trust LLC. Houston, Tx.	
☐ N351DD	99 King Air 350	FL-257	Dyson, Dyson & Dunn Inc. Winnetka, Il.	N257MM
☐ N351GC	91 King Air 350	FL-56	University of South Carolina, Columbia, SC.	N350DK
☐ N351GR	79 King Air E90	LW-324	Outlook Marketing LLC. Narrows, Va.	N2043C
☐ N351MP	00 King Air 350	FL-305	MAC Papers Inc. Jacksonville, Fl.	N3132M
☐ N351PC	00 Pilatus PC-12/45	351	Spur Leasing LLC. Evansville, In.	HB-FSD
☐ N351SA	92 King Air B200	BB-1423	Eric Stirling/Guardian Flight, Fairbanks, Ak.	P2-MBH
☐ N352BC	05 King Air 350	FL-463	Bear Creek Aviation LLC. Cincinnati, Oh.	N36933
☐ N352F	07 Kestrel F1C3	0001	Farnborought Aviationcraftcorp, Wilmington De.	
☐ N352GR	74 King Air E90	LW-93	Crow Aero Company LLC., Fort Payne, Al.	N655F
☐ N353KM	03 Pilatus PC-12/45	534	N353KM LLC. Carefree, Az.	HB-FSH
☐ N354AF	00 Pilatus PC-12/45	354	Alpha Flying Inc. Manchester, NH.	HB-FSF
☐ N355CL	98 King Air C90B	LJ-1520	Coastal Forest Resources Co. Weldon, NC.	N128JV
☐ N355DM	00 King Air 350	FL-320	Rioco Corp. McAllen, Tx.	N380MS
☐ N355ES	83 Conquest 1	425-0158	Leavenworth Excavating & Equipment, Leavenworth, Ks.	N25QL
☐ N355PM	01 PA-46-500TP Meridian	4697071	Santini Air LLC. Mooresville, NC.	
☐ N356AA	82 King Air B200C	BL-55	Aviation Advisors International Inc. Sarasota, Fl.	VH-FDA
☐ N356AJ	78 Mitsubishi MU-2P	381SA	R & J Ag Manufacturing Inc./Roger Shopbell LLC, Ashland, Oh.	N103RB
☐ N356F	01 TBM 700B	207	Aircraft Guaranty Title LLC. Houston, Tx. (trustor ?).	
☐ N357BB	90 King Air 350	FL-27	BDF Airgroup LLC. Addison, Tx.	(N73GB)
☐ N357CC	82 King Air F90	LA-180	Conklin Instrument Corp. Pleasant Valley, NY.	N999KK
☐ N357RL	03 King Air 350	FL-373	Korab Acquisitions LLC/TVPX Inc. Concord, Ma.	N6173K
☐ N357ST	81 Gulfstream 980	95074	Memphis Eagle Ltd. Dover, De.	(N123MZ)
☐ N358K	90 King Air C90A	LJ-1231	358K LLC. Omaha, Ne.	N931WC
☐ N359CV	01 Pilatus PC-12/45	382	Wen LLC. Spokane, Wa.	HB-FQB
☐ N359GP	84 Cheyenne II-XL	1166001	Great Plains Communications Inc. Blair, NE.	N835MW
☐ N359MB	02 King Air 350	FL-359	MasterBrand Cabinets Inc. Jasper, In.	
☐ N360CB	01 King Air 350	FL-336	KA 350 LLC., San Diego, Ca.	N4336P
☐ N360DA	99 Pilatus PC-12/45	270	On The Rise Aviation LLC. Dover, De.	(N880TR)
☐ N360EA	85 King Air B200	BB-1231	TransMontaigne Transport Inc. Englewood, Co.	OE-FJB
☐ N360MP	84 King Air C90A	LJ-1085	Aracel Inc. Tortola, BVI.	N720CT
☐ N360RA	79 MU-2 Marquise	740SA	T & A Aviation Inc. West Plains Mo.	XA-EFU
☐ N360X	01 King Air B200	BB-1783	Bank of Utah Trustee, Salt Lake City, Ut.	N625TA
☐ N361EA	83 King Air B200	BB-1103	Yakima King Fish II LLC/Fruit Packers Supply Yakima Wa.	N57SC

Reg	Yr	Type	c/n	Owner/Operator	Prev Regn
N361GB	95	Pilatus PC-12	132	Radio Flyer II Inc. Lincoln, Il.	N361DB
N361JA	76	Mitsubishi MU-2L	681	Flight Line Inc. Salt Lake City, Ut.	C-GJWM
N361JC	77	PA-31T Cheyenne II	7720062	Sandy Land Underground Water Distribution, Plains, Tx.	N68LM
N361MA	80	MU-2 Solitaire	429SA	Motors Management Group Inc. Richmond, Va.	N77DB
N361TD	87	King Air B200C	BL-128	Desa Air Inc. Dover, De.	N128TJ
N362D	78	King Air E90	LW-265	Jet Arizona Inc. Tucson, Az.	
N362DB	07	King Air 350	FL-571	BC Air LLC, Albuquerque, NM	
N362MC	78	King Air C90	LJ-760	IPLA Ownership Trust/Solomon Mark Ft Lauderdale Fl.	F-GHEM
N362SH	76	Rockwell 690A	11316	Flight Plan One LLC/Bay Cast Inc. Bay Cast, Mi.	(N690PB)
N363CA	01	King Air 350	FL-326	C W Avery Leasing Corp. Plainfield, Il.	N350MS
N363D	95	King Air B200	BB-1503	Wolfcreek Management LLC. Portland, Or.	N363K
N363EA	96	King Air B200	BB-1538	JA Investments Inc/Consolidated Biscuit Co. McComb, Oh.	PH-VMP
N364EA	80	King Air 200	BB-689	Omni Dynamic Aviation LLC. Fort Wayne, In.	N187MQ
N364WA	77	Rockwell 690B	11439	Aero Works LLC., Alpharetta, Ga.	D-IADH
N365CS	87	King Air 300	FA-120	J M Associates Inc., Little Rock, Ar.	N3025Z
N366FG	77	Rockwell 690B	11410	Inversiones Air Global CA. Caracas, Venezuela.	XB-DZP
N366GW	79	King Air E90	LW-320	Pioneer Air Inc. Peoria, Il.	N366JM
N366NC	96	King Air C90B	LJ-1444	NewCal Industries LLC. Pleasant Hill, Ca.	N1084N
N366SB	63	Fairchild F-27F	97	Beartooth Communications Inc. Helena, Mt.	N20W
N366SL	03	King Air 350	FL-366	The Rosenburg Co. San Francisco, Ca.	
N367EA	07	TBM 850	410	Jet Service of Iowa Inc., Peosta, Ia	
N367LF	78	King Air 200	BB-405	Life Logistics LLC. St Louis, Mo.	N350AC
N367RA	78	King Air 200	BB-367	October Investments LLC. Whitefish, Mt.	ZS-NPO
N368DC	00	Beech 1900D	UE-368	Dow Chemical Co. Midland, Mi.	
N368FA	80	King Air 200	BB-741	Jakma Air LLC. Marseilles, Il.	N75AH
N368PC	00	Pilatus PC-12/45	368	Flax Services Corp. Salt Lake City, Ut.	HB-FOU
N368RK	91	King Air C90A	LJ-1267	King Aviation Dallas Inc. Addison, Tx.	D-IEBE
N369F	89	King Air 300	FA-185	King Eire LLC. Woodside, Ca.	N341DB
N370AE	87	SA-227AT Merlin 4C	AT-506	GAS/Wilson Inc. Lake Zurich, Il.	N87FM
N370K	66	680V Turbo Commander	1570-25	Glenn G Riley. Santa Ana, Ca.	N222JK
N370LH	07	King Air B200GT	BY-37	Hawker Beechcraft Corp., Wichita, Ks.	
N370MA	78	Mitsubishi MU-2P	370SA	Robert Nass Inc. Asheville Regional, Pa.	N370AC
N370NA	02	King Air 350	FL-345	Fine Foods SA. Wilmington, De.	JA353N
N370U	96	King Air C90B	LJ-1428	University of Oklahoma, Norman, Ok.	N3242Z
N370X	69	SA-26AT Merlin 2B	T26-106	Twins Charter Aircraft Inc. Miami Beach, Fl.	
N372GT	01	Pilatus PC-12/45	372	Pacific Detroit Realty LLC. Portland, Or.	HB-FSV
N372JB	88	King Air 200	BB-719	B R Williams Trucking Inc. Oxford, Al.	N3722Y
N373CA	93	PA-42 Cheyenne III	8001037	CCH Aviation LLC. Great Falls, Va.	HK-3618W
N373KM	00	Pilatus PC-12/45	373	Pilatus Montana LLC. Cameron, Mt.	(N373GE)
N373LP	81	Conquest 1	425-0141	JAD Aviation Inc. Bloomington, Il.	D-IIGA
N373Q	81	PA-42 Cheyenne III	8001014	DeZavala Group LP. Edinburg, Tx.	C-GAKA
N373WP	06	King Air 350	FL-519	MPI Research Inc./Chase Equipment Leasing, Mattawan, Mi.	N3729Y
N374BH	05	King Air 350	FL-442	Core Air LLC/TIC Holdings Inc. Steamboat Springs, Co.	
N375AA	74	Rockwell 690A	11179	Miroslav Liska, Bend, Or.	N57179
N375AC	75	Mitsubishi MU-2M	327	Celco Constantine Engineering Laboratories, Wilmington, De.	N515MA
N375CA	74	Mitsubishi MU-2J	643	Realtime Consulting LLC., Winter Park, Fl.	N881DT
N375CP	05	King Air 350	FL-433	S & D Owner Inc., Dallas, Tx.	N24JJ
N375RD	00	PA-46-500TP Meridian	4697003	Richard Dumais, Richardson, Tx.	
N376KC	01	Pilatus PC-12/45	376	Kaiser Midwest Inc. Marble Hill, Mo.	HB-FSZ
N376NA	03	King Air 350	FL-376	Lawrence E Redman, Long Beach, Ca.	JA376N
N376RC	78	King Air 200	BB-376	BTD Inc/BAM Aircraft Leasing LLC./Business Air, Denton, Tx.	N409AC
N376WS	80	PA-31T Cheyenne II	8020064	Polar Star Co. Hodges, SC.	(N32WS)
N377CA	83	Conquest II	441-0289	Arturo Saldana, Coppell, Tx.	N88638
N377L	00	Pilatus PC-12/45	346	Fitch Jet Aviation LLC., Larkspur, Co.	HB-FRZ
N377NJ	68	Mitsubishi MU-2D	104	Turbine Aircraft Marketing Inc., San Angelo Tx.	N151JB
N377P	84	King Air C90A	LJ-1087	S.A. LLC., Hilton Head Island, SC.	N7252S
N378FC	06	TBM 850	378	TFC Management LLC. Houston, Tx.	
N378HH	01	Pilatus PC-12/45	378	Harrison Airplane Leasing LLC. Phoenix, Az.	HB-FPA
N378SF	78	King Air 200	BB-378	Jerri Trigg, Houston, Tx.	N200BP
N379JG	81	SA-226T Merlin 3B	T-414	Merlin Partners LLC, Salem Or.	N271DC
N379VM	73	King Air E90	LW-27	379VM LLC. Jeffco Airport, Co.	N999ES
N380TM	01	Pilatus PC-12/45	380	Mar Aviation Corp., Boardman, Oh.	N792SG
N381CR	87	Beech 1900C	UB-69	Joda LLC./Pineapple Air, Nassau, Bahamas	N331CR
N381PD	73	King Air C-12C	BC-14	Cx USA 8/06 to ?	N381PD
N381R	78	King Air 200	BB-385	Jack Air LLC. Morrison, Co.	N81RD
Reg	Yr	Type	c/n	Owner/Operator	Prev Regn

Reg	Yr Type	c/n	Owner/Operator	Prev Regn
N382MB	81 PA-31T Cheyenne II	8120057	Executive Aircraft Services Inc., Elizabethtown, NC.	N9087Y
N382ME	79 King Air 200	BB-436	Butler Aviation LLC., Butler, Pa.	N83KA
N382TW	75 King Air E90	LW-141	Flying Partners LLC/DeBoer Transportation Inc. Blenker, Wi.	TI-SFC
N383AA	72 King Air E90	LW-13	Clay County Air Inc. Success, Ar.	N21DJ
N383JP	80 King Air 200	BB-615	Moreland Aircraft LLC. Bakersfield, Ca.	RP-C704
N383SS	80 Conquest II	441-0161	Joseph Skilken & Co. Columbus, Oh.	N2721D
N385KA	85 King Air 300	FA-42	KA300 LLC., Scottsdale, Az.	N72DK
N385MC	82 King Air B200	BB-1017	McAninch Corp. Des Moines, Ia.	N200PH
N386CP	05 TBM 700C2	335	Columbia Properties Inc. Marietta, Ga.	N700ZE
N386GA	78 King Air C90	LJ-775	EFS Inc. Montgomery, Al.	HB-GIW
N386TH	06 King Air C90GT	LJ-1777	Oak Aviation/Haas Outdoors Industries, West Point, Ms.	N6178V
N387AS	95 King Air C90B	LJ-1417	Executive AirShare Corp. Wichita, Ks.	N3217X
N387CC	80 SA-226T Merlin 3B	T-360	Hiers Properties LLC. Hockessin, De.	N118BR
N387GC	01 King Air C90B	LJ-1655	Carlos Soto, Weston, Fl.	(N125AR)
N387W	01 Pilatus PC-12/45	387	State of Wisconsin, Madison, Wi.	HB-FQJ
N388NC	81 MU-2 Solitaire	452SA	Bayview Corporation, Vineland, NJ.	(D-IBBB)
N388PC	01 Pilatus PC-12/45	388	SDD Holdings Inc. Atlanta, Ga.	HB-FQE
N388SR	00 Pilatus PC-12/45	316	Sierra Romeo LLC, Ashland Or.	N102RR
N388TW	01 PA-46-500TP Meridian	4697018	James Gero, Rockwall, Tx.	
N389AS	96 King Air C90B	LJ-1438	Executive AirShare Corp. Wichita, Ks.	N3268M
N389RA	82 King Air B200C	BL-56	RidgeAire Inc., Jacksonville, Tx.	VT-EID
N389W	01 Pilatus PC-12/45	389	State of Wisconsin, Madison, Wi.	HB-FQN
N390MD	01 King Air 350	FL-333	Maryland State Police, Baltimore, Md.	N4483Y
N390PS	78 King Air E90	LW-279	Pro Air Inc/Progressive Swine Technologies, Columbus, Ne.	N390MT
N390SP	06 King Air B200	BB-1970	Arkansas State Police, Little Rock, Ar.	N7270Z
N391BT	81 King Air C90	LJ-983	Vector Aviation LLC. Jackson, Mi.	N491BT
N391EC	01 Pilatus PC-12/45	391	PC-12 Holding Inc. Santo Domingo, Dominican Republic.	HB-FQG
N391GM	80 SA-226T Merlin 3B	T-391	T F Aerial LLC. Pasadena, Ca.	F-GCTC
N391MT	03 King Air 350	FL-371	Maverick Tube Corp. Chesterfield, Mo.	N6171N
N392KC	78 King Air 200	BB-392	Fresh Air DeKalb LLC. Naperville, Il.	N392CT
N392TW	68 King Air B90	LJ-392	Victor Manuel Moncada, Medellin, Colombia.	N121HC
N392WC	01 Pilatus PC-12/45	392	Avant Aviation LLC. Shreveport, La.	HB-FQH
N393AF	01 Pilatus PC-12/45	393	Rigi Inc,Portsmouth, NH.	HB-FQI
N393CF	90 King Air 300LW	FA-214	J & J Black Diamond LLC. Vail, Co.	(N967JG)
N393JW	77 King Air 200	BB-292	Eric Stirling/Guardian Flight, Fairbanks, Ak.	(N393JM)
N394AL	68 King Air B90	LJ-394	Skydive Virginia Inc. McGaheysville, Va.	C-GASR
N394S	06 King Air 350	FL-442	Sunoco Inc. Philadelphia, Pa.	N7192X
N395AM	83 King Air B200	BB-1101	Air DB & B LLC. Sacramento, Ca.	N48CE
N395AS	99 King Air C90B	LJ-1575	Executive AirShare Corp. Wichita, Ks.	N971P
N395CA	84 Cheyenne II-XL	1166005	Cheyenne Air LLC. Ellensburg, Va.	HB-LRM
N395DR	81 PA-42 Cheyenne III	8001065	SCR Construction Inc. Richmond, Tx.	N742RB
N395KT	00 P-180 Avanti	1044	AvantAir Inc. Bedford,Ma	(N503RV)
N395MB	91 King Air 350	FL-39	Mammoth Beach LLC. El Segundo, Ca.	N390TT
N395PC	01 Pilatus PC-12/45	395	O'Brien Adventures LLC. Prescott, Az.	HB-FQP
N395SM	02 PA-46-500TP Meridian	4697129	Samuel Maness, Apollo Beach, Fl.	N302MM
N395W	01 Pilatus PC-12/45	394	State of Wisconsin, Madison, Wi.	HB-FQO
N396AS	99 King Air C90B	LJ-1540	Executive AirShare Corp. Wichita, Ks.	N600FL
N396AW	03 TBM 700C2	279	Gravity Aviation LLC, Chandler, Az.	N824RH
N396CA	82 King Air C90-1	LJ-1035	Willstaff Worldwide Staffing, Monroe, La.	F-GLJD
N396FW	80 PA-42 Cheyenne III	8001021	Southern Lady Inc. Lakeland, Fl.	C-FWAB
N396PS	69 SA-26AT Merlin 2B	T26-151	U R One Investments Inc. Bear, De.	C-GSWJ
N396SA	76 King Air C-12C	BC-23	Nolan Aviation LLC., Broomfield, Co.	N200LW
N397WM	88 King Air 300	FA-156	West Michigan Aviation Services, Grand Rapids, Mi.	N642BL
N398J	01 Pilatus PC-12/45	398	Oklahoma Cardiovascular Associates, Oklahoma City, Ok.	HB-FQL
N398SP	81 PA-31T Cheyenne 1	8104027	James D White, Bettendorf, Ia.	N681SW
N399AM	99 Pilatus PC-12/45	249	University of Utah Hospitals & Clinic, Salt Lake City, Ut.	(F-GTTT)
N399BM	78 King Air 200	BB-399	Baylor University, Waco, Tx.	F-GIRM
N399CW	98 King Air B200	BB-1646	Warren Manufacturing Inc. Birmingham, Al.	
N399MB	99 King Air C90B	LJ-1591	Tacoma Screw Products/TSP Leasing Tacoma, Wa.	JA 21EG
N399TW	83 King Air F90-1	LA-203	Trans West Aero LLC. La Jolla, Ca.	N42GA
N399WS	99 King Air C90B	LJ-1547	RMD Air LLC, Fresno Ca.	
N400AC	76 King Air B100	BE-12	Midlantic Jet Charters Inc. Atlantic City, NJ.	
N400AE	89 King Air 350	FL-2	Angmar Medical Holdings Inc. Arlington, Tx.	N400AL
N400AL	04 King Air 350	FL-428	Abbott Laboaratories Inc. Waukegan, Il.	N5128X
N400BW	98 Pilatus PC-12/45	224	RAW Inc. Raleigh, NC.	N224PB

Reg	Yr	Type	c/n	Owner/Operator	Prev Regn
☐ N400BX	76	King Air C90	LJ-686	R & J Aviation Inc. Sugar Grove, Il.	N100BT
☐ N400CM	76	PA-31T Cheyenne II	7620040	Aerial Surveys International LLC. Watkins, Co.	
☐ N400DC	69	SA-26AT Merlin 2B	T26-167	Parts & Turbines Inc. St Simons Island, Ga.	N5353M
☐ N400DG	68	SA-26T Merlin 2A	T26-9	Hodges Packing Co. Palestine, Tx.	N22EK
☐ N400DS	78	Rockwell 690B	11512	Starlight Leasing LLC. Appleton, Wi.	N81872
☐ N400GW	97	King Air B200	BB-1583	Whitman Properties LLC. Charleston, SC.	N424RA
☐ N400KW	78	King Air 200	BB-337	Prop Jocks Inc., Sylmar, Ca.	N600AM
☐ N400LJ	80	PA-31T Cheyenne 1	8004012	Alton Aviation LLC., West Lebanon, NH.	N41PN
☐ N400PS	79	MU-2 Solitaire	411SA	West Texas Executive Leasing Inc. San Angelo, Tx.	N8LC
☐ N400PT	98	PA-46-400TP Meridian	4697E1	Piper Aircraft Inc. Vero Beach, Fl.	
☐ N400RV	79	King Air C90	LJ-853	Quest Contracting Svcs Inc., West Palm Beach, Fl.	N6LD
☐ N400RX	73	Mitsubishi MU-2J	593	Intercontinental Jet Inc., Tulsa, Ok.	C-GJAV
☐ N400SG	74	Mitsubishi MU-2J	634	Pan American Importing Corp. Wilmington, De.	C-GODE
☐ N400VB	84	PA-42 Cheyenne 400LS	5527002	Kelleher Corp. San Rafael, Ca. (was 8427002).	N400PS
☐ N400WS	81	Cheyenne II-XL	8166044	Aspen Air Inc./Dura Bilt Products Inc. Albuquerque, NM.	N31KW
☐ N401BL	87	King Air 300	FA-125	Wells Fargo Bank NW NA., Salt Lake City, Ut.	N488GA
☐ N401CG	99	King Air B200	BB-1666	Cardinal Glass Industries Inc. Minnetonka, Mn.	N444MT
☐ N401CP	07	PA-46-500TP Meridian	4697316	Cantrell Leasing Inc., Glynn, Ga.	
☐ N401EM	81	King Air C90	LJ-950	Eagle Med/Ballard Aviation Inc. Wichita, Ks.	N108TT
☐ N401HC	88	King Air B200	BB-1294	Intermountain Health Care Services, Salt Lake City, Ut.	N294WT
☐ N401NS	85	King Air 300	FA-28	Naylor Inc. Atlanta, Ga.	N481NS
☐ N401PD	01	Pilatus PC-12/45	401	CAPC Equipment Rental LLC	HB-FQS
☐ N401SK	03	King Air B200	BB-1828	Florida Marine Transporters, Mandeville, La.	N61808
☐ N401SM	99	Pilatus PC-12/45	255	EPPS Air Service Inc. Atlanta, Ga.	HB-FRV
☐ N401VA	82	Cheyenne T-1040	8275001	Pro Aire Cargo & Consulting Inc, OshKosh Wi.	N2489Y
☐ N402AB	81	Gulfstream 840	11659	W W Farms Inc. Oxnard, Ca.	ZS-KYU
☐ N402BL	81	King Air F90	LA-130	Hastingwood Management LLP., Ilford, UK	N81SD
☐ N402CT	06	King Air B200	BB-1929	Forest River Inc. Elkhart, In.	N3729J
☐ N402EM	80	King Air C90	LJ-914	Ballard Aviation Inc. Wichita, Ks.	N914TT
☐ N402JL	04	King Air 350	FL-402	Health Systems Inc. Sikeston, Mo.	N6182Z
☐ N402KA	77	King Air 200	BB-296	Aviation Charter Services, Indianapolis, In.	N402CJ
☐ N402MM	99	PA-46-400TP Meridian	4697002	Piper Aircraft Inc. Vero Beach, Fl.	
☐ N403EM	82	King Air C90	LJ-1000	Ballard Aviation Inc. Wichita, Ks.	N982FA
☐ N404DP	81	King Air 200	BB-819	Palmer Aviation Leasing LLC. Germantown, Tn.	N500KA
☐ N404EW	89	King Air 300	FA-186	Allen Aviation LLC., Scottsdale, Az.	(N700FT)
☐ N404FA	82	King Air B200	BB-981	Joe Falk Motorsports/Falk Air Corp. Norfolk, Va.	N481BC
☐ N404GT	07	King Air B200GT	BY-4	G & D Transportation Inc., Morton Il.	N404GT
☐ N404J	02	King Air B200	BB-1793	JimsAir Aviation Services Inc. Lindberg Field-San Diego, Ca.	N5093X
☐ N404JP	82	King Air C90-1	LJ-1039	Parish Planes LLC. Tullahoma, Tn.	N6746S
☐ N404SC	79	King Air C90	LJ-843	Jay Hall Jr. Cheshire, Oh.	N843CP
☐ N404SS	97	Dornier 328-110	3090	BellSouth Corp. Atlanta-Fulton County, Ga.	D-CDYY
☐ N405DD	05	King Air C90B	LJ-1748	Creekstone Companies, Houston, Tx.	N36648
☐ N405EM	77	King Air C90	LJ-726	Ballard Aviation Inc. Wichita, Ks.	N434EM
☐ N405J	94	King Air 350	FL-112	JimsAir Aviation Services Inc. Lindberg Field-San Diego, Ca.	N850SJ
☐ N405PT	81	King Air B200	BB-930	Viking Aviation LLC/Construction Network Inc, Jonesboro, Ar.	N930SP
☐ N405SA	80	SA-226T Merlin 3B	T-329	Sequoia Air, Inglewood, Ca.	N626PS
☐ N406CP	81	Gulfstream 840	11655	Palumbo Aircraft Sales Inc. Uniontown, Oh.	YV-406CP
☐ N406GV	90	Reims/Cessna F406	F406-0049	Gussic Ventures LLC. Anchorage, Ak.	9M-PNS
☐ N406RL	99	King Air C90B	LJ-1574	Bristol Manufacturing Group/Pioneer LLC, Springfield Mo.	N406RL
☐ N406RS	79	PA-31T Cheyenne II	7920048	Bridge & Marine LLC., Jacksonville, Fl.	N404AF
☐ N406SD	91	Reims/Cessna F406	F406-0063	Bering Strait School District, Unalakleet, Ak.	PH-GUI
☐ N406SF	77	King Air E90	LW-218	New Mexico State University, Las Cruces, NM.	N700WD
☐ N407CF	07	King Air C90GT	LJ-1849	Air 4 LLC., Wilmington, NC.	N809P
☐ N407MA	81	MU-2 Marquise	1503SA	H & F Executive Aviation Inc. Wilmington, De.	
☐ N408SF	07	P-180 Avanti II	1137	SNOWWIS Aviation LLC. Siloam Ar.	
☐ N408SH	81	PA-31T Cheyenne 1	8104052	DGA Inc. Nebraska City, Ne.	N422HV
☐ N408WG	84	PA-42 Cheyenne 400LS	5527008	HLW LLC. Lexington, SC.	(N31WE)
☐ N409D	06	King Air 350	FL-497	DLD Holdings LLC/D L Davis & Co. Winston-Salem, NC.	N7197Y
☐ N409DH	81	King Air 200	BB-795	Roy DeLaRue Tours Inc., New York, NY	N825RT
☐ N409DR	01	Pilatus PC-12/45	377	Collett Transportation/Collett Land Co. Charlotte, NC.	N377PC
☐ N409LV	04	King Air 350	FL-409	Andrmar Air LLC. Las Vegas, Nv.	N6109U
☐ N409RA	79	King Air 200	BB-429	Turbo Air Inc. Boise, Id.	N574GS
☐ N410CA	81	Cheyenne II-XL	8166005	Waldinger Corp. Des Moines, Ia.	N127GP
☐ N410MC	78	King Air C90	LJ-761	Jack Tar Sea & Air LLC. Santa Barbara, Ca.	N25HB
☐ N410MF	79	Conquest II	441-0093	Ocean Mist Farms, Castroville, Ca.	N441K

Reg	Yr	Type	c/n	Owner/Operator	Prev Regn
☐ N410PT	07	King Air B200	BB-1978	Pact LLC., Plano, Tx.	N70118
☐ N410RE	74	King Air C-12L	BB-4	Commonwealth Aviation LLC. Hickory, NC.	N397SA
☐ N410SP	70	King Air A90	LM-136	Samaritan's Purse Inc. Boone, NC.	N7181Z
☐ N410TH	68	680W Turbo Commander	1790-20	Charles Bella, El Paso, Tx.	N5061E
☐ N410VE	81	Conquest 1	425-0097	Miami Air Corp. Wilmington, De.	N6849D
☐ N411BG	84	PA-42 Cheyenne 400LS	5527004	DP Air LLC. Portland, Or.	N4119B
☐ N411BL	79	King Air 200	BB-448	Butler Aviation Inc., Houma, La.	N700HM
☐ N411CC	95	King Air B200	BB-1520	Sunshine Aviation LLC. Roseburg, Or.	(N265EJ)
☐ N411DL	77	PA-31T Cheyenne II	7720057	Burt Aviation & Transportation LLC. Saginaw, Mi.	C-GGVB
☐ N411FT	69	King Air B90	LJ-443	WCA Transportation Services Inc. Coconut Creek, Fl.	N796K
☐ N411HA	70	King Air 100	B-21	RC Air LLC/RC Components Inc. Bowling Green, Ky.	N360C
☐ N411HB	07	PA-46-500TP Meridian	4697303	Piper Aircraft Inc. Vero Beach, Fl.	
☐ N411LM	77	PA-31T Cheyenne II	7720069	Brown Minneapolis Tank Company, Albuquerque, NM.	N45TX
☐ N411MV	00	Pilatus PC-12/45	344	Cowtown Investments LLC. Portola Valley, Ca.	HB-FRX
☐ N411RA	80	King Air 200	BB-712	Moe Air LLC/Moretz Sportswear, Newton, NC.	N200BM
☐ N411RJ	81	King Air F90	LA-108	EZ Acceptance Inc. San Diego, Ca.	N627AC
☐ N411RS	66	King Air 90	LJ-106	Sundance Aviation Inc. Yukon, Ok.	N271MB
☐ N412CB	05	King Air 350	FL-440	Bankers Capital Corp. Brandon, Ms.	N3040P
☐ N412MA	67	King Air A90	LJ-214	K & K Aircraft Inc. Bridgewater, Va.	N985AA
☐ N412SH	87	King Air B200	BB-1269	THD Properties LLC. Chicago, Il.	N21NV
☐ N414GN	75	King Air E90	LW-156	Newberg Flying Enterprises Inc. Chicago, Il.	(N5PC)
☐ N415HS	83	King Air F90-1	LA-210	Sogibo Inc. Wilmington, De.	N415RB
☐ N415PB	01	Pilatus PC-12/45	415	Mercury Travel Inc. Lakewood, Co.	HB-FRI
☐ N415RB	95	King Air B200	BB-1513	Barnhill Contracting Co. Tarboro, NC.	N3217N
☐ N415TM	01	King Air B200	BB-1762	Crouch Aire Corp. Seward, Ak.	N4362F
☐ N416AT	84	King Air B200	BB-1180	Ace Tomato Co. Manteca, Ca.	N221SP
☐ N416BK	79	King Air C90	LJ-816	King Taylor Inc. Brentwood, Tn.	N40PS
☐ N416DY	89	King Air 300	FA-197	Yancey Brothers Co. Austell, Ga.	N59AH
☐ N416LF	92	P-180 Avanti	1012	LDF Support Group Inc. Wichita, Ks.	N500GC
☐ N416MR	67	King Air A90	LJ-267	Flyboys LLC. Ephrata, Wa.	N416LF
☐ N416P	80	King Air F90	LA-67	Metro Aviation Inc. Shreveport, La.	N614ME
☐ N417AR	04	Pilatus PC-12/45	611	Greenway Air LLC. Orlando, Fl.	HB-FRL
☐ N417KC	01	Pilatus PC-12/45	417	Bedrock Aviation LLC. Holly, Mi.	HB-FRF
☐ N417RC	76	King Air 200	BB-188	Crossland Aviation LLC. Basalt, Co.	N4288S
☐ N417SH	06	King Air C90GT	LJ-1789	Ruby River Aviation LLC/Banks Hardwoods Inc. Elkhart, In.	
☐ N417VN	89	King Air C90A	LJ-1202	Il Delta Bravo LLC., Long Creek, Or.	HB-GIZ
☐ N418DR	97	Pilatus PC-12	192	DRG Technologies Inc. Omaha, Ne.	(N481DR)
☐ N418J	00	King Air B200	BB-1705	Griffin Investment Co. Findlay, Oh.	
☐ N418SP	70	King Air A90	LM-138	Missionary Aviation Repair Center, Soldotna, Ks.	N7191W
☐ N419R	78	PA-31T Cheyenne II	7820034	Reno Flying Service Inc. Reno, Nv.	N82249
☐ N419SC	80	Conquest II	441-0149	419 Aviation Inc. Inverness, Il.	N600VT
☐ N420AF	01	Pilatus PC-12/45	420	Alpha Flying Inc. Manchester, NH.	HB-FRJ
☐ N420DB	80	Conquest II	441-0129	Ernie Elliott Inc., Dawsonville, Ga.	(N441BD)
☐ N420DW	01	Pilatus PC-12/45	404	Richard Wikert, Fremont, Ne.	HB-FQU
☐ N420MA	82	Conquest 1	425-0116	RGS Investments Inc. Milwaukee, Wi.	(N425TS)
☐ N420PA	78	PA-42 Cheyenne III	7800001	Piper Aircraft Inc. Vero Beach, Fl.	
☐ N420TA	79	King Air 200	BB-420	Kohner Aviation Inc. Dover, De.	N210SU
☐ N421HV	91	King Air C90A	LJ-1266	Thermo King Sales & Service Inc. St Paul, Mn.	
☐ N422AS	04	King Air C90B	LJ-1714	ALL Star Advertising Agency Inc. Baton Rouge, La.	N6172Y
☐ N422GK	76	SA-226T Merlin 3A	T-260	Aircraft Guaranty Title LLC. Houston, Tx. Based Haguenau	LX-RSO
☐ N422MU	01	Pilatus PC-12/45	336	Chinook Inc. Colorado Springs, Co.	N336PC
☐ N422PM	95	King Air C90B	LJ-1412	Aerolease LLC./Weather Modification Inc., Fargo, ND.	N14GG
☐ N422Z	81	King Air F90	LA-135	Fremont Motor Co. Lander, Wy.	
☐ N423JB	82	Cheyenne II-XL	8166052	Golden State Air Charter LLC., Bakersfield, Ca.	D-IOKA
☐ N423TG	81	Conquest II	441-0200	Commercial Developers Inc. Wichita, Ks.	N313GA
☐ N423WA	01	Pilatus PC-12/45	423	SN Aero LLC. Anchorage, Ak.	HB-FRM
☐ N424BS	76	King Air 200	BB-179	Command Aircraft Parts & Recovery, Bunnell, Fl. (status ?).	N630DB
☐ N424CM	80	PA-31T Cheyenne 1	8004002	Alan L Brodkin PC. Irvine, Ca.	(N2499R)
☐ N424CP	82	King Air F90	LA-182	W C McQuaide Inc. Johnstown, Pa.	(N107MC)
☐ N424EM	93	King Air C90B	LJ-1351	Ballard Aviation Inc. Wichita, Ks.	N493JX
☐ N424MF	95	King Air C90B	LJ-1403	InvestAero LLC. Boca Raton, Fl.	N275FA
☐ N424PP	69	680W Turbo Commander	1821-35	Corona Aircraft Inc. Corona, Ca.	TG-DAM
☐ N424RA	02	King Air B200	BB-1797	Edward Rorer, Villanova, Pa.	N5097G
☐ N425AF	81	Conquest 1	425-0041	J.D. Leasing LLC., Wilmington, De.	ZS-MVW
☐ N425AL	81	Conquest 1	425-0100	Continental Aviation Services Inc. Naples, Fl.	N70HB

Reg	Yr Type	c/n	Owner/Operator	Prev Regn
❏ N425AP	80 King Air 200	BB-682	Tradewind Air LLC. Yorklyn, De.	N208JS
❏ N425AR	81 Conquest 1	425-0065	Robert Alan Eustace, Menlo Park, Ca.	N6844S
❏ N425AT	80 Conquest 1	425-0004	Med-Trade Inc. Northbrook, Il.	N425TF
❏ N425BA	81 Conquest 1	425-0046	Quad Fund Inc. Mount Pleasant, Tx.	(N911MM)
❏ N425BL	84 Conquest 1	425-0198	Bruce Lampert PC. Broomfield, Co.	N5PU
❏ N425BP	01 King Air B200	BB-1773	425 Aviation LLC., San Antonio, Tx.	N777SW
❏ N425BS	84 Conquest 1	425-0210	Golf & Juliet Travel LLC. Cincinnati, Oh.	N721VB
❏ N425CC	83 Conquest 1	425-0159	Yingling Aircraft Inc. Wichita, Ks.	N813ZM
❏ N425CL	84 Conquest 1	425-0206	ICM Inc. Colwich, Ks.	N12238
❏ N425CQ	83 Conquest 1	425-0173	Carriage Enterprises Inc. Wilmington, De.	N6873Q
❏ N425D	82 Conquest 1	425-0121	Smoore Inc/Titanium Luxury Club LLC. Scottsdale, Az.	N944JV
❏ N425DC	83 Conquest 1	425-0185	Kent Audio Visual/Kent Business Systems Inc. Wichita, Ks.	N6874L
❏ N425DD	81 Conquest 1	425-0083	NorCal Beverage Co. West Sacramento, Ca.	N6846X
❏ N425DH	81 Conquest 1	425-0066	Electronic Concepts Inc. Eatontown, NJ.	N6844T
❏ N425DM	81 Conquest 1	425-0098	Salt Creek LLC. Llano, Tx.	(N425TS)
❏ N425DR	84 Conquest 1	425-0199	Inter-City Air Ltd. Channel Islands.	VP-BDR
❏ N425DT	79 Rockwell 690B	11519	G & A Services Inc. Wilmington, De.	CP-2225
❏ N425E	81 Conquest 1	425-0096	Air Quest Aviation LLC.Granite Falls NC.	N425EA
❏ N425EA	81 Conquest 1	425-0063	Eagle Aviation Inc. West Columbia SC.	C-GDLG
❏ N425EC	80 MU-2 Marquise	793SA	WEC Ltd. Paradise Valley, Az.	HZ-AMA
❏ N425EM	83 Conquest 1	425-0164	Kudzu International Inc. Hagerstown, Md.	D-IJOY
❏ N425ET	81 Conquest 1	425-0072	DJT Inc. Lawton, Ok.	(N425TB)
❏ N425EZ	81 Conquest 1	425-0099	ICM Inc., Colwich, Ks.	N404EW
❏ N425GC	81 Conquest 1	425-0027	Agfest Enterprises LLC/Queens Flowers Corp. Miami, Fl.	VP-BNM
❏ N425GJ	81 Conquest 1	425-0029	Tri-County Builders Corp. Powell Butte, Or.	N926ES
❏ N425GM	81 Conquest 1	425-0033	Macrotech Polyseal Inc. Salt Lake City, Ut.	(N425GZ)
❏ N425HB	81 Conquest 1	425-0073	Conquest Aviation/Baker Donelson PC. Huntsville, Tn.	N550SC
❏ N425HD	82 Conquest 1	425-0113	Hiland Dairy Foods Co. Springfield, Mo.	N6851L
❏ N425HJ	83 Conquest 1	425-0169	DiMucci Companies/APD Developments LLC., Palatine, Il.	ZS-AMC
❏ N425JB	81 Conquest 1	425-0043	Betty MacGuire/MacGuire Aviation, Santa Teresa, NM.	N550SC
❏ N425JG	83 Conquest 1	425-0128	Twin City Enterprises Inc. El Paso, tx.	N444RR
❏ N425JH	82 Conquest 1	425-0124	MGP Ingredients Inc. Atchison, Ks.	N425DS
❏ N425JT	83 Conquest 1	425-0129	Joseph Thibodeau PC. Denver, Co.	N520RM
❏ N425KC	83 Conquest 1	425-0174	The Plumbers Warehouse, Carson, Ca.	N384MA
❏ N425KD	85 Conquest 1	425-0203	BDT LLC., Carbondale, Co.	N45TP
❏ N425LA	81 Conquest 1	425-0092	Cerretani Aviation Group LLC, Boulder	N40RD
❏ N425LC	81 Conquest 1	425-0054	Pro Air Services Inc. Bend, Or.	N425SM
❏ N425LG	82 Conquest 1	425-0107	ICM Inc. Colwich, Ks.	N1NL
❏ N425MM	81 Gulfstream 840	11699	Aardex Corp. Lakewood, Co.	XB-DYZ
❏ N425N	84 Conquest 1	425-0218	Tailwind LLC. Silver City, NM.	N425GV
❏ N425NC	84 Conquest 1	425-0207	John H Colle Jr., Pascagoula, Ms.	(N13EB)
❏ N425NP	86 Conquest 1	425-0224	JH Aircraft Management Inc. Jackson, Wy.	N850GM
❏ N425NW	81 Conquest 1	425-0070	Air Giant LLC. Watsonville, Ca.	N6854P
❏ N425PC	84 Conquest 1	425-0193	Kenair Aviation LLC/Nicewonder Group, Bristol, Va.	N214KC
❏ N425PG	85 Conquest 1	425-0200	425PG LLC. Dover, De.	N17HM
❏ N425PJ	83 Conquest 1	425-0157	Clyde Companies Inc., Orem, Ut.	(N68860)
❏ N425PL	81 Conquest 1	425-0010	Padilla Management Inc. Bow, Wa.	N813JL
❏ N425PN	85 Conquest 1	425-0214	421 Enterprises Inc. Woodstock, Ga.	N214LA
❏ N425PV	82 Conquest 1	425-0104	Westmoreland Mechanical Testing & Research, Latrobe, Pa.	N425MB
❏ N425RF	83 Conquest 1	425-0147	Edward L Flynn, Glendale, NY.	N500WD
❏ N425RM	83 Conquest 1	425-0180	Gallup Flying Service Inc., Gallup, NM.	N68731
❏ N425SF	81 Conquest 1	425-0037	Fowler Aircraft Sales & Leasing Inc. Columbus, Oh.	N6773L
❏ N425SL	85 Conquest 1	425-0236	Aircraft Guaranty Title LLC. Houston, Tx.	G-BNDY
❏ N425SP	83 Conquest 1	425-0184	Scope Leasing Inc. Columbus, Oh.	VH-JER
❏ N425SR	83 Conquest 1	425-0133	RBR Aircraft Inc. Albuquerque, NM.	(N83WF)
❏ N425SW	81 Conquest 1	425-0061	TJ Air Holdings Inc., Wilmington, De.	D-IAGT
❏ N425SX	82 Conquest 1	425-0106	Presidio Air Ventures LLC. Houston, Tx.	N425GA
❏ N425TB	81 Conquest 1	425-0068	Donnell Properties LLC. Wichita Falls, Tx.	(N425PF)
❏ N425TC	80 Conquest 1	425-0014	BFR LLC., Salem, Or.	(N6770W)
❏ N425TF	78 Mitsubishi MU-2N	725SA	Gregory Zielinski	C-FKIO
❏ N425TF	80 MU-2 Solitaire	425SA	Gregory M Zielinski, Lubbock, Tx.	N575CA
❏ N425TM	84 Conquest 1	425-0217	Six L's Packing Co. Clinton, NC.	(N526LS)
❏ N425TV	83 Conquest 1	425-0176	Conquest Aircraft Leasing LLC. Miami, Fl.	ZS-LDR
❏ N425TW	83 Conquest 1	425-0161	425TW LLC. Rexburg, Id.	N707NY
❏ N425TX	81 Conquest 1	425-0039	C Hadlai Hull, Chicago, Il.	D-INWG

Reg	Yr	Type	c/n	Owner/Operator	Prev Regn
N425WD	83	Conquest 1	425-0130	WMD Holdings, New York, NY.	N438H
N425WL	84	Conquest 1	425-0197	ICM Inc., Colwich, Ks.	N501
N425WT	83	Conquest 1	425-0175	Irwin International Inc. Corona, Ca.	(D-ILPC)
N425XP	81	Conquest 1	425-0064	Wingding Aviation LLC. Wilmington, De.	ZS-MIG
N425Z	83	Conquest 1	425-0186	Charles Christie Jr. Wichita Falls, Tx.	N425FG
N426EM	93	King Air C90B	LJ-1352	Ballard Aviation Inc. Wichita, Ks.	N494JY
N426HM	04	King Air C90B	LJ-1709	C & K Investment LLC. Tarrant, Al.	N744P
N426WF	06	King Air B200	BB-1953	Wellborn Forest Products Inc. Alexander City, Al.	
N427DD	78	PA-31T Cheyenne II	7820029	Dunagan Joint Property LLC. Huntsville, Al.	N78UA
N427DM	79	King Air C90	LJ-804	First Washington Management Group Inc. Dover, De.	N429DM
N427P	90	King Air B200	BB-1367	RB Air LLC/RDB Construction, Phoenix, Az.	N55HL
N427SE	06	King Air C90GT	LJ-1797	CB Aviation Inc. Gainesville, Fl.	
N427SP	73	SA-226AT Merlin 4	AT-018	River City Aviation, West Memphis, Ar.	N600TA
N427TA	77	PA-31T Cheyenne II	7720027	TAB LLC/Blacklidge Emulsions Inc. Gulfport, Ms.	XB-HGY
N427WA	01	Pilatus PC-12/45	427	Western Aircraft Inc. Boise, Id.	HB-FRP
N428CW	04	PA-46-500TP Meridian	4697201	Lexington Air Inc., Mansfield, Oh.	N851LC
N428DC	01	PA-46-500TP Meridian	4697124	Heritage Aircraft LLC. Indianapolis, In.	
N428V	76	King Air E90	LW-188	Winchester Air LLC. Laurel, Ms.	N68PM
N429AP	78	PA-31T Cheyenne II	7820076	Alan Pesch, Stonington, Ct.	N29CA
N429DM	81	King Air F90	LA-102	DKA Inc. Wilmington, De.	N44882
N429PC	01	Pilatus PC-12/45	429	J Air LLC., Davenport, Ia.	HB-FRR
N429PL	97	King Air B200	BB-1574	Learner Financial Corp. Walnut Creek, Ca.	(N429LF)
N429WM	81	MU-2 Marquise	1520SA	S & S Aviation Inc. Baltimore, Md.	N777MJ
N430JT	92	King Air B300C	FM-3	Lindsey Aviation Services, Haslet, Tx.	N8230Q
N430MC	81	King Air B200	BB-904	John DeNault/KJB Air, Fullerton, Ca.	(N202KC)
N430TW	06	King Air B200	BB-1935	NorAir LLC/Viking Construction Inc. Hayden, Id.	N3735C
N431CF	81	Cheyenne II-XL	8166002	John Gray Pontiac-Buick-GMC Inc., Paintsville, Ky.	C-FKEY
N431GW	80	PA-31T Cheyenne II	8020088	M C Aviation Inc. Barrington, Il.	N58GG
N431MC	85	PA-42 Cheyenne 400LS	5527031	Win Win Aviation LLC. Aspen, Co.	N41199
N431R	71	King Air 100	B-71	Vintage Props & Jets Inc. New Smyrna Beach, Fl.	N7771R
N431S	82	SA-227TT Merlin 3C	TT-431	B-Air LLC. Nashville, Tn.	N431SA
N431WC	01	Pilatus PC-12/45	431	Pelican Pacific Air LLC. Pleasanton, Ca.	HB-FRT
N431WJ	78	King Air 200	BB-431	World Jet Inc. Fort Lauderdale, Fl.	F-WQUQ
N432CV	95	Pilatus PC-12	119	Emjean Aviation Inc. Wilmington, De.	HB-FQM
N432MH	01	Pilatus PC-12/45	432	Magnum Hunter Production Inc.	N432PC
N432NA	59	Fairchild F-27F	35	Southeastern Oklahoma State University, Durant, Ok.	N768RL
N433HC	02	King Air B200	BB-1807	LJ-1381 Corp. Rio Pedras, PR.	N5007L
N434CA	82	CASA 212-200	286	Fayard Enterprises Inc. Louisburg, NC.	
N434JA	07	Pilatus PC-12/47	819	Jackson Air Charter LLC., Charlottesville, Va.	HB-FRH
N435A	67	King Air A90	LJ-229	Dodson International Parts Inc. Rantoul Ks.(Damaged 07/07)	
N435DM	99	TBM 700B	154	Miller Welding & Iron Works Inc. Washington, Il.	
N435PC	01	Pilatus PC-12/45	435	Bounty Air Leasing LLC. Coral Gables, Fl.	HB-FRV
N436CB	05	TBM 700C2	338	Bunting Equipment LLC. Selbyville, De.	N787CA
N437CF	66	King Air A90	LJ-140	Robert W Fields, Shelbyville, Tn.	N50GH
N437JB	03	King Air C90B	LJ-1687	Bill & Jodean Bradford Investments Inc. Dallas, Tx.	N6187L
N437WF	02	King Air B200	BB-962	Shae-Ron LLC. Edison, Ca.	N719HC
N438CA	98	King Air C90B	LJ-1541	Eagle Air Med Corp. Blanding, Ut.	
N438CR	79	King Air 200	BB-438	3 Lone Stars LLC. Arlington, Tx.	N438HT
N438GP	87	PA-42 Cheyenne 400LS	5527038	U S Marshals Service, Landover, Md.	YV- ??
N439PW	99	King Air C90B	LJ-1589	Paul Wood, Lake Forest, Il.	
N439WA	77	King Air E90	LW-216	Capital Air SC LLC. Spartanburg, SC.	N190DB
N439WC	02	Pilatus PC-12/45	439	Peninsular Capital Advisors LLC. Charlottesville, Va.	HB-FSD
N440CA	85	PA-42 Cheyenne IIIA	5501027	SunStarr Aviation LLC. Fond du Lac, Wi.	D-IHGO
N440CC	74	Rockwell 690A	11191	C F P & P Inc. Fort Vernon, In.	N616SD
N440DA	81	Conquest II	441-0207	Rue Educational Publishers, Clearwater, Fl.	G-FPLC
N440EA	07	TBM 850	447	EADS SOCATA North America, Pembroke Pines, Fl.	
N440EH	86	Conquest II	441-0358	Surdex Corp. Chesterfield, Mo.	N441FA
N440HC	82	Conquest 1	425-0145	Excel Family Partners LP., Scio, Oh.	N801ED
N440KA	97	King Air C90B	LJ-1499	Executive Beechcraft Inc. Kansas City Mo.	XB-MSF
N440KF	80	King Air C90	LJ-878	MJLG LLC. Nantucket, Ma.	N440KC
N440S	81	Cheyenne II-XL	8166016	Seneca Properties Inc. Sandusky, Oh.	N400XL
N440SM	70	King Air 100	B-44	TP Aviation LLC./American Door & Millwork Co., Sanford, Fl.	(N101PF)
N440ST	75	King Air 200	BB-65	Aero International Inc. El Paso, Tx.	(N901BR)
N440TP	65	King Air 90	LJ-17	Apex Aviation Group Inc. Southlake, Tx.	(N110AS)
N440WW	07	King Air B200GT	BY-5	Aztec Well Servicing Company inc.Aztec NM.	

Reg	Yr Type	c/n	Owner/Operator	Prev Regn
N441A	79 Conquest II	441-0094	David Clark, Redondo Beach, Ca.	N555GD
N441AB	83 Conquest II	441-0284	WDG Management Services LC. Vernon, Tx.	N6888C
N441AD	81 Conquest II	441-0226	Berkel & Co Contractors Inc. Bonner Springs, Ks.	N6281R
N441AE	82 Conquest II	441-0280	Aldridge Electric Inc. Libertyville, Il.	N986MC
N441AG	84 Conquest II	441-0327	Harvard Aviation Investment Corp. Las Vegas, Nv.	(N1209X)
N441AL	01 King Air B200	BB-1767	Aero Lease LLC/Summit Leasing Inc. Yakima, Wa.	N111JZ
N441AR	80 Conquest II	441-0148	Chrysalis 1 Inc. Fayetteville, Ar.	N170MA
N441BB	81 Conquest II	441-0217	Head Inc. Columbus, Oh.	N441WM
N441BD	79 Conquest II	441-0086	Fly-4-You Inc. Anchorage, Ak.	C-GLGE
N441BH	80 Conquest II	441-0145	AMT Services Leasing Co. Wilmington, De.	N31CR
N441BL	83 Conquest II	441-0322	Bravo Lima LLC. Newport Beach, Ca.	N536MA
N441BW	77 Conquest II	441-0034	Wisconsin Aviation Inc. Watertown, Wi.	(N248DJ)
N441CC	78 Conquest II	441-0008	Oregon Atlantic Aviation LLC. Eugene, Or.	N441CP
N441CG	95 King Air C90B	LJ-1398	Miami University, Oxford, Oh.	N996TT
N441CJ	80 Conquest II	441-0117	PFD Supply Corp. Carlinville, Il.	(N2623Z)
N441CR	83 Conquest 1	425-0149	Crowther Roofing/Flying Seas LLC. Fort Myers, Fl.	N425LD
N441CT	78 Conquest II	441-0048	Aberdeen Flying Service Inc. Aberdeen, SD.	N60FJ
N441CX	83 Conquest II	441-0305	Newport/Signal Air Inc. Costa Mesa, Ca.	N441FB
N441DB	83 Conquest II	441-0300	Alpha Victor Ltd. Dayton, Oh.	N68439
N441DD	84 Conquest II	441-0341	High Times Inc. Bentonville, Ar.	N441PM
N441DK	80 Conquest II	441-0176	Fly-4-You Inc. Anchorage, Ak.	N139ML
N441DN	84 Conquest II	441-0325	Shippers Air Corp. Quincey, Il.	N325CM
N441DR	77 Conquest II	441-0035	Tab Air, Los Banos, Ca.	G-FRAZ
N441DS	77 Conquest II	441-0028	Gable S Corporation, Broussard, La.	N36955
N441DZ	79 Conquest II	441-0089	Conquest Shares LLC. Liberal, Ks.	N90GC
N441E	83 Conquest II	441-0306	Star Builders, Princeton, WV	N66BZ
N441EB	78 Conquest II	441-0049	Plane Space Inc. West Palm Beach, Fl.	N441FW
N441EC	80 Conquest II	441-0179	BEE Aviation Inc. Sturgis, Ky.	N415PA
N441EE	79 Conquest II	441-0083	Flight Research Inc. Starkville, Ms.	N26BJ
N441EH	85 Conquest II	441-0351	Surdex Corp. Chesterfield, Mo.	N441PZ
N441EP	83 Conquest II	441-0283	CAAMS Inc., Stuart, Fl.	C-GMSL
N441F	77 Conquest II	441-0036	Rick's Key West, Key West, Fl.	N3AW
N441FP	92 King Air 350	FL-83	Flagstone King Air Holdings, Hamilton, Bermuda	VH-HPT
N441FS	83 Conquest II	441-0318	Executive Management Svcs/Air Golf II LLC, Indianapolis, In.	N300NK
N441G	81 Conquest II	441-0230	Robinson Manufacturing Co. Dayton, Tn.	N14PN
N441GA	82 Conquest II	441-0234	Richard Devirian, Torrance, Ca.	N42DT
N441HF	83 Conquest II	441-0315	Crusader Air LLC. Cleveland, Tn.	(N316CA)
N441HH	77 Conquest II	441-0007	Douglas H Herbert Performance Parts, Lincolnton, NC.	ZS-PES
N441HK	84 Conquest II	441-0336	Prosoft Technology Inc., Bakersfield, Ca.	N441JD
N441HS	84 Conquest II	441-0330	Phoenix Aircraft Sales & Rental Inc .Jacksonville, Fl.	(N747VB)
N441HT	79 Conquest II	441-0085	Wilkinson Rose Investments Inc. Beverly Hills Ca.	N347AR
N441JA	80 Conquest II	441-0137	Cheyenne Aviation Inc. Wilmington, De.	N301KB
N441JC	80 Conquest II	441-0156	Farmers Investment Co. Sahuarita, Az.	N829JQ
N441JK	81 Conquest II	441-0197	A L Stuart & Co. Stamford, Ct.	N8108Z
N441JR	83 Conquest II	441-0303	SR Aviation Inc. Wilmington, De.	N6860A
N441KM	78 Conquest II	441-0044	Kreuter Engineering Inc. New Paris, In.	N549GS
N441KP	78 Conquest II	441-0062	Alpha Victor Ltd. Dayton, Oh.	N76DA
N441LA	81 Conquest II	441-0210	Lee Aero LLC. Wichita, Ks.	N525MA
N441LB	78 Conquest II	441-0080	AirLink LLC/Concord Enterprises Inc. Lincoln, Ne.	N441BL
N441LS	85 Conquest II	441-0342	Liberty Steel Products Inc/Meander Air LLC. Jackson, Oh.	N30832
N441M	80 Conquest II	441-0122	Davandy LLC. St Louis, Mo.	(N441P)
N441MD	79 Conquest II	441-0103	Keystone Aerial Surveys Inc. Philadelphia, Pa.	N441CE
N441ME	83 Conquest II	441-0266	Scientific Flight Corp. Washington, DC.	N800YM
N441MJ	77 Conquest II	441-0024	Me LLC/Satellite Products Inc. Fort Payne Al.	YS-111N
N441MW	83 Conquest II	441-0286	First Port Air Inc. Omaha, Ne.	C-FUDY
N441ND	80 Conquest II	441-0123	Cyberdata Corp. Monterey, Ca.	(N441JH)
N441P	77 Conquest II	441-0032	Circle D Charter LLC., Mt. Eaton, Oh.	N441M
N441PG	82 Conquest II	441-0245	DPA LLC. Harlem, Mt.	C-GMSL
N441PN	85 Conquest II	441-0347	Pioneer Nursery, Visalia, Ca.	N1212K
N441PP	93 Conquest II	441-0292	Air Construction Inc. McKinney, Tx.	N666HC
N441PS	78 Conquest II	441-0045	S O Altfillisch Inc. Glendora, Ca.	N441JA
N441PW	82 Conquest II	441-0240	Four Star Greenhouse Sales Inc. Carleton, Mi.	N413PC
N441R	80 Conquest II	441-0163	Red Sea Nevada Inc. Henederson, Nv.	N38AA
N441RJ	80 Conquest II	441-0151	Hilltop Aviation LLC. Summit, NJ.	N2628M
N441RK	78 Conquest II	441-0074	Yingling Aircraft Inc. Wichita, Ks.	N1962J

Reg	Yr	Type	c/n	Owner/Operator	Prev Regn
☐ N441RS	81	Conquest II	441-0221	Donald P Johnson Trust, Laguna Beach, Ca.	N881CD
☐ N441S	83	Conquest II	441-0323	Fugro Geoservices Inc. Houston Tx.	N323JG
☐ N441SA	80	Conquest II	441-0172	Fly-4-You Inc. Anchorage, Ak.	N441VP
☐ N441SB	83	Conquest II	441-0301	Hondo LLC. Phoenix, Az.	N328VP
☐ N441SC	77	Conquest II	441-0012	Potts Air LLC., Sidney, Mt.	N36932
☐ N441SM	80	Conquest II	441-0134	Delta Southern Resource Leasing LLC. Baton Rouge, La.	N441DE
☐ N441ST	77	Conquest II	441-0014	RAL Enterprises Inc.	N441AA
☐ N441SX	82	Conquest II	441-0248	Pratt & Tobin PC. East Alton, Il.	N441JV
☐ N441TA	81	Conquest II	441-0204	Thomas Appleton, Hidden Hills, Ca.	N2727L
☐ N441TL	85	Conquest II	441-0357	Lantis Enterprises Inc., Spearfish, SD.	D-IOHL
☐ N441UC	85	Conquest II	441-0344	Unit Corp. Tulsa, Ok.	N441ML
☐ N441VB	80	Conquest II	441-0115	Avian Corp. Edina, Mn.	RP-C549
☐ N441VC	80	Conquest II	441-0192	Bell Aviation Inc, West Columbia,SC.	N441DW
☐ N441VH	81	Conquest II	441-0225	Satellite Aero Inc. Jackson, Wy.	N6854D
☐ N441WD	79	Conquest II	441-0107	JJA Holdings LLC. Birmingham, Al.	C-FGPK
☐ N441WJ	81	Conquest II	441-0194	WMJ Aviation LLC. Canton, Ga.	N26RF
☐ N441WL	78	Conquest II	441-0041	Lantis Enterprises Inc. Spearfish, SD.	N458HR
☐ N441WP	79	Conquest II	441-0098	Aero Transporte Nationale, Brownsville, Tx.	(N35DD)
☐ N441X	82	Conquest II	441-0254	M/V Forger Inc. Portland, Or.	N410MA
☐ N441YA	81	Conquest II	441-0231	Paxton Media Group Inc. Paducah, Ky.	HK-3647X
☐ N442JA	77	Conquest II	441-0013	Pegasus & Crew Inc. Fort Lauderdale, Fl.	N441BG
☐ N442JR	95	King Air B200	BB-1510	Don Ramatici Insurance Inc., Petaluma, Ca.	N208TS
☐ N442KA	79	King Air 200	BB-442	Nielsons Inc. Cortez, Co.	
☐ N443CL	79	King Air E90	LW-318	Ventana Aviation LLC. Salinas, Ca.	N943CL
☐ N443DW	83	Conquest II	441-0313	DWE Aviation Inc. Wilmington, NC.	N313DS
☐ N443H	80	Conquest 1	425-0002	Robert Hogue MD. Brownwood, Tx.	N74HR
☐ N443PE	89	BAe Jetstream 31	777	Petty Enterprises, Las Vegas, Nv.	N777JX
☐ N443TC	77	King Air B100	BE-20	Hanley Co. Knoxville, Tn.	N525WE
☐ N444AD	80	King Air 200	BB-733	Dept of Public Safety, Anchorage, Ak.	
☐ N444AK	84	Conquest II	441-0334	Triangle Aircraft LLC. Raleigh, NC.	N334FW
☐ N444BC	62	Gulfstream 1	96	Berry Contracting Inc. Corpus Christi, Tx.	N2NA
☐ N444BK	89	King Air B200	BB-1332	Koop Aviation BV. Groningen-Eelde, Holland.	D-ICSM
☐ N444BN	78	PA-31T Cheyenne II	7820028	Wildflower of Delaware LLC. Dover, De.	N82232
☐ N444CM	96	Pilatus PC-12	152	LJT Leasing LLC. Albertville, Mn.	HB-FRN
☐ N444CY	84	PA-42 Cheyenne IIIA	5501025	N444CY LLC. Johnston, Ia.	D-IHVA
☐ N444EB	79	King Air 200	BB-444	Herb Tobman, Las Vegas, Nv.	ZS-LZU
☐ N444EG	84	King Air 200	BB-624	FKM King Air LLC. Newport Beach, Ca.	N202BB
☐ N444ER	83	Cheyenne II-XL	8166071	Your Wings Inc., Palm Harbor, Fl.	N622AJ
☐ N444FT	00	Pilatus PC-12/45	322	Bluebird Air LLC. Louisville, Ky.	N124MK
☐ N444JV	00	TBM 700B	180	Rimrock Properties LLC. Billings, Mt.	N700VB
☐ N444KA	89	King Air B200	BB-1318	Carolina Turbine Sales Inc,Tyler Tx.	ZS-MMV
☐ N444KF	83	Conquest 1	425-0191	Fayette Investment LLC/Orion Investment Co. Fort Worth, Tx.	N1221N
☐ N444KK	83	King Air F90	LA-209	Darryl Unruh, Asheville, NC.	N6727U
☐ N444KU	82	King Air C90-1	LJ-1040	First Management Inc./TripleFour Ku LLC., Lawrence, Ks.	N115KU
☐ N444LB	82	SA-227TT Merlin 3C	TT-428A	SIR Family & Executive Charter Inc., Miami, Fl.	
☐ N444LN	81	PA-42 Cheyenne III	8001045	Wells Fargo Bank NW NA, Salt Lake City, Ut.	N169TC
☐ N444LP	02	King Air B200	BB-1816	BCS Produce Co. San Diego, Ca.	N5016K
☐ N444LR	96	King Air C90B	LJ-1447	Robert C Adler, Malibu, Ca.	N234ST
☐ N444PC	79	PA-31T Cheyenne II	7920066	Business Aircraft Center Inc. Danbury, Ct.	N111AM
☐ N444PS	74	King Air C90	LJ-615	Northwest Boring Co. Woodinville, Wa.	(N38DG)
☐ N444RC	75	PA-31T Cheyenne II	7520030	Four R C Corp. Baton Rouge, La.	N54959
☐ N444RK	83	King Air B100	BE-137	DeWaynes Quality Metal Coatings,Lexington Ky.	N65187
☐ N444RR	06	PA-46-500TP Meridian	4697278	Access Yacht Sales Inc. Key Largo, Fl.	N1040D
☐ N444SC	81	PA-42 Cheyenne III	8001034	PA42 LLC. Exeter, NH.	N74FB
☐ N444WC	82	Cheyenne II-XL	8166054	E S Wagner Co. Oregon, Oh.	N176RS
☐ N444WD	82	Gulfstream 1000	96006	FlyTo LLC. Indianapolis, In.	(N496MA)
☐ N444WF	82	MU-2 Marquise	1551SA	Marquise Enterprises LLC. Santa Clara, Ca.	N477MA
☐ N445CR	79	King Air C90	LJ-838	Claire Rice, Palm Desert, Ca.	N445DR
☐ N446AS	96	King Air C90B	LJ-1446	Executive AirShare Corp. Wichita, Ks.	N222NF
☐ N446JB	74	Rockwell 690A	11160	LaMair Aviation Corp. Wilmington, De.	N57092
☐ N447DB	01	King Air C90B	LJ-1656	Gulf Special Services Inc., Houston, Tx.	N656SA
☐ N447TF	03	King Air 350	FL-364	Continental Datalabel Inc. Elgin, Il.	N5084V
☐ N448CA	86	PA-42 Cheyenne 400LS	5527034	Tango Lima Aviation LLC. Terryville, Ct.	(N2UZ)
☐ N448CP	77	King Air E90	LW-232	CPL Aviation Inc. Bald Knob, Ar.	N112SB
☐ N449BK	81	MU-2 Solitaire	449SA	MGW Aviation Inc. Columbia, Tn.	N77DK

Reg	Yr	Type	c/n	Owner/Operator	Prev Regn
N449BY	02	Pilatus PC-12/45	449	Blue Yonder Airways LLC. Houston, Tx.	HB-FSH
N449CA	99	TBM 700B	150	Ascent Tech Services Inc. Parish, NY.	(N700EV)
N449LC	74	Rockwell 690A	11187	Blue Water Aviation Inc. Jupiter, Fl.	HC-BPX
N450CK	05	King Air 350	FL-464	Luther King Capital Management, Fort Worth, Tx.	N37164
N450CR	02	King Air 350	FL-340	Sierra Aviation LLC/Western Well Service, Taft, Ca.	HB-GJR
N450DW	01	King Air 350	FL-325	White Mountain Insurance Group. White River Junction, Vt.	N5025L
N450FS	76	Mitsubishi MU-2M	338	Northern Jet Sales LLC., Murfreesboro, Tn.	N456PS
N450HC	81	Cheyenne II-XL	8166021	Delaware Aviation LLC., Sidney, NY.	N300XL
N450LM	90	King Air 350	FL-5	Aircorp Inc. Anchorage Ak.	N450LM
N450MA	73	Mitsubishi MU-2J	587	Intercontinental Jet Inc., Tulsa, Ok.	N212BA
N450MW	84	PA-42 Cheyenne 400LS	5527013	Lofty LLC/Don Judkins Real Estate, Bakersfield, Ca.	N32KK
N450PC	02	Pilatus PC-12/45	450	Simbol Commercial Inc. Dallas, Tx.	HB-FSF
N450S	82	King Air 200	BB-1035	Griffing's Island Airlines Inc., Sandusky, Oh.	N7GA
N450WH	87	King Air B200	BB-1275	A T Williams Oil Co. Winston-Salem, NC.	N98RY
N451DM	00	Pilatus PC-12/45	350	Air Fox Hollow LLC. Menlo Park, Ca.	HB-FSC
N452GH	05	Pilatus PC-12/45	628	Crescent Real Estate Investors LLC. Palo Alto, Ca.	HB-FRV
N452MA	81	MU-2 Marquise	1533SA	Briggs Tobacco & Speciality Inc. Memphis, Tn.	
N452MD	02	Pilatus PC-12/45	452	MDR Aviation Inc. Columbia, Ms.	HB-FSK
N453PC	02	Pilatus PC-12/45	453	J & J Aviation LLC. Las Vegas, Nv.	HB-FSL
N454CA	81	PA-31T Cheyenne 1	8104053	SunStarr Aviation LLC. Fond du Lac, Wi.	G-JVAJ
N454DC	82	King Air B200	BB-995	F/90 LLC./Constructors West, Grand Junction, Co.	XA-RVJ
N454EA	78	Conquest II	441-0054	Topo Bird LLC. Yarmouth, Me.	C-GRSL
N454GC	80	King Air F90	LA-39	University of South Carolina, Columbia, SC.	N703JT
N454LF	98	King Air 350	FL-209	JAMM Aviation Inc. Columbus, Oh.	N2303B
N454P	94	King Air C90B	LJ-1372	McDowell Pharmaceutical LLC. Kansas City, Mo.	(N121EB)
N454PS	02	Pilatus PC-12/45	454	Shelaero LLC. De Kalb, Ga.	HB-FSM
N454TB	07	King Air 350	FL-554	KA 350 LLC., Center, Tx.	
N455DK	97	Pilatus PC-12/45	194	Doug Bradley Trucking Inc. Salina, Ks.	N216
N455JW	81	PA-42 Cheyenne III	8001040	Gas'N Shop Inc. Lincoln, Ne.	N456JW
N455LG	04	PA-46-500TP Meridian	4697203	Aero Aviation Enterprises LLC., Englewood, Co.	
N455MM	80	PA-31T Cheyenne II	8020087	Mike Miklus III Inc. Newark, De.	N26PJ
N455RS	05	PA-46-500TP Meridian	4697214	Meridian Transport LLC., Wilmington, De.	
N455SC	06	King Air 350	FL-500	Spartan Chemical Co. Swanton, Oh.	
N455SE	02	King Air 350	FL-356	BR Aircraft LLC. Sacramento, Ca.	N455SC
N455SG	01	PA-46-500TP Meridian	4697096	Graftaire LLC. Shreveport, La.	
N455WM	02	Pilatus PC-12/45	455	McClone Enterprises LLC. Shingle Spring, Ca.	HB-FSN
N456CS	76	King Air 200	BB-177	Xtreme Air LLC, New Iberia, La.	
N456ES	83	King Air B200	BB-1107	FordTex Aviation Inc. Taylor, Tx.	N564BC
N456FC	83	Conquest 1	425-0127	Lamar Leasing Co. Lamar, In.	N6882V
N456GT	82	Conquest II	441-0294	G T Aviation Inc. Wilmington, De.	N294VB
N456PC	02	Pilatus PC-12/45	456	Cummins Aviation LLC. Wilmington, De.	HB-FSQ
N456PF	78	King Air 200	BB-413	Cowan Watts Flying Service LLC. Pasco, Wa.	N2061B
N456PP	03	King Air C90B	LJ-1699	Air Montgomery (Guernsey) Ltd. Guernsey, Channel Islands.	N90KP
N456V	98	Pilatus PC-12/45	201	Conrad & Bischoff Inc., Idaho Falls, Id.	HB-FOM
N457C	07	PA-46-500TP Meridian	4697328	Flightline Group Inc. Tallahassee Fl.	
N457CP	67	King Air A90	LJ-275	Texas State Technical College, Waco, Tx.	N457SR
N457G	69	SA-26AT Merlin 2B	T26-150	National Flight Services Inc., Swanton, Oh.	N4257X
N457TG	80	PA-31T Cheyenne II	8020059	VT Air LLC. Corvalllis, Or.	N457TC
N458BB	85	MU-2 Solitaire	458SA	Beeline Flight Inc. Wilmington, De.	XB-FQM
N458DL	02	Pilatus PC-12/45	458	T J Leasing LLC., Bandera, Tx.	N458PC
N458Q	89	King Air 300	FA-181	Honcore Charters LLC. Los Angeles, Ca.	N456Q
N458TC	06	King Air B200	BB-1969	Tilt-Con Aviation LLC., Altamonte Springs, Fl.	N3729R
N459MA	02	TBM 700C2	259	Highlands Aviation LLC. Aspen, Co.	
N459PC	02	Pilatus PC-12/45	459	Alan Ross, Tulsa, Ok.	HB-FST
N459SA	85	MU-2 Solitaire	459SA	Solitaire Leasing LLC. Wilmington, De.	OY-CGW
N460FS	73	Mitsubishi MU-2K	280	R & J Enterprises of N Carolina, Murphy, NC.	N10BK
N460K	77	Rockwell 690B	11392	Two Builders & A Trucker LLC, Ocala Fl.	LV-MAG
N460PB	02	Pilatus PC-12/45	460	Travel Express Aviation/Plymouth Air LLC., Warrenville, Il.	HB-FSU
N461BB	01	PA-46-500TP Meridian	4697016	Aeroscape Investments & Research Inc. Orange Park, Fl.	
N461EP	03	King Air C90	LJ-1697	Ethanol Products LLC. Wichita, Ks.	N50847
N461LM	96	TBM 700	122	Royal Air LLC., Glenwood Springs, Co.	F-GLBJ
N461MA	74	Mitsubishi MU-2K	301	Good Aviation LLC. Grand Rapids, Mi.	N10T
N462MA	74	Mitsubishi MU-2K	302	Copper Station Holdings LLC. Columbia, SC.	
N462PC	02	Pilatus PC-12/45	462	NW Aircraft Sales & Leasing LLC. Scappoose, Or.	HB-FSW
N462PJ	06	PA-46-500TP Meridian	4697249	Aircraft Guaranty Title & Trust LLC. Houston, Tx.(trustor ?)	D-EXTP

Reg	Yr Type	c/n	Owner/Operator	Prev Regn
N463DC	76 SA-226T Merlin 3A	T-273	Jaime Hernandez, Brownsville, Tx.	N5390M
N463DN	81 PA-31T Cheyenne II	8120056	Gringo Management Co. Tortola, BVI.(Based Sion, Switzerland)	F-GGCH
N463DP	79 King Air 200	BB-463	Horsham Valley Airways Inc., Horsham, Pa.	VH-ITH
N463JB	92 King Air C90B	LJ-1310	Flying Fish Aviation LLC. Fountain Inn, SC.	C-GMBW
N463JT	02 Pilatus PC-12/45	463	Dealers Electric Equipment Leasing LLC., Waco, Tx.	HB-FRD
N465JB	92 King Air C90B	LJ-1304	Island Aviation LLC/Aviation Aviation Inc. Indianapolis, In.	C-GMBG
N465ME	05 PA-46-500TP Meridian	4697233	Markle Aviation LLC. Wilmington, De.	
N465PC	02 Pilatus PC-12/45	465	Fischer Industries Air LLC. Sebastian, Fl.	HB-FSY
N465SK	01 PA-46-500TP Meridian	4697013	Malibu Financial Corp. Dover, De.	
N465TP	05 PA-46-500TP Meridian	4697204	Black Ice LLC. Rancho Santa, Ca.	
N466DC	81 MU-2 Marquise	1528SA	Aerotel Inc. St Brooksville, Fl.	N60NB
N466MW	87 King Air B200	BB-1273	Shanair LLC/KA Partners LLC., Visalia, Ca.	N30486
N466SA	01 Pilatus PC-12/45	443	Timothy Hoiles, Colorado Springs Co.	HB-...
N467BC	99 King Air B200	BB-1647	Bright Coop Inc. Nacogdoches, Tx.	N50PU
N467BW	72 King Air A100	B-130	Rainbow International Airlines, St Thomas VI.	N83TM
N467JB	87 King Air 300	FA-137	Barnett Investments Inc. La Verne, Ca.	C-FTLB
N467MA	85 MU-2 Marquise	1567SA	Sydney Hope Ventures Inc. West Palm Beach Fl.	PT-LPB
N468BV	03 King Air 350	FL-369	BV Aviation LLC/Ball Ventures LLC. Idaho Falls, Id.	N103BE
N468SP	84 MU-2 Marquise	1566SA	Pace Inc. Plymouth Mi.	5Y-SPR
N469AF	02 Pilatus PC-12/45	469	Alpha Flying Inc. Manchester, NH.	HB-FQB
N469B	78 King Air C90	LJ-803	Water & Sewer Pipe Supply, Bridge City, La.	N75GA
N469BL	69 SA-26AT Merlin 2B	T26-139	AER Aviation Inc. Dallas, Tx.	C-FCAR
N469JB	80 King Air 200	BB-634	Solola Inc. Sparks, Nv.	OY-NUK
N469MA	82 MU-2 Marquise	1543SA	Via Air Inc. Charlotte, NC.	TF-FHM
N470AH	02 Pilatus PC-12/45	470	Brighton Aviation LLC. Boise, Id.	N470WA
N470KA	94 King Air 350	FL-109	Kerola Avn Inc./P I & I Motor Express Inc., Masury, Oh.	N434BW
N470MM	00 Beech 1900D	UE-394	Schwans Shared Services LLC. Marshall, Mn.	N41255
N470RJ	81 Conquest 1	425-0082	Northern Refrigerated Transport, Turlock, Ca.	N86EA
N470SC	90 King Air 350	FL-35	Poly-Foam International Inc. Fremont, Oh.	N550TP
N470TC	79 King Air 200	BB-424	MacAviation LLC. Jonesboro, Ar.	F-GMCR
N471CD	83 SA-227AT Merlin 4C	AT-549	Ashley Aire Inc. Upper Marlboro, Md.	89-1471
N473GG	78 PA-31T Cheyenne II	7820026	Dietrich Transport Inc. Norristown, Pa.	N570AB
N473PC	02 Pilatus PC-12/45	473	N473PC LLC. Spokane, Wa.	HB-FQD
N475JA	87 King Air C90A	LJ-1147	King Air LLC. Elizabeth, Co.	
N476D	02 Pilatus PC-12/45	476	Air Watkins LLC, Atlanta, Ga.	HB-FQG
N477AE	85 King Air 300	FA-84	Exodus Truck Systems Inc. Charlotte, NC.	N22BD
N477B	78 Conquest II	441-0055	Joplin Regional Stockyards Inc. Carthage, Mo.	HB-LFF
N477DD	81 MU-2 Solitaire	439SA	Tahoe Helicopters Inc. Bakersfield, Ca.	N439BA
N477HC	03 PA-46-500TP Meridian	4697171	Copperman Enterprises LLC. Naples, Fl.	
N477JM	79 King Air 200	BB-538	Cheryl H Walton, Indianapolis, In.	5N-AVH
N477PT	00 King Air C90B	LJ-1600	Puryear Aircraft Leasing LLC. Wilmington, NC.	N812LP
N478CR	97 King Air C90B	LJ-1474	ALG Aircraft LLC. Delano, Ca.	N205P
N479MA	82 MU-2 Marquise	1553SA	Gulf Group Transportation & Equipment Inc. Panama City, Fl.	
N479MM	82 PA-42 Cheyenne III	8001074	Central Arkansas Nursing Centers Inc. Fort Smith, Ar.	N423KC
N479SA	67 King Air A90	LJ-215	Ewing & Ewig Inc Corpus Christi, Tx.	N127HT
N479SW	79 PA-31T Cheyenne 1	7904047	Navajo Partners LLC. Wilmington, De.	
N479WB	81 King Air B200	BB-886	Flyguys Aviation LLC/GW Energy Inc.. Midland, Tx.	N146MD
N480AF	73 Mitsubishi MU-2K	248	Air 1st Aviation Companies Inc. Aiken, SC.	N725FN
N480BR	90 King Air B200	BB-1355	Raven Holdings LLC. Mesa, Az.	OH-WIB
N480K	79 Rockwell 690B	11543	SB Aircraft Sales, Boulder, Co.	(N117FA)
N480MA	82 MU-2 Marquise	1554SA	I M LLC. San Diego, Ca.	
N480TC	97 King Air B200	BB-1600	Cardinal AG Co. Eden Prairie, Mn.	
N480WH	02 Pilatus PC-12/45	480	Frank Howard No 1 LLC. Colorado Springs, Co.	HB-FQK
N481AF	73 Mitsubishi MU-2K	253	Air 1st Aviation Companies Inc. Aiken, SC.	N430DA
N481BR	06 King Air B200	BB-1967	BioReference Laboratories Inc. Elmwood Park, Nj.	
N481SW	81 PA-31T Cheyenne 1	8104016	Kent Companies, Midland, Tx.	
N482AF	73 Mitsubishi MU-2K	265	Air 1st Aviation Companies Inc. Aiken, SC.	N121CH
N483AF	73 Mitsubishi MU-2K	271	Air 1st Aviation Companies Inc. Aiken, SC.	N708DM
N484AF	74 Mitsubishi MU-2K	284	Air 1st Aviation Companies Inc. Aiken, SC.	N726FN
N484AS	80 PA-31T Cheyenne 1	8004055	AirSure Limited Properties Inc. Golden, Co.	N619RB
N484RJ	05 TBM 700C2	333	Aeroknot LLC. Boca Raton, Fl.	
N484SC	78 PA-31T Cheyenne II	7820022	Great Southwest Aviation Inc. Roswell, NM.	N9DK
N485AF	74 Mitsubishi MU-2K	308	Air 1st Aviation Companies Inc. Aiken, SC.	N709FN
N485AT	89 King Air C90A	LJ-1203	Advanced Technology Services Inc. Peoria, Il.	N115MZ
N485K	79 King Air 200	BB-485	Steven Aviation LLC. Wichita, Ks.	N120K

Reg	Yr	Type	c/n	Owner/Operator	Prev Regn
N485PC	03	Pilatus PC-12/45	485	Cheshire Leasing LLC. Fairview Park, Oh.	HB-FQS
N485R	80	King Air 200	BB-605	Native Trading Assoc. Hogansburg, NY.	N605EA
N486AF	75	Mitsubishi MU-2M	329	Air 1st Aviation Companies Inc. Aiken, SC.	N60AZ
N486PB	03	Pilatus PC-12/45	486	LRW Aviation LLC. Missoula, Mt.	HB-FQT
N487AF	76	Mitsubishi MU-2M	333	Air 1st Aviation Companies Inc. Aiken, SC.	N12SJ
N487JH	78	King Air B100	BE-43	MWP Properties/Blue Sky Ventures LLC., Lafayette, La.	N544FD
N487LM	03	Pilatus PC-12/45	517	J&L Air LLC., Greenwood Village, Co.	HB-FRT
N487PC	03	Pilatus PC-12/45	487	Abbey Leasing Co. Bonita Springs, Fl.	HB-FQU
N487TT	91	King Air 350	FL-67	Thompson Tractor Co. Birmingham, Al.	(N850TR)
N488FT	81	King Air F90	LA-137	Team Financial Inc. Birmingham, Al.	N200MW
N488JB	83	King Air B200	BB-1099	S.A.F.E. II LLC., San Antonio, Tx.	N60AA
N488XJ	98	King Air C90B	LJ-1527	Wilkes & McHugh PA. Tampa, Fl.	
N489JG	03	Pilatus PC-12/45	489	GCM Aviation LLC. Hillsborough, NJ.	HB-FQW
N490KQ	04	Kodiak 100	KD101	Quest Aircraft LLC. Sandpoint, Id. (Ff 16 Oct 2004)	
N490MA	74	Mitsubishi MU-2J	640	Paxson Communications Management Co. West Palm Beach, Fl.	
N490W	01	King Air C90B	LJ-1649	Aerolease LLC./Weather Modification Inc., Fargo, ND.	N4479W
N491JV	93	King Air C90B	LJ-1349	Omnione LLC. Albany, Or.	
N492B	07	TBM 850	452	EADS SOCATA North America, Pembroke Pines, Fl.	
N492PA	70	King Air B90	LJ-492	Air Shine LLC. Slaughters, Ky.	(N946WA)
N492WA	03	Pilatus PC-12/45	492	William Howard, Friday Harbor, Wa.	HB-FQZ
N493DT	78	King Air B100	BE-32	Sky Trek LLC/Coffman Specialities Inc. San Diego, Ca.	N1PN
N494MA	86	King Air 300	FA-108	Weir Street Leasing Inc. Vero Beach, Fl.	OY-LKT
N495DH	04	King Air 350	FL-404	Redwood Empire Disposal Inc., Petaluma, Ca.	HB-GJS
N495NM	78	King Air C90	LJ-781	Preferred Aviation/M&K Quality Truck Sales, Byron Center, Mi	N4953M
N495TM	97	King Air C90B	LJ-1495	Turbine Aircraft Marketing Inc. San Angelo, Tx.	D-IDIX
N495Y	04	King Air C90B	LJ-1707	Arkwest Aviation LLC. Danville, Ar.	
N497PC	03	Pilatus PC-12/45	497	US Customs & Border Protection, Washington, DC.	HB-F..
N498AC	77	King Air 200	BB-287	Pollard Aircraft Sales Inc., Southlake, Tx.	N429E
N499SW	80	King Air B100	BE-89	Stinger Welding Inc., Coolidge, Az.	C-GKNP
N500BG	04	Pilatus PC-12/45	600	Oakshire Aviation LLC, Yakima Wa.	N600PE
N500CR	80	King Air 200	BB-714	Horizon Air Inc. Lexington-Bluegrass, Ky.	N7CC
N500CS	81	King Air 200	BB-773	FML Beech Inc. Wilmington, De.	N83JE
N500EQ	94	King Air C90B	LJ-1387	Red Drive IV LLC. Houston, Tx.	N500ED
N500EW	81	Cheyenne II-XL	8166060	Performance Aircraft Leasing Lincolnshire Il.	N68MT
N500FC	97	King Air 350	FL-181	Fibres Aviation LLC/Fulghum Fibres Inc. Augusta, Ga.	N6789
N500FF	98	TBM 700	141	Evisair Corp. Wilmington, De.	
N500GN	75	King Air 200	BB-62	Downtown Travel /Adams Cabinet & App.,Shreveport, Ca.	N300GN
N500HG	06	King Air B200	BB-1954	Two Guys & A Plane Ltd/Hylant Group, Toledo, Oh.	N7054D
N500KD	80	King Air B100	BE-79	Winner Aviation Corp. Vienna, Oh.	N500JE
N500KR	77	King Air C90	LJ-708	NC State Bureau of Investigation, Raleigh, NC.	N500KS
N500KS	75	King Air 200	BB-59	Ken Schrader Racing Inc. Concord, NC.	N504WR
N500LM	84	PA-42 Cheyenne 400LS	5527016	James Smith, Kalispell, Mt.	
N500LP	83	King Air B200	BB-1141	Neal Hawthorn, Longview, Tx.	N66549
N500MS	75	King Air E90	LW-123	Mike Skinner Enterprises Inc. Greensboro, NC.	N121GW
N500MY	78	PA-31T Cheyenne 1	7804004	Tri Rotor Spray & Chemical, Ulysses, Ks.	N500MT
N500NG	94	King Air B200	BB-1483	Forecast Financial Inc. Westlake Village, Ca.	N572P
N500NK	03	Pilatus PC-12/45	500	Peoples Choice Consulting LLC. Irvine, Ca. (400th PC-12).	N500ZP
N500PB	81	Cheyenne II-XL	8166027	Broyhill Industries Inc. Lenoir, NC.	N2602Y
N500PJ	75	Mitsubishi MU-2L	668	Premier Jets Inc. Portland, Or.	N500RM
N500PM	84	PA-42 Cheyenne 400LS	5527021	PSM Holdings Inc., Orlando, Fl.	N248DJ
N500PV	79	King Air 200	BB-452	Pan Northern Air Services Sdn Bhd. Halim, Malaysia.	N500PR
N500QX	68	Mitsubishi MU-2F	133	Air 1st Aviation Companies Inc, Aiken SC.	N488GB
N500RJ	83	Conquest II	441-0302	Edward Jankowski, Mancos, Co.	N68599
N500RN	62	Gulfstream 1	95	USAF, 89th Operations Group, Andrews AFB. Md.	(N700MA)
N500SE	01	PA-46-500TP Meridian	4697118	Air FMS Inc. Galesburg, Il.	
N500SX	80	SA-226T Merlin 3B	T-366	Merlin Aviation Inc. Indianapolis, In.	N911JZ
N500VL	03	King Air 350	FL-383	WB Air Time LLC. Virginia Beach, Va.	N6183S
N500WF	81	King Air B200	BB-947	William Flowers, Dothan, Al.	G-FOOD
N500WY	06	Pilatus PC-12/47	762	M & N Equipment LLC., Casper, Wy.	HB-FSQ
N500XX	73	Mitsubishi MU-2K	250	JAM Aviation Inc. Quincy, Il.	N740FN
N501AR	03	PA-46-500TP Meridian	4697162	Warner Aviation Ltd. Cleveland, Oh.	N563MA
N501DU	81	King Air F90	LA-82	Herbert W Hardt., Bakersfield, Ca.	N501TD
N501EB	79	King Air 200	BB-422	Precision Holdings LLC. Kimberly, Id.	N551E
N501GS	81	King Air C90	LJ-964	North American Flight Services Inc., Ballston Spa, NY.	N595RC
N501HC	88	King Air B200	BB-1306	Intermountain Health Care Services, Salt Lake City, Ut.	N1553E

Reg	Yr Type	c/n	Owner/Operator	Prev Regn
☐ N501MS	74 King Air C90	LJ-626	J&R Air LLC/Chicago Adhesive Products Co. Romeoville, Il.	N500MS
☐ N501PB	03 Pilatus PC-12/45	501	Capital Holdings 121 LLC. Vero Beach, Fl.	HB-FRG
☐ N501PM	92 P-180 Avanti	1022	PM Aircraft Leasing LLC. Conroe, Tx.	F-GMCP
☐ N501SR	03 PA-46-500TP Meridian	4697165	Parker Equipment Rental LLC. Las Vegas, Nv.	N504SR
☐ N501WN	65 Gulfstream 1	165	Erin Miel Inc. Las Vegas, Nv.	N500WN
☐ N502BR	80 Conquest II	441-0135	U S Leasing & Financial Inc. Wilmington, De.	N93RK
☐ N502FS	85 CASA 212-200	294	Caribe-Rico Inc. Orlando, Fl.	N31BR
☐ N502NC	81 Conquest 1	425-0056	TWP Equipt Lsg LLC/TW Phillips Grading Inc., Dawsonville, Ga	N56DA
☐ N502SE	77 King Air C90	LJ-740	Aerolease LLC. Fargo, ND.	(N390YH)
☐ N503AB	70 King Air 100	B-18	Aero Transit Inc. Apple Valley, Ca.	(N901AT)
☐ N503B	78 Rockwell 690B	11503	Charles J Howard, Houston, Tx.	XB-IRY
☐ N503CB	82 King Air C90	LJ-997	CTB Inc. Goshen, In.	N1853T
☐ N503CG	97 Dornier 328-110	3086	Chip Ganassi/SABCO Racing, Mooresville, NC.	5N-SPD
☐ N503F	76 King Air 200	BB-185	RLD Leasing Inc. Downers Grove, Il.	N265EB
☐ N503LM	97 King Air 350	FL-182	Republican Transportation LLC, Corpus Christi, Tx.	(N128MG)
☐ N503M	66 King Air A90	LJ-158	Robert Spillman, Elyria, Oh.	(N900WM)
☐ N503P	79 King Air 200	BB-437	SOP Management LLC/Bill Smith Ford Inc. Southern Pines, NC.	N500MT
☐ N503RM	80 King Air 200	BB-673	Randy Marion Chevrolet Pontiac Buick, Mooresville, NC.	N502RH
☐ N503WJ	79 King Air 200	BB-503	Variety Wholesalers Inc. Raleigh, NC.	RP-C304
☐ N503WR	79 PA-31T Cheyenne 1	7904016	Bear Aviation Inc. Wilmington De.	N93CV
☐ N503WS	03 Pilatus PC-12/45	503	Priority Aircraft Inc. Blairsville, Pa.	N503PB
☐ N504CB	75 King Air E90	LW-125	M Richard Warner, Lufkin, Tx.	N543MB
☐ N504CE	05 King Air B200	BB-1897	Midamerican Energy Co, Des Moines Ia.	N897BM
☐ N504GF	83 King Air B200	BB-1156	Waffle House Inc. Norcross, Ga.	N66825
☐ N504SR	05 Pilatus PC-12/45	658	Synergy Aviation LLC. Missoula, Mt.	HB-FSS
☐ N504TF	04 King Air 350	FL-399	Teixeira Farms Inc. Santa Maria, Ca.	
☐ N505AK	83 Conquest 1	425-0160	82nd ABN Aviation LLC, Bear De.	N68865
☐ N505AM	81 King Air B200	BB-919	Flight Management Co/Dart Container Corp. Sarasota, Fl.	N160AD
☐ N505FK	73 King Air C-12C	BC-18	Monroe County Sheriffs Department, Key West, Fl.	N465MC
☐ N505FS	85 SA-227AT Merlin 4C	AT-591	F S Air Service Inc. Anchorage, Ak.	N176SW
☐ N505GM	77 SA-226T Merlin 3A	T-286	Range Fire Productions Inc., Vero Beach, Fl.	N226DD
☐ N505HC	82 Conquest II	441-0257	Span Construction & Engineering Inc. Madera, Ca.	N100YA
☐ N505MW	75 King Air E90	LW-155	Golden Eagle Associates Ltd. Dallas, Tx.	N505GA
☐ N505P	03 Pilatus PC-12/45	505	POMCO Equipment Inc. Syracuse, NY.	HB-FRK
☐ N505RT	68 680W Turbo Commander	1752-5	Twin City Leasing Corp. Kansas City, Mo.	N5051E
☐ N505WR	84 King Air 300	FA-15	J M Air Inc. Pinedale, Wy.	
☐ N506F	86 King Air C90A	LJ-1129	Park Avenue Group Inc. Stuart Fl.	N817F
☐ N506GT	80 King Air 200	BB-612	Foster Poultry Farms Inc. Livingston, Ca.	
☐ N506MV	99 King Air 350	FL-261	Foster Poultry Farms Inc. Livingston, Ca.	N350GT
☐ N507AZ	01 Pilatus PC-12/45	418	TMLR Holdings LLC., Eagle, Co.	N507AM
☐ N507BC	06 TBM 850	382	Eckles Leasing Inc. Blue Earth, Mn.	
☐ N507BE	80 King Air 200	BB-735	MP Leasing LLC. Vermillion, Mn.	N508JA
☐ N507DM	88 120ER Brasilia	120118	Jet Sales of Stuart LLC,Stuart Fl.	N500DE
☐ N507RC	03 Pilatus PC-12/45	507	Catbird Aviation LLC., Raleigh, NC.	N507PB
☐ N507W	67 King Air A90	LJ-269	Fall Air Inc. Missoula, Mt.	N788K
☐ N507WG*	82 King Air 350	FL-81	Whistler Investment Group, Raleigh, NC.	N507EB
☐ N508DW	79 King Air 200	BB-523	Air BP LLC. Wilmington, De.	N500DW
☐ N508GT	06 King Air C90GT	LJ-1775	TFH Aviation LLC/Micro Dynamics Group, Naperville, Il.	
☐ N508MV	81 King Air B200	BB-877	KAMV LLC. Stamford, Ct.	N711BU
☐ N509FP	04 King Air B200	BB-1886	Perdue Farms Inc. Salisbury, Md.	
☐ N509RH	95 SAAB 2000	030	Hendrick Motorsports Inc. Charlotte, NC.	N5125
☐ N510GS	99 King Air B200	BB-1746	Flyaway Inc. Fort Worth, Tx.	N518GS
☐ N510LA	07 King Air B200GT	BY-24	Hanger 4 LLC/Rennes Group, Green Bay, Wi.	
☐ N510LC	77 PA-31T Cheyenne II	7720068	Packless Industries/Packless Metal Hose, Waco, Tx.	(N69XX)
☐ N510ME	79 King Air E90	LW-312	CLAG LLC. Wichita Falls, Tx.	N505BG
☐ N510UF	04 King Air B200	BB-1872	United Fire & Casualty Co. Cedar Rapids, Ia.	N6172W
☐ N511AS	87 King Air B200	BB-1286	Textile Rubber & Chemical Co. Dalton, Ga.	N800GF
☐ N511D	97 King Air 350	FL-172	Bunn-O-Matic Corp. Springfield, Il.	
☐ N511DP	81 King Air 200C	BL-15	Air Med Services LLC. Lafayette, La.	N215AA
☐ N511KV	96 King Air C90B	LJ-1422	Raemarc Aviation LLC/ GQuest Technology LLC. Greensboro, NC.	N2123Y
☐ N511PB	03 Pilatus PC-12/45	511	Concept Support Services LLC. Sylvania, Oh.	HB-FRO
☐ N511RH	95 SAAB 2000	020	Hendrick Motorsports Inc. Charlotte, NC.	N5123
☐ N511RZ	93 King Air B200	BB-1458	Air Med Services LLC. Lafayette, La.	N457TQ
☐ N511SD	99 King Air B200	BB-1683	DashDale Aviation LLC. Fort Dodge, Ia.	
☐ N511TA	99 King Air B200	BB-1660	Air Med Services LLC, Lafayette La.	N40PJ

Reg	Yr	Type	c/n	Owner/Operator	Prev Regn
N512DC	02	King Air 350	FL-342	Colonial Coal Co. Prestonburg, Ky.	N4472S
N512FS	79	SA-226T Merlin 3B	T-299	F S Air Service Inc. Anchorage, Ak.	N55ZP
N512G	65	King Air 90	LJ-64	American Aircraft Inc. Newton, Ks.	N512Q
N512JD	66	680T Turbo Commander	1584-36	Ontrac Air Service, Eugene, Or.	N512JC
N512MM	06	PA-46-500TP Meridian	4697271	Lesley Warshaw Jr. Alexandria, La.	N271SE
N512RR	79	King Air C90	LJ-832	Ruhl Develpment LLC. Davenport, Ia.	N10QW
N513DM	82	MU-2 Marquise	1560SA	Incoe Corp. Troy, Mi.	N486MA
N513JM	91	King Air C90A	LJ-1274	Miles Aircraft LLC. Greensboro, NC.	N8099G
N513KL	81	King Air F90	LA-123	CSOKI Aviation Inc. Knoxville, Tn.	N211EC
N514GP	94	BAe Jetstream 41	41038	Georgia Pacific Corp. Atlanta, Ga.	N438JX
N514LK	06	King Air 350	FL-517	Spence Enterprises LLC., El Dorado Hills, Ca.	
N514NA	68	680W Turbo Commander	1772-10	NASA Langley Research Center, Hampton, Va.	83-24126
N514RD	79	King Air 200C	BL-5	Evergreen Helicopters Inc. McMinnville, Or.	N14RD
N514RS	94	2000A Starship	NC-51	Robert Scherer III, Charlotte, NC.	N6204U
N514TB	90	King Air B200	BB-1351	Hentzen Coatings Inc. Milwaukee, Wi.	N777JV
N515AF	03	Pilatus PC-12/45	515	Alpha Flying Inc. Manchester, NH.	HB-FRR
N515AM	80	Gulfstream 980	95008	Allen Myland Inc. Broomall, Pa.	N9761S
N515AS	72	King Air A100	B-90	Elias R V Morales, Valencia Caracobo, Venezuela.	(YV-2423P)
N515BA	79	King Air 200	BB-603	Middle Tennessee State University, Murfreesboro, Tn.	N70RB
N515BC	75	King Air E90	LW-121	Orion Medical Services/PCC Aviation LLC., Eugene, Or.	N500TR
N515CK	00	King Air B200	BB-1726	Whiskey Tango LLC/Basin Aviation, Midland, Tx.	N515CL
N515CP	84	King Air B200	BB-1175	Colemill Enterprises Inc. Nashville, Tn.	N515CR
N515GA	82	PA-31T Cheyenne 1	8104050	Ingram GP LLC. New Braunfels, Tx.	N49WA
N515KJ	72	King Air C90	LJ-566	MJK Aviation LLC Savannah, Ga.	N67PL
N515RC	84	PA-42 Cheyenne IIIA	5501018	Versa Air LLC., Racine, Wi.	N516GA
N515RP	00	Pilatus PC-12/45	330	Sunrise Community Inc. Miami, Fl.	HB-FRO
N516AF	70	Mitsubishi MU-2G	516	Air 1st Aviation Co, Aiken SC	VH-JES
N516WB	65	King Air 90	LJ-70	University of Alaska, Fairbanks, Ak.	N516W
N517AB	82	King Air F90	LA-176	Broin & Assocs Inc. Sioux Falls, SD.	N766RB
N517HP	79	Rockwell 690B	11517	B-H Sales Inc. Richmond, In.	N101RW
N518NA	67	King Air A90	LM-80	Lake Technical Institute, Watertown, SD.	66-18080
N518TS	86	King Air C90A	LJ-1130	Burdge Logistics LLC., Santa Fe Springs, Ca.	(N581TS)
N519CC	83	Gulfstream 1000	96068	Eagle Air Inc. Memphis, Tn.	N62GA
N519JG	95	SAAB 2000	017	Joe Gibbs Racing Inc. Huntersville, NC.	N.....
N519PC	03	Pilatus PC-12/45	519	Sierra Nevada Corp, Sparks Nv.	HB-FRU
N520DD	80	King Air 200	BB-738	Quail Creek Petroleum Management, Oklahoma City, Ok.	N66TS
N520DG	00	King Air B200	BB-1753	David R Webb Co. Edinburgh, In.	
N520HP	01	PA-46-500TP Meridian	4697012	Showtech Aviation Inc., Poway, Ca.	
N520JA	98	King Air C90B	LJ-1519	Cornerstone Air LLC., Winston Salem, NC.	N500VA
N520JG	68	Gulfstream 1	197	Joe Gibbs Racing Inc. Charlotte, NC.	N197RM
N520MC	75	King Air 200	BB-43	Mayo Aviation Inc. Englewood, Co.	N500UR
N521LB	77	King Air E90	LW-249	Monckton Byng Inc., Trustee, Wilmington, De.	N68CC
N521PC	03	Pilatus PC-12/45	521	Clover Mechanical LLC. Ottawa, Il.	HB-FRW
N521PM	77	PA-31T Cheyenne II	7720048	Exotic Car Club of America LLC, Methuen Ma.	N82163
N522AS	75	PA-31T Cheyenne II	7520007	Aerial Services Inc. Cedar Falls, Ia.	OH-PNT
N522DJ	04	Pilatus PC-12/45	539	DRJ Group Inc. Ocala, Fl.	N539PS
N522JP	91	King Air C90A	LJ-1289	Weather Modification Inc. Fargo, ND.	N1NP
N522MJ	74	King Air E90	LW-80	Shelton Flight LLC., Carson City, Nv.	N20LH
N522TG	80	King Air 200	BB-727	Alpha Technologies Inc./Blue Yonder Holding, Bellingham, Wa.	N1955E
N522WD	80	Conquest 1	425-0015	Grand Junction Aircraft Sales Inc., Grand Junction, Co.	N40RD
N523CJ	73	King Air E90	LW-40	Macon Aero Connections LLC. Macon, Ga.	N155CG
N523GM	98	King Air B200	BB-1598	Elliott Aviation Aircraft Sales Inc. Des Moines Ia.	N706TA
N523JL	03	Pilatus PC-12/45	523	Tradewind Aviation LLC. White Plains, NY.	HB-FRY
N523PD	79	PA-31T Cheyenne 1	7904044	Dennis Rulewicz, Jackson, Mi.	N23569
N523TH	89	King Air C90A	LJ-1219	Emma LLC. Waukee, Ia.	N367EA
N524AM	79	PA-31T Cheyenne II	7920039	Fairchild Holding SA. Geneva, Switzerland.	3A-MTD
N524CE	01	Pilatus PC-12/45	410	High Tech Floors LLC., White Marsh, Md.	N524CM
N524FS	80	King Air 200	BB-590	WFBNW NA/Littleton Overseas Inc. BVI.	F-GIDV
N524GM	01	King Air B200C	BL-142	N840GR Inc. Wilmington, De.	(N840GR)
N524GT	03	Pilatus PC-12/45	524	Airport Equipment Rentals Inc. Fairbanks, Ak.	HB-FRZ
N524MR	79	King Air 200	BB-524	Surrey Lodge LLC. Branson, Mo.	D-ILPC
N524PM	01	PA-46-500TP Meridian	4697024	Avion Equipment Leasing LLC, Helena Mt.	
N524TS	88	King Air C90A	LJ-1187	Flying Partners LLC. Baton Rouge, La.	(N15PT)
N525BC	99	King Air 350	FL-252	WCAT Air Corp. Midland, Tx.	N3252B
N525DF	00	King Air 350	FL-306	Ventex Operating Corp. Nocona, Tx.	

Reg	Yr	Type	c/n	Owner/Operator	Prev Regn
N525JK	67	King Air A90	LJ-305	Dynamic Aviation Group Inc. Bridgewater, Va.	N732NM
N525SK	83	King Air B200	BB-1148	ORRA Enterprises Inc. Wilmington, De.	N345MB
N525ZS	71	King Air 100	B-66	Unied States Dept. of Justice, Landover Md. (Seized)	HP-1411
N526RR	67	King Air A90	LJ-263	Aviation One of Florida Inc. Port Orange, Fl.	N526BT
N527AF	70	Mitsubishi MU-2G	527	Air 1st Aviation Companies Inc. Aiken, SC.	VH-MNU
N527CH	81	King Air B200	BB-899	Mitchell Patman Holdings LLC. Irving, Tx.	N1KA
N527DM	07	Pilatus PC-12/47	813	Aircraft Guaranty Corp., Houston, Tx.	HB-FRC
N527MA	01	PA-46-500TP Meridian	4697127	David Smith, Wadsworth, Oh.	
N527PB	03	Pilatus PC-12/45	527	Special Exploration Co. Stillwater, Ok.	HB-FSC
N527SE	07	King Air C90GT	LJ-1850	CB Aviation Inc., Gainesville, Fl.	
N528AF	70	Mitsubishi MU-2G	528	Air 1st Aviation Companies Inc. Aiken, SC.	VH-UZB
N528AM	85	King Air 300	FA-59	Sause Brothers Ocean Towing Co. Coos Bay, Or.	N7233U
N528EJ	03	Pilatus PC-12/45	528	EJ Leasing LLC. Fargo, ND.	HB-FSD
N528NA	61	King Air UC-12B	BJ-3	NASA, Hampton, Va.	161187
N528PM	05	Pilatus PC-12/45	653	Hypro Aviation LLC, Waterford Wi.	HB-FSO
N529JM	97	King Air C90B	LJ-1470	Mill Air Inc. Greenwich, Ct.	N118MB
N529NA	83	King Air B200	BB-1091	NASA Langley Research Center, Hampton, Va.	N9NA
N529PM	01	PA-46-500TP Meridian	4697029	Hi-Sonic Inc., Olathe, Ks.	
N529PS	03	Pilatus PC-12/45	529	Westgate Aviation LLC. Orlando, Fl.	N529PB
N530CH	92	King Air C90B	LJ-1322	DTR Ventures Inc. Windermere, Fl.	N500QT
N530HP	01	PA-46-500TP Meridian	4697101	High Performance Aircraft Inc., El Cajon, Ca.	
N530WC	03	Pilatus PC-12/45	530	Thursday Resources LLC. Tulsa, Ok.	HB-FSK
N531CB	83	King Air B100	BE-133	Big River Aviation LLC/Wood & Associates, Bonne Terre, Mo.	N531CM
N531CS	72	King Air C90	LJ-549	Southeastern Aviation LLC. Greensboro, NC.	N600DJ
N531MP	07	Pilatus PC-12/47	808	Passmore Aviation LLC., Pryor, Ok.	N808PC
N531SC	07	King Air B200GT	BY-20	Saddle Creek Corporation, Lakeland Fl.	
N531SW	99	King Air B200	BB-1656	Southwest Aircraft Charter LC. Mesa, Az.	N706TA
N532SW	85	King Air B200	BB-1228	Crown Aviation LLC/Bingham Equipment Co. Mesa, Az.	N85GA
N533GP	06	King Air 350	FL-507	Georgia-Pacific Corp., Atlanta, Ga.	
N533M	81	Conquest II	441-0222	Terra Diamond Industrial Inc. Salt Lake City, Ut.	N500GM
N533P	87	King Air B200	BB-1278	C W Parker Aviation LLC. Pinehurst, NC.	D-IAIR
N533PC	03	Pilatus PC-12/45	533	Chamberlain Development LLC. Tempe, Az.	HB-FSG
N533SS	76	King Air E90	LW-197	Sun South Aviation LLC., Oxford, Ms.	N228RA
N534M	98	Beech 1900D	UE-333	Menard Inc. Eau Claire, Wi.	N23235
N535BB	04	Pilatus PC-12/45	596	Flying Bar B LLC. Provo, Ut.	HB-FRH
N535JR	05	PA-46-500TP Meridian	4697253	Richbuilt Construction LLC. Boca Raton, Fl.	N253SE
N535KC	07	PA-46-500TP Meridian	4697335	Piper Aircraft Inc. Vero Beach, Fl.	
N535M	98	Beech 1900D	UE-332	Menard Inc. Eau Claire, Wi.	
N535MJ	04	Pilatus PC-12/45	535	Oxford Hill LLC. Westminster, Md.	HB-FSI
N535PN	88	King Air 300	FA-152	Bennie Air Inc., Phoenix, Az.	N20EW
N535WM	75	Mitsubishi MU-2L	655	Bankair Inc. West Columbia, SC.	N535MA
N536BW	04	King Air 350	FL-432	B & W Consulting LLC. Baton Rouge, La.	
N536M	98	Beech 1900D	UE-334	Menard Inc. Eau Claire, Wi.	
N536MR	07	King Air 350	FL-536	CFS Air LLC/Martin Product Sales LLC., Kilgore, Tx.	
N536RB	04	King Air B200	BB-1879	Paragon n'Flite LLC. Charleston, WV.	N36579
N537PC	04	Pilatus PC-12/45	537	Royce Leasing LLC. Indian Wells, Ca.	HB-F..
N538AM	86	King Air/Catpass 250	FA-107	Changer Inc. Greeneville, SC.	N538AS
N538BH	05	Pilatus PC-12/45	626	Mallard Haven LLC. Church Creek, Md.	HB-FRT
N539DP	65	King Air 90	LJ-53	Jorge Lopez, Caracas/Aircraft Guaranty LLC	N818MS
N540CB	87	King Air 300	FA-135	Pepco Inc. Rocky Mount, NC.	HB-GHY
N540GA	98	King Air C90B	LJ-1557	State of Georgia DoT, Atlanta, Ga.	N557SA
N540GC	81	Conquest 1	425-0026	Air Leb LLC. Tucson, Az.	N540GA
N540MA	01	King Air B200	BB-1765	EDT Towage Inc.NYC.	N3205Z
N540SP	73	King Air C-12C	BC-5	Baja Air Inc. California City, Ca.	73-22254
N540WJ	80	King Air F90	LA-54	World Jet Inc. Fort Lauderdale, Fl.	HK-2484
N541AA	82	King Air C90-1	LJ-1041	Platinum 23 Leasing Co. Fort Lauderdale, Fl.	PT-OVN
N541MC	67	King Air A90	LM-39	Jefferson County, Beaumont, Tx.	N7043Y
N541PB	04	Pilatus PC-12/45	541	Bureau of Immigration & Customs Enforcement, Washington, DC.	HB-FSO
N541RK	06	King Air C90GT	LJ-1779	Distributors Development, Schofield, Wi.	
N541SC	87	King Air 300	FA-138	King Air N541SC LLC. Los Banos, Ca.	N30757
N542KA	79	King Air 200	BB-542	Landmark Aviation LLC. Flowood, Ms.	N978GA
N543GA	99	King Air C90B	LJ-1558	State of Georgia DoT, Atlanta, Ga.	
N543GC	81	Conquest 1	425-0101	Kolberg-Pioneer Inc. Yankton SD.	N543GA
N543HC	00	King Air C90B	LJ-1620	Burk Royalty Co. Wichita Falls, Tx.	N3220E
N543JF	78	Mitsubishi MU-2P	389SA	Triple J Flying Inc. Olds, Ia.	N400ES

Reg	Yr Type	c/n	Owner/Operator	Prev Regn
N543PB	04 Pilatus PC-12/45	543	PC-12 LLC. Knoxville, Tn.	HB-FSQ
N543S	66 680T Turbo Commander	1556-14	Mark Lundell,Paradise Valley Az. (Sold?)	
N544AF	71 Mitsubishi MU-2G	544	Air 1st Aviation Companies Inc. Aiken, SC.	VH-KOF
N544CB	81 MU-2 Marquise	1536SA	Herrick & Co. Telluride, Co.	N157GA
N544GA	82 Gulfstream 900	15015	State of Georgia DoT, Atlanta, Ga.	N27MW
N544P	87 King Air B200	BB-1265	Precision Concrete Construction Inc. Alpharetta, Ga.	D-IAKK
N544UP	83 SA-227AT Merlin 4C	AT-544	Ameriflight Inc. Burbank, Ca.	N68TA
N545C	01 King Air C90B	LJ-1654	Executive Beechcraft Inc. Kansas City, Mo.	
N545KA	07 King Air 350	FL-545	Equipment Management Systems LLC, Ridgement Ms.	
N545LC	80 King Air 200	BB-339	Charlie Romeo LLC. Little Rock, Ar.	N339AJ
N546C	04 King Air C90B	LJ-1723	Farm Coast Credit, Visalia, Ca.	
N546MA	07 PA-46-500TP Meridian	4697331	Piper Aircraft Inc. Vero Beach, Fl.	
N546PB	04 Pilatus PC-12/45	546	Mountain State Equipment Leasing, Wodland Park, Co.	HB-FSL
N547AF	04 Pilatus PC-12/45	547	Alpha Flying Inc. Manchester, NH.	HB-FSS
N547GA	99 King Air C90B	LJ-1559	State of Georgia DoT, Atlanta, Ga.	
N547GC	81 Conquest 1	425-0084	Norton Packaging Inc. Hayward, Ca.	N547GA
N547TA	77 Mitsubishi MU-2P	364SA	Weissenburger Aviation Inc. Clive, Ia.	N749MA
N548UP	83 SA-227AT Merlin 4C	AT-548	Ameriflight Inc. Burbank, Ca.	N548SA
N549BR	79 King Air C90	LJ-809	Kendzicky Aviation LLC. Whitmore Lake, Mi.	N922DT
N549GA	00 King Air C90B	LJ-1613	State of Georgia DoT, Atlanta, Ga.	N5013J
N550BE	73 SA-226T Merlin 3	T-224	Cowboy Aviation LLC. Longmont, Co.	N5307M
N550GL	81 King Air 200	BB-781	The Sponsorship Services Group Inc. Archdale, NC.	N37NC
N550MM	81 Cheyenne II-XL	8166017	Lima Alpha Corp. Allentown, Pa.	N2536Y
N550SW	04 King Air C90B	LJ-1700	Chieftain LLC. Islamorada, Fl.	N923P
N551JL	81 King Air 200	BB-788	White Barron LLC/Post Warren Barker Law Firm, Pratt, Ks.	
N551TP	00 King Air 350	FL-303	Tecumseh Products Co. Tecumseh, Mi.	(N75WP)
N551VB	06 King Air 350	FL-503	Auto Central Services Inc., Sarasota, Fl.	N37026
N552JF	00 TBM 700B	184	Feat LLC., Hattiesburg, Ms.	N527TS
N552TP	00 King Air 350	FL-281	Blue Heron Aviation Inc., Longview, Wa.	
N552TT	83 King Air B200	BB-1159	Sunshine Airways of N O LLC. Metairie, La.	(D-IRUS)
N553AM	81 Conquest II	441-0219	Anderson Merchandisers Inc. Amarillo, Tx.	N555WA
N553CA	03 Pilatus PC-12/45	553	Pinnacle Jets LLC. Debary, Fl.	HB-FSV
N553CL	06 King Air 350	FL-504	Luck Stone Corporation, Manakin Sabot, Va.	N37040
N554CF	73 King Air E90	LW-66	Sky Clad Inc. Tampa Fl.	(N106TB)
N554VR	99 Pilatus PC-12/45	288	Cinco Aviation LLC, Los Angeles, Ca.	N777JX
N555AL	90 King Air C90A	LJ-1268	Data Systems International Inc. Overland Park, Ks.	N525P
N555AM	73 SA-226T Merlin 3	T-227	Edgewater Ventures LLC. Santa Monica, Ca.	N142NR
N555AT	81 PA-31T Cheyenne 1	8104054	MARKAY Enterprises Ltd. Wilmington, De.	N818SW
N555C	68 Mitsubishi MU-2F	129	ISD, Rivervalls, Mn.	N555S
N555CK	76 King Air C90	LJ-677	Schroeder Measurement Technologies, Dunedin, Fl.	N555WF
N555DX	85 King Air 300	FA-65	Gramling Brothers Inc./G3 LLC., Gramling, SC.	N332CP
N555EW	99 Pilatus PC-12/45	271	Safe Landings LLC. Billings, Mt.	HB-FSP
N555FD	90 King Air 300	FA-213	Moga Management LLC. Fairfax, Va.	N83RH
N555FT	80 Conquest II	441-0124	S & J Operating Co. Wichita Falls, Tx.	N2624N
N555FW	77 King Air E90	LW-248	Justin Brands Inc. Fort Worth, Tx.	N9FC
N555HJ	94 King Air C90B	LJ-1378	HJS Transport LLC. Newark, De.	N3083K
N555MS	80 King Air C90	LJ-872	Mott Oil Inc. Bessemer, Al.	N6668U
N555MT	77 Rockwell 690B	11418	Taylor Aircraft Holdings Inc. Short Hills, NJ.	N773CA
N555PE	04 Pilatus PC-12/45	555	Lindbergh Corp. Portland, Or.	HB-FSW
N555PM	76 PA-31T Cheyenne II	7620028	PH Aviation/Impact Fulfillment Services Inc. Burlington, NC.	N531PT
N555TZ	82 King Air F90	LA-189	Bobby Lloyd Inc/Aircraft FM LLC. Wichita Falls, Tx.	N107AJ
N555VE	79 Rockwell 690B	11546	Aircraft Guaranty Title LLC. Houston, Tx./Italian Coffee	YV1540
N555VW	93 King Air C90B	LJ-1330	John W Knapp, Chiloquin, Or.	N266F
N555WQ	00 King Air 350	FL-287	Iron Eagle Inc. Fayetteville, Ar.	N555WF
N555ZA	91 King Air 350	FL-48	Sunstream Air LLC. Portland, Or.	N309M
N556BA	97 King Air B200	BB-1556	Joint Advisory Services LLC. Myrtle Beach, SC.	YV-1031CP
N556HL	04 Pilatus PC-12/45	556	Sierra Nevada Corp., Sparks, Nv.	HB-FSX
N556UP	83 SA-227AT Merlin 4C	AT-556	Ameriflight Inc. Burbank, Ca.	N3113B
N557P	02 King Air C90B	LJ-1689	Atlantic Transportation Wilmington, Wilmington, NC.	
N558AC	68 SA-26AT Merlin 2B	T26-144	Haynie Enterprises Inc. Reno, Nv.	N913DM
N558AF	04 Pilatus PC-12/45	558	Alpha Flying Inc. Manchester, NH.	HB-FSY
N558BC	98 King Air 350	FL-223	Chain Electric Company/C-Y Aircraft LLC, Hattiesburg, Ms.	N787JB
N558KA	07 King Air 350	FL-558	Equipment Management Systems LLC, Ridgeland Ms.	
N559CA	01 TBM 700B	213	Fred Parsons, Alexandria, Va.	
N559CG	79 Rockwell 690B	11530	Kaymar SA. Fort Lauderdale, Fl.	N489GA

Reg	Yr Type	c/n	Owner/Operator	Prev Regn
N559PB	04 Pilatus PC-12/45	559	Key Equipment Finance Inc/Lane Airmotive LLC., Lakewood, Co.	HB-FSZ
N560UP	83 SA-227AT Merlin 4C	AT-560	Ameriflight Inc. Burbank, Ca.	N3113A
N561SS	79 King Air 200	BB-464	Horsham Valley Airways Inc., Horsham, Pa.	N79SE
N561ST	04 Pilatus PC-12/45	561	Lexa International Corp. Stamford, Ct.	HB-FQA
N561TC	76 Rockwell 690A	11315	KK Trucking	N34RT
N561UP	83 SA-227AT Merlin 4C	AT-561	Ameriflight Inc. Burbank, Ca.	N3113F
N562HP	03 PA-46-500TP Meridian	4697139	Steve & Carlota Assocs (SCA) LLC. Coronado, Ca.	
N562NA	97 Pilatus PC-12	174	Native Air Services Inc. Mesa, Az.	N174PC
N562PB	04 Pilatus PC-12/45	562	West Branch Air Services LLC. Alger, Mi.	HB-FQB
N563TM	04 Pilatus PC-12/45	563	Tight Wire LLC., San Antonio, Tx.	HB-FQC
N564AC	80 Conquest II	441-0147	Erickson Air Crane Inc. Central Point, Or.	N999BE
N564BC	07 King Air 350	FL-577	Hawker Beechcraft Corp., Wichita, Ks.	
N564CA	79 King Air B100	BE-58	Carver Aero Inc. Davenport, Ia.	N100P
N564KA	07 King Air 350	FL-564	RSE Company of Delaware Inc. Miami Fl.	
N565C	03 PA-46-500TP Meridian	4697173	Timeless Inc., Wilmington, De.	
N565HP	04 PA-46-500TP Meridian	4697211	Dana P Brent, Yuma, Az.	N777FX
N565M	85 Beech 1900C	UB-43	Raytheon Aircraft Co. Wichita, Ks.	N34GT
N566KA	89 King Air 300	FA-201	KCK Services LLC/Klinger Companies Inc., Sioux City, Ia.	N566KB
N566NA	97 King Air B200	BB-1566	Gulf Island Fabrication Inc. Houman, La.	LV-WYC
N566TC	83 King Air B200	BB-1145	Brokers International Ltd. Panora, Ia.	C6-TTC
N566UP	83 SA-227AT Merlin 4C	AT-566	Ameriflight Inc. Burbank, Ca.	N3113N
N567FH	04 Pilatus PC-12/45	567	Island Air Inc. Kalsipell, Mt.	HB-FQF
N567GJ	74 King Air E90	LW-95	Double Rainbow LLC/Crown Corr Inc. Gary, In.	OY-CFO
N567R	73 Rockwell 690	11051	Irvin Marx Jr. Dallas, Tx.	N500R
N567US	98 King Air B200	BB-1634	Arrow Trading Inc. Fort Lauderdale, Fl.	N567PK
N568HP	07 PA-46-500TP Meridian	4697306	RA Lotter Insurance Marketing Inc., Newport Beach, Ca.	
N568K	81 King Air B100	BE-106	SRI General Partner LLC. Houston, Tx.	(N59SS)
N568SA	99 King Air C90B	LJ-1568	S & S Seeds Inc. Carpinteria, Ca.	
N569AF	04 Pilatus PC-12/45	569	Alpha Flying, Manchester, NH.	HB-FQG
N569SG	82 King Air B200	BB-1084	Engineering & Professional Services Inc. Yorklyn, De.	N569SC
N569UP	83 SA-227AT Merlin 4C	AT-569	Ameriflight Inc. Burbank, Ca.	N31134
N571PC	04 Pilatus PC-12/45	571	D & A Investments LLC. Albuquerque, NM.	HB-FQI
N572BB	92 King Air C90B	LJ-1320	BBI Inc-Blue Beacon International Inc. Salina, Ks.	(N65GE)
N572M	78 King Air 200	BB-398	Carpau Corp. Tarpon Springs, Fl.	N929DM
N572PC	04 Pilatus PC-12/45	572	Ridge Air LLC. Lincoln, Ne.	HB-FQJ
N573G	82 SA-227AT Merlin 4C	AT-446	Ameriflight Inc. Burbank, Ca.	N3008L
N573MA	69 Mitsubishi MU-2F	162	Bohlke International Airways Inc. St Croix, USVI.	N875Q
N575C	71 King Air C90	LJ-532	David Lilly, Alentown, Pa.	N57SC
N575MX	05 King Air 350	FL-445	Queen Street PC-12 LLC. Tempe, Az.	N555ZT
N575PC	04 Pilatus PC-12/45	575	SDL Aero LLC., Phoenix, Az.	HB-FQL
N575RA	80 King Air 200	BB-575	J L M Air LLC. Clearwater, Fl.	D-IFUN
N576RG	04 Pilatus PC-12/45	576	Bob Air Acquisitions LLC. Concord, Ma.	HB-FQM
N577BE	85 King Air 300	FA-66	Ellsworth Management LLC. Steamboat Springs, Co.	N577BA
N577BF	04 Pilatus PC-12/45	577	Geoduck Aviation LLC. Seattle, Wa.	HB-FQN
N577D	70 King Air 100	B-22	Vintage Props & Jets Inc. New Smyrna Beach, Fl.	N577L
N577DC	67 King Air A90	LJ-308	Cosco Aviation Services, Crestview, Fl.	N970GA
N577PW	84 Conquest 1	425-0194	LA Aviation LLC. Daytona Beach, Fl.	N12214
N578DC	04 Pilatus PC-12/45	570	Nicholas Elliott & Jordan LLC. Tampa, Fl.	N570DC
N579MC	98 King Air 350	FL-230	Deer Horn Aviation LC. Midland, Tx.	N3059F
N579NC	95 TBM 700	102	NCC Aero LLC. Wilmington, De.	N88WF
N579PS	70 King Air B90	LJ-496	Missouri Aviation Partner/River Enterprises Inc Columbia, Mo	N878K
N580AF	73 Mitsubishi MU-2J	580	Intercontinental Jet Inc., Tulsa, Ok.	CP-2390
N580BK	82 King Air B200	BB-1000	John Newcombe Enterprises Inc. Blacksburg, Va.	N74RN
N580HP	07 PA-46-500TP Meridian	4697329	Robert J Reiger, Avila Beach Ca.	
N580PA	82 King Air F90	LA-158	Starfleet Marine Transportation, Mt Pleasant, SC.	N122SC
N580RA	73 King Air C90	LJ-580	Kelley Aviation Inc. Deer Park, Il.	(F-GFYI)
N580S	79 King Air B100	BE-77	Bott Radio Network Inc. Gravois Mills, Mo.	N55US
N581B	84 King Air C90A	LJ-1170	J G Boswell Co. Burbank, Ca.	N4131S
N581PC	04 Pilatus PC-12/45	581	Sierra Nevada Corp., Sparks, Nv.	HB-FQY
N581RJ	80 King Air F90	LA-14	AirMed Inc. Agusta Ga.	N205BC
N582C	03 TBM 700C2	274	Islander Aviation Inc., Wilmington, De.	
N582DT	04 Pilatus PC-12/45	582	CNB Aviation LLC., Miami, Fl.	HB-FQS
N582JF	74 SA-226AT Merlin 4A	AT-027	Jere Fabick, Milwaukee, Wi.	N824MD
N582SE	04 PA-46-500TP Meridian	4697188	Jerome V Banicki, Tempe, Az.	
N584JV	04 Pilatus PC-12/45	584	PLS Leasing LLC, Fargo Nd.	HB-FQS
Reg	Yr Type	c/n	Owner/Operator	Prev Regn

Reg	Yr	Type	c/n	Owner/Operator	Prev Regn
❏ N585CE	85	King Air B200	BB-1194	Ohmann Aviation Inc./Langley Payroll Plus Inc. Liberty, NC.	HK-4297X
❏ N585PA	81	Conquest 1	425-0047	Eagles Ridge NC LLC. Stuart, Fl.	5Y-KXU
❏ N585R	88	King Air C90A	LJ-1169	Baron Leasing Corp. Cresco, Pa.	N30844
❏ N586BC	85	King Air B200	BB-1223	Blue Cross & Blue Shield, Chattanooga, Tn.	N7231M
❏ N586DV	79	Rockwell 690B	11553	VAC1 LLC, Las Vegas Nv.	N27VG
❏ N586PB	04	Pilatus PC-12/45	586	Herin Aviation LLC., Corpus Christi, Tx.	HB-FQW
❏ N586TC	75	King Air C90	LJ-653	Focus Enterprises Inc. Valparaiso, In.	N585TC
❏ N586UC	83	King Air B200	BB-1118	PTS Aircraft Sales LLC. Canton, Oh.	N913PG
❏ N587M	68	King Air B90	LJ-361	CAB Air Inc. Cedartown, Ga.	N530M
❏ N587PB	95	King Air C90B	LJ-1408	Holmes II Excavation Inc. Munford, Al.	N749RN
❏ N588KC	04	Pilatus PC-12/45	588	RichSmith Air LLC. Little Rock, Ar.	HB-FRA
❏ N588KM	07	King Air C90GT	LJ-1871	Hawker Beechcraft Corp., Wichita, Ks.	
❏ N588SA	99	King Air C90B	LJ-1588	Eagle Air Med Corp. Blanding, Ut.	
❏ N588XJ	98	King Air C90B	LJ-1530	Harmon Foods Inc. Jacksonville, Fl.	
❏ N589AC	04	Pilatus PC-12/45	589	AC2 Aviation LLC. Livonia, Mi.	HB-FRB
❏ N589H	91	P-180 Avanti	1010	Western Airways Inc. Sugar Land, Tx.	(N1JW)
❏ N590GT	05	King Air C90GT	LJ-1759	CDM Leasing LLC. Shelby Township, Mi.	
❏ N590SA	68	King Air B90	LJ-401	X-Press Charter Services Inc. Longview, Tx.	N500NA
❏ N591AF	04	Pilatus PC-12/45	591	Alpha Flying Inc. Manchester, NH.	HB-F..
❏ N592Q	85	Conquest II	441-0361	Kelley Air Inc. Burlington, Ma.	N592G
❏ N593BJ	77	King Air 200	BB-297	H & O Aviation LLC. Wheeling, WV.	P2-IAH
❏ N593DJ	77	King Air 200	BB-277	SkyShare IV LLC. Fort Lauderdale, Fl.	N200AP
❏ N593MA	92	King Air 350	FL-68	McCardell Properties Inc. Auburn Hills, Mi.	N877V
❏ N593PC	04	Pilatus PC-12/45	593	U S Dept of Homeland Security, Washington, DC.	HB-FRE
❏ N594WA	04	Pilatus PC-12/45	594	Cari Consulting LLC., Covington, La.	HB-FRF
❏ N595TM	90	King Air C90A	LJ-1255	M & M Aero Group LLC., Easley, SC.	N55495
❏ N596CU	77	King Air C90	LJ-721	First Air Group Inc., Horseheads, NY.	N111AA
❏ N597CH	04	Pilatus PC-12/45	597	MSP LLC. Naples, Fl.	HB-F..
❏ N597MM	80	King Air 200	BB-720	SCT Corp/Sargent Corp. Stillwater, Me.	N208SW
❏ N597P	00	King Air C90B	LJ-1597	Flyby Aviation LLC. Wilmington, De.	LV-ZTP
❏ N598AC	92	King Air 350	FL-78	Iowa Land & Buidling Co. Cedar Rapids, Ia.	N551ES
❏ N598AT	01	PA-46-500TP Meridian	4697059	Advanced Technology Services Inc. Peoria, Il.	N84SH
❏ N598C	06	PA-46-500TP Meridian	4697275	Meridian Alliance LLC. Spring Valley, Ca.	
❏ N598MM	04	Pilatus PC-12/45	598	Macanair LLC. Edmonds, Wa.	N598HC
❏ N599HL	06	King Air C90GT	LJ-1762	Tigerpaw Investments LLC. Lakeland, Fl.	N762GT
❏ N599MC	07	King Air C90GT	LJ-1863	Hawker Beechcraft Corp., Wichita, Ks.	
❏ N599PB	04	Pilatus PC-12/45	599	Gen-Log LLC. Wilmington, De.	HB-F..
❏ N600AC	76	King Air E90	LW-185	N600AC LLC. Tucson, Az.	
❏ N600BF	67	King Air A90	LJ-193	James Vecchio, Grand Prairie, Tx.	N600BW
❏ N600CB	91	King Air 350	FL-38	Basha's - Chapman Group, Chandler, Az.	N350SR
❏ N600CX	74	King Air E90	LW-43	Michael Miller & Associates Inc. Alexandria, Va.	D-INAC
❏ N600FE	81	King Air C90	LJ-935	Richmor Aviation Inc. Hudson, NY.	N600FL
❏ N600KA	88	King Air 300	FA-143	Trend Service Inc., Lafayette, La.	N300KA
❏ N600KP	06	Pilatus PC-12/47	700	Katz Air Holdings LLC. Manhattan Beach, Ca.	HB-FQS
❏ N600MM	80	Gulfstream 980	95029	Bush Field Aircraft Co. Augusta, Ga.	(N700MM)
❏ N600RL	01	King Air B200	BB-1800	RML Aircraft Services LLC. Wichita, Ks.	N314FW
❏ N600WA	80	King Air F90	LA-71	Virginia Air Inc., Carson City, Nv.	(N576P)
❏ N600WM	80	King Air F90	LA-75	Cam-Trans Inc. La Crescenta, Ca.	N3686B
❏ N600WS	78	Rockwell 690B	11435	Sunbelt Communications Co. Las Vegas, Nv.	N200M
❏ N600WY	03	Pilatus PC-12/45	526	M & N Aviation, Casper, Wy.	N269AF
❏ N600YE	06	PA-46-500TP Meridian	4697250	York Excavating Inc., York, Pa.	N3120L
❏ N601BM	97	Pilatus PC-12	181	Butler Machinery Co. Fargo, Nd.	HB-FSB
❏ N601DM	79	King Air C90	LJ-825	Weisbrod & Weisbrod LLP. Dallas, Tx.	N11LS
❏ N601HT	00	Pilatus PC-12/45	337	CIGI Direct Insurance Services Inc. Salida, Co.	HB-FSJ
❏ N601JT	80	SA-226T Merlin 3B	T-319	Excalibur International Aviation Inc. Houston, Tx.	N808LB
❏ N601LM	72	King Air A100	B-116	David B Fields, Midland, Tx.	N100GV
❏ N601PC	76	King Air A100	B-225	Leavitt Group Enterprises Inc. Cedar City, Ut.	N723W
❏ N601SD	74	Mitsubishi MU-2J	610	Jefferson County Sheriff's Office, Beaumont, Tx.	N92ST
❏ N601TA	66	King Air A90	LJ-120	Turbine Power Inc. Bridgewater, Va.	N601T
❏ N601WT	82	Gulfstream 900	15016	Electroair Inc., Sodus, NY.	N950TJ
❏ N602BM	05	Pilatus PC-12/45	664	Butler Machinery Co. Fargo, Nd.	HB-FSY
❏ N602CN	81	King Air B200	BB-872	Chickasaw Nation, Ada, Ok.	N872BA
❏ N603PA	68	King Air B90	LJ-403	Blue Water Aircraft Inc. Wilmington, De.	(N603RE)
❏ N603TA	98	King Air B200	BB-1623	FF Aviation Investments LLC/OFI Property, Ventura, Ca.	(N250AJ)
❏ N603WM	89	King Air 300	FA-198	OneBeacon Insurance Co. Hanover, NH.	N16TB

Reg	Yr	Type	c/n	Owner/Operator	Prev Regn
N604MJ	02	King Air B200	BB-1801	Air Cana Corp. Santo Domingo, Dominican Republic.	N602MJ
N604RK	92	King Air B200	BB-1429	F & T Ventures LP. Odessa, Tx.	N80BT
N604WP	04	Pilatus PC-12/45	604	Rooney Consulting & Aviation Inc. Bandon, Or.	HB-FQG
N605EA	81	King Air F90	LA-129	Elliott Aviation Aircraft Sales Inc. Des Moines, Ia.	3A-MON
N605PC	04	Pilatus PC-12/45	605	Pacific Cataract and Laser Institute Inc., Chehalis, Wa.	(N705CC)
N605TQ	00	Pilatus PC-12/45	320	Tomcat Air LLP. Redington Beach, Fl.	N605TC
N606AJ	86	King Air B200	BB-1257	Aircraft Technical Service Inc. Van Nuys, Ca.	G-IJJB
N606DW	81	PA-31T Cheyenne II	8120038	D & L Aviation LLC. Phoenix, Az.	N300PV
N606WC	04	PA-46-500TP Meridian	4697176	E S Wagner Co. Oregon, Oh.	N164DB
N607AF	05	Pilatus PC-12/45	607	Alpha Flying Inc. Manchester, NH.	HB-F..
N607DK	81	King Air F90	LA-140	Trinity Lighting Inc. Jonesboro, Ar.	N190GM
N607MA	01	PA-46-500TP Meridian	4697107	John Moss, Wayland, Ma.	
N608SM	06	Pilatus PC-12/47	734	N412DP LLC., Huntersville, NC.	HB-FRS
N609BG	05	King Air 350	FL-468	Rensslear Iron & Steel Inc. Rensselaer, NY.	N6048L
N609SA	00	King Air C90B	LJ-1609	Seven Rivers Inc. Carlsbad, NM.	
N609TA	00	King Air B200	BB-1725	Comprehensive Logistics LLC/Wellcare Health Plans, Tampa.	
N609TW	06	Pilatus PC-12/47	712	D Consulting LLC. Westlake Village, Ca.	HB-FRB
N610CA	80	MU-2 Marquise	788SA	Bankair Inc. West Columbia, SC.	N277MA
N610GH	94	Pilatus PC-12	103	EPPS Air Service Inc. Atlanta, Ga.	HB-FOD
N610NK	05	Pilatus PC-12/45	610	Enkay Corp. Shreveport, La.	HB-FRJ
N610P	75	PA-31T Cheyenne II	7620002	Forrest Wood, Flippin, Ar.	N54977
N610RM	01	King Air B200	BB-1761	Barnstormers Aviation LLC. Eaton, Co.	N459DF
N610SC	06	King Air C90GT	LJ-1817	Southern Container Management Corp., Hauppauge, NY.	N610SC
N610TA	98	King Air B200	BB-1609	North Flight Inc. Traverse City, Mi.	(N260AJ)
N611	82	Gulfstream 900	15018	Department of the Interior, Boise, Id.	N5886N
N611AY	73	King Air C90	LJ-601	Frami Corp. Wilmington, De.	N99CD
N611DD	79	King Air C90	LJ-806	3030 Ltd. Allentown, Pa.	N105CG
N611GT	07	P-180 Avanti II	1148	Piaggio America Inc. West Palm Beach, Fl.	
N611MA	05	TBM 700C2	330	Glenn Abbett, La Crosse, In.	
N611ND	66	King Air A90	LM-11	K & K Aircraft Inc. Bridgewater, Va.	(N49K)
N611R	77	King Air E90	LW-244	Zim Air LLC. Okoboji, Ia.	OY-ASU
N611RR	80	PA-31T Cheyenne 1	8004006	Yellow Transportation services Inc. Milwaukee Wi.	(N611RP)
N612DT	60	Gulfstream 1	52	Mission Air Services LLC. San Antonio, Tx.	(N18TZ)
N612J	03	Pilatus PC-12/45	494	Kendall Jackson Wine Estates, Medford, Or.	N494PC
N612KC	97	Pilatus PC-12	173	TTX Air LLC, Sturgeon Bay Wi.	N173KS
N612SA	76	King Air C-12C	BC-29	Stanford & Associates Inc. Fredricksburg, Va.	(N42J)
N613BA	04	King Air 350	FL-396	Radar Acquisitions LLC, Concord Ma.	N351CR
N613BR	65	King Air 90	LJ-9	Alcovy Mountain Venture LLC. Monroe, Ga.	N649MC
N613HC	77	PA-31T Cheyenne II	7720053	Cross Island Cruising Inc. Dover, De.	(N779SW)
N613NA	98	Pilatus PC-12/45	197	Native Air Services Inc. Mesa, Az.	N197PC
N613RF	84	King Air C90A	LJ-1068	BATT Holdings LLC. Shreveport, La.	N666PC
N613TA	97	King Air B200	BB-1581	Townley Manufacturing Co. Candler, Fl.	N12MY
N614LD	05	Pilatus PC-12/45	614	Air Travel LLC. Oak Island, NC.	HB-FRQ
N614ML	92	King Air 350	FL-84	Oliver Aviation Inc/Love Box Co. Wichita, Ks.	N8084J
N614SA	00	King Air C90B	LJ-1614	Aircraft Guaranty Title LLC. Houston, Tx. (trustor ?).	
N615AA	67	King Air A90	LJ-298	McGee Industries LLC. Ridgecrest, Ca.	N788W
N615C	59	Gulfstream 1	16	Erin Miel Inc .Las Vegas, Nv.	N202HA
N615DP	76	Rockwell 690A	11317	Ray Aircraft Leasing LLC. Tuscaloosa, Al.	N615
N615SB	78	Rockwell 690B	11457	Clackamas Corner LLC. Lake Oswego, Or.	N691CP
N616EL	05	Pilatus PC-12/45	616	Empire LLC. Spokane, Wa.	HB-FRN
N616GB	81	King Air 200	BB-752	Business Aviation Services, Sioux Falls, SD	N300QW
N616MG	81	Conquest 1	425-0087	MidAir Pacific LLC. Eugene, Or.	N616CG
N616PS	80	SA-226T Merlin 3B	T-316	Valley River Leasing Inc., Murphy, NC.	N51DA
N617BB	70	Mitsubishi MU-2G	522	HDL Research Lab Inc. Brenham, Tx.	N147MA
N617DW	80	PA-31T Cheyenne 1	8004042	Abraham Melawer, Houston, Tx.	(N612AM)
N617KM	85	King Air C90A	LJ-1095	Carmel Aviation Inc., Las Vegas, Nv.	N850CE
N617MM	99	King Air C90B	LJ-1587	Eagle Air Med Corp. Blanding, Ut.	
N618	90	King Air B200	BB-1378	U S Department of the Interior, Boise, Id.	N5637Y
N618HG	07	King Air C90GT	LJ-1831	George D Hudgins, Nacogdoches, Tx.	N831EB
N618JL	05	Pilatus PC-12/45	618	Open Skies LLC. Mercer Island, Wa.	HB-FRR
N618JX	83	BAe Jetstream 31	618	KSC Enterprises Inc., Lake Mary, Fl.	N820JS
N618MA	05	PA-46-500TP Meridian	4697218	Differential Leasing LLC. Newark, De.	
N618RD	78	King Air E90	LW-301	Kyle N. Deaver, Waco, Tx.	N550P
N618ST	07	PA-46-500TP Meridian	4697318	Ascendancy Aviation LLC., Merritt Island, Fl.	
N618SW	81	Cheyenne II-XL	8166036	Hilton Development Corp. Rapid City, SD.	

Reg	Yr	Type	c/n	Owner/Operator	Prev Regn
N619AF	05	Pilatus PC-12/45	619	Alpha Flying Inc. Manchester, NH.	HB-F..
N619SH	05	King Air C90B	LJ-1737	WSC Leasing LLC/Blue Beacon International, Salina, Ks.	N36937
N620DB	79	PA-31T Cheyenne II	7920055	ALCO Plane LLC. Dover, De.	N23407
N620WA	05	Pilatus PC-12/45	620	Peak Aviation LLC. Wilson, Wy.	HB-FRO
N620WE	78	King Air C90	LJ-743	W H Ebert Corp. San Jose, Ca.	N161AC
N621TA	73	Mitsubishi MU-2J	605	BH Air LLC. El Paso, Tx.	XB-ARE
N621TB	68	King Air B90	LJ-334	Jason Tindal, Decatur, Al.	N722TS
N621TD	85	King Air C90A	LJ-1123	El Jefe Aviation Services Inc. Glyndon, Md.	N917BH
N622BB	84	PA-31T Cheyenne 1A	1104012	Wells Dairy Inc. Le Mars, Ia.	N284BB
N622KM	79	King Air 200	BB-491	K & M Equipment Co. Van Nuys, Ca.	N622DC
N622MM	83	Conquest 1	425-0187	Santa Fe Investments Inc. Wilmington, De.	(N425KA)
N622WW	05	Pilatus PC-12/45	622	Walker's Wings LLC. Ketchum, Id.	HB-FQX
N623AC	06	Pilatus PC-12/47	722	Claire Air Leasing Co LLC., Park City, Ut.	N12MC
N623BA	05	Pilatus PC-12/45	623	LMCO, Las Vegas, Nv.	HB-FRS
N623BB	67	King Air A90	LJ-277	Airshares Inc., Petersburg, Va.	N228CF
N623DT	07	King Air C90GT	LJ-1858	D/T Carson Enterprises Inc. Murrieta Ca.	
N623RT	01	TBM 700B	217	TMR Aircraft LLC. Fort Gibson, Ok.	N700ND
N623VP	81	King Air 200	BB-769	HKR&W LLC. Hilton Head Island, SC.	N769AJ
N624AF	05	Pilatus PC-12/45	624	Alpha Flying Inc. Manchester, NH.	HB-F..
N624CB	80	Conquest II	441-0166	Industrials International Inc. St Thomas, USVI.	I-GEFI
N624TS	06	Pilatus PC-12/47	724	Aerotomas LLC. Billings, Mt.	HB-FRK
N625GA	04	King Air B200	BB-1884	B R Consulting Inc. Sedona, Az.	
N625PP	73	King Air E90	LW-58	Pabian Outdoor-Southeast Inc., Gulf Breeze, Fl.	N350AT
N626AR	06	PA-46-500TP Meridian	4697286	Donnellan Aviation Inc., White Plains, NY.	
N626GT	07	King Air B200GT	BY-27	Hawker Beechcraft Corp., Wichita, Ks.	
N626MT	07	Pilatus PC-12/47	820	Retamco Aviation LLC., Roberts, Mt.	HB-FRI
N626SA	71	King Air 100	B-78	ArKo LLC. Lyndon Station, Wi.	RP-C282
N627DB	05	TBM 700C2	328	D A B Constructors Inc. Inglis, Fl.	N700ZC
N627FP	81	King Air B200	BB-928	HHV LLC, Barlett In.	N627FB
N627PC	84	PA-42 Cheyenne IIIA	5501010	De Vries Electric Inc., Pella, Ia.	N627KW
N628DS	82	King Air B200	BB-1013	Superior Air Charter Inc. Medford, Or.	N623DS
N628LD	07	King Air 350	FL-562	JH Equipment LLC, Bartlett Tx.	
N628MR	81	Conquest 1	425-0049	Richard Chevrolet Inc. Monterey, Ma.	N67EA
N629CD	66	King Air A90	LJ-173	JGM Air LLC. Destin, Fl.	N623R
N629DF	04	Pilatus PC-12/45	590	Delta Fox II LLC. Holland, Mi.	HB-F..
N629JG	03	King Air C90B	LJ-1688	POC LLC., Laurel, Mt.	
N629KC	05	PA-46-500TP Meridian	4697229	TCSI Inc. Strafford, Mo.	
N629MC	07	Pilatus PC-12/47	806	T & M Enterprises LLP, Portland, Or.	N806PE
N629MU	74	Mitsubishi MU-2J	629	Global Aircraft Industries of AZ LLC. Virginia, RSA.	ZS-NDM
N629RP	07	King Air B200	BB-1984	NRP Group LLC./Basche Properties II LLC., Cleveland, Oh.	N7184M
N629SC	72	King Air A100	B-137	Big Blue Inc. Fort Lauderdale, Fl.	PT-OVQ
N629SK	05	Pilatus PC-12/45	413	Karol Atmosfera LLC. Boston, Ma.	N413AF
N629TG	82	SA-227AT Merlin 4C	AT-427	Thomas Ganley, Brecksville, Oh.	N66GA
N629TM	74	Mitsubishi MU-2J	631	Dingman Marine Inc., Orlando, Fl.	(N621CG)
N630HA	74	Mitsubishi MU-2J	630	Turbine Aircraft Marketing Inc. San Angelo, Tx.	OY-BIS
N630MW	81	Cheyenne II-XL	8166011	Atwell Investments LC. Adel, Ia.	N218SW
N631BL	05	Pilatus PC-12/45	631	JD Aircraft LLC. Moncks Corner, SC.	HB-FRY
N631FA	78	SA-226AT Merlin 4A	AT-069	FirstAir Group Inc. Horseheads, NY.	(N558AC)
N631ME	04	King Air 350	FL-430	Marbob Energy Corp. Artesia, NM.	
N632DS	88	King Air 300	FA-141	Rockwell-Ditzler Assocs Inc. Houston, Tx.	N3080F
N633HC	04	King Air B200	BB-1852	Zenaida Avn LLC/Hintz Holman&Robillard, Berkeley Heights,NJ.	N6152L
N633ST	73	SA-226T Merlin 3	T-237	Bluebird Properties Inc. Sullivan, Mo.	C-FCPH
N633WC	81	PA-31T Cheyenne 1	8104036	Consolidated Concrete Co. Omaha, Ne.	N75BR
N634B	73	King Air C-12C	BC-19	Turbo Air Charter Inc. / Martin Aviation, Boise, Id.	73-22268
N634TT	86	King Air B200	BB-1252	Ted Taylor, Birmingham, Al.	N125GA
N635AF	77	King Air C90	LJ-736	Airhole LLC. Beaumont, Tx.	N19HT
N635B	77	King Air C-12C	BC-49	Fly By Knight LLC, Clearwater Fl.	77-22938
N635SF	03	King Air B200	BB-1847	Sanderson Farms Inc. Laurel, Ms.	N61847
N636B	77	King Air C-12C	BC-61	Kilne Process Systems Inc. Redding Pa.	77-22950
N636CR	81	PA-31T Cheyenne II	8120014	Camilo H Rodriguez P, Panama City, Panama.	(N322JD)
N637B	78	King Air C-12C	BC-62	Air Herrig LLC. Sarasota, Fl.	78-23126
N637JC	73	King Air 300	FA-116	Data Supplies Inc. Duluth, Ga.	N240S
N637PH	05	Pilatus PC-12/45	637	Capital Holdings 137 LLC. Wayzata, Mn.	HB-FSB
N637WG	74	Mitsubishi MU-2J	637	Bankair Inc. West Columbia, SC.	N951MS
N637WM	01	King Air B200	BB-1768	Wyoming Machinery Co. Casper, Wy.	N4268V

Reg	Yr Type	c/n	Owner/Operator	Prev Regn
N638AV	05 Pilatus PC-12/45	638	Air Volare LLC. Tallahassee, Fl.	VH-ZMM
N638D	68 King Air B90	LJ-424	Turbine Power Inc. Bridgewater, Va.	
N639B	78 King Air C-12C	BC-67	JetWest LLC. Monterey, Ca.	78-23131
N639KC	05 Pilatus PC-12/45	639	Kaiser Aviation LLC. Kieler, Wi.	HB-FSC
N640DF	92 King Air C90B	LJ-1312	Dr Richard Furman, Boone, NC.	N490J
N640MA	73 Mitsubishi MU-2J	590	Intercontinental Jet Inc., Tulsa, Ok.	N54US
N640MW	90 Beech 1900C-1	UC-1	Marvin Lumber & Cedar Co. Warroad, Mn.	N3114B
N640MY	05 Pilatus PC-12/45	640	Blue Yonder Aviation LLC. Castle Rock, Co.	HB-FRZ
N641MC	06 King Air 350	FL-495	McAninch Corp. Des Moines, Ia.	N71795
N641TK	05 Pilatus PC-12/45	641	T K Stanley Inc. Waynesboro, Ms.	HB-FSD
N641TS	80 King Air 200	BB-641	Eagle Creek Aviation Services Inc. Indianapolis, In.	N641TC
N642CT	99 Pilatus PC-12/45	246	America West Services LLC., Scottsdale, Az.	N6154F
N642DH	68 King Air B90	LJ-420	Diamond Airways Inc. Columbus, Oh.	N759KX
N642JL	85 King Air 300	FA-30	CorGar Air LLC. Coral Gables, Fl.	N70CR
N642PC	05 Pilatus PC-12/45	642	Jet One Inc./HLS Air Inc., San Diego, Ca.	HB-FSE
N642TD	78 King Air C90	LJ-766	Southwest Financial Inc. Garden City, Ks.	N44VC
N642TF	78 King Air 200	BB-363	Jett Aire Florida One Inc. West Palm Beach, Fl.	N96GA
N643BW	95 Pilatus PC-12	131	Wiley Equipment Leasing LLC., Newark, De.	N100WG
N643EA	01 King Air C90B	LJ-1643	PHM/Scott Companies, Monroe, La.	
N643JX	84 BAe Jetstream 31	643	Jetstream Air LLC., Smyrna, Tn.	N990AX
N643PC	05 Pilatus PC-12/45	643	TEDCO Inc. Tucson, Az.	HB-FSF
N644CB	04 King Air 350	FL-394	Cheney Bros Inc. Riviera Beach, Fl.	N246SE
N644EM	81 MU-2 Marquise	1534SA	Earle Martin, Houston, Tx.	N667AM
N644SD	05 Pilatus PC-12/45	644	SDJ Aviation LLC. Las Vegas, Nv.	HB-FSG
N644SP	76 King Air C90	LJ-696	4 Kings Aviation LLC/Rabbs Construction, Monticello, Ar.	(N525PC)
N645PC	05 Pilatus PC-12/45	645	Denver Aviation Partners LLC. Denver, Co.	HB-FSH
N646DR	80 King Air 200	BB-646	Anoka Air Charter/Wilderness Aircraft LLC. Minneapolis, Mn.	N646BM
N646KC	05 PA-46-500TP Meridian	4697224	Gary Crosseley Ford Inc. Liberty, Mo.	
N648JG	04 King Air C90	LJ-1706	Fortune Jet Group, Boca Raton, Fl.	N5066N
N649JC	80 King Air 200	BB-649	N649JC LLC., Atlanta, Ga.	N777JE
N649P	05 Pilatus PC-12/45	649	Capital Holdings 130 LLC. Chandler, Az.	HB-FSJ
N650BG	05 Pilatus PC-12/45	654	Hydro Mechanical Services LLC. Houston, Tx.	HB-FSP
N650DM	92 TBM 700	85	DVDMLS Inc. Moline, Il.	N702JP
N650JT	79 King Air B100	BE-60	Textile Rubber & Chemical Co. Dalton, Ga	(N650UT)
N650JW	83 King Air B200	BB-1126	Aircorp Inc., Anchorage, Ak.	C-FHJO
N650MC	05 Pilatus PC-12/45	650	CM Consulting LLC. Saratoga, Ca.	HB-FSN
N650RS	80 PA-31T Cheyenne II	8020071	Altitude Inc. Lakewood, Oh.	(N658RS)
N650WC	07 Pilatus PC-12/47	871	Pilatus Business Aircraft Ltd, Broomfield, Co.	HB-FQC
N651PB	05 Pilatus PC-12/45	651	Capital Holdings 145 LLC. Denver, Co.	HB-FSK
N652L	80 King Air E90	LW-329	Hartman Motor Sales Inc. Harrisonburg, Va.	F-GJBG
N653PC	94 Dornier 328-100	3027	Prince Transportation Inc. Holland, Mi.	D-CDHM
N653TB	80 King Air 200	BB-586	Community Financial Services Inc. Atlanta Ga.	ZS-MGG
N654BA	82 King Air B200C	BL-54	Department of the Air Force, McCarran, Nv.	N6563C
N654C	65 King Air 90	LJ-12	Turbine Power Inc. Bridgewater, Va.	N90MR
N654CW	07 TBM 850	439	EADS SOCATA North America, Pembroke Pines, Fl.	
N654FM	80 King Air 200	BB-654	BV Transportation LLC/Endeavor Capital, Portland, Or.	N17FS
N654JC	01 Pilatus PC-12/45	437	Jeticopter LLC. Mountain View, Ca.	HB-FRZ
N655BA	80 King Air 200	BB-655	Western Airways Inc. Sugar Land, Tx.	G-OGAT
N655JG	92 King Air B200	BB-1440	Jonda LLC., Sioux Falls, SD.	N8046H
N655MW	00 Beech 1900D	UE-377	Marvin Lumber & Cedar Co. Warroad, Mn.	N833CA
N655SC	99 King Air 350	FL-239	Standridge Color Corp. Social Circle, Ga.	N455SF
N656AF	05 Pilatus PC-12/45	656	Alpha Flying Inc. Manchester, NH.	HB-F..
N657PC	06 Pilatus PC-12/47	796	Reinbeck Motors Inc., Reinbeck, Ia.	HB-FQP
N657PP	03 King Air 350	FL-375	Peterson Tractor Co/Peterson Cat Inc. San Leandro, Ca.	N6175F
N659PC	69 Gulfstream 1	196	Conquest Air LLC. Sewickley, Pa.	N134PA
N660AA	06 King Air B200	BB-1949	Pelican Aircraft Inc. Nassau, Bahamas.	
N660GW	75 King Air C90	LJ-673	21F LLC., Nemo, SD.	N660JM
N660P	05 King Air 350	FL-454	Elta Systems Ltd., Arlington, Va.	
N660PB	90 King Air B200	BB-1364	William Wilson III, San Franciso, Ca.	N5510Y
N660WA	05 Pilatus PC-12/45	660	Missoula Air LLC. Jackson, Wy.	HB-FSV
N660WB	06 Pilatus PC-12/47	760	Newtown Aviation Inc. Waterford, Ireland.	HB-FSO
N660WM	06 King Air B200	BB-1944	Pelican Aircraft Inc. Nassau, Bahamas.	N37244
N661BA	83 King Air B200C	BL-61	Department of the Air Force, McCarran, Nv.	N6564C
N661DP	80 MU-2 Marquise	798SA	Great River Finance Co. La Grange, Mo.	VH-MIU
N661DW	92 TBM 700	61	Danwell Corp. Springfield, Il.	

Reg	Yr	Type	c/n	Owner/Operator	Prev Regn
N661TC	81	PA-31T Cheyenne II	8120022	Blue Goose Aviation LLC. Roseburg, Or.	N127AT
N661WP	04	Pilatus PC-12/45	578	Electro-Methods Holdings LLC. Windsor, Ct.	HB-FQO
N662BA	83	King Air B200C	BL-62	Department of the Air Force, McCarran, Nv.	N6566C
N662JS	76	King Air E90	LW-176	Hughes Flying Service Inc. Miami, Fl.	N70EA
N665CF	95	King Air C90B	LJ-1424	Coastal Flying Club LLC. Fort Worth, Tx.	D-IHBP
N665JK	75	King Air C90	LJ-665	Primecare Medical Inc. Penbrook, Pa.	EC-COK
N665KC	06	PA-46-500TP Meridian	4697265	Kansas City Aviation Center Inc. Olathe, Ks.	
N665MC	05	Pilatus PC-12/45	665	Grindstaff Aviation LLC. Crossville, Tn.	HB-FSZ
N665MW	00	King Air B200	BB-1737	Marvin Lumber & Cedar Co. Warroad, Mn.	N263MW
N665TM	81	Conquest II	441-0215	M Curve Aviation, Effingham, Il.	ZS-KPB
N666DC	73	King Air E90	LW-44	Blue Ash Industrial Supply Co. Cincinnati, Oh.	N166A
N666JK	81	PA-31T Cheyenne II	8120044	Powell Development Co. Kirkland, Wa.	(N40PD)
N666M	07	Pilatus PC-12/47	839	JJJ Aircraft LLC, Riverside, Ca.	HB-FRZ
N666MN	66	680T Turbo Commander	1568-24		N2637M
N666SP	74	Mitsubishi MU-2K	286	Air 1st Aviation Companies Inc. Aiken, SC.	(N66AW)
N667CC	03	King Air B200	BB-1827	Vulcan Steel Structures Inc. Adel, Ga.	N50807
N667RB	03	Pilatus PC-12/45	484	Rye Aviation Services Inc. Rye Beach, NH.	N484AF
N668K	01	King Air 350	FL-329	Aviaserv LLC/FLRT Inc. Van Nuys, Ca.	N350KA
N669AF	05	Pilatus PC-12/45	669	Alpha Flying Inc. Manchester, NH.	HB-F..
N669HS	69	SA-26AT Merlin 2B	T26-161	Smith Aviation Inc. Lyerly, Ga.	N59TP
N669WB	80	PA-31T Cheyenne 1	8004018	William Ball Family Trust, Scottsdale, Az.	N32JP
N670AT	69	King Air B90	LJ-481	Aurora Aviation Inc. Waco, Tx.	G-BVRS
N670TA	98	King Air B200	BB-1631	Rangeflyers Inc., Wichita, Ks.	N670DF
N670WH	05	Pilatus PC-12/45	670	Hawkins Aviation LLC. Boise, Id.	HB-FQC
N671LL	66	King Air A90	LJ-148	Aero Vision Internatioonal LLC., Muskegon, Mi.	N671L
N671PC	05	Pilatus PC-12/45	671	W Tango LLC. Corona del Mar, Ca.	HB-FQD
N672LS	68	King Air B90	LJ-369	Xtra Air LLC/Sturgis Interests Ltd., Houston, Tx.	N129RW
N672MM	07	King Air 350	FL-540	Biltmark Corporation, Wilmington, NC.	N540BK
N672PB	05	Pilatus PC-12/45	672	Sarabe Inc. Salisbury, Md.	HB-FQE
N672SD	05	Pilatus PC-12/45	666	Sweet Darling Sales Inc. Santa Cruz, Ca.	HB-FQA
N673PC	05	Pilatus PC-12/45	673	RLH Services LLC. Colorado Springs, Co.	HB-FQF
N674KC	05	Pilatus PC-12/45	674	D & D Aviation Inc. Grandview, Mo.	HB-FQG
N675BC	97	King Air 350	FL-178	Aviation Enterprises Inc.Wilmington De.	N675PC
N675PC	02	King Air 350	FL-352	Hederman Brothers Printing, Ridgeland, Ms.	N5152H
N676DM	71	681B Turbo Commander	6048	Daniela C Guerrieri, Bluffton, SC.	N911JM
N676J	76	King Air E90	LW-179	Integrity Aviation Inc. Worthington, Mn.	N211MH
N676PC	05	Pilatus PC-12/45	676	Prime Air LLC. Charlotte, NC.	HB-FQI
N677BC	75	King Air/Catpass 250	BB-86	PACTEC, Redlands, Ca.	TZ-ZBC
N677J	78	King Air E90	LW-294	RJA Corp-Richard J Andrews, Houston, Tx.	N9DF
N677JE	00	King Air B200	BB-1702	Air LLC. Huntingburg, In.	N581FM
N677KA	67	680V Turbo Commander	1677-60	H F Payne Construction Co. Monrovia, Md.	N2UL
N677WA	75	Rockwell 690A	11243	DJIC Inc., Danville, Ca.	(N911RX)
N678BK	76	Mitsubishi MU-2L	678	Intercontinental Jet Inc., Tulsa, Ok.	HK-2403
N678FA	99	King Air B200	BB-1678	PJK Oregon LLC., Eugene, Or.	HS-ADS
N678SS	82	King Air B200	BB-1021	Southern Systems Inc. Memphis, Tn.	N195KA
N679BK	76	Mitsubishi MU-2L	679	Intercontinental Jet Inc., Tulsa, Ok.	C-FYBN
N679FS	82	King Air C90-1	LJ-996	Frazee Aviation LLC. Tallahassee, Fl.	N502MS
N679PE	05	Pilatus PC-12/45	679	Premier International Holdings Ltd. Brownsville, Tx.	HB-F..
N680AS	95	BAe Jetstream 41	41030	Northstar Aviation LLC., Boca Raton, Fl.	N410JA
N680CB	06	King Air 350	FL-499	Airprop Inc./Ocean Hospitalities Inc., Portsmouth, NH.	N7199V
N680JD	68	680W Turbo Commander	1792-22	Michael Knudsen, Anaheim, Ca.	N43WL
N681EV	90	King Air C90A	LJ-1228	Soft Landing LLC. Pasco, Wa.	N190JS
N681GH	05	Pilatus PC-12/45	681	Quality Leasing Inc. Fort Walton, Fl.	HB-F..
N681HV	71	681B Turbo Commander	6049	Jet Crew Services Inc. Jensen Beach, Fl.	HC-BPY
N681SP	70	681 Turbo Commander	6027	Stanley Perkins, San Diego, Ca.	N548GQ
N682C	02	PA-46-500TP Meridian	4697130	South Shore Aviation Partners LLC. Wilmington, De.	
N682DR	76	King Air 200	BB-130	Air Services Inc. Traverse City, Mi.	N323MB
N682KA	76	King Air C90	LJ-682	J R Tomkinson Inc., Irvine, Ca.	N3980D
N683GW	02	King Air C90B	LJ-1683	Copart Auto Auctions Inc., Fairfield, Ca.	N6183A
N685BC	02	King Air 350	FL-355	Synovus Financial Corp, Columbus, Ga.	N6055H
N686AC	82	King Air B100	BE-127	The G W Van Keppel Co. Kansas City, Ks.	N666AC
N686CF	82	King Air B200	BB-1085	Cottonwood Investment Group LLC. Sleepy Eye, Mn.	N63686
N686GW	84	King Air C90A	LJ-1082	ABC AirGroup LLC/Concorde Companies, Tampa, Fl.	N666GW
N686PC	05	Pilatus PC-12/47	686	Jack Straw Development LLC. San Diego, Ca.	HB-FQM
N687AE	79	Conquest II	441-0287	AirEvac Services Inc. Lafayette, La.	N441DW

Reg	Yr	Type	c/n	Owner/Operator	Prev Regn
N687AF	05	Pilatus PC-12/47	687	Alpha Flying Inc. Manchester, NH.	HB-...
N687HB	76	Mitsubishi MU-2L	687	Golden Eagle Aviation LLC. Portsmouth, Va.	XB-ARF
N687L	66	680V Turbo Commander	1560-17	RAF Air Cargo Inc. Wilmington, De.	N419S
N688CP	79	PA-31T Cheyenne 1	7904028	Alvaro Manuel Pena Diaz, Dominican Republic.	N51FT
N688JB	90	King Air 350	FL-18	Costa Nursery Farms Inc. Goulds, Fl.	HK-3988X
N688LL	96	King Air C90B	LJ-1451	Conex International Corp. Jasper, Tx.	N3270V
N688RA	76	Mitsubishi MU-2L	688	Royal Air Freight Inc. Waterford, Mi.	N688MA
N688TM	67	680V Turbo Commander	1687-67	Boys from Dover LLC/Assurance Financial Ptnrs LLC,Miramar,Fl	N680FS
N689AE	83	Conquest II	441-0281	AirEvac Services Inc. Lafayette, La.	N6832C
N689BV	78	King Air 200	BB-338	Richmor Aviation Inc. Hudson, NY.	VR-BGN
N689PE	05	Pilatus PC-12/47	689	Rakid Aviation Inc. Torrejon, Spain.	HB-FQU
N690AC	79	Rockwell 690B	11527	Oregon Lifestyles Realty Inc. Bend, Or.	N81765
N690AH	73	Rockwell 690A	11119	Handmade Homes Inc. Enid, Ok.	XA-RTQ
N690AR	74	Rockwell 690A	11155	Reno Group Leasing LLC. Indianapolis, In.	N155TA
N690AS	76	Rockwell 690B	11277	Moro Aircraft Leasing Inc., Two Rivers, Ak.	N690AS
N690AT	74	Rockwell 690A	11202	Central Air Southwest, Kansas City, Mo.	N600PB
N690AX	77	Rockwell 690B	11384	David Miller, Palmer, Tx.	N690KC
N690BA	78	Rockwell 690B	11513	RAB Aviation Inc. Mantua, Oh.	(N690KG)
N690BG	77	Rockwell 690B	11381	William Greene, Elizabethton, Tn.	N46HA
N690BH	77	Rockwell 690B	11361	Bradley Howard, Van Nuys, Ca.	N100AM
N690BK	78	Rockwell 690B	11508	Accuforce Staffing Services/Staff Funds LLC., Kingsport, Tn.	N307CL
N690BM	76	Rockwell 690B	11311	William Latham, Haymarket, Va.	N57118
N690CC	77	Rockwell 690B	11379	Reuben C Setliff MD PC, Sioux Falls Sd.	
N690CF	74	Rockwell 690A	11168	N A Corp. Scappoose, Or.	N690AZ
N690CH	79	Rockwell 690B	11542	Borrego Air LLC. Bend, Or.	N76DT
N690CL	74	Rockwell 690A	11153	Centerline Aerospace Ltd., Thetford, Norfolk, UK.	N46663
N690CP	78	Rockwell 690B	11451	Three Sisters Corp. Monroeville, Pa.	N71MA
N690DB	74	Rockwell 690A	11226	Martin Container Inc/Swift Transportation Co. Phoenix, Az.	N717AP
N690DS	75	Rockwell 690A	11262	Title Financial Group, Blackfoot, Id.	N57104
N690E	84	PA-42 Cheyenne IIIA	5501020	Teufel Nursery Inc. Hillsboro, Or.	(N700LT)
N690EH	76	Rockwell 690A	11309	Surdex Corp. Chesterfield, Mo.	N2NQ
N690EM	73	Rockwell 690A	11125	Old Fort Inc. Dover, De.	N690AE
N690FD	77	Rockwell 690B	11393	Skyrent Aviation LLC., Wilmington, De.	N699GN
N690G	73	King Air E90	LW-34	Pepper Air LLC. Metairie, La.	(N387SC)
N690GF	76	Rockwell 690B	11357	GJF Enterprises Inc. Daytona Beach, Fl.	N690GH
N690GG	77	Rockwell 690B	11411	2141 Corp. Atlanta, Ga.	N95GR
N690GK	72	Rockwell 690	11031	La Mansion de Sarita Inc/N690 LLP. Fort Worth, Tx.	N84DT
N690GS	77	Rockwell 690B	11363	Byron C Hixon, Boise, Id.	N690JB
N690GZ	76	Rockwell 690B	11319	George Zimmermann, West Palm Beach, Fl.	N690AJ
N690HB	74	Rockwell 690A	11205	J Brooks LLC. Louisville, Ky.	N9007
N690HF	76	Rockwell 690A	11298	David Miller, Palmer, Tx.	(N80LE)
N690HM	74	Rockwell 690A	11159	U S Aircraft Leasing Inc. Dover, De.	N2ES
N690HS	78	Rockwell 690B	11431	M Morgan Holdings Inc. Wilmington, De.	N72RF
N690JH	79	Rockwell 690B	11529	Valencia Air Services LLC. San Juan, PR.	N226BP
N690JK	78	Rockwell 690B	11480	IESI TX GP Corp. Fort Worth, Tx.	N81799
N690L	97	King Air B200	BB-1573	Air Med Services LLC. Lafayette, La.	N702TA
N690LL	79	Rockwell 690B	11544	Baker Development Inc. Birmingham, Al.	N690BE
N690LN	77	Rockwell 690B	11415	Nuco Plastering & Stucco Inc., Phoenix, Az.	N730SS
N690LS	78	Rockwell 690B	11475	Office Management Systems Inc. Columbus, Ms.	N690CA
N690MG	77	Rockwell 690B	11423	Eagle Creek Aviation Services Inc. Indianapolis In.	N81674
N690PC	76	Rockwell 690A	11341	Powell Construction Company Inc., Johnson City, Tn.	N20BP
N690PT	75	Rockwell 690A	11252	D & J Benson Dairy, Amarillo, Tx.	(N690AR)
N690RA	72	Rockwell 690	11010	Turbo Joe Leasing LLC. Mesa, Az.	XA-RYF
N690RC	76	Rockwell 690A	11310	Proctor Enterprises of Louisiana Inc. Forest Hill, La.	N331JA
N690RD	77	Rockwell 690B	11350	Range Fire Productions Inc., Vero Beach, Fl.	HK-2051W
N690RK	73	Rockwell 690A	11138	Surry Chemicals Aviation LLC. Mount Airy, NC.	N690EC
N690RP	78	Rockwell 690B	11493	Andrew Foss, San Jose, Ca.	N1HR
N690SC	83	King Air B200	BB-1139	NE Construction Ltd., Lewisville, Tx.	N256BD
N690SD	76	Rockwell 690A	11287	Sedgwick County, Wichita, Ks.	N777HE
N690SG	74	Rockwell 690A	11146	Amber Aviation Inc. Beaver Creek, Oh.	F-OHJE
N690SM	76	Rockwell 690A	11337	First Wing Inc/The Estridge Companies, Carmel, In.	N1547A
N690SS	79	Rockwell 690B	11550	Arkie Flies Inc. Orlando, Fl.	N9LV
N690TC	77	Rockwell 690B	11385	B Fields Properties LLC. Poteau, Ok.	VH-EXT
N690TH	78	Rockwell 690B	11487	Atlanta Channel Inc. Panama City, Fl.	N690BB
N690TP	82	Gulfstream 900	15001	Seybert Arcraft LLC. Indianapolis, In.	N711DW

Reg	Yr Type	c/n	Owner/Operator	Prev Regn
N690TR	72 Rockwell 690	11034	Career Aviation Sales Inc. Oakdale, Ca.	EC-EFS
N690TW	85 PA-42 Cheyenne IIIA	5501026	Trans-West Inc. Denver, Co.	N31KF
N690WC	72 Rockwell 690	11017	V. J. Jet Corporation, Miami, Fl.	N101RQ
N690WD	74 Rockwell 690A	11176	JHH Aircraft Inc. Lancaster, Ca.	LV-LMU
N690WP	79 Rockwell 690B	11561	Bob Mitchell, Sallisaw, Ok.	N9196Q
N690WS	74 Rockwell 690A	11194	Burelbach Industries Corp. Rickreall, Or.	N953HF
N690XT	78 Rockwell 690B	11467	Eagle Creek Aviation Services Inc. Indianapolis In.	N690HT
N690XY	78 Rockwell 690B	11433	Mark W Peterson Lewiston Id.	(N690BW)
N691AS	90 King Air C90A	LJ-1240	3 Kings LLC. Portland, Or.	N1565X
N691PA	79 Rockwell 690B	11526	Macy-Lott Holdings LLC., Post, Tx.	N64EZ
N691PC	06 Pilatus PC-12/47	691	Sierra Nevada Corp., Sparks, Nv.	HB-FQO
N691SM	78 Rockwell 690A	11492	Seacol Inc/Watts Copy Systems Inc., Springfield, Il.	N643JW
N692BC	05 Pilatus PC-12/47	692	Connor Aviation LLC. Wilmington, De.	HB-FQP
N692M	77 King Air E90	LW-228	Suzie LLC. Wilmington, De.	N53BB
N692T	78 Rockwell 690B	11555	Delta Oil Inc. Wilmington, De.	N150SP
N692W	02 King Air C90B	LJ-1692	Claxton Poultry Farms/Norman W Fries Inc, Claxton, Ga.	
N693AT	05 Pilatus PC-12/47	693	Apex Aviation Partners LLC. Romeoville, Il.	HB-FSQ
N693MA	03 TBM 700C2	293	Currie Partners Inc. San Diego, Ca.	
N693PD	07 Pilatus PC-12/47	857	Aviate LLC, Atlanta, Ge.	HB-FSL
N693VM	75 Rockwell 690A	11234	Bryan Medlock Jr. Dallas, Tx.	N698CE
N694CT	03 King Air C90B	LJ-1694	Black Bear Reserve Equipment Co. Raleigh, NC.	N90KA
N694JB	86 King Air 300	FA-89	Barnett Investments Inc. La Verne, Ca.	LV-ZPY
N694KM	05 King Air B200	BB-1922	PMG Air LLC., New York, NY.	N837J
N695AB	81 Gulfstream 1000	96055	Maas Aircraft Lsg/JTM Provisions Co Inc., Harrison, Oh.	CP-2050
N695AM	82 Gulfstream 1000	96007	Red Fox Leasing Inc. Louisville, Ky.	(N6361U)
N695CT	85 Gulfstream 1000	96096	Challenge Tool & Manufacturing Inc. New Haven, In.	N44SD
N695EE	85 Gulfstream 1000B	96205	Eagle Creek Aviation Services Inc. Indianapolis, In.	N91575
N695FA	85 Gulfstream 1000	96077	Air O'Brien LLC/Blugrass Gas Sales, Anchorage, Ky.	N695DA
N695GG	82 Gulfstream 1000	96036	Golden Giant Building Systems Inc. Kenton, Oh.	N20GT
N695GH	85 Gulfstream 1000	96078	Wells Fargo Bank NW NA, Salt Lake City, Ut.	N85NM
N695GJ	82 Gulfstream 1000	96011	La Mansion Aviation Inc. Fort Worth, Tx.	N5422P
N695HT	82 Gulfstream 1000	96038	Farsight Technologies Inc. Las Vegas, Nv.	N707TS
N695JJ	76 King Air C90	LJ-695	Performance Energy Services LLC/Navajo Air LLC, Houma, La.	N93BB
N695KG	85 Gulfstream 1000B	96207	Klein Gilhousen, Bozeman, Mt.	N81432
N695MG	85 Gulfstream 1000B	96204	Goelst Corp/Goelst Aviation LLC. Winston-Salem, NC.	N30059
N695MM	82 Gulfstream 1000	96050	MMA Consulting Inc. Chestnut Hill, Ma.	N45LG
N695NC	82 Gulfstream 1000	96032	Aero Services EAP Inc. Fort Lauderdale, Fl.	VH-GAB
N695PC	00 Pilatus PC-12/45	305	Daetwyler Aircraft LLC. Huntersville, NC.	HB-FQS
N695QE	07 Pilatus PC-12/47	834	Soda Corners II LLC., Lathrop, Ca.	HB-FRV
N695RC	85 Gulfstream 1000	96087	Intermountain Crane Ltd LLC, Las Vegas Nv.	N722SG
N695WR	80 Gulfstream 980	95015	Rocky Mount Rental & Leasing Inc. Rocky Mount, NC.	N655PC
N695YP	84 Gulfstream 1000	96070	Golf Commander LLC. Perrysburg, Oh.	N7896G
N696JB	70 King Air 100	B-26	Dolph Briscoe Jr. Uvalde, Tx.	N610KR
N696RA	81 King Air F90	LA-87	Camacho Cigars Inc. Miami, Fl.	N200SC
N697MP	72 King Air C90	LJ-554	Air C & M Inc. Wilmington, De.	N697MB
N697P	85 King Air B200	BB-1217	Staker & Parson Companies, Klamath Falls, Or.	(N204GR)
N698GN	66 680V Turbo Commander	1589-40	Michael Franzblau, Los Angeles, Ca.	N699GN
N699AF	06 Pilatus PC-12/47	699	Alpha Flying Inc. Manchester, NH.	HB-...
N699AM	68 SA-26AT Merlin 2B	T26-101	Mid America Recycling, Des Moines, Ia.	N669SP
N699KM	75 SA-226T Merlin 3A	T-256	Lobo Well Service LLC. Park City, Ut.	(N226JP)
N699MW	85 King Air 300	FA-73	M A Inc. Oshkosh, Wi.	N408G
N699RK	79 SA-226T Merlin 3B	T-300	K'Berger Inc. Del Rio, Tx.	N193CS
N699SB	76 Rockwell 690A	11280	Bryant Racing Inc. Anaheim, Ca.	(N53AR)
N700AD	02 TBM 700C2	250	RKEFS LLC, Big Lake, Mn.	
N700AN	98 TBM 700	132	L S Ferguson/Commonwealth Eye Surgery, Lexington, Ky.	F-WWRO
N700AP	01 TBM 700B	190	Ron Amini, San Antonio, Tx.	N700VD
N700AQ	02 TBM 700C2	252	Hunter Corp. Santa Barbara, Ca.	
N700AZ	02 TBM 700C2	254	Elvaston Inc Trustee, Wilmington De.	
N700BA	80 King Air B100	BE-84	Jim Hawk Group Inc. Council Bluffs, Ia.	N300TN
N700BE	79 King Air 200	BB-528	Baercraft Leasing LLC. Merritt Island, Fl.	N203BC
N700BK	02 TBM 700C2	262	M H Ventures LLC. Wilmington, De.	
N700BN	01 TBM 700B	203	William Dixon Jr. Kentfield, Ca.	
N700BQ	04 TBM 700C2	298	Cuatro Aviation LLC. Los Angeles, Ca.	
N700BS	91 TBM 700	11	B & D Thermal Protection Consulting Inc. Daytona Beach, Fl.	N877PC
N700CB	00 TBM 700B	176	Fred Hibberd Jr. The Dalles, Or.	F-WWRO

Reg	Yr Type	c/n	Owner/Operator	Prev Regn
N700CC	96 TBM 700	113	Family Extended Care of Melbourne Inc. Hialeah, Fl.	F-OHBU
N700CF	96 TBM 700	123	James Findeiss, Fort Lauderdale, Fl.	N700TB
N700CL	03 TBM 700C2	266	Jupiter Equipment Leasing Inc. Garland, Tx.	
N700CP	76 King Air C90	LJ-700	Deep Rock resourses Inc. Dallas Tx.	N700FC
N700CS	95 TBM 700	109	Michael Rosenberg, Chapel Hill, NC.	
N700CT	02 TBM 700B	236	Vladigor Investments Inc. Van Nuys, Ca.	
N700CV	01 TBM 700B	221	Agnondas LLC. Palo Alto, Ca.	F-WWRJ
N700CZ	04 TBM 700C2	301	OKAY Sro. Brno, Czech Republic.	
N700DD	78 King Air E90	LW-288	Sammann Corp. Michigan City, In.	N717US
N700DE	91 TBM 700	4	Commercial Bag Co. Normal, Il.	N701MR
N700DH	74 King Air E90	LW-114	Avolare Enterprises LLC. Tucson, Az.	N89L
N700DM	04 TBM 700C2	305	Centennial Homes Inc. Novato, Ca.	(N700KD)
N700DQ	03 TBM 700C2	271	Tahoe Investments Inc. Los Altos Hills, Ca.	(D-FAJS)
N700DT	98 TBM 700	134	Delta Tango Corp. Whitefish, Mt.	F-WWRR
N700DZ	03 TBM 700C2	295	Timothy Diestel, Bend, Or.	
N700EG	03 TBM 700C2	284	JGG Management LLC. Oxnard, Ca.	
N700EJ	03 TBM 700C2	291	Comstock Crosser & Assocs Development LLC. Ca.	
N700EL	01 TBM 700B	209	Air Twinlite Inc. Dolls Grove, Ireland.	N701AR
N700EN	05 TBM 700C2	329	EYC Companies LLC., Raleigh, NC.	(N825KM)
N700ER	01 TBM 700B	198	Exchange Enterprise Group LLC. Indianapolis, In.	
N700EV	03 TBM 700C2	287	MG Air Transport LLC. Newport, NC.	
N700EZ	04 TBM 700C2	307	DBW Aviation LLC. Anaheim, Ca.	
N700FT	03 TBM 700C2	267	William Foster, Sherborn, Ma.	
N700GE	02 TBM 700C2	255	Corvis Aviation LLC. Flagstaff, Az.	
N700GJ	02 TBM 700B	241	RBL Aviation LLC. Carlsbad, Ca.	(N702RM)
N700GK	04 TBM 700C2	320	Garel Westall, Carlsbad, NM.	N700BD
N700GM	91 King Air C90A	LJ-1283	MICO Inc. North Mankata, Mn.	D-IHMW
N700GN	02 TBM 700C2	246	Twin Landfill Corp., Steamboat Springs, Co.	F-WWRJ
N700GQ	03 TBM 700C2	289	Dal Pezzo Aviation LLC. Fresno Ca.	
N700GT	03 TBM 700C2	276	Enstrom Candies Inc. Grand Junction, Co.	
N700GV	03 TBM 700C2	290	ADS Aviation LLC. Tulsa, Ok.	
N700GY	04 TBM 700C2	302	N700VB Inc Trustee, Wilmington, De.	D-FBFT
N700HD	04 TBM 700C2	313	Blettner Equipment Leasing LLC., Madison, Wi.	
N700HK	93 TBM 700	60	Daniel Lee, Wilson, Wy.	(N95DW)
N700HL	03 TBM 700C2	281	SAAIR LLC. Dover, Ma.	
N700HN	01 TBM 700B	204	Doyle Hartman, Aspen, Co.	
N700HY	03 TBM 700C2	278	Premier Aircraft Sales Inc., Fort Lauderdale, Fl.	(N702SB)
N700JD	03 TBM 700C2	264	Peter Goldschmidt, Duluth, Mn.	N700MZ
N700JV	02 TBM 700C2	245	Janzen Ventures Inc. Tulsa, Ok.	ZS-TBM
N700KD	04 TBM 700C2	322	Schneider Flight Services LLC. Durham, NC.	N700ZP
N700KH	01 TBM 700B	210	N700KH LLC. Dublin, Oh.	N708AV
N700KK	02 TBM 700B	243	Karl Corp/HK Aviation LLC. West Palm Beach, Fl.	N217DH
N700KM	99 TBM 700B	158	Frederick Croatti, Londonderry, NH.	
N700KP	02 TBM 700B	228	Midwest Equity Leasing LLC. Indianapolis, In.	
N700KV	04 TBM 700C2	296	Shephard Aviation Inc., Wilmington, De.	
N700KW	76 King Air 200	BB-115	Eastern Tennessee Subway Development, Kmoxville, Tn.	N335TM
N700L	82 Gulfstream 1000	96034	MAX 1 LLC. Aspen, Co.	(N24A)
N700LF	02 TBM 700C2	270	Sunbeam Aviation LLC. Wilmington, De.	(N700HS)
N700LL	93 TBM 700	86	Evergreen III LLC. Seattle, Wa.	
N700MK	02 TBM 700C2	251	Spring Brook Marina Inc. Seneca, Il.	F-WWRP
N700MV	91 TBM 700	13	Aircraft Guaranty Title LLC. Houston, Tx. (trustor ?).	(LX-JFB)
N700MX	91 TBM 700	14	Medex LLC. Middleton, Wi.	N292RG
N700NA	94 King Air B200	BB-1491	Penn State University, University Park, Pa.	JA8614
N700PC	80 Gulfstream 980	95023	James Lindsey Jr Family Trust, Van Nuys, Ca.	N888SF
N700PG	98 King Air 350	FL-233	Blue Cross & Blue Shield, Chattanooga, Tn.	N700PE
N700PL	05 Pilatus PC-12/45	657	Concepts West of Montana LLC. Missoula, Mt.	HB-FSR
N700PQ	77 Rockwell 690B	11389	Rogers Helicopters Inc. Clovis, Ca.	N700PC
N700PT	03 TBM 700C2	268	Links Aero LLC. Shalimar, Fl.	
N700PU	91 TBM 700	15	TBM Ventures LLC. Pendleton, Or.	
N700PV	01 TBM 700B	215	Aircraft Guaranty Title LLC. Houston, Tx. (trustor ?)	
N700PW	01 TBM 700B	211	David Lau, Watertown, Wi.	
N700PX	02 TBM 700C2	249	Unimax Aviation Inc. Portland, Or.	F-WWRK
N700QD	01 TBM 700B	174	Quest Diagnostics Inc. Teterboro, NJ.	F-GLBC
N700QT	05 TBM 700C2	337	River Run Equipment LLC. Ketchum, Id.	
N700RE	92 TBM 700	52	Electronic Industries Corp. Concord, NC.	N700PK

Reg	Yr Type	c/n	Owner/Operator	Prev Regn
N700RF	91 King Air C90A	LJ-1262	Pelico Inc/Anoka Air Charter Inc. Minneapolis, Mn.	N200HV
N700RG	78 PA-31T Cheyenne II	7820042	OFEK Holding Corp. Wilmington, De.	N400RT
N700RK	02 TBM 700C2	253	Kritser Equipment Leasing LLC. Colorado Springs, Co.	N700BH
N700RX	72 Mitsubishi MU-2K	241	Putnam County National Bank, Carmel, NY.	C-GJAV
N700S	01 TBM 700B	193	Stonehenge Aviation Inc. Wilmington, De.	
N700SB	96 King Air C90B	LJ-1433	Sanders Brothers Construction Co. Charleston, SC.	N100RU
N700SF	91 TBM 700	26	Air Frantz Inc. Greenwich, Ct.	
N700SL	02 TBM 700C2	257	Travel Equipment LLC. San Francisco, Ca.	
N700SX	05 TBM 700C2	325	Richard Bailey, Santa Rosa, Ca.	
N700SY	03 TBM 700C2	283	Camair LLC. Charlotte, NC.	
N700TF	77 King Air B100	BE-18	Top Flight Aviation LLC. Raleigh, NC.	N93AJ
N700TG	78 King Air C-12C	BC-75	Twin Cities Turboprop LLC. Auburn, Me.	N900RF
N700TJ	91 TBM 700	27	Flying Bees Aviation LLC. Columbus, Oh.	N700WD
N700TK	04 TBM 700C2	311	Lake Watch LLC. Roanoke, Va.	
N700TL	01 TBM 700B	227	SRQ/Jet Leasing LLC., Sarasota, Fl.	
N700U	03 King Air 350	FL-363	Ohio University, Athens, Oh.	N6043M
N700VA	02 TBM 700B	233	SOCATA Aircraft, Pembroke Pines, Fl. (status ?).	F-OIKI
N700VB	02 TBM 700B	237	Paul Castle Inc. Wilmington, De.	F-OIKJ
N700VF	81 PA-42 Cheyenne III	8001053	WBY Enterprises LLC. Jackson, Tn.	N543FM
N700VJ	00 TBM 700B	163	N700VJ LLC. Wilmington, De.	N700DN
N700VM	92 TBM 700	72	VMO Corp. Coral Gables, Fl.	
N700VX	96 TBM 700	118	KP Equipment LLC. Billings, Mt.	F-GLBI
N700WA	79 MU-2 Solitaire	400SA	Wemco Aviation Inc. Wilmington, De.	N40MZ
N700WB	05 TBM 700C2	324	UHV Sputtering Inc. Morgan Hill, Ca.	N700QT
N700WE	01 TBM 700B	214	Independence Associates LLC., Aspen, Co.	N703AV
N700WJ	81 Conquest 1	425-0036	Bighorn Airways Inc. Sheridan, Wy.	(N32TJ)
N700WK	00 TBM 700B	175	Riverton Air LLC. Wilmington, De.	D-FFBU
N700WT	93 TBM 700	91	Holt Aviation LLC. Mason City, Ia.	
N700YN	01 TBM 700B	222	California-Oregon Development LLC. Portland, Or.	F-WWRK
N700Z	05 King Air B200	BB-1920	Bramco Inc. Louisville, Ky.	N6178A
N700ZA	04 TBM 700C2	317	SC Meridian LLC. Rapid City, SD.	
N700ZF	05 TBM 700C2	336	Roof Management Ltd., Marysville, Oh.	
N700ZM	04 TBM 700C2	315	Montana Grille LLC., Bowling Green, Ky.	OE-EMS
N700ZR	93 TBM 700	87	Nova Aviation LLC. Fort Lauderdale, Fl.	N874RJ
N700ZZ	96 TBM 700	116	Tycor Leasing LLC. Tuscon, Az.	N116VL
N701AT	68 King Air B90	LJ-390	Elias R V Morales, Valencia Carabobo, Venezuela.	N701AT
N701AV	00 TBM 700B	179	Black Marlin Aviation LLC. Stuart, Fl.	(N69FR)
N701BN	61 Gulfstream 1	74	Battelle Pacific Northwest Laboratories, Pasco, Wa.	N5619D
N701CN	02 TBM 700C2	260	Clay Nordman, Merced, Ca.	N700XS
N701FC	00 King Air 350	FL-291	Forum Communications Co. Fargo, ND.	
N701JF	05 TBM 700C2	331	J Fergus Inc. Lewis Center, Oh.	N701MA
N701LT	95 TBM 700	107	Baker Aviation LLC. Versailles, Ky.	F-GLLL
N701MK	97 TBM 700	124	MAK Equipment Leasing LLC. Northampton, Pa.	N701PP
N701NC	78 King Air 200	BB-324	Omniflight Helicopters Inc., Addison, Tx.	N111SF
N701PT	80 PA-31T Cheyenne 1	8004008	Natoli Engineering Co. Chesterfield, Mo.	(N701DH)
N701QD	97 TBM 700B	126	Quest Diagnostics Inc. Teterboro, NJ.	N811SW
N701X	76 King Air E90	LW-165	Gold Aviation Services Inc. Fort Lauderdale, Fl.	N700DH
N701XP	79 King Air C90	LJ-826	Skyhammer Aviation LLC/Pittinger & Anderson Inc. Lincoln, Ne	(N20GT)
N702AA	01 TBM 700B	216	Lantech Leasing LLC. Louisville, Ky.	
N702AR	03 TBM 700C2	275	Carothers Equipment LLC., Water Valley, Ms.	
N702AV	00 TBM 700B	182	Panther Aviation LLC. Los Altos Hills, Ca.	
N702BM	91 TBM 700	2	Fabry Air Corp. Wilmington, De.	N100PB
N702DK	90 King Air C90A	LJ-1259	Cheyenne Ventures LLC. Richmond, Va.	N712JC
N702GS	00 TBM 700B	177	Monroe Group II Inc. Northbrook, Il.	F-WWRP
N702H	96 TBM 700	112	Anchor Equipment Leasing LLC. Cincinnati, Oh.	N12WY
N702MA	82 King Air B200	BB-1010	Michigan Aeronautics Commission, Lansing, Mi.	N62FC
N702MB	04 TBM 700C2	314	TBM 700 Inc. Wilmington, De.	
N702QD	00 TBM 700B	165	Quest Diagnostics Inc. Teterboro, NJ.	N700DY
N702RW	03 TBM 700C2	256	Wrenn Aircraft Inc. Waynesville, NC.	N700TB
N702TD	81 King Air B100	BE-110	Gorlin Aviation LLC/SpineMedica Inc., Marietta, Ga.	N702JL
N702XP	78 King Air E90	LW-266	H. D. Fowler Company Inc./Serenity Avn. LLC., Bellevue, Wa.	N215HC
N703DM	69 Mitsubishi MU-2F	138	Air 1st Aviation Companies Inc. Aiken, SC.	N252DC
N703HT	77 King Air 200	BB-228	Ray Anthony Crane Rental, West Mifflin, Pa.	N79KF
N703JR	76 King Air C-12C	BC-22	Jacksonville Sheriff's Department, Jacksonville, Fl.	N200NG
N703LW	79 King Air E90	LW-317	BBLC Assocs LLC. Parsippany, NJ.	N2062A

Reg	Yr	Type	c/n	Owner/Operator	Prev Regn
N703QD	99	TBM 700B	129	Quest Diagnostics Inc. Teterboro, NJ.	LX-JFC
N703RM	00	King Air B200	BB-1699	Rushmark Properties LLC. Fairfax, Va.	N3199B
N703TL	06	Pilatus PC-12/47	703	Ted Lamb Co. Prescott, Az.	HB-FQL
N703X	80	King Air 200	BB-737	First Air Leasing LLC/Lloyd Douglas Enter., Arlington, Tx.	N703X
N704QD	01	TBM 700B	188	Quest Diagnostics Inc. Teterboro, NJ.	
N705KC	05	Pilatus PC-12/45	635	Capital Holdings 129 LLC. Fort Lauderdale, Fl.	HB-F..
N705MA	06	PA-46-500TP Meridian	4697277	Kussman Air LLC., Columbus, In.	
N706AG	06	Pilatus PC-12/47	706	PC-XII LLC. Greensburg, In.	HB-FQV
N706DG	79	King Air 200	BB-548	Davis-Garvin Agency Inc/D-G Air LLC. Columbia, SC.	N78SC
N706DM	67	Mitsubishi MU-2B	038	Bush Field Aircraft Co. Augusta, Ga.	N8BL
N706KC	76	Rockwell 690A	11343	BRS Services Inc. Reno, Nv.	N706US
N707AF	78	Mitsubishi MU-2N	707SA	Gustl Spreng Enterprises Inc. Daytona Beach, Fl.	VH-NMU
N707AV	01	TBM 700B	197	Eleigh Aviation LLC. Carson City, Nv.	F-WWRK
N707CB	81	Conquest 1	425-0023	Flying High Ventures Inc. Sun River, Or.	N23AW
N707CV	81	PA-31T Cheyenne 1	8104013	Anaconda Land Dev Inc. San Juan, PR.	N212GM
N707FA	01	King Air 350	FL-337	Rodman Aviation LLC. Frisco, Tx.	N5037A
N707HM	06	King Air B200	BB-1939	Jeltin LLC/Hudson & Marshall Auctioneers, Dallas, Tx.	N3729N
N707KH	05	Pilatus PC-12/47	688	Sierra River Air Inc. Boise, Id.	HB-FQN
N707MA	83	Conquest II	441-0285	Caribbean Air & Marine Service, Memphis, Tn.	D-IIAA
N707ML	75	PA-31T Cheyenne II	7520017	Chaparral Leasing Inc. Topeka, Ks.	(N5RZ)
N707PC	04	King Air C90B	LJ-1703	Peyton S Carnes Jr., Wichita Falls, Tx.	N45PF
N707SS	71	King Air 100	B-81	Planes 4 Sale LLC/Casing Service & Equipt Inc. Houston, Tx.	N858B
N707TL	76	King Air E90	LW-173	Transworld Leasing Corp. San Antonio, Tx.	N1573L
N707WD	81	PA-31T Cheyenne II	8120103	Hafer & Assocs Corp. Phoenix, Az. (was 8120065).	N182TC
N708AF	06	Pilatus PC-12/47	708	Alpha Flying Inc. Manchester, NH.	HB-F..
N708DG	71	King Air C90	LJ-508	Hinds Community College, Raymond, Ms.	N706DG
N708EF	91	TBM 700	21	Mulligan Aviation, Annapolis, Md.	(N554CA)
N708PW	91	TBM 700	29	Third Moment Aviation LLC. NYC.	N700PW
N708WH	07	King Air B200GT	BY-7	Hollis & Span Contractors, Dothan Al.	
N709EA	92	King Air C90B	LJ-1309	Aerolease LLC./Weather Modification Inc., Fargo, ND.	C-GMBH
N709MC	00	TBM 700B	168	JMC Leasing Inc. St Petersburg, Fl.	
N709RB	06	Pilatus PC-12/47	709	LTA Air Express LLC, Saratogo, Wy.	HB-FQW
N710AS	72	King Air A100	B-127	Samoa Aviation Inc. Pago Pago, American Samoa.	C-GJVK
N710G	78	Mitsubishi MU-2N	710SA	Turbine Aircraft Marketing Inc. San Angelo, Tx.	I-MLST
N710JB	01	King Air B200	BB-1784	Sunset Leasing Inc. Sarasota, Fl.	N4484W
N710M	05	TBM 700C2	326	Derners of Melford Inc. Melford, Ia.	N700ZB
N710NC	78	King Air 200	BB-322	Ascension Aviation LLC. Gaylord, Mi.	N715MA
N711AW	00	King Air B200	BB-1708	Cutter Southwest Aircraft Sales LLC., Phoenix, Az.	N605TA
N711BN	73	King Air C90	LJ-588	Liberte Air Corp. St Croix, USVI.	N711BL
N711CQ	78	King Air C90	LJ-773	Nix Construction, Jonesboro, Ar.	N711CC
N711CR	74	King Air 200	BB-16	Pacific West Air LLC. Ramona, Ca.	N700CP
N711ER	81	PA-31T Cheyenne 1	8104056	Barlovento LLC. Dothan, Al.	(D-IAHM)
N711FN	81	Cheyenne II-XL	8166043	Desert LLC., Los Angeles, Ca.	N820SW
N711GE	81	Conquest II	441-0209	Flyingdog Inc. Wilmington De.	N2728G
N711GM	70	King Air 100	B-31	T & W Leasing, Mesquite, Tx.	N38HB
N711HV	77	King Air E90	LW-246	Kaden Airmotive Inc. Dallas, Tx.	N711NV
N711KB	80	King Air 200	BB-593	TIC Properties LLC. Jacksonville, Fl.	(N209JS)
N711KP	76	King Air C90	LJ-692	Peter Messina & Assocs Ltd. Itasca, Il.	(N692RC)
N711L	84	King Air F90-1	LA-222	U S Investments Ltd. Crystal Bay, Nv.	N69283
N711LD	81	PA-31T Cheyenne 1	8104040	Allegheny Industries Inc. Mount Airy, Md.	N981SR
N711MB	80	Conquest II	441-0116	Berry Plastics Acquisition Corp. Evansville, In.	N441GE
N711PB	77	Rockwell 690B	11356	Ohio Kentucky Oil Corp. Lexington, Ky.	N653PC
N711PM	02	TBM 700B	234	Lewis & Lewis Attorneys, Clarksdale, Ms.	N811SV
N711PN	06	Pilatus PC-12/47	711	Sierra Nevada Corp., Sparks, Nv.	HB-FQY
N711RD	79	PA-31T Cheyenne II	7920068	J E L Farms Ltd. Hale Center, Tx.	N40JC
N711RE	77	King Air A100	B-233	Tulip City Air Service Inc. Holland, Mi.	N99HE
N711RJ	94	King Air 350	FL-116	DG Financial Consulting Inc, Longview Tx.	D-CAAA
N711SB	01	PA-46-500TP Meridian	4697075	Cash South LLC. Georgetown, De.	
N711TN	80	King Air 200	BB-628	Francille Corp. Germantown, Tn.	N6739P
N711VK	69	Mitsubishi MU-2F	157	William D Fisher Enterprises LLC. Richmond, In.	N157AF
N711VM	79	King Air 200	BB-544	Walt Dickson, Frederick, SD.	N711VH
N711VN	90	King Air 350	FL-7	T & E Aviation Inc/Elco Inc. Bakersfield, Ca.	N7350C
N711VV	90	King Air B200	BB-1365	Maynard Aviation LLC. Hackensack, NJ.	N963GM
N712BC	02	Pilatus PC-12/45	448	SAH East Coast LLC. Teterboro, NJ.	HB-FSP
N712GJ	81	King Air B200	BB-840	Mark A Richardson, Casper, Wy.	N840RC

Reg	Yr Type	c/n	Owner/Operator	Prev Regn
N712RH	03 King Air B200	BB-1839	AMR Aviation LLC. Baton Rouge, La.	N5039X
N713RH	87 King Air B200	BB-1274	Falcon Air LLC. Olive Branch, Ms.	(N47AJ)
N715CA	81 PA-31T Cheyenne II	8120063	Giumarra Brothers Fruit Co. Los Angeles, Ca.	
N715CQ	92 King Air 200	BB-1421	International Muffler Co. Schulenberg, Tx.	(N538KB)
N715HL	99 Pilatus PC-12/45	292	Iliamna Air Taxi Inc. Iliamna, Ak.	N292PB
N715MC	91 TBM 700	30	Maiden Rock Aviation LLC. Bay City, Wi.	
N715RD	80 King Air 200	BB-707	Shull Management Inc. Banner Elk, NC.	N627BC
N715TL	04 Pilatus PC-12/45	548	TNH Leasing LLC. Iliamna, Ak.	HB-FST
N715V	95 TBM 700	108	DML Aviation LLC, Ann Arbour Mi.	(N555HN)
N715WA	73 King Air A100	B-168	Colemill Enterprises Inc. Nashville, Tn.	F-GFVM
N716AV	04 King Air B200	BB-1876	Snowy Range Aviation LLC. Cheyenne, Wy.	
N716CC	81 Conquest II	441-0213	J B F Inc. South Point, Oh.	N6851Y
N716MA	04 TBM 700C2	310	WRJ Inc. Clinton Township, Mi.	
N716SM	77 Conquest II	441-0004	Conquest Flight LLC. Merion Station, Pa.	N555JJ
N716TA	95 King Air B200	BB-1509	Grand-Air LLC/Ruffin Building Systems, Oak Grove, La.	N109NT
N716WA	80 PA-31T Cheyenne II	8020032	Westlog Inc./CAL-ORE Life Flight, Smith River, Ca.	(N414CW)
N717DC	87 King Air B200	BB-1261	Aircraft Unlimited Inc. Pierre, SD.	N2997N
N717ES	80 PA-42 Cheyenne III	8001004	Thompson Travel LLC. West Columbia, SC.	N42WZ
N717FM	98 King Air B200	BB-1611	Frazier Masonry Corp. Las Vegas, Nv.	HP-1515
N717JG	75 King Air C90	LJ-672	APL Leasing Ltd., Wilmington, De.	(N11AB)
N717LW	98 King Air B200	BB-1642	Greater Media Services Inc. Braintree, Ma.	N3051S
N717NC	06 Pilatus PC-12/47	717	Peco Aviation LLC., Cincinnati, Oh.	HB-FRF
N717PD	70 SA-26AT Merlin 2B	T26-178	CTS Air LLC., Shreveport, La.	N61775
N717PP	74 King Air E90	LW-74	Greenwood Group/Suzie LLC., Ponca City, Ok.	N71BX
N717PS	76 Mitsubishi MU-2L	686	Royal Air Freight Inc. Waterford, Mi.	N23RA
N717VE	98 King Air 350	FL-207	George Mitchell II, Midland, Tx.	N717VL
N717X	73 King Air C90	LJ-581	Bert Nelson, Dallas, Tx.	N717XP
N717Y	91 TBM 700	17	J H Van Zant II, Albany, Tx.	
N718EE	78 Mitsubishi MU-2N	718SA	Randall Wang, Arcadia Ca.	OK-HLB
N718JP	96 Pilatus PC-12	155	Pezold Air Charter LLC. Columbus, Ga.	N361FB
N718K	68 King Air B90	LJ-371	B90 King Group LLC. Austin, Tx.	
N718MB	91 King Air C90A	LJ-1287	MPW Industrial Services Group Inc. Hebron, Oh.	N881JT
N718RJ	97 King Air B200	BB-1597	AAA Cooper Transportation Corp. Dothan, Al.	
N719EA	92 King Air C90B	LJ-1319	AirSea Charters Inc. Omaha, Ne.	C-GMBZ
N719PC	06 Pilatus PC-12/47	719	Orchids Leasing LLC. Van Nuys, Ca.	HB-FRH
N720AM	99 King Air B200	BB-1663	Myers Aviation Co., Worcester, Pa.	N46BM
N720C	73 King Air A100	B-171	Oscar Charlie LLC. Hollywood, Md.	C-FJFH
N720JK	69 Mitsubishi MU-2F	154	Wolfhunter Aviation LLC. Kokomo, In.	(N81LJ)
N720MP	82 King Air B200	BB-1080	Idlewood Aviation Inc. Atlanta-DeKalb, Ga.	N72GG
N720RD	77 King Air C90	LJ-720	Stewart Mining Industries Inc. Vero Beach, Fl.	VT-EFP
N721AF	06 Pilatus PC-12/47	721	Alpha Flying Inc. Manchester, NH.	HB-F..
N721FC	68 Mitsubishi MU-2D	111	East Mississippi Community Co. Mayhew, Ms.	N858Q
N721PB	97 Pilatus PC-12	195	MOIP LLC. Boulder, Co.	N37DA
N721RD	80 King Air 200	BB-677	Drinkard Development Inc. Cullman, Al.	N200KK
N721SL	06 Pilatus PC-12/47	726	KBJ LLC, Scottsdale Az.	HB-FRL
N721SR	00 TBM 700B	181	122 Ventures Inc. Atlanta, Ga.	
N721TB	77 Rockwell 690B	11352	David C Poole Co. Greenville, SC.	N46JC
N722JB	01 King Air C90B	LJ-1652	JSB Aviation LLC. Wichita Falls, Tx.	N722JM
N722KP	96 King Air B200	BB-1545	Pearson Holdings LLC. Fort Lauderdale, Fl.	N286R
N722KR	84 King Air C90A	LJ-1065	Sunbird Aviation Inc. Belgrade, Mt.	N900LE
N722PM	06 King Air C90GT	LJ-1820	NINA, Paris, France	
N722SR	92 TBM 700	49	Go-Mav Inc. Simi Valley, Ca.	N567T
N722TR	81 King Air B200	BB-938	Gulf Coast Aviation Inc. Houston, Tx.	N132K
N722VB	81 King Air C90	LJ-987	T L Wallace Construction Co. Columbia, Ms.	N390L
N722WJ	80 King Air 200	BB-722	World Jet Inc. Fort Lauderdale, Fl.	F-HAAG
N723AC	76 Rockwell 690A	11249	Keystone Senior Capital Corp. Indianapolis, In.	N161JB
N723JP	79 PA-31T Cheyenne II	7920009	Missouri Forge Inc. Doniphan, Mo.	N723JR
N723KR	01 PA-46-500TP Meridian	4697033	Greater South Agency Inc. Columbia, SC.	
N724A	96 DHC 8-202	440	ARAMCO Associated Co. Houston, Tx.	C-GFBW
N724DM	98 TBM 700B	143	Air Men Inc. Concord, Ma.	N709DM
N724DR	00 King Air C90B	LJ-1612	Lands End Aviation LLC. Los Altos Hills, Ca.	N3212Y
N724HS	04 Pilatus PC-12/45	564	HS Holdings Group LLC. Oakland Park, Fl.	N564PB
N724KC	07 PA-46-500TP Meridian	4697324	Kansas City Aviation Centre Inc.Olathe, Ks.	
N724KH	96 King Air C90B	LJ-1426	Alliance Air Parts Inc., Oklahoma City, Ok.	N724KW
N724RN	01 TBM 700B	202	Ronald Nelson, Pasadena, Ca.	N709AV

Reg	Yr Type	c/n	Owner/Operator	Prev Regn
N725A	96 DHC 8-202	441	ARAMCO Associated Co. Houston, Tx.	C-GFCF
N725AR	80 King Air C90	LJ-879	Nuskyy, Birmingham, Al.	N6656D
N725JP	05 PA-46-500TP Meridian	4697243	Throttle Up LLC., Las Vegas, Nv.	
N725JT	81 MU-2 Solitaire	451SA	Corsair Enterprises Inc. Bamberg County, SC.	N1728S
N725MC	76 King Air 200	BB-169	N725MC Inc. Lafayette, Co.	N200KA
N725RA	80 King Air 200	BB-725	P & S Air Inc/Staley Inc. Little Rock, Ar.	TP-209
N725SV	78 Conquest II	441-0051	Sunview Air Inc. Delano, Ca.	N986SG
N726CB	00 King Air B200	BB-1750	Henry Broadcasting Nevada Inc. San Francisco, Ca.	N4150T
N726T	96 King Air 350	FL-149	B E & K Inc. Birmingham, Al.	N42ED
N727BW	81 King Air 200	BB-861	AUG Inc. Augusta, Ga.	N727DD
N727CC	82 Gulfstream 1000	96027	United States Aviation Underwriters, NYC.	N9947S
N727DL	85 SAAB 340A	036	Napleton Aviation Group,	ZS-ABM
N727DP	75 SA-226AT Merlin 4A	AT-039	Hellas Aviation LLC, Austin Tx.	N439BW
N727JA	77 Rockwell 690B	11399	Augustine Air LLC. Charlotte, NC.	N302WC
N727MT	78 King Air E90	LW-271	S V Leasing LLC. Princeton, NJ.	N123LN
N727PC	81 PA-42 Cheyenne III	8001025	Cheyenne Air LLC. Lafayette, La.	(D-IBTV)
N727RS	81 King Air B100	BE-112	Montana Sky Fly LLC. Hamilton, Mt.	N990SV
N727TP	81 MU-2 Marquise	1517SA	Ted Price Sr. Ventura, Ca.	(N321TP)
N728F	67 Mitsubishi MU-2B	019	Internet Jet Sales Ltd. White Milla, Pa.	N3551X
N728FN	74 Mitsubishi MU-2K	303	DGH P/L. Brunswick, VIC. Australia.	N728DM
N729AF	06 Pilatus PC-12/47	729	Alpha Flying Inc. Manchester, NH.	HB-F..
N729MS	76 King Air B100	BE-2	Mazak Properties Inc. Webster, Fl.	N43KA
N730EZ	06 King Air C90GT	LJ-1808	Med-Corp Health Services Inc., Muskogee, Ok.	N730EB
N730HM	99 King Air B200	BB-1648	Poet Research Inc/Broin & Assocs Inc. Sioux Falls, SD.	N788TA
N730MS	84 King Air B200	BB-1174	L-Mark LLC. Metairie, La.	(N696AC)
N730PT	77 PA-31T Cheyenne II	7720008	Twin Otter International Ltd. Las Vegas, Nv.	XA-HAY
N731BH	86 Conquest II	441-0360	Hubbard Air LLC. Berwyn, Pa.	N441RW
N731CA	05 TBM 700C2	332	Cool Stream LLC. NYC.	
N731CJ	79 MU-2 Marquise	731SA	Air 1st Aviation Companies Inc. Aiken SC.	N81FR
N731PB	80 Cheyenne II-XL	8166001	Pense Brothers Drilling Co. Frederickstown, Md.	N136SP
N731PC	06 Pilatus PC-12/47	731	Nicholas Services LLC. Blytheville, Ar.	HB-FRP
N731TM	91 TBM 700	5	Tango Mike Jets LLC., Wilmington, De.	N800GS
N733DC	96 Beech 1900D	UE-307	Niagara Mohawk Power Corp. Syracuse, NY.	N22761
N733P	01 PA-46-500TP Meridian	4697052	Angus Mercer, Charlotte, NC.	
N735MD	06 Pilatus PC-12/47	735	AKAYC AviationGroup LLC. Colleyville, Tx.	HB-FRT
N736P	85 King Air 300	FA-53	CSL 340 Corp. Truro, Ma.	
N737E	74 Rockwell 690A	11189	Green Fairways Inc. Chicago, Il.	(N300CG)
N738R	71 King Air C90	LJ-517	Pine Tree Aviation LLC. Boulder, Co.	N738RH
N739S	07 Pilatus PC-12/47	844	Lowrance Darrell J, Port Orange Fl.	HB-FSB
N739W	06 King Air B200	BB-1945	Watson Wings LLC/Watson Lumber Co. Mount Holly, Ar.	N7345S
N740AF	06 Pilatus PC-12/47	740	Aspen Furniture Designs Inc. Phoenix, Az.	HB-FRW
N740P	85 King Air B200	BB-1218	Navajo Nation, Window Rock, Az.	
N740PB	75 Mitsubishi MU-2L	657	Flight Line Inc. Watkins, Co.	N740PC
N740PC	85 King Air 300	FA-78	Oglethorpe Power Corp. Tucker, Ga.	N72479
N741FN	75 Mitsubishi MU-2L	658	Air 1st Aviation Company of Oklahoma, Tulsa, Ok.	N740DM
N741JP	05 King Air C90B	LJ-1756	Malco Leasing Corp	
N741JR	05 King Air B200	BB-1901	GTO Enterprises Inc/Packers of Indian River, Fort Pierce.	N3301M
N742GR	70 SA-26AT Merlin 2B	T26-172	Toys 4 Boys Inc. Beaumont, Tx.	N120FS
N742R	06 Pilatus PC-12/47	742	Riley Aviation Leasing LLC. Salt Lake City, Ut.	HB-FRZ
N743AE	06 Pilatus PC-12/47	743	PC-12 Ventures LLC. Mount Pleasant, SC.	HB-FSA
N744CH	78 Rockwell 690B	11470	CH Aviation Inc. Wilmington, De.	N86MP
N744DA	06 Pilatus PC-12/47	744	Best Wings LLC, Mishawaka In.	HB-FSB
N745EA	01 King Air B200	BB-1745	Wal-Mart Stores Inc. Rogers, Ar.	N615TA
N746KF	79 King Air 200	BB-473	Sierra 24 Leasing LLC. Fremont, Oh.	N510CB
N747AW	01 PA-46-500TP Meridian	4697037	N747AW Corp Trustee. Wilmington, De.	N123AD
N747BL	05 PA-46-500TP Meridian	4697226	Leone Aviation Inc, Armonk NY.	N3111K
N747HN	80 King Air 200	BB-658	JP Aviation LLC/Jim Parker Building Co Inc., Auburn, Al.	N127AP
N747KL	05 Pilatus PC-12/45	662	Lewis Aeronautical LLC. San Antonio, Tx.	HB-FSX
N747RE	77 PA-31T Cheyenne II	7720032	Weather Modification Inc. Fargo, ND.	(N748RL)
N747SY	82 MU-2 Marquise	1556SA	Yukon Flying Inc. Wilmington, De.	N277JR
N748LB	90 King Air B200	BB-1374	Beach Air LLC. Henderson, Nv.	N899HC
N748SB	01 King Air 350	FL-321	Nectar of the Gods Air Inc. San Juan, PR.	N541GA
N749FF	94 King Air B200	BB-1494	Family Foods Inc., Fayetteville, NC.	N3026H
N749GC	06 Pilatus PC-12/47	749	MRV Services LLC. Houston, Tx.	HB-FSG
N749L	79 SA-226T Merlin 3B	T-306	Liberty Air Inc. Bakersfield, Ca.	N226FC

Reg	Yr	Type	c/n	Owner/Operator	Prev Regn
N750CA	79	MU-2 Solitaire	407SA	Templeton Aircraft LLC. Washington, DC.	N979MA
N750FC	70	King Air 100	B-58	S & J Enterprises Inc. Fort Lauderdale, Fl.	C-FJLJ
N750HL	75	King Air 200	BB-48	HLMP Aviation Corporation, Miami Fl.	XC-AA38
N750KC	77	King Air 200	BB-224	Magnum Tool Co. Colorado Springs, Co.	N215PA
N750MD	04	King Air B200	BB-1878	Polet USA Inc., New York, NY.	N6078T
N750RC	74	King Air C90	LJ-640	Ferguson Aviation LLC. Linwood, NC.	N942M
N750TT	77	King Air 200	BB-215	Around The World Jet Charter Inc. Palm Springs, Ca.	ZS-NGC
N751BR	78	Rockwell 690B	11436	B & R Aviation LLC. Van Nuys, Ca.	N690FR
N751CM	05	TBM 700C2	339	Alto Vuelo LLC. Albuquerque, NM.	
N751J	91	TBM 700	25	Rocket Boy LLC. Las Vegas, Nv.	N751JB
N751KC	80	King Air C90	LJ-887	J A Peterson Enterprises Inc. Shawnee Mission, Ks.	N887CF
N752JS	06	Pilatus PC-12/47	752	SKA Consulting LLC. Westlake Village, Ca.	HB-FSH
N752MM	04	PA-46-500TP Meridian	4697192	SDCC Management Inc. Aubrey, Tx.	
N753C	06	PA-46-500TP Meridian	4697248	John Woodall, Dallas, Tx.	
N754SC	89	King Air B200	BB-1345	Paul R. Flowers, Dothan, Al.	N887JC
N754TW	78	King Air C90	LJ-754	Alcar Company/Eide Motors, Grand Forks,ND.	N303QC
N755DM	94	TBM 700	101	ISDM Inc. Prairie Village, Ks.	
N755EM	05	Pilatus PC-12/45	661	Sea Star Inc. Wetumpka, Al.	HB-FSW
N755HF	06	Pilatus PC-12/45	755	Joseph J Howley, Greenwich, Ct.	HB-F
N755JB	90	King Air B200	BB-1377	Commuter Air Technology Inc., Scottsdale, Az.	F-GNEG
N755MA	72	Mitsubishi MU-2J	553	Air 1st Aviation Company of Oklahoma, Tulsa, Ok.	N7034K
N755PG	90	TBM 700	1	Floyd Ventures LLC, Wilmington, De.	OE-ESM
N755Q	66	Mitsubishi MU-2F	131	PA Charter Inc. Gibsonia, Pa.	C6-BFA
N757ED	06	Pilatus PC-12/45	790	Edge Development Group LLC., Bend, Or.	HB-FQL
N757H	81	Conquest 1	425-0006	City Link Airlines, Silver City, NM.	C-GMSV
N758K	67	King Air A90	LJ-316	Kilo delta Enterprises Inc. Wiliamsburg Va.	XB-BZQ
N758PC	06	Pilatus PC-12/47	698	Jynair LLC. Portland, Or.	HB-FQR
N759A	96	DHC 8-202	435	ARAMCO Associated Co. Houston, Tx.	C-G...
N759AF	80	MU-2 Marquise	759SA	Golden Eagle Aviation LLC. Portsmouth, Va.	LV-ODZ
N759H	06	PA-46-500TP Meridian	4697245	Neljo Inc. Charlottesville, Va.	
N759PB	06	Pilatus PC-12/47	759	WFBNW NA. Salt Lake City, Ut. (trustor ?).	HB-F
N760MM	82	PA-42 Cheyenne III	8001102	Mawson & Mawson Inc. Langhorne, Pa.	N4114A
N760NP	75	King Air 200	BB-46	MEBE Inc. Oklahoma City, Ok.	N760NB
N761K	68	King Air B90	LJ-426	Jordan Foster Aviation Inc. Deland, Fl.	(N713JF)
N762GP	05	King Air B200	BB-1899	Global Industries Ltd. Sulphur, La.	N6199Y
N762JC	80	MU-2 Marquise	762SA	Briggs Aviation LLC./Platinum Services Inc., Dubuque, Ia.	OY-SUH
N762NB	81	King Air B200	BB-893	Sky High Air LLC. Orangeburg, SC.	
N762VM	87	SA-227AT Merlin 4C	AT-695B	F Major LLC. Houston, Tx.	N2709Z
N763LD	80	SA-226T Merlin 3B	T-313	Lucky Dog Holdings Inc. Boca Raton, Fl.	N326MS
N764CA	91	King Air B200	BB-1408	King Air 200 LLC/Carver Aero Inc. Muscatine, Ia.	N74RF
N765WA	81	King Air 200	BB-765	AV Enterprises Inc. Bozeman, Mt.	N242LC
N766LF	04	King Air B200	BB-1864	Luihn Food Systems Inc. Raleigh, NC.	N6084C
N766MA	78	Mitsubishi MU-2P	373SA	Frank Sanderson, Hampton, Va.	
N766RB	82	King Air F90	LA-196	Norman Black, Atlanta, Ga.	CC-CTE
N767CW	94	TBM 700	96	High Sierra Inc. Los Angeles, Ca.	
N767DM	81	Cheyenne II-XL	8166042	Snowbow Inc. Fairbanks, Ak.	N500XL
N767HP	99	TBM 700B	152	SOCATA Aircraft, Pembroke Pines, Fl.	
N767LD	68	King Air B90	LJ-425	Daytona Beach Aviation Leasing LLC., Port Orange, Fl.	N93WB
N767MC	73	King Air C90	LJ-595	New Life Aviation Group Inc. Laurelton, NY.	(N595AS)
N767TP	01	PA-46-500TP Meridian	4697036	Cross Development of Missouri, Wentzville, Mo.	
N767WF	78	King Air 200	BB-314	YNTA Inc. Wilmington, De.	N101BP
N767Z	78	Conquest II	441-0064	Mueller Aero Inc. Prairie du Sac, Wi.	N88823
N768MB	80	PA-31T Cheyenne 1	8004041	Hitch Enterprises Inc. Guymon, Ok.	N769MB
N769AF	06	Pilatus PC-12/47	769	Alpha Flying Inc. Manchester, NH.	HB-F..
N769BJ	97	King Air 350	FL-156	Air Progress LLC. Overland Park, Ks.	N350KG
N769CM	02	Pilatus PC-12/45	464	Pilatus PC-12 LLC. Park City, Ut.	N464WC
N769D	80	King Air F90	LA-52	Dailey Equipment Co. Jackson, Ms.	
N769GR	98	King Air C90B	LJ-1509	Rite Flite Aviation Ltd. Cleveland, Oh.	
N769JS	01	TBM 700B	187	West Coast Trens Inc. Huntington Beach, Ca.	
N769MB	79	King Air 200	BB-571	American Health Centers Inc. Parsons, Tn.	N702AS
N770AB	81	King Air B100	BE-121	AGB Management Inc., Warrenton, Va.	C-FAFZ
N770D	80	King Air B100	BE-90	Brodock Executive Air Inc. Utica, NY.	N67460
N770DC	00	TBM 700B	183	Broadway Two LLC. Dover, De.	
N770JH	90	King Air 350	FL-8	Skynight LLC/Skyview Cooling Co. Yuma, Az.	N124BB
N770MG	75	PA-31T Cheyenne II	7520029	Daugherty Petroleum Inc. Lexington, Ky.	N43SQ

Reg	Yr Type	c/n	Owner/Operator	Prev Regn
N770PB	94 King Air B200	BB-1498	Prosperity Bank, St Augustine, Fl.	N777AJ
N770PW	06 Pilatus PC-12/47	757	BD Capital Group LLC. Reno, Nv.	HB-FSL
N770RL	70 King Air 100	B-46	Sky King 101 LLC/Ra-Lin & Associates, Carrollton, Ga.	(N770RU)
N770RW	74 Mitsubishi MU-2J	627	The F4 Phantom II Corp. Santa Fe, NM.	5Y-BJX
N770SD	80 King Air F90	LA-72	Holiday Management Co. Evansville, In.	N90SK
N770SF	81 King Air B200	BB-916	Southern Pioneer Life Insurance Co. Trumann, Ar.	N770HM
N770VF	01 King Air C90B	LJ-1641	V F Management Co. Roanoke, Va.	N654P
N771BA	78 Rockwell 690B	11429	Eagle Creek Aviation Services Inc. Indianapolis, In.	N771BA
N771BL	05 PA-46-500TP Meridian	4697227	Den Asset Management LLC., Park City, Ut.	(N9021A)
N771CW	78 King Air B100	BE-52	Grand Prix Aviation LLC. Cordova, Tn.	N771S
N771FF	82 Gulfstream 900	15014	S E C Inc. Athens, Ga.	N5869N
N771HC	76 King Air 200	BB-147	Woolie Enterprises Inc., Oldsmar, Fl.	N777FL
N771HM	99 King Air 350	FL-262	HMHC Inc. Plymouth Meeting, Pa.	N725BA
N771JB	07 King Air C90GT	LJ-1848	Laurel Aviation Enterprises, St. James, NY.	
N771MG	98 King Air B200	BB-1636	Macy's Florida Inc. Opa Locka, Fl.	(N771SQ)
N771PA	83 King Air C90-1	LJ-1055	EJI Sales Inc. Montvale, NJ.	N303D
N771PD	01 King Air C90B	LJ-1635	Eagle Air Med Corp. Blanding, Ut.	N5035M
N771SW	77 PA-31T Cheyenne II	7720002	Western Kansas Ground Water Management, Scott City, Ks.	N505GP
N771XW	78 Conquest II	441-0065	Griffith Aviation Co ., Tulsa, Ok.	N777XW
N772AF	81 King Air B200	BB-1001	CKL Enterprises LLC. Pelham, Al.	N94QD
N772DA	80 MU-2 Marquise	772SA	EPPS Air Service Inc. Atlanta, Ga.	I-MPLT
N772MA	78 Mitsubishi MU-2P	382SA	Jetprop Inc. Waterloo, Ia.	
N772SL	78 SA-226T Merlin 3A	T-258	Jet Operators LLC. Dallas, Tx.	N828CM
N773	83 King Air F90-1	LA-214	Fickling & Co. Macon, Ga.	N77P
N773PW	79 King Air C90	LJ-864	Reed Ford Technology Inc. Pearl, Ms.	N199TD
N773S	67 King Air A90	LJ-283	Burke Management Services LLC. Huffman, Tx.	
N773SD	95 King Air C90B	LJ-1413	South Dakota DoT, Pierre, SD.	N573P
N773TC	05 TBM 700C2	312	Clark Aviation LLC. Basalt, Co.	F-GZRC
N773TP	00 King Air B200	BB-1722	Utah Aeronautical Operations, Salt Lake City, Ut.	
N773VA	85 King Air B200	BB-1195	Vader Aircraft Corporation, Ballston Spa, NY.	ZS-MCC
N774DK	96 Pilatus PC-12	167	Franklin M Orr Jr Trust, Stanford, Ca.	HB-FSC
N774GW	06 Pilatus PC-12/47	774	Pajaros LLC., Gresham, Or.	HB-FSZ
N774KV	81 Cheyenne II-XL	8166057	State of Nebraska, Lincoln, Ne.	N9168Y
N774MA	78 Mitsubishi MU-2P	384SA	Briggs Aviation LLC./Platinum Services Inc., Dubuque, Ia.	(N127RM)
N775CC	07 Pilatus PC-12/47	792	MGI Aircraftco LLC., Las Vegas, Nv.	HB-FQM
N775D	99 King Air C90B	LJ-1579	McLane Trailer Sales Inc. Poplar Bluff, Mo.	
N775DM	78 King Air C90	LJ-764	Antioch Air Corp. Jacksonville, Fl.	N201KA
N775MG	07 King Air 350	FL-553	Pearl Equipment LLC/M. G. Dyess Inc., Bassfield, Ms.	
N775SC	81 King Air 200	BB-808	National Railway Equipment Company, Mt. Vernon, Il.	N910EB
N776AF	06 Pilatus PC-12/47	776	Alpha Flying Inc. Manchester, NH.	HB-FQB
N776CC	72 Mitsubishi MU-2J	560	Loose Moose Aviation LLC. Wilmington, De.	N195MA
N776DC	77 King Air E90	LW-235	Suzie LLC. Wilmington, De.	C-FBCS
N776RM	94 TBM 700	98	776 Assocs MM LLC. Sarasota, Fl.	N700SP
N776RW	05 King Air B200	BB-1926	Reliance Well service Inc. Magnolia Ar.	N61726
N777AG	00 King Air B200	BB-1757	EMV Aircraft LLC., Destin, Fl.	N261BC
N777AJ	98 King Air B200	BB-1638	Horizon Timber Services Inc. Arkadelphia, Ar.	N777AG
N777AQ	80 King Air 200	BB-583	Pollard Aircraft Sales Inc., Southlake, Tx.	N777AG
N777AW	79 King Air 200	BB-536	Three C's LLC/Advanced Wireless Comms, Lakeville, Mn.	N33FM
N777CQ	06 Pilatus PC-12/47	754	LSAC Enterprises LLC. Port Washington, Wi.	HB-FSJ
N777EB	79 King Air C90	LJ-863	Sunshine Aviation LLC/Sunshine Homes Inc. Red Bay, Al.	N200SC
N777EL	79 Rockwell 690B	11538	Earl G. & Judith A Lunceford Trust, Hayden, Id.	N81701
N777FX	03 TBM 700C2	294	FX Luminaire/N777FX Aircraft LLC. San Diego, Ca.	N883CA
N777GF	72 King Air C90	LJ-564	Aeronca Inc. Middletown, Oh.	N246DA
N777GS	79 King Air A100	B-241	CJ Systems Aviation Group Inc. Allegheny County, Pa.	N777GF
N777HF	99 King Air B200	BB-1645	777MOC 1 LLC. Capitola, Ca.	N615WH
N777JZ	07 Pilatus PC-12/47	817	Bod Aviation LLC., Los Angeles, Ca.	HB-FRF
N777KA	78 King Air E90	LW-285	ATS Aircraft Sales Inc. Oneida Tn..	
N777LE	81 PA-31T Cheyenne II	8120104	Leading Edge Aviation Services Inc. Santa Ana. (was 8120069)	C-FZIC
N777LP	78 Mitsubishi MU-2N	719SA	Lincoln Leasing Co. Lincoln, Ne.	N911JE
N777MG	01 PA-46-500TP Meridian	4697066	Scotts Co. Marysville, Oh.	N5327Y
N777NP	65 King Air 90	LJ-67	APA Enterprises Inc. Poughskeepsie, NY.	(N21AM)
N777NV	81 Gulfstream 840	11680	Nevada Department of Transportation, Carson City, Nv.	N680WA
N777SS	80 King Air 200	BB-661	Leslie E Denherder, Bakersfield, Ca.	N111JW
N777VK	69 Mitsubishi MU-2F	179	Bill Austin Aircraft & Yacht Sales, Sparta, Tn.	N4WQ
N777WM	79 MU-2 Solitaire	397SA	Commodity Logistics LLC. Missoula, Mt.	N666SP

Reg	Yr Type	c/n	Owner/Operator	Prev Regn
N777YN	01 King Air C90B	LJ-1657	Black Raven Leasing LLC. Wilmington, De.	N777MN
N778DB	01 King Air C90B	LJ-1647	Kansas Aircraft Corp,New Century, Ks.	N169P
N778HA	81 PA-31T Cheyenne II	8120008	Wells Fargo Bank NW NA., Salt Lake City, Ut.	D-ICBH
N779AF	73 King Air E90	LW-51	Southern Air Services Inc. Tuscaloosa, Al.	N35CM
N779BZ	07 King Air B200	BB-1971	Biozyme Inc., St Joseph, Mo.	
N779CC	80 Conquest II	441-0155	Coastal Flying Club LLC. Austin, Tx.	XB-FND
N779DD	92 King Air C90A	LJ-1297	Basha's - Chapman Group, Chandler, Az.	N8239Q
N779JM	88 King Air C90A	LJ-1183	J & M Aviation Inc. Howell, Mi.	N482JA
N779M	80 SA-226T Merlin 3B	T-363	Tru-Truss Inc. Lacey, Wa.	(N155AM)
N779MJ	89 King Air C90A	LJ-1197	AM Management Inc. Iowa City, Ia.	N485JD
N779PC	06 Pilatus PC-12/47	779	Star Options Aviation Inc. Wilmington, De.	HB-FQB
N779VF	90 King Air C90A	LJ-1254	Fulling Mill LLC. Bronxville, NY.	N770VF
N780BP	73 Rockwell 690	11052	Long Star Air Service Inc. Miami, Fl.	N1230D
N780CA	06 P-180 Avanti II	1106	Eastlake Avanti LLC. Eastlake, Co.	
N780KB	05 King Air B200	BB-1924	Hawker Beechcrat Corp, Wichita Ks.	N700KB
N780RC	81 King Air 200	BB-780	D W Machine Products Inc. Highland, Il.	F-GIHK
N781CK	78 PA-31T Cheyenne II	7820056	Nailen Investments Inc. Dothan, Al.	N51RD
N781GT	06 King Air C90GT	LJ-1781	Ron Anderson Chevrolet Oldsmobile, Yulee, Fl.	
N781H	79 MU-2 Solitaire	409SA	Omni American Inc. Coatesville, Pa.	N78FS
N781PE	06 Pilatus PC-12/47	781	N5421 Foxtrot LLC, Wilmington De.	HB-FQD
N782MA	78 MU-2 Solitaire	390SA	Tri-Air LLC. Springfield, Mo.	
N783MA	78 Mitsubishi MU-2P	391SA	Mitchell Slayman, Bakersfield, Ca.	
N783MC	73 King Air C-12C	BC-2	U S Customs Service, Oklahoma City, Ok.	N7064B
N783PC	06 Pilatus PC-12/47	783	JHF Aviation LLC., Brentwood, Tn.	N783JJ
N783RS	80 Conquest II	441-0170	Ultra Wheel Co. Riverside, Ca.	N783ST
N784BK	06 Pilatus PC-12/47	784	Triple G Air LLC	HB-FQF
N784PF	81 Conquest 1	425-0018	N20PF LLC., Wilmington, De.	N20PF
N784RR	78 Conquest II	441-0078	Ranger Enterprises Inc., Rockford, Il.	N441KW
N785JH	00 P-180 Avanti	1036	Golden Falcon Aviation Inc Trustee, Wilmington, De.	N126PA
N785JP	04 King Air C90B	LJ-1710	Cherokee Nation Enterprses LLC, Stilwell Ok	
N785MA	03 TBM 700C2	280	Astro Aviation LLC. Waterford, Mi.	
N785PJ	05 PA-46-500TP Meridian	4697232	MCA-Plane LLC. Flint, Mi.	
N786AH	78 PA-31T Cheyenne II	7820053	SonFlight LLC. Andover, Ma.	C-GJJE
N786CB	76 King Air B100	BE-4	Western Wings Corp, Roseburg Or.	C6-BHV
N786DD	84 King Air B200	BB-1171	Lawrence Contracting Co. Gilberton, Pa.	N86DD
N786RM	99 King Air C90B	LJ-1545	Six Romeo Mike LLC. Billings, Mt.	N3145F
N786SR	82 King Air B200	BB-1016	North Slope Borough Search & Rescue, Barrow, Ak.	(N38AJ)
N786WM	06 Pilatus PC-12/47	786	Water Wings LLC., Phoenix, Az.	HB-FQH
N787K	66 King Air 90	LJ-102	Ameron-Enmar Finishes Division, Little Rock, Ar.	
N787LB	85 PA-42 Cheyenne IIIA	5501030	Lawrence Aviation Inc. Austin, Tx.	N637KC
N787TT	78 King Air C90	LJ-787	JCD-GP LLC. Center, Tx.	TC-NAZ
N788BB	76 PA-31T Cheyenne II	7620051	Slick Corp/AR Contractors, Fort Worth, Tx.	N631WF
N788JL	84 Conquest 1	425-0202	Priority Air Charter LLC. Kidron, Oh.	VH-EGQ
N788JR	88 120ER Brasilia	120095	Champion Air Inc., Mooresville, NC.	N138DE
N788KC	01 King Air C90B	LJ-1662	Mid-America Engine Inc., Olive Branch, Ms.	N313PT
N788RB	07 TBM 850	395	Blissco Inc., Tulsa, Ok.	N850RB
N788RR	00 TBM 700B	167	Kek Companies Inc., Portland, Or.	N788RB
N788SF	04 King Air B200	BB-1857	Suncrest Farms Inc. Van Nuys, Ca.	N5157G
N788SW	79 King Air E90	LW-327	Pollard Aircraft Sales Inc., Southlake, Tx.	G-JGAL
N789CH	79 PA-31T Cheyenne II	7920079	American Medflight Inc. Reno, Nv.	N555RC
N789CT	81 King Air B200	BB-907	Syl-Don LLC. Peoria, Il.	(N440KC)
N789G	62 Gulfstream 1	89	Friends of Yellow Tail Inc./Flair Builders LLC., Spring, Tx.	
N789KP	01 King Air C90B	LJ-1664	Northeast Executive Jet LLC. Reading, Ma.	N5064L
N789LL	03 King Air 350	FL-386	Leavitt Leasing Co. Los Angeles, Ca.	N5086P
N789SB	97 King Air 350	FL-143	Superior Industries International Inc. Fayetteville, Ar.	N2392S
N789WA	95 King Air C90B	LJ-1407	Dallas Jet International, Roanoke, Tx.	HB-GJF
N790A	82 King Air C90-1	LJ-1016	Ninety LLC/Butler Aviation Inc. Houma, La.	N790A
N790CA	05 TBM 700C2	341	Pokoik Enterprises Inc. Groton, Ct.	
N790GT	05 King Air C90GT	LJ-1761	Antonio Enriquez, Seattle, Wa.	
N790RB	78 King Air E90	LW-262	Gracie Aviation Inc.Ft Lauderdale Fl.	N7ZW
N790RV	07 King Air C90GT	LJ-1830	Robert V Voit, Scottsdale, Az.	N7030B
N790SD	79 PA-31T Cheyenne II	7920004	Silverwings Air Ambulance Ltd.. Silver City, NM.	N790SW
N790TB	99 TBM 700B	148	SOCATA Aircraft, Pembroke Pines, Fl.	(N700EV)
N791BP	07 King Air 350	FL-551	United States dept of Enerrgy, Portland Or.	
N791DC	91 King Air B200	BB-1402	Air Methods Corp/Deaconess Medical Center Inc. Billings, Mt.	N91CD

Reg	Yr Type	c/n	Owner/Operator	Prev Regn
N791EB	81 King Air 200	BB-791	TCAS Enterprises LLC. Colleyville, Tx.	TC-ACN
N792JM	88 King Air 300	FA-140	Jamestown Metal Marine Sales Inc. Boca Raton, Fl.	N117DR
N793DC	91 King Air B200	BB-1404	Air Methods Corp/Deaconess Medical Center Inc. Billings, Mt.	N93CD
N793P	07 King Air C90GT	LJ-1836	PBMJ LLC., Windber, Pa.	
N793WB	01 King Air 350	FL-324	Falcon Air Services LLC. Mesa, Az.	(N797WB)
N794A	84 PA-42 Cheyenne IIIA	5501015	Charlie Delta LLC. Erie, Co.	D-ILSW
N794AF	07 Pilatus PC-12/47	794	Clover Investors LLC., Manchester, NH.	
N794B	81 Conquest 1	425-0017	Forest Travel Agency Inc. Aventura, Fl.	N58CH
N794CE	79 King Air B100	BE-69	LMJ Inc. Wake Forest, NC.	N794WB
N794MA	80 MU-2 Marquise	794SA	West Texas Executive Leasing Inc. San Angelo, Tx.	N54CE
N795CA	79 King Air 200	BB-559	Plane South Leasing Inc. Dunwoody, Ga.	N559BM
N795PA	78 King Air 200	BB-328	Aircraft Acquisition LLC. Duluth, Ga.	(D-IDOL)
N795TB	84 SA-227TT Merlin 300	TT-483A	WFBNW NA. Salt Lake City, Ut. (trustor ?).	N328AJ
N797CF	78 King Air C90	LJ-797	Daedalus Inc/Business Aviation Services, Sioux Falls, SD.	N61GA
N797GM	06 Pilatus PC-12/47	747	797 Gulfmike LLC. Sheboygan, Wi.	HB-FSE
N797RW	80 Conquest II	441-0185	Tech II Inc. Springfield, Oh.	N999DF
N798K	66 King Air A90	LJ-178A	Randall Fortner, Eagle Creek, Or.	
N798RG	07 Pilatus PC-12/47	798	Air Group LLC., Louisville, Ky.	HB-FQR
N798WC	05 Pilatus PC-12/45	613	Land Sea Air Leasing Corp. Ward Cove, Ak.	HB-FRP
N799DD	72 King Air A100	B-102	Finkbeiner Aviation, Little Rock, Ar.	N777SD
N799GK	78 King Air C90	LJ-799	Duane Cotter, Weslaco, Tx.	ZP-TXE
N800BB	83 PA-31T Cheyenne 1	8104072	Anson Wood Products Inc., Mt. Gilead, NC.	N482TC
N800BJ	97 King Air 350	FL-184	Norsan Aviation LLC. Tucker, Ga.	(N100PX)
N800BK	81 King Air F90	LA-119	BK Aviation Inc. Grand Prairie, Tx.	(N800C)
N800BS	98 King Air B200	BB-1620	M & F Western Products Inc. Sulphur Springs, Tx.	
N800BY	72 Mitsubishi MU-2F	221	S & P Holdings LLC. Long Beach, Ms.	N800BR
N800CA	00 Beech 1900D	UE-383	Ruand Inc. Osage Beech, Mo.	N31686
N800CG	81 King Air 200	BB-826	American Mine Research Inc. Rocky Gap, Va.	N1CB
N800EB	79 PA-31T Cheyenne II	7920046	Southern Sky Inc. Miami, Fl.	N700LT
N800ED	76 Mitsubishi MU-2M	339	Rydal Services Inc. Rydal, Pa.	N6ONJ
N800GS	99 TBM 700B	149	HNP Air LLC. State College, Pa.	
N800HA	77 King Air 200	BB-220	Aircraft Trust & Financing Corp Tr. Ft Lauderdale Fl.	N75VF
N800KT	89 King Air B200	BB-1346	Justiss Oil Co. Jena, La.	
N800LD	78 SA-226T Merlin 3A	T-291	Glenn Air LLC Willis Tx.	N19SD
N800MK	96 King Air C90B	LJ-1460	Kohler-Stephens Ltd. Dallas, Tx.	N313MK
N800MM	81 SA-226T Merlin 3B	T-375	KLT Enterprises Inc/Public Safety Center, Eugene, Or.	(N98FT)
N800NR	87 King Air B200	BB-1262	A N Rusche Land & Investment LLC. Houston, Tx.	N90TM
N800PG	91 King Air C90A	LJ-1286	Bluegrass Tank & Equipment, Elizabethtown, Ky.	N301ER
N800PK	82 King Air B200	BB-982	King Air 982 LLC. Carlsbad-Palomar, Ca.	N800JR
N800RE	84 King Air 300	FA-7	EEI Holding Corp/Egizil Construction Inc. Springfield, Il.	N800EB
N800RP	74 King Air C90	LJ-628	Randolf S Martin Springfield, Il	F-GNUV
N800TS	82 King Air B200	BB-1032	Hales Company Inc., Clayton, NC.	N67FS
N800TT	82 King Air B200	BB-957	JENCO Inc. Greensboro, NC.	N200HW
N801BS	00 King Air C90B	LJ-1601	Stephen Parker, Odessa, Tx.	N903TS
N801CA	81 PA-31T Cheyenne 1	8104018	La Stella Corp. Pueblo, Co.	
N801EB	73 Rockwell 690A	11111	Ray Aircraft Leasing LLC. Tuscaloosa, Al.	XA-...
N801GG	80 King Air 200	BB-642	Lone Star Land & Cattle, Conroe, Tx.	N10BY
N801HL	80 PA-31T Cheyenne II	8020016	Eastern Mountain Air LLC. Dover, De.	N2355W
N801J	06 Pilatus PC-12/47	801	Goldeneye LLC., Harper Woods, Mi.	HB-FQT
N801JW	82 PA-42 Cheyenne III	8001072	Hortmont Aviation Services Inc. New Hope, Pa.	N63WA
N801KM	67 King Air A90	LJ-218	Covenant Sales & Leasing Inc. New Orleans, La.	N380M
N801NA	83 King Air B200	BB-1164	NASA, Edwards AFB. Ca.	N701NA
N801WA	01 PA-46-500TP Meridian	4697062	Radioflyer LLC, San Diego,Ca.	C-GEMO
N802AF	07 Pilatus PC-12/47	802	PRM Enterprises Inc., Manchester, NH.	HB-F
N802BS	01 King Air 350	FL-338	BancorpSouth Bank, Tupelo, Ms.	N3238S
N802DG	79 King Air C90	LJ-807	Hillsborough County Mosquito Control, Tampa, Fl.	N877WL
N802DJ	69 SA-26AT Merlin 2B	T26-117	Spartan Fleet Management Inc. Tryon, NC.	C-GYLP
N802GC	80 King Air B100	BE-96	Wisconsin Air Service LLC. Milwaukee, Wi.	N802RD
N802HS	95 Pilatus PC-12	118	Keystone Builders Resource Group Inc. Richmond, Va.	HB-FQL
N802M	87 King Air 300	FA-124	Midcountry Financial Corp. Macon, Ga.	N500FC
N802MJ	06 King Air B200	BB-1948	Panattoni Development, Monterey, Ca.	N36898
N802MM	03 PA-46-500TP Meridian	4697148	Renlim LLC. Atlanta, Fl.	
N802MW	82 PA-42 Cheyenne III	8001081	MIC-PLANE Inc. Baltimore, Md.	N881AM
N803HC	81 King Air F90	LA-99	H.J.King Air LLC/Mid-South Lumber Company, Lithonia, Ga.	N711KW
N804	80 King Air 200	BB-724	Transcom Services LLC. Pottsville, Pa.	(N200WB)

Reg	Yr Type	c/n	Owner/Operator	Prev Regn
N804C	84 Cheyenne II-XL	1166006	Northcoast Technologies, Chardon, Oh. (was s/n 1122001).	(N42RL)
N804GT	06 King Air C90GT	LJ-1804	Boardroom Aviation LLC.,/McKernan Packaging, Reno, Nv.	
N804JH	01 PA-46-500TP Meridian	4697044	Twin Landfill Corp. Laramie, Wy.	
N804ST	06 Pilatus PC-12/47	741	Double Black Diamond Aviation LLC., Corona Del Mar, Ca.	N531MP
N805C	01 King Air B200	BB-1751	Henner Revocable Trust, Pacifica, Ca.	N617TA
N806W	61 Gulfstream 1	67	U S Immigration & Naturalization Service, Pineville, La.	N5241Z
N807D	07 Pilatus PC-12/47	807	PK Services LLC., Wilmington, De.	HB-FQY
N807M	82 SA-227AT Merlin 4C	AT-454	Ameriflight Inc. Burbank, Ca.	N3013T
N807RS	00 King Air C90B	LJ-1602	Aerolease LLC./Weather Modification Inc., Fargo, ND.	(N700KB)
N807SM	07 King Air B200	BB-1989	Aurora Air Partners LLC., Canby, Or.	N989BK
N808DS	98 King Air B200	BB-1628	MT King Air LLC. Virginia Beach, Va.	
N808GU	66 680V Turbo Commander	1579-32	Kenneth Erickson, San Diego, Ca.	N6536V
N808NC	85 Gulfstream 1000	96085	Intermap Technologies Inc. Calgary, AB. Canada.	N205AB
N808NT	81 Gulfstream 980	95081	Eagle Air Inc. Memphis, Tn.	N888NT
N808SW	78 King Air C90	LJ-801	Sycamore Asset Mngmnt /Doyle Partners Air, Bakersfield, Ca.	TC-CSA
N808TC	83 King Air F90-1	LA-211	Valhalla Aviation Inc. Los Angeles, Ca.	N22SN
N808WD	99 King Air B200	BB-1685	State of Texas, Austin, Tx.	
N810CB	59 Gulfstream 1	23	Phoenix Air Group Inc. Cartersville, Ga.	N186PA
N810CM	80 King Air F90	LA-20	Crown Delaware Investments Corp. Irving, Tx.	N90ET
N810EC	81 Gulfstream 980	95071	Fini SA. (status ?).	N9823S
N810GW	82 King Air B200	BB-949	Appalachian Services Inc. Hazard, Ky.	N567JD
N810HM	83 PA-31T Cheyenne 1A	8304002	Basham, Boutwell, Miller, Gher & Assocs. Eastview, Ky.	N910HM
N810JB	76 King Air 200	BB-139	BS LLC. Vernon, In.	N170SP
N810K	82 King Air B200	BB-1045	ASI Holdings Inc. Albany, Ga.	N810V
N811FA	80 King Air 200	BB-678	Greenway Air LLC. Orlando, Fl.	N811VG
N811KC	79 King Air C90	LJ-869	Everbloom Growers Inc/PLH Leasing LLC., Homestead, Fl.	N732WJ
N811LC	89 King Air 300	FA-194	BEL Aviation LLC. Odessa, Tx.	(N811DC)
N811PC	07 Pilatus PC-12/47	811	TDM Partners LP., Yorba Linda, Ca.	HB-FRB
N811R	86 King Air C90A	LJ-1131	Precision Funding of Arkansas Inc. Little Rock, Ar.	N72508
N811SW	02 TBM 700C	240	Samir Wahby, Fort Dodge, Ia.	F-WWRO
N811VT	78 King Air 200	BB-323	Woolie Enterprises Inc. Oldsmar Fl.	N4430V
N812AC	66 King Air A90	LJ-123	Britannia Aircraft Ltd. Dover, De.	N815K
N812BJ	84 PA-42 Cheyenne 400LS	5527020	Skyview Unlimited LC. Hillsborough, Or.	N402TW
N812CP	81 King Air F90	LA-127	Alibi Air LLC., La Quinta, Ca.	YV-02CP
N812DP	75 King Air 200	BB-69	Vince Kovacevich, Fresno, Ca.	N204JS
N812KB	75 King Air E90	LW-144	Folly Aviation Inc. Boiling Springs, SC.	YV-66CP
N812P	65 King Air 90	LJ-2	Cascade Air Services Inc. Issaquah, Wa.	N812Q
N812PA	94 Pilatus PC-12	106	Priority Air Charter LLC, Kidron, Oh.	N82HR
N812PM	94 King Air 350	FL-119	SHP Arrow LLC./Georgetown Aviation Services, Austin, Tx.	N1558H
N813BL	79 King Air B100	BE-55	M-C Industries Inc. Topeka, Ks.	N546BZ
N813CF	81 PA-42 Cheyenne III	8001012	Fail Telecommunication Corp, Bay Springs Ms.	N813RA
N813JB	80 King Air C90	LJ-899	JWC Investments LLC. Denver, Co.	N6732V
N813JP	80 King Air 200	BB-715	CSG Aviation LLC. Columbus, Ga.	N140GA
N814CP	85 King Air C90A	LJ-1127	Cadach Aviation, Pompano Beach, Fl.	(N779JM)
N814G	66 King Air 90	LJ-104	Skydive Alabama, Vinemont Al.	(N819C)
N814SS	80 SA-226T Merlin 3B	T-314	Dallas Fort Worth Sarcoma Group, Dallas, Tx.	N963DC
N814TB	06 Pilatus PC-12/47	748	DB Aviation LLC. Aspen, Co.	HB-FSF
N814W	78 PA-31T Cheyenne II	7820073	Allen Lund Co. La Canada, Ca.	N7703L
N815AF	07 Pilatus PC-12/47	815	Bayboys LLC., Manchester, NH.	HB-F
N815CC	77 Rockwell 690B	11404	Monte Cluck, Gruver, Tx.	N205BL
N816BC	04 PA-46-500TP Meridian	4697195	Brett Lunger, Wilmington, De.	
N816BS	81 King Air 200	BB-778	816BS LLC. Lake Park, Fl.	N266RH
N816CM	81 PA-31T Cheyenne 1	8104009	Charli Papa LLC. Lincoln, Ne.	
N816DE	99 King Air 350	FL-232	Pennington Aviation Inc. Baton Rouge, La.	N816DK
N816PC	07 Pilatus PC-12/47	816	Wells Fargo Bank NW NA,, Salt Lake City, Ut.	HB-FRE
N816RL	76 King Air E90	LW-187	Peter Earp, Staverton, UK.	N66BP
N817BA	82 King Air B200	BB-956	Zane Bennett Galleries LLC. Santa Fe, NM.	PH-ECF
N817BB	80 King Air 200C	BL-13	Alberta Aircraft Leasing, Las Vegas, Nv.	C-FGPC
N817DP	87 King Air C90A	LJ-1156	Fain Group LLC. Cheyenne, Wy.	N18264
N817KA	07 King Air B300C	FM-17	Hawker Beechcraft Corp., Wichita, Ks.	
N818AG	01 King Air B200	BB-1771	Servicios Aereos Occidentales, Lima, Peru.	N4271V
N818BL	91 King Air B200	BB-1394	Brenmar Corp. Atlanta, Ga.	N625N
N818KA	07 King Air B300C	FM-18	Hawker Beechcraft Corp., Wichita, Ks.	
N818L	66 680V Turbo Commander	1558-16	Turcotte Enterprises Inc. Houston, Tx.	N818EC
N818PF	82 King Air B200	BB-1059	Patrick Farrah, Glenbrook, Nv.	N382AG

Reg	Yr Type	c/n	Owner/Operator	Prev Regn
N818PL	82 Conquest 1	425-0109	Telsmith Inc. Mequon, Wi.	N66LL
N818RA	97 Pilatus PC-12	179	H I S LLC. Los Altos Hills, Ca.	N179SS
N818WV	03 King Air 350	FL-381	Water Valley Land LLC. Longmont, Co.	N350PL
N819EE	97 King Air 350	FL-187	R & F Wings LLC/Raymours Furniture Co. Liverpool, NY.	N319EE
N819MH	77 King Air C90	LJ-735	Heritage Aviation LLC. Jacksonville, Fl.	N190TT
N819MK	77 PA-31T Cheyenne II	7720018	Century Turbines, Georgetown Tx.	3A-MBA
N819SW	81 PA-31T Cheyenne 1	8104059	Cedar Breaks Air LLC, Presho. Sd.	
N820CB	62 Gulfstream 1	93	AirSide Investors LLC. Wilmington, De.	N197PA
N820DM	07 PA-46-500TP Meridian	4697326	Piper Aircraft Inc. Vero Beach, Fl.	
N820RD	74 King Air E90	LW-82	Par Five Aviation LLC. Brookfield, Wi.	YV-O-MAC-
N820SM	04 TBM 700C2	316	Mehtaplane Properties LLC. Show Low, Az.	
N821CB	78 King Air B100	BE-35	Z Aviation LLC. Cary, NC.	N364BC
N821J	03 PA-46-500TP Meridian	4697172	Cornerstone Management Group LLC. Paris, Tn.	
N821MA	75 Mitsubishi MU-2N	661SA	Intercontinental Jet Inc, Tulsa Ok.	
N821PE	07 Pilatus PC-12/47	821	Sierra Nevada Corp., Sparks, Nv.	HB-FRJ
N821TB	84 King Air 300	FA-6	Schecher Aircraft Leasing Corp,Port Orange, Fl.	N64SS
N822BM	07 Pilatus PC-12/47	822	Malibu Partners LLC., Ocala, Fl.	HB-FRK
N822VK	90 King Air 300	FA-211	Villa Katharine LLC. Commerce, Ga.	N701JP
N823DB	81 Conquest 1	425-0086	Wright-Yost Holdings LLC, Idaho Falls, Id.	N40RN
N823EB	98 King Air 350	FL-227	Denison Aviation LLC. Indianapolis, In.	
N823SB	76 Rockwell 690A	11304	San Bernadino County Sheriff's Department, Rialto, Ca.	(N29AA)
N823SD	04 King Air 350	FL-390	Stafford Development Co. Tifton, Ga.	N777YC
N824AC	78 King Air E90	LW-291	Ecomate Air LLC Chesterfield Mo.	5U-ABV
N824JH	82 Cheyenne II-XL	8166040	Cloud Management Services LLC. Sarasota, Fl.	(N4DF)
N824S	82 King Air B200	BB-1064	BEP LLC/Bum Bros Materials Inc. Tuscaloosa, Al.	N129D
N824SM	07 Pilatus PC-12/47	824	In The Clear LLC, Ocala Fl.	HB-FRM
N824ST	98 King Air 350	FL-203	Speciality Retailers (TX) LP. Houston, Tx.	N877WA
N824VA	81 PA-31T Cheyenne 1	8104039	Elaine Matheson, Kennewick, Wa.	(N54EM)
N825B	82 Conquest 1	425-0123	Certified Leasing Co. Bakersfield, Ca.	N6882L
N825JG	89 King Air 300	FA-196	Strand Aviation Inc. Wilmington, De.	N325JG
N825K	66 King Air 90	LJ-91	Spirit Fighters Inc. Wilmington, De.	N2085W
N825KA	81 King Air 200	BB-825	Brock Enterprises Inc./Aviara LLP., Beaumont, Tx.	XC-FUS
N825KM	01 TBM 700B	224	Southern Palms Aviation LLC, Wilmington,De.	N9LE
N825P	06 King Air C90GT	LJ-1793	Smith Investments of Carolina Inc., North Myrtle Beach, SC.	
N825RL	83 King Air 200	BB-1108	Grulosa Inc. Sunrise, Fl.	XC-AA50
N825SD	96 King Air C90B	LJ-1449	Fluent Aviation LLC. Goldsboro, NC.	N72PK
N825SP	80 Conquest 1	441-0127	Lamm Aviation One LLC. Wilmington, De.	N322AN
N825ST	89 King Air B200	BB-1320	Weather Modification Inc. Fargo, ND.	N300LX
N825SW	82 Cheyenne II-XL	8166058	Hilton Enterprises Inc. Panama City, Fl.	
N825TT	06 King Air 350	FL-490	Cheyenne American Corp. Anaheim, Ca.	N37090
N826JM	90 King Air B200	BB-1358	Southland Airways LLC. Birmingham, Al.	N5682P
N826P	06 King Air C90GT	LJ-1813	LASR LLC., Penhook, Va.	
N826RM	80 PA-31T Cheyenne 1	8004033	Eighty-Eight Inc/Action Airlines Inc. Groton, Ct.	N855RM
N826TM	07 King Air C90GT	LJ-1857	TMG Aviation LLC, Deephaven Mn.	
N827CA	85 King Air 300	FA-43	Bell Aviation Inc. West Columbia SC.	N827CC
N827CC	05 King Air 350	FL-457	Calcot Ltd. Bakersfield, Ca.	N36957
N827CM	07 PA-46-500TP Meridian	4697310	Piper Aircraft Inc. Vero Beach, Fl.	
N827DL	86 King Air 300	FA-103	Equipos del Puerto SA. Guatemala City, Guatemala.	HP-1298
N827FM	67 King Air A90	LJ-292	South Aviation Inc. Fort Lauderdale, Fl.	LV-ZTO
N827HB	95 King Air 350	FL-129	Construction Co/Hill Brothers Leasing Co. Faulkner, Ms.	N46FL
N827HT	98 King Air B200	BB-1618	Horizon Timber Services Inc. Arkadelphia, Ar.	N1652
N827LP	79 PA-31T Cheyenne 1	7904048	Emerson Aviation Ltd. Huron, Oh.	N501PT
N827RM	82 King Air B100	BE-123	Chitwood & Chitwood Accounting, Chattanooga, Tn.	N55FR
N827T	66 King Air 90	LJ-83	Quest Aviation Inc. Fort White, Fl.	(YV-980P)
N827VG	02 TBM 700B	242	Mustang Enterprises Co. Santa Fe NM.	
N828AJ	04 King Air 350	FL-406	Air Jordan LLC. Newport News, Va.	
N828FC	96 King Air C90B	LJ-1436	Eagle Air Med Inc. Blanding,Ut.	N823FC
N828SG	81 Conquest 1	425-0122	Clasarant Aviation LLC. Lexington, SC.	N751JT
N828VV	07 Pilatus PC-12/47	826	Valley View Ventures LLC., Modesto, Ca.	HB-FRP
N829BC	91 TBM 700	31	Berry Companies Inc. Wichita, Ks.	N701PF
N829PE	07 Pilatus PC-12/47	829	Sierra Nevada Corp., Sparks, Nv.	HB-FRS
N831CH	80 PA-31T Cheyenne 1	8004047	BDE LLC. Palm Beach Gardens, Fl.	(N911DW)
N831E	01 King Air C90B	LJ-1650	Community Health Management, Orange Beach Al.	N5150K
N831KD	06 King Air B200	BB-1937	ITC-CS Inc. Tortola, BVI.	
N831PT	06 King Air 350	FL-487	Solitude Associates LLC. Gold River, Ca.	N7087U

Reg	Yr	Type	c/n	Owner/Operator	Prev Regn
N831TM	98	King Air B200	BB-1635	Jaqua Associates LLC. Laguna Beach, Ca.	N567A
N833RL	81	King Air 200	BB-833	BB833 Sales & Leasing Corp. Wilmington, De.	HP-1469
N835CC	83	Gulfstream 840	11730	State of New Mexico, Santa Fe, NM.	N28GA
N835MA	85	Conquest II	441-0343	Cook Aircraft Leasing Inc. Bloomington, In.	N12114
N836MA	78	SA-226AT Merlin 4A	AT-068	Javelin Conversions Inc. Houston, Tx.	(N26LE)
N838GT	07	King Air C90GT	LJ-1838	Dave Holt Inc/T&D Aviation LLC., bend, Or.	
N838PE	07	Pilatus PC-12/47	838	Sierra Nevada Corp., Sparks, Nv.	HB-FRY
N838RA	92	TBM 700	71	Chester Prior, Echo, Or.	N888RA
N840BC	81	Gulfstream 840	11663	Golden Eagle & Equipment & Leasing LLC. Buellton, Ca.	N840NB
N840CF	80	Gulfstream 840	11624	ABQ 421 LLC. Albuquerque, NM.	N840XL
N840CP	99	King Air B200	BB-1658	CPM Air, Burlingame, Ca.	N207CW
N840G	81	Gulfstream 840	11683	Sair LLC/S C Bodner Co. Indianapolis, In.	N171DR
N840GH	80	Gulfstream 840	11615	Green Aircraft Leasing Inc. Peoria, Il.	HC-BXT
N840JC	80	Gulfstream 840	11643	Semitool Inc. Kalispell, Mt.	(N5895K)
N840JK	81	Gulfstream 840	11697	Eagle Creek Aviation Services Inc. Indianapolis, In.	N840AA
N840JW	81	Gulfstream 840	11658	Westerman Ltd, Addison, Tx.	N840FK
N840KB	80	Gulfstream 840	11640	Thoroughbred Leasing Inc. Kingwood, WV.	N840VB
N840LC	80	Gulfstream 840	11647	Indiana Aircraft Sales Inc. Indianapolis, In.	HK-3460P
N840MA	74	Mitsubishi MU-2J	612	Air 1st Aviation Companies Inc. Aiken, SC.	N799MA
N840MD	81	Gulfstream 840	11693	Sunset Reef Aircraft Services, Middletown, Oh.	N79SA
N840MG	80	Gulfstream 840	11638	Grupo Texpasa SA. Guatemala City, Guatemala.	N3XY
N840NK	84	Gulfstream 840	11734	Implementation Leasing LLC. Carmel, In.	N600BM
N840PE	07	Pilatus PC-12/47	840	Sierra Nevada Corp., Sparks, Nv.	HB-FSA
N840PN	81	Gulfstream 840	11679	Pacific Network Air Ltd. UK.	ZS-SLL
N840PS	81	Gulfstream 840	11672	CHS Leasing LLC. Boca Raton, Fl.	N41462
N840SB	83	King Air F90-1	LA-202	Gantt Aviation Inc. Georgetown, Tx.	N777AS
N840SE	80	Gulfstream 840	11610	Maya Air LLC. Telluride, Co.	N840AA
N840SM	81	Gulfstream 840	11700	Sierra Mike LLC. Ruidoso, NM.	(N83SA)
N840TC	81	Gulfstream 840	11688	Select Interiors Holdings Ltd. Matching, UK.	XC-HAB
N840TW	81	Gulfstream 840	11689	Dover Leasing & Capital LLC., Wilmington, De.	N265JH
N840U	05	King Air B200	BB-1927	Candid Color Systems, Oklahoma City, Ok.	
N840V	82	Gulfstream 840	11727	Mid Kansas Agri Co. Pawnee Rock, Ks.	N5965K
N840VM	80	Gulfstream 840	11607	Commercial Aviation Services Inc. Miami, Fl.	N840EA
N842DS	79	King Air A100	B-244	Old Glory Inc. Tulsa, Ok.	N942DS
N842MA	07	TBM 850	424	Insight Technology Inc, Londonderry, NH	
N843BC	82	King Air B200	BB-1011	Comprehensive Blood & Cancer Center, Bakersfield, Ca.	N20SM
N843BH	01	TBM 700B	196	H & H Air Inc. Washington, In.	F-WWRI
N843FC	82	King Air B200	BB-1030	Food City Aviation LLC & Eagleair I & II LLC. Abingdon, Va.	N360SC
N843KA	07	King Air C90GT	LJ-1843	Aerolineas Ejecutivas SA., Toluca	
N844C	79	King Air C90	LJ-866	U S Silica Co. Berkeley Springs, WV.	N6664P
N844GT	07	Pilatus PC-12/47	825	Groendyke Transport Inc., Enid, Ok.	HB-FRN
N844MP	84	King Air B200	BB-1168	CV Aircraft Services LLC. Wilmington, De.	N179MC
N844MS	03	PA-46-500TP Meridian	4697168	Ed Smith, Goldthwaite, Tx.	N341MM
N844SC	81	Gulfstream 840	11701	BT-GS Aviation LLC. Baytown, Tx.	N50WF
N845TC	97	King Air B200	BB-1560	Flying Tuna LLC., Bloomington, In.	(N845TC)
N846BB	69	SA-26AT Merlin 2B	T26-149E	Merlin Wings LLC. Sandy, Ut.	N200BC
N846BE	84	King Air 300	FA-16	MD Airways Inc. Derby, Ks.	
N846CM	75	King Air 200	BB-18	PFY Aircraft Sales LLC. Collierville, Tn.	N346CM
N846PW	07	Pilatus PC-12/47	846	Parallel 35 Consulting LLC, Indio Ca.	HB-FRR
N846RD	04	PA-46-500TP Meridian	4697186	Richard Dietrich, Cleveland Heights, Oh.	
N846YT	81	Conquest II	441-0218	True Oil Co. Casper, Wy.	N41TA
N847BA	81	King Air 200	BB-847	Beech Transportation Inc/Aviation Charter, Eden Prairie, Mn.	OH-BIF
N847D	80	King Air B100	BE-91	Degol Aviation Inc. Altoona, Pa.	N717D
N847MA	07	TBM 850	434	EADS SOCATA North America, Pembroke Pines, Fl.	
N847TS	81	King Air 200	BB-864	Precept Research LLC. Dallas, Tx.	N92TC
N847YT	82	Conquest 1	425-0114	True Oil Co. Casper, Wy.	N68803
N848CE	76	Rockwell 690A	11303	CTS Aviation Inc. Climax, Mi.	N81409
N848NA	81	King Air 200	BB-848	BBKR LLC. Las Vegas, Nv.	RP-C267
N848PC	07	Pilatus PC-12/47	848	N412DP LLC, Charlotte NC.	HB-FSD
N849MA	07	TBM 850	412	Martin Lewis, Bloomington, Il.	
N850AA	06	TBM 850	399	Stevenson Leasing LLC., Kansas City, Ks.	
N850AB	06	TBM 850	381	RAB Leasing LLC, Bloomfield Hill Mi.	
N850AD	07	TBM 850	444	EADS SOCATA North America, Pembroke Pines, Fl.	
N850AG	07	TBM 850	414	ALS Aviation LLC., Culver City, Ca.	
N850AP	06	TBM 850	379	Soldream Air LLC. Tolland, Ct.	

Reg	Yr Type	c/n	Owner/Operator	Prev Regn
N850AR	06 TBM 850	386	Baron Real Estate Group LLC., Brookline, Ma.	F-WWRP
N850AT	82 King Air B200	BB-989	Mallard Aviation LLC. Lafayette, La.	N520D
N850AZ	06 TBM 850	384	MYAM LLC., Scottsdale, Az.	
N850BD	07 TBM 850	446	EADS SOCATA North America, Pembroke Pines, Fl.	
N850BG	06 TBM 850	367	850 B G LLC., Alton, NH.	N850CA
N850BK	81 King Air B200	BB-896	RPM Consulting LLC. Seguin, Tx.	N367EA
N850BQ	07 TBM 850	420	QM Automotive Group Inc. Miami Beach Fl.	N11T
N850BT	07 TBM 850	433	EADS SOCATA North America, Pembroke Pines, Fl.	
N850BZ	07 TBM 850	427	EADS SOCATA North America, Pembroke Pines, Fl.	
N850CB	07 Pilatus PC-12/47	850	CGB Aviation Leasing LLC, Ocala Fl.	HB-FSF
N850CW	06 TBM 850	376	Charles Walden, Corona del Mar, Ca.	
N850D	92 King Air 350	FL-70	L E Bell Construction Cc. Heflin, Al.	N350KC
N850DB	07 TBM 850	432	EADS SOCATA North America, Pembroke Pines, Fl.	
N850DD	06 TBM 850	370	Appleone LLC. Greenwood Village, Co.	
N850DL	06 TBM 850	354	Delta Lima LLC. Bayfield, Co.	
N850DP	06 TBM 850	423	51LG LLC, Rochester NY.	
N850GS	06 TBM 850	359	Winged Horse LLC. Anchorage, Ak.	
N850GX	07 TBM 850	435	EADS SOCATA North America, Pembroke Pines, Fl.	
N850JB	06 TBM 850	365	Serendipity Works Foundation, Paradise Valley, Az.	F-WWRN
N850JD	06 TBM 850	362	Juliette Delta LLC. Frankfort, In.	
N850JM	06 TBM 850	375	John Montgomery, Orinda, Ca.	
N850JR	06 TBM 850	348	BP Microsystems Leasing LLC., Kentfield, Ca.	N850AZ
N850JS	07 TBM 850	436	EADS SOCATA North America, Pembroke Pines, Fl.	
N850KL	06 TBM 850	398	Kevin C Landry, Boston, Ma.	
N850KM	07 TBM 850	407	Rohr Equipment Leasing LLC., Englewood, Co.	
N850L	06 TBM 850	347	Wildcat Air LLC. Franktown, Co.	
N850LD	07 TBM 850	417	Red Dragonfly LLC Riverside, Ct.	
N850LH	06 TBM 850	374	Liton Services Inc. Wilmington, De.	F-WWRR
N850LK	07 TBM 850	437	EADS SOCATA North America, Pembroke Pines, Fl.	
N850LW	07 TBM 850	403	San Sophia Aviation LLC., Carrollton, Ga.	N850LW
N850MA	06 TBM 850	350	R D Management LLC. Central City, Ne.	
N850MD	06 TBM 850	401	Desert Eagle Aviation inc. West Linn Or.	N850MD
N850PW	06 TBM 850	390	Cummins Mid South LLC, Jackson Ms.	
N850SB	06 TBM 850	357	Breaud Aviation LLC. Baton Rouge, La.	N850TX
N850TB	06 TBM 850	346	Aircraft Support LLC. Wilmington, De. (Fl 23 Jan 06).	F-WWRE
N850TG	06 TBM 850	361	850TG Investments LLC. Wilmington, De.	N850SC
N850U	06 TBM 850	380	UIS Aviation Services Inc., Pleasant Grove, Ut.	
N850WE	07 TBM 850	411	Greystone Aviation Inc., Newport Beach, Ca.	F-W.
N850WM	06 TBM 850	353	Patrick Alias, Sudbury, Ma.	
N850WT	07 TBM 850	430	EADS SOCATA North America, Pembroke Pines, Fl.	
N850XS	06 TBM 850	352	Mercury Aviation LLC. Hillsboro, Or.	
N851AF	07 Pilatus PC-12/47	851	KSN LLC, Portsmouth , Nh.	HB-FSR
N851BC	82 SA-227AT Merlin 4C	AT-495B	IBC Airways Inc. Miami, Fl.	(N9U)
N851GC	07 TBM 850	442	EADS SOCATA North America, Pembroke Pines, Fl.	
N851HB	07 King Air C90GT	LJ-1851	Hawker Beechcraft Corp., Wichita, Ks.	
N851KA	79 King Air C90	LJ-851	Beech Transportation Inc. Eden Prairie, Mn.	N4B
N851MA	06 TBM 850	392	Kabo Aviation LLC., Lexington, Ky.	
N851RM	00 Pilatus PC-12/45	360	Las Madronas Aviation LLC., Incline Village, Nv.	HB-FSL
N851TB	06 TBM 850	373	GTS Enterprises Inc. Canton, Ga.	
N851TC	06 King Air 350	FL-510	ITC Equipment LLC. Novi, Mi.	N7410L
N851WA	06 TBM 850	394	WA Aviation Inc Trustee, Wilmington, De.	
N852AL	98 Pilatus PC-12/45	213	Air Methods Corp/St Charles Medical Center Inc. Bend, Or.	N213WA
N852FR	07 Pilatus PC-12/47	852	F Rogers Corp, Livermore Ca.	HB-FSG
N852HB	07 King Air C90GT	LJ-1852	Hawker Beechcraft Corp., Wichita, Ks.	
N852JP	79 King Air 200	BB-516	Spectrum Aeronautical LLC. Cardiff by the Sea, Ca.	N281JH
N853AL	97 Pilatus PC-12	168	Air Methods Corp/St Charles Medical Center Inc. Bend, Or.	N168WA
N853MA	06 TBM 850	371	ASJ Aviation LLC. Burr Ridge, Il.	
N853WM	07 Pilatus PC-12/47	853	Formot Leasing LLC. Cncinnati Oh.	HB-FSH
N854AL	01 Pilatus PC-12/45	397	Air Methods Corp/Cascade Health Services, Oklahoma City, Ok.	N397WA
N854MA	06 TBM 850	368	Union Springs Aircraft LLC. Cincinnati, Oh.	
N855JL	81 PA-31T Cheyenne 1	8104045	Capsonic Automotive Inc. Elgin, Il.	N514M
N855MA	06 TBM 850	402	STS Inc., Wilmington, De.	
N856JT	74 Mitsubishi MU-2K	306	Joseph L Timmons Jr. Farmington, Ut.	N495MA
N856PC	07 Pilatus PC-12/47	856	Wells Fargo Bank NW NA,Salt Lake City Ut.	
N857EP	86 King Air B200	BB-1251	Blackhawk Aircraft Sales LLC., McGregor, Tx.	ZS-LTG

Reg	Yr Type	c/n	Owner/Operator	Prev Regn
❏ N857GA	79 King Air 200T	BT-11	Intermap Technologies Corp. Ottawa, ON. Canada. (was BB-573)	JA8815
❏ N858AC	84 Conquest II	441-0321	Storm Cat Air LLC., Spring Branch, Tx.	N441PJ
❏ N859GA	80 King Air 200T	BT-12	Global Aircraft Leasing Corp. Griffin, Ga. (was BB-591).	JA8816
❏ N859PL	07 Pilatus PC-12/47	859	Juniper Valley LLC, Salem, Or.	HB-FSM
❏ N859Q	68 Mitsubishi MU-2D	113	Leon County School Board, Tallahassee, Fl.	
❏ N860H	82 King Air B200	BB-1067	State of Ohio, Columbus, Oh.	N47MM
❏ N860MA	77 MU-2 Marquise	700SA	ZMP Corp. Huntsville, Al.	
❏ N860MH	77 King Air E90	LW-210	Livemercial Inc. Valparaiso, In.	N717TM
❏ N861FT	89 Reims/Cessna F406	F406-0034	Gussic Ventures LLC. Anchorage, Ak.	OO-LMO
❏ N861PP	03 Pilatus PC-12/45	510	PPC Excursions Inc. Harrisburg, Pa.	HB-FRN
❏ N862DD	77 King Air 200	BB-298	Drake & Drake Inc. Gravois Mills, Mo.	N5110
❏ N862RA	82 PA-31T Cheyenne 1	8104048	Air Pichon Corp. Santurce, PR.	N826CM
❏ N863RB	05 PA-46-500TP Meridian	4697213	Belleaire LLC., New Castle, De.	
❏ N865HR	77 King Air 200	BB-276	Holrob Investments LLC. Knoxville, Tx.	N7GU
❏ N865LR	06 King Air 350	FL-471	Equipment Management Systems LLC, Ridgeland Ms.	N865LS
❏ N865PT	00 King Air B200	BB-1709	FF Aviation Investments LLC. Ventura, Ca.	
❏ N866D	75 Mitsubishi MU-2L	656	McNeely Charter Service Inc. West Memphis, Az.	N666D
❏ N867MA	80 King Air F90	LA-65	Kenair Inc. West Palm Beach, Fl.	C-GMTI
❏ N867P	01 King Air C90B	LJ-1666	MTR Gaming Group Inc. Chester, WV.	
❏ N868MA	78 Mitsubishi MU-2N	708SA	Klaas Air LLC. Conway, Ar.	N15UD
❏ N868PE	07 Pilatus PC-12/47	868	Pilatus Business Aircraft Ltd, Broomfield, Co.	HB-FSZ
❏ N869AF	07 Pilatus PC-12/47	869	Pilatus Business Aircraft Ltd, Broomfield, Co.	HB-FQA
❏ N869D	71 Mitsubishi MU-2G	540	Turbine Aircraft Parts Inc. San Angelo, Tx.	(PT-...)
❏ N869P	77 Mitsubishi MU-2L	692	Triple C Aviation LLC., Lewes, De.	N623DC
❏ N870C	03 PA-46-500TP Meridian	4697159	Gardner Equipment Leasing LLC. Houston, Tx.	
❏ N870KC	07 Pilatus PC-12/47	870	Pilatus Business Aircraft Ltd, Broomfield, Co.	HB-FQB
❏ N871C	00 King Air B200	BB-1735	CAE II Ltd. Wilmington, De.	N612TA
❏ N871KS	91 King Air C90A	LJ-1277	Kansas State University, Salina, Ks.	N8012U
❏ N872CT	07 King Air 350	FL-555	WD Flooring LLC./Wisconsin Timber Assoc., Laona, Wi.	
❏ N873AF	85 King Air B200	BB-1200	Advance Food Co. Enid Ok.	N100LA
❏ N873K	68 King Air B90	LJ-344	Jose Gonzalez, Dorado, PR.	
❏ N873PC	07 Pilatus PC-12/47	873	PilatusBusiness Aircraft Ltd, Broomfeld Co.	HB-FQE
❏ N874CA	06 TBM 850	360	Zeliff Aviation LLC. Oakfield, NY.	
❏ N874CP	89 BAe Jetstream 32	874	CKU Aviation LLC., Dothan, Al.	N426AM
❏ N875DM	90 King Air B200	BB-1354	Adcap LLC. Wilmington, De.	N15JA
❏ N875RJ	05 Pilatus PC-12/45	646	Fredric Boswell, Amherst, NH.	HB-FSI
❏ N875SH	03 PA-46-500TP Meridian	4697174	N6104R LLC. Wilmington, De.	
❏ N876L	68 King Air B90	LJ-342	S K Oasis LLC. Redding, Ca.	XA-MIM
❏ N877RC	82 King Air B200	BB-978	KKM Holdings LLC. Naples, Fl.	N877RF
❏ N878JL	83 Conquest II	441-0293	Executive Turbine Sales Inc. Sarasota, Fl.	N293DR
❏ N878K	98 King Air C90B	LJ-1513	WEHCO Equipment Corp. Little Rock, Ar.	N600CF
❏ N878RA	75 King Air 200	BB-34	Ignition Inc., Fitzgerland, Ga.	N87BP
❏ N879SW	79 PA-31T Cheyenne 1	7904056	Cartex Production Inc. Paso Robles, Ca.	
❏ N880AC	82 MU-2 Marquise	1559SA	Lincoln Air Inc. Gettsburg, Pa.	HB-LQN
❏ N880H	73 King Air C90	LJ-596	State of Ohio, Columbus, Oh.	N2896W
❏ N880SW	80 PA-31T Cheyenne II	8020086	Escalante Aviation LLC, Miami Fl.	
❏ N880TC	82 PA-42 Cheyenne III	8001071	PeeJay Ventures Inc. Miami, Fl.	N108SB
❏ N881CS	81 King Air B200	BB-881	Fly by Knight LLC. Wilmington, De.	VH-USD
❏ N881JP	83 Conquest 1	425-0139	Colt Aviation Inc/E L Pruitt Co. Springfield, Il.	N320SS
❏ N881L	79 PA-31T Cheyenne II	7920090	Atlantic Aviation Group Inc. Miami, Fl.	N801L
❏ N881MC	06 King Air B200	BB-1930	Investors Management Corp. Raleigh, NC.	N5130V
❏ N882AC	77 Rockwell 690B	11375	Restrepo Aircraft Corp. Pompano Beach, Fl.	N412AC
❏ N882JP	81 King Air B200	BB-882	JPB Air LLC., Coronado, Ca.	N56AP
❏ N883BB	81 King Air B200	BB-883	Oregon 883 LLC. Roseburg, Or.	TC-YPI
❏ N883CR	92 TBM 700	83	Fourth LLC. Muskogee, Ok.	N883CA
❏ N883GB	07 King Air 350	FL-520	Integrys Energy Group Inc., Green Bay, Wi.	
❏ N883P	06 King Air 350	FL-508	Prince Air LLC/Prince Contracting Co. Palmetto, Fl.	N7208N
❏ N884D	81 Gulfstream 840	11696	Aerosales & Services Inc. Austin, Tx.	N88PD
❏ N884EA	07 King Air C90GT	LJ-1824	Caseys General Stores Inc, Ankeny Ia.	
❏ N884PG	76 King Air 200	BB-91	TCI Export LLC., Boise, Id.	N9CJ
❏ N885CA	06 TBM 850	363	Rand Insurance Inc. Riverside, Ct.	
❏ N885DS	07 PA-46-500TP Meridian	4697290	Donald Sher, Malibu, Ca.	N568HP
❏ N885RA	72 Rockwell 690	11012	Randsburg Corporation, Mesa, Az.	N921HB
❏ N886AC	00 King Air 350	FL-284	Ariel Corp. Mount Vernon, Oh.	N4484A
❏ N886MS	87 King Air 300	FA-131	Stihl Southwest Inc/SS Management LLC, Orlando Fl.	N87YQ

Reg	Yr Type	c/n	Owner/Operator	Prev Regn
N887TC	04 TBM 700C2	306	Western Aviation LLC., Yuma, Az.	(ZS-FEP)
N888AH	79 PA-31T Cheyenne 1	7904038	Contrail Inc. Bethlehem, Pa.	(N528KC)
N888AS	87 King Air 300LW	FA-136	San Tomo Partners, Stockton, Ca.	(N82HR)
N888AY	84 SA-227TT Merlin 3C	TT-489	Catterton Aviation II LLC. Greenwich, Ct.	N655PE
N888CG	95 Pilatus PC-12	127	UDP Holding Co. Rocksprings, Tx.	N33JQ
N888CV	78 PA-31T Cheyenne II	7820025	M D Aviation Ltd. Rockaway, NJ.	N888SV
N888DC	79 King Air 200	BB-454	South Atlantic Developers LLC. Hinesville, Ga.	
N888DS	69 Mitsubishi MU-2F	159	Dixie Continental Charter Group, Dover, De.	N30MA
N888ET	77 King Air 200	BB-258	Russcor Financial Inc. Scottsdale, Az.	N40PS
N888EX	77 King Air 200	BB-240	H & H Color Lab Inc., Raytown, Mo.	N888EM
N888FM	04 King Air 350	FL-418	SBL Services/Maines Paper & Food Service Inc. Conklin, NY.	
N888FV	99 King Air B200	BB-1682	King Air Partners LLC. Orlando, Fl.	N888FM
N888GD	04 King Air C90B	LJ-1713	New Global Aviation LLC/RMG Inc. Milton, Wv	N713EA
N888JS	85 Conquest 1	425-0215	BPR Management Corp. Denver, Co.	N1225D
N888LF	07 TBM 850	445	EADS SOCATA North America, Pembroke Pines, Fl.	
N888LG	81 PA-31T Cheyenne II	8120035	Marine Transportation Services Inc. Houston, Tx.	N888LB
N888MA	75 King Air C90	LJ-656	Sierra Air Center Inc., Livermore, Ca.	N15GA
N888PH	79 PA-31T Cheyenne 1	7904005	Colvin Stations Inc. Grants Pass Or.	N3WE
N888RH	79 MU-2 Marquise	737SA	Air 1st Aviation Companies Inc. Aiken, SC.	N315MA
N888SE	82 MU-2 Marquise	1549SA	Air 1st Aviation Companies Inc. Aiken, SC.	N475MA
N888WG	04 Pilatus PC-12/45	587	J & M Aircraft LLC. Aurora, Or.	HB-FQZ
N888WW	80 MU-2 Marquise	791SA	North West Holdings LLC. Mocksville, NC.	(N725SG)
N888ZC	03 King Air B200	BB-1844	Black River Construction Services, Black River Falls, Wi.	N99ML
N888ZT	79 King Air E90	LW-315	Pumpkin Patch Aviation LLC., Punta Gorda, Fl.	(N770MT)
N888ZX	83 King Air B200	BB-1140	Chaver Aviation Inc. Tulsa, Ok.	N42KA
N890LG	07 King Air C90GT	LJ-1854	Executive Beechcraft Inc. Kansas City, Mo.	
N891AA	89 King Air C90A	LJ-1221	Augusta Aviation Inc. Augusta, Ga.	N407GW
N892CA	07 TBM 850	408	Hampton Blue LLC., Highland Beach, Fl.	
N892SC	78 MU-2 Solitaire	392SA	Chartaire Inc., Colesburg, Ia.	N392P
N892WA	76 Rockwell 690A	11273	David Swetland, Cleveland, Oh.	I-TASA
N893CA	06 TBM 850	393	Well Air Inc., Brewster, NY.	
N893KB	80 MU-2 Solitaire	415SA	Select Homes Inc. Asheboro, NC.	N860SM
N893MC	98 King Air 350	FL-216	Midwest Air Services Inc. Fort Worth, Tx.	N898MC
N893SC	75 Mitsubishi MU-2P	321SA	Chartaire Inc., Colesburg, Ia.	N5LJ
N893WB	06 Pilatus PC-12/47	714	BFD LLC. Enid, Ok.	HB-FRC
N894EA	07 TBM 850	416	HLB Holdngs LLC, Omaha, Ne	
N895CA	94 King Air 350	FL-114	H L Chapman Pipeline Construction Co. Leander, Tx.	N616CK
N895FK	78 King Air C90	LJ-759	Cobb Aviation Services Inc. Macomb, Il.	N133E
N895MA	78 Mitsubishi MU-2N	723SA	Conair Inc./Lewis Drake & Assoc.Murray Ky.	
N895TT	85 King Air B200	BB-1239	Terry Corp. Jackson, Wy.	N833BK
N896CM	80 King Air 200	BB-668	Mike Vaughn Custom Sports Inc. Oxford, Mi.	N196PP
N896DR	80 PA-31T Cheyenne 1	8004050	V & F CB Services Inc. Fort Lauderdale, Fl.	N812CM
N896FM	86 Beech 1900C	UB-48	Intel Corp. Folsom, Ca.	N810BE
N896RJ	86 King Air 300	FA-90	RJ2 LLC/Endeavour Capital LLC. Portland, Or.	N544PS
N896SB	73 King Air A100	B-160	Rogers Helicopters Inc. Clovis, Ca.	OY-CCS
N897CA	06 TBM 850	377	Grand View Aviation LLC., Orchard Park, NY.	
N898CD	07 King Air 350	FL-556	Sunset Aviation Inc/Rare Air LLC., Novato, Ca.	N556KA
N898CM	80 King Air C90	LJ-898	N & M Management LLC. Hattiesburg, Ms.	LX-FRZ
N898WW	74 King Air E90	LW-103	Aero-Metric Inc/AeroMap US, Anchorage, Ak.	D-IDEA
N899D	68 King Air B90	LJ-386	Sun Charter LLC. St Petersburg, Fl.	N610K
N899MC	82 King Air B200	BB-998	Deer Horn Aviation LC. Midland, Tx.	N76PT
N899SD	81 King Air 200	BB-776	Sunridge Nurseries Inc. Bakersfield, Ca.	N500FP
N900AC	78 King Air E90	LW-282	Turbo Air Charter Inc. Boise, Id.	N50MB
N900CK	66 King Air 90	LJ-85	Island Bound LLC Clearwater, Fl.	N900CF
N900DZ	74 King Air C90	LJ-618	DLJ Aviation LLC. Little Rock, Ar.	N900DG
N900ET	84 Gulfstream 900	15037	Azucarera la Grecia SA. Honduras.	C-FAWG
N900HS	96 Pilatus PC-12	136	H-S Air Inc. Englewood, NJ.	N79CA
N900LL	81 Gulfstream 840	11687	Grace Equipment LLC. Bend, Or.	N90WE
N900M	82 MU-2 Marquise	1545SA	M & M Aircraft Inc. Cape Coral, Fl.	N471MA
N900MS	81 Conquest 1	425-0079	Quest One LLC. Hagerstown, Md.	N6846K
N900MT	83 King Air C90-1	LJ-1048	Schubert Public Affairs Inc. Sacramento, Ca.	N777HF
N900PL	05 King Air 350	FL-462	Big Sky Caravan LLC/Lodestar Inc. Ennis, Mt.	N23962
N900RD	77 King Air B100	BE-33	Chandler Aircraft Marketing Inc. Chandler, Tx.	(N232EB)
N900RH	81 King Air 200	BB-816	Rite-Hite Corp. Milwaukee, Wi.	N510G
N900RJ	66 680V Turbo Commander	1572-27	Michael Wood, McLean, Va.	(N713SP)

Reg	Yr	Type	c/n	Owner/Operator	Prev Regn
N900TV	69	Mitsubishi MU-2F	140	Dubois Anesthesia Assocs PC. Huntington, In.	N333RK
N900WC	80	King Air C90	LJ-907	Chandler Aviation Inc. Richmond, Va.	N900BE
N900WP	06	King Air 350	FL-496	TVPX Inc/MMM Acquisitions LLC. Caldera, Al.	N7196M
N900WS	06	King Air 350	FL-498	Triple Ace LLC. Shelby, Mt.	N36998
N900YH	73	Mitsubishi MU-2J	584	Styles Aviation Inc. NY.	N791MA
N901BK	71	King Air C90	LJ-521	Amerieast Inc. Columbus, Ga.	N70QZ
N901DM	01	PA-46-500TP Meridian	4697051	CRC Aviation Corp. Commack, NY.	
N901JB	82	King Air C90-1	LJ-1030	Globe Wholesale Inc. Tupelo, Ms.	N357HP
N901JS	04	King Air C90B	LJ-1726	Shewmaker Air LLC. Bentonville, Ar.	
N901MC	81	SA-226T Merlin 3B	T-369	McBee & Associates LLP. Dallas, Tx.	N1009Y
N901MT	84	PA-42 Cheyenne 400LS	5527011	McVean Trading & Investments, Memphis, Tn.	N86CR
N901PC	97	King Air C90B	LJ-1505	Transcontiental Capital Corp. Greenwich, Ct.	HC-BZD
N901PS	79	King Air F90	LA-5	F90X LLC., Modesto, Ca.	N602EB
N901SA	65	King Air 90	LJ-66	Colar Air Inc. San Juan, PR.	N1SA
N901SF	04	King Air B200	BB-1859	Silver Creek Management LLC/Singleton Investments LLC. Ca.	XA-SUL
N901TE	83	Gulfstream 900	15031	Etheridge Enterprises Inc. Jackson, Ms.	N471JS
N901TM	77	King Air E90	LW-227	Northwest Missouri Leasing LLC., Liberty, Mo.	N7ZP
N901TP	92	AP68TP-600 Viator	9001	Air Coulibri Inc. NYC.	I-BAML
N901TR	04	Pilatus PC-12/45	602	Northwest Flying Tigers LLC. Beverly Hills, Ca.	HB-F..
N901TS	96	King Air C90B	LJ-1458	R H K of Kansas Inc. Topeka, Ks.	N992WS
N901WL	68	King Air B90	LJ-410	W L Paris Enterprises Inc. Louisville, Ky.	N33CS
N902LT	97	King Air C90B	LJ-1480	G & S Aviation LLC. Austin, Tx.	
N902TS	96	King Air C90B	LJ-1459	Eagle Air Med Corporation Blanding Ut.	N994WS
N902XP	86	King Air C90A	LJ-1136	A & L Enterprise LLC. Urbandale, Ia.	N359JT
N903DC	78	Conquest II	441-0061	Rico Aviation LLC/Sanford Texas Ranch Inc. Amarillo, Tx.	N441MB
N903EH	82	BAe Jetstream 31	605	First Capital Group Inc. Albuquerque, NM.	N903FH
N903MA	04	TBM 700C2	308	Huse Aviation Corp. Bloomington, In.	
N903MD	68	King Air A90	LM-98	Maryland Dept of Agriculture, Annapolis, Md.	N7136M
N903P	93	King Air C90B	LJ-1344	Griffin Construction Co. Fort Smith, Ar.	N8220V
N903WD	77	Conquest II	441-0010	Prospect Aviation Corporation, Beaver Falls, Pa.	N20HC
N904DG	84	King Air B200	BB-1176	Resource Solutions & Logistical Supply, Cornelius, NC.	N81LC
N904DJ	72	King Air C90	LJ-561	AERS-Aircraft Engine Reconstruction Specialist, Prescott, Az	N777NW
N904DK	85	King Air C90A	LJ-1089	Weather Modification Inc. Fargo, ND.	N993RC
N904FH	83	BAe Jetstream 31	613	Coca-Cola Bottling Co. Chattanooga, Tn.	N331BA
N904HB	90	King Air C90A	LJ-1256	Louisiana Dept of Transportation, Baton Rouge, La.	
N904JG	06	King Air C90GT	LJ-1764	Jerome Gregoire, Austin, Tx.	
N904JP	85	King Air C90A	LJ-1121	Air South Inc., Jonesboro, Ar.	(N20LK)
N904MC	91	King Air 350	FL-44	Malco Leasing Corp/Reliant Air Charter, Danbury, Ct.	N90PR
N904P	88	King Air C90A	LJ-1181	Lock Haven Acft Sales/Lifeguard Air Ambulance, Pensacola,Fl.	RP-C1807
N904PA	06	King Air C90GT	LJ-1792	SAR Aviation LLC., Los Angeles, Ca.	
N904RB	85	King Air C90A	LJ-1088	Coil Construction Management Inc. Columbia, Mo.	N124MB
N904TH	02	King Air C90B	LJ-1680	Hughes Venture Group Inc. Princeton, Ky.	N74B
N904US	79	King Air C90	LJ-856	U S Energy Services Inc/Anoka Air Charter Inc. Minneapolis.	N904JS
N905GP	81	King Air 200	BB-789	Godwin Pumps of America Inc. Bridgeport, NJ.	N70KM
N905LC	84	PA-42 Cheyenne IIIA	5501022	reported stolen 1988. (status ?).	N4115K
N905TF	72	King Air E90	LW-6	CEI Inc. Scottsdale, Az.	N722M
N906HF	70	King Air A90	LM-140	Vanderwall Aircraft LLC. Peachtree City, Ga.	N7194P
N907DB	85	King Air 300	FA-85	DenBeste Transportation Inc. Windsor, Ca.	N112AB
N907G	81	King Air B200	BB-905	Script Care Ltd., Beaumont, Tx.	N185DH
N908BS	01	King Air B200	BB-1781	Avstar Inc., Seattle, Wa.	N34GN
N908GR	79	King Air C90	LJ-861	Myers Medical Equities Inc. Paterson, NJ.	N903GP
N908K	71	King Air C90	LJ-504	Church Management TC. Chattanooga, Tn.	(N479SJ)
N909BJ	06	Pilatus PC-12/47	694	Marlin Darlin Air LLC. Safety Harbor, Fl.	HB-FQQ
N909DD	00	King Air B200	BB-1695	Baron Charter Service LLC. Oklahoma City, Ok.	N915TL
N909GT	07	King Air B200GT	BY-9	Wells Fargo Bank NW NA, Salt Lake City Ut.	
N909P	04	PA-46-500TP Meridian	4697187	Green Plane LLC. Wisconsin Dells, Wi.	
N909PW	77	PA-31T Cheyenne II	7720060	Montalban Oil & Gas Operations Inc. Cut Bank, Mt.	N160NA
N910AJ	81	King Air B200	BB-910	L'Eagle Air II Inc. Key West, Fl.	ZS-LJA
N910BD	06	King Air 350	FL-483	DBS Air LLC. West Sacramento, Ca.	N36999
N910FC	81	Gulfstream 840	11682	GMR Aerial Surveys Inc/Photo Science, Lexington, Ky.	N910EC
N910HG	74	PA-31T Cheyenne II	7400009	Shipman & Associates LLP. Wilmington, NC.	N910HM
N910JP	78	PA-31T Cheyenne II	7820004	Kenneth C Landry, League City, Tx.	N33LD
N910KG	83	King Air B200	BB-1051	Smith-Mabry Co/GPS River Rock Products Co., Taft, Ca.	D-ICIR
N910NF	74	Mitsubishi MU-2J	623	Grace on Wings Inc., Plainfield, In.	N912NF
N911AZ	78	King Air E90	LW-300	State of Arizona, Phoenix, Az.	(N912AZ)

Reg	Yr Type	c/n	Owner/Operator	Prev Regn
☐ N911CF	80 King Air F90	LA-13	James Kirvida, Osceola, Wi.	N132AS
☐ N911CM	81 King Air 200	BB-820	Stratus Aviation LLC. Kansas City, Mo.	N369TA
☐ N911CX	79 King Air C90	LJ-830	Tri-State Careflight LLC., Bullhead City, Az.	N45PE
☐ N911FG	78 King Air C90	LJ-774	Aerolease LLC. Fargo, ND.	N911ND
☐ N911FN	76 King Air 200	LJ-688	United Capital Investment Group Inc., Laguna Niguel, Ca.	N195KQ
☐ N911MN	77 King Air 200	BB-229	Presentation Sisters Inc/McKennan Hospital, Sioux Falls, SD.	N904CM
☐ N911ND	80 King Air 200	BB-589	Jetlease LLC/Fargo Jet Center, Fargo, ND.	N553R
☐ N911PJ	80 Conquest II	441-0146	Horizons Inc. Rapid City, SD.	N146EA
☐ N911RL	70 King Air 100	B-55	PassNet Inc., Plymouth, Mn.	N4167P
☐ N911RX	92 King Air B200	BB-1425	Mediplane Inc., Santa Rosa, Ca.	N292SN
☐ N911SF	99 King Air B200	BB-1659	Whiskey Tango LLC. Midland, Tx.	
☐ N911TC	05 PA-46-500TP Meridian	4697238	Trinity Co. Lubbock, Tx.	
☐ N912JS	03 King Air B200	BB-1845	J & S Aviation Inc. Itasca, Il.	N5005V
☐ N912MF	79 King Air 200	BB-532	Metro Aviation Inc. Shreveport, La.	N16PX
☐ N912NM	97 Pilatus PC-12	169	Air Methods Corp. Peoria, Il.	N661DT
☐ N912SM	79 King Air 200	BB-478	St Mary's Hospital & Medical Center, Grand Junction, Co.	N789DS
☐ N912SV	88 King Air B200	BB-1299	St Vincent's Healthcare, Billings, Mt.	(N315SA)
☐ N913AL	99 Pilatus PC-12/45	266	Reliable Aircraft LLC. Terryville, Ct.	N112AF
☐ N913CR	78 PA-31T Cheyenne 1	7804003	Houston Helicopter Services LLC., Warner Robins, Ga.	N21JA
☐ N913DG	82 Conquest II	441-0246	Rico Aviation LLC/Sanford Texas Ranch Inc. Amarillo, Tx.	N913DC
☐ N914AS	82 PA-31T Cheyenne 1	8104066	Steier Inc/AAS Aviation Inc. Coral Gables, Fl.	D-IIXX
☐ N914BH	84 King Air 300	FA-21	Blackhawk Healthcare/Aline Development Corp. Austin, Tx.	N4600K
☐ N914CT	98 King Air B200	BB-1614	NGF Corp/Acclaim Entertainment Inc., Glen Cove, NY.	N2233Q
☐ N914JF	89 King Air 300	FA-191	Spectrum Group/J H F Aircraft Holdings LLC. Memphis, Tn.	(N881AR)
☐ N915CD	78 King Air C90	LJ-748	P & M Oasis Air LLC/SECO Manufacturing, Redding, Ca.	N974GA
☐ N915MR	00 King Air C90B	LJ-1637	Mobile Bay Air LLC. Theodore, Al.	N915MP
☐ N915RF	76 Mitsubishi MU-2L	677	Air 1st Aviation Companies Inc, Aiken,SC.	N2ND
☐ N916AD	06 Pilatus PC-12/47	756	Adventure Flyway LLC. Renton, Wa.	HB-FSK
☐ N916RT	82 Cheyenne II-XL	8166041	Newstone Aire LLC/Tiffin Aire Inc. Tiffin, Oh.	C-GFLL
☐ N916SJ	82 Conquest II	441-0243	JLS Group LLC. Milford, De.	N916AS
☐ N917CC	06 PA-46-500TP Meridian	4697259	DTC Aviation LLC. Naples, Fl.	
☐ N917TP	83 PA-31T Cheyenne 1	8104068	Terry R. Pruitt, College Station, Tx.	N456AC
☐ N917WA	85 King Air 300	FA-77	CajunFlight LLC. Rochester, NY.	N477JW
☐ N918FM	79 PA-31T Cheyenne 1	7904025	Fenton Motor Group, McAlester, Ok.	N531SW
☐ N918SA	80 King Air C90	LJ-918	Mid South Air LLC. Rogers, Ar.	(N950HS)
☐ N918TC	81 King Air B200	BB-918	Blue Sky Ventures LLC. Ogden, Ut.	ZS-NCH
☐ N918VS	76 King Air E90	LW-200	Pisces LLC. Tulsa, Ok.	N913VS
☐ N919AG	68 King Air B90	LJ-432	Papa Alpha Avn /Pollard Aircraft Sales Inc., Southlake, Tx.	N345LL
☐ N919CK	84 SA-227AT Merlin 4C	AT-585	Extant Aircraft Corp. Childress, Tx.	(F-....)
☐ N919CL	87 King Air C90A	LJ-1160	H&G 2006 LLC/Devorsetz Law Firm, Syracuse, NY.	N6031W
☐ N919EM	90 120ER Brasilia	120160	Gillett Evernham Motorsports, Statesville, NC.	N132PP
☐ N919HP	85 King Air 300	FA-81	King Three LLC. Baltimore, Md.	(N125JD)
☐ N919JP	74 King Air A100	B-202	Christus Health Northern Louisiana, Shreveport, La.	N45MF
☐ N919RE	80 King Air 200	BB-824	GEMS Aviation LLC/Evernham Motorsports LLC. Statesville, NC.	N824TT
☐ N920C	85 King Air 300	FA-54	G-Mc Aviation/Construction Engineers Consultant, Foley, Al.	N663AC
☐ N920TT	92 King Air C90B	LJ-1300	Pavilion Air LLC. Fresno, Ca.	C-GMBC
☐ N921AZ	88 King Air B200	BB-1287	Department of Public Safety, Phoenix, Az.	N713DH
☐ N921BS	94 King Air 350	FL-110	Old Dominion Aviation LLC. Hickory, NC.	N721BS
☐ N921ST	74 Rockwell 690A	11200	Aeronautical Technology Inc. Long Beach, Ca.	
☐ N922AA	82 King Air C90-1	LJ-1022	Winchester Express LLC., Fayetteville, Ar.	PT-OAB
☐ N922FM	72 Mitsubishi MU-2F	216	Oakton International Corp. Laporte, In.	N922ST
☐ N922HP	78 Conquest II	441-0027	Mapping Specialists of Tulsa Inc. Tulsa, Ok.	N900HA
☐ N922KV	81 Conquest 1	425-0052	Central Coast AG Rentals LLC. Salinas, Ca.	N425SG
☐ N922MM	04 King Air B200	BB-1866	Medico Inc. Ridgeland, Ms.	N6166Q
☐ N923AS	79 King Air 200	BB-541	Davis Construction Management, Fresno, Ca.	N113GW
☐ N923CR	84 King Air C90A	LJ-1074	Douglas Peacock Trust, Concord, Oh.	N6583K
☐ N923FP	02 King Air 350	FL-347	FMP Enterprises LLC. Yakima, Wa.	N350TL
☐ N923JK	91 King Air 350	FL-40	Sydney Aircraft Leasing LLC., Longview, Pa.	PT-WYO
☐ N924AC	79 King Air/Catpass 250	BB-483	Gulf Air LLC. Spring Hill, Fl.	N250FN
☐ N924BB	06 TBM 850	405	Bravo Bravo Investments LLC, Edina Mn.	N924BB
☐ N924JB	03 King Air B200	BB-1849	Hawker Beechcraft Corp., Wichita, Ks.	N924JD
☐ N924JP	72 TBM 700C2	277	PROMAG Retail Services LLC. Danville, Ca.	N700SN
☐ N924PC	72 Rockwell 690	11041	United CCM Corp. San Antonio, Tx. (status ?).	(N54MH)
☐ N924TT	92 King Air C90B	LJ-1301	Automotive Development Group/Carolina Avn., Mooresville, NC.	C-GMBD
☐ N925B	82 King Air B200	BB-1050	Atlantic Coast Leasing Corp. Rockport, Tx.	(N19KA)

Reg	Yr	Type	c/n	Owner/Operator	Prev Regn
N925ES	80	King Air C90	LJ-906	Flight Plan LLC., Meriden, Ks.	N957JF
N925GA	06	King Air B200	BB-1941	GEMI Trucking Inc., Eatonton, Ga.	N3191V
N925HW	01	Pilatus PC-12/45	444	HRPW Investments LLC., Gainesville, Ga.	HB-FSB
N925TK	92	P-180 Avanti	1021	TK Constructors Inc. Muncie, IN.	D-IPIA
N925X	63	King Air 90	LJ-1	Avionics Research Corp. Madison, Ms. Under restoration.	N26CH
N926FS	81	Conquest 1	425-0093	Ratcliff Ranch & Investment Co. Vinita, Ok.	N6848R
N926K	80	PA-31T Cheyenne 1	8004046	Cato Enterprises Inc. Lynn Haven, Fl.	PT-WNZ
N926LD	78	PA-31T Cheyenne II	7820047	Go Big LLC., Paradise Valley, Az.	N290T
N926PR	87	King Air 300	FA-127	FYK Corp. Jefferson, In.	N45BT
N926SC	80	Gulfstream 840	11622	S E Cone Jr. Hobbs, NM.	N49BB
N927BG	04	King Air B200	BB-1854	Dream Aviation LLC. Brandon, Ms.	N6194S
N927JC	80	King Air 200	BB-595	JLEE Industries LLC/REI Consultants Inc. Beaver, WV.	N528JJ
N927JT	91	King Air C90A	LJ-1263	JT Aero Management LLC/Bar G Feedyard, Hereford, Tx.	N927JJ
N927SM	82	Gulfstream 900	15013	ShamMach Air LLC. Shreveport, La.	N42SL
N928K	00	King Air C90B	LJ-1632	GB Auctions Inc. Spokane, Wa.	N928KG
N928KG	05	King Air B200	BB-1925	Stony Point Group Inc. Asheville, NC.	
N928TT	92	King Air C90B	LJ-1313	West Land Holdings LLC., Memphis, Tn.	C-GMBX
N929BW	98	King Air B200	BB-1630	Rieke Corp. Auburn, In.	
N929FD	99	King Air C90B	LJ-1585	Faust Distributing Co. Houston, Tx.	(N233SA)
N929SG	81	King Air 200	BB-834	Sierra Gulf Equipment LLC. Midland, Tx.	(N68MD)
N929TT	92	King Air C90B	LJ-1317	Creative Reality Group/GSL Air LLC. Miami, Fl.	C-GMBY
N930HM	05	PA-46-500TP Meridian	4697236	Ronald Hutchinson, Brookfield, Wi.	N111TN
N930K	67	King Air A90	LJ-294	FSG Air LLC/Medical Marketing Economics LLC. Oxford, Ms.	
N930MA	05	TBM 700C2	340	Hale Equities LLC, Wilmington De.	
N930MC	96	King Air C90B	LJ-1463	Corporate Flights LLC. South Bend, In.	N771SQ
N931GG	99	King Air C90B	LJ-1572	Bay Area/Diablo Petroleum Co. Salinas, Ca.	N33LA
N933CL	90	King Air 350	FL-19	SLFH Air LLCStephen L LaFrance Holdings Inc. Pine Bluff, Ar.	(N573P)
N933DG	83	PA-42 Cheyenne III	8001106	J B Air Inc. Manhattan, Ks.	N42KA
N933RT	82	King Air B200	BB-955	Phelps-Tointon Inc. Greeley, Co.	G-WILK
N933SE	00	Pilatus PC-12/45	375	Austin Encino Ltd. San Antonio, Tx.	N375PC
N934SH	77	King Air 200	BB-252	Construction Air LLC., Chattanooga, Tn.	N475U
N935AJ	81	King Air B200	BB-935	Carr Air LLC. Statesville, NC.	N500CY
N937D	81	PA-42 Cheyenne III	8001055	Red Baron Enterprises Inc. Dover, De.	N93BD
N938JW	01	PA-46-500TP Meridian	4697023	MHS Airplane LLC. Augusta, Ga.	
N938P	90	King Air C90A	LJ-1250	Account Control Technology Inc. Canoga Park, Ca.	F-GTRM
N939JB	79	PA-31T Cheyenne 1	7904039	SLIU Airplane LLC. Springfield, Mo.	HC-BNF
N939K	68	King Air B90	LJ-349	Mr Kent Raverty Acampo Ca.	
N939RK	77	King Air C90	LJ-725	Aero Mobil Inc. Wilmington, De.	D-IHDE
N940AC	80	Gulfstream 840	11629	Dr Stephen Ritland, Flagstaff, Az.	VH-NCM
N940HC	88	King Air B200	BB-1303	General Greene Investments Co. Greensboro, NC.	N1932H
N940MA	74	Mitsubishi MU-2J	615	Intercontinental Jet Inc., Tulsa, Ok.	N349MA
N940U	69	680W Turbo Commander	1843-42	F & F Automotive Inc. Valliant, Ok.	(YV-723P)
N941MA	79	MU-2 Marquise	744SA	EPPS Air Service Inc. Atlanta, Ga.	
N941S	79	MU-2 Marquise	738SA	HHK Safaris Inc. Wilmington, De.	N916MA
N942CE	00	King Air B200	BB-1731	Corporate Eagle Capital LLC. Waterford, Mi.	(N948CL)
N942CF	79	King Air 200	BB-494	GO Interests LLC., Manvel, Tx.	N942CE
N942ST	79	MU-2 Marquise	745SA	Bankair Inc. West Columbia, SC.	N942MA
N942TW	05	Pilatus PC-12/45	636	Zinfandel World Airlines LLC. Napa County, Ca.	HB-FSA
N943CA	03	TBM 700C2	273	Columbia Aircraft Sales Inc., Groton, Ct.	N703CA
N944BT	02	Pilatus PC-12/45	468	Cumulus Ltd. Salem, Or.	HB-FQA
N944C	01	King Air B200	BB-1749	Corporate Skyways Inc.Omaha Ne.	N616TA
N944CF	78	King Air 200	BB-326	Atlantic Coast Aviation LLC., Wallace, NC.	N944CE
N944K	69	King Air B90	LJ-467	Carmine Labriola Inc. Scarsdale, NY.	
N944LS	80	King Air 200	BB-604	Mid-America AG Network Inc. Wichita, Ks.	N944CC
N944RS	76	King Air E90	LW-177	Troy Fraser, Big Spring, Tx.	N2177L
N945SH	05	King Air 350	FL-458	Shelter General Insurance Co. Columbia, Mo.	
N945WS	72	King Air A100	B-94	Golden Wings Aviation Inc. Uniontown, Pa.	N12AQ
N946AM	79	King Air C90	LJ-815	Badger Sportswear Inc. Statesville, NC.	N2057N
N946CE	00	King Air B200	BB-1728	Corporate Eagle Capital LLC. Waterford, Mi.	
N946JJ	95	Pilatus PC-12	115	Betten Equipment Leasing Inc. Muskegon, Mi.	N398CA
N947AM	90	King Air C90A	LJ-1238	Badger Sportswear Inc. Statesville, NC.	N1553N
N948AM	89	King Air C90A	LJ-1210	Badger Sportswear Inc. Statesville, NC.	N1553D
N948CE	00	King Air B200	BB-1736	Corporate Eagle Capital LLC. Waterford, Mi.	N942CE
N948HB	80	King Air B100	BE-98	Fli Hi LLC/Flight Landata Inc., North Andover, Ma.	N753D
N949PC	06	King Air 350	FL-475	Pacific Coast Jet Charter Inc, Rancho Cordova, Ca.	N36975

Reg	Yr Type	c/n	Owner/Operator	Prev Regn
N949SW	78 King Air B100	BE-34	JR Davis Construction Company/Air JR LLC., Kissimmee, Fl.	N949SW
N950KA	06 Pilatus PC-12/47	730	Viluco Properties LLC. San Francisco, Ca.	HB-FRO
N950KM	04 Pilatus PC-12/45	540	Absoroka LLC., Colorado Springs, Co.	HB-FSN
N950MA	75 Mitsubishi MU-2L	671	Intercontinental Jet Inc., Tulsa, Ok.	N4203C
N950MB	90 King Air B200	BB-1372	Los Angeles Police Department, Van Nuys, Ca.	N5559X
N950MT	84 PA-42 Cheyenne IIIA	5501023	JTD Inc/John Tisdel Distributing Inc. Mason, Oh.	N932AK
N950TA	90 PA-42 Cheyenne IIIA	5501050	McNeil & Co. Cortland, NY.	JA8873
N950WA	06 TBM 850	404	Woodstock Aviation LLC., Santa Rosa, Ca.	N950WA
N951K	70 King Air 100	B-17	Rawhide Aircraft Inc., Troup, Tx.	
N951TB	05 PA-46-500TP Meridian	4697225	Moss Inc. Grand Junction, Co.	N3115C
N951TP	04 PA-46-500TP Meridian	4697175	Clover Crest II Inc., Marblehead, Ma.	N951TB
N953CM	07 PA-46-500TP Meridian	4697313	Burrill Resources Inc., Medford, Or.	
N954BL	06 King Air B200	BB-1951	B & L Motels Inc/Sarah & Clint LLC. Anchorage, Ak.	N7251U
N954BS	02 King Air C90B	LJ-1681	Desert Air LLC. Bend, Or.	N954BL
N954MS	98 King Air B200	BB-1649	Moss Supply Co. Charlotte, NC.	N154DF
N955RA	83 King Air F90	LA-201	Remington Products Co. Wadsworth, Oh.	N653LP
N956PC	00 Pilatus PC-12/45	323	Aeroshare 2 LLC, Salt Lake City Ut.	HB-FRF
N957CB	98 King Air B200	BB-1624	First National Bank & Trust Co. McAlester, Ok.	N1624B
N957JF	85 King Air F90	LA-236	Justice Flight LLC. Lebanon, Mo.	(N230RM)
N957ST	99 Pilatus PC-12/45	295	Seminole Tribe of Florida, Hollywood, Fl.	N295PC
N958JH	85 King Air C90A	LJ-1108	Jim Hankins Air Service Inc. Jackson, Ms.	N438SP
N959GM	81 King Air C90	LJ-971	Baercraft Leasing LLC. Merritt Island, Fl.	N959CM
N959MC	79 King Air C90	LJ-821	Midwest Corporate Aviation Inc. Wichita, Ks.	N821CT
N960JP	83 King Air B200	BB-1163	Have A Heart Leasing LLC. Chillicothe, Oh.	N200EW
N960V	80 King Air F90	LA-31	ImageAmerica Aviation Inc. St Louis, Mo.	N6675W
N961LL	99 King Air 350	FL-264	State of Illinois, Springfield, Il.	N2344H
N961PP	05 King Air 350	FL-447	Pinnacle Air Services Inc. Bloomington, In.	N37247
N962TT	81 King Air C90	LJ-962	W W Flying Club Inc. Brookhaven, Mn.	TC-MCK
N963BP	68 SA-26AT Merlin 2B	T26-114	Golden Isles Air LLC., St. Simons Island, Ga.	N1AQ
N963KA	77 King Air E90	LW-242	Fairway Leasing LLC. Bakersfield, Ca.	N95KA
N963P	06 King Air C90GT	LJ-1806	210 Destinations Co., Bethesda, Md.	
N964GB	82 King Air C90	LJ-1007	Great Escapes Aviation LLC. Fayetteville, NC.	N68PC
N964LB	91 King Air 350	FL-59	The Bergquist Co. Chanhassen, Mn.	N350JJ
N964RT	06 King Air B200	BB-1928	RT Ventures LLC/Healthfield Group Inc. Atlanta, Ga.	N3728E
N965LG	79 King Air C90	LW-204	Gulf Shore Air LLC. Williamstown, Ma.	N965LC
N965SB	01 PA-46-500TP Meridian	4697015	Brokers International Ltd. Panora, Ia.	
N967AB	07 Pilatus PC-12/47	843	Quixote Aviation Inc. Wilmington De.	HB-FSJ
N968MB	99 King Air B200	BB-1667	Gwinett Aviation Inc. Buford, Ga.	N600TA
N968T	79 King Air 200	BB-570	Urgent Care Services LLC. Slidell, La.	(N919LN)
N969MA	81 King Air B200	BB-894	Universal Air LLC. Columbia, SC.	(N894MA)
N970KK	85 King Air 300	FA-29	New South Communications Inc. Meridian, Ms.	N828JC
N970M	70 SA-226T Merlin 3	T-205	Madan Construction Co. Michigan City, In.	N20GC
N970NA	98 Pilatus PC-12/45	226	Native Air Services Inc. Mesa, Az.	N308NA
N970P	97 King Air C90B	LJ-1487	JNH LLC. Greencastle, Pa.	
N970PS	80 PA-31T Cheyenne II	8020023	Greg & Marilou Krech Trust, Huron, SD.	N611LM
N971JP	07 King Air 350	FL-565	John Portman & Assoc/AMC Inc. Atlanta Ga.	
N971LL	00 King Air 350	FL-267	State of Illinois, Springfield, Il.	N4167H
N971SC	93 King Air C90B	LJ-1343	Air Veronica LLC/New Horizons Communities, Port Royal, SC.	N8208C
N972BP	07 King Air B200GT	BY-10	Bonneville Power Administration Portland Or.	
N972SC	99 King Air 350	FL-258	SCANA Services Inc. Columbia, SC.	(N583SC)
N973BB	81 MU-2 Marquise	1509SA	Romeo Romeo Aviation Inc. Austria.	N973MA
N973GA	76 King Air C90	LJ-675	Rick Aviation Inc. Newport News, Va.	ZS-ODV
N973SC	03 King Air 350	FL-379	SCANA Corp. Columbia, SC.	N790P
N975TB	92 TBM 700	75	Stuart Shelk Jr. Powell Butte, Or.	N79RA
N976JT	76 King Air C90	LJ-699	Old Mill Aviation LLC., Taylors, SC.	
N976KC	80 King Air 200	BB-601	RWS Holdings LLC. Hickory, NC.	N6687H
N977AA	72 King Air C90	LJ-555	Maritime Sales & Leasing Inc. Newnan, Ga.	N108JD
N977DG	75 Rockwell 690A	11237	NextMed Management Services LLC., Tucson, Az.	N57237
N977G	81 PA-31T Cheyenne 1	8104065	Superior Gas Aviation LLC, Des Moines Ia.	N777G
N977GT	76 King Air 200	BB-141	Trovarsi LLC. Balch Springs, Tx.	N977LX
N977JC	80 Gulfstream 840	11641	Ace Inc. Winston-Salem, NC.	N850GA
N977MP	83 Conquest II	441-0310	Martin's Famous Pastry Shoppe Inc. Chambersburg, Pa.	N444KE
N977SB	72 King Air E90	LW-10	Glideco Leasing Inc. Fort Worth, Tx.	(N596PC)
N977XL	97 Pilatus PC-12/45	189	Aeronautical Charters Inc.	HB-FSX
N977XT	81 PA-42 Cheyenne III	8001008	R Y Timber Inc. Boise, Id.	N808CA

Reg	Yr	Type	c/n	Owner/Operator	Prev Regn
N980AK	80	Gulfstream 840	11636	Universal Pacific Investments Corp. Stateline, Nv.	N7649J
N980BC	00	King Air 350	FL-283	Poet LLC., Sioux Falls, SD.	N850NY
N980BH	80	Gulfstream 980	95002	Commander 980BH LC./Sheerin Charter Svs., San Antonio, Tx.	(N905BL)
N980CA	81	PA-31T Cheyenne 1	8104010	TLH Enterprises Inc. Corsicana, Tx.	
N980DT	81	Gulfstream 980	95048	Detroit Tool & Engineering Co. Lebanon, Mo.	N9800S
N980EA	80	Gulfstream 980	95031	Eagle Air Inc. Memphis, Tn. (now XC-HFW ?).	HP-1132P
N980EC	80	Gulfstream 980	95011	CPI-Airservice GmbH/Carlos de Pilar Group, Munich, Germany.	N9764S
N980GB	97	King Air B200	BB-1594	2 Guys Venture Corp. Farmingdale, NY.	N2132W
N980GR	81	Gulfstream 980	95049	Dash 10 LLC/Heyco Energy Group, Roswell, NM.	N3982C
N980GZ	81	Gulfstream 980	95063	Alken-Ziegler Inc. Kalkaska, Mi.	N980GM
N980HB	80	Gulfstream 980	95006	Holding & Barnes Group/HBC Aviation Inc. Southend, UK.	N171CT
N980MD	80	Gulfstream 980	95030	Air Operations International, Charlotte, NC.	N980AB
N980MH	81	Gulfstream 980	95078	JAC USA Inc.	JA8826
N980SA	80	Gulfstream 980	95012	Amstar Aviation, Dover, De.	YV-129P
N980WJ	81	Gulfstream 980	95061	World Jet Inc. Fort Lauderdale, Fl.	XC-PPF
N981AR	98	King Air 350	FL-199	Rockwell Forest Products, Pittsburgh, Pa.	
N981LL	99	King Air 350	FL-265	State of Illinois, Springfield, Il.	N3265T
N981WJ	81	Gulfstream 980	95045	World Jet Inc. Fort Lauderdale, Fl.	XC-AA98
N982GA	76	King Air 200	BB-149	Leestown Realty Group/Eastern King Air Svs, Centerport, NY.	D-IAHK
N982SB	98	King Air C90B	LJ-1518	Foster Hospitality Group LLC. Springfield, Mo.	
N982SS	98	King Air C90B	LJ-1523	Futrell Assocaites LLC. Raleigh, NC.	
N982TM	77	King Air 200	BB-226	Merlin Aviation LLC. St Louis, Mo.	N717SP
N983AJ	82	King Air B200	BB-983	Atlantic Bridge Aviation Ltd/Aircraft Guaranty Man. LLC Tx.	D-ISAZ
N983AR	99	King Air 350	FL-242	ET US Holdings LLC	
N983C	81	King Air 200	BB-755	Eric Stirling/Guardian Flight, Fairbanks, Ak.	N711AW
N983JB	05	King Air B200	BB-1904	Wing Air LLC/J B Coxwell Contracting Inc. Jacksonville, Fl.	N36644
N983K	66	King Air A90	LJ-169	Shadow Aviation, Reno, Nv.	N903K
N983TM	94	King Air 350	FL-94	Instrumental Technologies Inc. Warsaw, In.	N861CC
N984AA	68	King Air B90	LJ-429	Active Aero Charter, Detroit-Willow Run, Mi.	N811AA
N984MA	80	King Air C90	LJ-883	Montgomery Aviation Corp. Montgomery, Al.	(N527JD)
N984RE	80	MU-2 Marquise	787SA	EPPS Air Service Inc. Atlanta, Ga.	N267PC
N987B	80	King Air B100	BE-81	Nip & Tuck LLC. Carson City, Nv.	(N3737G)
N987GM	73	King Air E90	LW-65	Air Methods Corp/Flagstaff Medical Center Inc. Flagstaff, Az	N3065W
N987MA	68	Mitsubishi MU-2F	124	Fast Air Brokerage Inc. Miami, Fl.	N18UT
N988AE	80	Conquest II	441-0175	AirEvac Services Inc. Lafayette, La.	N2723A
N988C	03	TBM 700C2	282	Wood Farms Transportation Inc. Birmingham, Al.	
N988CC	79	King Air 200	BB-490	Jet Texas Assocs LLC. Georgetown, Tx.	N908RC
N988JR	78	King Air B100	BE-46	James River Coal Service Co. Richmond, Va.	N146BT
N988ME	92	King Air 350	FL-77	Flight Investors LP. Hagerstown, Md.	N4000K
N988MM	93	King Air B200	BB-1462	Nordic Aviation Contractor A/S. Skive, Denmark.	D-IWSH
N988SL	69	King Air B90	LJ-438	D N F Inc. Grand Rapids, Mi.	N900LS
N988V	07	TBM 850	429	EADS SOCATA North America, Pembroke Pines, Fl.	
N988XJ	99	King Air C90B	LJ-1566	Banana Trading Corp. Guatemala City, Guatemala.	
N989GM	74	King Air E90	LW-109	Dynamic Aviation Group Inc.Bridgewater, Va.	N388SC
N989LA	88	King Air B200	BB-1310	Davison Petroleum Products LLC. Ruston, La.	N16TF
N990CB	94	King Air C90B	LJ-1362	Fremont LLC. Springfield, Mo.	
N990CH	78	King Air C90	LJ-753	Duncan Aviation Inc. Lincoln, Ne.	N601SC
N990DP	01	PA-46-500TP Meridian	4697121	Amalgamated Aviation LLC., Hickory, NC	
N990DW	01	King Air C90B	LJ-1668	WSD LLC/Raven Aviation LLC., Coalinga, Ca.	N9DC
N990F	82	King Air F90	LA-164	Air Twerps Inc. Wilmington, De.	(F-GFDM)
N990GT	05	King Air C90GT	LJ-1768	JS Aviation LLC. Mesa, Az.	
N990KB	83	King Air C90-1	LJ-1046	Desert Air Inc. Phoenix, Az.	N90PU
N990L	88	King Air 300	FA-147	CL Aviation LLC/Levcor Inc. Houston, Tx.	N11GS
N990LR	78	PA-31T Cheyenne II	7820060	SMM Aviation Inc. Pascagoula, Ms.	XA-RMT
N990RS	93	P-180 Avanti	1015	Rainbow Sandals Retail Inc., San Clemente, Ca.	N181BG
N990SA	67	King Air A90	LJ-261	Summit Aviation Inc. Dallas, Tx.	N5115D
N990TF	99	King Air C90B	LJ-1548	South Dakota Dept of Transportation, Piere Sd.	N574P
N991GC	84	King Air F90-1	LA-224	Cumberland Corp. Kalispell, Mt.	N29GB
N991GT	06	King Air C90GT	LJ-1805	FL Ventures LLC., Scottsdale, Az.	
N991KA	81	King Air 200	BB-809	Belleview Transport Inc./Raider Investments, Belleview, Fl.	
N991LL	96	King Air 350	FL-142	State of Illinois, Springfield, Il.	N43676
N991SA	03	King Air C90B	LJ-1691	Westrade Air Services LLC. Houston, Tx.	N1072S
N991SU	77	King Air 200	BB-253	Iowa State University, Ames, Ia.	
N992MA	99	King Air 350	FL-271	Southwest Ford/Martrini Air LLC., Weatherford, Tx.	N999CY
N992TJ	82	King Air B200	BB-992	Republican Transportation LLC. Corpus Christi, Tx.	XB-MVG
					N340TT

Reg	Yr Type	c/n	Owner/Operator	Prev Regn
N992TT	80 PA-31T Cheyenne 1	8004019	Cellular Partners Inc. Hilton Head, SC.	D-ICGD
N993CB	98 King Air C90B	LJ-1550	Tri Counties Bank, Chico, Ca.	N261GB
N993RH	77 PA-31T Cheyenne II	7720066	BCS Group LLC,/List Advantage. Montgomery Al.	N888JM
N994DF	91 TBM 700	22	Cruz Adolph J, Trustee, Laguna Niguel, Ca.	D-FFBU
N994HP	01 King Air B200	BB-1766	Palmetto Express LLC. Lafayette, La.	N351N
N994ST	81 King Air F90	LA-83	Sharp Contracting Inc., Maryville, Tn.	N323DB
N995GT	06 King Air C90GT	LJ-1816	City Link Airlines, Hurley, NM.	
N995MS	81 King Air B200	BB-931	CAM Aviation Inc.Wilmington, De.	N6789
N995SA	79 King Air A100	B-246	Spitfire Sales & Leasing Inc. Goldsboro, NC.	N30SA
N995SC	83 PA-42 Cheyenne IIIA	5501004	Seneca Transportation LLC. Des Moines, Ia.	N775CA
N996AB	77 Rockwell 690B	11425	TTCN LLC., Sabinal, Tx.	ZP-TWV
N996KF	07 Pilatus PC-12/47	836	North Central Aviation LLC., New Richmond, Wi.	HB-FRX
N996LM	76 King Air 200	BB-157	Lockheed Martin Vought Systems Corp. Grand Prairie, Tx.	N93LV
N997JM	02 TBM 700C	244	Sunwave Aviation Inc. Wilmington, De.	LX-JFG
N997ME	82 King Air B100	BE-135	S Robert Davis, Charlotte, NC.	N135AR
N997RC	72 King Air U-21J	B-97	GK Aviation LLC., North Charleston, SC.	70-15910
N998AP	73 King Air C-12C	BC-8	Ameri-Air Leasing Corp. Sunny Isles, Fl.	HK-
N998BW	88 King Air 300	FA-149	Hoppin Air LLC Lexington Ky.	N64TE
N998JB	96 Pilatus PC-12/45	148	DA Plane LLC. Athens, Ga.	N2JB
N998LM	81 PA-31T Cheyenne II	8120006	Lightning Master Corp. Clearwater, Fl.	(N101TR)
N999DT	76 King Air 200	BB-138	Arkansas Bolt Co. Little Rock, Ar.	N925BQ
N999EG	81 King Air B200	BB-908	Transportation Holdings LLC. Owings Mills, Md.	N200TJ
N999ES	74 King Air C90	LJ-612	Cameron-Brooks Inc. Fredericksburg Tx.	N3112W
N999FG	79 Rockwell 690B	11535	SeaSpray Group LLC. Raleigh, NC.	N81709
N999G	73 King Air A100	B-144	Rapid City Regional Hospital, Rapid City, SD.	N999TB
N999GA	81 King Air B200	BB-929	Badger Airlines Inc. Milwaukee, Wi.	N81AJ
N999HW	91 King Air 350	FL-49	Franklyn Ventures II LLC. Newport Beach, Ca.	N350EB
N999MG	91 King Air 350	FL-65	Raytheon Aerospace Co. Madison, Ms.	N999MC
N999MM	07 King Air B200	BB-1997	Alder Air LLC./Washington Alder LLC., Mount Vernon, Wa.	
N999MX	82 SA-227AT Merlin 4C	AT-501	Vision Air Ltd. Nassau, Bahamas.	N3051H
N999NG	01 PA-46-500TP Meridian	4697022	Aerotech Flight Services, Framingham, Ma.	
N999NH	04 King Air C90B	LJ-1712	Nebraska Heart Institute PC. Lincoln, Ne.	N785P
N999RC	83 King Air F90-1	LA-208	Romeo Charlie Inc. Naples, Fl.	N901SA
N999RW	01 PA-46-500TP Meridian	4697037	RHW Enterprises Inc. Colorado Springs, Co.	
N999SE	80 King Air E90	LW-344	Sawdust Airlines Inc. Montoursville, Pa.	N888RT
N999SF	72 King Air E90	LW-5	ForSee Aviation LLC. Dalton, Ga.	N999SE
N999UP	82 MU-2 Marquise	1557SA	JPS Airtransport LLC. Bristol, NH.	N988RR
N999VB	80 King Air 200	BB-645	Cobb Aviation Services Inc., Macomb, Il.	N80GB
N999WW	80 MU-2 Marquise	790SA	SFG Commercial Aircraft Leasing Inc. South Bend In.	F-GEQM
N1007B	80 SA-226T Merlin 3B	T-327	Swearingen Aviation Corp. San Antonio, Tx.	
N1010V	81 SA-226T Merlin 3B	T-372	Transportation Systems Inc. Boise, Id.	
N1014V	80 SA-226T Merlin 3B	T-321	Air Wave LLC., Panama City Beach, Fl.	
N1031Y	96 King Air C90B	LJ-1431	Summerset Land Group, Greenwood, SC.	
N1032H	07 PA-46-500TP Meridian	4697302	Monee DR LLC., Missoula, Mt.	
N1039Y	70 SA-26AT Merlin 2B	T26-180E	Sheila DeForest, Pitt Meadows, Canada.	A2-KAM
N1052L	06 PA-46-500TP Meridian	4697269	Desoto Aviation Inc., Millersburg, Pa.	
N1052X	06 PA-46-500TP Meridian	4697270	M7 LLC. Idaho Falls, Id.	
N1056B	03 Pilatus PC-12/45	499	Jeffrey Arrowsmith, Saluda, Va.	HB-FRF
N1057L	96 King Air C90B	LJ-1457	Petro Air LLC. Monroe, La.	
N1061T	06 PA-46-500TP Meridian	4697274	Dunsirn Aviation LLC., Menasha, Wi.	
N1063F	06 PA-46-500TP Meridian	4697272	Plainco I LLC., Whitefish, Mt.	
N1063M	06 PA-46-500TP Meridian	4697280	Moren Transport North Sioux City SD.	
N1065Y	07 PA-46-500TP Meridian	4697295	Piper Aircraft Inc. Vero Beach, Fl.	
N1068K	96 King Air C90B	LJ-1448	Million Miles Aviation LLC.,Granite Bay, Ca.	
N1070F	96 King Air C90B	LJ-1440	DRP Aircraft Inc. Warren, Mi.	
N1071S	07 PA-46-500TP Meridian	4697298	Piper Aircraft Inc. Vero Beach, Fl.	
N1074G	96 King Air B200	BB-1534	Armstrong Family Trust, Scottsdale, Az.	
N1076K	96 King Air C90B	LJ-1461	Eagle Air Med Corp. Blanding, Ut.	(N83LS)
N1079D	96 King Air C90B	LJ-1462	Don Oppliger Trucking Inc/Jamie & Mary LLC. Clovis, NM.	
N1080Q	07 PA-46-500TP Meridian	4697321	Compass Rose Aviation LLC, Parker Co.	
N1083S	96 King Air C90B	LJ-1443	Scenic Aviation Inc. Blanding, Ut.	
N1089L	96 King Air C90B	LJ-1439	JMSSKY LLC. Flowood, Ms.	
N1092H	96 King Air C90B	LJ-1454	Stanhope-Seta UK Ltd. Blackbushe, UK.	
N1093Z	97 King Air B200	BB-1593	Group B-200 Inc /San Juan 55 Inc. San Juan PR	
N1095W	96 King Air C90B	LJ-1456	George Stieren, San Antonio, Tx.	

Reg	Yr	Type	c/n	Owner/Operator	Prev Regn
❏ N1100M	73	King Air E90	LW-25	Planes & Parts Enterprises LLC., Doral, Fl.	YV-..
❏ N1102K	97	King Air C90B	LJ-1465	Rough Brothers Inc. Cincinnati, Oh.	
❏ N1103G	97	King Air C90B	LJ-1475	Kenworth Inc. Birmingham, Al.	(N900KW)
❏ N1107W	97	King Air C90B	LJ-1477	W A S S Aviation LLC. St Robert, Mo.	
❏ N1110K	97	King Air C90B	LJ-1486	Peach Air Corp. Coral Gable, Fl.	
❏ N1114K	97	King Air B200	BB-1559	June & John Rogers/Sky Trek Aviation, Modesto, Ca.	
❏ N1114Z	98	King Air C90B	LJ-1514	Carefree Air LLC. San Jose, Ca.	
❏ N1118G	97	King Air B200	BB-1576	Southern Farm Bureau Casulaty Insurance Co. Ridgeland, Ms.	
❏ N1126J	97	King Air C90B	LJ-1483	Carlisle Mechanical & Welding Inc., Carlisle, Pa.	
❏ N1130D	07	Pilatus PC-12/47	823	Devonair Enterprises LLC., Rockford, Mi.	N823PE
❏ N1130J	97	King Air C90B	LJ-1467	B/W Air, Sheboygan, Wi.	
❏ N1135G	97	King Air C90B	LJ-1488	BCH Properties LLC. Wilmington, De.	
❏ N1154S	66	King Air 90	LJ-108	N1154S Inc. Wilmington, De.	
❏ N1162V	80	King Air 200	BB-711	Pre-Paid Legal Services Inc. Ada, Ok.	F-GILJ
❏ N1164F	82	MU-2 Marquise	1562SA	Velia Charters Inc. Irving Tx.	D-ICDG
❏ N1183G	79	PA-31T Cheyenne II	7920086	C A R Lease Corp. Brentwood, Tn.	OE-FMR
❏ N1194C	80	King Air 200	BB-679	Executive Aviation Services Inc. Rogers, Ar.	N256PL
❏ N1205S	79	King Air E90	LW-319	Standridge Color Corp. Social Circle, Ga.	N2065K
❏ N1207S	68	SA-26T Merlin 2A	T26-24	Henry Wurst Inc. Apex, NC.	
❏ N1208S	68	SA-26T Merlin 2A	T26-25	South Jersey Airways Inc. Atlantic City, NJ.	
❏ N1210S	68	SA-26T Merlin 2A	T26-27	Wepco Inc/Ridgley Aviation, Tyler, Tx.	
❏ N1210Z	85	Conquest II	441-0339	Nevada Conquest Aviation LP. Carson City, Nv.	(N441CP)
❏ N1212C	85	Conquest II	441-0346	Bil Mar Foods Inc. Muskegon, Mi.	
❏ N1221S	68	SA-26AT Merlin 2B	T26-109	PHASII LLC., Tempe, Az.	
❏ N1222B	82	Conquest 1	425-0060	Reid Dennis, Woodside, Ca.	N68436
❏ N1223B	85	Conquest 1	425-0201	Conquest Technology Associates LLC. Palo Alto, Ca.	(N888TP)
❏ N1224J	84	Conquest 1	425-0208	Lark Aviation Inc. Laguna Hills, Ca.	
❏ N1227J	85	Conquest 1	425-0229	Prairie Dog Aviation LC. Wichita, Ks.	
❏ N1250	86	King Air 300	FA-88	Alliance Laundry Systems LLC. Ripon, Wi.	N7255X
❏ N1253W	01	King Air 350	FL-330	Worthington Industries Inc. Columbus, Oh.	N350KA
❏ N1262K	85	Conquest 1	425-0234	Goldsteel Inc. Wilmingdon De.	
❏ N1290A	65	King Air 90	LJ-30	Turbine Power Inc. Bridgewater, Va.	N538M
❏ N1310T	74	King Air C90	LJ-617	PDQ Air, Lexington, Ky.	N65GH
❏ N1347Z	72	King Air A100	B-114	Westernair of Albuquerque Inc. Albuquerque, NM.	XC-FIX
❏ N1362N	76	King Air A100	B-230	CC Holding 500 Inc., Fort Lauderdale, Fl.	D-IKUL
❏ N1380	81	Cheyenne II-XL	8166008	American Trust & Savings Bank, Dubuque, Ia.	N35CA
❏ N1421Z	98	TBM 700	140	AAS Acquisitions LLC/TVPX Inc. Concord, Ma.	(N709DM)
❏ N1525C	92	King Air 350	FL-88	Cretex Companies Inc. Elk River, Mn.	N8288W
❏ N1542	05	King Air B200	BB-1916	Cook Canyon (GP) LLC Dallas, Tx.	N36916
❏ N1544V	94	King Air C90B	LJ-1366	ElanAir Inc/Heritage Flight, Burlington, Vt.	
❏ N1546	77	King Air C-12C	BC-58	U S Customs Service, Oklahoma City, Ok.	77-22947
❏ N1547	77	King Air C-12C	BC-50	U S Customs Service, Oklahoma City, Ok.	77-22939
❏ N1547V	88	King Air B200	BB-1307	South Dakota DoT, Pierre, SD.	
❏ N1548K	89	King Air 300	FA-179	Resort Transport/Integrated Marketing & Sales, Greenville.	
❏ N1549	77	King Air C-12C	BC-45	U S Customs Service, Oklahoma City, Ok.	77-22934
❏ N1551	76	King Air C-12C	BC-39	U S Customs Service, Oklahoma City, Ok.	76-22562
❏ N1551A	90	King Air 350	FL-24	Oso Rio LLC. Houston, Tx. (status ?).	N2SM
❏ N1551C	94	King Air C90B	LJ-1365	ElanAir Inc/Heritage Flight, Burlington, Vt.	
❏ N1551H	89	King Air C90A	LJ-1211	BancFirst, Oklahoma City, Ok.	
❏ N1552G	89	King Air C90A	LJ-1206	TIMMCO Holdings LLC. Edenton, NC.	
❏ N1553	76	King Air C-12C	BC-30	U S Customs Service, Oklahoma City, Ok.	76-22254
❏ N1553G	89	King Air C90A	LJ-1214	Avera Health, Sioux Falls, SD.	
❏ N1553M	89	King Air B200	BB-1328	Texas A & M University, College Station, Tx.	
❏ N1554	76	King Air JC-12C	BC-21	U S Customs Service, Oklahoma City, Ok.	76-22545
❏ N1558	73	King Air C-12C	BC-20	U S Customs Service, Oklahoma City, Ok.	73-22260
❏ N1559	73	King Air C-12C	BC-16	U S Customs Service, Oklahoma City, Ok.	73-22260
❏ N1559G	94	King Air B200	BB-1480	Horton Transportation Inc. Minneapolis, Mn.	
❏ N1560	73	King Air C-12C	BC-9	U S Customs Service, Oklahoma City, Ok.	73-22261
❏ N1560T	94	King Air C90B	LJ-1357	Black Oak Leasing LLC. La Crosse, Wi.	
❏ N1562H	97	King Air 350	FL-189	La Babia LLC. Wilmington, De.	
❏ N1564W	90	King Air C90A	LJ-1234	V J Coleman & Son, Ackerly, Tx.	
❏ N1567G	89	King Air C90A	LJ-1217	Hawk Aviation LLC/Crestwood Holdings Inc. Miami, Fl.	
❏ N1568X	94	King Air C90B	LJ-1368	CBEL Aviation Inc/Cherokee Brick & Tile Co. Macon, Ga.	
❏ N1655M	99	King Air B200	BB-1655	Michigan Aeronautics Commission, Lansing, Mi.	
❏ N1660W	78	King Air 200	BB-390	Central Flying Service Inc. Little Rock, Ar.	(N202MM)

Reg	Yr	Type	c/n	Owner/Operator	Prev Regn
N1667J	99	King Air B300C	FM-10	U S Department of Justice, Fort Worth, Tx.	N2328Q
N1685S	02	King Air C90B	LJ-1685	Baldini's Inc., Missoula, Mt.	
N1727S	81	MU-2 Marquise	1504SA	Bobby Hamilton Inc. Mount Juliet, Tn.	N541NC
N1790M	80	MU-2 Marquise	756SA	EPPS Air Service Inc. Atlanta, Ga.	N179CM
N1801B	74	King Air C90	LJ-634	Grover Aviation/Land Tejas Companies, Houston, Tx.	N19R
N1836H	81	King Air C90	LJ-990	Pacjets Ltd, Baraboo, Wi.	
N1840S	78	King Air E90	LW-263	Alice M Price, Baytown Tx.	N184JS
N1843S	83	Conquest II	441-0317	Berry GP Inc., Corpus Christi, Tx.	N1208J
N1845	01	King Air 350	FL-327	National City Bank, Highland Heights, Oh.	N5027X
N1848S	96	King Air C90B	LJ-1455	HCB Aircraft Inc. Tyler, Tx.	N1085V
N1850X	82	King Air B200	BB-946	Wings to Go Leasing Co. Doylestown, Pa.	
N1857F	82	King Air F90	LA-167	Cariva Inc. Perryton, Tx.	
N1865A	99	Beech 1900D	UE-361	Wachovia Bank of Georgia NA. Atlanta, Ga.	
N1875C	00	King Air C90B	LJ-1626	Star Cattle Company, Birmingham, Al.	N369RC
N1880C	02	King Air 350	FL-360	Clarkson Construction Co. Kansas City, Mo.	N5030D
N1883M	99	Beech 1900D	UE-354	Meijer Distribution Inc. Grand Rapids, Mi.	N30414
N1891S	84	King Air B200	BB-1153	SAN LLC. Knoxville, Tn.	N73MP
N1900C	88	Beech 1900C-1	UC-43	Raytheon Aircraft Credit Corp. Wichita, Ks.	N43GP
N1907W	70	SA-26AT Merlin 2B	T26-176	Minter Corp. St Simons Island, Ga.	N777PE
N1925L	83	King Air B200	BB-1094	SST Caravan LLC, North Oaks Mn.	N1925P
N1926A	81	King Air B200	BB-922	Arch Air 1 LLC. Philadelphia, Pa.	N80BT
N1928H	68	680W Turbo Commander	1789-19	Reed Kent Nixon, Aurora, Or.	(N260RC)
N1930P	79	MU-2 Solitaire	399SA	Superior Builders, St Joseph, Mi.	N9052Y
N1967H	92	TBM 700	46	Av Petro LLC, Albuquerque, Nm.	N701ES
N1968W	01	PA-46-500TP Meridian	4697115	Chewale Inc. McMinnville, Or.	N715MA
N1976J	75	PA-31T Cheyenne II	7520005	Lock Haven Aircraft Sales Inc. Lock Haven, Pa.	
N1978F	71	Mitsubishi MU-2F	212	International Aircraft Recovery, Fort Pierce, Fl.	YV-1978P
N1981S	81	Gulfstream 980	95047	Air Operations International, Charlotte, NC.	TG-...
N1983R	07	Pilatus PC-12/47	799	Blue Sky Air Services LLC., Wilmington, De..	HB-FQS
N1999G	68	King Air B90	LJ-319	Fayard Enterprises Inc. Louisburg, NC.	N845K
N2000E	66	King Air A90	LJ-172	Sussex Skydive LLC. Williamstown, NJ.	
N2025M	78	King Air 200	BB-384	Russcor Financial Inc., Scottsdale, Az.	
N2050A	79	King Air C90	LJ-813	Beech Transportation Inc/Aviation Charter, Eden Prairie, Mn.	N517PC
N2057C	79	King Air C90	LJ-827	King Cotton AG Inc. Corcoran, Ca.	
N2057S	79	King Air 200	BB-425	Whayne Supply Co. Louisville, Ky.	
N2100T	70	Mitsubishi MU-2F	182	Ranger Aviation Enterprises, Sonora, Tx.	N105MA
N2112V	06	King Air 350	FL-501	King Air FL 501 Inc., Fort Lauderdale, Fl.	N7001Z
N2141B	78	Rockwell 690B	11484	Amhurst Development Inc. Lewes, De.	G-BLPT
N2155B	72	Rockwell 690	11046	Metair LLC/Met Games LLC.Tulsa, Ok.	
N2164L	80	King Air F90	LA-79	Transport Aircraft Inc. Trenton, NJ.	XB-DQP
N2178F	98	King Air C90B	LJ-1508	Deer Horn Aviation LC. Midland, Tx.	
N2186L	76	King Air E90	LW-186	Gold Coast Logistics LLC. St Simons Island, Ga.	
N2192L	76	King Air E90	LW-192	Siller Brothers Inc. Yuba City, Ca.	
N2222C	04	Pilatus PC-12/45	542	Air Option Corp. Miami, Fl.	N542PB
N2225H	70	King Air 100	B-34	Integrity Air LLC. Traverse City, Mi.	HI-663CA
N2247R	84	PA-42 Cheyenne IIIA	5501005	Cheyenne IIIA Inc. Lawrenceville, Ga.	N5381X
N2274L	77	King Air E90	LW-213	Press Forge Co. Paramount, Ca.	
N2291F	98	King Air C90B	LJ-1521	NSP Aviation LLC. Statesville, NC.	
N2297C	97	King Air C90B	LJ-1497	Raviator Inc. Dallas, Tx.	
N2303P	69	SA-26AT Merlin 2B	T26-167E	HE Flyby LLC., Salt Lake City, Ut.	D-IBMD
N2310K	98	King Air C90B	LJ-1510	Jim's Supply Co. Bakersfield, Ca.	
N2315A	97	King Air 350	FL-171	Pizzagalli Construction Co. Burlington, Vt.	
N2315L	98	King Air C90B	LJ-1515	C & K Market Inc. Brookings, Or.	
N2325Y	98	King Air 350	FL-201	NFC Marketing Associates, Dallas, Tx.	
N2326J	98	King Air B200	BB-1606	Canales Bellair LLC., Corpus Christi, Tx.	N2326J
N2328E	98	King Air B200	BB-1608	Grouper LLC. Bozeman, Mt.	
N2341S	99	King Air 350	FL-241	Specsavers Aviation Ltd. Guernsey, C.I.	
N2348W	79	PA-31T Cheyenne 1	7904057	FGW Aviation LLC, Wilmington De.	
N2354Y	98	King Air C90B	LJ-1532	Utah Aeronautical Operations, Salt Lake City, Ut.	
N2356X	81	PA-31T Cheyenne 1	8104003	Pegasus II LLC. Wilmington, De.	
N2369V	80	PA-31T Cheyenne 1	8004035	Elsea Inc. Circleville, Oh.	
N2403X	81	PA-31T Cheyenne 1	8104014	W S Equipment Inc. Dover, De.	
N2415W	80	PA-31T Cheyenne 1	8004010	U S Nameplate Co. Naples, Fl.	
N2434V	84	PA-31T Cheyenne 1A	1104011	Forest Atlantic Air LLC., Wilmington, De.	
N2434W	84	PA-31T Cheyenne 1A	1104006	P J Nanavati, Springfield, Il.	

Reg	Yr	Type	c/n	Owner/Operator	Prev Regn
☐ N2435Y	81	PA-31T Cheyenne 1	8104049	Leonard A Framalin, Troy, Mi.	
☐ N2441K	78	Conquest II	441-0053	Golden Eagle Sales LLC. Overland Park, Ks.	N42MJ
☐ N2458W	80	PA-31T Cheyenne 1	8004017	Richard Karl, Tampa, Fl.	
☐ N2469V	80	PA-31T Cheyenne II	8020070	Casey-Fogli Concrete Contractors Inc. Belmont, Ca.	
☐ N2480X	81	PA-31T Cheyenne 1	8104026	Jane Air Inc. Wilmington, De.	
☐ N2519X	81	PA-31T Cheyenne 1	8104035	G & B Oil Co. Elkin, NC.	
☐ N2522V	80	PA-31T Cheyenne II	8020078	Mountain Air Services LLC. Greenwich, Ct.	
☐ N2535B	98	King Air 350	FL-224	Omega Air Inc. Long Beach, Ca.	N2217C
☐ N2552Y	82	PA-31T Cheyenne 1	8104061	STB Leasing LLC. Carnesville, Ga.	
☐ N2556R	80	PA-31T Cheyenne 1	8004003	Henderson Group Inc. Goodland, Tx.	
☐ N2587R	80	PA-31T Cheyenne 1	8004004	Hosteter Aviation LLC. Gentry, Ar.	
☐ N2722D	80	Conquest II	441-0168	USA Gasoline Corp. Agoura, Ca.	N2722D
☐ N2722Y	79	Conquest II	441-0173	AIA Inc/Reed Taylor, Lewiston, Id.	
☐ N2723X	80	Conquest II	441-0180	Eagle Aviation Inc. West Columbia, SC.	(N33AR)
☐ N2725N	80	Conquest II	441-0190	Wild Dells Air LLC. Wisconsin Dells, Wi.	
☐ N2748X	86	King Air B200	BB-1258	L Wood Aviation Inc, Georgetown Tx.	
☐ N2830S	78	King Air B100	BE-48	DeJarnette Enterprises Inc. Lee's Summit, Mo.	N5009M
☐ N2883	76	King Air 200	BB-144	Maxair Inc. Appleton, Wi.	N28S
☐ N3002S	66	King Air 90	LJ-103	Godwin Aircraft Inc. Memphis, Tn.	
☐ N3014C	07	PA-46-500TP Meridian	4697311	Des Moines Flying Service Inc., Des Moines, Ia.	
☐ N3030G	85	King Air C90A	LJ-1117	4079 Hotel Ltd. Toledo, Oh.	N3030C
☐ N3035P	98	King Air C90B	LJ-1535	ARB Inc. Lake Forest, Ca.	LV-ZNS
☐ N3035T	97	King Air C90B	LJ-1482	Canton Aviation LLC/A Altman Co. Canton, Oh.	
☐ N3051K	94	King Air B200	BB-1495	Wood Manufacturing Co. Flippin, Ar.	
☐ N3061J	07	PA-46-500TP Meridian	4697322	Des Moines Flying Service Inc, Des Moines Ia.	
☐ N3066W	98	King Air C90B	LJ-1536	Balco Aviation LLC. Pacheco, Ca.	
☐ N3068Z	99	King Air C90B	LJ-1544	Constructora Nacional SA. Guatemala City, Guatemala.	
☐ N3076W	73	King Air A100	B-176	Colemill Enterprises Inc. Nashville, Tn.	(N110VU)
☐ N3080F	99	King Air 350	FL-249	Equipment Management Systems LLC. Jackson, Ms.	
☐ N3084K	88	King Air 300	FA-160	The Durham Co. Lebanon, Mo.	
☐ N3088X	07	PA-46-500TP Meridian	4697323	Piper Aircraft Inc. Vero Beach, Fl.	
☐ N3092K	05	PA-46-500TP Meridian	4697223	Buck's Inc. Omaha, Ne.	N3092K
☐ N3096P	04	PA-46-500TP Meridian	4697178	MC Aircraft LLC. Las Vegas, Nv.	
☐ N3100K	69	King Air 100	B-1	Bushnell Aviation Inc. Baton Rouge, La. (status ?).	N3400K
☐ N3103A	04	PA-46-500TP Meridian	4697190	John P Zelbst, Lawton, Ok.	
☐ N3103L	06	King Air B200	BB-1933	NAC Aviation Ltd. Oxford, UK. (status ?).	
☐ N3110T	05	PA-46-500TP Meridian	4697221	George T Hampton Jr., Dudley, Mo.	
☐ N3115K	99	King Air 350	FL-315	FL350 Inc. Hato Rey, PR.	
☐ N3115M	04	PA-46-500TP Meridian	4697198	N3115MLLC, Akron Oh.	
☐ N3117S	05	PA-46-500TP Meridian	4697230	Front Range Radiation Oncology PC. Greenwood Village, Co.	
☐ N3117V	05	PA-46-500TP Meridian	4697234	Optisurance LLC, Addison, Tx.	
☐ N3120U	07	King Air B300C	FM-20	Hawker Beechcraft Corp., Wichita, Ks.	
☐ N3122Z	88	King Air 300	FA-162	Anheuser-Busch Companies Inc. St Louis, Mo.	
☐ N3123H	06	PA-46-500TP Meridian	4697242	Champ Systems Inc. Sacramento Ca.	
☐ N3128S	06	PA-46-500TP Meridian	4697251	Henderson Equipment Sales & Rental Inc. Grand Junction, Co.	
☐ N3129S	06	PA-46-500TP Meridian	4697256	DSK Air LLC. Hilton Head, SC.	
☐ N3129X	06	PA-46-500TP Meridian	4697246	Emerald Springs LLC., Missoula, Mt.	
☐ N3132A	06	PA-46-500TP Meridian	4697254	Delta Juliet Systems LLC. Chesterfield, Mo.	
☐ N3132V	06	PA-46-500TP Meridian	4697255	Piper Aircraft Inc. Vero Beach, Fl.	
☐ N3135Y	06	PA-46-500TP Meridian	4697258	Kansas City Aviation Center Inc. Olathe, Ks.	
☐ N3137T	06	PA-46-500TP Meridian	4697257	JJC Aviation LLC. Scottsdale, Az.	
☐ N3143T	99	King Air C90B	LJ-1543	Kansas Aircraft Corporation,New Century, Ks.	
☐ N3181	80	King Air 200	BB-637	The Shaw Consulting Group LLC. Fullerton, Ca.	(N409P)
☐ N3189D	07	King Air B200GT	BY-19	Horizon Group Inc. Boca Raton Fl.	
☐ N3190S	88	King Air C90A	LJ-1190	Banker Transportation/Banker Insulation Inc. Phoenix, Az.	
☐ N3195Q	00	King Air C90B	LJ-1595	ElanAir Inc/Heritage Flight, Burlington, Vt.	
☐ N3196K	94	King Air C90B	LJ-1384	Tampa Armature Works Inc. Tampa, Fl.	
☐ N3199Z	07	King Air B200	BB-1999	Hawker Beechcraft Corp., Wichita, Ks.	
☐ N3203P	70	681 Turbo Commander	6019	Marsh Aviation International, Mesa, Az.	C-GFAE
☐ N3206T	07	King Air B200GT	BY-6	Aerolineas Ejectivas S A, Toluca	
☐ N3213L	07	King Air B200GT	BY-13	Wells Fargo Bank NW NA, Salt Lake City, Ut.	
☐ N3216K	95	King Air C90B	LJ-1392	Hunt & Murt Aviation LLC., Paducah, Ky.	
☐ N3216U	95	King Air C90B	LJ-1397	Cemco Inc. Albuquerque, NM.	
☐ N3218P	95	King Air C90B	LJ-1411	Carlyle Aviation LLC. Atlanta, Ga.	N3218P
☐ N3220L	95	King Air C90B	LJ-1420	Pee Dee Aviation LLC. Florence, SC.	

Reg	Yr	Type	c/n	Owner/Operator	Prev Regn
N3221M	00	King Air C90B	LJ-1621	Eagle Air Med Corp. Blanding, Ut.	
N3223H	95	King Air C90A	LJ-1425	Georgia Department of Transportation, Atlanta, Ga.	(N54TF)
N3237S	88	King Air 300	FA-163	Western Wings Corporation, Roseburg, Or.	
N3246S	99	King Air C90B	LJ-1576	LBA Investments Inc. Dothan Al.	
N3250V	96	King Air B200	BB-1523	Standard Air News Inc. Fort Stockton, Tx.	
N3253Q	00	King Air 350	FL-293	Diamond Air Charter Inc/DB Aviation Inc. Waukegan, Il.	
N3254A	99	King Air 350	FL-254	Concho Energy Services LLC. Midland, Tx.	
N3262R	99	King Air C90B	LJ-1562	Scarab Enterprise LLC/Orosco & Assocs. Monterey, Ca.	
N3263C	96	King Air C90B	LJ-1432	Collins Timber LLC. Portland, Or.	
N3263N	99	King Air C90B	LJ-1563	Michael W Lattin, Elko, NV.	
N3272Q	07	King Air B300	FL-572	Hawker Beechcraft Corp., Wichita, Ks.	
N3292C	05	PA-46-500TP Meridian	4697210	Doverdel LLC. Wilmington, De.	N455RS
N3325H	02	PA-46-500TP Meridian	4697133	JBD LLC,Briarcliff Man NY.	N104ET
N3326Q	07	King Air B200GT	BY-26	Hawker Beechcraft Corp., Wichita, Ks.	
N3366K	07	King Air B300	FL-566	Polynesie Peries, Tahiti	
N3419S	07	King Air B300C	FM-19	Hawker Beechcraft Corp., Wichita, Ks.	
N3474P	07	King Air 350	FL-574	Hawker Beechcraft Corp., Wichita, Ks.	
N3474P	07	King Air 350	FL-581	Hawker Beechcraft Corp., Wichita, Ks.	
N3606T	70	King Air 100	B-30	Sunshine Aero Industries Inc. Crestview, Fl.	N360BT
N3620M	91	King Air B200	BB-1396	North Dakota State University, Fargo, ND.	N362EA
N3634K	67	King Air A90	LM-22	Dynamic Aviation Group Inc, Bridgewater Va.	CS-DCP
N3663B	80	King Air B100	BE-94	Newport Charter I LLC, Pawcatuk, Ct	
N3688P	80	King Air C90	LJ-915	FNB Investments LLC/Fly N Buy Aircraft Sales, Mesa, Az.	
N3690F	80	King Air C90	LJ-921	Advanced Design Systems LLC. Tuscaloosa, Al.	
N3695W	80	King Air C90	LJ-924	Fly High LLC. Tupelo, Ms.	
N3697F	80	King Air 200C	BL-14	Columbia Helicopters Inc. Aurora, Or.	
N3700M	80	King Air E90	LW-340	Boeing Co. Philadelphia, Pa.	
N3734Y	07	King Air C90GT	LJ-1834	Moem International Inc., Coral Gables, Fl.	
N3739C	91	King Air 350	FL-72	West Coast Charters LLC, Santa Ana ,Ca.	N3739C
N3805E	81	King Air C90	LJ-943	Mad Air LLC. Huntsville, Ar.	
N3809C	81	King Air F90	LA-112	Republic Refrigeration Inc. Monroe, NC.	
N3817H	81	King Air C90	LJ-938	James Jr Co. New Canaan, Ct.	
N3818C	76	King Air E90	LW-196	N3818C Training LLC. Carrollton. Tx.	N3813C
N3824V	81	King Air F90	LA-110	Donald A Hughes, Santa Barbara, Ca.	
N3867N	70	681 Turbo Commander	6010	Sierra American Corp. Dallas, Tx.	XB-PAO
N3869F	73	Rockwell 690A	11141	Dr Jeb James, Bay City, Tx.	N62366
N3929G	73	King Air E90	LW-55	Gale Investments Ltd. San Antonio, Tx.	XB-IEI
N3951F	75	PA-31T Cheyenne II	7520010	Barron Thomas Aviation Inc. Las Vegas, NM.	XA-JOF
N4000	77	King Air 200	BB-247	MCM Construction Inc. North Highlands, Ca.	N18347
N4009L	96	King Air B300C	FM-9	Stevens Express Leasing Inc. Memphis, Tn.	N10024
N4019	73	SA-226AT Merlin 4	AT-014	Orix Financial Services Inc. Kennesaw, Ga.	C-GSDR
N4042J	81	King Air B200	BB-874	Stevens Express Leasing Inc. Memphis, Tn.	N200GK
N4047C	76	King Air 200	BB-202	Flamingo Accent (USA) Inc., Wilmington, De.	N2425X
N4051X	69	SA-26AT Merlin 2B	T26-124	MerlinNX LLC Longmont Co.	
N4053H	01	King Air B200	BB-1774	Trustmark National Bank. Jackson, Ms.	
N4065D	75	Mitsubishi MU-2L	660	Intercontinental Jet Inc., Tulsa, Ok.	TF-FHL
N4100B	68	680W Turbo Commander	1803-25	Mid-State Drainage Products Inc. Port Gibson, Ms.	N5079E
N4100L	81	PA-42 Cheyenne III	8001061	Condor LC. Coon Rapids, Ia.	
N4107W	77	King Air E90	LW-238	Logom Aviation Inc. San Antonio, Tx.	N25TG
N4116Q	84	PA-42 Cheyenne IIIA	5501012	Lofty LLC/Don Judkins Real Estate, Bakersfield, Ca.	
N4116W	75	PA-31T Cheyenne II	7520032	Pace Aviation Ltd. Reno, Nv.	F-BXLC
N4146S	75	King Air C90	LJ-646	Barney Cam, Keystone Heights, Fl.	
N4170N	00	King Air 350	FL-270	Mercury Research & Surveying, Dover, De.	
N4174V	01	PA-46-500TP Meridian	4697014	GLR Aviation Inc. Milwaukee, Wi.	(OY-NEW)
N4180A	02	PA-46-500TP Meridian	4697151	North Park Transportation Co. Billigs, Mt.	
N4185L	01	PA-46-500TP Meridian	4697025	WDW Aviation Leasing Inc. Knoxville, Tn.	
N4195S	01	King Air B200	BB-1795	A I I Services Inc. Overland Park, Ks.	
N4200A	70	King Air 100	B-64	Vision Air Ltd. Nassau, Bahamas.	
N4209S	74	SA-226T Merlin 3	T-245	Merlin One Aircraft LLC,San Antonio Tx.	RP-C1261
N4216S	77	King Air E90	LW-211	Tica Investment Corp. San Diego, Ca.	N88RG
N4262X	69	SA-26AT Merlin 2B	T26-153	Latham Aviation Inc. Pelham, Al.	
N4270Y	01	King Air B200	BB-1770	DWO Enterprises, Rancho Santa Fe, Ca.	(N4SQ)
N4276Z	81	Conquest 1	425-0103	Midwest Medical Services/Complease LLC. Blaine, Mt.	C-GINT
N4298S	77	King Air 200	BB-198	Corporate Air Inc. Billings, Mt.	
N4298X	00	King Air C90B	LJ-1598	Great Texas Foods Inc. Nacogdoces, Tx.	

Reg	Yr	Type	c/n	Owner/Operator	Prev Regn
☐ N4368Y	00	King Air C90B	LJ-1599	Ray Plane LLC., Beaumont, Tx.	
☐ N4380Y	00	King Air 350	FL-280	Citrus World Inc. Lake Wales, Fl.	
☐ N4392K	01	King Air C90B	LJ-1642	Corporacion de Occidente SA. Guatemala City, Guatemala.	N4392K
☐ N4415F	02	King Air C90B	LJ-1675	Blue Star Properties LLC. Winston-Salem, NC.	
☐ N4415L	79	King Air B100	BE-67	Idaho State University, Pocatello, Id.	90-0060
☐ N4420F	82	Conquest 1	425-0053	Thane Hawkins Aviation Inc. White Bear Lake, Mn.	(D-IFLY)
☐ N4441T	80	Conquest II	441-0133	Godfrey Conveyor Company Inc., Elkhart, In.	N332S
☐ N4447W	74	King Air C90	LJ-627	Leavitt Group Enterprises Inc. Cedar City, Ut.	
☐ N4449Q	80	King Air C90	LJ-895	Warren Oil Co/Air-Care Inc. Rocky Mount, NC.	YV-355CP
☐ N4456A	02	King Air B200C	BL-143	Aviation Specialities Inc. Washington, DC.	
☐ N4466A	03	King Air B300C	FM-11	Aviation Specialities Inc. Washington, DC.	N6195A
☐ N4471M	02	King Air C90B	LJ-1671	ElanAir Inc/Heritage Flight, Burlington, Vt.	
☐ N4488L	95	King Air C90A	LJ-1423	Heart of America Management Co. Moline, Il.	N3253Q
☐ N4489A	02	King Air B200C	BL-145	Aviation Specialities Inc. Washington, DC.	
☐ N4490M	79	King Air B100	BE-64	ARCH Medical Service Inc. Engelwood, Co.	(N497SL)
☐ N4622E	68	680W Turbo Commander	1723-3	Montana Department of Highways, Helena, Mt. (was 1723-94).	
☐ N4679K	72	SA-226AT Merlin 4	AT-006	Hurley Aircraft, Yukon, Ok.	XC-UTF/TP
☐ N4679M	78	King Air 200	BB-343	Hawker Beechcraft Corp., Wichita, Ks.	
☐ N4717V	74	Rockwell 690A	11220	Cloud Splitter LLC. Columbia, Ca.	YV-236P
☐ N4757S	00	PA-46-500TP Meridian	4697006	Bombay Glass Corp. Depoe Bay, Or.	
☐ N4764A	88	King Air C90A	LJ-1161	M.K. Developers Inc., Naples, Fl.	N476JA
☐ N4776N	78	King Air C90	LJ-776	Zavala Airlines LLC. Dallas, Tx.	
☐ N4839R	06	PA-46-500TP Meridian	4697293	Flightline Group Inc., Tallahassee, Fl.	
☐ N4920Y	00	TBM 700B	169	Avex Inc.,Camarillo, Ca.	
☐ N4925T	04	King Air B200	BB-1870	Air Services LLC. Enterprise, Or.	N6170G
☐ N4947M	78	King Air C90	LJ-780	KCA of Montana LLC., Helena, Mt.	
☐ N4948W	65	King Air 90	LJ-31	Stewart-Davis International Inc. N Hollywood, Ca.	(N505M)
☐ N4950C	74	King Air C90	LJ-629	SkiAir LLC. Republic, Mo.	YV-39CP
☐ N5007	78	PA-31T Cheyenne II	7820061	Empire Airlines Inc. Lebanon, Mo.	N303KL
☐ N5016H	77	Rockwell 690B	11452	Waterland Holdings Ltd.	CS-ASG
☐ N5021S	03	King Air B200	BB-1821	RG Engineering, Santurce, PR.	
☐ N5025R	01	King Air C90B	LJ-1625	Standley-Bennett Inc. Lamar, Mo.	
☐ N5037W	00	King Air C90B	LJ-1630	Southland Sod Farms Operations Inc. Oxnard, Ca.	
☐ N5063K	01	King Air B200	BB-1763	Dairy Air LLC. Jerome, Id.	
☐ N5066N	92	King Air B300C	FM-7	Omega Air Inc. Long Beach, Ca.	N2789A
☐ N5067L	01	King Air C90B	LJ-1667	Hayes Aviation Inc., Franklin, Tn.	
☐ N5092S	02	King Air B200	BB-1802	Bonipak Produce/Bonita Packing Co. Santa Maria, Ca.	
☐ N5106F	02	King Air B200CT	BN-6	Raytheon Aircraft Co. Wichita, Ks.	
☐ N5107Z	02	King Air B200CT	BN-7	Raytheon Aircraft Co. Wichita, Ks.	
☐ N5111U	66	King Air A90	LJ-154	Aircraft Aloft LP/R Zadow & C Lingenfelser, Las Vegas, Nv.	N5111
☐ N5115H	04	King Air C90	LJ-1705	Sadler Air LLC. Lexington, Ky.	
☐ N5136V	76	PA-31T Cheyenne II	7620037	Field Tech Avionics Inst. Fort Worth, Tx.	C-GFIN
☐ N5139A	02	King Air B200C	BL-144	Aviation Specialities Inc. Washington, DC.	
☐ N5155A	02	King Air B200C	BL-146	Aviation Specialities Inc. Washington, DC.	
☐ N5166P	07	P-180 Avanti II	1129	Avanti2 LLC., Los Altos Hills, Ca.	
☐ N5215U	01	PA-46-500TP Meridian	4697068	Papillon Air LLC. Los Angeles, Ca.	
☐ N5245F	66	King Air 90	LJ-92	Marcelo Demaria Inc. Dover, De.	XC-FUR
☐ N5256S	99	King Air 350	FL-260	CVE Inc/Emmerson Enterprises, Scottsdale, Az.	(N350CE)
☐ N5317M	73	SA-226T Merlin 3	T-236	Aircraft R Us Corp. San Diego, Ca.	
☐ N5319K	01	PA-46-500TP Meridian	4697076	Northern Ventures LLC. Missoula, Mt.	
☐ N5320N	03	PA-46-500TP Meridian	4697153	Bridgelink Finance Inc/QuixoteInc.	
☐ N5322D	01	PA-46-500TP Meridian	4697074	Laugh Your Way America LLC., Green Bay, Wi.	
☐ N5322M	01	PA-46-500TP Meridian	4697021	Kansas City Aviation Center Inc.,Olathe, Ks.	(N555SZ)
☐ N5325P	01	PA-46-500TP Meridian	4697085	Diamond Resorts West LLC. Wilmington, De.	
☐ N5329Q	01	PA-46-500TP Meridian	4697097	Jaxon Enterprises, Redding, Ca.	
☐ N5333N	01	PA-46-500TP Meridian	4697084	AvantAir Inc. Clearwater, Fl.	
☐ N5335R	01	PA-46-500TP Meridian	4697100	Richard Rockefeller, Falmouth, Me.	
☐ N5337N	01	PA-46-500TP Meridian	4697102	Over & Out Inc. Clovis, NM.	
☐ N5338M	01	PA-46-500TP Meridian	4697103	Legacy SC Leasing LLC. Camano Island, Wa.	N803JH
☐ N5339G	01	PA-46-500TP Meridian	4697095	Klarity LLC. Great Falls, Mt.	
☐ N5339V	01	PA-46-500TP Meridian	4697110	Newton Rogers LLC. Wichita, Ks.	
☐ N5341C	02	PA-46-500TP Meridian	4697142	Skyridge Leasing LLC. Portland, Or.	
☐ N5347V	02	PA-46-500TP Meridian	4697126	Carter-Tate Leasing LLC. Savannah, Ga.	
☐ N5353V	02	PA-46-500TP Meridian	4697141	Riley W Kent, Hobbs NM.	
☐ N5355S	03	PA-46-500TP Meridian	4697136	Ramsey Pontiac Corp. Des Moines, Ia.	

Reg	Yr	Type	c/n	Owner/Operator	Prev Regn
N5356M	80	Gulfstream 980	95036	Mavax Ltd. Chesapeake, Va.	D-IOEB
N5358J	02	PA-46-500TP Meridian	4697140	Clifford Davis, Newport Beach, Ca.	
N5361A	02	PA-46-500TP Meridian	4697144	State Road 200 Aviation LLC, Ocala Fl.	
N5365D	03	PA-46-500TP Meridian	4697161	Verbena Investments 2 LLC. Las Vegas, Nv.	
N5431M	02	King Air C90B	LJ-1673	Jerry Nutt DDS. Destin, Fl.	N3251H
N5441M	77	SA-226T Merlin 3A	T-283	Worldwide Aircraft Services Inc. ,Springfield, Mo.	SE-GXV
N5450J	82	Gulfstream 1000	96024	Gallo Air Inc. Dover, De.	YV-484CP
N5462G	73	King Air E90	LW-69	Northwest Aircraft Leasing Corp. Wilmington, De.	N769AM
N5626Y	91	King Air 350	FL-43	Land Trends Inc. Joliet, Il.	
N5639K	90	King Air C90A	LJ-1239	Hap Taylor & Sons Inc. Bend, Or.	
N5641X	90	King Air C90A	LJ-1241	Beverly W. Bolin, Wichita Falls, Tx.	
N5655K	90	King Air 350	FL-12	Crescent Electric Supply Co. East Dubuque, Il.	(N491CE)
N5727	70	King Air 100	B-48	Vintage Props & Jets Inc. New Smyrna Beach, Fl.	N572
N5878K	80	Gulfstream 840	11626	Great Marbach Airlines Inc. Boca Raton, Fl.	
N5888K	92	King Air B300C	FM-6	Freelance Air Inc. Atlanta, Ga.	N80605
N5900K	80	Gulfstream 840	11648	Erwin Industries Inc. Hillsboro, Or.	
N5904A	04	Pilatus PC-12/45	583	Swiss Angel Aviation VI LLC. Christiansted, USVI.	HB-FQT
N5914K	81	Gulfstream 840	11662	Safeguards International Inc. Charlotte, NC.	OY-SVG
N5955K	81	Gulfstream 840	11703	Security Group Inc. Fort Pierce, Fl.	
N5956K	81	Gulfstream 840	11719	Leo Sullivan, O'Fallon, Il.	PT-LRQ
N6045S	79	King Air B100	BE-65	Executive Flight Service LLC. Danbury, Ct.	
N6069A	78	King Air 200	BB-357	Sigmon Properties LLC. Conover, NC.	N500DE
N6077X	02	King Air C90B	LJ-1677	Alper LP. Las Vegas, Nv.	(N444ES)
N6107A	78	PA-31T Cheyenne II	7820087	Barrwood Equipment Corp. Concord, NH.	
N6111V	04	King Air C90B	LJ-1711	Airplane 421 LLC. Yuma, Az.	
N6112G	04	King Air 350	FL-412	Metromont Leasing LLC. Spartanburg, SC.	(N626JP)
N6116N	04	King Air 350	FL-416	JNS Aircraft Sales LLC., Nara Visa, NM.	
N6137	65	King Air 90	LJ-47	Turbine Power Inc. Bridgewater, Va.	N613M
N6165Y	04	King Air 350	FL-405	Silver Air LLC. Hicksville, NY.	
N6173C	82	King Air C90-1	LJ-1014	Midwest Equipment of Morris Inc. Morris, Mn.	
N6175A	79	PA-31T Cheyenne II	7920011	Wells Fargo Bank NW NA, Salt Lake city Ut.	C-GHXG
N6182A	94	King Air B200	BB-1484	Colleen Corp. Philadelphia, Pa.	N200KA
N6190S	04	King Air C90B	LJ-1702	Justice Aviation LLC. Lexington, Ky.	
N6197C	06	King Air C90GT	LJ-1767	190 WB Aviation LLC. Lewes, De.	
N6207F	82	King Air C90-1	LJ-1017	Roche Fruit Co & J L Smith Co. Yakima, Wa.	
N6228Q	67	King Air A90	LJ-280	Cumberland Board of Vocational Education, Bridgeton, NJ.	N46G
N6271C	82	King Air B200	BB-1036	University of Texas, Austin, Tx.	
N6300F	04	King Air B200	BB-1865	GOMACO Corp/Godbersen Smith Construction Co. Ida Grove, Ia.	N6165Q
N6335F	82	King Air F90	LA-190	Dewane Investments LLC. Glendale, Az.	
N6356C	83	King Air C90-1	LJ-1052	Medical University of South Carolina, Charleston, SC.	
N6451D	82	King Air B200	BB-1009	U S Department of Energy, Las Vegas, Nv.	
N6492C	83	King Air C90-1	LJ-1050	Team Yamato LLC, Myrtle Beach,SC.	
N6507B	79	King Air 200	BB-498	U S Customs Service, Oklahoma City, Ok.	N23707
N6509F	79	King Air 200	BB-493	HAB Enterprises, Oklahoma City, Ok.	N6040W
N6531N	82	King Air B200	BB-1081	Bering Marine Corp. Seattle, Wa.	
N6563K	82	King Air C90-1	LJ-1032	Beech Transportation Inc/Aviation Charter, Eden Prairie, Mn.	
N6571S	76	King Air E90	LW-171	BCA Aviation Inc., Lavonia, Ga.	
N6590Y	90	Reims/Cessna F406	F406-0052	Gussic Ventures LLC. Anchorage, Ak.	
N6591F	90	Reims/Cessna F406	F406-0054	Gussic Ventures LLC. Anchorage, Ak.	
N6604L	83	King Air B200	BB-1121	Cubic Corp. San Diego, Ca.	
N6642K	84	King Air 300	FA-1	Hawker Beechcraft Corp., Wichita, Ks.	
N6644J	82	King Air B200	BB-1031	Equitable Energy Solutions Inc/H7 Aviation Inc San Diego Ca.	
N6646R	79	King Air C90	LJ-836	El Aero Services Inc. Elko, Nv.	
N6681S	79	King Air C90	LJ-850	Hawker Beechcraft Corporation, Wichita, Ks	
N6683W	83	King Air B200	BB-1154	Red Tail LLC. Lake Oswego, Or.	
N6684B	80	King Air 200	BB-631	J & D Aircraft Sales LLC., Pasco, Wa.	
N6692D	84	King Air C90A	LJ-1072	M & J Leasing LLC. Cameron, Wi.	
N6720Y	03	TBM 700C2	265	Robert Felland, Three Lakes, Wi.	(N700EV)
N6723Y	82	King Air C90-1	LJ-1013	R Thomas Development Inc. Lodi, Ca.	(SE-...)
N6728H	85	King Air B200	BB-1193	Eric Stirling/Guardian Flight, Fairbanks, Ak.	(N78GC)
N6754H	80	King Air C90	LJ-891	ACSS-Aviation Communication & Surveillance, Phoenix, Az.	(N450MT)
N6756P	80	King Air B100	BE-92	Permian Tank & Manufacturing Inc. Odessa, Tx.	
N6763K	84	King Air C90A	LJ-1064	Ellis Steel Company Inc., West Point, Ms.	
N6767M	83	Gulfstream 1000	96064	P A Bergner & Co. Peoria, Il.	OY-BPF
N6772P	81	Conquest 1	425-0022	Dave & Rick Good Partnership, Delphos, Oh.	

Reg	Yr	Type	c/n	Owner/Operator	Prev Regn
N6774Z	81	Conquest 1	425-0048	Ricarda Corp. Beatrice, Ne.	(N425E)
N6812W	85	King Air 300	FA-38	Diversified Energy Inc. Knoxville, Tn.	
N6818R	07	Pilatus PC-12/47	818	Robinson Air LLC., Everett, Wa.	HB-FRG
N6832M	83	Conquest II	441-0282	Firemans Fund Insurance Companies,	
N6840T	83	Conquest II	441-0299	Rains Aviation Ltd. Odessa, Tx.	
N6842D	01	TBM 700B	192	JF Edwards Construction Co., Geneseo, Il.	N71FF
N6844D	81	Conquest 1	425-0062	Financial Flyers II LLC. Petaluma, Ca.	
N6846S	81	Conquest 1	425-0081	C E Hamilton Trust, Silver City, NM.	
N6851G	82	Conquest 1	425-0112	Jack Bowles, Oklahoma City, Ok.	
N6851T	81	Conquest II	441-0211	Ward Leasing Co. Stamford, Ct.	
N6851X	81	Conquest II	441-0212	Superior Aviation Inc. Ford Airport-Kingsford, Mi.	
N6853T	81	Conquest II	441-0220	Escape Air Service Inc. Wilmington, De.	
N6855P	82	Conquest II	441-0233	Lantis Enterprises/Maverick Aviation LLC. Spearfish Sd.	
N6860C	83	Conquest II	441-0304	New Mexico State University, Las Cruces, NM.	YV-34CP
N6868C	07	TBM 850	415	N1968 LLC., Edwards, Co.	
N6885P	82	Conquest 1	425-0143	Walter Hartman, Camarillo, Ca.	
N6885S	82	Conquest 1	425-0144	State of Texas, Austin, Tx.	
N6886V	83	Conquest 1	425-0154	Marce Corporation, Covington, In.	
N6900K	78	Rockwell 690B	11441	Hartford Holding Corp. Naples, Fl.	ZS-KOG
N6971Z	05	Pilatus PC-12/45	629	Pairadice Air LLC. Beaumont, Tx.	HB-FRW
N7000B	66	King Air A90	LM-1	Dynamic AvLease Inc. Bridgewater, Va.	66-18000
N7000G	01	King Air B200	BB-1776	Ashprop LLC/Ashland Inc., Covington, Ky.	N23EH
N7007G	66	King Air A90	LM-2	Turbine Power Inc. Bridgewater, Va.	66-18001
N7010L	66	King Air A90	LM-7	Turbine Power Inc. Bridgewater, Va.	66-18006
N7014L	67	King Air A90	LM-10	Dynamic Aviation Group Inc. Bridgewater, Va.	66-18009
N7018F	66	King Air A90	LM-13	Turbine Power Inc. Bridgewater, Va.	66-18012
N7021Z	06	King Air 350	FL-521	Hawker Beechcraft Corp., Wichita, Ks.	
N7031K	82	Gulfstream 1000	96009	Eagle Air Inc. Memphis, Tn.	HK-3271
N7033U	05	King Air B300C	FM-13	Apex Aviation Inc. Haslet, Tx.	
N7036L	67	King Air A90	LM-26	Dynamic Aviation Group Inc. Bridgewater, Va.	66-18025
N7038Y	67	King Air A90	LM-28	Dynamic Aviation Group Inc. Bridgewater, Va.	66-18027
N7039T	67	King Air A90	LM-30	Dynamic Aviation Group Inc. Bridgewater, Va.	66-18029
N7043D	67	King Air A90	LM-35	Dynamic Aviation Group Inc. Bridgewater, Va.	66-18034
N7043N	67	King Air A90	LM-38	Dynamic Aviation Group Inc. Bridgewater, Va.	66-18037
N7047D	67	King Air A90	LM-41	Dynamic Aviation Group Inc. Bridgewater, Va.	66-18040
N7051K	67	King Air A90	LM-44	Dynamic Aviation Group Inc. Bridgewater, Va.	66-18043
N7052X	67	King Air A90	LM-45	Dynamic Aviation Group Inc. Bridgewater, Va.	66-18045
N7052Y	67	King Air A90	LM-47	Dynamic Aviation Group Inc. Bridgewater, Va.	66-18046
N7057A	81	Gulfstream 840	11664	MaLeCo, Salem, Or.	G-RNCO
N7062W	68	King Air A90	LM-49	Dynamic Aviation Group Inc. Bridgewater, Va.	66-18048
N7063D	68	King Air A90	LM-50	Dynamic Aviation Group Inc. Bridgewater, Va.	66-18049
N7064Q	67	King Air A90	LM-52	Dynamic Aviation Group Inc. Bridgewater, Va.	68-18051
N7066X	67	King Air A90	LM-54	Dynamic Aviation Group Inc. Bridgewater, Va.	66-18053
N7067S	67	King Air A90	LM-55	Dynamic Aviation Group Inc. Bridgewater, Va.	66-18054
N7069A	77	King Air C-12A	BC-54	U S Customs Service, Oklahoma City, Ok.	77-22943
N7069F	67	King Air A90	LM-56	Dynamic Aviation Group Inc. Bridgewater, Va.	66-18055
N7071H	67	King Air A90	LM-58	Dynamic Aviation Group Inc. Bridgewater, Va.	66-18057
N7074G	73	King Air C-12C	BC-17	U S Customs Service, Oklahoma City, Ok.	73-22266
N7078J	67	King Air A90	LM-67	Dynamic Aviation Group Inc. Bridgewater, Va.	66-18066
N7078L	67	King Air A90	LM-69	Dynamic Aviation Group Inc. Bridgewater, Va.	66-18068
N7079S	67	King Air A90	LM-70	Dynamic AvLease Inc. Bridgewater, Va.	67-18069
N7081L	67	King Air A90	LM-72	Alaska Aircraft Finance LLC. Anchorage, Ak.	67-18071
N7086V	06	King Air C90GT	LJ-1786	Western Inns Management of Oregon, Klamath Falls, Or.	
N7089Q	67	King Air A90	LM-77	Alaska Aircraft Finance LLC. Anchorage, Ak.	67-18076
N7092K	67	King Air A90	LM-83	Alaska Aircraft Finance LLC. Anchorage, Ak.	67-18083
N7101L	80	Gulfstream 980	95027	Southwest Jet Inc. Belton, Mo.	N83SA
N7112T	67	King Air A90	LM-88	Dynamic Aviation Group Inc. Bridgewater, Va.	66-18091
N7120P	67	King Air A90	LM-90	Dynamic Aviation Group Inc. Bridgewater, Va.	67-18094
N7126U	68	King Air A90	LM-93	Dynamic Aviation Group Inc. Bridgewater, Va.	66-18097
N7128H	68	King Air A90	LM-94	Dynamic Aviation Group Inc. Bridgewater, Va.	66-18098
N7130X	07	King Air 350	FL-530	Hawker Beechcraft Corp., Wichita, Ks.	
N7131Z	07	King Air 350	FL-531	Hawker Beechcraft Corp., Wichita, Ks.	
N7132Z	68	King Air A90	LM-95	Dynamic Aviation Group Inc. Bridgewater, Va.	66-18099
N7137G	68	King Air A90	LM-99	Dynamic Aviation Group Inc. Bridgewater, Va.	66-18103
N7139B	81	PA-42 Cheyenne III	8001042	Fly-Biz LLC. Zeeland, Mi.	N54568

Reg	Yr	Type	c/n	Owner/Operator	Prev Regn
☐ N7139Z	68	King Air A90	LM-101	Dynamic Aviation Group Inc. Bridgewater, Va.	66-18105
☐ N7146X	68	King Air A90	LM-104	Dynamic Aviation Group Inc. Bridgewater, Va.	67-18108
☐ N7155P	68	King Air A90	LM-107	Dynamic AvLease Inc. Bridgewater, Va.	67-18111
☐ N7155S	68	King Air A90	LM-112	Dynamic Aviation Group Inc. Bridgewater, Va.	67-18116
☐ N7157K	69	King Air A90	LM-115	Turbine Power Inc. Bridgewater, Va.	67-18119
☐ N7165J	69	King Air A90	LM-119	Dynamic Aviation Group Inc. Bridgewater, Va.	67-18123
☐ N7165Y	69	King Air A90	LM-120	Alaska Aircraft Finance LLC. Anchorage, Ak.	67-18124
☐ N7166P	79	King Air 200	BB-482	Manker Aerial Mapping Inc. Oklahoma City, Ok.	N6017
☐ N7169U	69	King Air A90	LM-122	Dynamic Aviation Group Inc. Bridgewater, Va.	67-18126
☐ N7169Z	69	King Air A90	LM-123	Dynamic Aviation Group Inc. Bridgewater, Va.	67-18127
☐ N7173K	69	King Air A90	LM-127	Dynamic Aviation Group Inc. Bridgewater, Va.	70-15893
☐ N7181E	69	King Air A90	LM-132	Dynamic Aviation Group Inc. Bridgewater, Va.	70-15898
☐ N7181H	69	King Air A90	LM-134	Dynamic Aviation Group Inc. Bridgewater, Va.	70-15900
☐ N7181J	69	King Air A90	LM-135	Dynamic Aviation Group Inc. Bridgewater, Va.	70-15901
☐ N7191N	06	King Air C90GT	LJ-1791	Wymair LLC/WXZ Development Inc., Fairview Park, Oh.	
☐ N7193M	69	King Air A90	LM-139	Dynamic Aviation Group Inc. Bridgewater, Va.	70-15905
☐ N7194Y	81	Cheyenne II-XL	8166064	Pan American Trading Co. Miami, Fl.	HC-BUS
☐ N7198B	70	King Air A90	LM-141	Dynamic Aviation Group Inc. Bridgewater, Va.	70-15907
☐ N7198S	70	King Air A90	LU-1	Dynamic AvLease Inc. Bridgewater, Va.	70-15875
☐ N7198Y	70	King Air A90	LU-2	Dynamic AvLease Inc. Bridgewater, Va.	70-15876
☐ N7199D	72	King Air A90	LU-6	Dynamic AvLease Inc. Bridgewater, Va.	70-15880
☐ N7199H	71	King Air A90	LU-7	Dynamic AvLease Inc. Bridgewater, Va.	70-15881
☐ N7199J	70	King Air A90	LU-8	Dynamic AvLease Inc. Bridgewater, Va.	70-15882
☐ N7199L	70	King Air A90	LU-9	Dynamic AvLease Inc. Bridgewater, Va.	70-15883
☐ N7199N	70	King Air A90	LU-10	Dynamic AvLease Inc. Bridgewater, Va.	70-15884
☐ N7199S	70	King Air A90	LU-11	Dynamic AvLease Inc. Bridgewater, Va.	70-15885
☐ N7201S	67	King Air A90	LM-61	Dynamic AvLease Inc. Bridgewater, Va.	66-18060
☐ N7201Z	68	King Air A90	LM-100	Dynamic Aviation Group Inc. Bridgewater, Va.	66-18104
☐ N7202Y	84	King Air 300	FA-12	McDonnell Douglas Corp. St Louis, Mo.	
☐ N7206E	85	King Air F90-1	LA-234	Stroeh Corporate Ventures Ltd. Incline Village, Nv.	
☐ N7223X	85	King Air C90A	LJ-1104	Gem City Properties LLC. Laramie, Wy.	
☐ N7228T	84	King Air 300	FA-20	Lonnie Pilgrim, Pittsburg, Tx.	
☐ N7230H	85	King Air C90A	LJ-1113	Frontier Spinning Mills LLC. Sanford, NC.	
☐ N7231P	85	King Air 300	FA-56	Genesis Financial Data Services, Colorado Springs, Co.	
☐ N7232R	83	King Air B200C	BL-69	U S Department of Energy, Albuquerque, NM.	N2811B
☐ N7233V	06	King Air 350	FL-523	Hawker Beechcraft Corp., Wichita, Ks.	
☐ N7247Y	73	King Air C-12C	BC-3	U S Customs Service, Oklahoma City, Ok.	73-22252
☐ N7250T	85	King Air B200	BB-1237	Puget Sound Energy, Bellevue, Wa.	
☐ N7256K	85	King Air B200	BB-1241	State of Texas, Austin, Tx.	
☐ N7277F	07	King Air C90GT	LJ-1837	Schuybroek Aviation Inc., Kampenhout, Belgium	
☐ N7282X	07	King Air C90GT	LJ-1832	Sky King Charters LLC/Eichel & Krone Co LPA, Cincinnati, Oh.	
☐ N7285Y	92	King Air B300C	FM-5	Lindsey Aviation Services, Haslet, Tx.	N56016
☐ N7368X	07	King Air 350	FL-538	N7368X Holdings LLC., Fort Lauderdale, Fl.	
☐ N7586Z	85	King Air 300	FA-71	Gould Aviation LLC. Aberdeen, SD.	ZS-LOI
☐ N7601L	77	Mitsubishi MU-2N	697SA	JCI Aviation Inc. Canadian, Tx.	N857MA
☐ N7610U	65	680V Turbo Commander	1458-10	Crystal Creek Ltd. New Orleans, La.	C-FHAP
☐ N7644R	68	King Air B90	LJ-335	Dynamic AvLease Inc. Bridgewater, Va.	
☐ N7736M	01	King Air C90B	LJ-1645	Magic Carpet Aviation Inc., Newcastle, Wy.	N345BH
☐ N7778T	05	PA-46-500TP Meridian	4697222	Tichenor McHenry Jr. Dallas, Tx.	
☐ N7931D	83	King Air C90-1	LJ-1049	Modern Aero Inc. d/b/a ASI-Aero Services, Eden Prairie, Ms.	
☐ N8001V	91	King Air C90A	LJ-1265	Rockwood LLC. Hobe Sound, Fl.	
☐ N8017M	92	King Air B200	BB-1438	Tucson Aeroservice Center Inc. Marana, Az.	
☐ N8021P	91	King Air C90A	LJ-1269	Contractors Material Co. Jackson, Ms.	
☐ N8061Q	69	680W Turbo Commander	1833-38	Irene C G Bitencourt, Caracas, Venezuela.	PT-KYY
☐ N8080Q	91	King Air 350	FL-54	GRM Group LLC. Greenville, SC.	
☐ N8083A	79	MU-2 Marquise	739SA	Dickerson Associates/MU-2 LLC., West Columbia, SC.	N707EZ
☐ N8096U	93	King Air C90B	LJ-1326	Alfalfa Aviation LLC. San Jose, Ca.	
☐ N8116N	91	King Air 350	FL-58	Hardy Boys Motorsports Inc. Dallas, Ga.	
☐ N8117N	76	King Air 200	BB-92	Sky Way Aircraft Inc. St Petersburg, Fl.	YV-....
☐ N8118R	75	King Air E90	LW-118	Kopp Clay Co. Malvern, Oh.	
☐ N8131F	76	PA-31T Cheyenne II	7620042	Scenic Airlines Inc. Las Vegas, Nv.	F-GAJC
☐ N8156Z	93	King Air C90B	LJ-1333	Brad Rogers, Tulsa Ok.	
☐ N8170J	80	King Air/Catpass 250	BB-728	Hlaf Aeta LLC. Sugarland, Tx.	C-GTGA
☐ N8210C	93	King Air C90B	LJ-1347	Choctaw Nation of Oklahoma, Durant, Ok.	
☐ N8244L	92	2000A Starship	NC-29	Radio Flyer LLC., Oklahoma City, Ok.	(N121GV)

Reg	Yr	Type	c/n	Owner/Operator	Prev Regn
☐ N8259Q	93	King Air C90B	LJ-1332	Craig Aviation LLC. Tempe, Az.	
☐ N8285Q	94	2000A Starship	NC-50	Starship Transport LLC. Newport Beach, Ca.	(N500CP)
☐ N8287E	94	King Air C90B	LJ-1356	Turbine Time LLC. Bakersfield, Ca.	
☐ N8421E	01	Pilatus PC-12/45	430	Viaplanes Ltd. Pryor, Ok.	HB-FRS
☐ N8484T	74	Mitsubishi MU-2J	617	Turbine Aircraft Marketing Inc. San Angelo, Tx.	EI-AWY
☐ N8838T	77	Conquest II	441-0003	F M Roberts, Miami, Fl.	N2899P
☐ N8870B	05	P-180 Avanti	1099	F B Air Holdings Inc. Naples, Fl.	
☐ N8887B	87	King Air C90A	LJ-1148	St Croix Acceptance Corp. St Croix, Wi.	N120RL
☐ N8897Y	81	SA-227AT Merlin 4C	AT-492	Career Aviation Academy Inc. Oakdale, Ca.	C-FJTA
☐ N8970N	79	Conquest II	441-0092	Martin Wagner, Wischstauden, Germany.	
☐ N8998W	98	King Air B200	BB-1637	Woolie Enterprises Inc, Oldsmar Fl.	N899RW
☐ N9029R	75	King Air E90	LW-132	Dairyland Power Corp. La Crosse, Wi.	
☐ N9032H	68	SA-26T Merlin 2A	T26-7	Napier Air Service Inc. Dothan, Al.	C-GGFJ
☐ N9059S	76	King Air E90	LW-159	State of New Mexico, Santa Fe, NM.	
☐ N9076S	77	King Air C90	LJ-715	Cadogan Properties Inc. Baton Rouge, La.	
☐ N9081R	79	King Air C90	LJ-859	Boulais Aviation Inc. Glendale, Az.	HR-AHJ
☐ N9085U	85	PA-42 Cheyenne IIIA	5501034	U S Customs Service, Oklahoma City, Ok.	
☐ N9091J	85	PA-42 Cheyenne IIIA	5501035	U S Customs Service, Oklahoma City, Ok.	
☐ N9116Q	86	PA-42 Cheyenne IIIA	5501037	U S Customs Service, Oklahoma City, Ok.	
☐ N9142B	86	PA-42 Cheyenne IIIA	5501038	U S Customs Service, Oklahoma City, Ok.	
☐ N9150T	84	PA-42 Cheyenne IIIA	5501024	U S Customs Service, Oklahoma City, Ok.	N41182
☐ N9159Y	84	PA-42 Cheyenne IIIA	5501028	Southern Arkansas University Tech, East Camden, Ar.	
☐ N9175N	73	Rockwell 690A	11071	Mark Todd LLC. Mesa, Az.	
☐ N9183C	83	PA-31T Cheyenne 1A	8304001	Peco Foods Inc. Gordo, Al.	
☐ N9223N	72	Rockwell 690	11023	BRS Services Inc. Reno, Nv.	
☐ N9266Y	84	PA-31T Cheyenne 1A	1104008	Mad River Enterprises Inc/Sampco Inc. Lenox, Ma.	
☐ N9279A	86	PA-42 Cheyenne IIIA	5501036	U S Customs Service, Oklahoma City, Ok.	
☐ N9331M	90	Beech 1900C-1	UC-139	Omicron Transportation Inc. Reading, Pa.	N1128M
☐ N9426	68	King Air B90	LJ-421	Equinox Administration Inc. Palm Harbour Fl.	
☐ N9442Q	72	King Air C90	LJ-542	AK Air LLC., Cheney, Wa.	
☐ N9450Q	72	King Air C90	LJ-550	Dr Bob Fischer, Hibbing, Mn.	XB-FRW
☐ N9683N	82	Conquest II	441-0255	CPC Aviation LLC/Henry Production Co. Lafayette, La.	N68587
☐ N9756S	80	Gulfstream 980	95003	Eagle Air Inc. Memphis, Tn.	N501NB
☐ N9767S	80	Gulfstream 980	95014	3MD Charter, Portland, Or.	(N321MD)
☐ N9812S	81	Gulfstream 980	95060	Aerographics Inc. Manassas, Va.	
☐ N9838Z	68	King Air B90	LJ-435	Skydive Midwest Aviation Inc. Louisburg, NC.	D-IHCH
☐ N9872C	76	King Air C90	LJ-698	Sierra Construction, Woodinville, Wa.	(N497P)
☐ N9898	98	King Air B200	BB-1627	Southern Electric Service Co. Greensboro, NC.	N744TA
☐ N9900	76	SA-226T Merlin 3A	T-266	Jet Operators LLC. Frisco, Tx.	(N97FT)
☐ N9901	66	King Air 90	LJ-93	Great Oaks Joint Vocational School District, Cincinnati, Oh.	N48A
☐ N9902S	82	Gulfstream 1000	96002	Hodge Electronics Inc. South Miami, Fl.	
☐ N9906S	82	Gulfstream 1000	96003	World Jet Inc. Fort Lauderdale, Fl.	HP-....
☐ N9942S	82	Gulfstream 1000	96022	Jerry Harvey, West Palm Beach, Fl.	
☐ N9945S	82	Gulfstream 1000	96025	Zuleta Services & Trading Co. Boca Raton, Fl.	
☐ N9948S	82	Gulfstream 1000	96028	Air Operations International, Charlotte, NC.	
☐ N9966S	82	Gulfstream 1000	96046	Franks Petroleum Inc. Shreveport, La. (status ?).	
☐ N9968S	82	Gulfstream 1000	96048	Eagle Air Inc. Memphis, Tn.	
☐ N9973S	82	Gulfstream 1000	96053	Ram-Air International Inc. Miami, Fl.	
☐ N10694	07	PA-46-500TP Meridian	4697297	Craig Ellingson, Clive, Ia.	
☐ N11692	78	King Air C90	LJ-772	Seven Bar Flying Service Inc. Albuquerque, NM.	F-GFBO
☐ N12244	84	Conquest 1	425-0213	D L S Inc. Fort Payne, Al.	
☐ N12268	85	Conquest 1	425-0227	Vector Group Aviation LLC. Santa Barbara, Ca.	
☐ N13622	78	Rockwell 690B	11469	Kenneth Vadnais, Santa Barbara, Ca.	F-GCMJ
☐ N14886	79	PA-31T Cheyenne 1	7904036	RMI Air LLC/Refuse Materials Inc. Ocilla, Ga.	N149CC
☐ N15234	89	King Air C90A	LJ-1194	Erickson Oil Products Inc. Hudson, Wi.	
☐ N15613	89	King Air 300	FA-193	Spencer Aviation Inc. Rockford, Il.	
☐ N16731	90	120ER Brasilia	120190	Dog Leg Transportation Co LLC., Sherrills Ford, NC.	
☐ N17573	77	King Air C90	LJ-714	Elliott Farms Ltd. Cutler, Ca.	
☐ N17792	78	King Air B100	BE-41	Bell Processing Inc. Wichita Falls, Tx	
☐ N18343	77	King Air E90	LW-243	Tule River Aero Industries Corp., Porterville, Ca.	
☐ N18471	82	King Air F90	LA-161	Polygon LLC. White Plains, NY.	
☐ N18481	82	Conquest 1	425-0105	George E Greer, Livonia Mi.	(N7711B)
☐ N22071	76	King Air 200	BB-111	Air Serv International Inc. Warrenton, Va.	N633EB
☐ N23243	79	PA-31T Cheyenne 1	7904017	ABC Aircraft LLC. Petoskey, Mi.	
☐ N23250	79	PA-31T Cheyenne 1	7904018	La Stella Corp. Pueblo, Co.	

Reg	Yr Type	c/n	Owner/Operator	Prev Regn
N23334	79 PA-31T Cheyenne 1	7904024	Laurens Aviation Company LLC., Columbia, SC.	TG-LIA
N23404	77 King Air A100	B-234	National Airplane Sales & Leasing, Bluffton, Oh.	
N23426	79 PA-31T Cheyenne 1	7904035	Selland Pontiac-GMC Inc. Moorhead, Mn.	
N23605	77 King Air A100	B-236	Edgar Artecona, Alvarado, Tx.	
N23646	79 PA-31T Cheyenne II	7920078	Dave's Construction Service, Reidsville, NC.	(PH-BAM)
N23718	79 PA-31T Cheyenne II	7920087	James Hodge Ford Lincoln Inc. Muskogee, Ok.	
N24203	78 King Air B100	BE-40	Fox Flite Inc. Tulsa, Ok.	
N25677	75 SA-226T Merlin 3A	T-254	Kolar Aviation Inc. Hudson, Oh.	N58018
N29997	87 King Air B200	BB-1268	Wallace Westwind Inc. Las Cruces, NM.	
N30397	03 PA-46-500TP Meridian	4697167	Applewood Development LLC. Bald Head Island, NC.	(N145TP)
N30854	74 Rockwell 690A	11229	Cornerstone Financial Enterprises, Van Nuys, Ca.	LV-LTO
N30898	05 PA-46-500TP Meridian	4697202	Goebel Paving Grading & Underground Inc. Petaluma, Ca.	
N30983	04 PA-46-500TP Meridian	4697189	Charles Schoenberger, Alamo, Ca.	
N31062	05 PA-46-500TP Meridian	4697208	Iport Leasing LLC., Mount Vernon, Wa.	
N31094	99 King Air B200	BB-1676	Parques Industriales Amista SA/AeroMaquila Inc. Del Rio, Tx.	
N31145	05 PA-46-500TP Meridian	4697215	Osadzinski Management LLC. Atherton, Ca.	
N31861	07 King Air C90GT	LJ-1861	Wells Fargo Bank NW NA	
N31869	07 King Air C90GT	LJ-1869	Hawker Beechcraft Corp., Wichita, Ks.	N31869
N31947	07 King Air C90GT	LJ-1847	Eye Fly Inc. Caldwell, NJ	N31947
N31967	07 King Air 350	FL-567	Wells Fargo Bank NW NA Salt Lake City, Ut.	
N31973	07 King Air B300	FL-573	Hawker Beechcraft Corp., Wichita, Ks.	
N32017	07 King Air B200GT	BY-17	Wells Fargo Bank NW NA, Salt Lake City, Ut.	
N32029	07 King Air B200GT	BY-29	Hawker Beechcraft Corp., Wichita, Ks.	
N32148	07 King Air B300	FL-568	Specialised Aircraft Services Inc. Wichita Ks.	
N32166	07 King Air B200GT	BY-16	Corporate Aircraft S.A. Roverdo	
N32229	65 King Air 90	LJ-49	John T Guthrie, Jr., Mountain View, Wy.	C-GNUX
N32238	00 King Air C90B	LJ-1580	Wells Fargo Bank NW NA, Salt Lake City Ut.	
N32928	07 King Air B200GT	BY-28	Hawker Beechcraft Corp., Wichita, Ks.	
N33122	07 King Air B200GT	BY-22	Hawker Beechcraft Corporation Wichita,Ks.	
N33226	07 King Air C90GT	LJ-1866	Hawker Beechcraft Corp., Wichita, Ks.	
N34003	07 King Air C90GT	LJ-1853	Wells Fargo Bank NW NA, Salt Lake City, Ut.	
N34008	07 King Air B200GT	BY-8	Wells Fargo Bank NW NA, Salt Lake City Ut.	N708WH
N34651	07 King Air B200GT	BY-21	Lider International Aviation Ltd. Nassau.	
N34923	07 King Air B200GT	BY-23	Corporate Aircraft S.A. Roverdo	
N36715	04 King Air 350	FL-415	Sundown Pastoral P/L. Broadbeach Waters, QLD. Australia.	
N36799	06 King Air C90GT	LJ-1769	Wells Fargo Bank Northwest NA.	
N36888	05 King Air C90GT	LJ-1788	WFBNW NA. Salt Lake City, Ut. (trustor ?).	
N36929	04 King Air C90B	LJ-1729	Translatin SA. Guatemala City, Guatemala.	
N36988	06 King Air 350	FL-488	Request Air Services LLC., Piney Flats, Tn.	
N37084	06 King Air 350	FL-482	Reliable Air Transport, Clinton, Md.	
N37093	06 King Air C90GT	LJ-1773	Durpanel SA. San Jose, Costa Rica.	
N37172	06 King Air 350	FL-472	Markoss Aviation Ltd. Biggin Hill, UK.	
N37198	06 King Air C90GT	LJ-1798	Suntrust Leasing Corp, Towson, Md.	N37198
N37200	06 King Air C90GT	LJ-1800	Klenk Holz AG., Oberrot, Germany	
N37222	04 King Air C90B	LJ-1722	WA Equioment Services LLC/Weismann Assocs LLC. NYC.	
N37390	90 King Air 350	FL-11	McEagle Aviation of Delaware LLC. O'Fallon, Mo.	N3739C
N37990	81 King Air F90	LA-101	IIIB LLC. Oskaloosa, Ia.	
N38280	81 King Air C90	LJ-953	O B Aircraft LLC. Tampa, Fl.	
N38381	81 King Air B200	BB-934	Wheels of Africa, Rand, RSA.	
N40191	99 Pilatus PC-12/45	248	Rivers Aviation LLC. Houston, Tx.	N652CA
N40593	97 King Air 350	FL-162	US Department of Justice, Fort Worth, Tx.	N1112Z
N43866	80 MU-2 Marquise	757SA	Pickett LLC., Huntsville, Al.	(N21MU)
N44776	80 Conquest II	441-0121	BCD Aviation LLC, Wilmington De.	N44776
N45818	73 SA-226T Merlin 3	T-235	U S Department of Justice, El Paso, Tx.	XC-UTE/TP
N50525	66 King Air A90	LJ-159	Wildcat Flying LLC. Larned, Ks.	86-0092
N50655	67 680V Turbo Commander	1714-88	Spur Aviation Services LC., Twin Falls, Id.	XB-CED
N51488	03 King Air B200CT	BN-8	Raytheon Aircraft Co. Wichita, Ks.	
N53235	01 PA-46-500TP Meridian	4697083	Mitchell Aviation Innovations LLC. Wayland, Ma.	
N53238	01 PA-46-500TP Meridian	4697086	Diederich Insurance Consulting Inc. Carbondale, Il.	
N53362	01 PA-46-500TP Meridian	4697109	Austin Aviation LLC. Gladwyne, Pa.	
N53369	01 PA-46-500TP Meridian	4697088	Maverick Country Stores Inc. Afton, Wy.	
N53401	02 PA-46-500TP Meridian	4697143	Lynch Leasing LLC. Jacksonville, Fl.	
N53516	02 PA-46-500TP Meridian	4697132	Delta Aircraft Holdings LLC. Wilmington, De.	
N53667	03 PA-46-500TP Meridian	4697158	Willson Consulting LLC. Naples, Fl.	
N54026	85 DHC 7-103	106	U S Department of Energy, Albuquerque, NM.	

Reg	Yr Type	c/n	Owner/Operator	Prev Regn
N54163	68 680W Turbo Commander	1774-12	Spur Aviation Services LLC Twin Falls Id.	N5416
N54199	03 PA-46-500TP Meridian	4697164	Gloria Franco, McAllen, Tx.	
N57112	75 Rockwell 690A	11263	Skystar Inc. Columbia, Ga.	
N57113	73 Rockwell 690A	11113	CSC Trust Co of Delaware. Wilmington, De.	
N57175	72 Rockwell 690	11004	Aero-Metric Engineering Inc. Sheboygan, Wi.	N37546
N57292	75 Rockwell 690A	11270	World Jet Inc. Fort Lauderdale, Fl.	
N58280	75 King Air 200	BB-61	TIPS Air Inc. San Antonio, Tx.	C-GSEP
N60887	07 PA-46-500TP Meridian	4697338	Piper Aircraft Inc. Vero Beach, Fl.	
N61228	82 King Air F90	LA-169	DA/PRO Rubber Inc. Tulsa, Ok.	
N61383	82 King Air C90A	LJ-1009	LWCR Transportation Inc. Minot, ND.	(N155RG)
N61698	03 King Air C90B	LJ-1698	Michael Wayne Investment Co. Virginia Beach, Va.	
N62300	81 King Air C90	LJ-989	Releco Ltd. High Point, NC.	(YV-442CP)
N62525	76 King Air C90	LJ-691	MRI Manufacturing & Research Inc. Tucson, Az.	JA8839
N62569	82 King Air B200	BB-1028	State of Texas, Austin, Tx.	
N63593	79 King Air 200	BB-552	James Latta, Fayetteville, Ar.	G-BGRD
N63791	83 King Air B200	BB-1100	Wells Fargo Bank NW NA, Salt Lake City Ut.	
N66000	78 King Air C-12C	BC-66	Department of the Army, Berryville, Va.	78-23130
N66804	80 King Air B100	BE-82	O.I.A. Enterprises LLC., Reno, Nv.	(N200JL)
N66820	79 King Air B100	BE-68	Bayport Air Co. Mobile, Al.	N6052C
N67511	80 King Air C90	LJ-888	Midwest Flight LLC. Tecumseh, Mi.	(N111GF)
N67726	81 Conquest 1	425-0030	Sky Cope LLC. Tulsa, Ok.	
N68734	84 Conquest 1	425-0182	Seanaire Inc. Midland Park, NJ.	
N69084	82 King Air F90	LA-157	MRS Management Inc. Rapid City, SD.	
N69301	84 King Air C90A	LJ-1079	Flying Mountains LLC. Steamboat Springs, Co.	
N70088	66 King Air A90	LM-6	Turbine Power Inc. Bridgewater, Va.	66-18005
N70189	06 King Air C90GT	LJ-1799	Wells Fargo Bank NW NA, Salt Lake City Ut.	
N70264	66 King Air A90	LM-17	Avlease Exchange Properties LLC., Bridgewater, Va.	66-18016
N70292	67 King Air A90	LM-18	Dynamic Aviation Group Inc. Bridgewater, Va.	66-18017
N70356	67 King Air A90	LM-25	Dynamic Aviation Group Inc. Bridgewater, Va.	66-18024
N70503	67 King Air A90	LM-43	Dynamic AvLease Inc. Bridgewater, Va.	66-18042
N70648	67 King Air A90	LM-53	Dynamic Aviation Group Inc. Bridgewater, Va.	66-18052
N70841	67 King Air A90	LM-73	Dynamic AvLease Inc. Bridgewater, Va.	67-18072
N70876	67 King Air A90	LM-75	Dynamic Aviation Group Inc. Bridgewater, Va.	66-18074
N70879	67 King Air A90	LM-76	Dynamic Aviation Group Inc. Bridgewater, Va.	66-18075
N70926	67 King Air A90	LM-84	Dynamic Aviation Group Inc. Bridgewater, Va.	67-18084
N70950	67 King Air A90	LM-86	Horstman Aviation LLC. Delphos, Oh.	67-18088
N71347	68 King Air A90	LM-96	Dynamic Aviation Group Inc. Bridgewater, Va.	66-18100
N71351	68 King Air A90	LM-97	Dynamic Aviation Group Inc. Bridgewater, Va.	66-18101
N71562	01 PA-46-500TP Meridian	4697081	Bryan Goodwin, Fort Smith Ar.	
N71581	68 King Air A90	LM-116	Dynamic Aviation Group Inc. Bridgewater, Va.	67-18120
N71597	68 King Air A90	LM-118	Dynamic Aviation Group Inc. Bridgewater, Va.	67-18122
N71797	69 King Air A90	LM-131	Dynamic Aviation Group Inc. Bridgewater, Va.	70-15897
N71878	06 King Air C90GT	LJ-1778	Wells Fargo Bank NW NA., Salt Lake City, Ut. (trustor ?).	
N71885	06 King Air 350	FL-485	Reliable Air Transport, Clinton, Md.	
N71966	07 King Air 350	FL-533	Hawker Beechcraft Corp., Wichita, Ks.	
N71982	70 King Air A90	LU-3	Dynamic Aviation Group Inc. Bridgewater, Va.	70-15877
N71992	70 King Air A90	LU-12	Dynamic AvLease Inc. Bridgewater, Va.	70-15886
N72470	73 King Air C-12C	BC-4	U S Customs Service, Oklahoma City, Ok.	73-22253
N72472	73 King Air C-12C	BC-11	U S Customs Service, Oklahoma City, Ok.	73-22263
N72476	74 King Air C-12C	BC-26	U S Customs Service, Oklahoma City, Ok.	76-22550
N72709	07 King Air C90GT	LJ-1839	South Bay Ltd, Anchorage	
N73380	06 King Air 350	FL-480	Powell & Simpson LLC, Wilmington De.	
N73415	06 King Air C90GT	LJ-1785	Consilux Consultoria e Construcoes Eletricas., Vista Alegre	
N73920	07 King Air C90GT	LJ-1840	Wells Fargo Bank NW NA, Salt Lake City, Ut.	
N74226	06 King Air 350	FL-522	Hawker Beechcraft Corp., Wichita, Ks.	
N75368	65 King Air 90	LJ-75	Bruffey Flying Inc. Rome, Ga.	C-GJBE
N77400	05 PA-46-500TP Meridian	4697206	Sky Bird Inc. Omaha, Ne.	
N81448	76 Rockwell 690A	11327	Lakin Law Firm, Wood River, Il.	
N81703	78 Rockwell 690B	11438	Frasca International Inc. Champaign, Il.	
N82094	77 PA-31T Cheyenne II	7720014	Jack Wall Aircraft Sales Inc. Memphis, Tn.	
N82156	77 PA-31T Cheyenne II	7720045	Gould Aviation LLC. Aberdeen, SC.	
N85516	93 Beech 1900D	UE-61	U S Department of State, Dulles, Va.	
N87699	81 King Air B200	BB-887	Sky King LLC/Optical Air Data Systems, Manassas, Va.	YV-2222P
N88598	82 Conquest II	441-0242	Circle D Charter LLC., Mt. Eaton, Oh.	N441WT
N88692	83 Conquest II	441-0290	Jim Jacobs, Great Barrington, Ma.	

Reg	Yr Type	c/n	Owner/Operator	Prev Regn
☐ N88727	82 Conquest II	441-0267	Conquest Flight Group LLC/Flex Flight LLC. Parker, Co.	
☐ N88834	82 Conquest II	441-0269	Victory Van Lines Inc/Jennair Aviation Inc. Staten Island.	N88834
☐ N91384	73 Rockwell 690A	11118	Airbourne Data Inc. Dover, De.	SE-FLN
☐ N96954	80 SA-226T Merlin 3B	T-311	Woodstead Enterprises LLC. The WoodInds, Tx.	N27563
Military				
☐ 05-0409	01 Pilatus PC-12/45	409	U-28A. HQ AFSOC. Hurlburt Field, Fl.	N922RG
☐ 05-0419	01 Pilatus PC-12/45	419	U-28A. HQ AFSOC. Hurlburt Field, Fl.	N419WA
☐ 05-0424	01 Pilatus PC-12/45	424	U-28A. HQ AFSOC. Hurlburt Field, Fl.	N424PB
☐ 05-0447	02 Pilatus PC-12/45	447	U-28A. HQ AFSOC. Hurlburt Field, Fl.	N447PC
☐ 05-0482	03 Pilatus PC-12/45	482	U-28A. HQ AFSOC. Hurlburt Field, Fl.	N482WA
☐ 05-0573	04 Pilatus PC-12/45	573	U-28A. HQ AFSOC. Hurlburt Field, Fl.	N666GT
☐ 05-52305	82 King Air B200	BB-924	U S Army, Fort Eustace, Va.	N107MG
☐ 07-21907	83 King Air B200	BB-1114	US Army Aviation & Missile Command, Fort Eustis, Va.	N872CA
☐ 161190	61 King Air UC-12B	BJ-6	U.S. Navy.	
☐ 161191	61 King Air UC-12B	BJ-7	U.S. Navy, Code 7E, NAS Jacksonville, Fl.	
☐ 161193	61 King Air UC-12B	BJ-9	U.S. Navy.	
☐ 161195	61 King Air UC-12B	BJ-11	U.S. Navy, Code 8F, NAS Guantanamo Bay, Cuba.	
☐ 161196	61 King Air UC-12B	BJ-12	U.S. Navy, Code 8N, NAS El Centro, Ca.	
☐ 161197	61 King Air UC-12B	BJ-13	U.S. Navy.	
☐ 161201	King Air UC-12B	BJ-17	U.S. Navy.	
☐ 161203	King Air UC-12B	BJ-19	U.S. Navy, Code 7C, NAS Norfolk, Va.	
☐ 161205	King Air UC-12B	BJ-21	U.S. Navy.	
☐ 161206	King Air UC-12B	BJ-22	U.S. Navy, Code 7G, NAS Whidbey Island, Wa.	
☐ 161306	King Air UC-12B	BJ-23	U.S. Navy.	
☐ 161309	King Air UC-12B	BJ-26	U.S. Navy.	
☐ 161310	King Air UC-12B	BJ-27	U.S. Navy.	
☐ 161312	King Air UC-12B	BJ-29	U.S. Navy.	
☐ 161313	King Air UC-12B	BJ-30	U.S. Navy.	
☐ 161315	King Air UC-12B	BJ-32	U.S. Navy.	
☐ 161316	King Air UC-12B	BJ-33	U.S. Navy.	
☐ 161318	King Air UC-12B	BJ-35	U.S. Navy.	
☐ 161319	King Air UC-12B	BJ-36	U.S. Navy.	
☐ 161320	King Air UC-12B	BJ-37	U.S. Navy.	
☐ 161323	King Air UC-12B	BJ-40	U.S. Navy, Code RW, VRC-30, NAS North Island, Ca.	
☐ 161324	King Air UC-12B	BJ-41	U.S. Navy.	
☐ 161325	King Air UC-12B	BJ-42	U.S. Marine Corps. Code 5D, MCAS New River, NC.	
☐ 161326	King Air UC-12B	BJ-43	U.S. Army, Code 7G, NAS Whidbey Island, Wa.	
☐ 161497	King Air UC-12B	BJ-45	U.S. Navy.	
☐ 161498	King Air UC-12B	BJ-46	U.S. Navy.	
☐ 161500	King Air UC-12B	BJ-48	U.S. Navy, Code 7E, NAS Jacksonville, Fl.	
☐ 161501	King Air UC-12B	BJ-49	U.S. Navy.	
☐ 161502	King Air UC-12B	BJ-50	U.S. Navy.	
☐ 161504	King Air UC-12B	BJ-52	U.S. Navy, Code 7B, NAS Atlanta, Ga.	
☐ 161505	King Air UC-12B	BJ-53	U.S. Navy.	
☐ 161507	King Air UC-12B	BJ-55	U.S. Marine Corps. Code 5D, MCAS New River, NC.	
☐ 161508	King Air UC-12B	BJ-56	U.S. Navy.	
☐ 161511	King Air UC-12B	BJ-59	U.S. Navy.	
☐ 161512	King Air UC-12B	BJ-60	U.S. Navy.	
☐ 161513	King Air UC-12B	BJ-61	U.S. Navy.	
☐ 161514	King Air UC-12B	BJ-62	U.S. Marine Corps.	
☐ 161515	King Air UC-12B	BJ-63	U.S. Navy, Code 5B, MCAS Beaufort, SC.	
☐ 161517	King Air UC-12B	BJ-65	U.S. Navy.	
☐ 161518	King Air UC-12B	BJ-66	U.S. Navy.	
☐ 163553	King Air UC-12F	BU-1	U.S. Navy, Code 8A, NAS Misawa, Japan.	
☐ 163554	King Air UC-12F	BU-2	U.S. Navy, Code 8A, NAF Atsugi, Japan.	
☐ 163555	King Air UC-12F	BU-3	U.S. Navy, Code 8A, NAF Atsugi, Japan.	
☐ 163556	King Air UC-12F	BU-4	U.S. Navy, Code 8A, NAF Atsugi, Japan.	
☐ 163557	King Air UC-12F	BU-5	U.S. Navy, Fleet Activities, Okinawa, Japan.	
☐ 163558	King Air UC-12F	BU-6	U.S. Navy. Iwakuni, Japan.	
☐ 163559	King Air UC-12F	BU-7	U.S. Navy, Iwakuni, Japan.	
☐ 163560	King Air UC-12F	BU-8	U.S. Navy, Okinawa, Japan.	
☐ 163561	King Air UC-12F	BU-9	U.S. Navy, Okinawa, Japan.	
☐ 163562	King Air UC-12F	BU-10	U.S. Navy, Japan.	
☐ 163563	King Air UC-12F	BU-11	U.S. Navy, Pacific Missile Range Facility, Barking Sands, Hi	
☐ 163836	King Air UC-12M	BV-1	U.S. Navy.	

Reg	Yr	Type	c/n	Owner/Operator	Prev Regn
☐ 163837		King Air UC-12M	BV-2	U.S. Navy.	
☐ 163838		King Air UC-12M	BV-3	U.S. Navy.	
☐ 163839		King Air UC-12M	BV-4	U.S. Navy, NS Rota, Spain.	
☐ 163840		King Air UC-12M	BV-5	U.S. Navy.	
☐ 163841		King Air UC-12M	BV-6	U.S. Navy.	
☐ 163842		King Air UC-12M	BV-7	U.S. Navy, NS Rota, Spain.	
☐ 163843		King Air UC-12M	BV-8	U.S. Navy.	
☐ 163844		King Air UC-12M	BV-9	U.S. Navy.	
☐ 163845		King Air UC-12M	BV-10	U.S. Navy.	
☐ 163846		King Air UC-12M	BV-11	Naval Research Laboratory, St Petersburg, Fl.	
☐ 66-15361	66	King Air A90	LJ-153	VC-6A, U S Army, White Sands Missile Range, Holloman AFB. NM	N901R
☐ 70-15908	72	King Air U-21J	B-95	U S Navy, Test Pilot School, NAS Patuxent River, Md.	
☐ 73-1208	73	King Air C-12C	BD-4	U S Army.	
☐ 73-1214	73	King Air C-12C	BD-10	USAF, U S Embassy Flight, Bangkok, Thailand.	
☐ 73-1215	73	King Air C-12C	BD-11	USAF, 412th Logistics Group, Edwards AFB. Ca.	
☐ 73-1216	73	King Air C-12C	BD-12	USAF,	
☐ 73-1217	73	King Air C-12C	BD-13	USAF, U S Embassy Flight, Manila, Philippines.	
☐ 73-1218	73	King Air C-12C	BD-14	USAF.	
☐ 73-22262	73	King Air C-12C	BC-10	U S Army, AEESB, NAS Lakehurst, NJ.	73-22262
☐ 76-0158	76	King Air C-12C	BD-15	USAF, Edwards AFB. Ca.	
☐ 76-0160	76	King Air C-12C	BD-17	USAF, U S Embassy Flight, Riyadh, Saudi Arabia.	
☐ 76-0161	76	King Air C-12C	BD-18	USAF, Edwards AFB. Ca.	
☐ 76-0162	76	King Air C-12C	BD-19	USAF.	
☐ 76-0164	76	King Air C-12C	BD-21	USAF, Military Training Mission, Dhahran, Saudi Arabia.	
☐ 76-0166	76	King Air C-12C	BD-23	USAF, 418th FLTS,	
☐ 76-0168	76	King Air C-12C	BD-25	USAF, U S Embassy Flight, Bogota, Colombia.	
☐ 76-0171	76	King Air C-12C	BD-28	USAF.	
☐ 76-0172	76	King Air C-12C	BD-29	USAF.	
☐ 76-22551	76	King Air C-12C	BC-27	Flight Safety Inc.	
☐ 76-22559	76	King Air C-12C	BC-36	U S Army, Flight Safety International,	
☐ 76-22561	76	King Air C-12C	BC-38	U S Army, Flight Safety International,	
☐ 76-22563	76	King Air C-12C	BC-40	U S Army, Fixed Wing Training Site, Clarksburg, WV.	(N7066D)
☐ 76-3239	76	King Air C-12C	BD-24	USAF.	76-0167
☐ 77-22932	77	King Air C-12C	BC-43	U S Army, Flight Safety International,	
☐ 77-22935	77	King Air C-12C	BC-46	U S Army, Flight Safety International,	
☐ 77-22941	77	King Air C-12A	BC-52	U S Army, Flight Safety International,	
☐ 77-22942	77	King Air C-12C	BC-53	U S Army.	
☐ 77-22944	77	King Air C-12C	BC-55	U S Army, Flight Safety International,	
☐ 77-22949	77	King Air C-12C	BC-60	U S Army, Flight Safety International,	
☐ 78-23128	78	King Air C-12C	BC-64	U S Army.	
☐ 78-23132	78	King Air C-12C	BC-68	U S Navy.	
☐ 78-23133	78	King Air JC-12C	BC-69	U S Navy.	
☐ 78-23135	78	King Air C-12C	BC-71	U S Army, Tuzla, Bosnia.	
☐ 78-23140	78	King Air JC-12D	BP-1	U S Army.	
☐ 78-23141	78	King Air RC-12D	GR-6	U S Army, B/304th MIB (Training), Libby AAF, Az. (was BP-2).	
☐ 78-23142	78	King Air RC-12D	GR-7	U S Army, 3rd MIB (AE), Camp Humphries, S Korea. (was BP-3).	
☐ 78-23143	78	King Air RC-12D	GR-8	U S Army. (was BP-4).	
☐ 78-23144	78	King Air RC-12D	GR-9	U S Army, 3rd MIB (AE), Camp Humphries, S Korea. (was BP-5).	
☐ 80-23371	78	King Air RC-12D	GR-2	U S Army, 3rd MIB (AE), Camp Humphries, S Korea. (was BP-12).	
☐ 80-23372	80	King Air RC-12G	FC-3	U S Army. (was BP-13)..	
☐ 80-23373	80	King Air RC-12D	GR-4	U S Army, B/1st MIB (AE), Wiesbaden, Germany. (was BP-14).	
☐ 80-23374	80	King Air RC-12D	GR-12	U S Army, 304th MIB (Training), Libby AAF, Az. (was BP-15).	
☐ 80-23375	80	King Air RC-12D	GR-5	U S Army. (was BP-16).	
☐ 80-23376	80	King Air RC-12D	GR-11	U S Army, B/15th MIB (AE), Robert Gray AAF, Tx. (was BP-17).	
☐ 80-23377	80	King Air RC-12D	GR-3	U S Army. (was BP-18).	
☐ 80-23378	80	King Air RC-12D	GR-13	U S Army, White Sands Missile Range, Holloman AFB. NM	
☐ 80-23379	80	King Air RC-12G	FC-1	U S Army. (was BP-20).	
☐ 80-23380	80	King Air RC-12G	FC-2	U S Army. (was BP-21).	
☐ 81-23541	81	King Air C-12D	BP-22	U S Army, USAARL,	
☐ 81-23542	81	King Air RC-12D	GR-1	U S Army. (was BP-23).	
☐ 81-23543	81	King Air C-12D	BP-24	U S Army.	
☐ 81-23544	81	King Air C-12D	BP-25	U S Army.	
☐ 81-23545	81	King Air C-12D	BP-26	U S Army.	
☐ 81-23546	81	King Air C-12D	BP-27	U S Army, OSACOM, Det 6, CT ARNG, Windsor Locks, Ct.	
☐ 82-23781	82	King Air C-12D	BP-29	U S Army, OSACOM, Hickam AFB. Hi.	

Reg	Yr Type	c/n	Owner/Operator	Prev Regn
☐ 82-23783	82 King Air C-12D	BP-31	U S Army, OSACOM, Det 23, RI ARNG, Quonset State Airport.	
☐ 82-23784	82 King Air C-12D	BP-32	U S Army, Flight Safety International,	
☐ 82-23785	82 King Air C-12D	BP-33	U S Army, Flight Safety International,	
☐ 83-0494	83 King Air C-12D	BP-40	USAF, U S Embassy Flight, Abidjan, Ivory Coast.	
☐ 83-0495	83 King Air C-12D	BP-41	USAF, U S Embassy Flight, Budapest, Hungary.	
☐ 83-0496	83 King Air C-12D	BP-42	USAF, U S Embassy Flight, Nairobi, Kenya.	
☐ 83-0497	83 King Air C-12D	BP-43	USAF, U S Embassy Flight, Buenos Aires, Argentina.	
☐ 83-0498	83 King Air C-12D	BP-44	USAF.	
☐ 83-0499	83 King Air C-12D	BP-45	USAF, U S Embassy Flight, La Paz, Bolivia.	
☐ 83-24145	83 King Air C-12D	BP-34	U S Army, OSACOM, Det 19, NJ ARNG, West Trenton, NJ.	
☐ 83-24146	83 King Air C-12D	BP-35	U S Army, OSACOM, Det 15, MI ARNG, Grand Ledge-Abrams, Mi.	
☐ 83-24147	83 King Air C-12D	BP-36	U S Army.	
☐ 83-24148	83 King Air C-12D	BP-37	U S Army, OSACOM, Gray AAF, Wa.	
☐ 83-24149	83 King Air C-12D	BP-38	U S Army.	
☐ 83-24150	83 King Air C-12D	BP-39	U S Army, Flight Safety International,	
☐ 83-24313	83 King Air RC-12H	GR-14	U S Army, B/3rd MIB (AE), Camp Humphreys, South Korea.	
☐ 83-24314	83 King Air RC-12H	GR-15	U S Army, B/3rd MIB (AE), Camp Humphreys, South Korea.	
☐ 83-24315	83 King Air RC-12H	GR-16	U S Army, B/3rd MIB (AE), Camp Humphreys, South Korea.	
☐ 83-24316	83 King Air RC-12D	GR-17	U S Army, B/3rd MIB (AE), Camp Humphreys, South Korea.	
☐ 83-24317	83 King Air RC-12H	GR-18	U S Army, B/3rd MIB (AE), Camp Humphreys, South Korea.	
☐ 83-24318	83 King Air RC-12H	GR-19	U S Army, B/3rd MIB (AE), Camp Humphreys, South Korea.	
☐ 84-0143	84 King Air C-12F	BL-73	U S Army.	
☐ 84-0144	84 King Air C-12F	BL-74	U S Army, Heidelberg, Germany.	N5801D
☐ 84-0145	84 King Air C-12F	BL-75	U S Army, OSACOM, Elmendorf AFB. Ak.	
☐ 84-0146	84 King Air C-12F	BL-76	U S Army, 204th MIB (AR), Biggs AAF, Tx.	
☐ 84-0147	84 King Air C-12F	BL-77	USAF, 3rd Wing, Elmendorf AFB. Ak	
☐ 84-0148	84 King Air C-12F	BL-78	USAF, 3rd Wing, Elmendorf AFB. Ak.	
☐ 84-0149	84 King Air C-12F	BL-79	U S Army, OSACOM, Elmendorf AFB. Ak.	
☐ 84-0150	84 King Air C-12F	BL-80	U S Army, OSACOM, Det 42, ND ARNG, Bismarck, ND.	
☐ 84-0151	84 King Air C-12F	BL-81	U S Army.	
☐ 84-0152	84 King Air C-12F	BL-82	U S Army, Heidelberg, Germany.	
☐ 84-0153	84 King Air C-12F	BL-83	U S Army, Heidelberg, Germany.	N58009
☐ 84-0154	84 King Air C-12F	BL-84	U S Army, Heidelberg, Germany.	
☐ 84-0155	84 King Air C-12F	BL-85	U S Army, Heidelberg, Germany.	
☐ 84-0156	84 King Air C-12U	BL-86	U S Army, Heidelberg, Germany.	
☐ 84-0157	84 King Air C-12U	BL-87	U S Army, Heidelberg, Germany.	
☐ 84-0158	84 King Air C-12U	BL-88	U S Army, HQ USEUCOM, Stuttgart, Germany.	
☐ 84-0159	84 King Air C-12F	BL-89	U S Army, OSACOM, Det 43, NE ARNG, Lincoln, Ne.	
☐ 84-0160	84 King Air C-12U	BL-90	U S Army, HQ USEUCOM, Stuttgart, Germany.	
☐ 84-0161	84 King Air C-12U	BL-91	U S Army, 6th Aviation Co. Vicenza, Italy.	
☐ 84-0162	84 King Air C-12U	BL-92	U S Army, 6th Aviation Co. Vicenza, Italy.	
☐ 84-0163	84 King Air C-12U	BL-93	U S Army, 204th MIB (AR), Biggs AAF, Tx.	
☐ 84-0164	84 King Air C-12F	BL-94	U S Army.	
☐ 84-0165	84 King Air C-12U	BL-95	U S Army.	
☐ 84-0166	84 King Air C-12F	BL-96	U S Army, A/6-52nd AVN, (TA), Seoul, South Korea.	
☐ 84-0167	84 King Air C-12F	BL-97	U S Army, A/6-52nd AVN, (TA), Seoul, South Korea.	
☐ 84-0168	84 King Air C-12F	BL-98	U S Army, A/6-52nd AVN, (TA), Seoul, South Korea.	
☐ 84-0170	84 King Air C-12F	BL-100	U S Army, A/6-52nd AVN, (TA), Seoul, South Korea.	
☐ 84-0171	84 King Air C-12F	BL-101	U S Army, OSACOM, Det 37, KS ARNG, Topeka, Ks.	
☐ 84-0172	84 King Air C-12F	BL-102	U S Army.	
☐ 84-0173	84 King Air C-12F	BL-103	U S Army, OSACOM, Det 46, OK ARNG, Norman, Ok.	
☐ 84-0174	84 King Air C-12F	BL-104	U S Army, OSACOM, Gray AAF, Wa.	
☐ 84-0175	84 King Air C-12F	BL-105	U S Army, OSACOM, Gray AAF, Wa.	N5803F
☐ 84-0176	84 King Air C-12F	BL-106	U S Army.	N5819T
☐ 84-0177	84 King Air C-12F	BL-107	U S Army, Det A C/2-228th AVN, USAR, MacDill AFB. Fl.	
☐ 84-0178	84 King Air C-12F	BL-108	U S Army.	
☐ 84-0179	84 King Air C-12F	BL-109	U S Army.	
☐ 84-0180	84 King Air C-12U	BL-110	U S Army, HQ USEUCOM, Stuttgart, Germany.	
☐ 84-0181	84 King Air C-12F	BL-111	U S Army, 204th MIB (AR), Biggs AAF, Tx.	
☐ 84-0182	84 King Air C-12F	BL-112	U S Army, OSACOM, Det 10, IN ARNG, Indianapolis, In.	
☐ 84-0484	84 King Air C-12F	BL-118	U S Army, OSACOM, Det 48, SD ARNG, Rapid City, SD.	
☐ 84-0485	84 King Air C-12F	BL-119	U S Army, OSACOM, Det 11, KY ARNG, Frankfort, Ky.	
☐ 84-0486	84 King Air C-12F	BL-120	U S Army, OSACOM, Det 47, OR ARNG, Salem, Or.	
☐ 84-0487	84 King Air C-12F	BL-121	U S Army, OSACOM, Det 53, WY ARNG, Cheyenne, Wy.	
☐ 84-0488	84 King Air C-12F	BL-122	U S Army, OSACOM, Elmendorf AFB. Ak.	
Reg	*Yr Type*	*c/n*	*Owner/Operator*	*Prev Regn*

Reg	Yr	Type	c/n	Owner/Operator	Prev Regn
☐ 84-0489	84 King Air C-12F	BL-123	U S Army, OSACOM, Det 45, NV ARNG, Reno, Nv.	
☐ 84-24375	84 King Air C-12D	BP-46	U S Army, Det A C/2-228th AVN, USAR, MacDill AFB. Fl.	
☐ 84-24376	84 King Air C-12D	BP-47	U S Army.	
☐ 84-24377	84 King Air C-12D	BP-48	U S Army.	
☐ 84-24378	84 King Air C-12D	BP-49	U S Army.	
☐ 84-24379	84 King Air C-12D	BP-50	U S Army, ARCENT, Dhahran, Saudi Arabia.	
☐ 84-24380	84 King Air C-12D	BP-51	U S Army, Det B C/2-228th Aviation (USAR), Sherman AAF, Ks.	
☐ 85-0147	85 King Air RC-12K	FE-1	U S Army, B/1st MIB (AE), Wiesbaden, Germany.	
☐ 85-0148	85 King Air RC-12K	FE-2	U S Army, B/1st MIB (AE), Wiesbaden, Germany.	
☐ 85-0149	85 King Air RC-12N	FE-3	U S Army, B/1st MIB (AE), Wiesbaden, Germany.	
☐ 85-0150	85 King Air RC-12K	FE-4	U S Army, B/1st MIB (AE), Wiesbaden, Germany.	
☐ 85-0152	85 King Air RC-12K	FE-6	U S Army, B/1st MIB (AE), Wiesbaden, Germany.	
☐ 85-0153	85 King Air RC-12K	FE-7	U S Army, B/1st MIB (AR), Wiesbaden, Germany.	
☐ 85-0155	85 King Air RC-12K	FE-9	U S Army, B/1st MIB (AR), Wiesbaden, Germany.	
☐ 85-1262	85 King Air C-12F	BP-53	U S Army, OSACOM, Det 25, TN ARNG, Smyrna, Tn.	
☐ 85-1263	85 King Air C-12F	BP-54	U S Army, OSACOM, Det 56, PR ARNG, San Juan, PR.	
☐ 85-1264	85 King Air C-12F	BP-55	U S Army, OSACOM, Davison AAF, Va.	
☐ 85-1265	85 King Air C-12F	BP-56	U S Army, OSACOM,	
☐ 85-1266	85 King Air C-12F	BP-57	U S Army, OSACOM, Davison AAF, Va.	
☐ 85-1267	85 King Air C-12F	BP-58	U S Army, OSACOM, Davison AAF, Va.	
☐ 85-1268	85 King Air C-12F	BP-59	U S Army, OSACOM, Davison AAF, Va.	
☐ 85-1270	85 King Air C-12F	BP-61	U S Army, OSACOM,	
☐ 85-1271	85 King Air C-12F	BP-62	U S Army, OSACOM, Det 59, UT ARNG, Salt Lake City No 2, Ut	
☐ 85-1272	85 King Air C-12F	BP-63	U S Army, OSACOM, Det 35, ID ARNG, Gowen Field-Boise, Id.	
☐ 86-0078	86 King Air C-12J	UD-1	USAF, 51st Fighter Wing, Osan AB. South Korea.	
☐ 86-0079	86 King Air C-12J	UD-2	USAF, HQ USEUCOM, Stuttgart, Germany.	
☐ 86-0080	86 King Air C-12J	UD-3	USAF, 46th Test Wing, Eglin AFB, Fl.	
☐ 86-0081	86 King Air C-12J	UD-4	USAF, 3rd Wing, Elmendorf AFB, Ak.	
☐ 86-0082	86 King Air C-12J	UD-5	U S Army, 78th Aviation Btn. NAF Atsugi, Japan.	
☐ 86-0083	86 King Air C-12J	UD-6	USAF, 51st Fighter Wing, Osan AB. South Korea.	
☐ 86-0084	86 King Air C-12F	BP-64	U S Army, OSACOM, Det 26, VA ARNG, Richmond-Byrd Field, Va.	
☐ 86-0085	86 King Air C-12F	BP-65	U S Army, OSACOM, Det 20, NY ARNG, Albany County, NY.	
☐ 86-0086	86 King Air C-12F	BP-66	U S Army, OSACOM, Det 32, CA ARNG, Mather AFB, Ca.	
☐ 86-0087	86 King Air C-12F	BP-67	U S Army, OSACOM, Det 22. PA ARNG, Fort Iniantown Gap, Pa.	
☐ 86-0088	86 King Air C-12F	BP-68	U S Army, OSACOM, Det 8, FL ARNG, St Augustine, Fl.	
☐ 86-0089	86 King Air C-12F	BP-69	U S Army, OSACOM, Det 36, IL ARNG, Decatur, Il.	
☐ 87-0160	87 King Air C-12F	BP-70	U S Army, OSACOM, Det 49, TX ARNG, Austin-Mueller Field, Tx.	
☐ 87-0161	87 King Air C-12F	BP-71	U S Army, OSACOM, Det 5, AL ARNG), Montgomery-Dannelly, Al.	
☐ 88-0325	88 King Air RC-12N	FE-10	U S Army, B/224th Military Intelligence Btn. Hunter AAF, Ga.	
☐ 88-0326	88 King Air RC-12N	FE-11	U S Army, B/224th Military Intelligence Btn. Hunter AAF, Ga.	
☐ 88-0327	88 King Air RC-12N	FE-12	U S Army, B/224th Military Intelligence Btn. Hunter AAF, Ga.	
☐ 89-0267	89 King Air RC-12N	FE-13	U S Army, B/224th Military Intelligence Btn. Hunter AAF, Ga.	
☐ 89-0268	89 King Air RC-12N	FE-14	U S Army, B/224th Military Intelligence Btn. Hunter AAF, Ga.	
☐ 89-0269	89 King Air RC-12N	FE-15	U S Army, B/224th Military Intelligence Btn. Hunter AAF, Ga.	
☐ 89-0270	89 King Air RC-12N	FE-16	U S Army, B/224th Military Intelligence Btn. Hunter AAF, Ga.	
☐ 89-0271	89 King Air RC-12N	FE-17	U S Army, B/224th Military Intelliegnce Btn. Hunter AAF, Ga.	
☐ 89-0273	89 King Air RC-12N	FE-19	U S Army, B/304th Military Intelliegnce Btn. Libby AAF, Az.	
☐ 89-0274	89 King Air RC-12N	FE-20	U S Army, B/304th Military Intelligence Btn. Libby AAF, Az.	
☐ 89-0275	89 King Air RC-12N	FE-21	U S Army, B/224th Military Intelligence Btn. Hunter AAF, Ga.	
☐ 89-0276	89 King Air RC-12N	FE-22	U S Army, B/224th Military Intelligence Btn. Hunter AAF, Ga.	
☐ 91-0516	91 King Air RC-12K	FE-23	U S Army, B/304th Military Intelligence Btn. Libby AAF, Az.	
☐ 91-0517	91 King Air RC-12K	FE-24	U S Army, B/304th Military Intelligence Btn. Libby AAF, Az.	
☐ 91-0518	91 King Air RC-12P	FE-25	U S Army.	
☐ 92-13120	92 King Air RC-12P	FE-26	U S Army.	
☐ 92-13121	92 King Air RC-12P	FE-27	U S Army.	
☐ 92-13122	92 King Air RC-12P	FE-28	U S Army.	
☐ 92-13123	92 King Air RC-12P	FE-29	U S Army.	
☐ 92-13124	92 King Air RC-12P	FE-30	U S Army.	
☐ 92-13125	92 King Air RC-12P	FE-31	U S Army.	
☐ 92-3327	92 King Air C-12F	BW-1	U S Army.	N2843B
☐ 92-3328	92 King Air C-12F	BW-2	U S Army.	N2844B
☐ 92-3329	92 King Air C-12F	BW-3	U S Army.	N2845B
☐ 93-0697	93 King Air RC-12P	FE-32	U S Army.	
☐ 93-0698	93 King Air RC-12P	FE-33	U S Army.	
☐ 93-0699	93 King Air RC-12P	FE-34	U S Army.	

Reg	Yr Type	c/n	Owner/Operator	Prev Regn
☐ 93-0700	93 King Air RC-12P	FE-35	U S Army.	
☐ 93-0701	93 King Air RC-12P	FE-36	U S Army.	
☐ 94-0315	94 King Air C-12R	BW-4	U S Army, Heidelberg, Germany.	
☐ 94-0316	94 King Air C-12R	BW-5	U S Army, Heidelberg, Germany.	
☐ 94-0317	94 King Air C-12R	BW-6	U S Army, Heidelberg, Germany.	
☐ 94-0318	94 King Air C-12R	BW-7	U S Army, Heidelberg, Germany.	
☐ 94-0319	94 King Air C-12R	BW-8	U S Army, Heidelberg, Germany.	
☐ 94-0320	94 King Air C-12R	BW-9	U S Army, B/2-228th AVN, USAR, McCoy AAF, Wi.	
☐ 94-0321	94 King Air C-12R	BW-10	U S Army, B/2-228th AVN, USAR, McCoy AAF, Wi.	
☐ 94-0322	94 King Air C-12R	BW-11	U S Army, OSACOM, Det 16, MS ARNG, Jackson, Ms.	
☐ 94-0323	94 King Air C-12R	BW-12	U S Army, OSACOM, Det 44, NM ARNG, Santa Fe, NM.	
☐ 94-0324	94 King Air C-12R	BW-13	U S Army, OSACOM, Det 31, AZ ARNG, Phoenix, Az.	
☐ 94-0325	94 King Air C-12R	BW-14	U S Army, OSACOM, Det 51, Camp Murray, Wa.	
☐ 94-0326	94 King Air C-12R	BW-15	U S Army, OSACOM, Det 41, MT ARNG, Helena, Mt.	
☐ 95-0088	95 King Air C-12R	BW-16	U S Army, Heidelberg, Germany.	
☐ 95-0089	95 King Air C-12R	BW-17	U S Army, A/2-228th AVN, USAR, Willow Grove JRB, Pa.	
☐ 95-0090	95 King Air C-12R	BW-18	U S Army, A/2-228th AVN, USAR, Willow Grove JRB, Pa.	
☐ 95-0091	95 King Air C-12R	BW-19	U S Army.	
☐ 95-0092	95 King Air C-12R	BW-20	U S Army, D/1-228th AVN, USAR, Los Alamitos, Ca.	
☐ 95-0093	95 King Air C-12R	BW-21	U S Army, D/1-228th AVN, USAR, Los Alamitos, Ca.	
☐ 95-0094	95 King Air C-12R	BW-22	U S Army, D/1-228th AVN, USAR, Los Alamitos, Ca.	
☐ 95-0095	95 King Air C-12R	BW-23	U S Army, D/1-228th AVN, USAR, Los Alamitos, Ca.	
☐ 95-0096	95 King Air C-12R	BW-24	U S Army, D/1-228th AVN, USAR, Los Alamitos, Ca.	
☐ 95-0097	95 King Air C-12R	BW-25	U S Army, B/2-228th AVN, USAR, McCoy AAF, Wi.	
☐ 95-0098	95 King Air C-12R	BW-26	U S Army, B/2-228th Aviation, Cairns AAF, Al.	
☐ 95-0099	95 King Air C-12R	BW-27	U S Army, D/1-228th AVN, USAR, Los Alamitos, Ca.	
☐ 95-0100	95 King Air C-12R	BW-28	U S Army, D/1-228th AVN, USAR, Los Alamitos, Ca.	
☐ 95-0101	98 King Air C-12R	BW-29	U S Army, A/2-228th AVN, USAR, Willow Grove JRB, Pa.	
☐ 96-0112	96 Beech C-12J	UE-256	U S Army, CBCDOM Flight Det. Phillips AAF, Md.	N10931
☐ N10AC	81 King Air B200	BB-858	Ogara Aviation Company, Las Vegas, Nv.	C-GDMU
☐ N102SK	93 King Air 350C	FN-1	Aerospace Trust Management LLC, Wilmington De.	T-721
☐ N399AS	83 King Air B200C	BL-65	U S Army, Aviation & Missile Command, Fort Eustis, Va.	N870CA
☐ N8079B	76 King Air C-12C	BD-20	USAF, Tinker AFB. Ok.	76-0123

OB = PERU   Total 30

Civil

Reg	Yr Type	c/n	Owner/Operator	Prev Regn
☐ OB-1146	78 SA-226AT Merlin 4A	AT-064E	Empresa Minera del Hierro,	OB-M-1146
☐ OB-1228	81 PA-31T Cheyenne II	8120048	Aerovias SA. Satipo.	OB-M-1228
☐ OB-1297	68 King Air B90	LJ-326	Aero Condor SA. Lima.	OB-T-1297
☐ OB-1308	79 PA-31T Cheyenne II	7920075	Videma SA-Compania de Taxi Aereo, Trujillo.	OB-S-1308
☐ OB-1364	68 King Air B90	LJ-330	Aero Condor SA. Lima.	N66MS
☐ OB-1365	81 PA-42 Cheyenne III	8001018	ATSA-Aero Transporte SA. Lima.	N19CD
☐ OB-1468	77 King Air 200	BB-193	TAS-Taxi Aereo Selva SRL. Lima.	N131MB
☐ OB-1509	75 King Air 200	BB-20	TAMSA-Transportes Aereos Maranon SA. Tarapoto. (stolen).	N9023R
☐ OB-1558	68 King Air B90	LJ-405	SAOSA-Servicios Aereos del Oriente SA. Pucallpa.	N68RT
☐ OB-1567	67 King Air A90	LJ-228	Air Atlantic SRL. Lima.	N946K
☐ OB-1593	69 King Air B90	LJ-477	Aero Condor SA. Lima.	N7777
☐ OB-1594	68 King Air B90	LJ-322	Aero Condor SA. Lima.	N45SC
☐ OB-1595	68 King Air B90	LJ-400	TATSA-Transporte Aereo Taxi SA. Lima.	N501PP
☐ OB-1629	81 PA-42 Cheyenne III	8001067	Aero Transporte CA. Lima.	N183CC
☐ OB-1630	81 PA-42 Cheyenne III	8001022	Aero Transporte CA. Lima.	N145CA
☐ OB-1633	78 PA-42 Cheyenne III	7801003	Aero Transporte CA. Lima.	N134KM
☐ OB-1687	81 PA-42 Cheyenne III	8001016	Aero Transporte CA. Lima.	N69PC
☐ OB-1714	81 PA-42 Cheyenne III	8001013	Servicios Aereos AQP SA. Lima.	(N827KR)
☐ OB-1803	78 PA-42 Cheyenne III	7800002		N911VJ

Military

Reg	Yr Type	c/n	Owner/Operator	Prev Regn
☐ AE-571	83 King Air B200CT	BN-2	Peruvian Navy, Esc 11, Lima-Callao. (was BL-58).	N6904Q
☐ AE-572	83 King Air B200CT	BN-3	Peruvian Navy, Esc 11, Lima-Callao. (was BL-59).	N2856B
☐ AE-573	83 King Air B200CT	BN-4	Peruvian Navy, Esc 11, Lima-Callao. (was BL-60).	N2790B
☐ AE-574	83 King Air B200T	BT-25	Peruvian Navy, Esc 11, Lima-Callao. (was BB-1096).	N2795B
☐ AE-575	83 King Air B200T	BT-26	Peruvian Navy, Esc 11, Lima-Callao. (was BB-1098).	N2826B
☐ EP-821	PA-31T Cheyenne	...	Peruvian Army, Lima.	
☐ EP-825	90 King Air 350	FL-21	Peruvian Army, Lima.	N666RH
☐ FAP-18	85 King Air 300	FA-41	FAP, Las Palmas-Lima.	HK-3495
☐ FAP-708	Rockwell 690	...	FAP, Las Palmas-Lima.	

☐ PNP-218	81 Gulfstream 980	95080	Policia Nacional del Peru, Lima.		N50ST
☐ PNP-230	73 King Air E90	LW-36	Policia Nacional del Peru, Lima.		OB-1598

OE = AUSTRIA   Total   16
Civil

☐ OE-BBB	79 King Air 200	BB-526	Federal Office for Meteorology & Survey, Vienna.		
☐ OE-EKD	96 Pilatus PC-12	142	Durst Aircraft Rental GmbH. Vienna.		HB-FRD
☐ OE-EMC	05 Pilatus PC-12/45	663	Michelfeit Sepp, Laxenburg.		HB-FQJ
☐ OE-EPC	03 Pilatus PC-12/45	536	Diamond Aircraft Industries GmbH. Neustadt.		(D-FAPC)
☐ OE-FBH	81 Conquest 1	425-0035	Ing Christian Koeing, Feldkirchen		N402NG
☐ OE-FDS	77 PA-31T Cheyenne II	7720056	Business Flugschule u Flugzeug GmbH. Vienna.		(N82169)
☐ OE-FHL	85 King Air C90A	LJ-1115	Airlink Luftverkehrs GmbH. Salzburg.		D-IBPE
☐ OE-FHM	91 King Air C90A	LJ-1284	EUROP STAR Aircraft GmbH. Villach.		N25GA
☐ OE-FIT	81 PA-42 Cheyenne III	8001048	Redair Luftfahrt GmbH., Mils		D-IMIM
☐ OE-FKG	80 PA-31T Cheyenne II	8020036	Airlink Luftverkehrs GmbH. Salzburg.		N30DJ
☐ OE-FKH	81 PA-31T Cheyenne 1	8104029	Airlink Luftverkehrs GmbH. Salzburg.		N803CA
☐ OE-FME	93 King Air 300LW	FA-228	Airlink Luftverkehrs GmbH. Salzburg.		(D-CAIR)
☐ OE-FOS	00 King Air B200	BB-1741	Inter Avia Flugbetrieb GmbH. St Georges Im Altergau.		D-IIAH
☐ OE-FRS	85 King Air C90A	LJ-1124	Jetalliance		N90EP
☐ OE-GBB	96 Dornier 328-100	3078	Tyrolean Jet Service GmbH. Vienna.		D-C...
☐ OE-KGB	01 PA-46-500TP Meridian	4697035	TITANEN Air Flugzeug GmbH. Vienna.		N77Y

OH = FINLAND   Total   10
Civil

☐ OH-ACN	76 Rockwell 690A	11301	Konekorhonen OY. Tikkakoski.		(N81405)
☐ OH-BAX	81 King Air C90	LJ-984	Scanwings OY. Helsinki.		LN-FOD
☐ OH-BCX	78 King Air C90	LJ-770	Metrojet OY/Scanwings OY., Vantaa.		N88CG
☐ OH-BEX	81 King Air C90	LJ-978	Aerial OY/Scanwings OY. Helsinki.		N725KR
☐ OH-BSA	89 King Air 300	FA-205	Finnair Aviation Institute, Pori.		N5672A
☐ OH-BSB	89 King Air 300	FA-206	Finnair Aviation Institute, Pori.		N5672J
☐ OH-KJJ	03 TBM 700C2	258	Fortel Kiinteistoet OY. Oulu.		
☐ OH-OTL	87 Reims/Cessna F406	F406-0015	Oulun Tilauslento OY. Oulu.		(LN-PBH)
☐ OH-PAY	88 PA-42 Cheyenne 400LS	5527040	Juris Economica OY. Helsinki.		JA8870
☐ OH-UTI	74 Rockwell 690A	11204	FM Kartta OY/Savair OY. Helsinki.		SE-GSR

OK = CZECH REPUBLIC / CZECHIA   Total   13
Civil

☐ OK-ATX	72 Mitsubishi MU-2K	239	Aerotaxi Sro. Prague.		N303AG
☐ OK-CTR	07 PA-46-500TP Meridian	4697320			
☐ OK-DSH	79 King Air C90	LJ-837	Delta System Air, Hradec Kralove.		N364D
☐ OK-EMA	00 Ibis Ae 270P Spirit	001	IBIS Aerospace Ltd. Prague. (Ff 25 Jul 00)		
☐ OK-EVA	04 Ibis Ae 270P Spirit	007	IBIS Aerospace Ltd. Prague.		
☐ OK-GTJ	92 King Air 300LW	FA-223	Time Air s r o, Prague.		D-IHHB
☐ OK-INA	03 Ibis Ae 270P Spirit	006	IBIS Aerospace Ltd. Prague.		
☐ OK-LFD	01 King Air 350	FL-322	Let's Fly Sro., Mosnov		D-CHGS
☐ OK-LIB	03 Ibis Ae 270P Spirit	005	IBIS Aerospace Ltd. Prague.		
☐ OK-MAG	77 King Air/Catpass 250	BB-221	Aerotaxi Sro. Prague.		PH-DDB
☐ OK-NET	07 PA-46-500TP Meridian	4697315	Piper Aircraft Inc. Vero Beach, Fl.		
☐ OK-OKL	81 PA-42 Cheyenne III	8001060	L-Consult Sro. Mnichovo Hradiste.		N631PC
☐ OK-VIP	06 PA-46-500TP Meridian	4697273	Piper OK a.s., Prague		N10656

OM = SLOVAKIA   Total   2
Civil

☐ OM-FLY	97 King Air B200	BB-1565	VIP Air, Bratislava		N685R
☐ OM-VIP	79 PA-31T Cheyenne II	7920002	VIP Air, Bratislava.		D-IXXX

OO = BELGIUM   Total   15
Civil

☐ OO-ASL	82 King Air B200C	BL-49	Air Service Liege NV, Antwerp		OK-LFB
☐ OO-GMJ	05 King Air 350	FL-460	ASL-Air Service Liege NV. Antwerp.		D-CGMI
☐ OO-IAL	81 King Air F90	LA-100	ASL-Air Service Liege NV. Antwerp.		D-IWAL
☐ OO-INN	94 King Air B200	BB-1500	Sky-Service NV/Latexco NV, Wevelgem.		RP-C1502
☐ OO-LAC	80 King Air B200C	BL-16	Sky-Service BV. Wevelgem.		F-GLTX
☐ OO-LET	94 King Air B200	BB-1473	ASL-Air Service Liege NV. Antwerp.		N8210X
☐ OO-ROB	77 Rockwell 690B	11409	G Velleman, Wevelgem.		N81646
☐ OO-SAD	70 King Air A90	LM-126	Cicade SA. Gosselies.		LX-RAD
☐ OO-SDU	03 King Air 350	FL-368	Bongrain Benelux SA. Breda, Holland.		N6068V

Reg   Yr   Type   c/n   Owner/Operator   Prev Regn

☐ OO-SKL	89 King Air B200	BB-1348	Sky-Service BV. Wevelgem.	D2-EST
☐ OO-SKM	91 King Air B200	BB-1407	Sky-Service BV. Wevelgem.	D2-ESQ
☐ OO-SXB	81 Xingu 121A	121040	Airventure BV. Antwerp. (status ?).	PT-MBH
☐ OO-SXC	81 Xingu 121A	121042	Airventure BV. Antwerp.	PT-MBJ
☐ OO-TBM	91 TBM 700A	3	Avia-Rent Wallonie ASBL, Gosselies	F-HBGC
☐ OO-VHV	79 King Air E90	LW-316	Sky-Service BV. Wevelgem.	N77WZ

OY = DENMARK Total 29
Civil

☐ OY-BHU	79 PA-31T Cheyenne 1	7904004	A/S Kongedybet, Copenhagen.	N131SW
☐ OY-BVS	68 King Air B90	LJ-418	Danish Air Transport A/S. Vamdrup.	(SE-LEN)
☐ OY-BVW	80 King Air 200	BB-705	Skandinavisk Motor A/S-Volkswagen, Brondby.	D-IBAB
☐ OY-CBP	77 King Air 200	BB-235	First Light ApS. Aarhus.	(N777MW)
☐ OY-CKP	82 King Air B200	BB-951	Cowi A/S. Lyngby.	LX-ALX
☐ OY-CVB	89 King Air 300	FA-175	Grakjaer A/S, Holstebro	N175NJ
☐ OY-EEF	97 King Air B200	BB-1548	Thrane & Thrane A/S. Roskilde.	
☐ OY-GEW	89 King Air 1300	BB-1342	ICRC/SAviation Assistance A/S. Roskilde.	VT-SAE
☐ OY-GSA	01 Pilatus PC-12/45	421	Widex ApS. Roskilde.	HB-FRN
☐ OY-JRN	78 King Air 200	BB-364	Ikaros Fly ApS. Roskilde.	F-GHYV
☐ OY-LAW	02 PA-46-500TP Meridian	4697138	Gefa GmbH/Air Alfa Aircraft Sales, Odense.	
☐ OY-LDA	02 PA-46-500TP Meridian	4697147	L Damsgaard Andersen,	
☐ OY-LLL	04 King Air B200	BB-1861	Lohfert & Lohfert A/S. Roskilde.	N50478
☐ OY-LMM	01 PA-46-500TP Meridian	4697108	Air Alpha Aircraft Sales A/S. Odense.	N480M
☐ OY-LSA	00 King Air C90B	LJ-1610	Peter Trane, Charlottenlund.	N44406
☐ OY-MEN	98 King Air 350	FL-229	Aviation Assistance A/S. Roskilde.	N9WV
☐ OY-MID	05 Pilatus PC-12/45	659	Midtair I/S, Herning	C-GPDJ
☐ OY-NUT	05 Pilatus PC-12/45	677	Execujet A/S. Roskilde.	HB-F..
☐ OY-PCL	99 King Air B200	BB-1675	Air Greenland A/S. Nuuk.	N2355Z
☐ OY-PEB	78 King Air 200	BB-309	Royal Unibrew A.S.	OY-PEB
☐ OY-PHD	05 PA-46-500TP Meridian	4697193	Air Alpha Aircraft Sales A/S. Odense.	
☐ OY-PKB	07 PA-46-500TP Meridian	4697309	Air Alpha A/S., Odense	N31136
☐ OY-PKC	07 PA-46-500TP Meridian	4697317	GEFA Gesellschaft Fur	
☐ OY-PPP	06 Pilatus PC-12/47	697	Baisden Ltd., Nicosia, Cyprus	(N909PP)
☐ OY-SBU	78 King Air C90	LJ-768	Danish Air Transport A/S / Felxa Group A/S. Vamdrup.	LN-KCG
☐ OY-SCI	03 Pilatus PC-12/45	496	Amicorp Denmark A/S. Copenhagen.	N496DT
☐ OY-TLP	02 P-180 Avanti	1060	Danish Crown SALG, OG Service A/S., Randers	F-HALE
☐ OY-TWO	07 Pilatus PC-12/47	863	Anpartsselskabet	HB-FSV
☐ OY-VIN	07 Pilatus PC-12/47	872	Air Alpha Aircraft Sales A/s, Odense	HB-FQD

PH = NETHERLANDS Total 25
Civil

☐ PH-	07 TBM 850	419	Salvagnini Nederland BV, Oistererwijk	
☐ PH-ATM	76 King Air/Catpass 250	BB-123	Skyline Aviation BV. Dan Helder.	D-IBIC
☐ PH-AXS	78 King Air E90	LW-297	Axess Aviation B.V., Amsterdam	LX-LTX
☐ PH-CLZ	04 TBM 700C2	299	Alibrent BV. Gravenhage.	F-OIKL
☐ PH-DIX	00 Pilatus PC-12/45	309	Din Air BV. Eindhoven.	HB-FRG
☐ PH-ECC	94 Pilatus PC-12	107	H.H. Jacobus, Aruba	N62JT
☐ PH-EEV	95 Dornier 328-110	3056	Elas Professional Services Network B.V., Valkenswaard	N438JS
☐ PH-EVY	98 Dornier 328-100	3095	SolidAir / Elas Professional Services Network, Schiphol	G-CJAC
☐ PH-FHB	06 PA-46-500TP Meridian	4697282	Faber Halbertsma Holding B.V., Eck en Wiel	N10803
☐ PH-HRK	06 P-180 Avanti II	1120	Rotterdam Private Air BV. Rotterdam.	
☐ PH-HUB	97 TBM 700A	127	Flying Thorn BV. Eindhoven.	F-OHBV
☐ PH-JFS	02 Pilatus PC-12/45	477	Eurofilters Holding BV. Overpelt, Belgium	HB-FPD
☐ PH-JOE	83 Conquest 1	425-0168	Westerheide Management & Consultancy BV. Arnhem.	G-BJYC
☐ PH-KBB	04 King Air C90	LJ-1718	Offshore Marine Consultants Ltd. Guernsey, C.I.	N720AF
☐ PH-MNZ	92 Dornier 228-212	8206	Kustwacht-Dutch Coastguard/Martinair Holland NV. Amsterdam.	D-CDIV
☐ PH-PIC	76 SA-226T Merlin 3A	T-267	Aerodata Remote Sensing B.V. Prinsenbeek	LX-PIX
☐ PH-SVY	80 PA-31T Cheyenne II	8020041	Slagboom en Peeters Luchtfotografie, Teuge.	N198AA
☐ PH-TCN	04 P-180 Avanti	1089	Plano di Volo/Van Gelder BV-Strovast, Rotterdam.	
☐ PH-TGA	07 TBM 850	428	Rembrand Van Rijn V O F, Eindhoven	
☐ PH-UKK	06 TBM 850	372	E.S. Management B.V., Roggel	N850WZ
☐ PH-XII	04 Pilatus PC-12/45	550	De Hondert Margen BV/Air Services UK Ltd. Rotterdam.	HB-...

Military

☐ U-01	81 Fokker 60UTA-N	20321	RNAF, 334 Squadron, Eindhoven. 'Marinus Van Meel'	PH-UTL
☐ U-03	95 Fokker 60UTA-N	20327	RNAF, 334 Squadron, Eindhoven. 'Jan Borghouts'	PH-UTP
☐ U-05	96 Fokker 50	20253	RNAF, 334 Squadron, Eindhoven. 'Fons Aler'	PH-KXO

Reg   Yr Type   c/n   Owner/Operator   Prev Regn

| ☐ U-06 | 96 Fokker 50 | 20287 | RNAF, 334 Squadron, Eindhoven. 'Robbie Wijting' | PH-MXI |

PJ = NETHERLANDS ANTILLES — Total 3

Civil
☐ PJ-...	83 Gulfstream 1000	96065	Zunoca Freezone NV. Curacao.	N46GA
☐ PJ-CEB	76 Rockwell 690A	11292	CEB Investments BV. Curacao.	HB-GEH
☐ PJ-NAF	82 Gulfstream 1000	96008	Jarbol Avia, Curacao.	N9917S

PK = INDONESIA — Total 24

Civil
☐ PK-AHA	96 TBM 700	119	Directorate of Civil Aviation, Jakarta.	F-OHBQ
☐ PK-AHC	96 TBM 700	120	Directorate of Civil Aviation, Jakarta.	F-OHBR
☐ PK-CAK	93 King Air B200C	BL-140	Directorate of Civil Aviation, Jakarta.	N82410
☐ PK-CAL	96 TBM 700	114	Directorate of Civil Aviation, Jakarta.	F-OHBS
☐ PK-CAM	96 TBM 700	121	Directorate of Civil Aviation, Jakarta.	F-OBHT
☐ PK-CDM	67 Gulfstream 1	177	Citra Aviation PT. Jakarta.	PK-CTE
☐ PK-DYR	78 PA-31T Cheyenne II	7820054	Deraya Air Taxi PT. Jakarta.	VH-MWT
☐ PK-JCA	92 King Air B200C	BL-138	Pura Group, Kudus.	VH-HPZ
☐ PK-ODR	80 Gulfstream 980	95019	Airfast Indonesia PT. Jakarta. (status ?).	N9772S
☐ PK-PTI	79 PA-31T Cheyenne II	7920084	Pelita Air, Jakarta.	N189GH
☐ PK-RGI	00 King Air B200	BB-1732	Eastindo, Jakarta.	N23268
☐ PK-RJA	68 Gulfstream 1	191	Pos Ekspres Prima, Jakarta. 'Anugerah II'	VH-JPJ
☐ PK-RJC	90 120ER Brasilia	120214	Premiair, Jakarta	EC-HSO
☐ PK-TRA	76 King Air 200	BB-113	Indonesia Air Transport, Jakarta.	
☐ PK-TRO	64 Gulfstream 1	130	Indonesia Air Transport, Jakarta.	N3416
☐ PK-TRW	96 Beech 1900D	UE-177	Mobil Oil/Indonesian Air Transport, Jakarta.	N3237H
☐ PK-TRX	96 Beech 1900D	UE-186	Mobil Oil/Indonesian Air Transport, Jakarta.	N3233J
☐ PK-UCG	06 Pilatus PC-12/47	795	Yajasi Aviation, Jayapura	VH-ZKM
☐ PK-VKA	80 King Air 200	BB-732	PENAS, Jakarta.	N3716D
☐ PK-VKB	81 King Air 200	BB-794	PENAS, Jakarta.	N3720U
☐ PK-VKY	67 King Air A90	LJ-197	PENAS, Jakarta.	N2510L
☐ PK-VKZ	67 King Air A90	LJ-189	PENAS, Jakarta.	N123KA

Military
| ☐ P-2033 | King Air B200 | ... | Indonesian Police, Jakarta. | |
| ☐ P-2066 | King Air B200 | ... | Indonesian Police, Jakarta. | |

PP = BRAZIL — Total 397

Civil
☐ PP-ACM	80 Xingu 121A	121021	Aerotaxi Abaete Ltda., Salvador, BA	PT-MAN
☐ PP-AMC	04 King Air C90GT	LJ-1727	Moinho Iguacu Agroindustrial, Rondonopolis, MG, Brazil	N690GT
☐ PP-AMJ	06 King Air C90GT	LJ-1772		N36688
☐ PP-BAF	01 King Air C90B	LJ-1646	SERMO Servicios de Mao Obra SC Ltda. Sao Paulo, SP.	N4446D
☐ PP-BER	05 Pilatus PC-12/45	655		N655PB
☐ PP-CBD	84 King Air B200	BB-1062	Rio Real Empreendimentos Ltda. Belo Horizonte, MG.	N985GA
☐ PP-COP	84 King Air C90B	LJ-1618	Cosan SA Industria Comercio, Piraccicaba, SP.	N5024W
☐ PP-CSE	85 King Air F90-1	LA-228	Covre Factoring Fomento Com Ltda.	N80WP
☐ PP-EHE	74 King Air C90	LJ-638	Caixego Caixa Econom do Estado Goias, Goiania, GO.	PT-KFV
☐ PP-EIC	81 Xingu 121A	121039	SEVOP Secretariat De Obras & Viacao Publicas	PT-MBG
☐ PP-EIJ	85 Xingu II 121A1	121094	Governo do Piaui	PT-MCH
☐ PP-EJG	91 King Air B200	BB-1410	State Government of Goias, Goiania, GO.	
☐ PP-EJO	85 King Air 300	FA-31	Governor do Estado do Minas Gerais, Belo Horizonte, MG.	PT-LNJ
☐ PP-EMN	80 Xingu 121A	121035	Governor of the State of Minas Gerais	PT-MBC
☐ PP-EOP	76 King Air 200	BB-137	State Government of Roraima, Boa Vista, RR.	PP-IKN
☐ PP-EPB	81 PA-42 Cheyenne III	8001035	State Government of Paraiba, Joao Pessoa, PB.	PT-OSX
☐ PP-EPD	86 King Air 300	FA-92	State Government of Amazonas, Manaus, AM.	PT-OSZ
☐ PP-EPS	96 King Air C90B	LJ-1442	State Government of Bahia, Salvador, BA.	PT-WNI
☐ PP-ERG	98 King Air B200	BB-1603	State Government of Rio Grande do Sol, Porte Alegre, RS.	PT-WRN
☐ PP-ETR	99 King Air C90B	LJ-1578	Para Governor do Estado,	N3178R
☐ PP-EUE	68 King Air B90	LJ-409	State Government of Parana, Curitiba, PR.	
☐ PP-FHE	82 Xingu II 121A1	121051	MIRAD - Min.da Reforma & do Desenvo Agrario	PT-FAY
☐ PP-FOY	73 King Air A100	B-142	Departamento de Policia Federal MJ, Brasilia, DF.	
☐ PP-JSC	00 King Air 350	FL-289	Sucocitrico Cutrale Ltda. Araraquara, SP.	N3189T
☐ PP-KKG	00 King Air 350	FL-288		(PP-KKK)
☐ PP-LCB	78 King Air C-12C	BC-65	Casa Bahia Comercial Ltda. Sao Paulo, SP.	N638B
☐ PP-LCQ	78 PA-31T Cheyenne II	7820046	MEDASA-Med Neto Dist de Alcool SA. Recife, PE.	N688CA
☐ PP-LOG	05 King Air 350	FL-434		N727MH

Reg   Yr   Type   c/n   Owner/Operator   Prev Regn

Reg	Yr	Type	c/n	Owner/Operator	Prev Regn
☐ PP-LOV	07	King Air B200	BB-1992		N992KA
☐ PP-PSC	96	120ER Brasilia	120313	Embraer	
☐ PP-SAM	06	Pilatus PC-12/47	785		N785PC
☐ PP-WCA	02	King Air C90B	LJ-1676	Csa Trading SA Vitoria	N771JC
☐ PR-...	75	King Air 200	BB-25	George de Sousa Pereira, Manauc.	N601CF
☐ PR-AAX	80	King Air 200	BB-736		N45CF
☐ PR-ACT	98	King Air B200	BB-1626		N2299W
☐ PR-ADM	04	King Air 350	FL-398	ADM do Brasil Ltda.	N6198N
☐ PR-AEF	03	King Air 350	FL-377	Fertipa Fertizantes do Para Ltda.	N6177F
☐ PR-AGM	05	Pilatus PC-12/45	667	Grupo Andre Maggi, Rondonopolis.	N667PE
☐ PR-AGR	05	Pilatus PC-12/45	652	Agrenco do Brasil SA. Cuiaba, MT.	N133N
☐ PR-AGV	04	King Air C90B	LJ-1725		N30025
☐ PR-APJ	00	King Air B200	BB-1755		N5055Q
☐ PR-ARC	05	King Air C90B	LJ-1739		N36839
☐ PR-ART	81	King Air 200	BB-806		N975SC
☐ PR-AVT	91	King Air C90A	LJ-1279		N611KA
☐ PR-BIO	06	King Air C90GT	LJ-1803		N71873
☐ PR-BLP	85	King Air B200	BB-1199	COC Empreeend Culturais Ltda.	N7203R
☐ PR-BOM	06	King Air C90GT	LJ-1763	Erai Maggi Scheffer, Rondondpolis, MG.	N61788
☐ PR-BTN	06	King Air B200	BB-1968	GECC/Bertin Ltda., Sao Paulo, Brazil	N70068
☐ PR-BTS	07	King Air C90GT	LJ-1827		N7207M
☐ PR-BZE	04	Pilatus PC-12/45	580		N150MX
☐ PR-CAR*	06	King Air C90GT	LJ-1826	Wells Fargo Bank NW NA., Salt Lake City, Ut.	(PR-DAH)
☐ PR-CCB	07	King Air 350	FL-541		N7101C
☐ PR-CCF	00	King Air C90B	LJ-1608	Itapemirim Taxi Aereo Ltda. Itapemirim, ES.	N4408U
☐ PR-CEB	06	King Air C90GT	LJ-1807	Avn Air LLC (GECC)/Equipav S.A., Sao Paulo, Brazil	N7007Y
☐ PR-CMI	04	King Air C90B	LJ-1715		N508CB
☐ PR-CVI	07	King Air B300	FL-550	Brazil	N750KA
☐ PR-DAH	06	King Air 350	FL-481	Dafra Da Amaz. Ind.Com De Motocic Ltd	N37318
☐ PR-DBR	81	Gulfstream 980	95069		D-IHUC
☐ PR-DHD	06	King Air C90GT	LJ-1825		N7125Y
☐ PR-DIN	06	King Air C90GT	LJ-1796		N71296
☐ PR-DOG	07	Pilatus PC-12/47	814	Avn Air LLC. (GECC)/Paulista de Construccoes e Comercio, SP	N814PC
☐ PR-EAO	05	King Air B200	BB-1912	Empreendimentos Agropecuarios Obras, Ibicui, Bahia.	N6132U
☐ PR-EDF	01	King Air 350	FL-335	Lider Taxi Aereo SA. Belo Horizonte, MG.	N5135N
☐ PR-EDP	01	King Air C90B	LJ-1672	Lider Taxi Aereo SA. Belo Horizonte, MG.	N5027R
☐ PR-EDW	80	King Air 200	BB-623		N6689D
☐ PR-FAG	89	Reims/Cessna F406	F406-0037		ZS-PPU
☐ PR-FAZ	02	King Air C90B	LJ-1674		N821CS
☐ PR-FIC	03	TBM 700C2	297	Usina Coruripe Acucar e Alcool SA.	N700HM
☐ PR-FKY	03	King Air C90B	LJ-1701	Lider Taxi Aereo SA. Belo Horizonte, MG.	N5134S
☐ PR-FRB	04	King Air B200	BB-1871	?	N917CB
☐ PR-GAB	07	TBM 850	418		N654CW
☐ PR-GFB	07	King Air C90GT	LJ-1821	Bertin Ltda/Onix Securities Trading Inc, Sao Paulo, Brazil	N7221Y
☐ PR-HRM	76	PA-31T Cheyenne II	7620053	LASA Engenhoria e Prospeccoes SA. Rio de Janeiro, RJ.	C-GHRM
☐ PR-IRB	05	King Air C90B	LJ-1743		N36883
☐ PR-JAG	06	King Air C90GT	LJ-1771	Jaguari Comercial E Agricola, Bela Vista,MS	N429K
☐ PR-JCA	07	King Air C90GT	LJ-1844	?	N1844B
☐ PR-JDB	04	King Air 350	FL-435	John Deere Brasil SA. Horizontina, RG.	N36635
☐ PR-JME	07	King Air C90GT	LJ-1841		N841TB
☐ PR-JQM	02	King Air C90B	LJ-1684	CEMAT, Cuiaba.	N5084J
☐ PR-JSP	78	King Air 200	BB-304	National Investments Leasing Inc.	N103PM
☐ PR-LIA	01	King Air B200	BB-1798	Lojas Americanos SA. Rio de Janeiro, RJ.	N577P
☐ PR-LJA	00	King Air 350	FL-290		N969MB
☐ PR-LJR	06	Pilatus PC-12/47	738		N738PE
☐ PR-LMT	07	King Air C90GT	LJ-1876		N
☐ PR-LPM	07	King Air B200	BB-1981		N7481P
☐ PR-MCE	04	King Air B200	BB-1890		N6190F
☐ PR-MFG	05	King Air C90B	LJ-1742	Marfrig Frigorficoes Comercio Alimen, Bataguassu, MG.	N36742
☐ PR-MLG	04	King Air B200	BB-1863	Lider Taxi Aereo SA. Belo Horizonte, MG.	N6203T
☐ PR-MLZ	01	King Air C90B	LJ-1644	Magazine Luiza SA. Franca, SP.	N90XP
☐ PR-MOZ	99	King Air 350	FL-237	Santa Colama Investimentos e Participacoes Ltda.	N115GB
☐ PR-MZP	92	King Air C90B	LJ-1311	Newberry Enterprises Inc. Georgetown, Grand Cayman.	N489JS
☐ PR-PIB	06	King Air C90GT	LJ-1784	Irmaos Biagi SA. Serana, SP.	N37124
☐ PR-PJC	66	King Air A90	LJ-181		PT-LBZ

Reg	Yr	Type	c/n	Owner/Operator	Prev Regn
☐ PR-RFB	99	King Air C90B	LJ-1546		N3071H
☐ PR-RHH	04	King Air C90B	LJ-1717	Bimco Properties Inc. Panama City, Panama.	N32217
☐ PR-RMA	03	King Air C90B	LJ-1693		N6193J
☐ PR-SDA	06	King Air C90GT	LJ-1770		N770WA
☐ PR-SGB	06	King Air C90GT	LJ-1794	Distribuicao Moveis Electrodomesticos, Cuiaba, MG.	N37324
☐ PR-SIA	91	King Air C90A	LJ-1272	Sukest Industria d'Alimentos e Farma Ltda.	N770AJ
☐ PR-TCA	96	King Air C90B	LJ-1441		D-IKMS
☐ PR-TIN	00	King Air C90B	LJ-1628	Visionary Ventures Inc.	N3228M
☐ PR-TLL	77	King Air C90	LJ-713	Lake Air Inc.	N114J
☐ PR-USA	02	King Air C90B	LJ-1679	Lider Taxi Aereo SA. Belo Horizonte, MG.	N4479M
☐ PR-UTI	78	Mitsubishi MU-2N	727SA		(PR-UTH)
☐ PR-VDQ	06	King Air B200	BB-1965	Minerva S/A	N68BK
☐ PR-XGT	07	King Air C90GT	LJ-1846		N846KA
☐ PR-XIB	01	King Air C90B	LJ-1639	Carpa Serrana Agropecuaria Rio Pardo, Serrano, SP.	N51139
☐ PT	81	King Air F90	LA-107		N700BK
☐ PT-	07	King Air B200GT	BY-15	Brazil?	
☐ PT-...	80	Gulfstream 980	95038	(status ?).	N91SA
☐ PT-...	77	Rockwell 690B	11391	EXBRA Impotacao e Exportacao Ltda. Sao Paulo, SP. (status ?)	N73MA
☐ PT-...	65	King Air 90	LJ-16	(status ?).	N51KA
☐ PT-...	67	680V Turbo Commander	1703-79	(status ?)	N161XX
☐ PT-ASN	85	King Air F90-1	LA-232	Ayrton Senna Prom. e Empreend. Ltda. Sao Paulo, SP.	D-IWPF
☐ PT-BOY	69	Mitsubishi MU-2F	145	Oeste Redes Aereas SA/ORA Taxi Aereo SA. Cuiaba, MT.	N769Q
☐ PT-BZW	69	Mitsubishi MU-2F	175	CITEP-Com. e Imp. T. Posses Ltda. Sao Caet. do Sul, SP.	N890Q
☐ PT-BZY	70	Mitsubishi MU-2F	188	Franca Taxi Aereo Ltda. Sao Luiz, MA.	N109MA
☐ PT-DEU	68	King Air B90	LJ-355	Claudiomar Vic Kehrnvald e Outro, Redencao, PA.	
☐ PT-DIQ	68	King Air B90	LJ-398	Umuarama Const. Terrap. Paviment Ltda. Araguaina, TO.	
☐ PT-DKV	70	King Air 100	B-43	Saenge Eng. de Saneam. e Edif Ltda. Sao Paulo, SP.	
☐ PT-DNP	70	King Air 100	B-56	Jorge Wady Cecilio, Goiania, GO.	
☐ PT-DTL	71	Mitsubishi MU-2F	196	SETE Taxi Aereo Ltda. Goiania, GO.	N116MA
☐ PT-FAX	82	Xingu 121A	121049	SUDENE - Superint. Do Desenvo. Do Nordeste	PT-MBR
☐ PT-FCM	97	King Air C90B	LJ-1471	Jatoba Agric Pec e Ind SA. Curitiba, PR.	N1099D
☐ PT-FFN	89	King Air 300	FA-174	Braulino Basilio Maia Filho, Aracatuba, SP.	N1543H
☐ PT-FFS	97	King Air B200	BB-1578	Gianni Franco Samaja, Sao Paulo, SP.	N330DR
☐ PT-FGB	91	King Air 350	FL-42	Berneck & Cia. Curitiba, PR.	N17NC
☐ PT-FRG	81	Xingu 121A	121044	DNER - Dep. Nacionales Estradas de Rodagem	PT-MBL
☐ PT-FSA	98	King Air 350	FL-221	Sattin SA. Adm e Participacoes, Sao Paulo, SP.	N221Z
☐ PT-IBE	71	King Air C90	LJ-531	Translima Taxi Aereo Ltda. Belo Horizonte, MG. (status ?).	
☐ PT-ICD	72	Mitsubishi MU-2F	215	Bens Tur Passaagens e Repres Ltda. Goiania, GO.	N181MA
☐ PT-ICP	72	King Air C90	LJ-558	Voar Taxi Aereo Ltda, Goiania, GO.	
☐ PT-IEC	72	681B Turbo Commander	6069	BCN Leasing Arrend. Mercantil SA. Baruerí, SP.	
☐ PT-IED	72	681B Turbo Commander	6070	MTP Industrial e Comercial Ltda.	
☐ PT-IGD	72	King Air E90	LW-9	Marcos Paixao de Araujo, Belo Horizonte, MG.	
☐ PT-JGA	73	Mitsubishi MU-2K	268	Maringa SA Cimento e Ferro-Liga, Sao Paulo, SP.	N314MA
☐ PT-JUB	93	King Air B200	BB-1455	RACC/	N8105Q
☐ PT-KGV	67	King Air A90	LJ-221	No Limits Taxi Aerea Ltda. Boituva, SP.	N38V
☐ PT-KME	75	PA-31T Cheyenne II	7520012	Lideranca Taxi Aereo Ltda. Brasilia, DF.	
☐ PT-KYF	61	Gulfstream 1	75	Jet Sul Taxi Aereo Ltda. Curitiba, PR.	N304K
☐ PT-LCE	81	King Air E90	LW-347	Edio Nogueira, Campinas, SP.	N3841V
☐ PT-LDA	72	Rockwell 690	11036	Representacaoes Seixas SA. Cpo. Eliseos, SP.	PT-FRC
☐ PT-LDL	72	Rockwell 690	11037	Taxi Aereo Marilia SA. Sao Paulo, SP.	PT-FRD
☐ PT-LER	81	King Air F90	LA-148	CTEEP-CiaTrans Energ Elet Paulista.	N1826P
☐ PT-LEW	72	Mitsubishi MU-2K	244	Aeronet Informatica Ltda. Imperatiz, MA. (status ?).	N400SM
☐ PT-LFX	74	Mitsubishi MU-2J	650	Redencao Taxi Aereo Ltda. Carlos Roberto Bueno, PA.	N990M
☐ PT-LHH	81	MU-2 Marquise	1508SA	AB Promocoes E P. Artist S/C Ltda. Anapolis, GO.	N618RT
☐ PT-LHJ	82	King Air C90	LJ-1010	Andre Luiz Sant Anna de Matto, Belo Horizonte, MG.	N6135Z
☐ PT-LHM	66	King Air 90	LJ-105	Aluisio Gregorio Motta Jr. Gurupi, TO.	PP-ENF
☐ PT-LHV	77	Rockwell 690B	11376	Omar Najar,	N81567
☐ PT-LHZ	75	King Air E90	LW-133	Luiz Rassi Jr. Goiania, GO.	(N52CB)
☐ PT-LIF	84	King Air F90-1	LA-223	ICAL-Industria de Calcinacao Ltda, S Jose da Lapa, MG.	N83KA
☐ PT-LIK	82	MU-2 Marquise	1546SA	Banco Cidade Leasing Arren. Merc. SA. Goiania, GO.	N472MA
☐ PT-LIR	80	MU-2 Solitaire	428SA	FRICOL-Frigorificos Colinas SA. Col. Tocantins, TO.	N124AX
☐ PT-LIS	79	MU-2 Marquise	749SA	Manuel Grzywacz Birembaum, Sao Paulo, SP.	N980MA
☐ PT-LJN	79	King Air A100	B-121	Santander Brasil Arrend. Mercantil, Baruerí, SP.	PP-EGK
☐ PT-LJS	85	MU-2 Marquise	1568SA	Uniair Taxi Aereo Ltda. Vitoria, ES.	N501MA
☐ PT-LLG	80	PA-31T Cheyenne II	8020054	Pabreulandia Agropastoril BC Ltda. Barra do Garcas, MG.	LV-OGB

Reg	Yr Type	c/n	Owner/Operator	Prev Regn
PT-LLO	89 King Air C90A	LJ-1225	Fatty Taxi Aereo Ltda. Sao Paulo, SP.	N1564M
PT-LLP	79 King Air F90	LA-7	Sao Joao Abrasivos e Minerios Ltda. Sao Joao da B Vista, SP.	N67RP
PT-LLR	81 King Air C90	LJ-946	Safra Leasing SA Arrend Mercantil. Sao Paulo, SP.	N3236T
PT-LLV	80 King Air C90	LJ-897	Realfort Distribuidora Ltda.	N758D
PT-LMD	67 Mitsubishi MU-2B	026	Taxi Aereo Marilia SA. Sao Paulo, SP.	N482G
PT-LMI	80 King Air C90	LJ-913	MACIFE-Materiais de Construcao SA. Taguatinga, DF.	N715AT
PT-LNG	81 PA-31T Cheyenne II	8120061	Marialdo Rangel dos Santos, Nova Andradina, MS.	N831CM
PT-LOH	68 Mitsubishi MU-2F	126	Belair Taxi Aereo Ltda. Belo Horizonte, MG.	N3917J
PT-LPD	88 King Air C90A	LJ-1173	CESP-Cia Energetica de Sao Paulo, Sao Paulo, SP.	
PT-LPG	87 King Air B200	BB-1271	A C Agro Mercantil SA. Paracatu, MG.	N3048U
PT-LPJ	82 King Air C90-1	LJ-1026	Carlos Roberto Alves, Belo Horizonte, MG.	N6364H
PT-LPL	80 King Air F90	LA-28	Construtora Jalk SA. Belo Horizonte, MG.	N90LL
PT-LPS	79 King Air C90	LJ-817	Construtora Emccamp Ltda. Belo Horizonte, MG.	N3981Y
PT-LQC	81 King Air F90	LA-132	Bandeirantes SA Arrend. Mercantil, Belo Horizonte, MG.	N38649
PT-LQD	79 King Air C90	LJ-844	Emival Ramos Caiado Filho, Brasilia, DF.	N707CV
PT-LQE	83 King Air C90-1	LJ-1056	Itapoan Taxi Aereo Ltda. Salvador, BA.	N90GH
PT-LRT	81 PA-31T Cheyenne II	8120040	Aerobert Emp. e Participacoes Ltda. Carapicuisa, SP.	N44TW
PT-LSE	84 King Air C90A	LJ-1063	TERCAM-Terraplen. Const. Inc. Ltda. Belo Horizonte, MG.	N76DS
PT-LSH	81 King Air F90	LA-94	Banespa SA. Sao Caef do Sul, SP.	N3735W
PT-LSO	78 King Air C90	LJ-794	Lider Taxi Aereo SA. Belo Horizonte, MG.	N57JB
PT-LSP	82 King Air F90	LA-197	Cia Cacique de Cafe Soluvel, Sao Paulo, SP.	YV-494CP
PT-LSQ	81 MU-2 Marquise	1530SA	Complemento Taxi Aereo Ltda. Sao Paulo, SP.	N449MA
PT-LTF	71 King Air C90	LJ-543	Ariba Aerotaxi Ltda. Belo Horizonte, MG.	N29791
PT-LTO	81 King Air F90	LA-156	Lider Taxi Aereo SA. Belo Horizonte, MG.	N1827F
PT-LTT	81 King Air F90	LA-103	Encalso Construcoes Ltda. Sao Jose do Rio Preto, SP.	N3802F
PT-LUF	75 King Air C90	LJ-651	Magazine Liliani SA. Imperatriz, MA.	N7300N
PT-LUJ	77 PA-31T Cheyenne II	7720039	Transjunior Transp. Comercio Ltda. Imperatriz, MA.	N1144Z
PT-LUT	84 King Air F90-1	LA-215	Locadora Brasal Ltda. Brasilia, DF.	N6730S
PT-LVI	79 King Air C90	LJ-834	Vigano Taxi Aereo Ltda. Belo Horizonte, MG.	N42QC
PT-LVK	89 King Air C90A	LJ-1201	Itapemirim Taxi Aereo Ltda. Itapemirim, ES.	(N486JA)
PT-LXI	80 King Air F90	LA-11	Jose Francisco da Cunha, Cabui Campinas, SP.	N18EH
PT-LXY	82 King Air F90	LA-195	Turim Taxi Aereo e Outro,	N70132
PT-LYK	88 King Air C90A	LJ-1188	Usina Santa Adelia SA. Jaboticabal, SP.	N1537H
PT-LYM	82 King Air F90	LA-185	Carioca Christ Nielsen Eng SA. Rio de Janeiro, RJ.	N61DH
PT-LYP	81 King Air F90	LA-126	Acucar e Alcool Osw. Rib. Mend. Ltda. Guaira, SP.	N3848V
PT-LYT	82 King Air C90-1	LJ-1037	Passaro Azul Taxi Aereo Ltda.	N283DP
PT-LYZ	79 King Air F90	LA-109	Novadata Sist. e Computacoes SA. Brasilia, DF.	N3806U
PT-LZA	74 King Air A100	B-200	Jet Sul Taxi Aereo Ltda. Curitiba, PR. (status ?).	PT-FOB
PT-LZB	79 PA-31T Cheyenne II	7920063	Nellitex Industria Textil Ltda. Americana, SP.	N23KF
PT-LZD	81 PA-42 Cheyenne III	8001038	Serafim Meneghel, Bandeirantes, PR.	LV-ONL
PT-LZH	79 King Air C90	LJ-808	Antonio de Donno,	(N711WT)
PT-LZR	79 PA-31T Cheyenne II	7920083	Nortox Agro Quimica SA. Arapongas, PR.	N31DC
PT-LZT	84 King Air F90-1	LA-216	Agropastoril Faz Caramuru Ltda.	N390D
PT-MAA	78 Xingu II 121A1	121001	RICO Taxi Aereo Ltda, Manaus, AM	PT-ZCT
PT-MAB	82 Xingu II 121A1	121007	BANJET Taxi Aereo Ltda, Belo Horizonte, MG	
PT-MAD	79 Xingu 121A	121010	Lider Taxi Aereo, Belo Horizonte, MG	
PT-MAL	80 Xingu II 121A1	121019	NHR Taxi Aereo Ltda, Sorocaba, SP	
PT-MAM	80 Xingu 121A	121020	ABC Taxi Aereo S.A., Uberlandia, MG	
PT-MAQ	80 Xingu II 121A1	121024	ABC Taxi Aereo S.A., Uberlandia, MG	
PT-MAV	80 Xingu 121A	121029	ABC Taxi Aereo S.A., Uberlandia, MG	
PT-MBF	06 King Air C90GT	LJ-1823		(PR-LOV)
PT-MCA	82 Xingu II 121A1	121058	Aerotaxi Abaete Ltda., Salvador, BA	
PT-MCM	85 King Air 300	FA-52	Conserva de Estradas Ltda. Belo Horizonte, MG.	N50KA
PT-MFL	82 PA-42 Cheyenne III	8001080	Fabio O Luchesi Advoc. Terras S/C. Sao Paulo, SP.	N882SW
PT-MFW	83 Cheyenne II-XL	8166067	Flysul Aerotaxi Ltda. Porto Alegre, RS.	(N67ER)
PT-MGZ	80 PA-31T Cheyenne II	8020058	TL Taxi Aereo Loc de Veiculos Ltda.	N236SR
PT-MJD	97 King Air B200	BB-1589	John Deere SA. Horizontina,	N2288B
PT-MJQ	99 King Air C90B	LJ-1564	Centrals Electr do Para SA. Belem, PA.	N3164R
PT-MMB	82 King Air B200	BB-971	Malharia Diana Ltda. Timbo, SC.	N503RH
PT-MMC	87 King Air 300	FA-113	Jet Sul Taxi Aereo Ltda. Curitiba, PR.	N299GS
PT-MMF	05 King Air B200	BB-1915	Usina Barra Grande de Lencois SA.	N37155
PT-MPN	78 Rockwell 690B	11465	Nome & Cia Ltda. Sarandi, PR.	CS-ASA
PT-MVJ	97 King Air C90B	LJ-1498	Claudino SA LJ de Departementos, Teresina, PI.	PT-WOZ
PT-OAJ	80 PA-31T Cheyenne 1	8004005	Osvaldo Raul Lunardi, Aracaju, SE.	N2594R
PT-OAM	80 PA-31T Cheyenne II	8020028	Sudameris Arrend. Mercantil SA. Sao Paulo, SP.	LV-OGG

Reg	Yr	Type	c/n	Owner/Operator	Prev Regn
PT-OBW	68	King Air B90	LJ-353	Alexandre Lacerda Biagi, Uberlandia, MG.	PT-FOA
PT-OCC	81	King Air C90	LJ-960	Constructora Eferco Ltda. Belo Horizonte, MG.	N3861H
PT-OCE	84	King Air F90-1	LA-217	Jose Maris Afonso, Belo Horizonte, MG.	N6756L
PT-OCI	82	King Air C90	LJ-998	Rodoban Transportes Terrest. e Aereos Ltda. Uberlandia, MG.	N17EN
PT-OCL	80	PA-31T Cheyenne II	8020033	Sudameris Arrend. Mercantil SA. Sao Paulo, SP.	N11WC
PT-OCT	72	King Air C90	LJ-567	Oceanair Aero Taxi Ltda.	PP-IAF
PT-OCY	79	King Air C90	LJ-847	Expresso Novalimense Ltda. Belo Horizonte, MG.	N317EC
PT-ODA	69	King Air B90	LJ-466	Ocean Air, Rio de Janeiro, RJ.	PP-IAG
PT-ODH	86	King Air C90A	LJ-1128	Macyr Meneghel Agropec. Uniao Ltda. Americana, SP.	N7248G
PT-ODM	81	PA-31T Cheyenne II	8120042	Eucatur Taxi Aereo Ltda. Cascavel, PR.	N131CC
PT-ODN	81	King Air F90	LA-85	EMSA/NTA-Nacional Taxi Aereo Ltda. Goiania, GO.	N3697P
PT-ODO	83	King Air F90-1	LA-213	EMSA/NTA-Nacional Taxi Aereo Ltda. Goiania, GO.	N77M
PT-ODR	80	PA-31T Cheyenne II	8020079	Co-operativa Centr. Oeste Catarinense, Chapeco, SC.	LV-OEU
PT-OED	80	PA-31T Cheyenne II	8020029	Fausto Jorge, Vera Cruz, SP.	(N661AE)
PT-OEP	82	King Air C90-1	LJ-1019	Lider Taxi Aereo SA. Belo Horizonte, MG.	N25AJ
PT-OFB	83	King Air F90	LA-200	Construtora Andrade Gutierrez SA. Belo Horizonte, MG.	N6685H
PT-OFC	72	King Air C90	LJ-534	Meier Transporte Coletivo Ltda.	N120JJ
PT-OFD	81	King Air F90	LA-118	Agropecuaria Rica SA. Cuiaba, MT.	N715GW
PT-OFF	91	King Air C90A	LJ-1264	Usina Matary SA. Recife, PE.	N5680Z
PT-OFH	79	PA-31T Cheyenne II	7920034	CQB Aviones Ltda. Jundiai, SP.	N29KR
PT-OFS	84	King Air F90-1	LA-225	Umuarama Const. Terrap. Paviment Ltda. Araguaina, TO.	N713DB
PT-OFY	85	King Air C90A	LJ-1094	U & M Construcao Pesada Ltda. Juiz de Fora, MG.	N7215L
PT-OHH	81	King Air C90	LJ-975	Joao Cesar Presotto, Guapore, RS.	N94SC
PT-OHK	80	MU-2 Marquise	774SA	Economico SA. Arrend. Mercantil, S Caet do Sul, SP.	N15ZM
PT-OHZ	82	King Air F90	LA-173	Colorado Auto Pecas Ltda. Goiania, GO.	N56TW
PT-OIF	80	King Air F90	LA-49	SOTAN-Soc. Taxi Aereo Nordeste Ltda. Maceio, AL.	N200BM
PT-OIP	77	Mitsubishi MU-2P	354SA	Lindolfo Gontijo Lucas, Manaus, AM.	N739MA
PT-OIU	71	King Air C90	LJ-515	VDL-Fomento Marcantil Ltda.	N953K
PT-OIY	81	MU-2 Solitaire	453SA	Co-op Arrozeira Extremo Sul Ltda. Pelotas, RS.	N24FJ
PT-OIZ	88	King Air C90A	LJ-1174	ICAL Energetica Ltda. Belo Horizonte, MG.	N31398
PT-OJA	81	King Air C90	LJ-952	TAF Linhas Aereas SA. Fortaleza, CE.	N4490L
PT-OJE	81	PA-31T Cheyenne II	8120031	Ciclotron Ind. Eletronica Ltda.	N628DE
PT-OJI	79	King Air C90	LJ-812	Mina Emp Imob e Agropastoris Ltda. Goiania, GO.	N627KP
PT-OJM	81	PA-31T Cheyenne II	8120070	EPAGRI SA. Florianopolis, SC.	N826SW
PT-OJQ	88	King Air 300	FA-154	Marina Taxi Aereo Ltda. Belo Horizonte, MG.	N1563K
PT-OJU	80	King Air C90	LJ-900	Felisberto Moutinho Rodrigues Jr. Osasco, SP.	N415MA
PT-OKL	82	PA-42 Cheyenne III	8001103	Sococo SA Industrias Alimenticias, Maceio, AL.	N4114D
PT-OKQ	89	King Air C90A	LJ-1195	Empresa Limpadora Centro Ltda. Barueri, SP.	N70PA
PT-OKT	81	PA-31T Cheyenne 1	8104041	Sementes Maggi Ltda. Rondonopolis, MT.	N805CA
PT-OLF	80	PA-31T Cheyenne 1	8004039	Olga Youssef Soloviov, Londrina, PR.	N500AQ
PT-OLI	84	King Air 300	FA-26	Citrosuco Paulista SA, Sao Paulo, SP.	N984CF
PT-OLP	84	King Air F90	LA-220	Maeda Taxi Aereo Ltda. Ituverava, SP.	N6837C
PT-OLQ	80	King Air C90	LJ-884	Jose Trujillo Rodriguez, Sao Paulo-Marte, SP.	N88RB
PT-OLW	81	King Air C90	LJ-985	Antonio Eustaquio Alves, Belo Horizonte, MG.	N409ND
PT-OLX	81	King Air C90	LJ-963	Emival Eterno da C Firma, Goiania, GO.	N38589
PT-OLZ	80	PA-31T Cheyenne II	8120005	Magim Rodriguez Jr.	N57656
PT-OMZ	89	King Air C90A	LJ-1220	Companhia Ferroligas Minas Gerais Ltda. Belo Horizonte, MG.	N5520X
PT-ONE	81	King Air F90	LA-144	Rio das Pedras Empreendimentos Ltda. Brasilia, DF.	(N300BF)
PT-ONJ	84	King Air C90	LJ-1078	EMSA/NTA-Nacional Taxi Aereo Ltda. Goiania, GO.	N78SR
PT-ONO	81	King Air F90	LA-92	Premier SA Partic e Administracao, Contagem, MG.	N3715T
PT-ONQ	82	King Air C90-1	LJ-1018	Gerson Neix,	N501LA
PT-ONU	81	King Air F90	LA-128	Construtora Gomes Lourenco Ltda. Campo Grande, MT.	N3867A
PT-OOS	78	Mitsubishi MU-2P	388SA	Agua Limpa Transportes Ltda. Rio Verde, GO.	N91CM
PT-OOT	82	King Air C90	LJ-995	ETA-Empresa de Taxi Aereo Ltda. Belo Horizonte, MG.	N1855H
PT-OOX	82	King Air F90	LA-162	Tecumseh do Brasil Ltda. Sao Carlos, SP.	N90BL
PT-OOY	80	King Air C90	LJ-882	Riana Taxi Aereo Ltda. Rio de Janeiro, RJ.	N181GA
PT-OPC	81	PA-31T Cheyenne II	8120010	Constr Villela e Carvalho Ltda.	(D-IIKW)
PT-OPD	80	King Air C90	LJ-920	Gama Indl. e Com. de Sec. e Molh. Ltda.Apar de Goiania, GO.	N42KA
PT-OPE	81	King Air C90	LJ-940	APEC-Assoc. Prudent. Educ. e Cultura, Pres. Prudente, SP.	N82P
PT-OPF	80	PA-31T Cheyenne II	8004038	Messias Rodrigues Talevi, Curitiba, PR.	N977CP
PT-OPH	76	PA-31T Cheyenne II	7620044	ATR-Travessia/Agroisa Agroindustrial Travessia, Recife, PE.	N92FC
PT-OPQ	80	PA-31T Cheyenne 1	8004007	Taxi Aereo Taroba Ltda. Cascavel, PR.	N2379W
PT-OPR	80	King Air C90	LJ-870	Banco Fibra SA. Sao Paulo, SP.	N500MB
PT-OQH	72	Rockwell 690	11011	Taxi Aereo Florianopolis Ltda. Florianopolis, SC.	N9211N
PT-OQP	69	King Air 100	B-7	Rubens Correia Coimbra, Penapolis, SP.	N800MD

Reg	Yr	Type	c/n	Owner/Operator	Prev Regn
☐ PT-OQQ	70	681 Turbo Commander	6021	Cia de Ind. Gerais Obras e Terras, Canoas, RS.	N10RN
☐ PT-OQS	82	King Air C90	LJ-1005	BIC Arrendamento Mercantil SA. Fortaleza, CE.	N6661J
☐ PT-OQY	85	Gulfstream 900	15038	Santa Barbara Taxi Aereo Ltda. Maringa, PR.	N77PK
☐ PT-ORB	92	King Air B200	BB-1435	INCOBRASA, Porto Alegre, RS.	N8050X
☐ PT-ORG	94	King Air C90B	LJ-1308	Santa Coloma Inv e Part SC Ltda.	
☐ PT-ORW	82	King Air C90	LJ-1004	Banco Bamerindos do Brasil SA. NYC. USA.	N45US
☐ PT-ORZ	90	King Air C90A	LJ-1233	Usina Alt. Alegre SA. Asucar e Alcool, Pres. Prudente, SP.	N113TP
☐ PT-OSI	81	King Air C90	LJ-936	SERMO Servicios de Mao Obra SC Ltda. Sao Paulo, SP.	N49FA
☐ PT-OSN	90	King Air C90A	LJ-1260	Usina Nova America SA. Sao Paulo, SP.	N5618Z
☐ PT-OSO	81	King Air C90	LJ-927	Tamandare Taxi Aereo Ltda. Teresina, PI.	N4492D
☐ PT-OSR	81	King Air 200	BB-784	Sudameris Arrend. Mercantil SA. Sao Paulo, SP.	N789H
☐ PT-OTA	82	King Air F90	LA-187	Fortaleza Sta Teres Emp Part Ltda. Belo Horizonte, MG.	N6416P
☐ PT-OTG	85	King Air C90A	LJ-1096	Empresa Gontijo de Transportes Ltda. Belo Horizonte, MG.	N7216H
☐ PT-OTI	90	King Air C90A	LJ-1237	Bompreco SA Supermercado do Nordeste, Recife, PE.	N338DR
☐ PT-OTV	81	PA-31T Cheyenne 1	8104017	Impres. Cia Bras. de Impr.e Prop. Sao Paulo, SP.	N4494U
☐ PT-OUF	81	King Air E90	LW-343	Macauba Citros Ltda. Curitiba, PR.	N3710Y
☐ PT-OUJ	81	King Air F90	LA-155	Tiquara Taxi Aereo Ltda. Recife, PE.	N155GA
☐ PT-OUL	66	King Air A90	LJ-125	Marcello Sergio R Costa e Outros, Boituva, SP.	N120JM
☐ PT-OUO	70	King Air B90	LJ-499	Jaime Valler, Campo Grande, MS.	N44454
☐ PT-OUX	81	King Air C90	LJ-937	Christiana Arcangeli, Sao Paulo, SP.	OY-BEK
☐ PT-OVB	81	PA-31T Cheyenne 1	8104051	Frigorifico Vale do Itajai Ltda. Itajai, SC.	N47TW
☐ PT-OVE	80	PA-31T Cheyenne 1	8004014	Altima Transp Rodoviarios Ltda.	N234PC
☐ PT-OVP	66	King Air A90	LJ-152	Plasticom-Plast Ind e Com Ltda. Goiania, GO.	N8180
☐ PT-OVW	77	Mitsubishi MU-2P	350SA	Air Bahia Taxi Aereo Ltda. Brasilia, DF.	N958MA
☐ PT-OVY	79	King Air C90	LJ-835	Chalet Agropecuaria Ltda. Corumba, MS.	N414AF
☐ PT-OXU	72	King Air C90	LJ-535	Pif Paf SA. Industria e Comercio, Belo Horizonte, MG.	N794K
☐ PT-OYN	84	King Air C90A	LJ-1081	Caribbean Participaoes Ltda.	N60CW
☐ PT-OZJ	81	King Air C90	LJ-951	Confederal Vig e Transp Valeres Ltda.	N511D
☐ PT-OZK	75	King Air 200	BB-45	Constructora Lima Araujo Ltda. Maceio, AL.	N46JK
☐ PT-OZL	93	King Air C90B	LJ-1341	Acucareira Zillor Lorenzett SA.	
☐ PT-OZN	80	PA-31T Cheyenne II	8020061	Irmaos Muffato e Cia Ltda. Cascavel, PR.	N711DH
☐ PT-OZP	82	King Air F90	LA-175	Safra Leasing SA Arrend Mercantil, Sao Paulo, SP.	N415GN
☐ PT-OZR	83	King Air C90-1	LJ-1059	Vector Taxi Aereo Ltda. Sao Paulo, SP.	N6581B
☐ PT-PAC	99	King Air C90B	LJ-1555	Caseli e Cia Ltda. Varzea Grande, MT.	N3205W
☐ PT-WAC	97	King Air 350	FL-177	A C Agro Mercantil SA. Paracatu, MG.	N2029Z
☐ PT-WAE	67	King Air A90	LJ-191	Joao Carlos Soares de Matos, Florianapolis, SC.	N737K
☐ PT-WAG	75	King Air E90	LW-138	Luis Alexandre Igayara, Rio de Janeiro, RJ.	N90GD
☐ PT-WAH	90	King Air C90A	LJ-1245	Henrique Duarte Prata, Sao Paulo-Marte, SP.	N5654E
☐ PT-WBQ	69	King Air B90	LJ-460	Nelson Cintra Ribeiro, Campo Grande, MS.	N113TT
☐ PT-WCS	94	King Air C90B	LJ-1377	MM Aerotaxi Ltda. Campinas-Viracopos, SP.	N3042K
☐ PT-WDU	78	King Air C90	LJ-791	MPE-Montagens e Projetos Especiais SA. Rio de Janeiro, RJ.	N791RC
☐ PT-WEF	81	PA-31T Cheyenne 1	8104034	Wellington Brasil Zucato,	N100GY
☐ PT-WEG	81	King Air B200	BB-875	EGESA-Empreend. Gerais de Eng. SA. Belo Horizonte, MG.	N313SC
☐ PT-WET	80	King Air F90	LA-78	Auguri Constructora Participacoes Ltda. Sao Paulo, SP..	N90MH
☐ PT-WFB	80	PA-31T Cheyenne II	8020048	Odilio Balbinotti, Maringa, PR.	N42EJ
☐ PT-WFN	93	King Air C90B	LJ-1346	Ambar AG de Eventos e Edit Ltda.	LV-WDP
☐ PT-WFQ	78	PA-31T Cheyenne II	7820049	Aguil Algodeira Gulmaraes Ltda. Recife, PR.	N689AC
☐ PT-WGJ	81	PA-31T Cheyenne II	8120101	Delta Nat Bank of New York, Curitiba, PR. (was 8120066).	N152CC
☐ PT-WGS	93	King Air B200	BB-1446	BB Leasing Co Ltda. Belo Horizonte, MG.	N5685X
☐ PT-WGU	94	King Air C90B	LJ-1363	Citicorp Leasing International Inc. Porto Alegre, RS.	N1534T
☐ PT-WHA	90	King Air C90A	LJ-1253	CONTERSA - Const. Terrap. e Saleam. Ltda. Goiania, GO.	N309P
☐ PT-WHN	81	PA-31T Cheyenne II	8104073	Irmaos Muffato e Cia Ltda. Cascavel, PR.	N9185Y
☐ PT-WHP	89	King Air C90A	LJ-1212	Leasing Bank of Boston SA. Goiania, GO.	N1551J
☐ PT-WIC	80	Gulfstream 840	11625	TAM/Banco Itamarati SA. Sao Paulo, SP.	N690HC
☐ PT-WIH	95	King Air C90B	LJ-1396	Coffee Holdings Inc. Varginha, MG.	N3218K
☐ PT-WIT	95	King Air C90SE	LJ-1394	Tecar Automavaic E A T Ltda. Goiania, GO.	N3217K
☐ PT-WIX	72	Mitsubishi MU-2F	232	Luiz Antonio Portelinha Bueno, Belem, PA.	N800HR
☐ PT-WJD	96	King Air C90B	LJ-1427	Frigorifico Independencia Ltda. Cajamar.	N3251E
☐ PT-WJF	94	King Air C90B	LJ-1386	Brasif Duty Free Shop Ltda. Rio de Janeiro, RJ.	N3165M
☐ PT-WKF	96	Pilatus PC-12	141	Flamingo Unimed AirTaxi Aereo Ltda. Sao Paulo, SP.	N141BL
☐ PT-WKN	97	King Air C90B	LJ-1494	Java Consultoria e Comercio Ltda. Rio Clara, SP.	N1135X
☐ PT-WLD	83	Gulfstream 900	15027	Plasutil Ind Com de Plasticos Ltda. Bauru, SP.	N900ST
☐ PT-WLJ	81	PA-31T Cheyenne II	8120011	Wagner Bisco e Outro,	N31FR
☐ PT-WLK	96	King Air B200	BB-1543	CEMIG-Cia Energetica de Minas Gerais, Belo Horizonte, MG.	N1082S
☐ PT-WMT	81	King Air C90	LJ-956	Industria de Madeiras Tozzo Ltda. Chapeco, SC.	N225AT

Reg   Yr Type   c/n   Owner/Operator   Prev Regn

Reg	Yr Type	c/n	Owner/Operator	Prev Regn
☐ PT-WMU	80 PA-31T Cheyenne 1	8004043	Lina Participacoes e Adm. Ltda. Tatui, SP.	N53WM
☐ PT-WMX	81 PA-31T Cheyenne 1	8104062	Fabrica de Pecas Elet. Delmar, Tatui, SP.	N2560Y
☐ PT-WNC	81 PA-31T Cheyenne II	8120020	Fabio da Silva Machado, Belo Horizonte, MG.	N56MC
☐ PT-WND	96 King Air 350	FL-141	Medley Industria Farmaceutica SA, Belo Horizonte, MG.	N1061Q
☐ PT-WNG	81 Cheyenne II-XL	8166049	Eicomon SA. Sao Paulo, SP.	(N57AF)
☐ PT-WNL	97 King Air 350	FL-159	Sementes Maggi Ltda. Rondonopolis, MT.	N1100N
☐ PT-WNN	97 King Air B200	BB-1558	UNIMED N N F C Trabajos Med. Ltda. Joao Pessoa.	N1108A
☐ PT-WNQ	97 King Air B200	BB-1584		N11355
☐ PT-WNS	83 MU-2 Marquise	1501SA	Dacunha SA. Sao Paulo, SP.	N43DC
☐ PT-WNW	85 King Air C90A	LJ-1092	Fox Distribuidora de Petroleo SA.	N11755
☐ PT-WOF	82 King Air B200	BB-986	Planfoto Distr Materials Fotograficos Ltda. Sao Paulo, SP.	N986TJ
☐ PT-WOR	81 PA-31T Cheyenne II	8120030	Transportes Guadalupe Ltda. Goiania, GO.	N199RC
☐ PT-WPN	91 King Air C90A	LJ-1294	Otto Baumgart Ind. Co. SA. Sao Paulo, SP.	N19BK
☐ PT-WPV	78 King Air B100	BE-45	Icaro Taxi Aereo Ltda. Brasilia, DF.	N263DC
☐ PT-WQW	99 King Air C90B	LJ-1577	Aleksander Carlos Manic, Curitiba, PR.	N4477N
☐ PT-WRA	94 King Air C90B	LJ-1385	GRANASA, Belo Horizonte, MG.	N3198K
☐ PT-WSI	97 King Air 350	FL-169	Simarelli Dist. de Petroleo Ltda. Cuiaba, CT.	N1099E
☐ PT-WSJ	96 King Air 350	FL-152	Jet Sul Taxi Aereo Ltda. Curitiba, PR.	N1092S
☐ PT-WST	78 Mitsubishi MU-2N	711SA	SETE Taxi Aereo Ltda. Goiania, GO.	N171CA
☐ PT-WSX	87 King Air B200	BB-1266	M & M Administracao e Particip Ltda. Londrina, PR.	N204MS
☐ PT-WTN	68 King Air B90	LJ-346	C Nacife Jr & Partner, Belo Horizonte, MG.	PP-EOC
☐ PT-WTU	97 King Air C90B	LJ-1491	Laboratorio Teuto Brasileiro Ltda.	N2316H
☐ PT-WTW	98 King Air 350	FL-205	Uniair Admin Part Serv Med Urg Ltda. Porte Alegre, RS.	(PT-WZC)
☐ PT-WUG	98 King Air C90B	LJ-1511	First Security Bank NA. Sao Paulo, SP.	N2311J
☐ PT-WUT	99 King Air 350	FL-240	Soc de Ens do Triangulo Ltda.	N3078T
☐ PT-WVI	93 King Air C90B	LJ-1331	INTA-Indaia Taxi Aereo Ltda. Recife, PE.	N8089J
☐ PT-WYT	78 Mitsubishi MU-2N	722SA	SETE Taxi Aereo Ltda. Goiania, GO.	N722MU
☐ PT-WZC	99 King Air C90B	LJ-1538	Uniair Admin Part Serv Med Urg Ltda. Porte Alegre, RS.	N3138B
☐ PT-XEG	84 King Air B200	BB-1190	Marca Agropecuaria Ltda. Barra do Garcas, MT.	N75GE
☐ PT-XHP	97 King Air C90B	LJ-1473	Henrique Duarte Prata, Sao Paulo-Marte, SP.	N1090X
☐ PT-XOC	82 PA-31T Cheyenne 1	8104064	Olga Intaschi Carvalho Cunha, Presidente Prudente, SP.	N502MM
☐ PT-XOU	97 King Air C90B	LJ-1501		N401TT
☐ PT-XOV	99 King Air C90B	LJ-1569	Vito Transportes Ltda. Contagem, MG.	N505P

Military

☐ 2002	87 120RT(VC-97)Brasilia	120040	Brazilian Air Force, ETA	
☐ 2003	88 120RT(VC-97)Brasilia	120055	Brazilian Air Force, ETA	
☐ 2004	88 120RT(VC-97)Brasilia	120066	Brazilian Air Force, ETA	
☐ 2650	78 Xingu 121E (VU-9)	121002	Brazilian Air Force, ETA	
☐ 2651	78 Xingu 121E (VU-9)	121003	Brazilian Air Force, ETA	
☐ 2652	78 Xingu 121E (VU-9)	121004	Brazilian Air Force, ETA	
☐ 2653	78 Xingu 121E (VU-9)	121005	Brazilian Air Force, ETA	
☐ 2654	78 Xingu 121E (VU-9)	121006	Brazilian Air Force, ETA	
☐ 2655	78 Xingu 121E (VU-9)	121008	Brazilian Air Force, ETA	
☐ 2656	84 Xingu 121E (VU-9)	121060	Brazilian Air Force, ETA	
☐ 2657	81 Xingu 121E (VU-9)	121037	Brazilian Air Force, ETA	PT-MBE

P2 = PAPUA NEW GUINEA   Total   8
Civil

☐ P2-CAA	79 King Air 200	BB-415	Department of Civil Aviation, Port Moresby.	P2-PNH
☐ P2-DRS	89 King Air C90A	LJ-1227	Tropicair Ltd., Port Moresby	N89KA
☐ P2-HCN	81 King Air 200C	BL-22	Hevi Lift (PNG) P/L. Mount Hagen.	P2-PJV
☐ P2-KSA	96 King Air B200	BB-1527	Regional Air P/L. Madang.	N170W
☐ P2-NTJ	82 King Air C90-1	LJ-1024	New Tribes Mission, Port Moresby.	VH-FOM
☐ P2-NTR	82 King Air C90-1	LJ-1021	New Tribes Mission, Port Moresby.	VH-FDZ
☐ P2-PNG	92 King Air 350	FL-79	Government Flying Unit, Port Moresby.	N8246Q
☐ P2-SIA	81 King Air 200C	BL-39	Summer Institute of Linguistics, Ukarumpa.	VH-FDR

P4 = ARUBA   Total   2
Civil

☐ P4-JML	61 Gulfstream 1	76	Transglobal AVV.	G-BRAL
☐ P4-SSI	97 King Air C90B	LJ-1476	Seahatch Laboratory NV. Maracaibo, Venezuela.	N1106M

RA = RUSSIA / RUSSIAN FEDERATION   Total   4
Civil

☐ RA-01500	07 Pilatus PC-12/47	803		
☐ RA-01509	06 Pilatus PC-12/47	745		HB-FSC

| Reg | Yr Type | c/n | Owner/Operator | Prev Regn |

☐ RA-14424	69 SA-26AT Merlin 2B	T26-152		N939C
☐ RF-14004	69 SA-26AT Merlin 2B	T26-129		N100SN

RP = PHILIPPINES Total 26
Civil

☐ RP-	07 King Air 350	FL-563		
☐ RP-C1728	94 King Air 350	FL-118	Philippine Long Distance Telephone Co. Manila.	N1555E
☐ RP-C1807	96 King Air 350	FL-153	Rikio Co. Ltd., Cebu City	N506P
☐ RP-C1978	71 King Air 100	B-77	Development Bank of the Philippines, Manila.	PI-C1978
☐ RP-C2100	91 King Air B200	BB-1405	Air Transportation Office, Manila.	N8129A
☐ RP-C2208	68 King Air B90	LJ-365	A M Areta Co. Manila.	N14VK
☐ RP-C223	75 King Air 200	BB-66	Ministry of Local Government of Philippines, Manila.	(N219DM)
☐ RP-C2296	98 King Air 350	FL-196	INAEC Aviation Corp. Manila.	N2296G
☐ RP-C2638	96 King Air 350	FL-137	United Laboratories Inc.	N1067S
☐ RP-C264	80 King Air 200	BB-692	Development Bank of the Philippines, Manila.	RP-C5139
☐ RP-C2850	96 King Air 350	FL-145	National Power Corp. Manila.	N1075G
☐ RP-C290	79 King Air C90	LJ-857	National Irrigation Administration, Manila.	N6064A
☐ RP-C291	79 King Air E90	LW-325	Lepanto Consolidated Mining Co.	N60575
☐ RP-C292	78 King Air E90	LW-277	Marcopper Mining Corp.	N4977M
☐ RP-C298	79 King Air E90	LW-302	Allied Banking Corp. Manila.	(N209DM)
☐ RP-C3500	96 King Air 350	FL-148	PNB Financial Center, Manila.	N3268H
☐ RP-C3885	96 King Air B200	BB-1532	Philippine Long Distance Telephone Co. Manila.	N3252X
☐ RP-C410	81 King Air F90	LA-136	(status ?).	RP-C410
☐ RP-C415	76 King Air E90	LW-190	Land Bank of the Philippines, Manila.	
☐ RP-C5129	78 King Air 200	BB-358	National Steel Corp. Manila.	
☐ RP-755	82 King Air B200	BB-975	United Coconut Planters Bank, Manila.	(N208DM)
☐ RP-C8299	96 BAe Jetstream 41	41080	Semirara Mining Corp., Makati City	N372UE
☐ RP-C8300	06 King Air 350	FL-505	Shoemart Inc., Manila	N37085
☐ RP-C879	75 King Air E90	LW-145	Philippine Airlines, Manila.	N122HC
☐ RP-C8853	96 King Air B200	BB-1529	Star Borne Chartered Corp. Manila.	N3261E

Military

☐ 11250	75 Rockwell 690A	11250	Government of Philippines, Manila.	N44WV

SE = SWEDEN Total 30
Civil

☐ SE-GHA	74 Mitsubishi MU-2K	283	SAAB Nyge-Aero AB. Skavsta.	N327MA
☐ SE-GHB	74 Mitsubishi MU-2K	287	SAAB Nyge-Aero AB. Skavsta.	N331MA
☐ SE-GHC	74 Mitsubishi MU-2K	289	SAAB Nyge-Aero AB. Skavsta.	N334MA
☐ SE-GHD	74 Mitsubishi MU-2K	293	SAAB Nyge-Aero AB. Skavsta.	N453MA
☐ SE-GHE	74 Mitsubishi MU-2K	294	SAAB Nyge-Aero AB. Skavsta.	N454MA
☐ SE-GHF	74 Mitsubishi MU-2K	299	SAAB Nyge-Aero AB. Skavsta.	N459MA
☐ SE-GHH	72 Mitsubishi MU-2F	222	SAAB Nyge-Aero AB. Skavsta.	N9PN
☐ SE-GSS	80 Gulfstream 840	11613	Wermlandsflyg AB., Torsby	LN-FWB
☐ SE-IIB	77 King Air C90	LJ-723	Varmforzinkning AB. Smilandsstehar.	OY-ASI
☐ SE-IOV	75 Mitsubishi MU-2M	337	SAAB Nyge-Aero AB. Skavsta.	N522MA
☐ SE-IOZ	75 Mitsubishi MU-2M	320	SAAB Nyge-Aero AB. Skavsta.	N641KE
☐ SE-IUA	76 Mitsubishi MU-2M	345	SAAB Nyge-Aero AB. Skavsta.	N730MP
☐ SE-IUV	81 Gulfstream 840	11681	Wermlandsflyg AB., Torsby	LN-FWA
☐ SE-IUX	80 King Air 200	BB-675	Nordkalottflyg AB/Barents Airlink, Lulea.	N26AD
☐ SE-IXC	85 King Air B200	BB-1210	SOS Flygambulans AB. Goteborg.	N7213J
☐ SE-KDK	81 King Air B200	BB-909	Bromma Air Maintenance AB. Stockholm-Bromma.	N171M
☐ SE-KFP	88 King Air B200C	BL-132	SOS Flygambulans AB. Goteborg.	
☐ SE-KOL	89 King Air 300LW	FA-189	Waltair i Linkoeping AB. Norrkoeping.	N8208B
☐ SE-KXM	79 King Air 200	BB-459	ELCON Finans A/S-Bromma Air Maintenance AB. Stockholm.	101002
☐ SE-LKY	86 King Air B200C	BL-127	NEX Time Jet AB/Nextjet, Stockholm.	D2-ESO
☐ SE-LLU	97 King Air 350	FL-175	Waltair i Linkoeping AB. Norrkoeping.	N1071S
☐ SE-LTL	80 King Air 200	BB-582	Barents Airlink/Nordkalottflyg AB. Lulea.	LN-MOA
☐ SE-LUB	78 PA-31T Cheyenne II	7820051	Foersaeljnings AB Balticum, Kristianstad.	OE-FBO
☐ SE-LVU	99 King Air B200	BB-1692	SEB Finans AB/Luftransport AB. Oestersund.	LN-MOO
☐ SE-LVV	96 King Air B200	BB-1537	SEB Finans AB/Luftransport AB. Oestersund.	LN-MON
☐ SE-LZU	73 Rockwell 690	11121	Wermlandsflyg AB., Torsby	LN-ACE
☐ SE-LZX	77 Rockwell 690B	11367	Wermlandsflyg AB., Torsby	LN-FAH
☐ SE-MAZ	96 King Air B200	BB-1522	SEB Finans AB./SOS Flygambulans, Stockholm	ZS-OBB

Military

☐ 100001	89 SAAB 340B/Tp 100	170	Swedish Air Force, Stockholm. (Code 001 of F16).	SE-F70
☐ 100006	98 SAAB 340B/Tp 100	431	Swedish Air Force, Stockholm. (Code 006 of F16).	SE-B31

Reg	Yr Type	c/n	Owner/Operator	Prev Regn

SP = POLAND   Total 8
Civil

☐ SP	07 King Air B200GT	BY-3	Aviation Asset Management SA	N803GT
☐ SP-FNS	96 King Air 350	FL-134	Prokom Investments SA/White Eagle Aviation, Gdynia.	N3252V
☐ SP-IKY	07 King Air B200	BB-1995	J. B. Investments Ltd., Konstancin Jeziorna, Poland	
☐ SP-KGW	80 King Air 200	BB-716	Kataro Anstalt/Libert, Katowice.	N765TC
☐ SP-KKH	81 PA-31T Cheyenne II	8120041	Transport Handel Uslugi Maria Komoro, Sztum.	N220SC
☐ SP-MXH	04 P-180 Avanti	1079	Lotnicze Pogotowie Ratunkowe, Szczecin.	
☐ SP-MXI	07 P-180 Avanti II	1124	Lotnicze Pogotowie Ratunkowe, Warsaw	
☐ SP-NEB	91 King Air C90A	LJ-1285	KGHM Polska Miedz SA ZH.	(F-GULM)

ST = SUDAN   Total 4
Civil

☐ ST-	85 Beech 1900C	UB-40	RAK Aviation (stored, Ras Al Khaimah)	N809BE
☐ ST-ANH	79 King Air C90	LJ-823	Sudan Airways Co. Khartoum.	N580C
☐ ST-BBA	78 King Air/Catpass 250	BB-341		ZS-LWM
☐ ST-SFS	79 King Air 200	BB-539	Sudan Airways Co. Khartoum.	N555SK

SU = EGYPT   Total 4
Civil

☐ SU-BAX	78 King Air 200	BB-353	Government of Egypt, Cairo.	SU-AYD
☐ SU-BNJ	99 King Air B200	BB-1664	Egyptian Air Ambulance, Cairo.	N3064J
☐ SU-MMN	06 King Air 350	FL-476	Alkan Establishment, Cairo.	N3726M
☐ SU-ZAA	94 King Air C90B	LJ-1353	Nuclear Materials Authority, Cairo.	N8292Y

SX = GREECE   Total 15
Civil

☐ SX-APJ	78 King Air 200	BB-401	Aviator Ltd. Athens.	OY-JAO
☐ SX-AVA	80 PA-31T Cheyenne II	8020026	3D Avionics, Thessaloniki.	N155DS
☐ SX-AVB	80 PA-31T Cheyenne II	8020027	3D Avionics, Thessaloniki.	(N248WW)
☐ SX-AVC	80 PA-31T Cheyenne II	8020038	3D Avionics, Thessaloniki.	N300HP
☐ SX-AVE	76 PA-31T Cheyenne II	7620018	3D Avionics, Thessaloniki.	N232PS
☐ SX-BGO	80 King Air C90	LJ-874	Life Line Aviation Ltd. Athens.	D-IFUN
☐ SX-BKY	93 King Air C90B	LJ-1334	Air Intersalonika, Thessalonika.	D-IIKY
☐ SX-ECG	78 King Air 200	BB-372	Civil Aviation Authority, Athens.	N4937M
☐ SX-FDC	77 PA-31T Cheyenne II	7720063	Piraeus Leasing SA, Athens	F-GFUV

Military

☐ 401	76 King Air C-12C	BC-34	Aeroporias Stratu-Army Aviation, Megara.	
☐ 402	00 King Air B200	BB-1733	Greek Army,	N3156L
☐ 403	00 King Air B200	BB-1744	Greek Army,	N3157F
☐ AC-21	00 Reims/Cessna F406	F406-0087	Hellenic Coast Guard,	F-GJJK
☐ AC-22	00 Reims/Cessna F406	F406-0088	Hellenic Coast Guard,	F-GJJN
☐ AC-23	00 Reims/Cessna F406	F406-0089	Hellenic Coast Guard,	F-GJJO

S2 = BANGLADESH   Total 2
Civil

☐ S2-AED	04 Pilatus PC-12/45	538	Lions Air AG. Dhaka.	HB-FPP

Military

☐ S3-BHN	84 PA-31T Cheyenne 1A	1104007	Government of Bangladesh, Dhaka.	N2436W

S5 = SLOVENIA   Total 2
Civil

☐ S5-CAE	80 Conquest II	441-0150	Smelt Air/GIO Business Aviation, Ljubljana.	SL-CAE
☐ S5-CMO	94 King Air C90B	LJ-1360	Alfa Histria/Kondorair, Portoroz.	N1560U

S7 = SEYCHELLES   Total 3
Civil

☐ S7-AAI	90 Reims/Cessna F406	F406-0051	Islands Development Co. Mahe.	(9V-...)
☐ S7-IDC	96 Beech 1900D	UE-212	Islands Development Co. Mahe.	N3217U
☐ S7-SMB	89 King Air B200	BB-1316	Seychelles Marketing Board, Mahe.	ZS-MFB

S9 = SAO TOME & PRINCIPE   Total 4
Civil

☐ S9-...	65 Gulfstream 1	167	Executive Jet Services, Mbabaue, Swaziland.	N717RA
☐ S9-BAA	98 King Air 350	FL-220	Golfo International Air Services SA/SAL Express. Sao Tome.	N3120X
☐ S9-CAM	97 King Air 350	FL-163	SONANGOL Aeronautica - Helipetrol, Luanda, Angola.	N1057Q
☐ S9-CAN	00 King Air 350	FL-294	SONAIR/Golfo International Air Services SA. Sao Tome.	N3214J

Reg   Yr Type   c/n   Owner/Operator   Prev Regn

TC = TURKEY

Total 17

Civil

☐ TC-AUT	74 King Air C90	LJ-622	Anadolu University Air Taxi, Eskisehir.	N104TT
☐ TC-AUV	73 King Air C90	LJ-587	Anadolu University Air Taxi, Eskisehir.	N61KA
☐ TC-FAH	85 PA-42 Cheyenne IIIA	5501033	THK-Turk Hava Kurumu, Ankara.	
☐ TC-FIR	82 King Air B200	BB-1082	Firat Aviation AS. Istanbul.	(N807BC)
☐ TC-IHC	78 King Air C90	LJ-771	IHC Aviation, Ankara.	N4774M
☐ TC-MSS	91 King Air C90A	LJ-1276	EMI-Erdem Mapping Information, Istanbul.	N8065R
☐ TC-OZD	94 King Air B200	BB-1496	Ozek Air, Bursa.	N3047L
☐ TC-TAT	97 King Air B200	BB-1568	Tatlises Air, Istanbul	D-ILLF
☐ TC-THK	85 PA-42 Cheyenne IIIA	5501031	THK-Turk Hava Kurumu, Ankara.	TC-FAG
☐ TC-UPS	75 SA-226AT Merlin 4A	AT-044	UPS-Uensped Paket Servisi, Istanbul. `Beril'	C-GGPT

Military

☐ 10010	91 King Air B200	BB-1409	Turkish Air Force,	
☐ 10011	91 King Air B200	BB-1411	Turkish Air Force,	
☐ 10012	91 King Air B200	BB-1413	Turkish Air Force,	
☐ 10013	91 King Air B200	BB-1414	Turkish Air Force,	
☐ 10014	91 King Air B200	BB-1415	Turkish Air Force,	
☐ 4005	92 King Air B200	BB-1434	Turkish Air Force,	N81148
☐ 4006	90 King Air B200	BB-1375	Turkish Air Force,	M-1375

TF = ICELAND

Total 4

Civil

☐ TF-FMS	85 King Air B200	BB-1221	Directorate of Civil Aviation, Reykjavik.	N7230U
☐ TF-MYX	83 King Air B200	BB-1136	Myflug HF. Myvatn.	LN-VIZ
☐ TF-ORD	91 Reims/Cessna F406	F406-0047	Eagle Air-Lysing hf/Ernir hf, Reykjavik.	D-IAAD
☐ TF-ORF	78 Conquest II	441-0057	Lysing Hf/Ernir Air Ehf, Reykjavik.	N441AK

TG = GUATEMALA

Total 26

Civil

☐ TG-	06 King Air C90GT	LJ-1822		N73220
☐ TG-	84 Cheyenne II-XL	1166007		N285KW
☐ TG-...	70 681 Turbo Commander	6036	Corporacion Internacional de Oportunidades, Guatemala City.	N681DC
☐ TG-...	74 Rockwell 690A	11162	Corp Hispano Americana Oportunidades, Guatemala City.	N777TE
☐ TG-...	74 Rockwell 690A	11175		N722EJ
☐ TG-...	73 SA-226T Merlin 3	T-240	Mynor Geovanni Ruballos Castro, Guatemala City.	N240NM
☐ TG-AMI	70 681 Turbo Commander	6032	Multillantas SA. Guatemala City.	N75GM
☐ TG-ASC	06 Pilatus PC-12/47	767	Aereo Ruta Maya SA, Guatemala City.	N767PB
☐ TG-BAQ	95 King Air C90B	LJ-1399	Credomatic de Guatemala SA. Guatemala City.	TG-BAC
☐ TG-COB	81 PA-31T Cheyenne II	8120003	COBIGUA, Guatemala City.	N57KW
☐ TG-EAB	80 PA-31T Cheyenne II	8020045	Compania de Jarabes y Bebidas La Mariposo SA. Guatemala City	N75CA
☐ TG-EME	94 King Air C90B	LJ-1364	Carlos Bruderer, Guatemala City.	TG-CGA
☐ TG-FYL	02 King Air B200	BB-1808	Industria Oleaginosa de Escuinita SA. Guatemala City.	N4488N
☐ TG-GAP	78 PA-31T Cheyenne II	7820058	Aceros Prefabricados SA. Guatemala City.	N82290
☐ TG-GOL	80 PA-31T Cheyenne II	8020003	FUMASA-Fumigadres Aereo SA. Guatemala City.	TG-OIL
☐ TG-HCR	80 PA-31T Cheyenne II	8020032	Hotel Caimo Real, Guatemala City.	N803SW
☐ TG-JYM	Conquest	...	noted Guatemala 7/06.	
☐ TG-LIA	81 PA-31T Cheyenne II	8120043	Aldan SA. Guatemala City.	N40H
☐ TG-OIL	01 King Air B200	BB-1794	FUMASA-Fumigadres Aeero SA. Guatemala City.	N250JJ
☐ TG-SAQ	94 King Air C90B	LJ-1373	Manuel Antonio Sanchez, Guatemala City.	TG-RWC
☐ TG-VAL	81 PA-31T Cheyenne II	8120045	Valores Aereos SA. Guatemala City.	N2441Y
☐ TG-VAS	78 King Air C90	LJ-782	Industria Oleaginosa de Escuinita SA. Guatemala City.	
☐ TG-WIZ	70 681 Turbo Commander	6022	Richard Stader Cater, Guatemala City.	C-GBIT

Military

☐ R-700	King Air	...	along with R-701/702/703 & 704 Guatemalan Air Force.	
☐ TG-CFA	82 King Air F90	LA-181	FAG/Guatemalan Air Force, Guatemala City.	HK-2888P
☐ TG-MDN-P	86 King Air 300	FA-105	FAG/Guatemala Air Force, Guatemala City.	TG-MDN

TI = COSTA RICA

Total 10

Civil

☐ TI-...	00 King Air C90B	LJ-1627	Raytheon Aircraft Co. Wichita, Ks.	N5027V
☐ TI-AWM	80 King Air F90	LA-76	Multiservicios del Sur SA. San Jose.	N781VC
☐ TI-AWN	75 PA-31T Cheyenne II	7520043	Carena de la Sur Ltda.	N29KL
☐ TI-AXM	Rockwell 690	...		
☐ TI-AXU	73 Rockwell 690A	11139		N7EV
☐ TI-AZI	97 King Air C90B	LJ-1468		N1134G

Reg   Yr   Type   c/n   Owner/Operator   Prev Regn

Reg	Yr Type	c/n	Owner/Operator	Prev Regn
☐ TI-AZO	77 King Air E90	LW-240		N500EA
☐ TI-BBN	77 King Air E90	LW-250	Nature Air	N321DM
☐ TI-MEL	81 Gulfstream 980	95056	Tecno Agricola SA. San Jose.	N980BM
☐ TI-TCT	75 King Air 200	BB-87	Teletica Canal 7 Television, San Jose.	N87GA

TJ = CAMEROON — Total 2
Civil

☐ TJ-AIM	81 Cheyenne II-XL	8166061	Societe SFID, Douala.	N983GA
☐ TJ-MJP	79 King Air E90	LW-321	SFID-Ste Forestiere Ind de la Doume, Douala.	EI-BHL

TL = CENTRAL AFRICAN REPUBLIC — Total 1
Civil

☐ TL-ADN	60 Gulfstream 1	42		3D-DOM

TN = CONGO BRAZZAVILLE — Total 2
Civil

☐ TN-	73 King Air C-12C	BD-5		N9008U
☐ TN-AFG	79 King Air E90	LW-326	Congolaise Industrielle des Bois, Brazzaville.	D-IHCE

TR = GABON — Total 3
Civil

☐ TR-...	06 King Air 350	FL-486	Comilog SA. Moanada.	N36886
☐ TR-LEQ	86 Reims/Cessna F406	F406-0007	Cie Equatoriale des Bois/Air Service Gabon, Libreville.	LX-LMS

Military

☐ TR-KJD	95 ATR 42F-300	131	Government of Gabon, Libreville.	(TR-KGP)

TT = CHAD — Total 1
Civil

☐ TT-AAF	95 Pilatus PC-12	128		JA8599

TU = IVORY COAST — Total 1
Civil

☐ TU-TJL	77 PA-31T Cheyenne II	7720033	Air Inter Ivoire, Abidjan.	N82152

TZ = MALI — Total 1
Civil

☐ TZ-ZBE	67 King Air A90	LM-64	Missionary Aviation Fellowship,	N70766

UN = KAZAKHSTAN — Total 3
Civil

☐ UN-	90 King Air C90A	LJ-1236		N905DR
☐ UN-	83 PA-42 Cheyenne III	8001105		N820BC
☐ UN-P3101	84 PA-31T Cheyenne 1A	1104010	GST Aero Aircompany, Almaty.	(N234PC)

UR = UKRAINE — Total 4
Civil

☐ UR-	93 King Air C90B	LJ-1348	Avia Star S.A.	N451A
☐ UR-CWA	91 King Air 350	FL-64	UKSATSE, Kerch	D-CAMM
☐ UR-CWB	91 King Air 350	FL-46	UKSATSE, Kerch.	D-CCBW
☐ UR-HBD	05 King Air 350	FL-469	Aerostar Ltd. Kiev.	N37069

VH = AUSTRALIA — Total 205
Civil

☐ VH-...	83 Cheyenne T-1040	8375001		N1194V
☐ VH-AAG	73 Rockwell 690A	11101	General Aviation Maintenance P/L. Essendon, VIC.	N57101
☐ VH-AMR	02 King Air B200	BB-1812	RFDS/Ambulance Service of NSW, Sydney, NSW.	VH-MSB
☐ VH-AMS	02 King Air B200	BB-1814	RFDS/Ambulance Service of NSW, Sydney, NSW.	VH-MVW
☐ VH-ATF	74 Rockwell 690A	11158	Jalgrid P/L. Maroochydore, QLD.	N57158
☐ VH-AYC	97 King Air B200	BB-1575	A C Airways P/L-Air Center Albury, Albury, NSW.	N501P
☐ VH-AZW	77 Conquest II	441-0026	Hardy Aviation (N.T.) P/L, Parap, NT.	VH-FWA
☐ VH-BUR	84 PA-42 Cheyenne 400LS	5527019	Burley Aircraft Trust, Sydney, NSW.	N1515H
☐ VH-BUW	81 PA-42 Cheyenne III	8001047	Central Air P/L. Cloverdale, WA.	VH-ISW
☐ VH-CBZ	81 King Air B200C	BL-38	Curtain Niugini Purchasing P/L. Townsville, QLD.	P2-CCB
☐ VH-CLT	74 Rockwell 690A	11152	Tasmanian Seafoods P/L. Smithton, Tasmania.	VH-NMT
☐ VH-CWO	84 King Air B200C	BL-72	Royal Flying Doctor Service, Port Hedland, WA.	N43CE
☐ VH-CZM	05 TBM 700C2	344	M D H P/L. Cloncurry, QLD.	F-OIKD
☐ VH-DTV	68 Mitsubishi MU-2F	132	Thomas Day, Romsey, VIC.	N756Q
☐ VH-DXD	75 PA-31T Cheyenne II	7520037	Betta Built, Toowoomba, QLD.	N111RF
☐ VH-DYN	80 King Air 200	BB-690	Sabstall P/L. Toowoomba, QLD.	VH-SKN

Reg	Yr Type	c/n	Owner/Operator	Prev Regn
VH-EEN	83 SA-227AT Merlin 4C	AT-563	Pel-Air Aviation P/L. Mascot, NSW.	N563UP
VH-EEO	83 SA-227AT Merlin 4C	AT-564	Pel-Air Aviation P/L. Mascot, NSW.	N564UP
VH-EEP	83 SA-227AT Merlin 4C	AT-567	Pel-Air Aviation P/L. Mascot, NSW.	N565UP
VH-EMJ	94 King Air C90B	LJ-1374	Lanstal P/L. Perth, WA.	N190CB
VH-EWQ	94 King Air 350	FL-122	Eastern Energy Services P/L. Toowoomba, QLD.	9M-DSL
VH-FDA	07 King Air B200	BB-1986	Royal Flying Doctor Service, Brisbane, QLD.	N986KA
VH-FDB	07 King Air B200	BB-1977	Royal Flying Doctor Service, Brisbane, QLD.	N7317A
VH-FDC	01 Pilatus PC-12/45	426	Royal Flying Doctor Service, Mount Isa, QLD. 'RFDS Mt Isa'	HB-F..
VH-FDD	99 King Air B200	BB-1697	Royal Flying Doctor Service, Mount Isa, QLD. 'RFDS Mt Isa'	N40483
VH-FDE	00 Pilatus PC-12/45	332	Royal Flying Doctor Service, Port Augusta, SA.	HB-F..
VH-FDF	99 King Air B200	BB-1696	Royal Flying Doctor Service, Cairns, QLD. 'RFDS Cairns'	N40481
VH-FDG	84 King Air B200	BB-1172	Royal Flying Doctor Service, Derby, WA. 'Alec McLaughlan'	G-OJGA
VH-FDI	82 King Air B200	BB-1037	Royal Flying Doctor Service, Brisbane. 'RFDS Brisbane'	VH-DAX
VH-FDJ	07 Pilatus PC-12/47	861	RFDSA. Adelaide	HB-FST
VH-FDK	02 Pilatus PC-12/45	466	Royal Flying Doctor Service, Adelaide, SA.	HB-FSZ
VH-FDM	01 Pilatus PC-12/45	428	Royal Flying Doctor Service, Charleville. 'RFDS Charleville'	HB-F..
VH-FDO	82 King Air B200	BB-1056	Royal Flying Doctor Service, Rockhampton. 'RFDS Rockhampton'	VH-RFX
VH-FDP	01 Pilatus PC-12/45	434	Royal Flying Doctor Service, Cairns, QLD. 'RFDS Cairns'	HB-F..
VH-FDR	04 King Air B200	BB-1881	Royal Flying Doctor Service, Brisbane, QLD.	N36801
VH-FDS	83 King Air 200C	BL-68	Royal Flying Doctor Service, Bundaberg. 'Marjorie Loveday'	N83GA
VH-FDT	07 King Air B200	BB-1990	Royal Flying Doctor Service, Brisbane, QLD.	N990KA
VH-FDW	04 King Air B200	BB-1880	Royal Flying Doctor Service, Brisbane, QLD.	N6180Q
VH-FDZ	04 King Air B200	BB-1882	Royal Flying Doctor Service, Brisbane, QLD.	N37082
VH-FGR	01 Pilatus PC-12/45	438	Royal Flying Doctor Service, Adelaide-West Beach, SA.	HB-FRW
VH-FGS	01 Pilatus PC-12/45	440	Royal Flying Doctor Service, Adelaide-West Beach, SA.	HB-FRX
VH-FGT	01 Pilatus PC-12/45	442	Royal Flying Doctor Service, Adelaide-West Beach, SA.	HB-FRY
VH-FII	80 King Air 200	BB-653	Pearl Aviation/Air Services Australia P/L. Brisbane, QLD.	VH-MXK
VH-FIX	93 King Air 350	FL-90	Pearl Aviation/Air Services Australia P/L. Brisbane, QLD.	D-CKRA
VH-FMC	95 Pilatus PC-12	109	Royal Flying Doctor Service, Port Augusta, SA.	
VH-FMF	95 Pilatus PC-12	110	Royal Flying Doctor Service, Port Augusta, SA.	
VH-FMP	95 Pilatus PC-12	122	Royal Flying Doctor Service, Alice Springs, NT.	HB-FQ.
VH-FMQ	79 Conquest II	441-0109	Skippers Aviation P/L. Perth, WA.	(N26226)
VH-FMW	95 Pilatus PC-12	123	Royal Flying Doctor Service, Alice Springs, NT.	HB-FQ.
VH-FMZ	96 Pilatus PC-12	138	Royal Flying Doctor Service, Alice Springs, NT.	HB-F..
VH-HIG	06 Pilatus PC-12/47	772	State of South Australia, Adelaide, SA.	HB-F..
VH-HLJ	82 King Air/Catpass 250	BB-945	Trailfinders P/L-Hinterland Aviation P/L. Cairns, QLD.	RP-C1577
VH-HMZ	77 Conquest II	441-0017	Scotts Agencies P/L. Mount Gambier, SA.	N500UW
VH-HPP	90 King Air B200C	BL-137	Eastern Energy Services P/L. Toowoomba, QLD.	ZS-NSD
VH-HWO	99 King Air B200	BB-1641	Royal Flying Doctor Service, Perth-Jandakot, WA.	N23355
VH-ICA	02 TBM 700C2	205	Austcom P/L. Melbourne, VIC.	N778C
VH-IOA	07 Pilatus PC-12/47	842	Milkwood Holdings PTY Ltd, Cooktown QLD.	VH-ZKM
VH-ITA	86 King Air B200	BB-1244	Awesome Aviation PTY LTD/Nantay PTY LTD., Perth, WA.	F-OINC
VH-ITH	78 King Air 200	BB-344	Interair P/L. Essendon, VIC.	N6297S
VH-IWO	98 King Air B200	BB-1639	Royal Flying Doctor Service, Kalgoorlie, WA.	N23352
VH-JET	96 King Air C90B	LJ-1464	Leppington Pastoral Co P/L. Camden, NSW.	N2040E
VH-JJR	82 King Air B200	BB-1019	General Flying Services P/L. Southland Centre, Vic.	VH-ARZ
VH-JLK	96 Pilatus PC-12	126	Acestar Holdings P/L. Perth, WA.	Z-KEN
VH-JLT	80 Conquest II	441-0138	Matthew Overell, Darwin, NT.	VH-KUZ
VH-JMU	02 Pilatus PC-12/45	445	Ocean Dynamics Air P/L, Ascot, QLD.	HB-FPN
VH-JSO	00 TBM 700B	173	Colin Joss & Co P/L. Albury, NSW.	N22WZ
VH-JVN	89 Reims/Cessna F406	F406-0033	Rossair Charter P/L. Adelaide, SA.	VH-RCB
VH-KFG	78 King Air C90	LJ-777	Karratha Flying Services P/L. Karratha, WA.	N9AN
VH-KFN	81 King Air 200C	BL-31	Rotor Lift P/L-Sky Trek P/L. Hobart, Tasmania.	N200LG
VH-KFT	93 TBM 700	92	Runge Aviation P/L. Brisbane, QLD.	F-OHBP
VH-KJD	05 King Air 350	FL-443	Driscoll Investments P/L-Executive Air, Kedron, QLD.	VH-KDT
VH-KQB	93 King Air C90A	LJ-1350	Raymond Cronin, Avenel, Vic.	JA007C
VH-KWO	01 Pilatus PC-12/45	363	Royal Flying Doctor Service, Perth-Jandakot, WA.	
VH-LAB	82 King Air B200T	BT-23	Air Affaires (Australia) P/L. Bankstown, NSW.	N312D
VH-LBA	78 Conquest II	441-0042	Jetcraft Aviation P/L. Archerfield, QLD.	N46MR
VH-LBC	82 Conquest II	441-0236	Jetcraft Aviation P/L. Archerfield, QLD.	VH-TFG
VH-LBD	83 Conquest II	441-0296	Aero Australia P/L. Gisborne, VIC.	N6838K
VH-LBX	78 Conquest II	441-0091	Skippers Aviation P/L. Perth, WA.	VH-AZY
VH-LBY	77 Conquest II	441-0023	Skippers Aviation P/L. Perth, WA.	VH-TFW
VH-LBZ	77 Conquest II	441-0038	Skippers Aviation P/L. Perth, WA.	VH-HWD
VH-LEM	79 Conquest II	441-0081	Fugro Spatial Soulutions P/L. Perth, WA.	N4490C

Reg	Yr	Type	c/n	Owner/Operator	Prev Regn
VH-LKB	77	King Air 200	BB-259	Australasian Jet P/L. Essendon, VIC.	VH-APA
VH-LKF	80	King Air 200	BB-660	Formula Aircraft P/L/Air Phoenix WA	N200TK
VH-LMC	83	Gulfstream 900	15026	McDonald Administration Services P/L., Gold Coast, Qld.	N995HP
VH-LNJ	81	King Air 200C	BL-41	Machjet P/L, Cooroy, QLD	VH-OYK
VH-LWO	99	King Air B200	BB-1643	Royal Flying Doctor Service, Perth-Jandakot, WA.	N23356
VH-LYG	82	King Air C90-1	LJ-1020	Michael Heine, Melbourne, VIC.	VH-LJG
VH-MLG	04	King Air 350	FL-389	Air Travel Australia P/L. Northland, VIC.	VH-WHP
VH-MQZ	06	King Air B200	BB-1961	Maroomba Airlines, Perth, WA.	N74061
VH-MRJ	06	TBM 850	389	Strategic Air Charter P/L., Central Park, VIC.	F-HBGD
VH-MSH	01	King Air B200	BB-1787	RFDS/Ambulance Service of NSW, Sydney, NSW.	N44857
VH-MSM	93	King Air B200	BB-1464	RFDS/Tasmania Ambulance Service, Launceston, Tasmania.	N133LC
VH-MSU	82	King Air 200C	BL-48	Royal Flying Doctor Service, Launceston. 'Philip H Bushell'	N1860B
VH-MSZ	81	King Air B200	BB-866	Royal Flying Doctor Service, Broken Hill, NSW. 'Fred Mckay'	ZK-PBG
VH-MVJ	03	King Air B200	BB-1842	RFDS/Ambulance Service of NSW, Sydney, NSW.	N50152
VH-MVL	89	King Air B200	BB-1333	Royal Flying Doctor Service, Broken Hill, NSW.	N1101W
VH-MVS	02	King Air B200	BB-1813	RFDS/Ambulance Service of NSW, Sydney, NSW.	N61913
VH-MVW	07	King Air B200	BB-1980	Royal Flying Doctor Service, Broken Hill, NSW	N980KA
VH-MVY	89	King Air B200	BB-1324	Royal Flying Doctor Service, Dubbo. 'Flying Doctor Society'	N7087N
VH-MWO	01	Pilatus PC-12/45	379	Royal Flying Doctor Service, Meekatharra, WA.	HB-F..
VH-MWQ	91	King Air B200	BB-1416	RFDS/Air Ambulance Victoria, Essendon, VIC.	VH-MSH
VH-MWU	92	King Air B200	BB-1418	RFDS/Air Ambulance Victoria, Essendon, VIC.	N131GA
VH-MWX	92	King Air B200	BB-1424	RFDS/Air Ambulance Victoria, Essendon, VIC.	N8236K
VH-MWZ	92	King Air B200	BB-1430	RFDS/Air Ambulance Victoria, Essendon, VIC.	VH-MSM
VH-NAX	79	Conquest II	441-0106	Rossair Charter P/L. Adelaide, SA.	(N441AF)
VH-NBT	71	681B Turbo Commander	6047	General Aviation Maintenance P/L. Essendon, VIC.	(VH-UJN)
VH-NMA	81	PA-42 Cheyenne III	8001066	Australasian Jet P/L. Essendon, VIC.	(N142AF)
VH-NSN	96	King Air B200	BB-1552	M Robertson/Orange Aviation P/L. Orange, NSW.	ZS-NZN
VH-NTE	79	King Air 200	BB-529	Pearl Aviation/NT Aerial Medical Service, Darwin, NT.	VH-SWP
VH-NTG	80	King Air 200C	BL-9	Pearl Aviation/NT Aerial Medical Service, Darwin, NT.	VH-KZL
VH-NTH	80	King Air 200C	BL-12	Pearl Aviation/NT Aerial Medical Service, Darwin, NT.	VH-SWO
VH-NTS	81	King Air 200C	BL-30	Pearl Aviation/NT Aerial Medical Service, Darwin, NT.	VH-TNQ
VH-NWO	01	Pilatus PC-12/45	396	Royal Flying Doctor Service, Meekatharra, WA.	HB-FQQ
VH-NYC	72	Rockwell 690	11026	General Aviation Maintenance P/L. Essendon, VIC.	N9226N
VH-OAA	79	Conquest II	441-0102	O'Connor's Air Services P/L. Mount Gambier, SA.	N4246Z
VH-OCS	77	Conquest II	441-0030	Rossair Charter P/L. Adelaide, SA.	N441MM
VH-OOI	07	Pilatus PC-12/47	827	Cockles P/L., Halls Head, WA.	
VH-OPM	79	Conquest II	441-0088	Warrnambool Bus & Motor Co P/L. Warrnambool, VIC.	VH-EVP
VH-OVC	80	SA-226T Merlin 3B	T-318	Shortstop Charter P/L. Essendon, VIC.	N318JC
VH-OWN	81	King Air B200	BB-936	Willmott Forests P/L. Melbourne, VIC.	N200NS
VH-OXF	02	King Air 350	FL-361	Gambamora Industries P/L. Coolangatta, QLD.	VH-KDX
VH-OYA	78	King Air 200	BB-365	Pearl Aviation/RAAF ARDU, Edinburgh, SA.	P2-SML
VH-OYD	82	King Air B200	BB-1041	Pearl Aviation Australia P/L. Darwin, NT.	N200BK
VH-OYE	78	King Air 200	BB-355	Pearl Aviation Australia P/L. Darwin, NT.	VH-SMB
VH-OYH	76	King Air 200	BB-148	Pearl Aviation Australia P/L. Darwin, NT.	VH-WNH
VH-OYT	79	King Air 200T	BT-6	AeroRescue P/L. Darwin, NT. (was BB-489).	VH-PPJ
VH-PCV	76	Rockwell 690A	11283	General Aviation Maintenance P/L. Essendon, VIC.	N57228
VH-PFK	00	King Air C90B	LJ-1586	ST Aerospace Engineers P/L. Singapore.	N15GZ
VH-PIL	98	Pilatus PC-12/45	231	Pegasus Air P/L. Sydney, NSW.	HB-FRB
VH-PSK	98	Beech 1900D	UE-311	Queensland Police Service, Brisbane, QLD.	N10984
VH-PYN	07	King Air 350	FL-525	Gulf Aircraft P/L, Brisbane, Qld.	N7185A
VH-RCI	83	SA-227TT Merlin 3C	TT-474	Hurlad P/L-Rich Air, Melbourne, VIC.	N75SC
VH-SAM	75	King Air C90	LJ-655	Rotor-Lift P/L. Hobart, Tasmania.	VH-NQH
VH-SBM	82	King Air B200	BB-964	FMR Investments Pty Ltd, Scarborough WA	VH-HTU
VH-SCQ	96	King Air 350	FL-150	Mandalay Holdings P/L. Brisbane, QLD.	VH-SGQ
VH-SGQ	05	King Air 350	FL-461	Queensland Government Air Wing, Kedron, QLD.	N36561
VH-SGT	75	King Air 200	BB-73	Network Aviation Australia, Perth, WA.	
VH-SGV	80	King Air 200	BB-718	Great Western Aviation P/L. Hamilton, QLD.	N6728N
VH-SKU	76	King Air 200	BB-165	D J & S J Barnard P/L-Skytrans, Cairns, QLD.	VH-XRF
VH-SMO	80	Conquest II	441-0132	Nantay P/L. Perth, WA.	VH-ANJ
VH-SMT	76	King Air 200	BB-162	Cx VH- 10/05 to ?	RP-C22
VH-SMZ	06	TBM 850	366	Strategic Air Charter P/L., Central Park, Vic.	N318EA
VH-SQH	77	King Air C90	LJ-730	Aviation Australia P/L. Eagle Farm, QLD.	N730WB
VH-SSD	71	SA-226T Merlin 3	T-213	Winrye Aviation P/L. (stored Bankstown).	N174SP
VH-SSL	71	SA-226T Merlin 3	T-210	Wettenhall Air Charter P/L. Denilquin, NSW.	N173SP
VH-SSM	71	SA-226T Merlin 3	T-204	Winrye Aviation P/L. Sydney-Bankstown, NSW.	VH-EGC

Reg	Yr Type	c/n	Owner/Operator	Prev Regn
☐ VH-TAM	80 King Air C90	LJ-919	Ad Astral Aviation Services P/L Belmont Wa.	ZS-LTZ
☐ VH-TAZ	77 Conquest II	441-0005	Tasair P/L. Hobart, Tasmania.	N441RZ
☐ VH-TFB	82 Conquest II	441-0260	Vee H Aviation P/L., Fyshwick, ACT	N68597
☐ VH-TLX	79 King Air 200	BB-550	Pearl Aviation Australia P/L. Darwin, NT.	P2-MBM
☐ VH-TPM	01 PA-46-500TP Meridian	4697089	Dromahair P/L. Tamworth, NSW.	
☐ VH-TSS	78 Rockwell 690B	11463	General Aviation Maintenance P/L. Essendon, VIC.	N101RG
☐ VH-UJG	73 Rockwell 690	11062	General Aviation Maintenance P/L. Essendon, VIC.	VH-NEY
☐ VH-URU	83 King Air B200	BB-1150	Heathgate Resources P/L. Adalaide, SA.	N103BG
☐ VH-UZA	82 SA-227AT Merlin 4C	AT-502	Jetcraft Aviation P/L. Archerfield, QLD.	VH-UUA
☐ VH-UZI	83 SA-227AT Merlin 4C	AT-570	Jetcraft Aviation P/L. Archerfield, QLD.	N570UP
☐ VH-VAT	98 Pilatus PC-12/45	203	Mandolin P/L., Sydney, NSW	ZS-AMS
☐ VH-VCB	79 King Air 200	BB-579	Peter Collings Holdings P/L.West Wing Avn P/L, Mt. Isa, QLD	P2-MML
☐ VH-VED	83 Conquest II	441-0272	Vee H Aviation P/L. Canberra, ACT.	N394G
☐ VH-VEH	82 Conquest II	441-0238	VEE H Aviation Pty Ltd, Fyshwick	N95TD
☐ VH-VEJ	82 Conquest II	441-0249	Vee H Aviation P/L. Canberra, ACT.	N911ER
☐ VH-VEM	80 Conquest II	441-0174	Vee H Aviation P/L. Canberra, ACT	VH-IJQ
☐ VH-VEW	82 Conquest II	441-0264	Vee H Aviation P/L. Canberra, ACT.	C-GSKH
☐ VH-VEZ	80 Conquest II	441-0182	Vee H Aviation P/L. Canberra, ACT.	VH-AZB
☐ VH-VWO	01 Pilatus PC-12/45	400	Royal Flying Doctor Service, Kalgoorlie, WA.	HB-FQR
☐ VH-WBI	05 Pilatus PC-12/45	617	Scrub Turkey Aero Trust, Fortitude Valley, QLD.	HB-F..
☐ VH-WCE	81 PA-42 Cheyenne III	8001033	Australasian Jet P/L. Essendon, VIC.	N582SW
☐ VH-WJY	04 King Air B200	BB-1875	Wagner Aviation P/L. Drayton North, QLD.	N6175U
☐ VH-WPE	06 Pilatus PC-12/47	704	Western Australia Police, Jandakot, WA.	HB-F..
☐ VH-WPY	06 Pilatus PC-12/47	720	Western Australia Police, Jandakot, WA.	HB-F..
☐ VH-WZN	82 King Air B200	BB-963	Lip-Air P/L, Cairns North, QLD	RP-C367
☐ VH-XBC	83 Conquest II	441-0297	Rossair Charter P/L, Adelaide, SA.	N441MT
☐ VH-XCB	94 King Air B200	BB-1472	Jandakot Flight Centre P/L 09/07	VH-MYO
☐ VH-XDB	79 King Air 200	BB-533	Network Aviation Australia, Perth, WA.	N87RK
☐ VH-XMD	77 Conquest II	441-0025	National Australia Bank Ltd. Melbourne, VIC.	N441HD
☐ VH-XMG	79 Conquest II	441-0130	Direct Air Charter (WA) P/L., Essendon, Vic.	VH-KDN
☐ VH-XMJ	80 Conquest II	441-0113	National Australia Bank Ltd. Melbourne, VIC.	N990AR
☐ VH-XTB	00 TBM 700B	166	Australian Aerospace, Milperra, NSW	9M-TBM
☐ VH-YDN	00 Pilatus PC-12/45	301	Northern Territory Police Air Wing, Darwin, NT.	HB-F..
☐ VH-YDO	95 Pilatus PC-12	102	Northern Territory Police Air Wing, Darwin. (was s/n P-04).	VH-NGC
☐ VH-YFD	80 Conquest II	441-0157	Tenix Aviation P/L., Export Park, SA./Rossair Charter Pty	(ZS-SMA)
☐ VH-YJG	76 Rockwell 690A	11308	General Aviation Maintenance P/L. Essendon, VIC.	N99WC
☐ VH-YJP	74 Rockwell 690A	11173	General Aviation Maintenance P/L. Essendon, VIC.	N950M
☐ VH-YWO	06 Pilatus PC-12/47	725	Royal Flying Doctor Service, Jamdakot, WA.	HB-F..
☐ VH-YZE	95 Reims/Cessna F406	F406-0076	Surveillance Australia P/L. Cairns, QLD.	VH-ZZE
☐ VH-YZF	95 Reims/Cessna F406	F406-0078	Surveillance Australia P/L. Broome, WA.	VH-ZZF
☐ VH-YZG	96 Reims/Cessna F406	F406-0079	Surveillance Australia P/L. Darwin, NT.	VH-ZZG
☐ VH-ZBD	07 Pilatus PC-12/47	837	Tom Browne Aviation P/L,Dubbo NSW	HB-FSI
☐ VH-ZEK	82 King Air B200	BB-1083	Silver Linings Aviation P/L. Bankstown, NSW.	N969
☐ VH-ZGS	06 King Air 350	FL-484	Storth P/L-Austrek Aviation P/L. Toowoomba, QLD.	N36984
☐ VH-ZMO	79 King Air 200	BB-470	Australasian Jet P/L. Essendon, VIC.	VH-CWE
☐ VH-ZOR	81 King Air 200	BB-762	JNP Enterprises PTY Ltd/Broome Air Services Pty Ltd	N762KA
☐ VH-ZOS	76 King Air 200	BB-145	Sunshine Air Services P/L. Mount Waverly, VIC.	N88CP
☐ VH-ZWO	02 Pilatus PC-12/45	467	Royal Flying Doctor Service, Perth-Jandakot, WA.	HB-FQM
Military				
☐ A32-339	01 King Air 350	FL-339	RAAF, 32 Sqn. East Sale, VIC.	VH-DHP
☐ A32-343	02 King Air 350	FL-343	RAAF, 32 Sqn. East Sale, VIC.	VH-JHP
☐ A32-346	02 King Air 350	FL-346	RAAF, 32 Sqn. East Sale, VIC.	VH-UHP
☐ A32-348	02 King Air 350	FL-348	RAAF, 32 Sqn. East Sale, VIC.	VH-VHP
☐ A32-349	02 King Air 350	FL-349	RAAF, 32 Sqn. East Sale, VIC.	VH-WHP
☐ A32-350	02 King Air 350	FL-350	RAAF, 32 Sqn. East Sale, VIC.	VH-XHP
☐ A32-351	02 King Air 350	FL-351	RAAF, 32 Sqn. East Sale, VIC.	VH-YHP
☐ A32-372	03 King Air 350	FL-372	RAAF, 32 Sqn. East Sale, VIC.	VH-PHP
☐ A32-426	04 King Air 350	FL-426	Royal Australian Army,	VH-XHP
☐ A32-437	05 King Air 350	FL-437	Royal Australian Army,	VH-YHP
☐ A32-439	05 King Air 350	FL-439	Royal Australian Army,	VH-ZHP

VN = VIETNAM   Total 1

Civil

| ☐ VN-B594 | 89 King Air B200 | BB-1329 | VASCO-Vietnam Air Services Co. | VH-SWC |

VP-B = BERMUDA Total 5
Civil

Reg	Yr Type	c/n	Owner/Operator	Prev Regn
☐ VP-BCT	85 Gulfstream 1000	96208	Control Techniques (Bermuda) Ltd. Blackpool, UK.	N695BE
☐ VP-BKW	79 King Air C90	LJ-805	David J Sewell, Ibadan, Nigeria.	VR-BKW
☐ VP-BLS	97 Pilatus PC-12	176	Bruno Schroder, Fairoaks, UK.	(N176BS)
☐ VP-BMK	89 King Air 300	FA-202	Mike-Fly Ltd. Triengen.	HB-GIP
☐ VP-BMZ	84 Gulfstream 900	15033	Aviatica Trading Co/Marlborough Fine Arts Ltd. Fairoaks, UK.	VR-BMZ

VP-C = CAYMAN ISLANDS Total 1
Civil

Reg	Yr Type	c/n	Owner/Operator	Prev Regn
☐ VP-CAY	82 Gulfstream 900	15011	(status ?). VP-CAY now on B 737 s/n 26286 wef 11/04.	VR-CAY

VQ-T = TURKS & CAICOS ISLANDS Total 1
Civil

Reg	Yr Type	c/n	Owner/Operator	Prev Regn
☐ VQ-TRT	85 King Air B200C	BL-125	Provo Air Center Ltd. Providenciales.	VH-BRF

VT = INDIA Total 81
Civil

Reg	Yr Type	c/n	Owner/Operator	Prev Regn
☐ VT	01 King Air B200	BB-1758		N619TA
☐ VT	99 King Air B200	BB-1700		N403J
☐ VT-ACD	05 King Air 350	FL-465	Aerial Services P/L. Mumbai.	N37065
☐ VT-AEL	01 King Air B200	BB-1788	M/S Adani Exports Ltd. Ahmeidabad.	N770M
☐ VT-AJV	87 King Air C90A	LJ-1159	Orient Flying School, Chennai.	N425SV
☐ VT-ASB	88 Reims/Cessna F406	F406-0031	Century Textiles & Industries Ltd. Mumbai.	D-IBOM
☐ VT-BSA	94 King Air B200	BB-1485	Border Security Force, Delhi.	N1509X
☐ VT-CIL	93 King Air B200	BB-1469	Coal India Ltd. Calcutta.	N82378
☐ VT-CTG	06 King Air B200	BB-1947	Govt of Chattisgarh, Raipur	N73817
☐ VT-DAF	97 King Air B200	BB-1563	Deccan Aviation, Jakkur	N204JT
☐ VT-DAR	99 Pilatus PC-12/45	251	Deccan Aviation P/L. Jakkur-Bangalore.	ZS-SRL
☐ VT-DAV	99 Pilatus PC-12/45	252	Deccan Aviation P/L. Jakkur-Bangalore.	ZS-SRM
☐ VT-DDS	05 King Air B200	BB-1896	Reliance Infrastructure Ltd. Mumbai.	N6196P
☐ VT-DEJ	95 King Air C90B	LJ-1404	Arrow Webtex Ltd., Pune	N3106P
☐ VT-EBB	94 King Air B200	BB-1486	National Remote Sensing Agency, Hyderabad.	N1542Z
☐ VT-EBG	05 King Air C90B	LJ-1752	Government of Bihar, Patna.	N6152Y
☐ VT-EFB	77 King Air C90	LJ-706	India Metals & Ferro Alloys Ltd. Orissa.	N23856
☐ VT-EFG	77 King Air C90	LJ-719	Government of Bihar, Patna.	N23917
☐ VT-EGR	81 King Air C90	LJ-967	Government of Maharashtra, Mumbai-Juhu.	N3832X
☐ VT-EHB	82 King Air B200	BB-972	Saraya Industries Ltd. New Delhi.	N18409
☐ VT-EHY	82 King Air C90	LJ-1008	Government of Punjab, Chandigarh.	N1842A
☐ VT-EJZ	85 King Air C90A	LJ-1100	EIH Ltd. Delhi.	N7219K
☐ VT-EMI	86 King Air C90A	LJ-1135	IGRUA-Indira Gandhi Rashtriya Uran Academy, Fursatganj.	N2602M
☐ VT-EMJ	86 King Air C90A	LJ-1137	IGRUA-Indira Gandhi Rashtriya Uran Academy, Fursatganj.	N6690N
☐ VT-ENL	86 King Air B200	BB-1248	Aviation Research Centre, Cuttack, Orissa.	N7256G
☐ VT-ENM	85 King Air B200	BB-1236	Aviation Research Centre, Cuttack, Orissa.	N72473
☐ VT-EPA	86 King Air B200	BB-1254	Aviation Research Centre, Cuttack, Orissa.	N2646K
☐ VT-EPY	87 King Air B200	BB-1277	Government of Maharashtra, Mumbai-Juhu.	N7241L
☐ VT-EQK	88 King Air B200	BB-1288	Air Works India Engineering Pvt Ltd. Mumbai.	N30850
☐ VT-EQN	88 King Air C90A	LJ-1167	Rajasthan State Flying School, Jaipur.	N31174
☐ VT-EQO	87 King Air C90A	LJ-1153	Alchemist Airways P/L., Chandigarh.	N70491
☐ VT-FAE	05 King Air B200	BB-1918	Honda Finance Ltd/Forum 1 Aviation Ltd. New Delhi.	N6118V
☐ VT-FIU	06 King Air 350	FL-478	Airports Authority of India, Safdarjung.	N6178N
☐ VT-GUJ	99 King Air B200	BB-1687	Gujarat Agro-Industries Ltd. Ahmebad.	N3117V
☐ VT-HIS	07 King Air B200	BB-1982	Hindustan Construction Co., Mumbai	N7022Y
☐ VT-HRA	05 King Air B200	BB-1906	Government of Haryana, Chandigarh.	N61806
☐ VT-HYA	94 King Air C90B	LJ-1376	SKB Infracons P/L. New Delhi.	N15542
☐ VT-JIL	99 King Air C90B	LJ-1573	Jaypee Ventures Ltd. Delhi.	N3203L
☐ VT-JKK	07 King Air 350	FL-552	Indamer Company P/L., Mumbai, India	N552KA
☐ VT-JPK	91 King Air C90A	LJ-1278	Aerial Services Pvt Ltd. Juhu.	N851GA
☐ VT-JRD	97 King Air C90B	LJ-1485		VT-JRD
☐ VT-JSL	06 Pilatus PC-12/47	782	India Flysafe Aviation Limited,	HB-FQQ
☐ VT-JVL	02 King Air B200	BB-1815	Jay Pee Ventures Ltd. New Delhi.	N5015M
☐ VT-KDA	00 Beech 1900D	UE-284	Reliance Travel & Transport Ltd. Mumbai.	N1129B
☐ VT-KPC	03 King Air C90B	LJ-1696	Finolex Industries Ltd. Pune.	N93QR
☐ VT-LJS	07 King Air 350	FL-526	Bharat Hotels Ltd., Gupkar, Srinigar	N3726V
☐ VT-LKK	05 King Air B200	BB-1895	Kirloskar Oil Engine Ltd. Pune.	N36995
☐ VT-LMW	07 King Air B200	BB-1998	Lakshmi Machine Works Ltd,	N998KA

Reg	Yr Type	c/n	Owner/Operator	Prev Regn
☐ VT-LNT	93 King Air B200	BB-1468	Larsen & Toubro Ltd. Mumbai.	N8230E
☐ VT-MEG	96 Pilatus PC-12	135	Mega Corporation, New Delhi	N999EP
☐ VT-MGJ	98 King Air 350	FL-192	Government of Maharashtra, Mumbai-Juhu.	N2192V
☐ VT-MPG	93 King Air B200	BB-1445	Flyjet Airways Pvt Ltd., Raipur	N8121M
☐ VT-MPT	01 King Air B200	BB-1775	Government of Madhya Pradesh, Bhopal.	N5075E
☐ VT-NEI	85 King Air C90A	LJ-1116	National Energy Processing Co/NEPC Micon Ltd. Madras.	N25AE
☐ VT-NKF	95 King Air C90B	LJ-1402	Force Motors Ltd. Pune.	N3234K
☐ VT-RAM	78 King Air C90	LJ-790	Lake Palace Hotels & Motels Ltd. Udaipur.	VT-EFZ
☐ VT-REL	00 King Air C90B	LJ-1604	Ran Air Services Ltd. New Delhi.	N928US
☐ VT-RJA	06 King Air B200	BB-1943	Government of Rajasthan, Jaipur.	N70143
☐ VT-RLL	94 King Air C90B	LJ-1369	Ran Air Services Ltd. New Delhi.	N3222K
☐ VT-RSB	89 King Air B200	BB-1317	Hindalco Industries Ltd/Birla Co. Mumbai.	N591EB
☐ VT-RSL	99 King Air C90B	LJ-1560	Ran Air Services Ltd. New Delhi.	N3160P
☐ VT-SAZ	03 King Air B200	BB-1831	Steel Authority of India, Delhi.	N61831
☐ VT-SDJ	97 King Air B200	BB-1567	Span Air P/L. New Delhi.	VT-CSK
☐ VT-SFL	97 King Air C90B	LJ-1496	TVS/Sundram Fasteners Ltd. Chennai.	N101SQ
☐ VT-SKM	06 King Air C90GT	LJ-1810	Bellary Iron Ores Pvt Ltd., Allipura, Bellary	N71650
☐ VT-SLK	91 King Air C90A	LJ-1270	Alchemist Airways P/L., Chandigarh.	N324AB
☐ VT-SRC	93 King Air B200C	BL-139	SRC Aviation Pte Ltd. New Delhi.	N65LW
☐ VT-SSL	05 King Air C90B	LJ-1751	Shamanur Sugars Limited, Davangere	N12LE
☐ VT-TAS	02 Pilatus PC-12/45	472	Tata Steel Ltd. New Delhi.	HB-FQO
☐ VT-TIS	95 King Air C90B	LJ-1393	Tata Steel Ltd. New Delhi.	N3217M
☐ VT-TOI	99 Beech 1900D	UE-353	Jubilant Enpro P/L. New Delhi.	D-CSAG
☐ VT-TVS	97 King Air B200	BB-1572	TVS Motor Co. Chennai.	N149SR
☐ VT-UAB	05 King Air B200	BB-1914	Government of Uttaranchal, Dehrudun.	N5114Z
☐ VT-UBA	77 King Air C90	LJ-711	McDowell & Co. Bangalore.	VT-EFE
☐ VT-UPA	94 King Air 300LW	FA-230	Government of Uttar Pradesh, Lucknow.	N80679
☐ VT-UPR	03 King Air B200	BB-1818	Government of Uttar Pradesh, Lucknow.	N5018F
☐ VT-UPZ	95 King Air C90B	LJ-1400	Government of Uttar Pradesh, Lucknow.	N3239K
☐ VT-VHL	87 King Air B200	BB-1267	Venkateshwara Hatcheries Group, Pun, Maharashtra.	N67GA
☐ VT-VSM	00 King Air B200	BB-1723	TVS Motor Co. Chennai.	N521DG
☐ VT-WFB	King Air	...	Indian Metals & Ferro Alloys Ltd.	
☐ VT-YUD	01 King Air B200	BB-1764	Essar Steel Pte Ltd. Mumbai.	ZS-PGB

Total 14

V5 = NAMIBIA
Civil

Reg	Yr Type	c/n	Owner/Operator	Prev Regn
☐ V5	95 Pilatus PC-12/45	125		ZS-ZEN
☐ V5-	79 Conquest II	441-0095		ZS-JMA
☐ V5-CCH	78 PA-31T Cheyenne II	7820085	Steel Construction/Corporate Charters CC. Windhoek.	N12HF
☐ V5-DHL	91 Reims/Cessna F406	F406-0062	DHL/Westair Wings Charters P/L. Windhoek.	N744C
☐ V5-EEZ	85 Reims/Cessna F406	F406-0004	Namibia Fisheries Protection, Windhoek. 'Sea Eagle'	F-WIVD
☐ V5-FMR	06 Reims/Cessna F406	F406-0093	Namibia Fisheries Protection	
☐ V5-LYZ	81 Conquest 1	425-0021	Wings Over Africa CC. Windhoek.	ZS-LYZ
☐ V5-MAC	79 Rockwell 690B	11557	Desert Air/Sossus Air Taxi, Windhoek.	N75WA
☐ V5-MDA	90 Reims/Cessna F406	F406-0058	Westair Wings Charters P/L. Windhoek.	ZS-OXE
☐ V5-MED	74 King Air E90	LW-87	Prosperity Africa Holdings,	9J-OGT
☐ V5-MFN	77 Rockwell 690B	11422		ZS-PFD
☐ V5-MGF	78 Rockwell 690A	11432	Ango Wings, Windhoek.	ZS-JRC
☐ V5-MJW	81 Conquest 1	425-0077	Eros Air P/L. Windhoek.	ZS-MJW
☐ V5-WAK	91 Reims/Cessna F406	F406-0048	DHL/Westair Wings Charters P/L. Windhoek.	G-FLYN

Total 269

XA = MEXICO
Civil

Reg	Yr Type	c/n	Owner/Operator	Prev Regn
☐ X.	77 PA-31T Cheyenne II	7720049	Universal Jet Rental de Mexico, Garza Garcia.	N82161
☐ XA	78 PA-31T Cheyenne II	7820077		N87SJ
☐ XA-	84 Conquest 1	425-0216		N216BJ
☐ XA-	79 Rockwell 690B	11537	Italian Coffee SA de CV., Puebla	N434CC
☐ XA-	89 King Air B200	BB-1322	Exportadora de Sal SA de CV., Guerrero Negro, BC.	N96GP
☐ XA-	75 SA-226T Merlin 3A	T-252		N600DL
☐ XA-	80 Gulfstream 840	11635	Taxis Aereos del Noroeste S.A., Sonora	N431MS
☐ XA-	74 SA-226T Merlin 3A	T-249		N777HZ
☐ XA-	06 Pilatus PC-12/47	775		N775PC
☐ XA-	07 Pilatus PC-12/47	832		N832PC
☐ XA-	06 King Air C90GT	LJ-1815		N3735M
☐ XA-	75 King Air 200	BB-49	Aero International Inc.	N222KA
☐ XA-	84 PA-42 Cheyenne 400LS	5527006	Aero WWG SA de CV., Puerto Penasco, SON, Mexico	N54DA

Reg	Yr	Type	c/n	Owner/Operator	Prev Regn
☐ XA-	07	King Air C90GT	LJ-1842		N842KA
☐ XA-	07	King Air C90GT	LJ-1829		N71839
☐ XA-	80	Conquest II	441-0139		C-GWCA
☐ XA-	80	King Air 200	BB-611		N25MR
☐ XA-	74	King Air 200	BB-6	Gerardo F Beltran Vargas, Mexico City.	N300TR
☐ XA-	84	PA-42 Cheyenne 400LS	5527007	Transportadora Egoba SA de CV, Queretaro	N531MC
☐ XA-	02	Pilatus PC-12/45	481	Vuelos Rapidos de Occidente SA de CV	N481TL
☐ XA-	05	Pilatus PC-12/45	680	Aerotron, Puerto Vallarta	N680PE
☐ XA-	81	Conquest II	441-0198	Arturo Sanchez Magallanes	N447WS
☐ XA-...	78	PA-31T Cheyenne II	7820032		N700PT
☐ XA-...	00	King Air C90B	LJ-1624	Aerolineas Ejecutivas SA. Toluca.	N4324K
☐ XA-...	78	Rockwell 690B	11455		N206BN
☐ XA-...	65	King Air 90	LJ-19		N821U
☐ XA-...	81	King Air B200	BB-915		N333RD
☐ XA-...	77	PA-31T Cheyenne II	7720055		N2157A
☐ XA-...	73	SA-226AT Merlin 4	AT-009		N479VK
☐ XA-...	67	King Air A90	LJ-287	Ruben Sanchez Martinez, Mig Hidalgo.	N502W
☐ XA-...	80	Conquest II	441-0153		N722GA
☐ XA-...	81	Cheyenne II-XL	8166025	Aviasur del Caribe,	N53WA
☐ XA-...	60	Gulfstream 1	38	Five Star Airplane Services SA. Naucalpan. (status ?).	N717RS
☐ XA-...	01	King Air B200	BB-1752	Aerolineas Ejecutivas SA. Toluca.	N5152G
☐ XA-...	76	PA-31T Cheyenne II	7620049		N37RL
☐ XA-...	67	King Air A90	LJ-200		N50RP
☐ XA-...	72	King Air E90	LW-14	Trans Caribbean Trust SA.	N4495N
☐ XA-...	79	Rockwell 690B	11549		N444NR
☐ XA-...	06	King Air B200	BB-1958		N37058
☐ XA-...	73	King Air A100	B-158		N62NC
☐ XA-...	65	Gulfstream 1	161		N925GC
☐ XA-...	00	Pilatus PC-12/45	333		N333PA
☐ XA-...	82	King Air F90	LA-193		N604DK
☐ XA-...	98	King Air C90B	LJ-1533		N628VK
☐ XA-...	85	Gulfstream 1000	96075		N6151W
☐ XA-...	68	King Air B90	LJ-399		N551AT
☐ XA-...	79	King Air 200	BB-610		N200VJ
☐ XA-...	80	King Air 200	BB-618		N269BW
☐ XA-...	79	King Air 200	BB-572	Francisco Zavaia Meza,	N898CA
☐ XA-...	79	Rockwell 690B	11548	Inmobilia Bahia Ensenada SA. Ensenada, BC.	N29KG
☐ XA-...	69	SA-26AT Merlin 2B	T26-158		M4260X
☐ XA-...	79	PA-31T Cheyenne 1	7904031	Rodolfo Chavaria Delgado,	N54EZ
☐ XA-...	82	King Air F90	LA-168		N43LA
☐ XA-...	80	King Air F90	LA-43		N6749E
☐ XA-...	77	SA-226T Merlin 3A	T-282		N956DS
☐ XA-...	05	King Air C90B	LJ-1753	GE Capital Leasing SA. Mexico City.	N37123
☐ XA-ABH	78	Rockwell 690B	11454	Aerotaxi Paba SA. Culiacan, Sinalao.	N81737
☐ XA-ACG	72	King Air C90	LJ-548		N800PW
☐ XA-ANS	04	P-180 Avanti	1088	Transportacion Aerea del Norte SA. Monterrey, NL.	N205PA
☐ XA-ASR	78	King Air 200	BB-395	Tomas Gonzales Sada y Pablo GL. Garza Garcia, NL.	XB-BRB
☐ XA-CAB	02	King Air 350	FL-341	Laboratorios Pisa SA.	N4471J
☐ XA-CHM	85	Gulfstream 900	15040	Chilchota Taxi Aereo SA. Coahuila. (status ?).	N4NT
☐ XA-CPR	05	King Air C90GT	LJ-1758		N390GT
☐ XA-DER	73	Rockwell 690	11060	Aerotaxis del Itsmo SA. Cuernavaca, Morelos.	N.....
☐ XA-EJS	84	PA-42 Cheyenne IIIA	5501008	Aeroservicios Azteca SA.	N777YP
☐ XA-FCV	99	King Air 350	FL-251	Aerolineas Ejecutivas SA. Toluca.	N3151H
☐ XA-GEC	82	King Air B200	BB-1086	Servicios Estatales Aeroportuarios, Guadalupe.	N200JM
☐ XA-GEM	75	Rockwell 690A	11267	Transportes Aereos Virva SA. Mexico City.	N57035
☐ XA-GFM	04	King Air B200	BB-1892		N3732K
☐ XA-HNG	79	PA-31T Cheyenne II	7920041	Mexhaga SA. Saltillo.	N66WJ
☐ XA-HPS	03	King Air B200	BB-1838	Aerolineas Ejecutivas SA. Toluca.	N5138Q
☐ XA-JAG	00	King Air C90B	LJ-1623	Aerolineas Ejecutivas SA. Toluca.	N5023T
☐ XA-JGR		Gulfstream 1	...	noted Acarigua, Venezuela 5/06.	
☐ XA-JOS	03	Pilatus PC-12/45	504		N504PB
☐ XA-LEK	81	Gulfstream 980	95042	Aerotux SA.	N9794S
☐ XA-LGT	80	King Air F90	LA-45	Aero Rentas de Coahuila SA. Coahuila.	N748GM
☐ XA-MSC	01	King Air C90B	LJ-1653		N653TF
☐ XA-NTC	77	Rockwell 690B	11370	Aerotaxi del Cabo SA.	XB-NTC

Reg	Yr	Type	c/n	Owner/Operator	Prev Regn
☐ XA-PCM	01	Pilatus PC-12/45	405		N405PB
☐ XA-PGT	76	PA-31T Cheyenne II	7620034	Aereo Rentas de Coahuila SA. Saltillo.	N7276C
☐ XA-PUY	72	Rockwell 690	11018	Aerovallarta SA. Puerto Vallarta, JAL.	N63PG
☐ XA-RCG	00	King Air 350	FL-277	Aerolineas Ejecutivas SA. Toluca.	N4477Q
☐ XA-RDS	05	King Air B200	BB-1907	Aerolineas Ejecutivas SA. Toluca.	N37307
☐ XA-RFH	05	King Air C90B	LJ-1741		N36741
☐ XA-RJB	65	Gulfstream 1	159	Aerolineas Damojh SA. Guadalajara.	G-BNKN
☐ XA-RLK	64	Gulfstream 1	138	Aero Guadalajara SA/Aerolineas Damojh SA. Guadalajara.	N126K
☐ XA-RMX	81	King Air 200	BB-814	Aerogisa SA. Saltillo.	N6VW
☐ XA-RNL	80	MU-2 Marquise	777SA	Servicios Aereos Interestatales SA. Del Norte, NL.	XB-DJX
☐ XA-RWR	79	PA-31T Cheyenne II	7920047	Aerolineas Comerciales SA. Michoacan.	N79CA
☐ XA-RXT	91	King Air C90A	LJ-1280	Aereo Servicios Saltillo SA. Saltillo.	
☐ XA-SAW	81	King Air F90	LA-95	Aero Quimmco SA. Monterrey.	XB-CGP
☐ XA-SFD	79	Rockwell 690B	11534	Aerolineas Villaverde SA. Cordoba.	XB-BGH
☐ XA-SHP	71	681B Turbo Commander	6063	GBM Aereo SA. Cuidad Acuna, Coahuila.	XB-HUL
☐ XA-TBT	64	Gulfstream 1	136	Industrial Minera Mexico SA.	XB-GAW
☐ XA-TJD	66	King Air A90	LM-16	Aeromover SA. San Luis Potosi.	N823SB
☐ XA-TJH	81	PA-42 Cheyenne III	8001039	Aerosan SA.	D-ICMC
☐ XA-TJN		King Air B200	...	noted Dallas 6/04.	
☐ XA-TLW	82	Conquest II	441-0237	Servicios Aereos de Chihuahua SA.	N700JG
☐ XA-TMP	80	King Air F90	LA-44	Aero Laguna SA. Torreon, Coah.	N244J
☐ XA-TOR	81	Gulfstream 840	11661	XABRE Aerolineas SA. Toluca.	N840DC
☐ XA-TQD	74	Rockwell 690A	11185		N690JB
☐ XA-TTR	98	King Air C90B	LJ-1524		N78XJ
☐ XA-TVO		King Air	...	& XB-GEC noted Toluca 9/05.	
☐ XA-TWB	81	King Air F90	LA-147		N722DR
☐ XA-TWZ	02	Pilatus PC-12/45	461		XA-PCM
☐ XA-TXK	73	King Air C90	LJ-584	Ecoturistica de Xcalak SA. Chetumal, Quintana Roo.	N73LK
☐ XA-UAO		Pilatus PC-12/45	...	& XA-URA noted Toluca 9/05.	
☐ XA-UBA	03	Pilatus PC-12/45	512	Servicios Aereos Poblanos SA.	N512PB
☐ XA-UES	04	Pilatus PC-12/45	585		N585PB
☐ XA-UET	05	King Air 350	FL-455	Aerolineas Ejecutivas SA. Toluca.	N6155U
☐ XA-UFN	06	Pilatus PC-12/47	701		N701PE
☐ XA-VIP	91	PA-42 Cheyenne IIIA	5501058	VIP Empresarial SA. Tamps.	N985TA
☐ XA-YAS	97	King Air C90B	LJ-1479	Aerolineas Ejecutivas SA. Toluca.	N1119U
☐ XA-ZEC	02	King Air B200	BB-1803	Aereo Servicios Jet SA. Guanajuato.	N5093G
☐ XB-...	78	PA-31T Cheyenne II	7820012	Marcelo Villareal Cantu, Monterrey, NL.	N781SW
☐ XB-...	69	680W Turbo Commander	1834-39		N200QT
☐ XB-...	72	King Air C90	LJ-536	Jose Luis Calzada, Mexico City.	N31WB
☐ XB-...	73	Mitsubishi MU-2K	273	Hugo Alvarez, Puebla.	N46MK
☐ XB-ACO	81	Gulfstream 980	95051	Procurad General de la Republica, Mexico City.	XC-HGG
☐ XB-AHK	00	King Air C90B	LJ-1593	Aerolineas Ejecutivas SA. Toluca.	N44693
☐ XB-AIN	90	PA-42 Cheyenne IIIA	5501048	Transportadora Egoba SA.	N948TA
☐ XB-ATC	85	Gulfstream 1000	96084	Procurad General de la Republica, Mexico City.	XC-HGW
☐ XB-AUR	70	681 Turbo Commander	6040	Salvador Navarro Diaz Barreiro,	N9097N
☐ XB-BED	74	Rockwell 690A	11188	Estacion Cuauhtemoc SPR.	XA-FIZ
☐ XB-CIO	68	King Air B90	LJ-387	Representaciones Cristaleria y Peltre de Zamora. (status ?).	N824K
☐ XB-DJN	70	681 Turbo Commander	6023	Gonzalez Trejo Alejandro, Mexico City.	XA-CAG
☐ XB-DMT	77	Rockwell 690B	11360	Carrillo Caraza Rene, Culiacan, Sinalao.	N100WC
☐ XB-DSH	80	Gulfstream 840	11631		XC-TXA
☐ XB-DTD	67	680W Turbo Commander	1788-18	Fernando Nunez Chavez, Durango.	XA-DII
☐ XB-DTW	80	Gulfstream 840	11650	Dulce V Gonzalez Garduno, Mexico City.	XA-JPA
☐ XB-ECT	82	Gulfstream 1000	96004	Francisco Lira Ortega, Ensenada, Baja California.	XA-LUV
☐ XB-EFZ	80	SA-226T Merlin 3B	T-328	Dist Int Productos Agricolas SA. Celaya.	N23X
☐ XB-EIH	74	Rockwell 690A	11214	Compras y Comisiones SA. Leon.	N57214
☐ XB-EWO	82	Conquest II	441-0235	Parson Meikle Joseph Richard, Nva Casas Grandes, Chihuahua.	N333GE
☐ XB-FMS	82	Conquest 1	425-0051	Arturo Armendariz Chaparr, Chihuahua.	XA-RLN
☐ XB-FMV	67	Mitsubishi MU-2B	034	Christian Esquino,	N28HR
☐ XB-FQC	74	Rockwell 690A	11144	Lin. de Producc. SA. Toluca.	XA-RAO
☐ XB-FSG	83	Cheyenne II-XL	8166047	Grupo Fralvar de Mexico SA. Mexico City.	N457SR
☐ XB-FXK	81	Conquest 1	425-0091	Jose Luis Franco Alvarez, Mexico City.	N68478
☐ XB-FXU	79	PA-31T Cheyenne 1	7904053	Krum SA. Del Norte, NL.	N2379R
☐ XB-FYD	73	Rockwell 690	11065	Gabriela Ortega Larraury, Del Norte, NL.	XB-CZX
☐ XB-GAL	84	PA-31T Cheyenne 1A	1104009		N9268Y
☐ XB-GBN	77	Conquest II	441-0021	Malva Inmobiliara SA. Queretaro.	XA-SKJ

Reg	Yr	Type	c/n	Owner/Operator	Prev Regn
XB-GCU	78	Rockwell 690B	11460	Fausto Bermudez Hernandez, Toluca.	N42DK
XB-GDS	77	Rockwell 690B	11371	Pascual Oyarvide Sanchez, Ciudad Valles, SLP.	XA-RMG
XB-GJL	73	Rockwell 690	11074	Manuel Vargas Ramirez, San Luis Rio Col, Baja California.	XB-AEL
XB-GMT	81	Gulfstream 840	11677	Vazquez Garcia Miguel Angel, Puebla, Chihuahua.	XB-GCV
XB-GQI	80	PA-31T Cheyenne 1	8004056	Rocha Fuentes Jorge Miguel, Del Norte, NL.	N8TH
XB-GTP	65	King Air 90	LJ-63		XA-MUR
XB-GVI	80	PA-31T Cheyenne II	8020008	Rodriguez Gracia Juan Gerardo, Del Norte, NL.	N165CA
XB-HCL	68	King Air B90	LJ-388	Pascual Oyarvide Sanchez, Ciudad Valles, SLP.	N93EJ
XB-HHA	84	King Air 300	FA-14	ALFACC SA.	N450AC
XB-HMI	99	King Air C90B	LJ-1549	G Morfin Villalpando,	N3076U
XB-HNA	79	PA-31T Cheyenne II	7920012	Constructora Brisa SA. Jalapa.	XB-RTG
XB-HOV	69	Mitsubishi MU-2F	156	Armando Alanis Rodriguez, Del Norte, NL.	N869Q
XB-HSE	74	Rockwell 690A	11225	TRC	XA-EOC
XB-IGJ		PA-31T Cheyenne	...	noted Toluca 9/05.	
XB-IHK	79	King Air 200	BB-423	Rafael Rodriguez Vale, Mexico City.	XB-HDY
XB-IHX	97	Pilatus PC-12	166		HB-FOL
XB-IKO	03	Pilatus PC-12/45	493		N493PB
XB-ILU	96	Pilatus PC-12	143	E Vazquez,	N6DQ
XB-ISC	74	Rockwell 690A	11145	(status ?).	N102JK
XB-JCT	76	King Air E90	LW-170		N555TT
XB-JER		Gulfstream 1	...	noted Acarigua, Venezuela 6/06.	
XB-JGU		Gulfstream 1	...	Global Air,	
XB-JLA	80	King Air E90	LW-333	Jose Lorca Avalos, San Luis Potosi.	N90BE
XB-JNC	83	PA-42 Cheyenne III	8001104	Industrias de Construcciones de Mexico SA.	N334FP
XB-JNN	89	King Air C90A	LJ-1199		N717RD
XB-JQC	72	SA-226T Merlin 3	T-220	Hock Construcciones SA de CV	N14TP
XB-JRF	82	King Air F90	LA-186	J M Rocha Fuentes,	N600SF
XB-JXY	73	SA-226T Merlin 3A	T-229		N78CS
XB-JYE	81	King Air 200	BB-873	Minera Penasquito SA. Zacatecas.	N529JA
XB-JZP	77	King Air 200	BB-225		N917BT
XB-KBC	06	King Air B200	BB-1932	Inmobiliara Archov SA.	N737EA
XB-KLY	79	Rockwell 690B	11563	Eduardo de la Vega Canelo, Culiacan.	N140CA
XB-LIJ	76	Mitsubishi MU-2M	341	Dirigir SA. Monterrey, NL.	N726MA
XB-NEB	73	Mitsubishi MU-2J	583	Administracion Central SA.	N287MA
XB-NUG	74	Mitsubishi MU-2J	619	Conductores Monterrey SA. Del Norte, NL.	N469MA
XB-PSG	84	PA-42 Cheyenne IIIA	5501019	Prisciliano Siller Garcia, Del Norte, NL.	N819PC
XB-REA	70	King Air 100	B-68	Negro Mex SA. (status ?).	XA-DEA
XB-RGG	73	King Air A100	B-170	Juan Jose Romo Lopez, ? Crashed Guatemala 11/07	XB-RGG
XB-RHO		King Air	...	noted Toluca 9/05, XA-TVO, XA-UET, XC-ORE noted Toluca 3/06.	
XB-RLM	79	PA-31T Cheyenne II	7920023	Pavimentos de la Laguna SA.	N793SW
XB-SCG	82	King Air C90	LJ-1003		N747SF
XB-SHH	77	Rockwell 690B	11406	Constructadora y Edificado Comal. Toluca.	XB-FKC
XB-TCT		King Air C90	...		
XB-TWL	77	Rockwell 690B	11382	Secretaria de Gobernacion, Mexico City.	XC-TAG
XB-WUI	69	King Air 100	B-4		N925BD
XB-XOI	70	Mitsubishi MU-2F	189	Roberto A Mariscal Saenz, Toluca.	N110MA
XB-ZRH	89	King Air 300	FA-203		N369MK
XC-AA12	82	Conquest II	441-0232	Procurad General de la Republica, Mexico City.	HK-3652
XC-AA27	81	Gulfstream 840	11652	Governor of the State of Sonora, Hermosillo. (status ?).	XC-HGJ
XC-AA29	80	Gulfstream 840	11606		ZP-.
XC-AA36	81	Gulfstream 840	11678	Governor of the State of Vera Cruz, Jalapa.	XC-HHY
XC-AA38		King Air B200	...	Procurad General de la Republica, Mexico City.	
XC-AA40		Gulfstream 840	...	Governor of the State of Tamaulipas, Ciudad Victoria	XC-HHK
XC-AA41		Conquest II	...	Procurad General de la Republica, Mexico City.	
XC-AA46	86	King Air 300LW	FA-95	Procurad General de la Republica, Mexico City.	HK-3536
XC-AA49	85	King Air 300	FA-83	PGR/Mexican Drug Enforcement Agency, Mexico City.	XC-HGV
XC-AA56	81	Gulfstream 840	11695	State Government of Baja California Norte.	XB-JIO
XC-AA62	81	Gulfstream 980	95068	Procurad General de la Republica, Mexico City.	HK-3409W
XC-AA67	80	Gulfstream 980	95000	Procurad General de la Republica, Mexico City.	YV-
XC-AA71	80	Conquest II	441-0189	Procurad General de la Republica, Mexico City.	HK-3595
XC-AA80	86	King Air 300	FA-74	Procurad General de la Republica, Mexico City.	HK-3519
XC-AA95		Conquest II	...	noted Toluca 9/05.	
XC-AGS	86	King Air C90A	LJ-1132	Governor of the State of Aguascalientes.	XA-GSM
XC-ALB	81	Gulfstream 980	95052		XC-AA94
XC-BCN	79	King Air 200	BB-435	Governor of the State of Baja California Norte.	XC-GOL

Reg	Yr	Type	c/n	Owner/Operator	Prev Regn
☐ XC-CGE		Conquest II	...	noted Toluca 3/06.	
☐ XC-CHI	97	King Air 300	FL-166	Governor of the State of Chihuahua.	N166FL
☐ XC-CTL	99	King Air B200	BB-1661		N2361C
☐ XC-DIJ	76	King Air 200	BB-100	Procurad General de la Republica, Mexico City.	N75KA
☐ XC-FIW	72	King Air A100	B-110	Secretariat of Communications & Transport, Mexico City.	
☐ XC-FOC	72	King Air C90	LJ-553	CIAAC-Centro Int de Adto de Aviacion Civil, Mexico City.	
☐ XC-FUY	73	King Air E90	LW-33	Direccion General de Aduanas, Monterrey.	
☐ XC-GAS	79	Rockwell 690B	11556	Direccion General de Carreteras Federales, Mexico City.	
☐ XC-GON	81	Conquest II	441-0224	Secretaria de Hacienda y Credito Publico, Mexico City.	N6854B
☐ XC-GOO	81	Conquest II	441-0208	Secretaria de Hacienda y Credito Publico, Mexico City.	N2728F
☐ XC-HFA	73	SA-226T Merlin 3	T-238	Governor of the State of Tamaulipas, Ciudad Victoria.	N130PC
☐ XC-HFN	82	Rockwell 1000	96043	Governor of the State of Chihuahua.	N9963S
☐ XC-HGH	81	Gulfstream 980	95072	Procurad General de la Republica, Mexico City.	HK-3492
☐ XC-HHH	80	Gulfstream 840	11649	Procurad General de la Republica, Mexico City.	HK-3448
☐ XC-HHS	78	Rockwell 690B	11450	Governor of the State of Sinalao, Culiacan.	N81729
☐ XC-HMO	79	Rockwell 690B	11560	Governor of the State of Sonora, Hermosillo.	(N690RB)
☐ XC-HUA	85	Gulfstream 1000	96091	Governor of the State of Oaxaca, Xoxocotlan.	XC-AA20
☐ XC-IFA		Rockwell 690	...	& XC-LIM, XC-ZCL & XA-AFI noted Toluca 3/06.	
☐ XC-JAL	77	Rockwell 690B	11417	Governor of the State of Jalisco, Guadalajara.	N81662
☐ XC-JCT	76	Rockwell 690A	11331	Fondo Nat. Fomento Al Turismo, Baja California Sur.	XB-ECX
☐ XC-JDB		Gulfstream 900	15009	Policia Federal Preventiva, Mexico City.	XC-AA39
☐ XC-LGE	83	Conquest II	441-0275	Comision Nacional de Agua, Mexico City.	XC-AA37
☐ XC-LHD	83	Gulfstream 1000	96056		XC-AA19
☐ XC-LIE	64	Gulfstream 1	148		C-FWAM
☐ XC-MLM	83	Gulfstream 900	15028	Governor of the State of Michoacan,	N5916N
☐ XC-NAY	73	Rockwell 690A	11115	Governor of the State of Nayarit, Tepic.	XB-XUC
☐ XC-OAX	81	Gulfstream 840	11656	Governor of the State of Oaxaca, Xoxocotlan.	(N5908K)
☐ XC-ONA	67	King Air A90	LJ-293	Cia S N P SA. Mexico City.	N793K
☐ XC-PFB		Gulfstream 980	95018	Policia Federal Preventiva, Mexico City.	N123LA
☐ XC-QET	80	PA-31T Cheyenne II	8020019	State Government of Queretaro.	N85CM
☐ XC-RAM	72	Rockwell 690	11021	Secretaria de Hacienda y Credito Publico, Mexico City.	
☐ XC-SAH	78	Rockwell 690B	11516	S.A.H.O.P. Mexico City.	
☐ XC-STA	78	Rockwell 690B	11447	TAF-Transporte Aereo Federal, Mexico City.	N81723
☐ XC-TAB	78	Rockwell 690B	11504	Governor of the State of Tabasco, Villahermosa.	N106SA
☐ XC-TAU	99	King Air B200	BB-1674		N404PT
☐ XC-TJN	99	King Air B200	BB-1681	Governor of the State of Vera Cruz. Jalapa.	XA-TJN
☐ XC-UAT	76	PA-31T Cheyenne II	7620046	Universidad Autonoma de Tamaulipas, Victoria.	N5432V
☐ XC-UJW		Rockwell 690	...	noted Cancun 6/06.	
☐ XC-UJX	77	Conquest II	441-0019		XC-AA74
☐ XC-VES	78	Rockwell 690B	11481	Governor of the State of Coahuila, Ramos Arizpe.	N126SA
☐ XC-VNC	60	Gulfstream 1	58	Procurad General de la Republica, Mexico City.	XA-TTU

Military

Reg	Yr	Type	c/n	Owner/Operator	Prev Regn
☐ 2206		Mitsubishi MU-2B	...	noted stored Santa Lucia 3/03.	
☐ 3918	82	Gulfstream 1000	96041	Mexican Air Force, Mexico City.	ETE-1318
☐ 3932	78	Rockwell 690B	11494	Mexican Air Force, Mexico City.	ETE-1332
☐ 3971		King Air B200	...	UETAAM, Mexico City. (noted 3/03).	
☐ 5201	88	King Air C90A	LJ-1166	Government of Mexico,	2201
☐ 5202	88	King Air C90A	LJ-1168	Government of Mexico,	2202
☐ 5203	88	King Air C90A	LJ-1171	Government of Mexico,	2203
☐ 5204	88	King Air C90A	LJ-1175	Government of Mexico,	2204
☐ 5205	88	King Air C90A	LJ-1176	Government of Mexico,	2205
☐ 5206		King Air C90	...	noted stored Santa Lucia 3/03.	
☐ ETE-1357		Mitsubishi MU-2B	...	noted stored Santa Lucia 3/03.	
☐ MT-214	82	Gulfstream 1000	96040	Mexican Navy, Mexico City.	N900JP
☐ MT-218	82	Gulfstream 1000	96013	Mexican Navy, Mexico City.	XC-HHZ
☐ MT-219	80	Gulfstream 980	95040	Mexican Navy, Mexico City.	XB-AOC
☐ MT-221	81	Gulfstream 980	95046	Mexican Navy, Mexico City.	XB-DSA
☐ MT-222	81	Gulfstream 980	95082	Mexican Navy, Mexico City.	HK-3453
☐ MT-223	68	Mitsubishi MU-2F	122	Mexican Navy, Mexico City.	N98MA
☐ MT-224	79	Conquest II	441-0101	Mexican Navy, Mexico City.	N412PW
☐ MU-1550	72	Mitsubishi MU-2J	566	Mexican Navy, Mexico City.	N210MA
☐ TP-216	82	Gulfstream 1000	96001	FAM, Government of Mexico, Mexico City.	XC-AA23

XT = BURKINA FASO Total 3
Military

☐ XT-MAX	80 King Air 200	BB-742	Government of Burkina Faso/Air Burkina, Ouagadougou.	G-BPWJ
☐ XT-MBA	80 King Air 200	BB-698	Government of Burkina Faso/Air Burkina, Ouagadougou.	N440CF
☐ XT-MBD	88 King Air B200	BB-1311	Burkina Faso Army, Ouagadougou.	N887FB

XU = CAMBODIA Total 1
Civil

| ☐ XU-HBB | 71 King Air C90 | LJ-510 | | F-GHBB |

YL = LATVIA Total 1
Civil

| ☐ YL- | 06 PA-46-500TP Meridian | 4697283 | | OY-PHZ |

YN = NICARAGUA Total 1
Military

| ☐ FAN-002 | 76 King Air C-12C | BC-37 | Fuerza Aérea - Ejército de Nicaragua | YV-.. |

YR = ROMANIA Total 3
Civil

☐ YR-CAA	92 King Air 350	FL-73	Civil Aviation Directorate, Bucharest.	(G-CCCB)
☐ YR-RLA	93 Beech 1900D	UE-69	LAR Romanian Airlines, Bucharest.	YR-AAK
☐ YR-RLB	93 Beech 1900D	UE-73	LAR Romanian Airlines, Bucharest.	YR-AAL

YS = EL SALVADOR Total 2
Civil

| ☐ YS-111N | 00 King Air B200 | BB-1707 | Corporacion CentroAmericana de Servicios de Navegacion Aerea | N205TS |
| ☐ YS-210P | King Air C90 | ... | noted Belize 1/06. | |

YU = SERBIA Total 4
Civil

☐ YU-BMM	80 PA-31T Cheyenne II	8020021	Government Flight Inspection, Belgrade.	(D-IOOO)
☐ YU-BPF	80 PA-31T Cheyenne II	8020006	JAT General Aviation, Belgrade.	N801CM
☐ YU-BPG	80 PA-31T Cheyenne II	8020012	JAT General Aviation, Belgrade.	N2328W
☐ YU-BPH	80 PA-31T Cheyenne II	8020063	JAT General Aviation, Belgrade.	N2389V

YV = VENEZUELA Total 314
Civil

☐ YV	81 Conquest II	441-0195	Compania de Inversiones El Ganje CA	N195FW
☐ YV	77 Rockwell 690B	11388	Servicios ECAE C.A., Caracas	N690ES
☐ YV	68 King Air B90	LJ-341		N83FM
☐ YV	75 King Air C90	LJ-649		N102AJ
☐ YV	75 King Air A100	B-209		N14CF
☐ YV	74 Rockwell 690A	11161	Maralac C.A.	N291RB
☐ YV	64 Gulfstream 1	129	Yacimientos California C.A., Caracas	N129AF
☐ YV	74 Rockwell 690A	11171		N690JJ
☐ YV	80 Gulfstream 980	95034		N980GM
☐ YV	94 King Air B200	BB-1479		(N47BW)
☐ YV	07 King Air C90GT	LJ-1828		N7328B
☐ YV	06 King Air C90GT	LJ-1787	Aviaservice International NV. Netherlands Antilles.	N71957
☐ YV	77 Conquest II	441-0001	Aeroservicios Avionorte S.A., Valencia, Carabobo	N983SM
☐ YV	67 King Air A90	LJ-270		N26540
☐ YV	81 SA-226T Merlin 3B	T-407		N402ML
☐ YV	79 King Air 200	BB-427	Importadora 763 CA. Caracas, Venezuela.	N101GQ
☐ YV-	79 King Air 200	BB-562	Transporte Aereo Del Ejecutivo Nacio, Venezuela	N120FN
☐ YV-	78 SA-226T Merlin 3A	T-290		N75RM
☐ YV-	80 King Air F90	LA-60	Toyama Maquinaria S.A. Valencia	N41WL
☐ YV-	77 Conquest II	441-0022	Supreme Year C.A.	N889DM
☐ YV-	76 King Air 200	BB-122		(N719HT)
☐ YV-...	82 SA-227AT Merlin 4C	AT-532	Air Trans CA. Caracas.	N3110B
☐ YV-...	70 SA-26AT Merlin 2B	T26-175		N499SP
☐ YV-...	77 King Air 200	BB-265	Servicios Tecnicos Maracaibo.	YV-141CP
☐ YV-...	84 Gulfstream 900	15034		N900DJ
☐ YV-...	82 Gulfstream 900	15012		YV-903P
☐ YV-...	79 King Air 200	BB-556		N79GA
☐ YV-...	81 Gulfstream 840	11694		N101KJ
☐ YV-...	79 Conquest II	441-0097	Dr Pedro Binaggia, Caracas.	N434AE

| Reg | Yr Type | c/n | Owner/Operator | Prev Regn |

Reg	Yr	Type	c/n	Owner/Operator	Prev Regn
☐ YV-....	80 Gulfstream 840	11632	Caraven SA. Caracas.		N711QP
☐ YV....	78 Conquest II	441-0040	Inversiones Pret a Porter CA. Caracas.		(N441RA)
☐ YV....	82 Conquest II	441-0259	Corporacion Avianturismo SA. Caracas.		N441CD
☐ YV-....	84 SA-227TT Merlin 3C	TT-507			N507TT
☐ YV-.	69 King Air B90	LJ-464	Edgar Heldes Garcia, Miranda.		N36DD
☐ YV-....	66 King Air A90	LJ-151			N28AB
☐ YV-.	75 King Air 200	BB-78			N694FC
☐ YV-.	66 King Air A90	LJ-130	Fabio Palmerini Munerato, Caracas.		N70UA
☐ YV-....	76 King Air 200	BB-133			N717HT
☐ YV-....	68 King Air B90	LJ-383	Pablo Rafael Vero, Valencia Carabobo.		N388MC
☐ YV-....	66 King Air A90	LJ-124			N6238N
☐ YV-....	69 SA-26AT Merlin 2B	T26-142	Victor Moucado,		N226HA
☐ YV-....	66 King Air A90	LJ-146			N77DA
☐ YV-....	71 King Air C90	LJ-503			N193A
☐ YV-....	95 King Air C90B	LJ-1388	Toyoandina SA. Trujillo.		N580AC
☐ YV-....	78 King Air 200	BB-391			N1969C
☐ YV-....	68 680W Turbo Commander	1762-8	Kenneth Mendez, Arturo Michelena.		N2755B
☐ YV-....	00 King Air B200	BB-1706	Aeroservicios Catatumbo SA. Maracaibo.		N3206M
☐ YV-....	77 Rockwell 690B	11413	Offshore Outsourcing Services International, Panama City.		N502DT
☐ YV-....	83 Conquest II	441-0319	Jhon Aurelio Tursini, Charallave, Venezuela.		N6412Q
☐ YV-....	79 King Air C90	LJ-810			N811GA
☐ YV-....	78 Conquest II	441-0060			N88598
☐ YV-....	69 Mitsubishi MU-2F	165			YV-1067P
☐ YV-....	75 King Air 200	BB-67			N78DV
☐ YV-....	68 King Air B90	LJ-374			N54CF
☐ YV-....	77 King Air 200	BB-279			N279CA
☐ YV-....	79 King Air 200	BB-507			N507K
☐ YV-....	67 King Air A90	LJ-224			N464AB
☐ YV-....	75 King Air 200	BB-31	Julio Gonzales, Caracas.		N600KW
☐ YV-....	68 King Air B90	LJ-396			N70SM
☐ YV-....	75 King Air 200	BB-51			5Y-BIR
☐ YV-....	66 King Air A90	LJ-147	Avioicaro, Caracas.		N198BC
☐ YV-....	76 King Air 200	BB-107	Daniel B Alejando, Caracas.		N115TT
☐ YV-....	67 King Air A90	LJ-240			N360D
☐ YV-....	85 King Air 300	FA-51			N20NK
☐ YV-....	66 King Air A90	LJ-167			N290RD
☐ YV-....	82 King Air B100	BE-128			(N56TJ)
☐ YV-....	77 King Air A100	B-231			N38P
☐ YV-....	76 King Air 200	BB-167			N300DK
☐ YV-....	81 King Air 200	BB-790			N64GA
☐ YV-....	67 King Air A90	LJ-222			(N901AS)
☐ YV-....	67 King Air A90	LJ-195	Hector Enrique Acosta, Caracas.		N98DD
☐ YV-....	69 King Air B90	LJ-452			N452TT
☐ YV-....	74 King Air 200	BB-17			N900CV
☐ YV-....	70 King Air B90	LJ-495			N71WH
☐ YV-....	81 King Air 200	BB-779			F-GEPY
☐ YV-....	68 King Air B90	LJ-357	(status ?).		N887KU
☐ YV-....	80 King Air 200	BB-613			N613JR
☐ YV-....	67 King Air A90	LJ-202			(N474DP)
☐ YV-....	62 Gulfstream 1	92			N3NA
☐ YV-....	59 Gulfstream 1	18	Mandel Teineira Vzgra, Caracas.		N48PA
☐ YV-....	79 Conquest II	441-0072	Corporacion Aerostar 521 CA. Caracas.		N441TF
☐ YV-....	80 Conquest II	441-0140	Inversiones Leasing Plane 2004, Caracas, Venezuela.		N604RR
☐ YV-....	67 King Air A90	LJ-266			N55LH
☐ YV-....	72 Rockwell 690	11030			N399GM
☐ YV-....	82 Conquest II	441-0250			N691AC
☐ YV-....	77 King Air C-12A	BC-51			N48JA
☐ YV-.....	71 King Air C90	LJ-511			N1UV
☐ YV0100	82 Gulfstream 1000	96016	Ministry of Transport & Communications, Caracas.		YV-O-MIF-1
☐ YV-0104	King Air B200	...			
☐ YV0106	74 King Air C-12L	BB-5	Servicio Autonomo de Transport Aereo, Caracas.		YV-O-SATA
☐ YV0115	78 Rockwell 690B	11500	Fondo Nacional Desarrollos Urbanos, Caracas.		YV-O-FDU-
☐ YV0138	91 King Air 350	FL-55			YV-112CP
☐ YV0145	74 Rockwell 690A	11198	Gabriel Matheus, Caracas.		YV-O-GPA1
☐ YV0149	81 Gulfstream 840	11657	CADAFE-CA de Administraciones y Fomento Electrico, Caracas.		YV-O-KWH-

Reg	Yr	Type	c/n	Owner/Operator	Prev Regn
☐ YV0154	80	Gulfstream 980	95010		ETE-1363
☐ YV-04CP	70	King Air 100	B-73		(N73PD)
☐ YV-1000CP	91	King Air C90A	LJ-1273		YV-2282P
☐ YV-1013P	80	King Air F90	LA-16	L F Mendoza Aristeguieta, Caracas.	YV-2289P
☐ YV1035	66	680V Turbo Commander	1538-5	Pro-Ambiente SA. Maturin, Monaga.	N100BP
☐ YV-1051P	80	King Air 200	BB-656		YV-2576P
☐ YV1054	78	King Air C90	LJ-786	Inversiones Angaz CA.	YV-972CP
☐ YV-105CP	81	Gulfstream 840	11685	(reported stolen ?)	N840BC
☐ YV1066	71	681B Turbo Commander	6061	Corporacion OK Inc CA. Caracas.	N520CS
☐ YV1085	77	Rockwell 690B	11390		YV-649P
☐ YV1159	79	King Air B100	BE-61		YV-903P
☐ YV1173	83	Gulfstream 900	15022		YV-521CP
☐ YV1177	75	Rockwell 690A	11245		YV-69CP
☐ YV1187	87	Reims/Cessna F406	F406-0022		YV-990CP
☐ YV-121CP	91	King Air B200	BB-1398	(reported stolen ?).	
☐ YV1239	75	King Air A100	B-214		N46BE
☐ YV1245	78	King Air C90	LJ-756		YV-172CP
☐ YV-124CP	77	PA-31T Cheyenne II	7720047	Agropecuaria Garza CA.	
☐ YV1257	73	King Air A100	B-161	Violeta Aviles Pernia, Charallave Miranda.	YV- 2615P
☐ YV1271	78	Rockwell 690B	11464	Arrendaven CA. Caracas.	YV-227CP
☐ YV-1300P	77	King Air 200	BB-282	(reported stolen ?).	YV-131CP
☐ YV1306	77	King Air A100	B-237		YV-1104CP
☐ YV1315	80	Gulfstream 840	11618		YV-39CP
☐ YV1325	81	Gulfstream 840	11698		YV-1102CP
☐ YV1348	73	Rockwell 690A	11131		N8535
☐ YV1349		King Air C90	...	noted Aruba 11/06.	
☐ YV1387	80	King Air 200	BB-602		N981LE
☐ YV1397	81	PA-31T Cheyenne II	8120013		YV-1995B
☐ YV-1402P	78	PA-31T Cheyenne II	7820067		N331PC
☐ YV-1405P	67	680V Turbo Commander	1719-90	Silvio Guedes,	YV-0-CVG-
☐ YV1412	82	SA-227TT Merlin 4C	TT-465	Servicios Aeronauticos de Oriente CA.	YV-695CP
☐ YV1443	79	PA-31T Cheyenne 1	7904013		YV-171P
☐ YV-144CP	77	Mitsubishi MU-2N	702SA		N862MA
☐ YV1456	78	Rockwell 690B	11490	Transporte Turbo Commander CA.	YV-918CP
☐ YV1459	74	Rockwell 690A	11207	Luis Enriquez Nunez,	YV-733P
☐ YV1465	77	King Air E90	LW-234	Aerotecnica SA. Caracas.	YV-118CP
☐ YV1486	70	King Air 100	B-16		YV-801CP
☐ YV-1500P	78	King Air E90	LW-270	Police Air Wing, Caracas.	
☐ YV-1507		King Air 100	...	(status ?).	
☐ YV1566		Rockwell 690A	...		
☐ YV-158CP	78	King Air C90	LJ-742		
☐ YV1595		King Air 90	...	noted Fort Lauderdale 2/06.	
☐ YV1599	68	King Air B90	LJ-370		YV-555CP-
☐ YV1603	00	King Air B200	BB-1712	Aviaservice CA. Caracas.	YV-639CP
☐ YV1607	81	King Air C90	LJ-973	Transportes Guyanes SA.	YV-436CP
☐ YV1617	82	Gulfstream 900	15017	DCA-Directorate of Civil Aeronautics, Caracas.	YV-880CP
☐ YV1632	77	Rockwell 690B	11377		YV-116CP
☐ YV1649	93	King Air C90B	LJ-1329		YV-1069CP
☐ YV1651		PA-31T Cheyenne	...		
☐ YV1676	04	P-180 Avanti	1086		I-BPAF
☐ YV-167CP	78	King Air C90	LJ-751	Artico SA.	
☐ YV1693	82	King Air F90	LA-174	Consorcio Industrial de Zulia, Caracas.	YV-702CP
☐ YV1694	99	King Air B200	BB-1671		YV-949CP
☐ YV1695	79	King Air C90	LJ-865	Vinccler CA.	YV-263CP
☐ YV1705	78	Conquest II	441-0063	Inversiones Salvador Salvatierra SA. Caracas.	YV-2390P
☐ YV1730	79	King Air 200	BB-440		YV-238CP
☐ YV1731	80	King Air 200	BB-598		YV-335CP
☐ YV1733	82	King Air B200	BB-1020		YV-488CP
☐ YV1750	84	Conquest 1	425-0189	Transporte Lucania CA. Valencia.	YV-2767P
☐ YV1753	78	Conquest II	441-0067	Servicios Aereos Tampa C.A.	YV-225CP
☐ YV1758	75	Rockwell 690A	11244		YV-109CP
☐ YV1777	83	Gulfstream 900	15032		YV-777CP
☐ YV-177T	76	SA-226T Merlin 3A	T-268		N502WC
☐ YV1787	75	Rockwell 690A	11264	Juan Otaola Pevan,	YV-01P
☐ YV1796	76	Rockwell 690A	11329		YV-86CP

Reg	Yr	Type	c/n	Owner/Operator	Prev Regn
☐ YV1835	82	Gulfstream 840	11725		YV-792CP
☐ YV1838	73	King Air A100	B-136		N700AT
☐ YV1839	88	King Air 300	FA-158	Inversiones Alas Bajas CA. Caracas.	YV-2401P
☐ YV1841	75	Rockwell 690A	11239	Benjamin Guillermo, Miami, Fl. USA.	YV-2317P
☐ YV1846	76	Rockwell 690A	11288	F Bermudez Motors CA. Caracas.	YV-192CP
☐ YV1851	84	Gulfstream 840	11735		YV-212P
☐ YV1857	85	Conquest II	441-0356		HK-3532
☐ YV-188CP	78	Rockwell 690B	11461		(N81763)
☐ YV1892	82	Gulfstream 840	11726	Inversiones Puerta Plata CA. Caracas.	YV-2505P
☐ YV1894	95	Beech 1900D	UE-157	Toyota Cars de Venezuela	YV-837CP
☐ YV189T	77	Rockwell 690B	11359		N690NA
☐ YV1909	77	King Air 200	BB-195	King Man SA. Panama City, Panama.	N5LE
☐ YV1923	82	SA-227TT Merlin 300	TT-447	Inversiones AGAP CA. Nueva Esparta.	YV-718CP
☐ YV1932	79	Rockwell 690B	11515		YV-2422P
☐ YV1957	83	Conquest 1	425-0162		YV-2263P
☐ YV1959	75	Rockwell 690A	11253	C Acosta, Caracas.	YV-2593P
☐ YV196T	79	King Air 200	BB-540	Wyngs Aviation CA. Caracas.	YV-946CP
☐ YV197T	00	King Air C90B	LJ-1605		YV-1074CP
☐ YV-1990P	75	PA-31T Cheyenne II	7520027		YV-08CP
☐ YV1994	79	Rockwell 690B	11547	Inversiones 12-6-86 CA. Caracas.	YV-532CP
☐ YV1998	78	Rockwell 690B	11483	MUTACA-Multitransporte Aereo CA. Caracas.	YV-218CP
☐ YV2001	79	Rockwell 690B	11532	Oficina Tecnica Vemef CA. Caracas.	YV-690P
☐ YV2006	78	PA-31T Cheyenne II	7820052		YV-194CP
☐ YV2009	78	Rockwell 690B	11499	Constructora Gualpac C.A., Caracas	N499WC
☐ YV2010	71	King Air 100	B-80	Antonio Korol, Caracas.	N424SW
☐ YV2020	81	Gulfstream 980	95084		YV-787CP
☐ YV-2034P	75	King Air C90	LJ-659		YV-410CP
☐ YV2037	76	Rockwell 690A	11325	Gustavo Jimenez Pocaterra,	YV-07CP
☐ YV2045	82	SA-227TT Merlin 3C	TT-459A		YV-292CP
☐ YV2048	78	Rockwell 690B	11448		N246MC
☐ YV-204CP	78	Rockwell 690B	11466		(N81769)
☐ YV2056	78	Rockwell 690B	11443		YV-1050P
☐ YV2078	84	King Air B200	BB-1157		RP-C5555
☐ YV2090	80	Gulfstream 980	95017	Inversiones 301 CA. Caracas.	YV-56CP
☐ YV2094	77	Rockwell 690B	11366		YV-775CP
☐ YV2099	80	Gulfstream 840	11603		YV-170CP
☐ YV2122	77	Rockwell 690B	11378		YV-143CP
☐ YV2129	71	King Air 100	B-83		YV-631CP
☐ YV2160	77	Rockwell 690B	11405	Transporte 454 SA. Caracas.	YV-454CP
☐ YV2175	81	Gulfstream 980	95058	Aeropetrol CA. Caracas.	YV-893CP
☐ YV2176	78	Rockwell 690B	11488		YV-243CP
☐ YV217T	79	PA-31T Cheyenne II	7920021		YV-723P
☐ YV2184	76	Rockwell 690A	11285		YV-81CP
☐ YV2188	77	Mitsubishi MU-2P	348SA		YV-2604P
☐ YV218T	01	King Air C90B	LJ-1659		YV-931CP
☐ YV2222	78	Rockwell 690B	11468		YV-2588P
☐ YV2226	77	King Air B100	BE-28		YV-127CP
☐ YV2229	74	Rockwell 690A	11180		YV-907CP
☐ YV-223CP	78	King Air C90	LJ-789	Trafi CA.	N2016L
☐ YV223T	78	Rockwell 690B	11472		YV-2694P
☐ YV2247	73	Rockwell 690A	11114	Servicios Aeronauticos 4 CA. Maracaibo.	YV-834CP
☐ YV2249	83	Gulfstream 900	15030		YV-822CP
☐ YV224T	80	Gulfstream 980	95009	Dr V G Ramirez,	YV-2566P
☐ YV2252	73	Rockwell 690	11061	Inversiones Regionales 001 CA. Caracas.	YV-854CP
☐ YV2256	75	Rockwell 690A	11228	Clover Internacional CA. Caracas.	YV-2812P
☐ YV-2280P	68	680W Turbo Commander	1804-26	John S Calcurian,	YV-O-INOS-
☐ YV228T	79	Conquest II	441-0100		N234CC
☐ YV-229CP	78	Rockwell 690B	11502		(N81842)
☐ YV2310	83	SA-227TT Merlin 3C	TT-468		YV-612CP
☐ YV-2323P	83	King Air B200C	BL-66		
☐ YV-2331P	78	PA-31T Cheyenne II	7820070	Boscolo Smeraldo Smeraldi, Caracas.	N6033A
☐ YV-2346P	81	Gulfstream 840	11671		YV-439CP
☐ YV-2365P	78	PA-31T Cheyenne II	7820037		N24E
☐ YV-2383P	70	681 Turbo Commander	6005		N35WA
☐ YV2392	06	King Air B200	BB-1966		N37066

Reg	Yr	Type	c/n	Owner/Operator	Prev Regn
YV-2404P	70	681 Turbo Commander	6029		N9074N
YV-242CP	80	SA-226T Merlin 3B	T-357	Transportes 242 CA. Caracas.	N30042
YV-2436P	68	680W Turbo Commander	1814-31	Diego Levine, Maracaibo.	N71AF
YV-2451P	77	PA-31T Cheyenne II	7720050	L Rosalen Hernandez, La Carlota.	YV-153CP
YV246T	79	Rockwell 690B	11539	Constructora La Pista CA. Caracas, Venezuela.	N729CC
YV-2475P	71	681B Turbo Commander	6052		N105SS
YV-2488P	74	Rockwell 690A	11190	Transporte Lehmacorp CA. Caracas.	N8KG
YV-2501P	70	681 Turbo Commander	6024	Julio Borges, Caracas.	N22WK
YV-251CP	79	PA-31T Cheyenne II	7920022	Multiservicios NISA CA.	
YV-257CP	79	King Air 200	BB-517	Inversiones Rizo CA. (status ?).	
YV-2584P	78	King Air 200	BB-316	Tocars SA. Caracas. (status ?).	YV-168CP
YV-2588P		Rockwell 690B	...		
YV-258CP	70	King Air B90	LJ-488	Molinpast CA. La Carlota.	YV-2229P
YV261T	78	SA-226T Merlin 3B	T-292		(N1AQ)
YV-262CP	84	SA-227TT Merlin 300	TT-521		D-IOOO
YV-2710P	80	King Air 200	BB-632		YV-1873P
YV-2812P		Rockwell 690A	...		
YV-2822P		PA-31T Cheyenne	...	(status ?).	
YV-2834P	78	King Air 200	BB-346	Hector Rafael Hernandez, Caracas. (status ?).	N747MB
YV-2835P	78	King Air C90	LJ-784	Atilio Yanez, Coro Esado Falcon.	N62SK
YV-290CP	80	King Air F90	LA-35	C A de Edificaciones - Resid D Paulo.	
YV-2710P	80	King Air 200	BB-632		
YV319T	78	Rockwell 690B	11471	Jose Pernia	(N622HC)
YV-326P	76	King Air E90	LW-172	G Bracho,	
YV-32P	89	King Air C90A	LJ-1191	Aviaservice CA. Caracas.	
YV-344P	67	680V Turbo Commander	1718-89		YV-340CP
YV-394CP	80	Gulfstream 840	11637	Construcciones Humboldt SA. Caracas.	(N5889K)
YV-401CP	81	King Air 200	BB-796	MUTACA-Multitransporte Aereo CA. Caracas.	
YV-403CP	81	King Air 200C	BL-23	Ministry of National Defence, Caracas.	
YV-407CP	81	Gulfstream 980	95067	(reported stolen ?).	(N9819S)
YV-42CP	80	King Air 350	FL-32	PDVSA Petroleo SA. Caracas.	YV-350CP
YV-465CP	72	King Air C90	LJ-556	(status ?)	YV-818P
YV-467CP	74	King Air E90	LW-94	SERVIVENSA-Servicios Avensa SA. Caracas.	N98ME
YV-472CP	83	SA-227TT Merlin 300	TT-471	Transporte Lux CA.	D-IISA
YV-492CP	82	Gulfstream 900	15006	(reported stolen ?)	N5852N
YV-505CP	82	Gulfstream 840	11723	(reported stolen ?).	YV-45CP
YV-516CP	79	King Air E90	LW-322	Servicios Avensa SA.	N600FC
YV-533P	81	Conquest II	441-0227	Jesus Romero,	N6854T
YV-536P	68	680W Turbo Commander	1813-30		YV-T-VTY
YV-53CP	83	Gulfstream 1000	96067		HK-3271
YV-581CP	80	Gulfstream 980	95007	Inversiones Torgo CA.	(N123RC)
YV-622CP	83	King Air F90-1	LA-207		N2DF
YV-627C	66	Gulfstream 1	170	TAAN-Transporte Aereo Andino SA. Caracas.	YV-620CP
YV-628C	66	Gulfstream 1	171	TAAN-Transporte Aereo Andino SA. Caracas.	YV-621CP
YV-660CP	95	King Air C90B	LJ-1401		N3270K
YV-663CP	77	Rockwell 690B	11358	MUTACA-Multitransporte Aereo CA. Caracas.	N810GF
YV-703CP	78	PA-31T Cheyenne II	7820008	Jose Manuel Aguilera,	N14MR
YV-706P	77	King Air E90	LW-208	DIM-Direccion Intelligencia Militar, Caracas.	
YV-710CP	79	SA-226T Merlin 3B	T-301	Aero Halcon 710 CA. Caracas.	N175WB
YV-740CP	82	SA-227TT Merlin 3C	TT-456		N3019U
YV-744CP	66	680T Turbo Commander	1685-66		YV-2435P
YV-770CP	81	SA-226T Merlin 3B	T-384		YV-2395P
YV-773CP	81	Gulfstream 840	11666	Margarita Aviacion Internacional CA. Margarita.	YV-626CP
YV-808CP	82	SA-227TT Merlin 3C	TT-435	Aero Centro de Servicios CA. Caracas.	N92RC
YV-820CP	68	680W Turbo Commander	1775-13	Executive CA. Caracas.	N9RN
YV-877CP	92	King Air B300C	FM-8	PDVSA Petroleo SA. Caracas.	N55684
YV-87CP	81	Gulfstream 840	11654	Aero Williams CA. Caracas.	N1NT
YV-886CP	82	King Air F90	LA-179	Banco Fomento Region de los Andes,	YV-486CP
YV-903CP	66	Gulfstream 1	173	Maria de Jesus Morano, Barcelona.	N173BT
YV-910CP	98	King Air 350	FL-206	Wyngs Aviation CA. Caracas.	N23227
YV-95CP	77	King Air B100	BE-19	Banco Nacional de Venezuela, Caracas.	
YV-980CP	80	Gulfstream 980	95028		N980CF
YV-980P	76	Rockwell 690A	11318		YV-98CP
YV-991CP	84	PA-42 Cheyenne 400LS	5527009		N941AA
YVO104	80	King Air 200	BB-701	Sistema Autonomo de Transporte y Servicio, Miranda.	YV-O-SATA
YV-O-BDA-3	76	Mitsubishi MU-2L	685	Agricultural Development State Bank,	N845MA

Reg	Yr Type	c/n	Owner/Operator	Prev Regn
☐ YV-O-CBL-5	80 King Air C90	LJ-889	State Government Ciudad Bolivar.	YV-354CP
☐ YV-O-IGV-1	77 SA-226T Merlin 3A	T-287		YV-693CP
☐ YV-O-MAC-2	79 PA-31T Cheyenne 1	7904040	Ministry of Agriculture, Caracas.	YV-239CP
☐ YV-O-MAR-1	76 Rockwell 690A	11323		YV-2437P
☐ YV-O-MIF-2	78 Rockwell 690B	11430	Ministry of Transport & Communications, Caracas.	YV-O-MTC-
☐ YV-O-MTC-5	76 Rockwell 690A	11281	Ministry of Transport & Communications, Caracas.	N57183
☐ YV-O-PTJ-2	83 King Air B200	BB-1092		YV-2352P
☐ YV-O-SATA-177	King Air 200	BB-223	Sistema Autonomo de Transporte y Servicio, Miranda.	YV-O-FMO-
☐ YV-O-SATA-277	King Air 200	BB-261	Sistema Autonomo de Transporte y Servicio, Miranda.	YV-791CP
☐ YV-O-SATA-377	King Air 200	BB-273	Sistema Autonomo de Transporte y Servicio, Miranda.	YV-O-FMO-
☐ YV-O-SATA-580	King Air 200	BB-731	Sistema Autonomo de Transporte y Servicio, Miranda.	YV-O-BIV-1
☐ YV-O-SATA-776	King Air E90	LW-189	Sistema Autonomo de Transporte y Servicio, Miranda.	YV-O-INV-3
☐ YV-O-SID-2	73 King Air A100	B-155	Siderurgica del Orinoco CA. Caracas.	

Military

Reg	Yr Type	c/n	Owner/Operator	Prev Regn
☐ 2840	79 King Air 200	BB-520	FAV, Caracas.	
☐ 3150	79 King Air 200	BB-522	FAV, Caracas.	
☐ 3240	81 King Air 200C	BL-19	FAV, Caracas.	
☐ 3280	81 King Air 200C	BL-18	FAV, Caracas.	
☐ ARBV-0212	81 King Air B200	BB-906	Venezuelan Navy	ARV-0212
☐ ARV-0201	78 King Air E90	LW-264	Venezuelan Navy, Caracas.	TR-0201
☐ EV-7702	77 King Air E90	LW-229	Venezuelan Army, Caracas.	
☐ EV-7910	79 King Air 200	BB-495	Venezuelan Army, Caracas.	
☐ GN-7593	75 King Air E90	LW-154	Venezuelan National Guard, Caracas.	N211DG
☐ GN-7839	78 King Air E90	LW-260	Venezuelan National Guard, Caracas.	
☐ GN-8270	82 King Air B200C	BL-51	Venezuelan National Guard, Caracas.	
☐ GN-8595	82 King Air B200	BB-980	Venezuelan National Guard, Caracas.	YV-466CP

Z = ZIMBABWE   Total   8

Civil

Reg	Yr Type	c/n	Owner/Operator	Prev Regn
☐ Z-AHL	77 King Air E90	LW-205	Debonair P/L., Harare	Z-DJF
☐ Z-DDD	92 Reims/Cessna F406	F406-0069	Government/Falcon Air, Harare.	F-GIOD
☐ Z-DDE	92 Reims/Cessna F406	F406-0068	Government/Falcon Air, Harare.	F-GIQC
☐ Z-DDF	93 Reims/Cessna F406	F406-0071	Government/Falcon Air, Harare.	F-GIQE
☐ Z-DDG	92 Reims/Cessna F406	F406-0067	Government/Falcon Air, Harare.	F-GEUG
☐ Z-LCS	79 King Air C90	LJ-848	EGAS Flight Academy of Zimbabwe, Harare.	TR-LCS
☐ Z-WRD	76 King Air C90	LJ-687	Delta Corp. Harare.	N127P
☐ Z-WSG	81 King Air 200	BB-748	Medical Air Rescue Service P/L. Harare.	N154BB

ZK = NEW ZEALAND   Total   15

Civil

Reg	Yr Type	c/n	Owner/Operator	Prev Regn
☐ ZK-KOH	70 Mitsubishi MU-2G	521	Helicopter Services (BOP) Ltd. Taupo.	VH-KOH
☐ ZK-LHL	83 Conquest 1	425-0171	Lakeland Helicopters (1989) Ltd. Rotorua.	N51CU
☐ ZK-MAN	90 King Air B200	BB-1366	Hawker Pacific NZ Ltd., Papakura	VH-IMP
☐ ZK-MKG	94 King Air C90SE	LJ-1367	Air Wanganui Commuter Ltd.	N111MU
☐ ZK-MOH	72 Rockwell 690	11006	NZ Aerial Mapping Ltd. Hastings.	HZ-SS1
☐ ZK-NFD	80 Conquest II	441-0141	Garden City Helicopters, Christchurch.	VH-CFD
☐ ZK-POD	77 PA-31T Cheyenne II	7720009	Cx ZK- 4/01 to ?	ZK-MPI
☐ ZK-PVB	76 Rockwell 690A	11321	New Zealand Aerial Mapping Ltd. Albany.	VH-DLK
☐ ZK-VAF	91 Reims/Cessna F406	F406-0057	Vincent Aviation Ltd. Wellington.	F-ODYZ
☐ ZK-XLC	86 Reims/Cessna F406	F406-0012	Kiwi Aviation Ltd, Gisbourne.	ZKVAA

Military

Reg	Yr Type	c/n	Owner/Operator	Prev Regn
☐ NZ1881	82 King Air B200	BB-1054	RNZAF, 42 Squadron, Ohakea.	ZK-KAB
☐ NZ1882	82 King Air B200	BB-1008	RNZAF, 42 Squadron, Ohakea.	ZK-KAC
☐ NZ1883	82 King Air B200	BB-1087	RNZAF, 42 Squadron, Ohakea.	ZK-KAD
☐ NZ1884	84 King Air B200	BB-1178	RNZAF, 42 Squadron, Ohakea.	ZK-KAF
☐ NZ1885	82 King Air B200	BB-968	RNZAF, 42 Squadron, Ohakea.	ZK-KAG

ZP = PARAGUAY   Total   16

Civil

Reg	Yr Type	c/n	Owner/Operator	Prev Regn
☐ ZP-...	85 Conquest 1	425-0223		N1226G
☐ ZP-...	81 Gulfstream 980	95053		N73DQ
☐ ZP-...	83 Gulfstream 900	15021	Carlos Alberto Matiauda, Asuncion.	N908TN
☐ ZP-...	82 SA-227TT Merlin 4C	TT-462A		N453CP
☐ ZP-...	80 Gulfstream 980	95035	Jesus Gutierrez, Asuncion.	N200JN
☐ ZP-TFV	Rockwell 690	...	noted Asuncion 9/05.	
☐ ZP-TIW	77 Rockwell 690B	11394		N531GK

Reg   Yr Type   c/n   Owner/Operator   Prev Regn

Reg	Yr Type	c/n	Owner/Operator	Prev Regn
☐ ZP-TJW	78 King Air E90	LW-284	GOYA S A C A. Asuncion.	N200WB
☐ ZP-TTU	80 Gulfstream 980	95021	Roberto Barchini,	ZP-PTU
☐ ZP-TWY	85 Gulfstream 1000	96095	Aero Commercial SRL. Asuncion.	N73DC
☐ ZP-TWZ	82 Gulfstream 900	15005	(status ?).	N5841N
☐ ZP-TXF	85 Gulfstream 1000	96079	Aero Commercial SRL. Asuncion.	N169CR
☐ ZP-TXG	85 Gulfstream 1000B	96203	Aero Commercial SRL. Asuncion.	N64JT
☐ ZP-TYI	80 PA-31T Cheyenne II	8020066	Itaipu Binacional, Asuncion.	N555HP
☐ ZP-TYZ	PA-42 Cheyenne	...	G Saba, Asuncion.	
☐ ZP-TZW	78 King Air E90	LW-261	Administracion Nacional de Electricidad, Asuncion.	N4283R

ZS = SOUTH AFRICA   Total   204
Civil

Reg	Yr Type	c/n	Owner/Operator	Prev Regn
☐ ZS-ACS	82 King Air B200	BB-961	Naturelink Charters P/L. Wonderboom.	A2-AHA
☐ ZS-AGI	02 Pilatus PC-12/45	471	Majuba Aviation P/L. Laneria.	HB-FQN
☐ ZS-ALD	82 King Air F90	LA-160	C T Van der Merwe Boerdery, Dendron.	N982SA
☐ ZS-ALX	62 Gulfstream 1	86	Tramon Air CC. Lanseria.	N10TB
☐ ZS-AMS	07 Pilatus PC-12/47	845	SA Red Cross Air Mercy Service, Cape Town	
☐ ZS-APS	06 Pilatus PC-12/47	771	South African Police Services, Wonderboom	HB-.
☐ ZS-ASB	81 King Air B200	BB-903	Turbine Air Partnership, Saxonwold	A2-BHM
☐ ZS-ASM	76 Conquest II	441-0698	SAM Aviation (PTY) Ltd., Saxonwold	5N-JBN
☐ ZS-AVH	06 Pilatus PC-12/47	713	Zulu Echo November P/L. Parklands.	HB-F..
☐ ZS-BCI	07 TBM 850	397	Bravo Capital Investments P/L., Sandton	F-OIKI
☐ ZS-BEB	97 Pilatus PC-12/45	180	The SARX Partnership, Lanseria.	HB-FSP
☐ ZS-CBL	00 King Air B200	BB-1742	NAC P/L. Lanseria.	N4288L
☐ ZS-CCK	07 King Air B200	BB-1987	Fourie's Poultry Farms P/L.,Potchefstrom.	N987KA
☐ ZS-COH	02 Pilatus PC-12	436	The Pilatus Partnership, Lanseria.	HB-...
☐ ZS-COP	89 King Air C90A	LJ-1204	South African Police Services, Wonderboom.	N1552D
☐ ZS-CPM	05 King Air B200	BB-1911	CPM Air Charter P/L. Capetown.	N36871
☐ ZS-CPX	81 Conquest 1	425-0071	ONZ Partnership, Lanseria.	N6845R
☐ ZS-CSC	82 King Air C90-1	LJ-1034	Manetrade 120 P/L. Northlands.	ZS-CPM
☐ ZS-CVH	81 King Air 200C	BL-32	Hands On Aviation P/L. Lanseria.	C9-ASX
☐ ZS-CWM	06 Pilatus PC-12/47	739	Ndzhakeni Investments P/L. Johannesburg.	HB-F..
☐ ZS-DAT	98 Pilatus PC-12/45	242	Hands on Aviation P/L. Lanseria.	HB-FR.
☐ ZS-DCG	01 PA-46-500TP Meridian	4697055	Goswell Developments P/L. Cato Ridge.	N53283
☐ ZS-DER	04 Pilatus PC-12/45	554	Blue Nightingale Trading 129 P/L. Nigel.	HB-...
☐ ZS-DLB	07 Pilatus PC-12/47	791	Pajair Trust, Knysna	HB-.
☐ ZS-DMM	97 Pilatus PC-12/45	198	Inyoni Partnership, Nelspruit.	HB-FQG
☐ ZS-DSL	79 King Air 200	BB-531	Cx ZS- 8/06 to ?	(PH-SKS)
☐ ZS-EFC	66 King Air A90	LJ-161	Fly In SA P/L. Lanseria.	ZS-IRJ
☐ ZS-FDR	85 King Air B200	BB-1234	Federal Air P/L. Durban.	N971LE
☐ ZS-FML	07 King Air 350	FL-534	First Quantum Minerals SA P/L., Rivonia	N71834
☐ ZS-FON	05 King Air C90B	LJ-1735	AVNA Aviation Partnership, Louterwater.	N36735
☐ ZS-FTG	05 Pilatus PC-12/45	615	Ferair CC. Capetown.	HB-F..
☐ ZS-GAA	07 Pilatus PC-12/47	858	Majuba Aviation PTY Ltd	HB-FSS
☐ ZS-GMC	07 Pilatus PC-12/47	797	Gem Diamond Technical Services, Northlands	HB-
☐ ZS-IAN	76 King Air E90	LW-169	Meeca Project CC. Lanseria.	N17SE
☐ ZS-JDD	07 Pilatus PC-12/47	805	Clapham Junction Trading (PTY), Stellenbosch	
☐ ZS-JIS	68 Gulfstream 1	193	King Air Services Partnership, Lanseria.	PK-TRN
☐ ZS-JRA	75 Rockwell 690A	11284	South African Weather Service, Pretoria.	N57273
☐ ZS-JRB	75 Rockwell 690A	11248	South African Weather Service, Pretoria.	N122K
☐ ZS-JRH	77 Rockwell 690B	11421	Trevor Lombard Aviation, Port Elizabeth.	N81672
☐ ZS-JSC	07 King Air B200	BB-1985	King Air Partnership, Houghton	N71850
☐ ZS-KGW	76 King Air 200	BB-381	Blue Moonlight Properties 82 P/L., Tzaneen	N4848M
☐ ZS-KLZ	80 King Air F90	LA-69	R Friedman, Franschhoek.	N6727C
☐ ZS-KMA	81 King Air C90	LJ-930	Flying Colours Aviation P/L. Port Elizabeth.	N3717J
☐ ZS-KSU	81 Conquest 1	425-0115	Cargo Carriers P/L. Johannesburg.	N68807
☐ ZS-KZI	81 King Air C90	LJ-959	B & E International P/L. Rand.	(D-IFIP)
☐ ZS-KZU	79 King Air 200	BB-416	Tafair Partnership P/L. Saxonwold.	N396DP
☐ ZS-KZY	82 Gulfstream 1000	96051	ESCOM-Electricity Supply Commission, Johannesburg.	N9971S
☐ ZS-KZZ	82 Gulfstream 1000	96052	Investec Bank Ltd. Johannesburg.	N9972S
☐ ZS-LAD	92 King Air 350	FL-75	National Airways Corporation P/L., Rand	D-COLA
☐ ZS-LAW	81 King Air B200	BB-889	Swiftflite Charter CC. Lanseria.	N3538K
☐ ZS-LBC	81 King Air F90	LA-122	B C Smither, Bryanston.	N3723N
☐ ZS-LEE	99 King Air C90B	LJ-1565	Gamont Development SA P/L. Three Rivers.	G-ERAD
☐ ZS-LFL	82 King Air C90-1	LJ-1033	Inter Air P/L-Theaco Road & Earthworks P/L. Vanderbijlpark.	N6717T

Reg	Yr	Type	c/n	Owner/Operator	Prev Regn
ZS-LFM	82	King Air B200	BB-954	Aircraft Africa Contracts Co P/L. Lanseria.	N1839S
ZS-LFU	82	King Air B200	BB-1018	Invicta Bearings P/L. Capetown.	3D-LKK
ZS-LFW	82	King Air B200	BB-999	King Air Services Partnership, Lanseria.	9Q-CPV
ZS-LIN	83	King Air C90-1	LJ-1053	Domberg Airways, Magaliessig.	N6891L
ZS-LRM	73	Rockwell 690A	11105	Commander Partnership, Lanseria.	A2-AIH
ZS-LRS	81	King Air 200C	BL-20	King Air Services Partnership, Melville	5Y-LRS
ZS-LSY	81	Cheyenne II-XL	8166031	Hendrik Casper Investments CC. Farrarmere.	V5-LSY
ZS-LTD	80	King Air F90	LA-63	C Troskie Vliegtuie, Cookhouse.	N3686V
ZS-LTF	74	King Air C90	LJ-613	Davy Foods P/L. Durban.	N3053W
ZS-LWD	81	King Air 200	BB-756	Mastermind Tobacco SA P/L. East London.	5Y-BWD
ZS-LYA	75	King Air 200	BB-26	NAC P/L. Lanseria.	N57FM
ZS-LZR	85	King Air C90A	LJ-1118	Crystal Air P/L. Bophuthatswana.	N937BC
ZS-MBZ	78	King Air C90	LJ-795	NAC P/L. Lanseria.	N551GA
ZS-MCA	72	King Air C90	LJ-551	500E Toerusting P/L. Pretoria.	ZS-XAC
ZS-MCO	07	King Air 350	FL-543	Manhattan Resources (PTY) Ltd., Benoni	N543KA
ZS-MES	82	King Air B200	BB-1038	Aircraft Africa Contracts Co P/L. Lanseria.	N223MH
ZS-MGF	74	Mitsubishi MU-2J	622	M I Da Silva, Sonpark.	(3D-AFH)
ZS-MHM	80	King Air F90	LA-47	Multimanaged Investments P/L. Isando.	N984GA
ZS-MIM	81	King Air 200	BB-846	Angolan Aircraft CC. Lanseria.	5Y-BKA
ZS-MIN	81	King Air B200	BB-941	Rossair Executive Air Charter P/L. Lanseria.	N36801
ZS-MKI	85	King Air C90A	LJ-1099	SPH Group P/L. Capetown.	Z-MKI
ZS-MSF	03	Pilatus PC-12/45	506	MSF Air Charter Co P/L. Sandton.	HB-
ZS-MSK	80	King Air 200	BB-597	Angolan Aircraft CC. Lanseria.	5Y-BJC
ZS-MTW	82	King Air B200	BB-1076	National Airways Corporation, Lanseria	C9-PMZ
ZS-MUM	68	King Air B90	LJ-408	Civair Helicopters CC. Capetown.	N481SA
ZS-NAW	82	King Air B200	BB-1027	Aircraft Africa Contracts P/L. Lanseria.	N40AB
ZS-NBJ	82	King Air B200	BB-1070	Investico Properties P/L. Helderberg.	SE-KND
ZS-NBO	80	King Air 200	BB-706	Smith Mining Equipment P/L. /Medair Charter, Lanseria	N25WD
ZS-NFO	80	King Air F90	LA-51	Shurlock International P/L. Pietermaritzburg.	N901NB
ZS-NHW	64	Gulfstream 1	141	Airquarius Air Charter P/L. Lanseria.	N800PA
ZS-NHX	78	King Air 200	BB-386	Vaal Mac Investments P/L. Vanderbijl Park.	N310GA
ZS-NKC	93	King Air B200	BB-1474	Metcash Aviation Services P/L. Lanseria.	N82010
ZS-NOW	92	King Air B200	BB-1427	Aviation Africa Partnership, Isando.	N8003U
ZS-NRR	77	King Air 200	BB-288	Permanne Investments P/L. Linkhills.	5Y-HHG
ZS-NTL	75	King Air 200	BB-85	Aircraft Africa Contracts Co P/L Lanseria.	V5-CIC
ZS-NTT	78	King Air 200	BB-350	Gideon Air P/L. Middelburg.	N125MS
ZS-NUF	79	King Air 200C	BL-4	Aviation Asset Management P/L. Lanseria.	V5-AAL
ZS-NVP	89	King Air B200	BB-1325	Rodo Investments P/L. Lanseria.	OY-LKH
ZS-NWC	74	King Air C90	LJ-625	J Robbertse Vervoer P/L. Hercules.	N50AB
ZS-NWK	75	King Air 200	BB-52	ZS-NWK P/L. Umhlanga Rocks.	N400AJ
ZS-NXH	75	King Air 200	BB-37	Ferox Investments P/L, Johannesburg	F-GPDV
ZS-NXI	77	King Air E90	LW-224	Phillips & Franks Second Hand Dealers CC. Boksburg.	D-IATA
ZS-NXT	95	King Air B200	BB-1502	Associated Managanese Mines, Northern Cape.	N1515E
ZS-NYE	77	King Air E90	LW-222	Barrange P/L. Fochville.	VH-MTG
ZS-NYK	96	BAe Jetstream 41	41095	Government of Kwazulu, Ulundi.	
ZS-NYM	96	Pilatus PC-12	147	NYM Partnership, Bryanston.	(ZS-FDS)
ZS-NZJ	80	King Air 200	BB-630	Out of the Blue Air Safaris P/L. Lanseria.	N630VB
ZS-OAE	75	King Air E90	LW-151	King Air Services Partnership, Lanseria.	TR-LVH
ZS-OAK	77	King Air 200	BB-197	Zelpy 2722 P/L. Lanseria.	(N12154)
ZS-OCI	76	King Air 200	BB-121	Manta Air P/L. Lanseria.	TR-LDX
ZS-ODI	96	King Air B200	BB-1542	Investage 17 P/L. Lanseria.	N202JT
ZS-ODU	94	King Air B200	BB-1476	Swiftflite Charter CC., Lanseria	N109GE
ZS-OEB	79	King Air 200T	BT-7	Baranza Air Services CC. (was BB-510).	(N853GA)
ZS-OED	83	King Air B200	BB-1149	King Air Services Partnership, Lanseria.	N200HF
ZS-OEE	88	Reims/Cessna F406	F406-0023	Fugro Airborne Surveys P/L.	V5-..
ZS-OFB	98	Pilatus PC-12/45	205	PC-XII Serial No 205 P/L. Benmore.	HB-F..
ZS-OFD	98	Pilatus PC-12/45	208	Hydro Holdings P/L. Wonderboom.	HB-F..
ZS-OHB	68	King Air B90	LJ-431	Freebird Aviation P/L. Lanseria.	9Q-CVT
ZS-OHE	89	Beech 1900C-1	UC-48	Solenta Aviation, Lanseria	9J-AFJ
ZS-OHR	75	King Air C90	LJ-669	Peter Vichos Trust, North Riding.	N971GA
ZS-ONB	75	Mitsubishi MU-2L	674	Saratoga Air Services CC. Lanseria.	N299HT
ZS-ONZ	81	Conquest 1	425-0075	C E Puckrin/Springgrove Air, Groenkloof.	ZS-PNP
ZS-OOE	59	Gulfstream 1	5	Merafe Aviation P/L. Randburg	F-GFGT
ZS-OSB	78	King Air 200	BB-327	Trans African Aviation Sales P/L. Lanseria.	N327CM
ZS-OSH	88	King Air 1300	BB-1296	EXG Investments P/L. Lanseria.	PH-DUS
Reg	Yr	Type	c/n	Owner/Operator	Prev Regn

Reg	Yr	Type	c/n	Owner/Operator	Prev Regn
ZS-OTK	82	King Air C90A	LJ-1193	Moyana Leisure P/L.	D2-ETJ
ZS-OTL	82	Cheyenne T-1040	8275011	Montina Boerdery Partnership, Dulwelskloof.	N2VZ
ZS-OTP	80	King Air 200	BB-683	N J Fronemann, Lanseria.	N2877K
ZS-OTS	83	King Air B200	BB-1113	ExDev P/L. Lanseria.	N745RL
ZS-OUI	80	King Air/Catpass 250	BB-688	Skyeinvest Administration P/L. Wynberg.	5R-MGH
ZS-OUO	01	PA-46-500TP Meridian	4697116	C D Wood, Orange Grove.	
ZS-OUP	82	Cheyenne T-1040	8275002	Flying Colours Aviation P/L. Port Elizabeth.	5Y-UAL
ZS-OUS	70	King Air 100	B-57	Lazercor 4 P/L. Port Elizebth.	N190CA
ZS-OUT	81	King Air 200	BB-764	JVS Air P/L. Lanseria.	LV-ONH
ZS-OVX	86	King Air B200	BB-1253	N J Fronemann, Lanseria.	A2-AEO
ZS-OYG	96	Beech 1900D	UE-230	Fourie's Poultry Farms P/L. Potchefstrom.	5N-BCQ
ZS-OYP	80	King Air 200	BB-594	Dezzo Trading 213 P/L. Durban.	N760BM
ZS-PAM	81	King Air 200	BB-813	Aircraft Africa Contracts Co P/L. Lanseria.	VH-IBF
ZS-PAZ	84	King Air 300	FA-25	Bonn Plant Hire P/L. Bon Accord.	N856GA
ZS-PBH	70	King Air 100	B-9	Warne Aviation P/L. Lanseria.	3C-PBH
ZS-PBS	81	PA-31T Cheyenne II	8120054	Semri Proprietary P/L. Louis Truchardt.	(N151CC)
ZS-PBT	84	Cheyenne II-XL	1166004	Eastern Charters P/L. Ermelo.	N90SC
ZS-PCH	04	King Air B200	BB-1856	C & L Air P/L. Makwassie.	N61956
ZS-PEA	81	King Air 200C	BL-29	Solenta Aviation P/L. Lanseria.	N500PH
ZS-PEI	01	King Air B200	BB-1789	Euro Coal P/L. Middleburg.	N4470B
ZS-PES	81	Conquest 1	425-0028	Peter Skeat/Ravencrest Property Holdings, Flamwood.	N425WB
ZS-PEZ	96	King Air B200	BB-1528	Booysen Bore Drilling Co P/L.	N528SA
ZS-PFA	68	King Air B90	LJ-395	Cenitor Management Holdings CC. Honeydew.	N81PG
ZS-PGW	81	King Air F90	LA-120	Desert Charm Trading 19 P/L. Sun Land.	N879PC
ZS-PGX	04	Pilatus PC-12/45	560	S African Red Cross Air Mercy Service, Cape Town.	HB-...
ZS-PHI	65	Gulfstream 1	164	Acas de Mocambique. 'Kruger Mpumalanga'	N290AS
ZS-PHJ	64	Gulfstream 1	134	Nelair Aviation Services P/L. Nelspruit.	3D-DUE
ZS-PHK	59	Gulfstream 1	25	Nelair Aviation Services P/L. Nelspruit.	3D-DLN
ZS-PJM	89	Beech 1900C-1	UC-76	Aircraft Africa Contracts Co P/L. Lanseria	N1568D
ZS-PKM	78	King Air 200	BB-382	Norse Air Charter P/L., Sandton	(N700E)
ZS-PLG	05	PA-46-500TP Meridian	4697199	Morisk Investments P/L. Lanseria.	N3095Q
ZS-PLJ	91	King Air B200	BB-1401	Naturelink Airlines P/L. Pretoria.	VH-YDH
ZS-PLK	93	King Air B200	BB-1463	Naturelink Airlines P/L. Pretoria.	VH-YEH
ZS-PLL	84	King Air B200	BB-1189	Naturelink Airlines P/L. Pretoria.	VH-KBH
ZS-PLY	80	King Air 200	BB-687	Medair Charter P/L, Lanseria	A2-MED
ZS-PMC	80	Conquest II	441-0162	Black Ginger 373 P/L. Lanseria.	LN-ABU
ZS-PNR	89	King Air B200	BB-1344	Pannar Air P/L. Greytown.?	N21PS
ZS-PNZ	80	King Air 200C	BL-8	Aircraft Africa Contracts Co P/L. Lanseria	5Y-NAX
ZS-PPG	97	King Air B200	BB-1562	Pick N' Pay (Gabriel Road) P/L. Capetown.	N203JT
ZS-PPZ	79	King Air 200	BB-419	Aircraft Africa Contracts Co P/L. Lanseria.	OY-BVB
ZS-PRA	89	King Air 1300	BB-1340	Aircraft Africa Contracts Co P/L. Lanseria.	OY-GMA
ZS-PRB	81	King Air 200C	BL-40	Aircraft Africa Contracts Co P/L. Lanseria.	OY-GEB
ZS-PRC	89	King Air 1300	BB-1341	Aircraft Africa Contracts Co P/L. Lanseria.	OY-GEU
ZS-PRK	06	Pilatus PC-12/47	690	Dewbury Trading 4 P/L. Tokai.	HB-F..
ZS-PRT	70	King Air C90	LJ-485	Blue Moonlight Properties 131, Germiston	9J-TAF
ZS-PRX	05	Pilatus PC-12/45	634	S African Red Cross Air Mercy Service, Cape Town.	HB-F..
ZS-PSP	80	King Air 200	BB-650	Nelair Aviation Services P/L. Nelspruit.	N740GL
ZS-PTX	06	Pilatus PC-12/47	695	S African Red Cross Air Mercy Service, Cape Town.	HB-F..
ZS-PUF	81	King Air 200	BB-867	Sheltam Rail Trust, Port Elizabeth.	N24AR
ZS-PXB	79	PA-31T Cheyenne II	7920056	Isiko Trading P/L., Ermelo	5U-ACC
ZS-PXF	07	King Air 350	FL-532	MTN Group Management Services, Cresta	N7262U
ZS-PXR	75	Rockwell 690A	11259	Joint Aid Management LLC/Jesus Alive Ministries, Honeydew	N425RR
ZS-PYD	81	Conquest 1	425-0067	Highveld Organic products Bryanston	5N-AMW
ZS-PZU	78	King Air 200	BB-315	Changing Altitudes P/L. Cape Town.	ZS-TAB
ZS-RAF	99	King Air B200	BB-1673	R A Foster, Lanseria.	N3173Y
ZS-RGS	85	Conquest II	441-0353	SAM Aviation (PTY) Ltd., Saxonwold	5N-ATR
ZS-SDO	99	Pilatus PC-12/45	282	ZS-SDO Aircraft P/L. Bedfordview.	(ZS-SDP)
ZS-SMC	94	King Air B200	BB-1489	AAA Investments P/L. Grahamstown.	N1563M
ZS-SMY	95	Pilatus PC-12	113	Chrome Loads P/L. Rustenburg.	N562GA
ZS-SPD	06	PA-46-500TP Meridian	4697266	Ropec Investments P/L. Rustenburg.	N10409
ZS-SRH	00	Pilatus PC-12/45	313	Tresso Trading 107 P/L. Capetown.	HB-F..
ZS-SRP	00	Pilatus PC-12/45	317	Manupont 127 P/L. Sunninghill.	5H-SRP
ZS-SRR	00	Pilatus PC-12/45	319	Summerset Charters P/L, Persequor Park	HB-F..
ZS-SSC	88	Reims/Cessna F406	F406-0032	Fugro Airborne Surveys P/L. Sunning Hill.	PH-CLE
ZS-SSD	88	Reims/Cessna F406	F406-0027	Fugro Airborne Surveys P/L. Sunning Hill.	D-ISHY

Reg	Yr Type	c/n	Owner/Operator	Prev Regn
☐ ZS-SSE	90 Reims/Cessna F406	F406-0043	Fugro Airborne Surveys P/L. Sunning Hill.	D-INUS
☐ ZS-TAY	07 PA-46-500TP Meridian	4697304	W Ferguson Investments CC., Bedfordview	N30953
☐ ZS-TBM	00 TBM 700B	164	The TBM 700 Air Charter Partnership, Pierre Van Ryneveld.	N164PG
☐ ZS-TGM	06 King Air B200	BB-1938	Tony Milligan Group P/L. Ladysmith.	N35788
☐ ZS-TIP	02 King Air B200	BB-1805	Karan Beef Freedlot, Heidelberg.	N4205G
☐ ZS-TKB	97 King Air C90B	LJ-1492	Alero Air Partnership, Kempton Park	N97CV
☐ ZS-TLA	01 Pilatus PC-12/45	383	Hernic Exploration P/L. Brits.	
☐ ZS-TNY	81 King Air B200	BB-914	Ferox Investments P/L. Lanseria.	5X-INS
☐ ZS-TOB	95 King Air B200	BB-1515	Kingsclere Trading P/L. Brooklyn.	N3235Z
☐ ZS-TSW	06 Pilatus PC-12/47	750	Tigair Aviation CC. Grand Central.	HB-F..
☐ ZS-TWP	06 King Air C90GT	LJ-1802	Merlin Aviation P/L, Marshalltown	N7102V
☐ ZS-XDG	77 King Air 200	BB-286	Aircraft Africa Contracts Co P/L. Lanseria.	7Q-NXB
☐ ZS-YEA	05 Pilatus PC-12/45	621	Richtrau No 46 P/L. Southdale.	HB-F...
☐ ZS-ZAZ	05 King Air 350	FL-459	John McCormick Family Trust, Clubview.	N36659
☐ ZS-ZOB	76 SA-226AT Merlin 4A	AT-051	WC Ferries CC,	TU-TOG
☐ ZS-ZXX	82 King Air B200	BB-1077	Matetsi Trust P/L. Parys.	(ZS-OGB)
Military				
☐ 651	82 King Air B200C	BL-45	SAAF, 41 Squadron, Waterkloof AFB.	ZS-LXS
☐ 652	81 King Air 200C	BL-34	SAAF, 41 Squadron, Waterkloof AFB.	ZS-LAY
☐ 653	87 King Air 300	FA-118	SAAF, 41 Squadron, Waterkloof AFB.	ZS-MHK
☐ 654	83 King Air B200C	BL-70	SAAF, 41 Squadron, Waterkloof AFB.	ZS-LNT
☐ 8030	97 Pilatus PC-12	145	SAAF, 41 Squadron, Waterkloof AFB.	HB-FRG

3A = MONACO Total 2
Civil

Reg	Yr Type	c/n	Owner/Operator	Prev Regn
☐ 3A-MIO	79 PA-31T Cheyenne II	7920001	Ljiljana Hennessy, Monaco.	I-NANE
☐ 3A-MSI	79 PA-31T Cheyenne 1	7904026	S Orlando, Cannes, France.	EX-EIM

3B = MAURITIUS Total 1
Civil

Reg	Yr Type	c/n	Owner/Operator	Prev Regn
☐ 3B-SKY	90 King Air B200	BB-1363	Unitex Finance Holding (Mauritius) Ltd. Port Louis.	N5503K

4R = SRI LANKA Total 2
Military

Reg	Yr Type	c/n	Owner/Operator	Prev Regn
☐ CR-842	84 King Air B200T	BT-30	4R-HVE, Sri Lankan Air Force, Colombo. (was BB-1185).	N6923L
☐ CR-843	88 King Air 1300	BB-1314	HISAR, 8 Light Transport Sqn. Ratmalana.	N4277E

4X = ISRAEL Total 29
Civil

Reg	Yr Type	c/n	Owner/Operator	Prev Regn
☐ 4X-CBF	81 PA-42 Cheyenne III	8001064	Z Danenberg, Sde Dov.	N932BF
☐ 4X-CBL	80 PA-31T Cheyenne II	8020080	Nesika Co Ltd. Herzlia.	N809SW
☐ 4X-CIC	82 PA-42 Cheyenne III	8001073	Moonair Aviation Ltd. Sde Dov.	N321CF
☐ 4X-CIZ	76 SA-226T Merlin 3B	T-271	Fast Link Ltd. Netanya.	N707PK
Military				
☐ 501	90 King Air B200	BB-1385	4X-FEA, IDFAF, Tel Aviv.	
☐ 504	90 King Air B200	BB-1386	4X-FEB, IDFAF, Tel Aviv.	N2872B
☐ 507	90 King Air B200	BB-1387	4X-FEC, IDFAF, Tel Aviv.	N2876B
☐ 510	90 King Air B200	BB-1388	4X-FED, IDFAF, Tel Aviv.	N2878B
☐ 622	00 King Air B200T	BT-39	IDFAF, Tel Aviv. (was BB-1684).	N32268
☐ 625	00 King Air B200T	BT-40	IDFAF, Tel Aviv. (was BB-1717).	N44717
☐ 629	00 King Air B200T	BT-41	IDFAF, Tel Aviv. (was BB-1721).	N44721
☐ 633	00 King Air B200T	BT-42	IDFAF, Tel Aviv. (was BB-1724).	N44724
☐ 636	00 King Air B200T	BT-43	IDFAF, Tel Aviv. (was BB-1727).	N42327
☐ 703	01 King Air B200CT	BN-5	IDFAF, Tel Aviv.	N5005M
☐ 719	03 King Air B200CT	BN-9	IDFAF, Tel Aviv.	N50969
☐ 722	02 King Air B200T	BT-44	IDFAF, Tel Aviv.	N51214
☐ 735	02 King Air B200T	BT-46	IDFAF, Tel Aviv.	N61346
☐ 842	02 King Air B200	BB-1806	IDFAF, Tel Aviv.	N4476Y
☐ 844	02 King Air B200	BB-1809	IDFAF, Tel Aviv.	N61369
☐ 848	02 King Air B200	BB-1811	IDFAF, Tel Aviv.	N51161
☐ 856	02 King Air B200	BB-1804	IDFAF, Tel Aviv.	N5104B
☐ 859	03 King Air B200	BB-1819	IDFAF, Tel Aviv.	N5019H
☐ 974	82 King Air RC-12D	BP-7	4X-FSA, IDFAF, Tel Aviv.	82-23638
☐ 977	82 King Air RC-12D	BP-8	4X-FSB, IDFAF, Tel Aviv.	82-23639
☐ 980	82 King Air RC-12D	BP-9	4X-FSC, IDFAF, Tel Aviv.	82-23640
☐ 982	82 King Air RC-12D	BP-10	4X-FSD, IDFAF, Tel Aviv.	82-23641
☐ 985	82 King Air RC-12D	BP-11	4X-FSE, IDFAF, Tel Aviv.	82-23642

☐ 987		King Air B200	FG-1	4X-FSF, IDFAF, Tel Aviv.	
☐ 990		King Air B200	FG-2	4X-FSG, IDFAF, Tel Aviv.	

5A = LIBYA *Total 5*
Civil

☐ 5A-DDT	79 King Air 200C	BL-1	Libyan Air Ambulance/Ministry of Health, Tripoli.	(F-GBLT)
☐ 5A-DDY	80 King Air 200C	BL-6	Libyan Air Ambulance/Ministry of Health, Tripoli.	
☐ 5A-DHZ	80 SA-226T Merlin 3B	T-345	Air Jamahiriya, Tripoli.	OO-HSC
☐ 5A-DJB	81 SA-226T Merlin 3B	T-388	Air Jamahiriya, Tripoli.	OO-XSC
☐ 5A-DKW	06 Reims/Cessna F406	F406-0092	Remote Sensing Centre, Biruni.	F-WWNP

5B = CYPRUS *Total 1*
Civil

☐ 5B-CJL	81 King Air C90	LJ-979	Dateline Overseas Ltd.	(D-IAAK)

5H = TANZANIA *Total 8*
Civil

☐ 5H-AWK	89 Reims/Cessna F406	F406-0030	Auric Air Services, Mwanza	5H-ANS
☐ 5H-PAY	89 Reims/Cessna F406	F406-0035	Precision Air Services Ltd., Arusha	S7-IDO
☐ 5H-RAS	86 Reims/Cessna F406	F406-0005	Regional Air Services Ltd. Arusha.	ZS-NNA
☐ 5H-SXB	89 Reims/Cessna F406	F406-0040	Nedbank Ltd/Safari Express, Arusha	ZS-OTT
☐ 5H-TZE	90 Reims/Cessna F406	F406-0046	Tanzanair, Dar es Salaam.	OY-PED
☐ 5H-TZX	85 King Air B200	BB-1196	Tanzanair, Dar es Salaam.	Z-ZLT
☐ 5H-WOW	91 Reims/Cessna F406	F406-0060	Air Excel Ltd. Arusha.	PH-GUG

Military

☐ JW9027	74 King Air A100	B-197	Tanzanian Air Force,	5X-UWT

5N = NIGERIA *Total 10*
Civil

☐ 5N-AMZ	78 King Air C90	LJ-755	Dumez (Nigeria) Ltd. Lagos. (status ?).	N9085S
☐ 5N-BHL	78 King Air 200	BB-387	Bristow Helicopters (Nigeria) Ltd. Lagos.	G-BFOL
☐ 5N-FLS	99 King Air 350	FL-246	Julius Berger Nigeria plc. Abuja.	D-CBIL
☐ 5N-FLY	00 King Air 350	FL-279	Julius Berger Nigeria plc. Abuja.	D-CIAO
☐ 5N-IHS	80 King Air 200	BB-663	Wings Aviation,	5N-AMT
☐ 5N-MGV		DHC 8-102	024	Aero Contractors Ltd. Lagos.	C-GMOK
☐ 5N-MPA	95 Beech 1900D	UE-149	Mobil Producing (Nigeria) Ltd. Lagos.	N3217L
☐ 5N-MPB	99 King Air 350	FL-238	Mobil Producing (Nigeria) Ltd. Lagos.	N2341R
☐ 5N-MPN	94 Beech 1900D	UE-77	Mobil Producing (Nigeria) Ltd. Lagos.	(N280KA)
☐ 5N-MPS	87 Dornier 228-201	8146	NEPA-National Electric Power Authority. (status ?).	D-CALO

5R = MADAGASCAR *Total 1*
Civil

☐ 5R-MIM	77 PA-31T Cheyenne II	7720059	Lycee Professionel St Exupery, Ivato.	N48AR

5T = MAURITANIA *Total 2*
Military

☐ 5T-MAB	81 PA-31T Cheyenne II	8120024	Mauritanian Air Force, Nouakchott.	N2470X
☐ 5T-MAC	81 PA-31T Cheyenne II	8120026	Mauritanian Air Force, Nouakchott.	N2483X

5V = TOGO *Total 3*
Civil

☐ 5V-...	78 PA-31T Cheyenne II	7820013		N813AR
☐ 5V-TTD	69 King Air B90	LJ-453	PEFACO Ltd. Lome.	(D-IAMX)

Military

☐ 5V-MCG	81 King Air B200	BB-857	Government of Togo, Lome.	N57AC

5X = UGANDA *Total 1*
Civil

☐ 5X-INS	99 King Air B200	BB-1650		N771TP

5Y = KENYA *Total 35*
Civil

☐ 5Y-	81 King Air 200	BB-837		ZS-LBD
☐ 5Y-	79 King Air 200	BB-525		ZS-MFC
☐ 5Y-...	78 King Air 200	BB-407		ZS-NUC
☐ 5Y-...	68 Gulfstream 1	190	Skyways Kenya Ltd. Nairobi. (status ?).	N190LE
☐ 5Y-BIX	90 Reims/Cessna F406	F406-0055	East African Air Charters Ltd. Nairobi.	N65912
☐ 5Y-BKN	87 Reims/Cessna F406	F406-0021	(status ?).	PH-FWG
☐ 5Y-BKT	77 King Air 200	BB-256	Queensway Air Services (K) Ltd. Nairobi.	(5Y-NTM)

Reg   Yr Type   c/n   Owner/Operator   Prev Regn

Reg	Yr Type	c/n	Owner/Operator	Prev Regn
☐ 5Y-BLA	80 King Air 200C	BL-10	ALS-Aircraft Leasing Services Ltd. Nairobi.	C-FAMB
☐ 5Y-BLR	60 Gulfstream 1	34	Skyways Kenya Ltd. Nairobi.	N34LE
☐ 5Y-BMA	76 King Air 200	BB-155	Skylink Aeromangement (K) Inc. Nairobi.	OY-GEH
☐ 5Y-BMC	77 King Air 200	BB-211	Skylink Aeromangement (K) Inc. Nairobi.	OY-BTR
☐ 5Y-BMR	61 Gulfstream 1	81	Skyways Kenya Ltd. Nairobi.	I-TASO
☐ 5Y-BMS	68 Gulfstream 1	194	Sincereways Kenya Ltd. Nairobi.	(FAV-8595)
☐ 5Y-BMY	78 Rockwell 690B	11474	Turbine Services Ltd. Nairobi.	5H-MTY
☐ 5Y-BSU	77 King Air 200	BB-222		ZS-KAA
☐ 5Y-BTL	73 Rockwell 690A	11103	James Gaunt, Nairobi.	N690CE
☐ 5Y-BVI	89 Beech 1900C-1	UC-55	Aviation Assistance A/S-UN, Nairobi.	OY-BVI
☐ 5Y-DDE	78 King Air 200	BB-379	IBIS Aviation Ltd. Nairobi.	G-ONEX
☐ 5Y-EKO	79 King Air 200C	BL-2	Air Bridge, Nairobi.	OY-BVE
☐ 5Y-HHA	82 King Air B200	BB-988	Blue Bird Aviation Ltd. Nairobi.	PH-LMC
☐ 5Y-HHE	79 King Air 200	BB-547	Blue Bird Aviation Ltd. Nairobi.	ZS-NIP
☐ 5Y-HHK	80 King Air 200	BB-696	Blue Bird Aviation Ltd. Nairobi.	5Y-TWB
☐ 5Y-HHM	83 King Air B200	BB-1152		(ZS-DSL)
☐ 5Y-JAI	79 King Air 200	BB-557	Capital Airlines Ltd. Nairobi.	OY-PAM
☐ 5Y-JJZ	83 King Air B200	BB-1127	Cerere AG. Nairobi.	G-BMNF
☐ 5Y-JMR	81 King Air 200C	BL-17	AD Aviation (Aircharters) Ltd. Nairobi.	(N76HM)
☐ 5Y-MAF	99 Pilatus PC-12/45	243	Mission Aviation Fellowship, Nairobi.	HB-FRN
☐ 5Y-MKM	89 Reims/Cessna F406	F406-0044		(LN-TED)
☐ 5Y-RJA	80 King Air 200	BB-619	Phoenix Aviation Ltd. Nairobi.	SE-KXN
☐ 5Y-SJB	79 King Air/Catpass 250	BB-467	East African Coffee Co. Nairobi.	5H-MUN
☐ 5Y-THS	80 King Air 200	BB-643		ZS-ALE
☐ 5Y-TWA	81 King Air 200	BB-803		5Y-TWA
☐ 5Y-TWC	81 King Air B200C	BL-37	Transworld Safaris (K) Ltd. Nairobi.	G-IFTB
☐ 5Y-XXX	58 Gulfstream 1	1	East African Express, Nairobi.	ZS-NVG
☐ 5Y-ZBK	00 King Air B200	BB-1714	ZB Air, Nairobi.	N3214D

6V = SENEGAL Total 1
Civil

☐ 6V-AGS	75 King Air 200	BB-28	Senegalair, Dakar.	F-GKPL

6Y = JAMAICA Total 1
Civil

☐ 6Y-JDB	77 Mitsubishi MU-2P	353SA	Aircraft & Engines Ltd. Grand Turk, Turks & Caicos Island.	6Y-JDB

7Q = MALAWI Total 1
Civil

☐ 7Q-YLT	03 Pilatus PC-12/45	525	Limbe Leaf Tobacco Co. Lilongwe.	ZS-PDZ

7T = ALGERIA Total 14
Civil

☐ 7T-VBE	93 King Air B200	BB-1453	National Institute of Cartography, Algiers.	N8153H
☐ 7T-VCV	72 King Air A100	B-93	ENESA/Air Algerie, Algiers.	N9369Q
☐ 7T-VRF	73 King Air A100	B-147	ENESA/Air Algerie, Algiers.	N1828W

Military

☐ 7T-VRI	76 King Air 200	BB-171	Ministry of Defence, Boufarik.	
☐ 7T-VRO	81 King Air 200	BB-807	Ministry of Defence, Boufarik.	
☐ 7T-VRS	81 King Air 200	BB-759	Ministry of Defence, Boufarik.	F-GCTC
☐ 7T-VRT	81 King Air 200	BB-775	Ministry of Defence, Boufarik.	F-GCTD
☐ 7T-WCF	94 King Air C90B	LJ-1359	Ministry of Defence, Algiers.	N8280K
☐ 7T-WCG	94 King Air C90B	LJ-1379	Ministry of Defence, Algiers.	N3122K
☐ 7T-WCH	94 King Air C90B	LJ-1380	Ministry of Defence, Algiers.	N3128K
☐ 7T-WRG	76 King Air 200	BB-184	Ministry of Defence, Boufarik.	
☐ 7T-WRH	76 King Air 200	BB-175	Ministry of Defence, Boufarik.	
☐ 7T-WRY	81 King Air 200T	BT-20	Ministry of Defence, Boufarik. (was BB-871).	7T-VRY
☐ 7T-WRZ	81 King Air 200T	BT-21	Ministry of Defence, Boufarik. (was BB-895).	7T-VRZ

9A = CROATIA Total 4
Civil

☐ 9A-BKB	07 King Air B200	BB-1983		N70783
☐ 9A-BOR	80 PA-31T Cheyenne 1	8004011	Delic Air, Pula	D-IBIW
☐ 9A-BZG	81 PA-31T Cheyenne 1	8104032	Geofoto, Zagreb.	D-IAPA

Military

☐ 014	PA-31T Cheyenne	...	Croatian Air Force, 27ETZ-Transport Aircraft Squadron,	

Reg Yr Type c/n Owner/Operator Prev Regn

9J = ZAMBIA   Total   8
Civil
☐ 9J-AAV	70 King Air B90	LJ-486	ZESCO Ltd-Zambia Electricity Supply Co Ltd. Lusaka.	A2-JZT
☐ 9J-DCF	73 King Air C90	LJ-575	Zambia Skyways Ltd. Lusaka.	N12RF
☐ 9J-MAS	98 Beech 1900D	UE-323	Roan Air Ltd. Lusaka.	N23047
☐ 9J-MBO	98 Beech 1900D	UE-319	Roan Air Ltd. Lusaka. 'Kaingo'	N23004
☐ 9J-MED	82 King Air B200	BB-1046		Z-APG
☐ 9J-STA	74 King Air E90	LW-116	Staravia Ltd. Lusaka.	TF-ELT
☐ 9J-YVZ	68 King Air B90	LJ-338	Eastern Safaris Ltd. Lusaka.	ZS-LWZ

Military
☐ AF602	70 BAe HS 748-2A	1688	Zambian Air Force,	

9M = MALAYSIA   Total   9
Civil
☐ 9M-DSR	93 TBM 700	69	Eurocopter Malaysia Sqn Bhd.	VH-ICO
☐ 9M-JPD	79 King Air 200T	BT-10	Directorate of Civil Aviation, Kuala Lumpur. (was BB-563).	N6065D
☐ 9M-JPL	06 King Air C90GT	LJ-1809	Upayapadu Sdn Bhd	N71909
☐ 9M-KNS	77 King Air 200	BB-294	Penerbangan Sabah/Sabah Air Pte Ltd. Kota Kinabalu.	N18494
☐ 9M-TDM	86 PA-42 Cheyenne 400LS	5527032	TDM Helling Sdn Bhd. Kuala Lumpur.	N425D

Military
☐ M41-01	93 King Air 200T	BT-35	Royal Malaysian Air Force, 16 Sku, Subang. (was BB-1448).	N15509
☐ M41-02	93 King Air 200T	BT-36	Royal Malaysian Air Force, 16 Sku, Subang. (was BB-1451).	N80024
☐ M41-03	93 King Air 200T	BT-37	Royal Malaysian Air Force, 16 Sku, Subang. (was BB-1454).	N80027
☐ M41-04	93 King Air 200T	BT-38	Royal Malaysian Air Force, 16 Sku, Subang. (was BB-1457).	N80048

9Q = CONGO KINSHASA   Total   8
Civil
☐ 9Q-CBU	71 681B Turbo Commander	6045		N9107N
☐ 9Q-CCG	74 King Air E90	LW-110	Inga Shaba, Kinshasa.	N8PC
☐ 9Q-CEM	72 King Air A100	B-105	Air Tropiques/Mimo,	ZS-TBS
☐ 9Q-CGL	70 681 Turbo Commander	6030	Cie Ciments Lacs,	D-IGAD
☐ 9Q-CKM	68 King Air B90	LJ-402	Fontshi Aviation Service, Kinshasa. 'Tshihuka'	ZS-IBE
☐ 9Q-COE	65 Gulfstream 1	156	ITAB Bionic Aviation,	(N159KK)
☐ 9Q-CRF	70 King Air 100	B-33	Forrest Air Co. Lumbumbashi.	N883K
☐ 9Q-CTG	80 King Air 200	BB-629	SCIBE Airlift, Kinshasa.	

* **Denotes reserved registration**

Total Props   10839

Business TurboProps - Written Off/Withdrawn From Use

C = CANADA

Civil

Reg	Yr	Type	c/n	Owner/Operator	Prev Regn
C-FANF	1969	SA-26T Merlin 2A	T26-32	Wfu. Parts at White Industries, Bates City, Mo. USA.	N742G
C-FATR	1970	681 Turbo Commander	6020	W/o St Andrews, Manitoba, Canada 3 Jan 93.	N114MR
C-FCAS	1965	King Air 90	LJ-23	W/o Sherrington, Canada. 1 May 79.	
C-FCAU	1965	King Air 90	LJ-24	W/o Nr Quebec City, PQ. Canada. 30 Aug 85.	
C-FCAV	1981	PA-42 Cheyenne III	8001006	Wfu. Cx C- 12/05.	N131RC
C-FCGJ	1967	King Air A90	LJ-231	Wfu. Cx C- 4/91.	
C-FCGX	1977	King Air/Catpass 250	BB-250	Wfu. Cx C- 6/04. Last located at Kamloops, BC. Canada.	N1008J
C-FDJQ	1971	King Air 100	B-84	Wfu.	TI-AYN
C-FEQB	1979	PA-31T Cheyenne II	7920071	Wfu. Located Calgary/Springbank, AB. Canada.	SX-ABU
C-FFEO	1967	680V Turbo Command	1693-72	W/o hangar fire Hamilton, ON. Canada. 15 Feb 93.	
C-FFYC	1969	SA-26T Merlin 2A	T26-36	W/o N E of Thompson, MT. Canada. 31 May 94.	N739G
C-FHBW	1968	King Air B90	LJ-336	Wfu. Located Aircraft Training School, Copenhagen, Denmark.	
C-FHYX	1970	SA-26AT Merlin 2B	T26-174	W/o ground fire, Canada. Oct 73.	
C-FKAL	1996	Pilatus PC-12	151	W/o Clarenville, NF. Canada. 18 May 98.	N151PB
C-FKIJ	1970	King Air 100	B-52	Wfu. Last located Kamloops, BC. Canada.	N8NP
C-FMAI	1973	King Air A100	B-145	Wfu. Last located Montgomery, Al. USA.	N380W
C-FMAR	1959	Gulfstream 1	3	Wfu. Parts at Montreal, PQ. Canada.	N703G
C-FMHB	1976	PA-31T Cheyenne II	7620023	Wfu. Located Calgary/Springbank, AB. Canada.	SX-ABT
C-FQMS	1967	Mitsubishi MU-2B	009	W/o Athabaska, Canada. 7 Apr 80.	HB-LEB
C-FRCL	1965	King Air 90	LJ-33	W/o Canada. 26 Aug 76.	N420G
C-FSSU	1980	King Air 200	BB-633	W/o hangar fire Quebec City, PQ. Canada. 10 Jan 93.	N650TJ
C-FTWO	1975	Mitsubishi MU-2L	672	W/o Terrace Airport, BC. Canada. 20 Dec 05.	N709US
C-FUAC	1965	King Air 90	LJ-3	Wfu. Located Vincennes University, In. USA.	
C-FVMH	1967	King Air A90	LJ-225	Wfu. Cx C- 8/91.	
C-GAMJ	1978	PA-31T Cheyenne II	7820063	W/o Haul Beach, NT. Canada. 17 Apr 89.	N82298
C-GAPK	1974	King Air A100	B-198	Wfu. Cx C- 8/06.	N712AS
C-GAPT	1975	PA-31T Cheyenne II	7620004	W/o Toronto, ON. Canada. 17 Oct 84.	
C-GARO	1972	King Air 200	BB-2	Wfu. Cx C- 4/97.	N200KP
C-GASW	1972	King Air A100	B-108	W/o Thunder Bay, ON. Canada. 14 Jun 99.	N110JJ
C-GBMI	1981	Conquest 1	425-0031	W/o La Rouche, PQ. Canada. 20 Nov 88.	N355MA
C-GBTI	1968	King Air B90	LJ-352	W/o Fort Frances, ON. Canada. 6 May 91.	VR-BHT
C-GBTI	1974	King Air E90	LW-111	Wfu. Parts at Griffin, Ga. USA.	N11GE
C-GBTS	1979	King Air B100	BE-73	W/o Muskoka, ON. Canada. 13 Apr 99.	N54CK
C-GCEV	1976	King Air 200	BB-153	W/o Sept-Iles Airport, PQ. Canada. 28 Jan 97.	N502AB
C-GCSL	1976	King Air 200	BB-118	W/o Quebec City, PQ. Canada. 10 Jan 93.	
C-GDOM	1968	King Air B90	LJ-368	W/o Fort Simpson, Canada. 16 Oct 88.	N1100D
C-GDSD	1975	SA-226T Merlin 3A	T-251	Wfu. Cx C- 12/92.	N711RD
C-GFFN	1974	King Air A100	B-190	W/o on approach Sandy Bay Airport 7.1.07	C-GNAR
C-GFKS	1979	King Air A100	B-247	Wfu. Reg canx 5/07 as Wfu	N153TC
C-GFRU	1976	Mitsubishi MU-2M	343	W/o Kelowna, BC. Canada. 18 Jan 82.	N728MA
C-GHSI	1975	PA-31T Cheyenne II	7520025	Wfu. Cx C- 11/95. Parts at White Industries, Bates City, Mo.	
C-GILM	1972	King Air A100	B-124	W/o Sioux Lookout, ON. Canada. 7 Dec 97.	N100SJ
C-GJNH	1966	680V Turbo Command	1587-38	Wfu. Cx C- 2/83.	N251B
C-GJPD	1979	PA-31T Cheyenne II	7920070	W/o hangar fire Quebec City, PQ. Canada. 10 Jan 93.	
C-GJUL	1975	King Air A100	B-218	W/o Chapleau, ON. Canada. 29 Nov 88.	N80MD
C-GJWW	1973	SA-226AT Merlin 4	AT-013	Wfu. Cx C- 8/88. Parts at Griffin, Ga. USA.	N720F
C-GKFG	1959	Gulfstream 1	22	Wfu. Located S Alberta Institute of Technology, Calgary.	N8BG
C-GKRL	1981	King Air B200	BB-878	W/o Fort McMurray, NB. Canada. 10 Dec 87.	G-BIPP
C-GLOW	1974	Mitsubishi MU-2J	624	W/o Edmonton, AB. Canada. 6 Dec 81.	N474MA
C-GNAK	1965	Gulfstream 1	154	W/o Linneas, Ne, USA. 19 Jul 00.	G-BNKO
C-GODI	1974	Mitsubishi MU-2J	649	W/o Portage la Prairie, MT. Canada. 28 May 77.	N530MA
C-GPCD	1975	King Air 200	BB-76	Wfu. Cx C- 4/06.	N500DR
C-GPIM	1980	PA-31T Cheyenne II	8020065	Wfu. Cx C- 2/04.	C-GNAM
C-GPIP	1977	PA-31T Cheyenne II	7720026	Wfu. Cx C- 1/93. Located Nr Lake City Airport, Fl. USA.	N82118
C-GPPN	1968	King Air B90	LJ-389	W/o Hudson's Bay, Canada. 22 Dec 84.	N745JB
C-GPTG	1968	Gulfstream 1	189	Wfu. Cx C- 3/01.	N776G
C-GPWR	1970	SA-26AT Merlin 2B	T26-160	Wfu. Parts at White Industries, Bates City, Mo. USA.	N38MJ
C-GQDD	1968	King Air B90	LJ-328	Wfu. Cx C- 5/87. Parts at Dodsons, Rantoul, Ks. USA.	N730K
C-GSID	1975	PA-31T Cheyenne II	7520042	W/o Kirkland Lake, ON. Canada. 18 Oct 87.	(N118L)
C-GSWB	1977	PA-31T Cheyenne II	7720013	W/o Montreal, PQ. Canada. 12 Nov 93. (parts at Bates City).	N82092

Reg	Yr	Type	c/n	Owner/Operator	Prev Regn
☐ C-GTDL	1963	Gulfstream 1	110	Wfu. Cx C- 5/86.	N533CS
☐ C-GTHN	1968	SA-26T Merlin 2A	T26-16	W/o Whale Cove, NT. Canada. 29 Jun 96.	N748G
☐ C-GVCE	1972	King Air A100	B-135	W/o Calgary, AB. Canada. 21 Nov 84.	N4GT
☐ C-GVCY	1971	SA-226AT Merlin 4	AT-003	Wfu. Cx C- 5/94. Parts at Dodsons, Rantoul, Ks. USA.	N5295M
☐ C-GWCY	1968	King Air B90	LJ-345	W/o Lynn Lake, Canada. Oct 81.	N550TS
☐ C-GWFM	1975	PA-31T Cheyenne II	7520041	Wfu. Cx C- 8/93.	N54972
☐ C-GWGP	1968	Mitsubishi MU-2D	109	Wfu.	N1AN
☐ C-GWSL	1975	SA-226AT Merlin 4A	AT-028	W/o St Hubert, PQ. Canada. 27 Dec 99.	N5341M
☐ C-GWSP	1973	SA-226AT Merlin 4	AT-010	Wfu. Cx C- 10/03.	N603L
☐ C-GYMR	1970	SA-26AT Merlin 2B	T26-177	W/o Fort Good Hope, NT. Canada. 12 Oct 88.	N83RS
☐ C-GYQT	1974	King Air A100	B-189	W/o Big Trout Lake, ON. Canada. 21 Feb 95.	N22220

CC = CHILE
Civil

Reg	Yr	Type	c/n	Owner/Operator	Prev Regn
☐ CC-COT	1967	King Air A90	LJ-227	W/o (details ?).	CC-PIR

CN = MOROCCO
Civil

Reg	Yr	Type	c/n	Owner/Operator	Prev Regn
☐ CN-CDE	1979	King Air 200	BB-567	W/o Casablanca, Morocco. 3 Nov 86.	

Military

Reg	Yr	Type	c/n	Owner/Operator	Prev Regn
☐ CNA-NA	1974	King Air A100	B-180	W/o Morocco. Oct 78.	

CP = BOLIVIA
Civil

Reg	Yr	Type	c/n	Owner/Operator	Prev Regn
☐ CP-1016	1973	Rockwell 690	11053	W/o La Paz, Bolivia. 9 Aug 93.	
☐ CP-1017	1972	Rockwell 690	11054	W/o Callao, Peru. 13 Feb 74.	
☐ CP-1106	1974	Rockwell 690A	11193	Wfu.	
☐ CP-1849	1982	King Air B200C	BL-52	W/o Santa Cruz, Bolivia. 14 Mar 84.	N6872X
☐ CP-2182	1973	Rockwell 690	11055	Wfu. Stolen.	N100MB
☐ CP-2287	1967	King Air A90	LJ-232	W/o Robore, Bolivia. 12 Apr 96.	N707EB
☐ CP-894	1970	681 Turbo Commander	6015	W/o Santa Cruz, Bolivia. 18 Jun 71.	N9066N

Military

Reg	Yr	Type	c/n	Owner/Operator	Prev Regn
☐ EB-002	1981	King Air 200C	BL-33	W/o 6 Dec 95.	FAB-002
☐ EB-003	1980	King Air C90	LJ-905	W/o 27 Nov 95.	YV-164CP
☐ FAB 006	1968	King Air B90	LJ-413	W/o La Paz, Bolivia. 26 Apr 79.	FAB 001
☐ FAB 023	1979	Rockwell 690B	11562	Wfu. Located La Paz, Bolivia.	HK-2996P

D = GERMANY
Civil

Reg	Yr	Type	c/n	Owner/Operator	Prev Regn
☐ D-CFMC	1986	King Air 300	FA-104	W/o Eichberg, Blumberg, Germany. 24 Oct 00.	(N494MA)
☐ D-CUNO	2000	King Air 350	FL-311	W/o Freiburg, Germany. 12 Jan 06.	N5011K
☐ D-IAAE	1978	Conquest II	441-0047	W/o Mount Orsa, Italy. 11 Jun 82.	(N36990)
☐ D-IAAY	1980	Conquest II	441-0144	W/o 6 Nov 80.	(N2627N)
☐ D-IAKS	1978	PA-31T Cheyenne II	7820048	W/o Borkum Island, Germany. 23 Jul 83.	OE-FOP
☐ D-IBAA	1983	Conquest 1	425-0163	W/o Hannover, Germany 24 Jan 96.	N66218
☐ D-IBAF	1976	King Air 200	BB-93	W/o Bourgas, Bulgaria. 27 Jul 77.	OE-FMC
☐ D-IBAR	1981	Gulfstream 980	95054	W/o Paderborn, Germany. 30 Jan 85.	(N9806S)
☐ D-IBDH	1992	King Air C90B	LJ-1307	W/o Accident Nr. Zhulyany, Ukrain	N8053U
☐ D-ICBC	1993	King Air 300	FA-227	W/o St Moritz-Samedan, Switzerland. 14 Feb 02.	(SP-FNH)
☐ D-ICEK	1981	Conquest 1	425-0055	W/o Aichstetten, Germany. 10 Dec 92.	N425VC
☐ D-IDDI	1979	PA-31T Cheyenne II	7920014	W/o Cologne, Germany. 5 Feb 93.	N792SW
☐ D-IEFW	1986	Conquest 1	425-0228	W/o Lake Constance, Switzerland. 24 Jan 94.	N1227A
☐ D-IEGA	1981	Conquest II	441-0193	W/o Ascheberg, Germany. 2 Apr 00. (at Rantoul, Ks.).	OE-FRZ
☐ D-IEWK	1976	SA-226AT Merlin 4A	AT-042	W/o Munich, Germany. 5 Feb 87.	OE-FTA
☐ D-IFSH	1982	PA-42 Cheyenne III	8001101	W/o Zurich, Switzerland. 28 Oct 03.	4X-CIM
☐ D-IGSW	1980	King Air 200	BB-669	W/o Keller Joch Mountain, Austria. 22 Nov 90.	N80GA
☐ D-IHAN	1979	MU-2 Solitaire	396SA	W/o Steinhausen, Germany. 9 Aug 79.	N788MA
☐ D-IHNA	1981	King Air C90	LJ-926	W/o Mindelheim, Germany. 27 May 94.	(D-IBBI)
☐ D-IHVI	1980	PA-31T Cheyenne II	8020007	W/o Southend, UK. 13 Mar 86.	N2529R
☐ D-IIWB	1980	PA-31T Cheyenne II	8020030	Wfu. Cx D- 2/96. Parts at Griffin, Ga. USA.	N37CA
☐ D-IKKS	1981	PA-31T Cheyenne II	8120034	W/o Concord, Ca. USA. 14 Jul 84.	F-GDCR
☐ D-IKOC	1978	Rockwell 690B	11498	W/o Paris, France. 21 Feb 81.	N131SA
☐ D-IKWP	1980	PA-31T Cheyenne 1	8004049	W/o Blieskastel, Germany. 10 Dec 88.	N5GW
☐ D-ILHA	1971	King Air C90	LJ-509	Wfu. Instructional airframe, Hamburg, Germany.	
☐ D-ILMA	1965	King Air 90	LJ-48	W/o Greven, Germany. 13 Aug 69.	
☐ D-ILNI	1966	King Air A90	LJ-116	W/o Milan, Italy. 21 Sep 67.	
☐ D-ILNU	1966	King Air A90	LJ-178	W/o Bremen, Germany. 16 Feb 67.	N798K

Reg	Yr	Type	c/n	Owner/Operator	Prev Regn
☐ D-ILRA	1980	PA-31T Cheyenne II	8020009	W/o Munich, Germany. 11 Aug 87.	N24HE
☐ D-ILSE	1969	SA-26AT Merlin 2B	T26-163E	W/o Stuttgart, Germany. 10 Apr 73.	F-BKML
☐ D-ILTU	1968	King Air B90	LJ-359	W/o Frankfurt, Germany. 22 Jan 71.	N7077N
☐ D-IMAY	1985	PA-42 Cheyenne 400L	5527024	W/o Nuremberg, Germany. 5 May 01.	(N400TM)
☐ D-IMON	1968	680W Turbo Command	1819-33	W/o Lake Walchensee, Germany. 27 Dec 78.	
☐ D-IMTT	1978	PA-31T Cheyenne II	7820041	Wfu. Parts at Dodsons, Ottawa, Ks. USA.	N82WC
☐ D-IMWH	1981	King Air F90	LA-114	W/o Dusseldorf, Germany. 6 Dec 87.	N313BH
☐ D-INIX	1972	Rockwell 690	11013	W/o Greenland. 21 Jun 72.	N9213N
☐ D-IOET	1973	Rockwell 690A	11142	W/o Luton, UK. 1 Dec 81.	
☐ D-IOFC	1978	PA-31T Cheyenne 1	7804011	W/o Borgo Ticino, Italy. 25 Mar 84.	

D2 = ANGOLA

Civil

Reg	Yr	Type	c/n	Owner/Operator	Prev Regn
☐ D2-ECH	1978	King Air 200	BB-345	W/o Cafunfo, Angola. 28 Jan 95.	F-GHCT
☐ D2-ECL	1975	King Air 200	BB-44	W/o Luanda, Angola. 28 May 97.	F-GHAL

EC = SPAIN

Civil

Reg	Yr	Type	c/n	Owner/Operator	Prev Regn
☐ EC-COI	1975	King Air C90	LJ-663	Wfu. Located Toledo-Ocana, Spain.	E22-7
☐ EC-COJ	1975	King Air C90	LJ-664	W/o Salamanca, Spain. 4 Oct 83.	E 22-8
☐ EC-DXG	1967	680V Turbo Command	1711-86	Wfu. Loacted Globalia Training Centre, Llucmajor, Mallorca.	N535SM
☐ EC-EAG	1968	680W Turbo Command	1776-14	Wfu.	N680W
☐ EC-EFH	1973	Rockwell 690A	11130	Wfu.	N111VS
☐ EC-EIH	1974	Rockwell 690A	11212	Wfu.	N690BT
☐ EC-EIL	1972	Rockwell 690	11007	Wfu.	N171TT
☐ EC-ERQ	1977	King Air 200	BB-218	W/o Banjul, Gambia. 9 Oct 97.	EC-351
☐ EC-ETH	1983	Conquest 1	425-0151	W/o Nr Malaga, Spain. 4 Sep 92.	N81798
☐ EC-EXQ	1964	Gulfstream 1	142	Wfu. Located Madrid-Barajas, Spain.	EC-461
☐ EC-EXS	1961	Gulfstream 1	64	Wfu. Located Madrid-Barajas, Spain.	EC-460
☐ EC-EZO	1960	Gulfstream 1	41	Wfu. Located at Madrid-Barajas, Spain.	EC-494
☐ EC-FFE	1976	Rockwell 690A	11344	W/o Warsaw-Okecie, Poland. 29 Nov 95.	N900FT
☐ EC-GDV	1976	SA-226AT Merlin 4A	AT-043	W/o Mediterranean Sea 10 Oct 01.	EC-975

Military

Reg	Yr	Type	c/n	Owner/Operator	Prev Regn
☐ E 22-02	1974	King Air C90	LJ-621	W/o Paria, Spain. 18 Feb 04.	EC-CHA
☐ E22-5	1974	King Air C90	LJ-623	W/o Salamanca, Spain. 1 Oct 80.	EC-CHB

EI = EIRE

Civil

Reg	Yr	Type	c/n	Owner/Operator	Prev Regn
☐ EI-BGL	1978	Rockwell 690B	11507	W/o Jevington, UK. 13 Nov 84.	N81850

EP = IRAN

Civil

Reg	Yr	Type	c/n	Owner/Operator	Prev Regn
☐ EP-AHN	1974	Rockwell 690A	11147	W/o.	
☐ EP-AKA	1972	681B Turbo Command	6065	Wfu. Located Aerospace Exhibition Centre, Tehran, Iran.	
☐ EP-AKB	1972	681B Turbo Command	6067	Wfu. Located Aerospace Exhibition Centre, Tehran, Iran.	

Military

Reg	Yr	Type	c/n	Owner/Operator	Prev Regn
☐ 5-59	1970	681 Turbo Commander	6009	Wfu. Located Tehran-Mehrabad.	N9059N
☐ IIN 501	1972	Rockwell 690	11049	W/o.	

F = FRANCE

Civil

Reg	Yr	Type	c/n	Owner/Operator	Prev Regn
☐ F-BNMC	1967	King Air A90	LJ-149	W/o Nr Marseilles, France. 28 Aug 97.	
☐ F-BSTM	1966	680V Turbo Command	1540-6	Wfu. Located Pelegry-Perpignan Museum, France.	F-WSTM
☐ F-BTDP	1972	King Air C90	LJ-560	W/o 17 Dec 74.	
☐ F-BTEE	1976	PA-31T Cheyenne II	7620045	Wfu. CoA expiry 16 Dec 92. Cx F- 10/00.	F-ODEE
☐ F-BUTS	1973	King Air E90	LW-68	Wfu. Cx F- 9/03. Parts at Dodsons, Rantoul, Ks. USA.	
☐ F-BUTV	1973	King Air C90	LJ-602	W/o. Destroyed by fire, France. 28 Jul 92.	
☐ F-BVET	1975	King Air 200	BB-21	Wfu. Cx F- 10/03.	
☐ F-BVRP	1975	King Air 200	BB-38	W/o Baiuyan, China. 4 Apr 83.	
☐ F-BVVM	1965	King Air 90	LJ-26	Wfu. Cx F- 4/94.	D-ILGK
☐ F-BXAR	1975	King Air C90	LJ-658	W/o. Ca. USA. Jan 79.	
☐ F-BXSF	1965	King Air 90	LJ-29	Wfu. Cx F- 3/93. Parts at Dodsons, Rantoul, Ks. USA.	D-ILMI
☐ F-GABV	1974	King Air E90	LW-102	W/o Alencon/Mount des Avaloirs, France. 1 May 98.	(F-GRCV)
☐ F-GAMP	1977	PA-31T Cheyenne II	7720029	Wfu. CoA expiry 23 Apr 93. Cx F- 10/00.	(N82122)
☐ F-GBDZ	1978	King Air E90	LW-295	W/o Paris, France. 15 Dec 82.	
☐ F-GBRD	1974	King Air E90	LW-91	W/o Barcelonette, France. 2 Nov 86.	N75DA
☐ F-GBRP	1978	King Air 200	BB-368	W/o Ribeauville, France. 17 Oct 80.	

☐ F-GCCC	1979	King Air 200	BB-504	W/o Bergamo, Italy. 26 Mar 84.	
☐ F-GCFH	1966	King Air A90	LJ-127	Wfu. Cx F- 8/96.	N72RD
☐ F-GCJS	1979	Mitsubishi MU-2P	406SA	Wfu. Cx F- 2/00.	N967MA
☐ F-GDHS	1981	MU-2 Marquise	1532SA	W/o Macey/Troyes, France. 21 May 91.	F-WDHS
☐ F-GDHV	1980	MU-2 Marquise	779SA	W/o Papeete, Tahiti. 27 May 94.	D-IFTG
☐ F-GDLE	1977	King Air 200	BB-230	W/o Moulins, France. 24 Nov 01.	G-BEHR
☐ F-GDMM	1965	King Air 90	LJ-54	Wfu. Cx F- 9/92.	N66WC
☐ F-GDPJ	1975	PA-31T Cheyenne II	7620006	W/o Paris, France. 12 Dec 84.	C-GDOW
☐ F-GDRT	1965	King Air 90	LJ-4	Wfu. CoA expiry 8/88, Cx F- 8/96.	TR-LBB
☐ F-GEBK	1976	SA-226T Merlin 3A	T-272	W/o Apr 85.	N49MJ
☐ F-GEDV	1966	King Air A90	LJ-150	Wfu. Last located Pontoise, France.	D-ICPD
☐ F-GEFR	1975	King Air A100	B-220	W/o Lille, France. 28 Aug 86.	N700K
☐ F-GEJV	1972	King Air A100	B-129	Wfu. Cx F- 10/05.	N235B
☐ F-GEJY	1972	SA-226T Merlin 3	T-222	Wfu. Located La Roche-Sur-Yon, France.	N5306M
☐ F-GEPE	1977	PA-31T Cheyenne II	7720031	Wfu. Instructional airframe Bodo, Norway.	HB-LIW
☐ F-GERA	1977	Mitsubishi MU-2N	701SA	W/o St Just, France. 16 Apr 88.	N468DB
☐ F-GERN	1979	King Air C90A	LJ-854	W/o St Broladre, France. 30 Dec 93.	N712D
☐ F-GFBF	1976	PA-31T Cheyenne II	7620054	Wfu. Cx F- 12/99.	N39518
☐ F-GFCQ	1964	Gulfstream 1	140	Wfu. Cx F- 4/98.	N92SA
☐ F-GFHR	1982	Conquest II	441-0252	W/o Saclay, France. 17 Nov 88.	N441CG
☐ F-GFIC	1960	Gulfstream 1	49	Wfu. Cx F- 4/98.	N456
☐ F-GFJF	1967	King Air A90	LJ-262	Wfu. CoA expiry 1/89, Cx F- 8/96.	N111ME
☐ F-GFMS	1979	SA-226T Merlin 3B	T-296	W/o Vannes, France. 7 Nov 87.	N245DA
☐ F-GGAM	1965	King Air 90	LJ-32	Wfu. Cx F- 15 May 98.	F-BTOK
☐ F-GGRZ	1979	MU-2 Solitaire	395SA	W/o 9 May 91.	N787MA
☐ F-GHBE	1979	King Air 200	BB-500	W/o 8 Feb 91.	N13HC
☐ F-GHFM	1977	King Air 200	BB-213	Wfu. Cx F- 4/96.	C-GBWC
☐ F-GHLD	1977	King Air/Catpass 250	BB-233	W/o Libreville, Gabon. 17 Dec 98.	N50JD
☐ F-GIAL	1981	King Air 200	BB-844	W/o Caen-Carpiquet, France. 9 Sep 99. (at Rantoul, Ks.).	SE-IGV
☐ F-GIIX	1964	Gulfstream 1	128	W/o Lyon-Satolas, France. 28 Jun 94.	G-BMSR
☐ F-GIML	1976	King Air E90	LW-180	W/o Reims-Prunay, France. 14 Nov 00.	N2180L
☐ F-GJCN	1980	King Air E90	LW-335	W/o 18 Aug 81.	
☐ F-GJGC	1963	Gulfstream 1	111	Wfu. Located Marseille-Marignane, France.	N3630
☐ F-GJJJ	1974	King Air A100	B-196	Wfu. Parts at Bates City, Mo. USA.	N773SK
☐ F-GJLH	1990	Reims/Cessna F406	F406-0056	W/o Strasbourg, France. Sep 93.	
☐ F-GJPL	1981	PA-31T Cheyenne II	8120029	W/o Azores, Atlantic Ocean. 5 Jun 90.	(D-IKHK)
☐ F-GLBC	1991	TBM 700	18	W/o France 15 Nov 91.	
☐ F-GLRA	1985	King Air C90A	LJ-1105	W/o Saumur, France. 19 Oct 94. Cx F- 10/95,	N72233
☐ F-GNGU	1963	Gulfstream 1	101	Wfu. Cx F- 4/98.	4X-ARV
☐ F-GOAE	1992	King Air B300C	FM-1	W/o Santiago, Spain. 7 Jun 01.	V5-RTZ
☐ F-GVPD	1992	King Air C90B	LJ-1321	W/o Besancon, France. 19 Oct 06.	LX-GNG
☐ F-GVRM	1966	King Air A90	LJ-121	W/o Montpellier, France. 24 Dec 04.	N948RM
☐ F-HDGC	1996	King Air C90B	LJ-1430	Wfu. Cx F- 9/06.	N178JM
☐ F-ODUK	1982	Conquest II	441-0270	W/o Faaa, Tahiti, French Polynesia. 4 Dec 90.	N441AC
☐ F-OHJL	1998	King Air B200	BB-1592	W/o Nr Faaa-Tahiti, French Polynesia. 16 Apr 04.	N6148X

G = GREAT BRITAIN

Civil

☐ G-ASXT	1964	Gulfstream 1	135	Wfu. Cx G- 4/89. Located Denver, Co. USA..	N755G
☐ G-BABX	1973	King Air A100	B-141	W/o Sturgate, UK. 12 Jan 77.	
☐ G-BGHR	1979	King Air 200	BB-508	W/o Tremblay, France. 25 Sep 79.	
☐ G-BHUL	1974	King Air E90	LW-383	W/o Goodwood, UK. 22 Apr 85.	N99855
☐ G-BKID	1973	King Air C90	LJ-604	W/o Copenhagen, Denmark. 26 Dec 83.	N1GV
☐ G-BLKP	1984	BAe Jetstream 31	634	Wfu 12/06	G-31-634
☐ G-BNAT	1974	King Air C90	LJ-614	W/o East Midlands, UK. 25 Jan 88.	G-OMET
☐ G-BNCE	1959	Gulfstream 1	9	Wfu. Located Dundee, Scotland.	N436M
☐ G-BOBX	1961	Gulfstream 1	77	Wfu.	9Q-CFK
☐ G-MDJI	1983	King Air B200	BB-1162	W/o Ottley Chevin Hill, UK. 19 Oct 87.	N71CS
☐ G-MOXY	1980	Conquest II	441-0154	W/o Blackbushe, UK. 26 Apr 87.	G-BHLN
☐ G-TWIG	1986	Reims/Cessna F406	F406-0014	W/o 37nm NW of Inverness, Scotland. 22 Oct 04.	PH-FWD
☐ G-WSJE	1979	King Air 200	BB-484	W/o Southend, UK. 12 Sep 87.	N84KA

HB = SWITZERLAND

Civil

☐ HB-...		King Air 200	...	W/o Kracow, Poland. 27 Aug 95.	
☐ HB-FOA	1991	Pilatus PC-12	P-01	Wfu. Cx HB- 31 Dec 96. Preserved at Pilatus HQ.	

| Reg | Yr | Type | c/n | Owner/Operator | Prev Regn |

Reg	Yr	Type	c/n	Owner/Operator	Prev Regn
☐ HB-FOJ	1996	Pilatus PC-12/45	158	W/o Brno, Czech Republic. 26 May 98.	
☐ HB-GDV	1968	King Air B90	LJ-433	W/o Kleinober, Austria. 24 Jan 86.	
☐ HB-LHT	1975	PA-31T Cheyenne II	7520003	W/o Shannon, Ireland. 12 Nov 76.	N66841
☐ HB-LLP	1980	MU-2 Marquise	767SA	W/o Basel, Switzerland. 3 Sep 94.	N251MA
☐ HB-LLS	1981	Conquest 1	425-0040	W/o Berne, Switzerland. 3 Mar 86.	N6775J

HC = ECUADOR
Military

Reg	Yr	Type	c/n	Owner/Operator	Prev Regn
☐ FAE-723	1980	King Air 200	BB-723	W/o Huey Rapingo Mountain, Ecuador 24 May 81.	HC-BHG

HI = DOMINICAN REPUBLIC
Civil

Reg	Yr	Type	c/n	Owner/Operator	Prev Regn
☐ HI-578SP	1989	King Air 300	FA-180	W/o Guatemala 21 Jan 90.	N1568E

HK = COLOMBIA
Civil

Reg	Yr	Type	c/n	Owner/Operator	Prev Regn
☐ HK-1771G	1974	Rockwell 690A	11217	Wfu. Located Bogota, Colombia.	N9227N
☐ HK-1805	1968	King Air B90	LJ-329	Wfu. Parts at Dodson's, Ottawa, Ks. USA.	N303X
☐ HK-1844P	1973	Rockwell 690	11056	Wfu. Located Charallave, Colombia.	HK-1844W
☐ HK-2217	1971	681B Turbo Command	6053	W/o Medellin, Colombia. 13 Mar 86.	HK-2217W
☐ HK-2245P	1976	Mitsubishi MU-2L	684	Wfu. Cx USA 8/95 as N600TN.	HK-2245W
☐ HK-2415	1973	Rockwell 690A	11100	W/o Bolivar Quay, Colombia. 8 Sep 91. (was s/n 11070).	N9200N
☐ HK-2438W	1979	SA-226T Merlin 3B	T-305	Wfu. Located at Catam AB. Bogota, Colombia.	N5658M
☐ HK-2451P	1980	PA-31T Cheyenne II	8020040	Wfu. Cx HK- 5/00.	
☐ HK-2478P	1980	Gulfstream 840	11609	W/o Riofrio, Venezuela. 15 Jun 90.	HK-2478W
☐ HK-2489	1980	King Air 200	BB-393	W/o Bogota, Colombia. 28 Oct 85.	N2014K
☐ HK-2532G	1967	Mitsubishi MU-2B	010	Wfu.	N4MA
☐ HK-2599P	1980	Gulfstream 840	11642	Wfu. Cx HK- 5/00.	HK-2599W
☐ HK-2674P	1981	PA-31T Cheyenne II	8120047	Wfu. Located Bogota, Colombia.	
☐ HK-2873W	1962	King Air C90	LJ-994	Wfu. Located Madrid AB. Colombia.	HK-2873
☐ HK-2907P	1981	Cheyenne II-XL	8166059	W/o Bocono, Venezuela. 13 Feb 00.	(N620AD)
☐ HK-3236P	1971	681B Turbo Command	6046	Wfu. Located Medellin, Colombia.	HK-3236X
☐ HK-3278	1984	Gulfstream 1000	96073	W/o Caqueta, Venezuela. 21 Mar 90.	N85DJ
☐ HK-3315X	1959	Gulfstream 1	24	W/o Nr Ibague, Colombia. 5 Feb 90.	N713US
☐ HK-3316X	1960	Gulfstream 1	59	W/o Monteira, Colombia. 2 May 90.	N11CZ
☐ HK-3330X	1962	Gulfstream 1	90	Wfu. Parts at Dodson's, Rantoul, Ks. USA.	N41JK
☐ HK-3337	1985	Conquest II	441-0354	Wfu. Located Bogota, Colombia.	HK-3337W
☐ HK-3614	1980	Conquest II	441-0178	Wfu. Cx HK- 5/00.	N446WS
☐ HK-4422X	1978	King Air 200	BB-377	W/o Crash After take off from Eldorado	N52GT

Military

Reg	Yr	Type	c/n	Owner/Operator	Prev Regn
☐ FAC-5180	1982	Gulfstream 1000	96044	Wfu. Located El Dorado AB. Colombia.	HK-2908

HL = KOREA
Civil

Reg	Yr	Type	c/n	Owner/Operator	Prev Regn
☐ HL5204	1991	PA-42 Cheyenne 400L	5527043	W/o Cheju, South Korea. 20 Mar 91.	N9226B
☐ HL5223	1971	681B Turbo Command	6057	W/o South Korea. 13 Sep 74.	N9130N

HS = THAILAND
Civil

Reg	Yr	Type	c/n	Owner/Operator	Prev Regn
☐ HS-TFB	1966	680T Turbo Command	1573-28	W/o Bangkok, Thailand. 22 Jul 84.	N80SS

Military

Reg	Yr	Type	c/n	Owner/Operator	Prev Regn
☐ 21-111	1977	SA-226AT Merlin 4A	AT-062E	W/o Thailand. 6 Nov 78.	
☐ 29-999	1978	SA-226AT Merlin 4A	AT-065	W/o Thailand. 20 Sep 82.	N5442M
☐ 348	1980	SA-226T Merlin 3B	T-348	Wfu.	N1009G
☐ 81491	1976	Rockwell 690A	11340	Wfu in Don Muang Museum	11340

I = ITALY
Civil

Reg	Yr	Type	c/n	Owner/Operator	Prev Regn
☐ I-....	1978	PA-31T Cheyenne II	7820059	Wfu. (status ?).	N11BC
☐ I-CODE	1981	PA-31T Cheyenne II	8120023	W/o Malindi, Kenya. 30 Dec 86.	N2468X
☐ I-FRUT	1979	MU-2 Solitaire	413SA	Wfu. Located Rotterdam, Holland.	N994MA
☐ I-IDMA	1980	MU-2 Marquise	769SA	W/o Sardinia. 24 Oct 89.	N57MS
☐ I-KWYR	1980	King Air C90	LJ-873	W/o Rome, Italy. 10 Feb 89.	N44TG
☐ I-MDDD	1964	Gulfstream 1	143	Wfu. CoA expiry 26 Sep 91.	N914P
☐ I-MGGG	1960	Gulfstream 1	51	Wfu. Located Geneva, Switzerland.	N90PM
☐ I-MLWT	1967	680T Turbo Command	1694-73	Wfu. CoA expiry 8 Nov 89.	N999WT
☐ I-PJAR	1987	P-180 Avanti	1002	Wfu. CoA expiry 3 Jun 95.	

Reg	Yr	Type	c/n	Owner/Operator	Prev Regn
☐ I-PJAV	1987	P-180 Avanti	1001	Wfu. CoA expiry 7 Dec 90.	
☐ I-POMO	1979	PA-31T Cheyenne 1	7904030	W/o Nr Piacenza, Italy. 6 Nov 06.	N601PT
☐ I-RWWW	1977	King Air E90	LW-220	Wfu. CoA expiry 8 Apr 90.	N17619
☐ I-TASB	1963	Gulfstream 1	105	Wfu. Located Bacong, Negros Oriental, Philippines.	N702G
☐ I-TASE	1975	Rockwell 690A	11260	Wfu. CoA expiry 9 Oct 95. Last located Bergamo, Italy.	(N891WA)
☐ I-TELM	1979	Rockwell 690B	11506	Wfu. CoA expiry 2 Mar 87.	D-IKAH

JA = JAPAN

Civil

Reg	Yr	Type	c/n	Owner/Operator	Prev Regn
☐ JA8604	1981	Gulfstream 980	95044	W/o 24 Mar 03.	N65664
☐ JA8620	1963	Mitsubishi MU-2A	001	Wfu.	
☐ JA8625	1963	Mitsubishi MU-2A	002	Wfu. Displayed at Osaka, Japan as 'KA1969'.	
☐ JA8626	1963	Mitsubishi MU-2A	003	Wfu. Displayed at Aerospace Museum Nagoya, Japan.	
☐ JA8627	1963	Mitsubishi MU-2B	004	Wfu. Cx JA 9/97.	
☐ JA8628	1963	Mitsubishi MU-2B	005	Wfu. Displayed at Tokyo-Narita, Japan.	
☐ JA8753	1970	Mitsubishi MU-2G	504	W/o Japan. 11 Mar 81.	
☐ JA8767	1970	Mitsubishi MU-2G	520	Wfu. Cx JA 12/85.	
☐ JA8770	1971	Mitsubishi MU-2F	195	Wfu. Displayed at Senda, Japan.	
☐ JA8783	1971	Mitsubishi MU-2G	546	Wfu. Cx JA 4/86.	
☐ JA8825	1981	King Air 200T	BT-19	W/o Fukuoka, Japan. 17 Feb 87. (was BB-823).	N3718N
☐ JA8896	1992	TBM 700	68	W/o Obihiro Airport, Japan. 26 Apr 96.	F-OHBI

Military

Reg	Yr	Type	c/n	Owner/Operator	Prev Regn
☐ 03-3207	1969	Mitsubishi MU-2S	907	W/o Japan. 2 Sep 70.	
☐ 03-3208	1970	Mitsubishi MU-2S	908	Wfu. (was s/n 186).	
☐ 13-3209	1971	Mitsubishi MU-2S	909	Wfu. Displayed at JASDF Hamamatsu, Japan. (was s/n 200).	
☐ 13-3210	1971	Mitsubishi MU-2S	910	Wfu. (was s/n 201).	
☐ 13-3211	1971	Mitsubishi MU-2S	911	Wfu. (was s/n 202).	
☐ 13-3212	1971	Mitsubishi MU-2S	912	Wfu. (was s/n 204).	
☐ 22-001	1967	Mitsubishi MU-2C	801	W/o Japan. 10 May 71. (was s/n 036).	
☐ 22002	1971	Mitsubishi LR-1	802	W/o Niikappu-tyo, Hokkaido, Japan. 14 Jun 77. (was s/n 203).	
☐ 22004	1972	Mitsubishi LR-1	804	Wfu. Located Mitsu-Seiki in Ichinomiya-cho, Hyogo.	
☐ 22005	1973	Mitsubishi LR-1	805	Wfu. (was s/n 275).	
☐ 22006	1974	Mitsubishi LR-1	806	Wfu. (was s/n 317).	
☐ 22011	1980	Mitsubishi LR-1	811	W/o Japan. 10 Aug 81. (was s/n 421).	
☐ 22012	1980	Mitsubishi LR-1	812	W/o 27km E of Miyako-jima, Japan. 7 Feb 90. (was s/n 422).	
☐ 23050	1990	King Air 350	FL-15	Wfu. Training airframe at JGSDF Utsunomiya Flying School.	N25KB
☐ 23-3213	1972	Mitsubishi MU-2F	913	Wfu. (was s/n 225).	
☐ 23-3214	1972	Mitsubishi MU-2E	914	Wfu. (was s/n 227).	
☐ 33-3215	1972	Mitsubishi MU-2E	915	Wfu. (was s/n 234).	
☐ 33-3216	1972	Mitsubishi MU-2E	916	Wfu. (was s/n 235).	
☐ 33-3217	1973	Mitsubishi MU-2E	917	Wfu. (was s/n 278).	
☐ 43-3218	1973	Mitsubishi MU-2E	918	Wfu. (was s/n 279).	
☐ 53-3219	1974	Mitsubishi MU-2E	919	W/o SW of Hamamatsu, Japan. 19 Oct 94. (was s/n 318).	
☐ 53-3271	1974	Mitsubishi MU-2J	951	Wfu. (was s/n 654).	
☐ 63-3220	1976	Mitsubishi MU-2E	920	Wfu. (was s/n 335).	
☐ 63-3221	1976	Mitsubishi MU-2E	921	Wfu. (was s/n 336).	
☐ 6801	1973	King Air TC90	LJ-597	Wfu. Gate Guardian.	N1845W
☐ 6802	1973	King Air TC90	LJ-598	Wfu. Located Tokushima AB.	N1846W
☐ 6803	1973	King Air TC90	LJ-599	Wfu. Located Hachinohe AB.	N1847W
☐ 6804	1975	King Air TC90	LJ-642	Wfu.	N7312R
☐ 6805	1975	King Air TC90	LJ-670	Wfu.	N9395
☐ 6806	1978	King Air TC90	LJ-778	Wfu.	N23780
☐ 6807	1979	King Air TC90	LJ-855	Wfu. Gate Guardian.	N6062X
☐ 73-3201	1968	Mitsubishi MU-2S	901	Wfu. Displayed at Kissa Hikojo tearooms, Hamamatsu.	
☐ 73-3202	1968	Mitsubishi MU-2S	902	Wfu. (was s/n 128).	
☐ 73-3222	1977	Mitsubishi MU-2E	922	Wfu. (was s/n 360).	
☐ 73-3272	1978	Mitsubishi MU-2J	952	Wfu. (was s/n 715).	
☐ 83-3203	1969	Mitsubishi MU-2S	903	Wfu. (was s/n 147).	
☐ 83-3204	1969	Mitsubishi MU-2S	904	Wfu. (was s/n 148).	
☐ 83-3273	1978	Mitsubishi MU-2J	953	Wfu. (was s/n 716).	
☐ 93-3205	1969	Mitsubishi MU-2S	905	W/o Japan. 11 Apr 73.	
☐ 93-3206	1969	Mitsubishi MU-2S	906	Wfu. (was s/n 176).	
☐ 93-3274	1978	Mitsubishi MU-2J	954	Wfu. (was s/n 717).	

LN = NORWAY

Civil

Reg	Yr	Type	c/n	Owner/Operator	Prev Regn
☐ LN-KBV	1979	PA-31T Cheyenne II	7920049	Wfu. fake marks LN-KBV at Sola, Norway 6/03.	F-GFVO
☐ LN-KCR	1978	King Air C90	LJ-793	W/o Skien, Norway. 2 Apr 87.	
☐ LN-MAH	1977	Conquest II	441-0002	Wfu. Parts at Dodsons, Rantoul, Ks. USA.	SE-IBI
☐ LN-PAG	1976	King Air 200	BB-119	Wfu. Cx LN- 7/92.	OY-AUJ
☐ LN-TSA	1978	King Air 200	BB-308	W/o Nr Gello, Norway. 19 March 93.	N98WP
☐ LN-VIP	1967	King Air A90	LJ-271	W/o Bodo, Norway. 28 Jun 68.	
☐ LN-VIP	1982	Conquest II	441-0279	W/o 11 Oct 85.	G-BJYB

LV = ARGENTINA

Civil

Reg	Yr	Type	c/n	Owner/Operator	Prev Regn
☐ LV-LDB	1972	681B Turbo Command	6064	Wfu.	LQ-LDB
☐ LV-LTA	1974	Rockwell 690A	11197	W/o Argentina. 26 Oct 75.	LV-PTI
☐ LV-MAV	1977	Rockwell 690B	11397	W/o Argentina. 12 Sep 84.	LV-PVM
☐ LV-MBR	1975	Rockwell 690A	11266	W/o Buenos Aires, Argentina. 14 Sep 80.	LV-PUV
☐ LV-MOC	1979	PA-31T Cheyenne II	7920031	W/o Buenos Aires, Argentina. 4 May 80.	LV-P..
☐ LV-MOD	1979	PA-31T Cheyenne II	7920033	Wfu. Parts at White Industries, Bates City, Mo. USA.	LV-P..
☐ LV-MOP	1979	MU-2 Marquise	742SA	W/o en route Neuquen-Bahia Blanca, Argentina. 4 May 95.	LV-PBY
☐ LV-MYY	1979	PA-31T Cheyenne II	7920085	W/o Buenos Aires, Argentina. 1 Feb 80.	LV-P..
☐ LV-OEV	1980	Gulfstream 840	11628	W/o 26 Aug 81.	LV-PHJ
☐ LV-PAC	1978	PA-31T Cheyenne II	7820065	W/o Lima, Peru. 14 Jul 78.	
☐ LV-WLW	1973	SA-226T Merlin 3	T-230	W/o Ushaia, Argentina. 4 Apr 96. (at Rantoul, Ks.).	N789B

Military

Reg	Yr	Type	c/n	Owner/Operator	Prev Regn
☐ 4-G-46/074	1979	King Air 200	BB-543	W/o Tierra del Fuego, Argentina. 15 May 86.	
☐ AE-177	1977	SA-226T Merlin 3A	T-277	W/o Argentina. 1982.	N5395M
☐ GN-705	1980	PA-31T Cheyenne II	8020092	W/o San Manual, General Villegas, Argentina. 6 Oct 95.	LV-OIF

LX = LUXEMBOURG

Civil

Reg	Yr	Type	c/n	Owner/Operator	Prev Regn
☐ LX-KTY	1968	King Air B90	LJ-339	W/o Nouadhibou Airport, Mauretania 3 Feb 04.	(F-GKTY)
☐ LX-NOP	1976	SA-226T Merlin 3A	T-259	Wfu.	CF-01

N = USA

Civil

Reg	Yr	Type	c/n	Owner/Operator	Prev Regn
☐ N1KA	1978	King Air 200	BB-411	W/o Mar 80.	
☐ N1MU	1973	Mitsubishi MU-2J	578	Wfu. Cx USA 12/02.	N578EH
☐ N1NR	1972	Rockwell 690	11024	W/o Wellsburg, WV. USA. 14 Aug 72.	
☐ N1PT	1971	King Air C90	LJ-505	Wfu. Parts at Dodsons, Rantoul, Ks. USA.	N886K
☐ N1VY	1972	Mitsubishi MU-2J	567	W/o Hilton Head, SC. USA. 1 Aug 01.	N1VN
☐ N1YC	1969	SA-26AT Merlin 2B	T26-131	Wfu. Cx USA 8/04.	N4251R
☐ N2CJ	1978	Mitsubishi MU-2N	726SA	W/o Santa Barbara, Ca. USA. 28 Jun 91.	N898MA
☐ N2DB	1972	Rockwell 690	11028	Wfu. Cx USA 9/06.	N9228N
☐ N2EP	1967	King Air A90	LJ-284	W/o Crestview, Fl. USA. 13 Nov 90.	
☐ N2GG	1969	King Air B90	LJ-462	W/o Joliet, Il. USA. 15 Feb 75.	N821K
☐ N2GT	1977	Mitsubishi MU-2P	367SA	Wfu. Cx USA 11/97. Parts at Bates City, Mo. USA.	N67GT
☐ N2MF	1966	King Air 90	LJ-96	W/o Houston, Tx. USA. 19 Mar 78.	N3PC
☐ N3CG	1967	680V Turbo Command	1680-62	Wfu. N Reg Cx 6/07 as destroyed/scrapped	N3CG
☐ N3ED	1968	Mitsubishi MU-2D	101	W/o Riverton, Wy. USA. 17 Jun 81.	N75MD
☐ N3GS	1978	King Air B100	BE-36	Wfu. Cx USA 4/93. Parts at Griffin, Ga. USA.	N200TV
☐ N3MU	1969	Mitsubishi MU-2F	143	Wfu. Parts at White Industries Inc. Bates City, Mo. USA.	N700MA
☐ N3RB	1971	SA-226T Merlin 3	T-214	W/o S of Grand Isle, La. USA. 17 Sep 85.	N7090
☐ N4BC	1970	SA-226T Merlin 3	T-205E	Wfu.	N1226S
☐ N4GN	1973	King Air E90	LW-38	W/o New York City, USA. 10 Mar 80.	N5000T
☐ N4NA	1965	Gulfstream 1	151	Wfu. Located Tucson, Az. USA.	NASA4
☐ N4TN	1968	Mitsubishi MU-2D	115	Wfu.	N102MA
☐ N4TS	1972	King Air C90	LJ-541	W/o Ossian, In. USA. 24 Oct 83.	N9314Q
☐ N4UB	1990	2000 Starship	NC-4	Wfu. Last located 10/04 at Marana, Az. USA.	N75WD
☐ N5AP	1973	Mitsubishi MU-2N	604	Wfu. Cx USA 8/01.	N300WT
☐ N5ER	1968	680W Turbo Command	1760-6	Wfu.	N177DC
☐ N5LN	1980	MU-2 Marquise	799SA	W/o Nr Rock, Ks. USA. 4 Nov 98.	N928VF
☐ N5NP	1970	681 Turbo Commander	6042	W/o Greenup, Ky. USA. 8 Mar 78.	N5NR
☐ N5NQ	1977	Mitsubishi MU-2P	356SA	Wfu.	N5NC
☐ N5NW	1973	Mitsubishi MU-2J	597	W/o Searcy, Ar. USA. 23 Jan 79.	N5MW
☐ N5WU	1974	King Air C90	LJ-635	W/o Newton, WV. USA. 16 Feb 98. (parts at Rantoul, Ks.).	N5GC
☐ N6JM	1979	PA-31T Cheyenne 1	7904011	W/o Baker, Nv. USA. 8 Aug 98.	N96MM

Reg	Yr	Type	c/n	Owner/Operator	Prev Regn
N6PE	1981	King Air B200	BB-856	W/o Nr Tulsa, Ok. USA. 8 Dec 04.	N1802H
N7GA	1972	King Air A100	B-119	W/o Williamstown, Ms. USA. 4 Aug 94.	OH-BKC
N8CC	1972	Mitsubishi MU-2J	569	W/o Bartlett, Tx. USA. 6 Jun 86. Cx USA 9/93.	N213MA
N8VB	1959	Gulfstream 1	12	Wfu. Parts at Dodson's, Rantoul, Ks. USA.	(XA-TBT)
N9JS	1969	Mitsubishi MU-2F	178	W/o Alpena, Mi. USA. 22 Apr 81.	N711SH
N9PU	1980	King Air F90	LA-57	W/o Ruidoso, NM. USA. 9 Dec 89.	HP-80SF
N9TW	1968	King Air B90	LJ-379	Wfu. Cx USA 5/01.	N73LC
N10AY	1965	King Air 90	LJ-88	Wfu.	(N90233)
N10DA	1972	Mitsubishi MU-2J	551	Wfu. Cx USA 7/01.	N3330K
N10TM	1969	King Air B90	LJ-476	W/o.Cr on app. Chattanooga, Tn. 20.9.07	N41AA
N10TN	1970	681 Turbo Commander	6037	Wfu.	N9090N
N11LG	1973	Mitsubishi MU-2J	595	Wfu. Cx USA 2/94.	N299MA
N11SS	1970	Mitsubishi MU-2G	518	W/o Hawesville, Ky. USA. 19 Jan 79.	N144MA
N11WU	1972	Mitsubishi MU-2J	565	Wfu. Cx USA 3/94.	N11WF
N12AB	1965	King Air 90	LJ-45	Wfu.	HB-GBK
N12EW	1974	Mitsubishi MU-2K	316	Wfu. Cx USA 10/94. Parts at White Industries, Mo. USA.	N77SS
N12GW	1959	Gulfstream 1	19	Wfu.	PK-WWG
N12KA	1973	King Air E90	LW-41	W/o Bloomington, Il. USA. 21 Jul 02.	N2AS
N12KV	1967	680V Turbo Command	1675-58	Wfu.	N12KW
N13RR	1976	Mitsubishi MU-2L	682	Wfu. Cx USA 3/04.	N13PR
N13TV	1974	Rockwell 690A	11148	Wfu. Cx USA 1/01.	(N2KC)
N14TK	1967	King Air A90	LJ-255	Wfu. Parts at White Industries, Bates City, Mo. USA.	N5113
N14VR	1991	2000 Starship	NC-22	Wfu. Last located 10/04 at Marana, Az. USA.	N14VP
N15NG	1980	King Air 200	BB-666	Wfu. Cx USA 3/04.	N15NA
N15SS	1978	PA-31T Cheyenne II	7820068	W/o Madison, In. USA. 30 Nov 81. (parts at Bates City.	N6027A
N15VC	1967	Mitsubishi MU-2B	023	Wfu. Reg cx 7/07 destroyed/scrapped	N15VC
N16CG	1980	MU-2 Solitaire	418SA	W/o The Woodlands, Tx. USA 1 May 01.	YV-11CP
N17AE	1980	King Air F90	LA-80	W/o Nashville, TN. USA. 24 Jan 01.	N614RG
N17CA	1964	Gulfstream 1C	123	Wfu. Parts at White Industries Inc. Bates City, Mo.	N2602M
N17JJ	1969	SA-26AT Merlin 2B	T26-166	Wfu. Cx USA 6/01.	N23X
N18LP	1967	King Air A90	LJ-278	Wfu. Cx USA 9/98. Parts at Dodsons, Rantoul, Ks. USA.	N741L
N18SE	1969	SA-26AT Merlin 2B	T26-134	Wfu.	N1UA
N18WP	1974	Mitsubishi MU-2J	648	Wfu.	N529MA
N20DL	1980	PA-31T Cheyenne 1	8004045	Wfu. Scrapped. N Reg cx 5/07	N20DL
N20FD	1989	King Air C90A	LJ-1213	Wfu. Parts at White Industries, Bates City, Mo. USA.	N1559T
N20HF	1960	Gulfstream 1	47	Wfu.	N20CC
N20PT	1969	SA-26AT Merlin 2B	T26-128	W/o Winchester, Va. USA. 18 Mar 94.	C-FBVI
N21LF	1982	Lear Fan	E003	Wfu. Located Frontiers of Flight Museum, Dallas, USA.	(N327ML)
N21MK	1967	Mitsubishi MU-2B	032	Wfu. Cx USA 12/94.	N707EB
N21PC	1974	Mitsubishi MU-2K	295	Wfu. Cx USA 9/95.	N455MA
N21VM	1971	Mitsubishi MU-2G	535	Wfu.	N159RS
N22CN	1979	PA-31T Cheyenne 1	7904049	W/o Nr Glendive, Mt. USA. 30 Nov 94.	N2368R
N22DW	1980	SA-226T Merlin 3B	T-317	W/o Teterboro, NJ. USA. 31 May 05.	N10143
N22EQ	1971	Mitsubishi MU-2F	192	Wfu. Cx USA 6/95.	N22LC
N22TE	1972	King Air A100	B-115	Wfu. Parts at White Industries, Bates City, Mo. USA.	N22T
N23CD	1969	Mitsubishi MU-2F	142	W/o El Paso, Tx. USA. 17 Oct 85.	N209MA
N23FL	1993	2000A Starship	NC-32	Wfu. Last located 3/05 at Marana, Az. USA.	N23FH
N23LS	1977	Rockwell 690B	11372	W/o.	N81557
N23UG	1963	Gulfstream 1	108	Wfu.	N1707Z
N24CV	1996	King Air B200	BB-1524	W/o Pacific Ocean off San Diego, Ca. USA. 24 May 00.	N1024A
N25ST	1971	King Air C90	LJ-507	W/o Gold Beach, Or. USA. 21 Aug 89.	N5PT
N26CA	1978	PA-31T Cheyenne II	7820062	Wfu.	(N82295)
N26JB	1969	SA-26AT Merlin 2B	T26-163	W/o Colorado, USA. 13 Feb 92.	N111SE
N26RA	1995	2000A Starship	NC-53	Wfu. Last located 6/06 at Marana, Az. USA.	N6MF
N26RT	1971	SA-226T Merlin 3	T-216	W/o Helsinki, Finland. 24 Feb 89.	N50PK
N27GP	1967	Mitsubishi MU-2B	027	W/o Schellville, Ca. USA. 13 Jul 82.	N57907
N27KM	1977	PA-31T Cheyenne II	7720051	Wfu. Reg cx 5/07. Aircraft scrapped	85-1609
N27MT		Rockwell 690B	11533	W/o Springfield, Mo. USA. 8 Oct 94.	N376RF
N27RA	1985	Beech 1900C	UB-37	W/o 125nm NW of Las Vegas, Nv. USA. 16 Mar 04.	N7214K
N28AD	1976	Rockwell 690A	11291	W/o Shepahua, Peru. 17 May 93.	
N28CG	1960	Gulfstream 1	50	Wfu.	N820CE
N28HF	1967	King Air A90	LM-82	Wfu. Located Ivy State Technical College, Terre Haute, In.	67-18082
N28SE	1967	King Air A90	LJ-239	W/o Apalachicola, Fl. USA. 30 Jun 85.	N28S
N29AA	1966	King Air 90	LJ-110	Wfu.	N695V
N30EM	1982	King Air B200	BB-958	W/o Rangeley, Me. USA. 22 Dec 00.	N82AJ
N30FL	1977	King Air C90	LJ-741	Wfu.	F-GFLD

Reg	Yr	Type	c/n	Owner/Operator	Prev Regn
N30GC	1973	King Air A100	B-177	w/o Crashed in Trees, Chino CA. 11/07	(N100BX)
N30LH	1994	2000A Starship	NC-47	Wfu. Last located 6/06 at Marana, Az. USA.	N64GQ
N30LT	2001	TBM 700B	201	W/o Nr Oxford-Kidlington, UK. 6 Dec 03.	
N30PC	1980	King Air 200	BB-702	W/o Pensacola, Fl. USA. 10 Apr 89.	
N30SG	1968	SA-26T Merlin 2A	T26-28	Wfu. Parts at White Industries, Bates City, Mo. USA.	N1212S
N30TF	1969	SA-26AT Merlin 2B	T26-162	W/o Cahokia, Il. USA. 16 Feb 03. (parts at Bates City).	C-FTEL
N31AT	1977	SA-226AT Merlin 4A	AT-057	Wfu. Parts at White Industries Inc. Bates City, Mo. USA.	N31264
N31CL	1967	Mitsubishi MU-2B	015	Wfu. Cx USA 4/96.	N707EB
N31XL	1981	Cheyenne II-XL	8166003	W/o Jackson, Tn. USA. 3 Jun 01.	
N32DF	1966	680V Turbo Command	1624-53	Wfu.	N1010M
N32HG	1976	King Air 200	BB-146	W/o New Castle, De. USA. 16 Jun 92.	N32CL
N32RL	1981	King Air B100	BE-117	W/o Gold Beach, Or. USA. 30 Sep 87.	
N33BJ	1977	PA-31T Cheyenne II	7720061	Wfu. Parts at White Industries, Bates City, Mo. USA.	
N33SE	1970	SA-26AT Merlin 2B	T26-170	Wfu. Cx USA 8/95.	N19SE
N33TF	1964	Gulfstream 1	133	Wfu. Parts at White Industries, Bates City, Mo. USA..	TU-VAC
N34F	1966	King Air A90	LJ-119	W/o 10 Mar 77. Parts at White Industries, Bates City, Mo.	N25CA
N34SM	1976	SA-226T Merlin 3A	T-263	W/o San Antonio, Tx. USA. 3 Feb 77.	N5377M
N34UA	1969	SA-26AT Merlin 2B	T26-145	Wfu. Cx USA 4/93.	
N35GT	1976	PA-31T Cheyenne II	7620030	Wfu. Parts at White Industries, Bates City, Mo. USA.	N300CM
N36CA	1979	PA-31T Cheyenne II	7920013	W/o Riviera, Az. USA. 8 Feb 84.	
N37AL	1979	MU-2 Marquise	752SA	Wfu. Parts at White Industries Inc. Bates City, Mo. USA.	N11WQ
N38B	1972	King Air 200	BB-1	Wfu. Cx USA 3/95.	
N38GP	1965	King Air 90	LJ-46	Wfu. Last located Deland, Fl. USA.	C-GZIZ
N39BC	1967	Mitsubishi MU-2B	020	Wfu. Parts at White Industries Inc. Bates City, Mo. USA.	N3552X
N39TU	1991	2000 Starship	NC-23	Wfu. Located Pima Museum, Tucson, Az. USA.	N39TW
N39YV	1975	King Air/Catpass 250	BB-39	W/o Pasadena, Ca. USA. 12 May 89.	N63JR
N40MP	1973	Rockwell 690A	11116	W/o Kingston, Ut. USA. 12 Nov 74.	
N40PP	1970	Mitsubishi MU-2G	515	Wfu.	N155WC
N40RM	1966	King Air A90	LJ-155	Wfu. Parts at White Industries, Bates City, Mo. USA.	N7HU
N41BE	1979	King Air A100	B-245	W/o Eveleth, Mn. USA. 25 Oct 02.	N41BP
N41DZ	1968	King Air B90	LJ-412	Wfu. Cx USA 12/98.	(N56K)
N41KA	1976	King Air B100	BE-1	Wfu. Cx USA 8/87. (was B-205).	
N41VC	1967	King Air A90	LJ-242	W/o Alice, Tx. USA. 12 Aug 97.	N812PS
N41WE	1978	King Air E90	LW-280	W/o Rawlins, Wy. USA. 11 Jan 05.	N4820M
N42CA	1964	Gulfstream 1	137	Wfu. Dismantled at Detroit Willow Run, Mi. Cx USA 4/95.	(N811CC)
N43DT	1965	King Air 90	LJ-6	Wfu. Cx USA 6/95. Parts at White Industries, Mo. USA.	C-GSFC
N43GT	1975	King Air C90	LJ-652	W/o Chamblee, Ga. USA. 1 Oct 89.	N4072S
N44MR	1973	Mitsubishi MU-2J	611	W/o Port Aransas, Tx. USA. 30 Nov 80. (parts at Bates City)	N344MA
N44UE	1973	King Air A100	B-140	W/o Atlanta, Ga. USA. 18 Jan 90. (parts at White Inds.).	N44UF
N45BS	1972	Mitsubishi MU-2J	558	W/o Carolina, PR. 15 Apr 02.	(N558BK)
N45EV	1971	Mitsubishi MU-2F	211	Wfu. Cx USA 6/95.	N123GS
N45MF	1977	King Air 200	BB-234	W/o collided with mountainous terrain, Belgrade, Mt. 6/2/07	N80PA
N45Q	1980	Gulfstream 840	11623	W/o Deadhorse, Al. USA.12 Oct 90.	N11EX
N45QC	1966	680T Turbo Command	1542-7	Wfu.	N45Q
N45RM	1976	King Air E90	LW-174	W/o Nr Yurimaguas, Peru. 1 Jul 92.	N21KE
N45TT	1967	King Air A90	LJ-312	W/o.N Reg Cx 7/07. Scrapped?	N675SB
N46DT	1965	King Air 90	LJ-7	Wfu. Parts at White Industries Inc. Bates City, Mo. USA.	C-GJBK
N46WA	1965	King Air 90	LJ-65	W/o Golfe du Lion-Marseilles, France. 13 Jan 94.	N981LE
N47CC	1978	PA-31T Cheyenne II	7820016	W/o Richlands, Va. USA. 29 Jul 81.	N82218
N47CK	1971	681B Turbo Command	6058	Wfu. Parts at White Industries, Mo. USA.	N4ME
N47CP	1981	PA-31T Cheyenne II	8120039	Wfu. Cx USA 8/90.	N2589X
N47LC	1973	King Air E90	LW-64	W/o.Crashed Carlsbad, Ca. 3.7.07	N213DS
N47R	1961	Gulfstream 1	69	Wfu. Located Pratt Community College, Ks. USA.	N47
N47WM	1979	King Air E90	LW-307	W/o NW Kingston, ON. Canada. 20 Jan 95.	N300EH
N48FL	1994	2000A Starship	NC-40	Wfu. Last located 10/04 at Marana, Az. USA.	N8300S
N49LL	1992	King Air C90B	LJ-1316	W/o Marble Canyon, Az. USA. 13 Jun 05.	N8114P
N50ES	1966	King Air 90	LJ-111	Wfu. Cx USA 5/96.	N27LR
N50JJ	1967	King Air A90	LJ-290	Wfu. Last located Montgomery, Al. USA.	N50JP
N50KV	1968	SA-26AT Merlin 2B	T26-115	W/o Lawrenceville, Ga. USA. 26 Apr 05.	N1223S
N50KW	1980	MU-2 Marquise	784SA	W/o Columbia, SC. USA. 19 Jan 96.	N785MA
N50LT	1977	King Air 200	BB-284	Wfu. Cx USA 9/97.	N25MK
N50PC	1970	King Air 100	B-19	W/o Birmingham, Al. USA. 1 Dec 74.	
N50VS	1978	Mitsubishi MU-2P	379SA	W/o Mansfield, Oh. USA. 2 Jan 89.	(N500V)
N53AD	1980	MU-2 Marquise	776SA	W/o Saratoga, Wy. USA. 5 Nov 81.	N262MA
N53LG	1979	Rockwell 690B	11523	W/o Nr Homerville, Ga. USA. 27 Mar 03.	N333PA
N55JS	1974	Rockwell 690A	11195	W/o W of Antlers, Ok. USA. 15 Oct 06.	N690DD

Reg	Yr	Type	c/n	Owner/Operator	Prev Regn
☐ N55MG	1967	King Air A90	LJ-303	W/o Charleston, SC. USA. 26 Nov 77.	N55MP
☐ N55MU	1993	2000A Starship	NC-30	Wfu. Last located 10/04 at Marana, Az. USA.	N55MP
☐ N55PC	1969	Mitsubishi MU-2F	146	Wfu. Cx USA 9/93.	(N78HC)
☐ N55ZM	1968	SA-26T Merlin 2A	T26-11	Wfu.	N55JM
☐ N56KA	1973	King Air E90	LW-46	Wfu. Cx USA 1/95. Parts at Dodsons, Rantoul, Ks. USA.	
☐ N57MM	1966	King Air A90	LJ-126	Wfu. Parts at White Industries, Bates City, Mo. USA.	N570M
☐ N57V	1967	King Air A90	LJ-264	W/o Washington, DC. USA. 25 Jan 75.	N573M
☐ N58FS	1969	SA-26AT Merlin 2B	T26-120	Wfu.	N74YC
☐ N59MD	1980	Conquest II	441-0177	W/o Derry, Pa. USA. 11 Nov 85.	
☐ N60AW	1980	PA-31T Cheyenne II	8020051	W/o Big Bear Lake, Ca. USA. 17 Feb 92.	N2343V
☐ N60BN	1969	Mitsubishi MU-2F	163	Wfu.	N6TN
☐ N60BT	1977	Mitsubishi MU-2P	358SA	W/o Edgartown, Ma. USA. 6 Oct 2000.	C-GIRO
☐ N60KG	1970	Mitsubishi MU-2G	511	Wfu. Cx USA 5/99.	N60KC
☐ N62BC	1976	PA-31T Cheyenne II	7620043	Wfu. Parts at White Industries, Bates City, Mo. USA.	N52BC
☐ N62BL	1978	King Air E90	LW-272	W/o New Roads, La. USA. 23 Jun 05.	(N301HC)
☐ N63XL	1981	Cheyenne II-XL	8166037	W/o Colorado Springs, Co. USA. 15 Sep 89.	D-IESW
☐ N64MD	1979	MU-2 Marquise	747SA	W/o Rapid City, SD. USA. 9 Feb 90.	N777ST
☐ N65CE	1960	Gulfstream 1	45	Wfu. Located Des Moines Educational Resource Center.	N329CT
☐ N65TD	1970	King Air 100	B-50	W/o Windsor, Ma. USA. 10 Dec 86.	N166TR
☐ N66CA	1979	PA-31T Cheyenne 1	7904055	W/o Mexico. 21 Apr 83.	
☐ N66KS	1971	SA-226T Merlin 3	T-209	W/o Bahamas. 9 Sep 86.	N400SU
☐ N66LM	1983	Conquest 1	425-0137	W/o Lakeland, Fl. USA. 11 Feb 92.	N6884L
☐ N66MF	1984	PA-42 Cheyenne IIIA	5501009	Wfu. Last located Montgomery, Al. USA.	N66MT
☐ N66U	1974	Mitsubishi MU-2K	309	W/o Hayden, Co. USA. 12 Sep 82.	N44RF
☐ N67SM	1970	Mitsubishi MU-2F	183	Wfu. CX USA 4/95.	N221KP
☐ N67TC	1974	Rockwell 690A	11233	Wfu. Cx USA 5/05.	HR-AAJ
☐ N68AM	1982	King Air F90	LA-172	Wfu. Cx USA 1/06.	(N808DS)
☐ N68KA	1981	King Air B200	BB-793	Wfu. Impounded by Mexican Government in 1986.	
☐ N68TG	1961	Gulfstream 1	68	W/o Tri Cities Airport, Bristol, Tn. USA. 15 Jul 83.	N7ZA
☐ N69BS	1991	TBM 700	10	W/o Spearfish, SD. USA. 4 Aug 98.	N19AP
☐ N69QJ	1973	Mitsubishi MU-2K	254	W/o Morristown, Tn. USA. 13 Nov 75.	N616AF
☐ N69TM	1976	Rockwell 690A	11322	W/o Nr Cashion, OK. USA. 12 Feb 95.	N4601L
☐ N70QR	1964	Gulfstream 1	144	Wfu. Cx USA 3/91.	N70CR
☐ N71CJ	1963	Gulfstream 1	107	Wfu. Last located Houston-Hobby, Tx. USA.	N71CR
☐ N71CR	1965	Gulfstream 1	163	W/o Addison, Tx. USA. 11 Jul 75.	N618M
☐ N71RD	1969	Gulfstream 1	322	Wfu. Parts at White Industries Inc. Bates City, Mo. USA.	N9QM
☐ N72B	1979	MU-2 Marquise	735SA	W/o Jefferson, Ga. USA. 24 Mar 83.	N913MA
☐ N72BS	1972	King Air A100	B-113	W/o Milville, NJ. USA. 2 Feb 85.	N9439Q
☐ N72VF	1975	Rockwell 690A	11242	W/o Yakima, Wa. USA. 12 Dec 97.	N72VT
☐ N73MW	1975	King Air 200	BB-22	W/o Kaduna, Nigeria. 28 Nov 05.	N7300R
☐ N74CC	1974	King Air C90	LJ-620	W/o Somerset, Ky. USA. 18 Jan 00.	
☐ N74EJ	1978	King Air 200	BB-340	W/o Dalton, Ga. USA. 14 Aug 97.	(N74PF)
☐ N74FB	1980	MU-2 Marquise	770SA	W/o Indianapolis, In. USA. 11 Sep 92.	N378RM
☐ N74LV	1982	King Air B200	BB-1074	Wfu. stolen 6 Mar 87. Cx USA 2/94.	C-GTDX
☐ N74MA	1969	King Air B90	LJ-479	Wfu. Cx USA 10/02.	(N502M)
☐ N74NL	1977	PA-31T Cheyenne II	7720010	W/o Lake County, In. USA. 30 Dec 86.	N2YP
☐ N74TD	1992	2000A Starship	NC-27	Wfu. Evergreen Aviation Museum, McMinnville, Or.	N74TF
☐ N75CF	1977	King Air E90	LW-212	W/o Beaufort, SC. USA. 19 Dec 99.	
☐ N75GC	1977	King Air C90	LJ-727	W/o Marathon, Fl. USA. 31 Jan 04.	N888BK
☐ N76BT	1966	680V Turbo Command	1567-23	Wfu. Cx USA 6/02.	N76D
☐ N76GM	1970	King Air B90	LJ-498	W/o Longmont, Co. USA. 23 Jan 97. (Parts at Rantoul, Ks.).	N100CQ
☐ N76ST	1967	SA-26T Merlin 2A	T26-4	Wfu. Parts at Dodson's, Rantoul, Ks. USA.	N700SC
☐ N77PR	1977	PA-31T Cheyenne II	7720006	Wfu. Cx USA 1/94.	N77CG
☐ N77SA	1983	Conquest II	441-0329	W/o Anchorage, Ak. USA. 28 Aug 05.	N12099
☐ N77TM	1968	Mitsubishi MU-2D	116	Wfu. Lake City, Fl. USA.	N862Q
☐ N78CP	1974	SA-226AT Merlin 4A	AT-029	Wfu. Parts at White Industries Inc. Bates City, Mo. USA.	N294A
☐ N78D	1966	680V Turbo Command	1580-33	W/o New Orleans, La. USA. 5 Dec 71.	
☐ N78L	1973	King Air A100	B-167	W/o Brookville, Fl. USA. 8 Nov 86.	N65HC
☐ N79BJ	1966	680V Turbo Command	1610-46	Wfu. Located Area Technical School, Atlanta, Ga. USA.	N79D
☐ N79HS	1961	Gulfstream 1	79	Wfu. Cx USA 9/92.	N190DM
☐ N80GP	1966	King Air WV	LJ-137	W/o Wheeling, WV. USA. 13 Nov 97.	N24PR
☐ N80JN	1974	Mitsubishi MU-2J	626	W/o.Destroyed 8/99. Sold to Ireland as parts 6/07	N80JN
☐ N80RD	1968	Gulfstream 1	198	W/o Houston, Tx. USA. 23 Aug 90.	N100C
☐ N81JN	1981	Gulfstream 840	11660	Wfu. Cx USA 11/05. Last located Mexico.	(N140WJ)
☐ N81MD	1974	King Air A100	B-203	W/o Lagos, Nigeria. 11 Aug 78.	N7373R
☐ N81SM	1981	PA-42 Cheyenne III	8001007	W/o Horseshoe Bay, Tx. USA. 7 Feb 87. Cx USA 9/95.	N51SM

Reg	Yr	Type	c/n	Owner/Operator	Prev Regn
☐ N81TR	1981	Gulfstream 840	11690	W/o Nr Denver, Co. USA. 23 Dec 92.	N5942K
☐ N82	1988	King Air 300	FF-17	W/o Nr Winchester Regional Airport, Va. USA. 26 Oct 93.	
☐ N82MA	1975	Mitsubishi MU-2L	665	W/o Nashville, Tn. USA. 6 Sep 90.	SX-AGQ
☐ N83MC	1973	Rockwell 690A	11124	Wfu. Cx USA 9/91.	(N83RV)
☐ N85BK	1981	King Air 200	BB-734	W/o Morlan, Ga. USA. 4 Dec 03. (parts to AAR, Griffin, Ga).	N85BC
☐ N85NL	1966	King Air 90	LJ-90	Wfu. Parts at Dodsons, Rantoul, Ks. USA.	N65NL
☐ N86SD	1980	MU-2 Marquise	765SA	W/o Dubuque, Ia. USA 19 Apr 93.	N984MA
☐ N87YB	1969	SA-26AT Merlin 2B	T26-130	W/o. Cx USA 3/98.	N87Y
☐ N88CA	1980	PA-31T Cheyenne II	8020081	Wfu. Cx USA 6/97.	C-GCNO
☐ N88CR	1971	King Air C90	LJ-514	W/o Houston, Tx. USA. 16 Jan 79.	N111HR
☐ N88LB	1974	PA-31T Cheyenne II	7400004	Wfu. Parts at White Industries, Bates City, Mo. USA.	N61DP
☐ N88TW	1976	King Air F90	LA-29	Wfu. Cx USA 4/01.	N667HE
☐ N88WZ	1967	680V Turbo Command	1713-87	Wfu.	N1123V
☐ N89CR	1972	Mitsubishi MU-2F	233	Wfu. Cx USA 7/99.	N5NE
☐ N89DA	1967	680V Turbo Command	1702-78	W/o Damphries, Jamaica. 15 Nov 82.	N89D
☐ N89JR	1967	King Air A90	LJ-185	Wfu. Parts at White Industries, Bates City, Mo. USA.	N769
☐ N90AF	1973	King Air E90	LW-29	W/o Cuzco, Peru. 26 Sep 93.	N1739W
☐ N90BB	1976	PA-31T Cheyenne II	7620027	Wfu. Parts at White Industries, Bates City, Mo. USA.	N82013
☐ N90BP	1977	King Air C90	LJ-718	Wfu. Cx USA 2/96.	
☐ N90DA	1972	King Air E90	LW-22	Wfu. Cx USA 10/03.	(OB-1602)
☐ N90JR	1967	King Air A90	LJ-211	Wfu. Cx USA 5/96. Parts at Dodsons, Ottawa, Ks. USA.	(D-ILKC)
☐ N90NY	1965	King Air 90	LJ-73	Wfu. Parts at White Industries, Bates City, Mo. USA.	N6GT
☐ N90RG	1972	King Air C90	LJ-546	W/o Pontiac, Mi. USA. 6 Aug 92.	N45BE
☐ N90SJ	1966	King Air A90	LJ-177	Wfu. Parts at White Industries, Bates City, Mo. USA.	N31NC
☐ N91G	1960	Gulfstream 1	37	W/o Houston, Tx. USA. 24 Sep 78.	N20S
☐ N91TW	1978	PA-31T Cheyenne II	7820078	W/o Delta, Ut. USA. 17 Jan 82.	
☐ N92JR	1967	Mitsubishi MU-2B	006	W/o Miami, Fl. USA. 13 May 81. (parts at White Inds.).	C-GMUA
☐ N93NB	1982	King Air B200	BB-970	Wfu. Cx USA 1/97.	N124CS
☐ N93NM	1982	Gulfstream 1000	96020	Wfu. Cx USA 11/05. Last located Mexico.	(N139WJ)
☐ N93UM	1971	Mitsubishi MU-2G	537	Wfu.	N161MA
☐ N94HD	1968	680W Turbo Command	1811-28	W/o Lucerne, Ca. USA. 11 Nov 78.	N94HC
☐ N94U	1981	King Air F90	LA-124	W/o Lynchburg, Va. USA. 24 Nov 00.	N13
☐ N95AC	1981	SA-226T Merlin 3B	T-381	Wfu. Last located Montgomery, Al. USA.	N80MJ
☐ N95MJ	1984	MU-2 Marquise	1564SA	W/o Egelsbach, Germany. 11 Jan 99.	N5PC
☐ N95UF	1966	King Air 90	LJ-78	Wfu. Last located at Deland, Fl. USA.	N730K
☐ N96JP	1972	Mitsubishi MU-2J	556	W/o Casper, Wy. USA. 6 Apr 93. Cx USA 7/94.	N33RH
☐ N96JS	1976	PA-31T Cheyenne II	7620021	Wfu. Parts at White Industries, Bates City, Mo. USA.	N131RG
☐ N96MA	1967	Mitsubishi MU-2B	011	Wfu.	N96MA
☐ N96WF	1996	Pilatus PC-12	139	Wfu. Cx USA 8/03.	HB-FRA
☐ N97AB	1970	SA-226T Merlin 3	T-203	W/o	N5273M
☐ N98AL	1968	Mitsubishi MU-2D	105	Wfu. Cx USA 2/96.	N2RA
☐ N98MK	1962	Gulfstream 1	98	Wfu. Parts at White Industries, Bates City, Mo. USA.	N29AY
☐ N100BE	1975	King Air A100	B-221	W/o Colorado Springs, Co. USA. 21 Dec 97. (at Rantoul, Ks.).	HZ-AFE
☐ N100CT	1966	680V Turbo Command	1618-50	W/o Bridgeport, Ct. USA. 3 Sep 84.	N4693E
☐ N100HC	1976	King Air 200	BB-98	W/o Greenville, Tx. USA. 12 Aug 85.	
☐ N100LB	1977	PA-31T Cheyenne II	7720021	Wfu. Parts at White Industries, Bates City, Mo. USA.	(N234C)
☐ N100NL	1969	SA-26AT Merlin 2B	T26-168	W/o Hot Springs, Va. USA. 16 Oct 71.	N20DE
☐ N100NX	1967	SA-26AT Merlin 2A	T26-3	Wfu. Parts at White Industries, Bates City, Mo. USA.	N100MX
☐ N100RN	1978	PA-31T Cheyenne II	7820091	W/o Utica, Wi. USA. 23 Feb 85.	N6121A
☐ N100SW	1971	Mitsubishi MU-2G	539	W/o between Miami & Atlanta, USA. 1 Apr 77. Cx USA 6/95.	N163MA
☐ N100TN	1975	PA-31T Cheyenne II	7520013	Wfu.	
☐ N101FB	1974	PA-31T Cheyenne II	7400007	Wfu. Parts at White Industries, Bates City, Mo. USA..	(N66836)
☐ N101GA	1965	King Air 90	LJ-11	W/o Royal, Ar. USA. 3 Jan 95.	N2JJ
☐ N101LR	1978	King Air C90	LJ-802	W/o Quito, Ecuador. 15 Sep 81.	
☐ N101XC	1967	King Air A90	LJ-219	Wfu. Parts at White Industries, Bates City, Mo. USA.	N52C
☐ N102JC	1997	Jetcruzer 500	001	Wfu. Cx USA 1/98.	
☐ N102RB	1972	King Air E90	LW-19	W/o Nr Otuzco, Julcan, Peru. 18 Mar 93.	N1716W
☐ N103RC	1975	Mitsubishi MU-2L	673	W/o West Memphis, Ar. USA. 22 Sep 05.	N4565E
☐ N104BR	1976	SA-226T Merlin 3A	T-269	W/o DuPage, Il. USA. 28 Aug 01.	N5039F
☐ N105FL	1989	King Air C90A	LJ-1215	W/o St Augustine, Fl. USA. 9 Apr 92.	
☐ N105MA	1968	Mitsubishi MU-2F	123	Wfu. Cx USA 6/95.	C-FHTL
☐ N106DP	1973	Mitsubishi MU-2J	571	Wfu. Cx USA 7/94.	N5HE
☐ N106EC	1968	SA-26T Merlin 2A	T26-34	Wfu. Parts at White Industries, Bates City, Mo. USA.	N96D
☐ N106MA	1970	Mitsubishi MU-2F	184	W/o Lake Texoma, Tx. USA. 7 May 91.	
☐ N107DC	1968	680W Turbo Command	1777-15	Wfu. Parts at Dodsons, Ottawa. Ks. USA.	N24099
☐ N107MA	1970	Mitsubishi MU-2F	185	Wfu. Cx USA 10/95. Parts at White Industries, Mo. USA.	

Reg	Yr	Type	c/n	Owner/Operator	Prev Regn
☐ N108SC	1971	Mitsubishi MU-2G	545	W/o Alamogordo, NM. 25 Jun 92.	N169MA
☐ N109P	1963	Gulfstream 1	109	Wfu. Cx USA 12/98.	N307AT
☐ N109TW	1971	Mitsubishi MU-2G	543	W/o Pago Pago, American Samoa. 22 Nov 81.	YV-1049P
☐ N110JK	1983	Cheyenne T-1040	8375005	Wfu. Cx USA 6/01.	PJ-WIG
☐ N110LT	1977	King Air C90	LJ-729	W/o Burlington, NC. USA. 13 Feb 90.	
☐ N110SL	1968	King Air B90	LJ-364	Wfu. Cx USA 8/98. Parts at Griffin, Ga. USA.	N555TB
☐ N111FL	1974	Rockwell 690A	11163	W/o Taos, NM. 29 Mar 92.	N9769S
☐ N111LA	1976	Rockwell 690A	11324	Wfu. Cx USA 7/92.	N81441
☐ N111PT	1968	SA-26T Merlin 2A	T26-15	Wfu.	N341T
☐ N111QL	1976	Rockwell 690A	11312	W/o Nacogdoches, Tx. USA. 17 Sep 83.	N1QL
☐ N111RC	1981	Conquest II	441-0188	Wfu. Cx USA 3/04.	N441GP
☐ N111WE	1966	680V Turbo Command	1593-41	Wfu.	N688NA
☐ N112SK	1974	Mitsubishi MU-2J	651	W/o Robert Lee, Tx. USA. 1 Dec 84.	N55KV
☐ N113TC	1965	King Air 90	LJ-22	W/o Knoxville, Tn. USA. 16 Jul 74.	N9502Q
☐ N114CM	1977	King Air C90	LJ-709	W/o Jackson, Wy. USA. 16 Jun 86.	N33TW
☐ N114CW	1966	King Air A90	LJ-114	Wfu. Cx USA 7/84.	N114KA
☐ N114K	1975	King Air E90	LW-122	W/o Mineral Wells, Tx. USA. 26 Oct 81.	VH-DDG
☐ N117EA	1980	Conquest II	441-0191	W/o ground fire, Pa. USA. 30 Nov 86.	C-GGMK
☐ N118LT	1960	Gulfstream 1	55	Wfu.	N9446E
☐ N119WM	1980	King Air 200	BB-662	W/o Salt Lake City, Ut. USA. 3 Mar 97.	N117WM
☐ N121BE	1980	PA-31T Cheyenne 1	8004036	W/o Great Falls, Mt. USA. 19 May 98.	N657DC
☐ N121CS	1981	PA-42 Cheyenne III	8001032	W/o Crashed near Prescott, Az. 18/10/06	N432R
☐ N121MA	1971	Mitsubishi MU-2F	206	Wfu.	
☐ N122G	1967	Mitsubishi MU-2B	033	Wfu.	N3563X
☐ N123AX	1972	Mitsubishi MU-2F	220	Wfu. Cx USA 10/94. Parts at White Industries, Mo. USA.	N123UA
☐ N123VC	1971	Mitsubishi MU-2F	214	Wfu. Located Technical School Vasteras-Hasslo, Sweden.	N129MA
☐ N125AB	1981	MU-2 Marquise	1531SA	Wfu. Cx USA 4/94.	N450MA
☐ N126AB	1969	Mitsubishi MU-2F	139	Wfu. Cx USA 8/01.	LV-WME
☐ N129D	1972	King Air A100	B-134	W/o Dieques, PR. USA. 17 Aug 83.	N84B
☐ N129GP	1967	King Air A90	LJ-216	W/o Endicott, NY. USA. 16 Apr 67.	
☐ N130AT	1980	King Air B100	BE-88	Wfu. Cx USA 8/95.	
☐ N131AF	1978	PA-31T Cheyenne II	7820005	Wfu. Parts at White Industries, Bates City, Mo. USA.	N5MC
☐ N132MA	1970	Mitsubishi MU-2G	503	W/o Atlantic City, NJ. USA. 16 Apr 72.	JA8739
☐ N133MA	1970	Mitsubishi MU-2G	506	W/o Rollinsville, Co. USA. 26 Dec 75.	
☐ N134MA	1970	Mitsubishi MU-2G	507	Wfu.	
☐ N135SP	1968	SA-26AT Merlin 2B	T26-111	Wfu. Located Long Beach, Ca. USA.	VH-CAH
☐ N136JC		Jetcruzer 500	003	Wfu. Cx USA 3/02.	
☐ N142LM	1965	King Air 90	LJ-28	Wfu.	N142L
☐ N142WJ	1980	Conquest II	441-0142	Wfu. N reg cx 6/07 as scrapped	XC-AA11
☐ N148CP	1976	King Air 200	BB-129	W/o Hampton, NY. USA. 9 Jun 85.	N143CP
☐ N149JA	1979	MU-2 Solitaire	402SA	Wfu. Cx USA 5/95. Parts at White Industries, Mo. USA.	N963MA
☐ N151BU	1966	King Air A90	LJ-183	Wfu. Cx USA 9/99.	C-FPCB
☐ N152BK	1982	MU-2 Marquise	1537SA	W/o Lewiston, Id. USA. 11 Feb 00.	OY-BHY
☐ N154MF	1967	Mitsubishi MU-2B	024	Wfu.	N111FN
☐ N154RH	1964	Gulfstream 1	132	Wfu. Cx USA 9/03.	N154NS
☐ N155AS	1973	Mitsubishi MU-2J	589	Wfu. Cx USA 4/06.	N155AS
☐ N155BM	2001	PA-46-500TP Meridian	4697053	W/o Daytona Beach, Fl. USA. 17 Dec 03.	N61PK
☐ N155MA	1967	Mitsubishi MU-2B	014	Wfu. Located Milwaukee Aerea Technical College, Wi. USA.	N4WD
☐ N155S	1965	King Air 90	LJ-14	Wfu. Stevenson Aviation & Aerospace Training, Winnipeg, MT.	D-ILTI
☐ N160TR	1979	PA-31T Cheyenne II	7920036	W/o Rieschweiler, Germany 12/2/07	N81918
☐ N161RS	1980	SA-226T Merlin 3B	T-341	Wfu. Parts at White Industries, Bates City, Mo. USA.	N61RS
☐ N163D	1967	680V Turbo Command	1701-77	Wfu.	N11CK
☐ N163SA	1979	PA-31T Cheyenne II	7920025	Wfu. Parts at White Industries Inc. Bates City, Mo. USA.	N6195A
☐ N165MA	1971	Mitsubishi MU-2G	541	W/o Lookout Mountain, Ga. USA. 20 Apr 82.	N165MA
☐ N165PA	1963	Gulfstream 1	119	Wfu. N Reg Cx 3/07	YV-28CP
☐ N167PA	1963	Gulfstream 1	117	Wfu. Last located Cartersville, Ga. USA. Cx USA 12/04.	YV-08CP
☐ N168PA	1963	Gulfstream 1	56	Wfu. Last located Cartersville, Ga. USA. Cx USA 12/04.	YV-46CP
☐ N171MA	1980	MU-2 Solitaire	431SA	W/o Nr Bunnell, Fl. USA. 25 Aug 06.	
☐ N171PC	1968	SA-26AT Merlin 2B	T26-103	Wfu. Parts at White Industries Inc. Bates City, Mo. USA.	N136SP
☐ N171TE	1966	King Air B90	LJ-180	W/o N of Haiti. 29 Nov 98.	N610W
☐ N173PA	1966	Gulfstream 1	175	Wfu. Cx USA 1/05.	YV-453CP
☐ N176BJ	1969	Mitsubishi MU-2F	144	Wfu. N reg cx 1/07 as scrapped.	N11KR
☐ N176CC	1976	PA-31T Cheyenne II	7620024	W/o Lamar, Co. USA. 2 Jun 78.	N82009
☐ N177MF	1970	SA-26AT Merlin 2B	T26-179	W/o Albany, Ky. USA. 3 Dec 80.	ZS-RTZ
☐ N178MA	1972	Mitsubishi MU-2J	554	W/o Raton, NM. USA. 25 Aug 78.	N178MA
☐ N180B	1973	King Air C90	LJ-569	Wfu. Parts at White Industries, Bates City, Mo. USA.	

Reg	Yr	Type	c/n	Owner/Operator	Prev Regn
N181CE	1993	2000A Starship	NC-31	Wfu. Last located 3/05 at Marana, Az. USA.	N1558S
N181LL	1969	King Air B90	LJ-440	Wfu. Cx USA 4/91.	N19HS
N181TG	1967	Gulfstream 1	181	W/o Nashville, Tn. USA. 1 Jun 85.	N25WL
N182	1972	Rockwell 690	11048	W/o Canton, Md. USA. 15 Jan 80.	N1NR
N183K	1961	Gulfstream 1	84	W/o Necoli, Colombia. 3 Jun 06.	N184K
N183MA	1972	Mitsubishi MU-2F	217	Wfu. Cx USA 1/07	
N184MA	1972	Mitsubishi MU-2F	218	W/o Fort Lauderdale, Fl. USA. 20 Jun 87.	
N187AF	1972	Mitsubishi MU-2F	187	W/o Cerillos, NM. USA. 10 Jun 01.	OY-DLM
N191A	1978	King Air C90	LJ-765	Wfu. Located Montgomery, Al. USA.	5N-WNL
N191DM	1966	King Air 90	LJ-100	Wfu. Cx USA 3/93. Parts at White Industries, Mo. USA.	N1NL
N191SA	1960	Gulfstream 1	61	Wfu. Parts at Dodsons, Rantoul, Ks. USA.	N734HR
N193GA	1974	King Air 200	BB-12	Wfu. Parts at Lake City, Fl. USA.	VH-NIH
N195B	1976	King Air E90	LW-195	Wfu. Parts at Dodsons, Rantoul, Ks. USA.	N195WF
N198MA	1972	Mitsubishi MU-2J	563	Wfu. Cx USA 1/07	
N198X	1998	TBM 700	138	W/o Lancaster Fox Airport, Ca. USA. 27 Dec 05.	N242CA
N199TA	1968	SA-26AT Merlin 2B	T26-110	W/o Del Rio, Tx. USA. 19 Jun 85.	N20TA
N200BE	1981	King Air 200	BB-832	W/o Rupert, WV. USA. 13 Jun 04.	N45BR
N200BR	1971	Mitsubishi MU-2F	205	W/o Provo, Ut. USA. 21 Dec 79.	N120MA
N200CM	1977	PA-31T Cheyenne II	7720004	Wfu. Parts at White Industries, Bates City, Mo. USA.	(N82073)
N200FD	1975	PA-31T Cheyenne II	7520040	W/o Lawrence, Ma. USA. 20 Mar 87.	N54971
N200HL	1968	Mitsubishi MU-2D	120	W/o New Orleans, La. USA. 20 Sep 74.	N284MA
N200MB	1979	King Air B100	BE-71	Wfu. Cx USA 3/93. Parts at White Industries, Mo. USA.	N66480
N200MR	1977	King Air 200	BB-219	Wfu. Parts at White Industries, Bates City, Mo. USA.	N884CA
N200PR	1983	Gulfstream 900	15029	W/o Price, Ut. USA. 7 May 86.	N36GA
N200RS	1985	PA-31T Cheyenne II	7520011	W/o St Louis, Mo. USA. 18 Jan 88.	N66844
N202JP	1975	PA-31T Cheyenne II	7520018	Wfu. Parts at White Industries, Bates City, Mo. USA.	N300WT
N204AJ	1970	King Air 100	B-10	W/o Houston, Tx. USA. 16 Sep 89.	N400BE
N206RF	1991	2000 Starship	NC-21	Wfu. Last located 3/05 at Marana, Az. USA.	N206R
N208MA	1967	Mitsubishi MU-2B	016	W/o Hays, Ks. USA. 3 Aug 79.	(N232LJ)
N208MS	1978	King Air 200	BB-400	W/o North Adams, Ma. USA. 6 Oct 99.	N999BT
N211X	1967	King Air A90	LJ-279	Wfu. Cx USA 9/91.	
N212CM	1966	680V Turbo Command	1626-54	Wfu.	N212CW
N212MA	1973	Mitsubishi MU-2K	262	Wfu. Cx USA 5/95.	N282MA
N213GA	1960	Gulfstream 1	48	Wfu.	G-AWYF
N214JB	1990	2000 Starship	NC-14	Wfu. Located Southern Museum of Flight, Birmingham, Al. USA.	N5674B
N217SB	1973	Mitsubishi MU-2J	586	Wfu. Cx USA 6/01.	N21AU
N218CS	1982	Cheyenne T-1040	8275016	W/o Stebbins, Ak. USA. 7 Apr 97.	C-GKIF
N220CS	1982	Cheyenne T-1040	8275013	W/o Nuiqsut, Ak. USA. 18 Sep 00.	C-GBDJ
N220F	1981	King Air C90	LJ-981	W/o East Greenwich, RI. USA. 27 Nov 85.	
N220MA	1981	MU-2 Solitaire	441SA	W/o Concord, NH. USA. 9 Jul 92.	N234BC
N221AP	1959	Gulfstream 1	6	Wfu. Cx USA 8/97.	S9-NAU
N221CH	1969	King Air E90	LJ-436	W/o Tucumari, NM. 15 May 01.	N309L
N221MA	1980	MU-2 Marquise	771SA	Wfu. Cx USA 8/06.	N248NW
N221MJ	1971	King Air C90	LJ-512	W/o Charleston, WV. USA. 4 Nov 75.	N659H
N221NC	1968	King Air B90	LJ-393	W/o Creede, Co. USA. 25 Jun 99. (parts at Bates City, Mo.).	(F-GSJL)
N225MS	1979	King Air 200	BB-496	Wfu. Cx USA 6/95 as stolen.	N180S
N226AT	1971	SA-226AT Merlin 4	AT-003E	Wfu.	N226TC
N227	1970	Mitsubishi MU-2G	510	Wfu. Cx USA 11/00.	N137MA
N229EM	1977	King Air C-12C	BC-59	Wfu. Last located Montgomery, Al. USA.	77-22948
N230E	1960	Gulfstream 1	36	Wfu. Last located El Mirage, Ca. USA.	N130A
N230TW	1969	King Air B90	LJ-445	W/o Nr Fort Drum, Fl. 5 Jan 94.	N70CS
N231RL	1981	King Air 200	BB-868	Wfu. Cx USA 3/97.	N3872K
N233MA	1973	Mitsubishi MU-2K	251	W/o McCleod, Tx. USA. 2 Sep 81.	
N234K	1976	PA-31T Cheyenne II	7620017	Wfu.	N57526
N234MA	1973	Mitsubishi MU-2K	252	W/o Jacksboro, Tx. USA. 26 Nov 79.	
N234MM	1963	Gulfstream 1	121	Wfu. Displayed at Disney-MGM Studio Theme Park, Orlando, Fl.	N732G
N239P	1969	SA-26AT Merlin 2B	T26-147	W/o Willoughby, Oh. USA. 29 Jan 70.	
N241DT	1973	SA-226T Merlin 3	T-242	W/o Santa Fe, NM. USA. 25 May 93.	N770U
N241FW	1982	Conquest II	441-0241	W/o Chicago, Il. USA. 23 Nov 86.	(N6856S)
N242DA	1965	King Air 90	LJ-20	Wfu. Parts at Dodson's, Rantoul, Ks. USA.	C-FMLC
N242DA	1970	King Air B90	LJ-484	Wfu. Parts at Dodsons, Rantoul, Ks. USA.	ZS-KLW
N242TC	1974	Rockwell 690A	11219	Wfu. Cx USA 12/02.	N50MP
N245CA	1961	Gulfstream 1C	83	Wfu. Parts at White Industries Inc. Bates City, Mo. USA.	N117GA
N245MA	1973	Mitsubishi MU-2J	576	Wfu.	
N250TJ	1981	PA-42 Cheyenne III	8001024	W/o Grand Junction, Co. USA. 31 Oct 92.	C-GRCY
N251M	1967	Mitsubishi MU-2B	013	W/o Gardner, Ks. USA. 9 Apr 79.	N3545X

Reg	Yr	Type	c/n	Owner/Operator	Prev Regn
N253TA	1991	2000 Starship	NC-10	Wfu. Last located 10/04 at Marana, Az. USA.	N1563Z
N254PW	1976	Rockwell 690A	11275	W/o Cadillac, Mi. USA. 10 Oct 85.	N952HE
N254TP	1973	Mitsubishi MU-2J	575	Wfu.	N7PW
N255C	1971	Mitsubishi MU-2G	536	Wfu.	N58BC
N256TM	1976	King Air 200	BB-96	W/o New Orleans, La. USA. 18 Apr 77.	
N257CG	2000	King Air B200	BB-1739	W/o Leominster, Ma. USA. 4 Apr 03.	N612TA
N261PL	1969	SA-26AT Merlin 2B	T26-121	Wfu.	N4252X
N266EB	1977	King Air 200	BB-266	W/o N Myrtle Beach, SC. USA. 2 Feb 06.	ZS-NNS
N269M	1985	Gulfstream 1000	96098	W/o Boca Raton, Fl. USA. 22 Jan 98.	N699GN
N269TA	1981	King Air 200	BB-749	Wfu. (aircraft stolen, de-registered 10/99).	N12KW
N270TC	1979	King Air C90	LJ-858	W/o Ronkonkoma, NY. 18 May 01.	F-GHFS
N271MA	1980	MU-2 Marquise	797SA	W/o Chicago, Il. USA. 16 Nov 88.	
N274MA	1980	MU-2 Marquise	786SA	W/o Tulsa, Ok. USA. 22 Feb 91.	
N275CA	1978	PA-31T Cheyenne II	7820089	Wfu.	XA-JGS
N275DP	1965	King Air 90	LJ-34	Wfu. Smithsonian 'Business Wings' exhibit 6/98-6/99.	N200SW
N275MA	1973	Mitsubishi MU-2K	255	W/o West Point, Va. USA. 5 Jan 85. (parts at Bates City).	
N278DU	1967	King Air A90	LJ-243	W/o Denver, Co. USA. 10 Jul 78.	N578DU
N287MN	1975	PA-31T Cheyenne II	7520004	Wfu. Parts at White Industries, Bates City, Mo. USA.	
N289MA	1973	Mitsubishi MU-2J	585	Wfu. Cx USA 10/94. Parts at White Industries, Mo. USA.	
N295X	1967	King Air A90	LJ-244	W/o Racine, Wi. USA. 1 May 72.	
N296A	1967	King Air A90	LJ-208	Wfu. Located Chenault Air Park, Lake Charles, La. USA.	N29SA
N296MA	1973	Mitsubishi MU-2J	592	W/o Coral Sea, Australia. 9 Dec 88.	
N298MA	1973	Mitsubishi MU-2J	594	Wfu. Cx USA 6/01.	
N299F	1973	Rockwell 690A	11112	W/o Calumet, Ok. USA. 27 May 78.	N57112
N300BD	1971	Mitsubishi MU-2G	547	Wfu.	N171MA
N300CP	1977	Rockwell 690B	11374	W/o South of Susanville, Ca. USA. 31 Dec 92.	N81562
N300CW	1980	MU-2 Marquise	795SA	W/o Putnam, Tx. USA. 14 Feb 90.	N287MA
N300HG	1966	King Air 90	LJ-94	Wfu. Parts at White Industries, Bates City, Mo. USA.	N300HC
N300KQ	1967	680V Turbo Command	1709-84	Wfu.	N300KC
N300MA	1973	Mitsubishi MU-2J	596	W/o Easton, Md. USA. 8 Feb 76.	
N300MC	1960	Gulfstream 1	32	Wfu. Cx USA 12/88.	N297X
N300PT	1973	SA-226T Merlin 3	T-233	Wfu. Cx USA 8/05.	N84LC
N300RX	1973	Mitsubishi MU-2J	572	Wfu. N Reg Cx 2/07	N986MA
N300SP	1976	King Air E90	LW-166	W/o Flagstaff, Az. USA. 31 Jan 96.	N26902
N300WC	1992	TBM 700	82	W/o Englewood, Co. USA. 26 Mar 01.	
N301DK	1968	King Air B90	LJ-372	W/o Dillinghan Airport, Mouleia, HI. USA. 22 May 99.	N301TS
N301KS	1985	King Air 300	FA-61	W/o Daytona Beach, Fl. USA. 14 Apr 04.	N7234E
N302WB	1972	Rockwell 690	11003	W/o Soto La Marina, Mexico. 16 Sep 03.	N72TT
N302X	1967	Mitsubishi MU-2B	030	Wfu.	N3561X
N303CA	1981	MU-2 Marquise	1518SA	W/o Rifle, Co. USA. 5 Mar 92. (Parts at Bates City, Mo.).	N678KM
N303MC	1981	Conquest 1	425-0034	W/o London, Ky. USA. 18 Jan 94.	N6773E
N304L	1968	Mitsubishi MU-2F	137	W/o March Harbour, Bahamas. 21 Apr 79.	N304LA
N304M	1968	SA-26T Merlin 2A	T26-8	Wfu.	
N307MA	1967	Mitsubishi MU-2B	007	W/o Las Vegas, Nv. USA. 28 Apr 80.	(D-IHFS)
N308PS	1974	King Air E90	LW-92	W/o Locust Grove, Ar. USA. 18 Nov 88.	N300PS
N309MA	1973	Mitsubishi MU-2J	602	W/o Smyrna, Tn. USA. 21 Sep 95.	
N311DS	1980	King Air F90	LA-41	Wfu.	N37JT
N311G	2001	King Air B200	BB-1760	W/o destroyed in crash in Guatemala 07/05	N4360N
N311LM	1977	PA-31T Cheyenne II	7720016	Wfu. Parts at White Industries, Bates City, Mo. USA.	C-FACM
N312MA	1973	Mitsubishi MU-2K	266	W/o Hillsboro, Or. USA. 24 May 05.	
N313BB	1970	Mitsubishi MU-2G	529	Wfu. Cx USA 4/94.	N3MP
N313PC	1971	Mitsubishi MU-2G	531	Wfu.	N155MA
N314SC	1982	Cheyenne T-1040	8275007	Wfu. Cx USA 12/06.	N9180Y
N316PR	1980	MU-2 Marquise	761SA	W/o Nr Fort Pierce, Fl. USA. 25 Jun 06.	N678RH
N318DH	1982	SA-227AT Merlin 4C	AT-469	W/o Beaver island, Mi. USA. 8 Feb 01.	C-GCAU
N319JG	1976	PA-31T Cheyenne II	7620056	Wfu.	N110DE
N320MA	1973	Mitsubishi MU-2K	274	Wfu.	(N10GE)
N321MA	1973	Mitsubishi MU-2K	276	W/o Double Springs, Al. USA. 4 Apr 77.	
N321MG	1973	Rockwell 690	11069	Wfu. Last located Malindi, Kenya.	(5Y-NCF)
N321MK	1991	2000 Starship	NC-20	Wfu. Last located 10/04 at Marana, Az. USA.	N8168S
N321ST	1974	Mitsubishi MU-2K	307	W/o Campbell Lake, Canada. 8 Sep 91.	N200TM
N321TP	1980	MU-2 Marquise	780SA	Wfu. Cx USA 5/95.	N16HA
N328CA	1963	Gulfstream 1C	116	Wfu. Parts at White Industries Inc. Bates City, Mo. USA.	N159AN
N330CB	1965	King Air 90	LJ-27	Wfu. Parts at Dodsons, Rantoul, Ks. USA.	N400PQ
N331AM	1966	King Air A90	LJ-144	Wfu. Parts at White Industries, Bates City, Mo. USA.	(N3DG)
N331H	1961	Gulfstream 1	70	Wfu. Parts at Dodsons, Rantoul, Ks. USA.	N770G

Reg	Yr	Type	c/n	Owner/Operator	Prev Regn
☐ N331MA	1980	MU-2 Marquise	768SA	Wfu. Cx USA 8/06.	N36MF
☐ N332K	1966	King Air 90	LJ-79	W/o Laredo, Tx. USA. 3 Sep 79.	N33JC
☐ N333BR	1968	Mitsubishi MU-2D	119	Wfu.	(N101ES)
☐ N333CA	1973	Rockwell 690A	11117	W/o Oklahoma City, Ok. USA. 22 Aug 73.	
☐ N333CS	1965	King Air 90	LJ-44	Wfu. Parts at White Industries, Bates City, Mo. USA.	XB-YAZ
☐ N333LM	1979	PA-31T Cheyenne II	7920052	W/o Malvern, Ar. USA. 29 May 96.	N333MZ
☐ N333MA	1974	Mitsubishi MU-2K	288	W/o Gander, Canada. 24 Mar 74.	
☐ N333WF	1978	Mitsubishi MU-2P	387SA	Wfu. N Reg Cx 2/07	N8TB
☐ N334DP	1984	King Air B200	BB-1188	W/o Fort Atkinson, Wi. USA. 16 Nov 87.	N334D
☐ N336SA	1980	SA-226T Merlin 3B	T-336	W/o Tx. USA. 19 Jan 82.	
☐ N338AS	1970	King Air B90	LJ-493	W/o West Palm Beach, Fl. USA. 3 Sep 99.	LV-WMD
☐ N339MA	1973	Mitsubishi MU-2J	607	Wfu.	(N200MK)
☐ N339W	1992	TBM 700	39	W/o Lake Tahow, Nv. USA. 29 Aug 92.	
☐ N340X	1968	SA-26T Merlin 2A	T26-17	Wfu. Parts at White Industries, Bates City, Mo. USA.	
☐ N345CA	1969	680W Turbo Command	1842-41	Wfu. Parts at White Industries, Bates City, Mo. USA.	N39480
☐ N345DF	1978	PA-31T Cheyenne II	7820088	Wfu. N reg cx 8/07 as aircraft scrapped	N4491C
☐ N345RD	1992	TBM 700	76	W/o Truckee, Ca. USA. 13 Mar 98.	
☐ N346K	1974	Mitsubishi MU-2K	292	Wfu.	N452MA
☐ N346MA	1973	Mitsubishi MU-2J	613	W/o Houston, Tx. USA. 14 Feb 80.	
☐ N360LL	1975	PA-31T Cheyenne II	7520036	W/o Nr Denver, Co. USA. 24 Jan 03.	HC-BXZ
☐ N363N	1967	King Air A90	LJ-236	Wfu. Parts at White Industries, Bates City, Mo. USA.	
☐ N369CD	1976	King Air E90	LW-162	Written off Ruidoso, NM 6.8.07	N36GS
☐ N371BG	1959	Gulfstream 1	4	Wfu.	N89DE
☐ N375A	1967	680V Turbo Command	1692-71	Wfu.	
☐ N385GA	1974	King Air 200	BB-15	Wfu. Cx USA 1/97.	ZS-MNF
☐ N386TM	1978	Mitsubishi MU-2P	386SA	W/o San Antonio, Tx. USA. 21 Jan 2000.	N999BE
☐ N388MC	1969	King Air B90	LJ-442	W/o Yazoo City, Ms. USA. 10 Jan 78.	(N745LP)
☐ N398DE	1986	King Air 300	FA-109	Wfu. Cx USA 12/00.	N364C
☐ N399T	1966	680T Turbo Command	1532-2	W/o Olathe, Ks. USA. 31 Jan 75.	HB-GEK
☐ N400AM	1968	King Air B90	LJ-354	W/o Burlington, Co. USA. 10 Sep 83.	(N506M)
☐ N400BG	1978	Conquest II	441-0069	W/o Dallas, Tx. USA. 1 Oct 85.	N441SE
☐ N400FA	1983	SA-227AT Merlin 4C	AT-557	Wfu.	
☐ N400KK	1968	Mitsubishi MU-2D	118	Wfu.	N100KK
☐ N400LP	1967	680V Turbo Command	1697-74	Wfu. Cx USA 4/99. Parts at White Industries, bates City, Mo.	N400LR
☐ N400N	1974	Rockwell 690A	11156	W/o Kelso, Wa. USA. 1 Dec 90.	N57077
☐ N400NL	1960	Gulfstream 1	62	Wfu.	N205M
☐ N400PT	1983	PA-42 Cheyenne 400L	5527001	Wfu. Cx USA 6/98. (was 8427001).	
☐ N400TR	1969	Mitsubishi MU-2F	161	Wfu. Cx USA 7/99.	N11LQ
☐ N401AS	1991	2000 Starship	NC-19	Wfu. Last located Community College, Salt Lake City, Ut.	N8025L
☐ N401MM	1999	PA-46-400TP Meridian	4697001	Wfu. Cx USA 12/05.	
☐ N403MM	1999	PA-46-400TP Meridian	4697E3	Wfu. Cx USA 12/05.	
☐ N409ET	1974	Rockwell 690A	11213	Wfu.	N925MC
☐ N410W	1965	King Air 90	LJ-39	Wfu. Parts at White Industries, Bates City, Mo. USA.	N410WA
☐ N411X	1969	SA-26AT Merlin 2B	T26-126	W/o Nashville, Tn. USA. 28 Mar 72. (at Rantoul, Ks.).	
☐ N418CD	1976	Mitsubishi MU-2M	344	Wfu. Cx USA 10/94. Parts at White Industries, Mo. USA.	N729MA
☐ N425AC	1980	Conquest 1	425-0009	W/o Natchez, Ms. USA. 18 Nov 81.	(N98896)
☐ N425BN	1981	Conquest 1	425-0057	W/o Las Vegas, Nv. USA. 11 Jan 92.	N67761
☐ N425EW	1983	Conquest 1	425-0150	W/o Nr MacArthur Airport, NY. 16 Dec 96.	(N68854)
☐ N425JP	1981	Conquest 1	425-0038	W/o.Reg cx as destroyed/scr following accident Menominee,Mi	N3FC
☐ N425K	1968	King Air B90	LJ-318	Wfu. Located Middle Georgia Technical Institute, W-Robins.	
☐ N425SC	1982	Conquest 1	425-0126	W/o Granby, Co. USA. 11 Jan 86.	N607DD
☐ N425SG	1983	Conquest 1	425-0166	W/o Lone Tree, Co. USA. 13 Aug 05.	(N802JH)
☐ N425TN	1984	Conquest 1	425-0196	W/o Harbor Springs, Mi.	(N196TM)
☐ N430C	1967	King Air A90	LJ-273	Wfu. Parts at Dodsons, Rantoul, Ks. USA. (as N5JR).	N585S
☐ N431G	1960	Gulfstream 1	29	Wfu. Located Toronto-Pearson, ON. Canada.	N222SE
☐ N432FA	1980	King Air 200	BB-592	W/o Green Bay, Wi. USA. 30 Jun 04.	N26SJ
☐ N439AF	1982	SA-227AT Merlin 4C	AT-439	Wfu. Cx USA 5/04.	N555GB
☐ N440D	1967	King Air A90	LJ-235	Wfu. Cx USA 5/99.	N7SD
☐ N440MA	1981	MU-2 Marquise	1524SA	W/o Scottsdale, Az. USA. 27 Jan 83.	
☐ N441AW	1981	Conquest II	441-0199	W/o Rio Grande, PR. USA. 5 Jan 02.	N441JG
☐ N441CA	1978	Conquest II	441-0046	Wfu. Cx USA 3/95.	(N36989)
☐ N441CC	1975	Conquest II	441-679	Wfu.	N7185C
☐ N441CD	1980	Conquest II	441-0131	W/o West Columbia, SC. USA. 15 Jan 86,	(N2625Y)
☐ N441CM	1980	Conquest II	441-0169	W/o Marble Falls, Tx. USA. 24 Dec 84.	N441CN
☐ N441KM	1981	Conquest II	441-0196	W/o St Louis, Mo. USA. 22 Nov 94. (parts at White Inds.).	N992TE
☐ N441MS	1978	Conquest II	441-0056	W/o Lakeland Linder Airport, Fl. USA. 2 Jan 97.	C-GDBB
Reg	Yr	Type	c/n	Owner/Operator	Prev Regn

Reg	Yr	Type	c/n	Owner/Operator	Prev Regn
N441NC	1979	Conquest II	441-0099	W/o Virginia, USA. 11 Jan 80.	N4106G
N441RB	1977	Conquest II	441-0029	Wfu.	(N36956)
N441W	1980	Conquest II	441-0181	W/o Birmingham, Al. USA. 10 Dec 03.	N81WS
N441W	1978	Conquest II	441-0052	W/o Walkers Cay, Fl. USA. 20 Apr 96. (at Rantoul, Ks.).	N441GM
N442TC	1968	King Air B90	LJ-332	Wfu. Parts at White Industries, Bates City, Mo. USA.	N440TC
N444AR	1972	Mitsubishi MU-2J	555	W/o Eagle, Co. USA. 18 Nov 81.	N444NR
N444GB	1966	680V Turbo Command	1565-21	W/o Keflavik, Iceland. 5 Aug 90.	(N444GP)
N444JV	1981	Conquest 1	425-0013	W/o San Jose, Ca. USA. 6 Mar 02.	(N117EE)
N444JW	1971	PA-31T Cheyenne II	7720015	W/o San Angelo, Tx. USA. 3 Dec 79. (parts at Dodsons)	N775SW
N444LM	1978	SA-226T Merlin 3B	T-295	W/o Livermore, Ca. USA. 3 May 85.	N4444F
N444PA	1977	Mitsubishi MU-2N	691SA	W/o Patterson, La. USA. 20 Oct 83.	N851MA
N444SR	1968	King Air B90	LJ-436	W/o Seal Beach, Ca. USA. 17 Feb 85.	N869K
N447AB	1972	Mitsubishi MU-2F	223	Wfu. Cx USA 7/94. Parts at Dodsons, Rantoul, Ks. USA.	N189MA
N451ES	2001	Pilatus PC-12/45	425	W/o Westphalia, Mo. USA. 14 Sep 02.	HB-FRO
N454MA	1981	MU-2 Marquise	1535SA	W/o Parker, Co. USA. 4 Aug 05.	
N456L	1976	King Air 200	BB-112	W/o Denver, Co. USA. 27 Mar 80.	
N466MA	1981	MU-2 Marquise	1540SA	W/o Burlington, Ct. USA. 19 Apr 84.	
N469JK	1967	King Air A90	LJ-274	Wfu. Parts at Lake City, Fl. USA.	N30AA
N473FW	1973	Mitsubishi MU-2K	269	Wfu. Cx USA 10/94. Parts at White Industries, Mo. USA.	(N473W)
N473MA	1982	MU-2 Marquise	1547SA	W/o North Adams, Ma. USA. 18 Mar 83.	
N474H	1969	King Air B90	LJ-474	Wfu. Parts at White Industries, Bates City, Mo. USA.	N14RA
N474U	1969	SA-26AT Merlin 2B	T26-133	Wfu. Cx USA 11/99. Parts at Lake City, Fl. USA.	N401NW
N477MD	2006	PA-46-500TP Meridian	4697264	W/o.Written Off 28.6.07 Wellsville, Mo.	
N480BC	1968	SA-26AT Merlin 2B	T26-108	Wfu. Parts at White Industries, Bates City, Mo. USA.	N122NK
N480CA	1980	PA-31T Cheyenne 1	8004051	W/o Toussus Le Noble, France. 2 Jan 04.	
N480K	1969	King Air B90	LJ-439	W/o Nr Bahamas. 27 Dec 71.	N480K
N483D	1967	King Air A90	LJ-212	Wfu. Cx USA 9/92.	N483G
N500AK	1984	SA-227TT Merlin 300	TT-527	W/o Sullivan County, Tn. USA 1 Apr 93.	N40EF
N500CP	1992	2000A Starship	NC-25	Wfu. Last located Orange County Santa Ana, Ca. USA.	N1553Y
N500GL	1973	Mitsubishi MU-2J	579	W/o Lajitas, Tx. USA. 19 Apr 81.	N441FS
N500JP	1970	681 Turbo Commander	6003	W/o Winnemucca, Nv. USA. 27 Jan 81.	C-FFDB
N500ML	1980	King Air B100	BE-78	W/o Jackson, Ms. USA. 13 Nov 97.	N3UL
N500PS	1972	Mitsubishi MU-2F	224	Wfu. Cx USA 1/07	N190MA
N500X	1967	King Air A90	LJ-199	W/o Galveston, Tx. USA. 26 Nov 69.	
N500X	1968	Mitsubishi MU-2D	114	Wfu. Located Bush Field Airport, Augusta, Ga. USA.	N908108
N501FS	1969	SA-26AT Merlin 2B	T26-146	W/o St George, Ak. USA. 7 Jul 98,	N7WY
N501M	1966	King Air A90	LJ-175	Wfu. Parts at White Industries, Bates City, Mo. USA.	N5ORM
N501RH	1981	King Air 200	BB-805	W/o Martinsville, Va. USA. 24 Oct 04.	N3812S
N503AA	1974	Mitsubishi MU-2J	633	Wfu. Cx USA 8/06.	(N56JS)
N504W	1968	SA-26AT Merlin 2B	T26-104	Wfu.	
N505SA	1967	Mitsubishi MU-2B	008	Wfu.	N224FW
N508GW	1968	SA-26T Merlin 2A	T26-35	Wfu. Instructional airframe Northrop University, Ca. USA.	N500DM
N511BF	1966	King Air A90	LJ-179	W/o Fentress, Tx. USA. 17 Oct 03.	N711CF
N512DM	1969	Mitsubishi MU-2F	155	Wfu. Cx USA 6/95.	N513DM
N513DC	1981	MU-2 Marquise	1513SA	W/o Eola, Il. USA. 5 Mar 86.	N275CA
N513NA	1970	Mitsubishi MU-2G	513	Wfu. Cx USA 6/95.	VH-UZD
N515AC	1990	2000 Starship	NC-16	Wfu. Last located Wichita BEC, Ks. USA.	N80KK
N515JS	1995	2000A Starship	NC-52	Wfu. Last located 6/06 at Marana, Az. USA.	N1564Q
N515WB	1977	PA-31T Cheyenne II	7720023	W/o Nr Columbus, Oh. USA. 2 Dec 93.	C-GGMD
N518DM	1967	King Air A90	LJ-251	W/o Marine City, Mi. USA. 31 Jul 99.	N516DM
N522RF	2001	PA-46-500TP Meridian	4697119	W/o Albuquerque, NM. USA. 7 Mar 03.	
N524SC	1970	King Air 100	B-37	Wfu. Cx USA 3/97. Parts at White Industries, Bates City, Mo.	N627L
N525MA	1976	Mitsubishi MU-2M	340	Wfu. Cx USA 11/94.	(N912DM)
N528WG	1976	King Air 200	BB-151	W/o Leonardstown, Md. USA. 12 Oct 06.	N98CM
N529N	1966	King Air 90	LJ-112	W/o Green Castle, Mo. USA. 11 Mar 66.	
N529V	1970	King Air B90	LJ-487	Wfu. Parts at White Industries, Bates City, Mo. USA.	N529M
N530N	1966	King Air A90	LJ-141	W/o USA. 1 May 93.	
N531MA	1968	Mitsubishi MU-2F	130	W/o Burlington, Vt. USA. 18 Feb 76.	N1173Z
N533DM	1974	Mitsubishi MU-2N	652SA	Wfu. Cx USA 8/06.	N533MA
N538EA	1981	MU-2 Marquise	1538SA	W/o Englewood, Ca. USA. 10 Dec 04.	N538MC
N539MA	1972	Mitsubishi MU-2J	552	Wfu. Cx USA 8/02.	N246W
N539SA	1983	SA-227AT Merlin 4C	AT-539	Wfu. Cx USA 5/86.	
N541F	1966	680V Turbo Command	1609-45	W/o Fort Lauderdale, Fl. USA. 3 Nov 90.	C-GPRO
N541W	1966	680T Turbo Command	1554-13	W/o Pompano Beach, Fl. USA. 3 Oct 70.	N5419
N542TW	1981	PA-42 Cheyenne III	8001052	W/o Charlotte, NC. USA. 28 Jun 85.	
N549LK	1967	Mitsubishi MU-2B	022	W/o Northfield, Oh. USA. 13 Oct 70.	N3554X

Reg	Yr	Type	c/n	Owner/Operator	Prev Regn
N550MA	1969	Mitsubishi MU-2F	169	Wfu. Cx USA 6/95.	N883Q
N551TR	1982	King Air B200	BB-1033	W/o 29 Jun 86.	N551TP
N555AM	1970	SA-226T Merlin 3	T-201	W/o Cameron, La. USA. 10 Jun 81.	N555DB
N555CH	1970	Mitsubishi MU-2G	508	Wfu. Cx USA 12/94.	N950MA
N555KG	1993	2000A Starship	NC-36	Wfu. Last located 10/04 at Marana, Az. USA.	XA-TNR
N558M	1974	Mitsubishi MU-2J	639	Wfu. Cx USA 7/94.	N550M
N561AF	1972	Mitsubishi MU-2J	561	Wfu. Cx USA 3/04.	VH-JMZ
N568H	1972	Rockwell 690	11027	W/o Los Angeles, Ca. USA. 26 Oct 76.	
N568UP	1983	SA-227AT Merlin 4C	AT-568	W/o London, Ky. USA. 31 Jan 85.	N568SA
N569H	1972	Rockwell 690	11029	Wfu. Located Technical School near Tara Field, Va. USA.	
N570AB	1975	PA-31T Cheyenne II	7520038	Wfu. Cx USA 6/89. Parts at White Industries, Bates City, Mo.	N54970
N571L	1966	King Air A90	LJ-135	Wfu. Parts at White Industries, Bates City, Mo. USA.	N571M
N575HC	1973	King Air E90	LW-67	W/o Pine Bluff, Ar. USA. 19 May 85.	N575HW
N577KA	1972	SA-226AT Merlin 4	AT-008	W/o Billings, Mt. USA. 7 May 86.	TR-LZS
N580BC	1961	Gulfstream 1	63	Wfu. Last located El Mirage, Ca. USA. Cx USA 7/03.	N144NK
N590DL	1975	PA-31T Cheyenne II	7520031	Wfu. Located Calgary Springbank Airport, AB. Canada.	SE-GLA
N590GM	1999	King Air C90B	LJ-1594	W/o Pagosa Springs Co. 4 Oct 07.	
N599TR	1965	Gulfstream 1	160	Wfu. Cx USA 5/06. Last located Lakeland, Fl. USA.	(N965CJ)
N600BV	1977	King Air 200	BB-254	W/o Madeira Island, Portugal. 12 Sep 03.	N600BW
N600CM	1977	PA-31T Cheyenne II	7720024	W/o Flat Rock, NC. USA. 23 Aug 85.	(N82116)
N600DM	1978	King Air 200	BB-414	Wfu. Cx USA 3/95.	N5VG
N600P	1968	SA-26T Merlin 2A	T26-6	Wfu. Parts at Dodsons, Rantoul, Ks. USA.	
N600TB	1973	Mitsubishi MU-2K	258	Wfu. Cx USA 6/95.	N278MA
N600WR	1976	PA-31T Cheyenne II	7620038	Wfu. Parts at Dodsons, Ottawa, Ks. USA.	N82028
N601G	1966	680T Turbo Command	1605-44	W/o Alphaha, Ga. USA. 8 Aug 76.	N6537V
N602PA	1966	680T Turbo Command	1534-3	Wfu. Cx USA 10/84.	N441LM
N602RM	1979	PA-31T Cheyenne II	7920081	W/o Deerfield, Va. USA. 1 Jul 99.	N600RM
N607DD	1975	PA-31T Cheyenne II	7520028	Wfu. Parts at White Industries, Bates City, Mo. USA.	VH-HMA
N611VP	1966	King Air A90	LJ-171	W/o Narssarsuaq, Greenland. May 88.	N755K
N616AS	1966	King Air A90	LJ-160	W/o West Jordan, Ut. USA. 19 Apr 97. (parts at Rantoul, Ks.)	N42CG
N616E	1967	680V Turbo Command	1707-82	Wfu. Cx USA 8/00.	N616MC
N616F	1966	King Air A90	LJ-165	W/o Lake Point, Ut. USA. 14 Jan 01.	N6HF
N617MS	1981	King Air 200C	BL-35	W/o Madisonville, Ky. USA. 24 Jun 87.	N26732
N618B	1975	Rockwell 690A	11232	Wfu. Cx USA 1/94. Parts at White Industries, Mo. USA.	N618
N618BB	1971	Mitsubishi MU-2G	533	Wfu. Cx USA 1/97. Parts at Bates City, Mo. USA.	C-FKCL
N623AW	1967	King Air A90	LJ-282	Wfu. Cx USA 8/05. Parts at White Industries, Bates City, Mo.	N853K
N626BL	1980	Lear Fan	E001	Wfu. Located Museum of Flight, Seattle, Wa. USA.	
N628MC	2003	Pilatus PC-12/45	516	Wfu. Triple B In Flight LLC., Seattle, Wa.	N629MC
N631DS	1994	2000A Starship	NC-44	Wfu. Last located 10/04 at Marana, Az. USA.	N1863Q
N631PT	1977	PA-31T Cheyenne II	7720001	W/o Harrisburg, Pa. USA. 24 Feb 77.	(N82065)
N631SR	1977	King Air 200	BB-244	W/o King Cove, Ak. USA. 15 Jul 81.	
N636SP	1977	SA-226T Merlin 3A	T-285	Wfu. Parts at Dodsons, Rantoul, Ks. USA.	N6SP
N636SW	1974	Mitsubishi MU-2J	636	Wfu. Cx USA 10/94. Parts at White Industries, Mo. USA.	N20PS
N638LD	1991	2000 Starship	NC-18	Wfu. Last located 4/03 at Marana, Az. USA.	N8246S
N638MA	1974	Mitsubishi MU-2J	638	Wfu. Cx USA 4/94.	N8LC
N641SE	1994	2000A Starship	NC-46	Wfu. Last located 6/06 at Marana, Az. USA.	N312KJ
N642WM	1969	SA-26AT Merlin 2B	T26-125	Wfu. Parts at Lake City, Fl. USA.	N393W
N648KA	1980	King Air 200	BB-648	W/o Bay View, Tx. USA. 10 Dec 04.	N17DW
N656A	1967	King Air A90	LJ-304	Wfu. Parts at White Industries, Bates City, Mo. USA.	
N660NR	2000	Pilatus PC-12/45	356	W/o Sea of Okhotsk, Western Pacific. 8 Jul 01.	HB-FSH
N660RB	1976	Rockwell 690A	11305	W/o Little Rock, Ar. USA. 17 May 88.	C-GIAB
N662DM	1972	Rockwell 690	11015	W/o Bridgeport, Ct. USA. 21 Jun 87.	N412FS
N666HB	1974	Mitsubishi MU-2K	281	Wfu. Cx USA 4/94.	N111PM
N666RK	1968	Mitsubishi MU-2D	110	Wfu.	N857Q
N666SE	1969	SA-26AT Merlin 2B	T26-154E	Wfu. Parts at White Industries, Bates City, Mo. USA.	N90874
N677WA	1978	Rockwell 690B	11473	Wfu.	5H-TAA
N680KM	1968	680W Turbo Command	1812-29	Wfu. Parts at White Industries, Bates City, Mo. USA.	N500NR
N680X	1968	680W Turbo Command	1778-16	Wfu.	C-GPNV
N686N	1964	680T Turbo Command	1473-1	Wfu. Cx USA 7/92.	(N48AD)
N688DC	1966	680T Turbo Command	1612-47	Wfu.	
N688SH	1966	680T Turbo Command	1597-42	Wfu. Cx USA 2/99.	N676MB
N690CB	1978	Rockwell 690B	11477	Wfu N Reg cx 3/07	C-FHNL
N690JC	1978	Rockwell 690B	11479	W/o Konowa, Ok. 25 Jun 92.	N51MF
N690JM	1973	Rockwell 690	11072	W/o Temecula, Ca. USA. 14 Oct 01.	RP-C1956
N690JP	1976	King Air C90	LJ-690	W/o Dallas, Tx. USA. 9 Oct 01. (parts at Rantoul, Ks.).	N80TB
N690RE	1976	Rockwell 690A	11271	Wfu. Cx USA 8/06.	N690RC

Reg	Yr	Type	c/n	Owner/Operator	Prev Regn
N690TB	1973	Rockwell 690A	11109	W/o Bishop, Ca. USA. 11 Aug 02.	N920AU
N690X	1969	SA-26AT Merlin 2B	T26-141	Wfu. Cx USA 6/91.	C-GHWM
N693PA	1977	Mitsubishi MU-2N	693SA	W/o Malad City, Id. USA. 15 Jan 96.	F-GHDS
N693PG	1971	SA-226T Merlin 3	T-207	W/o Chico, Ca. USA. 18 Sep 95.	N500QP
N696JB	1970	King Air 100	B-13	W/o Garner, Tx. USA. 28 Mar 90.	N100BW
N698X	1969	SA-26AT Merlin 2B	T26-137	W/o Jacksonville, Fl. USA. 27 Nov 03.	(N192GK)
N700AR	1991	TBM 700	23	W/o Moulins, France. 13 May 02.	F-GLBR
N700CM	1978	PA-31T Cheyenne II	7820007	W/o Jacksonville, Fl. USA. 9 Jan 86. (parts at Bates City).	
N700FN	1968	Mitsubishi MU-2F	127	Wfu.	N700DM
N700JW	1960	Gulfstream 1	53	Wfu. Cx USA 6/94. Parts at White Industries, Mo. USA.	(N701JW)
N700MB	1967	King Air A90	LJ-233	Wfu. Cx USA 6/05.	N100HT
N700NC	1972	King Air A100	B-138	Wfu. Cx USA 2/06. Last located MTW Aerospace Inc. Al. USA.	N600DK
N700PP	1992	TBM 700	59	W/o Leesburg, Va. USA. 1 Mar 03.	
N700R	1978	Rockwell 690B	11434	W/o hangar fire Pekin, Il.. USA. 25 Dec 85.	N113SA
N700SP	1972	King Air A100	B-92	W/o Hilton Head Island, SC. USA. 26 Apr 75.	N6739
N700SR	1974	Rockwell 690A	11164	W/o Cortez, Co. USA. 3 Jan 04.	N57152
N701DM	1969	Mitsubishi MU-2F	149	W/o Nr San Diego, Ca. USA. 28 Feb 89.	N8527Z
N701K	1979	MU-2 Solitaire	410SA	W/o Perry Sound, ON. Canada. 24 May 99.	N329WM
N701QR	1983	Conquest 1	425-0148	W/o Belgrade, Mt. USA. 29 Nov 05.	N425EK
N702FN	1973	Mitsubishi MU-2K	249	Wfu. Cx USA 8/94.	N702DM
N705G	1965	Gulfstream 1	152	Wfu.	OB-M-1235
N705QD	2001	TBM 700B	231	W/o Mobile, Al. USA. 24 Apr 03.	
N707BP	1976	Rockwell 690A	11326	Wfu. Cx USA 3/94.	N10VG
N707CE	1967	King Air A90	LJ-314	W/o Algeria. 29 May 90.	N971EL
N707WC	1967	King Air A90	LJ-188	W/o Cleveland, Oh. USA. 18 Oct 68.	N703K
N708G	1959	Gulfstream 1	8	Wfu. Located South of Houston-Hobby, Tx. USA.	
N709K	1966	King Air 90	LJ-97	Wfu. Parts at White Industries, Bates City, Mo. USA.	(N504M)
N710CA	1975	Mitsubishi MU-2L	669	Wfu.	TF-JMC
N711AH	1970	Mitsubishi MU-2G	523	W/o Glenwood Springs, Co. USA. 2 Mar 74.	N711
N711AH	1968	SA-26T Merlin 2A	T26-14	Wfu.	N952HE
N711FC	1971	King Air C90	LJ-516	W/o Columbia, SC. USA. 20 Dec 73.	N555RH
N711LL	1969	Mitsubishi MU-2F	180	Wfu. Cx USA 6/95.	N180SB
N711TB	1978	PA-31T Cheyenne II	7820031	Wfu. Parts at White Industries, Bates City, Mo. USA.	N82238
N711TT	1977	Rockwell 690B	11362	W/o Albuquerque, NM. USA. 8 Oct 87. (parts at Bates City).	N81537
N711TZ	1977	King Air E90	LW-226	W/o Kremmling, Co. USA. 19 Mar 03.	N976
N712CM	1967	King Air A90	LJ-311	W/o, Overstressed in flight Knock, Ireland 22.08.06	N712DB
N713GB	1971	Mitsubishi MU-2G	538	Wfu.	N77RZ
N713SP	1968	680W Turbo Command	1805-27	W/o Alexandria, La. USA. 4 Oct 79.	N5082E
N715G	1963	Gulfstream 1	118	Wfu.	
N715RA	1960	Gulfstream 1	31	Wfu.	C-FJFC
N716RA	1960	Gulfstream 1	43	Wfu. Cx USA 1/91.	N39289
N718RA	1966	Gulfstream 1	174	Wfu.	N7004B
N719RA	1960	Gulfstream 1	28	Wfu. Parts at Dodsons, Rantoul, Ks. USA.	N118X
N720K	1965	King Air 90	LJ-37	Wfu. Last located Deland, Fl. USA.	
N720X	1961	Gulfstream 1	73	W/o Arizona Desert, USA. Feb 87.	N207M
N721DM	1974	Mitsubishi MU-2K	312	Wfu. Parts at White Industries Inc. Bates City, Mo. USA.	N444RG
N721K	1965	King Air 90	LJ-43	Wfu. Cx USA 2/96. Parts at Dodsons, Rantoul, Ks. USA.	
N721RA	1961	Gulfstream 1	65	Wfu. Cx USA 11/88.	N641B
N722DM	1972	Mitsubishi MU-2K	245	Wfu. Parts at White Industries Inc. Bates City, Mo. USA.	N180SB
N722RA	1966	Gulfstream 1	168	Wfu. Cx USA 11/88.	N209T
N723RA	1959	Gulfstream 1	14	Wfu. Cx USA 11/88.	N1607Z
N724FN	1974	Mitsubishi MU-2K	300	Wfu. Cx USA 11/96. Parts at Bates City, Mo. USA.	N724DM
N724N	1966	King Air 90	LJ-82	W/o Leeville, La. USA. 22 Dec 79.	
N724RA	1963	Gulfstream 1	114	Wfu. Cx USA 1/89.	VH-WPA
N725MA	1973	Mitsubishi MU-2J	582	Wfu. Cx USA 6/01.	N155BA
N727DM	1972	Mitsubishi MU-2K	242	Wfu. Cx USA 3/94.	N211BA
N727MA	1976	Mitsubishi MU-2M	342	Wfu.	
N729FN	1974	Mitsubishi MU-2K	296	Wfu.	N729DM
N730SF	1973	Mitsubishi MU-2K	246	Wfu.	N228MA
N731KA	1977	King Air C90	LJ-731	Wfu. Parts at White Industries Inc. Bates City, Mo. USA.	N37PT
N735K	1965	King Air 90	LJ-35	Wfu. Located S Seattle Community College, Wa. USA.	
N737EF	1968	SA-26T Merlin 2A	T26-22	Wfu. Cx USA 3/93. Parts at White Industries, Mo. USA.	N999DT
N741P	1975	PA-31T Cheyenne II	7520020	W/o Jamaica. Oct 81. Parts at Bates City, Mo. USA.	N55SM
N741P	1977	PA-31T Cheyenne II	7720025	Wfu. Parts at White Industries, Bates City, Mo. USA.	(N710MA)
N742FN	1975	Mitsubishi MU-2L	670	W/o Edwards AFB, Ca. USA. 18 May 92.	N742DM
N743G	1961	Gulfstream 1	72	Wfu.	C-FNOC

Reg	Yr	Type	c/n	Owner/Operator	Prev Regn
N743K	1967	King Air A90	LJ-187	Wfu. Parts at White Industries, Bates City, Mo. USA.	N610K
N746G	1960	Gulfstream 1	46	Wfu.	
N747DN	2001	PA-46-500TP Meridian	4697038	Wfu. Cx USA 4/02.	
N747K	1965	King Air 90	LJ-51	Wfu. Cx USA 2/92. Parts at White Industries, Mo. USA.	
N747KF	1975	King Air 200	BB-70	Wfu. Cx USA 3/96.	N87JR
N750BR	1963	Gulfstream 1	99	W/o Nr Frankfurt, Germany. 13 Nov 88.	N364L
N750MA	1977	MU-2 Solitaire	365SA	W/o Fernandina Beach, Fl. USA. 19 Nov 81.	
N750Q	1967	Mitsubishi MU-2B	017	Wfu.South Florida Antiquities Museum Inc	N269AA
N750QQ	1968	Mitsubishi MU-2F	125	Wfu.	N71674
N751PC	1966	King Air A90	LJ-143	Wfu. Parts at White Industries Inc. Bates City, Mo. USA.	
N755AF	1980	MU-2 Marquise	755SA	W/o Baltimore, Md. USA. 14 May 04.	SE-KGO
N757Q	1969	Mitsubishi MU-2F	151	W/o Manning, SC. USA. 20 Nov 72.	
N758Q	1968	Mitsubishi MU-2F	134	W/o Trenton, NJ. USA. 15 Apr 69.	
N762JK	1992	TBM 700	62	Wfu. Parts at Dodsons, Ottawa, Ks. USA.	N45PM
N764Q	1969	Mitsubishi MU-2F	141	W/o Salisbury, Md. USA. 16 Jan 70.	N753Q
N765MA	1978	Mitsubishi MU-2P	372SA	W/o Bedford, Mn. USA. 28 Aug 78.	
N767K	1966	King Air A90	LJ-170	Wfu. Cx USA 8/88.	
N768H	2006	Pilatus PC-12/47	716	W/o Nr Big Timber Airport, Mt. USA. 24 Jun 06.	HB-FRE
N769WT	1989	King Air B200	BB-1319	W/o hangar fire George West, Tx. USA. 6 Sep 98.	(N366EA)
N770G	1999	Pilatus PC-12/45	299	W/o University Park, Pa. USA. 26 Mar 05.	HB-FPF
N770MA	1974	Mitsubishi MU-2J	625	Wfu. Cx USA 1/07	N22522
N772CB	1971	681B Turbo Command	6050	W/o Calhoun, Co. USA. 28 Mar 85.	N56MQ
N772K	1967	King Air A90	LJ-310	Wfu. Parts at Dodsons, Rantoul, Ks. USA.	
N776K	1965	King Air 90	LJ-56	Wfu. Parts at White Industries, Bates City, Mo. USA.	
N776L	1970	King Air 100	B-54	Wfu. Parts at Dodsons, Rantoul, Ks. USA.	N1776L
N777AT	1966	King Air A90	LJ-166	Wfu. Parts at White Industries, Bates City, Mo. USA.	N28J
N777EC	1973	King Air E90	LW-37	W/o NY State, USA. 7 Jan 79.	N1837W
N777JM	1978	PA-31T Cheyenne II	7820064	Wfu. Cx USA 5/94. Parts at White Industries, Bates City, Mo.	(N82301)
N777KU	1968	King Air B90	LJ-377	W/o Dodge City, Ks. USA. 17 Feb 04.	N8473N
N777KV	1977	PA-31T Cheyenne II	7720034	Wfu. Parts at White Industries Inc. Bates City, Mo. USA.	(N774KV)
N777MA	1972	Mitsubishi MU-2J	559	W/o Austin, Tx. USA. 18 Mar 77.	
N778HD	1979	PA-31T Cheyenne II	7920006	Wfu. Parts at White Industries, Bates City, Mo. USA.	
N780BF	1985	King Air 300	FA-70	W/o Cullman, Al. USA. 14 Jan 99.	(N66FB)
N784K	1968	King Air B90	LJ-427	Wfu. Located Griffin, Ga. USA.	
N786BP	1992	2000A Starship	NC-28	Wfu. Located Caloundra, NSW. Australia.	N82428
N791K	1967	King Air A90	LJ-253	W/o Portland, Me. USA. 13 Mar 73.	
N794CA	1981	PA-31T Cheyenne II	8120018	W/o Hobbs, NM. USA 4 Feb 02. (parts at Bates City).	N406TM
N795K	1966	King Air 90	LJ-95	Wfu. Located College of Aeronautics, La Guardia, NY. USA.	
N799V	1977	Rockwell 690B	11407	W/o Wichita, Ks. USA. 2 Nov 91.	N81643
N800AW	1981	SA-226T Merlin 3B	T-403	W/o Pontiac, Mi. USA. 10 Jan 88.	N4464V
N800BR	1981	Mitsubishi MU-2F	199	Wfu. Parts at Dodsons, Rantoul, Ks. USA.	N3RN
N800DH	1969	Mitsubishi MU-2F	166	Wfu. Cx USA 4/94.	N322GA
N800VT	1967	King Air A90	LJ-249	Wfu. Cx USA 12/95. Parts at White Industries, Mo. USA.	N800S
N800W	1980	PA-31T Cheyenne 1	8004032	Wfu. Parts at White Industries, Bates City, Mo. USA.	C-FDDD
N801BT	1978	SA-26T Merlin 2A	T26-18	Wfu. Cx USA 12/00.	N12NA
N801C	1976	PA-31T Cheyenne II	7620048	Wfu. Parts at White Industries, Bates City, Mo. USA.	(N414VM)
N801HD	1976	PA-31T Cheyenne II	7620031	W/o Beckley, WV. USA. 24 Nov 77.	N35RR
N802AC	1968	SA-26T Merlin 2A	T26-21	Wfu. Parts at Dodsons, Rantoul, Ks. USA.	N137RD
N803CC	1963	Gulfstream 1	112	Wfu. Cx USA 9/89.	N300PE
N803DJ	1968	SA-26AT Merlin 2B	T26-102	Wfu. Cx USA 8/02.	C-FBWU
N808W	1973	Mitsubishi MU-2J	609	W/o Patterson, La. USA. 14 Apr 85.	N508W
N814SW	1967	King Air A90	LJ-186	W/o Orange County Airport, Ca. USA. 16 Nov 96.	N881M
N816C	1965	King Air 90	LJ-42	Wfu. Parts at White Industries, Bates City, Mo. USA.	N81CC
N817SW	1981	PA-31T Cheyenne 1	8104044	Wfu. Cx USA 6/96.	
N823MA	1975	Mitsubishi MU-2L	663	Wfu. Cx USA 1/07	YV-409P
N830EM	1970	King Air 100	B-29	Wfu. Parts at White Industries Inc. Bates City, Mo. USA.	N8300E
N831PC	1980	PA-31T Cheyenne II	8020001	W/o West Palm Beach, Fl. USA. 1 Jun 83.	
N845JB	1962	Gulfstream 1	87	Wfu. Cx USA 9/97.	N87CE
N847	1973	Rockwell 690A	11140	W/o Chicago, Il. USA. 23 Apr 77.	
N847CE	1974	Rockwell 690A	11223	W/o Nemacolin, Pa. USA. 12 Sep 75.	N57223
N850MA	1977	Mitsubishi MU-2L	690	Wfu. Cx USA 4/94.	(N88DW)
N854Q	1968	Mitsubishi MU-2D	107	W/o Rochester, Mn. USA. 8 Jan 77.	N3571X
N855Q	1968	Mitsubishi MU-2D	108	Wfu. Cx USA 6/97.	N3572X
N859DD	1981	King Air B200	BB-859	W/o Jasper, Al. USA. 23 Jun 87.	N4935X
N861H	1964	Gulfstream 1	147	W/o Le Centre, Mn. USA. 11 Jul 67.	N774G
N861K	1969	King Air B90	LJ-471	Wfu. Cx USA 8/87.	

Reg	Yr	Type	c/n	Owner/Operator	Prev Regn
N863Q	1968	Mitsubishi MU-2D	117	Wfu. Cx USA 7/97.	
N866A	1967	King Air A90	LJ-201	Wfu. Cx USA 8/05.	(D-ILNY)
N866K	1965	King Air 90	LJ-76	Wfu. Cx USA 10/93.	N100AN
N866Q	1968	Mitsubishi MU-2F	121	Wfu. Cx USA 5/95.	
N869	1976	King Air 200	BB-174	W/o Chicago-Meigs, Il. USA. 11 Nov 99.	N69DD
N870MA	1972	King Air A100	B-109	Wfu. Cx USA 12/04.	N78MK
N872S	1969	SA-26AT Merlin 2B	T26-123	Wfu. Parts at White Industries, Bates City, Mo. USA.	N872D
N873Q	1969	Mitsubishi MU-2F	160	W/o Nashville, Tn. USA. 1 Nov 79.	
N877AQ	1965	King Air 90	LJ-41	Wfu. Parts at Dodsons, Rantoul, Ks. USA.	N877AG
N877Q	1969	Mitsubishi MU-2F	164	Wfu	
N878T	1967	King Air A90	LJ-246	W/o Big Piney, Tx. USA. 27 Feb 78.	
N880CA	1981	PA-31T Cheyenne II	8120001	Wfu. Cx USA 7/94.	
N882Q	1969	Mitsubishi MU-2F	168	W/o Cedillos, Mexico. 13 Jun 73.	
N885Q	1969	Mitsubishi MU-2F	172	Wfu. Cx USA 10/94. Parts at Bates City, Mo. USA.	
N887PE	1970	King Air 100	B-49	W/o Mayfield, Ky. USA. 15 Sep 89.	N887PL
N888DD	1967	680V Turbo Command	1679-61	Wfu. Cx USA 12/95.	N330LC
N888MA	1972	Mitsubishi MU-2J	550	W/o Neiva, Colombia. Feb 78.	N220SB
N888RJ	1971	Mitsubishi MU-2G	542	W/o New York, NY. USA. 5 Apr 77.	N166MA
N888TP	1982	MU-2 Marquise	1541SA	W/o Allentown, Pa. USA. 19 Jan 96. (Parts at Bates City, Mo.	N100TB
N892MA	1978	Mitsubishi MU-2N	721SA	Wfu. Cx USA 4/94.	
N895K	1965	King Air 90	LJ-25	W/o Billings, Mt. USA. 5 Aug 82.	
N898K	1967	King Air A90	LJ-198	Wfu. Cx USA 11/92.	C-GBFF
N900BP	1965	King Air 90	LJ-61	Wfu. Last located Columbus Bolton Field, Oh. USA.	N3078W
N906F	1964	Gulfstream 1	146	Wfu. Located Opa Locka, Fl. USA.	4X-JUD
N908CM	1977	King Air E90	LW-233	W/o Hotham Inlet, Ak. USA. 25 Aug 80.	
N911KA	1967	King Air A90	LJ-254	W/o Selmer, Tn. USA. 22 Jan 98. (parts at Rantoul, Ks.).	N781JT
N916PA	1979	King Air E90	LW-313	W/o Wiscassett, Mi. USA. 10 Jun 96.	N491KD
N917RG	1966	680V Turbo Command	1576-30	W/o Mazatlan, Mexico. Aug 76.	N1187Z
N919RD	1981	PA-31T Cheyenne 1	8104037	W/o Santa Fe, NM. USA. 16 Dec 99.	(N822WC)
N920C	1977	Conquest II	441-0020	W/o Gainesville, Ga. USA. 10 Aug 92. (parts at Griffin, Ga.)	N700AB
N920S	1971	Mitsubishi MU-2G	534	Wfu. N Reg Cx 2/07	(N78V)
N925TT	1980	King Air 200	BB-746	W/o Crashed into Buildings Salmon Id. 12/07	C-FMPE
N926S	1969	King Air B90	LJ-447	Wfu. Cx USA 2/06.	C-GSUN
N931SW	1976	PA-31T Cheyenne II	7620013	Wfu. Parts at White Industries, Bates City, Mo. USA.	CX-BLT
N932E	1966	680T Turbo Command	1588-39	W/o Kelso, Wa. USA. 11 Jul 84.	N932
N936K	1972	King Air C90	LJ-539	W/o Cedar Rapids, Ia. USA. 3 Jan 73.	
N940MA	1979	MU-2 Marquise	743SA	Wfu. Cx USA 6/95.	XB-PRO
N941K	1972	King Air A100	B-111	W/o Muscle Shoals, Al. USA. 22 Jun 78.	
N944CA	2001	TBM 700B	206	W/o on app to New Bedford, Ma. 3/2/07	(D-FAJS)
N948CC	1977	King Air E90	LW-236	W/o Reno, Nv. USA. 13 Mar 02.	N48V
N950	1968	SA-26T Merlin 2A	T26-370	Wfu. Cx USA 6/02.	N95D
N950TT	1973	SA-226T Merlin 3	T-225	W/o Byers, Co. USA. 20 Dec 97.	C-GRTL
N951HE	1968	680W Turbo Command	1751-4	Wfu. Located Memphis Area VoTec School, Tn. USA.	N951HF
N959L	1972	Mitsubishi MU-2J	570	Wfu. Cx USA 6/95.	N214MA
N960GK	1982	King Air B200	BB-960	Wfu. Parts at White Industries Inc. Bates City, Mo. USA.	(NZ1883)
N960M	1971	SA-226AT Merlin 4	AT-005	W/o Southern Pines, SC. USA. 14 Apr 75.	
N961G	1960	Gulfstream 1	30	Wfu. Cx USA 11/91.	N901G
N961JM	2002	PA-46-500TP Meridian	4697122	Wfu. Last located Montgomery, Al. USA.	(OY-LAW)
N962AT	1967	King Air A90	LJ-207	Wfu. Cx USA 3/03.	N383JC
N962BL	1966	680V Turbo Command	1562-16	Wfu. (as C-GFAF).	C-GFAF
N962MA	1979	MU-2 Solitaire	401SA	W/o New Orleans, La. USA. 23 Feb 80.	
N965MA	1979	MU-2 Solitaire	404SA	Wfu. Cx USA 10/96.	
N966MA	1979	MU-2 Solitaire	405SA	W/o Napa, Ca. USA. 11 Mar 2004.	N711TF
N969MA	1979	MU-2 Solitaire	409SA	W/o Ramsey, Mn. USA. 6 Dec 80.	
N974DC	1981	PA-31T Cheyenne II	8120027	Wfu. Cx USA 12/03.	N815SW
N982MA	1974	Mitsubishi MU-2K	314	Dbr. Accident Sao Paulo, Brazil 10 Jul 98 as PT-LTC.	PT-LTC
N987GM	1974	King Air E90	LW-98	W/o Tuba City, Az. USA. 31 May 89. (parts at White Inds.).	N439EE
N998VB	1978	King Air C90	LJ-785	W/o Tomahawk, Wi. USA. 31 Dec 96. (parts at Bates City).	N999VB
N999CR	1970	King Air 100	B-12	W/o Houston, Tx. USA. 18 Mar 91. (parts at White Industries)	N152X
N999FA	1975	Mitsubishi MU-2L	676	W/o Scottsdale, Az. USA. 20 Jul 96.	N90BC
N999P	1993	2000A Starship	NC-43	Wfu. Last located 6/06 at Marana, Az. USA.	N200ZS
N999PF	1974	SA-226T Merlin 3	T-247	Wfu. Cx USA 9/93.	N100T
N999RF	1990	2000 Starship	NC-9	Wfu. Last located 10/04 at Marana, Az. USA.	N2009W
N999TA	1970	Mitsubishi MU-2G	514	Wfu. Parts at White Industries Inc. Bates City, Mo. USA.	N514WG
N999WB	1970	Mitsubishi MU-2G	530	W/o Wayne, Il. USA. 30 Dec 97.	(N999TA)
N1008U	1980	SA-226T Merlin 3B	T-351	Wfu. Cx USA 8/02.	

Reg	Yr	Type	c/n	Owner/Operator	Prev Regn
N1011R	1979	SA-226T Merlin 3C	T-303E	W/o San Marcos, Tx., USA. 24 Mar 81.	
N1127D	1967	King Air A90	LJ-223	W/o Quincy, Il. USA. 19 Nov 96.	N1127M
N1154Z	1966	680V Turbo Command	1585-37	Wfu. Cx USA 2/83.	
N1171Z	1966	680V Turbo Command	1557-15	Wfu. Parts at White Industries, Bates City, Mo. USA.	
N1176W	1974	Rockwell 690A	11184	Wfu.	N110GM
N1184U	1976	King Air C-12C	BD-16	Wfu. Cx USA 12/02.	N60159
N1195Z	1966	680V Turbo Command	1575-29	W/o Atlanta, Ga. USA. 9 Dec 72.	
N1198S	1968	SA-26T Merlin 2A	T26-12	Wfu. Parts at White Industries, Bates City, Mo. USA.	C-GRDT
N1206S	1968	SA-26T Merlin 2A	T26-23	Wfu. Cx USA 9/93.	
N1210Y	1984	Conquest II	441-0338	W/o Maiduguri, Nigeria. 26 Sep 87.	
N1211C	1984	Conquest II	441-0340	Wfu. Cx USA 8/92.	
N1214S	1968	SA-26T Merlin 2A	T26-31	W/o Deadhorse, Ak. USA. 16 May 73.	
N1224S	1984	Conquest 1	425-0211	W/o Perkasie, Pa. USA. 17 Aug 97.	
N1224T	1984	Conquest 1	425-0212	Wfu. Cx USA 11/94.	
N1283	1976	King Air 200	BB-90	W/o Jackson, Wy. USA. 11 Sep 88.	
N1500X	1969	SA-26AT Merlin 2B	T26-127	Wfu. Cx USA 8/98.	
N1550S	1990	2000 Starship	NC-5	Wfu. Cx USA 4/00.	N42SR
N1552S	1990	2000 Starship	NC-12	Wfu. Last located 10/04 at Marana, Az. USA.	
N1553S	1990	2000 Starship	NC-13	Wfu. Last located 3/05 at Marana, Az. USA.	
N1556S	1990	2000 Starship	NC-6	Wfu. Cx USA 5/05.	
N1560S	1991	2000A Starship	NC-24	Wfu. Last located 10/04 at Marana, Az. USA.	
N1569S	1990	2000 Starship	NC-11	Wfu. Last located 10/04 at Marana, Az. USA.	
N1865D	1983	King Air B200	BB-1119	W/o Treasure Cay, Bahamas. 15 May 96.	N1865A
N1870S	1983	King Air B200	BB-1106	W/o Lake Tahoe, Nv. USA. 17 Jul 87.	N63882
N1879W	1981	Cheyenne II-XL	8166065	W/o Des Moines, Ia. USA. 29 Nov 90. (parts at Bates City).	N222XL
N1910L	1976	King Air B100	BE-10	W/o Midland, Tx. USA. 26 Nov 83.	
N2000S	1991	2000 Starship	NC-17	Wfu. Last located 3/05 at Marana, Az. USA.	N62KK
N2000S	1986	2000 Starship	NC-1	Wfu.	
N2019U	1978	King Air C90	LJ-792	W/o Nr St Mary's, Pa. USA. 14 Feb 85.	
N2029N	1978	King Air C90	LJ-798	W/o Houston, Tx. USA. 30 Dec 78.	
N2060M	1972	Mitsubishi MU-2J	564	Wfu.	N199MA
N2079A	1980	Conquest 1	425-0001	W/o Dayton, Oh. USA. 29 May 85.	
N2173Z	1967	680V Turbo Command	1704-80	Wfu. Cx USA 6/97.	C-GKFV
N2176D	1967	Mitsubishi MU-2B	028	Wfu. Located Thief River Falls Technical College, Mn.	CP-1962
N2181L	1976	King Air E90	LW-181	W/o Michigan City, In. USA. 7 Dec 80.	
N2301N	1967	SA-26T Merlin 2A	T26-2	W/o Olive Branch, Ms. USA. 22 Nov 78.	N500BW
N2336X	1981	PA-31T Cheyenne II	8120002	W/o Cody, Wy. USA. 20 May 87.	VH-IHK
N2400X	1965	King Air 90	LJ-18	W/o Akutan Island, Ak. USA. 17 Apr 76.	
N2406U	1971	Mitsubishi MU-2F	197	Wfu. Cx USA 1/01.	XA-GAL
N2484B	1979	Conquest II	441-0112	W/o Calexico, Mexico. 15 Nov 87.	HP-...
N2517X	1981	Cheyenne II-XL	8166004	W/o Springfield, Ky. USA. 16 Feb 82.	
N2566W	1980	PA-31T Cheyenne II	8020035	W/o Pontiac, Mi. USA. 19 Feb 81.	(N321SS)
N2601S	1967	SA-26T Merlin 2	T26-1	Wfu.	
N2643B	1971	681B Turbo Command	6060	Wfu.	9Q-CGE
N2646W	1978	Rockwell 690B	11496	Wfu. Parts at White Industries, Bates City, Mo. USA.	D-IKOA
N2727A	1981	Conquest II	441-0201	W/o Lander, Ey. USA. 29 Aug 86.	
N2755H	1966	680T Turbo Command	1628-55	W/o Jackson, Ms. USA. 7 Jul 80.	
N2937A	1981	Gulfstream 840	11670	W/o Wooster, Oh. USA. 31 Oct 84.	ZS-KZP
N3019W	1974	King Air C90	LJ-639	W/o Nr Munson, Fl. USA. 25 Jun 99.	
N3042S	1987	2000 Starship	NC-2	Wfu.	
N3107W	1988	King Air 300	FA-150	Wfu.	
N3177W	1974	King Air E90	LW-77	W/o Nueva Palestina, Peru. 31 May 93.	
N3199A	1995	King Air B200	BB-1499	Wfu.	
N3234S	1987	2000 Starship	NC-3	Wfu. Cx USA 1/01.	
N3333D	1967	King Air A90	LJ-259	W/o Itaguazurenda, Bolivia. 11 Oct 96.	N3333X
N3544X	1967	Mitsubishi MU-2B	012	Wfu.	
N3550X	1967	Mitsubishi MU-2B	018	W/o Springfield, Mo. USA. 21 Dec 68.	
N3560X	1967	Mitsubishi MU-2B	029	Wfu. Cx USA 9/93. Parts at Dodsons, Rantoul, Ks. USA.	
N3668P	1980	King Air B100	BE-95	Wfu. Parts at White Industries, Bates City, Mo. USA.	
N3804F	1981	King Air C90	LJ-947	W/o Gadsen, Al. USA. 5 Nov 89.	
N3833P	1968	680W Turbo Command	1761-7	Wfu.	C-GNYD
N3998Y	1980	PA-31T Cheyenne II	8020055	W/o Hobbs, NM. USA 31 Oct 02.	PH-TAX
N4089L	1978	Conquest 1	425-693	Wfu.	
N4202K	1973	Mitsubishi MU-2J	603	Wfu. Cx USA 7/94.	EC-EDK
N4207S	1977	King Air E90	LW-207	W/o Sitka, Al. USA. 31 Jul 77.	
N4284V	1973	Mitsubishi MU-2K	270	Wfu. Cx USA 3/95.	VH-MUO

Reg	Yr	Type	c/n	Owner/Operator	Prev Regn
N4392W	1974	King Air A100	B-192	Wfu. Last located MTW Aerospace Inc. Montgomery, Al.	
N4425W	1975	PA-31T Cheyenne II	7620009	Wfu. Parts at White Industries, Bates City, Mo. USA.	C-GIVM
N4463W	1974	King Air C90	LJ-633	W/o Beaufort, Ga. USA. 30 Nov 87.	
N4468M	1969	SA-26AT Merlin 2B	T26-119	Wfu. Parts at White Industries, Bates City, Mo. USA.	VH-CAJ
N4470H	1966	680T Turbo Command	1550-11	Wfu. Cx USA 8/84.	CF-SVJ
N4505B	1981	PA-42 Cheyenne III	8001015	Wfu. Cx USA 12/91.	
N4527E	1966	680V Turbo Command	1622-52	Wfu. Parts at White Industries, Bates City, Mo. USA.	
N4556E	1966	680T Turbo Command	1614-48	Wfu.	
N4594V	1973	Mitsubishi MU-2K	256	Wfu.	HZ-BIN
N4682E	1966	680V Turbo Command	1630-56	Wfu. Located Cincinnati Technical College, Oh. USA.	N4682E
N5058E	1968	680W Turbo Command	1787-17	W/o Atlanta, Ga. USA. 20 Nov 82.	
N5296M	1972	SA-226T Merlin 3	T-219	W/o Montreal, Canada. 10 Apr 73.	
N5329M	1974	SA-226T Merlin 3	T-243	W/o Bahamas. 3 Mar 77.	
N5549B	1992	2000 Starship	NC-15	Wfu. Last located 10/04 at Marana, Az. USA.	
N5589S	1969	Mitsubishi MU-2F	150	W/o Louisville, Ky. USA. 15 Dec 82.	C-FFER
N5805	1980	SA-226T Merlin 3B	T-324	Wfu. Located Hampton University, Newport News, Va. USA.	N77UU
N5860K	1980	Gulfstream 840	11608	W/o Patterson, La. USA. 13 Dec 81.	
N5889N	1982	Gulfstream 900	15019	Wfu. Cx USA 9/86.	
N5920C	1966	680T Turbo Command	1552-12	Wfu. Cx USA 6/69.	
N5926K	1981	Gulfstream 840	11674	W/o Freeport, Bahamas. 16 Oct 81.	
N5938K	1981	Gulfstream 840	11686	Wfu. Parts at White Industries, Bates City, Mo. USA.	
N5957K	1982	Gulfstream 840	11720	W/o 29 Mar 82.	
N6038A	1978	PA-31T Cheyenne II	7820072	W/o Swanton, Oh. USA. 31 Jan 92.	(N90TW)
N6040M	1979	King Air C90	LJ-840	W/o Indianapolis, In. USA. 5 Jun 79.	
N6069C	1967	King Air A90	LJ-291	Wfu. Parts at White Industries, Bates City, Mo. USA.	
N6123A	1978	PA-31T Cheyenne 1	7804008	W/o Baltimore, Md. USA. 22 Feb 79.	
N6134A	1978	PA-31T Cheyenne 1	7804006	W/o Graham, Tx. USA. 12 Nov 01.	
N6192A	1979	PA-31T Cheyenne 1	7904009	Wfu. Cx USA 2/96.	
N6200B	1967	King Air A90	LJ-250	Wfu. Parts at White Industries, Bates City, Mo. USA.	(N66FS)
N6272C	1982	King Air C90-1	LJ-1025	W/o Nr Azores. 18 Mar 82.	
N6280E	1982	King Air C90-1	LJ-1015	Wfu. Parts at Dodson's, Rantoul, Ks. USA.	
N6359U	1966	680T Turbo Command	1536-4	W/o Aspen, Co. USA. 22 Jan 70.	
N6514V	1966	680V Turbo Command	1581-34	Wfu.	
N6523V	1966	680V Turbo Command	1583-35	Wfu.	
N6540V	1966	680V Turbo Command	1571-26	Wfu. Located Portland Community College, Or. USA.	
N6569L	1974	Mitsubishi MU-2L	645	W/o De Funiak Springs, Fl. USA. 1 Sep 06.	YV-11CP
N6591L	1990	Reims/Cessna F406	F406-0053	W/o Barrow, Ak. USA. 17 Aug 03.	
N6600A	1978	PA-31T Cheyenne 1	7804001	Wfu.	
N6649P	1983	King Air B200	BB-1133	Wfu.	
N6653Z	1959	Gulfstream 1	21	Wfu. Cx USA 11/95.	XC-BIO
N6771Y	1981	Conquest 1	425-0019	W/o Sanford, Fl. USA. 11 Feb 88.	
N6774R	1981	Conquest 1	425-0045	W/o Newburgh, NY. USA. 12 Dec 83.	
N6843S	1975	King Air E90	LW-137	W/o Cordova, Ak. USA. 29 Nov 76.	
N6846D	1981	Conquest 1	425-0078	W/o Augusta, Ga. USA. 31 Jan 90.	(N6844V)
N6857E	1982	Conquest II	441-0244	W/o Muskegon, Mi. USA. 16 Jul 86.	
N6858S	1982	Conquest II	441-0253	W/o Flagstaff, Az. USA. 21 Feb 87.	
N6881S	1969	King Air B90	LJ-450	Wfu. Parts at Dodsons, Rantoul, Ks. USA., Ks.	N979LX
N6886D	1983	Conquest 1	425-0152	W/o Ithaca, NY. USA. 25 Feb 84.	
N7043G	1967	King Air A90	LM-37	W/o Tampa, Fl. USA. 12 Jun 06.	66-18036
N7138C	1969	King Air B90	LJ-446	Wfu. Cx USA 7/93. Parts at Dodson's, Rantoul, Ks. USA.	G-BLNA
N7377	1972	King Air A90	LJ-115	Wfu. Parts at White Industries, Bates City, Mo, USA.	N3OKS
N7388K	1990	2000 Starship	NC-7	Wfu. Last located 3/05 at Marana, Az. USA.	(N4NV)
N7400V	1975	King Air E90	LW-152	Wfu. Located Lima, Peru.	N9046G
N7500L	1969	PA-31T Cheyenne II	1	Wfu.	
N7603	1968	SA-26AT Merlin 2B	T26-112	Wfu. Parts at White Industries Inc. Bates City, Mo. USA.	N1222S
N7676L		PA-42 Cheyenne III	31-5003	Wfu.	
N8000Q	1992	2000A Starship	NC-26	Wfu. Last located 10/04 at Marana, Az. USA.	
N8042N	1967	680V Turbo Command	1720-91	Wfu.	OO-SKF
N8074S	1993	2000A Starship	NC-33	Wfu. Last located 3/05 Marana, Az. USA.	
N8092D	1979	King Air 200	BB-418	Wfu. Parts at White Industries, Bates City, Mo. USA.	CX-BOR
N8119S	1993	2000A Starship	NC-34	Wfu. Last located 10/04 Marana, Az. USA.	
N8149S	1993	2000A Starship	NC-35	Wfu. Last located 4/04 Marana, Az.USA.	
N8158X	1994	2000A Starship	NC-42	Wfu. Cx USA 9/04. Located Boeing Museum of Flight,	
N8194S	1994	2000A Starship	NC-37	Wfu. Last located 6/06 at Marana, Az. USA.	
N8196Q	1994	2000A Starship	NC-48	Wfu. Last located 10/04 at Marana, Az. USA.	
N8224Q	1995	2000A Starship	NC-49	Wfu. Located Staggerwing Museum, Tullahoma, Tn. USA.	XA-TQF

Reg	Yr	Type	c/n	Owner/Operator	Prev Regn
❏ N8280S	1994	2000A Starship	NC-38	Wfu. Last located 6/06 at Marana, Az. USA.	
❏ N8282S	1994	2000A Starship	NC-39	Wfu. Last located 10/04 at Marana, Az. USA.	
❏ N8283S	1994	2000A Starship	NC-41	Wfu. Located Kansas Aviation Museum, McConnell AFB. USA.	
❏ N8520L	1966	King Air A90	LJ-156	Wfu. Located Philadelphia, Pa. USA.	N22
❏ N9001N	1969	Rockwell 690	11000	W/o Rosedale, Ok. USA. 5 May 69.	
❏ N9003N	1969	680W Turbo Command	1828-36	Wfu.	N94490
❏ N9004N	1969	680W Turbo Command	1829-37	Wfu.	
❏ N9019N	1969	680W Turbo Command	1844-43	W/o Elkhart, In. USA. 28 Dec 71.	
❏ N9058N	1970	681 Turbo Commander	6008	Wfu. Located Broward Community College, Pembroke Pines, Fl.	YV-06CP
❏ N9060N	1970	681 Turbo Commander	6011	W/o Altus, Ok. USA. 25 Nov 70.	
❏ N9066N	1972	King Air C90	LJ-557	W/o Ciudad Constitucion, Peru. 12 Jul 94.	C-GQPC
❏ N9079S	1979	King Air F90	LA-1	Wfu. Cx USA 8/87.	
❏ N9129N	1971	681B Turbo Command	6056	W/o Mansfield, Oh. USA. 30 Nov 96.	
❏ N9150N	1973	Rockwell 690	11063	W/o Little America, Wy. USA. 25 Aug 84.	
❏ N9150R	1976	King Air 200	BB-181	Wfu. Parts at White Industries, Bates City, Mo. USA.	C-GPKK
❏ N9202N	1970	Rockwell 690	11002	W/o Bethany, Ok. USA. 26 Jun 70.	
❏ N9233T	1985	PA-42 Cheyenne IIIA	5501032	Wfu. Parts at White Industries Inc. Bates City, Mo. USA.	
❏ N9789S	1980	Gulfstream 980	95037	W/o Carlsbad, NM. USA. 12 May 82.	
❏ N9971F	1959	Gulfstream 1	17	Wfu.	C-FTPC
❏ N9971G	1977	Conquest II	441-0006	W/o Greensboro, Al. USA. 15 Nov 77.	(N441SA)
❏ N12117	1985	Conquest II	441-0345	Wfu. Used in development of Cessna 435 programme.	
❏ N17530	1977	King Air 200	BB-204	W/o Valparaiso. In. USA. 19 Oct 77.	
❏ N17690	1966	680V Turbo Command	1577-31	W/o Concord, Ca. USA. 3 Dec 85.	N17690
❏ N18260	1981	King Air B200	BB-900	W/o Piqua, Oh. USA. 24 Aug 01.	
❏ N23796	1977	King Air C90	LJ-737	W/o Pontiac, Il. USA. 23 Sep 77.	
❏ N24169	1978	King Air B100	BE-38	W/o Romeo, Mi. USA. 22 Nov 91.	
❏ N31434	1988	King Air C90A	LJ-1186	W/o Manaus, Brazil. 30 May 90.	
❏ N36941	1977	Conquest II	441-0018	W/o Butte, Mt. USA. 1 Apr 80.	
❏ N36962	1977	Conquest II	441-0033	W/o ground accident Mesa, Az. USA. Jan 84.	
❏ N41054	1983	Conquest 1	425-0172	W/o Idaho Falls, Id. USA. 10 Nov 00.	N425LS
❏ N45591	1970	Mitsubishi MU-2G	524	Wfu. Parts at White Industries Inc. Bates City, Mo. USA.	C-FGWF
❏ N46866	1973	Rockwell 690A	11108	Wfu. Cx USA 12/94. Parts at White Industries, Mo. USA.	HB-GFP
❏ N53070	1969	SA-26AT Merlin 2B	T26-155	Wfu.	C-GVCO
❏ N53328	2001	PA-46-500TP Meridian	4697098	W/o Palma, Spain. 19 Dec 02.	
❏ N54985	1975	PA-31T Cheyenne II	7620007	Wfu. Parts at White Industries, Bates City, Mo. USA.	(N76NL)
❏ N57096	1973	Rockwell 690A	11120	W/o 12 W of Anchorage, Ak. USA. 28 Jul 06.	
❏ N57133	1973	Rockwell 690A	11133	Wfu. Cx USA 12/92.	(N47EC)
❏ N57169	1974	Rockwell 690A	11203	W/o Jacksonville, Fl. USA. 24 Jun 87.	
❏ N57186	1974	Rockwell 690A	11186	W/o Independence, Ks. USA. 17 Nov 76.	
❏ N57233	1975	Rockwell 690A	11247	W/o Columbus, Oh. USA. 1 Oct 79.	
❏ N65103	1969	SA-26AT Merlin 2B	T26-140E	W/o Palo Alto, Ca. USA. 19 Oct 79.	D-IBMC
❏ N66534	1962	Gulfstream 1	85	Wfu. Cx USA 11/95.	XC-BAU
❏ N66847	1975	PA-31T Cheyenne II	7520019	Wfu. Parts at White Industries, Bates City, Mo. USA.	
❏ N80398	1978	Mitsubishi MU-2N	712SA	Wfu. Cx USA 3/95.	VH-SSL
❏ N81416	1976	Rockwell 690A	11306	W/o Winter Haven, Fl. USA. 14 Feb 83.	
❏ N81470	1976	Rockwell 690A	11335	Wfu. Cx USA 1/94. Parts at White Industries, Mo. USA.	
❏ N81502	1982	Gulfstream 1000	96000	W/o Chekotah, Ok. USA. 9 Oct 84.	
❏ N81521	1977	Rockwell 690B	11351	W/o Burns, Or. USA. 7 Jan 81.	
❏ N81601	1973	Mitsubishi MU-2J	577	Wfu. Cx USA 11/00.	C-FBAN
❏ N81628	1977	Rockwell 690B	11396	W/o White Plains, NY. USA. 22 Sep 90. (Parts at Bates City.)	
❏ N81717	1978	Rockwell 690B	11445	W/o Greenville, SC. USA. 17 Jan 84.	
❏ N82010	1976	PA-31T Cheyenne II	7620025	Wfu. Parts at White Industries, Bates City, Mo. USA.	(N820YL)
❏ N82123	1977	PA-31T Cheyenne II	7720030	Wfu. Parts at White Industries, Bates City, Mo. USA.	
❏ N82139	1977	PA-31T Cheyenne II	7720040	Wfu. Parts at White Industries, Bates City, Mo. USA.	N14BW
❏ N82271	1978	PA-31T Cheyenne II	7820044	W/o Pellston, Mi. USA. 13 May 78.	
❏ N82282	1978	PA-31T Cheyenne II	7820055	W/o Elyria, Oh. USA. 27 Apr 79. (Parts at White Inds.).	
❏ N88832	1979	Conquest II	441-0071	W/o Mexico. Sep 79.	
❏ N98949	1968	King Air B90	LJ-407	W/o Charlotte, Tx. USA. 5 May 82.	D-ILTP

Military

Reg	Yr	Type	c/n	Owner/Operator	Prev Regn
❏ 03	1962	Gulfstream 1	91	Wfu.	USCG 02
❏ 155722	1966	Gulfstream TC-4C	176	Wfu. Preserved Pensacola NAS. Fl. USA.	N798G
❏ 155723	1967	Gulfstream TC-4C	178	W/o Cherry Point, NC. USA. 16 Oct 75.	N778G
❏ 155724	1967	Gulfstream TC-4C	180	Wfu. At AMARC 10/94 as 4G002.	N786G
❏ 155725	1967	Gulfstream TC-4C	182	Wfu. At AMARC 5/00.	N762G
❏ 155726	1967	Gulfstream TC-4C	183	Wfu. At AMARC 5/00.	N766G
❏ 155727	1967	Gulfstream TC-4C	184	Wfu. At AMARC 10/94 as 4G004.	

Reg	Yr	Type	c/n	Owner/Operator	Prev Regn
☐ 155728	1967	Gulfstream TC-4C	185	Wfu. At AMARC 10/94 as 4G003.	
☐ 155729	1967	Gulfstream TC-4C	186	Wfu. At AMARC 10/94 as 4G001.	
☐ 155730	1967	Gulfstream TC-4C	187	Wfu. At AMARC 4/95 as 4G005.	
☐ 161185	1961	King Air UC-12B	BJ-1	Wfu.	
☐ 161186	1961	King Air UC-12B	BJ-2	Wfu. At AMARC 5G0011. (wef 6/97). (still there 5/06).	
☐ 161188	1961	King Air TC-12B	BJ-4	Wfu. At AMARC 5G0019. (wef 10/04). (still there 5/06).	
☐ 161189	1961	King Air UC-12B	BJ-5	W/o Nr Penscaloa, Fl. USA. 2 Jan 82.	
☐ 161192	1961	King Air UC-12B	BJ-8	Wfu. At AMARC 5G0020. (wef 4/05). (still there 5/06).	
☐ 161194	1961	King Air TC-12B	BJ-10	Wfu. At AMARC 5G0016. (wef 8/04). (still there 5/06).	
☐ 161198	1961	King Air UC-12B	BJ-14	Wfu. At AMARC 5G0005 9/96.	
☐ 161199	1961	King Air UC-12B	BJ-15	Wfu. At AMARC 5G0015. (wef 8/04). (still there 5/06).	
☐ 161200	1961	King Air UC-12B	BJ-16	Wfu. At AMARC 5G0021. (wef 5/05). (still there 5/06).	
☐ 161202	1961	King Air UC-12B	BJ-18	Wfu. At AMARC 5G0003. (wef 9/96).(still there 5/06).	
☐ 161204		King Air UC-12B	BJ-20	Wfu. At AMARC 5G0022. (wef 10/05). (still there 5/06).	
☐ 161307		King Air UC-12B	BJ-24	Wfu. At AMARC SG0025. (wef 1/06).	
☐ 161308	1961	King Air UC-12B	BJ-25	Wfu. At AMARC 5G0013. (wef 6/04). (still there 5/06).	
☐ 161311	1961	King Air UC-12B	BJ-28	Wfu. At AMARC 5G0001 9/96.	
☐ 161314	1961	King Air UC-12B	BJ-31	Wfu. At AMARC 5G0010.	
☐ 161317		King Air UC-12B	BJ-34	Wfu. At AMARC 5G0026. (wef 4/06).	
☐ 161321	1961	King Air UC-12B	BJ-38	Wfu. At AMARC 5G0007. (wef 12/96). (still there 5/06).	
☐ 161322	1961	King Air UC-12B	BJ-39	Wfu. At AMARC 5G0014. (wef 7/04). (still there 5/06).	
☐ 161327	1961	King Air UC-12B	BJ-44	Wfu.	
☐ 161499	1961	King Air UC-12B	BJ-47	Wfu. At AMARC 5G0004. (wef 9/96).(still there 5/06).	
☐ 161503		King Air UC-12B	BJ-51	Wfu. At AMARC 5G0024. (wef 12/05). (still there 5/06).	
☐ 161506	1961	King Air UC-12B	BJ-54	Wfu. At AMARC 5G0018. (wef 9/04). (still there 5/06).	
☐ 161509	1961	King Air UC-12B	BJ-57	Wfu. At AMARC 5G0008.	
☐ 161510		King Air UC-12B	BJ-58	Wfu. At AMARC 5G0028.	
☐ 161516	1961	King Air UC-12B	BJ-64	Wfu. At AMARC 5G0012. (wef 5/04). (still there 5/06).	
☐ 163564		King Air UC-12F	BU-12	Wfu. At AMARC 5G0023. (wef 11/05). (still there 5/06).	
☐ 163847		King Air UC-12M	BV-12	Wfu. At AMARC 5G0017. (wef 9/04). (still there 5/06).	
☐ 66-7943	1968	King Air C-6A	LJ-320	Wfu. Displayed at Wright-Patterson AFB.Oh.	N2085W
☐ 73-1210	1973	King Air C-12E	BD-6	Wfu. At AMARC CE0005. (wef 9/01). (still there 5/06).	
☐ 73-1211	1973	King Air C-12A	BD-7	W/o Nr Nadiz, Iran. 31 Jan 79.	
☐ 73-22250	1973	King Air C-12C	BC-1	Wfu. Located Fort Rucker, USA.	
☐ 73-22265	1973	King Air C-12C	BC-13	Wfu. Located Dothan, Al. USA.	
☐ 76-0165	1976	King Air C-12C	BD-22	W/o 14 Aug 02.	
☐ 76-0170	1976	King Air C-12C	BD-27	Wfu. At AMARC.	
☐ 76-0173	1976	King Air C-12C	BD-30	Wfu. At AMARC CE0007. (wef 9/01). (still there 5/06).	
☐ 84-0169	1984	King Air C-12F	BL-99	W/o Nr Camp Humphreys, South Korea. 12 Aug 03.	
☐ 85-0151	1985	King Air RC-12K	FE-5	W/o Sommerhausen, Germany. 6 Nov 98.	
☐ 85-0154	1985	King Air RC-12K	FE-8	W/o Nuremberg, Germany. 26 Mar 01.	
☐ 85-1261	1985	King Air C-12F	BP-52	W/o Juneau, Al. USA. 12 Nov 92.	
☐ 85-1269	1985	King Air C-12F	BP-60	W/o Brazil. 11 Jan 1992.	
☐ 86-0402	1958	Gulfstream 1	2	Wfu.	N39PP
☐ 89-0272	1989	King Air RC-12N	FE-18	W/o Ossabaw Island, Ca. USA. 16 Apr 97.	

OB = PERU

Civil

Reg	Yr	Type	c/n	Owner/Operator	Prev Regn
☐ OB-1176	1980	PA-31T Cheyenne II	8020010	W/o Tocache, Peru. 28 Feb 90.	OB-S-1176
☐ OB-1212	1974	Rockwell 690A	11222	W/o Uchiza, Peru. 7 May 92.	OB-M-1212
☐ OB-1219	1978	Mitsubishi MU-2N	730SA	W/o Progreso, Peru. 11 Apr 91.	OB-M-1219
☐ OB-1234	1981	PA-42 Cheyenne III	8001019	W/o San Rafael, Peru. 16 Sep 98.	OB-S-1234
☐ OB-1284	1974	Mitsubishi MU-2K	282	W/o Juanjui, Peru. 14 May 92.	N3MP
☐ OB-1305	1967	King Air A90	LJ-302	W/o S E Cuzco, Peru. 11 Oct 91.	OB-T-1305
☐ OB-1361	1969	King Air B90	LJ-451	W/o Uchiza, Peru. 27 Feb 91.	N896K
☐ OB-1362	1969	King Air B90	LJ-448	W/o Tomay Kichua, Peru. 31 Jul 90.	N428DN
☐ OB-1403	1977	PA-31T Cheyenne II	7720022	W/o Chacham Peak, Peru. 16 Jan 96.	N14LW
☐ OB-1420	1974	King Air E90	LW-106	W/o Palmapampa, Peru. 8 Mar 94.	SE-IIU
☐ OB-1700	1977	King Air/Catpass 250	BB-214	W/o Ventanilla, Peru. 18 Apr 05.	N26LE
☐ OB-932	1969	King Air B90	LJ-465	W/o Lima, Peru. 26 Jun 96.	OB-T-932
☐ OB-M-1003	1978	PA-31T Cheyenne II	7820057	W/o Cuzco, Peru. 26 Feb 81.	
☐ OB-M-1031	1972	Rockwell 690	11008	W/o Peru. 14 Feb 79.	(N9208N)

OD = LEBANON

Military

Reg	Yr	Type	c/n	Owner/Operator	Prev Regn
☐ L-701	1974	Rockwell 690A	11157	W/o Beirut, Lebanon. 1980.	N57086

OE = AUSTRIA
Civil

Reg	Yr	Type	c/n	Owner/Operator	Prev Regn
☐ OE-EDU	1992	TBM 700	73	W/o Nr Freiburg, Germany. 1 Apr 93.	
☐ OE-EHG	1991	TBM 700	28	Wfu. Cx OE- 3/96.	
☐ OE-FCS	1984	Gulfstream 900	15036	W/o Lake Constance, Switzerland. 23 Feb 89.	N45GA
☐ OE-FEM	1990	King Air 300LW	FA-210	W/o en route Salzburg-Krems, Austria 12 May 96.	D-IDLS
☐ OE-FGK	1980	PA-31T Cheyenne II	8020052	W/o Friedrichshafen, Germany. 8 Feb 92.	N700GC
☐ OE-FPS	1981	Conquest 1	425-0024	W/o Hannover, Germany. 8 Oct 91	D-IEAT
☐ OE-KDM	2001	PA-46-500TP Meridian	4697111	W/o Nr Ulenurme, Estonia. 24 Nov 06.	G-RKJT

OH = FINLAND
Civil

Reg	Yr	Type	c/n	Owner/Operator	Prev Regn
☐ OH-BKA	1970	King Air 100	B-39	wfu 10/07	HB-GEN
☐ OH-MIB	1971	Mitsubishi MU-2G	532	Wfu. Located Den Helder, Netherlands.	N30SA
☐ OH-MIC	1972	Mitsubishi MU-2J	557	Wfu. Cx OH- 10/01.	(N345SA)
☐ OH-PHA	1975	PA-31T Cheyenne II	7620001	Wfu. Instructional airframe Bardufoss, Norway.	OY-BSB

OK = CZECH REPUBLIC / CZECHIA
Civil

Reg	Yr	Type	c/n	Owner/Operator	Prev Regn
☐ OK-SAR	2002	Ibis Ae 270P Spirit	003	Wfu.	

OO = BELGIUM
Civil

Reg	Yr	Type	c/n	Owner/Operator	Prev Regn
☐ OO-TBW	1970	Mitsubishi MU-2G	526	W/o Angouleme, France. 15 Aug 76.	SE-FGG
☐ OO-TLS	1974	King Air A100	B-188	W/o Bacau, Romania. 8 Jan 94. (parts at Griffin, Ga. USA).	5X-UWS

Military

Reg	Yr	Type	c/n	Owner/Operator	Prev Regn
☐ CF-03	1976	SA-226T Merlin 3A	T-262	W/o Lille, France. 16 Apr 80.	N5375M

OY = DENMARK
Civil

Reg	Yr	Type	c/n	Owner/Operator	Prev Regn
☐ OY-ATW	1976	SA-226T Merlin 3A	T-261	W/o Gronholt, Denmark. 26 Apr 78.	N300TA
☐ OY-AUI	1974	SA-226AT Merlin 4	AT-015	W/o Copenhagen, Denmark. 12 Nov 82.	N223JC
☐ OY-AZA	1973	King Air C90	LJ-593	W/o Copenhagen, Denmark. 15 Jan 79.	N90KA
☐ OY-BEP	1981	King Air B200C	BL-43	W/o Roodt-Syr, Luxembourg. 18 Sep 82.	EI-BKV
☐ OY-BVA	1965	King Air 90	LJ-68	Wfu. PT-6 engine test-bed at Roskilde. Cx OY- 11/03.	D-IKAO
☐ OY-CGM	1981	Conquest II	441-0229	W/o Isortoq, Greenland. 11 Nov 90.	N68548

PH = NETHERLANDS
Civil

Reg	Yr	Type	c/n	Owner/Operator	Prev Regn
☐ PH-DRX	1982	MU-2 Marquise	1555SA	W/o Eindhoven, Holland. 12 Sep 88.	N481MA

Military

Reg	Yr	Type	c/n	Owner/Operator	Prev Regn
☐ U-02	1995	Fokker 60UTA-N	20324	Wfu. RNAF, 334 Squadron, Eindhoven. Willem Versteegh' (strd)	PH-UTN
☐ U-04	1995	Fokker 60UTA-N	20329	Wfu. RNAF, 334 Squadron, Eindhoven. 'Jules Zegers' (stored)	PH-UTR

PK = INDONESIA
Civil

Reg	Yr	Type	c/n	Owner/Operator	Prev Regn
☐ PK-PJH	1976	PA-31T Cheyenne II	7620015	Wfu.	9V-BHF
☐ PK-TRB	1976	King Air 200	BB-116	Wfu.	
☐ PK-TRL	1960	Gulfstream 1	60	Wfu. CoA expiry 10 Jun 98.	C-FIOM
☐ PK-TRM	1960	Gulfstream 1	57	Wfu.	N66JD

PP = BRAZIL
Civil

Reg	Yr	Type	c/n	Owner/Operator	Prev Regn
☐ PP-EFC	1972	King Air E90	LW-15	W/o Goiania, GO, Brazil. 30 May 00.	
☐ PP-FPP	1973	King Air E90	LW-56	Wfu. CofA expiry 13 Feb 94.	PT-FGA
☐ PT-DUX	1971	SA-226T Merlin 3	T-215	W/o Sao Paulo, Brazil. 27 Sep 71.	
☐ PT-IEE	1972	681B Turbo Command	6071	W/o Sao Paulo, SP. Brazil. 16 Dec 00.	
☐ PT-LJR	1981	King Air F90	LA-93	W/o Sao Pedro da Aldeia, Brazil. 2 Oct 88.	N1187K
☐ PT-LQS	1981	King Air C90	LJ-966	W/o Rondovia dos Imigrantes, Brazil. 17 Jul 00.	N181JH
☐ PT-LYI	1971	Mitsubishi MU-2F	213	Wfu. CoA expiry 29 Jan 93.	N100BR
☐ PT-OFG	1976	Rockwell 690A	11274	Wfu. CoA expiry 31 Mar 03.	N4432W
☐ PT-ORY	1981	King Air F90	LA-153	W/o Sao Paulo, Brazil. 3 Feb 93.	N200RA
☐ PT-OZY	1978	PA-31T Cheyenne II	7820030	W/o Nr Agua Comprida, MG. Brazil. 12 Jan 01.	N700TR
☐ PT-WHI	1979	PA-31T Cheyenne II	7920077	W/o Brazil. Oct 98.	LV-MZA

RP = PHILIPPINES

Civil

☐ RP-C202	1968	King Air B90	LJ-356	Wfu. Parts at Dodsons, Rantoul, Ks. USA.	PI-C202
☐ RP-C2340	1965	King Air 90	LJ-57	Wfu. Located Manila, Philippines.	N2340M
☐ RP-C710	1970	King Air 100	B-15	W/o San Jose, Philippines. 28 Nov 96.	PI-C710
☐ RP-C775	1972	681B Turbo Command	6066	Wfu. Located Army Museum Camp Aquino, Tarlac, Luzon.	N2NR
☐ RP-C990	1967	King Air A90	LJ-247	W/o Philipppines. 28 Jul 99.	

SE = SWEDEN

Civil

☐ SE-FGE	1970	681 Turbo Commander	6033	W/o Mestersvig, Greenland. 23 Jul 73.	N9086N
☐ SE-FGO	1968	Mitsubishi MU-2D	102	Wfu.	HB-LED
☐ SE-GHG	1970	Mitsubishi MU-2F	191	Wfu. Cx USA 5/01.	(HA-...)
☐ SE-GLB	1984	PA-31T Cheyenne II	7400002	Wfu.	OH-PNS
☐ SE-GUU	1969	King Air B90	LJ-470	W/o Sindal, Denmark. 15 Oct 85.	N490K
☐ SE-IHX	1983	Conquest II	441-0291	W/o 24 Mar 84.	N88707
☐ SE-IOU	1974	Mitsubishi MU-2K	304	W/o Sweden. 16 Feb 86.	N410MA
☐ SE-IOX	1976	Mitsubishi MU-2M	331	W/o Sweden. 15 Mar 86.	N3982L
☐ SE-KBX	1973	Mitsubishi MU-2K	247	Wfu.	N5TQ

Military

☐ 101001	1981	King Air 200C	BL-25	W/o Halmstad, Sweden. 24 Sep 90.	OY-CHE

SU = EGYPT

Civil

☐ SU-UAA	1995	King Air C90B	LJ-1418	W/o Inshas, Egypt. 10 Jun 00.	N3218X

SX = GREECE

Military

☐ P-9	1963	Gulfstream 1	120	Wfu. Preserved as '120' at Tatoi AFB. Greece.	

S9 = SAO TOME & PRINCIPE

Civil

☐ S9-NAA	1965	King Air 90	LJ-50	W/o 1988. Parts at White Industries, Bates City, Mo.	N75XA

TC = TURKEY

Civil

☐ TC-DBZ	1977	King Air C90	LJ-703	W/o 24/1/2000	TC-DBZ
☐ TC-DHA	1990	King Air 350	FL-37	W/o Istanbul, Turkey. 5 Dec 98.	N81604
☐ TC-LMK	1984	King Air C90A	LJ-1080	W/o Nr Bursa, Turkey. 21 Mar 00. (parts at Rantoul, Ks.).	N6931W
☐ TC-SMA	1966	Gulfstream 1	172	Wfu. Located Geneva, Switzerland.	N712RD

TN = CONGO BRAZZAVILLE

Civil

☐ TN-ADP	1974	SA-226AT Merlin 4A	AT-025	W/o Pointe Noire, Congo Republic. 11 Mar 94.	N52LB

TR = GABON

Civil

☐ TR-LYA	1977	King Air E90	LW-247	W/o Liberville, Gabon. Apr 78.	F-GAPO

TU = IVORY COAST

Civil

☐ TU-TJE	1976	King Air 200	BB-163	W/o Bouafle, Ivory Coast. 28 Jun 96.	

Military

☐ TU-VBB	1977	King Air 200	BB-295	W/o Touba, Ivory Coast. 21 Jun 90.	F-GAPV

VH = AUSTRALIA

Civil

☐ VH-AAV	1977	King Air 200	BB-245	W/o Sydney, Australia. 20 Feb 80.	A2-ABO
☐ VH-AAZ	1977	King Air 200	BB-241	W/o Bundaberg, QLD, Australia. 1991. Cx VH- 5/95.	N23915
☐ VH-AUP	1985	King Air B200C	BL-126	W/o Coffs Harbour, NSW. Australia. 15 May 03. (as VH-AMR).	VH-AMR
☐ VH-BBA	1980	MU-2 Marquise	782SA	W/o Leonora, WA. Australia. 16 Dec 88.	N269MA
☐ VH-BSS	1972	Rockwell 690	11044	W/o Botany Bay, NSW. Australia. 14 Jan 94.	N471SC
☐ VH-CCW	1977	PA-31T Cheyenne II	7720046	W/o Perth, Western Australia. 3 May 81.	N82175
☐ VH-CJP	1970	Mitsubishi MU-2G	505	W/o Cairns, QLD. Australia. 14 Nov 83.	HB-LEF
☐ VH-DRV	1978	PA-31T Cheyenne II	7820079	Wfu. Cx VH- 12/03.	N6109A
☐ VH-FLO	1963	Gulfstream 1	100	Wfu. Located Auckland, NZ.	N116K
☐ VH-FMN	1982	King Air 200C	BL-47	W/o Nr Mount Gambier, SA. Australia. 10 Dec 01.	N6334F

Reg   Yr   Type   c/n   Owner/Operator   Prev Regn

Reg	Yr	Type	c/n	Owner/Operator	Prev Regn
☐ VH-IAM	1970	Mitsubishi MU-2G	517	W/o Melbourne, Australia 21 Dec 94. (to N119BF for parts).	(N119BF)
☐ VH-IBC	1975	King Air 200	BB-74	W/o 1988.	N9730S
☐ VH-JWO	1970	681 Turbo Commander	6039	Wfu. Cx VH- 5/99. Located Essendon, VIC. Australia.	N420MA
☐ VH-KTE	1978	King Air 200	BB-320	W/o Adavale, Australia. 28 Aug 83.	N23786
☐ VH-LFH	1978	King Air E90	LW-255	W/o Nr Kingaroy, QLD. Australia. 25 Jul 90.	N258D
☐ VH-LQH	1975	King Air C90	LJ-644	W/o Toowoomba, QLD. Australia. 27 Nov 01.	N66CN
☐ VH-MLU	1981	MU-2 Marquise	1527SA	W/o Bargo, Australia. 24 May 83.	N445MA
☐ VH-MUA	1979	MU-2 Marquise	746SA	W/o Nr Meekatharra, WA. Australia. 26 Jan 90.	N943MA
☐ VH-NYB	1972	Rockwell 690	11039	Wfu. Cx VH- 4/94. Located Darwin, NT. Australia.	C-GICX
☐ VH-NYD	1970	681 Turbo Commander	6034	Wfu. Cx VH- 3/92. Located Darwin, NT. Australia.	N9087N
☐ VH-NYF	1970	681 Turbo Commander	6026	Wfu. Last located Moorabbin, VIC. Cx VH- 8/97.	N9024N
☐ VH-NYG	1970	681 Turbo Commander	6004	W/o Tamworth, Australia. 14 Feb 91.	N740ES
☐ VH-NYH	1970	681 Turbo Commander	6016	Wfu. Cx VH- 4/94. Located Darwin, NT. Australia.	N444JB
☐ VH-NYM	1967	Mitsubishi MU-2B	037	Wfu. Cx VH- 9/93.	VH-JWO
☐ VH-SKC	1975	King Air 200	BB-47	W/o Burketown, Queensland, Australia. 4 Sep 00.	RP-C200
☐ VH-SVQ	1977	Rockwell 690B	11380	W/o Tasman Sea, Australia. 2 Oct 94.	VH-FOZ
☐ VH-SWP	1975	SA-226AT Merlin 4A	AT-033	W/o Tamworth, NSW. Australia. 9 Mar 94.	(N.....)
☐ VH-TNP	1979	PA-31T Cheyenne II	7920026	W/o Benalla, VIC. Australia. 28 Jul 04.	VH-LJK
☐ VH-TNZ	1979	PA-31T Cheyenne II	7920064	W/o hangar explosion Moorabbin, Australia. 29 Sep 88	N23477
☐ VH-UZC	1970	Mitsubishi MU-2G	519	Wfu. Cx VH- 3/92.	ZK-EKZ
☐ VH-WMU	1970	Mitsubishi MU-2G	512	W/o Bathurst, Australia. 7 Nov 90. Cx USA as N318MA 6/95.	N318MA

VP-B = BERMUDA
Civil

Reg	Yr	Type	c/n	Owner/Operator	Prev Regn
☐ VP-BBK	1996	King Air B200	BB-1519	W/o Blackbushe, UK. 23 Dec 00.	VR-BBK

VQ-T = TURKS & CAICOS ISLANDS
Civil

Reg	Yr	Type	c/n	Owner/Operator	Prev Regn
☐ VQ-TIU	1989	King Air B200C	BL-131	W/o Major Hill, North Caicos 6/2/07	VH-BQR

VT = INDIA
Civil

Reg	Yr	Type	c/n	Owner/Operator	Prev Regn
☐ VT-EFF	1977	King Air C90	LJ-705	W/o Mainpuri, India. 30 Sep 01.	N2075L
☐ VT-EHK	1982	King Air B200	BB-985	W/o Nr Delhi Airport, India. 27 Aug 92.	N1841Z
☐ VT-EIE	1983	King Air B200C	BL-63	W/o Nr Buntar, India. 29 Jul 00.	N6921D
☐ VT-ELZ	1985	King Air F90-1	LA-233	W/o Bhilai, Madhra Pradesh, India. 3 Feb 98.	N72224
☐ VT-EOA	1987	King Air B200C	BL-129	W/o Delhi, India. 27 Aug 92.	N72401
☐ VT-EQM	1987	King Air 300	FA-128	W/o Nr Panvel, Bombay, India. 15 Jul 93.	N3029F
☐ VT-EUJ	1993	King Air B200	BB-1456	W/o Runda, Kulu Valley, India. 9 Jul 94.	N8090U
☐ VT-NEF	1980	King Air C90	LJ-890	W/o Dongar Pur Forest, India. 3 Feb 98. (at Rantoul, Ks.).	ZS-LOL

XA = MEXICO
Civil

Reg	Yr	Type	c/n	Owner/Operator	Prev Regn
☐ XA-DIS	1973	Mitsubishi MU-2J	608	W/o El Paso, Tx. USA. 20 Nov 83.	N340MA
☐ XA-EFN		Mitsubishi MU-2	...	Wfu. noted Toluca, Mexico 3/06.	
☐ XA-FOT	1966	King Air A90	LJ-168	W/o 15 Feb 78.	XB-BOF
☐ XA-IIW	1973	Rockwell 690	11050	Wfu.	XC-FUV
☐ XA-JUY	1973	Rockwell 690A	11170	Wfu.	XC-CAU
☐ XA-KUU	1972	Rockwell 690	11042	Wfu. Seen WFU 6/07 Fuselage only!	XA-KUU
☐ XA-LIG	1981	King Air 200	BB-802	W/o Poza Rica, Mexico. 5 May 84.	
☐ XA-MYR	1961	Gulfstream 1	71	Wfu. Last located Toluca, Mexico.	F-GFIB
☐ XA-TDJ	1964	Gulfstream 1	127	Wfu. Last located Merida, Mexico.	N717JP
☐ XB-AEA	1974	Rockwell 690A	11199	W/o Oklahoma City, Ok. USA. 1 Jan 80.	
☐ XB-AQQ	1974	Mitsubishi MU-2J	632	Wfu. Cx USA 6/97.	N995MA
☐ XB-CIJ	1959	Gulfstream 1	10	Wfu.	N1623Z
☐ XB-ESO	1959	Gulfstream 1	15	Wfu.	N26KW
☐ XB-LIJ	1973	Mitsubishi MU-2K	259	W/o Beloit, Ks. USA. 1975.	N279MA
☐ XB-NUV	1972	King Air A100	B-128	W/o San Luis Potosi, Mexico. 13 Oct 76.	N196B
☐ XB-QIY	1974	King Air E90	LW-113	W/o Monterrey, Mexico. 2 Mar 81.	XA-FEX
☐ XC-AA38	1980	Gulfstream 980	95020	W/o Nr Monterrey, Mexico. 19 Oct 92.	XC-HFX
☐ XC-AA48	1978	King Air 200	BB-369	Wfu. Parts at Dodson's, Rantoul, Ks. USA.	HK-3555
☐ XC-AA53	1967	Gulfstream 1	179	Wfu Acapulco	HK-3622
☐ XC-AA57	1963	Gulfstream 1	103	Wfu. Located Mexico City, Mexico.	PT-...
☐ XC-FEL	1968	Mitsubishi MU-2D	103	Wfu. Parts at White Industries, Bates City, Mo. (as N850Q).	XB-TIM
☐ XC-GEI	1961	Gulfstream 1	66	Wfu.	N111DR
☐ XC-ICP	1966	King Air A90	LJ-176	W/o Vera Cruz, Mexico. 28 Jan 73.	N5656A
☐ XC-PGR	1978	King Air 200	BB-317	W/o Otay Mesa, Mexico. 28 Oct 79.	

Military
☐ MT-217 1982 Gulfstream 1000 96026 Wfu. Located Vera Cruz, Mexico. HK-3157W

YV = VENEZUELA
Civil

Reg	Yr	Type	c/n	Owner/Operator	Prev Regn
☐ YV-....	1973	Rockwell 690A	11135	W/o Shot down whilst Drug running 2005	N744JD
☐ YV-1020	1963	Gulfstream 1	106	W/o. destroyed by Fuerza Aerea Colombiana. 26 Sep 05.	9XR-WR
☐ YV1081	1979	PA-31T Cheyenne II	7920018	W/o Estado Bolivar, Venezuela. 18 Nov 05.	N100KR
☐ YV-121CP	1965	Gulfstream 1	150	Wfu.	N777G
☐ YV-1700P	1967	King Air A90	LJ-205	W/o Adicora, venezuela. 13 Jun 98.	N707PR
☐ YV-174CP	1977	Mitsubishi MU-2L	695	W/o Caracas, Venezuela. 4 Jun 81.	N855MA
☐ YV-215CP	1978	PA-31T Cheyenne II	7820071	W/o Caracas, Venezuela. 4 Jun 81.	
☐ YV-2200P	1974	PA-31T Cheyenne II	7400006	W/o Newtown, Bahamas. 20 Jun 90.	YV-146CP
☐ YV-2466P	1973	King Air C90	LJ-591	W/o Nr Fort Lauderdale, Fl. USA. 16 Jun 01.	N108TT
☐ YV-246CP	1975	Rockwell 690A	11278	W/o Finca La Carolina, Colombia 13/1/07	N57176
☐ YV-2697P	1971	681 Turbo Commander	6044	W/o Nr Trujillo, Honduras. 6 Mar 06.	N529JC
☐ YV-2816P	1968	King Air B90	LJ-378	W/o La Carlota, Caracas, Venezuela. 15 Nov 04.	N320E
☐ YV-288CP	1979	King Air F90	LA-8	W/o Caracas, Venezuela. 8 May 84.	
☐ YV-299P	1965	King Air 90	LJ-72	W/o Higuerote, Miranda, Venezuela 31 Jan 79.	N901N
☐ YV-310CP	1980	Gulfstream 840	11645	W/o Nr Caracas, Venezuela. 27 Apr 96.	(N5897K)
☐ YV-385CP	1980	King Air 200	BB-740	W/o Nr Bimini, Bahamas. 20 Sep 99.	
☐ YV-426P	1976	King Air 200	BB-142	W/o Caracas, Venezuela. 4 Feb 82.	
☐ YV-597CP	1978	King Air 200	BB-394	W/o 12 Jan 89.	N223TC
☐ YV-652CP	1984	SA-227TT Merlin 3C	TT-515	Wfu. Last located Charallave, Venezuela.	N352SM
☐ YV-714CP	1967	680V Turbo Command	1689-69	W/o Cuchilla de la Marimona, Colombia. 3 Feb 06.	YV-843P
☐ YV-726CP	1976	King Air E90	LW-182	W/o Caracas, Venezuela. 27 Mar 94. (at Rantoul, Ks.).	YV-O-BIV-2
☐ YV-783CP	2000	King Air 350	FL-313	W/o Alto de Irapa, Edo Miranda, Venezuela. 24 May 05.	YV-2663P
☐ YV-94CP	1976	Mitsubishi MU-2M	347	W/o 1982.	YV-1050P
☐ YV-994P	1976	King Air C90	LJ-693	W/o Caracas, Venezuela. 4 Feb 82.	
☐ YV-O-106	1981	King Air 200	BB-770	W/o.Dbr accident en-route Miranda-Barinas 4/01	YV-O-SATA-6
☐ YV-O-MAR-	1967	680V Turbo Command	1683-64	W/o Venezuela 17 Aug 78.	YV-O-MOP-8
☐ YV-O-NCE-2	1976	King Air E90	LW-201	W/o Caracas, Venezuela. 13 Nov 95.	
☐ YV-T-ADJ	1973	King Air E90	LW-53	W/o Pratt, Ks. USA. 10 May 73.	

Military
☐ FAV.... 1974 King Air E90 LW-81 Wfu. Located Griffin, Ga. USA. YV-416P

ZS = SOUTH AFRICA
Civil

Reg	Yr	Type	c/n	Owner/Operator	Prev Regn
☐ ZS-IHZ	1970	King Air B90	LJ-497	W/o Capetown, South Africa. 26 Dec 92.	N9019Q
☐ ZS-INN	1971	King Air C90	LJ-523	Wfu. Cx ZS- 8/06.	V5-INN
☐ ZS-JRF	1978	Rockwell 690B	11491	W/o. Cx ZS- 16 Aug 93.	(N690RC)
☐ ZS-KMT	1980	King Air 200	BB-767	W/o Johannesburg, South Africa. 13 Apr 87.	N3717T
☐ ZS-KRS	1980	Gulfstream 840	11644	W/o South Africa. 16 Sep 81.	N5896K
☐ ZS-KVB	1980	Gulfstream 980	95005	W/o Nr Sishen, South Africa 20 Jun 84.	N9758S
☐ ZS-LNV	1983	King Air B200C	BL-71	W/o Steynsburg, South Africa. 10 May 97.	(N771D)
☐ ZS-LUC	1978	PA-31T Cheyenne II	7820092	W/o Welkom, South Africa. 26 Apr 89.	N777DL
☐ ZS-MGR	1975	King Air 200	BB-19	W/o Marunga, Angola. 21 Oct 95.	N221B
☐ ZS-MSG	1979	King Air B100	BE-75	W/o Vrede, South Africa. 23 Dec 94. Cx ZS- 6/95.	N814GT
☐ ZS-MSL	1981	King Air 200	BB-815	W/o Lome-Abidjan, Ivory Coast. 26 Jun 98.	N255AV
☐ ZS-NDH	1974	King Air C90	LJ-619	Wfu. Parts at Dodsons, Rantoul, Ks. USA.	5Y-MAL
☐ ZS-NEP	1981	King Air 200	BB-838	W/o Aminius nr Koudpan, Namibia. 28 Jun 93.	N14MF
☐ ZS-NRW	1977	King Air 200	BB-201	W/o Moz, South Africa. 28 Jun 04.	5Y-BKS
☐ ZS-NXY	1983	King Air C90-1	LJ-1058	W/o Sulkerbossstrand, South Africa. 13 Dec 96.	N6586K
☐ ZS-OFC	1998	Pilatus PC-12/45	206	W/o Nairobi, Kenya. 13 Feb 98.	HB-F..
☐ ZS-OIG	1989	Reims/Cessna F406	F406-0041	W/o Johannesburg, South Africa 3 Nov 01.	N563GA

Military
☐ SAAF16 1975 SA-226AT Merlin 4A AT-040 W/o Pretoria, South Africa. 14 July 82. (SAAF14)

Z3 = MACEDONIA
Civil

☐ Z3-BAB 1980 King Air 200 BB-652 W/o S of Sarajevo 26 Feb 04. (N88DA)

3C = EQUATORIAL GUINEA
Civil

☐ 3C-JJP Cheyenne T-1040 8275025 W/o N'Djamena, Chad. 14 Feb 01. 3C-JJP

5H = TANZANIA
Civil

☐ 5H-SCB	1983	Conquest 1	425-0183	W/o Nr Dar Es Salaam, Tanzania. 12 Jun 00.	VH-EGS
☐ 5H-TZC	1988	Reims/Cessna F406	F406-0028	W/o Muyowasi Tanzania. 13 Aug 02.	N7073C
☐ 5H-TZD	1988	Reims/Cessna F406	F406-0029	W/o Mount Palapala Morogoro, Tanzania. 24 Apr 96.	PH-FWI

5N = NIGERIA
Civil

☐ 5N-ATU	1966	King Air A90	LJ-136	Wfu. Located at Gamston, UK.	F-BFRE
☐ 5N-AUT	1975	PA-31T Cheyenne II	7520016	Wfu. Last located Groton, Ct. USA.	N101T

5R = MADAGASCAR
Civil

☐ 5R-MGV	1981	Conquest 1	425-0032	W/o Tulear, Malagasy Republic 25 Oct 06.	N44GB

5Y = KENYA
Civil

☐ 5Y-BIW	1981	King Air 200	BB-782	Wfu. Parts at Nairobi-Wilson, Kenya.	G-THUR
☐ 5Y-BLF	1964	Gulfstream 1	131	Wfu. Located Nairobi-Wilson, Kenya.	C-FRTT
☐ 5Y-EMJ	1965	Gulfstream 1	158	W/o Busia, Kenya. 24 Jan 03.	5Y-MIA
☐ 5Y-ING	1988	Reims/Cessna F406	F406-0024	W/o 12 Jun 95 Nairobi, Kenya.	PH-PEL
☐ 5Y-JET	1960	Gulfstream 1	44	Wfu. Located Nairobi-Wilson, Kenya.	F-GFGV
☐ 5Y-JJG	1985	Reims/Cessna F406	F406-0003	W/o Nairobi, Kenya. 8 Aug 94.	PH-ALK
☐ 5Y-JKB	1975	King Air 200	BB-72	W/o Crashed on game reserve	ZS-KJB
☐ 5Y-NAL	1989	Reims/Cessna F406	F406-0038	W/o Mar 94.	PH-ALX
☐ 5Y-NBB	1971	King Air C90	LJ-528	Wfu. Located Nairobi-Wilson, Kenya.	N883AV
☐ 5Y-TAL	1986	Reims/Cessna F406	F406-0009	Wfu. Last located Skive, Denmark.	PH-FWB
☐ 5Y-TNT	1971	SA-226T Merlin 3	T-211	W/o Nairobi-Wilson, Kenya. 1 Oct 92.	TN-ADO

6O = SOMALIA
Civil

☐ 6O-SBQ	1974	Rockwell 690A	11151	Wfu. Located Mombasa, Kenya.	3D-BYZ

7Q = MALAWI
Civil

☐ 7Q-YMM	1980	King Air C90	LJ-880	W/o Blantyre-Chileka, Malawi. 9 Nov 90. (at Rantoul, Ks.).	ZS-KLC

7T = ALGERIA
Civil

☐ 7T-VSH	1968	King Air B90	LJ-423	W/o Jan 76.	HB-GDT

9J = ZAMBIA
Civil

☐ 9J-GCF	1973	King Air C90	LJ-590	W/o Serenje, Zambia. 16 Aug 90.	N243L

9M = MALAYSIA
Civil

☐ 9M-CAM	1983	King Air B200T	BT-24	W/o Ipoh, Malaysia. 13 Dec 93.	9M-JPA

9Q = CONGO KINSHASA
Civil

☐ 9Q-...	1975	King Air C90	LJ-660	Wfu.	ZS-LXL
☐ 9Q-CAA	1974	Mitsubishi MU-2J	618	Wfu. Cx USA 7/94. Parts at Dodson's, Rantoul, Ks. USA.	9Q-CAA
☐ 9Q-CBD	1960	Gulfstream 1	35	Wfu. Cx 9Q- ?	N86MA
☐ 9Q-CBY	1960	Gulfstream 1	33	Wfu. Cx 9Q- ?	N23AH
☐ 9Q-CJB	1966	Gulfstream 1	155	Wfu & Cx 9Q- 1/96.	G-BMOW
☐ 9Q-CKZ	1970	King Air B90	LJ-494	Wfu. Last located Lumbumbashi, DRC. Cx 9Q- 10/96,	(N15LM)
☐ 9Q-COI	1979	SA-226T Merlin 3B	T-302	W/o Zaire. 6 Oct 83.	G-IIIB

Military

☐ 9T-MBD	1974	Mitsubishi MU-2J	620	W/o.	N470MA

Reg Yr Type c/n Owner/Operator Prev Regn

Business TurboProps
Cross-Reference by Construction Number

Aero Commander
Commander 680

C/N	Reg
1473-1	wfu
1532-2	w/o
1534-3	wfu
1536-4	w/o
1538-5	YV1035
1540-6	wfu
1542-7	wfu
1544-8	C-GSVQ
1546-9	C-FAXN
1721-1	N39AS
1722-2	N93RA
1723-3	N4622E
1751-4	wfu
1752-5	N505RT
1760-6	wfu
1761-7	wfu
1762-8	YV-....
1763-9	N200DT
1519-95	N175DB
1548-10	N7610U
1550-11	wfu
1552-12	wfu
1554-13	w/o
1556-14	N543S
1557-15	wfu
1558-16	N818L
1560-17	N687L
1562-18	wfu
1563-19	FAC-542
1564-20	EC-DSA
1565-21	w/o
1566-22	N292Z
1567-23	wfu
1568-24	N666MN
1570-25	N370K
1571-26	wfu
1572-27	N900RJ
1573-28	wfu
1575-29	w/o
1576-30	w/o
1577-31	w/o
1579-32	N808GU
1580-33	w/o
1581-34	wfu
1583-35	wfu
1584-36	N512JD
1585-37	wfu
1587-38	wfu
1588-39	w/o
1589-40	N698GN
1593-41	wfu
1597-42	wfu
1601-43	C-GFAB
1605-44	w/o
1609-45	w/o
1610-46	wfu
1612-47	wfu
1614-48	wfu
1616-49	N171AT
1618-50	w/o
1620-51	N11HM
1622-52	wfu
1624-53	wfu
1626-54	wfu
1628-55	w/o
1630-56	wfu
1632-57	HK-2285D
1675-58	w/o
1676-59	N66FV
1677-60	N677KA
1679-61	wfu
1680-62	wfu
1682-63	LV-OFX
1683-64	w/o
1684-65	D-IABC
1685-66	wfu
1687-67	wfu
1688-68	wfu
1689-69	w/o
1691-70	N47HM
1692-71	wfu
1693-72	w/o
1694-73	wfu
1697-74	wfu
1698-75	N20BM
1699-76	N29DE
1701-77	wfu
1702-78	w/o
1703-79	PT-...
1704-80	wfu
1705-81	N87BT
1707-82	wfu
1708-83	N200TB
1709-84	wfu
1710-85	N111SK
1711-86	wfu
1713-87	wfu
1714-88	N50655
1718-89	YV-344P
1719-90	YV-1405P
1720-91	wfu
1772-10	N514NA
1773-11	N11CT
1774-12	N54163
1775-13	YV-820CP
1776-14	wfu
1777-15	w/o
1778-16	w/o
1787-17	w/o
1788-18	XB-DTD
1789-19	N1928H
1790-20	N410TH
1791-21	N345TT
1792-22	N680JD
1793-23	N22ET
1802-24	N17JG
1803-25	N4100B
1804-26	YV-2280P
1805-27	w/o
1811-28	wfu
1812-29	wfu
1813-30	YV-536P
1814-31	YV-2436P
1818-32	N5RE
1819-33	w/o
1820-34	HP-1433
1821-35	N424PP
1828-36	wfu
1829-37	wfu
1833-38	N8061Q
1834-39	XB-...
1835-40	CP-1934
1842-41	wfu
1843-42	N940U
1844-43	w/o
1848-44	EP-FSS
1849-45	EP-FIA
1850-46	EP-FIB

Commander 681

C/N	Reg
6001	N22RT
6002	N6E
6003	N6VH
6004	w/o
6005	YV-2383P
6006	N113CT
6007	N68VH
6008	wfu
6009	wfu
6010	N3867N
6011	w/o
6012	EP-AGU
6013	N70RF
6014	HK-....
6015	w/o
6016	wfu
6018	N29PR
6019	N3203P
6020	w/o
6021	PT-OQQ
6022	TG-WIZ
6023	XB-DJN
6024	YV-2501P
6025	CP-2042
6026	wfu
6027	N681SP
6028	N100GL
6029	YV-2404P
6030	9Q-CGL
6032	TG-AMI
6033	w/o
6034	wfu
6035	HK-1977
6036	TG-...
6037	wfu
6038	N78CH
6039	wfu
6040	XB-AUR
6041	N25BE
6042	w/o
6043	HK-2376P
6044	w/o
6045	9Q-CBU
6046	wfu
6047	VH-NBT
6048	N676DM
6049	N681HV
6050	w/o
6051	N19MU
6052	YV-2475P
6053	w/o
6054	C-FCMJ
6055	N18KK
6056	w/o
6057	wfu
6058	wfu
6059	N30BG
6060	wfu
6061	YV1066
6062	5-280
6063	XA-SHP
6064	wfu
6065	wfu
6066	wfu
6067	wfu
6068	5-281
6069	PT-IEC
6070	PT-IED
6071	w/o
6072	5-282

British Aerospace
HS 748

C/N	Reg
1669	C-FAMO
1684	FAE-001
1688	AF602

Jetstream 31

C/N	Reg
605	N903EH
613	N904FH
618	N618JX
634	wfu
637	G-BRGN
643	N643JX
715	G-IJYS
739	C-GNGI
777	N443PE

Jetstream 41

C/N	Reg
41030	N680AS
41038	N514GP
41060	41060
41080	RP-C8299
41094	41094
41095	ZS-NYK
41102	B-HRS
41104	B-HRT

CASA
Casa 212

C/N	Reg
286	N434CA
294	N502FS
369	EB-50

Cessna
425 Conquest I

C/N	Reg
425-693	wfu
425-0001	w/o
425-0002	N443H
425-0003	G-KRMA
425-0004	N425AT
425-0005	N345TP
425-0006	N757H
425-0007	N67BA
425-0008	C-FKTL
425-0009	w/o
425-0010	N425PL
425-0011	A2-AHT
425-0012	N127BB
425-0013	w/o
425-0014	N425TC
425-0015	N522WD
425-0016	HB-LOE
425-0017	N794B
425-0018	N784PF
425-0019	w/o
425-0020	N55AC
425-0021	V5-LYZ
425-0022	N6772P
425-0023	N707CB
425-0024	w/o
425-0025	N83CH
425-0026	N540GC
425-0027	N425GC
425-0028	ZS-PES
425-0029	N425GJ
425-0030	N67726
425-0031	w/o
425-0032	w/o
425-0033	N425GM
425-0034	w/o
425-0035	OE-FBH
425-0036	N700WJ
425-0037	N425SF
425-0038	w/o
425-0039	N425TX
425-0040	w/o
425-0041	N425AF
425-0042	N1BM
425-0043	N425JB
425-0044	M-MANX
425-0045	w/o
425-0046	N425BA
425-0047	N585PA
425-0048	N6774Z
425-0049	N628MR
425-0050	N37PS
425-0051	XB-FMS
425-0052	N922KV
425-0053	N4420F
425-0054	N425LC
425-0055	w/o
425-0056	N502NC
425-0057	w/o
425-0058	N67JE
425-0059	F-GEFZ
425-0060	N1222B
425-0061	N425SW
425-0062	N6844D
425-0063	N425EA
425-0064	N425XP
425-0065	N425AR
425-0066	N425DH
425-0067	ZS-PYD
425-0068	N425TB
425-0069	N12NL
425-0070	N425NW
425-0071	ZS-CPX
425-0072	N425ET
425-0073	N425HB
425-0074	N10RM
425-0075	ZS-ONZ
425-0076	N14BM
425-0077	V5-MJW
425-0078	w/o
425-0079	N900MS
425-0080	C-GJHF
425-0081	N6846S
425-0082	N470RJ
425-0083	N425DD
425-0084	N547GC
425-0085	N71HE
425-0086	N823DB
425-0087	N616MG
425-0088	N35TY
425-0089	N73DW
425-0090	N90YA
425-0091	XB-FXK
425-0092	N425LA
425-0093	N926FS
425-0094	N105FC
425-0095	N8FR
425-0096	N425E
425-0097	N410VE
425-0098	N425DM
425-0099	N425EZ
425-0100	N425AL
425-0101	N543GC
425-0102	D-ICMF
425-0103	N4276Z
425-0104	N425PV
425-0105	N18481
425-0106	N425SX
425-0107	N425LG
425-0108	N70GM
425-0109	N818PL
425-0110	N114HL
425-0111	N77YP
425-0112	N6851G
425-0113	N425HD
425-0114	N847YT
425-0115	ZS-KSU
425-0116	N420MA
425-0117	N10FB
425-0118	HP-1544
425-0119	N7WF
425-0120	D-IPOS
425-0121	N425D
425-0122	N828SG
425-0123	N825B
425-0124	N425JH
425-0125	N125PG
425-0126	w/o
425-0127	N456FC
425-0128	N425JG
425-0129	N425JT
425-0130	N425WD
425-0131	N250GM
425-0132	N24TW
425-0133	N425SR
425-0134	N156GA
425-0135	N5CE
425-0136	N125SC
425-0137	w/o
425-0138	N39A
425-0139	N881JP
425-0140	N15ST
425-0141	N373LP

Serial	Reg	Serial	Reg	Serial	Reg	Serial	Reg	Serial	Reg
425-0142	N101CA	425-0225	N225DF	441-0070	N318AK	441-0153	XA-...	441-0236	VH-LBC
425-0143	N6885P	425-0226	N111KU	441-0071	w/o	441-0154	w/o	441-0237	XA-TLW
425-0144	N6885S	425-0227	N12268	441-0072	YV-....	441-0155	N779CC	441-0238	VH-VEH
425-0145	N440HC	425-0228	w/o	441-0073	D-IAAC	441-0156	N441JC	441-0239	HK-3615
425-0146	N146GW	425-0229	N1227J	441-0074	N441RK	441-0157	VH-YFD	441-0240	N441PW
425-0147	N425RF	425-0230	N98EP	441-0075	LV-MMY	441-0158	N3TK	441-0241	w/o
425-0148	w/o	425-0231	N127MC	441-0076	C-GPSQ	441-0159	N102NA	441-0242	N88598
425-0149	N441CR	425-0232	N75HW	441-0077	LV-MRU	441-0160	N47JR	441-0243	N916SJ
425-0150	w/o	425-0233	D-ICHS	441-0078	N784RR	441-0161	N383SS	441-0244	w/o
425-0151	w/o	425-0234	N1262K	441-0079	C-FWRL	441-0162	ZS-PMC	441-0245	N441PG
425-0152	w/o	425-0235	JA8855	441-0080	N441LB	441-0163	N441R	441-0246	N913DG
425-0153	N153JM	425-0236	N425SL	441-0081	VH-LEM	441-0164	N164GP	441-0247	N5HG
425-0154	N6886V	441 Conquest II		441-0082	LV-MRT	441-0165	EI-DMG	441-0248	N441SX
425-0155	N168MA	441-679	wfu	441-0083	N441EE	441-0166	N624CB	441-0249	VH-VEJ
425-0156	N17CP	441-0001	YV	441-0084	N84LJ	441-0167	N332DM	441-0250	YV-....
425-0157	N425PJ	441-0002	wfu	441-0085	N441HT	441-0168	N2722D	441-0251	HK-3573
425-0158	N355ES	441-0003	N8838T	441-0086	N441BD	441-0169	w/o	441-0252	w/o
425-0159	N425CC	441-0004	N716SM	441-0087	N687AE	441-0170	N783RS	441-0253	w/o
425-0160	N505AK	441-0005	VH-TAZ	441-0088	VH-OPM	441-0171	N14NW	441-0254	N441X
425-0161	N425TW	441-0006	w/o	441-0089	N441DZ	441-0172	N441SA	441-0255	N9683N
425-0162	YV1957	441-0007	N441HH	441-0090	N13NW	441-0173	N2722Y	441-0256	N256DD
425-0163	w/o	441-0008	N441CC	441-0091	VH-LBX	441-0174	VH-VEM	441-0257	N505HC
425-0164	N425EM	441-0009	N87WS	441-0092	N8970N	441-0175	N988AE	441-0258	N258VB
425-0165	N49GM	441-0010	N903WD	441-0093	N410MF	441-0176	N441DK	441-0259	YV....
425-0166	w/o	441-0011	N93HC	441-0094	N441A	441-0177	w/o	441-0260	VH-TFB
425-0167	C-GRHD	441-0012	N441SC	441-0095	V5-	441-0178	wfu	441-0261	HK-3512
425-0168	PH-JOE	441-0013	N442JA	441-0096	C-FJVR	441-0179	N441EC	441-0262	N50MF
425-0169	N425HJ	441-0014	N441ST	441-0097	YV-...	441-0180	N2723X	441-0263	N233RC
425-0170	N100CC	441-0015	N24PT	441-0098	N441WP	441-0181	w/o	441-0264	VH-VEW
425-0171	ZK-LHL	441-0016	HK-2390W	441-0099	w/o	441-0182	VH-VEZ	441-0265	C-FHSP
425-0172	w/o	441-0017	VH-HMZ	441-0100	YV228T	441-0183	N23EA	441-0266	N441ME
425-0173	N425CQ	441-0018	w/o	441-0101	MT-224	441-0184	N184VB	441-0267	N88727
425-0174	N425KC	441-0019	XC-UJX	441-0102	VH-OAA	441-0185	N797RW	441-0268	HC-BXH
425-0175	N425WT	441-0020	w/o	441-0103	N441MD	441-0186	N7NW	441-0269	N88834
425-0176	N425TV	441-0021	XB-GBN	441-0104	N273AZ	441-0187	N88GW	441-0270	w/o
425-0177	C-GSFF	441-0022	YV-	441-0105	N11MM	441-0188	wfu	441-0271	HK-3456W
425-0178	C-FVAX	441-0023	VH-LBY	441-0106	VH-NAX	441-0189	XC-AA71	441-0272	VH-VED
425-0179	N333UJ	441-0024	N441MJ	441-0107	N441WD	441-0190	N2725N	441-0273	HK-3009
425-0180	N425RM	441-0025	VH-XMD	441-0108	N108TJ	441-0191	w/o	441-0274	N322P
425-0181	N80PM	441-0026	VH-AZW	441-0109	VH-FMQ	441-0192	N441VC	441-0275	XC-LGE
425-0182	N68734	441-0027	N922HP	441-0110	HK-....	441-0193	w/o	441-0276	HK-3596
425-0183	w/o	441-0028	N441DS	441-0111	N59RT	441-0194	N441WJ	441-0277	HP-...
425-0184	N425SP	441-0029	wfu	441-0112	w/o	441-0195	YV	441-0278	N15DB
425-0185	N425DC	441-0030	VH-OCS	441-0113	VH-XMJ	441-0196	w/o	441-0279	w/o
425-0186	N425Z	441-0031	PNC-204	441-0114	HK-2538P	441-0197	N441JK	441-0280	N441AE
425-0187	N622MM	441-0032	N441P	441-0115	N441VB	441-0198	XA-	441-0281	N689AE
425-0188	N188DF	441-0033	w/o	441-0116	N711MB	441-0199	w/o	441-0282	N6832M
425-0189	YV1750	441-0034	N441BW	441-0117	N441CJ	441-0200	N423TG	441-0283	N441EP
425-0190	C-FKTN	441-0035	N441DR	441-0118	N14FJ	441-0201	w/o	441-0284	N441AB
425-0191	N444KF	441-0036	N441F	441-0119	N22CG	441-0202	N77ML	441-0285	N707MA
425-0192	C-FSEA	441-0037	N81PN	441-0120	C-FSKG	441-0203	N74GL	441-0286	N441MW
425-0193	N425PC	441-0038	VH-LBZ	441-0121	N44776	441-0204	N441TA	441-0287	HK-3540E
425-0194	N577PW	441-0039	N74BY	441-0122	N441M	441-0205	N295CE	441-0288	N77R
425-0195	N207RS	441-0040	YV....	441-0123	N441ND	441-0206	HK-3613	441-0289	N377CA
425-0196	w/o	441-0041	N441WL	441-0124	N555FT	441-0207	N440DA	441-0290	N88692
425-0197	N425WL	441-0042	VH-LBA	441-0125	N48BS	441-0208	XC-GOO	441-0291	w/o
425-0198	N425BL	441-0043	N43GT	441-0126	N337C	441-0209	N711GE	441-0292	N441PP
425-0199	N425DR	441-0044	N441KM	441-0127	N825SP	441-0210	N441LA	441-0293	N878JL
425-0200	N425PG	441-0045	N441PS	441-0128	N128EZ	441-0211	N6851T	441-0294	N456GT
425-0201	N1223B	441-0046	wfu	441-0129	N420DB	441-0212	N6851X	441-0295	N181MD
425-0202	N788JL	441-0047	w/o	441-0130	VH-XMG	441-0213	N716CC	441-0296	VH-LBD
425-0203	N425KD	441-0048	N441CT	441-0131	w/o	441-0214	C-GAGE	441-0297	VH-XBC
425-0204	N76SJ	441-0049	N441EB	441-0132	VH-SMO	441-0215	N665TM	441-0298	C-GCYB
425-0205	N111SU	441-0050	N83A	441-0133	N441T	441-0216	C-FNWC	441-0299	N6840T
425-0206	N425CL	441-0051	N725SV	441-0134	N441SM	441-0217	N441BB	441-0300	N441DB
425-0207	N425NC	441-0052	w/o	441-0135	N502BR	441-0218	N846YT	441-0301	N441SB
425-0208	N1224J	441-0053	N2441K	441-0136	N207SS	441-0219	N553AM	441-0302	N500RJ
425-0209	D-IDAX	441-0054	N454EA	441-0137	N441JA	441-0220	N6853T	441-0303	N441JR
425-0210	N425BS	441-0055	N477B	441-0138	VH-JLT	441-0221	N441RS	441-0304	N6860C
425-0211	w/o	441-0056	w/o	441-0139	XA-	441-0222	N533M	441-0305	N441CX
425-0212	wfu	441-0057	TF-ORF	441-0140	YV-...	441-0223	N92JQ	441-0306	N441E
425-0213	N12244	441-0058	C-GPSZ	441-0141	ZK-NFD	441-0224	XC-GON	441-0307	N2NC
425-0214	N425PN	441-0059	HK-3401	441-0142	wfu	441-0225	N441VH	441-0308	N33DE
425-0215	N888JS	441-0060	YV-....	441-0143	C-GPSR	441-0226	N441AD	441-0309	HK-3568
425-0216	XA-	441-0061	N903DC	441-0144	w/o	441-0227	YV-533P	441-0310	N977MP
425-0217	N425TM	441-0062	N441KP	441-0145	N441BH	441-0228	N880T	441-0311	N102AD
425-0218	N425N	441-0063	YV1705	441-0146	N911PJ	441-0229	w/o	441-0312	N331MP
425-0219	N232GM	441-0064	N767Z	441-0147	N564AC	441-0230	N441G	441-0313	N443DW
425-0220	N137CD	441-0065	N771XW	441-0148	N441AR	441-0231	N441YA	441-0314	C-GCIL
425-0221	C-GNEP	441-0066	N23NW	441-0149	N419SC	441-0232	XC-AA12	441-0315	N441HF
425-0222	D-	441-0067	YV1753	441-0150	S5-CAE	441-0233	N6855P	441-0316	C-FSFI
425-0223	ZP-...	441-0068	N3WM	441-0151	N441RJ	441-0234	N441GA	441-0317	N1843S
425-0224	N425NP	441-0069	w/o	441-0152	HK-3620X	441-0235	XB-EWO	441-0318	N441FS

441-0319	YV-....	F406-0036	G-MAFA	**328**		45	wfu	129	YV
441-0320	HK-3550	F406-0037	PR-FAG	3019	N328DC	46	wfu	130	PK-TRO
441-0321	N858AC	F406-0038	w/o	3024	N28CG	47	wfu	131	wfu
441-0322	N441BL	F406-0039	F-ZBBB	3027	N653PC	48	wfu	132	wfu
441-0323	N441S	F406-0040	5H-SXB	3034	N38CG	49	wfu	133	wfu
441-0324	HK-3611	F406-0041	w/o	3056	PH-EEV	50	wfu	134	ZS-PHJ
441-0325	N441DN	F406-0042	F-ZBCE	3078	OE-GBB	51	wfu	135	wfu
441-0326	N326RS	F406-0043	ZS-SSE	3086	N503CG	52	N612DT	136	XA-TBT
441-0327	N441AG	F406-0044	5Y-MKM	3090	N404SS	53	wfu	137	wfu
441-0328	HP-...	F406-0045	G-FIND	3095	PH-EVY	54	N164PA	138	XA-RLK
441-0329	w/o	F406-0046	5H-TZE	3109	C-FSCO	55	wfu	139	N196PA
441-0330	N441HS	F406-0047	TF-ORD	**Embraer**		56	wfu	140	wfu
441-0331	N68HS	F406-0048	V5-WAK	*Xingu 121A*		57	wfu	141	ZS-NHW
441-0332	HP-1189	F406-0049	N406GV	121010	PT-MAD	58	XC-VNC	142	wfu
441-0333	HK-3418	F406-0050	D-ICCC	121020	PT-MAM	59	w/o	143	wfu
441-0334	N444AK	F406-0051	S7-AAI	121021	PP-ACM	60	wfu	144	wfu
441-0335	HK-3497	F406-0052	N6590Y	121029	PT-MAV	61	wfu	145	HK-3580W
441-0336	N441HK	F406-0053	w/o	121035	PP-EMN	62	wfu	146	wfu
441-0337	N337KC	F406-0054	N6591R	121039	PP-EIC	63	wfu	147	w/o
441-0338	w/o	F406-0055	5Y-BIX	121040	OO-SXB	64	wfu	148	XC-LIE
441-0339	N1210Z	F406-0056	w/o	121042	OO-SXC	65	wfu	149	N192PA
441-0340	wfu	F406-0057	ZK-VAF	121044	PT-FRG	66	wfu	150	wfu
441-0341	N441DD	F406-0058	V5-MDA	121049	PT-FAX	67	N806W	151	wfu
441-0342	N441LS	F406-0059	AP-BFK	**Fokker**		68	w/o	152	wfu
441-0343	N835MA	F406-0060	5H-WOW	*F27*		69	wfu	153	N19BX
441-0344	N441UC	F406-0061	F-ZBGE	16	N406SD	70	wfu	154	w/o
441-0345	wfu	F406-0062	V5-DHL	35	N235KT	71	wfu	155	wfu
441-0346	N1212C	F406-0063	N406SD	97	N432NA	72	wfu	156	9Q-COE
441-0347	N441PN	F406-0064	G-SFPA	10281	N366SB	73	w/o	157	N94SA
441-0348	HK-3529	F406-0065	G-SFPB	20253	J 752	74	N701BN	158	w/o
441-0349	N274GC	F406-0066	F-ZBCG	20287	U-05	75	PT-KYF	159	XA-RJB
441-0350	AP-BCY	F406-0067	Z-DDG	20321	U-06	76	P4-JML	160	wfu
441-0351	N441EH	F406-0068	Z-DDE	20324	U-01	77	wfu	161	XA-...
441-0352	AP-BCQ	F406-0069	Z-DDD	20327	wfu	78	HK-3681	162	C-GPTA
441-0353	ZS-RGS	F406-0070	F-ZBCI	20329	U-03	79	wfu	163	w/o
441-0354	wfu	F406-0071	Z-DDF		wfu	80	D2-EXC	164	ZS-PHI
441-0355	D-ILYS	F406-0072	F-....	**Gulfstream**		81	5Y-BMR	165	N501WN
441-0356	YV1857	F406-0073	G-BVJT	*Gulfstream 1*		82	N12RW	166	D2-EXB
441-0357	N441TL	F406-0074	F-ZBCJ	1	5Y-XXX	83	wfu	167	S9-...
441-0358	N440EH	F406-0075	F-ZBCH	2	wfu	84	w/o	168	wfu
441-0359	N123ME	F406-0076	VH-YZE	3	wfu	85	wfu	169	N200AE
441-0360	N731BH	F406-0077	F-ZBCF	4	wfu	86	ZS-ALX	170	YV-627C
441-0361	N592Q	F406-0078	VH-YZF	5	ZS-OOE	87	wfu	171	YV-628C
441-0362	N36FR	F406-0079	VH-YZG	6	wfu	88	N195PA	172	wfu
441-0698	ZS-ASM	F406-0080	G-MAFB	7	N99EL	89	N789G	173	YV-903CP
Reims/Cessna 406		F406-0081	98-1001	8	wfu	90	wfu	174	wfu
F406-00..	98-1004	F406-0082	98-1002	9	wfu	91	wfu	175	wfu
F406-01	F-ZBFA	F406-0083	98-1003	10	wfu	92	YV-....	176	wfu
F406-0001	N17CK	F406-0084	98-1005	11	N7SL	93	N820CB	177	PK-CDM
F406-0002	D2-ECN	F406-0085	98-1006	12	wfu	94	N8E	178	w/o
F406-0003	w/o	F406-0086	F-ZBGA	14	wfu	95	N500RN	179	wfu
F406-0004	V5-EEZ	F406-0087	AC-21	15	wfu	96	N444BC	180	wfu
F406-0005	5H-RAS	F406-0088	AC-22	16	N615C	97	N184PA	181	wfu
F406-0006	F-ZBEP	F406-0089	AC-23	17	wfu	98	wfu	182	wfu
F406-0007	TR-LEQ	F406-0090	F-ZBGD	18	YV-....	99	w/o	183	wfu
F406-0008	F-WQUD	F406-0091	F-OSPJ	19	wfu	100	wfu	184	wfu
F406-0009	wfu	F406-0092	5A-DKW	20	N19FF	101	wfu	185	wfu
F406-0010	F-WQAY	F406-0093	V5-FMR	21	wfu	102	N11UN	186	wfu
F406-0011	D2-ECO	F406-0095	G-SFP.	22	wfu	103	wfu	187	wfu
F406-0012	ZK-XLC	**De Havilland**		23	N810CB	104	C-FHBO	188	C-FAWE
F406-0013	F-GRAZ	*DHC-6*		24	w/o	105	wfu	189	wfu
F406-0014	w/o	437	N143Z	25	ZS-PHK	106	w/o	190	5Y-...
F406-0015	OH-OTL	596	N16NG	26	N185PA	107	wfu	191	PK-RJA
F406-0016	D2-ECP	782	AP-BBR	27	N198PA	108	wfu	192	N171PA
F406-0017	F-ZBES	841	A6-MAR	28	wfu	109	wfu	193	ZS-JIS
F406-0018	G-LEAF	*DHC-7*		29	wfu	110	wfu	194	5Y-BMS
F406-0019	D2-ECQ	106	N54026	30	wfu	111	wfu	195	N190PA
F406-0020	G-TURF	*DHC-8*		31	wfu	112	wfu	196	N659PC
F406-0021	5Y-BKN	024	5N-MGV	32	wfu	114	wfu	197	N520JG
F406-0022	YV1187	391	HK-3997W	33	wfu	115	N61SB	198	w/o
F406-0023	ZS-OEE	435	N759A	34	5Y-BLR	116	wfu	199	N167PA
F406-0024	w/o	440	N724A	35	wfu	117	wfu	200	N159GS
F406-0025	F-ZBAB	441	N725A	36	wfu	118	wfu	322	wfu
F406-0026	F-OGOG	**Dornier**		37	w/o	119	wfu	323	HI-678CT
F406-0027	ZS-SSD	*228*		38	XA-...	120	wfu	*Gulfstream 1000*	
F406-0028	w/o	7028	A40-CQ	39	EC-EVJ	121	wfu	96000	w/o
F406-0029	w/o	8146	5N-MPS	40	N19TZ	122	F-GFEF	96001	TP-216
F406-0030	5H-AWK	8206	PH-MNZ	41	wfu	123	wfu	96002	N9902S
F406-0031	VT-ASB	8226	1112	42	TL-ADN	124	D2-EXD	96003	N9906S
F406-0032	ZS-SSC	8227	1113	43	wfu	125	N193PA	96004	XB-ECT
F406-0033	VH-JVN	8228	1114	44	wfu	126	N110RB	96005	N94PA
F406-0034	N861FT					127	wfu	96006	N444WD
F406-0035	5H-PAY					128	w/o	96007	N695AM

96008	PJ-NAF	96092	N211AD	11663	N840BC	15024	EJC-111	95063	N980GZ
96009	N7031K	96093	CX-...	11664	N7057A	15025	N29GA	95065	HK-3455
96010	HK-3239W	96094	N94EA	11665	N48BA	15026	VH-LMC	95066	EJC-115
96011	N695GJ	96095	ZP-TWY	11666	YV-773CP	15027	PT-WLD	95067	YV-407CP
96012	N95AB	96096	N695CT	11667	11667	15028	XC-MLM	95068	XC-AA62
96013	MT-218	96097	N112CE	11668	HK-3912	15029	w/o	95069	PR-DBR
96014	N51DM	96098	w/o	11669	HC-BUD	15030	YY2249	95070	JA8600
96015	N333UP	96099	HK-3283W	11670	w/o	15031	N901TE	95071	N810EC
96016	YV0100	96100	HK-3324P	11671	YV-2346P	15032	YV1777	95072	XC-HGH
96017	N17ZD	96201	N115GA	11672	N840PS	15033	VP-BMZ	95073	N200TT
96018	HK-3367	96202	N27VE	11673	HK-4065W	15034	YV-...	95074	N357ST
96019	N200DK	96203	ZP-TXG	11674	w/o	15035	N84LG	95075	HK-3407
96020	wfu	96204	N695MG	11675	N319BF	15036	w/o	95076	N76HH
96021	HK-3439	96205	N695EE	11676	N129TB	15037	N900ET	95077	N221K
96022	N9942S	96206	N224EZ	11677	XB-GMT	15038	PT-OQY	95078	N980MH
96023	HB-GHK	96207	N695KG	11678	XC-AA36	15039	N144JB	95079	HK-3481
96024	N5450J	96208	VP-BCT	11679	N840PN	15040	XA-CHM	95080	PNP-218
96025	N9945S	96209	N235GA	11680	N777NV	15041	N77HS	95081	N808NT
96026	wfu	96210	N238GA	11681	SE-IUV	15042	C-FGWT	95082	MT-222
96027	N727CC	Gulfstream 840		11682	N910FC	Gulfstream 980		95083	HK-3450
96028	N9948S	11600	N47TT	11683	N840G	95000	XC-AA67	95084	YV2020
96029	N79PH	11601	N63DU	11684	N51WF	95001	HK-...	Hawker Beechcraf	
96030	FAC-5198	11602	HK-...	11685	YV-105CP	95002	N980BH	Beech 1900C	
96031	HP-1149P	11603	YV2099	11686	wfu	95003	N9756S	UB-37	w/o
96032	N695NC	11604	HK-...	11687	N900LL	95004	FAB 030	UB-39	N2TS
96033	HK-3366X	11605	N125MM	11688	N840TC	95005	w/o	UB-40	ST-
96034	N700L	11606	XC-AA29	11689	N840TW	95006	N980HB	UB-43	N20RA
96035	N93MA	11607	N840VM	11690	w/o	95007	YV-581CP	UB-48	N565M
96036	N695GG	11608	w/o	11691	N32PH	95008	N515AM	UB-56	N896FM
96037	HK-3389P	11609	w/o	11692	C-FNRM	95009	YY224T	UB-64	N157PA
96038	N695HT	11610	N840SE	11693	N840MD	95010	YV0154	UB-68	N23BD
96039	HK-3060	11611	HK-3424	11694	YV-...	95011	N980EC	UB-69	C-FJDF
96040	MT-214	11612	LV-OEI	11695	XC-AA56	95012	N980SA	Beech 1900C-1	N381CR
96041	3918	11613	SE-GSS	11696	N884D	95013	N25TN		
96042	N303GM	11614	N74EF	11697	N840JK	95014	N9767S	UC-1	N640MW
96043	XC-HFN	11615	N840GH	11698	YV1325	95015	N695WR	UC-4	HZ-PC2
96044	wfu	11616	N133DL	11699	N425MM	95016	HK-3474	UC-43	N1900C
96045	HK-2909P	11617	N73EF	11700	N840SM	95017	YV2090	UC-48	ZS-OHE
96046	N9966S	11618	YV1315	11701	N844SC	95018	XC-PFB	UC-55	5Y-BVI
96047	HK-3390	11619	N72TB	11702	N64PS	95019	PK-ODR	UC-76	ZS-PJM
96048	N9968S	11620	HK-3680	11703	N5955K	95020	w/o	UC-139	N9331M
96049	HK-2951	11621	HP-...	11709	N97WT	95021	ZP-TTU	UC-169	0169
96050	N695MM	11622	N926SC	11719	N5956K	95022	HK-3484	UC-170	0170
96051	ZS-KZY	11623	w/o	11720	w/o	95023	N700PC	Beech 1900D	
96052	ZS-KZZ	11624	N840CF	11721	HK-3700	95024	N36JT	UE-12	N45AR
96053	N9973S	11625	PT-WIC	11722	HK-3447P	95025	N54UM	UE-27	N46AR
96054	N71MR	11626	N5878K	11723	YV-505CP	95026	HC-...	UE-61	N85516
96055	N695AB	11627	N88BJ	11724	N37SB	95027	N7101L	UE-63	C-GSWX
96056	XC-LHD	11628	w/o	11725	YV1835	95028	YV-980CP	UE-69	YR-RLA
96057	N34GA	11629	N940AC	11726	YV1892	95029	N600MM	UE-73	YR-RLB
96058	N36AG	11630	N106TT	11727	N840V	95030	N980MD	UE-77	5N-MPN
96059	HK-3391W	11631	XB-DSH	11728	HK-3385P	95031	N980EA	UE-149	5N-MPA
96060	FAH-006	11632	YV-...	11729	N67FE	95032	N265EX	UE-157	YV1894
96061	HK-3218	11633	HK-2495P	11730	N835CC	95033	N126M	UE-177	PK-TRW
96062	N12VA	11634	HC-BHU	11731	C-FNAO	95034	YV	UE-186	PK-TRX
96063	N83WA	11635	XA-...	11732	N8VL	95035	ZP-...	UE-212	S7-IDC
96064	N6767M	11636	N980AK	11733	11733	95036	N5356M	UE-230	ZS-OYG
96065	PJ-...	11637	YV-394CP	11734	N840NK	95037	w/o	UE-256	96-0112
96066	N54GA	11638	N840MG	11735	YV1851	95038	PT-...	UE-258	N28NG
96067	YV-53CP	11639	D-IUTA	Gulfstream 900		95039	D-IHSI	UE-284	VT-KDA
96068	N519CC	11640	N840KB	15001	N690TP	95040	MT-219	UE-288	T-729
96069	HK-3961X	11641	N977JC	15002	C-FSPM	95041	N218MS	UE-299	N305PC
96070	N695YP	11642	wfu	15003	HP-...	95042	XA-LEK	UE-303	N29NG
96071	N69GA	11643	N840JC	15004	HP-...	95043	HK-3461	UE-307	N733DC
96072	HK-3279	11644	w/o	15005	ZP-TWZ	95044	w/o	UE-311	VH-PSK
96073	w/o	11645	N165BC	15006	YV-492CP	95045	N981WJ	UE-317	HC-BYO
96074	HK-3253P	11646	N840LC	15007	N337DR	95046	MT-221	UE-319	9J-MBO
96075	XA-...	11647	N5900K	15008	N6BZ	95047	N1981S	UE-323	9J-MAS
96076	HK-3275	11648	XC-HHH	15009	XC-JDB	95048	N980DT	UE-324	A6-YST
96077	N695FA	11649	XB-DTW	15010	FAC-5454	95049	N980GR	UE-332	N535M
96078	N695GH	11650	HK-2601	15011	VP-CAY	95050	HK-3408	UE-333	N534M
96079	ZP-TXF	11651	XC-AA27	15012	YV-...	95051	XB-ACO	UE-334	N536M
96080	HK-4370X	11652	HK-3290P	15013	N927SM	95052	XC-ALB	UE-353	VT-TOI
96081	HP-...	11653	YV-87CP	15014	N771FF	95053	ZP-...	UE-354	N1883M
96082	HP-...	11654	N406CP	15015	N544GA	95054	w/o	UE-361	N1865A
96083	EJC-114	11655	XC-OAX	15016	N601WT	95055	FAC-5553	UE-368	N368CR
96084	XB-ATC	11656	YV0149	15017	YV1617	95056	TI-MEL	UE-371	CS-DOC
96085	N808NC	11657	N840JW	15018	N611	95057	HK-3444	UE-377	N655MW
96086	HK-3193	11658	N402AB	15019	wfu	95058	YV2175	UE-382	N27NG
96087	N695RC	11659	wfu	15020	C-GOVT	95059	HK-3819	UE-383	N800CA
96088	HK-3291P	11660	XA-TOR	15021	ZP-...	95060	N9812S	UE-392	N191CS
96089	N45RF	11661	N5914K	15022	YV1173	95061	N980WJ	UE-394	N470MM
96090	XC-HUA	11662		15023	HC-...	95062	HK-3406		

UE-423	A2-OLM	LJ-82	w/o	LJ-164	N17SA	LJ-246	w/o	LJ-329	wfu
King Air 90/C90/C90GT		LJ-83	N827T	LJ-165	w/o	LJ-247	w/o	LJ-330	OB-1364
LJ-1	N925X	LJ-84	C-FUFW	LJ-166	wfu	LJ-248	HK-....	LJ-331	F-GEXK
LJ-2	N812P	LJ-85	N900CK	LJ-167	YV-....	LJ-249	wfu	LJ-332	wfu
LJ-3	wfu	LJ-86	N17WT	LJ-168	w/o	LJ-250	wfu	LJ-333	LV-WRM
LJ-4	wfu	LJ-87	N98B	LJ-169	N983K	LJ-251	w/o	LJ-334	N621TB
LJ-5	HP-....	LJ-88	wfu	LJ-170	wfu	LJ-252	N33SB	LJ-335	N7644R
LJ-6	wfu	LJ-89	N195DP	LJ-171	w/o	LJ-253	wfu	LJ-336	wfu
LJ-7	wfu	LJ-90	wfu	LJ-172	N2000E	LJ-254	wfu	LJ-337	C-GHVR
LJ-8	N4RY	LJ-91	N825K	LJ-173	N629CD	LJ-255	wfu	LJ-338	9J-YVZ
LJ-9	N613BR	LJ-92	N5245F	LJ-174	N93RY	LJ-256	N256TA	LJ-339	w/o
LJ-10	N10JE	LJ-93	N9901	LJ-175	wfu	LJ-257	N299D	LJ-340	N240K
LJ-11	w/o	LJ-94	wfu	LJ-176	w/o	LJ-258	N123V	LJ-341	YV
LJ-12	N654C	LJ-95	wfu	LJ-177	wfu	LJ-259	w/o	LJ-342	N876L
LJ-13	C-FBPT	LJ-96	wfu	LJ-178	w/o	LJ-260	N96AG	LJ-343	N57AG
LJ-14	wfu	LJ-97	wfu	LJ-178A	N798K	LJ-261	N990SA	LJ-344	N873K
LJ-15	N37GP	LJ-98	F-GBPB	LJ-179	wfu	LJ-262	wfu	LJ-345	w/o
LJ-16	PT-....	LJ-99	N292A	LJ-180	w/o	LJ-263	N526RR	LJ-346	PT-WTN
LJ-17	N440TP	LJ-100	wfu	LJ-181	PR-PJC	LJ-264	N86MG	LJ-347	F-GFHO
LJ-18	w/o	LJ-101	N333G	LJ-182	N92WG	LJ-265	N10YP	LJ-348	C-GTMA
LJ-19	XA-....	LJ-102	N787K	LJ-183	wfu	LJ-266	YV-....	LJ-349	N939K
LJ-20	wfu	LJ-103	N3002S	LJ-184	HP-	LJ-267	N416MR	LJ-350	N7BF
LJ-21	N249PA	LJ-104	N814G	LJ-185	wfu	LJ-268	w/o	LJ-351	N90LG
LJ-22	w/o	LJ-105	PT-LHM	LJ-186	w/o	LJ-269	N507W	LJ-352	w/o
LJ-23	w/o	LJ-106	N411RS	LJ-187	wfu	LJ-270	YV	LJ-353	PT-OBW
LJ-24	w/o	LJ-107	N311SR	LJ-188	w/o	LJ-271	w/o	LJ-354	w/o
LJ-25	w/o	LJ-108	N1154S	LJ-189	PK-VKZ	LJ-272	N5Y	LJ-355	PT-DEU
LJ-26	wfu	LJ-109	N48XP	LJ-190	N216LJ	LJ-273	wfu	LJ-356	wfu
LJ-27	wfu	LJ-110	wfu	LJ-191	PT-WAE	LJ-274	wfu	LJ-357	YV-....
LJ-28	wfu	LJ-111	wfu	LJ-192	N15CT	LJ-275	N457CP	LJ-358	N60HT
LJ-29	wfu	LJ-112	w/o	LJ-193	N600BF	LJ-276	N90VP	LJ-359	w/o
LJ-30	N1290A	LJ-113	N105K	LJ-194	N55FY	LJ-277	N623BB	LJ-360	N125A
LJ-31	N4948W	LJ-114	wfu	LJ-195	YV-....	LJ-278	wfu	LJ-361	N587M
LJ-32	wfu	LJ-115	wfu	LJ-196	N348AC	LJ-279	wfu	LJ-362	N31SN
LJ-33	w/o	LJ-116	w/o	LJ-197	PK-VKY	LJ-280	N6228O	LJ-363	F-GICE
LJ-34	wfu	LJ-116A	N88SP	LJ-198	wfu	LJ-281	N39TE	LJ-364	wfu
LJ-35	wfu	LJ-117	N115PA	LJ-199	w/o	LJ-282	wfu	LJ-365	RP-C2208
LJ-36	N3DF	LJ-118	C-FCGE	LJ-200	XA-....	LJ-283	N773S	LJ-366	N68CD
LJ-37	wfu	LJ-119	w/o	LJ-201	wfu	LJ-284	w/o	LJ-367	N321DZ
LJ-38	N141RR	LJ-120	N601TA	LJ-202	YV-....	LJ-285	N98HB	LJ-368	w/o
LJ-39	wfu	LJ-121	w/o	LJ-203	C-FCGH	LJ-286	N43JT	LJ-369	N672LS
LJ-40	F-BTOP	LJ-122	HR-IAH	LJ-204	N52EL	LJ-287	XA-....	LJ-370	YV1599
LJ-41	wfu	LJ-123	N812AC	LJ-205	w/o	LJ-288	N270M	LJ-371	N718K
LJ-42	wfu	LJ-124	YV-....	LJ-206	F-GHDO	LJ-289	N5WG	LJ-372	w/o
LJ-43	wfu	LJ-125	PT-OUL	LJ-207	wfu	LJ-290	wfu	LJ-373	N275LE
LJ-44	wfu	LJ-126	wfu	LJ-208	wfu	LJ-291	wfu	LJ-374	YV-....
LJ-45	wfu	LJ-127	wfu	LJ-209	N54WW	LJ-292	N827FM	LJ-375	N101BS
LJ-46	wfu	LJ-128	F-BOSY	LJ-210	HK-....	LJ-293	XC-ONA	LJ-376	C-FMKD
LJ-47	N6137	LJ-129	N129LA	LJ-211	wfu	LJ-294	N930K	LJ-377	w/o
LJ-48	w/o	LJ-130	YV-....	LJ-212	wfu	LJ-295	N57EM	LJ-378	w/o
LJ-49	N32229	LJ-131	N80DG	LJ-213	N250U	LJ-296	HP-....	LJ-379	wfu
LJ-50	w/o	LJ-132	N290CC	LJ-214	N412MA	LJ-297	N140PA	LJ-380	N66AD
LJ-51	wfu	LJ-133	N90FA	LJ-215	N479SA	LJ-298	N615AA	LJ-381	N49GN
LJ-52	N134W	LJ-134	C-GLRR	LJ-216	wfu	LJ-299	N312VF	LJ-382	EC-GIJ
LJ-53	N539DP	LJ-135	wfu	LJ-217	CC-COT	LJ-300	N70VM	LJ-383	YV-....
LJ-54	wfu	LJ-136	wfu	LJ-218	N801KM	LJ-301	A9C-....	LJ-384	HP-....
LJ-55	HP-....	LJ-137	w/o	LJ-219	wfu	LJ-302	w/o	LJ-385	N130DM
LJ-56	wfu	LJ-138	N100UE	LJ-220	C-FCGI	LJ-303	w/o	LJ-386	N899D
LJ-57	wfu	LJ-139	N100WB	LJ-221	PT-KGV	LJ-304	wfu	LJ-387	XB-CIO
LJ-58	N58KA	LJ-140	N437CF	LJ-222	YV-....	LJ-305	N525JK	LJ-388	XB-HCL
LJ-59	N190BT	LJ-141	w/o	LJ-223	w/o	LJ-306	N124SA	LJ-389	w/o
LJ-60	N1WJ	LJ-142	N181NK	LJ-224	YV-....	LJ-307	N66RE	LJ-390	N701AT
LJ-61	wfu	LJ-143	wfu	LJ-225	wfu	LJ-308	N577DC	LJ-391	N55MG
LJ-62	N212WP	LJ-144	wfu	LJ-226	N271WN	LJ-309	C-FHWI	LJ-392	N392TW
LJ-63	XB-GTP	LJ-145	N45PR	LJ-227	w/o	LJ-310	wfu	LJ-393	w/o
LJ-64	N512G	LJ-146	YV-....	LJ-228	OB-1567	LJ-311	w/o	LJ-394	N394AL
LJ-65	w/o	LJ-147	YV-....	LJ-229	N435A	LJ-312	w/o	LJ-395	ZS-PFA
LJ-66	N901SA	LJ-148	N671LL	LJ-230	N77SS	LJ-313	C-FCGN	LJ-396	YV-....
LJ-67	N777NP	LJ-149	w/o	LJ-231	wfu	LJ-314	w/o	LJ-397	A6-SKY
LJ-68	wfu	LJ-150	wfu	LJ-232	w/o	LJ-315	N34HA	LJ-398	PT-DIQ
LJ-69	N190JL	LJ-151	YV-....	LJ-233	wfu	LJ-316	N758K	LJ-399	XA-....
LJ-70	N516WB	LJ-152	PT-OVP	LJ-234	N212D	LJ-317	N46AX	LJ-400	OB-1595
LJ-71	N110EL	LJ-153	66-15361	LJ-235	w/o	LJ-318	wfu	LJ-401	N590SA
LJ-72	w/o	LJ-154	N5111U	LJ-236	wfu	LJ-319	N1999G	LJ-402	9Q-CKM
LJ-73	wfu	LJ-155	wfu	LJ-237	N66GS	LJ-320	wfu	LJ-403	N603PA
LJ-74	N32FH	LJ-156	wfu	LJ-238	N6KZ	LJ-321	N223CH	LJ-404	N90NM
LJ-75	N75368	LJ-157	N90GN	LJ-239	w/o	LJ-322	OB-1594	LJ-405	OB-1558
LJ-76	wfu	LJ-158	N503M	LJ-240	YV-....	LJ-323	LV-VHR	LJ-406	N226JW
LJ-77	N58AC	LJ-159	N50525	LJ-241	N22BB	LJ-324	D2-EQC	LJ-407	w/o
LJ-78	wfu	LJ-160	w/o	LJ-242	w/o	LJ-325	C-FJHP	LJ-408	ZS-MUM
LJ-79	wfu	LJ-161	ZS-EFC	LJ-243	wfu	LJ-326	OB-1297	LJ-409	PP-EUE
LJ-80	D2-ALS	LJ-162	N198KA	LJ-244	w/o	LJ-327	G-OJRO	LJ-410	N901WL
LJ-81	N276VM	LJ-163	N20BL	LJ-245	N42CO	LJ-328	wfu	LJ-411	N14W

LJ-412	wfu	LJ-495	YV-....	LJ-580	N580RA	LJ-663	wfu	LJ-746	N322R
LJ-413	w/o	LJ-496	N579PS	LJ-581	N717X	LJ-664	w/o	LJ-747	N8MG
LJ-414	N57MA	LJ-497	w/o	LJ-582	N66KA	LJ-665	N665JK	LJ-748	N915CD
LJ-415	N87MM	LJ-498	w/o	LJ-583	N200TG	LJ-666	E 22-01	LJ-749	N90EJ
LJ-416	w/o	LJ-499	PT-OUO	LJ-584	XA-TXK	LJ-667	F-GQJD	LJ-750	N70FE
LJ-417	N44RG	LJ-500	C-GCFL	LJ-585	N14CP	LJ-668	HK-4357	LJ-751	YV-167CP
LJ-418	OY-BVS	LJ-501	N43WM	LJ-586	N60KA	LJ-669	ZS-OHR	LJ-752	FAC-5570
LJ-419	N11TN	LJ-502	N88HM	LJ-587	TC-AUV	LJ-670	wfu	LJ-753	N990DA
LJ-420	N642DH	LJ-503	YV-....	LJ-588	N711BN	LJ-671	N89FF	LJ-754	N754TW
LJ-421	N9426	LJ-504	N908K	LJ-589	N59KA	LJ-672	N717JG	LJ-755	5N-AMZ
LJ-422	C-GSFM	LJ-505	wfu	LJ-590	w/o	LJ-673	N660GW	LJ-756	YV1245
LJ-423	w/o	LJ-506	N32CC	LJ-591	w/o	LJ-674	N332DE	LJ-757	N104LC
LJ-424	N638D	LJ-507	w/o	LJ-592	N90EL	LJ-675	N973GA	LJ-758	N157CB
LJ-425	N767LD	LJ-508	N708DG	LJ-593	w/o	LJ-676	N26RE	LJ-759	N895FK
LJ-426	N761K	LJ-509	wfu	LJ-594	N90ZH	LJ-677	N555CK	LJ-760	N362MC
LJ-427	wfu	LJ-510	XU-HBB	LJ-595	N767MC	LJ-678	N150VE	LJ-761	N410MC
LJ-428	LV-VHO	LJ-511	YV-.....	LJ-596	N880H	LJ-679	N90MU	LJ-762	N350WA
LJ-429	N984AA	LJ-512	w/o	LJ-597	wfu	LJ-680	C-FNED	LJ-763	N9VC
LJ-430	N41WC	LJ-513	D-IFTC	LJ-598	wfu	LJ-681	N90PW	LJ-764	N775DM
LJ-431	ZS-OHB	LJ-514	w/o	LJ-599	wfu	LJ-682	N682KA	LJ-765	wfu
LJ-432	N919AG	LJ-515	PT-OIU	LJ-600	N73MC	LJ-683	N269SC	LJ-766	N642TD
LJ-433	w/o	LJ-516	w/o	LJ-601	N611AY	LJ-684	F-BXPY	LJ-767	N85DR
LJ-434	F-GFIR	LJ-517	N738R	LJ-602	w/o	LJ-685	C-FHLP	LJ-768	OY-SBU
LJ-435	N9838Z	LJ-518	F-ZBBF	LJ-603	E 22-04	LJ-686	N400BX	LJ-769	N24GJ
LJ-436	w/o	LJ-519	N290PA	LJ-604	w/o	LJ-687	Z-WRD	LJ-770	OH-BCX
LJ-437	N90DN	LJ-520	HP-...	LJ-605	E 22-03	LJ-688	N911FN	LJ-771	TC-IHC
LJ-438	N988SL	LJ-521	N901BK	LJ-606	N64KA	LJ-689	N100QT	LJ-772	N11692
LJ-439	w/o	LJ-522	F-BXAP	LJ-607	C-GKBB	LJ-690	w/o	LJ-773	N711CQ
LJ-440	wfu	LJ-523	wfu	LJ-608	E 22-..	LJ-691	N62525	LJ-774	N911FG
LJ-441	CC-CVZ	LJ-524	N19UM	LJ-609	C-GRSL	LJ-692	N711KP	LJ-775	N386GA
LJ-442	w/o	LJ-525	N90WJ	LJ-610	N89TM	LJ-693	w/o	LJ-776	N4776M
LJ-443	N411FT	LJ-526	N54EC	LJ-611	N65KA	LJ-694	N246CK	LJ-777	VH-KFG
LJ-444	N40BA	LJ-527	EC-GOY	LJ-612	N999ES	LJ-695	N695JJ	LJ-778	wfu
LJ-445	w/o	LJ-528	wfu	LJ-613	ZS-LTF	LJ-696	N644SP	LJ-779	N117MF
LJ-446	wfu	LJ-529	N290DP	LJ-614	w/o	LJ-697	N90AW	LJ-780	N4947M
LJ-447	wfu	LJ-530	N3KF	LJ-615	N444PS	LJ-698	N9872C	LJ-781	N495NM
LJ-448	wfu	LJ-531	PT-IBE	LJ-616	C-GMVP	LJ-699	N976JT	LJ-782	TG-VAS
LJ-449	LV-JJW	LJ-532	N575C	LJ-617	N1310T	LJ-700	N700CP	LJ-783	N197CC
LJ-450	wfu	LJ-533	N75RS	LJ-618	N900DZ	LJ-701	N90MV	LJ-784	YV-2835P
LJ-451	w/o	LJ-534	PT-OFC	LJ-619	wfu	LJ-702	N44HP	LJ-785	w/o
LJ-452	YV-....	LJ-535	PT-OXU	LJ-620	w/o	LJ-703	w/o	LJ-786	YV1054
LJ-453	5V-TTD	LJ-536	XB-...	LJ-621	w/o	LJ-704	N296AS	LJ-787	N787TT
LJ-454	N105RG	LJ-537	N101SS	LJ-622	TC-AUT	LJ-705	w/o	LJ-788	N107SC
LJ-455	HP-...	LJ-538	N65TA	LJ-623	w/o	LJ-706	VT-EFB	LJ-789	YV-223CP
LJ-456	F-GIFC	LJ-539	w/o	LJ-624	E 22-05	LJ-707	N122K	LJ-790	VT-RAM
LJ-457	N299MS	LJ-540	N123SK	LJ-625	ZS-NWC	LJ-708	N500KR	LJ-791	PT-WDU
LJ-458	HK-853W	LJ-541	w/o	LJ-626	N501MS	LJ-709	w/o	LJ-792	w/o
LJ-459	N9HW	LJ-542	N94420	LJ-627	N4447W	LJ-710	F-GJRK	LJ-793	w/o
LJ-460	PT-WBQ	LJ-543	PT-LTF	LJ-628	N800RP	LJ-711	VT-UBA	LJ-794	PT-LSO
LJ-461	N90WL	LJ-544	F-GHFE	LJ-629	N4950C	LJ-712	N85GW	LJ-795	ZS-MBZ
LJ-462	w/o	LJ-545	F-GHBD	LJ-630	N21SP	LJ-713	PR-TLL	LJ-796	N100V
LJ-463	N43MB	LJ-546	w/o	LJ-631	C-FLTC	LJ-714	N17573	LJ-797	N797CF
LJ-464	YV-....	LJ-548	XA-ACG	LJ-632	N71EN	LJ-715	N9076S	LJ-798	w/o
LJ-465	w/o	LJ-549	N531CS	LJ-633	w/o	LJ-716	N25DL	LJ-799	N799GK
LJ-466	PT-ODA	LJ-550	N94500	LJ-634	N1801B	LJ-717	F-GFHC	LJ-800	N60KW
LJ-467	N944K	LJ-551	ZS-MCA	LJ-635	w/o	LJ-718	wfu	LJ-801	N808SW
LJ-468	C-FNCN	LJ-552	N53EC	LJ-636	N66TL	LJ-719	VT-EFG	LJ-802	w/o
LJ-469	HK-....	LJ-553	XC-FOC	LJ-637	F-GCLD	LJ-720	N720RD	LJ-803	N469B
LJ-470	w/o	LJ-554	N697MP	LJ-638	PP-EHE	LJ-721	N596CU	LJ-804	N427DM
LJ-471	wfu	LJ-555	N977AA	LJ-639	w/o	LJ-722	N38RP	LJ-805	VP-BKW
LJ-472	N148Z	LJ-556	YV-465CP	LJ-640	N750RC	LJ-723	SE-IIB	LJ-806	N611DD
LJ-473	N90CB	LJ-557	w/o	LJ-641	N9UZ	LJ-724	N5TA	LJ-807	N802DG
LJ-474	wfu	LJ-558	wfu	LJ-642	wfu	LJ-725	N939RK	LJ-808	PT-LZH
LJ-475	N32BA	LJ-560	w/o	LJ-643	N96AH	LJ-726	N405EM	LJ-809	N549BR
LJ-476	w/o	LJ-561	N904DJ	LJ-644	w/o	LJ-727	w/o	LJ-810	YV-....
LJ-477	OB-1593	LJ-562	D-IIHA	LJ-645	N90CT	LJ-728	N291CC	LJ-811	N330V
LJ-478	N7TW	LJ-563	N139B	LJ-646	N4146S	LJ-729	w/o	LJ-812	PT-OJI
LJ-479	wfu	LJ-564	N777GF	LJ-647	D-IDAK	LJ-730	VH-SQH	LJ-813	N2050A
LJ-480	N2UV	LJ-565	N45RL	LJ-648	F-BXSL	LJ-731	wfu	LJ-814	N96DQ
LJ-481	N670AT	LJ-566	N515KJ	LJ-649	YV	LJ-732	N56DL	LJ-815	N946AM
LJ-482	F-BRNO	LJ-567	PT-OCT	LJ-650	N103BL	LJ-733	HK-44..	LJ-816	N416BK
LJ-483	N83TC	LJ-568	N108KU	LJ-651	PT-LUF	LJ-734	N284PM	LJ-817	PT-LPS
LJ-484	wfu	LJ-569	wfu	LJ-652	w/o	LJ-735	N819MH	LJ-818	N77NB
LJ-485	ZS-PRT	LJ-570	N73MH	LJ-653	N586TC	LJ-736	N635AF	LJ-819	G-RACI
LJ-486	9J-AAV	LJ-571	N183SA	LJ-654	N152WW	LJ-737	w/o	LJ-820	N100KB
LJ-487	wfu	LJ-572	N35TV	LJ-655	VH-SAM	LJ-738	N20WP	LJ-821	N959MC
LJ-488	YV-258CP	LJ-573	N90LB	LJ-656	N888MA	LJ-739	EJC-116	LJ-822	F-GBLU
LJ-489	LV-BDU	LJ-574	N318F	LJ-657	C-GTWW	LJ-740	N502SE	LJ-823	ST-ANH
LJ-490	N81AT	LJ-575	9J-DCF	LJ-658	w/o	LJ-741	wfu	LJ-824	N1MT
LJ-491	N88RP	LJ-576	N3GC	LJ-659	YV-2034P	LJ-742	YV-158CP	LJ-825	N601DM
LJ-492	N492PA	LJ-577	EC-HMA	LJ-660	wfu	LJ-743	N620WE	LJ-826	N701XP
LJ-493	w/o	LJ-578	N71KA	LJ-661	N90ME	LJ-744	N91TJ	LJ-827	N2057C
LJ-494	wfu	LJ-579	F-BVTB	LJ-662	N136PA	LJ-745	N37CN	LJ-828	F-GNMP

LJ-829	N98AR	LJ-912	N20	LJ-995	PT-OOT	LJ-1078	PT-ONJ	LJ-1161	N4764A
LJ-830	N911CX	LJ-913	PT-LMI	LJ-996	N679FS	LJ-1079	N69301	LJ-1162	C-FGXH
LJ-831	HK-3429W	LJ-914	N402EM	LJ-997	N503CB	LJ-1080	w/o	LJ-1163	HI-776SP
LJ-832	N512RR	LJ-915	N3688P	LJ-998	PT-OCI	LJ-1081	PT-OYN	LJ-1164	N104AJ
LJ-833	N85TB	LJ-916	6808	LJ-999	N333TL	LJ-1082	N686GW	LJ-1165	N39FB
LJ-834	PT-LVI	LJ-917	6809	LJ-1000	N403EM	LJ-1083	6819	LJ-1166	5201
LJ-835	PT-OVY	LJ-918	N918SA	LJ-1001	N91LW	LJ-1084	6820	LJ-1167	VT-EQN
LJ-836	N6646R	LJ-919	VH-TAM	LJ-1002	C-GAWA	LJ-1085	N360MP	LJ-1168	5202
LJ-837	OK-DSH	LJ-920	PT-OPD	LJ-1003	XB-SCG	LJ-1086	N105TC	LJ-1169	N585R
LJ-838	N445CR	LJ-921	N3690F	LJ-1004	PT-ORW	LJ-1087	N377P	LJ-1170	N581B
LJ-839	N299K	LJ-922	CN-TAX	LJ-1005	PT-OQS	LJ-1088	N904RB	LJ-1171	5203
LJ-840	w/o	LJ-923	N108JD	LJ-1006	N175AZ	LJ-1089	N904DK	LJ-1172	N32JP
LJ-841	N249CP	LJ-924	N3695W	LJ-1007	N964GB	LJ-1090	D-ILGI	LJ-1173	PT-LPD
LJ-842	A2-	LJ-925	N149CF	LJ-1008	VT-EHY	LJ-1091	N179MD	LJ-1174	PT-OIZ
LJ-843	N404SC	LJ-926	w/o	LJ-1009	N61383	LJ-1092	PT-WNW	LJ-1175	5204
LJ-844	PT-LQD	LJ-927	PT-OSO	LJ-1010	PT-LHJ	LJ-1093	N126WA	LJ-1176	5205
LJ-845	N28KP	LJ-928	N132AS	LJ-1011	N278SW	LJ-1094	PT-OFY	LJ-1177	C-FGXZ
LJ-846	N29TB	LJ-929	C-GCFB	LJ-1012	N278AB	LJ-1095	N617KM	LJ-1178	C-FGXJ
LJ-847	PT-OCY	LJ-930	ZS-KMA	LJ-1013	N6723Y	LJ-1096	PT-OTG	LJ-1179	C-FGXE
LJ-848	Z-LCS	LJ-931	D-IBMC	LJ-1014	N6173C	LJ-1097	N114DB	LJ-1180	LV-ROC
LJ-849	C-GCFZ	LJ-932	N34CE	LJ-1015	wfu	LJ-1098	F-HJCM	LJ-1181	N904P
LJ-850	N6681S	LJ-933	N3AT	LJ-1016	N790A	LJ-1099	ZS-MKI	LJ-1182	9301
LJ-851	N851KA	LJ-934	N101WR	LJ-1017	N6207F	LJ-1100	VT-EJZ	LJ-1183	N779JM
LJ-852	N90LF	LJ-935	N600FE	LJ-1018	PT-ONQ	LJ-1101	D-IFMI	LJ-1184	N149CM
LJ-853	N400RV	LJ-936	PT-OSI	LJ-1019	PT-OEP	LJ-1102	N109DT	LJ-1185	N50VP
LJ-854	w/o	LJ-937	PT-OUX	LJ-1020	VH-LYG	LJ-1103	N8GU	LJ-1186	w/o
LJ-855	wfu	LJ-938	N3817H	LJ-1021	P2-NTR	LJ-1104	N7223X	LJ-1187	N524TS
LJ-856	N904US	LJ-939	N94CD	LJ-1022	N922AA	LJ-1105	w/o	LJ-1188	PT-LYK
LJ-857	RP-C290	LJ-940	PT-OPE	LJ-1023	N332MS	LJ-1106	N222WJ	LJ-1189	C-FGXL
LJ-858	w/o	LJ-941	F-GEOU	LJ-1024	P2-NTJ	LJ-1107	N101BU	LJ-1190	N3190S
LJ-859	N9081R	LJ-942	N321AV	LJ-1025	w/o	LJ-1108	N958JH	LJ-1191	YV-32P
LJ-860	F-GBPZ	LJ-943	N3805E	LJ-1026	PT-LPJ	LJ-1109	N95PC	LJ-1192	C-FGXQ
LJ-861	N908GR	LJ-944	N9DA	LJ-1027	N83P	LJ-1110	6821	LJ-1193	ZS-OTK
LJ-862	N321FJ	LJ-945	N88GL	LJ-1028	LV-	LJ-1111	N96FA	LJ-1194	N15234
LJ-863	N777EB	LJ-946	PT-LLR	LJ-1029	N28TM	LJ-1112	N37XX	LJ-1195	PT-OKQ
LJ-864	N773PW	LJ-947	w/o	LJ-1030	N901JB	LJ-1113	N7230H	LJ-1196	N119SA
LJ-865	YV1695	LJ-948	N205MS	LJ-1031	N1GF	LJ-1114	N55WF	LJ-1197	N779MJ
LJ-866	N844C	LJ-949	N269JG	LJ-1032	N6563K	LJ-1115	OE-FHL	LJ-1198	JA
LJ-867	LX-APB	LJ-950	N401EM	LJ-1033	ZS-LFL	LJ-1116	VT-NEI	LJ-1199	XB-JNN
LJ-868	N139SC	LJ-951	PT-OZJ	LJ-1034	ZS-CSC	LJ-1117	N3030G	LJ-1200	C-FGXO
LJ-869	N811KC	LJ-952	PT-OJA	LJ-1035	N396CA	LJ-1118	ZS-LZR	LJ-1201	PT-LVK
LJ-870	PT-OPR	LJ-953	N38280	LJ-1036	N11SN	LJ-1119	N261GB	LJ-1202	N417VN
LJ-871	N290AJ	LJ-954	C9-ASK	LJ-1037	PT-LYT	LJ-1120	D-IKIN	LJ-1203	N485AT
LJ-872	N555MS	LJ-955	F-GIZB	LJ-1038	9102	LJ-1121	N904JP	LJ-1204	ZS-COP
LJ-873	w/o	LJ-956	PT-WMT	LJ-1039	N404JP	LJ-1122	N190EF	LJ-1205	N169DR
LJ-874	SX-BGO	LJ-957	HK-2596	LJ-1040	N444KU	LJ-1123	N621TD	LJ-1206	N1552G
LJ-875	N73PH	LJ-958	N11FT	LJ-1041	N541AA	LJ-1124	OE-FRS	LJ-1207	C-FGXS
LJ-876	N227DC	LJ-959	ZS-KZI	LJ-1042	6812	LJ-1125	N299VM	LJ-1208	N44GP
LJ-877	N300VA	LJ-960	PT-OCC	LJ-1043	6813	LJ-1126	N319MB	LJ-1209	N53TJ
LJ-878	N440KF	LJ-961	N16KM	LJ-1044	6814	LJ-1127	N814CP	LJ-1210	N948AM
LJ-879	N725AR	LJ-962	N962TT	LJ-1045	N84P	LJ-1128	PT-ODH	LJ-1211	N1551H
LJ-880	w/o	LJ-963	PT-OLX	LJ-1046	N990KB	LJ-1129	N506F	LJ-1212	PT-WHP
LJ-881	N32CM	LJ-964	N501GS	LJ-1047	6815	LJ-1130	N518TS	LJ-1213	wfu
LJ-882	PT-OOY	LJ-965	N205ST	LJ-1048	N900MT	LJ-1131	N811R	LJ-1214	N1553G
LJ-883	N984MA	LJ-966	w/o	LJ-1049	N7931D	LJ-1132	XC-AGS	LJ-1215	w/o
LJ-884	PT-OLQ	LJ-967	VT-EGR	LJ-1050	N6492C	LJ-1133	N77WM	LJ-1216	D-IEAH
LJ-885	N123LL	LJ-968	N277SW	LJ-1051	N111KA	LJ-1134	N303CA	LJ-1217	N1567G
LJ-886	C-GCFM	LJ-969	N77HE	LJ-1052	N6356C	LJ-1135	VT-EMI	LJ-1218	N224CC
LJ-887	N751KC	LJ-970	N121P	LJ-1053	ZS-LIN	LJ-1136	N902XP	LJ-1219	N523TH
LJ-888	N67511	LJ-971	N959GM	LJ-1054	N167BB	LJ-1137	VT-EMJ	LJ-1220	PT-OMZ
LJ-889	YV-O-CBL-!	LJ-972	HB-GJH	LJ-1055	N771PA	LJ-1138	D-ITCH	LJ-1221	N891AA
LJ-890	w/o	LJ-973	YV1607	LJ-1056	PT-LQE	LJ-1139	C-FGXG	LJ-1222	N322BR
LJ-891	N6754H	LJ-974	N55MN	LJ-1057	N47SW	LJ-1140	C-FGXU	LJ-1223	N191TP
LJ-892	HK-3277P	LJ-975	PT-OHH	LJ-1058	w/o	LJ-1141	JA8844	LJ-1224	F-GIDL
LJ-893	N16	LJ-976	6810	LJ-1059	PT-OZR	LJ-1142	JA8845	LJ-1225	PT-LLO
LJ-894	F-GCGA	LJ-977	D-IFHI	LJ-1060	6816	LJ-1143	JA8846	LJ-1226	F-GULM
LJ-895	N4449Q	LJ-978	OH-BEX	LJ-1061	6817	LJ-1144	JA8847	LJ-1227	P2-DRS
LJ-896	N17	LJ-979	5B-CJL	LJ-1062	6818	LJ-1145	JA8848	LJ-1228	N681EV
LJ-897	PT-LLV	LJ-980	6811	LJ-1063	PT-LSE	LJ-1146	6822	LJ-1229	N94MG
LJ-898	N898CM	LJ-981	w/o	LJ-1064	N6763K	LJ-1147	N475JA	LJ-1230	C-FGXT
LJ-899	N813JB	LJ-982	N102FK	LJ-1065	N722KR	LJ-1148	N8887B	LJ-1231	N358K
LJ-900	PT-OJU	LJ-983	N391BT	LJ-1066	F-	LJ-1149	JA8850	LJ-1232	N91KA
LJ-901	N93LP	LJ-984	OH-BAX	LJ-1067	N200TR	LJ-1150	JA8851	LJ-1233	PT-ORZ
LJ-902	N21	LJ-985	PT-OLW	LJ-1068	N613RF	LJ-1151	C-FGXX	LJ-1234	N1564W
LJ-903	N45SA	LJ-986	HC-...	LJ-1069	G-BMKD	LJ-1152	N252RC	LJ-1235	N92FC
LJ-904	N94HB	LJ-987	N722VB	LJ-1070	N210EC	LJ-1153	VT-EQO	LJ-1236	UN-
LJ-905	w/o	LJ-988	A2-DBH	LJ-1071	N68AJ	LJ-1154	N67CL	LJ-1237	PT-OTI
LJ-906	N925ES	LJ-989	N62300	LJ-1072	N6692D	LJ-1155	N32MT	LJ-1238	N947AM
LJ-907	N900WC	LJ-990	N1836H	LJ-1073	N120TT	LJ-1156	N817DP	LJ-1239	N5639K
LJ-908	N38TR	LJ-991	N19LW	LJ-1074	N923CR	LJ-1157	N85PH	LJ-1240	N691AS
LJ-909	N19	LJ-992	N305TT	LJ-1075	N120RP	LJ-1158	D-IHKM	LJ-1241	N5641X
LJ-910	N211PC	LJ-993	N81NA	LJ-1076	N86JG	LJ-1159	VT-AJV	LJ-1242	N88PD
LJ-911	N84TP	LJ-994	wfu	LJ-1077	D-IGKN	LJ-1160	N919CL	LJ-1243	N243JB

LJ-1244	N247MD	LJ-1327	D-IHHE	LJ-1410	N90CN	LJ-1493	N98WP	LJ-1576	N3246S
LJ-1245	PT-WAH	LJ-1328	F-GNEE	LJ-1411	N3218P	LJ-1494	PT-WKX	LJ-1577	PT-WQW
LJ-1246	N308MD	LJ-1329	YV1649	LJ-1412	N422PM	LJ-1495	N495TM	LJ-1578	PP-ETR
LJ-1247	D-IAAH	LJ-1330	N555VW	LJ-1413	N773SD	LJ-1496	VT-SFL	LJ-1579	N775D
LJ-1248	9302	LJ-1331	PT-WVI	LJ-1414	N344DP	LJ-1497	N2297C	LJ-1580	N32238
LJ-1249	9303	LJ-1332	N8259O	LJ-1415	N30CN	LJ-1498	PT-MVJ	LJ-1581	N326PT
LJ-1250	N938P	LJ-1333	N8156Z	LJ-1416	LV-WPB	LJ-1499	N440KA	LJ-1582	N46AE
LJ-1251	N87HB	LJ-1334	SX-BKY	LJ-1417	N387AS	LJ-1500	HP-1608	LJ-1583	D-IAVI
LJ-1252	N72TG	LJ-1335	6823	LJ-1418	w/o	LJ-1501	PT-XOU	LJ-1584	6828
LJ-1253	PT-WHA	LJ-1336	6824	LJ-1419	N257CQ	LJ-1502	N98KS	LJ-1585	N929FD
LJ-1254	N779VF	LJ-1337	6825	LJ-1420	N3220L	LJ-1503	N128SB	LJ-1586	VH-PFK
LJ-1255	N595TM	LJ-1338	6826	LJ-1421	N61GN	LJ-1504	N333BM	LJ-1587	N617MM
LJ-1256	N904HB	LJ-1339	6827	LJ-1422	N511KV	LJ-1505	N901PC	LJ-1588	N588SA
LJ-1257	N155A	LJ-1340	D-IIWB	LJ-1423	N4488L	LJ-1506	N54AM	LJ-1589	N439PW
LJ-1258	N111KC	LJ-1341	PT-OZL	LJ-1424	N665CF	LJ-1507	N202FG	LJ-1590	N13GZ
LJ-1259	N702DK	LJ-1342	C-FTPE	LJ-1425	N3223H	LJ-1508	N2178F	LJ-1591	N399MB
LJ-1260	PT-OSN	LJ-1343	N971SC	LJ-1426	N724KH	LJ-1509	N769GR	LJ-1592	6829
LJ-1261	N72GL	LJ-1344	N903P	LJ-1427	PT-WJD	LJ-1510	N2310K	LJ-1593	XB-AHK
LJ-1262	N700RF	LJ-1345	N43KM	LJ-1428	N370U	LJ-1511	PT-WUG	LJ-1594	w/o
LJ-1263	N927JT	LJ-1346	PT-WFN	LJ-1429	N96JF	LJ-1512	N38XJ	LJ-1595	N3195O
LJ-1264	PT-OFF	LJ-1347	N8210C	LJ-1430	wfu	LJ-1513	N878K	LJ-1596	6830
LJ-1265	N8001V	LJ-1348	UR-	LJ-1431	N1031Y	LJ-1514	N1114Z	LJ-1597	N597P
LJ-1266	N421HV	LJ-1349	N491JV	LJ-1432	N3263C	LJ-1515	N2315L	LJ-1598	N4298X
LJ-1267	N368RK	LJ-1350	VH-KQB	LJ-1433	N700SB	LJ-1516	N60VP	LJ-1599	N4368Y
LJ-1268	N555AL	LJ-1351	N424EM	LJ-1434	N313DW	LJ-1517	N90KS	LJ-1600	N477PT
LJ-1269	N8021P	LJ-1352	N426EM	LJ-1435	N16KW	LJ-1518	N982SB	LJ-1601	N801BS
LJ-1270	VT-SLK	LJ-1353	SU-ZAA	LJ-1436	N828FC	LJ-1519	N520JA	LJ-1602	N807RS
LJ-1271	N242NS	LJ-1354	LV-WJE	LJ-1437	N90PR	LJ-1520	N355CL	LJ-1603	N298D
LJ-1272	PR-SIA	LJ-1355	D-ISIX	LJ-1438	N389AS	LJ-1521	N2291F	LJ-1604	VT-REL
LJ-1273	YV-1000CP	LJ-1356	N8287E	LJ-1439	N1089L	LJ-1522	N98BK	LJ-1605	YV197T
LJ-1274	N513JM	LJ-1357	N1560T	LJ-1440	N1070F	LJ-1523	N982SS	LJ-1606	D-
LJ-1275	N275LA	LJ-1358	N94TK	LJ-1441	PR-TCA	LJ-1524	XA-TTR	LJ-1607	N73PG
LJ-1276	TC-MSS	LJ-1359	7T-WCF	LJ-1442	PP-EPS	LJ-1525	N88XJ	LJ-1608	PR-CCF
LJ-1277	N871KS	LJ-1360	S5-CMO	LJ-1443	N1083S	LJ-1526	LX-PRG	LJ-1609	N609SA
LJ-1278	VT-JPK	LJ-1361	F-HHAM	LJ-1444	N366NC	LJ-1527	N488XJ	LJ-1610	OY-LSA
LJ-1279	PR-AVT	LJ-1362	N990CB	LJ-1445	N90CH	LJ-1528	N20FD	LJ-1611	N322MR
LJ-1280	XA-RXT	LJ-1363	PT-WGU	LJ-1446	N446AS	LJ-1529	N66CK	LJ-1612	N724DR
LJ-1281	9304	LJ-1364	TG-EME	LJ-1447	N444LR	LJ-1530	N588XJ	LJ-1613	N549GA
LJ-1282	9305	LJ-1365	N1551C	LJ-1448	N1068K	LJ-1531	N150GW	LJ-1614	N614SA
LJ-1283	N700GM	LJ-1366	N1544V	LJ-1449	N825SD	LJ-1532	N2354Y	LJ-1615	N156MG
LJ-1284	OE-FHM	LJ-1367	ZK-MKG	LJ-1450	D-IWID	LJ-1533	XA-...	LJ-1616	N24DS
LJ-1285	SP-NEB	LJ-1368	N1568X	LJ-1451	N688LL	LJ-1534	N291DF	LJ-1617	LV-ARU
LJ-1286	N800PG	LJ-1369	VT-RLL	LJ-1452	N22FS	LJ-1535	N3035P	LJ-1618	PP-COP
LJ-1287	N718MB	LJ-1370	D-IHAH	LJ-1453	N25HB	LJ-1536	N3066W	LJ-1619	N67CO
LJ-1288	N27BM	LJ-1371	N34RF	LJ-1454	N1092H	LJ-1537	N299RP	LJ-1620	N543HC
LJ-1289	N522JP	LJ-1372	N454P	LJ-1455	N1848S	LJ-1538	PT-WZC	LJ-1621	N3221M
LJ-1290	JA8882	LJ-1373	TG-SAQ	LJ-1456	N1095W	LJ-1539	LX-PBL	LJ-1622	D-IDCV
LJ-1291	JA8883	LJ-1374	VH-EMJ	LJ-1457	N1057L	LJ-1540	N396AS	LJ-1623	XA-JAG
LJ-1292	JA8884	LJ-1375	N35HC	LJ-1458	N901TS	LJ-1541	N438CA	LJ-1624	XA-...
LJ-1293	N214P	LJ-1376	VT-HYA	LJ-1459	N902TS	LJ-1542	N330DB	LJ-1625	N5025R
LJ-1294	PT-WPN	LJ-1377	PT-WCS	LJ-1460	N800MK	LJ-1543	N3143T	LJ-1626	N1875C
LJ-1295	N191WB	LJ-1378	N555HJ	LJ-1461	N1076K	LJ-1544	N3068Z	LJ-1627	TI-...
LJ-1296	F-GLRZ	LJ-1379	7T-WCG	LJ-1462	N1079D	LJ-1545	N786RM	LJ-1628	PR-TIN
LJ-1297	N779DD	LJ-1380	7T-WCH	LJ-1463	N930MC	LJ-1546	PR-RFB	LJ-1629	N224JV
LJ-1298	N190SS	LJ-1381	N92BK	LJ-1464	VH-JET	LJ-1547	N399WS	LJ-1630	N5037W
LJ-1299	F-GNMA	LJ-1382	N96TH	LJ-1465	N1102K	LJ-1548	N990TF	LJ-1631	N86LD
LJ-1300	N920TT	LJ-1383	N118MF	LJ-1466	LV-WXC	LJ-1549	XB-HMI	LJ-1632	N928K
LJ-1301	N924TT	LJ-1384	N3196K	LJ-1467	N1130J	LJ-1550	N993CB	LJ-1633	N266RD
LJ-1302	N322TC	LJ-1385	PT-WRA	LJ-1468	TI-AZI	LJ-1551	D-INAS	LJ-1634	6831
LJ-1303	F-GMPM	LJ-1386	PT-WJF	LJ-1469	N97KA	LJ-1552	LQ-ZRB	LJ-1635	N771PD
LJ-1304	N465JB	LJ-1387	N500EQ	LJ-1470	N529JM	LJ-1553	N147TA	LJ-1636	6832
LJ-1305	C-GPNB	LJ-1388	YV-....	LJ-1471	PT-FCM	LJ-1554	N90RK	LJ-1637	N915MR
LJ-1306	N65CL	LJ-1389	N200U	LJ-1472	N100JD	LJ-1555	PT-PAC	LJ-1638	6833
LJ-1307	w/o	LJ-1390	N75PG	LJ-1473	PT-XHP	LJ-1556	CC-CVT	LJ-1639	PR-XIB
LJ-1308	PT-ORG	LJ-1391	F-GPLK	LJ-1474	N478CR	LJ-1557	N540GA	LJ-1640	N40XJ
LJ-1309	N709EA	LJ-1392	N3216K	LJ-1475	N1103G	LJ-1558	N543GA	LJ-1641	N770VF
LJ-1310	N463JB	LJ-1393	VT-TIS	LJ-1476	P4-SSI	LJ-1559	N547GA	LJ-1642	N4392K
LJ-1311	PR-MZP	LJ-1394	PT-WIT	LJ-1477	N1107W	LJ-1560	VT-RSL	LJ-1643	N643EA
LJ-1312	N640DF	LJ-1395	LV-WMG	LJ-1478	N200HV	LJ-1561	N100SM	LJ-1644	PR-MLZ
LJ-1313	N928TT	LJ-1396	PT-WIH	LJ-1479	XA-YAS	LJ-1562	N3262R	LJ-1645	N7736M
LJ-1314	N198PP	LJ-1397	N3216U	LJ-1480	N902LT	LJ-1563	N3263N	LJ-1646	PP-BAF
LJ-1315	D-IHSW	LJ-1398	N441CG	LJ-1481	N110PM	LJ-1564	PT-MJQ	LJ-1647	N778DB
LJ-1316	w/o	LJ-1399	TG-BAQ	LJ-1482	N3035T	LJ-1565	ZS-LEE	LJ-1648	HP-1500
LJ-1317	N929TT	LJ-1400	VT-UPZ	LJ-1483	N1126J	LJ-1566	N988XJ	LJ-1649	N490W
LJ-1318	N17KK	LJ-1401	YV-660CP	LJ-1484	N24YC	LJ-1567	JA01KA	LJ-1650	N831E
LJ-1319	N719EA	LJ-1402	VT-NKF	LJ-1485	VT-JRD	LJ-1568	N568SA	LJ-1651	N70VR
LJ-1320	N572BB	LJ-1403	N424MF	LJ-1486	N1110K	LJ-1569	PT-XOV	LJ-1652	N722JB
LJ-1321	w/o	LJ-1404	VT-DEJ	LJ-1487	N970P	LJ-1570	N300AW	LJ-1653	XA-MSC
LJ-1322	N530CH	LJ-1405	N59MS	LJ-1488	N1135G	LJ-1571	D-IDIX	LJ-1654	N545C
LJ-1323	D-IUDE	LJ-1406	N207P	LJ-1489	LV-YBP	LJ-1572	N931GG	LJ-1655	N387GC
LJ-1324	D-IKIM	LJ-1407	N789WA	LJ-1490	N197SC	LJ-1573	VT-JIL	LJ-1656	N447DB
LJ-1325	D-IHMV	LJ-1408	N587PB	LJ-1491	PT-WTU	LJ-1574	N406RL	LJ-1657	N777YN
LJ-1326	N8096U	LJ-1409	F-GKSP	LJ-1492	ZS-TKB	LJ-1575	N395AS	LJ-1658	N4YF

Serial	Reg	Serial	Reg	Serial	Reg	Serial	Reg	Serial	Reg
LJ-1659	YV218T	LJ-1742	PR-MFG	LJ-1825	PR-DHD	LM-31	N32P	LM-134	N7181H
LJ-1660	F-GTCR	LJ-1743	PR-IRB	LJ-1826	PR-CAR*	LM-32	N64C	LM-135	N7181J
LJ-1661	N199CG	LJ-1744	C-FMFR	LJ-1827	PR-BTS	LM-33	N84G	LM-136	N410SP
LJ-1662	N788KC	LJ-1745	C-FMFS	LJ-1828	YV	LM-34	N65JA	LM-137	N97D
LJ-1663	HP-	LJ-1746	C-FMFU	LJ-1829	XA-	LM-35	N7043D	LM-138	N418SP
LJ-1664	N789KP	LJ-1747	C-FMFX	LJ-1830	N790RV	LM-37	w/o	LM-139	N7193M
LJ-1665	N289RP	LJ-1748	N405DD	LJ-1831	N618HG	LM-38	N7043N	LM-140	N906HF
LJ-1666	N867P	LJ-1749	C-FMFY	LJ-1832	N7282X	LM-39	N541MC	LM-141	N7198B
LJ-1667	N5067L	LJ-1750	C-FMFZ	LJ-1833	D-IMAG	LM-41	N7047D	King Air E90	
LJ-1668	N990DW	LJ-1751	VT-SSL	LJ-1834	N3734Y	LM-43	N70503	LW-1	N190RM
LJ-1669	N126MM	LJ-1752	VT-EBG	LJ-1835	CC-CGS	LM-44	N7051K	LW-2	N100MW
LJ-1670	N70CM	LJ-1753	XA-...	LJ-1836	N793P	LM-45	N7052X	LW-3	F-GJAD
LJ-1671	N4471M	LJ-1754	N247CH	LJ-1837	N7277F	LM-47	N7052Y	LW-4	N77WF
LJ-1672	PR-EDP	LJ-1755	N97DA	LJ-1838	N838GT	LM-48	N37H	LW-5	N999SF
LJ-1673	N5431M	LJ-1756	N741JP	LJ-1839	N72709	LM-49	N7062W	LW-6	N905TF
LJ-1674	PR-FAZ	LJ-1757	N106ML	LJ-1840	N73920	LM-50	N7063D	LW-7	N51DN
LJ-1675	N4415F	LJ-1758	XA-CPR	LJ-1841	PR-JME	LM-51	N70U	LW-8	N132HS
LJ-1676	PP-WCA	LJ-1759	N590GT	LJ-1842	XA-	LM-52	N7064Q	LW-9	PT-IGD
LJ-1677	N6077X	LJ-1760	D-IBSG	LJ-1843	N843KA	LM-53	N70648	LW-10	N977SB
LJ-1678	N57WR	LJ-1761	N790GT	LJ-1844	PR-JCA	LM-54	N7066X	LW-11	N11DT
LJ-1679	PR-USA	LJ-1762	N599HL	LJ-1845	D-IHRG	LM-55	N7067S	LW-12	N12GJ
LJ-1680	N904TH	LJ-1763	PR-BOM	LJ-1846	PR-XGT	LM-56	N7069F	LW-13	N383AA
LJ-1681	N954BS	LJ-1764	N904JG	LJ-1847	N31947	LM-57	N75N	LW-14	XA-...
LJ-1682	N21LE	LJ-1765	N64GT	LJ-1848	N771JB	LM-58	N7071H	LW-15	w/o
LJ-1683	N683GW	LJ-1766	N74B	LJ-1849	N407CF	LM-59	N67B	LW-16	N43WS
LJ-1684	PR-JQM	LJ-1767	N6197V	LJ-1850	N527SE	LM-60	N87Q	LW-17	N259SC
LJ-1685	N1685S	LJ-1768	N990GT	LJ-1851	N851HB	LM-61	N7201S	LW-18	N22ER
LJ-1686	N272EA	LJ-1769	N36799	LJ-1852	N852HB	LM-64	TZ-ZBE	LW-19	w/o
LJ-1687	N437JB	LJ-1770	PR-SDA	LJ-1853	N34003	LM-67	N7078J	LW-20	N87CH
LJ-1688	N629JG	LJ-1771	PR-JAG	LJ-1854	N890LG	LM-68	N66W	LW-21	N121B
LJ-1689	N557P	LJ-1772	PP-AMJ	LJ-1855	N88DW	LM-69	N7078L	LW-22	wfu
LJ-1690	JA....	LJ-1773	N37093	LJ-1856	N271AK	LM-70	N7079S	LW-23	N345V
LJ-1691	N991SA	LJ-1774	N31JN	LJ-1857	N826TM	LM-72	N7081L	LW-24	N95LB
LJ-1692	N692W	LJ-1775	N508GT	LJ-1858	N623DT	LM-73	N70841	LW-25	N1100M
LJ-1693	PR-RMA	LJ-1776	N15UB	LJ-1859	N158J	LM-74	N62V	LW-26	00923
LJ-1694	N694CT	LJ-1777	N386TH	LJ-1860	N46MJ	LM-75	N70876	LW-27	N379VM
LJ-1695	N124LL	LJ-1778	N71878	LJ-1861	N31861	LM-76	N70879	LW-28	FAB 042
LJ-1696	VT-KPC	LJ-1779	N541RK	LJ-1862	N80KA	LM-77	N7089O	LW-29	w/o
LJ-1697	N461EP	LJ-1780	N51CT	LJ-1863	N599MC	LM-78	N78D	LW-30	N20WS
LJ-1698	N61698	LJ-1781	N781GT	LJ-1865	D-ITDK	LM-79	N80Y	LW-31	N90WT
LJ-1699	N456PP	LJ-1782	N155RG	LJ-1866	N33226	LM-80	N518NA	LW-32	N291MM
LJ-1700	N550SW	LJ-1783	N333TK	LJ-1869	N31869	LM-82	wfu	LW-33	XC-FUY
LJ-1701	PR-FKY	LJ-1784	PR-PIB	LJ-1871	N588KM	LM-83	N7092K	LW-34	N690G
LJ-1702	N6190S	LJ-1785	N73415	LJ-1876	PR-LMT	LM-84	N70926	LW-35	N14NM
LJ-1703	N707PC	LJ-1786	N7086V	King Air 90/C90/C90GT		LM-86	N70950	LW-36	PNP-230
LJ-1704	N50PD	LJ-1787	YV	LU-1	N7198S	LM-87	N65U	LW-37	w/o
LJ-1705	N5115H	LJ-1788	N36888	LU-2	N7198Y	LM-88	N7112T	LW-38	w/o
LJ-1706	N648JG	LJ-1789	N417SH	LU-3	N71982	LM-89	N41J	LW-39	HK-3907
LJ-1707	N495Y	LJ-1790	N125AR	LU-4	N94N	LM-90	N7120P	LW-40	N523CJ
LJ-1708	N170S	LJ-1791	N7191N	LU-5	N92S	LM-92	N61Q	LW-41	w/o
LJ-1709	N426HM	LJ-1792	N904PA	LU-6	N7199D	LM-93	N7126U	LW-42	N52KA
LJ-1710	N785JP	LJ-1793	N825P	LU-7	N7199H	LM-94	N7128H	LW-43	N600CX
LJ-1711	N6111V	LJ-1794	PR-SGB	LU-8	N7199J	LM-95	N7132Z	LW-44	N666DC
LJ-1712	N999NH	LJ-1795	N90GP	LU-9	N7199L	LM-96	N71347	LW-45	N200RM
LJ-1713	N888GD	LJ-1796	PR-DIN	LU-10	N7199N	LM-97	N71351	LW-46	wfu
LJ-1714	N422AS	LJ-1797	N427SE	LU-11	N7199S	LM-98	N903MD	LW-47	F-ASFA
LJ-1715	PR-CMI	LJ-1798	N37198	LU-12	N71992	LM-99	N7137G	LW-48	N22N
LJ-1716	D-IBBP	LJ-1799	N70189	LU-13	N96S	LM-100	N7201Z	LW-49	N12LA
LJ-1717	PR-RHH	LJ-1800	N37200	LU-15	N91S	LM-101	N7139Z	LW-50	N150TW
LJ-1718	PH-KBB	LJ-1801	HL5200	King Air A90		LM-103	N75V	LW-51	N779AF
LJ-1719	N304TC	LJ-1802	ZS-TWP	LM-1	N7000B	LM-104	N7146X	LW-52	N181Z
LJ-1720	N22HD	LJ-1803	PR-BIO	LM-2	N7007G	LM-105	N38F	LW-53	w/o
LJ-1721	N145AF	LJ-1804	N804GT	LM-5	N87E	LM-106	N39Q	LW-54	N77JX
LJ-1722	N37222	LJ-1805	N991GT	LM-6	N70088	LM-107	N7155P	LW-55	N3929G
LJ-1723	N546C	LJ-1806	N963P	LM-7	N7010L	LM-112	N7155S	LW-56	wfu
LJ-1724	N79PE	LJ-1807	PR-CEB	LM-8	N85Z	LM-113	N65V	LW-57	N88TR
LJ-1725	PR-AGV	LJ-1808	N730EZ	LM-9	N7014L	LM-115	N7157K	LW-58	N625PP
LJ-1726	N901JS	LJ-1809	9M-JPL	LM-10	N611ND	LM-116	N71581	LW-59	N290KA
LJ-1727	PP-AMC	LJ-1810	VT-SKM	LM-11	N7018F	LM-118	N71597	LW-60	N90PH
LJ-1728	N58GG	LJ-1811	N22CR	LM-13	N67X	LM-119	N7165J	LW-61	N129C
LJ-1729	N36929	LJ-1812	C-FPLZ	LM-14	N76Q	LM-120	N7165Y	LW-62	N26E
LJ-1730	LV-BDG	LJ-1813	N826P	LM-15	XA-TJD	LM-122	N7169U	LW-63	N93A
LJ-1731	N35HD	LJ-1814	C-FJTN	LM-16	N70264	LM-123	N7169Z	LW-64	w/o
LJ-1732	N52BG	LJ-1815	XA-	LM-17	N70292	LM-124	N89F	LW-65	N987GM
LJ-1733	M-OTOR	LJ-1816	N995GT	LM-19	N72L	LM-125	N95S	LW-66	N554CF
LJ-1734	N59GG	LJ-1817	N610SC	LM-21	N80R	LM-126	OO-SAD	LW-67	w/o
LJ-1735	ZS-FON	LJ-1818	N178EJ	LM-22	N3634K	LM-127	N7173K	LW-68	wfu
LJ-1736	N164WS	LJ-1819	LV-BIC	LM-24	N67K	LM-128	N93J	LW-69	N5462G
LJ-1737	N619SH	LJ-1820	N722PM	LM-25	N70356	LM-129	N99G	LW-70	LV-WZR
LJ-1738	N106DD	LJ-1821	PR-GFB	LM-26	N7036L	LM-130	N87V	LW-71	N121EG
LJ-1739	PR-ARC	LJ-1822	TG-	LM-28	N7038Y	LM-131	N71797	LW-72	N81HP
LJ-1740	C-FMFQ	LJ-1823	PT-MBF	LM-30	N7039T	LM-132	N7181E	LW-73	N111WA
LJ-1741	XA-RFH	LJ-1824	N884EA			LM-133	N94S	LW-74	N717PP

LW-75	N75LW	LW-158	N75JP	LW-241	N30KC	LW-324	N351GR	LA-59	N146FL
LW-76	N176TW	LW-159	N9059S	LW-242	N963KA	LW-325	RP-C291	LA-60	YV-
LW-77	w/o	LW-160	N53CE	LW-243	N18343	LW-326	TN-AFG	LA-61	N189JR
LW-78	N15WN	LW-161	F-BXON	LW-244	N611R	LW-327	N788SW	LA-62	F-GIFK
LW-79	N60BA	LW-162	w/o	LW-245	N3LS	LW-328	F-GJPD	LA-63	ZS-LTD
LW-80	N522MJ	LW-163	N34MF	LW-246	N711HV	LW-329	N652L	LA-64	N322GK
LW-81	wfu	LW-164	N200RE	LW-247	w/o	LW-330	LV-OBB	LA-65	N867MA
LW-82	N820RD	LW-165	N701X	LW-248	N555FW	LW-331	N54PT	LA-66	N90TP
LW-83	w/o	LW-166	w/o	LW-249	N521LB	LW-332	C-FJWU	LA-67	N416P
LW-84	N111JA	LW-167	N199PL	LW-250	TI-BBN	LW-333	XB-JLA	LA-68	N77PV
LW-85	N42PC	LW-168	N23EW	LW-251	F-GJCR	LW-334	N22TL	LA-69	ZS-KLZ
LW-86	F-GFDJ	LW-169	ZS-IAN	LW-252	N30CV	LW-335	w/o	LA-70	N119FJ
LW-87	V5-MED	LW-170	XB-JCT	LW-253	N43PC	LW-336	N21NM	LA-71	N600WA
LW-88	N29M	LW-171	N6571S	LW-254	N48W	LW-337	N290K	LA-72	N770SD
LW-89	N98HF	LW-172	YV-326P	LW-255	w/o	LW-338	N199DW	LA-73	N81GC
LW-90	HK-....	LW-173	N707TL	LW-256	N63BV	LW-339	N339KA	LA-74	N79EC
LW-91	w/o	LW-174	w/o	LW-257	N77CE	LW-340	N3700M	LA-75	N600WM
LW-92	w/o	LW-175	F-HAAA	LW-258	N203PC	LW-341	N341MH	LA-76	TI-AWM
LW-93	N352GR	LW-176	N662JS	LW-259	LV-WHV	LW-342	N90XS	LA-77	N277SP
LW-94	YV-467CP	LW-177	N944RS	LW-260	GN-7839	LW-343	PT-OUF	LA-78	PT-WET
LW-95	N567GJ	LW-178	HC-DAC	LW-261	ZP-TZW	LW-344	N999SE	LA-79	N2164L
LW-96	N214SC	LW-179	N676J	LW-262	N790RB	LW-345	N336JM	LA-80	w/o
LW-97	F-GESJ	LW-180	w/o	LW-263	N1840S	LW-346	N114WA	LA-81	C-FCDF
LW-98	w/o	LW-181	w/o	LW-264	ARV-0201	LW-347	PT-LCE	LA-82	N501DU
LW-99	N31WP	LW-182	w/o	LW-265	N362D	*King Air F90*		LA-83	N994ST
LW-100	N28MS	LW-183	HK-2491	LW-266	N702XP	LA-1	wfu	LA-84	HK-...
LW-101	N211CG	LW-184	N314MR	LW-267	N20S	LA-2	N49CH	LA-85	PT-ODN
LW-102	w/o	LW-185	N600AC	LW-268	N210YS	LA-3	N1MA	LA-86	N242LF
LW-103	N898WW	LW-186	N2186L	LW-269	N288CR	LA-4	HB-GJQ	LA-87	N696RA
LW-104	N123MH	LW-187	N816RL	LW-270	YV-1500P	LA-5	N901PS	LA-88	N6VJ
LW-105	N111FV	LW-188	N428V	LW-271	N727MT	LA-6	N111AA	LA-89	LV-ZPY
LW-106	w/o	LW-189	YV-O-SATA	LW-272	w/o	LA-7	PT-LLP	LA-90	N236JS
LW-107	N44MV	LW-190	RP-C415	LW-273	N273NA	LA-8	w/o	LA-91	N333WT
LW-108	N37HC	LW-191	N258JC	LW-274	N274KA	LA-9	N300TA	LA-92	PT-ONO
LW-109	N989GM	LW-192	N2192L	LW-275	N47BH	LA-10	N325WR	LA-93	w/o
LW-110	9Q-CCG	LW-193	N46RP	LW-276	N7TD	LA-11	PT-LXI	LA-94	PT-LSH
LW-111	wfu	LW-194	N117FH	LW-277	RP-C292	LA-12	N19RK	LA-95	XA-SAW
LW-112	N67PS	LW-195	wfu	LW-278	F-GHUV	LA-13	N911CF	LA-96	N47TE
LW-113	w/o	LW-196	N3818C	LW-279	N390PS	LA-14	N581RJ	LA-97	N114CW
LW-114	N700DH	LW-197	N533SS	LW-280	w/o	LA-15	N124BK	LA-98	N103CB
LW-115	N76SK	LW-198	N46BM	LW-281	N31A	LA-16	YV-1013P	LA-99	N803HC
LW-116	9J-STA	LW-199	F-GALZ	LW-282	N900AC	LA-17	N117TJ	LA-100	OO-IAL
LW-117	N10XJ	LW-200	N918VS	LW-283	N48TA	LA-18	N84JL	LA-101	N37990
LW-118	N8118R	LW-201	w/o	LW-284	ZP-TJW	LA-19	F-GETI	LA-102	N429DM
LW-119	N152D	LW-202	N65MS	LW-285	N777KA	LA-20	N810CM	LA-103	PT-LTT
LW-120	N99AC	LW-203	N203RD	LW-286	N155LS	LA-21	N66LP	LA-104	N90NA
LW-121	N515BC	LW-204	N965LG	LW-287	C-FNCB	LA-22	F-GHIV	LA-105	C-GVLH
LW-122	w/o	LW-205	Z-AHL	LW-288	N700DD	LA-23	N16BM	LA-106	N173PL
LW-123	N500MS	LW-206	N290MC	LW-289	N83WE	LA-24	N93KA	LA-107	PT
LW-124	N90BF	LW-207	w/o	LW-290	N60MH	LA-25	N128JP	LA-108	N411RJ
LW-125	N504CB	LW-208	YV-706P	LW-291	N824AC	LA-26	N96TT	LA-109	PT-LYZ
LW-126	N103AP	LW-209	N282DB	LW-292	N92DV	LA-27	N246CA	LA-110	N3824V
LW-127	N71WB	LW-210	N860MH	LW-293	N12AX	LA-28	PT-LPL	LA-111	N138RB
LW-128	N50EB	LW-211	N4216S	LW-294	N677J	LA-29	wfu	LA-112	N3809C
LW-129	LV-WFP	LW-212	w/o	LW-295	w/o	LA-30	N199BC	LA-113	C-GKSC
LW-130	N47AW	LW-213	N2274L	LW-296	F-GETJ	LA-31	N960V	LA-114	w/o
LW-131	N98PM	LW-214	N14SB	LW-297	PH-AXS	LA-32	N123CH	LA-115	F-GCTR
LW-132	N9029R	LW-215	N56HT	LW-298	N44GK	LA-33	N49PH	LA-116	N197AS
LW-133	PT-LHZ	LW-216	N439WA	LW-299	N127EC	LA-34	N57TM	LA-117	N120RC
LW-134	N55HC	LW-217	N16LH	LW-300	N911AZ	LA-35	YV-290CP	LA-118	PT-OFD
LW-135	LV-AYG	LW-218	N406SF	LW-301	N618RD	LA-36	N102WK	LA-119	N800BK
LW-136	G-ORTH	LW-219	N83FE	LW-302	RP-C298	LA-37	N30GT	LA-120	ZS-PGW
LW-137	w/o	LW-220	wfu	LW-303	N79CT	LA-38	N65MT	LA-121	N182CA
LW-138	PT-WAG	LW-221	N48VZ	LW-304	F-GMRN	LA-39	N454GC	LA-122	ZS-LBC
LW-139	N249WM	LW-222	ZS-NYE	LW-305	N111TC	LA-40	N66BS	LA-123	N513KL
LW-140	N1UC	LW-223	N333LE	LW-306	N67V	LA-41	wfu	LA-124	w/o
LW-141	N382TW	LW-224	ZS-NXI	LW-307	w/o	LA-42	N190FD	LA-125	N145MR
LW-142	N7WU	LW-225	N181CG	LW-308	N132DD	LA-43	XA-...	LA-126	PT-LYP
LW-143	N300MT	LW-226	w/o	LW-309	LN-ACY	LA-44	XA-TMP	LA-127	N812CP
LW-144	N812KB	LW-227	N901TM	LW-310	N10WG	LA-45	XA-LGT	LA-128	PT-ONU
LW-145	RP-C879	LW-228	N692M	LW-311	N282TC	LA-46	N208RC	LA-129	N605EA
LW-146	N41HH	LW-229	EV-7702	LW-312	N510ME	LA-47	ZS-MHM	LA-130	N402BL
LW-147	N28M	LW-230	N23W	LW-313	w/o	LA-48	N30NH	LA-131	N210AJ
LW-148	N80BT	LW-231	N304LG	LW-314	CP-	LA-49	PT-OIF	LA-132	PT-LQC
LW-149	N177MK	LW-232	N448CP	LW-315	N888ZT	LA-50	HB-GHD	LA-133	N31TL
LW-150	N100EC	LW-233	w/o	LW-316	OO-VHV	LA-51	ZS-NFO	LA-134	N90BD
LW-151	ZS-OAE	LW-234	YV1465	LW-317	N703LW	LA-52	N769D	LA-135	N422Z
LW-152	wfu	LW-235	N776DC	LW-318	N443CL	LA-53	N5AH	LA-136	RP-C410
LW-153	CC-DSN	LW-236	w/o	LW-319	N1205S	LA-54	N540WJ	LA-137	N488FT
LW-154	GN-7593	LW-237	N17NM	LW-320	N366GW	LA-55	N311GC	LA-138	N15
LW-155	N505MW	LW-238	N4107W	LW-321	TJ-MJP	LA-56	N68DK	LA-139	N94JD
LW-156	N414GN	LW-239	N25EN	LW-322	YV-516CP	LA-57	w/o	LA-140	N607DK
LW-157	N199TT	LW-240	TI-AZO	LW-323	N323HA	LA-58	N59EK	LA-141	F-GDAK

LA-142	N50AW	LA-225	PT-OFS	B-71	N431R	B-154	C-FONY	B-238	N1TR
LA-143	N69AD	LA-226	N16WG	B-72	C-FRKB	B-155	YV-O-SID-2	B-239	C-FSKA
LA-144	PT-ONE	LA-227	D-ISTB	B-73	YV-04CP	B-156	C-GDPI	B-240	N87CA
LA-145	N18	LA-228	PP-CSE	B-74	N74JV	B-157	C-GUPP	B-241	N777GS
LA-146	N90RT	LA-229	D-IRIS	B-75	N75LA	B-158	XA-...	B-242	IGM-240
LA-147	XA-TWB	LA-230	N111EN	B-76	C-GWWO	B-159	C-GLPG	B-243	C-FLRD
LA-148	PT-LER	LA-231	N78FB	B-77	RP-C1978	B-160	N896SB	B-244	N842DS
LA-149	N44PA	LA-232	PT-ASN	B-78	N626SA	B-161	YV1257	B-245	w/o
LA-150	N80M	LA-233	w/o	B-79	CC-CLY	B-162	N224LB	B-246	N955SA
LA-151	HK-3935W	LA-234	N7206E	B-80	YV2010	B-163	C-FASB	B-247	wfu
LA-152	N89CA	LA-235	N77WW	B-81	N707SS	B-164	C-FGIN	King Air B100	
LA-153	w/o	LA-236	N957JF	B-82	LV-WDO	B-165	C-FDJX	BE-1	wfu
LA-154	N90SB	King Air 100		B-83	YV2129	B-166	C-FAMU	BE-2	N729MS
LA-155	PT-OUJ	B-1	N3100K	B-84	wfu	B-167	w/o	BE-3	N150TJ
LA-156	PT-LTO	B-2	N211VP	B-85	C-GKBZ	B-168	N715WA	BE-4	N786CB
LA-157	N69084	B-3	C-FIDN	B-86	N53MD	B-169	C-FAPP	BE-5	N220AA
LA-158	N580PA	B-4	XB-WUI	B-87	N70JL	B-170	XB-RGG	BE-6	N24EM
LA-159	N222AG	B-5	N288RA	B-88	C-GJSU	B-171	N720C	BE-7	C-GVIK
LA-160	ZS-ALD	B-6	N122ZZ	B-89	C-FWYF	B-172	C-GIZX	BE-8	N45LU
LA-161	N18471	B-7	PT-OOP	B-90	N515AS	B-173	HP-1336AP	BE-9	N236CP
LA-162	PT-OOX	B-8	C-FDAM	B-91	F-GHHV	B-174	C-FTMA	BE-10	w/o
LA-163	N85PJ	B-9	ZS-PBH	B-92	w/o	B-175	C-GJHW	BE-11	N78DA
LA-164	N990F	B-10	w/o	B-93	7T-VCV	B-176	N3076W	BE-12	N400AC
LA-165	N300DM	B-11	N100KA	B-94	N945WS	B-177	w/o	BE-13	N93SF
LA-166	F-GFVN	B-12	w/o	B-95	70-15908	B-178	C-FNIF	BE-14	N68DA
LA-167	N1857F	B-13	w/o	B-96	C-FCAK	B-179	N127Z	BE-15	C-GDFJ
LA-168	XA-...	B-14	C-GJKS	B-97	N997RC	B-180	w/o	BE-16	C-FJDQ
LA-169	N61228	B-15	w/o	B-98	C-GHYT	B-181	CNA-NB	BE-17	C-FASN
LA-170	N314P	B-16	YV1486	B-99	N324EC	B-182	CNA-NC	BE-18	N700TF
LA-171	N46JX	B-17	N951K	B-100	C-GJBV	B-183	CNA-ND	BE-19	YV-95CP
LA-172	wfu	B-18	N503AB	B-101	N13K	B-184	C-FGNL	BE-20	N443TC
LA-173	PT-OHZ	B-19	w/o	B-102	N799DD	B-185	N220KW	BE-21	N60TJ
LA-174	YV1693	B-20	N195MA	B-103	C-FDOR	B-186	CNA-NE	BE-22	N213RJ*
LA-175	PT-OZP	B-21	N411HA	B-104	C-GAIK	B-187	CNA-NF	BE-23	N93D
LA-176	N517AB	B-22	N577D	B-105	9Q-CEM	B-188	w/o	BE-24	N234TK
LA-177	N127DC	B-23	C-GNCV	B-106	C-FDOS	B-189	w/o	BE-25	N125VH
LA-178	N178LA	B-24	C-GNAA	B-107	C-GNAJ	B-190	w/o	BE-26	C-GPRU
LA-179	YV-886CP	B-25	N136JH	B-108	w/o	B-191	C-GJBQ	BE-27	C-FIDC
LA-180	N357CC	B-26	N696JB	B-109	wfu	B-192	wfu	BE-28	YV2226
LA-181	TG-CFA	B-27	C-GWWA	B-110	XC-FIW	B-193	C-FAIP	BE-29	D-IDPL
LA-182	N424CP	B-28	C-FWYO	B-111	w/o	B-194	C-GHOC	BE-30	N111YF
LA-183	N90TD	B-29	wfu	B-112	C-FDOU	B-195	EC-CHE	BE-31	C-FAFS
LA-184	C-FCLH	B-30	N3606T	B-113	w/o	B-196	wfu	BE-32	N493DT
LA-185	PT-LYM	B-31	N711GM	B-114	N1347Z	B-197	JW9027	BE-33	N900RD
LA-186	XB-JRF	B-32	N122U	B-115	wfu	B-198	wfu	BE-34	N949SW
LA-187	PT-OTA	B-33	9Q-CRF	B-116	N601LM	B-199	F-GEXV	BE-35	N821CB
LA-188	N41AK	B-34	N2225H	B-117	C-FDOV	B-200	PT-LZA	BE-36	wfu
LA-189	N555TZ	B-35	C-GTLS	B-118	N18AH	B-201	C-GAVI	BE-37	N68MU
LA-190	N6335F	B-36	C-GXRX	B-119	w/o	B-202	N919JP	BE-38	w/o
LA-191	HK-4...	B-37	wfu	B-120	C-FDOY	B-203	w/o	BE-39	C-FSIK
LA-192	D-ITLL	B-38	C-FOOV	B-121	PT-LJN	B-204	C-FBGS	BE-40	N24203
LA-193	XA-...	B-39	wfu	B-122	C-FXAJ	B-206	C-FEYP	BE-41	N17792
LA-194	N27SE	B-40	C-FMXY	B-123	C-GJJF	B-207	C-FHGG	BE-42	N87NW
LA-195	PT-LXY	B-41	C-FAXE	B-124	w/o	B-208	N208SR	BE-43	N487JH
LA-196	N766RB	B-42	C-FAFD	B-125	C-FWRM	B-209	YV	BE-44	C-FPBC
LA-197	PT-LSP	B-43	PT-DKV	B-126	C-GASI	B-210	C-FEYT	BE-45	PT-WPV
LA-198	N198FM	B-44	N440SM	B-127	N710AS	B-211	C-GNEX	BE-46	N988JR
LA-199	N118MJ	B-45	C-GPCB	B-128	w/o	B-212	N15L	BE-47	N49E
LA-200	PT-OFB	B-46	N770RL	B-129	wfu	B-213	LN-AWA	BE-48	N2830S
LA-201	N955RA	B-47	C-FWYN	B-130	N467BW	B-214	YV1239	BE-49	C-GGKJ
LA-202	N840SB	B-48	N5727	B-131	C-FLRB	B-215	C-GPBA	BE-50	N136MB
LA-203	N399TW	B-49	w/o	B-132	C-FAIO	B-216	N28C	BE-51	N100TW
LA-204	N75MS	B-50	w/o	B-133	N22BJ	B-217	LN-AWB	BE-52	N771CW
LA-205	N205SM	B-51	C-FWPN	B-134	w/o	B-218	w/o	BE-53	N53TD
LA-206	N131SP	B-52	wfu	B-135	w/o	B-219	331	BE-54	N241CW
LA-207	YV-622CP	B-53	N153JA	B-136	YV1838	B-220	w/o	BE-55	N813BL
LA-208	N999RC	B-54	wfu	B-137	N629SC	B-221	w/o	BE-56	N98TA
LA-209	N444KK	B-55	N911RL	B-138	wfu	B-222	N232AL	BE-57	N75AP
LA-210	N415HS	B-56	PT-DNP	B-139	N247B	B-223	N223LH	BE-58	N564CA
LA-211	N808TC	B-57	ZS-OUS	B-140	w/o	B-224	C-FPLG	BE-59	C-FODC
LA-212	A2-AHV	B-58	N750FC	B-141	w/o	B-225	N601PC	BE-60	N650JT
LA-213	PT-ODO	B-59	C-FMWM	B-142	PP-FOY	B-226	N91RK	BE-61	YV1159
LA-214	N773	B-60	N54JW	B-143	C-GZUZ	B-227	C-	BE-62	N350TC
LA-215	PT-LUT	B-61	C-GSYN	B-144	N999G	B-228	F-GKEL	BE-63	N27CS
LA-216	PT-LZT	B-62	C-GKBQ	B-145	wfu	B-229	C-GMAG	BE-64	N4490M
LA-217	PT-OCE	B-63	C-FHKB	B-146	N200AJ	B-230	N1362N	BE-65	N6045S
LA-218	N299KP	B-64	N4200A	B-147	7T-VRF	B-231	YV-....	BE-66	N37PC
LA-219	N18CM	B-65	N102LF	B-148	C-GJLP	B-232	C-GKAJ	BE-67	N4415L
LA-220	PT-OLP	B-66	N525ZS	B-149	C-FLTS	B-233	N711RE	BE-68	N66820
LA-221	HK-3505	B-67	C-FWPG	B-150	F-GGLV	B-234	N23404	BE-69	N794CE
LA-222	N711L	B-68	XB-REA	B-151	C-FPAJ	B-235	C-GJLJ	BE-70	N120MG
LA-223	PT-LIF	B-69	N207SB	B-152	C-GISH	B-236	N23605	BE-71	wfu
LA-224	N991GC	B-70	N77PF	B-153	C-GYQK	B-237	YV1306	BE-72	C-FAFE

Serial	Reg	Serial	Reg	Serial	Reg	Serial	Reg	Serial	Reg
BE-73	w/o	BB-18	N846CM	BB-101	D2-EXW	BB-184	7T-WRG	BB-269	D-IICE
BE-74	N88FA	BB-19	w/o	BB-102	N200AF	BB-185	N503F	BB-271	N131TC
BE-75	w/o	BB-20	OB-1509	BB-103	N201CH	BB-187	C-GMRS	BB-272	N241CK
BE-76	N301TS	BB-21	wfu	BB-104	N40RA	BB-188	N417RC	BB-273	YV-O-SATA
BE-77	N580S	BB-22	w/o	BB-105	C-FKJI	BB-189	N56CC	BB-275	N8AM
BE-78	w/o	BB-23	N153ML	BB-106	N52SF	BB-190	C-FCGL	BB-275	C-GQNJ
BE-79	N500KD	BB-24	C-FCGB	BB-107	YV-....	BB-191	N200TP	BB-276	N865HR
BE-80	N93WT	BB-25	PR-...	BB-108	G-SAXN	BB-192	F-GLIF	BB-277	N593DJ
BE-81	N987B	BB-26	ZS-LYA	BB-109	N308RH	BB-193	OB-1468	BB-278	AP-CAA
BE-82	N66804	BB-27	C-GFOL	BB-110	N110BM	BB-194	HB-GIL	BB-279	YV-...
BE-83	N123BL	BB-28	6V-AGS	BB-111	N22071	BB-195	YV1909	BB-280	N280TT
BE-84	N700BA	BB-29	C-GKBN	BB-112	w/o	BB-196	HK-3995X	BB-281	C-FFAR
BE-85	N222LP	BB-30	G-ONAL	BB-113	PK-TRA	BB-197	ZS-OAK	BB-282	YV-1300P
BE-86	N264PA	BB-31	YV-....	BB-114	N300PW	BB-198	N4298S	BB-283	C-FATA
BE-87	N19DA	BB-32	N160SF	BB-115	N700KW	BB-199	F-GNPD	BB-284	wfu
BE-88	wfu	BB-33	HP-...	BB-116	wfu	BB-200	N2PY	BB-285	C-FKBU
BE-89	N499SW	BB-34	N878RA	BB-117	N21DE	BB-201	w/o	BB-286	ZS-XDG
BE-90	N770D	BB-35	N213UV	BB-118	w/o	BB-202	N4047C	BB-287	N498AC
BE-91	N847D	BB-36	N44UF	BB-119	wfu	BB-204	w/o	BB-288	ZS-NRR
BE-92	N6756P	BB-37	ZS-NXH	BB-120	C-GHOP	BB-205	N6PX	BB-289	N5ST
BE-93	N142JC	BB-38	w/o	BB-121	ZS-OCI	BB-206	N70AJ	BB-290	N290SJ
BE-94	N3663B	BB-39	w/o	BB-122	YV-...	BB-207	C-FCGW	BB-291	N291PA
BE-95	wfu	BB-40	N4TJ	BB-123	PH-ATM	BB-208	N62DL	BB-292	N393JW
BE-96	N802GC	BB-41	N200ZC	BB-124	C-GCET	BB-209	F-GPAS	BB-293	N200BT
BE-97	N97WD	BB-42	N66TJ	BB-125	N90PB	BB-210	G-FRYI	BB-294	9M-KNS
BE-98	N948HB	BB-43	N520MC	BB-126	D2-FFL	BB-211	5Y-BMC	BB-295	w/o
BE-99	C-GBVX	BB-44	w/o	BB-127	N200JL	BB-212	PNC-209	BB-296	N402KA
BE-100	N10AG	BB-45	PT-OZK	BB-128	HP-1591	BB-213	wfu	BB-297	N593BJ
BE-101	N311CM	BB-46	N760NP	BB-129	w/o	BB-214	w/o	BB-298	N862DD
BE-102	C-GNSC	BB-47	w/o	BB-130	N682DR	BB-215	N750TT	BB-299	N200FV
BE-103	N2TX	BB-48	N750HL	BB-131	N131SJ	BB-216	C-FAKN	BB-300	HP-...
BE-104	N67BS	BB-49	XA-	BB-132	HS-DCB	BB-217	C-FCGM	BB-301	C-FCGU
BE-105	C-FHSC	BB-50	N60SM	BB-133	YV-...	BB-218	w/o	BB-302	G-IMEA
BE-106	N568K	BB-51	YV-...	BB-134	N200EC	BB-219	wfu	BB-303	LX-JDP
BE-107	C-GPJL	BB-52	ZS-NWK	BB-135	HP-1598	BB-220	N800HA	BB-304	PR-JSP
BE-108	N108EB	BB-53	N280RA	BB-136	N57FT	BB-221	OK-MAG	BB-305	N11AB
BE-109	N105VY	BB-54	4-G-41/069	BB-137	PP-EOP	BB-222	5Y-BSU	BB-306	N230CS
BE-110	N702TD	BB-55	C-FDEB	BB-138	N999DT	BB-223	YV-O-SATA	BB-307	HB-GPG
BE-111	N118NL	BB-56	N44US	BB-139	N810JB	BB-224	N750KC	BB-308	w/o
BE-112	N727RS	BB-57	C-FAFT	BB-140	C-GPCP	BB-225	XB-JZP	BB-309	OY-PEB
BE-113	N88TL	BB-58	N60PD	BB-141	N977GT	BB-226	N982TM	BB-310	HK-...
BE-114	N125D	BB-59	N500KS	BB-142	w/o	BB-227	N335S	BB-311	HP-1512
BE-115	C-FIME	BB-60	HK-4108X	BB-143	N200CJ	BB-228	N703TT	BB-312	N127GA
BE-116	N116DG	BB-61	N58280	BB-144	N2883	BB-229	N911MN	BB-313	N30SE
BE-117	w/o	BB-62	N500GN	BB-145	VH-ZOS	BB-230	w/o	BB-314	N767WF
BE-118	N101SN	BB-63	HK-3705	BB-146	w/o	BB-231	C-FZVX	BB-315	ZS-PZU
BE-119	N188LL	BB-64	N56CD	BB-147	N771HC	BB-232	N162PA	BB-316	YV-2584P
BE-120	N110CE	BB-65	N440ST	BB-148	VH-OYH	BB-233	w/o	BB-317	w/o
BE-121	N770AB	BB-66	RP-C223	BB-149	N982GA	BB-234	w/o	BB-318	N49KC
BE-122	N54US	BB-67	YV-...	BB-150	N107FL	BB-235	OY-CBP	BB-319	N6HU
BE-123	N827RM	BB-68	C-GMWR	BB-151	w/o	BB-236	C-FCGC	BB-320	w/o
BE-124	N150YA	BB-69	N812DP	BB-152	N152TW	BB-237	HP-...	BB-321	N261AC
BE-125	N350TJ	BB-70	wfu	BB-153	w/o	BB-238	N200PH	BB-322	N710NC
BE-126	N248JH	BB-71	4-G-42/069	BB-154	N44KT	BB-239	F-GSIN	BB-323	N811VT
BE-127	N686AC	BB-72	w/o	BB-155	5Y-BMA	BB-240	N888EX	BB-324	N701NC
BE-128	YV-...	BB-73	VH-SGT	BB-156	N69CD	BB-241	w/o	BB-325	N65EB
BE-129	C-GSWF	BB-74	w/o	BB-157	N996LM	BB-242	N200RW	BB-326	N944CF
BE-130	N339JG	BB-75	HK-3936	BB-158	N81PF	BB-243	N43AJ	BB-327	ZS-OSB
BE-131	C-GSWG	BB-76	wfu	BB-159	C-FCGT	BB-244	w/o	BB-328	N795PA
BE-132	N150YR	BB-77	C-GWUY	BB-160	N160WJ	BB-245	w/o	BB-329	HP-...
BE-133	N531CB	BB-78	YV-...	BB-161	N114SB	BB-246	N200VA	BB-330	HP-...
BE-134	C-FOGP	BB-79	N1550S	BB-162	VH-SMT	BB-247	N4000	BB-331	G-FSEU
BE-135	N997ME	BB-80	F-GGMS	BB-163	w/o	BB-248	HK-3822	BB-332	N307DM
BE-136	N221TC	BB-81	N200FM	BB-164	HP-...	BB-249	C-GQJG	BB-333	HK-3941W
BE-137	N444RK	BB-82	LZ-YUK	BB-165	VH-SKU	BB-250	wfu	BB-334	D2-EBG
Super King Air 200		BB-83	N283KA	BB-166	N84CA	BB-251	F-GKCV	BB-335	N327RB
BB-1	wfu	BB-84	C-GFSB	BB-167	YV-...	BB-252	N934SH	BB-336	N311AV
BB-2	wfu	BB-85	ZS-NTL	BB-168	C-FOGY	BB-253	N991SU	BB-337	N400KW
BB-3	N24SP	BB-86	N677BC	BB-169	N725MC	BB-254	w/o	BB-338	N689BV
BB-4	N410RE	BB-87	TI-TCT	BB-170	C-GPEA	BB-255	HB-GJM	BB-339	N545LC
BB-5	YV0106	BB-88	N35	BB-171	7T-VRI	BB-256	5Y-BKT	BB-340	w/o
BB-6	XA-...	BB-89	N200WZ	BB-172	N94KC	BB-257	N257NA	BB-341	ST-BBA
BB-7	C-FBCN	BB-90	w/o	BB-173	N173RC	BB-258	N888ET	BB-342	O342
BB-8	N343CP	BB-91	N884PG	BB-174	w/o	BB-259	VH-LKB	BB-343	N4679M
BB-9	N200EZ	BB-92	N8117N	BB-175	7T-WRH	BB-260	N18CJ	BB-344	VH-ITH
BB-10	C-FALQ	BB-93	w/o	BB-176	N67GA	BB-261	YV-O-SATA	BB-345	w/o
BB-11	FAB 002	BB-94	N17HM	BB-177	N456CS	BB-262	EC-HHO	BB-346	YV-2834P
BB-12	wfu	BB-95	A2-AHZ	BB-178	N36CP	BB-263	N2U	BB-347	C-GJLI
BB-13	F-GIJB	BB-96	wfu	BB-179	N424BS	BB-264	C-FZNQ	BB-348	N28J
BB-14	C-GWWN	BB-97	w/o	BB-180	HK-4...	BB-265	YV-...	BB-349	F-GHLB
BB-15	wfu	BB-98	w/o	BB-181	wfu	BB-266	w/o	BB-350	ZS-NTT
BB-16	N711CR	BB-99	C-FSKO	BB-182	EC-GBB	BB-267	N8BG	BB-351	G-CEGR
BB-17	YV-...	BB-100	XC-DIJ	BB-183	N175SA	BB-268	C-GTUC	BB-352	HK-3922P

BB-353	SU-BAX	BB-437	N503P	BB-523	N508DW	BB-612	N506GT	BB-699	LV-OFT
BB-354	C-GDFT	BB-438	N438CR	BB-524	N524MR	BB-613	YV-....	BB-700	G-CGAW
BB-355	VH-OYE	BB-439	F-GGLN	BB-525	5Y-	BB-614	A2-KAS	BB-701	YVO104
BB-356	N79RR	BB-440	YV1730	BB-526	OE-BBB	BB-615	N383JP	BB-702	w/o
BB-357	N6069A	BB-441	N79CF	BB-527	C-FIFO	BB-616	F-GGMV	BB-703	HC-...
BB-358	RP-C5129	BB-442	N442KA	BB-528	N700BE	BB-617	HP-960P	BB-704	A2-AJK
BB-359	C-GDFN	BB-443	N71RG	BB-529	VH-NTE	BB-618	XA-...	BB-705	OY-BVW
BB-360	N18KA	BB-444	N444EB	BB-531	ZS-DSL	BB-619	5Y-RJA	BB-706	ZS-NBO
BB-361	N1HX	BB-445	N55SR	BB-532	N912MF	BB-620	D2-FEI	BB-707	N715RD
BB-362	HP-....	BB-446	N232JS	BB-533	VH-XDB	BB-621	N217CM	BB-708	N313EE
BB-363	N642TF	BB-447	LV-	BB-534	N12CF	BB-622	F-GHSV	BB-709	N71VT
BB-364	OY-JRN	BB-448	N411BL	BB-535	C-GOGT	BB-623	PR-EDW	BB-710	C-GCYN
BB-365	VH-OYA	BB-449	B-13152	BB-536	N777AW	BB-624	N444EG	BB-711	N1162V
BB-366	EC-IUV	BB-450	HK-3923X	BB-537	N5MK	BB-625	G-WVIP	BB-712	N411RA
BB-367	N367RA	BB-451	HB-GJI	BB-538	N477JM	BB-626	C9-ENH	BB-713	CN-CDN
BB-368	w/o	BB-452	N500PV	BB-539	ST-SFS	BB-628	N711TN	BB-714	N500CR
BB-369	wfu	BB-453	N23TC	BB-540	YV196T	BB-629	9Q-CTG	BB-715	N813JP
BB-370	N80RT	BB-454	N888DC	BB-541	N923AS	BB-630	ZS-NZJ	BB-716	SP-KGW
BB-371	N151EL	BB-455	C-GYDQ	BB-542	N542KA	BB-631	N6684B	BB-717	N77CA
BB-372	SX-ECG	BB-456	G-PFFN	BB-543	w/o	BB-632	YV-2710P	BB-718	VH-SGV
BB-373	N200FE	BB-457	N15KA	BB-544	N711VM	BB-633	w/o	BB-719	N372JB
BB-374	N111UT	BB-458	ANE-234	BB-545	D-ILIN	BB-634	N469JB	BB-720	N597MM
BB-375	N23ST	BB-459	SE-KXM	BB-546	4-G-47/074	BB-635	N30PH	BB-721	N8EF
BB-376	N376RC	BB-460	4-F-43/074	BB-547	5Y-HHE	BB-636	N127TA	BB-722	N722WJ
BB-377	w/o	BB-461	N313CT	BB-548	N706DG	BB-637	N3181	BB-723	w/o
BB-378	N378SF	BB-462	N220TT	BB-549	4-G-48/074	BB-638	N220JB	BB-724	N804
BB-379	5Y-DDE	BB-463	N463DP	BB-550	VH-TLX	BB-639	LV-WOS	BB-725	N725RA
BB-380	N323RR	BB-464	N561SS	BB-552	N63593	BB-640	CS-DDU	BB-726	G-CEGP
BB-381	ZS-KGW	BB-465	N31WC	BB-553	N326RT	BB-641	N641TS	BB-727	N522TG
BB-382	ZS-PKM	BB-466	N206P	BB-554	N5PX	BB-642	N801GG	BB-728	N8170J
BB-383	C-GZYO	BB-467	5Y-SJB	BB-555	EC-GHZ	BB-643	5Y-THS	BB-729	LV-WPM
BB-384	N2025M	BB-468	C-FEKB	BB-556	YV-...	BB-644	HP-....	BB-730	N108AL
BB-385	N381R	BB-470	VH-ZMO	BB-557	5Y-JAI	BB-645	N999VB	BB-731	YV-O-SATA
BB-386	ZS-NHX	BB-471	LV-RTC	BB-558	LV-WGP	BB-646	N646DR	BB-732	PK-VKA
BB-387	5N-BHL	BB-472	N305JS	BB-559	N795CA	BB-648	w/o	BB-733	N444AD
BB-388	N26BE	BB-473	N746KF	BB-560	F-GTEF	BB-649	N649JC	BB-734	w/o
BB-389	C-GKOX	BB-474	C-GCFF	BB-561	F-GULJ	BB-650	ZS-PSP	BB-735	N507BE
BB-390	N1660W	BB-475	N121LB	BB-562	YV-	BB-651	N141CT	BB-736	PR-AAX
BB-391	YV-...	BB-476	N203BS	BB-564	N42LJ	BB-652	w/o	BB-737	N703X
BB-392	N392KC	BB-477	N57GA	BB-565	N239PF	BB-653	VH-FII	BB-738	N520DD
BB-393	w/o	BB-478	N912SM	BB-566	N300HB	BB-654	N654FM	BB-739	N81RZ
BB-394	w/o	BB-479	C-GNBB	BB-567	w/o	BB-655	N655BA	BB-740	w/o
BB-395	XA-ASR	BB-480	D2-EMX	BB-568	G-BGRE	BB-656	YV-1051P	BB-741	N368FA
BB-396	N326AJ	BB-481	N84XP	BB-569	HP-	BB-657	N91MF	BB-742	XT-MAX
BB-397	F-GOCF	BB-482	N7166P	BB-570	N968T	BB-658	N747HN	BB-743	N28VU
BB-398	N572M	BB-483	N924AC	BB-571	N769MB	BB-659	C-GGAO	BB-744	F-GGLA
BB-399	N399BM	BB-484	w/o	BB-572	XA-...	BB-660	VH-LKF	BB-745	C-FSPN
BB-400	w/o	BB-485	N485K	BB-574	C-GZRX	BB-661	N777SS	BB-746	w/o
BB-401	SX-APJ	BB-486	N213PH	BB-575	N575RA	BB-662	w/o	BB-747	N63SK
BB-402	N182Z	BB-487	G-KVIP	BB-576	N53SP	BB-663	5N-IHS	BB-748	Z-WSG
BB-403	C-FGFZ	BB-488	4-G-45/074	BB-577	CN-CDF	BB-664	N280SC	BB-749	wfu
BB-404	N315MS	BB-490	N988CC	BB-578	N130CT	BB-666	wfu	BB-750	N81TF
BB-405	N367LF	BB-491	N622KM	BB-579	VH-VCB	BB-667	C-FWWQ	BB-751	N92JR
BB-406	F-GHOC	BB-492	N64DC	BB-580	ANE-233	BB-668	N896CM	BB-752	N616GB
BB-407	5Y-...	BB-493	N6509F	BB-581	N12NG	BB-669	w/o	BB-753	F-GERS
BB-409	N222LA	BB-494	N942CF	BB-582	SE-LTL	BB-670	N17VA	BB-754	N244JS
BB-410	N200PL	BB-495	EV-7910	BB-583	N777AQ	BB-671	C-GFSG	BB-755	N983C
BB-411	w/o	BB-496	wfu	BB-584	LN-MOB	BB-672	240	BB-756	ZS-LWD
BB-412	N316MS	BB-497	N72MM	BB-585	N143DE	BB-673	N503RM	BB-757	C-GBBS
BB-413	N456PF	BB-498	N6507B	BB-586	N653TB	BB-674	N51EE	BB-758	N20RE
BB-414	wfu	BB-499	C-GTJZ	BB-587	N247AF	BB-675	SE-IUX	BB-759	7T-VRS
BB-415	P2-CAA	BB-500	w/o	BB-588	G-OCEG	BB-676	F-GHVV	BB-760	N269ML
BB-416	ZS-KZU	BB-501	N38TJ	BB-589	N911ND	BB-677	N721RD	BB-761	N78CT
BB-417	N201KA	BB-502	N275X	BB-590	N524FS	BB-678	N811FA	BB-762	VH-ZOR
BB-418	wfu	BB-503	N503WJ	BB-592	w/o	BB-679	N1194C	BB-763	N56KA
BB-419	ZS-PPZ	BB-504	w/o	BB-593	N711KB	BB-680	N200WX	BB-764	ZS-OUT
BB-420	N420TA	BB-505	C-GKBP	BB-594	ZS-OYP	BB-681	F-GGPR	BB-765	N765WA
BB-421	A2-AEZ	BB-506	N8SV	BB-595	N927JC	BB-682	N425AP	BB-766	N52GP
BB-422	N501EB	BB-507	YV-...	BB-596	N72SE	BB-683	ZS-OTP	BB-767	w/o
BB-423	XB-IHK	BB-508	w/o	BB-597	ZS-MSK	BB-684	ZK457	BB-768	N219WC
BB-424	N470TC	BB-509	N72RL	BB-598	YV1731	BB-685	N29HF	BB-769	N623VP
BB-425	N2057S	BB-511	N202AJ	BB-599	N154BA	BB-686	N54TK	BB-770	w/o
BB-426	N70RD	BB-512	HK-	BB-600	N200BR	BB-687	ZS-PLY	BB-771	ANE-231
BB-427	YV	BB-513	C-GMOC	BB-601	N976KC	BB-688	ZS-OUI	BB-772	N111PV
BB-428	N106RH	BB-514	N335TA	BB-602	YV1387	BB-689	N364KA	BB-773	N500CS
BB-429	N409RA	BB-515	F-GKII	BB-603	N515BA	BB-690	VH-DYN	BB-774	N8NX
BB-430	N316GC	BB-516	N852JP	BB-604	N944LS	BB-691	N84CO	BB-775	7T-VRT
BB-431	N431WJ	BB-517	YV-257CP	BB-605	N485R	BB-692	RP-C264	BB-776	N899SD
BB-432	N200AU	BB-518	N83GA	BB-606	LV-WIO	BB-693	C-GXHN	BB-777	I-PIAH
BB-433	N94FG	BB-519	C-GCLQ	BB-607	D2-FFT	BB-694	EJC-117	BB-778	N816BS
BB-434	N50AJ	BB-520	2840	BB-608	N284K	BB-696	5Y-HHK	BB-779	YV-...
BB-435	XC-BCN	BB-521	N200QN	BB-610	XA-...	BB-697	N5UN	BB-780	N780RC
BB-436	N382ME	BB-522	3150	BB-611	XA-	BB-698	XT-MBA	BB-781	N550GL

BB-782	wfu	BB-867	ZS-PUF	BB-952	N185XP	BB-1036	N6271C	BB-1126	N650JW
BB-783	N25KA	BB-868	wfu	BB-953	N24GN	BB-1037	VH-FDI	BB-1127	5Y-JJZ
BB-784	PT-OSR	BB-869	N31FM	BB-954	ZS-LFM	BB-1038	ZS-MES	BB-1128	C-GGGQ
BB-785	N85FC	BB-870	LV-WEW	BB-955	N933RT	BB-1039	N124GA	BB-1129	C-GDHF
BB-786	N120P	BB-872	N602CN	BB-956	N817BA	BB-1040	N47DG	BB-1130	N209WC
BB-787	C-FZVW	BB-873	XB-JYE	BB-957	N800TT	BB-1041	VH-OYD	BB-1131	LV-AIY
BB-788	N551JL	BB-874	N4042J	BB-958	w/o	BB-1042	N142EB	BB-1132	N127MJ
BB-789	N905GP	BB-875	PT-WEG	BB-959	N81TL	BB-1043	N277JJ	BB-1133	wfu
BB-790	YV-....	BB-876	F-ZBFK/96	BB-960	wfu	BB-1044	G-SYGA	BB-1134	N27RC
BB-791	N791EB	BB-877	N508MV	BB-961	ZS-ACS	BB-1045	N810K	BB-1135	N74GS
BB-792	N110G	BB-878	w/o	BB-962	N437WF	BB-1046	9J-MED	BB-1136	TF-MYX
BB-793	wfu	BB-879	N4PT	BB-963	VH-WZN	BB-1047	N147NA	BB-1137	N333AP
BB-794	PK-VKB	BB-880	N53KA	BB-964	VH-SBM	BB-1048	G-FPLB	BB-1138	N29TV
BB-795	N409DH	BB-881	N881CS	BB-965	N300AJ	BB-1049	HK-4282X	BB-1139	N690SC
BB-796	YV-401CP	BB-882	N882JP	BB-966	G-BYCP	BB-1050	N925B	BB-1140	N888ZX
BB-797	G-BVMA	BB-883	N883BB	BB-967	N75ZT	BB-1051	N910KG	BB-1141	N500LP
BB-799	N269LS	BB-884	N49JG	BB-968	NZ1885	BB-1053	N132N	BB-1142	N68MY
BB-800	N1TX	BB-885	N146MH	BB-969	N96WC*	BB-1054	NZ1881	BB-1143	N23WS
BB-801	N244CH	BB-886	N479WB	BB-970	wfu	BB-1055	N6UD	BB-1144	LN-TWL
BB-802	w/o	BB-887	N87699	BB-971	PT-MMB	BB-1056	VH-FDO	BB-1145	N566TC
BB-803	5Y-TWA	BB-888	N70CU	BB-972	VT-EHB	BB-1057	N220TB	BB-1146	N194TR
BB-804	N174WB	BB-889	ZS-LAW	BB-973	C-FKCW	BB-1058	N250PW	BB-1147	N200BM
BB-805	w/o	BB-890	N100PY	BB-974	HK-3507	BB-1059	N818PF	BB-1148	N525SK
BB-806	PR-ART	BB-891	C-GHDP	BB-975	RP-C755	BB-1060	D2-FEG	BB-1149	ZS-OED
BB-807	7T-VRO	BB-892	N81LT	BB-976	N83PH	BB-1061	N200XC	BB-1150	VH-URU
BB-808	N775SC	BB-893	N762NB	BB-977	N125BK	BB-1062	PP-CBD	BB-1151	N151WT
BB-809	N991KA	BB-894	N969MA	BB-978	N877RC	BB-1063	N240CT	BB-1152	5Y-HHM
BB-810	N14TF	BB-896	N850BK	BB-979	C-FRMV	BB-1064	N824S	BB-1153	N1891S
BB-811	AEE-101	BB-897	D-IEFB	BB-980	GN-8595	BB-1065	N234KW	BB-1154	N6683W
BB-812	C-GJFY	BB-898	N212EJ	BB-981	N404FA	BB-1066	N50KG	BB-1155	N200UW
BB-813	ZS-PAM	BB-899	N527CH	BB-982	N800PK	BB-1067	N860H	BB-1156	N504GF
BB-814	XA-RMX	BB-900	w/o	BB-983	N983AJ	BB-1068	HK-3554	BB-1157	YV2078
BB-815	w/o	BB-901	N26UT	BB-984	HI-701SP	BB-1069	N145LG	BB-1158	G-JOAL
BB-816	N900RH	BB-902	N65TW	BB-985	w/o	BB-1070	ZS-NBJ	BB-1159	N552TT
BB-817	N56RT	BB-903	ZS-ASB	BB-986	PT-WOF	BB-1071	N14HG	BB-1160	N161GC
BB-818	N145JP	BB-904	N430MC	BB-987	N200HD	BB-1072	CNA-NG	BB-1161	N27CV
BB-819	N404DP	BB-905	N907G	BB-988	5Y-HHA	BB-1073	CNA-NH	BB-1162	w/o
BB-820	N911CM	BB-906	ARBV-0212	BB-989	N850AT	BB-1074	wfu	BB-1163	N960JP
BB-821	G-CLOW	BB-907	N789CT	BB-990	N208TC	BB-1075	N75LV	BB-1164	N801NA
BB-822	N250TM	BB-908	N999EG	BB-992	N992TJ	BB-1076	ZS-MTW	BB-1165	1165
BB-824	N919RE	BB-909	SE-KDK	BB-993	N32LJ	BB-1077	ZS-ZXX	BB-1166	N97SZ
BB-825	N825KA	BB-910	N910AJ	BB-994	N99LL	BB-1078	N129TT	BB-1167	N35GR
BB-826	N800CG	BB-911	N265EJ	BB-995	N454DC	BB-1079	N200NA	BB-1168	N844MP
BB-827	N20AE	BB-912	C-GFSH	BB-996	N48PA	BB-1080	N720MP	BB-1169	N40BC
BB-828	C-GJJT	BB-913	N9WR	BB-997	N7NA	BB-1081	N6531N	BB-1170	N55PC
BB-829	LN-NOA	BB-914	ZS-TNY	BB-998	N899MC	BB-1082	TC-FIR	BB-1171	N786DD
BB-830	N88MT	BB-915	XA-....	BB-999	ZS-LFW	BB-1083	VH-ZEK	BB-1172	VH-FDG
BB-831	F-OHCP	BB-916	N770SF	BB-1000	N580BK	BB-1084	N569SG	BB-1173	N3PX
BB-832	w/o	BB-917	N95TT	BB-1001	N772AF	BB-1085	N686CF	BB-1174	N730MS
BB-833	N833RL	BB-918	N918TC	BB-1002	N282CT	BB-1086	XA-GEC	BB-1175	N515CP
BB-834	N929SG	BB-919	N505AM	BB-1003	N58GA	BB-1087	NZ1883	BB-1176	N904DG
BB-835	N84PA	BB-920	F-GPAC	BB-1004	N104CX	BB-1088	N68FA	BB-1177	N193JC
BB-836	D2-EBF	BB-921	D-IKOB	BB-1005	D-ICKM	BB-1089	N87SA	BB-1178	NZ1884
BB-837	5Y-	BB-922	N1926A	BB-1006	CN-TPH	BB-1090	N49SK	BB-1179	N204WB
BB-838	w/o	BB-923	N316JP	BB-1007	C-FSKO	BB-1091	N529NA	BB-1180	N416AT
BB-839	N21FG	BB-924	05-52305	BB-1008	NZ1882	BB-1092	YV-O-PTJ-2	BB-1181	F-GJBS
BB-840	N712GJ	BB-925	N282SJ	BB-1009	N6451D	BB-1094	N1925L	BB-1182	N214PH
BB-841	N65KG	BB-926	N203LG	BB-1010	N702MA	BB-1095	N200DA	BB-1183	N91HT
BB-842	N204JS	BB-927	927	BB-1011	N843BC	BB-1099	N488JB	BB-1184	N93NP
BB-843	N211CP	BB-928	N627FP	BB-1012	N200MJ	BB-1100	N63791	BB-1186	N186EB
BB-844	w/o	BB-929	N999GA	BB-1013	N628DS	BB-1101	N395AM	BB-1187	N200SV
BB-845	EC-JJP	BB-930	N405PT	BB-1014	N239JV	BB-1102	F-ZBFJ/98	BB-1188	w/o
BB-846	ZS-MIM	BB-931	N995MS	BB-1015	N216RP	BB-1103	N361EA	BB-1189	ZS-PLL
BB-847	N847BA	BB-932	HB-GJX	BB-1016	N786SR	BB-1104	N162Q	BB-1190	PT-XEG
BB-848	N848NA	BB-933	D-IDRF	BB-1017	N385MC	BB-1106	w/o	BB-1191	N177CN
BB-849	N3DE	BB-934	N38381	BB-1018	ZS-LFU	BB-1107	N456ES	BB-1192	N61AP
BB-850	N3CR	BB-935	N935AJ	BB-1019	VH-JJR	BB-1108	N825RL	BB-1193	N6728H
BB-851	N208F	BB-936	VH-OWN	BB-1020	YV1733	BB-1109	C-FSKN	BB-1194	N585CE
BB-852	N46BR	BB-937	D2-ERK	BB-1021	N678SS	BB-1110	F-GSEB	BB-1195	N773VA
BB-853	C-GADI	BB-938	N722TR	BB-1022	C-GWGI	BB-1111	N83KA	BB-1196	5H-TZX
BB-854	HK-3214	BB-939	C-GGJF	BB-1023	N125NC	BB-1112	N311MP	BB-1197	N347D
BB-855	N199MH	BB-940	C-FZPW	BB-1024	HK-4343	BB-1113	ZS-OTS	BB-1198	N198DM
BB-856	w/o	BB-941	ZS-MIN	BB-1025	N22F	BB-1114	07-21907	BB-1199	PR-BLP
BB-857	5V-MCG	BB-942	N4OL	BB-1026	D2-FFK	BB-1115	C-FLRM	BB-1200	N873AF
BB-858	N10AC	BB-943	N280YR	BB-1027	ZS-NAW	BB-1116	F-GDJS	BB-1201	N53GA
BB-859	w/o	BB-944	D-	BB-1028	N62569	BB-1118	N586UC	BB-1202	N5NV
BB-860	N84PC	BB-945	VH-HLJ	BB-1029	N176M	BB-1119	w/o	BB-1203	N177LA
BB-861	N727BW	BB-946	N1850X	BB-1030	N843FC	BB-1120	N120NA	BB-1204	B-3551
BB-862	N207DB	BB-947	N500WF	BB-1031	N6644J	BB-1121	N6604L	BB-1205	B-3552
BB-863	N80WM	BB-948	N25CS	BB-1032	N800TS	BB-1122	N87CF	BB-1206	B-3553
BB-864	N847TS	BB-949	N810GW	BB-1033	w/o	BB-1123	N74ML	BB-1207	N3ZC
BB-865	N32SV	BB-950	N8NA	BB-1034	N185MV	BB-1124	I-ASMI	BB-1208	N200SE
BB-866	VH-MSZ	BB-951	OY-CKP	BB-1035	N450S	BB-1125	HS-KCH	BB-1209	N126SP

BB-1210	SE-IXC	BB-1295	G-WCCP	BB-1379	F-ZBMB/97	BB-1467	N95GA	BB-1550	N42SQ
BB-1211	N10EC	BB-1296	ZS-OSH	BB-1380	N200NR	BB-1468	VT-LNT	BB-1551	N151CF
BB-1212	N54FB	BB-1297	N23WJ	BB-1381	N151BG	BB-1469	VT-CIL	BB-1552	VH-NSN
BB-1213	N109MD	BB-1298	N36GS	BB-1382	N97WC	BB-1470	LN-MOI	BB-1553	N42FC
BB-1214	N200GS	BB-1299	N912SV	BB-1383	C-GXHG	BB-1471	N5TW	BB-1554	N38WV
BB-1215	N200KP	BB-1300	N313HS	BB-1384	C-GACN	BB-1472	VH-XCB	BB-1555	N288GS
BB-1216	N155AV	BB-1302	C-GXHS	BB-1385	501	BB-1473	OO-LET	BB-1556	N556BA
BB-1217	N697P	BB-1303	N940HC	BB-1386	504	BB-1474	ZS-NKC	BB-1557	G-SPOR
BB-1218	N740P	BB-1304	C-FPQQ	BB-1387	507	BB-1475	E3-AAJ	BB-1558	PT-WNN
BB-1219	N301HC	BB-1305	C-GXHR	BB-1388	510	BB-1476	ZS-ODU	BB-1559	N1114K
BB-1220	F-OIAN	BB-1306	N501HC	BB-1389	N277GE	BB-1477	N200PU	BB-1560	N845TC
BB-1221	TF-FMS	BB-1307	N1547V	BB-1390	F-GMGB	BB-1478	EC-JGB	BB-1561	F-HBRU
BB-1222	N126KA	BB-1308	N201NY	BB-1391	D2-ESP	BB-1479	YV	BB-1562	ZS-PPG
BB-1223	N586BC	BB-1309	C-GACA	BB-1392	HK-3704	BB-1480	N1559G	BB-1563	VT-DAF
BB-1224	C-FWXI	BB-1310	N989LA	BB-1393	N200VU	BB-1481	N200RS	BB-1564	EC-KHR
BB-1225	N119MC	BB-1311	XT-MBD	BB-1394	N818BL	BB-1482	N62FB	BB-1565	OM-FLY
BB-1226	N225WL	BB-1312	N312JC	BB-1395	N132MC	BB-1483	N500NG	BB-1566	N566NA
BB-1227	HK-3432	BB-1313	N88KE	BB-1396	N3620M	BB-1484	N6182A	BB-1567	VT-SDJ
BB-1228	N532SW	BB-1314	CR-843	BB-1397	N77HD	BB-1485	VT-BSA	BB-1568	TC-TAT
BB-1229	D-IBAD	BB-1315	HS-DCF	BB-1398	YV-121CP	BB-1486	VT-EBB	BB-1569	HB-GPH
BB-1230	N224P	BB-1316	S7-SMB	BB-1399	F-GJFE	BB-1487	N133K	BB-1570	G-ORJA
BB-1231	N360EA	BB-1317	VT-RSB	BB-1400	D-ICHG	BB-1488	N195CA	BB-1571	N80BC
BB-1232	C-GBYN	BB-1318	N444KA	BB-1401	ZS-PLJ	BB-1489	ZS-SMC	BB-1572	VT-TVS
BB-1233	N74AW	BB-1319	w/o	BB-1402	N791DC	BB-1490	N208AJ	BB-1573	N690L
BB-1234	ZS-FDR	BB-1320	N825ST	BB-1403	N147AA	BB-1491	N700NA	BB-1574	N429PL
BB-1235	N95CT	BB-1321	N133GA	BB-1404	N793DC	BB-1492	N44NL	BB-1575	VH-AYC
BB-1236	VT-ENM	BB-1322	XA-	BB-1405	RP-C2100	BB-1493	C-GHJF	BB-1576	N1118G
BB-1237	N7250T	BB-1323	N4KU	BB-1406	N212GA	BB-1494	N749FF	BB-1577	JA121N
BB-1238	N162GC	BB-1324	VH-MVY	BB-1407	OO-SKM	BB-1495	N3051K	BB-1578	PT-FFS
BB-1239	N895TT	BB-1325	ZS-NVP	BB-1408	N764CA	BB-1496	TC-OZD	BB-1579	C-GYSC
BB-1240	N200TK	BB-1326	N62WC	BB-1409	10010	BB-1497	N18AF	BB-1580	N345WV
BB-1241	N7256K	BB-1327	LN-BAA	BB-1410	PP-EJG	BB-1498	N770PB	BB-1581	N613TA
BB-1242	N242NA	BB-1328	N1553M	BB-1411	10011	BB-1499	wfu	BB-1582	N43TL
BB-1243	N200HX	BB-1329	VN-B594	BB-1412	N38VV	BB-1500	OO-INN	BB-1583	N400GW
BB-1244	VH-ITA	BB-1330	N92WC	BB-1413	10012	BB-1501	N200EG	BB-1584	PT-WNQ
BB-1245	N1MU	BB-1331	N88JH	BB-1414	10013	BB-1502	ZS-NXT	BB-1585	N200EJ
BB-1246	N207CM	BB-1332	N444BK	BB-1415	10014	BB-1503	N363D	BB-1586	N97WE
BB-1247	N48CS	BB-1333	VH-MVL	BB-1416	VH-MWQ	BB-1504	N50NA	BB-1587	N123ML
BB-1248	VT-ENL	BB-1334	LN-MOJ	BB-1417	LV-	BB-1505	HB-GJW	BB-1588	LV-YCS
BB-1249	N106GB	BB-1335	N335KW	BB-1418	VH-MWU	BB-1506	N75SR	BB-1589	PT-MJD
BB-1250	N88VN	BB-1336	N89UA	BB-1419	C-GNAX	BB-1507	C-GBBG	BB-1590	LN-MOT
BB-1251	N857EP	BB-1337	N330CS	BB-1420	N212LW	BB-1508	N288KM	BB-1591	D-IPSY
BB-1252	N634TT	BB-1338	C-GXHD	BB-1421	N715CQ	BB-1509	N716TA	BB-1592	w/o
BB-1253	ZS-OVX	BB-1339	C-GNAM	BB-1422	N125TS	BB-1510	N442JR	BB-1593	N1093Z
BB-1254	VT-EPA	BB-1340	ZS-PRA	BB-1423	N351SA	BB-1511	N56AY	BB-1594	N980GB
BB-1255	N152RP	BB-1341	ZS-PRC	BB-1424	VH-MWX	BB-1512	D2-EDD	BB-1595	LZ-BIZ
BB-1256	G-FPLE	BB-1342	OY-GEW	BB-1425	N911RX	BB-1513	N415RB	BB-1596	N82PK
BB-1257	N606AJ	BB-1343	C-GXHF	BB-1427	ZS-NOW	BB-1514	N31SV	BB-1597	N718RJ
BB-1258	N2748X	BB-1344	ZS-PNR	BB-1428	C-GFAD	BB-1515	ZS-TOB	BB-1598	N523GM
BB-1259	G-OMGI	BB-1345	N754SC	BB-1429	N604RK	BB-1516	N207HB	BB-1599	C-FGWR
BB-1260	N27GH	BB-1346	N800KT	BB-1430	VH-MWZ	BB-1517	D-IANA	BB-1600	N480TC
BB-1261	N717DC	BB-1347	F-GJFC	BB-1431	JA8705	BB-1518	G-MEGN	BB-1601	C-GLLS
BB-1262	N800NR	BB-1348	OO-SKL	BB-1432	N43TA	BB-1519	w/o	BB-1602	N203HQ
BB-1263	N20DH	BB-1349	N46CE	BB-1433	G-FPLD	BB-1520	N411CC	BB-1603	PP-ERG
BB-1265	N544P	BB-1350	N27HK	BB-1434	4005	BB-1521	LV-WOR	BB-1604	JA01EP
BB-1266	PT-WSX	BB-1351	N514TB	BB-1435	PT-ORB	BB-1522	SE-MAZ	BB-1605	N123AC
BB-1267	VT-VHL	BB-1352	OB-2	BB-1436	93303	BB-1523	N3250V	BB-1606	N2326J
BB-1268	N29997	BB-1353	A2-AGO	BB-1437	N34LT	BB-1524	w/o	BB-1607	F-GLRF
BB-1269	N412SH	BB-1354	N875DM	BB-1438	N8017M	BB-1525	N196SC	BB-1608	N2328E
BB-1270	F-GJFA	BB-1355	N480BR	BB-1439	N38JV	BB-1526	C-FSAT	BB-1609	N610TA
BB-1271	PT-LPG	BB-1356	N161RC	BB-1440	N655JG	BB-1527	P2-KSA	BB-1610	C-FSAO
BB-1272	N37GA	BB-1357	N299MK	BB-1441	93304	BB-1528	ZS-PEZ	BB-1611	N717FM
BB-1273	N466MW	BB-1358	N826JM	BB-1442	N128VT	BB-1529	RP-C8853	BB-1612	N200ND
BB-1274	N713RH	BB-1359	N90GA	BB-1443	93305	BB-1530	336	BB-1613	N209CM
BB-1275	N450WH	BB-1360	N326KW	BB-1444	N7PA	BB-1531	N16GF	BB-1614	N914CT
BB-1276	N14NG	BB-1361	N81DC	BB-1445	VT-MPG	BB-1532	RP-C3885	BB-1615	EJC-118
BB-1277	VT-EPY	BB-1362	D2-ECX	BB-1446	PT-WGS	BB-1533	N114HB	BB-1616	LV-YTB
BB-1278	N533P	BB-1363	3B-SKY	BB-1447	N70MN	BB-1534	N1074G	BB-1617	N200CY
BB-1279	N300TP	BB-1364	N660PB	BB-1449	LN-MOC	BB-1535	D-IBFT	BB-1618	N827HT
BB-1280	D-IBAR	BB-1365	N711VV	BB-1450	N213DB	BB-1536	N96CE	BB-1619	G-CDZT
BB-1281	C-FAMB	BB-1366	ZK-MAN	BB-1452	EJC-119	BB-1537	SE-LVV	BB-1620	N800BS
BB-1282	N200RR	BB-1367	N427P	BB-1453	7T-VBE	BB-1538	N363EA	BB-1621	N83FT
BB-1283	N113UL	BB-1368	N200EA	BB-1455	PT-JUB	BB-1539	N220AJ	BB-1622	N257YA
BB-1284	D-IBMP	BB-1369	LZ-ITV	BB-1456	w/o	BB-1540	N89WA	BB-1623	N603TA
BB-1285	N32WC	BB-1370	N79JS	BB-1458	N511RZ	BB-1541	N20LB	BB-1624	N957CB
BB-1286	N511AS	BB-1371	D2-EOJ	BB-1459	LN-MOD	BB-1542	ZS-ODI	BB-1625	N77CV
BB-1287	N921AZ	BB-1372	N950MB	BB-1460	LN-MOE	BB-1543	PT-WLK	BB-1626	PR-ACT
BB-1288	VT-EQK	BB-1373	N246PH	BB-1461	LN-MOF	BB-1544	F-OHJK	BB-1627	N9898
BB-1290	C-GNDR	BB-1374	N748LB	BB-1462	N988MM	BB-1545	N722KP	BB-1628	N808DS
BB-1291	N40PT	BB-1375	4006	BB-1463	ZS-PLK	BB-1546	C-GTDF	BB-1629	N300FL
BB-1292	N333TP	BB-1376	C-GNAK	BB-1464	VH-MSM	BB-1547	LN-SUZ	BB-1630	N929BW
BB-1293	N122TP	BB-1377	N755JB	BB-1465	LN-MOG	BB-1548	OY-EEF	BB-1631	N670TA
BB-1294	N401HC	BB-1378	N618	BB-1466	LN-MOH	BB-1549	G-MAMD	BB-1632	N12KR

BB-1633	D-IEDI	BB-1718	N13LY	BB-1804	856	BB-1889	N351CB	BB-1972	C-GSAH
BB-1634	N567US	BB-1719	N45SQ	BB-1805	ZS-TIP	BB-1890	PR-MCE	BB-1973	D-ITFC
BB-1635	N831TM	BB-1720	G-TAGH	BB-1806	842	BB-1891	N5AE	BB-1974	C-GSAU
BB-1636	N771MG	BB-1722	N773TP	BB-1807	N433HC	BB-1892	XA-GFM	BB-1975	I-MCAP
BB-1637	N8998W	BB-1723	VT-VSM	BB-1808	TG-FYL	BB-1893	N173TC	BB-1976	N23YR
BB-1638	N777AJ	BB-1725	N609TA	BB-1809	844	BB-1894	N63LB	BB-1977	VH-FDB
BB-1639	VH-IWO	BB-1726	N515CK	BB-1811	848	BB-1895	VT-LKK	BB-1978	N410PT
BB-1640	N25WC	BB-1728	N946CE	BB-1812	VH-AMR	BB-1896	VT-DDS	BB-1979	N337TB
BB-1641	VH-HWO	BB-1729	D-IBCB	BB-1813	VH-MVS	BB-1897	N504CE	BB-1980	VH-MVW
BB-1642	N717LW	BB-1730	N318CB	BB-1814	VH-AMS	BB-1898	F-HARR	BB-1981	PR-LPM
BB-1643	VH-LWO	BB-1731	N942CE	BB-1815	VT-JVL	BB-1899	N762GP	BB-1982	VT-HIS
BB-1644	PNC-225	BB-1732	PK-RGI	BB-1816	N444LP	BB-1900	N111LP	BB-1983	9A-BKB
BB-1645	N777HF	BB-1733	402	BB-1817	LV-ZZH	BB-1901	N741JR	BB-1984	N629RP
BB-1646	N399CW	BB-1734	G-MOUN	BB-1818	VT-UPR	BB-1902	HA-ACE	BB-1985	ZS-JSC
BB-1647	N467BC	BB-1735	N871C	BB-1819	859	BB-1903	N203PT	BB-1986	VH-FDA
BB-1648	N730HM	BB-1736	N948CE	BB-1820	N47RM	BB-1904	N983JB	BB-1987	ZS-CCK
BB-1649	N954MS	BB-1737	N665MW	BB-1821	N5021S	BB-1905	I-REEF	BB-1988	HS-ATS
BB-1650	5X-INS	BB-1738	C-GLFN	BB-1822	N203RC	BB-1906	VT-HRA	BB-1989	N807SM
BB-1651	N74RG	BB-1739	w/o	BB-1823	N299AL	BB-1907	XA-RDS	BB-1990	VH-FDT
BB-1652	LQ-ZRG	BB-1740	N170SE	BB-1824	N277WC	BB-1908	N204PT	BB-1991	N205TM
BB-1653	N346BA	BB-1741	OE-FOS	BB-1825	I-MTOP	BB-1909	N45RR	BB-1992	PP-LOV
BB-1654	D2-	BB-1742	ZS-CBL	BB-1826	N205SP	BB-1910	N228RC	BB-1993	N124EK
BB-1655	N1655M	BB-1743	N60AR	BB-1827	N667CC	BB-1911	ZS-CPM	BB-1994	LN-MMM
BB-1656	N531SW	BB-1744	403	BB-1828	N401SK	BB-1912	PR-EAO	BB-1995	SP-IKY
BB-1657	N300PU	BB-1745	N745EA	BB-1829	ZK450/J	BB-1913	N29PE	BB-1996	N20LH
BB-1658	N840CP	BB-1746	N510GS	BB-1830	ZK451/K	BB-1914	VT-UAB	BB-1997	N999MM
BB-1659	N911SF	BB-1747	G-SGEC	BB-1831	VT-SAZ	BB-1915	PT-MMF	BB-1998	VT-LMW
BB-1660	N511TA	BB-1748	C-GSAE	BB-1832	ZK452/L	BB-1916	N1542	BB-1999	N3199Z
BB-1661	XC-CTL	BB-1749	N944C	BB-1833	ZK453/M	BB-1917	D-IJAH	Super King Air 200C	
BB-1662	D-IVAN	BB-1750	N726CB	BB-1834	N1NP	BB-1918	VT-FAE	BL-1	5A-DDT
BB-1663	N720AM	BB-1751	N805C	BB-1835	ZK454/N	BB-1919	N205RA	BL-2	5Y-EKO
BB-1664	SU-BNJ	BB-1752	XA-...	BB-1836	ZK455/O	BB-1920	N700Z	BL-3	N39PH
BB-1665	N111MO	BB-1753	N520DG	BB-1837	ZK456/P	BB-1921	N224LM	BL-4	ZS-NUF
BB-1666	N401CG	BB-1754	N200WB	BB-1838	XA-HPS	BB-1922	N694KM	BL-5	N514RD
BB-1667	N968MB	BB-1755	PR-APJ	BB-1839	N712RH	BB-1923	HS-CNS	BL-6	5A-DDY
BB-1668	N214GB	BB-1756	N264SP	BB-1840	EC-IUX	BB-1924	N780KB	BL-7	HB-GJD
BB-1669	N115CT	BB-1757	N777AG	BB-1841	C-FGMG	BB-1925	N928KG	BL-8	ZS-PNZ
BB-1670	N327SE	BB-1758	VT	BB-1842	VH-MVJ	BB-1926	N776RW	BL-9	VH-NTG
BB-1671	YV1694	BB-1759	N95UT	BB-1843	N120FS	BB-1927	N840U	BL-10	5Y-BLA
BB-1672	D-IVIP	BB-1760	w/o	BB-1844	N888ZC	BB-1928	N964RT	BL-11	F-GRSO
BB-1673	ZS-RAF	BB-1761	N610RM	BB-1845	N912JS	BB-1929	N402CT	BL-12	VH-NTH
BB-1674	XC-TAU	BB-1762	N415TM	BB-1846	N10CW	BB-1930	N881MC	BL-13	N817BB
BB-1675	OY-PCL	BB-1763	N5063K	BB-1847	N635SF	BB-1931	G-KLYN	BL-14	N3697F
BB-1676	N31094	BB-1764	VT-YUD	BB-1848	N215HC	BB-1932	XB-KBC	BL-15	N511DP
BB-1677	N200HK	BB-1765	N540MA	BB-1849	N924JB	BB-1933	N3103L	BL-16	OO-LAC
BB-1678	N678FA	BB-1766	N994HP	BB-1850	N299AK	BB-1934	F-OIKM	BL-17	5Y-JMR
BB-1679	N55MP	BB-1767	N441AL	BB-1851	C6-MIP	BB-1935	N430TW	BL-18	3280
BB-1680	N299AV	BB-1768	N637WM	BB-1852	N633HC	BB-1936	LN-TRG	BL-19	3240
BB-1681	XC-TJN	BB-1769	N80VP	BB-1853	N93RR	BB-1937	N831KD	BL-20	ZS-LRS
BB-1682	N888FV	BB-1770	N4270Y	BB-1854	N927BG	BB-1938	ZS-TGM	BL-21	C9-ASV
BB-1683	N511SD	BB-1771	N818AG	BB-1855	N214TP	BB-1939	N707HM	BL-22	P2-HCN
BB-1685	N808WD	BB-1772	N28VM	BB-1856	ZS-PCH	BB-1940	C-GDVF	BL-23	YV-403CP
BB-1686	N52SZ	BB-1773	N425BP	BB-1857	N788SF	BB-1941	N925GA	BL-25	w/o
BB-1687	VT-GUJ	BB-1774	N4053H	BB-1858	N200HF	BB-1942	N321GC	BL-26	HP-....
BB-1688	N42LW	BB-1775	VT-MPT	BB-1859	N901SF	BB-1943	VT-RJA	BL-27	N44MR
BB-1689	N225TL	BB-1776	N7000G	BB-1860	G-PCOP	BB-1944	N660WM	BL-28	FAB 018
BB-1690	LV-ZYB	BB-1777	N33LA	BB-1861	OY-LLL	BB-1945	N739W	BL-29	ZS-PEA
BB-1691	N200NW	BB-1778	N1LF	BB-1862	N225WC	BB-1946	N31CG	BL-30	VH-NTS
BB-1692	SE-LVU	BB-1779	N282JD	BB-1863	PR-MLG	BB-1947	VT-CTG	BL-31	VH-KFN
BB-1693	G-GBMR	BB-1780	C-GSBC	BB-1864	N766LF	BB-1948	N802MJ	BL-32	ZS-CVH
BB-1694	N317RT	BB-1781	N908BS	BB-1865	N6300F	BB-1949	N660AA	BL-33	w/o
BB-1695	N909DD	BB-1782	N4NU	BB-1866	N922MM	BB-1950	N128AS	BL-34	652
BB-1696	VH-FDF	BB-1783	N360X	BB-1867	N119AR	BB-1951	N954BL	BL-35	w/o
BB-1697	VH-FDD	BB-1784	N710JB	BB-1868	LN-LTA	BB-1952	N87LN	BL-36	N111NS
BB-1698	F-GUFP	BB-1785	N101SG	BB-1869	N65GP	BB-1953	N426WF	BL-37	5Y-TWC
BB-1699	N703RM	BB-1786	N202FF	BB-1870	N4925T	BB-1954	N500HG	BL-38	VH-CBZ
BB-1700	VT	BB-1787	VH-MSH	BB-1871	PR-FRB	BB-1955	N215ML	BL-39	P2-SIA
BB-1701	JY-AW2	BB-1788	VT-AEL	BB-1872	N510UF	BB-1956	N95LM	BL-40	ZS-PRB
BB-1702	N677JE	BB-1789	ZS-PEI	BB-1873	N267CB	BB-1957	D-IRAR	BL-41	VH-LNJ
BB-1703	LV-ZTV	BB-1790	C-GSAV	BB-1874	F-HAMI	BB-1958	XA-...	BL-42	C-GIND
BB-1704	N68MN	BB-1791	N252CP	BB-1875	VH-WJY	BB-1959	N205PA	BL-43	w/o
BB-1705	N418J	BB-1792	EC-ILE	BB-1876	N716AV	BB-1960	N23HD	BL-44	C-GDPB
BB-1706	YV-....	BB-1793	N404J	BB-1877	LV-AXO	BB-1961	VH-MQZ	BL-45	651
BB-1707	YS-111N	BB-1794	TG-OIL	BB-1878	N750MD	BB-1962	C-GFSD	BL-46	N312ME
BB-1708	N711AW	BB-1795	N4195S	BB-1879	N536RB	BB-1963	C-GFSE	BL-47	w/o
BB-1709	N865PT	BB-1796	CC-CPB	BB-1880	VH-FDW	BB-1964	N50VM	BL-48	VH-MSU
BB-1710	N68FB	BB-1797	N424RA	BB-1881	VH-FDR	BB-1965	PR-VDQ	BL-49	OO-ASL
BB-1711	N44KA	BB-1798	PR-LIA	BB-1882	VH-FDZ	BB-1966	YV2392	BL-50	N150RL
BB-1712	YV1603	BB-1799	N102FG	BB-1884	N625GA	BB-1967	N481BR	BL-51	GN-8270
BB-1713	N96AM	BB-1800	N600RL	BB-1885	N204RA	BB-1968	PR-BTN	BL-52	w/o
BB-1714	5Y-ZBK	BB-1801	N604MJ	BB-1886	N509FP	BB-1969	N458TC	BL-53	N157A
BB-1715	G-CDFY	BB-1802	N5092S	BB-1887	F-HJPM	BB-1970	N390SP	BL-54	N654BA
BB-1716	D-IBFE	BB-1803	XA-ZEC	BB-1888	N187JP	BB-1971	N779BZ	BL-55	N356AA

576

BL-56	N389RA	BL-148	F-OIQL	**Super King Air B200**		FA-69	PNC-....	FA-154	PT-OJQ
BL-57	CNA-NI	BL-149	F-OIOK	FG-1	987	FA-70	w/o	FA-155	N66TG
BL-61	N661BA	BL-150	G-SASC	FG-2	990	FA-71	N7586Z	FA-156	N397WM
BL-62	N662BA	BL-151	G-SASD	**Super King Air B200CT**		FA-72	N82LP	FA-157	N350DW
BL-63	w/o	**Super King Air 200T**		BN-1	CC-DIV	FA-73	N699MW	FA-158	YV1839
BL-64	N188TC	BT-1	F-GALN	BN-2	AE-571	FA-74	XC-AA80	FA-159	PNC-208
BL-65	N399AS	BT-2	F-GALP	BN-3	AE-572	FA-75	ANE-232	FA-160	N3084K
BL-66	YV-2323P	BT-3	N2UW	BN-4	AE-573	FA-76	N1BK	FA-161	N221NM
BL-67	N70LG	BT-4	AU-871	BN-5	703	FA-77	N917WA	FA-162	N3122Z
BL-68	VH-FDS	BT-5	A2-MXI	BN-6	N5106F	FA-78	N740PC	FA-163	N3237S
BL-69	N7232R	BT-6	VH-OYT	BN-7	N5107Z	FA-79	N27KG	FA-164	N90WE
BL-70	654	BT-7	ZS-OEB	BN-8	N51488	FA-80	N300HH	FA-165	N4NF
BL-71	w/o	BT-8	D2-ERO	BN-9	719	FA-81	N919HP	FA-166	N166SA
BL-72	VH-CWO	BT-9	N120RL	**Super King Air 300**		FA-82	N15PX	FA-167	N19MC
BL-73	84-0143	BT-10	9M-JPD	FA-1	N6642B	FA-83	XC-AA49	FA-168	N300TN
BL-74	84-0144	BT-11	N857GA	FA-2	N251LL	FA-84	N477AE	FA-169	HK-3860
BL-75	84-0145	BT-12	N859GA	FA-3	N135MK	FA-85	N907DB	FA-170	HB-GHV
BL-76	84-0146	BT-13	N45E	FA-4	N111SS	FA-86	HK-3547	FA-171	N300PP
BL-77	84-0147	BT-14	N44U	FA-5	N313SA	FA-87	N301CG	FA-172	N28GC
BL-78	84-0148	BT-15	N45N	FA-6	N821TB	FA-88	N1250	FA-173	N30HV
BL-79	84-0149	BT-16	N130RL	FA-7	N800RE	FA-89	N694JB	FA-174	PT-FFN
BL-80	84-0150	BT-17	JA8824	FA-8	N52LP	FA-90	N896RJ	FA-175	OY-CVB
BL-81	84-0151	BT-18	D2-FMD	FA-9	N302NC	FA-91	N300MC	FA-176	N144AB
BL-82	84-0152	BT-19	w/o	FA-10	HK-3828	FA-92	PP-EPD	FA-177	N300RC
BL-83	84-0153	BT-20	7T-WRY	FA-11	N132CC	FA-93	N93GA	FA-178	N313BA
BL-84	84-0154	BT-21	7T-WRZ	FA-12	N7202Y	FA-94	LX-SEA	FA-179	N1548K
BL-85	84-0155	BT-22	N140RL	FA-13	N300PR	FA-95	XC-AA46	FA-180	w/o
BL-86	84-0156	BT-23	VH-LAB	FA-14	XB-HHA	FA-96	HK-3534	FA-181	N458Q
BL-87	84-0157	BT-24	w/o	FA-15	N505WR	FA-97	N97EB	FA-182	C-FWWK
BL-88	84-0158	BT-25	AE-574	FA-16	N846BE	FA-98	N306M	FA-183	C-FAKW
BL-89	84-0159	BT-26	AE-575	FA-17	N58ES	FA-99	HK-....	FA-184	D-IBER
BL-90	84-0160	BT-27	D-CACB	FA-18	N163BA	FA-100	HK-3648	FA-185	N369F
BL-91	84-0161	BT-28	JA8833	FA-19	N300TE	FA-101	HK-3654	FA-186	N404EW
BL-92	84-0162	BT-29	N120PR	FA-20	N7228T	FA-102	N195AL	FA-187	N350BF
BL-93	84-0163	BT-30	CR-842	FA-21	N914BH	FA-103	N827DL	FA-188	N156CH
BL-94	84-0164	BT-31	JA8854	FA-22	HK-....	FA-104	w/o	FA-189	SE-KOL
BL-95	84-0165	BT-32	JA8860	FA-23	N141SM	FA-105	TG-MDN-P	FA-190	N100AQ
BL-96	84-0166	BT-33	HP-1316	FA-24	N124CM	FA-106	N265PA	FA-191	N914JF
BL-97	84-0167	BT-34	F-GMLT	FA-25	ZS-PAZ	FA-107	N538AM	FA-192	D-C...
BL-98	84-0168	BT-35	M41-01	FA-26	PT-OLI	FA-108	N494MA	FA-193	N15613
BL-99	w/o	BT-36	M41-02	FA-27	N203RR	FA-109	wfu	FA-194	N811LC
BL-100	84-0170	BT-37	M41-03	FA-28	N401NS	FA-110	N313KY	FA-195	N195AE
BL-101	84-0171	BT-38	M41-04	FA-29	N970KK	FA-111	N305SA	FA-196	N825JG
BL-102	84-0172	BT-39	622	FA-30	N642JL	FA-112	N300SV	FA-197	N416DY
BL-103	84-0173	BT-40	625	FA-31	PP-EJO	FA-113	PT-MMC	FA-198	N603WM
BL-104	84-0174	BT-41	629	FA-32	N100BZ	FA-114	N239TT	FA-199	N199CE
BL-105	84-0175	BT-42	633	FA-33	N262SP	FA-115	N300CW	FA-200	N61KA
BL-106	84-0176	BT-43	636	FA-34	N100FL	FA-116	N637JC	FA-201	N566KA
BL-107	84-0177	BT-44	722	FA-35	N312DB	FA-117	N80BZ	FA-202	VP-BMK
BL-108	84-0178	BT-46	735	FA-36	N206K	FA-118	653	FA-203	XB-ZRH
BL-109	84-0179	**King Air B200GT**		FA-37	N2DB	FA-119	N118GW	FA-204	A6-
BL-110	84-0180	BY-1	LV-	FA-38	N6812W	FA-120	N365CS	FA-205	OH-BSA
BL-111	84-0181	BY-2	N175PL	FA-39	C-GHOG	FA-121	N92TX	FA-206	OH-BSB
BL-112	84-0182	BY-3	SP	FA-40	N52C	FA-122	N88RY	FA-207	CNA-NX
BL-118	84-0484	BY-4	N404GT	FA-41	FAP-18	FA-123	HP-1457	FA-208	CNA-NY
BL-119	84-0485	BY-5	N440WW	FA-42	N385KA	FA-124	N802M	FA-209	HP-1182
BL-120	84-0486	BY-6	N3206T	FA-43	N827CA	FA-125	N401BL	FA-210	w/o
BL-121	84-0487	BY-7	N708WH	FA-44	N20KW	FA-127	N926PR	FA-211	N822VK
BL-122	84-0488	BY-8	N34008	FA-45	N223JR	FA-128	w/o	FA-212	N54YC
BL-123	84-0489	BY-9	N909GT	FA-46	N123AF	FA-130	N3AH	FA-213	N555FD
BL-124	N149Z	BY-10	N972BP	FA-47	HK-3556P	FA-131	N886MS	FA-214	N393CF
BL-125	VQ-TRT	BY-11	N106PA	FA-48	N271BC	FA-132	N184D	FA-215	C-GTDB
BL-126	w/o	BY-12	LV-	FA-49	N312DE	FA-133	N153PE	FA-216	N312AR
BL-127	SE-LKY	BY-13	N3213L	FA-50	N214EC	FA-134	N38RY	FA-217	N79CB
BL-128	N361TD	BY-14	G-WATJ	FA-51	YV-....	FA-135	N540CB	FA-218	N193FS
BL-129	w/o	BY-15	PT-	FA-52	PT-MCM	FA-136	N888AS	FA-219	JA8881
BL-130	N130SC	BY-16	N32166	FA-53	N736P	FA-137	N467JB	FA-220	HB-GPI
BL-131	w/o	BY-17	N32017	FA-54	N920C	FA-138	N541SC	FA-221	LV-WLT
BL-132	SE-KFP	BY-18	N24HD	FA-55	N333WC	FA-139	N316RS	FA-222	LV-WMA
BL-133	N133US	BY-19	N3189D	FA-56	N7231P	FA-140	N792JM	FA-223	OK-GTJ
BL-134	N134WJ	BY-20	N531SC	FA-57	N75ME	FA-141	N632DS	FA-224	D-IFFB
BL-135	D2-ECY	BY-21	N34651	FA-58	N7RC	FA-142	N304JS	FA-225	CC-PWA
BL-136	N136AJ	BY-22	N33122	FA-59	N528AM	FA-143	N600KA	FA-226	F-GPRH
BL-137	VH-HPP	BY-23	N34923	FA-60	HP-1595	FA-144	N111EL	FA-227	w/o
BL-138	PK-JCA	BY-24	N510LA	FA-61	w/o	FA-145	N149CC	FA-228	OE-FME
BL-139	VT-SRC	BY-25	N99ML	FA-62	N103AD	FA-146	F-GICA	FA-229	LV-WIP
BL-140	PK-CAK	BY-26	N3326Q	FA-63	N35LW	FA-147	N990L	FA-230	VT-UPA
BL-141	LN-IDA	BY-27	N626GT	FA-64	N103CW	FA-148	N30FE	**Super King Air 300**	
BL-142	N524GM	BY-28	N32928	FA-65	N555DX	FA-149	N998BW	FF-1	N66
BL-143	N4456A	BY-29	N32029	FA-66	N577BE	FA-150	wfu	FF-2	N67
BL-144	N5139A	BY-37	N370LH	FA-67	N79TL	FA-151	N1MW	FF-3	N68
BL-145	N4489A			FA-68	N300SE	FA-152	N535PN	FA-4	N69
BL-146	N5155A					FA-153	N24BL	FF-5	N70

ID	Reg	ID	Reg	ID	Reg	ID	Reg	ID	Reg
FF-6	N71	FL-46	UR-CWB	FL-129	N827HB	FL-212	N350AB	FL-295	JA869A
FF-7	N72	FL-47	N350P	FL-130	D-CSKY	FL-213	N350JB	FL-296	N290AS
FF-8	N73	FL-48	N555ZA	FL-131	801	FL-214	N350CS	FL-297	JA870A
FF-9	N74	FL-49	N999HW	FL-132	825	FL-215	N160SM	FL-298	N151E
FF-10	N75	FL-50	N300TM	FL-133	N97DR	FL-216	N893MC	FL-299	N74KS
FF-11	N76	FL-51	N75WD	FL-134	SP-FNS	FL-217	N350BG	FL-300	F-GVLB
FF-12	N77	FL-52	B-00135	FL-135	N73WC	FL-218	JA866A	FL-301	F-GOSB
FF-13	N78	FL-53	HS-SLA	FL-136	N189MC	FL-219	N276JB	FL-302	N42ED
FF-14	N79	FL-54	N80800	FL-137	RP-C2638	FL-220	S9-BAA	FL-303	N551TP
FF-15	N80	FL-55	YV0138	FL-138	N311GM	FL-221	PT-FSA	FL-304	N60YP
FF-16	N81	FL-56	N351GC	FL-139	N60CM	FL-222	JA867A	FL-305	N351MP
FF-17	w/o	FL-57	N159JB	FL-140	N140WT	FL-223	N558BC	FL-306	N525DF
FF-18	N83	FL-58	N8116N	FL-141	PT-WND	FL-224	N2535B	FL-307	23054
FF-19	N84	FL-59	N964LB	FL-142	N991LL	FL-225	N57TX	FL-308	N64FB
Super King Air B300C		FL-60	N224CR	FL-143	N789SB	FL-226	N226K	FL-309	N143DK
FM-1	w/o	FL-61	N57KE	FL-144	N49WC	FL-227	N823EB	FL-310	LV-ZXX
FM-2	HP-2888	FL-62	C-FPWR	FL-145	RP-C2850	FL-228	N75WZ	FL-311	w/o
FM-3	N430JT	FL-63	N350DR	FL-146	2011	FL-229	OY-MEN	FL-312	N350JR
FM-4	N173S	FL-64	UR-CWA	FL-147	2012	FL-230	N579MC	FL-313	w/o
FM-5	N7285Y	FL-65	N999MG	FL-148	RP-C3500	FL-231	N103RN	FL-314	N350J
FM-6	N5888K	FL-66	N199Y	FL-149	N726T	FL-232	N816DE	FL-315	N3115K
FM-7	N5066N	FL-67	N487TT	FL-150	VH-SCQ	FL-233	N700PG	FL-316	N200VC
FM-8	YV-877CP	FL-68	N593MA	FL-151	HS-ITD	FL-234	C-FDTC	FL-317	C-FPCP
FM-9	N4009L	FL-69	N110HC	FL-152	PT-WSJ	FL-235	N325JM	FL-318	B-3583
FM-10	N1667J	FL-70	N850D	FL-153	RP-C1807	FL-236	C-GTEM	FL-319	N350TV
FM-11	N4466A	FL-71	N38H	FL-154	N57VA	FL-237	PR-MOZ	FL-320	N355DM
FM-12	N148AA	FL-72	N3739C	FL-155	N253AS	FL-238	5N-MPB	FL-321	N748SB
FM-13	N7033U	FL-73	YR-CAA	FL-156	N769BJ	FL-239	N655SC	FL-322	OK-LFD
FM-14	G-JENC	FL-74	N115TT	FL-157	N350LL	FL-240	PT-WUT	FL-323	N350KS
FM-15	C-GPNC	FL-75	ZS-LAD	FL-158	N10UN	FL-241	N2341S	FL-324	N793WB
FM-16	G-NICY	FL-76	D-CFMA	FL-159	PT-WNL	FL-242	N983AR	FL-325	N450DW
FM-17	N817KA	FL-77	N988ME	FL-160	N177GA	FL-243	N299AS	FL-326	N363CA
FM-18	N818KA	FL-78	N598AC	FL-161	N141K	FL-244	N171CP	FL-327	N1845
FM-19	N3419S	FL-79	P2-PNG	FL-162	N40593	FL-245	N328AJ	FL-328	EC-IBK
FM-20	N3120U	FL-80	F-GTEM	FL-163	S9-CAM	FL-246	5N-FLS	FL-329	N668K
FM-21	N68RF	FL-81	N507WG*	FL-164	N312RL	FL-247	N6JL	FL-330	N1253W
Super King Air 350		FL-82	N4YS	FL-165	N53TM	FL-248	N28PH	FL-331	23055
FL-1	N10TX	FL-83	N441FP	FL-166	XC-CHI	FL-249	N3080F	FL-332	N133NL
FL-2	N400AE	FL-84	N614ML	FL-167	N222PV	FL-250	N81PA	FL-333	N390MD
FL-3	N92TW	FL-85	ANE-235	FL-168	N17WC	FL-251	XA-FCV	FL-334	N350D
FL-4	N10K	FL-86	N27GE	FL-169	PT-WSI	FL-252	N525BC	FL-335	PR-EFF
FL-5	N450LM	FL-87	C-FMHD	FL-170	CN-RLE	FL-253	N350GL	FL-336	N360CB
FL-6	N350BS	FL-88	N1525C	FL-171	N2315A	FL-254	N3254A	FL-337	N707FA
FL-7	N711VN	FL-89	N145DC	FL-172	N511D	FL-255	D-COEB	FL-338	N802BS
FL-8	N770JH	FL-90	VH-FIX	FL-173	F-HJPD	FL-256	D-	FL-339	A32-339
FL-9	N1SC	FL-91	N143CE	FL-174	C-GFSA	FL-257	N351DD	FL-340	N450CR
FL-10	D2-FFO	FL-92	N141DA	FL-175	SE-LLU	FL-258	N972SC	FL-341	XA-CAB
FL-11	N37390	FL-93	N188MC	FL-176	23051	FL-259	N327R	FL-342	N512DC
FL-12	N5655K	FL-94	N983TM	FL-177	PT-WAC	FL-260	N5256S	FL-343	A32-343
FL-13	C-GJLK	FL-95	DF-103/C	FL-178	N675BC	FL-261	N506MV	FL-344	N72RE
FL-14	N350Q	FL-96	N60WC	FL-179	N350S	FL-262	N771HM	FL-345	N370NA
FL-15	wfu	FL-97	D-CFMB	FL-180	JA861A	FL-263	N102FL	FL-346	A32-346
FL-16	N350GA	FL-98	HP-	FL-181	N500FC	FL-264	N961LL	FL-347	N923FP
FL-17	C-GEAS	FL-99	N30SM	FL-182	N503LM	FL-265	N981LL	FL-348	A32-348
FL-18	N688JB	FL-100	N86GA	FL-183	F-GNOE	FL-266	23053	FL-349	A32-349
FL-19	N933CL	FL-101	D-CADN	FL-184	N800BJ	FL-267	N971LL	FL-350	A32-350
FL-20	N99U	FL-102	D2-ECW	FL-185	N2SM	FL-268	N49CL	FL-351	A32-351
FL-21	EP-825	FL-103	N113GF	FL-186	23052	FL-269	C-GOGS	FL-352	N675PC
FL-22	N350AJ	FL-104	N74RR	FL-187	N819EE	FL-270	N4170N	FL-353	C-GMEH
FL-23	N323DB	FL-105	N193RA	FL-188	JA862A	FL-271	N992MA	FL-354	C-FNIL
FL-24	N1551A	FL-106	C-GLOX	FL-189	N1562H	FL-272	C-GOIC	FL-355	N685BC
FL-25	N37TD	FL-107	N344L	FL-190	LV-YLC	FL-273	C-FVKC	FL-356	N455SE
FL-26	C-GNLA	FL-108	B-13153	FL-191	JA863A	FL-274	N64GG	FL-357	F-GKYY
FL-27	N357BB	FL-109	N470KA	FL-192	VT-MGJ	FL-275	N275BT	FL-359	N359MB
FL-28	N300KA	FL-110	N921BS	FL-193	JA864A	FL-276	D-CLOG	FL-360	N1880C
FL-29	N234KK	FL-111	B-3581	FL-194	HS-SLC	FL-277	XA-RCG	FL-361	VH-OXF
FL-30	N350DK	FL-112	N405J	FL-195	JA865A	FL-278	N350BW	FL-362	N270AB
FL-31	N126DS	FL-113	B-3582	FL-196	RP-C2296	FL-279	5N-FLY	FL-363	N700U
FL-32	YV-42CP	FL-114	N895CA	FL-197	N82WU	FL-280	N4380Y	FL-364	N447TF
FL-33	C-FRLD	FL-115	N5XM	FL-198	N221G	FL-281	N552TP	FL-365	N350RR
FL-34	N57SC	FL-116	N711RJ	FL-199	N981AR	FL-282	FAC-5746	FL-366	N366SL
FL-35	N470SC	FL-117	N43BG	FL-200	N76PM	FL-283	N980BC	FL-367	N160AC
FL-36	N96KA	FL-118	RP-C1728	FL-201	N2325Y	FL-284	N886AC	FL-368	OO-SDU
FL-37	w/o	FL-119	N812PM	FL-202	N350TF	FL-285	C-GRJZ	FL-369	N468BV
FL-38	N600CB	FL-120	F-GPGH	FL-203	N824ST	FL-286	G-BZNE	FL-370	N74TF
FL-39	N395MB	FL-121	N1PD	FL-204	N204W	FL-287	N555WQ	FL-371	N391MT
FL-40	N923JK	FL-122	VH-EWQ	FL-205	PT-WTW	FL-288	PP-KKG	FL-372	A32-372
FL-41	N350VM	FL-123	N350BD	FL-206	YV-910CP	FL-289	PP-JSC	FL-373	N357RL
FL-42	PT-FGB	FL-124	N235PB	FL-207	N717VE	FL-290	PR-LJA	FL-374	CN-...
FL-43	N5626Y	FL-125	C-FWPR	FL-208	N350JW	FL-291	N701FC	FL-375	N657PP
FL-44	N904MC	FL-126	N124EB	FL-209	N454LF	FL-292	JA868A	FL-376	N376NA
FL-45	N111SF	FL-127	N300LS	FL-210	N111M	FL-293	N3253Q	FL-377	PR-AEF
		FL-128	EC-GSQ	FL-211	N11TE	FL-294	S9-CAN	FL-378	N225CM

FL-379	N973SC	FL-463	N352BC	FL-546	N350AG	BC-47	N46X	BP-40	83-0494
FL-381	N818WV	FL-464	N450CK	FL-547	N111MD	BC-48	N45A	BP-41	83-0495
FL-382	23056	FL-465	VT-ACD	FL-548	D2-	BC-49	N635B	BP-42	83-0496
FL-383	N500VL	FL-466	N35VP	FL-549	N1VA	BC-50	N1547	BP-43	83-0497
FL-384	N350PJ	FL-467	N350PT	FL-550	PR-CVI	BC-51	YV-....	BP-44	83-0498
FL-385	C-GEJE	FL-468	N609BG	FL-551	N791BP	BC-52	77-22941	BP-45	83-0499
FL-386	N789LL	FL-469	UR-HBD	FL-552	VT-JKK	BC-53	77-22942	BP-46	84-24375
FL-387	N141CE	FL-470	N350MS	FL-553	N775MG	BC-54	N7069A	BP-47	84-24376
FL-388	N15EW	FL-471	N865LR	FL-554	N454TB	BC-55	77-22944	BP-48	84-24377
FL-389	VH-MLG	FL-472	N37172	FL-555	N872CT	BC-56	N46L	BP-49	84-24378
FL-390	N823SD	FL-473	D-CFMD	FL-556	N898CD	BC-57	N215HP	BP-50	84-24379
FL-391	N142CE	FL-474	N350SM	FL-557	D-C	BC-58	N1546	BP-51	84-24380
FL-392	N350CB	FL-475	N949PC	FL-558	N558KA	BC-59	wfu	BP-52	w/o
FL-393	N350HA	FL-476	SU-MMN	FL-559	N291B	BC-60	77-22949	BP-53	85-1262
FL-394	N644CB	FL-477	HB-GJP	FL-560	N350PX	BC-61	N636B	BP-54	85-1263
FL-395	HP-1555	FL-478	VT-FIU	FL-561	N350EB	BC-62	N637B	BP-55	85-1264
FL-396	N613BA	FL-479	C-GAEO	FL-562	N628LD	BC-63	HP-....	BP-56	85-1265
FL-397	N220CG	FL-480	N73380	FL-563	RP-	BC-64	78-23128	BP-57	85-1266
FL-398	PR-ADM	FL-481	PR-DAH	FL-564	N564KA	BC-65	PP-LCB	BP-58	85-1267
FL-399	N504TF	FL-482	N37084	FL-565	N971JP	BC-66	N66000	BP-59	85-1268
FL-400	N40GZ	FL-483	N910BD	FL-566	N3366K	BC-67	N639B	BP-60	w/o
FL-401	N319EE	FL-484	VH-ZGS	FL-567	N31967	BC-68	78-23132	BP-61	85-1270
FL-402	N402JL	FL-485	N71885	FL-568	N32148	BC-69	78-23133	BP-62	85-1271
FL-403	N100BE	FL-486	TR-...	FL-569	M-OORE	BC-70	N321F	BP-63	85-1272
FL-404	N495DH	FL-487	N831PT	FL-570	N268LB	BC-71	78-23135	BP-64	86-0084
FL-405	N6165Y	FL-488	N36988	FL-571	N362DB	BC-72	N30W	BP-65	86-0085
FL-406	N828AJ	FL-489	N200VJ	FL-572	N3272Q	BC-73	N200ET	BP-66	86-0086
FL-407	N160MW	FL-490	N825TT	FL-573	N31973	BC-74	N121TD	BP-67	86-0087
FL-408	N350MR	FL-491	N3AW	FL-574	N3474P	BC-75	N700TG	BP-68	86-0088
FL-409	N409LV	FL-492	N394S	FL-575	N350RV	BD-1	N11	BP-69	86-0089
FL-410	D-CWKM	FL-493	N30MC	FL-577	N564BC	BD-2	N49R	BP-70	87-0160
FL-411	N15WS	FL-494	CNA-NJ	FL-581	N3474P	BD-3	N311KB	BP-71	87-0161
FL-412	N6112G	FL-495	N641MC	FL-585	N350RV	BD-4	73-1208	King Air C-12J	
FL-413	N350TT	FL-496	N900WP	Super King Air 350C		BD-5	TN-	UD-1	86-0078
FL-414	N19GR	FL-497	N409D	FN-1	N102SK	BD-6	wfu	UD-2	86-0079
FL-415	N36715	FL-498	N900WS	King Air C-12C		BD-7	w/o	UD-3	86-0080
FL-416	N6116N	FL-499	N680CB	BC-1	wfu	BD-8	N12	UD-4	86-0081
FL-417	N8YN	FL-500	N455SC	BC-2	N783MC	BD-9	N121CA	UD-5	86-0082
FL-418	N888FM	FL-501	N2112V	BC-3	N7247Y	BD-10	73-1214	UD-6	86-0083
FL-419	AP-...	FL-502	C-GBCE	BC-4	N72470	BD-11	73-1215	King Air C-12R	
FL-420	LV-BAN	FL-503	N551VB	BC-5	N540SP	BD-12	73-1216	BW-1	92-3327
FL-421	N350FW	FL-504	N553CL	BC-6	N34UP	BD-13	73-1217	BW-2	92-3328
FL-422	N350K	FL-505	RP-C8300	BC-7	N40R	BD-14	73-1218	BW-3	92-3329
FL-423	N5RF	FL-506	G-POWB	BC-8	N998AP	BD-15	76-0158	BW-4	94-0315
FL-424	N106ER	FL-507	N533GP	BC-9	N1560	BD-16	wfu	BW-5	94-0316
FL-425	JA02EP	FL-508	N883P	BC-10	73-22262	BD-17	76-0160	BW-6	94-0317
FL-426	A32-426	FL-509	N92TH	BC-11	N72472	BD-18	76-0161	BW-7	94-0318
FL-427	N345DG	FL-510	N851TC	BC-12	N48A	BD-19	76-0162	BW-8	94-0319
FL-428	N400AL	FL-511	C-GKOS	BC-13	wfu	BD-20	N8079B	BW-9	94-0320
FL-429	HP-1588	FL-512	N114RG	BC-14	N381PD	BD-21	76-0164	BW-10	94-0321
FL-430	N631ME	FL-513	N189CB	BC-15	N222DM	BD-22	w/o	BW-11	94-0322
FL-431	N75PX	FL-514	N350LM	BC-16	N1559	BD-23	76-0166	BW-12	94-0323
FL-432	N536BW	FL-515	D-CRAO	BC-17	N7074G	BD-24	76-3239	BW-13	94-0324
FL-433	N375CP	FL-516	N350RK	BC-18	N505FK	BD-25	76-0168	BW-14	94-0325
FL-434	PP-LOG	FL-517	N514LK	BC-19	N634B	BD-26	N49K	BW-15	94-0326
FL-435	PR-JDB	FL-518	N273TA	BC-20	N1558	BD-27	wfu	BW-16	95-0088
FL-436	N83KB	FL-519	N373WP	BC-21	N1554	BD-28	76-0171	BW-17	95-0089
FL-437	A32-437	FL-520	N883GB	BC-22	N703JR	BD-29	76-0172	BW-18	95-0090
FL-438	G-SERC	FL-521	N7021Z	BC-23	N396SA	BD-30	wfu	BW-19	95-0091
FL-439	A32-439	FL-522	N74226	BC-24	N145MJ	King Air C-12D/F		BW-20	95-0092
FL-440	N412CB	FL-523	N7233V	BC-25	N200NY	BP-1	78-23140	BW-21	95-0093
FL-441	N246SD	FL-524	N141L	BC-26	N72476	BP-7	974	BW-22	95-0094
FL-442	N3748H	FL-525	VH-PYN	BC-27	76-22551	BP-8	977	BW-23	95-0095
FL-443	VH-KJD	FL-526	VT-LJS	BC-28	N42Z	BP-9	980	BW-24	95-0096
FL-444	AP-...	FL-527	N1WV	BC-29	N612SA	BP-10	982	BW-25	95-0097
FL-445	N575MX	FL-528	N350MG	BC-30	N1553	BP-11	985	BW-26	95-0098
FL-446	N60DL	FL-529	N214WL	BC-31	N41R	BP-22	81-23541	BW-27	95-0099
FL-447	N961PP	FL-530	N7130X	BC-32	N2MP	BP-23	81-23543	BW-28	95-0100
FL-448	N122RG	FL-531	N7131Z	BC-33	N225LH	BP-25	81-23544	BW-29	95-0101
FL-449	N73WW	FL-532	ZS-PXF	BC-34	401	BP-26	81-23545	King Air RC-12D/H	
FL-450	C-GCGB	FL-533	N71966	BC-35	N283B	BP-27	81-23546	GR-1	81-23542
FL-451	JA377N	FL-534	ZS-FML	BC-36	76-22559	BP-28	N301PT	GR-2	80-23371
FL-452	CN-RLL	FL-535	HB-GJT	BC-37	FAN-002	BP-29	82-23781	GR-3	80-23377
FL-453	N62AZ	FL-536	N536MR	BC-38	76-22561	BP-30	N302PT	GR-4	80-23373
FL-454	N660P	FL-537	N2VA	BC-39	N1551	BP-31	82-23783	GR-5	80-23375
FL-455	XA-UET	FL-538	N7368X	BC-40	76-22563	BP-32	82-23784	GR-6	78-23141
FL-456	N316W	FL-539	N350NY	BC-41	N101CS	BP-33	82-23785	GR-7	78-23142
FL-457	N827CC	FL-540	N672MM	BC-42	N1SP	BP-34	83-24145	GR-8	78-23143
FL-458	N945SH	FL-541	PR-CCB	BC-43	77-22932	BP-35	83-24146	GR-9	78-23144
FL-459	ZS-ZAZ	FL-542	N304BP	BC-44	N258AG	BP-36	83-24147	GR-10	N321P
FL-460	OO-GMJ	FL-543	ZS-MCO	BC-45	N1549	BP-37	83-24148	GR-11	80-23376
FL-461	VH-SGQ	FL-544	N64TR	BC-46	77-22935	BP-38	83-24149	GR-12	80-23374
FL-462	N900PL	FL-545	N545KA			BP-39	83-24150		

GR-13	80-23378	BJ-34	wfu	NC-23	wfu	105	wfu	198	N91MM
GR-14	83-24313	BJ-35	161318	NC-24	wfu	106	N28DC	199	wfu
GR-15	83-24314	BJ-36	161319	NC-25	wfu	107	w/o	205	w/o
GR-16	83-24315	BJ-37	161320	NC-26	wfu	108	wfu	206	wfu
GR-17	83-24316	BJ-38	wfu	NC-27	wfu	109	wfu	207	N122MA
GR-18	83-24317	BJ-39	wfu	NC-28	wfu	110	wfu	208	N111HF
GR-19	83-24318	BJ-40	161323	NC-29	N8244L	111	N721FC	209	N35JL
King Air RC-12G		BJ-41	161324	NC-30	wfu	113	N859Q	210	N38BE
FC-1	80-23379	BJ-42	161325	NC-31	wfu	114	wfu	211	wfu
FC-2	80-23380	BJ-43	161326	NC-32	wfu	115	wfu	212	N1978P
FC-3	80-23372	BJ-44	wfu	NC-33	wfu	116	wfu	213	wfu
King Air RC-12K/N/P		BJ-45	161497	NC-34	wfu	117	wfu	214	wfu
FE-1	85-0147	BJ-46	161498	NC-35	wfu	118	wfu	215	PT-ICD
FE-2	85-0148	BJ-47	wfu	NC-36	wfu	119	wfu	216	N922FM
FE-3	85-0149	BJ-48	161500	NC-37	wfu	120	w/o	217	wfu
FE-4	85-0150	BJ-49	161501	NC-38	wfu	121	wfu	218	w/o
FE-5	w/o	BJ-50	161502	NC-39	wfu	122	MT-223	219	N185MA
FE-6	85-0152	BJ-51	wfu	NC-40	wfu	123	wfu	220	wfu
FE-7	85-0153	BJ-52	161504	NC-41	wfu	124	N987MA	221	N800BY
FE-8	w/o	BJ-53	161505	NC-42	wfu	125	wfu	222	SE-GHH
FE-9	85-0155	BJ-54	wfu	NC-43	wfu	126	PT-LOH	223	wfu
FE-10	88-0325	BJ-55	161507	NC-44	wfu	127	wfu	224	wfu
FE-11	88-0326	BJ-56	161508	NC-45	N45FL	129	N555C	226	N107SB
FE-12	88-0327	BJ-57	wfu	NC-46	wfu	130	w/o	228	N228WP
FE-13	89-0267	BJ-58	wfu	NC-47	wfu	131	N755Q	229	N100CF
FE-14	89-0268	BJ-59	161511	NC-48	wfu	132	VH-DTV	231	N346VL
FE-15	89-0269	BJ-60	161512	NC-49	wfu	133	N500QX	232	PT-WIX
FE-16	89-0270	BJ-61	161513	NC-50	N8285Q	134	w/o	233	wfu
FE-17	89-0271	BJ-62	161514	NC-51	N514RS	135	N54CK	239	OK-ATX
FE-18	w/o	BJ-63	161515	NC-52	wfu	136	N115AP	240	N64LG
FE-19	89-0273	BJ-64	wfu	NC-53	wfu	137	w/o	241	N700RX
FE-20	89-0274	BJ-65	161517	**Ibis**		138	N703DM	242	wfu
FE-21	89-0275	BJ-66	161518	**AE270P**		139	wfu	243	N250AF
FE-22	89-0276	**King Air UC-12F**		001	OK-EMA	140	N900TV	244	PT-LEW
FE-23	91-0516	BU-1	163553	003	w/o	141	w/o	245	wfu
FE-24	91-0517	BU-2	163554	005	OK-LIB	142	w/o	246	wfu
FE-25	91-0518	BU-3	163555	006	OK-INA	143	wfu	247	wfu
FE-26	92-13120	BU-4	163556	007	OK-EVA	144	wfu	248	N480AF
FE-27	92-13121	BU-5	163557	**Mitsubishi**		145	PT-BOY	249	wfu
FE-28	92-13122	BU-6	163558	**MU-2/LR-1**		146	wfu	250	N500XX
FE-29	92-13123	BU-7	163559	001	wfu	149	w/o	251	w/o
FE-30	92-13124	BU-8	163560	002	wfu	150	w/o	252	w/o
FE-31	92-13125	BU-9	163561	003	wfu	151	w/o	253	N481AF
FE-32	93-0697	BU-10	163562	004	wfu	154	N720JK	254	w/o
FE-33	93-0698	BU-11	163563	005	wfu	155	wfu	255	w/o
FE-34	93-0699	BU-12	wfu	006	w/o	156	XB-HOV	256	wfu
FE-35	93-0700	**King Air UC-12M**		007	wfu	157	N711VK	257	N344KL
FE-36	93-0701	BV-1	163836	008	wfu	158	N22MZ	258	wfu
King Air UC-12B		BV-2	163837	009	w/o	159	N888DS	259	w/o
BJ-1	wfu	BV-3	163838	010	wfu	160	w/o	260	N50ET
BJ-2	wfu	BV-4	163839	011	wfu	161	wfu	261	N281MA
BJ-3	N528NA	BV-5	163840	012	wfu	162	N573MA	262	wfu
BJ-4	wfu	BV-6	163841	013	w/o	163	wfu	263	N30RR
BJ-5	w/o	BV-7	163842	014	wfu	164	wfu	264	N38AF
BJ-6	161190	BV-8	163843	015	wfu	165	YV-....	265	N482AF
BJ-7	161191	BV-9	163844	016	w/o	166	wfu	266	w/o
BJ-8	wfu	BV-10	163845	017	wfu	167	N310MA	267	N59RW
BJ-9	161193	BV-11	163846	018	w/o	168	w/o	268	PT-JGA
BJ-10	wfu	BV-12	wfu	019	N728F	169	wfu	269	wfu
BJ-11	161195	**Starship**		020	wfu	170	N58CA	270	wfu
BJ-12	161196	NC-1	wfu	021	HR-...	172	wfu	271	N483AF
BJ-13	161197	NC-2	wfu	022	w/o	173	N18BF	272	N272MC
BJ-14	wfu	NC-3	wfu	023	wfu	174	N52CD	273	XB-...
BJ-15	wfu	NC-4	wfu	024	wfu	175	PT-BZW	274	wfu
BJ-16	wfu	NC-5	wfu	025	N2GZ	177	N12RA	276	w/o
BJ-17	161201	NC-6	wfu	026	PT-LMD	178	w/o	277	N3GT
BJ-18	wfu	NC-7	wfu	027	w/o	179	N777VK	280	N460FS
BJ-19	161203	NC-8	N10TQ	028	wfu	180	wfu	281	wfu
BJ-20	wfu	NC-9	wfu	029	wfu	182	N2100T	282	w/o
BJ-21	161205	NC-10	wfu	030	wfu	183	wfu	283	SE-GHA
BJ-22	161206	NC-11	wfu	031	N31WM	184	w/o	284	N484AF
BJ-23	161306	NC-12	wfu	032	wfu	185	wfu	285	N11SJ
BJ-24	wfu	NC-13	wfu	033	wfu	187	w/o	286	N666SP
BJ-25	wfu	NC-14	wfu	034	XB-FMV	188	PT-BZY	287	SE-GHB
BJ-26	161309	NC-15	wfu	035	N36G	189	XB-XOI	288	w/o
BJ-27	161310	NC-16	wfu	037	wfu	190	N140CM	289	SE-GHC
BJ-28	wfu	NC-17	wfu	038	N706DM	191	wfu	290	N14YS
BJ-29	161312	NC-18	wfu	101	w/o	192	wfu	291	N291MB
BJ-30	161313	NC-19	wfu	102	wfu	193	N8PC	292	wfu
BJ-31	wfu	NC-20	wfu	103	wfu	194	HI-	293	SE-GHD
BJ-32	161315	NC-21	wfu	104	N377NJ	195	wfu	294	SE-GHE
BJ-33	161316	NC-22	wfu			196	PT-DTL	295	wfu
						197	wfu	296	wfu

297	N7DD	390SA	N782MA	524	wfu	607	wfu	691SA	w/o
298	N188RM	391SA	N783MA	525	C-FTML	608	w/o	692	N869P
299	SE-GHF	392SA	N892SC	526	w/o	609	w/o	693SA	w/o
300	wfu	393SA	N82WC	527	N527AF	610	N601SD	694	N13YS
301	N461MA	395SA	w/o	528	N528AF	611	w/o	695	w/o
302	N462MA	396SA	w/o	529	wfu	612	N840MA	696	N301GM
303	N728FN	397SA	N777WM	530	w/o	613	w/o	697SA	N7601L
304	w/o	398SA	N61GJ	531	wfu	614	N21JA	698SA	N187SB
305	N50K	399SA	N1930P	532	w/o	615	N940MA	699SA	N32EC
306	N856JT	400SA	N700WA	533	wfu	616	N110MA	700SA	N860MA
307	w/o	401SA	w/o	534	wfu	617	N8484T	701SA	w/o
308	N485AF	402SA	wfu	535	wfu	618	wfu	702SA	YV-144CP
309	w/o	403SA	N264KW	536	w/o	619	XB-NUG	703SA	N338CM
310	N324GM	404SA	wfu	537	wfu	620	w/o	704SA	LV-MGC
311	N311RN	405SA	w/o	538	wfu	621	HK-2120P	705SA	N24WC
312	wfu	406SA	wfu	539	w/o	622	ZS-MGF	706SA	C-FJEL
313SA	N100KE	407SA	N750CA	540	N869D	623	N910NF	707SA	N707AF
314	w/o	408SA	w/o	541	w/o	624	w/o	708SA	N868MA
315	N99SR	409SA	N781H	542	wfu	625	wfu	709SA	N105WM
316	wfu	410SA	w/o	543	wfu	626	w/o	710SA	N710G
319	N54PC	411SA	N400PS	544	N544AF	627	N770RW	711SA	PT-WST
320	SE-IOZ	412SA	N25GM	545	w/o	628	C-FROW	712SA	wfu
321SA	N893SC	413SA	wfu	546	wfu	629	N629MU	713SA	N89DR
322	N40KC	414SA	N73MA	547	wfu	630	N630HA	714SA	N222FA
323	N216CD	415SA	N893KB	548	N200RX	631	N629TM	718SA	N718EE
324	N143JA	416SA	N44AX	549	C-FTOO	632	wfu	719SA	N777LP
325	N325MA	417SA	N61JB	550	w/o	633	wfu	720SA	N3UN
326	N165MA	418SA	w/o	551	wfu	634	N400SG	721SA	wfu
327	N375AC	419SA	N52MA	552	wfu	635	EC-GOK	722SA	PT-WYT
328	N305DS	420SA	D-IKKY	553	N755MA	636	wfu	723SA	N895MA
329	N486AF	423SA	N100NP	554	w/o	637	N637WG	724SA	N223JB
330	N261WB	424SA	N157MA	555	w/o	638	wfu	725SA	N425TF
331	w/o	425SA	N425TF	556	wfu	639	wfu	726SA	w/o
332	N333TX	426SA	N36AT	557	wfu	640	N490MA	727SA	PR-UTI
333	N487AF	427SA	N40AM	558	w/o	641	N211BE	728SA	N9NB
337	SE-IOV	428SA	PT-LIR	559	wfu	642	N74TC	729SA	N61BA
338	N450FS	429SA	N361MA	560	N776CC	643	N375CA	730SA	w/o
339	N800ED	430SA	N66FF	561	wfu	644	LV-WJY	731SA	N731CJ
340	wfu	431SA	w/o	562	N66CY	645	w/o	732SA	N80HH
341	XB-LIJ	432SA	N44VR	563	wfu	646	N118P	733SA	N15ET
342	wfu	433SA	N5LC	564	wfu	647	N44KU	734SA	N271TW
343	w/o	434SA	C-FGEM	565	wfu	648	wfu	735SA	w/o
344	wfu	435SA	N104JB	566	MU-1550	649	w/o	736SA	N175CA
345	SE-IUA	436SA	N62CN	567	wfu	650	PT-LFX	737SA	N888RH
346	N10UT	437SA	N145FS	568	N334EB	651	w/o	738SA	N941S
347	w/o	438SA	N10VU	569	w/o	652SA	wfu	739SA	N8083A
348SA	YV2188	439SA	N477DD	570	wfu	653	N129DW	740SA	N360RA
349SA	N316EN	440SA	N219MA	571	wfu	655	N535WM	741SA	N193AA
350SA	PT-OVW	441SA	w/o	572	wfu	656	N866D	742SA	w/o
351SA	N10MR	446SA	N15TR	573	N260CB	657	N740PB	743SA	wfu
352SA	D-IAHT	447SA	N48NP	574	N19GU	658	N741FN	744SA	N941MA
353SA	6Y-JDB	448SA	N68CL	575	wfu	659	N6KF	745SA	N942ST
354SA	PT-OIP	449SA	N449BK	576	wfu	660	N4065D	746SA	w/o
355SA	N29WD	450SA	N220N	577	wfu	661SA	N821MA	747SA	w/o
356SA	wfu	451SA	N725JT	578	wfu	662	C-FFFG	748SA	N102BX
357SA	N21HP	452SA	N388NC	579	w/o	663	wfu	749SA	PT-LIS
358SA	w/o	453SA	PT-OIY	580	N580AF	664	N59KS	750SA	N130MS
361SA	LV-MCV	454SA	N19GA	581	N93AH	665	w/o	751SA	N117H
362SA	N140CP	458SA	N458BB	582	wfu	666	N207BA	752SA	wfu
363SA	N110GC	459SA	N459SA	583	XB-NEB	667	N305CW	753SA	N174MA
364SA	N547TA	501	JA8737	584	N900YH	668	N500PJ	754SA	N46AK
365SA	w/o	502	N211RV	585	wfu	669	wfu	755SA	w/o
366SA	N2RA	503	w/o	586	wfu	670	w/o	756SA	N1790M
367SA	wfu	504	w/o	587	N450MA	671	N950MA	757SA	N43866
368SA	N78WD	505	w/o	588	N37KK	672	w/o	758SA	N261MA
369SA	N24PE	506	w/o	589	wfu	673	w/o	759SA	N759AF
370SA	N370MA	507	wfu	590	N640MA	674	ZS-ONB	760SA	N322TA
371SA	N30MA	508	wfu	591	N99BT	675	N68TN	761SA	w/o
372SA	w/o	509	N154WC	592	w/o	676	w/o	762SA	N762JC
373SA	N766MA	510	wfu	593	N400RX	677	N915RF	763SA	C-GEHS
374SA	N122CK	511	wfu	594	wfu	678	N678BK	764SA	N196MA
375SA	N81MF	512	wfu	595	wfu	679	N679BK	765SA	w/o
379SA	w/o	513	wfu	596	w/o	680	N201UV	766SA	N6KE
380SA	N333RK	514	wfu	597	wfu	681	N361JA	767SA	w/o
381SA	N356AJ	515	wfu	598	N15YS	682	wfu	768SA	wfu
382SA	N772MA	516	N516AF	599	N22XY	683	C-FIFE	769SA	w/o
383SA	N40JJ	517	w/o	600	N113SD	684	wfu	770SA	w/o
384SA	N774MA	518	wfu	601	C-FROM	685	YV-O-BDA-	771SA	wfu
385SA	N52WM	519	wfu	602	w/o	686	N717PS	772SA	N772DA
386SA	w/o	520	wfu	603	wfu	687	N687HB	773SA	N350RG
387SA	wfu	521	ZK-KOH	604	wfu	688	N688RA	774SA	PT-OHK
388SA	PT-OOS	522	N617BB	605	N621TA	689SA	N112MA	775SA	N70KC
389SA	N543JF	523	w/o	606	C-FOUR	690	wfu	776SA	w/o

777SA	XA-RNL	1510SA	N17HG	1019	N121WH	1102	N137SL	132	N361GB
778SA	N10HT	1511SA	N3MA	1020	N113SL	1103	N138SL	133	LV-ZSX
779SA	w/o	1512SA	N60FL	1021	N925TK	1104	N139SL	134	HB-FOG
780SA	wfu	1513SA	w/o	1022	N501PM	1105	HB-LTZ	135	VT-MEG
781SA	N60KC	1514SA	N14VL	1023	MM62159	1106	N780CA	136	N900HS
782SA	w/o	1515SA	LY-ZDV	1024	MM62160	1107	N140SL	137	N116AF
783SA	C-FFSS	1516SA	N89SC	1025	MM62161	1108	N108SL	138	VH-FMZ
784SA	w/o	1517SA	N727TP	1026	MM62167	1109	N143SL	139	wfu
785SA	C-GAMC	1518SA	w/o	1027	MM62168	1110	F-HBAI	140	N2YF
786SA	w/o	1519SA	N33EW	1028	MM62162	1111	N150SL	141	PT-WKF
787SA	N984RE	1520SA	N429WM	1029	MM62163	1112	F-HALF	142	OE-EKD
788SA	N610CA	1521SA	C-FRWK	1030	MM62164	1113	MM62247	143	XB-ILU
789SA	N21CJ	1522SA	N78PK	1031	MM62169	1114	MM62246	144	N312PC
790SA	N999WW	1523SA	C-FHMA	1032	I-DPCR	1115	N156SL	145	8030
791SA	N888WW	1524SA	w/o	1033	I-DPCS	1116	N157SL	146	N146PC
792SA	N34AL	1525SA	N35RR	1034	D-IZZY	1117	C-GCOM	147	ZS-NYM
793SA	N425EC	1526SA	N44MX	1035	I-FXRB	1118	MM62248	148	N998JB
794SA	N794MA	1527SA	w/o	1036	N785JH	1119	N158SL	149	N74AX
795SA	w/o	1528SA	N466DC	1037	C-GJMM	1120	PH-HRK	150	N94FE
796SA	C-GGDC	1529SA	N132BK	1038	N122PA	1121	N159SL	151	w/o
797SA	w/o	1530SA	PT-LSQ	1039	N39GK	1122	N124PA	152	N444CM
798SA	N661DP	1531SA	wfu	1040	I-BCOM	1123	F-GPKN	153	N153PB
799SA	w/o	1532SA	w/o	1041	MM62199	1124	SP-MXI	154	N217EB
801	w/o	1533SA	N452MA	1042	HB-LTE	1125	D-IIVA	155	N718JP
802	w/o	1534SA	N644EM	1043	N180HM	1126	MM62249	156	N156SB
803	22003	1535SA	w/o	1044	N395KT	1127	N160SL	157	HB-FOI
804	wfu	1536SA	N544CB	1045	I-FXRC	1128	N161SL	158	w/o
805	wfu	1537SA	w/o	1046	N29JS	1129	N5166P	159	C-GBTL
806	wfu	1538SA	w/o	1047	MM62200	1130	N162SL	160	N55BK
807	22007	1539SA	N42AF	1048	N105GP	1131	N163SL	161	N161AJ
808	22008	1540SA	w/o	1049	I-FXRE	1132	F-GPKO	162	N162PB
809	22009	1541SA	w/o	1050	N50WG	1133	C-GPII	163	N49LM
810	22010	1542SA	N4R	1051	N61GT	1134	N164SL	164	C-FMPA
811	w/o	1543SA	N469MA	1052	N102SL	1135	N165SL	165	N10PF
812	w/o	1544SA	N215MH	1053	MM62201	1136	N167SL	166	XB-IHX
813	22013	1545SA	N900M	1054	N153SL	1137	N408SF	167	N774DK
814	22014	1546SA	PT-LIK	1055	C-FSTP	1138	I-PREE	168	N853AL
815	22015	1547SA	w/o	1056	D-IJET	1139	N168SL	169	N912NM
816	22016	1548SA	N8RW	1057	C-GPDJ	1140	N169SL	170	C-GBXW
817	22017	1549SA	N888SE	1058	MM62202	1141	N172SL	171	N129AG
818	22018	1550SA	C-GZNS	1059	N103SL	1145	N145GS	172	N172PB
819	22019	1551SA	N444WF	1060	OY-TLP	1146	N173SL	173	N612KC
820	22020	1552SA	N246W	1061	C-GWRK	1147	N175SL	174	N562NA
901	wfu	1553SA	N479MA	1062	N133PA	1148	N611GT	175	N118AF
902	wfu	1554SA	N480MA	1063	N130EM	1149	N24XJ	176	VP-BLS
903	wfu	1555SA	w/o	1064	F-GZPE	1150	N176XL	177	EC-JXM
904	wfu	1556SA	N747SY	1065	C-GFOX	1151	N178SL	178	C-GKAY
905	w/o	1557SA	N999UP	1066	HB-LTN			179	N818RA
906	wfu	1558SA	N157CA	1067	I-FXRD	**Pilatus**		180	ZS-BEB
907	w/o	1559SA	N880AC	1068	N105SL	*PC-12/12M/Spectre*		181	N601BM
908	wfu	1560SA	N513DM	1069	C-GJOL	P-01	wfu	182	C-FOPD
909	wfu	1561SA	N64MD	1070	N106SL	P-02	HB-FOB	183	N183PC
910	wfu	1562SA	N1164F	1071	MM62203	101	N312BC	184	C-GMPE
911	wfu	1563SA	N7HN	1072	C-GPIA	102	VH-YDO	185	N185PB
912	wfu	1564SA	w/o	1073	N107SL	103	N610GH	186	N121PH
913	wfu	1565SA	N100BY	1074	C-GWII	104	N51WN	187	C-GAWP
914	wfu	1566SA	N468SP	1075	MM62205	105	N95NW	188	N188PC
915	wfu	1567SA	N467MA	1076	MM62212	106	N812PA	189	N977XL
916	wfu	1568SA	PT-LJS	1077	N149SL	107	PH-ECC	190	N190PE
917	wfu	1569SA	N222HH	1078	I-DVFM	108	LX-SKY	191	N48PG
918	wfu	**Partenavia**		1079	SP-MXH	109	VH-FMC	192	N418DR
919	w/o	*AP68TP-600*		1080	N23RF	110	VH-FMF	193	C-GDGD
920	wfu	9001	N901TP	1081	I-BPAE	111	N222CM	194	N455DK
921	wfu	**Piaggio**		1082	MM62204	112	N263RS	195	N721PB
922	wfu	*P-180 Avanti/II*		1083	N147SL	113	ZS-SMY	196	C-GRJP
923	83-3223	1001	wfu	1084	N130SL	114	N121RF	197	N613NA
924	83-3224	1002	wfu	1085	MM62211	115	N946JJ	198	ZS-DMM
925	93-3225	1004	N180BP	1086	YV1676	116	N116SK	199	N199WF
926	23-3226	1006	N111VR	1087	MM62206	117	N12FA	200	C-GRMS
927	23-3227	1007	C-FNGA	1088	XA-ANS	118	N802HS	201	N456V
951	wfu	1008	N109MS	1089	PH-TCN	119	N432CV	202	C-FSRK
952	wfu	1009	C-GLEM	1090	MM62213	120	N15EK	203	VH-VAT
953	wfu	1010	N589H	1091	N146SL	121	HB-FOT	204	C-FKUL
954	wfu	1011	N128SL	1092	N109SL	122	VH-FMP	205	ZS-OFB
1501SA	PT-WNS	1012	N416LF	1093	N145SL	123	VH-FMW	206	w/o
1502SA	N71DP	1013	N155SL	1094	I-CFPA	124	N124UV	207	C-GVKC
1503SA	N407MA	1014	N152SL	1095	C-GKWO	125	V5	208	ZS-OFD
1504SA	N1727S	1015	N990RS	1096	MM62207	126	VH-JLK	209	N108JC
1505SA	N321GM	1016	D-IGOB	1097	N131SL	127	N888CG	210	N210PT
1506SA	N160SP	1017	N17PA	1098	N132SL	128	TT-AAF	211	C-FVPK
1507SA	N308TC	1018	N180AV	1099	N8870B	129	N129JW	212	N212PB
1508SA	PT-LHH			1100	N134SL	130	N1TC	213	N852AL
1509SA	N973BB			1101	N136SL	131	N643BW	214	C-GRDC

582

215	N321MX	298	N64WF	381	I-LOAN	464	N769CM	547	N547AF
216	N216KC	299	w/o	382	N359CV	465	N465PC	548	N715TL
217	N25EP	300	N77ZA	383	ZS-TLA	466	VH-FDK	549	EC-JFO
218	N218WA	301	VH-YDN	384	N14RD	467	VH-ZWO	550	PH-XII
219	N219PC	302	N302PB	385	N7ZT	468	N944BT	551	HB-FPI
220	N224JD	303	N303JD	386	HB-FOY	469	N469AF	552	N152PC
221	N221PC	304	N304PT	387	N387W	470	N470AH	553	N553CA
222	C-FIJV	305	N695PC	388	N388PC	471	ZS-AGI	554	ZS-DER
223	N317NA	306	N271SS	389	N389W	472	VT-TAS	555	N555PE
224	N400BW	307	C-FKVL	390	N12DZ	473	N473PC	556	N556HL
225	N69FG	308	C-GKNR	391	N391EC	474	N57LT	557	N4TF
226	N970NA	309	PH-DIX	392	N392WC	475	C-GLCE	558	N558AF
227	C-FYZS	310	N166SB	393	N393AF	476	N476D	559	N559PB
228	N12JD	311	C-GMPY	394	N395W	477	PH-JFS	560	ZS-PGX
229	C-FMPO	312	N142LT	395	N395PC	478	N26VW	561	N561ST
230	N230PG	313	ZS-SRH	396	VH-NWO	479	HB-FPE	562	N562PB
231	VH-PIL	314	C-FMPE	397	N854AL	480	N480WH	563	N563TM
232	N242JH	315	C-FMPW	398	N398J	481	XA-...	564	N724HS
233	C-FKRB	316	N388SR	399	C-FPCI	482	05-0482	565	N65AF
234	C-FAJV	317	ZS-SRP	400	VH-VWO	483	N281WB	566	C-GPLT
235	N105MW	318	N318MT	401	N401PD	484	N667RB	567	N567FH
236	N299AM	319	ZS-SRR	402	N22LP	485	N485PC	568	G-CCWY
237	C-GBJV	320	N605TQ	403	N128CM	486	N486PB	569	N569AF
238	C-GRBA	321	N321PL	404	N420DW	487	N487PC	570	N578DC
239	C-GMPI	322	N444FT	405	XA-PCM	488	N56EZ	571	N571PC
240	C-FCJV	323	N956PC	406	F-GRAJ	489	N489JG	572	N572PC
241	N316PM	324	C-FKSL	407	HB-FPW	490	N324SC	573	05-0573
242	ZS-DAT	325	N325MW	408	N82HR	491	C-GPAI	574	LX-JFI
243	5Y-MAF	326	N337TP	409	05-0409	492	N492WA	575	N575PC
244	C-GEOW	327	N327JZ	410	N524CE	493	XB-IKO	576	N576RG
245	C-GKPL	328	N328JP	411	HB-FOW	494	N612J	577	N577BF
246	N642CT	329	N329NG	412	G-ILMD	495	N83AJ	578	N661WP
247	HB-FPL	330	N515RP	413	N629SK	496	OY-SCI	579	D-FAPC
248	N40191	331	C-FASP	414	N226N	497	N497PC	580	PR-BZE
249	N399AM	332	VH-FDE	415	N415PB	498	EC-ISH	581	N581PC
250	C-FKPI	333	XA-...	416	C-FASF	499	N1056B	582	N582DT
251	VT-DAR	334	HB-FOX	417	N417KC	500	N500NK	583	N5904A
252	VT-DAV	335	N335WH	418	N507AZ	501	N501PB	584	N543JV
253	N253PC	336	N422MU	419	05-0419	502	N124PS	585	XA-UES
254	C-FYUT	337	N601HT	420	N420AF	503	N503WS	586	N586PB
255	N401SM	338	N338PC	421	OY-GSA	504	XA-JOS	587	N888WG
256	F-GJFG	339	C-FGFL	422	HB-FPC	505	N505P	588	N588KC
257	N92AG	340	N343CW	423	N423WA	506	ZS-MSF	589	N589AC
258	C-FPCN	341	N58VS	424	05-0424	507	N507RC	590	N629DF
259	N62GA	342	N2JB	425	w/o	508	M-ICKY	591	N591AF
260	N260HS	343	HB-FVZ	426	VH-FDC	509	N4TS	592	N26KH
261	N33JA	344	N411MV	427	N427WA	510	N861PP	593	N593PC
262	N199CM	345	N345RF	428	VH-FDM	511	N511PB	594	N594WA
263	N65TB	346	N377L	429	N429PC	512	XA-UBA	595	N212LT
264	N264WF	347	N347KC	430	N8421E	513	EC-KFK	596	N535BB
265	N68PK	348	N348PC	431	N431WC	514	N156SW	597	N597CH
266	N913AL	349	HB-FOQ	432	N432MH	515	N515AF	598	N598MM
267	N267WF	350	N451DM	433	C-FPCZ	516	wfu	599	N599PB
268	C-GFIL	351	N351PC	434	VH-FDP	517	N487LM	600	N500BG
269	N269PB	352	I-TOPS	435	N435PC	518	020	601	N154DF
270	N360DA	353	C-FASR	436	ZS-COH	519	N519PC	602	N901TR
271	N555EW	354	N354AF	437	N654JC	520	N234RG	603	C-GPCO
272	C-GMPZ	355	N5DM	438	VH-FGR	521	N521PC	604	N604WP
273	N273AF	356	w/o	439	N439WC	522	LX-JFH	605	N605PC
274	C-GMPW	357	C-GZGZ	440	VH-FGS	523	N523JL	606	N21AU
275	C-FKPA	358	C-FVPC	441	N216TM	524	N524GT	607	N607AF
276	C-FPCL	359	F-GVJB	442	VH-FGT	525	7Q-YLT	608	HB-FPS
277	N277PC	360	N851RM	443	N466SA	526	N600WY	609	G-INTO
278	N278WC	361	C-FIAS	444	N925HW	527	N527PB	610	N610NK
279	N167AR	362	N326PA	445	VH-JMU	528	N528EJ	611	N417AR
280	C-FWAV	363	VH-KWO	446	N131JN	529	N529PS	612	C-FQMM
281	N100YC	364	N220CL	447	05-0447	530	N530WC	613	N798WC
282	ZS-SDO	365	C-GSLC	448	N712BC	531	LX-LAB	614	N614LD
283	C-FMPB	366	HB-FOS	449	N449BY	532	N7YR	615	ZS-FTG
284	N191SP	367	N45PM	450	N450PC	533	N533PC	616	N616EL
285	N88NT	368	N368PC	451	C-FKPX	534	N353KM	617	VH-WBI
286	N123CF	369	N128GH	452	N452MD	535	N535MJ	618	N618JL
287	N287PC	370	N78PG	453	N453PC	536	OE-EPC	619	N619AF
288	N554VR	371	N71TP	454	N454PS	537	N537PC	620	N620WA
289	N289PB	372	N372GT	455	N455WM	538	S2-AED	621	ZS-YEA
290	N6FZ	373	N373KM	456	N456PC	539	N522DJ	622	N622WW
291	HB-FOP	374	C-GMPP	457	N327YR	540	N950KM	623	N623BA
292	N715HL	375	N933SE	458	N458DL	541	N541PB	624	N624AF
293	C-GFLA	376	N376KC	459	N459PC	542	N2222C	625	CS-DIQ
294	GN-810	377	N409DR	460	N460PB	543	N543PB	626	N538BH
295	N957ST	378	N378HH	461	XA-TWZ	544	HB-FPR	627	N1RH
296	C-FMPN	379	VH-MWO	462	N462PC	545	HB-FPT	628	N452GH
297	N269AB	380	N380TM	463	N463JT	546	N546PB	629	N6971Z

630	N292P	713	ZS-AVH	796	N657PC	879	HB-FQK	8004005	PT-OAJ
631	N631BL	714	N893WB	797	ZS-GMC	880	HB-FQL	8004006	N611RR
632	G-PVPC	715	N227NS	798	N798RG	882	HB-FQN	8004007	PT-OPQ
633	D-FCGH	716	w/o	799	N1983R	883	HB-FQO	8004008	N701PT
634	ZS-PRX	717	N717NC	800	C-FMDF	884	HB-FQP	8004009	N98GF
635	N705KC	718	N324BK	801	N801J	885	HB-FQR	8004010	N2415W
636	N942TW	719	N719PC	802	N802AF	1001	HB-FVB	8004011	9A-BOR
637	N637PH	720	VH-WPY	803	RA-01500	1002	HB-FVC	8004012	N400LJ
638	N638AV	721	N721AF	804	N236WR	**Piper**		8004013	N31MB
639	N639KC	722	N623AC	805	ZS-JDD	*Cheyenne I*		8004014	PT-OVE
640	N640MY	723	HB-FRJ	806	N629MC			8004015	N244AB
641	N641TK	724	N624TS	807	N807D	7804001	wfu	8004016	N75TW
642	N642PC	725	VH-YWO	808	N531MP	7804002	N200TS	8004017	N2458W
643	N643PC	726	N721SL	809	N36EG	7804003	N913CR	8004018	N669WB
644	N644SD	727	C-GBMF	810	N184TH	7804004	N500MY	8004019	N992TT
645	N645PC	728	I-CNDB	811	N811PC	7804005	N96MA	8004020	N166WT
646	N875RJ	729	N729AF	812	LX-JFM	7804006	w/o	8004021	N49AC
647	N320PW	730	N950KA	813	N527DM	7804007	N17CE	8004022	N141GA
648	G-OLTT	731	N731PC	814	PR-DOG	7804008	w/o	8004023	N52HL
649	N649P	732	G-ZUMO	815	N815AF	7804009	N331KB	8004024	I-SASA
650	N650MC	733	N326V	816	N816PC	7804010	N7VR	8004025	N314DD
651	N651PB	734	N608SM	817	N777JZ	7804011	w/o	8004026	N314GK
652	PR-AGR	735	N735MD	818	N6818R	7904001	N195AA	8004027	N73BG
653	N528PM	736	N72EA	819	N434JA	7904002	N119RL	8004028	N300CE
654	N650BG	737	N52NK	820	N626MT	7904003	N37PJ	8004029	N93CN
655	PP-BER	738	PR-LJR	821	N821PE	7904004	OY-BHU	8004030	N66TW
656	N656AF	739	ZS-CWM	822	N822BM	7904005	N888PH	8004031	N60JW
657	N700PL	740	N740AF	823	N1130D	7904006	N300WP	8004032	wfu
658	N504SR	741	N804ST	824	N824SM	7904007	N231SW	8004033	N826RM
659	OY-MID	742	N742R	825	N844GT	7904008	C-GTMM	8004034	N82TW
660	N660WA	743	N743AE	826	N828VV	7904009	wfu	8004035	N2369V
661	N755EM	744	N744DA	827	VH-OOI	7904010	N212HH	8004036	w/o
662	N747KL	745	RA-01509	828	N144MF	7904011	w/o	8004037	N114JR
663	OE-EMC	746	N325FS	829	N829PE	7904012	N4RX	8004038	PT-OPF
664	N602BM	747	N797GM	830	G-WINT	7904013	YV1443	8004039	PT-OLF
665	N665MC	748	N814TB	831	N4DF	7904014	HB-LLK	8004040	N219SC
666	N672SD	749	N749GC	832	XA-	7904015	N131DF	8004041	N768MB
667	PR-AGM	750	ZS-TSW	833	HB-FVA	7904016	N503WR	8004042	N617DW
668	N212PK	751	LX-DNI	834	N695OE	7904017	N23243	8004043	PT-WMU
669	N669AF	752	N752JS	835	N100MS	7904018	N23250	8004044	HB-LQP
670	N670WH	753	N92CA	836	N996KF	7904019	N70TJ	8004045	wfu
671	N671PC	754	N777CQ	837	VH-ZBD	7904020	N187SC	8004046	N926K
672	N672PB	755	N755HF	838	N838PE	7904021	N232DH	8004047	N831CH
673	N673PC	756	N916AD	839	N666M	7904022	N165KC	8004048	N55JP
674	N674KC	757	N770PW	840	N840PE	7904023	N52PF	8004049	w/o
675	C-GRCN	758	N56RJ	841	HB-FSP	7904024	N23334	8004050	N896DR
676	N676PC	759	N759PB	842	VH-IOA	7904025	N918FM	8004051	w/o
677	OY-NUT	760	N660WB	843	N967AD	7904026	3A-MSI	8004052	D-IRVK
678	LX-JFJ	761	D-FINE	844	N739S	7904027	N98TG	8004053	D-ILCE
679	N679PE	762	N500WY	845	ZS-AMS	7904028	N688CP	8004054	N51RM
680	XA-	763	N16VK	846	N846PW	7904029	N93SH	8004055	N484AS
681	N681GH	764	N26KR	847	D-FFHZ	7904030	w/o	8004056	XB-GOI
682	G-MATX	765	CX-FCS	848	N848PC	7904031	XA-...	8004057	N316WB
683	LX-JFK	766	N214CS	849	C-GMLF	7904032	N60KV	8104001	N181SW
684	D-FHGN	767	TG-ASC	850	N850CB	7904033	N29ORS	8104002	CC-PNS
685	HB-FPY	768	C-FMPF	851	N851AF	7904034	N334CA	8104003	N2356X
686	N686PC	769	N769AF	852	N852FR	7904035	N23426	8104004	N70GW
687	N687AF	770	N35WA	853	N853WM	7904036	N14886	8104005	N199MA
688	N707KH	771	ZS-APS	854	N12AG	7904037	N200FB	8104006	N37TW
689	N689PE	772	VH-HIG	855	LX-JFN	7904038	N888AH	8104007	HK-....
690	ZS-PRK	773	D-FIBI	856	N856PC	7904039	N939JB	8104008	N38TW
691	N691PC	774	N774GW	857	N693PD	7904040	YV-O-MAC-	8104009	N816CM
692	N692BC	775	XA-	858	ZS-GAA	7904041	N301TA	8104010	N980CA
693	N693AT	776	N776AF	859	N859PL	7904042	N129LC	8104011	N329KK
694	N909BJ	777	N72DZ	860	N116TH	7904043	N70TW	8104012	N39TL
695	ZS-PTX	778	HB-FVV	861	VH-FDJ	7904044	N523PD	8104013	N707CV
696	N126BK	779	N779PC	862	HB-FSU	7904045	LV-MYX	8104014	N2403X
697	OY-PPP	780	N48GA	863	OY-TWO	7904046	N222SL	8104015	N105MA
698	N758PC	781	N781PE	864	HB-FSO	7904047	N479SW	8104016	N481SW
699	N699AF	782	VT-JSL	865	HB-FSW	7904048	N827LP	8104017	PT-OTV
700	N600KP	783	N783PC	866	N866PE	7904049	w/o	8104018	N801CA
701	XA-UFN	784	N784BK	867	G-OCLE	7904050	N222GW	8104019	N191MA
702	HB-FPZ	785	PP-SAM	868	N868PE	7904051	N165SW	8104020	N26JB
703	N703TL	786	N786WM	869	N869AF	7904052	N137CW	8104021	N112BB
704	VH-WPE	787	N220JP	870	N870KC	7904053	XB-FXU	8104022	N300SR
705	N1CW	788	D-FATN	871	N650WC	7904054	CC-PHM	8104023	CC-PWH
706	N706AG	789	C-GFLN	872	OY-VIN	7904055	w/o	8104024	N225CA
707	C-GODE	790	N757ED	873	N873PC	7904056	N879SW	8104025	N880M
708	N708AF	791	ZS-DLB	874	N874AF	7904057	N2348W	8104026	N2480X
709	N709RB	792	N775CC	875	N178MH	8004001	N10CS	8104027	N398SP
710	G-TRAT	793	N96MV	876	HB-FQH	8004002	N424CM	8104028	N38RE
711	N711PN	794	N794AF	877	HB-FQI	8004003	N2556P	8104029	OE-FKH
712	N609TW	795	PK-UCG	878	HB-FQJ	8004004	N2587R	8104030	N47GW

8104031	N90VM	7520012	PT-KME	7620052	N220FS	7820009	N131PC	7820092	w/o
8104032	9A-BZG	7520013	wfu	7620053	PR-HRM	7820010	F-GRPS	7920001	3A-MIO
8104033	N94EG	7520014	FAC-5739	7620054	wfu	7820011	HA-SIT	7920002	OM-VIP
8104034	PT-WEF	7520015	C-FYBV	7620055	N55R	7820012	XB-...	7920003	N225WW
8104035	N2519X	7520016	wfu	7620056	wfu	7820013	5V-...	7920004	N790SD
8104036	N633WC	7520017	N707ML	7620057	N200VE	7820014	N18ZX	7920005	CC-PLL
8104037	w/o	7520018	wfu	7720001	w/o	7820015	F-GHTA	7920006	wfu
8104038	N27BF	7520019	wfu	7720002	N771SW	7820016	w/o	7920007	N22WF
8104039	N824VA	7520020	w/o	7720003	N34HM	7820017	HB-LRV	7920008	C-GVKA
8104040	N711LD	7520021	C-GKPC	7720004	wfu	7820018	CC-CIW	7920009	N723JP
8104041	PT-OKT	7520022	LV-LTV	7720005	N28BG	7820019	N31ET	7920010	D-IOTT
8104042	N5RB	7520023	N40TT	7720006	wfu	7820020	CC-PZB	7920011	N6175A
8104043	N247LM	7520024	C-GPNP	7720007	N99VA	7820021	N182ME	7920012	XB-HNA
8104044	wfu	7520025	wfu	7720008	N730PT	7820022	N484SC	7920013	w/o
8104045	N855JL	7520026	N181DC	7720009	ZK-POD	7820023	C-GGPS	7920014	w/o
8104046	N221RC	7520027	YV-1990P	7720010	w/o	7820024	N155CA	7920015	N200PG
8104047	N83MG	7520028	wfu	7720011	N20WL	7820025	N888CV	7920016	N161XX*
8104048	N862RA	7520029	N770MG	7720012	N119EB	7820026	N473GG	7920017	LV-MNR
8104049	N2435Y	7520030	N444RC	7720013	w/o	7820027	LX-RST	7920018	w/o
8104050	N515GA	7520031	wfu	7720014	N82094	7820028	N444BN	7920019	N20TN
8104051	PT-OVB	7520032	N4116W	7720015	w/o	7820029	N427DD	7920020	N39EH
8104052	N408SH	7520033	I-CGAT	7720016	wfu	7820030	w/o	7920021	YV217T
8104053	N454CA	7520034	I-HYDR	7720017	C-	7820031	wfu	7920022	YV-251CP
8104054	N555AT	7520035	N17TU	7720018	N819MK	7820032	XA-...	7920023	XB-RLM
8104055	D-ISIG	7520036	w/o	7720019	N135CL	7820033	N63CA	7920024	N159DG
8104056	N711ER	7520037	VH-DXD	7720020	N37HB	7820034	N419R	7920025	wfu
8104057	D-IHJK	7520038	wfu	7720021	wfu	7820035	CC-CMH	7920026	w/o
8104058	N277DG	7520039	C-GJPT	7720022	w/o	7820036	N202HC	7920027	N31ZS
8104059	N819SW	7520040	w/o	7720023	w/o	7820037	YV-2365P	7920028	N123EA
8104060	N14PX	7520041	wfu	7720024	w/o	7820038	C-GVKK	7920029	N68BJ
8104061	N2552Y	7520042	w/o	7720025	wfu	7820039	N233PS	7920030	N89JA
8104062	PT-WMX	7520043	TI-AWN	7720026	wfu	7820040	N98TB	7920031	w/o
8104063	CC-PBT	7620001	wfu	7720027	N427TA	7820041	wfu	7920032	N88BC
8104064	PT-XOC	7620002	N610P	7720028	N171JP	7820042	N700RG	7920033	wfu
8104065	N977G	7620003	LV-LZO	7720029	wfu	7820043	N44DT	7920034	PT-OFH
8104066	N914AS	7620004	w/o	7720030	wfu	7820044	w/o	7920035	N111KV
8104067	LX-ACR	7620005	I-PALS	7720031	wfu	7820045	I-CGTT	7920036	w/o
8104068	N917TP	7620006	w/o	7720032	N747RE	7820046	PP-LCO	7920037	N53AM
8104070	CC-CBD	7620007	wfu	7720033	TU-TJL	7820047	N926LD	7920038	N333XX
8104071	CC-CWD	7620008	C-GMEJ	7720034	wfu	7820048	w/o	7920039	N524AM
8104072	N800BB	7620009	wfu	7720035	N200NB	7820049	PT-WFQ	7920040	N80CP
8104073	PT-WHN	7620010	C-GXBF	7720036	F-GGRV	7820050	N250TT	7920041	XA-HNG
8104101	N75WA	7620011	F-GFEA	7720037	N112BL	7820051	SE-LUB	7920042	N28CA
Cheyenne 1A		7620012	C9-JTP	7720038	N77NL	7820052	YV2006	7920043	N47CA
1104004	N90WW	7620013	wfu	7720039	PT-LUJ	7820053	N786AH	7920044	N90WG
1104005	N58AM	7620014	N98AT	7720040	wfu	7820054	PK-DYR	7920045	C-FGWA
1104006	N2434W	7620015	wfu	7720041	F-ODGS	7820055	w/o	7920046	N800EB
1104007	S3-BHN	7620016	C-GTFP	7720042	F-GJPE	7820056	N781CK	7920047	XA-RWR
1104008	N9266Y	7620017	wfu	7720043	N80MA	7820057	w/o	7920048	N406RS
1104009	XB-GAL	7620018	SX-AVE	7720044	LV-BCU	7820058	TG-GAP	7920049	wfu
1104010	UN-P3101	7620019	C-GMDF	7720045	N82156	7820059	wfu	7920050	LV-MOE
1104011	N2434V	7620020	F-BXSK	7720046	w/o	7820060	N990LR	7920051	N97TW
1104012	N622BB	7620021	wfu	7720047	YV-124CP	7820061	N5007	7920052	w/o
1104013	N48AM	7620022	LV-BCR	7720048	N521PM	7820062	wfu	7920053	CC-CYT
1104014	D-ILGA	7620023	wfu	7720049	X.	7820063	w/o	7920054	N187CP
1104015	D-IEMR	7620024	w/o	7720050	YV-2451P	7820064	wfu	7920055	N620DB
1104016	D-IFHZ	7620025	wfu	7720051	wfu	7820065	w/o	7920056	ZS-PXB
1104017	N85KG	7620026	C-GXCD	7720052	C-GXTC	7820066	D-IKEW	7920057	N52TT
8304001	N9183C	7620027	wfu	7720053	N613HC	7820067	YV-1402P	7920058	CC-CAO
8304002	N810HM	7620028	N555PM	7720054	N30DU	7820068	w/o	7920059	N25MG
8304003	N84CF	7620029	C-GNWD	7720055	XA-...	7820069	N155MC	7920060	N81WE
Cheyenne II		7620030	wfu	7720056	OE-FDS	7820070	YV-2331P	7920061	N44HT
1	wfu	7620031	w/o	7720057	N411BL	7820071	w/o	7920062	N78CA
7400002	wfu	7620032	F-GALD	7720058	C-FFNV	7820072	w/o	7920063	PT-LZB
7400003	N231PT	7620033	C-FNYM	7720059	5R-MIM	7820073	N814W	7920064	w/o
7400004	wfu	7620034	XA-PGT	7720060	N909PW	7820074	N274SB	7920065	LV-OAP
7400005	N10BQ	7620035	LV-BCT	7720061	wfu	7820075	N75TF	7920066	N444PC
7400006	w/o	7620036	C-GNDI	7720062	N361JC	7820076	N429AP	7920067	N74TW
7400007	wfu	7620037	N5136V	7720063	SX-FDC	7820077	XA	7920068	N711RD
7400008	N227TM	7620038	wfu	7720064	N211AE	7820078	w/o	7920069	C-FCEF
7400009	N910HG	7620039	C-FWUT	7720065	LV-MDG	7820079	wfu	7920070	w/o
7520001	N234K	7620040	N400CM	7720066	N993RH	7820080	N5D	7920071	wfu
7520002	F-GFLE	7620041	N67DW	7720067	F-GHJV	7820081	N2DS	7920072	CC-CZC
7520003	w/o	7620042	N8131F	7720068	N510LC	7820082	N7FL	7920073	EC-DHF
7520004	wfu	7620043	wfu	7720069	N411LM	7820083	N53TA	7920074	N24DD
7520005	N1976J	7620044	PT-OPH	7820001	N115PC	7820084	N100WQ	7920075	OB-1308
7520006	N49NM	7620045	wfu	7820002	C-FRJE	7820085	V5-CCH	7920076	HK-2347
7520007	N522AS	7620046	XC-UAT	7820003	N55GD	7820086	N186GA	7920077	w/o
7520008	C-GNKP	7620047	N111CT	7820004	N910JP	7820087	N6107A	7920078	N23646
7520009	N113RC	7620048	wfu	7820005	wfu	7820088	wfu	7920079	N789CH
7520010	N3951F	7620049	XA-...	7820006	LV-BCP	7820089	wfu	7920080	LV-MTU
7520011	w/o	7620050	N2FJ	7820007	w/o	7820090	N32KW	7920081	w/o
		7620051	N788BB	7820008	YV-703CP	7820091	w/o	7920082	CC-PNA

7920083	PT-LZR	8020072	N83CA	8120063	N715CA	8166067	PT-MFW	8001070	N82PG
7920084	PK-PTI	8020073	N100CM	8120064	F-GLRP	8166068	N328KK	8001071	N880TC
7920085	w/o	8020074	N62E	8120068	N43WH	8166069	C-GBFO	8001072	N801JW
7920086	N1183G	8020075	N36TW	8120070	PT-OJM	8166070	CC-CPR	8001073	4X-CIC
7920087	N23718	8020076	N29LA	8120101	PT-WGJ	8166071	N444ER	8001074	N479MM
7920088	HK-....	8020077	HK-2585P	8120102	D-INNN	8166072	HK-3117W	8001075	HK-3693X
7920089	N171AF	8020078	N2522V	8120103	N707WD	8166075	N83XL	8001078	N28DA
7920090	N881L	8020079	PT-ODR	8120104	N777LE	8166076	N57KC	8001079	N22UP
7920091	N26SL	8020080	4X-CBL	**Cheyenne II-XL**		**Cheyenne III**		8001080	PT-MFL
7920092	N108NL	8020081	wfu	1166001	N359GP	31-5003	wfu	8001081	N802MW
7920093	N99KF	8020082	N82PC	1166002	CC-PML	7800001	N420PA	8001101	w/o
7920094	F-GPBF	8020083	HB-LNL	1166003	EC-JRF	7800002	OB-1803	8001102	N760MM
8020001	w/o	8020084	F-ODMM	1166004	ZS-PBT	7801003	OB-1633	8001103	PT-OKL
8020002	N333P	8020085	N154CA	1166005	N395CA	7801004	N48RA	8001104	XB-JNC
8020003	TG-GOL	8020086	N880SW	1166006	N804C	8001001	N51KC	8001105	UN-
8020004	N23WP	8020087	N455MM	1166007	TG-	8001002	D-IONE	8001106	N933DG
8020005	N25ND	8020088	N431GW	1166008	N150TK	8001003	N242RA	**Cheyenne IIIA**	
8020006	YU-BPF	8020089	N333TN	8166001	N731PB	8001004	N717ES	5501003	N29TF
8020007	w/o	8020090	C-51	8166002	N431CF	8001005	N113WC	5501004	N995SC
8020008	XB-GVI	8020091	HB-LTI	8166003	w/o	8001006	wfu	5501005	N2247R
8020009	w/o	8020092	w/o	8166004	w/o	8001007	w/o	5501006	N236RC
8020010	w/o	8120001	wfu	8166005	N410CA	8001008	N977XT	5501007	D-IXXX
8020011	N90FS	8120002	w/o	8166006	N282PC	8001009	LV-BEI	5501008	XA-EJS
8020012	YU-BPG	8120003	TG-COB	8166007	N303TS	8001010	N133FM	5501009	wfu
8020013	LV-OGF	8120004	N139CS	8166008	N1380	8001011	D-IABA	5501010	N627PC
8020014	N137JE	8120005	PT-OLZ	8166009	N248J	8001012	N813CF	5501011	G-GZRP
8020015	HP-809	8120006	N998LM	8166010	N200XL	8001013	OB-1714	5501012	N4116Q
8020016	N801HL	8120007	N55KW	8166011	N630MW	8001014	N373Q	5501013	N90TW
8020017	D-IKET	8120008	N778HA	8166012	N321LB	8001015	wfu	5501014	D-IFSH
8020018	N108UC	8120009	N85GC	8166013	G-FCED	8001016	OB-1687	5501015	N794A
8020019	XC-QET	8120010	PT-OPC	8166014	N15KW	8001017	N175AA	5501016	N313BB
8020020	N118WC	8120011	PT-WLJ	8166015	N192TB	8001018	OB-1365	5501017	N75LS
8020021	YU-BMM	8120012	C-FJVB	8166016	N440S	8001019	w/o	5501018	N515RC
8020022	N38VT	8120013	YV1397	8166017	N550MM	8001020	N332SM	5501019	XB-PSG
8020023	N970PS	8120014	N636CR	8166018	C-FWCP	8001021	N396FW	5501020	N690E
8020024	N151GS	8120015	HB-LUF	8166019	HK-2749P	8001022	OB-1630	5501021	N141TC
8020025	N4WF	8120016	N311AC	8166020	N22YC	8001023	N69PC	5501022	N905LC
8020026	SX-AVA	8120017	CP-1678	8166021	N450HC	8001024	w/o	5501023	N950MT
8020027	SX-AVB	8120018	w/o	8166022	N3RK	8001025	N727PC	5501024	N9150T
8020028	PT-OAM	8120019	HC-BIF	8166023	N88B	8001026	LV-APF	5501025	N444CY
8020029	PT-OED	8120020	PT-WNC	8166024	N58PL	8001027	N112BC	5501026	N690TW
8020030	wfu	8120021	N85HB	8166025	XA-...	8001028	N190CA	5501027	N440CA
8020031	N47JF	8120022	N661TC	8166026	N28WN	8001029	N238PC	5501028	N9159Y
8020032	TG-HCR	8120023	w/o	8166027	N500PB	8001030	C-GPSB	5501029	D-IDBU
8020033	PT-OCL	8120024	5T-MAB	8166028	C-FJAK	8001031	N123AG	5501030	N787LB
8020034	N97PC	8120025	N51JK	8166029	N66JC	8001032	w/o	5501031	TC-THK
8020035	w/o	8120026	5T-MAC	8166030	C-FCEC	8001033	VH-WCE	5501032	wfu
8020036	OE-FKG	8120027	wfu	8166031	ZS-LSY	8001034	N444SC	5501033	TC-FAH
8020037	F-GIII	8120028	CC-CYB	8166032	N225PT	8001035	PP-EPB	5501034	N9085U
8020038	SX-AVC	8120029	w/o	8166033	G-CHEY	8001036	N8RY	5501035	N9091J
8020039	N63CM	8120030	PT-WOR	8166034	N82XL	8001037	N373CA	5501036	N9279A
8020040	wfu	8120031	PT-OJE	8166035	HK-3074P	8001038	PT-LZD	5501037	N9116Q
8020041	PH-SVY	8120032	HK-2631G	8166036	N618SW	8001039	XA-TJH	5501038	N9142B
8020042	N716WA	8120033	D-IBSA	8166037	w/o	8001040	N455JW	5501039	FAC-5743
8020043	HK-3472X	8120034	w/o	8166038	CC-PVE	8001041	N176FB	5501040	N95SA
8020044	F-GCLH	8120035	N888LG	8166039	N120SK	8001042	N7139B	5501041	D-IOSA
8020045	TG-EAB	8120036	N33MS	8166040	N824JH	8001043	F-GXES	5501042	D-IOSB
8020046	N302TA	8120037	HK-2642P	8166041	N916RT	8001044	LV-WXG	5501043	D-IOSC
8020047	HK-2455	8120038	N606DW	8166042	N767DM	8001045	N444LN	5501044	D-IOSD
8020048	PT-WFB	8120039	wfu	8166043	N711FN	8001046	N75AW	5501045	D-ITRI
8020049	N15UE	8120040	PT-LRT	8166044	N400WS	8001047	VH-BUW	5501046	D-ITWO
8020050	N91TS	8120041	SP-KKH	8166045	N237PC	8001048	OE-FIT	5501047	D-IAAE
8020051	w/o	8120042	PT-ODM	8166046	N107PC	8001049	N95VR	5501048	XB-AIN
8020052	w/o	8120043	TG-LIA	8166047	XB-FSG	8001050	N116JP	5501049	N121LN
8020053	C-GTTS	8120044	N666JK	8166048	C-FGSX	8001051	N5PA	5501050	N950TA
8020054	PT-LLG	8120045	TG-VAL	8166049	PT-WNG	8001052	w/o	5501051	B-3621
8020055	w/o	8120046	N178CD	8166050	HB-LNX	8001053	N700VF	5501052	B-3622
8020056	N314TD	8120047	wfu	8166051	N287CB	8001054	N94EW	5501053	N102AE
8020057	N22DT	8120048	OB-1228	8166052	N423JB	8001055	N937D	5501054	D-IAWB
8020058	PT-MGZ	8120049	CC-PJH	8166053	HK-2963	8001056	HR-JFA	5501055	D-IDIA
8020059	N457TG	8120050	N33MC	8166054	N444WC	8001057	N158TJ	5501056	B-3624
8020060	N112ED	8120051	HK-3043P	8166055	N85EM	8001058	N157LL	5501057	C-GSAA
8020061	PT-OZN	8120052	D-IFGN	8166056	EC-IPZ	8001059	HK-2772P	5501058	XA-VIP
8020062	N8CF	8120053	N87YP	8166057	N774KV	8001060	OK-OKL	5501059	B-3625
8020063	YU-BPH	8120054	ZS-PBS	8166058	N825SW	8001061	N4100L	5501060	B-3626
8020064	N376WS	8120055	N49B	8166059	w/o	8001062	FAC-5744	8301001	D-IHLA
8020065	wfu	8120056	N463DN	8166060	N500EW	8001063	C-GBOT	8301002	N75FL
8020066	ZP-TYI	8120057	N382MB	8166061	TJ-AIM	8001064	4X-CBF	**Cheyenne 400LS**	
8020067	N42CV	8120058	CC-CFP	8166062	N312MT	8001065	N395DR	5527001	wfu
8020068	N350ST	8120059	N18KW	8166063	N151MP	8001066	VH-NMA	5527002	N400VB
8020069	CC-PZX	8120060	N31HL	8166064	N7194Y	8001067	OB-1629	5527003	N40FK
8020070	N2469V	8120061	PT-LNG	8166065	w/o	8001068	HK-2684X	5527004	N411BG
8020071	N650RS	8120062	HK-4179X	8166066	C-FWPT	8001069	N5SY		

Serial	Reg	Serial	Reg	Serial	Reg	Serial	Reg	Serial	Reg
5527005	N85SL	4697024	N524PM	4697107	N607MA	4697192	N752MM	4697275	N598C
5527006	XA-	4697025	N4185L	4697108	OY-LMM	4697193	OY-PHD	4697276	D-ERAH
5527007	XA-	4697026	N184AE	4697109	N53362	4697194	HB-PQX	4697277	N705MA
5527008	N408WG	4697027	N62LT	4697110	N5339V	4697195	N816BC	4697278	N444RR
5527009	YV-991CP	4697028	N264B	4697111	w/o	4697196	N27DK	4697279	N279ST
5527010	LN-LYY	4697029	N529PM	4697112	N1RQ	4697197	N343RR	4697280	N1063M
5527011	N901MT	4697030	N117PW	4697113	N26KC	4697198	N3115M	4697281	N281SE
5527012	N321LH	4697031	N45PJ	4697114	C-GMYM	4697199	ZS-PLG	4697282	PH-FHB
5527013	N450MW	4697032	N125WZ	4697115	N1968W	4697200	C-GNSS	4697283	YL-
5527014	N144PL	4697033	N723KR	4697116	ZS-OUO	4697201	N428CW	4697286	N626AR
5527015	N42QB	4697034	N154DR	4697117	N211EZ	4697202	N30898	4697287	C-GCOL
5527016	N500LM	4697035	OE-KGB	4697118	N500SE	4697203	N455LG	4697289	N58BT
5527017	N46HL	4697036	N767TP	4697119	w/o	4697204	N465TP	4697290	N885DS
5527018	D-IYYY	4697037	N999RW	4697120	N91KM	4697205	N43MN	4697291	EC-
5527019	VH-BUR	4697038	wfu	4697121	N990DP	4697206	N77400	4697292	C-GUXL
5527020	N812BJ	4697039	N226DL	4697122	wfu	4697207	N46ME	4697293	N4839R
5527021	N500PM	4697040	N262MM	4697123	N32CK	4697208	N31062	4697294	N299MA
5527022	D-IQAS	4697041	N134G	4697124	N428DC	4697209	N209ST	4697295	N1065Y
5527023	LN-ACV	4697042	N59WF	4697125	D-EICO	4697210	N3292C	4697296	N296ST
5527024	w/o	4697043	N301D	4697126	N5347V	4697211	N565HP	4697297	N10694
5527025	N332SA	4697044	N804JH	4697127	N527MA	4697212	N49LG	4697298	N1071S
5527026	JA8253	4697045	N93LL	4697128	N85TK	4697213	N863RB	4697299	D-FMOR
5527027	N46FD	4697046	N46PV	4697129	N395SM	4697214	N455RS	4697300	N169CA
5527028	HB-LTM	4697047	N120WW	4697130	N682C	4697215	N31145	4697301	N95KW
5527029	N40MV	4697048	N32KE	4697132	N53516	4697216	N32CA	4697302	N1032H
5527030	D-IEXP	4697049	N215SD	4697133	N3325H	4697217	N142EE	4697303	N411HB
5527031	N431MC	4697050	D-EALL	4697134	N46WE	4697218	N618MA	4697304	ZS-TAY
5527032	9M-TDM	4697051	N901DM	4697135	N135FL	4697219	N123TS	4697305	N305DG
5527033	HK-3451	4697052	N733P	4697136	N5355S	4697220	N10ST	4697306	N568HP
5527034	N448CA	4697053	w/o	4697138	OY-LAW	4697221	N3110T	4697307	N153TC
5527035	JA8867	4697054	N46PL	4697139	N562HP	4697222	N7778T	4697308	N308ST
5527036	N34ER	4697055	ZS-DCG	4697140	N5358J	4697223	N3092K	4697309	OY-PKB
5527037	LQ-BLU	4697056	N76MG	4697141	N5353V	4697224	N646KC	4697310	N827CM
5527038	N438GP	4697057	N120SL	4697142	N5341C	4697225	N951TB	4697311	N3014C
5527039	N37KW	4697058	N97LL	4697143	N53401	4697226	N747BL	4697312	N113T
5527040	OH-PAY	4697059	N598AT	4697144	N5361A	4697227	N771BL	4697313	N953CM
5527041	N4WE	4697060	C-FIPO	4697145	N5PP	4697228	N186PS	4697314	N168CA
5527043	w/o	4697061	D-ECRB	4697146	N231CM	4697229	N629KC	4697315	OK-NET
5527044	N313PC	4697062	N801WA	4697147	OY-LDA	4697230	N3117S	4697316	N401CP

Cheyenne T-1040

Serial	Reg
4697063	D-ECBE	4697148	N802MM	4697231	N53KB	4697317	OY-PKC
8275001	N401VA	4697064	N164ST	4697149	N303JW	4697232	N785PJ	4697318	N618ST
8275002	ZS-OUP	4697065	N129EJ	4697150	N241PM	4697233	N465ME	4697319	N287MA
8275005	N219CS	4697066	N777MG	4697151	N4180A	4697234	N3117V	4697320	OK-CTR
8275006	N311SC	4697067	N8UM	4697152	G-DERK	4697235	N118JV	4697321	N1080Q
8275007	wfu	4697068	N5215U	4697153	N5320N	4697236	N930HM	4697322	N3061J
8275008	N223CS	4697069	N310JM	4697154	N6DM	4697237	N237ST	4697323	N3088X
8275011	ZS-OTL	4697070	D-ESSS	4697155	N338DB	4697238	N911TC	4697324	N724KC
8275013	w/o	4697071	N355PM	4697156	N248DA	4697239	N188CE	4697325	D-
8275014	N217CS	4697072	N135JM	4697157	N235TW	4697240	G-CEJB	4697326	N820DM
8275015	HK-2926P	4697073	N282SW	4697158	N53667	4697241	N45FF	4697327	N71SE
8275016	w/o	4697074	N5322D	4697159	N870C	4697242	N3123H	4697328	N457C
8275025	N304SC	4697075	N711SB	4697160	N81BL	4697243	N725JP	4697329	N580HP
8375001	VH-...	4697076	N5319K	4697161	N5365D	4697244	N219GR	4697330	N111RC
8375005	wfu	4697077	N19CX	4697162	N501AR	4697245	N759H	4697331	N546MA

PA-46-500TP Meridian

Serial	Reg
4697078	G-DERI	4697163	N78CC	4697246	N3129X	4697333	N63SE
4697E1	N400PT	4697079	D-EPUS	4697164	N54199	4697247	N2QE	4697334	N334ST
4697E3	wfu	4697080	N73YP	4697165	N501SR	4697248	N753C	4697335	N535KC
4608058	F-GHRR	4697081	N71562	4697166	N145DP	4697249	N462PJ	4697336	N220JL
4697001	wfu	4697082	N55ZG	4697167	N30397	4697250	N600YE	4697337	N194JL
4697002	N402MM	4697083	N53235	4697168	N844MS	4697251	N3128S	4697338	N60887
4697003	N375RD	4697084	N5333N	4697169	N134M	4697252	N168RV	4697339	C-GHVM
4697004	N250SA	4697085	N5325P	4697170	EC-IVZ	4697253	N535JR		

Rockwell Commander

Serial	Reg
4697086	N53238	4697171	N477HC	4697254	N3132A		
4697005	N43VM	4697087	N184RB	4697172	N821J	4697255	N3132V	11000	w/o
4697006	N4757S	4697088	N53369	4697173	N565C	4697256	N3129S	11001	N41T
4697007	N17LH	4697089	VH-TPM	4697174	N875SH	4697257	N3137T	11002	w/o
4697008	N89ST	4697090	N46WK	4697175	N951TP	4697258	N3135Y	11003	w/o
4697009	N209KC	4697091	C-FHVM	4697176	N606WC	4697259	N917CC	11004	N57175
4697010	N333MM	4697092	N14GV	4697177	N62WM	4697260	N260GF	11005	HK-2055
4697011	N67BW	4697093	N53PK	4697178	N3096P	4697261	C-GVJV	11006	ZK-MOH
4697012	N520HP	4697094	N337TF	4697179	N29LH	4697262	N281DD	11007	wfu
4697013	N465SK	4697095	N5339G	4697180	N187JD	4697263	N172MA	11008	w/o
4697014	N4174V	4697096	N455SG	4697181	N175WB	4697264	w/o	11009	N25BD
4697015	N965SB	4697097	N53290	4697182	N152AL	4697265	N665KC	11010	N690RA
4697016	N461BB	4697098	w/o	4697183	N220UM	4697266	ZS-SPD	11011	PT-OQH
4697017	N747AW	4697099	N199CP	4697184	N294DR	4697267	N345WT	11012	N885RA
4697018	N388TW	4697100	N5335R	4697185	C-GLER	4697268	C-FMKK	11013	w/o
4697019	D-EPKD	4697101	N530HP	4697186	N846RD	4697269	N1052L	11014	HK-1982
4697020	N255DW	4697102	N5337N	4697187	N909P	4697270	N1052X	11015	w/o
4697021	N5322M	4697103	N5338M	4697188	N582SE	4697271	N512MM	11016	C-GKDZ
4697022	N999NG	4697104	N104BH	4697189	N30983	4697272	N1063F	11017	N690WC
4697023	N938JW	4697105	D-EVER	4697190	N3103A	4697273	OK-VIP	11018	XA-PUY
		4697106	N225MA	4697191	N28NK	4697274	N1061T		

11019	LV-LEY	11123	N112EF	11206	N74GB	11289	N95JM	11377	YV1632
11020	C-GZON	11124	wfu	11207	YV1459	11290	N290PF	11378	YV2122
11021	XC-RAM	11125	N690EM	11208	N76EC	11291	w/o	11379	N690CC
11022	LV-BCJ	11126	N132JH	11209	HP-1607	11292	PJ-CEB	11380	w/o
11023	N9223N	11127	N17HF	11210	N70MD	11293	6-3202	11381	N690BG
11024	w/o	11128	HK-2282P	11211	D-IBAG	11294	5-4035	11382	XB-TWL
11025	C-FZRQ	11129	N37BW	11212	wfu	11295	5-4036	11383	N45AZ
11026	VH-NYC	11130	wfu	11213	wfu	11296	HK-2414P	11384	N690AX
11027	w/o	11131	YV1348	11214	XB-EIH	11297	N208CL	11385	N690TC
11028	wfu	11132	D2-EAA	11215	N32GA	11298	N690HF	11386	HK-...
11029	wfu	11133	wfu	11216	HK-1770G	11299	N121JW	11387	N44NC
11030	YV-....	11134	C-GHWF	11217	wfu	11300	N80TB	11388	YV
11031	N690GK	11135	w/o	11218	N75U	11301	OH-ACN	11389	N700PQ
11032	C-GFPP	11136	N318TK	11219	wfu	11302	HR-CEM	11390	YV1085
11033	HK-2281	11137	N331RC	11220	N4717V	11303	N848CE	11391	PT-...
11034	N690TR	11138	N690RK	11221	HK-3514	11304	N823SB	11392	N460K
11035	C-GJFO	11139	TI-AXU	11222	w/o	11305	w/o	11393	N690FD
11036	PT-LDA	11140	w/o	11223	w/o	11306	w/o	11394	ZP-TIW
11037	PT-LDL	11141	N3869F	11224	N200JQ	11307	C-FMFP	11395	CP-2266
11038	N33WG	11142	w/o	11225	XB-HSE	11308	VH-YJG	11396	w/o
11039	wfu	11143	EP-AHL	11226	N690DB	11309	N690EH	11397	w/o
11040	C-FAKP	11144	XB-FQC	11227	N50DX	11310	N690RC	11398	LV-MAW
11041	N924PC	11145	XB-ISC	11228	YV2256	11311	N690BM	11399	N727JA
11042	wfu	11146	N690SG	11229	N30854	11312	w/o	11400	N25CE
11043	N71VE	11147	w/o	11230	LV-LTY	11313	N245CF	11401	N78NA
11044	w/o	11148	wfu	11231	N115AB	11314	HK-3656	11402	N345CM
11045	EP-AGV	11149	N57RS	11232	wfu	11315	N561TC	11403	N127AA
11046	N2155B	11150	N333HC	11233	wfu	11316	N362SH	11404	N815CC
11047	EP-AGW	11151	wfu	11234	N693VM	11317	N615DP	11405	YV2160
11048	w/o	11152	VH-CLT	11235	N122AV	11318	YV-980P	11406	XB-SHH
11049	w/o	11153	N690CL	11236	LV-LRH	11319	N690GZ	11407	w/o
11050	wfu	11154	N31DV	11237	N977DG	11320	N98PJ	11408	N79BE
11051	N567R	11155	N690AR	11238	LV-LTB	11321	ZK-PVB	11409	OO-ROB
11052	N780BP	11156	w/o	11239	YV1841	11322	w/o	11410	N366FG
11053	w/o	11157	w/o	11240	F-BXAS	11323	YV-O-MAR·	11411	N690GG
11054	w/o	11158	VH-ATF	11241	LV-LTC	11324	wfu	11412	LV-MBY
11055	wfu	11159	N690HM	11242	w/o	11325	YV2037	11413	YV-....
11056	wfu	11160	N446JB	11243	N677WA	11326	wfu	11414	N93ME
11057	C-GWEW	11161	YV	11244	YV1758	11327	N81448	11415	N690LN
11058	EC-HNH	11162	TG-...	11245	YV1177	11328	EC-DXA	11416	N108SA
11059	HK-3465P	11163	w/o	11246	LV-LZL	11329	YV1796	11417	XC-JAL
11060	XA-DER	11164	w/o	11247	w/o	11330	N112EM	11418	N555MT
11061	YV2252	11165	HK-3466	11248	ZS-JRB	11331	XC-JCT	11419	LV-BNA
11062	VH-UJG	11166	C-GRRO	11249	N723AC	11332	N32PR	11420	N60DB
11063	w/o	11167	C-FIIL	11250	11250	11333	5-4037	11421	ZS-JRH
11064	N83G	11168	N690CF	11251	N251ES	11334	5-4038	11422	V5-MFN
11065	XB-FYD	11169	N38WA	11252	N690PT	11335	wfu	11423	N690MG
11066	N68TD	11170	wfu	11253	YV1959	11336	N3WU	11424	N38LM
11067	FAB 028	11171	YV	11254	N24GT	11337	N690SM	11425	N996AB
11068	C-GGOO	11172	N60BM	11255	HK-3314W	11338	N222ME	11426	N9KG
11069	wfu	11173	VH-YJP	11256	EP-KCD	11339	N32WS	11427	N55WJ
11070	N9175N	11174	N66GW	11257	N121FM	11340	wfu	11428	N91CT
11071	wfu	11175	TG-...	11258	LV-LTX	11341	N690PC	11429	N771BA
11072	w/o	11176	N690WD	11259	ZS-PXR	11342	N76WA	11430	YV-O-MIF-2
11073	HP-....	11177	N15CD	11260	wfu	11343	N706KC	11431	N690HS
11074	XB-GJL	11178	N57EG	11261	LV-LTU	11344	w/o	11432	V5-MGF
11075	EP-AKI	11179	N375AA	11262	N690DS	11350	N690RD	11433	N690XY
11076	5-2501	11180	YV2229	11263	N57112	11351	w/o	11434	w/o
11077	4-901	11181	6-3201	11264	YV1787	11352	N721TB	11435	N600WS
11078	4-902	11182	EP-AHM	11265	I-MAGJ	11353	N31WD	11436	N751BR
11079	4-903	11183	5-2505	11266	w/o	11354	HK-4323	11437	N167R
11100	w/o	11184	wfu	11267	XA-GEM	11355	N303G	11438	N81703
11101	VH-AAG	11185	wfu	11268	LV-LZM	11356	N711PB	11439	N364WA
11102	HP-....	11186	XA-TQD	11269	N4PZ	11357	N690GF	11440	N20ME
11103	5Y-BTL	11187	w/o	11270	N57292	11358	YV-663CP	11441	N6900K
11104	C-GAAL	11188	N449LC	11271	wfu	11359	YV189T	11442	LV-MDN
11105	ZS-LRM	11189	XB-BED	11272	N90AT	11360	XB-DMT	11443	YV2056
11106	C-FCZZ	11190	N737E	11273	N892WA	11361	N690BH	11444	N318WA
11107	CP-2467	11191	YV-2488P	11274	wfu	11362	w/o	11445	w/o
11108	wfu	11192	N440CC	11275	w/o	11363	N690GS	11446	C-FMCX
11109	w/o	11193	C-GDCL	11276	N118CR	11364	HK-2291X	11447	XC-STA
11110	HK-3597	11194	wfu	11277	N690AS	11365	HK-3561	11448	YV2048
11111	N801EB	11195	N690WS	11278	w/o	11366	YV2094	11449	N28TC
11112	w/o	11196	w/o	11279	C-GEOS	11367	SE-LZX	11450	XC-HHS
11113	N57113	11197	N52PY	11280	N699SB	11368	HP-77PE	11451	N690CP
11114	YV2247	11198	w/o	11281	YV-O-MTC-	11369	N1VQ	11452	N5016H
11115	XC-NAY	11199	YV0145	11282	N20EB	11370	XA-NTC	11453	HK-2218W
11116	w/o	11200	w/o	11283	VH-PCV	11371	XB-GDS	11454	XA-ABH
11117	w/o	11201	N921ST	11284	ZS-JRA	11372	w/o	11455	XA-...
11118	N91384	11202	N24CC	11285	YV2184	11373	N279DD	11456	N267RD
11119	N690AH	11203	N690AT	11286	N286AF	11374	w/o	11457	N615SB
11120	w/o	11204	w/o	11287	N690SD	11375	N882AC	11458	N98AJ
11121	SE-LZU	11205	OH-UTI	11288	YV1846	11376	PT-LHV	11459	N40WG
11122	HK-3147X								

11460	XB-GCU	11543	N480K	35	35	138	w/o	222	N700YN
11461	YV-188CP	11544	N690LL	38	JA8894	139	F-MABS	223	C-GITC
11462	N225MM	11545	N32BW	39	w/o	140	N1421Z	224	N825KM
11463	VH-TSS	11546	N555VE	46	N1967H	141	N500FF	225	N70LR
11464	YV1271	11547	YV1994	49	N722SR	142	D-FNRE	226	N226PB
11465	PT-MPN	11548	XA-...	50	N84HS	143	N724DM	227	N700TL
11466	YV-204CP	11549	XA-...	52	N700RE	144	N144JT	228	N700KP
11467	N690XT	11550	N690SS	53	C-GTBM	145	F-GTJM	229	N123ZC
11468	YV2222	11551	N253JM	57	N57SL	146	F-RAXR	230	N324JS
11469	N13622	11552	N37RR	59	w/o	147	F-RAXS	231	w/o
11470	N744CH	11553	N586DV	60	N700HK	148	N790TB	232	EI-TBM
11471	YV319T	11554	N107GL	61	N661DW	149	N800GS	233	N700VA
11472	YV223T	11555	N692T	62	wfu	150	N449CA	234	N711PM
11473	wfu	11556	XC-GAS	63	LX-JFA	151	N70LT	235	N335MA
11474	5Y-BMY	11557	V5-MAC	67	N62LM	152	N767HP	236	N700CT
11475	N690LS	11558	LV-MYA	68	w/o	153	N4MD	237	N700VB
11476	N330ES	11559	N40SM	69	9M-DSR	154	N435DM	238	C-GBCO
11477	wfu	11560	XC-HMO	70	70	155	N321CW	239	N115KC
11478	N36JF	11561	N690WP	71	N838RA	156	F-MABT	240	N811SW
11479	w/o	11562	wfu	72	N700VM	157	D-FALF	241	N700GJ
11480	N690JK	11563	XB-KLY	73	w/o	158	N700KM	242	N827VG
11481	XC-VES	11564	CP-2224	74	N93BN	159	F-MABU	243	N700KK
11482	G-CECN	11565	HP-...	75	N975TB	160	F-MABV	244	N997JM
11483	YV1998	11566	N186E	76	w/o	161	N18SR	245	N700JV
11484	N2141B	**SAAB**		77	F-RAXD	162	D-FGYY	246	N700GN
11485	N173DB	*SAAB 2000*		78	F-RAXE	163	N700VJ	247	N15SB
11486	N94AC			80	80	164	ZS-TBM	248	N220MA
11487	N690TH	017	N519JG	82	w/o	165	N702QD	249	N700PX
11488	YV2176	020	N511RH	83	N883CR	166	VH-XTB	250	N700AD
11489	HK-2551P	030	N509RH	84	N228CX	167	N788RR	251	N700MK
11490	YV1456	031	SE-LOG	85	N650DM	168	N709MC	252	N700AQ
11491	w/o	034	N166GC	86	N700LL	169	N4920Y	253	N700RK
11492	N691SM	051	JA003G	87	N700ZR	170	N58HP	254	N700AZ
11493	N690RP	054	JA004G	88	N217DC	171	N129AG	255	N700GE
11494	3932	*SAAB 340*		89	N5BR	172	N70PH	256	N702RW
11495	N130TT	022	N340SS	90	N57HQ	173	VH-JSO	257	N700SL
11496	wfu	029	N184K	91	N700WT	174	N700QD	258	OH-KJJ
11497	C-FNWD	036	N727DL	92	VH-KFT	175	N700WK	259	N459MA
11498	w/o	050	N44KS	93	F-RAXL	176	N700CB	260	N701CN
11499	YV2009	170	100001	94	94	177	N702GS	261	G-MCMC
11500	YV0115	385	JA8951	95	F-RAXH	178	C-FPBL	262	N700BK
11501	N12DE	405	JA8952	96	N767CW	179	N701AV	263	N263CW
11502	YV-229CP	431	100006	97	N300AE	180	N444JV	264	N700JD
11503	N503B	**Socata**		98	N776RM	181	N721SR	265	N6720Y
11504	XC-TAB	*TBM 700*		99	F-MABO	182	N702AV	266	N700CL
11505	N36SW			100	F-MABP	183	N770DC	267	N700FT
11506	wfu	1	N755PG	101	N755DM	184	N552JF	268	N700PT
11507	w/o	01	F-WTBM	102	N579NC	185	LX-JFL	269	F-WWRI
11508	N690BK	02	F-WKPG	103	F-RAXI	186	D-FIVE	270	N700LF
11509	N78TT	03	F-WKDL	104	F-RAXJ	187	N769JS	271	N700DQ
11510	N61TS	2	N702BM	105	F-RAXK	188	N704QD	272	N272MA
11511	N87WZ	3	OO-TBM	106	F-ZVMN	190	N700AP	273	N943CA
11512	N400DS	4	N700DE	107	N701LT	191	C-GRBV	274	N582C
11513	N690BA	5	N731TM	108	N715V	192	N6842D	275	N702AR
11514	N20MA	6	N157JB	109	N700CS	193	N700S	276	N700GT
11515	YV1932	7	N138JM	110	F-RAXP	194	N19SG	277	N924JP
11516	XC-SAH	8	N56WF	111	F-RAXM	195	HB-KFR	278	N700HY
11517	N517HP	9	N5HT	112	N702H	196	N843BH	279	N396AW
11518	N25RZ	10	w/o	113	N700CC	197	N707AV	280	N785MA
11519	N425DT	11	N700BS	114	PK-CAL	198	N700ER	281	N700HL
11520	N47EP	12	EC-FPF	115	F-MABQ	199	LX-JFD	282	N988C
11521	N7KS	13	N700MV	116	N700ZZ	200	N275CA	283	N700SY
11522	N84GU	14	N700MX	117	F-RAXN	201	w/o	284	N700EG
11523	w/o	15	N700PU	118	N700VX	202	N724RN	285	N90CP
11524	N22CK	16	N283BS	119	PK-AHA	203	N700BN	286	N9EE
11525	HK-3379W	17	N717Y	120	PK-AHC	204	N700HN	287	N700EV
11526	N691PA	18	w/o	121	PK-CAM	205	VH-ICA	288	D-FKAI
11527	N690AC	19	C-GBTS	122	N461LM	206	w/o	289	N700GQ
11528	N15SF	20	N50ST	123	N700CF	207	N356F	290	N700GV
11529	N690JH	21	N708EF	124	N701MK	208	LX-JFE	291	N700EJ
11530	N559CG	22	N994DF	125	F-RAXO	209	N700EL	292	N262J
11531	N244MP	23	w/o	126	N701QD	210	N700KH	293	N693MA
11532	YV2001	24	D-FOOO	127	PH-HUB	211	N700PW	294	N777FX
11533	w/o	25	N751J	128	N63TP	212	LX-JFF	295	N700DZ
11534	XA-SFD	26	N700SF	129	N703QD	213	N559CA	296	N700KV
11535	N999FG	27	N700TJ	130	D-FSJP	214	N700WE	297	PR-FIC
11536	N260WE	28	wfu	131	F-RAXQ	215	N700PV	298	N700BQ
11537	XA-	29	N708PW	132	N700AN	216	N702AA	299	PH-CLZ
11538	N777EL	30	N715MC	133	N98NF	217	N623RT	300	N300AZ
11539	YV246T	31	N829BC	134	N700DT	218	HB-KOL	301	N700CZ
11540	N67CG	32	F-GLBZ	135	N88U	219	F-GMLV	302	N700GY
11541	N270DP	33	F-RAXA	136	F-MABR	220	N2WF	303	N210CL
11542	N690CH	34	N8EG	137	D-FIRE	221	N700CV	304	N8KF

#	Reg	#	Reg	#	Reg	#	Reg	#	Reg
305	N700DM	387	D-FBFS	T26-24	N1207S	T26-164	N164BT	T-263	w/o
306	N887TC	388	N220JM	T26-25	N1208S	T26-165	N160EA	T-264	F-GZJM
307	N700EZ	389	VH-MRJ	T26-26	N269PM	T26-166	wfu	T-265	LX-NRJ
308	N903MA	390	N850PW	T26-27	N1210S	T26-167	N400DC	T-266	N9900
309	N101NX	391	LX-JFL	T26-28	wfu	T26-167E	N2303P	T-267	PH-PIC
310	N716MA	392	N851MA	T26-29	N187Z	T26-168	w/o	T-268	YV-177T
311	N700TK	393	N893CA	T26-30	wfu	T26-169	N102DY	T-269	w/o
312	N773TC	394	N851WA	T26-31	w/o	T26-170	w/o	T-270	N226SR
313	N700HD	395	N788RB	T26-32	wfu	T26-171E	C-GRBF	T-271	4X-CIZ
314	N702MB	396	N85JE	T26-33	N121KB	T26-172	N742GR	T-272	w/o
315	N700ZM	397	ZS-BCI	T26-34	wfu	T26-172E	C-FCAW	T-273	N463DC
316	N820SM	398	N850KL	T26-35	wfu	T26-173	N22NR	T-274	C-FAMF
317	N700ZA	399	N850AA	T26-36	w/o	T26-174	w/o	T-275	AE-176
318	N12MA	400	N32WZ	**Merlin 2B**		T26-175	YV-...	T-276	F-
319	N319TB	401	N850MD	T26-100	N333F	T26-176	N1907W	T-277	w/o
320	N700GK	402	N855MA	T26-101	N699AM	T26-177	w/o	T-278	N303MA
321	F-HBCF	403	N850LW	T26-102	wfu	T26-178	N717PD	T-279	N279M
322	N700KD	404	N950WA	T26-103	wfu	T26-179	w/o	T-280	AE-178
323	N223EA	405	N924BB	T26-104	wfu	T26-180E	N1039Y	T-281	AE-179
324	N700WB	406	N223JG	T26-105	N345T	**Merlin 3/3A/3B**		T-282	XA-...
325	N700SX	407	N850KM	T26-106	N370X	T-201	w/o	T-283	N5441M
326	N710M	408	N892CA	T26-107	N158CA	T-202	D-....	T-284	N154L
327	N300CX	409	N63DL	T26-108	wfu	T-203	w/o	T-285	wfu
328	N627DB	410	N367EA	T26-109	N1221S	T-204	VH-SSM	T-286	N505GM
329	N700EN	411	N850WE	T26-110	w/o	T-205	N970M	T-287	YV-O-IGV-1
330	N611MA	412	N849MA	T26-111	wfu	T-205E	wfu	T-288	HP-1069
331	N701JF	413	D-FGPE	T26-112	wfu	T-206	N46NA	T-289	N104TA
332	N731CA	414	N850AG	T26-113	HP-1136AP	T-207	w/o	T-290	YV-
333	N484RJ	415	N6868C	T26-114	N963BP	T-208	N269DE	T-291	N800LD
334	N334JR	416	N894EA	T26-115	w/o	T-209	w/o	T-292	YV261T
335	N386CP	417	N850LD	T26-116	N96RL	T-210	VH-SSL	T-293	F-GGVG
336	N700ZF	418	PR-GAB	T26-117	N802DJ	T-211	w/o	T-294	LN-HTD
337	N700QT	419	PH-	T26-118	N12WC	T-212	N222MV	T-295	w/o
338	N436CB	420	N850BQ	T26-119	wfu	T-213	VH-SSD	T-296	w/o
339	N751CM	421	LZ-TBM	T26-120	wfu	T-214	w/o	T-297	N127WD
340	N930MA	422	LX-JFO	T26-121	wfu	T-215	w/o	T-298	F-GLPT
341	N790CA	423	N850DP	T26-122	C-GBZM	T-216	w/o	T-299	N512FS
342	HB-KHC	424	N842MA	T26-123	wfu	T-217	N224HR	T-300	N699RK
343	N71EE	425	N302RJ	T26-124	N4051X	T-218	N75MX	T-301	YV-710CP
344	VH-CZM	426	HB-KHP	T26-125	wfu	T-219	w/o	T-302	w/o
345	I-TICO	427	N850BZ	T26-126	w/o	T-220	XB-JQC	T-303	N96VC
TBM 850		428	PH-TGA	T26-127	wfu	T-221	N22EQ	T-304	N76CC
346	N850TB	429	N988V	T26-128	w/o	T-222	wfu	T-305	wfu
347	N850L	430	N850WT	T26-129	RF-14004	T-223	N263CM	T-306	N749L
348	N850JR	432	N850DB	T26-130	wfu	T-224	N550BE	T-307	N307PA
349	HB-KOR	433	N850BT	T26-131	wfu	T-225	w/o	T-308	N50MT
350	N850MA	434	N847MA	T26-132	HA-SIP	T-226	N70FC	T-309	N60NH
351	N351CK	435	N850GX	T26-133	wfu	T-227	N555AM	T-310	N49H
352	N850XS	436	N850JS	T26-134	w/o	T-228	N290TA	T-311	N96954
353	N850WM	437	N850LK	T26-135	N213SC	T-229	XB-JXY	T-312	F-GRNT
354	N850DL	438	N294PJ	T26-136	N137CP	T-230	w/o	T-313	N763LD
355	C-GMET	439	N654CW	T26-137	w/o	T-231	N46SA	T-314	N814SS
356	N257JM	442	N851GC	T26-138	N73HC	T-232	LV-WIR	T-315	N50LG
357	N850SB	443	N22MY	T26-139	N469BL	T-233	wfu	T-316	N616PS
358	N37SV	444	N850AD	T26-140	N321PH	T-234	N101MC	T-317	w/o
359	N850GS	445	N888LF	T26-140E	w/o	T-235	N45818	T-318	VH-OVC
360	N874CA	446	N850BD	T26-141	wfu	T-236	N5317M	T-319	N601JT
361	N850TG	447	N440EA	T26-142	YV-....	T-237	N633ST	T-320	HK-2479W
362	N850JD	452	N492B	T26-143	LV-RZB	T-238	XC-HFA	T-321	N1014V
363	N885CA	**Swearingen**		T26-144	N558AC	T-239	N239DR	T-322	D-IDEA
364	N226RA	**Merlin 2A**		T26-145	wfu	T-240	TG-...	T-323	N329HS
365	N850JB	T26-1	wfu	T26-146	w/o	T-241	N23AE	T-324	wfu
366	VH-SMZ	T26-2	w/o	T26-147	w/o	T-242	w/o	T-325	N100CE
367	N850BG	T26-3	wfu	T26-148	N200MH	T-243	w/o	T-326	N300AL
368	N854MA	T26-4	wfu	T26-149	EC-GJZ	T-244	N244SA	T-327	N1007B
369	N288CC	T26-5	N201SM	T26-149E	N846BB	T-245	N4209S	T-328	XB-EFZ
370	N850DD	T26-6	wfu	T26-150	N457G	T-246	N43CB	T-329	N405SA
371	N853MA	T26-7	N9032H	T26-151	N396PS	T-247	wfu	T-330	N113GS
372	PH-UKK	T26-8	wfu	T26-152	RA-14424	T-248	N104EM	T-331	N331GM
373	N851TB	T26-9	N400DG	T26-153	N4262X	T-249	XA-	T-332	N46KC
374	N850LH	T26-11	wfu	T26-154	N20KV	T-250	N125WG	T-336	w/o
375	N850JM	T26-12	wfu	T26-154E	wfu	T-251	wfu	T-339	N339RW
376	N850CW	T26-14	wfu	T26-155	wfu	T-252	XA-	T-341	wfu
377	N897CA	T26-15	wfu	T26-156	N30HS	T-253	HK-....	T-342	LN-SFT
378	N378FC	T26-16	w/o	T26-157	N20EF	T-254	N25677	T-345	5A-DHZ
379	N850AP	T26-17	wfu	T26-158	XA-...	T-255	N9NZ	T-348	wfu
380	N850U	T26-18	wfu	T26-158E	N8KT	T-256	N699KM	T-351	w/o
381	N850AB	T26-19	C-FSVC	T26-159	N66MD	T-257	N39MS	T-354	N200SN
382	N507BC	T26-20	C-GLKA	T26-160	wfu	T-258	N772SL	T-357	YV-242CP
383	F-GSCF	T26-21	wfu	T26-161	N669HS	T-259	wfu	T-360	N387CC
384	N850AZ	T26-22	wfu	T26-162	w/o	T-260	N422GK	T-363	N779M
385	N74MA	T26-23	wfu	T26-163	w/o	T-261	w/o	T-366	N500SX
386	N850AR			T26-163E	w/o	T-262	w/o	T-369	N901MC

T-372	N1010V	AT-034	N54GP
T-375	N800MM	AT-035	I-NARC
T-378	N98UC	AT-036	LV-WNC
T-381	wfu	AT-037	N202WS
T-384	YV-770CP	AT-038	EC-JCV
T-387	N36LC	AT-039	N727DP
T-388	5A-DJB	AT-040	w/o
T-391	N391GM	AT-041	EC-GBI
T-394	N59EZ	AT-042	w/o
T-397	N38TA	AT-043	w/o
T-400	N350MC	AT-044	TC-UPS
T-403	w/o	AT-051	ZS-ZOB
T-405	N120TM	AT-057	wfu
T-407	YV	AT-058	I-NARW
T-410	N299EC	AT-062	EC-GFK
T-414	N379JG	AT-062E	w/o
T-417	N12MF	AT-063	AE-181
Merlin 3C		AT-064	AE-182
T-303E	w/o	AT-064E	OB-1146
TT-421	N75X	AT-065	w/o
TT-424	N266M	AT-066	EC-JQC
TT-426A	N2GL	AT-067	N120SC
TT-428A	N444LB	AT-068	N836MA
TT-431	N431S	AT-069	N631FA
TT-433	N123LH	AT-071	60501
TT-435	YV-808CP	AT-071E	AE-180
TT-438	N53DA	AT-072	60502
TT-441	N6UP	AT-073	60503
TT-444	N227TT	AT-074	EC-HBF
TT-447	YV1923	Merlin 4C	
TT-450	N99JW	AT-423	F-GHVF
TT-453	N31JV	AT-427	N629TG
TT-456	YV-740CP	AT-434	HZ-SN8
TT-459A	YV2045	AT-439	wfu
TT-462A	ZP-...	AT-440B	D-CBIN
TT-465	YV1412	AT-446	N573G
TT-468	YV2310	AT-452	N45MW
TT-471	YV-472CP	AT-454	N807M
TT-474	VH-RCI	AT-461	N120FA
TT-477	N227JT	AT-464	N313D
TT-480	N81WS	AT-469	w/o
TT-483A	N795TB	AT-492	N8897Y
TT-486A	N1MN	AT-493	D-CNAY
TT-489	N888AY	AT-495B	N851BC
TT-507	YV-....	AT-501	N999MX
TT-512A	D-IBHL	AT-502	VH-UZA
TT-515	wfu	AT-506	N370AE
TT-518	N213PA	AT-511	D-CCCC
TT-521	YV-262CP	AT-532	YV-...
TT-527	w/o	AT-539	wfu
TT-529	D-IMWK	AT-544	N544UP
TT-534	N90GT	AT-548	N548UP
TT-536	N17VV	AT-549	N471CD
TT-541	N112CS	AT-556	N556UP
Merlin 4		AT-557	wfu
AT-002	C-GTMW	AT-560	N560UP
AT-003	wfu	AT-561	N561UP
AT-003E	wfu	AT-563	VH-EEN
AT-004	N94CE	AT-564	VH-EEO
AT-005	w/o	AT-566	N566UP
AT-006	N4679K	AT-567	VH-EEP
AT-007	HZ-SN6	AT-568	w/o
AT-008	w/o	AT-569	N569UP
AT-009	XA-...	AT-570	VH-UZI
AT-010	wfu	AT-577	N120JM
AT-011	C-	AT-585	N919CK
AT-012	F-GERP	AT-591	N505FS
AT-013	wfu	AT-602B	N240DH
AT-014	N4019	AT-607B	N241DH
AT-015	w/o	AT-608B	N242DH
AT-016	JA8828	AT-609B	N243DH
AT-017	C-GPCL	AT-618B	N244DH
AT-018	N427SP	AT-624B	N245DH
AT-020	I-NARB	AT-625B	N246DH
AT-025	w/o	AT-626B	N247DH
AT-027	N582JF	AT-630B	N248DH
AT-028	w/o	AT-631B	N249DH
AT-029	wfu	AT-695B	N762VM
AT-030	N69ST		
AT-031	F-GMTO		
AT-032	N90NH		
AT-033	w/o		

Biz-Jet Database

If you need more information then call us for a quote.

We can supply a database updated monthly or a simple report.

Demo available to download on
www.buchairuk.co.uk

Data Includes:

Registration
Registration Country
Construction Number
Aircraft Type
Engine Manufacturer
Engine Model
Year of manufacturer
Base of Operation
Operator/Owners Name
Operator/Owners Address
Contact
Telephone Number
Fax Number
Purchase date
History of Aircraft

BUCHair UK Ltd, 78 High Street,
Reigate, Surrey, RH2 9AP
Tele: +44 (0)1737 224747   Fax: +44 (0)1737 226777
Email sales@buchairuk.co.uk

OD-KMI   JetStar 2 (now HB-JGK)   photo: Jean-Luc Altherr

N990PA   Sabreliner 65   photo: Jarrod Wilkening

HB-VCN   Sabreliner 65   photo: Barry Ambrose BIZAV

AP-MIR		Challenger 601			photo: Jean-Luc Altherr

VP-CRR		Challenger 601-3A		photo: Jean-Luc Altherr

OE-IFG		Global Express			photo: Jean-Luc Altherr

LZ-YUN Challenger 604 photo: Barry Ambrose BIZAV

G-PRKR Challenger 604 photo: Jean-Luc Altherr

G-TAGA Challenger 604 photo: Jean-Luc Altherr

OE-IPK　　　　Challenger 604　　　　　　　　photo: Barry Ambrose BIZAV

N521FX　　　　Challenger 300　　　　　　　　photo: Woifgang Zilske

7T-VCW　　　　HS 125/700B　　　　　　　　photo: Barry Ambrose BIZAV

RA-02850   HS 125/700B   photo: Jean-Luc Altherr

VP-BMM   Hawker 850XP   photo: Thomas Niepel

ZS-PCY   Hawker 850XP   photo: Barry Ambrose BIZAV

N900LD   Hawker 900XP   photo: Barry Ambrose BIZAV

N97FL   Astra 1125 SPX   photo: Barry Ambrose BIZAV

C6-JET   Astra 1125 SPX   photo: Thomas Niepel

T7-VII   Citation VII   photo: Barry Ambrose BIZAV

OY-CKE   Citation VII   photo: Jean-Luc Altherr

OK-SLX   Citation Excel   photo: Barry Ambrose BIZAV

A9C-BXJ   Citation Excel XLS   photo: Jean-Luc Altherr

N562DB   Citation Excel XLS   photo: Thomas Niepel

TC-TMA   Citation Bravo   photo: Thomas Niepel

N61YP   CitationJet   photo: Bill Shull

OE-FGL   CitationJet CJ-2   photo: Thomas Niepel

M-ELON   CitationJet CJ-3   photo: Barry Ambrose BIZAV

N680GG   Citation Sovereign   photo: Barry Ambrose BIZAV

PR-SPR   Citation Sovereign   photo: Barry Ambrose BIZAV

SU-SMA   Citation Sovereign   photo: Jean-Luc Altherr

N931QS Citation X photo: Barry Ambrose BIZAV

N777FL Gulfstream G150 photo: Dick Milne

N662GA Gulfstream G550 photo: Barry Ambrose BIZAV
(now EC-KLS)

N939KM   Gulfstream G3   photo: Dick Milne

XA-CHR   Gulfstream G4SP   photo: Jean-Luc Altherr

N408QS   Gulfstream G4SP   photo: Barry Ambrose BIZAV

F-HAIR　　　　　Falcon 50　　　　　　　　　　　　photo: Thomas Niepel

N90TH　　　　　Falcon 900C　　　　　　　　　　　photo: Barry Ambrose BIZAV

N910MW　　　　Falcon 900EX　　　　　　　　　　photo: Barry Ambrose BIZAV

G-GALX   Falcon 900EX EASY   photo: Barry Ambrose BIZAV

N844UP   Falcon 2000   photo: Bill Shull

VP-BGG   Falcon 7X   photo: Barry Ambrose BIZAV

N28MJ   Learjet 35A   photo: Barry Ambrose BIZAV

G-ZXZX   Learjet 45   photo: Thomas Niepel

G-MEET   Learjet 40   photo: Barry Ambrose BIZAV

EI-VIV   Learjet 60   photo: Jean-Luc Altherr

D-AONE   Legacy 600   photo: Barry Ambrose BIZAV

N88B   Learjet 24   photo: Dick Milne
(Pima Museum)